lonely planet

China

Caroline Liou
Marie Cambon
Alexander English
Thomas Huhti
Korina Miller
Bradley Wong

LONELY PLANET PUBLICATIONS
Melbourne • Oakland • London • Paris

60°E
80°E
100°E

Ural River

Omsk

Novosibirsk

Krasnoyarsk

Yenisey

River

SAYAN MOUNTAINS

ASTANA

Qaraghandy

ARAL
SEA

KAZAKHSTAN

Balkhash Lake

AL TAI

Syr Darya River

Ishim River

Irtysh River

Amu

Darya

River

ALMATY

Ürümqi

Turpan

TASHKENT

BISHKEK

UZBEKISTAN

KYRGYZSTAN

XINJIANG

Dunhuang

Kashgar

TAJIKISTAN

DUSHANBE

Tarim Basin

KUNLAN SHAN

Qinghai Hu
(Qinghai
Lake)

AFGHANISTAN

Under administration
of China

Golmud

QINGHAI

KABUL

ISLAMABAD

PLATEAU
OF TIBET

Xiwu

Rawalpindi

Lahore

HIMALAYA

TIBET

Indus River

Mt
Everest
(8848m)

Shigatse

Lhasa

PAKISTAN

DELHI

NEPAL

Karachi

Jaipur

Agra

KATHMANDU

THIMPHU

BHUTAN

Ganges

Lucknow

Deccan

Varanasi

Patna

River

BANGLADESH

Ahmedabad

INDIA

Calcutta

DHAKA

MYANMAR

Chittagong

Mandalay

River

Bhubaneswar

ARABIAN
SEA

Mumbai (Bombay)

Godavari River

BAY OF
BENGAL

Ayeyarwady

Thanlwin River

120°E   140°E

Baikal Lake

Irkutsk

Ulan Ude

HEILONGJIANG

Manzhouli

Manchurian Plain

Yichun

Qiqihar   Jixi

Daqing   ⊙ **Haerbin**

ULAAN BAATAR

Xilinhot

JILIN

Jilin

⊙ **Changchun**

MONGOLIA

Erenhot

Badaojiang

Shenyang

LIAONING

Jinzhou   Anshan

Chengde

Dandong

P'YONGYANG

NORTH KOREA

Gobi Desert

Baotou

Hohhot

HEBEI

BEIJING

Datong

TIANJIN

⊙ **Tianjin**

Dalian

SOUTH KOREA

SEOUL

INNER MONGOLIA

Huang He

Wuhai

Shijiazhuang

Pusan

(Yellow River)

Taiyuan

Qingdao

Kwangju

Vladivostok

40°N

JAPAN

TOKYO

Nagoya

Kyoto ⊙

Osaka

Hiroshima

SEA OF JAPAN (East Sea)

Sapporo

Sendai

Yinchuan

Wuwei

NINGXIA

Xining

Lanzhou

GANSU

Xi'an

SHANXI

Anyang

Zhengzhou

Ji'nan

Shijiusuo

SHANDONG

Luoyang

Xuzhou

YELLOW SEA

JIANGSU

SHAANXI

HENAN

Bozhou

Nanyang

ANHUI

Nanjing

Suzhou

SHANGHAI

Hefei

Yangzhou

Shanghai

Ningbo

Songpan

HUBEI

Wuhan

Yichang

Hangzhou

Chengdu

SICHUAN

Emeishan

Leshan

CHONGQING

⊙ **Chongqing**

Changsha

ZHEJIANG

Jingdezhen

Wenzhou

EAST CHINA SEA

Naha

Nanchang

JIANGXI

FUJIAN

HUNAN

Pingxiang

Hengyang

Nanping

Fuzhou

Guiyang

GUIZHOU

Ganzhou

Quanzhou

Xiamen

TAIPEI

PACIFIC OCEAN

Tainan

Xiaguan (Dali City)

Guilin

Guangzhou

Foshan

Shenzhen

TAIWAN

20°N

GUANGDONG

Kunming

GUANGXI

Liuzhou

Wuzhou

MACAU

HONG KONG

Shantou

YUNNAN

Nanning

HANOI

Haiphong

Haikou

Hainan Dao

SOUTH CHINA SEA

PHILIPPINE SEA

Laoag

Baguio

PHILIPPINES

LAOS

THAILAND

VIENTIANE

VIETNAM

MANILA

Lucena

Khabarovsk

Amur River

Yangzi River

The external boundaries of India on this map have not been authenticated and may not be correct

0   250   500 km

China
7th edition – September 2000
First published – October 1984

Published by
Lonely Planet Publications Pty Ltd A.C.N. 005 607 983
192 Burwood Rd, Hawthorn, Victoria 3122, Australia

Lonely Planet Offices
Australia PO Box 617, Hawthorn, Victoria 3122
USA 150 Linden St, Oakland, CA 94607
UK 10a Spring Place, London NW5 3BH
France 1 rue du Dahomey, 75011 Paris

Photographs
Many of the images in this guide are available for licensing from
Lonely Planet Images.
email: lpi@lonelyplanet.com.au

Front cover photograph
A new restaurant opens in Hong Kong (Jon Davison)

ISBN 0 86442 755 7

Printed by SNP Offset (M) Sdn Bhd

Printed in Malaysia

Although the authors and Lonely Planet try to make the information as accurate as possible, we accept no responsibility for any loss, injury or inconvenience sustained by anyone using this book.

Contents – Text

THE AUTHORS   12

FOREWORD   16

INTRODUCTION   19

FACTS ABOUT CHINA   21

History 21
Highlights in China 31
Getaways 31
Historic Architecture &
Foreign Concessions 31
Sacred Mountains &
Nature Reserves 33
Spectacular Sights 35
Outdoor Activities 36
Geography 46
Climate 48
Ecology & Environment 50
Flora & Fauna 52
Government & Politics 54
Economy 56
Population & People 56
Education 59
Arts 60
Society & Conduct 70
Religion 72

FACTS FOR THE VISITOR   79

Planning 79
Responsible Tourism 81
Suggested Itineraries 81
Visas & Documents 82
Embassies 85
Customs 86
Money 87
Post & Communications 89
Books 93
Internet Resources 95
Films 96
Newspapers & Magazines 96
Radio & TV 97
Video Systems 97
Photography & Video 97
Time 98
Electricity 98
Weights & Measures 99
Laundry 99
Health 99
Toilets 114
Women Travellers 115
Gay & Lesbian Travellers 115
Disabled Travellers 116
Senior Travellers 116
Travel With Children 117
Useful Organisations 117
Dangers 118
Annoyances 119
Legal Matters 121
PSB 123
Business Hours 124
Public Holidays & Special
Events 125
Activities 126
Courses 131
Work 131
Moving to China 132
Accommodation 132
Entertainment 136
Spectator Sports 136
Shopping 137

CHINESE CUISINE   139

The Northern School 140
The Eastern School 141
The Western School 143
The Southern School 145
Food Etiquette 146
Uyghur Food 147
Drinks 148

GETTING THERE & AWAY   150

Air 150
Land 156
Trans-Siberian Railway 160
Sea 164
Organised Tours 165

GETTING AROUND   168

Air 168
Bus 169
Train 171
Car & Motorcycle 175
Bicycle 176
Hitching 178
Boat 179
Local Transport 179
Organised Tours 181

BĚIJĪNG   183

History 183
Orientation 186
Information 186
National Buildings &
Monuments 188
Parks & Gardens 198

Museums & Galleries 200
Temples & Mosques 201
Other Places to See 203
Places to Stay 208
Places to Stay – Budget 208
Places to Stay – Mid-Range ..210
Places to Stay – Top End 211

Places to Eat 213
Entertainment 217
Shopping 220
Getting There & Away 222
Getting Around 224
Around Běijīng 228
The Great Wall 228

Shísán Líng 238
Qīng Dōng Líng 239
Tánzhè Sì 239
Peking Man Site 240
Shídù 240

TIĀNJĪN 242

Around Tiānjīn 255
Tánggū 255

Jìxiàn 257
Pán Shān 258

Tiānzūn Gé 258
Wǔqīng 258

HÉBĚI 259

Shíjiāzhuāng 259
Around Shíjiāzhuāng 262

Chéngdé 263
Běidàihé 269

Qínhuángdǎo 272
Shānhǎiguān 272

SHĀNDŌNG 276

Jǐ'nán 278
Around Jǐ'nán 283
Tài Shān 283
Tài'ān 288
Around Tài'ān 291

Qūfú 291
Zōuxiàn 297
Línzī 297
Qīngdǎo 298
Around Qīngdǎo 304

Yāntái 305
Pénglái 308
Wēihǎi 309

JIĀNGSŪ 310

Nánjīng 310
Around Nánjīng 326
Zhènjiāng 327
Yángzhōu 329

Yíxīng Xiàn 334
Dīngshān 335
Sūzhōu 341
Around Sūzhōu 350

Xúzhōu 353
Liányúngǎng 355

ĀNHUĪ 357

Héféi 357
Bózhōu 361
Túnxī 366

Around Túnxī 367
Jiǔhuá Shān 367
Wúhú 369

Guìchí 369

SHÀNGHǍI 370

History 370
Government 371
Economy 372
Orientation 373
Information 374

The Bund 377
French Concession 378
Things to See 378
Pǔdōng Xīnqū 385
Places to Stay 387

Places to Eat 391
Entertainment 393
Shopping 395
Getting There & Away 397
Getting Around 399

ZHÈJIĀNG 401

Hángzhōu 401
Shàoxīng 410
Around Shàoxīng 413

Níngbō 413
Pǔtuóshān 416
Xīkǒu 419

Wēnzhōu 420
Tiāntái Shān 422
Chún'ān Xiàn 422

FÚJIÀN 423

Fúzhōu 423
Xiàmén 428
Gǔlàng Yǔ 429

Yǒngdìng 434
Quánzhōu 434
Around Quánzhōu 436

Méizhōu 437
Wǔyí Shān 437

LIÁONÍNG 440

Shěnyáng 440
Around Shěnyáng 447
Dàlián 448

Around Dàlián 455
Bīngyù Gōu 456
Dāndōng 456

Around Dāndōng 459

JÍLÍN 460

Chángchūn 460
Jílín 465

Around Jilin 468
Chángbái Shān 468

Around Chángbái Shān 472

HĒILÓNGJIĀNG 473

Hāěrbīn 473
Around Hāěrbīn 483
Mǔdānjiāng 483
Jìngpò Hú 483

Suífēnhé 484
Wǔdàlián Chí 485
Hēilóngjiāng Biānjìng 486
Qíqíhā'ěr 488

Zhālóng Zìrán
Bǎohùqū 488

SHĀNXĪ 491

Tàiyuán 491
Around Tàiyuán 495
Píngyáo 496

Ruìchéng 498
Yùnchéng 498
Wǔtái Shān & Táihuái 499

Dàtóng 502
Around Dàtóng 505

SHĀNXĪ (SHAANXI) 508

Xī'ān 508
Around Xī'ān 519

Xiányáng 522
Yán'ān 526

Yúlín 529

HÉNÁN 531

Zhèngzhōu 532
Sōng Shān 536
Luòyáng 539

Lóngmén Shíkū 543
Ānyáng 544
Around Ānyáng 545

Jīgōng Shān 546
Kāifēng 546

HÚBĚI 551

Wǔhàn 551
Wǔdāng Shān 560

Shénnóngjià 561
Yíchāng 561

JIĀNGXĪ 566

Jiǔjiāng 574
Lúshān 576

Yīngtán 578
Jǐnggāng Shān 578

HÚNÁN 581

Chángshā 581
Zhūzhōu 592
Yuèyáng 592

Héngyáng 594
Héng Shān 595
Huáihuà 596

Wǔlíngyuán & Zhāngjiājiè ..596
Měngdònghé 599

HONG KONG 601

History & Politics 601
Orientation 603
Information 603
Activities 611
Organised Tours 612
Getting There & Away 612

Getting Around 616
Kowloon 619
Places to Stay 622
Shopping 626
Hong Kong Island 627
Places to Stay 635

Shopping 638
New Territories 638
Places to Stay 639
Outlying Islands 640

MACAU 643

Language 644	Places to Stay 654	Getting There & Away 658
Information 644	Places to Eat 656	Getting Around 659
Things to See 649	Entertainment 657	
Special Events 651	Shopping 658	

GUǍNGDŌNG 661

Guǎngzhōu 663	Zhūhǎi 688	Around Zhàoqìng 696
Around Guǎngzhōu 680	Around Zhūhǎi 692	Zhànjiāng 696
Shēnzhèn 683	Zhōngshān 693	Shàntóu 699
Around Shēnzhèn 688	Around Zhōngshān 693	Around Shàntóu 702
Hǔmén 688	Zhàoqìng 693	Cháozhōu 702

HǍINÁN DǍO 704

History 704	Hǎikǒu 707	Sānyà 712
Climate 704	Wénchāng 711	Tōngzhá 715
Population & People 704	Xīnglóng 711	Qióngzhōng 716
Orientation 705	Xīncūn 711	

GUǍNGXĪ 717

Nánníng 719	Yángshuò 736	Liǔzhōu 745
Around Nánníng 723	Around Yángshuò 740	Wúzhōu 748
Guìlín 727	Lóngshèng 741	
Around Guìlín 735	Sānjiāng 744	

GUÌZHŌU 752

History 752	Around Ānshùn 761	Chóng'ān 767
Festivals 752	Western Guìzhōu 763	Kǎilǐ to Lìpíng 767
Guìyáng 753	Kǎilǐ 764	Lìpíng to Guìlín 767
Ānshùn 759	Around Kǎilǐ 766	Zūnyì 767

YÚNNÁN 770

History 770	Zhōngdiàn 817	Bǎoshān Region 835
Kūnmíng 772	Around Zhōngdiàn 819	Bǎoshān 836
Around Kūnmíng 786	Déqīn 819	Around Bǎoshān 838
Shí Lín 790	Around Déqīn 820	Téngchōng 838
Lùnán 793	Xīshuāngbǎnnà	Around Téngchōng 840
Xiàguān 793	Region 820	Déhóng Region 842
Around Xiàguān 794	Special Events 822	Yíngjiāng 842
Dàlǐ 795	Sīmáo 822	Ruìlì 843
Around Dàlǐ 801	Jǐnghóng 822	Around Ruìlì 846
Dàlǐ to Lìjiāng 802	Around Jǐnghóng 829	Wǎndīng 847
Lìjiāng 803	Dàměnglóng 832	Mángshì 849
Around Lìjiāng 810	Around Dàměnglóng 834	

CHÓNGQÌNG 851

Chóngqìng City 851	Dàzú Xiàn 860

CRUISING DOWNRIVER 863

Tickets 863	Fares 864	The Route 865
Classes 864	Food 864	

SÌCHUĀN 870

Chéngdū 872
Around Chéngdū 888
Éméi Shān 891
Lèshān 898
Méishān 903
Western Sichuān & The Road
to Tibet 903
Kāngdìng 904
Around Kāngdìng 906

Móxī 906
Hǎiluógōu Bīngchuān
Gōngyuán 907
Lúdìng 909
Sìchuān-Tibet Highway –
Northern Route 910
Sìchuān-Tibet Highway –
Southern Route 911
Northern Sìchuān 913

Sōngpān 914
Huánglóng 916
Jiǔzhài Gōu 917
Nánpíng 920
Chéngdū to Xiàhé 921

XĪNJIĀNG 922

Ürümqi 925
Around Ürümqi 932
Dàhéyàn 932
Turpan 933
Around Turpan 935
Around Kùchē 939
South-West Xīnjiāng –
Kashgaria 940

Kashgar 940
Karakoram Highway 950
Southern Silk Road 950
Yengisar 951
Yarkand 951
Karghilik 952
Hotan 953
Hotan to Golmud 955

Northen Xīnjiāng 955
Bù'ěrjīn 955
Jímǔnǎi 958
Tǎchéng 958
Yīníng 959
Around Yīníng 961

GĀNSÙ 962

Lánzhōu 962
Around Lánzhōu 968
Línxià 969
Xiàhé 970
Around Xiàhé 973
Hézuò 973

Lǎngmùsì 974
Hexi Corridor 974
Jiāyùguān 974
Around Jiāyùguān 976
Liǔyuán 977
Dūnhuáng 978

Around Dūnhuáng 981
Eastern Gānsù 984
Píngliáng 984
Around Píngliáng 985
Màijī Shān & Tiānshuǐ 985
Luòmén 987

NÍNGXIÀ 989

Yínchuān 989
Around Yínchuān 994

Zhōngwèi 994
Around Zhōngwèi 996

Gùyuán 997

INNER MONGOLIA 999

History 999
Hohhot 1002
Around Hohhot 1005
The Grasslands 1005

Bāotóu 1006
Around Bāotóu 1009
Dōngshèng 1010
Around Dōngshèng 1011

Hǎilāěr 1011
Mǎnzhōulǐ 1012
Around Mǎnzhōulǐ 1014
Xanadu 1014

TIBET 1015

History 1015
Trekking 1017
Travel Restrictions 1018
What to Bring 1018
Dangers & Annoyances 1018
Getting Around 1019

Lhasa 1019
Around Lhasa 1027
Yarlung Valley 1028
Yamdrok-Tso Lake 1029
Gyantse 1029
Shigatse 1029

Sakya 1032
Rongphu Monastery &
Everest Base Camp 1032
Tingri 1032
Zhangmu 1033
Zhangmu to Kodari 1033

QĪNGHǍI 1034

Xīníng 1036
Around Xīníng 1039

Golmud 1041
Getting to Tibet 1042

6 Contents – Text

LANGUAGE   1044

Mandarin 1044   Portuguese 1054
Cantonese 1052   Tibetan 1056

GLOSSARY   1059

People 1062   Historical Events 1065

THIS BOOK   1066

ACKNOWLEDGMENTS   1067

INDEX   1077

Text 1077   Boxed Text 1087

MAP LEGEND   back page

METRIC CONVERSION   inside back cover

Contents – Maps

GETTING THERE & AWAY

Sea Routes.........................164

GETTING AROUND

Domestic Airfares...............168

BĚIJĪNG

Běijīng Municipality 185	Central Běijīng 204	Huànghuā Great Wall
Běijīng 194	Běijīng Subway Routes.......227	Walking Routes 232

TIĀNJĪN

Tiānjīn Municipality 243	Central Tiānjīn 246
Tiānjīn 244	Tánggū 256

HÉBĚI

Héběi...................................260	Běidàihé, Qínhuángdǎo &	Shānhǎiguān 273
Shíjiāzhuāng.......................261	Shānhǎiguān 270	
Chéngdé 264	Běidàihé..............................271	

SHĀNDŌNG

Shāndōng 277	Tài'ān 288	Yāntái 306
Jǐ'nán..................................280	Qūfù 292	
Tài Shān..............................284	Qīngdǎo 300	

JIĀNGSŪ

Jiāngsū................................311	Wúxī 338	Zhōuzhuāng........................352
Nánjīng 316	Around Wúxī & Tài Hú 340	Xúzhōu 354
Zhènjiāng............................328	Sūzhōu 342	
Yángzhōu 332	Around Sūzhōu 350	

ĀNHUĪ

Ānhuī...................................358	Héféi 360	Huáng Shān........................363

SHÀNGHǍI

Shànghǎi Municipality 372	Shànghǎi 374	Central Shànghǎi 380

ZHÈJIĀNG

Zhèjiāng..............................402	Shàoxīng 412	Pǔtuóshān 418
Hángzhōu 404	Níngbō.................................414	Wēnzhōu.............................420

FÚJIÀN

Fújiàn..................................424	Xiàmén & Gǔlàng Yǔ 430
Fúzhōu.................................426	Quánzhōu 436

LIÁONÍNG

Liáoníng...............................441	Dàlián 452	Dāndōng 458
Shěnyáng.............................444	Around Dàlián 456	

8 Contents – Maps

JÍLÍN

Jílín 461
Chángchūn 462
Jílín 466
Tiān Chí & Chángbái Shān .. 469

HĒILÓNGJIĀNG

Hēilóngjiāng 474
Hāěrbīn 478

SHĀNXĪ

Shānxī 492
Tàiyuán 494
Wǔtái Shān 499
Táihuái 500
Dàtóng 502

SHĀNXĪ (SHAANXI)

Shānxī 509
Xī'ān 514
Around Xī'ān 520
Huá Shān 525
Yán'ān 528

HÉNÁN

Hénán 532
Zhèngzhōu 534
Around Zhèngzhōu 537
Luòyáng 540
Kāifēng 548

HÚBĚI

Húběi 552
Wǔhàn 554
Yíchāng 562

JIĀNGXĪ

Jiāngxī 567
Nánchāng 568
Jǐngdézhèn 572
Jiǔjiāng 574
Lúshān 576

HÚNÁN

Húnán 582
Chángshā 584
Sháoshān 588
Yuèyáng 592
Wǔlíngyuán Scenic Area ... 597

HONG KONG

Hong Kong 606
Hong Kong Districts 609
Kowloon 620
Central Hong Kong 628
Wanchai & Causeway Bay .. 632

MACAU

Macau Peninsula 646
Central Macau 652

GUǍNGDŌNG

Guǎngdōng 662
Shāmiàn Dǎo 666
Guǎngzhōu 670
Fóshān 682
Shēnzhèn 684
Zhūhǎi 690
Zhàoqìng 694
Dǐnghú Shān 697
Zhànjiāng 698
Shàntóu 700
Cháozhōu 702

HǍINÁN DǍO

Hǎinán Dǎo 706
Hǎikǒu 708
Sānyà 714

GUǍNGXĪ

Guǎngxī 718
Nánníng 720
Guìlín 730
Yángshuò 736
Around Yángshuò 740
Lóngjǐ Tītián 742
Lóngshèng 743
Liǔzhōu 746
Wúzhōu 748

GUÌZHŌU

Guìzhōu 753	Ānshùn 760	Zūnyì 768
Guìyáng 754	Kǎilǐ 765	

YÚNNÁN

Yúnnán 771	Dàlǐ & Ěrhǎi Hú 801	Jǐnghóng 824
Kūnmíng 778	Lìjiāng 804	Bǎoshān 836
Around Kūnmíng	Lìjiāng – Old Town............808	Téngchōng............840
(Diān Chí) 788	Around Lìjiāng 811	Ruìlì 844
Shí Lín (Stone Forest)............791	Zhōngdiàn 817	Wǎndīng 848
Dàlǐ 796	Xīshuāngbǎnnà 821	Mángshì............849

CHÓNGQÌNG

Chóngqìng Municipality......852	Chóngqìng............854	

CRUISING DOWNRIVER

Cháng Jiāng (Chóngqìng to Shànghǎi)............866		

SÌCHUĀN

Sìchuān 871	Dūjiāngyàn 890	Sōngpān 914
Chéngdū 877	Éméi Shān 894	Jiǔzhài Gōu 918
Qīngchéng Shān 888	Lèshān 900	

XĪNJIĀNG

Xīnjiāng 923	Around Turpan............936	Yīníng 960
Ürümqi 926	Kashgar 942	
Turpan 934	Bù'ěrjīn 956	

GĀNSÙ

Gānsù 963	Xiàhé & Lābǔlèng Sì............972	Dūnhuáng 978
Lánzhōu............964	Jiāyùguān............975	Tiānshuǐ............986

NÍNGXIÀ

Níngxià 990	Yínchuān 992	Zhōngwèi............995

INNER MONGOLIA

Inner Mongolia 1000	East Bāotóu 1007	
Hohhot 1004	West Bāotóu 1008	

TIBET

Tibet 1016	Barkhor Area 1024	
Lhasa............1022	Shigatse 1030	

QĪNGHǍI

Qīnghǎi 1035	Xīníng 1036	Golmud 1042

MAP INDEX

RUSSIA

KAZAKHSTAN

MONGOLIA

Bu'erjin
p956

Yining p960

KYRGYZSTAN

Ürümqi p926

Turpan p934
Around Turpan
p936

XINJIANG

GANSU

Kashgar p942

Dunhuang
p978

Jiayuguan
p975

Xining p103

Lanzhou
p964

Golmud p1042

Xiahe &
Labuleng Si
(Labrang
Monastery)
p972

QINGHAI

Jiuzhai Gou p918
Songpan p914

PROVINCE MAPS

Anhui p358
Beijing
  Municipality p185
Chongqing
  Municipality p852
Fujian p424
Gansu p963
Guangdong p662
Guangxi p718
Guizhou p753
Hainan Dao p706
Hebei p260
Heilongjiang p474
Henan p532
Hong Kong p606
Hubei p552
Hunan p582
Inner Mongolia p1000
Jiangsu p311
Jiangxi p567
Jilin p461
Liaoning p441
Macau p646
Ningxia p990
Qinghai p1035
Shaanxi p509
Shandong p277
Shanghai
  Municipality p372
Shanxi p492
Sichuan p871
Tibet p1016
Tianjin
  Municipality p243
Xinjiang p923
Yunnan p771
Zhejiang p402

TIBET

SICHUAN

Chengdu p877

Lhasa p1022
Barkhor Area p1024

Qingcheng Shan
p888

Dujiangyan p890

Shigatse p1030

Emei Shan p894
Leshan p900

NEPAL

BHUTAN

Zhongdian
p817

INDIA

Lijiang p804
Lijiang Old Town p808
Around Lijiang p811

Kunming p778
Around Kunming
(Dian Chi) p788

INDIA

BANGLADESH

Baoshan p836
Tengchong p840

Dali p796
Dali & Erhai Hu
p801

Shilin
(Stone Forest)
p791

Rulli p844
Wanding p848
Mangshi p849

YUNNAN

Bay of Bengal

MYANMAR

Xishuangbanna p821
Jinghong p824

LAOS

THAILAND

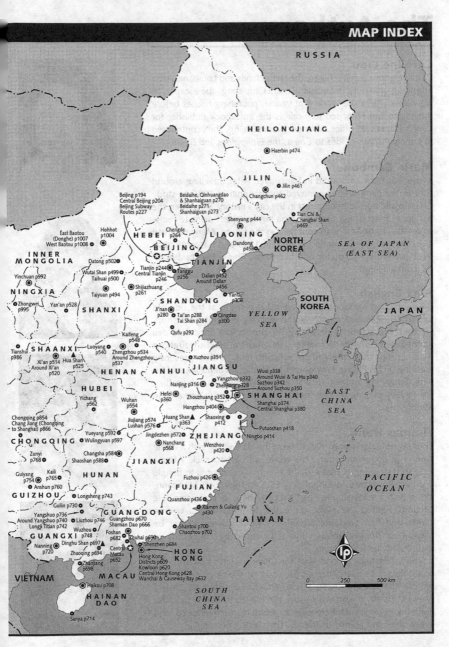

MAP INDEX

The Authors

Caroline Liou

Caroline grew up in Michigan, the Netherlands and Louisiana. After attending university in Louisiana and Hong Kong, she escaped to New York where she worked at various publishing houses before moving to San Francisco to work as the guidebook publisher for Lonely Planet's US office. She now lives in Běijīng. She's contributed to Lonely Planet's guides to *China*, the *Philippines* and *Beijing*.

Marie Cambon

Marie was born and raised in Vancouver. After travelling around Asia in the early 80s, she moved to Shànghǎi in 1986 to study Chinese and pursue her interest in the city's history. Since then she has spent most of her time in China but has great plans to rediscover the North American continent in the future. Marie received a master's degree in communication in 1993 and has worked as freelance writer, translator and filmmaker. This is her third book for Lonely Planet.

Alex English

Brought up in Melbourne, Alex got his first job at the ripe old age of 10, selling newspapers and working in a butcher's shop. He then spent four years eating the profits in a chocolate deli at Melbourne's Victoria market. Alex has travelled throughout Asia, Europe and the Indian subcontinent, and is presently working on his PhD in Environmental Studies. When Alex and his wife, Eunkyong and son, Oscar, are not roaming the globe they are usually playing on the swings at a local park in Seoul or in Melbourne.

Thomas Huhti

Thomas Huhti hails from Wisconsin in the US and still calls it home when not barrelling around the world with a backpack. After a long stint studying in East Asia, he eventually managed to finagle a university degree in Linguistics, ESL, and (almost) Mandarin, along with a fellowship to head back to China for two years. He circumnavigated the globe thereafter to jump-start a writing career and flee graduate school. He would always rather be playing ice hockey, though this is balanced by epic bouts of loafing, movies and reading.

This is Thomas' second stint for China; he also co-wrote the first edition of Lonely Planet's *South-West China* guide, helped update the latest *Canada* guide, and has assisted on Lonely Planet's *Thailand* and *Myanmar*. He has contributed to other guidebooks on French Polynesia, Baja and Northern Mexico, and every nook and cranny of the US. He is a dog person.

Korina Miller

Korina lived the first 18 years of her life on Vancouver Island. Since then she hasn't lived in any one place for longer than 10 months, managing to take in parts of Japan, India, Egypt, Europe and South America as well as squeezing in a degree in Communications and Canadian Studies. In 1997 she spent six months in Shànghǎi and Líjiāng as an intern researching cooperatives and ecotourism. She has recently begun studying for an MA in Migration Studies and is living happily ever after with a fellow nomad she picked up in a Brighton discoteque and eloped with to a beach in Tobago. This is Korina's first book for LP.

Bradley Wong

A California native, Brad Wong's interest in China started in 1993 when he visited Guǎngzhōu on his first trip to the country, dined on cheap dim sum and searched for his grandparents' village.

Since then, he has completed a 2000-kilometre solo bicycle trek from Běijīng to Húnán, tumbled into a countryside commode in Hénán, cleared overgrown rice fields with peasants and met some unfriendly baboons on a sacred Buddhist mountain.

A journalist by training, Brad most recently worked for the *Pacific Daily News on Guam*, where he covered politics and illegal immigration. He also has worked for the *Salinas Californian* and the *Congressional Quarterly Weekly Report* in Washington, DC. He has contributed essays about China and travelling to two anthologies, including one from Lonely Planet. He also was a contributing writer for Lonely Planet's *USA* guide.

He has studied Chinese at Jinan University in Guǎngzhōu and is continuing his studies at the Beijing Language and Culture University.

FROM THE AUTHORS

Caroline Special thanks to Amy, William, Evie and Max Soileau, for always having an open door. *Duo xie* to many others who helped out in immeasurable ways: NBC bureau chief and long-term Běijīng resident Chris Billing, for his companionship, humour and insight into how things really work in Běijīng; Amanda Hudson for offering me a respite from Běijīng's mean streets; Julia Cheung, partner in crime in exploring Běijīng's nightlife and shopping scene; my good friend Judy Xing; Ye Lin of BTG (a shining example that CTS really can help out); Su Li; and Alex English for helping to wrap up the stray ends. Thanks also to Calum Macleod and Zhang Lijia, Kaiser Kuo and the staff of ChinaNow.com, Chang Enlai and William Lindesay for their valuable insights and contributions to the book. Finally, a huge pat on the back for LP staff without whose expertise this book could never have been put together: Greg Alford, Martin Heng, Lara Morcombe, Leanne, Lucy and Tim.

14 The Authors

Alex Thanks to all the infinite number of patient and polite Chinese who endured my many inquisitions from Yīníng to Mǎnzhōulì. A nod of appreciation to the many taxi drivers for acting as local tourist offices. Thanks also to the resourceful Bokhi and her wonderful family for setting us on our way in the best shape; Lao Xu and Wu Laoshi in Sūzhōu for their humour and care; Ablimit (Elvis), for his help in Kashgar; Bradley Mayhew for holding up Western Xīnjiāng; Sarah Walters for her company along a dark Yellow dirt road; Caroline Liou for looking after a very dirty and smelly drover; and of course all the team of cartos, editors and seniors for their endurance with a sometimes curly book. The biggest thanks have to go to my favourite travelling companions, Eunkyong and Oscar – thanks guys!

Marie Once again I would like to thank Jolanda Jonkhart and Ron Gluckman for giving me a great place to stay in Hong Kong. Praise goes to Randy Schuks for putting up with my bad temper in Fújiàn and northern Guǎngdōng. Thanks also to Nancy Norton Tomasko, Rocky at Phoenix, Neil Gough of *Clueless in Guangzhou*, Bradley Mayhew, Grace Chen, Maria Barbieri, Jenny Wang, OJ Tang, Xiao Zhou and Lao Chen, Kyoko Hirooka, Yukio Okuda, Tess Johnston, the Macau Tourist Association and reader Yiqun Chen who cleared up a very urgent matter regarding a misplaced northern fish delicacy mistakenly attributed to be Hángzhōu cuisine.

Tom The following accumulated boatloads of karma either proffering information or possessing unvanquishable good humour as travel partners: Lilia Cai and Neil Gough and the folks at Anna's Art Cafe (Yángshuò); Wu Zhongfu (Nánníng); the folks at the Dongba House (Líjiāng); Kevin Leung, Yan Dan, Clotilde and Axel, Lynn van Eck, Yvonee Wolters and John Pettus (Zhōngdiàn, Déqīn and/or Sōngpān); Bradley Berman (Chéngdū); and Brian Buschay (Éméi Shān, hope the knee's OK). Most of all, I dearly miss my longtime friends Azhu, Bex, Sara, Amei, Awen, and particularly Derek John (Mat) Matthewson (all Jǐnghóng) along with Pan Hai Bin (Nánníng). And finally, a tip of the ballcap to the irrepressibly cheerful, optimistic Ms Ma and her boyfriend Hot Springs, both of whom made the long, long Déqīn travail so worthwhile in the end; I'm certain it was their attitude alone that forced all malignant weather aside. A nod to all the readers who took the time to write in; it really helps us! And a special thank you to Hyeon, for absolutely everything.

Once again, thanks to the durability of modern personal stereos and the artistry of Dou Wei, Jimmy Lafave, Husker Du, the Gufs (Milwaukee), Tsuyoshi Nagabuchi and Walt Whitman. And thank you to the wonderful people of China. Your curiosity, eagerness to help, and especially willingness to smile are unparalleled.

Korina A thousand thank yous to Marie Cambon for introducing me to the world of Lonely Planet, for the home away from home and for helping me to keep my sense of humour. A huge thank you to Kristen Odijk for the opportunity, to Jen Jones for getting me there, to Rosa Wang for her help with translations, to Trisha Purchas for taking my photo, to the tomato farmer of Lìxī for getting me to the train on time, and to all of the people I met en route for answering my incessant number of questions. A very special thank you to my family for their boundless support and to Paul ... for everything.

Bradley Much thanks goes out to everyone who has helped me better understand the world's most populous country.

My participation in this project would not have been possible without the generosity of my former editors at the *Pacific Daily News on Guam*. They gave me a three-month sabbatical to pursue this opportunity.

Also, I would still be a reader rather than a writer of Lonely Planet books if it wasn't for the great help and support from Caroline Liou, who I accidentally met at a Vietnamese restaurant in Oakland, California, a few years ago.

And my appreciation goes to Greg Alford, Martin Heng and the Melbourne office staff for their patience and assistance.

Much thanks to the numerous tourism officials and residents who gave me insight into a particular city or area, specifically Zhai Yan for the wonderful tour of Jǐngzhēn's porcelain industry, Cheng Hong Qing for insights about Wǔhàn, Wei Min for background on Húběi and Chen Zhong Jee and Mr Ho for their explanations about Sōng Shān.

And to my friends Mary Chang, Martin Dare, Masahiro Umeda, Norman Mah, Kenneth Chen, Henry Chen, Sylvia Chen and Liu Dan: our discussions were great and the company was the best. Thanks for the help.

Of course, my parents, sister and relatives have been – and still are – the best.

In the future, I hope more people will be able to travel the globe.

Foreword

ABOUT LONELY PLANET GUIDEBOOKS

The story begins with a classic travel adventure: Tony and Maureen Wheeler's 1972 journey across Europe and Asia to Australia. Useful information about the overland trail did not exist at that time, so Tony and Maureen published the first Lonely Planet guidebook to meet a growing need.

From a kitchen table, then from a tiny office in Melbourne (Australia), Lonely Planet has become the largest independent travel publisher in the world, an international company with offices in Melbourne, Oakland (USA), London (UK) and Paris (France).

Today Lonely Planet guidebooks cover the globe. There is an ever-growing list of books and there's information in a variety of forms and media. Some things haven't changed. The main aim is still to help make it possible for adventurous travellers to get out there – to explore and better understand the world.

At Lonely Planet we believe travellers can make a positive contribution to the countries they visit – if they respect their host communities and spend their money wisely. Since 1986 a percentage of the income from each book has been donated to aid projects and human rights campaigns.

Updates Lonely Planet thoroughly updates each guidebook as often as possible. This usually means there are around two years between editions, although for more unusual or more stable destinations the gap can be longer. Check the imprint page (following the colour map at the beginning of the book) for publication dates.

Between editions up-to-date information is available in two free newsletters – the paper *Planet Talk* and email *Comet* (to subscribe, contact any Lonely Planet office) – and on our Web site at www.lonelyplanet.com. The *Upgrades* section of the Web site covers a number of important and volatile destinations and is regularly updated by Lonely Planet authors. *Scoop* covers news and current affairs relevant to travellers. And, lastly, the *Thorn Tree* bulletin board and *Postcards* section of the site carry unverified, but fascinating, reports from travellers.

Correspondence The process of creating new editions begins with the letters, postcards and emails received from travellers. This correspondence often includes suggestions, criticisms and comments about the current editions. Interesting excerpts are immediately passed on via newsletters and the Web site, and everything goes to our authors to be verified when they're researching on the road. We're keen to get more feedback from organisations or individuals who represent communities visited by travellers.

> Lonely Planet gathers information for everyone who's curious about the planet – and especially for those who explore it first-hand. Through guidebooks, phrasebooks, activity guides, maps, literature, newsletters, image library, TV series and Web site we act as an information exchange for a worldwide community of travellers.

Research Authors aim to gather sufficient practical information to enable travellers to make informed choices and to make the mechanics of a journey run smoothly. They also research historical and cultural background to help enrich the travel experience and allow travellers to understand and respond appropriately to cultural and environmental issues.

Authors don't stay in every hotel because that would mean spending a couple of months in each medium-sized city and, no, they don't eat at every restaurant because that would mean stretching belts beyond capacity. They do visit hotels and restaurants to check standards and prices, but feedback based on readers' direct experiences can be very helpful.

Many of our authors work undercover, others aren't so secretive. None of them accept freebies in exchange for positive write-ups. And none of our guidebooks contain any advertising.

Production Authors submit their raw manuscripts and maps to offices in Australia, USA, UK or France. Editors and cartographers – all experienced travellers themselves – then begin the process of assembling the pieces. When the book finally hits the shops, some things are already out of date, we start getting feedback from readers and the process begins again …

WARNING & REQUEST

Things change – prices go up, schedules change, good places go bad and bad places go bankrupt – nothing stays the same. So, if you find things better or worse, recently opened or long since closed, please tell us and help make the next edition even more accurate and useful. We genuinely value all the feedback we receive. Julie Young coordinates a well travelled team that reads and acknowledges every letter, postcard and email and ensures that every morsel of information finds its way to the appropriate authors, editors and cartographers for verification.

Everyone who writes to us will find their name in the next edition of the appropriate guidebook. They will also receive the latest issue of *Planet Talk*, our quarterly printed newsletter, or *Comet*, our monthly email newsletter. Subscriptions to both newsletters are free. The very best contributions will be rewarded with a free guidebook.

Excerpts from your correspondence may appear in new editions of Lonely Planet guidebooks, the Lonely Planet Web site, *Planet Talk* or *Comet*, so please let us know if you *don't* want your letter published or your name acknowledged.

Send all correspondence to the Lonely Planet office closest to you:

Australia: PO Box 617, Hawthorn, Victoria 3122
USA: 150 Linden St, Oakland, CA 94607
UK: 10A Spring Place, London NW5 3BH
France: 1 rue du Dahomey, 75011 Paris

Or email us at: talk2us@lonelyplanet.com.au

For news, views and updates see our Web site: www.lonelyplanet.com

HOW TO USE A LONELY PLANET GUIDEBOOK

The best way to use a Lonely Planet guidebook is any way you choose. At Lonely Planet we believe the most memorable travel experiences are often those that are unexpected, and the finest discoveries are those you make yourself. Guidebooks are not intended to be used as if they provide a detailed set of infallible instructions!

Contents All Lonely Planet guidebooks follow roughly the same format. The Facts about the Destination chapters or sections give background information ranging from history to weather. Facts for the Visitor gives practical information on issues like visas and health. Getting There & Away gives a brief starting point for researching travel to and from the destination. Getting Around gives an overview of the transport options when you arrive.

The peculiar demands of each destination determine how subsequent chapters are broken up, but some things remain constant. We always start with background, then proceed to sights, places to stay, places to eat, entertainment, getting there and away, and getting around information – in that order.

Heading Hierarchy Lonely Planet headings are used in a strict hierarchical structure that can be visualised as a set of Russian dolls. Each heading (and its following text) is encompassed by any preceding heading that is higher on the hierarchical ladder.

Entry Points We do not assume guidebooks will be read from beginning to end, but that people will dip into them. The traditional entry points are the list of contents and the index. In addition, however, some books have a complete list of maps and an index map illustrating map coverage.

There may also be a colour map that shows highlights. These highlights are dealt with in greater detail in the Facts for the Visitor chapter, along with planning questions and suggested itineraries. Each chapter covering a geographical region usually begins with a locator map and another list of highlights. Once you find something of interest in a list of highlights, turn to the index.

Maps Maps play a crucial role in Lonely Planet guidebooks and include a huge amount of information. A legend is printed on the back page. We seek to have complete consistency between maps and text, and to have every important place in the text captured on a map. Map key numbers usually start in the top left corner.

Although inclusion in a guidebook usually implies a recommendation we cannot list every good place. Exclusion does not necessarily imply criticism. In fact there are a number of reasons why we might exclude a place – sometimes it is simply inappropriate to encourage an influx of travellers.

Introduction

As a travel destination China offers an endless diversity of historical and architectural masterpieces and impressive natural landscapes. It is home to one of the world's longest continuous civilisations, with a rich heritage of art, architecture and language. It's a land of picturesque rural landscapes, crowded urban cityscapes and captivating beauty – from the windswept plains of the Gobi Desert to Guìzhōu's fascinating karst hills, from the notorious northern face of Mt Everest to volcanic crater lakes.

Historically, the 20th century wreaked massive change and upheaval upon the Chinese. Two revolutions – the first ended the Qing dynasty and the second saw the Chinese Communist Party (CCP) rise to power – broke down centuries-old traditions, such as the reliance on extensive family structures and Confucian ethics. For a country that refined its culture so gradually that it seemed clothed in a cloak of immutability, the past 100 years have been a watershed. Now, as the celebrations that marked the 50th anniversary of the People's Republic of China (PRC) fade from memory, the momentum continues.

Growing economic prosperity has been the single most important shift in the past two decades and China is reaping the benefits of Deng Xiaoping's economic reforms. Privatisation and the influx of foreign capital has funded modernisation programs and provided access to modern technology. While on the one hand the sheer size and potential of China's consumer market has gained the attention of foreign firms, on the other the importation of foreign technology and ideas has fostered an admiration for global culture within the country. Western food, dress, art, film and music have infiltrated China on a massive scale. In the large cities on the eastern seaboard, the nouveau riche dress in the latest European fashions, drive Mercedes-Benz's, collect household whitegoods, dine on haute cuisine and dance to the latest beats in all-night discos.

As with most change, there is a downside. The rise of a new wealthy class has widened the gap between the haves and the have-nots. While GDP per head in China's richer east coast averages over US$1000, in it's poorest province, Guìzhōu, GDP per head is a meagre US$280 per year. While city dwellers move ahead economically, the other two-thirds of China's population live in rural areas. Rural peasants and workers in search of economic salvation are streaming into the large cities where they face certain discrimination. The many who are unable to find legitimate work are reduced to begging, prostitution, petty and organised crime. The dismantling of unprofitable state-owned companies have resulted in a rise in unemployment. These problems have been compounded by a growth in corruption that spreads from the lowest-ranking officials right up to party leaders. Politically, the CCP has been inflexible in its resistance to moves for political freedom; human rights violations continue to draw the attention of the world's media. Population growth, untrammelled industrialisation and poor resource management have had devastating effects on the environment, particularly on natural habitats and species diversity, and air and water quality.

Tourism, however, has bloomed in this new economic climate. Hotels, restaurants, Internet cafes, tour operators and theme parks are sprouting everywhere. At the same time, Party officials are realising the monetary benefits of restoring and protecting cultural and natural sights. Problems that plagued travellers in the recent past, such as the dual-pricing system, are fast disappearing, making travel in China is more accessible and comfortable.

Be aware, however, that travel in China can be overwhelming, with language the single most difficult barrier to overcome. This guidebook has undertaken to facilitate the ease with which you master some basic Chinese by providing tonal marks wherever possible. Familiarising yourself with the Chinese words for hotel, restaurant, park, temple, station and so on will make getting around a little easier and, hopefully, will lead to greater interaction with Chinese people.

Facts about China

HISTORY
Mythological Beginnings

The Chinese claim a history of 5000 years, but early 'records' are of a mythological and legendary nature. The very existence of the Xia dynasty, documented in early Chinese histories as the first Chinese dynasty, still awaits archaeological verification.

According to legend, the Xia dynasty was preceded by three sovereigns and five emperors. The first of the three sovereigns, Fuxi, is usually depicted alongside his wife and sister, the goddess Nügua. The two are human from the waist up, but have the tails of dragons. Nügua is credited with having fashioned human beings from clay and having created the institution of marriage, while Fuxi bestowed the gifts of hunting, fishing and animal husbandry.

The ox-headed Shennong, another of the three sovereigns, bestowed agriculture and knowledge of the medicinal properties of plants on the Chinese.

The five emperors (like the three sovereigns) are also credited with having founded certain key elements of the Chinese cultural tradition. For example, the first of them, Huang Di, is said to have brought the agricultural calendar, boats, armour and pottery to the Chinese people. A later emperor, Shun, devised the writing brush. Dynastic rule commenced when the same Shun abdicated in favour of Yu, the first emperor of the Xia.

Xia & Shang Dynasties

Many historians believe that the Xia dynasty actually may have existed, although not in the terms depicted in Chinese mythology. The dynasty is claimed to have held power for nearly five centuries from 2200 to 1700 BC, before becoming corrupt and being overthrown by the Shang.

There is more evidence of the existence of the Shang than of the Xia. Archaeological finds have shown for certain that a state existed in the Huáng Hé (Yellow River) plain in the present provinces of Shāndōng, Shānxī and Shaanxi, and that it held power from 1554 to 1045 BC. It was an agricultural society that practised a form of ancestor worship. It was also marked by the presence of what seems to be a caste of high priests who practised divination using so-called oracle bones. Associated with ancestor worship and divination are the Shang bronze vessels, the surfaces of which are covered with extraordinarily detailed linear designs. Like the Xia before it, the Shang dynasty fell prey to corruption and degeneracy, and was toppled by the Zhou.

Zhou Dynasty

Like the Shang before it, little is known with any great certainty about the Zhou dynasty (1100–221 BC). It is thought that they were a nomadic tribe who came under the influence of the Shang and later displaced it. The Zhou capital was known as Hao and was near Chāng'ān (present-day Xī'ān), the site that was to become the imperial seat of power for many subsequent Chinese dynasties. The Zhou also established another power centre close to present-day Luòyáng in Hénán, from where they governed the subjugated Shang. The Zhou social structure seems to have been heavily influenced by the Shang, from whom they inherited the practices of divination and ancestor worship.

Historians generally divide the Zhou period into the Western Zhou (1100–771 BC) and the Eastern Zhou (770–221 BC). The demarcation point is the sacking of the traditional Zhou capital of Hao by barbarian tribes, the transfer of power to Luòyáng and a loss of effective control by the Zhou over its feudatory states. Nevertheless, Zhou nobles remained symbolic heads of state over a land of warring kingdoms until 221 BC, when they were displaced by the Qin.

The Eastern Zhou, though riven by strife, is thought of as the crucible of Chinese culture. The traditional Chinese division of the period into the Spring and Autumn period (722–481 BC) and the Warring States period (453–221 BC) doesn't follow any historical logic, but rather refers to the periods covered by two historical books of the same names, written during the period, which were to become cornerstones of the classical education system until the Qing collapsed in 1911.

The *Spring & Autumn Annals* is traditionally ascribed to Confucius (551–479 BC), a scholar who wandered from state to state during these troubled times in search of a ruler who would put his ideas for the perfect state into practice.

Mandate of Heaven The Zhou period is important for the establishment of some of the most enduring Chinese political concepts. Foremost is the 'mandate of heaven', in which heaven gives wise and virtuous leaders a mandate to rule and removes it from those who are evil and corrupt. It was a concept that was later extended to incorporate the Taoist theory that heaven expresses disapproval of bad rulers through natural disasters such as earthquakes, floods and plagues of locusts.

In keeping with this was the idea that heaven also expressed its displeasure with corrupt rulers through rebellion and withdrawal of support by the ruled. This has been referred to as the 'right to rebellion'. It is a slippery concept, because the right to rebellion could only be confirmed by success.

Nevertheless, rebellious expressions of heaven's will were an essential ingredient in China's dynastic cycle, and mark an essential difference with, say, Japan, where the authority of the imperial family derives from a single lineage that, according to legend, can be traced back to the Sun goddess.

Qin Dynasty

The tenuous authority of the Zhou ended in the 3rd century BC, when the state of Qin united the Chinese, for the first time, into a single empire. The First Exalted Emperor Qin Shihuang ruled only from 221 to 207 BC, and is remembered above all for his tyranny and cruelty. At the same time, the Qin dynasty developed administrative institutions that were to remain features of the Chinese state for the following 2000 years.

The state of Qin grew in power during the 5th and 4th centuries BC. In 246 BC the state conquered present-day Sìchuān and proceeded to do likewise with the remaining kingdoms that stood in its way. By 221 BC the Qin was victorious, and Qin Shihuang fashioned his conquests into an empire, giving himself the newly coined title *huángdì*, or emperor.

The Qin dynasty's chief historical legacy was its strong centralised control. It divided its territory into provincial units administered by centrally appointed scholars. Weights and measures and the writing system were standardised. All books inimical to the laws of the state were burnt in accordance with imperial edict. Construction of what much later was to become the Great Wall was undertaken largely by conscripts, of whom countless numbers perished.

Qin Shihuang's heir to the imperial throne proved ineffectual and, shaken by rebellion, the Qin capital near Chāng'ān fell to an army led by the commoner Liu Bang in 207 BC. Liu lost no time in taking the title of emperor and establishing the Han dynasty.

Han Dynasty

The Han dynasty ruled China from 206 BC to AD 220. While it held the reins of power less tightly than the preceding Qin, it nevertheless maintained many of the institutions of the dynasty that it followed. Its history is complicated by the fact that it is often divided into a Western Han and an Eastern Han, with an interregnum of 14 years (AD 9–23), during which the country was governed by the Xin.

The Western Han was a period of consolidation, notable for the true establishment of the Chinese state and the military extension of the empire's borders. The Eastern Han, after a brief period of stability, fell prey to a process of a weakening and decentralisation of power that in AD 220 saw the abdication of the last of the Han emperors and the beginning of some 400 years of turmoil.

Foreign Contacts The expansion of the Han brought the Chinese into contact with the 'barbarians' that encircled their world. As a matter of course, this contact brought both military conflict and commercial gains.

To the north, the Xiongnu (a name given to various nomadic tribes of central Asia) posed the greatest threat to China. Military expeditions were sent against these tribes, initially with much success. This in turn provided the Chinese with access to central Asia, opening up the routes that carried Chinese silk as far afield as Rome.

On the diplomatic front, links were formed with central Asian tribes, and the great Chinese explorer Zhang Qian provided the authorities with information on the possibilities of trade and alliances in northern India. During the same period, Chinese influence percolated into areas that were later to become known as Vietnam and Korea.

Decentralisation of Power

From the collapse of the Han dynasty in AD 220 until the establishment of the Sui in AD 581, China was riven by more than four centuries of internal conflict with some of the most terrible wars in the nation's history. Curiously, however, the turmoil still allowed for a widespread flowering of Buddhism and the arts.

Chinese historians refer to this period as the Wei, Jin and Southern & Northern dynasties. This is a simplification. Altogether 19 kingdoms and fiefdoms competed for power in the period of 316–439 alone. Initially the country divided into three large kingdoms; the Wei governed the area roughly north of the Cháng Jiāng (Yangzi River) while the south was represented by the Wu to the east and the Shu to the west (Sìchuān Province is still often referred to as Shu).

The Wei lasted little more than 40 years. Its successor, the Western Jin, fared not much better. By 306 its capital, Luòyáng, had fallen to Xiongnu horsemen, issuing in 150 years of bloodshed as non-Han tribes fought each other for absolute power. In the 5th century the Tuoba tribe eliminated its rivals in the north, and its Sinisised rulers set about consolidating their position through such measures as land reform. But they were to fall too, and the north divided into Eastern and Western Wei.

The Western Wei, although numerically weaker than its rival in the north, set up an efficient administrative system and disbanded Buddhist temples, confiscating much of the faith's accumulated wealth in the process. In 577 it defeated the Eastern Wei, and in 581 one of its own generals seized power and established the Sui dynasty. By 589 the Sui had southern China, and the country was once again reunified under a single government.

Sui Dynasty

The Sui dynasty (589–618) was short-lived, but its accomplishments were many. Yang Jian, the Chinese-Tuoba general who established the dynasty, was given the title Wendi, the 'Cultivated Emperor'. He began administrative reform, modelling much of it on the earlier Han institutions; the civil service was strengthened at the expense of aristocratic privilege; and land reform was undertaken. All of this, along with revisions of the law code, was to serve as the basis for the institutions of the Tang dynasty that followed fast on the heels of the Sui's collapse.

The Sui went into rapid decline under the rule of Wendi's son, Yangdi. His massive public works in restoring strategically important sections of the Great Wall and establishing the Grand Canal (which did much to achieve the economic cohesion of China) were clearly aimed at strengthening the empire. However, his three unsuccessful incursions onto Korean soil put an enormous burden on the national coffers and fanned the flames of revolt.

Tang Dynasty

Faced with disastrous military setbacks in Korea and revolt on the streets, Yangdi was assassinated by one of his high officials. Meanwhile, another Sui official, posted in the border garrison of Tàiyuán, turned his troops back on the capital. His name was Li Yuan (known posthumously as Gaozu) and he was to establish the Tang dynasty (618–907), commonly regarded by the Chinese as the most glorious period in their history.

Gaozu's grab at dynastic succession was not without contest, and it was to take 10 years before the last of his rivals was defeated. Once this was achieved, however, the Tang set about putting the house in order. A pyramidical administration was established, with the emperor at its head, two policy-formulating ministries and a Department of State Affairs below this, followed in turn by nine courts and six boards dealing with specific administrative areas. In a move to discourage the development of regional power bases, the empire was divided into 300 prefectures (zhōu) and 1500 counties (xiàn), a regional breakdown that persists to this day.

The accession of Gaozu's son, Taizong (600–49), to the imperial throne saw a continuation of the early Tang successes. Military conquests re-established Chinese control of the silk routes and contributed to an influx of traders, producing an unprecedented 'internationalisation' of Chinese society.

The major cities of Xī'ān, Luòyáng and Guǎngzhōu, as well as many other trading centres, were all home to foreign communities. Mainly from central Asia, these communities brought with them new religions, food, music and artistic traditions. Later in the Tang dynasty, foreign contact was extended to Persia, India, Malaysia, Indonesia and Japan. By the 9th century the city of Guǎngzhōu was estimated to have a foreign population of 100,000.

Buddhism also flourished under the Tang. Chinese pilgrims, notably the famous wanderer Xuan Zang, made their way to India, bringing back with them Buddhist scriptures that in their turn brought about a Buddhist renewal. Translation, which until this time had extensively Sinicised difficult Buddhist concepts, was undertaken with a new rigour, and Chinese Buddhist texts increased vastly in number. One of the consequences of this, however, was a schism in the Buddhist faith.

In reaction to the complexity of many Buddhist texts being translated from Sanskrit, the Chan school (more famously known by its Japanese name, Zen) arose. Chan looked to bypass the complexities of scriptural study through discipline and meditation, while another Buddhist phenomenon, the Pure Land school (later to become the most important form of Chinese Buddhism), concerned itself with attaining the 'Western Paradise'.

For the Chinese, the apex of Tang dynastic glory was the reign of Xuanzong (685–761), known also by the title Minghuang, or the 'Radiant Emperor'. His capital of Chāng'ān was one of the greatest cities in the world, with a population of over one million. His court was a magnet to scholars and artists throughout the country, and home for a time to writers such as Du Fu and Li Bai, perhaps China's two most famous poets. His reign similarly saw a flourishing of the arts, dance and music, as well as a remarkable religious diversity.

Some might say that all this artistic activity was an indication that the empire was beginning to go a bit soft at the core. Xuanzong's increasing preoccupation with the arts, Tantric Buddhism, Taoism, one of his consorts, Yang Guifei, and whatever else captured his fancy, meant that the affairs of state were largely left to his administrators.

An Lushun, a general in the north-east, took this opportunity to build up a huge power base in the region, and before long (755) he made his move on the rest of China. The fighting, which dragged on for nearly 10 years, overran the capital and caused massive dislocations of people and millions of deaths. Although Tang forces regained control of the empire, it was the beginning of the end for the Tang.

Anarchy & Discord

Tang power gradually weakened during the 8th and 9th centuries. In the north-west, Tibetan warriors overran Tang garrisons, while to the south the Nanzhao kingdom centred in Dàlǐ, Yúnnán, posed a serious threat to Sìchuān. Meanwhile, in the Chinese heartland of the Cháng Jiāng (Yangzi River) region and Zhèjiāng, heavy taxes and a series of calamities engendered wide-ranging discontent that culminated in Huang Zhao, the head of a loose grouping of bandit groups, ransacking the capital.

From 907 to 959, until the establishment of the Song dynasty, China was once again racked by wars between contenders for the mandate of heaven. It is a period often referred to as the Five Dynasties and Ten Kingdoms period.

Song Dynasty

In 959 Zhao Kuangyin, the leader of the palace corps of one of the so-called Five Dynasties (the Later Zhou), usurped power from a seven-year-old head of state. By 976 he had conquered the dozen or so other kingdoms that stood in the way to reunifying China and established yet another dynasty: the Song (960–1279).

The Song is generally divided into the Northern Song (960–1126) and the Southern Song (1127–1279). The reason behind this division lies with the Juchen Jin dynasty, which took control of the north from 1126 and drove the Song from its capital of Kāifēng to the southern capital of Hángzhōu.

Despite the continual threat of powerful forces on its borders (the Tibetan/Tangut Xixia kingdom, the Mongol Liao dynasty and the Juchen Jin dynasty), the Song is memorable for its strong centralised government, a renewal of Confucian learning, a restoration of the examination system that fostered a civilian-dominated bureaucracy, and what has been referred to as a commercial revolution.

The economic progress of the Song period can be attributed in large part to dramatically increased agricultural production. Land reclamation, new rice strains and improved agricultural techniques and tools all played a role in this development. At the same time improvements in the transport infrastructure, the rise of a merchant class and the introduction of paper money facilitated the growth of wider markets. This commercial revolution allowed for the growth of more urban centres nourished by the influx of goods from around the country.

When Marco Polo arrived in China in the 13th century he found prosperous cities on a grander scale than those he was used to at home in Europe. Historians point to the Song dynasty as the turning point in China's development of an urban culture.

Mongol Reign (Yuan Dynasty)

Beyond the Great Wall lay the Gobi Desert. Beyond that lay only slightly more hospitable grassland stretching all the way from Manchuria to Hungary and inhabited by nomadic Turkic and Mongol tribes who endured a harsh life as shepherds and horse breeders. The Mongols, despised for what was considered their ignorance and poverty, occasionally went to war with the Chinese, but had always been defeated.

In 1206, after about 20 years of internal war, Genghis Khan united the roaming Mongol tribes into a new national entity: the 'Blue Mongols', under the protection of the 'heavenly sky'. In 1211 he turned his attention on China, penetrated the Great Wall two years later and then took Běijīng in 1215. Stubborn resistance from the Chinese rulers, conflict within the Mongolian camp and campaigns in Russia delayed the conquest of Song China for many years. Not until 1279 did the grandson of Genghis, Kublai Khan, bring southern China under his sway and establish the Yuan dynasty (1271–1368). The China ruled by Kublai was the vastest empire the world has ever seen.

The Mongols established two capitals: a summer capital of Shangdu in Inner Mongolia and a winter capital of Dadu, or, as it's now known, Běijīng. They made many administrative changes to the Chinese court; the major difference from the Song being the militarisation of administrative organs. Another major feature of the Yuan dynasty was that the Chinese became 3rd and 4th class citizens in their own country. Society was split into four categories, with the Mongols first, their central Asian allies next, northern Chinese third and southern Chinese last.

The Mongols were harsh in administering their rule, but on the economic front at least they were less interfering than the Chinese dynasties that had preceded them. More work was carried out on China's canal system and roads, offering a further stimulus to trade. The commercial revolution that had gathered pace in the Song continued unabated in the Yuan, with inter-regional and even international trade flourishing. Taxes were heavy, however, except for those of Mongol descent who were exempt.

Despite internal intrigues and widespread Chinese disaffection with their Mongol rulers, the grip of the Yuan dynasty over its vast empire remained strong almost until the very end. By the middle of the 14th century, however, the country had become convulsed by rebellion. Chief among the rebel groups were the Red Turbans, who were guided in their mission by a belief structure of diverse religious sources, ranging from Buddhism to Manichaeism, Taoism and Confucianism. By 1367 Zhu Yuanzhang, originally an orphan and Buddhist novice, had climbed to the top of the rebel leadership, and in 1368 he established the Ming dynasty and restored Chinese rule.

Ming Dynasty

Upon founding the Ming dynasty (1368–1644), Zhu Yuanzhang took the name of Hongwu. He established his capital in Nánjīng, but in 1402 Yongle (strictly speaking the third, but effectively the second, Ming emperor) set about building a new seat of imperial power on the site of the old Yuan capital in Běijīng.

In 1420 Běijīng was designated the first capital and Nánjīng designated the second (their names mean 'Northern Capital' and 'Southern Capital' respectively).

Hongwu is remembered for his despotism (he had some 10,000 scholars and their families put to death in two paranoid purges of his administration), but he was also a strong leader who did much to set China back on its feet in the aftermath of the Yuan collapse. This consolidation was continued by Yongle. He ruled less autocratically, running the court bureaucracy with a steadier hand than Hongwu, and he carried out effective campaigns in protection of the Great Wall against the Mongols.

During Yongle's reign, China developed into a strong maritime nation. Zheng He, a eunuch general of Muslim descent, undertook seven great expeditions to South-East Asia, Persia, Arabia and even eastern Africa.

In the final years of Ming rule, official corruption, excessive eunuch power, intellectual conservatism and costly wars in defence of Korea (and ultimately China itself) against Japan's Toyotomi Hideyoshi brought the nation to virtual bankruptcy. A famine in Shaanxi, coupled with governmental neglect, was the spark for a massive peasant rebellion that brought the Ming rule to a close.

Qing Dynasty

The Manchus to the north had long been growing in power, and looked with keen interest to the convulsions of rebellion in their huge neighbour. Taking advantage of the turmoil in China, they launched an invasion. Initially held back by the Great Wall, they were allowed to pass by a Ming general, who saw an alliance with the Manchus as the only hope for defeating the peasant rebel armies that now threatened Běijīng itself.

The Manchus lost no time in inflicting a decisive defeat on the peasant forces, and in June 1644 they marched into the Ming capital and made it their own. They proclaimed their new dynasty the Qing (1644–1911), although it was to be four decades before they finally cleared the south of Ming loyalist forces and pacified the whole country. Today's 'triads' in China (the modern secret societies generally thought to be involved in criminal activity, especially drug trafficking) are actually the descendants of secret societies originally set up to resist the Manchus.

Although the Manchus concentrated power in their own hands and alienated the Han Chinese, the reign of the early Qing emperors from 1663 to 1796 was a period of great prosperity. The throne was occupied by three of the most able rulers China has known: Kangxi, Yongzheng and Qianlong. The Qing expanded the empire to its greatest limits since the Han dynasty, bringing Mongolia and Tibet under Qing suzerainty. Reduced taxation and massive flood control and irrigation projects benefited the peasants.

One problem was that the first three emperors' exceptional competence led to a concentration of power in their hands that none of their successors was a match for. Like the Mongols, the Manchu rulers succumbed to the ways of the Chinese and soon became culturally indistinguishable from them, modelling their government on the Ming dynasty. Thus the isolationism and intellectual conservatism of the Ming was passed on to the Qing.

China continued to be an inward-looking nation, oblivious to the technological and scientific revolutions taking place in Europe. The coming of Europeans to China hastened the fall of the Qing and helped mould the China we know today.

Coming of the West

The first European ships to anchor off the shores of China, in 1516, were Portuguese. Although by 1557 they had set up a trade mission in Macau, it was not until 1760 that other European powers – the British, Dutch and Spanish – gained secure access to Chinese markets via a base in Guǎngzhōu. All trade was carried out via a monopolistic guild known as the Cohong; the same guild mediated all non-commercial dealings with the Chinese empire, effectively keeping foreigners at a long arm's length from the political centre in Běijīng.

Trade flourished under the auspices of the Cohong – in China's favour. British purchases of tea, silk and porcelain far outweighed Chinese purchases of wool and spices. In 1773, the British East India Company, acting on behalf of King George III's government, sent an envoy bearing gifts and protected by a man-of-war and support vessels to the Emperor, requesting greater trade for Britain and to set up diplomatic residence in Běijīng, thereby avoiding the restrictions of the Cohong. The Emperor Qianlong sent an edict to George III rejecting the proposals, stating that China had little need for foreign commodities and that for an envoy to remain at the capital would be of little advantage to Britain and would upset the harmony of the Chinese Celestial Empire. The venture had cost the British

East India Company a great deal of money. The company, however, had found one foreign commodity that would in subsequent years alter the balance of trade – opium. Despite imperial declarations of war against drugs, opium addiction in China skyrocketed and with it so did sales – from 1000 chests in 1773 to 23,570 in 1832. One chest contained approximately 150 pounds of opium.

After much imperial vacillation and hand-wringing, in March 1839 Lin Zexiu, an official of great personal integrity, was dispatched to Guǎngzhōu to put a stop to the illegal traffic once and for all. He acted promptly, demanding and eventually getting some 20,000 chests of opium stored by the British in Guǎngzhōu. This, along with several other minor incidents, was just the pretext that hawkish elements in the British government needed to win support for military action against China. In 1840 a British naval force assembled in Macau and moved up the coast to Beihe, not far from Běijīng. The Opium War was on.

For the Chinese, the conflicts centred on the opium trade were a fiasco from start to finish. While the Qing court managed to fob the first British force off with a treaty that neither side ended up recognising, increasing British frustration soon led to an attack on Chinese positions close to Guǎngzhōu.

The resulting treaty ceded Hong Kong to the British and called for indemnities of Y6,000,000 and the full resumption of trade. The furious Qing emperor refused to recognise the treaty, and in 1841 British forces once again headed up the coast, taking Fújiàn and eastern Zhèjiāng. They settled in for the winter and, in the spring of 1842, their numbers swollen with reinforcements, they moved up the Cháng Jiāng (Yangzi River) duly dispatching all comers. With British guns trained on Nánjīng, the Qing fighting spirit evaporated, and they reluctantly signed the humiliating Treaty of Nanjing.

Decline of the Qing

Internal rebellions like the Nian and the Taiping (Daibing) weakened the stability of the Qing emperors. The increased presence of missionaries had also fuelled hatred against 'foreign devils', which led to further rebellion throughout the provinces. A growing population combined with the scarcity of arable land added to internal pressures against the Qing rulers. There was also a decline in the general calibre and strength of the emperors, which can be seen by the increasing influence in the period from 1856 to 1908 of the Emperor Xianfeng's favourite consort, Cixi. As the Dowager Empress, Cixi, exerted a great deal of influence on politics as coregent for her nephew, Guangxu, in the period from 1875 to 1908.

Cixi saw all attempts to reform the ancient institutions of the empire as a threat to the conservative power base of her government. In short, it was poorly equipped to adapt to the demands of dynamic western powers who refused to enter into relations with China as mere vassals. Reforming elements within the Qing were perpetually thwarted; rural poverty and western influence were factors in promoting civil unrest that emerged in four major rebellions in the mid-19th century.

The western powers embarked on a landgrabbing spree that carved China up into 'spheres of influence'. The first to go were China's colonial 'possessions'. A war with France from 1883 to 1885 ended Chinese suzerainty in Indo-China and allowed the French to maintain control of Vietnam and eventually gain control of Laos and Cambodia. The British occupied Burma (Myanmar). In 1895 Japan forced the Chinese out of Korea and made them cede Taiwan. By 1898 the European powers were on the verge of carving up China and having her for dinner – a feast that was thwarted only by a US proposal for an 'open-door' policy that would leave China open to trade with any foreign power.

In the face of so much national humiliation it was inevitable that rebellions aiming to overthrow the Qing would emerge. The first major rebellion was the Taiping. Led by Hong Xiuquan, a native of Guǎngdōng and a failed scholar whose encounters with western missionaries had led him to believe

he was the younger brother of Jesus, the rebellion commanded forces of 600,000 men and 500,000 women.

The Taipings owed much of their ideology to Christianity. They forbade gambling, opium, tobacco and alcohol; advocated agricultural reform; and outlawed footbinding for women, prostitution and slavery. Ironically, they were defeated by a coalition of Qing and western forces – the Europeans preferring to deal with a corrupt and weak Qing government than a powerful, united China governed by the Taipings.

The second major rebellion to rock China was that of the Righteous Harmonious Fists, or Boxers. They emerged in Shāndōng in 1898 out of secret societies who trained in martial arts. The Boxers were fanatically anti-foreign, saw 1900 as the dawn of the new age and believed themselves invincible to the bullets of the foreign forces. Poorly organised, the Boxers roamed in bands attacking Chinese Christians and foreign missionaries. The Empress Dowager attempted to ride the tide of anti-foreign feeling by declaring war on the foreign powers in 1900. In the event, a combined British, US, French, Japanese and Russian force of 20,000 troops defeated the Boxers, the empress fled to Xī'ān and the foreign forces levied yet another massive indemnity on the Qing government and demanded that their troops be stationed in Běijīng to protect their embassies.

Fall of the Qing

With the defeat of the Boxers, even the Empress Dowager realised that China was too weak to survive without reform. But, while the civil service examinations based on irrelevant 1000-year-old Confucian doctrines were abolished, other court-sponsored reforms proved to be a sham. Furthermore, by now secret societies aimed at bringing down the Qing dynasty were numerous, even overseas where they were set up by disaffected Chinese who had left their homeland.

To make matters worse for the Qing, in 1908 the Empress Dowager died and the two-year-old Emperor Puyi ascended to the throne. The Qing was now rudderless, and quickly collapsed in two events: the Railway Protection Movement and the Wuchang Uprising of 1911.

The Railway Protection Movement grew out of public anger at new railways being financed and built by foreigners. Chinese investors were barred from these railway ventures, which the public felt should have been in Chinese control, not in the hands of foreigners. Plans to construct lines to provincial centres using local funds soon collapsed, and the despairing Qing government adopted a policy of nationalisation and foreign loans to do the work. Opposition by vested interests and provincial leaders soon fanned violence that spread and took on an anti-Qing nature. The violence was worst in Sìchuān, and troops were taken from the Wuchang garrison in Wǔhàn to quell the disturbances.

As it happened, revolutionaries in Wǔhàn, coordinated by Sun Yatsen's Tokyo-based Alliance Society, were already planning an uprising in concert with disaffected Chinese troops. A bomb accidentally exploded in Wǔhàn, which drew the authorities, attention to a list of the names of revolutionaries. This forced the revolutionaries to take action sooner than intended on 10/10/1911 – the Double Tenth. The revolutionaries were quickly able to take control of Wǔhàn and ride on the back of the large-scale Railway Protection uprisings to victory over all China.

Two months later representatives from 17 provinces throughout China gathered in Nánjīng to establish the Provisional Republican Government of China. China's long dynastic cycle had come to an end.

Early Days of the Republic

The Provisional Republican Government was set up on 10 October 1911 (a date that is still celebrated in Taiwan as 'Double Tenth') by Sun Yatsen (who was not in China at the time) and Li Yuanhong, a military commander in Wuchang. Lacking the power to force a Manchu abdication, they had no choice but to call on the assistance of Yuan Shikai, head of the imperial army and the same man the Manchus had called on to put down the republican uprisings.

The republicans promised Yuan Shikai the presidency if he could negotiate the abdication of the Emperor, which he achieved. The favour cost the republicans dearly. Yuan Shikai placed himself at the head of the republican movement and forced Sun Yatsen's resignation.

Yuan lost no time in dissolving the Provisional Republican Government and amending the constitution to make himself president for life.

When this met with regional opposition, he took the natural next step in 1915 of declaring an imperial restoration and pronouncing himself China's latest emperor. Yúnnán seceded, taking Guǎngxī, Guìzhōu and much of the rest of the south with it. Forces were sent to bring the breakaway provinces back into the imperial ambit, and in the confusion Yuan himself passed away. What followed was a virtual warlord era, with no single power strong enough to hold the country together until the communists established the People's Republic of China (PRC) in 1949.

Intellectual Revolution

Chinese intellectuals had been probing the inadequacies of the old Confucian order and looking for a path to steer China into the 20th century ever since early contact with the west, but a sense of lost possibilities with the collapse of the republican government and the start of a new period of social decay lent an urgency to their worries in the early years of the 1900s. Intellectuals and students were also supported by a sense of nationalism that had been slowly growing in force since the late years of the Qing.

Beijing University became a hotbed of intellectual dissent, attracting scholars from all over China (even Mao Zedong was present in his capacity as library assistant). They were merciless in their criticisms of orthodox Chinese society. Some explored ideas of social Darwinism, the *Communist Manifesto* was translated into Chinese and became the basis for countless discussion groups, others favoured anarchism, and all looked keenly to events unfolding in Russia, where revolutionaries had taken power.

The catalyst for the demonstrations that became known as the May Fourth Movement was the decision of the Allies in Versailles to pass defeated Germany's rights in Shāndōng over to the Japanese. A huge public outcry ensued and on 4 May 1919 students took to the streets in a protest that combined a sense of nationalist outrage with demands for modernisation. Mass strike action in support of the students took place throughout China. Although the disturbances were quelled and many of the ringleaders temporarily imprisoned, the May Fourth incident is considered a watershed in contemporary Chinese history.

Perhaps most interesting today is the way in which the student protests at Tiānánmén in 1989 echoed the slogans and catchcries of the 1919 protests. Students bearing placards marked with 'Mr Science' and 'Mr Democracy' in 1989 were harking back to 1919, when the same slogans were used – perhaps, in fine Chinese tradition, seeking the authority of historical precedent.

Kuomintang & Communists

After initial setbacks, Sun Yatsen and the Kuomintang (also known as the Guomindang, KMT or Nationalist Party), which had emerged as the dominant political force after the fall of the Qing dynasty, managed to establish a secure base in southern China, and began training a National Revolutionary Army (NRA) with which to challenge the northern warlords.

Talks between representatives of the Soviet Communist International (Comintern) – the international body dedicated to world revolution – and prominent Chinese Marxists eventually resulted in several Chinese Marxist groups banding together to form a Chinese Communist Party (which became the CCP) at a meeting in Shànghǎi in 1921.

The Comintern, from 1922, encouraged the CCP to ally with the Kuomintang, probably motivated more by the hope of forming a buttress against Japanese expansionism than by the promise of a Soviet-style revolution in China. The union was short lived. After Sun Yatsen's death in 1925 a power struggle emerged in the Kuomintang between those sympathetic to the communists and those who – headed by Chiang Kaishek – favoured a capitalist state dominated by a wealthy elite and supported by a military dictatorship.

Shànghǎi Coup

Chiang Kaishek attempted to put an end to growing communist influence during the 1926 Northern Expedition, which set out to wrest power from the remaining warlords. With Chiang as commander in chief, NRA forces took Wǔhàn and Nánchāng, and prepared to move on Shànghǎi.

As NRA troops advanced on the city, Shànghǎi workers were called upon to strike and take over key installations. Having lured the communists out of the woodwork, Chiang let loose a reign of terror against the communists and their sympathisers.

With the help of Shànghǎi's underworld leaders (green gang) and with financial backing from Shànghǎi bankers and foreigners, Chiang armed hundreds of gangsters, dressed them in Kuomintang uniforms and launched a surprise attack overnight on the workers' militia. About 5000 Shànghǎi communists were killed. They were easily identified by the red stain on their necks from their red cotton clothing. Massacres of communists and various anti-Chiang factions followed in other Chinese cities. Zhou Enlai managed to escape by a hair's breadth. Another prominent CCP leader, Li Dazhao, was executed by slow strangulation.

Kuomintang Government

By the middle of 1928 the Northern Expedition had reached Běijīng and a national government was established, with Chiang holding both military and political leadership. Nevertheless, only about half of the country was under the direct control of the Kuomintang; the rest was ruled by local warlords.

China's social problems were many: child slave labour in factories; domestic slavery and prostitution; destitute and starving dying on the streets; and strikes ruthlessly suppressed by foreign and Chinese factory owners. In the face of such endemic social

(continued on page 37)

HIGHLIGHTS IN CHINA

Getaways

Unlike the South-East Asian trail, which seems to harbour some little getaway with travellers' breakfasts, walks, waterfalls and fabulous beaches at every turn, in China such retreats are few and far between. There are, however, a couple of places that have achieved legendary status on the travel circuit.

Yángshuò

This village is set amid the famous karst scenery of Guìlín in Guǎngxī. The surrounding countryside alone, which can be explored by bicycle, makes Yángshuò worth a stay of a few days. There are also river trips along the Lí Jiāng, buzzing rural markets, imposing caves to explore, cheap accommodation and banana pancakes for breakfast. What more could you ask for?

Líjiāng

Home to the matriarchal Naxi minority in Yúnnán, Líjiāng's exotic old town has survived over two centuries and is a picturesque maze of cobbled streets, exquisite old wooden buildings, gushing canals and lively markets.

Xīshuāngbǎnnà

In Yúnnán, on the border with Laos and Myanmar, Xīshuāngbǎnnà is adored by backpackers. It is a region of lush rainforest and subtropical weather, and is home to many of Yúnnán's ethnic groups.

Historic Architecture & Foreign Concessions

Dynasties have risen and fallen for at least a few millennia in China. Nevertheless, there's not as much imperial debris about as you might expect. Dynasties rarely fell gracefully, with imperial decline generally marked by rampaging peasant uprisings and pillaging armies led by turncoat generals. Add to this the assault on the past led by the Cultural Revolution and the rapid modernisation and urbanisation of the nation over the past 15 years, and it's a wonder there's anything left to see. Fortunately there is – some spectacular palaces and ruins that give an insight into the opulence of China's past.

But by the end of the 19th century the weakness of the Qing government allowed the European powers to grab a large number of 'foreign concessions'. Much of the old architecture is still standing, now often functioning as schools and government offices. In some cities, such buildings are being torn down and replaced with hastily thrown together high-rises. In other cities, such as Guǎngzhōu and Shànghǎi, some of the concession buildings are being gentrified.

The Forbidden City

This Běijīng palace of Ming and Qing emperors, their eunuch servants, princesses and harems, was off-limits to ordinary Chinese citizens for 500 years. The original plans for the site laid out the buildings in keeping with yin and yang, to balance the negative with the positive. What remains is the largest and best-preserved cluster of ancient buildings in China.

The Summer Palace

Originally used as a summer residence, this palace was established in the late Qing period. Much of the area is lake and parklands and it is one of the most pleasant places in Běijīng to visit.

The Great Wall

Běijīng is the jumping-off point for the Great Wall, China's most famous imperial legacy, which stretches from Shānhǎi Guān on the east coast to Jiāyùguān in the Gobi Desert. The wall is the only man-made structure visible from the moon and is one of China's most impressive sights. The wall can actually be viewed from many places, but most visitors approach it from Běijīng.

Bìshǔshānzhuāng

This summer palace in Chéngdé, Héběi, has a throne room and the full range of court trappings. It was established in 1703 by Emperor Kangxi and eventually became a quasi-government seat rather than a summer villa. By 1790, during the reign of Kangxi's grandson, Qianlong, it had grown to the size of Běijīng's Summer Palace and the Forbidden City combined. Chéngdé is now on UNESCO's World Heritage list.

Potala Palace

Dominating the skyline of Lhasa in Tibet, the dazzling Potala Palace was once the centre of the Tibetan government and the winter residence of the Dalai Lama. The Potala is one of the architectural wonders of the world, with the immense construction standing 13 storeys tall and containing thousands of rooms, shrines and statues.

Mínggù Gōng

These are the ruins of the Ming Palace in Nánjīng, which is said to have been a magnificent structure after which the Imperial Palace in Běijīng was modelled.

The Bund

China's most famous collection of European architecture is lined up facing the water in Shànghǎi. The buildings are a vagabond assortment of neoclassical 1930s downtown New York styles, with a pompous touch of monumental antiquity thrown in for good measure.

French Concession

Although parts of Frenchtown are derelict and falling in swathes to modern building projects, the French Concession also turns up some delightful architectural surprises. You can see some of the best old

GLENN BEANLAND

BRADLEY MAYHEW

Top: The Forbidden City in Běijīng gives an insight into the splendour of Imperial China.

Middle: The ethnic diversity of China is another of its fascinating aspects. In South-West Guìzhōu a Miao woman visits the local market with her child.

Bottom: Hēilóng Tán in Yúnnán offers spectacular views of the surrounding mountains.

DIANA MAYFIELD

Highlights in China

GLENN BEANLAND

MARTIN MOOS

Top: The glorious Qing architecture of the Summer Palace in Běijīng

Bottom: The Great Wall at Sīmǎtái, China's most legendary and breathtaking sight

JULIET COOMBE

Top: The legendary peaks of Huáng Shān in Ānhuī form one of China's most popular attractions.

Bottom: Customs House: one of the grand architectural features of The Bund in Shànghǎi

BRADLEY MAYHEW

Highlights in China

GLENN BEANLAND

MARTIN MOOS

MARTIN MOOS

Top: Contemplate the majesty of Běijīng's Summer Palace across the water of Kūnmíng Hú.

Middle: The Yúngāng Shíkū Buddhist caves in Shānxī showcase the artistic ingenuity of their craftsmen.

Bottom: Camel trekking across the hauntingly barren desert dunes around Dūnhuáng in Gānsù

architecture here, from Art Deco apartment complexes to neo-classical mansions and villas with quaint balconies and doorways.

Shāmiàn Dǎo
Guǎngzhōu is home to China's earliest foreign concession, and has an unexpectedly peaceful enclave of European buildings on Shāmiàn Dǎo. The colonial buildings are in varying states of decaying disrepair and shining renovation, and make a great place to wander around.

Gǔlàng Yǔ
This island in Xiàmén has one of China's most charming collections of colonial architecture. The fact that there are no motorised vehicles on the small island makes this one of the only places in the country where it is possible to take peaceful walks and appreciate the buildings at leisure.

Qīngdǎo
Qīngdǎo, in Shāndōng, was ceded to the Germans in 1898, and by 1904 the brewery was in place, along with countless villas and administrative buildings. Qīngdǎo's architectural attractions are scattered, as modern construction has taken its toll on the city's charms, but there are enough remaining to make a visit worthwhile.

Tiānjīn
In 1858 Tiānjīn became a treaty port for the British. By the turn of the century French, Germans, Italians, Belgians and Japanese had also arrived. The result is a remarkable potpourri of architectural styles divided up into concessions.

Sacred Mountains & Nature Reserves
Eulogised through the centuries in countless paintings and poems, the sacred mountains of China were once places of pilgrimage; the vastness of the towering peaks inspired the climber with a sense of the frailty of human existence. Dotted along the well-marked trails are poems, inscriptions and temples. The chief attraction is, inevitably, sunrise at the summit, where crowds gather to gaze on the 'sea of clouds'.

Héng Shān
This holy Taoist peak in Húnán was once where kings and emperors hunted and made sacrifices to heaven and earth. Today, Buddhists and Taoists live here peacefully and there is a smattering of temples amid the picturesque serenity.

Tài Shān
Tài Shān, in Shāndōng, is the most revered of the five sacred Taoist mountains of China. The mountain is shrouded in mystique and legend – imperial sacrifices were offered from its summit and upon climbing its heights it's easy to understand why. You don't need to be an experienced hiker to climb Tài Shān; it can easily be ascended and descended in a day, with sunrise the major attraction.

Sōng Shān

In Taoism, Sōng Shān is considered the central axis of the five sacred mountains, symbolising earth in the religion's belief that five elements make up the world. The 70 tree-covered peaks, in Hénán, can be visited as a day trip from Luòyáng and Zhèngzhōu.

Éméi Shān

The original temple structures on this mountain in Sìchuān date back as far as the advent of Buddhism itself in China. The two-day Éméi Shān hike offers beautiful views and spectacular sunsets. Fir trees, pines and cedars clothe the slopes; lofty crags, cloud-kissing precipices, butterflies and azaleas together form a nature reserve of sorts. The mountain is sprinkled with the surviving temples that offer refuge to hikers and pilgrims.

Wǔtái Shān

Centred on the beautiful monastic village of Táihuái in Shānxī, this holy Buddhist area contains some beautiful alpine scenery, architecturally superb temples and peaceful mountain trails.

Pǔtuóshān

The charming island of Pǔtuóshān in Zhèjiāng is also a sacred Buddhist mountain. It's blessed with ancient temples and pagodas, pleasant beaches, rolling hills, arched bridges and narrow alleys; and is home to fishing boats, artisans and monks. The island has no cars so is a tranquil oasis on which to escape the hustle-bustle.

Huáng Shān

This mountain in Ānhuī is probably the country's most famous landscape attraction. With its gnarled pines, craggy rocks and a rolling sea of clouds, it's evocative of a Chinese ink painting. Huáng Shān's highlight is the sunrise: a 'sea' of low clouds blanketing the valley to the north with 'island' peaks hazily reaching for the heavens. Huáng Shān is extremely sacred in China and the ambition of many is to scale its heights.

Jiǔhuá Shān

The other holy mountain in Ānhuī has less spectacular scenery but a quieter and more spiritual atmosphere. Jiǔhuá Shān is an important place for believers to come and bless the souls of the recently deceased to ensure them a passage to Buddhist heaven.

Chángbái Shān

This is China's largest nature reserve, covering 210,000 hectares of dense, virgin forest. The wild and remote area in Jílín is home to a wide variety of animal and plant life. The prime scenic spot is Tiān Chí, a huge volcanic crater lake at the summit of the mountain.

Dǐnghú Shān

This mountain range in Guǎngdōng offers a myriad of walks among dense forest, pools, springs, ponds, temples, nunneries and charming scenery.

Hānàsī Hú

Mountains and forests and a diverse range of flora and fauna surround this alpine lagoon in the Altai region at the northernmost tip of Xīnjiāng. The area is inhabited by semi-nomadic Kazakhs and Mongolians and there are plenty of opportunities for hiking.

Jiǔzhài Gōu

This spectacular nature reserve in Sìchuān is scattered with high alpine peaks, hundreds of clear lakes and lush forests. Jiǔzhài Gōu was first settled by ethnic Tibetans and their traditions can still be seen in the shrines, prayer wheels and prayer flags that decorate the region.

Mèngdá Tiān Chí

This beautiful and relatively little visited nature reserve is on the upper reaches of the Huáng Hé (Yellow River) in Qīnghǎi. Tiān Chí is the main drawcard and is a lake sacred to the local Tibetans and Sala Muslims, set in a lush valley of verdant alpine forest.

Sānchàhé

In Xīshuāngbǎnnà, Yúnnán, this nature reserve of dense jungle and rainforest is home to many endemic species of tropical flora and fauna, including the banyan and umbrella trees, wild tigers, leopards, elephants and golden-haired monkeys.

Zhālóng

Zhālóng is an enormous wetlands and bird-watching area in Hēilóngjiāng and is the protected breeding area of the red-crowned crane. Some 236 different species of bird are found in the reserve, including storks, swans, geese, ducks, herons, harriers, grebes and egrets.

Zhāngjiājiè (Wǔlíngyuán)

Zhāngjiājiè is a nature reserve in Húnán that encompasses dramatic, splintering karst mountain scenery rivalling Guìlín and Yángshuò in Guǎngxi.

Spectacular Sights

Tombs in Nánjīng

Construction of Zhōngshān Líng, an immense Ming-style tomb mausoleum, began a year after the death of Sun Yatsen. The finished product has become a pilgrimage for people wishing to pay their respects to the father of modern China. Míng Xiàolíng, the Tomb of Hong Wu, is another impressive mausoleum lying on the southern slope of Zǐjīn Shān.

Army of Terracotta Warriors

In 1974 an exciting archaeological discovery of underground vaults eventually yielded thousands of life-size terracotta soldiers and their horses in battle formation. The warriors are 2000 years old, are amazingly well preserved and form one of China's most intriguing and popular historical sights.

Mògāo Kū

These caves, set into desert cliffs above a river valley in Gānsù, are the most impressive and best-preserved examples of Buddhist cave art anywhere in China. Some 492 grottoes are still standing and they contain religious art depicting 1000 years of history.

Yúngāng Shíkū

The Yúngāng Buddhist caves are next to the pass near Dàtóng leading to Inner Mongolia. They contain over 50,000 statues and stretch for about 1km east to west. The incredible artwork shows influences of the many foreign craftsmen, from India and Central Asia, who worked on the grottoes. On top of the mountain ridge are the remains of a 17th-century Qing dynasty fortress.

Dà Fó

The Grand Buddha in Lèshān, Sìchuān, is the largest buddha in the world. At 71m high, it is carved into a red sandstone cliff face overlooking the confluence of the Dadu and Min Rivers. Work on this enormous figure took over 90 years and its sheer size and the monumentality of the artistic feat are breathtaking.

Outdoor Activities

Longing to rejuvenate your polluted urban senses and commune with nature? For travellers seeking to air their respiratory organs, China offers some excellent opportunities.

Hiking

The popular Hǔtiào Xiá, in Yúnnán, offers hikes through one of the deepest gorges in the world. Éméi Shān, the sacred Buddhist mountain in Sìchuān, is another popular hiking spot. Hiking on the **Great Wall** around Běijīng is an experience no visitor to China should miss. A favourite one-day hike, which takes you through unrestored parts of the Wall, is from Jīnshānlǐng to Sīmǎtái. The Tibetan settlement of **Jiǔzhài Gōu** nature reserve in Sìchuān offers dazzling alpine scenery; and in Xīnjiāng, **Hānàsī Hú** (Hanas Lake) nature reserve is also spectacular.

Horse Treks

Horse trek operators in **Sōngpān**, Sìchuān, guide you through pristine and peaceful valleys and forests, and the glacier park of **Hǎiluó Gōu** also inspires treks along its glacier trails. The grasslands of Inner Mongolia, such as at **Mǎnzhōulǐ**, and the area around **Tiān Chí**, a small, deep-blue lake in Xīnjiāng, also offer fantastic opportunities for horse trekking.

Cycling

A bicycle trip through backwoods China is yet another excellent way of escaping to the outdoors. Unless you're an experienced cyclist, you may want to consider hooking up with a tour company if you're interested in a long-distance ride. Backroads (www.backroads.com) and Bike China (www.bikechina.com) are a couple of possibilities.

(continued from page 30)

malaise, Chiang became obsessed with countering the influence of the communists.

Civil War

After the massacre of 1927, the communists were divided between an insurrectionary policy of targeting large urban centres and one of basing its rebellion in the countryside. After costly defeats in Nánchāng and Chángshā, the tide of opinion started to shift towards Mao Zedong, who, along with Zhu De, had established his forces in the Jǐnggāng Shān, on the border of Jiāngxī and Húnán, and who advocated rural-based revolt.

Communist-led uprisings in other parts of the country met with some success. However, the communist armies were still small and hampered by limited resources. They adopted a strategy of guerrilla warfare, emphasising mobility and deployment of forces for short attacks on the enemy, followed by swift separation once the attack was over. Pitched battles were avoided except where their force was overwhelmingly superior. The strategy was summed up in a four line slogan:

The enemy advances, we retreat;
The enemy camps, we harass;
The enemy tires, we attack;
The enemy retreats, we pursue.

By 1930, the ragged communist forces had turned into an army of perhaps 40,000, which presented such a serious challenge to the Kuomintang that Chiang waged extermination campaigns against them. He was defeated each time, and the communist army continued to expand its territory.

The Long March

Chiang's fifth extermination campaign began in October 1933, when the communists suddenly changed their strategy. Mao and Zhu's authority was being undermined by other members of the party who advocated meeting Chiang's troops in pitched battles, but this strategy proved disastrous. By October 1934 the communists had suffered heavy losses and were hemmed into a small area in Jiāngxī.

On the brink of defeat, the communists decided to retreat from Jiāngxī and march north to Shaanxi. In China's northern mountains the communists controlled an area which spread across Shaanxi, Gānsù and Níngxià, held by troops commanded by an ex-Kuomintang officer who had sided with the communists after the 1927 massacre.

There was not one 'Long March' but several, as various communist armies in the south made their way to Shaanxi. The most famous was the march from Jiāngxī Province that began in October 1934, took a year to complete and covered 8000km over some of the world's most inhospitable terrain. On the way the communists confiscated the property of officials, landlords and tax-collectors, redistributed the land to the peasants, armed thousands of peasants with weapons captured from the Kuomintang and left soldiers behind to organise guerrilla groups to harass the enemy.

Of the 90,000 people who started out in Jiāngxī only 20,000 made it to Shaanxi. Fatigue, sickness, exposure, enemy attacks and desertion all took their toll.

The march proved, however, that the Chinese peasants could fight if they were given a method, an organisation, leadership, hope and weapons. It brought together many people who later held top positions after 1949, including Mao Zedong, Zhou Enlai, Zhu De, Lin Biao, Deng Xiaoping and Liu Shaoqi. It also established Mao as the paramount leader of the Chinese communist movement; during the march a meeting of the CCP hierarchy recognised Mao's overall leadership, and he assumed supreme responsibility for strategy.

Japanese Invasion

In September 1931 the Japanese took advantage of the confusion in China to invade and occupy Manchuria, setting up a puppet state with the last Chinese emperor, Puyi, as the symbolic head. Chiang, still obsessed with the threat of the communists, went ahead with his fifth extermination drive: 'pacification first, resistance later' was his slogan.

The communists had other plans. In late 1936 in Xī'ān they convinced Chiang's own generals to take him hostage, and an anti-Japanese alliance was formed after negotiations with Zhou Enlai – the foremost diplomat negotiator for the CCP. But it did little to halt the advance of the Japanese, who in 1937 launched an all-out invasion; by 1939 they had overrun most of eastern China, forcing the Kuomintang to retreat west to Chóngqìng.

In 1941 the Japanese assault on Pearl Harbor brought the Americans into the conflict. Hoping to use Chiang's troops to tie down as many Japanese as possible, the Americans instead found Chiang actively avoiding conflict, saving his troops for renewed attacks on the communists once the Americans had defeated the Japanese. The US general Joseph Stilwell, who was sent to China in 1942 by President Roosevelt to improve the combat effectiveness of the Chinese army, concluded that 'the Chinese government was a structure based on fear and favour in the hands of an ignorant, arbitrary and stubborn man ...' and that its military effort since 1938 was 'practically zero'.

Defeat of the Kuomintang

The Kuomintang-communist alliance had collapsed by 1941 and by the end of WWII China was in the grip of an all-out civil war. The 900,000-strong communist army was backed by the militia and several million active supporters. With the surrender of Japan in 1945, a dramatic power struggle began as the Kuomintang and communist forces gathered in Manchuria for the final showdown.

By 1948 the communists had captured so much US-supplied Kuomintang equipment and had recruited so many Kuomintang soldiers that they equalled the Kuomintang in both numbers and supplies. Three great battles were fought in 1948 and 1949 in which the Kuomintang were defeated and hundreds of thousands of Kuomintang troops joined the communists. The communists moved south and crossed the Cháng Jiāng (Yangzi River); by October all the major cities in southern China had fallen to them.

In Běijīng on 1 October 1949, Mao Zedong proclaimed the foundation of the People's Republic of China (Zhonghua Renmin Gongheguo). Chiang Kaishek fled to the island of Formosa (Taiwan), taking with him the entire gold reserves of the country and what was left of his air force and navy. Some two million refugees and soldiers from the mainland crowded onto the island. To prevent an attack from the mainland, President Truman ordered a protective US naval blockade.

The USA continued to recognise Chiang's delusion of being the legitimate ruler of all China. To most of the world, China was nicknamed 'mainland China' (Zhōngguó dàlù), which was basically China excluding Hong Kong, Macau and Taiwan.

Early Years of the PRC

The PRC began its days as a bankrupt nation. The economy was in chaos due to rampant inflation and a legacy of economic mismanagement left by the KMT. The country had just 19,200km of railways and 76,800km of useable roads – all in bad condition. Irrigation works had broken down and livestock and animal populations were greatly reduced. Industrial production had fallen during the Japanese bombing and occupation to half that of the prewar period and agricultural output plummeted.

With the communist takeover, China seemed to become a different country. Unified by the elation of victory and the immensity of the task before them, and further bonded by the Korean War and the necessity to defend the new regime from possible US invasion, the communists made the 1950s a dynamic period. They embarked upon land reform, recognised the role of women, and restored the economy by curbing inflation. The drive to become a great nation quickly was awesome.

By 1953 inflation had been halted, industrial production had been restored to prewar levels and the land had been confiscated from the landlords and redistributed to the peasants. On the basis of earlier Soviet models, the Chinese embarked on a massive five-year plan that was successful in lifting production on most fronts.

At the same time, the party increased its social control by organising the people according to their work units *(dānwèi)* and dividing the country into 21 provinces, five autonomous regions, two municipalities (Běijīng and Shànghǎi) and around 2200 county governments with jurisdiction over approximately one million party sub-branches.

Hundred Flowers

While the early years of the PRC enjoyed rapid economic development, immense problems remained in the social sphere, particularly with regard to the question of intellectuals. Many Kuomintang intellectuals had stayed on rather than flee to Taiwan, and still more overseas Chinese, many of them highly qualified, returned to China soon after its 'liberation' to help in the enormous task of reconstruction. Returning Chinese and those of suspect backgrounds were given extensive re-education courses in special universities put aside for the purpose, and were required to write a self-critical 'autobiography' before graduating. For many it was a traumatic experience.

Meanwhile, writers, artists and film-makers were subject to strict ideological controls guided by Mao's writings on art during the Yán'ān period (the time Mao spent in Yán'ān after the Long March). The issue came to a head around the figure of a writer, Hu Feng, who, in response to an easing of these controls in the early years of the first five-year plan, spoke out about the use of Marxist values in judging creative work. He soon became the object of nationwide criticism and was accused of being in the employ of the Kuomintang. He was tried and imprisoned (where he remained until 1979). Before long a witch-hunt was on in artistic circles for evidence of further 'Hu Fengism'.

In the upper echelons of the party itself opinions were divided as to how to deal with the problem of the intellectuals. But Mao, along with Zhou Enlai and other influential figures, felt that the party's work had been so successful that it could roll with a little criticism, and in a closed session Mao put forward the idea of 'letting a hundred flowers bloom' in the arts and 'a hundred schools of thought contend' in the sciences.

It was to be a full year before Mao's ideas were officially sanctioned in April 1957, but once they were, intellectuals around the country responded with glee. Complaints poured in on everything from party corruption to control of artistic expression, from the unavailability of foreign literature to low standards of living; but most of all, criticisms focused on the CCP monopoly on power and the abuses that went with it.

The party quickly had second thoughts about the flowers, and an anti-rightist campaign was launched. Within six months 300,000 intellectuals had been branded rightists, removed from their jobs and, in many cases, incarcerated or sent to labour camps for thought reform.

The Great Leap Forward

The first five-year plan had produced satisfactory results on the industrial front, but growth of agricultural yields had been a disappointingly low 3.8%. The state now faced the difficult problem of how to increase agricultural production to meet the needs of urban populations coalescing around industrialised areas.

As with the question of dealing with intellectuals, the party leadership was divided on how to respond. Some, such as Zhou Enlai, favoured an agricultural incentive system. Mao favoured mass mobilisation of the country and inspirational exhortations that he believed would jump-start the economy into first-world standards overnight.

In the end it was Mao who won the day, and the Chinese embarked on a radical program of creating massive agricultural communes and drawing large numbers of people both from the country and urban areas into enormous water control and irrigation projects. In Mao's view revolutionary zeal and mass cooperative effort could overcome any obstacle and transform the Chinese landscape into a productive paradise. At the same time Mao criticised the earlier emphasis on heavy industry, which had required the support and assistance of Russian engineers, and pushed for small local industry to be developed in the communes, with profits going back into agricultural development.

China embarked on one of the greatest failed economic experiments in human history. The communists tried to abolish money and all private property, and told everyone to build backyard blast furnaces to increase steel production. Lacking iron ore, peasants had to melt down farm tools, pots, pans and doorknobs to meet their quota of steel 'production'.

Chinese villages have for centuries suffered from a lack of wood for cooking and construction, but the blast furnaces suddenly created a huge new demand for fuel. Furniture, doors and even wooden buildings had to be demolished to feed the hungry fires. Villages that proudly met their quota for steel production soon discovered that the steel produced was basically worthless.

Despite the enthusiastic forecasts for agricultural production, at the end of the day there was little incentive to work in the fields. Large numbers of rural workers engaged in the worthless blast furnaces project resulted in a massive slump in grain output. Bad weather in 1959 and the withdrawal of Soviet aid in 1960 made matters worse.

All effort was made to cover up the ensuing disaster and no foreign assistance was sought. China plunged into a famine of staggering proportions – an estimated 30 million Chinese starved to death (some put the figure at 60 million). As a result of the failure of the Great Leap Forward, Mao resigned his position as head of state, but remained as Chairman of the Communist Party.

Sino-Soviet Split

Droughts and floods were beyond even Mao's ability to control, but he played no small part in the Great Leap Forward and the Sino-Soviet dispute that led to the withdrawal of Soviet aid. Basically Mao's problems with the USSR stemmed from the latter's policy of peaceful coexistence with the USA, Khrushchev's de-Stalinisation speech and what Mao generally felt to be the increasingly revisionist nature of the Soviet leadership. Sino-Soviet relations became ever frostier when Khrushchev reneged on a promise to provide China with a prototype atomic bomb and sided with the Indians in a Sino-Indian border dispute.

In 1960 the Soviets removed all their 1390 foreign experts working in China. With the experts went the blueprints for some 600 projects that the two powers had been working on together, including China's nuclear bomb program. In 1969, the Soviet and Chinese armies briefly clashed in a territorial dispute over obscure Zhenbao (Treasure) Island on the border of Siberia and north-east China.

The Cultural Revolution

Although the official scapegoats were the Gang of Four, most non-partisan scholars now agree that the prime mover in the Cultural Revolution was Mao. The Cultural Revolution (1966–70) was an attempt to create new socialist structures overnight via the process of revolution, which, as the writer Richard Evans in his book *Deng Xiaoping and the Making of Modern China* states, 'Mao saw as having its own redemptive value'.

Mao's extreme views, his recent disastrous policy decisions and his opposition to bureaucratisation led to his increasing isolation within the party. In response, he set about to cultivate a personality cult with the assistance largely of Lin Biao, the minister of defence and head of the People's Liberation Army (PLA).

In the early 1960s, Lin had a collection of Mao's sayings compiled into a book that was to become known simply as the 'little red book', although its real title was *Quotations from Chairman Mao*. The book became the subject of study sessions for all PLA troops and was extended into the general education system.

The Cultural Revolution began when a play was released, which although set in an earlier era of Chinese history, criticised Mao. Mao launched a purge of the arts with the assistance of his wife, Jiang Qing, an erstwhile Shànghǎi B-grade movie star. The launching site was a play by Wu Han, *The Dismissal of Hai Rui from Office*. The play's depiction of an upright Song official defying the authorities in defence of the people's rights was felt to be a direct reference to Mao's dismissal of Peng Dehuai, the army marshal who had dared to raise his voice in protest against the Great Leap Forward. The work was attacked on strict Marxist ideological grounds and battle lines were drawn within the party on how to deal with the problem.

The result was that Mao's opponents were purged and simultaneously wall posters went up at Beijing University attacking the university administration. Mao officially sanctioned the wall posters and criticisms of party members by university staff and students, and before long students were being issued red armbands and taking to the streets. The Red Guards (hóng-wèibīng) had been born. By August 1966 Mao was reviewing mass parades of the Red Guards, chanting and waving copies of his little red book.

Nothing was sacred in the brutal onslaught of the Red Guards as they went on the rampage through the country. Universities and secondary schools were shut down; intellectuals, writers and artists were dismissed, killed, persecuted or sent to labour in the countryside; publication of scientific, artistic, literary and cultural periodicals ceased; temples were ransacked and monasteries disbanded; and many physical reminders of China's 'feudal', 'exploitative' or 'capitalist' past (including temples, monuments and works of art) were destroyed.

By the end of January 1967 the PLA had been ordered to break up all 'counter-revolutionary organisations' – an edict that was interpreted by the PLA as all groups with interests contrary to their own. Thousands of Chinese were killed in the ensuing struggles – particularly in Sìchuān and in Wǔhàn where the PLA took on a coalition of 400,000 Red Guards and workers' groups, killing more than 1000 people. The struggles continued through to September 1967, and even Mao and Jiang Qing began to feel that enough was enough. 'Ultra-left tendencies' were condemned and the PLA was championed as the sole agent of 'proletarian dictatorship'.

The Cultural Revolution took a new turn as the Red Guards slipped from power and the PLA began its own reign of terror. The so-called Campaign to Purify Class Ranks was carried out by Workers' Mao-Thought Propaganda Teams on anyone with a remotely suspect background – this could mean anything from having a college education to having a distant cousin who lived overseas. Those who needed re-education were sent to schools in the countryside that combined intensive study and self-criticism with hard labour.

Repercussions Like most of Mao's well intentioned experiments, the Cultural Revolution was a disaster of vast proportions. One of the few elements to benefit was the PLA, which ended up with a deeper penetration of most government organisations. Vast numbers of Chinese were victims of the revolution.

A major victim of the Cultural Revolution was the man who had done so much to get it started: Lin Biao. In the aftermath of the Cultural Revolution, Mao was troubled by the powers of the PLA and demanded self-criticisms from senior PLA officers. It is thought that a desperate Lin Biao sought support for an assassination attempt on Mao and, failing to find it, fled with his family to the USSR in a Trident jet. The 'renegade and traitor', as the Chinese press labelled him, died when his plane crashed in Mongolia on 13 September 1971.

Post Cultural Revolution Years

Some measure of political stability returned during the years immediately following the Cultural Revolution. Zhou Enlai exercised the most influence in the day-to-day governing of China and, among other things, worked towards restoring China's trade and diplomatic contacts with the outside world. In 1972 US President Richard Nixon visited Běijīng and improved relations between the USA and the PRC.

In 1973, Deng Xiaoping, vilified as China's 'No 2 Capitalist Roader' during the Cultural Revolution, returned to power. Nevertheless, Běijīng politics remained factional and divided. On the one side was Zhou, Deng and a faction of 'moderates' or 'pragmatists', and on the other were the 'radicals', 'leftists' or 'Maoists' led by Jiang Qing. As Zhou's health declined, the radicals gradually gained the upper hand.

By the time of Zhou's death in January 1976, Hua Guofeng, Mao's chosen protege, was made acting premier and Deng (under attack again from Madame Mao) disappeared from public view.

Tiānānmén Incident

The death of Zhou Enlai and public anger at Jiang Qing and her clique culminated in the Tiānānmén Incident of March 1976. During the Qing Ming Festival, when Chinese traditionally honour the dead, crowds began to gather in Tiānānmén Square to lay wreaths for Zhou, recite poems, make speeches and brandish posters. The content of the speeches, poems and banners was as much critical of Jiang as it was eulogistic of Zhou.

The Politburo met in an emergency session and, with the approval of Mao, branded the gathering counter-revolutionary. On 5 April, when an attempt was made to remove the wreaths from the square, the crowd fought with police and police vehicles were burnt. The square was occupied by some 30,000 militia during the night and the remaining several hundred protesters were beaten and arrested. The incident was blamed on Deng, who was relieved of all his posts and fled to Guǎngzhōu, before disappearing altogether.

Mao's Death & the Gang of Four

Mao had been a sick man for many years. In 1974 he was diagnosed as having Lou Gehrig's disease, an extremely rare motor-neuron disorder that leads quickly to death. For the last few years of his life he was immobilised, fed through a tube into his nasal passage and his speech was indecipherable. On 8 September 1976 he died.

Mao's annointed successor was Hua Guofeng, who had started his days in relative obscurity as a party leader in Mao's home county and whom Mao had cultivated and elevated to the giddy heights of premier and party chairman.

At first Hua temporised over dealing with Jiang Qing and the three other leaders of her clique (Zhang Chunqiao, Wang Hongwen and Yao Wenyuan) who had come to be known as the Gang of Four. But when the gang announced their opposition to Hua, he acted with the Politburo to have them arrested on 6 October. There were celebrations throughout China when the news was formally announced three weeks later.

The Gang did not to come to trial until 1980, and when it took place it provided a bizarre spectacle, with the blame for the entire Cultural Revolution falling on their shoulders. Jiang Qing remained unrepentant, hurling abuse at her judges and holding famously to the line that she 'was Chairman Mao's dog – whoever he told me to bite, I bit'. Its meaning was not lost on most Chinese, and privately whispers circulated that the problem had been not a Gang of Four, but a 'Gang of Five'. Jiang Qing's death sentence was commuted and she lived under house arrest until 1991, when she committed suicide by hanging.

Third Coming of Deng

In the middle of 1977 Deng Xiaoping returned to power for the third time and was appointed to the positions of vice-premier, vice-chairman of the party and chief of staff of the PLA. His next step was to remove Hua Guofeng. In September 1980 Hua relinquished the post of premier to Zhao Ziyang, a long-standing member of the CCP whose economic reforms in Sìchuān in the mid-1970s overcame the province's bankrupt economy and food shortages and won him Deng's favour. In June 1981 Hu Yaobang, a protege of Deng's for several decades, was named party chairman in place of Hua.

Final power now passed to the collective leadership of the six-member Standing Committee of the CCP, which included Deng, Hu and Zhao. The China they took over was racked with problems, a backward country in desperate need of modernisation. Ways had to be found to rejuvenate and replace an aged leadership (themselves) and to overcome the possibility of a leftist backlash. The wasteful and destructive power struggles that had plagued the CCP since its inception had to be eliminated.

The need for order had to be reconciled with the popular desire for more freedom; those with responsibility had to be rewarded, but watched over in case of misuse of privilege; the crisis of faith in the communist ideology had to be overcome; and a regime now dependent on the power of the police and military for its authority had to be legitimised.

1980s – Economics in Command

With Deng at the helm, China set a course of pragmatic reforms towards economic reconstruction. In rural China, the so-called 'Responsibility System' allowed agricultural households and factories to sell their quota surpluses on the open market. And in coastal China, Special Economic Zones (SEZs) were established at Zhūhǎi (next to Macau), Shēnzhèn (next to Hong Kong) and Shàntóu and Xiàmén (both just across the Taiwan Strait from Taiwan). The results have been nothing short of spectacular: over the past 15 years China has managed average annual growth rates of 9%.

In communist China, however, the rush of economic reform has generated very little in the way of political reform. In fact, the reforms of the past 15 years might be thought of as a trade-off: increased economic opportunities in return for a continued communist monopoly on power. The party – one way or another – controls virtually every facet of public life: it is accountable to nobody but itself; it controls the army; and it controls the government, the courts and industry. In short, very little gets done in China without the approval of the party. It is hardly surprising that official corruption has become a major problem.

Along with the communist autocracy and its attendant corruption, the other spectre haunting China was inflation, which hit 30% in the late 1980s. Corruption and inflation had between them led to widespread social unrest and a call for the return of the 'good old days under Mao', and in 1989 resulted in the demonstrations that were put down in the Tiānānmén massacre.

Tiānānmén Massacre

The immediate catalyst of the protests of 1989 was the death of Hu Yaobang, a reforming element and protege of Deng's who had been attacked and forced to resign by hardliners in early 1987. Behind the scenes, double-digit inflation, rampant official corruption and a purge of reformist party members like Hu had given rise to massive social discontent. On 22 April 1989, a week after Hu's death, China's leaders gathered in the Hall of the People for an official mourning service. Outside, approximately 150,000 students and other activists held an unofficial service that soon became a massive pro-democracy protest.

All through April, crowds continued to fill Tiānānmén Square, and by the middle of May protesters in and around the square had swelled to nearly one million. Workers and even members of the police force joined in. Protests erupted in at least 20 other cities. Approximately 3000 students staged a hunger strike for democracy in the square. Railway workers assisted students travelling to Běijīng by allowing them free rides on the trains.

Students enrolled at Běijīng's Art Institute constructed the 'Goddess of Democracy' in Tiānānmén Square – a statue that bore a striking resemblance to America's Statue of Liberty. The students made speeches demanding a free press and an end to corruption and nepotism. Huge pro-democracy demonstrations in Hong Kong, Macau and Taiwan lent support. The arrival of the foreign press corps turned the 'Běijīng Spring' into the media event of 1989.

Throughout much of May, the CCP was unable to quell the protests, and the imminent arrival of Mikhail Gorbachev for the first Sino-Soviet summit since 1959 precluded the use of arms to dispel the crowds. On 20 May, however, immediately after Gorbachev's departure, martial law was declared, and by 2 June, 350,000 troops had been deployed around Běijīng. In the early hours of the morning on 4 June the 27th Army division attacked. Other units loyal to Deng were also employed. Heavy tanks and armoured vehicles made short work of the barricades, crushing anyone who got in their way, while troops with automatic weapons strafed the crowds on the streets. The number of deaths that resulted from the action is widely disputed. Eyewitness accounts have indicated that hundreds died in the square alone, and it's likely that fighting in the streets around the square and in the suburbs of Běijīng may have led to several thousand casualties. Hospitals were filled to overflowing, PLA troops are said to have refused to allow doctors to treat their patients, and rumours circulated of mass graves.

The truth will probably never be known. What is certain is that the party lost whatever remaining moral authority it had in the action, and will no doubt one day have to deal with widespread recriminations. Indeed, much of China's current political repression may indeed be motivated by fear among the leadership that they could, in the future, be put on trial for the massacre at Tiānánmén Square.

Hong Kong & Macau

In 1984 a Sino-British agreement allowed for the reversion of Hong Kong to China in 1997. The original 'unequal' Treaty of Nanjing (1842) foisted on China by Britain at the end of the Opium War had ceded Hong Kong to the British 'in perpetuity', but the New Territories adjoining Kowloon were 'leased' to the British for 99 years in 1898. In the event, Britain agreed to hand the entire colony, lock, stock and skyscrapers, back to China when the lease on the New Territories expired.

The transition of power was not entirely smooth. According to the terms of the 1984 agreement, Hong Kong's transfer to Chinese rule was to take place under the concept of 'one country, two systems'. The implementation of this system was laid out in the Basic Law, which promised the former colony a 'high degree of autonomy' as a Special Administrative Region (SAR). Following the handover, however, the Chinese government scrapped the entire democratically elected Legislative Council (LEGCO) and replaced it with a legislature

appointed by Běijīng. This was not entirely unexpected: Běijīng had always maintained that the elections, hastily called by the British after almost a century of completely undemocratic colonial administration, represented a rather hypocritical thumbing of the nose. While not ignoring the differences in the legal and political freedoms enjoyed in the respective countries, one can't help but see Běijīng's point.

Since the handover, Hong Kong's biggest controversy, which sparked widespread protest in the region, were comments by a top Chinese cabinet official criticising a ruling by the Court of Final Appeal stating that offspring of a Hong Kong permanent resident had the right of abode in Hong Kong. The comments were viewed as interfering in Hong Kong's judicial system. Still, in the three years since the handover, Hong Kong remains relatively stable, with business recovering from the Asian economic crisis of the late 1990s. Hong Kong's Běijīng-approved leader, Chief Executive Tung Chee-hwa, although given to making remarks such as telling democrats to 'forget Tiānánmén', remains rather uncontroversial.

Macau was the oldest European settlement in the east until 20 December 1999, when it was returned to the People's Republic of China. As in Hong Kong, a new Basic Law was established for the Macau SAR, enacted by the PRC's National People's Congress, and acts as a mini-constitution, prescribing the systems to be practised in the SAR. Similar to the arrangement with Hong Kong, Macau will govern itself for a period of 50 years and Portuguese will remain one of the official languages. However, it is assumed that the provisions of the Basic Law will ensure the implementation of the policies of the mainland government with regard to Macau. Prior to the handover, Edmund Ho Hau Wah was chosen as Chief Executive.

Taiwan

The Kuomintang (KMT, now known as the Nationalist Party) government of Chiang Kaishek fled to Taiwan in 1949 following the communist takeover and has been there ever since, getting steadily richer. Its foreign currency reserves are among the world's largest. Following the election on 18 March 2000, when the Democratic Progressive Party (DPP) wrested power from the KMT after half a century of rule, it is arguably the most democratic of the 'Four Little Tigers', or 'Dragons' as the Chinese refer to them (the others are South Korea, Singapore and Hong Kong).

The people of Taiwan have been watching the Chinese takeover of Hong Kong and Macau with trepidation. Their concern is not merely political: Taiwanese media reports on the eve of the handover of Macau put the amount of Taiwan investment in the fledgling SAR as high as US$1 billion, with over 1500 Taiwan-based firms choosing to use Macau as a springboard for their mainland operations. According to Taiwan's Mainland Affairs Council (MAC), 63% of passengers passing through Macau International Airport in 1999, that is more than 1.4 million trips, originated in Taiwan.

But the main concern of Taiwanese people was expressed by the former chairman of the MAC, Su Chi, in an interview with Taiwan's *China Times*, when he said that Běijīng had long been touting a 'Hong Kong and Macau first, Taiwan later' strategy in its efforts to persuade Taiwan into accepting its 'one country, two systems' unification formula. The problem is a simple one. The KMT occupied Taiwan while maintaining the fiction that they were the legitimate government of all China (the Republic of China, or ROC). The communists, for their part, maintain that Taiwan is a province of China (the People's Republic of China, or PRC). The only thing that both sides could agree on was that China should be reunited 'very soon'.

With the pro-independence DPP looking likely to win only the second direct presidential poll (the first was in 1996), following a split in the ruling Nationalist Party prior to the March election, thinly veiled threats of military action emerged from no less a figure than Chinese Premier Zhu Rongji. Nonetheless, two factors in particular resulted in victory for the DPP's Chen Shui-bian: dissatisfaction with corruption and with half a century during which the interests of KMT refugees (about 13% of the population) were put above those of native Taiwanese whose ancestors migrated centuries ago (about 73% of the population). Above all, this election shows the determination of the Taiwanese to control their own destiny having been pawns in the communist–KMT struggle for half a century. In this respect, there are those who believe China's stance actually helped boost Chen's vote.

Military action, of course, was not taken. Instead, Běijīng is adopting a wait-and-see approach. Indeed, it is difficult to see what else they could do barring a full-scale invasion, which would inevitably involve the USA. Despite sabre-rattling, it is notable that there was no repeat of China's 'missile testing' prior to the 1996 election, which brought two US aircraft carriers to the region. During the election campaign Chen, for his part, deliberately played down his party's pro-independence stance and made it clear he was willing to be pragmatic, if not conciliatory, with regard to unification. Since the election, it appears the clause advocating independence may be dropped from the party's charter, while Chen himself is eager to go to Běijīng for talks and has already offered to open direct lines of communication with the mainland that have been closed for 50 years.

Holding It Together

Overall, the Deng years brought political stability and rising living standards, but Deng died in early 1997. Jiang Zemin heads both the government and the party as state president and Communist Party general secretary. But Jiang's power is held in place by a fragile web of alliances and compromises. The reality is that China has never had a system for orderly succession.

Faced with a looming inner-party power struggle and an overall situation of increasingly uneven economic development, both Chinese and foreign experts voice concerns that the problems facing the current regime make it ripe for radical change, if not total collapse. It has become fashionable to quote the first paragraph of *Romance of the Three Kingdoms*, a classic novel that describes the struggles to reunify the empire during the Three Kingdoms period: 'The empire, long united, must divide; long divided, must unite. Thus it has always been'.

But the party so far has managed to keep a lid on things. As other communist governments crumbled and its neighbours were consumed by the Asian economic crisis, China has come through relatively unscathed. But at what price has this 'stability' come? Chinese people have no official means through which to vent dissatisfaction with the system. The party has a habit of crushing any form of organisation outside itself, pre-empting any source of threat to its stability. Dissidents who attempted to register a democratic political party were quickly given harsh jail terms; members of Falun Gong, a seemingly innocuous meditation sect, suffered a countrywide crackdown which banned the practice and resulted in the arrest and 're-education' of its members, which numbered in the millions. The crackdown was in fact the largest purge of party members since the Tiānānmén massacre, as many Falun Gong followers were also party, PLA and security force members.

There are signs of attempts by the party to address social unrest, including (yet another) widely publicised anti-corruption campaign targeting shady government bureaucrats. Village elections in rural China continue, and there's even discussion that this taste of democracy could extend to the township level.

Ironically, however, if the western press is not announcing the impending collapse of China (with its attendant consequences for the world economy), it is warning of the dangers of an ascending and newly empowered China. China has the world's largest military and has nuclear capability. The party even celebrated its 50th anniversary by parading its weapons arsenal down Běijīng's main thoroughfare in a showcase of its military might. Both the USA and China's Asian neighbours are watching the situation with intense interest.

The next few years will be critical for China. Relations with the USA reached crisis point after the bombing of the Chinese embassy in Belgrade, while ongoing disputes over trade issues and human rights threatens China's export industries. The dismantling of the unprofitable state sector and dealing with the resulting unemployment remains an ongoing challenge. Paradoxically, China's entry into the WTO, long pursued by Běijīng, and the further opening up of China's economy could potentially threaten its fragile stability.

GEOGRAPHY

China is bounded to the north by deserts and to the west by the inhospitable Tibet-Qīnghǎi Plateau. The Han Chinese, who first built their civilisation around the Huáng Hé (Yellow River), moved south and east towards the sea. The Han did not develop as a maritime people so expansion was halted at the coast; they found themselves in control of a vast plain cut off from the rest of the world by oceans, mountains and deserts.

China is the third largest country in the world, after Russia and Canada, and has an area of 9.5 million sq km. Only half of China is occupied by Han Chinese; the rest is inhabited by Mongols, Tibetans, Uyghurs and a host of other 'national minorities' who occupy the periphery of China. The existence of numerous minority languages is why maps of China often have two spellings for the same place – one spelling being the minority language, the other being Chinese. For example, Kashgar is the same place as Kashi.

From the capital, Běijīng, the government rules 21 provinces and the five 'autonomous regions' of Inner Mongolia, Níngxià, Xīnjiāng, Guǎngxī and Tibet. The 'special municipalities' of Běijīng, Tiānjīn, Shànghǎi and most recently Chóngqìng are administered directly by the central government.

Taiwan, Hong Kong and Macau are all firmly regarded by the PRC as Chinese territory. Hong Kong was returned to Chinese

A Tale of Two Rivers

China's two major rivers are the Cháng Jiāng (Yangzi River) and the Huáng Hé (Yellow River). The Cháng Jiāng, surpassed in length only by the Amazon and the Nile, ís by far the more important. Commencing in the Tanggulashan mountains in south-west Qīnghǎi near the Tibetan border, it descends in an easterly direction to the sea near Shànghǎi for 6400km. Its watershed of almost 2 million sq km – 20% of China's land mass – supports a population of 400 million people. In the Red Basin area in Sìchuān alone, it nourishes more people than the combined populations of England and France.

Its initial descent from 6000m-high mountains is perilous. When a Chinese photographer called Yao Mao-shu tried to navigate the length of the river from its source in 1985, he completed only one-sixth of the journey before plunging to his death in a steep gorge where the currents run at 60km/h. In the following year, after a further attempt was abandoned, a Chinese team managed to complete the task, but only after four men were lost in the gorges and rapids.

The Middle River, as the central third is called, and the Lower River, below Wǔhàn – the Grain Basket of China, and a popular area for boat tours – have been profoundly important in China's development. Marco Polo travelled in the lower Cháng Jiāng region in the 13th century. He was astonished at the volume of navigation and trading in that area. For centuries, junks, sampans and other vessels have carried commodities such as rice, salt, silk, tea and oil on its waters. Of course, the river's advantages have been offset by problems of floods, which periodically inundate millions of hectares and destroy hundreds of thousands of lives.

The more northerly of the two, the Huáng Hé, is a very different river. Whereas the Cháng Jiāng is fondly referred to as the Long River, China's Main Street and China's Lifeline, the Huáng Hé is called China's Sorrow and the World's Muddiest River. It flows through yellow powdery soil known as loess, which has been deposited by monsoons and cyclones that howl across Inner Asian deserts. Because of its height above the surrounding plains, the east-west section receives no water from tributaries – unlike the Cháng Jiāng, which has more than 700 tributaries. As a result, it has flooded frequently and radically changed its course. It has carried little river traffic. Its volume is only one-tenth of that of the Cháng Jiāng. The loess soil on its banks can be used to build cave-like housing structures, such as those used by Mao Zedong and his followers between 1936 and 1947, but these are very vulnerable to seismic movement. In 1920, 300,000 people were buried in this area following an earthquake.

sovereignty in 1997 and Macau was handed over in 1999. There is conflict with Vietnam concerning sovereignty over the Nansha and Xisha island groups in the South China Sea; Vietnam claims both and has occupied some of the Nansha Islands. In 1989 the Chinese took some of these islands from Vietnam by force. Other disputed islands in the Nansha group are also claimed by the Philippines, Taiwan and Malaysia.

China's topography varies from mountainous regions with towering peaks to flat, featureless plains. The land surface is a bit like a staircase descending from west to east. At the top of the staircase are the plateaus of Tibet and Qīnghǎi in the southwest, averaging 4500m above sea level. Tibet is referred to as the 'Roof of the World'. At the southern rim of the plateau is the Himalayan mountain range, with peaks averaging 6000m high; 40 peaks rise 7000m or more. Mt Everest, known to the Chinese as Qomolangma Feng, lies on the China-Nepal border.

Melting snow and ice from the mountains of western China and the Tibet-Qīnghǎi Plateau provides the headwaters for many of the country's largest rivers: the Cháng Jiāng (Yangzi River), Huáng Hé (Yellow River), Láncāng Jiāng (Mekong River) and Nu Jiāng (Salween River). The latter runs from eastern Tibet into Yúnnán and on into Myanmar.

The Tarim Basin is the largest inland basin in the world and is the site of the Xīnjiāng Autonomous Region. Here you'll find the Taklamakan Desert (the largest in China) as well as China's largest shifting salt lake, Lop Nur (Luóbù Pō), where nuclear bombs are tested. The Tarim Basin is bordered to the north by the Tiān Shān mountains.

To the east of this range is the low-lying Turpan Depression, known as the 'Oasis of Fire', which is the hottest place in China. The Junggar Basin lies in the far north of Xīnjiāng Province, beyond the Tiān Shān range.

As you cross the mountains on the eastern edge of this second step of the topographical staircase, the altitude drops to less than 1000m above sea level. Here, forming the third step, are the plains of the Cháng Jiāng (Yangzi River) valley and northern and eastern China. These plains – the homeland of the Han Chinese, their 'Middle Kingdom' – are the most important agricultural areas of the country and the most heavily populated. It should be remembered that two-thirds of China is mountain, desert or otherwise unfit for cultivation. If you exclude the largely barren regions of Inner Mongolia, Xīnjiāng and the Tibet-Qīnghǎi Plateau from the remaining third, all that remains for cultivation is a meagre 15% or 20% of land area. Only this to feed more than a billion people!

In such a vast country, the waterways have taken on a central role as communication and trading links. Most of China's rivers flow east. At 6300km long, the Cháng Jiāng is the longest river in China and the third longest in the world after the Nile and the Amazon.

The Huáng Hé (Yellow River), about 5460km long and the second longest river in China, is the birthplace of Chinese civilisation. The third great waterway of China, the Grand Canal, is the longest artificial canal in the world. It originally stretched for 1800km from Hángzhōu in south China to Běijīng in the north. Today, however, most of the Grand Canal is silted over and no longer navigable.

CLIMATE

China has a lot of it. Spread over such a vast area, the country is subject to the worst extremes in weather, from the bitterly cold to the unbearably hot. There isn't really an 'ideal' time to visit the country, so use the following information as a rough guide to avoid temperature extremes. The warmest regions in winter are found in the south and south-west in areas such as Xīshuāngbǎnnà in Yúnnán, the southern coast and the island of Hǎinán Dǎo. In summer, high spots like Éméi Shān in Sìchuān are a welcome relief from the heat.

North

Winters in the north fall between December and March and are incredibly cold. Běijīng's temperature doesn't rise above 0°C (32°F), although it will generally be dry and sunny. North of the Great Wall, into Inner Mongolia or Hēilóngjiāng, it's much colder with temperatures dropping to -40°C (-40°F), and you'll see the curious sight of sand dunes covered in snow.

Summer in the north is around May to August. Běijīng temperatures can rise to 38°C (100°F) or more. July and August are also the rainy months in this city. In both the north and south most of the rain falls during summer.

Spring and autumn are the best times for visiting the north. Daytime temperatures range from 20°C to 30°C (68°F to 86°F) and there is less rain. Although it can be quite hot during the day, nights can be bitterly cold and bring frost.

Central

In the Cháng Jiāng (Yangzi River) valley area (including Shànghǎi) summers are long, hot and humid. Wǔhàn, Chóngqìng and Nánjīng have been dubbed 'the three furnaces' by the Chinese. You can expect very high temperatures any time between April and October.

Winters are short and cold, with temperatures dipping well below freezing – almost as cold as Běijīng. It can also be wet and miserable at any time apart from summer. While it is impossible to pinpoint an ideal time to visit, spring and autumn are probably best.

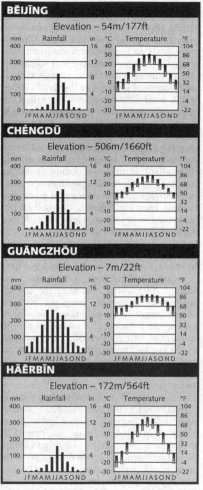

BĚIJĪNG
Elevation – 54m/177ft

KŪNMÍNG
Elevation – 1891m/6204ft

CHÉNGDŪ
Elevation – 506m/1660ft

LHASA
Elevation – 3658m/12,001ft

GUǍNGZHŌU
Elevation – 7m/22ft

SHÀNGHǍI
Elevation – 5m/16ft

HĀ̌ERBĪN
Elevation – 172m/564ft

ÜRÜMQI
Elevation – 918m/3011ft

South

In the far south, around Guǎngzhōu, the hot, humid periods last from around April to September, and temperatures can rise to 38°C (100°F). This is also the rainy season. Typhoons are liable to hit the south-east coast between July and September.

There is a short winter from January to March. It's nowhere near as cold as in the north, but temperature statistics don't really indicate just how cold it can get, so bring warm clothes.

Autumn and spring can be good times to visit the south, with day temperatures in the 20°C to 25°C (68°F to 75°F) range. However, it can also be miserably wet and cold, with perpetual rain or drizzle, so be prepared for all weather.

North-West

It gets hot in summer, but at least it's dry. The desert regions can be scorching in the daytime. Turpan, which sits in a depression 150m below sea level, more than deserves the title of the 'hottest place in China', with maximums of around 47°C (117°F).

In winter this region is as formidably cold as the rest of northern China. In Ürümqi the average temperature in January is around -10°C (14°F), with minimums down to almost -30°C (-22°F). Temperatures in Turpan are only slightly more favourable to human existence.

Tibet

In Tibet it's easy to get the impression that all four seasons have been compressed into one day. Temperatures can vary from below zero during the evening and early morning to a sizzling 38°C (100°F) at midday, but it always feels remarkably cool in the shade.

Winter brings intense cold and fierce winds. Snowfall is far less common in Tibet than the name 'Land of Snows' implies – it's an arid place and the sun is quick to melt off snowfalls. Rainfall is scarcest in the north and west of Tibet. Northern monsoons can sweep across the plains for days on end, often whipping up dust storms, sandstorms, snowstorms, or (rarely) rainstorms.

ECOLOGY & ENVIRONMENT

If you think that travelling abroad is like getting a breath of fresh air, you'd better not look at the facts and figures on China's environment. Like other developing countries, China's economic boom has come at the expense of controls on air pollution, land clearing, deforestation, endangered species and rural and industrial waste. China's huge population combined with geographical factors make its environmental problems infinitely more massive than that of other nations.

Prior to the reforms that began in 1978, environmental concerns were more likely to be dismissed as a bourgeois conspiracy. For a country that has constantly been going through an enormity of social change and development, it is surprising that there is much of an environment left to be concerned about. A recent phenomenon, however, is the government allowing Chinese individuals to legally form environmental groups, which in turn have had some success in raising public awareness of various environmental issues. The floods of 1998 in which over 3600 people were killed (in large part due to deforestation), brought much attention to the issue. Even Jiang Zemin, state president and CCP general secretary, has publicly called for action on the environment, ordering officials to 'pay close attention to co-ordinating economic construction efforts with population control and resource and environmental protection efforts.' How and whether this will be implemented is yet another arduous task facing the Chinese government.

Energy Use & Air Pollution

Nine out of 10 of the world's most polluted cities are found in China, and it is estimated that by 2005 China may have the not-so-prestigious status of being the world's largest source of air pollution. The land of the bicycle is facing stiff competition with an increase of cars and trucks on the road, which is exacerbating the already poor air quality of most Chinese cities.

Most of the major cities lie smothered under great canopies of smog. Tests conducted by the World Health Organisation (WHO) and China's National Environmental Protection Agency showed levels of airborne suspended particles average 526 micrograms per sq metre in northern China (WHO recommends a safe limit of 60 to 90 micrograms per sq metre). The first problem is coal. It provides for some 70% of China's energy needs and around 900 million tonnes of it go up in smoke every year. Some of it comes back to earth in the form of acid rain. This heavy reliance on coal has lead to an estimated 40% of the country being affected by acid rain. Even Korea and Japan have been airing their concerns about damage to their forests from acid rain that is believed to have come from China. Renewable energy use is still in its infant stages in China, with most of the resources going into hydro power. The main problem is that renewable energy is uncompetitive against an unsustainable and heavily subsidised coal power industry.

Desertification & Land Use

China has been combating the spread of its deserts for more than 40 years via aggressive afforestation programs. They have met with mixed success, as they're continually hampered by the ongoing stress placed on the land by overgrazing and irrigation. Nevertheless, forest coverage has doubled since 1949.

Every year large dust storms blow across Korea and Japan from China's loess plateau. The main cause of these storms is the desertification of large parts of northern and western China due to a lack of sustainable land management. China has been trying to avoid future drought and soil erosion through a system of afforestation. Unfortunately this has been hampered by the expansion of cash crops, particularly rubber, into old-growth forests by cash-strapped villages.

Water & Wetlands

China's rivers and wetlands face a great deal of pressure from draining and reclamation, as well as pollution from untreated industrial liquids, domestic sewerage, human waste and chemicals. It is estimated that China annually dumps three billion tonnes of untreated water into the ocean via its rivers. Some reports indicate that half the population is supplied with polluted water. This poor quality water, coupled with often acute water shortages, is creating significant environmental health hazards.

Environment versus Development

While its easy to point fingers at China's environmental record, the reality is that a big contributor to the environmental problems of developing nations are industrialised countries with high rates of consumption shifting their manufacturing base to developing countries with lower environmental protection standards. As the developing nation struggles to meet the basic human needs of its people, the economic necessity of resource exploitation more often than not prevails over badly managed conservation policies.

The good news is that the Chinese are acutely aware of both the short- and long-term effects of continuing degradation of grassland, forest, cropland, aquatic and coastal ecosystems. However, the problem lies in the low priority given to environmental and conservation issues in the light of the emphasis on continued expansion and development of the agricultural, industrial and energy resource base.

Two dramatic examples of this are the construction of the Sānxiá (Three Gorges) Dam on the Cháng Jiāng (Yangzi River) and the Xiaolangdi Dam on the Huáng Hé (Yellow River). Both dams promise much, but the realities of such grand schemes may be harder to fulfil.

Culture

China is faced with the pressing problem of protecting its dwindling cultural heritage from the pressures of economic advancement. Traditionally, the communist authorities have viewed most cultural relics as memories of the tyranny and oppression of the past and therefore destroyed or let them go to waste. However, Běijīng has recently switched to a policy of attempting to salvage remaining structures of historical and cultural importance in a nationalistic bid to embody the country's grand history. With an increase in cultural tourism, there will be more incentive to preserve important sites due to the resulting cash flow.

Global Implications

The impact of China's environmental problems doesn't stop at the country's borders – acid rain, desert sand storms, and silted and polluted rivers are all too familiar to China's neighbours. Across the north of China, rampaging natural fires are believed to consume more than 200 million tonnes of coal a year, further exacerbating China's contribution to global warming.

Education

None of these environmental hazards is good for anyone's health, and the government has made noises about taking action.

The problem is not that China lacks legislation designed to curb the worst excesses of industry (the central government recently established 230 new environmental standards), but that these laws are rarely enforced. It's not unusual to see huge billboards proclaiming the need to 'Preserve the Environment for Future Generations' plonked right next to huge industrial complexes belching out plumes of viscous-looking smoke and oozing untreated waste into a nearby river.

The countryside is feeling the pressure too, with pesticide poisoning becoming more prevalent. There has also been a move away from traditional farming methods towards the increased reliance on costly and hazardous fertilisers and pesticides.

The compelling economic pressure to exploit nature is exacerbated by a lack of awareness and education on the part of the masses. This translates into a lack of concern, although recent surveys suggest that a large proportion of the urban population is unhappy with the current state of the environment. The government is tackling the issue with radio and television campaigns that include publicising the names of companies and industries responsible for polluting the environment. There has also been an increase in the severity of penalties for violating China's conservation laws, with the death penalty and life sentences not uncommon. However, it must be said that there is still very little room for debating the issues in the media.

For the most part, the Chinese people seem to be taking the attitude that China can get rich and dirty, and then spend some of the proceeds on cleaning up. It's a time-honoured tradition around the world, but then China (the world's most populous nation) is unique in the grand scale it's abusing the environment. If the environment continues to be a secondary concern, then China's economic development may be severely retarded in the new millennium.

FLORA & FAUNA

China is endowed with an extremely diverse range of natural vegetation and animal life. There are about 30,000 species of seed plants and 2500 species of forest trees, representing a large variety of genera, many of which are indigenous to China. Unfortunately, human beings have had a considerable impact and much of China's rich natural heritage is rare, endangered or extinct. Many animals are officially protected, though illegal hunting and trapping continues. A bigger challenge is habitat destruction, caused by encroaching agriculture, urbanisation and industrial pollution. To the government's credit, more than 900 nature reserves have been established protecting about 7% of China's land area.

Flora

One of China's most famous plants must be bamboo. There are actually more than 300 species of bamboo plant covering about 3% of the total forest area in China. Most of this bamboo is located in the sub-tropical zones south of the Cháng Jiāng (Yangzi River). The plant is not only valued by the giant panda, but cultivated for use as a building material and food.

Many other well-known plants are indigenous to China, including the azalea, rhododendron, lotus flower, magnolia, ginkgo, maple, birch, poplar and spruce. The variety and intermixture of temperate and tropical plants in China is best understood by comparing the vegetation of Jílín Province in the semifrigid north and Hǎinán Province in the tropical south. It would be difficult to find one common plant species shared by the two provinces with the exception of a few weeds.

China's diversity of ecosystems supports an equivalent range of flora: the tropical forests of South China; the desert and steppe vegetation of north-western China; the taiga coniferous forests of the border areas adjoining Russia; and the mangrove swamps along the shores of the South China Sea. Tropical and temperate coniferous forests with broad-leaved evergreen and deciduous plants prevail in the southern provinces of Hǎinán, Yúnnán and Guǎngxī, whereas vast areas of desolate and very sparse salt-tolerant and drought-resistant vegetation prevails in the arid north-west. Along the borders of the Gobi Desert are wide plains of grasslands and just across to the north-east are the last great tracts of forests in China.

Fauna

China's wealth of vegetation and variety of landscapes has fostered the development of a great diversity of fauna.

In spite of the odds against them, a number of rare animals continue to survive in small and remote areas of China. Notable among such survivors are the small species of alligator in central and eastern China, the giant salamander in western China, and the Cháng Jiāng (Yangzi River) dolphin. The diversity of fauna is perhaps greatest in the valleys and ranges of Sìchuān and Tibet and it is here that the giant panda is confined.

Perhaps no animal better represents both the beauty and the struggle of wildlife in China than the panda. These splendid animals are endangered by a combination of hunting, habitat encroachment and natural disasters. Through a number of joint programs run by Chinese and overseas agencies, animals like the giant panda and the Cháng Jiāng dolphin are receiving more attention and protection, which will hopefully guarantee their survival.

Throughout the Chinese mountains, takin (or goat antelope), wild yaks, argali sheep, numerous species of pheasants, and a variety of laughing thrushes may be found. The extreme north-eastern part of China is inhabited by some interesting mammals, such as reindeer, moose, musk deer, bears, sables and tigers.

This region also features considerable birdlife, such as cranes, ducks, bustards, swans and herons. Good bird-watching possibilities exist, especially in the spring. Some good places for this activity include the nature reserve, Zhālóng, in Hēilóngjiāng; Qīnghǎi Hú in Qīnghǎi; and Póyáng Hú in northern Jiāngxī, China's largest freshwater lake.

For sheer diversity of flora and fauna, the tropical south of Yúnnán Province, particularly the area around Xīshuāngbǎnnà, is one of the richest in China. This region provides habitats for the parrot, hornbill, slender loris, gibbon, snub-nosed monkey, and herds of wild Indian elephants.

If you're interested in delving further into China's flora and fauna, two good books on the subject are *Living Treasures* by Tang Xiyang and *The Natural History of China* by Zhao Ji et al.

Cruelty to Animals

While China's treatment of animals is not the best, it's not the worst either. Travellers most frequently come up against hard reality when they visit some of the markets, many of which resemble take-away zoos. The southern provinces of Guǎngdōng and Guǎngxī are particularly notable for the wide selection of unusual still-living delicacies on offer – dogs, cats, rats, snakes, monkeys, scorpions, lizards, turtles and other exotica.

In western countries, shoppers are usually shielded from the messy business of slaughtering animals, but in China it's often done right in front of the customer – for larger animals, a swift blow on the head with a club is the usual means of execution.

Things can get nasty down on the farm – the way in which deer are confined in dark hovels is not very humane. The notorious bear-bile extraction industry has come in for particularly virulent condemnation by animal rights activists.

Endangered Species

China's endangered plants and animal list is depressingly long. Animals on the list include the giant panda, snow leopard, Cháng Jiāng dolphin, South China tiger, chiru antelope, crested ibis, Asian elephant, golden monkey, red-crowned crane and black-crowned crane, to name just a few.

Unprotected forest areas are diminishing due to intensive farmland cultivation, the reclaiming of wetlands, damming of rivers, industrial and rural waste, and desertification. All these factors put more pressure on isolated populations.

Most of China's endangered species are found in and adjoining the 900 or so protected nature reserves. The problems of monitoring and managing the reserves, as well as adjacent areas, are complicated by a complex network of government departments.

Nature Reserves

Despite a history of resource, population and pollution pressures, China has an incredibly diverse range of natural escapes scattered across the country. In fact in 2000, China had a total of 926 nature reserves covering over 7% of its total surface area. These parks offer the traveller an incredible variety of landscapes and a rich diversity of flora and fauna.

Some notable ones include: Jiǔzhàigōu in Sìchuān Province, Zhāngjiājiè in Húnán Province and Chángbái Shān in Jílín Province. Most of China's sacred mountains (including Pǔtuóshān, Wǔtái Shān, Éméi Shān, Huá Shān and Jiǔhuá Shān) have also been converted into nature reserves.

Though the prospect for increasing the total number of nature reserves looks good, environmentalists shouldn't cheer too loudly since most of China's parklands are under heavy pressure from commercial development.

GOVERNMENT & POLITICS

Precious little is known about the inner workings of the Chinese government, but what is known is that the entire monolithic structure, from grassroots work units to the upper echelons of political power, is controlled by the Communist Party.

Power in China is by no means visible in the form of appointed leaders and designated institutions, as could be seen in the case of Deng Xiaoping, who before his death remained the most powerful man in China even when he was officially retired and held no official titles whatsoever.

The highest authority rests with the Standing Committee of the CCP Politburo. The Politburo comprises 25 members and below it is the 210-member Central Committee, made up of younger party members and provincial party leaders. At grassroots level the party forms a parallel system to the administrations in the army, universities, government and industries. Real authority is exercised by the party representatives at each level in these organisations. They, in turn, are responsible to the party officials in the hierarchy above them, thus ensuring strict central control.

The day-to-day running of the country lies with the State Council, which is directly under the control of the CCP. The State Council is headed by the premier and beneath the premier are four vice-premiers, 10 state councillors, a secretary-general, 45 ministers and various other agencies. The State Council implements the decisions made by the Politburo: it draws up quotas, assesses planning, establishes priorities and organises finances. The ministries include Public Security, Education, Defence, Culture, Forestry, Railways, Tourism, Minority Affairs, Radio & TV, the Bank of China and Family Planning.

Rubber-stamping the decisions of the CCP leadership is the National People's Congress (NPC). It comprises a 'democratic alliance' of both party members and non-party members who include intellectuals, technicians and industrial managers. In theory they are empowered to amend the constitution and to choose the premier and members of the State Council. The catch is that all these office-holders must first be recommended by the Central Committee, and thus the NPC is only an approving body.

The Chinese government is also equipped with a massive bureaucracy. The term 'cadre' is usually applied to bureaucrats, and their monopoly on power means that wide-ranging perks are a privilege of rank for all and sundry – from the lowliest clerks to the shadowy puppet masters of Zhongnanhai. China's bureaucratic tradition is a long one.

At grassroots level, the basic unit of social organisation outside the family is the work unit (dānwèi). Every Chinese person is theoretically a member of one, whether he or she works in a hospital, a school, an office, a factory or a village, although increasingly Chinese nowadays slip through the net by being self-employed or working in a private operation. For those who are members, tight controls are exercised by the leaders of the unit to which they belong.

The work unit is a perfect organ of social control and little proceeds without it. It approves marriages and divorces and even childbirth. It assigns housing, sets salaries, handles mail, recruits party members, keeps files on each unit member, arranges transfers to other jobs or other parts of the country, and gives permission to travel abroad. The work unit's control extends into every part of the individual's life.

The wild card in the system is the army. Comprising land forces, the navy and the air force, it has a total of around 2.9 million members. China is divided into seven military regions, each with its own military leadership – in some cases with strong regional affiliations.

A breakdown of central power might result in a return to the warlordism of the early 20th century or a unified putsch by the PLA. In any event, the PLA is a force to be reckoned with.

Political Dissidence & Repression

The brutal massacre in Tiānānmén Square in 1989 focused world attention on China's political repression, but it was not the end of the story. In the mid-1990s there were a few cases of high-profile, relatively organised dissent. In mid-1995, 12 petitions had been signed by prominent intellectuals, largely calling for greater freedom of speech and, specifically, a re-evaluation of the Tiānānmén Square protests.

The petitions resulted predictably in a round of arrests, and at the time of writing the hardliners seemed to be reasserting themselves and China was cracking down once again. Wang Dan, a leader in the Tiānānmén Square protests, was re-arrested in 1996 and sentenced to 11 years in prison. Wei Jingsheng received another 14-year sentence. In 1997 two dissidents in Shēnzhèn (Li Wenming and Guo Baosheng) were each sentenced to three years in prison. Many other dissidents are being

held under house arrest. And in 1998 dissidents who tried to form a democratic political party were sentenced to 13-year and 11-year prison terms. In Xīnjiāng, several Muslim separatists were executed for taking part in an anti-Běijīng protest.

One of the great problems of Chinese dissenters is that they rarely find much to agree on. The ringleaders of the Tiānānmén protests, most of whom fled the country in the wake of the massacre, have failed to organise as a group outside China, and some of them have given up politics entirely; Wuer Kaixi, famously captured on TV arguing it out with Li Peng, was last seen running a Sizzler-style steak bar in California.

Other prominent foreign based dissidents such as Fang Lizhi and Liu Binyan are considered too old and too removed from current events in China to really matter to many young dissidents. It's fair to say that, for the moment, China has successfully crushed any organised resistance to the government.

Democracy?

While the previous description of China's government makes it appear anything but democratic, there is one curious anomaly – local governments for villages with a population under 10,000. In the 1990s, a little-noticed reform permitted small villages to elect their own leaders. Recently there's even been discussion that this taste of democracy could extend to the township level.

Optimists have pointed to this reform, suggesting it's the beginning of a major movement towards democracy throughout China. Believers in this scenario predict that China will continue to democratise as the leadership is gradually handed over to the younger generation. The fact that more and more young Chinese have had the chance to travel, live, work and study in the west should encourage this trend.

Pessimists note the case of Hong Kong, whose democratically elected Legislative Council was dismissed the day the British handed over the colony to China. The world will no doubt be watching with bated breath to see if the dragon can be tamed by a foreign notion called democracy.

ECONOMY

Under Mao, China's economy was a prisoner to ideology and incompetence. The reign of Deng Xiaoping (essentially 1977 to 1997) has been a period of reforms. The moribund Maoist economy has been dramatically reinvigorated. In short, Deng chose a pragmatic approach to achieving the so-called 'Four Modernisations': namely, modernisation of China's industry, agriculture, defence, and science and technology.

Rural China was the birthplace of Deng's pioneering economic reforms. Having been forcibly collectivised during the Mao era, the 'household responsibility system' of the late 1970s allowed farmers to sell whatever they wanted on the free market after government quotas had been filled. Productivity rose and a new era of plenty was heralded for rural China.

Unfortunately, rural earnings lag far behind urban incomes. Increased mechanisation and fertiliser use has increased productivity, but has also led to a scarcity of work – there are perhaps as many as 100 million farm labourers without regular employment. Rural industries (factories in the countryside) have absorbed some of the surplus agricultural workers, but as many as 15 million peasants a year flock to the coastal cities every year in the hope of finding employment – often they end up working long hours in poorly paid factory or construction jobs.

After two decades of high growth, China's economy is now slowing and unemployment is on the rise. The state's current aim to restructure inefficient state-owned enterprises is costing millions of jobs and is leading to social unrest among laid-off workers, many of whom feel the government has abandoned them to the market economy. In an attempt to stimulate the economy, the government has turned to pouring money into public works projects. But consumers, worried about layoffs, are holding on to their money. Privatisation as a means of reviving the state sector has also been scaled back, basically out of fear by the party that further privatisation would undermine its rule.

Chinese leaders hope that WTO membership will spur the economy. In the short term, however, membership would certainly mean more factory closings and unemployment. In the longer term, it's hoped that it will increase imports and exports, force state industries into the market and revive foreign investment. Pessimists take the view that the government's hesitancy to reform its state enterprises at a faster rate and its unwillingness to nurture the private sector will drive China to crisis point. Optimists point out that China's policy of gradual economic reform has basically worked well so far and has allowed China to come out unscathed from Asia's economic crisis.

POPULATION & PEOPLE

The official figures for 1999 show mainland China (excluding Taiwan) with a population of 1.26 billion people. Officially, only 30% of the total population is classified as urban, which is low by any standards (Australia's population is 86% urban). The figures are changing though, as the countryside urbanises and farmers abandon the land and migrate into the cities in search of work.

The huge population has to be fed with the produce of around 15% to 20% of the land they live on – the sum total of China's arable land. The rest is barren wasteland or can only be lightly grazed. Much of the productive land is also vulnerable to flood and drought caused by the vagaries of China's summer monsoons or unruly rivers.

Worse still, China's arable land is shrinking at an alarming rate. Industrialisation, urbanisation and erosion are robbing the country of valuable farmland while the population continues to grow. The Malthusian prospect of an ever-growing population, with an ever-shrinking capacity to feed itself, led the government to promote a limited birth control program in the 1950s, but this was abandoned during the Cultural Revolution. The responsibility lies with Mao Zedong, whose decision was probably his greatest mistake. He believed that birth control was a capitalist plot to make China weak and that the country would find

Sherry Liu

I went to America in 1986. Unlike most of the ambitious young people who wanted to study or find work, I left China to follow the man I loved.

Sadly, our marriage didn't work out, though I gained in other ways. Since law was the only free course on offer I enrolled at law school and mastered English by attending class. In my first few years in America, I faced an identity and value crisis. America seemed so much more civilised than China, with a greater material life. Fellow Chinese envied my success as a lawyer but I knew I was never assigned any major cases. I sound ungrateful as the firm was good to me, but half my brain was asleep.

I thought I loved my own country, but its society was so mismanaged, I had to stay abroad. Gradually I became reconciled with myself, though ego prevented me from doing China-related work. When Motorola knocked on my door in 1995, I had been away from China for 10 years, but my friends persuaded me it makes sense to use one's best strength.

OXFORD UNIVERSITY PRESS

A few weeks after my return [to China], my American boss handed me all the documents on our marathon negotiations with a Chinese partner for a pager joint-venture in Shànghǎi. I was left on my own, under pressure to reach a deal before a deadline that meant millions of dollars in tax breaks. Each side had different agendas, but at dawn on the third day we reached an acceptable consensus, just in time.

I soon realised that knowing how to function in China is in my blood. I feel like a mediator bridging the two cultures, or 'a fish in water', as the Chinese say. China is a socialist country, meaning the government is heavily involved in almost everything. In the West, you largely do business on your own. 'Don't panic!' I tell Western multinationals. 'Make an informed decision and sleep with it.' It is up to me to effect that compromise. A giant like Motorola cannot afford to stand around and wait.

I believe foreign investment does have a positive impact in China, because foreign companies require greater transparency, meaning no closed-door decisions. Tremendous progress *has* been made in China's legal system, though there is a long way to go. Problems include consistency, interpretation and enforcement. Court verdicts should be based on right and wrong, not who knows who, or offers the bigger bribe.

I usually come over as a patriot since I always try to defend China. Despite the frustrations of living and working here, I see China in a better light as I remember what its past was like. I can't blame the millions of Chinese in America who don't want to come back. It is only human nature to seek a better life. Fortunately, as China opens up and gradually enters the world family, there are more opportunities here. I didn't see it so clearly until my own return.

**Abridged from *China Remembers* by Zhang Lijia and Calum MacLeod,
an oral history of the PRC, published by Oxford University Press (1999)**

strength in a large population. His ideas very much reflected his background of the peasant farmer for whom many hands make light work in the fields. It wasn't until 1973 that a nationwide birth-control program was instituted, with each couple permitted to have just one child.

The original plan was to limit growth to 1.25 billion people by the year 2000, hold that figure steady somehow, and allow birth control and natural mortality to reduce the population to 700 million, which China's leaders estimate would be ideal. Current projections, however, indicate that China's population will be close on 1.5 billion by the year 2010, and that the present population could double within 50 years.

In recent years the main thrust of the campaign in the cities has been to encourage couples to sign a one-child pledge by offering them an extra month's salary per year until the child is 14, plus housing normally reserved for a family of four (a promise sometimes not kept because of the housing shortage). If the couple have a second child then the privileges are rescinded, and penalties such as demotion at work or even loss of job are imposed. If a woman has an abortion it entitles her to a vacation with pay.

Birth-control measures appear to be working in the cities, but it's difficult to say what's happening in the villages or if the target of zero growth can ever be reached. The catch is that Chinese agriculture still relies on human muscle and farmers still find it desirable to have many children. As is the case in China regarding the implementation of government policies and laws, enforcement varies with the enforcer: some local officials have been known to resort to forced abortions, confiscation of property and other coercive means, while others look the other way.

On the other hand, families who do abide by the one-child policy will often go to great lengths to make sure their child is male. This is particularly true in rural China, where the ancient custom of female infanticide continues to this day. In parts of China, this is creating a serious imbalance of the sexes. One survey in Shaanxi

Province, for example, determined that 145 male infants were being born for every 100 females. The overall average for China is 114 males for every 100 females.

If China's one-child policy does succeed, one looming consequence will be a rapidly ageing population. The baby boom generated by Mao's policies has created a population that is today overwhelmingly young. The baby bust of the one-child policy will create the opposite. In the 1990s, less than 5% of the population supported an elderly person; by 2050 it is estimated that almost 50% of the population will do so. Only when the birth and death rates are in balance (and China is able to re-adopt a two-child policy) will the population be reasonably middle-aged.

Han Chinese make up about 93% of the population; the rest is composed of China's 55 officially recognised ethnic minorities. China actually claims that there are 56 by creating the somewhat bogus 'Gaoshan' minority in Taiwan. It's 'somewhat bogus' because the nine aboriginal tribes in Taiwan all reject the label 'Gaoshan', which Běijīng has assigned to them, and because many Taiwanese do not agree that Taiwan is part of China.

Although minorities account for about 7% of the population, they are distributed over some 50% of Chinese-controlled territory, mostly in the sensitive border regions. Minority separatism has always been a threat to the stability of China, particularly among the Uyghurs and the Tibetans, who have poor and often volatile relations with the Han Chinese. The minority regions provide China with the greater part of its livestock and hold vast untapped deposits of minerals.

Maintaining amicable relations with the minorities has been a continuous problem for the Han Chinese. Tibet and Xīnjiāng are heavily garrisoned by Chinese troops, partly to protect China's borders and partly to prevent rebellion among the local population.

The Chinese government has also set up special training centres, like the National Minorities Institute in Běijīng, to train minority cadres for these regions. Since 1976 the government has tried to diffuse discontent by relaxing some of its grasp on the day-to-day

Wives for Sale

As China continues to shed the austerities of the hardline communist years, many of the old ways are returning. The Chinese are going back to their temples, burning paper money for their ancestors, playing mahjong and, in time-honoured tradition, the sale of wives in rural China is once again coming back into fashion.

Outlawed by Mao and effectively suppressed after 1949, the trafficking of women reappeared in China with Deng Xiaoping's reforms of the late 1970s that relaxed controls and opened the country to the market economy. Current statistics of the practice vary wildly. A state-run newspaper reported in 1999 that police had rescued 23,000 abducted women between 1996 and 1998 and arrested 26,000 people for trafficking women. Given that the number of arrested exceeds the number rescued, it is not surprising that many assume the number of women sold into marriage is much higher than the figure given, perhaps double according to one Chinese journalist.

The demand for wives in rural areas has increased over the past decade as many women leave poor villages in search of work in nearby cities. The one-child policy and traditional preference for baby boys has led to high rates of selective abortions and infanticide, which has further imbalanced the ratio of women to men. In the countryside there is approximately 130 males for every 100 females. To tip the scales, it is often cheaper for a man to buy a wife for between Y2000 and Y4000 than to pay upwards of Y10,000 for betrothal gifts.

Women, who are often under the age of 20, are either lured by traffickers with promises of work or are often abducted at knife-point. Many are drugged and raped and resold a number of times. While an increasing number of these women are escaping (or attempting to), this had led to the practice of cutting the tendons in the women's feet and ankles to stop them from running away. Family members and neighbours often support the buyers by guarding over the newly acquired 'wife'. Other women are prevented from reporting what has happened to them for reasons of shame or because local authorities are in cahoots with the traffickers.

While the Chinese government reports that strong efforts are being made to stamp out the selling of women and have made attempts to hammer it home through public executions of traffickers, there appears to be little evidence that the practise is diminishing.

life of the minority peoples, in particular allowing temples and mosques closed during the Cultural Revolution to reopen.

EDUCATION

China records an official literacy rate of 80%, which is above average for a third world country, but still far short of developed country standards. Many minority people cannot read Chinese characters, but may be literate in their own native scripts.

In theory, China still upholds the Confucian system in which one gains entrance to the best schools through competitive examinations rather than connections. In practice, money and political connections definitely help. Getting one's child into an elite school is the dream of every Chinese parent, but only about 1% of applicants are so lucky.

Until very recently, all education right through to university level was 100% state-funded. In return, university graduates must accept whatever job the state wishes to assign them. However, the past few years has seen a radical new experiment – students can pay their own way through school and are then free to take a job of their own choosing. Of course, most Chinese cannot afford this, although some manage by borrowing money from their relatives.

China has belatedly recognised the economic value of having an educated population at least semi-fluent in various foreign languages. English is by far the most popular foreign language, and there's many young Chinese who will be anxious to practice.

If you want to meet English-speaking Chinese then go to the 'English corners' that have developed in many large Chinese cities. Usually held on a Sunday morning in a convenient park, Chinese people who speak, or are learning, English gather to practise the language. Also seek out the 'English Salons' – evening get-togethers at which the Chinese practise English, listen to lectures or hold debates in English.

ARTS

Many of China's ancient art treasures were ransacked or razed to the ground during the Cultural Revolution. Precious pottery, calligraphy and embroidery was defaced or destroyed.

Fortunately, since the early 1970s a great deal of work has been done to restore what was destroyed in the Cultural Revolution. Initially, restoration was carried out only on major attractions with foreign tourism in mind, but with local tourism emerging as a major money-spinner in the 1990s tourist attractions all over China are having cash pumped into them. On a less positive note, China's cultural and artistic tourist attractions have often been tackily restored and are swarming with pushy souvenir entrepreneurs advertising with loud speakers.

Music

Traditional Chinese musical instruments include the two-stringed fiddle *(èrhú)*, three-stringed flute *(sānxián)*, four-stringed banjo *(yuèqín)*, two-stringed viola *(húqín)*, vertical flute *(dòngxiāo)*, horizontal flute *(dízi)*, piccolo *(bāngdí)*, four-stringed lute *(pípa)*, zither *(gǔzhēng)*, ceremonial trumpet *(suǒnà)* and ceremonial gongs *(dàluó)*.

Popular Music

China is beginning to develop a thriving music industry. Much of it is heavily influenced by the already well established music industries in Taiwan and Hong Kong, but these are in turn influenced by western musical trends, as the recent popularity of Cantonese rap and Taiwanese-language rock experiments have shown.

China has generally been slow in developing a market for western music (much of what is available in the shops is of the Car-

penters ilk), but the advent of satellite TV (now widely available) and the popularity of MTV and Channel V, broadcast via Hong Kong's Star TV network, is set to change all that.

China's first concert featuring a foreign rock group was in April 1985, when the British group Wham! performed. The audience remained sedate – music fans who dared to get up and dance in the aisles were hauled off by the PSB. Since then, things have become more liberal and China has produced some notable local bands.

Běijīng seems to be the hard rock and heavy metal capital of China. Cui Jian was a pioneer in bringing real rock and roll to China in the late 1980s, and he is still active – in 1997 he even did a concert in Taiwan. More recently popular is Li Jie. Cobra (Yǎnjìngshé) is an all-woman rock band from Beijing. Recent years have even spawned a number of heavy metal bands, better known ones being Tang Dynasty (Táng Cháo), Black Panther (Hēi Bào) and Reincarnation (Lúnhuí).

Ceramics

Earthenware production has a long history in China. As many as 8000 years ago Chinese tribes were making artefacts with clay. The primitive 'Yangshao' culture (which existed along the Huáng Hé) is noted for its distinctive pottery painted with flowers, fish, animals, human faces and geometric designs. Around 3500 BC the 'Longshanoid' culture (first found near the village of Lóngshān in Shāndōng) was making white pottery and eggshell-thin black pottery.

Pottery making was well advanced by the Shang period; the most important development occurred around the middle of the dynasty with the manufacture of a greenish glaze applied to stoneware artefacts. During the Han dynasty the custom of glazing pottery became fairly common. However, the production of terracotta items – made from a mixture of sand and clay, fired to produce a reddish-brown colour and left unglazed – continued.

During the Southern and Northern Song dynasties, a type of pottery halfway between Han glazed pottery and true porcelain was

Běijīng Music Scene

Rock music flourishes amid adversity, and Běijīng serves it up in abundance. The grit, the unforgiving climate, the dehumanising concrete and the dislocating pace of change in the capital create a climate in which rock music has thrived. Sneers, snarls, scowls – the essential vocab of rock body language – are learned easily from the surly cabbies that prowl Běijīng's dusty streets. Unlike the milder and more genteel cities of the South like Shànghǎi and Guǎngzhōu, where syrupy Hong Kong and Taiwan pop idols still rule the airwaves, Běijīng has a flourishing rock scene that offers up everything from cerebral progressive to head-banging metal, funk to punk, slam to glam.

Beginning in the mid-1980s, as cassette players became commonplace and as increasing numbers of foreign students' tape collections were duplicated and circulated, rock gained a small but dedicated following. At first, expats formed bands with young Chinese musicians, but by 1988 home-grown outfits like Black Panther (Hēi Bào) and May Day (Wu Yue Tian) were playing shows not only in Běijīng but in the provinces as well. My own ex-band, Tang Dynasty (Táng Cháo), often rode the rails to remote venues where we slogged it out loud and lo-fi before bewildered audiences who gaped with hands as often as not clapped to their ears. Yaogun Yue (literally 'rock-roll music') was still mysterious: 'I see lots of rocking,' commented one puzzled observer in Inner Mongolia, 'but where's the rolling?'.

Undaunted, the rockers plowed forward, and a handful of bands managed to get signed with foreign labels in the early 1990s: pop-rockers Black Panther signed with JVC, and progressive metalists Tang Dynasty with Taiwan's Rock Records. In the last five or six years, Běijīng has witnessed an explosion of new rock talent.

While Běijīng 's post-Cui Jian rock musicians generally ostensibly bristle at the tendency of westerner observers to pigeonhole them as anti-authoritarian rebels, they're not above pandering to the west when it can get them media attention. The attention that the Běijīng bands have received in the international media has, some might argue, given them an exaggerated sense of self-importance, and many have become complacent. Cities like Kūnmíng and Chéngdū have, in the meantime, produced some fresh, original talent that may one day topple Běijīng's rock monopoly.

Punk seems to be all the rage in Běijīng these days, and true to the genre's spirit, PRC punkers abjure good musicianship and build their careers on three chords, knee-jerk iconoclasm, body art and hair dye. Whatever you might think of bands like Anarchy Jerks, 69, Reflector and Brain Failure, the punks are admittedly a healthy antidote to formulaic glitter-rock love balladeers like Zero (Ling Dian) and Black Panther, who remain locked in the Bon Jovi mould.

While Běijīng has its share of poser punks and soulless pop rockers, there's not inconsiderable talent in the capital. My personal favorites are Overload (Chaozai), a hard-edged guitar rock band with metal roots, and Thin Man (Shou Ren), a super-tight hard funk ensemble. Also noteworthy are Zi Yue (Confucius Sez, a band that combines splendid chops with dry, wry Běijīng wit) and Cold Blooded Animals (Lengxue Dongwu), a sinister and grungy power trio.

Kaiser Kuo
(former lead guitarist in Tang Dynasty)

produced. The proto-porcelain was made by mixing clay with quartz and the mineral feldspar to make a hard, smooth-surfaced vessel. Feldspar was mixed with traces of iron to produce an olive-green glaze.

Chinese pottery reached its artistic peak under the Song rulers. During this time true porcelain was developed. It was made of fine kaolin clay and was white, thin and translucent. Porcelain was produced under the Yuan, but gradually lost the delicacy and near-perfection of the Song products. However, it was probably during the Yuan dynasty that 'blue-and-white' porcelain made its first appearance. Another noted invention was mono-coloured porcelain in ferrous red, black or dark blue. A new range of mono-coloured vessels was developed under the Qing.

During the Qing period the production of coloured porcelain continued with the addition of new colours and glazes and more complex decorations. This was the age of true painted porcelain, decorated with delicate landscapes, birds and flowers. Elaborate designs and brilliant colouring became the fashion. Porcelain imitations of other materials, such as gold and silver, mother of pearl, jade, bronze, wood and bamboo, also became popular.

Bronze Vessels

Bronze is an alloy whose chief elements are copper, tin and lead. Tradition ascribes the first casting of bronze to the legendary Xia dynasty of 5000 years ago.

The Shang dynasty ruler and the aristocracy are believed to have used a large number of bronze vessels for sacrificial offerings of food and wine. Zhou dynasty bronze vessels tend to have long messages in ideographic characters; they describe wars, rewards, ceremonial events and the appointment of officials.

Bronze mirrors were used as early as the Shang dynasty and had already developed into an artistic form by the Warring States period. Ceramics gradually replaced bronze utensils by Han times, but bronze mirrors were not displaced by glass mirrors until the Qing dynasty. The backs of bronze mirrors were inscribed with wishes for good fortune and protection from evil influence. Post-Han writings are full of fantastic stories of the supernatural powers of mirrors. One of them relates the tale of Yin Zhongwen, who held a mirror to look at himself, but found that his face was not reflected – soon after, he was executed.

Jade

The jade stone has been revered in China since Neolithic times. Jade was firstly utilised for tools because of its hardness and strength, but later appeared on ornaments

and ceremonial vessels for its decorative properties. In the periods of the Qin and Han dynasties, people began to believe that jade was empowered with magical and life-giving properties, and began to bury their dead with jadeware. Opulent jade suits, meant to prevent decomposition, have been found in Han tombs, whilst Taoist alchemists, hoping to become immortal, ate elixirs of powdered jade. Jade was also considered a guardian against disease and evil spirits, and even now pillowcases can be purchased in Chinese department stores with jade squares attached to ward off disease.

Jade's value lies not just in its scarcity, but depends also on its hardness and the skill with which it has been carved. While the pure white form is the most highly valued, the stone varies in translucency and colour, including many shades of green, brown and black.

Funerary Objects

As early as Neolithic times (9000–6000 BC), offerings of pottery vessels and stone tools or weapons were placed in graves to accompany the departed.

During the Shang dynasty, precious objects such as bronze ritual vessels, weapons and jade were buried with the dead. Dogs, horses and even human beings were sacrificed for burial in the tombs of great rulers. When this practice was abandoned, replicas (usually in pottery) were made of human beings, animals and precious objects. A whole repertoire of objects was produced especially for burial, making symbolic provision for the dead without wasting wealth or making human sacrifice.

Burial objects made of earthenware were very popular from the 1st to the 8th centuries AD. During the Han dynasty, pottery figures were cast in moulds and painted in bright colours after firing. Statues of attendants, entertainers, musicians, acrobats and jugglers were made, as well as models of granaries, watchtowers, pigpens, stoves and various other things.

Close trade links with the west were illustrated among these models by the appearance among funerary objects of the two-humped Bactrian camel, which carried merchandise along the Silk Road. Warriors with west Asian faces and heavy beards appeared as funerary objects during the Northern Wei dynasty.

The cosmopolitan life of Tang China was illustrated by its funerary wares; western and central Asians flocked to the capital at Cháng'ān and were portrayed in figurines of merchants, attendants, warriors, grooms, musicians and dancers. Tall western horses with long legs, introduced to China from central Asia at the beginning of the 1st century BC, were also popular subjects for tomb figurines.

Other funerary objects commonly seen in Chinese museums are fearsome military figures dressed in full armour, often trampling oxen underfoot. The figures may have served as tomb guardians and may represent the four heavenly kings. These kings guard the four quarters of the universe and protect the state; they have been assimilated into Buddhism and you see statues of them in Buddhist temples.

Guardian spirits are some of the strangest funerary objects. A common one has bird wings, elephant ears, a human face, the body of a lion and the legs and hooves of a deer or horse, all rolled into one.

Literature

China has a rich literary tradition. Unfortunately – barring many years of intensive study – much of it is inaccessible to western readers. Many of the most important Chinese classics are available in translation, but much of the Chinese literary heritage (particularly its poetry) is untranslatable, although scholars persevere.

The essential point to bear in mind when discussing Chinese literature is that prior to the 20th century there were two literary traditions: the classical and the vernacular. The classical tradition was the Chinese equivalent of a literary canon. The classical canon, largely Confucian in nature, consisted of a core of texts written in ancient Chinese that had to be mastered thoroughly by all aspirants to the Chinese civil service, and was the backbone of the Chinese education system – it was nearly indecipherable to the masses. The vernacular tradition arose in the Ming dynasty and consisted largely of prose epics written for entertainment.

For western readers it is the vernacular texts, precursors of the contemporary Chinese novel and short story, that are probably of more interest. Most of them are available in translation and provide a fascinating insight into life in China centuries past.

Perhaps the three most famous early 'novels' are: *The Water Margin* (Shuǐhǔ Zhuàn), also translated as *Rebels of the Marsh*; *The Dream of the Red Chamber* (Hónglóu Mèng), also translated as *The Dream of Red Mansions* and *The Story of the Stone*; and *Journey to the West* (Xīyóu Jì).

Another classic is the *Jin Ping Mei*, a racy story about a wealthy Chinese man and his six wives – it's banned in China, but available elsewhere in English. *The I Ching (Jìjing)*, or *Book of Changes*, is used to predict the future, but is regarded by the Chinese (and New Agers) as an ancient source of wisdom. *The Art of War (Bīngfǎ)* by Sun Tzu (Sūnzǐ) was studied by Mao and is still required reading for modern military strategists in the west.

By the early 19th century, western novels had begun to appear in Chinese translations in increasing numbers. Chinese intellectuals began to look at their own literary traditions more critically, in particular the classical one, which was markedly different in form from the Chinese that was spoken by modern Chinese. Calls for a national literature based on vernacular Chinese rather than the stultifying classical language grew in intensity.

The first of the major Chinese writers to write in colloquial Chinese as understood by the masses was Lu Xun (1881–1936), and for this reason he is regarded by many as the father of modern Chinese literature. Most of his works were short stories that looked critically at the Chinese inability to drag its nation into the 20th century. His first set of short stories was entitled *Call to Arms (Nàhǎn)* and included his most famous tale *The True Story of Ah Q*. His second collection was entitled *Wandering*, and his last collection was called *Old Tales Retold*.

Lao She (1899–1966), another important early novelist, also produced an allegorical work in *Cat City*, but is famous most of all for *The Rickshaw Boy*, a book that has been translated many times into English. It is a social critique of the living conditions of rickshaw drivers in Běijīng. Lao She died from wounds inflicted by zealous Red Guards during the Cultural Revolution.

Literary creativity in post-1949 China was greatly hampered by ideological controls. Mao's 'Yan'an Talks on Art & Literature' edict basically reduced literature to the status of a revolutionary tool, and writers were extolled to seek out ideal forms and to find the 'typical in the individual'. Works that did not show peasants triumphing over huge odds were considered not inspirational enough and condemned as bourgeois.

There has been increased creative freedom in the Chinese literary scene in the years following the Cultural Revolution, but it remains an area in which the government maintains careful vigilance. Most writers belong to state-sponsored literary guilds and many write on salary. Naturally they are careful not to bite the hand that feeds them.

Wang Meng was born in Běijīng in 1934 and his writings have touched on all sorts of sensitive topics including reform, elections, family, politics and technology. He was labelled a 'rightest' in 1957 because one of his short stories, 'The Young Newcomer in the Organisation Department', mildly criticised bureaucracy. In 1963 he was forced to move to a labour camp in rural Xīnjiāng where he spent the next 16 years. His 'rightest' label was officially removed in 1979 and he was allowed to take up writing again. He was given the prestigious job of Minister of Culture in 1986, but was forced to step down in the wake of the 1989 democracy protests in Tiānānmén Square. However, he was later appointed vice-chairman of the Chinese Writers' Association. Wang Meng has authored a number of excellent stories including *The Stubborn Porridge*, *A Winter's Topic*, *The Butterfly* and *Kitty*.

Ba Jin is the pen name of Li Feigan who was born in 1904 and is reportedly still alive.

He studied in Paris and translated some French works into Chinese, but become well known for his own novels which he produced in the 1930s and 1940s. He was brutally persecuted during the Cultural Revolution, but managed to survive. His best-known works include *Family*, *Autumn*, *Spring*, *Garden of Repose* and *Bitter Cold Nights*.

Shen Congwen (1902–88) lived in Húnán and his fiction reflects the lifestyle in that region. More than 20 of his best stories have been gathered into the book *Imperfect Paradise*, published in English by the University of Hawaii Press.

One of the most interesting writers in contemporary China is Zhang Xianliang, whose book *Half of Man Is Woman* was extremely controversial for its sexual content. Most western readers find Zhang's sexual politics highly suspect, but his book, now published by Penguin, is worth reading all the same.

Some of the work of another writer, Wang Shuo, has been translated into English. Much of his work has been adapted for film and he is popular with the younger generation. For the authorities, however, his stories about disaffected urban youth, gambling, prostitution and confidence tricksters are considered a bad influence.

Blood Red Dusk by Lao Gui (literally 'old devil') is available in English by Panda (the Chinese publisher). It's a fascinatingly cynical account of the Cultural Revolution years.

Feng Jicai is a writer who has enjoyed great success in China with stories like *The Magic Ponytail* and *A Short Man & His Tall Wife*, which have a satirical magic realist touch to them. His often horrific account of the Cultural Revolution, *Voices from the Whirlwind*, is a collection of anonymous personal accounts of those turbulent years and has recently been published in English by Pantheon Books.

For a recap of some of the latest trends in Chinese literature, look out for a copy of *The Lost Boat: Avant Garde Fiction from China*, edited by Henry YH Zhao (Wellsweep Press, 1994). It has samples from what Zhao identifies as the three main strands in Chinese literature since 1986.

Bookshops Finding any of the above books in non-Chinese editions takes perseverance. The Foreign Languages Bookstores and Friendship Stores in Běijīng and Shànghǎi are the cheapest places to find foreign-language editions of Chinese literature. Some bookstores in Hong Kong also have excellent collections, although prices are higher than elsewhere in China. For information on the exact location of bookstores in China, see the relevant destination chapters in this book.

Taiwan is another good source, although you won't find much there from mainland China. Some made-in-China books are exported to western countries and sold at vastly inflated prices. You can search in the various Chinatowns around the world, although mostly what you'll find are titles printed in Chinese.

The USA seems to have the most complete collections of English-language books about China, probably because of the large number of ethnic Chinese living there. Some of the US-based bookshops can be accessed online and will do mail orders to other countries.

If you're searching for Chinese literature, you can check out the following:

China China National Publishing Industry Trading Corporation (☎ 10-6421-5031, 6421-5793, fax 6421-4540 – for journal subscriptions only), 504 Anhuali, Andingmenwai (PO Box 782), Běijīng, 100011, China

France L'Harmattan (☎ 1 46 34 13 71), 21 rue des Écoles, in the Latin Quarter
Le Tiers Mythe (☎ 1 43 26 72 70), 21 rue Cujas

Taiwan Eslite (☎ 02-2773-0095), 2nd floor, 245 Tunhua South Rd, Section 1 (near Jenai Rd), Taipei. This is Taiwan's largest bookshop.
Caves Books (☎ 02-2537-1666), 103 Chungshan North Rd, Section 2, Taipei

UK Stanford's Bookshop (☎ 020-7836 1915), 12-14 Long Acre, London WC2E 9LP. It's one of the best shops of its kind in the UK.
The Travel Bookshop (☎ 020-7229 5260), 13 Blenheim Cres, London W11 2EE. This is another good source of travel literature.

USA China Books & Periodicals Inc (☎ 415-282-2994, fax 282-0994), 2929 24th St, San Francisco, CA 94110. www.chinabooks.com
The Asia Society's Bookstore, 725 Park Ave (at 70th St), New York City, NY

Architecture

China's architectural history, parallelling that of the Chinese empire and stretching back more than 3000 years, is one of the longest of any civilisation. However throughout this long history, building forms have remained surprisingly static. The practice of rebuilding and resurrecting ideas from the past means that traditionalism has long been one of China's most dominant architectural features. Within this traditionalism though, there are a huge variety of built forms, from the imperial structures of Běijīng, to the lingering colonial buildings of Shànghǎi, to temple architecture, and to the more modern building forms now practised all across China.

Across all these various built forms, from the lowliest village homestead to the largest imperial palace, certain basic principles have long been respected. The use of symmetry and axes, and the orientation of buildings and structures towards the south, are long-standing architectural ideas still practiced today. In plan, the basic layout for many building types consists of a walled compound, housing one or more structures. Many different materials and finishes can be seen throughout Chinese architecture – wood, rammed earth, masonry, stone, thatch, tiles, plaster, paint – with the choice dependant on a range of factors including function, cost, availability and aesthetics.

History It is difficult to define all but the broadest characteristics of early Chinese architecture as we have few surviving structures dating from before the 8th century AD. Many early buildings were constructed in wood, which has long since disappeared, and architecture of a more durable nature was often destroyed by war. Much of what is known has been gathered from references to building in literature, song, and artwork.

Until the Lord of Qin became first emperor around 220 BC and unified China under a centralised system, there was no such thing as a Chinese national architecture. He built large and impressively decorated structures, fusing regional architecture into a single imperial style as a sign of national greatness. During this period there were many great achievements in building, including the beginnings of what would later become the Great Wall. This emphasis on monumental building as a symbol of wealth and power continued during the Han dynasty (AD 206–20), not always to the liking of the poor, who still lived under thatch.

After the Han's collapse, a period of decentralisation followed during which Buddhism spread across China, bringing with it a foreign decorative influence and vastly increasing the numbers of pagodas and grottoes across the country.

The Sui dynasty (AD 589–618) once again united China at a time when architects were afforded one of the highest civic standings. This era saw a flurry of building activity in a period characterised by expansion and rebuilding, including the restoration of some parts of the Great Wall, and the beginnings of the Grand Canal.

It is from the successive Tang (AD 618–907) and Song dynasties (AD 960–1279) that the first surviving structures appear, many of these masonry pagodas based on square plans. The use of colour, both as a decorative and protective element, became more detailed during these dynasties. The Song were overrun by the Mongols of the late 13th century, who contributed little of their own culture to architecture, instead choosing to imitate and rebuild the style of the Chinese.

Běijīng was the long-standing capital during the Ming and Qing dynasties (1368–1911). The Forbidden City, on which construction began in 1406, showcases the architecture of the time. It is also one of the few palaces of any dynasty to survive in relatively intact form. In it we can see the epitome of the traditional Chinese architectural ideas of monumentality and symmetry, with strong use of colour and decoration. The Qing dynasty, originating with the invading Manchus from the north, followed Chinese style and like the Mongols, brought little of their own influence in terms of architecture. The coming of the west in the 18th century was to hasten the demise of the last of the dynasties, and led to the entering of a new architectural influence and a profound change in building design and construction.

Western Influence & Modern Architecture It was as early as the 15th century that the first foreign traders, the Portuguese, came into contact with China, but it was not until the establishment of trading headquarters and banks in the late 18th century that a colonial influence in architecture made its presence felt. The Portuguese, Germans, British, Dutch, Spanish and Russians, among others, established communities and constructed buildings using foreign architects and Chinese craftsmen. These buildings from the late 18th and 19th centuries were often in the Classical Revival style, originally constructed in brick and timber, and later, in steel and concrete.

There are many examples of foreign-designed buildings from this time (mostly banks, large-scale residences, offices, and churches) in Chinese cities such as Shànghǎi, Macau, Guǎngzhōu, Tiānjīn, Hāěrbīn and Qīngdǎo. Although traditional-style Chinese architecture was still retained by the Qing government for use in state and religious architecture and the courtyard house still dominated domestically, western architecture combined with Chinese decoration began to be used by the Qing for more functional buildings.

It was not until the 20th century, however, that Chinese architects designed western-style buildings themselves, at first using the Classical Revival style. The first overseas trained Chinese architects returned to China in the 1920s, bringing with them new ideas after exposure to some of the architectural movements that were popular in the west. Foreign styles such as the International Style, characterised by sleek, clean lines, flat roofs, and materials such as steel and glass, had appeared in Shànghǎi by the 1940s. There was for some time a push to revive the traditional Chinese style, but this proved uneconomical and was eventually abandoned. Over the past decade as China's doors have more fully opened, many buildings have been built by both Chinese and foreign architects alike that completely depart from Chinese traditional forms.

Religious Architecture The centre of prayer for the main Chinese religions of Buddhism, Taoism and Confucianism, is the temple. Generally there is no set time for prayer and no communal service, except for funerals. Worshippers enter the temple whenever they want to make offerings, pray for help or give thanks.

Externally, there is little difference between the temples for these faiths. The large roof is the dominant feature, and is usually decorated with figures of divinities and lucky symbols such as dragons or carp. Stone lions often guard the temple entrance. Beyond is the main hall with an altar table, and depending on the size and wealth of the temple, there may be side altars and adjoining rooms with shrines to different gods, chapels for prayers to the dead, and displays of funerary plaques. There are also living quarters for the temple keepers. Colours also play a significant role in temple architecture, with red, gold or yellow, and green the dominant colours. Red represents joy, green signifies harmony, while yellow and gold herald heavenly glory. White stands for purity and is also the colour of death. Grey and black are the colours of disaster and grief.

The most visually striking feature of the Buddhist temple is the pagoda. This tall, symbolic feature was probably introduced from India along with Buddhism around 1st century AD. Pagodas were often built to house religious artefacts and documents, or to commemorate important events, or to store the ashes of the deceased. Earlier Buddhist temples usually combine a pagoda with a hall-style temple. Later style temples, without pagodas, consist of buildings arranged around a courtyard and originate from the form and planning of palaces and residences. Around the 4th century, the construction of Buddhist cave temples began. The caves at Lóngmén near Luòyáng, at Mògāo near Dūnhuáng, and at Yúngāng near Dàtóng, are some of the finest examples.

French and Jesuit missionaries introduced Christian religious architecture to China around the 18th century. Many of the resulting churches utilised the European styles of the Baroque and Gothic, while others blended a western structure with traditional Chinese decorative styles. Islamic architecture may also be found across China, most of it dating after the 14th century and influenced by Central Asian styles, and again, often combined with local Chinese style.

For those interested in finding out more about Chinese architecture, a detailed reference is *The Art and Architecture of China* by Laurence Sickman and Alexander Soper. Also worthwhile reading (before you go, as this won't fit in your backpack!) are the relevant sections of Sir Bannister Fletcher's weighty but comprehensive tome *A History of Architecture*.

Film

While most travellers in China manage to get to at least one opera or acrobatics performance, few get around to seeing any Chinese films. Part of the problem of course is purely linguistic – films are usually dull when you can't follow the dialogue. Still, a number of Chinese releases have enjoyed success at western film festivals and art house cinemas, and these are always subtitled into English.

Much of the early post-1949 film work was ideologically motivated – heroic workers and peasants battling (and emerging victorious) against evil foreigners and Kuomintang devils. As can be expected, the years of the Cultural Revolution did nothing to improve this state of affairs.

The major turning point took place with the graduation of the first intake of students since the end of the Cultural Revolution from the Beijing Film Academy in 1982. This group of adventurous directors, the most well known of whom are Zhang Yimou, Chen Kaige, Wu Ziniu and Tian

Zhuangzhuang, became known collectively as the 'Fifth Generation'. The new directors of the 1990s have been dubbed the 'Sixth Generation' and include such people as He Jianjun, Jiang Wen, Ning Ying, Wu Wenguang and Zhang Yuan.

Both the Fifth- and Sixth-Generation directors have constantly run into problems with the authorities, and the most controversial works get clipped by censors or banned outright. The government has even retaliated against 'troublesome' directors by denying them film to work with, or revoking their passports so they cannot attend foreign film festivals.

Tragedy is a central element of Chinese art films, and plots tend to move slowly. Ge You is arguably China's most popular actor and Gong Li the most popular actress.

The first film by the Fifth Generation directors to come to the attention of film buffs in the west was *Yellow Earth* (*Huáng Tǔdì*; 1984) by Chen Kaige. Chen's most notable work was *Farewell My Concubine* (1993). Other movies by Chen include *Life on a String* and *The Big Parade*.

Zhang Yimou made *Red Sorghum* (*Hóng Gāoliang*; 1987), a film that was adventurous by Chinese standards in portraying an illicit love affair against the backdrop of the Sino-Japanese War. Zhang has emerged as China's foremost director (and sometimes cameraman) with award-winning releases such as *The One & the Eight* (1984), *The Story of Qiu Ju* (1991), *The Old Well* (1987), *To Live* (*Huózhe*; 1994), *Ju Dou* (1990), *Raise the Red Lantern* (1991) and *Shanghai Triad* (1995). Gong Li has appeared in most of Zhang's films.

Huang Jianxin directed *Stand Up, Don't Bend Over* and *The Black Cannon Incident* (*Hēipào Shìjiàn*; 1986). The latter is without a doubt the sharpest satire released by any of the Fifth Generation directors.

Tian Zhuangzhuang directed The *Blue Kite* (*Lán Fēng-zheng*; 1993), a Cultural Revolution tragedy that is banned in China. Other notable films include: *Swan Song*, the tragic story of a Cantonese opera composer who dies neglected after his best work is stolen and made famous by a music student; *The Horse Thief*, a haunting story set in Tibet; and *The Women from the Lake of Scented Souls*, which portrays the unhappiness of a woman who runs a sesame-oil mill. For information on the Hong Kong film industry, see the boxed text 'From Kung Fu to Cannes' in that chapter.

Theatre

Chinese theatre draws on very different traditions from western theatre. The crucial difference is the importance of music to Chinese theatre, and thus it is usually referred to as opera. Contemporary Chinese theatre, of which the most famous is Běijīng opera, has a continuous history of some 900 years, having evolved from a convergence of comic and balladic traditions in the Northern Song period. From this beginning, Chinese opera has been the meeting ground for a disparate range of forms: acrobatics, martial arts, poetic arias and stylised dance.

Operas were usually performed by travelling troupes whose social status was very low in traditional Chinese society. In fact, their status was on a par with prostitutes and slaves and their children barred from social advancement by a government decree that made them ineligible to participate in public-service examinations. Chinese law also forbade mixed-sex performances, forcing actors to act out roles of the opposite sex. Opera troupes were frequently associated with homosexuality in the public imagination, contributing further to their 'untouchable' social status.

Despite this, opera remained a popular form of entertainment, although it was considered unworthy of the attention of the scholar class. Performances were considered an obligatory adjunct to New Year celebrations and marriages, and sometimes to funerals and ancestral ceremonies.

Opera performances usually take place on a bare stage, with the actors taking on stylised roles that are instantly recognisable to the audience. The four major roles are the female role, the male role, the 'painted-face' role (for gods and warriors) and the clown.

Calligraphy

Unique to Asian cultures, calligraphy is both a practical written language and a highly skilled art form. Traditionally it has been regarded in China as the highest form of artistic expression. The basic tools, commonly referred to as 'the four treasures of the scholar's study', are paper, ink, inkstone (on which the ink is mixed) and brush. These materials, which are shared by Chinese painters, reflect the close relationship between Chinese painting and calligraphy.

Written Chinese is not an alphabetic language but rather a series of characters. Chinese characters began as basic representations of objects, similar to hieroglyphs, called pictographs. These pictographs developed over time to become more and more stylised, and were later combined together to describe more complex and abstract meanings, with additional elements included to indicate pronunciation. From this base, countless calligraphic styles have developed over the years, resulting in a rich variety of graphic forms. Earlier styles of calligraphy, such as the *zhuan* or Seal Script dating from the Western Zhou dynasty, lean towards a squarer, more formal style. A more flowing, cursive style of calligraphy was later developed to counter the need for a quicker writing style. The later styles of calligraphy, the *kaishu* (regular script), *xingshu* (running hand), and *caoshu* (grass writing or cursive hand), are sometimes evocatively compared to a person standing, walking and running.

Calligraphy is still an extremely popular pastime in China and a major area of study. It can be seen all over China – on documents, artworks, in temples, adorning the walls of caves, and on the sides of mountains and monuments.

Painting

Chinese painting is the art of brush and ink applied onto *xuan* paper, or silk. The basic tools are those of calligraphy, which has influenced painting in both its style and theory. A painting, like calligraphy, may be achieved in a very short time, but only following much thought and a total conception of the piece in the artist's mind beforehand. The brush line, which varies in thickness and tone, is the important feature of a Chinese painting, along with calligraphy itself, which is usually incorporated in the form of an inscription or poem along with the artist's seal. Shading is regarded as a foreign technique (introduced to China via Buddhist art from central Asia between the 3rd and 6th centuries) and colour plays only a minor symbolic and decorative role.

From the Han dynasty until the end of the Tang dynasty, the human figure occupied the dominant position in Chinese painting, as it did in pre-modern European art. Figure painting flourished against a Confucian background, illustrating moral themes. The practice of seeking out places of natural beauty and communing with nature first became popular among Taoist poets and painters, and landscape painting for its own sake started in the 4th and 5th centuries. By the 9th century the interest of artists began to shift away from figures and the separate genre of flower-and-bird painting developed, with a subject matter covering a large range of animals, birds, flowers and fruit. From the 11th century onwards, landscape was to dominate Chinese painting. Later, a group of painters known as the Individualists exerted influence towards the end of the Ming dynasty with unusual compositions and brushwork that diverged from traditional techniques, however it was not until the 20th century that there was any real departure from native traditions.

When the communists came to power, much of the country's artistic talent was turned to glorifying the revolution and bombarding the masses with political slogans. Colourful billboards of Mao waving to cheering crowds holding up the little red book were popular, as were giant Mao statues standing above smaller statues of enthusiastic workers and soldiers. Since the late 1970s, the Chinese art scene has gradually recovered. The work of traditionally influenced painters can be seen for sale in shops and galleries all over China, while in the major cities a flourishing avant-garde scene has emerged. The work of Chinese painters has been arguably more innovative and dissident than that of writers, possibly because the political implications are harder to interpret by the authorities. Art collecting has become a fashionable hobby among China's new rich, and many of China's young artists have exhibited work overseas to critical acclaim.

SOCIETY & CONDUCT
Traditional Culture

Chinese culture literally took a beating during the Cultural Revolution – the country has yet to recover completely. It should be noted that there is a cultural gap between Hong Kong and Macau and the rest of China. Hong Kong and Macau, while outwardly more modern, are also more traditionally Chinese because the Cultural Revolution didn't have such an effect there.

Some of the more notable aspects of traditional Chinese culture are mentioned below.

Face 'Face' could be loosely defined as 'status', 'ego' or 'self-respect' and is by no means alien to foreigners. Essentially it's about avoiding being made to look stupid or being forced to back down in front of others.

A negotiated settlement of differences that provides benefits to both parties is always preferable to confrontation. Outright confrontation should be reserved as a last resort (Chinese are not shy of using it) and problems should first be tackled with smiling persistence – if one tack fails, try another.

Handling Paper If you want to impress your Chinese hosts, always use both hands when presenting them with a piece of paper

Fēngshuǐ

Fēngshuǐ, literally meaning 'wind and water', is a collection of ancient geomantic principles that supports the existence of bodies of water and configurations of land forms that direct the flow of universal qi (vital energy or cosmic currents). With the help of a fengshui master this qi can be successfully courted to maximise a person's wealth, happiness, longevity and procreation, however, at the same time, a negative flow of qi may bring on disaster.

One reason for fēngshuǐ's success may be that wealth (cai), happiness (fu), long life (shou) and healthy offspring (zi) are the four major concerns of fengshui and parallel the general concerns of the Chinese population.

Pagodas, temples, houses and even whole cities and villages have been located and built so as to be in harmony with the surrounding landscape. Even a household will try and maximise its own benefits by placing the family's house, tomb, business or furniture in an appropriate location so as to receive the optimum qi. The positioning of such a structure will determine the lasting wellbeing of the inhabitants; good placement should result in good fortune.

Fēngshuǐ cosmology has been used to select the most auspicious site of cities as far back as the 3rd or 4th century. Yet, fēngshuǐ as a tradition has been constantly attacked throughout Chinese history – by imperialists, nationalists and communists alike. Despite the aggressive actions of this century, it has survived and prospered among the people. While Chinese geomancy is inherently conservative, especially in architecture, accusations of disturbances to the natural balance of fengshui have been often vented by peasants against the state. Even during the early stages of European and Japanese expansion into China, many Chinese were incensed at the disturbances caused by the construction of train lines and over-shadowing churches to their happy balance of seemingly hidden powers in the surrounding geography. The Chinese called for the removal of the offending steeples and the redirecting of train lines so as to be more in harmony with the local fengshui.

Fēngshuǐ has its origins on the mainland of China, but during the last century it has been more closely associated with Singapore, Hong Kong, Taiwan and the overseas Chinese communities. This is mainly due to the way the communist regime has exploited fēngshuǐ as a means of securing power

(this includes namecards). This gesture shows respect.

Fortune Telling Being a fortune teller was not the safest of occupations during the Cultural Revolution. Most of them either quickly changed their profession or spent 20 years breaking rocks at a labour camp in Qīnghǎi.

It's a different case in Hong Kong and Macau. The lucrative business of fortune telling is how many temples in Hong Kong and Macau pay their bills. Palmists (who also read your face) set up in some of the night markets.

Dos & Don'ts

Speaking Frankly People often don't say what they think, but rather what they think you want to hear or what will save face for

them. Thus, for example, a staff member at an airport or airline office may tell you that your flight will be here 'very soon' even if they know the flight will be delayed for two days.

Smiling A smile doesn't always mean happiness. Some Chinese people smile when they are embarrassed or worried. This explains the situation where the foreign tourist is ranting and raving at the staff in the hotel lobby, while the person behind the desk stands there grinning from ear to ear.

Guānxì Within their daily life, Chinese people often have to compete for goods or services in short supply and many have been assigned jobs for which they have zero interest and often no training. Those who have *guānxì* (connections) usually get what

Fēngshuǐ

for some, while breaking the fengshui of others. During the Cultural Revolution the authorities set about the systematic destruction of graves, ancestral halls, shrines and tablets to destroy the peasants' links with their ancestors and clans. The authorities classified the practice of fēngshuǐ as illegal and yet at the same time used fēngshuǐ to punish those of a 'bad-class' background, by destroying their ancestors' tombs and cremating the bones to truncate the family lines.

A fēngshuǐ master or geomancer is normally trained by his father and passes his skills down through the generations. When called upon to inspect a prospective housing or grave site, the master usually brings along his compass *(loupan)* and calendar *(nongli)* and after a little scrutiny, involving the consultation of his tools of trade and an inspection of the nearby landscape to locate the Green Dragon and White Tiger, decides the most favourable location. Then a combination of dates including, say the birth of the owner, is included in the analysis to decide upon the starting date for construction.

This is a simplistic summary of a trade that draws more on intuition and practical experience than books of learning. However, if a geomancer is in possession of a fēngshuǐ manual or calendar then he would have an advantage over many others who rely purely on oral and practical training.

The geomancer is also often called upon to aid in the determination of appropriate marriage and funeral dates, as well as to write 'prayers' to protect and bring good fortune upon a household.

During the past two decades rural China has seen a building boom that has not only increased the demand for optimal qi sites, but also put the pressure on possible disturbances to the fengshui of the neighbours. The demand for the fēngshuǐ master has seen a recent increase in areas outside the placement of a house or grave. Today, households are more likely to call on the mysterious powers of the geomancer for advice on how to realign the fēngshuǐ of households that have been afflicted by premature death, sickness, poor business performance and mental disease.

So what do you do if you require the services of a fēngshuǐ master? The current situation in mainland China is a lot more tolerant of geomancers and a cash payment would be generally appreciated for services rendered, but don't bargain too hard as it may disturb the fragile qi.

they want because the connections network is, of course, reciprocal.

Obtaining goods or services through connections is informally referred to as 'going through the back door' *(zǒu hòu mén)*. Cadres are well placed for this activity; foreigners will have to resort to some sort of gift giving (bribery?) to achieve the same result.

Negotiate Over Dinner If you're planning to cut any business deals in China, you'd best invite the relevant officials or business partners to dinner. Proposals that were 'impossible' a few hours earlier can suddenly become very possible when discussed over a plate of Běijīng duck and a bottle of Johnny Walker.

Gift Giving This is a complicated issue with the Chinese. It's good manners when visiting people at their homes to bring some sort of gift, especially if you've been invited for a meal. Fruit or flowers are OK, or a box of chocolates. Money is not generally appropriate (and indeed would be an insult). Imported goods have much prestige value and will help you win points in the face game.

One of the reasons to give gifts is to build some connections (see 'Guānxì' previously).

Tobacco Diplomacy At least in the case of male-to-male relationships, it is always polite to offer a cigarette when meeting somebody. You are under no obligation to smoke, but if refusing always remember to do so politely with a smile and a wave of the hand.

When offering a cigarette to someone, you must extend the open pack with a cigarette protruding from it – it would be impolite to remove a single cigarette from the pack and hand it over.

When dealing with officialdom, cigarettes make an excellent subtle bribe. To really curry favour, you could then perhaps tell the official to 'just keep the pack, I'm trying to quit smoking'.

If you want to engage in this sort of tobacco diplomacy, prestigious foreign brands like Marlboro and 555 are almost mandatory.

Greater China

The official party line is that Taiwan is a part of China, even if the Taiwanese don't happen to agree. Ditto for Tibet and the Spratly Islands. The educational system also pounds this into everyone's head. The authorities are constantly warning of plots by foreign imperialists and 'splitists' who want to divide and weaken China.

In short, if you have any pro-independence sentiments about Tibet and Taiwan (or Xīnjiāng for that matter), you'd best keep them to yourself.

RELIGION

Chinese religion has been influenced by three great streams of human thought: Taoism, Confucianism and Buddhism. Although each has separate origins, all three have been inextricably entwined in popular Chinese religion along with ancient animist beliefs. The founders of Taoism, Confucianism and Buddhism have been deified. The Chinese worship them and their disciples as fervently as they worship their own ancestors and a pantheon of gods and spirits.

Taoism

It is said that Taoism (Dào jiào) is the only true 'home-grown' Chinese religion – Buddhism was imported from India and Confucianism is mainly a philosophy. According to tradition, the founder of Taoism was a man known as Laotzu (Lǎozǐ), whose name has been variously misspelled in western literature as 'Laotse' and 'Laotze'. He is said to have been born around the year 604 BC, but there is some doubt that he ever lived at all. Almost nothing is known about him, not even his real name. Laotzu translates as the 'Old One' or the 'Grand Old Master'. It's widely believed that Laotzu was the keeper of the government archives in a western state of China, and that Confucius consulted with him.

At the end of his life, Laotzu is said to have climbed on a water buffalo and ridden west towards what is now Tibet, in search of solitude for his last few years. On the way, he was asked to leave behind a record of his beliefs. The product was a

Chinese Zodiac

Astrology has a long history in China and is integrated with religious beliefs. As in the western system of astrology, there are 12 zodiac signs; however, unlike the western system, your sign is based on the year rather than the month in which you were born. Still, this is a simplification. The exact day and time of birth is also carefully considered in charting an astrological path.

If you want to know your sign in the Chinese zodiac, look up your year of birth in the chart, though it's a little more complicated than this because Chinese astrology goes by the lunar calendar. The Chinese Lunar New Year usually falls in late January or early February, so the first month will be included in the year before. Future years are included here so you'll know what's coming:

Rat	Ox/Cow	Tiger	Rabbit	Dragon	Snake
1924	1925	1926	1927	1928	1929
1936	1937	1938	1939	1940	1941
1948	1949	1950	1951	1952	1953
1960	1961	1962	1963	1964	1965
1972	1973	1974	1975	1976	1977
1984	1985	1986	1987	1988	1989
1996	1997	1998	1999	2000	2001

Horse	Goat	Monkey	Rooster	Dog	Pig
1930	1931	1932	1933	1934	1935
1942	1943	1944	1945	1946	1947
1954	1955	1956	1957	1958	1959
1966	1967	1968	1969	1970	1971
1978	1979	1980	1981	1982	1983
1990	1991	1992	1993	1994	1995
2002	2003	2004	2005	2006	2007

slim volume of only 5000 characters, the *Tao Te Ching* (*Dao De Jing*) or *The Way & Its Power*. He then rode off on his buffalo. It's doubtful that Laotzu ever intended his philosophy to become a religion.

Chuangtzu (Zhuāngzǐ), who lived between 399 BC and 295 BC, picked up where Laotzu left off. Chuangtzu is regarded as the greatest of all Taoist writers and *The Book of Chuangtzu* is still required

reading for anyone trying to make sense of Taoism. However, like Laotzu, Chuangtzu was a philosopher and was not actually trying to establish a religion.

Credit for turning Taoism into a religion is generally given to Zhang Daoling, who formally established his Celestial Masters movement in 143 BC.

At the centre of Taoism is the concept of *dao*. Dao cannot be perceived because it exceeds senses, thoughts and imagination; it can be known only through mystical insight, that cannot be expressed with words. Dao is the way of the universe, the driving power in nature, the order behind all life, the spirit which cannot be exhausted. Dao is the way people should order their lives to keep in harmony with the natural order of the universe.

Just as there have been different interpretations of the 'way', there have also been different interpretations of *de* – the power of the universe. This has led to the development of three distinct forms of Taoism in China.

Taoism later split into two divisions, the 'Cult of the Immortals' and 'The Way of the Heavenly Teacher'. The Cult of the Immortals offered immortality through meditation, exercise, alchemy and various other techniques. The Way of the Heavenly Teacher had many gods, ceremonies, saints, special diets to prolong life and offerings to the ghosts. As time passed, Taoism increasingly became wrapped up in the supernatural, self-mutilation, witchcraft, exorcism, fortune telling, magic and ritualism. Taoists eventually produced a collection of over 1400 baffling scriptures known as the *Daozang*.

Taoism today has been much embraced in the west by New Agers, parapsychologists and others who offer their own various interpretations of what Laotzu and Chuangtzu were really trying to tell us.

Confucianism

More a philosophy than a religion, Confucianism (Rújiā Sīxiǎng) has nevertheless become intertwined with Chinese religious beliefs.

With the exception of Mao, the one name that has become synonymous with China is Confucius (Kǒngzǐ). He was born of a poor family around 551 BC, in what is now Shāndōng. His ambition was to hold a high government office and to reorder society through the administrative apparatus. At most he seems to have had several insignificant government posts, a few followers and a permanently blocked career.

At the age of 50 he perceived his divine mission, and for the next 13 years tramped from state to state offering unsolicited advice to rulers on how to improve their governing, while looking for an opportunity to put his own ideas into practice. That opportunity never came, and he returned to his own state to spend the last five years of his life teaching and editing classical literature. He died in 479 BC, aged 72.

The glorification of Confucius began after his death. Mencius (372–289 BC), or Mengzi, helped raise Confucian ideals into the national consciousness with the publication of *The Book of Mencius*.

Eventually, Confucian philosophy permeated every level of Chinese society. To hold government office presupposed a knowledge of the Confucian classics, and spoken proverbs trickled down to the illiterate masses.

During the Han dynasty Confucianism effectively became the state religion – the teachings were made the basic discipline for training government officials and remained so until almost the end of the Qing dynasty in 1911.

In the 7th and 8th centuries temples and shrines were built in memory of Confucius and his original disciples. During the Song dynasty the Confucian bible, the *Analects*, became the basis of all education.

It is not hard to see why Confucianism took hold in China. Confucianism defines codes of conduct and patterns of obedience. Women obey and defer to men, younger brothers to elder brothers, and sons to fathers. Respect flows upwards, from young to old, from subject to ruler. Certainly, any reigning Chinese emperor would quickly see the merits of encouraging such a system.

All people paid homage to the emperor, who was regarded as the embodiment of Confucian wisdom and virtue – the head of the great family-nation. For centuries administration under the emperor lay in the hands of a small Confucian scholar class. In theory anyone who passed the examinations qualified, but in practice the monopoly of power was held by the educated upper classes.

There has never been a rigid code of law, because Confucianism rejected the idea that conduct could be enforced by some organisation; taking legal action implied an incapacity to work things out by negotiation. The result, however, was arbitrary justice and oppression by those who held power. Dynasties rose and fell, but the Confucian pattern never changed. Indeed, it still holds true in today's China.

The family retains its central place as the basic unit of society; Confucianism reinforced this idea, but did not invent it. The key to family order is filial piety – children's respect for and duty towards their parents. Teaming up with traditional superstition, Confucianism reinforced the practice of ancestor worship. Confucius himself is worshipped and temples are built for him. The strict codes of obedience were held together by these concepts of filial piety and ancestor worship, as well as by the concept of 'face' – to let down the family or group is a great shame for Chinese.

In its early years, Confucianism was regarded as a radical philosophy, but over the centuries it has come to be seen as conservative and reactionary. Confucius was strongly denounced by the communists as yet another incorrigible link to the bourgeois past. During the Cultural Revolution, Confucian temples, statues and Confucianists themselves took quite a beating at the hands of rampaging Red Guards. However, in recent years the Chinese government has softened its stance, perhaps recognising that Confucianism can still be an effective instrument of social control. Confucian temples (particularly the ones at Qūfù in Shāndōng Province) are now being restored.

Buddhism

Buddhism (Fó Jiào) was founded in India by Siddhartha Gautama (563–483 BC) of the Sakyas. Siddhartha was his given name, Gautama his surname and Sakya the name of the clan to which his family belonged.

The story goes that although he was a prince brought up in luxury, Siddhartha became discontented with the world when he was confronted with the sights of old age, sickness and death. He despaired of finding fulfilment on the physical level, since the body was inescapably subject to these weaknesses.

Around the age of 30 Siddhartha broke from the material world and sought 'enlightenment' by following various yogic disciplines. After several failed attempts he devoted the final phase of his search to intensive contemplation. One evening, sitting beneath a banyan tree, he slipped into deep meditation and emerged having achieved enlightenment. His title 'Buddha' means 'the awakened' or 'the enlightened one'.

Buddha founded an order of monks and preached his ideas for the next four decades until his death. To his followers he was known as Sakyamuni, the 'silent sage of the Sakya clan', because of the unfathomable mystery that surrounded him. It is said that Gautama Buddha was not the first buddha, but the fourth, and will not be the last.

The cornerstone of Buddhist philosophy is the view that all life is suffering. Everyone is subject to the traumas of birth, sickness, decrepitude and death; to what they most dread (an incurable disease or an ineradicable personal weakness); and to separation from what they love.

The cause of suffering is desire – specifically the desires of the body and the desire for personal fulfilment. Happiness can only be achieved if these desires are overcome, and this requires following the 'eightfold path'. By following this path the Buddhist aims to attain nirvana. Volumes have been written in attempts to define nirvana; the *suttas* (discourses of the Buddha) simply say that it's a state of complete freedom from greed, anger, ignorance and the various other 'fetters' of existence.

The first branch of the eightfold path is 'right understanding': the recognition that life is suffering, that suffering is caused by desire for personal gratification and that suffering can be overcome. The second branch is 'right-mindedness': cultivating a mind free from sensuous desire, ill will and cruelty. The remaining branches of the path require that one refrain from abuse and deceit; that one show kindness and avoid self-seeking in all actions; that one develop virtues and curb passions; and that one practise meditation.

Buddhism developed in China from the 3rd to 6th centuries AD. In the middle of the 1st century AD the religion gained the interest of the Han emperor Ming. He sent a mission to the west, which returned in AD 67 with Buddhist scriptures, two Indian monks and images of the Buddha.

Centuries later, other Chinese monks like Xuan Zang journeyed to India and returned with Buddhist scriptures that were then translated from the original Sanskrit. Buddhist monasteries and temples sprang up everywhere in China, and played a similar role to the churches and monasteries of medieval Europe – functioning as guesthouses, hospitals and orphanages for travellers and refugees. Gifts from the faithful allowed them to amass considerable wealth and set up money-lending enterprises and pawnshops. These pawnshops functioned as unofficial banks for the poor right up to the mid-20th century.

The Buddha wrote nothing; the Buddhist writings that have come down to us date from about 150 years after his death. By the time these texts came out, divisions had already appeared within Buddhism. Some writers tried to emphasise the Buddha's break with Hinduism, while others tried to minimise it. At some stage Buddhism split into two major schools: Theravada and Mahayana.

The Theravada or 'doctrine of the elders' school (also called Hinayana or 'little vehicle' by non-Theravadins) holds that the path to nirvana is an individual pursuit. It centres on monks and nuns who make the search for nirvana a full-time profession. This school maintains that people are alone in the world and must tread the path to nirvana on their own; buddhas can only show the way. The Theravada school is the Buddhism of Sri Lanka, Myanmar, Thailand, Laos and Cambodia.

The Mahayana, or 'big vehicle', school holds that since all existence is one, the fate of the individual is linked to the fate of others. The Buddha did not just point the way and float off into his own nirvana, but continues to offer spiritual help to others seeking nirvana. The Mahayana school is the Buddhism of Vietnam, Japan, Tibet, Korea, Mongolia and China.

Mahayana Buddhism is replete with innumerable heavens, hells and descriptions of nirvana. Prayers are addressed to the Buddha and combined with elaborate ritual. There are deities and bodhisattvas – a rank of supernatural beings in their last incarnation before nirvana. Temples are filled with images such as the future buddha, Maitreya (often portrayed as fat and happy over his coming promotion) and Amitabha (a saviour who rewards the faithful with admission to a Christian-like paradise). The ritual, tradition and superstition that Buddha rejected came tumbling back in with a vengeance.

In Tibet and areas of Gānsù, Sìchuān and Yúnnán, a unique form of the Mahayana school is practised: Tantric or Lamaist Buddhism (Lǎmā Jiào). Tantric Buddhism, often called *Vajrayana* or 'thunderbolt vehicle' by its followers, has been practised since the early 7th century AD and is heavily influenced by Tibet's pre-Buddhist Bon religion, which relied on priests or shamans to placate spirits, gods and demons.

Generally speaking, it is much more mystical than other forms of Buddhism, relying heavily on *mudras* (ritual postures), *mantras* (sacred speech), *yantras* (sacred art) and secret initiation rites. Priests called *lamas* are believed to be reincarnations of highly evolved beings; the Dalai Lama is the supreme patriarch of Tibetan Buddhism.

Islam

The founder of Islam (Yīsīlán Jiào) was the Arab prophet Mohammed. Strictly speaking, Muslims believe it was not Mohammed who shaped the religion but God, and Mohammed merely transmitted it from God to his people. To call the religion 'Mohammedanism' is also incorrect, since it implies that the religion centres around Mohammed and not around God. The proper name of the religion is Islam, derived from the word *salam*, which primarily means 'peace', and in a secondary sense 'surrender' or 'submission'. The full connotation is something like 'the peace that comes by surrendering to God'. The corresponding adjective is 'Muslim'.

The prophet was born around AD 570 and came to be called Mohammed, meaning 'highly praised'. His ancestry is traditionally traced back to Abraham, who had two wives, Hagar and Sarah. Hagar gave birth to Ishmael, and Sarah had a son named Isaac. Sarah demanded that Hagar and Ishmael be banished from the tribe. According to Islam's holy book, the Koran, Ishmael went to Mecca, where his line of descendants can be traced down to Mohammed. There have been other true prophets before Mohammed, but he is regarded as the culmination of them and the last.

Mohammed said that there is only one God, Allah. The name derives from joining *al*, which means 'the', with *Illah*, which means 'God'. His uncompromising monotheism conflicted with the pantheism and idolatry of the Arabs. His moral teachings and vision of a universal brotherhood conflicted with what he believed was a corrupt social order based on class divisions.

The initial reaction to his teachings was hostile. He and his followers were forced to flee from Mecca to Medina in 622, where Mohammed built up a political base and an army that eventually defeated Mecca and brought all of Arabia under his control. He died in 632, two years after taking Mecca. By the time a century had passed the Arab Muslims had built a huge empire that stretched all the way from Persia to Spain. Although the Arabs were eventually supplanted by the Turks, the strength of Islam has continued to the present day.

Islam was brought to China peacefully. Arab traders who landed on the southern coast of China established their mosques in great maritime cities like Guǎngzhōu and Quánzhōu, and Muslim merchants travelling the Silk Road to China won converts among the Han Chinese in the north of the country. There are also large populations of Muslim Uyghur people (of Turkic descent), whose ancestors first moved into China's Xīnjiāng region during the Tang dynasty.

Christianity

The earliest record of Christianity (Jīdū Jiào) in China dates back to the Nestorians, a Syrian Christian sect. They first appeared in China in the 7th century when a Syrian named Raban presented Christian scriptures to the imperial court at Chāng'ān. This event and the construction of a Nestorian monastery in Chāng'ān are recorded on a large stone stele made in AD 781, now displayed in the Shǎnxī Lìshǐ Bówùguǎn (Shaanxi History Museum) in Xī'ān.

The next major Christian group to arrive in China were the Jesuits. The priests Matteo Ricci and Michael Ruggieri were permitted to set up base at Zhàoqìng in Guǎngdōng in the 1580s, and eventually made it to the imperial court in Běijīng. Large numbers of Catholic and Protestant missionaries established themselves in China following the intrusion into China by the western powers in the 19th century. Christians are estimated to comprise about 1% of China's population.

Judaism

Kāifēng in Hénán Province has been the home of the largest community of Chinese Jews. Their religious beliefs of Judaism (Yóutài Jiào) and almost all the customs associated with them have died out, yet the descendants of the original Jews still consider themselves Jewish. Just how the Jews got to China is unknown. They may have come as traders and merchants along the Silk Road when Kāifēng was the capital of China, or they may have emigrated from India. For more details, see the Kāifēng section in the Hénán chapter.

Religion & Communism

Today the Chinese communist government professes atheism. It considers religion to be base superstition, a remnant of old China used by the ruling classes to keep power. This is in line with the Marxist belief that religion is the 'opiate of the people'.

Nevertheless, in an effort to improve relations with the Muslim, Buddhist and Lamaist minorities, in 1982 the Chinese government amended its constitution to allow freedom of religion. However, only atheists are permitted to be members of the CCP. Since almost all of China's 55 minority groups adhere to one religion or another, this rule precludes most of them from becoming party members.

Traditional Chinese religious beliefs took a battering during the Cultural Revolution when monasteries were disbanded, temples were destroyed and the monks were sometimes killed or sent to the fields to labour. Traditional Chinese religion is strong in places like Macau, Hong Kong and Taiwan, but in mainland China the temples and monasteries are pale shadows of their former selves.

Since the death of Mao, the Chinese government has allowed many temples (sometimes with their own contingent of monks and novices) to reopen as active places of worship. All religious activity is firmly under state control and many of the monks are caretakers within renovated shells of monasteries, which serve principally as tourist attractions.

Confucius has often been used as a political symbol, his role 'redefined' to suit the needs of the time. At the end of the 19th century he was upheld as a symbol of reform because he had worked for reform in his own day. After the fall of the Qing dynasty, Chinese intellectuals vehemently opposed him as a symbol of a conservative and backward China. In the 1930s he was used by Chiang Kaishek and the Kuomintang as a guide to proper, traditional values. Today Confucius is back in favour, with the Chinese government seeing much to be admired in the neo-Confucianist authoritarianism espoused by Lee Kuan Yew of Singapore.

Christianity is still officially frowned upon by the government as a form of spiritual pollution, but nevertheless you can see new churches being built. What the Chinese government does, however, is make it difficult for Chinese Christians to affiliate with fellow Christians in the west. Churches are placed under the control of the government: the Three-Self Patriotic Movement was set up as an umbrella organisation for the Protestant churches, and the Catholic Patriotic Association was set up to replace Rome as the leader of the Catholic churches.

Proselytising is forbidden and western missionaries are routinely denied visas to enter China – those who enter on tourist visas but are caught proselytising on the sly are unceremoniously booted out.

There is much friction between the government and the Chinese Catholic church because the church refuses to disown the Pope as its leader. For this reason, the Vatican maintains diplomatic relations with Taiwan, much to China's consternation.

Muslims are believed to be the largest identifiable religious group still active in China today, numbering perhaps 2% to 3% of the nation's population. The government has not published official figures of the number of Buddhists, but they must be substantial since most Tibetans, Mongolians and Dai people follow Buddhism. There are around three million Catholics and four million Protestants. It's impossible to determine the number of Taoists, but the number of Taoist priests is very small.

Of all people in China, the Tibetan Buddhists felt the brunt of Mao's Cultural Revolution. The Dalai Lama and his entourage fled to India in 1959 when the Tibetan rebellion was put down by Chinese troops. During the Cultural Revolution the monasteries were disbanded (some were levelled to the ground) and the theocracy, which had governed Tibet for centuries, was wiped out overnight. Some Tibetan temples and monasteries have been reopened and the Tibetan religion is still a very powerful force among the people.

Facts for the Visitor

PLANNING

When to Go

Local tourism has taken off in a big way in China, and in the summer months, when it hits its peak, getting around and finding accommodation can become quite a headache.

Winter is obviously the quietest time of year to get about and there are good discounts on hotels, but the weather can be frigid. Spring and autumn are the best months to be on the road.

See the Climate section in the Facts about the Country chapter for information on seasonal weather variations throughout China.

Major public holidays are to be avoided if possible. Chinese New Year is a terrible time of year to be travelling.

Maps

Top quality maps of almost every Chinese city – even many small towns – are readily available. Some of these show incredible detail – bus routes (including names of bus stops), the locations of hotels, shops and so on. City maps normally cost only Y2 to Y4 – the cost may be partly subsidised by advertisements.

Maps are most easily purchased from bookstalls or street vendors around train and bus stations, from branches of the Xinhua Bookstore or from hotel front desks. Unfortunately maps are almost always in Chinese. It is only in tourist centres that you will find English-language maps.

The places to look for English-language editions are hotel gift shops, Friendship Stores (Yǒuyì Shāngdiàn) and sometimes the foreign-language bookshops. There are also a few atlases – these cover only major cities and tourist sites. Most are in Chinese, but there are a few English editions around – English-language editions invariably cost more than the Chinese equivalents.

There seems to be no central place in China where you can go to purchase maps for the entire country. The selection at the Foreign Languages Bookstore, on Wangfu-jing Dajie in Běijīng, is decent, but hardly comprehensive.

Some of the most detailed maps of China available in the west are the aerial survey 'Operational Navigation Charts' (Series ONC). These are prepared and published by the Defence Mapping Agency Aerospace Center, St Louis Air Force Station, Missouri 63118, USA. Cyclists and mountaineers have recommended these highly. In the UK you can obtain these maps from Stanfords Map Centre (☎ 020-7836 1321), 12-14 Long Acre, London WC2E 9LP, or from the Map Shop (☎ 06-846 3146), AT Atkinson & Partner, 15 High St, Upton-on-Severn, Worcestershire, WR8 OHJ.

Australians can contact Mapland (☎ 03-9670 4383) at 372 Little Bourke St in Melbourne, or the Travel Bookshop (☎ 02-9241 3554) at 20 Bridge St in Sydney.

In France see Ulysse (☎ 1 43 25 17 35) at 26 rue Saint Louis en l'Île, or IGN (☎ 01 43 98 80 00) at 107 rue de la Boetie in Paris.

Lonely Planet publishes a *Hong Kong City Map*. Nelles publishes good detailed regional maps of China, and Berndtson has an excellent detailed *Beijing* map.

What to Bring

If you are only travelling to a single destination, eg Běijīng or Shànghǎi, a suitcase will do. For others, a backpack is still the best carrying container. Many packs these days are lockable, otherwise you can make it a bit more thief-proof by sewing on tabs so you can padlock it shut. It's worth paying the money for a strong, good-quality pack as it's much more likely to withstand the rigours of Chinese travel.

An alternative is a large, soft, zip bag with a wide shoulder strap. This is obviously not an option if you plan to do any trekking.

If you are undertaking a longer trip, whatever you carry your gear in, the usual budget travellers' rule applies – bring as little as possible.

China is pretty informal about clothing, although fashionable clothing is in vogue in Hong Kong, Běijīng and Shànghǎi. Shorts and T-shirts are respectable summer wear, but try to look clean. Flip-flops (thongs) and sandals are OK. Clothing is one of the best cheap buys in China, so don't feel compelled to bring everything from home.

If you're travelling in the north of China at the height of winter, prepare yourself for incredible cold. Good down jackets are available in China, but it's hard to find good quality boots (at least in larger sizes). A reasonable clothes list would include:

- underwear and swimming gear
- one pair of cotton trousers
- one pair of shorts
- one long cotton skirt (women)
- a few T-shirts or lightweight shirts
- sweater for cool nights in the hills
- one pair of sneakers or shoes
- socks
- sandals
- flip-flops (thongs) – handy to wear when showering
- lightweight jacket or raincoat
- a set of 'dress up' clothes
- a hat

Bedding Hotels provide copious bedding during the winter months, as do the sleeper carriages on trains. A sleeping bag, although a hassle to carry, can come in handy. You can use it to spread over unsavoury-looking hotel bedding, as a cushion on hard train seats, and as a seat for long waits on railway platforms. If you are planning on camping or spending time in the hills (especially during the cool season) a sleeping bag is essential. A sheet sleeping bag will suffice if you are going to be spending all your time in hot, tropical places.

Toiletries Soap, toothpaste, shampoo and other toiletries are readily available. Outside the major cities, some items are hard to find, such as shaving cream, decent razor blades, mosquito repellent, deodorant, dental floss, tampons and contact lens solution. Bring condoms with you, as the quality of locally made condoms may be suspect. Antibacterial hand gel (the kind that you don't need to use with water) comes in handy as public bathrooms don't have hand-washing facilities.

Miscellaneous Items See the Health section later in this chapter for a medical kit check list. Some handy items to stow away in your pack could include the following:

- a padlock, especially for budget travellers – most cheap hotels and quite a number of mid-range places have doors locked by a flimsy latch and padlock. You'll find having your own sturdy lock on the door does wonders for your peace of mind.
- a knife (preferably Swiss Army) – it has a whole range of uses, such as peeling fruit etc.
- a sarong – can be used as a bed sheet, an item of clothing, an emergency towel and a pillow.
- insect repellent, a box of mosquito coils or an electric mosquito zapper.
- a torch (flashlight) and/or candles
- a voltage stabiliser – for those travellers who may be bringing sensitive electronic equipment.
- moisture-impregnated disposable tissues – for your hands and face
- a spare set of glasses and your spectacle prescription. If you wear contact lenses, bring enough solution to last your trip.
- earplugs (to shut out the din in some hotels) and a sleeping mask
- a sun hat and sunglasses
- a water bottle – it should always be by your side.
- high-factor sunscreen
- string – useful as a makeshift clothes line (double-strand nylon is good to secure your clothes if you have no pegs). You can buy small, inexpensive sachets of washing powder everywhere.
- a pair of binoculars – if you plan to be bird-watching and wildlife-spotting
- a high-pitched whistle – some women carry them as a possible deterrent to would-be assailants.

You may want to consider taking along gifts for locals you meet in your travels. English books and magazines are appreciated by those who are studying the language. Stamps make good gifts; the Chinese are avid collectors, congregating outside the philatelic sections of the post offices and dealing on the footpath. Odd-looking foreign coins and currency are appreciated. Foreign postcards are sought after, and pictures of you and your family make popular gifts.

RESPONSIBLE TOURISM

Common sense and courtesy go a long way when you are travelling. Think about the impact you may be having on the environment and the people who inhabit it. One very simple way of minimising your impact is to reduce the amount of plastic you use. Bring your own cup rather than using disposable plastic ones; recycle plastic bags; try and recycle plastic drinking bottles, or purify your water.

As exotic and tempting as they may be, avoid buying products that further endanger threatened species and habitats.

SUGGESTED ITINERARIES

Unless you have a couple of years up your sleeve and inexhaustible funds, you are only going to be able to see a small part of China on any one trip. It's a good idea to have a loose itinerary to follow. The following suggestions assume you have at least four weeks in China (see the Xīnjiāng chapter for details on the Silk Road).

Běijīng to Tibet via Xī'ān

This route has emerged as a very popular one with many travellers, particularly those arriving overland from Europe by train and heading for Nepal and India via Tibet. The great thing about this route is that it gives you the best of China's historical sights (Běijīng and Xī'ān) and at the same time gives you an opportunity to travel out into China's remote and sparsely populated western regions.

Běijīng, Xī'ān and Lhasa are the main attractions on this route. En route to Xī'ān, you can also visit Dàtóng and Tàiyuán, although they are not particularly pleasant cities. Xīníng is worth a day or so, mainly for the nearby lamasery of Tǎ'ěr Sì. The less time spent in Golmud, the better. From Lhasa, it is possible to travel on to Nepal via the Tibetan temple towns of Gyantse, Shigatse and Sakya, and cross the border at Zhangmu – some travellers make a detour to the Everest base camp. The journey from Lhasa to Kathmandu is a once-in-a-lifetime trip.

Běijīng to Hong Kong via the South-West

There are many variations on this route, depending on how much time you have and how much you enjoy travelling on Chinese trains (or, more to the point, trying to get tickets for the trains).

A stopover in Kūnmíng allows travellers to explore Yúnnán, which is arguably the most exotic of China's provinces – rich in ethnic colour and some of the best scenery in all China. From Kūnmíng, many travellers also opt to travel on to Chéngdū (via Dàlǐ and Lìjiāng).

From Chéngdū there are many options: onwards to Chóngqìng and down the Cháng Jiāng (Yangzi River) to Shànghǎi or Wǔhàn, or on to Guìzhōu and Guìlín and then to Hong Kong. You can speed things up on this route with a flight or two.

Hong Kong to Kūnmíng via Guìlín

This has long been China's most favoured backpacker trail. The standard routine is a brief stay in Guǎngzhōu (one or two nights), followed by a ferry to Wúzhōu, and from there a direct bus to Yángshuò. Many travellers are seduced into spending much longer than they planned in Yángshuò.

Onward travel to Kūnmíng can be undertaken by train or by plane. From Kūnmíng there is a wide range of choices – south to the regional areas of Xīshuāngbǎnnà and Déhóng or north-west to Lìjiāng. Other possibilities include flights from Kūnmíng to Chiang Mai or Bangkok in Thailand, or taking a train to Hanoi in Vietnam.

Cháng Jiāng (Yangzi River) Routes

Cruises on the Cháng Jiāng have long been touted as one of China's premier attractions. In reality they get mixed reports.

The most interesting part of the Cháng Jiāng is the section between Chóngqìng and Wǔhàn; the section east of here, between Wǔhàn and Shànghǎi, is of little interest (the river gets so wide you cannot even see its shores).

Gānsù–Sìchuān Route

This scenic route travels along the eastern edge of the Tibetan mountains and is usually done in several stages, stopping at Xiàhé, Hézuò, Lǎngmùsì, Zöigê and Sōngpān – a trip taking at least four days. For travel in this area you'll need People's Insurance Company of China (PICC) insurance.

On a highland plateau two hours further south in Sìchuān is Zöigê, from where it's possible to make a side trip to Jiǔzhàigōu National Park. Road conditions worsen noticeably once you cross from Gānsù into Sìchuān, and from Lǎngmùsì it's a bumpy four hours to Zöigê.

From Zöigê it's a full day's journey by bus south to Chéngdū, although many opt to break up the journey with a stay in Sōngpān. For more information on these areas, see the Sìchuān chapter.

North-East Route

Visit the former treaty port of Dàlián, an up-and-coming metropolis, then head north to what used to be Manchuria and the cities of Shěnyáng, Chángchūn and Hāěrbīn. It's a region that seems like a combination of Canadian prairies, rust belt heavy industry, leftover traces of Japanese colonialism and undeniable Russian influences. Apart from the cities, it's also possible to try and commune with nature (always an elusive prospect in China) in the Chángbái Shān and Zhālóng nature reserves. The north-east also offers a true winter experience, including skiing and -30°C (-22°F) weather, and during the summer is a good place to go and escape the heat while the rest of China bakes. You could keep heading north to the grasslands of Mǎnzhōulǐ in Inner Mongolia and on to Siberia or Europe along the Trans-Siberian Railway.

VISAS & DOCUMENTS
Passport

You must have a passport with you all of the time; it is the most basic travel document. The Chinese government requires that your passport be valid for at least six months after the expiry date of your visa. You'll need at least one entire blank page in your passport for the visa.

If you lose your passport, you should certainly have some ID card with your photo – many embassies require this before issuing a new passport.

Visas

A visa is required for the People's Republic of China (PRC), but at the time of writing, visas were not required for most western nationals to visit Hong Kong or Macau. A new visa policy allows foreigners from 17 countries (Australia, Austria, Belgium, Canada, France, Germany, Greece, Italy, Japan, Korea, Luxembourg, Netherlands, New Zealand, Portugal, Singapore, Spain and the United States) to enter Shànghǎi (through Pudong or Hongqiao airports) without a visa and stay up to 48 hours. Plans are afoot to extend this new policy to other cities.

There are six types of visas, as follows:

Type	Description	Chinese name
L	Travel	lǚxíng
F	Business or Student (less than 6 months)	fǎngwèn
D	Resident	dìngjū
G	Transit	guòjìng
X	Long-term Student	liúxué
Z	Working	rènzhí

For most travellers, the type of visa is 'L', from the Chinese word for travel (lǚxíng). This letter is stamped right on the visa.

Visas are readily available from Chinese embassies and consulates in most western and many other countries. A standard 30-day, single-entry visa from most Chinese embassies abroad can be issued in three to five working days. You can get an application form in person at the embassy or consulate or obtain one on line at Web sites such as www.cbw.com/tourism. A visa mailed to you will take up to three weeks. Rather than going through an embassy or consulate, you can also make arrangements at some travel agencies, especially Chinese government-owned agencies (such as CITS and CTS), which have overseas representatives. Visa applications require one photo.

You can easily get a visa in Hong Kong. The standard 30-day visa can be obtained from almost any travel agency. The cheapest visas are available from the Visa Office (☎ 2827 1881) at the Ministry of Foreign Affairs of the PRC, 5th floor, Low Block, China Resources Building, 26 Harbour Rd, Wanchai. For next-day service, a 30-day to three-month single-entry visa is HK$100 or HK$150 for a double-entry visa. It's an extra HK$150 for same-day service. US passport holders, unless of Chinese descent, must pay an extra HK$160. It also has a photo service for HK$30. The office is open Monday to Friday from 9 am to 12.30 pm and from 2 to 5 pm, and on Saturday until 12.30 pm.

If you need more than three months or a multiple-entry visa, head to one of the branches of CTS in Hong Kong or Macau. Prices range from HK$160 for a single-entry, 90-day visa issued in three days to HK$1300 for a six-month, multiple-entry visa. Some Hong Kong travel agencies can also get you 60- and 90-day, and multiple-entry visas. Try Sky Fortune Travel & Tours (☎ 2301 1082), 15th floor, Cameron Centre, 57-59 Chatham Rd South, Tsimshatsui, Kowloon.

A 30-day visa is activated on the date you enter China, and must be used within three months of the date of issue. The 60-day and 90-day visas are activated on the date they are issued.

Visas valid for more than 30 days are usually difficult to obtain anywhere other than in Hong Kong.

Multiple-entry visas allow you to enter and leave the country an unlimited number of times and are available through CTS and some travel agencies in Hong Kong and Macau. The cheapest multiple-entry visas cost HK$350 and are valid for 90 days; six-month multiple-entry visas cost HK$500 for next-day pick-up or HK$600 for same day pick-up. The latter are business or short-term student (F) visas.

It is possible to obtain single-entry visas at the border at Shēnzhèn and Zhūhǎi. Unfortunately, they are valid for travel only within the Shēnzhèn Special Economic Zone or the Zhūhǎi Special Economic Zone respectively, and the price of HK$360 is hardly worth it. Furthermore, you might not get the full 30 days.

See the Land section in the Getting There & Away chapter for information on visas for travelling on the Trans-Siberian Railway.

Visa Extensions Visa extensions are handled by the Foreign Affairs Branch of the local Public Security Bureau (PSB; Gōngānjú) – the police force. Government travel organisations, like CITS, have nothing to do with extensions, so don't bother asking. Extensions can cost nothing for some, but Y250 for most nationalities.

The situation with visa extensions seems to change frequently. Recently, travellers who entered China with a 30-day visa have been able to renew their visa twice (30 days each time, so the total stay is up to 90 days) without any problem.

It's also possible to get visa extensions, without going outside China, through private visa services in Běijīng. The legality of these services is questionable, and most of them seem to operate through private connections with the PSB. The typical cost for a six-month, multiple-entry F visa is Y3000 and up, and can take anywhere from a couple days to a couple weeks. These services are also useful in changing a student X visa to an F visa, which is usually difficult to do. Although some foreigners have used these services without incident, you are taking a risk. Don't hand over your payment until after your visa has been successfully extended. Look in the classified section of *City Edition*, *Beijing Scene* or *Metro* for listings of these services; it's wise to ask around for a personal recommendation from someone who has actually recently used one of the services.

The penalty of overstaying your visa in China is Y500 *per day*! Many travellers have reported having trouble with officials who read the 'valid until' date on their visa incorrectly. For a one-month tourist (L) visa, the 'valid until' date is the date by which you must enter the country, not the date upon which your visa expires. Your visa expires the number of days that your visa is valid for after the date of entry into China (but note that you must enter China within three months of the date the visa was

issued). Sixty- and 90-day visas are activated on the day they are issued.

Photocopies

If you're thinking about working or studying
in China, photocopies of university diplomas,
transcripts and letters of recommendation
could prove helpful.

Married couples should have a copy of
their marriage certificate. Especially in small
towns, you may have to produce a marriage
certificate in order to share a room in a hotel
with your spouse. This practice is randomly
enforced with both locals and foreigners.

A photocopy of your passport is also a
good idea.

Travel Permits

In the early 1980s only 130 places in China
were officially open to foreign tourists.
Nowadays 1330 places are open for travel –
most of the country, except for certain remote border areas, especially those inhabited
by ethnic minorities.

Most of the places described in this book
are open to foreigners, but one incident (like
a riot in Xīnjiāng or Tibet) can cause new
permit regulations to be issued overnight.
Even worse is the fact that some small towns
in China require these permits for the sole
reason to extract fines from any foreigners
who show up without one (Kǎilǐ in Húnán
Province is one such example). To find out
about latest restrictions, it's best to check
with the police in provincial capitals, but
don't be surprised if even they can't tell you.

To travel to closed places you officially
require an Alien Travel Permit (tōngxíng
zhèng). The police have wide discretion in
issuing a permit to a closed place. However,
the choice of open places is now so extensive that most travellers won't need to apply.
Foreign academics and researchers wanting
to poke around remote areas usually need
the right credentials or letter of introduction
(jièshào xìn).

Travel permits can be demanded from
you at hotel registration desks, boat or bus
ticket offices and unusual areas during spot
checks by police. If you're off the track, but
heading towards a destination for which

you have a permit, the police may stop you
and revoke your permit.

The permit also lists the modes of transport you're allowed to take: plane, train,
ship or car – and if a particular mode is
crossed out then you can't use it. If a mode
is cancelled it can be reinstated at the next
police station, but that may be for only a
single trip from point A to point B. You
could try and carry on regardless – though
if caught, you face losing your permit.

If you manage to get a permit for an unusual destination, the best strategy is to get to
that destination as fast as you can (by plane if
possible). Local police do not have to honour
the permit and can cancel it and send you
back. Take your time getting back – you're
less likely to be hassled if you're returning to
civilisation. Transit points usually don't require a permit, and you can stay the night.

Travel Insurance

Although you may have medical insurance
in your own country, it is probably not valid
in China. But ask your insurance company
anyway – you *might* already be covered.

A travel insurance policy to cover theft,
loss and medical problems is a good idea.
Some policies offer lower and higher med-
ical-expense options; the higher ones are
chiefly for countries such as the USA,
which have extremely high medical costs.
There is a wide variety of policies available,
so check the small print.

Some policies specifically exclude 'dangerous activities', which can include scuba
diving, motorcycling, even trekking. A locally acquired motorcycle licence is not
valid under some policies.

Check that the policy covers ambu-
lances or an emergency flight home. If you
have to claim later make sure you keep all
documentation.

Driving Licence

As a tourist, you are not allowed to drive in
China. An International Driving Permit is
not recognised by the Chinese authorities.

Foreign residents in China are allowed to
drive, although they're governed by a different set of regulations. A Chinese driver's

licence is required, and getting it will be much easier if you bring along a valid licence from your home country. If you do not have a licence from home, you'll have to take a driving course in China, as well as the driving test itself – two hassles best avoided.

Before you can obtain your Chinese licence, you must first secure a residence permit (see the entry on Resident Permits later in this chapter). Then you must hand in your native country's drivers' licence – the police keep this licence and issue you with a Chinese one. When you leave China, you must turn in your Chinese licence and your native country's licence will then be returned to you. Just to complicate things, you need to prove you have a car before the Chinese licence can be issued! Foreign residents may face restrictions on where they can drive – ask the local police how far you are permitted to drive from your place of residence.

Student & Youth Cards

If you are studying in China, you'll be issued a student card by your school. These are occasionally useful to get a discount on admission fees.

International student cards and youth cards can sometimes get you a discount on international flights to China. However, these cards are unlikely to get you any discounts in China itself.

Resident Permits

The 'green card' is a residence permit, issued to English teachers, foreign experts and long-term students who live in China. The green card is not really a card, but resembles a small passport. Green cards are issued for one year and must be renewed annually. If you lose your card, you'll pay a hefty fee to have it replaced.

Besides having to have all the right paperwork, you must also pass a health exam to obtain a resident permit. The cost of the health exam is Y350 for students to Y650 for foreigners working in China. Bring your passport and two photos. You're also not supposed to eat or drink prior to having the test. Besides a general health exam, ECG and an x-ray, you will be tested for HIV.

The staff use disposable syringes, which are unwrapped in front of you; if you bring your own syringe they generally refuse to use it unless you adamantly insist.

EMBASSIES
Chinese Embassies

Addresses of China's embassies and consulates in major cities overseas include:

Australia (☎ 02-6273 4780, 6273 4781) 15 Coronation Drive, Yarralumla, Canberra ACT 2600
Consulates: Melbourne, Perth and Sydney
Canada (☎ 613-789 3434) 515 St Patrick St, Ottawa, Ontario K1N 5H3
Consulates: Toronto, Vancouver
France (☎ 01 47 36 77 90) 9 Avenue V Cresson, 92130 Issy les Moulineaux
Italy (☎ 06-3630 8534, 3630 3856) Via Della Camilluccia 613, 00135 Roma
Consulate: Milan
Japan (☎ 03-3403 3380, 3403 3065) 3-4-33 Moto-Azabu, Minato-ku, Tokyo 106
Consulates: Fukuoka, Osaka and Sapporo
Netherlands (☎ 070-355 1515) Adriaan Goekooplaan 7, 2517 JX, The Hague
New Zealand (☎ 04-587 0407) 104A Korokoro Rd, Petone, Wellington
Consulate: Auckland
Singapore (☎ 734 3361) 70 Dalvey Rd
South Korea (☎ 319 5101) 83 Myŏng-dong 2-ga, Chunggu, Seoul
Sweden (☎ 08-767 87 40, 767 40 83) Ringvagen 56, 18134 Lidings
UK (☎ 020-7636 9756) 31 Portland Place, London, W1N 5AG
USA (☎ 202-338-6688, ✉ visa@china-embassy.org) Room 110, 2201 Wisconsin Ave NW, Washington, DC 20007
Consulates: Chicago, Houston, Los Angeles, New York and San Francisco

Foreign Embassies in China

In Běijīng there are two main embassy compounds – Jianguomenwai and Sānlǐtún.

The following embassies are situated in Jianguomenwai, east of the Forbidden City:

India (☎ 6532 1908, fax 6532 4684) 1 Ritan Donglu
Ireland (☎ 6532 2691, fax 6532 2168) 3 Ritan Donglu
Israel (☎ 6505 2970, fax 6505 0328) Room 405, West Wing, China World Trade Centre, 1 Jianguomenwai Dajie

Japan (☎ 6532 2361, fax 6532 4625)
7 Ritan Lu
Mongolia (☎ 6532 1203, fax 6532 5045)
2 Xiushui Beijie
New Zealand (☎ 6532 2731, fax 6532 4317)
1 Ritan Dong Erjie
North Korea (☎ 6532 1186, fax 6532 6056)
Ritan Beilu
Philippines (☎ 6532 1872, fax 6532 3761)
23 Xiushui Beijie
Singapore (☎ 6532 3926, fax 6532 2215)
1 Xiushui Beijie
Thailand (☎ 6532 1903, fax 6532 1748)
40 Guanghua Lu
UK (☎ 6532 1961, fax 6532 1937)
11 Guanghua Lu
USA (☎ 6532 3831, fax 6532 6057)
3 Xiushui Beijie
Vietnam (☎ 6532 5414, fax 6532 5720)
32 Guanghua Lu

The Sānlǐtún Compound, north-east of the
Forbidden City, is home to the following
embassies:

Australia (☎ 6532 2331, fax 6532 6957)
21 Dongzhimenwai Dajie
Cambodia (☎ 6532 1889, fax 6532 3507)
9 Dongzhimenwai Dajie
Canada (☎ 6532 3536, fax 6532 4072)
19 Dongzhimenwai Dajie
France (☎ 6539 1300, fax 6539 1301)
Unit 1015, Tower A, 21 Gong Ti Beilu,
Chaoyangqu
Germany (☎ 6532 2161, fax 6532 5336)
17 Dongzhimenwai Dajie
Italy (☎ 6532 2131, fax 6532 4676)
2 Sanlitun Dong Erjie
Kazakstan (☎ 6532 6182, fax 6532 6183)
9 Sanlitun Dong Liujie
Malaysia (☎ 6532 2531, fax 6532 5032)
13 Dongzhimenwai Dajie
Myanmar (Burma) (☎ 6532 1584, fax 6532
1344) 6 Dongzhimenwai Dajie
Nepal (☎ 6532 1795, fax 6532 3251) 1 Sanlitun
Xi Liujie
Netherlands (☎ 6532 1131, fax 6532 4689)
4 Liangmahe Nanlu
Pakistan (☎ 6532 2504)
1 Dongzhimenwai Dajie
Russia (☎ 6532 1267, fax 6532 4853)
4 Dongzhimen Beizhongjie, west of the
Sānlǐtún Compound in a separate compound
South Korea (☎ 6532 0290, fax 6532 6778)
9 Sanlitun Dong Silu
Sweden (☎ 6532 3331, fax 6532 2909)
3 Dongzhimenwai Dajie

Consulates In Shànghǎi there are consulates
for Australia, Austria, Canada, France, Germany, India, Italy, Japan, the Netherlands,
New Zealand, Russia, Singapore, Sweden,
the UK and the USA.

In Guǎngzhōu, there are consulates for
Australia, France, Thailand, the USA and
Vietnam. There is a US consulate in Shěnyáng, in Liáoníng. In Kūnmíng there are
consulates for Laos, Myanmar and Thailand. Keep in mind that these consulates
aren't always able (or willing) to issue
visas. You're best off getting visas for these
countries before you leave your home country or in Běijīng. See the relevant destination chapters for details.

CUSTOMS

Chinese border crossings have gone from
being severely traumatic to exceedingly
easy. There are clearly marked 'green channels' and 'red channels'; take the red channel only if you have something to declare.

You're allowed to import 400 cigarettes
(or the equivalent in tobacco products), 2L
of alcoholic drink and 50g of gold or silver. Importation of fresh fruit is prohibited. You can legally bring in or take out
only Y6000 in Chinese currency. There are
no restrictions on foreign currency except
that you should declare any cash that exceeds US$5000 (or its equivalent in an-
other currency).

A very peculiar restriction is the Y300
limit (Y200 if going to Hong Kong or
Macau) on taking herbal medicines out of
the country.

Cultural relics, handicrafts, gold and silver ornaments, and jewellery purchased in
China have to be shown to customs on leaving. If these items are deemed to be 'cultural
treasures', they will be confiscated. All bags
are x-rayed, and some foreigners have had
nearly worthless pottery and paintings (on
sale in any tourist shop) seized by overzealous customs agents.

It's illegal to import any printed material,
film, tapes etc 'detrimental to China's politics, economy, culture and ethics'. But
don't be too concerned about what you take
to read.

As you leave China, any tapes, manuscripts, books etc 'which contain state secrets or are otherwise prohibited for export' can be seized.

MONEY
Costs
How much will a trip to China cost? That's largely up to the degree of comfort you need. It also depends on how much travelling you do, and what parts of China you visit. Eastern China, for example, is much more expensive than the west.

Eastern China (basically everywhere between Hēilóngjiāng and Hǎinán Dǎo) has become very difficult to do on a shoestring. Outside the major cities of Běijīng, Guǎngzhōu and Shànghǎi, it is very unusual to come across dorm accommodation, and in many cities accommodation rates start at US$25 to US$35 for a double (singles are rarely available).

Food costs remain reasonable throughout China, but if you are careful they can be as little as US$5 per day. Transport costs can be kept to a minimum by travelling by bus wherever possible or by travelling hard-seat on the train. In other words, travelling through the booming coastal cities of China for less than US$35 per day is quite a challenge.

Western China, however, remains relatively inexpensive. Popular backpacker destinations such as Yúnnán, Sìchuān, Guǎngxī, Gānsù, Xīnjiāng, Qīnghǎi and Tibet abound in budget accommodation and cheap eats. Generally, keeping costs down to US$25 per day is not too difficult. The main drain on the savings will be the long train journeys, on which generally only the hardiest of travellers can face hard-seat.

On average, mid-range hotels will cost around US$35 to US$50 for a double with air-con, bathroom, TV etc. It is usually possible to eat well in hotel restaurants for around US$5 to US$10.

Transport costs have decreased by about 10% to 20% since the duel-pricing system was abolished. Train travel is very reasonable, and generally costs about half the price of flying. For sample train fares see the Getting Around section in the Běijīng chapter, and for domestic airfares see the Getting Around chapter.

Top-end travel in China? It's possible to hit the major attractions of the country staying in five-star hotels (US$100 and up for a double), flying long distances, taking taxis to and from airports, dining on Chinese haute cuisine and enjoying a few drinks in the lobby bar in the evenings for between US$200 and US$250 per day.

Carrying Money
A money belt or pockets sewn inside your clothes is the safest way to carry money. Velcro tabs sewn to seal your pockets shut will also help thwart roving hands.

Keeping all your eggs in one basket is not advised – guard against possible loss by leaving a small stash of money (say US$100) in your hotel room or buried in your backpack, with a record of the travellers cheque serial numbers and a photocopy of your passport.

Cash
A lot of Chinese vendors and taxi drivers cannot make change for even a Y50 note, so stock up on Y10 bills at the nearest bank.

Counterfeit bills are a problem in China. Very few Chinese will accept a Y50 or Y100 bill without first checking to see whether or not it's a fake. Notes that are old and tattered are also sometimes hard to spend. If you are having problems with a note, exchange it for a new one or small change at the Bank of China – counterfeits, however, will be confiscated.

Local Chinese have a variety of methods for checking bills. First of all, they look for the watermark – obviously, if it doesn't have one it's a fake. Many locals maintain that colours tend to be more pronounced in counterfeit notes and the drawn lines less distinct. The texture of a note is also a telltale sign – counterfeits tend to be smoother than authentic bills.

Travellers Cheques
Besides the advantage of safety, travellers cheques are useful to carry in China because the exchange rate is actually more favourable than what you get for cash.

Cheques from most of the world's leading banks and issuing agencies are now acceptable in China – stick to the major companies such as Thomas Cook, American Express (Amex) and Citibank.

ATMs

Most automated teller machines (ATMs) in most Chinese cities only work with the Chinese banking system and foreign cards will be rejected. Exceptions are Běijīng, Shànghǎi, Guǎngzhōu, Shēnzhèn and, of course, Hong Kong, where you'll find ATMs advertising international bank settlement systems such as GlobalAccess, Cirrus, Interlink, Plus, Star, Accel, The Exchange and Explore. The rear side of your ATM card should tell you which systems will work with your card. Visa, MasterCard and Amex will work in many of these cities' ATMs as well. Don't, however, rely solely on withdrawing cash from ATMs in China as it can often be difficult to find an ATM that is working properly. The maximum cash withdrawal per day is Y2500.

Credit Cards

Plastic is gaining more acceptance in China for use by foreign visitors in major tourist cities. Useful cards include Visa, MasterCard, Amex and JCB. They can be used in most mid-range and top-end hotels, Friendship Stores and some department stores. You still can't use credit cards to buy train tickets, but recently more and more travel agents are able to accept credit cards for flights.

Credit card cash advances have become fairly routine at head branches of the Bank of China, even in places as remote as Lhasa. Bear in mind, however, that a 4% commission is generally deducted and usually the minimum advance is Y1200.

International Transfers

Except when in Hong Kong and Macau, having money sent to you in China is a time-consuming and frustrating task that is best avoided. If dealing with the Bank of China, the process can take weeks, although it can be much faster at CITIC Bank.

China Courier Service Corporation (a joint-venture with Western Union Financial Services in the USA) is very fast and efficient. In Běijīng, there is a branch (☎ 63 18 4313) at 7 Dongdan Jie in Qianmen (in the post office). In Shànghǎi, Shanghai EMS (☎ 6356 8129, 1 Sichuan Beilu) acts as an agent for Western Union.

Currency

The Chinese currency is known as Renminbi (RMB), or 'People's Money'. Formally the basic unit of RMB is the *yuán*, which is divided into ten *jiao*, which is again divided into ten *fen*. Colloquially, the yuán is referred to as *kuài* and jiǎo as *máo*. The fen has so little value these days that it is rarely used.

The Bank of China issues RMB bills in denominations of one, two, five, 10, 50 and 100 yuán. Coins are in denominations of one yuán, five jiǎo and one, two and five fen. There are still a lot of paper versions of the coins floating around, but it is likely that these will gradually disappear in favour of the coins.

Hong Kong's currency is the Hong Kong dollar and Macau's is the *pataca*. Both currencies are worth about 7% more than Renminbi.

Currency Exchange

Exchange rates for Chinese RMB are as follows:

country	unit		yuan
Australia	A$1	=	Y5.32
Canada	C$1	=	Y5.45
euro	€1	=	Y7.94
France	FF1	=	Y1.25
Germany	DM1	=	Y4.20
Hong Kong	HK$1	=	Y1.04
Japan	¥1	=	Y0.067
UK	UK£1	=	Y12.57
USA	US$1	=	Y8.07

Changing Money

Foreign currency and travellers cheques can be changed at border crossings, international airports, major branches of the Bank of China, tourist hotels, some Friendship Stores and some large department stores. Top-end hotels will generally change money for hotel guests only. The official rate is given almost everywhere, so there is little need to shop around looking for the best deal.

Australian, Canadian, US, UK, Hong Kong, Japanese and most Western European currencies are accepted in China. In some of the backwaters, it may be hard to change lesser known currencies – US dollars are still the easiest to change.

Keep at least a few of your exchange receipts. You will need them if you want to exchange any remaining RMB you have at the end of your trip. Those travelling to Hong Kong can change RMB for Hong Kong dollars there.

Bank Accounts

Foreigners can open bank accounts in China – both RMB and US dollar accounts (the latter only at special foreign-exchange banks). You do not need to have resident status – a tourist visa is sufficient. Virtually every foreigner working in China will tell you that CITIC is far better to do business with than the Bank of China. It's basically more efficient and well-versed in handling international credit card transactions, including accepting personal cheques against your Amex.

Black Market

The abolition of Foreign Exchange Certificates (FEC) in 1994 basically knocked China's flourishing black market on its head. But thanks to China's thriving smuggling rings (who need US dollars to carry on their business transactions), you can still change money on the black market in major cities at rates substantially better than those offered by the banks. Your best bet is to ask a foreign resident or someone you trust for a recommendation on a 'reputable' moneychanger. Generally speaking, though, it's inadvisable to change money on the streets given the risk of short-changing, rip-offs and the abundance of counterfeit currency floating about.

Tipping & Bargaining

In China almost no-one asks for tips. When tips are offered, they are offered *before* you get the service, not after – that will ensure (hopefully) that you get better service.

Since foreigners are so frequently overcharged in China, bargaining becomes essential. You can bargain in shops, hotels, taxis (unless they use their meter), with most people – but not everywhere. In large shops where prices are clearly marked, there is usually no latitude for bargaining (although if you ask the staff sometimes can give you a 10% discount). In small shops and street stalls, bargaining is expected, but there is one important rule to follow – be polite.

You should keep in mind that entrepreneurs are in business to make money – they aren't going to sell anything to you at a loss. Your goal should be to pay the Chinese price, as opposed to the foreigners' price – if you can do that, you've done well.

Taxes

Although big hotels and top-end restaurants may add a tax or 'service charge' of 10% or more, all other consumer taxes are included in the price tag.

POST & COMMUNICATIONS
Postal Rates

Postage for domestic letters up to 20g is Y0.50; domestic postcards are Y0.30. International airmail postal rates follow:

letters (weight)	international	HK, Macau & Taiwan	Asia-Pacific
0–20g	Y5.40	Y2.50	Y4.70
21–100g	Y11.40	Y5.00	Y9.80
101–250g	Y21.80	Y9.50	Y18.60
251–500g	Y40.80	Y17.70	Y34.80
501g–1kg	Y76.70	Y32.70	Y65.30
1–2kg	Y124.00	Y56.80	Y105.00
Postcards	Y4.20	Y2.00	Y3.70
Aerograms	Y5.20	Y1.80	Y4.50

There are discounts for printed matter and small packets. Maximum weight is 30kg. Most post offices offer materials for packaging, including padded envelopes, boxes and heavy brown paper.

Post offices are very picky about how you pack things; don't finalise your packing until the thing has got its last customs clearance.

If you have a receipt for the goods, put it in the box when you're mailing it, since it may be opened again by customs further down the line.

EMS Domestic Express Mail Service (EMS) parcels up to 200g cost Y15; each additional 200g costs Y5. For international EMS, the charges vary according to country. Some sample minimal rates (up to 500g parcels) are as follows:

country/region	cost
Asia (South)	Y255
Asia (South-East)	Y150
Australia	Y195
Europe (Eastern)	Y382
Europe (Western)	Y232
Hong Kong & Macau	Y95
Japan & Korea	Y115
Middle East	Y375
North America	Y217
South America	Y262

Registration Fees The registration fee for letters, printed matter and packets is Y3. Acknowledgement of receipt is Y3 per article.

Sending Mail

The international postal service seems efficient, and airmail letters and postcards will probably take around five to 10 days to reach their destinations. If possible, write the country of destination in Chinese, as this should speed up the delivery. Domestic post is amazingly fast – perhaps one or two days from Guǎngzhōu to Běijīng. Within a city it may be delivered the same day it's sent.

As well as the local post offices, there are branch post offices in just about all the major tourist hotels where you can send letters, packets and parcels. Even at cheap hotels you can usually post letters from the front desk – reliability varies, but in general it's OK. In some places, you may only be able to post printed matter from these branch offices. Other parcels may require a customs form attached at the town's main post office, where their contents will be checked.

The post office requires that you use an envelope of an approved size. If you bring envelopes from abroad, these might not meet the standard. They will still be delivered, but given low priority and will take a long time to arrive at the intended destination.

Private Carriers There are a number of foreign private couriers in China that offer international express posting of documents and parcels. None of these private carriers is cheap, but they're fast and secure. In major cities these companies have a pick-up service as well as drop-off centres, so call their offices for the latest details.

The major players in this market are United Parcel Service, DHL, Federal Express and TNT Skypak. See the relevant destination chapter to find the courier office nearest you.

Receiving Mail

There are fairly reliable poste restante services in just about every city and town. The collection system differs from place to place, but one thing all post offices seem to agree on is the Y1 to Y2.30 charge for each item of poste restante mail you collect. Remember, you will need your passport to be able to retrieve your letters or parcels.

Some major tourist hotels will hold mail for their guests, but this is a less reliable option. Receiving a parcel from abroad is a bit complicated. The mail carrier will not deliver the parcel to your address – what you get is a slip of paper (in Chinese only). Bring this to the post office (indicated on the paper) along with your passport – the parcel will be opened and inspected in front of you. As long as it contains nothing nasty you will then be allowed to take it. One good thing about this system is that it mostly eliminates the possibility of your goods being pinched by corrupt customs officials.

Officially, China forbids certain items from being mailed to it – the regulations specifically prohibit 'reactionary books, magazines and propaganda materials, obscene or immoral articles'. You also cannot mail Chinese currency abroad or receive it by post.

Telephone

China's phone system is undergoing a major overhaul and, given the size of the task, it has so far been reasonably successful. Both international and domestic calls can be made with a minimum of fuss from your hotel room and card phones are increasingly widespread.

Most hotel rooms are equipped with phones from which local calls are free. Alternatively, local calls can be made from public pay phones or from privately run phone booths (there's one of these on every corner nowadays). Long-distance domestic calls can also be made from the phone booths, but not usually international calls. In the lobbies of many hotels, the reception desks have a similar system – free calls for guests, Y1 for non-guests, and long-distance calls are charged by the minute.

You can place both domestic and international long-distance phone calls from main telecommunications offices. Generally you pay a deposit of Y200 and are given a card with the number of the phone booth you call from. The call is timed by computer, charged by the minute and a receipt will be provided.

Domestic long-distance rates in China vary according to distance, but are cheap. International calls are expensive, although in larger cities, with the introduction of IP cards, this is quickly changing (see Phone Cards following). Rates for station-to-station calls to most countries in the world are around Y20 per minute. There is a minimum charge of three minutes. Reverse-charge calls are often cheaper than calls paid for in China. Time the call yourself – the operator will not break in to tell you that your minimum period of three minutes is approaching. After you hang up, the operator will ring back to tell you how much it cost. There is no call cancellation fee.

If you are expecting a call – either international or domestic – try to advise the caller beforehand of your hotel room number. The operators frequently have difficulty understanding western names and the hotel receptionist may not be able to locate you. If this can't be done, then try to inform the operator that you are expecting the call and write down your name and room number.

The country code to use to access China is ☎ 86.

Phone Cards   There's a wide range of local and international phonecards. Lonely Planet's eKno Communication Card is aimed specifically at independent travellers and provides budget international calls, a range of messaging services, free email and travel information – for local calls, you're usually better off with a local card. You can join online at www.ekno.lonelyplanet.com, or by phone from China by dialling ☎ 10800-180-0073. Once you have joined, to use eKno from China, dial ☎ 10800-180-0072. Check the eKno Web site for joining and access numbers from other countries and updates on super budget local access numbers and new features.

With the recent introduction of the IP (Internet Phone) system, international call rates have plunged by about 25% to Y4.80 per minute and Y1.50 per minute to Hong Kong, Macau and Taiwan. The service is currently only available in 25 cities in China, including Běijīng and Shànghǎi. To take advantage of these rates, you have to buy an IP card, which are usually available in increments of Y100. Unfortunately the cards aren't easily obtainable, requiring delivery or having to search out an outlet in remote areas, although you can increasingly buy them in Internet cafes. You dial a local number, then punch in your account number, followed by the number you wish to call. English-language service is usually available.

Regular card phones are also found in hotel lobbies and in most telecommunications buildings. They're about double the price of IP rates, although they've also come down substantially from former IDD rates. Note that most phone cards can only be used in the province where you buy them. Smartcards can be used throughout China, provided you can find a Smartcard phone.

Direct Dialling and Collect Calls   The international access code in China is ☎ 00.

Add the country code, then the local area code (omitting the 0 before it) and the number you want to reach. Another option is to dial the home country direct dial number (☎ 108), which puts you straight through to a local operator there. You can then make a reverse-charge (collect) call or a credit-card call with a telephone credit card valid in the destination country.

Dialling codes include:

country	direct dial	country direct
Australia	☎ 00-61	☎ 108-61
Canada	☎ 00-1	☎ 108-1
Hong Kong	☎ 00-852	☎ 108-852
Japan	☎ 00-81	☎ 108-81
Netherlands	☎ 00-31	☎ 108-31
New Zealand	☎ 00-64	☎ 108-64
UK	☎ 00-44	☎ 108-44
USA	☎ 00-1	☎ 108-1*

* For the USA you can dial ☎ 108-11 (AT&T), ☎ 108-12 (MCI) or ☎ 108-13 (Sprint)

Essential Numbers There are several telephone numbers that are the same for all major cities. However, only international assistance is likely to have English-speaking operators:

directory	number
International assistance	☎ 115
Local directory assistance	☎ 114
Long-distance assistance	☎ 113/173
Police hotline	☎ 110
Fire hotline	☎ 119

Mobile Phones Unless your phone is on the US network, your mobile phone should work in China. Mobile phones are popular in China, especially in big cities. There are over 10 million subscribers, in part because it's actually cheaper to buy a mobile phone than to get a conventional phone installed. If you want to get a Chinese SIM card, the cost is Y2000 for one that accepts international calls or Y600 for local service. Usage rate is an additional 3 jiǎo per minute. If you have a Chinese SIM card, you can make overseas calls for Y4.80 per minute by first dialling ☎ 17901, ☎ 17911, ☎ 17921 or ☎ 17931,

followed by 00, the country code then the number you want to call. You will be billed accordingly.

Fax & Email
Email has taken off in China. Not only will you find Internet cafes in all tourist destinations, but they're also springing up in small towns. The cheapest way to keep in touch while on the road is to sign up for a free email account with Hotmail (www.hotmail.com), Rocketmail (www.rocketmail.com) or Yahoo (www.yahoo.com) and access your account from an Internet cafe. These services are free, but you have to put up with advertising. If you're willing to spend US$15 per year, you can get all your email forwarded to any address of your choice by signing up with Pobox (www.pobox.com) – this service can also be used to block advertising and mail bombs.

If you want to use a foreign-based Internet Service Provider (ISP) (eg Compuserve), you may have a bit of trouble accessing it from China.

If you're travelling with a portable computer and modem and wish to avoid Internet cafes, you can set up a local Internet account for about Y100, plus Y4 to Y8 per hour. Note that it can be risky to attach your modem to the phone in your hotel room and dial out through the switchboard – if the switchboard is digital (as opposed to analog) you risk frying your modem. Ironically, this is a bigger problem at newer hotels – old hotels usually have analog equipment. Konexx (www.konexx.com) sells a device called a 'mobile konnector' that not only protects the modem, but also allows you to hook up to the phone's handset cord.

You do have to put up with some censorship – the Chinese government has blocked access to sites that peddle pornography or contain political content deemed unsuitable for the masses (such as CNN's Web site). Also, connections are often agonisingly slow. Nevertheless, you can get quite a lot of useful work done on the Internet. China Telecom offers Internet service in major cities. Internet service providers in Běijīng include:

Beijing Telecommunications Admin (☎ 010-6306 0779) 11 Xichangan Jie, www.bta.net.cn

Eastnet (☎ 010-6529 2268) Lufthansa Center Department Store (computer section)
Unicom-Sparkice (☎ 010-6505 2288 ext 6206, ✉ cafe@unicom.com.cn) 2nd floor, China World

BOOKS

Fathoming the enigma of China is such a monumental task that the need for 'China-watchers' and their publications will probably never dry up. Indeed, just keeping up with the never-ending flood of conjecture would be a full-time job in itself. Be aware that a book might be a hardcover rarity in one country while it's readily available in paperback in another. The following is just an abbreviated tour of the highlights.

Lonely Planet

Lonely Planet guides to the region include *Beijing, Central Asia, Hong Kong & Macau, Shanghai, South-West China* and *Tibet*. There are phrasebooks covering Mandarin, Cantonese, Tibetan, Central Asian languages and Arabic. Also published by Lonely Planet are *Read This First: Asia & India*, *Healthy Travel Asia & India* and *Chasing Rickshaws*.

Guidebooks

The Hong Kong publisher Odyssey is gradually producing a series of illustrated provincial guides to China. To date there are guides to Yúnnán, Guìzhōu, Sìchuān, Shànghǎi, Xī'ān and Běijīng. There is less emphasis on the kind of practical travel information you find in Lonely Planet guides, but they are attractively packaged and provide good background reading.

It is worth keeping an eye out for reprints of old guidebooks to China. Oxford has rereleased *In Search of Old Peking* by LC Arlington and William Lewisohn, which is a wonderfully detailed guide to a world that is now long gone.

Travel Tales

From Heaven Lake by Vikram Seth, follows Seth's journey from Xīnjiāng to Tibet and on to Delhi. Another possibility is *Danziger's Travels* by Nick Danziger – a good 'Silk Road' book that takes quite a long time to get to China.

China by Bike: Taiwan, Hong Kong, China's East Coast by Roger Grigsby, is just what the title implies.

The greatest backpacker of all time was, of course, Marco Polo. Author Ronald Latham published *Marco Polo, The Travels* in 1958, and it's still available as a Penguin reprint.

History & Politics

The most comprehensive history available is the *Cambridge History of China*. The series runs to 15 volumes and traces Chinese history from its earliest beginnings to 1982.

A far more practical overview for travellers is *The Walled Kingdom: A History of China from 2000 BC to the Present* by Witold Rodzinsky. It should be available in a handy paperback edition of around 450 pages.

The best recent history of modern China is Jonathan Spence's *The Search for Modern China*. It comprehensively covers China's history from the late Ming dynasty through to the Tiānānmén Massacre, in lively prose that is a pleasure to read. Spence's *The Gate of Heavenly Peace: The Chinese and Their Revolution, 1895–1980*, a history of ideas and personalities, is also recommended.

The Great Chinese Revolution 1800–1985 by John King Fairbank is another highly rated modern history.

A political history of the Deng years has already appeared in *Burying Mao* by Richard Baum. For anyone seriously interested in China's stop-go reforms of the last 20 years, this is the book to read. Merle Goldman also looks at the tortuous course of democratic reform in *Sowing the Seeds of Democracy in China: Political Reform in the Deng Xiaoping Era*.

Hungry Ghosts: Mao's Secret Famine by Jasper Becker is perhaps the best book on the disastrous Great Leap Forward. The book focuses on the 1958–62 famine that killed up to 30 million people.

It is worth picking up a copy of *The Soong Dynasty* by Sterling Seagrave for a racy account of the bad old days under the Kuomintang.

China's takeover of Hong Kong still stirs up strong feelings. Mark Roberti contributes in his *The Fall of Hong Kong – China's Triumph and Britain's Betrayal*.

General

Insights *Wild Swans* by Jung Chang is one of the more ambitious of the long line of autobiographical 'I survived China, but only just' books. *Life and Death in Shanghai* by Nien Cheng focuses largely on the Cultural Revolution and is also recommended.

Red Azalea by Anchee Min is a strange and racy account of what it was like to grow up in the Cultural Revolution.

Less riveting, perhaps, is a fine account of life in rural China in *Mr China's Son: A Villager's Life* by He Liuyi.

State of the nation accounts of contemporary Chinese politics and society by western scholars and journalists are thick on the ground and tend to become repetitive if you read too many of them. One of the best is *China Wakes* by Nicholas D Kristof and Sheryl Wudunn. Orville Schell has also been diligently tracking China's awakening in several books, the latest being *Mandate of Heaven*.

Another interesting account is Canadian journalist Jan Wong's *Red China Blues*. The book spans the author's experiences from being a pro-communist foreign student in China during the Cultural Revolution to her stint as a foreign correspondent during the massacre at Tiānānmén.

For an insight into Chinese society, check out Perry Link's *Evening Chats in Beijing*. It's intelligent, well written and packed with illuminating insights and observations drawn from a long career of writing and thinking about China.

Real China: From Cannibalism to Karaoke by John Gittings is informative and entertaining, even if the title is unfortunate.

China Remembers by Calum MacLeod and Lijia Zhang is an excellent collection of short essays by Chinese whose lives exemplify China in the last 50 years.

Human Rights *Eighteen Layers of Hell: Stories from the Chinese Gulag* by Kate Saunders blows the lid off China's human rights violations.

Harry Wu, imprisoned by Chinese authorities for 19 years, exposes China's *láogǎi* (forced labour camps) in his eloquently written *Bitter Winds: A Memoir of My Years in China's Gulag*. Wu returned to China again in 1995 and was immediately arrested and tried for espionage, but was expelled after intervention by the US congress and President Clinton. He wrote about that experience in his sequel, *Troublemaker: One Man's Crusade Against China's Cruelty*.

The smuggled prison letters of dissident Wei Jingsheng have been collected and published in *The Courage to Stand Alone: Letters from Prison and Other Writings*, edited by Kristina Torgeson.

Some earlier works, not out of print, can be tracked down in libraries. Two such examples are *Prisoner of Mao* (1976) by Bao Ruo-Wang and *Seeds of Fire – Chinese Voices of Conscience* (1989), edited by Geremie Barmé and John Minford.

Biography Biographical appraisals of China's shadowy leaders are immensely popular. Mao, of course, has been the subject of countless biographies. The classic is *Red Star over China* by Edgar Snow, but it was his personal physician, Zhisui Li, who finally exposed the world's most famous dictator cum pop icon. Li's *The Private Life of Chairman Mao* is absolutely compelling in its account of Mao as a domineering manipulator who hypocritically flouted the authoritarian and puritanical rules he foisted on his people – fascinating stuff.

Mao gets similar treatment in *The New Emperors* by Harrison E Salisbury. The book covers the lives of Mao and Deng, but the bulk of the book is devoted to Mao, while Deng remains quite elusive.

Richard Evans has written the excellent *Deng Xiaoping and the Making of Modern China*, which has a particularly good synopsis of the events leading up to the killings in Tiānānmén Square in 1989.

Fiction *The Good Earth* by Pearl S Buck has become a classic. Ms Buck lived most of her life in 19th-century China and was a prolific writer. Some of her lesser known books are still in print, including *Sons – Good Earth Trilogy Volume 2*, *The Big Wave*, *The Child Who Never Grew*, *Dragon Seed*, *East Wind: West Wind*, *A House Divided*, *Imperial Woman*, *Kinfolk*, *The House of Earth Volume 9*, *The Living Reed*, *The Mother*, *Pavilion of Women*, *Peony*, *The Three Daughters of Madame Liang*, *Little Red* and *The Promise*.

Manchu Palaces: A Novel by Jeanne Larsen is the story of Lotus, a woman struggling to secure a job for herself in the Forbidden City during the 18th-century Manchu dynasty.

The work of Jonathan Spence occupies an unusual space somewhere between biography, fiction and history. *The Memory Palace of Matteo Ricci* is a study of the most famous Jesuit to take up residence in China. *The Question of Hu* and *Emperor of China: Self-Portrait of K'ang Hsi* are also highly recommended.

Rose Crossing by Nicholas Jose is a quirky account of a chance encounter of a 17th-century English naturalist and a eunuch of the deposed Ming court on a deserted island.

The Chinese-American writers Maxine Hong Kingston and Amy Tan have both written books about the experiences of immigrant Chinese in the USA. Although their novels are not directly about China, they reveal a great deal about Chinese relationships and customs. Look out for Kingston's *The Woman Warrior* and *China Men*, or Tan's *The Kitchen God's Wife* and *The Joy Luck Club*.

Finally, all of Peter Hopkirk's books are worth reading. None of them deals with China specifically, but in *The Great Game*, *Foreign Devils on the Silk Road* and *Trespassers on the Roof of the World* Hopkirk writes breezily of 19th-century international espionage, exploration, pilfering of lost art treasures and the struggle for territorial domination at the far-flung edges of the Chinese empire in Xīnjiāng (Chinese Turkestan, as it was then known) and Tibet.

INTERNET RESOURCES

Lonely Planet has information on China on its Internet site at www.lonelyplanet.com.au.

Other recommended China travel, arts and entertainment-related Web sites include:

Art Scene China: Contemporary Chinese Art Gallery An online art gallery featuring a wide selection of artworks by well-established and up-and-coming artists from throughout China. www.artscenechina.com

Beijing Scene An English-language entertainment tabloid with news on culture, travel and employment. www.beijingscene.com

Chinese-Art A site covering both traditional and contemporary Chinese art. www.chinese-art.com

China Avante-Garde: Contemporary Chinese Art An art advisory service specialising in the acquisition of important works of contemporary Chinese art. www.china-avantgarde.com

Chinese Business World: China Travel Guide The Chinese Business World China travel guide with a hotel and flight booking facility. www.cbw.com/tourism

China Now – The Ultimate Guide to City Life in China A site featuring columns, travel information, nightlife and restaurant listings, and classified ads. www.chinanow.com

Inside China General and business news on China, Hong Kong and Taiwan. www.insidechina.com

SurfChina An online search engine for China with a wide range of links to other China travel-related sites. www.surfchina.com/html/travel.html

Virtual China A site focussing on China-related financial and technology news. www.virtualchina.com

Other recommended China-related Web sites worth taking a look at include:

Beijing Language and Culture University The Web site of the university that provides foreign students with an education in Chinese language and culture. www.blcu.edu.cn

Beijing Normal University Email this address for information on studying at Beijing Normal University
✉ isp@bnu.edu.cn

China Daily Web Site Coverage on economy, politics, social events, culture, life, arts and sport. www.chinadaily.com.cn

China Online: The Information Network for China Focuses on Chinese business and economic news.
www.chinaonline.com

Muzi Carries general information and news about China.
www.muzi.net

Sinopolis Daily China news and information, includes articles translated into English from the Chinese press.
www.sinopolis.com

Zhaopin A huge database of jobs in China.
www.zhaopin.com

Zhongwen: Chinese Characters and Culture Includes a pinyin chat room and an online dictionary of Chinese characters.
www.zhongwen.com

You can also check out Amnesty International's Web site at www.amnesty.org or get its China report in print. Perhaps a more immediate Web site is run by Support Democracy in China at www.christusrex .org/www1/sdc/sdchome.html.

FILMS

Movies produced by westerners and filmed in China are thin on the ground, largely because the Chinese government has a habit of demanding huge fees for the privilege. Still, there are a few that have become well-known classics.

The definitive classic is *The Last Emperor*, released in 1988 by Columbia Pictures and directed by Bernardo Bertolucci.

American-Chinese author Amy Tan has seen some of her books made into films – *The Joy Luck Club* gives some useful insights into Chinese culture; however, much of the action takes place in California.

On the other hand, documentaries about China are numerous. *The Gate of Heavenly Peace* by Carma Hinton and Richard Gordon covers the democracy protests and bloodshed at Tiānānmén Square in 1989. Another serious documentary is *The Dying Rooms* by Kate Blewett and Britain's Channel Four.

NEWSPAPERS & MAGAZINES
Chinese-Language Publications

Newspapers in China contain little hard news. Mostly, they are devoted to sloganeering and editorialising.

When Hong Kong residents held a candlelight vigil for the students who were massacred by communist troops in Tiānānmén Square, the Chinese press showed the photo with the caption, 'Hong Kong people are expressing their joy and happy feelings at being reunited with the motherland', and when the Chinese embassy in Belgrade was bombed by NATO, media temporarily withheld the US apology, fanning the flames of public outrage.

There are more than 2000 national and provincial newspapers in China. The main one is *Renmin Ribao (People's Daily)*, with nationwide circulation. The Letters to the Editor section in the *People's Daily* provides something of a measure of public opinion, and complaints are sometimes followed up by reporters. However, the sports page usually attracts the most interest. Every city in China will have its own local version of the *People's Daily* and, like the banner publication, they tend to serve chiefly as a propaganda vehicle.

At the other end of the scale is China's version of the gutter press – several hundred 'unhealthy papers' and magazines hawked on street corners and bus stations in major cities with nude or violent photos and stories about sex, crime, witchcraft, miracle cures and UFOs. These have been severely criticised by the government for their obscene and racy content. They are also extremely popular.

There are also about 40 newspapers for the minority nationalities.

Foreign-Language Publications

China publishes various newspapers, books and magazines in a number of European and Asian languages. The *China Daily* is China's official English-language newspaper and is available in most major cities – it even makes its way as far as Lhasa, though usually a couple of weeks out of date. The *Shanghai Star* is available in Shànghǎi only (sadly, since it's better than the *China Daily*). Běijīng, Shànghǎi, Guǎngzhōu and Kūnmíng have English-language 'what's on' type magazines basically published by and for expats.

Paper Propaganda

Apart from the mass media, the public notice board retains its place as an important means of educating the people or influencing public opinion. Other people who want to get a message across glue up big wall posters (*dàzibào*, or 'big character posters') in public places.

This is a traditional form of communicating ideas in China. If the content catches the attention of even a few people then word-of-mouth can spread it very quickly. Deng Xiaoping personally removed from China's constitution the right to put up wall posters.

Public notice boards abound in China. Two of the most common subjects are crime and accidents. In China it's no-holds-barred – before-and-after photos of executed criminals are plugged up on these boards along with a description of their heinous offences. Other memorable photos include people squashed by trucks, blown up by fireworks or fried after smoking cigarettes near open petrol tanks. Other popular themes include industrial safety and family planning. Inspiring slogans such as 'The PLA Protects the People' or 'Follow the Socialist Road to Happiness' are also common.

Imported Publications

In large cities like Běijīng, Shànghǎi and Guǎngzhōu, it's fairly easy to score copies of popular imported English-language magazines like *Time*, *Newsweek*, *Far Eastern Economic Review* and the *Economist*. It is also usually possible to find European magazines such as *Le Point* and *Der Spiegel*.

Foreign newspapers like the *Asian Wall Street Journal* and *International Herald-Tribune* are also available. Imported periodicals are most readily available from the big tourist hotels, though a few Friendship Stores also stock copies.

To China's credit, foreign-language magazines and newspapers are seldom, if ever, censored, even when they contain stories critical of China. Of course, a different set of rules applies to Chinese-language publications from Taiwan – essentially, these cannot be distributed in China without special permission.

RADIO & TV

Domestic radio broadcasting is controlled by the Central People's Broadcasting Station (CPBS). Broadcasts are made in *pǔtōnghuà* (standard Chinese speech) plus local dialects and minority languages.

There are also broadcasts to Taiwan in *pǔtōnghuà* and Fujianese, and Cantonese broadcasts for residents of Guǎngdōng, Hong Kong and Macau.

Radio Beijing is China's overseas radio service and broadcasts in about 40 foreign languages, as well as in *pǔtōnghuà* and several local dialects.

If you want to keep up with the world news, a short-wave radio receiver (through which you can receive Voice of America and BBC news) would be worth bringing with you. You can buy these in China, but the ones from Hong Kong are usually more compact and better quality.

Chinese Central Television (CCTV) began broadcasting in 1958, and colour transmission began in 1973. Major cities may have a second local channel, like Beijing Television (BTV).

Hong Kong's STAR TV broadcasts via satellite to China. There are both Chinese- and English-language shows, and a few are worth watching. CNN is also available in certain designated areas.

VIDEO SYSTEMS

China subscribes to the PAL broadcasting standard, the same as Australia, New Zealand, the UK and most of Europe. Competing systems not used in China include SECAM (France, Germany, Luxembourg) and NTSC (Canada, Japan and the USA). However, VCDs and DVDs are much more widely used in China than videotapes.

PHOTOGRAPHY & VIDEO
Film & Equipment

Imported film and cameras are expensive, but major Japanese companies like Fuji and Konica now have factories in China – this has brought film prices down to what you'd pay in the west. Cameras are still mostly pricey, although there are some made-in-China models.

While colour print film is available almost everywhere, it's almost always 100 ASA (21 DIN). Slide film can be found in big cities only (look for it in Friendship Stores and major camera shops). It's even harder to find B&W film, but speciality camera shops sometimes carry it.

Finding the special lithium batteries used by many cameras is generally not a problem, but it would be wise to bring a couple of spares.

You're allowed to bring in 8mm movie cameras; 16mm or professional equipment may cause concern with customs. Motion picture film is next to impossible to find in China.

Video

Video cameras were once subject to shaky regulations, but there seems to be no problem now, at least with the cheap camcorders that tourists carry. A large professional video camera might raise eyebrows – the Chinese government is especially paranoid about foreign TV crews filming unauthorised documentaries.

For the average video hobbyist, the biggest problem is recharging your batteries – bring all the adaptors you can, and remember that it's 220V.

Restrictions

Photography from planes and photographs of airports, military installations, harbour facilities and railroad terminals are prohibited; bridges may also be a touchy subject. With the possible exception of military installations, these rules are rarely enforced.

Photography most definitely is prohibited, however, in many museums, at archaeological sites and in some temples. It also prevents valuable works of art from being damaged by countless flash photos. There should be a sign in English advising of such restrictions, but ask if you're not sure.

If you're caught taking photos where you shouldn't, generally the film is ripped out of your camera. Make sure you start with a new roll if you don't want to lose any previous shots.

Photographing People

If you have befriended a local, he or she is generally more than happy to be a model. Candid shots of people, however, are viewed with suspicion by many Chinese – why is that foreigner taking my picture? The idea of using photography as a creative outlet is alien to most Chinese, for whom cameras are used to snap friends and family at get-togethers or posed in front of tourist sights. Make contact with people you want to photograph – often a smile and a wave will do the trick.

Airport Security

Most x-ray machines in China's airports are marked 'film safe', and this seems to be the case. However, films with a very high ASA rating could be fogged by repeated exposures to x-rays – you may wish to hand carry such films rather than zap it with rays.

As elsewhere in the world, airport security personnel don't want you taking photographs and they're especially protective about the area around the x-ray machines.

TIME

Time throughout China is set to Běijīng time, which is eight hours ahead of GMT/UTC. When it's noon in Běijīng it's also noon in far-off Lhasa, Ürümqi and all other parts of the country. Since the sun doesn't cooperate with Běijīng's whims, people in China's far west follow a later work schedule so they don't have to commute two hours before dawn.

When it's noon in Běijīng the time in other cities around the world is:

Hong Kong	noon
Sydney	2 pm
Wellington	4 pm
Los Angeles	8 pm
Montreal	11 pm
New York	11 pm
London	4 am
Frankfurt	5 am
Paris	5 am
Rome	5 am

ELECTRICITY

Electricity is 220V, 50 cycles AC. For the most part, you can safely travel with two types of plugs – two flat pins (like American plugs, but without the ground wire) and three pronged angled pins (like Australian plugs).

Conversion plugs are easily purchased in China's major cities, but are more difficult to find elsewhere. Battery chargers are widely available, but these are generally the bulky style that are not suitable for travelling.

Many Chinese cities experience sudden blackouts, especially in summer due to the increasing use of air-conditioning. It is very helpful to have a torch (flashlight) for such occasions.

WEIGHTS & MEASURES

The metric system is widely used in China. However, the traditional Chinese measures are often used for domestic transactions and you may come across them. The following equations will help:

metric	Chinese
1m *(mǐ)*	3 *chi*
1km *(gōnglǐ)*	2 *lǐ*
1L *(gōngshēng)*	1 *gōngshēng*
1kg *(gōngjīn)*	2 *jīn*

LAUNDRY

Each floor of just about every hotel in China has a service desk, usually near the elevators. The attendant's job is to clean the rooms, make the beds and collect and deliver laundry. Almost all tourist hotels have a laundry service, and if you hand in clothes one day you should get them back a day or two later. If the hotel doesn't have a laundry, they can usually direct you to one. Hotel laundry services tend to be expensive and you might wind up doing what many travellers do – hand-washing your own clothes.

HEALTH

Although China presents a few particular health hazards that require your attention, overall it's a healthier place to travel than many other parts of the world. Large cities like Běijīng and Shànghǎi have decent medical facilities, but problems are encountered in isolated areas such as Inner Mongolia, Tibet or Xīnjiāng.

Medical services are generally very cheap in China, although random foreigner surcharges may be exacted. These surcharges often mean that foreigners get better service, while Chinese patients usually have to wait for hours in long queues.

In case of accident or illness, it's best just to get a taxi and go to the hospital directly – try to avoid dealing with the authorities (police and military) if possible.

As elsewhere in Asia, the Chinese do not have Rh-negative blood and their blood banks don't store it.

Predeparture Planning

Immunisations For some countries no immunisations are necessary, but the further off the beaten track you go the more necessary it is to take precautions.

Plan ahead for getting your vaccinations: some of them require an initial shot followed by a booster, while some vaccinations should not be given together. It is recommended you seek medical advice at least six weeks before travel. Note that some vaccinations should not be given during pregnancy or to people with allergies discuss this with your doctor.

The only vaccination requirement for travellers to China is yellow fever if coming from an infected area (parts of Africa and South America). There is no risk of yellow fever in China.

In some countries immunisations are available from airports or government health centres – ask travel agents or airline offices.

Record all vaccinations on an International Health Certificate, available from your doctor or government health department.

Discuss your requirements with your doctor, but vaccinations you should consider for this trip include:

Cholera This vaccine is not recommended: protection is poor, immunisation lasts only six months and it's contraindicated during pregnancy. Furthermore, China doesn't have a big problem with cholera.

Diphtheria & Tetanus Everyone should make sure they are up to date with these

Medical Kit Check List

Following is a list of items you should consider including in your medical kit – consult your pharmacist for brands available in your country.

☐ **Aspirin** or **paracetamol** (acetaminophen in the USA) – for pain or fever

☐ **Antihistamine** – for allergies, eg hay fever; to ease the itch from insect bites or stings; and to prevent motion sickness

☐ **Antibiotics** – consider including these if you're travelling well off the beaten track; see your doctor, as they must be prescribed, and carry the prescription with you

☐ **Loperamide** or **diphenoxylate** – 'blockers' for diarrhoea

☐ **Prochlorperazine** or **metaclopramide** for nausea and vomiting

☐ **Rehydration mixture** – to prevent dehydration, eg due to severe diarrhoea; particularly important when travelling with children

☐ **Insect repellent, sunscreen, lip balm** and **eye drops**

☐ **Calamine lotion**, **sting relief spray** or **aloe vera** – to ease irritation from sunburn and insect bites or stings

☐ **Antifungal cream** or **powder** – for fungal skin infections and thrush

☐ **Antiseptic** (such as povidone-iodine) – for cuts and grazes

☐ **Bandages, Band-Aids (plasters)** and other wound dressings

☐ **Water purification tablets** or **iodine**

☐ **Scissors, tweezers** and a **thermometer** (note that mercury thermometers are prohibited by airlines)

☐ **Syringes** and **needles** – in case you need injections in a country with medical hygiene problems. Ask your doctor for a note explaining why you have them.

☐ **Cold** and **flu tablets**, **throat lozenges** and **nasal decongestant**

☐ **Multivitamins** – consider for long trips, when dietary vitamin intake may be inadequate

vaccinations. After an initial course of three injections, boosters are necessary every 10 years.

Hepatitis A All travellers to China should be protected against this common disease. Hepatitis A is the most common travel-acquired illness, but can be prevented by vaccination. The hepatitis A vaccine gives good protection for at least a year (longer if you have a booster). Alternatively, you can have immunoglobulin, which protects you for a limited time only and carries a theoretical though minuscule risk (in western countries) of blood-borne diseases like HIV. A combined hepatitis A and typhoid vaccine has recently become available.

Hepatitis B China is one of the world's great reservoirs of hepatitis B infection. The vaccination is recommended (especially for long-term travellers) and involves three injections, the quickest course being over three weeks and a booster at 12 months. A combined hepatitis A and B vaccine is available.

Japanese B Encephalitis This mosquito-borne disease is a risk for travellers to rural areas of China. Consider the vaccination if you're spending a month or longer in a high-risk area, making repeated trips to a risky area or visiting during an epidemic (usually associated with the rainy season). It involves three injections over 30 days.

The vaccine is expensive and has been associated with serious allergic reactions so the decision to have it should be balanced against the risk of contracting the illness.

Polio Polio is a very serious, easily transmitted disease, still prevalent in many developing countries. Everyone should keep up to date with this vaccination. A booster every 10 years maintains immunity.

Rabies With rabies, you have the choice of having the immunisation either before you go (called pre-exposure) or just if you're unlucky enough to get bitten (post-exposure). Preexposure vaccination involves receiving a course of three injections over a period of a month before you leave. This primes your system against rabies, giving you some, but not complete, protection against it. If you then get bitten by a suspect animal, you will need to have two boosters to prevent rabies developing.

If you didn't have pre-exposure vaccination, you will need the full course of rabies vaccination (five injections over a month) as well as an immediate injection of rabies antibodies. However this can be difficult to obtain in China; and even it's available it might be best to avoid blood products.

Consider having pre-exposure rabies vaccination if you're going to be travelling through China for more than three months or if you're going to be handling animals. Children are at particular risk of being bitten, so may need to be vaccinated even if you're going for only a short time.

Tuberculosis The risk of TB to travellers is usually very low. For those who will be living with or closely associated with local people in high risk areas in China, there may be some risk.

As most healthy adults do not develop symptoms, a skin test before and after travel to determine whether exposure has occurred may be considered. A vaccination is recommended for children living in these areas for three months or more.

Typhoid Travellers to China are at risk for this disease, especially if travelling to smaller cities, villages or rural areas. The vaccine is available either as an injection or as capsules to be taken orally.

Malaria Medication If you're travelling to malarial areas in China, you'll need to take measures to avoid getting this serious, potentially fatal disease. Antimalarial drugs do not prevent you from being infected but kill the malaria parasites during a stage in their development and significantly reduce the risk of becoming very ill or dying.

Expert advice on medication should be sought, as there are many factors to consider, including the area to be visited, the risk of exposure to malaria-carrying mosquitoes, the side effects of medication, your medical history and whether you are a child or adult or pregnant.

Travellers to isolated areas in China may like to carry a treatment dose of medication for use if symptoms occur.

Health Insurance Make sure that you have adequate health insurance. See the Travel Insurance entry under Visas & Documents earlier in this chapter.

Travel Health Guides *Where There Is No Doctor* by David Werner is useful, though intended for people going to work in an underdeveloped country rather than for the average traveller. Lonely Planet's *Travel with Children* by Maureen Wheeler gives a run down on health precautions to be taken with kids, or if you're pregnant and travelling. *Healthy Travel Asia & India* is another comprehensive Lonely Planet title.

There are also a number of excellent travel health sites on the Internet. From the Lonely Planet home page there are links at www .lonelyplanet.com/weblinks/wlprep.htm to the World Health Organisation and the US Centers for Disease Control & Prevention.

Other Preparations Make sure you're healthy before you start travelling. If you are going on a long trip make sure your teeth are OK. If you wear glasses take a spare pair and your prescription.

If you require a particular medication take an adequate supply, as it may not be available locally. Take part of the packaging showing the generic name, rather than the brand, which will make getting replacements easier. It's a good idea to have a legible prescription or letter from your doctor to show that you legally use the medication to avoid any problems.

Basic Rules

Food It's generally agreed that food, not water, is the most common source of gut troubles in travellers. We can't tell you exactly what to avoid in every situation because there are so many variables, but we can give you some guidelines to help you decide what's likely to be less safe and therefore better avoided:

- How food is prepared is more important than where it's prepared – a plate of noodles cooked in a steaming hot wok in front of you at a street stall is probably safer than food left out on display in an upmarket hotel buffet.
- Heating kills germs, so food that's served piping hot is likely to be safer than lukewarm or cold food, especially food that's been sitting around; note that freezing doesn't kill germs.
- Fruit and vegetables are difficult to clean (and may be contaminated where they are grown), but they should be safe if they're peeled or cooked.
- Well-cooked meat and seafood should be OK; raw or lightly cooked meat and seafood can be a source of parasites.
- Tinned food or milk, or powdered milk, is usually safe (check 'best before' dates if necessary).
- You'll be delighted to know that all forms of bread and cakes are usually safe, although it's best to avoid cream-filled goodies if you can, as microorganisms such as salmonella love cream.
- Popular eating places have an incentive to provide safe food to keep the customers coming.
- Your stomach's natural defences (mainly acid) can cope with small amounts of contaminated foods – if you're not sure about something, don't pig out on it!

And here are a few cautions to bear in mind:

- The more food has been handled (peeled, sliced, arranged), the more likely it may have been contaminated by unwashed hands.
- Good food can be contaminated by dirty dishes or cutlery, blenders used for making fruit juices are often suspect.
- Food that looks and smells delicious can still be seething with microorganisms.
- Hot spices don't make food safe, just more palatable.
- Salads are best avoided because they are hard to clean adequately and they are often contaminated with bug-containing dirt.
- Fruit juices and other drinks may be diluted with unsafe water.
- Unpasteurised and unboiled milk and dairy products should be avoided (more likely in rural areas) as unpasteurised milk can transmit diseases (including TB and salmonella); boiling unpasteurised milk makes it safe to drink.
- Be wary of food, including ice cream, that has been kept frozen, and may have thawed and been refrozen.

- Avoid raw fish, meat and seafood because of the risk of parasites.
- Most restaurants use disposable chopsticks, but consider carrying your own chopsticks for the occasional restaurant that doesn't.

Water Tap water is not considered safe to drink (or brush your teeth with) anywhere in China except Hong Kong. On the other hand, in most cities it's chlorinated and probably won't kill you. You need to be really careful in remote areas like Tibet, especially when drinking surface water. If you don't know for certain that the water is safe, then assume the worst.

Bottled water or soft drinks are fine.

Water Purification You've got to pay attention to water purification if you're going to be camping or hiking. The simplest way of purifying water is to boil it thoroughly. Vigorous boiling for a few minutes should be satisfactory; however, at high altitudes water boils at a lower temperature, so germs are less likely to be killed. Boil it longer in these environments.

In China, flasks of boiled water are provided outside most hotel rooms daily. With this you can safely make your own tea.

Consider purchasing a water filter for a long trip. There are two main kinds of filter. Total filters take out all parasites, bacteria and viruses, and make water safe to drink. They are often expensive, but they can be more cost effective than buying bottled water.

Simple filters (which can even be a nylon mesh bag) take out dirt and larger foreign bodies (but not the smaller foreign bodies such as viruses) from the water so that chemical solutions work much more effectively; if water is dirty, chemical solutions may not work at all.

It's very important when buying a filter to read the specifications, so that you know exactly what it removes from the water and what it doesn't.

Simple filtering will not remove all dangerous organisms, so if you cannot boil water it should be treated chemically. Chlorine tablets (Puritabs, Steritabs or other

Nutrition

If your diet is poor or limited in variety, if you're travelling hard and fast and therefore missing meals or if you simply lose your appetite, you can soon start to lose weight and place your health at risk.

Make sure your diet is well balanced. Cooked eggs, tofu, beans, lentils (dhal in India) and nuts are all safe ways to get protein. Fruit you can peel (bananas, oranges or mandarins for example) is usually safe (melons can harbour bacteria in their flesh and are best avoided) and a good source of vitamins. Try to eat plenty of grains (including rice) and bread. Remember that although food is generally safer if it is cooked well, overcooked food loses much of its nutritional value. If your diet isn't well balanced or if your food intake is insufficient, it's a good idea to take vitamin and iron pills.

In hot climates make sure you drink enough – don't rely on feeling thirsty to indicate when you should drink. Not needing to urinate or small amounts of very dark yellow urine is a danger sign. Always carry a water bottle with you on long trips. Excessive sweating can lead to loss of salt and therefore muscle cramping. Salt tablets are not a good idea as a preventative, but in places where salt is not used much, adding salt to food can help.

brand names) will kill many pathogens, but not those causing giardiasis and amoebic dysentery.

Iodine is very effective in purifying water and is available in tablet form (such as Potable Aqua), but follow the directions carefully and remember that too much iodine can be harmful. Iodine tastes as bad as it sounds.

Medical Problems & Treatment

Self-diagnosis and treatment can be risky, so wherever possible seek qualified help. Although we do give drug dosages in this section, they are for emergency use only.

A five-star hotel can usually recommend a good place to go for medical advice. In some places standards of medical attention are so low that for some ailments the best advice is to get on a plane and go to Běijīng, Shànghǎi or Hong Kong.

Antibiotics should ideally be administered only under medical supervision. Take only the recommended dose at the prescribed intervals and use the whole course, even if the illness seems to be cured earlier. Stop immediately if there are any serious reactions and don't use the antibiotic at all if you are unsure that you have the correct one.

Some people are allergic to commonly prescribed antibiotics such as penicillin or sulpha drugs; carry this information when travelling (eg on a bracelet).

Environmental Hazards

Altitude Sickness Lack of oxygen at high altitudes (over 2500m) affects most people to some extent. There are bus journeys in Tibet, Qīnghǎi and Xīnjiāng where the road goes over 5000m. Acclimatising to such extreme elevations takes several weeks at least, but most travellers come up from sea level very fast – a bad move! If you ever have a chance to experience acute mountain sickness (AMS), you won't forget it.

Symptoms of AMS usually develop during the first 24 hours at altitude, but may be delayed up to three weeks. Mild symptoms include headache, lethargy, dizziness, difficulty sleeping and loss of appetite. AMS may become more severe without warning and can be fatal.

These mild symptoms are unpleasant, but a far more serious complication is high-altitude pulmonary oedema. This is usually seen only at elevations above 3000m about 24 to 72 hours after ascent.

Symptoms include coughing up frothy sputum, which usually progresses from white to pink to bloody. A rattling sound in the chest can be heard, often without a stethoscope. The symptoms might be mistaken for

Everyday Health

Normal body temperature is up to 37°C (98.6°F); more than 2°C (4°F) higher indicates a high fever. The normal adult pulse rate is 60 to 100 per minute (children 80 to 100, babies 100 to 140). As a general rule the pulse increases about 20 beats per minute for each 1°C (2°F) rise in fever.

Respiration (breathing) rate is also an indicator of illness. Count the number of breaths per minute: between 12 and 20 is normal for adults and older children (up to 30 for younger children, 40 for babies). People with a high fever or serious respiratory illness breathe more quickly than normal. More than 40 shallow breaths a minute may indicate pneumonia.

pneumonia, but the suddenness of their appearance in a rapidly ascending climber should make you suspect pulmonary oedema. *This is a medical emergency!* Coma and death can follow rapidly – the only effective treatment is to get the victim to a lower elevation as soon as possible.

Treat mild symptoms by resting at the same altitude until recovery, usually a day or two. Painkillers can be taken for headaches. If symptoms persist or become worse, however, *immediate descent is necessary*; even 500m can help. Drug treatments should never be used to avoid descent or to enable further ascent.

The drugs acetazolamide (Diamox) and dexamethasone have been recommended for prevention of AMS. They can reduce the symptoms, but they also mask warning signs; severe and fatal AMS has occurred in people taking these drugs. In general they are not recommended for travellers.

To prevent acute mountain sickness:

• Ascend slowly – have frequent rest days, spending two to three nights at each rise of 1000m. If you reach a high altitude by trekking, acclimatisation takes place gradually and you are less likely to be affected than if you fly directly to a higher altitude.
• It is always wise to sleep at a lower altitude than the greatest height reached during the day. Also,

once above 3000m, care should be taken not to increase the sleeping altitude by more than 300m per day.
• Drink extra fluids. The mountain air is dry and cold and moisture is lost as you breathe.
• Eat light, high-carbohydrate meals for more energy.
• Avoid alcohol as it may increase the risk of dehydration.
• Avoid sedatives.

Fungal Infections Fungal infections such as ringworm occur more commonly in hot weather and are usually found on the scalp, between the toes (athlete's foot) or fingers, in the groin (jock itch or crotch rot) and on the body. You get ringworm (which is a fungal infection, not a worm) from infected animals or by walking on damp areas, like shower floors.

To prevent fungal infections wear loose, comfortable clothes, avoid artificial fibres, wash frequently and dry carefully (especially between the toes, the groin area and under the breasts).

If you do get an infection, wash the infected area daily with a disinfectant or medicated soap and water, and rinse and dry well. Apply an antifungal cream or powder like clotrimazole, ketoconazole, miconazole, nystatin, tebinafine or amorolfine. If you don't have that, then try plain old talcum powder – it's better than nothing. Try to expose the infected area to air or sunlight as much as possible and wash all towels and underwear in hot water, changing them often.

Heat Exhaustion Dehydration or salt deficiency can cause heat exhaustion. Take time to acclimatise to high temperatures, drink sufficient liquids and do not do anything too physically demanding.

Salt deficiency is characterised by fatigue, lethargy, headaches, giddiness and muscle cramps; salt tablets may help.

Anhydrotic heat exhaustion, caused by an inability to sweat, is quite rare. It is likely to strike people who have been in a hot climate for some time, rather than newcomers.

Heatstroke This serious, occasionally fatal, condition can occur if the body's heat-regulating mechanism breaks down and the body temperature rises to dangerous levels. Long, continuous periods of exposure to high temperatures can leave you vulnerable to heat stroke.

The symptoms are feeling unwell, not sweating very much or at all and a high body temperature (39°C to 41°C or 102°F to 106°F). Where sweating has ceased the skin becomes flushed and red. Severe, throbbing headaches and lack of coordination will also occur, and the sufferer may be confused or aggressive. Eventually the victim will become delirious or convulse. Hospitalisation is essential, but in the interim get victims out of the sun, remove their clothing, cover them with a wet sheet or towel and then fan continually. Give fluids if they are conscious.

Hypothermia This is when your body starts to lose the battle to maintain your body heat in cold conditions and your core body temperature starts to fall. Be aware that you don't need incredibly low temperatures to become hypothermic.

If you are trekking at high altitudes or simply taking a long bus trip over mountains, particularly at night, be aware. In Tibet it can go from being mildly warm to blisteringly cold in a manner of minutes – blizzards have a way of just coming out of nowhere. If you're out walking, cycling or hitching, this can be more than inconvenient.

It is best to dress in layers; silk, wool and some of the new artificial fibres are all good insulating materials. A hat is important, as a lot of heat is lost through the head. A strong, waterproof outer layer and a space blanket are essential. Carry basic supplies, including food (along with some chocolate to generate heat quickly) and fluid to drink.

Symptoms of hypothermia are exhaustion, numb skin (particularly the toes and fingers), shivering, slurred speech, irrational or violent behaviour, lethargy, stumbling, dizzy spells, muscle cramps and violent bursts of energy. Irrationality may take the form of sufferers claiming they are warm and trying to take off their clothes.

To treat mild hypothermia, first get the person out of the wind and/or rain, remove their clothing if it's wet and replace it with dry, warm clothing. Give them hot liquids – not alcohol – and some high-kilojoule, easily digestible food. Do not rub victims, instead allow them to slowly warm themselves. This should be enough to treat the early stages of hypothermia. The early recognition and treatment of mild hypothermia is the only way to prevent severe hypothermia, which is a critical condition.

Frostbite This is a severe condition that can cause loss of limbs and (on the face) disfigurement for life. Although you'll feel little or no pain when the tissue is frozen, it becomes excruciating when the wound thaws out. Ironically, the condition is not unlike a third-degree burn. Prevention is by far the best cure – if you must travel in intense cold, protect your limbs with fur-lined boots and mittens, and wear a parka and a ski mask.

Motion Sickness Eating lightly before and during a trip will reduce the chances of motion sickness.

If you are prone to motion sickness try to find a place that minimises disturbance – near the wing on aircraft, close to midships on boats, near the centre on buses. Fresh air usually helps; reading and cigarette smoke don't. Commercial motion sickness preparations, which can cause drowsiness, have to be taken before the trip commences. Ginger (available in capsule form) and peppermint (including mint-flavoured sweets) are natural preventatives.

Prickly Heat Prickly heat is an itchy rash caused by excessive perspiration trapped under the skin. The pores of the skin get clogged, causing painful swelling. It usually strikes people who have just arrived in a hot climate. Keeping cool, bathing often, using a mild talcum powder or resorting to air-conditioning may help until you acclimatise.

Sunburn It's very easy to get sunburnt at high elevations (Tibet), in the deserts (Xīnjiāng) or the tropics (Hǎinán Dǎo). Use a sunscreen, hat, and barrier cream for your nose and lips. Calamine lotion is good for mild sunburn. Protect your eyes with good quality sunglasses, particularly if you will be near water, sand or snow.

Infectious Diseases

China Syndrome Upper respiratory tract infections (URTIs), or the common cold, are the most common ailment to afflict visitors to China. The Chinese call it *gǎnmào* and it is a particular problem here – transmission rates are high because of the crowding and the cold.

China also has a special relationship with the influenza virus. You may not remember the notorious 'Hong Kong flu' of 1968, but you may have heard of the more recent 'Shànghǎi flu'(1989) and 'bird flu' (1997–98) epidemics. There have been various other influenza strains named after Chinese cities. This is because China is the production house for new strains of influenza virus. The reason for this is thought to be the proximity in which people live to ducks and pigs, which are reservoirs for the two other main populations of the virus. This provides the opportunity for the viruses to chop and change, reappearing in different forms or strains.

During winter, practically the entire population of 1.3 billion is stricken with gǎnmào. URTIs are aggravated by cold weather, poor nutrition and China's notorious air pollution. Smoking makes it worse, and half the population of China smokes. Overcrowded conditions increase the opportunity for infection. Another reason is that Chinese people spit a lot, which helps spread the disease. It's a vicious circle: they're sick because they spit and they spit because they're sick.

Winter visitors to China should bring a few favourite cold remedies. These can easily be purchased from any good pharmacy in Hong Kong or Macau. Such items can be found elsewhere in China, but with considerably more difficulty.

Symptoms of influenza include fever, weakness, sore throat and a feeling of malaise. Any URTI, including influenza, can lead to complications such as bronchitis and pneumonia, which may need to be treated with antibiotics. Seek medical help in this situation. Finally, if you can't get well in China, leave the country and take a nice holiday on a warm beach in Thailand.

Diarrhoea Travellers' diarrhoea *(lā dùzi)* has been around a long time – even Marco Polo had it. A change of water, food or climate can all cause the runs; diarrhoea caused by contaminated food or water is more serious. Despite all your precautions you may still get a mild bout of travellers' diarrhoea, but a few rushed toilet trips with no other symptoms is not indicative of a serious problem.

Dehydration is the main danger with any diarrhoea, which can occur quite quickly in children or the elderly. Under all circumstances *fluid replacement* (at least equal to the volume being lost) is the most important thing to remember. Soda water or soft drinks allowed to go flat and diluted 50% with clean water are good. With severe diarrhoea a rehydrating solution is preferable to replace minerals and salts lost.

Commercially available oral rehydration salts (ORS) are very useful; add them to boiled or bottled water. In an emergency you can make up a solution of six teaspoons of sugar and a half teaspoon of salt to a litre of boiled or bottled water.

You need to drink at least the same volume of fluid that you are losing in bowel movements and vomiting. Urine is the best guide to the adequacy of replacement – if you have small amounts of concentrated urine, you need to drink more. Keep drinking small amounts often. Stick to a bland diet as you recover.

Gut paralysing drugs can be used to bring relief from the symptoms, although they do not actually cure the problem. Only use these drugs if you do not have access to toilets eg if you *must* travel. For children under 12 years Lomotil and Imodium are not recommended. Do not use these drugs if the person has a high fever or is severely dehydrated.

In certain situations antibiotics may be required: diarrhoea with blood or mucus (dysentery), any diarrhoea with fever, watery diarrhoea with fever and lethargy, persistent diarrhoea not improving after 48 hours and severe diarrhoea. In these situations Imodium or Lomotil should be avoided.

A stool test is necessary to diagnose which kind of dysentery you have, so you should seek medical help urgently in this situation. Where this is not possible the recommended drugs for dysentery are norfloxacin 400mg twice daily for three days or ciprofloxacin 500mg twice daily for five days. These are not recommended for children or pregnant women. The drug of choice for children would be co-trimoxazole (Bactrim, Septrin, Resprim) with dosage dependent on weight. A five-day course is given. Ampicillin or amoxycillin may be given in pregnancy, but medical care is necessary.

Amoebic dysentery is characterised by a gradual onset of symptoms; fever may not be present. It will persist until treated and can recur and cause other health problems.

Giardiasis is another type of diarrhoea. The parasite causing this intestinal disorder is present in contaminated water. The symptoms are stomach cramps, nausea, a bloated stomach, watery, foul-smelling diarrhoea, and frequent gas.

Giardiasis can appear several weeks after exposure to the parasite. The symptoms may disappear for a few days and then return; this can go on for several weeks. Tinidazole, known as Fasigyn, or metronidazole (Flagyl) are the recommended drugs. Treatment is a 2g single dose of Fasigyn or 250mg of Flagyl three times daily for five to 10 days.

Acupuncture

Chinese acupuncture (zhēnjiŭ) has received enthusiastic reviews from its many satisfied patients. Of course, one should be wary of overblown claims. Acupuncture is not likely to cure terminal cancer or heart disease, but it is of genuine therapeutic value in the treatment of chronic back pain, migraine headaches, arthritis and other ailments.

Acupuncture is a technique employing needles that are inserted into various points of the body. As many as 2000 points for needle insertion have been identified, but only about 150 are commonly used. In former times, needles were probably made from bamboo, gold, silver, copper or tin. These days, only stainless steel needles of hairlike thinness are used, causing very little pain when inserted.

One of the most amazing demonstrations of acupuncture's power is that major surgery can be performed using acupuncture alone as the anaesthetic. The acupuncture needle is inserted into the patient and a small electric current is passed through the needle. The current is supplied by an ordinary torch battery.

The exact mechanism by which acupuncture works is not fully understood by modern medical science. Chinese practitioners have their own theories, but it is by no means certain they really know either. Needles are inserted into various points of the body, each point believed by the acupuncturist to correspond to a particular organ, joint, gland or other part of the body. These points are believed to be connected to the particular area being treated by an 'energy channel', also translated as a 'meridian'. By means not fully understood, it seems the needle can block pain transmission along the meridian. No matter how it works, many report satisfactory results.

Acupuncture is practised in hospitals of traditional Chinese medicine, which can be found all over China. Some hospitals in major cities like Guǎngzhōu, Běijīng and Shànghǎi also train westerners in the technique. And if you need some emergency acupuncture, even hotels (upmarket ones, at least) provide such services at their in-house clinics.

If you're (justifiably) concerned about catching hepatitis or HIV from contaminated acupuncture needles, you might consider buying your own before undergoing treatment. Good quality needles are available in major cities in China. Needles come in a bewildering variety of gauges – try to determine from your acupuncturist which type to buy.

Hepatitis Hepatitis is a general term for inflammation of the liver. The disease comes in A, B, C and E strains. It is a common disease worldwide. The symptoms are fever, chills, headache, fatigue, feelings of weakness and aches and pains, followed by loss of appetite, nausea, vomiting, abdominal pain, dark urine, light-coloured faeces, jaundiced (yellow) skin and the whites of the eyes may turn yellow.

Hepatitis A is transmitted by contaminated food and drinking water. The disease poses a real threat to the western traveller. You should seek medical advice, but there is not much you can do apart from resting, drinking lots of fluids, eating lightly and avoiding

Chinese Herbal Medicine

Chinese medicine encompasses a basic philosophy on life that stresses that it's better to stay healthy than to take medicines. Longevity has been has been attributed to keeping an even temper, eating a balanced diet, exercising regularly and getting a good sleep. Chinese herbal medicine *(zhōng yào)* is also 'holistic' in that it seeks to treat the whole body rather than focusing on a particular organ or disease. Herbal medicine, along with acupuncture, is the most common medical system in China.

Chinese medicine has evolved over thousands of years from practices originally employed by ancient peoples. While its origins lie in legend, evidence of early medical practises have been found on bones inscribed during the Shang dynasty and on treatises excavated from ancient tombs. A pharmaceutical system was established in the Song dynasty that standardised the practice of medicine, and Chinese medicine made early headway into immunology by developing a method of immunisation against smallpox during the 17th century.

Today, it's common to see herbalists' shops lined with small drawers filled with various ingredients. These ingredients range from the ordinary (such as ginseng) to the exotic (snake gall bladder or powdered deer antler). The ingredients all undergo preparation such as baking, roasting or simmering before being consumed – the precise process being determined by the disease.

Chinese medicine seems to work best for the relief of unpleasant symptoms (pain, sore throat etc) and for some long-term conditions that resist western medicines, such as migraine headaches, asthma and chronic backache. While many of the herbs seem to work, remember that herbs are not miracle drugs.

Another benefit of Chinese medicine is that there are relatively few side effects. Nevertheless, herbs are still medicines, not candy, and there is no need to take them if you're feeling fine to begin with – in fact, some herbs are mildly toxic and if taken over a long period of time can actually damage the liver and other organs.

Before shopping for herbs, keep in mind that although a broad-spectrum remedy, such as snake gall bladder, may be good for treating colds, there are many different types of colds. The best way to treat a cold with herbal medicine is to see a Chinese doctor and get a specific prescription. Otherwise, the herbs you take may not be the most appropriate for your condition. However, if you can't get to a doctor, you can just try your luck at the pharmacy.

If you visit a Chinese doctor, you might be surprised by what he or she discovers about your body. For example, the doctor will almost certainly take your pulse as it's believed that your pulse will indicate the state of your health. They then may tell you that you have a slippery pulse or perhaps a thready pulse. Chinese doctors have identified more than 30 different kinds of pulses. The doctor may then examine your tongue to see if it is slippery, dry, pale or greasy, or has a thick coating or maybe no coating at all. The doctor, having discovered that you have wet heat, as evidenced by a slippery pulse and a red greasy tongue, will prescribe the herbs for your condition.

fatty foods. People who have had hepatitis should avoid alcohol for some time after the illness, as the liver needs time to recover.

Hepatitis E is transmitted in the same way and can be very serious in pregnant women.

There are almost 300 million chronic carriers of *hepatitis B* in the world. It is spread through contact with infected blood, blood products or body fluids, for example through sexual contact, unsterilised needles and blood transfusions, or contact with blood via small breaks in the skin. Other risk situations include having a shave, a tattoo, or having your body pierced with contaminated equipment.

The symptoms of type B may be more severe and may lead to long-term problems.

Chinese Herbal Medicine

If you spend a good deal of time on buses and boats, you'll get to see how the Chinese deal with motion sickness, nausea and headaches – usually by smearing liniments on their stomach or head. Look for White Flower Oil (Bái Huā Yóu), probably the most popular brand. A variation on the theme are salves, the most famous being Tiger Balm, which originated in Hong Kong. And should you strain yourself carrying a heavy backpack around, try applying 'sticky dog skin plaster' (góupí gāoyào) to your sore muscles. You might be relieved to

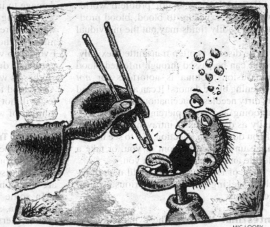

MIC LOOBY

know that these days it's no longer made from real dog skin.

Beware of quackery – there is one Chinese herbal medicine, for instance, which pregnant women take to ensure that their foetus will develop into a boy. Other herbal tonics promise to boost your IQ or sexual prowess and to cure baldness. All sorts of overblown claims have been made for herbal medicines, especially by those who make and sell them. Most of these miracle herbs are expensive, and the promised results have never been confirmed by any scientific studies. Yet some gullible westerners have persuaded themselves that Chinese herbs can cure any disease. A visit to any of China's hospitals will quickly shatter this myth.

Counterfeiting is another problem. Everything gets copied in China, and the problem extends even to medications. If the herbs you take seem to be totally ineffective, it may be because you've bought sugar pills rather than medicine.

Another point to be wary of when taking herbal medicine is the tendency of some manufacturers to falsely claim that their product contains numerous potent and expensive ingredients. For example, some herbal formulas may list rhinoceros horn as an ingredient. Rhinoceros horn, widely acclaimed by herbalists as a cure for fever, is practically impossible to buy. Any formula listing rhinoceros horn may, at best, contain water buffalo horn. In any case, the rhino is a rare and endangered species.

Hepatitis D is spread in the same way, but the risk is mainly in shared needles.

Hepatitis C can lead to chronic liver disease. The virus is spread by contact with blood – usually via contaminated transfusions or shared needles. Avoiding these is the only means of prevention.

HIV/AIDS Infection with the human immunodeficiency virus (HIV), may develop into acquired immune deficiency syndrome (AIDS). HIV is a major problem worldwide. Any exposure to blood, blood products or bodily fluids may put the individual at risk.

The disease is often transmitted sexually, but it can be passed through infected blood transfusions; China is notorious for *not* screening blood donors! It can also be spread by dirty needles – vaccinations, acupuncture, tattooing and body piercing can be potentially as dangerous as intravenous drug use. If you do need an injection, ask to see the syringe unwrapped in front of you, or take a needle and syringe pack with you.

Fear of HIV infection should never preclude seeking treatment for serious medical conditions.

Intestinal Worms These parasites are most common in rural, tropical areas. The different worms have different ways of infecting people. Some may be ingested with food, including undercooked meat, and some enter through your skin.

Infestations may not show up for some time, and although they are generally not serious, if left untreated some can cause severe health problems later.

Consider having a stool test when you return home to check for these and determine the appropriate treatment.

Schistosomiasis Also known as bilharzia, this disease is found in the central Cháng Jiāng (Yangzi River) basin. It is carried in water by minute worms which infect certain varieties of freshwater snails found in rivers, streams, lakes and particularly behind dams. The worms multiply and are eventually discharged into the water.

The worm enters through the skin and attaches itself to your intestines or bladder. The first symptom may be a tingling and sometimes a light rash around the area where it entered. Weeks later a high fever may develop.

Once the disease is established, abdominal pain and blood in the urine are other signs. The infection often causes no symptoms until the disease is well established (several months to years after exposure) and damage to internal organs irreversible.

Avoiding swimming or bathing in fresh water where bilharzia is present – this is the main method of preventing the disease. Even deep water can be infected. If you do get wet, dry off quickly and dry your clothes as well.

A blood test is the most reliable, but the test will not show positive in results until a number of weeks after exposure.

Sexually Transmitted Diseases Gonorrhoea, herpes and syphilis are among these diseases; sores, blisters or rashes around the genitals, discharges or pain when urinating are common symptoms.

In some STDs, such as wart virus or chlamydia, symptoms may be less marked or not observed at all, especially in women. Syphilis symptoms eventually disappear completely, but the disease continues and can cause severe problems in later years. While abstinence from sexual contact is the only 100% effective prevention, using condoms is also effective. The treatment of gonorrhoea and syphilis is with antibiotics.

The different sexually transmitted diseases all require specific antibiotics. There is no cure for herpes or AIDS.

Tuberculosis China has traditionally had a high rate of TB infection, and there is now a worldwide resurgence of this severe disease.

It is a bacterial infection which is usually transmitted from person to person through coughing, but may be transmitted via the consumption of unpasteurised milk. Milk that has been boiled is safe to drink, and the souring of milk to make yoghurt or cheese also kills the bacilli.

Travellers are usually not at great risk as close household contact with the infected person is usually required before the disease is passed on.

Typhoid Typhoid fever is a dangerous gut infection caused by contaminated water and food. As with cholera, it tends to occur in summer in areas that have had severe flooding. Medical help must be sought.

Early symptoms are a headache, body aches and a fever which rises a little each day until it is around 40°C (104°F) or more. The victim's pulse is often slow relative to the degree of fever present – unlike a normal fever where the pulse increases. There may also be vomiting, abdominal pain, diarrhoea or constipation.

In the second week the high fever and slow pulse continue and a few pink spots may appear on the body; trembling, weight loss, delirium, weakness and dehydration may occur.

Complications such as pneumonia, perforated bowel or meningitis also may occur.

Sufferers of TB should be kept cool and hydrated. Cipro-floxacin 750mg twice a day for 10 days is good for adults.

Chloramphenicol is recommended in many countries. The adult dosage is two 250mg capsules, four times a day. Children aged between eight and 12 years should have half the adult dose; and younger children one-third the adult dose.

Insect-Borne Diseases

Filariasis, Dengue fever, Japanese B encephalitis, leishmaniasis and typhus are all insect-borne diseases, but they do not pose a great risk to travellers. For more information on them, see the Less Common Diseases entry later in this section.

Malaria Malaria has been nearly eradicated in China and is not generally a risk for travellers visiting the cities. It is found predominantly in rural areas in the south-western region – principally Guǎngdōng, Guìzhōu, Yúnnán, Hǎinán, Sìchuān and Fújiàn.

Transmission occurs mainly during summer in most risk areas, but occurs year-round in Hǎinán and Yúnnán. If you are travelling to rural Hǎinán or peripheral Yúnnán it is important to take anti-malarial tablets and to take steps to avoid mosquito bites.

The symptoms of this serious and potentially fatal disease range from fever, chills and sweating, headache, diarrhoea and abdominal pains to a vague feeling of ill-health.

Seek medical help immediately if malaria is suspected. Without treatment malaria can rapidly become more serious and can be fatal.

If medical care is not available, malaria tablets can be used for treatment. You need to use a malaria tablet which is different to the one you were taking when you contracted malaria.

The treatment dosages are mefloquine (three 250mg tablets and a further two six hours later) or fansidar (single dose of three tablets). If you were previously taking mefloquine and cannot obtain fansidar, then alternatives are halofantrine (three doses of two 250mg tablets every six hours) or quinine sulphate (600mg every six hours). There is a greater risk of side effects with these dosages than in normal use if used with mefloquine, so medical advice is preferable. Travellers are advised to prevent mosquito bites at all times. The main messages are:

- wear light-coloured clothing
- wear long pants and long-sleeved shirts
- use mosquito repellents containing the compound DEET on exposed areas (overuse of DEET may be harmful, especially to children, but it's considered preferable to being bitten by disease-transmitting mosquitoes)
- avoid wearing perfumes or aftershave
- use a mosquito net impregnated with mosquito repellent (permethrin) – it may be worth taking your own
- impregnating clothes with permethrin effectively deters mosquitoes and other insects

Cuts, Bites & Stings

Bedbugs & Lice Bedbugs live in various places, but particularly in dirty mattresses and bedding. Spots of blood on bedclothes or on the wall could be an indication that perhaps you ought to find another hotel. Alternatively, you can fight the little buggers with insecticide. Bedbugs leave itchy bites in neat rows. Calamine lotion or Stingose spray may help.

All lice cause itching and discomfort. They make themselves at home in your hair (head lice), your clothing (body lice) or in your pubic hair (crabs). You catch lice through direct contact with infected people or by sharing combs, clothing and the like. Chemical powder or shampoo treatment will kill the lice and infected clothing should then be washed in very hot water.

Insect Bites & Stings Ant bites, bee and wasp stings are usually painful rather than dangerous, but it's another story if you're allergic. People who are allergic to them may develop severe breathing difficulties and require urgent medical attention.

People who have this allergy usually are aware of it, and should carry a kit containing an antihistamine and epinephrine.

Cuts & Scratches Wash well and treat any cut with an antiseptic such as povidone-iodine. Where possible avoid bandages and Band-Aids, which can keep wounds wet.

Ticks You should always check all over your body if you have been walking through a potentially tick-infested area as ticks can cause skin infections and other more serious diseases.

If a tick is found attached, press down around the tick's head with tweezers, grab the head and gently pull upwards. Avoid pulling the rear of the body as this may squeeze the tick's gut contents through the attached mouth parts into the skin, increasing the risk of infection and disease.

Smearing chemicals on the tick will not make it let go and is not recommended.

Snakes China has a variety of poisonous snakes, the most famous being cobras. *All* sea snakes are poisonous and are readily identified by their flat tails, but opportunities for ocean swimming in China are few and far between.

Thanks to American cowboy movies, people often associate snakes with the desert, but they are in fact most common in forested areas, where they have far more to eat.

Snakes are not generally aggressive with creatures larger than themselves – they won't chase after you, but they can get nasty if you corner or step on them. To minimise your chances of being bitten always wear boots, socks and long trousers when walking through undergrowth where snakes may be present. Don't put your hands into holes and crevices, and be careful when collecting firewood.

Snake bites do not cause instantaneous death and antivenenes are usually available. Keep the victim calm and still, wrap the bitten limb tightly, as you would for a sprained ankle, and then attach a splint to immobilise it. Then seek medical help, if possible bringing the dead snake for identification. Don't attempt to catch the snake if there is a possibility of being bitten again. Tourniquets and sucking out the poison are now comprehensively discredited.

Less Common Diseases

Cholera The bacteria responsible for this disease are carried in contaminated food or water. This is the worst of the watery diarrhoeas and medical help should be sought.

China does not have a serious problem with this, but there can be outbreaks during floods (the Huáng Hé (Yellow River) basin is notorious). Floods and corresponding cholera outbreaks are generally widely reported, so you can avoid such problem areas.

Fluid replacement is the most vital treatment – the risk of dehydration is severe as you may lose up to 20L a day. If there is a delay in getting to hospital then begin taking tetracycline. The adult dose is 250mg four times daily. It is not recommended for children under nine nor for pregnant women.

Tetracycline may help to shorten the illness, but adequate fluids are required to save lives.

Dengue Fever Occurring in parts of southern China, this mosquito-spread disease can be fatal in children. There is no preventative drug available. A sudden onset of fever, headaches and severe joint and muscle pains are the first signs before a rash develops. Recovery may be prolonged.

Filariasis This is a mosquito-transmitted parasitic infection found in many parts of Africa, Asia, Central and South America, and the Pacific. Possible symptoms include fever, pain and swelling of the lymph glands; inflammation of lymph drainage areas; swelling of a limb or the scrotum; skin rashes and blindness.

Treatment is available to eliminate the parasites from the body, but some of the damage already caused by the infection may not be reversible. Medical advice should be obtained promptly if filariasis is suspected.

Japanese B Encephalitis This viral infection of the brain is transmitted by mosquitoes. Most cases occur in rural areas as the virus exists in pigs and wading birds.

Symptoms include fever, headache and alteration in consciousness. Hospitalisation is needed for correct diagnosis and treatment. There is a high mortality rate among those who have symptoms; of those who survive many are intellectually disabled.

Leishmaniasis A group of parasitic diseases transmitted by sandfly bites, which are in China, as well as many parts of the Middle East, Africa, India, Central and South America and the Mediterranean.

Cutaneous leishmaniasis affects the skin tissue causing ulceration and disfigurement and visceral leishmaniasis affects the internal organs. Seek medical advice as laboratory testing is required for diagnosis and correct treatment.

Avoiding sandfly bites is the best precaution. Bites are usually painless, itchy and are yet another reason to cover up and apply repellent.

Rabies Rabies is a fatal viral infection found in many countries and is caused by a bite or scratch by an infected animal, such as a dog, cat or monkey. Any bite, scratch or even lick from a warm-blooded, furry animal should be cleaned immediately and thoroughly. Scrub with soap and running water, and then clean with an alcohol or iodine solution.

If there is any possibility that the animal is infected, medical help should be sought immediately to prevent the onset of symptoms and death. In a person who has not been immunised against rabies this involves having six injections over 28 days starting as soon as possible after the exposure.

Tetanus Tetanus occurs when a wound becomes infected by a germ which lives in soil and in the faeces of horses and other animals.

It enters the body via breaks in the skin. All wounds should be cleaned promptly and adequately and an antiseptic cream or solution applied. Use antibiotics if the wound becomes hot, throbs or pus is seen.

The first symptom may be discomfort in swallowing, or stiffening of the jaw and neck; this is followed by painful convulsions of the jaw and whole body. The disease can be fatal.

Typhus Typhus is spread by ticks, mites or lice. It begins with fever, chills, headache and muscle pains followed a few days later by a body rash. There is often a large painful sore at the site of the bite and nearby lymph nodes are swollen and painful.

Typhus can be treated under medical supervision. Seek local advice on areas where ticks pose a danger and always check your skin and hair carefully for ticks after walking in a danger area such as a tropical forest.

A strong insect repellent can help, and serious walkers in tick areas should consider having their boots and trousers impregnated with benzyl benzoate and dibutylphthalate.

Women's Health

Gynaecological Problems Sexually transmitted diseases are a major cause of vaginal problems. Symptoms include a smelly discharge, painful intercourse and sometimes a burning sensation when urinating. Male sexual partners must also be treated.

Medical attention should be sought and remember in addition to these diseases HIV or hepatitis B may also be acquired during exposure. Besides abstinence, the best thing is to practise safe sex using condoms.

Antibiotic use, synthetic underwear, sweating and contraceptive pills can lead to fungal vaginal infections when travelling in hot climates. Maintaining good personal hygiene, and wearing loose-fitting clothes and cotton underwear will help prevent these infections.

Fungal infections, characterised by a rash, itch and discharge, can be treated with a vinegar or lemon-juice douche, or with yoghurt. Nystatin, miconazole or clotrimazole pessaries or vaginal cream are the usual prescribed treatment.

Pregnancy It is not advisable to travel to some places while pregnant as some vaccinations normally used to prevent serious diseases are not advisable in pregnancy, eg yellow fever. In addition, some diseases are much more serious for the mother (and may increase the risk of a stillborn child) in pregnancy, eg malaria.

Most miscarriages occur during the first three months of pregnancy. Miscarriage is not uncommon, and can occasionally lead to severe bleeding. The last three months should also be spent within reasonable distance of good medical care. A baby born as early as 24 weeks stands a chance of survival, but only in a good modern hospital.

Pregnant women should avoid all unnecessary medication, though vaccinations and malarial prophylactics should still be taken where needed. Additional care should be taken to prevent illness and particular attention should be paid to diet and nutrition. Alcohol and nicotine, for example, should be avoided.

TOILETS

Some travellers have given up eating (for a while at least) just to avoid having to use Chinese toilets. Unfortunately, unless your stay in China is extremely brief, you'll have to learn to cope.

Public toilets in China are hardly the healthiest-looking places – basically they're holes in the ground or ditches over which you squat. Many cannot be flushed at all while others are flushed with a conveniently placed bucket of water. Public toilets can

often be found in train stations and the side streets of the cities and towns – many now charge a fee of one or two jiǎo. Some have very low partitions (without doors) between the individual holes and some have none. Toilet paper is never provided – always keep a stash with you. Dormitory-style hotel rooms are also not equipped with toilet paper.

While it takes some practice to get proficient at balancing yourself over a squat toilet, at least you don't need to worry about whether the toilet seat is clean. Furthermore, experts who study such things claim that the squatting position is better for your digestive system. Tourist hotels have international-style 'sit-down' toilets, a luxury you will come to appreciate. The issue of

女 Nǚ: woman, female, feminine
The character for woman, or feminine, has changed over time. Earlier versions depicted more submissive poses. In the modern version, tradition prevails, but the submissiveness has vanished. A woman, unlike her husband and sons, is still to be found around the house, where she can be seen striding around doing household chores, often with a baby strapped to her back.

男 Nán: man, male, masculine
The character for male, or masculine, is a combination of the characters for field (above) and strength (below). Traditionally, the males of the household would exert their strength in the fields. Their daily tasks included planting and harvesting crops, and tending to their livestock.

what to do with used toilet paper has caused some concern. One traveller writes:

We are still not sure about the toilet paper ... in two hotels they have been angry with us for flushing down the paper in the toilet. In other places it seems quite OK though.

In general, the wastebasket next to the toilet is where you should throw the toilet paper. The sewerage systems in many hotels cannot handle toilet paper. This is especially true in old hotels where the antiquated plumbing system was designed in the pre-toilet paper era. Also, in rural areas there is no sewage treatment plant – the waste empties into an septic tank and toilet paper will really create a mess in there. Be considerate and throw the paper in the wastebasket.

WOMEN TRAVELLERS

Principles of decorum and respect for women are deeply ingrained in Chinese culture. Despite the Confucianist sense of superiority accorded men, Chinese women often call the shots and wield a tremendous amount of influence (especially within marriage). There is a strong sense of balance between men and women.

In general, foreign women are unlikely to suffer serious sexual harassment in China, but there have been reports of problems in Xīnjiāng. Wherever you are, it's worth noticing what local women are wearing and how they are behaving and making a bit of an effort to fit in, as you would in any other foreign country.

GAY & LESBIAN TRAVELLERS

The official attitude to gays and lesbians in China is ambiguous, with responses ranging from draconian penalties to tacit acceptance.

Certainly there is greater tolerance in the big cities than in the more conservative countryside. However, even the big cities are not good places for gays and lesbians to be open about their sexual orientation in public, as police or local officials might respond to this 'provocation' with a crackdown on local meeting places.

In 1996 the British organisation War on Want reported that China was jailing gays

---

Gender Games

It's been said before that China is one of the safest places in Asia – if not the world – for foreign women to travel by themselves. This may not be quite as true as it was a decade ago, particularly in places like Běijīng (beware of lecherous taxi drivers), but the changes are not dramatic. The stares, shrieks, whistles and excruciating 'hellos' that burst forth at the spectacle of a foreigner may have the occasional lascivious slant (note it's a melodious whistle as opposed to the standard American wolf call), but this is generally more annoying than actually threatening. Indeed, you are in greater danger of being robbed in China than being sexually assaulted.

In many instances, the Chinese people – both women and men – will look out for your safety; there is also the fact that it's rare to find yourself in a situation where there are no other people around. In any situation, however, it is clearly better to give your intuition the benefit of the doubt if things don't feel right.

It's worth remembering that many people in China, particularly men, have the impression that westerners treat sex as casually as shaking hands. Remember too that the Chinese press never tires of pointing out western sexual decadence. On the other hand, don't be fooled into thinking that the condescending deference often given to foreigners is gender-blind. Despite the rhetoric of the revolution, Chinese women do not share the same equality as men. And as a female foreigner, neither do you.

Marie Cambon

---

for up to five years for 'disturbances against the social order' (a violation of Penal Code section 158). Other gays are reportedly treated with electric shocks to 'cure' their homosexuality.

Similarly, Chinese writers and film producers who try to deal with the topic of homosexuality routinely see their works banned.

On the other hand, there are many recognised gay discos, bars and pubs in the big cities that appear to function without official harassment, although they tend to keep a fairly low profile (see individual city entries for listings of these venues).

Check out www.utopia-asia.com/tipschin.htm or www.gaychina.com for tips on travelling in China.

DISABLED TRAVELLERS

China has few facilities geared for the disabled. But that doesn't necessarily make it out of bounds for those who do have a physical disability (and a sense of adventure). On the plus side, most hotels have lifts, so booking ground-floor hotel rooms is not essential. In bigger cities, some hotels at the four- and five-star level have specially designed rooms for people with physical disabilities.

On the other hand, just getting up the steps to enter the hotel lobby could present a challenge. People whose sight, hearing or walking ability is impaired must be extremely cautious of the traffic, which almost never yields to pedestrians. Travelling by car or taxi is probably the safest transport option.

Not surprisingly, Hong Kong is more user-friendly to the disabled than the rest of China. However, Hong Kong presents some substantial obstacles of its own such as the stairs at the subway stations, narrow crowded footpaths and steep hills.

Get in touch with your national support organisation (the 'travel officer' if there is one) before leaving home. They often have travel literature for holiday planning and can put you in touch with travel agents who specialise in tours for the disabled.

In the UK the Royal Association for Disability & Rehabilitation (☎ 020-7250 3222, fax 7250 0212), at 12 City Forum, 250 City Rd, London EC1V 8AF, produces three holiday fact packs for disabled travellers.

In the USA, contact the Society for the Advancement of Travel for the Handicapped (SATH; ☎ 212-447 7284) at 347 Fifth Ave No 610, New York, NY 10016.

In France try the CNFLRH (☎ 1 53 80 66 66) at 236 bis rue de Tolbiac, Paris.

SENIOR TRAVELLERS

In China, older people are revered. To be called elderly is a compliment, a tribute to your maturity and wisdom. China even has legislation to reinforce the duty of children to support their parents. On the rare occasions when children have lapsed in this respect, their omissions have resulted in prison sentences.

If you do decide to be adventurous, try getting up early in the morning once or twice. Go out in the streets. There you will see mature Chinese citizens enjoying themselves performing *taijiquan* (tai chi) and other exercises. Go into the parks on weekends and you will hear seniors singing beautiful Chinese songs. You may return to your own country wishing that its people regarded old age as an achievement, not merely as something preferable to the alternative.

The senior traveller who is adventurous and healthy should not find China too daunting. But a few precautions and preparations will make your trip more pleasant.

Never pass up the opportunity to use a toilet. In China, you need to add, 'especially if it's an international-style toilet'. If you have travelled in other parts of Asia, you will have encountered squat toilets. If not, and you are less flexible in your joints than you used to be, you should limit your first visit to China to the large cities, and stay in hotels that have international-style toilets. But when you venture out, you may have to use squat toilets, not always in private. Some readers suggest that you take a stool with you, to help you manage the squat toilets. Certainly it would be useful if you could lay your hands on a light but strong collapsible stool.

If the thought of using squat toilets, sometimes in public, troubles you, consider taking part in a conducted tour for mature travellers. CITS organises group tours for seniors. There are also private travel agencies, such as Saga Holidays in the UK, which specialise in tours for seniors.

Lonely Planet's *Read this First: Asia and India* has chapters on Niche Travellers (including Senior Travellers) and on Health. You should consult your doctor about vaccinations before you go to China. But the larger cities are reasonably safe and healthy places.

First-class travel on trains is comfortable, and taxis are an alternative to crowded buses and subways. You should aim to travel in the shoulder season, when the tourist areas are less crowded, and the weather is more benign. Běijīng and Shànghǎi can be uncomfortably hot in the middle of summer and unpleasantly cold in winter.

TRAVEL WITH CHILDREN

One of the greatest advantages of travelling with children is that you appear almost normal to the locals. This opens up many more opportunities for conversing with the Chinese and therefore understanding their life, even if all they want is to have an opportunity to play with your kids.

There still remains a strong curiosity among many Chinese towards foreigners and this curiosity is only increased when there are foreign children involved. Don't be surprised if a complete stranger picks up your child or takes them from your arms. Children are often seen as common property for all to share.

The treatment you'll receive, if travelling with a young child or baby, can often make life a lot easier in China. People will give up seats, help you through a crowd, make extra allowances and in general treat you as a VIP.

Chinese cities tend to have zoos, spacious parks with rowing boats and amusement parks with lots of cotton candy, Ferris wheels, flashing lights and merry-go-rounds. For older children, travellers' centres like Yángshuò – with everything from watching video movies in the cafes to floating down the river in truck inner tubes – will probably be the highlight of a China visit.

Chinese food seems to go down all right with most foreign children. It's ideal, however, to prepare children beforehand, by making Chinese-style meals or by taking them to Chinese restaurants so that their palate makes the necessary adjustments, especially to hot spices like chilli. Also consider taking along dry foods to provide a sense of continuity and comfort, and a set of plastic cutlery for each child – coping with chopsticks could well be overwhelming. Baby food is often available, but the Chinese prefer the sweeter varieties and nearly everything is processed and has had sugar

added. Breast feeding is the safest and best way to get around.

Basics like nappies, bottles, creams, medicine, clothing, dummies and other paraphernalia are available in all larger provincial capitals. Sometimes the range and quality is limited, but at other times surprisingly good.

Travel in China tends to be uncomfortable and very slow, involving long distances by train, often in hard-seat carriages where everyone smokes and spits. As one travelling parent suggested, fly now and then to overcome the enormous distances.

Probably the biggest dangers are the roads (look both ways and watch out for holes), the profusion of dangerous objects (open electric wires) and the flu. If you can avoid these, then your child will come away with very fond and enjoyable memories of their China sojourn.

USEFUL ORGANISATIONS

English-language cultural and social organisations are thin on the ground in China, and counselling services are virtually nonexistent. For counselling services, try a medical centre that provides services to foreigners. Embassies and consulates sometimes sponsor cultural events. Business-related organisations are more prolific.

Alcoholics Anonymous (☎ 6462 9199, 6465 1561) AA meets three times a week in Běijīng.

American Chamber of Commerce (☎ 8519 1920), Suite 1903, China Resources Bldg, 8 Jianguomen Beijie, Běijīng 10005. It provides a forum for foreign businesses in China and publishes an annual directory of individual and corporate members. It has a Web site at www.amcham-china.org.cn.

British Chamber of Commerce (☎ 6504 4752, ✉ info@britaininchina.com), 31 Technical Club, 15 Guanghuali, Jianguomenwai, Běijīng 0100020. It offers its members assistance in doing business in China and publishes a directory of individual and corporate members.

China Brief (☎ 8652 1309), 24 Xiehe Hutong, Waijiao Bujie, Běijīng 10005. It publishes a newsletter on development projects in China as well as a directory of NGOs in China. It has a Web site at www.chinadevelopmentbrief.com.

DANGERS
Crime

Outwardly, China is booming, with gleaming new skyscrapers, superhighways and department stores bulging with the latest consumer goods. Yet beneath the consumerism and glittering office towers is poverty on a massive scale. The cities are filled with poor people, often newly arrived from the countryside and desperate to find work. Not everyone gets a job, and some turn to crime.

Although crime is certainly on the rise in China, the scary reports in the press tend to exaggerate the dangers. Providing you are sensible, keep your wits about you and make it difficult for thieves to get at your belongings, you shouldn't have any problems.

Pickpocketing is the most common form of theft and the one you need to carefully guard against. The wholesale theft of luggage is unusual (unless you leave it lying around unattended), but razoring of bags and pockets in crowded places like buses is fairly common. Certain cities are worse than others – Guăngzhōu, Guìyáng and Xī'ān are notorious.

The high risk areas in China are train and bus stations, city and long-distance buses and hard-seat sections of trains. The hard-seat sections of trains in particular can become very anarchic with the onset of darkness – they are sometimes worked by gangs who use knives to persuade travellers to hand over their valuables. Some foreign travellers who have tried to resist have been stabbed in incidents such as these.

Be careful in public toilets – quite a few foreigners have laid aside their valuables, squatted down to business, and then straightened up to find someone has absconded with the lot.

Hotels are generally safe. There are attendants on every floor keeping an eye on the rooms and safeguarding the keys. Dormitories obviously require more care. Don't be overly trusting of your fellow travellers – many of them are considerably less than honest. All hotels have safes and storage areas for valuables – use them. Don't leave anything you can't do without (passport, travellers cheques, money, air tickets etc) lying around in dormitories.

Small padlocks are useful for backpacks and some dodgy hotel rooms. Bicycle chain locks (preferably not Chinese-made) are handy not only for hired bikes, but for attaching backpacks to railings or luggage racks. The trendy waist-pouches often used by Hong Kong residents are definitely *not* advisable for valuables. Street tailors are skilled at sewing inside pockets to trousers, jackets and shirts usually for a few yuán, and these can even be sealed with zippers.

Loss Reports If something of yours is stolen, you should report it immediately to the nearest Foreign Affairs Branch of the PSB. Staff will ask you to fill in a loss report before investigating the case and sometimes even recovering the stolen goods.

If you have travel insurance (highly recommended), it is essential to obtain a loss report so you can claim compensation. Be warned, however, many travellers have found Foreign Affairs officials very unwilling to provide one. Be prepared to spend many hours, perhaps even several days, organising it.

Violence

Street fighting in China is extremely common, yet it seldom leads to serious injury – mostly there's just lots of arm-waving, screaming and threats.

The reasons are generally simple enough – people are pushing and shoving their way to the front of a queue, the traffic is forever noisily colliding and finally someone just flips out. Don't get involved.

Many Chinese carry knives (at least the men do), but these are seldom used for anything other than slicing bread. Guns are impossible to buy legally (there is a small black market in military pistols though). That having been said, there have been cases of armed robbery by gangs on trains – knives are the usual weapons. The police have tried to crack down on this and there have been arrests and executions of offenders. The chance of it happening to you is small and you need not let this deter you from riding the train, but it's a good idea to be aware that it can happen.

ANNOYANCES
Lăowài!

Get outside the cosmopolitan centres of Guăngzhōu, Shànghăi and Běijīng and you will hear the exclamation 'lăowài', or alternatively 'Hello, lăowài, hello'. You'll probably hear this a couple of dozen times a day. Lăo means 'old' in Chinese and is a mark of respect; wài means 'outside'. Together they constitute the most polite word the Chinese have for 'foreigner'.

Chinese speakers will hear it used in many ways – sometimes with a thick overlay of irony that undermines the respect implied in the word – but generally it is used in startled surprise at suddenly encountering a foreigner in a world that is overwhelmingly Chinese.

There is no point getting annoyed by it. If you answer by saying hello, they (the audience) will often as not break into hysterical laughter.

Noise

In recent years the Chinese government has launched an anti-noise pollution campaign. Look out for billboards emblazoned with a huge crossed-through ear presiding over busy intersections swarming with honking traffic. The government is on a loser with this one. The Chinese are generally much more tolerant of noise than most foreigners. People watch TV at ear-shattering volumes, drivers habitually lean on the horn, telephone conversations are conducted in high-decibel rapid-fire screams and most of China seems to wake uncomplainingly to the sound of jackhammers and earth-moving vehicles. If it's peace and quiet you want, head for a remote part of China – try the desert in Xīnjiāng, or a mountain-top in Tibet.

Spitting

When China first opened to foreign tourism, many foreign travellers were shocked by the spitting, which was conducted noisily by everyone everywhere.

Up in Smoke

Both Mao Zedong and Deng Xiaoping were chain smokers, and both lived to a ripe old age. Nevertheless, awareness of tobacco's harmful effects are sinking in. The Chinese government is beginning to make good on a long-held promise to do something about public smoking, banning cigarettes in airports and many railway stations. Overall, however, the authorities have a real battle on their hands.

In rural China smokers are very cavalier towards non-smokers, and buses and trains are generally thick with wafting cigarette smoke. Smokers in buses often toss their burning butts into the aisles where they continue to smoulder and occasionally start fires. Tossing lit cigarette butts out of bus windows is also common, with little regard about where they might land. Hotel rooms are often covered in cigarette burns – many guests grind their cigarettes into the carpet.

As with drinking hard liquor, smoking in public has traditionally been a male activity, though more women are starting to smoke. If you cannot tolerate smoking in crowded public places like buses and restaurants, you will either have to leave the country or buy a gas mask – the Chinese will be positively offended if you tell them not to smoke.

For smokers, on the other hand, the good news is that cigarettes are cheap (around US$1 per pack for foreign brands) and you can smoke almost anywhere. Chinese cigarettes are a mixed bag. The cheapest brands can cost less than Y2, while the best brands (such as Red Pagoda Mountain – *hongtashan*) cost double the most expensive foreign cigarettes.

Campaigns to stamp out the practice have been reasonably successful in the major urban centres – there is less public spitting in Guăngzhōu, Shànghăi and Běijīng these days (some areas impose a Y50 fine), but out in the country it is still a national sport.

Apart from the fact that it is very unpleasant to be stuck in, say, a bus with 50 people who feel compelled to pave the floor with gob, the spitting also spreads the flu (see the Health section for further details).

Racism

There is no racism in China because we don't have any black people.

Student, Chengdu University

Racism in China is a knotty problem. Most Chinese will swear blind that neither they nor their government is racist. But then very few Chinese you meet will have thought very deeply about the issue, and the Chinese government doesn't allow public debate on China's racist policies and attitudes. But, of course, as in most other countries around the world, racism is alive and kicking in China.

The Chinese are a proud people. Being Chinese links the individual to a long historical lineage, for the most part of which, Chinese believe, their country was the centre of the world. Being Chinese is often defined by blood, not nationality (and where does that leave China's ethnic minorities?). Take the dual-pricing system (remnants of which still exist here and there). Whether it is motivated by greed or not, it is fundamentally racist, especially since exceptions can be made for 'overseas Chinese' (that is, anyone who looks Chinese and claims to be of Chinese ancestry). But most Chinese don't see this as racism – to them, it's simply the rules.

Then there's the interesting case of non-Chinese Hong Kong residents. There are many 'foreigners' who were born in Hong Kong and hold Hong Kong passports, and in fact have never lived anywhere else. Some are one-half Chinese or one-quarter Chinese, but Běijīng flatly refused to grant citizenship to anyone who was not of 'pure Chinese descent'. In other words, racial purity was the deciding factor, not place of birth. This rendered all these people stateless in July 1997. Like others born in Hong Kong, they hold 'British National Overseas' (BNO) passports, which allows them to travel, but gives them no right of abode in Britain. Since a BNO passport does not confer nationality, the non-Chinese Hong Kong residents are now stateless. The 30,000 Hong Kong–born Indians are the largest affected group, but there are many others born in Hong Kong who have 'mixed blood' and are thus racially unqualified to become Chinese citizens.

Gripes aside, foreigners in China are generally treated well. It is very unusual to encounter direct racism in the form of insults (although it does happen) or be refused service in China (except to be excluded from 'Chinese-only hotels'). It does help, however, if you are from a predominantly white and prosperous nation. Other Asians and blacks often encounter discrimination in China. The most famous outright racist incident occurred in 1988 when Chinese students in Nánjīng took to the streets to protest black overseas students dating local Chinese women.

When a Chinese tells you that racism is a 'foreign problem', bear in mind that homosexuality too is a 'foreign problem' – in fact almost everything the Chinese government considers 'unhealthy' is a foreign problem. And if that sounds a little racist, it isn't, because there's no racism in China.

Queues

Forget queues. In China a large number of people with a common goal (a bus seat, a train ticket etc) generally form a surging mass. It is one of the more exhausting parts of China travel, and sometimes it is worth paying extra in order to be able to avoid train and bus stations. Otherwise, take a deep breath and leap in with everyone else.

Beggars

In major cities, beggars often target westerners and are found in areas where they congregate (such as near the Silk Market and Sānlítún in Běijīng). Children, likely under the supervision of a nearby adult who will collect the cash, are often the most aggressive – you practically have to be removed with a crowbar once they've seized your trouser leg. There have even been stories of children being kidnapped, taken hundreds of kilometres from their homes and forced into these begging gangs.

Prostitution

Prostitution seems to be on the rise in China. If you are male and staying in a hotel, chances are high that you'll either receive a phone call from a prostitute asking if you'd like a 'massage' or prostitutes will actually come knocking on your hotel room door in the middle of the night. It's also not uncommon for men to be approached by prostitutes on the streets, in certain bars and karaoke lounges and even in office buildings. A polite *búyào* ('no') should be enough to deter them.

LEGAL MATTERS
Legal System

China has improved its legal system significantly since the introduction of the policy of 'opening up to the outside world' in the late 1970s. When the People's Republic of China was founded in 1949, its new government abolished the law drafted by the previous government and claimed to establish a new legal system for the whole people. However, the drafting of the new laws was interrupted by the Chinese Communist

Party's internal political movements during the first 30 years of the PRC. For instance, during the Cultural Revolution from 1966 to 1976, there was a legal vacuum in China as its law enforcement agencies were smashed. Judges and lawyers either changed their professions or were sent to the countryside for re-education. Drafting of new laws and establishing the legal system were only re-started after the end of the Cultural Revolution.

China's legal system is closer to a Civil Law System than a Common Law System as its creative law-making is undertaken by legislature, not by judges. In the past 20 years many pieces of law have been enacted covering contract, labour, intellectual property, foreign exchange control, customs, taxation, banking, consumer protection, bankruptcy, dispute resolution etc. Chinese people are relying more and more on laws

Visiting the Basic People's Court

On a recent visit to China, I was lucky to be invited with a group of visiting law students to observe a trial in progress. Our hosts assured us that things were looking up in the Chinese criminal justice system. Accused persons were now entitled to be represented by counsel. If the accused could not afford legal counsel, the trial judge had power to direct a lawyer to act for the defence.

In the case that we observed – a trial for car theft and assault – the accused did indeed have legal representation. His counsel looked a little lonely as she sat at her desk, one of only three people on the stage who were not attired in military uniform. When the court opened, the three judges marched in, resplendent in uniforms appropriate for top-ranking military brass: smart officer-style caps, epaulettes with gold stars on their shoulders and so on. I then noticed that the two prosecutors were also wearing military uniforms. A slightly different shade of khaki, perhaps. But I wondered how I would feel if I were defence counsel, dressed in civvies, with the prosecution and the court all manifestly part of the same establishment.

The performers were clearly conscious of the presence of the audience, which included a large contingent of visitors from Hong Kong. At one stage, the prosecutor was vilifying the accused, who had been shown the screwdriver that had been employed as a weapon in the assault. He had denied that it was his screwdriver. In the course of her denunciation, the prosecutor declared that the accused was so brazen that he had even denied his culpability in the presence of such a large audience!

This was the Basic People's Court, the lowest in the Chinese judicial hierarchy. It operated with efficiency and with what some would regard as a refreshing concern for the rights of the victim, who remained seated at a special desk throughout the short trial.

We were escorted out of the court at the conclusion of the evidence and legal argument. It took a few days of persistent inquiry to ascertain the outcome of the trial. Rather predictably, the accused had been convicted. He had been sentenced to four years' jail, a result within the range that might be expected in the British, Canadian or Australian systems.

Graham Fricke QC

to govern their civil and commercial activities. Legal concepts have been recognised and accepted gradually by the Chinese people. Before the economic and legal reforms, individual Chinese people were not allowed to engage in commercial activities such as opening their own businesses or selling their own hand-made or home-grown products directly in the market. Private ownership and self-employment did not exist. Administrative procedures and decisions were used to deal with the relationship between the state and the individuals. Neighbourhood and village mediation committees were the main organisations handling disputes between individual citizens. Nowadays, enacted legislation, courts, arbitration commissions and private law firms play dominant roles in resolving civil and commercial disputes in China.

Foreign-Related Legal Matters

There are laws that deal specifically with foreign businesspeople and tourists. Under these laws, foreigners and their legitimate interests are protected. Foreign investors have been granted preferential treatment for choosing China as their investment destination. For example, a lower tax rate and some tax holidays are available to foreign investors who set up joint ventures in China. Import duty exemptions and tax refunds are granted to foreign investment in high technology and export-oriented industries.

Individual foreign travellers have been treated as equally as the local Chinese in many respects. For example, foreigners are no longer required to use a special currency certificate. The Foreign Exchange Certificate was abolished and foreigners use the Chinese currency, Renminbi, to buy goods and pay for services. In addition, foreign tourists do not pay a higher fare if they want to travel by train or plane. Friendship Stores, which were exclusively opened for foreigners, still exist but are open to locals as well. The prices in the Friendship Stores are now more compatible as people can go elsewhere to shop.

Foreigners are required to respect Chinese law and social order while they invest or travel in China. If foreigners breach Chinese law, they are prosecuted like the locals. If they commit crimes in Chinese territory, they will be punished in accordance with the China's Criminal Law. The foreigner's home country may request the extradition of the foreigner from China. However, it is up to the Chinese government whether the criminal will be extradited.

In China's court system, there are four levels hierarchically. At local county or district level is the basic people's court. At municipal level, there are intermediate people's courts, and at the provincial level is the higher people's court. At the top, is the supreme people's court. If a foreigner is involved in a legal dispute, he or she can take the matter to an intermediate people's court at municipal level or above. A people's court at basic level has no jurisdiction over a matter related to foreigners. If foreign travellers run into legal troubles in China, they should contact their embassies or consulates in China for assistance. If foreign investors are involved in legal disputes, they should contact their lawyers in their home country and in China for legal advice.

Over one hundred foreign law firms had received permits to open offices in China by 1999. Most of these foreign law firms are located in Běijīng or Shànghǎi and mainly focus on civil and commercial matters. Foreign lawyers are not permitted to act on behalf of their clients in the people's courts, however, they are permitted to act on behalf of their clients in the arbitration proceedings of an arbitration commission. In addition, parties to an arbitration proceeding can appoint foreigners as their arbitrators. The arbitration proceeding can be conducted in a foreign language as well. For instance, the proceedings of the China International Economic and Trade Arbitration Commission can be conducted completely in English or any other foreign language chosen by the parties. Interpreters and translators may not be necessary in a foreign language arbitration proceeding. From these points of view, it is advisable to take your disputes to an arbitration commission or a conciliation centre for resolution rather than taking the matter to a court.

Travellers should take extra care to comply with Chinese law as it may not be complete or transparent in some areas. Inconsistency exists between the national law and regional regulations. Corruption occurs in the judicial system, which affects law enforcement. For instance, if a traveller has a dispute with a local person whose relative is a judge of the regional intermediate people's court, he or she has to be very cautious about the outcome of their court case as the court may deliver the judgement in favour of the Chinese party because of the special relation. If the local Chinese's relative is a senior party or government official, the judgement may be delivered in favour of the Chinese party as the judge may be pressured by the party or government official. Sometimes, judges and lawyers may protect illegitimate local interests by ignoring national law, which grants equal treatment to both Chinese and foreigners in China. Therefore, sometimes the written law is not enforced properly or consistently. It has taken China about 20 years to establish a modern legal system. It will take a longer period for China to improve its law enforcement.

Drugs

In the past 20 years, drugs and drug control have become a big issue in China. According to the International Narcotics Control Board's annual report, China is the only country that has witnessed a rise in heroin seizures, from 3.8 tons in 1994 to 7.0 tons in 1998. If this trend continues, China may become one of the world's biggest consumers of heroin. The Chinese government has realised that China has become both a conduit for international drug trafficking and a consumer of drugs. Thus, the Chinese government places great emphasis on fighting drugs and drug-related crimes.

According to China's Ministry of Public Security, in the first half of 1999, the police cracked down on more than 110,000 drug-related cases and arrested nearly 140,000 suspects. Nowadays, the Chinese government is making an effort to involve and support international cooperation in controlling drugs. The government's other major task is

to help drug addicts quit their habit by establishing and expanding drug rehabilitation centres. Officials from the Ministry of Public Security claim that the government has helped 320,000 drug addicts kick their habit by compulsory means and has re-educated 210,000 addicts through labour since 1997.

If a traveller is arrested with drugs, he or she will be punished in accordance with the provisions of the Criminal Code of the PRC (Section 7 of Chapter 6 of Part II of the Criminal Code). Depending upon the seriousness of the case, the offender can be sentenced to three to 15 years imprisonment for trafficking, selling, transporting or manufacturing drugs. Some serious offenders will be jailed for life or even subject to the death sentence. Conditions vary in different prisons. Most prisons are located in rural or isolated areas. Prisoners engage in labour work daily.

PSB

Among the many striking Chinese sayings, a particularly applicable one is 'With one monkey in the way, not even 10,000 men can pass'. For foreigners and Chinese alike, the major monkey governing everyday life in China is the Public Security Bureau (PSB; Gōngānjú).

The PSB is the name given to China's police, both uniformed and plainclothes. Its responsibilities include suppression of political dissidence, crime detection, mediating family quarrels and directing traffic. A related force is the Chinese People's Armed Police Force (CPAPF), which was formed several years ago to absorb cuts in the People's Liberation Army (PLA). The Foreign Affairs Branch (wài shì kē) of the PSB deals with foreigners. This branch (also known as the 'entry-exit' branch) is responsible for issuing visa extensions and Alien Travel Permits.

The PSB is responsible for introducing and enforcing regulations concerning foreigners. So, for example, they bear responsibility for exclusion of foreigners from certain hotels. If this means you get stuck for a place to stay, they can offer advice. Don't pester them with trivia or try to 'use' them to bully a point with a local street vendor. Do turn to them for mediation in serious disputes with

Kill the Rooster to Frighten the Monkey

'To get rich is glorious,' Deng once famously said. But in the scramble for glory, more and more Chinese are turning to crime. Locals all over the country fret at the increasing incidence of theft and kidnappings. Crime, they mutter, extends from railway station platforms to the corridors of power. No-one is immune to temptation in get-rich-quick China. In mid-1995, the vice-mayor of Běijīng committed suicide while under investigation for fraud. Chen Xitong, the Běijīng Communist Party chief, was sacked for corruption. Even former 'model workers' are being arrested on charges of extortion and murder.

Cracking down on crime is a priority for the government if it is to stay in power. Official corruption was a major factor in the Tiānānmén crisis, and most Chinese claim that the problem is worse now than it was then. Widely publicised arrests and drives against corruption are met with public cynicism: the problem is the government itself. Its monopolistic hold on power and brokering of all business deals puts it in a perfect cream-skimming position. Besides, privilege for high officials and their relatives is an age-old tradition in China.

High officials caught with their fingers in the civic pocket sometimes face lengthy jail terms, but often get away with a stern rebuke and a temporary demotion. For less well-connected criminals it is often the firing squad.

Meanwhile, widespread unemployment and social disaffection is leading to a growing problem in juvenile crime. Murder, rape and theft head the list of juvenile crimes. The official view is that Chinese youngsters are victims of 'spiritual pollution' – influenced by the western disease of greed and general depravity.

Justice in China is for the most part the domain of the police, who also decide the penalty. The ultimate penalty is execution, which serves the purpose of 'killing the rooster to frighten the monkey' or, to phrase this in official terms, 'it is good to have some people executed so as to educate others'. Before execution, the prisoner is typically paraded through the streets on the back of a truck. The standard manner of execution is a bullet in the back of the head, often at a mass gathering in some sports stadium. Afterwards a mugshot and maybe even a photo of the dead body gets plugged up on a public notice board.

The prisoner's family often has to pay the cost of imprisonment, as well as the cost of the bullet. Other means of fundraising include selling the prisoner's organs to hospitals in Hong Kong for transplant purposes.

hotels, restaurants, taxi drivers etc. This often works since the PSB wields godlike power – especially in remote areas. When confronted by the PSB most Chinese follow orders without a dispute for fear of being carted off and never heard from again.

There are a few ways you can inadvertently have an unpleasant run-in with the PSB. The most common way is to overstay your visa. Another possibility is being in a closed area without a permit – fortunately, these days there aren't too many places left in China that require travel permits.

Foreign males who are suspected of being 'too friendly' with Chinese women could have trouble with the PSB.

If you're a foreign resident, the same problem could occur if you drive your car or motorcycle too far from your authorised home. Foreign businesspeople have complained about the local PSB demanding payoffs.

BUSINESS HOURS

China officially converted to a five-day work week in 1995, although some businesses still force their workers to put in six days. Banks, offices and government departments are normally open Monday to Friday. As a rough guide only, they open around 8.30 am, close for one to two hours in the middle of the day, then reopen until 5 or 6 pm. Saturday and Sunday are both public holidays, but most museums stay open on weekends and make up for this by closing on Monday and/or another day mid-week.

Travel agencies, Friendship Stores, the foreign-exchange counters in the tourist hotels and some of the local branches of the Bank of China have similar opening hours, but are generally open on Saturday and Sunday as well (at least in the morning).

Many parks, zoos and monuments have similar opening hours and are also open on weekends and often at night. Shows at cinemas and theatres end around 9.30 to 10 pm.

Restaurants keep long hours and it is always possible to find something to eat at any hour of the day, especially around train and bus stations.

Long-distance bus stations and train stations open their ticket offices around 5 or 5.30 am, before the first trains and buses pull out. Apart from a one- or two-hour break in the middle of the day, they often stay open until midnight.

PUBLIC HOLIDAYS & SPECIAL EVENTS

The PRC has nine national holidays, as follows (Hong Kong and Macau have different holidays):

public holiday	date
New Year's Day	1 January
Spring Festival (Chinese New Year)	February
International Women's Day	8 March
International Labour Day	1 May
Youth Day	4 May
International Children's Day	1 June
Birthday of the Chinese Communist Party	1 July
Anniversary of the founding of the PLA	1 August
National Day	1 October

Hanging around the appropriate temples at certain times will reward you with special ceremonies and colourful events.

Special prayers are held at Buddhist and Taoist temples on days when the moon is either full or just the thinnest sliver. According to the Chinese lunar calendar, these days fall on the 15th and 16th days of the lunar month and on the last (30th) day of the month just ending and the 1st day of the new month.

Other notable times when temples are liveliest include:

February
Spring Festival (Chūn Jié)
This is otherwise known as Chinese New Year and starts on the first day of the first month in the lunar calendar. Although officially lasting only three days, many people take a week off work. Be warned: this is China's biggest holiday and all transport and hotels are booked solid. Although the demand for accommodation skyrockets, many hotels close down at this time and prices rise steeply. If you can't avoid being in China at this time, then book your room in advance and sit tight until the chaos is over! The Chinese New Year will fall on the following dates: 24 January 2001, 12 February 2002 and 1 February 2003.

Lantern Festival (Yuánxiāo Jié)
It's not a public holiday, but it is very colourful. People take the time to make (or buy) paper lanterns and walk around the streets in the evening holding them. It falls on the 15th day of the 1st moon, and will be celebrated on the following dates: 7 February 2001, 26 February 2002 and 16 February 2003.

March/April
Guanyin's Birthday (Guānshìyīn Shēngrì)
The birthday of Guanyin, the goddess of mercy, is a good time to visit Taoist temples. Guanyin's birthday is the 19th day of the 2nd moon and will fall on the following dates: 13 March 2001, 1 April 2002 and 21 March 2003.

April
Tomb Sweeping Day (Qīng Míng Jié)
A day for worshipping ancestors; people visit the graves of their departed relatives and clean the site. They often place flowers on the tomb and burn ghost money for the departed. It falls on 5 April in the Gregorian calendar in most years, or 4 April in leap years.

Water-Splashing Festival (Pō Shuǐ Jié)
Held in the Xīshuāngbǎnnà in Yúnnán, this event falls around mid-April (usually 13 to 15 April). The purpose is to wash away the dirt, sorrow and demons of the old year and bring in the happiness of the new. The event gets staged more often now for tourists.

April/May
Mazu's Birthday (Māzushēngrì)
Mazu, goddess of the sea, is the friend of all fishing crews. She's called Mazu in Fújiàn Province and Taiwan. The name gets changed to Tianhou in Guǎngdōng, and in Hong Kong the spelling is 'Tin Hau'. Her birthday is widely celebrated at Taoist temples in coastal regions as far south as Vietnam. Mazu's birthday is on the 23rd day of the 3rd moon, and will fall on the following dates: 16 April 2001, 5 May 2002 and 24 April 2003.

June
Dragon Boat Festival (Duānwǔ Jié)
This is the time to see dragon boat races. It's a fun holiday despite the fact that it commemorates the sad tale of Chu Yuan, a 3rd century BC poet-statesman who hurled himself into the mythological Mi Lo river in Húnán to protest against the corrupt government. This holiday falls on the 5th day of the 5th lunar month, which corresponds to the following dates: 25 June 2001, 15 June 2002 and 4 June 2003.

August
Ghost Month (Guǐ Yuè)
The devout believe that during this time the ghosts from hell walk the earth and it is a dangerous time to travel, go swimming, get married or move to a new house. If someone dies during this month, the body will be preserved and the funeral and burial will be performed the following month. The Chinese government officially denounces Ghost Month as a lot of superstitious nonsense. The Ghost Month is the 7th lunar month, or really just the first 15 days. The first day of the Ghost Month will fall on the following dates: 19 August 2001, 9 August 2002 and 29 July 2003.

September/October
Mid-Autumn Festival (Zhōngqiū Jié)
This is also known as the Moon Festival, and is the time to eat tasty moon cakes. Gazing at the moon and lighting fireworks are popular activities, and it's also a traditional holiday for lovers. The festival takes place on the 15th day of the 8th moon, and will be celebrated on the following dates: 12 September 2000, 1 October 2001, 21 September 2002 and 11 September 2003.

September
Birthday of Confucius (Kǒngzi Shēngrì)
The birthday of the great sage occurs on 28 September of the Gregorian calendar. This is an interesting time to visit Qūfù in Shāndōng, the birthplace of Confucius. On the other hand, all hotels in town are likely to be booked out at this time. A ceremony is held at the Confucius Temple starting around 4 am.

ACTIVITIES
Adventure Sports
Western China in particular offers the type of topography to entice mountaineers, white-water rafters, hang-gliding enthusiasts and others who want to pursue their adventurous hobbies in some of the world's highest mountains.

The problem, as always, is the faceless, sombre figures known collectively as 'the authorities'. High-ranking cadres, the PSB, the military, CITS and others in China with the power to extort money know a good business opportunity when they see it. Foreigners have been asked for outrageous sums of money for mountaineering and rafting permits. The amount demanded varies considerably depending on who you're dealing with, and the price is always negotiable.

In many cases, it's doubtful that the law really requires a permit. A Chinese person may climb the same mountain as you without having any authorisation at all and it may be perfectly legal. But many local governments simply make up the law as they go along.

In general, when foreigners do something that is deemed unusual – and hang-gliding, bungy jumping, kayaking and the like are unusual in China – a permit will be required and a fee will be charged. The more unusual the activity, the higher the fee demanded.

Hiking
As opposed to mountaineering (which requires equipment such as ropes and ice axes), normal hiking activities can usually be pursued without permits. The Chinese idea of hiking is often different from the western concept – most of the peaks climbed are hardly wilderness areas. You can expect an admission gate (charging a fee), handrails, concrete steps, Chinese characters painted on the rocks, temples, pavilions, trailside souvenir vendors, loudspeakers

Chinese Martial Arts

Often misinterpreted, Chinese martial arts teach an approach to life that stresses patience, endurance, magnanimity and humility. The following is a thumbnail sketch of a few of the arts that you may see while travelling in China.

Taijiquan – Supreme Ultimate Fist

The most popular martial art in the world, *taijiquan* or tai chi, is generally practised in China by the elderly, who find it invaluable for flexibility, good circulation, leg strength and good balance. A major part of studying taijiquan is the development of *qi*, or energy, which can be used for healing, or in fighting.

The most popular form of taijiquan is the Yang style, which is not too difficult to learn in its simplified form (though the full form has 108 postures and takes 20 minutes to perform) and is not strenuous. Other styles, such as the Chen style, call for a wider array of skills as the postures are painfully low and the kicks high, so endurance and flexibility are important. Chen style is popular with younger exponents and clearly has its roots in Shaolin, mixing slow movements with fast, snappy punches. Other styles include the Sun and Wu styles.

After learning the empty hand form (a smooth, continuous set of movements), the practitioner goes on to learn weapons forms, generally including the taiji sword and maybe the taiji pole, depending on the skills of the teacher. Practitioners can also be trained in the use of other weapons.

A student of taijiquan will be introduced to pushing hands, a two-person exercise that opens the door to the fighting side of taijiquan. Pushing hands teaches students how to interpret the force of their opponents and to react accordingly. The correct interpretation of, and reaction to, force is the main weapon in the taiji armoury. Resistance to force is educated out of the student and instead a yielding to pressure is trained. Through yielding, force can be controlled and redirected away from the target; this aspect is very hard to train as it goes against natural inclinations to resist force with force. The highest point of taijiquan, being able to evade all attacks, is reserved for a precious few who have devoted themselves to the art. If fighting or self-defence is what you are after, learn karate, kickboxing or *wing chun*, which emphasise the martial aspect.

Nonetheless, for those who learn taijiquan, the art promises a lifelong interest that constantly surprises with its lessons in re-educating the body. Strength, speed, suppleness and health are all physical benefits enjoyed by students of taijiquan, and the slow movements promote relaxation as an antidote to stress.

Wing Chun

Invented by a Buddhist nun, Ng Mui, who taught her skills to a young girl called Wing Chun, this is a ferocious and dynamic system that promises reasonably quick results for those learning. This was the style that taught film star Bruce Lee how to move.

Wing chun emphasises speed rather than strength. Evasion, subterfuge and rapid strikes are the hallmarks of the wing chun system. The forms are simple and direct, doing away with the pretty flourishes that characterise other styles.

The theory of wing chun is enshrined in its 'centre-line theory', which draws an imaginary line down the human body and centres all attacks and blocks on that line. The line runs through the sensitive regions: eyes, nose, lips, mouth, throat, heart, solar plexus and groin. Any blow that lands on any of these points is debilitating and dangerous. None of the blocks stray beyond the width of the shoulders, as this limits the range of possible attacks. This gives the forms of wing chun its distinctive simplicity. The sweeps of western boxers are removed and instead the punch takes its strength mainly from the shoulders, elbows and wrist. Punches are delivered with great rapidity in

Chinese Martial Arts

a straight line, along the shortest distances between the puncher and the punched. A two-person training routine called *chi sau*, or sticking hands, teaches the student how to be soft in response to attacks; softness promotes relaxation in the practitioner and fosters speed in counterattacking.

Weapons in the wing chun arsenal include the twin wing chun butterfly knives, which are sharp and heavy, and an extremely long pole, which requires considerable strength to handle with skill.

Despite being an excellent system for self-defence, wing chun practitioners are often over-confident and cocky, which is contrary to the spirit of the system. Wing chun forms are not especially strenuous and often do not build up the stamina necessary for students who want to fight professionally. For your average punter, however, the study of wing chun can provide a whole range of useful skills.

Bagua Zhang – Eight-Trigram Boxing

This intriguing art is probably one of the strangest to witness, and is certainly one of the most esoteric. In fact, *bagua* fighters were feared among Chinese boxers for their ferocity and unorthodox moves. The practitioner wheels around in a circle, changing speed and direction, occasionally kicking or thrusting out a palm strike. This is the art of *bagua zhang*, or eight-trigram boxing, one of the soft or internal styles of Chinese boxing.

Eight-trigram boxing draws its inspiration from the trigrams (an arrangement of three broken and unbroken black lines) of the classic *Book of Changes* or *I Ching*. The trigrams are often arranged in circular form and it is this pattern that is traced out by the bagua walker.

The practitioner of bagua zhang must display all the skills of subterfuge, evasion, speed and unpredictability, which are the motifs of this style. Force is generally not met with force, but deflected by circular movements – circular forms are the mainstay of all movements. Arcing, twisting, twining and spinning, reflect a circular pattern that is as natural as the orbits and shape of the planets.

A further hallmark of the style is the exclusive use of the palm instead of the fist as the main striking weapon. This may appear strange and even ineffectual, but in fact the palm can transmit a surprising amount of power. The palm can also be better protected than the fist, as it is cushioned by muscle. The fist has to transmit the power of a punch through a myriad of bones, which have to be correctly aligned to avoid damage. If you had to punch a brick wall as hard as you could, would you use your fist or your palm?

The art of bagua zhang is deeply esoteric and almost off-limits to non-Chinese. There are practitioners who teach foreigners, but they are not nearly as prolific as teachers of bagua's sister art, taijiquan. Anyone who finds a teacher of worth must be prepared for an intense schooling in a difficult art. Those who do become proficient in bagua zhang will inherit a disappearing legacy of old China.

Xingyi Quan – Body-Mind Boxing

Xingyi quan is another soft, or internal martial art, which is often mentioned in the same breath as taijiquan, despite being different in many ways. Like taijiquan the training emphasises the development of qi, or energy; however, the movements of xingyi quan are dynamic and powerful, and the fighting philosophy is not passive, like that of taijiquan.

spewing forth advertisements, camel rides, photo props, restaurants and perhaps a hotel or two.

Hiking areas of this sort include some of China's famous mountains like Tài Shān and Éméi Shān. Still, it can be good fun and exercise, and it's part of the 'China experience'.

Camel & Horse Riding

The venues are not numerous, but China does offer some opportunities of this sort. Camel rides for tourists have become popular pastimes in places like Inner Mongolia or the deserts around Dūnhuáng (Gānsù).

Chinese Martial Arts

Possibly the oldest martial art still in existence in China, xingyi quan was developed in imitation of the fighting techniques and spirit of twelve animals. There are different schools of xingyi quan, which promote different animal styles, but the standard form consists of the dragon, tiger, horse, monkey, chicken, harrier, Chinese ostrich, swallow, eagle, bear, water lizard and snake. Each animal must be understood in terms of its shape and intention or idea.

Before studying the animal forms, the student must start with the five punches that are the building blocks of xingyi quan. The five punches are *pi*, *beng*, *zuan*, *pao* and *heng*; each one must be studied in turn until perfected. In general, each punch is practised while stepping up and down in a straight line and then put together into a linking set.

Each punch represents one of the five elements of Chinese philosophy – pi (metal), beng (wood), zuan (water), pao (fire) and heng (earth). The punches reflect the cycle of conquest and creation implicit in the life of the five elements: fire conquers metal, metal conquers wood, wood conquers earth, earth conquers water and water conquers fire. Alternatively, fire produces earth, earth produces metal, metal produces water, water produces wood and wood produces fire.

Xingyi quan is performed in a relaxed state, emphasising a calm but observant mind. The movements are quick, intelligent and direct, assisted to their target by a body that must unite all its movements into a threaded whole. Training in the art is punishing and consists of many postures that must be held for a long time in order to develop qi. Attacks are generally met with force rather than with evasive manoeuvring. Like bagua zhang, teachers of xingyi quan are hard to find and are often reticent about the art.

Other Martial Arts

There are dozens of other martial art styles in existence in China, and each style reflects its own fighting philosophy and spirit. You can take your pick according to your persuasion: drunken boxing, white crane boxing, white eyebrow boxing, monkey boxing, tiger boxing, five ancestors boxing and many, many more. Each style is a distillation of fighting experience and contains a deep and rewarding link with the past.

An enthusiastic martial arts student at Shàolín Sì, one of China's most famous monastery training centres, in Hénán.

More common are the photo-prop camels and horses (you dress up like Genghis Khan, mount your steed and have your photo taken). There are chances for beautiful trips by horses in the mountains of Xīnjiāng, or for that matter in the hills west of Běijīng. Costs are negotiable, but in general, the further away from a big city you are, the cheaper it gets.

Exercise & Gymnastics

Swimming pools, gymnasiums and weight-lifting rooms are popular ways to keep fit and enjoy yourself. While swimming pools and gymnasiums exist for the Chinese public, they are generally overcrowded and in poor condition. You'll find better facilities at the tourist hotels, but of course they won't be free (unless you're a guest at the hotel).

For a fee, most hotels in big cities like Běijīng permit non-guests to join their 'health club', which entitles you to use the workout rooms, pools, saunas or tennis courts. This is not a bad idea if you're staying for a month or more – monthly membership fees typically start at around Y850 and there are discounts for married couples and families. There are even bigger discounts if you sign up for six months or more.

Massage

Legitimate massage (as opposed to prostitution) has traditionally been performed by blind people in China. The Chinese can take credit for developing many of the best massage techniques that are still employed today.

Most five-star hotels have massage services at five-star prices (typically Y300 per hour). Rates are around Y50 per hour at small specialist massage clinics, but you'll need a Chinese person to direct you to one.

Winter Sports

Běijīng's lakes freeze over for a couple of months during winter and ice skating becomes feasible. Further north in Hāěrbīn, January temperatures dip to -40°C (-40°F) and ice-boat racing is a favourite pastime for those who can afford it. North-east China is also the venue for skiing, both the downhill and cross-country varieties. Those who have tried it, however, say that the slopes are mostly only suitable for beginners.

Skiing and ice skating demand specialised shoes. If you have big feet you'll often have difficulty finding the right size and therefore may need to bring your own equipment. If you have small or average size feet, you shouldn't have any trouble renting ice skates at skating rinks and skiing equipment at resorts.

Therapeutic Massage

Massage (ànmó) has a long history in China. It's an effective technique for treating a variety of painful ailments, such as chronic back pain and sore muscles. To be most effective, a massage should be administered by someone who has studied the techniques. An acupuncturist who also practises massage would be ideal.

Traditional Chinese massage is somewhat different from the increasingly popular do-it-yourself techniques practised by people in the west. One traditional Chinese technique employs suction cups made of bamboo placed on the patient's skin. A burning piece of alcohol-soaked cotton is briefly put inside the cup to drive out the air before it is applied. As the cup cools, a partial vacuum is produced, leaving a nasty-looking but harmless red circular mark on the skin. The mark goes away in a few days. Other methods include blood-letting and scraping the skin with coins or porcelain soup spoons.

A related technique is called moxibustion. Various types of herbs, rolled into what looks like a ball of fluffy cotton, are held close to the skin and ignited. A slight variation of this method is to place the herbs on a slice of ginger and then ignite them. The idea is to apply the maximum amount of heat possible without burning the patient. This heat treatment is supposed to be good for such diseases as arthritis.

There is no real need to subject yourself to such extensive treatment if you would just like a straight massage to relieve normal aches and pains. Many big tourist hotels in China offer massage facilities, but the rates charged are excessive – around Y180 per hour and up. You can do much better than that by inquiring locally. Alternatively, look out for the blind masseuses that work on the streets in many Chinese cities.

Golf

Golf courses have invaded the suburbs of Běijīng, Shànghǎi and Guǎngzhōu. As elsewhere, it's a sport of the well-to-do, but that seems to be even more true in China. While green fees are similar to what you'd pay in the west, the cost is astronomical compared with the typical Chinese salary.

COURSES

As China continues to experiment with capitalism, universities have found it increasingly necessary to raise their own funds and not depend so much on state largesse. For this reason, most universities welcome fee-paying foreign students.

Most of the courses offered are Chinese-language study, but other options include Chinese medicine, acupuncture, music and brush painting. If you've got the cash, almost anything is possible.

A bottom-end quote for four hours of instruction per day, five days a week, is around US$1200 per semester, and perhaps half that for a six-week summer session. For these rates, the teacher to student ratio is typically 1:25. A semester lasts about four months, with the Spring semester starting just after Chinese New Year and the Autumn semester starting in mid-September. Dormitory housing starts at around US$15 a day for a private room, or half that amount to share. There have been complaints from students that universities try to hit foreigners with all sorts of hidden surcharges – 'study licences', health certificates and so on. Other schools try to coerce you into teaching English for little or nothing.

If possible, don't pay anything in advance – show up at the school to assess the situation yourself and talk to other foreign students to see if they're satisfied. Although schools claim you must register in advance, if you show up a day or two before classes begin you'll usually be allowed to register. An exception to this is Beijing University and Beijing Language and Culture University, where classes fill up early, so registration is necessary. Once you've handed over the cash, don't expect a refund.

WORK
Teaching English

There are opportunities to teach English and other foreign languages, or even other technical skills if you're qualified. Teaching in China is not a way to get rich – the pay is roughly Y1200 to Y2500 a month. While this is better than what the average urban Chinese worker earns, it won't get you far after you've left China. There are usually some fringe benefits like free or low-cost housing and special ID cards that get you discounts at some hotels.

In order to qualify for the high end of the salary range, you need to be declared a 'foreign expert'. It's not totally clear what makes you an expert, but points in your favour could include holding a graduate degree, a Teacher of English as a Second Language (TESL) certificate, other credentials and/or experience. The final decision is made by the State Bureau for Foreign Experts.

It's become fairly typical for universities to pressure foreigners into working excessive hours. A maximum teaching load should be 20 hours per week, and even this is a lot – you can insist on no more than 15 and some teachers get away with 10. Chinese professors teach far fewer hours than this – some hardly show up for class at all since they often have outside business interests.

The main reason to work in China is to experience the country at a level not ordinarily available to travellers. Unfortunately, just how close you will be able to get to the Chinese people depends on what the local PSB allows. In some towns where the local PSB is almost hysterical about evil foreign 'spiritual pollution', your students may be prohibited from having any contact with you beyond the classroom, although you may secretly meet them far away from the campus.

Foreign teachers are typically forced to live in separate apartments or dormitories – Chinese students wishing to visit you at your room may be turned away at the reception desk, or they may be required to register their name, ID number and purpose of their visit. Since many people are reluctant to draw attention to themselves like this, they may be unwilling to visit you at all.

In other words, teaching in China can be a lonely experience unless you spend all your free time in the company of other expats, but this deprives you of the 'foreign experience' you may be seeking. A lot depends on where you'll be teaching – things are fairly open in

Shànghǎi, but it's a different story in the hinterlands of Gānsù Province.

Two topics that cannot be discussed in the classroom are politics and religion. Foreigners teaching in China have reported spies being placed in their classrooms. Other teachers have found microphones hidden in their dormitory rooms (one fellow we know took revenge by attaching his Walkman to the microphone wires and blasting the snoops with punk music!).

Rules change – China is opening up, and some provinces are liberalising faster than others. In the city where you live, you may find that conditions are better than those that are described here.

If you are interested in working in China, contact a Chinese embassy or one of the universities directly.

Doing Business

In bureaucratic China, even simple things can be made difficult – renting property, getting licences, hiring employees, paying taxes etc can generate mind-boggling quantities of red tape. Many foreign business people who have worked in China say that success is usually the result of dogged persistence and finding cooperative officials.

Even when you think you've got everything all agreed to on paper, don't be surprised if things go awry when you put your agreements into practice. It's not uncommon for your Chinese joint-venture partner to change the terms of the agreement once business has commenced. Your copyrights, patents and trademarks may be pirated. Your rent and property taxes may suddenly be raised, and your Chinese employees (who know your company's secrets) may simultaneously walk out and start working for a new state-run company just across the street producing exactly same goods as you do. While the business climate has improved in recent years, there are still 1001 things that can go wrong.

If you have any intention of doing business in China, be it buying, selling or investing, it's worth knowing that most towns and – in large cities – many neighbourhoods have a Commerce Office (Shāngyè Jú). If you approach one of these offices for assistance, the reaction you get can vary from enthusiastic welcome to bureaucratic inertia. In case of a dispute (the goods you ordered are not what was delivered etc), the Commerce Office could assist you, provided that it is willing.

Anyone thinking of doing serious business in China and setting up a company is advised to do some research before going ahead. In particular, talk to other foreigners who are already doing business in China.

MOVING TO CHINA

If you're going to be moving heavy items like furniture or all your household goods, you will need the services of an international mover or freight forwarder. In Běijīng you can try Global Silverhawk Limited (☎ 6767 5566, fax 8769 4013, @ global@public .bta.net.cn) or Crown Worldwide (☎ 6585 0640, fax 6585 0648, @ general.cnbjg@ crownworldwide.com).

In Hong Kong there's Asian Express (☎ 28 93 1000) and Jardine International (☎ 2563 6653).

In Shànghǎi you can try calling Crown Worldwide (☎ 6472 0254, @ cnshg@ crownworldwide.com). Most of these companies have branch offices serving other major cities in China.

ACCOMMODATION

In the more developed parts of China, hotel prices have risen so high that it's no cheaper than travelling in Europe or the USA. In more isolated regions like Inner Mongolia or Qīnghǎi it's still pretty cheap, but the trend is clear – prices are rising everywhere.

On the other hand, quality has improved – rooms are more luxurious, service has improved and hotel staff are friendlier and more used to dealing with foreigners than a few years ago. In the past, it was common for the staff to simply deny that rooms were available even when the hotel was empty.

When you check into a hotel, there is usually a question on the registration form asking what type of visa you have. Most travellers aren't sure how to answer. For most, the type of visa is 'L', from the Chi-

宾馆 **Bīnguǎn: guesthouse, hotel, restaurant**
The top of this character is a roof, and underneath it is the character for soldier. It has been suggested that all *bīnguǎn* (guesthouses and hotels) are guarded by a soldier under a small roof. The first part of guǎn means food. The second part originally meant official residence (notice the roof) and later came to mean any public building. A building open to the public that serves food is another way of expressing the idea of restaurant or hotel.

饭店 **Fàndiàn: restaurant, hotel**
Fàn, meaning cooked rice, comes from the character for food in combination with the phonetic for 'to return', a reference to a hand returning to the mouth in the process of eating. In earlier times, a *diàn* was an earth platform in a hall, used at banquets to put empty goblets and food on. The earth platform forms part of a building, so the top of the character is a type of house. Underneath is the actual platform with things placed on it. As a diàn is somewhere people put things, a place to display goods is also called diàn, as in *shāngdiàn* (shop). A *fàndiàn*, literally a food shop, may even offer you a bed!

餐厅 **Cāntīng: restaurant, dining hall**
This is an amalgamation of two characters: *cān*, meaning food, meal or eat, and *tīng*, meaning hall or room. In ancient times, the top left part of cān meant tongue and mouth, and the top right was like a hand. The bottom part of the character represents a food bowl; thus the hand is putting food into the mouth. In the traditional writing for tīng, the top of the character meant a cliff or cave where people reside. The bottom part of this character means person(s). Thus, tīng is a place where people gather, for example, to hold functions.

nese word for travel (*lǚxíng*). For a full list of visa categories, see the Visas & Documents section earlier in this chapter.

Reservations
It's possible to book rooms in advance at upmarket hotels through overseas branches of CITS, CTS, other travel agencies or online (see the Internet Resources section earlier). Often you actually get a discount by booking through an agency – the walk-in rate is higher. Airports at major cities often have hotel booking counters that offer discounted rates.

Camping
You have to get a long way from civilisation before camping becomes feasible in China. Camping within sight of a town or village in most parts of China would probably result in a swift visit by the PSB. Wilderness camping is more appealing, but most such areas in China require special permits and are difficult

to reach. Many travellers have camped successfully in Tibet and remote north-western Sichuān.

The trick is to select a couple of likely places about half an hour before sunset, but keep moving (by bicycle, foot or whatever) and then backtrack so you can get away from the road at the chosen spot just after darkness falls. Be sure to get up around sunrise and leave before sightseeing locals take an interest.

Rental Accommodation
If you're going to be working for the Chinese government as a teacher or other type of foreign expert, then you'll almost certainly be provided with low-cost housing. Conditions probably won't be luxurious, but it will be cheap or even free.

Foreign students also are usually offered decent accommodation by their schools, although the price can vary from very reasonable to totally ridiculous.

If you're visiting Chinese friends for any length of time, their work unit may be able to provide you with temporary accommodation at low cost. Alternatively, you could live with your Chinese friends – in the recent past this was prohibited, but now it seems to be OK almost everywhere in China.

The news is not good for those coming to China to do business or work for a foreign company. The cheap subsidised apartments available to the Chinese are generally not open to foreigners, which leaves you with two choices – living in a hotel or renting a luxury flat in a compound specifically designated for foreigners.

If you live in a hotel, you might be able to negotiate a discount for a long-term stay, but that's not guaranteed. As for luxury flats and villas, monthly rents start at around US$2000 and reach US$5000 or more.

Considering the sky-high rents, buying a flat or villa might seem like a good idea for companies with the cash. It is actually possible, but the rules vary from city to city. In Xiàmén, for example, only overseas Chinese are permitted to buy luxury villas – real estate speculators from Taiwan do a roaring trade. Shēnzhèn has long been in the business of selling flats to Hong Kong residents, who in turn rent them out to others. Foreigners can buy flats in Běijīng (at astronomical prices), and doing this can actually gain you a residence permit. In most cases, buying actually means that you own the property for 75 years, after which it reverts to the state.

It's possible to live in Chinese housing or move in with a Chinese family and simply pay rent. In Běijīng expect to pay as little as Y1200 for a small one-bedroom up to Y4500 or more for a larger place. Families typically charge around Y1000 for a room. Although new policies allowing foreigners to legally live in Chinese housing have recently been enacted, landlords often refuse to register their foreign tenants (either they haven't heard of the new laws or are distrustful of them). If you're not registered by your landlord, then you will be subjected to periodic sweeps during which your landlord will warn you to stay away for a few days. Of course, none of the above applies in Hong Kong and Macau where you are mostly free to live where you like.

University Accommodation

In theory, university dormitories are for students, teachers and their guests, or others with business at the university. In practice, universities are trying to make money, and they are simply entering into the hotel business just like many other state-run organisations.

Especially along China's east coast and in major cities, staying in a university dorm can often be one of your cheapest options. Many universities will rent out vacant dorm rooms in the foreign student dormitory. Universities also sometimes have actual hotels, although the prices are usually on a par with regular budget hotels. One problem that you may have to contend with is that many university dormitories have restrictions – lights out by 10 pm and doors locked, no visitors in your room etc.

Hostels

Unlike Europe or Australia, an International Youth Hostel Federation card won't get you far in China. Basically you can choose from staying at the Mt Davis Hostel in Hong Kong or the Vila Dom Bosco Hostel in Macau. There are, however, dormitories (duō rén fáng) in most of China's major tourist destinations.

Where dormitories do exist, the staff at hotel reception desks are often reluctant to tell you. Try a little friendly forcefulness. If this doesn't work, you have no choice but to look elsewhere – there are many cities in China where dormitory accommodation is just not available to foreigners.

Guesthouses

In China guesthouses (bīnguǎn) are usually enormous government-run hotels, often with many wings in spacious grounds. Most of them were set up in the 1950s for travelling government officials and overseas dignitaries. Most of these were renovated during the 1990s and are being rented out as midrange accommodation – you no longer have to be a government official or dignitary.

Chinese guesthouses are most definitely not the kind of inexpensive, family-run guesthouses you find all over Thailand, Indonesia and other parts of Asia.

Hotels

There is no shortage of hotels in China. The problem comes if you are on a budget. In many parts of China, finding a room for less than US$25 a night can be an ordeal. Often inexpensive accommodation is in fact available – if you are Chinese. For foreigners, there are generally rules (enforced by the PSB) concerning which hotels you may or may not stay in, and of course the only ones open to foreigners are the expensive ones.

On the other hand, for travellers on mid-range budgets, China's hotels have improved immensely. Service standards are better, the toilets may actually flush and sometimes there are even minibars and 24-hour hot water. Unless you are in a four- or five-star joint venture, however, it is wise not to expect too much, no matter how much you are spending. Many of the finer details of the hotel business still elude Chinese management and staff.

If you're studying in the PRC, you can sometimes get a discount on room prices. Students usually have to show their government-issued 'green card', which should entitle them to pay the same price as local Chinese. However, these days many hotels charge the same price to foreigners and locals, in which case the green card is of no help at all.

If you are really stuck for a place to stay, it may help to phone or visit the local PSB and explain your problem. Just as the PSB makes the rules, the PSB can break them – a hotel not approved for foreigners can be granted a temporary reprieve by the PSB and all it takes is a phone call from the right official. Unfortunately, getting such an exemption is not the usual practice.

Some definitions of hotel terminology are in order. The vast majority of rooms in China are 'twins', which means two single beds placed in one room. A 'single room' (one bed per room) is a rarity, although you may occasionally stumble across one. The

western concept of a 'double room' (a room with one large double bed shared by two people) is also extremely rare in China. In most cases, your choice will be between a twin room *(shuāng rén fáng)* or a suite *(tàofáng)*, the latter obviously being more expensive. However, in most cases two people are allowed to occupy a twin room for the same price as one person, so sharing is one good way to cut expenses.

Most hotels have an attendant on every floor. The attendant keeps an eye on the hotel guests. This is partly to prevent theft and partly to stop you from bringing locals back for the night (this is not a joke).

To conserve energy, in many cheaper hotels hot water for bathing is available only in the evening – sometimes only for a few hours – or once every three days. It's worth asking when or if the hot water will be turned on.

The policy at every hotel in China is to require that you check out by noon to avoid being charged extra. If you check out between noon and 6 pm there is a charge of 50% of the room price – after 6 pm you have to pay for another full night.

Almost every hotel has a left-luggage room *(jìcún chù* or *xínglǐ bǎoguān)*, and in many hotels there is such a room on every floor. If you are a guest in the hotel, use of the left-luggage room might be free (but not always).

Something to be prepared for is lack of privacy – what happens is that you're sitting starkers in your hotel room, the key suddenly turns in the door and the room attendant casually wanders in. Don't expect anyone to knock before entering. Some of the better hotels have a bolt that will lock the door from the inside, but most budget hotels are not so well equipped. Your best protection is to prop a chair against the door.

In a big city like Běijīng or Shànghǎi, it's wise to call ahead first to see if there are any vacant rooms. Of course, at budget hotels there's only a slight chance that the person answering the phone will speak anything other than Chinese. When the hotel operator answers, ask to speak to the service desk *(zǒng fúwù tái)* and then ask 'Do you have a vacancy?' *(yǒu méiyǒu kōng fángjiān)*, to which they'll either reply *yǒu* (have) or *méiyǒu* (don't have).

The Chinese method of designating floors is the same as that used in the USA, but different from, say, Australia's. What would be the ground floor in Australia is the 1st floor in China, the 1st is the 2nd, and so on.

ENTERTAINMENT

As on all other fronts, China's entertainment options are improving rapidly. Bars, discos and karaoke parlours are springing up in all the major cities and more cultural entertainment is also being performed.

Cinemas

Upmarket hotels have in-house English-language movies, but elsewhere the situation is fairly dire. The few foreign movies that are shown in China are dubbed into Chinese. Hong Kong movies at least usually have inventive English subtitles – 'she my sister you call watermelon fool!' – and can be entertaining when you are in the mood for historical kung fu epics and fast-paced police dramas.

Discos

Discos have taken China by storm. In rural China, not many Chinese are really sure of the appropriate moves to make to a pounding bass, and it's not unusual to see huge crowds dancing in formation, everyone looking over their shoulders to see what everyone else is doing. But in cities like Guǎngzhōu, Shànghǎi and Běijīng, there are disco complexes (look out for the JJ chain) where the music and the dancers are hip to the latest international trends. See the entertainment entries for Guǎngzhōu, Shànghǎi and Běijīng for some suggestions.

Karaoke

If you don't know what karaoke *(kǎlā OK)* is by now, China will be a rude awakening. This is *the* entertainment option for moneyed Chinese. Even the plebs are leaping in, yodelling in search of a melody at roadside karaoke stalls.

The CCP propaganda department has weighed in with suitably proletarian sing-along hits, Chinese business people from Hǎinán to Hēilóngjiāng slug back the XO and caterwaul with hostesses on their knees, and no doubt Party leaders get together for wine and songs after a hard day at the office sentencing dissidents and keeping the economic miracle on track. 'Let's get together and sing some songs' is what Chinese say to each other when it's time to unwind.

Much maligned by westerners, karaoke can be fun with enough drinks under your belt and with the right people. It's not unusual for inebriated westerners who claim to hate karaoke to have to be pried loose from the microphone once they get going.

Warning One thing to watch out for in karaoke parlours is rip-offs. In some heavily touristed areas, young women work as touts. You may not even realise that they are touts – they will 'invite' any likely looking male to join them at a nearby karaoke bar, but no sooner than the bottle of XO is ordered then the woman 'disappears' and the hapless male is presented with a bill for US$200.

It is not sensible to accept invitations to clubs from young women on the streets. In clubs themselves, if you invite a hostess to sit with you, it is going to cost you money – the same rules apply in China as anywhere else in the world of paid entertainment and sex.

Crosstalk

Back in the days before karaoke and MTV, the Chinese had to entertain themselves with pun-laden stand-up comedy acts and story-telling. This is known as *xiàngshēng* (crosstalk). Unfortunately, you'd have to be extremely fluent at Mandarin to make any sense out of this – it's extremely difficult to translate because it relies to a great extent on Chinese sound-alike words. Much of the unintelligible noise emanating from the loudspeaker on the trains and buses is just this sort of crosstalk.

SPECTATOR SPORTS

If there is any spectator sport the Chinese have a true passion for, it's soccer. Games are devoutly covered in the mass media and it's possible to see live matches when the team comes to Běijīng. China has dreams of eventually taking the World Cup, and the government has been throwing money into the project by importing players and coaches. The season runs approximately from April to November.

Although it hasn't quite fired the Chinese imagination the way soccer has, basketball does provide entertainment during the long winter when playing outdoors means risking frostbite. China's professional league, the China Basketball Association (CBA), even recruits players from the USA.

Perhaps of more interest to foreigners are international sporting events. Běijīng hosted the Asian Games in 1990 and China has thrown in bids (so far unsuccessfully) to host the Olympic Games.

SHOPPING

The Chinese produce some interesting items for export – tea, clothing and Silkworm missiles (the latter not generally for sale to the public).

Gone are the days of ration cards and empty department stores – China is in the grip of a consumer revolution. The new China looks more and more like the old Hong Kong by the day. However, it's still sensible to save your shopping for imported electronic consumer items for Hong Kong and Macau – import duties are still too high in the rest of China. For most visitors, shopping in China is restricted to souvenirs.

The so-called 'Friendship Stores' (not notable for friendly staff) were set up to cater to foreign needs back in the days when ordinary Chinese basically had no access to imported luxury items. It is a measure of just how far China has come when you think how, just 10 years ago, many Chinese dreamed of simply getting through the doors of a Friendship Store.

Nowadays, Friendship Stores are an anachronism and have become one of the many chains of department stores stacked to the rafters with consumer goodies. However, the Friendship Stores are still useful in that they carry foreign reading matter not easily

obtainable elsewhere in China, and there are usually some staff who can speak English. Some Friendship Stores are good venues for finding souvenirs, and can even arrange shipping back to your home country.

The regular Chinese department stores all stock a broad range of cheap, everyday consumer items. They are definitely worth checking out.

Hotel gift shops are still useful to pick up western and Japanese slide film and imported magazines, among other things. On the whole, they tend to be expensive places for shopping, but can be a lifesaver when you're desperate for something to read.

Blankets spread on the pavement and pushcarts in the alleys – this is where you find the lowest prices. In street markets, all sales are final; forget about warranties and, no, they don't accept Amex. Nevertheless, the markets are interesting, but be prepared to bargain hard.

Service standards have been steadily improving in China over the past few years. In the recent past it was usual to be ignored by shop assistants as they read comics and chatted over jam jars of tea. Now with some real competition, shops are pushing their staff to be polite and attend to customers. The authorities have gotten in on the act, with public campaigns urging workers in service industries not to spit and to try smiling at customers. Even railway staff now manage the occasional tight-lipped smile as they toss passengers a rice-box lunch for the afternoon meal.

Antiques

Many of the Friendship Stores have antique sections and some cities have antique shops, but in the case of genuine antiques you can forget about bargains. Chinese are very savvy when it comes to their own cultural heritage. Only antiques that have been cleared for sale to foreigners may be taken out of the country.

When you buy an item over 100 years old it will come with an official red wax seal attached. This seal does *not* necessarily indicate that the item is an antique though. A Canadian who bought 'real' jade for Y1500

More Than Meets the Eye ...

Once upon a time in China you got what you paid for. If the sales clerk said it was top-quality jade then it was top-quality jade. Times have changed – now there are all sorts of cheap forgeries and imitations about, from Tibetan jewellery to Qing coins, phoney Marlboro cigarettes, fake Sony Walkmans (complete with fake Maxell cassette tapes), imitation Rolex watches, even fake Garden biscuits (Garden Bakeries is Hong Kong's biggest seller of bread, cakes and biscuits).

China has implemented a major crackdown on counterfeiting, although efforts have been directed mainly towards items that flout international intellectual copyright laws: CDs, pirated software and the like. It's a big country, however, and there are still a lot of illegal consumer goods out there.

At the same time, the government has to contend with more localised problems: the manufacture of fake train tickets, fake lottery tickets and fake Y100 notes. Cadres frequently pad their expense accounts with fake receipts – one of the many reasons why state-run companies are losing money.

Take care if you are forking out a large sum for something. Watch out for counterfeit Y100 notes. And if you are after genuine antiques, try to get an official certificate of verification – just make sure the ink is dry.

at a Friendship Store in Guìlín later discovered in Hong Kong that it was a plastic fake. After six months of copious correspondence and investigation, the Guìlín Tourism Bureau refunded the money. (Note, however, that while Friendship Stores around the country are generally accountable for their goods and will give refunds, this is not the norm. At all other stores in China, once you've handed over your cash it's gone for good.) You'll also get a receipt of sale, which you must show to customs when you leave the country; otherwise the antique will be confiscated. Imitation antiques are sold everywhere. Some museum shops sell replicas, usually at extravagant prices.

Stamps & Coins

China issues quite an array of beautiful stamps that are generally sold at post offices in the hotels. Outside many of the post offices you'll find amateur philatelists with books full of stamps for sale; it can be extraordinarily hard bargaining with these enthusiasts! Stamps issued during the Cultural Revolution make interesting souvenirs, but these rare items are no longer cheap. Old coins are often sold at major tourist sites, but many are forgeries.

Paintings & Scrolls

Watercolours, oils, woodblock prints, calligraphy – there is a lot of art for sale in China. Tourist centres like Guìlín, Sūzhōu, Běijīng and Shànghǎi are good places to look out for paintings.

Prices are usually very reasonable – even some of the high quality work available in galleries. In the eyes of connoisseurs, the scrolls selling for Y200 are usually rubbish, but remain popular purchases all the same.

Oddities

If plaster statues are to your liking, the opportunities to stock up in China are abundant. Fat buddhas appear everywhere, and 60cm-high Venus de Milos and multi-armed gods with flashing lights are not uncommon.

Lots of shops sell medicinal herbs and spices. Export tea is sold in extravagantly decorated tins – you can often get a better deal buying the same thing at train stations.

CHINESE CUISINE

One of the most common greetings used by Chinese everywhere is, 'Chī fànle ma?' Although this is usually translated as 'Have you eaten yet?', which is taken to show the significance of food in Chinese culture, the literal translation – 'Have you eaten rice yet?' – reveals the importance of rice in the development of Chinese culture. In fact, fàn may be more loosely translated as 'grain' – as opposed to cài, which literally means 'vegetable' and, by extension, any accompaniment to grain in a meal. The principle that a proper meal is based around a staple grain dates back at least to the Shang dynasty (1554–1045 BC) and remains fundamental to Chinese cuisine wherever it is found.

The dichotomy between fàn and cài also shows how the principles of balance and harmony, Yin and Yang, are applied in everyday life. Most vegetables and fruits are Yin foods, generally moist or soft, and are meant to have a cooling effect, nurturing the feminine aspect of our nature. (Contrary to what you might expect, post-natal mothers should not eat Yin foods.) Yang foods – fried, spicy or with red meat – are warming and nourish the masculine side of our nature. Any meal should not only harmonise a variety of tastes, but also provide a balance between cooling and warming foods. Historically, though, fàn (grain) has played a more important role than cài; one of the highest compliments that can be paid to a dish is that it 'helps the rice go down' (hsai fàn).

Cooking in China is divided into four schools: the Northern, Eastern, Western and Southern. The differences among them arose not only from geographical and climatic differences, but also from historical and cultural circumstances. Ironically, it was not until China was under threat from the Jurchen Mongols in the 12th century, when the Song court fled south of the Cháng Jiāng (Yangzi River), that these regional cuisines were codified and developed. Widespread urbanisation, made possible by the commercialisation of agriculture and food distribution, gave rise to the restaurant industry, which in turn facilitated the development of the regional cuisines. A further impetus was provided by demand from the merchants and bureaucrats who constantly travelled the kingdom.

The Mongol conquest of the north, China's wheat bowl, also precipitated the shift to rice as the main staple. This was a significant change, as rice is the best source of nutritionally balanced calories and can therefore support more people from a given area than any other crop. Improved communications, notably the building of the Grand Canal to link many of China's innumerable waterways, allowed food to be brought from and supplied to any part of the kingdom.

During the Ming dynasty (1368–1644), the restaurant industry continued to flourish. At this time, the court kitchens in the Forbidden City alone are reputed to have employed 5000 people. Refrigeration – blocks of ice were cut from northern rivers and lakes in winter and stored in deep caves for use in summer – allowed further diversification and use of products out of season. The last significant development in Chinese cuisine, however, took place in the Qing dynasty (1644–1911), when crops were introduced from the New World. Maize, sweet potatoes and peanuts – which flourished in climates where rice, wheat and millet wouldn't grow – made life possible in formerly uninhabitable areas. The other significant import from the New World was red chillies, which are not only a spice, but also a concentrated source of vitamins A and C.

The Northern School

In the north, the fàn is traditionally wheat or millet rather than rice. Its most common incarnations are as *jiǎozi* (steamed dumplings) and *chūnjuan* (spring rolls), while arguably the most famous Chinese dish of all, Běijīng duck, is also served with typical northern ingredients: wheat pancakes, spring onions and fermented bean paste. The range of cài is limited in the north, so there is a heavy reliance on freshwater fish and chicken; cabbage is ubiquitous and seems to fill any available space on trains, buses and lorries in the winter.

JULIET COOMBE

Not surprisingly, the influence of the Mongols is felt most strongly in the north and two of the region's most famous culinary exports – Mongolian barbecue and Mongolian hotpot – are adaptations from Mongol field kitchens. Animals that were hunted on horseback could be dismembered and cooked with wild vegetables and onions using soldiers' iron shields on top of hot coals as primitive barbecues. Alternatively, each soldier could use their helmet as a pot, filling it with water, meat, condiments and vegetables to taste. Mutton is now the main ingredient in Mongolian hotpot.

Roasting was once considered rather barbaric in other parts of China, and is still more common in the north. The main methods of cooking in the northern style, though, are steaming, baking and 'explode-frying'. The last of these is the most common, historically because of the scarcity of fuel and, more recently, due to the introduction of the peanut, which thrives in the north and produces an abundance of oil. Although northern-style food has a reputation for being unsophisticated and bland, it has the benefit of being filling and therefore well suited to the cold climate.

Ānhuī 安徽

Smoked shad with tea	*Máofēng xūn shíyú*	毛峰熏鲥鱼
Stewed Mandarin fish with mutton	*yú yǎo yáng*	鱼咬羊
Stewed preserved Mandarin fish	*yān xiān guìyú*	腌鲜鳜鱼
Steamed crab with roe and shrimp	*xiè huáng xiā zhōng*	蟹黄虾盅
Preserved crab in Chinese wine	*Túnxī zuì xiè*	屯溪醉蟹
Deep-fried mutton	*jiāo zhá yángròu*	焦炸羊肉
Blanched smoked chicken	*shēng xūn zǐ jī*	生熏子鸡
Chicken wrapped in lotus leaf	*qīngxiāng shā wǔ jī*	清香沙梧鸡
Steamed pigeon with yam	*Huángshān dùn gē*	黄山炖鸽
Deep-fried and stewed bean curd with pork and shrimp	*hóngwǔ dòufu*	洪武豆腐

Shāndōng 山东

Steamed shrimp, chicken and dried scallops	xiùqiú gānbèi	绣球干贝
Stewed sea cucumber with scallion	cōng shāo hǎishēn	葱烧海参
Hot and sour fish egg and coriander soup	huì wūguī dan	烩乌龟蛋
Salty and sour flounder and scallion soup	kuà dùn mùyú	侉炖目鱼
Deep-fried sweet and sour carp	tángcù lǐyù	糖醋鲤鱼
Hot and sour Mandarin fish and scallion soup	cù jiāo guiyú	醋椒鳜鱼
Stir-fried pork tenderloin with coriander	yuán bào lǐjī	芫爆里脊
Stir-fried pig's tripe and kidney	yóu bào shuāng cuì	油爆双脆
Spicy braised pig's intestine	jiǔ zhuǎn dàcháng	九转大肠
Stir-fried chicken, fish and bamboo shoots	zāo līu sān bái	糟熘三白
Steamed and fried pork, shrimp and bamboo shoot balls	sì xǐ wánzi	四喜丸子
Stir-fried chicken and jelly fish	chǎo jī sī zhé tóu	炒鸡丝蜇头
Stir-fried chicken with egg white	fúróng jī piàn	芙蓉鸡片
Stir-fried chicken with bamboo shoots	jiàng bào jī dīng	酱爆鸡丁
Steamed bean curd, minced pork and black fungus	bó shān dòufu xiāng	博山豆腐箱
Boiled lotus seeds with sugar crystal	bīngtáng liánzǐ	冰糖莲子
Deep-fried and stewed bean curd, egg and shrimp	guō tā dòufu hé	锅塌豆腐盒
Sliced bean curd with Chinese cabbage	sān měi dòufu	三美豆腐
Deep-fried egg yolk with essence of banana	xiāngjiāo guō zhá	香蕉锅炸
Sweet and crispy deep-fried apple	bāsī píngguǒ	拔丝苹果

The Eastern School

The eastern region – blessed with the bounty of the Cháng Jiāng and its tributaries, a subtropical climate, fertile soil and a coastline – has long been a mecca for gastronomes. The Southern Song capital of Hángzhōu, on the banks of Xī Hú (West Lake) with its abundant fish, including the highly esteemed silver carp, is the birthplace of the restaurant industry. At least one restaurant, the Lóuwàiyóu, has survived the intervening 800 years. Sūzhōu is equally famous for its cuisine, which has been eulogised by generations of poets.

A vast variety of ingredients and condiments is available, which has led to a wide diversity of cuisine within the region. Explode-frying is used here, too, but not as much as the form of frying known as archetypally Chinese throughout the world: stir-frying in a wok. Another eastern style of cooking that has been exported to the rest of the world (from Fújiàn via Taiwan) is the red-stew, in which meat is simmered slowly in dark soy sauce, sugar and spices. Indeed, many Fújiàn dishes rely on a heavy, meaty stock for their distinctive flavour. Nonetheless, it is in this region that Chinese vegetarian cuisine reached its apex, partly thanks to the availability of fresh ingredients and partly to the specialisation of generations of chefs. As might be expected, seasoning is light to allow the natural flavours of the fresh ingredients to be fully appreciated.

GLENN BEANLAND

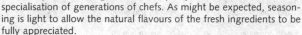

Jiāngsū 江苏

Stir-fried clam, water chestnut and mushroom	tiānxià dìyī xiān	天下第一鲜
Steamed crab	qīngzhēng dàzháxiè	清蒸大闸蟹
Deep-fried Mandarin fish with shrimp and bamboo shoots	sōngshǔ guìyú	松鼠鳜鱼
Hot and sour fish soup	cùliū guìyú	醋溜鳜鱼
Boiled fish liver with bamboo shoots	qīngtāng tū fèi	清汤秃肺
Fish tail stew	qīngyú shuǎi shuǐ	青鱼甩水
Deep-fried and stewed eel	Wúxī cuì shàn	无锡脆鳝
Carp and water shield	chúncài cuān tángyú piàn	莼菜汆塘鱼片
Blanched eel tail	qiàng hǔ wěi	炝虎尾
Braised carp head	chāi huì liányú tóu	拆烩鲢鱼头
Deep-fried pork with pea shoots	biān dǎ kū sū	扁大枯酥
Braised pork and crab meat balls	xiè fěn shīzi tóu	蟹粉狮子头
Boiled pig's trotters	Zhènjiāng yáo ròu	镇江肴肉
Salty and sweet stewed spareribs	Wúxī ròu gútou	无锡肉骨头
Braised duck and pigeon	sān tào yā	三套鸭
Roasted hen with ham, pork and mushrooms	jiàohuā jī	叫花鸡
Steamed turtle and chicken	bàwáng bié jī	霸王别姬
Boiled egg, stewed with minced pork	shénxiān dàn	神仙蛋
Stir-fried duck's giblets with chicken	měirén gān	美人肝
Shredded chicken with bean curd soup	wénsì dòufu	文思豆腐

Fújiàn 福建

Braised shark's fin with scallops and sea cucumber	*fó tiào qiáng*	佛跳墙
Steamed sturgeon	*bābǎo fúróng xún*	八宝芙蓉鲟
Fried eel	*jiān zāo mànyú*	煎糟鳗鱼
Roast Mandarin fish	*cōng yóu kǎo yú*	葱油烤鱼
Fish ball soup with eel, shrimp and pork	*qīxīng yú wán tāng*	七星鱼丸汤
Steamed pork with dried mustard	*cài gān kòu ròu*	菜干扣肉
Stewed frog with mushrooms	*yóu mèn shílín*	油焖石鳞
Steamed bird's nest with shredded chicken	*jī sī yànwō*	鸡丝燕窝
Chicken with glutinous rice	*jiā hé cuì pí jī*	嘉禾脆皮鸡
Chicken skin and mushroom soup	*jī pí mógu tāng*	鸡皮蘑菇汤

Zhèjiāng (Hángzhōu) 浙江（杭州）

Mandarin fish soup with ham and mushrooms	*Sòngsǎo yú gēng*	宋嫂鱼羹
Stewed sweet and sour fish	*Xīhú cù yú*	西湖醋鱼
Stewed yellowfin croaker with potherb mustard	*xuěcài dàtāng huángyú*	雪菜大汤黄鱼
Stir-fried eel with onion	*níng shì shànyú*	宁式鳝鱼
Stir-fried shrimp in tea	*lóngjīng xiārén*	龙井虾仁
Stewed pork	*dōngpō ròu*	东坡肉
Steamed pork wrapped in lotus leaf	*héyè fěnzhēng ròu*	荷叶粉蒸肉
Boiled chicken	*qīngtāng yuè jī*	清汤越鸡
Water shield soup	*Xīhú chúncài tāng*	西湖莼菜汤
Stewed bamboo shoots	*yóu mèn chūn sǔn*	油焖春笋

The Western School

The Western School is renowned most for its use of the red chilli, introduced by Spanish traders in the early Qing dynasty. While northern foods evolved to provide lasting satisfaction in a cold climate, Sìchuān dishes tend to dry out the body through perspiration, which helps it adjust to the intense humidity. Again, with a subtropical climate and the aid of an irrigation system supplied by the Mín Hé for over two millennia, fresh ingredients are available year-round, although not in the abundance or variety found in the east or south of the country. Pork, poultry, legumes and soybeans are the most commonly used cài, supplemented by a variety of wild condiments and mountain products, such as mushrooms and other fungi, as well as bamboo shoots. Seasonings are heavy: the red chilli is often used in conjunction with Sìchuān peppercorns, garlic, ginger and onions. Apart from its medicinal and nutritional values, fiery seasonings stimulate the palate and help the fàn go down in a province where the choice of cài is quite limited. Meat, particularly in Húnán, is marinated, pickled or otherwise processed before cooking, which is generally by stir- or explode-frying.

The cuisine of the Eastern School has a reputation as being down-to-earth, rather like the inhabitants of the region. Mao Zedong hailed from Húnán and remained fond of the hot foods from his native province throughout his life. However, it was due to the nationalists in the civil war that Sìchuān cuisine gained international recognition. Fleeing the Japanese in 1937, the nationalist government took refuge in Chóngqìng until the end of the war in Asia. On its return to Nánjīng and Shànghǎi, thousands of Sìchuān chefs were brought along. Most of them continued on to Taiwan when the nationalist government was forced to flee once more, and from there spread out across the globe.

BRADLEY MAYHEW

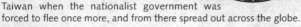

Sìchuān 四川

Stewed sea cucumber with pork and soybean sprouts	jiācháng hǎishēn	家常海参
Stewed carp with ham with hot and sweet sauce	gānshāo yán lǐ	干烧岩鲤
Stewed eel with garlic	dàsuàn shàn duàn	大蒜鳝段
Stewed beef with innards in a hot sauce	fūqī fèi piàn	夫妻肺片
Boiled and stir-fried pork with salty and hot sauce	huíguō ròu	回锅肉
Boiled pork with minced garlic	suàn ní bái ròu	蒜泥白肉
Stir-fried pork tenderloin with crispy rice	guōbā ròu piàn	锅巴肉片
Stir-fried pork, bamboo shoots and black fungus	yú xiāng ròu sī	鱼香肉丝
Fried and boiled beef, garlic sprouts and celery	shuǐ zhǔ niúròu	水煮牛肉
Stir-fried beef and celery with chilli	gānbiān niúròu sī	干煸牛肉丝
Braised oxtail in wine	qīngdùn niú wěi	清炖牛尾
Stir-fried pork or beef tenderloin with tuber mustard	zhàcài ròu sī	榨菜肉丝
Boiled chicken in a hot sauce	bàngbang jī	棒棒鸡
Stir-fried chicken with peanuts	gōngbǎo jī dīng	宫保鸡丁
Stir-fried chicken with hot Sichuān pepper	huājiāo jī dīng	花椒鸡丁
Chicken and ham soup	jī dòuhuā	鸡豆花
Stewed chicken wings in red wine	guìfēi jī chì	贵妃鸡翅
Deep-fried and stewed vermicelli and minced beef	mǎyǐ shàng shù	蚂蚁上树
Stewed bean curd and minced beef	mápó dòufu	麻婆豆腐
Chinese cabbage soup	kāishuǐ báicài	开水白菜

Top: Local farmers in Dàlǐ harvest their crops.

Middle & Bottom: Market stalls in Líjiāng display their fresh produce.

HILARY ADELE SMITH

KRAIG LIEB

MARIE CAMBON

Top & Middle: Eating at street stalls is a cheap and tasty way of sampling local fare, which ranges from noodles in Běijīng to sizzling Dai specialities in Měnghǎi, Yúnnán.

Bottom: Wake up in Shàoxīng, Zhèjiāng, and indulge in onion pancakes for breakfast.

Vendors show off their spectacular noodle-making skills on the streets of Běijīng

Variation in food across the different regions of China is vast. A local of Xiàhé in the north-eastern province of Gānsù grinds spices; a Uyghur man carefully weighs his watermelon in Xīnjiāng; and a Uyghur woman sells her beautifully decorated bread in Kashgar, Xīnjiāng.

Húnán 湖南

Stir-fried and steamed sea cucumber with chicken and duck	*hǎishēn zhēng pén*	海参蒸盆
Boiled sliced fish	*húdié piāo hǎi*	蝴蝶飘海
Roasted Mandarin fish	*wǎng yóu chāshāo guìyú*	网油叉烧鳜鱼
Braised turtle with pork	*dòngtíng jīn guī*	洞庭金龟
Steamed pork with preserved soybeans	*zǒu yóu dòuchǐ kòu ròu*	走油豆豉扣肉
Stewed preserved pork	*xiāngxī suān ròu*	湘西酸肉
Steamed dried preserved pork with chicken and carp	*làwèi hé zhēng*	腊味合蒸
Stir-fried chicken with chilli	*málà zǐ jī*	麻辣子鸡
Steamed and stir-fried chestnut with cabbage	*bǎnlì shāo càixīn*	板栗烧菜心
Lotus seeds and crystal sugar soup	*bīngtáng xiāng lián*	冰糖湘莲

The Southern School

The food from this region is the most common form of Chinese food found in the western world, as most overseas Chinese have their roots in the Guǎngdōng region. The humid climate and heavy rainfall mean that rice has been a staple here since the Chinese first came to the region in the Han era (206–220 BC). The Southern School benefits from a cornucopia of ingredients to choose from, and in the south the choices are exotic. Stir-frying is the most favoured method of cooking, closely followed by steaming. Dim sum, now a worldwide Sunday institution, originated in this region; to go *yám cha* (Cantonese for 'drink tea') still provides most overseas Chinese communities with the opportunity to get together.

Not only are the ingredients more varied than elsewhere in China, methods of preparation also reach their peak of sophistication in the south, where the appearance and texture of foods are prized alongside their freshness. Such refinement is a far cry from the austere cuisine of the north and the earthy fare of the west. Consequently, the southerners' gourmandising and exotic tastes – for dogs, cats, raccoons, monkeys, lizards and rats – have earned them a long-established reputation around China.

Guǎngdōng (Cantonese) 广东

Stewed shark's fin with pork and chicken feet	*hóngshāo dà qún chì*	红烧大群翅
Steamed lobster	*shēng chuī lóngxiā*	生炊龙虾
Stir-fried crab with ginger and scallions	*jiāng cōng chǎo xiè*	姜葱炒蟹

Stewed abalone with bamboo shoots and oyster sauce	háoyóu wǎng bào piàn	蚝油网鲍片
Blanched prawns with shredded scallion	bái zhuó xiā	白灼虾
Stir-fried prawns with coriander and chilli	jiāo yán xiā	椒盐虾
Roast pork with sweet syrup	mì zhī chāshāo	蜜汁叉烧
Sweet and sour deep-fried pork with pineapple	bōluó gǔlǎo ròu	菠萝咕唠肉
Stir-fried beef with bamboo shoots in oyster sauce	háoyóu niúròu	蚝油牛肉
Stir-fried beef tenderloin with black pepper	tiěbǎn hēi jiāo niúliǔ	铁板黑椒牛排
Smoked chicken with tea and sugar	tàiyé jī	太爷鸡
Salt-baked chicken	dōngjiāng yán jú jī	东江盐焗鸡
Stir-fried snake meat with mushrooms and bamboo shoots	wǔcǎi chǎo shé sī	五彩炒蛇丝
Stir-fried ham and milk	dàliáng chǎo xiān nǎi	大良炒鲜奶
Boiled chicken with scallion and peppercorn	bái qiē jī	白切鸡
Boiled chicken with ham and bok choy	jīnhuá yùshù jī	金华玉树鸡
Stir-fried dog meat with garlic	yuán bāo gǒu ròu	原煲狗肉
Stir-fried and stewed sweet potato leaves and straw mushrooms	hù guó cài	护国菜
Steamed white gourd with duck, ham and shrimp	dōngguā zhōng	冬瓜盅
Deep-fried and stewed noodles with shrimp and mushrooms	gānshāo yīfǔ miàn	干烧伊府面

Food Etiquette

Eating Chinese-style is well-established in the west and wouldn't faze most people these days. It's a rewarding way to eat for many reasons. First, eating together really does mean sharing food since all diners eat cài from communal bowls, making it much more of a social event than western-style eating (and arguably contributing to closer family bonds). On the one hand, no one wants to appear greedy by taking too much and depriving others. On the other, people can eat as much or as little as they want from each bowl, according to their own taste, without offending the host. This method of serving even allows people to select combinations of foods to eat together to suit their own taste, particularly when a variety of sauces and dips are provided as accompaniments.

Although Chinese restaurants have a reputation in the west for being noisy, tasteless and basic (Formica tables, tacky calendars and plastic chopsticks), this only shows that westerners don't appreciate the same things when going out to eat. While most westerners need to feel they've got value for money by the quality of the ambience and service, for most Chinese the quality of the food is paramount. Good restaurants gain a reputation solely for the quality of their food, no matter what the decor and no matter how far out of the way.

However, there are a few dos and don'ts in Chinese food etiquette, mostly applicable only when you dine with Chinese. The most important is probably who pays the bill: although you are expected to try to pay, you shouldn't argue too hard as the one who extended the invitation will inevitably foot the bill. Going Dutch is unheard of except among the closest of friends. Other things to remember are to fill your neighbours' tea cups when they are empty, as yours will be by them. You can thank the pourer by tapping your middle finger on the table gently. On no account serve yourself tea without serving others first. Don't place your chopsticks in your rice while you are doing something else; this makes the bowl reminiscent of an offering to the dead and is regarded as very bad form. Finally, in deference to the importance of fàn in Chinese history and culture, it is considered impolite to leave rice in your individual bowl at the end of a meal, especially if all cài dishes have been eaten. Even today, Chinese children are admonished to eat their rice as western children are told to eat their greens.

Uyghur Food

Uyghur cuisine reflects the influences of Xīnjiāng's chequered past. Yet, despite centuries of sporadic Chinese and Mongol rule, the strongest influence on ingredients and methods is still Turkic or Middle Eastern, which is evident in the reliance on mutton for protein (roughly, cài) and wheat for the staple grain (fàn). When rice is eaten, it is often in the Central Asian version of pilau (plov). Nevertheless, the influence of Chinese culinary styles and ingredients makes it probably the most enjoyable region of Central Asia in which to eat.

Uyghur bread resembles Arabic khoubz (Indian nan) and is baked in ovens based on the tanour (Indian tandoor) model. It is often eaten straight from the oven and sprinkled with poppy seeds, sesame seeds or fennel. Uyghur bakers also make excellent bagels (girde nan). Wheat is also used for a variety of noodles. Laghman (lāmián in Chinese) are the most common: al dente, thick and topped with a combination of spicy mutton, peppers, tomatoes, eggplant, green beans and garlic. Suoman are noodle squares fried with tomatoes peppers garlic and meat, sometimes quite spicy. Suoman goshsiz is the vegetarian variety.

Kebabs are common, as they are throughout the Middle East and Central Asia, both shashlik- and tandoori-style. Samsas or samsis are the Uyghur version of samosas: baked envelopes of meat. Hotan and Kashgar specialise in huge meat pies called daman or (gosh girde). Meat often makes an appearance inside dumplings (chuchura), which can be steamed or fried.

Xīnjiāng is justly famous for its fruit; its apricots, grapes, watermelons, sweet melons and raisins can be found all over China. The best grapes in China come from Turpan, while Hami melons have gained an international reputation for their sweetness.

CRAIG PERSHOUSE

Drinks

Nonalcoholic Drinks

Tea is the most commonly served brew in the PRC. The origins of tea-drinking are obscure, but legend has it that it was first cultivated in China about 4000 years ago in the modern-day province of Sìchuān. Although black (fermented) tea is produced in China, principally in the Huáng Shān area (Ānhuī), green (unfermented) is by far the most widely drunk. Indian and Sri Lankan black tea is available only in international supermarkets. Familiar brands of instant coffee are for sale everywhere, but fresh-brewed coffee is virtually unknown.

Sugary Chinese soft drinks are cheap and ubiquitous. Jianlibao is a soft drink made with honey rather than sugar. Lychee-flavoured carbonated drinks are unique to China and seem to be a favourite with foreign travellers.

A surprising treat is fresh sweet yoghurt, available in many parts of China. It's typically sold in what looks like small milk bottles and is drunk with a straw rather than eaten with a spoon. Fresh milk is rare, but you can buy imported UHT milk from supermarkets in big cities.

Coca-Cola, first introduced to China by American soldiers in 1927, is now produced locally. Chinese attempts at making similar brews include TianFu Cola, which has a recipe based on the root of herbaceous peony.

Alcoholic Drinks

If tea is the most popular drink in the PRC, then beer must be number two. By any standards the top brands are good. The best known is Tsingtao, made with a mineral water that gives it a sparkling quality. It's essentially a German beer since the town of Qīngdǎo (formerly spelled 'Tsingtao'), where it's made, was once a German concession and the Chinese inherited the brewery. Experts claim that draft Tsingtao tastes much better than the bottled stuff. Local brews are found in all the major cities of China. Notable brands that are worth a taste include Zhujiang in Guǎngzhōu and Yanjing in Běijīng. San Miguel has a brewery in Guǎngzhōu, so you can enjoy this 'imported' beer at Chinese prices.

China has cultivated vines and produced wine for an estimated 4000 years. Chinese wine-producing techniques differ from those of the west. Quality-conscious wine producers in western countries work on the idea that the lower the yield the higher the quality of the wine produced. But Chinese farmers cultivate every possible square centimetre of earth; they encourage their vines to yield heavily and also plant peanuts between the rows of vines as a cover crop for half the year. The peanuts sap much of the nutrient from the soil, and in cooler years the large grape crop fails to ripen sufficiently to produce good wine.

Western producers try to prevent oxidation in their wines, but oxidation produces a flavour that Chinese tipplers find desirable and go to great lengths to achieve. Chinese diners are also keen on wines with different herbs and other materials soaked in them, which they drink for their health and for restorative or aphrodisiac qualities.

The word 'wine' gets rather loosely translated – many Chinese 'wines' are in fact spirits. Rice wine is intended mainly for cooking rather than drinking.

Hejie Jiu (lizard wine) is produced in the southern province of Guǎngxī; each bottle contains one dead lizard suspended perpendicularly in the clear liquid.

Wine with dead bees or pickled snakes is also desirable for its alleged tonic properties – in general, the more poisonous the creature, the more potent the tonic effects.

Tibetans have an interesting brew called *chang*, a brew made from barley. Mongolians serve sour-tasting *koumiss*, made of fermented mare's milk with lots of salt added. *Maotai*, a favourite of Chinese drinkers, is a spirit made from sorghum (a type of millet) and used for toasts at banquets.

Getting There & Away

AIR
Airports & Airlines

Hong Kong, Běijīng and Shànghǎi are China's main international air gateways. While in the past the cheapest way to get to China has been via Hong Kong, these days there is not that much variation in fares to Hong Kong and the mainland cities.

The Civil Aviation Administration of China (CAAC; Zhōngguó Mín Yong Háng Kong Zong Ju) acts as China's civil aviation authority. Although it operates a few uneconomical services, most flights are run by one of China's 30 or so airlines, only a handful of which operate international flights. Although their safety record has been fairly poor in the past, it is improving: China has seen only two fatal accidents in the past six years. Air China, China's national flag carrier, has a 45-year safe-flying record.

Buying Tickets

Stiff competition has resulted in widespread discounting on air tickets – which is good news for travellers! Passengers flying in economy can usually manage some sort of discount, but unless you buy carefully and flexibly, it is still possible to end up paying exorbitant amounts for a journey.

For long-term travel there are plenty of discount tickets that are valid for 12 months, allowing multiple stopovers with open dates. When you're looking for bargain air fares, go to a travel agent rather than directly to the airline. Airlines do occasionally have promotional fares and special offers, but generally they only sell fares at the official listed price.

The days when some travel agents would routinely fleece travellers by running off with their money are, happily, almost over. Paying by credit card generally offers protection as most card issuers provide refunds if you can prove you didn't get what you paid for. Similar protection can be obtained by buying a ticket from a bonded agent,

such as one covered by the Air Transport Operators License (ATOL) scheme in the UK. Agents who only accept cash should hand over the tickets straight away and not tell you to 'come back tomorrow'. After you've made a booking or paid your deposit, call the airline and confirm that the booking was made. It's generally not advisable to send money (even cheques) through the post unless the agent is very well established – some travellers have reported being ripped off by fly-by-night mail-order ticket agents.

You may decide to pay more than the rock-bottom fare by opting for the safety of a better known travel agent. Firms such as STA Travel, which has offices worldwide, Council Travel in the USA and USIT Campus (formerly Campus Travel) in the UK are not going to disappear overnight and they do offer competitive prices to most destinations.

If you purchase a ticket and later want to make changes to your route or get a refund, you need to contact the original travel agent. Airlines only issue refunds to the purchaser of a ticket – usually the travel agent who bought the ticket on your behalf. Many travellers change their routes halfway through their trips, so think carefully before you buy a ticket that is not easily refunded.

Buying Tickets On Line Many airlines offer some excellent fares to Web surfers. They may sell seats by auction or simply cut prices to reflect the reduced cost of electronic selling. Numerous travel agents around the world have Web sites, which can make the Internet a quick and easy way to compare prices, a good start for when you're ready to start negotiating with your favourite travel agency. Online ticket sales work well if you are doing a simple one-way or return trip on specified dates. However, online superfast fare generators are no substitute for a travel agent who knows all about special deals, has strategies for avoiding layovers and can offer advice on everything from the airline that has the best vegetarian food to the best travel insurance to bundle with your ticket. Some Web sites for airlines are:

Aeroflot
www.aeroflot.org
Air Macau
www.airmacau.com.mo
Alitalia
www.alitalia.com
All Nippon Airways
www.ana.co.jp
American Airlines
www.aa.com
Asiana Airlines
www.asiana.co.kr
Austrian Airlines
www.aua.com
British Airways
www.british-airways.com
CAAC
www.caft.com
Canadian Airlines International
www.CdnAir.ca
Dragonair
www.dragonair.com

Ethiopian Airlines
www.ethiopianairlines.com
Finnair
www.finnair.fi
Japan Airlines
www.jal.co.jp
KLM–Royal Dutch Airlines
www.klm.nl
Korean Air
www.koreanair.com
LOT Polish Airlines
www.lot.com
Lufthansa Airlines
www.lufthansa.com
Malaysia Airlines
www.malaysia-airlines.com.my
Northwest Airlines
www.nwa.com
Pakistan International Airlines
www.fly-pia.com
Qantas Airways
www.qantas.com.au
Scandinavian Airlines
www.scandinavian.net
Singapore Airlines
www.singaporeair.com
Swissair
www.swissair.com
Tarom
tarom.digiro.net
Thai Airways International
www.thaiairways.com
Turkish Airlines
www.turkishairlines.com
United Airlines
www.ual.com
Virgin Atlantic
www.fly.virgin.com

Another useful Web site with good deals on flights to China from Canada and the USA is Fly China at www.flychina.com.

Departure Tax

If leaving China by air, the departure tax is Y90. This has to be paid in local currency, so be sure you have enough yuan to avoid a last-minute scramble at the airport money-changing booth.

The USA

Discount travel agents in the USA are known as consolidators (although you won't see a sign on the door saying consolidator). San Francisco is the ticket-consolidator capital of America, although some good deals can be found in Los Angeles, New York and other big cities. Consolidators can be found through the *Yellow Pages* or the major daily newspapers. The *New York Times*, the *Los Angeles Times*, the *Chicago Tribune* and the *San Francisco Examiner* all produce weekly travel sections in which you will find a number of travel agency ads.

Council Travel, America's largest student travel organisation, has around 60 offices in the USA; its head office (☎ 800-226 8624) is at 205 E 42 St, New York, NY 10017. Call it for the office nearest you or visit its Web site at www.ciee.org. STA Travel (☎ 800-777 0112) has offices in Boston, Chicago, Miami, New York, Philadelphia, San Francisco and other major cities. Call the toll-free ☎ 800 number for office locations or visit its Web site at www.statravel.com.

From the US west coast, low-season return fares to Hong Kong or Běijīng start at around US$750 with Korean Air, Northwest Airlines and United Airlines. Fares increase dramatically during summer and the Chinese New Year. From New York to Běijīng or Hong Kong, low-season return fares start at around US$890 with Korean Air, Northwest Airlines and United Airlines.

Canada

Canadian discount air ticket sellers are also known as consolidators and their air fares tend to be about 10% higher than those sold in the USA. The *Globe and Mail*, the *Toronto Star*, the *Montreal Gazette* and the *Vancouver Sun* carry travel agent ads and are a good place to look for cheap fares. Travel CUTS (☎ 800-667 2887) is Canada's national student travel agency and has offices in all major cities. Its Web address is www.travelcuts.com.

From Canada, fares to Hong Kong are often higher than those to Běijīng. Canadian Airlines, Air China and China Eastern sometimes run super-cheap fares. Return low-season fares between Vancouver and Běijīng start at around US$800.

Australia

Quite a few travel offices specialise in discount air tickets. Some travel agents, particularly smaller ones, advertise cheap air fares in the travel sections of weekend newspapers, such as the *Age* in Melbourne and the *Sydney Morning Herald.*

Two well known agents for cheap fares are STA Travel and Flight Centre. STA Travel (☎ 03-9349 2411) has its main office at 224 Faraday St, Carlton, Victoria, 3053, and offices in all major cities and on many university campuses. Call ☎ 131 776 Australia-wide for the location of your nearest branch or visit its Web site at www.statravel.com.au.

Flight Centre (☎ 131 600 Australia-wide) has a central office at 82 Elizabeth St, Sydney, and there are dozens of offices throughout Australia. Its Web address is www.flightcentre.com.au. From Australia, Hong Kong is a popular destination and is also the closest entry point into China. Although it's a shorter flight, fares from Australia to Hong Kong are generally not that much cheaper than fares to Běijīng or Shànghǎi. Low-season return fares to either Shànghǎi or Běijīng from the east coast of Australia start at around A$989, with fares to Hong Kong starting from A$980.

New Zealand

The *New Zealand Herald* has a travel section in which travel agents advertise fares. Flight Centre (☎ 09-309 6171) has a large central office in Auckland at National Bank Towers, corner Queen and Darby Sts, and many branches throughout the country. STA Travel (☎ 09-309 0458) has its main office at 10 High St, Auckland, and has other offices in Auckland as well as in Hamilton, Palmerston North, Wellington, Christchurch and Dunedin. The Web address is www.statravel.com.au.

International arlines such as Malaysia Airlines, Thai Airways International and Qantas Airways have return fares from Auckland to Hong Kong for around NZ$1355 during the low season. Return low-season fares to Běijīng start at NZ$1645 with Malaysia Airlines.

Air Travel Glossary

Cancellation Penalties If you have to cancel or change a discounted ticket, there are often heavy penalties involved; insurance can sometimes be taken out against these penalties. Some airlines impose penalties on regular tickets as well, particularly against 'no-show' passengers.

Courier Fares Businesses often need to send urgent documents or freight securely and quickly. Courier companies hire people to accompany the package through customs and, in return, offer a discount ticket which is sometimes a phenomenal bargain. However, you may have to surrender all your baggage allowance and take only carry-on luggage.

Full Fares Airlines traditionally offer 1st class (coded F), business class (coded J) and economy class (coded Y) tickets. These days there are so many promotional and discounted fares available that few passengers pay full economy fare.

Lost Tickets If you lose your airline ticket an airline will usually treat it like a travellers cheque and, after inquiries, issue you with another one. Legally, however, an airline is entitled to treat it like cash and if you lose it then it's gone forever. Take good care of your tickets.

Onward Tickets An entry requirement for many countries is that you have a ticket out of the country. If you're unsure of your next move, the easiest solution is to buy the cheapest onward ticket to a neighbouring country or a ticket from a reliable airline which can later be refunded if you do not use it.

Open-Jaw Tickets These are return tickets where you fly out to one place but return from another. If available, this can save you backtracking to your arrival point.

Overbooking Since every flight has some passengers who fail to show up, airlines often book more passengers than they have seats. Usually excess passengers make up for the no-shows, but occasionally somebody gets 'bumped' onto the next available flight. Guess who it is most likely to be? The passengers who check in late.

Promotional Fares These are officially discounted fares, available from travel agencies or direct from the airline.

Reconfirmation If you don't reconfirm your flight at least 72 hours prior to departure, the airline may delete your name from the passenger list. Ring to find out if your airline requires reconfirmation.

Restrictions Discounted tickets often have various restrictions on them – such as needing to be paid for in advance and incurring a penalty to be altered. Others are restrictions on the minimum and maximum period you must be away.

Round-the-World Tickets RTW tickets give you a limited period (usually a year) in which to circumnavigate the globe. You can go anywhere the carrying airlines go, as long as you don't backtrack. The number of stopovers or total number of separate flights is decided before you set off and they usually cost a bit more than a basic return flight.

Transferred Tickets Airline tickets cannot be transferred from one person to another. Travellers sometimes try to sell the return half of their ticket, but officials can ask you to prove that you are the person named on the ticket. On an international flight tickets are compared with passports.

Travel Periods Ticket prices vary with the time of year. There is a low (off-peak) season and a high (peak) season, and often a low-shoulder season and a high-shoulder season as well. Usually the fare depends on your outward flight – if you depart in the high season and return in the low season, you pay the high-season fare.

The UK

Airline ticket discounters are known as bucket shops in the UK. Despite the somewhat disreputable name, there is nothing under-the-counter about them. Discount air travel is big business in London. Advertisements for many travel agents appear in the travel pages of the weekend broadsheets, such as the *Independent on Saturday* and the *Sunday Times*. Look out for free magazines such as *TNT*, which are widely available in London – start by looking outside the main train and underground stations.

For students or travellers under 26, popular travel agencies in the UK include STA Travel (☎ 020-7361 6161), which has an office at 86 Old Brompton Rd, London SW7 3LQ, and other offices in London and Manchester. Visit its Web site at www .statravel.co.uk. USIT Campus Travel (☎ 020-7730 3402), 52 Grosvenor Gardens, London SW1WOAG, has branches throughout the UK. The Web address is www.usitca mpus.com. Both of these agencies sell tickets to all travellers but cater especially to young people and students.

Other recommended bucket shops include: Trailfinders (☎ 020-7938 3939), 194 Kensington High St, London W8 7RG; Bridge the World (☎ 020-7734 7447), 4 Regent Place, London W1R 5FB; and Flightbookers (☎ 020-7757 2000), 177-178 Tottenham Court Rd, London W1P 9LF.

From the UK, low-season return fares to either Běijīng or Hong Kong start at £430 with Gulf Air, Air France and Sabena.

Western Europe

Though London is the travel-discount capital of Europe, there are several other cities in which you will find a range of good deals. Generally there is not much variation in air fare prices from the main European cities. The major airlines and travel agents generally have a number of deals on offer, so shop around.

Across Europe many travel agencies have ties with STA Travel, where cheap tickets can be purchased and STA-issued tickets can be altered (usually for a US$25

fee). Outlets in major cities include: Voyages Wasteels (☎ 08 03 88 70 04 from within France, fax 01 43 25 46 25), 11 rue Dupuytren, 756006 Paris; STA Travel (☎ 030-311 0950, fax 313 0948), Goethestrasse 73, 10625 Berlin; Passaggi (☎ 06-474 0923, fax 482 7436), Stazione Termini FS, Gelleria Di Tesla, Rome; and ISYTS (☎ 01-322 1267, fax 323 3767), 11 Nikis St, Upper Floor, Syntagma Square, Athens.

France has a network of student travel agencies that can supply discount tickets to travellers of all ages. OTU Voyages (☎ 01 44 41 38 50) has a central Paris office at 39 Ave Georges Bernanos (5e) and another 42 offices around the country. The Web address is www.otu.fr. Acceuil des Jeunes en France (☎ 01 42 77 87 80), 119 rue Saint Martin (4e), is another popular discount travel agency.

General travel agencies in Paris that offer some of the best services and deals include Nouvelles Frontières (☎ 08 03 33 33 33), 5 Ave de l'Opéra (1er), which has a Web address at www.nouvelles-frontieres.com; and Voyageurs du Monde (☎ 01 42 86 16 00) at 55 rue Sainte Anne (2e).

Belgium, Switzerland and the Netherlands are also good places for buying discount air tickets. In Belgium, Acotra Student Travel Agency (☎ 02- 512 86 07), at rue de la Madeline, Brussels, and WATS Reizen (☎ 03-226 16 26), at de Keyserlei 44, Antwerp, are both well-known agencies. In Switzerland, SSR Voyages (☎ 01-297 11 11) specialises in student, youth and budget fares. In Zurich there is a branch at Leonhardstrasse 10 and there are branches in most major cities. The Web address is www.ssr.ch.

In the Netherlands NBBS Reizen is the official student travel agency. You can find it in Amsterdam (☎ 020-624 09 89), at Rokin 6,6 and there are several other agencies around the city. Another recommended travel agent in Amsterdam is Malibu Travel (☎ 020-626 32 30), at Prinsengracht 230.

Russia

Air China and Aeroflot have direct flights connecting Běijīng and Moscow. Return flights cost US$1203. Xinjiang Airlines also has a flights from Ürümqi to Moscow for US$927 one-way.

Japan

There are many flight options available for travel between Japan and China. Air China and Japan Airlines have several flights per week from Tokyo and Osaka to Běijīng and Hong Kong. There are also flights that travel from Japan to most other major cities in China, including Dàlián, Shànghǎi and Qīngdǎo.

In Tokyo, try STA Travel (☎ 03-5485 8380), in the Star Plaza Aoyama Building, 1-10-3 Shibuya.

One-way fares from Tokyo to Běijīng start at around US$650. Air China has the cheapest fares from Tokyo to Hong Kong. Expect to pay, with a stopover in Taipei, around US$470 for a one-way fare.

Kazakhstan

Xinjiang Airlines has two flights per week between Ürümqi in Xīnjiāng province and Almaty. The one-way fare is $US155.

Kyrgyzstan

Kyrgyzstan Airlines has twice-weekly flights between Ürümqi and Bishkek. The one-way fare is US$190.

Mongolia

MIAT-Mongolian Airlines and Air China run flights between Běijīng and Ulaan Baatar. A one-way fare is US$210. It can sometimes take a week to get a ticket and the flight schedule is considerably reduced during the winter months. There are also two flights per week to Ulaan Baatar from Hohhot (US$172 one-way) with MIAT Mongolian Airlines.

Myanmar (Burma)

Air China has two flights a week from Yangon to Běijīng, with a stopover in Kūnmíng, for US$660 one-way. In the reverse direction, you can join the flight in Kūnmíng, but you must have a visa for Myanmar – available at the Myanmar consulate in Kūnmíng.

Nepal

Royal Nepal Airlines operates flights that run between Kathmandu and Shànghǎi (US$790 one-way) and Hong Kong (US$508 one-way).

China Southwest Airlines has three flights per week (two per week in the low season) between Lhasa and Kathmandu for US$228 one-way. You will not be able to purchase this ticket to Lhasa unless you already have a Tibetan Tourism Bureau permit.

North Korea

There are two flights weekly between Běijīng and P'yŏngyang with Koryo Air for US$154 one-way.

Pakistan

Air China and Pakistan International Airlines have weekly direct flights from Běijīng to Karachi, costing US$1013 oneway. There are cheaper flights available via Bangkok. There are also two flights per week between Ürümqi and Islamabad on Xinjiang Airlines for US$210 one-way.

Singapore

In Singapore, STA Travel (☎ 737 7188), in the Orchard Parade Hotel, 1 Tanglin Rd, offers competitive discount fares for Asian destinations and beyond. Singapore, like Bangkok, has hundreds of travel agents, so you can compare prices on flights. Chinatown Point shopping centre, on New Bridge Rd, has a good selection of travel agents.

One-way fares to Běijīng are around US$750, while fares to Hong Kong start at US$550.

South Korea

Discount travel agencies in Seoul include: Joy Travel Service (☎ 776 9871, fax 756 5342), 10th floor, 24-2 Mukyo-dong, Chung-gu, Seoul (directly behind City Hall); and discounters on the 5th floor of the YMCA building on Chongno 2-ga (next to Chonggak subway station).

Air China and Korean Air have several flights per week between Seoul and Běijīng,

Paging Passenger Li

Of all the various problems that afflict China, one of the oddest is the fact that the country is running out of names.

Unlike the west, where name-giving got a new lease of life in the 1960s (think of rock star Prince, who changed his name to an ideogram which has no pronunciation), China has got stuck in a bit of a rut on the moniker front. Chinese academics point out that parents have to be more inventive with their kids' names if China is not to slip into a social quagmire of widespread mistaken identities.

Some Chinese people have four character names (two characters for the surname and two for the given name). Unfortunately, such people are the rare exception. The majority has just a one character surname and either one or two characters for the given name. On paper, China today has around 3100 surnames. Unfortunately, a quarter of the population of China share just five surnames: Li, Wang, Zhang, Liu and Chen. In Běijīng alone, it's estimated that there are over 5000 individuals named Zhang Li and Liu Hui. With 1.25 billion people nationwide, it's not hard to see why so many people wind up with exactly the same name.

The problem is particularly acute in big cities, where thousands of people may share the same surname and given name, written in exactly the same characters. Chinese newspaper reports frequently bemoan wrongful arrests, bank account errors and unwanted surgery performed – all due to instances of mistaken identity.

The Chinese authorities constantly wring their hands in desperation at finding a solution. Academics have been consulted, and have proposed various ideas such as requiring children to adopt the surnames of both parents. Another proposal is to resurrect some of the 8000 surnames that were once in use in China, but have now become extinct – perhaps the authorities will assign them just like ID card numbers. Yet the easiest and undoubtedly most popular solution does not seem to have occurred to the authorities – how about just allowing individuals to change their name to whatever suits their fancy?

Hong Kong, Shànghǎi, Shěnyáng and Qīngdǎo. One-way fares from Seoul to Běijīng and Shànghǎi are around US$210.

Thailand

Khao San Rd in Bangkok is the budget-travellers headquarters. Bangkok has a number of excellent travel agents but there are also some suspect ones; ask the advice of other travellers before handing over your cash. STA Travel (☎ 02-236 0262), 33 Surawong Rd, is a good and reliable place to start.

One-way fares from Bangkok to Běijīng are about US$300. Other one-way fares from Bangkok include Hong Kong for around US$200, Chéngdū for US$255 and Shànghǎi for US$240.

Uzbekistan

From Běijīng there are twice-weekly flights to Tashkent with Uzbekistan Airways. One-way fares are around US$500.

Vietnam

China Southern Airlines and Vietnam Airlines fly between China and Vietnam. The only direct flight is between Ho Chi Minh City and Guǎngzhōu. One-way fares are US$362. One-way fares from Běijīng to Hanoi, via Hong Kong, are US$382.

LAND

If you're starting from Europe or Asia, it's possible to travel all the way to China. There are numerous interesting routes, including the Trans-Siberian Railway trek from Europe or the China-Vietnam, Tibet-Nepal, Xīnjiāng-Pakistan and Xīnjiāng-Kazakhstan border crossings.

Border Crossings

China shares land borders with 14 countries: Afghanistan, Bhutan, India, Kazakhstan, Kyrgyzstan, Laos, Mongolia, Myanmar, Nepal, North Korea, Pakistan,

Russia, Tajikistan and Vietnam. China also has official border crossings between its special administrative regions, Hong Kong and Macau. The borders with Afghanistan, Bhutan and India are closed.

Kazakhstan

A year-round road crosses from Ürümqi in China to Almaty via the border post at Khorgos and Zharkent (formerly Panfilov). Buses run Monday to Saturday in each direction, taking about 24 hours, with no stops except for food and toilets. Bring some food: If the bus is running late, you may get pretty hungry. The cost is about US$50 and crossing the border shouldn't really be a problem as long as you have a valid Kazakhstan visa.

The Ürümqi buses bypass Yīníng (Xīnjiāng), about 100km from the border and the largest town en route, so if you want to stop off here or at Sàilĭmù Hú (also in Xīnjiāng) you can take a daily Almaty-Yīníng bus for US$30.

There are two other China-Kazakhstan crossings farther north, at Tacheng (Bakhty in Kazakhstan) and Jeminay (Maykapchigay on the Kazak side). The Jeminay crossing is the more reliable of the two, though neither is all that reliable.

Foreigners can only cross the border at Dostyq by rail, taking the 2nd or soft-class Genghis Khan Express. Trains leave Monday and Saturday from Ürümqi to Almaty. The journey takes a very slow 35 hours, eight of which are spent at the Chinese and Kazak customs, and the hard sleeper fare is around Y400. At the Ürümqi train station there's a special ticket window for these trains, inside the large waiting room in the main building. It's only open Monday, and Thursday to Saturday, 10 am to 1 pm and 3 to 7 pm. You will, of course, need a visa for Kazakhstan. There's no guarantee of a restaurant car so bring your own food and drink and share, as everyone else does.

Kyrgyzstan

From at least June to September it's possible to cross the dramatic 3752m Torugart Pass on a rough road from Kashgar into Kyrgyzs-

tan. Chinese and Kyrgyz buses run over the pass but foreigners are forbidden from taking the bus and have to arrange their own pricey transport, at least on the China side.

Even the most painstaking arrangements can be thwarted by logistical gridlock on the China side or by unpredictable border closures (eg, for holidays or snow).

Another warm-weather crossing is now open for commerce, from Kashgar via Irkeshtam to Osh, but so far not for individual tourists.

Laos

From the Měnglà district in China's southern Yúnnán province it is legal to enter Laos via Boten in Luang Nam Tha province if you possess a valid Lao visa. From Boten there are morning and afternoon buses onward to the provincial capitals of Luang Nam Tha and Udomxai, three and four hours away, respectively.

The Lao consulate in Kūnmíng, Yúnnán, issues both seven-day transit and 15-day tourist visas for Laos. These cost US$35 and US$40, respectively, and take four to five days to process. You must bring three photos and you may need a visa from a third country (such as Thailand) stamped in your passport. The majority of travellers from Kūnmíng go via Jǐnghóng to Měnglà and thence to the border at Mohan. As the bus journey from Jǐnghóng will take the better part of the day, you will probably have to stay overnight at Měnglà. See the Kūnmíng section in the Yúnnán chapter for more information on visas.

Myanmar (Burma)

Originally built to supply the forces of Chiang Kaishek in his struggle against the Japanese, the famous Burma Road runs from Kūnmíng, in China's Yúnnán province, to the city of Lashio. Nowadays the road is open to travellers carrying permits for the region north of Lashio, although you can only legally cross the border in one direction – from the Chinese side (Ruìlì) into Myanmar via Mu-se in the northern Shan State. This appears to be possible only if you book a visa-and-transport package from Chinese travel agencies in Kūnmíng. Once across the border at Mu-se, you can continue on to Lashio and farther south to Mandalay and Yangon.

A second route, a little farther north-west from Lwaigyai to Bhamo, is also open in the same direction. You cannot legally leave Myanmar by either route.

Nepal

The 920km road connecting Lhasa with Kathmandu is known as the Friendship Hwy. It's a spectacular trip over high passes and across the Tibetan plateau, the highest point being La Lungla Pass (5200m).

If the weather's good, you'll get a fine view of Mt Everest from the Tibetan village of Tingri. By far the most popular option for the trip is renting a 4WD through a hotel or travel agency and then sorting out a private itinerary with the driver.

When travelling from Nepal to Lhasa, foreigners must arrange transport through tour agencies in Kathmandu. If you already have a Chinese visa, you could try turning up at the border and organising a permit in Zhangmu. This is a gamble, however, as the rules and regulations change hourly. The occasional traveller slips through (even a couple on bicycles). At Zhangmu you can hunt around for buses, minibuses, 4WDs or trucks heading towards Lhasa.

North Korea

Visas are difficult to arrange to North Korea and at the time of writing it was totally impossible for US and South Korean citizens.

There are twice weekly trains between Běijīng and P'yŏngyang.

Pakistan

The exciting trip on the Karakoram Hwy, over the 4800m Khunjerab Pass and what is said to be the world's highest public international highway, is an excellent way to get to or from Chinese Central Asia. There are regular bus and 4WD services when the pass is open – normally May to early November. See Lonely Planet's *Karakoram Highway* guide and the Xīnjiāng chapter in this book for more information.

Russia

The Russian border is 9km from Mǎnzhōulǐ and is reputedly quite reliable and sees a lot of traffic. Officially, the only public transport that crosses the border is the Trans-Manchurian, but there are ample opportunities for picking up a lift preferably in Mǎnzhōulǐ or at the border. A taxi to the border from Mǎnzhōulǐ costs Y10.

Tajikistan

There are grand plans to build a road from near Murgab in eastern Tajikistan to near Bulunkul on the China side, to link up with the Karakoram Hwy to Pakistan. It will take years (if not decades) for this to happen and even then, for the first few years at least, this will be for local traffic only.

Vietnam

In the finest bureaucratic tradition, travellers require a special visa for entering Vietnam overland from China. These visas cost double and take twice as long to issue as the normal tourist visas needed for entering Vietnam by air. Travellers who have tried to use a standard visa to enter Vietnam overland from China have fared poorly, and it no longer seems possible to bribe your way in.

Exiting from Vietnam to China is much simpler. The Chinese don't require anything more than a standard tourist visa, and Chinese visas do not indicate entry or exit points. However, your Vietnamese visa must have the correct exit point marked on it, a change that can easily be made in Hanoi. Ironically, it seems to be possible to bribe your way out.

The Vietnam-China border crossing is open from 7 am to 4 pm, Vietnam time, or 8 am to 5 pm, China time. Set your watch when you cross the border – the time in China is one hour later than in Vietnam. Neither country observes daylight savings time. There are currently two border checkpoints, detailed below, where foreigners are permitted to cross between Vietnam and China.

Friendship Pass The busiest border crossing is at the Vietnamese town of Dong Dang, 164km north-east of Hanoi. The closest Chinese town to the border is Píng-xiáng, but it's about 10km north of the actual border gate. The crossing point (Friendship Pass) is known as Huu Nghi Quan in Vietnamese or Yǒuyì Guān in Chinese.

Dong Dang is an obscure town. The nearest city is Lang Son, 18km to the south. Buses and minibuses on the Hanoi-Lang Son route are frequent. The cheapest way to cover the 18km between Dong Dang and Lang Son is to hire a motorbike for US$1.50. There are also minibuses cruising the streets looking for passengers. Just make sure they take you to Huu Nghi Quan and not to the other nearby checkpoint – this is the only one where foreigners can cross.

There is a customs checkpoint between Lang Son and Dong Dang. Sometimes there are long delays here while officials gleefully rip apart the luggage of Vietnamese and Chinese travellers. For this reason, a motorbike might prove faster than a van since you won't have to wait for your fellow passengers to be searched. Note that this is only a problem when you're heading south towards Lang Son, not the other way.

On the Chinese side, it's a 20-minute drive from the border to Píngxiáng by bus or share taxi – the cost for the latter is US$3. Píngxiáng is connected by train to Nánníng, capital of China's Guǎngxī province. Trains to Nánníng depart Píngxiáng at 8 am and 1.30 pm. More frequent are the buses (once every 30 minutes), which take four hours to make the journey and cost US$4.

There is a walk of 600m between the Vietnamese and Chinese border posts.

A word of caution – because train tickets to China are expensive in Hanoi, travellers have bought a ticket to Dong Dang, walked across the border and then bought a Chinese train ticket on the Chinese side. This isn't the best way because it's several kilometres from Dong Dang to Friendship Pass, and you'll have to hire someone to take you by motorbike. If you're going by train, it's better to buy a ticket from Hanoi to Píngxiáng, and then in Píngxiáng get the ticket to Nánníng or beyond.

Trains on the Hanoi-Dong Dang route run according to the following schedule:

Train No	depart Dong Dang	arrive Hanoi
HD4	8.30 am	8.00 pm
HD2	5.40 pm	1.50 am

Train No	depart Hanoi	arrive Dong Dang
HD3	5.00 am	1.30 pm
HD1	10.00 pm	5.10 am

There is also a twice-weekly international train running between Běijīng and Hanoi, which stops at the Friendship Pass. You can board or exit the train at numerous stations in China. The entire Běijīng-Hanoi run is 2951km and takes approximately 55 hours, including a three-hour delay (if you're lucky) at the border checkpoint. Schedules are subject to change, but at present train No 5 departs Běijīng at 8.30 am on Monday and Friday, arriving in Hanoi at 11.30 am on Wednesday and Sunday, respectively. Going the other way, train No 6 departs Hanoi at 2 pm on Wednesday and Saturday, arriving in Běijīng at 5.42 pm on Friday and Monday, respectively. The complete schedule follows.

station	to Hanoi train No 5	to Běijīng train No 6
Běijīng	8.30 am	5.42 pm
Shíjiāzhuāng	1.32 pm	2.34 pm
Zhèngzhōu	5.25 pm	10.37 am
Hànkǒu (Wǔhàn)	10.41 pm	5.26 am
Wǔchāng (Wǔhàn)	11.02 pm	4.59 am
Chángshā	2.52 am	1.10 am
Héngyáng	4.57 am	11.04 pm
Yǒngzhōu	7.10 am	8.49 pm
Guìlín North	10.26 am	5.33 pm
Guìlín	10.52 am	5.12 pm
Liǔzhōu	1.26 pm	2.19 pm
Nánníng	5.39 pm	10.30 pm
Píngxiáng	12.04 am	12.59 am
Dong Dang	3.30 am*	8.30 pm*
Hanoi	11.30 am*	2.00 pm*

* Vietnamese time

Lao Cai-Hékǒu A 762km metre-gauge railway, inaugurated in 1910, links Hanoi with Kūnmíng. The bordertown on the Vietnamese side is Lao Cai, 294km from Hanoi. On the Chinese side, the bordertown is called Hékǒu, 468km from Kūnmíng.

Vietnamese and Chinese authorities have started a direct international train service between Hanoi and Kūnmíng. The schedule is as follows:

station	to Hanoi	to Kūnmíng
Kūnmíng	2.45 pm	6.00 am
Yì Liáng	4.50 pm	3.31 am
Kāi Yuán	10.45 pm	9.32 pm
Kékǒu	7.20 am	9.30 am
Lao Cai	7.40 am	7.00 am
Hanoi	8.20 pm	9.30 pm

Domestic trains run daily on both sides of the border. On the Chinese side, Kūnmíng-Hékǒu takes about 16 hours. Trains depart and arrive at Kūnmíng's north train station according to the following schedule:

Train No	depart Kūnmíng	arrive Hékǒu
313	9.30 pm	1.55 pm

Train No	depart Hékǒu	arrive Kūnmíng
314	2.45 pm	7.50 am

On the Vietnamese side, trains run according to the following schedule:

Train No	depart Lao Cai	arrive Hanoi
LC4	9.40 am	8.10 pm
LC2	6.00 pm	4.10 am

Train No	depart Hanoi	arrive Lao Cai
LC3	5.10 am	3.35 pm
LC1	9.45 pm	7.55 am

Mong Cai-Dōngxīng Vietnam's third, but little known, border crossing is at Mong Cai in the north-east corner of the country, just opposite the Chinese city of Dōngxīng. Officially only Vietnamese and Chinese citizens may cross here.

TRANS-SIBERIAN RAILWAY

The Trans-Siberian Railway and connecting routes comprise one of the most famous, romantic and potentially enjoyable of the world's great train journeys. Rolling out of Europe and into Asia, through eight time zones and over 9289km of taiga, steppe and desert, the Trans-Siberian makes all other train rides seem like once around the block with Thomas the Tank Engine.

There is some confusion of terms here as there are, in fact, three railways. The 'true' Trans-Siberian line runs from Moscow to Vladivostok. But the routes traditionally referred to as the Trans-Siberian Railway are the two branches that veer off the main line in eastern Siberia to make a beeline for Běijīng.

Most readers of this book will not be interested in the first option since it excludes China – your decision is basically between the Trans-Manchurian or the Trans-Mongolian; however, it makes little difference. The Trans-Mongolian (Běijīng-Moscow, 7865km) is marginally faster, but requires you to purchase an additional visa and endure another border crossing, although you do at least get to see the Mongolian countryside roll past your window. The Trans-Manchurian is longer (Běijīng-Moscow, 9001km).

Trans-Mongolian Railway

This branch line has been open since the mid-1950s and has become the rail route most synonymous with the 'Trans-Siberian' tag.

The Trans-Mongolian travels north to the Mongolian border at Erenhot, 842km from Běijīng. The train continues to Ulaan Baatar before reaching the last stop in Mongolia, Sukhe Bator.

From the Russian border town of Naushki, the train travels to Ulan Ude, where it connects with the Trans-Siberian line,

The Trans-Mongolian leaves Běijīng every Wednesday.

Trans-Manchurian Railway

From Běijīng, this train travels north through the cities of Shānhǎiguān, Shěnyáng and Hāěrbīn before arriving at the border post Mǎnzhōulǐ, 935km from Běijīng. Zabaykal'sk is the Russian border post and the train continues from here to Tarskaya, where it connects with the Trans-Siberian line.

The Trans-Manchurian leaves Běijīng every Saturday.

Classes of Travel

The standard accommodation on all long-distance, Trans-Siberian–related trains is in 2nd-class carriages. On the Chinese trains, 1st class has softer beds but hardly any more space than 2nd class and is not worth the considerably higher fare. The real luxury comes with Chinese deluxe class, which has roomy, wood-panelled two-berth compartments with a sofa, and a shower cubicle shared with the adjacent compartment.

Other than in the deluxe class on the Chinese train, there are no showers in any category.

Costs

In the past, the Trans-Siberian routes represented one of the cheapest ways of travelling one-third of the way around the world. These days, however, with airline companies in desperate competition and slashing prices, that's no longer the case. The standard foreigner price of a Moscow-Běijīng ticket is Y1602 for 2nd class on the Trans-Mongolian, and Y1825 on the Trans-Manchurian route.

Visas

Trans-Siberian travellers will need Russian and Mongolian visas if they take the Trans-Mongolian, as well as a Chinese visa. It's safer to obtain all visas in your home country before setting out. Some tour companies arrange visas as part of their package.

Russian A transit visa issued in Běijīng will usually give you three or four days in Moscow at the end of your journey. In Běijīng, the Russian embassy (☎ 010-6532 2051, visa section ☎ 6532 1267) is at 4 Dongzhimennei Beizhongjie, just off Dongzhimennei Dajie. A transit or tourist visa costs US$50 and takes one week to

process; US$80 for one- to two-day express service; or US$120 for one-hour service. There is a consular fee on top of the standard processing charge that varies dramatically with citizenship. You will need three photos, your passport and the exact money in dollars. For a transit visa, you will also need a valid entry visa for a third country plus a through ticket from Russia to the third country. Consular hours are Monday to Friday from 9 to 11.30 am.

In Ulaan Baatar, the Russian embassy (☎ 326 037, fax 327 018) is at Enkh Taivny Örgön Chölöö. Visas take about two days to process and sponsors/invitations from within Russia are required. The consular section is open Monday, Wednesday and Friday from 9.30 am to 12.30 pm and 2.30 to 5.30 pm.

Mongolian If you are travelling on the Trans-Mongolian train, you will need some kind of Mongolian visa. These come in two forms: transit or tourist. A transit visa (valid for seven days) is easy enough to get (just present a through-ticket and a visa for your onward destination). The situation regarding visas changes regularly, so check with a Mongolian embassy or consulate.

In Běijīng, the Mongolian embassy (☎ 010-6532 1203) is at 2 Xiushui Beilu, Jianguomenwai. The visa section is open Monday to Friday from 9 to 11.30 am and 2 to 3.30 pm.

A transit visa generally costs US$30 and takes three days to issue, or US$60 for same-day or next-day service. Tourist visas cost US$40, or US$60 for express service. Visas are free for Finnish and Indian nationals. All Mongolian embassies shut down for the week of National Day (Naadam), which officially falls around 11 to 13 July.

Books

The Trans-Siberian Handbook by Bryn Thomas covers in some detail the major settlements along the line. Also recommended is *Red Express* (out of print) by Michael Cordell & Peter Solness, a lavish photo album produced to accompany the

Australian TV series of the same name. It examines life in ex-communist realms from East Berlin to China, following the route of the railway.

What to Bring
The list of extra travelling essentials for a Trans-Siberian jaunt includes toilet paper, a plug for the toilet sink, some soft, slip-on footwear like thongs (flip-flops) or Chinese cloth sandals, and loose, comfortable pants like tracksuit or shell-suit trousers. You won't need a sleeping bag.

Boiling water is always available at the end of each carriage. There's a dining car attached to most long-distance trains, and at each stop you'll find clusters of kiosks and locals selling home produce, so it isn't necessary to bring too much in the way of food. Juice or water in a plastic bottle is a good idea.

Baggage Space
There is a luggage bin underneath each of the lower berths and there is a limit of 35kg per passenger.

Passengers with excess baggage are supposed to present it (along with passport, ticket and customs entry declaration) the day before departure at the Luggage Shipment Office, which is on the right-hand side of the main train station in Běijīng. The excess is charged at about US$11 per 10kg, with a maximum excess of 40kg allowed.

Time Zones
Officially, China and Mongolia only have one time zone, five hours later than Moscow time. Local time is thus unchanged from Běijīng to Irkutsk, except in late April or early May and again in September, when you may find a one-hour shift at the border. This is because of differences in switching to daylight-saving time.

Food & Drink
The dining cars are changed at each border, so en route to Moscow you get Russian, Chinese and possibly Mongolian versions. There's no menu and no choice, but what you normally get is a number of stir-fried dishes with rice, and this set meal costs about US$6. Dining cars are open from approximately 9 am to 9 pm local time.

In the dining car there's often a table of pot noodles, chocolate, beer, juice and the like being peddled by the staff. The prices are inflated and there's nothing that isn't available from the station kiosks.

Border Formalities
Border stops can take anything between one and six hours as customs officials go through the travelling warehouses that are the Chinese traders' compartments. For foreign travellers the procedure is uncomplicated: passports, visas and currency forms are examined, and baggage searches are rare (for this reason you may be approached by a trader and asked to carry their bag across the border – this is not a good idea).

At the Chinese-Mongolian and Chinese-Russian borders, about two hours are spent hoisting the train aloft so that its bogies can be changed (the old Soviet Union used a wider gauge of track than its neighbours). If you're riding the Trans-Mongolian and want to witness this odd operation, stay on the train when it disgorges its passengers at Erlian station, on the Chinese side of the China-Mongolia border. The train then pulls into a large shed 500m away. Get off before the staff lock the doors. It's OK to walk around and take photos, then stroll back down the line to the station.

Safety
Common sense applies. Don't leave valuables lying about, and don't leave hand baggage unattended in a compartment while you get off at a station. A few years ago the Trans-Mongolian had quite a bad reputation, but militia now ride the trains and matters have improved. For added safety, lock your cabins from the inside.

Buying Tickets
From Australasia In Australia, Gateway Travel (☎ 02-9745 3333, fax 9745 3237), 48 The Boulevarde, Strathfield, NSW, 2135, offers 2nd-class through-tickets on the Trans-Manchurian and the Trans-

Mongolian for A$460 and A$460, respectively, as well as some stopover packages. Its Web site is at www.russian-gateway.com.au.

Sundowners (☎ 03-9600 1934, fax 9642 5838), Suite 15, Lonsdale Court, 600 Lonsdale St, Melbourne, Victoria, 3000, offers a variety of 16- to 30-day package tours, as well as unescorted packages with stopovers.

The New Zealand based operator Suntravel (☎ 09-525 3074, fax 525 3065, ☻ suntravel@suntravl.com), 407 Great South Rd, PO Box 12-424, Penrose, Auckland, has 'basic express packages'. A 17-day trip from Běijīng to St Petersburg, with stays along the way, costs NZ$2573 on the Trans-Mongolian and NZ$2299 on the Trans-Manchurian.

From Canada Exotik Tours (☎ 514-284 3324, fax 843 5493, ☻ exotiktours@exotiktours.com), 1117 Ste-Catherine O, Suite 806, Montreal, Quebec H3B 1H9, offers two nine- and eight-day Moscow-Běijīng packages on the Trans-Mongolian and Trans-Manchurian routes for US$600 and US$680, respectively.

From Germany Lernidee Reisen (☎ 030-786 5056, fax 786 5596), Duden Strasse 78, 10965 Berlin, sells 2nd-class tickets: Běijīng-Moscow (DM775), Moscow-Běijīng (DM735), Běijīng-Ulaan Baatar (DM335), Ulaan Baatar-Běijīng (DM295), Ulaan Baatar-Moscow (DM540) and Moscow-Ulaan Baatar (DM585).

Travel Service Asia (☎ 7351-37 3210, fax 37 3211, ☻ TSA-Reisen@t-online.de), Schmelzweg 10, 88400 Biberach/Riss, offers package tours on the Trans-Mongolian and Trans-Manchurian routes. A 14-day trip from Moscow via Irkutsk, Ulaan Baatar and Běijīng, with two nights in Moscow, two nights in Irkutsk and two nights in Ulaan Baatar, costs DM1730. Check out its Web site at www.travel-service-asia.de.

From China In Běijīng you can buy tickets from the China International Travel Service (CITS; Zhōngguó Guójì Lǚxíngshè; ☎ 6515 0093 ext 35) office in the Beijing Tourist Building, at 28 Jianguomenwai,

opposite the Gloria Plaza Hotel. Hard sleeper tickets on the Trans-Mongolian are Y1602 and on the Trans-Manchurian are Y1825. Tickets don't include the necessary visas; you'll need to arrange these for yourself.

If you want a package that includes train tickets, visas and hotel, try Moonsky Star in Hong Kong (also known as Monkey Business; ☎ 852-2723 1376, fax 2723 6653, ☻ MonkeyHK@compuserve.com), Flat 6, 4th floor, E-block, Chungking Mansions, 36-44 Nathan Rd, Tsimshatsui, Kowloon, or in Běijīng (☎ 8610-6356 2126, fax 6356 2127, ☻ MonkeyChina@compuserve.com), Capital Forbidden City Hotel, 48 Guanganmen Nanjie, South Building, 3rd floor, Xuanwu District, 100054. The company has a lot of experience in booking Trans-Siberian trains for independent travellers. A basic, 2nd-class, nonstop ticket from Běijīng to Moscow, including the first night in Moscow, costs US$375 (plus the cost of the visa, which varies according to nationality) on the Trans-Manchurian or US$345 (plus the cost of the visa) on the Trans-Mongolian. Monkey Business also offers various packages with stopovers in destinations along the way. For example, for a two-day stopover in Lake Baikal and in Ulaan Baatar, the price is US$675.

There are other ticket agencies in Hong Kong worth calling. You might try Time Travel (☎ 852-2366 6222, fax 2739 5413), Block A, 16th floor, Chungking Mansions, 40 Nathan Rd, Tsimshatsui, Kowloon.

From Russia The Travellers Guesthouse/IRO Travel (☎ 095-971 4059, ☎ 280 8562, fax 280 7686, ☻ tgh@glasnet .ru), ulitsa Bolshaya Pereyaslavskaya 50, 10th floor, Moscow 129401, sells Trans-Mongolian tickets for Moscow-Běijīng for US$200, plus US$20 for each stopover. Along the route, it also offers homestays in Russia and hostels in Mongolia for US$15 to US$25 a night.

From the UK The China Travel Service (☎ 020-7836 9911, fax 7836 3121, ☻ CTS@ctsuk.com), 7 Upper St Martins Lane, London WC2H 9DL, sells tickets on all the routes, with meals and two days lodging at the start and end of the journey, for £170 to £492, depending on the route, the class and the time of travel.

Intourist Travel (☎ 020-7538 8600, fax 7538 5967), Intourist House, 219 Marsh Wall, London E14 9PD, offers Trans-Manchurian and Trans-Mongolian packages from £566 to £731. Its Web site is at www.intourus.demon.co.uk.

Steppes East (☎ 01285-81 0267, fax 81 0693), Castle Eaton, Swindon, Wiltshire SN6 6JU, has 13-day, individually tailored Trans-Mongolian packages for about £930. On the Web it can be found at www.steppes east.co.uk.

From the USA White Nights (☎/fax 916-979 9381, ✉ wnights@concourse.net), 610 Sierra Drive, Sacramento, CA 95864, offers Moscow-Běijīng tickets from US$311 and Moscow-Vladivostok from US$582. It also offers visa support.

SEA
Hong Kong
There are numerous ships plying the waters between Hong Kong and the mainland, the most useful being the boats to Guǎngzhōu. See the Getting There & Away section of the Hong Kong chapter for details.

Japan
Osaka/Yokohama to Shànghǎi The Japan-China International Ferry service connects Shànghǎi and Osaka/Yokohama. The *Suzhou Hao* departs once weekly (heading for Osaka one week and to Yokohama the next week) and takes two days. It's kind of empty during the low season, but can be crowded during summer. Fares depend on class – from a low of US$140 all the way up to a staggering US$1600 for a luxury suite (but there is no surcharge for luggage). Departures from Shànghǎi are every Tuesday, while departures from Japan are every Friday. For information ring the shipping company's office in Tokyo (☎ 03-5202 5781, fax 5202 5792), Osaka (☎ 06-232 0131, fax 232 0211) or Shànghǎi (☎ 021-6535 1713). The address

SEA ROUTES

of the shipping office in Shànghǎi is at 1 Jinling Donglu.

Kōbe to Tiānjīn Another ship runs from Kōbe to Tánggū (near Tiānjīn). Departures from Kōbe are every Thursday at noon, arriving in Tánggū the next day. Economy/1st class tickets cost US$250/350, or pay US$1400 for your very own stateroom. The food on this boat gets poor reviews so bring a few emergency munchies.

Tickets can be bought in Tiānjīn from the shipping office (☎ 2331 2283) at 89 Munan Dao, Hepingqu, or at the port in Tánggū (☎ 2938 3961). In Kōbe, the office is at the port (☎ 078-321 5791, fax 321 5793).

Korea
Travelling from Korea, international ferries connect the South Korean port of Inch'ŏn with Wēihǎi, Qīngdǎo, Tiānjīn, Dàlián, Shànghǎi and Dāndōng. Wēihǎi and Qīngdǎo are in Shāndōng (the closest province to South Korea) and boats are operated by the Weidong Ferry Company. Tiānjīn is close to Běijīng and boats are run by the Jinchon Ferry Company. The boats have (horrors) a karaoke lounge.

The phone numbers for Weidong Ferry Company are: Seoul (☎ 711 9111); Inch'ŏn (☎ 886 6171); Wēihǎi (☎ 0896-522 6173); and Qīngdǎo (☎ 0532-280 3574).

Phone numbers for Jinchon Ferry Company are: Seoul (☎ 517 8671); Inch'ŏn (☎ 887 3963); and Tiānjīn (☎ 022-2331 6049). In Seoul, tickets for any boats to China can be bought from the International Travel Association (ITA; ☎ 777 6722), Room 707, 7th floor, Daehan Ilbo Building, 340 Taepyonglo 2-ga, Chung-gu, Seoul. Prices range from US$88 to US$300, and depending on the destination, boats leave anywhere from once a week to three times a week.

For the Tiānjīn ferry only, you can also get tickets in Seoul from Taeya Travel (☎ 514 6226, 342 4200), in Kangnam-gu by the Shinsa subway station. In China, tickets can be bought cheaply at the pier, or from CITS (for a very *steep* premium). The cheapest price is Y800 for a dorm bed.

To reach the International Ferry Terminal from Seoul, take the Seoul-Inch'ŏn commuter train (subway line 1 from the city centre) and get off at the Tonginch'ŏn station. The train ride takes 50 minutes. From Tonginch'ŏn station it's either a 45-minute walk or five-minute taxi ride to the ferry terminal.

Inch'ŏn to Wēihǎi The trip takes approximately 17 hours. Departures from Wēihǎi are Wednesday, Friday and Sunday at 5 pm. Departures from Inch'ŏn are on Tuesday, Thursday and Saturday at 5 pm. The fares are 2nd class US$100; 1st class US$140; royal class US$180; and royal suite class US$300. There is a 5% discount on a round-trip ticket.

Wēihǎi is no place to hang around, so if you arrive there it's best to hop on the first bus to Qīngdǎo. If that's not available, take a bus to Yāntái and then to Qīngdǎo.

Inch'ŏn to Qīngdǎo Boats for Inch'ŏn leave on Monday and Thursday at 4 pm, take 20 hours and tickets cost Y1100. Boats leave Inch'ŏn twice a week. For details check with the Weidong Ferry Company in

Seoul (☎ 711 9111), Inch'ŏn (☎ 886 6171) or Qīngdǎo (☎ 280 3574).

Inch'ŏn to Tiānjīn The schedule for this ferry is a little irregular. It departs once every four or five days, usually on a Monday, Wednesday or Friday. The journey takes a minimum of 28 hours. Departures from Tiānjīn are at 10 am. The boat departs Inch'ŏn at 1 pm. The fares are 3B class US$120, 3A class US$140, 2B class US$150, 2A class US$160, 1st class US$180 and VIP class US$230.

The boat doesn't dock at Tiānjīn proper, but rather at the nearby port of Tánggū. Accommodation in Tiānjīn is outrageously expensive, but Tánggū has at least one economical accommodation option, the Seamen's Hotel. Tánggū has trains and minibuses directly to Běijīng.

Third class on the boat is a huge vault with around 80 beds and horrid toilets.

Russia
From Fǔyuǎn, a small port on the Amur River in north-eastern China, a hydrofoil sails every other day to Khabarovsk, but it's not certain whether foreigners can cross the border (legally) here.

ORGANISED TOURS
There are literally hundreds of tour operators who can organise tours to China. If your time is limited but your budget isn't, tours can save you a lot of time and energy.

Tours organised in China with CITS get recommended by only a few, but they are worth considering for day trips and excursions or getting to places that have limited transport options.

There is also an increasing number of private tour companies in China, giving you a few more choices, including Sunshine Tours (☎ 6586 8069, fax 6586 8077, ✉ sunpress@ public.bta.net.cn), based in Běijīng. Check out www.sinotravel.com for tour information. If you're interested in biking tours, check out Bike China, a Yúnnán-based company with a Web site at www.bikechina.com.

While there are many companies that can organise straightforward sightseeing tours of China, listed here are some companies that offer more adventurous or special interest tours.

Australia

Tailwinds Bicycle Touring (☎ 02-6249 6634; ℮ goactive@ozemail.com.au) 1st floor, Garema Centre, Bunda St, Canberra, ACT 2601

Intrepid Adventure Travel (☎ 1300 360 667) 13 Spring St, Fitzroy, Victoria 3065, offers small, off-the-usual-tourist-track group tours. Web site: www.intrepidtravel.com.au

Peregrine Adventures (☎ 03-9662 2700) 258 Lonsdale St, Melbourne, Victoria 3000, offers walking, hiking and cycling tours. Web site: www.peregrine.net.au

World Expeditions (☎ 02-9264 3366) 3rd floor, 441 Kent St, Sydney, NSW 2000, offers adventure and cultural tours for small groups. Web site: www.worldexpeditions.com.au

UK

Explore Worldwide (☎ 01252 760000) 1, Fredrick St, Aldershot, Hampshire GU11 1LQ, offers small group adventure tours. Web site: www.explore.co.uk

Imaginative Traveller (☎ 020-8742 3113) 14 Barley Mow Passage, London W4 4PH, offers cycling and walking tours. Web site: www.imaginative-traveller.com

Naturetrek (☎ 01962 733051) Cheriton Mill, Cheriton Alresford, Hampshire SO24 0NG, offers birdwatching and botanical tours. Web site: www.naturetrek.co.uk

USA

Boojum Expeditions (☎ 1-800-287-0125, 406-587-0125) 14543 Kelly Canyon Rd, Bozeman, MT 59715, offers horseback and cycling trips in Mongolia and Tibet. Web site: www.boojumx.com

Earth River Expeditions (☎ 914-626-2665) 180 Towpath Rd, Accord, NY 12404, offers rafting and trekking tours. Web site: www.earthriver.com

Voyagers International (☎ 607-273-4321) PO Box 915, Ithaca, NY 14851, offers photography tours. Web site: www.voyagers.com

Overseas Adventure Travel (☎ 800-493-6824) tours place an emphasis on culture and wilderness. Web site: www.oattravel.com

REI (☎ 800-426-4840, 253-891-2500) Sumner, WA 98352, offers hiking and cycling tours. Web site: www.rei.com

Wilderness Travel (☎ 510-558-2488, 800-368-2794) 1102 Ninth St, Berkeley, CA 94710, offers Silk Road tours. Web site: www.wildernesstravel.com

Chinese Travel Agents Abroad

For information on offices in Hong Kong and Macau see the relevant chapters.

CITS Outside China and Hong Kong, CITS is usually known as the China National Tourist Office (CNTO). CITS (or CNTO) representatives include:

Australia
CNTO (☎ 02-9299 4057, fax 9290 1958) 19th floor, 44 Market St, Sydney NSW 2000
France
Office du Tourisme de Chine (☎ 1 44 21 82 82, fax 44 21 81 00) 116 Avenue des Champs Elysees, 75008, Paris
Germany
CNTO (☎ 069-520 135, fax 528 490) Ilkenhansstr 6, D-60433 Frankfurt am Main
Israel
CNTO (☎ 03-522 6272, fax 522 6281) 19 Frishman St, PO Box 3281, Tel-Aviv 61030
Japan
China National Tourist Administration (☎ 03-3433 1461, fax 3433 8653) 6th floor, Hamamatsu-cho Bldg, 1-27-13 Hamamatsu-cho, Minato-ku, Tokyo
Singapore
CNTO (☎ 221 8681, fax 221 9267) 1 Shenton Way, No 17-05 Robina House, Singapore 0106
UK
CNTO (☎ 020-7935 9787, fax 7487 5842) 4 Glenworth St, London NW1
USA
CNTO Los Angeles Branch (☎ 818-545 7504, fax 545 7506) Suite 201, 333 West Broadway, Glendale CA 91204
New York Branch (☎ 212-760 9700, fax 760 8809) Suite 6413, Empire State Bldg, 350 Fifth Ave, New York, NY 10118

CTS Overseas representatives include the following:

Australia
(☎ 02-9211 2633, fax 9281 3595) Ground floor, 757-9 George St, Sydney, NSW 2000
Canada
Vancouver: (☎ 800-663 1126, 604-872 8787,

fax 873 2823) 556 West Broadway, BC V5Z
1E9; (☎ 800-387 6622, 416-979 8993,
fax 979 8220)
Toronto: Suite 306, 438 University Ave, Box
28, Ontario M5G 2K8

France
(☎ 1 44 51 55 66, fax 44 51 55 60) 32 Rue
Vignon, 75009, Paris

Germany
Frankfurt am Main: (☎ 69-223 8522, fax 223
2324) Düsseldorfer Strasse 14, D-60329,
Berlin: (☎ 30-393 4068, fax 391 8085)
Beusselstrasse 5, D-10553,

Japan
(☎ 03-3273 5512, fax 3273 2667) 103 Buyoo
Bldg, 3-8-16, Nihombashi, Chuo-ku, Tokyo

Malaysia
(☎ 03-201 8888, fax 201 3268) Ground floor,
112-4 Jalan Pudu, 55100, Kuala Lumpur

Philippines
(☎ 02-733 1274, fax 733 1431) 801-3 Gandara
St (corner Espeleta St), Santa Cruz, Manila

Singapore
(☎ 532 9988; fax 535 4912) 1 Park Rd,
No 03-49 to 52, People's Park Complex,
Singapore, 059108

South Korea
(☎ 02-566 9361, fax 557 0021) 8th floor,
Chung Oh Bldg, 164-3 Samsung-dong,
Kangnam-gu, Seoul

Thailand
(☎ 02-226 0041, fax 226 4701) 559 Yao-waraj
Rd, Sampuntawang, Bangkok 10100

UK
(☎ 020-7836 9911, fax 836 3121) CTS House,
7 Upper St, Martins Lane, London WC2H
9DL

USA
Main Office: (☎ 800-332-2831/415-398-6627,
fax 398-6669, ✉ info@chinatravelservice
.com) Lower floor, 575 Sutter St, San Francisco, CA 94102
Los Angeles Branch: (☎ 818-457-8668, fax
457-8955, ✉ USCTSLA@aol.com) Suite 303,
US CTS Bldg, 119 South Atlantic Blvd,
Monterey Park, CA 91754

Getting Around

For information on Hong Kong and Macau see those chapters.

AIR

The Civil Aviation Administration of China (CAAC) is the civil aviation authority for numerous airlines, including Air China, China Eastern, China Southern, China Northern, China Southwest, China Northwest, Great Wall, Shanghai, Shenzhen, Sichuan, Xiamen, Xinjiang, Yunnan and several others.

CAAC publishes a combined international and domestic timetable in both English and Chinese in April and November each year. These can be bought at some airports and CAAC offices in China for Y12, but are free in Hong Kong at the CAAC office and airport service counter. Individual airlines also publish timetables. You can buy these from ticket offices throughout China.

More and more booking offices have been computerised over recent years. These offices allow you to purchase a ticket to or from any other destination on the computer reservation system. If the city you want to fly from is not on the system, however, you'll have to wait until you get there to buy your ticket from the local booking office.

You need to show your passport when reserving or purchasing a ticket, and you definitely need it to board the aircraft. Some airports will even check your Chinese visa, and if it's expired you will be prohibited from boarding.

Business class tickets cost 25% more than economy class, and 1st class tickets cost an

DOMESTIC AIRFARES

Major air routes in China.
One-way economy airfares in RMB (yuan).
Note these fares are subject to change.

extra 60%. Children over 12 are charged adult fares. You can use credit cards at most CAAC offices and travel agents.

There is no such thing as discounting no matter where you buy your tickets. Travel agents charge you full fare, plus extra commission for their services. The service desks in better hotels (three-star and up) can reserve and even purchase air tickets for you with a little advance notice.

There is an airport tax of Y50 on domestic flights.

Cancellation fees depend on how long before departure you cancel. On domestic flights, if you cancel 24 to 48 hours before departure you lose 5% of the fare; if you cancel between two and 24 hours before the flight you lose 10%; and if you cancel less than two hours before the flight you lose 20%. If you don't show up for a domestic flight, you are entitled to a refund of 50%.

When purchasing a ticket, you may be asked to buy insurance. It's certainly not compulsory though some staff give the impression it is – the amount you can claim is pathetically low.

On domestic and international flights the free baggage allowance for an adult passenger is 20kg in economy class and 30kg in 1st class. You are also allowed 5kg of hand luggage, though this is rarely weighed. The charge for excess baggage is 1% of the full fare for each kilogram.

On domestic flights, you might get a real meal if you're flying on an Airbus or Boeing, but if the plane is Soviet built there will be no facilities for hot food.

When exiting aircraft in China, everyone grabs their hand luggage and storms for the door before the aircraft even rolls to a stop. It's best to sit back and let them fight it out.

BUS

Long-distance buses are one of the best means of getting around the country. Services are extensive and main roads are usually bumpy, but passable. Also, since the buses stop every so often in small towns and villages, you get to see parts of the countryside you wouldn't see if you travelled by train. Of course, the buses provide

stops in places you had never counted on visiting: breakdowns are frequent.

Safety is another consideration. Accidents are frequent, especially on winding mountain roads. Foreigners have been injured and killed in bus crashes.

The shock absorbers on Chinese buses are poor (or nonexistent), and for this reason try to avoid sitting at the rear of the bus if possible. The Chinese tend to know this, and there is much competition for seats at the front of the bus.

Many long-distance buses are equipped with tape players and stereo speakers that allow the drivers to blast out your eardrums with music – select a seat as far away from the speakers as possible and bring earplugs.

Chinese law requires drivers to announce their presence to cyclists, and for this they use a tweeter for preliminaries, a bugle or bullhorn if they get annoyed and an ear-wrenching air horn when they're really stirred up.

While the roads in China and the general condition of the buses have improved in recent years, traffic is getting worse. For the

Navigating Cities on Foot

At first glance, Chinese street names can be a little bewildering, with name changes common every few hundred metres. The good news is that there is some logic to it, and a little basic Chinese will help to make navigating much easier.

Many road names are compound words made up of a series of directions that place the road in context with all others in the city. Compass directions are particularly common in road names. The directions are: běi (north), nán (south), dōng (east) and xī (west). So Dong Lu literally means East Road.

Other words which regularly crop up are zhōng (central) and huan (ring, as in ring road). If you bring them together with some basic numerals, you could have Dongsanhuan Nanlu, which literally means 'east third ring south road' or the south-eastern part of the third ring road.

Trips to Traumatise

Foreign regulars on Chinese buses develop a kind of 1000-yard stare that betrays the tattered fragments of what we call innocence. They display the 'been there, done that' mentality of the veteran – they cross the road without looking (even in Guǎngzhōu), fly on Friday the 13th and smoke 60 a day (even Temple of Heaven brand). They have eluded death and feel chosen, somehow. Life is not the same after a long-distance bus trip in China; it is a rite of passage, a journey into the heart of darkness, a life on the edge and to some, I am sure, a drug that must be regularly imbibed.

I remember one bus ride in particular that I would rather forget, crammed as I was into a Bruegel-esque carnival of sweaty peasants, pigs, chickens, farm tools and other bucolic delights on the hulking leviathan of a Chinese bus that wound its way along a mountainous road to Dàlǐ, in Yúnnán, sheer walls on one side and plunging ravines on the other.

The driver drove like Mr Death himself – I half expected him to wheel around and start scything away at the nearest passenger. If the road ahead was obstructed by an ever-so-slightly-slower moving vehicle, he'd be up with his full weight on the gas pedal like a deranged jockey. Our bus would creep by the other like two sprinting snails, around countless bends in the road and blind corners. You'd find yourself standing up, white-knuckle grip on your traveller's Bible, screaming the increasingly shrill mantra 'come on, come on'. Eventually the driver would slump back in his seat and light a victory cigarette and our bus would ease by, slotting into the hard-won gap in front. Five minutes later the other bus would pass on the inside, and the process would repeat itself.

We passed the site where a car had taken a plunge over the side of the road. A group of motorists stood looking down into the ravine, hands on hips, at the point where a set of tyre tracks were neatly clipped off at the edge of the tarmac. I'm sure I heard the driver chuckle up front. Further on we passed a minibus with its roof ripped off, and an old man sat in the back singing a ditty to himself and counting his oranges in a basket. The roof was 50m further up the road. There was that chuckle again.

I remember getting to Lìjiāng and leafing through the travellers' book in Pete's Cafe (during its heyday), and coming across an entry from one poor bloke who had been in a minibus accident in the locality. The distillation of his experience yielded the tragic advice to 'sit at the back of the bus, so that when there is a collision you will have time to slow down before you hit the windscreen'.

Damian Harper

most part bus travel is a rather slow means of transport, although if there's a major highway along your travel route buses can be faster than trains. It's safe to estimate times for bus journeys by calculating the distance against a speed of 25km/h. Things are slowed further by driving techniques – drivers are loath to change gears and appear to prefer to almost stop on a slope rather than changing from third into second.

Petrol-saving ploys include techniques such as getting up to the highest speed possible and then coasting to a near standstill. Bus engines are switched off for stops of any kind, even if it's only for a matter of seconds.

Classes

In recent years night buses have become increasingly frequent. These services get mixed reviews – they are more dangerous and it's difficult to sleep on a crowded jolting bus. On popular routes, sleeper buses (wòpù qìchē) have been introduced – they are usually double the price of a normal bus service, but many travellers swear by them. Some have comfortable reclining seats, while others have two-tier bunks.

Privately owned minibuses are increasingly competing with public buses on medium-length routes. Although they're often a bit cramped, you always get a seat (or at least a knee to sit on), though you often have to bargain to get the Chinese price. Officially the prices should be the same but there have been many reports of foreigners being overcharged (though this should gradually change for the better over the next few years). Drivers will sometimes try to make you pay extra for bulky luggage.

Backpacks are a nightmare to stow on buses as there's little space under the seats and the overhead racks are hardly big enough to accommodate a loaf of bread. If you intend doing a lot of bus travel, then travel light! In China, unlike other Asian countries, people do not ride on the roof, although luggage is sometimes stowed there.

Tickets

It's a good idea to buy your ticket a day in advance. All seats are numbered. While some hotels and travel agents book bus tickets, it's often cheaper, easier and less error-prone to head for the bus station and do it yourself.

Bus stations are often large affairs with numerous ticket windows and waiting halls. There is a special symbol for a bus station that appears on local maps and is meant to resemble the bus steering wheel. The symbol is:

Costs

The cost of bus travel all depends on the quality of the bus and the mode of transport. Upper berths are cheaper than lower berths, and local buses are cheaper than expresses.

With meals, it's a mixed bag. If you don't want to rely on your driver's choice of restaurant, stock up on sufficient munchies before you board the bus.

TRAIN

Although crowded, trains are the best way to get around in reasonable speed and comfort. The network covers every province except Tibet, and that's not for want of trying (experts have advised the Chinese that it is impossible to build a line up to Lhasa – it would involve drilling tunnels through ice). There is

an estimated 52,000km of railway lines in China, most of which was built after 1949.

The safety record of the train system is good. Other than getting your luggage pinched or dying from shock when you see the toilets, there isn't much danger. However, the Chinese have a habit of throwing rubbish out the windows even as the train moves through a station. Avoid standing too close to a passing train.

Most train stations require that luggage be x-rayed before entering the waiting area.

Just about all train stations have left-luggage rooms (jìcún chù) where you can safely dump your bags for about Y2 to Y4.

Buying train tickets in China is a mixed bag. At some train stations you have to push and shove just to get to the ticket window, while at others, railway staff bend over backwards to assist foreigners (particularly if you smile and behave friendly). Even when all the sleepers are supposedly full, they sometimes manage to find one for foreigners, so it pays to be nice. Unfortunately, many foreigners take out their frustrations on the railway staff – this just makes it tough for all who follow.

Classes

In communist China there are no classes; instead you have hard seat, hard sleeper, soft seat and soft sleeper.

Hard Seat Except on the trains that serve some of the branch or more obscure lines, hard seat is in fact padded, but you'll get little sleep on the upright seats. Since hard seat is often the only thing the locals can afford, it's usually packed to the gills, the lights stay on all night, passengers spit on the floor, you can carve the smoke in the air and the carriage speakers endlessly drone news, weather, good tidings and music. Hard seat on tourist or express trains is more pleasant and less crowded.

Hard seat is OK for a day trip, but beyond that the enjoyment of your journey will be dependent on your comfort threshold.

Hard Sleeper These are comfortable and only a fixed number of people are allowed in the sleeper carriage. The carriage is made up of doorless compartments with half a dozen bunks in three tiers. Sheets, pillows and blankets are provided. The best bunk to get is a middle one since the lower one can be invaded by all and sundry who use it as a seat during the day, while the top one has little headroom. The top bunks are also where the cigarette smoke floats about (although increasingly smoking is not being allowed on trains) and they are close to the loudspeakers.

Lights and speakers in hard sleeper go out at around 9.30 to 10 pm. Competition for hard sleepers has become keen in recent years, and you'll be lucky to get one on short notice.

Soft Seat On shorter journeys (such as Shēnzhèn to Guǎngzhōu) some trains have soft-seat carriages. The seats are comfortable and overcrowding is not permitted. Smoking is prohibited, but if you want to smoke you can do so by going out into the corridor between cars. Soft seat costs about the same as hard sleeper. Unfortunately, soft-seat cars are a rarity.

Soft Sleeper Soft sleeper is luxurious travel, with four comfortable bunks in a closed compartment – complete with straps to keep the person on the top bunk from falling off in the middle of the night, wood panelling, potted plants, lace curtains, teacups, semi-clean washrooms, carpets and often air-con.

Soft sleeper costs twice as much as hard sleeper, and sometimes as much as flying. It's usually easier to purchase soft rather than hard sleeper because few ordinary Chinese can afford it.

Train Types

Train composition varies from line to line and also from day to night, and largely depends on the demand for sleepers on that line. If the journey time is more than 12 hours then the train qualifies for a dining car. The dining car often separates the hard-seat from the hard-sleeper and soft-sleeper carriages.

The conductor is in a little booth in a hard-seat carriage in the middle of the train – usually carriage No 7, 8 or 9 (all carriages are numbered on the outside). Coal-fired samovars are found in the ends of the hard-class sections, and from these you can draw a supply of hot water. However, on long trips the water often runs out.

Different types of trains are usually recognisable by the train number:

Nos 1–299 The 'special express' (*tèkuài*) trains are usually diesel hauled. They have all classes and there is a surcharge for speed and superior facilities. With a few exceptions, the international trains are included in this group.

Nos Y1–Y299 The 'travel' (*yóu*) class trains are the same as the aforementioned, though with lots more hard sleeper cars.

Nos K1–K299 The 'fast speed' (*kuàisù*) trains are another variation on the above theme. This class of train is the quickest and most luxurious.

Nos Z1–Z100 The 'standard high speed' (*zhǔngāosù*) are especially fast trains only operated on the Guǎngzhōu-Kowloon line.

Nos 300–599 The 'direct express' (*zhíkuài*) trains make more stops than the special expresses. They have soft and hard sleepers, but fewer of them. The speed surcharge is half that of the special expresses, but the difference in overall price is minimal.

Nos 600–699 The 'fast passenger' (*kuàikè*) trains take short suburban routes like Shànghǎi-Sùzhōu. You won't find sleepers on these.

Nos 700–799 The 'direct passenger' (*zhíkè*) trains are slow, and stop at everything they can find. They may even have hard wooden seats and no sleepers. The trains have antique fittings, lamps and wood panelling, and are usually steam powered. There is no speed surcharge as there is no speed.

Nos 800–999 The 'passenger' (*kè*) trains are also slowpokes, but at least have hard sleepers.

Apart from speed, the numbers don't really tell you much about the train. As a general rule, the outbound and inbound trains have matching numbers; thus train Nos 79 and 80 divide into No 79 leaving Shànghǎi and travelling to Kūnmíng, and No 80 leaving Kūnmíng and travelling to Shànghǎi.

Reservations & Tickets

Buying hard-seat tickets at short notice is usually no hassle, although you will not always be successful in getting a reserved seat.

If you try to buy a sleeper ticket at the train station and the clerk says *méi yǒu* (not have), you'll have to seek the assistance of a travel agent. This can mean China International Travel Service (CITS; Zhōngguó Guójì Lǚxíngshè), China Travel Service (CTS; Zhōngguó Lǚxíngshè), China Youth Travel Service (CYTS; Zhōngguó Qīngnián Lǚxíngshè) or the travel booking desk in your hotel. However, many CITS and CTS offices no longer do rail bookings. Most hotels have an in-house travel agent who can obtain train tickets. You'll pay a service charge of around Y40.

If you can't get a ticket for a popular route, you could try buying a ticket for somewhere two or three stops after your intended destination. Ask the ticket seller to write a note to the conductor, asking them to give you your ticket back early (this is necessary in sleeper trains, where the conductor exchanges your ticket for a plastic or metal chit; you get your original ticket back to exit the train station).

Tickets for sleepers can usually be obtained in major cities, but not in quiet backwaters. There is a five-day, advance-purchase limit.

You can buy tickets either on the night before departure or the day of departure from the train station. This often involves formidably long queues. Some stations are surprisingly well run, but others are bedlam. The best stations now have computers that spit out tickets quickly and efficiently, resulting in queues that move fast. Hard-seat tickets bought on the same day will usually be unreserved. If there are no seats, you'll either have to stand or find a place for your bum among the peanut shells, cigarette butts and spittle.

Platform Tickets An alternative to all the above is not to bother with a ticket at all and simply walk on to the train. To do this, you need to buy a platform ticket (*zhàntái piào*). These are available from the station's information booth for a few jiǎo. You then buy your ticket on the train.

This method is usually more hassle than it's worth, but may be necessary if you arrive at the station without enough time to get your ticket.

Getting Aboard As soon as the train pulls into the station, all hell breaks loose. In the hope of getting a seat, hard-seat passengers charge at the train, often pushing exiting passengers back inside.

If you have a reserved seat or sleeper, you can let the crowd fight it out for a while, then peacefully find your carriage and claim your rightful place. If you don't have a reserved seat, you're going to have to join the fray. The sensible option is to head for either the very front or the very rear of the train. Most passengers attack the middle of the train – the part closest to the platform entrance gate.

Upgrading If you get on the train with an unreserved seating ticket, you can seek out the conductor (who will usually be in the first hard-seat car) and upgrade (*bǔpiào*) yourself to a hard sleeper, soft seat or soft sleeper if there are any available. If you get to the upgrade conductor before that train departs, leave your name on a list of those waiting to upgrade. Once the train departs the conductor will hand out tickets in list order. On some trains it's easy to do, but others are notoriously crowded. A lot of intermediary stations along the railway lines can't issue sleepers, making upgrading the only alternative to hard seat.

If the sleeper carriages are full then you may have to wait until someone gets off. That sleeper may only be available to you until the next major station, but you may be able to get several hours of sleep. The price will be calculated for the distance that you travelled in the sleeper.

If upgrading fails and you can't bear the thought of hard seat, head for the dining car. You will probably have to buy a seat for Y10, but it is sometimes worth it.

Ticket Validity Tickets are valid for three days, depending on the distance travelled. On a cardboard ticket the number of days is

Běi: north
This character is a representation of two people back-to-back, and literally means 'in the opposite direction'. The derivation is from a representation of a defeated army, in which the vanquished soldiers were depicted in the act of turning around and running away. In ancient times south was named first; the opposite of south was consequently called, simply, opposite: běi.

 Nán: south
The top of this character was formerly a representation of grass or trees growing. When plants face the sun, they grow lush and vigorously and, since China is in the northern hemisphere, in Chinese thinking the south faces the sun. Thus, the character means south.

 Dōng: east
Each day, without fail, the sun rises from the east. It is no surprise, then, that when the ancient Chinese were looking for a way to represent east, the sun made up part of the picture. The other component of the character for east means tree: as the sun rises, it can be seen through the trees.

 Xī: west
The original pictograph for west showed a bird's nest since, as the sun sets in the west, birds can be seen settling in to roost. Over time, the character came to show a bird sitting atop its nest rather than the nest alone. It's easy to see how the modern character was derived from this ideograph.

 Zhōng: centre, middle
This character has been through some modifications over the centuries, but essentially remains the same as the original pictograph. It shows an arrow hitting the bull's-eye of a target and passing right through the centre.

printed at the bottom left-hand corner. If you go 250km it's valid for two days; 500km, three days; 1000km, four days; 2000km, six days; and 2500km, seven days.

If you miss your train, your ticket is not refundable. However, if you return your ticket at least two hours before departure, you should be able to get an 80% refund. If you're travelling two weeks before or after the Spring Festival (the high season), you must return your ticket at least six hours before departure for a 50% refund.

Timetables

There are train timetables in Chinese, but no matter how fluent your Chinese, the timetables are excruciatingly detailed and it's a drag working your way through them.

Even the Chinese complain about this. Thinner versions listing the main trains can sometimes be bought at major train stations. Hotel reception desks and CITS offices have copies of the timetable for trains out of their city or town.

A few Web sites are popping up that have train schedules. The government-run Web site (Chinese-language only) at www.train .cei.gov.cn features a train schedule database, as well as ticket-booking capability, or try www.travelinchina.com.

Costs

Calculation of train prices is a complex affair based on the length of the journey and the speed of the train. There are a few variables, such as air-con charges or whether a child occupies a berth or not, but nothing worth worrying about. The express surcharge is the same regardless of what class you use on the train. Soft-sleeper on international trains (and the *Hong Kong–Beijing Express*) can clean your wallet out quickly.

Food is available on the trains and at stations. It's not gourmet style, but the prices are certainly reasonable. Aside from the dining cars, railway staff regularly walk through the trains with pushcarts offering *miàn* (instant noodles), *miànbāo* (bread), *héfàn* (boxed rice lunches), *huǒtuǐ* (bologna), *píjiǔ* (beer), *kuàng quán shuǐ* (mineral water) and *qìshuǐ* (soft drinks). After about 8 pm, when meals are over, you can probably wander back into the dining car. The staff may want to get rid of you, but if you just sit down and have a beer it may be OK.

CAR & MOTORCYCLE

For those who would like to tour China by car or motorbike, the news is bleak – basically it's impossible unless you go with a large group accompanied by Public Security Bureau (PSB; Gōngānjú) the whole way, apply for permits months in advance and pay through the nose for the privilege. It's not like India, where you can simply buy a motorbike and head off on your own. So if you're hoping to ship in your motorcycle or car or to buy one when you get to

China and drive around independently, you can forget about it.

If you're visiting China on a L (tourist) visa, you cannot (legally) drive in China. Foreign residents (for example, those on a X, Z or D visa) may drive in China after obtaining a Chinese drivers' licence. However, there are often restrictions on how far you can drive from your place of residence – the local PSB can inform you of the latest regulations. As with driving a car, foreigners can drive motorcycles if they are a resident of China and have a Chinese motorcycle licence.

On the other hand, it's easy enough to book a car with a driver. Basically, this is just a standard long-distance taxi. Travel

---

Stunt Driving

Aside from breakdown, there are sometimes other difficulties which could delay your journey. One German traveller taking a bus from Wúzhōu to Yángshuò was surprised when his bus started competing with the bus ahead for roadside passengers. After getting up perilously close to its rear bumper and blasting furiously on an armoury of horns, his driver managed, in a hair-raising exhibition of reckless abandon and dare-devilry, to sweep around the opposition on a blind bend and be first to get to a group of prospective passengers just around the corner. The other driver, determined not to let his fellow get away with such deviously unsporting behaviour, pulled up and started thumping him through the window.

A decisive knock-out proving elusive in such cramped quarters, the two soon leapt out of their buses to continue the punch-up on the roadside. Things were beginning to look grim for the German's driver, when a wailing siren announced the arrival of the boys in green. Without even a glance at the passengers of the two buses, they handcuffed the two drivers, threw them unceremoniously into the back of their van and drove off. It was five hours before new drivers were dispatched to the scene of the crime.

agencies like CITS or even hotel booking desks can make the arrangements. They generally ask excessive fees – the name of the game is to negotiate. If you can communicate in Chinese or find someone to translate, it's not particularly difficult to find a private taxi driver to take you wherever you like for less than half of CITS rates.

Road Rules

You're more likely to get fined for illegal parking than speeding. Indeed, with China's gridlock traffic, opportunities for speeding are swiftly vanishing.

If you travel much around China, you'll periodically encounter road blocks where the police stop every vehicle and impose arbitrary fines for driving with sunglasses, driving without sunglasses etc. The fine must be paid on the spot or the vehicle will be impounded. Basically, these are fundraising events.

Rental

Tourists are not yet permitted to rent either cars or motorbikes. Rental companies do exist, but they are only for the domestic market or for foreigners armed with a Chinese drivers' licence.

Purchase

Only legal residents of China can purchase a motor vehicle. The whole procedure is plagued by bureaucracy, with lots of little fees to be paid along the way.

The licence plates issued to foreigners are different from those issued to Chinese, and this is a big hassle. Since the licence plates go with the car, this essentially means that a foreigner wanting to buy a used car must buy it from another foreigner.

BICYCLE

Probably the first time the Chinese saw a pneumatic-tyred bicycle was when a pair of Americans called Allen and Sachtleben bumbled into Běijīng around 1891 after a three-year journey from Istanbul. They wrote a book about it called *Across Asia on a Bicycle*. The novelty was well received by

the Qing court, and the boy-emperor Puyi was given to tearing around the Forbidden City on a cycle.

Today there are over 300 million bikes in China, more than can be found in any other country. Some are made for export, but most are for domestic use.

The traditional Chinese bicycle and tricycle are workhorses, used to carry anything up to a 100kg slaughtered pig or a couch.

In western countries, travel agencies organising bicycle trips advertise in cycling magazines. Bicycle clubs can contact CITS (or its competitors) for information about organising a trip. See Organised Tours in the Getting There & Away chapter for a list of tour operators.

Rental

There are bicycle hire shops that cater to foreigners in most traveller centres. In touristy places like Yángshuò, it's even possible to rent mountain bikes, but elsewhere it's usually the old black clunkers. The majority of hire places operate out of hotels popular with foreigners, but there are also many independent hire shops. Even in towns with little tourist traffic there are often hire shops catering to Chinese who are passing through. Surprisingly, medium-size cities often have better bicycle-rental facilities than large metropolises.

Day hire, 24-hour hire or hire by the hour are the norm. It's possible to hire for a stretch of several days, so touring is possible if the bike is in good condition. Rates for westerners are typically Y2 per hour or Y10 to Y20 per day – the price depends more on competition than anything else. Some big hotels charge ridiculous rates.

If you hire over a long period you should be able to reduce the rate. Most hire places will ask you for a deposit of anything up to Y500 and to leave some sort of ID. Sometimes the staff will ask for your passport. Give them some other ID instead, like a student card or a drivers' licence.

If you're planning to stay in one place for more than about five weeks, it's probably cheaper to buy your own bike and either sell it or give it to a friend when you leave.

The ever-watchful eye of Chairman Mao, Líjiāng

JULIET COOMBE

Working in the fields in Jǐnghóng, Yúnnán

KRAIG LIEB

Morning *tàijíquán* in Jǐngshān Gōngyuán, Běijīng

HILARY ADELE SMITH

A small Xīshuāngbǎnnà local enjoys her noodles.

CRAIG PERSHOUSE

Village local in Báishā, Yúnnán

KRAIG LIEB

Uyghur chilli transaction, Kashgar bazaar, Xīnjiāng

CRAIG PERSHOUSE

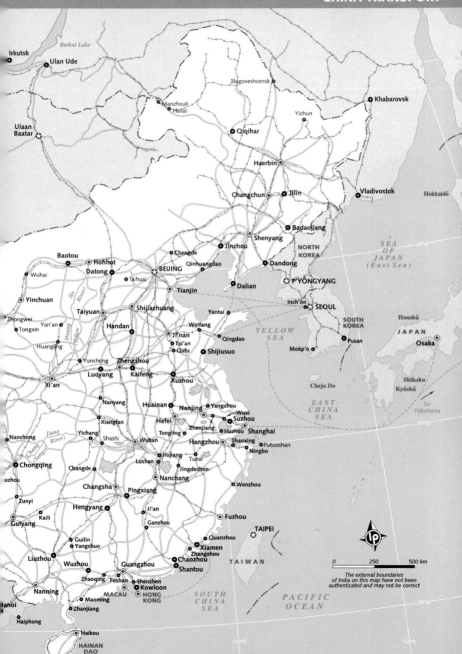

A long day in Zhèngzhōu, Hénán

Colourful cloth at the Kashgar bazaar, Xīnjiāng

Hani women at Měnghùn's lively Sunday market

Snap! (Hénán)

A ride to school, Běijīng style

Mastering martial arts at Shàolín Sì in Hénán

Before taking a bike, check the brakes, get the tyres pumped up hard and make sure that none of the moving parts are about to fall off. Get the saddle raised to maximum leg power. It's also worth tying something on the bike – a handkerchief, for example – to identify your bicycle amid the zillions at the bicycle racks.

A bike licence is obligatory for Chinese, but is not necessary for a foreigner. Some cities have bicycle licence plates, and in Běijīng the bikes owned by foreigners have special licence plates so they can't be sold to a Chinese (although most foreigners don't bother to register their bikes). Bike-repair shops are everywhere and repairs are cheap (about Y10), but overcharging of foreigners is common – ask first. Outdoor bicycle repair stalls are found on every other corner in larger cities, and repairs are very cheap – from 3 jiǎo to pump up your tyres to Y10 to fix a bent wheel rim.

Purchase

Some travellers have saved themselves the bother of bringing bikes across the border by buying mountain bikes or racers in China. A run-of-the-mill Flying Pigeon costs about Y300. Some brands are acceptable quality and are even exported. For information on specific shops see the Hong Kong and Běijīng chapters.

Touring

The legalities of cycling from town to town are open to conjecture. There is no national law in China that prohibits foreigners from riding bicycles. Basically, the problem is that of 'open' and 'closed' areas. It's illegal for foreigners to visit closed areas without a permit. Fair enough, but foreigners can transit a closed area – that is, you can travel by train or bus through a closed area as long as you don't exit the vehicle in this 'forbidden zone'. The question is: Should riding a bicycle through a closed area be classified as 'transiting' or 'visiting' it?

Chinese law is as clear as mud on this issue. Most of the time, the police won't bother you, but some officials just can't stand seeing foreigners bicycling through

---

街 **Lù: road, street, way, path**
In ancient times, the left side of this character meant both leg and foot, although it refers only to foot now. The upper part of the right side of the character also meant foot in times gone by, while the lower part referred to a special location. Thus the character as a whole can be interpreted as 'feet heading towards a special place'. How do they get there? By finding a path or road.

路 **Jiē: road, street**
The radical of this character, the two parts of which appear at the side, means to go. Sandwiched between them the repeated phonetic, which means soil, suggests the ground on which one goes; that is, a street or road.

China – they expect you to be travelling by taxi and tour bus. After all, foreigners are universally regarded as rich and bicycles are meant for poor peasants. Most Chinese can't figure out why foreigners would even want to cycle around China.

If you get caught in a closed area, it is unlikely to be while you are on the road. The law keeps firm tabs on transients via hotels. If you're staying overnight in an open place, but you are suspected of having passed through a closed area, the police may pull a raid on your hotel. You can be hauled down to the police station where you have to submit to a lengthy interrogation, sign a confession and pay a fine. Fines vary from Y50 to whatever they think you can afford. There is some latitude for bargaining in these situations, and you should request a receipt (shōujù). Don't expect police to give you any tips on which areas are closed and which are open – they seldom know themselves.

Camping is possible if you can find a spare blade of grass. The trick is to select a couple of likely places about half an hour before sunset, keep pedalling and then backtrack so you can pull off the road at the chosen spot just after darkness falls.

It's essential to have a kickstand for parking. A bell, headlight and reflector are good ideas. Make sure everything is bolted down, otherwise you'll invite theft. Adhesive reflector strips get ripped off.

Hazards

Night riding is particularly hazardous. Many drivers in China only use their headlights to flash them on and off as a warning for cyclists up ahead to get out of the way. On country roads, look out for those UFO-style walking tractors, which often have no headlights at all.

Your fellow cyclists are another factor in the hazard equation. Be prepared for cyclists to suddenly swerve in front of you, to come hurtling out of a side road or even to head straight towards you against the flow of the traffic. Chinese bicycles are rarely equipped with lights.

In most larger towns and cities bicycles should be parked at designated places on the pavement. This will generally be a roped-off enclosure, and bicycle-rack attendants will give you a token when you park there. It can cost from 1 jiǎo to Y1. If you don't use this service, you may return to find that your bike has been 'towed' away. Confiscated, illegally parked bicycles make their way to the police station. There will be a fine in retrieving it, although it shouldn't bankrupt you.

Bicycle theft does occur. The bicycle racks with their attendants help prevent this, but keep your bike off the streets at night, or at least within the hotel gates. If the hotel has no grounds then take the bike up to your room. Most hired bicycles have a lock around the rear wheel that can be pried open with a screwdriver in seconds. It would be better buying and using a cable lock, widely available from shops in China, but your best bet is to bring along a secure lock from your home country. You should definitely use your own lock when renting a bike.

Off the Road

Most travellers who bring bikes take at least a couple of breaks from the rigours of the road, during which they use some other means of transport. The best option is the bus. It is generally no problem stowing bikes on the roofs of buses and there is seldom a charge involved. Air and train transport are more problematic.

Bikes are not cheap to transport on trains: they can cost as much as a hard-seat fare. It's cheaper on boats, if you can find one. Trains have quotas for the number of bikes they may transport. As a foreigner you will get preferential treatment in the luggage compartment and the bike will go on the first available train. But your bike won't arrive at the same time as you unless you send it on a couple of days in advance. At the other end it is held in storage for three days free, and then incurs a small charge.

The procedure for putting a bike on a train and getting it at the other end is as follows:

- Railway personnel would like to see a train ticket for yourself (not entirely essential).
- Go to the baggage transport section of the station. Get a white slip and fill it out to get the two or three tags for registration. Then fill out a form (it's in Chinese, but just fill it out in English) that reads: 'Number/to station x/send goods person/receive goods person/total number of goods/from station y'.
- Take the white slip to another counter, where you pay and are given a blue slip.
- At the other end (after delays of up to three days for transporting a bike) you present the blue slip and get a white slip in return. This means your bike has arrived. The procedure could take from 20 minutes to an hour depending on who's around. If you lose that blue slip you'll have trouble reclaiming your bike.

The best bet for getting your bike on a bus is to get to the station early and put it on the roof. Strictly speaking, there should not be a charge for this, but in practice the driver will generally try to get you to pay.

Transporting your bike by plane can be expensive, but it's often less complicated than by train. Some cyclists have not been charged; others have had to pay 1% of their fare per kilogram of excess weight.

HITCHING

Hitching is never entirely safe in any country in the world, and we don't recommend it. Travellers who decide to hitch should understand that they are taking a small but potentially serious risk. People who do choose to hitch will be safer if they travel in pairs and let someone know where they are planning to go.

Many people have hitchhiked in China, and some have been amazingly successful. It's not officially sanctioned and the same dangers that apply elsewhere in the world also apply in China. Exercise caution, and if you're in any doubt as to the intentions of your prospective driver, say no.

Hitching in China is rarely free, and passengers are expected to offer at least a tip. Some drivers might even ask for an unreasonable amount of money, so try to establish a figure early to avoid problems later. Even when a price is agreed upon, don't be surprised if the driver raises it when you arrive at your destination and creates a big scene (with a big crowd) if you don't cough up the extra cash. Indeed, he or she may even pull this scam halfway through the trip, and if you don't pay up then you get kicked out in the middle of nowhere.

In other words, don't think of hitching as a means to save money – it will rarely be any cheaper than the bus. The main reason to do it is to get to isolated outposts where public transport is poor. There is, of course, some joy in meeting the locals this way, but communicating is certain to be a problem if you don't speak Chinese.

The best way to get a lift is to head out to main roads on the outskirts of town. There are usually lots of trucks on the roads, and even postal trucks and army convoys are worth trying. There is no Chinese signal for hitching, so just try waving down the trucks.

BOAT

For better or worse, China's boats are disappearing fast. Many services have been cancelled – victims of improved bus and air transport. In coastal areas, you're most likely to use a boat to reach offshore islands like Pǔtuóshān or Hǎinán Dǎo.

The Yāntái-Dàlián ferry will likely survive because it saves hundreds of kilometres

of overland travel. For the same reason, the Shànghǎi-Níngbō service will probably continue to operate, but elsewhere the outlook for coastal passenger ships is not too good.

There are also several inland shipping routes worth considering, but these are also vanishing. For details of each trip see the appropriate sections in this book.

The best known river trip is the three-day boat ride along the Cháng Jiāng (Yangzi River) from Chóngqìng to Wǔhàn. The Guǎngzhōu to Wúzhōu route along the Xī Hé (West River) is popular with low-budget travellers as it is the cheapest way to get from Guǎngzhōu to Guìlín and Yángshuò, disembarking at Wúzhōu and then continuing on by bus to Guìlín or Yángshuò. The Lí Jiāng boat trip from Guìlín to Yángshuò is a popular tourist ride that takes six hours.

You can also travel the Grand Canal from Hángzhōu to Sūzhōu on a tourist boat. There are no longer passenger boats on the Huáng Hé (Yellow River).

There are still a number of popular boats between Hong Kong and the rest of China, but services are getting fewer. See the Getting There & Away section of the Hong Kong chapter for details.

LOCAL TRANSPORT

Long-distance transport in China is not really a problem – the dilemma occurs when you finally make it to your destination. As in US and Australian cities where the car is the key to movement, the bicycle is the key in China and if you don't have one, life is more difficult. Walking is not usually recommended, since Chinese cities tend to be very spread out.

Bus

Apart from bikes, buses are the most common means of getting around in the cities. Services are fairly extensive and the buses go to most places. The problem is that they are almost always packed. If an empty bus pulls in at a stop then a battle for seats ensues. Even more aggravating is the slowness of the traffic. You just have to be patient, never expect anything to move rapidly, and allow lots of time to get to the train station to catch your train. One consolation is that buses are cheap – rarely more than Y1.

Good maps of Chinese cities and bus routes are readily available and are often sold by hawkers outside the train stations. When you get on a bus, point to where you want to go on the map, and the conductor (who is seated near the door) will sell you the right ticket. They usually tell you where to get off, provided they remember.

You may be offered a seat in a crowded bus, although this is now a rarity. If that peculiarly Chinese politeness does manifest itself and you're offered a seat, it's best to accept as a refusal may offend. Whatever you do, smile and be appreciative.

Taxi

Taxis cruise the streets in most large cities, but elsewhere they may simply congregate at likely spots (such as bus stations) and hassle every foreigner who walks past.

You can always summon a taxi from the tourist hotels, which sometimes have separate booking desks. You can hire them for a single trip or on a daily basis – the latter is worth considering if there's a group of people who can split the cost. Some of the tourist hotels also have minibuses on hand.

While most taxis have meters, they are a pure formality (except in large cities) and usually only get switched on by accident. Sometimes you're better off without the meter – as elsewhere in the world, taxi drivers don't mind taking you for a 20km ride to a place just across the street. Taxi prices should be negotiated before you get into the taxi, and bargaining is usual (but keep it friendly as nastiness on your part will result in a higher price!). Don't be surprised if the driver attempts to change the price when you arrive, claiming that you 'misunderstood' what he said. If you want to get nasty, *this* is the time to do it. If your spoken Chinese is less than perfect, write the price down clearly and make sure the driver agrees at the start to avoid 'misunderstandings' later.

It's important to realise that most Chinese cities impose limitations on the number of passengers that a taxi can carry. The limit is usually four, though minibuses can take more, and drivers are usually unwilling to break the rules and risk trouble with the police.

We witnessed a vicious argument in Běijīng between eight foreigners and a taxi driver – the driver refused to take all eight people in one trip, saying it was illegal and he could get into trouble. He was willing to make two trips, but the foreigners figured that was just his way of trying to charge double and therefore rip them off. The driver was, in fact, telling the truth.

Motorcycle Taxi

The deal is that you get a ride on the back of someone's motorcycle for about half the price of what a regular four-wheeled taxi would charge. If you turn a blind eye to the hazards, this is a quick and cheap way of getting around. You must wear a helmet – the driver will provide one. Obviously, there is no meter, so fares must be agreed to in advance.

Motor-Tricycle

The motor-tricycle (sānlún mótuōchē) – for want of a better name – is an enclosed three-wheeled vehicle with a driver at the front, a small motorbike engine below and seats for two passengers behind. They tend to congregate outside the train and bus stations in larger towns and cities. Some of these vehicles have trays at the rear with bench seats along the sides so that four or more people can be accommodated.

Pedicab

A pedicab (sānlúnchē) is a pedal-powered tricycle with a seat to carry passengers. Chinese pedicabs have the driver in front and passenger seats in the back.

Pedicabs are gradually disappearing in China, victims of the combustion engine. However, pedicabs congregate outside train and bus stations or hotels in parts of China. In a few places, pedicabs cruise the streets in large numbers (Lhasa, for example).

Unfortunately, some drivers are aggressive. A reasonable fare will be quoted, but when you arrive at your destination it'll be multiplied by 10. Another tactic is to quote

Pedicabs Versus Rickshaws

A rickshaw is a two-wheeled passenger cart pulled by a man on foot. It was invented in Japan, where the word *jin-rikusha* means 'human-powered vehicle'. It was introduced into China in the late 19th century, where it was called *yángchē* (foreign vehicle).

The rickshaw eventually became a symbol of human exploitation – one person pulling another in a cart – and disappeared from China in the 1950s. Its replacement, the pedicab – sometimes mistakenly called a rickshaw – is a tricycle with a seat for one or two passengers.

you a price like Y10 and then demand US$10 – the driver claims that you 'misunderstood'. Yet another tactic is for the driver to bring you halfway and demand more payment to bring you to your destination.

ORGANISED TOURS

Some of the one-day tours are reasonably priced and might be worth the cost as they can save you a lot of trouble. Some remote spots are difficult to reach and a tour might well be your only option.

Some tours are very informal and even popular with budget travellers. For example, at Turpan in Xīnjiāng Province, many travellers do a one-day tour by minibus of the surrounding countryside. The minibus drivers hang around the hotels and solicit business, so there is no need to get involved with CITS or other agencies.

Another low-cost option is to go on a tour with a local Chinese group. A number of travellers use this option in Běijīng, for example, to reach the Great Wall. The tour bus could be an old rattletrap and you'll get to visit a few souvenir shops (which invariably pay under-the-table commissions to the bus drivers), but these tours can be interesting if you keep a sense of humour about it. Don't expect the guides to speak anything but Chinese – possibly just the local dialect.

Sometimes the buses will whiz through interesting spots and make long stops at dull

places for the requisite photo sessions. You might have difficulty getting a ticket if your Chinese isn't good and they think you're too much trouble. The Chinese tours are often booked through hotel service desks or from private travel agencies. In some cases, there is an established tour bus meeting spot – you just roll up in the morning and hop on board.

CITS

The China International Travel Service (CITS; Zhōngguó Guójì Lǚxíngshè) deals with China's foreign tourist hordes, and mainly concerns itself with organising and making travel arrangements for group tours. CITS existed as far back as 1954, when there were few customers; now they're inundated with a couple of hundred thousand foreign tourists a year. Unfortunately, after 40 years of being in business, CITS has still not gotten its act totally together.

Nowadays, travellers make their way around China without ever having to deal with CITS. In many remote regions, CITS does not offer much in the way of services. In other places, CITS may sell hard-to-get-hold-of train tickets or tickets for the opera or acrobatics or perhaps provide tours of rural villages or factories. It really all depends on where you are.

There will usually be a small service charge added on to the price of any train, boat or plane tickets purchased through CITS.

CITS is a frequent target of ire for all kinds of reasons: rudeness, inefficiency, laziness and even fraud. Bear in mind, however, that service varies enormously from office to office. Expect the worst, but be prepared to be pleasantly surprised.

CTS

The China Travel Service (CTS; Zhōngguó Lǚxíngshè) was originally set up to handle tourists from Hong Kong, Macau and Taiwan and foreign nationals of Chinese descent. These days your gene pool and nationality make little difference – CTS has now become a keen competitor with CITS.

Many foreigners use the CTS offices in Hong Kong and Macau to obtain visas and book trains, planes, hovercraft and other transport to China.

CTS can sometimes get you a better deal on hotels booked through their office than you could obtain on your own (of course, this does not apply to budget accommodation such as backpackers' dormitories).

CYTS

The name China Youth Travel Service (CYTS; Zhōngguó Qīngnián Lǔxíngshè)

implies that this is some sort of student organisation, but these days CYTS performs essentially the same services as CITS and CTS. Being a smaller organisation, CYTS seems to try harder to compete against the big league. This could result in better service, but not necessarily lower prices.

CYTS is mostly interested in tour groups, but individual travellers could find it useful for booking air tickets or sleepers on the trains.

Běijīng 北京

☎ 010 • pop 12,167,000

'The mountains are high and the emperor is far away' says an ancient Chinese proverb, meaning that the further one moves from Běijīng's grasp, the better. Běijīng, capital of the People's Republic of China (PRC), is where they move the cogs and wheels of the Chinese universe.

Those who have slugged it out in hard-seat trains and ramshackle buses through the poverty-stricken interior of China appreciate the creature comforts of Běijīng. The city boasts some of China's best restaurants and recreation facilities, and palatial hotels fit for an emperor. Foreigners who have passed their time only in Běijīng without seeing the rest of China come away with the impression that everything is hunky-dory in the PRC.

Whatever impression you come away with, Běijīng is not a realistic window on China. Especially after its facelift prior to the PRC's 50th anniversary, it's too much of a cosmetic showcase to qualify. However, with a bit of effort you can get out of the make-up department: In between the wide boulevards, high-rises and militaristic structures are some historical and cultural treasures.

HISTORY

Although the area south-west of the city was inhabited by cave dwellers some 500,000 years ago, the earliest records of settlements in Běijīng date from around 1000 BC. The city developed as a frontier trading town for the Mongols, Koreans and tribes from Shāndōng and central China. By the Warring States Period it had grown to be the capital of the Yan kingdom. The town underwent a number of changes as it acquired new warlords – the Khitan Mongols and the Manchurian Juchen tribes among them. During the Liao dynasty, Běijīng was referred to as Yanjing (capital of Yan), and this is the name used for Běijīng's most popular beer.

Highlights

Population: 12.6 million
Area: 16,800 sq km

• The Forbidden City, the centre of power in the Middle Kingdom for more than 500 years
• Tiāntán (Temple of Heaven), a perfect example of Ming architecture and the symbol of Běijīng
• The Summer Palace, the lovely gardens of China's imperial rulers in a stunning setting beside Kūnmíng Hu
• The Great Wall, ancient China's greatest public works project and now the nation's leading tourist attraction
• The *hútòngs*, Běijīng's traditional neighbourhoods

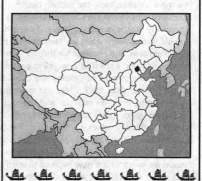

Běijīng's history really gets under way in AD 1215, the year Genghis Khan set fire to Yanjing and slaughtered everything in sight. From the ashes emerged Dadu (Great Capital), alias Khanbaliq, the Khan's town. By 1279 Genghis Khan's grandson Kublai had made himself ruler of most of Asia, and Khanbaliq was his capital. With a lull in the fighting from 1280 to 1300, foreigners managed to drop in along the Silk Road for tea with the Great Khan. The mercenary

Xiao Liangyu

I am one of Běijīng's 3 million 'floating population'. We might be second-class citizens here, yet life is much better than back in the village. Mine is called Xi-aocun in Ānhuī, a beautiful place encircled by rivers and hills. But the reality is that it's very poor.

OXFORD UNIVERSITY PRESS

The only families that had money to build new houses were those with family members who worked as migrants. So, I decided to go to the city to work. At 18, I got work through the friend of a friend as a builder in Hénán. The job was no easier than my usual toil in the fields – we worked up to 12 hours a day, eating and sleeping in harsh conditions – but the pay was much better.

I saved enough to return home to get married at Chinese New Year in 1992. A cousin who had 'made it' suggested I try my luck in the capital, so I took my new wife to Běijīng. We rented a tiny room in Lan-qiying, north-west of the city. So many migrants from Ānhuī settled there it's also known as Ānhuī village.

We opened a food stall selling *youtiao* (fried dough sticks) for breakfast at a busy junction. Before long, I learned that many fellow Ānhuī workers were in a more lucrative line – the rubbish business. With help from friends, I earned a very desirable position as a rubbish man in Qinghua University.

I ride my tricycle across the university's residential area, singing out loudly 'collecting reeee-jects! Any old books, newspapers for sale? Bottles, caaardboard?' Some items have a fixed price, such as aluminium cans, and I bargain for the rest. After sorting out the rubbish I collect, like a soldier counting war trophies, I sell it at a recycling centre. Honestly, no local would like to be a rubbish man. My clothes are shabby, hair messy and dusty. But it's actually not a bad business. I buy plastic bottles for 5 fen and sell for 7.5 fen, and make 5 to 10 fen from each aluminium can.

Small profit, but it all adds up, and I can sell big items like stoves or washing machines for 50% more than I paid. I earn something between Y1000 to Y1500 every month. I dare say my income is more than many urban workers. I'll do my best to give my son a good education so he can find a decent job. If you have money and education, who dares to look down on you?

Yet it's harder now to make good money as a rubbish man and I'm looking at other possibilities. I heard we migrants are now allowed to learn to drive. One friend vaguely promised me a job as a truck driver if I had a licence, so I'm going to enrol at a driving school. My dream is to drive a Liberation model truck, in a pair of clean white gloves. The salary may not be much higher, but a truck driver sounds much better than a rubbish man!

Abridged from *China Remembers* by Zhang Lijia and Calum MacLeod, published by Oxford University Press (1999)

Zhu Yanhang led an uprising in 1368, taking over the city and ushering in the Ming dynasty. The city was renamed Beiping (Northern Peace) and for the next 35 years the capital was shifted south to Nánjīng.

In the early 1400s Zhu's son Yongle shuffled the court back to Beiping and renamed it Běijīng (Northern Capital). Many of the structures like the Forbidden City and Tiāntán were built in Yongle's reign.

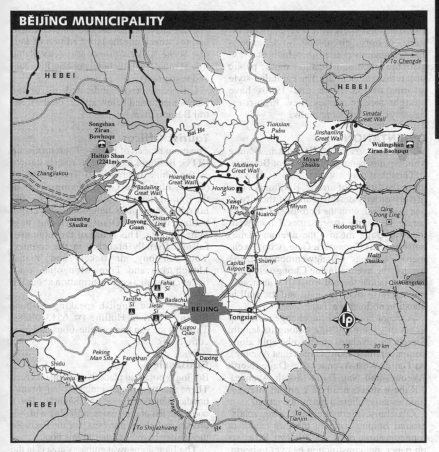

BĚIJĪNG MUNICIPALITY

The first change of government came with the Manchus, who invaded China and established the Qing dynasty. Under them, and particularly during the reigns of the emperors Kangxi and Qianlong, Běijīng was expanded and renovated, and summer palaces, pagodas and temples were built.

In the last 120 years of the Qing dynasty, Běijīng, and subsequently China, were subjected to power struggles, invaders and the chaos they caused: the Anglo-French troops who in 1860 marched in and burnt the Old Summer Palace to the ground; the corrupt regime under Empress Dowager Cixi; the

Boxers; General Yuan Shikai; the warlords; the Japanese who occupied the city in 1937; and the Kuomintang after the Japanese defeat. Běijīng changed hands again in January 1949 when People's Liberation Army (PLA) troops entered the city. On 1 October of that year Mao proclaimed a 'People's Republic' to an audience of some 500,000 citizens in Tiānānmén Square.

Like the emperors before them, the communists have significantly altered the face of Běijīng to suit their own image. Down came the commemorative arches, while blocks of buildings were reduced to rubble to widen major boulevards. From 1950 to 1952 the outer walls were levelled in the interests of traffic circulation. Soviet experts and technicians poured in, which may explain the Stalinesque features on the public structures that went up. The capitalist-style reforms of the 1980s and 1990s have brought foreign money, new high-rises, freeways and shopping malls.

ORIENTATION

With a total area of 16,800 sq km, Běijīng Municipality is roughly the size of Belgium.

Though it may not appear so to the visitor in the turmoil of arrival, Běijīng is a city of very orderly design. Think of the city as one giant grid, with the Forbidden City at its centre. As for the street names: Chongwenmenwai Dajie means 'the avenue (dajie) outside (wai) Chongwen Gate (Chongwenmen)', whereas Chongwenmennei Dajie means 'the avenue inside Chongwen Gate' (that is, inside the old wall). It's an academic exercise since the gate and the wall in question no longer exist.

A major boulevard can change names up to six or even eight times along its length. Streets and avenues can also be split along compass points: Dong Dajie (East Avenue), Xi Dajie (West Avenue), Bei Dajie (North Avenue) and Nan Dajie (South Avenue). All these streets head off from an intersection, usually where a gate once stood.

Officially, there are four 'ring roads' around Běijīng, circling the city centre in four concentric rings. A Fifth Ring Rd exists on paper, but construction has yet to begin.

Maps

English-language maps of Běijīng are generally handed out free at the big hotels. They're often part of an advertising supplement for various companies whose locations are, of course, also shown on the map. It's better to fork out a few yuan for a bilingual map that shows bus routes. These are available from the Friendship Store and hotel gift shops.

If you can deal with Chinese-language maps, you'll find a wide variety from which to choose. You can pick these up at train stations or at any streetside news stalls for Y3.

INFORMATION

For the latest restaurant and entertainment listings, check out the latest edition of *Beijing Scene*, *City Edition* or *Metro*, available free at most five-star hotels or Sānlǐtún bars and restaurants.

Unless otherwise indicated, all of the places mentioned below appear on the Central Běijīng map.

Tourist Offices

The main branch of Beijing Tourism Group (BTG; Běijīng Lǚxíngshè; formerly known as the China International Travel Service (CITS; Zhōngguó Guójì Lǚxíngshè) is at the Beijing Tourist Building (☎ 6515 8562, fax 6515 8603) at 28 Jianguomenwai Dajie, behind the New Otani Hotel and near Scitech Plaza. This is one of the more useful and friendly branches in the country. You can buy air tickets and Trans-Manchurian and Trans-Mongolian train tickets, as well as get information about the city.

There is an English-speaking 24-hour Beijing Tourism Hotline (☎ 6513 0828). This service can answer questions and hear complaints.

Embassies

Běijīng is not a bad place to stock up on visas. There are two major embassy neighbourhoods: Jiànguóménwài and Sānlǐtún. For a complete list of embassies in Běijīng with addresses and phone numbers, see the Facts for the Visitor chapter earlier in this book.

The Jiànguóménwài embassy area is in the vicinity of the Friendship Store, east of the city centre. The Sānlǐtún embassy cluster is several kilometres to the north-east, near the Great Wall Sheraton Hotel.

Money

All hotels – even most budget ones – can change travellers cheques or US dollars.

If you want to cash travellers cheques and receive US dollars in return (necessary if you're going to Russia or Mongolia), this can be done at CITIC at the International Building (Guójì Dàshà), adjacent to the Friendship Store at 19 Jianguomenwai

Dajie. CITIC will advance cash on major international credit cards.

There is a useful branch of the Bank of China in Xindongan Plaza – just to the east of the Forbidden City on Wangfujing Dajie near the Foreign Languages Bookstore – which offers many of the same services as CITIC but is less efficient.

You can change US dollars on the black market for a much better exchange rate than in the banks (at the time of writing the bank rate was Y8.03 to one US dollar, whereas the black market rate was Y8.82). There are money changers on Sānlǐtún's bar street – try one of the stalls in the clothing market with things hanging down obscuring the view inside. Some of the restaurants around universities with large numbers of foreign students also change money. Of course changing money this way is not without risk; your best bet is to ask one of Běijīng's foreign residents to recommend a particular vendor with whom to change money.

Post & Communications

The international post and communications building is on Jianguomenwai Dajie, not far from the Friendship Store. It's open Monday to Friday from 8 am to 6 pm and 9 am to 5 pm for international package pick-up (be sure to bring your passport). All letters and parcels marked 'Poste Restante, GPO Beijing' will wind up here. The staff even file poste restante letters in alphabetical order, a rare occurrence in China, but you pay for all this efficiency – there is a Y1.50 fee charged for each letter received.

There are a number of private couriers that offer international express posting of documents and parcels. The major ones are:

United Parcel Service (☎ 6593 2932) Unit A, 1st floor, Tower B, Beijing Kelun Bldg, 12A Guanghua Lu, Chaoyang District
DHL (☎ 6466 2211, fax 6467 7826) 45 Xinyuan Jie, Chaoyang District. There are also branches in the Kempinski Hotel and China World Trade Centre
Federal Express (☎ 800 810 2338, 6561 2003) Hanwei Bldg, 7 Guanghua Lu, Chaoyang District. There's also a branch in the Golden Land Bldg, next to the 21st Century Hotel

TNT Skypak (☎ 6465 2227, fax 6462 4018) 8A Xiangheyuan Zhongli, Chaoyang

Email & Internet Access

The Sparkice Internet Cafe (Shíhuá Wǎngluò Kafei Shi; ☎ 6833 5225, ☻ cafesparkice.co.cn), in the west wing of the Capital Gymnasium (west of Běijīng Dòngwùyuán), charges Y30 per hour for use of its machines. It's open daily from 10 am to 10 pm. There are branches of Sparkice in the China World Trade Centre at 1 Jianguomenwai Dajie and on the campus of Beijing Normal University. Internet cafes can also be found outside the south gate of Qinghua University and outside the south gate of the Beijing Language and Culture University. Although the computers aren't as well kept and as fast as Sparkice's, the Benk Internet Cafe (☎ 6507 2814, 59 Dongdaqiao Lu, ☻ beak@public.bta.net.cn) is conveniently located just around the corner from the Silk Market.

Libraries

The massive Beijing Library (☎ 6841 5566), at 39 Baishiqiao Lu, Haidian District, west of the Běijīng Dòngwùyuán, has foreign periodicals and foreign books reading rooms. Although foreigners aren't allowed to check books out, you can buy a day pass for Y1 on the third floor. You can also access the Internet here or watch Chinese and international films and listen to Chinese pop on the third floor. The library is open daily 9 am to 5 pm. Various embassies also have small libraries in English and other languages. Some of the more useful embassy libraries include the American Center for Educational Exchange (☎ 6597 3242), at Room 2801, Jīngguǎng Xīn Shìjie Fàndiàn, Hujialou, in Chaoyang District, and the Cultural & Educational Section of the British Embassy (☎ 6590 6903), on the 4th floor of the British Embassy Annex, Landmark Tower, 8 Dongsanhuan Beilu, also in Chaoyang District.

PSB

The Public Security Bureau (PSB; Gōngānjú; ☎ 6404 7799) has an office at 2 Andingmen Dongdajie, about 300m east of the Yōnghé

Gōng. It's open 8.30 am to noon and 1 to 5 pm Monday to Saturday. The visa office is on the 2nd floor.

Medical Services

Asia Emergency Assistance (AEA; ☎ 6462 9100, fax 6462 9111), at 1 Xingfu Sancun Bei Jie, behind the German embassy, has the largest clientele within the foreign community. The staff are mostly expats, and emergency service is available 24 hours. AEA offers emergency evacuation from China for the critically ill. The International Medical Centre (☎ 6465 1561, fax 6465 1560) is in the Lufthansa Centre at 50 Liangmaqiao Lu. Emergency service is available 24 hours, but it's a good idea to call first for an appointment. The Hong Kong International Medical Clinic (Gǎng Aò Zhōgxīn; ☎ 6501 2288 ext 2345, fax 6502 3426), on the 3rd floor of the Hong Kong Macau Center (also known as the Swissôtel), has a 24-hour medical and dental clinic, including obstetrical/gynaecological services. The staff can also do immunisations here. Prices are more reasonable than those at AEA and the International Medical Centre.

Much cheaper than going to foreigners clinics are Chinese hospitals that cater to foreigners. Beijing Union Medical Hospital (Xiéhé Yīyuàn; ☎ 6529 6114, 53 Dongdan Beidajie) has the reputation of being the best in the country. There is a foreigners and high-level cadres only wing in the back building.

If you're looking for a herbal remedy for your ailment (there are cures for everything from a low sex-drive to cold sores), the Beijing Traditional Chinese Medicine Hospital (Běijīng Zhōng Yīyīyuàn; ☎ 6401 6677, 23 Meishuguan Houjie) has a foreigners clinic on the 3rd floor. There's a pharmacy on the Ground floor, where thousands of herbs are stored.

NATIONAL BUILDINGS & MONUMENTS
Forbidden City 紫禁城

The Forbidden City (Zǐjìn Chéng, so called because it was off limits for 500 years, is the largest and best-preserved cluster of an-

---

The Power of Eunuchs

An interesting feature of the Ming dynasty, and one that was principal in its eventual decline, was the ever-increasing power and number of eunuchs in the imperial court. Eunuchs, generally castrated at a young age by their families in the hope that they would attain the imperial court, had been employed by Chinese emperors as early as the Han dynasty. Traditionally, their role was to serve the needs of the emperor and his harem in parts of the imperial palace that were off limits to all adult males barring the emperor himself.

By the early Ming, the number of eunuchs in the service of the emperor was already 10,000 and, despite imperial edicts forbidding their access to political power, they continued to grow in influence and numbers throughout the Ming.

Certain eunuchs (perhaps the most infamous of whom is Wei Zhongxian, who practically ruled all of China in the 1620s) assumed dictatorial power and siphoned off massive fortunes while their emperors frolicked with their consorts.

In the late years of Ming rule, eunuchs probably numbered somewhere between 70,000 and 100,000 and exercised enormous control over the nation.

---

cient buildings in China. It was home to two dynasties of emperors, the Ming and the Qing, who didn't stray from this pleasure dome unless they absolutely had to.

The Běijīng authorities insist on calling this place the Palace Museum (Gùgōng). Whatever its official name, it's open daily from 8.30 am to 5 pm, with the last admission tickets sold at 3.30 pm. Two hundred years ago the admission price would have been instant death, but this has dropped considerably to Y30 or Y50 if you want admission to all the special exhibition halls. Rental of a cassette tape for a self-guided tour (recorded by Roger Moore of 007 fame) is another Y30 plus a deposit (such as your passport). For the tape to make sense you must enter the Forbidden City

Bĕijīng's Forbidden City: the secluded and palatial realm of Ming and Qing emperors.

from the south gate and exit from the north. The tape is available in a large number of languages.

It's worth mentioning that many foreigners get the Forbidden City entrance confused with the gate, Tiānānmén, because the two are physically attached and there are no signs in English. As a result, some people wind up purchasing the Tiānānmén admission ticket by mistake, not realising that this only gains admission to the upstairs portion of the gate. To find the Forbidden City ticket booths, keep walking north until you can't walk any further without paying.

The basic layout for the city was established between 1406 and 1420 by Emperor Yongle, commanding battalions of up to a million labourers. From this palace the emperors governed China, often rather erratically as they tended to become lost in this self-contained little world and allocated real power to the court eunuchs. One emperor devoted his entire career to carpentry – when an earthquake struck (an ominous sign for an emperor) he was delighted, since it gave him a chance to renovate.

The buildings now seen are mostly post-18th century, as with a lot of restored or re-built structures around Bĕijīng. The palace was constantly going up in flames; a lantern festival combined with a sudden gust of wind from the Gobi desert would easily do the trick, as would a fireworks display. Fires were also deliberately lit by court eunuchs and officials who could get rich off the repair bills. The moat around the palace, now used for boating, came in handy since the local fire brigade was considered too lowly to quench the royal flames. In 1664 the Manchus stormed in and burned the palace to the ground.

It was not just the buildings that went up in smoke, but rare books, paintings and scrolls. In this century there have been two major lootings of the palace: first by Japanese forces, and second by the Kuomintang, who, on the eve of the communist takeover in 1949, removed thousands of crates of relics to Taiwan, where they are now on display in Taipei's National Palace Museum. The gaps have been filled by treasures (old, newly discovered and fake) from other parts of China. Of these treasures, only a small percentage is on display. Plans are afoot to construct an underground museum in order to exhibit more of the collection.

Tiānānmén Square 天安门广场

This vast desert of pavement is the heart of Běijīng. Tiānānmén Guǎngchǎng, is Mao's creation, as is Chang'an Jie leading up to it. During the Cultural Revolution, the chairman, wearing a Red Guard armband, reviewed parades of up to a million people here. In 1976 another million people jammed the square to pay their last respects to him. In 1989 army tanks and soldiers cut down pro-democracy demonstrators.

Today (if the weather is conducive) the square is a place for people to lounge around in the evening and to fly decorated kites and balloons for the kiddies. Surrounding or studding the square is a strange mishmash of monuments past and present: Tiānānmén (Gate of Heavenly Peace), the Zhōngguó Gémìng Lìshǐ Bówùguǎn (Chinese Revolution History Museum), the Great Hall of the People, Qián Mén (Front Gate), the Mao Mausoleum and the Rénmín Yīngxióng Jìniànbēi (Monument to the People's Heroes). Under construction on the west side of the Great Hall of the People (and due for completion in 2002) is the new National Theatre. After a year and a half long international competition, the Central Committee chose a design by French architect Paul Andreau, whose glass and titanium edifice has been compared to an egg, a bubble and an emperor's grave mound.

If you get up early you can watch the **flag-raising ceremony** at sunrise, performed by a troop of PLA soldiers drilled to march at precisely 108 paces per minute, 75cm per pace. The same ceremony in reverse gets performed at sunset, but you can hardly see the soldiers for the throngs gathered to watch. A digital sign on the square announces the times for the sunrise ceremony for the next two days. The square was renovated in 1999 in preparation for the 50th anniversary of the PRC. The grey cement slabs were replaced by pink granite ones (the old slabs are now being used at China's first drive-in movie theatre) and grass lawns now adorn portions of the square. Super megawatt light bulbs now light up the square at night, so be sure to bring along your sunglasses.

Bicycles cannot be ridden across Tiānānmén Square (apparently tanks are OK), but you can walk the bike. Traffic is one way for north-south avenues on either side of the square.

Tiānānmén 天安门
Gate of Heavenly Peace

Tiānānmén is a national symbol. The gate was built in the 15th century and restored in the 17th. From imperial days it functioned as a rostrum for proclaiming to the assembled masses. There are five doors to the gate, and in front of it are seven bridges spanning a stream. Each of these bridges was restricted in its use and only the emperor could use the central door and bridge.

It was from the gate that Mao proclaimed the People's Republic on 1 October 1949. The dominating feature is the gigantic portrait of Mao – the required backdrop for any photo the Chinese take of themselves at the gate. To the left of the portrait is a slogan 'Long Live the People's Republic of China' and to the right 'Long Live the Unity of the Peoples of the World'.

You pass through Tiānānmén on your way into the Forbidden City (assuming you enter from the southern side). There is no

Mén: door, gate
The former character is easily recognisable as a double door that swings open from the middle, reminiscent of the half-doors of saloons in old westerns. The modern character for door represents an open door or doorway – easier to write, but perhaps also indicating the importance of charity in these acquisitive, get-ahead times.

fee for walking through the gate, but to go upstairs and look down on the square costs a whopping Y30 for foreigners, or Y10 for Chinese. It's hardly worth it – you can get a similar view of the square from inside Qián Mén for a quarter of the price.

Qián Mén 前门地铁站
Front Gate

Silent sentinel to the changing times, Qián Mén sits on the southern side of Tiānānmén Square. Qián Mén guarded the wall division between the ancient Inner City and the outer suburban zone and dates back to the reign of Emperor Yongle in the 15th century. With the disappearance of the city walls, the gate sits out of context, but it's still impressive.

Qián Mén actually consists of two gates. The southern one is called Jiàn Lóu (Arrow Tower) and the rear one is called Zhōngyáng Mén or Chéng Lóu. You can go upstairs into Zhōngyáng Mén.

Great Hall of the People
人民大会堂

The Great Hall of the People (Rénmín Dàhuìtáng) is the venue of the rubber-stamp legislature, the National People's Congress. It's open to the public when the Congress is not sitting – to earn some hard currency it's even rented out occasionally to foreigners for conventions! These are the halls of power, many of them named after provinces and regions of China and decorated appropriately. You can see the 5000-seat banquet room where US President Richard Nixon dined in 1972, and the 10,000-seat auditorium with the familiar red star embedded in a galaxy of lights in the ceiling. There's a sort of museum-like atmosphere in the Great Hall, with *objets d'art* donated by the provinces, plus a snack bar and a restaurant.

The hall is on the western side of Tiānānmén Square and admission is Y35.

Rénmín Yīngxióng Jìniànbēi
人民英雄纪念碑
Monument to the People's Heroes

On the southern side of Tiānānmén Square, the Monument to the People's Heroes was completed in 1958 and stands on the site of the old Outer Palace Gate.

The 36m obelisk, made of Qīngdǎo granite, bears bas-relief carvings of key revolutionary events (one relief shows the Chinese destroying opium in the 19th century), as well as appropriate calligraphy from Mao Zedong and Zhou Enlai.

Mao Zedong Mausoleum
毛主席纪念堂

Chairman Mao died in September 1976 and his mausoleum (Máo Zhǔxí Jìniàntáng) was constructed shortly thereafter.

Commonly known to Běijīng expats as the 'Maosoleum', this enormous building is located just behind the Rénmín Yīngxióng Jìniànbēi in Tiānānmén Square.

However history judges Mao, his impact on its course was enormous. Easy as it now is to vilify his deeds and excesses, many Chinese show deep respect when confronted with the physical presence of the man. CITS guides freely quote the old 7:3 ratio on Mao that first surfaced in 1976 – Mao was 70% right and 30% wrong (what, one wonders, are the figures for CITS itself?) and this is now the official Party line.

The mausoleum is open daily from 8.30 to 11.30 am. Entry is free, though you have to pay Y10 to check your bags and camera (the baggage check is across the street from the mausoleum, next to the Zhōngguó Lìshǐ Bówùguǎn). Join the enormous queue of Chinese sightseers, but don't expect more than a quick glimpse of the body as you file past the sarcophagus. At certain times of year the body requires maintenance and is not on view.

Whatever Mao might have done to the Chinese economy while he was alive, sales of Mao memorabilia are certainly giving the free market a boost these days. At the souvenir stalls near the mausoleum you can pick up Chairman Mao key rings, thermometers, face towels, handkerchiefs, sun visors, address books and cartons of cigarettes (a comment on his chain-smoking?).

Zhōngnánhǎi 中南海

Just west of the Forbidden City is China's new forbidden city, Zhōngnánhǎi. The

On Your Bike

It's Běijīng's broad avenues, tree-lined side streets and narrow *hútòngs* (atmospheric, winding alleyways, some of which date back 500 years) that lend the city its unique character. A taxi goes either too quickly for you to catch the details, or too slowly to sustain interest. Chronic traffic jams can make bicycle travel not just more adventurous, but more efficient as well.

Běijīng city is a sprawling metropolis with six million inhabitants, but it is flat and ideal for cycling. Much of Běijīng life is lived on the street, too. For an evening's entertainment, people fly kites or throw frisbees in Tiānānmén Square. Elsewhere, under the Imperial Palace walls, young people dance to rock, and older ones gather for ballroom dancing. Clusters of neighbours squat under streetlights to gossip and play cards. Street stalls offer kitchenware, silk, vegetables, noodles and even banquets. Repairmen, upholsterers and house painters jostle on footpaths with their tool boxes.

You may cycle past dentists extracting teeth, barbers doing short-back-and-sides, teenage boys shooting pool, old men taking constitutionals, caged birds in hand. Magicians, 'miracle medicine' salesmen and all sorts of other street performers compete for attention. Tables spill out of restaurants onto the pavement, and brawlers tumble out of bars and karaoke clubs.

Cars, trucks, motorcycles and buses caught in the hideous traffic jams of the inner city rev their motors impatiently. Tempers flare and great bouts of cursing and counter-cursing add to the commotion.

The bustle can seem daunting. But you quickly work out how to weave around the horse-drawn carts and negotiate the buses and trams that seem to dip into the bike lanes from nowhere. You learn that crossing large intersections is best done in clusters; opportunistic alliances that are tight as the traffic policemen's white gloves. You find that, unless it's very late, there's almost nowhere you can break down, or get a flat, that's too far from the roadside stand of an itinerant bicycle repairman. With luck, you won't discover that the easiest way to get into a fight in Běijīng is to run into another bicycle.

There are places in Běijīng that really only ought to be seen by bicycle; places of such magic that only the breeze on your face convinces you they're for real. One is the moat around the Forbidden City, traversable around the eastern side of the palace. On one side of the path the clay-red wall of the Imperial Palace, with its crenellated battlements, rears up. Ornamental guard towers with flying eaves and roofs of gold jag into view at each corner. On the other, through weeping willows, you see lotuses and fishermen lounging as pleasure boats stir up ripples on the still water of the moat. Fabulous by day, the moat is enchanting by night. If you start at the front of the palace, by Tiānānmén Square, when you come out the back you're just a short ride to the even more spectacular 'back lakes' – Houhai and Shishahai.

Villas that once belonged to princes (now the abodes of the communist nomenklatura) line these man-made lakes, along with sprawling dazayuar, labyrinthine courtyard houses shared by dozens of families. The majestic Drum Tower, where once imperial timekeepers beat out the hours of the day, looms over the scene. In summer, the paths are lively with strollers, lovers and locals trying their luck with rod and reel. In winter, a blanket of snow freshens the Běijīng grey; no sooner does the lake freeze over than it swarms with skaters.

Linda Jaivin

Linda Jaivin is a writer and translator. Her books include Confessions of an S&M Virgin, Eat Me **and** Rock n Roll Babes from Outer Space.

palace's interior is off limits to tourists, but you can gawk at the entrance. The compound was first built between the 10th and 13th centuries as a sort of playground for the emperors and their retinues. It was expanded during Ming times, but most of the present buildings only date from the Qing dynasty.

Empress Dowager Cixi once lived here; after the failure of the 1898 reform movement she imprisoned Emperor Guangxu in the Impregnating Vitality Hall where, ironically, he later died. After the overthrow of the imperial government and the establishment of the republic, it served as the site of the presidential palace.

Since the founding of the People's Republic in 1949, Zhōngnánhǎi has been the site of the residence and offices of the highest-ranking members of the Communist Party.

Summer Palace 颐和园

One of the finest sights in Bĕijīng, the Summer Palace (Yíhéyuán) includes an immense park that tends to pack out badly during the summer months. The site had long been a royal garden and was considerably enlarged and embellished by Emperor Qianlong in the 18th century.

The park was later abandoned, but Empress Dowager Cixi began rebuilding in 1888 with money supposedly intended for the construction of a modern navy. She did restore a marble boat that sits immobile at the edge of the lake: it was fitted out with several large mirrors and the empress used to dine there at the lakeside.

In 1900 foreign troops, annoyed by the Boxer Rebellion, had a go at torching the Summer Palace. Restorations took place a few years later and a major renovation occurred after 1949, by which time the palace had once again fallen into disrepair.

The original palace was used as a summer residence. It was divided into four sections: court reception, residences, temples and strolling or sightseeing areas. Three-quarters of the park is occupied by Kūnmíng Hú (Kunming Lake), and most items of structural interest are towards the eastern or northern gates.

The main building is the **Rénshòudiàn** (Benevolence and Longevity Hall), just off the lake towards the east gate. It houses a hardwood throne and has a courtyard with bronze animals. It was here that the emperor-in-residence handled state affairs and received envoys.

Along the north shore of the lake is the **Chángláng** (Long Corridor), which runs for

The grand opulence of the Hall of Audience in the grounds of Bĕijīng's Old Summer Palace; the building was destroyed by British and French troops in 1860.

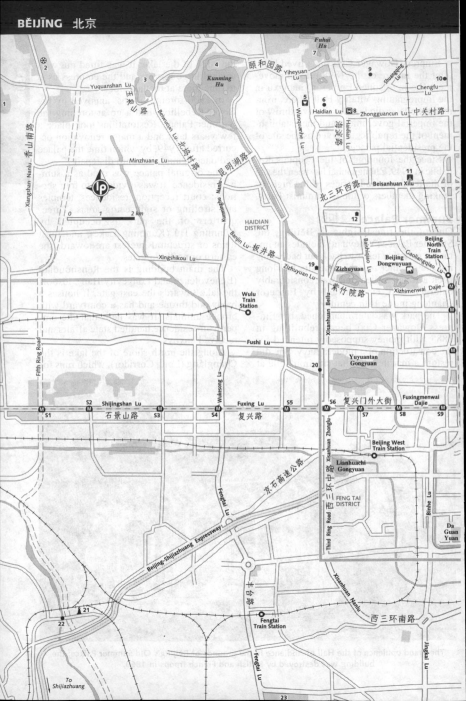

Map labels

颐和园路

Yiheyuan Lu

Kunming Hu 昆明湖

Fuhai Hu

Yuquanshan Lu

玉泉山路

Xiangshan Nanlu 香山南路

Minzhuang Lu

Renwucun Lu

北坞村路

Kunminghu Nanlu

昆明湖路

Minzhuang Lu

HAIDIAN DISTRICT

Banjin Lu 板井路

Xingshikou Lu

Zhizhuyuan Lu

Wulu Train Station

Fushi Lu

Fengtai Lu

Fifth Ring Road

Shijingshan Lu 石景山路

Wukesong Lu

Fuxing Lu

复兴路

京石高速公路 Beijing-Shijiazhuang Expressway

丰台路 Fengtai Lu

Fengtai Train Station

To Shijiazhuang

Wanquanhe Lu

Haidian Lu

Haidian Lu 海淀路

Zhongguancun Lu 中关村路

Chengfu Lu

Shuangqing Lu

北三环西路

Beisanhuan Xilu

Baishiqiao Lu

Gaoliangqiao Lu

Beijing North Train Station

Zizhuyuan

Beijing Dongwuyuan

紫竹院路

Zizhuyuan Lu

Xizhimenwai Dajie

Xisanhuan Beilu

Yuyuantan Gongyuan

复兴门外大街 Fuxingmenwai Dajie

Fuxingmenwai Dajie

Xisanhuan Zhonglu

西三环中路

Beijing West Train Station

Lianhuachi Gongyuan

FENG TAI DISTRICT

Third Ring Road 西三环路

Binhe Lu

Da Guan Yuan

Xisanhuan Nanlu 西三环南路

Jingkai Lu

Markers

1, 2, 3, 4, 5, 6, 7, 8, 9, 10, 11, 12, 19, 20, 21, 22, 23

S1, S2, S3, S4, S5, S6, S7, S8, S9

To Airport &
M'venpick Hotel

Guangshun Beidajie

Shuidujichang Expressway 首都机场高速公路

16

Juxianqiao Lu

北四环东路

CHAOYANG
DISTRICT

To Badaling &
Shisan Ling

Badaling Expressway

安定路

Fourth Ring Road

Beisihuan Zhonglu

北四环中路

14

15

Anding Lu

Huixin Dongjie

Beisihuan Donglu

Nanhuqu Lu

Beisihuan Donglu

Shuangyi Lu

Shuangyi Lu

北三环中路

Third Ring Road

Beisanhuan Zhonglu

13

Liangmaqiao Lu

17

*Shuidui
Hu*

Chaoyang
Park

Hepingli Train
Station

Ditan
Gongyuan

Beisanhuan Donglu

Deshengmen
Xidajie

德胜门西大街

Second Ring Road

S25 **S26** **S27** **S28**

18

Nongzhanguan Nanlu
农展馆南路

Tuanjiehu
Gongyuan

XICHENG
DISTRICT

S24

S23

DONGCHENG
DISTRICT

S29

东三环北路

S22

*Beihai
Hu*

Jingshan
Gongyuan

Jingshan
Qianjie

S30

Chaoyang Lu

Fuxingmennei
Dajie

Xidan Beidajie

*Zhonghai
Hu*

Forbidden
City

Wangfujing Dajie

Dongsanhuan Beilu

Dongsi Nandajie

S31

S10

Xichang'an Jie

S11

S12

Tiananmen
Square

S13

S14

Jianguomennei
Dajie

Jianguomenwai
Dajie

Jingtong Expressway 京通快速公路

S37

S36

S35

S34

Qianmen Dongdajie

Qianmen Dajie

S15

S32

S16

S17

S18

S19

S20

S21

S33

Beijing
Train
Station

CHONGWEN
DISTRICT

Dongsanhuan Zhonglu

Guangqu Lu

Guang'anmennei Dajie

XUANWU
DISTRICT

Tiantan Lu

Tiantan Donglu

Longtan
Gongyuan

Guangqumen
Nanbinhe Lu

Dongsanhuan Nanlu

Huagong Lu

Taoranting
Gongyuan

*Tiantan
Gongyuan*

You'anmen
Dongbinhe Lu

Beijing South
Train Station

Yongdingmen
Dongbinhe Lu

Zuo'anmen Xibinhe Lu

Puhuangyu Lu

See Central Beijing Map Pages 204–5

Anlelin Lu
安乐林路

Nansanhuan
Zhonglu

24

Majiapu Donglu

马家堡东路

25

26

27

28

Nanyuan Lu

Nansanhuan Donglu 南三环东路

Nansanhuan Xilu

Beijing-Tianjin Expressway

Dayangfang Lu

京津高速公路

To
Tianjin

BĚIJĪNG

PLACES TO STAY

12 Friendship Hotel
友谊宾馆

16 Holiday Inn Lido;
Watson's
丽都假日饭店;
屈臣氏

17 21st Century Hotel
Foreign Student
Dormitory
二十一世纪饭店

19 Shangri-La Hotel
香格里拉饭店

24 Lihuá Fàndiàn
丽华饭店

25 Jīnghuá Fàndiàn
京华饭店

26 Hǎixīng Dàjiǔdiàn
海兴大酒店

OTHER

1 Xiāngshān Gōngyuán
香山公园

2 Běijīng Zhíwùyuán
北京植物园

3 Yùquán Shān
玉泉山

4 Summer Palace
颐和园

5 Solutions
解决

6 Beijing University
北京大学

7 Old Summer Palace
圆明园遗址

8 Zhōngguāncūn Bus Stop
中关村(公共汽车站)

9 Qinghua University
清华大学

10 Beijing Language and
Culture University

11 Dàzhōng Sì
大钟寺

13 Běijiāo (Déshèngmén)
Long-Distance
Bus Station
北郊(德胜门)
长途汽车站

14 Zhōnghuá Mínzú Yuán
中华民族园

15 Asian Games Village
亚运村

18 Yáogǔnlè
摇滚乐

20 TV Tower
电视塔

21 Memorial Hall of the
War of Resistance
Against Japan
抗日战争纪念馆

22 Lúgōu Qiáo
卢沟桥

23 World Park
世界公园

27 Hǎihùtún Long-Distance
Bus Station
海户屯公共汽车站

28 Zhàogōngkǒu Bus
Station
赵公口汽车站

SUBWAY STATIONS

S1 Bājiǎocūn
八角村地铁站

S2 Bābǎoshān
八宝山地铁站

S3 Yùquánlù
玉泉路地铁站

S4 Wǔkēsōng
五棵松地铁站

S5 Wànshòulù
万寿路地铁站

S6 Gōngzhǔfén
公主坟地铁站

S7 Jūnshìbówùguǎn
军事博物馆地铁站

S8 Mùxīdì
木樨地地铁站

S9 Nánlǐshìlù
南礼士路地铁站

S10 Fùxīngmén
复兴门地铁站

S11 Xīdān
西单地铁站

S12 Tiān'ānménxī
天安门西地铁站

S13 Tiān'ānméndōng
天安门东地铁站

S14 Wángfǔjǐng
王府井地铁站

S15 Dōngdān
东单地铁站

S16 Jiànguómén
建国门地铁站

S17 Yǒng'ānlǐ
永安里地铁站

S18 Guómào
国贸地铁站

S19 Dàwàngqiáo
大望桥地铁站

S20 Sìhuìxī
四惠西地铁站

S21 Sìhuìdōng
四惠东地铁站

S22 Fùchéngmén
阜城门地铁站

S23 Chēgōngzhuāng
车公庄地铁站

S24 Xīzhímén
西直门地铁站

S25 Jīshuǐtán
积水潭地铁站

S26 Gǔlóu
鼓楼地铁站

S27 Āndìngmén
安定门地铁站

S28 Yōnghégōng
雍和宫地铁站

S29 Dōngzhímén
东直门地铁站

S30 Dōngsìshítiáo
东四十条地铁站

S31 Cháoyángmén
朝阳门地铁站

S32 Běijīng Zhàn
(Běijīng Train Station)
北京站

S33 Chóngwénmén
崇文门地铁站

S34 Qiánmén
前门地铁站

S35 Hépíngmén
和平门地铁站

S36 Xuānwǔmén
宣武门地铁站

S37 Chángchūnjiē
长春街地铁站

more than 700m and is decorated with mythical scenes. If the paint looks new it's because a lot of pictures were whitewashed during the Cultural Revolution.

On artificial Wànshòu Shān (Longevity Hill) are a number of temples. The **Páiyún Diàn** (Cloud Dispelling Hall) on the western slopes is one of the few structures to escape destruction by Anglo-French forces. It contains some elaborate bronzes. At the top of the hill sits the **Huìhái Sì** (Sea of Wisdom Temple), made of glazed tiles; good views of the lake can be had from this spot.

Other sights are largely associated with Empress Cixi, like the place where she kept Emperor Guangxu under house arrest, the place where she celebrated her birthdays, and exhibitions of her furniture and memorabilia. A kitsch atmosphere pervades this 'museum': tourists can have their photos taken in imperial dress.

Another noteworthy feature of the Summer Palace is the 17-arch bridge spanning 150m to **Nánhú Dǎo** (South Lake Island). On the mainland side is a beautiful bronze ox. Also note the **Yùdài Qiáo** (Jade Belt Bridge) on the mid-west side of the lake and the **Héqù Yuán** (Harmonious Interest Garden), which is a copy of a Wúxī garden, at the north-eastern end.

Currently under construction is a new Cultural Relics Hall, built to house the Summer Palace's huge collection of Qing dynasty art, including: jade, bronze and porcelainware; furniture; books and calligraphy.

You can get around the lake by hiring a small motorboat or rowing boat. Boating and swimming are popular pastimes for the locals, and skating is possible in winter. As with the Forbidden City moat, it used to be a common practice to cut slabs of ice from the lake in winter and store them for summer use.

The park is about 12km north-west of the centre of Běijīng. The easiest way to get there on public transport is to take the subway to Xīzhímén (close to the zoo), then a minibus. Bus No 332 from the zoo is slower but will get you there eventually. Lots of minibuses return to the city centre from the Summer Palace, but get the price and destination settled before departure. You can

also get there by bicycle; it takes about 1½ to two hours from the centre of town. Rather than taking the main roads, it's far more pleasant to cycle along the road following the Běijīng-Mìyún Diversion Canal.

Admission is Y45; this ticket does *not* get you into everything, as there are some additional fees inside. Admission for Chinese is Y20; foreigners need to be a Běijīng resident with valid ID to get this price.

Old Summer Palace 圆明园遗址

Located north-west of the city centre (see the Běijīng map), the original Summer Palace (Yuánmíng Yuán) was laid out in the 12th century. By the reign of Emperor Qianlong it had developed into a set of interlocking gardens. Qianlong set the Jesuits to work as architects for European-style palaces for the gardens, incorporating elaborate fountains and baroque statuary.

During the Second Opium War (1860), British and French troops destroyed the palace and sent the booty abroad. Since the Chinese pavilions and temples were made of wood they did not survive the fires, but a marble facade, some broken columns and traces of the fountains remain.

Once a favourite picnic spot for foreigners living in the capital and for Chinese couples seeking a bit of privacy, the Old Summer Palace nowadays takes on the feel of a tourist circus – crowded, with music blasted by loudspeakers over the entire grounds. There's even a dinosaur park.

The site covers a huge area – some 2.5km from east to west – so be prepared to do some walking. There are three entrance gates to the compound, all on the southern side. The western section is the main area, **Yuánmíng Yuán** (Perfection and Brightness Garden). The southern compound is the **Wànchūn Yuán** (10,000 Spring Garden). The eastern section is the **Chángchūn Yuán** (Eternal Spring Garden) – it's here that you'll find the **European Garden** with its Great Fountain Ruins, considered the best-preserved relic in the palace and featured prominently on postcards.

To get to the Old Summer Palace, take minibus 375 from the Xīzhímén subway station. Minibuses also connect the new Summer Palace with the old one, or a taxi will take you for Y10.

Admission is Y10; the grounds are open daily from 7 am to 7 pm.

PARKS & GARDENS
Yùquán Shān 玉泉山
Jade Spring Mountain

About 2.5km west of the Summer Palace is Yùquán Shān, an area only recently developed as a park. The spring's name is derived from the water's clear, jade-like, crystalline appearance. During the Ming and Qing dynasties mineral water from the spring was sent daily to the Forbidden City to quench the emperor's thirst. It was believed the water had a tonic effect.

Yùquán Shān sports the usual temples, pagodas and pavilions. At the base of the mountain is the **Míngjìng Yuán** (Garden of Light and Tranquillity).

Xiāngshān Gōngyuán 香山公园
Fragrant Hills Park

Easily within striking distance of the Summer Palace are the Xī Shān (Western Hills), another former villa-resort of the emperors. The part of Xī Shān closest to Běijīng is known as Xiāng Shān (Fragrant Hills). This is the last stop for the city buses – if you want to get further into the mountains, you'll have to walk, cycle or take a taxi.

You can either scramble up the slopes to the top of **Xiānglú Fēng** (Incense-Burner Peak) or take the crowded chairlift. From the peak you get an all-embracing view of the countryside. The chairlift is a good way to get up the mountain, and from the summit you can hike further into the Western Hills and leave the crowds behind.

Within walking distance of the North Gate of Xiāngshān Gōngyuán is the **Bìyún Sì** (Azure Clouds Temple), the landmark of which is the **Liúlí Tǎ** (Diamond Throne Pagoda). Of Indian design, it consists of a raised platform with a central pagoda and stupas around it. The temple was built in 1366, and was expanded in the 18th century with the addition of the Hall of Arhats, containing 500 statues representing disciples of Buddha.

Sun Yatsen's coffin was placed in the temple in 1925 before moving to Nánjīng.

There are a few ways to get to Xiāng Shān by public transport: bus No 333 from the Summer Palace, bus No 360 from the zoo or bus No 318 from Píngguǒyuán (the last stop in the west on the subway).

Xiāngshān Zhíwùyuán 香山植物园
Fragrant Hills Botanical Gardens

About 2km east of Xiāngshān Gōngyuán is Xiāngshān Zhíwùyuán (Botanical Gardens). While not spectacular, the gardens are a botanist's delight and a pleasant place for a stroll. At the northern end of the gardens is the **Wòfó Sì** (Sleeping Buddha Temple).

Jǐngshān Gōngyuán 景山公园
Prospect Hill Park

Just to the north of the Forbidden City is Jǐngshān Gōngyuán, which contains an artificial mound made of earth excavated to create the palace moat. If you clamber to the pavilions at the top of this regal pleasure garden you will get a magnificent panorama of the capital and a great overview of the russet roofing of the Forbidden City.

On the eastern side of the park a locust tree stands in the place where the last of the Ming emperors, Chongzhen, hanged himself after slaying his family, rather than see the palace razed by the Manchus. The hill supposedly protects the palace from the evil spirits – or dust storms – from the north.

Gōngyuán: park
公园 The top of gōng means opposite, and underneath is the character for private; thus, it means public. A park in China now is a public park, whereas there weren't any gōngyuán, as such, in China before 1911.

The outside of yuán indicates something surrounded by a type of fence. Inside the fence is a character that means flowers and trees growing, and curved bridges – all of which are found inside a typical Chinese garden.

Entrance to Jǐngshān Gōngyuán is a modest 30 jiǎo, or you can pay more than 30 times as much for a souvenir 'tourist passport ticket' – fortunately, this is optional.

Běihǎi Gōngyuán 北海公园
North Sea Park

Approached by four gates, and just northwest of the Forbidden City, Běihǎi Gōngyuán is the former playground of the emperors. The park covers an area of 68 hectares, more than half of which is a lake. The island in the lower middle is composed of the heaped earth excavated to create the lake – some attribute this to Kublai Khan.

The site is associated with the Great Khan's palace, the navel of Běijīng before the creation of the Forbidden City. All that remains of the Khan's court is a large jar made of green jade, in the Round City near the southern entrance.

From the 12th century onwards, Běihǎi Gōngyuán was landscaped with artificial hills, pavilions, halls, temples and covered walkways. Dominating Jade Islet on the lake, the 36m-high **White Dagoba** was originally built in 1651 for a visit by the Dalai Lama and was rebuilt in 1741.

On the north-eastern shore of the islet is the handsome, double-tiered **Huàláng** (Painted Gallery). Near the boat dock is the Fángshàn Fànzhuāng, a restaurant that dishes up imperial recipes that were favoured by Empress Cixi. She liked 120-course dinners with about 30 kinds of desserts (see Places to Eat later in this chapter).

The main attraction on the northern side is the **Jiǔlóng Bì** (Nine Dragon Screen), 5m high and 27m long, made of coloured glazed tiles. The screen, standing at the entrance to a temple that has disappeared, was built to scare off evil spirits. To the southwest of the boat dock on this side is the **Wǔlóng Diàn** (Five Dragon Pavilion), dating from 1651.

Běihǎi Gōngyuán is a relaxing place to stroll around, grab a snack, sip a beer, rent a rowing boat or, as the Chinese do, cuddle on a bench in the evening. It's crowded on weekends. Some people dive into the lake when no-one's around, but swimming is not permitted. In winter there's ice skating. Admission is Y5 and it's open daily 7 am to 7 pm.

Tiāntán Gōngyuán 天坛公园
Temple of Heaven Park

The most perfect example of Ming architecture, **Tiāntán** or **Temple of Heaven** has come to symbolise Běijīng. Its lines appear on countless pieces of tourist literature and as a brand name for a wide range of products from Tiger Balm to plumbing fixtures. It is set in the 267-hectare Tiāntán Gōngyuán, with four gates at the compass points and bounded by walls to the north and east. It originally functioned as a vast stage for solemn rites performed by the Son of Heaven, who came here to pray for good harvests, seek divine clearance and atone for the sins of the people.

The temples, seen in aerial perspective, are round and the bases are square, deriving from the ancient Chinese belief that heaven is round, and the earth is square. Thus the northern end of the park is semi-circular and the southern end is square.

The 5m-high **Yuánqiū** (Round Altar) was constructed in 1530 and rebuilt in 1740. It is composed of white marble arrayed in three tiers, and its geometry revolves around the imperial number nine. Odd numbers were considered heavenly, and nine is the largest single-digit odd number. The top tier, thought to symbolise heaven, has nine rings of stones, each composed of multiples of nine stones, so that the ninth ring has 81 stones. The number of stairs and balustrades are also multiples of nine. If you stand in the centre of the upper terrace and say something, the sound waves are bounced off the marble balustrades, amplifying your voice (nine times?).

Just north of the altar, surrounding the entrance to the Imperial Vault of Heaven, is the **Huíyīnbì** (Echo Wall), 65m in diameter. A whisper can travel clearly from one end to your friend's ear at the other – that is, if there's not a tour group in the middle.

The octagonal **Imperial Vault of Heaven** was built at the same time as the Round Altar, and is structured along the lines of the older Hall of Prayer for Good Harvests. It used to contain tablets of the emperor's ancestors, which were used in the winter solstice ceremony. Proceeding up from the Imperial Vault is a walkway: to the left is a molehill composed of excess dirt dumped from digging air-raid shelters, and to the right is a rash of souvenir shops.

The dominant feature of the whole complex is the **Qǐnián Diàn** (Hall of Prayer for Good Harvests), a magnificent piece mounted on a three-tiered marble terrace. Amazingly, the wooden pillars ingeniously support the ceiling without nails or cement – for a building 38m high and 30m in diameter, that's quite an accomplishment. Built in 1420, the Hall was burnt to cinders in 1889 and heads rolled in apportioning blame. A faithful reproduction based on Ming architectural methods was erected the following year. Admission is Y14 and it's open daily from 8.30 am to 4.30 pm.

MUSEUMS & GALLERIES
Zhōngguó Lìshǐ Bówùguǎn
中国历史博物馆
National Museum of Chinese History
If you don't count the Forbidden City and other palaces, this, the Zhōngguó Lìshǐ Bówùguǎn, is Běijīng's largest museum. It is housed in a sombre building on the eastern side of Tiānānmén Square, and access was long thwarted by special permission requirements. From 1966 to 1978 the museum was closed so that history could be revised in the light of recent events. There are actually two museums here – the Museum of History and the Museum of the Revolution.

Well worth a visit is the Museum of History, which contains artefacts and cultural relics (many of them copies) from prehistoric times to 1919, subdivided into sections on primitive communal groups, slavery, feudalism, and capitalism and imperialism, laced with Marxist commentary. Don't miss the Han dynasty jade burial suit, worn by Prince Huai. It consists of over 1200 small jade plates sewn together with gold thread.

Only about a third of the relics have English explanations, although an audio guide in English is available for Y40 (plus a Y400 deposit).

博物馆 Bówùguǎn: museum
Bó means a large number or abundant, plentiful. The left side is the number 10, which stands for a large number. The right part means everywhere or a wide area. Wù is a thing, an object or matter. The left side, meaning cattle, stands for big animals, among other things. The right side is the phonetic for this word. A thing (ie, an object) in Chinese means anything other than a human.

The Zhōngguó Gémìng Lìshǐ Bówùguǎn (Chinese Revolution History Museum) is divided into five sections: the founding of the CCP (1919–21), the first civil war (1924–27), the second civil war (1927–37), the resistance against Japan (1937–45) and the third civil war (1945–49). There are English explanations throughout the museum.

It's open Tuesday to Sunday from 8.30 am to 3.30 pm and admission costs Y5 for the Museum of Chinese History and Y3 for the Museum of the Revolution.

Jūnshì Bówùguǎn 军事博物馆
Military Museum
Perhaps more to the point than the Zhōngguó Gémìng Lìshǐ Bówùguǎn, Jūnshì Bówùguǎn traces the genesis of the PLA from 1927 to the present and has some interesting exhibits: pictures of Mao in the early days, Socialist realist sculptures, captured US tanks from the Korean War, and other tools of destruction. Explanations are mostly in Chinese, although the third floor, which has an exhibit on the history of war in China, has English explanations.

The museum is open from 8.30 am to 4 pm daily and admission is Y5. It is on Fuxing Lu on the western side of the city; to get there take the subway to Jūnshìbówùguǎn station.

Zìrán Bówùguǎn 自然博物馆
Natural History Museum
The four main exhibition halls of the large Zìrán Bówùguǎn are devoted to flora, fauna,

ancient fauna and human evolution. Some of the more memorable exhibits include a human cadaver cut in half to show the insides and complete dinosaur skeletons. There is also plenty of pickled wildlife, although nothing worse than what you see for sale in some of the street markets.

Some of the exhibits were donated by the British Museum, the American Museum of Natural History and other foreign sources.

The Zìrán Bówùguǎn is in the Tiānqiáo area, just north of the west gate of Tiāntán Gōngyuán. Admission is Y15. The museum is open daily from 8.30 am until 5 pm.

Zhōngguó Měishùguǎn 中国美术馆
China Art Gallery

Back in the post-Liberation days, one of the safest hobbies for an artist was to retouch classical-type landscapes with red flags, belching factory chimneys or bright red tractors. Times have changed and the modern art scene is alive, though the Zhōngguó Měishùguǎn more reflects the scene of days gone by. However, at times, very good exhibitions of current work (including photo displays) are held in an adjacent gallery.

The gallery is just north-east of the Forbidden City on Chaoyangmennei Dajie. It's open Tuesday to Sunday from 9 am to 4 pm. Admission is Y4.

Sòng Qìnglíng Gùjū 宋庆龄故居
Madam Song's Residence

Madam Song was the second wife of Dr Sun Yatsen, who went on to become the first president of the Republic of China. After 1981, Madam Song's large residence was transformed into a museum dedicated to her memory and to that of Dr Sun. The layout of the residence is original and on display are personal items and pictures of historical interest.

The museum is on the northern side of Shíshà Hòuhǎi Hú. It is open Tuesday to Sunday from 9 am to 4.30 pm. Admission is Y10.

Gǔdài Jiànzhù Bówùguǎn
古代建筑博物馆
Museum of Ancient Architecture

Housed on the site of the Xiannong Alter, where Ming and Qing emperors once made sacrifices to the gods, this museum has displays housed in a large courtyard-style building. Exhibits give overviews (with English explanations) of architectural features of Chinese cities, palaces, altars, monasteries, temples & mosques, residences, gardens and mausoleums. Stone and wood carvings and other pieces from these structures are on display, along with photos of Chinese masterpieces in each of these categories.

The museum (☎ 6301 7620) is just southeast of the Qiánmén Fàndiàn at 21 Dongjinglu. It's open daily, except Monday, from 9 am to 4 pm.

TEMPLES & MOSQUES
Yōnghé Gōng 雍和宫
Lama Temple

The Yōnghé Gōng is by far the most colourful temple in Běijīng – beautiful gardens, stunning frescoes and tapestries, and incredible carpentry. Get to this one before you're 'templed out' – it won't chew up your day.

The Yōnghé Gōng is the most renowned Tibetan Buddhist temple in China, outside Tibet itself. North-west of the city centre toward Andingmen Dongdajie, it became the official residence of Count Yin Zhen after extensive renovation. There was nothing unusual in that, but in 1723 he was promoted to emperor and moved to the Forbidden City. His name was changed to Yong Zheng, and his former residence became Yonghe Palace. In 1744 it was converted into a lamasery and became a residence for large numbers of monks from Mongolia and Tibet.

In 1949 the Yōnghé Gōng was declared protected as a major historical relic. Miraculously it survived the Cultural Revolution without scars. In 1979 a large amount of money was spent on repairs and it was restocked with several dozen novices from Inner Mongolia – a token move on the part of the government to back up its claim that the Yōnghé Gōng is a 'symbol of religious freedom, national unity and stability in China'. The novices study Tibetan language and the secret practices of the Gelukpa Sect.

No photography is permitted inside the temple buildings (tempting as it is). The monks, and the postcard industry, are sensitive to the reproduction of Buddha images. The temple is open daily, except Monday, from 9 am to 4.30 pm and admission is Y15. You can get there by subway to the Yōnghégōng station.

Kǒng Miào & Guózǐjiān
孔庙与国子监
Confucian Temple & Imperial College

Just down the *hútòng* (alley) opposite the gates of the Yōnghé Gōng is the former Kǒng Miào and Guózǐjiān.

The Kǒng Miào is the second largest Confucian temple in China, after the one at Qūfù. The temple was reopened in 1981 after some mysterious use as a high-official residence and is now used as a museum. The forest of steles in the temple courtyard look forlorn. The steles record the names of those successful in the civil service examinations (possibly the world's first) of the imperial court.

The Guózǐjiān was the place where the emperor expounded the Confucian classics to an audience of thousands of kneeling students, professors and court officials – an annual rite. Built by the grandson of Kublai Khan in 1306, the former college was the only institution of its kind in China; it's now the **Capital Library**.

The temple is run down and sees few tourists, but is a good place to get away from the hordes at the Yōnghé Gōng. Among the museum's displays is a suit of long underwear completely covered with tiny characters – a student's cheat sheet for passing the exam.

The museum is open daily from 8.30 am to 5 pm; admission is Y10.

Dōngyuè Sì 东岳寺

Built in the Yuan dynasty, Dōngyuè Sì is a recently restored Taoist temple in the middle of the Chaoyang district.

The huge courtyard is surrounded on all sides with heavenly departments, each in charge of different aspects of existence. Worried about your finances? Make a de-

posit at the Department for Bestowing Material Happiness. Concerned about China's environment? Pay a visit to the Department of the Preservation of Wilderness. Life-sized painted clay figures – many of which are half animal, painted in garish colours, donning menacing expressions and brandishing painful-looking weapons – depict each department. There are also English explanations of each department's function.

Dōngyuè Sì is located on Chaoyangmenwai Dajie, about 200m east of Full Link Plaza on the opposite side of the street. Admission is Y10.

Dàzhōng Sì 大钟寺
Great Bell Temple

The Dàzhōng Sì houses the biggest bell in China, 6.75m tall and weighing a hefty 46.5 tonnes. The bell is inscribed with Buddhist sutras, comprising over 227,000 Chinese characters.

The bell was cast during the reign of Ming Emperor Yongle in 1406 and the tower was built in 1733. Getting the bell from the foundry to the temple proved difficult: a shallow canal was built and when it froze over in winter the bell was moved across the ice by sled.

Within the grounds of the monastery are several other buildings (besides the Bell Tower itself). These include the **Guanyin Hall**, the **Sutra-keeping Tower**, the **Main Buddha Hall** and the **Four Devas Hall**. This monastery is one of the most popular in Běijīng and was reopened in 1980.

Dàzhōng Sì is along the north-western part of the Third Ring Rd (Beisanhuan Xilu; see the Běijīng map).

Báitǎ Sì 白塔寺
White Dagoba Temple

The dagoba of the Báitǎ Sì can be spotted from the top of Jǐng Shān and is similar (and close) to the one in Běihǎi Gōngyuán. It was used as a factory during the Cultural Revolution, but reopened after restoration in 1980. The dagoba dates back to Kublai Khan's days and is now just a historical monument. It lies off Fuchengmennei Dajie.

Guǎngjì Sì 广济寺
Universal Rescue Temple

The Guǎngjì Sì is on the north-western side of the Xisi Beidajie intersection with Fuchengmennei Dajie, to the east of the Báitǎ Sì. It's in good condition and is the headquarters of the Chinese Buddhist Association. It is claimed to contain some of the finest Buddhist statues in China.

Dōngsì Qīngzhēn Sì 东四清真寺
East Four Islam Mosque

This is one of two functioning mosques in Běijīng, the other being Niújiē Lǐbài Sì. It's to the east of Jǐngshān Gōngyuán at 13 Dongsi Nandajie, just south of the intersection with Chaoyangmennei Dajie.

Niújiē Lǐbài Sì 牛街礼拜寺
Ox Street Mosque

In the south-western sector of Běijīng (Xuanwu District), south of Guang'anmennei Dajie, is a Muslim residential area with a handsome mosque facing Mecca. Built in 996, the mosque is the city's oldest and largest. The ornate main prayer hall (open to men only) dominates the courtyard; the small and plain women's prayer hall is off to the rear. Famous guests include Mohammed Ali, who visited the mosque while in Běijīng. Open daily from 8 am until sunset; admission is free for Muslims or Y10 otherwise.

Fǎyuán Sì 法源寺
Source of Law Temple

This temple was originally constructed in the 7th century and is still going strong. It's now the China Buddhism College. A visit here is like going to a college campus – students playing ping pong during the break and hanging out and chatting – except the students are monks dressed in Buddhist yellow robes. Don't miss the hall at the very back of the temple, which houses an unusual copper Buddha seated upon a thousand-petal lotus flower. From the entrance of Niújiē Lǐbài Sì, walk left 100m then turn left into the first *hútòng* (alley). Follow the hútòng for about 10 minutes and you'll arrive at Fǎyuán Sì. The temple is open Thursday to Tuesday from 8.30 to 11.20 am and 1.30 to 3.30 pm. Admission is Y5.

Báiyún Guàn 白云观
White Cloud Temple

Báiyún Guàn is south-west of town. It was once the Taoist centre of northern China and is now the most active Taoist temple in Běijīng. Check a map for directions. Walk south on Baiyun Lu and cross the moat. Continue south along Baiyun Lu and turn into a curving street on the left; follow it for 250m to the temple entrance. Inside are several courtyards, including a pool, a bridge, several halls of worship and Taoist motifs. The temple is open 8.30 am to 4.30 pm daily; Y8 admission.

OTHER PLACES TO SEE
Gōngwáng Fǔ 恭王府
Prince Gong's Residence

To find Gōngwáng Fǔ, you have to get off the main roads into the small alleys running around the Shisha Qianhai Lakes. Gōngwáng Fǔ is more or less at the centre of the arc created by the lakes running from north to south. It's reputed to be the model for the mansion in Tsao Hsueh-Chin's (Cao Xueqin) 18th century classic, *A Dream of Red Mansions*. It's one of the largest private residential compounds in Běijīng, with a layout of nine courtyards, high walls and elaborate gardens. Prince Gong was the son of a Qing emperor. It is open daily 8.30 am to 4.30 pm. Admission is Y5.

Gǔ Lóu & Zhōng Lóu 鼓楼，钟楼
Drum Tower & Bell Tower

The Gǔ Lóu was built in 1420 and has several drums, which were beaten to mark the hours of the day – in effect the Big Ben of Běijīng. Time was kept with a water clock. The tower is located on Gulou Dongdajie, 1km north of Jǐngshān Gōngyuán.

Behind the Gǔ Lóu, down an alley further north, is the Zhōng Lóu. This tower was built at the same time as the Gǔ Lóu, but burnt down. The present structure dates from the 18th century. It is open daily from 9 am to 4.30 pm. Admission is Y10.

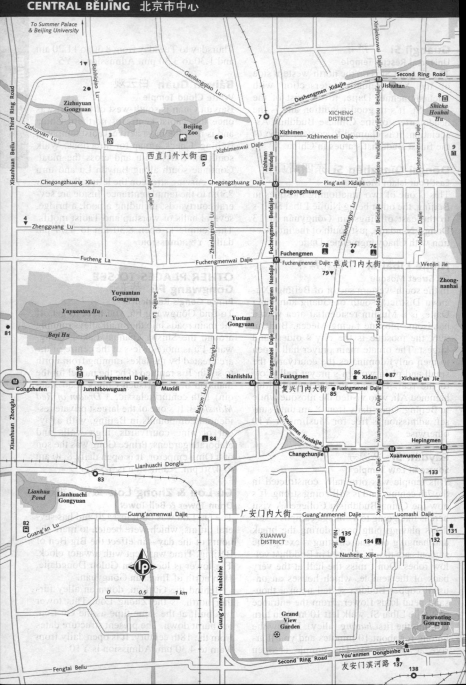

To Summer Palace
& Beijing University

Second Ring Road

Gaoliangqiao Lu

Deshengmen Xidajie

1 ▼

Bashiqiao Lu

2 ●

Zizhuyuan
Gongyuan

Beijing
Zoo

Zizhuyuan Lu

3 🏛

5 🏛

西直门外大街

Xizhimenwai Dajie

Sanlihe Dajie

Chegongzhuang Xilu

Chegongzhuang Dajie

Zhengguang Lu

Xisanhuan Beilu — Third Ring Road

4 ▼

Fucheng La

Fuchengmenwai Dajie

Yuyuantan
Gongyuan

Yuyuantan Hu

Bayi Hu

81 ●

Sanlihe Lu

Zhanlanguan Lu

Yuetan
Gongyuan

Xizhimen

Xizhimennei Dajie

Xizhimen
Nandajie

Chegongzhuang

Ping'anli Xidajie

Chegongzhuang

Fuchengmen Beidajie

Fuchengmen

Zhaodengyu Lu

Fuchengmennei Dajie 阜成门内大街

Fuchengmen Nandajie

Fuxingmennei Dajie

Jishuitan

8 ●
Shicha
Houhai
Hu

XICHENG
DISTRICT

9 ●

Deshengmennei Dajie

Xinjiekou Nandajie

Xisi Beidajie

Xinjiekouxi Dajie

78 ● 77 ● 76 ●

79 ▼

Wenjin Jie

Xishiku Dajie

Zhong-
nanhai

80 🏛

Fuxingmennei Dajie

Gongzhufen

Junshibowuguan

Muxidi

Nanlishilu

Sanlihe Donglu

Bayun Lu

Fuxingmen

Fuxingmenbei Dajie

Xidan Beidajie

86 ● Xidan

87 ●

85 ●

Xichang'an Jie

Fuxingmennei Dajie 复兴门内大街 ● Fuxingmennei Dajie

Xuanwumennei Dajie

84 🏛

Xisanhuan Zhonglu

Lianhuachi Donglu

83 ●

Fuxingmen Nandajie

Hepingmen

Changchunjie

Xuanwumen

133 ●

Lianhua
Pond

Lianhuachi
Gongyuan

Guang'anmenwai Dajie

82 ●

Guang'an Lu

广安门内大街 — Guang'anmennei Dajie

Guang'anmen Nanbinhe Lu

Xuanwumenwai Dajie

XUANWU
DISTRICT

Luomashi Dajie

Niu Jie

135 ●

134 🏛

Nanheng Xijie

131 ●

132 ●

Grand
View
Garden ❁

Taoranting
Gongyuan

136 ●

You'anmen Dongbinhe Lu

137 ●

138 ●

Fengtai Beilu

Second Ring Road

友安门滨河路

0   0.5   1 km

Deshengmen Xidajie

Xizhimennei Dajie

7 ●

Ande Lu

Ditan
Gongyuan

17

To
Airport &
M'venpick
Hotel

27

28
29

Andingmen Xidajie
安定门东大街

Andingmen Dongdajie

25 26

30

Gulou

Andingmen

Yonghegong

18   19

31

15   16

20

Dongzhimenwai Xiejie

东三环北路

11   12

Jiaodaokou
Dongdajie

Dongzhimennei Dajie

Dongzhimen

22
23
24

Sanlitun
Embassy
Area

32

Gulou Dongdajie

Dongzhimenwai Dajie

21

DONGCHENG
DISTRICT

14

46

Dongsanhuan Beilu

Shicha
Qianhai
Hu

13

Di'anmen Dongdajie
地安门东大街

Dongsishitiao

35   34

33

D'anmen Xidajie

47

45   44

36
37   38

39

Beihai
Gongyuan

74

48

49

43

41   40

75

Meishuguan
Dongjie

Workers
Stadium

42

Beihai
Hu

Jingshan
Gongyuan

73

50

52

Tuanjiehu
Gongyuan

Jingshan Qianjie

Chaoyangmennei Dajie

Chaoyangmen

51

Zhong-
nanhai
Hu

72

60

59

Chaoyangmenwai Dajie
朝阳门外大街

53

Forbidden
City

70

71

Dengshi Kou Jie

58

55

Ritan
Gongyuan

57

56

67   68

69

61

62
63
64

Zhongshan
Gongyuan

66

65

Dong Dan

96

Jianguomen

101

103

104

105   106

107
108

Tiananmen XI

88

93   94

95

Jianguomennei Dajie

102

Jianguomenwai
Dajie

89

92

Tiananmen
Dong

Wangfujing

建国门内大街

97

98
99
100

Yong An Li

Guo Mao

Tiananmen
Square

91

Beijing Zhan

109

90

Qianmen Dongdajie

117

CHONGWEN
DISTRICT

120   Qianmen

Chongwenmen

121

119   118

Dazhalan Jie

122
123

Zhushikou Dongdajie

Guangqumennei Dajie

Guangqumenwai Dajie

124

Zhushikou Xidajie

110

125

天坛路

Tiantan Lu

116

115   Tiyuguan Lu

Guangming Lu

Jinsong Lu

130

113

Longtan Lu

Beiwei Lu

129

126

114

Tiantan
Gongyuan

Longtan
Gongyuan

111

127

128

Yongdingmen
Xibinhe Lu

Yongdingmen Dongbinhe Lu

Zuo'anmen Xibinhe Lu

Zuo'an Lu

112

Beihai Lu

PLACES TO STAY

10 Zhúyuán Bīnguǎn
竹园宾馆

13 Lǚsōngyuán Bīnguǎn
侣松园宾馆

14 Yóuhǎo Bīnguǎn
友好宾馆

25 Huádū Fàndiàn
华都饭店

26 Kūnlún Fàndiàn
昆仑饭店

27 Hilton Hotel
希尔顿大酒店

30 Kempinski Hotel;
Lufthansa Centre;
International Medical
Centre
凯宾斯基饭店
燕沙商城

31 Great Wall Sheraton
长城饭店

41 City Hotel
城市宾馆

42 Gōngtǐ Bīnguǎn
工体宾馆

46 Red House

49 Swissôtel; Hong Kong
Medical Clinic
瑞士酒店

53 Jingguang New
World Hotel
京广新世界饭店

58 Rìtán Bīnguǎn
日坛宾馆

61 Hǎoyuán Bīnguǎn
好园宾馆

62 Hépíng Bīnguǎn
和平宾馆

63 Palace Hotel
王府饭店

64 Central Academy of
Arts Dormitory
中央美术学院
留学生宿舍

70 Fāngyuán Bīnguǎn
芳园宾馆

86 Mínzú Fàndiàn
民族饭店

93 Grand Hotel Běijīng
贵宾楼饭店

94 Beijing Hotel
北京饭店

96 International Club Hotel
国际俱乐部饭店

102 Scitech Hotel;
Scitech Plaza
赛特饭店；
赛特购物中心

105 Jiànguó Fàndiàn
建国饭店

106 Jīnglún Fàndiàn;
Sìhéxuān Fàndiàn
京伦饭店；四合轩饭

107 Kerry Centre Hotel
嘉里中心饭店

108 China World Hotel;
Sparkice Internet Cafe;
Trader's Hotel
中国大饭店

111 Lèyóu Fàndiàn
乐游饭店

113 Tiāntán Tǐyù Bīnguǎn
天坛体育宾馆

114 Tiāntán Hàoyuán Bīnguǎn
天坛昊园宾馆

124 Yuǎndōng Fàndiàn
远东饭店

129 Fènglóng Bīnguǎn
风龙宾馆

130 Běiwěi Fàndiàn
北纬饭店

131 Qiánmén Fàndiàn
前门饭店

136 Xiāoxiāng Dàjiǔdiàn
潇湘大酒店

137 Qiáoyuán Fàndiàn
侨园饭店

PLACES TO EAT

1 Wēigōngcūn
魏公村

4 Jiǔhuāshān Kǎoyādiàn
九花山烤鸭店

17 Tángēnyuàn Shífáng
坛根院食坊

23 Green Tea House
紫云茗

29 Jīnshānchéng Chóngqìng
Càiguǎn
金山城重庆菜馆

33 1,001 Nights
一千零一夜餐厅

37 Dàchéng Yónghé
大成永和

48 Red Capital Club
新红资

50 Metro Cafe
美特糕

55 Phrik Thai
京港泰式美食

57 Xǐhéyǎjū Cāntīng
義和雅居餐厅

60 Afanti
美特糕

68 Dōngānmén Night
Market
东安门夜市

69 The Courtyard
四合轩

71 Lǜ Tiānshǐ Fàndiàn
绿天使饭店

75 Fāngshān Fànzhuāng
芳山饭店

79 Néngrénjū
能仁居

109 Huángchéng Lǎomā
皇城老妈

116 Beijing Noodle King
老北京炸酱面大王

118 Lìchún Kǎoyādiàn
利纯烤鸭店

119 Qiánmén Quànjùdé
Kǎoyādiàn
前门全聚德烤鸭店

123 Dìyīlóu Fàndiàn
第一楼饭店

125 Gōngdélín Sùcàiguǎn
功德林素菜馆

MUSEUMS & GALLERIES

8 Sòng Qìnglíng Gùjū
宋庆龄故居

9 Gōngwáng Fǔ
恭王府

73 Zhōngguó Měishùguǎn
中国美术馆

80 Jūnshì Bówùguǎn
军事博物馆

91 Mao Zedong Mausoleum;
Rénmín Yīngxióng
Jìniànbēi
毛主席纪念堂；
人民英雄纪念碑

92 Zhōngguó Lìshǐ Bówùguǎn
中国历史博物馆

97 Gǔguān Xiàngtái
古观象台

126 Zìrán Bówùguǎn
自然博物馆

128 Gǔdài Jiànzhù Bówùguǎn
古代建筑博物馆

TEMPLES & MOSQUES
15 Kǒng Miào
孔庙
16 Yōnghé Gōng
雍和宫
51 Dōngyuè Sì
东岳寺
72 Dōngsì Qīngzhēn Sì
东四清真寺
76 Guǎngjì Sì
广济寺
78 Báitǎ Sì
白塔寺
84 Báiyún Guàn
白云观
134 Fǎyuán Sì
法源寺
135 Niújiē Lǐbài Sì
牛街礼拜寺

SHOPPING
52 Extreme Beyond
探险野营登山装备
专卖店
66 Xīndōngān Plaza;
Bank of China
新东安市场;中国银
67 Foreign Languages
Bookstore
外文书店
77 Adam & Eve Health
Centre
北京市亚当夏娃
保健中心
103 Friendship Store; CITIC
友谊商店;国际大厦
104 Xiùshuǐ Shìchǎng
秀水东街
112 Pānjiāyuán Market
潘家园市场
115 Hóngqiáo Market
红桥市场
122 Dàchàlàn
大栅栏街
133 Liúlíchǎng
琉璃厂

ENTERTAINMENT
28 Keep In Touch
保持联络酒吧
32 CD Cafe
CD咖啡室
34 Public Space
35 Half and Half

36 Butterfly Bar
38 The Den
40 Hidden Tree; Jam House
隐蔽的树
43 Havana Cafe
45 Club Vogue
47 Poly Plaza
保利大厦
54 Cháoyáng Dàjùchǎng
朝阳剧场
56 Hot Spot
热点
85 Sānwèi Bookstore &
Teahouse
三味书屋
121 Zhèngyǐcí Dàxìlóu
正乙祠大戏楼
132 Húguǎng Huìguǎn
湖广会馆

OTHER
2 Beijing Library
北京图书馆
3 Sparkice Internet Cafe;
Capital Gymnasium
实华网络咖啡室;
首都体育馆
5 Zhanlanguan Lu Tour
Bus Station
展览馆路旅游车
售票处
6 Beijing Exhibition Centre
北京展览馆
7 Běijīng North (Xīzhímén)
Train Station
北京北火车站
11 Zhōng Lóu
钟楼
12 Gǔ Lóu
鼓楼
18 PSB
公安局外事科
19 Russian Embassy
苏联大使馆
20 Dōngzhímén Long-
Distance Bus Station
东直门长途汽车站
21 Australian & Canadian
Embassies
澳大利亚大使馆
加拿大大使馆
22 Tǎyuán Diplomatic
Building
塔园外交办公楼

24 Asia Emergency Assistance
39 Zhàolóng Hotel
兆龙饭店
44 Tibet Dipper Photo Service
西藏北斗星图片总社
59 Full Link Plaza
丰联广场
65 Beijing Union
Medical Hospital
北京协和医院
74 Beijing Traditional
Chinese Medicine Hospital
北京中医院
81 Xīnxīng Fàndiàn
新兴饭店
82 Liánhuāchí Bus Station
莲花池长途汽车站
83 Běijīng West Train Station
北京西火车站
87 Aviation Building
(CAAC & Airport Bus)
民航营业大厦
88 Tiānānmén
天安门
89 Great Hall of the People
人民大会堂
90 Qiánmén Tour Bus Station
前门旅游车发车站
95 Oriental Plaza
东方广场
98 Gloria Plaza Hotel
凯莱大酒店
99 Tourism Building
(BTG, formerly CITS)
旅游大厦
100 New Otani Hotel
长富宫
101 International Post &
Communications
国际邮电局
110 Mǎjuàn Long-Distance
Bus Station
马圈长途汽车站
117 Běijīng Train Station
北京火车站
120 Qián Mén
前门
127 Tiānqiáo Bus Station
天桥汽车站
138 Běijīng South
(Yǒngdìngmén) Train
Station
北京南站
(永定门火车站)

Gǔguān Xiàngtái 古观象台
Ancient Observatory

One of Běijīng's oddities is the ancient observatory mounted on the battlements of a watchtower, forlornly overlooking the traffic-clogged Second Ring Rd near Jianguomennei Dajie.

The observatory dates back to Kublai Khan's days, when it was north of the present site. The Great Khan, as well as later Ming and Qing emperors, relied heavily on astrologers before making any move.

The present observatory was built from 1437 to 1446, not only to facilitate astrological predictions, but also to aid seafaring navigators. Navigational equipment is displayed downstairs. On the roof is a variety of astronomical instruments designed by the Jesuits.

The observatory is open Wednesday to Sunday from 9 to 11 am and from 1 to 4 pm.

Lúgōu Qiáo 卢沟桥
Reed Moat Bridge

Described by the great traveller himself, the 260m-long Lúgōu Qiáo, or **Marco Polo Bridge**, is made of grey marble and has more than 250 marble balustrades supporting 485 carved stone lions. First built in 1192, the original arches were washed away in the 17th century. The bridge is a composite of different eras (it was widened in 1969) and spans the river, Yǒngdìng Hé, near the little town of Wǎnpíng.

Long before CITS, Emperor Qianlong did his bit to promote the bridge. In 1751 he put his calligraphy to use and wrote 'Morning Moon Over Lugou Bridge', now engraved into stone tablets on the site. On the opposite bank is a monument to the emperor's inspection of the Yǒngdìng Hé.

Despite the praises of Marco Polo and Emperor Qianlong, the bridge wouldn't have rated more than a footnote in Chinese history were it not for the famed Marco Polo Bridge Incident, which ignited a full-scale war with Japan. On 7 July 1937, Japanese troops illegally occupied a railway junction outside Wǎnpíng. Japanese and Chinese soldiers started shooting, and that gave Japan enough of an excuse to at-

tack and occupy Běijīng. The Marco Polo Bridge Incident is considered by many as the date of China's entry into WWII.

A relatively recent addition to this ancient site is the **Memorial Hall of the War of Resistance Against Japan**, built in 1987. Also on the site are the **Wanping Castle**, the **Daiwáng Sì** and a tourist hotel.

The bridge is 16km from the city centre and getting there is difficult. You can get to the bridge by taking bus No 339 from Liánhuāchí bus station south-west of the city centre. Another option is bus No 309, which can be picked up at Líulí Qiáo; get off the bus at Xīdáokǒu and the bridge is just ahead.

Běijīng Dòngwùyuán 北京动物园
Beijing Zoo

With the exception of the well-tended pandas, the zoo is mostly a downer – no attempt has been made to re-create natural environments for the animals, and they live in tiny cages with little shade or water. Getting to the zoo is easy enough – take the subway to the Xīzhímén station. From there, it's a 15-minute walk to the west or a short ride on any of the trolleybuses. Open daily 7.30 am to 6 pm. Admission is Y7 (or Y5 not including the panda house).

PLACES TO STAY

If you arrive in town without hotel reservations and are planning to stay in a mid-range or top-end hotel, stop by the airport hotel reservations counter, which has been known to get discounts of up to 50% off rack rates. The counter is located just outside the arrivals area, after you pass through customs.

PLACES TO STAY – BUDGET

The good news is that dormitory hotels in Běijīng seem to be proliferating; the bad news is that they're still mostly in the southern part of town, far from the city centre. For the sake of definition, any hotel where a double can be had for less than Y200 in the high season is considered 'budget.' Dorm beds in the high season average around Y35.

Běijīng Area

The following places to stay all appear on the Běijīng map.

At present, the *Jīnghuá Fàndiàn* (☎ 6722 2211, Nansanhuan Zhonglu, Yongdingmenwai) is in vogue with backpackers. Although it's on the southern part of the Third Ring Rd, far from the city centre, and despite complaints of exceptionally unfriendly service, it's a good place to get travel information, rent bicycles and book trips to the Great Wall. Dorm beds cost Y35 in a four-bed room, or Y26 in a 30-bed room. Twins are Y180. Bus Nos 2 and 17 from Qián Mén drop you off nearby. From Běijīng west train station, take the Fangzhuang bus to Yangqiao. When you walk out of the station go right and you'll see several bus queues. The Fangzhuang bus is inside the bus yard. The ride is about 30 minutes. After you cross over a small (and smelly) river you'll see a McDonald's. After the bus turns left get off at the first top. The Jīnghuá is about 50m in the direction the bus is headed.

Just around the corner from the Jīnghuá is the *Hǎixīng Dàjiǔdiàn* (Sea Star Hotel; ☎ 6721 8855, fax 6722 7915, 166 Haihutun, Yongwai). Dorm beds are Y35 and twins cost Y180. The rooms are even nicer than at the Jīnghuá, but they tend to fill up faster.

Also close by, the *Lìhuá Fàndiàn* (☎ 6721 1144, 71 Yangqiao, Yongdingmenwai) is another well-established backpackers' haven. Dorms cost Y35 and twins are Y198. Bus No 14, from Xīdān and Hépíngmén subway stations, is the easiest way to get there.

Central Běijīng

Unless otherwise indicated, the following places to stay all appear on the Central Běijīng map.

The *Yuǎndōng Fàndiàn* (Far East Hotel; ☎ 6301 8811, fax 6301 8233, 90 Tieshuxie Jie, Qianmenwai) has a fine location among Běijīng's hútòngs. Tieshuxie Jie is in fact the western end of Dàchìlàn (south-west of Qián Mén). Twins cost Y298 to Y398. It also has cheerless doubles in the basement for Y160 (shared bath). To get here head south on Nanxinhua Jie. About

200m after you pass Líulíchǎng you'll see a sign (in English) on the right-hand side of the street saying Far East Hotel. Follow the hútòng for about 50m; the four-storey hotel is on the right. The Y298 rooms are often fully booked so try to call ahead.

Gaining in popularity is the *Fènglóng Bīnguǎn* (Feng Long Youth Hostel; ☎ 6357 5314, ✉ jian.min@hotmail.com). It's slightly closer to the centre of town than the Jīnghuá Fàndiàn. Here dorm beds are Y40 in a small four-bed room with bath and doubles for Y180. It also has a friendly tourist office that offers overnight trips to Sīmǎtái (Y90), bike rental and Internet access. From Běijīng train station take bus 20 or 54, and from Běijīng West train station take bus 122 to Běijīng South train station (Yǒngdìngmén). The hostel is on the opposite side of Second Ring Rd.

Near the Fènglóng Bīnguǎn, the *Qiáoyuán Fàndiàn* (☎ 6301 2244, fax 6303 0119, 135 Youanmen Dongbinhe Lu) also offers dorm beds for Y30 in a 10-bed room or Y60 in a two-bed room with bath. Although the rooms are passable, its solitary location gives it a feeling of isolation.

The *Fāngyuán Bīnguǎn* (☎ 6525 6331, fax 6513 8549, 36 Dengshikou Xijie) deserves a plug even though it's relatively undiscovered by travellers. Its very central location off Wangfujing Jie is a big plus. The staff are pretty friendly and the hotel is well run. Twins cost Y177 and Y217.

The *Lǔsōngyuán Bīnguǎn* (☎ 6401 1116, 6404 0436, fax 6403 0418, 22 Banchang Hutong), north of the Forbidden City, is superb. Built by a Mongolian general in the Qing dynasty, this courtyard hotel has atmosphere. Its location among the hútòngs makes a good base for exploring the city. The staff are very friendly. You can also rent bikes here for Y30 per day. Dorm beds are Y100, singles/doubles are Y250/450. If you want a double bed book ahead as the hotel only has two (the rest of the rooms have two single beds). The dormitory is currently the only one in China officially recognised by the International Youth Hostel Federation. There is a small sign (in English) on Andingmennei Dajie. The hotel is about 50m down the alley. Take bus 104 from Běijīng train station to the Bei Bingma Si bus stop. Walk a short distance south then turn right down the first alley.

An OK budget option in the centre of the city is the **Gōngtǐ Bīnguǎn** (☎ 6501 6655), located in the east side of the Gōngréntǐ Yuchang (Workers' Stadium). Doubles with shared bath start at Y140. The hotel is a bit run down, but it's conveniently located in the heart of Běijīng's bar scene. Of course, if a sports match or concert is taking place in the stadium prepare for lots of noise.

It's sometimes possible to stay in foreign student dormitories if there are empty rooms. The **Central Academy of Arts Dormitory** (Zhōngyāng Měishù Xuéyuàn Liúxuéshēng Sùshè; ☎ 6513 0926, 8th floor, 5 Xiaowei Hutong) is very centrally located behind the Palace Hotel in Wángfǔjǐng and has been known to rent out doubles (shared bath) for Y120. As space is very limited, it's a good idea to call ahead. From the Palace Hotel walk west and turn left down the first small street (if you've hit Xindongan Plaza then you've gone too far). The dormitory is about 50m down on the right. Enter the second door.

The **21st Century Hotel Foreign Student Dormitory** (Èrshíyī Shìjì Fàndiàn; ☎ 6460 9911 ext 6101, 40 Liangmaqiao Lu), on the Běijīng map, has also been known to rent rooms out to travellers. Dorm rooms here are pretty comfortable, with air-con and private bath. Basement rooms are Y83 per person.

PLACES TO STAY – MID-RANGE

Following are hotels with twin rooms in the Y200 to Y600 range. It's worth considering staying in a courtyard hotel, which mostly fall in this range. Staying in one of these is a good way to experience a more traditionally Chinese atmosphere; all of the courtyard hotels are located amid Běijīng's few remaining hutongs (alleyways) and offer a quiet escape from the city.

Bargaining for a room is possible in some cases – politely ask for a 'discount'. Many travellers negotiate discounts of 30% or more, at least during the winter low season.

Each of the following hotels appears on the Central Běijīng map.

The **Hǎoyuán Bīnguǎn** (☎ 6512 5557, fax 6512 5557, 53 Shijia Hutong) is a quiet courtyard hotel about a 10-minute walk from Wángfǔjǐng's main drag. Comfortable, clean rooms are Y360 for a twin. To get here go north on Dongdan Dajie. About 25m before Dengshikou Dajie, you'll see a small alley – Shijia hutong – leading off to the right. The hotel is about 50m down the alley on your left. You can't miss the big red gates guarded by two stone lions.

Tiāntán Hàoyuán Bīnguǎn (☎ 6701 4499, fax 6701 2404, 9A Tiantan Donglu), a well-kept courtyard hotel a short distance south of the east gate of Tiāntán Gōngyuán, has recently renovated doubles for Y480 and suites for Y880. Of Běijīng's courtyard hotels, this is the best maintained and most stylish, and considering the location it's excellent value.

Also near the Tiāntán or Temple of Heaven, the **Tiāntán Tǐyù Bīnguǎn** (Tiantan Sports Hotel; ☎ 6701 3388, fax 6701 5388, 10 Tiyuguan Lu) was recently renovated. Clean, good value (though characterless) doubles are Y268.

The **Běiwěi Fàndiàn** (☎ 6301 2266, fax 6301 1366, 13 Xijing Lu), on the western side of Tiāntán Gōngyuán, has recently renovated, clean rooms. Singles are Y180 and doubles are Y232.

Also in the area, very close to the west gate of the Tiāntán, the newly opened **Xiāoxiāng Dàjiǔdiàn** (☎ 8316 1188, fax 6303 0690, 42 Beiwai Lu) is a standard hotel, but as rooms are new it's extremely clean. Doubles start at Y480, but staff are quick to offer a 40% discount.

Just around the corner from Pānjiāyuán market (aka the Dirt Market), the small **Lèyóu Fàndiàn** (☎ 6771 2266, fax 6771 1636, 13 Dongsanhuan Nanlu) is nothing special, but rooms are clean and in good shape. Standard doubles start at Y288.

In a hútòng just off Jiaodaokou, the **Yóuhǎo Bīnguǎn** (☎ 6403 1114, fax 6401 4603, 7 Houyuansi) was once the residence of Chiang Kaishek, and after 1949 the site of the Yugoslav Embassy. Today it's a nice but slightly run-down courtyard hotel. Singles are Y288 and doubles are Y380.

West of the Gǔ Lóu, the **Zhúyuán Bīnguǎn** (*Bamboo Garden Hotel;* ☎ *6403 2229, fax 6401 2633, 24 Xiaoshiqiao Hutong*) is a largish hotel surrounding four interconnected courtyards with a traditional Chinese rock garden and bamboo groves. Small doubles are Y380, while more spacious doubles with a balcony overlooking the garden are Y580. Y1200 will get you the suite decorated with Ming-style furniture.

The **Qiánmén Fàndiàn** (☎ *6301 6688, fax 6301 3883, 175 Yong'an Lu*), southwest of Qián Mén, has standard twins for Y630. This large hotel is a favourite of package tour groups.

The newly opened **Red House** (☎ *6416 7500;* ✉ *redhouse@ht.rol.cn.net, 10 Taipingzhuang Dajie, Dongzhimenwai*) has a convenient location near Běijīng's expat area, Sānlǐtún. Suites are available for both long- and short-term rental. Prices start at Y300, and all rooms have a kitchen and cable TV. At the time of writing, dormitory space was being installed – call or email ahead for confirmation. Major credit cards are accepted here as well. It has a Web site at www.redhouse.com.cn.

PLACES TO STAY – TOP END

Keeping up with the top-end hotels in Běijīng is like skiing uphill. No sooner does one extravaganza open its doors than the ground-breaking ceremony is held for an even more luxurious pleasure palace. For definition purposes, anything costing over Y700 for a standard twin room is called 'top end'. Listed are a selection of Běijīng's top five-star hotels, followed by good-value, centrally located three- and four-star hotels. As rates for five-star hotels are given in US dollars, that's what we've listed here. Keep in mind that there is usually a 15% service charge on top of the room rate. As with mid-range hotels, discounts of 30% or more are often available if you ask. Unless otherwise indicated, all hotels appear on the Central Běijīng map.

Among Běijīng's swanky five-star hotels, you couldn't do better than the **Grand Hotel Beijing** (*Guìbīnlóu Fàndiàn;* ☎ *6513 0057, fax 6513 0050,* ✉ *sales@mail.grandhotelbeijing.com.cn, 35 Dong Chang'an Jie*). Standard twins are US$275, while rooms overlooking the Forbidden City start at US$300. Rooms are decorated with Chinese-style furniture, with an East-meets-West theme. The hotel boasts the bar with the best view of the city – the 10th floor has outdoor tables overlooking Chang'an Jie and the Forbidden City. Also, the hotel couldn't be more centrally located, just a few minutes' walk from Tiānānmén Square and the Forbidden City to the east and Wángfǔjǐng, Běijīng's premiere shopping area, to the west.

The **International Club Hotel** (*Guójì Jùlèbù Fàndiàn;* ☎ *6460 6688, 21 Jianguomen Dajie*) rivals the Grand Hotel as Běijīng's most luxurious hotel. Rooms are on the small side but are elegantly decorated and include a huge jacuzzi-style bathtub. The hotel has a small British-style bar called the Press Club; one of Běijīng's best Italian restaurants, Danieli's; and a scrumptious Sunday brunch.

Also considered by many as Běijīng's top hotel is the **Palace Hotel** (*Wángfǔ Fàndiàn;* ☎ *6512 8899, fax 6512 9050,* ✉ *tph@peninsula.com, 8 Jinyu Hutong, Wangfujing Dajie*). It's right around the corner from Běijīng's first indoor shopping mall, Xindongan Plaza. Doubles start at US$320, but there is usually a 'promotional price' available, bringing the price down to around US$192.

The **China World Hotel** (*Zhōngguó Dàfàndiàn;* ☎ *6505 2266, fax 6505 4323, 1 Jianguomenwai Dajie*), inside China World Trade Centre, is another five-star hotel in contention for the title of Běijīng's most upmarket lodging. Standard double rooms start at US$205.

The **Hilton Hotel** (*Xīěrdùn Fàndiàn;* ☎ *6466 2288, fax 6465 3052, 1 Dongfang Lu, Dongsanhuan Beilu*) has twins for US$109. This typical up-market hotel has a well-equipped gym and an excellent Cajun restaurant, Lousiana.

The **Kūnlún Fàndiàn** (☎ *6500 3388, fax 6506 8424, 2 Xinyuan Nanlu*) has standard twins for US$130. The top floor has a revolving restaurant and bar with excellent views of the city.

The *Kempinski Hotel (Kǎibīnsījī Fàndiàn;* ☎ *6465 3388, fax 6465 3366, Lufthansa Centre, 50 Liangmaqiao Lu)* has standard twins beginning at US$135. The hotel has a great location, next door to the Lufthansa shopping centre and across the street from a string of small but excellent local restaurants – choose from Italian, Japanese, Korean Sìchuān or Húnán cuisines. The hotel also has one of Běijīng's best gyms and a good deli and bakery.

The *Great Wall Sheraton (Chángchéng Fàndiàn;* ☎ *6500 5566, fax 6590 5398, 10 Dongsanhuan Beilu)* has standard twins for US$220, although it usually has a promotional rate of US$115. This is one of the city's first international hotels – when it was built, wide open spaces surrounded the hotel. Now the Hard Rock Cafe is next door and other upscale hotels, shops and restaurants sprawl in all directions.

The three-star *City Hotel (Chéngshì Bīnguǎn;* ☎ *6500 7799, fax 6500 7668, 4 Gongti Donglu)* is next to one of Běijīng's most popular nightclubs, the Den. Doubles are Y600.

Swissôtel (Ruìshì Jiǔdiàn; ☎ *6501 2288, fax 6501 2501,* ☻ *swissotel@chinamail .com, Dongsishitiao Li Jiao Qiao),* just outside the Dōngsìshítiáo subway station, has standard doubles starting at US$115. It has an excellent gym and swimming pool. A bank of China with an international access ATM is on the 2nd floor.

The *Jingguang New World Hotel (Jīngguǎng Xīn Shìjiè Fàndiàn;* ☎ *6501 8888, fax 6501 3333),* in Hujialou, has twins starting at US$90. This was once Běijīng's tallest building with 52 floors.

The three-star *Rìtán Bīnguǎn (*☎ *6512 5588, fax 6512 8671,1 Ritan Lu),* near Rìtán Gōngyuán, is next to the Russian fur market. The hotel is a favourite of Russian businesspeople. Standard twins cost Y660.

The four-star *Hépíng Bīnguǎn (Peace Hotel;* ☎ *6512 8833, fax 6512 6863, 3 Jinyu Hutong, Wangfujing Dajie)* has twins starting at Y750.

The *Beijing Hotel (Běijīng Fàndiàn;* ☎ *6513 7766, fax 6513 7307,* ☻ *business@ chinabeijinghotel.com.cn, 33 East Chang'an Avenue),* opened in 1900, is Běijīng's oldest hotel. Famous guests include Zhou Enlai and Edgar Snow. At the time of writing a new west wing, slated to open at the end of 2000, was under construction. Hotel conditions are up to par, but there isn't much in the way of charm or style. Twin rooms start at US$160 and suites are US$300 to US$350.

The four-star *Scitech Hotel (Sàitè Fàndiàn;* ☎ *6512 3388, fax 6512 3542,* ☻ *sthotel1@sw.com.cn, 22 Jianguomenwai Dajie)* has twins for US$70. The hotel has an excellent location; it's across the street from the Friendship Store, a short walk east to the Silk Market.

The *Jiànguó Fàndiàn (*☎ *6500 2233, fax 6500 2871,* ☻ *sales@hoteljianguo.com, 5 Jianguomenwai Dajie)* is a four-star hotel that has standard twins starting at US$92. It has a reputation for being good value for money and has a very cosy atmosphere.

The *Jīnglún Fàndiàn (*☎ *6500 2266, fax 6500 2022,* ☻ *jinglun@public3.bta.net.cn, 3 Jianguomenwai Dajie)* has twins starting at US$98. Rooms here aren't quite up to the standard of other four-star hotels. However, there's an excellent Běijīng-style restaurant on the 4th floor.

The *Kerry Centre Hotel (Jiāi Fàndiàn;* ☎ *6561 8833, fax 6561 2626, 1 Guanghua Lu)* is the latest addition to Běijīng's collection of five-star hotels. Standard rooms start at US$170. It's located next to the China World Trade Center.

The four-star *Trader's Hotel (Gúomào Fàndiàn;* ☎ *6505 2277, 6505 0818, 1 Jianguomenwai Dajie)* is a good, lower-priced alternative to staying that the China World Hotel, which is next door. Doubles start at US$140.

The *Mínzú Fàndiàn (*☎ *6601 4466, fax 6601 4849, 51 Fuxingmennei Dajie),* west of CAAC and east of Fùxīngmén subway, has twins for US$85 to US$128 and suites for US$144 to $198.

The following hotels are marked on the Běijīng map:

The *Holiday Inn Lido* (*Lìdū Jiàrì Fàndiàn;* ☎ 6437 6688, fax 6437 6237, Jichang Lu, Jiangtai Lu), on the road to the airport, has standard twins starting at US$76. Although isolated from the city centre, there's a small shopping mall attached to the hotel as well as an 'antique' market across the street.

The *Friendship Hotel* (*Yōuyí Bīnguǎn;* ☎ 6849 8888, fax 6831 4661, 3 Baishiqiao Lu), built in the 1950s to house 'foreign experts,' is a sprawling garden-style hotel that has managed to retain its old-style charm. It boasts Běijīng's nicest outdoor swimming pool. Twins start at US$80.

The *Shangri-La Hotel* (*Xiānggé Lǐlā Fàndiàn;* ☎ 6841 2211, fax 6841 8006, 29 Zhizhuyuan Lu), in Haidian District, has rooms starting at US$120.

At Capital airport, the four-star *Mövenpick Hotel* (*Guódū Dàfàndiàn;* ☎ 6456 5588, fax 6456 5678) has twins starting at US$135. Amenities include some excellent tennis courts, a great gym and a large outdoor swimming pool.

PLACES TO EAT

There are so many eateries and so much diversity of cuisine around the capital that it's hard to imagine China ever experienced a famine. On the other hand, eating on a budget is becoming more difficult. While there are still plenty of back-alley cafes and pushcarts where you can grab a cheap meal, the days are gone when any backpacker could afford to visit an upmarket restaurant and rub elbows with Běijīng's well-fed cadres.

If you do have a meal in one of the upmarket restaurants, be aware that rice is generally considered a fairly plebeian dish – a final 'fill-you-up' to be ignored until the 'real food' is finished. So, unless you act like a barbarian and demand some rice at the beginning of the meal, it will probably only appear towards the end of the meal. Unless otherwise indicated all of the following places to eat can be found on the Central Běijīng map.

For a comprehensive list of restaurants, check *City Edition*.

Chinese Food

Northern cuisine specialities include Beijing duck, Mongolian hotpot, Muslim barbecue and imperial dishes. Popular street fare includes dumplings, noodles and steamed buns.

Cheap Eats The hútòngs are so packed with small eateries and food stalls that it would take a book larger than this one to list them all. A special mention should go to the night market, *Dōngānmén Yèshì*, which gets going from around 6 to 9 pm daily. All sorts of exotic eats from street stalls are available, including deep-fried scorpion, grasshopper or caterpillar kebabs. It's also a good place to try typical street food, like *málàtàng* (spicy soup), *zòngzi* (sticky rice in lotus leaves) or *jiānbǐng* (Chinese crepes). The night market is at the northern end of Wángfǔjǐng near Xindongan Plaza.

Beijing Duck Beijing duck, the capital's most famous invention, is now a production line of sorts. Your meal starts at one of the farms around Běijīng where the duck is fattened with grain and soybean paste. The ripe duck is lacquered with molasses, pumped with air, filled with boiling water, dried, and then roasted over a fruitwood fire. The result, force-fed or not, is delicious. The duck is served in stages. First comes boneless meat and crispy skin with a side dish of shallots, plum sauce and crepes, then duck soup made of bones and all the other parts of the duck except the quack.

Tucked in a hútòng in East Qián Mén, *Lìchún Kǎoyādiàn* (*Lichun Roast Duck Restaurant;* ☎ 6702 5681, Beixiangfeng Hutong, Zhengyi Lu Nankou) is a tiny restaurant squeezed into a typical Běijīng courtyard house. It's worth it to come here for the atmosphere alone, and the duck isn't bad either. It only has a few tables and the owners insist that you make reservations. From Qianmen Dongdajie, walk east till you hit Zhengyi Lu. Turn right onto Zhengyi Lu; at the end of Zhengyi Lu turn right, then take your first left. Follow the alleyway to the end, then turn right, then take your first left. Take the next left, and the duck restaurant is at the end of this alley. If all the zigzagging gets you lost, ask the locals to point you in the right direction – just ask for the *kǎo-yādiàn*.

Jiǔhuāshān *(Jiuhua Shan Roast Duck Restaurant;* ☎ *6848 3481, 55 Zhengguang Lu)*, behind the Ziyu Hotel, serves the Capital's most delicious roast duck. *Kaoya* lovers say this is how roast duck should be done: crispy skin cooked just right so all the fat has dripped out. Although it's in Haidian, a bit of a trek from the city centre, and the atmosphere is nothing special (a brightly lit cavernous hall with big tables), the duck here is worth the effort. A whole duck is Y88.

Otherwise known as the 'Old Duck', the **Qiánmén Quànjùdé Kǎoyādiàn** *(Qianmen Quanjude Roast Duck Restaurant;* ☎ *6511 2418, 32 Qianmen Dajie)* is one of the oldest restaurants in the capital, dating back to 1864. The atmosphere here is definitely touristy, complete with duck souvenirs, from stuffed animals to baseball caps with big duck bills, for sale at the entrance. Despite its marketing efforts, it's still a good place to try roast duck. Now there's a dozen or so branches across the city. Price depends on which section of the restaurant you sit in. Ducks here go for Y108 or Y168.

Other Běijīng Cuisine *Tángēnyuàn Shífáng (*☎ *6427 3356, A1 Ditan Dongmenwai)* serves up some of Běijīng's most authentic local food – try the *má dòufu* (tofu paste), *mènsūyú* (fried and pickled fish), *zìmǐ zhōu* (purple porridge). Patrons spit on the floor and smoke while they're eating as they watch cross-talk, Peking opera and acrobats on stage at this not-to-be-missed eatery just outside the east gate of the park Dìtán Gōngyuán. It even has rickshaws waiting at the park gate to take customers up to the front door. Yes, it's a tourist trap, but prices are extremely reasonable and its noisy and crowded atmosphere makes for a fun night out if you go with the flow.

More refined in atmosphere and lighter on the grease, the **Sìhéxuān Fàndiàn** *(Si He Xuan Restaurant;* ☎ *6500 2266, 3 Jianguomenwai Dajie)*, on the 4th floor of the

Jīnglún Fàndiàn, serves fresh and delicious street fare such as *bāozi* (steamed buns), *jiǎozi* (dumplings) and *zhōu* (rice porridge) at reasonable prices in a restaurant designed to look like a courtyard house. It's open till 2.30 am, a rarity in Běijīng.

The **Dìyīlóu Fàndiàn** *(First Floor Restaurant;* ☎ *6303 0268, 83 Qianmen Dajie)* has the best *tāng bāo* (soup buns) around, and for only Y9 per bamboo steamer. Other typical, simple Běijīng dishes to try are *xiǎo cōng bàn dòufu* (scallion tofu; Y3) and *liáng bàn huáng guā* (cold cucumber; Y4).

Just north of the east gate of the Tiāntán and across from Hóngqiáo market, **Beijing Noodle King** *(Lǎo Běijīng Zhàjiàngmiàn Dàwáng;* ☎ *6705 6705, 29 Chongwenwai Dajie)* is the place to try *zhá jiàng miàn* – thick, warm noodles mixed with thin slices of cucumber, scallions, turnip and beans along with black bean sauce (Y8 per bowl). The waiters make a ruckus with the clanging of plates as they mix the vegetables into the noodles at your table.

If you're in the mood for dumplings day or night, **Jìn Māo Jiǎozichéng** *(Golden Cat Dumpling City;* ☎ *8598 5011)*, next to the east gate of Tuánjiéhú Gōngyuán, serves over a dozen varieties of dumplings, from pumpkin (this author's favourite) to donkeymeat to the standard pork-filled. Order dumplings by the *liang* (about Y3.50 for five dumplings). The restaurant is in a courtyard house, so you can sit outside when the weather cooperates. It's open 24 hours.

Also open 24 hours, and conveniently located near the Sānlǐtún's bar street (Sanlitun Lu) on Gongti Dongu, is **Dàchéng Yǒnghé** *(Yonghe Soy Milk City)*, where you can get typical Chinese breakfast fare. The fluorescent lighting is a bit glaring at 3 am, but the *dòujiāng* (soybean milk; Y2), *yóutiáo* (fried dough stick; Y2), *zóngzi* (sticky rice in lotus leaves; Y4), *húntun* (wonton soup; Y8) and *jiǎozi* (Y6) taste great. It also has an English menu.

Imperial Imperial food (*gōngtíng cài* or *mǎnhàn dàcān*) is food fit for an emperor and will clean your wallet out very quickly.

In 1982 a group of Běijīng chefs set about reviving the imperial pastry recipes, and even went so far as to chase up the last emperor Pu Yi's brother to try their creations on.

Běijīng's most elaborate imperial cuisine is served up in the *Fángshàn Fànzhuāng* (☎ 6401 1889), located in a pavilion overlooking the lake in Běihǎi Gōngyuán (enter through either the west or south gate). Set menus range from Y100 to Y500 per person. All dishes are elaborately prepared, and range from delicately filled pastries to sea cucumber with deer tendon, peppery inkfish's egg soup and camel paw with scallion (no, it's not a real camel paw). The Y500 menu will get you rare delicacies such as bird's nest soup, abalone and turtle meat. Reservations are a must.

Mongolian Hotpot Mongolian hotpot is a winter dish. A brass pot with charcoal inside it is placed at the centre of the table and you cook thick strips of mutton and vegetables, fondue fashion, spicing as you like. Look for the symbol shaped like the hotpot on little food stalls and restaurants in the hútòngs. Standard hotpot fare includes *yángròu* (mutton), *fěnsī* (rice noodles), *bōcài* (spinach), *báicài* (cabbage), *tǔdòu* (potato), *dòufu* (tofu) and *mógū* (mushrooms).

Běijīng's most renowned hotpot restaurant is *Néngrénjū* (☎ 6601 2560, 5 Taipingqiao, Baitasi, Xicheng). In winter this place is packed with loyal patrons so come early.

Sìchuān Famous for its fiery *làzi jī* (pepper chicken), *Jīnshānchéng Chóngqìng Càiguǎn* (*Golden Hill City Restaurant;* ☎ 6464 0945, 52 Liangjiu Lu), across from the Kempinski Hotel, is a great place to eat Sìchuān food. Other excellent dishes include *sōngshǔ guìyú* (deep-fried squirrel fish and sweet-and-sour sauce), *zhútǒng féiniú* (steamed beef in a bamboo tube), *gānbiān sìjìdòu* (crisp-fried green beans) and if you still have room, the *básī pínggu* (toffee apples).

A favourite of Běijīng expats, *Xīhéyǎjū Cāntīng* (☎ 6506 7643), at the north-east corner of Rìtán Gōngyuán, commonly referred to as the Rìtán Gōngyuán Restaurant, serves up reliably tasty dishes in a courtyard-style restaurant. Try standard Sìchuān fare like *mápò dòufu* (tofu) and *gōngbǎo jīdīng* (chicken with peanuts). The eclectic menu also has Shāndōng and Cantonese food.

Huángchègg Lǎoma (☎ 6779 8801, 39 Qingfengzhazhou) has excellent Sìchuān hotpot in airy, elegant surroundings. Sìchuān hotpot differs from Mongolian in that the pot, which looks like a yinyang symbol, is divided into two sides – on hot and one not so hot. Don't miss the *jiǔsìrúhóngbǎoshí* (a thick red liquor with 'medicinal' qualities).

Uyghur Muslim barbecue is dirt cheap if you know the right place to look for it. The right place is Wēigōngcūn, in Haidian, just north of the Beijing Library. This is where Běijīng's Uyghur minority congregates. Gānjiākǒu, south of here, used to be the more popular Uyghur neighbourhood, but sadly the restaurants here were demolished due to street widening (part of the city's scheme to fix the city up in preparation for the PRC's 50th anniversary). Although there are some signs of life emerging from the rubble, at the time of writing only a couple of small restaurants had reopened their doors.

Wēigōngcūn is a pleasant little street lined with tiny, family-owned restaurants that serve up the usual Uyghur fare: *náng* (flatbread), *sānpào tái* or *bābǎo chá* (sweet Uyghur tea), some vegetable dishes, *miàn* (noodles) and *ròuchuàn* (kebabs). The street also has a couple of Dai and Tibetan restaurants.

Běijīng's most popular Xīnjiāng restaurant is *Afanti* (☎ 6527 2288, 2 Houguaibang Hutong, Chaoyangmennei Dajie). It's famous for its table dancing, which wondrously takes place every night of the week. Xīnjiāng folk music and traditionally dressed dancers get the atmosphere going. It's best to come here in a big group, and to make reservations.

Vegetarian The Yángzhōu-style *Gōngdélín Sùcàiguǎn* (*Gongdelin Vegetarian Restaurant;* ☎ 6511 2542, 158 Qianmen Nandajie) is probably the best vegetarian restaurant in the city. It serves up wonderful vegie food with names to match. How about the 'peacock in pride' or 'the fire is singeing the snow-capped mountains'? It's open daily from 10.30 am to 8.30 pm.

The *Lǚ Tiānshǐ Fàndiàn* (*Green Angel Vegetarian Restaurant;* ☎ 6524 2476, 57 *Dengshikou Dajie*) serves similar fare, but in cleaner, brighter, more peaceful surroundings (and with slightly higher prices). A crystal shop and small vegetarian grocery occupy the 1st floor. Mount the staircase to the restaurant on the 2nd floor and you will be greeted by photos of famous vegetarians – Socrates, Einstein, Plato, Darwin … and Paul Newman. Specialties include Beijing duck, meatballs and broccoli, and sweet and sour fish with pine nuts (all fashioned by vegies only). Be sure to check the prices on the menu (in English) before letting the staff make suggestions for the best dishes.

Cantonese No self-respecting tourist hotel in Běijīng is without a Cantonese restaurant dishing up dim sum to their Hong Kong clientele. Remember that dim sum is for breakfast and lunch only – at night it's mostly seafood. The *Gloria Plaza Hotel* (*Kàilái Fàndiàn*) is well-known for its excellent dim sum – expect to wait for a table. Restaurants in the *Hilton* and *Huádū Fàndiàn* (next to the Kūnlún Fàndiàn) also serve good dim sum.

Fusion If you're looking for upscale dining, Běijīng has a few exceptional restaurants worth trying. The following restaurants all serve Chinese-influenced food, but with a modern twist (hence the subheading). Reservations are necessary; expect to pay around Y200 per person.

Běijīng's most chic restaurant is *The Courtyard* (☎ 6526 8881, 95 Donghuamen Dajie). It has a stunning view of the Forbidden City (the restaurant is just outside the east gate) and its surrounding moat. There's also a modern art gallery downstairs and a cosy cigar room upstairs.

Hidden away down a quiet hútòng is the *Red Capital Club* (*Xīnhóngzī Jùlèbù;*

☎ 6402 7150 during the daytime, 8401 8886 at night and on weekends, 66 Dongsi Jiu Tiao). It's in a meticulously restored courtyard house, with traditional Chinese decor. Every dish has a myth that goes along with it, so be prepared to spend at least a ½ hour reading the menu (it's in English). Look for the big red doors with no sign.

A beautiful little place for lunch or dinner is the *Green Tea House* (☎ 6468 5903, 54 Tayuancun, Sānlǐtún). This tiny Chinese-style tea house is lavishly decorated and its refined dishes and teas are exceptional. But the real reason to come here is the food presentation – truly works of art.

Non-Chinese Food

If you're looking for a break from Chinese food, Běijīng won't let you down. You can eat just about any type of cuisine from around the world here.

If you're craving Italian food, *Metro Cafe* (☎ 6552 7828, 6 Gongti Xilu) won't let you down. It has a fine selection of delicious homemade pastas and sauces at reasonable (but not dirt cheap) prices.

1,001 Nights (☎ 6532 4050), across from the Zhàolóng Hotel on Gongrentiyuchang Beilu, serves excellent Middle Eastern food 24 hours, including *baba ganoush* (eggplant dip), hummus and *schwarma* (meat and salad wrapped in bread).

Back in Asia, *Phrik Thai* (☎ 6586 9726, Guan Dong Dian Lu), a short distance west of the Jīngguǎng Fàndiàn on Chaoyangmen Dajie, is a tiny restaurant that serves delicious Thai food at reasonable prices.

Fast Food Since *Kentucky Fried Chicken* (*KFC; Kěndéjī Jiāxiāng Jī*) opened its doors in 1987 fast food has invaded Běijīng in a big way. At the time of its opening of the Běijīng branch, it was the largest KFC in the world. The colonel's smiling face is still just across the street from Mao's mausoleum in Tiānānmén Square – if this doesn't make the late Chairman turn over in his grave, nothing will. Just to give you an idea, here's a partial list of fast food chains found around Běijīng: Dairy Queen, Dunkin' Donuts, TGI Friday's, Popeye's, Subway,

Pizza Hut, Schlotsky's, the ubiquitous Mc-Donald's and Starbucks, the city's latest invader.

Chinese bread is about as tasty as a dried-out sponge, but a few entrepreneurs in Běijīng have started to introduce edible baked goods to the masses. One fine effort in this direction is *Bella's*, where you can get freshly baked bread and pastries (try the cinnamon ring), along with a pretty decent cafe latte or espresso. There are outlets on Sānlǐtún's bar street, next to Kylin Plaza on Gongrentiyuchang Beilu.

Another place to look is in some of the big hotels – a few have sent the staff off to Europe for a wintertime crash course in making German black bread and Danish pastries. Unfortunately, hotel prices tend to be high. The deli in the *Holiday Inn Lido* (see the Běijīng map) stocks delectable chocolate cake, sourdough bread and other requisite baked goods, but it's certainly not cheap.

Supermarkets One of the best-stocked supermarkets is in the basement of *Scitech Plaza*, a department store on the southern side of Jianguomenwai Dajie.

On the eastern fringe of Jiàngúoménwài is the China World Trade Centre; go down into the basement to find a fully fledged *Wellcome supermarket* imported lock, stock and shopping cart from Hong Kong. The Wellcome slogan 'low everyday prices' doesn't quite describe the situation in Běijīng, but you'll find all the familiar goodies right down to the 'No Frills Dried Lemon Peel'.

Just next to the CITIC building is the *Friendship Store*. When you enter the building turn sharply right to find the food section. The supermarket is decidedly mediocre, but you can find all the basic necessities.

Just north of the Great Wall Sheraton is the enormous *Lufthansa Centre* – yes, it is a ticket office for a German airline, but also a multi-storey shopping mall. There is a fine supermarket in the basement chock-a-block with imported goods.

Pub Grub If the truth be told, the majority of westerners in Běijīng rarely indulge in dim sum, Beijing duck or Mongolian hot-pot. The fact is that, outside of breakfast, most foreigners are drawn towards a collection of pubs in the Sānlǐtún and Jiàngúoménwài areas. Since these are great socialising spots often with outdoor tables, live music and closing times hovering around 2 am, we've listed these places in the following 'Entertainment' section.

ENTERTAINMENT

Check out *Beijing Scene* for the latest on entertainment in the capital. Its 'Picks' section highlights some of the more worthwhile events taking place each week. Unless otherwise indicated, all venues appear on the Central Běijīng map.

Acrobatics

Two thousand years old, and one of the few art forms condoned by Mao, acrobatics *(tèjì biǎoyǎn)* is the best entertainment deal in town.

Good places to catch an acrobatics show are *Poly Plaza (Bǎolì Dàshà Jùyuàn;* ☎ *6500 1188 ext 5127, 14 Dongzhimennan Dajie)*, where the China Acrobatics Troupe takes the stage nightly at 7:15pm. The *Cháoyáng Dàjùchǎng (Chaoyang Theatre;* ☎ *6507 2421, 36 Dongsanhuan Beilu),* at Chaoyang Beilu in the north-eastern part of Běijīng, runs shows from 7.15 to 8.45 pm. Tickets to either venue are Y80.

Běijīng Opera

Originally an ancient temple, the ornately decorated *Zhèngyǐcí Dàxìlóu (Zhengyici Theatre;* ☎ *6303 3104, 220 Xiheyan Dajie, Hepingmenwai)* is the oldest wooden theatre in the country and is the best place in the city to experience this traditional art form. The theatre was restored by a private businessman with an interest in reviving the dying art and reopened in 1995 after a long period of disrepair. Three years later the theatre was summarily closed after the owner couldn't afford its hefty rent and then reopened under new management a few months later. The theatre has nightly performances from 7.30 to 9 pm; tickets are Y50.

Similarly decorated, with balconies surrounding the canopied stage, the *Huguang*

Běijīng Opera

It used to be the Marx Brothers, the Gang of Four and the Red Ballet – but it's back to the classics again these days. Běijīng opera (*píngjù*) is one of the many forms of the art and the most famous, but it only has a short history. The year 1790 is the key date given; in that year a provincial troupe performed before Emperor Qianlong on his 80th birthday. The form was popularised in the west by the actor Mei Lanfang (1894–1961) who is said to have influenced Charlie Chaplin.

Běijīng opera bears little resemblance to its European counterpart. The mixture of singing, dancing, speaking, mime, acrobatics and dancing can go on for five or six hours, but two hours is more usual.

There are four types of actors' roles: the *sheng*, *dan*, *jing* and *chou*. The sheng are the leading male actors and they play scholars, officials, warriors and the like. The dan are the female roles, but are usually played by men (Mei Lanfang always played a dan role). The jing are the painted-face roles, and they represent warriors, heroes, statesmen, adventurers and demons. The chou is basically the clown.

Language is often archaic Chinese and the screeching music is searing to western ears, but the costumes and make-up are magnificent. The action that really catches the western eye is a swift battle sequence – the female warriors involved are trained acrobats who leap, twirl and somersault into attack. It's not unlike boarding a Běijīng bus during rush hour.

Catching at least one Běijīng opera is almost mandatory for visitors to the capital.

Guild Hall (☎ *6351 8284, 3 Hufangqiao Lu*) stages performances nightly from 7.15 to 8.40 pm. The theatre is the site where the Kuomintang, led by Dr Sun Yatsen, was established in 1912. Tickets range from Y20 (for a back table) to Y150.

The **Líyuán Jùchǎng** (*Liyuan Theatre;* ☎ *6301 6688 ext 8860*), in the Qiánmén Fàndiàn also puts on regular live performances. Though nice, the theatre is of the sterile, movie-theatre variety; it's much more interesting to see Běijīng opera in a traditional setting.

Bars

Referred to by locals as the 'Bar Street,' Sanlitun Lu is basically considered the centre of expat life in Běijīng. There are actually two main bar streets in Sānlǐtún – the main one that runs between Gongrentiyuchang Beilu and Dongzhimenwai, and a smaller alleyway that runs south from Gongrentiyuchang Beilu. The alleyway, also known as Sanlitun Nanlu, is between Sanlitun Lu and Gongrentiyuchang Donglu (look for the neon green 'Nashville' sign across from Kylin Plaza).

Although rumours constantly circulate that Sanlitun Lu is going to be shut down, bars on this street are still going strong. Pretty much right in the middle of the street is **Public Space** (☎ *6416 0759*), a popular place that plays good music and attracts a good crowd. You can also grab a late dinner here – try the warm salmon salad (Y45).

On Sanlitun Nanlu, **Hidden Tree** (☎ *6509 3642*) has a wide selection of Belgian beers, some on tap, and serves decent Greek food. **Jam House** (☎ *6506 3845*) has a pleasant outdoor rooftop space, and live music downstairs.

Gay venues include **Half and Half** (☎ *6416 6919*), down a narrow alley to the east of Kylin Plaza, and **Butterfly Bar** on Sanlitun Lu.

Discos & Clubs

The latest addition to Běijīng's nightlife scene is the monolithic **Yáoguè** (*Rock & Roll;* ☎ *6592 9856*), a huge neon-lit strip of clubs and bars at the south gate of Cháoyáng Gōngyuán; see Běijīng map. If you want to party with the locals, this is the place to come.

Owned by the PLA, **Rè Diǎn** (*Hot Spot;* ☎ *6501 9955, Dongsanhuan Lu*) is a relatively long-standing haven for Běijīng clubbers. The night club is well-known for its cage dancers.

In the Sānlǐtún area, *The Den* (☎ *6592 6290*), next to the City Hotel, *Havana Cafe* (☎ *6586 6166*), north gate of Gongrentiyuchang and *Club Vogue* (☎ *1300 113 5089, Gongrentiyuchang Donglu*), a half block north of Gongrentiyuchang Beilu – look for the red doors with no sign – are all popular hang-outs with dance floors and decent music. The Den and Havana Cafe mostly pack in the expat crowd, while Club Vogue is the place to be seen if you're a Chinese model or musician. In Haidian, *Solutions* (☎ *6255 8877*), across from Beida's west gate (see the Běijīng map), is a popular hang-out for the foreign student crowd.

Live Music

Běijīng has a lively and varied live music scene. In the mood for punk, rock, jazz, folk, alternative, classical or reggae? There's a good chance of seeing whatever type of music fits your mood almost any night of the week.

On Sanlitun Nanlu, *Jam House* (☎ *6506 3845*) is a laid-back dive with live music most nights of the week. *Keep in Touch*, down an alley across from the Kempinski Hotel, has a small stage but is where you can see some of Běijīng's, if not China's, top bands, like Tang dynasty, the all-female band Cobra and Thin Man. Another good venue to see live music is the *Busy Bee Bar* (☎ *6402 5788, 208 Dongsi Beidajie*). If you're in the mood for Jazz, try *CD Cafe* (☎ *6501 8877 ext 3032*), on the east side of East Third Ring Rd. Red velvet curtains frame the stage at this bordering on swanky jazz joint.

Sānwèi Bookstore & Teahouse (☎ *6601 3204, 60 Fuxingmennei Dajie*), opposite the Mínzú Fàndiàn, has a small bookshop on the ground floor, but hidden on the 2nd floor is a charming Chinese teahouse. Chinese classical music is provided on Saturday night from 8.30 to 10.30 pm. Admission is Y30.

Theme Parks

China's largest theme park is *World Park* (Shìjiè Gōngyuán). Chinese who can't afford

The Karaoke Phenomenon

Nowadays karaoke requires little in the way of introduction, even in the west. The word 'karaoke' is a combination of the Japanese words *kara*, meaning 'empty', and *oke*, a Japanese contraction of the English word 'orchestra'. The idea is simple enough: the voice track is removed from a particular song, providing the audience with a do-it-yourself pop hit.

From small-time beginnings in Japan, karaoke first took Taiwan and Hong Kong by storm, and then inevitably slipped into China. Today it has become one of the main recreational activities for locals. It's easy to recognise a karaoke parlour: they are usually lit up in neon and have a Chinese sign with the characters for *kǎlā* (a phonetic rendering of the Japanese) followed by the English letters 'OK'. Sometimes clubs can be identified by the acronym KTV – 'karaoke television'. The latter normally have private booths.

It's actually worth checking out a karaoke parlour or two while you are in Běijīng, though they are generally not cheap. There are two menus: one for the drinks and one for the songs. Don't expect much in the way of English songs. It usually costs around Y10 to get up on stage and sing a song, and the locals clamour for the opportunity. It doesn't matter how badly you sing. You'll get a polite round of applause from the audience when you finish, probably a rapturous round of applause if you are a foreigner.

A recent development is the poor-person's karaoke bar, a TV (a video with a bouncing ball following the lyrics) set up by the roadside, where you pay a few jiao to sing into a small PA system. The Chinese government, with characteristic market savvy, has responded to the karaoke boom by setting up a department to produce karaoke numbers that give the public an opportunity to musically express their burning ardour for the Communist Party. Perversely, everyone seems to prefer singing Rod Stewart numbers and the latest Taiwanese and Hong Kong pop hits.

an overseas holiday come here to visit the Eiffel Tower, the pyramids of Egypt and America's Statue of Liberty. Of course, these reproductions are somewhat smaller than the originals. The park is south-west of the centre, about 3km south of Fēngtái train station (see the Běijīng map). If you don't plan to travel by taxi, you'll have to take a bus to Fēngtái train station and a minibus from there to the park. Bus Nos 309 (from the Běijīng West train station) and 406 (from the Asian Games Village) can also get you there.

If World Park is where you go to see reproductions of famous buildings, then the *Zhōnghuá Mínzú Yuán* (China Ethnic Minorities Park) is where you go to see reproductions of China's 56 ethnic minorities. Han Chinese dress up in minority costumes and pretend to be Tibetans or Mongolians. Tourists can do the same (for a fee) to capture that memorable photo to show the loved ones back home. The landscape is also dotted with small-scale imitations of famous Chinese scenic spots such as a fake Jiuzhaigou Dragon Waterfall. The park is in the north of Běijīng (see the Běijīng map), and double-decker bus No 2 goes there. The park is open daily from 8 am to 10 pm and admission costs Y60.

SHOPPING
The following is a description of some shopping districts and bargains to be had.

Wángfǔjǐng   王府井
This prestigious shopping street is just east of the Forbidden City. It's a solid block of stores and a favourite haunt of locals and tourists. The area was recently done up, complete with a pedestrian walkway, as part of the government's beautification of Běijīng for the 50th anniversary of the PRC.

Wángfǔjǐng is home to Běijīng's first multi-storey megamall – Xindongan Plaza. Of prime interest to foreign travellers is the Foreign Languages Bookstore. There's a small English-language section, where you can stock up on Chinese-language textbooks and other miscellaneous titles like coffee-table books and cookbooks. It also

carries a small selection of travel guides (including a few Lonely Planet titles).

Dàchìlàn   大栅栏
Dàchìlàn is a hútòng running west from the northern end of Qián Mén, near Tiānānmén Square. It's a heady jumble of silk shops, department stores, theatres, herbal medicine, food and clothing specialists and some unusual architecture.

Dàchìlàn has a remnant medieval flavour to it, a hangover from the days when hútòngs sold specialised products – one would sell lace, another lanterns, another jade. This one used to be called Silk Street. Dàchìlàn is still *the* place to buy silk. The Beijing Silk Store (☎ 6301 6658, 5 Zhubaoshi, Qianmen Dajie) has the best selection, while Ruifuxiang (☎ 6303 2808, 5 Dazhalan) is also good. The name Dàchìlàn refers to a wicket-gate that was closed at night to keep prowlers out.

Líulíchǎng   琉璃厂
Not far to the west of Dàchìlàn is Líulíchǎng, Běijīng's antique street. In imperial Běijīng, shops and theatres were not permitted near the city centre, but Líulíchǎng was outside the gates. Many of the city's oldest shops can be found along or near this crowded hútòng.

Although it's been a shopping area for quite some time, only relatively recently has it been dressed up for foreign tourists. The stores here are all designed to look like an ancient Chinese village. The vast majority of the shops at Líulíchǎng are run by the government, but that doesn't mean they are honest. Prices are mostly outrageous, but Líulíchǎng is worth a look – some of the art books and drawings are a good deal and not easily found elsewhere. This is a good place to buy a chop; with some bargaining you can get one for Y30 and have it engraved for Y10.

Jiànguóménwài   建国门外
The Friendship Store (Yǒuyì Shāngdiàn; ☎ 6500 3311), at 17 Jianguomenwai Dajie, is the largest store of this type in the land, stocking both touristy souvenirs and everyday useful items. It's been superseded by newer shopping malls, but the book and

Mao Mania

Although he's been dead for 20 years, the legacy of Mao Zedong continues to play a major role in the contemporary political life of China and, indeed, for many mainland Chinese Mao has made the leap from emperor to god-like status.

What is more intriguing, perhaps, is how Mao has captivated the imagination beyond China's borders in a guise that is far less politically defined: 'Like, wouldn't it be cool to have matching Mao earrings?'. Maybe it all began with Andy Warhol's 1972 silkscreen portrait after Nixon's visit to China that put the chairman up alongside pop icons like Marilyn Monroe and made him fashionable, for it can't be denied that the Mao image today, along with other artefacts associated with the Cultural Revolution, has a certain trendy cachet in Hong Kong, Japan and the west. Of course, China experienced its own resurgence of Maoist kitsch in the early 90s, yet this was seen as a nostalgic and even spiritual response to disillusionment with the current leadership and uncertainty about changes brought by the economic reforms.

The fascination with Mao outside of the local context is a little more baffling, especially when seen in the light of historical realities. Compared with Mao, it's hard to think of other dictators in world history that have made such a splash in the souvenir market – Mao badges, Mao's little red books, miniature Mao statues, Mao lighters and Mao T-shirts have all done a brisk trade since China's opening in the early 1980s.

It does beg the question: how can anybody with more than a passing understanding of Mao's role in Chinese history really feel comfortable walking around wearing a Mao T-shirt? It's difficult to see a similar currency among tourists for souvenirs featuring Hitler or Stalin. Perhaps the difference is that the international community, and most certainly the mainland Chinese government, have not repudiated Mao's value as the leader of China after 1949, but this does not make his crimes against humanity any less abhorrent.

Not many foreign tourists seemed interested in buying a Deng Xiaoping T-shirt after the crackdown on demonstrators in the 1989 Tiananmen Massacre. Yet that single incident pales almost into insignificance when one considers many of the events which occurred under Mao's leadership – the mass slaughter of Chinese soldiers during the Korean War, the anti-rightist purge during the One Hundred Flowers campaign, the famine following the Great Leap Forward where as many as 30 million people (if not more) died of starvation, and finally the brutality and devastation of the Cultural Revolution, from which China has yet to recover.

The complete demystification of Mao may never take place in China and no doubt he will occupy a sacred place for many years to come. Outside of China, however, Mao's image might have less appeal as an item of popular recognition if there was a greater awareness about his role in Chinese history. No matter how compelling he may appear in the official portrait hanging above the entrance to the Forbidden City, there's nothing like a good dose of Mao stories to turn you off the chairman forever.

magazine section is a gold mine for travellers starved of anything to read.

The Xiùshuǐ Shìchǎng (Silk Market) is on the northern side of Jiànguóménwài between the Friendship Store and the Jiānguó Fàndiàn. This is the place to buy brand-name clothing, shoes and purses (the Gap, North Face, Prada, etc.), but be aware that most of the stuff here is fake. Go early to avoid crowds and forget it on Sunday. Bar-

gaining is imperative, although it's often a struggle because of all the foreign tourists willing to throw money around like water. Rumours abound of the market being shut down and moved indoors, but at the time of writing it was still thriving.

Sānlǐtún
There's another clothing market on Sanlitun Lu. It sells similar things to the Silk

Market, but it's much smaller and less crowded. It's generally a pleasant place to stroll (except for the CD and VCD sales-people who accost you every few feet), with cafes and bars just across the street. If you are interested in buying rip-off CDs, don't pay more than Y10. VCDs go for Y15 each, although quality is not usually very good.

Markets
Absolutely not to be missed is the Pānjiāyuán market, also known as the Dirt Market. It takes place on Saturday and Sunday only. The market gets going around 6 am and winds down around 3 pm, although many vendors start packing up around noon; the earlier you get there the better. For sale in the covered section are all kinds of 'antiques' (most are reproductions) and knick-knacks: ceramics, wooden chests, Yíxīng teapots, Cultural Revolution memorabilia, Mao alarm clocks, Tibetan carpets, scrolls, reproductions of 1920s cigarette ads, Chinese furniture etc, but you have to bargain for everything here. Outside the covered section anything goes. Those on the hunt for true antiques usually start here; this is where countryfolk hawk all kinds of things, and collectors dream of lifting a true antique from an unsuspecting farmer for next to nothing. To get here head south on East Third Ring Rd (if you're coming from, say, the Jiànguóménwài area) and exit just before Panjiayuanqiao. The market, surrounded by a tall wall, is about 100m west, on your left.

If you can't make it to Pānjiāyuán, Hóngqiáo is open daily and is a decent alternative to pick up 'antiques' on the 3rd floor. Also known as the pearl market, Hóngqiáo is where you can pick up real pearls (of varying quality) for dirt-cheap prices. The pearl vendors are on the third floor. The 2nd floor has a huge selection of fake designers including Prada, Gucci and Louis Vuitton. The first floor has every conceivable kind of everyday item, from nail clippers to pots and pans. Hóngqiáo is across the street from the east gate of the Tiāntán (Temple of Heaven).

Miscellaneous
If there's anything you think is impossible to buy in Běijīng, check out Watson's (Qūchénshì), in the Holiday Inn Lido on the road heading out towards the airport, and Full Link Plaza, on Chaoyangmennei Dajie. This place sells every vitamin known to humanity, sun screen (UV) lotion, beauty creams, tampons and the widest selection of condoms in Běijīng.

In addition to condoms, the Adam & Eve Health Centre (Yǎdāng Xiàwá Bǎojiàn Zhōngxīn; ☎ 6617 3708), China's first sex shop, sells everything from three-penis wine (a virility drug of course) and all shapes and sizes of vibrators (including one in the shape of a woman astride a beaver) to the all-inclusive Bedside Orgy Kit.

For outdoor gear, Extreme Beyond (☎ 6506 5121) sells high-quality, real (ie, not fake) goods, including brand-name backpacks, Gore-Tex jackets, sleeping bags and hiking boots. Prices are a little steep, but are still well below what you'd pay at home. Even though it's a shop, you can bargain here.

A reliable place to get photos developed is the Tibet Dipper Photo Service (Xīzàng Běidǒuxīng Túpiànzǒngshè; ☎ 6415 0710). Professional photographers get photos and slides developed here, but the shop also caters to regular folks.

GETTING THERE & AWAY
Air
Běijīng has direct air connections to most major cities in the world. Many travellers make use of the direct Běijīng-Hong Kong flights on CAAC or Dragonair. Economy class one-way/return tickets cost Y2750/3880. Flights tend to be heavily booked, especially on Dragonair. It's cheaper to fly from Guǎngzhōu (one way Y1360) and Shēnzhèn (one way Y1400), which are both near Hong Kong and have daily direct flights to Běijīng.

For more information about international flights to Běijīng, see the Getting There & Away chapter earlier in this book.

The CAAC aerial web spreads out in every conceivable direction, with daily flights to most destinations. For the most current information, get a CAAC timetable. Domestic flights connect Běijīng to the following cities:

Bāotóu (Y470; one hour; Wednesday), Chángshā (Y970; two hours; daily), Chéngdū (Y1150; two hours and 20 minutes; daily), Chóngqìng (Y1250; 2¼ hours; daily), Dàlián (Y570; one hour and 10 minutes; daily), Fúzhōu (Y1240; 2½ hours; daily), Guǎngzhōu (Y1360; two hours and 50 minutes; daily), Guìlín (Y1430; 4¼ hours; daily), Hāěrbīn, Hǎikǒu (Y1800; three hours and 40 minutes), Hǎilāěr (Y920; two hours; four times weekly), Hángzhōu (Y920; 50 minutes; daily), Hong Kong (Y2710; three hours; daily), Hohhot (Y400; one hour; daily), Jǐ'nán (Y500; one hour; daily), Kūnmíng (Y1450; four hours; daily), Nánchāng (Y1040; two hours; daily), Nánjīng (Y810; one hour and 35 minutes; daily), Nánníng (Y1640; three hours and 25 minutes; daily), Níngbō (Y940; two hours and 10 minutes; daily), Shànghǎi (Y900; two hours; daily), Shàntóu (Y1460; three hours; daily), Shěnyáng (Y560; one hour; daily), Shēnzhèn (Y1400; three hours; daily), Tàiyuán (Y470; 50 minutes; daily), Ulanhot (Y610; two hours and 20 minutes; twice weekly), Wēnzhōu (Y1240; two hours; daily), Wǔhàn (Y860; two hours; daily), Xiàmén (Y1370; 2½ hours; daily), Xī'ān (Y840; 1½ hours; daily), Xilinhot (Y340; 50 minutes; twice weekly), Yanji (Y900; one hour and 40 minutes; four times weekly), Zhèngzhōu (Y550; one hour and 10 minutes; daily)

CAAC goes by a variety of aliases (Air China, China Eastern Airlines etc), but you can buy tickets for all of them at the Aviation Building (Mínháng Dàshà; ☎ 6601 3336 for domestic, ☎ 6601 6667 for international) at 15 Xichang'an Jie, Xicheng District. You can purchase the same tickets at any travel agent or business centre. Domestic plane ticket prices are regulated so they're the same price no matter where you buy them.

The individual offices of other airlines are:

Aeroflot (☎ 6500 2412) Jīnglún Fàndiàn, 3 Jianguomenwai Dajie
Air France (☎ 6588 1388) Room 512, China World Trade Center, 1 Jianguomenwai Dajie
Air Macau (☎ 6515 8988) Room 807, Scitech Tower, 22 Jianguomenwai Dajie

Alitalia (☎ 6561 0375) Room 143, Jiànguó Fàndiàn, 5 Jianguomenwai Dajie
All Nippon Airways (☎ 6590 9191) Room 1510, China World Trade Center, 1 Jianguomenwai Dajie
American Airlines (☎ 6517 1788) c/o Beijing Tradewinds, 114 International Club, 11 Ritan Lu
Asiana Airlines (☎ 6468 4000) Room 134, Jiànguó Fàndiàn, 5 Jianguomenwai Dajie
Austrian Airlines (☎ 6462 2161) Great Wall Sheraton Hotel, 10 Dongsanhuan Beilu
British Airways (☎ 6512 4070) Room 210, 2nd floor, Scitech Tower, 22 Jianguomenwai Dajie
Canadian Airlines International (☎ 6468 2001) Unit C201, Lufthansa Centre, 50 Liangmaqiao Lu
Dragonair (☎ 6518 2533) 1st floor, L107, China World Trade Center, 1 Jianguomenwai Dajie
El Al Israel Airlines (☎ 6597 4512) Room 2906, Jīngguǎng Xīn Shìjie Fàndiàn
Ethiopian Airlines (☎ 6505 0134) Room 0506, China World Trade Center, 1 Jianguomenwai Dajie
Finnair (☎ 6512 7180) Room 204, Scitech Tower, 22 Jianguomenwai Dajie
Garuda Indonesia (☎ 6505 2901) Unit L116A, West Wing, China World Trade Center, 1 Jianguomenwai Dajie
Japan Airlines (☎ 6513 0888) Ground floor, Changfugong Office Bldg, Hotel New Otani, 26A Jianguomenwai Dajie
KLM – Royal Dutch Airlines (☎ 6505 3505) Suite 104, China World Trade Center, 1 Jianguomenwai Dajie
Korean Air (☎ 6505 0088) Room 401, West Wing, China World Trade Center, 1 Jianguomenwai Dajie
LOT Polish Airlines (☎ 6500 7215) Room 2002, Chains City Hotel, 4 Gongren Tiyuchang Donglu
Lufthansa Airlines (☎ 6465 4488) S101, Lufthansa Centre, 50 Liangmaqiao Lu
Malaysia Airlines (☎ 6505 2681) W115A/B Level One, West Wing Office Block, China World Trade Center, 1 Jianguomenwai Dajie
Mongolian Airlines (☎ 6507 9297) Jīnglún Fàndiàn, Jianguomenwai Dajie
Northwest Airlines (☎ 6505 3505) Room 104, China World Trade Center, 1 Jianguomenwai Dajie
Pakistan International Airlines (☎ 6505 1681) Room 617, China World Trade Center, 1 Jianguomenwai Dajie
Qantas Airways (☎ 6467 3337) Suite S120, Ground floor, East Wing Office Bldg,

Kempinski Hotel, Lufthansa Centre, 50 Liangmaqiao Lu

Scandinavian Airlines (☎ 6518 3738) 18th floor, Scitech Tower, 22 Jianguomenwai Dajie

Singapore Airlines (☎ 6505 2233) Room 109, China World Trade Center, 1 Jianguomenwai Dajie

Swissair (☎ 6512 3555) Room 201, Scitech Tower, 22 Jianguomenwai Dajie

Tarom (☎ 6500 2233 ext 111) Jiànguó Fàndiàn, 5 Jianguomenwai Dajie

Thai Airways International (☎ 6460 8899) S102B Lufthansa Centre, 50 Liangmaqiao Lu

United Airlines (☎ 6463 1111) Lufthansa Centre, 50 Liangmaqiao Lu

Yugoslav Airlines (☎ 6590 3388 ext 447) Room 414, Kūnlún Fàndiàn, 2 Xinyuan Nanlu

Bus

Many foreigners don't think so, but you can indeed arrive in or depart from Běijīng by bus. The advantage over the train (besides cost) is that it's easier to get a seat on a bus. Sleeper buses are widely available and certainly recommended for those long overnight journeys. In general, arriving by bus is easier than departing, mainly because when leaving it's confusing to try and figure out which bus station has the bus you need.

The basic rule is that long-distance bus stations are on the perimeter of the city in the direction you want to go. The four major ones are at Dōngzhímén (north-east), Hǎihùtún (south; see the Běijīng map), Běijiāo (north – also called Déshèngmén; see the Běijīng map) and Mǎjuàn (east). Near the entrance to the Běijīng-Tiānjīn Expressway is the Zhàogōngkǒu bus station (see the Běijīng map) where you get buses to (surprise) Tiānjīn. The Tiānqiáo bus station (western side of Tiāntán Gōngyuán) and Líanhūachí bus station (south-west of the city) are two places where you can get buses to sites south-west of Běijīng.

In addition, there are a few small bus stations where tour buses and minibuses gather (usually just in the morning) looking for passengers heading to the Great Wall and other sites in the outlying areas. The most important of these is the Qián Mén bus station (which has two parts) just to the south-west of Tiānānmén Square.

Train

Foreigners arriving or departing by train do so at Běijīng's main train station (Běijīng huǒchē zhàn) south-east of the Forbidden City or Běijīng West train station (Běijīng xī zhàn), near Líanhūachí Gōngyuán. It's the largest train station in China.

There are also two other stations of significance in the city, Běijīng South train station (Yǒngdìngmén; see Běijīng map) and Běijīng North train station (Xīzhímén) on the Second Ring Rd.

There are special ticketing windows for foreigners at Běijīng and Běijīng West stations, although they're now also open to Chinese – look for the small sign in English saying 'International Passenger Booking Office'. The ticketing office is open daily from 5.30 to 7.30 am and 8 am to 5.30 pm, and from 7 pm to 12.30 am. The Běijīng West train station office is open 24 hours. Those are the official times, but foreigners have often found the staff to arrive late and leave early. Whether or not you get a ticket here is pot luck – sometimes the staff are friendly and helpful, at other times they are belligerent. Tickets can be booked five or six days in advance. Your chances of getting a sleeper (hard or soft) are good if you book ahead.

See the following table for approximate travel times and train fares out of Běijīng for hard seat, hard sleeper and soft sleeper. Variations may arise because of variations in routes taken by different trains: For example, the journey to Shanghai can take between 17 and 25 hours depending on the train.

GETTING AROUND
To/From the Airport

The airport is 27km from the Forbidden City, but add another 10km if you're going to the southern end of town where most of the budget hotels are.

At the airport you'll be presented with a bewildering choice of buses all congregating by the main exit. In fact, almost any bus that gets you to a subway station will do. Inside the airport terminal is the service desk that sells tickets. All buses into town cost Y16, so just plop down the money and tell

REIMUND ZUNDE

The colour, sound and energy of Běijīng opera

JEAN ROBERT

The closed doors of the Forbidden City

HILARY ADELE SMITH

Traditional wedding carriage

LEE FOSTER

On guard: marching soldiers in the Forbidden City

Gōngwáng Fǔ, the Běijīng residence of Prince Gong

Snow play in Běijīng

Travel Times & Train Fares from Běijīng

Destination	Soft Sleeper (Y)	Hard Sleeper (Y)	Hard Seat (Y)	Soft Seat (Y)	Approx Travel Time (hours)
Bǎotóu	–	169	112	85	23
Běidàihé	–	–	62	–	3
Chángchūn	397	249	137	–	17
Chángshā	529	345	191	–	16
Chéngdé	–	–	41	61	5
Chéngdū	642	418	231	–	32
Chóngqìng	658	430	238	–	32
Dàlián	369	237	122	–	19
Dāndōng	400	263	143	–	15
Dàtóng	159	108	54	–	7
Fúzhōu	705	458	253	–	35
Guǎngzhōu	705	458	253	–	24
Guìlín	658	429	237	–	24
Hángzhōu	554	363	200	–	16
Hā'ěrbīn	442	290	158	–	14
Hohhot	254	170	92	–	11
Hong Kong	1027	777	–	–	28
Jǐ'nán	205	128	73	114	5
Kūnmíng	890	578	320	–	49
Lánzhōu	600	390	215	–	29
Luòyáng	184	117	53	–	12
Nánjīng	417	274	150	–	12
Nánníng	770	499	276	–	31
Qīngdǎo	326	215	116	184	17
Qíqíhā'ěr	529	345	191	–	16
Shànghǎi	499	327	179	–	15
Shěnyáng	286	191	103	–	9
Shēnzhèn	720	467	257	–	33
Shíjiāzhuāng	–	–	40	–	3
Sūzhōu	472	309	170	268	15
Tài'ān	241	149	92	–	7
Tàiyuán	224	149	79	–	11
Tángshān	–	–	20	33	3
Tiānjīn	–	–	25	40	1.5
Ürümqi	1006	652	363	–	60
Xī'ān	417	274	150	–	15
Xīníng	658	430	238	–	33
Yínchuān	292	188	94	–	22
Zhèngzhōu	264	175	94	–	8

them where you want to go – somebody outside can direct you towards the right bus.

One company called 'Airbus' currently operates two routes. Route A goes to

Běijīng train station and this is probably the most popular bus with travellers. Route B goes to the Xīnxīng Fàndiàn on the western side of town near Yùyuántán Líanhūachí.

Both of these buses can drop you at a subway station.

The Anle Bus Company offers three routes. The most popular route is to Xīdān, which is close to the CAAC office west of the Forbidden City. Another route is to Zhōngguāncūn, which is in north-west Běijīng. The third route is to the art gallery, Zhōngguó Měishùguǎn, north of the central area Wángfǔjīng.

The official schedule for all of the above buses is once every 30 minutes between 5.30 am and 7 pm, but during peak hours they put on additional buses.

A taxi (using its meter) should cost only about Y85 from the airport to the centre. Be aware of rip-off taxi drivers who approach you inside the terminal and ask something like Y250 for the trip – don't even talk to them, just go outside and get in the taxi queue just outside the arrival area. Drivers will also expect you to pay the Y10 toll if you take the airport expressway.

Bus

There are a mind-boggling number of buses plying Běijīng's traffic-choked boulevards. Destinations are written in Chinese only and figuring out the system will take patience – it's considerably easier if you score a bus map. The buses are packed at the best of times, and during the rush hour it's armpits and elbows all round.

Buses run from around 5 am to 11 pm, and the stops are few and far between. It's important to work out how many stops you need to go before boarding.

Buses are routed through landmarks and key intersections, and if you can pick out the head and tail of the route you can get a good idea of where the monster will travel. Major stations are situated near long-distance junctions: the main Běijīng train station, Dōngzhímén, Hǎihùtún, Yǒngdìngmén and Qián Mén. Běijīng Dòngwùyuán (Beijing Zoo) has the biggest pile-up, with about 15 bus lines, since it's where inner and outer Běijīng converge.

One- and two-digit bus numbers are city core; 100-series buses are trolleys and 300-series are suburban lines. If you work out

how to combine bus and subway connections the subway will speed up part of the trip.

Double-decker Bus The double-deckers are special two-tiered buses for tourists and upper-crust locals. They run in a circle around the city centre. The cost is Y2 but you are spared the traumas of normal public buses – passengers are guaranteed a seat! The following routes hit major points around the city:

1 Běijīng West train station, heading east on Fuxingmen Dajie, Xichang'an Jie, Dongchang'an Jie, Jianguomenei Dajie, Jianguomenwai Dajie, Jianguo Lu and terminating at a major bus stop called Bawangfen (intersection of Jianguo Lu and Xidawang Lu).

2 Qián Mén, north on Dongdan Beidajie, Dongsi Nandajie, Dongsi Beidajie, Yōnghé Gōng, Zhōnghuá Mínzú Yuán (Ethnic Minorities Park), Asian Games Village.

3 Jijia Temple (the south-west extremity of the Third Ring Rd), Dà Guān Yuán (Grand View Garden), Lèyóu Fàndiàn, Jingguang New World Hotel, Tuánjiéhú Gōngyuán, Agricultural Exhibition Centre, Lufthansa Centre.

4 Běijīng Dòngwùyuán, Exhibition Centre, Second Ring Rd, Holiday Inn Downtown, Yuetan Gōngyuán, Fuxingmen Dajie flyover, Qianmen Xidajie, Qián Mén.

6 Guofang University, Agricultural University, Beijing University, Qinghua West Gate, People's University, Wēigōngcūn, Zhōnghuá Mínzú Yuán, Běijīng Library, Ganjiakou, Yùyuāntán, Jūnshì Bówùguǎn, Běijīng West train station

Subway

The subway (dì tiě) is definitely the best way to travel around. The Underground Dragon can move at up to 70km per hour – a jaguar compared with the lumbering buses. The subway system made its debut in 1969 for Chinese only (foreigners gained admission in 1980). After nearly three decades the trains are showing their age – it's a pale shadow to Shànghǎi's spiffy new subway system.

To recognise a subway station ((dì tiě) zhàn), look for the subway symbol, which is a blue English capital 'D' with a circle around it. Another way of recognising a

BĚIJĪNG SUBWAY ROUTES

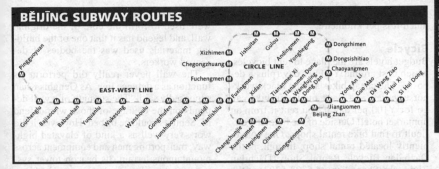

subway station is to look for an enormous cluster of bicycles.

Trains run at a frequency of one every few minutes during peak times. It can get very crowded, but it sure beats the buses! The carriages have seats for 60 and standing room for 200. The subway is open from 5 am to 11 pm; platform signs are in Chinese characters and pinyin.

There are two established lines, the Circle Line and the East-West Line. A third line opened in 1999. This third line (Fuba line) currently doesn't connect with the older lines, although the plan is for it to connect to Xīdān by late 2000. The Fuba line is open from 6.30 am to 9.30 pm. The fare is a flat Y3 regardless of distance on the Circle Line and East-West Line and Y2 for the third line.

Circle Line This 16km line presently has 18 stations: Běijīng train station, Jiànguómén, Cháoyángmén, Dōngsìshítiáo, Dōngzhímén, Yōnghégōng, Āndìngmén, Gǔlóu, Jīshuǐtán, Xīzhímén (the north train station and zoo), Chēgōngzhuāng, Fùchéngmén, Fùxīngmén, Chàngchūnjiē, Hépíngmén, Qiánmén and Chóngwénmén.

East-West Line This line has 12 stops and runs from Xīdān to Píngguǒyuán, which is – no, not the capital of North Korea – a western suburb of Běijīng, the name meaning Apple Orchard (the apple trees have unfortunately long since vanished). It takes 40 minutes to traverse the length of the line. The stops are Xīdān, Fùxīngmén, Nánlìshìlù,

Mùxīdì, Jūnshì Bówùguǎn, Gōngzhǔfén, Wànshòulù, Wǔkēsōng, Yùquánlù, Bābǎoshān, Bājiǎocūn, Gúchénglù and Píngguǒyuán. Fùxīngmén is where the Circle Line meets the East-West Line and there is no additional fare to make the transfer.

Fuba Line This is the line on the eastern side of the East-West line. The first stop is at the north-west corner of Tiānānmén Square and the last stop is in the eastern suburbs of the city. Stops include Tiān'ānménxī, Tiān'anméndōng, Wángfǔjǐng, Dōngdān, Yǒng'ānlǐ, Guómào, Dàwàngqiáo, Sìhuìxī, and Sìhuìdōng.

Taxi

With the number of taxis in the city reaching close to 100,000, finding one is only a problem during rush hours and rain storms.

Taxis come in different classes. The bottom of the pecking order once belonged to the yellow microbuses known as *miàndī* or 'bread taxis' (because they're shaped like a loaf of bread), although they've recently been phased out because they don't meet Běijīng's new pollution standards. *Xiali* taxis are now the most economical at Y1.20 per kilometre (Y10 for the first 5km). Next are the Y1.60 taxis (Y10 for the first 4km). Top of the line are the petrol-guzzling limousine taxis which cost Y10 for the first 4km and Y2 for each kilometre thereafter. Between 11 pm and 6 am there is a 20% surcharge added to the flagfall metered fare. There's a small red sticker on the side rear window of every taxi that tells you how much it is per kilometre.

Bicycle

Budget hotels are the place to rent bicycles, which cost around Y10 per day (plus a deposit). The cheap bikes are the black workhorse variety – a sleek mountain bike can go for Y100 per day if you rent it from an upmarket hotel! Outside of the hotel it's difficult to find bike rental shops. One conveniently located rental shop, though, is the Dazhalan Bicycle Rental Shop (Dachilan Zixingche Shangdian; ☎ 6303 5303) at the western end of Dachilan (right next to the gate at the end of the street). You can rent a bike here for Y10 per day plus a Y100 to Y300 deposit (depending on the type of bike you rent). The shop is open daily 9 am to 6.30 pm. When renting a bike it's safest to use your own lock in order to prevent bicycle theft.

Good quality bikes can be bought from Giant (☎ 6403 4537) at 77 Jiaodaokou Dongdajie.

The increase in traffic in recent years has made biking along major thoroughfares dangerous and nerve-racking. However, cycling through Běijīng's hútòngs is still an experience not to be missed. (See the boxed text 'On Your Bike'.)

Around Běijīng

THE GREAT WALL

Also known to the Chinese as the '10,000 Li Wall', the Great Wall (Chángchéng) stretches from Shānhǎi Guān on the east coast to Jiāyù Guān in the Gobi Desert.

Standard histories emphasise the unity of the wall. The 'original' wall was begun 2000 years ago during the Qin dynasty (221–207 BC), when China was unified under Emperor Qin Shihuang. Separate walls, constructed by independent kingdoms to keep out marauding nomads, were linked up. The effort required hundreds of thousands of workers, many of them political prisoners, and 10 years of hard labour under General Meng Tian. An estimated

180 million cubic metres of rammed earth were used to form the core of the original wall, and legend has it that one of the building materials used was the bodies of deceased workers.

The wall never really did perform its function as a defence line. As Genghis Khan supposedly said, 'The strength of a wall depends on the courage of those who defend it'. Sentries could be bribed. However, it did work very well as a kind of elevated highway, transporting men and equipment across mountainous terrain. Its beacon tower system, using smoke signals generated by burning wolves' dung, transmitted news of enemy movements quickly back to the capital. To the west was Jiāyù Guān, an important link on the Silk Road, where there was a customs post of sorts and where unwanted Chinese were ejected through the gates to face the terrifying wild west.

During the Ming dynasty a determined effort was made to rehash the whole project, this time facing it with bricks and stone slabs – some 60 million cubic metres of them. This project took over 100 years, and the costs in human effort and resources were phenomenal.

The wall was largely forgotten after that. Lengthy sections of it have returned to dust and the wall might have disappeared totally had it not been rescued by the tourist industry. Several important sections have recently been rebuilt, fitted out with souvenir shops, restaurants and amusement park rides, and formally opened to the public. The most touristed area of the Wall by far is Bādálǐng. Also renovated but less touristed are Sīmǎtái and Jīnshānlǐng. But to truly appreciate the Wall's magnificence, seeing the Wall *au naturel*, such as at Huánghuāchéng, is well worth the effort.

Bādálǐng 八达岭

The majority of visitors see the Great Wall at Bādálǐng, 70km north-west of Běijīng at an elevation of 1000m. This section of the wall (called Bādálǐng Chángchéng) was restored in 1957, with the addition of guard rails. Since the 1980s Bādálǐng has become

Standing for over 2000 years, the Great Wall is China's most spectacular attraction.

exceedingly crowded so a cable car was added to smooth the flow of tourist traffic.

The Great Wall Circle Vision Theatre was opened in 1990. It is a 360-degree amphitheatre showing 15-minute films about the Great Wall.

There is an admission fee of Y25, which also gets you into the Zhōngguó Chángchéng Bówùguǎn (China Great Wall Museum). You can spend plenty more for a tacky 'I Climbed the Great Wall' T-shirt, a talking panda doll, a cuckoo clock that plays 'The East Is Red' or a plastic reclining buddha statue with a light bulb in its mouth.

Getting There & Away CITS, CTS, big hotels and everyone else in the tourist business does a tour to Bādálǐng. Prices border on the ridiculous, with some hotels asking over Y300 per person.

There are inexpensive Chinese tour buses to Bādálǐng, although they usually combine Bādálǐng with a visit to the Shísān Líng (Ming Tombs) as well as a detour to a herbal medicine or souvenir shop. Big tour buses leave from across the street from the southwest corner of Tiānānmén Square between 6.30 and 10 am – for Y50 they'll bring you to the Great Wall at Bādálǐng and the Shísān Líng. Smaller buses leave for the same destinations from the south end of Tiānānmén Square (to the west of McDonald's) at 8 and 9.30 am for Y40. Plan about nine hours for the trip. A tour bus (No 4) also leaves from Zhanlanguan, directly across the street from the entrance to the zoo. They leave around 8 am and return around 6 pm and go to Bādálǐng and Shísān Líng. Cost is Y36, but the buses aren't as new and comfortable as the ones that leave from Qián Mén. Probably the cheapest way to get to Bādálǐng is to take minibus No 919 (Y10) from Déshèngmén (next to the Jīshuǐtán subway stop). Buses leave every ¼ hour (or as they fill up) starting from 5.30 am; the last bus leaves Bādálǐng for Běijīng at 6.30 pm.

A taxi to the wall and back will cost a minimum of Y400 for an eight-hour hire with a maximum of four passengers.

Mùtiányù 慕田峪
To take some of the pressure off crowded Bādálǐng, a second site for Great Wall viewing was opened at Mùtiányù, 90km

Conserving the Great Wall

Built to defend the Middle Kingdom from Mongol attack, the Great Wall north of Běijīng is now under modern attack, from hordes of environmentally-unaware day trippers riding in Jettas and Santanas, tossing their picnic garbage, letting off earth-shaking fireworks and etching their inglorious names on its 400-year-old bricks.

No longer self-protected by its inaccessibility – most sections are within three-hour's drive for Běijīng's ¾ million private car owners – the arrival of the fun-seeking nouveau riche at once-forgotten sections of Wall has made tourism development a high priority of local farmers and township bureaucrats eager to impress the party elite with their ability to 'relieve poverty'. Each would like their section of Wall to become the next Bādálǐng, but only bigger and 'better', with more cablecars and tourist kitch, the trademarks of domestic tourism.

But the Great Wall not only belongs to China, someone cries, it is a UNESCO World Heritage Site, and surely that ensures its preservation? In theory yes, but in reality, the designation shrouds the Wall under a false cloak of security. The Great Wall, actually many Great Walls built by many dynasties over a 2500-year-long period, and extending for more than 50,000km across 17 provinces, autonomous regions and municipalities, is the world's most extensive outdoor museum – without a curator. It is neither protected by any specific laws, nor managed as a relic or resource by any special office.

William Lindesay – author of *Hiking on History: Exploring Beijing's Great Wall*, Oxford **University Press**

north-east of Běijīng. It didn't take long before armadas of Japanese tour buses began to congregate, and today this part of the wall (called Mùtiányù Chángchéng) is almost as much of a carnival as Bādálǐng. Admission is Y20.

Getting There & Away From Dōngzhímén bus station take a bus No 916 to Huairou (Y4; one hour), then change for a bus for Mùtiányù.

Jūyōng Guān　居庸关
Juyong Pass

Originally constructed in the 5th century and rebuilt by the Ming, this section of the Wall was considered one of the most strategically important because of its position as a link to Běijīng. However, this section has been thoroughly renovated to point where you don't feel as if you're walking on a part of history. Still, if you're in a hurry, it's the closest section of the Wall to Běijīng. You can do the steep and somewhat strenuous circuit in under two hours.

Admission to the Great Wall at Jūyōng Guān is Y25.

Getting There & Away Approximately 50km northwest of Běijīng, Jūyōng Guān is on the road to Bādálǐng (Bādálǐng is another ¼ hour further down the road). Take minibus No 919 (Y10) from Déshèngmén (next to the Jīshuǐtán subway stop). Buses headed to Bādálǐng leave every ¼ hour (or as they fill up) starting from 5.30 am; be sure to let the bus driver know you want to be dropped off at Jūyōng Guān Chángchéng.

Sīmǎtái　司马台

In sharp contrast to the over-restored wall at Bādálǐng and Mùtiányù is Sīmǎtái. This 19km section of wall mostly still remains in its pristine crumbling condition. However, things are changing. The first danger sign was the T-shirt vendors, who set up shop around 1994, and then a loudspeaker, which now bellows music and 'nature sounds' to increase your enjoyment of the Wall. In 1996 a cable car (Y40) was installed. Sīmǎtái, however, is still generally an enjoyable outing.

The Sīmǎtái section of the wall dates from the Ming dynasty and has some unusual features, like 'obstacle-walls' – walls-within-walls used for defending against enemies who'd already scaled the Great Wall. There are 135 watchtowers at Sīmǎtái, the highest of which is Wàngjīng Lóu. Small cannon have been discovered in this area, as well as evidence of rocket-type weapons such as flying knives and flying swords.

Sīmǎtái is not for the faint-hearted: this section of the wall is very steep. A few slopes have a 70-degree incline and you need both hands free, so bring a day-pack to hold your camera and other essentials. One narrow section of footpath has a 500m drop, so it's no place for acrophobics. The steepness and sheer drops, however, do help keep out the riffraff.

In the early 1970s a nearby PLA unit destroyed about 3km of the wall to build barracks, setting an example for the locals who used stones from the wall to build houses. In 1979 the same unit was ordered to rebuild the section they tore down.

Admission to the site at Sīmǎtái costs Y20.

Getting There & Away Sīmǎtái is 110km north-east of Běijīng. From Dōngzhímén bus station take a minibus to Mìyún (1¼ hours; Y6). From Mìyún hire a *miandi* for Y70 roundtrip (about ¼ hour one way) or you could hire the miandi for Y30 one way and try to catch a tour bus from Sīmǎtái back to Běijīng (about Y30).

For budget travellers, the best deal around is offered through the Jīnghuá Fàndiàn – Y60 for the return journey by minibus. Ring its booking office (☎ 6722 2211) for more details. The Fēnglóng Bīnguǎn (☎ 6357 5314) offers tours for Y70, although the staff need a minimum of six people. Hiring a taxi from Běijīng for the day costs about Y400.

Jīnshānlǐng 金山岭
Though not as steep (and therefore not as impressive) as Sīmǎtái, the Great Wall at Jīnshānlǐng (Jīnshānlǐng Chángchéng) is considerably less developed than any of the sites previously mentioned. This section of the wall has been renovated and souvenir vendors have moved in, but so far there is no cable car and visitors are relatively few. Many of the tourists stopping here are on an excursion between Běijīng and Chéngdé in

Héběi, with Jīnshānlǐng thrown in as a brief stop-off.

Perhaps the most interesting thing about Jīnshānlǐng is that it's the starting point for a hike to Sīmǎtái (see 'Walking the Wild Wall'). You can do the walk in the opposite direction, but getting a ride back to Běijīng from Sīmǎtái is easier than from Jīnshānlǐng. Of course, getting a ride should be no problem if you've made arrangements with your driver to pick you up (and didn't pay him in advance). The distance between Jīnshānlǐng and Sīmǎtái is only about 10km, but it takes nearly four hours because the trail is steep and stony. Admission to the Great Wall at Jīnshānlǐng is Y40.

Getting There & Away From Dōngzhímén bus station you can take a minibus to Mìyún (Y6; 1¼ hour), and from Mìyún hire a miandi for Y80 a return trip (1 hour each way).

Huánghuā
For a genuine Wild Wall hike that is easy to access and close to Běijīng, the Huánghuā Cháng Chéng (Yellow Flower Fortress) section is ideal (see 'Walking the Wild Wall'). The Great Wall at Huánghuā clings to a high hillside adjacent to a reservoir. Around 60km north of Běijīng, Huánghuā is a classic and well-preserved example of Ming defence with high and wide ramparts, intact parapets and sturdy beacon towers.

It is said that one Lord Cai was responsible for building this section, and he was meticulous about its quality. Each *cùn* (inch) of the Wall represented a whole day's work of one labourer. When the Ministry of War heard that his lordship's efforts had been so extravagant, he was beheaded and his family lost their privileges and fell into disgrace. Years later, a general judged Lord Cai's Wall to be one of the best and he had to be official posthumously rehabilitated.

Places to Stay & Eat The large building near the dam is a training centre (☎ 6165-1134). Its accommodation isn't officially

(continued on page 238)

Walking the Wild Wall

Away from the heavily touristed areas of the Great Wall, long sections stride across the region's lofty mountain ranges. This 'Wild Wall' is remote, lonely, unspoilt, overgrown and crumbling. There are no tickets, no signposts, no hassles from trinket-sellers, no coach parks or garbage to spoil the view. Travellers can trek up narrow footpaths winding uphill from tiny villages in Běijīng 's backwoods and discover what for many may turn out to be the ultimate China experience. Here are three walks, the first two from Huánghuā, about 60km north of Běijīng; the third between Jīnshānlíng and Sīmǎtái Village. The walks coincide at Zhùangdàokǒu Guān (Zhuangdaokou Pass). See the relevant Getting There and Away sections for details about access.

Huánghuā to Zhùangdàokǒu Guān (4km; Three-Hour Loop)

The obvious place to start this walk is at the point where the Wall meets the road in Huánghuā Town. However, since the Wall is in quite a poor state there, it's easier to walk about 100m to the south.

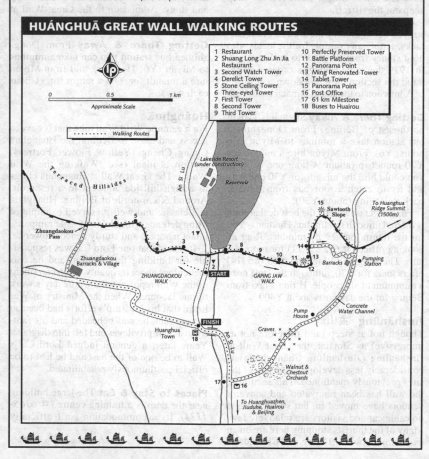

HUÁNGHUĀ GREAT WALL WALKING ROUTES

1 Restaurant	10 Perfectly Preserved Tower
2 Shuang Long Zhu Jin Jia Restaurant	11 Battle Platform
	12 Panorama Point
3 Second Watch Tower	13 Ming Renovated Tower
4 Derelict Tower	14 Tablet Tower
5 Stone Ceiling Tower	15 Panorama Point
6 Three-eyed Tower	16 Post Office
7 First Tower	17 61 km Milestone
8 Second Tower	18 Buses to Huairou
9 Third Tower	

0   0.5   1 km
Approximate Scale

········· Walking Routes

Walking the Wild Wall

After passing a small, deep quarry and old toilet, you'll see a well-trodden path leaving the road-side and heading up a creek. The path keeps to the left-hand side of the creek and is clear and easy to follow. After about 300m it starts to veer towards the Wall, and fades among the terraces, but your first target is in sight.

Second Watch Tower To get to this tower (the first, lower tower is derelict) make your way to an arched entrance just past the tower itself. As you pass through the archway, straight ahead is an engraved tablet embedded in the Wall. It details construction of a 150-*zhàng* (3.333m) length of Wall in the seventh year of the Wanli period (1579) by a group of commanders and their workforce. The name of the stonemason who carved the tablet, Wu Zongye, is in the bottom left-hand corner.

The tower itself has three windows along both its northern and southern faces. Locals describe towers by referring to the number of openings along one face, referring to them as *kēng* (holes) or *yǎn* (eyes). So this tower is a three-hole or three-eyed tower, sān kēng lóu or sān yǎn lóu. It once had a wooden roof which supported a second-story structure, but its central area is open to the sky. You can see holes in the course of brick (half a metre above archway apexes) where roof–floor beams were positioned.

Leaving the tower, make your way west along the ramparts towards a derelict tower. From this high point you get panoramic views of the area.

Derelict Tower Looking east, the Huánghuā Shuǐkù (Huanghua Reservoir) is in full view. Beyond the reservoir, four towers dot the Wall on its lower slopes, while a roofless battle platform can be seen near the summit. The Wall then turns north and plunges out of sight. It reappears with a side view of the inverted, U-shaped stretch of Wall known as the Gaping Jaw. Further on, the Wall can be seen snaking up the Huánghuā ridge.

Looking north, a few seemingly solitary watchtowers can be seen in the vicinity of Fènghúangtúo Shān (1530m). They are connected by walls, but they are small in scale and of inferior quality.

Looking south, you can see Huánghuā town and the wide river valley leading towards Huánghuāzhèn. The view starkly illustrates the strategic nature of the pass between the mountains here.

From the corner tower the Wall swings north, running level through conifer woods before turning west again and dropping to a three-eyed tower, notable for its stone ceiling.

Stone Ceiling Tower Large slabs of igneous rock have been incorporated into the ceiling of this tower. Normally, rock was used only in foundations, with bricks employed throughout the upper levels. Given that the slabs are almost 1m long and about 40cm wide, it's difficult to explain their use; the effort required to hoist such heavy slabs into position would have been considerable.

Leave the tower through the western door and follow the Wall as it drops through a thick conifer plantation. The parapets around here are in poor condition and the Wall's pavement is overgrown and, in some places, totally derelict. After 200m and another three-eyed tower, the ramparts cross a small valley where a pass, or gate, in the Wall once existed. In compensation for the condition of the ramparts here, the gate is in excellent condition.

Zhùangdàokǒu Guān This pass, a passageway through the Wall, is about 2.5m wide in the form of a brick archway founded on large igneous blocks. It is most striking for its engraved tablets which are different on either side of the archway. The tablet on the southern side features three large characters zhuang dao kou from right to left. The smaller characters record the name of the official who put the tablet in place, Liu Xun, and the date, in the fifth year of the Wanli reign (1577). Farmers

Walking the Wild Wall

continue to use this gate to reach terraced hillsides beyond the Wall to tend their fruit trees or coppice conifers for firewood.

The tablet on the northern face, also dated 1577, bears three large characters which read from right to left Zhèn Lǔ Guān (Suppress Captives Pass).

Zhùangdàokǒu was originally fortified in 1404, during the early years of the Ming dynasty. It was one of three passes (along with Jūyōng Guān at Bādálǐng and Gǔběikǒu in the north-east) deemed to be critical in blocking large Mongol armies on horseback and preventing them from reaching the capital easily. Between these passes, where sturdy walls and towers were built, there were only lines of watchtowers and beacon towers. It was left to later dynasties to connect them with walls.

Zhùangdàokǒu Guān to Zhùangdàokǒu Village From the archway turn south and follow the path down hill. It is about 500m to the village of Zhùangdàokǒu, a marvellous little settlement half nestled within the walls of an ancient barracks. The path is as old as the pass itself, linking the barracks with the Wall.

As you enter the village, the barracks is the large walled structure on the left; it's possible to climb its wall at the near corner. It averages seven courses of stone blocks in height, and the blocks are of the same provenance and shape as those used as foundations for the Wall. About half the foundation of the structure remains; it now encloses some farmhouses.

From the top of its walls you can see carved granite water spouts protruding from inside. All other structures, and half the walls, have been removed – probably during the Cultural Revolution.

Village to Bus Stop or Restaurant Follow your nose down through the narrow alleyways (note the Cultural Revolution slogans in yellow and faded images of Mao's head on crumbling plaster walls) to the southern edge of the village, then turn left at the bank of the stream and follow the main road for 1km to a T-junction. Buses for Huairou and Chāngpíng leave from here. Turn left here if you want to return to the starting point, or refuel at the Shuang Long Zhu Jiu Jia restaurant (literally, 'Pair of Dragons Playing with a Pearl Alcohol House').

Huánghuā to Gaping Jaw (4km; Four-Hour Loop)
From the restaurant walk north for 50m and cross the top of the dam holding back Huánghuā Shuǐkù. The dam occupies the site of the main Huánghuā Mén (Huanghua Gate) – only the foundations of this once-glorious structure remain.

From the far end of the dam, climb up the footpath on the northern side and enter the First Tower through one of its north-facing windows.

It is a short, steep climb to the Second Tower. Parapets have fallen down, locals have removed the bricks, and they have also taken away bricks which topped the stone block foundations of the rampart. The Wall drops in height before climbing to the Third Tower. This is a conventional shape – more of a quadrangle than an oblong – and is offset well to the north.

Perfectly Preserved Tower A gradual 200m climb takes you to the Fourth Tower. It is quite standard in shape, and is in exceptionally good condition. The ramparts before and beyond the tower are also in excellent condition (with parapets still standing and brickwork intact) as are its upper storey battlements and loopholes.

The tower is a three-eyed structure with its central area open to the sky. On the floor of the tower is an engraving dating from the Longqing period (1567–72). At the time of writing, a wooden ladder in the tower gave access the tower's top storey. Just outside the eastern door of the tower there's

Walking the Wild Wall

a flight of steps cut down into the ramparts and leading to a perfectly preserved granite archway. On the Wall facing the archway is a gap that once housed a tablet.

Battle Platform Exiting the tower, the ramparts climb to a short steep section featuring small observation platforms in front of a large battle platform. This is like a roofless watchtower, asymmetrically offset to the north for observation and enfilading (flanking) fire. Within its parapets are two rows of loopholes, each topped with bricks of different designs. The platform, close to the summit, commands a strategic position for cannon fire to the valley below.

From the battle platform, the Wall reaches the summit and then turns north to a tower which provides a fine place for views of the area.

Panorama Point Looking north, you can see the distinctive shape of the section of the Wall called Gaping Jaw. Looking east, the Wall streaks up the Huánghuā ridge towards the summit. From the south, the ridge profile looks like a camel's back and is called, 'the camel's back which breaks the wind'. Heading north, the ramparts lead to a well-preserved four-eyed tower.

Ming-Renovated Tower In good light, the colour of the top half-dozen courses of bricks, especially on the southern face of the tower, appears to differ from the rest. Inside, some parts of the brickwork seem to have been repaired with mortar of a different colour. These features suggest that the top of the tower was rebuilt and other parts inside were repaired. The reason why these efforts were made is open to debate. It is unlikely that the tower, in such a dominant, high position was attacked and damaged. It is more likely that the tower dates from the early Ming and was repaired in the later Ming, or that it was damaged by an earthquake and repaired.

Tablet Tower About 100m downhill is another fine four-eyed tower. Just before the tower there are steps down from the Wall leading through an archway off the Wall and down the gully.

The second chamber on the right (south) houses an engraved tablet from the third year of the Longqing period (1570). It is etched with 206 characters and edged with a simple vine design.

You now have two options. The shorter route is to leave by the southern door, exit the Wall via the steps and archway, and head down the gully path to the valley floor. This is route is easy and reaches the valley by a small water-pumping station.

If you feel like a longer walk, leave the tower by the north door and walk around the Gaping Jaw and its steep eastern limb, called Sawtooth Slope. This option will appeal to those who enjoy a scramble as the Sawtooth Slope (named for its zigzag profile) is an extremely steep and slippery descent. It is possible to continue east along Huánghuā ridge, but it's a tough hike that's very steep and challenging.

Barracks Both routes end up at the pumping station. From there you can walk about 50m southwest to a barracks. The structure's south-facing wall has an intact archway, and all four of its perimeter walls are standing. The barracks once housed up to 200 men stationed to guard this section of the Wall, taking advantage of a sheltered position and a water source.

To the Main Road To return to the main road, walk south on the stony track which swings gradually to the west, crossing a concrete-channelled waterway after about 600m. There is a small pump house, nearby on the right, and a fork off and up a bank to the right (west). Avoid this and keep

Walking the Wild Wall

on the main track, passing conical grave mounds on either side of the track and walking through walnut and chestnut orchards.

The track swings right all the time and eventually hits the road by a post office and beside the 61km milestone of the An Si Lu. Head north to the bridge for transport to Huáiróu and Chāngpíng.

Jīnshānlǐng to Sīmǎtái Village (9km; Five-Hour Loop)

In order to match the following descriptions with the actual features, it is *vital* to track your progress and know your tower number. To this end, a comment, minor or major, is made about all 30 towers on the hike.

Wall access is at Zhùandàokǒu Guān, at the top of an avenue of restaurants at Jīnshānlǐng. At the top of the street go straight ahead, passing in front of the quadrangular siheyuan, then toilets, on the right. It is 300m up to Tower 30 in the dip. Turn left (east) towards Sīmǎtái and proceed several hundred metres uphill to the T-junction.

T-Junction Panorama Point A 150m spur or 'tail wall' that leads to the left (north) was built to command a ridge that provided attackers with an easy route up to the Wall. On the hillside in the immediate foreground (east) are the low remains of the Northern Qi dynasty (AD 550–77) Great Wall. (More of the same Wall can be seen at the end of this hike.)

Following the Wall's route east, its watchtower-dotted outline can be seen snaking along the Jīnshānlǐng ridge and descending toward Sīmǎtái Shuǐkù in the valley. It then climbs further east up the Sīmǎtái ridge.

From the T-junction it's a short walk up to Tower 29, the highest on the first part of the hike. En route you pass through a series of zhang qiang or barrier walls. These are rebuilt – see the giveaway grey bricks – but ahead are many originals. They functioned as shields for guarding forces in the event of raiders mounting the Wall.

Tower 29 is extensively reconstructed. Off to the right is a storehouse building now rented by local photographer Zhou Wanping whose pictures are worth checking out.

Walk downhill to the shell-like ruins of Tower 28. Originally containing much wood that has rotted, the structure collapsed. In the masonry are holes where wooden timbers and floorboards were once positioned. A further 100m downhill is a battle platform where cannon, installed on the Wall from c. 1610, were positioned. There is a path off to the left leading back to the entrance.

Tower 27 has tubular archways, one of three internal tower styles found here. The others are angular chambers and domed structures.

Drainage En route to Tower 26, note the drainage system to channel water off the Wall. Good drainage was vital to ensure that the fill's stones and mortar did not become saturated, act as a slurry and cause washouts. Channel bricks and damming stones guide rainfall toward pavement-level sluices, which also double-up as observation holes (loopholes). Under the sluice, bricks were carved to ease the water's passage down the Wall.

Just before Tower 26 are more barrier walls. The tower had a wooden roof structure, which, like others of the same material, have rotted, collapsed and become derelict shells. Tower 25 is perched on a large outcrop of bare rock.

Tower 24 is the type of brick-roofed structure that survives well. Outside, reconstruction ends and the wild Wall begins. In Tower 23 there are many timber holes and other impressions in the masonry where beams and posts were positioned. Between Tower 23 and Tower 22 are eight barrier walls. Beyond Tower 22 are 15 more. The foot of the next slope has been completely washed out, leaving only the north-facing wall upright. This is a good place to view the Wall in cross-section.

Walking the Wild Wall

Beyond is Tower 21, a derelict wooden structure. A further variation of loophole style can be seen in its parapets; this time they are of pyramidal shape.

Fifty metres out of Tower 21 is another major washout – a classic example of hydrostatic pressures causing the Wall's collapse. Tower 20 retains a rare trace of fossilised wood in its north-western corner.

Fossilised Wood & Pottery Fragments Tower 19 is brick roofed with tubular archways. Tower 18 is 100 m further on. In its north-west lower corner, another fragment of fossilised wood is exposed. Fragments of pottery storage jars for water and grain, glazed and unglazed, can be found among the ruins here. The tower was probably used for foodstuffs.

There are more barrier walls between Towers 18 and 17. Tower 17 is very derelict. Between Towers 17 and 16, on the inside (south-facing) wall are two gaps where engraved tablets were once positioned. Tower 16 has good tubular arched ceilings and a fine granite archway entrance. Tower 15 was a wooden structure; it has timber holes but little else of interest.

Tower 14 is a 'five-eyed tower', having five windows along its longest face. There are also fine boltholes inside the door of its north-west entrance.

Dome Ceiling & Relief Tablet The floor of Tower 13's central chamber is square while its roof is dome shaped, divided into eight segments with a small octagonal opening at its apex. Around the dome chamber are four tubular arched corridors. On the upper storey, but difficult to access, is a relief tablet depicting a qilin, a mythical beast symbolising good administration. This tower was used by a military official probably in command of the whole Jīnshānlǐng Wall.

Stamped Bricks Between Towers 13 and 12 are hundreds of in situ bricks stamped with characters contained within a long rectangular cartouche and reading:

Quadrant Dome Tower Tower 12's central chamber is roofed with a fine dome divided into four quadrants. In its surrounding arched, tubular corridors is a stele base upon which an engraved tablet was once positioned. The tower's granite doorways and window sills, with hollows for hinges to turn, remain in good condition.

Between Towers 12 and 11 there are more stamped bricks on the inside of the ramparts. Through Tower 11, which is in fine condition with tubular arches, the ramparts en route to Tower 10 have a gap on the inside of the north-facing parapet where a tablet was once positioned. Tower 10 has three tubular arches; the central one is much wider than the flanking two.

From Tower 10 it is a steep descent to Tower 9, which has a good granite doorway facing westward. Inside is yet another example of architectural design variation – the angular chamber. Also, while the central chamber is wide, flanking ones are narrow.

Out of Tower 9, parapets are broken down and the pavement is loose. Terraces to the south (right) of the Wall contain its bricks. In the lower storey of Tower 8 are cane mat marks imprinted on dark-brown mud. This 'plaster' was added for insulation in winter and indicates that those manning the Wall were willing and allowed to make improvements to their frontier homes for the sake of comfort. About 5% of ceiling space is still 'insulated'.

Although it's a steep descent down to Tower 7, look out for stampings on the loose bricks. Tower 7 is a derelict shell structure, open to the sky.

One hundred metres out of Tower 7, on the south parapet, are a few solitary stamped bricks in situ. Tower 6 was a wooden structure. Broken tiles from its roof can be found in the rubble. Out of Tower 6 is a steep downhill section that has resulted in a classic washout at the foot of the slope. Take the lower

Walking the Wild Wall

path on the southern side rather than threading your way along the narrow, crumbling Wall-top path. From Tower 6, it is 150m downhill to the start of the rebuilt Wall that leads from Tower 5 eastwards.

View of Northern Qi Great Wall From Tower 4, further remains of the Northern Qi Great Wall can be seen on the mountain ridge to the south. The remains are most noticeable beyond (west of) the newly built road and two short telegraph poles. This mid-6th century Wall stretched from north of Běijīng to Dàtóng in the west. There is no way through Tower 2. Leave the Wall before the tower and follow the footpath below. Rejoin the Wall and continue down, leaving it again before Tower 1. Cross the bridge and follow the rocky road down to Sīmǎtái village.

William Lindesay
William Lindesay has walked the length of the Wall, from Jiāyùguān to Shānhǎiguān. These walks are based on his second book on the Wall, *Hiking on History: Exploring Beijing's Great Wall*, due to be published by Oxford University Press.

(continued from page 231)

open to the public or foreigners, but try your luck. If they allow you to stay, they charge Y135 per person, including meals. The tiny, family-run *'Lonely Planet' Hotel* (nothing to do with us) has two very basic rooms for Y40 per night.

If you want to spend a night on the Wall, it's possible to sleep in a watch tower. It's unlikely that the PSB would bother you, but we can't predict their reaction.

The *Shuang Long Zhu Jiu Jia* restaurant, just south of the Wall, is run by a local family and serves a wide variety of cheap dishes. There's another restaurant north of the Wall, on the left-hand side of the road, serving similar fare. Otherwise, there is a string of restaurants on An Si Lu in Huánghuāzhen.

Getting There & Away There is no direct bus to Huánghuā, but there are two indirect routes. The first option is to take a public bus or minibus to Húairóu from Dōngzhímén long-distance bus station in Běijīng (near the subway station of the same name). Bus No 916 leaves every 15 minutes from 5.30 am to 6.30 pm (Y4) and takes just over an hour to get to Húairóu. Minibuses adopt the same number (916) and run the same route a little quicker for Y5. Let the bus driver know your intended destination is Huánghuāchéng so they can

tell you where to get off the bus once you reach Húairóu. From Húairóu you can take a minibus directly to Huánghuāchéng (Y4, 40 minutes) or hire a miandi from Húairóu to Huánghuāchéng for Y60 round trip. For an additional Y60, you can hire a miandi all the way back to the third ring road in Běijīng (most miandis don't have the permission to Běijīng).

SHÍSĀN LÍNG 十三陵
Thirteen Tombs

About an hour and half north-west of Běijīng lies the final resting place of 13 of the 16 Ming emperors. The 40 sq km area, known as the Shísān Líng (Thirteen Tombs), also known as the Ming Tombs, is a charming stretch of rolling countryside dotted with tombs and small villages and farms. Open to the public are three completely renovated tombs – Cháng Líng, Dìng Líng and Zhào Líng. Cháng Líng and Dìng Líng are surrounded by sprawling concrete parking lots inundated with big tour buses. Much quieter is Zhào Líng; and the small countryside village next to it is worth a stroll around. The rest of the tombs are in various states of dilapidation, and are sealed off by locked gates. However, these are more worth exploring, although to see them you either have to jump the fence (which is against the law) or convince the grounds keeper to let you in. When the weather's good Běijīng expats often picnic out at tombs such as De Líng.

The road leading up to the tombs is a 7km stretch called 'spirit way'. It starts with a triumphal arch, then goes through the Great Palace Gate, where once officials had to dismount, and passes a **giant tortoise** (made in 1425) which bears the largest stele in China. This is followed by a guard of 12 sets of **stone animals**. Admission to Cháng Líng is Y20, Dìng Líng is Y26 and Zhào Líng is Y20.

Getting There & Away

The tombs lie 50km north-west of Běijīng and a few kilometres from the town of Chāngpíng. Tour buses usually combine them with a visit to the Great Wall at Bādálǐng. Big tour buses leave from across the street from the south-west corner of Tiānānmén Square between 6.30 and 10 am – for Y50 they'll bring you to the Great Wall at Bādálǐng and the Shísān Líng. Smaller buses leave for the same destinations from the south end of Tiānānmén Square (to the west of McDonald's) at 8 and 9.30 am for Y40. Plan about nine hours for the trip. A tour bus (No 4) also leaves from Zhanlanguan, directly across the street from the entrance to the zoo. They leave around 8 am and return around 6 pm and go to Bādálǐng and Shísān Líng. Cost is Y36, but the buses aren't as new and comfortable as the ones that leave from Qián Mén.

If you don't want to combine the trip with Bādálǐng and if you'd like to see tombs other than Cháng Líng or Dìng Líng, you can take minibus No 345 from Déshèngmén to Chāngpíng; you can wave down the mini-bus just outside the Jīshuǐtán subway exit. The trip to Chāngpíng takes about an hour (Y6). Alternatively, you can take a large air-conditioned bus (No 845) from Xīzhímén (just outside the Xīzhímén subway stop) to Chāngpíng (Y7). From Chāngpíng you can hire a miandi for Y60 for a half day. It's about a 10-minute ride from Chāngpíng to the entrance to the Shísān Líng. This is a good way to get around and explore the unrenovated tombs.

QĪNG DŌNG LÍNG 清东陵
Eastern Qing Tombs

The area of the Qīng Dōng Líng could be called Death Valley, housing as it does five emperors, 14 empresses and 136 imperial consorts. In the mountains ringing the valley are buried princes, dukes, imperial nurses and more.

Emperor Qianlong (1711–99) started preparations when he was 30, and by the time he was 88 he had used up 90 tonnes of his silver. His resting place covers half a square kilometre. Some of the beamless stone chambers are decorated with Tibetan and Sanskrit sutras, and the doors bear bas-relief bodhisattvas.

Empress Dowager Cixi also got a head start. Her tomb, Dingdong, was completed some three decades before her death. The phoenix (symbol of the empress) appears above that of the dragon (the emperor's symbol) in the artwork at the front of the tomb – not side by side as on other tombs. Both tombs were plundered in the 1920s.

Located in Zūnhuà County, 125km east of Běijīng, the Qīng Dōng Líng offer a lot more to see than the Shísān Líng, although you may be a little jaded after the Forbidden City.

Getting There & Away

Unfortunately, getting there by public bus is difficult and involves changing buses a few times along the way. Tour buses are considerably more comfortable than the local rattletraps and take about two hours to get there; you then have about three hours on site. Some people prefer to go from Tiānjīn.

TÁNZHÈ SÌ 潭柘寺
Cudrania Pool Temple

About 45km directly west of Běijīng is Tánzhè Sì, the largest of all the Běijīng temples, occupying an area 260m by 160m. The Buddhist complex has a long history dating back to the 3rd century (Jin dynasty); structural modifications date from the Liao, Tang, Ming and Qing dynasties, so the temple has a number of features – dragon decorations, mythical animal sculptures and grimacing gods – no longer found in temples in the capital.

The temple takes its name from its proximity to the Lóng Tán (Dragon Pool) and some rare cudrania (zhè) trees. Locals come to the Lóng Tán to pray for rain during droughts. The cudrania trees nourish silkworms and provide a yellow dye. The bark of the tree is believed to cure women of sterility, which may explain why there are so few of these trees left at the temple entrance.

The temple complex is open daily from 8.30 am until 6 pm.

Getting There & Away
One option is to take bus No 15 from Zhanlanguan (across from the zoo) three stops to where it meets up with bus No 336. Take bus No 336 to Méngtóugōu, and from there you can hire a taxi. Alternatively, you can take the subway to Píngguǒyuán, bus No 336 to Hétān and then a numberless bus to the temple.

PEKING MAN SITE
Deemed a Unesco World Heritage Site, Zhōukǒudiàn is the site where remains of primitive people who lived here half a million years ago were excavated. In the 1920s and 1930s, a major archaeological excavation unearthed skullcaps, stone tools and animal bones believed to be 500,000 to 230,000 years old. Unfortunately, research on Peking Man's skull was never carried out because the skullcap and other remains mysteriously disappeared on the eve of the Japanese invasion during an attempt to smuggle them to the United States. Subsequent digs resulted in more remains, but nothing as substantial as Peking Man.

Today there's not much to see here. There's an 'Apeman Cave' on a hill above the village, several lesser caves and some dig sites. There is also a fossil exhibition hall (with English explanations) that displays several artefacts; some are models, others are the real thing. There are three sections to the exhibition hall: pre-human history, the life and times of Peking Man and recent anthropological research. On display are ceramic models, stone tools and the skeletons of prehistoric creatures.

The exhibition hall is open daily from 8.30 am to 4.30 pm, but check before you go. Admission is Y20.

Getting There & Away
Zhōukǒudiàn is 48km south-west of Běijīng. Bus 917 from Tiānqiáo bus station (western side of Tiāntán Gōngyuán) goes to Fángshān (one hour) from where you can take a bus (No 2) or taxi to the site (6km). If combined with a trip to Tánzhè Sì and Lúgōu Qiáo (Marco Polo Bridge), approaching the site by taxi is not unreasonable.

SHÍDÙ 十渡
About 110km south-west of Běijīng city, Shídù is Běijīng's answer to Guìlín. Its pinnacle-shaped rock formations, pleasant, small rivers and general beauty make it a favourite spot with expats. Shídù means 'ten ferries' or 'ten crossings': before the new road and bridges were built, travellers had to cross the Juma River 10 times while travelling along the gorge from Zhangfang and Shídù village.

Places to Stay
The Lóngshān Fàndiàn is a small, family-run place of the simple wooden bed variety opposite the train station. Foreigners aren't officially allowed to stay here, although it may be possible to convince them to let you spend the night. In the town of Shídù, along the main road about 1½ km from the train station is the Yíshūlóu Fàndiàn (☎ 6134 9988). When you see a two-storey building with red lanterns in front you've found it. The hotel is on the 2nd floor, above the restaurant. Simple but clean rooms are Y40 per person. Down near Jiudu (the 'ninth ferry'), next to the bungee jumping platform, is the large Shānguāng Lóu (☎ 6134 0762), where rooms go for Y290. There's also a camping ground here, conveniently located on a flood-plain. In Liùdù, nicely located on the river and away from any amusement facilities, is the Dōngzhèng Bīnguǎn (☎ 6134 0791), where clean standard rooms are Y240.

Getting There & Away

Getting to Shídù is fastest by train, but there are only two departures daily, from the Běijīng South train station (Yŏngdìngmén), which is probably the only chance you'll have to use this station. If you take the morning train, the trip can be done in one day.

The schedule from Yŏngdìngmén to Shídù is as follows:

No	From	To	Depart	Arrive
795	Yŏngdìngmén	Shídù	6.38 am	8.49 am
897	Yŏngdìngmén	Shídù	5.40 pm	8.11 pm

The schedule from Shídù to Yŏngdìngmén is as follows:

No	From	To	Depart	Arrive
796	Shídù	Yŏngdìngmén	7.40 pm	10.01 pm
898	Shídù	Yŏngdìngmén	9.10 am	11.37 am

Tiānjīn 天津

Like Běijīng, Shànghǎi and most recently Chóngqìng, Tiānjīn belongs to no province – it's a special municipality, which gives it a degree of autonomy, but it's also closely administered by the central government. The city is nicknamed 'Shànghǎi of the North', a reference to its history as a foreign concession, its heavy industrial output, its large port and its Europeanised architecture. Foreigners who live there now often call it 'TJ' – an abbreviation which mystifies the Chinese.

One of the specialties of the place is the two day kite-flying festival held in early April or late September. For business people, the big event of the year is the Tiānjīn Export Commodities Fair held every March. It's for invited guests only – to get an invitation, contact the China International Travel Service (CITS; Zhōngguó Guójì Lǚxíngshè) or the China Travel Service (CTS; Zhōngguó Lǚxíngshè) well in advance.

The hotels are as expensive as Běijīng's (but lack dormitories), so budget travellers tend to give the place a miss. However, you can travel down to Tiānjīn from Běijīng in just 1½ hours, and one full day in this city is really quite enough.

History

The city's fortunes are, and always have been, linked to those of Běijīng. When the Mongols established Běijīng as the capital in the 13th century, Tiānjīn first rose to prominence as a grain-storage point. Pending remodelling of the Grand Canal by Kublai Khan, the grain was shipped along the Cháng Jiāng (Yangzi River), out into the open sea, up to Tiānjīn, and then through to Běijīng. With the Grand Canal fully functional as far as Běijīng, Tiānjīn was at the intersection of both inland and port navigation routes. By the 15th century, the town was a walled garrison.

For the sea-faring western nations, Tiānjīn was a trading bottleneck too good to be passed up. In 1856 Chinese soldiers

Highlights

Area: 11,300 sq km
Population: 9.5 million

- The Gǔwán Shìchǎng antique market, one of China's most outstanding markets, particularly on a Sunday
- Tiānjīn's 19th-century European buildings, poignant reminders of a not-too-distant past
- Strolling, shopping and eating

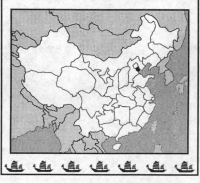

boarded the *Arrow*, a boat flying the British flag, ostensibly in search of pirates. This was as much of an excuse as the British and the French needed. Their gunboats attacked the forts outside Tiānjīn, forcing the Chinese to sign the Treaty of Tianjin (1858), which opened the port up to foreign trade and also legalised the sale of opium.

Understandably, the Chinese were reluctant to honour this treaty, which led the British and French to resort to further violence. In 1860 British troops bombarded Tiānjīn in an attempt to coerce the Chinese into signing another treaty.

The English and French settled in. Between the years 1895 and 1900 they were joined by the Japanese, Germans, Austro-Hungarians, Italians and Belgians. Each of these concessions was a self-contained

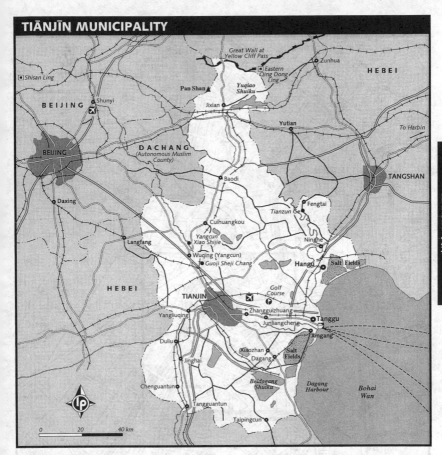

TIĀNJĪN MUNICIPALITY

world with its own prison, school, barracks and hospital.

This life was disrupted only in 1870 when the locals attacked the French-run orphanage and killed, among others, 10 of the nuns – apparently the Chinese thought the children were being kidnapped. Thirty years later, during the Boxer Rebellion, the foreign powers levelled the walls of the old Chinese city.

Meanwhile, the European presence stimulated trade and industry, including salt, textiles and glass manufacture. Heavy silting of the Hǎi Hé (Sea River) led to the con-struction of a new harbour 50km downstream at Tánggū. The opening of this new harbour meant that Tiānjīn lost its bustling-port character.

Since 1949 Tiānjīn has been a centre for major industrialisation and it produces a wide range of consumer goods. Brand-name products from Tiānjīn are favoured within China for their quality – from Flying Pigeon bicycles to Seagull watches.

Orientation

Like Běijīng, Tiānjīn is a large, sprawling municipality of which most is rural. The

TIĀNJĪN 天津

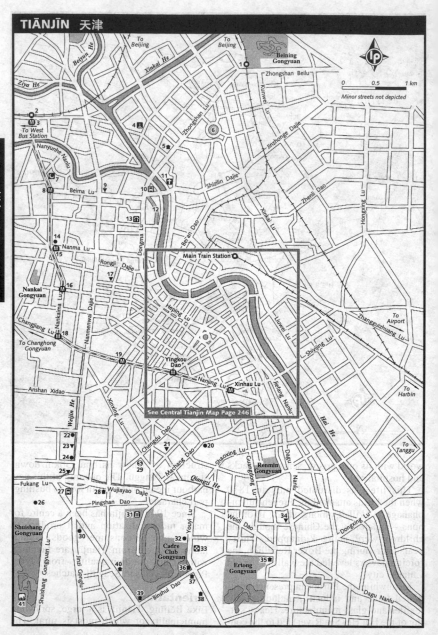

TIĀNJĪN 天津

To Beijing

To Beijing

Beining Gongyuan

Beiyun He

Ziya He

Xinkai He

Zhongshan Beilu

0   0.5   1 km

Minor streets not depicted

2
M 3
To West Bus Station

Nanyunhe Nanlu

Zhongshan Lu

Kunwei

Jinzhonghe Dajie

Hongxing Lu

4

5

Shizilin Dajie

11

10

C 7

8 M   Beima Lu

9

Zhenli Dao

Xinkai Lu

12

13

Dongma Dao

Beian Dao

14
M
15   Nanma Lu

Rongji Dajie

Main Train Station

17

Nankai Gongyuan

16 M

Nankaima Lu

Heping Lu

To Airport

Zhangguizhuang Lu

Nammenwai Dajie

Changjiang Lu

18 M

Liuwei Lu

L Shiying Lu

To Changhong Gongyuan

19 M

Yingkou Dao

Nanjing Lu   Xinhau Lu

M

Jintang Nanlu

Anshan Xidao

Wejin He

Xinxing Lu

To Harbin

See Central Tianjin Map Page 246

Hai He

To Tanggu

22
23
24

Chengdu Dao

21

20

Shaoxing Lu

Guangong Lu

Renmin Gongyuan

Dagu Nanlu

25

Fukang Lu

27

28   Wujiayao Dajie

29

Qiangzi He

Machang Dao

Dongxing Lu

26   Pingshan Dao

Youyi Lu

Weidi Dao

34

31

32

Cadre Club Gongyuan

33

Shuishang Gongyuan

30

40

36

35   Ertong Gongyuan

Shuishang Gongyuan Lu

Jintai Gonglu

37

Binshui Dao

39

38

Dagu Nanlu

41

TIĀNJĪN

PLACES TO STAY
5　Tianjin Holiday Inn
　　假日饭店
28　Caesar's Palace Hotel
　　凯撒皇宫大酒店
35　Park Hotel
　　乐园饭店
36　Tianjin Grand Hotel
　　天津宾馆
37　Crystal Palace Hotel
　　水晶宫饭店
38　Geneva Hotel
　　津利华大酒店
39　Dickson Hotel
　　带蔷酒店
40　Sheraton Hotel
　　喜来登大酒店

PLACES TO EAT
9　Ěrduǒyǎn Zhágāodiàn
　　耳朵眼炸糕店
17　Shípǐn Jiē
　　食品街
21　Broadway Cafe
　　贵宾楼西餐厅
23　Alibaba Restaurant; Nuts
　　阿里巴巴酒家
25　Korean Hotpot
　　Restaurants
　　韩国火锅餐厅

34　Máhuā
　　桂发祥麻花店

OTHER
1　North Train Station
　　北火车站
2　West Train Station
　　西火车站
4　Dàbēi Yuàn
　　大悲院
6　Zhōngshān Gōngyuán
　　中山公园
7　Qīngzhēn Sì
　　清真寺
10　North-East Bus Station
　　东北角发车站
11　Wànghǎilóu Cathedral
　　望海楼教堂
12　Gǔwénhuà Jiē
　　古文化街
13　Wén Miào
　　文庙
14　Carrefour
　　家乐福
20　Foreign Language Institute
　　外国语学院
22　Tianjin University
　　天津大学
24　Nankai University
　　南开大学

26　Zhōu Ēnlái Jìniànguǎn
　　周恩来纪念馆
27　South Bus Station
　　八里台发车站
29　Bank of China
　　中国银行
30　Diànshì Tǎ
　　电视塔
31　Zìrán Bówùguǎn
　　自然博物馆
32　CITS
　　中国国际旅行社
33　Friendship Store
　　友谊商店
41　Zoo
　　动物园

SUBWAY STATIONS
3　Xī Dìtiězhàn
　　西地铁站
8　Xīběijiǎo Dìtiězhàn
　　西北角地铁站
15　Xīnánjiǎo Dìtiězhàn
　　西南角地铁站
16　Èrwěi Lù Dìtiězhàn
　　二纬路地铁站
18　Hǎiguāng Sì Dìtiězhàn
　　海光寺地铁站
19　Ānshāndào Dìtiězhàn
　　鞍山道地铁站

TIĀNJĪN 天津

population of Tiānjīn's city and suburbs is some five million, although the municipality itself takes in a total of more than 10 million.

Information

The *Tianjin Telegraph*, a monthly newsletter put out by and for expats, has restaurant and bar reviews. You can pick it up for free at expat hangouts like City Slicker Saloon, Cozy Cafe and upmarket hotels. The Tiānjīn Tourism Bureau (☎ 2835 4860, fax 2835 2324) is at 18 Youyi Lu (almost opposite the Friendship Store). Just next door at 22 Youyi Lu, is CITS (☎ 2835 8499, fax 2835 2619).

The Public Security Bureau (PSB; Gōngānjú) is at 30 Tangshan Dao, and the Bank of China is at 80 Jiefang Beilu.

Post & Communications You'll find the Dongzhan Post Office next to the main train station; overseas parcels can be mailed and long-distance phone calls can be made here. For letters, there is another post office on Jiefang Beilu, a short walk north of the New World Astor Hotel.

A private courier, DHL (☎ 2430 3388, fax 2430 5577), is at 35 Liujing Lu.

Internet cafes are found on the Nankai and Tianjin university campuses. There's also a Sparkice Internet cafe in the Imperial Palace Hotel.

The telephone code for Tiānjīn is ☎ 022.

Gǔwán Shìchǎng　古玩市场
Antique Market

Depending on your tastes, the antique market is the best sight in Tiānjīn, even if

TIĀNJĪN 天津

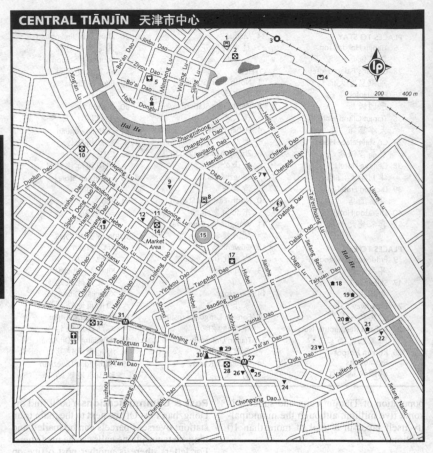

CENTRAL TIĀNJĪN 天津市中心

you're not into collecting second-hand memorabilia. In every direction, vendors spread blankets along the *hútòngs* (narrow alleyways) making it a fascinating place to stroll around. Among the many items on sale are stamps, silver coins, silverware, porcelain, clocks, photos of Mao, Cultural Revolution memorabilia and old books.

According to the locals, much of what is on display at the antique market was seized during the Cultural Revolution and warehoused – the government is now slowly selling the stuff off to vendors who, in turn, resell it in Tiānjīn. These goods supposedly

come from all over China. Many of the items carry stickers on the back indicating when, where and from whom the goods were seized.

Just why everything wasn't all immediately destroyed is subject to speculation – possibly it was to be used as evidence at political trials, or maybe some official was a closet antique buff. Of course, not all that you see is real – there are fake antiques, fake stickers and so on.

The market is best on Sunday (although even then it doesn't rival Běijīng's Pānjiāyuán antique market for sheer size

CENTRAL TIĀNJĪN

PLACES TO STAY

6 Ocean Hotel
远洋宾馆

18 Imperial Palace Hotel
天津皇宫饭店

19 New World Astor Hotel
利顺德大饭店

20 Tianjin First Hotel
天津第一饭店

21 Hyatt Hotel
凯悦饭店

29 Friendship Hotel
友谊宾馆

PLACES TO EAT

7 Sgt Pepper's Music Hall Grill and Bar
沙金音乐西餐厅

9 Dēngyíng Lóu Grand Restaurant
登瀛楼饭店

12 Gǒubùlǐ
狗不理总店

22 Cosy Cafe & Bar
客思特西餐酒吧

23 Kiessling's Bakery
天津起士林

24 City Slicker Saloon
老外!牛仔餐厅

26 Rùnliáng Cāntīng
润良餐饮

OTHER

1 Buses to Běijīng
往北京汽车站

2 Wing On Department Store
永安百货

3 Main Train Station
天津火车站

4 Dōngzhàn Post Office
东站邮局

5 Kānghǎo
康好娱乐城

8 Bus Station No 1 (To Tánggū)
一路汽车站(往塘沽)

10 Tiānjīn Department Store
百货大楼

11 Shopping Area
购物区

13 Gǔwán Shìchǎng
古玩市场

14 Bīnjiāng Shangsha Department Store
滨江商厦

15 Zhōngxīn Gōngyuán
中心公园

16 Bank of China
中国银行

17 PSB
公安局外事科

25 International Building
国际大厦

28 Isetan Department Store
伊势丹百货

30 Kàngzhèn Jìniànbēi
抗震纪念碑

32 International Market
国际商场

33 Xīkāi Jiàotáng
西开教堂

SUBWAY STATIONS

27 Xīnhuá Lù Dìtiězhàn
新华路地铁站

31 Yíngkǒudào Dìtiězhàn
营口道地铁站

and selection). On weekdays there are very few vendors; Saturday is better but still with not as many vendors as on Sunday. It's open from 7.30 am to around 3 pm – get there at 8 am for the widest selection.

Gǔwénhuà Jiē 古文化街
Ancient Culture Street

The Gǔwénhuà Jiē is an attempt to recreate the appearance of an ancient Chinese city. Besides the traditional buildings, the street is lined with vendors plugging every imaginable type of cultural goody including Chinese scrolls, paintings and chops (name seals). Pirated CDs are also widely available. On certain public holidays, street operas are staged here.

Within the confines of the street is the small **Tiānhòu Gōng** (Heaven Queen Temple). Tiānhòu (Heaven Queen) is the goddess of the sea, and is known by various names in different parts of China (Matsu in Taiwan and Tin Hau in Hong Kong). It is claimed that Tiānjīn's Tiānhòu Gōng was built in 1326, but it has seen a bit of renovation since then.

The Gǔwénhuà Jiē is a major drawcard for tourists, both foreign and local, and is as worthwhile a place to stroll around in search of 'antiques' as the Gǔwán Shìchǎng. The street is in the north-western part of town.

Wén Miào 文庙
Confucius Temple

On the northern side of Dongmennei Dajie, one block west of the Gǔ Wénhuà Jiē, is Tiānjīn's Wén Miào. The temple was built in 1463 during the Ming dynasty then, along with Confucianists in general, took a beating during the Cultural Revolution. In 1993 the buildings were restored and opened to the public.

Qīngzhēn Sì   清真寺
Great Mosque

Although it has a distinctly Chinese look, this large mosque is an active place of worship for Tiānjīn's Muslim community. The mosque is on Dafeng Lu, not far south of the west train station.

Dàbēi Yuàn   大悲院
Monastery of Deep Compassion

One of the city's largest and best preserved temples, Dàbēi Yuàn was built between 1611 and 1644, expanded in 1940, battered during the Cultural Revolution and finally restored in 1980.

The temple is on Tianwei Lu, in the northern part of the city.

Catholic Church

This is one of the most bizarre-looking Catholic churches (Xīkāi Jiàotáng) you're likely to see. Situated on the southern end of Binjiang Dao, the twin onion domes form a dramatic backdrop to the 'Coca-Cola Bridge' (a pedestrian overpass crossing Nanjing Lu). It's definitely worth a look. Church services are now permitted again on Sundays, which is about the only time you'll have a chance to look inside.

Kàngzhèn Jìniànbēi   抗震纪念碑
Earthquake Memorial

Opposite the Friendship Hotel on Nanjing Lu is a curious, pyramid-shaped memorial. Although there's not much to see here, the memorial is a pointed reminder of the horrific events of 28 July 1976, when an earthquake registering eight on the Richter scale struck north-eastern China. The epicentre was at Tángshān and Tiānjīn was severely affected – the city was closed to tourists for two years. The earthquake measured 8.0 on the Richter scale and more than 240,000 were killed (a fifth of Tángshān's population) and 160,000 seriously injured. It was the greatest natural disaster of the decade.

Hǎihé Gōngyuán   海河公园
Sea River Park

Stroll along the banks of the Hǎi Hé (a popular pastime with the locals) and see photo booths, fishing, early-morning *taijiquan* (tai chi), opera-singing practice and old men toting birdcages. The Hǎi Hé esplanades have a peculiarly Parisian feel, in part due to the fact that some of the railing and bridge work is French.

The river water isn't so pure that you'd want to drink it, but an attempt has been made to clean it up, and trees have been planted along the embankments. Tiānjīn's industrial pollution horrors are further downstream and are not included in the tour.

It's not Venice, but there are tourist boat cruises on the Hǎi Hé that leave from a dock not far from the New World Astor Hotel. The boats cater to Chinese tourists more than foreigners and therefore tend to run mainly during summer weekends and other holiday periods.

At the northern end of town are half a dozen smaller rivers and canals that branch off the Hǎi Hé. One vantage point is at the park Xigu Gōngyuán. Take bus No 5, which runs from near the main train station and passes by the west train station.

Shuǐshàng Gōngyuán   水上公园
Water Park

This large park is in the south-western corner of town, not far from the Diànshì Tǎ. The name in Chinese means water park – more than half the surface area is a lake. The major activity here is renting row boats and pedal boats.

It's one of the more relaxed places in busy Tiānjīn, although not on weekends when the locals descend on the place like cadres at a banquet. The park features a Japanese-style floating garden and a fairly decent zoo.

Getting to the park from the main train station requires two buses. Bus No 8 to the last stop gets you close. From there, catch bus No 54, also to the last stop, just outside the park entrance.

Museums

There are five or so museums in Tiānjīn and none are really worth the trouble unless you're an enthusiast. The **Zìrán Bówùguǎn**

(Natural History Museum) is down the fossil-end of town at 206 Machang Dao.

The **Lìshǐ Bówùguǎn** (History Museum), is on the south-eastern side of the Hǎi Hé. It sits at the edge of a triangular park called the **Dì Èr Gōngrén Wénhuà Gōng** (No 2 Workers' Cultural Palace) and contains 'historical and revolutionary relics of the Tiānjīn area'.

Guǎngdōng Hùi Guǎn (Guǎngdōng Guild Hall), also known as the Museum of Opera, is considered of historical relevance because Dr Sun Yatsen gave an important speech there in 1922.

Zhōu Ēnlái Jìniànguǎn
周恩来纪念馆
Zhou Enlai Memorial Hall

Zhou Enlai grew up in Shàoxīng in Zhèjiāng, but he attended school in Tiānjīn, so his classroom is enshrined and there are photos and other memorabilia from his youth (1913–17). The memorial is next to Shuǐshàng Gōngyuán in the south-western corner of town near the Diànshì Tǎ. From the main train station, take bus No 8 to Bā Lǐ Tái and then bus No 54 to the memorial hall. Admission is Y10.

Streetscapes

Far more engrossing than any of the preceding is the fact that Tiānjīn itself is a museum of European architecture from the turn of the 20th century. One minute you're in little Vienna, turn a corner and you could be in a London street, hop off a bus and you're looking at some vintage French wrought-iron gates or a neo-Gothic cathedral. Unfortunately, recent post-modern architectural horrors are starting to impact on Tiānjīn's skyline. Poking out of the post-earthquake shanty rubble is an ever-increasing number of high-rise castles made of glass and steel. The streets around Munan Dao, as well as Jiefang Lu, are particularly pleasant areas to stroll around.

Nevertheless, if you're a connoisseur of architecture, go no further – Tiānjīn is a textbook of just about every style imaginable. Of course, things have been renamed, and anyone with a sense of humour will be amused

by some of the uses to which the bastions of the European well-to-do have been put.

Chinatown

Sorry, but we couldn't resist this misnomer. The old Chinese sector can easily be identified on the bus map as a rectangle with buses running around the perimeter. Roughly, the boundary roads are: Beima (North Horse), Nanma (South Horse), Xima (West Horse) and Dongma (East Horse). Originally there was one main north-south street, crossing an east-west one within that walled rectangle.

In this area you can spend time fruitfully exploring the lanes and side streets where traditional architecture remains, and perhaps even find a dilapidated temple or two. Basically, though, this is a people-watching place, where you can get glimpses of daily life through doorways. All along the way are opportunities to shop, window shop and eat to your heart's content.

Places to Stay – Budget

Although Tiānjīn has many reasonably priced hotels, the PSB has deemed most of these off limits to foreigners.

The cheapest places open to foreigners are the guesthouses at Nankai and Tianjin universities. **Tiānjīn Dàxué Zhuānjiā Lóu** (Tianjin University Qinyuan Hotel; ☎ 2740 7711, fax 2335 8714) has very clean doubles for Y166, including breakfast. The **Tiānjīn Dàxué Liú Xué Sheng Lóu** (Tianjin University Foreign Students' Dormitory; ☎ 2740 4373) has rooms starting at Y126. Not as well kept are the foreign students dormitories at Nankai University. There are two buildings offering accommodation. **Nánkāi Dàxué Yìyuánsùshè Èrhàolóu** (Nankai University Building 2; ☎ 2350 1832) has doubles on the grotty side for Y150, while the newer and better **Nánkāi Dàxué Yìyuánsùshè Sìhàolóu** (Building 4; ☎ 2350 5335) has doubles for Y200.

Places to Stay – Mid-Range

A 15% service charge is added to the prices quoted for Tiānjīn's hotels. Standard rates are listed, although most places will give at least a 30% discount.

TIĀNJĪN 天津

Look no further than the *Imperial Palace Hotel* (*Tiānjīn Huánggōng Fàndiàn;* ☎ 2379 0888, fax 2379 0222, 177 Jiefang Beilu) for mid-range accommodation. This Singapore joint venture is housed in a beautiful and cozy building that was originally built by a British merchant in 1923 and recently renovated. It has a great Thai dinner buffet on Friday and Saturday for Y36. There's also the Sparkice Internet cafe open from 2 to 10 pm for Y20 per hour. The rooms start at Y581, including breakfast; during the low season a 45% discount isn't hard to get.

The *Park Hotel* (*Lèyuán Fàndiàn;* ☎ 2830 9815, fax 2830 2042, 1 Leyuan Lu) is (surprise) next to a park. Standard twins cost Y480 and singles are Y316.

Caesar's Palace Hotel (*Kǎisǎ Huánggōng Dàjiǔdiàn;* ☎ 2337 6381, fax 2337 4922, 4 Qixiangtai Nanlu, Hexi District) is no relation to the same-named Las Vegas pleasure palace. Standard twins cost Y650.

The *Friendship Hotel* (*Yǒuyì Bīnguǎn;* ☎ 2331 0372, 94 Nanjing Lu) has doubles starting at Y500.

The *Tianjin First Hotel* (*Tiānjīn Dìyī Fàndiàn;* ☎ 2330 9988, fax 2312 3000, 158 Jiefang Beilu), opposite the Hyatt, boasts a bit of old world charm. Standard rooms start at Y400 and suites at Y687.

Places to Stay – Top End

You can bask in luxury at the *Hyatt Hotel* (*Kǎiyuè Fàndiàn;* ☎ 2331 8888, fax 2331 1234, 219 Jiefang Beilu). Standard rooms are US$109, or US$90 on the weekends.

The *New World Astor Hotel* (*Lìshùndé Fàndiàn;* ☎ 2331 1688, fax 2331 6282, 33 Tai'erzhuang Lu) dates from early this century and, like the Tianjin First Hotel, retains the feel of foreign concession days (although it's been completely refurbished). Twins start at Y1105 and suites at Y1700.

Another of swanky hotel is the *Crystal Palace Hotel* (*Shuǐjīnggōng Fàndiàn;* ☎ 2835 6886, fax 2835 8886, 28 Youyi Lu). Facilities include a swimming pool, a tennis court, a health club and a French restaurant. Standard rooms start at US$100.

The *Sheraton Hotel* (*Xǐláidēng Dàjiǔdiàn;* ☎ 2334 3388, fax 2335 8740, sheraton@mail.zlnet.com.cn, Zijinshan Lu) is in the south part of Tiānjīn. The hotel dishes up 281 rooms priced between Y1500 and Y1750, plus 49 suites ranging from Y3125 to Y6250. To that, add another 15% surcharge, but if it helps the buffet breakfast is thrown in free. Guests also qualify for a free copy of the *South China Morning Post*.

In the vicinity of Gǔwénhuà Jiē, the *Tianjin Holiday Inn* (*Jiàrì Fàndiàn;* ☎ 2628 8888, fax 2628 6666, hotel@mail.hitianjin.com, 288 Zhongshan Lu) has doubles starting at US$130.

The latest addition to Tiānjīn's collection of upmarket hotels is the *Ocean Hotel* (*Yuǎnyáng Bīnguǎn;* ☎ 2420 5518, fax 2420 5516, ohtj@shell.tjvan.net.cn, 5 Ocean Square), located a short walk from the train station. Single rooms start at US$48 and doubles at US$88 (although discounts bring rooms under Y500).

The *Geneva Hotel* (*Jīnlìhuá Dàjiǔdiàn;* ☎ 2835 2222, fax 2835 9855, 32 Youyi Lu) is hidden behind the World Economy & Trade Exhibition Centre (one of the most perverse architectural nightmares in China). However, the hotel is fine, and twins start at Y660.

The *Dickson Hotel* (*Dàichéng Jiǔdiàn;* ☎ 2836 4888, fax 2836 5018, dickson@shell.tjvan.net.cn, 18 Binshui Dao) is another reasonable upmarket hotel. Standard twins start at US$155.

The *Tianjin Grand Hotel* (*Tiānjīn Bīnguǎn;* ☎ 2835 9000, fax 2835 9822, Youyi Lu) is indeed grand and houses 1000 beds in two high-rise blocks. It's benefited from considerable renovation since it was first built in 1960, and prices have been hiked up to Y640 for twins.

Places to Eat

Chinese *Shípǐn Jiē (Food Street)* is a covered alley with two levels of restaurants. Old places close and new ones open all the time, but there are approximately 40 to 50 restaurants on each level. You need to check prices – some of the food stalls are dirt cheap, but a few upmarket restaurants are almost absurdly expensive. You can find some real exotica here, like snake (expensive), dog meat (cheap) and eels (mid-range). Mexican food fans take note: there are bags of nacho chips for sale. Shípǐn Jiē is a couple of blocks south of Nanma Lu, about 1km west of the centre. Just one block north of Food Street is Rongji Dajie, an alley that also boasts its fair share of restaurants.

Between Changchun Dao and Binjiang Dao is **Gǒubùlǐ** (☎ 2730 2540, 77 Shandong Lu) the king of the dumpling shops with a century-old history. The house speciality is bāozi (steamed dough bun), filled with high-grade pork, spices and gravy. You can also get bāozi with special fillings like chicken, shrimp or their delicious shūcài bāozi (vegetarian dumplings) – be prepared to wait 10 to 15 minutes. A set meal, including soup, pickled vegetables and eight dumplings is Y13 to Y18, depending on the filling. The baozi here truly are exceptional not only for the better quality ingredients but also because they aren't greasy (a rarity in these parts). Frozen versions of this product can be bought from grocery stores all over Tiānjīn.

Another Tiānjīn institution is the **Dēng Yǐng Lóu Grand Restaurant** (94 Binjiang Dao). This shop is not quite a century old (it

started in 1913) and it specialises in Shāndōng cuisine, including roast duck. This is also a good place to come for Tiānjīn-style breakfast. Specialties include cùjiāo huóyú (live fish hot and sour soup), fúróng xièhuàng (crab roe mixed with egg white) and Tiānjīn-style jīnmèn sān wèir xiā (three-eaten prawns).

A permanent cake box clipped onto a bicycle rack is one of the eccentricities of Tiānjīn residents and a prerequisite for a visit to friends. Yángcūn rice-flour cake is a pastry that has been produced in Wǔqīng County suburbs since the Ming dynasty. It's made from rice and white sugar.

The **Ěrduǒyǎn Zhágāodiàn** (Eardrum Fried Spongecake Shop) takes its name from its proximity to Eardrum Lane. This shop specialises in cakes made from rice powder, sugar and bean paste, all fried in sesame oil. These special cakes have been named (you guessed it) 'eardrum fried spongecake'.

Another Tiānjīn speciality that takes its name from a shop's location is the **Máhuā** (18th Street Dough-Twists). The street seems to have been renamed 'Love Your Country Street' (àiguó dào), and the famous

Capitalist Road

Advertising for the foreign market is one area in which the Chinese still stumble. A Chinese-produced TV advertisement shown in Paris for Chinese furs treated viewers to the bloody business of skinning, and to refrigerated cadavers, before the usual parade of fur-clad models down the catwalk.

It would be fun to handle the advertising campaigns for China's more charming brand names. There's Pansy underwear (for men), or you can pamper your stud with Horse Head facial tissues. Wake up in the morning with a Golden Cock alarm clock (since renamed Golden Rooster). You can start your breakfast with a glass of Billion Strong Pulpy C Orange Drink, or finish your meal with a cup of Imperial Concubine Tea. For your trusty portable radio it may be best to stay away from White Elephant batteries, but you might try the space-age Moon Rabbit variety. Long March car tyres should prove durable, but what about the ginseng product with the fatal name of Gensenocide?

Out of the psychedelic 60s comes White Rabbit candy. Flying Baby toilet paper seems to have been discontinued, but you might still be able to find a pack of Puke cigarettes. The characters for Coca-Cola translate as 'tastes good, tastes happy', but the Chinese must have thought they were really on to something good when the 'Coke Adds Life' slogan got mistranslated and claimed that it could raise the dead. And as a sign of the times, one enterprising food vendor has started a chain store named 'Capitalist Road'.

Condoms provide fertile ground for creative name-branding. Asia Good Oil is an inventive local product name, while Huan Bao Multifunction Condoms gets you thinking – just how many functions are there for a condom?

shop is also referred to as Guìfā Xiáng Máhuādiàn. However, the dough-twists made from sugar, sesame, nuts and vanilla can be bought all over town – try the shops at the train station.

Kiessling's Bakery (Qǐshílín Cāntīng; 33 Zhejiang Lu), built by the Austrians in 1911 during the foreign concession days, is a Tiānjīn institution. However, you needn't go there, as the cakes are distributed all around the city at various shops and restaurants.

Foreign residents of Tiānjīn with a bit of cash like to pig out every Sunday at the *Sheraton Hotel*, which does a mean buffet from 11 am until 2 pm. It costs Y120 (no student cards are accepted), so don't eat breakfast if you want to get the maximum benefit.

Should you wish to fortify a main meal, an ice cream or a coffee, Tiānjīn produces a variety of liquid substances. There's Kafei-jiu, which approximates to Kahlua, and Sekijiu, which is halfway between vodka and rocket fuel.

Hotpot Korean hotpot *(huǒguō)* seems to be a very big hit with Tiānjīn's expats. There is a whole string of cheap but good Korean restaurants underneath the flyover on Fukang Lu, near Nankai University in the south-western part of town.

The *Rùnliáng Cāntīng (☎ 2311 5998, 182 Xinhua Lu)*, across from the International Building (Guójì Dàshà), is a good place to try Tiānjīn-style hotpot.

International Popular with local expats, the *Broadway Cafe (Guìbīnlóu Xīcāntīng; ☎ 2330 0541 or 130 0130 7877, 74 Munan Dao)* serves steaks and other hearty western fare. At the time of writing plans were afoot for a move to a larger location on Ti Yuan Bei, near the Diànshì Tǎ. An Irish pub, coffee bar and outdoor patio were also in the works for the new location.

The *City Slicker Saloon (Lǎowài Niúzǎi Cāntīng; ☎ 2313 0278, 55 Nanjing Lu)* specialises in Tex-Mex fare, including fajitas, chilli dogs, barbecue ribs, nachos and salsa. The friendly owners will make you feel at home amid the bizarre country & western-style decor.

The *Cosy Cafe & Bar (Kèsītè Xīcān Jiǔbā; ☎ 2837 2349)* is an expat haven. The atmosphere is very western, the menu is in English, there is MTV and popcorn is served at the beginning of every meal. The cafe has an unusual location, hidden underneath the Daguangming Bridge by the Hyatt Hotel. It also has a second, larger branch next to the Friendship Store on Youyi Lu.

Sgt Pepper's Music Hall Grill & Bar (Shājìn Yīnyuè Xīcāntīng; ☎ 2312 8138, 62 Jiefang Beilu) serves up western-style bar food, although this place is more a bar (with live music) than a restaurant.

Within Nankai University is *Alibaba Restaurant (Ālǐbābā Jiǔjiā; ☎ 2350 5613)*. Indian and international food (at under Y20) are the specialties here. The restaurant doubles as an unofficial pub for foreigners studying in Tiānjīn, and stays open very late.

The *Sheraton Hotel* has a small grocery shop that sells such rare items as cheese, cereal and Diet Coke. It's not in the main building, so go into the lobby and ask.

Entertainment

The most happening bar in town is *Sgt Pepper's Music Hall Grill & Bar* (see details in Places to Eat). Its in-house Filipino band packs in a mixed crowd, from well-heeled locals to expats to foreign students. There's no cover charge but it has a Y60 minimum per person, although it's not strictly enforced. *City Slicker Saloon, Cozy Cafe* and *Alibaba* are also happening nightspots. Around the corner from Alibaba is *Nuts (☎ 2350 8457)*, a hip little hole in the wall popular with foreign students at Nankai and Tianjin universities.

If you're looking for a disco, *Kānghǎo* is the in place to go. It's packed to the hilt with young Chinese hipsters. The cover charge is Y10 for women and Y20 for guys.

Computer nerds can try the *Internet Cafe (Shūxiāng Yuán)* across the main road from the foreign student's dormitory on the campus of Nankai University.

Shopping

A shopping trip to Tiānjīn will dispel any doubts about China's commitment to the textile trade. Only Hong Kong can match Tiānjīn for the amount of clothing on sale, and much of Hong Kong's supply originates in Tiānjīn. Although the selection isn't as good, shopping here is significantly cheaper than in Běijīng.

The shopping street to stroll along is Binjiang Dao, with alleyways and other commercial streets gathered around it there's something like eight whole blocks of concentrated shopping. Binjiang Dao itself is a pedestrian street, and you can find just about anything in the many boutiques, curio stores and emporiums. The area is particularly lively between 5 and 8 pm, when the streets are thronged with shoppers and theatre-goers.

Parallel to Binjiang Dao (starting from the southern end) there are more than 100 street stalls selling mostly clothing, plus many more permanent-looking stores. Also at the southern end is Tiānjīn's most up-market department store, Isetan, a Japanese department store.

Adjacent to the main train station is the Wing On department store (Yǒng'ān Bǎihuò), a branch of the Hong Kong company. It's knee-deep in everything from silk stockings to woollen overcoats.

Another massive shopping drag extends from the west train station south via Beima Lu, where it meets another shopping drag called Dongma Lu coming from the north train station. The sprawl of shops snakes down the length of Heping Lu as far as Zhōngxīn Gōngyuán (Central Park). Carrefour, the French supermarket chain, has a branch at 138 Dongma Lu. The street between Carrefour and Gǔwénhuà Jiē also has good shopping.

Also worth looking into is the Friendship Store (Yǒuyì Shāngdiàn), on Youyi Lu at the southern end of town. The ground floor has a notable supermarket.

Specialties Tiānjīn is considered famous for its carpets. If you're serious about carpets (and that's serious money!) the best bet is to get to a factory outlet. There are eight carpet factories in the Tiānjīn Municipality. Making the carpets by hand is a long and te-

dious process – some of the larger ones can take a proficient weaver over a year to complete. Patterns range from traditional to modern. Tianjin Carpets Import-Export Corporation (☎ 2830 0894) is at 45 Baoding Dao in the Heping District. The Tiānjīn Carpet Corporation (☎ 2830 0894) is at 5 Xinweidi Dao in the Hexi District.

Clay figurines are another local speciality. The terracotta figures originated in the 19th century with the work of Zhang Mingshan; his fifth-generation descendants train new craftspeople. The small figures take themes from human or deity sources and the emphasis is on realistic emotional expressions. Master Zhang was reputedly so skilful that he carried clay up his sleeves on visits to the theatre and came away with clay opera stars in his pockets. In 1900, during the Boxer Rebellion, western troops came across satirical versions of themselves correct down to the last detail in uniforms. These voodoo dolls were ordered to be removed from the marketplace immediately! The workshop is at 270 Machang Dao, Hexi District (southern end of Tiānjīn). The Art Gallery on Jiefang Lu has a collection of earlier Zhang family figurines. You can also buy brightly painted clay figurines on Gǔ Wénhuà Jiē.

Tiānjīn is also known for its New Year posters, which first appeared in the 17th century in the town of Yángliǔqīng, 15km west of Tiānjīn proper. Woodblock prints are hand-coloured, and are considered to bring good luck and happiness when posted on the front door during the Lunar New Year – OK if you like Day-Glo pictures of fat babies. Rarer are the varieties that have historical, deity or folk-tale representations.

Getting There & Away

Air The Civil Aviation Administration of China (CAAC; Zhōngguó Mínháng; ☎ 2330 1556) is at 113 Nanjing Lu. Korean Air (☎ 2319 0088 ext 2800), Dragon Air (☎ 2311 0191) and the Tiānjīn Air-Sales Agency (☎ 2330 3480), which can book flights on most airlines, have booking offices in the International Building (Guójì Dàshà) at 75 Nanjing Lu. CITS can also book tickets on most airlines.

Korean Air flies the Tiānjīn-Seoul route. Dragonair and CAAC both offer daily direct flights between Hong Kong and Tiānjīn. Tiānjīn has flights to most major cities in China.

Bus The opening of the Běijīng-Tiānjīn Expressway has made bus travel a good alternative to taking the train. Buses to Běijīng depart from in front of Tiānjīn's main train station (Y30; 1½ hours). In Běijīng, catch the bus to Tiānjīn from the Zhaogongkou bus station on the southern side of town, but be careful you get a bus to Tiānjīn train station (Tiānjīn huǒchē zhàn) and not to the outlying districts of Kāifā or Tánggū (unless you want to go to Tánggū). Buses run roughly every half hour throughout the day.

There are four long-distance bus stations, with buses running to places that the average foreign traveller may have little interest in. Bus station No 1 (Yīlù qìchē zhàn) is opposite the Bohai Hotel and is the place to get buses to Tánggū.

Other bus stations are usually located at intervals along the direction of travel. The south bus station (Bālǐtái fāchē zhàn) is on the north-eastern edge of Shuǐshàng Gōngyuán, which is south-west of the city centre – this is where you get buses to points south. The west bus station (Xīzhàn fāchē zhàn) is at 2 Xiqing Dao, near Tiānjīn's west train station.

Of possible interest to travellers is the north-east bus station (Dōngběijiǎo fāchē zhàn), which has the most destinations and the largest ticket office. It's very close to the Gǔ Wénhuà Jiē, just west of the Hǎi Hé in the north of Tiānjīn. Bus No 24 from the city centre will land you in the general vicinity. From the north-east bus station you can get buses to Jìxiàn. If you're the sort of person who likes to see everything along the way, a road route worth considering is from Tiānjīn to Běijīng via Jìxiàn.

Train Tiānjīn is a major north-south train junction with frequent trains to Běijīng, extensive links with the north-eastern provinces, and lines southwards to Jì'nán, Nánjīng, Shànghǎi, Fúzhōu, Héféi, Yāntái, Qīngdǎo and Shíjiāzhuāng.

There are three train stations in Tiānjīn: main, north and west. Ascertain the correct station. For most trains you'll want the main train station. Some trains stop at both the main and west stations, and some only go through the west train station (particularly those originating in Běijīng and heading south). Trains heading for north-eastern China often stop at the north train station.

If you have to alight at the west train station, bus No 24 connects the west train station with the main train station, passing through the central shopping district.

The main train station has a 'soft-seat booking office' that foreigners can use even for hard-seat tickets. To find it, go into the main station entrance (by the x-ray machines) and up the escalator to the 2nd floor – it's off to the right. There are usually no queues.

Express trains take just under 1½ hours for the trip between Tiānjīn and Běijīng. Local trains take about two hours.

Boat Tiānjīn's harbour is Tánggū, 50km (30 minutes by train or an hour by bus) from Tiānjīn proper. This is one of China's major ports, offering a number of possibilities for arriving and departing by boat. See the Tánggū section later in this chapter for details.

Getting Around

To/From the Airport From the city centre, it's about 15km to Tiānjīn's Zhāngguìzhuāng airport. Taxis ask for Y30 or more for the trip, and there is a bus from the CAAC ticket office. For airport information call ☎ 2490 2950.

Bus Key local transport junctions are the areas around the three train stations. The main train station has the biggest collection: bus Nos 24, 27 and 13, and further out toward the river are Nos 2, 5, 25, 28 and 96. At the west train station are bus Nos 24, 10 and 31 (Nos 11 and 37 run past the west train station); and at the north train station are bus Nos 1, 7 and 12.

Another major bus station point is around Zhōngxīn Gōngyuán, at the edge of the central shopping district. From here you'll get bus Nos 11 and 94, and nearby are bus Nos 9, 20 and 37. To the north of Zhōngxin Gōngyuán are bus Nos 1, 91, 92 and 93.

A useful bus to know is the bus No 24, which runs between the main and west stations 24 hours a day. Also noteworthy is bus No 8 – it starts at the main train station then zigzags across town before finally terminating at Nankai University in the southern part of town. From the main train station bus No 13 passes by Sgt Pepper's, the Hyatt, the Foreign Language Institute, the Friendship Store (on Youyi Lu) and the Crystal Palace Hotel.

With the exception of bus No 24, buses run from 5 am to 11 pm.

Train The subway (dìxià tiělù) can be useful – it runs all the way from Nanjing Lu to the west train station and costs Y1 per ride. Tiānjīn's subway opened in 1982 and has seen no improvement since then; the cars shuttle back and forth on a single track.

There's nothing to see down in the depths except the subterranean bathroom tiling, but it saves some trauma with the buses.

Taxi Taxis can be found most readily near the train station and around tourist hotels. Most drivers prefer not to use the meters, but the fare is generally Y10 to anywhere within the city centre.

Around Tiānjīn

Tiānjīn can be used as a staging point for trips directly north to Jìxiàn and to the Great Wall at Yellow Cliff Pass, as well as Zūnhuà, Tángshān and Běidàihé in Héběi. It's also a launching pad for roaring into the north-east (Manchuria).

TÁNGGŪ 塘沽
There are three harbours on the Tiānjīn Municipality stretch of coastline: Hàngū (north), Tánggū-Xīngǎng (centre) and Dàgǎng (south). Tánggū is about 50km from Tiānjīn proper. The Japanese began the construction of an artificial harbour during their occupation (1937–45) and it was completed by the communists in 1952, with further expansions in 1976 for container cargo. The Tánggū-Xīngǎng port now handles one of the largest volumes of goods of any port in China.

This is one of China's major international seaports, kept open by ice-breakers in winter. The harbour is where 'friends from all over the world' come to drop anchor.

As for sightseeing, the best advice we can give is to go no further than the ferry pier – the further you go, the worse it gets. Tánggū is a forest of cranes, containers and smokestacks – it's no place to linger.

Nevertheless, you will find foreigners lingering here – not travellers, but business people. Tánggū is booming and many export-oriented industries have set up shop here. The chief focus of all this activity is the **Tianjin Economic & Development Area** (Jīngjì Jìshù Kāifāqū), or TEDA (Tàidà). Should you decide to wander around this area in the northern part of Tánggū, you'll see plenty of factories, but also expensive residences and shops catering for the predominantly foreign and overseas Chinese investors and technical experts.

If you insist on seeking out some touristy sights, the city's most famous 'scenic spot' in town is **Dàgū Pàotái** (Dagu Fort), on the southern bank of the Hǎi Hé. The fort was built during the Ming dynasty, some time between 1522 and 1567. The purpose was to protect Tiānjīn from foreign invasions. It may have worked for a while, but considering how easily the Europeans overran the place during the 19th century, it was not exactly a smashing success.

The most happening area of town is **Nánhuò Shìchǎng** (Nanhuo Market), just south of the train station. The sprawling market is brimming over with stalls selling anything from fake Luis Vuitton purses to squid on a stick. If you need to catch a quick meal or fritter away some time while waiting for a boat this is the place to come.

An infinitely more refined place to while away some time is the **Tàidà Dāngdài Yìshù Bówùguǎn** (TEDA Contemporary Art Museum; ☎ 2532 0088 ext 817), on the 3rd

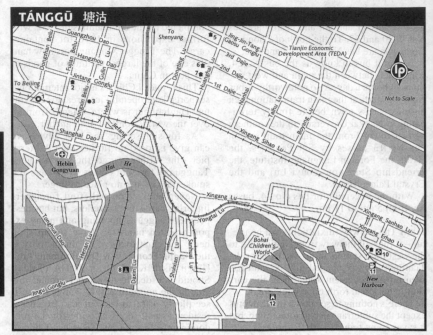

TÁNGGŪ 塘沽

To Shenyang
Jing-Jin-Tang Gaosu Gonglu
Tianjin Economic Development Area (TEDA)
Guangzhou Dao
Fujian Beilu
Hangzhou Dao
Dongtian Beilu
Jintang Gonglu
Guilin
Zhongxin Beilu
Hebei Lu
3rd Dàjiē
2nd Dàjiē
1st Dàjiē
Dongting Lu
Huanghai
Nanhai Lu
Taihu Lu
Boyang Lu
To Beijing
Shanghai Dao
Jiefang Lu
Xingang Sihao Lu
Hebin Gongyuan
Hai He
Xingang Lu
Yongtai Lu
Tonghua Dao
Henan Lu
Daxin Lu
Shuikun Lu
Sanhuai Lu
Xingang Sanhao Lu
Xingang Erhao Lu
Bohai Children's World
Jingu Gonglu
New Harbour
Not to Scale

TÁNGGŪ

1 Tánggū Train Station 塘沽火车站	5 DD Centre; Tàidà Dāngdài Yìshù Bówùguǎn 大地中心;泰达当代艺术博物馆	8 Cháoyīn Sì 潮音寺
2 Shènglì Bīnguǎn 胜利宾馆		9 Guójì Hǎiyuán Jùlèbù 国际海员俱乐部
3 Nánhuò Shìchǎng 南货市场	6 TEDA Hotel International 泰达国际	10 Friendship Store 友谊商店
4 Tánggū Hospital 塘沽医院	7 Jīnfān Dàshà 金帆大厦	11 Passenger Ferry Terminal 天津港客运站
		12 Dàgū Pàotái 大沽炮台

floor of the DD Centre (Dàdì Zhōngxīn). The two room gallery exhibits the works of some of China's most up and coming contemporary artists. It's open from 10 am to 4 pm Tuesday to Saturday.

For reasons not fully understood (by us), Tánggū has a very heavy public security presence. Many of the cops are in plain clothes, but if you're astute you'll notice the PSB vehicles – they have long, white li-

cence plates with black lettering, except for the first two letters, which are red. For what it's worth, there is a local rumour that Tánggū is the PSB headquarters.

Places to Stay

As in Tiānjīn, you can forget about dormitories and cheap hotels (although also like Tiānjīn, 30 to 40% discounts are easy to negotiate). If arriving in Tánggū by ship, it's

Buddhist monks at Qíyuán Sì, perched on the sacred peaks of Jiǔhuá Shān in Ānhuī

The lion's protective gaze guards the entrance of Lónghuá Tǎ in Shànghǎi.

The charming Venetian-style canals of Shàoxīng in Zhèjiāng

Returning from work in the fields of Ānhuī

best to hop on the first train to Běijīng or Běidàihé.

Most travellers stay at the *Guójì Hǎiyuán Jùlèbù (International Seamen's Club; ☎ 2579 3204)*. The simple reason for this is because it's within walking distance of the ferry pier. Unfortunately, for this same reason, it is often full just when you are most likely to need a room here. Slightly grotty but OK doubles are Y160.

The closest hotel to the main train station accepting foreigners is the bland *Shènglì Bīnguǎn (Victory Hotel; ☎ 2534 5833, 11 Jintang Lu)*. Standard twins cost Y398.

In TEDA, the three-star *Jīnfān Dàshà (Golden Sail Hotel; ☎ 2532 6666, 49 1st Dajie at Huanghai Lu)* has standard twins for Y280, including breakfast. Tánggū's most upmarket hotel is the *TEDA Hotel International (Tàidà Guójì Jiǔdiàn; ☎ 2532 6000, fax 2532 6216, 8 2nd Dajie at Huanghai Lu)*, a bizarre castle-like monstrosity. This is where most international business people stay. Standard rooms start at Y695. The *DD Centre (Dàdì Zhōngxīn; ☎ 2532 0088 ext 876, 26 Jieda Lu at 3rd Dajie)*, a hotel and office complex, has standard rooms starting at Y500, including an American breakfast buffet. Amenities include a swimming pool and a health club.

Getting There & Away

There are minibuses to Tánggū from Tiānjīn's south bus station. The trip costs Y5 and takes one hour. In Tánggū, departures are from the main train station and also from Nánhuò Shìchǎng. Buses leave when full – about once every 30 minutes throughout the day.

The main railway line to north-eastern China runs from Běijīng to Hāěrbīn via Tiānjīn and Tánggū. In other words, it's a heavily travelled route with frequent services. Trains cover the 50km from Tiānjīn to Tánggū in just 30 minutes. The route passes by saltworks that furnish roughly a quarter of the nation's salt.

Tánggū's harbour has been renamed New Harbour (Xīngǎng) – you catch ferries at the New Harbour passenger ferry terminal (Xīngǎng kèyùn zhàn).

For travellers, probably the most interesting ships are the international passenger ferries. One plies the route between Inch'ǒn (South Korea) and Tiānjīn, while another goes to Kobe, Japan. See the Getting There & Away chapter for more details about prices and times.

Boats to Dàlián depart daily and the journey takes 13 to16 hours. Because of the large number of passengers on the boats, it's recommended that you stick to 4th class or higher (tickets Y129 to Y705. The liners are comfortable, can take up to 1000 passengers, and are equipped with a bar, restaurant and movies.

Tickets can be purchased at Tánggū port opposite the Tánggu Theatre, but if you're in Tiānjīn it's safer to buy in advance. In Tiānjīn, tickets can be bought at 1 Pukou Dao (☎ 2339 4290). Difficult to find, Pukou Dao is a short distance south of the Hyatt and runs west off Tai'erzhuang Lu and is roughly on the same latitude as the enormous smokestack that stands on the opposite side of the river.

JÌXIÀN 蓟县

Rated as one of the 'northern suburbs' of Tiānjīn, although it's actually 120km from Tiānjīn city, the Jìxiàn area is about 90km due east of Běijīng.

Near the city's west gate is the 1000 year-old **Dúlè Sì** (Temple of Solitary Joy). The main multi-storey wooden structure, the Avalokitesvara Pavilion, qualifies as the oldest such structure in China. It houses a 16m-high statue of a bodhisattva with 10 heads that rates as one of China's largest terracotta statues. The buddha dates back to the Liao dynasty and the murals inside are from the Ming dynasty. The complex has been restored in the interests of tourism.

Just east of Jìxiàn is **Yúqiáo Shuǐkù** (Yuqiao Reservoir), easily the most attractive body of water (not counting the sea) in Tiānjīn Municipality.

Getting There & Away

One way of getting to Jìxiàn is to join a tour from Běijīng to the Qīng Dōng Líng (Eastern Qing Tombs) and Zūnhuà (see the

Around Běijīng section in the Běijīng chapter for details). However, this will normally only give you a brief lunch stop in Jìxiàn before pushing on to the tombs. There are also regular long-distance buses from Běijīng.

Buses from Tiānjīn's north-east bus station go to Jìxiàn and take about two hours. There is also a direct Tiānjīn-Jìxiàn train link.

PÁN SHĀN 盘山

To the north-west of Jìxiàn is Pán Shān, a collection of hills ranked among the 15 famous mountains of China. Emperor Qianlong was claimed to have been so taken with the place that he swore he never would have gone south of the Cháng Jiāng (Yangzi River) had he known Pán Shān was so beautiful.

The emperor aside, don't expect the Himalayas. Nevertheless, it's still a lovely area, dotted with trees, springs, streams, temples, pavilions and various other ornaments. On the summit of the peak is the Dingguang Stupa. There are 72 temples here.

The hills are 12km north-west of Jìxiàn, 150km north of Tiānjīn and 40km west of the Qīng Dōng Líng in Héběi. A suburban-type train runs to Jìxiàn from Tiānjīn; you can also get there by bus from Tiānjīn's north-east bus station to Jìxiàn, and from Jìxiàn change to a bus for Pán Shān.

GREAT WALL AT YELLOW CLIFF PASS 黄崖关长城

At the very northern tip of Tiānjīn Municipality (bordering Héběi) is Huángyá Guān or Yellow Cliff Pass. This is where Tiānjīn residents head to view the Great Wall. This section of the wall is 41km long before it crumbles away on each end – the part open to tourists was restored in 1984.

Some new features have been added to the original structures, including the **Bāguà Chéng** (Eight Diagrams Labyrinth), **Chángchéng Bówùguǎn** (Great Wall Museum), **Shíkèbēi Lín** (Forest of Steles) and **Shuǐ Guān** (Water Pass).

Getting There & Away

Huángyá Guān is 140km north of Tiānjīn city. Buses go to the wall mostly on weekends, with early-morning departures from

Tiānjīn's north-east bus station or sometimes from the main train station. Alternatively, take a bus to Jìxiàn, and from there change to a bus headed to the Wall.

TIĀNZŪN GÉ
Heaven Respect Pavilion

You'd have to be a real temple and pavilion enthusiast to come way out here to see this place. Nevertheless, it's rated as one of Tiānjīn's big sights.

The Tiānzūn Gé is three-storeys tall – locals are proud to tell you that the pavilion remained standing when everything else nearby was reduced to rubble by the 1976 Tángshān earthquake.

The pavilion is located near Fēngtái in Ninghe County, on the eastern border of Tiānjīn Municipality and Héběi. Buses to Fēngtái depart from Tiānjīn's north-east bus station.

WŬQĪNG 武清

Within the country seat of Wǔqīng County, the town of Wǔqīng (also called Yángcūn) is nothing to get excited about. However, it is home to the **Yángcūn Xiǎo Shìjiè** (Yángcūn Mini-World). This latest addition to Tiānjīn's tourist potpourri was formerly known as the Yongyang Ancient Gardens and was a recreated Han dynasty village. That didn't go over too well, so it's been transformed into a model of 170 famous landscapes around the globe each reduced to miniature size. Some of the models are one fifteenth of life size, while others had to be shrunk to one thirtieth of the original.

Perhaps of greater interest to frustrated travellers is the **Guójì Shèjī Cháng** (International Shooting Range; ☎ 2934 5757). It's operated by Norinco, China's weapons manufacturer, which is in fact run by the PLA.

A more benign activity practised here is table tennis (don't shoot at the balls) and Wǔqīng was the host of the 43rd World Table Tennis Championships.

Wǔqīng is about 30km north of central Tiānjīn and just off the Běijīng-Tiānjīn expressway. Catch a bus Tiānjīn's north-east bus station.

Hébĕi 河北

Wrapping itself around the centrally administered municipalities of Běijīng and Tiānjīn is the province of Hébĕi. It is often viewed either as an extension of Běijīng, the red-tape maker, or of Tiānjīn, the industrial powerhouse. This is not far off the mark since, geographically speaking, Běijīng and Tiānjīn take up a fair piece of the pie. In fact, Tiānjīn used to be the capital of Hébĕi. However, following Tiānjīn's inclusion into the central government administration, it was replaced by the next largest city, Shíjiāzhuāng.

Topographically, Hébĕi falls into two distinct parts: the mountain tableland to the north, where the Great Wall runs, and the monotonous southern plain. The region's agriculture, which is mainly wheat and cotton, is hampered by dust storms, droughts (five years in a row from 1972 to 1977) and flooding. These natural disasters should give you an idea of the weather. It's scorching and humid in summer, and freezing in winter, with dust fallout in spring and heavy rains in July and August.

Coal is Hébĕi's main resource and most of it is shipped through Qínhuángdǎo, a thriving port town with iron, steel and machine industries.

The attractions for travellers are the beach resort of Běidàihé and the town of Chéngdé, with its grand palaces and temples. Shíjiāzhuāng, the capital city, is not a major drawcard.

The best thing to see in Hébĕi is the Great Wall, which spans the province before meeting the sea at Shānhǎiguān.

Highlights

Capital: Shíjiāzhuāng
Population: 64.9 million
Area: 190,000 sq km

- Chéngdé, the 18th-century imperial resort, with its collection of replicas of minority architecture
- The beachside resort of Běidàihé, where well-heeled Chinese holiday-makers get away from Běijīng's stifling heat

way network constructed in this century brought the town relative prosperity and a consequent population explosion.

Shíjiāzhuāng has the biggest People's Liberation Army (PLA) officer training school in China; the school is about 2km west of the city. After the Běijīng protests and subsequent killings in 1989, all the new students at Beijing University were taken to this re-education camp for a one year indoctrination.

For an industrial city known chiefly for its smokestacks, Shíjiāzhuāng tries hard to keep the streets litter free – a crime as slight as a discarded pistachio nut incurred this author a fine of Y10. For some travellers Shíjiāzhuāng might be a useful transit point, but it's no place to linger and take in the sights.

SHÍJIĀZHUĀNG 石家庄

☎ 0311 • pop 8,601,900

Shíjiāzhuāng is a railway junction town about 250km south-west of Běijīng and, in spite of being the capital of the province, it could be considered a bit of a cultural desert. At the turn of the 20th century it was just a small village with 500 inhabitants and a handful of buildings. The rail-

HÉBĚI 河北

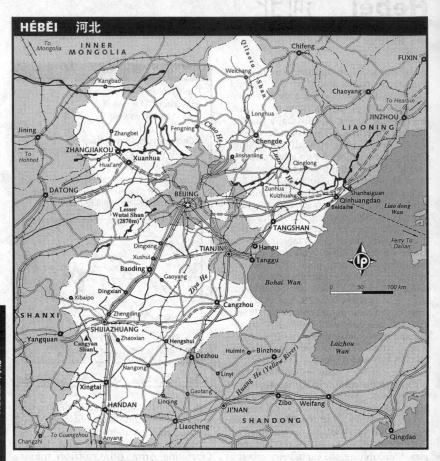

Lièshì Língyuán 烈士陵园

Revolutionary Martyrs' Mausoleum

Lièshì Língyuán (☎ 702 3028) is on Zhongshan Lu, west of the train station. The guerrilla doctor Norman Bethune (1890–1939) is interred here, and there is a memorial and a photo and drawing display depicting his life and works.

Following the communists' victory in 1949, Bethune (Bái qiú'ēn) became the most famous foreigner in China since Marco Polo. Even today, most Chinese don't know who Marco Polo is, but they all know Bethune. He goes down in modern Chinese history as the man who served as a surgeon with the Eighth Route Army in the war against Japan, having previously served with the Spanish communist forces against Franco and his German Nazi allies.

Bethune is eulogised in the reading of Mao Zedong Thought – 'We must all learn the spirit of absolute selflessness from Dr Norman Bethune'.

In China, 'Bethune' is also synonymous with 'Canada' – it's about all the Chinese tend to know about the country, and bringing up the name makes for instant friendships if you're Canadian.

SHÍJIĀZHUĀNG 石家庄

SHÍJIĀZHUĀNG

PLACES TO STAY
4 Báilín Dàshà
  柏林大厦
6 Yínquán Fàndiàn
  银泉饭店
9 Wǔjǐng Bīnguǎn
  武警宾馆
11 Guójì Dàshà
  国际大厦
15 Héběi Bīnguǎn; CITS; CTS
  河北宾馆; 中国国际
  旅行社; 中国旅行社

OTHER
1 Lièshì Língyuán
  沂芇嘤
2 Post Office
  邮局
3 Train Station
  火车站
5 Airport Centre
  (CAAC)
  河北华联旅行社
7 Yǒng'ān Shìchǎng
  永安步行商业街

8 Central Long-Distance
  Bus Station
  长途汽车站
10 Xiáyàng Long-Distance
  Bus Station
  向阳长途汽车站
12 Héběi Shěng Bówùguǎn
  河北省博物馆
13 TV Tower
  电视台
14 Teachers' University
  师范大学

Buried in the cemetery are more than 700 army cadres and heroes who died in various battles including the resistance against Japan, the War of Liberation, and the Korean War.

The area around the Lièshì Língyuán is a large park, and in the central alley contains an impressive pair of bronze Jin dynasty lions that date from 1185. There is also a statue of Dr Norman Bethune in the courtyard of the Bethune International Peace Hospital, which is a little way to the west of the cemetery.

Héběi Shěng Bówùguǎn
河北省博物馆
Hebei Provincial Museum

This large museum (☎ 604 5642) is opposite the Guójì Dàshà. All explanations are in Chinese. The museum is at 4 Dong Gajie and is open daily except Monday from 8 to 11.30 am and 2 to 5.30 pm.

Places to Stay

Wǔjǐng Bīnguǎn (☎ 862 6002, 49 Shengli Nanlu) is the cheapest place that accepts foreigners – the reason why it can take foreigners may have something to do with the fact that the building is owned by the military. Good doubles with private bath are Y80. The building is on Guangming Lu, just behind the train station. When you exit the station, turn left and walk to Yuhua Lu – use the underpass to get past the railway tracks then up the steps (to your left) to reach Guangming Lu. As yet, the hotel has no English sign.

The best deal in the area around the train station is the *Băilín Dàshà* (☎ 702 1398, 24 Chezhan Jie). The rooms are very clean and the staff are extremely courteous. A single with bath costs Y198 and a double with private bath is Y240.

The *Yínquán Fàndiàn (Silver Spring Hotel;* ☎ 702 6981, 12 Zhanqian Jie) is a short distance south of the train station. Although not as well kept as the Băilín, it has decent doubles for Y128.

There are two fancy hotels in town. The *Héběi Bīnguăn (Hebei Grand Hotel;* ☎ 581 5961, fax 581 4092, 23 Yucai Jie) is a fully renovated guesthouse and is the darling of tour groups. Rooms at the back start at Y380 and spiffier rooms in the main building start at Y568. The hotel is near the No 6 bus stop. The *Guójì Dàshà (International Hotel;* ☎ 604 7888, fax 603 4787, 23 Chang'an Xilu) has long been a haven for elderly tour groups. The rooms are surprisingly good value, with doubles from Y290 to Y690.

Places to Eat
Close to the Yínquán Fàndiàn is a long commercial street called *Yǒng'ān Shìchǎng.* Here you'll find lots of good eats at rock-bottom prices from both street stalls and restaurants.

Getting There & Away
The Civil Aviation Administration of China (CAAC; Zhōngguó Mínháng) connects Shíjiāzhuāng to:

Chóngqìng (two flights weekly), Guǎngzhōu (five), Hohhot (two), Kūnmíng (two), Nánjīng (two), Qínhuángdǎo (two), Shànghǎi (seven), Shēnzhèn (two), Wēnzhōu (two), Xiàmén (two).

Shíjiāzhuāng is a major rail hub with comprehensive connections. There are lines to Běijīng (three hours), Tàiyuán (five hours), Dézhōu (five hours) and Guǎngzhōu (thirty-plus hours).

To reach most sights outside of town you need to take a bus from the central long-distance bus station, which is next to the train station, to minibus stations scattered on the outskirts of town.

Getting Around
To/From the Airport Shíjiāzhuāng's airport is 40km from town. The CAAC bus costs Y25 and departs from the Airport Centre (booking office), opposite the train station. The bus schedule changes daily, so check with the office for departure times. There are two or three buses per day, with the first leaving at around 5.40 am and the last leaving at around 5 pm. A taxi to the airport will cost about Y100 and the ride takes about an hour.

Bus Within the city there are 10 bus lines. If you're headed to one of the minibus stations hold on to your belongings as you exit the bus. The Píngshān station in particular is one to look out for: as you exit the bus, minibus drivers try to pull you onto their bus while thieves grab at your belongings.

AROUND SHÍJIĀZHUĀNG
Although there's nothing spectacular in this part of Héběi, but there are a few places that may be worth a visit.

Zhèngdìng 正定
☎ 0311
This town, 18km north of Shíjiāzhuāng, has several magnificent temples and monasteries. The largest and oldest is the monastery, **Lóngxīng Sì**, noted for its huge, 20m-high bronze buddha dating back almost 1000 years to the Song dynasty. The multi-armed statue is housed in the **Cí ēn Sì** (Temple of Great Mercy), an impressive structure with red and yellow galleries.

Bus No 201 from the Central long-distance bus station travels to the temples; the ride takes about an hour.

Zhàozhōu Qiáo 赵州桥
Zhaozhou Bridge

This bridge is in Zhaoxian County, about 40km south-east of Shíjiāzhuāng and 2km south of Zhaoxian town. It has spanned the river, Jiǎo Hé, for 1400 years and is China's oldest standing bridge. Historians consider this bridge a masterpiece and rank it among China's most important contributions to architecture. The world's first segmental bridge (ie, it's arch is a segment of a circle, as opposed to a complete semi-circle), it predates bridges of this kind throughout the world by 800 years.

Zhàozhōu Qiáo is exceptional in that not only does it still stand but it's in remarkable shape. It is 50m long and 9.6m wide, with a span of 37m. Twenty-two stone posts are topped with carvings of dragons and mythical creatures, with the centre slab featuring a magnificent *taotie* (an offspring of a dragon). Credit for this daring piece of engineering goes to Li Chun, but according to legend the master mason Lu Ban constructed it overnight. Astounded immortals, refusing to believe that this was possible, arrived to test the bridge. One immortal had a wagon, another had a donkey, and they asked Lu Ban if it was possible for them both to cross at the same time. He nodded. Halfway across, the bridge started to shake and Lu Ban rushed into the water to stabilise it. This resulted in donkey-prints, wheel-prints and hand-prints being left on the bridge (there are actually two small indentations about half-way across the bridge). Admission is Y10. Several more old stone bridges are to be found in Zhaoxian County.

From the Central long-distance bus station take bus No 3 to the Hua Xia long-distance bus station. From there take a minibus to Zhaoxian (Y6, one hour). From Zhaoxian there are no public buses to the bridge, but there are plenty of taxis willing to take you (Y15 return).

Cāngyán Shān 苍岩山
Cangyan Mountain

About 45km south-west of Shíjiāzhuāng is a scenic area of woods, valleys and steep cliffs dotted with pagodas and temples. The novelty here is a bizarre, double-roofed hall sitting on a stone-arch bridge spanning a precipitous gorge. It is known as the **Hanging Palace**, and is reached by a 300-step stairway. The palace dates from the Sui dynasty. On the surrounding slopes are other ancient halls.

Xībǎipō 西柏坡
Patriotic Education Base

In Píngshān County, 80km north-west of Shíjiāzhuāng, was the base from which Mao Zedong, Zhou Enlai and Zhu De directed the northern campaign against the Kuomintang from 1947 to 1948. The original site of Xībǎipō village was submerged by the reservoir Gǎngnán Shuǐkù and it's been replaced by a massive tourist trap, a favourite excursion for bus loads of PLA enlistees. In 1977 a **Gémìng Jìniàn Bówùguǎn** (Revolutionary Memorial Museum) was erected, along with several monuments scattered across the grounds and even a hotel. This is *the* place to pick up tacky Mao memorabilia – you name it and souvenir hawkers will surely have it – with Mao's portrait imprinted on it of course.

To get there from Shíjiāzhuāng take bus No 8 from the Central long-distance bus station. Get off at the bus at the Píngshān minibus stop (about 20 minutes) and take a minibus to its terminus in Píngshān (Y5, one hour). From there switch to a minibus headed to Nánpíng and get off at Xībǎipō (Y8, one hour). The Xībǎipō is open daily from 8 am to 6 pm and admission is Y15.

CHÉNGDÉ 承德

☎ 0314 • pop 700,000

Chéngdé is an 18th century imperial resort area 255km from Běijīng. Once known as Jehol, it boasts the remnants of the largest regal gardens in China.

Chéngdé was an obscure town until 1703 when Emperor Kangxi began building a summer palace, with a throne room and the full range of court trappings. More than a home away from home, Chéngdé became a sort of government seat, since where the emperor went his seat went too. Kangxi called his summer creation Bìshǔ

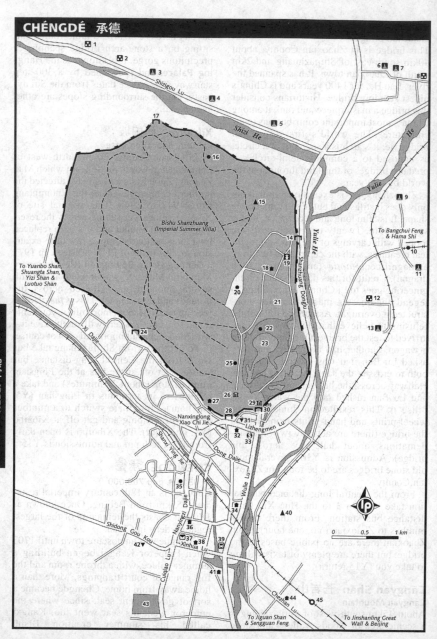

CHÉNGDÉ 承德

CHÉNGDÉ

PLACES TO STAY

18 Měnggǔbāo Dùjiàcūn
蒙古包渡假村

27 Qíwànglóu Bīnguǎn
绮望楼宾馆

32 Mountain Villa Hotel
山庄宾馆

34 Wàijiāo Rényuán Bīnguǎn
外交人员宾馆

36 Chéngdé Bīnguǎn
承德宾馆

38 Xīnhuá Fàndiàn
新华饭店

41 Yúnshān Fàndiàn
云山饭店

44 Huìlóng Dàshà
会龙大厦

PLACES TO EAT

31 Jīnbào Chāoshì Měishí
金豹超市美食

42 Chángshèng Fàndiàn
常胜饭店

OTHER

1 Luóhàn Táng
(Arhat Hall Ruins)
罗汉堂

2 Guǎng'ān Sì (Ruins)
广安寺

3 Shūxiàng Sì
殊像寺

4 Pǔtuózōngshèngzhī Miào
普陀宗圣之庙

5 Xūmífúshòuzhī Miào
须弥福寿之庙

6 Pǔníng Sì
普宁寺

7 Pǔyòu Sì
普佑寺

8 Guǎngyuán Sì
(Ruins)
广缘寺

9 Ānyuǎn Sì
安远庙

10 Chairlift
棒槌峰索道

11 Pǔlè Sì
普乐寺

12 Pǔshàn Sì
(Ruins)
溥善寺

13 Pǔrén Sì
溥仁寺

14 Huìdíjí Mén
惠迪吉门

15 Běizhěn Shuāngfēng
(Beizhen Twin Peaks)
北枕双峰

16 Gǔjù Tíng
(Ancient Pavilion)
古俱亭

17 Xīběi Mén
(North-West Gate)
西北门

19 Yǒngyòusì Tǎ
永佑寺塔

20 Wénjīn Gé
文津阁

21 Wànshù Yuán
(Forest Grove)
万树园

22 Yǔ Lóu
雨楼

23 Rúyì Zhōu (Ideal Island)
如意洲

24 Bìfēng Mén
碧峰门

25 Fāngyuánjū
(Fragrant Garden House)
芳园居

26 Zhèng Gōng
正宫

28 Lìzhèng Mén
丽正门

29 Dōng Gōng (East Palace)
东宫

30 Déhuì Mén
德汇门

33 Bank of China
中国银行

35 Xinhua Bookstore
新华书店

37 Post Office
邮局

39 Long-Distance Bus Station
长途汽车站

40 Luóhàn Shān
罗汉山

43 Lièshì Jìniànguǎn
革命烈士纪念馆

45 Train Station
火车站

Shānzhuāng (Imperial Summer Villa or Fleeing-the-Heat Mountain Villa).

By 1790, during the reign of Kangxi's grandson Qianlong, it had grown to the size of Běijīng's Summer Palace and the Forbidden City combined. Qianlong extended an idea started by Kangxi, to build replicas of minority architecture in order to make envoys feel comfortable. In particular he was keen on promoting Tibetan and Mongolian Lamaism, which had proved to be a useful way of debilitating the Mongols. The Mongolian branch of Lamaism required one male in every family to become a monk – a convenient method of channelling manpower and damaging the Mongol economy.

This explains the Tibetan and Mongolian features of the monasteries north of the Bìshǔ Shānzhuāng, one of them is a replica of the Potala Palace in Lhasa.

So much for business – the rest was the emperor's pleasure, which included the usual bouts of hunting and feasting. Occasionally the outer world would make a rude intrusion into this dream life. In 1793 British emissary Lord Macartney arrived and sought to open trade with China. Qianlong dismissed him with the statement that China possessed all things and had no need for trade.

Today, Chéngdé has slipped back into being the provincial town it once was, its grandeur long decayed, and its monks and emperors long gone. The current population of 700,000 is engaged in mining, light industry and tourism.

During the Cultural Revolution, the priceless remnants of Qing dynasty culture were allowed to go to seed – palaces and monasteries became tattered, Buddhist statues were disfigured, windows were bricked up, columns reduced to stumps and so on.

All this is being restored, in some cases from the base up, in the interests of promoting tourism. Chéngdé is now on UNESCO's World Heritage list, which will hopefully increase its chances of being authentically restored.

Compared to other Chinese cities its size, Chéngdé's dusty, small-town ambience is nice enough and there's some quiet hiking in the rolling countryside.

Information

The Bank of China is near the Mountain Villa Hotel and the post office is further south on Nanyingzi Lu. The Public Security Bureau (PSB; Gōngānjú; ☎ 223 091) is on Wulie Lu.

Bìshŭ Shānzhuāng 避暑山庄
Imperial Summer Villa

This park covers 590 hectares and is bounded by a 10km wall. Emperor Kangxi decreed that there would be 36 'beauty spots' in Jehol; Qianlong delineated 36 more. That makes a total of 72, but where are they? At the northern end of the gardens the pavilions were destroyed by warlords and Japanese invaders, and even the forests have suffered cutbacks. The park is on the dull side, and hasn't been very well maintained.

With a good deal of imagination you can perhaps detect traces of the original scheme of things, with landscaping borrowed from the southern gardens of Sūzhōu, Hángzhōu and Jiāxīng, and from the Mongolian grasslands. There is even a feature for resurrecting the moon, should it not be around – a pool shows a crescent moon created by the reflection of a hole in surrounding rocks.

Passing through Lizhèng Mén, the main gate, you arrive at the **Zhèng Gōng** (Front Palace), a modest version of Bĕijīng's palace. It contains the main throne hall, the Hall of Simplicity & Sincerity, built of an aromatic hardwood called *nanmu* and now a museum displaying royal memorabilia, arms, clothing and other accoutrements. The emperor's bedrooms are fully furnished. Around to the side is a door without an exterior handle (to ensure privacy and security for the emperor), through which the lucky bed partner for the night was ushered before being stripped and searched by eunuchs.

The double storey **Yŭ Lóu** (Misty Rain Tower), on the north-western side of the main lake, was an imperial study. Further north is the **Wénjīn Gé** (Wenjin Chamber), built in 1773 to house a copy of the *Sikuquanshu*, a major anthology of classics, history, philosophy and literature commissioned by Qianlong. The anthology took 10 years to put together. Four copies were made, but three have disappeared; the fourth is in Bĕijīng.

About 90% of the compound is taken up by lakes, hills, mini-forests and plains, with the odd vantage-point pavilion. At the northern part of the park the emperors reviewed displays of archery, equestrian skills and fireworks. Horses were also chosen and tested here before hunting sorties. Yurts were set up on the mock-Mongolian prairies (a throne, of course, installed in the emperor's yurt) and picnics were held for minority princes. The park is open from 5.30 am to 6.30 pm and admission is Y50.

Wàibā Miào 外八庙
Eight Outer Temples

Outside the walls of the imperial garden, to the north and north-east, are several former temples and monasteries. The number started at 11 many years ago, then plummeted to five (destroyed by Japanese bombers and the Cultural Revolution), although four others still exist in various states of disrepair. The Wàibā Miào are from 3km to 5km from the garden's front gate; bus No 6 taken to the north-eastern corner will drop you in the vicinity.

The surviving temples were all built between 1750 and 1780. The Chinese-style **Pǔrén Sì** and the vaguely Shanxi-style **Shūxiàng Sì** have been totally rebuilt. The most popular (and most crowded) temples are **Pǔtuózōngshèngzhī Miào** and **Pǔníng Sì**, which houses the amazing multiple-armed Goddess of Mercy. Get there in the early morning when the air is crisp and cool and the sun is shining on the front of the temples – it's the best time to take photos. Some of the temples are listed here in clockwise order. Unless otherwise noted, admission is Y20 and opening hours are 8 am to 5.30 pm.

Pǔtuózōngshèngzhī Miào (Temple of Potaraka Doctrine) 普陀宗圣之庙 Pǔtuózōngshèng, the largest of the Chéngdé temples, is a mini-facsimile of Lhasa's Potala Palace. It was built for the chieftains from Xīnjiāng, Qīnghǎi, Mongolia and Tibet to celebrate Qianlong's 60th birthday and was also a site for religious assemblies. It's a solid-looking fortress that has been almost completely renovated. Notice the stone column in the courtyard inscribed in Chinese, Tibetan, Mongol and Manchu scripts. The main hall is housed at the very top, surrounded by several small pavilions (most of which now house souvenir stalls); the climb to the top is worth it for the views.

Xūmǐfúshòuzhī Miào 须弭福寿之庙 **(Temple of Sumeru, Happiness and Longevity)** Xūmǐfúshòu was built in honour of the sixth Panchen Lama, who stayed here in 1781. It incorporates elements of Tibetan and Han architecture and is an imitation of a temple in Shigatse, Tibet. At the highest point is a hall with eight gilded copper dragons commanding the roof ridges, and behind that sits a glazed-tile pagoda.

Pǔníng Sì 普宁寺 **(Temple of Universal Tranquillity)** Pǔníng is also modelled on a Tibetan temple. It was built to commemorate Qianlong's victory over Mongol tribes when the subjugated leaders were invited to Chéngdé. A stele relating the victory is inscribed in Tibetan, Mongol, Chinese and Manchu. The main feature is a towering 22m wooden statue of Guanyin, the Goddess of Mercy. She has 42 arms with an eye on each palm and each hand holds a musical instrument. The temple appears to be used as an active place of worship. You can catch bus No 6 from in front of the Mountain Villa Hotel to Pǔníng.

Ānyuǎn Sì 安远庙 **(Far Spreading Peace Temple)** Ānyuǎn is a copy of the Gurza temple in Xīnjiāng. Only the main hall remains and it contains Buddhist frescoes in a very sad state.

Pǔlè Sì 普乐寺 **(Temple of Universal Happiness)** Pǔlè Sì was built in 1776 for visits of minority envoys (Kazaks among them). It's in much better shape than the other temples and has been retiled and repainted. At the rear of the temple is the unusual Round Pavilion (currently being renovated), reminiscent of Běijīng's Tiāntán (Temple of Heaven).

It's a 30-minute hike to **Bàngchuí Fēng** (Club Rock) from Pǔlè – the rock is said to resemble a club used for beating laundry dry. Nearby is **Hámá Shí** (Toad Rock). There is pleasant hiking, good scenery and commanding views of the area. You can save yourself a steep climb to the base of Bàngchuí Fēng and Hámá Shí by taking the chairlift, but it's more fun to walk if you're reasonably fit. Bus No 10 will take you to Pǔlè Sì.

Other Hills
Other hills that are regarded as famous beauty spots (and possibly climbable) include: **Luóhàn Shān** (Arhat Hill), almost in the centre of town; **Sēngguān Fēng** (Monk's Hat Peak), 4km south of town; **Yuánbǎo Shān** (Ingot Hill), 10km southwest of town; **Shuāngtǎ Shān** (Twin Pagoda Hill), 15km to the south-west; **Yǐzi Shān** (Chair Mountain), 14km to the south-west; **Luòtuó Shān** (Camel Mountain), 20km south-west; and **Jīguān Shān** (Cockscomb Hill), 15km south-east.

Jīnshānlǐng 金山岭
It's a good two-hour, 113km drive from the centre of Chéngdé to the Great Wall at

HÉBĚI 河北

Jīnshānlǐng, but some travellers like to do it. It's in the direction of Bĕijīng, and if you're travelling by car or bus then you could stop off here on a Bĕijīng-Chéngdé excursion. Admission is Y40.

It is possible to hike (about four hours) along the wall between Jīnshānlǐng and Sìmătái. For information about the Great Wall at Jīnshānlǐng, see the Bĕijīng chapter.

Organised Tours

The only practical way to see all the sights in one day is to take a tour by minibus. Most of these tours start out at 8 am. The cheapest bus tours cost Y30 (check at the Mountain Villa Hotel), but are Chinese-speaking only; a personal tour costs about Y100.

Pricey tours are available from the China International Travel Service (CITS; Zhōngguó Guójì Lǚxíngshè) in Bĕijīng. A complete two-day tour to Chéngdé costs around Y3000 for one person, but it gets cheaper as the size of the group increases.

Places to Stay

As soon as you arrive at the train station – or even on the train itself – hotel touts will be waiting for you. If you go with them you'll get a free ride to your hotel; at the hotel you pay the standard rate and the touts get a commission.

The Stalinist architecture at the *Mountain Villa Hotel* (Shānzhuāng Bīnguǎn; ☎ 202 3501, fax 202 2457, 127 Xiaonanmen Lu) evokes mixed reactions, but this place gets good reviews from travellers. Standard twins are Y240 and Y480. The best deal is the doubles in the back part of the hotel for Y140. The more expensive rooms are large enough to hold a party in – perhaps that's why they come equipped with mahjong tables. Take bus No 7 from the train station and from there it's a short walk.

The *Chéngdé Bīnguǎn* (☎ 202 3157, 33 Nanyingzi Dajie) is a reliable cheapie with doubles for Y90, Y100 and Y120. Although the rooms are a bit smelly and worn on the edges, it's decent for the price. It's also conveniently located in front of a night market. Bus No 7 from the train station drops you right outside the hotel.

The *Xīnhuá Fàndiàn* (☎ 206 3181, 4 Xinhua Lu) has nondescript rooms for Y70, Y210 and Y300. The higher priced rooms aren't worth the extra cost.

Near the train station, the recently renovated *Huìlóng Dàshà* (☎ 208 5369, 1 Xinjuzhai, Chezhan Lu) has clean, modern rooms starting at Y200.

In the top-end range, the *Wàijiāo Rényuán Bīnguǎn* (Guesthouse for Diplomatic Missions; ☎ 202 1976, Wulie Lu), although clean and modern, is nothing special. Standard twins are Y380 and suites are Y780. The *Yúnshān Fàndiàn* (☎ 215 6171, fax 215 3256, 6 Nanyuan Donglu) is one of the better hotels in town and a favourite with tour groups. The brochure enthusiastically proclaims 'Let warm and pleasure accompany you everywhere hope excellent service in Yunshan give you happy memory'. You'd probably have a happier memory if prices were lower; standard rooms are Y440.

There are two hotels just within the walls of the Bìshǔ Shānzhuāng. On the western side is the *Qǐwànglóu Bīnguǎn* (☎ 202 4385), built in Qing dynasty style with palatial gardens. It has a pleasant, quiet atmosphere, and there's space to sit out in the gardens. Twins cost Y500. Further north, on the eastern side, is the desolate *Ménggǔbāo Dùjiàcūn* (Mongolian Yurt Hotel; ☎ 216 3094), where you can stay in a drab concrete yurt for Y260 and Y290.

Places to Eat

Chéngdé's local specialty is wild game – deer and pheasant. A good place to try it, at moderate prices, are the restaurants on Shidonggou Kou. Try the *Chángshèng Fàndiàn* where you can get a half portion of juicy *shān jī dīng* (pheasant) or *lùròu* (deer) for Y30.

Across from the Mountain Villa Hotel is the bright and cavernous restaurant *Jīnbaò Chāoshì Měishí* (Golden Leopard Super Delicious) where you can choose fresh, uncooked dishes and the staff will cook them up for you. A huge, super delicious plate of vegies is Y8, fish Y18 and tofu Y4. For street food or a quick meal, try the restaurants along Shanxiying Jie (at the northern end of Nanyingzi Lu) or Nanxinglong Xiao Chi Jie (across from the Lizhèng Mén, the main gate of the Bìshǔ Shānzhuāng), where you can get a heaped plate of *jiǎozi* (dumplings) for Y5.

Getting There & Away

Bus Although most travellers go by train, buses are now a viable alternative. Buses from Chéngdé to Běijīng (Y30, 3½ hours) leave every 20 minutes. For an extra Y5 you can take a comfortable air-conditioned bus, which leave Chéngdé for Běijīng at 9.20 am, and 2.40 and 4.20 pm.

Train There are trains connecting Chéngdé to Běijīng, and also to Shěnyáng in Liáoníng. Most comfortable is the *Běijīng-Chéngdé express* (train Nos 225 and 226) which has a plush soft-seat section – it's no smoking and tea is served to passengers for a small fee. The one-way trip takes less than five hours and costs Y41. The slower trains, although half the price, take over seven hours. The schedule is as follows:

Běijīng to Chéngdé

Train No	Depart	Arrive
225	7.25 am	11.25 pm
591	1.23 pm	6.31 pm
613	11.40 pm	4.37 am
853	4.10 pm	11.17 pm

Chéngdé to Běijīng

Train No	Depart	Arrive
226	2.40 pm	6.38 pm
592	6.01 am	11.40 am
614	10.29 pm	4.02 am
854	6.36 am	1.39 pm

Shěnyáng to Chéngdé

Train No	Depart	Arrive
520/521	7.50 am	9.44 pm
592	4.04 pm	6.01 am

Chéngdé to Shěnyáng

Train No	Depart	Arrive
519/522	7.01 am	8.38 pm
593	6.47 pm	8.43 am

Getting Around

Taxis and motor-tricycles are widely available – bargaining is necessary, especially with the tricycles. Taxis are Y5 at flagfall, which should get you to most destinations in town. There are half a dozen minibus lines, but the only ones you'll probably need to use are the No 7 from the station to the Chéngdé Bīnguǎn, and the No 6 to the Wàibā Miào grouped at the north-eastern end of town. The service is infrequent – you might have to wait 30 minutes or more.

Another good way to get around town and to the Wàibā Miào is on a bicycle. You can rent bicycles at the Yúnshān Fàndiàn for Y20 per day, plus a Y300 deposit.

BĚIDÀIHÉ 北戴河
☎ 0355

A 35km stretch of coastline on China's east coast, the Běidàihé, Qínhuángdǎo & Shānhǎiguān region borders the Bó Hǎi (Bo Sea). The seaside resort of Běidàihé was built by westerners, but is now popular with the Chinese. The simple fishing village was transformed when English railway engineers stumbled across it in the 1890s. Diplomats, missionaries and business people from the Tiānjīn concessions and the Běijīng legations hastily built villas and cottages in order to indulge in the new bathing fad.

The original golf courses, bars and cabarets have disappeared, although there are signs that these will be revived in the interests of the nouvelle bourgeoisie. The cream of China's leaders congregate at the summer villas, also continuing a tradition – Jiang Qing and Lin Biao had villas here and Li Peng and Jiang Zemin currently have heavily guarded residences along the seaside on the road between Běidàihé and Nádàihé. Although government elite have summer homes here, Běidàihé is very much a resort for ordinary, albeit comparatively well-healed, Chinese. During the summer high season (May to October), Běidàihé comes alive with vacationers who crowd the beaches, eat at the numerous outdoor seafood restaurants and stroll the night markets well into the night.

BĚIDÀIHÉ, QÍNHUÁNGDǍO & SHĀNHǍIGUĀN
北戴河、秦皇岛、山海关

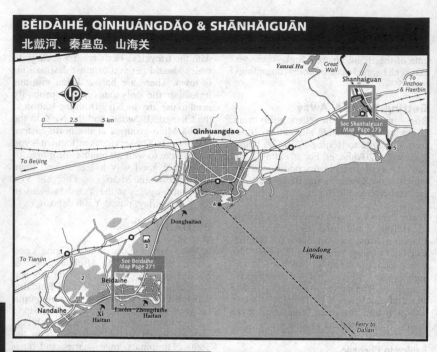

BĚIDÀIHÉ, QÍNHUÁNGDǍO & SHĀNHǍIGUĀN

1 Běidàihé Train Station
  北戴河火车站
2 Liánfēngshān Gōngyuán
  联峰山公园
3 Hǎibīn Guójiāsēnlín Gōngyuán;
  Yěshēng Dòngwùyuán
  海滨国家森林公园;
  野生动物园
4 Qínhuángdǎo Gǎng
  秦皇岛港
5 Lǎolóngtóu
  老龙头

Just to make sure nothing nasty comes by in the water, there are shark nets. Army members and working heroes are rewarded with two week vacations at Běidàihé. There are many sanatoriums where patients can get away from the noise of the city.

The average June temperature is 21°C (70°F). In January, by contrast, temperatures rest at −5°C (23°F).

Things to See
There are various hikes to vantage points with expansive views of villas or the coast. The **Wànghǎi Tíng** (Sea-Viewing Pavilion) is at the park, **Liánfēngshān Gōngyuán**, about 1.5km north of **Zhōngdàihé Hǎitān** (Middle Beach), which is halfway between Běidàihé and Nándàihé. Right on the shoreline, at **Gēziwō Gōngyuán** (Pigeon's Nest Park) is the **Wànghǎi Tíng** (Eagle Pavilion). **Lǎohǔ** (Tiger Rocks) is a popular place to watch the sunrise. At the eastern end of Běidàihé is the **Bìluó Tǎ** (Emerald Shell Tower).

The tide at the **Dōng Hǎitān** (East Beach) recedes dramatically and tribes of kelp collectors and shell-pickers descend upon the sands. In the high season you can even be photographed in cardboard-cutout racing boats, with the sea as a backdrop.

BĔIDÀIHÉ 北戴河

BĔIDÀIHÉ

1 Minibus Stop
中巴站
2 Bus Station
海滨汽车站
3 Post Office
邮局
4 Zhōnghăitān
Bīnguăn
中海滩宾馆
5 Hăibīn Mătou
海滨码头

6 Yŏuyì Jiŭdiàn Bīnguăn
友谊酒店宾馆
7 Hăixiān Cāntīng
海鲜餐厅
8 Yuèhuá Bīnguăn
悦华宾馆
9 Guesthouse for
Diplomatic Missions
外交人员宾馆
10 Kiessling's Restaurant
起士林餐厅

11 Bank of China
中国银行
12 Guóhăi Bīnguăn
国海宾馆
13 Tiĕjiàn
Dùjiàcūn
铁建度假村
14 Biluó Tă
碧螺塔
15 Wànghăi Tíng
望海亭

To the south-west of Bĕidàihé is Nándàihé, an up-and-coming resort that is already starting to look tacky. It lacks the seaside resort atmosphere of its older cousin, and there's really no reason to visit.

Places to Stay

Many places are open for business only during the brief summer season (May to Octo-

ber), and many cheaper hotels do not accept foreigners.

Although newer, splashier hotels have sprung up around town, the **Guesthouse for Diplomatic Missions** (*Wàijiāo Rényuán Bīnguăn*; ☎ 404 1287, 6532 4336 in Bĕijīng, 1 Baosanlu) is still the most appealing place to stay. You can actually relax outdoors here – the guesthouse has its own small but private beach and some of the rooms have outdoor porches. In the high season the place can get pretty boisterous, with fellow guests playing mahjong or blaring their TV late into the night. At the moment the cheapest rooms are Y300 in July and August, and Y200 in May, June, September and October (it's closed the rest of the year). Standard rooms with a porch are Y550 in the low season and Y720 in the high season.

Right in town is the *Friendship Hotel* (*Yǒuyì Jiǔdiàn Bīnguǎn;* ☎ *404 1613),* where small but clean and comfortable rooms are Y260. Next door is the *Friendship Restaurant,* which serves a tasty traditional Chinese breakfast.

The newish *Zhōnghǎitān Bīnguǎn (Central Beach Hotel;* ☎ *404 1445 ext 1002)* is a fairly nondescript hotel enclosed within a wall with guarded gates. Clean, recently renovated doubles range from Y420 to Y680.

Smack in the centre of town is the *Yuèhuá Bīnguǎn* (☎ *404 0470, 100 Dongjing Lu),* one of Bĕidàihé's newest top-end hotels. Standard doubles start at Y450. Bĕidàihé's most upmarket hotel is the *Guóhǎi Bīnguǎn* (☎ *409 8500, 154 Dongjing Lu),* opposite the beach, where doubles start at Y680. The rooms have balconies and the hotel's facilities include a tennis court. Next door is yet another top-end hotel, the *Tièjiàn Dùjiàcūn* (☎ *335 5590),* where characterless but clean and modern doubles start at Y480.

Few foreigners stay in Nándàihé, although the cheapest rooms around can be found at the *Nándàihé Yǒuyì Bīnguǎn (Nándàihé Friendship Hotel;* ☎ *405 1091, 12 Youyi Lu).* This little hotel has dorm beds in slightly drab triple rooms for Y15. The *Nándàihé Bīnguǎn* (☎ *405 0160, 8 Guangming Lu)* is a supposedly upmarket hotel that's actually nothing special, although it's one of the few hotels in the area that accepts foreigners. Standard rooms start at Y440.

Places to Eat

A whole string of seafood restaurants are along Bao Erlu, near the beach. You won't have to look for them, as the persistent restaurant owners will be looking for you. You can choose your meal from the wide variety of mysterious sea creatures kept alive in buckets in front of most restaurants.

Near the Wàijiāo Rényuán Bīnguǎn is *Kiessling's Restaurant (Qìshìlín Cāntīng),* a relative of the Tiānjīn branch, which only operates from June to August. It serves both Chinese and international food (although there's no English menu) and has some pleasant outdoor seating. On Saturday evening the *Wàijiāo Rényuán Bīnguǎn* has an outdoor barbecue starting at 6.30 pm, where you can dine on all sorts of roasted beasts for Y18 per serve.

QÍNHUÁNGDĂO 秦皇岛
pop 2,618,700

Qínhuángdăo is a teeming port city with few tourist attractions. Compared to neighbouring Shānhǎiguān and Bĕidàihé, which have a tourist-town feel, Qínhuángdăo is a thriving commercial city, complete with shopping centres and even a McDonald's. It has an ice-free harbour.

Water pollution makes this beach *not* the place to get your feet wet. The locals will be the first to suggest that you move along to Bĕidàihé or Shānhǎiguān.

SHĀNHǍIGUĀN 山海关
Shānhǎiguān is where the Great Wall meets the sea. In the 1980s this part of the wall had nearly returned to dust, but it has been rebuilt and is now a first-rate tourist drawcard. On summer weekends there are throngs of camera-clicking Bĕijīng residents, but things are much mellower during the winter months. The scenic hills to the north offer a possible refuge from the chaos.

Shānhǎiguān was a garrison town with a square fortress, four gates at the compass points an d two major avenues running between the gates. The present village is within the substantial remains of the old walled enclosure. Just 10 years ago, Shānhǎiguān was a city of considerable charm, with narrow *hútòngs* (narrow alleyways) and traditional Chinese houses enclosed within the city walls. Although there are still a few remnants of the old city, much of it was been replaced with functional brick and tile structures or uninspired imitations of the old style. However, within the city walls pedestrians still outnumber cars, which makes it a pleasant place to stroll around.

The Wall

There are three places to walk on the wall in the Shānhăiguān vicinity. Unfortunately, if you've come here hoping to do some lonely walks along less visited parts of the wall you'll be disappointed – the wall here has either been completely rebuilt and turned into a carnival-like tourist attraction or has virtually crumbled away. It is possible to walk on some unrenovated parts of the wall, although you'd have to drive two hours north-east of the city.

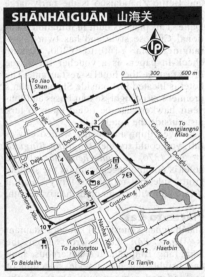

Tiānxià Dìyī Guān 天下第一关 (First Pass Under Heaven) Also known as the Dōng Mén (East Gate), this Ming dynasty grand structure is topped with a two storey, double-roofed tower and was rebuilt in 1639.

The calligraphy at the top (attributed to the scholar Xiao Xian) reads 'First Pass Under Heaven'. The words reflect the Chinese custom of dividing the world into civilised China and the 'barbarians'. The barbarians got the better of civilised China when they stormed this gate in 1644.

A Y20 ticket buys you admission to the top of the wall, and from this vantage point you can see decayed sections trailing off into the mountains. At the watchtower there are souvenir shops selling handkerchiefs, and a parked camel waiting for photos. How about a pair of 'Wooden Chopsticks' or some 'Brave Lucky Jewellery'?

Across the street the **Chángchéng Bówùguăn** (Great Wall Museum) displays armour, dress, weaponry and photographs.

Lăolóngtóu 老龙头 (Old Dragon Head) This is where the Great Wall meets the sea. What you see now was reconstructed in the late 1980s – the original wall has long since crumbled away. The name is derived from the legendary carved dragon head that once faced the ocean.

There are beaches on either side of the wall where you can swim and there's also an amusement park. It's 4km south of Shānhăiguān, catch bus No 23 from the South Gate; admission is Y30.

Jiāo Shān (Horned Hill) A half-hour walk (3km) outside the North Gate brings you to

SHĀNHĂIGUĀN

1 Bĕijiē Zhāodàisuŏ
   北街招待所
2 Jīngshān
   Bīnguăn
   京山宾馆
3 Tiānxià Dìyī Guān
   天下第一关
4 Street Market
   南大商业街

5 Chángchéng
   Bówùguăn
   长城博物馆
6 Jīguān Zhāodàisuŏ
   机关招待所
7 Bank of China
   中国银行
8 Post Office
   邮局

9 Yùfáng Xiăochī
   裕丰小吃
10 Wàng Yàn Lóu
   Fàndiàn
   望雁楼饭店
11 Dōngfāng Bīnguăn
   东方宾馆
12 Train Station
   火车站

HÉBĔI 河北

yet another section of the Great Wall that has been rebuilt. Jiăo Shān is where the Great Wall passes over its first high peak. It's a steep climb from the bottom, or you can take the chairlift that deposits you about a 10-minute walk west of the wall. The Qixian Monastery, said to have once served as a retreat for scholars, is also in the area. Admission to the hill and monastery is Y5.

Yànsāi Hú
Yansai Lake
Just 6km to the north-west of Shānhăiguān, the lake is also known as Shíhé Shuĭkù (Stone River Reservoir). The reservoir is 4km to 5km long and boat trips are available for tourists.

Mèngjiāngnǚ Miào 孟姜女庙
Mengjiangnu Temple
Mèngjiāngnǚ Miào is a Song-Ming reconstruction 6 km east of Shānhăiguān (with regular buses from the South Gate). It has coloured sculptures of Lady Meng and her maids and calligraphy on Looking for Husband Rock. The story is famous in China:

Meng's husband, Wan, was press-ganged into wall building because his views conflicted with those of Emperor Qin Shihuang. When winter came the beautiful Meng Jiang set off to take her husband warm clothing, only to discover that he had died from the backbreaking labour. Meng tearfully wandered the Great Wall, thinking only of finding Wan's bones to give him a decent burial. The wall, a sensitive soul, was so upset that it collapsed, revealing the skeleton entombed within. Overcome with grief, Meng hurled herself into the sea from a conveniently placed boulder.

Chángshòu Shān 长寿山
Longevity Mountain
This area has interesting rock formations and potential as a nice place for a hike. However, as with other Shānhăiguān sights, it's been transformed into a tourist spectacle with stone statues carved into rock faces and concrete paths herding tourists around the various rock formations. It's 9km northeast of Shānhăiguān; take bus No 26 from the South Gate.

Places to Stay
Within Shānhăiguān's hútòngs are a couple fine places to stay. The newly opened *Jīguān Zhāodàisuǒ (Official Hotel; ☎ 505 4888, 17 Dongxi Tiao)* is in a large courtyard house located down a quiet hútòng. Doubles with common bath are Y100 or Y130 with bath. During the high season this place fills up, so try to call ahead. Similarly atmospheric, although run down, is the *Běijiē Zhāodàisuǒ (☎ 505 1680, 2 Mujia Hutong)*. Twins cost Y100, but if you ask for a dormitory the staff will put you in with another traveller at Y50 per bed.

More upmarket but somewhat lacking in the quiet charm of the Jīguān Zhāodàisuǒ and Běijiē Zhāodàisuǒ is the fairly large *Jīngshān Bīnguǎn (☎ 505 1130)*, on Dong Dajie. This place is built in imitation traditional Chinese style and has twin rooms ranging from Y140 to Y300. Among check-in papers is a voucher for a free breakfast at the hotel's restaurant. The hotel is located just outside Shānhăiguān's premier tourist sight, so tour buses and souvenir hawkers can be relied upon to lurk just outside the hotel.

If everything inside the walled city is full, you could try the *Dōngfāng Bīnguǎn (☎ 505 1376, 33 Guancheng Nanlu)*. The hotel is nothing special and on the slightly grotty side, but rooms are fairly cheap at Y45/Y160 with common bath/private bath.

Places to Eat
Shānhăiguān's most well known restaurant is *Wàng Yàn Lóu*, across from the Dōngfāng Bīnguǎn. It's cavernous, loud and bright, but has a wide selection of seafood and a menu with photos of the dishes. A few doors in from the South Gate on Nan Dajie, *Yùfāng Xiăochī* serves delicious jiaozi.

Getting There & Away
Air Qínhuángdǎo's little airport offers flights to:

Cháoyáng (three per week), Dàlián (four), Nánjīng (two), Shànghǎi (two), Tàiyuán (two) and Yāntái (three)

Train The three train stations of Běidàihé, Qínhuángdǎo and Shānhǎiguān are accessible from Běijīng, Tiānjīn or Shěnyáng (Liáoníng). The trains are frequent, but don't always stop at all three stations or always arrive at convenient hours.

One factor to consider is that the hotels at Shānhǎiguān are within walking distance of the train station, whereas at Běidàihé the nearest hotel is at least 10km from the station. This is no problem if you arrive during daylight or early evening – there are plenty of minibuses meeting incoming trains at Běidàihé train station. However, you can't count on this at night and a taxi could be quite expensive. If you're going to arrive in the dead of night, it's better to do so at Shānhǎiguān.

The fastest trains take three hours to Běidàihé from Běijīng, and an extra hour to Shānhǎiguān. From Shěnyáng to Shānhǎiguān is a five hour trip. Tiānjīn is three to four hours away.

Alternatively, you could get a train that stops at Qínhuángdǎo and then take a minibus from there to Běidàihé or Shānhǎiguān.

Bus Although there are long-distance buses between Běidàihé, Qínhuángdǎo and Shānhǎiguān and Běijīng, most travellers go by train. You can take a direct bus from Chéngdé to Qínhuángdǎo (Y60; seven hours).

Boat Passenger boats leave from the port in Qínhuángdǎo to Dàlián every even-numbered day at 6 pm, arriving in Dàlián at 7 am. Fares range from Y100 to Y629, depending on how fancy a cabin you want.

Getting Around

Bus Minibuses are fast and cheap and can be flagged down easily. At the Běidàihé train station you'll be greeted by numerous screaming minibus drivers. Look for one that screams 'haibin' (the beach). To be more specific, tell him you want to get off at the Běidàihé bus station (Hǎibīn qìchē zhàn). The fare varies, but should be around Y3. Watch out for the minibus drivers who like to drop foreigners off at the front door of their hotel for an extra Y20 or so – the regular fare is Y3, so you're paying an extra Y17 to go one more block. Other drivers may take you to a hotel you didn't want in the hope of getting a commission from the hotel owners.

On all other minibuses, the fare is Y2. The main routes are Běidàihé bus station to Qínhuángdǎo train station, and Qínhuángdǎo train station to Shānhǎiguān.

Buses connect Běidàihé, Shānhǎiguān and Qinhuangdao. These generally run every 30 minutes from around 6 or 6.30 am to around 6.30 pm (not guaranteed after 6 pm). Some of the useful public bus routes are:

No 5 Běidàihé train station to Běidàihé Zhōngdàihe Hǎitān (½ hour)

Nos 3 & 4 Běidàihé to Qínhuángdǎo (¾ hour), then to Shānhǎiguān (another ¼ hour)

Nándàihé is a little harder to reach, but bus Nos 5 and 22 go there from the Běidàihé bus station.

Motor-Tricycles These are popular in Shānhǎiguān. It's Y2 to anywhere within town.

Bicycle Shānhǎiguān and Běidàihé are good places to explore by bike. Ask at your hotel about bike-rental outlets; if nothing else, someone on the hotel staff may rent you their own bike.

HÉBĚI 河北

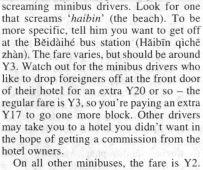

Shāndōng 山东

Across the Yellow Sea from South Korea, Shāndōng has a history that can be traced back to the origins of the Chinese state: Confucius, China's great social philosopher, was born here and lived out his days in Lu, one of the small states in the south of today's province (the Chinese character for Lu is still associated with Shāndōng). His ideas were further championed by the great Confucian philosopher Mencius, who hailed from the same region.

From the earliest record of civilisation in the province (furnished by the black pottery remains of the Lóngshān culture), Shāndōng has had a tumultuous history. It was victim to the capricious temperament of the oft-flooding Huáng Hé (Yellow River), which finishes its long journey from tributaries in Qīnghǎi here, emptying into the Bó Hǎi (Bo Sea). The consequences included mass death, starvation and a ruined provincial economy. In more recent years, Shāndōng has suffered the humiliation of foreign encroachment upon its territory.

In 1899 the Huáng Hé (also aptly named 'China's Sorrow') flooded the entire Shāndōng plain; a sad irony in view of the two scorching droughts that had swept the area that same year and the year before. The flood followed a long period of economic depression, a sudden influx of demobilised troops in 1895 after China's humiliating defeat by Japan in Korea, and droves of refugees from the south moving north to escape famines, floods and drought.

To top it all off, the Europeans arrived with their peculiar ways (Qīngdǎo was snatched by the Germans, and the British obtained a lease for Wēihǎi). Their activities included the building of railroads and some feverish missionary work, which the Chinese believed angered the gods and spirits and meddled with the sacred laws of feng shui.

All this created a perfect breeding ground for rebellion, and in the closing years of the 19th century the Boxers arose out of Shāndōng, armed with magical spells and

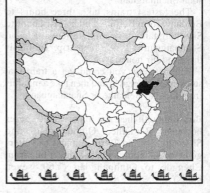

broadswords, which they thought would protect them from the west's hail of bullets.

The port of Qīngdǎo fell into the clutches of the Germans in 1898; the Germans added an industrial infrastructure, cobbled streets and Bavarian architecture. This development still gives Qīngdǎo an economic momentum. Today, Jǐ'nán, the provincial capital, plays second fiddle to Qīngdǎo's tune. Other economic foci in the province include Shengli Oilfield, which is China's second-largest producer of oil. By 1994 Shāndōng was ranked among the top four provincial economies in China (alongside Guǎngdōng, Jiāngsū and Sìchuān).

The sights of Qūfù and Tài Shān, the most revered of China's sacred mountains,

SHĀNDŌNG 山东

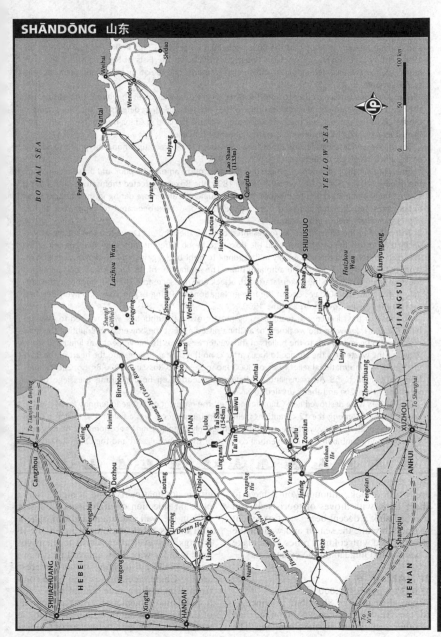

SHĀNDŌNG 山东

BO HAI SEA

YELLOW SEA

The Fists of Righteousness & Harmony

The popular movement known as the Boxer Rebellion erupted in China in the last few years of the 19th century. The Boxers, or Yihetuan (loosely translated as the Fists of Righteousness and Harmony), were a loose confederation of anti-foreign elements that took their beliefs and practices from secret societies.

Many reasons fused together to spur the Boxers on to the massacres they were to perform. The strongest was resentment of foreigners due to the recent humiliating defeats for the Qing court at the hands of the powers, but there was also the scramble for land in China by the 'barbarians', and the general dislike of Christian missionaries and their practices.

There was a widespread feeling that China was about to be sliced up among the powers and Chinese culture trampled underfoot.

Emerging initially in Shāndōng, where they found support among the poor and those reeling from the flooding of the Huáng Hé (Yellow River) in 1899, the Boxers protected themselves with charms, superstitions and martial arts techniques. They gradually became more daring in their attacks upon missionaries and their families, and eventually espoused a creed dedicated to wiping out all foreigners, or 'hairy men' (and women).

The policy of the Qing court (as represented by Cixi, the Empress Dowager) toward the Boxers vacillated. At first the court considered the Boxers to be no different from the usual peasant uprisings, but later viewed them as an ally in its agenda to fight back against the foreign powers and restore the integrity of the Manchu administration. The aspirations of the Qing court soon paralleled those of the rebels when the Boxers started to attack and massacre foreigners at random in the capital, and the famous 50-day siege of the foreign legations in Běijīng began. Cixi effectively declared war on the foreign powers on 21 June 1900.

The folly of this alliance was recognised by most provincial authorities, who refused to rally behind the court, knowing the weakness of a China pitted against the powers and doubting the Boxers claims to be impervious to the bullets of the westerners. Thus the movement was limited in scale, allowing the westerners the chance to focus attacks on the capital, Běijīng, and the heart of the Boxers' cause. An international relief force of 8000 Japanese, 4800 Russians, 3000 British, 2100 Americans, 800 French, 58 Austrians and 53 Italians descended on Běijīng, lifting the siege of the legations, while Cixi and the court fled to Xī'ān.

The Boxers were destroyed and China found itself the recipient of a huge indemnity known as the Boxer Protocol. Among the 12 conditions included in the protocol was a bill of 450 million taels of gold (to be paid off yearly with interest), which effectively crippled China's economy for many years. This indemnity contributed to the eventual collapse of the Manchu court and the Qing dynasty.

are worth a look, although you'll have to share them with droves of tourists. If you want to sink a decent beer, scoff excellent seafood, breathe the sea air and wander the streets filled with colonial relics, then make a beeline to Qīngdǎo on the coast.

JǏ'NÁN 济南
☎ 0531 • pop 5,492,000

Jǐ'nán, the capital of Shāndōng province, is for most travellers a transit point on the road to other destinations around Shāndōng. The city is not unattractive and at night offers a pleasant selection of night markets, lights, hole-in-the-wall restaurants and atmosphere.

Jǐ'nán is most commonly noted for its springs, however after a visit to them you may wonder why. Downplayed in Jǐ'nán's tourist pitch, but perhaps of more interest, are the Chinese celebrities who have come from Jǐ'nán. Bian Que, founder of traditional Chinese medicine, Zou Yan, founder of the Yin and Yang five element school, as well as Zhou Yongnian, founder of Chinese public libraries, all herald from these parts. In addition, Jǐ'nán has been home to a great number of nationally and internationally recognised writers.

The area has been inhabited for at least 4000 years, and some of the earliest reminders of this are the eggshell-thin pieces of black pottery unearthed in the town of Lóngshān, 30km east of Jǐ'nán. These provide the first link in an unbroken chain of tradition and artistic endeavour that culminated in the beautifully crafted ceramics of later dynasties.

Modern development in Jǐ'nán stems from 1899, when construction of the Jǐ'nán to Qīngdǎo railway line began. When completed in 1904, the line gave the city a major communications role. The Germans had a concession near the train station after Jǐ'nán was opened up to foreign trade in 1906. The huge German building on Jing Yilu opposite the Shāndōng Bīnguǎn now houses a railway sub-office; it is made of the same stone, and in the same style, as much of the architecture in Qīngdǎo.

Information

Money The Bank of China is at 22 Luoyuan Jie, south of Hēihǔ Quán (Black Tiger Spring). There are exchange services available at many of the top-end hotels.

Post & Communications The post office can be found on the corner of Jing Erlu and Wei Erlu. China Telecom is located on Gongqingtuan Lu, west of Wǔlóng Chí and Bàotū Quán (see the Springs section later). You can only make telephone calls from this branch.

China Telecom also offers Internet access on the 5th storey of the Silver Plaza on Luoyuan Jie. Access is Y5 per hour for students (no ID required!) and Y10 for others. Opening hours are from 9 am to 9pm.

Travel Agencies There is a branch of China International Travel Service (CITS; Zhōngguó Guójì Lǚxíngshè; ☎ 260 0777) at 102 Jing Shilu, near the Botanical Gardens. The China Travel Service (CTS; Zhōngguó Lǚxíngshè; ☎ 296 7401, fax 296 5261) at 9

Qianfoshan Dong Erlu is inconveniently located east of the Shāndōng Shěng Bówùguǎn (see later); however the staff are extremely helpful. Head to the Hong Kong and Macau office on the 2nd floor for English-speaking staff. To reach the office take bus No 51 to Jing Shilu and then transfer to bus No 68.

PSB The Public Security Bureau (PSB; Gōngānjú) is in a white-tiled building on the east corner of Jing Sanlu and Wei Wulu.

Qiānfó Shān
Thousand Buddha Mountain

The statues here were disfigured or disappeared during the Cultural Revolution, but new ones are gradually being added. There's also a grotto with copies of the four famous Buddhist caves of China; entry costs Y15.

A cable car can take you to the top of the mountain for a further Y18 (return). Qiānfó Shān is on the south side of town; entry is Y10. Bus No 51 from the train station goes there as do bus Nos 2, 31 and 68 from the city centre – get off at Qianfoshan Lu.

Shāndōng Shěng Bówùguǎn
山东省博物馆
Shandong Provincial Museum

The museum is next door to Qiānfó Shān. Its displays give you a quick overview of the history of Shāndōng, as well as a taste of some local art. There is also an interesting exhibit of musical instruments. The museum is open from 8 to 11 am and from 2 to 5 pm. Admission is Y20.

Dàmíng Hú 大明湖
Big Brilliant Lake

The park surrounding this lake has small temples, gardens, an amusement park and, for military aircraft enthusiasts, the preserved shell of a MiG fighter. Otherwise the lake is populated by tour groups.

You can enter the park at three points: in the north-east, the south-west or at the southern end, off Daminghu Lu. The southern end of the park is connected to the rest of the park by small ferry boats (Y3). Entry to the park costs Y12.

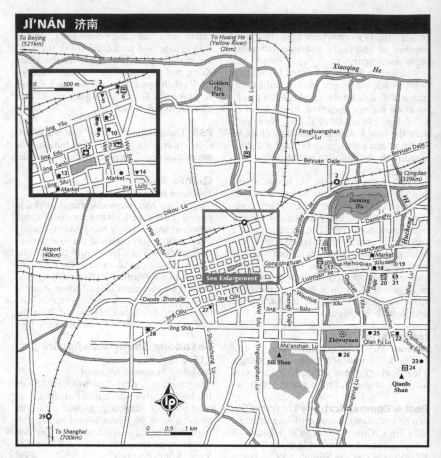

JǏ'NÁN 济南

To Beijing (521km)

To Huang He (Yellow River) (2km)

Xiaoqing He

Golden Ox Park

500 m

3

4

6

Fenghuangshan Lu

Jing Yilu

7

8

9

10

Beiyuan Dajie

Beiyuan Dajie

To Qingdao (339km)

Jing Erlu

12

Wei Erlu

Wei Sanlu

2

Daming Hu

Daminghu Lu

Hucheng He

Jing Sanlu

Jing Silu

13

14

Market

Market

Jing Liulu

Xishunhe Jie

Quancheng Lu

Market

Dikou Lu

Wei Shi'erlu

1

15

Heihuquan Xilu

19

Airport (40km)

Gongqingtuan Lu

16

17

18

See Enlargement

Luoyuan Jie

20

21

Daode Zhongjie

Jing Qilu

Shengli Dajie

Wenhua

27

Xilu

Lishan Lu

Jing Qilu

Wei Erlu

Jing

Balu

Qiantang Lu

Jing Shilu

Shuninchang Lu

Yingxiongshan Lu

Shengeng Lu

Ma'anshan Lu

Zhiwuyuan

Qian Fu Lu

Qianfoshan Dong Lu

28

25

23

24

Sili Shan

26

Qianfo Shan

29

To Shanghai (700km)

0   0.5   1 km

Springs

Jǐ'nán's 100-plus springs are often quoted as the main attraction of the city, but, before you jump in a cab, be warned that the only time they display any vestige of activity is during the rainy season in August.

The three main springs are **Wǔlóng Chí** (Five Dragon Pool), **Bàotū Quán** (Gushing-from-the-Ground Spring) and **Hēihǔ Quán** (Black Tiger Spring). During the rainy season, Hēihǔ Quán is a popular source of 'clean' water. All three are within walking distance of each other, south of Dàmíng Hú, in the centre of the city.

Lǐ Qīngzhào Cí 李清照祠
Hall to Commemorate Li Qingzhao

A native of Jǐ'nán, Li Qingzhao remains a popular cult figure in Chinese literary circles; she is seen as the most significant and definitely the most famous female poet of the Song dynasty (see the boxed text 'The Song Poet').

The hall, next to Bàotū Quán (Gushing-from-the-Ground Spring), was built in 1956 in a style that emulates traditional Chinese architecture. Around the courtyard there are halls that contain portraits of Li Qingzhao and extracts of her work.

JǏ'NÁN

PLACES TO STAY
4 Jǐ'nán Tiělǔ Dàshā
Jiǔdiàn
济南铁路大厦酒店
7 Guìdū Dàjiǔdiàn
贵都大酒店
8 Shāndōng Bīnguǎn
山东宾馆
9 Shāndōng
Lóngqiāntán
Jiǔdiàn
山东龙千潭酒店
10 Xíxíjū Jiēdàichù
习习居接待处
13 Jǐ'nán Fàndiàn
济南饭店
18 Quánchéng
Dàfàndiàn
泉城饭店
22 Qílǔ Bīnguǎn
齐鲁宾馆、
26 Nánjiāo Bīnguǎn
南郊宾馆

PLACES TO EAT
5 Tiānlóng Kuàicān
天龙快餐

14 Jùfēngdé
Fàndiàn
聚丰德饭店
27 Yuèdū Jiǔlóu
粤都酒楼

OTHER
1 Long-Distance
Bus Station
长途汽车站
2 East Train Station
火车东站
3 Jǐ'nán Train
Station
济南火车站
6 Tiānqiáo Bus
Station
天桥汽车站
11 Main Post
Office
邮局
12 PSB
公安局外事科
15 Wǔlóng Chí
五龙潭公园
16 Telecom
中国电信

17 Bàotū Quán ;
CAAC;
LT Qīngzhào Cí
趵突
中国民航
清照祠
19 Hēihǔ Quán
黑虎泉
20 Silver Plaza
(Internet)
网吧
21 Bank of China
中国银行
23 CTS
中国旅行社
24 Shāndōng Shěng
Bówùguǎn
山东省博物馆
25 CITS;
Shandong Airlines
中国国际旅行社；
山东航空公司
28 China Eastern
Airlines
东方航空公司
29 Jǐ'nan South Train Station
济南南站

Places to Stay

Just a stone's throw from the Jǐ'nán train station is the **Shāndōng Bīnguǎn** (☎ 692 5881, fax 691 0797), a cheap place with doubles for Y150 to Y160.

South of the Shāndōng Bīnguǎn is the newly opened **Shāndōng Lòngqiāntán Jiǔdiàn** (☎ 605 7777, fax 605 5678, 11 Wei Sanlu). Doubles cost Y180 to Y280.

Across the street is the **Xíxíjū Jiēdàichǔ** (☎ 605 7886), with doubles starting at Y168.

Looking like an asylum from Victorian England is the **Jǐ'nán Fàndiàn** (☎ 793 8981, 240 Jing Silu), half a block west of Wei Liulu on Jing Silu. The reception is in the building to your far right as you enter through the gate. Double rooms cost Y288.

North of the public square of the Jǐ'nán train station is the **Jǐ'nán Tiělǔ Dàshà Jiǔdiàn** (Jǐ'nán Railway Hotel; ☎ 601 2118, fax 601 2188), a three-star option. Doubles cost Y280 to Y680.

Also close to the train station is the **Guìdū Dàjiǔdiàn** (☎ 690 0888, fax 690 0999, 1 Shengping Lu). Double rooms cost from Y278 to Y498.

The plush **Nánjiāo Bīnguǎn** (☎ 295 3931, fax 295 3957, 2 Ma'anshan Lu), to the south of the Botanical Gardens, has singles/doubles for Y310/380 and suites from Y480 to Y680. The hotel was, so the story goes, constructed for an impending visit by Mao, who then decided to skip Jǐ'nán.

Surrounded by the parched springs of Jǐ'nán is the **Quánchéng Dàfàndiàn** (☎ 692 1911, fax 692 3187, 2 Nanmen Dajie), which is a three-star hotel with standard facilities. Doubles start at Y380 and deluxe suites cost Y650.

Next to the Qiānfóshān is the **Qílǔ Bīnguǎn** (☎ 296 6888, fax 296 7676, 8

SHĀNDŌNG 山东

The Song Poet

Li Qingzhao is famed for her elegant language, strong imagery and, perhaps most importantly, her ability to remain unpretentious in her poetry. Only 70 of Li's poems have survived despite the fact that she wrote continuously throughout her lifetime. As the most celebrated female poet of the Song dynasty, she has a large following of literary buffs, especially in her hometown of Jǐ'nán.

Born in 1084 into the privileged world of a scholar's family, Li Qingzhao was able to cultivate her love for poetry from a young age. Her early poems are characterised by her carefree leisure and love for beauty and life.

In 1126 Li's life changed dramatically. Having fled with her family from the advancing Jin army, and with the death of her husband at the same time, Li was forced to leave her life of luxury behind. Although her writing becomes dark and melancholy, it was during this period that she created some of her most powerful poetry.

Alone in the Night
    The warm rain and pure wind
    Have just freed the willows from
    The ice. As I watch the peach trees,
    Spring rises from my heart and blooms on
    My cheeks. My mind is unsteady,
    As if I were drunk. I try
    To write a poem in which
    My tears will flow together
    With your tears. My rouge is stale.
    My hairpins are too heavy.
    I throw myself across my
    Gold cushions, wrapped in my lonely
    Doubled quilt, and crush the phoenixes
    In my headdress. Alone, deep
    In bitter loneliness, without
    Even a good dream, I lie,
    Trimming the lamp in the passing night.

Qianfoshan Lu), the prime tourist hotel in town. Doubles start at Y580 and suites at Y980. You can reach the hotel by bus No 51 from the Jǐ'nán train station.

Places to Eat

Jǐ'nán is swamped with restaurants. The area around the Jǐ'nán train station is the best place to seek out cheap eats – it's dotted with bargain places selling Shāndōng and Sìchuān food. Chinese fast food can be found directly opposite the train station at the *Tiānlóng Kuàicān*; a meal for two can cost as little as Y12. Try the *guōtiē* (fried dumplings).

Decent Cantonese cuisine is served at the *Yuèdū Jiǔlóu*, at the south-eastern intersection of Jing Qilu and Wei Balu. You can choose from plates of prepared but uncooked food, which are arranged on chilled shelves. You know what you are getting and the food is good. A similar Shāndōng-style restaurant can be found at the *Shāndōng Lòngqiāntàn Jiǔdiàn*.

Good Beijing duck and a range of Shāndōng cuisine can be had at *Jùfēngdé Fàndiàn*, at the intersection of Jing Wulu and Wei Erlu. For pizza and seafood at reasonable prices, try the *Guìdū Dàjiǔdiàn*.

There are a number of *markets* in Jǐ'nán where you can fill up on kebabs for around Y5. Try the alley off Jing Wulu, between Wei Erlu and Wei Sanlu. Also head down Wei Qilu or Nanmen Dajie off Quancheng Lu. The main shopping drag, Quancheng Lu, is also lined with restaurants of every size and description.

International-style *bars*, *cafes* and *restaurants* are opening on Qianfoshan Lu, leading up to Qiānfó Shān. Expect to pay international-style prices.

Getting There & Away

Air There are three flights a week (Sunday, Tuesday and Friday) between Hong Kong and Jǐ'nán (Y2550). Domestic flights are available between Jǐ'nán and all major Chinese cities. Destinations include Běijīng (Y500; daily), Shànghǎi (Y610; daily) and Guǎngzhōu (Y1270; daily).

An office of the Civil Aviation Administration of China (CAAC; Zhōngguó Mínháng; ☎ 601 8145) is opposite the southern entrance to Bàotū Quán on Luoyuan Jie. China Eastern Airlines (☎ 796 4445, 796 6824) is at 408 Jing Shilu. Both offices sell the same tickets. The Shandong Airlines booking office is in the same office as CITS and you'll find China Southwest Airlines (☎ 691 1082) in the Quánchéng Dàjiǔdiàn. Larger hotels can also supply airline tickets.

Bus Jǐ'nán has at least three bus stations. The main long-distance bus station (chángtú qìchē zhàn) in the north of town has buses to Běijīng and Qīngdǎo (Y50; five hours). The Tiānqiáo bus station (tiānqiáo qìchē zhàn) is next door to the main train station and has minibuses to Tài'ān (Y10; 1½ hours). Minibuses to Tài'ān also depart from the huge parking lot in front of the train station. There is another minibus station in front of the east train station (huǒchē dōngzhàn) for minibuses to Qūfù and the rural areas near Jǐ'nán.

Train Be aware that there are two train stations in Jǐ'nán: most trains use the main train station (jǐ'nán huǒchē zhàn), but a handful arrive and depart from the east train station (huǒchē dōngzhàn).

Jǐ'nán is a major link in the east China rail system. From Jǐ'nán there are direct trains to Běijīng (nine hours) and Shànghǎi. Trains heading south pass through nearby Tài'ān (1¼ hours). Direct trains go to Chángchūn (Y102) in Jílín and to Qīngdǎo (Y31), Yāntái (Y38) and Tiānjīn. Other destinations include Hángzhōu and Hāěrbīn (Y95). There are also direct Qīngdǎo-Jǐ'nán-Xī'ān-Xīníng trains.

Getting Around
To/From the Airport Flights depart from the Xijiao airport, 40km west of the city – a new freeway makes it possible to cover the distance in just 40 minutes. You can catch an airport bus from the CAAC ticket office. A taxi will cost around Y130.

Bus & Taxi Bus No 4 connects the long-distance bus station with the main train station. Bus No 51 runs from the main train station, through the centre of town and then south past Bàotū Quán to Qiānfó Shān. Bus No 11 will take you from the train station to Dàmíng Hú. Taxis cost Y6 for the first 3km.

AROUND JǏ'NÁN
Sìmén Tǎ 四门塔
Four Gate Pagoda
Near the village of Liubu, 33km south-east of Jǐ'nán, are some of the oldest Buddhist structures in Shāndōng. Shentong Monastery holds the Sìméntǎ, which dates back to the 6th century and is possibly the oldest stone pagoda in China.

The **Lónghǔ Tǎ** (Pagoda of the Dragon and the Tiger) was built during the Tang dynasty. It stands close to the Shentong Monastery and is surrounded by stupas. Higher up is the **Qiānfó Yá** (Thousand Buddha Cliff), which displays carved grottoes containing buddhas.

To reach Sìmén Tǎ, catch bus No 22 from Daguanyuan Lu and Jingsu Lu. CTS can also arrange tours.

TÀI SHĀN 泰山
Southern Chinese say they have 'myriad mountains, rivers and geniuses' while those from Shāndōng retort that they have 'one mountain, one river and one saint', with the implication that they have the last word on each: Tài Shān, the Huáng Hé (Yellow River) and Confucius. Tài Shān is the most revered of the five sacred Taoist mountains of China. Once upon a time, imperial sacrifices to heaven and earth were offered from its summit, although only five of China's many emperors ever climbed Tài Shān: however, Emperor Qianlong of the Qing dynasty scaled it 11 times. From its heights Confucius uttered the dictum 'The world is small'; Mao lumbered up and commented 'The East is Red'. You too can climb up and say 'I'm knackered'.

Today the mountain is a victim of its popularity: pilgrims run the gauntlet of hoarse T-shirt and trinket sellers; sections of the mountain echo to the strains of karaoke; devotees fling empty water bottles and film wrappers into the gullies and rivers, festooning the sacred mount with trash. Nevertheless, if you set out early on a weekday morning you will experience a serenity that will make the hike worth it.

Tài Shān is a unique experience – its supernatural allure (legend, religion and history rolled into one) drags in the Chinese in droves. The Princess of the Azure Clouds (Bixia), a Taoist deity whose presence permeates the temples dotted along the route, is a powerful cult figure for the rural women of Shāndōng and beyond. Tribes of wiry grandmothers trot up the steps with surprising ease, their target the cluster of temples at the summit where they burn money and incense, praying for their progeny (and their blisters). It's said that if you climb Tài Shān you'll live to be 100, and some of the grandmothers look pretty close to that already! Sun-worshippers – foreign and Chinese – also muster wide-eyed on the peak, straining for the first flickers of dawn. In ancient Chinese tradition, it was believed that the sun began its westward journey from Tài Shān.

Tài Shān is not a major climb, but with 6660 steps to the summit, it can be gruelling. Nevertheless, many porters with callused shoulders and misshapen backs make the journey, plodding ever upwards with crates of drinks, bedding and the occasional Chinese tourist. One wonders how many backs were broken in the building of the temples and stone stairs on Tài Shān – a massive undertaking accomplished without any mechanical aids.

Climate
Bear in mind that weather conditions on the mountain vary considerably compared with Tài'ān. Clouds and mist frequently envelop the mountain, particularly in summer. The best times to visit are in spring and autumn when the humidity is low, although old-timers say that the clearest weather is from early October onwards. In winter the weather is often fine, but very cold. The tourist season peaks from May to October.

On average, there are 16 fine days in spring, eight in summer, 28 in autumn and 35 in winter. Due to weather changes, you're advised to carry warm clothing with you, no matter what the season. The summit can be very cold, windy and wet; army overcoats are available there for rental. If you don't have a waterproof coat, you can buy one (a converted dustbin liner) from one of the ubiquitous vendors.

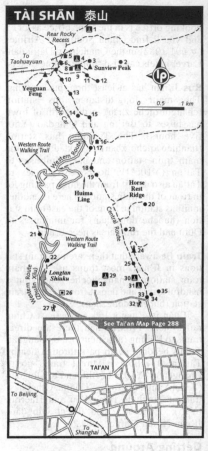

Climbing Tài Shān
The town of Tài'ān lies at the foot of Tài Shān and is the gateway to the mountain (see the Tài'ān section in this chapter). Entry costs Y35 off-season (January, February, November and December) and Y50 the remainder of the year. The admission fee includes Y1 insurance.

On Foot Spending the night on the mountain is possible halfway up at Zhōngtiān Mén (Midway Gate to Heaven) and on the summit. Allow two hours for climbing between each of these points – a total of eight

TÀI SHĀN

PLACES TO STAY

5 Nántiānmén Bīnguǎn
南天门宾馆

6 Xiānjū Fàndiàn
仙居饭店

8 Shénqì Bīnguǎn
神憩宾馆

16 Yùyèquán
Bīnguǎn
玉液泉宾馆

OTHER

1 Hòushí Wù
(Rear Temple)
后石坞

2 Diànshì Tǎ
电视塔

3 Gǒngběi Shí
拱北石

4 Yùhuáng Dǐng; Wúzì Bēi
玉皇顶;
无字碑

7 Nántiān Mén
南天门

9 Bìxiá Cí
碧霞祠

10 Kāixiān Fáng
开仙坊

11 Xiānrù Qiáo
(Bridge of the Gods)
仙人桥

12 Zhānlǔ Tái (Terrace)
占鲁台

13 Duìsōng Tíng ;
Yíngkè Sōng
对松亭 ;
迎客松

14 Wǔsōng Tíng
五松亭

15 Yúnbù Qiáo
(Cloud Bridge)
云步桥

17 Zhōngtiān Mén;
Cable Car
中天门
空中索道

18 Bùtiān Qiáo
(Skywalk Bridge)
步天桥

19 Hútiān Gé
(Pavilion)
壶天阁

20 Jīng Shíshàngǔ
经石山谷

21 Chángshòu Qiáo;
Hēilóng Tán
长寿桥 ;
黑龙潭

22 Ticket Booth
售票处

23 Dǒumǔ Guān
(Hall)
斗母宫

24 Gémìng Lièshì
Jìniànguǎn
(Monument to
Revolutionary Heroes)
革命烈士纪念碑

25 Wànxiān Lóu
(10,000 Immortals Pavilion)
万仙楼

26 Feng Yuxiang Língmù
(Tomb);
Dàzhòng Qiáo
(Everyman's Bridge)
冯玉祥陵墓;大众桥

27 Trailhead for Western
Route
(No 3 Bus West
Station or No 2 Bus)
三路汽车西终点站

28 Pǔzhào Sì
普照寺

29 Jìniàn Sì
纪念寺

30 Hóng Mén
红门

31 Guāndì Miào
关帝庙

32 Trailhead for
Central Route
(No 3 Bus
East Terminal)
三路汽车东终点站

33 Tiānxià Dìyīmén;
Ticket Booth
天下第一门;售票处

34 Yúnmǔ Chí
(Cloud Empress Pool)
云母池

35 Hǔshān Shuǐkù
(Tiger Mountain Reservoir)
虎山水库

hours up and down, at the minimum. Allowing several more hours would make the climb less strenuous and give you more time to look around.

If you want to see the sunrise, then dump your gear at the train station or at a guesthouse in Tài'ān and time your ascent so that you'll reach the summit before sundown. Stay overnight at one of the summit guesthouses and get up early the next morning for the famed sunrise, which may or may not make its appearance. It is possible to scale the mountain at night and some Chinese do this, timing it so that they arrive before sunrise. The way is lit by lamps, but it

is advisable to take a torch, as well as warm clothes, food and water.

There are two main paths up the mountain: the central route and the western route, converging midway at Zhōngtiān Mén. Most people slog up the central route (which used to be the imperial route and is littered with cultural relics) and head down (usually by bus) along the western route. Other trails run through orchards and woods. Tài Shān is 1545m above sea level, with a climbing distance of 7.5km from base to summit on the central route. The elevation change from Zhōngtiān Mén to the summit is approximately 600m. The route is populated by stalls and individuals selling fruit, buns, water, tea eggs, trinkets and so forth.

By Minibus & Cable Car Several times each morning, minibuses run from the Tài'ān train station to Zhōngtiān Mén, halfway up Tài Shān. Frequent buses come down the mountain until 5 pm (Y11); however, as this is the favoured option for getting back to Tài'ān, you may have to wait several buses for a seat.

It's about a five minute walk from Zhōngtiān Mén to the cable car (kōng zhōng suǒ dào), which holds 30 passengers and takes eight minutes to travel from Zhōngtiān Mén to Yùeguān Fēng (Moon View Peak), near Nántiān Mén (South Gate to Heaven). The fare is Y45 up and Y30 down. Be warned, if you climb Tài Shān in the high season or at weekends, the queues here may force you to wait for up to two hours for a cable car. Check the length of the queue first before you buy a ticket, as getting a refund is tricky.

The same applies when you want to descend from the summit; fortunately, there is another, far more efficient cable car (Y40) that only carries six passengers and is as regular as clockwork. It takes you from north of Nántiān Mén down to Taóhūa Yuán (Peach Blossom Park), a scenic area behind Tài Shān that is also well worth exploring. From here you can take a minibus to Tài'ān, which takes about 40 minutes (Y15). You can reverse this process by first taking a minibus from Tài'ān train station to Taóhūa Yuán and then ascending by cable car.

Central Route On this route you'll see a bewildering catalogue of bridges, trees, rivers, gullies, towers, inscriptions, caves, pavilions and temples. Tài Shān, in fact, functions as an outdoor museum of calligraphic art, with the prize items being the **Jīng Shíshāngǔ** (Rock Valley Scripture) along the first section of the walk and the **Gōngbēi Shí** (North Prayer Rock), which commemorates an imperial sacrifice, at the summit. Lost on most foreigners are the literary allusions, word games and analogies spelt out by the characters decorating the journey.

The climb proper begins at **Tiānxià Diyīmén** (No 1 Archway Under Heaven), at the mountain base. Behind that is a stone archway overgrown with wisteria and inscribed 'the place where Confucius began to climb'. **Hóng Mén** (Red Gate Palace), with its wine-coloured walls, is the first of a series of temples dedicated to the Princess of the Azure Clouds, daughter of the god of Tài Shān. Following the temple is **Dǒumǔ Guān**, a hall that was first constructed in 1542 and given the more magical name of 'Dragon Spring Nunnery'.

Continuing through the tunnel of cypresses known as Cypress Cave is **Húimǎ Lǐng**, where Emperor Zhen Zong had to dismount and continue by sedan chair because his horse refused to go further. Another emperor rode a white mule up and down the mountain and the beast died soon after the descent; it was posthumously given the title of general and its tomb is on the mountain.

Zhōngtiān Mén (Midway Gate to Heaven) is the second celestial gate. From here you can look north to the distant stream of the faithful on the final stretch to the summit. A little way on is **Wǔsōng Tíng** (Five Pine Pavilion) where, in 219 BC, Emperor Qin Shihuang was overtaken by a violent storm and was sheltered by the kind pines. He promoted them to the 5th rank of minister.

From here you set out upon **The Path of Eighteen Bends** that will eventually lead you to the summit. En route you'll pass **Dùisōng Tíng** (Opposing Pines Pavilion) and the **Yíngkè Sōng** (Welcoming Pine), with a branch extended as if to shake hands. Beyond that is the **Kāixiān Fáng** (Archway to Immortality). It was believed that those passing through it would become celestial beings. From here to the summit, emperors were carried in sedan chairs – eat your hearts out!

The final leg-wobbling stretch takes you to **Nántiān Mén**, the third celestial gate.

On arrival at the *dàidǐng* (summit) you will see the **Diànshì Tǎ** (Wavelength Pavilion), which is a radio and weather station, and the **Journey to the Stars Gondola** (cable car). If you continue along Paradise Rd, you'll come to **Sunview Peak**.

The march ends at the **Bìxiá Cí** (Azure Clouds Temple), where small offerings of one sort or another are made to a bronze statue, once richly decorated. The iron tiling on the buildings is intended to prevent damage by strong winds, and on the bronze eaves are *chiwen* (ornaments meant to protect against fire). The temple is absolutely splendid, with its location in the clouds, but its guardians are a trifle touchy about you wandering around, and parts of it are inaccessible. The bronze statuette of the Princess of the Azure Clouds is in the main hall.

Perched on the highest point (1545m) of the Tài Shān plateau is **Yùhuáng Dīng** (Jade Emperor Temple), with a bronze statue of a Taoist deity. In the courtyard is a rock inscribed with the elevation of the mountain. In front of the temple is the one piece of calligraphy that you really can appreciate – the **Wúzì Bēi** (Wordless Monument). This one will leave you speechless. One story goes that it was set up by Emperor Wu 2100 years ago – he wasn't satisfied with what his scribes came up with, so he left it to the viewer's imagination.

The main sunrise vantage point is **Gǒngběi Shí**; if you're lucky, visibility extends to over 200km, as far as the coast. The sunset slides over the Huáng Hé (Yellow River) side. At the rear of the mountain is **Rear Rocky Recess**, one of the better known spots for viewing pine trees; there are some ruins tangled in the foliage. It's a good place to ramble and lose the crowds for a while.

Western Route The most popular way to descend the mountain is by bus via the western route. The footpath and road intercept at a number of points and are often one and the same. Given the amount of traffic, you might prefer to hop on a bus rather than inhale its exhaust. If you do hike down, the trail is not always clearly marked. (Note that buses will not stop for you once they have left Zhōngtiān Mén.)

Either by bus or foot, the western route treats you to considerable variation in scenery, with orchards, pools and flowering plants that make traditional Chinese paintings seem incredibly realistic. Along this

route there is nothing to note in the way of structures. The major scenic attraction is **Hēilóng Tán** (Black Dragon Pool), which is just below **Chángshòu Qiáo** (Longevity Bridge) and is fed by a small waterfall. Swimming in the waters are rare, red-scaled carp, which are occasionally cooked for the rich. Mythical tales revolve around this pool, which is said to be the site of underground carp palaces and of magic herbs that turn people into beasts.

An enjoyable way to end the hike is with a visit to the monastery, **Pǔzhào Sì**, founded 1500 years ago along the base of the mountain. Entry to the monastery is Y5.

Places to Stay & Eat

The *Yūyèquán Bīnguǎn (Spring Guesthouse;* ☎ *822 674)* is a halfway house at Zhōngtiān Mén – the only one that accepts foreigners. Rooms are nothing special but cheap at Y50 per person.

The summit of Tài Shān is rapidly turning into a town in its own right with restaurants, shops and hotels. The *Nántiānmén Bīnguǎn (☎ 833 0988, fax 823 5204)* is located in the north-east of the summit, towards Rear Rocky Recess, in a newly developing lane of shops. The hotel has doubles/triples from Y120/140.

The *Xiānjū Fàndiàn (☎ 823 9984, fax 822 6877)*, just to the east of Nántiān Mén, has dorm beds for Y60 per person or doubles with private bath for Y160.

Finally, the *Shénqì Bīnguǎn (☎ 822 3866)* is a three star hotel on the summit with singles/doubles/triples for Y580/680/880. There are also suites for Y6800, which is expensive, but you're paying for the view. The hotel provides extra blankets and rents out People's Liberation Army-style overcoats. There's even an alarm bell that tells you when to get up for sunrise.

If you wonder where all those amazing old women go, it seems that there are lodgings – possibly former monasteries – tucked down side trails. They are off limits to foreigners.

There is no fear of a food shortage on Tài Shān; the central route is dotted with teahouses, stalls, vendors and restaurants. Your pockets are likely to feel emptier than your stomach, but keep in mind that all supplies are carried up by foot and that the prices rise as you do.

TÀI'ĀN 泰安
☎ 0538 • pop 5,328,100

Tài'ān is the gateway town to the sacred Tài Shān, a place most Chinese would like to visit at least once in their lifetime. You'll probably need the better part of a day to take in the mountain, so be prepared to spend the night.

On an incidental note, Tài'ān is the home town of Jiang Qing, Mao's fourth wife, ex-film actor and notorious spearhead of the Gang of Four, on whom all of China's ills are sometimes blamed. She was later airbrushed out of Chinese history and committed suicide in May 1991.

Orientation & Information
The Xinhua Bookstore on Qingnian Lu has a selection of maps covering the areas of Tài'ān and Shāndōng. Street vendors sell numerous Tài Shān maps, none of which are in English.

The main branch of the Bank of China is on Hongmen Lu, north of Dàizōng Archway. The main post office is on Shengping Jie, across the road from the PSB. There is also a post office on Daizong Lu, east of the Tàishān Dàjiǔdiàn (Grand Hotel).

A couple of doors down from the CTS office is an unnamed computer office (☎ 823 6464) that provides Internet access for Y8 per hour. The office claims to be open 24 hours – except when it's closed; call ahead.

The CITS office (☎ 833 6182), 22 Hongmen Lu, is in a compound just north of Dàizōng Archway. The CTS office (☎ 821 1754) at 1145 Hushan Lu, is north off Shenping Jie. Both offices can arrange air and train tickets.

The PSB (☎ 822 4004) is south-west of the Dài Miào on Shengping Jie.

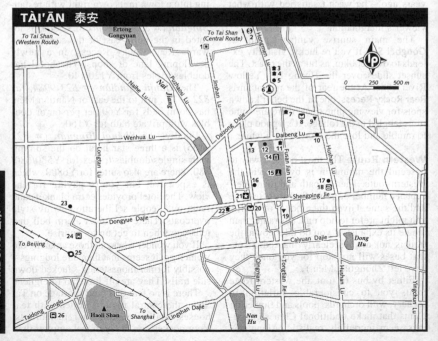

Dài Miào 岱庙

This huge temple complex is in the centre of town, with Tài Shān as a background. Traditionally a pilgrimage stop on the road to the sacred mountain (and a resting spot for hiking emperors), the temple was also the site of huge sacrifices to the god of Tài Shān. The complex covers an area of 96,000 sq metres and is enclosed by high walls. The main hall is the **Tiankuang** (Temple of Heavenly Blessing), dating back to AD 1009. It is some 22m high and is constructed of wood with double-eaved yellow tiling.

The Tiankuang was the first built of the 'big three' halls (the others being Hall of Supreme Harmony at the Forbidden City and Dacheng Hall at Qūfù). The poorly lit interior has a 62m-long fresco running west to east depicting Emperor Zhen Zong as the god of Tài Shān. Zhen Zong 'raised' the god of Tài Shān to a status equal to his own. You'll find a 7m-high stele to celebrate this in the western courtyard.

The fresco has been painstakingly retouched by artisans of succeeding dynasties and, although recently restored, is in poor shape – but a majestic concept nonetheless.

You may also be rewarded with music, dance and theatre in front of the hall.

The temple complex has been repeatedly restored, however in the late 1920s it was stripped of its statues and transformed into offices and shops. Later it suffered damage under the Kuomintang. It now functions as an **open-air museum** with a forest of 200-odd steles. One inscribed stone, originally at the summit of Tài Shān, is believed to be over 2000 years old (Qin dynasty). It can be seen at the Eastern Imperial Hall, along with a small collection of imperial sacrificial vessels.

Around the courtyards are ancient, twisted cypresses, gingkos and acacias. Some of the cypresses appear partially ossified. There is a cypress in front of Tiankuang under which visitors can indulge in a game of luck. A person is blindfolded and made to walk around a rock three times anticlockwise and three times clockwise. They then try to grope towards the cypress, 20 steps away, and invariably miss every time.

Entrance to the temple is at the southern end of Hongmen Lu, on Daibeng Lu. Tickets cost Y15 and the temple is open daily from 7.30 am to 6.30 pm.

TÀI'ĀN

PLACES TO STAY

3 Institute of Mining and Technology Guesthouse
山东矿业学会招待所

4 Tàishān Bīnguǎn
泰山宾馆

7 Tàishān Dàjiǔdiàn
泰山大酒店

11 Yùzuò Bīnguǎn
御座宾馆

22 Huáqiáo Dàshà
华侨大厦

PLACES TO EAT

9 Chángxiāng Shuǐjiǎoguǎn
常香水饺馆

13 California Beef Noodles King USA
美国加州牛肉面

19 Huìbīn Cāntīng
惠宾餐厅

OTHER

1 Martyrs' Tomb
烈士陵园

2 Bank of China
中国银行

5 CITS
中国国 事眯狸

6 Dàizōng Archway
岱宗坊

8 Post Office
邮电局

10 Pedestrian Food Market

12 Entrance to Dài Miào
岱庙入口处

14 Bówùguǎn
博物馆

15 Dài Miào
岱庙

16 Xinhua Bookstore
新华书店

17 CTS
中国旅行社

18 Internet Office
网吧

20 Main Post Office
总邮局

21 PSB
公安局外事科

23 China Eastern Airlines Booking Office
东方航空公司售票处

24 Minibuses to Jǐ'nán; Bus No 3 (to Tài Shān)
往济南汽车;三路汽车
（往泰山）

25 Train Station
火车站

26 Long-Distance Bus Station
长途汽车站

Places to Stay

Budget travellers should head for the *Shāndōng Institute of Mining and Technology Guesthouse (Kuàngyè Xuéhuì Zhāodàisuǒ; ☎ 833 2577, fax 821 4564)*. It has friendly staff and is excellent value. Clean, four-bed dorms go for Y25 to Y35 per person and spacious, bright doubles with private bath cost Y60. The guesthouse is at the foot of Tài Shān, giving you easy access for an early start.

Next door is the three-star *Tàishān Bīnguǎn (☎ 822 4678, fax 822 1432)*, which has beds in three-bed dorms for Y50. Doubles cost Y300. At the time of writing it was under major renovation. To get to both guesthouses, take bus No 3 heading east from the train station. Get off just before Dàizōng Archway.

Clustered around the train station are a number of hotels to which touts will be more than happy to drag you, but few take foreigners.

Next door to the Dài Miào, the three-star *Yòuzuò Bīnguǎn* has average doubles for Y280. The location is good but the place feels neglected.

The *Tàishān Dàjiǔdiàn (Tàishān Grand Hotel; ☎ 822 7211, 210 Daizhong Dajie)* has doubles for Y180 to Y380 or suites for Y480. The poshest hotel in town is the *Huáqiáo Dàshà (Overseas Chinese Hotel; ☎ 822 8112, fax 822 8171)* on Dongyue Dajie. Equipped with four-star facilities, standard doubles cost US$45 to US$85 and suites US$110.

Places to Eat

Tài'ān doesn't have a great selection of places to eat, but there is some good food around. *Chángxiāng Shuǐjiǎoguǎn (Changxiang Dumpling Restaurant; 193 Hushan Lu)*, near Daizong Dajie, does excellent *jiaozi* (dumplings) and sweet and sour dishes. Also try the *California Beef Noodles King USA (Měiguó Jiāzhōu Niúròumiàn)* near the Dài Miào, where a bowl of *niúròumiàn* (beef noodles) will cost just Y6. It does an excellent vegetarian version too.

One of the best treats in town is the *Huìbīn Cāntīng (Duck Restaurant)*, south of the Dài Miào. There's no English sign; look for the big restaurant with a cartoon duck on the window. You can get a whole Běijīng duck for Y50, expertly carved in front of you by the chef – a bargain.

For more expensive cuisine, the *Huáqiáo Dàshà* caters for the international palate, with a selection of western and Chinese dishes in its many restaurants.

Getting There & Away

Bus Tài'ān can be approached by road from either Jǐ'nán or Qūfù and is worth combining with a trip to the latter. The Tài'ān to Qūfù buses depart from the main long-distance bus stations in both cities (two hours; leaving roughly every hour). The highway is in good condition.

Although there are a few large public buses connecting Tài'ān to Jǐ'nán, these are overcrowded horrors and you're better off travelling by minibus (Y10; 1½ hours). In Jǐ'nán, departures are from the Tiānqiáo bus station or the parking lot in front of the main long-distance bus station. In Tài'ān, minibuses to Jǐ'nán depart from in front of the train station.

Train There are more than 20 express trains running daily through Tài'ān, with links to Běijīng (nine hours), Hāěrbīn, Jǐ'nán (1¼ hours), Nánjīng (nine hours), Qīngdǎo (9½ hours), Shànghǎi, Shěnyáng, Xī'ān and Zhèngzhōu (11 hours). Some special express trains from Jǐ'nán don't stop at Tài'ān. Check schedules to avoid arriving at some unpleasant hour.

Tài'ān and Tài Shān make good stopovers on the way south from Qīngdǎo to Qūfù and Shànghǎi.

Getting Around

Getting around is easy. The long-distance bus station is just south of the train station, so all local transport is directed towards these two terminals.

There are three main bus routes. Bus No 3 runs from the Tài Shān central route trailhead to the western route trailhead via the train station. Bus Nos 1 and 2 also end up near the train station. Minibuses run on the same routes and are more comfortable, but they will leave the station only when full. You can commandeer a minibus and use it as a taxi.

Taxis and pedicabs can be found outside the train station – the drivers can be overly keen and some may overcharge. Most destinations around town cost Y10 to Y12. The ubiquitous yellow mini-vans, called *huangchong* (yellow insects), are the same price as taxis.

AROUND TÀI'ĀN
Língyán Sì 灵岩寺
Divine Rock Temple

This temple is set in mountainous terrain in Changqing County, 30km from Tài'ān, at the northern foot of Tài Shān. It used to be a large monastery that served many dynasties (the Tang, Song and Yuan, among others) and housed 500 monks in its heyday. On view is a forest of 200 stupas and a nine storey octagonal pagoda, as well as the **Qiānfó Diàn** (Thousand Buddha Temple), which contains 40 fine, highly individualised clay arhats – the best Buddhist statues in Shāndōng.

Buses to Língyán Sì depart from in front of the train station in Tài'ān. Catch one that is heading to Jǐ'nán and ask the driver to let you off at the temple. You'll be let off about 30 minutes up the road from the temple. From there it's a 15-minute taxi ride (Y10) followed by a 10-minute walk up the hill. Entry costs Y31.

QŪFÙ 曲阜
☎ 0537

Of monumental significance to the Chinese is Qūfù, birthplace of Confucius, with its harmonies of carved stone, timber and fine imperial architecture. Following a 2000-year-old tradition, there are two fairs a year in Qūfù – in spring and autumn – when the place comes alive with craftspeople, healers, acrobats, peddlers and peasants. It also hosts a huge party on 28 September to mark Confucius' birthday.

Unfortunately, Qūfù has suffered a blight of tourism; prepare to be hassled by pedicab drivers and souvenir vendors.

Information

The Bank of China is around the corner from the post office, on Dongmen Dajie. The main post office is just north of Gǔ Lòu (Drum Tower), on Gulou Dajie.

Don't be fooled by the giant CITS sign near Língxīngmén (Star Gate); it's nothing more than a billboard. The office is in the south of town, off Dacheng Lu (☎ 441 5315, fax 441 2492) at 1 Sheng Lu. The PSB is also south of town, in a brick building on the corner of Weyutai Lu and Hundao Jie. It's best reached by taxi.

Kǒng Miào 孔庙
Confucius Temple

The temple started out as a simple memorial hall and mushroomed into a complex one-fifth the size of the Qūfù town centre. Huge extensions during the Ming and Qing dynasties are mainly responsible for its present scale. The main entrance is **Língxīng Mén** in the south, which leads through a series of portals emblazoned with calligraphy. The third entrance gateway, the **Arch of the Spirit of the Universe** has four bluish, painted figures that refer to the doctrines of Confucius as heavenly bodies that move in circles without end.

Magnificent gnarled, twisting pines occupy the spaces between the buildings and rows of steles in the courtyards to the Kǒng Miào. There are more than 1000 steles in the temple grounds, with inscriptions from Han to Qing times – the largest such collection in China. The creatures bearing the tablets of praise are *bixi* (dragon offspring), legendary for their strength.

The tablets at Qūfù are noted for their fine calligraphy; a rubbing once formed part of the dowry for a descendant of Confucius. In earlier dynasties, women were not allowed to set foot in the temple grounds; one tablet records the visit of Emperor Wuzong of the Yuan dynasty who brought his sister along – the first woman ever to enter the Kǒng Miào.

Roughly halfway along the north-south axis is the **Great Pavilion of the Constellation of Scholars**, a triple-roofed, Jin dynasty wooden structure of ceremonial

SHĀNDŌNG 山东

QŪFÙ 曲阜

To Tai'an (65km) & Ji'nan (150km)

Kong Lin

Zu Sui He

Erlin Men

Dalin Men

Highway 104

Eternal Spring Archway

Huancheng Xilu

Lindao Lu

0   200   400 m
Approximate Scale

Yanen Xilu

Yanen Donglu

5

Bei Men Dajie

Houzuo Jie

6   Yanmiao Jie

Tianguandi Jie

Shuyuan Jie

Kong Miao

7

Dongmen Dajie

8

9   10

Ximen   Dajie

11   Queli Jie   Wumaci Jie

13   12

Zhonglou Jie

14

Queli Jie

Gulou Dajie

Nanmen Dajie

Ancient Pool

Banbi Jie

15

Shen Dao

Nanma Dao

Jingxuan Lu

To Shao Hao Ling (4km) & Train Station (6km)

Dacheng Lu

16

To Yanzhou (16km)

To CITS

17   18

Bingzha Lu

Zhougongmiao Jie

3

4

To PSB & Zouxian (23km)

Hundao Lu

QŪFÙ

PLACES TO STAY

5 Jīnfǔ Bīnguǎn
金府宾馆

12 Quèlǐ Bīnshè
阙里宾舍

17 Lǚyóu Bīnguǎn
旅游宾馆

18 Kǒngfǔ Fàndiàn
孔府饭店

OTHER

1 Tomb of Confucius
孔子墓

2 Bike Rental
自行车出租

3 Ruins of the
Ancient Lu
State
鲁国址

4 Zhōugōng
Miào
周公庙

6 Yánhuí Miào
颜回庙

7 Post Office
邮局

8 Kǒng Fǔ
孔府

9 Gǔ Lòu
鼓楼

10 Bank of China
中国银行

11 Xinhua
Bookstore
新华书店

13 Zhōng Lòu
(Bell Tower)
钟楼

14 Restaurants;
Street Market
餐厅;商业街

15 Língxīng Mén
棂星门

16 Bus Station
汽车站

importance. Further north through Dacheng Gate and to the right is a juniper planted by Confucius. The small Xingtan Pavilion up from that commemorates the spot where Confucius is said to have taught under the shade of an apricot tree.

The core of the Confucian complex is **Dacheng Hall**, which, in its present form, dates from 1724; it towers 31m on a white marble terrace. The Kong family imported glazed yellow tiling for the halls in the Kǒng Miào, and special stones were brought in from Xīshān. The craftspeople carved the dragon-coiled columns so expertly that they had to be covered with red silk when Emperor Qianlong came to Qūfù lest he felt that the Forbidden City's Taihe Hall paled in comparison. The superb stone they are carved from is called 'fish roe stone'.

The hall was used for unusual rites in honour of Confucius. At the beginning of the seasons and on the great sage's birthday, booming drums, bronze bells and musical stones sounded from the hall as dozens of officials in silk robes engaged in 'dignified dancing' and chanting by torchlight. The rare collection of musical instruments is displayed, but the massive stone statue of the bearded philosopher has disappeared – presumably another casualty of the Cultural Revolution.

At the extreme northern end of the Kǒng Miào is **Shengji Dian**, a memorial hall containing a series of stones engraved with scenes from the life of Confucius and tales about him. They are copies of an older set which date back to 1592.

In the eastern compound of the Kǒng Miào, behind the Hall of Poetry & Rites, is **Confucius' Well** (a Song-Ming reconstruction) and the **Lu Wall**, where the ninth descendant of Confucius hid the sacred texts during the anti-Confucian persecutions of Emperor Qin Shihuang. The books were discovered again during the Han dynasty (206 BC–AD 220) and led to a lengthy scholastic dispute between those who followed a reconstructed version of the last books and those who supported the teachings in the rediscovered ones.

Entry costs Y20. Opening hours are from 8 am to 4.30 pm daily.

Kǒng Fǔ 孔府
Confucius Mansions

Situated to the east of the Kǒng Miào, the Kǒng Fǔ dates from the 16th century (Ming dynasty), with more recent patchwork. The place is a maze of 450 halls, rooms and buildings, and getting around it requires a compass – there are all kinds of side passages to which servants were once restricted.

The Kǒng Fǔ is the most sumptuous aristocratic lodgings in China, which is indicative of the Kong family's former great power. From the Han to the Qing dynasties,

SHĀNDŌNG 山东

Confucianism

Qūfù is the birth and death place of the sage Confucius (551–479 BC) whose impact was not felt during his own lifetime. He lived in abject poverty and hardly put pen to paper, but his teachings were recorded by dedicated followers in *The Analects of Confucius*. His descendants, the Kong family, fared considerably better.

Confucian ethics were adopted by subsequent rulers to keep the populace in line and Confucian temples were set up in numerous towns. Qūfù acquired the status of a holy place, with the direct descendants of Confucius as its guardian angels.

The original Confucian temple at Qūfù (dating from 478 BC) was enlarged, remodelled, added to, taken away from and rebuilt. The majority of the present buildings are from the Ming dynasty. In 1513 armed bands sacked the temple and the Kong residence, and walls were built around the town from 1522 to 1567 to fortify it. These walls were recently removed, but vestiges of Ming town planning, like the Drum and Bell towers, remain.

More a code that defined hierarchical relationships than a religion, Confucianism has had a great impact on Chinese culture. It teaches that son must respect father, wife must respect husband, commoner must respect official, official must respect ruler, and so on. The essence of its teachings are obedience, respect, selflessness and working for the common good.

You would think that this code would have fitted nicely into the new order of communism; however, it was swept aside because of its connections with the past. Confucius was seen as a kind of misguided feudal educator, and clan ties and ancestor-worship were viewed as a threat. In 1948 Confucius' direct heir, the first-born son of the 77th generation of the Kong family, fled to Taiwan, breaking a 2500-year tradition of Kong residence in Qūfù.

During the Cultural Revolution the emphasis shifted to the youth of China (even if they were led by an old man). A popular anti-Confucian campaign was instigated and Confucius lost face. Many of the statues at Qūfù also lost face (literally) amid cries of 'Down with Confucius, down with his wife!'. In the late 1960s a contingent of Red Guards descended on the sleepy town of Qūfù, burning, defacing and destroying. Other Confucian edifices around the country were also attacked. The leader of the guards who ransacked Qūfù was Tan Houlan. She was jailed in 1978 and was not tried until 1982. The Confucius family archives appear to have survived intact.

In 1979 the Qūfù temples were reopened and millions of yuan were allocated for renovations and repairs. Tourism is now the name of the game; if a temple hasn't got fresh paint, new pillars, replaced tiling or stonework, and a souvenir shop or photo merchant with a great sage cardboard cutout, they'll get around to it soon. Some of the buildings even have electricity, with speakers hooked up to the eaves playing soothing flute music. One fifth of Qūfù's residents are again claiming to be descendants of the great sage, though incense-burning, mound-burial and ancestor-worship are not consistent with the party line.

While the current popularity of the great sage is undeniable, it is debatable as to what extent his teachings are taking fresh root in China. The majority of devotees around Qūfù are middle-aged or elderly, suggesting that the comeback of Confucianism is more likely a reemergence of beliefs never effectively squashed by the communists. Nevertheless, Confucian ethics (though not by that name) are finding their way back into the Shāndōng school system, presumably to instil some civic mindedness. Students are encouraged once again to respect their teachers, elders, neighbours and family.

Chinese scholars are also making careful statements reaffirming the significance of Confucious' historical role and suggesting that the 'progressive' aspects of his work were even cited in the writings of Mao Zedong. Confucius too, it seems, can be rehabilitated.

the descendants of Confucius were ennobled and granted privileges by the emperors. They lived like kings themselves, with 180-course meals, servants and consorts. Confucius even picked up some posthumous honours.

The town of Qūfù grew around the Kŏng Fŭ and was an autonomous estate administered by the Kongs, who had powers of taxation and execution. Emperors could drop in to visit – the Ceremonial Gate near the south entrance was opened only for this event. Because of this royal protection, copious quantities of furniture, ceramics, artefacts, customary and personal effects survived and some may be viewed. The Kong family archives are a rich legacy and also survived. Extensive renovations of the complex have been made.

The Kŏng Fŭ is built on an 'interrupted' north to south axis. Grouped by the south gate are the former administrative offices (taxes, edicts, rites, registration and examination halls). To the north on the axis is **Neizhai Men**, a special gate that seals off the residential quarters (used for weddings, banquets and private functions). East of Neizhai Men is the **Tower of Refuge**, where the Kong clan could gather if the peasants turned nasty. It has an iron-lined ceiling on the ground floor, and a removable staircase to the 1st floor. Grouped to the west of the main axis are former recreational facilities (studies, guestrooms, libraries and small temples). To the east is the odd kitchen, ancestral temple and the family branch apartments. Far to the north is a spacious garden with rockeries, ponds and bamboo groves. Kong Decheng, the last of the family line, lived in the Kŏng Fŭ until 1948, when he hightailed it to Taiwan.

Kŏng Fŭ is open from 8 am to 4.30 pm daily; admission is Y20.

Kŏng Lín   孔林
Confucian Forest

North of the Kŏng Fŭ, about 2km up Lindao Lu, is the Kŏng Lín, the largest artificial park and best preserved cemetery in China. This timeworn route has a kind of 'spirit way' lined with ancient cypresses.

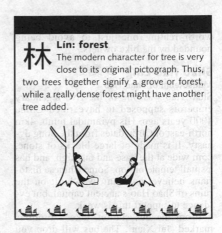

Lín: forest

The modern character for tree is very close to its original pictograph. Thus, two trees together signify a grove or forest, while a really dense forest might have another tree added.

To reach the forest takes about 30 minutes by foot, 15 minutes by pedicab, or you can attempt to catch the infrequent bus No 1. On the way, look into the **Yánhuí Miào** (Yanhui Temple; Y5), which is off to the right and has a spectacular dragon head embedded in the ceiling of the main hall, plus a pottery collection. The route to the forest passes through the **Eternal Spring Archway**, its stone lintels are decorated with coiled dragons, flying phoenixes and galloping horses dating from 1594 (Ming dynasty). Visitors, who needed permission to enter Kŏng Lín, had to dismount at the Dalín Mén (Forest Gates).

The pine and cypress forest of over 20,000 trees (it is said that each of Confucius' students planted a tree from his birthplace) covers 200 hectares and is bounded by a wall 10km long. Confucius and his descendants are buried here. Flanking the approach to **Confucius' tomb** are pairs of stone panthers, griffins and larger-than-life guardians. The Confucian barrow is a simple grass mound enclosed by a low wall, and faced with a Ming dynasty stele. His sons are buried nearby. Scattered through the forest are dozens of temples and pavilions, and hundreds of sculptures, tablets and tombstones. Even today, descendants of Confucius can still be buried in the Kŏng Lín.

The forest is open from 7.30 am to 6 pm and entry costs Y10. There is a bike rental place just outside the gates, allowing you to tour the forest on wheels for Y5. It's almost worth renting one just to avoid being hounded by the bike owners.

Shào Hào Líng 少昊陵
Mausoleum of Shao Hao

Shào Hào was one of the five legendary emperors supposed to have ruled China 4000 years ago. His pyramidal tomb, 4km north-east of Qūfù, dates from the Song dynasty. It is made of large blocks of stone, 25m wide at the base and 6m high, and has a small temple on top. Some Chinese historians believe that Qūfù was built on the ruins of Shào Hào's ancient capital, but evidence to support this is weak.

From the bus station, take a minibus marked 'Jui Xian'. The bus will drop you 300m south of the tomb.

Places to Stay

There are cheap guesthouses in Qūfù that may take you, but they are fickle. What's more, they are often difficult to find; they display only Chinese signs – try one of the touts lingering near the bus station.

The budget option open to foreigners is the *Kǒngfǔ Fàndiàn (Confucius Mansions Hotel;* ☎ 441 2686, fax 441 3786, 9 Datong Lu), where dorm beds cost Y60 and doubles start at Y140. You can enter the hotel off Jingxuan Lu or Datong Lu; you'll find the hotel at the back of the complex. Try to get a room at the front of the hotel rather than at the back, which neighbours the karaoke bar. Hot water is available after 7.30 pm.

The traditional Chinese architecture of the *Quèlǐ Bīnshè (*☎ 441 1300, fax 441 2022, 1 Queli Jie)* blends in with the adjacent Kǒng Miào. The hotel has comprehensive facilities and singles/doubles for Y298/398.

The *Lǚyóu Bīnguǎn (*☎ 441 1625, fax 441 6207, 1 Dacheng Lu)* is a decent hotel diagonally opposite the bus station; it has doubles from Y180 to Y240 and suites for Y800.

North of town, en route to the Kǒng Lín, the *Jīnfǔ Bīnguǎn (Mansions Hotel;* ☎ 441 3469, fax 441 3209)* has reasonable doubles/triples for Y180/300.

Places to Eat

There is plenty of good food in Qūfù. Restaurants are clustered on the roads leading from the Gǔ Lòu (Drum Tower). Wumaci Jie, east off Gulou Dajie, turns into a huge *food market* in the evenings. Here you can eat fresh seafood at some of the fanciest food stalls (complete with white table cloths) in China. The market continues south onto Nanmen Dajie, where the locals eat. There you can squat at a low table and consume an enormous and delicious plate of fried noodles for Y2.50.

The *Confucius Restaurant* in the Kǒngfǔ Fàndiàn serves reasonable food. The *Quèlǐ Bīnshè* offers excellent, if somewhat pricey set evening meals of local culinary specialities. You might also be treated to live entertainment.

Sankong (Three Confucius) beer is the local brew.

Getting There & Away

Bus Minibuses regularly shuttle between the train station in nearby Yǔnzhōu and the bus station in Qūfù (Y7; 20 minutes), departing when packed. Minibuses run as late as 11 pm if there are passengers. Minibuses will also serve as taxis if you pay them enough.

From the bus station, buses depart frequently (one per hour) for Tài'ān and Jǐ'nán.

To find the minibus station in Yǔnzhōu, walk straight ahead as you exit the train station, cross the parking lot and turn right. The bus station is 50m down the road on the left.

Train When a railway project for Qūfù was first brought up, the Kong family petitioned for a change of routes, claiming that the trains would disturb Confucius' tomb. They won and the nearest tracks were routed to Yǔnzhōu, 16km to the west of Qūfù. Eventually, the railway builders constructed another station about 6km east of Qūfù, but only slow trains stop here, so it is more convenient to go to Yǔnzhōu. From Yǔnzhōu, it's a 20-minute bus ride to Qūfù, with minibuses departing when full.

Ask for a Qūfù ticket and if the clerk says *méi yǒu* (don't have), try 'Yǔnzhōu'. Yǔnzhōu is on the line from Běijīng to

Shànghǎi. There's a fair selection of trains to destinations including Tài'ān (two hours), Jǐ'nán (three hours), Xúzhōu (2½ hours), Nánjīng (seven hours) and Kāifēng (nine hours). Some special express trains don't stop here; others arrive at inconvenient times like midnight.

Getting Around

There are only two bus lines and service is not frequent. Probably most useful for travellers is bus No 1, which travels along Gulou Dajie and Lindao Lu, connecting the bus station with the Kǒng Lín. Bus No 2 travels from east to west along Jingxuan Lu.

Pedicabs, bizarre motor-tricycles and decorated tourist horse-carts (Y15 to the Kǒng Lín for the latter) swarm around, but expect to haggle.

ZŌUXIÀN 邹县

Zōuxiàn is a good place to visit as it's far more relaxed than Qūfù. This is the home town of Mencius (372–289 BC), who is regarded as the first great Confucian philosopher. He developed many of the ideas of Confucianism as they were later understood.

Zōuxiàn's Líng Xīng Mén (Spiritual Star Temple) and Yàshèng Fǔ (Temple of the Second Sage) are at the southern end of town, about a 20-minute walk from the bus station. Excellently restored, these two quiet temples contain wonderful murals from AD 800, beautiful gardens and the tomb of Mencius and his descendants.

A Y15 ticket gets you into both temples, which are next door to one another. To reach the temples, head right out of the bus station and take the first left until you reach a T-junction. Turn right and then left onto Yashengmiao Jie. En route you'll pass through a lively *food market*.

Zōuxiàn is 23km south of Qūfù and can be visited as a day trip by train from Yǔnzhōu or by bus from Qūfù. From Qūfù, buses leave frequently from the main station for the 35-minute ride.

LÍNZĪ 临淄

As you step off the train in Línzī, it may be difficult to imagine that what you see before

you was once a booming centre. During the Eastern Zhou dynasty (770–221 BC), this area flourished as the capital of the Ch'i state. Throughout the Han period (206 BC–AD 220) it was designated the chief administrative centre of Shāndōng and, after a slight slump, Línzī prospered again during the Qi (AD 479–502). Today, Línzī's claim to fame is based on the excavation of a pit of horses dating back some 2500 years. The horses you'll see here are not only older than those excavated in Xī'ān, but they are also the remains of real animals.

So far, 600 horse skeletons have been discovered. As horses and chariots indicated the strength of the state, it's not surprising that they were buried (their throats slashed first) in the course of their master's funeral. At the Mù Xùn Mǎ Kēng (Dongzhou Tomb of Sacrificial Objects) in Línzī, about 90 horse skeletons are on display in a large pit. To reach the museum from the train station, take minibus No 26. It will drop you 2km north of the museum. From there you can hitch a ride or stretch your legs in the countryside for another half hour.

En route, bus No 26 passes the new Lìshǐ Búowǔguǎn (History Museum), which houses an excellent exhibit of the life and times of the early Zhou dynasty, during which Emperor Wu encouraged over 100 schools of thought. The exhibit includes an intricate model of a Zhou village. Admission to the museum is Y20.

Línzī is on the bus route and train line between Jǐ'nán and Qīngdǎo. If you start out early enough, it can be visited as a stopover between the two. Store your luggage at the small shop inside the train station. Be warned that it is nearly impossible to get transport out of Línzī after 4.30 pm, so double check train and bus times when you arrive. If you do spend the night, the friendly *Guójì Fàndiàn* (International Hotel), two blocks north of the train station on the left, has comfortable doubles for Y50 per person.

Línzī is a prefecture of Zībó, which lies 20km to its west. Zībó is a major coal-mining centre of over two million people, noted for its glassworks and pottery.

QĪNGDĂO 青岛

☎ 0532 • pop 6,954,400

Perched on the southern seaboard of the Shāndōng peninsula, the picturesque town of Qīngdǎo (Green Island) is a welcome breather from the clogging conformity of socialist town planning. Its German legacy more or less intact, Qīngdǎo takes pride in its Bavarian appearance – the Chinese call the town 'China's Switzerland'. With its cool sea breezes, (relatively) clear air, balmy evenings (in summer) and excellent seafood, this is where party cadres come to build sand castles, lick ice cream and dream of retirement.

Qīngdǎo was a simple fishing village until the Kaiser Wilhelm II set his sights on it. When two German missionaries were killed in the Boxer Rebellion, the Kaiser jumped on the opportunity to declare an international crisis. The obvious solution was for China's Manchu government to hand over Qīngdǎo. In 1898 China ceded the town to Germany for 99 years. Under German administration, the famous Qīngdǎo Píjiǔchǎng (brewery) opened in 1903, electric lighting was installed, missions and a university were established, the railway to Jǐ'nán was built, a garrison of 2000 men was deployed, and a naval base was established.

In 1914 the Japanese moved into town after the successful joint Anglo-Japanese naval bombardment of the port. Japan's position in Qīngdǎo was strengthened by the Treaty of Versailles and they held the city until 1922 when it was ceded back to the Kuomintang. The Japanese returned in 1938, after the start of the Sino-Japanese war, and occupied the town until defeated in 1945.

Qīngdǎo is now China's fourth-largest port and the second largest city in Shāndōng. Booming industry and an entrepreneurial spirit have successfully carried the city into the 21st century.

Orientation

Qīngdǎo is situated on a peninsula with small bays and beaches along the southern coastline. These coastal areas and the Central district have great charm. The northern and eastern districts are industrial zones and the west is home to the shipping industry.

Information

Money The main branch of the Bank of China is east of town in the World Trade Centre at 6 Zhanshan Dalu; however you can also change money in any of the large hotels in town.

Post & Communications The main post office is on Zhongshan Lu. There is a second office further south, near the CAAC office. China Telecom has recently opened an Internet office at 3 Anhui Lu, on the corner of Guangxi Lu. At the time of writing, a private telephone line in Qīngdǎo was needed to get online but it shouldn't be long before it provides public access. In the meantime, try major hotels such as the Shangri-la, but expect to pay high prices.

Travel Agencies There is a CITS counter (☎ 287 9215) at 9 Nanhai Lu in the Hùiquán Wángcháo Dàjiǔdiàn (Huiquan Dynasty Hotel), but the staff are not particularly helpful to individual travellers. On the fourth storey of the run-down building directly behind the hotel is the CITS business office. The staff may seem surprised to find you here but are considerably more helpful. Alternatively, you can try CITS Outbound Department (☎ 389 5591), 1 Wushenguan Lu, which is around the corner in the Wushenguan Hotel. You can book tours of the brewery, shell-carving factory and locomotive factory both here and at the counter in the Hùiquán Wángcháo Dàjiǔdiàn.

PSB The PSB (☎ 286 2787) is a block west of Zhongshan Lu, near Feicheng Lu. The office is in an unnumbered grey building on the west side of the street.

Things to See

The wonderful castle-like villa at the eastern end of the No 2 Bathing Beach is **Huàshí Lóu**, the former German governor's residence and a replica of a German palace. Built in 1903, it is said to have cost 2,450,000 taels of silver. When Kaiser Wilhelm II got the bill, he immediately recalled the extravagant governor and sacked him. The Chinese call it the 'Chiang Kaishek

Building' as the generalissimo secretly stayed here in 1947. Around the back is a terrace where the German governor used to play tennis with his lackeys and the garage where they used to park the Mercedes. It's well worth the Y5 entry fee to patrol the gardens, the reception rooms and climb to the roof for an excellent view of the sea.

To the right of Xìnhàoshān Gōngyuán remains one of Qīngdǎo's most astounding pieces of German architecture, the **Xìnhàoshān Yíng Bīnguǎn** (Xinhao Hill Hotel). The German governor and Chairman Mao both stayed here, although not simultaneously. Take a peek at the interior, which has a gorgeous wooden staircase and balcony – the German grand piano was made in 1876.

The twin-spired **Tiānzhǔ Jiàotáng** (Catholic Church), up a steep hill off Zhongshan Lu, is an imposing edifice with a light bulb-encrusted cross on the roof. The crosses were torn off the steeples during the Cultural Revolution, but God-fearing locals rescued them and buried them in the hills. The church still has regular Sunday services. The area around the church is rich in architectural textures and is worth exploring. A daily **fish market**, featuring colourful exotica from the depths, sets up on the cobbled street of Feicheng Lu, which leads up to the church.

The other main church is the **Jīdū Jiàotáng** (Protestant Church), opposite the southwestern entrance to **Xìnhàoshān Gōngyuán**. This German structure is simple yet attractive; the white clock face on the green tower is still inscribed with the manufacturer's name. If you knock on the door, the Chinese priest will probably show you around and inform you that he has a congregation of 1000 people every Sunday. The interior is typically spartan, but worth a look.

For a colourful and exhaustive account of Qīngdǎo's historic architecture, turn to *Far from Home: Western Architecture in China's Northern Treaty Ports* by Tess Johnston & Deke Erh.

Beaches

Qīngdǎo is famous for its six beaches, which are extremely popular with the Chinese. The beaches are not bad and can make for a pleasant stroll, but don't go expecting a surfers' paradise. June to September is the main swimming season, when 60,000 to 70,000 sunseekers gather on the sand. The beaches are sheltered and are equipped with changing sheds. Shark nets, lifeguards, lifeboat patrols and medical stations provide safety.

Close to the train station is the **No 6 Bathing Beach**. This is a lively area in the morning, jostling with *taijiquan* (tai chi) practitioners, frisbee throwers and joggers. This beach neighbours **Zhàn Qiáo**, a pier that reaches out into the bay and has the eight-sided pavilion, **Huílán Gé**, at its end. The pier is a famous landmark that crops up on the label of Tsingtao beer. Beyond, you can see the **lighthouse** on Xiǎo Qīng Dǎo (Little Green Island), which lends its name to Qīngdǎo. Next to the jetty there are boat ticket vendors for tours around the bay and beyond (Y10).

Continuing east, around the headland and the lighthouse, is **Lǔ Xùn Gōngyuán**, a park where hard-sell types will attempt to entice you into lightning tours of the beaches on their speedboats (Y60).

The sand of **No 1 Bathing Beach** is coarsegrained, engulfed in seaweed and bordered by concrete beach huts and bizarre statues of dolphins. Past the **Hùiquán Wángcháo Dàjiǔdiàn** (Huiquan Dynasty Hotel) and the Ocean Research Institute is **Bādàguān** (Eight Passes Area), well known for its sanatoriums and exclusive guesthouses. The spas are scattered in lush wooded zones off the coast, and each street is lined with a different tree or flower, including maple, myrtle, peach, snowpine or crab apple. This is a lovely area in which to stroll.

As you head out of Bādàguān, Nos 2 and 3 bathing beaches are just east, and the villas lining the headlands are exquisite. **No 2 Bathing Beach** is cleaner, quieter and more sheltered than **No 1 Bathing Beach**.

Parks

Qīngdǎo has a splendid collection of parks that are worth exploring. Wandering from park to park down Qīngdǎo's lovely streets is an excellent way of escaping the bustle.

QĪNGDǍO 青岛

To Shangri-La
Hotel, Bank of
China & Lao Shan
(40km)

36 ☐
37 ●

Dongfang ☐

No 3
Bathing
Beach

Cape
Taiping

Taiping Wan

Hong Kong Lu

Taipingjiao Lu

Yan'an Sanlu

Taipingshan
Gongyuan

Dianshi Ta

Zhongshan
Gongyuan

Weihai Lu

Mushuguan Lu

Shenzi Haiguan Lu

38 ☐
35

No 2
Bathing
Beach

34 ●

Yan'an Yilu

Zoo ☐

Bada-guan

33 ●

Wendeng

Qingdaoshan
Gongyuan

Oixia Lu

32 ●

Nathal L

No 1
Bathing
Beach

Huiquan Wan

Liaoning

Zhushuishan
Gongyuan

Huangtai Lu

Daxue Lu

31 ●
☐ 29

Lu Xun
Gongyuan

To Airport

To Ji'nan

Xihing Lu

Liaoning Lu

Xinhaoshan
Gongyuan

27 ●
28 ☐

26 ●

Laiyang Lu

Longshan Lu

Jiangsu Lu

Rehe Lu

12 ●

Hunan Lu

YELLOW SEA

Baoyou Lu

Jiaozhou Lu

11 ●
9 ☐
8 ☐
10 ●
13 ●
14 ●
15 ●

Dexan Lu

23 ☐
22 24

Taiping Lu

24 ●
25 ●

Qingdao Wan

30 ✴

1 ●
2 ●
3 ●

5 ●
6 ●

Jinan Lu

Henen Lu

Hubei Lu

16 ●

Zhongshan Lu

Guang Xilu

No 6
Bathing
Beach

Night
Market

Zhongang
Harbour

Qufu Lu

17 ●

Tai'an Lu

27 ●

Quan Xilu

20 ●

19 ●

Yunnan Lu

Feixan Lu

Guizhou Lu

Xilingxia Lu

Shexuan Lu

Jiaozhou Wan

18 ☐

Sichuan Lu

Tuandao Wan

1 km
0.5
0

QĪNGDǍO

PLACES TO STAY

1 Hépíng Bīnguǎn
和平宾馆

2 Yǒuyì Bīnguǎn;
Store
友谊宾馆.商店

10 Qīngdǎo Fàndiàn
青岛饭店

16 Fótáo Bīnguǎn
佛桃宾馆

22 Zhànqiáo Bīnguǎn
栈桥宾馆

28 Xìnhàoshān Yíng
Bīnguǎn
信号山迎宾馆

31 Yínhǎi Huāyuán
Fàndiàn
银海花园饭店

32 Huìyuán Fàndiàn
汇原饭店

37 Hǎitiān Dàjiǔdiàn
海天大酒店

PLACES TO EAT

7 Chūnhélóu Fàndiàn
春和楼饭店

8 Qīnghǎi Mùsīlín
Fànzhuāng
青海穆斯林饭庄

9 Rìběn Liàolī
日本料理

19 Hǎoshìjiè Hǎishàng
Huánggōng
好世界海上皇宫

20 California Beef Noodles
King USA
美国加洲牛肉面

OTHER

3 Passenger Ferry
Terminal
青岛港客运站

4 Qīngdǎo Píjiǔchǎng
青岛啤酒厂

5 Foreign Language
Bookstore
外文书店

6 Xinhua Bookstore
新华书店

11 Tiānzhǔ Jiàotáng
天主教堂

12 Guānhǎi Shān
Gōngyuán
观海山公园

13 Main Post Office
邮电局

14 CAAC
中国航空公司

15 PSB
公安局外事科

17 Train Station; Tiědào Dàshà
火车站.铁道大厦

18 Local Ferry
青岛轮渡站

21 Long-Distance
Buses
长途汽车站

23 Telecom Internet
中国电信网吧

24 Zhàn Qiáo
栈桥

25 Huílán Gé
回澜阁

26 Jīdū Jiàotáng
基督教堂

27 Longshan
Underground
Market
龙山地下商场

29 Qīngdǎo Bówùguǎn
青岛博物馆

30 Xiǎo Qīng Dǎo
小青岛

33 CITS (Huiquan
Dynasty Hotel)
中国国际旅行社

34 CITS Outbound
Department
青岛中国国际旅行社

35 Huāshí Lóu
花石

36 Zhànshān Sì
湛山寺

The charm of **Guānhǎishān Gōngyuán** lies in finding it – the route winds up a small hill through restful lanes; the park is at the top. Although small, the park used to be a golf course for the Germans. The white trigrams marked on the paving stones at the top are for the practise of a secretive martial art called *bagua zhang* (eight trigram boxing).

Down the hill and to the east is **Xìn-hàoshān Gōngyuán**, whose summit is graced with the carbuncular towers known as the *mógu lóu* (mushroom buildings). Beneath the park is the Lóngshān Dìxià Shāngyè (Longshan Underground Market), a tunnel complex given over to selling tacky clothes. Minibus No 26 can take you to Xìn-hàoshān Gōngyuán.

North of the Hùiquán Wángcháo Dàjiǔdiàn (Huiquan Dynasty Hotel) is **Zhōngshān Gōngyuán**, which covers 80 hectares, has a teahouse and temple and in springtime is a heavily wooded profusion of flowering shrubs and plants.

The mountainous area north-east of Zhōngshān Gōngyuán is called **Tàipíngshān Gōngyuán**, an area of walking paths, pavilions and the best area in town for hiking. In the centre of the park is the **Diànshì Tǎ** (TV tower), which has an express lift up to fabulous views of the city (Y40). You can reach the tower via cable car (Y10). Also within the park is Qīngdǎo's largest temple, **Zhànshān Sì**. Built in 1934, it is the latest Tiantai Buddhist temple in China and is

SHĀNDŌNG 山东

currently used by the growing number of practising Buddhists in Qīngdǎo as well as by the 20 monks in residence. The temple has a number of dramatic, sandalwood buddhas covered in gold foil and is well worth the Y5 entry fee.

Just west of Tàipíngshān Gōngyuán is **Qīngdǎoshān Gōngyuán**. A notable feature of this hilly park is **Jīngshān Pàotái** (Jingshan Fort).

Qīngdǎo Píjiǔchǎng 青岛啤酒厂
Tsingtao Brewery

The brewery is tucked into the industrial part of town, inland and east of the Zhōnggǎng harbour. Tsingtao beer has gained a worldwide following.

The brewery was established early this century by the Germans who still supply the parts for modernisation of the system. The flavour of the finest brew in Asia comes from the mineral waters of nearby Láo Shān. Unfortunately, unless you are on a tour it's almost impossible to get into the brewery for a look. Tours can be booked at CITS in Qīngdǎo.

Special Events

The summer months see Qīngdǎo overrun with tourists, particularly in the second and third weeks of July, when the annual trade fair is held. Another festival to look out for is the beer festival in August. Gardeners may be interested to note that Qīngdǎo's radish festival is in January, the cherry festival in May and the grape festival in September (Qīngdǎo is a major producer of wine).

Places to Stay – Budget

If you arrive during July's trade fair, be prepared to be forced into expensive accommodation. Also be warned that many hotels shut down during winter. Call ahead to make sure you won't be greeted by a locked door.

The *Tiědào Dàshà (Railway Hotel;* ☎ 286 9963, 2 Tai'an Lu) is the ugly duckling that adjoins the train station. Dorm beds cost from Y45. If these are fully booked, there are standard doubles for Y200 to Y280.

The *Fótáo Bīnguǎn (* ☎ *287 1581, 13 Tai'an Lu)*, just north of the train station on Tai'an Lu, has dorms for Y35 and cubby hole singles/doubles for Y40/128.

The *Yǒuyì Bīnguǎn (Friendship Hotel;* ☎ *282 8165)* is next door to the passenger ferry terminal on Xinjiang Lu. Dorm beds in two- or four-bed rooms cost Y40; doubles cost Y80 to Y160. To get here from the train station, take bus No 8, which passes the hotel. Alternatively, a taxi costs Y7.

The *Hépíng Bīnguǎn (Peace Hotel;* ☎ *282 7851, fax 282 7691, 10 Xin Jiang Lu)* is down an alley to the east of the passenger ferry terminal – almost behind the Yǒuyì Bīnguǎn. Basic doubles/triples cost Y80/100; doubles with bath cost Y185.

Finally, not far from No 1 Bathing Beach, the *Huìyuán Fàndiàn (* ☎ *288 4233, 1 Qixia Lu)* has cheap, average singles/doubles for Y120/180. From the train station, take the No 6 bus to the Xiǎoyúshān Gōngyuán stop. A taxi costs Y7.

Places to Stay – Mid-Range

Near Lu Xun Gōngyuán and No 1 Bathing Beach is the *Yinhǎi Huāyuán Fàndiàn (Yinhai Garden Hotel;* ☎ *296 7556, 5 Nanhai Lu)*. With views of the ocean, it's reasonably priced at Y238 for a double with private bath.

The *Qīngdǎo Fàndiàn (* ☎ *289 1888, 53 Zhongshan Lu)* has its entrance on Qufu Lu. It has recently been refurbished, however the gloss is skin deep and the tack shows through. Singles/doubles cost Y352/448. A cheaper and more down-at-heel hotel of the same name is next door where singles/doubles cost Y178/200.

Most touts at the train station will attempt to drag you off to the *Zhànqiáo Bīnguǎn (* ☎ *287 0502, fax 288 8666, 31 Taiping Lu)*. The location next to the beach and in the heart of town is great, but it's noisy. Rooms cost Y298 to Y598.

Places to Stay – Top End

Qīngdǎo is swarming with top-end accommodation, most of it overpriced. However, the *Hǎitiān Dàjiǔdiàn (* ☎ *287 1888, fax 387 1777, 48 Xianggang Xi Lu)* offers good value for money with singles/doubles, some with ocean views, for US$100/110 to US$138/148. Rates include breakfast, airport shuttle and newspapers.

East of town, you'll find the newly opened **Shangri-La Hotel** (Xiānggélǐlā Jiǔdiàn; ☎ 388 3838, fax 388 6860, 9 Zhanliugan Lu). Rooms are plush and prices include limo service to and from the airport, laundry, breakfast and a 6 pm check out. Singles/doubles cost US$155/175 to US$210/230; suites cost US$290 to US$1500.

Probably the hotel with the most character and history is the **Xìnhàoshān Yíng Bīnguǎn** (Xinhao Hill Hotel; ☎ 286 6209, fax 286 1985, 26 Longshan Lu), next to Xìnhào Shan Gōngyuán. A converted former German mansion, it is splendid inside and out. Doubles start at Y600. The hotel closes during the low season (October to May). Call ahead to make certain that someone is around.

Places to Eat
Qīngdǎo is overrun with good food. The locals are crazy about kebabs, which is understandable as they are delicious! You can buy them for Y1.50 from the ubiquitous street stalls – they are usually made from zhūròuchuàn (pork) or sometimes from yángròuchuàn (lamb); you get about five chunks per skewer, all cooked to a crisp. You can get them là (spicy) or bùlà (not spicy). Another local favourite is diànkǎo yóuyú (squid on a stick). The street stalls usually sell beer and soft drinks and provide you with a stool to perch on while you feast. Go for the popular stalls where the crowds gather (especially on Zhongshan Lu).

The waterfront area is brimming with restaurants, from No 6 Bathing Beach almost all the way to No 1 Bathing Beach. The area around No 1 Bathing Beach is the best place to find cheap eats. Any of the seaside restaurants serve up fresh seafood. The gǎ la (mussels) are excellent, and a plate of these will cost you about Y12. Hǎiluó (sea snails) are also popular, and cost Y20 per plate.

South-west of the train station on Feixian Lu are a number of reasonably priced restaurants, including a branch of the ever growing chain **California Beef Noodles King USA** (Měiguo Jiāzhōu Niuròumiàn), where you can slurp down a huge bowl of noodles for under Y10.

Just up the road from the very prominent KFC is the **Qīnghǎi Mùsīlín Fànzhuāng** (Qīnghǎi Muslim Restaurant; 31 Dexian Lu). There's no English sign, but you can't miss the Arabic script. There's also no English menu, but try the yángròu pàomó, a dish that involves breaking chapatti-like bread into a bowl and then adding a mutton broth – delicious and cheap.

A couple of doors down is the **Rìběn Liàolǐ** (Sushi Bar; ☎ 287 9279, 41 Dexuan Lu), which has decently priced, tasty, Japanese fare, friendly service and a comfortable atmosphere.

More expensive options include the **Chūnhélóu Fàndiàn** (☎ 282 7371, 146 Zhongshan Lu), which is one of Qīngdǎo's most famous eateries. The **revolving restaurant** in Tàipíngshān Gōngyuán's TV tower offers reasonable food and great views of Qīngdǎo, although the lift to the restaurant costs Y40. The food has a pre-set charge of Y60 per person.

Looking just like Australia's Opera House, the **Hǎishìjiè Hǎishàng Huánggōng** (Good World Seaside Palace; 2 Xilingxia Lu) has fresh and fancy seafood for Y50 to Y200.

The **Shangri-la Hotel** offers a weekend dim-sum buffet breakfast from 8 to 10 am for Y52 per person (plus 15% service charge).

Shopping
Along Xilingxia Lu on the western side of No 6 Bathing Beach is a lively night market that can meet any tourist's shopping needs. If you're looking for higher quality (and prices), visit the Arts & Crafts Store at 212 Zhongshan Lu.

Getting There & Away
Air The CAAC office (☎ 287 0057) is at 29 Zhongshan Lu. The booking office of China Eastern Airlines (☎ 287 0215) is adjacent to the Hùiyuán Dàjiǔdiàn (see Places to Stay

SHĀNDŌNG 山东

earlier). Korean Air and All Nippon Airways are in the Hǎitiān Dàjiǔdiàn (see Places to Stay earlier). Larger hotels also have airline ticket offices. The Qīngdǎo airport inquiries numbers are ☎ 484 3331 and ☎ 484 2139.

There are five flights a week between Qīngdǎo and Hong Kong (Y2560) and there are also daily flights to Seoul (Y1700) with Korean Air. Air Macau flies three times a week to Macau (Y2120) and All Nippon Airways has four flights a week to both Osaka (Y3950) and Fukuoka (Y3350).

Destinations in China include Shànghǎi, Běijīng, Hāěrbīn, Shěnyáng, Kūnmíng and Dàlián (Y430).

Bus Buses and minibuses depart from the area next to the massive Hualian Building, just across from the train station. The ticket office is a little difficult to spot; it's in a converted minibus camouflaged among the buses.

Minibuses to Yāntái (Y30; three hours; leaving every ½ hour) depart from 7 am to 5 pm. From 6 am to 6 pm, there are departures every ½ hour to Jǐ'nán (Y50; five hours); it is faster than going by train. Daily sleeper buses to Shànghǎi (Y160; 16 hours) leave at 10.30 am, noon and 1 pm. There is one daily sleeper to Běijīng (Y120; 22 hours) leaving at 10 am.

Train All trains from Qīngdǎo go through the provincial capital of Jǐ'nán, except for the direct Qīngdǎo to Yāntái trains. One train goes daily to Yāntái (Y22; four hours), leaving Qīngdǎo at 2.40 pm. There are direct trains to Jǐ'nán (Y31), Běijīng (Y200), Guǎngzhōu (Y300) and Shànghǎi (Y280; 20 hours); but in summer you may consider a cheaper journey by boat to Shànghǎi. Sleeper fares can be bought with some persistence at the train station, giving you lots of time to check out the wonderful old German ticket office.

Boat Regular boats run between Qīngdǎo and Inch'ǒn in South Korea. Departures from Qīngdǎo are on Monday and Thursday at 4 pm (Y740; 20 hours). There is also a boat to Shànghǎi (Y240; 26 hours) that runs from the last week of June until the end of September, leaving at noon on even days of the month.

The boat service to Dàlián has been suspended, so the best way to get there is to take the train or bus to Yāntái and then continue by boat. (See the Yāntái section later in this chapter for details.)

Getting Around

To/From the Airport Qīngdǎo's antiquated airport is 30km north from the city. Taxi drivers ask Y100 (or whatever they think you might possibly pay) for the journey. Buses leave from the CAAC office between 6 am and 5 pm (Y10; hourly).

Bus Most transport needs can be catered for by the bus No 6 route, which starts at the northern end of Zhongshan Lu, runs along it to within a few blocks of the train station and then east to the area above No 3 Bathing Beach. Bus No 26 from the train station runs along the coast and past Zhōngshān Gōngyuán before heading north at the end of No 3 Bathing Beach. Minibuses also follow these routes (Y2).

Taxi Qīngdǎo taxis are among the cheapest in China; Y7 will get you almost anywhere around town.

AROUND QĪNGDǍO

Láo Shān, 40km east of Qīngdǎo, is a famous Taoist retreat with cable-car facilities, temples and waterfalls. Covering some 400 sq km, this is where Láo Shān mineral water starts its life and it's an excellent place to go hiking or climbing. The mountain is associated with Taoist legend and myth, with the central attraction being the Song dynasty **Tàiqīng Gōng** (Great Purity Palace). This Taoist monastery was established by the first Song emperor as a place to perform Taoist rites to save the souls of the dead. It's located a third of the way up Láo Shān, at the top of the first cable car, and just off the main walking path. Admission is Y3. Due north of the Tàiqīng Gōng is **Jiǔ Shuǐ**, noted for its numerous streams and waterfalls.

From the Tàiqīng Gōng, there are paths leading to the summit of Láo Shān. Three quarters of the way up to the summit, at the top of the second cable car, you have the option of ascending either through a cave or by stairs. The cave is amazing but requires you to crawl, climb steep ladders and cross narrow suspension bridges – all of this in the pitch black together with masses of tourists. Bring a torch. If you suffer vertigo or claustrophobia, you'd be better off taking the stairs.

Entry to Láo Shān is Y30. The cable car up the first half of the mountain costs Y15 with a ride up the second half costing Y20. From Qīngdǎo, bus No 304 runs to Láo Shān (Y9; two hours) with the first leaving from Taiping Lu at approximately 6.20 am. Tour buses to Láo Shān (Y25 return) also ply the streets of Qīngdǎo from 6 am onwards, returning at 5 pm. You are more likely to get a seat on a tour bus; public transport however, gives you the flexibility of returning when you like.

About 30 minutes by boat from Qīngdǎo and a further 40 minutes by bus is the beach of **Huángdǎo** (Yellow Island). Once the secret of locals, it is quickly becoming popular with tour groups. It remains, however, quieter and cleaner than Qīngdǎo's beaches. The ferry (Y5.50) leaves from the terminal (Qīngdǎo Lúndùzhàn) to the west of the train station. The first departure is at 6.30 am with the final boat returning at 9 pm. Once you reach the island, take bus No 1 to its terminus (Y2.50).

YĀNTÁI 烟台
☎ 0535 • pop 6,414,900

Yāntái is a busy ice-free port on the northern coast of the Shāndōng peninsula. It's not the most exciting town and the main reason for coming here is to take a boat to Dàlián or South Korea. However, as few tourists take the time to explore Yāntái, those who do can expect a warm welcome from friendly locals. There are a number of parks and an excellent museum to fill the day.

Note the signs posted on the way into town that read 'No whistling in built-up areas'. This is an attempt to decrease noise pollution; the law forbids the use of vehicle horns in town. The result is a somewhat eerie quiet in Yāntái's traffic clogged streets.

Like Qīngdǎo, Yāntái started life as a defence outpost and fishing village. It opened for foreign trade in 1862, but had no foreign concessions. Several nations, Japan and the USA among them, had trading establishments here and Yāntái was something of a resort area at one time. Since 1949 the port and naval base at Yāntái have been expanded and, apart from fishing and trading, the town is a major producer of wines, spirits and fruits. Yāntái means Smoke Terrace: wolf-dung fires were lit on the headland to warn fishing fleets of approaching pirates.

Information
The main branch of the Bank of China is at 166 Jie Fang Lu, on the corner of Sanma Lu. There is also a branch across from the train station where you can sometimes exchange US dollars.

The main post office is on the roundabout at the junction of Nan Dajie and Dahaiyang Lu. A second branch can be found on the corner of Nan Dajie and Xinanhe Lu.

At the time of writing, China Telecom was in the process of opening an office at 29 Haigang Lu, where it will offer public access to the Internet. Opening hours are 8 am to 5 pm.

There is a branch of CTS (☎ 608 5654) at 96 Beima Lu, near the train station, where you can book ferry and airline tickets. The main CTS office (☎ 622 4431) is in the crumbling edifice behind the Huàqiáo Bīnguǎn.

The PSB (☎ 624 5817) at 90 Tongshi Lu is south of town, past Nánshān Gōngyuán.

Yāntái Bówùguǎn 博物馆
Yantai Museum
The Yāntái Bówùguǎn is definitely worth a visit, as it is housed in a guild hall that was built by merchants and sailors as a place of worship to Linmo, the Sea God. Linmo was a strong cult figure of the 18th century; it is believed she appeared as a vision to fishermen who were lost at sea, leading them safely to shore.

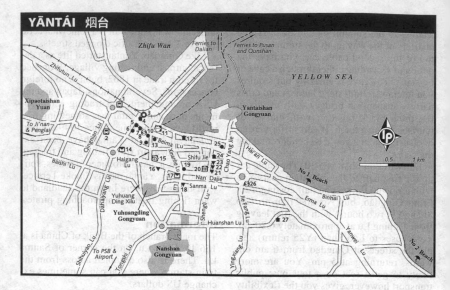

YĀNTÁI 烟台

The main hall of the museum is known as the 'Travelling Palace of the Goddess' as it was originally designed and finished in Guǎngzhōu and then shipped to Yāntái for assembly. Beyond the hall, at the centre of the courtyard, is the museum's most fascinating piece of architecture: a brightly and intricately decorated gate. Supported by 14 pillars, the gate is a collage of hundreds of carved and painted figures, flowers, beasts, phoenixes and animals. The carvings depict battle scenes and folk stories including *Stories for Three Kingdoms* and *The Eight Immortals who Crossed the Sea* (see the Boxed Text 'The Immortal Eight'). As you pass through the gate, you'll encounter two stone pillars on which are carved coiling dragons.

At the southern end of the museum is a theatrical stage that was first made in Heosin, Fújiàn and shipped to Yāntái. Apparently Linmo wasn't particularly fond of that stage as it was lost at sea and had to be reconstructed in Yāntái. The stage continues to be used for performances to celebrate Linmo's birthday and anniversary of deification. On these days you can join the celebrations. Entry to the museum is Y5.

Parks

Yāntái has a number of parks where you can escape for an afternoon. **Nánshān Gōngyuán** (Y3), south of town, is the largest and most popular, especially with families. It has a zoo, amusement park and pond. You can rent boats to row around the pond.

For a more peaceful retreat, try **Yùhuángdǐng Gōngyuán**, in the centre of Yāntái, with its quiet trails, 600-year-old Taoist temple, archway, pavilion and pagoda. The park is known as Lesser Pénglái – and that it is: less money, people and noise! Entry is Y5 and it is open from 6 am to 6 pm.

On the north coast is **Yàntáishān Gōngyuán**, where you can hang out with the local fisherfolk.

Places to Stay

The two options for budget travellers are equally unpleasant. The *Jǐnxiáng Dàjiǔdiàn (Golden Shell Hotel;* ☎ *621 6495, 173 Beima Lu)* is a 10-minute walk from the train station. The first building you come to has cheap doubles from Y128 to Y200 and triples for Y228. The rooms improve as you climb the stairs; but even hiking to the top floor doesn't ensure escape from the cockroach infestation. In the

YĀNTÁI

PLACES TO STAY

4 Yāntái Tiĕdào Dàshà;
China Southwest Airlines
铁道大厦;
西南航空公司

5 Yóudiàn Bīnguǎn
邮电宾馆

7 Gǎngchéng Bīnguǎn
港城宾馆

12 Jīnxiáng Dàjiǔdiàn
金翔大酒店

24 Tàipíngyáng Dàjiǔdiàn
太平洋大酒店

27 Huàqiáo Bīnguǎn; CTS
华侨宾馆;中国旅行社

PLACES TO EAT

16 Fāngkuài Shāokǎo
方块烧烤

18 Ravioli King of New Sun
新太饺子王

21 Carvel
凯菲冰淇淋专卖店

22 California Beef Noodles
King USA
美国加洲牛肉面

23 Hǎoxiānglái Cāntīng
好香来餐厅

OTHER

1 Buses to Pénglái
去蓬莱车站

2 Long-Distance
Bus Station
长途汽车站

3 Train Station
火车站

6 CAAC
中国民航

8 Bank of China
中国银行

9 Friendship Store
友谊商店

10 International
Seamen's Club
国际海员俱乐部

11 Boat Ticket Office;
Departures
烟台港客运站

13 CTS
中国旅行社

14 Main Post
Office
电信大楼

15 China Telecom
中国电信

17 Post Office
邮局

19 Shandong
Airlines
山东航空公司

20 Yāntái
Bówùguǎn
博物馆

25 Foreign Languages
Bookstore
外文书店

26 Bank of China
中国银行

newer and plusher building next door, doubles cost Y188 to Y300.

Directly across the street from the train station is the *Gǎngchéng Bīnguǎn* (☎ 628 3888). Doubles start at Y138. While the hotel seems to be slightly less popular with the cockroaches, the noisy International Seaman's Club is next door. The racket that surrounds it in the wee hours of the morning leaves you with little likelihood of sleep.

To the right as you exit the train station is the newly renovated *Yāntái Tiĕdào Dàshà* (Yāntái Railway Mansion; ☎ 625 6588, 135 Beima Lu), with decently priced doubles from Y200. Across the street is the new *Yóudiàn Fàndiàn* (Post & Telecom Hotel; ☎ 628 8888), with standard rooms from Y280 to Y998.

The *Huàqiáo Bīnguǎn* (Overseas Chinese Guesthouse; ☎ 622 4431) was closed for renovation at the time of writing, but will offer doubles with sea views for Y300, so it's worth checking out. The hotel is east of town and can be reached on bus No 7.

The most upmarket hotel in Yāntái is the *Tàipíngyáng Dàjiǔdiàn (Shāndōng Pacific Hotel; ☎ 620 6888, fax 621 5204, 74 Shifu Lu)*, which features a bowling alley, billiards room and other four-star facilities. It has doubles from Y660.

Places to Eat

The train station area has a reasonable selection of restaurants; head east down Beima Lu for Korean food. Across the street from the train station is a maze of *market alleys* where you can buy fruit, dried snacks and meals. Be sure to ask the price before you dig in.

Across the street from the Tàipíngyáng Dàjiǔdiàn is *Hǎoxiānglái Cāntīng*, a busy restaurant that serves Chinese and international cuisine. Around the corner on Shengli Lu, you'll find the *California Beef Noodles King USA (Mĕiguo Jiāzhōu Niuròumiàn)*, where you can buy huge, cheap bowls of piping hot noodles.

The *Ravioli King of New Sun (Xīntài Jiǎozīwáng)* is a deservedly popular joint on Xinanhe Lu, but don't go expecting Italian fare; the ravioli it specialises in is *jiaozi* (dumplings). Meals start at Y14.

SHĀNDŌNG 山东

The most popular spot for kebabs is the hole-in-the-wall *Fāngkuài Shāokǎo*, on the corner of Side Lu and Nan Dajie, beneath the pedestrian overpass. The crowds here can be unbelievable.

For all of your ice cream needs, including floats, cakes and shakes, head to *Carvel (Kǎifēi Bīngqílín Zhuānmàidiàn)*, across from the museum on Shengli Lu.

Getting There & Away

Air Flights leave daily, except Monday, for Seoul (Y1990), and on Tuesday and Saturday for Hong Kong (Y1700). There are daily flights to Běijīng and Shànghǎi and three flights a week to Guǎngzhōu. Flight bookings can be made at CTS or at the CAAC office (☎ 624 1330) at 6 Dahaiyang Lu. Shandong Airlines' (☎ 662 2737) main booking office is on the corner of Nan Dajie and Xinanhe Lu and China Southwest Airlines (☎ 625 0919) is at the western end of the Yāntái Tiědào Dàshà (see Places to Stay earlier).

Bus There are frequent minibuses between Yāntái and Qīngdǎo (Y30; three hours; departing approximately every ½ hour). In both cities, buses congregate in front of the train stations and depart when full. Frequent minibuses to Pénglái (Y8) depart from the bus station on the corner of Bei Malu and Qingnian Lu, about a five-minute walk west of the train station.

Train The Yāntái to Qīngdǎo train (Y22; four hours; departing daily at 8.53 am) terminates in Qīngdǎo – it does not carry on to Jǐ'nán. Two trains daily terminate in Jǐ'nán (Y38), leaving Yāntái at 9.52 am and 5.27 pm. Trains depart daily for Běijīng (Y67) at 9.08 pm and Shànghǎi (Y88) at 2.08 pm.

Boat At the passenger ferry terminal near the train station, it is possible to book tickets for express boats to Dàlián (Y170; three hours; departing daily at 8.30 and 10 am and 12.30 and 2 pm). There are also slow boats to Dàlián (Y123; seven hours; departing daily at 8, 8.30 and 10 am). The service to Tiānjīn has been cancelled indefinitely.

Boats to Pusan in South Korea (US$120 to US$360) leave every Thursday at 11 am. Another destination in Korea is Qunshan; boats leave every Monday (US$100 to US$300).

Getting Around

The airport is approximately 20km south of town. Airport buses (Y10; 25 minutes; 15km; departing hourly) leave from the CAAC office from 6 am to 5.40 pm.

Bus No 7 runs through the city from east to west, passing Yuhuang Gōngyuán, Nánshān Gōngyuán and the Huàqiáo Bīnguǎn. Bus No 3 does a loop of town, running past the train station, south down Xinan Lu and west on Yohuang Dingxi Lu. To reach the east coast take bus No 10. Taxis cost Y8 to anywhere in town.

PÉNGLÁI 蓬莱

About 65km north-west of Yāntái is Pénglái and the coastal castle of **Pénglái Gé**, a place of the gods often referred to in Chinese mythology. China's ancient legend of the Eight Immortals Crossing the Sea originated here (see the boxed text 'The Immortal Eight'.) Pénglái Gé is perched on a cliff top overlooking the sea and is about 1000 years old. Here you can discover a fascinating array of castles and temples, and enjoy wonderful views of fishing boat flotillas. Many of the temples, walls and pavilions are delightfully overgrown with ivy and creepers. It's popular with tour groups, so you need to be in the mood for crowds to enjoy a day at Pénglái. The castle now has a cable car, laser-gun park and theatre. Entry costs Y50.

Besides the castle, Pénglái is famous for an **optical illusion** that the locals claim appears every few decades. The last full mirage seen from the castle was in July 1981, when two islands appeared with roads, trees, buildings, people and vehicles. This phenomenon apparently lasted about 40 minutes.

If you decide to stay the night in Pénglái, the *Péngxiáng Dàshà* (☎ 565 6788, 135 Zhongguo Pénglái Beilu) is a 15-minute walk to the right as you exit the bus station. Doubles cost Y200.

Pénglái is easily visited as a day trip from Yāntái (Y8; 1½ hours).

The Immortal Eight

In the days before mere mortals could reach it, Pénglái was home to the Eight Immortals. At that time, Pénglái was one of 108 Taoist paradises; the air was scented not by yams, puffed wheat and tea eggs, but by millions of pearl blossoms and trees of coral. Birds and animals that lingered nearby were as white as clouds and the palace was surrounded by a weightless sea, uncrossable by mortals (even ticket vendors!). Eight palaces, each atop a peak, housed the eight immortal residents.

Born of an ancient Taoist myth, the Eight Immortals have become the superheroes of Chinese folktales. Their antics and adventures provide humorous stories that convey beauty and happiness. Models for those who renounced the material world to find a more spiritual way of living, the Eight Immortals were destined to travel together for an eternity, performing and witnessing wonders.

Each of the eight gained their immortality by different means, with their identities based on varying degrees of fact. Lan Kai He, for example, was a destitute woman who is believed to have been carried to heaven and granted immortality for the purpose of protecting of the poor. He Xiangsu, the goddess of housekeepers, was a woman of the 7th century who ground up a gemstone and gained immortality by drinking its juice.

Zhang Guo, an 8th century eccentric, traversed the earth on a magic donkey that he could fold up and store in his pocket. Lu Dongbin was a prince, also of the 8th century, who envisioned his life of royalty ending in banishment by the court and decided to beat them to it by renouncing his life and thereby achieving immortality.

Han Xiang was a philosopher of the 9th century who fell from a sacred peach tree and was granted immortality just moments before crashing to the ground. Han Zhongli, once an army officer and official of the state, retired to the life of a hermit. While dabbling in a little alchemy, the wall of his cave split open and a box of the elixir of eternal life appeared.

It is said that Li Xuan, otherwise known as 'Iron Crutch', was granted immortality in one of two ways: either by a female goddess who found him limping and begging next to her bath and evidently took a fancy to him, or by the Taoist philosopher Nan Yang who was cremated on the sixth rather than the prescribed seventh day, leaving his lingering soul to assume the body of Li, a nearby beggar. In either case, Li is portrayed as the god of the disabled. Finally, Kao Guojiu, the brother of the 11th century Empress Kao, became so disgusted by the corruption of the courts that he took to the mountains and learned the ways of the immortal from Li Xuan.

The Immortal Eight have remained a popular source of artistic inspiration since the 12th century. Each has a characteristic possession that is generally included in any artistic depiction. Han Zhongli, for example, carries a fan with which he is capable of reviving the souls of the dead. The other seven possessions are a drum, castanets, a ladle, pipe, flute, a basket of flowers and a gourd in which Li Xuan carries his elixir.

WĒIHĂI 威海

☎ 05451 • pop 2,450,900

About 60km east of Yāntái is the obscure port city of Wēihǎi. The British had a concession here, though little remains today to remind you of its colonial heritage.

The only reason to go to Wēihǎi is to avail yourself of its passenger ferry service to Inch'ŏn in South Korea, although you can also do this in Qīngdǎo. The boat leaves at 5 pm on Wednesday, Friday and Sunday, arriving in Inch'ŏn at 8 am the next day.

There are a variety of ticket prices (2nd class costs Y930, the suite costs Y3360). In the other direction, the boat leaves Inch'ŏn for Wēihǎi at 6 pm on Tuesday, Thursday and Saturday, arriving in Wēihǎi at 8 am.

If you arrive in Wēihǎi without having purchased a ferry ticket in advance, the place to go is CITS (☎ 522 6210), 44 Dongcheng Lu. Minibuses run from the long-distance bus station in Wēihǎi directly to Yāntái, Qīngdǎo and Jǐ'nán. Sleeper coaches also run to Shànghǎi and Běijīng.

Jiāngsū 江苏

Blessed with China's most productive land, Jiāngsū is symbolic of agricultural abundance and has long been known as 'the land of fish and rice' – the original Chinese character for the province contained these two pictographs. The southern part of Jiāngsū lies within the Cháng Jiāng (Yangzi River) Basin, a tapestry landscape of greens, yellows and blues contrasting with whitewashed farmhouses. Woven into this countryside is a dense concentration of towns and cities with one of the highest levels of industrial output in China.

As far back as the 16th century, the towns on the Grand Canal (Dà Yùnhé) set up industrial bases for silk production and grain storage, and are still ahead of the rest of the nation. While heavy industry is based in Nánjīng and Wúxī, the other towns concentrate more on light industry, machinery and textiles. They're major producers of electronics and computer components, and haven't been blotted out by the scourges of coal mining or steelworks.

Today, southern Jiāngsū is increasingly being drawn into the ever-expanding economy of nearby Shànghǎi, aided in part by an expressway between Nánjīng and Shànghǎi. It's one of the most rapidly developing provinces in China, evident in the fast rate of construction in the major cities.

The stretch from Nánjīng down to Hángzhōu in Zhèjiāng is heavily touristed. North of the Cháng Jiāng (Yangzi River) is a complete contrast with comparatively snail-paced development that has left it lagging behind the rest of the province. In the north the major port is situated at Liányúngǎng and there's a large coal works in Xúzhōu.

Jiāngsū is hot and humid in summer, yet has overcoat temperatures in winter (when visibility can drop to zero). Rain or drizzle can be prevalent in winter, but it's gentle rain, adding a misty, soft touch to the land. The natural colours can be spectacular in spring. Heavy rains fall in spring and summer, but autumn is fairly dry.

Highlights

Capital: Nánjīng
Population: 70.2 million
Area: 102,600 sq km

- Nánjīng's Zǐjīn Shān (Purple Mountain), with its wealth of historical sights
- Sūzhōu, a city of canals and beautiful traditional gardens, despite the ravages of redevelopment
- Zhōuzhuāng, a beautifully preserved riverside village known as the new Venice of China and recently recognised as an International Heritage Site

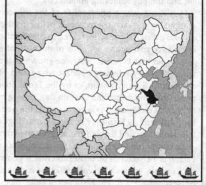

NÁNJĪNG 南京

☎ 025 • pop 5,298,200

Nánjīng is one of China's more attractive major cities. It sports a long historical heritage and has twice served briefly as the nation's capital, firstly in the early years of the Ming dynasty (AD 1368–1644) and secondly as the capital of the Republic of China in the early years of the 20th century. Most of Nánjīng's major attractions are reminders of the city's former glory under the Ming.

Like many other major Chinese cities, Nánjīng is swiftly developing; cranes dominate the skyline as skyscrapers are constructed at a blistering pace. Nánjīng is home

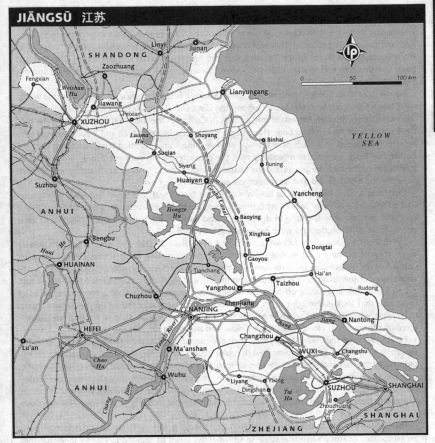

JIĀNGSŪ 江苏

to several colleges and universities and a large foreign student population. There is an abundance of international-style restaurants, a lively nightlife and access to just about any amenity from around the world.

Just east of the city is Zǐjīn Shān (Purple Mountain), where it's possible to spend a pleasant day hiking and swimming.

History

The Nánjīng area has been inhabited for about 5000 years, and a number of prehistoric sites have been discovered in or around the city. Recorded history, however,

begins in the Warring States Period (453–221 BC), when Nánjīng emerged as a strategic object of conflict. The arrival of a victorious Qin dynasty (221–207 BC) put an end to this, allowing Nánjīng to prosper as a major administrative centre.

The city's fortunes took a turn for the worse in the 6th century when it was successively rocked by floods, fires, peasant rebellions and military conquest. With the advent of the Sui dynasty (AD 589–618) and the establishment of Xī'ān as imperial capital, Nánjīng was razed and its historical heritage reduced to ruins. Although it

The Heavenly Kingdom of the Taiping

The Taiping Rebellion that occured in the middle of the 19th century ranks among the most frenzied and calamitous periods in Chinese history. What made it more remarkable was its creed: that Hong Xiuquan, the leader of the Taipings, was the brother of Jesus and the son of God. He had been sent down to exterminate 'demons' – who (coincidentally) were personified by the Qing dynasty and its supporters.

Born into a Hakka family in eastern Guǎngxī and having failed the official examinations that would have taken him onto the career ladder among the Qing elite, Hong Xiuquan first came into contact with Christianity through Protestant missionaries in Canton in the mid-1830s. After failing the official examinations for the third time, Hong had a dream of a bearded man and a younger man who he later interpreted, in a flash of realisation after reading some Christian tracts, as being God the Father and Jesus, his son. He repeatedly read the character for his surname 'Hong' in the Chinese translation of the bible he possessed; the character means 'flood' and he made strong associations between the biblical flood and his mission on earth to wipe out evil.

Collecting around him a flock of believers attracted by his zeal, self-belief and drive, Hong soon had a formidable army of faithful who sought to establish the Heavenly Kingdom of Great Peace on earth, overthrowing the Qing in the process. God was the one true god and traditional Chinese beliefs (such as Confucianism) were heretical and wayward.

By 1850, Hong Xiuquan's followers numbered more than 20,000 and were a capable military force, regimented by a strict morality that forbade opium smoking, took serious measures against corruption and established separate camps to divide the sexes. A communal treasury was set up to take charge of the finances of the Taiping community and legal and agrarian reforms followed suit.

Led by capable and daring officers, the Taiping army dispatched itself on a remarkable series of conquests that took it through Húnán, Húběi and Ānhuī, eventually setting up the Taiping capital in Nánjīng, which fell to the rebels in March 1853. The Manchu population of Nánjīng was slaughtered in affirmation of Hong's plan to rid China, and the world, of demons.

For 11 years the Taiping held sway over their conquered domain, with Hong ruling over all as the Heavenly King. Hong further regimented the rules governing the Taiping faithful, creating a society ordered by spartan and inflexible decrees all intent on eliminating inequality. However, the forces that were to destroy the Heavenly Kingdom soon emerged in a power struggle among the leadership of the Taiping. Eventually this resulted in the murder of those in positions of great influence, along with their supporters. Hong reasserted his authority, but in doing so eliminated his most useful advisers.

The Taiping's failure to take Peking (Běijīng) and Shànghǎi was partly because the foreign powers (suspicious of Hong's heretical strain of Christianity) failed to respond to Hong's faith that they would not support the Qing. The Taiping's economic strategies similarly failed, and the strict codes of conduct left many bitter and complaining; Hong also failed to align himself and his cause with other contemporaneous anti-Qing rebellions. All of these factors led to an erosion of the power and influence of the Taiping.

Qing soldiers, led by Zeng Guofan, eventually retook Nánjīng in 1864, soon after Hong Xiuquan's death. Zeng Guofan reported to the emperor that none of the 100,000 rebels in Nánjīng surrendered, but instead took their own lives.

The fanaticism of the Taiping was incredible, and despite its strongly anti-Manchu character, the event clearly questions the theory that Christianity has no place in China. Even though Hong arrogated upon himself the heretical (to Protestants and Catholics) title of son of God, the Taiping were responsible for, among other things, a vast translation and publishing program of Christian scriptures and writings, and it was their aim to spread these ultimately to the four corners of the earth.

enjoyed a period of prosperity under the long-lived Tang dynasty, it gradually slipped into obscurity.

Then in 1356, a peasant rebellion led by Zhu Yuanzhang against the Mongol Yuan dynasty (AD 1271–1368) was successful. The peasants captured Nánjīng and 12 years later claimed the Yuan capital, Běijīng. Zhu Yuanzhang took the name of Hong Wu and set himself up as the first emperor of the Ming dynasty, with Nánjīng as its capital. A massive palace was built and huge walls were erected around the city.

Nánjīng's glory as imperial capital was short-lived. In 1420, the third Ming emperor, Yong Le, moved the capital back to Běijīng. From this time, Nánjīng's fortunes variously rose and declined as a regional centre, but it was not until the 19th and 20th centuries that the city again entered the centre stage of Chinese history.

In the 19th century, the Opium Wars brought the British to Nánjīng and it was here that the first of the 'unequal treaties' were signed, opening several Chinese ports to foreign trade, forcing China to pay a huge war indemnity, and officially ceding the island of Hong Kong to Britain. Just a few years later, Nánjīng became the Taiping capital during the Taiping Rebellion (1851–64), which succeeded in taking over most of southern China. In 1864, the combined forces of the Qing army, British army and various European and US mercenaries surrounded the city. They laid siege for seven months, before finally capturing it and slaughtering the Taiping defenders.

In the 20th century, Nánjīng has been the capital of the Republic of China; the site of the worst war atrocity in Japan's assault on China (the 1937 'Rape of Nánjīng' in which as many as 300,000 people may have died); and the Kuomintang capital from 1928 to 1937 and 1945 to 1949, before the communists 'liberated' the city and made China their own.

Orientation

Nánjīng lies entirely on the southern bank of the Cháng Jiāng (Yangzi River), bounded in the east by Zǐjīn Shān. The cen-

tre of town is a traffic circle called Xinjiekou, where some of the hotels, including the Jīnlíng Fàndiàn, and most tourist facilities are located. Nánjīng train station and the main long-distance bus station are in the far north of the city.

The historical sights, including the Zhōngshān Líng (Sun Yatsen Mausoleum), Línggǔ Sì (Sharp Valley Temple) and the tomb of the first Ming Emperor Hong Wu, are on Zǐjīn Shān, on Nánjīng's eastern fringe.

The city has experienced long periods of prosperity, evident in the numerous buildings that successive rulers built – their tombs, steles, pagodas, temples and niches lay scattered throughout the city. If you can get hold of a copy, *In Search of Old Nanking* by Barry Till & Paula Swart (Joint Publishing Company, Hong Kong, 1982) will give you a thorough rundown. Unfortunately, much has been destroyed or allowed to crumble into ruins.

Maps Several different versions of local maps are available from the Foreign Language Bookstore, as well as newspaper kiosks and street hawkers around Nánjīng. Many of these city maps contain local bus routes. A number of upscale hotels, including the Jīnlíng Fàndiàn and Hilton, give out free English-language maps of the city.

Information

Money The main branch of the Bank of China (☎ 4456688) is at 29 Hong Wu Lu, just south of Zhongshan Donglu. You can also change money at the Jīnlíng Fàndiàn and other top-end hotels.

Post & Communications The main post office is at the corner of Beijing Donglu and Zhongyang Lu. The more upmarket tourist hotels also offer postal services. The main China Telecom office is on the northeast corner of the Gǔ Lóu (Drum Tower) traffic circle and is open daily from 8 am to 10 pm.

Email & Internet Access China Telecom's Internet Cafe is on Zhongshan Beilu,

Broken as Jade

'How could historical facts written in blood be concealed by lies written in ink?' questioned a Chinese commentator article written in 1982. The article continued:

Your 'samurai' forebears used innocent Chinese to test bacteriological warfare, used them as living targets. They dismembered and chopped up Chinese captives who were tied to trees. You forced Chinese to dig holes and bury themselves alive. You adopted such savage means as the 'iron maiden', pulling out fingernails, branding, belly cutting, electric grinding and flesh eating to persecute Chinese compatriots.

The article was published as part of a Chinese protest against the approval and publication of Japanese school textbooks that severely downplayed Japan's brutality during its invasion into China between 1937 and 1945, in particular, its attack on Nánjīng. As part of the Chinese protest, a media campaign of photos and reports was launched. This campaign rekindled fear and hostility towards the Japanese both in those Chinese who had survived the invasion as well as in younger generations.

In 1945, with the Chinese army comparatively weak and under-funded and the Japanese army on the horizon, the invasion into and occupation of Nánjīng by Japan appeared imminent. As it packed up and fled, the Chinese government encouraged the people of Nánjīng to stay, saying: 'All those who have blood and breath in them must feel that they wish to be broken as jade rather than remain whole as tile'. To reinforce this statement, the gates to the city were locked, trapping over half a million citizens inside. Nevertheless, thousands of civilians attempted to follow the retreating government by escaping through Xiaguan Men, the only gate in the city wall that remained unlocked. Leading up to the gate was a 70-foot tunnel inside of which reigned panic and mayhem. In the resulting chaos and collisions, thousands of people were suffocated, burned or trampled to death.

What followed in Nánjīng was six weeks of continuous, unfathomable victimisation of civilians to an extent that had yet to be witnessed in modern warfare. During Japan's occupation of Nánjīng, between 300,000 and 400,000 Chinese civilians were killed, either in group massacres or individual murders. Within the first month, at least 20,000 women between the ages of 11 and 76 were brutally raped. Women who attempted to refuse or children who interfered were often bayoneted or shot. It has been reported by those involved that the atrocities committed in Nánjīng were condoned and encouraged by the Japanese officers in command as acceptable and expected military procedure.

The Japanese, however, underestimated the courageousness and strength of the Chinese people. Instead of breaking the people's will, the invasion only served to fuel a sense of identity and determination. Those who did not die – broken as jade – survived to fight back.

Given the brutality of Japan's invasion into Nánjīng, it is not at all surprising that the Chinese protested it being airbrushed from Japanese textbooks. Equally disturbing as Japan's misrepresentation of the brutality is the rest of the world's apparent aversion to it. The Rape of Nánjīng is conspicuously absent from many world history books. Despite this, it is hoped that a growing awareness of the Rape of Nánjīng will help to prevent such atrocities from occurring again. As the ancient Chinese proverb says, 'Past experience, if not forgotten, is a guide for the future' ('Qian shi bu wang hou shi zhi shi').

west of the Holiday Inn, and offers Internet access for Y12 per hour. You can also get online in the Internet bar on the ground floor of the Nanjing University Foreign Students Dormitory (see Places to Stay). The

Internet bar is open 9.30 am to 1.30 am and costs 2 jiǎo per minute.

Travel Agencies The China International Travel Service (CITS; Zhōngguó Guójì

Lǚxíngshè; ☎ 342 8999, fax 342 8954, @ otcitsnj.col.co.cn) at 202/1 Zhongshan Beilu, can arrange air, train and boat tickets, although there's a service charge for each ticket.

Ming City Wall

Nánjīng enjoyed its golden years under the Ming dynasty, and there are numerous remnants of the period. One of the most impressive is the Ming city wall measuring over 33km – the longest city wall ever built in the world. About two-thirds of it still stands. It was built between 1366 and 1386, by more than 200,000 labourers.

The layout is irregular, an exception to the usual square walls of these times, as much of it is built on the foundations of earlier walls, which took advantage of strategic hills. Averaging 12m high and 7m wide at the top, the wall was built of bricks supplied from five Chinese provinces. Each brick had stamped on it the place it came from, the overseer's name and rank, the brickmaker's name and sometimes the date. This was to ensure that the bricks were well made; if they broke they had to be replaced.

Just east of the Nánjīng Bówùguǎn (Nánjīng Museum) is a section of the wall that you can wander along with steps leading up to it from the road. You can walk along the top only as far as Qián Hú (Front Lake), where a section of wall has collapsed into the water. Venturing too close to the collapsed portion is not advised; one reader reported that while at this section of the wall he was detained by police and his film confiscated due to the sensitive nature of a nearby military base.

Ming City Gates

Some of the original 13 Ming city gates remain, including Zhōngyāng Mén (Centre Entreat Gate) in the north and Zhōnghuá Mén (Brilliant Middle Gate) in the south. The city gates were heavily fortified and, rather than being the usual weak points of the defences, they were defensive strongholds. The Zhōnghuá Mén has four rows of gates, making it almost impregnable; it could house a garrison of 3000 soldiers in vaults in the front gate building. Today some of these vaults are used as souvenir shops. Zhōnghuá Mén can be visited, but Zhōngyāng Mén is now used as a barracks.

Míng Gùgōng 明故宫
Ming Palace Ruins

Built by Hong Wu, Míng Gùgōng is said to have been a magnificent structure after which the Imperial Palace in Běijīng was modelled. Virtually all that remains of it is five marble bridges lying side by side, known as the Wǔlóng Qiáo (Five Dragon Bridges); the old ruined gate called Wu Mén; and the enormous column bases of the palace buildings.

The palace suffered two major fires in its first century and was allowed to fall into ruins after the Ming court moved to Běijīng. It was later looted by the Manchus and then, during the Taiping Rebellion, bombardments by Qing and western troops finished it off.

You can reach the Míng Gùgōng by bus No 1; entry is Y1.

Early Remains

Nánjīng has been inhabited since prehistoric times. Remains of a prehistoric culture have been found at the site of today's Gǔ Lóu (Drum Tower), in the centre of the city, and in surrounding areas. About 200 sites of small clan communities, mainly represented by pottery and bronze artefacts dating back to the late Shang and Zhou dynasties, have been found on both sides of the Cháng Jiāng (Yangzi River).

In AD 212, towards the end of the Eastern Han period, the military commander in charge of the Nánjīng region built a citadel on Qīngling Shān in the west of Nánjīng. At that time the mountain was referred to as Shítou Shān (Stone Head Mountain) and so the citadel became known as the Shítou Dūshì (Stone City). The wall measured over 10km in circumference. Today, some of the red sandstone foundations can still be seen.

Gǔ Lóu 鼓楼
Drum Tower

Built in 1382, the Gǔ Lóu lies roughly in the centre of Nánjīng, on a traffic circle on

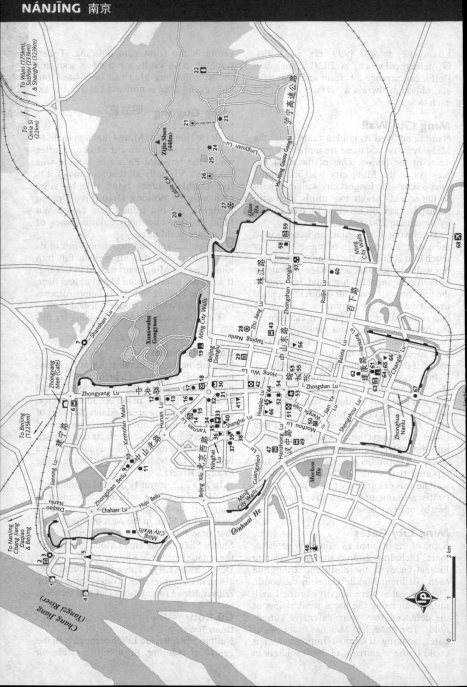

PLACES TO STAY

8 Dīngshān Huāyuán Jiǔdiàn
丁山花园酒店

10 Hóngqiáo Fàndiàn
虹桥饭店

11 Nánjīng Fàndiàn
南京饭店

12 Xuánwǔ Fàndiàn
玄武饭店

15 Nanjing Holiday Inn
怡华假日酒店

16 Jiāngsū Dàjiǔdiàn
江苏大酒店

24 Nanjing International
Conference Centre
南京国际会议大酒

34 Jīnglì Jiǔdiàn
晶丽酒店

35 Nanjing University Foreign
Students Dormitory
南京大学
外国留学生宿舍

37 Nanjing Normal University;
Nanshan Hotel
南京师范大学
南山宾馆

38 Gǔnándū Fàndiàn
古南都饭店

44 Zhōngxīn Dàjiǔdiàn
中心大酒店

52 Jīnlíng Fàndiàn
金陵饭店

58 Hilton Hotel
希尔顿饭店

61 Zhuàngyuánlóu Jiǔdiàn
状元楼酒店

62 Yuèhuá Dàjiǔdiàn
悦华大酒店

PLACES TO EAT

36 Swede & Kraut
老外乐

39 Skyway Bakery & Deli
云中食品店

40 Jack's Place; Pizza Express;
Family Cafe; Coffee & Tea
杰克店

41 Wǔzhōu Jiǔjiā
梧州酒家

45 Rendezvous Bistro
亲密爱人面包房,酒吧

46 Henry's Home Cafe
亨利之家

56 Sichuān Jiǔjiā
四川酒家

65 Lǎozhèngxīng Càiguǎn
老正兴菜馆

66 Wǎnqíng Lóu
晚晴楼

LAKES & GARDENS

25 Zǐxiá Hú; Míng Xiàolíng
Fēngjǐngqū
紫霞湖

27 Zhíwù Yuán
植物园

28 Xú Yuán
南京煦园

MONUMENTS & TOMBS

5 Dùjiāng Jìniànbēi
渡江纪念碑

21 Zhōngshān Líng
中山陵

26 Míng Xiàolíng
明孝陵

48 Memorial of the Nanjing
Massacre
大屠杀纪念馆

MUSEUMS & GALLERIES

2 Nánjīng Tiáoyuē Shǐliào
Chénlièguǎn
南京条约史料陈列馆

29 Jiāngsū Měishùguǎn
江苏美术馆

59 Nánjīng Bówùguǎn
南京博物院

63 Tàipíng Tiānguó Lìshǐ
Bówùguǎn
太平天国历史博物馆

PAGODAS & TEMPLES

17 Zhōng Lóu
钟楼

19 Jīmíng Sì
鸡鸣塔

22 Línggǔ Sì
灵谷塔

32 Gǔ Lóu
鼓楼

64 Fūzǐ Miào
夫子庙

TRANSPORT

1 No 4 Dock
四号码头

3 Nánjīng West Train Station
南京西站

4 Zhōngshān Dock
中山码头

6 Long-Distance Bus Station
长途汽车站

7 Nánjīng Train Station
南京火车站

31 China Eastern Airlines
Booking Office
东方航空售票处

43 Hanfu Jie Bus Station
汉府街汽车站

47 Minibuses to Zhènjiāng
and Yángzhōu
往镇江、扬州
小公共汽车

49 Minibus to Airport
小公共汽车往机场车

54 Xinjiekou Traffic Circle
新街口

60 CAAC
中国民航.

68 Nánjīng Airport
南京机场

OTHER

9 CITS
中国国际旅行社

13 Foreign Languages
Bookstore
外文书店

14 China Telecom Internet
中国电信网吧

18 China Telecom
中国电信

20 Zǐjīnshān Observatory
紫金山天文台

23 Zhōngshānlíng Yīnyuè Tái
中山陵音乐台

30 Main Post Office
邮电局

33 Catch 22
凯琪22

42 Zhongshan Department
Store
中山百货

50 Cháotiān Gōng
朝天宫

51 GE Shopping Centre
金鹰商场

53 PSB
公安局

55 Bank of China
中国银行

57 Míng Gùgōng
明故宫

67 Zhōnghuá Mén
中华门

Běijīng Xilu. Drums were usually beaten to give directions for the change of the night watches and, in rare instances, to warn the populace of impending danger. Only one large drum remains today. The tower is open daily from 8 am to midnight; entry is free.

Zhōng Lóu 钟楼
Bell Tower

North-east of the Gǔ Lóu, the Zhōng Lóu houses an enormous – you guessed it – bell, cast in 1388 and originally situated in a pavilion on the western side of the Gǔ Lóu. The present tower dates from 1889 and is a small two-storey pavilion with a pointed roof and upturned eaves. The tower is surrounded by a garden and teahouse that remain open late into the evening.

Cháotiān Gōng 朝天宫
Heaven Dynasty Palace

Cháotiān Gōng was originally established in the Ming dynasty as a school for educating noble children in court etiquette. Most of today's buildings, including the centrepiece of the palace, a Confucius temple, date from 1866 when the whole complex was rebuilt. Today the buildings are being used for a range of endeavours, including a *qigong* institute and a pottery centre.

Next to the eastern entrance of the palace, off Wangfu Dajie, is the **Jiāngsū Shěng Kūnjùyuàn** (Jiāngsū Province Kunju Theatre), where excellent – if rather infrequent – performances are held. *Kunju* is a regional form of classical Chinese opera that developed in the Sūzhōu-Hángzhōu-Nánjīng triangle. It is similar to, but slower than, Peking opera and is performed with colourful and elaborate costumes.

You can enter the palace off Mochou Lu. To reach it, take bus No 4 and get off two stops west of Xinjiekou. Entry to the palace is Y10.

Tàipíng Tiānguó Lìshǐ Bówùguǎn 太平天国历史博物馆
Taiping Heavenly Kingdom History Museum

Hong Xiuquan, the leader of the Taipings, had a palace built in Nánjīng, but the building was completely destroyed when

Nánjīng was taken in 1864. All that remains is a stone boat in an ornamental lake in what is now the Xú Yuán (Balmy Garden).

Palace or no palace, the Taiping enthusiasts have still managed to find a home for a museum, displaying maps showing the northward progress of the Taiping army from Guǎngdōng, Hong Xiuquan's seals, Taiping coins, weapons, and texts that describe the Taiping laws on agrarian reform, social law and cultural policy. Other texts describe divisions in the Taiping leadership, the attacks by the Manchus and foreigners, and the fall of Nánjīng in 1864. Most of the the original literature is kept in Běijīng.

The museum is off Zhonghua Nanlu and is open daily from 7 am to 5 pm; entry costs Y6.

Nánjīng Bówùguǎn 南京博物馆
Nanjing Museum

Just inside the eastern city walls on Zhongshan Donglu, the Nánjīng Bówùguǎn houses an array of artefacts from Neolithic times right through to the communist period. The main building was constructed in 1933 in the style of an ancient temple with yellow-glazed tiles, red-lacquered gates and columns. A brand-new complex, similar in design to the first, has recently been opened.

The museum houses an interesting exhibit of a burial suit made of small rectangles of jade sewn together with silver thread, dating from the Eastern Han dynasty (AD 25–220) and excavated from a tomb discovered in the city of Xúzhōu in northern Jiāngsū. Other exhibits include bricks with the inscriptions of their makers and overseers from the Ming city wall, drawings of old Nánjīng, an early Qing mural of old Sūzhōu and relics from the Taiping Rebellion. The museum is open daily from 9 to 11.45 am and 1.30 to 4.45 pm. Entry costs Y10 from Monday to Friday and Y5 on weekends and holidays.

Nánjīng Tiáoyuē Shǐliào Chénlièguǎn 南京条约史料陈列馆
Nanjing Treaty History Museum

This museum houses a small collection of photographs, maps and newspaper clippings (no English captions) related to the

Nánjīng Treaties. The real reason to come here is the building itself, which is where the first of the 'unequal treaties' was signed.

The museum is in the Jing Hai Temple, near the west train station, on Chao Yue Lu off Re Hou Lu. To get there catch bus No 13 to Sanxi Lu or bus No 31 or 16 to the Cháng Jiāng Dàqiáo (Yangzi Bridge). The museum is open daily from 8.30 am to 5 pm.

Memorial of the Nánjīng Massacre

The exhibits at the **Dàtúshā Jìniànguǎn** (Memorial Hall) document the atrocities committed by Japanese soldiers against the civilian population during the occupation of Nánjīng in 1937. (See boxed text 'Broken as Jade'.) They include pictures of actual executions, many taken by Japanese army photographers, and a gruesome viewing hall built over a mass grave of massacre victims. Also on display is furniture used at the signing of Japan's surrender to China – the disproportionately smaller and lower table and chairs given to the Japanese officers carried an unmistakable message. Many of the captions are in Chinese only but the photographs, skeletons and displays tell their own haunting stories.

The exhibits conclude on a more optimistic note, with a final room dedicated to the post-1945 Sino-Japanese reconciliation. The memorial hall is open daily from 8.30 am to 5 pm and entry costs Y8. It's in the city's south-western suburbs on bus route No 7, 37 or 41.

Dùjiāng Jìniànbēi 渡江纪念碑

Monument to the Crossing of the Yangzi River
In the north-west of the city on Zhongshan Beilu, this monument, erected in April 1979, commemorates the crossing of the river on 23 April 1949 and the capture of Nánjīng from the Kuomintang by the communist army. The characters on the monument are in the calligraphy of Deng Xiaoping.

Xuánwǔhú Gōngyuán 玄武湖公园

Profound Military Lake Park
This park is almost entirely covered by the waters of a large urban lake, but you can walk along causeways or take a boat out to its central forested islands.

A long path goes around the shores of Xuánwǔ Hú (Profound Military Lake), following alongside the old city walls for much of its length. The park, however, has an urban feel to it; if you're looking to get away from it all this is not the place to do it.

You can enter Xuánwǔhú Gōngyuán from the main gate off Zhongyang Lu or just west of Jiming Temple. The park is open daily from 6.30 am to 11 pm; entry is Y15.

Nánjīng Cháng Jiāng Dàqiáo 南京长江大桥

Yangzi River Bridge
One of the great achievements of the communists, and one of which they are justifiably proud, is the Cháng Jiāng Dàqiáo at Nánjīng. Opened on 23 December 1968, it's one of the longest bridges in China – a double-decker with a 4500m-long road on top and a railway line below.

Apparently the bridge was designed and built entirely by the Chinese after the Russians marched out and took the designs with them in 1960. Given the immensity of the construction it is an impressive engineering feat, before which there was no direct rail link between Běijīng and Shànghǎi. You can reach the bridge by bus No 16 or 31.

Fūzǐ Miào 夫子庙

Man and Son Temple
Located in the south of the city in a pedestrian zone on Gong Yuan Zie, at the core of Fūzǐ Miào is the site of an ancient Confucius temple that was a centre of Confucian study for more than 1500 years. Fūzǐ Miào has been damaged and rebuilt repeatedly, and what you see here today are newly restored late Qing dynasty structures or wholly new buildings reconstructed in traditional style. The main **Kǒng Miào** (Temple of Confucius) is behind them on the small square in front of the canal. A five-minute walk northwest from here are the **Dìgúode Kǎoshì Lǐtáng** (Imperial Examination Halls), where scholars spent months – or years – in tiny cells studying Confucian classics in preparation for civil service examinations.

Zhou Peikun

I might not have become a *getihu* (small businessman) if my work unit had taken me back when I came out of jail in 1984. I desperately needed money. The only way out was business.

It wasn't easy to start one. We were so poor nobody dared lend us any money. A colleague of my father finally lent me Y400, with high interest. We decided to sell 'hatched eggs', a delicacy loved by Nánjīng people. I got up at midnight and rode a borrowed tricycle 50km to a chicken farm on the north bank of the Cháng Jiāng (Yangzi River). At midnight the next day, I reached home again with 500 *jin* of eggs. Then we boiled and sold the rest at a busy junction. The whole family span like machines without rest.

In one month we made just over Y1000, no small amount for the time! But the egg business was too exhausting. From egg profits, we bought a sugar-cane crusher. It looks insignificant, but selling sugar-cane juice was quite lucrative. One jin of cane made two cups of juice that sold for 30 fen, but the sugarcane cost only 6 fen per jin. Again, that 24-fen profit required lots of work to locate, buy, transport, wash, peel and chop the cane. My wife knew the rural suburbs well so we always found cheap, good quality suppliers.

Eight months later we expanded into the fruit business, which needed more capital and space. I became a proper getihu, licensed to sell fruit at Fūzǐ Miào (Confucius Temple). My brother and some friends tried to stop me, for a getihu was not a well-respected profession. Few people would give up 'decent' jobs to become one and the overall quality of getihu at that time was poor. When I first sold eggs on the street, I felt embarrassed, and lowered my head if I saw people I knew. Gradually, I overcame the feeling. I was making clean money with my own two hands.

Fūzǐ Miào, a tourist spot known throughout China, is ideal for fruit as it's surrounded by residential areas. Competition was intense. To stand out, I was always the first to introduce the season's new fruits, and at very high prices. Watermelon was my favourite: popular and long-lasting. To be the earliest buyer, I slept in the melon fields far from Nánjīng, and sold them all night long. I always kept myself busy cleaning and polishing the fruit, lining them up nicely. These rules sound so simple, but not everyone follows them.

I've no regrets about the path I chose. How much can my former colleagues at the factory earn now? Perhaps Y700 to Y800 per month, maximum Y1000 for the most skilled workers. In our profession, people like to play down their wealth, for tax reasons among others. Let me boast just once – I've got a million yuan to play with. Twenty years' reform and opening up have changed people's concepts – they care more about money and less about social status. Nowadays, it's not so bad to be a getihu.

Abridged from *China Remembers* by Zhang Lijia and Calum MacLeod, published by Oxford University Press (1999)

Today, the area surrounding Fūzǐ Miào has become Nánjīng's main amusement quarter and is a particularly lively and crowded place on weekends and public holidays. There are restaurants, souvenir shops, tacky side-shows in old halls and a bookseller stocking ancient Chinese manuscripts. Buildings surrounding the canal on the small square are lit up at night, adding to the area's kitsch ambience. This atmosphere extends into the Confucius temple itself, which now houses a tacky display of dressed-up mannequins.

Fūzǐ Miào is open from 8 am to 9 pm and entry costs Y15. From the docks, you can reach the Fūzǐ Miào area by trolley-bus No 31 and from Xīnjiēkǒu by bus No 1. Bus No 7 also runs alongside Fūzǐ Miào.

Xú Yuán 南京煦园
Balmy Garden

This site served as the Tiānwáng Fǔ (Heavenly King Presidential Residence) during the Ming dynasty. It was also here that Hong Xiuquan and his fellow Taiping leaders set up house and the location has since been used by Sun Yatsen's provincial government, the Nationalist Government and, most recently, as the Presidential Palace of the Republic of China. The garden is home to a number of halls that include the offices used by Dr. Sun himself for a month in 1912. There is also a classical Ming garden here, complete with Hong Xiuquan's marble boat. The gardens are open daily from 8 am to 5 pm and are located at 292 Changjiang Lu, just east of Taiping Beilu.

Jiāngsū Měishùguǎn 江苏美术馆
Jiangsu Art Gallery

Down the street from the Xú Yuán is the obscure Jiāngsū Měishùguǎn. This small hall displays the works of local painters in frequently changing exhibitions. The gallery is open from 8 to 11.30 am and 2 to 5 pm; admission is Y2.

Lièshì Mùdì 烈士墓地
Martyr's Cemetery

Also known as Yǔhūa Tái, this pleasant park is in the south of the city. Once the Kuom-

---

美术馆 **Měishùguǎn: gallery**

Měi, meaning beautiful or admirable, is itself an amalgamation of the characters for big and sheep. While not perhaps in line with modern western thinking, a grown up who has learned the gentle manner of a sheep is regarded in traditional Chinese thinking as admirable.

The traditional form for shù (skills, art) is 術, from which only the middle part remains in the simplified character. If we take out 术 from the traditional form, it becomes 行, which is like a crossroads. As anyone visiting Běijīng or Shànghǎi will testify, the ability to cross the road in heavy traffic is a type of skill, or to some extent an art form!

---

intang's execution grounds, the communists have turned it into a garden dedicated to revolutionaries who lost their lives here. Along with a large monument, there is an exhibition hall in the garden that provides a brief history of the revolutionaries. Captions are in Chinese only. Admission is Y4.

Zǐjīn Shān 紫金山
Purple Mountain

Most of Nánjīng's historical sights are scattered over the southern slopes of this forested hill at the city's eastern fringe. It is possible to take a half hour cable car ride (Y20/35 one way/return) up to the top of the 400m hill for a panoramic, if somewhat hazy, view of Nánjīng, or you can walk up the stone path that runs beneath the cable cars. On the way down you can visit the **observatory**, located 350m up the hill. On display at the observatory are bronze astronomical instruments from the Ming dynasty. The observatory is open daily during daylight; entry is Y6.

Bus No 9 will take you from the city centre to Zhōngshān Líng (Sun Yatsen's Mausoleum), at the centre of Zǐjīn Shān. From there, bus No 20 runs between all of the sites on the hill, operating from 8 am to 5 pm and costing Y2 per ride.

Zhōngshān Líng 中山陵 (Sun Yatsen Mausoleum) As the hordes of tourists indicate, for many Chinese, a visit to Sun Yatsen's tomb is something of a pilgrimage. Sun is recognised by the communists and the Kuomintang alike as the father of modern China. He died in Běijīng in 1925, leaving behind an unstable Chinese republic. He had wished to be buried in Nánjīng, no doubt with greater simplicity than the Ming-style tomb that his successors built for him. Nevertheless, less than a year after his death, construction of this immense mausoleum began.

The tomb itself lies at the top of an enormous stone stairway, 323m long and 70m wide. At the start of the path stands a stone gateway built of Fújiàn marble, with a roof of blue-glazed tiles. The blue and white of the mausoleum were meant to symbolise the white sun on the blue background of the Kuomintang flag.

The crypt is at the top of the steps at the rear of the memorial chamber. A tablet hanging across the threshold is inscribed with the 'Three Principles of the People', as formulated by Dr Sun: nationalism, democracy and people's livelihood. Inside is a seated statue of Dr Sun. The walls are carved with the complete text of the *Outline of Principles for the Establishment of the Nation* put forward by the Nationalist government. A prostrate marble statue of Sun seals his coffin. Entry to Zhōngshān Líng costs Y15.

Zhōngshānlíng Yīnyuè Tái (Open Air Music Hall) 中山陵音乐台 Just east of the Zhōngshān Líng, this outdoor auditorium was built in 1932 and can hold up to 3000 people. A peaceful place to escape the crowds, you can relax here among the trees, fountains and manicured lawns, listening to recorded classical music drifting from hidden speakers and the sounds of the rivalling birds. Entry is Y3.

Míng Xiàolíng 明孝陵 (Tomb of Hong Wu) This tomb also lies on the southern slope of Zǐjīn Shān. Construction began in 1381 and was finished in 1383; the emperor died at the age of 71 in 1398. The first section of the avenue leading up to the mausoleum is lined with stone statues of lions, camels, elephants and horses. There's also a mythical animal called a *xiezhi*, which has a mane and a single horn on its head; and a *qilin* which has a scaly body, a cow's tail, deer's hooves and one horn.

As you enter the first courtyard, a paved pathway leads to a pavilion housing several steles. The next gate leads to a large courtyard where you'll find the **Línghún Tǎ** (Altar Tower or Soul Tower) – a mammoth rectangular stone structure. To get to the top of the tower, go to the stairway in the middle. Behind the tower is a wall, 350m in diameter, which surrounds a huge earth mound. Beneath this mound is the tomb vault of Hong Wu, which has not been excavated. Entry costs Y10.

Línggǔ Sì 灵谷寺 (Spirit Valley Temple) One of the most interesting buildings in Nánjīng is the **Beamless Hall**. In 1381, when Hong Wu was building his tomb, he had a temple on the site torn down and rebuilt a few kilometres to the east. Of this temple only the Beamless Hall (so called because it is built entirely of bricks) remains. The structure has an interesting vaulted ceiling and a large stone platform where Buddhist statues used to be seated. In the 1930s the hall was turned into a memorial to those who died in the 1926–28 revolution. One of the inscriptions on the inside wall is the old Kuomintang national anthem.

A road leads either side of the Beamless Hall and up two flights of steps to the **Pine Wind Pavilion**, originally dedicated to the goddess of mercy as part of the Línggǔ Sì. Today it houses a small shop and teahouse.

The Línggǔ Sì itself and its memorial hall to Xuan Zang is close by; after you pass through the Beamless Hall, turn right and follow the pathway. Xuan Zang was the Buddhist monk who travelled to India and brought back the Buddhist scriptures. Inside the memorial hall is a 13-storey wooden pagoda model that contains part of his skull, a sacrificial table and a portrait of the monk. It costs Y10 to enter the temple.

Close by is the **Línggǔ Tǎ** (Spirit Valley Pagoda). This nine-storey, 60m-high, octagonal building was built in the 1930s under the direction of a US architect as a memorial to Kuomintang members who died in the 1926–28 revolution.

Míng Xiàolíng Fēngjǐngqū (Scenic Spot of Ming Xiaoling) 明孝陵风景区

Just west of the Zhōngshān Líng, this quiet area has a tree-lined, stone pathway that winds around pavilions and picnic grounds and ends at Zǐxiá Hú (Purple Dawn Lake), a small lake that you can swim in – a very relaxing way to spend a hot afternoon. Entrance to the area costs Y10.

Zhíwù Yuán 植物园 (Botanical Gardens)

These gardens, beneath Zǐjīn Shān, were established in 1929. Covering over 186 hectares, the gardens display more than 3000 plant species and include rose, medicinal plant and bonsai gardens. Entry costs Y15.

Places to Stay – Budget

The cheapest beds in town are at the *Nanjing University Foreign Students Dormitory* (Nánjīng Dàxué Wàiguó Liúxuéshēng Sùshè), a 20-storey white-tiled building on Shanghai Lu, just south of Beijing Xilu. Dorm beds in double rooms with communal facilities, including kitchen, cost Y44 per person. Beds in a double with attached bathroom cost Y200 (for one or two people). The best way to reach the dormitory is to take bus No 13 from the train station or the long-distance bus station (get off at the intersection of Beijing Xilu and Shanghai Lu).

A 10-minute walk from the Nanjing University dormitory is the *Nanjing Normal University Nanshan Hotel* (Nánjīng Shīfàn Dàxué Nánshān Bīnguǎn; fax 373 8174). It's slightly more expensive, but its location in the middle of the campus is quiet and relaxing. Just outside the main gates of the university are several inexpensive streetfood vendors. Doubles with shower start at Y50 per person. To get there from the Nanjing University dorm, walk south along Shanghai Lu. Turn right into the second or third alleyway, then take the first road left to the main gate of Nanjing Normal University (next to a McDonald's). The dormitory is inside the campus compound, to the left of the large grassy quadrangle.

Places to Stay – Mid-Range

Most Nánjīng accommodation is middle to top end in price; in fact, it's fairly difficult to find a decent room for under Y350.

On a pretty, tree-lined street close to Nanjing University is the *Jīnglì Jiǔdiàn* (☎ 331 0818, 7 Běijīng Xilu). It's a new place and offers singles/doubles starting at Y380/575 with all the amenities of a luxury hotel.

One block north is the *Jiāngsū Dàjiǔdiàn* (☎ 332 9888, fax 332 0888, 28 Zhongshan Beilu). This 34-storey high-rise has the amenities of an upmarket hotel and is good value with standard double rooms starting at Y420.

The *Yuèhuá Dàjiǔdiàn* (☎ 221 3888, fax 221 3995), across from the Zhuàngyuánlóu Jiǔdiàn (Mandarin Garden Hotel), has standard rooms from Y360. The rooms are clean, but slightly run-down, but the hotel's location in Fūzǐ Miào makes it a fairly good deal.

The *Hóngqiáo Fàndiàn* (☎ 340 0888, fax 342 0756, 202 Zhongshan Beilu) caters largely to tour groups. Nevertheless, it also has a good location near the heart of Nánjīng's shopping district at relatively reasonable prices. Doubles cost from Y280 to Y580.

Places to Stay – Top End

The *Xuánwǔ Fàndiàn* (☎ 335 8888, fax 663 9624, 193 Zhong Yang Lu), a tower block opposite the Jiāngsū Exhibition Hall, is one of the cheaper top-end options. It may not quite hit the spot as a luxury hotel, but the smaller corner rooms are good value at Y450. Standard doubles start at Y650. There's also a rotating restaurant at the top of the hotel.

Behind a restaurant and across the road from the Hóngqiáo Fàndiàn is the city's oldest tourist establishment, the *Nánjīng Fàndiàn* (☎ 341 1888, fax 342 2261, 259 Zhongshan Beilu). Its newly renovated rooms start at US$78, although there are some older rooms still available for US$40.

The **Zhuàngyuánlóu Jiǔdiàn** (Mandarin Garden Hotel; ☎ 220 2555, fax 220 1876, 9 Zhuang Yuan Lu) has single rooms from Y730 and doubles from Y996. The most useful thing about this new luxury hotel is its location in the northern part of Fūzǐ Miào.

The 36-storey **Jīnlíng Fàndiàn** (☎ 471 1888, fax 470 4141, ✉ hotel@jinlinghot el-nanjing.com), at Xinjiekou, is the best and most well known of Nánjīng's top-end hotels. Standard doubles begin at US$170 with suites priced at US$2000. The hotel's numerous amenities include a sauna, a fitness centre and a swimming pool, and at street level there's a shopping arcade.

Popular with foreign tour groups is the **Dīngshān Huāyuán Jiǔdiàn** (Dingshan Garden Hotel; ☎ 880 2888, fax 882 1729, 90 Chahaer Lu), which offers standard doubles for Y815. There's a great view of the city and Xuánwǔ Hú (Profound Military Lake) from here, but it's somewhat inconveniently located outside of the city centre. The hotel does, however, provide free and frequent shuttle buses to and from the airport, the train station and the city centre. A new five-star building promising even more fantastic views is due to open in 2000.

Two standard luxury hotels are the **Gǔnándū Fàndiàn** (Grand Hotel; ☎ 331 1999, fax 331 9498, 208 Guangzhou Lu), near Nanjing Normal University, and the **Zhōngxīn Dàjiǔdiàn** (Central Hotel; ☎ 440 0888, fax 441 4194, 75 Zhongshan Lu), near the corner of Huaqiao Lu. Both have doubles from US$100.

The **Hilton Hotel** (Xīěrdùn Fàndiàn; ☎ 480 8888, fax 480 9999, 319 Zhongshan Donglu) and the **Nanjing Holiday Inn** (Nánjīng Yìhuájiàkì Jiǔdiàn; ☎ 330 8888, fax 330 9898, 45 Zhongshan Lu) have both recently opened in Nánjīng, providing two top-end standbys. The Hilton Hotel is located next to the Nánjīng Bówùguǎn at the eastern edge of town, just inside the city wall. Standard rooms start at Y1406. The Holiday Inn offers doubles from US$120 plus 15% tax and is located on Zhongshan Beilu.

For those interested in staying on the forested slopes of Zǐjīn Shān, the **Nanjing International Conference Centre** (Nánjīng

Guójì Huìyì Dàjiǔ; ☎ 443 0888, fax 443 9255, ✉ ichon@public1.ptt.js.cn) has twin rooms from Y800. The hotel is south of Zhōngshān Líng, next to the over priced Undersea World. As well as being easily accessible to many of Nánjīng's major tourist sites, if not Nánjīng itself, the hotel offers bowling alleys, tennis courts, a sauna, an indoor golf centre, a swimming pool and fine living.

Places to Eat

Some of Nánjīng's livelier eating houses are in the Fūzǐ Miào quarter. The **Lǎozhèngxīng Càiguǎn** (119 Gongyuan Jie), just east of Fūzǐ Miào's main square by the river, serves typical lower Cháng Jiāng (Yangzi River) cuisine and was a favourite of Kuomintang officers before the war.

On the opposite side of the river, Qínhuái Hé, from Fūzǐ Miào's main square is **Wǎnqíng Lóu** (☎ 224 9877). Here you can try delicious Nánjīng dim sum – a pre-set, 20-dish, dim sum feast costs Y60 and is definitely good value. There are also a number of teahouses above the shops in this area that offer excellent night views of Fūzǐ Miào.

Anyone who has arrived in Nánjīng from the backwoods of China and wants to forget all about local delicacies can head over to one of the cluster of restaurants that have sprung up around Nanjing University to cater to adventurous locals and foreign students. Down the alley on the southern side of the Nanjing University Foreign Students Dormitory, east off Shanghai Lu, are several cheap places to eat including **Pizza Express**, **Jack's Place**, **Family Café** and **Dukes Restaurant**. You'll also find a number of cheap Chinese restaurants down this alley. A few doors south of the dormitory, on Shanghai Lu, is a branch of **Coffee & Tea**, which is fairly pricey but open late serving snacks and fresh filter coffee.

The place to go for cheap street food is just outside the main gate of Nanjing Normal University on Ninghai Lu. **Street stalls** and **restaurants** serve dumplings and steamed buns and tasty bowls of noodles. Also in this area is **Swede & Kraut** (Lǎowàilè; ☎ 663 8020, 2nd Floor, 137

Ninghai Lu). It serves great home-made bread and pasta, and vegetarian, chicken and steak dishes. A 20% discount is given to students. Opened in co-operation with Swede & Kraut, *Skyway Bakery & Deli* (☎ *663 4834, 3-6 Hankou Lu)* is just around the corner and serves fresh bread, cakes, coffee and Italian ice cream.

Henry's Home Cafe (Hēnglìzhījiā; ☎ *470 1292, 33 Huaqiao Lu)* is west off Zhongshan Lu. This place has very friendly service and occasionally shows movies. It serves pasta, pizza, *fajitas* (Mexican tortilla wraps) and steak dishes.

The *Wǔzhōu Jiǔjiā (Tree House)* has moved to a new location on Xiao Fen Ziao (first alley north of Guangzhou Lu off Zhongshan Lu). Once known as the Sprite Outlet, this place is popular with foreigners and locals. The food is cheap and there's an English menu. Also in this area is *Rendezvous Bistro (*☎ *472 1657, 59-1 Juan Jia Ziao),* selling cakes, pastries, fresh bread as well as Greek, Italian and Mexican cuisine. The bistro is on the first lane west of the Zhōngxīn Dàjiǔdiàn (Central Hotel), running parallel with Zhongshan Lu.

Worth visiting more for the view than for its food is the *vegetarian restaurant* at Jiming Temple, high on a hill overlooking Xuánwǔhú Gōngyuán. It's very cheap and is open daily from 8 am to 5.30 pm, although you must arrive before 5 pm to enter. Admission to the temple is Y4.

A good place to sample local specialities is the *Sìchuān Jiǔjiā (*☎ *664 3651).* Here, Nánjīng pressed duck is slathered with roasted salt, steeped in clear brine, baked dry and then kept under cover for some time; the finished product should have a creamy-coloured skin and red, tender flesh.

Entertainment

Nánjīng has an active nightlife and a range of bars, pubs and discos to choose from. The best place to ask about entertainment is at the foreign student dormitories where you'll find recent advertisements and posters. *Catch 22,* in the alley south of Nanjing University Foreign Students Dormitory, is popular with students and often has live music.

Shopping

There is little you can't buy in Nánjīng from designer clothing to trinket souvenirs. Hunan Lu has a late night market and is lined with shops and stalls. The area surrounding Fūzǐ Miào is a pedestrian zone with souvenirs and antiques for sale. Around Hanzhong Lu and Zhongshan Lu you'll find a number of major department stores including Zhongshan department store and GE shopping centre.

Getting There & Away

Air Nánjīng has regular air connections to all major Chinese cities. There are also daily flights to/from Hong Kong.

The main office for the Civil Aviation Administration of China (CAAC; Zhōngguó Mínháng; ☎ 664 9275) is at 52 Ruijin Lu (near the terminal of bus route No 4), but you can also buy tickets at the CITS and CTS offices or at most of the top-end hotels. China Eastern Airlines has daily flights to Hong Kong; its office is just north of Xinjiekou. Dragon Air (☎ 332 8000) also has daily flights to Hong Kong; there's an agent in the CITS office.

Bus The long-distance bus station is west of the main train station, south-east of the wide-bridged intersection with Zhongyang Lu. It's a big chaotic place and even if you can read the posted information (in Chinese) it is all wildly inaccurate. Have the name of the place you want to go written in Chinese. You can also buy bus tickets at a bus ticket office (☎ 334 3966) at 204 Zhongshan Beilu, near CITS. There are direct buses to destinations all over Jiāngsū and to major destinations around China. The new expressway between Nánjīng and Shànghǎi, and Nánjīng and Liányúngǎng has made transport by bus much quicker than before.

Faster and somewhat more expensive minibuses for Zhènjiāng (one hour) and Yángzhōu (1½ hours) leave from a station on Hanzhong Lu. Take local bus No 13 north to reach the long-distance bus station and south to reach the minibus station.

Train Nánjīng is a major stop on the Běijīng to Shànghǎi railway line, and the station is mayhem; there are several trains a day in both directions. Heading eastwards from Nánjīng, the line to Shànghǎi connects with Zhènjiāng, Chángzhōu, Wúxī and Sūzhōu.

An efficient daily express service runs between Nánjīng and Shànghǎi, using two modern double-decker trains. Train T1 runs directly to Shànghǎi, while T2 stops at Wúxī. The Y215 and Y216 also stop at Sūzhōu. Train numbers starting with T are the most luxurious and Y is considered second best (regular trains have numbers only). All cars are air-conditioned and a no-smoking rule is vigorously enforced.

There is no direct rail link to Hángzhōu; you have to go via Shànghǎi. Alternatively, there is a direct bus from Nánjīng to Hángzhōu. Likewise, to get to Guǎngzhōu by rail you must change trains at Shànghǎi.

Heading west, there is a direct rail link to the port of Wúhú on the Cháng Jiāng (Yangzi River). If you want to go further west along the river, then the most sensible thing to do is take the ferry.

You can buy train tickets at CITS or the train ticket office on Zhongshan Lu, just south of the China Eastern Airlines booking office. The office is open daily from 8 am to 12 pm and 1 to 5 pm.

Boat There are several departures daily from Nánjīng's Cháng Jiāng (Yangzi River) port down river (eastward) to Shànghǎi and upriver (westward) to Wǔhàn (two days), including a few boats to Chóngqìng (five days). Most ferries leave from No 4 dock (sìhào mǎtóu), a kilometre north of Zhongshan dock, which is at the western end of Zhongshan Beilu. Tickets can be purchased from the CITS office on Zhongshan Beilu. For full details on Cháng Jiāng (Yangzi River) cruises, see the Chongqing chapter.

Getting Around
To/From the Airport Nánjīng airport is approximately one hour south of the city. There is a minibus service that departs from outside the Sheraton Hotel on Hanzhong Lu. Tickets cost Y20 and the buses depart when full. Many of the hotels also have

hourly shuttle buses that run to and from the airport. Taxis charge exorbitant prices up to and beyond Y100.

Local Transport Taxis cruise the streets of Nánjīng and are very cheap – most destinations in the city are Y7, but make sure that the meter is switched on. You can get around in motor-tricycles as well; be sure to agree on a price beforehand. Private minibuses ply the main thoroughfares; wave one down and ride for Y1.

You can get to Xinjiekou, in the heart of town, by jumping on bus No 1 or 33 from the train station, or No 10 or 34 from the Cháng Jiāng (Yangzi River) docks. Many local maps contain bus routes. Buses cost Y1 per ride.

AROUND NÁNJĪNG
Qīxiá Sì 栖霞山
Morning of Birds Temple
This temple, 22km north-east of Nánjīng, was founded by the Buddhist monk Shao Shezhai, during the Southern Qi dynasty, and is still an active place of worship. Qīxiá has long been one of China's most important monasteries, and even today is one of the largest Buddhist seminaries in the country. There are two main temple halls: the **Maitreya Hall**, with a statue of the Maitreya Buddha sitting cross-legged at the entrance, and behind this the **Vairocana Hall**, housing a 5m-tall statue of Vairocana.

Behind the temple is the **Qiānfó Xuányá** (Thousand Buddha Cliff). Several small caves housing stone statues are carved into the hillside, the earliest of which dates from the Qi dynasty (AD 479–502), although there are others from succeeding dynasties through to the Ming. There is also a small stone pagoda built in AD 601, and rebuilt during the late Tang period. The upper part has engraved sutras and carvings of the Buddha; around the base, each of the pagoda's eight sides depicts Sakyamuni.

You can reach Qīxiá from Nánjīng by public bus from the Gǔ Lóu (Drum Tower) bus station or by private minibus from in front of the Nánjīng train station. It's about a one hour ride.

Yángshān Bēicái
Yangshan Quarry

The quarry at Yángshān, 25km east of Nánjīng, was the source of most of the stone blocks cut for the Míng Gùgōng (Ming Palace) and statues of the Ming tombs. The attraction here is a massive tablet partially hewn from the rock. Had the tablet been finished it would have been almost 15m wide, 4m thick and 45m high! The base stone was to be 6.5m high and 13m long.

One story goes that Ming dynasty Emperor Hong Wu wished to place the enormous tablet on the top of Zǐjīn Shān. The gods had promised their assistance to move it, but when they saw the size of the tablet, even they gave up and Hong Wu had to abandon the project. It seems, however, that Yong Le, the son of Hong Wu, ordered the tablet to be carved; he planned to erect it at his father's tomb. When the tablet was almost finished he realised there was no way it could be moved.

You can get to Yángshān from the bus station on Hanfu Jie (east of Xinjiekou) on bus No 9 or 20. Buses to the thermal-springs resort at Tangshanzhen pass Yángshān on the way.

ZHÈNJIĀNG 镇江
☎ 0511 • pop 2,654,100

Just an hour from Nánjīng, Zhènjiāng is a town of over 2 million people. The main attraction is Jīnshān Gōngyuán (see later), where an active Buddhist temple attracts large crowds of worshippers.

The Daxi Lu area, the oldest part of the city, is an interesting area to wander around.

Information
The main branch of the Bank of China is on Zhongshan Lu, just east of the intersection with Jiefang Lu. The main telecommunications and post office is on Dian Li Lu, on the corner of Xinma Lu. There are a number of other post offices around town including one on Jiefang Lu and another across from the train station. The Guójì Fàndiàn (see Places to Stay later) gives out free English maps or you can buy the Chinese version at the train station or bus station.

Jīnshān Gōngyuán 金山公园
Gold Hill Park

Jīnshān Gōngyuán packs in the crowds who congest the flights of stairs that lead up through a Buddhist temple Jīnshān to the seven-storey octagonal Cishou Pagoda.

The temple gains its name from a Chan Master who is said to have come into copious amounts of gold *(jin)* after opening the gates at the entrance of the park. There are four caves at the mount; of these **Fáhǎi** (Buddhist Sea) and **Báilóng** (White Dragon) feature in the Chinese fairy tale *The Story of the White Snake*. Take bus No 2 to Jīnshān (this is the last stop). The temple is open from 6 am to 6 pm and tickets cost Y20.

Jiāo Shān 焦山
Jade Hill

Known as Jade Hill because of its dark green foliage, Jiāo Shān is to the east of Zhènjiāng on a small island. There's good hiking here with a number of pavilions along the way to the top of the 150m-high mount, from where Xijiang Tower gives a view of activity on the Cháng Jiāng (Yangzi River). At the base of Jiāo Shān is an active monastery. Tickets to enter the area cost Y9.

To get to Jiāo Shān take bus No 4 to the terminal. From there it's a short walk and a boat ride (Y4), or you can take a cable car to the top of the hill (Y15), walk down and take the boat back.

Běigùshān Gōngyuán 北固山公园
North Hill Park

Also on the No 4 bus route, this park is home to **Gānlù Sì** (Pleasant Land Temple), which features a Song dynasty pagoda. The pagoda was once six storeys, but was reduced to four by overzealous Red Guards during the Cultural Revolution.

Bówùguǎn 博物馆
Museum

Between Jīnshān Gōngyuán and the centre of town is the old British consulate, now converted into a museum. It houses pottery, bronzes, gold, silver, Tang dynasty paintings, and photographs and memorabilia of the Sino-Japanese war. The ornate, red- and

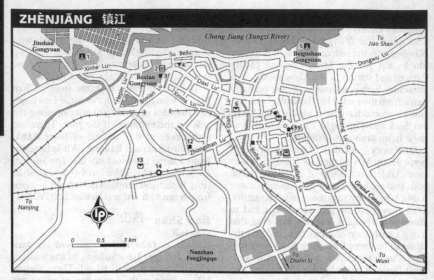

ZHÈNJIĀNG 镇江

black-brick building, situated atop a small hill, is a fascinating sight in contrast to the surrounding area.

Bus No 2 lets you off close to the museum. The museum costs Y5 and is closed Wednesday and Thursday.

Daxi Lu & Song Jie Area
Well worth investigating on foot is the area surrounding the museum, the oldest section of Zhènjiāng. Winding cobblestone alleys give views over a maze of tiled rooftops and meander down to boat docks on the Cháng Jiāng (Yangzi River).

The staircase to the east of the museum leads to Song Lu, where a small stone pagoda above an archway is said to date from the Yuan dynasty.

Zhúlín Sì
Bamboo Forest Temple
At the southern end of town, in an area known as Nánshān Fēngjǐngqū (South Hill Scenic Park) is the Zhúlín Sì. As temples go, it won't qualify as the biggest or best in China, but its setting among the trees and hills makes it a relaxing spot.

You can reach Zhúlín Sì by bus No 15.

Places to Stay
The *Jīngkǒu Fàndiàn* (☎ 522 4866, fax 523 0056, 407 Zhongshan Donglu) is one of the cheapest options around; it has doubles for Y120 in the old wing or standard renovated doubles from Y480. Although the hotel appears somewhat grotty from the outside, inside it's clean and quite comfortable. Enter the hotel from Binhe Lu, an alley off Zhongshan Lu, on the east side of the river. The alley is marked by a large gateway bearing the name of the hotel.

Not far from the station is the *Zhènjiāng Bīnguǎn* (☎ 523 3888 fax 523 1055, 92 Zhongshan Xilu), which has standard doubles from US$30 in an older building, or US$60 in the new building at the front.

The *Dàhuángjiā Jiǔdiàn* (Royal Hotel; ☎ 527 1438, 35 Boxian Lu) is in a great location in the old section of town. White columns, gold statues and wrought iron decorate the front, making it a bizarre sight. Inside, the maze of halls and rooms is cloaked in an eerie atmosphere. Nevertheless, doubles with a balcony, though somewhat shabby, are a good deal at Y100. The hotel is a 15-minute ride from the train station on bus No 2.

ZHÈNJIĀNG

PLACES TO STAY & EAT
3 Dàhuángjiā Jiǔdiàn
大皇家酒店
4 Yànchūn Jiǔlóu
宴春酒楼
10 Guójì Fàndiàn
国际饭店
11 Jīngkǒu Fàndiàn
京口饭店
12 Zhènjiāng
Bīnguǎn
镇江宾馆

MUSEUM & TEMPLES
1 Jīnshān Sì
金山寺
2 Zhènjiāng
Bówùguǎn
博物馆
5 Gānlù Sì
甘露寺

OTHER
6 Telecommunications
and Post Office
邮电局

7 Gōngyìpǐn Dàlóu
工艺品大楼
8 Post Office
邮局
9 Bank of China
中国银行
13 Post Office
邮局
14 Train Station
火车站
15 Long-Distance Bus Station
汽车站

The new *Guójì Fàndiàn (International Hotel; ☎ 502 1888, fax 502 1777, 218 Jie Fang Lu)*, on the south-east corner with Zhongshan Lu, has the most upmarket standard rooms in town; prices start at US$60.

Places to Eat
The most famous restaurant in town is *Yànchūn Jiǔlóu (☎ 527 1615, 17 Renmin Lane)*, in an alley north of Daxi Lu. The 1st floor serves wonton soup and other dim sum. The 2nd floor serves cold dim sum and other local specialities, along with eight treasures tea. Hot water for the tea is poured by an attendant standing several feet away from your table, using a kettle with a very long spout. The 1st floor is open from 3 to 6.30 pm and the 2nd floor is open from 11 am to 1.30 pm and 5 to 8.30 pm.

Shopping
There's a very fine Gōngyìpǐn Dàlóu (Arts & Crafts Shop; ☎ 522 2332) at 191 Jiefang Beilu which stocks embroidery, porcelain, jade and other artefacts as well as antiques. The shop is open from 9 am to 6.30 pm.

Getting There & Away
Bus The long-distance bus station is in the south-eastern corner of the city centre on Jiefang Lu. There are hourly buses from Zhènjiāng to Nánjīng (one hour) and Wúxī (two hours) and a bus and ferry combination to Yángzhōu (one hour). You can get more frequent buses to Yángzhōu from the eastern side of the main train station.

Train Zhènjiāng is on the main Nánjīng to Shànghǎi line. It's 3½ hours by fast train to Shànghǎi and an hour to Nánjīng. Although some of the special express trains don't stop at Zhènjiāng, there is a grand choice of schedules. Most hotels offer a train booking service and can book sleepers.

Getting Around
Almost all the transport (local buses, buses to Yángzhōu, taxis, pedicabs and motortricycles) is close to the train station.

Bus No 2 is a convenient tour bus. It travels east from the station along Zhongshan Lu to the city centre where you'll find department stores and the post office. It then swings west past the museum and continues on to the terminal at Jīnshān Gōngyuán. Bus No 4, which crosses the No 2 route in the city centre on Jiefang Lu, runs to Ganlu Temple and Jiāo Shān in the east.

YÁNGZHŌU 扬州
☎ 0514 • pop 4,461,400
Yángzhōu, near the junction of the Grand Canal (Dà Yùnhé) and the Cháng Jiāng (Yangzi River), was once an economic and cultural centre of southern China. It was home to scholars, painters, storytellers, poets and merchants in the Sui and Tang dynasties.

Today Yángzhōu is a pleasant, small city with broad, tree-lined boulevards dotted with canals, bridges and gardens. While it's not the major attraction that local tourist literature might have you believe, Yángzhōu

The Grand Canal

The world's longest canal, the Grand Canal (Dà Yùnhé) once meandered almost 1800km from Běijīng to Hángzhōu and is a striking example of China's sophisticated engineering prowess. Today perhaps half of it remains seasonally navigable. The party claims that, since liberation, large-scale dredging has made the navigable length 1100km. However, canal depths are up to 3m and canal widths can narrow to less than 9m. Put these facts together, think about some of the old stone bridges spanning the route, and you come to the conclusion that it is restricted to fairly small, flat-bottomed vessels.

The progress of the Grand Canal's construction spanned many centuries. The first 85km were completed in 495 BC, but the mammoth task of linking the Huáng Hé (Yellow River) and the Cháng Jiāng (Yangzi River) was undertaken during Sui times by a massive conscripted labour force between AD 605 and 609. It was developed again during the Yuan dynasty (1271–1368). The canal enabled the government to capitalise on the growing wealth of the Cháng Jiāng basin and to ship supplies from south to north.

Sections of the canal have been silted up for centuries, however, the canal comes into its own south of the Cháng Jiāng, where concern for tourism has ensured year-round navigation. The Jiang-nan section of the canal (Hángzhōu, Sūzhōu, Wúxī, Chángzhōu, Zhèjiāng) is a skein of canals, rivers and branching lakes.

Passenger services on the canal have dwindled to a trickle; they are unpopular with locals now that there are faster ways to get around. If you want a canal journey, the only option (apart from chartering your own boat) is the overnight service that travels between Hángzhōu and Sūzhōu. By all accounts it's a very pleasant trip, and improvements have been made on the much-maligned sanitation front. (See the Sūzhōu Getting There & Away section in this chapter for more details.)

has an enjoyable atmosphere and is a worthwhile break from Jiāngsū's bigger centres of Nánjīng and Sūzhōu. The main attraction, Shòuxī Hú (Slender West Lake), tends to get swamped with tour groups but the other sights remain quiet enough. Yángzhōu has enough sights to keep the traveller busy for a couple days or can be visited on a day trip from Nánjīng; on a good run it only takes 1½ hours by bus.

Information

CTS (☎ 734 5777), on Shita Lu, sells maps and train and air tickets. The main branch of the Bank of China is just across the street from CTS and the new post and China Telecom office is a block west.

Canals

Yángzhōu once had 24 stone bridges spanning its network of canals. Although the modern bridges are concrete, they can still offer good vantage points from which to view canal life.

You might like to investigate the environs a short way out of town. The Grand Canal actually passes a little to the east of Yángzhōu. The bus No 2 station in the north-east is a boat dock on the river. Bus Nos 4 and 9 run over a bridge on the canal. There are also two ship locks to the south of Yángzhōu.

Gè Yuán 个园

On Dongguan Lu, this garden was landscaped by the painter Shi Tao for an officer of the Qing court. Shi Tao was an expert at making artificial rocks; the composition here suggests the four seasons. The entrance is on Yanfu Donglu and tickets cost Y12.

Hé Yuán 何园

Also known as Jixiao Mountain Villa, Hé Yuán was built in the 19th century. This garden contains rockeries, ponds, pavilions and walls inscribed with classical poetry; entry costs Y8.

Xī Yuán 西园
West Garden

This park offers a quiet escape along a small canal with birds and blossoms. Within the park are 25 designated scenic spots including archways, bridges, a marble boat and the meeting of three rivers. At the southern end of the park is a garden containing well over 200 bonsai-style potted plants. The garden also serves as a potted plant research centre and, in the outlying buildings, you can see the gardeners at work.

Wénfēng Tǎ
Beacon of Scripture Pagoda

This graffiti-ridden pagoda is in an eerie state of disrepair. It offers a bird's-eye view of the flotsam, jetsam and sampans along the Grand Canal. Made of brick and wood, it's been rebuilt several times. The pagoda is a 10-minute walk from the east bus station.

Shòuxīhú Gōngyuán 瘦西湖公园
Slender West Lake Park

This is the top scenic spot in Yángzhōu and is in the western suburbs on the route of bus No 5. Shòuxī Hú (Slender West Lake) is a slim version of Xī Hú (West Lake) in Hángzhōu. Mass local tourism has done much to restore this garden and, if you are lucky enough to visit it on a quiet day, it's a worthwhile excursion.

Shòuxīhú Gōngyuán offers an imperial dragon-boat ferry, a restaurant and a white dagoba (dome-shaped shrine) modelled after the one in Běihǎi Gōngyuán in Běijīng. The highlight is the triple-arched, Wǔtíng Qiáo (Five Pavilion Bridge) that was built in 1757.

Emperor Qianlong's fishing platform is also in the park. It is said that the local divers used to put fish on the emperor's hook so he'd think it was good luck and provide funding for the town.

The park is open until 6.30 pm but ticket sales stop at 5.45 pm. Admission is Y25. There are two entrances; the southern entrance is close to the Hóngqiáo Bīnguǎn and the northern entrance is close to Dàmíng Sì.

Dàmíng Sì 大明寺
Great Brightness Temple

Emperor Qianlong renamed this temple Fǎjìng Sì (Silence of the Law Temple) in 1765 when he visited. The monastery was founded more than 1000 years ago and was subsequently destroyed and rebuilt. Then it was destroyed right down to its foundations during the Taiping Rebellion; what you see today is a 1934 reconstruction.

The original temple is credited to the Tang dynasty monk Jianzhen, who studied sculpture, architecture, fine arts and medicine, as well as Buddhism. In AD 742 two Japanese monks invited him to Japan for missionary work. It turned out to be mission impossible. Jianzhen made five attempts to get there, failing due to storms. On the fifth attempt he ended up in Hǎinán. On the sixth trip, aged 66, he finally arrived. He stayed in Japan for 10 years and died there in AD 763. Later, the Japanese made a lacquer statue of Jianzhen, which in 1980 was sent to Yángzhōu.

The Chinese have a wooden copy of this statue on display at the Jianzhen Memorial Hall. Modelled after the chief hall of the Toshodai Temple in Nara (Japan), the Jianzhen Memorial Hall was built in 1974 at Dàmíng Sì and was financed by Japanese contributions. Special exchanges are made between Nara and Yángzhōu; even Deng Xiaoping, returning from a trip to Japan, came to the Yángzhōu monastery to strengthen renewed links between the two countries.

Near the monastery is Píngshān Táng (Flat Hill Hall), the former residence of the Song dynasty writer Ouyang Xiu, who served in Yángzhōu. Also nearby are the **Martyr's Shrine** and ruins from the Tang dynasty. To the east of Dàmíng Sì you'll find the **Hànmù Bówùguǎn** (Han Dynasty Tomb Museum).

You can reach Dàmíng Sì by taking bus No 5 to Wǔtíng Qiáo; it's then a 10-minute walk north. The Hànmù Bówùguǎn can be reached by bus No 3.

Pǔhādīng Mùyuán 普哈丁墓园
Tomb of Puhaddin

This tomb contains documentation of China's contact with the Muslims. It's on the eastern bank of a canal on the bus No 2

YÁNGZHŌU 扬州

route. Puhaddin came to China during the Yuan dynasty (AD 1271–1368) to spread the Muslim faith. There is also a mosque here, however it has been closed indefinitely for renovations.

Yángzhōu Shì Bówùguǎn
扬州市博物馆
Yangzhou City Museum

This museum lies to the west of Guoqing Lu, near the Xīyuán Fàndiàn. It's in a temple originally dedicated to Shi Kefa, a Ming dynasty official who refused to succumb to his new Qing masters and was executed.

On display are large wooden coffins dating to the Han and Northern Song dynasties, a 1000-year-old wooden boat and a Han dynasty jade funeral suit. Inside the grounds, the museum is surrounded by an antique market. Opening hours are from 8 am to 5 pm and admission is free.

Places to Stay

On the Yángzhōu Teacher's College campus, across from the southern entrance to Shòuxī Hú, is the **Hóngqiáo Bīnguǎn** (☎ 797 5275). Clean, standard doubles are good value at Y160 and triples go for Y180.

YÁNGZHŌU

PLACES TO STAY & EAT

7 Gébì Huàláng Kāfēi
戈壁画廊咖啡
8 Hóngqiáo Bīnguǎn
虹桥宾馆
10 Xīyuán Fàndiàn
西园饭店
12 Yángzhōu Bīnguǎn
扬州宾馆
15 Lántiān Dàshà
蓝天大厦
20 Càigēnxiāng Fàndiàn
菜根香饭店
22 Fùchūn Cháshè
富春茶社
23 Gònghéchūn Jiǎomiàndiàn
共和春饺面店

MUSEUMS, TEMPLES & GARDENS

2 Hànmù Bówùguǎn
汉墓博物馆
3 Píngshān Táng
平山堂
9 Xī Yuán
西园
11 Yángzhōu Shì Bówùguǎn
扬州市博物馆
13 Gè Yuán
个园
24 Hé Yuán
何园

OTHER

1 Tang Dynasty Ruins
唐城遗址
4 Martyrs' Shrine
烈士墓

5 Píngshān Táng
平山堂
6 Shòuxīh Entrance
瘦西湖
14 Bank of China
中国银行
16 CTS
中国旅行社
17 Post & China Telecom Office
邮政电信局
18 Bank of China (Main Branch)
中国银行 (大同支行)
19 Pǔhādīng Mùyuán
普哈丁墓园
21 Xinhua Bookstore
新华书店
25 Long-Distance Bus Station
扬州汽车站

From the bus station take bus No 3 to the corner of Huaihai Lu and Yanfu Lu. From there it's about a 10-minute walk west. Follow the canal and take the first right over a stone bridge and then the first left onto Da Hongqiao Lu. After crossing over a second stone bridge turn left. Enter through the gate in the white wall.

The town's two main hotels are both located behind the museum. The garden-style **Xīyuán Fàndiàn** (☎ 734 4888, fax 723 3870, 1 Fengle Shang Lu) is said to have been constructed on the site of Qianlong's imperial villa. Twins are priced at Y218 while doubles are at Y256 in the older building while standards go for Y620 in the new main building.

Next door, the **Yángzhōu Bīnguǎn** (☎ 734 2611, fax 734 3599, 5 Fengle Shan Lu) has standard doubles from Y198.

The newer **Lántiān Dàshà** (☎ 736 0000, fax 731 4101), on Wenhe Lu, has singles/doubles starting at Y220/280.

Places to Eat

The most famous culinary export of Yángzhōu is Yángzhōu fried rice and, as most travellers who have tried it will confirm, it tastes just like fried rice – don't expect too much.

The **Fùchūn Cháshè**, on a lane just off Guoqing Lu, is the place to go to sip tea and eat local snacks. Order *sǔn ròu zhēng jiǎo* for a delicious sampling of *jiǎozi* (dumplings) and *bāozi* (steamed buns). There's also a new branch of the Fùchūn Cháshè next to Gè Yuán.

The **Càigēnxiāng Fàndiàn** is one of Yángzhōu's more famous establishments. It's the place to go to try local delicacies, but it's not the place to be if you have no-one to help share the costs.

Although somewhat lacking in atmosphere, the **Gònghéchūn Jiǎomiàndàin** is a dumpling and noodle restaurant in the south of town, on Ganquan Lu, and is a better option for inexpensive dining.

Across the street from the Xu Yuán is the **Gébì Huàláng Kāfēi** (Gobi Café & Gallery; 26 Da Hongqiao Lu), which displays paintings and sculptures from local artists and serves a delicious variety of snacks, cocktails and drinks. Try the melon milk tea or Vienna cappuccino. The cafe also has games, magazines and mellow music and is a wonderful place to while away a couple of hours.

Getting There & Away

Both planes and trains give Yángzhōu a miss, which perhaps explains why the city is missing out on China's current tourist and industrial tidal wave. The nearest airport is in Nánjīng and the closest train station is in Zhènjiāng. From Yángzhōu there are buses to Nánjīng (1½ to two hours), Wúxī, Sūzhōu and Shànghǎi, most via Zhènjiāng. Buses to Nánjīng depart from the west bus station.

Minibuses from Zhènjiāng (1½ hours) run every 15 minutes and depart from the eastern side of Zhènjiāng train station. Buses from Zhènjiāng and Nánjīng first stop at the Yángzhōu west bus station but stay on the bus and get off at the east bus station, which is closer to the centre of town. Buses cross over the Cháng Jiāng (Yangzi River) on a ferry.

Getting Around

Most of the sights are at the edge of town. If you're in a hurry, you might consider commandeering a taxi. The central area can easily be covered on foot. Bus Nos 1, 2, 3, 5, 6 and 7 all terminate near the east long-distance bus station.

Bus No 1 runs from the east bus station, up Guoqing Lu, and then loops around the perimeter of the inside canal, returning just north of the east bus station. Bus No 4 is an east to west bus and goes along Ganquan Lu. Bus Nos 8 and 16 connect the east and west bus stations.

YÍXĪNG XIÀN 宜兴县
Yixing County

Yíxīng Xiàn is famed for its tea utensils, in particular its pots. Delicious tea can be made in an aged Yíxīng teapot simply by adding hot water, or so it is claimed. The potteries of Yíxīng, especially in Dīngshān, are a popular excursion for Chinese tourists but see very few foreign visitors.

The town of Yíxīng is *not* an attraction, although most visitors end up passing through the place en route to the nearby karst caves or to Dīngshān.

Shíhuī Yándòng 石灰岩洞
Karst Caves

There are karst caves to the south-west of Yíxīng township, and if you are in the area, it is worth visiting one of them. Despite the standard selection of coloured neon that lights the interior of the caves, you will likely be required to rent a rather useless torch (flashlight) for Y5 to Y10; it's far better to bring your own. The caves are cold and slippery so take a jacket and wear sturdy footwear.

To reach the caves from Yíxīng, hop on a bus to Dīngshān. Buses head for Dīngshān via a number of routes; double check with the driver that the bus actually passes the caves.

Shànjuǎn Dòng This cave is embedded in Lúoyán Shān (Snail Shell Hill), 27km south-west of Yíxīng. It covers an area of roughly 5000 sq metres. Entry is via the middle cave, a stone hall with a 1000m floor space. From here you can mount a staircase to the snail's shell, the upper cave, or wander down to the lower caves and the water cave. In the water cave, you can jump in a rowing boat for a 120m ride to the exit called 'Suddenly See the Light'.

The cave is about midway between Yíxīng and Dīngshān (about a 10-minute bus ride). The bus will let you off at a crossroad; from there it's another 20-minute minibus ride west. Admission to the cave is Y28.

Zhānggōng Dòng Nineteen kilometres south of Yíxīng town, Zhānggōng Dòng is the most impressive of the three caves. It's similar in scale to Shànjuǎn Dòng, but it offers more possibilities for visitors to explore smaller caves.

From inside you scale a small hill called Yufeng Shān then emerge at the top amid a temple from which there is a splendid view of the surrounding countryside with hamlets stretching as far as the lake, Tài Hú.

The cave is about a 15-minute ride from Yíxīng on the road to Dīngshān. From there you must take a minibus or motorcycle taxi a further 10 minutes off the main road. Admission is Y25.

Línggǔ Dòng Three kilometres down the road from Zhānggōng Dòng, Línggǔ is the largest and least explored of the three caves. The cave has six large halls arrayed roughly in a semicircle.

Near the Línggǔ Dòng is the **Yánxiàn Cáchǎng** (Yanxian Tea Plantation), with bushel-lots laid out like fat caterpillars stretching into the horizon. The trip is worth it for the tea fields alone.

To get to Línggǔ follow the directions to Zhānggōng Dòng. Línggǔ is a further five-minute taxi ride down the road from Zhānggōng. Admission is Y20.

Yíxīng Táocí Bówùguǎn
宜兴陶瓷博物
Ceramics Museum

Located along the road to Dīngshān, a couple of minutes walk from the turn off for Zhānggōng Dòng, this museum displays examples of Yíxīng pottery through the ages, beginning 6000 years ago and carrying through to present day. Admission is Y10.

Places to Stay

The **Yíxīng Fàndiàn** (☎ 2179 2811) is at the end of Renmin Lu on the southern edge of Yíxīng town. Quiet, pleasant doubles cost Y200 to Y260. To reach the hotel take minibus No 6 from the bus terminal. On foot, it's a half hour walk; head three blocks straight ahead from the bus station and turn right onto Renmin Lu. The hotel is a further 15 minutes down the road on the right.

In the city centre, the smaller **Táodū Dàfàndiàn** (☎ 790 9348, fax 790 9149, 134 Renmin Nan Lu) offers reasonable doubles and triples for Y240. Take bus No 1 from the bus station.

The most upmarket hotel in town is the 24-storey **Yíxīng Guójì Fàndiàn** (International Hotel Yíxīng; ☎ 791 6888, fax 790 0767, 52 Tongzhenguan Lu). The hotel has singles for Y300 and doubles from Y360 to Y420. Bus No 1 from the bus station passes the hotel.

Getting There & Around

There are buses from Yíxīng to Wúxī (1½ hours), Shànghǎi, Nánjīng, Sūzhōu and Hángzhōu.

Private minibuses ply the streets of Yíxīng and all terminate in the bus stations of either Yíxīng town or Dīngshān. There are frequent connections between the two stations.

DĪNGSHĀN

Dīngshān is the pottery centre of Yíxīng Xiàn and has enjoyed that reputation since the Qin and Han dynasties; some of the scenes you can witness here, especially at the loading dock that leads into Tài Hú, are timeless.

Almost every local family is engaged in the manufacture of ceramics and at least half of the houses are made of the stuff. The area is extremely dusty and everywhere you look there are vehicles hauling rocks from the mountains outside of town.

Dīngshān is about 15km south of Yíxīng town and has two dozen ceramics factories producing more than 2000 varieties of pottery – quite an output for a population of 100,000. Among the array of products are the ceramic tables and garbage bins that you find around China, huge jars used to store oil and grain, the famed Yíxīng teapots, and the glazed tiling and ceramic frescoes that are desperately needed as spare parts for tourist attractions – the Forbidden City in Běijīng is one of the customers. The ornamental rocks that you see in Chinese gardens are also made here.

Dīngshān's pottery factories and occasional exhibition spaces are scattered around town; you'd do best to hire a taxi if you want to see everything. There are a host of factories in the east of town however many require prior arrangements for a visit. Perhaps the most enjoyable way to get a first hand look at Yíxīng's pottery production is by following the innumerable loaded down junks along the canals, taking you through the back streets lined with pottery packed shops and loading docks.

As of yet, there are no hotels in Dīngshān that can host foreigners so if you want to stay in the area, Yíxīng is your only option.

Getting There & Away

There are direct buses from Dīngshān to Yíxīng, departing every 20 minutes for the

Judging a Yíxīng Teapot

Buying a teapot in Dīngshān or the surrounding area can be a memorable experience. To help convince you of the high quality of their teapots, shopkeepers can be extremely animated. You'll encounter shopkeepers standing on the pot, blowing through its spout, striking a match on it, showing you that the inside is the same colour as the outside or rubbing their hand against the side and showing you their palm. Unfortunately, none of these antics give you much of an indication of whether a pot is good quality.

So what should you look for? First, make sure the teapot is stable – the body, spout, handle, lid and knob should all be balanced. Also, the lid should be deep-seated and firm (it shouldn't rattle or jam). The clay should be naturally shiny and slightly rough rather than glazed smooth. Finally, ask if you can put water in the pot; the water should shoot out straight from the spout instead of dribbling.

Prices can range wildly, from just a few dollars to US$20,000 for a pot made by a renowned artist. Some say that unless you are buying a teapot made by a well known artist, don't pay more than Y30. You may want to visit the Yíxīng Táocí Bówùguǎn (Ceramics Museum), located between Yíxīng and Dīngshān, to view high-quality teapots before venturing to the market across the street where a dizzying variety of generally low-quality teapots are for sale.

20-minute journey. Transfer in Yíxīng for buses to Wúxī, Zhènjiāng and Nánjīng.

WÚXĪ & TÀI HÚ 无锡与太湖
☎ 0510 • pop 4,322,900

Wúxī and Tài Hú are possible stopovers between Sūzhōu and Nánjīng. Wúxī itself has little to recommend it (a typical sprawling Chinese urban development with some dirty industry thrown in for good measure). Nearby Tài Hú is easily accessible from Wúxī, however, as it continues to be an extremely popular destination for tourists, its mediocre sights are more than a little overrun.

Tài Hú is a freshwater lake with a total area of 2200 sq km and an average depth of 2m. There are some 90 islands, large and small, within it, and more than 30 varieties of fish. The fishing industry in the area is very active.

Orientation & Information

The city centre of Wúxī is ringed by Jiefang Lu. The train station and main bus station are about a 10-minute walk north of Jiefang Beilu. A network of canals cuts through the city, including the Grand Canal.

The Bank of China is on Jiankang Lu, half a block south off Renmin Zhonglu.

The post office is on the corner of Renmin Zhonglu and Jiankang Lu. At the western end of the post office is a China Telecom office that offers public access to the Internet for Y20 per hour. The office is open daily from 8 am to 5 pm.

CTS (☎ 230 1249, fax 230 1960, @ WCTSCAA@public1.wx.js.cn) is in the building of the Zhōnglǔ Dàjiǔdiàn (CTS Grand Hotel) at 88 Station Lu, across the street from the train station. Look for the IATA sign. The office sells train and bus tickets, international plane tickets and transport to Shànghǎi's Hongqiao Airport.

Xīhuì Gōngyuán
West Favoured Park

The vast Xīhuì Gōngyuán is west of the city. The highest point in the park, Xī Shān (West Hill) is 75m above sea level. If you climb the **Lóngguāng Tǎ** (Dragon Light Pagoda), the seven-storey octagonal structure at the top of the hill, you'll be able to take in a panorama of Wúxī and Tài Hú. The brick and wood pagoda was built during the Ming dynasty, burned down during the Qing dynasty and rebuilt many years later. For an even greater view, take the chairlift (Y22), which is 1km into Huì Shān (Kind Hill).

The park itself is turning into an amusement ground complete with children's rides, games, loud speakers, souvenir stalls and a small zoo. You'll also find a large artificial lake and a cave that burrows for 500m from the eastern to the western side of the park. Despite all of this added glitz, the park continues to be a place where families and couples come to stroll away the afternoon. By exploring the western section, which rambles into Huì Shān, it is still possible to find a peaceful spot.

Within the park there is a total of 18 historical and cultural sights including the Huìshān Sì (Kind Hill Temple), once a Buddhist monastery, and an azalea garden with over 300 different species. On the western side of the park you'll find the famous Ming dynasty **Jìchàng Yuán** (Carefree Garden) – 'Ming' refers to the garden layout as the buildings are recent.

To get to Xīhuì Gōngyuán, you can take bus No 2 or 10. Entry costs Y15 and many of the gardens, the zoo and amusements charge an additional yuan or two.

Méi Yuán 梅园
Plum Garden
Once a small peach garden built during the Qing dynasty, this has since been renovated, re-landscaped and expanded. It is renowned for its thousands of red plum trees that blossom in the spring. The highest point is Méi Tǎ (Plum Pagoda), with views of Tài Hú. The garden is across the street from the Wúxī bus No 2 terminus and entry costs Y15.

Lǐ Yuán 蠡园
Carp Garden
Often crowded, this garden is geared for school children's excursions and tour groups. A wander through the garden provides a tour of the tacky concrete labyrinth of fish ponds, walkways, mini-bridges, a mini-pagoda, and souvenir vendors hawking garish plaster and gilded figurines. Inside the garden, on the shore of Tài Hú, is a tour-boat dock for cruises to other points. Entry to the garden is Y20.

Yuán Tóuzhǔ 鼋头渚
Turtle Head Isle
So named because it appears to be shaped like the head of a turtle, Yuán Tóuzhǔ is not actually an island, but a peninsula. This is the scenic strolling area where you can walk a circuit of the park and watch the junks on Tài Hú.

The entrance at the southern end of the park is just north of Bao Jie Bridge. This end of the park is rather peaceful with a lovely narrow road leading up to **Guāngmíng Tíng** (Brightness Pavilion), which is the highest point of Yuán Tóuzhǔ offering all-round vistas. The northern end of the park is overflowing with tourists and school children, souvenir stalls and restaurants. Located at this end is **Chángchūn Qiáo** (Perpetual Spring Bridge) as well as a small lighthouse. The architecture here, like that in the Lǐ Yuán, is mostly reproductions of classical styles. Inland from the lighthouse is *Chenglan (Clear Ripples Hall)*, a very nice teahouse from where you can sip tea with a view of the lake. North-west of the lighthouse is the pier where you can catch ferries to Sānshān (Three Hills Isles).

To get to Yuán Tóuzhǔ, take bus No 1 or 820 from the north bus station in Wúxī (½ hour) which lets you off at Bao Jie Bridge. From here you can walk or take a taxi to the southern entrance of the park. Alternatively, from the same bus station, take bus No 2 to its terminus (½ hour), then a small high-speed boat (Y20) or a taxi over the bridge to the northern entrance of the park. You can buy tickets for the boat from a kiosk in front of the Tài Hú Amusement Park.

Admission to Yuán Tóuzhǔ and Sānshān is Y35 (the ferry to Sānshān is included). You can purchase a Y45 ticket that includes entrance to the park and allows you to ride a train around the park's perimeter. If you enter by taxi from the southern entrance, an additional Y10 charge is levied.

Sānshān 三山
Three Hills Isles
Sānshān is an island park a couple of kilometres south-west of Yuán Tóuzhǔ. Vantage points at the top look back toward Yuán Tóuzhǔ and you can work out if it really does look like a turtle head or not. The islands are home to a number of pavilions and temples as well as three large buddha statues, the smallest measuring over 16m high. Watch out for the monkeys that inhabit the isles.

WÚXĪ 无锡

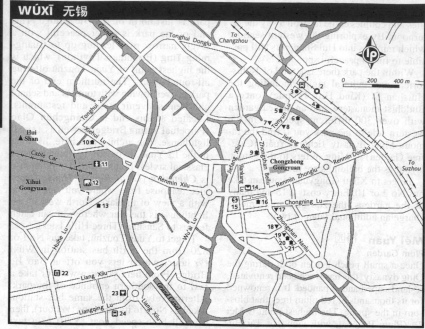

Wúxī Bówùguǎn 博物馆
Wuxi Museum

It doesn't appear that this museum sees many independent travellers but as long as you arrive between 8.30 am and 4.30 pm, you'll soon find an employee who is more than happy to unlock the door. The museum contains over 200 historical articles and craft works from over the past 6000 years, looking at the development of the local culture and its interaction with neighbouring counties. The museum is on the 2nd floor at 71 Huilte Lu. Entry is Y10.

Places to Stay – Budget
Qinggongye University Foreign Experts Hotel (Qīnggōngyè Dàxué Zhuānjiālóu; ☎ *586 1034),* on Huihe Lu, has rooms with private bath in the foreign students' dormitory. The rooms are somewhat dreary but comfortable and at Y60 per person, including a huge breakfast, they are a great deal. From the train station take bus No 2. After

crossing the Grand Canal get off at the second stop. The university is 200m further, on the other side of the street.

Touts around the train station will take travellers to the *Jīnhuá Dàfàndiàn (*☎ *272 0612, fax 271 1092, 9 Liangxi Lu),* where singles/doubles/triples are Y160/200/240. The rooms are slightly run-down, but clean. To get there, cross the bridge across the street from the train station then take the first small street on your left.

The *Jīngshānlóu Fàndiàn (*☎ *370 8888, fax 370 6081, 5 Xihui Lu),* east of the Grand Canal, has comfortable doubles from US$38. Bus No 10 from the train station stops directly outside.

Places to Stay – Mid-Range
The *Tiānmǎ Dàjiǔdiàn (*☎ *272 7668, fax 272 7878, 18 Liangxi Lu)* has doubles for Y350. To get there follow the same directions to the Jīnhuá Dàfàndiàn, but turn right after the bridge.

WÚXĪ

PLACES TO STAY

4 Zhōnglǚ Dàjiǔdiàn;
   CTS

5 Tiānmǎ Dàjiǔdiàn
   天马大酒店

6 Jǐnhuá Dàfàndiàn
   锦华大饭店

9 Sheraton Hotel
   喜来登大饭店

10 Jǐngshānlóu Fàndiàn
   景山楼饭店

13 Qinggongye
   University Foreign
   Experts Hotel
   轻工业大学专家楼

16 New World Courtyard
   Merriot Hotel
   新世界万怡酒店

20 Xīn Liángxī Dàjiǔdiàn
   新梁溪大酒店

21 Liángxī Fàndiàn
   梁溪饭店

PLACES TO EAT

7 Food Market
   食品市场

8 Zhōngguó Fàndiàn
   中国饭店

17 Wúxī Kǎoyāguǎn
   无锡烤鸭馆

18 Wángxìngjì
   王兴记

19 NYHT
   南洋皇亭

OTHER

1 North Bus
   Station
   无锡汽车客运中心站

2 Train Station
   火车站

3 Bicycle Rental
   租自行车店

11 Lóngguāng Tǎ
   龙光塔

12 Zoo
   动物园

14 Main Post Office;
   China Telecom Internet
   市邮电局；
   中国电信互联网

15 Bank of China
   中国银行

22 Wúxī Bówùguǎn
   博物馆

23 Barberry's Pub Cafe

24 South Bus Station
   无锡汽车站

Closer to the city centre is the **Liángxī Fàndiàn** (☎ 272 6812, fax 271 9174, 63 Zhongshan Nan Lu). Doubles start at Y340, including breakfast for one person. Take bus No 12 from the train station.

The **Tàihú Yīng Yuán** (Tai Hu Lake Cherry Resort; ☎ 588 1888, fax 588 1666) is at the northern end of Yuán Tóuzhǔ (Turtle Head Isle). Beautiful, brand-new singles begin at Y388 and doubles at Y398. To get there take bus No 2 from the train station to its terminus and then a five-minute taxi ride to the hotel. Be prepared to pay the park entrance fee.

Places to Stay – Top End

Nondescript, plush hotels are sprouting up all over the city. **Zhōnglǚ Dàjiǔdiàn (CTS Grand Hotel**; ☎ 230 0888, fax 230 2213, 88 Station Lu), directly across the street from the train station, has standard doubles from Y480 to Y880.

Within the city centre, the **Xīn Liángxī Dàjiǔdiàn (New Liangxi Grand Hotel**; ☎ 272 6878, fax 270 1207, 65 Zhongshan Lu) also has doubles starting at Y480. Bus No 12 from the train station will drop you in front of the hotel.

Located behind the New World department store, on the corner of Renmin Lu and Zhongshan Lu, the **New World Courtyard Merriot Hotel** (Xīnshìjiè Wànyí Jiǔdiàn; ☎ 276 2888, fax 276 3388, 335 Zhongshan Lu) has doubles from US$70. This hotel is also on bus route No 12.

The brand-new **Sheraton Hotel** (Xǐláidēng Dàjiǔdiàn; ☎ 272 1888, fax 275 2781, 443 Zhongshan Lu) has immaculate doubles beginning at Y888 during the week or Y688 on weekends. Prices include one breakfast. The hotel is next to Garden City Mall.

On Tài Hú, 12km from the train station, is the **Húbīn Fàndiàn** (☎ 510 1888, fax 510 2637, Li Yuan Garden). Standard rooms range from Y328 to Y680, depending on the view. From the main bus station in Wúxī take bus No 1 or 820.

Places to Eat

Wúxī has no shortage of restaurants. For an excellent and economical lunch try the **Zhōngguó Fàndiàn**, just south of the train station. One entrance leads into an à la carte dining area, but look for the entrance off Ton Yun Lu for the rough and ready section

JIĀNGSŪ 江苏

AROUND WÚXĪ & TÀI HÚ

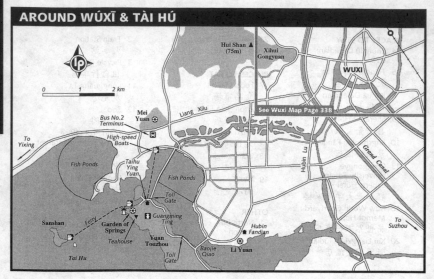

Hui Shan (75m) ▲
Xihui Gongyuan
WUXI
See Wuxi Map Page 338
0 1 2 km
Bus No.2 Terminus
Mei Yuan
Liang Xilu
High-speed Boats
To Yixing
Fish Ponds
Taihu Ying Yuan
Fish Ponds
Toll Gate
Hubin Lu
Grand Canal
Guangqing Ting
Sanshan
Ferry
Garden of Springs
Teahouse
Yuan Touzhou
Hubin Fandian
To Suzhou
Tai Hu
Toll Gate
Baojie Qiao
Li Yuan

where dumplings are served – ask for *xiǎolóngbāo*.

A block south and across the street, you'll find an excellent *food market* with fresh noodles, vegies, seafood, tea, cooked meat, baked goods and all the chicken feet you could possibly wish for. The market is buried behind the clothing market on the corner of Ton Yun and Jiefang Lu.

Another place worth popping into is the cafeteria-style *Wángxìngjì*, which is in the city centre on Zhongshan Nanlu. This place is famous for its *húntun* (a kind of ravioli served in soup) – it's very good and very cheap too. Dim sum is served in an adjoining room. Unfortunately, the restaurant has nothing for vegetarians. On the next block, however, the *NYHT* (*Nán Yáng Huáng Tíng;* ☎ 273 4701, 85 Zhongshan Nanlu) is a self-serve restaurant with good food for reasonable prices and lots of vegie dishes.

Popular with wealthy locals and expats is the *Wúxī Kǎoyāguǎn* (*Wúxī Roast Duck*), also on Zhongshan Lu. Prices are steep and the atmosphere stuffy.

If you are staying east of the Grand Canal, a number of *hole-in-the-wall restaurants* are clustered around the entrance to the Qinggongye University (see Places to Stay). These restaurants are popular with students for their cheap meals.

Entertainment
Near the south bus station there are a few pubs, including *Barberry's Pub Cafe* (*3 Liangxi Lu*), which is popular with expats and foreign students.

Shopping
Silk products and embroidery are good buys. There are also a large number of clay figurines for sale that may appeal to some tastes and other's sense of humour. A local folk art, the figurines take many forms and shapes, but are most commonly modelled after famous opera stars. Look out for models of obese infants – symbols of fortune and happiness.

Every Sunday there is a *Yù Shìchǎng* (Jade Market), which sells jade and local handicrafts, including *Yíxīng teapots*. It's near *Jīnhuá Dàfàndiàn* (see Places to Stay earlier) and the train station.

Getting There & Away
The north bus station, next to the train station, is where most long distance buses depart.

There is another bus station down on Liangqing Lu, but it has fewer services. Frequent direct buses to Yíxīng (1½ hours) leave from the south bus station only.

There are direct buses to Shànghǎi (two hours), Sūzhōu (¾ hour), Yíxīng (one hour) and Zhènjiāng (1½ hours). For Dīngshān change buses in Yíxīng and for Yángzhōu transfer in Zhènjiāng.

Wúxī is on the line from Běijīng to Shànghǎi, with frequent express and special-express trains. About every two hours there are trains to Sūzhōu (40 minutes), Shànghǎi (1¾ hours) and Nánjīng (2¾ hours).

Foreigners are supposed to buy their train tickets from Window No 2. There is a soft-seat waiting room for those travelling via this class.

Getting Around

There are about 15 local bus lines. Bus 2 runs from the train station, along Jiefang Lu, across two bridges to Xīhuì Gōngyuán, then way out to Méi Yuán. Bus No 2 almost crosses the bus No 1 route at the square, Gōngnóngbīng Guǎngchǎng.

Bus No 1 starts on Gongnongbing Lu and runs to the Húbīn Fàndiàn, Lǐ Yuán and across the bridge to Yuán Tóuzhǔ.

A good tour bus is No 10, which does a long loop around the northern part of the city area, taking in four bridges, Xīhuì Gōngyuán and the shopping strip of Renmin Lu.

To rent a bike, head down the lane directly across the street from the north bus station and turn right down the first adjoining alley. One day on a somewhat unsteady bike will cost you Y6.

SŪZHŌU 苏州

☎ 0512 • pop 5,749,900

Jiāngsū's most famous attraction, Sūzhōu is a famed silk production centre and a celebrated retreat brimming with gardens and canals. However, this hasn't done anything to hold back the gathering tide of urban renewal. Unfortunately, much of the city's charm is being swept away by new road, housing and hotel developments. Nevertheless, a wander through the charming gardens and what remain of its cobbled alleys makes a visit to Sūzhōu worthwhile.

Sūzhōu's gardens are looked upon as works of art – a fusion of nature, architecture, poetry and painting designed to ease, move or assist the mind.

History

Dating back some 2500 years, Sūzhōu is one of the oldest towns in the Yangzi Basin. With the completion of the Grand Canal in the Sui dynasty, Sūzhōu found itself strategically located on a major trading route, and the city's fortunes and size grew rapidly.

Sūzhōu flourished as a centre of shipping and grain storage, bustling with merchants and artisans. By the 12th century the town had attained its present dimensions, and if you consult the map, you'll see the layout of the old town.

The city walls, a rectangle enclosed by moats, were pierced by six gates (north, south, two in the east and two in the west). Crisscrossing the city were six north-south canals and 14 east-west canals. Although the walls have largely disappeared and a fair proportion of the canals have been plugged, central Sūzhōu retains some of its 'Renaissance' character.

A legend was spun about Sūzhōu through tales of beautiful women with mellifluous voices, and through the famous proverb 'In heaven there is paradise, on earth Sūzhōu and Hángzhōu'. The story picks up when Marco Polo arrived in 1276. He added the adjectives 'great' and 'noble', although he reserved his finer epithets for Hángzhōu.

By the 14th century Sūzhōu had established itself as China's leading silk producer. Aristocrats, pleasure-seekers, famous scholars, actors and painters were attracted to the city, constructing villas and garden retreats for themselves.

At the height of Sūzhōu's development in the 16th century, the gardens, large and small, numbered over 100. If we mark time here, we arrive at the town's tourist formula today – 'Garden City, Venice of the East', a medieval mix of woodblock guilds and embroidery societies, whitewashed housing, cobbled streets, tree-lined avenues and canals.

JIĀNGSŪ 江苏

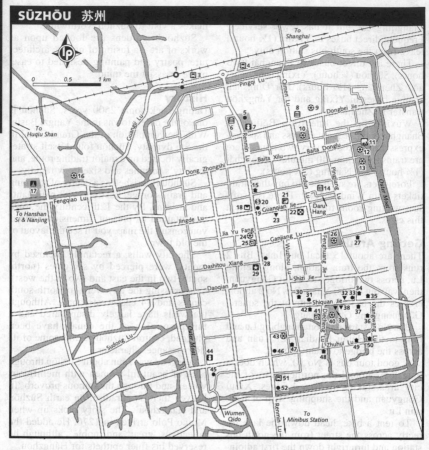

SŪZHŌU 苏州

The wretched workers of the silk sweat-shops, protesting against paltry wages and the injustices of the contract hire system, were staging violent strikes even as far back as the 15th century, and the landlords shifted as a result. In 1860 Taiping troops took the town without a blow. In 1896 Sūzhōu was opened to foreign trade, with Japanese and international concessions. During WWII, it was occupied by the Japanese and then by the Kuomintang. Somehow Sūzhōu slipped through the worst ravages of the Cultural Revolution relatively unscathed.

Information

Tourist Office Sūzhōu has one branch of CITS (☎ 522 2223) that acts as a genuine tourist office. It's is in a separate building to the right as you enter the grounds of the Sūzhōu Fàndiàn compound.

Money The Bank of China is at 490 Renmin Lu, but all of the major tourist hotels also have foreign-exchange counters.

Post & Communications The post office is on the corner of Renmin Lu and Jingde Lu.

SŪZHŌU

PLACES TO STAY

15 Huáqiáo Dàjiǔdiàn
    华侨大酒店
27 Gloria Plaza Hotel
    凯莱大酒店
30 Nánlín Fàndiàn
    南林饭店
34 Yíngfēng Bīnguǎn
    迎凤宾馆
35 Dōngwú Fàndiàn
    东吴饭店
36 Gūsū Fàndiàn
    姑苏饭店
37 Sūzhōu Fàndiàn; CITS
    苏州饭店;
    中国国际旅行社
42 Nányuán Bīnguǎn
    南园宾馆
47 Cānglàng Bīnguǎn
    沧浪宾馆
48 Yǒuyí Bīnguǎn
    友谊宾馆
49 Zhúhuī Fàndiàn
    竹辉宾馆
50 Xiāngwáng Bīnguǎn
    相王宾馆

PLACES TO EAT

22 Suzhou Shangsha
    Department Store
    苏州商厦
23 Sōnghè Lóu
    松鹤楼
32 Yángyáng Shuǐjiǎoguǎn
    洋洋水饺馆
38 Lǎodàkěyǐ
    老大可以
39 Yǒnghé Dòujiāng
    永和豆浆

GARDENS

9 Zhuōzhèng Yuán
    拙政园

10 Shīzi Lín
    狮子林
12 Dōng Yuán
    东园
13 Ǒu Yuán
    (Coupling Garden)
    耦园
16 Liú Yuán
    留园
24 Yí Yuán
    怡园
26 Shuāngtǎ Yuàn
    双塔院
40 Wǎngshī Yuán
    网师园
43 Cānglàng Tíng
    沧浪亭

MUSEUMS

6 Sūzhōu Sīchóu
    Bówùguǎn
    丝绸博物馆
8 Sūzhōu Bówùguǎn
    苏州博物馆
14 Xìqǔ Bówùguǎn
    戏曲博物馆

TEMPLES & PAGODAS

7 Běisì Tǎ
    北寺塔
17 Xīyuán Sì
    西园寺
21 Xuánmiào Guàn
    玄妙观
44 Ruìguāng Tǎ
    瑞光塔

TRANSPORT

1 Train Station; CITS
    火车站;
    中国国际旅行社
2 Boat Tours
    游船游览

3 Local Buses
    当地汽车
4 Long-Distance
    Bus Station
    南门汽车站
5 Bicycle Rental
    租自行车店
28 China Eastern Airlines
    Booking Office
    东方航空售票处
31 CITS
    中国国际旅行社
33 Bicycle Rental
    租自行车店
51 Long-Distance
    Bus Station
    南门汽车站
52 Grand Canal Boats
    Ticket Office
    轮船站

OTHER

11 Zoo
    动物园
18 Post Office
    邮局
19 Sūzhōu Shípǐn
    Dàshà
    苏州食品大厦
20 Bank of China
    中国银行
25 China Telecom
    Internet
    电信网络
29 PSB
    公安局
41 Internet Bar
    必胜网吧
45 Pán Mén
    盘门
46 Foreign Languages
    Bookstore
    外文书店

Email & Internet Access While a number of places in Sūzhōu advertise Internet access, the majority are either perpetually closed or else their connection is not functioning. In its office on the corner of Renmin Lu and Ganjiang Lu, China Telecom offers public access to the Internet through a number of new computers. The price is Y18 per hour and it's open daily from 8 am to 10 pm. Also try the funky Internet Bar (Xiàndàifén; ☎ 519 5497) on Dai Cheng Ziao Lu, where you enjoy a cocktail while you email. It's open from noon until 2 am and rates are Y20 per hour.

Travel Agencies There is a second CITS branch (see Tourist Office earlier for the main branch) at the train station and a third, that handles international airline tickets, in the east of the Nánlín Fàndiàn complex (see Places to Stay later).

PSB The PSB office is at 7 Dashitou Xiang, on the corner of Renmin Lu. Enter through a red door on Renmin Lu.

Běisì Tǎ 北寺塔
North Temple Pagoda

The Běisì Tǎ is the tallest pagoda south of the Cháng Jiāng (Yangzi River) – at nine storeys it dominates the northern end of Renmin Lu. You can climb it for a fine aerial view of the town and the farmland beyond, where tea, rice and wheat are grown. The factory chimneys (the new pagodas of Sūzhōu) loom on the outskirts, hovering within the haze and smoke they create.

The temple complex goes back 1700 years and was originally a residence. The pagoda has been burnt, built and rebuilt. Made of wood, it dates from the 17th century. Off to the side is **Nanmu Hall**, which was rebuilt in the Ming dynasty with some of its features imported from elsewhere. There is a teahouse with a small garden out the back.

Běisì Tǎ is open from 8 am to 5.30 pm and entry costs Y7.

Sūzhōu Bówùguǎn 苏州博物馆
Suzhou Museum

Found east of the Zhuózhèng Yuán (Humble Administrator's Garden), the Sūzhōu Bówùguǎn was once the residence of Taiping leader, Li Xiucheng.

The museum offers some interesting old maps, including those of the Grand Canal, Sūzhōu, and heaven and earth. It also houses Qing dynasty steles forbidding workers' strikes, and relics such as funerary objects, porcelain bowls and bronze swords unearthed or rescued from various sites around the Sūzhōu District. There are no English captions.

The museum is open daily from 8.30 am to 4 pm; entry costs Y5.

Sūzhōu Sīchóu Bówùguǎn 苏州丝绸博物馆
Suzhou Silk Museum

Highly recommended by many, this museum houses a number of fascinating exhibitions that provide a thorough history of Sūzhōu's silk industry over the past 4000 years. Exhibits include a section on old looms and weaving techniques and a room with live silk worms in various stages of life. A second building displays clothing made of silk from the early 1900s. Many of the captions and explanations are in both Chinese and English.

The museum is open from 9 am to 5 pm; tickets cost Y7.

Xuánmiào Guàn 玄妙观
Temple of Mystery

The heart of what was once Sūzhōu Bazaar – an area that is being rapidly developed – is the Taoist Xuánmiào Guàn. It was founded during the Jin dynasty in the 3rd century AD and laid out from AD 275–279, with additions during the Song dynasty.

From the Qing dynasty onwards, the bazaar fanned out from the temple with tradespeople and travelling performers using the grounds. The enormous **Sanqing Hall**, supported by 60 pillars and capped by a double roof with upturned eaves, dates from 1181. It was burnt and seriously damaged in the 19th century. During the Cultural Revolution the Red Guards squatted here and it was later transformed into a library. Today the temple is surrounded by a street market and Sūzhōu's main shopping district, Guanqian Jie.

Entry to Xuánmiào Guàn is Y10 and it's open daily from 9 am to 6 pm.

Xìqǔ Bówùguǎn 戏曲博物馆
Museum of Opera & Theatre

In the old city of Sūzhōu, this small museum is worth going to for the surrounding area of small cobblestone lanes lined with stalls selling vegetables and inexpensive snacks. The museum houses a moveable stage, old musical instruments, costumes and photos of famous performers. From Linden Lu go east on Daru Hang. At the end of the road go right, then take the first left.

Zhuózhèng Yuán 拙政园
Humble Administrator's Garden

Many consider this to be one of Sūzhōu's best gardens, second only to the Wǎngshī Yuán (Garden of the Master of the Nets).

Dating back to the early 1500s, this garden's 5 hectares feature streams, ponds, bridges and islands of bamboo. There's also a teahouse and a small museum that explains Chinese landscape gardening concepts. In the same area are the Sūzhōu Bówùguǎn and several silk mills. The garden is open daily from 7.30 am to 5.30 pm; entry costs Y30.

Shīzi Lín 狮子林
Lion Grove

Just around the corner from the Zhuózhèng Yuán, this 1 hectare grove was constructed in 1350 by the monk Tian Ru and other disciples as a memorial to their master, Zhi Zheng. The garden has rockeries that evoke the forms of lions. The walls of the labyrinth of tunnels bear calligraphy from famous chisels. It's open daily from 7.30 am to 5.30 pm; admission is Y10.

Yí Yuán 怡园
Garden of Harmony

A small Qing dynasty garden owned by an official called Gu Wenbin, this one is quite young for a Sūzhōu garden. It has assimilated many of the features of other gardens and blended them into a style of its own. In the east are buildings and courtyards. The western section has pools with coloured pebbles, rockeries, hillocks and pavilions. Opening times are 7.30 am to 5.30 pm; entry to the garden is off Renmin Lu and admission is Y4.

Cānglàng Tíng 沧浪亭
Blue Wave Pavilion

A bit on the wild side with winding creeks and luxuriant trees, this is one of the oldest gardens in Sūzhōu. The buildings date from the 11th century, although they have been rebuilt on numerous occasions since.

Originally the home of a prince, the property passed into the hands of the scholar Su Zimei, who gave it its name. This 1 hectare garden attempts to create optical illusions with the scenery both outside and inside – you look from the pool immediately outside to the distant hills. **Míngdào Táng** (Enlightened Way Hall), the largest building, is said to have been a site for delivery of lectures during the Ming dynasty. Close by, on the other side of Renmin Lu, is the former Confucius Temple.

The garden opens from 7.30 am to 5.30 pm; entry costs Y5. The entrance is off Renmin Lu and is signposted as 'Surging Wave' Pavilion.

Wǎngshī Yuán 网师园
Garden of the Master of the Nets

This is the smallest garden in Sūzhōu – half the size of the Cānglàng Tíng and one-tenth the size of the Zhuózhèng Yuán. It's small and hard to find, but well worth the trouble as it's better than all the others combined.

This garden was laid out in the 12th century, abandoned, then restored in the 18th century as part of the residence of a retired official. According to one story, he announced that he'd had enough of bureaucracy and would rather be a fisherman. Another explanation of the name is that it was simply near Wangshi Lu. The eastern part of the garden is the residential area – originally with side rooms for sedan-chair lackeys, guest reception and living quarters. The central part is the main garden. The western part is an inner garden where a courtyard contains the **Diànchūn Yí** (Spring Rear Cottage), the master's study. This section and the study, with its Ming-style furniture and palace lanterns, was duplicated and unveiled at the Metropolitan Museum of Art in New York in 1981.

A miniature model of the whole garden, using Qingtian jade, Yingde rocks, Ānhuī paper, Sūzhōu silk and incorporating the halls, kiosks, ponds, blossoms and rare plants of the original design, was produced especially for a display at the Pompidou Centre in Paris in 1982.

The most striking feature of this garden is its use of space. Despite its size, the scale of the buildings is large, but nothing appears cramped. A section of the buildings is

Sūzhōu's Gardens

The key elements of these famous gardens are rocks and water. Just like the Zen gardens of Japan, there are surprisingly few flowers and no fountains. Although these gardens were designed to perfection, they were intended to give the illusion of a natural scene consisting of only moss, sand and rock. These microcosms were laid out by master crafts-people and have changed hands many times over the centuries.

The gardens suffered a setback during the Taiping Rebellion in the 1860s, and under subsequent foreign domination of Sūzhōu. Efforts were made to restore them in the 1950s, but during the so-called Horticultural Revolution gardeners downed tools, as flowers were frowned upon.

In 1979 the Suzhou Garden Society was formed, and an export company was set up to promote Sūzhōu-designed gardens. A number of the gardens have been renovated and opened to the public.

used by a co-operative of woodblock artists who find the peaceful atmosphere congenial to work.

There are two entrances to the garden. The first is off Shiquan Jie, next door to Yǒnghé Dòujiāng (Yong He Soya-Bean Milk Shop). The second is via a narrow alley just west of the Sūzhōu Fàndiàn. Going east on Shiquan Lu, take a right onto Daichengqiao Lu, then left down the first alley. It's open daily from 7.30 am to 5.30 pm; entry costs Y10.

Liú Yuán 留园
Garden for Lingering In
Extending over an area of 3 hectares, Liú Yuán is one of the largest gardens in Sūzhōu, noted for its adroit partitioning with building complexes.

The garden dates from the Ming dynasty and managed to escape destruction during the Taiping Rebellion. A 700m covered walkway connects the major scenic spots, and the windows have carefully selected

perspectives. The walkway is inlaid with calligraphy from celebrated masters and the garden has a wealth of potted plants. There is also a rock from Tài Hú located outside **Yuanyang** (Mandarin Duck Hall); at 6½m high you couldn't miss it if you tried.

The garden is about 3km west of the old city walls. Bus No 5 will take you there via bridges that look down on the busy water traffic. Catch the bus on Renmin Lu, near the Bank of China.

Xīyuán Sì
West Garden Temple
Approximately 500m west of the Liúyuán, this temple was built on the site of a garden laid out at the same time as the Liú Yuán and then donated to the Buddhist community. The temple was destroyed in the 19th century and entirely rebuilt; it contains some expressive Buddhist statues.

Hánshān Sì 寒山寺
Cold Mountain Temple
One kilometre west of the Liúyuán, this temple was named after the poet-monk Hanshan, who lived in the 7th century. It was repeatedly burnt down and rebuilt, and was once the site of lively local trading in silk, wood and grain. Not far from its saffron walls lies the Grand Canal. Today, the temple holds little of interest except for a stele by poet Zhang Ji immortalising both the nearby Maple Bridge and the temple bell (since removed to Japan). However, the fine walls and the humpback bridge are worth seeing.

Bus Nos 30 and 31 will take you close to the temple but it's easiest to catch bus No 5 to the Liú Yuán and walk the final kilometre west.

Hǔqiū Shān 虎丘山
Tiger Hill
In the far north-west of town, Hǔqiū Shān is extremely popular with local tourists. The hill itself is artificial, and is the final resting place of He Lu, founding father of Sūzhōu. He Lu died in the 6th century BC and myths have coalesced around him – he is said to have been buried with a collection of 3000 swords and to be guarded by a white tiger.

Built in the 10th century, the leaning **Yúnyán Tǎ** (Cloud Rock Pagoda) stands atop Hǔqiū Shān. The octagonal seven-storey pagoda is built entirely of brick, an innovation in Chinese architecture at the time. The pagoda began tilting over 400 years ago, and today the highest point is displaced over 2m from its original position.

To get to Hǔqiū Shān, take bus No 5 to its terminus. Admission is Y30.

Pán Mén 盘门三景
Coiled Gate

In the south-western corner of the city, straddling the outer moat, this stretch of the city wall contains Sūzhōu's only remaining original city gate. From the top of the gate there are good views of the moat, surrounding houses and **Ruìguāng Tǎ** (Auspicious Light Pagoda), a crumbling pagoda that dates from the 3rd century AD and is reputedly the oldest pagoda in Jiāngsū.

Near the southern end of Renmin Lu, cross over the humpbacked bridge, Wúmén Qiáo, and follow the ramp down its right side. This will bring you to Nan Men Lu, which you can follow right to the gate. The gate and its surrounding buildings are open from 8 am to 5 pm. Admission costs Y8.

Boat Tours

By the canal, south of the train station (opposite the soft-seat waiting room), you can hire a boat that will take you along the canal either south to Pán Mén or north to Hǔqiū Shān. If you are with a group the cost is Y30, or if you hire a boat alone it's Y150. The trip takes about an hour. Boats depart from the Foreign Travellers Transportation Company Pier (Wàishì Lǚyóu Chēchuán Gōngsī Mǎtóu; ☎ 752 6931).

Places to Stay

Sūzhōu has very little to offer in the way of cheap accommodation. However, depending on the season, it is often possible to bargain room prices down. Don't be immediately deterred by the posted rates.

Hotel touts outside Sūzhōu's train station, especially those with pedicabs, can be extremely aggressive. They will offer a ridiculously cheap fare to your destination and then, once you are loaded into their pedicab, claim that the hotel you have chosen has been bulldozed or burnt to the ground. They will then insist on taking you to a hotel of their choice. The problem is that their choice is often not as cheap as they claim or doesn't accept foreigners.

A couple of hours later you may still not have found a place to stay and instead be stuck with a large taxi bill.

Places to Stay – Budget

The **Yíngfēng Bīnguǎn** (☎ 530 6291), over a small footbridge opposite the Sūzhōu Fàndiàn, offers doubles with bath for Y160. Walk through Yíng Feng restaurant to find the hotel. Don't be put off by the hotel's grotty exterior or drab lobby; rooms are clean and quite nice, some looking onto a central garden.

The **Dōngwú Fàndiàn** (☎ 519 443), run by Sūzhōu University International Cultural Exchange Institute, has clean, air-conditioned singles for Y140 and doubles for Y200, all with shared bath. From Renmin Lu head east down Shiquan Jie; the guesthouse is on the left just past the Sūzhōu Fàndiàn.

The **Nánlín Fàndiàn** (see Places to Stay – Top End) has very nice doubles with private bath in an older building for Y178. Unfortunately the karaoke bar is also in this building. You can also try the **Yǒuyì Bīnguǎn** (see Places to Stay – Mid-Range), which has standard doubles in its older building beginning at Y160.

The **Cānglàng Bīnguǎn** (☎ 520 1557, fax 510 3285, 53 Wuqueqiao), south of Shiquan Jie, has somewhat unkept doubles for Y180, triples for Y225 and quads for Y240.

Places to Stay – Mid-Range

Head to the south-eastern corner of town for mid-range accommodation.

The **Xiāngwáng Bīnguǎn** (☎ 529 1162, fax 529 1182, 118 Zhuhui Lu) offers standard doubles with bath for Y220 or Y280. The hotel is at the eastern end of Zhuhui Lu, on the corner of Xiangwang Lu.

Just north of Guanqian Jie, the **Huáqiáo Dàjiǔdiàn** (Overseas Chinese Hotel; ☎ 720

2883, 518 Renmin Lu) has rather drab standard doubles for Y300.

The *Yŏuyì Bīnguăn (Friendship Hotel;* ☎ *529 1601, fax 520 6221)* has opened a brand-new building with clean, air-conditioned singles for Y380 and doubles for Y400. The hotel is on Zhuhui Lu, at the intersection with Diachengqiao Lu.

The *Nánlín Fàndiàn (*☎ *519 6333, fax 519 1028, 20 Gunxiufang Shiquan Jie)* has pleasant gardens and caters to foreign tour groups. Doubles in its new building cost Y270 to Y450. The hotel also has upmarket suites from Y600 to Y1200. Enter the hotel complex off Shiquan Lu.

Places to Stay – Top End
The number of top-end hotels in Sūzhōu is quickly growing as is the number of mid-range hotels upgrading and charging top-end prices.

Recently reopened after renovations, the *Gūsū Fàndiàn (*☎ *520 0566, fax 519 9727, 5 Xiangwang Lu)* has singles starting at Y380 and doubles for Y480. A 10% service charge is also added.

The *Sūzhōu Fàndiàn (*☎ *520 4646, fax 520 4015, 115 Shiquan Jie)* is a sprawling place that does a brisk trade in tour groups. Doubles start at Y450. Further along Shiquan Jie, the *Nányuán Bīnguăn (*☎ *519 7661, fax 519 8806, 249 Shiquan Jie)* is inside a walled garden compound. Doubles with breakfast begin at Y480.

The *Zhúhuī Fàndiàn (Bamboo Grove Hotel;* ☎ *520 5601, fax 520 8778)*, on Zhuhui Lu, is the pick of Sūzhōu's top-end accommodation with all the facilities you would expect of a five-star hotel. Room rates start at Y590 for a double, including one breakfast.

Close to the old city of Sūzhōu, the upmarket *Gloria Plaza Hotel (Kăilái Dàjiŭdiàn;* ☎ *521 8508, fax 521 8533, 535 Ganjiang Lu)* also has five-star service with rooms starting at Y765.

Places to Eat
Sūzhōu is a tourist town, and consequently there is no shortage of places dishing up local and tourist cuisine. Shiquan Jie, between Daichengqiao Lu and Xiangwang Lu, is lined

with *bars*, *restaurants* and *bakeries*. Open 24 hours is the *Yŏnghé Dòujiāng (Yonghe Soya-Bean Milk Shop; 167 Shiquan Jie)*, next door to the entrance of Wăngshī Yuán. It serves tasty rice, noodle and soup dishes; for breakfast there is *dòujiāng* (sweet soya bean milk) and *yóutiáo* (fried bread sticks).

A little further east along Shiquan Jie, try the *Lăodàkèyĭ (*☎ *510 0598, 173 Shiquan Jie)* for fresh seafood straight from the aquarium. Across the street and further east is the *Yángyáng Shuĭjiăoguăn (Authentic Chinese Dumpling House;* ☎ *519 2728, 144 Shiquan Jie)*. With fresh dumplings, snails and vegie dishes for very reasonable prices, it is extremely popular. Share tables with locals and sip tea from a beer glass. Try upstairs for more seating if downstairs is full.

If you're on a tight budget, try the food courts of the ever-growing number of department stores at the southern end of Renmin Lu. You can fill up for Y5 in the food court on the 3rd floor of the *Sūzhōu Shāngshà department store (57-69 Guanqian Jie)*. Buy food tickets at the entrance, then redeem them by choosing from the wide array of Chinese dishes and desserts, including dumplings, steamed buns, snails and 100-year-old eggs. It's hard to miss this large store, with its ornate tiled roof.

A half block north of Yí Yuán is Jia Yu Fang, a street lined with several fairly upmarket *Chinese restaurants*.

If money is no object, you might try the *Sōnghè Lóu (141 Guanqian Jie)*, rated as the most famous restaurant in Sūzhōu: Emperor Qianlong is said to have eaten there. The large variety of dishes includes squirrel fish, plain steamed prawns, braised eel, pork with pine nuts, butterfly-shaped sea cucumber, watermelon chicken and spicy duck. The waiter may insist that you be parcelled off to the special 'tour bus' cubicle at the back where an English menu awaits. The Sōnghè Lóu runs from Guanqian Jie to an alley behind, where tour minibuses pull up. Travellers give the restaurant mixed reviews.

Entertainment
Very popular is the nightly performance of dance and song at Wăngshī Yuán. The

audience moves from pavilion to pavilion to watch a variety of traditional Chinese performing arts. The show lasts from 7.30 to 10.30 pm and tickets can be bought from CITS for Y60. Alternatively, turn up shortly before the performance and buy your ticket on the spot.

Shopping

Sūzhōu-style embroidery, calligraphy, paintings, sandalwood fans, writing brushes and silk underclothes are for sale nearly everywhere. For good quality items at competitive rates, shop along Shiquan Jie, east off Renmin Lu. The street is lined with shops with names like 'Mysterious Holy Things', and 'Han & Tibetan Shop'.

For silk try the cloth shops on Guanqian Jie; most cloth shops have tailors on hand who can make simple clothing in about three days. Next to Xuánmiào Guàn there's a night market that sells very reasonably priced silk.

The Sūzhōu Shípǐng Dàshà (Suzhou Food Centre; 246 Renmin Lu) sells all kinds of local, traditional specialities and teas in bulk.

The newsagent in the Zhúhuī Fàndiàn has a good selection of foreign books. The Foreign Language Bookstore at 44 Renmin Lu, just south of Cānglàng Tíng, also has a small selection of English paperbacks.

Getting There & Away

Air Sūzhōu does not have an airport, but China Eastern Airlines (Dōngfāng Hángkōng Gōngsī; ☎ 522 2788) has a ticket office at 192 Renmin Lu for booking flights out of Shànghǎi. For international tickets, you can also try Sūzhōu CITS Travel and Air Services (Sūzhōu Gúolǚ Hángkōng Lǚyòufúwú Gōngsī; ☎ 529 5199) at the eastern end of the Nánlín Fàndiàn complex. The office is open daily from 8.30 am to 4.30 pm.

Bus There are three long-distance bus stations in Sūzhōu. The main one is at the northern end of Renmin Lu, next to the train station, and a second at the southern end of Renmin Lu. Both have connections between Sūzhōu and just about every major place in the region, including Shànghǎi, Hángzhōu, Wúxī, Yángzhōu and Yíxīng. A third station, further south on Renmin Lu, has similar connections with private minibuses that are slightly cheaper but run less frequently than from the other two stations.

Travelling by bus on the new Nánjīng to Sūzhōu highway takes about the same amount of time as the train, but tickets are generally slightly more expensive.

Train Sūzhōu is on the railway line from Nánjīng to Shànghǎi. To Shànghǎi takes about 50 minutes, to Wúxī 40 minutes and to Nánjīng 3¼ hours. For long-distance sleepers, ask your hotel or try CITS.

Boat There are boats along the Grand Canal to Hángzhōu. It's basically only foreigners and overseas Chinese who use them these days – locals prefer to travel by bus or train.

Boats from Sūzhōu to Hángzhōu depart daily at 5.30 pm and arrive the next morning at 7 am. Officially, you can only purchase tickets at the 'civilisation unit' window at the boat booking office. Prices there are Y190 for a sleeper in a four-berth room or Y280 in a double berth. Ask, however, at your hotel; some hotels will purchase tickets for guests at a much cheaper rate.

Getting Around

Bus The main thoroughfare is Renmin Lu with the train and main bus stations just off the northern end, and a large boat dock and another long-distance bus station at the southern end.

Bus No 1 runs the length of Renmin Lu and bus No 2 is a kind of around-the-city bus. Bus No 5 is a good east to west bus and can be picked up in either direction on Renmin Lu near the Bank of China or Huáqiáo Dàjiǔdiàn (see Places to Stay earlier). Bus No 4 runs from Changmen directly east along Baita Lu, turns south and runs past the eastern end of Guanqian Jie and then on to the Sūzhōu Fàndiàn.

Taxi Taxis and pedicabs congregate outside the main train station, down by the boat dock at the southern end of Renmin Lu, and at Jingmen (Nanxin Bridge) at the western end of Jingde Lu. They also tend to hover around tourist hotels. Drivers generally use their meters. Like elsewhere in China, the pedicab drivers can be fairly aggressive. Expect to barter hard.

Bicycle There are several bicycle rental shops scattered around the city. The one across from the Sūzhōu Sīchóu Bówùguǎn (Silk Museum) offers the best rates at Y10 per day however, with only ten bikes for hire, they disappear quickly. There are two more shops across from the Sūzhōu Fàndiàn and another next to CITS at the train station, all of which charge between Y15 and Y30 per day, plus deposit.

AROUND SŪZHŌU
Grand Canal 大运河
The Grand Canal (Dà Yùnhé) proper cuts to the west and south of Sūzhōu, within a 10km range of the town. Suburban bus Nos 13, 14, 15 and 16 will get you there. In the north-west, bus No 11 follows the canal for a fair distance, taking you on a tour of the enchanting countryside. Hop off the bus once you find yourself a nice bridge on which you can perch and watch the world of the canal float by. Parking yourself for too long could make you the main tourist attraction.

Bǎodài Qiáo
Precious Belt Bridge
With 53 arches, this is considered one of China's best bridges. It straddles the Grand Canal, and is a popular spot with fisherfolk. The three central humpbacks of the bridge are larger to allow boats through. The bridge is no longer used for traffic – a modern one has been built alongside it.

Bǎodài Qiáo is thought to be a Tang dynasty construction named after Wang Zhongshu, a local prefect who sold his precious belt to pay for the bridge's construction for the benefit of his people.

The bridge is south-east of Sūzhōu. You can get there by taxi or a 40-minute bike ride. Head south on Renmin Lu, past the south moat, then left at the TV towers.

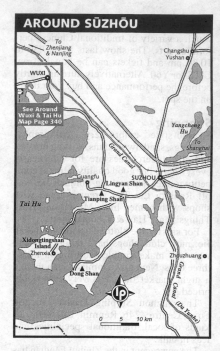

AROUND SŪZHŌU

Tài Hú Area
The towns surrounding Sūzhōu provide ample opportunity for a visit to Tài Hú and the countryside beyond the lake. **Língyán Shān** (Spirit Rock Hill), 15km from Sūzhōu, is home to an active Buddhist monastery; **Tiānpíng Shān** (Quiet Heaven Hill), 18km from Sūzhōu, is famous for its medicinal spring waters; and **Guāngfú**, 25km west of Sūzhōu, borders the lake with an ancient seven-storey pagoda.

Dōng Shān (East Hill), 40km west of Sūzhōu, is surrounded by the lake on three sides and noted for its gardens and the **Zǐjīnān** (Purple Gold Nunnery) that contains 16 coloured clay icons.

To see eroded Tài Hú rocks 'harvested' for landscaping, visit **Xīdòngtíngshān Dǎo** (South-East Enduring Hills Island), located 60km south-west of Sūzhōu.

Head 50km north-east to **Chángshú**, known for its lace making and **Yúshān** with its nine-storey Song Pagoda.

All of these destinations can be reached by long-distance buses from the station at the southern end of Renmin Lu (north of the bridge) or the minibus station located south, over the moat, on Renmin Lu.

ZHŌUZHUĀNG 周庄

Set in the countryside 38km south-east of Sūzhōu, Zhōuzhuāng offers a step back in time into what is believed to be the first water town of China. Established over 900 years ago, Zhōuzhuāng boasts 14 bridges and over 60% of its buildings are from the Yuan, Ming and Qing dynasties. Zhōuzhuāng also has a huge tourism industry and is extremely popular with Chinese tourists yet surprisingly untouched by those from abroad. Despite the crowds, a day in Zhōuzhuāng is definitely worthwhile. The cobbled lanes of the Old Town are pedestrianised and picturesque, confirmed by the many painters seated alongside the canals. Many of the locals continue to go about their day, sitting on their steps and making lace or fishing in the canals with cormorants.

Orientation & Information

The bus will let you off north-west of the Old Town. To find the Old Town, head east on Quangong Lu and take the first left onto Quanfu Lu. Maps are available at many stalls inside the Old Town.

Directly across from the bus station is the Zhouzhuang Travel Service. As of yet, the PSB has not established itself in Zhōuzhuāng. It is also not the most convenient town to change money or to post a letter. The Yúnhǎi Dùjiàcūn (see Places to Stay later) may provide these services, but to be on the safe side, take care of such business before arriving.

Things to See

Entrance to the Old Town of Zhōuzhuāng is through the Gǔběi Lóu (Ancient Memorial Archway). South of the archway, Zhōuzhuāng's narrow cobbled alleys are entirely pedestrianised. Within the Old Town are ten sights including temples, gardens and the former homes of officers from the Qing and Ming dynasties, many of

which are still inhabited by artisans and workers today.

The Shěn Tīng (Hall of Shen's Residence) is considered the best of these houses, containing seven courtyards and over 100 rooms, each connected to a main hall. Inside, wood carvers and weavers are hard at work. South of here, the Zhāng Tīng (Hall of Zhang's Residence) dates back over 500 years and was home to a local officer. This house has six courtyards and over 70 rooms. Running through the residence is the Rùojìng Hé (Footpath River).

Other former residences to visit in Zhōuzhuāng include Yèchǔcāng Zhu (Former Residence of Yechucang), Mí Lóu (Mi House), Zé Tīng (Hall of Ze's Residence) and the Zhěn'gù Táng (Solid Faith Hall).

At the southern end of town, Quánfú Sì (Temple of Total Well-being) contains 21 gold buddhas plus one large bronze buddha measuring over 5m in height. The temple is surrounded by pagodas and courtyard buildings, extending into Nánhú Yuán (South Lake Garden). This garden was built for Zhang Jiying, a literary man of the Jin dynasty, and consists of bridges crisscrossing over the water.

The Zhōuzhuāng Bówùguǎn (Zhōuzhuāng Museum) is home to nearly 1000 artefacts including a number from the local fishing and artisan industries. South of the museum is the Chéngxū Dàoyuàn (Garden of Clear and Empty Paths), with a Taoist Temple that was built during the Song dynasty.

All of the sights in Zhōuzhuāng can be visited on one ticket for Y35, which is available at the entrance to any of the sights; all sights close at 5 pm. Almost all of the signs and captions within the sights are in Chinese only but you're more than likely to be befriended by a number of Chinese tourists who may be willing to be your tour guides.

For a Boat Tour of the canal, head south of the Shuāng Qiáo (Double Bridge) on Nan Shijie in the south-west of town. Half-hour trips cost Y60 per boat, which hold up to eight people.

Note the imposing Quánfú Tǎ (Pagoda of Total Well-being) just north of the Old

Town. The pagoda was built in 1987 in order to hide the water tower in preparation for the tourism boom promoted by the provincial government. The campaign seems to have been an enormous success, with Zhōuzhuāng recently declared an International Heritage Site by the United Nations.

Places to Stay

Zhōuzhuāng can easily be visited on a day trip from either Sūzhōu or Shànghǎi or as a stop over between the two. If you are planning to spend the night here, there is no shortage of rooms.

The *Fountaineblean Double Bridge Holiday Inn* (*Fēndān Shuāngqiáo Dùjiàcūn;* ☎ *721 1549*) has the cheapest doubles in town for Y200. The rooms are somewhat shabby but the location in the Old Town with a view of the water more than make up for it. To find the hotel, head south on Nan Shijie and take the first left after the Shěn Tīng.

Just north of the bus station is the upscale *Yunhai Holiday Villa* (*Yúnhǎi Dùjiàcūn;* ☎ *721 1977, 5 Daqiao Lu*). Standard rooms start at a reasonable Y220 and villas range from Y350 to Y1800.

Places to Eat

The central area of the Old Town is home to a great number of nondescript *restaurants* catering to tour groups at astronomical prices. For more reasonable prices try the southern end of Nan Shijie and Nan Hujie, on either side of the canal between Longxing Bridge and Baoen Bridge. The eastern side of this canal has a number of *restaurants* with outdoor seating. You can also find *cheap eats* in the small restaurants between Zhenfeng and Puqing Bridges, at the western end of town.

Just north of the pagoda, on Quanfu Lu, is a large fruit and *vegetable market*.

Shopping

A number of local specialities are available in Zhōuzhuāng, including woven goods, wood carvings, sweets, lace and Yíxīng teapots. Of particular notice are the locally harvested fresh water pearls. These are avail-

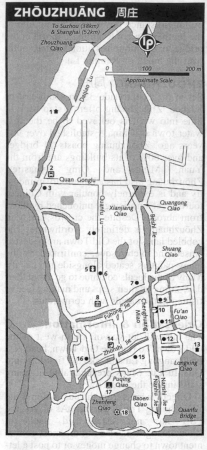

able at extremely reasonable prices in every form from traditional jewellery to animal and pagoda shapes and even face powder.

Getting There & Away

Six buses run daily between Sūzhōu's north bus station and Zhōuzhuāng (1¼ hours). The first leaves Sūzhōu at 7.10 am with the last bus returning to Sūzhōu at 4.40 pm.

From Shànghǎi, two buses depart daily from the Hutai Lu bus station at 9.30 am and 1 pm (Y17; two hours). The last bus returning to Shànghǎi from Zhōuzhuāng leaves at 4.30 pm.

ZHŌUZHUĀNG

PLACES TO STAY & EAT
1 Yúnhǎi Dùjiàcūn
云海渡假村
4 Vegetable Market
蔬菜市场
13 Fontaineblean Double
Bridge Holiday Inn
枫丹双桥渡假村

MUSEUM & HALLS
7 Zhēn'gù Táng
贞固堂
8 Zhōuzhuāng Bówùguǎn
周庄博物馆
9 Zhāng Tīng
张厅

11 Zé Tīng
迮厅
12 Shěn Tīng
沈厅

**OTHER THINGS TO
SEE**
5 Quánfú Tǎ
全福塔
6 Gǔbēi Lóu
古碑楼
14 Chéngxū
Dàoyuàn
澄虚道院
15 Yèchǔcāng Zhu
叶楚伧故居

16 Mí Lóu
迷楼
17 Quánfú Sì
全福寺
18 Nánhú Yuán
南湖园

OTHER
2 Bus Station
汽车站
3 Zhouzhuang
Travel Service
周庄旅行社
10 Boat Tours
游船游览

XÚZHŌU 徐州

☎ 0516 • pop 8,671,600

At the junction of four provinces (Hénán, Ānhuī, Shāndōng and Jiāngsū), Xúzhōu has a recorded history of more than 2000 years and is the birthplace of Liu Bang, the first emperor of the Han dynasty. More than 200 wars have been fought in the area, the most recent being one of the three major battles between the Kuomintang and the communists (the former lost). Being a fairly ordinary city, few travellers bother to make Xúzhōu a stopover. Nevertheless, it is a major railway junction and you may wish to break up your train journey with a day spent visiting the sites and pleasant parks which Xúzhōu has to offer.

Orientation

Xúzhōu's main drag, Huaihai Lu, runs east-west, with the train station at its eastern most end. Both Zhongshan Lu in the west and Fuxin Lu in the east run north-south and intersect with Huaihai Lu. The parks and major sites are located at the southern end of town.

Information

You'll find the Bank of China on Jiangsu Lu. Many of the top-end hotels also have currency exchanges. The China Telecom office is on the southern side of Huihai Lu, seven blocks west from the train station.

There is also a post office on Hauihai Lu, across the street and a block further east from the Telecom office. The main post office is on Tong Shan Lu, east of Fuxin Lu.

CITS and CTS (☎ 373 5525, fax 373 7256) share office quarters at 45-3 Zhongshan Lu, a block and a half south of Huaihai Lu. You can purchase transport tickets here.

The PSB is on Jiefang Lu, south of Huaihai Lu and Zhongshan Lu.

Xúzhōu Bīngmǎyǒng Bówùguǎn

徐州兵马俑博物馆

Xuzhou Terracotta Army Museum

This museum contains a miniature army of terracotta soldiers and horses (each under 40cm) that are more than 2000 years old. Discovered in 1984, four pits display 3000 well preserved clay horses, foot soldiers, chariot soldiers, archers and servants all headed by a commander, and all with varying facial expressions. The army dates from the Han dynasty and is believed to have been built to guard the tomb of a general or warrior prince. It's open daily from 8.30 am to 4.30 pm; admission is Y10. It's in the south-eastern corner of the city. To reach it, take bus No 5 and get off at the two stone lions that mark the entrance to the museum.

Things to See

Next door to the Xúzhōu Bīngmǎyǒng Bówùguǎn is the **Xīhàn Chǔwáng Líng**

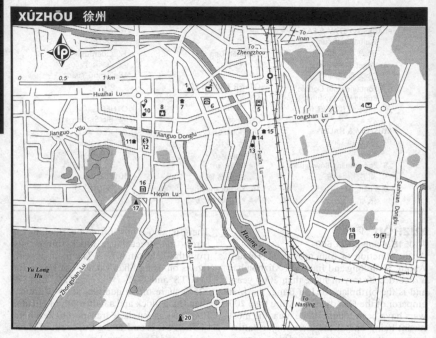

XÚZHŌU 徐州

(Han Dynasty Tomb), the tomb of the third Chu duke, Liu Wu. The tomb is 117m long, covering an area of 850 sq metres, with a number of underground rooms including a stable, kitchen, armoury, bathroom, coffin room and antechambers for the prince and princess. This is where the jade burial suit, on display in the Nánjīng Bówùguǎn, was discovered. Entry costs Y20. The Gūishān Hànmù is a further 100m down the road from the Xúzhōu Bīngmǎyǒng Bówùguǎn (see the previous section for details on how to get there).

Half the scenery of Xúzhōu is found on **Yúnlóng Shān** (Dragon in the Clouds Hill) and, for a mere Y3, it is a pleasant place to spend an afternoon. Located at the southern end of town, the park's stone trails and steps will lead you past the **Xīnghūa Sì** (Temple of Abundance), several pavilions, and a stone carving from the Northern Wei dynasty. Set in a grotto off the mountainside is a giant gilded buddha head, the statue of

the Sakyamuni Buddha. After entering the park, follow the trail up the righthand side of the hill to avoid the souvenir hawkers and to explore the quieter regions. You can continue along the trail for about 1km to a **pagoda** that offers an all-round vista of the city and surrounding area.

The park is open daily from 6 am to 6.30 pm. Bus Nos 2 and 11 run between the train station and the park.

Directly across the street from the park, the brand-new **Xúzhōu Bówùguǎn** (Xuzhou Museum) opened in the summer of 1999 with exhibitions of historical artefacts from the surrounding region.

Neighbouring Yúnlóng Shān, to the south-east, is a further 40 hectares of park filled with pine and cypress trees. At the southern edge is the **Huáihǎi Zhànyì Lièshì Jìniàntǎ** (Monument to Huaihai Campaign Martyrs), a revolutionary war memorial and obelisk. The Huaihai battle was a decisive one fought by the People's Liberation Army

XÚZHŌU

PLACES TO STAY & EAT
7 Huāyuán Fàndiàn
   花园饭店
9 Kāngshīfù Miànguǎn
   康师傅面馆
11 Zhōngshān Fàndiàn
   中山饭店
13 Market
   市场
14 Yángguāng Dàjiǔdiàn
   阳光大酒店
15 Jīnxīyuán Bīnguǎn
   津西缘宾馆

SIGHTS
16 Xúzhou Bówùguǎn
   徐州博物馆

17 Yúnlóng Shān
   云龙山
18 Xúzhōu Bīngmǎyǒng
   Bówùguǎn
   徐州兵马俑博物馆
19 Xīhàn Chǔwáng Líng
   西汉楚王陵
20 Huáihǎi Zhànyì
   Lièshì Jìniàntǎ
   淮海战役烈士纪念塔

OTHER
1 Foreign Languages
   Book Store
   外文书店
2 Post Office
   邮局

3 Train Station
   火车站
4 Main Post Office
   邮局
5 Long-Distance Bus
   Station
   长途汽车站
6 China Telecom
   中国电信
8 PSB
   公安局外事科
10 CTS;
   CITS
   中国旅行社；
   中国国际旅行社
12 Bank of China
   中国银行

(PLA) from November 1948 to January 1949. The nearby Memorial Hall contains an extensive collection of weaponry. The park is on the route of bus No 11.

Places to Stay

For foreigners, the selection of accommodation in Xúzhōu is sparse, especially if you're on a budget. However, have a look around. As in much of China, new buildings are shooting into the skyline at lightening pace and a number of them are bound to be foreign-friendly hotels.

The *Jīngxīyuán Bīnguǎn* (☎ 380 3695, 129 Jianguo Lu) is two blocks south from the train station on the corner of Fuxin Lu. Rundown doubles start at Y180 and are the cheapest in town. Across the street, the *Yángguāng Dàjiǔdiàn* (Sunshine Hotel; ☎ 380 0168, fax 380 2474, 219 Jianguo Lu) has much newer and brighter doubles from Y288.

The *Zhōngshān Fàndiàn* (☎ 569 8900, fax 569 2233, 80 Zhongshan Lu) has doubles from Y260 to Y328 and suites for Y628. The hotel is three and a half blocks south of Huaihai Lu.

The *Huāyuán Fàndiàn* (Garden Hotel; ☎ 373 8740, fax 372 2905, 1 Jiefang Lu), in the centre of town, has comfortable doubles for Y380 or Y428.

Places to Eat

Kāngshīfù Miànguǎn serves beer and big bowls of piping hot noodles. You'll find it on the east side of Zhongshan Lu, half a block south of Huaihai Lu.

The alley running along the east side of the Huáng Hé (Yellow River), south of Jianguo Lu, has a *market* filled with stalls selling fruit, baked bread, stir fries and noodles. Fill up for a bargain with views of the water.

Getting There & Away

Airline tickets to Běijīng (Y550) are available from CTS or the China Eastern Airline booking office (☎ 373 3777) at the southern end of the Hāuyuán Fàndiàn complex.

Buses to Qūfù, Tiān, Jǐ'nán, Nánjīng and Liányúngǎng can be found at the long-distance bus station, located just south of the train station.

Xúzhōu is at the junction of two major train lines. There are frequent trains to Běijīng, Nánjīng and Liányúngǎng. The train station is located in the north-eastern corner of the city.

LIÁNYÚNGǍNG 连云港
☎ 0518 • pop 4,372,500
Few travellers find themselves passing through this out of the way, dusty city.

However, should you end up here with time to kill, there are a couple of sights to pass the time.

Orientation & Information

The town is divided into port and city sections with Yúntái Shān (Cloud Terrace Hill), the 'scenic spot', overlooking the ocean. Maps are available from the main bus and train stations.

The Bank of China is located on Hailian Lu, 150m east of its intersection with Tongguan Lu. The post office is just off Hailian Lu, about a 10-minute walk east of Tongguan Lu.

Things to See

Fifteen kilometres south of the city is **Huāguǒ Shān** (Flowers and Fruit Mountain), a 625m-high mountain reputed to be the inspiration for the mountain of the same name in the Ming dynasty classic *Journey to the West* (although three other places make the same claim).

About a third of the way up the mountain there's a 1300-year-old Taoist monastery, **Sānyuán Gōng** (Three Element Monastery), where there are two impressive 1000-year-old gingko trees. A short walk up a footpath from the monastery is **Shuǐlián Dòng** (Water Curtain Cave), the fictional home of Sun Wukong, the King of the Monkeys. A number of footpaths wind around this picturesque mountain, making it a pleasant place for hiking.

You can take a minibus (Y3; ½ hour) from 103 Tongguan Lu, just south of Jiefang Lu. The first bus leaves at 8 am.

The other major sight near Liányúngǎng is **Kǒngwàng Shān** (Keyhole Vista Hill), where there are over a hundred 2000-year-old (Eastern Han) stone carvings. The road to this hill ends at a small temple. Take the path to the south-west of the temple, down to the cliff-side carvings. Look for sculptures of a toad and an elephant in a nearby field, which also date from the Eastern Han dynasty.

Kǒngwàng Shān is located about 2km south of the city. Unfortunately there is no public transport to the temple. You can reach it via a 20-minute taxi ride.

Places to Stay

The hotel situation in Liányúngǎng is not too rosy; rooms tend to be overpriced and dim and, to make matters worse, few hotels accept foreigners. None of the rooms are exceptional for value or quality.

There is a small selection of hotels accepting foreigners along Tongguan Lu, south-east of the main train and bus stations. To reach Tongguan Lu, take bus No 23 or 8 from the train station.

Heading south, the first one you'll reach is the *Xiě Ěrdēng Fàndiàn* (☎ 552 0026, 76 Tongguan Lu). The hotel is on the east side of the road, opposite the Agricultural Bank of China. Doubles cost Y130.

The *Kāngpíng Jiǔdiàn* (☎ 551 1888, fax 550 0888, 220 Tongguan Lu) is a few doors down, with doubles including breakfast from Y135. The hotel is currently under renovation so the rooms may be somewhat brighter and cleaner (and pricier) in the future.

East off Tongguan Lu, on the corner of Hailian Lu, the *Lónghǎi Fàndiàn* (☎ 541 2511, 11 Tongguan Lu) has doubles from Y180.

Getting There & Away

The main bus and train stations are next to each other in the north-western corner of the city. The airport is approximately 30km west of the city.

Buses along the eastern coast connect Liányúngǎng with Shànghǎi and Qīngdǎo. A good highway connects Liányúngǎng and Nánjīng.

If you're travelling to or from Xúzhōu by train, a branch line runs east to Liányúngǎng (three hours). Get off the train at Xinpu, the station closest to the city centre.

CAAC and other domestic airlines fly between Liányúngǎng and Běijīng, Guǎngzhōu and Shànghǎi. You can purchase air tickets to Běijīng (Y550; twice weekly) from the travel agency inside the Lónghǎi Fàndiàn (see Places to Stay earlier).

Ānhuī 安徽

Ānhuī offers travellers the opportunity to climb the legendary Huáng Shān, explore Ming and Qing dynasty merchant homes, and experience the Buddhist spirituality of holy Jiǔhuá Shān.

The historical and tourist sights of Ānhuī are concentrated in the south, and are more accessible from Hángzhōu or Shànghǎi than from the provincial capital, Héféi. For travellers cruising the Cháng Jiāng (Yangzi River), the ports of Guìchí and Wúhú are convenient jumping-off points to southern destinations.

The provincial borders of Ānhuī were defined by the Qing government and, except for a few changes to the boundary with Jiāngsū, have remained unchanged. Northern Ānhuī forms part of the North China Plain, which the Han Chinese settled in large numbers during the Han dynasty. The Cháng Jiāng cuts through the southern quarter of Ānhuī and the area south of the river was not settled until the 7th and 8th centuries.

HÉFÉI 合肥
☎ 0551 • pop 4,223,100

Prior to 1949 Héféi was a quiet market town but it has since boomed into an industrial centre. It's a pleasant, friendly city with lively markets. While there are few cultural or historical attractions, the parks and lakes that circle the city centre are ideal for relaxing walks.

Héféi is home to the University of Science and Technology (Zhōngguó Kēxué Jìshù Dàxué), where one of China's more famous dissidents, Fang Lizhi, was vice president until he sought asylum in the west after the 1989 massacre at Tiānānmén.

Orientation
Shengli Lu leads down to the Nánféi Hé then meets up with Shouchun Lu.

Changjiang Lu is the main commercial street and cuts east-west through the city. Most accommodation is either in the city centre or on Meishan Lu, overlooking the pond, Yǔhuā.

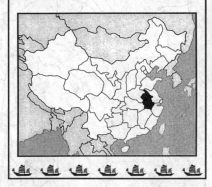

Information
The Bank of China is at 155 Changjiang Lu, although hotels such as the Ānhuī Fàndiàn and the new Holiday Inn will also change money. There is a post office on Changjiang Lu next to the City department store.

Email junkies can log on at the business centre at the Ānhuī Fàndiàn (Y15 per 15 minutes) and at the Changjiang Lu post office (Y8 per hour) on the 2nd floor.

China International Travel Service (CITS; Zhōngguó Guójì Lǚxíngshè; ☎ 281 2384) is in a tiled building at 153 Meishan Lu, beside the Ānhuī Fàndiàn. Staff members are helpful and speak English.

The Public Security Bureau (PSB; Gōngānjú) is on Shouchun Lu's northern side, west of the intersection with Fuyang Lu.

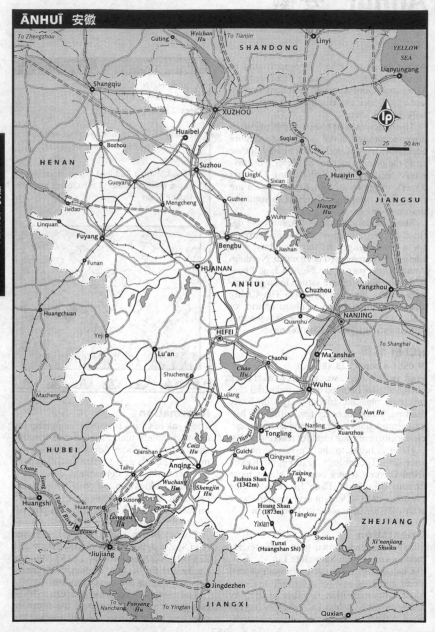

Things to See & Do

Pleasant parks can be found around town. Located in the north-east, **Xiāoyáojīn Gōngyuán** is the most expansive and has a small, rather depressing zoo. **Bāohé Gōngyuán** is to the south and is nicer, with small tombs and a temple.

The small **Míngjiāo Sì** (Bright Teaching Temple) sits 5m above ground, across from Xiāoyáojīn Gōngyuán. Built in early AD 500, the temple saw military skirmishes a few centuries later when troops from the Wu and Wei kingdoms fought in the area. It's off an alley near Shouchun Lu and across from a karaoke bar; admission is Y5.

Finally, there's the **Ānhuī Shěng Bówùguàn**, which is one of the better provincial museums; entry is Y10.

Places to Stay

Two inexpensive hotels near the cluster of bus stations accept foreigners.

The **Yínlù Dàjiǔdiàn** (☎ 429 6303, fax 429 5506, 1 Shouchun Lu) is on the triangle where Huaihe Lu crosses the river to intersect with Ma'anshan Lu – about a 10-minute walk from the bus stations. Clean air-con twins cost Y188. The hotel lobby is above a restaurant.

Though far from the city centre, the *Aò Xīng Bīnguǎn* (☎ 261 8183) is a bargain. It's on Mingguang Lu, about 200m north-west from the intersection with Shengli Lu. Singles/twins without bath are Y80/50. Twins with attached bath are Y140 and Y160.

In the south, the *University of Science and Technology* (Zhōngguó Kēxué Jìshù Dàxué) rents rooms in the *Foreign Experts' Building* (Zhuānjiālóu; ☎ 360 2585). Beds are Y50 with shared bathrooms, and twins with bath are Y130/150. The building is located in the university's eastern section. Take bus No 1 from the train station to the university bus stop, which is opposite the university entrance. Enter here and go down the main street, turn left at the first road and then left again. The guesthouse is a grey building with five floors.

The *Huáqiáo Fàndiàn* (Overseas Chinese Hotel; ☎ 265 2221, fax 264 2861, 68 Changjiang Lu) is centrally located and has twins for Y420. Foreigners are allowed to stay in B block, which is located at the back.

The four-star *Ānhuī Fàndiàn* (☎ 281 1818, fax 281 7583, 18 Meishan Lu) is a grab at elegance with a health centre and a bowling alley. The rooms range from Y660 to Y930 and are subject to a 15% service charge.

Within the grounds of the Ānhuī Fàndiàn, the *Fùháo Dàjiǔdiàn* offers clean doubles, with bath and buffet breakfast, starting at Y148. The contact details are the same as the Ānhuī Fàndiàn.

The city's other upscale hotel is the new *Holiday Inn* (Gǔjǐngjìarì Jiǔdiàn; ☎ 429 1188, fax 429 1166, 1104 Changjiang Lu). Located at the intersection of Shengli Lu and Shochun Lu, near the Yínlù Dàjiǔdiàn, it has twins for Y1000, a swimming pool and a health club.

Places to Eat

There are several reasonable sidewalk *restaurants* in the Anqing Lu area and behind the Bank of China on Changjiang Lu. A variety of noodles, bread and dumplings can satisfy the budget traveller's appetite for Y1 to Y3.

The *Aò Xīng Bīnguǎn* cooks up cheap meals but lacks an English menu. Fried rice and egg is Y6; a pitcher of beer is Y20.

Getting There & Around

Air Héféi has daily flights to Běijīng (Y790; 1½ hours), Guǎngzhōu (Y830; 1½ hours), Huáng Shān (Y330; 30 minutes) and Shànghǎi (Y390; 40 minutes), plus less regular flights to Chéngdū (Y970; two hours), Fúzhōu (Y580; 1½ hours), Hángzhōu (Y370; one hour), Kūnmíng (Y1330; three hours), Wǔhàn (Y290; 40 minutes), Xī'ān (Y690; two hours) and Hong Kong (Y1560; two hours).

Bookings can be made at the China Eastern Airlines office (☎ 282 2357) at 246 Jinzhai Lu. Reservations can also be made through CITS at the advance train ticket booking office on the north side of Changjiang Lu at the Jinzhai Lu intersection.

Taking a taxi (Y15; 30 minutes) is the best way to the airport, which is about 11km south of the city centre.

ĀNHUĪ 安徽

ĀNHUĪ 安徽

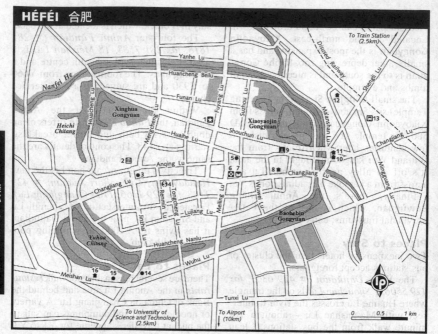

HÉFÉI 合肥

HÉFÉI

1 PSB
公安局

2 Ānhuī Shěng Bówùguǎn
省博物馆

3 Train Ticket Office
火车预售票处

4 Bank of China
中国银行

5 Foreign Languages Bookstore
外文书店

6 City Department Store
市百货大楼

7 Post Office
市邮电局

8 Huáqiáo Fàndiàn
华侨饭店

9 Míngjiāo Sì
明教寺

10 Holiday Inn, Gǔjǐng
假日大酒店，古井

11 Yínlù Dàjiǔdiàn
银路大酒店

12 Aò Xīng Bīnguǎn
澳星宾馆

13 Long-Distance Bus Stations
长途汽车站

14 China Eastern Airlines
东方航空售票处

15 CITS
中国国际旅行社

16 Ānhuī Fàndiàn; Fùháo Dàjiǔdiàn
安徽饭店；富豪大酒店

Bus A cluster of long-distance bus stations is located north of the Changjiang Lu and Mingguang Lu intersection in the city's east. There are daily departures to Hángzhōu (Y132; eight hours), Wǔhàn (Y140; 10 hours) and Huáng Shān (Y55; seven hours).

The freeway to Nánjīng has shortened travel times considerably; air-con buses take 2½ hours to Nánjīng (Y55) and six hours for the trip to Shànghǎi (Y145). Similarly, the freeway connection south to Jiǔjiāng (Y70), in Jiāngxī, allows for an eight-hour journey.

Frequent minibuses also depart for Wúhú (Y27); the trip takes 2½ hours.

Train The train station is 4km north-east from the city centre. Trains go to Shànghǎi (Y180; 8½ hours), Běijīng (Y300; 18 hours), Zhèngzhōu (Y97; 10½ hours, via Kāifēng), Xiàmén (Y220; 38 hours), Bózhōu (Y27; five hours) and Jiǔjiāng (Y50; six hours).

Hard-seat tickets can be purchased at the station ticket office. Try your luck with hard-sleeper tickets at windows Nos 14 and 15, or soft sleeper at window No 13. The advance ticket booking office, where you can book sleepers three days in advance, is better. It's on the northern side of Changjiang Lu, at the intersection with Jinzhai Lu, and is open daily.

CITS can also book sleepers, but the staff need a week's notice.

BÓZHŌU 亳州
☎ 0558

Bózhōu lies in Ānhuī's far north-west, near Hénán. It has been one of the most important trading centres for traditional medicine in central China, attracting merchants and Chinese herbalists from a wide area.

Things to See

Bózhōu's main attraction is its **Zhōngyào Shìchǎng** (Medicinal Market). Wander through the hustle bustle and you'll see mounds of pressed herbs, roots, rocks, minerals, wasp nests, animal skins, tortoise shells, dried insects and snakes – it's not for the faint-hearted. The market is in a large, white-tiled exhibition hall on Mulan Lu, near the train station.

The **Cáocāo Yùnbīngdào** (Underground Pass) is a 600m-long subterranean passageway parallel to Renmin Zhonglu. The famous Han general Cao Cao built it as a secret route for soldiers to surprise the enemy. You can walk through the damp tunnel; entry is Y10.

The **Huāxì Lóu** (Flower Play Temple) features an ornate tiled gate that was built in the Qing dynasty. There is a small museum that features a Han dynasty burial suit made

from pieces of jade with silver thread. It's in the north-east section of town.

Places to Stay

Most places seem willing to accept foreigners. The *Bózhōu Bīnguǎn* (☎ 552 4841) is on Banjie Lu off Xinhua Lu in the middle of town. Twins cost Y220, but bargaining may get the cost down to Y160. There are grotty twins for Y160.

About 100m up from the Bózhōu Bīnguǎn, north towards Heping Lu, the *Lìdū Dàshà* (☎ 552 3008, 180 Xinhua Lu) has beds in clean doubles with bath for Y60. Triples without bath are Y40.

The *Gǔjǐng Dàjiǔdiàn* (☎ 552 1298, fax 552 3244, 105 Chaoling Nanlu) is a white-tiled attempt at modern architecture on the main corner, 1km south of the long-distance bus station. Doubles range from Y138 to Y198.

Getting There & Away

Buses primarily go to Zhèngzhōu (Y50; four hours) and Héféi (Y50; four hours); other than that you'll have to wait for buses heading to other cities.

Bózhōu is on the Zhèngzhōu-Héféi train line, but trains stop here at inconvenient hours – either very early in the morning or around midnight.

A daily train to Héféi (Y30; five hours) leaves at 7 am from the train station, which is about 4km south-east of the city.

HUÁNG SHĀN 黄山
Yellow Mountain ☎ 0559

Huáng Shān is the name of the 72-peak mountain range in Ānhuī's south, 280km west of the coastal city of Hángzhōu. For the Chinese, Huáng Shān, along with Guìlín, is probably the country's most famous landscape attraction.

Orientation & Information

Buses from Túnxī drop you off in Tāngkǒu, the main village at the mountain's foot, or at the terminal near **Huángshān Mén** (Yellow Mountain Gate) in upper Tāngkǒu. Maps, raincoats, food and accommodation are available here.

Huáng Shān – A Tradition of Tranquillity and Inspiration

In good weather Huáng Shān is truly spectacular, and the surrounding countryside, with its traditional villages and patchwork paddy fields, is among the most beautiful in China. Huáng Shān has a 1200-year history as a tourist attraction. Countless painters and poets have trudged around the range, seeking inspiration and bestowing the peaks with fanciful names such as Nine Dragons, Taoist Priest, Ox Nose, Fairy Capital and Hunchback.

Today, the reclusive artists seeking an inspirational retreat from the hustle and bustle of the temporal world have been replaced by crowds of tourists, who bring the hustle and bustle with them. Still, with a little effort, you might be rewarded with a small moment of tranquillity, and the views are quite breathtaking.

Some travellers have escaped the well-trodden tourist trails and returned thrilled with what they discovered. It is also worth noting that, given the amount of people who pass through this area, the park management does a commendable job trying to keep the place litter-free.

The highest peak is Liánhuā Fēng (Lotus Flower Peak) at 1864m, followed by Guāngmíng Dǐng (Bright Summit Peak) and Tiāndū Fēng (Heavenly Capital Peak). Some 30 peaks rise above 1500m.

There's expensive accommodation near the hot springs, which are 4km further up the valley. The road ends halfway up the mountain at the Yúngǔsì cable car station (890m above sea level), where the eastern steps begin. Other hotels are scattered on trails around the summit area.

Another cable car goes from **Yùpíng Fēng** (Jade Screen Peak) area to just above the hot springs resort. A third cable car approaches Huáng Shān from the north-west going to **Sōnglín Fēng** (Pine Forest Peak) and is accessible from the southern side of Taiping reservoir.

The Bank of China is next to the Huángshān Bīnguǎn in the hot springs area. The Táoyán Bīnguǎn can also change money.

Routes to the Summit

There are three basic routes to the top: the short, hard way (eastern steps); the longer, harder way (western steps); and the very short, easy way (cable car). The eastern steps lead up below the Yúngǔsì cable car line and the western steps lead up from the parking lot near the **Cíguāng Gé** (Mercy Light Temple), about 3km above the hot springs. Another cable car also goes from here to Yùpíng Fēng area, bringing you about halfway up the mountain.

Regardless of how you ascend Huáng Shān, you'll have to pay a Y65 entrance fee.

Pay at the eastern steps near the Yúngǔsì cable car station or where the western steps begin. Minibuses run to both places from Tāngkǒu for Y10.

Make sure to pack enough water, food and appropriate clothing before you take your first step toward the summit. Bottled water and food prices increase the higher you go. The market under the stone bridge in Tāngkǒu has a good selection of food at affordable prices.

Eastern Steps The 7.5km eastern steps route can be climbed comfortably in about three hours. It's a killer if you push yourself too hard, but it's definitely easier than the western steps.

Purists can extend the eastern steps climb by several hours by starting from Huángshān Mén, where a stepped path crosses the road at several points before connecting with the main eastern steps trail at the Yúngǔsì cable car station.

If you have time, the recommended route is a 10-hour circuit hike taking the eastern steps to the top and descending to the hot springs resort via the western steps. Don't underestimate the hardship involved. While cut-stone stairways make climbing a little easier, the extremely steep gradients will turn even an experienced walker's legs to jelly in about seven hours.

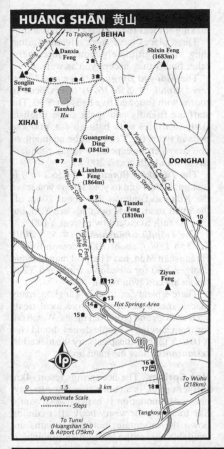

HUÁNG SHĀN 黄山

To Taiping
Taiping Cable Car
BEIHAI

▲ Danxia Feng
Shixin Feng (1683m) ▲

▲ Songlin Feng

Tianhai Hu

XIHAI

Guangming Ding (1841m)

DONGHAI

Yungusi Temple Cable Car

Eastern Steps

▲ Lianhua Feng (1864m)

Western Steps

▲ Tiandu Feng (1810m)

Taiping Feng Cable Car

Taohua He

Ziyun Feng ▲

Hot Springs Area

To Wuhu (218km)

0   1.5   3 km
Approximate Scale
·········· Steps

To Tunxi (Huangshan Shi) & Airport (75km)

Tangkou

Western Steps The 15km western steps route has some stellar scenery, following a precarious route hewn out of the sheer rock cliffs. But it's twice as long and strenuous as the eastern steps and much easier to enjoy if you're clambering down rather than gasping your way up.

The western steps descent begins at the **Fēilái Shí** (Flying Rock), a rectangular boulder perched on an outcrop half an hour from the Běihǎi Bīnguǎn, and goes over **Guāngmíng Dǐng** (Bright Summit Peak), where there is an odd-shaped weather station and a hotel.

Not to be missed on the western steps is the exhilaratingly steep and exposed stairway to **Tiāndū Fēng** (Heavenly Capital Peak), directly adjacent to the Yùpínglóu Bīnguǎn. Young lovers bring locks engraved with their names up here and fix them to the chain railings, symbolising that they're 'locked' together. The western path continues past the **Bànshān Sì** (Mid-Level Temple) and back to the hot springs resort.

Halfway between the Bànshān Sì and the hot springs resort is a parking lot with waiting minibuses. For Y10, you can skip the last 1½ hours of walking and get a lift to the hot springs resort.

Cable Car The eight-minute cable car ride from Yúngǔ Sì (Cloud Valley Temple) is the least painful way up. For Y10, minibuses take you from Huángshān Mén to the Yúngǔsì station. From here the one-way cable car fare is Y50. Either arrive very

ĀNHUĪ 安徽

HUÁNG SHĀN

1 Qīngliáng Tái 清凉台	7 Báiyúnlóu Bīnguǎn 白云楼宾馆	13 Huángshān Bīnguǎn 黄山宾馆
2 Shīlín Fàndiàn 狮林饭店	8 Tiānhǎi Bīnguǎn 天海宾馆	14 Huángshān Wénquán Dàjiǔdiàn 黄山温泉大酒店
3 Běihǎi Bīnguǎn 北海宾馆	9 Yùpínglóu Bīnguǎn 玉屏楼宾馆	15 Táoyuán Bīnguǎn 桃源宾馆
4 Xīhǎi Bīnguǎn 西海宾馆	10 Yúngǔ Shānzhuāng 云谷山庄	16 Huángshān Mén 黄山门
5 Báiyún Bīnguǎn 白云宾馆	11 Bànshān Sì 半山寺	17 Long-Distance Bus Station 长途汽车站
6 Fēilái Shí 飞来石	12 Cíguāng Gé 慈光阁	18 Tiāndū Fēng 天都峰

early in the day (the service starts at 5.30 am) or later in the day (if you're staying overnight). Queues of more than one hour are the norm. In high season, many people wait up to three hours for a ride – you may as well walk.

There's another cable car station that goes from just below the Yùpínglóu Bīnguǎn to the parking lot above the hot springs resort. Tickets are Y50.

Guides

Guides are unnecessary since the mountain paths are easy to follow. However, CITS can organise an English-speaking guide for around Y400 per day. Private individuals sometimes offer their services as guides, but often speak no English beyond 'hello'. The truly decadent might make their ascent in a sedan chair strung between bamboo poles and bounced (literally) along by two porters. The price? Around Y400 one way or Y1000 for the day, depending on your bargaining skills.

On the Summit

Paved trails meander around the lookout points on the summit. Imagine a Chinese ink landscape and you'll know what the Chinese are referring to in their admiration – gnarled pines, craggy rocks, a rolling sea of clouds.

Huáng Shān's highlight is the Běihǎi sunrise: a 'sea' of low clouds blanketing the valley to the north with 'island' peaks hazily reaching for the heavens. **Qīngliáng Tái** (Refreshing Terrace) is five minutes from the Běihǎi Bīnguǎn and attracts sunrise crowds (hotels supply thick padded jackets for the occasion). It's communal sightseeing at its best. The noise generated by several hundred tourists is almost as incredible as the sunrise itself. Fortunately, most people return to eat breakfast shortly afterwards, leaving you to enjoy the mountains in peace.

Places to Stay & Eat

Huáng Shān has five locations with hotels and restaurants. Prices and bed availability vary according to season.

Tāngkǒu Tāngkǒu has affordable hotels, making it ideal for a Huáng Shān assault.

Three places have signs advertising that they can legitimately house foreigners; other hotels may accept you as well.

The **Xiāoyáo Bīnguǎn** *(Free and Unfettered Hotel;* ☎ *556 1679)* offers beds in rooms with four and five beds for Y30. The staff are friendly and speak some English. Beds in triples with bath go for Y60 and beds in twins for Y100. But be adamant, or you may get an expensive room. Standard twins with bath cost Y200.

The **Tāngkǒu Bīnguǎn** *(☎ 556 2400)* is just up the hill and to your left as you leave the Xiāoyáo Bīnguǎn. It's about 200m off the main road. Beds in quads are Y50, but may be full. Standard twins cost Y100.

The **Tiāndū Shānzhuāng** *(☎ 556 2160, fax 556 1590),* about 700m downhill from Huángshān Mén, has a helpful manager and charges Y60 for a bed in a triple and Y240 for an air-con twin room.

There's plenty of food in Tāngkǒu, many places specialise in expensive local treats such as frogs and preserved meats. Watch out for overcharging – simple dishes should cost Y10 to Y15. For cheap eats, try the makeshift *restaurants* under the main bridge.

Hot Springs The hot springs resort, 4km further uphill, is an attractive place to stay, but accommodation is expensive. If you'd like to soak your weary body after coming down the mountain, hot spring baths are available next to the Huángshān Bīnguǎn. A tourist book claims the water helps prevent health and skin ailments. A private bath is Y50 and a communal bath is Y30. There's also a swimming pool. The ticket includes a bathing suit. It's open from 8 am to 8 pm.

The **Huángshān Bīnguǎn** *(☎ 556 2357, fax 556 2121)* has twins with shower and air-con starting at Y340. If you're a student, the manager may rent you a bed for Y50. Guests can also use the hotel-run hot spring next door.

Across the bridge, the **Huángshān Wénquán Dàjiǔdiàn** *(☎ 556 2197, fax 556 2511)* rents twins for Y480, although bargaining may help. Up the hillside is the overpriced *Táoyuán Bīnguǎn (Peach Blossom Hotel;* ☎ *556 2666, fax 556 2888)* with twins from US$57 to US$72 and suites starting at US$120.

The Huángshān Wénquán Dàjiǔdiàn and Táoyuán Bīnguǎn have *restaurants*; as in Tāngkǒu, restaurant touts look for hungry travellers. Watch out for overcharging.

Yungusi Cable Car Station The *Yúngǔ Shānzhuāng* (☎ *556 2466, fax 556 2346)* is probably the best place to stay if you have the money and want a secluded, if somewhat inconvenient, setting within the pine and bamboo forest. It's down the steps from the car park in front of the cable car station. Twins are Y580, and the luxury suites go for Y4200.

Summit Area Ideally, a Huáng Shān visit should include a stay on the summit.

The cheapest place near the top is the *Shílín Fàndiàn* (☎ *556 4040),* which has beds in dorms for Y60 and Y100 and twins with bath for Y520. It's a short walk down from the Běihǎi Bīnguǎn.

The *Běihǎi Bīnguǎn* (☎ *556 2552, fax 556 2996)* is overpriced but comfortable and provides the best location for seeing the sunrise. Twins are Y680 to Y830 and beds in quads with attached bath are Y150.

The *Xīhǎi Bīnguǎn* (☎ *556 2712, fax 556 2988),* further west along the trail, is a real 'mountain hotel' designed by Swedish architects. Twins start at Y560. All rooms have heating and 24-hour hot water.

The *Báiyún Bīnguǎn (White Cloud Hotel;* ☎ *556 1708, fax 556 1602)* is up from Tiānhǎi Hú (Heavenly Sea Lake) and west of the Xīhǎi Bīnguǎn. Standard twins start at Y580.

The Xīhǎi and Běihǎi Bīnguǎns have bars and restaurants serving international and Chinese food, but as these tend to cater to tour groups, it's sometimes difficult to get service outside meal times. There are cheaper restaurants nearby.

Western Steps The *Tiānhǎi Bīnguǎn* (☎ *556 2201)* is the highest on the western steps and is just down from Guāngmíng

Dǐng (Bright Summer Peak), beside the path on your left as you come down the mountain. Twins with bath cost Y400 and beds in very basic dorms cost Y100.

If you want more luxury, take the turnoff to the right from the main path (if heading down the mountain) to the *Báiyúnlóu Bīnguǎn* (☎ *556 1341).* This hotel should not be confused with the Báiyún Bīnguǎn mentioned earlier (Báiyún means 'white cloud'). It's secluded and set on the mountain's edge. Beds in twins, triples and quads with attached bathrooms are Y340/200/120.

Further down the mountain, at a spectacular 1660m-high lookout near Tiāndū Fēng (Heavenly Capital Peak), is the *Yùpínglóu Bīnguǎn (Jade Screen Tower Hotel;* ☎ *556 2317, fax 556 2258).* The rates and conditions reflect its relative inaccessibility: a twin is Y520 and dormitory beds cost Y120. Washing arrangements are basic and be prepared for water shortages.

At 1340m, is the small *Bànshān Sì (Mid-Level Temple;* ☎ *556 2264).* It has bunk beds in small rooms for Y60.

There are few eating options on this route. Considering its location, the Yùpínglóu Bīnguǎn has a cheap dining hall beside its courtyard, and a better restaurant upstairs. The Bànshān Sì has a teahouse serving simple meals.

Getting There & Away
A paved road means that buses from Túnxī (Huángshān Shì) now take around 1½ hours to reach Huángshān Mén. On a sunny day, the countryside leading to Tāngkǒu is beautiful. Minibuses to Túnxī leave from the bridge area in Tāngkǒu; tickets are Y10.

In summer, other direct buses to Tāngkǒu come from Héféi (seven hours), Shànghǎi (12 hours), Sūzhōu (11 hours) and Jǐngdézhèn (six hours). There are also buses from Jiǔhuá Shān (four hours) and the Cháng Jiāng (Yangzi River) ports of Wúhú (four hours) and Guìchí (five hours). The Tāngkǒu bus station is just below Huángshān Mén.

It's possible to travel by air or train to Túnxī; see the following Túnxī section for further details.

ĀNHUĪ 安徽

Getting Around

Minibuses provide the easiest and cheapest way to get around Huáng Shān, although they usually don't budge until there are enough people on board. In the morning, they ferry people to the eastern and western steps. You can usually find minibuses on Tāngkǒu's streets, but they congregate on the highway across the bridge. Likewise, minibuses wait at the bottom of mountain routes in the afternoon. Minivan taxis abound; you'll have to bargain.

TÚNXĪ 屯溪

☎ 0559 • pop 1,464,400

The old trading town of Túnxī (Huángshān Shì) is roughly 70km south-east from Huáng Shān. As its new Chinese name (meaning Huángshān City) implies, Túnxī is the main springboard for Huáng Shān. It's also a pleasant town to explore for a day.

Information

The Bank of China is at 9 Xinan Lu, opposite the Xinhua Bookstore.

CITS (☎ 251 2771) is at 6 Xizhen Lu, on the 3rd floor of the building opposite the Huāxī Fàndiàn. It can arrange English-speaking guides for tours of Huáng Shān and the surrounding area.

The PSB is in the eastern section of Túnxī, at 108 Changgan Lu.

Places to Stay & Eat

Several Túnxī hotels, especially the cheaper ones, don't accept foreigners.

The *Sēnlín Jiǔdiàn* (☎ 252 0750) is the cheapest place near the train station that will accept foreigners. Twins and triples with bath are Y160/180. It's west of the roundabout in front of the train station. Next door on the corner is the Changying Hotel, which has an English sign but does not accept foreigners.

Another hotel near the train station is the three-star *Huángshān Jīngwěi Jiǔdiàn* (☎ 253 8188, fax 251 7178, 18 Qianyuan Beilu), on the south-eastern corner of the main street running past the train station. Standard rooms are Y400, but the staff may part with one for Y240.

Across from the Huángshān Jīngwěi Jiǔdiàn, on the south-western corner of the main street, the *Jiāngnán Dàjiǔdiàn* (☎ 251 1067, 25-7 Qianyuan Beilu) has twins for Y160 and Y200.

Near the Héng Jiāng (Traversing River), in the town's old part south-west of the train station, the *Huāxī Fàndiàn* (☎ 251 4312, fax 251 4990, 1 Xijiang Jie) has twins for Y280. It's pleasantly located where the two rivers, Héng Jiāng and Xīnān Jiāng, meet.

The *Huangshan International Hotel* (*Huángshān Guójì Dàjiǔdiàn*; ☎ 252 6999, fax 251 2087, 31 Huashan Lu) is the best place to stay if you have cash to splash about. Twins start at Y680.

There are *restaurants* and *food stalls* around the train station and the fare is not bad. The Huangshan International Hotel has an international-style restaurant.

Shopping

Running a block in from the river, Lao Jie (Old Street) is a souvenir street lined with wood stores and buildings from the Song dynasty. Besides the usual trinkets, you can also buy goods similar to those at the Shànghǎi antique market – prices may be lower here, especially for antique furniture.

While tourists swarm the area during the high season, an early morning stroll through this narrow pedestrian and commercial street can be like stepping into China's past.

Getting There & Away

Air There are flights from Túnxī to Běijīng (Y870; two hours; weekly), Guǎngzhōu (Y770; 1½ hours; daily), Héféi (Y330; 30 minutes; five times weekly), Shànghǎi (Y460; one hour; daily), Hong Kong (Y1750; two hours; weekly) and less frequent flights to other cities.

The CAAC office (☎ 953 4111) is on Huangshan Lu beside the International Hotel. A taxi to the airport, 5km away, will cost about Y25. You can book airline tickets at outlets near the train station.

Bus The long-distance bus station in Túnxī is 400m east of the train station. Buses run between Túnxī and Tāngkǒu. There are also buses to Shànghǎi, Hángzhōu, Héféi, Nánjīng and Jǐngdézhèn.

Train Trains from Héféi and Nánjīng via Wúhú pass through Túnxī. For connections from southern destinations, first go to Yīngtán in Jiāngxī and change trains there. Northern destinations are at the train station's window No 2 and southern destinations at window No 3. You can book sleeper tickets at the window in the courtyard's far end, which is reached through a doorway to the right as you exit the waiting room. The waiting room is next to the main ticket office.

If you're planning to leave from Túnxī after visiting Huáng Shān, it's a good idea to book your ticket early. CITS may have difficulty booking sleepers on short notice. The travel agency in the Sēnlín Jiǔdiàn can also book sleepers for a Y50 fee.

AROUND TÚNXĪ
Shèxiàn & Yīxiàn
屯溪、歙县和黟县附近地区
☎ 0559

The dazzling and romantic landscape around Huáng Shān abounds with crop fields, road-side markets and classical Chinese residential architecture. The towns of Shèxiàn and Yīxiàn, near Túnxī, are famous for old, narrow streets, memorial arches (*páifāng*) and merchant homes with open courtyards and fine wood carvings.

Formerly known as Huizhou, this region produced many wealthy merchants during the Ming and Qing dynasties who returned with trade profits to build houses in their home towns. Both Shèxiàn and Yīxiàn can be visited as day trips from Túnxī, although to see Yīxiàn's sights, you'll need a travel permit (Y50) from either the PSB in Túnxī, or have one arranged by CITS.

The **Tángyuè Páifāng Qún** (Memorial Arches of Tangyue) are 1.5km off the highway on the way to Shèxiàn; you can get off the bus and walk or take a motor-tricycle.

In Shèxiàn, the street area known as Doushan Jie, in the old town centre, has a fine collection of houses in narrow, stone-lined alleys. There's a good Y8 guided tour that takes you inside the houses.

Cheng Jiben (☎ 651 1378) is an extremely helpful local teacher with impeccable English who may be available for a tour. He's an ordinary citizen, so please be respectful of his time and offer him a tip after the tour.

At Yīxiàn there are three main villages, **Xīdì**, **Hóngcūn** and **Nánpíng**, all located outside the main town. The best way to see them is to hire a minivan taxi in Yīxiàn. Foreigners normally need a travel permit to enter the villages, but if you don't have one, your taxi driver might be able to help you with a little incentive.

Xīdì had nine memorial arches of which one remains. The rest were destroyed during the Cultural Revolution and this one survived because Mao slogans covered it.

Nánpíng was the location for Zhang Yimou's acclaimed film *Judou* and the set has been preserved for tourists, along with photographs of the production. Several houses have exquisite wood carvings, although many of the human figures were decapitated by Red Guards during the Cultural Revolution. Entry to each of the villages is about Y20.

Getting There & Away
From Túnxī, Shèxiàn is 15km north-east and Yīxiàn is 35km north-west.

You can catch minibuses to both towns from the bus station or near the roundabout in front of Túnxī train station, where the ticket-collectors lean out the doors of passing buses and call out the town names. Tickets to Shèxiàn are Y4 and the trip takes 30 minutes. The Y7 journey to Yīxiàn takes one hour.

JIŬHUÁ SHĀN 九华山
Nine Brilliant Mountains ☎ 0566
To avoid Huáng Shān's carnival crowds, skip it in favour of Jiǔhuá Shān, a holy mountain with less spectacular scenery but with a quieter and more spiritual atmosphere.

With 99 peaks and an elevation of 1342m, Jiǔhuá Shān is one of China's four sacred Buddhist mountains (the others are Pǔtuóshān in Zhèjiāng, Éméi Shān in Sìchuān and Wǔtái Shān in Shānxī).

Third-century Taoist monks built thatched temples at Jiǔhuá Shān, but with the rise of Buddhism, stone monasteries gradually replaced them.

Jiǔhuá Shān owes its importance to Kim Kiao Kak (Jīn Qiáojué), a Korean Buddhist disciple who arrived in China in AD 720 and founded a worshipping place for Ksitigarbha, the guardian of the earth. Pilgrims flock to Jiǔhuá Shān for the annual festivities held on the anniversary of Kim's death, which falls on the 30th day of the 7th lunar month. The mountain apparently received its name after the poet, Li Bai, was so moved by seeing nine peaks that he wrote that they help hold the world and the heaven together.

In its heyday, during the Tang dynasty, as many as 3000 monks and nuns, living in more than 150 monasteries, worshipped at Jiǔhuá Shān. Today only 70 temples and monasteries remain, but a palpable feeling of spirituality still permeates the place, something often lacking at China's other 'holy' sites.

Jiǔhuá Shān is also an important place for believers to come and bless the souls of the recently deceased to ensure them a passage to Buddhist heaven.

Orientation & Information

Jiǔhuá is a village that lies 600m above sea level, about halfway up the mountain (or, as the locals say, at roughly navel height in a giant Buddha's potbelly). The bus stops below the main gate where you pay an entrance fee (Y45 between March and November; Y35 the rest of the year).

From here, Jiuhua Jie, the narrow main street, leads up past restaurants, souvenir stalls and hotels. The village square is built around a pond along a side street that leads to the right.

As you continue on the street, China Travel Service (CTS; Zhōngguó Lǚxíngshè; ☎ 501 1588) has an office on the 3rd floor of 135 Beimai Xintun Lu, near a school field, and offers tours for Y30 per day. The Bank of China is at 65 Huachen Lu, near Dàbēi Lóu. As you exit the temple, turn left, take your first right and then another right.

Things to Do

Hiking up the ridge behind Qíyuán Sì, at the bottom of Jiuhua Jie, leads you to the Bǎisuì Gōng, known as the Longevity Palace.

From there, walk south along the ridge until you reach two paths, a western one that leads to town or an eastern one that dips into a pleasant valley and continues to the peak, Tiāntái Zhèng Dǐng. The walk to the peak is about four hours and along the way small temples, nunneries and restaurants line the path.

From the valley, a cable car (Y51/88 one-way/return) whisks passengers to the peak. For information on the mountain paths, several Chinese-language maps, can be bought in the village. Exploring the village, talking to the monks and listening to their soothing chanting can be very relaxing.

Places to Stay & Eat

The beautiful palace-style monastery, *Qíyuán Sì* (☎ 501 1281), sits at the bottom of the village. It has basic dorm beds for Y5 or more comfortable beds for Y20. You may have difficulty staying here if you can't speak Chinese.

The monks might recommend the hotel within the monastery, the *Fójiào Bīnguǎn* (Buddhism Hotel; ☎ 501 1608). Beds in rooms for six persons with shared bath cost Y60. Standard twins are Y100/180 without/with toilet.

Across from the monastery is the *Jùlóng Bīnguǎn* (☎ 501 1368, fax 501 1022), a standard Chinese tourist operation with helpful staff and passable, comfortable twins with bath for Y180. If it's empty, ask for a discount. Better twins are on the hotel's upper floors and start at Y320.

The *Jiǔhuá Shān Zhōnglóu Fàndiàn* (Bell Tower Hotel; ☎ 501 1251, fax 501 1363), at the top of the main street, is a better option. Twins cost Y140 with bath. Beds in triples without bath are Y20, if you can get one.

Behind the Jiǔhuá Shān Zhōnglóu Fàndiàn to the left is the family-run *Nányuàn Lǚguǎn* (☎ 501 1122). Set amid trees, it has clean twins and basic washing facilities for Y25 per bed. It's at the bottom of the trail leading down from the ridge.

On the path to the peak, nestled in the valley, are spartan guesthouses that allow you to experience the mountain at night and to watch misty clouds cling to the treetops. The washing facilities and wood beds are very basic and the toilets are outside.

The *Fènghuángsōng Mínyuán Dàjiǔdiàn* (☎ 501 2097), east of the 1400-year-old 'phoenix' tree, offers beds for Y10. The *Qīng Yǎ Fàndiàn* (☎ 501 1700), further up the mountain, has beds from Y10 to Y20. From the village, it takes about two hours to hike to both places.

For meals, try the *Jùlóng Bīnguǎn's* Y30 set dinner *(tào cān)*, which is tasty and worth the price.

Getting There & Away

There are two daily buses to Jiǔhuá Shān from Huáng Shān via Qīngyáng (Y25, four hours) that follow the road alongside the Taiping Reservoir. There are also buses to Shànghǎi (Y55; 10 hours), Nánjīng (Y50; four hours), Wúhú (Y20; three hours) and Guìchí (Y8; 1½ hours).

WÚHÚ 芜湖
☎ 0553 • pop 2,139,500

Wúhú is a Cháng Jiāng (Yangzi River) port and railway junction. Railway lines branch off south to Túnxī, east to Shànghǎi (via Nánjīng) and, from the northern bank of the

river, north to Héféi. There are also buses from Wúhú to Huáng Shān (five hours) and Jiǔhuá Shān (five hours).

Places to Stay

There are pricey and budget hotels near the long-distance bus station. The *Wúhú Yíngkèsōng Dàjiǔdiàn* (☎ 311 7788, fax 385 1799, 2 Zhan Guangchang) has twins for Y268. The *Dōngyuàn Bīnguǎn* (☎ 382 9041) offers twins from Y60 to Y150.

The *Gǎnlǒng Bīnguǎn* (☎ 383 1319) has good river views and is to the right as you exit the ferry terminal. Twins and triples with bath and air-con are Y60/30. Bus No 4 from the train and bus stations drops you off near the terminal.

GUÌCHÍ 贵池
☎ 0566

To the west of Wúhú is the Cháng Jiāng port of Guìchí, which has buses to Huáng Shān (five hours) and Jiǔhuá Shān (1½ hours). Ferries also go between Wúhú & Guìchí. The trip takes about five hours. (For details on Cháng Jiāng cruises, see the Chóngqìng chapter.)

Places to Stay

The *Jiǔzi Bīnguǎn* (☎ 202 2648, 2 Tanjiang Nanlu) is to your left as you exit the bus station. Twins with bath cost Y128 and single beds are Y67. The bus station is a short motor-trike ride from the dock.

ĀNHUĪ 安徽

Shànghǎi 上海

Whore of the Orient, Paris of the East; city of quick riches, ill-gotten gains and fortunes lost on the tumble of dice; the domain of adventurers, swindlers, gamblers, drug runners, idle rich, dandies, tycoons, missionaries, gangsters and backstreet pimps; the city that plots revolution and dances as the revolution shoots its way into town – Shànghǎi was a dark memory during the long years of forgetting that the communists visited upon their new China; the city's seductive aura that so beguiled the western mind was snuffed out.

Shànghǎi put away its dancing shoes in 1949. The masses began shuffling to a different tune – the dour strains of Marxist-Leninism and the wail of the factory siren; and all through these years of oblivion, the architects of this social experiment firmly wedged one foot against the door on Shànghǎi's past; until finally the effort started to tell.

Today Shànghǎi has reawakened and is busy snapping the dust off its cummerbund. This is a city typifying the huge disparities of modern China – monumental building projects push skywards, glinting department stores swing open their doors to the stylish elite, while child beggars, prostitutes and the impoverished congregate among the champagne corks and burst balloons of the night before. History is returning to haunt Shànghǎi and, at the same time, to put it squarely back on the map.

As the pulse of this metropolis quickens, its steps are firmer, and at this point we make an apology. A lot of what you read in this guide will have changed by the time you have this book in your hands. The booming metropolis of Shànghǎi is evolving at a pace so unmatched by any other Chinese city that even the morning ritual of flinging open one's hotel curtains reveals new facets to the skyline and new sounds on the streets. Shànghǎi is racing full-speed towards the future and has little time for yesterday.

Highlights

Population: 14.2 million
Area: 6200 sq km

- The Bund, the single most evocative symbol of the 'Paris of the East'

- Nanjing Lu, where socialism with Chinese characteristics shakes hands with shop-till-you-drop commercialism

- Getting lost on the backstreets of Frenchtown

- Yù Yuán Shāngchéng (Yu Gardens Bazaar), tacky but fun, with some delicious lunch time snacks

History

As anyone who wanders along the Bund or through the backstreets of Frenchtown can see, Shànghǎi (the name means 'by the sea') is a western invention. As the gateway to the Cháng Jiāng (Yangzi River), it was an ideal trading port. When the British opened their first concession in 1842, after the first Opium War, it was little more than a small town supported by fishing and weaving. The British changed all that.

The French followed in 1847, an International Settlement was established in 1863 and the Japanese arrived in 1895 – the city was parcelled up into autonomous settlements, immune from Chinese law. It became in effect China's first fully fledged Special Economic Zone.

By 1853 Shànghǎi had overtaken all other Chinese ports. Mid-18th century Shànghǎi had a population of just 50,000; by 1900 the figure had jumped to one million. By the 1930s the city claimed some 60,000 foreign residents and was the busiest international port in Asia. Shànghǎi had more motor vehicles than all the rest of China put together and the largest buildings in the east.

This city that was built on the trade of opium, silk and tea, also lured the world's great houses of finance, who descended on the city to erect grand palaces of plenty. Shànghǎi became a byword for exploitation and vice; its countless opium dens, gambling joints and brothels managed by gangs were at the heart of Shànghǎi life. Guarding it all were the American, French and Italian marines, British Tommies and Japanese bluejackets.

Foreign ships and submarines patrolled the Cháng Jiāng (Yangzi River) and Huángpǔ Jiāng (Huangpu River) and the coasts of China. They patrolled the biggest single foreign investment anywhere in the world – the British alone had £400 million sunk into the place.

After Chiang Kaishek's coup against the communists in 1927, the Kuomintang cooperated closely with the foreign police and the Shànghǎi gangs, and with Chinese and foreign factory owners, to suppress labour unrest.

The settlement police, run by the British, arrested Chinese labour leaders and handed them over to the Kuomintang for imprisonment or execution, and the Shànghǎi gangs were repeatedly called in to 'mediate' disputes inside the settlement.

If it was the Chinese who supported the whole giddy structure of Shànghǎi, worked as beasts of burden and provided the muscle in Shànghǎi's port and factories, it was simultaneously the Chinese who provided the weak link.

Exploited in workhouse conditions, crippled by hunger and poverty, sold into slavery, excluded from the high life and the parks created by the foreigners, the poor of Shànghǎi had a voracious appetite for radical opinion. The Chinese Communist Party (CCP) was formed here in 1921 and, after numerous setbacks, 'liberated' the city in 1949.

The communists eradicated the slums, rehabilitated the city's hundreds of thousands of opium addicts, and eliminated child and slave labour. These were staggering achievements.

Unfortunately, they also put Shànghǎi to sleep. The wake-up call came in 1990 when the central government started throwing money at the municipality, and the city hasn't looked back since.

Climate

The best times to visit Shànghǎi are spring and autumn. In winter temperatures can drop well below freezing and there is often a blanket of drizzle. Summers are hot and humid with temperatures as high as 40°C (104°F). So, in short, you'll need silk long johns and down jackets for winter, an ice block for each armpit in summer and an umbrella wouldn't go astray in either season.

Government

Shànghǎi has always courted extremism in politics and has been an accurate barometer for the mood of the nation. Radical intellectuals and students, provoked by the startling inequalities between rich and poor, were perfect receptacles for the many foreign opinions circulating in the concessions. The meeting that founded the Chinese Communist Party (CCP) was held here back in 1921. Mao Zedong also cast the first stone of the Cultural Revolution in Shànghǎi, by publishing in the city's newspapers a piece of political rhetoric he had been unable to get published in Běijīng.

Most extraordinarily, during the Cultural Revolution, a People's Commune was set up in Shànghǎi, modelled on the Paris Commune of the 19th century. (The Paris Commune was set up in 1871 and controlled Paris for two months. It planned to introduce socialist reforms such as turning over management of factories to workers' associations.) The Shànghǎi Commune lasted

SHÀNGHǍI 上海

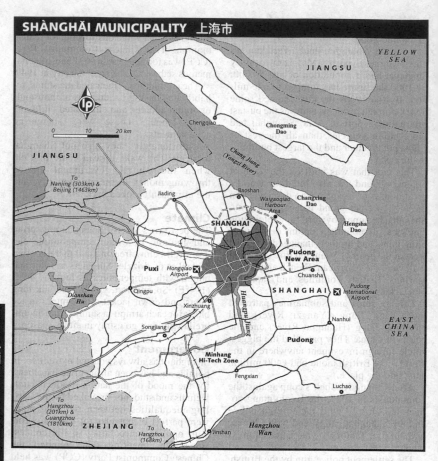

SHÀNGHǍI MUNICIPALITY 上海市

just three weeks before Mao ordered the army to put an end to it.

The so-called Gang of Four (see the History section in the Facts about the Country chapter) had its power base in Shànghǎi. The campaign to criticise Confucius and Mencius (Mengzi) was started here in 1969, before it became nationwide in 1973 and was linked to Lin Biao.

The city's influence now ripples through the whole of the party apparatus to the top: President Jiang Zemin is Shànghǎi's ex-Party chief and premier Zhu Rongji and minister Wu Bangguo also hail from the municipality. Furthermore, Hong Kong's new chief executive, Tung Chee-hwa, is a Shànghǎi man.

Economy

Shànghǎi's long malaise came to an abrupt end in 1990, with the announcement of plans to develop Pǔdōng, on the eastern side of the Huángpǔ Jiāng, although there have since been teething problems. Property values soared in the early 1990s, but overbuilding has created a glut of office space and real estate prices dropped in most sectors towards the end that decade.

Nevertheless, Shànghǎi's goal is to become a major financial centre along with its emerging economic strength. Lùjiāzuǐ, the area that faces off the Bund on the Pǔdōng side of the Huángpǔ Jiāng, is taking shape as a modern high-rise counterpoint to the austere, old-world structures on the Bund.

Shànghǎi has a unique opportunity, and the savvy with which locals have grabbed it have many shaking their heads knowingly, saying that Shànghǎi always had the potential to be a great city. Massive freeway projects crisscross the city, the metro system is proceeding apace, and the indications are that this forward planning will circumvent the infrastructure problems that face other Asian cities such as Bangkok, Jakarta and Taipei.

Shànghǎi's burgeoning economy, its leadership and its intrinsic self-confidence have put it miles ahead of other cities in China. Neither Běijīng nor Guǎngzhōu can match the superficial, gilt-edged feel of modernity that covers the city. Shànghǎi authorities know that tourism makes money, so it spends a little bringing it in; this simple logic is apparently lost on the rest of the country. In this respect it has some of the best services in China, which compared to most international centres still isn't saying much.

Fuelled by the gushing enthusiasm of both foreign and local propaganda, Shànghǎi is at times gripped in a hyped-up vision that is in danger of crumpling against the sheer reality of managing a city of this size and complexity. Moreover, the visionaries seem to forget there is more to a great city than gleaming buildings and metro systems. Public discourse and critique of the economy and its relationship to culture and politics is as lacking in Shànghǎi today as private telephones were two decades ago.

Nothing would satisfy the central government more than for Shànghǎi to replace Hong Kong as China's frontier on the future, swinging the spotlight of attention from the ex-colony on to a home-grown success story. Indeed, great strides have taken place in achieving this goal. But there's still a long way to go.

Population

Shànghǎi's population figure is deceptive since it takes into account the whole municipal area of 6340 sq km.

Nevertheless, the central core of some 220 sq km has more than 7.5 million people, which must rate as one of the highest population densities in China, if not the world.

Orientation

Shànghǎi municipality covers a substantial area, but the city proper is a more modest size. Within the municipality is the island of Chóngmíng. It's part of the Cháng Jiāng (Yangzi River) delta and is worth a footnote because it's the second largest island in China (or third if you recognise China's claim to Taiwan).

Broadly, central Shànghǎi is divided into two areas: Pǔdōng (east of the Huángpǔ Jiāng) and Pǔxī (west of the Huángpǔ Jiāng). The First Ring Road does a long elliptical loop around the city centre proper, which includes all of commercial west-side Shànghǎi, the Lùjiāzuǐ Finance and Trade Zone and the Jīnqiáo Export Processing Zone of Pǔdōng.

A second (outer) ring road will link Hóngqiáo Airport (in the west of town) with the new Wàigāoqiáo Free Trade Zone, a port on the Cháng Jiāng (Yangzi River) in Pǔdōng.

For visitors, the attractions of Shànghǎi are in Pǔxī. Here you will find the Bund, the shopping streets, the former foreign concessions, hotels, restaurants, sights and nightclubs.

In the central district (around Nanjing Lu) the provincial names run north-south, and the city names run east-west. Some roads are split by compass points, such as Sichuan Nanlu (Sichuan South Rd) and Sichuan Beilu (Sichuan North Rd). Some of the monstrously long roads are split by sectors, such as Zhongshan Dong Erlu and Zhongshan Dong Yilu, which mean Zhongshan East 2nd Rd and Zhongshan East 1st Rd.

There are four main areas of interest in the city: the Bund from Sūzhōu Hé (Sūzhōu Creek) to the Shànghǎi Harbour Passenger Terminal at Shiliupu Wharf (Shíliùpù

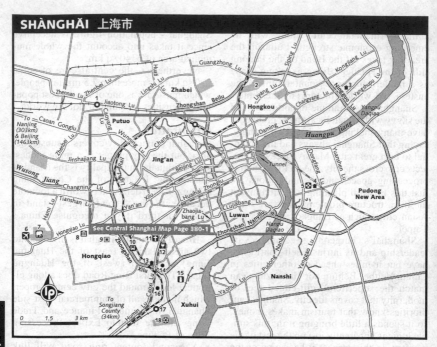

SHANGHAI 上海市

Mǎtóu); Nanjing Donglu (a very colourful neighbourhood); Frenchtown, which includes Huaihai Zhonglu and Ruijin Lu (an even more colourful neighbourhood); and the Yùfó Sì (Jade Buddha Temple) and the side trip along Sūzhōu Creek.

Maps English maps of Shànghǎi are available at the Foreign Languages Bookstore (see Bookshops later in this section), the Jinjiang Hotel bookshop and occasionally from street hawkers. Watch out for the map sellers on the Bund who squawk 'English map' (the only English they know), but when you look at them they are usually just a maze of characters. The best of the bunch is the bilingual *Shanghai Official Tourist Map*, which is produced by the Shanghai Municipal Tourism Administration. It's usually available at the Tourist Information Centres listed in the Tourist Offices section.

Maps of Shànghǎi are available in Hong Kong and abroad. Periplus publishes a map

of Shànghǎi that's also sold in the Foreign Languages Bookstore.

Information

Tourist Offices Shànghǎi operates Tourist Information Centres, located in the metro station at Shànghǎi train station (Shànghǎi zhàn), another at the metro station in Rénmín Guǎngchǎng (People's Square; ☎ 6438 1693) and a third in the international arrivals hall of Hóngqiáo Airport (☎ 6268 8899 ext 56750). The staff are professional and polite and will provide free maps to Shànghǎi in a wide array of languages, including English, Japanese, Korean and French. The assistants are keen to speak English and are very helpful.

The Tourist Hotline (☎ 6252 0000) has a useful English-language service.

There are a couple of superb Web sites offering up-to-date travel and entertainment information on Shànghǎi. Check out www .shanghai-ed.com or www.shangai-abc.com.

SHÀNGHǍI

PLACES TO STAY

3   Changyang Hotel
   长阳饭店

4   New Asia Tomson Hotel
   新亚汤臣大酒店

13   Huating Hotel
   and Towers
   华亭宾馆

SIGHTS

2   Hóngkǒu Gōngyuán;
   Lǔ Xùn Líng
   虹口公园;
   鲁迅陵

7   Shànghǎi
   Dòngwùyuán
   上海动物园

8   Liú Hǎisù
   Měishùguǎn
   刘海粟美术馆

9   Wànguó Gōngmù;
   Sòng Qìnglíng
   Língyuán
   万国公墓、
   宋庆龄陵园

11   St Ignatius
   Cathedral
   天主教堂

15   Lónghuá Tǎ
   龙华塔

16   Cáoxī Gōngyuán
   漕溪公园

18   Shànghǎi Zhíwùyuán
   植物园

OTHER

1   West Train Station
   上海西站

5   Nextage Department Store
   新世纪商厦

6   Hóngqiáo Airport
   虹桥机场

10   Western District Bus Station
   西区汽车站

12   JBL Dance Pub
   南丹信息

14   Shanghai Stadium;
   Sightseeing Bus Centre
   上海体育场;
   旅游集散中心

17   South Train Station
   上海南站

That's Shanghai is a useful magazine and it has a Web site at www.thatsshanghai.com.

Foreign Consulates   There is a growing band of consulates in Shànghǎi. If you're doing the Trans-Siberian journey and have booked a definite departure date, it's much better to get your Russian visa here than face the horrible queues at the Russian embassy in Běijīng.

Your own country's consulate is worth a visit – not just if you've lost your passport, but also for up-to-date newspapers from home.

Australia (☎ 6433 4604, fax 6437 6669) Room 401, Shanghai Centre, 1376 Nanjing Xilu

Canada (☎ 6279 8400, fax 6279 8401) Suite 604, West Tower, Shanghai Centre, 1376 Nanjing Xilu

France (☎ 6437 7414, fax 6433 9437) 21-23 floor, Qihua Tower, 1375 Huaihai Zhonglu

Germany (☎ 6433 6951, fax 6471 4448) 181 Yongfu Lu

Japan (☎ 6278 0788, fax 6278 8988) 8 Wan-shan Lu, Hóngqiáo

New Zealand (☎ 6471 1108, fax 6431 0226) 15A, Qihua Tower, 1375 Huaihai Zhonglu

Russia (☎ 6324 2682, fax 6306 9982) 20 Huangpu Lu

South Korea (☎ 6219 6417, fax 6219 6918) 4th floor, International Trade Centre, 2200 Yan'an Xilu

UK (☎ 6279 7650, fax 6279 7651) 3rd floor, Room 301, Shanghai Centre, 1376 Nanjing Xilu

USA (☎ 6433 6880, fax 6433 4122) 1469 Huaihai Zhonglu

Money   There are money-changing counters at almost every hotel, even cheapies like the Pujiang Hotel. Credit cards are more readily accepted in Shànghǎi than in other parts of China.

Most tourist hotels will accept major credit cards such as Visa, American Express, MasterCard, Diners and JCB, as will banks and Friendship Stores (and related tourist outlets like the Shanghai Antique and Curio Store).

The enormous Bank of China right next to the Peace Hotel tends to get crowded, but is better organised than Chinese banks elsewhere around the country (it's worth a peek for its grand interior). There's a branch of Citibank next door on the Bund that is open 24 hours for ATM withdrawal. ATMs accepting most major cards are located at various branches of the Bank of China scattered throughout the city and also at the Industrial and Commercial Bank of China (ICBC) and China Construction Bank.

American Express (☎ 6279 8082) has an office at Room 206, Retail Plaza, Shanghai Centre, 1376 Nanjing Xilu.

Post & Communications   The larger tourist hotels have post offices from where

SHÀNGHǍI 上海

you can mail letters and small packages, and this is by far the most convenient option.

Shànghǎi's phone code is ☎ 021.

The international post and telecommunications office is at the corner of Sichuan Beilu and Bei Suzhou Lu. The section for international parcels is in the same building, along with poste restante, but entered around the corner at 395 Tiantong Lu. There are large telecommunication offices at 1761 Sichuan Beilu and 1200 Yanan Donglu.

Express parcel and document service is available with several foreign carriers. Contact DHL (☎ 6536 2900), UPS (☎ 6248 6060), Federal Express (☎ 6275 0808) or TNT Skypak (☎ 6421 1111).

Long-distance phone calls can be placed from hotel rooms and don't take long to get through. Long-distance calls can also be made from the post office next to the Peace Hotel on Nanjing Donglu; international telegrams and telexes also can be sent from here. Phone cards available from the telecommunication office are useful, but usually don't work with hotel phones. For the international operator dial ☎ 103.

Internet Resources A number of hotels in Shànghǎi provide Internet services, but they are usually a little pricey. The Shanghai Library, at 1555 Huaihai Zhonglu, has terminals on the ground floor. It's open from 9 am to 6 pm daily and costs Y5 per hour. Bring your passport for ID. The massive Book City, at 465 Fuzhou Lu, has an Internet cafe on the 2nd floor, charging Y7 per half hour. It's open daily from 9.30 am to 6.45 pm and until 9 pm from Friday to Sunday.

The 3C+T Internet Café, at 238 Shanxi Nanlu, close to the Parkson department store, is open daily from 10 am until after midnight and charges Y15 per hour, though you're expected to buy a drink.

Travel Agencies The main office of China International Travel Service (CITS; Zhōngguó Guójì Lǚxíngshè; ☎ 6323 8749) is in Room 610 on the 6th Floor of 1277 Beijing Xilu. Another CITS office that can handle most ticketing services is on the 1st floor of the Guangming Building, at 2 Jinling

Donglu. There's another CITS office on Nanjing Donglu near the Peace Hotel, but it's mostly for booking airline tickets.

Train, plane and boat tickets can be booked at the Beijing Xilu and Jinling Donglu offices, subject to availability. CITS will often need at least three days to get tickets for destinations further than Hángzhōu or Sūzhōu. A service charge of Y10 is added. If you're in a hurry, try your hotel or one of the other booking options mentioned in the Getting There & Away section later in this chapter.

Boat tickets are easier to book at CITS, but often a lot more expensive than doing it yourself across the road at the boat ticketing office.

Bookshops Shànghǎi is one of the better places in China to stock up on reading fodder. Coupled with the tourist hotel bookshops, Shànghǎi's bookshops have a reasonable, if gagged, selection.

The main Foreign Languages Bookstore is at 390 Fuzhou Lu. The 1st floor has a good but pricey range of maps and the 2nd floor has a range of western literature that breaks the usual Jane Austen mould and has begun offering more interesting contemporary English reading material. It's a good place to stock up on books if you're heading for a long haul in other parts of China. Fuzhou Lu has traditionally been the bookshop street of Shànghǎi and is well worth a stroll.

The Shànghǎi Bówùguǎn (Shanghai Museum) bookshop has an excellent range of books on Chinese art, architecture, ceramics and calligraphy and is definitely worth a visit if you are in the museum. It also has a wide selection of cards and slides.

Get a copy of Pan Ling's *In Search of Old Shanghai* for a rundown on who was who and what was what back in the bad old days.

For where they lived, consult *A Last Look: Western Architecture in Old Shanghai* by Tess Johnston & Deke Erh, which offers a fascinating photographic record of buildings in the city. Keep an eye out for their newest book on the old French Concession. These books are usually available at the Shànghǎi Bówùguǎn bookshop or visit the Old China Hand Reading Room

(☎/fax 6473 2526), at 27 Shaoxing Lu, which is run by Deke Erh. Besides their series of books on western architecture in China, the bookshop-cum-cafe has a whole range of books on art, architecture and culture.

Newspapers & Magazines A small range of foreign newspapers and magazines is available from the larger tourist hotels (eg Park, Jinjiang, Hilton) and some shops.

Publications include the *Wall Street Journal, International Herald Tribune, Asiaweek, South China Morning Post*, the *Economist, Time* and *Newsweek*. They are expensive, however, with *Newsweek* and *Time* usually costing about Y35.

Back in the late '90s, life for foreigners in Shànghǎi improved considerably with the appearance of three entertainment publications edited and compiled by native speakers of English. There were some shaky beginnings and changeovers as the authorities tried to come to terms with these upstart foreigners creating their own publications, which was no small feat in a country that controls its media with an iron fist. Nothing controversial, of course, but at least they are *interesting* to read.

The most comprehensive is the monthly magazine *That's Shanghai*, closely followed by the weekly paper, *Travel China: Shanghai Edition*. The monthly *Shanghai Talk*, put out by Ismay Publications, was undergoing some changes at the time of writing and may be under a different name by the time you read this. If you want to know what's going on in Shànghǎi, check these out. They're free and available in most of the western-style bars and restaurants and some hotels.

Medical Services Shànghǎi is credited with the best medical facilities and most advanced medical knowledge in China. Hospital treatment is available at the Huashan Hospital (☎ 6248 9999), at 12 Wulumuqi Zhonglu, which has a Hong Kong joint-venture section catering to those who can pay for more luxurious care; and at the Shanghai First People's Hospital (☎ 6324 3852) at 585 Jiulong Lu in Hongkou. For an ambulance, call the Shanghai Emergency Centre (☎ 6324 4010) at 68 Haining Lu.

World Link (☎ 6279 7688, fax 6279 7698) offers private medical care and can be found at Suite 203 in the Shanghai Centre.

The New Pioneer Medical Centre (☎ 6469 3898, fax 6469 3897) has similar services, as well as dental care. It's on the 2nd floor of the Ge Ru Building at 910 Heng Shan Lu, in the Xújiāhuì area, near St Ignatius Cathedral.

PSB The Public Security Bureau (Gōngānjú; ☎ 6357 6666) has an office at 333 Wusong Lu, near the intersection with Kunshan Lu.

The Bund

The Bund (Wàitān) is an Anglo-Indian term for the embankment of a muddy waterfront. The term is apt: mud bedevils Shànghǎi. Between 1920 (when the problem was first noticed) and 1965, the city sank several metres. Water was pumped back into the ground, but the Venetian threat remains. Concrete rafts are used as foundations for high-rises in this spongy mass.

Its muddy predicament aside, the Bund is symbolic of Shànghǎi. In faraway Kashgar and Lhasa, local Chinese pose for photographs in front of oil-painted Bund facades. Constant throngs of Chinese and foreign tourists pad past the porticos of the Bund's grand edifices with maps in hand. The buildings themselves loom serenely, oblivious to the march of revolutions; a vagabond assortment of neoclassical 1930s downtown New York styles, with a pompous touch of monumental antiquity thrown in for good measure.

To the Europeans, the Bund was Shànghǎi's Wall Street, a place of feverish trading, of fortunes made and lost. One of the most famous traders was Jardine Matheson & Company. In 1848 Jardine's purchased the first land offered for sale to foreigners in Shanghai and set up shop shortly after, dealing in opium and tea. The company grew into one of the great hongs (a 'hong' is literally a business firm), and today it owns just about half of Hong Kong.

SHÀNGHǍI 上海

At the north-western end of the Bund were the British Public Gardens (now called Huángpǔ Gōngyuán). Famously, a sign at the entrance announced 'No Dogs or Chinese Allowed'. Or at least that is how posterity remembers it; in actual fact the restrictions on Chinese and dogs were listed in separate clauses of a whole bevy of restrictions on undesirables. The slight, however, will probably never be forgotten.

The Bund today is in the process of yet another transformation. The building identified by a crowning dome is the old Hongkong & Shanghai Bank, completed in 1921 with much pomp and ceremony. For many years it housed the Shanghai People's Municipal Government and was off-limits to curious travellers. Now it belongs to the Pudong Development Bank. Other Bund fixtures are being sold off, and will no doubt be dusted off and cleaned up.

The statues that once lined the Bund no longer exist but you can get an idea of what things used to look like from photos on display at the **Waìtān Lìshǐ Bówùguǎn** (Bund History Museum), at the north end of Huángpǔ Gōngyuán.

The Tung Feng Hotel, at the bottom of the Bund near Shiliupu Wharf, only hints at its former grandeur and conveys nothing of its former exclusivity. It was once home to the Shanghai Club, the snootiest little gang this side of Trafalgar Square. Membership was confined to upper-crust male Brits. They sat around the club's 110-foot bar (the longest in the world at the time), sipping chilled champagne and comparing fortunes. The hotel has closed down for the time being.

What Was What

Until recently, Shànghǎi was a vast museum, housing an inheritance of foreign trophies. Now, with both eyes on the future, Shànghǎi wants a face-lift. While state-protected landmark buildings on the Bund and elsewhere are safe from the ball-and-chain, in other parts of town chunks of history are giving way to department stores and office blocks.

Shànghǎi is shackled to a past it is both suspicious and proud of, so who knows what the city will look like by the next century. But as the Chinese like to say, '*Jiùde búqù, xīnde bùlái*' ('if the old doesn't go, the new won't come').

For the time being, old Shànghǎi can still be enjoyed. The ancient buildings have an old-world grumpiness about them, scowling at the fresh-faced upstarts surrounding them. The **Chinese city**, for example, is still a maze of narrow lanes, lined with closely packed houses and laundry hanging from windows. It lies on the south-western bank of the Huángpǔ Jiāng, bounded to the north by Jinling Donglu and to the south by Zhonghua Lu. The **Yù Yuán** (Yu Gardens) are in this part of town and are well worth a visit.

The **International Settlement** (Shànghǎi Zūjiè), in its time a brave new world of co-operation between the British, Europeans and Americans (the Japanese were also included, but were considered suspect), cuts a broad swathe through the north of the city centre. It extends from the intersection of Yan'an Xilu and Nanjing Xilu north to Sūzhōu Hé and east to the Huángpǔ Jiāng. Nanjing Lu and the Bund shared pride of place in this settlement. South of Yan'an Lu and squeezed north of the Chinese city was the **French Concession** (Fǎguó Zūjiè). Yan'an Lu was known as Avenue Foch in the west, and Avenue Edward VII in the east; the French strip of the Bund (south of Yan'an Lu) was known as the Quai de France. Despite the names, there were never all that many French people in the concession – 90% of the residents were Chinese, and the most numerous foreigners were Russians. Nevertheless, Frenchtown remains one of the most interesting parts of Shànghǎi. The premier district (around the Jinjiang Hotel and on Huaihai Lu) is once again being gentrified, and department stores have opened up everywhere in the last few years. But for Frenchtown at its best, simply strike off on the side streets that head south off Yan'an Lu (see Frenchtown later in this section for more information).

Nanjing Lu & the Central District

Nanjing Donglu, from the Peace to the Park hotels, has long been China's golden mile, though its glamour has slipped a few notches in the last 15 years. Hoping to bring back its former glory, the city began a massive renovation project in the late 1990s, turning Nanjing Lu into a pedestrian-only shopping extravaganza from Henan Lu to Xizang Lu.

Nanjing Xilu takes over where Nanjing Donglu ducks beside **Rénmín Gōngyuán** (People's Park). The park and the adjacent Rénmín Guǎngchǎng were once the site of the Shanghai Racecourse and now proudly displays the Shànghǎi Bówùguǎn, the Grand Theatre and a rather drab municipal government building. Nanjing Xilu itself was previously Bubbling Well Rd, the natural spring having been long sealed over.

The crowds are less intense as you head west along Nanjing Xilu, past the former Shanghai Race Club and previous site of the Shanghai Library, that is now slated to become the new home of the Shànghǎi Měishùguǎn (Shanghai Art Museum). Beyond the Chengdu Lu Expressway, which thunders down the centre of Shànghǎi, Nanjing Xilu gives way to office blocks and more shops and hotels, all of which join forces in the impressive Shanghai Centre and Soviet-era Shanghai Exhibition Centre opposite.

Frenchtown

The core of Frenchtown (Fǎguó Zūjiè), the former French Concession, is the area around Huaihai Lu and the Jinjiang Hotel. Huaihai Lu is the shopper's Pǔdōng, a glittering alternative to worn Nanjing Lu; huge department stores have gone up such as Isetan, Printemps and Parkson as well as others. The area around the Jinjiang Hotel and Jinjiang Tower is littered with cafes, boutiques and the odd antique shop.

On side streets off Huaihai Lu, from roughly Siming Lu all the way west to Huashan Lu, is some of the best old architecture, from old Art-Deco apartment complexes to neo-classical mansions and villas with quaint balconies and doorways.

Site of the 1st National Congress of the CCP 一大会址

The CCP was founded in July 1921 in a French Concession building at 76 Xingye Lu. Given the significance of the occasion, the museum (Zhōnggòng Yīdàhuìzhǐ) has a very low profile. There are some photographs and the like with English captions. Opening hours are 8.30 to 11 am and 1 to 4 pm, and it's closed Monday and Thursday mornings. Entry is Y3.

Shànghǎi Bówùguǎn (Shanghai Museum)

This stunning new building was built in 1994 at a cost of Y570 million, and can be seen as a completely new approach to museum design in China. Shànghǎi Bówùguǎn is symbolic of the many changes that are afoot in China – gone are airy corridors, dry exhibits, yawning security guards and stale air – the new Shànghǎi Bówùguǎn is as impressive outside as in.

Designed to recall the shape of an ancient Chinese *ding* vessel, this architectural statement is home to one of the most impressive collections of art in China, making it a must-see.

Take your pick from the galleries that house some fantastic specimens – from the archaic green patina of the Ancient Chinese Bronze Gallery through the silent solemnity of the Chinese Sculpture Gallery, from the exquisite beauty of the ceramics in the Zande Lou Gallery to the measured and timeless flourishes captured in the Chinese Calligraphy Gallery. Chinese painting, seals, jade, Ming and Qing furniture, coins and ethnic art are also on offer, intelligently displayed in well-lit galleries. Furthermore, the exhibits are generously spaced out, giving you the opportunity to stroll leisurely and unhurriedly through the galleries.

While guiding you through the craft of millennia, the museum simultaneously takes you through the pages of Chinese history. Expect to spend half if not the whole day here.

Originally located on Henan Nanlu, the museum can now be found at 201 Renmin Dadao, near Rénmín Guǎngchǎng metro station, and is open daily from 9 am to 5 pm; entrance is Y20.

West Train Station

Hutai Lu Long-Distance Bus Station

Zhongtan Lu Station

Zhenping Lu Station

Putuo

Putuo Gongyuan

Caoyang Gongyuan

Caoyang Lu Station

Suzhou He

Jinshajiang Lu Station

154

155

Jing'an

南京西路

Jing'ansi

Changning

Changning Lu Station

Changning

153

128

延安中路

Xuanhua Lu

Anhua Lu

127

Hu Xi Stadium

Yanan Xilu Station

152

Yan'an Xilu

Yan'an Xilu

129

淮海中路

Ding Xiang Yuan

Fuxing Xilu

126

130 132

131

125

124

123

133

Taojiang Lu

135 137

134 136

142 140

143 141

144

145

138

139

151

Hongqiao Lu Station

149

150

Huaihai Xilu

146

148 147

Hengshan Lu

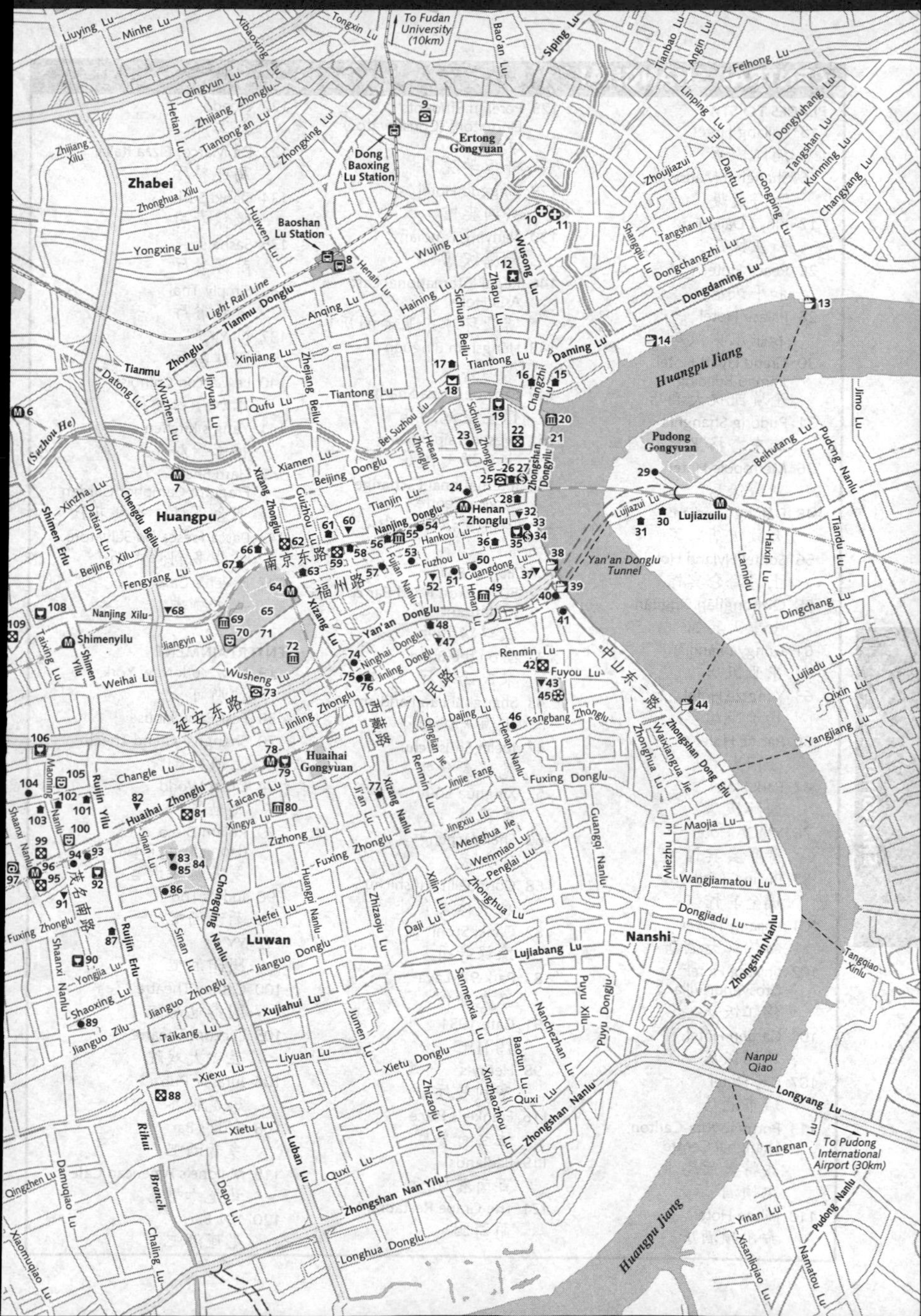

To Fudan University (10km)
Liuying Lu
Minhe Lu
Xibaoxing Lu
Tongxin Lu
Bao'an Lu
Siping Lu
Tianbao Lu
Anqin Lu
Feihong Lu
Qingyun Lu
Zhijiang Zhonglu
Tiantong'an Lu
Hetian Lu
Zhijiang Xilu
Zhongxing Lu
Dong Baoxing Lu Station
Ertong Gongyuan
Linping Lu
Dongyuhang Lu
Tangshan Lu
Kunming Lu
Gongping Lu
Dantu Lu
Zhoujiazui Lu
Changyang Lu
Zhabei
Zhonghua Xilu
Huiwen Lu
Baoshan Lu Station
Yongxing Lu
Wujing Lu
Wusong Lu
Tangshan Lu
Shangqiu Lu
Dongchangzhi Lu
Henan Lu
Haining Lu
Sichuan Beilu
Zhapu Lu
Dongdaming Lu
Light Rail Line
Tianmu Donglu
Anqing Lu
Tianmu Zhonglu
Xinjiang Lu
Zhejiang Beilu
Tiantong Lu
Daming Lu
Changzhi Lu
Huangpu Jiang
Datong Lu
Wuzhen Lu
Jinyuan Lu
Qufu Lu
Tiantong Lu
Bei Suzhou Lu
Henan Zhonglu
Sichuan Zhonglu
Zhongshan Dongyilu
Jimo Lu
Pudong Gongyuan
Beihutang Lu
Pudong Nanlu
(Suzhou He)
Xiamen Lu
Beijing Donglu
Xizang Zhonglu
Guizhou Lu
Tianjin Lu
Xinzha Lu
Chengdu Beilu
Huangpu
Shimen Erlu
Datian Lu
Nanjing Donglu
Henan Zhonglu
Hankou Lu
Lujiazui Lu
Lujiazuilu
Haixin Lu
Tiandu Lu
Lannidu Lu
Beijing Xilu
南京东路
Fuzhou Lu
Fujian Nanlu
Guangdong Lu
Yan'an Donglu Tunnel
Fengyang Lu
福州路
Henan Lu
Dingchang Lu
Nanjing Xilu
Xizang Lu
Yan'an Donglu
Taixing Lu
Shimenyilu
Shimen Yilu
Jiangyin Lu
Ninghai Donglu
Jinling Donglu
Renmin Lu
Fuyou Lu
Lujiadu Lu
Qixin Lu
Weihai Lu
Wusheng Lu
中山东二路
人民路
Jinling Zhonglu
西藏南路
Dajing Lu
Fangbang Zhonglu
Henan Nanlu
Zhonghua Lu
Waixiangua Jie
Zhongshan Dong Erlu
Yangjiang Lu
延安东路
Qingfen Jie
Renmin Lu
Huaihai Gongyuan
Jinjie Fang
Fuxing Donglu
Maoming Nanlu
Ruijin Yilu
Changle Lu
Huaihai Zhonglu
Taicang Lu
Xingya Lu
Ji'an Lu
Xizang Nanlu
Jingxiu Lu
Menghua Jie
Guangqi Nanlu
Maojia Lu
Miezhu Lu
Shaanxi Nanlu
Sinan Lu
Zizhong Lu
Fuxing Zhonglu
Wenmiao Lu
Penglai Lu
Wangjiamatou Lu
茂名南路
Chongqing Nanlu
Huangpi Nanlu
Zhizaoju Lu
Xilin Lu
Zhonghua Lu
Dongjiadu Lu
Fuxing Zhonglu
Hefei Lu
Daji Lu
Ruijin Erlu
Shaanxi Nanlu
Luwan
Jianguo Donglu
Nanshi
Lujiabang Lu
Zhongshan Nanlu
Tanggiao Xinlu
Yongjia Lu
Sinan Lu
Shaoxing Lu
Jianguo Zhonglu
Xujiahui Lu
Jumen Lu
Sanmenxia Lu
Puyu Xilu
Puyu Donglu
Nanchezhan Lu
Jianguo Zilu
Taikang Lu
Liyuan Lu
Xietu Donglu
Baotun Lu
Nanpu Qiao
Xiexu Lu
Zhizaoju Lu
Xinzhaozhou Lu
Quxi Lu
Longyang Lu
Xietu Lu
Zhongshan Nanlu
Rihui Branch
Luban Lu
To Pudong International Airport (30km)
Tangnan Lu
Qingzhen Lu
Damuqiao Lu
Quxi Lu
Zhongshan Nan Yilu
Dapu Lu
Huangpu Jiang
Yinan Lu
Pudong Nanlu
Xiaomuqiao Lu
Chaling Lu
Longhua Donglu
Xisanliqiao Lu
Namatou Lu

CENTRAL SHÀNGHǍI

PLACES TO STAY

15 Pujiang Hotel
浦江饭店
16 Shanghai Mansions
上海大厦
17 Xīnyǎ Dàjiǔdiàn
新亚饭店
26 Peace Hotel
和平饭店
28 Palace Hotel
和平汇中饭店
30 Grand Hyatt Hotel;
Jinmao Building
金贸凯悦大酒店
31 Pudong Shangrila
浦东香格里拉大酒店
36 Metropole Hotel
新城饭店
48 Dàfàng Fàndiàn
大放饭店
56 Sofitel Hyland Hotel
上海海仑宾馆
58 Qīzhòngtiān Bīnguǎn
七重天宾馆
61 Dōngyà Fàndiàn
东亚饭店
63 Yangtze Hotel
杨子饭店
66 Pacific Hotel
金门大酒店
67 Park Hotel
国际饭店
76 YMCA Hotel
青年会宾馆
87 Ruijin Guesthouse
瑞金宾馆
101 Jinjiang Tower
新锦江大酒店
102 Jinjiang Hotel;
Grosvenor Villa
锦江饭店
103 Garden Hotel
花园饭店
107 City Hotel
城市酒店
113 Portman Ritz-Carlton;
Shanghai Centre
波特曼丽思卡
尔顿酒
118 Hilton Hotel
希尔顿酒店

123 Foreign Students'
Dormitory (Conservatory
of Music)
音乐学院
129 Xingguo Hotel
兴国宾馆
130 Nányīng Fàndiàn
南鹰饭店
146 Regal International East
Asia Hotel
富豪环球东亚大酒店1
148 Héngshān Bīnguǎn
衡山宾馆
149 Crowne-Plaza Shanghai
银星皇冠酒店
151 Westin Taipingyang
太平洋大饭店
154 International Exchange
Service Centre
国际交流服务中心

PLACES TO EAT

32 50 Hankou Road Bar &
Restaurant
汉口路50号
37 M on the Bund
米氏西餐厅
43 Shànghǎi Lǎo Fàndiàn
上海老饭店
47 Juélín Shùshíchù
觉林素食处
52 Xìnghǔa Lóu
杏花楼
60 Shěndàchéng
沈大成
68 Gōngdélín Shūshíchù
功德林素食处
82 Ganki Sushi
缘禄寿司
83 Park 97; Lava
派克餐馆
91 Cafe 1931
1931吧
98 Henry's
亨利餐厅
116 Frankie's Place
法兰奇餐厅
119 Badlands
百岗餐厅
121 The Grape Restaurant
葡萄园

122 Ooedo
大江户
128 Da Marco; Pizza Italia
马可餐厅;
134 Ganki Sushi
缘禄寿司
135 Sasha's
萨莎餐厅
136 Simply Thai
天泰餐厅
137 Ali YY
阿建餐厅
140 Le Garcon Chinoise
乐加尔松餐厅
141 Yang's Kitchen
杨家厨房
142 Harn Sheh;
Fragrant Camphor Garden
寒舍茶坊; 香樟花园
143 Pasca Fresca Da Salvatore
沙华多利意式面食
147 Keven's Café
凯文咖啡

ENTERTAINMENT

19 New York New York
迪斯可
35 Fest Brew House
70 Shanghai Grand Theatre
上海大剧院
74 Great World
大世界
79 Rojam Disco
(Hong Kong Plaza)
罗尖姆娱乐宫
90 Judy's Too
菊迪酒吧
92 YY's
阴阳酒吧
100 Cathay Theatre
国泰电影院
105 Lyceum Theatre
兰心大戏院
106 Jurassic Pub
恐龙世界
108 Eddy's Bar
乡音酒吧
115 Malone's American Cafe
马龙咖啡店
120 101 Bar
星座酒吧

SHÀNGHǍI 上海

CENTRAL SHÀNGHǍI

124 Paulaner Bauhaus
宝莱纳餐厅

126 Cotton Club
棉花俱乐部

133 O'Malleys Bar
欧玛莉酒吧

144 Real Love
真爱酒吧

150 Goya's
戈雅酒吧

SHOPPING

22 Friendship Store
友谊商店

24 Guànlóng
(Photo Supplies)
冠龙照相器材商店

42 Shanghai Tourist
Shopping Emporium
上海旅游购物商场

46 Fangbang Lu Antique
Market
方浜路古玩市场

50 Shanghai Antique and
Curio Store
上海文物市场

51 China Science and
Technology Book
Company
中国科技图书公司

53 Foreign Languages
Bookstore
外文书店

54 Xinhua Bookstore
新华书店

57 Book City
书城

59 Hualian Department
Store
华联商厦

62 No 1 Department Store
第一百货

77 Dongtai Lu Antique
Market
东台路古玩市场

81 Isetan Department Store
伊势丹

93 Watson's Pharmacy
屈臣氏

95 Printemps Department
Store
上海巴黎春天百货

99 Parkson Department Store
百盛百货

109 Westgate Mall
梅龙镇广场

110 Jingdezhen Porcelain
Artware
景德镇瓷器店

138 YMCA Bike Shop
青年车行

PARKS & GARDENS

21 Huángpǔ Gōngyuán
黄浦公园

45 Yù Yuán Shāngchéng
豫园商城

65 Rénmín Gōngyuán
人民公园

84 Fùxīng Gōngyuán
复兴公园

117 Jìng'ān Gōngyuán
静安公园

152 Tiānshān Gōngyuán
天山公园

153 Zhōngshān Gōngyuán
中山公园

155 Chángfēng Gōngyuán
长风公园

SIGHTS

1 Yùfó Sì
玉佛寺

20 Wàitān Lìshǐ Bówùguǎn
外滩历史博物馆

29 Oriental Pearl Tower
东方明珠电视塔

33 Customs House
海关楼

49 Shànghǎi Zìrán Bówùguǎn
上海自然博物馆

55 Zhōngguó Gǔdài Xìng
Wénhuà Zhǎnlǎn
中国古代性文化展览

69 Shànghǎi Měishùguǎn
上海美术馆

72 Shànghǎi Bówùguǎn
上海博物馆

80 Site of 1st National
Congress of CCP
一大会址

85 ShanghART
香格纳画廊

86 Sūn Zhōngshān Gùjū
孙中山故居

139 Shànghǎi Huàyuàn
上海画院

TRANSPORT

2 Longmen Hotel
(Train Ticketing Office)
龙门饭店

3 Shànghǎi Train Station
火车站

4 Train Station (Metro);
Tourist Information Centre
火车站（地铁站）

5 Hengfeng Lu Long-
Distance Bus Station
恒丰路客运站

6 Hangzhou Lu Station
(Metro)
杭州路站

7 Xinzha Lu Station
(Metro)
新闸路站

8 Gongxing Lu Long-
Distance Bus Station
公兴路长途汽车站

13 Gongpinglu Wharf
公平路码头

14 International Ferry
Terminal
外虹桥码头

23 Train Ticket Booking
Service
火车售票处

38 Huángpǔ Jiāng Tour
Boats Dock
黄浦上游船

39 Ferries to Pǔdōng
码头（至浦东）

41 Boat Ticketing Office
船售票处

44 Shiliupu Wharf
十六铺码头

64 Renmin Square Station
(Metro);
Tourist Information Centre
人民广场站

75 Train Ticket Booking
Service
鸪笼燮贝

78 Huangpi Nanlu Station
(Metro)
黄陂南路站

SHÀNGHǍI 上海

CENTRAL SHÀNGHǍI

96 Shaanxi Nanlu Station
(Metro)
陕西南路站

111 China Eastern Airlines
(CAAC)
民航售票处

125 Changshu Lu Station
(Metro)
常熟路站

145 Hengshan Lu Station
(Metro)
衡山路站

OTHER

9 China Telecom
中国电信

10 Shanghai First People's
Hospital
上海市第一人民医院

11 Shanghai Emergency
Centre
上海市医疗急救中心

12 PSB
公安局

18 International Post Office
国际邮局

25 International Telephone;
Gino Cafe
国际长途电话;
季诺意大利餐厅

27 Bank of China;
Citibank
中国银行;
花旗银行

34 Pudong Development
Bank
浦东发展银行

40 CITS
中国国际旅行社

71 Rénmín
Guǎngchǎng
人民广场

73 China Telecom
中国电信

88 Haixing Plaza
海兴广场

89 Old China Hand
Reading Room
老汉书店

94 Huangshan Tea Company
黄山茶业公司

97 3C+T Internet Café
浦罗国际网络广场

104 JJ Dickson Centre
锦江迪生商厦

112 Shanghai Exhibition
Centre
上海展览中心

114 CITS
中国国际旅行社

127 Huashan Hospital
华山医院

131 Shanghai Library
上海图书馆

132 US Consulate
美国领事馆

SHÀNGHǍI 上海

Sūn Zhōngshān Gùjū 孙中山故居
Sun Yatsen's Residence

China is simply brimming with Sun Yatsen memorabilia, and here is one of his former residences at 7 Xianshan Lu, formerly the rue Molière. He lived here for six years, supported by overseas Chinese funds. After Sun's death, his wife, Song Qingling (1893–1981), continued to live here until 1937, constantly watched by Kuomintang plain-clothes police and French police. The two-storey house is set back from the street and furnished as it was back in Sun's days, even though it was looted by the Japanese.

The entry price of Y8 gets you a brief tour of the house. It is open daily from 9 am to 4.30 pm.

Yù Yuán Shāngchéng 豫园市场
Yu Gardens Bazaar

At the north-eastern end of the old Chinese city, the Yù Yuán Shāngchéng is one of Shànghǎi's premier sights and is well worth a visit. Try not to visit on the weekend, though, as the crowds are pressing to say the least. See the Places to Eat section for details on the bazaar's justifiably famous and delicious snacks.

The Pan family, rich Ming dynasty officials, founded the gardens. The gardens took 18 years (from 1559 to 1577) to be nurtured into existence and were snuffed out by a bombardment during the Opium War in 1842. The gardens took another trashing during French reprisals for attacks on their nearby concession by Taiping rebels. Today they have been restored and are worth visiting to see a fine example of Ming garden design. Opening hours are 8.30 am to 5 pm daily. Entry is Y15.

The **Chénghuáng Miào** (Temple of the Town Gods) and **Laǒ Jiē** (Old Street), which is known more prosaically as Fangbang Zhonglu, are recently restored attractions in the bazaar area. The temple and the street, together with the Yù Yuán Shāngchéng itself, present a rather Disneyland version of historical China. In this district more than 100 speciality shops and restaurants jostle shoulders over narrow laneways and small squares in a mock 'olde Cathay' setting. It's a great stop for lunch and also handy for souvenir shopping.

Yùfó Sì 玉佛寺
Jade Buddha Temple

The Yùfó Sì is one of Shànghǎi's few Buddhist temples. It is active and attracts large numbers of visitors – largely local and overseas Chinese tourists.

Built between 1911 and 1918, the centrepiece is a 2m-high white jade buddha around which the temple was built. The story goes that a monk from Pǔtuóshān travelled to Myanmar (Burma) via Tibet, lugged the buddha back to its present site and then went off in search of alms to build a temple for it.

This seated buddha, encrusted with jewels, is said to weigh 1000kg. A smaller buddha from the same shipment reclines on a mahogany couch.

No photography is permitted. The temple closes for lunch between noon and 1 pm, and is open daily except on special occasions such as the Lunar New Year in February, when some 20,000 Chinese Buddhists descend on the place. Admission is Y5.

The temple is in the north-west of town, near the intersection of Anyuan Lu and Jiangning Lu. One way to get there is to take the metro out to Shànghǎi train station and then walk (about 1km) or take a taxi or motor-tricycle.

Bus No 19 runs from around the corner of Shanghai Mansions, along Tiantong Lu and eventually on past the temple.

Pǔdōng Xīnqū 浦东新区
Pudong New Area

Larger than Shànghǎi itself, the Pǔdōng Xīnqū is on the eastern bank of the Huángpǔ Jiāng. Before 1990 – when development plans were first announced – Pǔdōng constituted 350 sq km of boggy farmland supplying vegetables to Shànghǎi's markets. Now the vegies are grown elsewhere as Pǔdōng has become a Special Economic Zone (SEZ).

Shànghǎi's second metro line connects Pǔdōng with Pǔxī and was opened at the end of 1999. The Wàigāoqiáo harbour area is being upgraded into a major container port and work has begun on the US$2 billion Pǔdōng airport, which will eventually supplement Hóngqiáo airport. The first international flights began relocating there in late 1999.

The gargantuan economic strides in Pǔdōng have created a vast city out of nothing, but culture was never an issue. Its purpose is the creation of wealth. The tourist will, for the most part, feel dwarfed and alienated by the scale of the place, and attractions are few and far between.

The **Oriental Pearl Tower** (Dōngfāng Míngzhū), which resembles an inverted hypodermic, is a uniquely uninspiring piece of architecture, although the views of Shànghǎi from its lookout halfway up are sensational. The drawback is that you have to queue forever to get into the high-speed elevator and the privilege costs Y50 (Y100 if you want to go to the top bauble). The nearby Jinmao Building also has an observation deck (Y50) at the 88th floor. You're better off spending your money in the coffee shop of the Grand Hyatt on the 54th floor or, even better, the Cloud Nine Bar on the 87th floor.

The **Shànghǎi Lìshǐ Bówùguǎn** (Shanghai History Museum) was in the process of relocating from Hóngqiáo to the Oriental Pearl Tower at the time of writing. The pair of bronze lions that once stood outside the Hongkong & Shanghai Bank are now housed here as well as many other artefacts from old Shànghǎi. It's worth checking out if you feel like going back in time.

Other Sights

South-west of central Shànghǎi, close to the Huángpǔ Jiāng, is the **Lónghuá Tǎ** (Longhua Pagoda). It's said to date from the 10th century and has recently been restored for tourism. The easiest way there is to take the metro to the Caobao Lu metro station, then walk or take a taxi to the pagoda from Caobao Lu, or take the metro to Xújiāhuì and take bus No 44 right to the temple.

The Xújiāhuì area, bordering the western end of Frenchtown, once had a Jesuit settlement with an observatory (which is still in use). **St Ignatius Cathedral**, whose spires were lopped off by Red Guards, has been restored and is open once again for Catholic services. It's at 158 Puxi Lu, in the Xújiāhuì district; the best way to get there is to take the metro to Xújiāhuì station, and then it's a short walk south to the church.

Further south-west of the Lónghuá Tǎ are the **Shànghǎi Zhíwùyuán** (Shanghai Botanical Gardens), which has an exquisite collection of plants, including 9000 examples of bonsai, and miniature landscapes with trees and rockery cultivated with meticulous care.

The **Shanghai Exhibition Centre** (Shànghǎi Zhǎnlǎn Zhōngxī) is south of the Shanghai Centre. Architectural buffs will appreciate the monumentality and unsubtle, bold Bolshevik strokes – there was a time when Pǔdōng was set to look like this. There are irregular displays of local industrial wares and heavy machinery.

Out near Hóngqiáo airport is **Shànghǎi Dōngwǔyuán** (Shanghai Zoo), which has a roller-skating rink, a children's playground and other recreational facilities; to get there, take the No 831 bus from Jinling Lu off the Bund (Y4) or bus No 505 from Rénmín Guǎngchǎng. To the west of the zoo is the former **Sassoon Villa** (see the boxed text 'The Cathay Hotel' later).

On the way to the town of Jiāxìng, by rail or road, is Sōngjiāng Xiàn (Songjiang County), 30km south-west of Shànghǎi. The place is older than Shànghǎi itself. On the mountain of Tiānmǎ Shān, in Sōngjiāng Xiàn, is the **Hùzhū Tǎ**, a pagoda built in AD 1079. It's the leaning tower of China, with an inclination now exceeding the tower at Pisa by 1.5°. The 19m-high tower started tilting 200 years ago. The nearby hill of Shé Shān is crowned by the beautiful **Basilica of Notre Dame**, a Catholic church completed in 1935.

Buses go to Shé Shān and Tiānmǎ Shān from the Western District bus station (xīqūzhàn) at 555 Wuzhong Lu. Bus No 113 terminates there from Shànghǎi train station. Another way to get to Shé Shān from Shànghǎi is from the Sightseeing Bus Centre (Lǚyóu Jísàn Zhōngxīn); not to be confused with the Jinjiang Hotel sightseeing bus, which is inside the west entrance of the Shanghai Stadium, at 666 Tianyaoqiao

The Chinese Circus

Circus acts in China go back 2000 years to the original Middle Kingdom. Effects are obtained using simple props such as sticks, plates, eggs and chairs. Apart from the acrobatics, there's magic, vaudeville, drama, clowning, music, conjuring, dance and mime thrown into a complete performance. Happily, it's an art that actually gained from the communist takeover and did not suffer during the Cultural Revolution. Performers used to have the status of gypsies, but now it's 'people's art'.

Most of the provinces have their own performing troupes, sponsored by government agencies, industrial complexes, the army or rural administrations. About 80 troupes are active in China and they're much in demand. You'll also see more bare legs, star-spangled costumes and rouge in one acrobat show than you'll see anywhere else in China.

Acts vary from troupe to troupe. Some traditional acts haven't changed over the centuries, while others have incorporated roller skates and motorbikes. One time-proven act that's hard to follow is the 'Balancing in Pairs', with one man balanced upside down on the head of another and mimicking every movement of the partner below, mirror image, even drinking a glass of water!

Hoop jumping is another: four hoops are stacked on top of each other and the person going through the very top hoop may attempt a backflip with a simultaneous body twist.

The 'Peacock Displaying Its Feathers' involves an array of people balanced on one bicycle. According to the Guinness Book of Records, a Shànghǎi troupe holds the record at 13 people, though apparently a Wǔhàn troupe has done 14.

The 'Pagoda of Bowls' is a balancing act where the performer, usually a woman, does everything with her torso except tie it in knots, all the while casually balancing a stack of porcelain bowls on foot, head or both – and perhaps also balancing on a partner.

Lu. Buses to Shé Shān area and its theme park leave frequently and cost Y10.

Huángpǔ Jiāng River Trip
黄浦江游览船

The Huángpǔ Jiāng offers some remarkable views of the Bund and the riverfront activity. Huángpǔ Jiāng tour boats (☎ 6374 4461) depart from the dock on the Bund, a few blocks south of the Peace Hotel, at 219-39 Zhongshan Dong Erlu. The one-hour cruise is Y25 or Y35 and takes in Yángpu Dà Qiáo (Yangpu Bridge); while the two- and 3½-hour cruises have several classes, ranging in price from Y35 to Y100. The more expensive tickets include refreshments. Depending on your enthusiasm for loading cranes, the night cruises are more scenic, though the boat traffic during the day is interesting. The 3½-hour excursion is a 60km round trip, northwards up the Huángpǔ Jiāng to the junction with the Cháng Jiāng (Yangzi River) and back again along the same route.

Departure times vary depending on which trip it is, but there are morning, afternoon and evening departures for all three categories.

Shànghǎi is one of the world's largest ports; 2000 ocean-going ships and about 15,000 river steamers load and unload here every year. The tour boat passes an enormous variety of craft – freighters, bulk carriers, roll-on roll-off ships, sculling sampans, giant praying-mantis cranes, the occasional junk and Chinese navy vessels (which aren't supposed to be photographed).

Things to See & Do

Shànghǎi has a number of art galleries, museums and exhibition sites that are worth visiting, and new venues have been appearing on the scene each year. The Liú Hǎisù Měishùguǎn (Liu Haisu Art Gallery; ☎ 6270 1018), named in honour the late Liu Haisu, a well-known artist of traditional Chinese painting, hosts both local and international exhibitions. It's located at 1660 Hongqiao Lu, in the Gǔběi area, and is open daily from 9 am to 4 pm. The Shànghǎi Huàyuàn (Shanghai Academy of Chinese Painting; ☎ 6474 9977 ext 217), at 197 Yueyang Lu, features local and western artists in its shows.

For cutting-edge works by modern Chinese artists, the place to go in Shànghǎi is ShanghART (Xiānggénà Huàlíng; ☎ 6359 3923), situated at the Gaolan Lu entrance to Fùxīng Gōngyuán. (Fùxīng Park). Opened in the late '90s by Lorenz Helbing, a Swiss art dealer, the gallery has become a much needed public arena for some of the most exciting examples of artistic expression coming out of China today. It's open daily from 10 am to 7 pm and has new shows roughly every month. Check out the gallery's Web site at www.shanghart.com.

The long-awaited opening of the new location of the Shànghǎi Měishùguǎn (Shanghai Art Museum; ☎ 6327 8593) was expected to take place in the spring of 2000. Its new premises is at 325 Nanjing Lu.

There's nothing particularly spectacular at the Shànghǎi Zìrán Bówùguǎn (Shanghai Natural History Museum; ☎ 6321 3548), though it may be of marginal interst for hard-core zoologists, taxidermists and dinosaur fans. For a more gripping display of natural history, visit the Zhōngguó Gǔdài Xìng Wénhuà Zhǎnlǎn (Museum of Chinese Sex Culture; ☎ 6351 4381). Curated by Liu Dalin a professor of sexology, the museum first opened as a temporary exhibition in 1999 but proved so popular it has remained open. Exhibits range from the sacred to the profane, and come from Professor Liu's personal collection. For anyone interested in the history of the dildo and bound feet, among other things, there's a treasure trove of interesting stuff here. The museum is open daily from 10 am to 9 pm and entry is Y30. To get there, head a few steps east of the Sofitel Hotel and go down the small alley by the Sincere Building at 479 Nanjing Donglu; the museum is on the 8th floor.

Places to Stay – Budget

Shànghǎi has some of the highest real estate values in China, and lower-end accommodation has felt the squeeze for a while now. Oversupply has brought the prices down slightly. While there are no real cheap hotels, however, there are a few that represent value for money.

Take note that budget accommodation can be swamped during the summer and on holidays, leaving you with little choice but to upgrade to pricey doubles that cost Y300 or more.

The distinguished **Pujiang Hotel** (*Pǔjiāng Fàndiàn;* ☎ 6324 6388, fax 6324 3179, 15 Huangpu Lu*) was originally called the Astor House Hotel and was Shànghǎi's first hotel. This is *the* place for those counting their shekels – it's central, has loads of style and the rooms are vast. Although the galleries upstairs look like they belong in a Victorian asylum, there's a nobility about the place that makes Y55 for a dorm bed a bargain and a half. Doubles start at Y300. From the Bund, it's a short walk across the Wàibáidù Qiáo (Garden Bridge) and Sūzhōu Creek.

The newly renovated **YMCA Hotel** (*Qīngniánhuì Bīnguǎn;* ☎ 6326 1040, fax 6320 1957, 123 Xizang Nanlu*) is another option with dormitories, and it's close to Rénmín Guǎngchǎng. Bunk beds in clean four-person rooms with bath and air-con are US$15 per bed. Rooms are more pricey, starting at US$55.

The **Foreign Students' Dormitory** (*Liúxuéshēng Lóu;* ☎ 6437 2577, 20 Fenyang Lu*), at the Shanghai Conservatory of Music, is an old stand-by with a great location off Huaihai Zhonglu. Unfortunately, it's often fully booked. Rooms with shared bath and fan are Y80 and Y200 with bath and air-con. It's a short walk from the Changshu Lu metro station. To find the rooms walk through the entrance to the conservatory and bear left.

While somewhat out of the way, the foreign student dormitory at East China Normal University also has reasonably priced rooms. The **International Exchange Service Centre** (*Guójì Jiāoliú Fúwú Zhōngxīn;* ☎ 6257 9241, fax 6257 1813, 3663 Zhongshan Beilu*) has rooms with bath and air-con for Y150. The university is located north-west of the city centre off Zhongshan Beilu. To find the foreign student building go through the main gate, cross two bridges then turn left.

In the north-east, also a little out of the way, is the excellent **Changyang Hotel** (*Chángyáng Fàndiàn;* ☎ 6543 4890, fax 6543 0986, 1800 Changyang Lu*). Doubles/triples are Y210/Y270, but push for a discount, which was as high as 50% at the time of writing. Bus No 22 from the Bund area runs right past the hotel.

Places to Stay – Mid-Range

Mid-range accommodation in Shànghǎi will cost between Y300 and Y400 for a double, but discounts can often bring these prices down to Y250 or so. If you're landing at the airport, try the Shanghai Travel Service (☎ 6268 3683), which has booths in both the international and domestic arrival halls. It has a list of hotels offering discounts.

The **Qīzhòngtiān Bīnguǎn** (*Seventh Heaven Hotel;* ☎ 6322 0777 ext 701, fax 6351 7193, 627 Nanjing Donglu*) is right in the thick of things on Nanjing Donglu, by the Hualian department store. It doesn't look like much from the outside but the interior was renovated in 1999. Small, clean singles and doubles start at Y280 and Y300. The reception is on the 7th floor. Across the street the **Dōngyà Fàndiàn** (*East Asia Hotel;* ☎ 6322 3233, fax 6322 4598, 680 Nanjing Donglu*) is more pricey and not that great. The reception is on the 2nd floor through a clothing store. Singles and doubles start at Y357.

The **Yangtze Hotel** (*Yángzǐ Fàndiàn;* ☎ 6351 7880, fax 6351 6974, 740 Hankou Lu*) is right behind the Protestant church that faces Rénmín Gōngyuán. The hotel was built back in 1934 and the exterior is largely unchanged, including the wonderful Art Nouveau balconies. Singles are good value at Y360, but doubles start at Y520.

Down near the Bund, the **Metropole Hotel** (*Xīnchéng Fàndiàn;* ☎ 6321 3030, fax 6321 7365, 180 Jiangxi Lu*) was once a grand old hotel and some of the old touches remain. Singles/doubles start at Y380/Y400, but a 30% discount is available. The deluxe rooms are in the Y580 range, but have the old polished wooden floors.

Tucked away from the fashionable districts, but close to the Bund nevertheless, the unpretentious **Dàfāng Fàndiàn** (☎ 6326 0505, fax 6311 4542, 33 Fujian Lu) is friendly and has singles/doubles for Y308/Y418, but again, 30% discounts were available, which make this quite a good deal. It's just south of the Yanan overpass, accessible by the pedestrian bridge.

Near the main post office in Hongkou, but also within walking distance of the Bund, the thirties-era **Xīnyà Dàjiǔdiàn** (New Asia Hotel; ☎ 6324 2210, 6356 6816, 422 Tiantong Lu) has singles and doubles in the US$40 to US$50 range, but discounts can also bring this price down. Extension renovations inside have taken away some of its historical feel.

The **Nányīng Fàndiàn** (☎ 6437 8188, fax 6437 8593, 1720 Huaihai Zhonglu) is in the south-western part of the city. Very comfortable doubles cost Y388 and discounts are available.

Places to Stay – Top End

Shànghǎi is virtually built up from hotels in the top-end (over Y400) category, though some of them have discounts that bring them into mid-range prices. Top-end hotels generally fall into two categories: the noble and aristocratic hotels of old Shànghǎi and the slick new towers bursting with modern amenities. Most of the hotels listed below add on a 10% or 15% service charge.

Business travellers will probably opt for modern facilities like the Portman Ritz-Carlton, Hilton or the imposing Grand Hyatt in Pǔdōng. Those with a sense of history might want to stay at one of the more urbane options, such as the Peace Hotel, where they can wrap themselves in nostalgia and fumble for the bell-pull in the middle of the night.

Interior renovations have robbed the Park Hotel, Shanghai Mansions and Jinjiang Hotel of character and history, but if there's one place left in Shànghǎi that will give you a sense of the past, it's the old Cathay, now known as the **Peace Hotel** (Hépíng Fàndiàn; ☎ 6321 6888, fax 6329 0300, 20 Nanjing Donglu), which rises up majestically from the Bund. On the ground floor of

---

The Cathay Hotel

The Peace Hotel is a ghostly reminder of the immense wealth of Victor Sassoon. From a Baghdad Jewish family, Sassoon made millions out of the opium trade and then ploughed it back into Shànghǎi real estate and horses.

Sassoon's quote of the day was 'There is only one race greater than the Jews, and that's the Derby'. His office-cum-hotel was completed in 1930 and was known as Sassoon House, incorporating the Cathay Hotel. From the top floors Victor commanded his real estate – he is estimated to have owned 1900 buildings in Shànghǎi.

Like the Taj in Bombay, the Stanley Raffles in Singapore and the Peninsula in Hong Kong, the Cathay was the place to stay in Shànghǎi. Sassoon himself resided in what is now the VIP section, which is below the green pyramidal tower, complete with Tudor panelling. He also maintained a Tudor-style villa out near Hóngqiáo airport, just west of the zoo. The likes of Noel Coward (who wrote Private Lives in the Cathay) wined and dined in the hotel's Tower Restaurant.

Back in 1949 the Kuomintang strayed into the place, awaiting the arrival of the communists. A western writer of the time records an incident in which 50 Kuomintang arrived, carrying their pots and pans, vegetables and firewood, and one soldier was overheard asking where to billet the mules. After the communists took over the city, the troops were billeted in places like the Picardie (now the Héngshān Bīnguǎn on the outskirts of the city), where they spent hours experimenting with the elevators, used bidets as face-showers and washed rice in the toilets – which was all very well until someone pulled the chain.

In 1953 foreigners tried to give the Cathay to the Chinese Communist Party in return for exit visas. The government refused at first, but finally accepted after the payment of 'back taxes'.

SHÀNGHǍI 上海

this 12-storey edifice is a sumptuous lobby, restaurants, shops, a bookshop, bank, barber, bar and rooftop cafe. Some travellers have rightly pointed out, however, that in terms of service, this hotel is way overpriced. Singles/doubles are US$120/160 and, if that's not enough, there are suites starting at US$250. The national deluxe suites (US$520) are laid out in 1930s Art Deco style to represent the concessions of the time – French, British, American and Japanese, not to mention Chinese. Across from the Peace Hotel is its annex, the older *Peace Palace Hotel (Hépíng Huìzhōng Fàndiàn;* ☎ *6329 1888, fax 6329 7979, 23 Nanjing Donglu),* which has similar rates.

Across Sūzhōu Hé from the Bund, *Shanghai Mansions (Shànghǎi Dàshà;* ☎ *6324 6260, fax 6306 5147, 20 Bei Suzhou Lu)* is another old hotel with great views. Formerly called the Broadway Mansions, this was a block of apartments used to house American officers just after WWII. Standard double rooms (no singles) start at Y850 but a 30% discount may be available

The *Park Hotel (Guójì Fàndiàn;* ☎ *6327 5225, fax 6327 6958, 170 Nanjing Xilu)* overlooks Rénmín Gōngyuán. Erected in 1934, the building is one of Shànghǎi's best examples of Art Deco architecture from the city's cultural peak. With recent renovations, however, the interior has lost all its old-world charm. Singles are US$80 and US$100, while doubles start at US$150. The rooms are quite comfortable and the service is efficient.

A couple of doors down, the *Pacific Hotel (Jīnmén Dàjiǔdiàn;* ☎ *6327 6226, fax 6372 3634, 108 Nanjing Xilu)* has a fabulously opulent foyer and is more economical than the Park Hotel. Singles start at US$55 and doubles cost US$70 to US$95.

The traditional-style *Jinjiang Hotel (Jǐnjiāng Fàndiàn;* ☎ *6258 2582, fax 6472 5588, 59 Maoming Nanlu)* underwent massive renovations in 1999. Rooms in the north building are in the Y1300 range, but it's still possible to find less expensive rooms for Y600 in the south building. The lavish *Grosvenor Villa (Guìbīn Loú),* in the southernmost part of the complex, is very

luxurious, with standard rooms for US$200. Adjacent to the older complex, the *Jinjiang Tower (Xīn Jǐnjiāng Dàjiǔdiàn;* ☎ *6433 4488, fax 6415 0045, 161 Changle Lu)* is an ugly glass skyscraper. Standard rooms start at US$210, but discounts can bring that down to US$98.

Other historical options are the *Ruijin Guesthouse (Ruìjīn Bīnguǎn;* ☎ *6472 5222, fax 6472 2277, 118 Ruijin Erlu)* and *Xingguo Hotel (Xīngguó Bīnguǎn;* ☎ *6212 9070, fax 6251 2145, 72 Xingguo Lu),* both of which have elegant grounds and separate old mansions with large rooms and suites. The Ruijin Guesthouse has singles/doubles for Y400/Y650, and suites ranging from Y1200 to Y3200. Doubles at the Xingguo Hotel start at Y680 and suites range from Y1100 to Y2000. Both hotels were offering discounts of 20% to 30%.

The newest and brightest star on the Shànghǎi hotel horizon has to be the *Grand Hyatt Hotel (Jīnmaò Kǎiyuè Dàjiǔdiàn;* ☎ *5830 3338, fax 5830 8838, 177 Lujiazui Lu).* It starts on the 54th floor of the Jinmao Building in Pǔdōng and goes up another 33 storeys. Doubles start at US$280, but nobody ever pays that much do they?

The *Pudong Shangrila (Pǔdōng Xiānggélǐlā Dàjiǔdiàn;* ☎ *6882 6888, fax 6882 0160, 33 Fucheng Lu)* doesn't quite have the height, but is equally elegant with standard singles and doubles starting at US$220 and US$240.

The *Shanghai New Asia Tomson Hotel (Shànghǎi Xīnyà Tāngchén Dàjiǔdiàn;* ☎ *5831 8888, fax 5831 7777, 777 Zhangyang Lu)* is a little more east, in the heart of Pǔdōng, near the Nextage department store. Singles and doubles start at US$180 but rooms were available for US$80 for a promotional discount.

Back across the Huángpǔ Jiāng there is a whole slew of modern five-star hotels. The *Portman Ritz-Carlton (Botèmàn Lìsī Kǎerùn Jiǔdiàn;* ☎ *6279 8888, fax 6279 8800, 1376 Nanjing Xilu)* is in the massive Shanghai Centre. Rooms start at US$230. The elegant Japanese-run *Garden Hotel (Huāyuán Fandiàn;* ☎ *6415 1111, fax 6415 8866, 58 Maoming Lu)* has similar rates and nicer grounds: on the site of the old French Club, across from the Jinjiang Hotel.

The *Regal International East Asia Hotel* (Fùháo Huánqiú Dōngyà Jiǔdiàn; ☎ 6415 5588, fax 6445 8899, 516 Hengshan Lu) is another new five-star addition to Shànghǎi's hotel scene. Rooms start at US$200, but have been discounted as low as US$90. Similarly, the *Hilton Hotel* (Jìng'ān Xī Ěrdùn Jiǔdiàn; ☎ 6248 0000, fax 6248 3848, 250 Huashan Lu) has rooms starting at US$230, but were offering 50% discounts.

The former Sheraton and first 'modern' hotel to appear in Shànghǎi in 1987, has now been handed over completely to local management. The *Huating Hotel and Towers* (Huátíng Bīnguǎn; ☎ 6439 1000, fax 6255 0830, 1200 Caoxi Beilu) has singles/doubles starting at US$215/US$235. Likewise, what used to be the Holiday Inn is now known only as the *Crowne-Plaza Shanghai* (Yínxīng Huángguǎn Jiǔdiàn; ☎ 6280 8888, fax 6280 3353, 388 Panyu Lu). Rooms start at US$210, but 50% discounts are available.

There's a cluster of hotels in Hóngqiáo, including the elegant *Westin Taipingyang* (Wēisītīng Tàipíngyáng; ☎ 6275 8888, fax 6275 5420, 5 Zunyi Nanlu). Standard rooms are US$210, but it was offering rates slashed more than 50%. At the other end of town near the Bund, the *Sofitel Hyland Hotel* (Hǎilún Bīnguǎn; ☎ 6351 5888, fax 6351 4088, 505 Nanjing Donglu) has rooms starting at US$190, with more than a 50% discount off these prices available.

Discounts on some of the locally-run four-star hotels with prime locations are good value. The *Héngshān Bīnguǎn* (☎ 6437 7050, fax 6433 5732, 534 Hengshan Lu) is overpriced at Y902 for a double, but worthwhile when rooms are discounted to Y580. The same goes for the *City Hotel* (Chéngshì Jiǔdiàn; ☎ 6255 1133, fax 6255 0211, 5-7 Shanxi Nanlu), which has rooms starting at Y980 discounted to more than 50% for Y380.

Places to Eat

Like everything else in Shànghǎi, the restaurant industry has witnessed an upheaval over the last five years. Keep your eyes open for the new restaurants that are springing up with increasing frequency. The side streets around town all feature small restaurants serving cheap, local food.

Also look out for Shànghǎi's favourite dumpling, *xiǎolóngbāo*, which is copied everywhere else in China, but is only true to form here. For Y5, you should get a steamer with four of these. They are wonderful, but there's an art to eating them – they're full of scalding oil. In the Bund area, Sichuan Zhonglu is a good place to look, as are the side streets in the old French Concession.

The Bund Area & Nanjing Lu For cheap eats near the Pujiang Hotel try the Zhapu Lu food street for all kinds of eats. Ask for *xiǎolóngbāo*.

Near the Bund itself there are a number of restaurants catering to local tourists, and none of them is very good. A new development, however, is the number of elegant western restaurants staking out territory along the famous skyline. For the latest trends in international cuisine, Michelle Garnaut has taken her renowned skills to create *M on the Bund* (Mǐshì Xīcāntīng; ☎ 6350 9988, 20 Guangdong Lu), on the 7th floor of the Huaxia Bank. There's a magnificent terrace view of the Bund and if you don't feel like dinner, it's worth having a drink at least.

The *50 Hankou Road Bar & Restaurant* (Hànkǒu Lù Wǔshí Hào; ☎ 6323 8383, 50 Hankou Lu) serves up hearty western meals in an eclectic atmosphere. For good, if somewhat overpriced, generic Chinese food, the *Dragon-Phoenix Hall* (Lóngfèng Tīng; ☎ 6321 6888, 20 Nanjing Lu), on the 8th floor of the Peace Hotel, comes with superb views and unpretentious service.

On Fuzhou Lu, the *Xìnghuā Lóu* (☎ 6355 3777, 343 Fuzhou Lu) serves quality dim sum and was established in the reign the Qing emperor who ruled from 1851 to 1861.

Nanjing Donglu is not what it used to be when it comes to restaurants, and many of the old establishments have moved; *Shěndàchéng* (☎ 6322 5615, 636 Nanjing

SHÀNGHǍI 上海

Donglu) still clings to the corner of Zhejiang Zhonglu and Nanjing Donglu, opposite the Dōngyà Fàndiàn; it serves up Shànghǎi snacks and dumplings.

Yù Yuán Shāngchéng Area If for no other reason than you are hungry, it is worth heading down to the Yù Yuán Shāngchéng (Yù Yuán Bazaar) for the excellent snack food that ranks among the best in China.

These snacks are available in the big-name Yù Yuán Shāngchéng restaurants such as the *Shànghǎi Lǎo Fàndiàn* (*Old Shanghai Restaurant; ☎ 6328 2782, 242 Fuyou Lu*), which is located on the south side of the street opposite the Shanghai Tourist Shopping Emporium, near the entrance of the Yù Yuán Shāngchéng; and the *Green Wave Gallery* (*Lǜbōláng Cāntīng; ☎ 6328 0602, 115 Yuyuan Lu*), which is on the south side of the pond. These places tend to charge extortionate amounts for food that is only marginally better than the stuff served downstairs by street vendors. There's one advantage: they do have English menus.

Certain stalls are famed for a particular snack, and these inevitably have long queues snaking from the counters, such as the *Nánxiáng Mántoúdiàn* (*Nanxiang Steamed Bun Restaurant; ☎ 6326 5265, 87 Yuyuan Lu*), which is on the east side of the pond, opposite the Húxīntíng teahouse.

Old French Concession Area This area is rapidly emerging as the best part of town for places to eat, with a wide variety of food styles to suit every pocket.

For good, reasonable Chinese *Yang's Kitchen* (*Yángjiā Chúfáng; ☎ 6431 3028, 3 Nong 9, Hengshan Lu*) can't be beat. The *níngfēngmì jiānruǎnjī* (lemon chicken) is delicious and the *roùmò qiéguā jiābǐng* (stewed eggplant with pork mince), that you roll up in little pancakes, is out of this world. It's down a small lane at 9 Hengshan Lu.

One of the most enduring private Chinese restaurants from the 1980s, the reliable *Grape Restaurant* (*Pútáo Yuán; ☎ 6472 0486, 55 Xinle Lu*) still packs in the crowds in its premises beside the old Orthodox church by Xiangyang Lu. Further down

Xinle Lu, *Henry's Restaurant* (*Hēnglì Cāntīng; ☎ 6473 3448, 8 Xinle Lu*) also serves Shanghaiese-style food in a retro 1920s atmosphere.

Western-style restaurants abound, especially around Hengshan Lu. Ensconced in a house that was once part of the Soong family complex, *Sashas* (*Sàshā Cāntīng; ☎ 6474 6166, 9 Dongping Lu*) has a great outside barbecue. The bar-cum-restaurant *Badlands* (*Bǎigǎng Cāntīng; ☎ 6466 7788, 895 Julu Lu*) is an old favourite for good-value nachos, tacos and burritos. For reasonable and authentic American breakfasts, try *Kevin's Café* (*Kǎiwén Kāfēi; 525 Hengshan Lu*).

If you're looking for fashionable people and food, *Park 97* (*Paìkè Cānguǎn; ☎ 6318 0785, 2 Gaolan Lu*) at the entrance to Fùxīng Gōngyuán, is the Shànghǎi incarnation of Hong Kong's 1997 Group. It also has a popular Spanish tapas bar called *Lava*. For a more sedate atmosphere and French cuisine, *Le Garcon Chinois* (*Lè Jiā'ěrsōng Cāntīng; ☎ 6431 3005*) is a nicely renovated house and yard tucked in the lane on the way to Yang's Kitchen. The cakes baked on the premises are especially good, along with the coffee.

Shànghǎi has a lot of Italian restaurants. One of the best, according to those in the know, is *Da Marco* (*Mǎkè Cāntīng; ☎ 6210 4495, Jīnqiáo Huāyuán (Golden Bridge Garden), 103 Dong Zhu An Bang Lu*), somewhat removed from the former French Concession area proper. Next door, *Pizza Italia* (*Yìdàlì Bǐsà; ☎ 6226 6137*) is said to have the best pizza in Shànghǎi, no small accomplishment, and the best prices, at Y10 a slice or Y40 for a 12-inch pizza. Bus No 44 from Xújiāhuì takes you relatively close. Get off at the intersection of Yuyuan Lu and Jiangsu Lu. Bus No 20 takes you to the same place from the Bund.

For cheap, reasonable, no-frills Italian, *Pasta Fresca Da Salvatore* (*Shāhúadūolì Yìdàlì Miànshì; ☎ 6473 0772*) has a number of outlets in Shànghǎi, but the one at 4 Hengshan Lu is conveniently located by the metro station.

Shànghǎi also has a growing number of Asian restaurants. Everyone raves about

Simply Thai (Tiāntài Cāntīng; ☎ 6445 9551, 5-C Dongping Lu) for it's delicious, inexpensive dishes. Next door, *Ali Y Y (Ā' Jiàn Cāntīng; ☎ 6415 4191)* serves up cheap Xīnjiāng-style food such as kebabs, noodles and unleavened bread.

Indian restaurants are slowly establishing themselves, in the footsteps of the *Tandoor Indian Restaurant* (Yìndù Cāntīng; ☎ 6472 5494) found in the south arcade of the Jinjiang Hotel. Both the food and decor are excellent, if a little pricey. The *Hazara* (☎ 6466 4328), also known as *Face*, in the Ruijin Guesthouse, gets rave reviews.

For a friendly atmosphere and Malaysian-style Chinese food, try *Frankie's Place* (Fǎlánqí Cāntīng; ☎ 6247 0886, 118 Changde Lu), a little outside the former French Concession area, near the Shanghai Centre.

There are too many Japanese restaurants in Shànghǎi to list here, but one of the best is *Ooedo* (Dà Jiānghù; ☎ 6467 3332, 30 Donghu Lu), which offers a delicious all-you-can-eat sushi buffet and other dishes for Y200. At the other end of the buffet spectrum, sushi and other snacks of the conveyor-belt variety are served up for Y58 per person by the two outlets of *Ganki Sushi*, located at 29 Dongping Lu and 668 Huaihai Lu.

Vegetarian Food Vegetarianism became something of a snobbish fad in Shànghǎi at one time; it was linked to Taoist and Buddhist groups, then to the underworld, and surfaced on the tables of restaurants as creations shaped like flowers or animals.

Khi Vehdu, who ran the Jìng'ān Sì (Temple of Quiet Tranquillity) in the 1930s, was one of the most celebrated exponents. The nearly 2m-tall abbot had a large following and each of his seven concubines had a house and a car. The Jing'an Temple was eventually divested of its Buddhist statues and turned into a factory.

The *Gōngdélín Shūshíchù* (Gōngdélín Vegetarian Restaurant; ☎ 6327 0218, 445 Nanjing Xilu) is probably Shànghǎi's most famous vegetarian restaurant. All the food is designed to resemble meat, and is convincingly prepared. It is open until midnight.

The food and atmosphere are well worth exploring, even if you are not a vegetarian.

The *Juélín Shūshíchù* (☎ 6326 0115, 250 Jinling Donglu) is another vegetarian restaurant. It closes early at 7.30 pm. Lunch runs from 11 am to 1.30 pm.

If you're visiting the Yùfó Sì, you can also have a vegetarian lunch there.

Tea & Coffee Houses Shànghǎi is one of the best places in China to find some quiet place to sip coffee or tea and write a letter or just relax. One of the nicest places is *Cafe 1931* (Yijiǔsānyī Bā; ☎ 6472 5264, 112 Maoming Lu), a small cafe outfitted with a 1930s theme, serving coffee, tea and small meals. If you're trekking through the city and need some refreshment, look for *Gino Café* (Jìnuò Yìdàlì Cāntīng), which has grown to have six branches in the city. There's a useful one down near the Peace Hotel, at 66 Nanjing Donglu.

There are also a number of Taiwanese-style teahouses around town. One of the most famous is *Harn Sheh* (Hánshè Cháfāng), which features a cornucopia of bizarre and delicious beverages. Its branch at 10 Hengshan Lu is called *Fragrant Camphor Garden* (Xiāngzhāng Huāyuán) and is a nice place to relax.

At the Yù Yuán, one of the best places to sit and look over the mob below is in the ornate *Húxīntíng* (Mid-Lake Pavilion Teahouse. It's open daily from 8.30 am to 10 pm.

Entertainment

Shànghǎi is emerging as the most spiritually polluted city in China. All the old evils are creeping back with a vengeance. Over the last couple of years there's been an explosion of nightlife options, with everything from the incredibly sleazy to the marginally chic. None of it comes cheaply, however. A night on the town in Shànghǎi is comparable to a night out in Hong Kong or Taipei.

Bars & Clubs There's a lot to choose from in Shànghǎi's scene, and venues open and close all the time. Check out the Shànghǎi entertainment magazines for guidance. One thing stays the same, however; drinks at

SHÀNGHǍI 上海

most of the popular bars in Shànghǎi are expensive, so if you're looking to save money, have a few stiff ones at the local corner stall before venturing in.

The *Hard Rock Café* (*Yìngshí Jùlèbù;* ☎ 6279 8133), outside the Shanghai Centre, offers all the usuals – buffalo wings, barbecue ribs and BLT sandwiches, all to a backdrop of live bands and music memorabilia. Close by, *Malone's American Café* (*Mǎlóng Měishì Jiǔlóu;* ☎ 6247 2400, 257 Tongren Lu*) is popular. It also serves breakfast.

Three bars in Shànghǎi brew their own beer. *Fest Brew House* (*Wàitān Píjiǔ Zǒngtuì;* ☎ 6321 8447, 11 Hankou Lu*) is a pleasant place down near the Bund. A few blocks up Nanjing Lu you can also enjoy good beer at the *Hyland 505 Brauhaus*, in the Sofitel Hotel. The *Paulaner Bauhaus* (*Bǎoláinà Cāntīng;* ☎ 6474 5700, 150 Fengyang Lu*) is the grand master of the Shànghǎi microbreweries. A pint of wheat beer will also set you back about Y80.

Although it doesn't brew its own, *O'Malley's* (*Oūmǎlì Jiǔbā;* ☎ 6474 4533, 42 Taojiang Lu*) brought up the standards of beer drinking considerably when it introduced draught Guinness and Kilkenny beers to Shànghǎi residents. It still remains one of the most popular places to hang out, either on the large lawn in good weather, or inside within the old world pub atmosphere.

In a different vein altogether is the *Jurassic Pub* (*Kǒnglóng Shìjiè;* ☎ 6258 3758, 8 Maoming Nanlu*), a dinosaur theme bar, complete with an over-arching brontosaurus skeleton, live squawking parrots and dino-skull urinals in the gents. For the cigar and martini set, try *Goya's* (*Gēyǎ Jiǔbā;* ☎ 6280 1256, 359 Xinhua Lu*), near the Crowne-Plaza Hotel.

One of the best bars for live music is the *Cotton Club* (*Miánhuā Jùlèbù;* ☎ 6437 7110, 1428 Huaihai Lu*), a comfortable, unassuming place that mostly features blues bands. The *Peace Hotel bar* features an ancient jazz band that has been strumming since time immemorial, but it's doubtful whether it's worth the Y42 cover charge.

Shànghǎi has a few venues that cater to gay patrons, but as elsewhere in China, it's wise to be discreet. Men or women, gay or straight, are welcome at the places listed below. *Eddy's Bar* (*Xiāngxīn Jiǔbā; 860 Nanjing Lu*) is a friendly place patronised by a mix of young professionals, expats and Asians from neighbouring countries. Look for the red sign at the entrance to the alley. The *101 Bar* (*Xīngzuò Jiǔbā;* ☎ 5404 7719, 98 Xinle Lu*) is a discreet place that has recently opened. For dancing, try the *JBL Dance Pub* (*Nándān Xìnxǐ;* ☎ 6427 1337, 256 Nandan Donglu*) in Xújiāhuì.

Discos Shànghǎi is beginning to pull in some top-notch DJs from abroad and there are a lot of popular dance venues. The dance floor starts pumping after midnight in the basement at *YY's* (*Yīngyáng;* ☎ 6431 2668, 125 Nanchang Lu*), or you can enjoy a drink in the tasteful bar upstairs. Two larger places popular with local clubbers that are worth trying are *Rojam Disco* (*Lúojiānmǔ Yúlègōng;* ☎ 6390 7181, 4th floor, Hong Kong Plaza, 283 Huaihai Zhonglu*) and *Real Love* (*Zhēn'ài Jiǔbā* ☎ 6473 3182, 10 Hengshan Lu*).

Down by the Bund, *New York New York* (*Niǔyūe Dísīkè;* ☎ 6321 6097, 146 Huqiu Lu*), located in an old movie theatre, has faded somewhat since the heady days of the mid-1990s, but it's still worth a look. A bar during the weekdays, *Judy's Too* (*Júdí Jiǔbā;* ☎ 6473 1417, 176 Maoming Nanlu*) is insanely crowded on the weekends and is usually a lot of fun.

Performing Arts Along with Běijīng, Shànghǎi is one of the great cultural centres of China. Unfortunately, Běijīng and Cantonese opera and Chinese drama (which is often an extravagant display of costumes, make-up and acrobatics) are almost exclusively delivered in Chinese and therefore inaccessible to most foreigners.

Traditional Chinese drama and opera and interpretations of western opera, ballet and theatre are presented by such establishments as the *Shanghai Opera House* (*Shànghǎi Gējù Yuàn*), the *Shanghai Ballet Troupe* (*Shànghǎi Bālěiwǔ Tuán*) and the *Shanghai Theatre Academy* (*Shànghǎi*

Xìjù Xuéyuàn). Classical music is performed by the *Shanghai Symphony Orchestra (Shànghǎi Jiāoxiǎng Yùetuán)* as well as visiting orchestras and local chamber groups. Look for what's playing at the new *Shanghai Grand Theatre (Shànghǎi Dà Jùyùan; ☎ 6372 8701),* in Rénmín Guǎngchǎng, which features both national and international opera and theatre. Ticket prices start at Y120.

For cheaper, if less sophisticated fare, check out the *Great World (Shànghǎi Dà Shìjìe; ☎ 6326 3760, 1 Xizang Zhonglu),* the wedding cake building near Rénmín Guǎngchǎng (at the Yanan Lu intersection), which was once the famous and salacious Great World in pre-1949 Shànghǎi. There's a potpourri of performances available on different stages: opera, acrobatics and magic, but no strip shows yet.

The *Conservatory of Music (Yīnyuè Xuéyuàn; ☎ 6437 2577),* at 20 Fenyang Lu off Huaihai Zhonglu in Frenchtown, often has classical music performances. Chamber music is also played weekly at the *Jing An Hotel (☎ 6248 1888, 370 Huashan Lu),* located next to the Hilton Hotel

Cinemas Foreign movies are generally dubbed into Chinese and Chinese movies very rarely have English subtitles but there are exceptions at the multiplexes *Golden Cinema Haixing (Jīahúa Hǎixīng Yǐngchéng; ☎ 6418 7034, Haixing Plaza, 1 Ruijin Nanlu)* and *Studio City (Huányì Diànyǐng Chéng; ☎ 6218 2173, Westgate Mall, 1038 Nanjing Xilu).* Some of the bars, such as Judy's Too, also have movie showings.

Acrobatics Chinese acrobatic troupes are among the best in the world, and Shànghǎi is a good place to see a performance. The *Shanghai Acrobatics Troupe (Shànghǎi Zájì Tuán)* has performances at the Shanghai Centre (☎ 6279 8663) every night at 7.30 pm. Tickets sell for around Y60. Acrobatic shows can also be seen at *Lyceum Theatre (Lánxīn jùyùan; ☎ 6217 8530, 57 Maoming Nanlu),* an old Shànghǎi theatre across from the Jinjiang Hotel.

Shopping

Shànghǎi offers a plethora of choice for the shopper: all Chinese products and popular souvenirs find their way here. The city is catching up with commercial centres like Hong Kong, but it still has a long way to go. The traditional shopping streets were always Nanjing Lu and Huaihai Lu, but now it seems almost every side street is full of boutiques and shops.

Department Stores Shànghǎi has some of the best department stores in China, including the flashy western and Japanese-style outlets that are probably of more interest to Shànghǎi residents than to visitors. On the other hand, if you can find your size, there are sometimes good fashion deals in some of the department stores.

The *Hualian department store (Húalían Shāngshà),* formerly called No 10, and before that Wing On, at 635 Nanjing Donglu, and the *No 1 department store (Dìyī Bǎihùo Shāngdiàn),* at 830 Nanjing Donglu, are fascinating places to browse in if you can stand the crowds.

Asia's largest department store is *Nextage (Xīnshìjì Shāngshà),* which is second in size only to Macy's, on the corner of Pudong Lu and Zhangyang Lu in Pǔdōng. There are 150 retail outlets selling from 100,000 sq metres of floor space to countless customers.

Finally, the *Friendship Store* is a great place to pick up last-minute souvenirs, and the lack of crowds make it a pleasant place to browse at your leisure. It's located on Beijing Xilu, near Sūzhōu Creek.

Supermarkets & Pharmacies If you're craving anything from home or need western pharmaceutical items, the best place to stock up is the Shanghai Centre. The former Wellcome supermarket is now called *The Market* and is packed with imported biscuits, chocolates, pasta, cheeses and beverages. There's also a *Park 'n' Shop* in the basement of the Parkson department store, on the corner of Huaihai Lu and Shanxi Nanlu. The French chain *Carrefour (Jīalèfú)* also has branches in Gǔběi and Pǔdōng, but generally you can find most things in the growing number of Shànghǎi's local supermarkets.

Also in the Shanghai Centre is a branch of **Watson's** (*Qūchénshì*), a pharmacy with cosmetics, over-the-counter medicines and health products. Watson's has another branch just down from the Cathay Theatre, on Huaihai Zhonglu. Neither of these places is cheap – prices are similar to those you would pay in Hong Kong.

Photographic Supplies For photographic supplies, check the shops in the major hotels. Shànghǎi is one of the few places in China where slide film is readily available. Shànghǎi's foremost photographic supplies shop is **Guànlóng**, at 190 Nanjing Donglu, where you can also get slide film.

Porcelain The best place to find decent porcelain is the Shànghǎi Bówùguǎn. The shop there sells imitations of the pieces displayed in the Zande Lou Gallery (within the Shànghǎi Bówùguǎn); the imitations are fine specimens and far superior to the mediocre pieces you see in the tourist shops. However, be prepared to pay a hefty whack.

There's a variety of more prosaic porcelain for sale at the **Jingdezhen Porcelain Artware Shop** (*Jǐngdézhèn Cíqì Diàn*) on the corner of Nanjing-Xilu and Shanxi Nanlu. They also have pricey speciality items as well.

The Yù Yuán Shāngchéng is also a good place to rummage around in the hope you might find a gem or two; if you are hunting for rare pieces, you will not need reminding that the market is flooded with fakes.

Souvenirs & Antiques On the arts and crafts, souvenirs and antiques front, one of the best places to go is the Yù Yuán Shāngchéng. There are a number of shops here selling ceramics, 'antique' posters, pocket watches, paintings and a host of other collectibles. Haggle hard as it's all overpriced – if you wander around you will see the same stuff at a variety of prices which means a lot of it is fake.

Expensive alternatives are the designated tourist shops, which are for the large part haggle-free zones. Their range is good, but again, there's a lot of rubbish so you need a shrewd eye if you don't want to pay too much over the **Shanghai Tourist Shopping Emporium** (*Shànghǎi Lǚyóu Gòuwù Shāngchéng*) at 239 Fuyou Lu (in the Yù Yuán Shāngchéng area); another is the **Shanghai Antique and Curio Store** (*Shànghǎi Wénwù Shāngdiàn;* ☎ 6321 2864), at 192–246 Guangdong Lu. You can also try the various antique stalls on Dongtai Lu, a block west of Xizang Nanlu and on Fangbang Lu (dolled up as Shànghǎi's 'old street'), near the Yù Yuán Shāngchéng.

Tea & Teapots Tea and the dainty teapots and cups used by the Chinese make excellent gifts, and Shànghǎi is a good place to buy them. The Yù Yuán Shāngchéng is one of the best places in Shànghǎi to make purchases. Otherwise, look out for the exclusive **Shanghai Huangshan Tea Company** (*Shànghǎi Huángshān Cháyè Gōngsī*) at 853 Huaihai Zhonglu. Prices can be surprisingly reasonable. Yíxīng ware, the most valued of all Chinese teapots, is available here.

Clothing & Shoes Tall people may have difficulty finding large sizes in Shànghǎi, but it's a shopping paradise for smaller folks. The **market** on Huating Lu, off Huaihai Lu near the intersection with Changshu Lu, is open during the day and is packed with people and stalls selling cheap clothes. Try Maoming Lu and Shanxi Nanlu for various boutiques, as well as Nanjing Lu and Huaihai Lu of course. Shanxi Nanlu north of Huaihai Lu is packed with small shoe stores and good prices.

Outdoor Gear Some of the department stores, street markets and sporting goods stores have backpacks and sleeping bags, though you'll have to search a bit to find good hiking boots. Try **Sport City**, on the 5th floor of the Westgate Mall at 1038 Nanjing Xilu, for outdoor gear.

If you're bicycling through Shànghǎi and need that crucial missing part, call the **YMCA Bike Shop** (*Qīngnián Chēháng*), also known as **Wolf's Mountain Bike Club**

(☎ 1380 195 3000), at 485 Yongjia Lu, between Yueyang and Taiyuan Lu.

Getting There & Away

Shànghǎi has rail and air connections to places all over China, ferries travelling up the Cháng Jiāng (Yangzi River), many boats along the coast, and buses to destinations in adjoining provinces.

Air Civil Aviation Administration of China (CAAC; Zhōngguó Mínháng) international destinations include Bangkok, Brussels, Hong Kong, London, Los Angeles, Madrid, Munich, Nagasaki, Nagoya, New York, Osaka, Paris, San Francisco, Singapore, Sydney, Tokyo, Toronto and Vancouver. Dragonair also flies between Shànghǎi and Hong Kong (Y1320). Northwest Airlines and United Airlines fly to the USA; Canadian Airlines International can get you to Canada; and Qantas Airways can fly you to Australia. Virgin Atlantic opened up a direct flight to London in 1999. International departure tax is Y90.

Daily (usually several times daily) domestic flights connect Shànghǎi to every major city in China. Prices include Běijīng (Y900), Guǎngzhōu (Y1020) and Guìlín (Y1040). Minor cities are less likely to have daily flights, but the chances are there will be at least one flight a week, probably more, to Shànghǎi. The domestic departure tax is Y50.

China Eastern Airlines' main office (☎ 6247 5953 for domestic, ☎ 6247 2255 for international) is at 200 Yan'an Zhonglu, and is open 24 hours a day. There are also ticket sales counters at most of the major hotels around town and at the main CITS office in the Guangming Building. The following airlines have offices in Shànghǎi.

Aeroflot (☎ 6415 6936) East Lake Hotel, Donghu Lu
Air France (☎ 6360 6688) Room 1301, Novel Plaza, 128 Nanjing Xilu
All Nippon Airways (☎ 6279 7000) 2nd floor, East Wing, Shanghai Centre, 1376 Nanjing Xilu
Canadian Airlines International (☎ 6375 8899) Suite 702, Central Plaza, Huangpi Beilu
Dragonair (☎ 6279 8099) Room 202, 2nd floor, Shanghai Centre, 1376 Nanjing Xilu

Japan Airlines (☎ 6472 3000) 2nd floor, Ruijin Building, 205 Maoming Lu
Korean Air (☎ 6275 6000) 1st floor, Office Tower, Yangtze Hotel, 2099 Yanan Xilu
Lufthansa Airlines (☎ 6248 1100) Shanghai Hilton Hotel, 250 Huashan Lu
Malaysia Airlines (☎ 6279 8657) Suite 209, East Wing, Shanghai Centre, 1376 Nanjing Xilu
Northwest Airlines (☎ 6279 8009) Suite 204, Level 2, East Building, Shanghai Centre, 1376 Nanjing Xilu
Qantas Airways (☎ 6279 8660) Suite 203A, West Wing, Shanghai Centre, 1376 Nanjing Xilu
Singapore Airlines (☎ 6279 8000) Room 208, East Wing, Shanghai Centre, 1376 Nanjing Xilu
Thai Airways International (☎ 6279 7170) 2nd floor, West Building, Shanghai Centre, 1376 Nanjing Xilu
United Airlines (☎ 6279 8010) Suite 204, West Building, Shanghai Centre, 1376 Nanjing Xilu
Virgin Atlantic (☎ 5353 4600) Room 221-23, 12 Zhongshan Dong Yilu

Bus There are a few long-distance bus stations in Shànghǎi but the most useful for the traveller is probably the one on the corner of Hutai Lu and Zhongshan Beilu, north of Shànghǎi train station. Deluxe buses leave for Hángzhōu (Y54; two hours), Sūzhōu (Y28; one hour), Nánjīng (Y87; 31 hours), Shàoxīng (Y70; three hours) and Níngbō (Y96; four hours). Buses also leave from 270 Hengfeng Lu for the above destinations, which is within walking distance of the Hanzhong Lu metro station. Buses to Sūzhōu and Hángzhōu also leave from the parking lot directly in front of the domestic arrival hall at the airport.

There are four buses a day to Zhōuzhuāng (Y18; one hour), but you have to go to the bus station at 80 Gongxing Lu, near Shànghǎi's old train station. Bus No 65 from the Bund passes nearby. Buses to Zhōuzhuāng also leave from the Sightseeing Bus Centre near the west entrance to the Shànghǎi Stadium, at 666 Tianyaoqiao Lu. Tickets are Y22.

Train Shànghǎi is at the junction of the Běijīng-Shànghǎi and Běijīng-Hángzhōu train lines. Since these branch off in various

SHÀNGHĂI 上海

directions, many parts of the country can be reached by direct train from Shànghǎi. The problem is getting hold of tickets.

There are many options for buying train tickets in Shànghǎi. At Shànghǎi train station, the easiest is the counter in the soft seat waiting room for current and next day tickets. It's open from 7 am to 9 pm, with breaks for lunch and dinner. Another convenient place is at the Longmen Hotel, a short walk west of Shànghǎi train station. You can book sleepers up to four days in advance and there's a Y5 service charge.

In town, CITS books tickets for a Y10 service charge. You can also book train tickets across the street at 1 Jinling Donglu (Y5 service charge). Train ticket outlets are at also at 230 Beijing Donglu and 121 Xizang Nanlu, and are open daily from 7.30 am to 5 pm.

Most trains depart and arrive at Shànghǎi train station (Shànghǎi zhàn; see the Central Shànghǎi map), but some depart and arrive at the west train station (xī zhàn; see the Shànghǎi Municipality map). Be sure to find out which one you should leave from. Trains to Hángzhōu also leave from Meilong station, behind the Hongmei Lu metro station in the southwest suburbs, and take one hour and 40 minutes.

Travel times from Shànghǎi are: Běijīng (15 hours), Fúzhōu (21 hours), Guǎngzhōu (26 hours), Guìlín (31 hours), Hángzhōu (two hours), Huángshān (12 hours), Kūnmíng (56 hours), Nánjīng (three hours), Qīngdǎo (20 hours) and Xī'ān (24 hours).

There are special double-decker 'tourist trains' operating between Shànghǎi and Hángzhōu, and Shànghǎi and Nánjīng (with stops at Wúxī, Sūzhōu, Hángzhōu and Zhènjiāng). They are all comfortable softseat trains and smoking is forbidden; attendants bring around drinks and food and, if you're going to Hángzhōu or Nánjīng, it is even possible to book your hotel room aboard the train.

Boat Boats are definitely one of the best ways of leaving Shànghǎi and they're often also the cheapest. For destinations on the coast or inland on the Cháng Jiāng (Yangzi River), they may even sometimes be faster than trains, which have to take rather circuitous routes. Smaller, grottier boats handle numerous inland shipping routes.

Boat tickets can be bought from CITS, which charges a commission, or from the ticket office at 1 Jinling Donglu, so it's best to compare prices before you fork out to CITS. You can also buy boat tickets at the Shiliupu Wharf, 111 Zhongshan Dong Erlu, on the Bund.

Weekly ferries to Inchon in Korea and twice a week boats to Osaka and Kobe in Japan depart from the international passenger terminal to the east of Shanghai Mansions, at 1 Taiping Lu. Passengers are requested to be at the harbour three hours before departure. Tickets can be bought from CITS or from the 2nd floor ticket office at 1 Jinling Donglu. Tickets to Korea (46 hours) range from Y750 to VIP cabins for Y2500. Tickets to Japan (45 hours) range from Y1300 to Y6500.

Boats to Pǔtuóshān (12 hours) depart every day at 6 pm. Tickets cost Y38 to Y269, depending on the class. A five-hour rapid ferry service also has buses departing daily at 8 am and 10.50 am from Shiliupu Wharf and costs Y153 or Y180 deluxe. It's roughly a two-hour bus ride to the wharf and then a three-hour boat ride.

The main destinations of ferries up the Cháng Jiāng from Shànghǎi are Nántōng, Nánjīng, Wúhú, Guìchí, Jiǔjiuāng and Wǔhàn. From Wǔhàn you can change to another ferry that will take you to Chóngqìng. If you're only going as far west as Nánjīng, take the train, which is much faster than the boat. Daily departures are from Shiliupu Wharf. (For full details on Cháng Jiāng cruises, see the Chóngqìng chapter.)

If money is more important than time, the most sensible way to head west from Shànghǎi is along the river. Wǔhàn, for example, is over 1500km by rail from Shànghǎi. For about half the hard-sleeper train fare you can get a berth in 4th class on the boat. For a bit more than a hard-sleeper ticket on a train you'd probably be able to get a bed in a two-person cabin on the boat.

There are also daily boats to Dàlián (36 hours) with tickets ranging from Y133 to

Y340. Boats to Qīngdǎo leave roughly five times a week, but check with the Jingling Lu office. The trip takes about 26 hours and tickets cost between Y151 and Y231.

Getting Around

Shànghǎi is not a walker's dream. There are some fascinating areas to stroll around, but new road developments, building sites and shocking traffic conditions conspire to make walking an exhausting and often stressful experience.

The buses, too, are hard work; they're not easy to figure out, and difficult to squeeze into and out of, though things have improved with some of the routes offering deluxe air-con vehicles (Y2). The metro system, on the other hand, is a dream. The No 1 line does a north-south sprint through central Shànghǎi while the newer No 2 line runs from Zhōngshān Gōngyuán (Sun Yatsen Park), along Nanjing Lu and across to Pǔdōng. Tickets are between Y3 and Y4 depending on the distance. A light rail system running from Shànghǎi's south train station towards Fudan University is scheduled to open in the near future. Travellers with money to spare can at least hop into a taxi.

To/From the Airport Hóngqiáo Airport (☎ 6268 8899) is 18km from the Bund and getting there takes about 30 minutes if you're lucky, or over an hour if you're not. You can get bus No 505 from Rénmín Guǎngchǎng all the way to the airport, or No 911 (double-decker) from Huaihai Zhonglu.

Bus No 831 also speeds to the airport from Jinling Lu, just off the Bund. There is a bus from the CAAC office on Yan'an Lu to the airport. Tickets are Y5 and it is directly in front of the domestic arrival hall. Major hotels like the Jinjiang have an airport shuttle. Taxis from the centre of town cost approximately Y50, depending on the kind of taxi, the route taken and the traffic conditions.

At the time of writing, the new international airport in Pǔdōng (☎ 3848 4500) was not yet completed, but expect most non-Chinese international airlines to be arriving there by the time you read this. Just to be sure, however, check your ticket. Bus No 1

(Y18) runs between Hóngqiáo and Pǔdōng airports, bus No 2 (Y19) runs from Pǔdōng airport to a stop opposite the Portman Ritz-Carlton and bus No 5 (Y18) goes to Shànghǎi train station. A taxi to Pǔdōng airport from the city centre will cost around Y130.

Tour Bus If you want to see Shànghǎi in a hurry, or you want to go to Pǔdōng, then the best way is to jump aboard one of the red Jinjiang Shanghai Tour buses that leave every half hour from the Jinjiang Hotel on Maoming Nanlu (immediately in front of the old French Club, which is part of the Garden Hotel). They are comfortable, speedy and cheap, with a one day ticket costing Y18. They stop at a number of tourist destinations, including Rénmín Guǎngchǎng, the Oriental Pearl Tower in Pǔdōng and Nánpǔ Qiáo (South River Bridge), and then return to the Jinjiang Hotel. You can get off, go and see the sight and wait for the next bus to come along and pick you up, using the same ticket.

Bus Buses are often packed to the hilt and, at times, impossible to board. The closest thing to revolutionary fervour in Shànghǎi today is the rush-hour bus ambushes. Once on board, keep your valuables tucked away since pickpocketing is easy under such conditions, and foreigners make juicy targets.

Contrary to popular belief, buses are not colour coded. Routes 1 to 30 are for trolleybuses (now supplemented by regular buses). Buses 1 to 199 operate from 5 am to 11 pm. Buses in the 200 and 400 series are peak-hour buses, and 300 series buses provide all-night service. Suburban and long-distance buses don't carry numbers – the destination is in characters. Some useful bus routes are listed below, though with the new metro line in operation, it may be easier to take that route.

No 20 This bus takes you to Rénmín Guǎngchǎng from the Bund.

No 61 This bus starts from the intersection of Wusong Lu and Tiantong Lu, past the PSB. No 55 from the Bund also goes by the PSB.

No 64 This bus gets you to Shànghǎi train station from the Pujiang Hotel. Catch it near the Pujiang Hotel on Beijing Donglu, close to the intersection

SHÀNGHǍI 上海

with Sichuan Zhonglu. The ride takes 20 to 30 minutes.

No 65 Runs from northeast of Shànghǎi train station, passes Shanghai Mansions, crosses Wàibáidù Qiáo (Garden Bridge), and then heads directly south along the Bund (Zhongshan Lu) as far as the Bund can go. It passes near long-distance bus station on Gongxing Lu.

No 42 This bus starts from the Bund at Guangdong Lu and passes up along Renmin Lu close to the Yù Yuán, then up Huaihai Lu, up Xiangyang Lu then to Xújiāhuì and terminating at the Shànghǎi Stadium.

No 19 This bus links the Bund area to the Yùfó Sì area. Catch it at the intersection of Tiantong Lu and Sichuan Beilu.

No 112 This bus zig-zags north from the south end of Rénmín Guǎngchǎng to Nanjing Xilu, down Shimen Erlu to Beijing Xilu then up Jiangning Lu to the Yùfó Sì.

No 11 This bus travels the ring road around the old Chinese city.

No 71 This bus can get you to the CAAC office, from which you can catch the airport bus. Catch No 71 from Yan'an Donglu close to the Bund.

No 831 This bus goes all the way from Jinling Lu, around the corner from the Bund, to the airport via Huanghai Zhonglu.

No 904 This bus goes from Shànghǎi train station past the Shanghai Mansions, down to the Bund to the Shiliupu Wharf and ends up at Nánpǔ Qiáo.

No 903 This bus goes from Shànghǎi train station past the Portman Ritz-Carlton and the Hilton Hotel to the Shànghǎi Stadium.

No 911 This bus leaves from Zhonghua Lu near the intersection with Fuxing Zhonglu, within walking distance of the Bund, and goes up Huaihai Lu then proceeds to the zoo.

Train   The second part of the Shànghǎi metro is being constructed at a feverish pace. The first section runs from Shànghǎi train station in the north through Rénmín Guǎngchǎng and down to the Xinzhuang metro station in the southern part of town.

A second line has been constructed which will eventually connect Hóngqiáo and Pǔdōng airports (running east-west through the centre of town). The first part of this line opened in late 1999 and runs from Zhōngshān Gōngyuán to Longyang Lu in Pǔdōng. Tickets are Y3 for up to 13 stops and Y4 after that.

Trains run from 5 am to 10 pm – once every nine minutes at rush hours and every 12 minutes during off-peak hours.

Taxi   Shànghǎi taxis are reasonably cheap and easy to flag down. Fares vary slightly depending on the taxi – flag fall is Y10 or Y8 depending on the size of the vehicle.

Hotel Transport   Most large, opulent hotels have a free shuttle bus to the Bund and the airport for their guests.

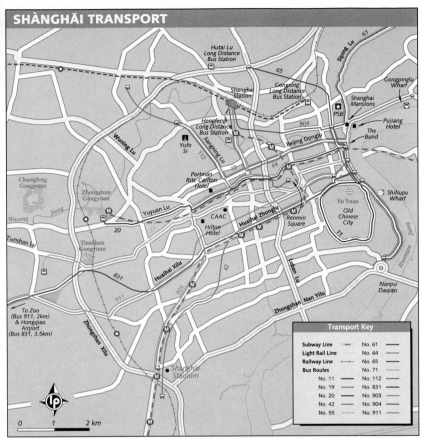

SHÀNGHǍI TRANSPORT

Hutai Lu
Long Distance
Bus Station

65

Siping Lu 67

Gongpinglu
Wharf

Shanghai
Station

Gongxing
Long Distance
Bus Station

Shanghai
Mansions

904

PSB

Pujiang
Hotel

Hengfeng
Long Distance
Bus Station

Beijing Donglu

The
Bund

Wuning Lu

Yufo
Si

Jiangning Lu

112

64

49

Changfeng
Gongyuan

Portman
Ritz-Carlton
Hotel

Shiliupu
Wharf

Zhongshan
Gongyuan

Yu Yuan

Old
Chinese
City

Wusong

Jiang

Yuyuan Lu

CAAC

Huaihai Zhonglu

Renmin
Square

11

20

Tianshan Lu

Tianshan
Gongyuan

Hilton
Hotel

Luban Lu

Nanpu
Daqiao

Huaihai Xilu

42

Huaihai Xilu

831

903

911

Zhongshan Nan Yilu

To Zoo
(Bus 911, 2km)
& Hongqiao
Airport
(Bus 831, 3.5km)

Zhongshan Xilu

Shanghai
Stadium

Transport Key

Subway Line	No. 61
Light Rail Line	No. 64
Railway Line	No. 65
Bus Routes	No. 71
No. 11	No. 112
No. 19	No. 831
No. 20	No. 903
No. 42	No. 904
No. 55	No. 911

0   1   2 km

BRADLEY MAYHEW

理 使 爾 自

BRADLEY MAYHEW

Modern: Shànghǎi's Oriental Pearl Tower overlooks the riverfront activity of the Huángpǔ Jiāng
Classic: Detail of a Christian church in Shànghǎi

Ancient gate in Tiānjīn's Gǔwénhuà Jiē

In Shànghǎi, young dancers celebrate the handover of Macau to China.

Cycling hard in Sūzhōu, Jiāngsū

Zhèjiāng 浙江

Zhèjiāng is one of the smallest provinces in China, but its longtime prosperity has always made it more important than its size might indicate.

The region is mainly divided between the area north of Hángzhōu, which is part of the lush Cháng Jiāng (Yangzi River) delta cut with rivers and canals, and the mountainous area to the south, which continues the rugged terrain of Fújiàn. The jagged coastline of Zhèjiāng has 18,000 islands – more than any other province.

Intensely cultivated for a thousand years, northern Zhèjiāng has lost most of its natural vegetation and is a flat, featureless plain with a dense network of waterways, canals and irrigation channels. The Grand Canal also ends here – Zhèjiāng was part of the great southern granary from which food was shipped to the depleted areas of the north.

The growth of Zhèjiāng's towns was based on their proximity to the sea and to some of China's most productive farmland. Hángzhōu, Níngbō and Shàoxīng have all been important trading centres and ports since the 7th and 8th centuries. Their growth was accelerated when, in the 12th century, the Song dynasty moved court to Hángzhōu in the wake of an invasion from the north.

Níngbō was opened up as a treaty port in the 1840s, only to fall under the shadow of its great northern competitor, Shànghǎi. Chiang Kaishek was born near Níngbō, and in the 1920s Zhèjiāng became a centre of power for the Kuomintang.

Silk was always a popular export and today Zhèjiāng, producing a third of China's raw silk, brocade and satin, is known as the 'land of silk'. The province is also famous for its tea production.

Hángzhōu is the provincial capital. To the south-east of the city are several places you can visit without backtracking. The major destination for travellers, however, is the island of Pǔtuóshān, with its monasteries, nunneries, crags, beaches, myths and legends.

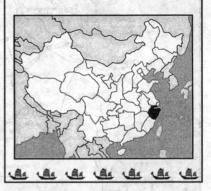

Highlights

Capital: Hángzhōu
Population: 43.6 million
Area: 101,800 sq km

- Hángzhōu's Xī Hú (West Lake), one of China's most famous attractions
- Pǔtuóshān, a rapidly developing but still magical getaway dotted with temples, pavilions and caves

HÁNGZHŌU 杭州
☎ 0571 • pop 6,079,600

'In heaven there is paradise, on earth Sūzhōu and Hángzhōu'. So runs one of China's oldest tourist blurbs. For the Chinese, Hángzhōu (along with Guìlín) is the country's most famous tourist attraction. Indeed, you can book your hotel room from on board the train as you ease into Hángzhōu train station, while announcements on the platform welcome you to the 'tourist capital of China'. Droves of tour groups descend on the city during all seasons, peaking on holidays and weekends and resulting in a blight of tacky tourist amenities and costly hotels. But don't despair: even this tourist excess has not diminished the beauty of Hángzhōu's Xī Hú (West Lake) area.

ZHÈJIĀNG 浙江

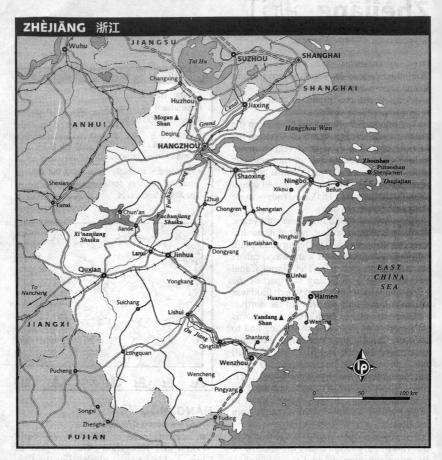

ZHÈJIĀNG 浙江

History

Hángzhōu's history goes back to the start of the Qin dynasty (221 BC). By the time Marco Polo passed through the city in the 13th century he described it as one of the most splendid in the world.

Although Hángzhōu prospered greatly after it was linked with the Grand Canal in AD 610, it really came into its own after the Song dynasty was overthrown by the invading Juchen, predecessors of the Manchus.

The Song capital of Kāifēng, along with the emperor and the leaders of the imperial court, was captured by the Juchen in 1126.

The rest of the Song court fled south, finally settling in Hángzhōu and establishing it as the capital of the Southern Song dynasty.

China had gone through an economic revolution in the preceding years, producing huge and prosperous cities, an advanced economy and a flourishing inter-regional trade. With the Juchen invasion, the centre of this revolution was pushed south from the Huáng Hé (Yellow River) Valley to the lower Cháng Jiāng Valley and to the coast between the Cháng Jiāng and Guǎngzhōu.

While the north remained in the hands of the invaders (who rapidly became Sinicised), in the south Hángzhōu became the hub of the Chinese state. The court, the military, the civil officials and merchants all congregated in Hángzhōu, the population of which rose from half a million to 1.75 million by 1275. The city's large population and its proximity to the ocean promoted the growth of river and sea trade, and of ship building and other naval industries.

When the Mongols swept into China they established their court at Běijīng. Hángzhōu, however, retained its status as a prosperous commercial city. It did take a beating in the Taiping Rebellion: in 1861 the Taipings laid siege to the city and captured it, but two years later the imperial armies took it back. These campaigns reduced almost the entire city to ashes, led to the deaths of over half a million of its residents through disease, starvation and warfare, and finally ended Hángzhōu's significance as a commercial and trading centre.

Few monuments survived the devastation, and most of those that did became victims of the Red Guards a century later during the Cultural Revolution. Much of what may be seen in Hángzhōu today is of fairly recent construction.

Orientation

Hángzhōu is bounded to the south by the Qiántáng Jiāng and to the west by hills. Between the hills and the urban area is the large Xī Hú, the region's premier scenic attraction. The eastern shore of the lake is the developed touristy district; the western shore is quieter.

Information

Tourist Office At the intersection of Yan'an Lu and Jiefang Lu there's the Hángzhōu Tourist Information Centre where you can pick up a map in English and Chinese. It also has tours of Hángzhōu for Y20.

Money The main Bank of China branch is at 140 Yan'an Lu, near Qingchun Lu, and is open daily from 8 am to 6 pm.

Post & Communications The post office and China Telecom office are opposite

each other on Yan'an Lu. An Internet service is available for Y18 per hour on the 3rd floor of the Jiefang Lu department store, open daily from 9 am to 9 pm.

Travel Agencies The China International Travel Service (CITS; Zhōngguó Guójì Lǚxíngshè; ☎ 515 2888) has an office at 1 Beishan Lu in a charming old building, Wànghú Lóu, near the north end of the Baidi Causeway. It deals mainly with tour groups and is not very useful for the individual traveller, who is better off going to the China Travel Service (CTS; Zhōngguó Lǚxíngshè; ☎ 707 4401, fax 702 0588) beside the Huáqiáo Fàndiàn.

Bookshops The Foreign Languages Bookstore at 34 Hubin Lu has good maps, including some in English. It also has a surprisingly good collection of English novels on the 2nd floor.

PSB The Public Security Bureau (PSB; Gōngānjú; ☎ 707 6677 ext 22641) is at 35 Huagang Xiang, a street off Huagang Lu.

A Close Shave

Língyǐn Sì might have been razed for good during the Cultural Revolution but, for the intervention of Zhou Enlai. Accounts vary as to what exactly happened, but it seems there was a confrontation between those who wanted to save the temple and those who wanted to destroy it.

The matter eventually went all the way up to Zhou, who gave the order to save both the temple and the sculptures on the rock face opposite. This is hardly surprising considering that Zhou gave the final nod of approval way back in 1953 for the carving of the huge buddha inside the temple, and twice allocated funds for the statue's completion. The monks, however, were sent to work in the fields.

In the early 1970s a few of the elderly and invalid monks were allowed to come back and live out their last few years in a small outbuilding on the hillside behind the temple.

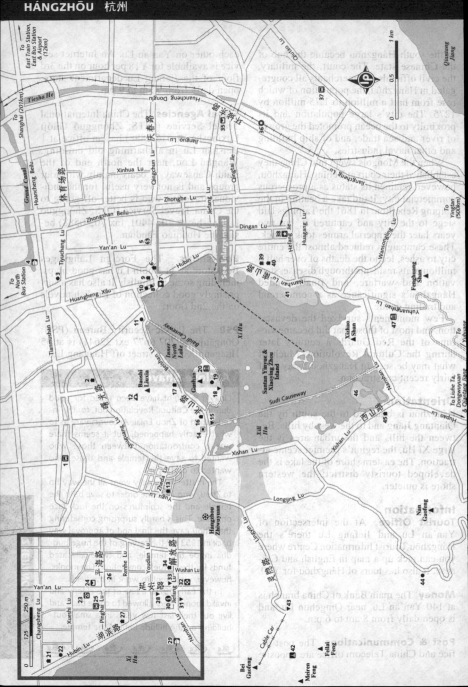

HÁNGZHŌU

PLACES TO STAY

2 Huánglóng Fàndiàn
黄龙饭店

6 Haihua Novotel Hotel
海华大酒店

9 Wànghú Bīnguǎn
望湖宾馆

13 Foreign Student Dormitory
外国留学生楼

16 Hangzhou Shangri-La Hotel
杭州香格里拉饭店

17 Xīnxīn Fàndiàn
新新饭店

21 Huáqiáo Fàndiàn; CTS
华侨饭店;
中国旅行社

27 Xīhú Fàndiàn
西湖饭店

34 Xīnqiáo Fàndiàn
新桥饭店

39 International Art Centre Inn
中国美术学院
国际培训中心

40 China Academy of Art Foreign Student Dormitory
中国美术学院
外事招待所

45 Huāgǎng Fàndiàn
花港饭店

PLACES TO EAT

8 Häagen Dazs
哈根达斯

15 Shānwàishān Càiguǎn
山外山菜馆

18 Lóuwàilóu Càiguǎn
楼外楼菜馆

28 Kǎoyā Diàn
烤鸭店

31 Croissants de France
可颂坊

33 Mr Pizza
密斯明斯特比萨

43 Tiānwàitiān Càiguǎn
天外天菜馆

OTHER

1 West Bus Station
长途汽车西站

3 CAAC
民航售票处

4 Hángzhōu Passenger Wharf
客运码头

5 Bank of China
中国银行

7 Casablanca Country Pub
卡萨布兰卡乡村俱乐

10 Foreign Languages Bookstore
外文书店

11 CITS
中国国际旅行社

12 Huánglóng Dòng (Yellow Dragon Cave)
黄龙洞

14 Yuè Fēi Mù
岳飞墓

19 Zhōngshān Gōngyuán
中山公园

20 Zhèjiāng Bówùguǎn
浙江省博物馆

22 Paradise Rock
天上人间

23 China Telecom
国际长途电话

24 Post Office
邮局

25 Bus No 308 to Liùhé Tǎ
308路车至六和塔

26 Market Street
市场

29 Boats to Sāntán Yìnyuè
船至三潭印月

30 Tourist Information Centre
旅游咨询服务中心

32 Jiefang Lu Department Store
解放路百货商店

35 Main Post Office
邮电局

36 Train Station
火车站

37 South Bus Station
长途汽车南站

38 PSB
公安局

41 Liǔlàngwènyīng Gōngyuán
柳浪问莺公园

42 Língyǐn Sì
灵隐寺

44 Lóngjǐng (Dragon Well)
龙井

46 Huāgǎng Guānyú
花港观鱼

47 Zhōngguó Sīchóu Bówùguǎn
中国丝绸博物馆

Língyǐn Sì 灵隐寺
Temple of the Soul's Retreat

Língyǐn Sì, roughly translated as either Temple of Inspired Seclusion or Temple of the Soul's Retreat, is really Hángzhōu's main attraction.

It was built in AD 326 and, due to war and calamity, has been destroyed and restored no fewer than 16 times.

The present buildings are restorations of Qing dynasty structures. The Hall of the Four Heavenly Guardians at the front of the temple is inscribed with the couplet, 'cloud forest Buddhist temple', penned by the Qing emperor Kangxi, who was a frequent visitor to Hángzhōu and was inspired on one occasion by the sight of the temple in the mist and trees.

Inside the hall is a statue of the laughing Buddha who can 'endure everything unendurable in the world and laugh at every laughable person in the world'.

ZHÈJIĀNG 浙江

Behind this hall is the Great Hall, where you'll find the magnificent 20m-high statue of Siddhartha Gautama. Based on a Tang dynasty original, it was sculpted in 1956 from 24 blocks of camphor wood.

Behind the giant statue is a startling montage of 150 small figures which charts the journey of 53 children on the road to buddhahood; also represented are Ji Gong, a famous monk who secretly ate meat, and a character known as the 'mad monk'. During the time of the Five Dynasties about 3000 monks lived here.

The place is normally crawling with tourists. Bus No 7, 507 (both from the train station) or 505 (from the zoo) go to the station at the foot of the hills west of Hángzhōu. Behind the Língyǐn Sì is **Běi Gāofēng** (Northern Peak), which can be scaled via cable car. From the summit there are sweeping views across the lake and city.

Zhèjiāng Shěng
Bówùguǎn 浙江省博物馆
Zhejiang Provincial Museum
On Gǔ Shān (Solitary Hill Island), a short walk from the Shangri-La Hotel, these buildings were part of the holiday palace of Emperor Qianlong in the 18th century.

Mainly a natural history museum, it contains both a whale and dinosaur skeleton.

Yuè Fēi Mù 岳飞墓
Mausoleum of General Yue Fei
During the 12th century, when China was attacked by Juchen invaders from the north, General Yue Fei (1103–41) was commander of the Song armies.

Despite his successes against the invaders, he was recalled to the Song court where he was executed after being deceived by Qin Hui, a treacherous court official. More than 20 years later, in 1163, Song emperor Gao Zong exonerated Yue Fei and had his corpse reburied at the present site.

Chinese tourists traditionally cursed and spat upon the iron statues of Qin Hui and his wife, Wang Shi, but now they have to do it surreptitiously since, though it might be hard to believe, spitting is against the law in China.

The Mausoleum of General Yue Fei is in a compound bounded by a red-brick wall a few minutes' walk west of the Hangzhou Shangri-La Hotel. It was ransacked during the Cultural Revolution, but has since been restored. Inside is a large statue of the general and the words, 'return the mountains and rivers to us', a reference to his patriotism and resistance to the Juchen.

Liùhé Tǎ 六和塔
Six Harmonies Pagoda
To the south-west of the city stands an enormous rail-and-road bridge that spans the Qiántáng Jiāng. Close by is the 60m-high octagonal Liùhé Tǎ. The pagoda also served as a lighthouse, and was supposed to have the magical power to halt the tidal bore that thundered up the Qiántáng Jiāng in mid-September every year.

Behind the pagoda is a charming walk through terraces dotted with sculptures, bells, shrines and inscriptions. Take bus No 308 from Yan'an Lu.

Xī Hú 西湖
West Lake
There are 36 lakes in China called Xī Hú, but this one is by far the most famous. Indeed it is the West Lake from which all other west lakes take their name.

Xī Hú is the symbol of Hángzhōu, and can make for a pleasant outing, though some of its charm has fallen victim to the plundering of tour groups and tacky facilities. Twilight and evening can be a better time to view the lake, especially when it is layered with mist.

Xī Hú was originally a lagoon adjoining the Qiántáng Jiāng. In the 8th century the governor of Hángzhōu had it dredged; later a dike was built that cut it off from the river completely. The resulting lake is about 3km long and a bit under 3km wide. Two causeways, the Báidī and the Sūdī, split the lake into sections.

The causeways each have a number of arched bridges, large enough for small boats and ferries to pass under. The sights are scattered around the lake; a motley collection of gardens, bridges and pavilions.

Many have literary associations that are unfortunately lost on most foreigners.

The largest island in the lake is **Gǔ Shān** (Solitary Hill Island) – the location of the **Zhèjiāng Shěng Bówùguǎn, Zhōngshān Gōngyuán** and the restaurant **Lóuwàilóu Càiguǎn**. The Baidi causeway links the island to the mainland.

Most of the other sights are connected with famous people who once lived there – poets, emperors who visited (Hángzhōu was very popular with the ruling elite) or Chinese patriots. **Huāgǎng Guānyú** (Red Carp Pond) is a chief attraction, home to a few thousand red carp and studded with earthen islets.

Hángzhōu's **Zhíwùyuán** (Botanical Gardens) even have a sequoia pine presented by Richard Nixon on his 1972 visit.

From **Xiǎoyíng Zhōu** (Lesser Ocean Island; also known as Lesser Ying Zhou) on the lake you can look over at **Sāntán Yìnyuè** (Three Pools Mirroring the Moon), a string of three small towers in the water, each of which has five holes that release shafts of candlelight on the night of the moon cake festival in mid-autumn, when the moon is full.

If you want to contemplate the moon in the privacy of your own boat there are a couple of places around the lake where you can hire paddle boats and go for a slow spin. Boats can also be chartered for a lake cruise from the small docks along the eastern side of the lake.

Other Sights

The **Dòngwùyuán** (zoo) is on the west side of Hupao Lu on the way to Liùhé Tǎ (Six Harmonies Pagoda). It has Manchurian tigers, larger than their southern counterparts and a protected species.

Travellers have recommended the **Zhōngguó Sīchóu Bówùguǎn** (China Silk Museum) on Yuhuangshan Lu. There are good displays of silk samples, and on the history and processes of silk production. English-speaking tour guides are available. Entry is Y5 and bus No 31 goes by the museum.

About 60km north of Hángzhōu is **Mògān Shān**. Pleasantly cool at the height of summer, Mogan Shan was developed as a resort for Europeans living in Shànghǎi and Hángzhōu during the colonial era. It's well worth visiting and staying in one of the old villas.

To reach Mogan Shan, take a minibus from the north bus station (Y15; 1½ hours); there is a selection of hotels there, with doubles starting at Y250.

Places to Stay – Budget

Fortunately, Hángzhōu's hotel prices have dropped slightly from the dizzy heights of the early and mid-'90s but budget accommodation is still hard to come by. It's a good idea to avoid the high season, weekends and holidays.

The **China Academy of Art Foreign Student Dormitory** (*Zhōngguó Měishù Xuéyuàn Wàishì Zhaòdaìsuǒ*; ☎ 702 3415) has a great location on Nanshan Lu. The rooms are somewhat dilapidated, Y120 for doubles with air-con and bath, but the setting more than makes up for that.

The **Foreign Student Dormitory** (*Liúxuéshēng Lóu*; ☎ 799 6092) of Zhejiang University has rooms for the same price, but its location isn't as convenient. It's a white four-storey building down a small lane off Zheda Lu, the main road heading into the university. Bus No 16 takes you there.

The cheapest budget option is the **Xīhú Fàndiàn** (☎ 706 6933, fax 706 6151, 80 Renhe Lu). It has singles/doubles/triples with shared bath and fan for Y80/100/120 and air-con (no bath) singles/doubles for Y140/170. Singles/doubles with air-con and bath are Y220/280.

Places to Stay – Mid-Range

Hángzhōu accommodation is pretty much priced in the mid-range to top-end bracket. As always, ask for a discount.

The **International Art Centre Inn** (*Zhōngguó Měishù Xuéyuàn Guójì Péixùn Zhōngxīn*; ☎ 571 7070, 220 Nanshan Lu) is beside the entrance to the China Academy of Art. Comfortable doubles are Y380 and larger doubles are Y398. Discounts of up to 30% are available.

The **Huāgǎng Fàndiàn** (☎ 799 8899, fax 796 2481, 4 Xishan Lu) is set on beautiful grounds on the western side of Xī Hú. Standard doubles start at Y450, but at the time of writing discounts of 50% were being offered. The *Xīnxīn Fàndiàn* (☎ 798 7101, fax 705 3263, 58 Beishan Lu), also has a pleasant, if less serene, location on the north edge of Xī Hú. Lake-view doubles are Y572 and hillside view rooms are Y528, but discounts up to 40% are available.

On the eastern side of the lake, the *Huáqiáo Fàndiàn (Hángzhōu Overseas Chinese Hotel;* ☎ 707 4401, fax 707 4978, 15 Hubin Lu)* was recently renovated and, while a little overpriced, is in a convenient location and has good facilities. Doubles start at Y450.

The *Xīnqiáo Fàndiàn* (☎ 707 6688, fax 707 1428, 176 Jiefang Lu) is still within walking distance of Xī Hú, but is a little uninspired. Singles/doubles start at Y520/590.

Places to Stay – Top End
There's no shortage of top-end hotels in Hángzhōu, but the most elegant and romantic place is the *Hangzhou Shangri-La Hotel (Hángzhōu Xiānggé Lǐlā Fàndiàn;* ☎ 707 7951, fax 707 3545, 78 Beishan Lu). Also called the Hángzhōu Fàndiàn, it's on the northern side of the lake, next to the Yuè Fēi Mù and surrounded by spacious forested grounds. Doubles here start at Y1600 (plus a 15% service charge). If you can't afford to stay there, at least go there for a drink or a wander around.

The comfortable and efficient *Haihua Novotel Hotel (Hǎihuá Dàjiǔdiàn;* ☎ 721 5888, fax 721 5108, 298 Qingchun Lu) is very good value, with rooms starting at US$85 and lake-view rooms for US$105. The restaurants are excellent and the facilities superb. Nearby, the *Wànghú Bīnguǎn* (☎ 707 1024, fax 707 1350) is a large hotel with a whole range of rooms, some as cheap as Y350. Standard doubles are Y980.

Another massive place is the *Huánglóng Fàndiàn (Yellow Dragon Hotel;* ☎ 799 8833, fax 799 8090), which has overpriced rooms starting at US$130. Maybe that's why it's offering 45% discounts. It's also a bit of a hike to the lake.

Places to Eat
Hángzhōu's most famous restaurant is the *Lóuwàilóu Càiguǎn* on Gǔ Shān, right on Xī Hú. Apart from excellent views of the lake, however, its fame has gone to its head and made the chefs complacent. You're better off trying some of the famous local dishes such as *xīhú cùyú* (Xī Hú fish in sweet and sour sauce) at other establishments, which have better cooks and more reasonable prices. Try the *Shānwàishān Càiguǎn* (☎ 796 5450), near the Yuè Fēi Mù or the *Tiānwàitiān Càiguǎn* (☎ 798 6621) beside the entrance to the Língyǐn Sì.

Dishes to look out for are *dōngpō ròu*, pork slices flavoured with Shàoxīng wine and named after the Song dynasty poet Sudong Po and another local delicacy that apparently was a firm favourite with the Qianlong emperor, *shāguō yútóu dòufu* (earthenware pot fish-head tofu).

For Chinese cheap eats, check out Yan'an Lu, a street to the east of Hubin Lu. Parallel to Yan'an Lu further east, Wushan Lu is a haven for bargain restaurants with snappy service; there are a few popular dumpling restaurants here.

You can order a la carte cheaply at the *Kǎoyā Diàn (Roast Duck Restaurant)* if you can read the menu. Otherwise ask for the Běijīng duck (*kǎoyā*). Y36 will get you half a duck (enough for two). Downstairs is the cheaper, more down-at-heel option while upstairs is pricier.

Top-end hotels dish out a wide range of superior cuisine. The Haihua Novotel Hotel features a fine western restaurant in the form of *Le Paris*. Most of the hotels also have bakeries. There's a *Croissants de France* on Jiefang Lu and an elegant *Häagen Dazs* outlet on Hubin Lu.

You can find *KFC* at various locations, as well as other fast-food outlets like *Mr Pizza* on the corner of Jiefang Lu and Yan'an Lu.

Entertainment
There are a couple of bars on the north-eastern side of Xī Hú. A rustic place on the lakeshore, the *Casablanca Country Pub*, opens at 6 pm, and down the road past the

Huáqiáo Fàndiàn there's the *Paradise Rock Pub and Restaurant*.

Shopping

Hángzhōu is well known for its tea, in particular Longjing green tea (grown in the Lóngjǐng area, south-west of Xī Hú), and also silk, fans and, of all things, scissors.

Shops around the lake sell all of these, but at high, touristy prices. One of the best places to look, however, is the market street on Wushan Lu in the evenings. Stalls go up in the early evening and are piled high with a fascinating confusion of collectables. Fake ceramics jostle with Chairman Mao memorabilia, ancient pewter tobacco pipes, silk shirts and pirated CDs. Get the gloves off and bargain hard if anything catches your eye. For silk, try Xinhua Lu, a couple of blocks east of Zhongshan Lu. In the market, make sure you check that the silk is genuine and not a polyester clone (it should feel smooth and soft between your thumb and finger).

Getting There & Away

Air The Civil Aviation Administration of China (CAAC; Zhōngguó Mínháng; ☎ 515 4259) has an office at 390 Tiyuchang Lu. Dragonair (☎ 799 8833 ext 6061) has a representative in the Huánglóng Fàndiàn on Shuguang Lu.

Both Air China and Dragonair offer daily flights to/from Hong Kong for Y1230 (discounted rate).

Hángzhōu has regular domestic connections with all major Chinese cities. There are several flights a day to Běijīng (Y920) and Guǎngzhōu (Y840).

Bus Numerous bus services go to and from Hángzhōu, but all three long-distance stations are located outside the city. The north bus station on Mogan Lu has deluxe (Y98; five hours) and economy (Y50; seven hours) buses to Nánjīng and other points in Jiāngsū. Buses to Mògān Shān also leave from here or you can take a minibus to Déqīng (Y9) and proceed from there.

Buses for Qiāndǎohú (Y26; four hours) and Huáng Shān (Y52; seven hours) leave

from the west bus station on Tianmushan Lu. The east bus station is the most comprehensive with frequent deluxe buses to Shànghǎi (Y54; two hours), Shàoxīng (Y18.50; one hour) and Níngbō (Y42; two hours). Economy buses are cheaper, but slower.

Buses to Tiāntái Shān also leave from here. Sleepers are Y50 and economy buses are Y27. The trip takes about six hours.

Train There are trains from Hángzhōu to Fúzhōu, Xiàmén, Nánchāng, Shànghǎi and Guǎngzhōu, and east to the towns of Shàoxīng and Níngbō. For most trains to the north you must first go to Shànghǎi, but there is a direct train to Běijīng, which takes 16 hours. Trains to Guǎngzhōu take 24 hours. In 1998, the Jīnhuá to Wēnzhōu train line, which connects Hángzhōu with Wēnzhōu, was completed. Express trains from Hong Kong to Shànghǎi also stop at Hángzhōu every second day.

Some trains arrive and depart from the Hángzhōu East station; check your ticket. At the time of writing, Hángzhōu's main station was having a complete overhaul and all trains were being diverted to the absolute chaos of the Hángzhōu east station. This situation should be remedied by the time you read this.

Fast trains from Hángzhōu to Shànghǎi make the trip in two hours with some trains continuing through to Sūzhōu. Another convenient way to get to Shànghǎi is from the Hángzhōu east station to Méilǒng, the train station behind the Hongmei Lu subway stop in Shànghǎi. Fast trains do the trip in one hour and 40 minutes.

It can be a bit difficult to book sleepers in Hángzhōu at the train station, especially to Běijīng. CTS will book sleepers for a Y40 service charge.

Boat You can get to both Wúxī and Sūzhōu by boat up the Grand Canal from Hángzhōu. There's one boat daily for Sūzhōu, leaving at 5.30 pm, and one leaving for Wúxī at 6 pm. Both trips take 13 hours. Economy class in a cabin of four people costs Y65. There are also deluxe cabins with four-person beds, at Y88 per bed, and two-person cabins for Y130 per bed. Buy tickets at the wharf just north off Huancheng Beilu.

Travellers have mixed opinions about this trip. Although it's more romantic to arrive in a place by boat, keep in mind that most of the journey is in darkness.

Getting Around

To/From the Airport Hángzhōu's airport is 15km from the city centre; taxi drivers ask around Y50 for the trip. Shuttle buses leave from the CAAC office. Tickets are Y5.

Bus Bus No 7 is very useful as it connects the main train station to the major hotel area on the eastern side of the lake. Of course, it doesn't do you much good if your train arrives at the Hángzhōu east station; take bus No 11 or 31, which will bring you close to the Xī Hú area. Bus No 15 connects the north and west bus stations to the northwest area of Xī Hú. Bus No 27 is useful for getting between the eastern and western sides of the lake.

Taxi Metered taxis are ubiquitous. Keep a map handy and watch out for lengthy detours. Prices for taxis depend on the size of the vehicle. Rates are cheap; figure on around Y10 to Y12 from the main train station to Hubin Lu.

Bicycle Bicycle rentals are available in a few places and are the best way to get around. Probably the most convenient place is the outlet beside the Huáqiáo Fàndiàn. Rentals are Y6 per hour and a deposit of Y300 to Y400 is required. The small kiosk near the China Academy of Art Foreign Student Dormitory also rents bikes.

Check out the bikes before you take off, especially the brakes.

Boat The boating industry on Xī Hú is the usual throng of boat operators jostling with each other to get you on board; just stand on the eastern shore and they will home in on you. Often the ordeal of bargaining for a private boat can take away some of the charm of the actual ride, but sometimes it's worth the splurge. Larger boats also leave the eastern shore, taking visitors out to the islands for Y16.

SHÀOXĪNG 绍兴
☎ 0575 • pop 4,289,400

Just 67km south-east of Hángzhōu, Shàoxīng is the centre of the waterway system on the northern Zhèjiāng plain. The waterways are part of the city's charm – and although we wouldn't go as far as the tourist brochures, which sing the praises of 'China's Venice', Shàoxīng does have atmosphere, with its rivers (subject to flooding), canals, boats and arched bridges.

Shàoxīng is the birthplace of many important intellectual and artistic figures in China's modern history, including China's first great modern novelist, Lu Xun. It's also the home of Shàoxīng wine, though many travellers might conclude that this is definitely an acquired taste.

Since early times, Shàoxīng has been an administrative centre and an important agricultural market town. It was capital of the Yue Kingdom 770–211 BC.

Orientation

Encircled by large bodies of water and rivers, and crossed by canals, Shàoxīng is a pleasant place to explore by a combination of bicycle, pedicab or foot. One of the nicest walks is along the lane called Longshan Houjie behind the Shàoxīng Hotel that meanders beside the canal. The hill in Fǔshān Gōngyuán behind the hotel is also a good place for shady walks.

Information

Major hotels can change money for guests. The main branch of the Bank of China is at 201 Renmin Zhonglu and there's another one at 472 Jiefang Beilu. Both change travellers cheques.

The China Telecom building is on Dong Jie near the intersection with Xinjian Beilu. The Tiger Computer Store at 156–162 Hechang Tang in the south-west section of the city has Internet services for Y7 per hour. It's open from 8.30 am to the wee hours of the morning.

The CITS office (☎ 515 6426, fax 516 5766) is grouped with a number of other travel agencies at 368 Fushan Xilu. You can find maps at the Xinhua Bookstore and at small shops near the major hotels.

The PSB (☎ 865 1333 ext 2104) is about 1km east of the city centre on Renmin Donglu, near the intersection of Huiyong Lu.

Lǔ Xùn Gùjū 鲁迅故居
Lu Xun's Former Home
Lu Xun (1881–1936), one of China's best-known modern writers and influential author of such stories as *Diary of a Madman* and *Medicine*, was born in Shàoxīng and lived here until he went abroad to study. He later returned to China, teaching at Guǎngzhōu's Zhongshan University in 1927. He was forced to hide out in Shànghǎi's French Concession when the Kuomintang decided his books were too dangerous. His tomb is in Shànghǎi.

You can visit Lǔ Xùn Gùjū, at 208 Lu Xun Zhonglu, where his living quarters are faithfully preserved. At the same site, on Lu Xun Zhonglu, is the **Lǔ Xùn Jìniànguǎn** (Lu Xun Memorial Hall). Opposite is the school where the novelist and essayist was a pupil (his desk is still there). Entry is Y7.

This area is a treat, not just for the buildings associated with Lu Xun, but also for its scenic charm; wander around here and follow the river south along Fuhe Jie (which runs parallel with Jiefang Nanlu towards Xiánhēng Dàjiǔdiàn) for delightful views of Shàoxīng.

Fuhe Jie is home to **Tonglian Antique Market**, which consists of rows of antique stalls and shops selling ceramics and calligraphy. It makes for a lovely walk beside stone walls and arched bridges.

Yǔ Líng 禹陵
King Yu's Mausoleum
According to legend, the first Chinese dynasty held power from the 21st to the 16th century BC, and its founder was King Yu, who is credited with having engineered massive flood-control projects.

A temple and mausoleum complex to honour the great-grandfather of China was first constructed in the 6th century and has been added to over the centuries. Yǔ Líng, King Yu's Mausoleum, is composed of several parts: the huge 24m-tall Main Hall, the Memorial Hall, the Wǔ Mén (Meridian Gate) and Gǒu Lóu. A statue of Yu graces the Main Hall.

A No 2 bus will get you to Yǔ Líng from the train station area (get off at the last stop). See the following Dōng Hú entry for boat transport from Yǔ Líng to the lake.

Zhōu Ēnlái Zǔjū 周恩来祖居
Zhou Enlai's Ancestral Home
Zhou Enlai was born in the small town of Huái Ān in Jiāngsū, but his ancestral home was here in Shàoxīng. Other historical figures, such as the enlightened educator Cai Yuanpei and pioneering woman revolutionary Qiu Jin, have also had their former residences turned into museums.

Dōng Hú 东湖
East Lake
Dōng Hú, an attractive place of sculpted rock formations, is around 6km east of the city centre. There is a temple (Dōnghú Sì) by the lake. Take a No 1 bus to the last stop. You can hire a 'pedal boat', a local form of transport, from Dōng Hú to Yǔ Líng and other sights. The trip takes around one hour and costs Y80, depending on your bargaining skills.

Places to Stay
Few budget travellers visit Shàoxīng, but it has some of the cheapest budget accommodation in east China. The tiny and unpretentious *Dàzhòng Lǚguǎn* (☎ 512 5821, 45 Xiaoshan Jie) in a small lane off Jiefang Bĕilu, looks like it shouldn't take foreigners, but does. Rooms are Y16 with a fan, and the bathroom is shared. No-one speaks English, but the staff are very welcoming.

The *Shàoxīng Lǚguǎn* (☎ 514 7314, 213 Jiefang Bĕilu) is another budget option with singles and doubles with fan and shared bath for Y32 and Y50. Triples are Y66, doubles with bath Y120, and air-con is an extra Y20. It's a clean, basic, and friendly place, with the only drawback being the noisy traffic.

ZHÈJIĀNG 浙江

SHÀOXĪNG 绍兴

The **Shàoxīng Fàndiàn** (☎ 515 5888, fax 515 5565, 9 Huanshan Lu) has a whole range of rooms starting with rather grotty doubles for Y300 to much more pleasant rooms for Y550. A 40% discount makes this place a good mid-range option and while the rooms are a little musty, the grounds and location are hard to beat.

Nearby, the **Lóngshān Bīnguǎn** (☎ 515 5515, fax 515 5308) has some cheap singles and doubles on offer for Y200 and Y210, as well as nicer standard rooms for Y400 that were available for a 40% discount at the time of writing.

The **Huáqiáo Fàndiàn** (Overseas Chinese Hotel; ☎ 513 2323, 91-5 Shangda Lu) has some real cheapies with fan and shared bath for Y76, as well as standard doubles for Y200 and Y258.

For more upmarket accommodation, the four-star **Xiánhēng Dàjiǔdiàn** (☎ 806 8688, fax 805 1028, 680 Jiefang Nanlu) has doubles starting at Y398 and deluxe suites for Y600 and Y800. A 20% discount was available at the time of writing. Located in the southern part of town, the hotel's facilities include a tennis court, swimming pool, western restaurant and coffee shop.

SHÀOXĪNG

PLACES TO STAY

5 Huáqiáo Fàndiàn
华侨饭店

6 Dàzhòng Lǚguǎn
大众旅馆

7 Shàoxīng Lǚguǎn
绍兴旅馆

9 Shàoxīng Fàndiàn
绍兴饭店

10 Lóngshān Bīnguǎn
龙山宾馆

OTHER

1 Train Station
火车站

2 TV Tower
电视塔

3 Jièzhū Sì
戒珠寺

4 Cai Yuanpei's Former
Residence
蔡元培故居

8 City Hall
市政府

11 CITS
中国国际旅行社

12 Wànghǎi Tíng
望海亭

13 Dàshàn Tǎ
大善塔

14 Xinhua Bookstore
新华书店

15 Zhōu Ēnlái Zǔjū
周恩来祖居

16 Bāzì Qiáo
(Eight-Character Bridge)
八字桥

17 Bank of China
中国银行

18 Night Food Stalls
肖夜街

19 Bank of China
(Main Branch)
中国银行

20 Tonglian Antique
Market
通联故玩市场

21 Lǔ Xùn Gùjū;
Lǔ Xùn Jiniànguǎn
鲁迅故居

22 Sanwei Ancient Library
三味书屋

Places to Eat

Adventurous types can try the *food stalls* that go up at night on the intersection of Dong Jie and Jiefang Beilu. It's a case of pointing at what others are eating and ordering, and the food is dirt cheap.

If you wonder what the smell of old, unwashed socks is, it's *chòudòufu* (smelly tofu), which is all the rage in Shàoxīng. If this doesn't tempt you there's always the *KFC* on Jiefang Beilu.

Decent Sìchuān, Shàoxīng and Cantonese cuisine can be found at the *Xiānhēng Dàjiǔdiàn*; it also dishes up western food at its *Tulip Western Restaurant*. The misnamed *Xī Cāntīng (Western Restaurant)* in the Shàoxīng Fàndiàn actually serves up good, generic Chinese food and has an English menu.

Getting There & Away

Hángzhōu-Níngbō trains and buses all stop in Shàoxīng. Luxury buses speed to Níngbō (Y38) in 1½ hours from the long-distance bus station. Buses to Hángzhōu (Y18.50) take an hour and to Shànghǎi (Y56.60) take three hours.

Getting Around

The bus system in Shàoxīng is fairly straightforward. Bus No 1 leaves from the train station down Jiefang Lu and bus No 8 goes down Zhongxing Lu close to the centre of the city from the long-distance bus station.

Taxis are cheap, starting at Y7, and pedicabs marginally cheaper. The best way to get around is by bicycle, available for rent in a couple of places on Jiefang Beilu. Try the place on the north-west side of the Chengbei bridge. Rentals are Y3 per hour with a Y300 deposit required.

AROUND SHÀOXĪNG

Considered one of Shàoxīng's 'must see' spots, the **Lán Tíng** (Orchid Pavilion) does not get many foreign visitors. There are actually several that are worth visiting if you don't mind the trek out there. The gardens were built in AD 1548.

Lán Tíng is around 10km south-west of the city and is reached by bus No 3.

NÍNGBŌ 宁波

☎ 0574 • pop 5,333,100

Like Shàoxīng, Níngbō rose to prominence in the 7th and 8th centuries as a trading port. Ships carrying Zhèjiāng's exports sailed from here to Japan, the Ryukyu islands and along the Chinese coast.

By the 16th century the Portuguese had established themselves as entrepreneurs in the trade between Japan and China, since

ZHÈJIĀNG 浙江

NÍNGBŌ 宁波

the Chinese were forbidden to deal directly with the Japanese.

Although Níngbō was officially opened to western traders after the first Opium War, its once-flourishing trade gradually declined as Shànghǎi boomed. By that time the Níngbō traders had taken their money to Shànghǎi and formed the basis of its wealthy Chinese business community.

Níngbō today is a bustling city with fishing, textiles and food processing as its primary industries. Travellers come here mainly in transit on the way to nearby Pǔtuóshān, one of Zhèjiāng's premier tourist attractions.

Information

The post office is just south of the Xīnjiāng Qiáo, where the Fènghùa Jiāng forks into the Yúyáo and Yǒng Rivers. Internet services are available at a pleasant teahouse above the Xinhua Bookstore in a traditional-style building near the KFC on Zhongshan Xilu. It's open from 8 am to midnight and charges Y10 per hour.

For travel tickets go to the ticketing office (☎ 730 2711) at the Nányuàn Fàndiàn (see Places to Stay later).

The PSB (☎ 736 2934 ext 1923) east of town on Zhongxing Lu at the intersection of

NÍNGBŌ

PLACES TO STAY
14 Níngbō Fàndiàn
　宁波饭店
15 Níngbō Hǎiyuán Guójì
　国际海员俱乐部
16 International Seamen's
　Club
　亚洲花园宾馆
17 Asia Garden Hotel
　宁波华侨饭店
21 Nányuàn Fàndiàn
　南苑饭店
22 Yúnhǎi Bīnguǎn
　云海宾馆

OTHER
1 Zoo
　动物园
2 North Train Station
　火车北站

3 Radio & TV Tower
　电台发射塔
4 Zhōngshān Gōngyuán
　中山公园
5 North Bus Station
　汽车北站
6 Passenger Ferry Terminal
　轮船码头
7 Catholic Church
　天主教堂
8 East Bus Station
　汽车东站
9 Main Post Office
　邮电局
10 City Hall
　市政府
11 Internet Teahouse;
　Xinhua Bookstore
　因特网茶艺馆
　新华书店

12 Bank of China
　中国银行
13 Tiānyī Gé
　天一阁
18 South Bus
　Station
　汽车南站
19 Train Station
　火车南站
20 Minibuses to Xīkǒu
　往溪口小公共汽车
23 Chenghuangmiao
　Shopping Complex
　城隍庙商场
24 Bank of China
　中国银行
25 PSB
　公安局外事科
26 CAAC
　中国民航

Baizhang Lu. The main branch of the Bank of China is on Yaohang Jie and another smaller branch is on Zhongshan Xilu.

Things to See

Yuè Hú (Moon Lake) makes for a pleasant walk in the right weather, though the whole place was being redesigned at the time of writing. Just west of the lake is the **Tiānyī Gé**, a pavilion built during the Ming dynasty and considered to be China's oldest existing private library.

If you are near the passenger ferry terminal, the old Portuguese **Catholic Church** (Tiānzhǔ Jiàotáng) is well worth a visit. It was built in 1628, destroyed and rebuilt in the 19th century. It's an active church, with a Mediterranean-style whitewashed interior displaying prints of the fourteen Stations of the Cross, colourful icons and a vaulted ceiling. The whole impression is a meticulous preservation of European Catholicism. The church is at 40 Zhongma Lu, just a few minutes' walk down from the ferry terminal.

Places to Stay

Níngbō is not exactly a Mecca for budget travellers but the large discounts available

make it very good value for mid-range prices. The **International Seamen's Club** (*Níngbō Guójì Hǎiyuán Jùlèbù;* ☎ 711 6882, fax 713 1725, 68 Mayuan Lu) has doubles and triples for Y98 and Y108 with bath and air-con. The building and rooms are marginal but it's livable. Slightly better rooms are Y168 and Y198. The hotel is within walking distance from the train and bus stations.

Hidden off in a back building, the **Níngbō Huáqiáo Fàndiàn** (☎ 729 3175, fax 729 4790, 130 Liuting Jie) has economy singles/doubles for Y160/Y180, with a discount available. The newly renovated section has standard doubles for Y500, but at the time of writing a 50% discount was being offered.

The **Yúnhǎi Bīnguǎn** (☎ 730 2288, fax 730 8794, 2 Changchun Lu) has doubles starting at Y250 (discounted to Y200), but the Y388 rooms are much nicer and were discounted to Y220.

The large **Níngbō Fàndiàn** (☎ 712 1688, fax 712 1668, 65 Mayuan Lu) is nicely located by the Hucheng Canal. Singles start at Y270 but the Y480 doubles discounted to Y248 are the best value. Directly in front,

ZHÈJIĀNG 浙江

the *Asia Garden Hotel* (*Yàzhōu Huāyuán Bīnguǎn;* ☎ *711 6888, fax 711 2138*) is also good value, with singles/doubles for Y320/Y380 available with a 30% discount. Both the Níngbō and Yàzhōu Huāyuán hotels have comfortable restaurants, quite a rare thing in Níngbō.

The best place to stay in Níngbō is the *Nányuàn Fàndiàn* (☎ *729 5678, fax 729 7788, 2 Lingqiao Lu*), a five-star establishment that opened in May 1999. Standard doubles were Y900, available for a 45% discount; cheaper rooms for Y398 are in another building.

Places to Eat

Despite its size, Níngbō really suffers from having nowhere decent to eat. Your best bet is to try the places adjoining the hotels, such as the popular buffet offered by the *Níngbō Fàndiàn* for Y50. The *Nányuàn Fàndiàn* also has a number of restaurants to choose from, as well as a good value buffet breakfast in the lobby bar for Y58 and western lunches and dinners in the hotel's pub.

Getting There & Away

Air The CAAC ticket office (☎ 742 7888) is at 91 Xingning Lu. There are daily flights to Hong Kong and most major Chinese cities have air connections with Níngbō.

Bus The main long-distance bus station is beside the train station. Deluxe buses leave frequently for Shànghǎi (Y90; four hours), Hángzhōu (Y42; one hour and 40 minutes) and Shàoxīng (Y38; one hour and 10 minutes). Economy buses to Wēnzhōu are Y85 (eight hours) and sleeper buses are Y109 (six hours). Minibuses to Xīkǒu depart from the small street running south-east from the train station. Tickets cost Y6 and the trip takes about an hour.

Train Train services between Shànghǎi and Níngbō are very frequent though it's still faster to take a deluxe bus. It's not too difficult to book tickets at the train station, but try your hotel, or the booking service in the Nányuàn Fàndiàn. The staff will add on an extra service charge.

Boat Overnight ferries go to Shànghǎi (12 hours) from the passenger ferry terminal (Lúnchuán Mǎtóu) north-east of the city centre. Ticket prices range from Y151 for 2nd class to Y36 for a seat. Fast boats do the trip in six hours, departing from ports outside Níngbō, but a bus takes passengers from the Níngbō ferry terminal. Tickets are Y60.

Slow boats to Pǔtuóshān depart from the passenger ferry terminal and take about five hours, with tickets ranging from Y21 to Y52. Frequent fast boats to Pǔtuóshān take 2½ hours, which includes a 1½-hour bus ride. Tickets are Y51.

The ferry terminal is poorly serviced by public buses. It's best to take a taxi, which will cost about Y20 to most of the hotels.

Getting Around

Níngbō's Lishe airport is a 20-minute ride from town. Airport buses leave from the CAAC office and cost Y5. A taxi should cost around Y30.

Taxis are fairly cheap, starting at Y10 and Y8 for the smaller compacts.

PǓTUÓSHĀN 普陀山
☎ 0580

Pǔtuóshān is the China we all dream about – temples, pagodas, arched bridges, narrow alleys, fishing boats, artisans and monks – and the China we see on postcards and in coffee-table books. Here you feel miles away from the hustle and bustle that characterise modern Chinese cities.

The best way to see the island is to amble about from temple to crag and from beach to monastery, rather than rush about like the tour groups. The serenity of the island lies in its relaxed pace, and that is an essential element if you want to enjoy the place to its utmost.

While there is no need to see everything, you can jump aboard one of the numerous minibuses that charge across the island stopping at the sights for Y2.50 to Y4.

The two large beaches, **Bǎibùshā** (One Hundred Step Beach) and **Qiānbùshā** (One Thousand Step Beach) on the east of the island, are attractive and largely unspoilt, although you have to pay to get in (Y12). Go at twilight when the ticket office is empty and there's a better atmosphere. **Fányīn Dòng** (Sanskrit Tidings Cave), on the far eastern tip of the island, has a temple dedicated to Guanyin perched between two cliffs with a seagull's view of craggy rocks and crashing waves.

The area around the **Pǔjìchán Sì** (Puji Temple) is a treat, and from here it is easy to plan an attack on the rest of the island. Most of the minibuses go via here.

Other sights to look out for are: **Lóng Tóu** (Dragon Head), **Hòu'ào Shā**, **Gǎng Dūn** (Ridge Mound), **Pǔtuó É'ěr** (Putuo Goose's Ear), **Hùijìchán Sì** (Wisdom Benefit Meditation Temple), **Gǔfó Dòng** (Ancient Buddhist Cave), **Xiāngyún Tíng** (Fragrant Cloud Pavilion), **Shàncái Dòng** (Wisdom and Wealth Cave), **Yángzhī Dòng** (Poplar Branch Convent), **Chaóyáng Dòng**, **Xiānrén Dòng** (Fairy's Cave), **Dūobǎo Tǎ** (Many Treasures Pagoda), **Xītīan Dòng** (Western Sky Cave), **Nántīan Mén** (South Sky Gate), **Jīn Shā** (Golden Beach), **Bùkěnqù Gūanyīn Yùan** (Cannot Agree to Leave Guanyin Hall) and **Gūanyīn Tiào** (Guanyin Leap).

There's a Y40 entrance fee to the island itself upon arrival, which does not include entry fees to other sights.

There's a post office west of Pǔjì Sì and a Bank of China further west down the road.

Places to Stay

It's difficult to provide reliable information on Pǔtuóshān's accommodation as prices vary seasonally and according to demand. There's nothing in the way of budget accommodation, and many hotels do not take foreigners. If you're coming from Shànghǎi, it may be worthwhile to book accommodation through a travel agency. A barrage of touts meets each ferry and you can always try your luck with them.

The *Xīlín Fàndiàn* (☎ 609 1303, fax 609 1199) is about 10m to the left of the Pǔjì Sì when facing the temple. It has pleasant rooms in a courtyard, with doubles starting at Y248. A 20% discount is available on weekdays. Further up the road from here, the *Xīlái Xiǎozhuāng* (Xilei; ☎ 609 1812, 609 1023) is a large place with restaurants

and shops. The cheapest rooms start at Y468 and it was offering a 30% discount.

The *Jīnpíng Shānzhuāng* (Jinping Mountain Villa; ☎ 609 1500, fax 609 1698) has a nice location near the Fǎyúchán Sì, but its cheaper doubles for Y300 are not very inviting, even with a 30% discount. Nicer rooms with a veranda go for Y480.

The *Qiánhé Shānzhuāng* (Qianhe Mountain Villa; ☎ 609 1630) is in a new building with comfortable rooms starting at Y386, but it's often full.

The best and newest hotel in Pǔtuóshān is the immaculate *Huáguāng Shānzhuāng* (Huagang Mountain Villa; ☎ 609 2667, fax 609 2537) near the Fǎyúchán Sì – it's also the best place to go for a romantic getaway. Standard doubles with sea-view verandas are Y680. Rooms without verandas are Y580 and deluxe singles are Y880. A 40% discount is offered on weekdays.

Places to Eat

Most of the hotel food is both expensive and appalling in Pǔtuóshān, so avoid it and head for the *seafood restaurants* down near the boat ticket office.

A good place serving Shànghǎi-style snacks and a variety of teas is the *Pǔtuóshān Cháyìguǎn (Putuoshan Tea House)* on the south-west side of the pond in front of Pǔjì Sì. It also has a breakfast.

Getting There & Away

Pǔtuóshān is accessible by boat from either Níngbō or Shànghǎi, but Níngbō is closer and offers more frequent services. Air services from Běijīng and Shànghǎi fly into a new airport on the larger island of Zhūjiājiān, a five-minute boat ride to the south.

To/From Shànghǎi Two daily night boats leave Pǔtuóshān at 4 and 5 pm for the 12-hour voyage to Shànghǎi. Tickets range from Y38 to around Y269; it's easy to upgrade once you are on board. Frequent fast boats leave Pǔtuóshān to either the port of Jinshan or Luchao, where passengers are then bussed to Shiliupu Wharf on the Bund. About three hours are spent on the boat and one to two hours on the bus. Tickets range from Y155

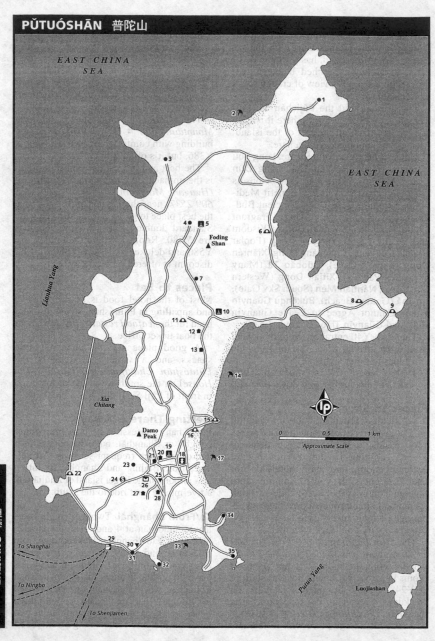

PǓTUÓSHĀN 普陀山

EAST CHINA SEA

EAST CHINA SEA

Liánhua Yáng

Foding Shan

Xia Chitang

Damo Peak

To Shanghai

To Ningbo

To Shenjiamen

Pǔtuó Yáng

Luojiashan

Approximate Scale

PǓTUÓSHĀN

PLACES TO STAY
12 Jǐnpíng Shānzhuāng
    锦屏山庄
13 Huáguāng Shānzhuāng
    华光山庄
20 Xīlín Fàndiàn
    锡麟饭店
21 Xīlái Xiǎozhuāng
    西来小庄
27 Qiánhé Shānzhuāng
    千荷山庄
28 Sānshèngtáng
    Fàndiàn
    三圣堂饭店

PLACES TO EAT
25 Pǔtuóshān
    Cháyìguǎn
    普陀山茶艺馆
30 Restaurants
    餐厅

OTHER
1 Lóng Tóu
    龙头
2 Hòu'ào Shā
    后岙沙

3 Gǎng Dūn
    岗墩
4 Pǔtuó É'ěr Lì
    普陀鹅耳枥
5 Huìjìchán Sì
    慧济禅寺
6 Gǔfó Dòng
    古佛洞
7 Xiāngyún Tíng
    香云亭
8 Shàncái Dòng
    善财洞
9 Fànyīn Dòng
    笠舳
10 Fǎyǔchán Sì
    法雨禅寺
11 Yángzhī Dòng
    杨枝庵
14 Qiānbùshā
    千步沙
15 Cháoyáng Dòng
    朝阳洞
16 Xiānrén Dòng
    仙人洞
17 Bǎibùshā
    百步沙

18 Duōbǎo Tǎ
    多宝塔
19 Pǔjìchán Sì
    普济禅寺
22 Xītiān Dòng
    西天洞
23 Administrative Office
    管理局
24 Bank of China
    中国银行
26 Post Office
    邮电局
29 Passenger Ferry
    Terminal
    轮船码头
31 Boat Ticket Office
    轮船售票处
32 Nántiān Mén
    南天门
33 Jīn Shā
    金沙
34 Bùkěnqù
    Guānyīn Yuàn
    不肯去观音院
35 Guānyīn Tiào
    观音跳

to Y180. Keep in mind that this can be a rough trip for those prone to seasickness. See the Getting There & Away section of the Shànghǎi chapter for information on how to reach Pǔtuóshān from Shànghǎi.

To/From Níngbō The simplest way to go to Pǔtuóshān is the fast ferry, with frequent departures from Níngbō's passenger ferry terminal *(lúnchuán mǎtóu)*. The trip takes about three hours, with an hour on the boat and two hours by bus to Níngbō, depending on which port you go to. Tickets are Y51. A slow boat from Níngbō takes five hours. Tickets range from Y21 to Y52.

Ferries leave every ¼ hour to Pǔtuóshān's neighbouring island of Zhūjiājiān. Tickets are Y12.50.

Getting Around
Walking is the most relaxing option if you have time, but if not minibuses zip from the ferry terminal to Pǔjì Sì (Y3), from where you can change to other buses going to other sights. It's also pleasant to walk up to Fódǐng Shān (Buddhist Summit Mountain) from a trail at Fǎyǔchán Sì. For the less physically inclined there's a cable car available for Y25.

XĪKǑU 西口

About 60km south of Níngbō is the small town of Xīkǒu, the home of Chiang Kaishek. Despite local rumours that Chiang's body was secretly returned to China in order to bury it at Xīkǒu, his remains in fact still reside in Taiwan at Cihu, which is south of Taipei. Chiang's relatives have persistently maintained that when the Kuomintang 'retakes the mainland', the body will be returned to its proper resting place at Xīkǒu. See the Níngbō Getting There & Away section for information on getting to Xīkǒu.

WĒNZHŌU 温州

☎ 0577 • pop 7,083,500

Wēnzhōu is basically a stopover on the eastern coast, famous for its people emigrating to France and Italy and, perhaps because of that connection, an abundance of shoe factories. Unless you're in the shoe business, Wēnzhōu offers the curious traveller little more than crushed expectations. It's very much for those in transit and does not offer much in the way of sights.

Information

An Internet service is available in the gleaming new China Telecom building at the corner of Liming Lu and Huancheng Donglu. It's open daily from 8 am to 5.30 pm and charges Y10 per hour.

There's a CITS office (☎ 825 2523) on Xiaonan Lu that can book air tickets and arrange tours. The PSB office (☎ 821 0851) is at the end of a small lane called Xigong Jie, north of Guangchang Lu.

Things to See

The only scenic site is Jiāngxīn Dǎo or Jiāngxīn Gūyǔ (Heart of the River Island) in the middle of the Oū Jiāng. The island is a park dotted with pagodas, a lake and footbridges. It can be easily reached by ferry (Y5) from the Máháng pier (Máháng mǎtóu) on Wangjiang Xilu.

It's also interesting to explore the older streets south of Guangchang Lu.

Places to Stay

Many of the cheaper places don't take foreigners in Wēnzhōu. One exception is the *Xìnghuācūn Fàndiàn (☎ 852 8588, 83 Lucheng Lu)*. Basic singles/doubles/triples are Y24/26/28 with fan and shared bath. The Y44 doubles with air-con and bath are excellent value. There's a 10% 'building fee' added on. There's no English sign, but it's a grungy white five-storey building flanked by cheap clothing stores, about 100m south-east of the west bus station.

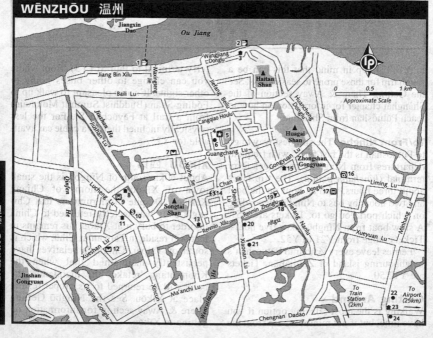

WĒNZHŌU 温州

Another fairly reasonable place is the **Dōng'ōu Dàshà** (☎ 818 7901, fax 818 5875, 1 Wangjiang Donglu) with singles for Y178 and doubles for Y190 and Y220, located down near the river.

A good mid-range option is the **Húbīn Fàndiàn** (☎ 822 7961, fax 821 0600, 1 Youyongqiao Lu) beside the tree-lined Jiǔshān Hé. Standard singles and doubles start at Y337, and 15% discounts are available.

Nearby, the **Huáqiáo Fàndiàn** (☎ 822 3911, fax 822 9656, 17 Xinhe Jie) is another reasonable option when the staff aren't renovating the ceilings. Singles/doubles start at Y319/Y374, but ask for a discount. The free breakfast and dinner are inedible, and the free swimming pool isn't that appealing either.

The **Wēnzhōu Dàjiǔdiàn** (☎ 882 2222, fax 881 2133, 61 Gongyuan Lu) is in a lively part of town adjacent to Zhōngshān Gōngyuán. Doubles start at Y280.

There are a number of upmarket hotels in Wēnzhōu. One of the best is the **Wenzhou International Hotel** (Wēnzhōu Guójì Dàjiǔdiàn; ☎ 825 1111, 825 8888, 1 Renmin Zhonglu), a four-star hotel with restaurants, a swimming pool and in-house movies. Doubles start at Y438 and include breakfast. Less central, but with many amenities, including a good western-style coffee shop, the **Dynasty Hotel** (Wángcháo **Dàjiǔdiàn**; ☎ 837 8888, fax 833 8208, 18 Minhang Lu) has standard rooms starting at Y750, with a 30% discount available.

Places to Eat

Not surprisingly, for a port, Wēnzhōu is known for its seafood and there are numerous restaurants near the west bus station. There's a **KFC** on Renmin Zhonglu; look for better restaurants here and on Jiefang Beilu.

One place to try out in Wēnzhōu is the elegant **Café de Champselysees** (Xiāngxièlìshè Xīcāntīng; ☎ 825 1318), on the 2nd floor of the Huanqiu Building on Jiefang Beilu. European and Chinese food are served as well as coffee. Look for the mock colonial facade.

Getting There & Away

Air CAAC (☎ 833 3197) is in the south-east section of town. Wēnzhōu has reasonably good connections with other Chinese cities, but the airport is notoriously bad for heavy fog – pilots often end up flying at ridiculously low altitudes trying to find the runway.

Bus Wēnzhōu has two main bus stations, west and south, with the former offering more destinations. As a general rule, if you're heading south, take the south station; north or west, take the west station.

WENZHŌU

PLACES TO STAY
3 Dōng'ōu Dàshà
   东瓯大厦
8 Húbīn Fàndiàn
   湖滨饭店
11 Xìnghuācūn Fàndiàn
   杏花村饭店
13 Huáqiáo Fàndiàn
   华侨饭店
15 Wēnzhōu Dàjiǔdiàn
   温州大酒店
18 Wenzhou International Hotel
   温州国际大酒店
23 Dynasty Hotel
   王朝大酒店

OTHER
1 Máháng Pier
   麻行码头
2 Passenger Ferry Terminal
   温州港客运站
4 PSB
   公安局
5 Rénmín Guǎngchǎng
   人民广场
6 City Hall
   市政府
7 Post & Telephone Office
   邮电局
9 West Bus Station
   汽车西站
10 Bank of China
   中国银行

12 Post Office
   邮局
14 Bank of China
   中国银行
16 China Telecom & Internet
   中国电信
17 South Bus Station
   汽车南站
19 Café de Champselysees
   麻行码
20 CITS
   中国国际旅行社
21 Train Ticket Booking Office
   火车预售票处
22 Wenzhou Sports Center
   温州体育馆
24 CAAC

ZHEJIANG 浙江

Buses to Fúzhōu (Y145; 10 hours) leave from the south station. For long-haul destinations, you're better off taking the train.

Train A train line was completed to Wēnzhōu via Jīnhuá in 1998 connecting the city to Hángzhōu, Shànghǎi and Běijīng. The train station is to the south of the city. Take bus No 5 or 27 from the city centre. Alternatively, a taxi to the station will cost around Y15.

CITS doesn't book train tickets, but try your hotel, or the little outlet near the CITS on Xiaonan Lu. A Y10 service charge is added.

Getting Around

Wēnzhōu airport is 27km south-west of town and taxis charge between Y80 and Y100 for the trip. Bus No 301 can take you there from Renmin Lu. A bus also goes from CAAC for Y10.

Taxis are cheap (Y10 to most destinations) and easy to flag down.

TIĀNTÁI SHĀN 天台山
Heavenly Terrace Mountain

Tiāntái Shān is noted for its many Buddhist monasteries, which date back to the 6th century. While the mountain itself may not be considered sacred, it's very important as the home of the Tiāntái Buddhist sect, which is heavily influenced by Taoism.

From Tiāntái it's a 3.5km hike to the **Góuqīng Sì** (Gouqing Monastery) at the foot of the mountain (you can stay overnight here). From the monastery a road leads 25km to **Hùadǐng Fēng** (Huading Peak), (over 1100m high), where a small village has been built. On alternate days public buses run up to Huadingfeng. From here you can continue by foot for 1km or 2km to the **Bàijīngtái Sì** (Praying the Scriptures Terrace Temple) on the summit of the mountain.

On the other days the bus goes to different parts of the mountain, passing **Shíliáng Fēipù** (Shiliang Waterfall). From the waterfall it's a good 5km to 6km walk along a series of small paths to **Hùadǐng Fēng**.

Tiāntái Shān is in the east of Zhèjiāng. Buses link it with Hángzhōu, Shàoxīng, Níngbō and Wēnzhōu.

CHÚN'ĀN XIÀN 淳安县
Chun'an County
☎ 0571

Chún'ān Xiàn, in western Zhèjiāng, is known for its Lake of a Thousand Islands, a reservoir created in 1958.

One route to Huáng Shān in Ānhuī that's worth investigating would be a trip starting from Hángzhōu. Take a bus to Qiāndǎohú (Y26; four hours) and from there take a boat to the south-west tip of the lake, where a road connects up to a highway going from Zhèjiāng to Huáng Shān.

Fújiàn 福建

The coastal region of Fújiàn, known in English as Fukien or Hokkien, has been part of the Chinese empire since the Qin dynasty (221–207 BC), when it was known as Min.

Sea trade transformed the region from a frontier into one of the centres of the Chinese world. During the Song and Yuan dynasties, the coastal city of Quánzhōu was one of the main ports of call on the maritime silk route, along which travelled not only silk, but textiles, precious stones, porcelain and a host of other valuables. The city was home to more than 100,000 Arab merchants, missionaries and travellers.

Despite a decline in the province's fortunes after the Ming dynasty restricted maritime commerce in the 15th century, the resourcefulness of the Fújiàn people proved itself in the huge numbers that emigrated to South-East Asia. Ports like Xiàmén were stepping stones for Chinese people heading for Taiwan, Singapore, the Philippines, Malaysia and Indonesia. This diaspora forged overseas links that have continued from the 16th century to today, contributing much to the modern character of the province.

Nowadays, many descendants of the original emigrants send money to Fújiàn, and the Chinese government is trying to build up a sense of patriotism in overseas Chinese to get them to invest more money in their 'homeland'.

Just as most Hong Kong residents trace their cultural roots to Guǎngdōng, most Taiwanese consider Fújiàn to be their ancestral home. Fújiàn's local dialect, Minnanhua (south-of-the-Min-River-language), is essentially the same as Taiwanese, although both places officially speak Mandarin Chinese. Not surprisingly, the Taiwanese are the biggest investors in Fújiàn and the most frequent visitors.

FÚZHŌU 福州
☎ 0591 • pop 5,748,500

Capital of Fújiàn province, Fúzhōu is an industrial hinterland, choked with concrete

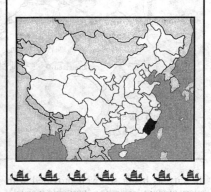

Highlights

Capital: Fúzhōu
Population: 31.8 million
Area: 120,000 sq km

- Xiàmén's island of Gǔlàng Yǔ, one of China's most charming pockets of colonial architecture
- Nánpǔtuó Sì, a fascinating temple just outside Xiàmén
- The earth buildings of the Hakka people in remote south-western Fújiàn
- The walled town of Chóngwǔ, not far from Quánzhōu
- Wǔyí Shān, a protected mountain area with scenic rock peaks

dust and shorn of interest. It can serve as an overnight pit-stop for travellers en route to Xiàmén, Quánzhōu or Wǔyí Shān, but offers few diversions.

History
Fúzhōu dates back to the 3rd century AD, when it was known as Yecheng ('smelting city'). Later it emerged as a major commercial port specialising in the export of tea.

Marco Polo, passing through Fúzhōu towards the end of the 13th century, described

FÚJIÀN 福建

the city as being so 'well provided with every amenity' as to be a 'veritable marvel'. While those amenities may still exist, 'marvel' is hardly the word to describe Fúzhōu these days.

Fúzhōu is second only to Xiàmén as a centre of Taiwanese investment. The money that the town has attracted is reflected in a lot of pricey new hotels and restaurants.

Orientation
Fúzhōu's city centre sprawls northward from the Mǐn Jiāng (Min River). Walking from one end of town to the other will take you more than an hour.

The train station is situated in the northeast of town, while most of the accommodation is on Wuyi Lu and Wusi Lu, sandwiched between Hualin Lu and Gutian Lu.

Information
The main Bank of China is near the intersection of Wusi Lu and Hudong Lu. It changes travellers cheques and is open daily from 8 am to 6 pm. Another branch is near the KFC on Gutian Lu. The post and China Telecom building is on the corner of Dong

Jie and Bayiqi Lu. A private courier, DHL
(☎ 781 1111), operates just up from the
Táiwān Fàndiàn on Hualin Lu. There's a
China Telecom Internet cafe on Jintai Lu,
near the Wuyi Beilu intersection. Open
from 8 am to 10 pm, it's located on the 2nd
floor and charges Y10 per hour.

A large China Travel Service (CTS;
Zhōngguó Lǔxíngshè; ☎ 753 6250) is at
128 Wusi Lu in front of the Huáqiáo Dàshà.
It can book plane tickets and has a number
of tours to areas in Fújiàn, but it doesn't
book train tickets.

The Public Security Bureau (PSB;
Gōngānjú; ☎ 782 1104) is at 107 Beihuan
Zhonglu, opposite the Sports Centre in the
northern part of town.

Things to See

Fúzhōu's sights are minor attractions and
the city has few places of historical interest.
The areas worth seeing are mainly scattered
about, which makes travel between them
difficult.

In the centre of town a vast **Maó Zhǔxí
Xiàng** (Mao Zedong Statue), framed by two
neon advertisements, presides over a sea of
cyclists. The statue was erected to commemorate the 9th National Congress of the Communist Party where Maoism was enshrined
as the new state religion and Lin Biao was
officially declared Mao's successor.

Right behind Mao is the **Yúshān
Fēngjǐngqū** (Yu Mountain Scenic Area),
which has some remains of the old city
walls and is a pleasant place for a stroll.

In the north-west of Fúzhōu is **Xīhú
Gōngyuán** (West Lake Park), on Hubin Lu,
where you'll find the **Fújiàn Shěng
Bówùguǎn** (Fujian Provincial Museum).
Next to the lake is the zoo, home to an unremarkable collection of animals, and
Xióngmāo Shìjiè (Panda World) where you
can watch this protected species riding bicycles and 'eating western food'. Entry is Y16.

Immediately east of the town, on **Gǔ
Shān** (Drum Hill), is **Yǒngquán Sì** (Gushing
Spring Monastery). The hill takes its name
from a large, drum-shaped rock at the summit that apparently makes a racket when
it's rainy and windy. The monastery dates

back 1000 years and is said to house a collection of 30,000 Buddhist scriptures of
which 657 are written in blood. Bus No 39
can take you there from Wuyi Zhonglu or
from Gutian Lu.

Places to Stay – Budget

Budget travellers are better off not staying in
Fúzhōu. Cheap hotels near the train station
were not taking foreigners at the time of
writing, but you can always try your luck.

The **Tiānfú Dàjiǔdiàn** (☎ 781 2328, fax
781 2308, 138 Wusi Lu) is reasonable value
with singles/doubles for Y188/268.

Places to Stay – Mid-Range

Most of Fúzhōu's hotels are mid-range in
price. The **Dōnghú Bīnguǎn** (☎ 755 7755,
fax 755 5519, 73 Dongda Lu) is a large,
well-equipped place with a swimming pool
and a whole range of rooms. Standard doubles in its No 2 building are Y230 and Y280
and the other buildings have doubles starting
at Y400. Discounts of 15% are available.

Similar to the Dōnghú in style, the
Huáqiáo Dàshà (Overseas Chinese Hotel;
☎ 755 7603, fax 755 0648), on Wusi Lu, has
doubles starting at Y350 and offers discounts of 25%. A less attractive mid-range
option in the north part of town is the
Táiwān Fàndiàn (☎ 781 8666), on Hualin
Lu, which claims it will have guests registered and settled in their rooms in five minutes! The rooms aren't that great, however,
with singles/doubles for Y279/297.

The more upmarket **Mǐnjiāng Fàndiàn**
(☎ 755 7895, 755 1489), on Wusi Lu south
of Hudong Lu, has standard doubles for
Y380 and Y440, as well as more expensive
rooms and suites. The lobby is quite attractive, with a coffee shop decorated with boat
hulls and the oddly-named 'floating bar'.
Perhaps it's named for the patrons who float
out the door after one too many.

Places to Stay – Top End

The impressive **Success Link International Hotel** (Chénglóng Guójì Dàjiǔdiàn;
☎ 782 2888, fax 782 1888, 252 Wusi Lu)
has standard doubles starting at Y578 and
suites starting at Y1088. The hotel features

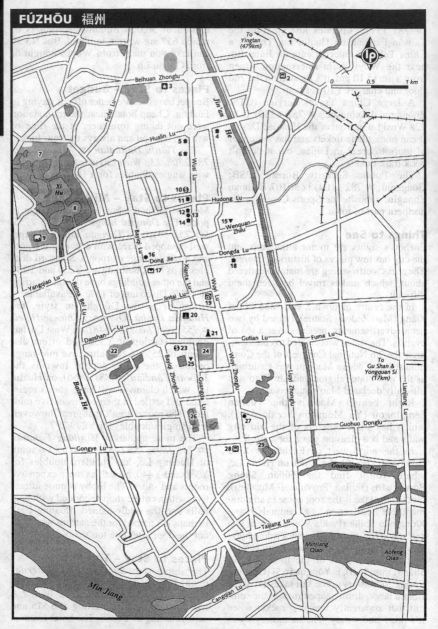

FÚZHŌU 福州

FÚZHŌU

PLACES TO STAY

4 Táiwān Fàndiàn
台湾饭店

5 Success Link
International Hotel
成龙国际大酒店

6 Hot Spring Hotel
温泉大饭店

11 Tiānfú Dàjiŭdiàn
天福大酒店

12 Mĭnjiāng Fàndiàn
闽江饭店

14 Huáqiáo Dàshà
华侨大厦

18 Dōnghú Bīnguǎn
东胡宾馆

PLACES TO EAT

15 Nóngjiā Fànzhuàng
农家饭庄

25 Shànghǎi Xīcāntīng
上海西餐厅

OTHER

1 Train Station
火车站

2 North
Long-Distance
Bus Station
长途汽车北站

3 PSB
公安局

7 Zuǒhǎi Gōngyuán
左海公园

8 Xīhú Gōngyuán;
Fújiàn Shěng
Bówùguǎn
西湖公园;
省博物馆

9 Dòngwùyuán
(Zoo)
动物园

10 Bank of China
中国银行

13 China Travel Service
中国旅行社

16 Lìdá Dàshà
(Train Ticket Booking
Office)
利达大厦

17 Post & Telephone
Building
邮电大楼

19 Yīntèwǎngba
(Internet Cafe)
因特网吧

20 Fǎhǎi Sì
法海寺

21 Máo Zhŭxí Xiàng
毛主席像

22 Yúshān
Fēngjǐngqū
于山风景区

23 Bank of China
中国银行

24 Wŭyī
Guǎngchǎng
五一广场

26 Chátíng Gōngyuán
(Tea Pavilion Park)
茶亭公园

27 CAAC
民航售票处

28 South
Long-Distance
Bus Station
福州汽车南站

29 Nán Gōngyuán
(South Park)
南公园

---

a billiards room, a sauna and a weights room. Nearby on Wusi Lu, the *Hot Spring Hotel* (*Wēnquán Dàfàndiàn;* ☎ 785 1818, fax 783 5150, 218 Wusi Lu) has all the facilities expected in a five-star hotel, as well as natural hot spring water in the bathrooms. Standard rooms start at Y988 and comfortable suites start at Y1780.

Places to Eat

Digging up cheap eats is no problem in Fúzhōu. The best place to head is Wenquan Zhilu, which is full of restaurants and bars. For reasonable Chinese food in a lively atmosphere, try the *Nóngjiā Fànzhuàng*. A plate of *háoyóu niúròu* (beef with oyster sauce) goes for Y12 and *Yángzhōu chǎofàn* (Yangzhou fried rice) is Y6. Pitchers of draught beer are popular, but the best thing about this place is the home-made *mǐjiǔ* (rice wine) at Y15 a pitcher.

The *Shànghǎi Xīcāntīng*, opposite Wŭyī Guǎngchǎng (Wuyi Square) on Guangda Lu, is part of a chain and serves excellent dim sum and *xiǎolóng bāo* (Shànghǎi dumplings); just point at what takes your fancy from the plates and steamers as they come round on trolleys.

Getting There & Away

Air The Civil Aviation Administration of China (CAAC; Zhōngguó Mínháng; ☎ 334 5988) has an office on Wuyi Lu. The Dōnghú Bīnguǎn also has a large air ticketing centre. Daily flights are available to major destinations such as Běijīng (Y1240; 2½ hours) Guǎngzhōu (Y660; one hour), Shànghǎi (Y620; 70 minutes), Hong Kong (Y1130; 80 minutes) and Wŭyí Shān (Y380; 30 minutes).

Bus There are two long-distance bus stations in town: a long-distance bus station in the north near the train station, and one at the southern end of town, down from the CAAC office. Buses head north and south to all important destinations in Fújiàn and Zhèjiāng and the bus stations have services to the same destinations. Economy buses are cheaper but often less direct.

There are buses to Guǎngzhōu (Y246; 18 hours), Shànghǎi (Y247; 24 hours), Wēnzhōu (Y151; 10 hours), Quánzhōu (Y60; 3½ hours) and Xiàmén (Y50; six hours). Deluxe buses to Guǎngzhōu (Y280; 16 hours) and Shēnzhèn (Y260; 13 hours) depart from the south bus station. Luxury buses travel to Xiàmén (Y80; 4½ hours) and depart from the north bus station and direct buses to Hong Kong (Y334; 15 hours) leave from both stations. Night buses leave the north bus station for Wǔyí Shān (Y90; eight hours) but it's much more comfortable to take the day train.

Train The railway line from Fúzhōu heads north-west and connects the city with the main Shànghǎi-Guǎngzhōu line at the Yīngtán junction. A branch line splits from the Fúzhōu-Yīngtán line and goes to Xiàmén. In 1998 a new line was completed that travels to Wǔyí Shān. Tickets are Y47 for a hard seat and the trip takes just under seven hours.

There are direct trains from Fúzhōu to Běijīng, Shànghǎi, Nánchāng and Xiàmén. The rail route to Xiàmén is circuitous, so you're better off taking the bus. It's fairly easy to buy tickets at the train station, which is a good 100m to the left of the main train station building, when you are facing the station. Many of the hotels will book train tickets for a service fee and there's also a ticket outlet in town in the entrance of the Lida Building (Lìdá Dàshà), opposite the post office, which is open from 8 am to 5 pm daily.

Getting Around

Fúzhōu is a sprawling city, which makes it difficult to get around by foot. A taxi ride starts at around Y10. There's a good bus network and bus maps are available at the train station or at the hotels. Bus No 51 travels from the train station along Wuyi Lu; and bus No 8 reaches the Xī Hú (West Lake) from Gutian Lu.

XIÀMÉN 厦门

☎ 0592 • pop 1,246,700

Xiàmén, or at least the part that huddles the harbour, has a relaxing charm.

The neighbouring island of Gǔlàng Yǔ is an enchanting retreat of meandering lanes and shaded backstreets, set in an architectural twilight of colonial villas and crumbling remains. It's well worth spending a day or so exploring the place.

History

Xiàmén, also known as Amoy, was founded around the mid-14th century, in the early years of the Ming dynasty. A town had been in existence at the site since the Song dynasty, but the Ming built the city walls and established Xiàmén as a major seaport and commercial centre.

In the 17th century it became a place of refuge for the Ming rulers fleeing the Manchu invaders. Xiàmén and nearby Jīnmén were bases for the Ming armies who, under the command of the pirate-general Koxinga, had as their battle-cry, 'resist the Qing and restore the Ming'.

The Portuguese arrived in the 16th century, followed by the British in the 17th century and later by the French and the Dutch, all of whom attempted to establish Xiàmén as a trade port. They all met with very limited success.

The port was closed to foreigners in the 1750s and it was not until the Opium War that the tide turned. In August 1841 a British naval force of 38 ships carrying artillery and soldiers sailed into Xiàmén harbour, forcing the port to open. Xiàmén then became one of the first treaty ports.

Japanese and western powers followed soon after, establishing consulates and making the island of Gǔlàng Yǔ a foreign enclave. Xiàmén turned Japanese in 1938 and remained that way until 1945.

Just offshore from Xiàmén, the islands of Jīnmén and Xiǎo Jīnmén have been occupied by Taiwanese Nationalist troops since the communist takeover in 1949. When the People's Liberation Army (PLA) began bombing them in 1958, the USA's mutual security pact with Taiwan very nearly led to war between China and the USA. Tensions remain high. When China conducted missile tests off Taiwan's shores in early 1996, the USA reacted by sending ships to the area, and Taiwanese forces dug in further. Taiwan spends huge amounts on defence in a bid to tip the balance.

Not that you will sense any of this in Xiàmén itself. It's a vibrant place, with shops packed with all kinds of consumer goodies.

Orientation

The town of Xiàmén is on the island of the same name. It's connected to the mainland by a long causeway bearing a railway line, road and footpath.

The interesting part of Xiàmén is the western (waterfront) district, directly opposite the small island of Gǔlàng Yǔ. This is the old area of town, known for its quaint architecture, parks and winding streets.

The central district includes the train station. Everything within a kilometre east of the train station is regarded as the eastern district. Both the central and eastern districts are soulless places, a jumble of high-rises and featureless, numbing architecture.

Information

The Bank of China is at 10 Zhongshan Lu, near the Lùjiāng Dàshà. A branch of the Hongkong Bank is also located just behind the Bank of China. There's an American Express office (☎ 212 0268) in Room 212 on the 2nd floor of the Holiday Inn. China Telecom runs an Internet cafe near Xiamen University, on Yanwu Jie. It's open daily from 10 am to 11 pm and charges Y10 per hour. Xiàmén's main post office is on the corner of Xinhua Lu and Zhongshan Lu.

There are several China International Travel Service (CITS; Zhōngguó Guójì Lǚxíngshè) offices around town. Probably the most convenient is the one next door to the Bank of China on Zhongshan Lu, next to the harbour (☎ 212 6917). Travellers have recommended Mr. Wu, who speaks English well and is very helpful with arranging tickets and tours – he can be accessed at CITS. Xiàmén wants to make tourists happy and has a complaints hotline (☎ 800 8582 ext 36).

There's a large PSB complex opposite the post office, and the visa section (☎ 226 2203) is located in the north-east section, near the entrance on Gongyuan Xilu.

GǓLÀNG YǓ 鼓浪屿
Gulang Island

A five-minute boat trip takes you to this sleepy island of winding paths, creeper-laden trees, Christian cemeteries and almost Mediterranean flavours. By 1860, the foreign powers had well-established residencies on Gǔlàng Yǔ and, as the years rolled by, churches, hospitals, post and telegraph offices, libraries, hotels and consulates were built.

In 1903 the island was officially designated an International Foreign Settlement, and a municipal council with a police force of Sikhs was established to govern it. Today, memories of the settlement linger in the charming colonial buildings that blanket the island and the sound of classical piano wafting from shuttered windows. Many of China's most celebrated musicians have come from Gǔlàng Yǔ.

The best way to enjoy Gǔlàng Yǔ is to wander among the streets, absorbing the charm and character of the place. Exploration is easy, and even the walk up to **Rìguāng Yán** (Sunlight Rock) – the highest point on Gǔlàng Yǔ (93m) – is a leisurely climb. On a clear day you can see the island of Jīnmén.

The large colonial building at the foot of Rìguāng Yán is the **Koxinga Memorial Hall** (Zhèngchénggōng Jìniànguǎn). Inside is an exhibition that is partly dedicated to the Dutch in Taiwan, and partly to Koxinga's throwing them out. The hall is open daily from around 8 to 11 am and 2 to 5 pm.

Near the ferry pier, **Xiàmén Hǎidǐ Shìjiè** (Xiamen Seaworld) is open from 8.30 am to 7 pm (entry Y60).

Ferries to Gǔlàng Yǔ leave from the pier just west of Xiàmén's Lùjiāng Dàshà. The trip is free going over, or Y1 for the top deck. From Gǔlàng Yǔ, tickets are Y1 for the bottom deck and Y2 for the top.

There are no cars on Gǔlàng Yǔ, but electric buggies buzz around the island for Y30.

XIÀMÉN & GǓLÀNG YǓ 厦门、鼓浪屿

Nánpǔtuó Sì 南普陀寺
Southern Buddhist Temple

On the southern outskirts of Xiàmén town, this Buddhist temple was built more than 1000 years ago during the Tang dynasty. It was ruined in a battle during the Ming dynasty, but rebuilt during the Qing dynasty.

Entering the temple through **Tiānwáng Diàn** (Heavenly King Hall) you are met by the laughing buddha *(mílèfó)*, with the four heavenly kings on either side. The classical Chinese inscription reads: 'When entering, regard the buddha and afterwards pay your respects to the four kings of heaven'.

Behind the laughing buddha is Wei Tuo, a Buddhist deity who safeguards the doctrine. He holds a stick that points to the ground, indicating that the temple is rich and can provide visiting monks with board and lodging (if the stick is held horizontally it means the temple is poor and is a polite way of saying find somewhere else to stay).

Behind this is a courtyard and on either side are the drum and bell towers. In front of the courtyard is **Dàxióngbǎo Diàn** (Great Heroic Treasure Hall), a two-storey building containing three buddhas that represent Buddha in his past, present and future lives.

XIÀMÉN & GǓLÀNG YǓ

PLACES TO STAY

3 Xiamen Plaza Hotel
东南亚大酒店
5 Singapore Hotel
新加坡酒店
7 Xiàmén Bīnguǎn
厦门宾馆
10 Xiáxī Lǚshè
霞溪旅社
11 Xīnqiáo Jiǔdiàn
新侨酒店
13 Lùjiāng Dàshà
鹭江大厦
16 Holiday Inn
假日皇冠海景大酒店
22 Lìzhīdǎo Jiǔdiàn
丽之岛酒店
24 Gǔlàngyǔ Bīnguǎn
鼓浪屿宾馆
32 Xiamen University Hotel
厦门大学国际学术
交流中心
34 Càiqīngjié Lóu
蔡清洁楼

PLACES TO EAT

30 Dàfāng Sùcàiguǎn
大方素菜馆

31 Gōngdé Sùcàiguǎn
功德素菜馆

OTHER

1 Long-Distance
Bus Station
长途汽车站
2 Friendship Store
友谊商场
4 Train Station
厦门火车站
6 Zhōngshān
Gōngyuán
中山公园
8 PSB
公安局外事科
9 Main Post &
Telephone Office
邮电局
12 Xinhua Bookstore
新华书店
14 Ferry Terminal
(to Gǔlàng Yǔ)
轮渡码头
(往鼓浪屿)
15 Bank of China;
CITS
中国银行,
中国国际旅行社

17 Heping Pier
(to Hong Kong)
和平码头
(往香港)
18 Ferry Terminal
(to Xiàmén)
轮渡码头
(往厦门)
19 Bówùguǎn
博物馆
20 Bank of China
中国银行
21 Xiàmén Hǎidǐ Shìjiè
厦门海底世界
23 Yīnyuè Tīng
(Musical Hall)
音乐厅
25 Rìguāng Yán
日光岩
26 Koxinga Memorial Hall
郑成功纪念馆
27 Statue of Koxinga
郑成功塑像
28 Nánpǔtuó Sì
南普陀寺
29 Internet Cafe
因特网吧
33 Xiamen University
厦门大学

The biography of Buddha and the story of Xuan Zang, the monk who made the pilgrimage to India to bring back the Buddhist scriptures, are carved on the lotus-flower base of the buddha figure. In the corridors flanking the temple are the 18 arhats (monks who reach nirvana) in their customary positions.

The **Dàbēi Diàn** (Great Compassion Hall) contains four statues of Guanyin (the goddess of compassion). The original hall was made of wood, but was destroyed by fire in 1928. Worshippers cast divining sticks at the feet of the statues to seek heavenly guidance.

The temple has a vegetarian restaurant in a nice shady courtyard where you can dine in the company of resident monks. Bus No 1 from the train station or bus No 2 from the ferry terminal both go to the temple.

Xiamen University

Xiamen University (Xiàmén Dàxué) is next to Nánpǔtuó Sì and was established with overseas Chinese funds. It features an attractive lake and makes for a pleasant stroll. The campus entrance is next to the stop for bus No 1. At the southern entrance to the university there's a pleasant beach, which is also the terminus for bus No 2.

Places to Stay

The western district around the harbour and university area has the best sights, food and atmosphere. Anything further east is inconvenient. By far the best area to stay is on Gǔlàng Yǔ. It lacks any real budget places but it will make your stay in Xiàmén both memorable and relaxing.

Around the first week of September every year a large investment fair takes place in

Xiàmén and accommodation prices go up. It can be hard to find a room during this time.

Places to Stay – Budget

The *Xiàxī Lǚshè* (☎ *202 4859, fax 202 3015*), down a small lane west off Zhongshan Lu, combines economy with an excellent location. It has a wide range of rooms, starting with singles/doubles for Y34/56 with fan and shared bath. Cheap doubles sans bathroom are available for Y74; swisher doubles with bath and air-con are Y130. There's an extra Y12 tax for foreigners. Bus No 21 from the train station takes you there. A taxi from either the train or bus station costs Y10.

On Gǔlàng Yǔ, the quaintly named *Lìzhīdǎo Jiǔdiàn* (*Beautiful Island Hotel of Gulangyu; ☎ 206 3309, fax 206 331, 133 Longtou Lu*) is airy, bright and clean and has cosy rooms from Y120 (without window) to Y168 (with window). The *Gǔlàngyǔ Bīnguǎn* (☎ *206 3856*) is the former property of an overseas Chinese businessman from Indonesia. Three mansions are surrounded by ancient banyan trees. Unfortunately the rooms are overpriced and aren't very well maintained, but the setting makes up for this. The cheapest doubles start at Y240.

The *Overseas Student Dormitory* (*Càiqīngjié Lóu; ☎ 208 4528, fax 208 6774*) at Xiamen University has singles/doubles/triples for Y120/150/170, though rooms are usually taken up by foreign students from September to June. You can get there from the university's south gate. Walk uphill for about 100m then take a left and keep your eyes open for a purple 10-storey building.

The *Singapore Hotel* (*Xīnjiāpō Jiǔdiàn; ☎ 202 6668, fax 202 5950*) is conveniently located next to Zhōngshān Gōngyuán (Sun Yatsen Park). Small doubles are available for Y190 and larger rooms are Y235.

Places to Stay – Mid-Range

Most accommodation in Xiàmén is mid-range, shading into top end. It's really only worth considering the hotels near the harbour. The *Lùjiāng Dàshà* (☎ *202 2922, fax 202 4644*) has a prime location opposite the

Gǔlàng Yǔ ferry terminal. It's a 1940s Chinese-style building that often has good deals. Standard doubles are Y535, but it also has some cheaper singles for Y320 (add a 10% service charge).

The *Xiàmén Bīnguǎn* (☎ *202 2265, fax 202 1765*) is a stately place with a certain colonial elegance. Doubles start at Y530.

The *Xīnqiáo Jiǔdiàn* (☎ *203 8883, fax 203 8765, 444 Zhongshan Lu*) is a classy old place with singles/doubles for Y350/450, plus a Y10 addition for air-con. Discounts up to 40% are available.

Another mid-range option is just inside the north gate of Xiamen University. The *Xiamen University Hotel* (*Xiàmén Dàxué Xuéshù Jiāoliú Zhōngxīn; ☎ 208 7783, 208 6116*) has standard doubles for Y390 and cheaper older rooms for Y260.

Places to Stay – Top End

There is a wide range of top-end accommodation in Xiàmén, but much of it is badly located in the eastern part of town.

The best place to stay is the *Holiday Inn* (*Jiàrì Huángguān Hǎijǐng Dàjiǔdiàn; ☎ 202 3333, fax 203 6666, 12-8 Zhenhai Lu*). Standard doubles start at US$160. It also has some of the best international and Chinese restaurants in town.

Another top-end hotel, the *Marco Polo Hotel* (*Mǎgē Bōluó Dōngfāng Dàjiǔdiàn; ☎ 509 1888, fax 509 2888, 8 Jianye Lu*), has standard rooms starting at US$160, which can be discounted as low as US$85. Similarly, the *Xiamen Mandarin Hotel* (*Xiàmén Měilìhuá Dàjiǔdiàn; ☎ 603 1666, fax 602 1814, Xinglong Lu*) has discounts for standard rooms that are normally US$180.

Beside the train station, the *Xiamen Plaza Hotel* (*Xiàmén Dōngnányà Dàjiǔdiàn; ☎ 505 8888, fax 505 8899*) is worth checking out for discounts of more than 50% for its listed Y918 rooms.

Places to Eat

Xiàmén is brimming with places to eat. All the alleys off Zhongshan Lu harbour cheap eats. Head down Jukou Jie, near the intersection with Siming Lu, which offers a plethora of Sìchuān restaurants.

Businesses compete for space along the towering sacred peaks of Huá Shān in Shaanxi.

Shopping in the rain in Luòyáng, Hénán

The ancient city walls that encompass the great city of Xī'ān, Shaanxi

A quick snip in a Yuèyáng alley, Húnán

Near the university there are good, cheap, attractive restaurants lining Siming Nanlu and Yanwu Jie. Two vegetarian restaurants are the *Dàfāng Sùcàiguǎn* (☎ 209 3236) and the *Gōngdé Sùcàiguǎn*. Try the monk's vegetables *(luóhàn zhāifàn)*.

The Holiday Inn has a good coffee shop, a bakery and an Italian restaurant. Xiàmén also has its share of good bakeries scattered around, as well as the usual range of fast-food outlets.

Gǔlàng Yǔ is the place to go for seafood. Fresh is best and the meals swim around in buckets and trays outside the restaurants, but they're not cheap. For budget eats, wander up the hill a little from the Gǔlàngyǔ Bīnguǎn, to the square formed by an intersection of roads.

Getting There & Away

Air Xiàmén Airlines is the main airline under the CAAC banner in this part of China. There are innumerable ticket offices around town, many of which are in the larger hotels like the Holiday Inn. Ask at your hotel.

CAAC has flights to Hong Kong, Kuala Lumpur, Manila, Penang and Singapore. Silk Air (☎ 205 3280) flies to Singapore and has an office in the Holiday Inn. All Nippon Airways (☎ 573 2888) flies to Osaka and has ticketing agents at the Holiday Inn and Lùjiāng Dàshà. Dragonair (☎ 202 5433) is located in the Marco Polo Hotel.

Xiàmén airport has flights to all major domestic destinations around China, including Wǔyí Shān (Y470) four times a week.

Bus Deluxe and economy buses leave from the long-distance bus station and the ferry terminal. Destinations include Fúzhōu (Y80), Quánzhōu (Y32; 1½ hours) and Shàntóu (Y100; five hours). Departures are frequent and there are express buses to Guǎngzhōu (Y200; 12 hours), Shēnzhèn (Y180; nine hours) and Hong Kong (Y350; 10 hours). Buses also make the trips inland to Lóngyán (Y44; three hours) and Yǒngdìng (Y37; five hours).

Train Fújiàn has a meagre rail system. There's a line from Guǎngzhōu to Shàntóu (close to the Fújiàn border), but still no link-up with any cities in Fújiàn. The line from Xiàmén heads north and connects with the main Shànghǎi-to-Guǎngzhōu line at the Yīngtán junction. Another line runs from Yīngtán to Fúzhōu.

From Xiàmén there are direct trains to destinations including Hángzhōu (Y250; 23 hours), Shànghǎi (Y300; 25 hours) and Běijīng (Y390; 39 hours). Trains to Wǔyí Shān take 14 hours and a hard sleeper is Y142. The train to Fúzhōu takes a circuitous route – the bus is cheaper and quicker. It's fairly painless to book tickets at the train station. CITS will make bookings for a Y35 service fee.

Boat Ships to Hong Kong leave from the Amoy Port Administration passenger terminal at Heping Pier on Tongwen Lu, about 10 minutes walk from the Lùjiāng Dàshà. There's a ticket office at the terminal.

The boat leaves every Wednesday at 5 pm and takes 19 hours. The fares are:

Class	Fare
VIP	Y670
1st class	Y470
2nd class	Y430
3rd class	Y390
Seat	Y340

Getting Around

The airport is 15km north-east of the waterfront district, or about 8km from the eastern district. Taxis cost around Y35. Bus No 27 travels from the airport to the ferry terminal via the train station.

Frequent minibuses run between the train station and ferry terminal for Y1. Buses to Xiamen University go from the train station (bus No 1) and from the ferry terminal (bus No 2). Taxis are cheap, starting at Y7.

AROUND XIÀMÉN

The **Jíměi Xuéxiào Cūn** (Jimei School Village) is a much-touted tourist attraction on the mainland north of Xiàmén Island. The

FUJIÀN 福建

Cūn: village

The left radical of *cūn* is *mù*, which means trees or wood; the right side means inch, measurement or regulations. In ancient China, a household with an acre of land would have grown mulberry trees for silk worms. Therefore, surrounding people's homes there would have been trees, especially mulberry trees. Thus, a village is somewhere trees are planted according to rules and regulations!

school was set up in 1913 by Tan Kahkee, a native of the area who migrated to Singapore and became a wealthy industrialist. He returned some of that wealth to the mother country, and the school now has around 20,000 students.

The Chinese architecture has a certain appeal and the waters in front of the school are the site of a dragon-boat race at the feast of Quyuan (usually happening around mid-June). Bus Nos 66 and 67 to Jíměi leave from near the waterfront on the corner of Zhongshan Lu and Tonqen Lu (Y3/5 without/with air-con).

YŎNGDÌNG 永定
☎ 0597

Yŏngdìng is an out-of-the-way place in south-west Fújiàn. Set in a rural area dominated by small mountains and farmland, it wouldn't be worth a footnote, but for its unusual architecture. Known as 'earth buildings' *(tǔlóu)*, these large, circular edifices resemble fortresses and were probably designed for defence. They were built by the Hakka, one of China's ethnic minorities.

Coming from Hénán in northern China, the Hakka people first moved to the Guăngdōng and Fújiàn provinces in the south to escape severe persecution in their homelands. The name Hakka means 'guests'; today Hakka communities are scattered all over South-East Asia.

There are no *tǔlóu* in Yŏngdìng itself, which is a particularly ugly town. One of the main buildings sought out by visitors is the Zhènchénglo, 43km north-east of Yŏngdìng in Húkēng. Frequent minibuses travel there from the Yŏngdìng bus station (Y7; 1½ hours). You can get to Yŏngdìng by bus from Guăngdōng or Xiàmén (Y37; five hours) or Lóngyán (Y7/15 without/with air-con; one hour).

QUÁNZHŌU 泉州
☎ 0595 • pop 6,501,300

Quánzhōu was once a great port city and an instrumental stop on the maritime silk route. Marco Polo, back in the 13th century, called it Zaiton and informed his readers that '... it is one of the two ports in the world with the biggest flow of merchandise'. It's slipped a few pegs since then, but Quánzhōu still has a few products of note, including the creamy-white *dehua* (or 'blanc-de-Chine' as it is known in the west) porcelain figures, and locally crafted puppets.

Prettier and cleaner than Fúzhōu, Quánzhōu's prime attraction is Kāiyuán Sì, offering a relaxing retreat.

Orientation & Information
The long-distance bus station is in the southern corner of the city on the intersection of Wenling Lu and Quanxiu Jie.

The Kāiyuán Sì is in the north-west of town on the corner of Xinhua Lu and Xi Jie, 2km from the bus station.

The PSB office (☎ 218 0308) and post office are on Dong Jie. There's a Bank of China branch on Jiuyi Jie, but for travellers cheques you have to go to the main branch on Fengze Lu.

Things to See
Kāiyuán Sì (Kaiyuan Temple) is distinguished by its pair of tall **pagodas** and the

huge grounds in which it is set. Originally called Liánhūa Sì (Lotus Temple), construction began in AD 686, and in AD 738 was changed to the name of Kāiyuán during the reign of the famous Tang emperor Tang Minghuang, who ruled at the height of the Tang dynasty.

It was founded in the 7th century during the Tang dynasty, but reached its peak during Song times when 1000 monks lived there. The present buildings, including the pagodas and the main hall, are more recent. The main courtyard is the refuge of some huge, ancient trees, one of which has a drooping branch supported by a carved pillar.

Within the grounds of Kāiyuán Sì, behind the eastern pagoda, is a **museum** containing the enormous hull of a Song dynasty seagoing junk, which was excavated near Quánzhōu. The temple is on Xi Jie, in the north-western part of town. A ride by mini-van taxi from the bus station will cost Y6.

There are some charming little side streets off Xi Jie; if you're staying in a hotel in the south of Quánzhōu get a pedicab to Kāiyuán Sì and the driver will probably take you down the maze of winding streets that lead there.

Quánzhōu is studded with small temples and can make for an interesting ramble. The **Qīngjìng Sì** (Peaceful Mosque), on Tumen Jie, is evidence of the once large Muslim community and while not spectacular, is worth visiting.

Places to Stay

There is nothing particularly cheap in Quánzhōu, but the *Huáqiáo Zhìjiā (Overseas Chinese Home; ☎ 228 3559, 228 3560)* on Wenling Lu, has some of the cheapest rooms. Singles/doubles/triples are Y150/130/180. The *Jiànfú Dàshà (☎ 228 3511)*, next door, was recently renovated and has comfortable rooms starting at Y296 and suites for Y450. Discounts of up to 40% are possible.

Close to the bus station, the *Jīnzhōu Dàjiǔdiàn (☎ 258 6788, 258 1011, Quanxiu Jie)* has small doubles for Y200 and better

ones for Y260 (with a possible 35% discount).

The best value in Quánzhōu is at the three-star *Huáqiáo Dàshà (Overseas Chinese Hotel; ☎ 228 2192, fax 228 4612)*. The north building has doubles starting at Y350 and up, while the much nicer south building has recently renovated doubles for Y540, as well as some cheaper doubles for as low as Y190. The best part of this hotel, however, is the location and varied facilities, such as a swimming pool, a bowling alley and restaurants.

Places to Eat

The are loads of small restaurants and bakeries in the area surrounding Kāiyuán Sì. A nightly food market also sets up near Guānye Miào (Guanye Temple) off Tumen Jie.

One of the best places to eat in Quánzhōu is at the Quánzhōu Huáqiáo Dàshà's (see Places to Stay earlier) *Tángrén Shíjie (Tang Dynasty Chinese Specialty Restaurant)*. Set up like an indoor food street, you can pick and choose from a variety of delicious and reasonably priced cooked items.

Getting There, Away & Around

The long-distance bus station has buses to destinations as far away as Shànghǎi and Guǎngzhōu. From Xiàmén Quánzhōu is a two-hour trip along the freeway on deluxe buses (Y32). Economy buses do the trip for Y18 but are slower.

Likewise, deluxe buses travel to Fúzhōu (Y60) in 3½ hours while economy (Y33) buses take five hours. Trains travel from Quánzhōu to Wǔyí Shān (Y148, sleepers; 15 hours), leaving from a station 7km east of the city centre.

You can also book tickets for trains originating in Xiàmén or Fúzhōu at two outlets near Tóngfó Sì (Brass Buddha Temple). One is directly across from the Huáqiáo Dàshà and the other is across from the Bank of China.

Quánzhōu has some useful buses, but minivan taxis are very cheap and can take you most places for Y6.

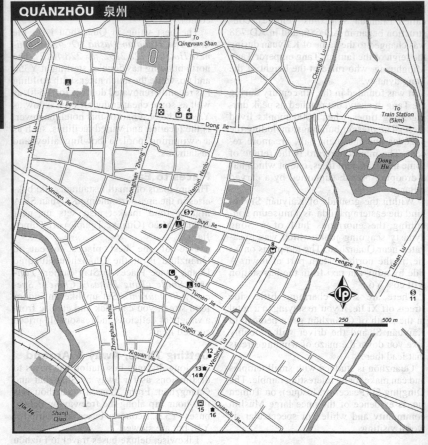

QUÁNZHŌU 泉州

AROUND QUÁNZHŌU
Qīngyuán Shān 青原山
Pure Water-Source Mountains

Qīngyuán Shān is a reasonably scenic mountain area scattered with a few caves, tombs and statues.

The **Qīngyuán Dòng** (Buddhist Caves) in the mountain were destroyed during the Cultural Revolution, although some people still pray in front of the spaces where the statues used to be.

This area was once the site of violent armed confrontations between two Red Guard factions.

Also found on the mountain is the 'rock that moves'. It's one of these nicely shaped and balanced rocks that wobbles when you give it a nudge; supposedly to see it move you have to place a stick or a piece of straw lengthways between the rock and the ground and watch it bend as someone pushes on the rock.

The largest statue on the mountain is a stubby Song dynasty effigy of Laotzu, legendary founder of Taoism. Locals say Kuomintang troops used the statue for target practice, but there's no sign of bullet holes.

QUÁNZHŌU

PLACES TO STAY
- 5 Huáqiáo Dàshà;
Tángrén Shíjiē
华侨大厦；
- 13 Jiànfú Dàshà
建福大厦
- 14 Huáqiáo Zhījiā
华侨之家
- 16 Jīnzhōu Dàjiǔdiàn
金州大酒店

OTHER
- 1 Kāiyuán Sì
开元寺

- 2 Zhonglou
Department
Store
钟楼百货
- 3 Post &
Telecommunications
Building
邮电局
- 4 PSB
公安局
- 6 Tóngfó Sì
铜佛寺
- 7 Bank of China
中国银行

- 8 Post &
Telecommunications
Building
邮电局
- 9 Qīngjìng Sì
清净寺
- 10 Guānyuè Miào
关岳庙
- 11 Bank of China
中国银行
- 12 Xinhua Bookstore
新华书店
- 15 Long-Distance Bus Station
泉州汽车站

Getting There & Away

From Quánzhōu, bus No 3 by the clock tower at the intersection between Xi Jie and Zhongshan Lu goes to Qīngyuán Shān.

Chóngwǔ 崇武

One of China's best preserved walled cities, Chóngwǔ is a little-visited marvel, on the coast to the east of Quánzhōu. The granite city walls are around 2.5km long and average 7m in height. Scattered around the walls are 1304 battlements; there are four gates into the city.

The town wall was built in 1387 by the Ming government as a front line defence against marauding Japanese pirates, and it has survived the last 600 years remarkably well. Koxinga also took refuge here in his battle against Qing forces. The surrounding area is full of stone-carving workshops.

Frequent minibuses depart Quánzhōu's bus station to nearby Huì'ān (Y5; 45 minutes). From there yellow minivans (Y5) and minibuses (Y4) make the short hop to Chóngwǔ.

MÉIZHŌU 湄州

About halfway between Quánzhōu and Fúzhōu is the county of Pútián. Just offshore is the island of Méizhōu, known for its scenic beauty and dotted with temples.

Taoists credit Méizhōu as being the birthplace of Mazu, goddess of the sea. Mazu is known by a number of names: Tin Hau in

Hong Kong, Thien Hau in Vietnam, and so on. As protector of sailors and fishing folk, she enjoys VIP status in coastal provinces like Fújiàn.

Mazu's birthday is celebrated according to the lunar calendar, on the 23rd day of the third moon, and at this time the island comes alive with worshippers. In summer, it's also a popular spot for Taiwanese tourists.

You reach Méizhōu by taking a bus to Pútián city, then a minibus to Wénjiā on the Zhōngwén peninsula and a ferry to the island. The temple is simply called the **Māzǔ Miào** (Mazu Temple).

WǓYÍ SHĀN 武夷山
☎ 0599

In the far north-west corner of Fújiàn is Wǔyí Shān, an attractive region of rivers, crags and forests. It recently became a protected area and is certainly worth visiting if you want to get away from towns and cities. Unfortunately, it is also a prime tourist spot and is home to glib-tongued hustlers and would-be guides pursuing tourists in motorised tricycles. It can get crowded during holiday times; the low season (when it's cold) can be a good time to visit.

The scenic area lies on the west bank of the stream, Chóngyáng Xī, and some of the accommodation is located along its shore. Most of the hotels are concentrated in the *resort district (dùjiàqū)* on the east side of the river. The main settlement is Wǔyíshān city, about

FÚJIÀN 福建

10km to the north-east, with the train station and airport roughly half-way between.

Information

CTS (☎ 525 2819) is at the bottom of the driveway leading up to the Wǔyí Shānzhuāng (Wuyi Mountain Villa), which is on the west side of the river. It can book train and plane tickets. Most of the hotels will also book tickets. The main Bank of China in Wǔyíshān city is on Wujiu Lu and can change travellers cheques. Maps of the Wǔyí Shān area are available at small bookshops in the resort district.

Things to See

The main reason to visit Wǔyí Shān is to walk up to the sheer rock peaks that jut skywards and take a trip down the Jiǔqū Hé (Nine Twists River) on bamboo rafts. The main entrance is at Wǔyí Gōng, near the confluence of the Chongyang and Jiǔqū Rivers. An entrance fee of Y71 gets you into all other sights, or you can pay individually at each entrance. Tickets are usually in the vicinity of Y17 to Y30. One way to get around the entrance fees is to visit places at 6 am before the ticket booths open. It's also a good way to get a jump on the crowds.

A couple of nice walks are the 530m Dàwáng Fēng (Great King Peak), accessed through the main entrance, and 410m Tiānyoú Fēng (Heavenly Tour Peak), where an entrance is reached by road up the Jiǔqū Hé. Trails within the scenic area connect all the major sites. At the northern end of the scenic area, the Shǔlián Dòng (Water Curtain Cave) is a cleft in the rock about one third of the way up a 100m cliff face. If it's not dry, water plunges over the top of the cliff creating a curtain of spray.

One of the highlights for visitors is floating down the Jiǔqū Hé, which is named for the 'nine twists' (jiǔqū) of its meandering form. Bamboo rafts are fitted with rattan chairs and depart from Xīngcūn, a short bus ride west of the resort area. The trip down the river takes over an hour and boats run from 8 am to 1.30 pm. Tickets are Y60.

One of the mysteries of Wǔyí Shān is the cavities carved out of the rock faces at great heights that once held boat-shaped coffins. Scientists have dated some of these artefacts as being as old as 4000 years old. If you're taking the raft down the river, it's possible to see some remnants of these coffins on the west cliff face of the third meander or 'twist', also known as Xiǎozàngshān Fēng (Small Storing Place Peak).

Places to Stay

There's a whole range of accommodation in Wǔyí Shān, mostly concentrated on the east side of the river. Consequently, the west side is quieter.

There are a few cheap places that accept foreigners scattered on the west bank immediately across from the main bridge spanning the Chongyang River. Try the Aìhú Bīnguǎn (☎ 525 2268), the first in line after you cross over the bridge. Small, basic doubles and triples are Y160 and Y210.

One of the nicest places in Wǔyí Shān, with secluded and peaceful grounds is the Wǔyí Shānzhuāng (Wuyi Mountain Villa; ☎ 525 1888, fax 525 2567). Double rooms start at Y280 and discounts are available mid-week.

The east bank area is packed with hotels. At the southern end of the district, the Lántíng Fàndiàn (☎ 525 2880, fax 525 2569) has comfortable rooms with balconies and scenic views. Doubles start at Y338, but it's possible to get discounts mid-week. There's an outdoor swimming pool, though it's a bit scummy, and a very good restaurant.

The Guómáo Dàjiǔdiàn (International Trade Hotel; ☎ 525 2521, fax 525 2891) has some of the best amenities, including a western restaurant, but the surroundings are a little austere. Standard doubles start at Y480.

Getting There & Away

Wǔyí Shān is serviced by flights from Běijīng (Y1080; two hours), Shànghǎi (Y530; one hour), Fúzhōu (Y380; 35 minutes), Xiàmén (Y470; 50 minutes), Guǎngzhōu (Y710; one hour and 35 minutes) and Hong Kong (Y1380; two hours). Direct trains go to Wǔyí Shān from Fúzhōu, Quánzhōu and Xiàmén. See the Getting There & Away section of those cities for details.

The long-distance bus station is in the north-west part of Wǔyíshān city. Daily buses go south to Fúzhōu (Y90; eight hours) and north-east to Wēnzhōu (Y125; 12 hours). There are frequent buses to Nánpíng (Y37; three hours) and north to Shàgráo (Y23; two hours) in Jiāngxī. It's possible to book train tickets at CTS for trains stopping in Shàowǔ, which head to other destinations such as Shànghǎi, Běijīng, etc. There are frequent buses to Shàowǔ (Y15; 1½ hours) from Wǔyíshān

city that also stop in the resort district. The road traverses some nice countryside.

Getting Around

A public bus shuttles between Wǔyíshān city and the resort district, and there are minibuses between Wǔyíshān city and Xīngcūn.

Expect to pay about Y10 for a motorised trishaw from the resort district to most of the other scenic area entrances. Minivan taxis are also plentiful. A ride from the train station or airport to the resort district will cost about Y20.

Liáoníng 辽宁

Once the southernmost province of Manchuria, Liáoníng continues to gleam with a nugget or two of Manchu history. Visitors today, however, are drawn to this province by its beaches, hiking and, most often, by its dynamic city life. Those intrigued by borders or hoping to get a glimpse into North Korea may also enjoy the pilgrimage to Dāndōng, situated across Yālù Jiāng (Green Duck River) from this neighbouring country.

The enticing refuge of Dàlián is Liáoníng's most popular destination for travellers. Nicknamed 'the Hong Kong of the North', Dàlián is an innovative and fast-developing city complemented by beautiful historic architecture, relatively clean streets and surrounding parklands. This city alone makes a trip to Liáoníng worthwhile, even if it's the only part of China's north-east that you visit.

SHĚNYÁNG 沈阳
☎ 024 • pop 6,738,000

Shěnyáng was a Mongol trading centre from as far back as the 11th century, becoming the capital of the Manchu empire in the 17th century. With the Manchu conquest of Běijīng in 1644, Shěnyáng became a secondary capital under the Manchu name of Mukden, and a centre of the ginseng trade.

Industrialisation was introduced by the Russians, who occupied the city at the turn of the century, and continued by the Japanese, the victors of the Russo-Japanese War (1904–05) who fought the last major land battle of the war in Shěnyáng. Throughout its history, Shěnyáng has rapidly changed hands, in turn dominated by warlords, the Japanese (1931), the Russians (1945), the Kuomintang (1946) and the Chinese Communist Party (1948). At the end of WWII, the city was looted of its industrial hardware.

Shěnyáng is, for the most part, a grim mess of socialist town planning, solidified by ice in winter and roasting in summer. History buffs will find solace in some well

Highlights

Capital: Shěnyáng
Population: 41.1 million
Area: 145,700 sq km

- Běi Líng in Shěnyáng, the burial place of the founder of the Qing dynasty that dates back to the start of the Manchu era
- The dynamic port city of Dàlián, with its sea breezes and relaxed atmosphere
- Dāndōng, the gateway to North Korea

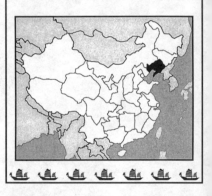

preserved relics of the Manchu era while most other travellers would consider it wise to leap-frog Shěnyáng for more pleasant and interesting destinations.

Orientation

Shěnyáng is built on the typical north-south axis of the Qing dynasty, bordered to the south by the Hún Hé (Muddy River). While accommodation is conveniently located around the train stations, the sights are scattered all over the city.

Information

Consulates Shěnyáng's US consulate (☎ 322 1198, fax 282 0074) is at 52 Shisi Wei Lu in the Heping District. Next door is

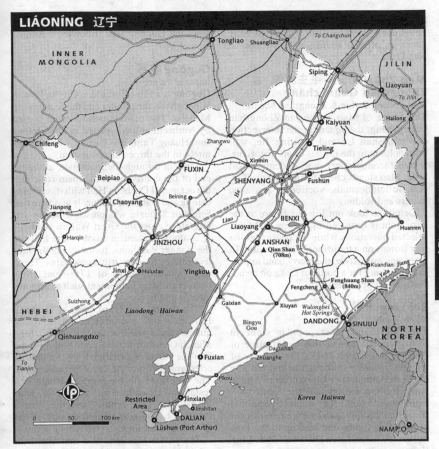

LIÁONÍNG 辽宁

INNER MONGOLIA

JILIN

HEBEI

NORTH KOREA

To Changchun

Tongliao
Shuangliao
Siping
Liaoyuan
To Jilin
Hailong
Kaiyuan
Zhangwu
Xinmin
Tieling
Chifeng
FUXIN
SHENYANG
Fushun
Beipiao
Beining
BENXI
Jianping
Chaoyang
Liaoyang
Huanren
Harqin
Liao
He
ANSHAN
Qian Shan
(708m)
Kuandian Jiang
Yalu
JINZHOU
Jinxi
Huludao
Yingkou
Fenghuang Shan
(840m)
Fengcheng
Suizhong
Gaixian
Xiuyan
Liaodong Haiwan
Bingyu Gou
Wulongbei Hot Springs
DANDONG
SINUIJU
Qinhuangdao
Dagushan
To Tianjin
Fuxian
Zhuanghe
Pikou
Korea Haiwan
NORTH KOREA
Restricted Area
Jinxian
Jinshitan
DALIAN
NAMP'O
Lüshun (Port Arthur)

0   50   100 km

the Japanese consulate (☎ 322 7490). If you're thinking of heading out of China via Dāndōng, there is a North Korean consulate (☎ 685 2742) in Shěnyáng, however visas are more likely to be obtained in Běijīng.

Money The main branch of the Bank of China is at 253 Shifu Lu. There is also a branch conveniently located in Room 301 of the Traders Shopping Centre, next to the Traders Hotel.

Post & Communications The main post office is in the Yóuzhèng Dàshà Bīnguǎn;

most large hotels also have postal facilities. At the time of writing, there was no public Internet access but check about the current situation with major hotels and China Telecom, which currently provides private line access only.

PSB The Public Security Bureau (PSB; Gōngānjú) is at 66 Bei San Jing Jie, near the south-west corner with Shi-Yi Wei Lu.

Travel Agent You'll find the China International Travel Service (CITS; Zhōngguó Guójì Lǚxíngshè; ☎ 612 2445, fax 680

8772) in a building about 100m north of the Fènghuáng Fàndiàn (see Places to Stay later); its official address is 113 Huanghe Nan Dajie.

Maó Zhǔxí Xiàng 毛主席像 & Zhōngshān Guǎngchǎng
Mao Zedong Statue & Zhongshan Square

This statue of Mao Zedong in Zhōngshān Guǎngchǎng, the square at the intersection of Zhongshan Lu and Nanjing Jie, will bring a lump to the throats of art historians, socialist iconographers and students of bad taste. Mao stands cheerily aloft, flanked by ecstatic intellectuals, vociferous peasants, miners and soldiers.

Details to look out for: the figure at the very front is thrusting up a copy of Mao's selected quotations while the peasant at the rear stomps on a traditional Chinese lion. In true tragicomic style, the merry band appear to be reaching for a bottle of Coke on an advertisement opposite.

Běi Líng 北陵
North Tomb

The finest and most popular sight in Shěnyáng, Běi Líng is the burial place of Huang Taiji (1592–1643), the founder of the Qing dynasty (although he did not live to see the conquest of China). Set in a huge park, Běilíng Gōngyuán, the tomb took eight years to build. The impressive animal statues on the approach to it are reminiscent of the Ming tombs and lead up to the central grassy mound area known as Zhāo Líng (Luminous Tomb).

Dōng Líng 东陵
East Tomb

Also known as Fu Líng, Dōng Líng is set in a forested area 8km from Shěnyáng. Entombed here, along with his mistress, is Nurhachi, grandfather of Emperor Shunzhi, who launched the Manchu invasion of China in 1644.

Started in 1626, construction of the tomb took several years to complete, with subsequent additions and renovations. This small tomb is perched on a wooded hilltop overlooking a river.

To get to Dōng Líng take bus No 218 from the Gùgōng (see following). Admission is Y6.

Gùgōng 故宫
Imperial Palace

Gùgōng is a mini-Forbidden City in layout, although it's far smaller and the features are Manchu. The main structures were started by Nurhachi and completed in 1636 by his son, Huang Taiji. It is currently and indefinitely in the throes of restoration.

Straight through the main gate, at the far end of the courtyard, is the main structure: the octagonal Dazheng Hall with its coffered ceiling and elaborate throne. It was here that Emperor Shunzhi was crowned before setting off to cross the Great Wall in 1644.

In the courtyard in front of the hall are the Banner Pavilions, formerly administrative offices used by tribal chieftains. These now house displays of 17th- and 18th-century military equipment such as armour, swords and bows.

The central courtyard, west of Dazheng Hall, contains a conference hall, living quarters and some shamanist structures (one Manchu custom was to pour boiling wine into the ear of a sacrificial pig, so that its cries would attract the devotees' ancestors). The courtyard on the western fringe is a residential area added on by Emperor Qianlong in the 18th century and the Wensu Pavilion to the rear housed a copy of the Qianlong anthology.

The palace functions as a museum, with exhibitions of ivory and jade artefacts, furniture, and Ming and Qing paintings. There is also a decent display of enamels and ceramics and an excellent collection of musical instruments. Exhibit captions are in Chinese.

You'll find the palace in the oldest section of the city; take bus No 7 from Shěnyáng's south train station. Admission is Y25.

Běi Tǎ 北塔
North Pagoda

Although Běi Tǎ is located in the haze of nearby industry, this small oasis is nevertheless worth a visit. This is the only pagoda

Chen Liyan

All of a sudden, I became a laid off worker. It was late 1997 when we were summoned to a meeting and heard that all those aged above 37 must take early retirement and 55% of their salaries. At first I tried to refuse, then I heard those who were laid off later might receive no money at all. Life around the factory had seemed normal as we were paid every month, unlike many other factories. I even enjoyed free lunches there until the very day I left.

Staying at home that winter was the worst time I ever experienced. I had worked for the Shenyang Textile Factory for nearly 20 years. I was not highly skilled, but I did my best. For many years, I worked all three shifts, standing in front of the spindles to connect the broken threads. But that was it. Twenty years before the normal retirement age and I was stuck at home, so stressed that my health suffered for a long time.

OXFORD UNIVERSITY PRESS

I looked around for a job, but it was far from easy. I went to a job fair, but women over 35 years old without any particular skill and low education simply had no chance. I don't mean to be choosy, but some jobs are just not suitable. People suggested I deliver newspapers, but I can't bike very well; a family needed a nanny for a one-year-old baby, but that was too much responsibility. A relative eventually found me a job washing clothes at a laundry. I liked the job as the Y300 salary was not bad with regular working hours. But the business soon went bust. I had to start all over again.

A month later I was hired by the neighbourhood committee to patrol Ningbo Rd and tell peddlers to move to the nearby central market. It's an effort to keep the area tidy, and the market can also charge administration fees, but it's cold standing in the streets all day, and sometimes I get threatened. My monthly salary is only Y200 and I work every day of the week. If I want the weekend off, the salary is only Y150! The salary is all I get now. When I worked at the factory, I received free medical care, a monthly bonus, and subsidies for showers and haircuts.

I daren't think about the future. My husband could be made redundant at any time. We have a son at school and tuition is increasingly expensive. I've been paid Y170 per month by my old factory so far, but for how long, I have no idea. Falling to this degree, I don't know who to blame, except myself for being unlucky. Sometimes when I watch TV dramas about laid-off workers, how they became more successful in their new careers after overcoming the depression of being laid off, I wish it could happen in my life. But I know it's impossible.

Abridged from *China Remembers*, by Zhang Lijia & Calum MacLeod, published by Oxford University Press (1999)

left intact of the four that once marked the boundaries of the city. Tourism has rekindled an interest in it which has led to a clean-up and new paint job of the both the pagoda and its accompanying halls.

The main hall features magnificently painted murals of deities – slightly gruesome but amazing none the less. Within a second hall is a panelled painting of Shěnyáng, dated from 1665. The detail is

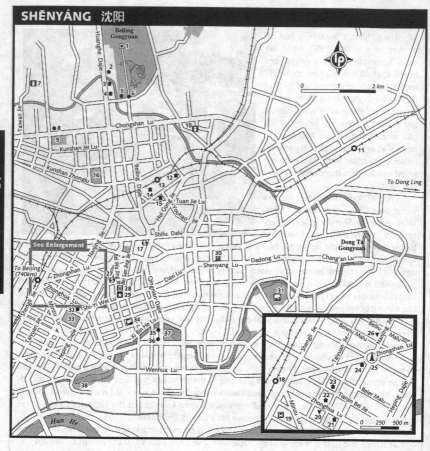

SHĚNYÁNG 沈阳

minute, giving you a glimpse into homes, courts and street life. The final hall contains a buddha at his finest – big, gold and jovial with a belly to boot.

Entry to the pagoda is down an unmarked lane off Chongshan Lu. Take bus No 328 from either the north or south train station or No 213 from Běi Líng. Entry is Y5; it's open from 8.30 am to 4.30 pm.

Wúgòu Jìngguāng Shělì Tǎ
Pagoda of Buddhist Ashes
West of Běi Líng, Wúgòu Shěguāng Jìnlì Tǎ is home to a 13m-high, 13-storey brick

pagoda dating back to AD 1044. The adjacent temple has been developed into a small museum exhibiting photos of stupas from throughout China as well as relics removed from the interior of the pagoda.

This place is quiet – perhaps even a little too quiet. The dust is settling, the upkeep is lacking and the bored attendant obliged to follow you from room to room is quite unnerving.

Officially given the English name of 'Pagoda of Buddhist Ashes', the ticket for the temple ironically reads 'Stupa Without Worldly Dust and Dirt'.

SHĚNYÁNG

PLACES TO STAY & EAT
- 3 Fènghuáng Fàndiàn
  凤凰饭店
- 4 Liáoníng Dàshà
  辽宁大厦
- 12 Dōngfāng Dàshà
  东方大厦
- 14 Yóuzhèng Dàshà Bīnguǎn;
  Main Post Office
  邮政大厦宾馆、
  邮电局
- 15 Gloria Plaza Hotel
  凯莱大酒店
- 20 Food Fair
  美食城
- 21 New World Courtyard
  新世界酒店
- 22 Traders Hotel;
  Traders Shopping Centre
  商贸饭店、商贸中心
- 23 Dōngběi Fàndiàn
  东北饭店
- 24 Liáoníng Bīnguǎn
  辽宁宾馆
- 26 Curry Shop
  山小室咖喱快餐

OTHER
- 1 Běi Líng
  北陵

- 2 CITS
  中国国际旅行社
- 5 Aeroflot
- 6 Park Entrance
  公园门口
- 7 Wúgòu Jìnggūcīng Shěli Tǎ
  无垢净光舍利塔
- 8 Liáoníng Dàxué
  辽宁大学
- 9 Bǎiniǎo Gōngyuán
  百鸟公园
- 10 Běi Tǎ
  北塔
- 11 East Train Station
  东站
- 13 North Train Station;
  Shěntiě Dàshà
  北火车站；
  沈铁大厦宾馆
- 16 Bitáng Gōngyuán
  碧塘公园
- 17 Bank of China
  中国银行
- 18 South Train Station
  火车南站
- 19 South Long-Distance
  Bus Station
  长途汽车南站

- 25 Maó Zhǔxí Xiàng
  毛主席像
- 27 Bank of China
  中国银行
- 28 Liáoníng Shěng
  Bówùguǎn
  辽宁省博物馆
- 29 PSB
  公安局外事科
- 30 Gùgōng
  故宫
- 31 Dòngwùyuán (Zoo)
  动物园
- 32 CAAC
  中国民航
- 33 Zhongshan Gongyuán
  中山公园
- 34 US Consulate;
  Japanese Consulate
  美国领事馆
- 35 TV Tower; Foreign
  Languages Bookstore
  电视塔、
  外文书店
- 36 Běifāng Túshū Chéng
  北方图书城
- 37 Qīngnián Gōngyuán
  青年公园
- 38 Nánhú Gōngyuán
  南湖公园

To reach the pagoda, take bus No 15 from Běi Líng and get off at the corner of Taiwan Jie and Kunshan Je Lu. From here, walk north, cross the bridge and hang a right. The temple is a three-minute walk north of here, down an alley on the right. Look for a red gate.

Liáoníng Shéng Buówùguǎn
省博物馆
Liaoning Provincial Museum
This huge museum houses diverse artefacts collected from throughout Liáoníng – from fossils and bones to jade and teacups.

On the ground floor is an interesting display of before and after photographs of the city; the architecture of Shěnyáng in the early 1900s and the modern delights of shopping centres and McDonalds' that have replaced it.

Admission is Y8 and it's open daily from 9 am to 5 pm. The entrance to the museum is on Shi Wei Lu, just off Bei Wu Jing Jie.

Places to Stay
If you arrive at Shěnyáng's north train station, the cheapest and place to stay is the *Yóuzhèng Dàshà Bīnguǎn* (☎ 252 8717) where prices for doubles range from Y98 to Y206. Even more conveniently located is the *Shěntiě Dàshà (Railway Hotel; ☎ 252 2888)*. If you can convince them you're Chinese, dorm beds are available for Y40; if not, doubles start at Y120.

To the east of the north train station is the *Dōngfāng Dàshà (☎ 252 7388, fax 252 4520, 112 Beizhan Lu).* It looks like it should be expensive, but doubles/triples/suites start at Y138/168/198.

The **Dōngběi Fàndiàn** (☎ 383 8120, fax 340 4972, 100 Tianjin Beijie) is a huge old hotel not far from the south train station and in the main shopping zone. Singles/doubles are good value at Y150/Y210.

The giant statue of Mao in Zhōngshān Guǎngchǎng faces the castle-like **Liáoníng Bīnguǎn** (☎ 383 9166, fax 383 9103). Full of character, this hotel was built in 1927 by the Japanese and boasts art nouveau windows and a billiard room with slate tables – in short, old but elegant. Singles/doubles are Y240/360.

The **Liáoníng Dàshà** (☎ 680 9502, 105 Huanghe Dajie) is near Běi Líng (North Tomb). This enormous Soviet-style place has echo-chamber acoustics and somewhat resembles Communist Party headquarters (maybe it is). Rooms rates range from Y280 to Y380 for a double and suites start at around Y980.

The **Fènghuáng Fàndiàn** (Phoenix Hotel; ☎ 680 5858, fax 680 7207, 109 Huanghe Dajie, ❷ ppd@mx.sy.cei.gov.cn) is just north of the Liáoníng Dàshà. This is a major staging area for tour groups, and offers all the modern amenities and prices to go with this. Single/double rooms are Y415/458 and suites range from Y780 to Y1190.

The **Gloria Plaza Hotel** (Kǎilái Dàjiǔdiàn; ☎ 252 8855, fax 252 8533, 32 Yingbin Jie) has opened across from the north train station and offers luxury rooms starting at Y498. Another new hotel in town is the five-star **New World Courtyard** (Xīnshìjiè Wànyí Jiǔdiàn; ☎ 386 9888, fax 386 0018, 2 Nanjing Nan Jie, ❷ nwhs2@ sy.col.co.cn). Doubles are plush and should be for Y1033. It may be possible to negotiate a discount of up to 40%.

Across the street, the **Traders Hotel** (Shāngmào Fàndiàn; ☎ 341 2288, fax 341 3838, 68 Zhonghua Lu) is the plushest accommodation in town. This place is owned by, and indistinguishable from, the Shangri-La hotel chain. Top-notch standards in all aspects of hotel management can be expected and the facilities are excellent. Superior doubles will cost US$165 and the 'Presidential Suite' is US$1200.

Places to Eat

Both the north and south train stations are cheap restaurant zones. The market, **Zhōngshān Shìchǎng**, west off Zhongshan on Beiliu Malu, has a multitude of snacks, fruit and evening food stalls.

Also in this area, the **Curry Shop** (Shānxiǎoshí Kālí Kuàicān; ☎ 341 7213) serves excellent noodles and vegie or meat dishes at good prices. You'll find it on Nanjing Jie, just south of Beiliu Malu.

On the 2nd floor of the building across from the Traders Shopping Centre is a *food fair* (měi shíchéng) with a decent selection of Chinese and Japanese cuisine.

A few doors down, the New World Courtyard Hotel has a delicatessen with fresh filter coffee, croissants and banana bread. The Traders Hotel offers a wide variety of international cuisine, including Korean and western food.

Shopping

Next to, and part of, the Traders Hotel is the Traders Shopping Centre, a three-storey emporium of international names like Dunhill, Esprit and Sisley. In the same area is Taiyuan Jie, the major shopping street of Shěnyáng, where you can stock up on the latest clothing at Giordano and Bossini. This area is also filled with side streets of stalls and markets where you'll find reasonably priced goods.

The **Běifāng Túshū Chéng** (Northern Book Town), next to the North Tower in the south of Shěnyáng, is the local foreign bookshop with an OK selection of music and maps.

Getting There & Away

Air The office of the Civil Aviation Administration of China (CAAC; Zhōngguó Mínháng; ☎ 323 3835) is at 117 Zhonghua Lu in the Heping District. Air China runs four flights a week between Shěnyáng and Hong Kong (Y3230). There are also flights to Seoul (Y2160) and Irkutsk (Y2230).

There are a huge number of domestic destinations, including Běijīng (Y560), Shànghǎi (Y1040), Hāěrbīn (Y410) and Shēnzhèn (Y1820).

Aeroflot (☎ 611 5482) has a ticket office on the 2nd floor of the Taishan Hotel and also offers flights to Irkutsk. Compared with a direct Moscow-Běijīng flight, a combined Moscow-Irkutsk-Shěnyáng-Běijīng air ticket offers considerable savings.

CITS (☎ 680 6961) also has a booking office in the Fènghuáng Fàndiàn (see Places to Stay earlier).

Bus If you come out of the south train station (a Byzantine structure with a miniature tank on a pillar in front of it) and cross over the pedestrian overpass, you'll be confronted with a line of buses; this is the south long-distance bus station. Services include two buses a day to Tiānjīn (Y60/100 seat/sleeper), three a day to Dàlián (Y78) and two departures a day to Běijīng (Y130 sleepers). There are also regular departures to Ānshùn (Y12).

There are also departures from directly in front of the south train station, which include Běijīng (Y75/130 seat/sleeper) and Chángchūn (Y35/50 seat/sleeper). Similar destinations are also serviced by buses departing from the north train station.

Train The situation with train stations is tricky as there is a north station (běi zhàn) and a south station (nán zhàn). The east train station is a local station, used mainly for freight. Arriving is not usually a problem as many trains that arrive at one station will carry on to the next after a short stop. However, if you are departing from Shěnyáng by train, double check as to which station you need.

Buying sleepers anywhere in the northeast is a headache, and Shěnyáng is no exception; it is advisable to purchase your ongoing ticket as soon as you arrive.

Generally, the south train station includes trains to Hāěrbīn (Y52), Chángchūn (Y34), Ānshùn (Y8), Dāndōng (Y18), Tonghua (Y22), Běijīng (Y48) and Tiānjīn (Y40), while express trains go from the north train station to places including Guǎngzhōu and Shànghǎi.

Regular minibuses ply the route between the south and north train stations.

Getting Around

Although Shěnyáng has lots of buses and routes, the city is sprawling and getting anywhere by public transport is likely to require at least one transfer. Maps of the bus routes are sold at the train stations.

Bus No 138 runs between the north and south train stations and then north past the Běi Tǎ (North Pagoda). Bus No 207 runs from the south train station and east to the TV tower.

Taxis cost Y7 for the first 4km. A trip between the two train stations will cost you Y10.

AROUND SHĚNYÁNG
Qiān Shān 千山

These hills are about 80km south of Shěnyáng. The name is an abbreviation for Qiānlián Shān (Thousand Lotuses Mountain). You can hike around the hills, which have a scattering of Tang, Ming and Qing temples. The mountain itself gets very crowded on Sunday and public holidays. It is steep in parts and takes about three hours to reach the summit.

At the southern foot of the mountain (approached along a different bus route) are the hot springs, **Tanggangzi Wēnquán**. The last Qing emperor, Puyi, used to bathe here with

---

Thousand Lotuses Mountain

According to legend, there was once a fairy who wanted to bring spring to the world by embroidering pretty clouds on lotuses. Just as she was making the 999th lotus, the gods found it, accused her of stealing the clouds and had her arrested.

The fairy put up a fight and during the struggle all the lotuses dropped to earth, where they immediately turned into green hills. In memory of the fairy, people began to call the mountain Qiānlián Shān (Thousand Lotuses Mountain), or just Qiān Shān.

Later, a monk arrived and actually counted the peaks and discovered there were only 999, so he built an artificial one to make a round number.

his empresses. Today Tanggangzi's hot springs are piped into ordinary baths for ordinary folk. There is a sanatorium that offers accommodation for those with lingering diseases, as well as for those who just want to linger.

Getting There & Away Regular buses from Shěnyáng's south long-distance bus station leave for Ānshùn (Y11), 60km away, where you change buses to Qiān Shān. The whole journey takes 2½ hours. The bus drops you off at the entrance to the park, Qiānshān Gōngyuán.

Maps can be bought from hawkers near the gate or from the ticket office.

DÀLIÁN 大连
☎ 411 • pop 5,403,600

Dàlián has been known by several names – Dalny, Dairen, Lüshun and Luda. Today, Lüshun (formerly Port Arthur) is the part further south, and Lüshun and Dàlián comprise Lüda. A military base is located at Lüshun and, considered a 'sensitive zone', the area is off limits to foreigners.

In the late 19th century the western powers were busy carving up pieces of China for themselves. To the outrage of Tsar Nicholas II, Japan gained the Liáodōng Peninsula under an 1895 treaty (after defeating Chinese battleships off Port Arthur in 1894). Nicholas II gained the support of the French and Germans and not only managed to get the Japanese to withdraw from Dàlián, but

---

Warning

Do not attempt to head south-west, past Xīnghǎi Gōngyuán. This area, including Lüshun (Port Arthur), is considered a military sensitive zone and off limits to all foreigners. While CITS in Dàlián does not seem to be aware of this situation and will encourage you to visit Lüshun, you're likely to see little more than the inside of Lüshun's PSB office, which is not worth the price of the train ticket to get there. If you are tempted to head in this direction, check with the PSB in Dàlián to see if the situation has changed.

---

also to receive it as a Russian concession in 1898. From there, Russia set about constructing a port as an alternative to the only partially ice-free port of Vladivostok.

Itching for a war with Japan (to whip up nationalist feelings at home and distract from internal difficulties), the Tsar pushed the two countries to the brink of war in 1904. However, Nicholas II underestimated the strength of the Japanese navy who pre-emptively attacked Port Arthur in February 1904, crippling and blockading the Russian fleet. The Russians lurched from one blunder to another, culminating in the serious defeat of the Russian Baltic Fleet off Korea in May 1905. The same year, Dàlián passed back into Japanese hands, and the Japanese completed the port facilities in 1930. Finally, in 1945, the Soviet Union reoccupied Dàlián and did not withdraw until 10 years later.

Today, Dàlián has the largest harbour in the north-east, and is also one of the most prosperous cities in China. Crisscrossed by old, colourful trams, the city exhibits some wonderful architecture and has refreshing acres of grass and lawns.

Dàlián also harbours a large number of credited 'intellectuals' and an extremely successful and popular soccer team. Next to the sea, the weather in Dàlián tends to be much warmer than in other areas of Liáoníng, with the summer months particularly pleasant. Perhaps because of this, Dàlián also has a noticeably relaxed pace and it often feels as if the entire city is on holiday.

Orientation

Dàlián is perched on the Liáodōng Peninsula and borders the Yellow Sea to the north. Many of the sights can be found in the eastern part of town around the square, Zhōngshān Guǎngchǎng. The ferry terminal is in the east of the city and the Dàlián train station is centrally located.

The main shopping zones and sights are not far from each other and the scale of Dàlián is such that walking about is both reasonably easy and an enjoyable way to explore the city.

Information

Money The permanent home of the Bank of China is the stately green-roofed building at 9 Zhongshan Guangchang. The building is currently under renovation and, in the meantime, the bank has taken up temporary residence across the square on Yan'an Lu.

Next door to the Shangri-La Hotel, the Hong Kong & Shanghai Banking Corporation has an ATM accepting Cirrus, Plus, Mastercard, Visa and Global Access cards.

Post & Communications The main post and telephone office is on the corner of Changjiang Lu and Shanghai Lu. Most of the large hotels also provide postal services.

Email & Internet Access China Telecom offers Internet access between 9 am and 5 pm in an office on Shanghai Lu, across from the post office. The charge is 0.3 jiǎo per minute and the server is incredibly fast.

There is also an Internet cafe, 21°C (Ershíyī Shìjiwǎng) on the corner of Qi Qi Jie and Ji Fang Lu. There you can sip a beer or coffee at any hour of the day and surf the web to your heart's content for Y10 per hour.

Visit Dalian, a free monthly English magazine, lists a range of things to see and do. It can be a useful guide although it seems more concerned with being impressive than informative. The magazine is randomly available on request from some large hotels, such as the Furama Hotel

Travel Agencies CITS (☎ 368 7843) is at 1 Changtong Jie, on the western side of the park, Láodòng Gōngyuán (Workers Movement Park), not far from the Mínháng Dàshà (Civil Aviation Hotel) and CAAC. The office is officially on the 4th floor, however, if the staff can't help you there, try the Dalian Overseas Tourism Corporation (☎ 368 0857, fax 368 7831), on the 5th floor, which can help with tours including summer trips to Bīngyù Gōu.

PSB The PSB is on the corner of Yan'an Lu, south of Zhōngshān Guǎngchǎng.

Zhōngshān Guǎngchǎng 中山广场
Zhongshan Square

Zhōngshān Guǎngchǎng is the hub of Dàlián – a panorama of grand buildings encircling a roundabout. The square (in fact a circle) in the middle comes alive at night with ambient music and lights – half of the city turns up to dance and play badminton. You'll find the crowds back again the next morning, practising everything from *taijiquan* (tai chi) to ballroom dancing.

The classical edifice opposite the excellent Dàlián Bīnguǎn is the People's Cultural Hall. The Bank of China is next door in the triple green-domed building. Other historic buildings around the square have been converted to kindergartens, hotels and government offices.

Recently built structures in the area have been designed to harmonise with Zhōngshān Guǎngchǎng, testimony to the adulation it receives from locals and architects.

Rénmín Guǎngchǎng 人民广场
People's Square

Formerly known as Stalin Square, this huge square displays a monstrous effigy of a Russian soldier, usually crowned with pigeons.

Behind the statue is a new residential development designed in the Russo-European style that can be seen all over Dàlián. Some truly horrendous crimes against good taste conspire on either flank in the form of government buildings.

Bus No 15 can take you to Rénmín Guǎngchǎng from Zhōngshān Guǎngchǎng (Y0.5). On the way, you will pass **Yǒuhǎo Guǎngchǎng** (Good Friend Square), which has a vast spheroid that's illuminated like a giant disco ball at night.

Places to Stay – Budget

As anyone can see, Dàlián has Shànghǎi as its model and that includes the exorbitant hotel prices. Cheapies are generally off limits to those of a foreign disposition, however following a tout from the train station may lead you to an accepting and acceptable bargain. Prices quoted here are low season. Expect prices to go up during

Northern Warlords

Once known as Manchuria, north-eastern China has historically been the birthplace of conquerors. Perhaps it was the harsh climate that caused the Mongols and Manchus to turn their sights southwards.

At the turn of the 20th century Manchuria was a sparsely populated region, but it had rich, largely untapped resources. Both the Russians and the Japanese eyed it enviously. After the Chinese were defeated by the Japanese in the Sino-Japanese War of 1894–95, the Liáoníng Peninsula was ceded to Japan. Japan's strength alarmed the other foreign powers, Russia among them, and Japan was forced to hand the peninsula back to China. As a reward for this intervention, the Russians were allowed to build a railway across Manchuria to their treaty port of Port Arthur (Lüshun), near present-day Dàlián. The Russians moved troops in with the railway, and for the next 10 years effectively controlled north-eastern China.

The Russo-Japanese War of 1904–05 put an end to Russia's domination of Manchuria. Overall control of Manchuria moved into the hands of Zhang Zuolin, a bandit-leader in control of a large and well-organised private army. By the time the Qing dynasty fell, he had the power of life and death in southern Manchuria, and between 1926 and 1928 ran a regional government recognised by foreign powers.

Zhang's policy had been to limit Japan's economic and political expansion, and eventually to break Japan's influence entirely. But by the 1920s the militarist Japanese government was ready to take a hard line on China.

Zhang Zuolin was killed by the Japanese in a bomb attack, and control of Manchuria passed to his son, Zhang Xueliang, with the blessing of the Kuomintang.

The Japanese invasion of Manchuria began in September 1931, and the weak Kuomintang government in Nánjīng couldn't do anything about it. Chiang Kaishek was too obsessed with his annihilation campaigns against the communists to challenge the Japanese militarily. Manchuria fell to the Japanese, who renamed it the independent state of Manchukuo – a Japanese puppet state. The exploitation of the region began in earnest: heavy industry was established and extensive railway lines were laid.

The Japanese occupation of Manchuria was a fateful move for the Chinese communist forces locked up in Shaanxi. The invasion forced Zhang Xueliang and his Dōngběi (North-Eastern) army out of Manchuria – these troops were eventually moved into central China to fight the communists. Up until the mid-1930s Zhang's loyalty to Chiang Kaishek never wavered, but he gradually became convinced that Chiang's promises to cede no more territory to Japan and to recover the Manchurian homeland were empty ones. Zhang made a secret truce with the communists, and when Chiang Kaishek flew to Xī'ān in December 1936 to organise yet another extermination campaign against the communists, Zhang had Chiang arrested. Chiang was released only after agreeing to call off the extermination campaign and to form an alliance with the communists to resist the Japanese. Chiang never forgave Zhang and later had him arrested and taken to Taiwan as a prisoner – he wasn't permitted to leave Taiwan until 1992.

summer and look for discounts during the dead of winter.

One delightful relic of the Russian era exists just over the railway bridge in the form of the *Dàlián Shènglì Dàjiǔdiàn (Dalian Victory Hotel;* ☎ *281 8032, 61 Shanghai Lu).* The staff are friendly and the rooms are clean although slightly noisy. Dorms in triples

without bath go for Y30 or Y50 with bath. If you head up Shanghai Lu from Zhōngshān Guǎngchǎng, it's the quaint old building on your right after crossing the railway bridge.

Places to Stay – Mid-Range
The Foreign Experts' Hotel (Zhuānjiā Gongyù Bīnguǎn; ☎ *280 1199, fax 263*

Northern Warlords

As WWII came to an end, the north-east suddenly became the focus of a renewed confrontation between the communist and Kuomintang troops. At the Potsdam Conference of July 1945 it was decided that all Japanese forces in Manchuria and North Korea would surrender to the Soviet army; those stationed elsewhere would surrender to the Kuomintang.

After the A-bombs obliterated Hiroshima and Nagasaki in August 1945 and forced the Japanese government to surrender, the Soviet armies moved into Manchuria, engaging the Japanese armies in a brief but bloody conflict. The Americans started transporting Kuomintang troops by air and sea to the north, where they could oversee the surrender of Japanese forces and regain control of north and central China. The US navy moved in to Qīngdǎo and landed 53,000 marines to protect the railways leading to Běijīng and Tiānjīn and the coal mines that supplied those railways.

The communists, still in a shaky truce with the Kuomintang, also joined the rush for position. Although Chiang Kaishek told them to remain where they were, the communist troops marched to Manchuria on foot, picking up arms from abandoned Japanese depots as they went. Other communist forces went north by sea from Shāndōng. In November 1945 the Kuomintang attacked the communists even while US-organised peace negotiations were taking place between the two. That attack put an end to the talks.

The communists occupied the countryside, setting in motion their land-reform policies, which quickly built up support among the peasants. There was a tremendous growth of mass support for the communists, and the force of 100,000 regulars who had marched into Manchuria rapidly grew to 300,000, as soldiers of the old Manchurian armies that had been forcibly incorporated into the Japanese armies flocked to join them. Within two years the Red Army had grown to 1½ million combat troops and four million support personnel.

On the other side, although the Kuomintang troops numbered three million and had Soviet and US arms and support, its soldiers had nothing to fight for and either deserted or went over to the communists, who took them in by the thousands. The Kuomintang armies were led by generals Chiang had chosen for their personal loyalty to him rather than for their military competence; Chiang ignored the suggestions of the US military advisers who he himself had asked for.

In 1948 the communists took the initiative in Manchuria. Strengthened by the recruitment of Kuomintang soldiers and the capture of US equipment, the communists became both the numerical and material equal of the Kuomintang. Three great battles led by Lin Biao in Manchuria decided the outcome. In the first battle, in August 1948, the Kuomintang lost 500,000 people. In the second battle (from November 1948 to January 1949) whole Kuomintang divisions went over to the communists, who took 327,000 prisoners. In all, the Kuomintang lost seven generals through fighting, capture or desertion, and seven divisional commanders crossed sides. The third decisive battle was fought in the area around Běijīng and Tiānjīn; Tiānjīn fell on 23 January and another 500,000 troops came across to the communist camp. It was these victories that sealed the fate of the Kuomintang and allowed the communists to drive southwards.

9958, 110 Dàlián Shizhongshanqu Nanshan Lu), located within the University of Foreign Languages campus at the southern end of town, has comfortable twin rooms for Y253 or doubles for Y360. Each floor has a public kitchen. To reach the hotel take bus No 23 to its terminus and then, heading west (the same direction the bus was heading

in), take the second left. The hotel is at the far end of the campus – someone should be able to direct you.

The **Dōngfāng Fàndiàn** (☎ 263 4161, fax 263 6859, 28 Zhongshan Lu) is not far from the train station. Doubles start at Y248. The hotel is popular with Russian tourists and is often full.

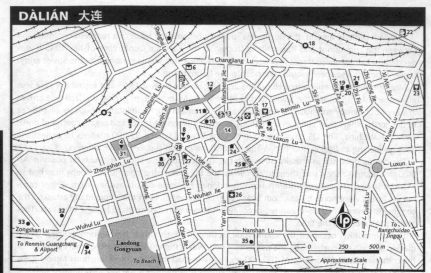

DÀLIÁN 大连

The **Dàlián Fàndiàn** (☎ 263 3171, fax 280 4197, 6 Shanghai Lu) looks like an old 1930s warehouse and has singles starting at Y218 and doubles from Y328. This is not the same hotel as the more illustrious example of the same name on Zhōngshān Guǎngchǎng.

Near Zhōngshān Guǎngchǎng, the **Gloria Plaza Hotel** (Kǎilái Dàjiǔdiàn; ☎ 280 8855, fax 280 8533, 5 Yide Jie, @ gih.beijing@gloriahotels.com) is not quite up to par with the rest of the Gloria chain. Standard doubles are Y298 to Y368 and suites are Y658 (plus 15% service).

Places to Stay – Top End

The **Dàlián Bīnguǎn** (☎ 263 3111, fax 263 3111, 4 Zhongshan Guangchang) is easily recognisable by the wrought iron entrance that leads to a fabulous marbled interior. This hotel was used in a scene in the movie *The Last Emperor*. Treat yourself to an emperor's double (Y400).

Just behind the Dàlián Bīnguǎn is the **Bólǎn Dàjiǔdiàn** (Grand Hotel; ☎ 280 6161, fax 280 6980, 1 Jie Fang Jie). It isn't very grand inside, although the prices certainly are – singles/doubles are US$78/88.

East from Zhōngshān Guǎngchǎng, the **Guójì Dàjiǔdiàn** (International Hotel; ☎ 263 8238, fax 263 0008, 9 Renmin Lu) has doubles for Y680 and suites for Y780 (plus 15% service).

The new **Bohai Pearl Hotel** (Bóhǎi Míngzhū Fàndiàn; ☎ 265 0888, fax 263 4480, 8 Shénglí Guǎngchǎng) is next to the train station. Plush singles run at Y730 with doubles starting at Y898. In an attempt to establish itself in Dàlián's competitive hotel market, the hotel seems to offer a permanent 30% discount.

The five-star **Furama Hotel** (Fùlìhuá Dàjiǔdiàn; ☎ 263 0888, fax 280 4455, 60 Renmin Lu, @ framahtlpub@dl.inpta.net.cn) is an excellent hotel. Featuring an Executive floor, the hotel has standard doubles for Y490; the presidential suite is a mere Y21,750. Prices include breakfast but not the 15% service charge. The hotel comes complete with its own Cartier and Dunhill outlets.

The newly opened **Dalian Shangri-La Hotel** (Dàlián Xiāngge Lǐlā Dàjiǔdiàn; ☎ 252 5000, fax 252 5050) is just next door. It has all you'd expect from a five-star hotel for US$190 to US$1200.

DÀLIÁN

PLACES TO STAY
1 Dàlián Shènglì
   Dàjiǔdiàn
   大连胜利大酒店
3 Bóhǎi Pearl
   Hotel
   渤海明珠大酒店
11 Dàlián Fàndiàn
   大连饭店
16 Guójí Dàjiǔdiàn
   国际大酒店
19 Furama Hotel
   富丽华大酒店
21 Dalian
   Shangri-La
   大连香格里拉饭店
24 Dàlián Bīnguǎn
   大连宾馆
25 Bólǎn Dàjiǔdiàn
   博览大酒店
27 Gloria Plaza Hotel
   凯莱大酒店
30 Dōngfāng Fàndiàn
   东方饭店
36 Foreign Expert's
   Hotel;
   University of Foreign
   Languages
   专家公寓宾馆;
   外国语大学

PLACES TO EAT
4 Hollywood Studio
   好莱坞影城
8 Pizza King Italian
   Restaurant
   比萨王意大利餐厅
9 Williams Burger
   美国威廉士堡
12 Dàchóngqìng Jiǔlóu
   大重庆酒楼
29 Wángmázǐ Dàpáidàng
   王麻子大排档

OTHER
2 Dàlián Train Station;
   Long-Distance Bus Station
   大连火车站、
   长途汽车站
5 Diànxìn Wǎngba (Internet)
   电信网吧
6 Post Office
   邮局
7 Dalian Foreign Languages
   Bookstore; Golden Voice
   外文书店;
   金嗓子唱片店
10 Xinhua Bookstore
   新华书店
13 Bank of China
   中国银行

14 Zhōngshān Guǎngchǎng
   中山广场
15 Friendship Shopping
   Centre
   友谊商城
17 Greenery Beerhouse
   君悦来啤酒屋
18 East Train Station
   大连东站
20 Dragon Air
   港龙航空
22 Ferry Passenger Terminal
   大连港客运站
23 JJ's Nightclub
   JJ'S俱乐部
26 PSB
   公安局外事科
28 Yǒuhǎo Guǎngchǎng
   友好广场
31 Shènglì Guǎngchǎng
   胜利广场
32 CAAC
   中国民航
33 All Nippon Airways
   全日空
34 CITS
   中国国际旅行社
35 21°C
   二十一世纪网络咖啡

Out of town is the **Bàngchuídǎo Bīnguǎn** (☎ 263 5131), which is set in a beautiful area by the east coast. Many top-ranking party members and cadres stay here. It's next to a beach and it can only be reached by taxi. Be sure to call ahead to check that the hotel is open and has rooms available.

Places to Eat

Tianjin Jie is a great area for small, cheap restaurants that specialise in fried dumplings and pancakes. The area around Youhou Lu is especially popular with students. In particular, try **Wóngmázǐ Dàpáidàng** (☎ 265 3356) on the corner of Xiang Qian Jie and Zhongshan Lu. It's a lively place where students hang out for hours on end. Grill kebabs at your table or

dig into a hotpot and wash it down with cheap beer. The beer brewed in Dàlián is good; try Keller, which has a hoppy taste that's a cut above the rest.

For a more upmarket version, try **Dàchóngqìng Jiǔlóu**, a Sìchuān hotpot restaurant that is very popular in winter. You can divide the hotpot into spicy and mild and proceed to dip shreds of yángròu (lamb), zhūròu (pork), mógu (mushrooms), dòufu (tofu), pángxiè (crab) and whatever else into the scalding broth. Be warned that the crabs usually turn up on the table alive. The food is not cheap (Y120 for two), but it's tasty and affordable if you're in a group. You'll find the restaurant at the eastern end of Tianjin Jie.

Reasonable Italian food including pizza, pasta, soups and salads, can be found at

Pizza King Italian Restaurant (Yìdàli'bǐsà Bìngdiàn; ☎ *280 6888, 122 Youhao Lu),* a much classier restaurant than its name implies.

Recently opened in Shénglí Guǎngchǎng, *Hollywood Studio (Hǎoláiwūyǐng Chéng;* ☎ *250 2777, fax 250 2723, 28 Shénglí Guǎngchǎng)* is the new hang-out for trendy Dalianese. The décor and menu are modelled after the Hard Rock Café, as are its prices.

Around the University of Foreign Languages is another area with hole in the wall *restaurants, bakeries* and *cafes,* catering more to students than foreigners.

For fast food, try *Williams Burger (Wēilián Shǐbào),* on Yǒuhǎo Guǎngchǎng, a Chinese version of McDonalds, or any of the cheap buffets along Tianjin Jie – greasy but good! At the other end of the market, the Bóhǎi, Shangri-La and Furama Hotels all have excellent international and Chinese cuisine.

Entertainment

Dàlián has enjoyed an increase in bars, pubs and clubs in recent years. A lot of these are targeted at the Japanese business divisions who loosen their ties and sweep through the city. Other venues aim more at younger folk.

The area around the square, Yǒuhǎo Guǎngchǎng, is worth exploring for small bars and late night coffee shops. You'll find similar places around the University of Foreign Languages. *21 C°,* the local Internet bar, is open 24 hours and serves tasty snacks, beer and cocktails in a warm atmosphere.

The *Casablanca Café and Bar (*☎ *264 6598, 35 Renmin Lu)* caters to expats (the bar is only open in the evenings). You'll find it on Renmin Lu, down a small alley on the south side of the street. Also on Renmin Lu, on the left as you come down from Zhōngshān Guǎngchǎng, is the *Greenery Beerhouse (*☎ *263 7285),* which is an extremely mellow place that serves international snacks as well as beer. Budweiser and Tennents are Y20 a bottle.

JJ's, the nightclub chain, has a club in the Shenjiang Entertainment Centre (Shēnjiāng Yúlèzhōngxīn), at the northern end of Wuwu Lu.

Surrounding Yǒuhǎo Guǎngchǎng are a number of movie theatres showing both Chinese and American films.

Shopping

Tianjin Jie is the main shopping thoroughfare in Dàlián and is a huge jumble of shops and stalls. Also located here is the giant new Dalian Foreign Languages Bookstore as well as possibly the best-stocked music shop in China, Golden Voice (Jīnsǎngzi).

Just on the left down Renmin Lu, coming out of Zhōngshān Guǎngchǎng, is the Friendship Shopping Centre with big-name goods and a wide selection of imported spirits.

Getting There & Away

Air Dàlián has domestic and international air connections. Air China and Dragonair have flights to Hong Kong for Y2590. Air China and All Nippon Airways fly to Osaka (Y2410), Fukuoka, Sendai and Tokyo (Y2970). Air China also flies to Seoul (Y1890). The huge range of domestic flights include Běijīng (Y570), Shànghǎi (Y850) and Guǎngzhōu (Y1640).

CAAC (☎ 362 4451) is at 143 Zhongshan Lu, next door to the Mínháng Dàshà (Civil Aviation Hotel; also known as Dalian Royal Hotel). The office is open from 8 am to 7.30 pm. Dragonair has an office next door to the Furama Hotel, and All Nippon Airways is located in the Senmao Building, across from the Children's Hospital on Zhongshan Lu.

Bus The long-distance bus station is located south-west of town and services nearby rural areas only. Buses to most long-distance destinations leave from the square in front of the Dàlián train station. There are buses to Shěnyáng (Y45) and the odd overnight coach to Běijīng (Y130). Buses to Dāndōng (Y60) take nine hours and leave every 15 minutes between 4.50 am and 9.30 am. Other destinations include Tiānjīn and Hāěrbīn.

There is also a private bus station just next to CITS. Book your ticket peacefully the day before or arrive at the last minute and be ready for a fight.

Train Mayhem! There is no information counter at the train station and apparently not nearly enough ticket counters. Have your destination, preferred travel dates and seat-class written down. Armed with this, brave the crowds and buy your ticket as early as possible. Most departures are from Dàlián train station (huǒchēzhàn) rather than from the Dàlián east train station (dōng zhàn).

Ten trains leave daily for Shěnyáng (Y55/80 seat/sleeper), the first leaving at 7.30 am. If you're lucky enough to catch an express train, you'll arrive four hours later, otherwise the trip takes six hours. There are two overnight trains to Dāndōng (Y47/105 seat/sleeper) leaving at 7.30 pm and arriving at 5.30 am. Other destinations include Běijīng, Hāěrbīn, Chángchūn and Jílín.

Boat Tickets can be bought at the ferry terminal in the east of Dàlián. Tickets are also sold at a booth in front of the train station. Boats are a sensible way to leave Dàlián as the trains and buses are a long haul.

There is an international service to Inch'on in South Korea that leaves on Tuesday and Friday at 11 am. Tickets range from US$96 to US$184.

Two boats to Shànghǎi leave on even days of the month. The first departs at 2 pm (40 hours), with ticket prices ranging from Y120 to Y254. The second and faster boat leaves at 6 pm (32 hours) and costs Y460.

There are four express departures to Yāntái (Y120) daily. Boats depart at 8 am, 10 am, 12.30 pm and 2 pm for the 3½-hour journey. Slower boats also cover the route for Y98 to Y150. There is also a daily boat to Wēihǎi (Y106), leaving at 8.30 pm. Boats to Tánggū (the port of Tiānjīn) depart on even days of the month at 4.30 pm and on odd days of the month at 3 pm. Tickets range from Y140 to Y258. Ferry services to Qīngdǎo have been discontinued.

Bus No 13 travels from the train station to the passenger ferry terminal.

Getting Around

The central district of Dàlián is not large and can mostly be covered on foot, although you may have to resort to using the bus, depending on where you are staying. At the time of writing there were no bicycle hire outlets.

The airport is 12km from the city centre and can be reached on bus No 701 from Zhōngshān Guǎngchǎng. A taxi from the airport to the city centre will cost about Y30.

The city of Dàlián has splashed out big money upgrading its fleet of buses and they are now among the best in China. Bus No 13 runs from the train station to the passenger ferry terminal. Bus No 23 runs south down Yan'an Lu. Colourful trams also glide around the city and run until 11 pm. Minibuses follow the same routes and charge Y2.

Taxis in Dàlián will cost about Y15 for most places in the city.

AROUND DÀLIÁN
Parks & Beaches

Surrounding parklands, beaches and health resorts are the main attractions for many visitors to Dàlián. Five kilometres to the south-east is the scenic area, **Bàngchuídǎo Jǐngqū**, which has an attractive pebbly beach as you can only get there by taxi and it's mainly visited by those staying at the Bàngchuídǎo Bīnguǎn (see the Dàlián Places to Stay section earlier).

A good idea, if the weather's fine, is to head out there by cab and then follow the coastal road on foot to **Lǎohǔtān Gōngyuán**. This stretch of coastline provides some excellent views of the ragged cliffs and crashing waves. From Lǎohǔtān Gōngyuán you can return to Dàlián by bus No 2 or 712.

The best beach is the small **Fùjiāzhuāng Hǎishuǐ Yùchǎng**, which has fine sand and rocky outcrops. The bay is deep and is excellent for swimming, but has few facilities. The beach is a fair way out of town, take bus No 401.

Five kilometres to the south-west of the city is **Xīnghǎi Gōngyuán**, which also has a popular beach. Inside the park is Dàlián's Ocean World, which has an exorbitant Y110 entrance fee. Take bus No 406 or tram No 202 from the city centre.

LIÁONÍNG 辽宁

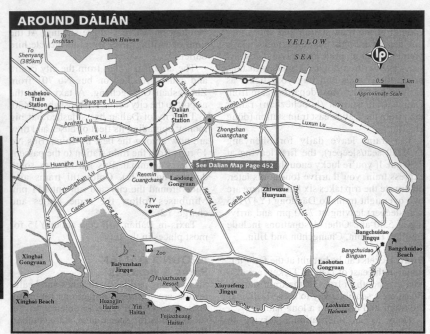

AROUND DÀLIÁN

Jīnshítān (Golden Stone Beach), 60km north of Dàlián, has a number of natural scenic wonders and is an attractive beach area with splendid coves and rock formations. There is also a golf course, cross-country motorcycling, an amusement park and hunting grounds within a forest. Locally, the area is euphemistically called 'Little Guìlín'. Buses to Jīnshítān leave from the square in front of the Dàlián train station.

BĪNGYÙ GŌU
Bingyu Valley

CITS claims this valley is Liáoníng's answer to Guìlín and Yángshuò. It has a number of towering, vertical rock formations with a river meandering between them. It's pretty, but it's not likely to replace Guìlín on the travellers' circuit. Still, if you're more interested in finding some silence than sights, you may want to check it out.

The valley is 250km north-east of Dàlián. Take a bus from the square in front of the

Dàlián train station to Zhuānghé (Y30), a town about three hours east of Dàlián, halfway to Dāndōng. From there take another bus to Bīngyù Fēngjǐnqū, which is a scenic area a further 1½ hours down the road. Alternatively, you can take a train from Dàlián to Zhuānghé (Y20) and then take a bus.

A 15-minute walk from the river, the *Furama Hotel* (*Fùlìhua Dàjiǔdiàn;* ☎ 822 0237) offers three-star accommodation with doubles for Y480. Reservations can be made at the *Fùlìhua Dàjiǔdiàn* (☎ 263 0888) in Dàlián. Villas along the river are also available at similar prices; ask at the CITS for information and reservations.

DĀNDŌNG 丹东

☎ 0415 • pop 2,394,900

Dāndōng lies at the border of Liáoníng and North Korea. Dāndōng's tourist industry thrives on the views of North Korea across the Yālù Jiāng (Green Duck River).

Unfortunately, these views only offer what can barely be considered a glimpse into North Korea and many travellers depart disappointed. Some travellers come here to continue onwards to Tonghua and the Chángbái Shān nature reserve in Jílín.

If you are planning to go to Sinuiju on the other side of the Yālù Jiāng, don't get your hopes up. Foreigners can join tour groups to P'yŏngyang, but are not allowed into Sinuiju. (At the time of writing, American, Israeli and South Korean nationals were not being issued with North Korean visas.) Even going to P'yŏngyang from Dāndōng via CITS means a wait of 25 days (two weeks at least) for the paperwork to grind its way through the vast cogs of the North Korean bureaucracy. You could try applying for a visa in the North Korean embassy in Shěnyáng or Běijīng, which will likely prove quicker.

Information

The CITS office (☎ 212 7721) is the big building on your right as you exit the train station.

The PSB is located in a huge tiled building, one block north-east of Shiwei Lu, on Jiangcheng Dajie.

The Bank of China's main branch is on Da'an Jie, at the corner of Erwei Lu.

The post office is on Wuyi Jie, at the corner of Qiwei Lu.

North Korean Border

A view of this border (Běi Cháoxiǎn Biānjiè) can enjoyed from Yālùjiāng Gōngyuán (Green Duck River Park). This park is a favourite picnic site for visiting Chinese tourists. It's peppered with photographers trying to squeeze family members into the standard 'I visited the Sino-Korean border' shot.

The original steel-span bridge was 'accidentally' strafed in 1950 by the Americans, who also accidentally bombed the airstrip at Dāndōng. The Koreans have dismantled this bridge as far as the mid-river boundary line. All that's left is a row of support columns on the Korean side and half a bridge (still showing shrapnel pockmarks)

on the Chinese side. You can wander along what's left of it for Y10. Along the way are photographs of the bridge's construction and destruction. The Sino-Korean Friendship Bridge runs parallel to the remains of the old one.

Those without a North Korean visa can get pretty close to the country by trotting down to the Yālùjiāng Gōngyuán and jumping onto a **boat cruise** (guānguāng chuán). Don't bother with the large boats (Y6) as they are a waste of time – you have to wait for them to fill up with passengers (which tends to take forever) and the trip is laborious.

Board one of the speed boats (Y13) and zip along the river right up flush with the North Korean side. You are not supposed to take photos, but everyone does. North Korea is largely hidden by a man-made embankment and there isn't much to see. Nevertheless, if you're wanting to visit North Korea, this may well be as close as you get. If you keep paying the pilot, he will take you as far as you want, but once you are beyond the outskirts of Sinuiju, there's even less to see.

Kàngměi Yuáncháo Jìniànguǎn
抗美援朝纪念馆

Museum to Commemorate US Aggression

With everything from statistics to shrapnel, this museum offers the Chinese and North Korean perspectives of the war with the United States. Almost all captions are in Chinese and Korean, however the visual displays are interesting. Don't miss the Chinese propaganda leaflets that were dropped across enemy lines.

The museum is in the north-east of town, just across the tracks from the stadium. Entrance to the compound is Y2. It contains the North Korean War Memorial Column (easily spotted from the road below) and a number of tanks and planes. Admission into the museum itself is a further Y20. It's open daily from 8 am to 5.30 pm however tickets are only sold until 4.30 pm.

To reach the museum, take bus No 21 from the train station and get off just past the stadium. Cross the tracks and walk east towards the Memorial Column.

LIÁONÍNG 辽宁

Other Sights

A huge Máo Zhǔxí Xiàng (Chairman Mao Statue) greets you as you exit the train station. The Jǐnjiāngshān Gōngyuán, in the north-west of Dāndōng, is a pleasant park that offers a panoramic view of the city and North Korea.

Places to Stay

If you arrive at the bus station looking for a cheap bed, head to the train station where touts will greet you with offers of rooms for under Y20.

The *Jiāo Tōng Dàshà* (☎ 213 2777), adjoining the bus station on its east side, is the cheapest hotel officially accepting foreigners. Beds in somewhat dim, three-bed dorms cost Y35 each and doubles range from Y160 to Y200.

One step up in both price and quality is the *Yóudiàn Fàndiàn (Post and Telecommunications Hotel;* ☎ 216 6888, fax 213 5988, 78 Qi Wei Lu). Singles go for Y198 and doubles for Y218.

The *Yālù Jiāng Dàshà* (☎ 212 5901, fax 212 6180, 87 Jiuwei Lu) is a standard two-star establishment that strives to look a cut above the rest, but doesn't quite make it. Prices are steep, with singles going for Y420 and standard rooms ranging from Y368 to Y420. Enter off Jiu Wei Lu unless you're interested in checking out the latest fashions in terry cloth – the entrance on Da'an Lu leads to the sauna and the lobby is filled with lounging Chinese business men letting off some steam.

Places to Eat

There are a number of restaurants opposite Sīdàlín Gōngyuán (Stalin Park) that serve fresh seafood and both Chinese and Korean cuisine. The *Rì Yuè Tán (Sun & Moon Pool Restaurant;* ☎ 345 6789) is justifiably popular. Choose six different dishes of vegies, meat and seafood to dip into a scalding broth for Y138; it's enough to feed four or five people.

The *Hóngmǎ Xībǐndiàn (Red Horse Western Cake House; Qi Wei Lu)*, across from the post office, serves pizza, hamburgers and pastries as well as Corona,

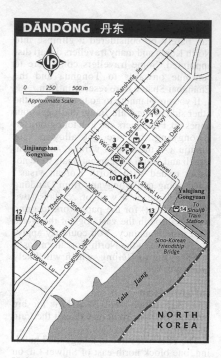

Heineken, imported wine and freshly brewed coffee.

Each evening, the *Yālù Jiāng Hotel* has a huge bargain buffet of Chinese and Korean cuisine for Y35.

Getting There & Away

Air There are connections to Běijīng, Shànghǎi, Shēnzhèn and Guǎngzhōu. The CAAC office (☎ 617 6655) can be found on Da'an Jie, not far from the Yālù Jiāng Dàshà.

Bus The bus station is on Shiwei Lu, not far from the train station. A bus leaves daily for Tonghua at 6.30 am and takes nine hours. As there is only one bus per day and it is often full, book your ticket as soon as you arrive in Dāndōng. Buses to Dàlián leave at 5.30, 6 and 8.40 am and 4 pm and take seven hours. There are also daily buses to Shěnyáng and Chángchūng and buses every other day to Hāěrbīn.

DĀNDŌNG

1	Bank of China 中国银行	7	Xinhua Bookstore 新华书店	11	CITS 中国国际旅行社
2	CAAC 中国民航	8	Long-Distance Bus Station; Jiāo Tōng Dàshà 长途汽车站; 交通大厦	12	Kàngměi Yuáncháo Jìniànguǎn (Museum to Commemerate US Aggression) 抗美援朝纪念馆
3	Yālù Jiāng Dàshà 鸭绿江大厦	9	PSB 公安局外事科	13	Riyùetán Cāntīng 日月潭餐厅
4	Post Office 邮局	10	Train Station 丹东火车站	14	Tour Boat Pier 旅游码头
5	Yóudiàn Fàndiàn 邮电饭店				
6	Hóngmǎ Xībǐngdiàn 红马西饼店				

Train There are direct trains to Dāndōng from Shěnyáng and Chángchūn. The trains from Moscow to P'yǒngyang and Běijīng to P'yǒngyang pass through Dāndōng; if you have the requisite visa, you can jump on the train and head for P'yǒngyang for US$19.

AROUND DĀNDŌNG

About 52km north-west of Dāndōng is the town of Fèngchéng. The nearby mountain **Fènghuáng Shān** (Phoenix Emperor Mountain) is 840m high and dotted with temples, monasteries and pagodas from the Tang, Ming and Qing dynasties. The Fenghuang Mountain Temple Fair takes place in April and attracts thousands of people. Fènghuáng Shān is one hour from Dāndōng by either train or bus. The express train does not stop here, but does give you a great view of the mountain from the window.

Also north of Dāndōng are the **Wǔlóngbèi Wēnquán**. You can reach these hot springs on a 20km bus ride from Dāndōng's main bus station. Hotel accommodation is available near the springs.

Dàgū Shān (Lonely Mountain) is about 90km south-west of Dāndōng, en route to Dàlián, close to the town of Gūshān. There are several groups of Taoist temples here dating from the Tang dynasty.

Jílín 吉林

Bordering Russia, North Korea and Inner Mongolia, Jílín is part of the historic territory of the Manchus, founders of the Qing dynasty (1644–1911). Industrialised under the Japanese who seized Manchuria and shaped it into the puppet state of Manchukuo (1931–1945), Jílín's main attraction for tourists is Tiān Chí (Heaven Pool). This volcanic lake is only accessible for a few months of the year, when its sublime landscape is revealed by the receding snow and ice.

CHÁNGCHŪN 长春
☎ 0431 • pop 6,837,900

Chángchūn was developed by the Japanese as the capital of Manchukuo (known as Hsin-king) between 1933 and 1945. In 1945 the Russians arrived in Chángchūn on a looting spree. When they departed in 1946, the Kuomintang moved in to occupy the cities of the north-east, only to find themselves surrounded by the communists in the countryside. The communists had assembled a formidable array of scrounged and captured weaponry – even former Japanese tanks and US jeeps. The communists took over the city in 1948.

With Soviet assistance, China's first car-manufacturing plant was set up here in the 1950s, starting with 95-horsepower Jiefang (Liberation) trucks, and moving on to make bigger and better vehicles like the now-defunct Red Flag limousines. If you have ever wondered why every other car in China's cities is a Volkswagen, the answer is that the company has a factory in Chángchūn (as well as one in Shànghǎi).

There is little reason to linger in Chángchūn. The sights are few and uninspiring; it mainly functions as a transit point for travellers.

Orientation

The city sprawls from north to south, which makes transportation between points arduous. Roughly bisected from north to south

Highlights

Capital: Chángchūn
Population: 23.8 million
Area: 187,000 sq km

- Tiān Chí, a volcanic crater lake in the stunning Chángbái Shān – China's largest nature reserve
- Sōnghuāhú Qīngshān and Běidàhú, two of China's leading ski resort areas
- The Yánbiān Cháoxiān (Korean Autonomous Prefecture), where you can get a taste of Korean culture in rural China

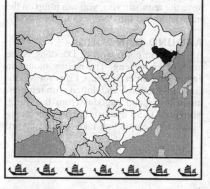

by the Yītōng Hé, most of the facilities and places of interest can be found on the western side of the river. The long-distance bus station and train station are in the north of the city.

Information

Money The main branch of the Bank of China is in the Yinmao Building on Xinmin Dajie, next door to Chángbái Shān Bīnguǎn.

Post & Communications The post office is in an attractive old building on Renmin Dajie, south of the train station. There is also another post office next to the train station.

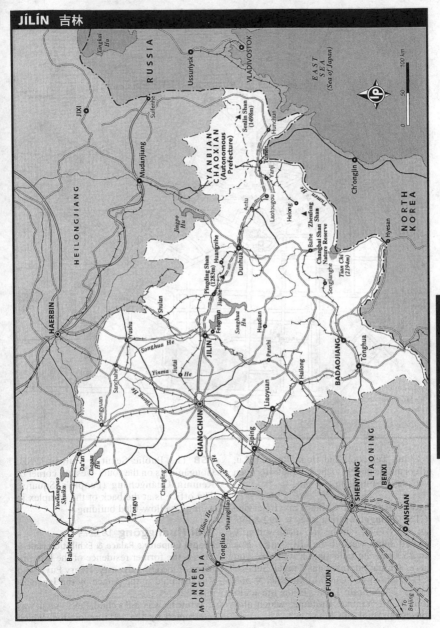

CHÁNGCHŪN 长春

China Telecom, 2nd floor, Renmin Lu, offers public access to the Internet. It's open weekdays from 8 am to 4 pm.

Travel Agencies China Travel Service (CTS; Zhōngguó Lǚxíngshè; ☎ 892 8466, fax 892 8712), Jianshe Jie, inconveniently located south-west of the city centre. Bus No 25 from the train station will take you there. China International Travel Service (CITS; Zhōngguó Guójì Lǚxíngshè; ☎ 565 6313), 14 Xinmin Dajie, is on the main floor of the Yinmao Building, which also houses the Bank of China.

PSB The Public Security Bureau (PSB; Gōngānjú) is on the south-western corner of Rénmín Guǎngchǎng (People's Square). The office is at the back of the complex in a dingy, yellow-tiled building.

Wěi Huánggōng 伪皇宫
Puppet Emperor's Palace & Exhibition Hall
This is the former residence of the last emperor of the Qing dynasty, Henry Puyi, who was installed in the palace by the Japanese in 1932.

While he was still a child, Puyi's reign was interrupted by the 1911 revolution, which

CHÁNGCHŪN

PLACES TO STAY

4 Chángchūn Shì
Chángdiàn Lǚshè
长春市长电旅社

6 Chūnyí Bīnguǎn
春谊宾馆

12 Yuèfǔ Dàjiǔdiàn
乐府大酒店

17 Shangri-La Hotel
香格里拉大酒店

18 Chángchūn Bīnguǎn
长春宾馆

25 Chángbáishān Bīnguǎn
长白山宾馆

PLACES TO EAT

13 Wǔhuán Guǎngchǎng
五环广场

16 Běijīng Kǎoyā
北京烤鸭

22 French Bakery
红磨坊

26 Xīnjiāng Màimàití
Miànguǎn
新疆买买提面馆

OTHER

1 Railway
Carriage
Factory
客车工厂

2 Train Station;
Tiělián Dàshà
火车站;
铁联大厦

3 Post Office
邮局

5 Underground
Shopping Mall
春华商城

7 Long-Distance
Bus Station
长途汽车站

8 Changchun
Shopping
Centre
长春商业城

9 Wěi
Huánggōng
伪皇宫

10 Post Office
邮电局

11 China Telecom
(Internet)
中国电信（网吧）

14 Government Buildings
市政府

15 CAAC
中国民航

19 PSB
公安局外事科

20 CTS
中国旅行社

21 Foreign Language
Bookstore
外文书店

23 Bank of China;
CITS
中国银行；
中国国际旅行社

24 Film Studio
长春电影制片厂

27 Zoo
动物园

28 Changchun
University
东北师大

installed the Republic. After living in exile for many years, Puyi was commandeered by the Japanese as the 'puppet emperor' of Manchukuo in 1934. Captured by the Russians at the end of WWII, Puyi returned to China in 1959 and died in 1967, thus ending a life which had largely been governed by others. His story was the basis for the award-winning film *The Last Emperor*.

The palace is a place of threadbare carpets and sad memories. Puyi's study, bedroom, temple, his wife's quarters and his lover's quarters are all on view. Extracts from his diary are stapled to the walls (chronicling his unhappiness in love and life), alongside period photos of the luckless Puyi and his entourage. History buffs will love it, but all the captions are in Chinese. At the back of the palace is a grisly exhibition of Japanese atrocities in Manchuria.

The palace is open from 9 am to 3.50 pm; entry is Y10. Shower caps are issued to be worn on visitor's feet to protect the carpet.

Bus No 10 goes to the palace from the train station.

Nánhú Gōngyuán   南湖公园

This park is the largest in the city. It has ponds, pavilions and wooden bridges. From the train station, take bus No 62 or 25, or bus No 13 from Rénmín Guǎngchǎng. Admission is Y6.

Film Studio

Those expecting Hollywood, or even Bollywood, will vent a few yawns sauntering around the sprawling estate of the film studio, **Chángchūn Diànyǐng Zhìpiànchǎng**. Documentaries and low-budget flicks are made here, but most of what's on show is tacky and vapid.

It's Y5 for basic entry and thence each spectacle has its own entry fee, or you can buy an all-inclusive ticket for Y75. Bus No 13 goes to the studio from Rénmín Guǎngchǎng.

JÍLÍN 吉林

Places to Stay

Touts will hound you at the station. Tag along if you're looking for a bargain, as most of Chángchūn's cheap hotels are off limits to foreigners. One budget hotel budget that may accept foreign travellers is the friendly *Chángchūn Shì Chángdiàn Liǔshè* (☎ 272 6361), just around the corner from the train station. Doubles with very basic shared bath start at Y40. The rooms are tiny and simple but clean. The hotel is a little tricky to find – head right out of the train station and look for a 24-hour chemist on the left side of the street. The hotel is directly opposite it, up a once-red carpeted staircase.

Tiělián Dàshà (*Railway Hotel;* ☎ 272 9381) is at the eastern end of the train station. Dorm beds range from Y25 to Y70 per person and triples cost Y180. Huge doubles with private bath cost Y260. Also conveniently located is the *Chūnyí Bīnguǎn* (☎ 279 9966, fax 896 0171, 2 Renmin Jie), one block south of the train station. Doubles range from Y180 to Y260 or you can splurge on the presidential suite for Y5800.

Chángchūn Bīnguǎn (☎ 892 9920, fax 892 2033, 18 Xinhua Lu) near Rénmín Guǎngchǎng has basic doubles starting at Y238.

Near Nánhú Gōngyuán is *Chángbái Shān Bīnguǎn* (☎ 566 9911, fax 564 3194, 16 Xinmin Jie). Doubles cost Y298 or Y360, including breakfast. The hotel is inconveniently located; take bus No 25 or 62 from the train station.

A better deal can be had at *Yuèfǔ Dàjiǔdiàn* (*Paradise Hotel;* ☎ 271 7071, fax 271 5709, 46 Renmin Jie, ✉ Yfh@Public .cc.jl.cn), opposite Shènglì Gōngyuán. Fairly plush singles/doubles/triples start at Y248/298/348. Depending on the season, the more expensive rooms are sometimes available at half-price.

The most upmarket hotel in Chángchūn is the *Shangri-La Hotel* (*Xiānggélǐlā Jiǔdiàn;* ☎ 898 1818, fax 898 1919, 9 Xi'an Lu), which offers sterling service and accommodation. Doubles start at US$160 or the presidential suite is available at US$1200. At the time of writing the *Max Court Hotel* was about to open next door to the Shangri-

La, and will likely provide some stiff competition and (hopefully) competitive rates.

Places to Eat

Běijīng Kǎoyā (*Xi'an Lu*) serves excellent Beijing Duck among other dishes. It's not that cheap, with half a duck priced at about Y40, but the food and service is great. The chef nonchalantly carves the duck in front of you with a few expert flicks of the wrist. You'll find the restaurant west of the Shangri-La Hotel on Xi'an Lu.

On the street running along the northern edge of Shènglì Gōngyuán are a number of upscale seafood and hot-pot *restaurants*. The street itself is a *market* lined with stalls selling steamed rolls, snacks and kebabs. At the western end of this market is the *Wǔhuán Guǎngchǎng* (*Olympic Plaza*), which houses Korean, Japanese and seafood restaurants as well as a sports bar and excellent grocery store. After you've finished filling up, check out the indoor tennis courts, bowling alley, sauna and disco.

South of the city, between Renmin Dajie and Mudan Jie, is a hotbed of *restaurants*. In particular, explore Guilin Jie, a main shopping street and hang-out for students. At the western end is *Xīnjiāng Mǎimǎití Miànguǎn* (*Xin Jiang Mai Mai Ti Noodles Restaurant*) a Muslim restaurant where Frank, the friendly proprietor, serves up excellent middle eastern dishes. At the other end of the same street is the *French Bakery* (*Hóng Mò Fǎng;* ☎ 562 3994, 33 Guilin Jie), a popular cafe for expats and foreign students, where you can sip cappuccinos and espressos and savour baguettes, turnovers and chocolate croissants.

Getting There & Away

Air The Civil Aviation Administration of China (CAAC; Zhōngguó Mínháng; ☎ 272 5001), 2nd floor, China Construction Bank, is south of Shènglì Gōngyuán, across from a large, momentous building that is also the provincial headquarters for the Communist Party. The entrance to CAAC is off an alley down the western side of the building.

There is a flight on Tuesday to Hong Kong (Y2860), daily flights to Seoul

(Y2160) except for Saturday, and flights on Wednesday to Vladivostok (Y1330). Domestic destinations include Běijīng (Y770), Shànghǎi (Y1280), Shēnzhèn (Y1990) and Guǎngzhōu (Y1950).

Bus The long-distance bus station (kèyùn zhōngxīn) is behind Chūnyí Bīnguǎn. You can catch buses from here to Jílín. The first bus departs at 5 am and then another leaves every 15 minutes (Y15; 2½ hours).

Train There are frequent trains to Hāěrbīn (Y23) and Jílín (Y11). Other destinations include Běijīng (Y445), Tiānjīn (Y83), Dàlián (Y61), Shànghǎi (Y156), Jǐ'nán (Y102) and Nánjīng (Y140).

An overnight train travels to Tumen – this is the train for Chángbái Shān and Tiān Chí (get off the train at Dunhua station).

Getting Around

Chángchūn airport is only a few kilometres to the east of the city centre; CAAC provides a shuttle bus to the airport from its ticket office (Y5).

Bus No 6 runs through the centre of town, between the train station and Nánhú Gōngyuán. Bus No 10 runs east from the train station to Wěi Huánggōng and bus No 25 heads south from the station, along the western edge of town. Taxis congregate outside the train station and Yuèfǔ Dàjiǔdiàn (see Places to Stay earlier).

JÍLÍN 吉林

☎ 0432 • pop 4,276,300

The city of Jílín, originally established as a fortress in 1673, was severely damaged during WWII and suffered wholesale looting by Russian soldiers.

Despite the industrial nature of the city, Jílín is noted for its winter scenery, which challenges the backdrop of workers' flats and factories. At any other time of year, unless you are manic about meteorites, there is little to draw you to Jílín.

Information

The Bank of China is next to Yínhé Dàshà on Sonngjiang Lu. The main post office is on Jiangnan Jie, north of Jílín Bridge, and the PSB is on Běijīng Lu, just north of the Catholic Church.

CITS (☎ 245 7721), 4 Jiangwan Lu, is on the second floor of Jiāngchéng Bīnguǎn. CTS (☎ 245 9204), 2 Jiangwan Lu, is at the front of the Dōngguān Bīnguǎn complex.

Ice-Rimmed Trees

The banks of the Sōnghuā Jiāng offer up a spectacular wonderland scene during the winter months when the branches of pine and willow trees are covered in needle-like hoarfrost. This unusual tourist attraction is created by the Fengman Hydroelectric Station. Built by the Japanese, disassembled by the Russians and then reassembled by the Chinese, this station fuels three large chemical plants. Water passing from the artificial Sōnghuā Hú through the power plant becomes a warm steamy current that merges with the Sōnghuā Jiāng and prevents it from freezing. Overnight, vapour rising from the river meets the -20°C (-4°F) air temperature, causing the display.

During the Lunar New Year (late January to mid-February), hordes of Japanese and overseas Chinese come for the icicle show. However, while the trees may be the most popular sight in town, the 20km stretch from the lake to the city centre provides ample viewing for all. The best time to catch this sight is in the morning. The stretch of the river in from of the Dōngguān Bīnguǎn (see Places to Stay later) is a good place to start.

Wén Miào 文庙

This temple is also known as the Confucius Temple (Kǒng Miào). Temples dedicated to Confucius were built so that the great sage would bestow good luck on local hopefuls taking the notoriously difficult imperial examinations (huìkǎo).

An exhibition details the huìkǎo, describing how examinees were confined to solitary cells during examinations. Examples of ingenious cheating devices are on show, including undershirts covered in minuscule characters (worn despite the risk that the ultimate penalty for cheating was death). The

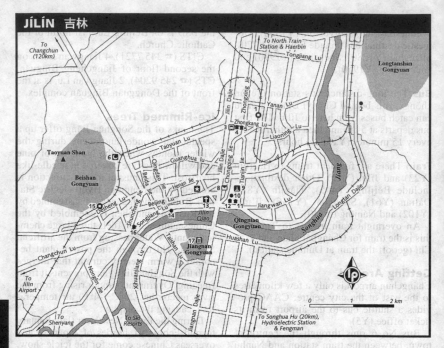

JÍLÍN 吉林

To Changchun (120km)

Taoyuan Shan

Beishan Gongyuán

To North Train Station & Haerbin

Tongjiang Lu

Longtanshan Gongyuán

Zhongkang Lu

Yanan Lu

Liaoning Lu

Jílín Dàjie

Zhongxing Jie

Taoyuan Lu

Guanghua lu

Qingdao

Beida

Henan Jie

Jílín Dàjie

Chongqing Jie

Tianjin Jie

Jiangwan Dàjie

Songhua Jiàng

Beijing Lu

Desheng Lu

Shuncheng Lu

Songjiang Lu

Jílín Qiáo

Qingnian Gongyuán

Huashan Lu

Songhua   Longtan Dàjie

To Jílín Airport

Changchun Lu

Norljin Jie

Xihuanjiang Jie

Jiangnan Gongyuán

Xihuanjiang Jie

Taidan Lu

To Shenyang

To Ski Resorts

Jiangnan Dàjie

To Songhua Hu (20km), Hydroelectric Station & Fengman

0   1   2 km

LP

---

temple to Confucius features statues of the sage, his favourite students and Mencius (the Confucian philosopher). Also arrayed are a host of sacrificial animal figures.

Entrance to the temple is off Jiangwan Lu, next to Jiāngchéng Bīnguǎn (see Places to Stay later). Admission is Y10 and it's open daily from 8.30 am to 3.30 pm. Take bus No 13 from the main train station.

Běishān Gōngyuán 北山公园

If you need a little exercise, go to Běishān Gōngyuán, a hilly area on the western side of town with temples, pavilions, forests and footpaths. The scenery is mellow enough and is certainly preferable to Jílín's industrial smokestacks. On the western side of the park is **Taoyuan Shan**, which is worth a short hike.

Bus No 7 from the train station terminates in front of the park entrance. If you're on a local train, Běishān train station is near the park.

Catholic Church

This Catholic Church (Tiānzhǔ Jiàotáng), built in 1917, has become a symbol of Jílín city. The church was completely ransacked during the Cultural Revolution, and its small library of religious works was also torched. In 1980 the church re-opened and now holds regular services.

The church is not far from Dōngguān Bīnguǎn, on the northern bank of the Sōnghūa Jiāng.

Yúnshí Yǔ Bówùguǎn
Meteorite Shower Museum

In March 1976 the Jílín area received a heavy meteorite shower, and the largest meteor fragment is on view in this museum. Apparently it's the largest chunk anywhere in the world, weighing in at 1770kg. The museum is open Monday to Saturday from 8.30 am to 4 pm and Sunday from 8.30 am to 3 pm, and admission is Y10. Take bus No 3 from outside Dōngguān Bīnguǎn.

JÍLÍN

PLACES TO STAY	OTHER	
4 Jiāotōng Bīnguǎn 交通宾馆	1 Main Train Station 吉林火车站	9 Wén Miào 文庙
5 Jílín Guójì Fàndiàn 吉林国际饭店	2 Lóngtánshān Deer Farm 龙潭山鹿场	10 CAAC 中国民航
11 Jiāngchéng Bīnguǎn; CITS 江城宾馆, 中国国际旅行社	3 Long-Distance Bus Station 岔路乡汽车站	13 Catholic Church 天主教堂
12 Dōngguān Bīnguǎn; CTS 东关宾馆; 中国旅行社中国民航	6 Mosque 清真寺	14 City Hall 市政府
16 Yínhé Dàshà; Bank of China 银河大厦;中国银行	7 PSB 公安局外事科	15 Běishān Train Station 北山火车站
	8 Post Office 邮局	17 Yǔnshí Yǔ Bówùguǎn 陨石雨博物馆

Festival

Jílín, like Hāěrbīn, has an **Ice Lantern Festival** (Bīngdēng Jié), held at Jiāngnán Gōngyuán on the southern side of the Sōnghūa Jiāng. Locals claim that Jílín invented the Ice Lantern Festival and Hāěrbīn copied it (Hāěrbīn's festival is much more famous though, so it's probably sour grapes). Other attractions in the park during winter time include an **ice-skating rink**.

Places to Stay

There are no cheap hotels open to foreigners in Jílín, and the lowest prices are midrange. Getting hold of a cheap room during January and February is tricky, as the city is bristling with icicle watchers. The rates quoted are off season – expect large increases when snow flakes start to fall.

The most convenient option is **Jiāotōng Bīnguǎn** (Traffic Hotel; ☎ 255 8891, fax 253 8149, 6 Zhongkang Lu), next door to the long distance bus station. Singles/twins cost Y200/280 and triples are a deal at Y240.

If Jiāotōng Bīnguǎn is full, head to **Dōngguān Bīnguǎn** (☎ 245 4272, fax 244 5208, 2 Jiangwan Lu) for threadbare doubles from Y220 to Y280. Take bus No 3 from the train station.

Next door to Dōngguān Bīnguǎn is the upmarket **Jiāngchéng Bīnguǎn** (☎ 245 7721, fax 245 8973, 4 Jiangwan Lu). This hotel mainly takes tour groups. The cheap-

est doubles are Y240, and triples/suites cost Y270/480.

The **Yínhé Dàshà** (Milky Way Hotel; ☎ 484 1780, fax 484 1621, 79 Songjiang Lu) is a reasonable option, although its quite a hike from the main train station. It's a good deal if you get one of the standard or triple rooms for Y380; suites cost Y580. Take bus No 1 and ask the driver to tell you when the bus has reached the Línjiāngmén stop by the bridge over the river, which is very close to the hotel.

Jílín Guójì Fàndiàn (Jilin International Hotel; ☎ 292 9818, fax 255 3788, 20 Zhongxing Jie) is the most upmarket option in town. Conveniently located between the train and bus station, three-star singles/doubles/triples cost Y320/420/360.

There are advertisements around town for a **Jílín Hilton Hotel**, but it has yet to make an appearance.

Places to Eat

There is little to report in the way of a local cuisine; hotel proprietors will be stumped to give you a recommendation. Even the area around the train station is unusually absent of restaurants. If you head south of the station on Chongqing Jie, you will happen upon a number of rather nondescript *restaurants*, *cafes* and *street stalls*.

The restaurant on the second floor of **Dōngguān Bīnguǎn** serves reasonable food, as does the Chinese/Western restaurant in *Jílín Guójì Fàndiàn*. There are a number of seafood and hot-pot *restaurants* on Shuncheng Jie, behind the Yínhé Dàshà, which cater to tour groups. Alternatively, you can munch of kebabs sold from *vendors* on the southern side of Jílín Bridge, while you watch families fly kites in the park.

Getting There & Away

Air CAAC (☎ 245 4260) is at 1 Chongqing Jie, behind Dōngguān Bīnguǎn. There are flights between Jílín and Běijīng (Y760), Shànghǎi (Y1170) and Guǎngzhōu (Y1940).

Bus The long-distance bus station (chà lù xiāng) is one long block west of the train station. There are buses between Jílín and Chángchūn every 15 minutes throughout the day (2½ hours). A daily bus departs at 2.15 pm for Hāěrbīn and, if there is demand, a second bus departs at 4.30 pm (six hours). One bus a day leaves for Dunhua at 9 am; change at Dunhua to reach Báihé and Tiān Chí. There are also services to Shěnyáng.

Train The main train station is in the north of the city. There is a regular direct train service between Jílín and Chángchūn with the last train departing at 4 pm. There are two direct trains to Hāěrbīn (four hours), departing at 4.55 am and 8 am. There are also services to Tumen (via Dunhua), Shěnyáng and Dàlián. There are also direct trains to Běijīng and Tiānjīn, but tickets have to be bought well in advance if you hope to nab a sleeper. It's easier to go to Chángchūn and organise it from there.

Getting Around

Jílín's airport is about 10km west of the city. A taxi will cost you about Y50. Private minibuses leave the airport following flight arrivals, but the service doesn't operate the other way. Shuttle buses run from CAAC to the airport once a day at 11.30am, and cost Y5.

There's usually a virtual taxi festival happening around the train station. Taxi fares are a flat Y20 to anywhere within the city.

AROUND JÍLÍN
Ski Resorts

Located 25km south-east of Jílín, east of Fengman, the slopes Sōnghuā Hú Qīngshān reach an elevation of 934m. Opened in 1982 with an emphasis on beginners, the ski resort, **Sōnghuā Hú Qīngshān Huáxuě Chǎng**, has progressed in line with its skiers and now offers both intermediate slopes and a 5km section for cross-country fans. Other features are its 270m main piste, a 1800m cableway, a 2km practice piste and a ski jump.

The ski season runs from approximately December to February, depending on the weather's co-operation. The resort has equipment rental, a cafe, restaurant and shopping arcade. Entry to the resort is Y50. You can reach it by bus No 9 from the main train station.

For those who find this all a little too tame, **Tonghua**, in the southern part of the province, has ski slopes fit for competitions of champions.

Běidàhú Huáxuě Chǎng, 20km from Jílín, is perhaps the best place in China to practice the art of sliding downhill. A day of skiing will cost you Y500. Ski rental and accommodation are both available at the resort. Unfortunately the only way to reach Běidàhú is by taxi (Y60).

CHÁNGBÁI SHĀN 长白山
Ever-White Mountains ☎ 0439

Chángbái Shān is China's largest **nature reserve**, covering 210,000 hectares of dense, virgin forest.

Because of elevation changes there is a wide variation in animal and plant life in the reserve. From 700 to 1000m above sea level there are mixed coniferous and broad-leaf trees (including white birch and Korean pines); from 1000 to 1800m, there are cold-resistant coniferous trees such as dragon spruce and fir; from 1800 to 2000m is a third forest belt; and above 2000m the landscape is alpine tundra – treeless and windy.

For the budding natural scientist there's plenty to investigate. Some 300 medicinal plants grow within the reserve (including winter daphne, Asia bell and wild ginseng); and entomologists will have a field day by

TIĀN CHÍ & CHÁNGBÁI SHĀN
天池与长白山

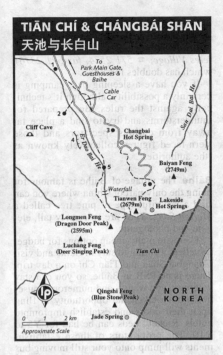

TIĀN CHÍ & CHÁNGBÁI SHĀN

1 Báishān Skating Rink
白山冰场
2 Xiǎo Tiānchí
小天池
3 Fēng Kǒu (Wind Gap)
风口
4 Sàiqí Yá
(Chess Match Cliff)
赛棋崖
5 Guān Qiáo
(Crest Bridge)
冠桥
6 Tiānchí
Meteorological
Observatory
天池气象站

the shores of Tiān Chí at the end of June, when the snow finally melts and an explosion of insect life results. Some very shy animal species also make their home in the mountain range (the rarer ones being protected cranes, deer and Manchurian tigers).

Facilities for the more bold include hot springs, a skating rink, cable car and walking trails. Admission through the main gate of the park is Y35 plus a further Y25 to get up to the Tiān Chí.

Tiān Chí 天池
Heaven Pool
Tiān Chí is a volcanic crater lake at an elevation of 2194m and is by far the most popular sight at Chángbái Shān. The lake is 5km from north to south, 3.5km from east to west, and 13km in circumference. It's surrounded by jagged rock outcrops and 16 mountainous peaks; the highest is Báiyán Fēng (White Rock Peak), which soars to 2749m. Èrdàobái Hé runs off the lake, with

a rumbling 68m waterfall that is the source of the Sōnghūa Jiāng and Tumen Hé. The lake is also said to be home to a monster that has yet to be photographed (see the boxed text 'Myths and Mists of Tiān Chí').

Between 11 am and noon, tour buses roll up to disgorge day-trippers who pose heroically for photos in front of the waterfall, stampede up the mountain (one-hour hike), take a lakeside breather and then rush down again between 1 and 2 pm. The beauty of the place is badly marred by picnic detritus, smashed glass and discarded film wrappers. Even so, there are opportunities to leave the crowds behind and spend a couple of peaceful and sublime days hiking around.

Keeping the boxed text 'Beware of the Border' in mind, if you're planning to hike off the beaten tourist trail, it's also advisable to bring dried food, sunscreen lotion and other medical supplies, good hiking gear and to hike in a group. High altitude weather is very fickle; no matter how warm and sunny it is in the morning, sudden high winds, rain, hail and dramatic drops in temperature are entirely possible by afternoon. The peaks are often covered in cloud by around the 1000m mark.

For those just keen to see the lake, you can rent overcoats and waterproofs from the scrum of women encircling you as you get off the bus at Tiān Chí. Construction helmets are issued to protect tourists from falling rocks.

Beware of the Border

Hiking at Tiān Chí is limited not only by the sharp peaks and their rock-strewn debris but also by the fact that the lake overlaps the Chinese-North Korean border. As recently as 1998, a British tourist was held for a month in a North Korean prison after unknowingly crossing the border while attempting to take a stroll around the circumference of the lake. This is an easy thing to do as the border is either not clearly marked or not indicated at all.

To make matters worse, there are no detailed maps of the area available. Approximately one third of the lake, the south-eastern corner, is on the North Korean side and off-limits. Do not venture east of Báiyán Fēng (White Rock Peak) or the Lakeside Hot Springs at Tiān Chí's summit. If you have any suspicions that you are nearing the border or are at all unsure as to where exactly it lies, do not proceed any further!

Places to Stay

There are also a growing number of places to stay in the Chángbái Shān region; however, most are tacky tour group hotels and require you to fork out big time. With competition on the rise and the majority of tourists visiting the park on day trips, you may be able to bargain prices down to Y200 per person, and some of these hotels are even beginning to offer dorm beds for Y50. If you plan to stay for a couple of days, staying in a dorm will likely prove cheaper than basing yourself in Báihé and returning daily. The problem of which hotels have dorms and whether or not they're open to foreigners seems as much determined by mood as by demand. Call ahead or take your chances.

Chángbái Shān Tiānchí Bīnguǎn (☎ 574 2069), by the main Tiān Chí gate, is a tasteless villa-style hotel frequented by South Koreans. Doubles start at Y500. Nearby, the *Chángbái Shān Dùjuān Shānzhuāng* (*Mount Changbai Cuckoo Villa;* ☎ 571 2574, fax 571 2376), is Swiss chateau-style, complete with hot spring baths, cheesy night club and ski hire. Doubles cost Y445. Much of the same can be found at the *Chángbái Shān Yùndòngyuán Cūn* (*Changbai Athletes Village;* ☎ 571 2574, fax 571 2376), which has doubles for Y485.

If you have a sleeping bag, camping is certainly a possibility, although it's technically against the rules. Be prepared for thunderstorms and try to find a place far away from curious spectators and those stern-faced figures collectively known as 'the authorities'.

Báihé The village of Báihé is famous for being the only part of China where you can find a beautiful type of pine tree called a *Meiren Song.* They are extremely tall, elegant and photogenic.

There are many cheap options for budget travellers wanting to stay in Báihé and visit Chángbái Shān and Tiān Chí on a day trip. There is no PSB in Báihé, so you can stay wherever you want – and numerous households have taken the opportunity to fling open their doors and establish impromptu hotels. Rickety beds can be had for Y5 to Y10. The proprietors of these establishments will jump onto your still moving bus or train and attempt to drag you home.

If you choose to opt out of this exchange, you can head for *Tiělù Zhāodàisuǒ* (☎ 571 1189), which has four-bed spacious dorms for Y13 per person or simple, clean doubles for Y50. The hotel is operated by the folks at the train station and is directly to the right as you exit the station.

On the left as you exit the train station is the official hotel of Báihé, the *Báiyún Bīnguǎn* (☎ 571 2545), with beds for Y100 per person.

Getting There & Away

The *only* season when there's public transport access (when the road from Báihé to Chángbái Shān isn't iced over) is from June to September. Telephone one of the hotels in the area to get a weather check and status report to avoid trekking out to be met by a white out.

There are two main directions from which you can tackle Chángbái Shān; one is

Myths and Mists of Tiān Chí

The enchanting scenery at Tiān Chí (Heaven Pool) would not be complete in the Chinese world without a legend or mystery of some sort. Of the many myths attached to the region, the most intriguing is the origin of the Manchu race.

Three heavenly nymphs descended to the lake in search of earthly pleasure. They took a dip in the lake, and while they were frolicking in the water, along came a magic magpie and dropped a red berry on the dress of one of the nymphs. When she picked it up to smell it, the berry flew through her lips. She became pregnant and gave birth to a handsome boy with an instant gift of the gab. He went on to foster the Manchus and their dynasty.

Dragons and other things that go bump in the night were believed to have sprung from the lake. In fact, they're still believed to do so. There have been intermittent sightings of unidentified swimming objects – China's very own Loch Ness beasts and aquatic yetis. Tiān Chí is the deepest alpine lake in China at a depth estimated at between 200m and 350m. It is frozen over in winter and temperatures are well below zero, so it would take a pretty hardy monster to make this place home (even plankton can't). Sightings from the Chinese and North Korean sides point to a black bear, fond of swimming and oblivious to the paperwork necessary for crossing these tight borders.

On a more profound and heartfelt note, Chinese couples throw coins into the lake, pledging that their love will remain as deep and lasting as Tiān Chí.

---

from Shěnyáng to Báihé, via Tonghua, and the other is from Dunhua to Báihé (it is also possible to fly to Yanji, then backtrack to Antu and get a bus to Báihé, but this is very expensive).

The route via Tonghua is preferable as you can, if you want, arrive early in the day in Báihé and tackle the mountain on the same day. There are two trains per day from Tonghua to Báihé, departing at 8.40 am and 9.40 pm. From Báihé, trains depart for Tonghua at 7.10 am and 10.55pm (277km; 9½ hours). Sleepers/seats cost Y78/29.

From Dāndōng, there are buses to Tonghua departing at 6.40 am (9 hours) and regular buses to Tonghua from Shěnyáng. If you have to spend the night in Tonghua, the *Guómào Dàjiǔdiàn*, opposite the train station, has dorm beds/doubles for Y16/52.

If you opt for the route via Dunhua, there are six buses a day from Dunhua to Báihé (Y17), with the earliest bus leaving at 7.45 am (four hours). There are direct trains to Dunhua from both Chángchūn and Jílín. Alternatively, you can take the train to Tumen and get off at Dunhua. Dunhua has many places where you can stay for the night, including the *Zhōnghuá Yìchūn Bīnguǎn*

(☎ 622 8541), west of the long-distance bus station, which has doubles for Y160.

To catch a bus from Báihé to Dunhua, walk to the end of the road facing the train station, past all the restaurants and pine trees, and buy tickets in the shop directly facing you. Buses to Dunhua stop here.

If you arrive at Báihé in the evening, you will have missed all possible transport and will have to stay the night there (see Places to Stay earlier). If you arrive in the morning, you can jump on to one of the minibuses that race up to the mountain (the service stops at noon).

Getting Around

Buses leave for Chángbái Shān from the square in front of the train station at Báihé from about 6 am to noon. They cost Y40 which includes the return trip, allowing you a few hours to scramble up to the lake and back again.

If you want more time to hike around and you're in a group, it's worth considering hiring a car with a driver for the trip (just pop into one of the restaurants in Báihé and ask, as some of the restaurant owners provide transport). The driver will wait for you to return from the lake and will also offer to drive you to the highest accessible peak (by road) for an additional fee. It is worth doing this if the weather is fine – the view is spectacular.

Hiring a jeep to Tiān Chí for a group should cost around Y300, however, expect to barter with drivers who may attempt to double this price. Always agree on a price before you set out. Be aware that both the buses and the hired cars will drop you off at a point where it is still another hour's hike to the lake.

No buses cover the route from Báihé when there's snow and ice, but you may find a local driver who can navigate the icy roads with tire chains. This will probably set you back a small fortune and maybe the odd broken rib, followed by the possibility of frostbite, so weigh it up carefully.

AROUND CHÁNGBÁI SHĀN
Yánbiān Cháoxiǎn 延边朝鲜
Korean Autonomous Prefecture
The Chángbái Shān region presents possibilities for shaking off the cities and traipsing through the wilderness – and there are certainly some good reasons for doing so, including virgin forest and babbling brooks, and some rough travel and trails.

This area, the Yánbiān Cháoxiǎn, has China's greatest concentration of Korean and Han-Korean groups. The majority inhabit

the border areas north and north-east of Báihé, extending up to Yanji. While the local people of Korean decent are often indistinguishable in dress and appearance from their Chinese counterparts, many of their traditions continue to link them to their heritage. If you visit this area around mid-August, you can join in the **Old People Festival**. These Korean-Chinese are a hospitable, lively lot who will dish up huge portions of spiced, cold noodles and dog meat while singing, dancing and drinking you under the table.

The green mountains here provide more dramatic scenery than Jílín's flatter areas to the north and west. Trains and buses pass through countless villages where you can catch glimpses of everyday life off the tourist trail.

Getting around by train is safer than braving the winding roads by bus. Apart from public buses, the only other means of vehicle transport is by hiring a private jeep (and driver) or by hitching a lift on a logging truck.

Off the main track, the trains are puffing black dragons. The fittings are old and the trains have no sleepers. Trains running east from Dunhua to Tumen pass through Antu, Laotougou and Yanji from where you can also connect north to Hēilóngjiāng.

Hēilóngjiāng 黑龙江

Hēilóngjiāng (Black Dragon River) is China's northernmost province and is known for its subarctic climate. Come January, with its -30°C (-22°F) weather and howling Siberian gales, the locals sensibly huddle round their stoves, swathed in thickly padded clothing and blankets, quaffing the local firewater. Activity slows to a crunch in this snowflake-spitting weather, while the animals bypass the season completely by hibernating.

Welcome, believe it or not, to the tourist season. Inquisitive Hong Kong and Taiwanese tourists fly up to fulfil their childhood ambition of seeing snow, and are reputedly so blown away by the cold that they never set foot north of the Tropic of Cancer again. Don't be put off – if you come prepared for weather conditions similar to winter on Pluto, the city of Hāěrbīn offers a sparkling spectacle of ice-encrusted Russian buildings, winter sports and its famous Ice Lantern Festival. The months of May to September open up the rest of the province to exploration.

Mòhé, in northern Hēilóngjiāng, holds the record for China's lowest plunge of the thermometer, a mere -52.3°C (-61.1°F). As a result of living in these conditions, the people of Hēilóngjiāng are hewn from rough material and have a reputation for being hardy and bellicose. It's worth noting that the hard stuff available on shelves all over Hāěrbīn is called 'hand grenade', which comes in an appropriately shaped bottle. It may not be for connoisseurs of wines and spirits, but it is possibly a collector's item nonetheless.

HĀĚRBĪN 哈尔滨
☎ 0451 · pop 9,149,100

Originally a quiet village on the Sōnghūa Hé, Hāěrbīn derives its name from *alejin*, the Manchu word for 'honour' or 'fame'.

In 1896 the Russians negotiated a contract to build a railway line from Vladivostok to Hāěrbīn and Dàlián. The Russian

imprint on the town remained in one way or another until the end of WWII. By 1904 the 'rail concession' was in place, and with it came other Russian demands on Manchuria. These were stalled by the Russo-Japanese War (1904–05) and, with the Russian defeat, the Japanese gained control of the railway.

473

HĒILÓNGJIĀNG 黑龙江

In 1917 large numbers of Russian refugees flocked to Hāěrbīn, fleeing the Bolsheviks. The Japanese occupied the city in 1932, and in 1945 the Soviet army wrested it back and held it until 1946 when, as agreed by Chiang Kaishek and Stalin, Kuomintang troops were finally installed.

Hāěrbīn today is largely an industrial city but improving relations with Russia have resulted in flourishing trade and a mini-boom in cross-border tourism. The vast majority of foreign faces on the streets of Hāěrbīn today are Russian; the Chinese call them *lǎo máozi* (hairy ones). They will no doubt call you this as well, or speak to you in Russian, rather than Chinese or English.

The Russians generally come over to holiday and to buy all manner of consumer goods: clothing, coffee and cosmetics. They also bring with them all manner of items that will fetch a price in China, including Russian army surplus (for 'surplus' read 'anything that sells'), including night-vision goggles and possibly the odd warhead.

Hāěrbīn was once a graceful Chinese city and continues to possess a number of architectural gems handed down from the Russian era. The recent success in the tourism

The Magical Root

With properties considered almost mystical throughout much of the world, ginseng has been used for medicinal purposes in China for well over 2000 years. Although this pronged root is found and grown all over China, that which comes from Manchuria is thought by many to be of the highest quality.

Ginseng belongs to the 'chi' category of herbs that are used to restore and rebuild organs and tissues, energising the entire body. Over the years the popularity of ginseng has spread, as has its uses. You'll most commonly spot ginseng being used as a curative tea, good for sore throats and coughs, however its uses extend far beyond that: fatigue, convalescence, debility, lack of energy, shock, stress, weakened immunity, chronic diseases ... you name it and it's not unlikely that ginseng is the answer. Women giving birth are given a chunk of it to chew on, as are the ill on their deathbed in the belief that ginseng's power as a source of vital energy will revitalise them. Ginseng is not administered to people with severe fever or infection as the herb is said to be so potent that it will give strength to the illness rather than the ill.

For the sceptical, scientific research has confirmed ginseng's positive effects on the body although exactly how ginseng manages this remains something of a mystery. Western scientists have made up their own category to fit ginseng into: 'adaptogens'. Adaptogens affect the way in which the body's hormones and nerves respond to their environment. In this way, ginseng works to increase your ability to adapt to and survive stressful conditions – perhaps a helpful hint while travelling around China.

industry has spurred the restoration of some of the old Russian neighbourhoods; however, Hāěrbīn's allure is slowly being overwhelmed by giant, glitzy buildings and the fast pace and pollution of city life. Enjoy what's left of its charm while it lasts.

Orientation

In the north is the Sōnghuā Hé, separating the city from Tàiyángdǎo Gōngyuán (Sun Island Park). The Dàolǐqū district, in the section towards the banks of the Sōnghuā Hé, houses the main shopping zone of Hāěrbīn and displays most of the historical buildings that give the city its character.

The main train station is in the centre of town, surrounded by a cluster of hotels.

Information

Tourist Office Potentially useful and conveniently located is the China Haerbin Overseas Tourist Corporation (Hǎiwài Lǚyóu Gōngsī; ☎ 461 5846, fax 461 4259), 89 Zhongyang Dajie, on the 2nd floor of the charming Mǎdiěěrh Bīnguǎn. It can arrange all sorts of tours and activities including hunting, skiing, and 'cold water' fishing on

the vast lake Xīngkǎi Hú in the east of the province.

Money The Bank of China is at 19 Hongjun Jie, near the Guójì Fàndiàn. Any of the large hotels will change money.

Post & Communications The main post office is on the corner of Dongda Zhijie and Fendou Lu. A second office is located next to the train station, and a third on Zhongyang Dajie. The main telephone office is also on Fendou Lu, north of the main post office.

China Telecom has an Internet office at 90 Xidazhi Jie, next to the Haerbin Polytech University. It isn't signposted, but you'll find it at the end of the hall on the ground floor. The server is snail-paced, but access is cheap at Y3 per hour.

It's far easier to get comfortable at Telecom's Internet bar on Zhongyang Dajie where you can watch videos while your server chugs along. Access here is still cheap at Y5 per hour. The office is open from 9 am to 8 pm. To find the office, follow the outdoor stairs down to the dungeon of the office on the corner of Zhongyang

Dajie and Xi 5 Dao Jie (one block north of Mǎdiēěrh Bīnguǎn).

Travel Agencies China International Travel Service (CITS; Zhōngguó Guójì Lǚxíngshè; ☎ 232 4114, fax 230 2476), 11th floor, 95-1 Zhongshan Lu, has found a new home near the train station. It can provide you with train and airline tickets and organise boating and skiing tours during the high season.

PSB The Public Security Bureau (PSB; Gōngānjú) is on Duan Jie, west off Zhongyang Dajie.

Dàolǐqū 道里区

Put wandering around the market areas and the streets high on your list. There's a very different kind of architectural presence in Hāěrbīn – Russian spires, cupolas, scalloped turrets and cobblestone streets. Walking along Zhongyang Dajie and the side streets that run off it in the heart of the Dàolǐqū area is like wandering through a living museum. There are thirteen preserved buildings, each with a plaque stating when it was built and a brief history of its use.

Church of St Sophia

Hāěrbīn has many Orthodox churches (dōngzhèng jiàotáng), the majority of which were ransacked during the Cultural Revolution and have since fallen into disrepair.

The Church of St Sophia (Shèng Suǒfēiyà Jiàotáng), built by the Russians in 1907, has had it's exterior restored. It's in the heart of the city centre, extending into an open square. The square provides an enjoyable place to people-watch while listening to the classical Russian music that drifts from the church. Impromptu performances are often held here in the summer months.

The interior of the church has also been restored but left in its original state as much as possible. The result is subtle and beautiful and well worth a look. The church now houses the **Haerbin Architecture Arts Centre**, which displays a photographic trail of Hāěrbīn's history from its infancy through

its various foreign occupations. A very interesting visit.

The church is on the north-east corner of Zhaolin Jie and Toulong Jie, one block south of Shitou Dajie. Entry costs Y10.

Sīdàlín Gōngyuán 斯大林公园
Stalin Park

Sīdàlín Gōngyuán, a perambulating zone down by the river, is dotted with statues and recreation clubs for the locals. The promenade is constructed along a 42km embankment that was built to curb the unruly Sōnghuā Hé. The bizarre **Fánghóng Shènglì Jìniàntǎ** (Flood Control Monument) was built in 1958 to celebrate the embankment's victory in holding back the river, as well as to commemorate the thousands of people who had previously died in the Sōnghuā's floods.

A resort feel holds sway in summer, with ice-cream stands, photo booths and boating trips along the river. Vendors sell plates of *hélúo* (steamed river snails), crickets in cages and boat tickets across to Tàiyángdǎo Gōngyuán and along the Sōnghuā Hé.

The Sōnghuā Hé itself comes alive in winter with **ice-skating, ice-hockey, tobogganing** and even **ice sailing** (vessels sail on the ice surface, assisted by wind power, and reach speeds of 30 km/h). Equipment for each of these sports can be hired. Slightly madder folk astound onlookers by swimming in gaps in the ice.

The area west of the passenger ferry terminal is a popular place for Hāěrbīn's older residents to spend time sipping tea, dancing, singing, playing music and mahjong and chatting up a storm.

Tàiyángdǎo Gōngyuán 太阳岛公园
Sun Island Park

Facing Sīdàlín Gōngyuán and a ferry trip away is Tàiyángdǎo Gōngyuán, a sanatorium/recreational zone covering 3800 hectares. The main draw of the area is Tàiyángdǎo Gōngyuán, which has gardens, forested areas and a 'water world'. Short helicopter flights from the park over Hāěrbīn cost Y150. In the summer the area is alive with both flora and tour groups. In the winter it has something of a neglected feel about it, but provides a peaceful getaway.

Boat tickets are available in Sīdàlín Gōngyuán. Buy a ticket from one of the government-run boat ticket vendors (*guóyíng chuánpiào*), whose dock is directly north of Fánghóng Shènglì Jìniàntǎ. These tickets only cost Y1, while the private operators will fleece you. You can also take a cable car to Tàiyángdǎo Gōngyuán from the end of Tongjiang Jie. Tickets cost Y20/30 one way/return.

Dōngběi Hǔ Lìnyuán 东北虎林园
Siberia Tiger Park

The mission of the Dōngběi Hǔ Lìnyuán is to study, breed, release and ultimately save the Manchurian tiger from extinction. However, while you are definitely promised a very up-close look at the 11 captive cats,

those who are not too keen on zoos might best give this supposed sanctuary a miss. The fenced off field feels far too small for these beasts, never mind the touring minibuses whose drivers blare their horns and play chicken with the cats to the delight of the tourists. If you visit at feeding time, you may even have the special treat of witnessing the tigers pounce on their dinner of doomed cows.

As you fall under the watchful eyes of these defeated looking, dusty tigers, you can't help but wonder how the park is preparing the animals for the wild.

Tickets for the park cost Y33 and entitle you to a 20-minute bus tour within the fenced-off field as well as entry into a small museum. To reach the park, take bus No 85, which will drop you a 15-minute walk, or Y3 pedicab ride, from the entrance.

Species under Threat

Also known as the Amur, Siberian and North-Eastern China tiger, the Manchurian tiger has long been resident in China. Believed to be the ancestor of all tiger species, the Manchurian tiger began its trek south from the arctic circle and northern Siberia several million years ago. Today it makes its home in eastern Russia, North Korea and north-eastern China.

The Manchurian tiger is one of the rarest as well as the largest of all tiger sub-species. The average male can grow up to four metres long, with a healthy weight of 300kg. The comforts of captivity can increase this weight to over 500kg. But have no fear – it is extremely unlikely that you will run into one of these beasts in the wilds of China. In 1998 it was estimated that the number of Manchurian tigers had depleted to somewhere between 360 and 406, with only 30 to 35 of those roaming freely in China. Given first-grade protection by the Chinese government and recognised as one of the most endangered species worldwide by the World Wide Fund for Nature, the situation of the Manchurian tiger remains perilous. This is the result of the encroachment of cities and pollution on the tigers' territory as well as the lucrative business of poaching. The bones of the tiger, in particular the thigh bones, are highly prized in traditional Chinese medicine, while tiger skins also fetch a hefty price on the black market. One tiger can earn up to 10 years' income for a Chinese poacher.

In response to the Manchurian tigers' plight, the Chinese government has set up a number of breeding centres, including Dōngběi Hǔlìn Yuán (Siberian Tiger Park) outside Hāěrbīn. Currently home to over 70 tigers, the purpose of centres like this one is to restore the natural population of the tigers by breeding them and reintroducing them into the wild. However, conservationists stress the need for minimal human contact with tigers, and for the centres to emulate as much as possible the life that the tigers will face once released. It has been argued that China's breeding centres, which see bus loads of tourists snapping photos of the cats munching on their dinners of cows and chickens, will produce tigers with a taste for livestock and who will associate people and vehicles with feeding time. It is believed that this may render them more suitable for a life of drive-through fast food than one in the great outdoors. Until the first captive tiger is set free, the fate of China's Manchurian tigers – and the local livestock and vehicle owners – remains unknown.

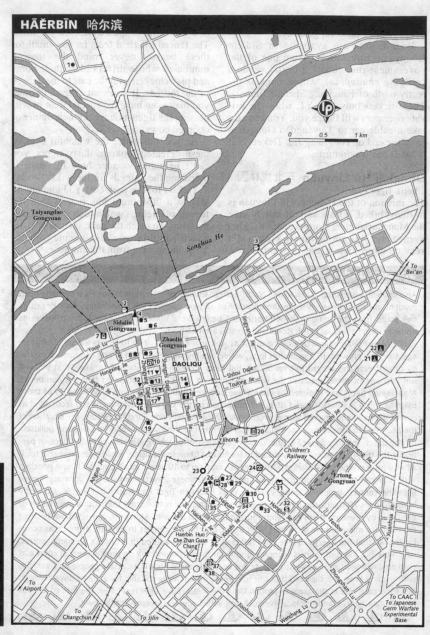

HĀĚRBĪN 哈尔滨

HĀĚRBĪN

PLACES TO STAY

5 Sōnghuājiāng
   Kǎilái Shāngwù Jiǔdiàn
   松花江凯莱商务酒店
6 Mínzú Bīnguǎn
   民族宾馆
8 Zhōngdà Dàjiǔdiàn
   中大大酒店
9 Jīngǔ Fàndiàn
   金谷饭店
13 Mǎdiě'ěr Bīnguǎn
   马迭尔宾馆
19 Holiday Inn
   万达假日酒店
25 Kūnlún Fàndiàn
   昆仑饭店
27 Běiyuàn Fàndiàn
   北苑饭店
29 Gōngānjú Zhāodàisuǒ
   公安局招待所
30 Huáqiáo Fàndiàn
   华侨饭店
33 Guójì Fàndiàn; CAAC
   国际饭店
35 Tiānzhú Bīnguǎn
   天竹宾馆

PLACES TO EAT

11 Portman Bar
   波特曼西餐厅

12 Huáméi Xī Cāntīng
   华梅西餐厅
15 Pizza Mai
   比萨麦
17 Lǎodū Yīchù
   老都一处

OTHER

1 Dōngběi Hǔ Línyuán
   东北虎林园
2 Ferries to Tàiyángdǎo
   Gōngyuán
   太阳岛游览船
3 Passenger Ferry Terminal
   游船渡口
4 Fánghóng Shènglì Jìniàntǎ
   防洪胜利纪念塔
7 Cable Car
   览车
10 Internet
   网吧
14 Foreign Languages
   Bookstore
   外文书店
16 PSB
   公安局外事科
18 Church of St Sophia;
   Haerbin Architecture Arts
   Centre
   圣索菲亚教堂

20 Dōngběi Lièshì Guǎn
   (Martyrs' Museum)
   东北烈士馆
21 Jí Lè Sì
   吉乐寺
22 Tǎ Yuàn
   塔院
23 Main Train Station
   哈尔滨火车站
24 Telephone Office
   电信局
26 CITS
   中国国际旅行社
28 Long-Distance
   Bus Station
   公路客运站
31 Main Post Office
   总邮局
32 Bank of China
   中国银行
34 Shěng
   Bówùguǎn
   省博物馆
36 Mao Statue
   毛主席像
37 Internet
   网吧
38 Haerbin Polytech
   University
   哈尔滨工业大学

You can also combine the trip with a visit to Tàiyángdǎo Gōngyuán's gardens from where you can head back to Sīdàlín Gōngyuán via ferry. Minibuses/taxis running between the gardens and Dōngběi Hǔ Línyuán cost Y10 per person. You'll get a better deal going from Dōngběi Hǔ Línyuán to the gardens rather than vice versa.

Jí Lè Sì 吉乐寺
Temple of Bliss

Located at the eastern end of Dongda Zhijie, the deserted feel of the Jí Lè Sì is defied by the active Buddhist community in residence. Inside the temple are a number of statues including Mílēifó (Maitreya), the Buddha yet-to-come, whose arrival will bring paradise on earth. Entry costs Y6. The gate closes at 4.30 pm at which time, if you're already inside, you can discreetly catch the monks in ceremonial action.

Tǎ Yùan 塔院
Pagoda Courtyard

Next door to the Jí Lè Sì is Tǎ Yùan, the largest temple in Hēilóngjiāng. The temple was under restoration at the time of writing, but was still open to visitors. Gates close at 4 pm; admission is Y5.

Both temples can be reached by taking bus No 14 from the southern end of Zhongyang Dajie to its terminus.

Értóng Gōngyuán 儿童公园
Children's Park

The Értóng Tiěgǔl (Children's Railway) in the Értóng Gōngyuán was built in 1956. It has 2km of track that is plied by a miniature

HĒILÓNGJIĀNG 黑龙江

diesel, pulling seven cars with seating for 200; the round trip from 'Běijīng' to 'Hāěrbīn' takes 20 minutes. The train driver, ticket collectors, rail guards and support personnel are all kids under the age of 13.

You can take your kids there on bus No 8 from the southern end of Zhongyang Dajie; get off at Fendou Lu. The park is open daily, with Sunday often particularly crowded.

Germ Warfare Base

If you haven't visited concentration camps such as Belsen or Auschwitz, a similar lesson in the extreme horrors of war can be learnt at the **Japanese Germ Warfare Experimental Base – 731 Division** (Rìběn Xìjūn Shíyàn Jīdì – 731 Bùduì).

In 1939 the Japanese army set up a top-secret, germ-warfare research centre in Hāěrbīn. Japanese medical experts experimented on prisoners of war, including Chinese, Soviet, Korean, Mongolian and British prisoners. Over 4000 people were exterminated in bestial fashion: some were frozen or infected with bubonic plague, others were injected with syphilis and many were roasted alive in furnaces.

When the Soviets took back Hāěrbīn in 1945, the Japanese blew up the base. The secret could have remained buried forever, but a tenacious Japanese journalist dragged out the truth in the 1980s.

The Japanese medical profession was rocked by the news that some of its leading members had a criminal past that had hitherto escaped detection. Another disturbing angle to the story was the claim that the Americans had granted freedom to the perpetrators of these crimes in return for their research data.

As you walk into the museum, a sign in Chinese states rather ironically: 'The friendship between the Japanese and Chinese people is everlasting'. The exhibition consists of only two small rooms plus a nearby vestige of the original base. All captions are in Chinese only; if you are unable to read them, it is questionable whether or not the long haul out to the museum is worth it.

The museum is 20km south of the city, on the corner of Xinjiang Da Jie and Xingjian Jie; take bus No 338 from the main train station. The museum is open from 8.30 to 11.30 am and 1 to 4 pm; admission is Y10.

Festivals

If you don't mind the cold, then you shouldn't miss Hāěrbīn's main drawcard, the **Ice Lantern Festival** (Bīngdēng Jié) held in Zhaōlín Yùan. Officially, it's held from 5 January to 15 February, although in reality it may start a week earlier and glisten into March.

Fanciful sculptures are produced in the shapes of animals, plants, buildings or motifs taken from legends. Some of the larger sculptures have included a miniature Great Wall of China and a scaled-down Forbidden City. At night the sculptures are illuminated from the inside with coloured lights, turning the place into a temporary fantasy land. Ticket prices vary from year to year, but are costly.

In winter you can reach the park by a 20-minute walk over the frozen river or a Y10 ride on a horse-drawn sleigh. Sleigh drivers will also take you to swimming holes for Y100. Brrrrrrr...

In warmer times, there's the **Haerbin Music Festival** (Yīnyuè Juì) a 12-day event that takes place in July.

Places to Stay

During Hāěrbīn's Ice Lantern Festival hotel prices are at least 20% higher than those listed here, and rooms of any sort can be difficult to find.

As you exit the train station, you will be pounced upon by hotel touts who will drag you off to cheap dives nearby. If you're in search of budget accommodation then tag along, but scope the room first. These rooms are most often off limits to foreigners and, as they are in direct competition with the PSB's own hostel, the police appear to be clamping down. Be warned that at any moment you may be asked to leave by hotel owners who suddenly remember (or are reminded) that they cannot accommodate foreigners.

If what you're looking for is a cheap, comfortable bed, you're better off heading straight for the PSB's imaginatively named *Gōngānjú Zhāodàisuǒ (Hostel of the PSB;* ☎ *642-8560 8000)*. The hostel has moved from its previous seedy location to a somewhat less seedy spot just around the corner from the train station. Clean, large three-bed dorms are a great deal at Y38, including breakfast. Doubles are available at Y120. The staff is unbelievably friendly although, not surprisingly, it takes even more than the usual mass of paperwork to check-in.

As you exit the main train station, just off to your right is the 19-storey *Tiānzhú Bīnguǎn* (☎ *363 7261, fax 364 3720, 6 Songhuajiang Jie)*. This well-located place is a favourite haunt of visiting Russians. Doubles/triples start at Y120/180; prices include breakfast, although you may need to remind the staff of this. Similarly besieged by Russian contingents is the *Běiyuàn Fàndiàn* (☎ *364 2545)*, directly facing the train station. Doubles start at Y130.

Huáqiáo Fàndiàn (Overseas Chinese Hotel; ☎ *364 1476, fax 364 0916, 52 Hongjun Jie)* is within walking distance of the main train station. A refuge of Hong Kong residents and southerners coming to build snowmen in Hāěrbīn, it's often full. Doubles start at Y200.

The *Guójì Fàndiàn (International Hotel;* ☎ *366 9698, fax 362 5651)* is just off Hongjun Jie and just over a kilometre from the train station. Overpriced singles are Y200 and doubles are Y260, but breakfast is thrown in free as a consolation.

If you want to stay in the Dàolǐqū area without paying exorbitant prices, check out the *Zhōngdà Dàjiǔdiàn* (☎ *463 8888, 40 Zongyang Lu)*. The rooms are slightly run down but reasonable at Y238. From the windows you can look down on Zhongyang Dajie.

Across the street is the new *Jīngǔ Fàndiàn* (☎ *469 8700, fax 469 8458, 185 Zhongyang Dajie)*, which provides three-star facilities with doubles starting at Y480.

Mǎdiēěrh Bīnguǎn (Modern Hotel; ☎ *461 5846, fax 461 4997, 89 Zongyang Dajie)* is in a stunning location in Dàolǐqū. Built in 1906, it's a wonderful hotel, full of character and style and friendly staff. The rooms are lovely with singles for Y220 (although the staff may let two people squeeze in), and doubles/triples for Y418/308.

Half a block from Sīdàlín Gōngyuán is *Sōnghuājiāng Kǎilái Shāngwù Jiǔdiàn (Songhuajiang Gloria Inn;* ☎ *463 8855, fax 463 8533, 257 Zhongyang Dajie)*. It offers decent rooms and service in a prime location, with prices to match. Rooms start at Y588, although prices are negotiable during low seasons.

Around the corner is *Mínzú Bīnguǎn (Nationality Hotel;* ☎ *467 4338, fax 467 4058, 111 Youyi Lu)*. Although it's seen better days, it's worth checking out for its cheap deals brought on by the stiff competition in the area. During the low season, you may get standard rooms priced at Y620 for as low as Y200.

Just on the cusp of Hāěrbīn's attractive Dàolǐqū district is the *Holiday Inn (Wàndá Jiàrì Jiǔdiàn;* ☎ *422 6666, fax 422 1661, 90 Jingwei Jie)*. The hotel is for those in need of four-star service and expert hotel management, plus a decent range of restaurants. Rooms start at Y814.

To the immediate south-west of the train station is the new *Kūnlún Fàndiàn* (☎ *360 6688, fax 360 0888, 8 Tielu Jie)*. Facilities include an indoor pool, sauna and six restaurants. Standards start at Y640 to Y1145, plus a 15% service charge.

Places to Eat

Lanterns hang above the entrance to every restaurant – a practice almost exclusive to Hāěrbīn. It's actually a rating system – the more lanterns, the higher the standard and price. Red lanterns mean Chinese food, and blue denotes pork-free cuisine from the Muslim Hui minority (mainly lamb dishes).

Hāěrbīn has also long been famous for expensive culinary exotica, such as grilled bear paws, deer nostrils and Siberian tiger testicles. Fortunately, Běijīng now takes a dim view of serving up endangered species and substitutes have taken their place.

In Hāěrbīn you'll encounter sausages galore. This culinary art has developed alongside the growth in Russian tourism and has become something of a trademark of

Hāěrbīn. Shop windows are filled with lengths of sausages, popular with both locals and Russian visitors alike.

A stroll down Zhongyang Dajie will present you with endless restaurant options. As a rule of thumb, the prices tend to go down as you venture further south. You'll find a number of *bakeries* that serve fresh bread, croissants and pastries, as well as *pubs* where you can sample the local beer, 'Hapi'. There are also a number of fast-food outlets specialising in everything from burgers to *jiǎozi* (dumplings).

Just off Zhongyang Dajie on Shitou Dajie is the *Lǎodǔ Yīchù*, a well known dumpling restaurant. A large plateful will cost you Y26. Around the corner at *Pizza Mai (Bǐ Sà Mài; 154 Shanzhi Dàjie)*, feast on cheap pizzas, spaghetti, Tuscany bread, quesadillas, soups and salads.

The more expensive *Portman Bar (Bōtèmàn Xīcāntīng)* is in a square just around the corner from Mǎdiēěrh Bīnguǎn. It serves western cuisine including fresh seafood and pasta, all to be washed down with jugs of red wine.

Despite the name, *Huáméi Xīcāntīng (Huamei Western Restaurant; ☎ 461 7368)*, just opposite Mǎdiēěrh Bīnguǎn on Zhongyang Dajie, is the place to go for Russian food.

Getting There & Away

Air Civil Aviation Administration of China (CAAC; Zhōngguó Mínháng; ☎ 262 7070) can be found in the hotel of the same name at 101 Zhongshan Lu. It also has a more conveniently located ticketing office next to Guójì Fàndiàn on Hongjun Jie. China Travel Service (CTS; Zhōngguó Lǚxíngshè; ☎ 364 0916) also has a ticketing office in Huáqiáo Fàndiàn. There are frequent flights to Seoul (Y2680) and twice weekly flights to Hong Kong (Y320). CAAC offers international flights to Khabarovsk (Y1250) in Siberia and twice-weekly flights to Vladivostok (Y1330).

A huge number of domestic destinations can be reached from Hāěrbīn including Běijīng (Y770), Shànghǎi (Y1410), Guǎngzhōu (Y2030), Shēnzhèn (Y1970) and Shěnyáng (Y410).

Bus The main long-distance bus station is located directly opposite the train station. Destinations include Jílín (10 am; Y30), Jiāmùsī (Y70 sleeper), Shěnyáng (Y103 sleeper), Qíqíhā'ěr (8 am; Y55) and Dàlián (no sleeper available).

Train A vast number of destinations include Suífēnhé (Y165 sleeper), Chángchūn (Y33; four hours), Dàlián (Y125), Běijīng (Y158; 18 hours) and Jí'nán (Y95). Rail connections to Qíqíhā'ěr (Y37), Mǔdānjiāng (Y35) and Jiāmùsī (Y40) are regular but slow.

For travellers on the Trans-Siberian Railway, Hāěrbīn is a possible starting or finishing point, but it is very tricky to get hold of tickets. For more information try CITS, the China Haerbin Overseas Tourist Corporation or ask directly at the train station.

Boat At the time of writing, the ferry service departing from Hāěrbīn has been suspended but is scheduled to resume running in the summer of 2000. Check with the passenger ferry terminal for more information. In previous years, boats have run to Jiāmùsī from late May to late October. In Jiāmùsī you can change ferries and carry on to Tóngjiāng.

Getting Around

To/From the Airport Hāěrbīn's airport is 46km from town and the journey takes at least one hour, half of which is spent in the traffic-clogged streets near the city centre.

Shuttle buses depart for the airport from the CAAC office south-east of town on Zhongshan Lu and cost Y10; buy tickets on the bus, not inside the office. Buses depart about 2½ hours before scheduled flight departure times. The CAAC shuttle bus is far preferable to taxis, which charge around Y150 to reach the airport.

Bus Hāěrbīn's many buses start running at 5 am and finish at 10 pm (9.30 pm in winter). Trolleybus Nos 101 and 103 can take you from Sīdàlín Gōngyuán to the train station. Minibuses also follow this route and cost Y2.

Boat The government ferry can take you from Sīdàlín Gōngyuán to Tàiyángdǎo

Gōngyuán for Y1 (see Tàiyángdǎo Gōngyuán for more information). Tickets are also available in Sīdàlín Gōngyuán for boat cruises up and down the Sōnghuā Hé (Y30).

AROUND HÁĚRBĪN
Ski Resorts
The **Yùquán hunting grounds**, 65km from Hāěrbīn, offer skiing facilities most appreciated by beginners. If you do want to go hunting, you pay per animal slaughtered, rather than an entrance fee. Inquire in Hāěrbīn at the China Haerbin Overseas Tourist Corporation or ask at CITS.

Yābùli, about 200km (four hours by train) east of Hāěrbīn, was the site of the 1996 Asian Winter Games. Dagoukui Mountain, the actual **ski area**, is a 25km jeep ride from the main town.

Ski passes (including equipment) run from Y260 per day to Y750 for 3 days. There is also a 200m chute that you can slide down for Y100. In the summer the area is popular for hiking.

Information and room bookings can be organised in Hāěrbīn (☎ 345 5088). CITS offers tours to the area that include transport, skiing, horseback riding and a ride down the 'chute'; however, unless you are in a group, these tours are extremely pricey.

Places to Stay
Fēngchē Shānzhuāng (Windmill Hotel; ☎ 345 5168) in Yābùli offers three-star accommodation at the bottom of the ski hill. Prices vary with season and day; a double room on a weekday in low season will cost Y340 while, on a weekend in high season, the same room will cost Y980. The hotel also has a youth compartment *(qīngnǐan gāngyù)* with beds for Y240/480 in low/high season. You can book by phone of through CITS in Hāěrbīn.

MŬDĀNJIĀNG 牡丹江
☎ 0453
A nondescript city of more than one million people, Mŭdānjiāng's main interest to independent travellers is its function as a staging post for visits to nearby Jìngpò Hú (Mirror Lake).

Information
The Bank of China is two blocks south of the train station, on the east side of Taiping Lu; follow the road directly opposite the train station. Three blocks past the bank, on the same side of the road, you'll find the post office.

CTS has an office in the squat barracks, behind Běishān Bīnguǎn. The PSB office is two blocks east of the train station on Guang Hua Jie; head left out of the station.

Places to Stay
Běishān Bīnguǎn (☎ *652 5788, fax 652 4670, 1 Xidiming Jie)* is on the corner of Xinhua Lu, just south of the park and about 1km north of the train station. While the hotel does have dorm beds for Y80, it's not too keen on renting them to foreigners and is likely to charge a 100% surcharge. You're better off taking a double for Y160. You can reach the hotel by taking a five-minute ride on bus No 2 or 14 heading west (right) from the train station.

The other hotel that accepts foreigners is *Mǔdānjiāng Bīnguǎn (*☎ *622 5633, fax 622 7947, 85 Guanghua Jie)*, with doubles for Y265. The hotel is 1km down the road to the left as you exit the train station, or head east on bus No 1.

Getting There & Away
The usual approach to Mŭdānjiāng is by rail from Hāěrbīn. There are also rail connections with Suífēnhé, Tumen, Jiāmùsī and Dōngjīng.

There are flights from Mŭdānjiāng to Běijīng and other cities. The long distance buses arrive and depart from in front of the train station. Regular departures link Mŭdānjiāng to Tumen, Jamusi and Dōngjīng.

JÌNGPÒ HÚ 镜泊湖
Mirror Lake
Covering an area of 90 sq km and 45km in length, the clear reflections of the tree-lined coast and many small islands within this lake leave no question as to why it has been so-named. It is extremely popular with visiting Russians and the area has

been developed as a resort with hotels, recreation centres and even a post office.

Apart from speeding about from island to islet by boat, or turning off the beaten path and escaping into the woods that ring the lake, the main visitor pastime is fishing. The season is from June to August, and tackle and boats can be hired (prices are negotiable). Different varieties of carp (silver, black, red-tailed and crucian) are the trophies.

Nearby, **Diaoshuilou Waterfall**, spanning 20m in height and 40m in width, is an attractive spectacle that swells in size during the rainy season. Some foreigners like to come here and amaze the locals by diving into the pools.

Unfortunately, the area has relinquished much of its majesty to the tourist industry, which has pock-marked the surrounding greenery with resorts and hotels and polluted the air with the screeching sounds of karaoke. The summer months constitute a battle between vendors of every conceivable shape and size who prey off the visiting hordes.

Visiting the lake during low season, from October to May, however, provides a relatively peaceful getaway. Both spring and autumn are pleasant and attractive times to visit, with the opportunity to wander around a lake free of speedboats. The low season sees the disappearance of not only the majority of vendors and tourists, but also of the PSB. This means your chances of getting a bargain bed are much greater. Be warned, however, that many hotels and restaurants shut down during the low season. Entry to the area costs Y20.

Places to Stay
A number of hotels encircle the lake, though many of them are out of bounds to foreigners. The bus will drop you in front of the *Shanzhuang Binguan* (☎ 627 0012), a bright blue building trimmed with red. It has the cheapest rooms at the lake, with dorm beds for Y20. Unfortunately, the karaoke machine is extremely loud and the toilets are a five-minute walk up the road. To offset this, the owners are very cheerful and may invite you to warm up in the evenings on their *kàng* (heatable brick bed).

The new *Yōudìanjǔ Bīnguǎn* (☎ 627 0088) is the best deal in town. Simple rooms with private bath and a view of the lake go for Y150 per person.

The *Jìng-Bóhú Bīnguǎn* (*Jingbo Lake Hotel;* ☎ 627 0091), which also calls itself the 'Presidential Building', is the most up-market option, however, the rooms are way overpriced at Y480 per person.

Getting There & Away
The best approach is by rail from Hāěrbīn. First take a train to Mǔdānjiāng (Y42) and then change trains to Dōngjīng (Y7; 1¼ hours). From there, it's one hour by minibus (Y7) to the lake.

From June to September, three buses run daily from Mǔdānjiāng train station to Dōngjīng. Buses depart between 6 and 7 am (two hours).

Dōngjīng is connected by train to Suífēnhé with one train departing for the seven-hour journey at 7.40 pm. There are also slow connections to Jiāmùsī (6.40 am; 10 hours) and Tumen (12.20 pm; six hours).

If you are on a tour of the lakes of the north-east, it is possible to take the bus from Báihé, near Tiān Chí in Jílín, to Dūnhuáng and from there take the bus to Dōngjīng. The bus from Dūnhuáng will pass Jìngpò Hú, but it is better to carry on to Dōngjīng and backtrack as you will be dropped off miles from any transport at the edge of the lake. If you are headed to Dūnhuáng from Dōngjīng, a daily bus departs at 7.30 am (Y34).

SUÍFĒNHÉ 绥芬河
☎ 0453
This town achieved commercial importance in 1903 with the opening of the South Manchurian Railway, a vital link in the original Trans-Siberian route running from Vladivostok to Moscow via Manchuria. The role of Suífēnhé faded, however, when the railway was later rerouted via Khabarovsk to Vladivostok and Nakhodka.

After the demise of the USSR in 1991, Suífēnhé has, like other borderland outposts, enjoyed a spasmodic growth in cross-border trade and tourism. Yet the self-flattering nickname of 'Little Moscow of the East' harbours little, if any, truth. Other than shop signs printed in Russian, one or two dilapidated Russian-style buildings and a whole lot of Russians themselves, you'll be hard pressed to find anything in Suífēnhé to remind you of its pre-revolutionary days.

Unless you plan on joining the Russian tourists on a shopping spree through the many tacky department stores or are crossing the border into Russia, there is little in Suífēnhé to justify the long journey required to reach it. If you are hoping to continue on into Russia, you will need to have organised a Russian visa in Běijīng and, if you plan to re-enter China, a re-entry visa as well.

Information
The Bank of China is at 41 Shan Cheng Lu, across from the main square. You'll find the post office in a large, Russian relic building, on the corner of Jing Xin Jie and Guang Hua Lu, behind the church. The PSB is at 20 Xin Kai Jie, uphill from the train station.

Places to Stay
Suífēnhé has many hotels offering cheap rooms of poor quality, which mostly cater to Russian tour groups. The first hotel you will come to, 200m directly uphill from the train station, is the **Zhuān Yòng Bīnguǎn** (☎ 392 0300). Slightly shabby singles with bath cost Y60, while much nicer doubles go for Y120.

If you continue up the hill, passing to left of the church, you'll find the 'official' foreign guesthouse, **Dōngxīng Dàjiǔdiàn** (☎ 392 5430). Dorm beds cost Y50 and doubles range from Y128 to Y300. The hotel is on the corner of Ying Xin Jie and Guang Hua Lu.

Even further up the hill, on the corner of Tong Tian Lu and Xin Hua Jie, is the **Hùidájiàrì Jiǔdiàn** (☎ 392 1630). Rooms here cost a little more, but are much nicer. Doubles range from Y200 to Y260 and suites begin at Y300.

Getting There & Away
The Hāěrbīn to Suífēnhé train leaves Hāěrbīn at 9.15 pm, passing through Mǔdānjiāng around 3.45 am and arriving in Suífēnhé at 7.25 am.

There is a morning departure from Suífēnhé to Hāěrbīn, arriving at Mǔdānjiāng at 1.28 pm, as well as a night train departing for Hāěrbīn at 8.20 pm, arriving at 7.07 am.

An international passenger train departs for Vladivostok at 9.30 am, Monday to Saturday and 10.30 am on Sunday. This train passes through Pogranichny (Grodekovo). Pogranichny is a small town that borders China near Suífēnhé, 210km from Vladivostok. Pogranichny is also connected by bus and taxi with Ussuriysk and Vladivostok.

WÚDÀLIÁN CHÍ 五大连池
Five Large Connected Lakes
Wúdàlián Chí is a nature reserve and health spot that has also been turned into a 'volcano museum'. Despite being voted one of the top 40 sights in China in 1992, Wúdàlián Chí is still primarily the province of geologists, volcanologists and the infirm, and sees few tourists apart from the tour groups arriving by the bus load in the summer.

This area, in the north of the province, has a long history of volcanic activity. The most recent eruptions occurred in 1719 and 1720, when lava from craters blocked the nearby Běi Hé and formed the series of barrier lakes. The malodorous mineral springs are the source of legendary cures and thus the main attraction for the hordes of chronically ill people who slurp the waters or slap mud onto themselves.

As for the volcanoes themselves, don't come expecting Krakatoa. Basically, the volcano museum has steam fumaroles, hot springs and a little geothermal activity here and there, but not much else. The museum is approximately 10km north of the traffic circle, where the bus will drop you. Motorised rickshaws will affix themselves to you and begin their bargaining at Y50 for a return trip. Entrance to the lakes and museum is Y35.

To liven up the scenery, there is a year-round ice lantern festival. The **ice sculptures** are in caves that have a steady temperature of -10°C (14°F), even during summer. Coloured lights in the sculptures create a psychedelic effect. The caves are approximately 8km east of the main traffic circle; entry is Y10. Taxis can be hired to do a 20km loop of the area, taking in both the lakes and caves. Bargaining begins at Y100.

A month long 'water drinking festival' is held at the start of May every year by the local Daur minority. Activities include music, dance and unbridled drinking of the local waters.

There are over 40 sanatoriums in town with beds ranging from Y30 to Y60. The most prominent is a giant, new yellow building on the north-east corner of the traffic circle. Many sanatoriums close during the low season (September to May), however, the *Lóngquán Bīnguǎn (Dragon Spring Hotel;* ☎ 722 2426) is open year-round. Rooms with private bath cost Y50 per person.

If you plan to stay in Bei'an, the *Tiānlóngdà Jiǔdiàn* (☎ 666 4818) has comfortable, clean and very reasonable doubles for Y84, or Y184 with private bath. The hotel is located directly across the street from the train station.

To reach Wǔdàlián Chí, take a six hour train ride northwards from Hāěrbīn to Bei'an. From Bei'an, there are four buses departing daily for Wǔdàlián Chí (5.50 and 10.30 am, 12.40 and 3.30 pm). The last bus returning to Bei'an departs from Wǔdàlián Chí at 3.30 pm (Y13). The journey takes you through scenic countryside and a number of villages. You can also reach Wǔdàlián Chí from Hēihé in the north or Qíqíhǎ'ěr in the south-west.

HĒILÓNGJIĀNG BIĀNJÌNG 黑龙江边境

Black Dragon River Borderlands

Much of the north-eastern border between China and Siberia follows the course of the Hēilóng Jiāng (Black Dragon River), also known to the Russians as the Amur River. Along the border it is possible to see Siberian forests and the dwindling settlements of northern tribes, such as the Daur, Ewenki, Hezhen and Oroqen. (See the boxed text 'The Oroqen'.)

Currently, most foreigners require permits to visit the area – international borders

and ethnic minority areas are sensitive places. Check the current situation with the PSB. CITS in Hāěrbīn are likely to encourage you to head off north regardless, claiming that a physical similarity to the Russians is permit enough. The PSB, however, do not agree and it is not advisable to follow the advise of CITS unless you are willing to undertake a very long journey at risk of being sent straight back.

Due to the problem with permits, boat tours along the Sōnghūa Hé have ceased. Nevertheless, as areas are continuously falling in and out of restrictions, check with CITS or the China Haerbin Overseas Tourist Corporation as to whether or not the tours have resumed.

Assuming that you have at least two weeks to spare, are flexible about transport and have your permits in order, an independent trip should be viable during the summer – take a small medical kit and insect repellent. Apart from the boat, Hēihé, Mòhé and Tóngjiāng can be reached by combinations of train and bus transport.

Mòhé 漠河

Natural wonders are the attraction in China's northernmost town, which is sometimes known as the Arctic of China. In mid-June, the sun is visible in the sky for as long as 22 hours. The aurora borealis (northern lights) are another colourful phenomenon at Mòhé. China's lowest absolute temperature of -52.3°C (-62°F) was recorded here in 1965, so not surprisingly on a normal winter day a temperature of -40°C is common.

During May 1987 the area was devastated by China's worst forest fire in living memory. The towns of Mòhé and Xilinji were completely gutted, more than 200 people died and over one million hectares of forest were destroyed.

Getting to Mòhé requires a train trip north from Jagdaqi to Gulian, followed by a 34km bus ride.

Hēihé 黑河

☎ 0456

Hēihé's claim to fame is that it borders Russia. Due to the recent thawing in relations

The Oroqen

The Oroqen minority, scattered over a vast area of north-western Hēilóngjiāng and Inner Mongolia, traditionally lived as nomadic forest hunters. Today it's hard to determine how much of Oroqen culture has remained intact. Official publications trumpet stories of a wondrous change from primitive nomadism to settled consumerism, complete with satellite TV.

Although the Oroqens' lifestyle may be rapidly changing, they continue to maintain their own language as well as much of their unique lifestyle and traditions. Largely self-sufficient people, they make their boots, clothes and sleeping bags from deerskins, and their baskets, eating utensils and canoes from birch bark. Their traditional tent, the *xianrenzhu*, is covered with birch bark in the summer and deerskin in the winter. The diet of the Oroqen consists mainly of wild plants, fish and meat that often preserved by drying and smoking. Raw deer liver, washed down with fermented mare's milk, is a particularly popular dish! Increasingly, the Oroqen are lumbermen and agriculturists while many continue to raise reindeer and hunt. A major source of income is deer hunting since a deer's embryo, antlers, penis and tail are highly prized in Chinese medicine.

Traditional Oroqen beliefs are based in shamanism. The Oroqen trace their roots back to a hunter and a sky-maiden who conceived a child by urinating on the same rock crevice. This crevice then sealed until the sky-maiden returned to blow spirit breath upon it. Out hatched the first Oroqen who followed a life of free-spirited hunting.

A belief in spirits also extends to the animal world. The bear, for example, holds great spiritual significance for the Oroqen. If a bear is killed, which would be most likely in self-defence, a complicated rite is performed to ask the bear's forgiveness and its bones are spread on a tall frame of willow branches. This 'wind burial' is also the traditional funeral for a human.

Recommended reading includes, *The Oroqens – China's Nomadic Hunters* by Qiu Pu. It's very informative, provided you skip the political salad dressing.

between the two countries, there is a steadily increasing amount of cross-border trade and even a fledgling tourist industry. Chinese tour groups are now able to cross the border to Blagoveshchensk, a large Russian port opposite Hēihé. Street stalls in Hēihé sell Russian army greatcoats, boots, helmets, binoculars and other military surplus.

There are problems for foreigners wishing to visit Blagoveshchensk. A Russian tourist visa is needed, and a re-entry visa for China is also necessary. All this must be arranged in Běijīng, not in Hēihé. In theory, one could cross the border at Blagoveshchensk and take a train to link up with the Trans-Siberian Railway at Belogorsk, 109km away, continue to Moscow and then on to Europe. This would require a Russian tourist visa.

Those without a Russian visa can console themselves with hour-long cruises of the Hēilóng Jiāng from Hēihé (Y10); binoculars can be rented on board.

The main hotel in Hēihé that accepts foreigners is the **Hēihé Guójì Fàndiàn** (*Hēihé International Hotel;* ☎ 227 013, *48 Wangsu Jie*); doubles are Y230.

Daily trains run to and from Hāěrbīn, but be aware that the train station is 5km from Hēihé and tickets for Hāěrbīn must be bought in the city centre, from the ticket office at the junction between Xinghua Jie and Guandu Lu. Buses also run to and from Hēihé from Hāěrbīn, Bei'an, Wǔdàlián Chí and Qíqíhā'ěr. During summer months, boats also connect Hēihé with Mòhé and Tóngjiāng.

Tóngjiāng 同江
☎ 0454

Tóngjiāng lies at the junction of the Sōnghuā and Hēilóng rivers. They swell to a combined width of 10km, but their respective colours, black for the Hēilóng and yellow for the Sōnghuā, don't mix until later.

The Hezhen minority, a mere 1300 people, lives almost entirely from fishing. A local delicacy is sliced, raw fish with a spicy vinegar sauce. Apart from carp and salmon, the real whopper here is the huso sturgeon (*huáng yú*), which can grow as long as 3m and weigh up to 500kg!

Trains reach nearby Fujin, from where buses connect with Tóngjiāng. It has boat connections with Hēihé and boat and bus connections with Jiāmùsī. At the time of writing, boat connections with Hāěrbīn were suspended until at least the summer of 2000.

QÍQÍHĀ'ĚR 齐齐哈尔
☎ 0452 • pop 5,510,000

Qíqíhā'ěr was established in 1684 and is one of the oldest settlements in the northeast. Its name is taken from the Daur word for 'borderland'. As the gateway to Zhālóng Zìrán Bǎohùqū (Zhalong Nature Reserve), a bird-watching area 35km south-east, Qíqíhā'ěr acts as a springboard rather than as a tourist destination in itself. The town is industrialised, with a population of more than one million, and produces locomotives, mining equipment, steel, machine tools and motor vehicles. There's not much to see here – a **zoo**, the riverside and the **ice-carving festival** from January to March.

Highest and lowest temperatures over the year achieve a nice symmetry with 39°C (102.2F) in July and -39°C (-38.2°F) in January.

Information
Money The Bank of China is on the corner of Bukui Dajie and Longhua Lu; head straight out of the train station to the T-intersection in the road; the bank will be on your left.

Post & Communications As you exit the train station you'll see the post office to the right. China Telecom is also in this office and offers public Internet access.

Travel Agencies CITS (☎ 271 5836) is in the Húbīn Fàndiàn. It also has offices (☎ 272 2584) around the back of the hotel where friendly staff can provide you with advice about the best times and places for bird-watching. CITS runs tours to the bird reserve (see the Zhālóng Zìrán Bǎohùqū section).

PSB The PSB is on Bukui Dajie, just north of Longhua Lu.

Places to Stay
Húbīn Fàndiàn (☎ 271 3121, 4 Wenhua Dajie) is one of the cheapest places that accepts foreigners; doubles are Y180. An alternative is the *Hèchéng Bīnguǎn (Crane City Hotel;* ☎ 272 2541, fax 271 3367), which has doubles from Y230 to Y280. The hotel is located behind Húbīn Fàndiàn; follow the path around the right side of Húbīn Fàndiàn. You can reach both hotels on tram No 15 from the train station.

Getting There & Away
There are flights between Qíqíhā'ěr and Běijīng, Dàlián, Guǎngzhōu, Shànghǎi and Shěnyáng. Qíqíhā'ěr is linked directly by rail to Běijīng (about 22 hours) via Hāěrbīn (about four hours).

Qíqíhā'ěr is also connected by rail to the northern towns of Bei'an and Hēihé. Trains to Bei'an depart at 6 am and 8.30 am. There is a night train to Hēihé, passing through Bei'an at 2.40 am. Look after your valuables when travelling this route, as it is notorious for theft.

While it's easier to purchase train tickets, there are also buses to Hāěrbīn. If you miss the morning trains to Bei'an, a bus departs from the eastern bus station (nearest the train station) at noon (Y32). The road is in poor condition and the bumpy journey takes eight hours.

ZHĀLÓNG ZÌRÁN BĂOHÙQŪ 扎龙自然保护区
Zhalong Nature Reserve
This nature reserve is at the north-west tip of a giant marsh, and is made up of about 210,000 hectares of wetlands. It lies strategically on a bird-migration path that extends from the Russian Arctic, around the Gobi Desert and down into South-East Asia. Some 236 different species of bird are found in the reserve, including storks,

Rare Cranes Find Sanctuary

The Zhālóng Zìrán Bǎohùqū, one of China's first nature reserves, was set up in 1979. In 1981 the Chinese Ministry of Forestry invited Dr George Archibald (director of the International Crane Foundation – ICF) and Wolf Brehm (director of Vogelpark Walsrode, Germany) to help set up a crane centre at Zhālóng.

Of the 15 species of cranes in the world, eight are found in China and six are found at Zhālóng. Four of the species that migrate here are on the endangered list: the red-crowned crane, the white-naped crane, the Siberian crane and the hooded crane. Both the red-crowned and white-naped cranes breed at Zhālóng (as do the common and demoiselle cranes), while hooded and Siberian cranes use Zhālóng as a stopover.

The centre of attention is the red-crowned crane, a fragile creature whose numbers at Zhālóng (estimated to be only 100 in 1979) were threatened by drainage of the wetlands for farming. The near-extinct bird is, ironically, the ancient symbol of immortality and has long been a symbol of longevity and good luck in the Chinese, Korean and Japanese cultures. With some help from overseas experts, the ecosystem at Zhālóng has been studied and improved, and the number of these rare birds has risen.

Several hand-reared (domesticated) red-crowned and white-naped cranes are kept in a pen at the sanctuary for viewing and study.

On the eve of their 'long march' southwards in October, large numbers of cranes can be seen wheeling around, as if in farewell. The birds have been banded to unlock the mystery of their winter migration grounds (in either Korea or southern China).

Since the establishment of the ICF, George Archibald and Ron Sauey have managed to create a 'crane bank' in Wisconsin, USA, stocking 14 of the 15 known species. They've even convinced the North Koreans to set up bird reserves in the mine-studded demilitarised zone between North and South Korea, and the travel baggage of these two countries includes suitcases full of Siberian crane-eggs picked up in Moscow (on one trip a chick hatched en route was nicknamed 'Aeroflot'). Last on the egg list for the ICF is the black-necked crane, whose home is in remote Tibet and for whom captive breeding may be the final hope.

swans, geese, ducks, herons, harriers, grebes and egrets. The tens of thousands of winged migrants arrive from April to May, rear their young from June to August and depart from September to October.

Birds will be birds – they value their privacy. While some of the red-crowned cranes are more than 1.5m tall, the reed cover is taller. The best time to visit is in spring, before the reeds have a chance to grow, however, as this is low tourist season, it's more difficult (and expensive) to arrange tours.

For the patient binoculared and rubber-booted ornithologist, day tours are offered by CITS in Qíqíhā'ěr (approximately Y100 per person plus Y160 for a return bus). The Zhālóng Bīnguǎn also offers tours through the freshwater marshes in flat-bottom boats during the summer months.

Even if you're not a bird fan, a trip into this very peaceful countryside will be bliss to those who have been traipsing around China's cities. Without doing a tour, you can wander the marshes and nearby villages. Be warned: the mosquitoes are almost as big as and definitely more plentiful than the birds – take repellent!

Entry into the reserve is Y10 for locals; expect a 100% increase for foreigners. If you are entering by public bus, get off at the toll booth and buy your own ticket rather than leaving the task to the driver, who is likely to add on an additional commission.

Places to Stay

The somewhat run-down *Zhālóng Bīnguǎn* has rooms with negotiable prices. Doubles begin at around Y100 to Y120 during the

HĒILÓNGJIĀNG 黑龙江

low season and rise during the summer months (June to September). Arriving in low season, you might find that you're the only guest – the silence is bliss!

As an alternative, you can stay on the bus and head into town, where locals will sometimes offer beds for Y10 or Y20.

Getting There & Away

Zhālóng is linked to Qíqíhā'ěr by a fairly good road, but there's not much traffic along it. Buses travel to Zhālóng (Y5; 1½ hours) from the bus station at the western end of Longhua Lu in Qíqíhā'ěr. The departures are at around 6 am and 1.30 and 4.30 pm.

Buses tend to leave Qíqíhā'ěr late and Zhālóng early; the schedule is very approximate so show up early if you don't want to miss your bus.

There are also infrequent minibuses that cover this route (Y3).

Shānxī 山西

Shānxī was one of the earliest centres of Chinese civilisation and formed the state of Qin. After Qin Shihuang unified the Chinese states in 221 BC, the northern part of Shānxī became the key defensive bulwark between the Chinese and the nomadic tribes to the north.

Despite the Great Wall, the nomadic tribes still managed to break through and used Shānxī as a base for their conquest of the Middle Kingdom.

When the Tang dynasty fell in the 9th century, the political centre of China moved away from the north-west. Shānxī went into a rapid economic decline, although its importance in the northern defence network remained paramount.

It was not until the intrusion of foreign powers into China that industrialisation truly got under way. When the Japanese invaded China in the 1930s they carried out development of industry and coal mining around the capital of Tàiyuán. True to form, Shānxī was a bastion of resistance to this invasion from the north, this time through the communist guerrillas who operated in the mountainous regions.

After 1949, the communist government began to exploit Shānxī's mineral and ore deposits, and developed Dàtóng and Tàiyuán as major industrial centres. China's biggest coal mines can be found near these cities, and the province accounts for a third of China's known iron and coal deposits.

Shānxī means West of the Mountains, the mountains being the Taihang Range, which forms the province's eastern border. To the west it is bordered by the Huáng Hé (Yellow River). The province's population of about 31 million people is surprisingly small by Chinese standards, unless you consider the fact that almost 70% of the province is mountainous.

Along with its mineral deposits, Shānxī is rich in history. This is especially true of the northern half, which is a virtual gold mine of temples, monasteries and cave-temples – a

Highlights

Capital: Tàiyuán
Population: 31.1 million
Area: 156,000 sq km

- The Buddhist caves of Yúngāng Shíkū, a stunning array of China's oldest sculptures
- The 1400-year-old monastery Xuánkōng Sì, an architectural feat 75km south-east of Dàtóng
- Táihuái, a peaceful monastic village in the picturesque Wǔtái Shān mountain range

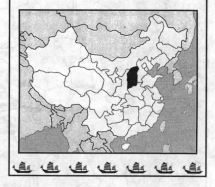

reminder that this was once the political and cultural centre of China. Among these, the main attraction for travellers are the Buddhist caves of Yúngāng Shíkū at Dàtóng and the Buddhist mountain of Wǔtái Shān.

TÀIYUÁN 太原
☎ 0351 • pop 2,932,800

Tàiyuán, provincial capital and industrial sprawl often shrouded in fog, has a few attractions, but little to make it worth a special trip. It is, however, more cosmopolitan than its northern neighbour, Dàtóng.

The first settlements on the site of modern-day Tàiyuán date back 2500 years. By

SHĀNXĪ 山西

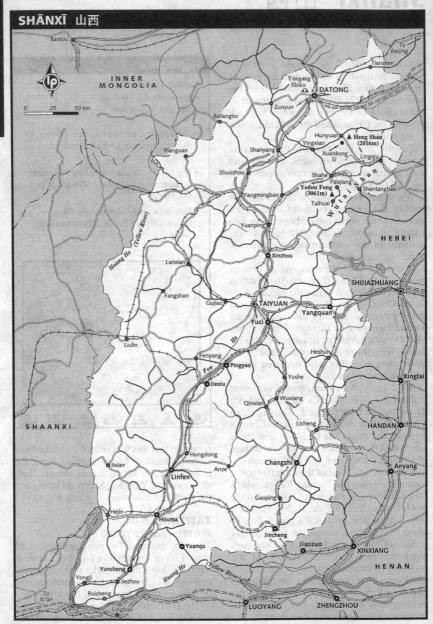

SHĀNXĪ 山西

the 13th century it had developed into what Marco Polo referred to as 'a prosperous city, a great centre of trade and industry'. But it was also the site of constant armed conflict, sitting squarely on the path by which successive northern invaders entered China. There were once 27 temples here dedicated to the god of war.

Today, the city looks much like its modern counterparts Zhèngzhōu and Luòyáng, with wide, tree-lined avenues and large residential blocks. The main street Yingze Dajie, easily mistaken for a runway, runs west from the train station. Hotels and banks line the street, with clothing shops and restaurants crowded around the side streets. There is a lively night market on Liuxiang Nanlu, selling lots of clothing, shoes, music and bric-a-brac.

Information

China International Travel Service (Zhōng-guó Guójì Lǔxíngshè; CITS; ☎ 407 4209) is at 282 Yingze Dajie, next door to the Bank of China.

The Public Security Bureau (Gōngānjú; PSB) has a foreign affairs office at 9 Hou-jia Lane, near Wǔyī Guǎngchǎng (May 1st Square).

The most convenient Bank of China is just west of the train station on Yingze Dajie, next door to the Huáyùan Bīnguǎn. The main branch is also on Yingze Dajie, west of Jiefang Lu. Both can change money, including travellers cheques.

The post and telephone office is diagonally opposite the train station. The post office is open from 8 am until 8 pm daily and the telecom office operates 24 hours a day. The main telecom office is at the western end of Yingze Dajie. An Internet cafe (wǎngbā) wasn't up and running when we visited, but should be by the time you read this. Ask at the telephone office for details.

Chóngshàn Sì 崇善寺
Chongshan Temple
This Buddhist monastery was built towards the end of the 14th century on the site of a monastery that is said to date back to the 6th or 7th century. The main hall contains three impressive statues; the central figure is

Guanyin, the goddess of mercy with 1000 hands and eyes.

Beautifully illustrated book covers show scenes from the life of Buddha. Also on display are some Buddhist scriptures of the Song, Yuan, Ming and Qing dynasties. The monastery is on a side street running east off Wuyi Lu. Opening hours are 8 am to 5 pm daily and entry costs Y4.

Shuāngtǎ Sì
Twin Pagoda Temple
This temple has two Ming dynasty pagodas, each a 13-storey octagonal structure almost 55m high. It is possible to climb one of the pagodas, but it is only recommended for those who enjoy dark, slippery spiral stairs. The pagodas are built entirely of bricks carved with brackets and cornices to imitate ancient Chinese wooden pagodas.

The best way to get there is by bike. Ride along Chaoyang Jie for about 750m, turn right and then continue south for 1.5km. Otherwise, catch a taxi (Y6). It's open daily from 8 am to 5 pm and entry costs Y6.

Shānxī Shěng Bówùguǎn
省博物馆
Shanxi Provincial Museum
The museum is located in two separate sections. The main museum is on Qifeng Jie, north-west of Wǔyī Guǎngchǎng. It's housed in the Chúnyáng Gōng (Chunyang Palace), which used to be a temple for offering sacrifices to the Taoist priest Lu Dongbin, who lived during the Tang dynasty. The second section is on Wenmiao Xiang, south of Chóngshàn Sì. The museum is housed in attractive Ming period buildings and was once a Confucan temple (wén-miào). Both museums should be open by the time you read this after recent restoration works. They are open daily from 9 am to 6 pm and entry to each museum costs Y3.

Places to Stay
Tàiyuán has an abundance of accommodation, mostly congregated around the train and bus stations. Officially, many budget hostels cannot accept foreigners, but seem willing to take the occasional backpacker.

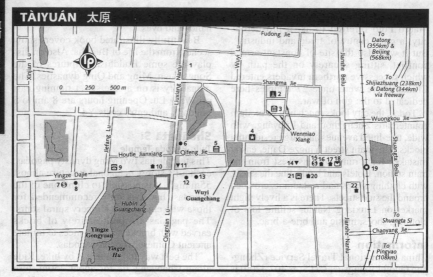

TÀIYUÁN 太原

You might try *Tiánhé Dàshà* (☎ 407 5054, 11 Gongyu Lane) on a small street leading south from the train station. It has dorm beds in quads/triples for Y15/22 and twins with attached bath for Y120. There are a few similar places around the train station where you may be able to talk your way into a cheap dorm bed.

The cheapest official option is the *Chángtài Fàndiàn* (☎ 403 4960, fax 403 4931), about 400m west of the train station on Yingze Dajie. It has dorm beds in triples for Y33 and twins with common bathroom from Y78 to Y88. The hotel is reasonably clean and certainly fresher than the Tiánhé. There are cheaper dorms in the building behind, but it may not be willing to take foreigners.

There are plenty of middle to top-end hotels in Tàiyuán offering similar services for the same price. One of the better value places is the *Diànlì Dàshà (Electric Power Hotel;* ☎ 404 1784, fax 404 0777), about 300m west of the train station on Yingze Dajie. Singles/twins are Y150/160, which is a pretty good price for Tàiyuán.

Failing that, the next best option is the *Huáyuàn Bīnguǎn* (☎ 404 6201), which is also on the north side of Yingze Dajie, but

closer to the train station. Clean and comfortable twins with private bath are Y188.

Further west along Yingze Dajie is the *Yíngzé Bīnguǎn* (☎ 404 3211, fax 404 3784), which incorporates two massive buildings. The east block has cheaper rooms, but only for Chinese guests. The west block is a glittering four-star hotel, complete with sauna, gym, medical clinic and swimming pool. Twins cost Y530, plus 10% service charge, and come equipped with refrigerators and English-language satellite TV.

Places to Eat

On the Tàiyuán street-food menu are local favourites like *zhūjiǎo* (pigs' trotters) stewed in cauldrons, and a savoury pancake called *làobǐng*. The local variant of Chinese noodles, called *liángpí*, is often served in steaming bowls of spicy soup.

Directly opposite the bus station on Yingze Dajie, between a massage parlour and a sex shop, is a *jiǎozi diàu (dumpling shop)* where a plate of dumplings (Y6) will warm your belly before or after a long bus trip. Good cheap noodles (Y3) can be found at *Liúnánmiàn Shíguǎn*, on Liuxiang

TÀIYUÁN

PLACES TO STAY
10 Yíngzé Bīnguǎn
    迎泽宾馆
16 Huáyùan Bīnguǎn
    华苑宾馆
17 Diànlì Dàshà
    电力大厦
20 Chángtài Fàndiàn
    长泰饭店
22 Tiánhé Dàshà
    天和大厦

PLACES TO EAT
11 Liǔnánmiàn Shíguǎn
    柳南面食馆
14 Jiǎozi Diàu
    饺子店

OTHER
1   Night Market
    夜市场
2   Chóngshàn Sì
    崇善寺
3   Shānxī (Section 2)
    Shěng Bówùguǎn
    省博物馆
4   PSB
    公安局
5   Shānxī (Section 1)
    Shěng Bówùguǎn
    省博物馆
6   Huayu
    Supermarket
7   Bank of China
    中国银行

8   CITS
    中国国际旅行社
9   Telecom Office
    电信局
12 Airline Booking Office
    通航售票处
13 Train Booking Office
    火车售票处
15 Bank of China
    中国银行
18 Post & Telephone Office
    邮电大楼
19 Train Station
    火车站
21 Long-Distance Bus Station
    长途汽车站

Nanlu (next to the children's clothing shop), about 100m north of Yingze Dajie.

Most of Tàiyuán's hotels also have tasty and reasonably priced restaurants. Those craving western food could try the buffet at the Yíngzé Bīnguǎn.

Getting There & Away

Air The airline booking office (☎ 404 2903) is at 158 Yingze Dajie and is open daily from 8 am to 8 pm. Useful flights include Běijīng (Y470; daily), Chéngdū (Y910; thrice weekly), Guǎngzhōu (Y1140; daily), Shànghǎi (Y960; daily) and Xī'ān (Y450; four times weekly). There are also flights to most other major domestic destinations.

Bus Iveco buses to Dàtóng (Y50; five hours) leave hourly from the long-distance bus station and from outside the southern end of the train station. There are three buses to Wǔtái Shān (Y43; four hours) from the bus station leaving at 9.15, 11.15 am and 1.30 pm. Private Iveco buses (Y43) and minibuses (Y22) leave from the northern end of the train station when full.

From in front of the west side of the long-distance bus station there are express buses travelling to Běijīng (Y120; six hours) every half hour from 7 am to 11.20 pm. There are also departures every day to

Zhèngzhōu from the bus station and the southern end of the train station.

Train It's fairly easy getting sleeper tickets for trains originating from Tàiyuán, but difficult for those that don't. There is a special foreigners' ticket window (No ·14) at the train station where you can buy same-day tickets; it's open daily from 8.30 to 11.30 am and 2.30 to 6.30 pm.

For advance purchases go to the train booking office at 138 Yingze Dajie, which is open daily from 8 am to 7 pm. Services starting off from Tàiyuán include express trains to Běijīng (eight hours), Chéngdū (30 hours), Dàtóng (seven hours), Luòyáng (12 hours), Zhèngzhōu (10 hours) and Shànghǎi (22 hours).

If you're headed to Xī'ān, your best bets are train Nos 535 and 485 as both trains start from Tàiyuán.

AROUND TÀIYUÁN
Jìncí Sì 晋祠寺

This ancient Buddhist temple is at the source of the Jìn Hé, by Xuánwàng Hill, 25km south-west of Tàiyuán. It's thought that the original buildings were constructed between AD 1023 and 1032, but there have been numerous additions and restorations over the centuries, right up to Qing times.

As you enter the temple compound the first major structure is the Mirror Terrace, a Ming building used as an open-air theatre. The name is used in the figurative sense to denote the reflection of life in drama.

Zhibo's Canal cuts through the temple complex and lies west of the Mirror Terrace. Spanning this canal is the Huixian (Meet the Immortals) Bridge, which provides access to the Terrace for Iron Statues, which displays figures cast in AD 1097.

Further back is the Goddess Mother Hall, the oldest wooden building in the city and one of the most interesting in the temple complex. Inside are 42 Song dynasty clay figures of maidservants standing around a large seated statue of the sacred lady, said to be the mother of Prince Shuyu of the ancient Zhou dynasty.

Next to the Goddess Mother Hall is the Zhou Cypress, an unusual tree which has supposedly been growing at an angle of about 30° for the last 900 years.

In the north of the temple grounds is the Zhenguan Baohan Pavilion, which houses four stone steles inscribed with the handwriting of the Tang emperor Tai Zong. In the south of the temple grounds is the Sacred Relics Pagoda, a seven-storey octagonal building constructed at the end of the 7th century.

The temple is open daily from 8 am to 6 pm and entry costs Y15. To get to Jìncí Sì catch a No 8 minibus from in front of Tàiyuán's train station. The ride takes one hour and costs Y2.

Qiáo Jiā Dàyuàn　乔家大院
Qiao Family Courtyard House

This is the sight where Zhang Yimou's film *Raise the Red Lantern*, starring Gong Li, was filmed. This extensive Qing dynasty courtyard house complex was built by Qiao Guifa, a small-time tea and beancurd merchant who rose to riches. The ornate complex consists of six courtyards, containing over 300 rooms and on display are Qing dynasty curios and furniture.

To get here take any Píngyáo-bound minibus. On the right-hand side of the highway you'll see red lanterns and a large gate

marking the complex. It's 40km west of Tàiyuán. Admission is Y28.

Shuānglín Sì　双林寺

This monastery, 110km south-west of Tàiyuán, is well worth the effort. It contains exquisite painted clay figurines and statues dating from the Song, Yuan, Ming and Qing dynasties. Most of the present buildings date from the Ming and Qing dynasties, while most of the sculptures are from the Song and Yuan dynasties. There are around 2000 figurines in total. The monastery is open daily and entry costs Y12.

PÍNGYÁO　平遥
☎ 0354 • pop 40,000

Surrounded by a completely intact 6km Ming dynasty city wall (claimed to be the last remaining one in China), Píngyáo is an exceptionally well-preserved traditional Han Chinese city. Its ancient narrow, small temples and courtyard houses offer a rare glimpse into the architectural styles and town planning of imperial China.

Located on the old route between Běijīng and Xī'ān, Píngyáo was a thriving merchant town during the Ming and Qing dynasties. It was here that China's earliest *tongs* (banks) were set up and Píngyáo rose to be the financial headquarters of all of China during the Qing dynasty. After its heyday the city fell into poverty, and without the cash to modernise, Píngyáo's streets remained unchanged.

Tourism is changing this small town fast. Until a couple of years ago, Píngyáo saw few visitors. Now visitors are arriving in ever increasing numbers, especially domestic tourists. Although there are complaints of conservation workers slapping on coats of paint instead of employing proper techniques, so far general over-restoration ha not taken place and several hundred homes have been deemed cultural relics thus protected from being demolished or radically altered. In 1997 Píngyáo was inscribed as a UNESCO World Heritage Site.

A good, although crowded, time to visit Píngyáo is during the Lantern Festival (15 days after Chinese New Year, during the full moon). Red lanterns are hung outside the doors of residences, and every year a small, country-style parade takes place. Locals munching on sugar cane and candied fruit flood the streets and vendors sell *yuàn xiāo*, a traditional round white snack (which symbolises the moon) made of glutinous rice flour filled with a sweet sesame and walnut paste and served in soup.

Things to See & Do

The city's main drag is Nan Dajie. Several 'antique' shops line the street; most sell common pottery and bronzeware that is found at 'antique' markets around China. In the middle of the street (and marking the centre of town) is the Town Building. At a whopping 18.5m, it's the tallest building in the city. You can see over the tiled roofs of the entire city from the top (admission Y5). At 109 Ming Qing Jie is the **Furniture Museum**. This Qing-style courtyard house, with its elaborately carved wooden window frames, is a typical example of a home of a wealthy financier of the time. Admission is Y13 (an additional Y20 for a guided tour).

Not to be missed is the **Rishengchang Financial House Museum** on Xi Dajie (admission Y10). In the late 18th century a man named Li Daquan opened a small dye shop here. His business prospered and he opened branches as far away as Sìchuān. As sales grew, it became increasingly difficult for Li to collect profits from all the branches. His solution was to introduce a system of checks and deposits, and the home office in Píngyáo essentially became a financial agent for the company, and eventually, for other businesses, individuals and the Qing government.

The bank prospered for over 100 years, and at its height had 57 branches around China. The Japanese invasion and civil strife in the 1930s, along with increased competition from foreign banks, forced its decline and eventual closure. The museum has over 100 rooms, including offices, living quarters and a kitchen, as well as several old cheques.

The ancient city wall, originally erected in the Zhou dynasty (827–728 BC), com-pletely surrounds the city. Most of what you'll see now was actually built during the Ming dynasty; notice the stamped bricks below your feet. The outer portion of the wall has a few shell marks, remnants of the Japanese invasion in the 1930s. If you ascend the wall at the north gate, you can hire a pedicab to pedal you around the wall. Admission is Y15.

Exploring Píngyáo streets, you'll come across several other small museums housed in traditional courtyard houses, temples and even a Catholic church. Museums aside, wandering the streets and back alleyways is the real reason to come here. The main commercial streets are filled with locals selling traditional Chinese snacks – candied or dried fruit, all manner of nuts and seeds, fruit and sugarcane. Wandering the small, dirt back streets, reveals the courtyard houses of some of today's residents, with fading ornately carved wooden entrances and window frames.

Places to Stay & Eat

There are a few traditional courtyard-style hotels within the city walls, and a few modern hotels outside the wall (which lack atmosphere). A popular hotel is the *Jin Cheng Hotel* (☎ 568 0944, 62 Ming Qing Jie), located in a nicely restored courtyard house. Slightly musty doubles with bath and 24-hour hot water are Y100. It also has singles with shared bath for Y60. In the front of the hotel is a popular *restaurant*, where you can eat local fare such as *shuǐ jianbāo* (fried pork-filled bread) and *dòu miàn jiān bǐng* (fried pancake with string beans).

Getting Around

Píngyáo can be easily navigated on foot, or you can rent a bike for the day at one of the shops on Xi Dajie.

Getting There & Away

Train Most visitors arrive on a day trip from Tàiyuán, or overnight from Běijīng. Train No 605 leaves Běijīng West train station daily at 7.31 pm and arrives in Píngyáo at 6.39 am. Hardsleeper is Y93. Although several trains depart Píngyáo for Běijīng, tickets are extremely limited, so returning to Běijīng your best bet is to take a minibus to Tàiyuán. Train No Y220 departs Tàiyuán for Běijīng at 9 pm and arrives at Běijīng train station at 7 am. Hardsleeper is Y145.

From Tàiyuán, train No 675 departs at 11.41 am and arrives in Píngyáo at 1.28 pm. The No 676 heads back from Píngyáo to Tàiyuán at 6.42 pm.

Bus Minibuses wait outside the Tàiyuán train station and leave for Píngyáo (and vice versa) as they fill up (Y11; 1½ hours). You can also take a bus to Běijīng from across the street from the train station in Tàiyuán. The overnight bus departs at 10.30 pm and arrives in Běijīng at 5 am (Y120).

RUÌCHÉNG 芮城
☎ 0359
At Ruìchéng, 93km south of Yùnchéng, is **Yǒnglè Taoist Temple**, which has valuable frescoes dating from the Tang and Song dynasties. In the 1960s the temple was moved to Ruìchéng from its original site beside the Huáng Hé (Yellow River), when the Sānménxià Dam was built. The temple is 3km directly south from the main intersection.

The surrounding area is quite charming, with many people continuing to live in simple cave dwellings.

Places to Stay
Shíliáng Zhāodàisuǒ (Grain Hostel) is opposite the bus station and has clean dorms from Y6. The rooms with attached bathrooms are not worth Y30, as there is hardly ever any water. If this place doesn't suffice, then head back into town to the more upmarket *Ruìchéng Bīnguǎn*.

Getting There & Away
From Yùnchéng's long-distance bus station there are half-hourly departures to Ruìchéng (Y8; 2½ hours). On the way, the bus passes Jièzhōu before climbing the cool subalpine slopes of Zhōngtiao Shān. It is also possible to hop on this bus in Jièzhōu, but you will need to catch a motor tricycle back to the main road from Guāndì Miào from where you can just wave the bus down.

From Ruìchéng there are early-morning buses to both Luòyáng and Xī'ān via Huá Shān, starting at 6.30 am.

YÙNCHÉNG 运城
☎ 0359
Yùnchéng is in the south-western corner of Shānxī, near where the Huáng Hé (Yellow River) completes its great sweep through far northern China and begins to flow eastwards. The small city is famed for the gutsy little orange tractors that are assembled here and often seen chugging along country roads.

At Jièzhōu, 18km south of Yùnchéng, is the large **Guāndì Miào**. This temple was originally constructed during the Sui dynasty, but was destroyed by fire in AD 1702 and subsequently rebuilt. Bus No 11 from Yùnchéng train station terminates at the Guāndì Miào. The trip takes 40 minutes and costs Y2. The temple is open daily and entry costs Y20.

Places to Stay
Tiědào Dàshà (☎ 206 8899) has new and clean rooms with friendly staff. Comfortable singles with common shower or a bed in a triple with attached bath are both Y50. The hotel is to the right as you exit the train station.

Huáxià Dàjiǔdiàn (☎ 208 0239), directly opposite the train station, has reasonable dorms starting from Y15 and beds in a twin/triple with attached bath for Y50/40.

Getting There & Away
Yùnchéng is on the Tàiyuán-Xī'ān train lines; all trains, including daily express trains, stop here.

There are direct bus connections from Yùnchéng to Luòyáng (Y20; six hours), leaving every half hour between 7 am and 4.30 pm from the bus station. If you're lucky you will get an Iveco, which completes the trip in 3½ hours. There are also Iveco buses to Xī'ān (Y35) departing halfhourly. Both the buses and trains to Xī'ān pass by Huá Shān.

The bus station is a five-minute walk south from the train station on the right.

WǓTÁI SHĀN 五台山 & TÁIHUÁI

Wǔtái Shān (Five-terrace Mountain), centred on the beautiful monastic village of Táihuái, is one of China's sacred Buddhist mountain areas. Táihuái lies deep in an alpine valley enclosed by the five peaks of Wǔtái Shān, the highest of which is the 3058m northern peak, Yèdǒu Fēng, known as the roof of northern China. Táihuái itself has 15 or so old temples and monasteries, and some 20 others dot the surrounding mountainsides.

The relative inaccessibility of Wǔtái Shān spared it the worst of the Cultural Revolution. Improved roads have now made it possible to reach Táihuái in at least five hours from either Dàtóng or Tàiyuán, and the area sees a steady flow of tourists, which rises to a flood in July and August. But at other times of the year it's a charming, relaxing spot. Between October and March, it is often below freezing, and even in summer the temperature drops rapidly at night, so make sure you take appropriate clothing.

In addition to the temples, the surrounding scenery is great, and there are quite a few mountain trails leading out from near Táihuái.

Information

CITS (☎ 654 2142) is at 18 Mingqing Jie, a small road on the western side of the river Qīngshuǐ Hé, south of Táihuái village. There is a smaller, more convenient branch on the southern side of the lane that is opposite the Tàiyuán bus stop. The staff arrange tours of the outlying temples, but unless you want an English-speaking guide, you can take one of the Chinese tours from Táihuái for far less money (see Organised Tours later in this section).

If you need to reach the PSB for any reason, talk to the owner of the hotel you're staying at.

The Bank of China can only change major currencies. Some of the expensive tourist hotels south of town have money-changing facilities, but you may have to be a guest to use them, especially if you are wanting to change travellers cheques.

Temples

You'd have to either be a sincerely devout Buddhist or utterly temple-crazed to take in

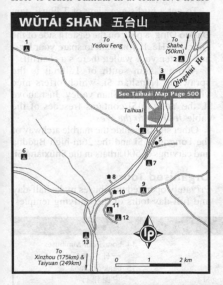

WǓTÁI SHĀN 五台山

To Yedou Feng
To Shahe (50km)
Qingshui Hé
See Taihuái Map Page 500
Taihuái
To Xinzhou (175km) & Taiyuan (249km)
0   1   2 km

WǓTÁI SHĀN

1 Fēnglín Sì 风林寺	6 Lóngquán Sì 龙泉寺	10 Qīxiánggé Bīnguǎn 栖贤阁宾馆
2 Bìshān Sì 碧山寺	7 Pǔhuà Sì 普化寺	11 Nánshān Sì 南山寺
3 Qīfó Sì 七佛寺	8 Yǒuyì Bīnguǎn 友谊宾馆	12 Yòuguó Sì 佑国寺
4 Shūxiàng Sì 殊像寺	9 Guānyīn Dòng (Temple) 观音洞	13 Zhènhǎi Sì 镇海寺
5 CITS 中国国际旅行社		

every temple and monastery in the Wǔtái Shān area. Most people will probably just stroll around Táihuái, although there are some outside town that are worth visiting.

Tǎyuàn Sì with its large, white, bottle-shaped pagoda built during the Ming dynasty is the most prominent temple in Táihuái. The **Xiǎntōng Sì** has seven rows of halls, totalling over 400 rooms. The **Luóhòu**

Sì contains a large wooden lotus flower with eight petals, on each of which sits a carved Buddhist figure; the big flower is attached to a rotating disk so that when it turns, the petals open up and the figures appear.

Just next door, the small **Guǎngrén Sì**, run by Tibetan and Mongolian monks, contains some fine examples of early Qing woodcarvings.

For a more secluded, spiritual visit, try the **Cífú Sì**, several hundred metres beyond the Pǔsàdǐng Sì on the ridge overlooking the town. Here there are no hawkers, just a few pleasant monks, one or two of whom speak English.

To get a bird's-eye view of Táihuái, you can make the somewhat strenuous trek up to **Dàiluó Dǐng**, a peak on the eastern side of the Qīngshuǐ Hé. If you want to spare your legs, and lighten your wallet, there's a chairlift.

About 2.5km south of Táihuái is the sprawling **Nánshān Sì**, which offers nice views of the Wǔtái Shān valley. Just above it, the **Yòuguó Sì** contains frescoes of the fable *Journey to the West*.

Other sights include the marble archway of the **Lóngquán Sì** and the 26m-high Buddha and carvings of 500 arhats in the **Shūxiàng Sì**.

Organised Tours

Privately operated minibuses make half-day and full-day tours of the outlying temples.

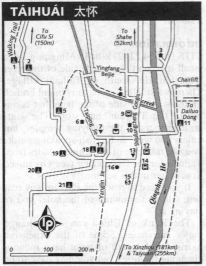

TÁIHUÁI 太怀

To Cifu Si (150m)
Walking Trail
To Shahe (52km)
Yingfang Beijie
Chairlift
creek
Tafping Jie
To Dailuo Dong
Shijiangzheng Gonglu
Jie
Yanglin Jie
Qingshui He
To Xinzhou (181km) & Taiyuan (255km)
0 100 200 m

TÁIHUÁI

PLACES TO STAY
3 Jīnfēng Fàndiàn
金峰饭店
4 Dōngfēng Bīnguǎn
东风宾馆
6 Gōngyì Měishù Zhāodàisuǒ
工艺美术招待所
10 Wǔtáishān Bīnguǎn
五台山宾馆

PLACES TO EAT
7 Railway Restaurant
13 Noodle Stands
路边面摊

OTHER
1 Pǔsàdǐng Sì
菩萨顶寺
2 Guǎngzōng Sì
广宗寺
5 Yuánzhào Sì
园照寺
8 Post Office
邮政局
9 Public Buses to Dàtóng
大同国营汽车站
11 Shàncái Dòng (Temple)
善财洞
12 Public Buses to Tàiyuán
太原国营汽车站

14 Local Tour Minibuses
一日游中巴站
15 Bank of China
中国银行
16 CITS
中国国际旅行社
17 Guǎngrén Sì
广仁寺
18 Luóhòu Sì
罗侯寺
19 Xiǎntōng Sì
显通寺
20 Tǎyuàn Sì
塔院寺
21 Wànfó Sì
万佛寺

A sample route might include Qīfó, Guānyīn Dòng, Shūxiàng, Lóngquán and Yòuguó temples and Nánshān Sì, among others. For a group of four to six people, this kind of tour costs Y50 per person, but if there is a larger number of tourists taking the same bus you may only have to pay Y40.

Show up at the local tour minibus stop between 7 and 7.30 am: after that most of the tourists will be gone, making it hard to join a tour.

Places to Stay

Táihuái is teeming with hostels and hotels that cater mainly to local tourists, although many seem willing to take the occasional foreigner. In any case, there are a few that are actually allowed to have foreign guests, which at least means you don't have to worry about being kicked out in the middle of the night by the PSB. Rates for all hotels generally go up around 40% during the high season (July to August).

The cheapest official option is the **Dōngfēng Bīnguǎn** (☎ 654 2524), a blue-tiled building on a small lane north of the creek. It has drab dorms with beds for Y20 to Y40, and twins with a bath for Y80. In winter, dorm beds go for Y10 and twins for Y40 with attached bathroom. The catch: the hotel doesn't have any water until late April.

The **Gōngyì Měishù Zhāodàisuǒ** (Wǔtái Shān Arts and Crafts Hotel; ☎ 654 2531, 25 Taiping Jie), has clean twins with private bath for Y100.

The large **Wǔtáishān Bīnguǎn** (No 2 Reception Centre; ☎ 654 2342) on Shijuliangcheng Gonglu, has cosy twins for Y100 in the middle building. There are also twins/triples with bathroom for Y140/150 and more comfortable twins and triples in the new building for Y240.

Just across the bridge to the north of the Dàiluó Dǐng chairlift is the **Jīnfēng Fàndiàn**, which has twins and triples with bathroom for Y120. There are dorm beds (Y20) in the west wing, but they are reserved for the Chinese. The privilege of the east wing is fresher blankets, but this may have changed by the time you visit.

Wǔtái Shān's luxury hotels are several kilometres south of the village. Every year more are being built. The best choice is probably the **Qīxiángé Bīnguǎn** (☎ 654 2400, fax 654 2183), which enjoys a peaceful setting at the foot of the mountains, and is a short walk from Nánshān Sì. Nicely furnished doubles/twins cost Y280/380 and triples with shared bath are Y160. If you require a living room and a study to go with your bedroom, the luxury suite is Y1080.

Back towards Táihuái, **Yǒuyì Bīnguǎn** (Friendship Hotel; ☎ 654 2678, fax 654 2123), one of the official tourist spots, charges a ridiculous Y480 for twins and Y456 for singles – definitely not worth it.

Places to Eat

Táihuái has almost as many small restaurants as it does hotels, and again they are largely similar. Prices tend to be higher here, as nearly all food has to be trucked in from the plains. Except for the pricey tourist hotels, there's not an English menu to be found in the area.

The **Railway Restaurant** on Taiping Jie has good food and the prices are reasonable. There is no English sign, but look out for the railway symbol or the karaoke/youth club opposite.

There are noodle stands just off the main road north of the Tàiyuán bus station serving tasty liáng pí, fried noodles, fried rice, dumplings etc. A bowl of noodles should cost around Y3.

Getting There & Away

There is now a park entrance fee of Y50 that both Chinese and foreigners have to pay before entering Wǔtái Shān. Genuine card-carrying Tibetan pilgrims are exempted.

From Dàtóng, there's one bus during summer to Wǔtái Shān departing from the new bus station at 7 am. The trip, via Húnyuán, Shāhé and over the scenic pass near Yèdǒufēng, takes five hours (Y30).

From Táihuái, buses to Dàtóng (Y30) leave from the northern part of the village. There is one departure daily, at 6.30 am. The bus will usually stop off at **Xuánkōng Sì** (Hanging Monastery) for 30 minutes, but always check before you buy your ticket. Public buses to Tàiyuán (Y43) leave at 6 and 7 am and 2 pm from a small stop near the middle of the village.

Private buses and minibuses (Y22) also make the run to Tàiyuán. Most leave in the morning, although sometimes there are afternoon departures. Private buses generally loiter between the two public bus stops.

Getting Around
Táihuái town can be covered on foot, and you can make pleasant day hikes out to some of the temples in the surrounding area.

DÀTÓNG 大同
☎ 0352 • pop 2,696,800

Dàtóng's chief attraction is the nearby **Yúngāng Shíkū** (Yungang Buddhist Caves). The city itself is not very attractive, although it has a few interesting historical sights. An ancient imperial capital, modern Dàtóng has little to show for its former greatness. It's crowded, polluted and industrial, but local authorities have been trying to spruce it up the recently and it's turning into a pretty lively place, with rows of upmarket shops and restaurants.

History
In the 5th century AD, the Toba, a Turkic-speaking people, succeeded in unifying all of northern China and forming the Northern Wei dynasty. Adopting Chinese ways, they saw trade, agriculture and Buddhism flourish. Their capital was Dàtóng. It remained as such until AD 494, when the court moved to Luòyáng.

Orientation
The pivotal point of Dàtóng is **Hóngqí Guǎngchǎng** (Red Flag Square) at the intersection of Da Xijie and Xinjian Nanlu. Apart from the Yúngāng Shíkū, the historic sights such as **Huáyán Sì** and the **Jiǔlóng Bì** (Nine Dragon Screen) are inside the crumbling old **city walls**. This is where you'll also find most of the shops and nightlife.

At Dàtóng's northern end is the train station, and several of the few hotels open to foreigners.

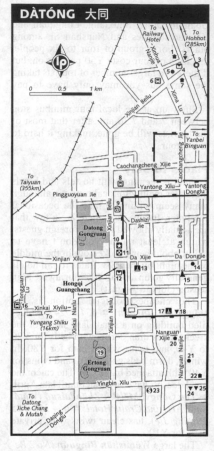

DÀTÓNG 大同

You can pick up tourist maps from hawkers around the train station; some have a little English.

Information
Dàtóng has two CITS offices: a branch at the train station and another at the Yúngāng Bīnguǎn (☎ 510 1326). The staff broker accommodation, can purchase train tickets and run regular tours of the city and Yúngāng Shíkū. In addition to informative English-language tours, it also has French speaking guides. Many readers have found the staff very helpful and friendly.

DÀTÓNG

PLACES TO STAY
1 Hóngqí Dàfàndiàn
红旗大饭店
7 Fēitiān Bīnguǎn
飞天宾馆
22 Yúngāng Bīnguǎn; CITS
云冈宾馆,
中国国际旅行社

PLACES TO EAT
2 Chēzhàn Kuàicān
车站快餐
18 Yǒnghé Dàjiǔdiàn
永和大酒店
24 Yǒnghé Hóngqí Měishíchéng
永和红旗美食城
25 Jiǔlóng Dàjiǔdiàn
九龙大酒店

OTHER
3 Train Station; CITS
火车站;
中国国际旅行社
4 Post & Telephone Office
邮电局
5 Bike Rental
6 Old (North) Bus Station
汽车北站(旧站)
8 New Bus Station
新汽车站
9 Wǎngbā (Internet Cafe)
网吧
10 PSB
公安局
11 Department Store
百货大楼
12 Main Post & Telephone Office
邮电大楼
13 Huáyán Sì
华严寺

14 Jiǔlóng Bì
九龙壁
15 Gǔ Lóu (Drum Tower)
鼓楼
16 Xīnkāilǐ Bus Station (for Yúngāng Shíkū)
新开里汽车站
17 Shànhuà Sì
善化寺
19 Datong Stadium
大同体育场
20 Advance Train Booking Office
鸹翠な燮贝
21 Foreign Languages Bookstore
外文书店
23 Bank of China (Main Branch)
中国银行(大同支行)

The Bank of China's main branch on Yingbin Xilu is the only place to change travellers cheques, unless you're staying at the Yúngāng Bīnguǎn.

The main post and telephone office is south of Hóngqí Guǎngchǎng with the clock tower at the intersection of Da Xijie and Xinjian Nanlu.

Internet access (wǎngbā) is available for Y10 an hour on the ground floor of a small building on Xinjian Beilu, just north of Pingguoyuan Jie.

The PSB office is on Xinjian Beilu, north of the large department store.

Jiǔlóng Bì 九龙壁
Nine Dragon Screen

This is one of Dàtóng's several 'dragon screens' – tiled walls depicting fire-breathing dragons. The Jiǔlóng Bì was originally part of the gate of the palace of Ming dynasty emperor Ming Taizhu's 13th son, and is 8m high, over 45m long and 2m thick.

The Jiǔlóng Bì is a short distance east of the intersection of Da Dongjie and Da Beijie; you can get there on bus No 4 from the train station. It's open daily from 8 am to 6.30 pm and entry costs Y3.

Huáyán Sì 华严寺

This monastery is on the western side of the old city. The original monastery dates back to AD 1140 and the reign of Emperor Tian Ju'an of the Jin dynasty.

Mahavira Hall is one of the largest Buddhist halls still standing in China. In the centre of the hall are five gilded Ming dynasty buddhas seated on lotus thrones. Around them stand Bodhisattvas, soldiers and mandarins. The ceiling is decorated with colourful paintings originally dating from the Ming and Qing dynasties, but recently restored and supported by massive wooden beams.

Bojiajiaocang Hall (Hall for the Conservation of Buddhist Scriptures of the Bojia Order) is smaller but more interesting than the main hall. It contains 29 coloured clay figures made during the Liao dynasty (AD 907–1125), representing the Buddha and Bodhisattvas. The figures give the monastery a touch of magic lacking in other restored temples.

Huáyán Sì is about 500m east of the post office at the end of Xiasipo Lane, which runs south off Da Xijie. Bus No 4 passes here. When we visited, the buildings were receiving timely repairs. When they reopen entry should cost about Y15.

Shànhuà Sì 善化寺

This temple is in the south of Dàtóng just within the old city walls. Built during the Tang dynasty, it was destroyed by fire during a war at the end of the Liao dynasty.

In AD 1128 more than 80 halls and pavilions were rebuilt, and further restoration was done during the Ming dynasty. The main hall contains statues of 24 divine generals. There is a small dragon screen within the monastery grounds. The temple is open daily from 8.30 am to 6 pm and admission costs Y6.

Dàtóng Jīchē Chǎng 大同机车厂
Datong Locomotive Factory

This factory was the last in China to make steam engines for the main train lines. In 1989 it finally switched to diesel and electric engines. However, the factory maintains a museum housing several steam locomotives. After wandering through the factory you enjoy the ultimate train-buff fantasy – a ride in the cabin of one of the locomotives.

The factory is on the city's south-western outskirts. You can only see it as part of a CITS tour. It's rare that large groups wish to go, but CITS will arrange small group tours for about Y100 per person.

Places to Stay

Officially, Dàtóng offers little for the budget traveller. The cheapest deal you can get is a dorm bed for Y40, and you may need to book through CITS at the train station to get this price.

Fēitiān Bīnguǎn (☎ 281 5117), just across from the southern end of the train station, asks Y100 for very average twins with attached bath. It offers Chinese customers a bed with bath for Y60. If you book through CITS you can get a dorm bed for Y40. The same deal goes for the *Railway*

Hotel, which is about 850m north of the train station. It also has some of the Y40 dorm beds that CITS organise.

At the southern end of town is the *Yúngāng Bīnguǎn* (☎ 502 1601), or rather their building No 2, which is in the same grounds as the three-star hotel. It has dorm beds for Y50 with TV and armchairs and is clean and the staff are friendly. The entrance is to the right as you enter the main gate. To get there catch bus No 15 from the train station and get off at *shizhengfu* stop and then walk another five minutes east, otherwise catch a taxi for Y10.

Opposite the Fēitiān Bīnguǎn lies the *Hóngqí Dàfàndiàn* (☎ 281 6823, fax 281 6671), a good mid-range choice. Reasonably clean twins go for Y170, and the price includes three meals a day and an evening plate of fruit, a rather rare perk.

Yànběi Bīnguǎn (☎ 602 4116, fax 602 7287) is a clean and modern place on Yuhe Beilu, about 2km south-east of the train station. It has twins from Y260 to Y400. It's a 10-minute walk from the train station or Y6 in a taxi.

Places to Eat

Yǒnghé Dàjiǔdiàn is well regarded by Dàtóng's locals as the best restaurant in Shānxī. Lunch and dinner crowds provide a glimpse of Dàtóng's upper crust. Ask for some local specialities or try its delicious Běijīng duck.

The same owner has another restaurant, *Yǒnghé Hóngqí Měishíchéng*, which is opposite the Yúngāng Bīnguǎn. Just next door is the *Jiǔlóng Dàjiǔdiàn (Nine Dragon Restaurant)* which also has tasty food at reasonable prices. All three restaurants have English menus.

At the opposite end of the spectrum, next to the train station, is *Chēzhàn Kuàicān*. It's a tiny, five-table affair serving tasty and cheap noodles and dumplings. A Y12 plate of dumplings is enough for two people.

The *Hóngqí Dàfàndiàn's restaurant*, not the canteen, is pretty good, and is quite reasonably priced. However, it is often booked out on weekends with rowdy wedding banquets that are best avoided.

Getting There & Away

Air Dàtóng's airport is still on the drawing board after the military airport closed down due to insufficient demand. If or when it is built, it will be less than 10km south of the city and will have flights to Běijīng, Shànghǎi and Guǎngzhōu.

Bus Dàtóng has two bus stations: the old, or north station, near the train station, and the new station on Yantong Xilu. Departures mostly start from the new station and pass by the old one before heading out, although some routes have separate departures from each station.

Daily buses to Tàiyuán leave the new station and take six hours (Y50). Privately run buses to Tàiyuán also leave frequently throughout the day from in front of the train station. Iveco buses make the trip in approximately five hours and cost Y50, whereas minibuses and sleepers are cheaper (Y20/30, respectively) but they are slower and less reliable.

There is one daily bus to Wǔtái Shān (Y30; five hours) from May to September leaving the new station at 7 am. There are daily departures from the old station, usually early in the morning, but times vary according to the season.

Train A train line north-east to Běijīng and a northern line to Inner and Outer Mongolia meet in a Y-junction at Dàtóng. Trans-Siberian trains via Ulaan Baatar come through here.

There are daily express trains to Běijīng (seven hours), Lánzhōu (24 hours), Hohhot (five hours), Tàiyuán (seven hours) and Xī'ān (18 hours). Tickets to Xī'ān can be hard to get, mainly because there's only one direct train, No 475.

The train station sells day-of-departure tickets only. If you want to buy sleeper or advance tickets try the advance booking office at the corner of Nanguan Nanjie and Nanguan Xijie. Failing that, try upgrading once you are on board or contact the staff at CITS who might be able to get you a ticket: they charge a Y40 commission per hardsleeper berth.

AROUND DÀTÓNG
Yúngāng Shíkū 云岗石窟
Cloud Ridge Caves

These are the main reason most people make it to Dàtóng. The caves are cut into the southern cliffs of Wǔzhōu Shān, 16km west of Dàtóng, next to the pass leading to Inner Mongolia. The caves contain over 50,000 statues and stretch for about 1km east to west.

On top of the mountain ridge are the remains of a huge, mud-brick 17th-century Qing dynasty fortress. As you approach the caves you'll see the truncated pyramids, which were once the watchtowers. Sadly, many of the caves suffer damage from coal and other pollution, largely a result of the neighbouring coal mine. At the time of writing, most of the coal trucks were being diverted to a back road, making the trip more pleasant.

The caves are open daily from 8.30 am to 5.30 pm and entry costs Y20 (or Y35 during summer). There are no guides at the caves, but there are good English descriptions and explanations throughout. For details, see the boxed text 'Bodhisattvas, Dragons & Celestial Beings'.

Getting There & Away

Bus No 3 (Y1.5) from the terminal at Xīnkāilǐ, on the western edge of Dàtóng, goes past Yúngāng Shíkū. You can get to Xīnkāilǐ on bus No 4 from the train station or bus No 17 from opposite the main Bank of China. From Xīnkāilǐ it's about a 25-minute ride to the caves.

Many travellers take a CITS tour out to the caves, which costs Y100 per person (minimum of five people). The tour also includes the Xuánkōng Sì and a visit to some local cave dwellings.

Xuánkōng Sì 悬空寺
Hanging Monastery

This monastery is just outside the town of Húnyuán, 65km south-east of Dàtóng. Built precariously on sheer cliffs above Jīnlóng Canyon, the monastery dates back more than 1400 years. Its halls and pavilions were built along the contours of the cliff

Bodhisattvas, Dragons & Celestial Beings

Most of the caves of the Yúngāng Shíkū were carved during the Northern Wei dynasty between AD 460 and 494. Yúngāng (Cloud Ridge) is the highest part of Wǔzhōu Shān's sandstone range and is on the north bank of the river of the same name. The Wei rulers once came here to pray to the gods for rain.

The caves appear to have been modelled on the Dúnhuáng Shíkū in Gānsù, which were dug in the 4th century AD and are some of the oldest in China. At Dúnhuáng the statues are terracotta since the rock was too soft to be carved, but here at Dàtóng are some of the oldest examples of stone sculpture to be seen in China. Various foreign influences can be seen in the caves: there are Persian and Byzantine weapons, Greek tridents, and images of the Indian Hindu gods Vishnu and Shiva. The Chinese style is reflected in the robust Bodhisattvas, dragons and flying *apsaras* (celestial beings rather like angels).

Work on the Yúngāng Shíkū fizzled out when the Northern Wei moved their capital to Luòyáng in AD 494. In the 11th and 12th centuries the Liao dynasty, founded by northern invaders, saw to some repairs and restoration. More repairs to the caves were carried out during the Qing dynasty. From east to west the caves fall into three major groups, although their numbering has little to do with the order in which they were constructed.

Caves 1–4

These early caves, with their characteristic square floor plan, are at the far eastern end, and are separated from the others. Caves 1 and 2 contain carved pagodas. Cave 3 is the largest in this group, although it contains only a seated buddha flanked by two Bodhisattvas.

Caves 5–13

Yúngāng art is at its best in this group, especially in caves 5 and 6, which boast walls of wonderfully carved Buddhist tales and processions. Cave 5 also contains a colossal seated buddha almost 17m high. Cave 6 contains a richly carved pagoda, and an entrance flanked by fierce guardians. In the centre of the rear chamber stands a two-storey pagoda-pillar about 15m high. On the lower part of the pagoda are four niches with carved images, including one of the Maitreya Buddha (the future Buddha). Gautama Buddha's life story from birth to his attainment of nirvana is carved in the east, south and west walls of the cave and on two sides of the pagoda.

Caves 7 and 8 are linked and contain carvings with Hindu influences. Shiva, with eight arms and three heads, and seated on a bull, is on one side of the entrance to cave 8. On the other side is the multifaced Indra, perched on a peacock. Caves 9 and 10 are notable for their front pillars and figures bearing musical instruments. These instruments appear again in cave 12, while cave 13 has a 15m-high buddha statue, its right hand propped up by a figurine.

Caves 16–20

These caves were carved in about AD 460 and the buddha in each one represents an emperor from the Northern Wei dynasty. The buddha in cave 18 represents Emperor Taiwu, who was once a great patron of Buddhism, but later (through the influence of a minister) came to favour Taoism.

After a revolt that he blamed on the Buddhists, Taiwu ordered the destruction of Buddhist statues, monasteries and temples, and the persecution of Buddhists. This lasted from AD 446 to 452, when Taiwu was murdered. His son is said to have died of a broken heart, having been unable to prevent his father's atrocities, and was posthumously awarded the title of emperor.

Taiwu's grandson (and successor) Emperor Wencheng, who restored Buddhism to the dynasty, is represented by the 14m-high seated buddha of cave 20.

Cave 21 and onwards are small, in poor condition and can't compare to their better preserved counterparts.

face using the natural hollows and outcrops. The buildings are connected by corridors, bridges and boardwalks and contain bronze, iron and stone statues of gods and buddhas.

Notable is the Three Religions Hall where Buddha, Laotzu and Confucius sit side by side. Some long-overdue repairs have been made to the monastery in recent years and some sections have been closed off. It's open daily and entry costs Y21.

The CITS tour to the Yúngāng Shíkū will include the Xuánkōng Sì. Chinese tours costing Y35 and taking four to five hours leave from both the old and new bus stations from 7.30 to 8.30 am.

You can also take a public or private bus from Dàtóng to Húnyuán, just 5km from the Xuánkōng Sì. Public buses to Húnyuán, leave from the old bus station at 7 am, take two hours and cost Y5. Private minibuses

leave from near the bus station and cost Y8. A taxi from Húnyuán, to the monastery costs Y30 return. The last bus back from Húnyuán, leaves at around 4 pm. Another option is the bus to Wǔtái Shān, which goes directly past the monastery and may stop for half an hour.

Mù Tǎ 木塔
Wooden Pagoda

This 11th-century pagoda at Yìngxiàn, 70km south of Dàtóng, is one of the oldest wooden buildings in the world. It's said that not a single nail was used in the construction of the nine-storey, 97m structure.

Tours of the Xuánkōng Sì sometimes include the Mù Tǎ. You can also get there by taking a minibus from near the old bus station in Dàtóng (Y8; two hours). It's open every day.

Shaanxi (Shǎnxī) 陕西

The northern part of Shaanxi is one of the oldest settled regions of China, with remains of human habitation dating back to prehistoric times. This was the homeland of the Zhou people, who eventually conquered the Shang and established their rule over much of northern China. It was also the homeland of the Qin, who ruled from their capital of Xiányáng near modern-day Xī'ān and formed the first dynasty to rule over all of eastern China.

Shaanxi remained the political heart of China until the 9th century. The great Sui and Tang capital of Chāng'ān (Xī'ān) was built there and the province was a crossroads on the trading routes from eastern China to central Asia.

With the migration of the imperial court to pastures further east, Shaanxi's fortunes declined. Rebellions afflicted the territory from 1340 to 1368, again from 1620 to 1644, and finally in the mid-19th century, when the great Muslim rebellion left tens of thousands of the province's Muslims dead. Five million people died in the famine from 1876 to 1878, and another three million in the famines of 1915, 1921 and 1928.

It was probably the dismal condition of the Shaanxi peasants that provided the communists such willing support in the province in the late 1920s and during the subsequent civil war. From their base at Yán'ān the communist leaders directed the war against the Kuomintang and later against the Japanese, before being forced to evacuate in the wake of a Kuomintang attack in 1947.

Some 35 million people live in Shaanxi, mostly in the central and southern regions. The northern area of the province is a plateau covered with a thick layer of wind-blown loess soil, which masks the original landforms. Deeply eroded, the landscape has deep ravines and almost vertical cliff faces.

The Great Wall in the far north of the province is something of a cultural barrier, beyond which agriculture and human existence were always precarious ventures.

Highlights

Capital: Xi'an
Population: 35.4 million
Area: 205,000 sq km

- The Army of Terracotta Warriors, one of China's premier attractions
- Huá Shān, one of the less-touristed sacred mountains
- Xī'ān, with its cultural sites, great food and interesting mix of Chinese and Islamic cultures

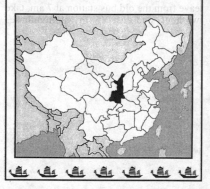

Like so much of China, this region is rich in natural resources, particularly coal and oil. The Wèi Hé, a branch of the Huáng Hé (Yellow River), cuts across the middle of the province. This fertile belt became a centre of Chinese civilisation.

The south of the province is quite different from the north; it's a comparatively lush, mountainous area with a mild climate.

XĪ'ĀN 西安
☎ 029 • pop 6,620, 600

Xī'ān once vied with Rome and later Constantinople for the title of greatest city in the world. Over a period of 2000 years Xī'ān has seen the rise and fall of numerous Chinese dynasties, and the monuments and

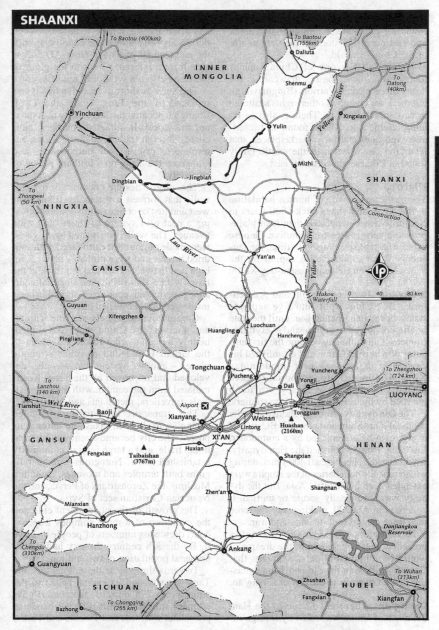

archaeological sites in the city and the surrounding plain are a reminder that once upon a time Xī'ān stood at the very centre of the Chinese world.

Today Xī'ān is one of China's major tourist attractions. The big drawcard is the Army of Terracotta Warriors (Bīngmǎyǒng), but there are countless other sights scattered in and around the city. There is also an Islamic element to Xī'ān, found in tucked-away mosques and busy marketplaces, that lends the city a touch of the exotic rarely found in Chinese cities further east.

History

The earliest evidence of human habitation in the Xī'ān area dates back 6000 years to Neolithic times, when the then lush plains proved a perfect area for primitive Chinese tribes to establish villages. In time, the legendary Zhou established a capital on the banks of the Fèn Hé near present-day Xī'ān.

Xiányáng Between the 5th and 3rd centuries BC, China split into five separate states locked in perpetual war, until the state of Qin conquered everyone and everything. Emperor Qin Shihuang became the first emperor of a unified China and established his capital at Xiányáng, near modern-day Xī'ān. His longing for immortality gave posterity a remarkable legacy – a tomb guarded by thousands of terracotta soldiers.

The Qin dynasty crumbled shortly after the death of Qin Shihuang. In 207 BC it was overthrown by a revolt led by a commoner, Liu Pang. Pang established the Han dynasty, which lasted a phenomenal 400 years, during which time the boundaries of the empire were extended deep into central Asia. But the dynasty was never really secure or unified. It collapsed in AD 220, making way for more than three centuries of disunity and war.

Nevertheless, the Han empire set a precedent that lingered on in the dreams of would-be empire builders, a dream that came to fruition in the Sui and Tang dynasties, which ruled from the city of Chāng'ān.

Chāng'ān After the collapse of the Han, the north of China was ruled by foreign invaders, and the south by a series of weak and short-lived Chinese dynasties. When the Sui dynasty united the country, it built the new capital of Chāng'ān in AD 582 as a deliberate reference back to the glory of the Han period, a symbol of reunification.

The Sui was short lived and in 618 it was replaced by the Tang. Under the Tang, Chāng'ān became the largest city in Asia, if not the world. It attracted courtiers, merchants, foreign traders, soldiers, artists, entertainers, priests and bureaucrats, and embarked the Tang on a brilliant period of creativity.

The city's design encompassed outer walls that formed a rectangle, 10km east-west and just over 8km north-south, enclosing a neat grid system of streets and wide avenues. The walls, punctuated by 11 gates, were made of pounded earth faced with sun-dried bricks, and were probably about 5.5m high and between 5.5m and 9m thick at the base. Within these walls the imperial court and government conducted their business inside yet another walled city.

Communications between the capital and the rest of China were developed, mainly by canals that linked Chāng'ān to the Grand Canal and to other strategic places – another system that was also developed and improved by the Tang. Roads radiated from the capital, with inns for officials, travellers, merchants and pilgrims.

This transport infrastructure enabled Chāng'ān to draw in taxes and enforce its power. The city became a centre of international trade, and a large foreign community established itself. Numerous foreign religions built temples and mosques, including Muslims, the Zoroastrians of Persia, and the Nestorian Christian sect of Syria.

The growth of the government elite and the evolution of a more complex imperial court drew vast numbers of people to serve it. By the 8th century the city had a phenomenal population of two million.

Towards the end of the 8th century the Tang dynasty and its capital began to decline. From 775 onwards the central government suffered reverses at the hands of provincial warlords and Tibetan and Turkic invaders. The setbacks exposed weaknesses in the empire, and although the Tang still maintained overall supremacy, they gradually lost control of the transport networks and the tax-collection system on which their power depended.

The Tang dynasty fell in AD 907 and China once again broke up into a number of independent states. Chāng'ān was eventually relegated to the role of a regional centre.

Orientation

Xī'ān retains the same rectangular shape that characterised Chāng'ān, with streets and avenues laid out in a neat grid pattern.

The central block of the modern city is bounded by the city walls. The centre of town is the enormous Zhōng Lóu (Bell Tower), and from here run Xī'ān's four major streets: Bei, Nan, Dong and Xi Dajie. The train station stands at the north-eastern edge of the central city block. Jiefang Lu runs south from the station to intersect with Dong Dajie.

Most of the tourist facilities can be found either along or in the vicinity of Jiefang Lu or along Xi Dajie and Dong Dajie. However, many of the city's sights like the Shǎnxī Lìshǐ Bówùguǎn, the Dàyàn Tǎ and Xiǎoyàn Tǎ, and Bànpō Bówùguǎn are outside the central block.

Further afield on the plains surrounding Xī'ān are sights such as the Xiányáng Shì Bówùguǎn, Fǎmén Sì, the Qín Shǐhuáng Líng and the Army of Terracotta Warriors near Líntóng.

Maps Pick up a copy of the widely available *Xī'ān Tourist Map*. A bilingual production, it is exhaustive in its listings and is regularly updated – even the bus routes are correct.

Information

Tourist Offices Xī'ān actually has a tourist information centre, rather than the old standby of the China International Travel Service (CITS; Zhōngguó Guójì Lǚxíngshè). The Xī'ān Tourist Information Services Centre (☎ 745 5043) is just next to the Jiěfàng Fàndiàn in front of the train station and is open daily from 7.30 am to 8 pm. It offers friendly and free advice on bus routes, accommodation and also runs daily Eastern and Western tours. (See Organised Tours under Xiánguáng later in this chapter.)

PSB The Public Security Bureau (PSB; Gōngānjú; ☎ 723 4500 ext 51810) at 138 Xi Dajie, is a five-minute walk west of the Zhōng Lóu. It's open Monday to Friday from 8 am to noon and 3 to 6 pm.

Money The main branch of the Bank of China is at 223 Jiefang Lu, just up from Dong Wulu. It's open Monday to Friday from 8.30 to 11.45 am and 2 to 5.30 pm and on weekends from 9 am to 3 pm. There's also a branch on Dong Dajie where foreigners can change cash and travellers cheques.

Post & Communications The main post office is opposite the Zhōng Lóu on Bei Dajie. Hours are 8.30 am to 8 pm daily. China Telecom is next to Zhōnglóu Guǎngchǎng (Bell Tower Square), opposite the post office. It has an Internet bar on the 2nd floor that charges Y18 an hour. There is another post and telephone office just opposite the train station next to the Jiěfàng Fàndiàn.

Travel Agencies One of the best choices in town is Golden Bridge Travel (☎ 725 7975, fax 725 8863), on the 2nd floor of the Bell Tower Hotel. The staff are friendly and are willing to dole out information even if you don't end up using their services.

John's Information Cafe chain has opened an office in Xī'ān inside the Rénmín Dàshà Gōngyù. Just across the road, the staff at Mum's Home Cooking and Dad's Home Cooking run Eastern Tours and can also provide some useful information about getting to major sights in the area.

CITS (☎ 524 1864) has an office on Chang'an Lu, a short walk south of Youyi Xilu. It mainly organises tours, although other services such as rail ticket bookings are available.

Zhōng Lóu 钟楼
Bell Tower

The Zhōng Lóu is a huge building in the centre of Xī'ān that is entered through an underpass on the north side of the tower. The original tower was built in the late 14th century, but it was rebuilt at the present location in 1739 during the Qing dynasty. A large iron bell in the tower used to mark the time each day, hence the name. There are musical performances inside the tower every afternoon. Entry costs Y15.

Gǔ Lóu 鼓楼
Drum Tower

The Gǔ Lóu, a smaller building to the west of the Zhōng Lóu, marks the Muslim quarter of Xī'ān. Entrance is Y12 and opening hours are 8 am to 6 pm. Běiyáunmèn is an interesting restored street of traders and craftspeople running directly north from the Gǔ Lóu.

Chéngqiáng 城墙
City Walls

Xī'ān is one of the few cities in China where old city walls are still visible. The walls were built on the foundations of the walls of the Tang Forbidden City during the reign of Hong Wu, first emperor of the Ming dynasty.

They form a rectangle with a circumference of 14km. On each side of the wall is a gateway, and over each stand three towers. At each of the four corners is a watchtower, and the top of the wall is punctuated with defensive towers. The wall is 12m high, with a width at the top of 12m to 14m and at the base of 15m to 18m.

Air-raid shelters were hollowed out of the walls when the Japanese bombed the city, and during the Cultural Revolution caves were dug to store grain. Most sections have been restored or even rebuilt, but others have disappeared completely (although they're still shown on the maps), so unfortunately it's not possible to walk right around Xī'ān along the city walls.

There are a number of access ramps up to the wall, some of which are located just east of the train station, near Heping Lu and at

Nán Mén (South Gate), beside the Bēilín Bówùguǎn. There are also some obscure steps at the eastern end of the south wall. The wall is open until 10 pm during summer and tickets cost around Y8.

Dàyàn Tǎ 大雁塔
Big Goose Pagoda

This pagoda stands in what was formerly the Temple of Great Maternal Grace in the south of Xī'ān. The temple was built around AD 648 by Emperor Gao Zong (the third emperor of the Tang dynasty) when he was still crown prince, in memory of his deceased mother. The buildings that stand today date from the Qing dynasty and were built in a Ming style.

The original pagoda was built in AD 652 with only five storeys, but it has been renovated, restored and added to many times. It was built to house the Buddhist scriptures brought back from India by the travelling monk Xuan Zang, who then set about translating them into 1335 Chinese volumes. This impressive, fortress-like wood-and-brick building rises to 64m. You can climb to the top for a view of the countryside and the city.

The Dàyàn Tǎ is at the end of Yanta Lu, at the southern edge of Xī'ān. Bus No 41 from the train station goes straight there. The entrance is on the southern side of the temple grounds. Entry is Y15 and another Y5 to climb the pagoda.

On the eastern side of the temple is the **Tángdài Yìshù Bówùguǎn** (Tang Dynasty Arts Museum) with a collection specifically devoted to the Tang period in Xī'ān. Entry is Y15. Both the pagoda and museum are open from 8.30 am to 5.30 pm.

Xiǎoyàn Tǎ 小雁塔
Little Goose Pagoda

The Xiǎoyàn Tǎ is in the pleasant grounds of the Jiànfú Sì. The top of the pagoda was shaken off by an earthquake in the middle of the 16th century, but the rest of the 43m-high structure is intact.

The Jiànfú Sì was originally built in AD 684 as a site to hold prayers to bless the afterlife of the late Emperor Gao Zong. The pagoda, a rather delicate building of 15 progressively smaller tiers, was built from AD 707 to 709 and housed Buddhist scriptures brought back from India by another pilgrim.

You can get to the Xiǎoyàn Tǎ on bus No 3, which runs from the train station through the Nán Mén of the old city and down Nanguan Zhengjie. The pagoda is on Youyi Xilu, just west of the intersection with Nanguan Zhengjie.

Entry to the grounds is Y5 or Y10 if you want to climb to the top of the pagoda for a panorama of Xī'ān's apartment blocks and smokestacks. It's open from 8.30 am to 5 pm.

Dàqīngzhēn Sì 大清真寺
Great Mosque

This is among the largest mosques in China. The present buildings only date back to the middle of the 18th century, although the mosque might have been established several hundred years earlier.

It stands north-west of the Gǔ Lóu and is built in a Chinese architectural style with most of the grounds taken up by gardens. Still an active place of worship, the mosque holds several prayer services each day.

The mosque is open from 8 am to 7.30 pm. The courtyard of the mosque can be visited, but only Muslims may enter the prayer hall. Entry is Y12.

The Dàqīngzhēn Sì is a five-minute walk from the Gǔ Lóu: go under the arch, then take the second tiny lane leading left to a small side street. From here the mosque is a few steps along to the right past souvenir shops.

Shǎnxī Lìshǐ Bówùguǎn
陕西历史博物馆
Shaanxi History Museum

Built in huge, classical Tang style (modern-day white tile mania however remains predominant), the museum was opened in 1992 and is rated as one of the best museums in China. The collection is chronologically arranged and includes material previously housed in the Provincial Museum, although many objects have never been on permanent display before.

The ground floor section deals with China's prehistory and the early dynastic period, starting with Palaeolithic Langtian Man and the more recent New Stone Age settlements at Líntóng and Bànpō between 7000 and 5000 years ago. Particularly impressive are several enormous Shang and Western Zhou dynasty bronze cooking tripods, Qin burial objects, bronze arrows and crossbows, and four original terracotta warrior statues taken from near the Qín Shǐhuáng Líng.

Upstairs, the second section is devoted to Han, Western Wei and Northern Zhou dynasty relics. There are some interesting goose-shaped bronze lamps and a set of forged-iron transmission gears, which are surprisingly advanced for their time.

The third section has mainly artefacts from the Sui, Tang, Ming and Qing dynasties. The major advances in ceramic-making techniques during this period are most evident, with intricately crafted terracotta horses and camels, fine pale-green glazed *misi* pottery and Buddhist-inspired Tang dynasty statues.

The final section, in the basement, is devoted to various exhibitions, which are worthy of a browse, but often lack English explanations.

To get there from the train station, take bus No 5 or 14. Photography is allowed but you must deposit (free of charge) any hand luggage in the lockers provided. Foreigners are required to enter through a special entrance (gift shop) to the west, which entails the privilege of paying an extra Y5. Admission is Y30 or Y12 for students. English guided tours are available for Y60 (or free in winter), although most exhibits include labels and explanations in English. Guides are available from an office (honoured guest reception room) to the far right of the main entrance. The museum is open daily from 8.30 am to 5.30 pm.

Bēilín Bówùguǎn 碑林博物馆
Forest of Steles Museum

Once the Temple of Confucius, the museum houses a fine collection devoted largely to the history of the Silk Road. Among the artefacts is a tiger-shaped tally from the Warring States Period, inscribed

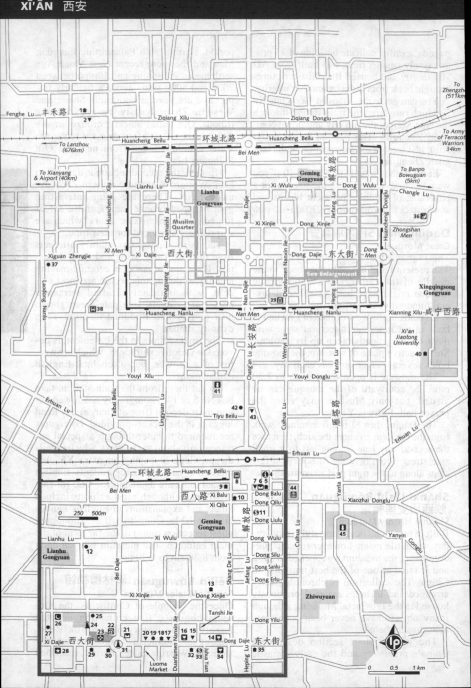

XĪ'ĀN

PLACES TO STAY

1   Rénmín Dàshà Gōngyù;
    John's Information Cafe
    人民大厦公寓
5   Jiěfàng Fàndiàn
    解放饭店
9   Shàngdé Bīnguǎn
    尚德宾馆
10 Guānghuá Jiǔdiàn
    光华酒店
13 Rénmín Dàshà
    人民大厦
18 YMCA Hotel
    青年会宾馆
29 Lìjīng Jiǔdiàn
    丽晶酒店
30 Bell Tower Hotel; Golden
    Bridge Travel
    钟楼饭店
32 Hotel Royal Xi'an
    西安皇城宾馆
35 Hyatt Regency Xi'an
    西安凯悦饭店
40 Èrshíwǔhào Sùshè
    二十五号宿舍

PLACES TO EAT

2   Mum's Home Cooking;
    Dad's Home Cooking
7   Jiěfàng Měishí Guǎngchǎng
    解放美食广场
15 Báiyúnzhāng Jiǎoziguǎn
    白云章饺子馆
17 Wángfǔ Cānyǐn

20 Wǔyī Fàndiàn
    五一饭店
43 Wèiwèi Jiǎoziguǎn
    味味饺子馆

OTHER

3   Train Station
    火车站
4   Xi'an Tourist Information
    Services Centre
    旅游资问服务中心
6   Post and Telephone Office
    邮电局
8   Long-Distance Bus Station
    长途汽车站
11 Bank of China
    中国银行
12 Advance Rail Booking
    Office;
    ICBC Bank
    铁路售票处;工商银行
14 Old Gun Club
    老枪酒吧
16 1+1
19 Foreign Languages
    Bookstore
    外文书店
21 Main Post Office
    邮电大楼
22 China Telecom Internet Bar
    中国电信网吧
23 Zhōnglóu Guǎngchǎng;
    Century Ginwa Shopping
    Centre; Beer Garden
    钟鼓楼广场；世纪金花

24 Gǔ Lóu
    鼓楼
25 Běiyuánmén
26 Dàqīngzhēn Sì
    大清真寺
27 Chénghuáng Miào
    城隍庙
28 PSB
    公安局外事科
31 Zhōng Lóu
    钟楼
33 Bank of
    China
    中国银行
34 Fashion Bar
    服喜会酒吧
36 Bāxiān Ān
    八仙安
37 CAAC
    民航售票处
38 Xī'ān West Bus
    Station
    西安汽车西站
39 Běilín Bówùguǎn
    碑林博物馆
41 Xiǎoyàn Tǎ;
    Jiànfú Sì
    小雁塔；荐福寺
42 CITS
    中国国际旅行社
44 Shǎnxī Lìshǐ Bówùguǎn
    陕西历史博物馆
45 Dàyàn Tǎ
    大雁塔

SHAANXI 陕西

with ancient Chinese characters and probably used to convey messages or orders from one military commander to another.

One of the more extraordinary exhibits is the Běilín (Forest of Steles), the heaviest collection of books in the world. The earliest of these 2300 large engraved stone tablets dates from the Han dynasty.

Most interesting is the Popular Stele of Daiqin Nestorianism, which can be recognised by the small cross at the top and is engraved in AD 781 to mark the opening of a Nestorian church. The Nestorians were an early Christian sect who differed from orthodox Christianity in their belief that Christ's human and divine natures were quite distinct.

Other tablets include the Ming De Shou Ji Stele, which records the peasant uprising led by Li Zhicheng against the Ming, and the 114 Stone Classics of Kaichen, from the Tang dynasty, inscribed with 13 ancient classics and historical records.

All of the important exhibits have labels in English or you can pay Y100 for an English guide. The museum entrance is on a side street that runs west off Baishulin Lu, close to the Nán Mén of the old city wall. It's open from 8 am to 6 pm and admission is Y20. The buildings and streets around the museum have been tastefully renovated in Ming style and there are quite a few street stalls selling their wares.

Muslim Quarter

This area near the Dàqīngzhēn Sì has retained much of its original character. The backstreets to the north and west of the mosque have been home to the city's Hui community for centuries.

Walking through the narrow laneways lined with old mud-brick houses, you pass butcher shops, sesame oil factories, smaller mosques hidden behind enormous wooden doors and proud, stringy-bearded men wearing white skullcaps. Good streets to explore are Nanyuan Men, Huajue Xiang and Damaishi Jie, which runs north off Xi Dajie through an interesting Islamic food market.

Bāxiān Ān 八仙安
Temple of the Eight Immortals

This is Xī'ān's largest Taoist establishment and an active place of worship. Scenes from Taoist mythology are painted around the temple courtyard.

To get there take bus No 10, 11, 28 or 42 east along Changle Lu and get off two stops past the city walls, then continue 100m on foot and turn right (south) under a green-painted iron gateway into a market lane. Follow this, turning briefly right then left again into another small street leading past the temple. The entrance is on the southern side of the temple grounds. You can also reach the temple by following the street running directly east from Zhōngshān Mén.

Places to Stay – Budget

For such a major travel destination, Xī'ān has a depressingly limited selection of true budget spots. For several years the main backpacker crash pad has been **Rénmín Dàshà Gōngyù** (Flats of Renmin Hotel; ☎ 624 0349, 9 Fenghe Lu), about 4km north-west of the city centre. It's not a convenient location, and the hotel's popularity stems solely from its *relatively* cheap dorm beds and the presence of three traveller cafes, where you can meet other travellers and fill up on banana pancakes.

Beds in quads (with free breakfast) go for Y40, while more comfortable twins with bathroom cost Y160. All rooms have air-con, which is a bonus during Xī'ān's sweltering summer. There's supposedly 24-hour hot water, bicycle rental and a relatively cheap laundry service. Rooms aren't particularly clean and the toilets sometimes look like they were last cleaned during the Ming dynasty. If no-one from one of the restaurants meets you at the station, take bus No 9 and ask to be let off at Fenghe Lu. A taxi from the station costs Y10. Minibus No 501 runs from in front of Rénmín Dàshà Gōngyù to the city centre and the Zhōng Lóu (Y1.50).

Just opposite the bus station and around the corner from the train station is the **Shàngdé Bīnguǎn** (☎ 742 6164, fax 742 7787), where a bed in a triple/quad costs Y30/25 with common showers. Twins range from Y138 to Y168. It has cheap bicycle rental and a reliable laundry service.

Also around the corner from the train station is the **Guānghuá Jiǔdiàn** (☎ 742 4546). It has dorm beds for Y35 and Y40 and twins for Y180 and Y198, which is not bad value for central Xī'ān.

Xi'an Jiaotong University (Xī'ān Jiāotōng Dàxué) has a foreign student building in **Èrshíwǔhào Sùshè** (No 25 dorm; ☎ 326 8813), which has very comfortable and clean twins for Y81 or Y99 with TV and air-con. Give it a ring first before you head out there. The university is just south-east of the city wall on Ganning Xilu and is best reached on bus No 705 from the train station. After you hop off the bus, pass through the main gate of the university and turn right, walk on for about 200m and turn left at the long straight road. Walk all the way to the end and the building is on the other side of the basketball court. It's about a 10-minute walk. Taxis are allowed on campus for a gate fee of Y3.

Places to Stay – Mid-Range

The **Jiěfàng Fàndiàn** (☎ 742 8946, fax 742 2617), diagonally across the wide square to your left as you leave the train station, has a convenient location, which is the deciding factor for some travellers. Comfortable twins cost Y240, triples Y280 and quads Y320. There are also cheaper twins in the older wing at the back for Y180.

The enormous *Rénmín Dàshà (People's Hotel;* ☎ *721 5111, fax 721 8152, 319 Dong Xinjie)* was designed in early 1950s Stalinist architectural style (with Chinese characteristics) and has been renovated into a fairly upmarket accommodation option. The cheapest twins (which do look quite nice) cost Y300 and the suites are Y650. The hotel sits in between two monolithic derelict buildings on Dong Xinjie.

The *YMCA Hotel (Qīngniánhuì Bīnguǎn,* ☎ *726 2288, fax 727 5830, 339 Dong Dajie)* is a friendly place with twins for Y268 and suites for Y488. Breakfast is free. The hotel is down an obscure lane off Dongda Jie.

The *Lìjīng Jiǔdiàn (*☎ *728 8731, fax 728 8731, 6 Xi Dajie)* is just opposite the Zhōnglóu Guǎngchǎng and is very central. Small singles are Y240 and very comfy twins are Y280. If you need a place to unwind away from the noise and pollution, it has a very pleasant tea garden on the 4th floor.

Places to Stay – Top End
This is the category most Xī'ān hotels aim for, and there are dozens of choices. Here are some that stand out from the crowd.

For location and luxury you can't beat the *Hyatt Regency Xi'an (Kǎiyuè Fàndiàn,* ☎ *723 1234, fax 721 6799).* Its service and facilities have garnered it a five-star rating, and it's just a few minutes walk to Xī'ān's restaurant and nightlife scene. Standard twins are US$130, and luxury twins are US$150. Regency club rooms, which are better equipped for business travellers, are US$170 per night. It also has Internet access on the 2nd floor. Don't forget to add a 15% service charge on room rates and all food and services.

Also enjoying a fine location, and a bit cheaper, is the four-star *Hotel Royal Xi'an (Xī'ān Huángchéng Bīnguǎn;* ☎ *723 5311, fax 723 5887),* which is a member of Japan's Nikko Hotels group. Twin rooms start at Y688, while suites cost Y1750, although both of these rooms are usually discounted to Y450 and Y1500, respectively (including service charge).

The prize for best position among Xī'ān's hotels has to go to the *Bell Tower Hotel (Zhōnglóu Fàndiàn;* ☎ *727 9200, fax 721 8767,* @ *bth@sein.sxgb.com.cn).* Managed by the Holiday Inn group, it's quite a pleasant place, and is among the more reasonably priced top-end choices with rates starting at Y680. The service and amenities don't match the Hyatt or other luxury hotels, but should still make for a comfortable stay.

Places to Eat
There's a lot of good street food in Xī'ān. In winter the entire population seems to get by on endless bowls of noodles, but at other times of the year there are all kinds of delicious snacks to be had.

Much of the local street food is of Islamic origin, and some common dishes are: *fěnrèròu,* made by frying chopped mutton in a wok with fine-ground wheat; *héletiáo,* dark brown sorghum or buckwheat noodles; and *ròujiāmó,* fried pork or beef stuffed in pita bread, sometimes with green peppers and cumin.

Another dish worth trying is *yángròu pàomó,* a soup dish that involves breaking (or grating) a flat loaf of bread into a bowl and adding a delicious mutton stock. You will first be served a bowl and one or two pieces of flat bread: try and break the bread into tiny chunks, the better to absorb the broth.

The cheap ground floor restaurant in the *Wǔyī Fàndiàn* is good for staple northern Chinese food like pork dumplings and hearty bowls of noodles. It's popular with locals and always busy.

The *Wèiwèi Jiǎoziguǎn (61 Chang'an Beilu)* is just across the road from CITS and serves up a good range of tasty dumplings. Two people can eat on Y10 worth of dumplings.

The *Wángfǔ Cānyǐn* is just to the east and is similar to the Wǔyī Fàndiàn with point and eat canteen-style food. Head upstairs to the 2nd floor and try some of the specials. The *wángfǔ zhásūpái* (home style ribs), *xiāngjiān yínxuěyú* (fish) and *měiwéi páigǔbāo* (rib soup) are all very tasty.

Good for dumplings is the *Báiyúnzhāng Jiǎoziguǎn,* diagonally opposite the Hotel

Royal Xi'an. Mutton or beef dumplings are made fresh, and they are well worth the wait.

The *Jiěfàng Měishí Guǎngchǎng* is opposite the train station and is a convenient place to fill up after a long train journey. The food is nothing special, but it's cheap and ordering is easy: just point and choose.

Around the Rénmín Dàshà Gōngyù, the travellers' restaurant scene centres on three establishments: *Dad's Home Cooking*, *Mum's Home Cooking* and *John's Information Cafe*. The competition between these three is fierce. Service and food are almost exactly the same, so spread your business around if possible. All are pleasant places to meet up with other backpackers, trade travellers' tales and knock back more beer than is good for you.

During the warmer months, a beer garden is set up in Zhōnglóu Guǎngchǎng. It's a pleasant place to rest your weary feet and have a cold drink.

Entertainment

Although not on a par with Běijīng or Shànghǎi, Xī'ān does have an increasingly lively nightlife scene. In addition to the usual karaoke and hostess clubs, a number of small bars featuring live music have sprung up, and are worth popping into.

The *Old Gun Club* (*Lǎoqiāng Jiǔbā*), on Dong Dajie, is one of the friendliest and relaxing spots, and has live folk/rock music (Chinese and western) nightly.

Also on Dong Dajie are *1+1* (*Yījiāyī*) and the *Fashion Bar* (*Fúxǐhuì Jiǔbā*), which are both very popular nightclubs that draw large crowds on weekends.

Shopping

Huajue Xiang is a narrow alley running beside the Dàqīngzhēn Sì with many small souvenir and 'antique' shops – they're great for browsing. This is one of the best places in China to pick up souvenirs like name chops or a pair of chiming steel balls. Bargaining is the order of the day.

An interesting place to visit is the **Chénghuáng Miào** (City God's Temple), an old-style wooden structure that possibly dates from the early Qing period. It's actually no longer a temple, but now houses a small wares market that looks like the China of the early 1980s: lots of older consumer goods, some interesting porcelain ware, Chinese musical instruments and calligraphy implements.

The temple is a 10-minute walk west of the Gǔ Lóu at the end of a long covered market running north off Xi Dajie. There's no English sign, so look for the large red Chinese characters above the entrance immediately east of the Xijing Hotel.

Around town you'll also find worthy conversation pieces like carved-stone ink trays used in Chinese calligraphy and a wide range of jade products from earrings to cigarette holders. There are plenty of silks too, but you're probably better off buying these closer to their source (Sūzhōu, Shànghǎi etc). Street hawkers sell delicate miniature wire furniture and ingenious little folded bamboo-leaf insects such as crickets and cicadas, which make cheap and attractive souvenirs.

If you're interested in Chinese and Buddhist classical music, there's an interesting selection at the Xiǎoyàn Tǎ.

Getting There & Away

Air Xī'ān is one of the best-connected cities in China – it's possible to fly to almost any major Chinese destination, as well as several international ones.

China Northwest Airlines (☎ 870 2299) is somewhat inconveniently located on the south-eastern corner of Xiguan Zhengjie and Laodong Lu, 1.5km from Xī Mén (West Gate). Office hours are 8 am to 9 pm daily. There are numerous other outlets around town, as well as most hotels, which normally sell plane tickets and are more centrally located.

Daily flights include Běijīng (Y840), Chéngdū (Y500), Guǎngzhōu (Y1190) and Shànghǎi (Y1260).

On the international front, there are flights to Hong Kong with both Dragonair and China Northwest. Dragonair (☎ 426 9288) has an office in the lobby of the Sheraton Hotel.

China Northwest also has flights to Macau, and to Nagoya and Hiroshima in Japan.

Bus The most central long-distance bus station is opposite Xī'ān's train station. From here you can get buses to Huá Shān (Y12; four hours) and Yán'ān (Y30; eight hours), as well as sleeper buses to more distant destinations such as Zhèngzhōu (Y93; 12 hours), Luòyáng (Y58; 10 hours) and Yínchuān (Y110; 15 hours).

Buses to Zhèngzhōu leave around noon and to Luòyáng at 3.30 and 4.30 pm, while sleepers to Yínchuān leave hourly from 12.30 pm to 6.30 pm. Xī'ān's west bus station is on Huancheng Nanlu, west of the Nán Mén.

If you're headed to Huáshān village, private minibuses leave when full from the east parking lot in front of the train station from 7 am to 6 pm. If they go via the highway the ride takes 2½ hours and costs Y20.

Train There are direct trains from Xī'ān to Běijīng (14 hours), Chéngdū (27 hours), Guǎngzhōu (17 hours), Héféi, Korla, Qīngdǎo, Shànghǎi, Tàiyuán, Ürümqi and Wǔhàn. For Chóngqìng and Kūnmíng change at Chéngdū.

For travellers to Luòyáng and Zhèngzhōu, there is a day air-con tourist train (No Y201) that only takes 8½ hours to reach Zhèngzhōu.

While you can sometimes get same-day tickets in the main ticket hall, most counters will probably refer you to the foreigners' ticket window on the 2nd level: look for the staircase near the English sign directing foreigners and overseas Chinese to the 1st floor. You'll need to bring your passport in order to register at the small window at the western end of the 2nd level. The ticket clerk will then give you a registration slip that you take to window No 2, at the eastern end of the floor: this is where you actually buy the ticket. The foreigners' window is open from 8.30 to 11.30 am and from 2.30 to 5.30 pm. Be aware that it often closes early, especially on weekends.

There's an Advance Rail Booking Office inside the ICBC Bank on Jiefang Lu, south of Xi Wulu, but it only sells tickets for trains starting from Xī'ān. CITS can organise tickets with a minimum of fuss, providing you give two or three days' notice.

Getting Around

To/From the Airport Xī'ān's Xiguan airport is around 40km north-west of Xī'ān. China Northwest Airlines runs shuttle buses hourly from 5 am to 6 pm between the airport and its Xī'ān booking centre (Y15; 50 minutes), from where you can pick up a taxi or local bus to your hotel.

Small Daihatsu taxis charge at least Y70 in either direction, while larger Santanas cost around Y100.

Xī'ān's packed public buses are a pickpocket's paradise, so watch your wallet when you ride them. More comfortable minibuses run on the same routes and charges are around Y2 for most central destinations.

Local buses go to all the major sights in and around the city, such as Bànpō Bówùguǎn and the Army of Terracotta Warriors.

Taxis are abundant and reasonably cheap: flag fall is around Y6, although short trips around town are a set Y5.

Bicycle hire is available at the Rénmín Dàshà Gōngyù and Bell Tower Hotel for around Y1 to Y2 per hour.

AROUND XĪ'ĀN

Most of the really interesting sights are outside the city. The two biggest drawcards are the Army of Terracotta Warriors near the Qín Shǐhuáng Líng, and the Bànpō Bówùguǎn.

Army of Terracotta Warriors

Ranking up there with the Great Wall and the Forbidden City as one of China's top historical sights, the 2000-year-old Army of Terracotta Warriors (Bīngmǎyǒng) remains stunningly well preserved: a perpetually vigilant force standing guard over an ancient imperial necropolis. In 1974 peasants digging a well uncovered what turned out to be perhaps the major archaeological

AROUND XĪ'ĀN

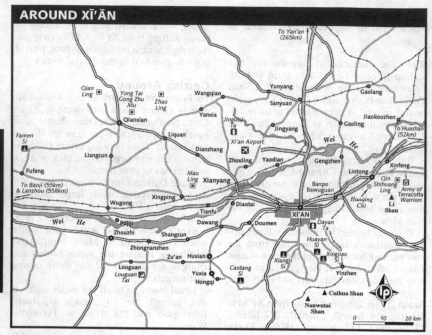

discovery of the 20th century: an underground vault of earth and timber that eventually yielded thousands of life-size terracotta soldiers and their horses in battle formation. In 1976 two other smaller vaults were discovered close to the first one.

The first underground vault measures about 210m east to west and 60m from north to south. The pit varies in depth from 5m to 7m. Walls were built running east to west at intervals of 3m, forming corridors. In these corridors, on floors laid with grey brick, are arranged the terracotta figures. Pillars and beams once supported a roof.

The 6000 terracotta figures of warriors and horses face east in a rectangular battle array. The vanguard appears to be three rows of 210 crossbow and longbow bearers who stand at the easternmost end of the army. Close behind is the main force of armoured soldiers holding spears, dagger-axes and other long-shaft weapons, accompanied by 35 horse-drawn chariots

(the latter, made of wood, have long-since disintegrated). Every figure differs in facial features and expressions.

The horsemen are shown wearing tight-sleeved outer robes, short coats of chain mail and wind-proof caps. The archers have bodies and limbs positioned in strict accordance with an ancient book on the art of war. There is speculation that the sculptors used fellow workers, or even themselves, as models for the warriors' faces.

Many of the figures originally held real weapons of the day, and over 10,000 pieces have been sorted to date. Bronze swords were worn by the figures representing the generals and other senior officers. Surface treatment made the swords resistant to rust and corrosion so that after being buried for more than 2000 years they were still sharp. The weapons are now kept in storage, out of public view.

The second vault, excavated in 1976, contained about 1000 figures. The third vault contained only 68 warriors and one war chariot, and appeared to be the command post for the soldiers in the other vaults. Archaeologists believe the warriors discovered so far may be part of an even larger terracotta army still buried around Qín Shǐhuáng Líng (Tomb of Qin Shihuang). Excavation of the entire complex and the tomb itself could take decades.

Almost as impressive is a pair of bronze chariots and horses unearthed in 1980 just 20m west of the Qín Shǐhuáng Líng and now housed in the Qín Yǒng Bówùguǎn, a small museum within the enclosure of the warriors site.

Visitors are not permitted to take photos at the site, unless they pay for the privilege or are a world leader. People who break this rule can expect to have their film confiscated. If you decide to take a few sly shots and get caught, try to remember that the attendants are just doing their job.

Entrance costs Y55 to see the vaults, the museum, and the *Circle Vision* documentary on the warriors and their excavation. Hours for all the exhibits are from 8.30 am to 5.30 pm daily.

Getting There & Away You can see the site as part of a tour from Xī'ān (see Organised Tours under Xiángyáng later in this chapter). Alternatively, it is possible to do it yourself by public bus. From the parking lot just east of the train station take bus No 306 or 307 (Y5), which travel via Huáqīng Chí. Bus No 307 does the return journey to Xī'ān via Bànpō Bówùguǎn.

Qín Shǐhuáng Líng　秦始皇陵
Tomb of Qin Shihuang

It may not amount to much as a tourist attraction, but in its time the Qín Shǐhuáng Líng must have been one of the grandest mausoleums the world had ever seen.

In the year 246 BC, at the age of 13, Ying Zheng ascended the throne of the state of Qin and assumed the title 'Shi Huang', or First Emperor. One by one he defeated his enemies, until in 221 BC the last of them fell. Qin Shihuang united the country, and standardised the currency and written script.

On the down side, he acquired a reputation for purges, mass book-burning parties, enforced labour in massive construction projects, and other tyrannical behaviour. His rule lasted until his death in 210 BC. His son only held out for four years, before being overthrown by the revolt that established the Han dynasty.

Historical accounts describe Qin's tomb as containing palaces filled with precious stones and ingenious defences against intruders. It housed ceilings vaulted with pearls, statues of gold and silver, and rivers of mercury. It is said that the artisans who brought it all into being were buried alive within, taking its secrets with them.

Despite the legends and impressive statistics, basically all there is to see nowadays is a mound. Unless you have a good sense for Chinese history this place probably won't do much for you. If you are interested, the tomb is about 1.5km east of the Army of Terracotta Warriors, and can be reached by bus No 306 or 307. Entry costs Y12,

Huáqīng Chí　华清池
Huaqing Pool

The Huáqīng Chí is 30km east of Xī'ān below Lí Shān (Black Horse Mountain). Water from hot springs is funnelled into public bathhouses, which have 60 pools accommodating 400 people.

During the Tang dynasty these natural hot baths were a favoured retreat of emperors and their concubines. The Huáqīng Chí leaves most visitors cold. If you don't fancy strolling around the gardens with swarms of excited tourists, try the museum up the road or take a walk on one of the paths leading up through the forest behind the complex.

There is a Taoist temple on Lí Shān dedicated to the 'Old Mother' Nu Wa, who created the human race and patched up cracks in the sky after a catastrophe. On the mountain's summit are beacon towers built for defence during the Han dynasty. A cable car will whiz you up there for Y25, and Y20 to come down. Admission to Huáqīng Chí is Y30.

Bus No 306 or 307, which run from the Xī'ān train station to the Army of Terracotta Warriors, stop at Huáqīng Chí.

Bànpō Bówùguǎn 半坡博物馆
Banpo Neolithic Village

Officially rated as Xī'ān's No 2 attraction, surpassed only by the Army of Terracotta Warriors, the Bànpō Bówùguǎn gets mixed reports. The general consensus is that it's tacky and boring, but the occasional traveller comes away singing its praises.

The best advice is to limit your visit to Bànpō Bówùguǎn and avoid the adjacent Matriarchal Clan Village, where matriarchs in Neolithic garb, high heels and stockings merely reinforce the feeling that you're in modern, not ancient, China.

Bànpō is the earliest example of 'Yangshao culture', named after the village where the first of these was discovered. It appears to have been occupied from 4500 BC until around 3750 BC. The village was discovered in 1953 and is on the eastern bank of the river, Chǎn Hé, in a suburb of Xī'ān.

A large hall has been built over what was part of the residential area of the village, and there are adjacent buildings housing pottery and other artefacts. Pottery found south of Qínlíng Shān has suggested that even earlier agricultural villages may have existed here.

The Bànpō ruins are divided into three parts: a pottery-manufacturing area, a residential area and a cemetery. These include the remains of 45 houses or other buildings, over 200 storage cellars, six pottery kilns and 250 graves.

The residential part of the village was surrounded by an artificial moat, 300m long, about 2m deep and 2m wide. It protected the village from attacks by wild animals and from the effects of heavy rainfall in what was originally a hot and humid environment. To the east of the residential area is the pottery kiln centre. To the north of the village lies the cemetery, where the adult dead were buried along with funerary objects like earthen pots. The children were buried in earthen pots close to the houses.

The Bànpō Bówùguǎn is open daily from 8 am to 6.30 pm and entry costs Y20.

Getting There & Away

The Eastern Tour to the Army of Terracotta Warriors usually includes Bànpō Bówùguǎn.

Independent travellers generally visit by way of electric bus No 105 from the train station.

XIÁNYÁNG 咸阳
☎ 0910 • pop 4,730,500

This little town is half an hour's bus ride from Xī'ān. The chief attraction is **Xiányáng Shì Bówùguǎn** (Xiányáng City Museum), which houses a remarkable collection of 3000 miniature terracotta soldiers and horses, discovered in 1965, excavated from a Han dynasty tomb. Each figure is about half a metre high. Admission is Y20 and the museum is open from 8 am to 6 pm.

Getting There & Away

To get to Xiányáng Shì Bówùguǎn from Xī'ān, take bus No 611 from the train station to the bus station and then get bus No 59. Get off at the bus station in Xiányáng. Up ahead on the left-hand side of the road you'll see a clock tower. Turn right at this intersection and then left at Xining Jie.

The museum is housed in a former Ming dynasty Confucian temple on Zhongshan Jie, which is a continuation of Xining Jie. The entrance is flanked by two stone lions. It's about a 20-minute walk from the bus station.

Imperial Tombs

Apart from the Qín Shǐhuáng Líng, a large number of other imperial tombs dot the Guānzhōng plain surrounding Xī'ān. The easiest way to get there is by tour from Xī'ān (see the Organised Tours section later in this section for details).

In these tombs are buried the emperors of numerous dynasties, as well as empresses, concubines, government officials and high-ranking military leaders. Construction of an emperor's tomb often began within a few years of his ascension to the throne and did not finish until he died.

Entry to the tombs ranges from Y15 to Y30; they are open from 8.30 am to 5 pm.

Zhāo Líng (Zhao Tomb) The Zhāo Líng set the custom of building imperial tombs on mountain slopes, breaking the tradition of building tombs on the plains with an artificial hill over them. This burial ground on Jiǔzong Shān, 70km north-west of Xī'ān, belongs to the second Tang emperor, Tai Zong, who died in AD 649.

Of the 18 imperial mausoleums on the Guānzhōng plain, this is probably the most representative. With the mountain at the centre, the tomb fans out to the south-east and south-west. Within its confines are 167 lesser tombs of the emperor's relatives and high-ranking military and government officials. Burying other people in the same park as the emperor was a custom dating back to the Han dynasty.

Buried in the sacrificial altar of the tomb were six statues known as the 'Six Steeds of Zhaoling', representing the horses that the emperor used during his wars of conquest. Some of the statues have been relocated to museums in Xī'ān.

Qián Líng (Qian Tomb) This is one of the most impressive tombs, 85km north-west of Xī'ān in Liáng Shān. This is the joint resting place of Tang Emperor Gao Zong and his wife Empress Wu Zetian.

Gao Zong ascended the throne in AD 650 after the death of his father, Emperor Tai Zong. Empress Wu, actually a concubine of Tai Zong, also caught the fancy of his son, who made her his empress. Gao died in AD 683, and the following year Empress Wu dethroned her husband's successor, Emperor Zhong Zong. She reigned as an all-powerful monarch until her death around AD 705.

The tomb consists of three peaks; the two on the southern side are artificial, but the higher northern peak is natural and is the main part of the tomb. Walls originally surrounded the tomb, but these are gone. South-west of the tomb are 17 smaller tombs of officials.

The grounds of the imperial tomb boast a number of large stone sculptures of animals and officers of the imperial guard. There are 61 (now headless) statues of the leaders of minority peoples of China and of the representatives of friendly nations who attended the emperor's funeral. The two steles on the ground each stand more than 6m high. The Wúzi Bēi (Wordless Stele) is a blank tablet;

one story goes that it symbolises Empress Wu's absolute power, which she considered inexpressible in words.

Zhāng Huái Mù (Prince Zhang Huai's Tomb) Zhang was the second son of Emperor Gao Zong and Empress Wu. For some reason the prince was exiled to Sìchuān in AD 683 and died the following year, aged only 31.

Empress Wu posthumously rehabilitated him. His remains were brought to Xī'ān after Emperor Zhong Zong regained power. Tomb paintings show horsemen playing polo, but these and other paintings are in a terrible state.

Yǒng Tài Gōng Zhǔ Mù (Princess Yong Tai's Tomb) Near Zhāng Huái Mù is the Yǒng Tài Gōng Zhǔ Mù, which features tomb paintings depicting palace servants. The line engravings on the stone outer coffin are extraordinarily graceful.

Yong Tai was a granddaughter of Tang Emperor Gao Zong, and the seventh daughter of Emperor Zhong Zong. She was put to death by Empress Wu in AD 701, but was rehabilitated posthumously by Emperor Zhong Zong after he regained power.

Mào Líng (Mao Tomb) The Mào Líng, 40km from Xī'ān, is the resting place of Emperor Wu, the most powerful ruler of the Han dynasty, who died in 87 BC. The cone-shaped mound of rammed earth is almost 47m high, and is the largest of the Han imperial tombs. A wall used to enclose the mausoleum, but now only the ruins of the gates on the eastern, western and northern sides remain.

It is recorded that the emperor was entombed clad in jade clothes sewn with gold thread with a jade cicada in his mouth. Apparently buried with him were live animals and an abundance of jewels.

Fǎmén Sì
Doorway Temple
Fǎmén Sì, 115km north-west of Xī'ān, was built during the Eastern Han dynasty in about AD 200.

SHAANXI 陕西

In 1981, after torrential rains had weakened the temple's ancient brick structure, the entire western side of the 12-storey pagoda collapsed. The subsequent restoration work produced a sensational discovery. Below the pagoda in a sealed crypt (built during the Tang dynasty to contain four sacred finger bones of the Buddha, known as *sarira*) were over 1000 sacrificial objects and royal offerings, including stone-tablet Buddhist scriptures, gold and silver items and some 27,000 coins. These relics had been completely forgotten for over 1000 years.

A museum housing part of the collection has been built on the site. After the excavations had finished the temple was reconstructed in its original form.

The best way to visit Fǎmén Sì is to take a Western Tour from Xī'ān (see the following Organised Tours section). Some tours don't include the temple so check before you book. Admission prices are Y15 to the temple, Y20 to the crypt and Y18 to the museum; the pagoda itself is not open to the public.

Organised Tours

One-day tours allow you to see all the sights around Xī'ān more quickly and conveniently than if you arranged one yourself. Itineraries differ somewhat, but there are two basic tours: a 'Western Tour' and an 'Eastern Tour'. There are also Chinese tours that leave from the square in front of the train station.

Travel agency tours are more expensive than those run by other operators, but the train station operators don't leave until they have enough people and tend to give you less time at each place and more time at other 'attractions'.

Eastern Tour The Eastern Tour (Dōngxiàn Yóulǎn) is the most popular as it includes the Army of Terracotta Warriors as well as the Qín Shǐhuáng Líng, Bànpō Bówùguǎn and Huáqīng Chí.

CITS offers a Eastern Tour for Y280, including lunch and all entry tickets: it also throws in a visit to the Dàyàn Tǎ. The coach leaves Xī'ān around 9 am and returns by 5 pm. An English-speaking guide is provided

and you usually get two hours at the warriors and Qín Shǐhuáng Líng.

The Xi'an Tourist Information Services Centre runs daily tours that depart from the office at the train station from 7.30 to 8.30 am. The Eastern Tour includes 10 stops and costs Y44. For a little extra the staff may provide you with an English-speaking guide.

Essentially the same tour can be done for far less by taking one of the Chinese minibus tours; you can buy tickets for Y44 at a kiosk in front of the train station. Travellers have mixed reports about these tours and have sometimes come away with a deeper understanding of contemporary Chinese culture, rather than Chinese history.

Western Tour The longer Western Tour (Xīxiàn Yóulǎn) includes the Xiányáng Shì Bówùguǎn, some of the imperial tombs, the Qián Líng and sometimes also Fǎmén Sì.

It's far less popular than the Eastern Tour and consequently you may have to wait a couple of days for CITS to organise enough people. Otherwise contact the tourist bureau's office at the station, which seems to run the most frequent tours. Its Western Tour visits seven locations and costs Y54.

HUÁ SHĀN 华山

The 2200m-high granite peaks of Huá Shān, 120km east of Xī'ān, tower above the plains to the north, forming one of China's sacred mountain areas. The tough climb to the top rewards you with stunning views and weary limbs.

There are now three different choices for climbing the mountain, all of which meet up at the **Běi Fēng** (North Peak), the first of four summit peaks. Two of these routes start from the eastern base of the mountain at the cable car terminus. If your legs aren't feeling up to the task, an Austrian-built cable car can get you to the Běi Fēng in 10 scenic minutes (Y55/Y100 one way/return). The second route works its way under the cable car route and takes a sweaty two hours.

The third route is the traditional and most popular route and the one that will leave the most memories, both physical and psychological. A 6km path leads to the Běi Fēng from the town of Huáshān. The first 4km are pretty easy going, but after that it's all steep stairs, and from Bĕi Fēng on to the other summits its also fairly strenuous. But the scenery is great; along **Cānglóng Fēng** (Green Dragon Ridge), which connects the Bĕi Fēng with **Dōng Fēng** (East Peak), **Nán Fēng** (South Peak) and **Xī Fēng** (West Peak), the way has been cut along a narrow rock ridge with impressive sheer cliffs on either side.

The Nán Fēng is the highest at 2160m, but all three rear peaks afford great views when the weather cooperates.

From Huáshān village, at the base of the mountain, it usually takes between three to five hours to reach the Bĕi Fēng, and another

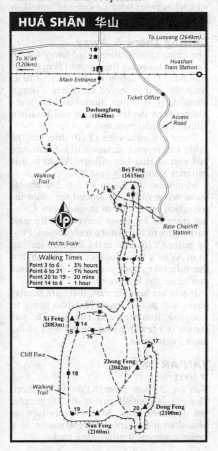

HUÁ SHĀN 华山

PLACES TO STAY

1 Xīyuè Bīnguǎn
   西岳宾馆
2 Huáxiá Dàjiǔdiàn
   华夏大酒店
4 Máonǚ Dòng
   毛女洞
6 Bĕifēng Fàndiàn
   北峰饭店
12 Diànlì Bīnguǎn
   电力宾馆
14 Xīfēng Lǚshè
   西峰旅社
16 Zhènyuè Gōng
   镇岳宫
18 Liàndān Lú
   炼丹炉
20 Dōngfēng Bīnguǎn
   东峰宾馆

OTHER

3 Yùquán Sì
   玉泉寺
5 Qúnxiān Tái
   群仙台
7 Jùxiān Tái
   聚仙台
8 Cānglóng Fēng
   苍龙峰
9 Wǔyún Fēng
   五云峰
10 Fēiyú Lǐng
   飞鱼岭
11 Hóngshēng Tái
   鸿声台
13 Jīnsuǒ Guān
   金锁关
15 Jùlíng Zú
   巨灵足
17 Yǐnfèng Tíng
   引风亭
19 Yǎngtiān Chí
   仰天池
21 Xiàqí Tíng
   下棋亭

hour or so to get to any one of the others. Several narrow and almost vertical 'bottleneck' sections can be dangerous when the route is crowded, particularly under wet or icy conditions.

There is accommodation on the mountain, most of it quite basic and overpriced, but it does allow you to start in the afternoon, spend the night and catch the sunrise from either Dōng Fēng or Nán Fēng. Many tourists actually make the climb at night, aided by torches (flashlights) and countless tea and refreshment stands. The idea is to start off at around 11 pm to midnight, which should get you to Dōng Fēng at sunrise. In summer this is certainly a much cooler option, but you do miss the scenery on the way up.

The gate ticket price is Y50. When heading out from Huáshān village, be careful not to hit the trail via the Yùquán Sì (Jade Fountain Temple), unless you're interested in seeing it, and paying another Y8 entry fee. There's a path that skirts the temple to the left and reconnects with the main Huá Shān trail.

Places to Stay & Eat

Just over 4km up the mountain trail at Maónǚ Dòng (Hairy Woman Cave) is a *small hostel* with very basic rooms, all with shared bath. Rates range from Y20 for a bed in a 10-person dorm to Y35 in a twin. Although nothing special, it's a good place to stop off for the night, especially if you arrive at Huáshān later in the day.

The next place is the *Běifēng Fàndiàn*, just below the Běi Fēng, which has twins/quads with private bath for Y240/280 and beds in 30-person dorms for Y25.

The best value accommodation is the pleasant *hostel* at Zhènyuè Gōng, which sits in the valley between the rear peaks. Despite lacking the view, it does receive the morning sun and is centrally located. It has clean and basic dorm beds from Y20 to Y50.

All the summits have accommodation of one sort or another. The *Xīfēng Lǚshè* sits atop the Xī Fēng and has dorm beds for Y30. Beds in twins are Y120. Also on the Xī Fēng is the *Diànlì Bīnguǎn* (☎ 216 2970), which provides all the creature comforts. Twins/triples with attached bath are a ridiculous Y980.

On Dōng Fēng is the *Dōngfēng Bīnguǎn*, which charges a usurious Y60 for a mat and blanket in the grimy and draughty attic.

There are plenty of cheap places to stay in Huáshān village along the road leading up to the trailhead and Yùquán Sì.

The *Huáxià Dàjiǔdiàn* has beds in fairly clean quads with shared bath for Y25. It's 100m from the main intersection on the right heading towards the Huá Shān trailhead.

At the main intersection is the *Xīyuè Bīnguǎn* (☎ 436 4741, fax 436 4559), which has twins with air-con and bathroom for Y218 and triples for Y320.

Getting There & Away

The nearest train station is at Mèngyuán, on the Xī'ān-Luòyáng line, about 15km east of Huáshān. This station is also referred to as Huáshān, and is served by nearly a dozen trains daily in either direction. Minibuses run between the train station and Huáshān village (Y3; 30 minutes).

There are minibuses (Y10) direct to the cable car from a separate ticket entrance just east of Huáshān village. A taxi to this entrance should only cost Y5.

Minibuses to Xī'ān (Y20; 2½ hours) leave when full from around the main intersection from 7 am to around 6 pm. Coming from Xī'ān, buses leave from the east parking lot in front of the train station. Public buses (Y15) also make the run, leaving from Xī'ān's long-distance bus station, but the ride takes four hours, as these buses don't take the highway.

If you are heading east, there are regular buses that pass through Huáshān going to Luòyáng, Ruìchéng and Tàiyuán. The bus station is a few hundred metres west of the main intersection.

YÁN'ĀN 延安
☎ 0911

Yán'ān, 270km from Xī'ān in northern Shaanxi, is a small city of 40,000 people, but together with Mao's birthplace at Sháoshān it has special significance as a major communist pilgrimage spot.

Between 1936 and 1947 this was the headquarters of the fledgling Chinese Communist Party. The Long March from Jiāngxī ended in 1936 when the communists reached the northern Shaanxi town of Wúqí. The following year they moved their base to Yán'ān.

Apart from the revolution history sites, there's not a whole lot to see in Yán'ān, although just making it up to this remote section of the province is in itself pretty interesting. Despite its status as the 'birthplace' of the revolution, Yán'ān has been largely neglected by the Chinese government, and it remains a fairly poor, underdeveloped place.

Even Mao himself turned his back on Yán'ān: after living here for nearly a decade, he left in 1947, never to revisit. Today, as the revolutionary spirit gradually fades, fewer Chinese and foreign visitors make it to Yán'ān.

Orientation

Yán'ān is spread out along a Y-shaped valley formed where the east and west branches of the Yán Hé meet. The town centre is clustered around this junction, while the old communist army headquarters is at Yángjiālǐng on the north-western outskirts of Yán'ān. The train station is at the far southern end of town, 4.5km from the centre. For a bird's eye view of Yán'ān head up to the revolving restaurant on the top floor of the Yàshèng Dàjiǔdiàn.

Information

The PSB can be found inside the Yán'ān Bīnguǎn on Zhangxin Jie. The Bank of China is inconveniently located in the north of town on Beiguan Jie. The post and telephone office is on Zhangxin Jie. In addition to the usual services there is an Internet bar inside the telephone section. Hours are 8 am to 6 pm.

CITS (☎ 231 7859) has an office in the Bǎiyuè Fàndiàn (see Places to Stay & Eat).

Things to See

During their extended stay, the communist leadership moved house quite a bit within Yán'ān. As a result there are numerous former headquarters sites.

One of the most interesting is the **Yángjiālǐng Gémìng Jiùzhǐ** (Yangjialing Revolution Headquarters Site), 3km northwest of the town centre. Here you can see the assembly hall where the first Central Committee meetings were held, including the 7th national plenum, which formally confirmed Mao as the leader of the party and the revolution.

Nearby are simple dugouts built into the loess earth where Mao, Zhu De, Zhou Enlai and other senior communist leaders lived, worked and wrote. Further uphill are caves that used to house the secretariat, propaganda and personnel offices. Admission to the site is Y10 and hours are 8 am to 5 pm.

About 1km south-east of here is the **Yán'ān Gémìng Jiniànguǎn** (Yan'an Revolution Museum), which has an extensive collection of revolutionary paraphernalia – old uniforms, weaponry and many photographs and illustrations. There's even a stuffed horse that was allegedly ridden by Mao himself. Unfortunately there are no English labels. The museum is open daily from 7.30 am to 6 pm and entry costs Y10.

Just a few minutes walk south is the last site occupied by the communist leadership in Yán'ān, the **Wángjiāpíng Gémìng Jiùzhǐ** (Wangjiaping Revolution Headquarters Site). There's not quite as much to see here, although it's interesting to note the improvement in living standards enjoyed by Mao and top-ranking comrades. Entry costs Y8 and hours are 7.30 am to 6 pm daily.

All the above stops can be reached by taking bus No 1, which runs from the train station along the road east of the river and then heads up Zaoyuan Lu. Just ask the conductor to drop you off at the respective site. Bus No 8 also passes by all these places and can be caught from the bridge, Dà Qiáo.

More accessible from the city is the **Fènghuángshān Gémìng Jiùzhǐ** (Fenghuangshan Revolution Headquarters Site), about 100m north of the post office. This was the first site occupied by the communists after their move to Yán'ān, as reflected by the relatively primitive lodgings of the leading cadres. Entry is Y5 and hours are 7.30 am to 8 pm.

SHAANXI 陕西

The **Bǎo Tǎ** (Treasure Pagoda), built during the Song dynasty, stands on a prominent hillside south-east of the river junction. Entry costs Y10, plus an additional Y5 to climb the pagoda, which is open from 7 am to 8 pm daily.

Qīngliáng Shān is a pleasant hillside park with some nice trails and a few sights, including a **Wànfó Dòng** (Ten Thousand Buddha Cave) dug into the sandstone cliff beside the river. The cave has relatively intact Buddhist statues and wall inscriptions. The park is open daily from 7 am to 8 pm and entry is Y10.

Places to Stay & Eat

The *Jiālíng Bīnguǎn* (☎ 231 5470), on the eastern side of town, is not supposed to accept foreigners, but you may be able to talk your way in. If so, you can get dorm beds for Y26 and slightly dingy but comfortable twins with private bath for Y120.

The *Yàshèng Dàjiǔdiàn* (☎ 213 2778) in the centre of town is Yán'ān's fanciest hotel. Stylish twins start at Y198 and suites are Y380. There is even a rotating restaurant on the top floor.

The *Bǎiyuè Fàndiàn* (☎ 211 2159) is a more modest affair with dorm beds for Y25/30 and air-con twins for Y120. There is hot water from 7 to 8 am and then again from 8 to 11 pm. The hotel is just north of the post office.

The best food in town is claimed to be found in the Yàshèng Dàjiǔdiàn's *Rotating Restaurant*. The restaurant is on the top floor of the hotel and serves both Chinese and western food.

If you have to do any banking, then drop into the popular *Zhōngyuàn Dàjiǔdiàn*, which is just next door. If you can put up with the tacky elevator music, it serves up a tasty bowl of *niúròu shāozi*, a kind of spaghetti bolognese.

Markets set up on both sides of Dà Qiáo during the day and in the evening with lots of tea tables. The locals while away the day here, chewing pumpkin seeds and playing chess. Noodles are the order of the day.

There are a few good restaurants opposite the bus station serving cheap and tasty meals.

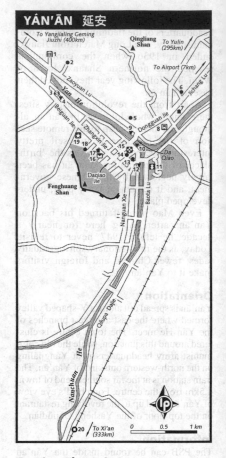

YÁN'ĀN 延安

Getting There & Away

Air There are weekly flights to Xī'ān (Y380) and Běijīng (Y800) every Thursday.

The airline booking office (☎ 211 3854) is on Jichang Lu, diagonally opposite the Jiālíng Bīnguǎn, and is open daily from 8 am to noon and 2.30 to 5.30 pm. A free bus service connects the office with the airport, 7km north-east of the city.

Bus Heading to Xī'ān, buses run every half to one hour from 6 to 11.30 am. The ride takes nine hours and costs Y37 (Y53 for a sleeper). The schedule is the same in

YÁN'ĀN

PLACES TO STAY & EAT

4 Zhōngyuàn Dàjiǔdiàn
中苑大酒店

7 Jiālǐng Bīnguǎn
嘉岭宾馆

9 Night Market
夜市

10 Night Market
夜市

12 Night Market
夜市

13 Yàshèng Dàjiǔdiàn;
Rotating Restaurant
亚圣大酒店

17 Bǎiyuè Fàndiàn;
CITS
百悦饭店；
中国国际旅行社

OTHER

1 Yán'ān Géming
Jìniànguǎn
延安革命纪念馆

2 Wángjiāpíng
Géming Jiùzhǐ
王家坪革命旧址

3 Bank of
China
中国银行

5 Qīngliáng Shān
Entry Gate
清凉山售票口

6 CAAC
民航售票处

8 Long-Distance
Bus Station
延安汽车站

11 Bǎo Tǎ
宝塔

14 Xīnhuá Bookstore
新华书店

15 Yan'an Department Store
延安百货大楼

16 Post & Telecom Office
Internet Bar
邮电大楼

18 Fènghuángshān
Géming Jiùzhǐ
凤凰山革命旧址

19 PSB;
Yán'ān Bīnguǎn
公安局外事科；
延安宾馆

20 Train Station
火车站

SHAANXI 陕西

the reverse direction. There is also a comfy express bus (Y79; six hours) at 9.15 am. Otherwise, there are share taxis (Santanas) to Xī'ān that take four hours and cost Y100 or Y120 for the front seat.

From Yán'ān there is a morning (9.40 am) and night (7.30 pm) bus to Yúlín (Y43; eight hours) and an express bus at 2.30 pm (Y61). Heading west, there are three daily departures to Yínchuān, in Níngxià (Y45; 12 hours) at 2.40, 5.30 am and 4.30 pm.

Train A train line links Yán'ān with Xī'ān via an interesting route along the Luo Hé. There are daily trains in either direction: an overnight service (No 661/2) that leaves both Xī'ān and Yán'ān at 10.20 pm (7½ hours), and a day train (No 845/6) that departs either station around 10.10 am (nine hours).

Getting sleeper tickets to Yán'ān is usually no problem, but getting them back can be quite difficult: either get down to the station by 3 pm to line up for the overnight train, or try the foyer of the large hotel opposite the bus station at 9 am. A taxi from the train station into town costs Y10.

YÚLÍN 榆林
☎ 0912

Yúlín lies on the fringe of Inner Mongolia's Mu Us Desert in far northern Shaanxi.

During the Ming dynasty, Yúlín was a fortified garrison town and patrol post serving the Great Wall.

Yúlín's remoteness and relative poverty have kept the old town somewhat insulated from the 'white-tile' trend in Chinese architecture, which is rapidly destroying what remains of the country's older buildings. Along the narrow brick lanes near the unrestored Zhōng Lóu (Bell Tower) are traditional family houses with tiny courtyards hidden behind low enclosure walls and old stone gates. The city's old Ming walls are mainly still standing, although in places their original outer brick layer has been removed.

A large three-tiered **fortress** and **Zhènbēi Tái** (Beacon Tower) lie 7.5km north of town.

Places to Stay & Eat

The *Yúlín Bīnguǎn* (☎ 328 3971, fax 328 3970), on Xinjian Lu, just north of the city walls, is the official tour group and conference hotel, and is therefore often full. Singles are Y160 and twins range from Y120 to Y160. It also has beds in twins/triples with a shower for Y50/40. The hotels dining hall is not bad and quite cheap.

The *Yúxī Dàjiǔdiàn* (☎ 328 0492), on Renmin Lu, has beds in triples with attached bath from Y25 and comfortable twins for Y90 and Y130. The staff might try and add on a foreigners surcharge, but just remain polite but firm and they should back down.

Getting There & Away

There are daily flights to Xī'ān (Y580) and there's one direct sleeper bus daily between Xī'ān and Yúlín (Y90; 15 hours), but it's more convenient and less tiring to stop in

Yán'ān. There are also three buses each day between Yán'ān and Yúlín (Y43; eight hours).

There is one daily bus at 5.30 am to Yínchuān (Y46; 14 hours) following a route close to the Great Wall. There are also half-hourly buses to Dàliǔtǎ, from where you can catch a train to Dōngshèng and Bāotóu in Inner Mongolia.

Hénán 河南

Hénán, or at least its northern tip where the Huáng Hé (Yellow River) crosses, is allegedly where it all began. The beginnings of Chinese civilisation can be traced back about 3500 years, when primitive settlements here began to coalesce into a true urban sprawl.

Today, Hénán is one of China's smallest provinces but also the most densely populated. Its 90 million people – about a third the population of the USA – jostle for living space and train tickets.

History

It was long thought that tribes who migrated from western Asia founded the Shang dynasty (c. 1700–1100 BC). Shang dynasty settlement excavations in Hénán, however, have shown these towns to be built on the sites of even more ancient settlements. The Shang probably emerged from a continuous line of development that reaches back into prehistoric times.

The first archaeological evidence of the Shang period was discovered near Ānyáng in northern Hénán. However, the first Shang capital, perhaps dating back 3800 years, is believed to have been at Yanshi, west of modern-day Zhèngzhōu. Around the mid-14th century BC, the capital is believed to have moved to Zhèngzhōu, where its ancient city walls are still visible. Many Shang settlements have also been found outside the walled area. Later the capital moved to Yīn, near the modern town of Ānyáng to the north.

The only clues as to what Shang society was like are found in the remnants of their cities, in divining bones inscribed with a primitive form of Chinese writing and in ancient Chinese literary texts. Apart from the Zhèngzhōu walls, all that has survived of their cities are the buildings' pounded-earth foundations, stone-lined trenches where wooden poles once supported thatched roofs, and pits used for storage or as underground houses.

Highlights

Capital: Zhèngzhōu
Population: 91.7 million
Area: 167,000 sq km

- Kāifēng, a delightful blast from the past
- Shàolín Sì, a monastery for those with an interest in kung fu
- Lóngmén Shíkū, the Buddhist caves near Luòyáng

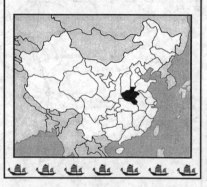

Hénán again occupied centre stage during the Song dynasty (AD 960–1279), but political power deserted it when the government fled south from its capital at Kāifēng following a 12th-century invasion from the north. Nevertheless, with a large population on the fertile (although periodically flood-ravaged) plains of the unruly Huáng Hé, Hénán remained an important agricultural area.

Hénán's urban centres dwindled in importance and population with the demise of the Song dynasty. It was not until the 1949 communist victory that they again expanded. Zhèngzhōu was transformed into a sizeable industrial city, as was Luòyáng. Kāifēng and Ānyáng, however, have been slower to respond to the call of the hammer and anvil.

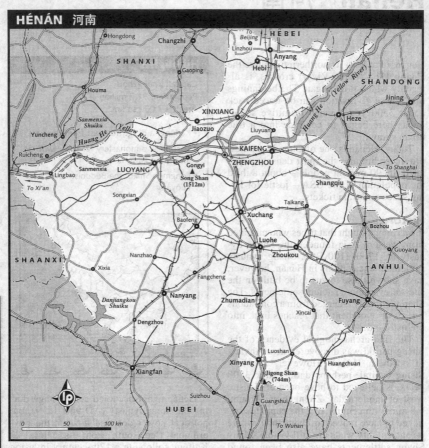

HÉNÁN 河南

ZHÈNGZHŌU 郑州

☎ 0371 • pop 5,973,300

Provincial capital of Hénán since 1949,
Zhèngzhōu is a sprawling paradigm of ill-
conceived town planning. It sports broad,
neatly intersecting boulevards, a people's
park, a towering anachronistic Mao statue
and a new provincial museum.

While Zhèngzhōu lags behind Guǎngzhōu
and Shànghǎi, it is valiantly holding up its
end in the latest Chinese revolution with a
high-tech science park on the town's outskirts. Zhèngzhōu is at best an overnight stop
en route to more worthwhile attractions.

Orientation

All places with interest for travellers lie east
of the railway line.

The town's liveliest part is around the
restaurants and markets near the train and
bus stations. North-east of the train station,
five roads converge at the prominent tower
of Èrqī Tǎ to form a messy traffic circle that
marks Zhèngzhōu's commercial centre. Erqi
Lu runs north from the Èrqī Tǎ to intersect
with Jinshui Lu near Rénmín Gōngyuán.
The new Hénán Shěng Bówùguǎn is in the
city's north along Nongye Lu; the Holiday
Inn is east on Jinshui Lu.

Information

The Bank of China is at 16 Huayuankou Lu in the city's northern section. The branch on Jinshui Lu, across the T-junction with Chengdong Lu, also will change travellers cheques and cash. The post and China Telecom telecommunications centre is in the building at the far right of the square as you exit the train station. The business centre at the Novotel International Hotel Zhèngzhōu offers email service for Y2.5 per minute.

China International Travel Service (CITS; Zhōngguó Guójì Lǚxíngshè; ☎ 595 2072, ✉ lhm@public.zz.ha.cn) has an office at 15 Jinshui Lu; English is spoken at the CITS European and American department (☎ 595 4501). The Public Security Bureau (PSB; Gōngānjú) is at 70 Erqi Lu, near the intersection with Xili Lu.

Shang Dynasty Ruins

On Zhèngzhōu's eastern outskirts lie the remains of an ancient city from the Shang period (Shāng Dài Yízhǐ). Long, high mounds of earth indicate where the city walls used to be, although roads now cut through them. This is one of the earliest relics of Chinese urban life.

Excavations here, and at other Shang sites, suggest that a 'typical' Shang city consisted of a central walled area containing large buildings (presumably government buildings or the residences of important people, used for ceremonial occasions) surrounded by villages. Each village specialised in a product such as pottery, metal-work, wine or textiles. The village dwellings were mostly semi-underground pit houses, while the buildings in the centre were rectangular and above ground.

Excavations have also uncovered Shang tombs. These are rectangular pits with ramps or steps leading down to a burial chamber where the coffin was placed and surrounded with funerary objects such as bronze weapons, helmets, musical instruments, inscribed oracle bones and silk fabrics. Some also contained the skeletons of sacrificial animals and humans. Study of these human skeletons suggests they were

of a different ethnic origin from the Shang – possibly prisoners of war. This and other evidence suggest that Shang society was an aristocratic dictatorship with the emperor/father-figure at the apex and did not enslave its own people.

Ruins are at two sites. The portion that still has some of the wall standing is in the city's south-eastern section. Bus No 2 stops nearby, get off at the stop called Dōng Mén Kǒu (East Gate). Bus No 3 runs near the old Shang city. The other ruins are in **Zǐjīngshān Gōngyuán** near the Novotel Hotel.

Hénán Shěng Bówùguǎn
河南省博物馆
Henan Provincial Museum

The provincial museum, housed in an impressive new building, is in the city's northern section on Nongye Lu across from the intersection with Jingqi Lu.

It exhibits artefacts discovered in Hénán, including some from the Shang period. There's also an exhibition on the 7 February revolt. The **Èrqī Tǎ** (7 February Memorial Tower) in Zhèngzhōu's centre, commemorates the bloody suppression of a 1923 strike organised by workers maintaining the Wǔhàn-Běijīng railway.

Huáng Hé 黄河
Yellow River

The Huáng Hé is 24km north of Zhèngzhōu. The road passes near Huāyuánkǒu village, where in April 1938 Kuomintang general Chiang Kaishek ordered his troops to blow up the river dykes to halt the Japanese advance. This desperately ruthless tactic was successful for a few weeks; it also drowned about one million Chinese people and left another 11 million homeless and starving.

The United States helped repair the dyke in 1947 and today the point where it was breached has an irrigation sluice gate and Mao's instruction, 'Control the Huáng Hé', etched into the embankment. The river has always been regarded as 'China's sorrow' because of its propensity to flood. It carries masses of silt from the loess plains and deposits them on the riverbed, causing the water to overflow the banks. Consequently,

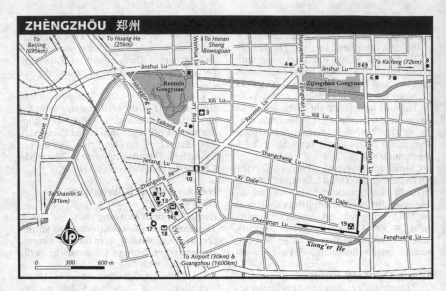

ZHÈNGZHŌU 郑州

peasants have built the dykes higher and higher each century. As a result, parts of the river flow along an elevated channel that is sometimes more than 15m in height.

The building of upstream dams and irrigation canals to divert the flow have helped partially control the river.

Bus No 16 goes to the Huáng Hé Gōngyuán (Yellow River Park) from outside the Zhèngzhōu Fàndiàn.

Places to Stay

As you exit the train station, *Jīnyángguāng Dàjiǔdiàn* (*Golden Sunshine Hotel;* ☎ 696 9999, fax 699 9534, 86 Erma Lu) is on your left. It's an upmarket place but has comfortable air-con singles/doubles for Y40/60. Standard twins go for Y160. There are more expensive rooms, which tour groups often occupy. Lower-level rooms are noisier because of the station.

Opposite the train station, near several shops, is *Zhōngyuán Dàshà* (☎ 696 6172), a cavernous white tower with rooms in two adjoining hotels. Both are a bit run-down, but handy if you're in transit. There are twins for Y80, and singles/twins with bath and air-con are Y100.

The *Zhèngzhōu Fàndiàn* (☎ 696 9941, fax 696 1673, 8 Xinglong Jie) is across the street and to the left as you leave the train station. Basic doubles without bath are Y80. Standard twins with bath are Y130 and Y160.

Not far from the station near the Èrqī Tǎ, the *Èrqī Bīnguǎn* (☎ 696 1169, 168 Jiefang Lu) has doubles for Y80 and Y130 with bath.

The marble-festooned *Hóngshānhú Jiǔdiàn* (*Red Coral Hotel;* ☎ 698 6688, fax 699 3222, 20 Erma Lu), has singles/twins for Y480/760. Bargaining may drop singles/doubles to Y312/368. The hotel also offers a free Chinese-style breakfast with each room, and there's a swimming pool.

The *Yǒuyì Bīnguǎn* (*Friendship Hotel;* ☎ 622 8807, fax 622 4728, 96 Jinshui Lu) has clean twins from Y308 to Y348. Cheaper twins without bath are Y70, or Y100 with bath. A taxi to the hotel from the train station should cost Y6.

In the city's eastern suburbs is the *Novotel International Hotel* (*Yàgāo Guójì Fàndiàn;* ☎ 595 6600, fax 599 7818, 114 Jinshui Lu). Rooms start at Y470 for a twin, plus a 15% service charge.

The *Holiday Inn Crowne Plaza* (*Huángguān Jiàrì Bīnguǎn;* ☎ 595 0055,

ZHÈNGZHŌU

PLACES TO STAY & EAT
1 Yŏuyì Bīnguăn
   友谊宾馆
6 Novotel International Hotel
   河南雅高国际饭店
7 Holiday Inn Crowne Plaza
   郑州皇冠假日宾馆
10 Èrqī Bīnguăn
   二七宾馆
11 Hóngshānhú Jiŭdiàn
   红珊瑚酒店
12 Zhèngzhōu Fàndiàn
   郑州饭店
13 Canteen
   餐厅

14 Jīnyángguāng Dàjiŭdiàn
   金阳光大酒店
16 Zhōngyuán Dàshà
   中原大厦

OTHER
2 Advance Booking Office
   (Train Tickets)
   火车预售票处
3 PSB
   公安局外事科
4 CITS
   中国国际旅行社
5 Bank of China
   中国银行

8 CAAC
   中国民航售票处
9 Èrqī Tă
   二七塔
15 Long-Distance
   Bus Station
   长途汽车站
17 Train Station
   火车站
18 Post & Telecom
   Office
   邮政大楼
19 Shang Dynasty
   Ruins
   商代遗址

fax 599 0770) is next door. This place started life as the Russian Foreign Experts' Hotel back in the 1950s but has been renovated and is now managed by the Holiday Inn group. Rates start from US$103 for singles and US$118 for twins, which includes a 20% service charge.

Places to Eat
Like other parts of north-western China, the restaurants in Zhèngzhōu dish up bowls of opaque noodles called *liáng fĕn*. Give them a try with a tossing of vinegar or hot chilli.

Opposite the Jīnyángguāng Dàjiŭdiàn, there's a *canteen* of no discernible name that has noodle, dumpling and rice dishes to choose from behind the counter.

The classier restaurants are clustered at the fashionable end of town, on Jinshui Lu between Chengdong Lu and Huayuankou Lu. The Holiday Inn has a *patisserie* and an international *restaurant* serving reasonably inexpensive hamburgers and steaks.

Getting There & Away
Air The Civil Aviation Administration of China (CAAC; Zhōngguó Mínháng; ☎ 599 1111) has an office and hotel at 3 Jinshui Lu, but there are ticket outlets scattered throughout town. The new airport is about 30km south of the city centre. An airport shuttle bus (Y15; 40 minutes) leaves from

the CAAC office throughout the day. A taxi to the airport costs around Y80 to 100.

From Zhèngzhōu there are flights to more than 20 Chinese cities. Daily services include Bĕijīng (Y550), Guăngzhōu (Y1080) and Shànghăi (Y640), and there are less frequent flights to Guìlín (Y960), Kūnmíng (Y1010), Wŭhàn (Y410), Qīngdăo (Y680), Chéngdū (Y760) and even Ürümqi (Y1740). There are also two flights a week to Hong Kong (Y1980).

Bus From the long-distance bus station (opposite the train station), comfortable aircon Iveco minibuses go to Luòyáng (Y23; two hours), leaving every 20 minutes and plying the freeway between Zhèngzhōu and Luòyáng.

Ordinary buses (Y17; 2½ hours) take the old road. Buses leave every half hour for the trip to Ānyáng (Y30; four hours). Buses to Kāifēng (Y10) don't take the freeway, so the trip takes about an hour. There are also overnight sleeping-berth coaches *(wòpùchē)* to Bĕijīng (Y150; 7½ hours), Shànghăi (Y170; 16 hours), Wŭhàn (Y80; 10 hours, Xī'ān (Y100; 10 hours) and other destinations, although trains are better. Minibuses for Shàolín (Y10; two hours) leave from the bus station and in front of the train station. However, some buses may only go to Dēngfēng, but you can catch a bus to Shàolín from there.

HÉNÁN 河南

Train Zhèngzhōu is a crucial junction in the Chinese rail network, and numerous trains run via the city, so you could find yourself here 'in transit' for a few hours. The train station ticket office is often crowded and tickets are easier to buy at the advance booking office at 134 Erqi Lu. CITS and many hotels also book tickets.

Express trains do the journey to Běijīng (Y180; 8½ hours), and trains also go to Guǎngzhōu (Y350; 20 hours), Luòyáng (Y20; two hours), Shànghǎi (Y230; 11 to 14 hours), Wǔhàn (Y55; 6½ hours), overnight to Xī'ān (Y100; 12 hours) and Tàiyuán (Y390; 12 hours). The Běijīng-Kowloon express train also stops in Zhèngzhōu.

Travellers to Xī'ān are best off taking the faster, two-tiered 'tourist train' (Y100) that leaves Zhèngzhōu daily at 11.02 am and arrives in Xī'ān just before 8 pm.

Getting Around
Since most sights and tourist facilities are away from the city centre, the bus system, which is pretty straightforward, is the best bet.

Bus No 2 goes from the train station to the Novotel, while the No 3 runs near the Shang city ruins.

Taxis are readily available. The red ones have meters, but drivers rarely use them (most journeys around town should be Y10 to Y15); minivan taxis generally cost between Y7 and Y10.

SŌNG SHĀN 嵩山
☎ 0371
Three main peaks and two areas – Shàolín Sì and Dēngfēng – comprise Sōng Shān, which rises to 1512m above the sea and sits about 80km west of Zhèngzhōu.

In Taoism, Sōng Shān is considered the central mountain, symbolising earth in the religion's belief that five elements make up the world. Legend says that Taoists searched throughout China for mountains to match these crucial elements. They came up with Héng Shān in Héběi for wood, Héng Shān in Húnán for fire, Tài Shān in Shāndōng for water and Huá Shān in Shaanxi for metal. Sōng Shān occupies the axis – directly under heaven.

Cave Dwellings

The road between Zhèngzhōu and Luòyáng provides a unique opportunity to see some of China's cave dwellings. Over 100 million Chinese people live in cave houses cut into dry embankments, or in houses where the hillside makes up one or more walls. These are not peculiar to Hénán Province: a third of these dwellings are found in the dry loess plain.

Some communities use both caves and houses; the former are warmer in winter and cooler in summer, but also tend to be darker and less ventilated than ordinary houses. Sometimes a large square pit is dug first and then caves are hollowed into the four sides of the pit. A well is sunk in the middle of the yard to prevent flooding during heavy rains. Other caves, such as those at Yán'ān, are dug into the side of a cliff face.

The floors, walls and ceilings of these cave dwellings are made of loess, a fine yellowish-brown soil which is soft and thick and makes good building material. The front wall may be made of loess, mud-brick, concrete, bricks or wood, depending on the availability of materials. Ceilings are shaped according to the quality of the loess. If it is hard then the ceiling may be arched; if not, the ceiling may rise to a point. Besides the doors and windows in the front wall, additional vents may let in light and air.

While kung fu's popularity draws crowds to Shàolín Sì during the high season, it's possible to eke out an alternative visit by spending the night and trekking the area for some peace and quiet.

Shàolín Sì 少林寺
China's most famous martial arts tradition was developed by Buddhist monks at Shàolín Sì, 80km west of Zhèngzhōu.

Each year, thousands of Chinese enrol at Shàolín's martial art schools. Enthusiastic trainees, many as young as five, can often be seen in the monastery grounds ramming a javelin through their imaginary opponent's body or gracefully kicking into a sparring dummy with enough force to wind an elephant.

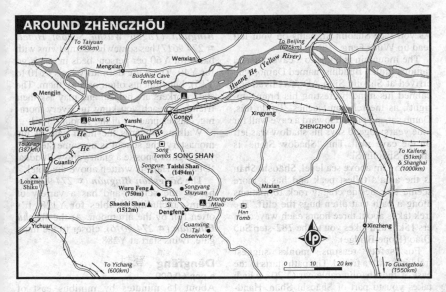

AROUND ZHÈNGZHŌU

To Taiyuan (450km)

To Beijing (675km)

Mengxian

Wenxian

Huang He (Yellow River)

Buddhist Cave Temples

Mengjin

Xingyang

ZHENGZHOU

Baima Si   Yanshi   Gongyi

LUOYANG

Luo He   Yiluo He

To Xi'an (387km)

Yi He

Guanlin

Song Tombs   Taishi Shan (1494m)

SONG SHAN

To Kaifeng (51km) & Shanghai (1000km)

Songyue Ta

Longmen Shiku

Wuru Feng (750m)

Songyang Shuyuan

Shaolin Si

Zhongyue Miao

Mixian

Shaoshi Shan (1512m)

Dengfeng

Yichuan

Guanxing Tai Observatory

Han Tomb

Xinzheng

To Yichang (600km)

0   10   20 km

To Guangzhou (1550km)

HÉNÁN 河南

Some students have found stardom from years of practicing the control of their minds and bodies; one teacher's young son has struck it big and appeared in Hong Kong martial arts movies.

After graduation, many students become police officers, security guards or physical education teachers.

According to legend, Shàolín was founded in the 5th century AD by an Indian monk, Bodhidharma, who preached Chan (Zen) Buddhism. Apparently, for relief between long periods of meditation, Bodhidharma's disciples imitated the natural motions of birds and animals, developing these exercises over the centuries into a form of unarmed combat.

The monks have supposedly intervened continually throughout China's many wars and uprisings – always on the side of righteousness, naturally. Perhaps as a result, their monastery has suffered repeated sackings. The most recent episodes were in 1928, when a local warlord, Shi Yousan, torched almost all the temple's buildings, and in the early 1970s, courtesy of the Red Guards.

In spite of fires and vandalism, many of the monastery buildings are still standing, although most have had any original charm restored out of them. One interesting sight is the **Shàolín Tǎlín** (Forest of Dagobas) outside the walls past the temple; each of the 244 dagobas (dome-shaped shrines containing Buddhist relics), some dating back to the Tang dynasty, was built in memory of a monk.

Nowadays Shàolín is a tourist trap catering to tourists who are bussed in every day. The main area is thick with food stalls, street photographers and souvenir shops. Try to visit on a weekday when there are fewer people.

The main gate ticket is Y40 and includes a small map and a panoramic film in Chinese that is screened in the building near the entrance.

The film's highlight is watching monks use their minds and muscles to withstand having logs rammed into their stomachs and suspend themselves from rope nooses – using only their chins. One monk even uses his teeth to pick up a wooden table and serve tea to others.

Trekking It's possible to escape the din of tourists and souvenir hawkers by climbing some mountains and breathing the fresh air. As you face Shàolín Sì, paths on your left lead up Wǔrǔ Fēng.

The mountain is home to a cave where a famous Indian Buddhist named Damo, who arrived at Shàolín Sì in AD 527, lived and calmed his mind by resting his brain 'upright', as the religion teaches. To do this, Damo sat and prayed toward a cave wall for nine years; legend says his shadow was left on the cave wall. This 'Shadow Stone' is still at Shàolín Sì.

At 1512m above sea level, Shǎoshì Shān is the area's tallest peak and has a more scenic trek beside craggy rock formations along a path that often hugs the cliff. The trek takes about three hours each way, covers 15km and takes you to the 782-step Suǒ Qiáo (Rope Bridge).

For safety reasons, monks suggest trekking with a friend. The path starts to the east of the Shàolín cable car (Y20), which takes you to part of Shǎoshì Shān. Hand-drawn maps in Chinese are available at souvenir stalls.

Kung Fu Classes If you're striving to be the next Jackie Chan, an instructor can teach you the ways in a day-long class. The **Shàolín Monastery Wǔshù Institute at Tǎgōu** (☎ 274 9617, ✉ wushu@shaolinkungfu.com), with a Web site at www.shaolinkungfu.com, is supposedly Shàolín's oldest and largest school with 7000 students. Its one-day class (Y180) includes lodging; ask at the school's hotel. The Wǔshù Bīnguǎn's package goes for Y500 and includes lodging and three meals.

If your body isn't limber enough to spiral in the air and kick above your head, you can watch youngsters who have practiced for years. While students practice throughout the day, you may be able to snag a free look in a school courtyard or indoor hall. If all is quiet, the Wǔshù Bīnguǎn gives demonstrations for Y50.

Places to Stay It's possible to spend the night at Shàolín and hopefully avoid – at least for a bit – the high season's congested atmosphere.

The *Tǎgōu Wǔshù Xuéxiào Jiāoxué Bīnguǎn (Tagou Wushu School Hotel;* ☎ 274 9617) has somewhat damp twins with baths for Y60 per person; beds in quads go for Y40. There are dormitory beds (Y10 to Y15), but students often occupy them. The staff workers are helpful and may ask their friends to teach you kung fu. Every morning, classes practise in the school's yard.

Walking towards the main gate of the monastery, the school is up some steps on your right, opposite a giant yellow Buddha. 'Dharma Hall' is written above the hotel.

The *Sōngshān Bīnguǎn* (☎ 274 9050) is beside the school and has a variety of rooms, including doubles for Y128. It's often full by the afternoon. At the *Wǔshù Bīnguǎn* (☎ 274 9016), closer to the main gate, twins start at Y288.

Dēngfēng 登封
● pop 60,000

About 15 minutes by minibus east of Shàolín Sì lies Dēngfēng, which has Tàishì Shān towering behind it.

The area is home to some noteworthy historical attractions. If Shàolín Sì is crowded, this somewhat sleepy mountain town serves as an alternative destination.

Excluding any trekking, Dēngfēng's sights can be seen independently within two days. CITS (☎ 287 2137) at 48 Zhongyue Dajie has helpful, English-speaking staff.

Things to See & Do
Built during the Qin dynasty, Zhōngyuè Miào remains a popular draw and is modelled after the Forbidden City in Běijīng.

The temple originally served as a place to worship the god of the central mountain Sōng Shān. But the temple's significance eventually meshed with Taoism, whose adherents dubbed Sōng Shān the earth's centre. Inside the elaborate, red temple with 12 courtyards is a tablet illustrating the location of all of the Taoist sacred mountains.

The temple is 4km east of the city centre; take green bus No 2.

Twelve kilometres south-east of the city is the **Guānxīng Tāi Observatory**, China's oldest surviving observatory. In AD 1276, the emperor ordered two astronomers to chart a calendar by watching the sun's shadow. After observing from the stone tower, they came back in AD 1280 with a mapping of 365 days, five hours, 49 minutes and 12 seconds, which differs from modern calculations by only 26 seconds.

Regular southbound buses can take you there; catch them from any large intersection in the south-east of the city. The observatory is off an alley.

In Dēngfēng's north-west, the famous Sōngyáng Shūyuàn (Songyang Academy) sits at Tàishì Shān's base and contains a 4500-year-old cypress tree, China's oldest.

Nearby is the Sōngyuè Tǎ (Central High Mountain Pagoda). Built in AD 520, during the Northern Wei dynasty, it's the country's oldest pagoda and has been restored.

Take bus No 2 west and then north to the academy, which is the last stop. From there, take a motor-tricycle taxi to the pagoda; the ride should cost Y10 to Y15. The sites are open daily from 8 am to 6 pm. Entrance to each one is Y10.

North of Dēngfēng 1494m-high Tàishì Shān provides another trekking opportunity. Area maps show trails leading to the summit.

Places to Stay & Eat

The upmarket Shàolín Guójì Dàjiǔdiàn (☎ 286 6188, fax 287 1448, 16 Shaolin Lu), in the east of the city, rents clean, comfortable twins for Y240. Bargaining may help. Some rooms have views of Tàishì Shān.

About half a block west, the cheaper Liángyè Bīnguǎn (☎ 287 1791, 28 Shaolin Lu) has twins/triples with bath for Y88/68 per person.

Yùshàn Zhāi Cāntīng (42 Zhongyue Dajie), next to CITS, serves delicious food and is frequented by workers who are curious about foreigners. Dishes range from Y10 to Y100.

Getting There & Away

Sōng Shān is well off the major road between Zhèngzhōu and Luòyáng. Buses from these cities go to both Shàolín and Dēngfēng, more often Shàolín,

because of its popularity. Tickets cost Y10 from Zhèngzhōu and Y8 from Luòyáng.

In Shàolín, Iveco minibuses to Zhèngzhōu (Y20) and Luòyáng (Y20) wait for passengers in the parking lot opposite the Shàolín Tǎlín and at the town's major intersection. The Dēngfēng bus station is on western Zhongyue Dajie.

Many Zhèngzhōu hotels have day tours (Y40) to Shàolín, including sites along the way but excluding entrance fees.

LUÒYÁNG 洛阳

☎ 0379 • pop 6,070,200

Founded in during the Xia dynasty, Luòyáng was the capital of 13 dynasties until the Northern Song dynasty moved its capital to Kāifēng in the 10th century AD. In the 12th century, Juchen invaders from the north stormed and sacked Luòyáng, which never quite recovered.

For centuries it languished with only memories of greatness. By the 1920s it had just 20,000 inhabitants. The communists brought life back to Luòyáng, constructing an industrial city that now houses more than a million people.

Today, it's hard to imagine that Luòyáng was once the centre of the Chinese world and home to more than 1300 Buddhist temples. There are reminders of Luòyáng's historical greatness scattered about town, but the main attraction are the caves (Lóngmén Shíkū) 16km out of town.

Orientation

Luòyáng is spread across the northern bank of the Luò Hé. Luòyáng train station, a large white-tiled building with a loud chiming clock, is in the city's north. Luòyáng's chief thoroughfare is Zhongzhou Lu, which meets Jinguyuan Lu leading down from the train station at a central T-intersection.

The old city is in the town's eastern part, beyond the old west gate at Xiguan, where sections of the original walls can still be seen. Throughout the maze of narrow streets and winding laneways stand many older houses. Using the Wén Fēng Tǎ as a landmark, it's a great area to explore on foot or by bicycle.

LUÒYÁNG 洛阳

Information

The CITS office (☎ 432 3212) is on Changjiang Lu, diagonally opposite Xīyuàn Gōngyuán, not far from the Yǒuyì Bīnguǎn. But it's far from the train station. There's also a branch at the Mǔdan Dàjiǔdiàn. CTS (☎ 485 6535) has an office across from the hotel. The PSB is on the corner of Kaixuan Lu and Tiyuchang Lu.

The Bank of China is at 439 Zhongzhou Zhonglu. The branch opposite the Yǒuyì Shāngdiàn (Friendship Store) will only exchange cash. The main post and China Telecom telephone office is at the T-junction of Zhongzhou Lu and Jinguyuan Lu and has an email service for Y18 per hour.

Báimǎ Sì 白马寺
White Horse Temple

Founded in the 1st century AD, Báimǎ Sì was the first Buddhist temple constructed on Chinese soil. Today, Ming and Qing structures stand at the site of the original temple.

Five hundred years before the journey of Xuan Zhuang, the Tang dynasty monk whose travels are fancifully immortalised in the classic *Journey to the West*, two envoys of the Han dynasty court went in search of Buddhist scriptures.

In Afghanistan, they met two Indian monks and together they returned to Luòyáng. The story goes that they carried Buddhist scriptures and statues on the backs of two white horses. In due course the temple was founded to house the scriptures and statues, and it was named after the horses.

The temple is 13km east of Luòyáng and can get crowded with tourists and hawkers. The sensible way to get there is to take a minibus from the area around the train and bus station for Y5. Alternatively, take bus No 5 or No 9 to Xiguan traffic circle at the edge of the old city walls and then walk east to the stop for bus No 56, which will take you to the temple. Entry is Y18.

LUÒYÁNG

PLACES TO STAY	OTHER	8 PSB
2 Tiān Xiāng Fàndiàn 天香饭店	1 Train Station 火车站	公安局
13 Peony Hotel 牡丹饭店	3 Long-Distance Bus Station 长途汽车站	9 Bank of China (Main Branch) 中国银行
14 Huāchéng Fàndiàn 花城饭店	4 Xī Guān (West Gate) 西关	10 Luòyáng Bówùguǎn 洛阳博物馆
16 Yǒuyì Bīnguǎn 友谊宾馆	5 Night Market 南大街夜市	11 CTS 中国旅行社
17 Xīn Yǒuyì Bīnguǎn 新友谊宾馆	6 Wén Fēng Tǎ 文峰塔	12 Bank of China 中国银行
	7 Post Office 邮电局	15 Yǒuyì Shāngdiàn 友谊商店
		18 CITS 中国国际旅行社

Wángchéng Gōngyuán
King City Park

The Jiàn Hé runs through the park. In the north-western section, across the river, there's a tiny, depressing zoo. There's also an underground 'theme park' with moving dinosaur models and an assortment of polystyrene ghouls.

The Peony Festival, centred on Wángchéng Gōngyuán, is held from 15 to 25 April when thousands of tourists descend on Luòyáng to view the peony flowers. If nature fails to provide sufficiently resplendent blooms, fake peonies are attached to the bushes.

Luòyáng Bówùguǎn 洛阳博物馆
Luoyang Museum

The museum is next to Wángchéng Gōngyuán and houses early bronzes, Tang figurines and implements from the Stone Age. There are some eye-catching pieces, especially in jade, and there are brief English captions for some exhibits. Catch bus No 2 from the train station.

Luòyáng Gǔmù Bówùguǎn
洛阳古墓博物馆
Luoyang Museum of Ancient Tombs

This is a new museum that has a number of restored tombs ranging from the Han to the Song dynasties and includes the Han tombs formerly located in Wángchéng Gōngyuán. The museum is underground and consists of brick-lined vaults with painted murals, carvings and burial items that were discovered when the tombs were excavated. There are a few English captions. Entry is Y12.

The museum is on the road to the airport, north of the city. Take bus No 83 from the stop opposite the long-distance bus station and ask the driver to let you off at the turnoff to the museum. A minivan taxi will take you there for Y10.

Places to Stay

Tiān Xiāng Fàndiàn (☎ 394 0600, 56 Jinguyuan Lu) has singles/twins without bath for Y45/44 and air-con twins with bath for Y130. The staff may refuse to rent you an inexpensive room.

The *Huāchéng Fàndiàn* (☎ 485 7115, 49 Zhongzhou Xilu) has twins (no bath) Y40 and twins/triples with bath for Y80/135. Bus Nos 11, 54 and 103 run past it, get off at the stop after the Mǔdan Dàjiǔdiàn.

In the west of town, on Xiyuan Lu, are two Friendship Hotels. Catering to tour groups, both have twins starting at Y388 (plus Y15 tax). The older of the two, *Yǒuyì Bīnguǎn (Friendship Hotel;* ☎ 491 2780, fax 491 3808, 6 Xiyuan Lu) is a better deal and has a swimming pool. *Xīn Yǒuyì Bīnguǎn (New Friendship Hotel;* ☎ 493 1445, fax 491 2328, 6 Xiyuan Lu) is down the road and has doubles for Y498. Bus No 103 from the train station terminates close to the hotels (get off at the seventh stop). For a taxi, expect to pay

HÉNÁN 河南

Gǒngyì Shì

Gǒngyì Shì (Gǒngyì City), formerly called Gongxian County, is between Zhèngzhōu and Luòyáng and is home to a fascinating series of Buddhist caves and tombs built by the Northern Song emperors. Construction of the caves began in AD 517 and additions continued through the Eastern and Western Wei, Tang and Song dynasties. Today there are 256 shrines containing more than 7700 Buddhist figures.

The Sòng Líng (Song Tombs) are scattered over an area of 30 sq km, and within them repose seven of the nine Northern Song emperors (the other two were carted off by the Jin armies who overthrew the Northern Song in the 12th century). Some 800 years on, all that remain of the tombs are ruins, burial mounds and the statues which, amidst fields of wheat, line the sacred avenues leading up to the ruins. About 700 stone statues are still standing, and together they comprise the main attraction of the tombs. The statues illustrate a progression of styles, from the simplicity of late-Tang forms to the life-like depiction of public figures and animals.

Buses running on the old highway (not the freeway) from Luòyáng to Gǒngyì pass by one of the Sòng Líng sites. You can get off the bus there and visit the tombs, or you can continue on into Gǒngyì and hire a taxi to visit both the tombs and the Shíkūsì (Buddhist Caves). It's possible to do this in half a day; expect to pay about Y80 for the taxi. If you're coming from the direction of Zhèngzhōu, get off at Gǒngyì.

Entry to the Sòng Líng and Shíkūsì is Y5. From Gǒngyì there are frequent buses to Luòyáng and Zhèngzhōu.

around Y30 from Luòyáng airport or Y15 to Y20 from the main train station.

Peony Hotel (*Mǔdan Dàjiǔdiàn;* ☎ 485 6699, fax 485 6999, 15 Zhongzhou Xilu) is a high-rise joint venture. It's popular with foreign tourists, although it falls short of delivering international standards. Room rates start at Y550, plus 5% tax.

Larger, more luxurious hotels are expected to open soon – if they haven't already.

Places to Eat

Luòyáng is far enough west to give the local street food a slight Islamic touch. Cheap snacks include *jiǎnpào*, small fried pastries filled with chopped herbs and Chinese garlic, and *dòushāgāo*, a sweet 'cake' made from ground yellow peas and jujubes (Chinese dates), sold by street vendors for about Y0.50 a slice.

At night, the lively *street market* at the intersection of Nan Dajie and Zhongzhou Donglu in the city's east is a good alternative to staying in the railway area. Look for *shāguō*, a kind of meat and vegetable casserole cooked with bean noodles in a small earthenware pot.

The Tiān Xiāng Fàndiàn has a good restaurant with an English menu; nearby restaurants also have English menus. You'll find better 'sit-down' *restaurants* along Zhongzhou Lu. The Mǔdan Dàjiǔdiàn has a *coffee shop* with passable international-style meals.

Getting There & Away

Air Luòyáng is not well connected by air (consider flying into or out of Zhèngzhōu). The Mǔdan Dàjiǔdiàn has a small ground-floor travel office, as do the Tiān Xiāng Fàndiàn and the Yǒuyì Bīnguǎn.

There are flights to Dàlián (Y740) and Chéngdū (Y680).

Bus The long-distance bus station is diagonally opposite the main train station. Aircon Iveco buses do the trip to Zhèngzhōu on the freeway in about two hours for Y23, departing every 20 minutes. There are also ordinary buses to Zhèngzhōu (Y15; two hours). Buses to Shàolín depart every half hour (Y8; two hours); slow buses to Dēngfēng (Y10) take two hours. You can also get direct buses to Ānyáng (Y46; five hours) and Ruìchéng in south-western Shǎnxī (Y23; eight hours) from here.

Coach buses with sleeping berths leave in the evening from outside the train station for Běijīng (Y188; nine hours), Xī'ān (Y60;

10 hours), Tàiyuán (Y80; 11 hours), Wǔhàn (Y80; 15 hours) and Guǎngzhōu (Y260; 30 hours). There are also frequent minibuses to Gǒngyì Shì (Y7; one hour).

Train Direct trains go to Běijīng (Y112; 13 hours), Shànghǎi (Y246; 18 hours) and Xī'ān (Y61; eight hours). Note that there is also a two-tiered tourist train running between Zhèngzhōu and Xī'ān daily – it stops in Luòyáng en route to Xī'ān at 12.25 pm and arrives in Xī'ān around 7 pm the same day.

There are some direct trains north to Tàiyuán (Y108; 14 hours) and south to Xiāngfán (7½ hours) and Yíchāng (Y110; 13 hours). Yíchāng is a port on the Cháng Jiāng (Yangzi River), where you can pick up the Chóngqìng-Wǔhàn ferry.

Getting Around

The airport is 12km north of the city. Bus No 83 (Y1) leaves from the stop opposite the long-distance bus station to the airport. A taxi ride will cost about Y25 from the train station.

You can rent bicycles on the corner of Daonan Lu and Jinguyuan Lu, across the street from the train station, for Y5 a day. But check your bicycle carefully; the frame of ours broke within an hour. Red cabs and yellow minivan taxis are abundant and should cost about Y10. The bus system is also less crowded than other Chinese cities.

LÓNGMÉN SHÍKŪ 龙门石窟
Dragon Gate Grottoes

In AD 494 the Northern Wei dynasty moved its capital from Dàtóng to Luòyáng. At Dàtóng the dynasty had built the impressive Yúngāng Shíkū. Now in Luòyáng, the dynasty commenced work on the Lóngmén Shíkū. Over the next 200 years, more than 100,000 images and statues of Buddha and his disciples were carved into the cliff walls on the banks of the Yī Hé, 16km south of the city. The caves of Luòyáng, Dūnhuáng and Dàtóng represent the peak of Buddhist cave art.

Much damage was done to the sculptures at Luòyáng during the 19th and 20th centuries by western souvenir hunters who

beheaded just about every figure they could lay their saws on. These heads now grace the museums and private paperweight collections of Europe and North America. Among these were two murals that were entirely removed and can now be seen at the Metropolitan Museum of Art in New York and the Atkinson Museum in Kansas City. The Cultural Revolution also took its toll when the Red Guards arrived with hammers – the Ten Thousand Buddha Cave was particularly damaged during this period.

The art of Buddhist cave sculpture largely came to an end around the middle of the 9th century as the Tang dynasty declined. Persecution of foreign religions in China began, with Buddhism as the prime target. Although Buddhist art and sculpture continued in China, it never reached the heights it had enjoyed previously.

Bīnyáng Sān Dòng 宾阳三洞
Three Binyang Caves

The main Lóngmén Shíkū are on the Yī Hé's western bank. They stretch out along the cliff face on a north-south axis. The three Bīnyáng caves are at the northern end, closest to the entrance. Construction began on all under the Northern Wei dynasty and, although two were finished during the Sui and Tang dynasties, the statues all display the benevolent expressions that characterised the Northern Wei style.

Wànfó Dòng 万佛洞
Ten Thousand Buddha Cave

Just south of the Bīnyáng Dòng is the Tang dynasty Wànfó Dòng, built in AD 680. In addition to the legions of tiny bas-relief Buddhas that give the cave its name, there is a fine big buddha and images of celestial dancers.

Other images include musicians playing the flute, the *pípá* (a plucked stringed instrument), the cymbals and the *zheng* (a 13–14–stringed harp).

Liánhuā Dòng 莲花洞
Lotus Flower Cave

This cave was carved in AD 527 during the Northern Wei dynasty and has a large standing buddha, now faceless. On the ceiling are wispy *apsaras* (celestial nymphs) drifting around a central lotus flower. A common symbol in Buddhist art, the lotus flower represents purity and serenity.

Fèngxiān Sì 奉先寺
Ancestor Worshipping Temple
This is the largest structure at Lóngmén and contains the best works of art. It was built between AD 672 and 675, during the Tang dynasty. The roof is gone and the figures lie exposed to the elements. Tang figures tend to be more three-dimensional than the Northern Wei figures, standing out in high relief and rather freer from their stone backdrop.

Their expressions and poses also appear to be more natural, but unlike the otherworldly figures of the Northern Wei, the Tang figures are meant to be awesome.

The seated central buddha is 17m high and is thought to be Vairocana, the supreme, omnipresent divinity. The face is thought to be modelled on that of the all-powerful Empress Wu Zetian of the Tang dynasty.

As you face the buddha, to the left are statues of the disciple Ananda and a bodhisattva wearing a crown, a tassel and a string of pearls.

To the right are statues (or remains) of another disciple, a Bodhisattva, a heavenly guardian trampling on a spirit and a guardian of the buddha.

Yàofāng Dòng 药方洞
Medical Prescription Cave
South of the Fèngxiān Sì is the tiny Yàofāng Dòng. The entrance to this cave is filled with 6th-century stone steles inscribed with remedies for common ailments.

Gǔyáng Dòng 古阳洞
Earliest Cave
Adjacent to the Yàofāng Dòng is the much larger Gǔyáng Dòng, cut between AD 495 and 575. It's a narrow, high-roofed cave featuring a buddha statue and a profusion of sculptures, particularly of flying apsaras. This was probably the first cave of the Lóngmén group to be built.

Shíkū Dòng 石窟洞
Carved Cave
The Shíkū Dòng was constructed during the Northern Wei dynasty. This is the last major cave in the Lóngmén complex and it features intricate carvings depicting religious processions.

Getting There & Away
The Lóngmén Shíkū are 13km south of town and can be reached from the Luòyáng train station area by bus No 81 or from the Yǒuyì Bīnguǎn by bus No 60, which leaves from the stop opposite the hotel. Bus No 53 from the Xiguan traffic circle also goes past the caves. Minibuses go to the caves from the train and bus station area for Y2. Get off before the bus crosses the bridge and walk down the steps to the entrance.

Entry has soared to Y55. The caves are open daily from 6 am to 8 pm. It's good to go in the early morning to avoid the crowds and enjoy the best light as the morning sun hits the cliff side. To get a comprehensive view, cross the river and view the caves from the other side.

ĀNYÁNG 安阳
☎ 0372 • pop 5,076,600
Ānyáng is north of the Huáng Hé near the Hénán-Héběi border. As a result of significant archaeological discoveries, Ānyáng is now believed to be the site of Yīn, the last capital of the ancient Shang dynasty and one of the first centres of an urban-based Chinese civilisation.

Peasants working near Ānyáng in the late 19th century unearthed pieces of polished bone inscribed with an ancient form of Chinese writing that turned out to be divining bones with questions addressed to the spirits and ancestors. Other inscriptions were found on tortoise shells and on bronze objects, suggesting that the late Shang capital once stood here in the 14th century BC.

The discoveries attracted the attention of archaeologists, although it was not until the late 1920s that excavations uncovered ancient tombs, the ruins of a royal palace, and workshops and houses – proof that the legendary Shang dynasty had indeed existed.

Yīnxū Bówùgyuàn 殷墟博物院
Museum of the Yin Ruins

There is a museum at the Yīn site, but its collection is disappointingly limited. It includes reassembled pottery, oracle bone fragments and jade and bronze artefacts. There are no English captions, and it's a bit mystifying unless you're really into this stuff.

Bus No 1 from near the corner of Jiefang Lu and Zhangde Lu goes past the museum turn-off, then you have to walk across the railway tracks and head along the river until you come to the museum. It's open daily from 8 am to 6 pm; admission is Y10.

Yuán Shìkǎi Mù 袁世凯墓
Tomb of Yuan Shikai

A more recent remnant of Chinese history is the tomb of Yuan Shikai. He had it built in the style of the tomb of the American Civil War general and president, Ulysses S Grant, with some Chinese touches. It reflects, more than anything else perhaps, the Napoleonic aspirations of this man who started out as a Qing military official and eventually supported Sun Yatsen, only to wrest the presidency from him and attempt a restoration of the imperial system, crowning himself emperor in 1916! His coup was short-lived, however, and he was buried shortly afterwards in this tomb of his own design. It's 3km east of the Yīn museum; you can take bus No 2 from the train station. Get off at the bridge and walk north to the site. Entry is Y10.

Other Sights

It's well worth walking around the town's old section, a few blocks east of the train station and south of Jiefang Lu. For a view of the city, climb the **Wén Feng Tǎ**, a hexagonal Buddhist tower topped by a stupa.

Places to Stay & Eat

Fēnghuáng Dàjiǔdiàn (☎ 592 7207), on Jiefang Lu near its intersection with Xihuancheng Lu, charges Y70 for grotty twins without bath and Y96 for twins with bath and air-con. There is a good restaurant on the ground floor; beware of rats visiting your room during the night!

Ānyáng Bīnguǎn (☎ 592 2219, fax 592 2244, 1 Youyi Lu), up the road and across the street, is a nicer place to stay. Twins with bath start at Y138.

There are *restaurants* in the old town, particularly on Hongqi Lu, south of Jiefang Lu near the restored gate tower.

Getting There & Away

From Ānyáng long-distance bus station there are connections to Zhèngzhōu (Y30; four hours), Lìnzhoūshí (Y65; two hours), Tàiyuán (Y90; a rough 10-hour ride across the Tàiháng Shān) and Luòyáng (Y46; five hours). The long-distance bus station is a large orange-tiled building close to the train station. Turn right down the street after exiting the train station. Ānyáng is on the main Běijīng-Zhèngzhōu railway line and most express trains stop here.

AROUND ĀNYÁNG

About 50km west of Ānyáng, in the Tàiháng Shān foothills close to Hénán's border with Shǎnxī, lies **Línxiàn County**, although the name of the main town has been changed to Lìnzhoū Shí (Lìnzhoū City).

Línxiàn is a rural area that ranks with Sháoshān as one of the 'holy' places of Maoism because of the famous **Hóngqí Qú** (Red Flag Canal). To irrigate the district, a river was rerouted through a tunnel beneath a mountain and then along a new bed built on the side of steep cliffs. The communists insist that this colossal job, carried out during the Cultural Revolution, was done entirely by the toiling masses without the help of engineers and machines.

The statistics are impressive: 1500km of canal were dug, hills were levelled, 134 tunnels were pierced, 150 aqueducts were constructed and enough earth was displaced to build a road 1m high, 6m wide and 4000km long. All this was supposedly done by hand in keeping with Mao's vision of a self-reliant China.

There are daily buses from Ānyáng to Chángzhì in Shǎnxī that go past the canal site. An alternative route is to take a bus to Lìnzhoūshí and then transfer to another bus to the canal.

HÉNÁN 河南

JĪGŌNG SHĀN 鸡公山

Rooster Mountain ☎ 0376

Jīgōng Shān, on the Hénán-Húběi border, was developed as a hill station resort by American missionaries in the early 20th century. It soon became popular with westerners living in Hànkǒu in Wǔhàn as a relief from the hot summers. Like Lú Shān in Jiāngxī, it's full of old European-style stone houses and has a refreshing setting but is smaller and less inundated with tourists.

Jīgōng Shān is dominated by **Bàoxiǎo Fēng** (Dawn Heralding Peak), a large stone outcrop resembling a crowing rooster, which is how Jīgōng Shān got its name. Climb to the top for a nice view of the surrounding area. Across the valley to the east, the former **American School** (Měiguóshì Dàlóu) is well preserved and worth a look. To the south, **Chiang Kaishek's Air Raid Shelter** (Jiǎng Jièshí Fángkōng Dòng) is part of his former residence and is open to visitors. The main village in Jīgōng Shān, known as **Nánjiē**, is on the western flank of the mountain overlooking the Běijīng-Zhèngzhōu railway.

The entry fee to Jīgōng Shān is Y50; it's open daily.

Places to Stay & Eat

Although less crowded than Lú Shān, Jīgōng Shān is a popular weekend getaway for tourists from Wǔhàn and Zhèngzhōu and there are many hotels.

On the road to the main peak, *Yúnzhōng Gōngyuán Zhāo-Dàisuǒ (Yunzhong Park Guesthouse;* ☎ *691 2033)* is an old stone villa with grotty triples (Y20 per bed) and basic washing facilities.

Further up the hill, *Yúnzhōng Bīnguǎn* (☎ *691 2033)* has beds in clean twins/triples with bath for Y90/Y60. The suites are Y360 and have terrific views.

Yǒuyì Bīnguǎn (Friendship Hotel; ☎ *691 2091)* is near Chiang Kaishek's former house and has twins with bath for Y180 and dorm beds for Y30.

All these hotels have *restaurants*. Nánjiē village also has a number of private restaurants with beds upstairs for Y20.

Getting There & Away

The station for Jīgōng Shān (with the same name) is on the Běijīng-Zhèngzhōu railway line. Normally you can take a train from Wǔhàn (four hours), but when we were there services had been temporarily suspended. They may have resumed. Buses from Wǔhàn leave from the Hànkǒu long-distance bus station and take about four hours. There are frequent minibuses to Xìnyáng (45 minutes), from where it's easy to catch trains to Wǔhàn or Zhèngzhōu.

It's 11km from the train station to Jīgōng Shān and minibuses make the trip for Y5. It's also possible to approach Jīgōng Shān from the south-east where a cable car takes people up for Y10/20 one-way/return.

KĀIFĒNG 开封

☎ 0378 • pop 5,573,300

Once the prosperous imperial capital of China during the Northern Song dynasty (AD 960–1126), Kāifēng is a charming city. It doesn't see a great deal of tourist traffic, and it deserves more than it gets. Kāifēng has been somewhat left behind in China's modernisation drive. While the locals tut with embarrassment about the lack of fast-food outfits and five-star hotels, for the foreign visitor there is much in Kāifēng that has disappeared from other parts of China.

It would be a good idea to get there soon, however. Even Kāifēng is slowly being nudged into the modern world. Whole blocks are being demolished to make way for the dreams of China's civic planners. The old city walls surround Kāifēng on all sides, but roads or new buildings frequently breach them.

Kāifēng was the first city in China where Jews settled when arrived, via India, during the Song dynasty. A small Christian community also lives in Kāifēng alongside a much larger local Muslim minority; you may see churches and mosques in Kāifēng's backstreets.

Orientation

The long-distance bus station and the train station are both outside (about 1km south) the old city walls; the rest of Kāifēng is

Kāifēng's Israelites

Father Nicola Trigault translated and published the diaries of the Jesuit priest Matteo Ricci in 1615, and based on these diaries he gives an account of a meeting between Ricci and a Jew from Kāifēng. The Jew was on his way to Běijīng to take part in the imperial examinations, and Trigault writes:

When he (Ricci) brought the visitor back to the house and began to question him as to his identity, it gradually dawned upon him that he was talking with a believer in the ancient Jewish law. The man admitted that he was an Israelite, but he knew no such word as 'Jew'.

Ricci found out from the visitor that there were 10 or 12 families of Israelites in Kāifēng. A 'magnificent' synagogue had been built there and the five books of Moses had been preserved in the synagogue in scroll form for more than 500 years.

The visitor was familiar with the stories of the Old Testament, and some of the followers, he said, were expert in the Hebrew language. He also told Ricci that in a province which Trigault refers to as 'Cequian' at the capital of 'Hamcheu' there was a far greater number of Israelite families than at Kāifēng, and that there were others scattered about. Ricci sent one of his Chinese converts to Kāifēng, where he confirmed the visitor's story.

Today several hundred descendants of the original Jews live in Kāifēng and though they still consider themselves Jewish, the religious beliefs and customs associated with Judaism have almost completely died out. The original synagogue was destroyed in a Huáng Hé (Yellow River) flood in 1642. It was rebuilt but destroyed by floods again in the 1850s. This time there was no money to rebuild it. Christian missionaries 'rescued' the temple's scrolls and prayer books in the late 19th century, and these are now in libraries in Israel, Canada and the USA.

---

mostly within the walled area. The city's pivotal point is the Sihou Jie and Madao Jie intersection; the famed street market here is particularly lively at night. The surrounding restaurants, shops and houses are of mainly traditional Chinese wooden architecture. Nearby is the Kāifēng Bīnguǎn and the Dà Xiàngguó Sì.

Information

The Bank of China is on Gulou Jie diagonally opposite the Dàjīntái Lügуǎn. Money also can be changed at the Dōngjīng Dàfàndiàn. There are post and China Telecom offices near the corner of Zhongshan Lu and Ziyou Lu, and on the corner of Mujiaqiao Jie and Wusheng Jiao Jie.

CITS (☎ 595 5130) has an office at 14 Yingbin Lu, next to the Dōngjīng Dàfàndiàn. The PSB is at 14 Shengfu Jie on the southern side of the street at the Zhongshan Lu corner.

More information about Jews in the region is available from the Kaifeng Institute for Research on the History of Chinese Jews (☎ 393 2178 ext 8010). The office is at the city museum.

Dà Xiàngguó Sì 大相国寺

This temple is next to a large Chinese-style market. Founded in AD 555, but frequently rebuilt over the following 1000 years, Dà Xiàngguó Sì was completely destroyed in the early 1640s when rebels opened the Huáng Hé's dykes, destroying the temple and the city. The temple was renovated in 1671 during the Qing dynasty. The temple is open daily from 8 am to 6 pm; entry costs Y15.

Tiě Tǎ 铁塔
Iron Pagoda

Built in the 11th century, the Tiě Tǎ is actually made of normal bricks, but covered in specially coloured tiles that look like iron. You can climb to the top of this impressive structure. The tiles on the lower levels have damaged buddha images.

HÉNÁN 河南

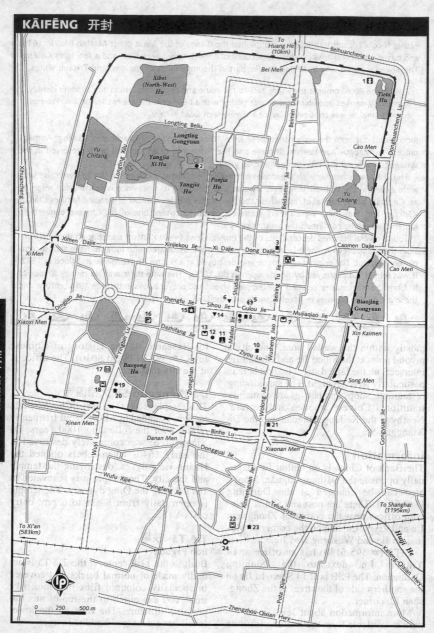

KĀIFĒNG 开封

Xibei
(North-West)
Hu

To Huang He
(10km)

Beihuancheng Lu

Bei Men

Tieta
Hu

1

Dongbuancheng Lu

Beimen Dajie

Cao Men

Longting Beilu

Longting
Gongyuan

Longting Xilu

Yu
Chitang

Yangjia
Xi Hu

2

Yangjia
Hu

Panjia
Hu

Beidaomen Jie

Yu
Chitang

Xhuancheng Lu

Ximen Dajie

Xi Men

Xinjiekou Jie

Xi Dajie

Dong Dajie

Caomen Dajie

Dong Dajie

3

Beixing Tu Jie

4

Cao Men

Dingliao Jie

Xiaoxi Men

Shengfu Jie

Sihou Jie

6

5

Gulou Jie

Bianjing
Gongyuan

Xin Kaimen

Shudian Jie

Madao Jie

Wusheng Jiao Jie

Mujiaqiao Jie

7

Yingbin Lu

16

15

14

8

9

Dazhifang Jie

13

12

11

Baogong
Hu

17

18

19

20

10

Ziyou Lu

Zhongshan Lu

Song Men

Wolong Lu

Xinan Men

Danan Men

Binhe Lu

21

Xiaonan Men

Dongguai Jie

Wu Lu

Wufu Xijie

Siyingfang Jie

Ximenguan Jie

To Shanghai
(1195km)

Telubeiyan Jie

To Xi'an
(583km)

Pota Xijie

Huaji He

Kaifeng-Qixian Hwy

22

23

24

Zhengzhou-Qixian Hwy

0   250   500 m

HÉNÁN 河南

KĀIFĒNG

PLACES TO STAY

3 Biànjīng Fàndiàn
汴京饭店

8 Dàjīntái Lǚguǎn
大金台旅馆

10 Kāifēng Bīnguǎn
开封宾馆

20 Dōngjīng Dàfàndiàn
东京大饭店

21 Téngfēi Bīnguǎn
腾飞宾馆

23 Biàndà Lǚshè
汴大旅社

PLACES TO EAT

6 Jiǎozi Guǎn
饺子馆

14 Dìyīlóu Bāozi Guǎn
第一楼包子馆

OTHER

1 Tiě Tǎ
铁塔

2 Lóng Tíng
龙亭

4 Kaifeng Synagogue
开封犹太教堂遗址

5 Bank of China
中国银行

7 Post & Telecom
Office
邮电局

9 Night Market
鼓楼夜市

11 Dà Xiàngguó Sì
大相国寺

12 Dà Xiàngguó Sì
Market
大相国寺市场

13 Post & Telecom
Office
邮电局

15 PSB
公安局

16 Yánqìng Guàn
延庆观

17 Kāifēng Bówùguǎn
开封博物馆

18 Western Long-Distance
Bus Station
长途汽车西站

19 CITS
中国国际旅行社

22 Southern Long-Distance
Bus Station
长途汽车南站

24 Train Station
火车站

Take bus No 3 near the long-distance bus station to the route terminus; it's a short walk to the park's entrance from there. Entry to the park is Y15; it's an additional Y3 to climb the pagoda, which is open daily from 8 am to 6 pm.

Other Sights

The large local museum, **Kāifēng Bówùguǎn**, on Yingbin Lu, just south-west of Bāogōng Hú, is now virtually empty (apart from a workmanlike display on Kāifēng's revolutionary history) – 'no money', the staff complain. The museum apparently has a Jewish stele and other artefacts from early settlers. Entry is Y5.

Lóngtíng Gōngyuán (Y15) is largely covered by lakes; on its drier northern rim near the **Lóng Tíng** (Dragon Pavilion) itself there's a small children's fun park with sideshows and bumper-car rides; old men often sit here playing Chinese chess in the shade.

The small Taoist temple, **Yánqìng Guàn**, has interesting architecture and a 13m-high pagoda. Admission is Y6.

Unfortunately, there is almost nothing left of the **Kaifeng Synagogue** (see the boxed text 'Kāifēng's Israelites' in this chapter) now the boiler room of the No 4 People's Hospital. You can see the remains of an iron

cover over an old well, which still has water. The staff at the hospital have seen so many visitors coming through, they'll know what you're looking for. The hospital is diagonally opposite the Biànjīng Fàndiàn on Beixing Tu Jie, on the route for bus No 3.

You can visit the **Huáng Hé** (Yellow River), about 10km north of the city, although there isn't much to see because the water level is so low these days. To get there, take bus No 6 from the bus station near the Tiě Tǎ to Liǔyánkǒu. It only does the trip twice a day, so a taxi might be better (Y50, including the return trip). About 1km east of where the bus terminates, there's a statue called the **Tiě Niú** (Iron Rhinoceros) which dates from the Ming dynasty and was meant to guard against floods.

Places to Stay

Kāifēng is rare in modern China – it's a place where independent travellers get a wider range of accommodation than those with lots of money to throw around and there seem to be no constraints on where foreigners can stay.

Biàndà Lǚshè (☎ 565 3163, 397 Xinmenguan Jie) is the white, four-storey building you see to the left as you leave the bus station. It's very basic inside (none of the rooms has a private bathroom), but has singles/twins from Y20/30, so you can hardly complain.

North of the station, right inside the city wall, is **Téngfēi Bīnguǎn** (☎ 596 7479, 218 Wolong Jie). Popular with Korean students, the hotel has beds from Y20 (triple with shared bathroom) to Y50 (double with bath).

One good place is **Dàjīntái Lüguǎn** (☎ 595 6677, 23 Gulou Jie), nearly opposite the Bank of China. It has a central yet quiet location in a small courtyard just behind the street front and offers twins with bath (including 24-hour hot water) for Y120. No-frills twins are available from Y20 and Y60. The staff could be friendlier.

Biànjīng Fàndiàn (☎ 288 6699, fax 288 2449, 109 Dong Dajie) is on the corner of Dong Dajie and Beixing Tu Jie, in the Muslim quarter. It lacks character but the rooms are clean. There's also a popular restaurant in the back of the hotel compound. Singles/twins with bath and air-con are Y160/140, and triples cost Y60 per person. Dorm beds go for Y25. To get there take bus No 3 from the long-distance bus station and get off at the sixth stop.

Kāifēng Bīnguǎn (☎ 595 5589, fax 595 3086, 66 Ziyou Lu), right in the town's centre, is a Russian-built structure, but done in the rather ornate style of traditional Chinese architecture. Twins and triples range from Y180 to Y240 in the pleb wings. There are more upmarket rooms in Building 2, where twins start at Y378. There's also a range of suites starting at Y420.

South of Baogong Park on Yīngbin Lu is **Dōngjīng Dàfàndiàn** (☎ 398 9388, fax 595 6661, 99 Yingbin Lu). It's a Chinese attempt to bring international comfort to the weary traveller. The staff speak some English. Twins in the newer rooms are Y228 and Y268. There are also twins for Y80 in the older rooms, but you can do better elsewhere. Bus No 9 from the train station goes past here. The hotel is opposite the western long-distance bus station.

Places to Eat

Despite its small size, Kāifēng offers some gastronomical delights, especially at the famed **night market** near the corner of Gulou Jie and Madao Jie. Worth sampling there is *ròuhé*, a local snack of fried vegetables and pork (or mutton in its Islamic version) stuffed into a 'pocket' of flat bread.

With a big bottle of beer costing Y2, this is the place to table hop and try the different small eats (*xiǎo chī*), such as hand-pulled and shaved noodles, roasted mutton served on metal skewers and dumplings.

As its name suggests, the government-run **Jiǎozi Guǎn** specialises in *jiǎozi* (dumplings). The dumplings here are tasty and inexpensive. Upstairs there's a much wider selection of dishes. It's on the corner of Shudian Lu and Sihou Jie in a three-storey traditional Chinese building with a quaint old wooden balcony where there are good views of the bustling night market.

The **Dìyīlóu Bāozi Guǎn** on Sihou Jie comes recommended and specialises in steamed buns. Try the *xiǎolóng bāo* (small buns filled with pork) for Y5. It's diagonally opposite the Jiǎozi Guǎn.

Getting There & Away

Bus Cars, minibuses and buses to Zhèngzhōu collect passengers at the bus station for Y15, Y9.50 and Y7 respectively. The western bus station, opposite the Dōngjīng Dàfàndiàn, has minibuses (Y15) and cars (Y15). Minibuses go to Luòyáng and do the trip on the freeway in 2½ hours for Y30.

From the southern bus station in front of the train station, there are three daily buses to Ānyáng (Y25; five hours) via Zhèngzhōu and irregular bus service to Bózhōu (Y22; six hours) in Ānhuī.

Train Kāifēng lies on the railway line between Xī'ān and Shànghǎi and trains are frequent. Expresses to Zhèngzhōu take about 1½ hours; to Shànghǎi, 13 hours; and to Xī'ān, nine hours. You can also get trains south to Bózhōu and Héféi in Ānhuī from here; departure times are inconvenient.

Getting Around

Buses are less crowded than other Chinese cities and travel to major tourist areas. Pedicabs and taxis are also available and congregate around the bus and train stations.

Húběi 湖北

Site of the great industrial city and river port of Wǔhàn, dissected by the Cháng Jiāng (Yangzi River) and its many tributaries, and supporting nearly 60 million people, Húběi is one of China's most important provinces. For most travellers, however, it's mainly a transit point, or the end point of the Cháng Jiāng cruise down from Chóngqìng (see the Chóngqìng chapter for full details).

The province actually comprises two quite different areas. The eastern two-thirds is a low-lying plain drained by the Cháng Jiāng and its main northern tributary, the Hàn Shǔi, while the western third is an area of rugged highlands with small cultivated valleys and basins dividing Húběi from Sìchuān.

The plain was settled by the Han Chinese in 1000 BC. Around the 7th century AD it was intensively settled and by the 11th century it was producing a rice surplus. In the late 19th century it was the first area in the Chinese interior to undergo considerable industrialisation.

WǓHÀN 武汉
☎ 027 • pop 7,239,000

Not many people go out of their way to get to Wǔhàn, but a lot of people pass through the place since it's the terminus of the Cháng Jiāng (Yangzi River) ferries from Chóngqìng. Livelier, less grimy and more modern than Chóngqìng, Wǔhàn is now enjoying a boom in foreign and local investment that may help it catch up to the comparatively sparkling, cosmopolitan citadels of Nánjīng and Shànghǎi.

Greater Wǔhàn's population is 7.2 million, making the city one of China's largest. It's actually a conglomeration of what were once three independent cities: Wǔchāng, Hànkǒu and Hànyáng.

Wǔchāng was established during the Han dynasty, became a regional capital under the Wu Kingdom and is now the provincial capital. It used to be a walled city, but the walls have long since gone. Hànkǒu was a village and became an important military

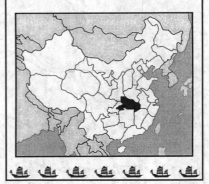

stronghold curing the Song dynasty. By the Ming dynasty it has been transformed into one of China's four major commercial cities. The Treaty of Nanjing opened it to foreign trade. There were five foreign concession areas in Hànkǒu – British, German, Russian, French and Japanese – all grouped around present-day Zhongshan Dadao.

With the completion of the Běijīng-Wǔhàn railway in the 1904, Hànkǒu continued to expand. A reconstruction effort started in 1895, following the Sino-Japanese War, sparked the initial expansion.

HÚBĚI 湖北

Many of the European-style buildings from the concession era have remained – particularly Russian buildings, along Yanjiang Dadao on the north-eastern bank of the Cháng Jiāng, and British, French and German structures, on Zhongshan Dadao. Government offices now occupy what were once the foreign banks, department stores and private residences. These European buildings and the density of development give Hànkǒu an unusually cosmopolitan atmosphere.

Hànyáng, which dates back to about AD 600, has long been outstripped by neighbouring Hànkǒu and today is the province's smallest municipality. During the second half of the 19th century it was developed for heavy industry, and in 1891 became home to the first modern iron and steel plant in China. This was followed during the early 1900s by a string of riverside factories.

The 1930s depression and the Japanese invasion ruined Hànyáng's heavy industry, and since the communists gained power the main economic activity has been light industry.

Orientation

Wǔhàn is the only city on the Cháng Jiāng that can truly be said to lie on both sides of the river. From Wǔchāng on the south-eastern bank, the city spreads across the Cháng Jiāng to Hànkǒu and Hànyáng, the two separated by the smaller Hàn Shǔi.

Two bridges cross the Cháng Jiāng: an older one in the south and a new one to the north. A shorter bridge spans the Hàn Shǔi linking Hànyáng with Hànkǒu. Ferries and speedboats cross the rivers continuously throughout the day.

The city's real centre is Hànkǒu, especially the area around Zhongshan Dadao, although 'central' Wǔhàn seems to be shifting gradually northwards, across Jiefang Dadao, Hànkǒu's principal thoroughfare. Most of Hànkǒu's hotels, department stores, restaurants and street markets are within this sector, which is surrounded by quieter residential areas.

The area around the Jianghan Lu and Zhongshan Lu intersection is lively, particularly during the evening when the night markets open. Hànkǒu has an enormous

train station 5km north-west of town. There is an older disused station north-west on the Zhongshan Dadao and Chezhan Lu intersection. The main Wǔhàn ferry terminal is also in Hànkǒu.

The Tiānhé international airport is about 30km north of Hànkǒu.

On the other side of the river, Wǔchāng is a modern district with long, wide avenues lined with drab concrete blocks of flats, businesses and restaurants. Many recreational areas and the Húběi Shěng Bówùguǎn are on the Wǔchāng side of the river. The city's second train station is in Wǔchāng.

City maps of varying quality are on sale around Wǔhàn; try the Xinhua Bookstore and the larger hotels.

Information

Money The Bank of China's main branch is in an ornate old concession-era building on the corner of Zhongshan Dadao and Jianghan Lu in Hànkǒu. The major tourist hotels also have money changing services.

Post & Communications The main post office is on Zhongshan Dadao near the Bank of China. If you're at the Chángjiāng Dàjiǔdiàn or Hànkǒu Fàndiàn, there is a convenient post office on the corner of Qingnian Lu and Hangkong Lu. Long-distance telephone calls can be made from China Telecom phones throughout the city. One convenient phone office is on the 2nd Floor of the Wǔhàn Xīn Mínzhòng Lèyuán, a popular shopping centre in a yellow concession-era building at 608 Zhongshan Dadao.

Email & Internet Access Travellers can send and retrieve email messages at the Internet Bar (Wànwéi Wǎngbā), which charges Y4 per hour. The bar is on the third floor of the Wǔhàn Xīn Mínzhòng Lèyuán. Internet prices drop to Y2 per hour at the China Telecom office one floor below. Another China Telecom office is on the 1st Floor of 51 Tianjin Lu and charges Y18 per hour.

Travel Agencies The helpful China International Travel Service (CITS; Zhōngguó

WŬHÀN 武汉

To Beijing (1231km)

To Xiangfan (334km)

Fazhan Dadao

Fazhan Dadao

To Tianhe International Airport (30km)

Jiefang Gongyuan

Wuhan Chang Jiang Er Qiao

To Shanghai (1043km)

Huangxiaohe Lu

Jianhe Dadao

Zhongshan Dadao

Sanyangqiao Lu

Qingnian Lu

Hankou

Bei Hu

Taibei Lu

Oliciang Lu

Xuangang Lu

Dazhi Lu

Taibei Yilu

Jianghan Beilu

Jiefang Dadao

Hankong Lu

Kinhua Lu

Zhongshan Gongyuan

Qianjin Lu

Zhongren Lu

Chongren Lu

Jiefang Dadao

Shundao Jie

Baohua Jie

Zhongshan Dadao

Hanzheng Jie

Wusheng Lu

Nanjing Lu

Lanjiang Dadao

Minsheng Lu

Chang Jiang (Yangzi River)

Han Shui

Yue Hu

Sha Hu

To Mao Zedong Bieshu & Hubeisheng Bowuguan (2.7km)

Cuiweilheng Lu

Lanjiang Lu

Yaolu Dr

Wuhan Changjiang Da Qiao

Hanyang

Yingwu Dadao

Minzhu Lu

Jiefang Lu

Minzhu Lu

Zhongan Lu

To Bayi Lu & Dong Hu (East Lake)

Wuluo Lu

Wuchang

Ziyang Lu

Zhongshan Lu

Ziyang Hu

Shai Hu

To Wuhan University

To Guangzhou (1064km)

Nanhu Hu

0   0.5   1 km

WǓHÀN

PLACES TO STAY

3　Shènglì Fàndiàn
　　胜利饭店
6　Jiāng Hàn Fàndiàn
　　江汉饭店
7　Xiéli Bīnguǎn
　　协力宾馆
16　Yínfēng Bīnguǎn
　　银丰宾馆
19　Xuángōng Fàndiàn
　　璇宫饭店
21　Holiday Inn
　　武汉天安假日酒店
22　Mèngtiān Hú Bīnguǎn
　　梦天湖宾馆
25　Xinhuá Jiǔdiàn
　　新华酒店
26　New World Courtyard
　　Wuhan
　　新世界万怡酒店
28　Chángjiāng Dàjiǔdiàn
　　长江大酒店
32　Holiday Inn Riverside
　　晴川假日酒店
40　Jiǔzhōu Fàndiàn
　　九洲饭店
41　Hánghǎi Bīnguǎn
　　航海宾馆

PLACES TO EAT

9　Lǎotōngchéng Jiǔlóu
　　老通城酒楼
20　Míng Diǎn Kāfēi Yǔ Chá
　　名典咖啡与茶

OTHER

1　New Hànkǒu Train
　　Station
　　汉口新火车站
2　PSB
　　公安局外事科
4　Old Hànkǒu Train
　　Station (disused)
　　汉口旧火车站
5　Měiměi Jiǔba
　　美美酒吧
8　China Telecom
　　中国电信
10　Advance Booking Office
　　(Train Tickets)
　　火车预售票处
11　Bank of China
　　中国银行
12　CTS
　　中国国际旅行社
13　Wǔhàn Ferry Terminal;
　　Huáyuán Yángguāng
　　Jiǔdiàn
　　武汉港客运站
　　华源阳光酒店
14　Hànkǒu–Wǔchāng Ferries
　　汉口武昌渡船
15　Wǔhàn Xin Mínzhòng
　　Lèyuán;
　　China Telecom;
　　Internet
　　武汉新民众乐园；
　　中国电信
17　Xinhua Bookstore
　　新华书店

18　Main Post Office
　　邮局
23　Long-Distance
　　Bus Station
　　长途汽车站
24　CITS
　　中国国际旅行社
27　China Southern Airlines
　　中国南方航空公司
29　CAAC
　　中国民航售票处
30　Hànyáng
　　Train Station
　　汉阳火车站
31　Guīyuán Sì
　　归园寺
33　Zhonghua Lu Pier
　　中华路码头
34　Huánghè Lóu
　　(Yellow Crane Tower)
　　黄鹤楼
35　Former Headquarters of
　　the Wuchang Uprising
　　武昌起义纪念馆
36　Wǔchāng Long-Distance
　　Bus Station
　　武昌长途汽车站
37　Jīnghàn Dàshà
　　京汉大厦
38　China Southern Airlines
　　中国南方航空公司
39　Wǔchāng
　　Train Station
　　武昌火车站

Guójì Lǚxíngshè; ☎ 8578 4125, ✉ hbcits@public.wh.hb.cn) is in Hànkǒu at 26 Taibei Yilu, diagonally opposite the New World Courtyard Wuhan. There's an enclosed parking lot outside and the building entrance has a CITS sign. Take the lift to the 7th floor. Bus No 9 stops near the western end of Taibei Yilu on Xinhua Lu: from there it's a five-minute walk.

Across from the Wǔhàn ferry terminal is a China Travel Service (CTS; Zhōngguó Lǚxíngshè; ☎ 8285 5259, ✉ mosso@public.wh.hb.cn) office, at 142 Yanjiang Dadao, that offers the usual services and has staff members that speak English.

PSB The PSB is at 306 Shengli Jie, a 10-minute walk north-east of the Shènglì Fàndiàn (see Places to Stay later).

Wǔhàn Chángjiāng Dàqiáo
武汉长江大桥
Wuhan Yangzi River Big Bridge
Wǔchāng and Hànyáng are linked by this great bridge (1100m long and 80m high). The 1957 completion of the bridge marked one of communist China's first great engineering achievements. Until then all traffic had to be laboriously ferried across the river. A second trans–Cháng Jiāng bridge in northern Wǔhàn was completed in mid-1995.

Húběi Shěng Bówùguǎn
湖北省博物馆
Hubei Provincial Museum

This museum is a must if you're interested in archaeology and is worth a look even if you're not. In 1999, a new building was opened to house a large collection of artefacts from the Zenghouyi Tomb, which was unearthed in 1978 on the outskirts of the city of Suízhōu, about two-thirds of the way to Xiāngfán from Wǔhàn.

The tomb dates from around 433 BC, in the Warring States Period. The male internee, whose surname is Yi, was buried with about 7000 of his favourite artefacts, including bronze ritual vessels, weapons, horse and chariot equipment, bamboo instruments, utensils, and gold and jade objects.

One of the most fascinating finds was a two-tone, seven-note scale of bronze bells. The 64 elaborate bells are played using hammer-like objects and poles. The entire bell set has intricate carvings and warrior figures serving as bases and shows that a musical scale existed in ancient China.

There are musical performances throughout the day on duplicate bells, and the Chinese performers introduce each song in English. Various examples of musical recordings are for sale at a museum counter.

The museum has informative photographs and English captions. Entry is Y10; open daily from 8.30 am to noon and 2 to 4 pm.

The museum is beside Dōng Hú (East Lake) in Wǔchāng, one of the most pleasant areas in Wǔhàn. Take bus No 14 from the Zhonghua Lu ferry pier (the dock closest to the old bridge) to the last stop, then walk back along the road about 10 minutes, where there's a sign for Mao Zedong's villa. The museum is down that road.

Day Trip In summer you can do a scenic day trip that includes the museum, taking a ferry over from Hànkǒu to the Zhonghua Lu pier in Wǔchāng, then boarding bus No 36 to Mó Shān. Take another ferry across the lake to Dōnghú Gōngyuán (East Lake Park), walk to the museum, then get bus No 14 to Huánghè Lóu (Yellow Crane Tower), and finally get a ferry back to Hànkǒu.

Máo Zédōng Biéshù   毛泽东别墅
Mao Zedong Villa

If you've just arrived from Húnán, you may have had enough of Mao by now. If not, stroll through the Chairman's bucolic hideaway here (Y10).

The villa tour takes in his living quarters, offices, private swimming pool and a meeting room where key decisions were made during the Cultural Revolution. Mao stayed here more than 20 times between 1960 and 1974, including nearly 18 months between 1966 and 1969. The pleasant tree-filled grounds have become a haven for a variety of birds. To get there, keep going past the provincial museum for about 10 minutes: there are signs to show you the way.

Wuhan University

Wuhan University (Wǔhàn Dàxué), beside Luojia Hill in Wǔchāng, was founded in 1913, and many of the charming campus buildings originate from that period.

The university was the site of the 1967 'Wǔhàn Incident' – a protracted battle during the Cultural Revolution with machine gun nests on top of the library and supply tunnels dug through the hill. For a bit of Cultural Revolution nostalgia take bus No 12 to the terminus.

Other Things to See

Doubling as a curiosity shop and active Buddhist temple, the Guīyuán Sì has buildings dating from the late Ming and early Qing dynasties. The main attractions are statues of Buddha's disciples in an array of comical poses. A few years ago the statues were out in the open, and the incense smoke and sunshine filtering through the sky-lights gave the temple a rare magic. Alas, no longer. The incense is considered a fire hazard, so now visitors have to make do with unlit offerings; entry is Y3.

To get there, take bus No 45 down Zhongshan Dadao and over the Hàn Shuǐ bridge; there's a stop near the McDonald's within walking distance of the temple. The temple is on Cuiweiheng Lu at the junction with Cuiwei Lu. A trinket market sets up along Cuiwei Lu.

A former military observation post, the **Huánghè Lóu**, sits at the southern end of the Wǔhàn Chángjiāng Dàqiáo and is one of Wǔhàn's noted landmarks. Standing over 51m high, the five-level tower is more of a tourist trap today. Entrance is Y30. The double-decker bus No 64 loops the city and stops near the tower.

At the beginning of Wuluo Lu below the Huánghè Lóu, there is a small square with a statue of Sun Yatsen. Behind the statue is a colonial-style red brick building that is the **former headquarters of the Wuchang uprising** (Xīnhàigémìng Wǔchāng Qǐyì Jìniànguǎn) of 10 October 1911, which marked the end of the Qing dynasty. Sun Yatsen wasn't even in China at that time, but he returned as president of the new republic. The exhibit is rather pathetic, but the building is interesting. Entry is Y10.

Places to Stay – Budget

Many budget places in Wǔhàn have closed their doors to foreigners. But in early 2000 some mid-range hotels were offering significant discounts. While a bit difficult to get to, accommodation at the universities is the cheapest. The **Foreign Student Dormitory** (Liúxuéshēnglóu; ☎ 8768 2813) at Wuhan University has spartan rooms for Y30 per bed. New dorms are expected, if they're not already up and prices may increase.

Up the road from there, the **Foreign Experts Guesthouse** (Wàiguó Zhuānjiā Zhāodàisuǒ; ☎ 8768 2930) has large twin rooms with attached bath and air-con for Y180. Both these places will accept travellers, but it's best to phone first. They are located in the eastern part of the campus and it's a long 20-minute slog up the hill. You might be better off hiring a motorcycle with side-car at the entrance that will take you up for Y8. Wuhan University is located in Wǔchāng's eastern end. Bus No 12 from Zhonghua Lu pier will take you there.

A far more convenient choice in Wǔchāng is **Hánghǎi Bīnguǎn** (Marine Hotel; ☎ 8804 3395, fax 8807 8717, 460 Zhongshan Lu), which is diagonally opposite the train station and underneath the overpass on Zhongshan Lu. The manager,

Cheng Hongqing, is friendly and helpful and may give you a tour of the city. Singles/doubles with bath are Y110/130.

The **Jīnghàn Dàshà** (Chinese Capital Hotel; ☎ 8782 5700, fax 8736 7885, 442 Wuluo Lu) is next to the long-distance bus station in Wǔchāng. The hotel offers some good deals with singles/twins with bath for Y128/148.

In Hànkǒu, next to the bus station is the **Mèngtiān Hú Bīnguǎn** (Mengtian Lake Hotel; ☎ 8571 6595 ext 8888, 1305 Jiefang Dadao). The somewhat cavernous rooms look like former karaoke parlours with beds, but the prices – especially for solo travellers – are right. Singles/doubles with shared bath are Y78/118.

Places to Stay – Mid-Range

Given its prime location in Hànkǒu, the **Huáyuán Yángguāng Jiǔdiàn** (Magnificent Sunshine Hotel; ☎ 8280 1366, fax 8283 4128, 997 Zhongshan Dadao) is a decent place to stay. Singles and doubles with bath cost Y288, but the staff may give you either for Y150.

In central Hànkǒu, the renovated **Xīnhuá Jiǔdiàn** (☎ 8579 0333, 162 Jianghan Beilu) is on a side street off Jianghan Beilu just around the corner from Xinhua Lu. The hotel has air-con doubles/triples without bath for Y128/180 and doubles/triples with bath for Y268/348.

Just north of and opposite the Wǔhàn ferry terminal, **Xiélì Bīnguǎn** (☎ 8280 3903, 2 Tianjin Lu) has decent twins for Y200. It's handy for those late-night Cháng Jiāng cruise arrivals.

Shènglì Fàndiàn (Victory Hotel; ☎ 8270 7241, fax 8270 7604, 1 Siwei Lu), an old British-built guesthouse on the corner of Shengli Jie and Siwei Lu, has standard twins for US$37. It's a bit out of the way, but there are buses along Shengli Jie.

Costing a bit more, but definitely worth it, is **Yínfēng Bīnguǎn** (☎ 8568 0711, fax 8564 8511, 400 Zhongshan Dadao). Twins are Y318/348 and feature clean wooden floors, sparkling bathrooms and great water pressure for showers. Depending on the season, the hotel may lower its rates.

Over in Wǔchāng and very convenient to the train station, *Jiǔzhōu Fàndiàn* (☎ *8804 2120, fax 8804 2784)* has twins for Y168. The hotel is at the far left of the square as you exit the station.

Places to Stay – Top End

Jiāng Hàn Fàndiàn (☎ *8281 1600, fax 8281 4342, 245 Shengli Jie)*, near the disused Hànkǒu train station, is the place to stay if you can afford it. Built by the French in 1914 as the Demin Hotel, it's a former French embassy and one of the best examples of colonial architecture in this part of China. The interior is impressive. Rates range from US$80 for a twin to US$280 for a suite, plus a 15% surcharge. The hotel has its own post office, shops and an excellent restaurant.

Chángjiāng Dàjiǔdiàn (☎ *8363 2828, fax 8364 4110, 1131 Jiefnag Dadao)*, on the corner of Jiefang Dadao and Qingnian Lu, has singles/doubles starting at Y280/380 (plus 15%). The hotel is quite good, but this intersection now resembles a freeway junction due to an adjacent noisy traffic overpass.

Xuángōng Fàndiàn (☎ *8281 0365, fax 8281 6942, 57 Jianghan Yi Lu)* conveniently located in Wǔhàn's city centre offers clean singles/doubles with bath and balconies for Y380/480. Negotiating will help. The hotel occupies a British-designed building; the only setback is street noise at night.

Although inconveniently located, the plain-looking *New World Courtyard Wuhan* (*Xīnshìjiè Wànyí Jiǔdiàn;* ☎ *8578 7968, fax 8578 9171, 9 Taibei Yilu)* offers three-star service and twins for US$109 (plus 15%). Prices seem negotiable. It's a good spot for international food (see Places to Eat following).

Holiday Inn (*Jiàrì Jiǔdiàn;* ☎ *8586 7888, fax 8584 5353, 868 Jiefang Dadao)* is the best hotel in town; standard singles/twins are US$120/130. It's about 100m southwest of the intersection with Jianghan Lu.

Holiday Inn also manages the revamped *Holiday Inn Riverside* (*Qíngchuān Jiàrì Jiǔdiàn;* ☎ *8471 6688, fax 8471 6181, 88 Xima Chang Jie)*, in a prime location on the edge of the river north of the old Cháng Jiāng bridge in Hànyáng.

Places to Eat

Wǔhàn has some pretty good eating houses in all price ranges. Popular local snacks include fresh catfish from the nearby Dōng Hú and charcoal-grilled whole pigeons served with a sprinkling of chilli. You can try some of these dishes on the *floating restaurants* at the end of Bayi Lu on the shore of Dōng Hú, where you can pick your catfish before they cook it.

Good streets for *night food* are Minsheng Lu and Jianghan Lu, both running off Zhongshan Dadao. If you have a craving for western food, there's no better spot than the New World Courtyard Wuhan's coffee shop; prices at the Holiday Inn are also reasonable.

Bakeries with crunchy rolls and French bread are also fairly common. There's a good one in the lobby of the Holiday Inn on Jiefang Dadao.

The *Lǎotōngchéng Jiǔlóu* at 1 Dazhi Lu on the corner with Zhongshan Dadao is a bustling canteen and a great place to people watch. It serves a tasty snack called *dòupí,* which looks like a stuffed omelette but is actually made with a bean curd base – its name translates as 'bean skin' – and is served rolled around a filling of rice and diced meat, vegetables *(shuāngdōng dòupí)* or egg *(dànguāng dòupí)*.

The Lǎotōngchéng was apparently a favourite of Mao's, although presumably he didn't have to push and shove with the proletariat to get his dòupí. Dòupí is no great delicacy, but at Y4 a serving you can't go wrong.

Entertainment

Wǔhàn nightlife has taken off with discos and nightclubs opening all over Hànkǒu. The new *Měiměi Jiǔbā (Meimei Bar)* on Xianggang Lu is the latest rage. At the Xianggang Lu and Jiefang Dadao intersection, walk north for about 10 minutes; the club is on your left.

Caffeine lovers will enjoy the numerous cafes that have sprouted up around the city. Try the Taiwanese-run *Míng Diǎn Kāfēi*

Yǔ Chá (Ming Dian Coffee Lounge, ☎ 8583 2256, 35 Jiefang Dadao). Located near the Holiday Inn and rows of teahouses, the upmarket Míng Diǎn pours espresso for Y22 and cappuccino for Y28. There are other cafes on the corner of Tianjin Lu and Yanjiang Dadao.

Getting There & Away

The best way of getting to eastern destinations such as Nánjīng and Shànghǎi is by air or river ferry, rather than the circuitous rail route.

Air The main CAAC ticket office is at 151 Liji Beilu in Hànkǒu, but it's better to go to the China Southern Airlines (☎ 8361 1756) outlet at 1 Hangkong Lu right near the Chángjiāng Dàjiǔdiàn. In Wǔchāng there is a China Southern Airlines office (☎ 8764 5121) at 586 Wulou Lu. The arilines offers air connections to virtually all major cities in China, including daily flights to Běijīng (Y860), Guǎngzhōu (Y740), Kūnmíng (Y1050), Shànghǎi (Y650) and Shēnzhèn (Y780); and several each week to Chéngdū (Y750), Fúzhōu (Y620), Hong Kong (Y1550) and Xī'ān (Y550).

You can also find a number of air ticket outlets in the area around the Wǔchāng train station.

Bus The main long-distance bus station is in Hànkǒu on Jiefang Dadao, between Xinhua Lu and Jianghan Lu. Buses to Wǔdāng Shān leave from the Wǔchāng bus station, which is south-east of Zhongshan Lu on Wuluo Lu, and marked by a pedestrian bridge crossing. From Hànkǒu there are daily departures to Chángshā (Y82; five hours), Nánchāng (Y110; 10 hours), Zhèngzhōu (Y90; 12 hours) and Shànghǎi (Y305; 16 hours).

One good way to get to Yíchāng is on a comfortable air-con bus run by the Jielong bus company, that leave every hour (Y98). The journey takes four hours on the freeway. A Korean joint-venture bus company, Hanguang, operates Daewoo buses that leave for Yíchāng every hour for Y88. Smaller Iveco buses do the same trip for Y72.

You can also get buses to Yíchāng, Wǔdāng Shān (Y87; nine hours), Shànghǎi (Y305; 16 hours) and other destinations from Wǔchāng bus station.

For travellers disembarking from the Wǔhàn ferry terminal, long-distance buses are waiting at the terminal's car park and go to Shànghǎi (Y306; 16 hours) Héféi (Y150; seven hours), Jiǔjiāng (Y80; four hours) and Nánjīng (Y190; nine hours) as well as other cities. As you enter the terminal's waiting hall, the booking office is to your right.

Train Wǔhàn is on the main Běijīng-Guǎngzhōu line; express trains to Kūnmíng, Xī'ān and Lánzhōu run via the city. Most trains that go through Wǔhàn stop at both Hànkǒu and Wǔchāng train stations. Note that many southbound trains originating in Wǔhàn, including trains to Wǔdāng Shān (Y150; 12 hours), depart from Wǔchāng station rather than Hànkǒu.

At Hànkǒu station, hard and soft sleepers must be booked in the small ticket office between the waiting hall and the main ticket office.

There is also a train ticket office at 24 Baohua Jie in central Hànkǒu where Zhongshan Dadao briefly divides into Baohua Jie at the intersection with Nanjing Lu. You can book sleepers three days in advance.

Note that many southbound trains originating at Wǔhàn depart from Wǔchāng station rather than Hànkǒu. Tickets for these must be bought at Wǔchāng. Window 18 is for foreigners, but you can go to any window. CITS can book sleepers for a Y50 service charge.

The Běijīng-Kowloon express train also goes through Wǔchāng, but it does not stop in Hànkǒu.

Some sample hard-sleeper tickets are Běijīng (Y281; 12 hours), Guǎngzhōu (Y257; 17 hours), Guìlín (Y212; 12 hours), Kūnmíng (Y394; 24 hours), Shànghǎi (Y262; seven hours) and Xī'ān (Y215; 16 hours).

Boat You can catch ferries from Wǔhàn along the Cháng Jiāng, either east to Shànghǎi or west to Chóngqìng (see the 'Downriver on the Cháng Jiāng (Yangzi

River)' section in the Chóngqìng chapter
for full details).

Getting Around
To/From the Airport Buses to Tiānhé international airport (Y10; 40 minutes) leave
12 times a day from the China Southern
Airlines office on Hangkong Lu and five
times daily from the office on Wuluo Lu in
Wǔchāng. A taxi to the airport should cost
about Y80 and take half an hour; enterprising taxi drivers may try to undercut the airport bus and offer a ride for Y20.

Bus & Ferry Bus routes crisscross the city,
but getting where you want to go may mean
changing at least once. A useful bus is the
No 38, which passes the Jiāng Hàn Fàndiàn
to and from the new Hànkǒu train station.
Bus No 9 runs from the train station down
Xinhua Lu to the Wǔhàn ferry terminal.

In Wǔchāng, bus No 12 runs from Wuhan
University to the Zhonghua Lu ferry pier,
and bus Nos 503 and 601 go from the
Hànkǒu ferry terminal across to Wǔchāng.
Motor-tricycles and pedicabs wait outside
the main train stations and the Wǔhàn ferry
terminal, as well as the smaller ferry docks.

The Hànkǒu-Wǔchāng ferries are normally a more convenient, and always a much
faster, way of crossing the river. The large
boats take 20 minutes to make the crossing,
while smaller speedboats, which carry around
15 people, do it in five minutes for Y5.

WǓDĀNG SHĀN 武当山
☎ 0719
The Wǔdāng mountains stretch for 400km
across north-western Húběi and are sacred
to Taoists. Situated south-east of Shíyǎn,
the highest summit is the 1612m Tiānzhù
Fēng, which translates as 'Pillar Propping
Up the Sky' or 'Heavenly Pillar Peak'.

A number of Taoist temples were built on
the range during the construction sprees of
Ming emperors Cheng Zu and Zhen Wu.
Noted temples include the Jīn Diàn on
Tiānzhù Fēng, which was built entirely of
gilded copper in 1416; the hall contains a
bronze statue of Zhen Wu, who became a
Taoist deity.

The Zǐxiāo Gōng (Purple Cloud Temple)
stands on Zhǎnqí Fēng (Soaring Flag Peak),
and the Nanyan Gōng perches on the South
Cliff. Wǔdāng Shān is also famous for the
Wǔdāng Shān-style of martial arts developed here, and there are numerous schools
in and around the town.

The train station is called Wǔdāng Shān,
but the town used to go by the name of
Laoying. The entrance gate to the mountain
is about 1km east of the town; entry costs
Y21 and it's another Y10 to view the Jīn
Diàn (Golden Hall) when you get to the top.

It's 10km from the entrance gate to the
parking lot up the mountain, then another
two hours hike up to Tiānzhù Fēng. There
are walking paths up from the entrance gate,
but most people take a minivan taxi up to
the parking lot for Y10. At the time of writing a cable car was being constructed.

Places to Stay & Eat
On the main street of Wǔdāng Shān town,
directly down from the train station,
Xuánwǔ Dàjiǔdiàn (☎ 566 6013), on
Laobai Lu, has beds in twins with bath for
Y20 per bed and twins from Y60 to 100.
There's no English sign, but it's right be-
side an ornate Chinese-style arch.

The best value in town is *Laǒyīng
Fàndiàn* (☎ 566 5347), which has clean
twins/triples for Y60/50 per bed. It's located on the main street east of the Yongle
Lu intersection.

At the end of Yongle Lu, beside the martial arts school, *Wǔdāngshān Bīnguǎn*
(☎ 566 5548, 33 Yongle Lu) is the town's
most luxurious place. Twins cost Y180.

You can also stay on the mountain.
Jīndǐng Lǚguǎn, below the temple on
Tiānzhù Fēng, has beds in twins/triples for
Y60/40, as well as bunk beds for Y25.
Bathroom and eating facilities are basic, but
there are fantastic views and you might
meet the resident Taoist priests.

Down at the parking lot, the best place to
stay is *Bǎihuì Shānzhuāng* with nice twins
for Y78 and Y120.

In town, there are a couple of good *private restaurants* on Yongle Lu near its intersection with the main road.

Getting There & Away

Wǔdāng Shān is on the railway line from Wǔhàn to Chóngqìng, but few trains stop and you may have to take a bus to Shíyàn (one hour). There are daily trains from Wǔhàn and Xiāngfán. There are also sleeper buses to Wǔhàn (12 hours) leaving from the bus station that is diagonally opposite the Xuánwǔ Dàjiǔdiàn.

Minibuses to Shíyàn go up and down the main street collecting passengers; tickets cost Y5.

SHÉNNÓNGJIÀ 神农架
☎ 0719

The Shénnóngjià district in remote northwestern Húběi has the wildest scenery in the province. With heavily forested mountains of fir, pine and hemlock – including something rare in China, old-growth stands – the area is known as a treasure trove of more than 1300 species of medicinal plants. Indeed, the name for the area roughly translates as 'Shennong's Ladder' to commemorate a legendary emperor, Shennong, believed to be the founder of herbal medicine and agriculture. According to the legend, he heard about some special plants growing high on a precipice, so he cut down a great tree and used it as a ladder to reach the plants, which he added to his medical collection.

As part of a more modern legend, Shénnóngjià is also famous for the sightings of wild, ape-like creatures – a Chinese equivalent of the Himalayan yeti or the North American bigfoot. The stories are interesting, but the creatures seem to be able to distinguish between peasants and scientists – molesting the former and evading the latter. Nevertheless, there is a small base station set up in the reserve with displays of 'evidence' of sightings. More real, but just as elusive perhaps, are leopards, bears, wild boars and monkeys (including the endangered golden snub-nosed monkey) that reportedly inhabit the area.

Foreigners are at least allowed into the area of the Shénnóngjià district near the town of Mùyúpíng, 200km north-west of Yíchāng. There are two high peaks in the area, Shénnóngjià Shān at 3105m and Lǎojūn Shān at 2936m. It's a six-hour bus ride to Mùyúpíng from Yíchāng, or you can take a boat to Xiāngxī (five hours) on the Three Gorges (Sānxiá) and from there it's a 90km ride to Mùyúpíng. From Mùyúpíng you will have to hire a car to get into the reserve.

The CITS in Yíchāng arranges a three-day tour that includes visits to botanical sites, rafting and Shénnóngjià Shān, but be prepared to pay up to Y2000 per person. The tour includes accommodation, although much of the time is taken up with transportation. Other travel agencies around the train station in Yíchāng also offer tours to Shénnóngjià, but you should specify the Mùyúpíng area unless you want some adventures with the police.

It may be possible to visit Sōngbǎi, an area in the Shénnóngjià reserve that has been off limits to foreigners in the past. In early 2000 the Yíchāng CITS was uncertain if foreigners needed a travel permit. The staff suggested checking with the PSB in Yíchāng or Mùyúpíng. Take care: if you do need a permit and are caught without one, expect a Y1000 fine and to be ejected from the area.

YÍCHĀNG 宜昌
☎ 0717 • pop 3,996,700

Just below the famous Three Gorges (Sānxiá), Yíchāng is the gateway to the upper Cháng Jiāng (Yangzi River) and was a walled town as long ago as the Sui dynasty. The city was opened to foreign trade in 1877 by a treaty between Britain and China, and a concession area was set up along the riverfront south-east of the old city.

Today Yíchāng is best known as the gateway city to the massive and controversial Three Gorges hydroelectric project being built at Sandouping, 40km upstream. Because it helps generate electricity for the area, the Gezhou Dam on the city's western end has also made Yíchāng noteworthy. Crews are also at work to complete a second bridge across the Cháng Jiāng which is expected to be finished in 2001.

A steady flow of Cháng Jiāng tourists passing through town is also swelling local coffers. Unless you have a special fondness

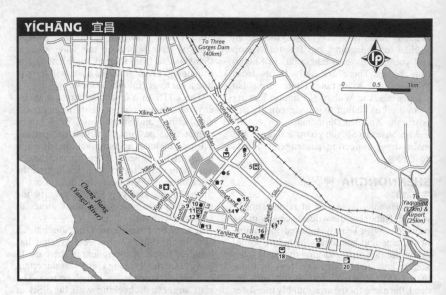

YÍCHĀNG 宜昌

for dams, there's really not much worth seeing in Yíchāng, but it's a useful jumping-off point for more interesting places.

Information

You can change money at the Bank of China on Shengli Silu near the Dàgōng Fàndiàn. The main post office is at the corner of Yunji Lu and Yiling Dadao.

The new CITS office (☎ 622 0837) is at 18 Longkang Lu, though residents still call the street by its old name, Kangzhuang Lu. CITS offers tours of the Three Gorges that include rafting trips (Y280 per person), but you will need at least four people for a tour.

The China Telecom office at the corner of Jiefang Lu and Fusui Lu offers Internet use for Y3 per hour.

Three Gorges Dam

Dam enthusiasts and people who like being around large rock-crushing equipment will enjoy taking a look at the construction site of the Three Gorges Dam (Sānxiá Shuǐlì Shūniǔ Gōngchéng), which is expected to be completed in 2009.

To get there, take yellow minibus No 4 (Y1) from outside the train station until it

arrives at the bus No 8 terminus. Bus No 8 (Y18 return) takes 40 minutes to reach the construction site and the drops you off at the dam's south-western end. Minibuses (Y20 return) and motorcycle taxis (Y10 return) can take you up the cement road to see the project; alternatively you can walk up the paved road.

Places to Stay

Between the Yíchāng ferry terminal and the Dàgōngqiáo ferry and bus facility is the economical *Wài Tān Fàndiàn Zhāodàisuǒ* (☎ 622 4532, 148 Yanjiang Dadao). Beds range from Y15 to 55 per person. Some rooms have heating and bathrooms and others don't. The staff only speak Chinese but are friendly and helpful; look for the hotel's name in red characters on a silver background.

About 1km west of the Dàgōngqiáo terminal is the better *Yíng Jiāng Bīnguǎn* (☎ 623 0743, 55 Erma Lu). Tidy twins start at Y118, but the staff may drop the price to Y80.

Just down the steps from the train station and to the south-east, the *Yángguāng Dàjiǔdiàn* (Sunshine Hotel; ☎ 644 6075, fax 644 6086, 1 Yunji Lu) is a good deal and

YÍCHĀNG

PLACES TO STAY & EAT	OTHER	9 Market
3 Yángguāng Dàjiǔdiàn 阳光大酒店	1 Sānxiá Bīnguǎn 三峡宾馆	市场
		10 CITS Air & Train Ticket
7 Táohuālíng Bīnguǎn 桃花岭饭店	2 Train Station	Centre 国际旅行社票务中心
12 Neptune Coffee 海王星咖啡	火车站	11 China Telecom 中国电信
13 Yíng Jiāng Bīnguǎn 迎江宾馆	4 Post Office 邮局	15 CITS 中国国际旅行社
14 Běijīng Jiǎoziguǎn 北京饺子馆	5 Long-Distance Bus Station 长途汽车站	17 Bank of China 中国银行
16 Yichang International Hotel 宜昌国际大酒店	6 China Southern Airlines	18 Dàgōngqiáo Bus & Ferry Terminal
19 Wài Tān Fàndiàn Zhāodàisuǒ	中国南方航空公司	大公桥客运站
外滩饭店招待所	8 PSB 公安局	20 Yíchāng Ferry Terminal 宜昌港

has clean, although slightly tattered, twins starting at Y100. There are other hotels around here that are also worth trying.

One luxury hotel with a great deal is the recently renovated *Táohuālíng Bīnguǎn* (☎ 643 6666 fax 623 8888, 29 Yunji Lu) in the middle of town. Nice twins with wooden floors start at Y398, plus 10% service charge. But the unheated twins with Chinese toilets (Y120) in an annex building are a great deal given the location. The hotel also has a bowling alley, swimming pool and very nice grounds.

Towering over the Cháng Jiāng, the *Yichang International Hotel* (☎ *Yíchāng Guójì Dàjiǔdiàn; ☎ 622 2888, fax 622 8186, 127 Yanjiang Lu)*, with a revolving restaurant at its top, is the city's newest luxury palace. Standard doubles start at Y428.

Places to Eat

Yíchāng has a variety of restaurants around town. For coffee, pizza or salad, visit the relaxing and somewhat surreal *Neptune Coffee (Hǎi Wáng Xīng Kāfēi; ☎ 622 9934, 40 Fusui Lu)*. The restaurant opened in 1999 and is popular with locals, though the Chinese-style pizzas are dry. The place does have a catch: it claims Chinese peasants first introduced pizza to Marco Polo, who returned to Italy in AD 1300 with the idea.

Near the Táohuālíng Bīnguǎn, the bustling *Běijīng Jiǎoziguǎn (28 Longkang Lu)* serves

up dumplings and an array of northern-style cold dishes. There is also a lively *night market* for dining on Taozhu Lu.

Getting There & Away

Air Yíchāng's airport is 25km south-east of the city centre and has flights to Běijīng (Y1040), Shēnzhèn (YY790), Shànghǎi (Y860) and other cities. There are a several ticket offices around town, especially near the train station and ferry terminals. There's a helpful China Southern Airlines office (☎ 625 1538) at 21 Yunji Lu.

CITS (☎ 622 8915) has a ticket centre that books flights and train tickets at 2 Erma Lu.

Bus The main long-distance bus station is south of the train station along Dongshan Dadao. There are also long-distance services from the two ferry terminals on Yanjiang Dadao. The Korean joint-venture Hanguang air-con bus to Wǔhàn (Y88; four hours) leaves from the main bus station every hour. There is also a bus to Mùyúpíng (Y46; six hours). The Jielong bus service to Wǔhàn (Y98) departs from the Dàgōngqiáo terminal; and Iveco buses to Wǔhàn(Y72) leave from the Yíchāng ferry terminal. Buses to Shànghǎi should cost around Y300 and take about 24 hours.

Train Yíchāng's train station is at the T-intersection of Dongshan Dadao and Yunji

The Three Gorges Dam

When completed in about 2009, the Three Gorges Dam (Sānxiá Shuǐlì Shūnjiǔ Gōngchéng) will be the world's largest water storage reservoir. A cherished vision since the early years of Republican China, long before the communists came to power, the dam proposal was finally given the go-ahead by the current government only in 1992, and one of its staunchest supporters from the beginning was Li Peng. This colossal project involves the construction of a 2km, 185m-high dam wall across the Cháng Jiāng (Yangzi River) at Sandouping, 38km upstream from the existing Gezhou Dam. The project aims to supply electricity, to improve the river's navigability and to protect against flooding. If all goes according to schedule, the gap will have closed by now, although the water level is not expected rise significantly for a few more years.

The Three Gorges Dam is a cornerstone in government efforts to channel economic growth from the dynamic coastal provinces towards the more 'backward' Chinese hinterland. The dam's hydro-electric production – reckoned to equal almost one-fifth of China's current generating capacity – is intended to power the continuing industrialisation of the upper Cháng Jiāng Basin.

Navigation upriver from Yíchāng has always been hindered by unfavourable conditions for shipping. Although passing the dam itself will be an inconvenience – the Three Gorges Dam will have five passage locks compared with just one lock on the Gezhou Dam – the navigability of the upper Cháng Jiāng will be drastically improved by the widening of shipping lanes and the creation of a more constant water level within the new lake. Inundation will eliminate strong river currents, and obstacles dangerous to navigation such as sand bars and submerged rocks will disappear completely.

At least as important will be the dam's role in flood control. The Cháng Jiāng is prone to repeated flooding, which has often resulted in great loss of life. Several catastrophic floods have occurred this century, in 1931, 1935, 1954 and more recently in 1991, when more than 2000 people are believed to have perished.

However, the massive scale of the Three Gorges Dam project has caused disquiet among environmentalists and economists, arousing some of the most outspoken criticism of government policy in China since 1989. Protests also centre on what will be a significant loss of cultural artefacts and important sites marking various periods of China's cultural history. Despite an ambitious plan of relocation and preservation, time is running out and the technocrats in charge of the dam project have not given this issue the attention it deserves.

The social and environmental implications of the dam, which will create a vast 550km-long lake stretching deep into Sìchuān, are profound indeed. When the back-waters build up behind the dam wall, the great inland port of Chóngqìng will become the world's first metropolis situated on the banks of a major artificial lake.

An estimated two million people living in the inundated areas will need to be relocated. Some destruction of the natural and scenic splendour of the Three Gorges is unavoidable. Boat trips of the Three Gorges are running overtime as local and foreign tourists rush to see one of China's most famous sights before the concrete slabs begin to spell the demise of a great river.

Construction of the dam will be enormously expensive, with a final cost probably in the vicinity of US$20 billion. Economists both in China and abroad have warned that it may be imprudent for the government to concentrate such investment into one single project.

Fears about the dam project were also heightened when information was released about two dams that collapsed in Hénán in 1975. After 20 years as a state secret, it is now apparent that as many as 230,000 people died in the catastrophe. Planners insist that the Three Gorges Dam will be constructed according to safety regulations that would make a similar disaster impossible – still, the collapse of the walls holding back the world's largest storage reservoir in one of the world's most densely populated area is a thought that must give even the most gung-ho supporters of the Three Gorges project nightmares.

Lu. The ticket office is on your left as you approach the main building.

Train service has improved in the past few years with trains going to Běijīng (Y318; 22 hours), Zhèngzhōu (Y190; 12 hours), Xī'ān (Y171; 20 hours), Huáihuà (Y66; 11 hours) and Guǎngzhōu (Y329; 25 hours). From Yíchāng, the best way to get to Zhāngjiājiè in Húnán is by train. The seven-hour journey costs Y60.

Boat All passing river ferries stop at the larger Yíchāng ferry terminal or the Dàgōngqiáo bus and ferry terminal. Travellers often find the two-day trip through the gorges between Chóngqìng and Yíchāng quite long enough, and some disembark or board here rather than spend an extra day on the river between Yíchāng and Wǔhàn.

There is also a hydrofoil service that goes to Wanxian in Sìchuān at the western end of the Three Gorges; the trip takes six hours.

Tickets are Y195. A hydrofoil goes to Chóngqìng; the 12-hour trip costs Y380. Tickets can be purchased at either of the ferry terminals.

For full details on Cháng Jiāng cruises, see the 'Downriver on the Cháng Jiāng (Yangzi River)' section in the Chóngqìng chapter. While both ferry terminals sell tickets east and west on the Cháng Jiāng, the larger Yíchāng ferry terminal is a better place to purchase tickets because it offers more service to destinations, especially east to Shànghǎi.

Getting Around

The airport bus (Y20; half hour) leaves from the Sānxiá Bīnguǎn. A taxi to the airport should cost Y60. Yíchāng's city centre is small enough that you can walk to many places. Bus Nos 3 and 4 (Y1) run from Yunji Lu, near the train station, to the ferry terminals. Motorcycles taxis (Y5) and taxis (Y10) are also available.

Jiāngxī 江西

Tucked between some of China's wealthier cities and provinces, south-eastern Jiāngxī sees few foreign visitors, which is part of its allure for independent travellers.

Jiāngxī entered the Chinese empire at an early date, but remained sparsely populated until the 8th century. Before this the main expansion of Han Chinese had been from the north into Húnán and Guǎngdōng. The Grand Canal was built from the 7th century onwards, it opened up the south-eastern regions and made Jiāngxī an important transit point on the trade route from Guǎngdōng.

Peasants settled in Jiāngxī between the 8th and 13th centuries. The development of industries such as silver mining and tea growing allowed the formation of a wealthy Jiāngxī merchant class. By the 19th century, however, the province's role as a major transport route from Guǎngzhōu was reduced by the opening of coastal ports to foreign shipping, which forced the Chinese junk trade to decline.

Jiāngxī also has Jǐnggāng Shān, one of the most famous communist guerrilla bases that travellers can visit. It was only after several years of war that the Kuomintang were able to drive the communists out onto their 'Long March' to Shaanxi.

NÁNCHĀNG 南昌

☎ 0791 • pop 4,078,900

A city of squat, box-like buildings, Nánchāng has a rhythm similar to other crowded metropolises in the new China – congested roads with horns blaring and locals hawking their goods.

The city's characters mean 'southern prosperity', but expensive hotel rooms and a lack of tourist attractions prompt many travellers to use this provincial capital as nothing more than a stopover, especially during cold, drizzly and grey days.

There are places to visit though, and the city's cramped backstreets and markets are interesting to explore.

Highlights

Capital: Nánchāng
Population: 41.1 million
Area: 166,600 sq km

- Jǐngdézhèn, China's most famous area for the production of porcelain and ceramics
- Lúshān, a hill resort where mountain vistas have inspired communist leaders and artists alike

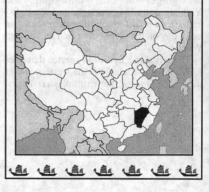

History

In modern Chinese history, Nánchāng is best remembered for the communist-led uprising of 1 August 1927.

After Chiang Kaishek staged his massacre of communists in March 1927, what was left of the Communist Party fled underground. At the time, urban revolution dominated Party ideology.

Kuomintang Army troops led by communist officers happened to be concentrated around Nánchāng at the time, and an opportunity for a successful insurrection appeared possible.

On 1 August (known as *bāyī* in Chinese) 30,000 troops led by Zhou Enlai and Zhu De seized the city and held it for several days until loyalists to the Nánjīng regime drove them out.

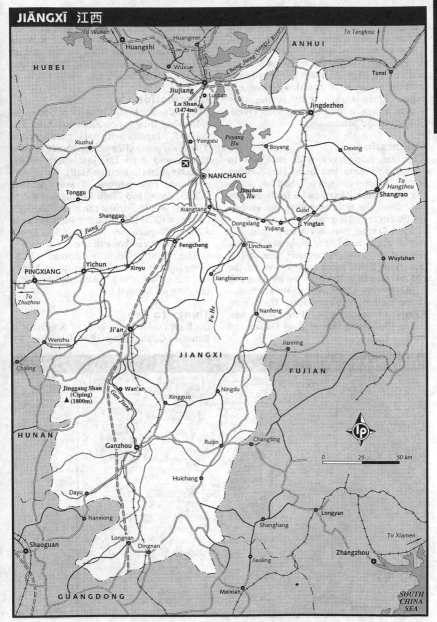

JIĀNGXĪ 江西

To Wuhan
Huangshi
Huangmei
ANHUI
To Tangkou
HUBEI
Wuxue
Tunxi
Chang Jiang (Yangzi River)
Jiujiang
Lushan
Jingdezhen
Lu Shan
(1474m)
Xiushui
Yongxiu
Poyang
Hu
Boyang
Dexing
Tonggu
NANCHANG
To
Hangzhou
Junshan
Hu
Shangrao
Shanggao
Xiangtang
Guixi
Jin Jiang
Dongxiang
Yujiang
Yingtan
Fengcheng
Yichun
Xinyu
Linchuan
Wuyishan
PINGXIANG
To
Zhuzhou
Jiangbiancun
Fu He
Nanfeng
JIANGXI
Ji'an
Jianning
Wenzhu
FUJIAN
Chaling
Jinggang Shan
(Ciping)
(1800m)
Wan'an
Ningdu
Xingguo
HUNAN
Gan Jiang
Ruijin
Changting
0   25   50 km
Ganzhou
Dayu
Huichang
Nanxiong
Longyan
To Xiamen
Shaoguan
Longnan
Dingnan
Shanghang
Zhangzhou
Jiaoling
GUANGDONG
Meixian
SOUTH
CHINA
SEA

The revolt was largely a fiasco, but the gathering of soldiers marked the beginning of the communist army in Chinese history. The army retreated south from Nánchāng to Guǎngdōng, but Zhu De led some soldiers and circled back to Jiāngxī to join forces with the ragtag army that Mao Zedong had organised in Húnán. From there, they sought refuge in the Jǐnggǎng Shān (Well-Shaped Ridge Mountains).

Orientation

The Gàn Jiāng is a river that lies to Nánchāng's north, and the Fǔ Hé (Comfort River), which branches off the Gan, sits to the city's west. Zhanqian Lu leads directly west from the train station to the Fushan traffic circle and overpass.

Bayi Dadao goes north-west from the traffic circle and is the main north-south artery through the city; another main strip is Yangming Beilu, which cuts east-west to the old and new Bayi Bridges over the Gan Hé.

Most tourist sights and facilities are on or in the vicinity of Bayi Dadao. The square Rénmín Guǎngchǎng sits at the town's centre, at the intersection of Bayi Dadao and Beijing Lu.

Maps Maps (Y5) are sold around the bus and train stations, and at the Xinhua Bookstores on Bayi Dadao: one at Rénmín Guǎngchǎng and the other on the western side of the street between the long-distance bus station and the Fushan traffic circle.

Information

The main Bank of China is opposite the Nánchāng Bīnguǎn on Zhanqian Xilu. The Jiāngxī Bīnguǎn will only change cash. There's a post office on the corner of Bayi Dadao and Ruzi Lu, just south of the Zhǎnlǎnguǎn (Exhibition Hall).

China International Travel Service (CITS; Zhōngguó Guójì Lǚxíngshè; ☎ 626 3437) is at 171 Fuzhou Lu; a smaller CITS office (☎ 622 1131) is on the 4th floor of the Jiāngxī Bīnguǎn (see Places to Stay later). Many hotels can book tickets.

The Public Security Bureau (PSB; Gōngānjú) is about 100m north of Minde Lu, the office is in a cream-tiled high-rise building on Shengli Lu.

Things to See

On Bayi Dadao in the heart of Nánchāng is **Rénmín Guǎngchǎng** (People's Square).

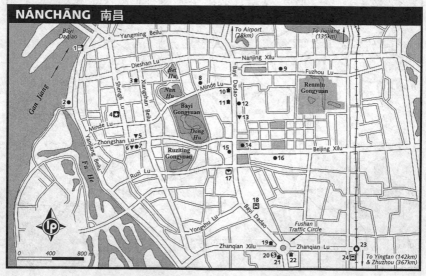

NÁNCHĀNG 南昌

Here you'll find the **Bāyī Jìniàn Tǎ** (Monument to the Martyrs), a sculpture of red-tiled flags and a stone column topped with a rifle and fixed bayonet. Opposite the square is the **Zhǎnlǎnguǎn** (Exhibition Hall), an immense building with a giant red star – a nostalgic tribute to Stalinist architecture now cluttered with advertising billboards.

The city's pride is the towering **Téngwáng Gé** (Jumping King Pavilion), erected in 1989, allegedly on the site of 28 previous reconstructions. Originally built during the Tang period, the nine-storey granite pavilion overlooks the Fǔ Hé and houses exhibition rooms with paintings, teahouses and the inevitable souvenir shop.

On the top floor is a traditional Chinese music and dance theatre with performances throughout the day.

The pavilion is open daily from 8 am to 5.30 pm. Entry is Y30 and includes a souvenir coin.

Other sights include the **Gémìng Lièshì Jìniànguǎn** (Memorial Hall to the Martyrs of the Revolution), on Bayi Dadao, north of Rénmín Guǎngchǎng. The hall's exhibits are in Chinese, but the archival photos from the 1920s to 1940s are worth the Y3 admission.

The **Residence of Zhou Enlai & Zhu De** (Zhōu Enlái Hé Zhū Dé Jiùjū), on Minde Lu, and the **Former Headquarters of the Nanchang Uprising** (Bāyī Nánchāng Qǐyì Jìniànguǎn), near the corner of Shengli Lu and Zhongshan Lu, are now museums.

Places to Stay

The best deal in Nánchāng is the *Xiàngshān Fàndiàn* (☎ 678 1402 ext 2800, 222 Xiangshan Beilu), although it's far from the bus and train stations. Triples with attached bath and air-con cost Y156, but the hotel will rent one bed for Y56. Twins range from Y160 to Y220. Take bus No 5 for nine stops from the train station; the bus stop is diagonally opposite the hotel entrance. There's no English sign, but look for a courtyard and the hotel disco (Y28), which the staff say is popular.

Around the Fushan traffic circle there are three hotels that are close to the train and bus stations. The massive *Nánchāng Bīnguǎn* (☎ 621 9698, 16 Bayi Dadao) has clean, comfortable twins for Y180 and triples for Y260.

The *Póyánghú Dàjiǔdiàn* (☎ 647 1188, fax 647 1177, 1128 Jinggang Shan Dadao), on the traffic circle's south-western side, is

---

NÁNCHĀNG

PLACES TO STAY
3 Xiàngshān Fàndiàn
 象山宾馆
10 Jiāngxī Bīnguǎn; CITS
 江西宾馆;
 中国国际旅行社
11 Jiāngxī Fàndiàn
 江西饭店
19 Nánchāng Bīnguǎn
 南昌宾馆
21 Póyánghú Dàjiǔdiàn
 鄱阳湖大酒店
22 Jiǔzhōu Dàjiǔdiàn
 九洲大酒店

PLACES TO EAT
5 Rosa Bakery
 罗沙蛋糕
6 St Hark Country Chicken
 美国胜哈客乡村炸鸡

13 Kěkě Kāfēi
 Bīngqílín Chéng
 可可咖啡冰淇淋城

OTHER
1 Nánchāng Port
 南昌港客运站
2 Téngwáng Gé
 腾王阁
4 PSB
 公安局外事科
7 Former Headquarters
 of the Nanchang
 Uprising
 八一南昌起义纪念馆
8 Residence of
 Zhou Enlai
 & Zhu De
 周恩来和朱德旧居
9 CITS
 中国国际旅行社

12 Gémìng Lièshì
 Jìniànguǎn
 革命烈士纪念馆
14 Rénmín Guǎngchǎng
 人民广场
15 Zhǎnlǎnguǎn
 展览馆
16 CAAC
 中国民航
17 Post Office
 邮电局
18 Long-Distance
 Bus Station
 长途汽车站
20 Bank of China
 中国银行
23 Train Station
 火车站
24 Minibuses to Jiǔjiāng
 往九江小型车

plush, with marble floors and an exercise room. It has twins for Y240 and triples for Y340. Both have attached baths.

The *Jiǔzhōu Dàjiǔdiàn (Lucky Hotel;* ☎ 610 8840, fax 621 9733, 25 Zhanqian Lu) may still be undergoing renovation, but its twins with bath and air-con cost Y238. The manager may part with one for Y180.

In the city centre, the *Jiāngxī Bīnguǎn* (☎ 622 1131, fax 622 4388, 368 Bayi Dadao) is popular with foreigners. The exterior is a relic of early 1960s socialist architecture, but the interior has a lot of marble and is quite shiny. Standard twins start at Y770, but the hotel may give a 50% discount, depending on the season.

The *Jiāngxī Fàndiàn* (☎ 621 2123, 356 Bayi Dadao) is a large complex around the corner. Triples are Y210 per room with air-con. Singles cost Y180, and twins with attached bath are Y120/210.

Places to Eat

As usual, the train station area is good for cheap eats. For street snacks try *xiànbǐng* (fried pancakes stuffed with vegetables). The ones cooked in electric fryers are less oily than the deep-fried variety.

The adventurous seekers of local cuisine may want to eat under the Fushan traffic circle, where entrepreneurs with woks and tricycles fry up tasty meat, tofu and other vegetable dishes for Y3, and you can sit at tables in the street.

Also on Bayi Dadao, near the traffic circle, there are several bakeries. One popular one on Zhongshan Lu, opposite the Former Headquarters of the Nanchang Uprising, is the Hong Kong-style chain, *Rosa Bakery (Luóshā Dàngāo)*, which has good bread and cakes.

For fast food try the Taiwanese-run *St Hark Country Chicken (Měiguó Shènghākè Xiāngcūn Zhájī; 378 Zhongshan Lu)*, near the intersection with Shengli Lu. The staff will want to speak English with you. The Jiāngxī Bīnguǎn also has international-style food and English menus.

The city has a pseudo-western coffeehouse, where travellers can unwind. The *Kěkě Kāfēi Bīngqílín Chéng* is on the 2nd floor of a building on Bayi Dadao, a few minutes south of the Gémìng Lièshì Jìniànguǎn. The menu has coffee (Y18), ice cream (Y28) and tea (Y8).

Getting There & Away

Air   The new Chāngběi airport is 28km north of the city. Flights go to Běijīng (Y1040), Guǎngzhōu (Y580), Hong Kong (Y1370), Kūnmíng (Y940), Níngbō (Y440), Shànghǎi (Y570), Wēnzhōu (Y490) and Xī'ān (Y810).

The main office of the Civil Aviation Administration of China (CAAC; Zhōngguó Mínháng; ☎ 627 8246) is at 37 Beijing Xilu, near Rénmín Guǎngchǎng, but the Fushan traffic circle and Zhanqian Lu near the train station also have travel agencies.

Chinese Eastern Airlines (☎ 627 0881) is at 87 Minde Lu, opposite the Jiāngxī Bīnguǎn.

Bus   Nánchāng's long-distance bus station is on Bayi Dadao, between Rénmín Guǎngchǎng and the Fushan traffic circle. Air-con buses go twice a day to Chángshā (Y75 to Y82; eight hours), Jiǔjiāng (Y35; 1½ hours) and the porcelain-producing centre of Jǐngdézhèn (Y32; 6½ hours). There are also buses to Jǐnggāng Shān (Y60 to Y74; nine hours) in Jiāngxī's south-western mountains, Lúshān hill station (Y37; 2½ hours) to the north and Guǎngzhōu (Y135; 15 hours). The bus station is open daily from 4 am to 10 pm.

Minibuses to Jiǔjiāng (Y20) run throughout the day and depart from the train station. Tickets for sleeper buses to various destinations, such as Guǎngzhōu (18 hours) or Shēnzhèn (20 hours) are available on the right as you exit the train station.

Train   Nánchāng lies off the main Guǎngzhōu-Shànghǎi railway line, but most trains make the detour north via the city. There are direct trains to Fúzhōu (Y100; 10 hours) once daily. Express trains run daily to the Cháng Jiāng (Yangzi River) port of Jiǔjiāng (Y22; 2½ hours), although the freeway to Jiǔjiāng makes it quicker and cheaper to do the trip by bus.

Boat The small Nánchāng ferry terminal is south of the two Bayi Bridges. An alternate route to Jǐngdézhèn is to catch a 6.30 am boat across the lake Póyáng Hú to Bōyáng, then a bus to Jǐngdézhèn. Tickets are Y26, and the trip takes seven hours to Bōyáng, then another two hours to Jǐngdézhèn. There are two daily fast boats that do the trip in three hours; tickets cost Y61. In summer, tourist cruise boats also leave from here.

Getting Around
Buses to the airport (Y15; 40 minutes) leave from the main CAAC office. A taxi will cost about Y100.

From the train station, the most useful public transport routes are bus No 2, which goes up Bayi Dadao past the long-distance bus station, and bus No 5, which runs north along Xiangshan Beilu. Motor-tricycles and meter taxis are available.

JǏNGDÉZHÈN 景德镇
☎ 0798 ● pop 1,404,700

An ancient town with many narrow streets and wooden buildings, Jǐngdézhèn manufactures the country's much-coveted porcelain. The city continues to be a major ceramics producer and attracts numerous buyers, especially from Hong Kong and Singapore.

Mass production may be comprising quality so purchasing good items depends on which factory made the porcelain and how much money you want to spend. The process of making fine porcelain dates back to the Song dynasty and is quite fascinating to observe.

The city has some charming back alleys but chimney stacks belching out coal from firing kilns dominate the city skyline, making the outskirts depressing.

In the 12th century the Song dynasty fled south after an invasion from the north. The Song court moved to Hángzhōu and the imperial potters moved to Jǐngdézhèn, near Gāolǐng village and the rich supply of Gāolǐng clay. The area also started producing pottery because locals noticed the clay's strength. Folk artists and rivers in the area assisted with production and transportation.

Today, the ceramics industry employs about 60% of Jǐngdézhèn's residents.

Orientation
Most of Jǐngdézhèn is flat and lies on the eastern bank of the Chang Jiāng (Yangzi River), and the main arteries are Zhongshan Lu and Zhushan Lu. Maps are available from newspaper stands, the Xinhua Bookstore and around the bus and train stations. The city centre can be walked easily.

Information
The CITS office (☎ 822 3925, 822 2939 for English speakers) is at 21 Lianshe Beilu, north of the Jǐngdézhèn Fàndiàn. The post office is on Zhushan Lu. The Bank of China is on Maanshan Lu, towards the train station.

Things to See & Do
The tiny side streets leading off Zhongshan Lu, particularly those in the older area between Zhongshan Lu and the river, are good for wandering.

Porcelain and ceramic lovers will enjoy Jǐngdézhèn's museums. To view exquisite vases, bowls and plates, try the **Táocí Guǎn** (Museum of Porcelain) on Lianshe Beilu, north of the CITS office. It houses a variety of beautifully painted porcelain from the Song, Ming and Qing dynasties and the post-1949 era. Entry is Y10.

The **Táocí Lìshǐ Bówùguǎn** (Museum of Ceramic History) is on the city's western edge. Its stone-and-wood structures house a modest collection taken from ancient kiln sites. There's a popular teahouse in the back near a lake.

As you face the museum, the **Gǔyáo Cíchǎng** (Ancient Pottery Factory) is to your right. It's a workshop where craftsmen demonstrate traditional Qing and Ming porcelain-making technology of moulding and baking.

The process takes about four days and has remained virtually unchanged since its inception. The ancient structures make it fascinating to watch, even though the factory is touristy.

To get there take bus No 3 past the long-distance bus station to the terminus near

Cidu Dadao. Walk under the stone gate and follow the road through forest and tea groves for about 800m to the museum entrance. From the city centre, a taxi will cost about Y10 and entry to the museum costs Y10. An additional Y10 is charged for entry to the Gǔyáo Cíchǎng.

There are **pottery factories** throughout the city, some of which were government run.

One small factory known for good quality duplicates from the Yuan, Ming and Qing dynasties is the Jingdezhen Jiayang Ceramics (Jiāyáng Táocí Yǒuxiàn Gōngsī; ☎ 844 1200), located in the city's eastern suburbs at 356 Chaoyang Lu. Vice Director Huang Yun Peng is the porcelain expert here. Bus No 3 heads east on Dong Erlu and goes by the factory. It may be more convenient to take a taxi.

To better understand porcelain, CITS has helpful English-speaking guides. A half-day tour costs Y100 and is worth it. Tours may include the city's museums, the **Yìshù Táochǎng** (Art Porcelain Factory), the **Měidiāo Táochǎng** (Porcelain Sculpture Factory) or the modern **Wèimín Táochǎng** (Weimin Porcelain Factory). Confirm with the CITS staff as to where you'll go because you may not see workers at all the factories.

Places to Stay

A central and inexpensive place is the **Jǐngdézhèn Fàndiàn** (☎ 822 2301, 1 Zhushan Lu). Its cheapest twins cost Y52 and have cement floors and leaky bathrooms. There are better ones for Y240. It's about a five-minute walk from the train station, and bus No 2 travels past the hotel.

The train station area is noisy but offers some deals. The inappropriately named **Wényuàn Dàfàndiàn** (Wen Yuan Grand Hotel; ☎ 822 4898) is next to the station and has singles for Y65 and doubles for Y90. There are cheaper rooms, but the staff may refuse to rent them to you. If you're a good negotiator, a bed in a triple is Y40.

The most luxurious hotel is the **Jǐngdézhèn Bīnguǎn** (☎ 822 5010, fax 822 6416, 60 Fengjin Lu), near Lianhuatang Lu. The three-star hotel is near a quiet lake park about 15 minutes' walk from the town

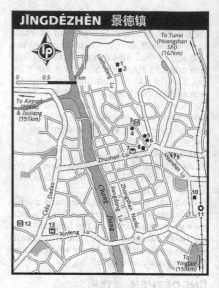

JĪNGDÉZHÈN 景德镇

centre. Porcelain-buyers often stay there. Prices range from Y280 to Y480 for an aircon twin with TV, phone and refrigerator. It has restaurants, a post office and a money-changing counter.

In the shadow of that guesthouse is the two-star **Jǐngdézhèn Bīnguǎn** (☎ 822 4927). This is the older place right behind the guesthouse; twins range from Y160 to Y220. It's a trifle run down but reasonable.

Places to Eat

There is no shortage of cheap eats in Jǐngdézhèn, particularly the tasty thick rice noodles known locally as liángbàn mǐfěn. At night there's a lively market area with restaurants near the Jǐngdézhèn Fàndiàn.

While it may not always have electricity, the delicious **Huáyuán Jiǔzhuàng** (China Garden Restaurant; ☎ 821 7879), next to the Táo Cí Guǎn on Lianshe Beilu, is known for its tofu dishes at reasonable prices. The restaurant has an eclectic English menu with french fries, eel and deep-fried frog.

Shopping

Porcelain is sold everywhere, piled on pavements, lined up on street stalls and

JǏNGDÉZHÈN

PLACES TO STAY	OTHER	7 Post Office
1 Jǐngdézhèn Bīnguǎn 景德镇宾馆	3 Táocí Guǎn; Huáyuán Jiǔzhuāng 陶瓷馆; 华园酒壮	邮电局 9 Bank of China 中国银行 11 Train Station;
2 Jǐngdézhèn Bīnguǎn 景德镇宾馆	4 CITS 中国国际旅行社	Long-Distance Bus Station 火车站;长途汽车站
8 Jǐngdézhèn Fàndiàn 景德镇饭店	5 CAAC Ticket Office 中国民航	12 Táocí Lìshǐ Bówùguǎn; Gǔyáo Cíchǎng 陶瓷历史博物馆;
10 Wényuàn Dàfàndiàn 文苑大饭店	6 Xinhua Bookstore 新华书店	古窑瓷厂 13 Long-Distance Bus Station 长途汽车站

tucked away in antique shops, particularly those on Lianshe Beilu, up from the Jǐngdézhèn Fàndiàn.

The Porcelain Friendship Store (Yǒuyì Shāngdiàn) is at 13 Zhushan Lu, but the market opposite the Jǐngdézhèn Fàndiàn is a good alternative. Huge blue and white summer teapots sell for Y15 or you can purchase a 2m-high mega-vase for Y1000 and up. Also worth checking out are the hand-painted *cíbǎn* (tiles) that come in a variety of sizes and prices. Dinner sets are also a bargain, ranging from Y60 to Y90.

Getting There & Away
Jǐngdézhèn is a bit of a transportation bottle-neck, but the situation has improved with the Luójiā airport and expanded bus service.

Air Luójiā airport is 10km north-west of the city. There is a CAAC ticket office on Lianshe Beilu across from the Jǐngdézhèn Fàndiàn and just up from the Xinhua Bookstore. Flights only go to Shànghǎi (Y400), Guǎngzhōu (Y690) and Běijīng (Y1000).

Bus The minibus service to Jiǔjiāng and Nánchāng is convenient and leaves from the northern end of Maanshan Lu, two minutes' walk from the Jǐngdézhèn Fàndiàn. The hotel also sells minibus tickets to Nánchāng.

The long-distance bus station has services to Yīngtán (Y25; four hours), Jiǔjiāng (Y25; 4½ hours) and Nánchāng (Y32; 6½

hours), as well as Shànghǎi (Y88; 16 hours) and Hángzhōu (Y60; 10 hours). Buses to Túnxī (Huáng Shān Shì) take about four hours (Y30). Another long-distance bus station near the train station has similar routes.

Train Jǐngdézhèn train station is like a deserted crypt, and there is little in the way of tickets available either. Everything but hard-seat tickets, which should suffice for short hauls, is reserved for those with connections with the ticket sellers.

For longer trips, it may be worth calling CITS, where you can organise hard-sleeper and soft-sleeper tickets, although you may have to book a few days in advance.

If you're heading north there are trains to Shànghǎi (Y122; 17 hours) and Nánjīng (Y86; seven hours) via Túnxī, the gateway to the legendary Huáng Shān (Y13; four hours) and Wúhú (Y31; five hours).

There is train service to Nánchāng (Y22; 5½ hours), but for better connections, go to the railway junction at Yīngtán (Y12; three hours).

Getting Around
There is no direct bus to the airport, but a taxi should cost Y30 from the city centre. Bus No 2 crawls at a snail's pace from the long-distance bus station, through the town centre past the Jǐngdézhèn Fàndiàn and out to the train station. Taxis are reasonable, but you may have to bargain. There are also pedicabs, motor-tricycles and motorcycles for hire.

JIǓJIĀNG 九江

☎ 0792 • pop 4,376,900

Jiǔjiāng is a stopover on the road to Lúshān; if you're travelling from Nánchāng, you can safely miss the city by taking a bus directly to Lúshān. Travellers arriving in Jiǔjiāng by ferry from Chóngqìng or Shànghǎi may need to stay overnight.

Situated close to Póyáng Hú (Poyang Lake), which drains into the Cháng Jiāng (Yangzi River), Jiǔjiāng has been a port since ancient times. Once a leading market town for tea and rice in southern China, it opened to foreign trade in 1862. The city eventually developed into a port serving nearby Húběi and Ānhuī. Today Jiǔjiāng is a medium-sized city, second in importance to Nánchāng on a provincial level.

Orientation

Jiǔjiāng stretches along the southern bank of the Cháng Jiāng. Two interconnected lakes divide the older north-eastern part of the city from a newer industrial sprawl to the south. The long-distance bus station is on the city's eastern side, the train station is on the city's southern edge and the main river port is conveniently close to the heart of town.

Information

There's a friendly CITS office (☎ 858 1974) on the 2nd floor of a building in the courtyard of the Nánhú Bīnguǎn. The main Bank of China is at 52 Xunyang Lu, which is on the eastern side of Nánmén Hú (South Gate Lake) at the south-eastern intersection of Nanhu Lu and Xunyang Lu. The post office is close to the intersection of Jiaotong Lu and Xunyang Lu.

Things to See

The small Néngrén Sì (Benevolent Temple) on Yuliang Nanlu has a disused Yuan dynasty pagoda and garden. About 20 monks returned to the temple in 1988 after it closed during the Cultural Revolution. On the same street, at the corner with Gantang Nanlu, is an old Catholic church that reopened in 1984.

A **museum** (bówùguǎn) is housed in quaint old buildings on **Yānshuǐ Tíng**, a tiny

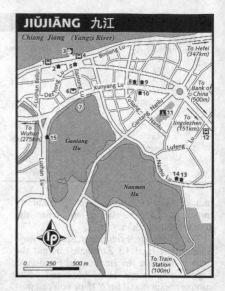

JIǓJIĀNG 九江

Chiang Jiang (Yangzi River)

island in Gāntáng Hú. It's near the town centre and a bridge connects it to the shore. It contains some interesting photographs of Jiǔjiāng during the treaty port days. There are no English captions. Entry costs Y5.

Places to Stay

One inexpensive place is the super basic *Zhígōng Dàshà* (☎ 811 1918, 44 Jiaotong Lu). As you leave the ferry terminal, it's a few minutes directly south on your left, before the Yānshuǐ Tíng. Beds in quads are Y20, singles cost Y40 and doubles are Y50.

A better deal is the *Běigǎng Bīnguǎn* (☎ 822 5582), conveniently located on Binjiang Lu opposite the ferry terminal. It has twins/triples for Y180/240 with air-con.

There are other mid-range hotels on Xunyang Lu about 10 minutes' walk from the ferry terminal. The *Wǔzhōu Fàndiàn* (☎ 811 3796, 86 Xunyang Lu) has good value singles for Y180 and twins for Y200. Beside it, the *Kuānglú Bīnguǎn* (☎ 822 8893, fax 822 1249, 88 Xunyang Lu) has similar prices, with singles/twins at Y150/Y180.

Across the street, the *Báilù Bīnguǎn* (*White Deer Hotel;* ☎ 822 2818, fax 822

JIǓJIĀNG

PLACES TO STAY
2 Běigǎng Bīnguǎn
   北港宾馆
5 Zhígōng Dàshà
   职工大厦
8 Wǔzhōu
   Fàndiàn
   五洲饭店
9 Kuānglú Bīnguǎn
   匡庐宾馆
10 Báilù Bīnguǎn
   白鹿宾馆

13 Jiǔjiāng Bīnguǎn
   九江宾馆
14 Nánhú Bīnguǎn;
   CITS
   南湖宾馆;
   中国国际旅行社
15 Jiǔlóng Bīnguǎn; CAAC
   九龙宾馆;中国民航

OTHER
1 Minibuses to Nánchāng
   往南昌小型车

3 Cháng Jiāng Ferry Terminal
   轮船客运码头
4 Minibuses to Lúshān
   往庐山小型车
6 Post Office
   邮局
7 Yānshuǐ Tíng; Bówùguǎn
   烟水亭、博物馆
11 Néngrén Sì
   能仁寺
12 Long-Distance Bus Station
   长途汽车站

1915, 133 Xunyang Lu) is a Chinese version of a luxury hotel with twins from Y245 to Y285 and suites for Y485. The Báilù also has tours to Lúshān – see the following Lúshān section for details.

At the western end of Xunyang Lu, the ***Jiǔlóng Bīnguǎn** (☎ 823 6779, fax 822 8634, 75 Lushan Lu)* has twins for Y220, but try bargaining.

Further from the harbour in a pleasant setting on the shores of Nánmén Hú, the ***Nánhú Bīnguǎn** (☎ 858 5042, 28 Nanhu Lu)* has twins for Y140 and Y180. The hotel was closed for renovations at the time of research, but was expected to re-open Foreigners may be required to pay a 50% surcharge.

Next door, the ***Jiǔjiāng Bīnguǎn** (☎ 856 0018, fax 856 6677, 30 Nanhu Lu)* is the city's best hotel with standard twins for Y380 and various suites starting at Y500. Foreigners pay a Y100 surcharge.

If you arrive late at night by train, the tall ***Jīngjiu Dàjiǔdiàn** (☎ 856 5918, 366 Changhong Lu)* offers inexpensive and clean rooms. Basic triples with shared bath cost Y90, but you can get one bed for Y30. Better twins with bath are Y168. The hotel is about a 10-minute walk east of the station.

Getting There & Away

Air Jiǔjiāng's airport closed in 1999, so the best way to get there by air is to use Nánchāng's new Chāngběi airport. There are no direct buses from the airport to Jiǔjiāng; travellers will have to take a bus from Nánchāng.

Bus Minibuses for Lúshān leave frequently from the car park next to the ferry terminal. Scheduled public buses to Lúshān leave from the long-distance bus station between 7.30 am and 1.30 pm. The fare for all Lúshān buses is about Y10.

Several hotels offer guided one-day tours of Lúshān for Y100. You can buy tickets for the same tour from the parking lot in front of the ferry terminal.

Minibuses depart for Jǐngdézhèn (Y25) every half hour from the long-distance bus station. The 4½ hour trip includes a short ferry ride across Póyáng Hú. There are frequent buses to Nánchāng (Y25; 1½ hours) and to Wǔhàn (Y65; four hours), among other places.

Minibuses to Nánchāng (Y35; 1½ hours) can also be picked up at the car park in front of the ferry terminal and at the train station.

Train There are several Jiǔjiāng-Nánchāng express trains each day (Y22; 1½ hours). Jiǔjiāng's train station is in the city's southern section.

A Jiǔjiāng-Héféi railway link opened in 1995 and the journey takes 4½ hours.

Boat Most long-distance boats plying the Cháng Jiāng stop in Jiǔjiāng. Tickets up-river to Chóngqìng cost Y635 (2nd class),

Y266 (3rd class) and Y191 (4th class); downriver fares to Shànghǎi are Y269 (2nd class), Y123 (3rd class) and Y85 (4th class). First class exists only on the Wǔhàn to Chóngqìng route.

Getting Around

Bus No 1 and minibuses (Y1) ply the route between Xunyang Lu, the long-distance bus station and the train station. Pedicabs and motor-tricycles are at the bus and train stations and the dock. The fare is around Y3 but this can be negotiated.

LÚSHĀN 庐山
☎ 0792

European and American settlers in the late 19th century established Lúshān, or Kuling as English speakers called it, as a refreshing escape from lowland China's hot and sweaty summers.

They left a fascinating hotchpotch of colonial buildings, from stone cottages reminiscent of southern Germany to small French-style churches and more grandiose hotels built in classical Victorian style.

Lúshān can be cold and shrouded in heavy fog, and during the summer tourists swarm the area. But on the right day, the fog can make for a picturesque blanket over the town. If you arrive on a clear, uncrowded day, stay for some trekking and fresh mountain air.

For the Chinese, Lúshān is rich with significance. Its mountain vistas have been the subject of poems and paintings, and it has seen some historical, epoch-making events. China's post-1949 revolutionaries found Lúshān's cool uplands ideal for Party conferences. In 1959 the Central Committee of the Communist Party held its fateful meeting, which eventually ended in Peng Denhuai's dismissal, sent Mao almost into a political wilderness and provided the seeds for the rise and fall of Liu Shaoqi and Deng Xiaoping.

In 1970, after Mao regained power, another meeting was held in Lúshān, this time of the Politburo. Exactly what happened is shrouded in as much mist as the mountains, but it seems that Lin Biao clashed with

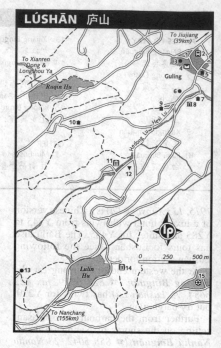

Mao, opposed his policies of *rapprochement* with the USA and probably proposed continuing the Cultural Revolution's xenophobic policies. Whatever happened, Lin was dead the following year.

Orientation & Information

The arrival point in Lúshān is the charming resort village of Gǔlǐng, perched 1167m high at the range's northern end. Two kilometres before Gǔlǐng is the entrance gate, where you must pay a Y50 fee.

Gǔlǐng village has shops and the post office, the bank and the long-distance bus station. Scores of tourist hotels, sanatoriums and factory work-units' holiday hostels sit in the surrounding hills.

The CITS office (☎ 828 2497), uphill from the Lúshān Bīnguǎn, is well organised and helpful.

Detailed maps showing roads and walking tracks are available from shops and hawkers in Gǔlǐng.

LÚSHĀN

PLACES TO STAY & EAT	OTHER	8 Měilú Biéshù
5 Gǔlǐng Fàndiàn	1 Jiēxīn Gōngyuán	美庐别墅
牯岭饭店	街心公园	11 Rénmín Jùyuàn
7 Lúshān Biéshù Cūn	2 Long-Distance Bus Station	人民剧院
庐山别墅村	长途汽车站	13 Sānbǎoshù
9 Lúshān Bīnguǎn	3 Xinhua Bookstore	三宝树
庐山宾馆	新华书店	14 Lúshān
10 Yúnzhōng Bīnguǎn	4 Post Office; Bank	Bówùguǎn
云中宾馆	邮局;银行	博物馆
12 Sānhé Fàndiàn	6 CITS	15 Zhíwù Yuán
三和饭店	中国国际旅行社	植物园

Things to See

Lúshān has enough attractions to keep you there for a couple of days. While it costs Y10 to visit most tourist attractions, an alternative is to skip these and explore the mountain roads and paths on your own.

Built by Chiang Kaishek in the 1930s as a summer getaway, Měilú Biéshù (Meilu Villa) was named after the general's wife, Song Meiling. It's not a particularly grand house but interesting to visit. Although the original gardens were probably more spacious and better maintained than today, the villa has been kept much as it was. There are interesting items on display, like the kerosene-operated American fridge.

The Rénmín Jùyuàn (People's Hall), built in 1936 and the venue for the Communist Party's historic 1959 and 1970 get-togethers, is now a museum. On display are photos of Mao, Zhou and other Party elite taking it easy between meetings.

At Lúshān's north-western rim, the land falls away abruptly to give some spectacular views across Jiāngxī's densely settled plains. A long walking track south around these precipitous slopes passes the cave, Xiānrén Dòng, and continues to Lóngshǒu Yá (Dragon Head Cliff), a natural rock platform tilted above a vertical drop of hundreds of metres.

Chinese visitors enjoy the Sānbǎoshù (Three Ancient Trees), not far by foot from Lúlín Hú (Lulin Lake). Five hundred years ago Buddhist monks planted a ginko and two cedar trees near their temple. Tourists used to climb the branches to have their photos taken, but a fence now protects the trees from this indignity.

The Lúshān Bówùguǎn (Lushan Museum) beside Lúlín Hú commemorates the historic 1970 Communist Party meeting with a photo collection and Mao's huge bed. Scrolls and inscribed steles displaying Li Bai's poetry and calligraphy can be seen. Unfortunately, the English explanations are limited.

The Zhíwù Yuán (Botanical Garden) is mainly devoted to subalpine tropical plants that thrive in the cooler highland climate. In the open gardens there are rhododendrons, camellias and conifers.

Organised Tours

From Jiǔjiāng, return day trips cost Y100 and give you about five hours in Lushan; the Báilù Bīnguǎn in Jiǔjiāng gives tours. Tours normally include pavilions, a nature hike and the museum and are more enjoyable if you bring a friend.

Places to Stay

Hotel prices vary according to season. During the low season (from October to May), when it's cold, drizzly and miserable, few people stay overnight and there are good deals.

In the height of summer, budget travellers can forget about Lúshān – it's probably cheaper to do a day trip from Jiǔjiāng, unless you want to be based on the mountain.

Most places open to foreigners are more upmarket, but it's worth checking around Gǔlǐng for a bargain; locals will approach you. You can also book villa accommodation through CITS.

The centrally located **Gǔlǐng Fàndiàn** (☎ 828 2200, fax 828 2209, 104 Hedong Lu) used to be reasonable, but prices have increased. It's right in Gǔlǐng village around the corner from the bank, shops, restaurants and bus station. Twins with attached bath are Y200 during the off season and Y400 during the high season. The hotel may rent a single bed for Y100 during the low season.

Three other places are worth considering. The **Lúshān Bīnguǎn** ☎ 828 2060, fax 828 2843, 446 Hexi Lu) is a large three-star colonial-era hotel now managed as a joint venture. It has twins ranging from Y120 to Y580.

Lúshān Biéshù Cūn (☎ 828 2927, fax 828 8946, 182 Hedong Lu) has cottages scattered throughout a lovely old pine forest. Suites range from Y480 to Y3000, and there's usually a 20% discount in the low season.

Yúnzhōng Bīnguǎn (☎ 828 5420, fax 828 28535, 49 Xiangshan Lu) rents villas and rooms in villas for Y360 and up.

Places to Eat
Remember that Lúshān is a tourist attraction for Chinese, who like to spend big on meals; if you're on a budget, check the prices first.

Don't expect any English menus, but you will find one of sorts at the **Sānhé Fàndiàn**, run by Mr Liu, a transplanted Shànghǎi local. It's housed in a quaint little stone building with blue windows, and it's on the road to the Rénmín Jùyuàn. There are vegetarian and meat dishes for reasonable prices, including a delicious lemon chicken for Y28.

Getting There & Around
In summer, daily buses go to Nánchāng (Y35l two hours) and Jiǔjiāng (Y7; one hour), but from November to late March direct buses to Nánchāng are sporadic.

Minibuses to Jiǔjiāng also congregate opposite the long-distance bus station on the road heading towards Jiǔjiāng. During the tourist season, numbers can be high, so arrive early to get a room.

If you like country walking, exploring Jiǔjiāng on foot is ideal. Paths and small roads criss-cross Lúshān, so getting around

is easy. If time is short, consider hiring a taxi to visit sights and walking back.

YĪNGTÁN 鹰潭
☎ 0792 • pop 1,025,800
Nánchāng is north of the Shànghǎi-Guǎngzhōu railway line and although most trains make the short detour to Nánchāng, you may have to catch some at Yīngtán, a railway junction town. If you're here, the river area near the old town is worth exploring. You might try getting a boat to the other side.

Places to Stay
The **Huáqiáo Fàndiàn** (Overseas Chinese Hotel; ☎ 622 1344, fax 622 1149, 21 Zhanjiang Lu) is the large 15-storey building on the main street down from the station. Standard twins are Y288. There are cheaper hotels on the same street.

Getting There & Away
The long-distance bus station is opposite the train station. There are buses to Jǐngdézhèn (Y35; four hours) and Nánchāng (Y35; 2½ hours).

There are trains from Yīngtán to Fúzhōu (9½ hours), Guǎngzhōu (16 hours), Shànghǎi (11½ hours) and Xiàmén (15 hours). Trains to Nánchāng take two hours and there is also a branch line to Jǐngdézhèn (2½ hours) via Guixi.

JǏNGGĀNG SHĀN 井冈山
☎ 0792
With its tree-lined streets and misty mountain range, Jǐnggāng Shān provides a welcome respite from China's congested, noisy cities.

But from June to October Jǐnggāng Shān can be packed with tourists who come to view the area's famous mountains (some of which appear on the Y100 note), tranquil waterfalls and Red Army war sites.

Historically, this remote 500-peak region in the Luóxiāo Shān (Clouds on Display Mountains) along the Húnán-Jiāngxī border played a crucial role in the early communist movement. It's been dubbed the 'Cradle of the Chinese Revolution'.

After suffering a string of defeats in an urban-based revolution, Mao led 900 men into these hills in 1927. Other companies of the battered communist army led by Zhu De joined them a year later. From here, Mao launched the 'Long March' into Shaanxi.

Orientation & Information

Cíping (also called Jǐnggāng Shān), the main township, is nestled around a small lake in the mountains, 820m above the sea. Hotels, restaurants and the bus station are within easy walking distance.

The local China Travel Service (CTS; Zhōngguó Lǚxíngshè; ☎ 655 2504) is on 2 Tianjie Road, across from the Jǐnggāngshān Bīnguǎn. Some English is spoken there. The Bank of China is on 6 Nanshan Lu on the lake's south-eastern end.

The town has roadside signs listing emergency phone numbers, including the PSB (☎ 655 2360) and medical help (☎ 655 2595).

For an English-language tourist brochure (Y2) or a map showing hiking trails in the hills (Y2), try the Xinhua Bookstore in the Cuihu Hotel on Hong Jun Nanlu. Hotels also sell maps.

Local companies give tours – expect them to knock on your door. Your hotel may be able to help you hire a van for about Y100 to tour major sites, but be careful of overcharging. CTS provides tours for Y300.

Things to See

Jǐnggāng Shān is a major scenic area with large expanses of natural highland forest and numerous attractions devoted to the Civil War. The area has square-stemmed bamboo and some 26 kinds of alpine azaleas that bloom from late April.

At Wǔlóng Tán (Five Dragon Pools), 7km north-west of town, five cascading waterfalls, as well as vista points and well marked cement paths, make for a refreshing day-long trek. There's also a cave that communist troops used as a hospital during the Civil War.

If you start early, you'll avoid the tourist onslaught. The total hike can take six hours (three hours each way) and there are signs in English. Admission is Y20.

A reliable transportation option is to hire a van to take you there early in the morning and pick you up in the afternoon. A few sporadic minibuses (Y3) leave from the bus station.

The watching post, Huángyángjiè, sits to the west. At 1300m above sea level, the mountainous scenic area offers stunning views on a clear day. In 1928 the outnumbered Red Army defended the area from Nationalist attacks. Entry is Y7.

Standing 1438m above sea level, Wǔzhǐ Fēng (Five Fingers Peak) is to the south – it features on the back of the Y100 banknote. The Wǔlóng Tán have better hiking paths, though.

The Jǐnggāngshān Gémìng Bówùguǎn (Jinggangshan Revolutionary Museum) is devoted to the Kuomintang and communists' struggle for control of the Húnán-Jiāngxī area in the late 1920s. Explanations are in Chinese, but the collection is visual enough. Admission is Y8.

The Gémìng Jiùzhǐqún (Former Revolutionary Quarters) in Cíping served as the communist command centre between 1927 and 1928, and Mao lived temporarily in one of the five mud-brick buildings. Entry is Y5.

The town has the Diāosù Yuán (Sculpture Park), but the Y15 entrance fee is steep unless you like statues of young communist martyrs. All of the sites are open daily from 8 am to noon and from 2 to 5 pm.

Adventurous trekkers can venture into the surrounding mountains for self-guided walks on dirt trails. Local maps from the Xinhua Bookstore show trails and are mediocre. You'll have to ask locals where they start.

Places to Stay & Eat

Just about every building in town is a hotel, but different hotel managers gave different answers as to whether the inexpensive ones accept foreigners.

As you exit the long-distance bus station, turn left and make a sharp right along Tongmu Ling Lu, where hotels range from Y35 to Y200 per night.

The *Yuándǐng Bīnguǎn* (☎ 655 2246, 10 *Tongmu Ling Lu*) is almost immediately to your left as you leave the bus station. It charges Y70 per person for a passable twin, Y50 per person for a triple and Y35 per person for a quad. The rooms are basic and have squat toilets.

The *Jǐnggāngshān Fàndiàn* (☎ 655 2328, 1 Xinshi Chang Lu) is down the road and provides clean, basic accommodation. Four-bed dorms with bath go for Y40, and twins with attached bath for Y80. Beds are also available in triples with attached bath for Y50 each.

The other *Jǐnggāngshān Bīnguǎn* (☎ 655 2272, fax 655 2221, 10 Hongjun Beilu) is where the Party top brass chose to stay – Mao Zedong, Lin Biao, Deng Xiaoping and Li Peng have all stayed here. This hotel is expensive – Y200 and up for a twin – and there is a mind-boggling variety of rooms and villas. The manager speaks English.

The hotel is a 15-minute walk from the bus station; go down Tongmu Ling Lu, turn right at the first road, and then right again. There's no English sign on the main entrance to the driveway.

Up the road from the Jǐnggāngshān Bīnguǎn, on Hongjun Beilu, is another monolithic enterprise. The *Jǐnggāngshān Dàshà* (Jǐnggāngshān Plaza; ☎ 655 2251, fax 655 2428) is a huge stone villa. A sign also refers to the hotel as the Jinggangshan Grand Hotel. It's popular with tour groups on government-sponsored jaunts, and rooms are often unavailable. Twins are Y120/200. Beds in dorms are available for Y20 and Y25 Prices go up by about 20% during the high season.

There are good cheap *restaurants* on the main street down from the bus station. The restaurant in the Yuán Dǐng Bīnguǎn is cheap and serves tasty food. For something a bit more romantic, try the place on the island in the middle of the lake.

Shopping

Stalls in the town centre sell different bamboo products – some are tacky – but there are nice summer mats and comfortable rocking chairs. These products can be found all over south-central China, but the chairs are a good buy here, ranging from Y15 to Y70. Mats sell for Y90.

Getting There & Away

From Nánchāng there are direct buses to Jǐnggāng Shān each day (seven to nine hours). It's a pleasant ride with scenes of lush countryside, high bamboo fences, old stone bridges, water buffalo and flocks of ducks in rice paddies.

From Jǐnggāng Shān, there are buses to Nánchāng at 6.30 am and 7 pm daily. The trip costs Y61 and there are also sleeper buses for Y71.

It's possible to take sleeper buses to Chángshā in Húnán (Y70; nine to 10 hours).

From Jǐnggāng Shān, you may have to transfer buses in Jíán in Jiāngxī (Y23 to Y31; three hours). If you arrive in Jíán from Chángshā, it's possible to go directly by bus to Jǐnggāng Shān.

Don't be confused with the Jǐnggāng Shān train station, which is in Tàihé, a town south of Jíán. From the Tàihé station, you'll have to take a bus or taxi to the town centre and catch a long-distance bus to Jǐnggāng Shān (three hours).

Because buses leave in the morning, you may have to spend the night. If possible, give Tàihé a miss.

Húnán 湖南

Húnán has many notable attractions. The Zhāngjiājiè nature reserve in the west offers jutting mountain scenery, rivalling the karst peaks of Guǎngxī. Sháoshān, the birthplace of Mao Zedong, is an interesting, beautiful and relaxing village. South of Chángshā, visitors can ascend Héng Shān, a Buddhist and Taoist sacred mountain. In the north, the port city of Yuèyáng is a major stop for Cháng Jiāng (Yangzi River) cruises and has a lively atmosphere.

The province occupies some of China's richest land. Between the 8th and the 11th centuries, the population increased fivefold, spurred on by a prosperous agricultural industry and southerly migrations. Under the Ming and Qing dynasties it was one of the empire's granaries, and vast quantities of rice were shipped to the depleted north.

By the 19th century, Húnán began to suffer from the pressure of population. Land shortage and landlordism led to widespread unrest among Chinese farmers and hill-dwelling minorities. This increasingly desperate economic situation led to the massive Taiping Rebellion of the mid-19th century and the communist movement of the 1920s.

The communists found strong support among Húnán's peasants and established a refuge on the mountainous Húnán-Jiāngxī border in 1927. Several prominent communist leaders were born in Húnán: Mao Zedong, Liu Shaoqi, Peng Dehuai and Hu Yaobang. Hua Guofeng, a Shānxī native, became an important provincial leader in Húnán.

Most of Húnán's residents are Han Chinese, but hill-dwelling minorities occupy the border regions. They include the Miao, Tujia, Dong (a people related to the Thais and Lao) and Yao. In Húnán's far north, there's a pocket of Uyghurs.

CHÁNGSHĀ 长沙
☎ 0731 • pop 5,719,100

The site of Chángshā has been inhabited for 3000 years. By the Warring States Period a large town had been established. The town

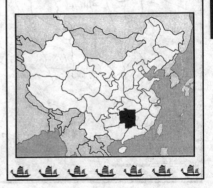

owes its prosperity to its location on the fertile Húnán plains and on the Xiáng Jiāng, where it grew as a major agricultural trading centre.

In 1904 the city opened to foreign trade as a result of the 1903 Treaty of Shanghai between Japan and China. The 'most-favoured nation' principle allowed foreigners to establish themselves in Chángshā, and large numbers of Europeans and Americans arrived to build factories, churches and schools. Yale University started a college here, which eventually became a medical centre.

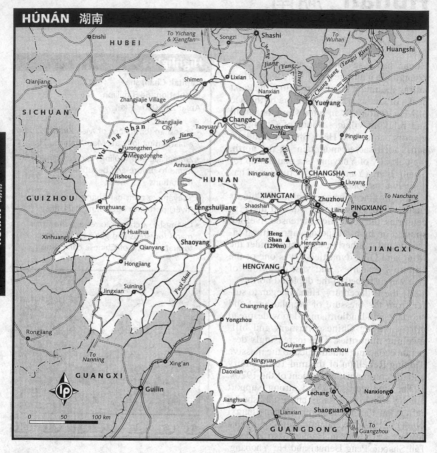

HÚNÁN 湖南

Orientation

Most of Chángshā lies on the eastern bank of the Xiáng Jiāng (Xiang River). The train station is in the city's far east. From the station, Wuyi Lu leads to the river, neatly separating the city's northern and southern sections.

From Wuyi Lu, you cross the Xiáng Jiāng bridge to the western bank, passing over Júzi Zhōu (Long Island) in the middle of the river. Most major attractions are located east of the river. City maps are on sale at kiosks around the train station and in hotel shops.

Information

Money The Bank of China is next to the CAAC office on Wuyi Donglu. You can also change money at the Xiángjiāng and Fúróng Bīnguǎns.

Post & Communications The main post and China Telecom office is on Wuyi Zhonglu near the intersection of Yingbin Lu. There is another post office immediately to your right as you leave the train station.

Email & Internet Access The Huá Tiān Dàjiǔdiàn (see Places to Stay later) has a business centre with Internet access for Y2 per hour.

Travel Agencies The China International Travel Service (CITS; Zhōngguó Guójì Lǚxíngshè; ☎ 228 0184) has an office at 46 Wuyi Donglu, about half a block west of the train station. The CITS Europe and America Department (☎ 228 0439, ✉ citsamer@ public.cs.hn.cn) has friendly, multilingual staff and is located on the 11th floor of the Xiaoyuan Dàshà on Wuyi Lu. There's also a CITS office where English is spoken next to the Fúróng Bīnguǎn. The Xiāngjiāng Bīnguǎn and Huá Tiān Dàjiǔdiàn can assist with transport bookings.

PSB The Public Security Bureau (PSB; Gōngānjú) is in a cream-tiled building on Huangxing Lu, at the western end of town just south of Jiefang Xilu.

Húnán Shěng Bówùguǎn 省博物馆
Hunan Provincial Museum
The museum is on Dongfeng Lu within walking distance of the Xiāngjiāng Bīnguǎn. The exhibits chronicle revolutionary history and two buildings are devoted to the 2100-year-old Western Han tombs at Mǎwángduī, some 5km east of the city, which were fully excavated by 1974.

Not to be missed are the mummified remains of a Han dynasty woman. Her preserved body, which was discovered wrapped in more than 20 layers of silk and linen, is housed in the basement. The organs have been removed and are on display. Another building houses the enormous solid outer timber casks.

Large quantities of silk garments and fabrics were found in the tomb, as well as stockings, shoes and gloves. One interesting object is a painting on silk depicting the underworld, earth and heaven.

The Húnán Shěng Bówùguǎn is open Monday to Friday from 8 am to noon and 2.30 to 5 pm, and on weekends from 8.30 am to 5 pm; entry is Y16. From the intersection of Yingbin Lu and Wuyi Zhonglu, bus No 3 heads north on Dongfeng Lu past the museum.

Maoist Pilgrimage Spots
Scattered about the city are Maoist pilgrimage spots. The **Hunan No 1 Teachers' Training School** (Dìyī Shīfàn Xuéxiào) is where Mao attended classes between 1913 and 1918, and where he returned as a teacher and principal from 1920 to 1922. The school was destroyed during the civil war but has since been restored. Follow the arrows for a self-guided tour of Mao's dormitory, study areas, halls where he held some of his first political meetings and even an open-air bathing well where he enjoyed taking cold baths. There's a quote from him above the well, where he said it was a good way to 'exercise fearlessness'.

The school is still in use, so you can see China's educational system in action. Take bus No 1 bus from outside the Xiāngjiāng Bīnguǎn or the train station; entry is Y6.

The **Former Office of the Hunan Communist Party Committee** (Zhōng Gòng Xiāngqū Wěiyuánhuì Jiùzhǐ) is now a museum that includes Mao's living quarters and photos and historical items from the 1920s. Within the museum grounds there's a long wall with carved large-scale versions of Mao's poems, showing his characteristic expansive brushstrokes. The entrance is on Bayi Lu and on the route of bus No 1; the museum is open daily and admission is Y10.

Léi Fēng Jìniànguǎn 雷锋纪念馆
Lei Feng Memorial Museum
If you like communist propaganda or just Chinese communists, visit the Léi Fēng Jìniànguǎn (☎ 810 5014), an hour's bus ride west of Chángshā.

Lei Feng was a soldier who the communists lionised in 1963, one year after he died in a traffic accident at age 22, as a model worker, party member and all-round communist citizen. His feats included washing his fellow soldiers' laundry, helping old ladies cross the street and getting people up-to-date on party doctrine.

The museum exhibits a group of photos featuring Lei smiling over a washtub of dirty socks and cartoon-like renderings of him and his parents facing down evil landlords and Japanese invaders.

HÚNÁN 湖南

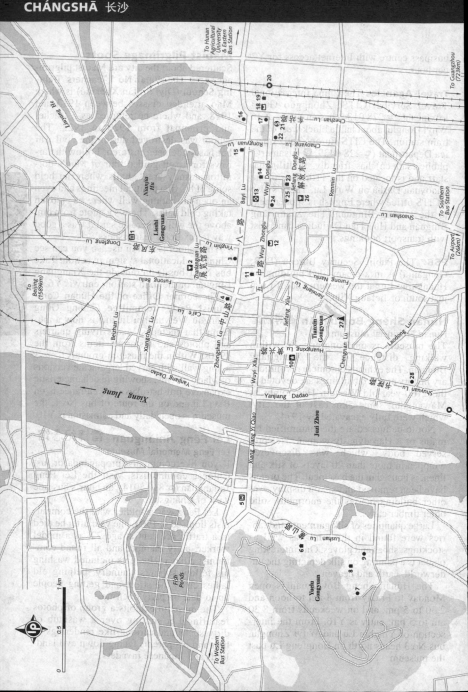

To Hunan Agricultural University & Eastern Bus Station

Liuyang He

To Guangzhou (723km)

20

18 19
16
17
车站路 Chezhan Lu
21
22
15 Rongyuan Lu
朝阳路 Chaoyang Lu
14
13 Wuyi Donglu
25 23
解放东路 Jiefang Donglu-
Bayi Lu
24
26
Renmin Lu
Shaoshan Lu
To Southern Bus Station

Niujia Hu

Lieshi Gongyuan

1
Dongfeng Lu
东风路

To Beijing (1589km)

2
展览馆路 Zhanlanguan Lu
Yingbin Lu
3
八一路
Wuyi Zhonglu
12
Furong Nanlu

11
Furong Beilu

4
Cai'e Lu
Zhongshan Lu 中山路
五一中路 Wuyi Zhonglu

Beizhan Lu
Xiangchun Lu

Wuyi xilu
Zhongshan Lu
解放西路 Jiefang Xilu
Jianxing Lu

10
Tianxin Gongyuan
27
Chengnan Lu
Laodong Lu

28
Shuyuan Lu

Yanjiang Dadao

Xiang Jiang 湘江

Juzi Zhou

Yanjiang Dadao

湘江一桥 Xiang Jiang Yi Qiao

5

Lushan Lu
6
9
8
7
Yuelu Gongyuan
岳麓山

Fish Ponds

To Western Bus Station

To Airport (26km)

N

1 km

0   0.5

CHÁNGSHĀ

PLACES TO STAY & EAT

4 Xiāngjiāng
Bīnguǎn
湘江宾馆

6 Húnán Shīfàn Dàxué
Zhuānjiālóu
湖南师范大学专家楼

8 Wàngjiāng Lóu
望江楼

11 Xiǎotiān'é Dàjiǔdiàn;
John's Café
小天鹅大酒店

14 Fúróng Bīnguǎn;
CITS
芙蓉宾馆,
中国国际旅行社

15 Nánhǎi Bīnguǎn
南海宾馆

19 Chēzhàn Dàshà
车站大厦

23 Huá Tiān Dàjiǔdiàn
华天大酒店

25 Do Do Fun
Coffeehouse
豆豆坊咖啡

OTHER

1 Húnán Shěng
Bówùguǎn
省博物馆

2 JJ's Disco
湖南太空世界
娱乐中心

3 Former Office
of the Hunan
Communist Party
Committee
中共湘区委员会旧址

5 Róngwānzhèn Bus
Terminus
溶湾镇终站

7 Àiwǎn Tíng
爱晚亭

9 Yuelu Academy
岳麓书院

10 PSB
公安局

12 Main Post &
China Telecom
Office
邮电局

13 Friendship Store
友谊商店

16 Hunan Embroidery
Research Institute
湖南省湘绣研究所

17 CITS
中国国际旅行社

18 Post Office
邮局

20 Train Station
火车站

21 Bank of China
中国银行

22 CAAC
中国民航售票处

24 Xinhua Bookstore
新华书店

26 Hot Rock Pub
滚石的吧

27 Tiānxīn Gé
天心阁

28 Hunan No 1 Teachers'
Training School
第一师范学校

To get there, take bus No 12 from the train station to the terminus at Róngwānzhèn, where you can switch to minibus No 15, which makes its final stop just south of the museum; entry is Y4.

Other Sights

Yuèlù Gōngyuán (Bottom of the High Mountain Park) is a pleasant place to visit on the western bank of the Xiáng Jiāng, along with **Hunan University** (Húnán Dàxué). The university evolved from the site of the **Yuelu Academy** (Yuèlù Shūyuàn), which was established during the Song dynasty for scholars to prepare for civil examinations. In 1903 the Confucian classics were replaced by more practical subjects as the Qing government attempted to reform education to foster modernisation. In 1926 Húnán Dàxué was established. The Yuèlù Academy lies on the hillside behind the Mao statue. There's a teahouse inside and a good Chinese bookshop in the back; entry is Y14.

From the university you can hike to the **Àiwǎn Tíng** (Loving Dusk Pavilion), to get a good view of the town. **Júzi Zhōu** (Long Island), or Long Sandbank, from which Chángshā takes its name, lies in the middle of the Xiáng Jiāng. To get to the university, take bus No 202 from Wuyi Xilu or the train station and get off at the last stop, past the Mao statue.

The only remaining part of the old city walls is **Tiānxīn Gé** (Heart of Heaven Pavilion), south-west of Jiefang Lu, which is an interesting area to explore.

Places to Stay

Unhappily for independent travellers, city hotels that accept foreigners are mostly upmarket. The cheapest option is university accommodation; the only drawback is getting there.

The *Húnán Shīfàn Dàxué Zhuānjiālóu (Hunan Normal University Foreign Experts' Building;* ☎ *887 2211)* has beds in twin rooms with bath from Y70 to Y80. It's best to phone first because it's often full. The university is located north of Hunan University, below Yuèlù Gōngyuán on the western side of the river. Take bus No 202 and ask the driver to let you off at *shīfàn dàxué*. From the university entrance, it's about a 750m slog uphill to a white building with a circular driveway. You might want to take a taxi from the entrance.

The *Húnán Nóngyè Dàxué Waìbīnlóu* (*Hunan Agricultural University Guesthouse; ☎ 461 8060*) has beds for Y60 in pleasant twin rooms with balconies and private bathrooms. Again, it's better to phone about vacancies. The university is located in the eastern outskirts past the eastern long-distance bus station. Take bus or minibus No 110 from the south car park beside the train station. The university is the last stop, about a 40-minute ride. From the entrance, walk straight beside the playing field, turn left at the first intersection, then right and left again at the small garden circle. Go straight for about 75m. At the bottom of some stairs, there's an English sign for the guesthouse.

In the city centre, one good deal is the conveniently located, navy-run *Nánhǎi Bīnguǎn* (*☎ 229 7888, fax 229 6771, 1 Rongyuan Lu*). It has clean, comfortable twins for Y200. The *Fúróng Bīnguǎn* (*Lotus Hotel; ☎ 440 1888, fax 446 5175, 128 Wuyi Donglu*) has singles and twins for Y268/298.

On the northern side of the train station, the *Chēzhàn Dàshà* (*☎ 229 3366, 1 Wuyi Donglu*) has decent twins/triples for Y138/148 and the staff can book your train tickets. The hotel even has a doorway to the platform, just before the exit gate. If you're taking a train, this one is hard to beat. But the hotel is often full.

The *Xiāngjiāng Bīnguǎn* (*☎ 440 8888, fax 444 8285, 36 Zhongshan Lu*) has ordinary twins available for Y150 and better ones for Y260. The more expensive rooms have a 10% service charge but include a free Chinese-style breakfast. To get there from the train station, take bus No 1, which stops near the hotel driveway.

While far from the city centre, one quiet place is the *Wàngjiāng Lóu* (*☎ 882 1246, fax 882 4287*) at Hunan University. Rooms start at Y160 and twins/triples with attached

bath are Y240/360. It's in a red-brick building on the hillside tucked behind the Yuèlù Academy. It's a good idea to phone ahead.

The *Xiǎotiān'é Dàjiǔdiàn* (*Cygnet Hotel; ☎ 441 0400, fax 442 3698, 178 Wuyi Zhonglu*) is a three-star joint venture on the corner of Wuyi Zhonglu and the Furong Lu overpass. Standard twins are listed at Y458, but they may be available for Y268, plus a 14% service charge.

The best luxury place in town is the five-star *Huá Tiān Dàjiǔdiàn* (*☎ 444 2888, fax 444 2270, 380 Jiefang Donglu*), just off Shaoshan Lu. Business travellers praise the Huá Tiān for its clean rooms. Rates range from US$98 for a standard twin room to US$446 for a deluxe suite. All rooms come with a 15% service charge.

Places to Eat

Hunanese food uses plenty of chilli and hot spices. There are several good fast-food places on Chezhan Lu, just south of the train station, and there are street-side stalls at night on Chaoyang Lu, near the CAAC office.

The Huá Tiān Dàjiǔdiàn's *coffee shop* has standard international fare for reasonable prices. Next door to the hotel, the *Oasis* (*Ōuxiāng Wū*) is a Taiwan-style coffee house with good-value meals of meat, rice and vegetables for Y35, including tea or coffee.

The Xiǎotiān'é Dàjiǔdiàn has an international bar and restaurant called *John's Cafe* (*Wànlóng Xīcāntīng; ☎ 441 0400 ext 797, 178 Wuyi Zhonglu*), which serves draught beer and steak dishes.

The adventurous might like to sample *bīngláng* (betel nut), which is sold at street stalls. When chewed, the woody flesh, which has an overpowering, spicy-sweet taste, produces a mild, semi-narcotic effect.

For the coffee lover, the *Do Do Fun Coffeehouse* (*Dòudòufáng Kāfēi; 398 Jiefang Lu*) is a quiet Western-style coffeehouse serving espresso (Y18), cappuccino (Y18) and iced coffee (Y20). It's across the street from the Hot Rock Pub.

There are Taiwan-style bars and teahouses in the vicinity of Jiefang Donglu and Chaoyang Lu.

Entertainment

To boogie the night away with the fashionable set, head to the *Hot Rock Pub (Gǔshí Debā)*, the city's trendiest disco, at the corner of Jiefang Donglu and Shaoshan Lu. There's no cover charge, but you have to purchase Y40 worth of drinks.

Another boogie palace is *JJ's* disco, which is near the Zhǎnlǎnguǎn (Exhibition Hall) on Zhanlanguan Lu; entry is Y50.

In the new Chángshā, it's possible to check email, relax over a cup of fresh brew and then groove at a flashy disco – all within kilometres of where Mao studied and contemplated the plight of the rich and poor.

Shopping

Chángshā offers some exquisite embroidered items at the aptly named Hunan Embroidery Research Institute (Húnánshěng Xiāngxiù Yánjiūsuǒ; ☎ 229 1821) in a courtyard at 70 Bayi Lu. The factory is geared for tour groups, but the items include pictures of sacred mountains, bamboo scenes and goldfish. Prices start at Y980.

Getting There & Away

Air The main office for the Civil Aviation Administration of China (CAAC; Zhōngguó Mínháng; ☎ 411 9821) is at 5 Wuyi Donglu, one block west of the train station. The Fúróng Bīnguǎn also has a CAAC booking office. From Chángshā, there are flights almost daily to Běijīng (Y970), Chéngdū (Y730), Guǎngzhōu (Y550), Kūnmíng (Y760), Shànghǎi (Y710) and Xī'ān (Y710).

There are also flights to Hong Kong (Y1300) daily except for Wednesday and Sunday. The airport is 26km from the city centre and CAAC shuttle buses leave about two hours before scheduled flights. The fare is Y13.

Bus The city's three long-distance bus stations are all inconveniently located outside the city centre. The general rule is that buses heading west depart from the western bus station; points east and north depart from the eastern bus station; and for the south, it's the southern bus station. You can reach all the bus stations from the train station, which has a public bus and minibus service.

To get to the eastern bus station, take bus No 26 from the train station; for the western bus station No 212 or 213; and for the southern bus station No 102, 103 or 107. Buses for Yuèyáng (Y22; 2½ hours), Nánchāng (Y75; eight hours) and Nánjīng (Y256; 20 hours) leave from the eastern bus station. Buses for Huáihuà (Y99; 11 hours) and Zhāngjiājiè (Y93; seven to 11 hours) leave from the western bus station.

Buses for Sháoshān (Y20; 2½ hours), Héng Shān (Y19; three hours) and Guǎngzhōu (Y91; 15 hours) leave from the southern bus station. All the stations are open from 6 am to at least 9 pm. Minibuses from the train station to Yuèyáng cost Y20.

Train There are two Guǎngzhōu-Chángshā-Běijīng express trains daily in each direction and a daily train to Shànghǎi (Y300; 20 hours). Other important routes via Chángshā are Běijīng-Guìlín-Kūnmíng and Guǎngzhōu-Xī'ān-Lánzhōu. Not all trains to Shànghǎi, Kūnmíng and Guìlín stop in Chángshā, so it may be necessary to go to Zhūzhōu first and change there.

If you're heading to Hong Kong, you can take an overnight Chángshā-Shēnzhèn air-conditioned express train that gets into Shēnzhèn around 9.30 am. A hard-sleeper berth costs around Y300. The Běijīng-Kowloon express train also passes through Chángshā. There is a daily train to Sháoshān (Y17) that leaves at 7.25 am. Counter No 6 at the Chángshā train station is for foreigners, but you can also book tickets with CITS for a Y40 service charge.

SHÁOSHĀN 韶山

☎ 0732

Although small, Sháoshān, about 130km south-west of Chángshā, looms large in significance to Chinese communism as Mao Zedong's birthplace. In the 1960s during the Cultural Revolution's headier days, three million pilgrims came here each year, and a railway line and paved road from Chángshā were built to transport them.

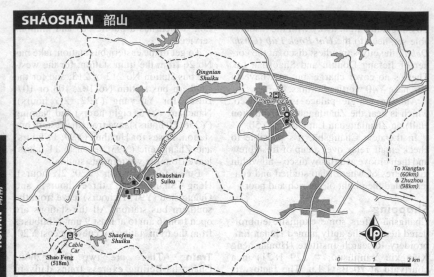

SHÁOSHĀN 韶山

Qingnian
Shuiku

Shaoshan Suiku

Shaoshan Lu

Yingbin Lu

Chupun Lu

To Xiangtan
(60km)
& Zhuzhou
(98km)

Shaofeng
Shuiku

Cable
Car

Shao Feng
(518m)

0   1   2 km

After Mao's death the numbers declined. But as memories of the Cultural Revolution's excesses gradually fade, the village has seen a tourist revival. In 1993, Sháoshān celebrated the centenary of Mao's birth.

Considering the tourists who have passed through since it became a national shrine, Sháoshān is hardly typical of Chinese villages. Despite tourism's impact, the countryside has retained its charm. Traditional adobe houses dot this landscape of mountains and lush rice paddies.

Apart from its historical significance, Sháoshān is a great place to get away from big cities, although the atmosphere is somewhat compromised by loudspeakers blaring out recordings of Mao's speeches.

Orientation

Sháoshān has two parts: the new town clustered around the train and bus stations and the original Sháoshān village about 5km away.

From the train station, or the main road, there are minibuses to village sites. Motorcycle taxis also meet the train from Chángshā. The minibus to the village should only cost Y1.50, but some drivers may want more money. Normally, they proceed directly to the Dī Shuǐ Dòng (Dripping Water Cave), so make sure you tell the driver you want to stop at the village. Some minibuses will take you to the key sites for Y10. The long-distance bus station is on Yingbin Lu, just north of the train station.

Máo Zédōng Gùjū
毛泽东同志故居
Mao's Childhood House
This fairly large structure with mud walls and a thatched roof is the village's principal shrine. It's no different from millions of other mud-brick dwellings in China, except for its former occupant, its painstaking restoration and the People's Liberation Army guard.

Exhibits include kitchen utensils, original furnishings, bedding and photos of Mao's parents. It's open daily; entry is Y3.

Máo Zédōng Jìniànguǎn
毛泽东同志纪念馆
Museum of Comrade Mao
The museum opened in 1967 during the Cultural Revolution. Unfortunately there are no English captions, but the exhibits are graphic enough. One highlight is the computer

SHÁOSHĀN

1 Dī Shuǐ Dòng
   滴水洞
2 Long-Distance Bus Station
   长途汽车站
3 Train Station
   火车站
4 Yínfēng Bīnguǎn
   银峰宾馆
5 Máo Zédōng Gùjū
   毛泽东同志故居
6 Sháoshān Bīnguǎn
   韶山宾
7 Máo Zédōng Jìniànguǎn
   毛泽东同志纪念馆
8 Hóngrì Fàndiàn
   红日饭店
9 Cable Car Station
   韶峰游览索道

vendors, who can create digital reproductions of you lighting Mao's cigarette or shaking his hand. The museum is open daily; admission is Y7.

Other Sights

Fancy a Chinese fan that unfolds to reveal a jolly profile of the Chairman? How about a red cigarette lighter with his portrait that plays 'The East is Red' when you flick it open? If you came looking for Mao souvenirs, you can drop your cash at the three **tourist markets**, which are uphill from his childhood house; near the Sháoshān Bīnguǎn; and at the Dī Shuǐ Dòng site. All should satiate any craving for Maoist kitsch. There is also more conventional Maobilia such as badges, rings, busts, statues and the Mao portrait good-luck charms that Chinese drivers attach to their car mirrors.

Dī Shuǐ Dòng (Dripping Water Cave) is 3km up from Sháoshān village. Retreating to his native Sháoshān in June 1966, Mao lived in this cave for 11 days, probably thinking up new slogans for the Cultural Revolution that had just begun. Nearby are the Mao clan's family tombs. Buses to the cave leave from the car park opposite the Sháoshān Bīnguǎn.

Sháo Fēng (Shao Peak) is the conical-shaped mountain visible from the village.

The summit has a lookout pavilion, and the 'forest of steles' on the lower slopes has stone tablets engraved with Mao's poems. The area is less frequented than other Sháoshān sites and has pleasant paths through pine forests and stands of bamboo.

From Sháoshān village take a minibus south to the end of the road at the cable car station, or hop aboard a motorcycle taxi for about Y5. Hiking to the top takes about an hour or you can take the cable car for Y20.

Places to Stay & Eat

The upmarket **Sháoshān Bīnguǎn** (☎ 568 5127) is on the main street into town across from the car park. Rooms start at Y240 and triples go for Y280. A hotel extension (☎ 568 5064) is around the corner to the right, up a small hill, and has nice grounds, although the reception, with its portraits of Marx, Mao et al, is rather austere.

Up the road from the Mao statue is the cheaper **Hóngrì Fàndiàn**, which is popular with backpackers. It's a small, family-run hotel with basic accommodation. Beds in small dorms are Y10 and twins without bath are Y30. The family also dishes up some tasty meals.

Meals are a bit pricey in Sháoshān because food must be shipped in to meet tourist demand. There are **restaurants** on the road across from the Sháoshān Bīnguǎn and to the left of the Hóngrì Fàndiàn.

In the new town, south of the train station, the **Yínfēng Bīnguǎn** (☎ 568 1080) has beds in triples with attached bath and air-con for Y50 and twins for Y168.

Getting There & Away

Bus Chángshā has several buses a day to Sháoshān (Y20; 2½ hours), leaving from the southern bus station from 8 am onwards. From the Sháoshān bus station there are buses to Chángshā daily. There may be others leaving from the village throughout the day, just keep an eye out near the Sháoshān Bīnguǎn. There are also frequent minibuses to Xiāngtán (Y6; 1½ hours). From there you can catch a train or bus to Chángshā or Huáihuà. Buses also go to Héng Shān.

Mao Zedong

Mao was Húnán's main export. He was born in the Húnánese village of Sháoshān, not far from Chángshā, in 1893. His father was a poor peasant who had been forced to join the army because of heavy debts. After several years of service he returned to Sháoshān and by careful saving, through small trading and other enterprises, managed to buy back his land.

As 'middle' peasants, Mao's family owned enough land to produce a surplus of rice with which they were able to buy more land. This raised them to the status of 'rich' peasants. Mao began studying in the local primary school when he was eight years old and remained at school until the age of 13, while working on the farm and keeping accounts for his father's business. His father continued to accumulate wealth (or what was considered a fortune in the little village) by buying mortgages on other people's land.

Several incidents influenced Mao around this time. A famine in Húnán and a subsequent uprising of starving people in Chángshā ended in the execution of the leaders by the Manchu governor. This left a lasting impression on Mao, who '... felt that there with the rebels were ordinary people like my own family and I deeply resented the injustice in the treatment given to them'. He was also influenced by a band of rebels who had taken to the hills around Sháoshān to defy the landlords and the government, and by a radical teacher at the local primary school who opposed Buddhism and wanted people to convert their temples into schools.

At the age of 16 Mao left Sháoshān to enter middle school in Chángshā, his first stop on the path to power. At this time he was not yet an anti-monarchist. He felt, however, even at an early age, that the country was in desperate need of reform. He was fascinated by stories of the ancient rulers of China, and learned something of foreign history and geography.

In Chángshā, Mao was first exposed to the ideas of revolutionaries and reformers active in China, he heard of Sun Yatsen's revolutionary secret society and read about the abortive Canton Uprising of 1911. Later that year an army uprising in Wǔhàn quickly spread and the Qing dynasty collapsed. Yuan Shikai made his grab for power and the country appeared to be slipping into civil war. Mao joined the regular army, but resigned six months later, thinking the revolution was over when Sun handed the presidency to Yuan and the war between the north and south of China did not take place.

Mao became an avid reader of newspapers and from these was introduced to socialism. He decided to become a teacher and enrolled in the Hunan No 1 Teachers' Training School, where he was a student for five years. During his time at the school, he inserted an advertisement in a Chángshā newspaper 'inviting young men interested in patriotic work to make contact with me ...'. Among them was Liu Shaoqi, who later became president of the Peoples Republic of China (PRC); Xiao Chen, who became a founding member of the Chinese Communist Party (CCP); and Li Lisan.

'At this time', says Mao, 'my mind was a curious mixture of ideas of liberalism, democratic reformism and utopian socialism ... and I was definitely anti-militarist and anti-imperialist.' Mao graduated from the teachers' training school in 1918 and went to Běijīng, where he worked as an assistant librarian at Beijing University. In Běijīng he met future co-founders of the Chinese Communist Party: the student leader Zhang Guodao, Professor Chen Duxiu and university librarian Li Dazhao. Chen and Li are regarded as the founders of Chinese communism. It was Li who gave Mao a job and first introduced him to the serious study of Marxism.

Mao found in Marxist theory a program for reform and revolution in China. On returning to Chángshā, he became increasingly active in communist politics. He became editor of the *Xiang River Review*, a radical Húnán students' newspaper, and also took up a post as a teacher. In 1920 he was organising workers for the first time and from that year onwards considered himself a Marxist. In

Mao Zedong

1921 Mao went to Shànghǎi to attend the founding meeting of the Chinese Communist Party. Later he helped organise the first provincial branch of the CCP in Húnán, and by the middle of 1922 the CCP had organised trade unions among the workers and students.

Orthodox Marxist philosophy saw revolution spreading from the cities as it had in the Soviet Union. The peasants, ignored through the ages by poets, scholars and political soothsayers, had likewise been ignored by the communists; however, Mao took a different stance and saw the peasants as the lifeblood of the revolution. The party had done very little work among them, but in 1925 Mao began to organise peasant trade unions. This aroused the wrath of the landlords and Mao had to flee to Guǎngzhōu (Canton), where the Kuomintang and communists held power in alliance with each other. Mao proposed a radical redistribution of the land to help the peasants, and supported (and probably initiated) the demands of the Húnán peasants' union to confiscate large landholdings. Probably at this stage he foresaw the need to organise and arm them for a struggle against the landlords.

In April 1927 Chiang Kaishek launched his massacre of the communists. The party sent Mao to Chángshā to organise what became known as the 'Autumn Harvest Uprising'. By 1 September units of a peasant-worker army had been formed, with troops drawn from the peasantry, Héngyáng miners and rebel Kuomintang soldiers. Mao's army moved south through Húnán and climbed up into the peaks of Jǐnggāng Shān to embark on a guerrilla war against the Kuomintang. This action eventually culminated in the 1949 communist takeover.

Mao became the new chairman of the PRC, and was to retain the title until his death in 1976. Faced with a country exhausted from civil war, yet jubilant with victory, Mao embarked on a number of radical campaigns to repair his war-ravaged country. During the formative years of the Chinese communist state, Mao was inclined to conform to the Stalinist model of 'constructing socialism'. In the mid-1950s, however, he and his advisers became more disillusioned with the Soviets and began to implement Mao's preferred peasant-based and decentralised socialist development. The outcome was the ill-fated Great Leap Forward and, later, the Cultural Revolution (for details, see the History section in the Facts about the Country chapter at the beginning of this book).

The current regime in Běijīng still remembers Mao as being 70% correct and 30% wrong, and for many Chinese they will never forget both sides of their Chairman. The feelings towards Mao today are complex and contradictory. He is hated for the torturous memories and experiences that he dragged many Chinese through, but at the same time, he is revered like a god who united the Chinese people and put China on the map as a world power. For many Chinese he will always be remembered as the 'Great Leader', 'Great Teacher', 'Great Helmsman', 'Great Commander-in-chief' and 'supremely beloved Chairman Mao'.

Despite the ever-present image of Mao looking down upon Tiānānmén Square, the most common position Mao holds is hanging from the rear view mirror of Běijīng's taxis. As China moves away from its revolutionary past and into its current capitalist zeal, Mao has slowly been replaced by his successors – and has been transformed from the people's idol into a saint who will protect them from a crash or financial bankruptcy.

Detailed biographies of Mao Zedong include Ross Terrill's *Mao*, Jerome Ch'en's *Mao and the Chinese Revolution* and Stuart R Schram's *Mao Tse-tung*.

An interesting account of Mao's earlier years is recorded in Edgar Snow's *Red Star Over China*. The five-volume *Selected Works of Mao Tse-tung* provide an abundant collection of materials on Mao Zedong's thoughts.

HÚNÁN 湖南

Train   There is one train daily from Chángshā. It leaves at 7.25 am and departs from Sháoshān station at 4.16 pm, so you can do Sháoshān as a day trip. The one-way fare is Y17 and the hard-seat journey takes about three hours.

ZHŪZHŌU   株州
☎ 0733 • pop 3,656,500

Formerly a small market town, Zhūzhōu underwent rapid industrialisation following the completion of the Guǎngzhōu-Wǔhàn railway line in 1937. As a major railway junction and port city on the Xiāng Jiāng, Zhūzhōu developed into an important coal and freight reloading point and manufacturing centre. Most travellers stop here to change trains, but the city has some pleasant areas.

Places to Stay
The *Qìngyún Dàshà* (☎ 822 2222, fax 822 5356), opposite the train station, has triples for Y170 and twins for Y240 and up, which includes a free breakfast.

Another option is the *Zhūzhōu Bīnguǎn* (☎ 821 9888, fax 821 0399), on Xinhua Xilu. Clean triples are Y278. Twins with attached bath start at Y308. To get there from the train station head right past the Qìngyún Dàshà. At the next main intersection turn left and continue past the traffic roundabout. The hotel is just before the bridge off a little side street to the right.

Getting There & Away
Zhūzhōu is at the junction of the Běijīng-Guǎngzhōu and the Shànghǎi-Kūnmíng railway lines. From Chángshā it's one hour by express train.

The bus station on Xinhua Xilu has buses to Xiāngtán, which has buses to Sháoshān. It's a 15-minute walk to the train station: turn right and cross the railway bridge, then turn left again at the next intersection.

YUÈYÁNG   岳阳
☎ 0730 • pop 5,103,500

Yuèyáng is a port of call for river ferries plying the Cháng Jiāng (Yangzi River) between Chóngqìng and Wǔhàn. The Wǔhàn-

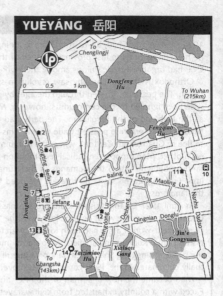

Guǎngzhōu railway passes through this small provincial city, so if you're heading to Guǎngzhōu you can get off the boat here instead of going to Wǔhàn.

Orientation & Information
Yuèyáng is situated south of the Cháng Jiāng on the north-eastern shore of Dòngtíng Hú, where the lake flows into the river. Yuèyáng has two separate sections. Yuèyáng proper is really the southern part, where you'll find the train and bus stations, many hotels and sights. Some 17km away to the north at Chénglíngjī is the city's main port. Most Cháng Jiāng ferries dock here, but there are two smaller local docks in the main (southern) part of Yuèyáng, where long-distance ferries also call in.

CITS (☎ 823 2010) is in the courtyard of the Yúnmèng Bīnguǎn, at 25 Chengdong Lu. Boat and train tickets can be booked at the ticket office of the Yuèyáng Bīnguǎn.

Things to See
Yuèyáng has a 'port city' and working-class atmosphere, and its narrow, old backstreets are a colourful contrast to China's modernisation drive.

YUÈYÁNG

1 Yuèyáng Lóu Ferry Dock 岳阳楼轮船客运站	6 Yuèyáng Bīnguǎn 岳阳宾馆	11 Dáhuá Dàjiǔdiàn 达华大酒店
2 Xuělián Bīnguǎn 雪莲宾馆	7 Nányuèpō Dock 南岳坡码头	12 Yúnmèng Bīnguǎn; CITS 云梦宾馆; 中国国际旅行社
3 Yuèyáng Lóu 岳阳楼	8 Dài Jiā Cūn 傣家村	
4 Yuèyáng Lóu Bīnguǎn 岳阳楼宾馆	9 Train Station 火车站	13 Cí Shì Tǎ 慈氏塔
5 Bùbùgāo Dàjiǔdiàn 步步高大酒店	10 Long-Distance Bus Station 长途汽车站	14 Former Train Station 旧火车站

HÚNÁN 湖南

The city's chief landmark is the **Yuèyáng Lóu** (Yueyang Tower), a temple complex constructed during the Tang dynasty and subsequently rebuilt. Housed within the tower is a gold replica of the complex. The park is something of a mecca for Japanese tourists, apparently because of a famous poem written in its praise which Japanese kids learn at school. However, it may not be worth the Y21 entrance fee.

For some fascinating exploring, head to the **Cí Shì Tǎ** (Loving Clan Pagoda), a brick tower dating back to 1242. To get there, take bus No 22 down Baling Lu to the lake, get off and walk south on Dongting Nanlu. Keep to the left so the buildings don't block your view and, after about 10 minutes, you'll see the pagoda, which lies up a lane to the right in a residential courtyard.

Dongting Nanlu and the old railway area also have some of Yuèyáng's oldest and most interesting streets, with vegetable markets, brown brick buildings and fish drying on poles.

Yuèyáng borders the enormous 3900 sq km **Dòngtīng Hú** (Dongting Lake), which is China's second largest body of fresh water. There are several islands in the lake; the most famous is **Jūnshān Dǎo** (Junshan Island), where *yínzhēn chá* (silver needle tea) is grown. When the tea is added to hot water, it's supposed to remain on the surface, sticking up like tiny needles and emitting a fragrant odour.

You can board boats for the 45-minute ride to Jūnshān Dǎo at either Nányuèpō dock (Nányuèpō mǎtóu), centrally located at the end of Baling Lu (bus No 22 more or less gets you there), or at the Yuèyáng Lóu ferry dock (Yuèyáng Lóu lúnchuán kèyùnzhàn), just north of the Yuèyáng Lóu on Dongting Beilu. The latter has more frequent departures.

For both docks, the earliest boats Jūnshān Dǎo leave around 7.30 am, and the last boat from the island departs at 4.30 pm. The return fare is Y15, and it's worth a visit for the tea plantations and other farming. Once you get off the boat be prepared for an entrance fee of Y32. There are also fast boats that get there in 10 minutes for Y30 return.

Places to Stay

Probably the best deal in town is the basic *Xuělián Bīnguǎn* (☎ 832 1633), on Dongting Beilu just north of Yuèyáng Lóu. Beds in quads cost Y20 and Y25; beds in twins with attached bath cost from Y35 to Y75. Probably the best value are the beds in 2nd floor twins for Y40. The hotel has central air-conditioning and expensive rooms have heat in winter. The hotel and surrounding buildings are of quaint traditional Chinese architecture and are in a scenic part of town. There's no English sign advertising the place, but look for white Chinese characters on a green billboard. From the train station, take bus No 22 to the Yuèyáng Lóu and walk north a few minutes.

South of the train station, on the southwestern side of the overpass roundabout on Nanhu Dadao, the *Dàhuá Dàjiǔdiàn* (☎ 824 1001) has twins/triples with bathrooms and air-con for Y108/Y118. As the station is a long way east of the lake's shore, this place is really only convenient if you need to catch an early train.

On a side street just off Dongting Beilu, the *Yuèyáng Lóu Bīnguǎn* (☎ 832 1288, 57 *Dongting Beilu*) is a friendly place offering twins and triples with bath for Y148/188. Bus No 22 to the Yuèyáng Lóu will get you there. The *Yúnmèng Bīnguǎn* (☎ 822 1115, 25 *Chengdong Lu*) is east of the lakeshore and across the railway tracks. It has twins for Y200 and triples for Y190/210.

The classiest and probably most central place in town is the three-star *Yuèyáng Bīnguǎn* (☎ 832 0011, fax 832 0235, 26 *Dongting Beilu*). Singles/twins cost Y168/248 and up. From the train station, take bus No 22 or 10 and get off after turning right onto Dongting Beilu. Another more luxurious hotel is expected to open soon, if it hasn't done so already.

Places to Eat

There are good fish and seafood restaurants, particularly on Dongting Beilu, which also has cheap spots for dumplings, noodles and breakfast. You can get refreshing drinks, ice cream and meals at the *Bùbùgāo Dàjiǔjiàn (High-stepping Restaurant)*. The friendly owners serve some tasty dishes. They also serve *bābǎo chá*, which is 'eight-treasure' spiced and fruity tea. The restaurant is across from the Yuèyáng Bīnguǎn.

Somewhat far from home, but tasty nevertheless, is the *Dǎi Jiā Cūn*, specialising in Dǎi minority food from Yúnnán. Try the *bōluó fàn* (rice served up in a carved-out pineapple) for Y20, or the *héyè dòufu* (tofu wrapped in lotus leaves) for Y25. It's on the corner of Jiefang Lu and Nanzheng Jie, which leads into Dongting Nanlu. The entrance is done up in rustic wood with waterwheels as decoration. The restaurant also has cultural dance performances for your dining entertainment. There are *food stalls* and small *restaurants* near the Nányuèpō dock and just south of the new train station.

Shopping

'Silver needle tea' remains a popular souvenir to amaze friends back home. It's not cheap – the best quality goes for Y120 for 50g – but you can buy the same amount of lesser quality for Y48. It's sold around

town, but try the shop across from the Yuèyáng Lóu.

Getting There & Away

Yuèyáng is on the main Guǎngzhōu-Běijīng railway line. There are trains to Wǔhàn (Y33; four hours), Chángshā (Y26; two hours) and Guǎngzhōu (Y200; 12 hours). There are also daily buses to Chángshā (Y31; 2½ hours) and Wǔhàn (Y60; four hours) from the long-distance bus station.

Most of the large Cháng Jiāng ferries dock at Yuèyáng's northern port at Chenglingji. Private minibuses to Yuèyáng train station regularly meet arriving boats. Bus Nos 1 and 22, which leave from an intersection about 200m inland from the ferry terminal, also take you to the trains.

There are usually four boats daily to Chóngqìng from Chenglingji. Boats to Wǔhàn leave twice daily, in the morning. The Yuèyáng Lóu ferry dock usually has one to two departures daily in either direction. Although boats are less frequent, sailing from the Yuèyáng Lóu ferry dock is more convenient if you're in town, not to mention aesthetically more pleasing: Chenglingji is drab.

Upriver to Chóngqìng usually takes four days. Chinese ticket prices from Yuèyáng are: 2nd class, Y478; 3rd class, Y202; and 4th class, Y145. Although not available on all boats, there are also 1st-class cabins for Y952. Sailing to Chóngqìng, prices out of Chenglingji are a bit lower.

Downriver to Wǔhàn normally takes under 10 hours. Chinese ticket prices from Yuèyáng are: 2nd class, Y100; 3rd class, Y48; and 4th class, Y36.

You can book train and boat tickets at the Yuèyáng Bīnguǎn ticket counter and at CITS. For more information on the Chóngqìng to Shànghǎi boat trip, see the 'Downriver on the Cháng Jiāng (Yangzi River)' section in the Chóngqìng chapter.

HÉNGYÁNG 衡阳
☎ 0730 • pop 6,924,200

Héngyáng is Húnán's second largest city. It's on the railway junction where the Guìlín-Chángshā and Běijīng-Guǎngzhōu lines intersect, and travellers from Guǎngzhōu to Guìlín often find themselves here between train connections.

Héngyáng has important lead and zinc-mining industries, but was badly damaged during WWII. Despite post-1949 reconstruction, it still lags noticeably behind its northern neighbour, Zhūzhōu.

The CITS (☎ 825 4160) office has some obliging English speakers and is around the corner from the Yànchéng Bīnguǎn at 26 Huancheng Nanlu. The office can book train tickets and arrange a guided visit to Héng Shān.

Places to Stay & Eat

Héngyáng is strict about where foreigners can stay. Close to the train station is the **Huíyàn Bīnguǎn** (☎ *833 2331, 26 Guangdong Lu*), which charges Y188 for a nice twin room with wooden floors. From the train station it's a 10-minute walk straight along the main road.

Across the river, another accommodation option is the **Yànchéng Bīnguǎn** (☎ *822 6921, 91 Jiefang Lu*), where twins start at Y248. Bus No 1 runs past the hotel, but a taxi might be best for the first time, as the main sign is in Chinese and it may be difficult to find.

The Huíyàn Bīnguǎn has a restaurant that serves great steamed dumplings and other fairly cheap dishes. Check prices first though, as it has seafood delights priced at Y200 and up.

Shān: hill, mountain

This character can be seen either as a mountain range with three peaks or as a mountain in its own right, with its peak in the middle. Either way, it is one of the simplest to remember!

Getting There & Away

Héngyáng is a major railway junction with trains to Wǔhàn, Guǎngzhōu and Guìlín, among other places. Trains to Chángshā take 2½ hours and hard seats cost Y28. Buses for Chángshā (Y40; three hours) leave once an hour.

There's also a bus to Jǐnggāng Shān (Y44; six hours) in Jiāngxī, departing at 6.20 am. To get to the long-distance bus station, take bus No 1 from the train station to the last stop on Jiefang Lu. Buses also go to Héng Shān (Y12; one hour).

HÉNG SHĀN 衡山
☎ 0734

Héng Shān is one of China's holy mountains, shooting up 1290m above sea level and covering 400km. About 100km south of Chángshā, it is also known as Nányuè Shān (Southern High Mountain), and is where kings and emperors once hunted and made sacrifices to heaven and earth.

Today Buddhists and Taoists live peacefully on the mountain and Chinese tourists flock here, especially during the summer, to pray before the gods. While there are more scenic and famous mountains in China, Héng Shān still makes for an interesting visit.

Zhùróng Diàn (Wishing Harmony Palace), built during the Ming dynasty, sits atop the mountain and is the resting place of Zhu Rong, an official 'in charge of' fire during one of China's early periods who used to hunt on Héng Shān. Taoists believe fire is a critical element in the world and selected Héng Shān to represent fire.

Orientation & Information

Héng Shān's main street is Dongshan Lu, which runs west to east and starts once you pass the town's archway. There are a few English-language maps on sale for Y2; try some of the shops and hotels on Dongshan Lu. The Héngyáng CITS office (☎ 825 4160), where English is spoken, can help arrange a guide, but one is not necessary.

As you leave Dongshan Lu and the archway, the Bank of China is on your left, at 37 Hengshan Lu. As you enter the archway, the post office is about a block down on your left. The PSB office is at Xi Waijie, or about a block south of Dongshan Lu.

To get to Héng Shān, follow Dongshan Lu until it curves to your right. **Hiking** on the paved road or marked paths to **Zhùróng Fēng** (Wishing Harmony Peak), the mountain's highest point, takes four hours by foot and another four hours to descend. The time excludes visiting the monasteries, temples, villas and gardens that dot Héng Shān.

If time is crucial, hire a motorcycle taxi to whizz you to the top, which should cost between Y30 to Y50. There's also a cable car that starts midway on the mountain and goes nearly to the top, which costs Y30. Entrance to the mountain is Y30.

Places to Stay & Eat

Héng Shān's numerous hotels on Dongshan Lu range from basic to comfortable. The cheapest option is to sleep in an extra room over a restaurant.

The tiny *Jiāchéng Jiŭlóu (110 Dongshan Lu)* is inexpensive and serves tasty dumplings and dishes. It also rents four beds for Y30 each per night. The friendly owners don't speak English, but they'll get the idea if you're looking for cheap lodging. There's no heat in the basic rooms and you must share a bathroom.

Don't be surprised if other restaurant owners offer you rooms as you eat.

At Héng Shān's base, in a dirt lot near souvenir hawkers, there's the *Fùháo Dàjiŭdiàn (☎ 566 2392, Banbian Jie)*. It has nice twins for Y60 in its main building. If those are unavailable, the staff may put you in more spartan triples for the same price. Nicer triples start at Y120.

The *Nóngyè Bīnguǎn (Agricultural Bank of China Hotel; ☎ 566 6491, 19 Zhurong Lu)* sits at the intersection of Dongshan Lu and Zhurong Lu and across the street from more expensive hotels. It has basic triples for Y88 and nicer twins with bath for Y138.

Midway on Héng Shān, the *Zǐzhúlín Bīnguǎn (☎ 566 1400)* offers basic twins with stunning vistas for Y140. Dormitory rooms in the back range from Y20 to Y30, but the plain wood beds don't look stable.

The guesthouse is near some restaurants off the main mountain road and dirt bend. A motorcycle taxi is probably the best way to get there, and it's best to call about vacancies.

For food, there are plenty of street-side *restaurants* on Dongshan Lu.

Getting There & Away

From the archway on Dongshan Lu, turn right and the long-distance bus station is a few minutes walk across the street on your left. It's the gateway to Héng Shān and also has buses to Chángshā (Y28; three hours) and Héngyáng (Y12; one hour). Arriving buses may drop you at Dongshan Lu.

HUÁIHUÀ 怀化
☎ 0745 • pop 4,766,200

Huáihuà is a drab town built around a railway junction in western Húnán. Most people use it as a transit point to or from Zhāngjiājiè, Yaqueling or Liŭzōu.

The *Tiědào Bīnguǎn (Railway Hotel; ☎ 225 1888)* is the first hotel on your right as you exit the train station. It has twins/triples for Y188/Y150. A much better deal is the *Tiānfù Fàndiàn (☎ 225 1988)*, which is right beside the Tiědào Bīnguǎn. Twins go for Y90, Y150 and up.

The *Lìdū Bīnguǎn (☎ 223 8888, fax 223 9988, 156 Yingfeng Xilu)* has standard twins for Y268. Turn left at the first intersection off the main street leading from the train station and walk about 50m.

Getting There & Away

Běijīng-Kūnmíng, Chéngdū-Guǎngzhōu and Shànghǎi-Chóngqìng express trains run via Huáihuà. There are also a number of slower trains from Guìyáng, Guǎngzhōu, Zhèngzhōu and Liŭzōu, terminating in Huáihuà.

There is a daily train to Zhāngjiājiè (5½ hours) that leaves at 11.25 am. You can also catch a train to Sānjiāng (5½ hours) in northern Guǎngxī.

WǓLÍNGYUÁN & ZHĀNGJIĀJIÈ
武陵源   张家界
☎ 0744 • pop 1,537,700

Parts of the Wǔlíng Shān mountains in north-western Húnán were set aside in 1982 as nature reserves collectively known as the Wǔlíngyuán Fēngjǐngqū (Scenic Area), encompassing the localities of Zhāngjiājiè, Tiānzǐshān and Suǒxīyù. Zhāngjiājiè is the best known, and many Chinese refer to this area by that name.

The first area of its kind in China, Wǔlíngyuán is home to three minority peoples – the Tujia, Miao and Bai – who continue to speak their languages and maintain their traditional cultures.

The mountains have gradually eroded to form a spectacular landscape of craggy peaks and huge rock columns rising out of the luxuriant subtropical forest. There are waterfalls, limestone caves (including Asia's largest chamber), fresh clear streams, and rivers suitable for organised rafting trips. It's a relaxing place to rest and recouperate and there are many short and extended hikes available.

Several towns serve as access points to Wǔlíngyuán, but the most popular gateways

are **Zhāngjiājiè Shì** (the city formerly known as Dayong) and **Zhāngjiājiè Cún** (village). The city is near the railway line, while Zhāngjiājiè Cún is situated nearly 600m above sea level in the Wuling foothills, surrounded by sheer cliffs and vertical rock outcrops.

A fee of Y62 must be paid at the Zhāngjiājiè forest reserve's main entrance just past the village. Chinese maps showing walking trails, some with sites marked in English, are on sale in Zhāngjiājiè city and village. The scenery is spectacular, but don't expect to view it alone: Wǔlíngyuán is a major national tourist area and is usually swarming with tour groups.

An airport is furthering tourism, and more hotels and karaoke nightspots are being added to the already considerable number both inside and outside the park. Locals who serve as guides will approach you, but you don't really need one. Just follow the crowds up the mountain paths.

HÚNÁN 湖南

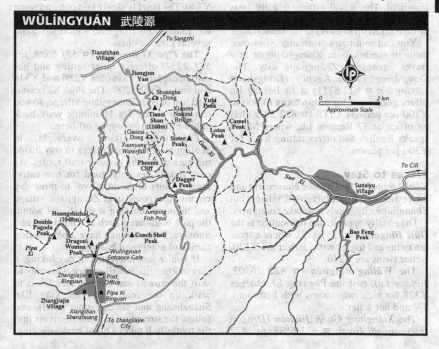

WǓLÍNGYUÁN 武陵源

HÚNÁN 湖南

Things to See & Do

The highest area closest to Zhāngjiājiè village is **Huángshízhài** and, at 1048m, it's a strenuous hike up 3878 stone steps. Like other sights that require a certain amount of exertion in China, a cable car is being built for the less physically inclined.

In the northern section of the reserve, **Tiānzǐ Shān** (Tianzi Peak) is another good hike. Like Huáng Shān, every rock, crag and gully has been given an elaborate name.

Organised tours to the park and Jiǔtiān Dòng (Jiutian Cave) often include a **rafting trip** (piāolǘ), or you can join a tour and just do the rafting trip. While there are good white-water rafting possibilities north-west of Zhāngjiājiè near the Húběi border, you'll have to make special arrangements for the equipment and transport.

In Wǔlíngyuán, most of the rivers the tours go on are pretty tame, so don't expect great thrills; still, it's a good way to get away from the crowds and the scenery is beautiful. The actual rafting usually lasts about two hours with about the same amount of time taken up in travel to the launch area.

You can join tours or arrange your own through the hotels in Zhāngjiājiè or at a travel agency in Zhāngjiājiè city. The Dongsheng Travel Agency (Dōngshēng Lüxíngshè; ☎ 822 8711) at 18 Jiefang Lu offers good rates for group tours (Y600 to Y700 per person). CITS (☎ 822 2928) has an office at 37 Renmin Lu, where Mr Li speaks English and offers rafting tours for Y300 per person.

Places to Stay

You'll probably find it more convenient and interesting to stay in Zhāngjiājiè village, but Zhāngjiājiè city hotels also take foreigners.

Diagonally opposite the bus station is the *Dūlè Bīnguǎn* (☎ 822 2872), where a spartan twins and triples with shower are Y120. Better twins are Y240.

The *Wǔlíng Bīnguǎn* (☎ 822 26302, Jiefang Lu), past the Pǔguāng Sí, charges Y328 for nice twin rooms with bathroom, TV and hot water.

The *Xiánglóng Guójì Jiǔdiàn* (Dragon International Hotel; ☎ 822 6888, fax 822 2935, 46 Jiefang Lu)* is a glittering marble and chrome establishment masquerading as a four-star hotel. The cheapest rooms are twins in the older wing at Y477. In the renovated building twins start at Y764, plus a 15% service charge.

In Zhāngjiājiè village most places accept foreigners. Just uphill from where the buses stop is the *Zhāngjiājiè Bīnguǎn* (☎ 571 2388), which has basic but clean twins for Y150. The hotel has a three star addition next door that offers more upmarket air-con twins for Y300. It also has beds for Y75 in dorms, but you will have to push to get these. The hotel can also book train tickets three days in advance.

Better value can be found at the *Xiāngdiàn Shānzhuāng* (Xiāngdiàn Mountain Inn; ☎ 571 2266, fax 571 2172), uphill from the bridge, 50m off the main road. This hotel has beds in clean twins and triples with attached bathrooms for Y300. There are also more luxurious twins for Y340. The hotel is nicely laid out, and some rooms have balconies. It's also quieter than the Zhāngjiājiè Bīnguǎn, which sits amid several karaoke clubs.

The *Pípā Xī Bīnguǎn* (☎ 571 8888, fax 571 2257) offers a quiet setting and has somewhat fancy twins for Y280 and Y348 and suites for Y1200. The Pípā Xī is situated just outside Zhāngjiājiè village, so you can save yourself a 10-minute walk back uphill by getting dropped off here.

For those hiking overnight in Wǔlíngyuán, there are places to stay inside the park along the popular trail routes. As park tickets are only good for one entry, local visitors often do a two- to three-day circuit hike, going in at Zhāngjiājiè village and hiking or bussing it to villages within the park boundaries such as Tiānzǐshān and Suǒxīyù, both of which have a bewildering choice of hotels and hostels.

If you're just interested in day hiking, a stay in Zhāngjiājiè will suffice. One way to skirt the crowds and the entrance fee is to walk up the road past the Xiāngdiàn Shānzhuāng and several other hotels, and follow the stream up past the reservoir into the foothills. It takes a bit of bushwhacking, but there are nice views and some peace and quiet in which to enjoy them. There are poisonous snakes in the area, so take care if you take this route.

Places to Eat

There are simple *eating houses* scattered around the village, and the better hotels also have *restaurants*. The places on the other side of the small stream opposite the Zhāngjiājiè Bīnguǎn on the road towards the park entrance have good *húndùn* dumplings.

In Zhāngjiānjiè village, the **Bābǐ Q Taíwāncūn Cāntīng** *(Taiwan Barbecue Village;* ☎ *823 5595)*, on the corner of Tianmen Lu and Jiaochang Lu, has a great atmosphere and good meals featuring barbecued chicken. Draught beer is available in the afternoon and evening. Mr Ding, who is of Tujia nationality, started the restaurant. He was born in Taiwan where his father retreated with Kuomintang troops after 1949.

Shopping

A good buy in Zhāngjiājiè are the tightly woven baskets with a simple black line pattern that Tujia women carry on their backs. You can find the baskets at markets in Zhāngjiājiè city and on Huilong Lu, west of Beizheng Lu. These aren't the coloured baskets sold to tourists but the real thing, and cost about Y20. Also available are other items such as wooden buckets and bamboo cradles.

Getting There & Away

There are flights linking Zhāngjiājiè city with Běijīng (Y1060), Chángshā (460), Chóngqìng (460), Guǎngzhōu (Y750), Shànghǎi (Y1060), Wǔhàn (Y460) and Shēnzhèn (Y750).

There are direct trains from Zhāngjiājiè city to Chángshā (Y98; 16 hours), Zhèngzhōu (Y110; 30 hours) and Guǎngzhōu (Y319; 24 hours). The Chángshā train leaves around 6.30 pm and gets you in the next morning at 10.30 am. You can also get trains from the Cháng Jiāng port of Yíchāng that pass through Zhāngjiājiè on their way to Huáihuà, including the daily train from Xiāngfán in Húběi that passes through

Sānjiāng and terminates at Liǔzōu in Guǎngxī. The CTS in Zhāngjiājiè city (☎ 822 7718) is opposite the Xiánglóng Guójì Jiǔdiàn on Jiefang Lu. The staff can book hard and soft sleepers, as well as air tickets.

Buses leave the Zhāngjiājiè city bus station for Chángshā in the early morning. The seven-hour trip costs Y62 and Y84 for air-con buses. Sleeper buses are also available for Y62, leaving at around 5, 6 and 7 pm and arriving in Chángshā seven hours later.

Minibuses to Zhāngjiājiè village (Y10; one hour) pick up incoming passengers at the car park in front of the train station. The minibuses stop at the bus station in Zhāngjiājiè city, which lies across the river, 14km from the train station. They then continue on to the Zhāngjiājiè village. At the Zhāngjiājiè city bus station, you can also get buses to Tiānzǐshān and Suǒxīyù villages.

MĚNGDÒNGHÉ
☎ 0744

An hour and a half south of Zhāngjiājiè by train, Měngdònghé is nestled between the hills and rivers of western Húnán.

From here you can take a 45-minute boat ride to Wáng Cūn, which is better known as **Fúróngzhèn** (Hibiscus Town). It was the location for Xie Jin's 1986 film of the same name. The film, adapted from Gu Hua's novel *A Town Called Hibiscus*, portrayed how the political turbulence of the 1950s and 1960s unsettled the lives of ordinary villagers. It turned the town into a tourist destination; unfortunately, the stone streets and wooden buildings came out much better on film than in real life. Today, the village has little character and dilapidated buildings.

One reason to visit Fúróngzhèn is for **rafting**. Trips here are better organised than in Zhāngjiājiè and you can buy tickets at the rafting ticket office at the dock. The cost is Y70 and includes transport to the launch site. Be prepared to get wet. Vendors in the village sell plastic ponchos and bags. There's also a private museum of **Tujia Culture** in an old house on the main street that's worth visiting.

Places to Stay & Eat

Up the stone steps and to the left side of the main street of the village, a private establishment with the wonderful name of *Tiānxià Dìyī Jiǔlóu (First Snail Under Heaven Restaurant;* ☎ 585 3418) has small clean rooms upstairs for Y8, although washing facilities are basic. The staff can also arrange tickets for the rafting trip, and throw in a free hat as well.

On the stream's southern side, there's the *Tīngtāo Shānzhuāng* (☎ 585 3372), which has singles/twins with attached bath for Y128/156.

It's obvious where you should go if you enjoy eating snails. There are other restaurants lining the main street. In the film *Hibiscus Town* the main protagonist is renowned for making *mǐdòufu*, a tasty snack that looks like cubes of tofu, but is actually milled rice flour topped with pickles and chilli sauce. The stalls down by the dock sell it for about Y2.

Getting There & Away

Trains from Zhāngjiājiè, Huáihuà and Liǔzōu all stop in Měngdònghé. From the train station, walk down the steps to the ferry boat dock. Tickets to Fúróngzhèn are Y4, but beware of overcharging. Boats go back to the train station roughly an hour before the train arrives.

Hong Kong 香港

☎ 0852 • pop 6,149,000

Hong Kong is a curious anomaly. It's an energetic paragon of the virtues of capitalism and yet is now part of what is officially the largest communist country in the world. A British colony since the middle of the 19th century, Hong Kong was handed back to China on 1 July 1997 amid much fanfare and anticipation.

Despite its return to the 'motherland', Hong Kong's political and economic system is still significantly different from that of the People's Republic of China (PRC). Thus, much of what you've read elsewhere in this book (about visas, currency, accommodation, international phone calls etc) does not apply to Hong Kong.

Most visitors should have few problems getting around Hong Kong – English is widely spoken and most street signs are bilingual. If you've been brushing up on your Mandarin, be aware that it is spoken by less than half the population – most speak Cantonese as their native tongue. On the other hand, Mandarin is currently in vogue and so many people are studying it since the handover that it's often a good bet to try it out.

HISTORY & POLITICS
Hong Kong must stand as one of the more successful results of drug dealing. The drug was opium and the runners were backed by the British government. European trade with China goes back more than 400 years. As the trade mushroomed during the 18th century and European demand for Chinese tea and silk grew, the balance of trade became more and more unfavourable to the Europeans – until they started to run opium into the country.

The Middle Kingdom was, understandably, upset at this turn of events and attempted to throw the foreigners out. Opium was affecting the economy to an alarming degree and creating a society of addicts. The war of words ended when British gunboats were sent in. There were only two of

---

Highlights

Population: 6.15 million
Area: 1092 sq km

- A sampan ride in Aberdeen harbour
- Riding the Peak Tram to Victoria Peak
- A delicious dim sum feast in a top-notch restaurant
- Retail therapy in the many shopping centres

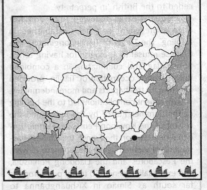

---

them, but they managed to demolish a Chinese fleet of 29 ships. The ensuing first Opium War went much the same way and, at its close in 1841, the island of Hong Kong was ceded to the British.

Following the Second Opium War in 1860, Britain took possession of the Kowloon Peninsula. Finally, in 1898, a 99-year lease was granted for the New Territories. What would happen after the lease ended in 1997 was the subject of considerable speculation. Although the British supposedly had possession of Hong Kong Island and the Kowloon Peninsula for all eternity, it was pretty clear that if they handed back the New Territories, China would want the rest as well.

In late 1984, an agreement was reached: China would take over the entire colony in 1997, but Hong Kong's unique free enterprise

Unequal Treaties

The first of the many unequal treaties foisted on the Chinese by the Europeans (and later the Japanese) was the Treaty of Nanjing. It brought the Opium wars to a close with a humiliating slap in the face for the Qing court.

According to its terms (there were 12 articles altogether) the ports of Guǎngzhōu, Xiàmén, Fúzhōu, Níngbō and Shànghǎi were to be opened to foreign trade; British consuls were to be established in each of the open ports; an indemnity of 21 million Mexican dollars was to be paid to the British; the Cohong was to be disbanded; and, perhaps most humiliating, Hong Kong was to be ceded to the British 'in perpetuity'.

Unequal treaties followed thick and fast once a precedent had been established in Nánjīng. The Treaty of Tianjin, originating in a Chinese refusal to apologise for having torn a British flag and culminating in a combined British-French occupation of Tiānjīn, provided a further 10 treaty ports and more indemnities.

Subsequent complications led to the burning of the Summer Palace by the British and the ceding of the Kowloon Peninsula. Further unequal treaties won the French the Chinese vassal state of Vietnam, gave the Japanese Taiwan, the Pescadores and the Liaodong Peninsula, and eventually opened 50 treaty ports from as far south as Sīmáo in Xīshuāngbǎnnà to Manzhouli on the Russian frontier.

In the space of some 50 years or so, a spate of unequal treaties effectively turned China into a colony of the imperial forces of the day.

economy would be maintained for at least 50 years. Hong Kong would become a Special Administrative Region (SAR) of China with the official slogan, 'One country, two systems'.

China repeatedly reassured Hong Kong's population that 'nothing will change', but few believed this. Well aware of China's previous record of broken promises and harsh political repression, Hong Kongers began looking for escape routes, especially after the 1989 massacre in Tiānānmén Square.

Nervousness about 1997 also caused capital to flee to safe havens overseas. A belated attempt by Britain to increase the number of democratically elected members of Hong Kong's Legislative Council (LEGCO) caused China to threaten to dismiss the council and appoint leaders approved by Běijīng. During the lead up to the handover, denunciations of Britain by the Chinese leadership bordered on the hysterical.

The last governor and instigator of the reforms, Chris Patten, was vilified as China's No 1 enemy. Despite protests up to the last minute, LEGCO was dissolved days before the handover and on 1 July the new Provisional Legislative Council took office, composed of Hong Kong representatives appointed by Běijīng. Former shipping magnate, Tung Chee-hwa, himself a refugee to Hong Kong after 1949, was given the post of Chief Executive.

The transition took place smoothly, but months after the handover Hong Kong was hit with the so called 'Asian flu' economic crisis that paralysed many Asian economies at the end of 1997. Tourism also dropped considerably. By the end of 1999, after two years of record unemployment figures and a slowdown in growth, Hong Kong's economy was beginning to recover.

The first incident to test the degree of autonomy Hong Kong has from Běijīng occurred in January 1999, when Hong Kong's Court of Final Appeal argued that mainland Chinese applying for residency in Hong Kong could be granted legal status if one of their parents was a Hong Kong resident. The Hong Kong government did not agree, and asked Běijīng for support in disallowing the court's decision. Běijīng complied.

The crux of the problem was just how many 'offspring' from mainland China might immigrate to Hong Kong; the government estimated that it would be well over a million people. Regardless of whether or not immigrants would aid or hinder Hong Kong's prosperity, many observers were concerned that letting Běijīng overrule the court's appeal of the law did not bode well for future issues and judicial procedures based in democratic process.

There's a strong sense of pride among the people of Hong Kong that they are no longer a colony of Britain, combined with a new consciousness about being Chinese. The gulf between China and Hong Kong in education, public services, lifestyle, language and economy, however, makes the twinning of these two entities almost absurd. At this point in time, it's very difficult to see what Hong Kong will become, other than to suggest its position as a dynamic, prosperous city may fade, and be gradually overshadowed by Shànghǎi. Yet, it will be Hong Kong expertise and experience that contributes the most to mainland China, and indeed, to its own demise. In that sense, it may be that the former colony has got the raw end of the deal.

ORIENTATION

Hong Kong's 1070 sq km are divided into four main areas – Kowloon, Hong Kong Island, the New Territories and the outlying islands.

Hong Kong Island is the economic heart of the colony, but comprises only 7% of Hong Kong's land area. Kowloon is the densely populated peninsula to the north – the southern tip of the Kowloon Peninsula is Tsimshatsui, where herds of tourists congregate. The New Territories, which officially include the outlying islands, occupy 91% of Hong Kong's land area. Much of it is rural and charming, but tourists seldom take the time to visit this scenic part of Hong Kong.

INFORMATION
Tourist Offices

The enterprising Hong Kong Tourist Association (HKTA) is definitely worth a visit. The staff are efficient and helpful and have loads of printed information – most of which is free, including a comprehensive guidebook.

You can call the HKTA hotline (☎ 2508 1234) from 8 am to 6 pm Monday to Friday or 9 am to 5 pm on weekends and holidays. If HKTA hasn't got it covered in its brochures, the staff will do their best to answer any of your questions, including shopping advice and inquiries about retailers who are HKTA members.

HKTA also has general and specialised tours (such as an innovative 'cooking tour' which includes classes, and a 'family insight' tour of public housing estates) as well as brochures on walks you can do independently. Tour prices range from HK$275 to HK$450, with a discount for seniors and children. For those interested in history, pick up the association's excellent brochure on museums and heritage in Hong Kong.

HKTA's Web site is at www.hkta.org. Overseas branches of the HKTA can be found in most European and Asian countries, as well as Australia, New Zealand and the USA.

China Travel Agents in Hong Kong

The China Travel Service (CTS; ☎ 2851 1700 hotline, @ ctsdmdhkstar.com) has numerous outlets around Hong Kong. It's a good place to get visas and book tickets to China.

The two main branches are: Kowloon (☎ 2315 7188, fax 2721 7757) 1st floor, Alpha House, 27-33 Nathan Rd, Tsimshatsui (enter from Peking Rd); and Central (☎ 2853 3888, fax 2854 1383) 4th floor, CTS House, 78-83 Connaught Rd.

The China International Travel Service (CITS; ☎ 2732 5888, fax 2721 7154).) has a branch at New Mandarin Plaza, Tower A, 12th floor, 14 Science Museum Rd, Tsimshatsui East.

Foreign Consulates

Hong Kong is a good place to pick up a visa for elsewhere or to replace a stolen or expired passport. There is still some uncertainty surrounding the fate of the Chung Hwa Travel Service, which issues visas for Taiwan, but it was still functioning at the time of writing. The following consulates could come in handy:

Australia (☎ 2827 8881) 23rd and 24th floor, Harbour Centre, 25 Harbour Rd, Wanchai
Canada (☎ 2810 4321) 11th-14th floor, Tower One, Exchange Square, 8 Connaught Place, Central
France (☎ 2529 4316) 26th floor, Tower Two, Admiralty Centre, 18 Harcourt Rd, Central

HONG KONG 香港

India (☎ 2527 2186) Unit A, 26th floor, United Centre, 95 Queensway, Central
Indonesia (☎ 2890 4421) 6-8 Keswick St and 127 Leighton Rd, Causeway Bay
Japan (☎ 2522 1184) Exchange Square, Central
Malaysia (☎ 2527 0921) 24th floor, Malaysia Bldg, 50 Gloucester Rd, Wanchai
Nepal (☎ 2667 7813) Room 1206, Concordia Plaza, 1 Science Museum Rd, Tsimshatsui
New Zealand (☎ 2525 5044) Suite 6501, Central Plaza, 18 Harbour Rd, Wanchai
Philippines (☎ 2823 8500) Room 602, United Centre, 95 Queensway, Central
Singapore (☎ 2527 2212) Room 901, Tower One, Admiralty Centre, 18 Harcourt Rd, Central
South Korea (☎ 2529 4141) 5th floor, Far East Finance Centre, 16 Harcourt Rd, Central
Taiwan (☎ 2525 8315) Chung Hwa Travel Service, 4th floor, Lippo Tower, 89 Queensway, Central
Thailand (☎ 2521 6481) 8th floor, Fairmont House, 8 Cotton Tree Drive, Central
UK (☎ 2901 3111) 1 Supreme Court Rd, Central

USA (☎ 2523 9011) 26 Garden Rd, Central
Vietnam (☎ 2591 4517) Visa Office, 15th floor, Great Smart Tower, 230 Wanchai Rd, Wanchai

Visas

Even under Chinese rule, most visitors to Hong Kong still do not need a visa. But beware – these visa regulations could change in the next few years.

British passport holders are permitted to stay visa-free for six months, but this can be expected to change and they are no longer given the automatic right to work.

Citizens of most Western European nations, Canada and USA can stay for three months. Visitors from Mexico are allowed one month. Visas are still required for Eastern Europeans and citizens of communist countries (including mainland China, where a special travel permit is still required). Visas for Hong Kong are now issued through Chinese consulates.

Life After the Handover

What's changed for the traveller to Hong Kong, now it's reverted to Chinese control (becoming the Hong Kong Special Administrative Region)? While the situation may change in the future, the short answer is 'not much'. Some of the changes are:

Consulates The British have opened up a new consulate, while the Australian, Canadian and other Commonwealth-country commissions will become consulates.

Currency The Chinese government has promised to honour Hong Kong's capitalist system and way of life for the next 50 years; thus Hong Kong's currency does not change.

Emergencies Free emergency medical service for visitors is no longer available – everyone now pays. The UK/Hong Kong Reciprocal Health Arrangement also ended with the handover: Brits should now have travel insurance for Hong Kong.

Flag The new flag (a white Bauhinia flower with five red stars on a red field) replaces the Union Jack.

Holidays Queen Elizabeth's birthday will no longer be celebrated from 1998; neither will Remembrance Day. Holidays now celebrate the handover of Hong Kong at the beginning of July and Victory over Japan Day (18 August).

Names Victoria Park may be renamed Hong Kong Central Park; most names that included the word Royal will lose that title and be known without it, eg The Royal Post Office becomes The Post Office.

Transport A new express train between Kowloon and Beijing began service in July 1997, taking about 30 hours.

Visas Many Hong Kong travel agencies arrange visas to mainland China. The border between Hong Kong and mainland China will remain in place.

For tourist visa extensions, you should inquire at the Immigration Department (☎ 2824 6111) at 2nd floor, Wanchai Tower Two, 7 Gloucester Rd, Wanchai. In general, it does not like to grant extensions unless there are special circumstances – cancelled flights, illness, registration in a legitimate course of study, legal employment, marriage to a local etc.

Hong Kong is still the best place to pick up a visa for China, and this will probably continue for a while. See the Facts for the Visitor chapter in this book.

Money

Costs Hong Kong is an expensive place to visit but prices actually dropped in 1999. If you stay in dormitories, eat budget meals and valiantly resist the strong urge to shop, you can survive (just barely) on under HK$250 per day. However, most travellers will spend more.

In general, tipping is not expected in Hong Kong. A 10% service charge is usually added to restaurant bills in upmarket establishments, and this is a mandatory 'tip'. In taxis you should round the fare up to the nearest HK$0.50 or dollar.

If you shop for cameras, electronics and other big ticket items in the Tsimshatsui tourist zone, bargaining is essential because the shops will try to charge double. However, bargaining is *not* the norm in Hong Kong. It's only normal in places where tourists congregate.

Out in the suburban shopping malls or in the street markets of Mongkok and Shamshuipo, everything has a price tag and there is little scope for bargaining. Always try to bargain for your accommodation, however, if you're staying at a private guesthouse or smaller hotel.

Currency Exchange The unit of currency in Hong Kong is the HK dollar, which is divided into 100 cents. Bills are issued in denominations of $10, $20, $50, $100, $500 and $1000. Coins are issued in denominations of $5, $2, $1, 50 cents, 20 cents and 10 cents. Exchange rates at the time of publication were as follows:

Exchange Rates

country	unit		HK$
Australia	A$1	=	HK$4.65
Canada	C$1	=	HK$5.28
China	Y1	=	HK$0.94
euro	€	=	HK$7.46
France	FF1	=	HK$1.14
Germany	DM1	=	HK$3.82
Japan	¥100	=	HK$7.42
New Zealand	NZ$1	=	HK$3.87
UK	UK£1	=	HK$12.37
USA	US$1	=	HK$7.78

Hong Kong has no exchange controls – locals and foreigners can send large quantities of money in or out as they please with no restrictions, and even play the local stock market while they're at it.

Hong Kong is, in fact, the financial centre of Asia simply because it is so unregulated. Whether or not China will interfere with this financial freedom in the coming years is the big question that keeps bankers awake at night.

Hong Kong is also a dream come true for money changing. All major and many minor foreign currencies can be exchanged. Foreigners can open bank accounts in various currencies (or in gold!), and international telegraphic transfers are fast and efficient. International credit cards are readily accepted.

Banks give the best exchange rates, but they vary from bank to bank. Excellent rates can be found at Wing Lung Bank, 4 Carnarvon Rd, Tsimshatsui, opposite the New Astor Hotel. It also charges the lowest fee for the service, HK$30 per transaction. There's also an automatic exchange machine outside, although the rates won't be as good as in the bank.

Another good bank for changing money is the Hang Seng Bank, which has numerous branches all over the city (the small branches in the Mass Transit Railway (MTR) stations do not change money). However, the Hang Seng charges HK$50 per transaction, so the rates are good only if you change more than US$200. Its parent company, the Hong Kong Bank, offers slightly lower rates.

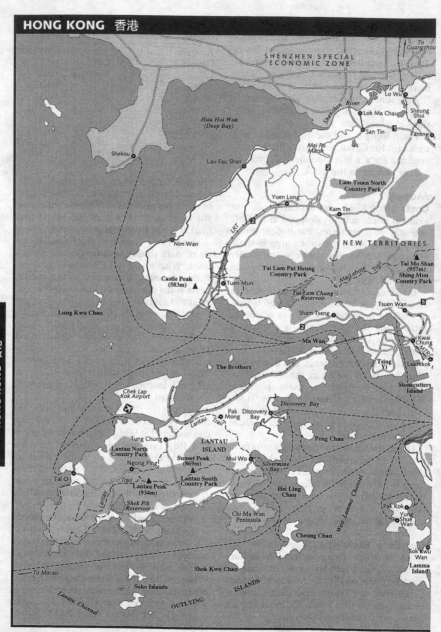

HONG KONG 香港

SHENZHEN SPECIAL
ECONOMIC ZONE

To
Guangzhou

Lo Wu

Lok Ma Chau

Sheung
Shui

Shenzhen River

San Tin

1

Fanling

Shekou

Hau Hoi Wan
(Deep Bay)

Mai Po
Marsh

Lau Fau Shan

2

Lam Tsuen North
Country Park

Yuen Long

Kam Tin

Nim Wan

LRT

NEW TERRITORIES

Tai Lam Pat Heung
Country Park

Tai Mo Shan
(957m)
Shing Mun
Country Park

Castle Peak
(583m)

Tuen Mun

Maclehose Trail

Tai Lam Chung
Reservoir

Tsuen Wan

5

Lung Kwu Chau

Sham Tseng

Kwai
Chung

Ma Wan

Tsing
Yi

Laichikok

The Brothers

Stonecutters
Island

Chek Lap
Kok Airport

Discovery Bay

Pak
Mong

Discovery
Bay

Lantau Trail

Tung Chung

LANTAU
ISLAND

Peng Chau

Lantau North
Country Park

Sunset Peak
(869m)

Mui Wo

Silvermine
Bay

Ngong Ping

Lantau South
Country Park

Hei Ling
Chau

Tai O

Trail

Lantau Peak
(934m)

Lantau

Shek Pik
Reservoir

Chi Ma Wan
Peninsula

Pak Kok

Yung
Shue
Wan

West Lamma Channel

Cheung Chau

To Macau

Sok Kwu
Wan

Lamma
Island

Lantau Channel

Shek Kwu Chau

ISLANDS

Soko Islands

OUTLYING

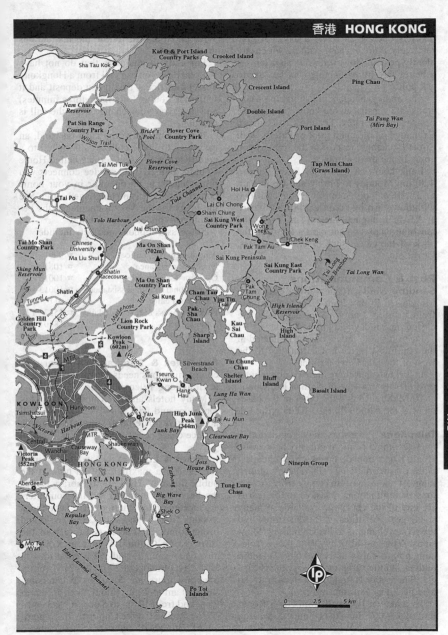

香港 **HONG KONG**

Sha Tau Kok
Kat O & Port Island
Country Parks
Crooked Island
Crescent Island
Ping Chau
Nam Chung
Reservoir
Pat Sin Range
Country Park
Bride's
Pool
Plover Cove
Country Park
Double Island
Port Island
Tai Pang Wan
(Mirs Bay)
Wilson Trail
Tai Mei Tuk
Plover Cove
Reservoir
Tolo Channel
Tap Mun Chau
(Grass Island)
Tai Po
Hoi Ha
Tolo Harbour
Lai Chi Chong
Sham Chung
Nai Chung
Sai Kung West
Country Park
Wong
Shek
Tai Mo Shan
Country Park
Chinese
University
Ma Liu Shui
Ma On Shan
(702m)
Pak Tam Au
Chek Keng
Shing Mun
Reservoir
Shatin
Racecourse
Sai Kung Peninsula
Sai Kung East
Country Park
Tai Long
Wan Beaches
Tai Long Wan
Tunnel
Shatin
Ma On Shan
Country Park
Sai Kung
Pak
Tam
Chung
High Island
Reservoir
Golden Hill
Country Park
KCR
Lion Rock
Country Park
Cham Tau
Chau
Yim Tin
Tsai
Pak
Sha
Chau
Kau
Sai
Chau
High
Island
Kowloon
Peak
(602m)
Wilson Trail
Sharp
Island
MacLehose Trail
MTR
Tseung
Kwan
Silverstrand
Beach
Tiu Chung
Chau
Shelter
Island
Bluff
Island
Basalt Island
KOWLOON
Hunghom
Hang
Hau
Lung Ha Wan
Tsimshatsui
Yau
Tong
High Junk
Peak
(344m)
Tai Au Mun
Victoria
Harbour
Junk Bay
Clearwater Bay
MTR
Central
Wanchai
Causeway
Bay
Shaukeiwan
Victoria
Peak
(552m)
HONG KONG
ISLAND
Joss
House Bay
Ninepin Group
Aberdeen
Big Wave
Bay
Tung Lung
Chau
Repulse
Bay
Shek O
Stanley
Tathong
Channel
Mo Tat
Wan
East Lamma Channel
Po Toi
Islands
0   2.5   5 km

Licensed moneychangers in the tourist districts operate 24 hours a day, but give relatively poor exchange rates, which are clearly posted. However, you can often get a better rate by bargaining (but be sure to ask politely).

The moneychangers in Chungking Mansions in Tsimshatsui are known to give the best exchange rates. Try the City Foreign Exchange on the main floor or Patel's Wall Street Exchange, just off to the right as you come in the main entrance.

Bank hours are generally from 9 am to 4.30 pm Monday to Friday and from 9 am to 12.30 pm on Saturday. You can also withdraw cash by credit card or bank card at ATMs throughout the city, as long as the machine displays your card's logo (on the back of the card), such as Global Access, Cirrus etc.

Post & Communications

Sending Mail   All post offices are open Monday to Friday from 8 am to 6 pm and from 8 am to 2 pm on Saturday. They are closed on Sunday and public holidays.

Poste restante letters can be collected at the main post office in Central, just to the west of the Star Ferry terminal.

In Tsimshatsui there are two convenient post offices just east of Nathan Rd. One is at 10 Middle Rd and the other in the basement of the Albion Plaza, 2-6 Granville Rd.

Telephone   Price wars and deregulation in the telecommunications industry have made Hong Kong one of the world's cheapest place for international calls. There's quite a range of phone cards to choose from, in various denominations. Masaya phone cards are one of the cheapest, available at many small grocery stores, 7-Eleven stores and the moneychangers in the Chungking Mansions. You can also buy Hongkong Telecom phone cards at Hongkong Telecom outlets, but they aren't necessary the cheapest. There's a Hongkong Telecom at 10 Middle Rd in Tsimshatsui.

To make an IDD call from Hong Kong, first dial ☎ 001, then the country code, area code and number. When calling Hong Kong from abroad, the country code is ☎ 852. With phone cards, follow the instructions on the card.

For calls to countries that do not have IDD service, you can call from a Hongkong Telecom office – first pay a deposit and it will hook you up (minimum three minutes) and give you your change after the call is completed.

If you don't have the cash on hand, an easy way to make collect calls or bill to a credit card is to use a service called Home Country Direct. This service connects you immediately to an operator in your home country, so there is no language barrier. See the Facts for the Visitor chapter at the beginning of this book for details.

Some useful phone numbers include:

Ambulance, fire, police	☎ 999
Directory assistance	☎ 1081
Operator-assisted calls	☎ 10010
International dialling assistance	☎ 10013
Credit card calls	☎ 011
Police business & taxi complaints	☎ 2527 7177
Time	☎ 18501
Weather	☎ 1878066

Fax, Telex & Telegraph   All your telecommunications needs can be taken care of at Hongkong Telecom offices.

Many hotels and even hostels have fax machines and will allow you to both send and receive material for quite reasonable service charges.

Internet & Email   You can use terminals for free for a maximum of an hour at the public libraries. The Central Library is near the Star Ferry terminal and the computers are located on the 9th floor. It's a good idea to book first by phone (☎ 2921 2675) and bring some ID. The Arts Library in the Hong Kong Cultural Centre in Kowloon also has terminals and it's a good idea to book by phone (☎ 2734 2042). Library opening hours are Monday to Thursday from 10 am to 7 pm, Friday from 10 am to 9 pm and from 10 am to 5 pm on weekends.

The Pacific Coffee Company has a number of outlets with Internet access scattered around Hong Kong. There's one in the International Finance Centre above Hong Kong station and one in Kowloon in the Gateway Two mall beside the City Super, an upmarket food market. The Bookworm Café, on Lamma Island, also has one terminal. Charges are usually around HK$50 per hour.

Many of the guesthouses also have Internet services.

Travel Agencies
There are lots of travel agencies in Hong Kong and some agencies offering competitive prices include:

Phoenix Services (☎ 2722 7378, fax 2369 8884) Room 7A, 7th floor, Milton Mansion, 96 Nathan Rd, Tsimshatsui.
Shoestring Travel (☎ 2723 2306, fax 2721 2085) Flat A, 4th floor, Alpha House, 27-33 Nathan Rd, Tsimshatsui.
Traveller Services (☎ 2375 2222, fax 2375 2233) 1012 Silvercord Tower One, 30 Canton Rd, Tsimshatsui.
Web site: www.traveller.com.hk

One of the cheapest places to get visas for China is at the Hung Shing Travel Service

(☎ 2369 3188, fax 2369 3293), Room 711, New East Ocean Centre, 9 Science Museum Rd, Tsimshatsui East.

Bookshops
Hong Kong is an excellent place to stock up on books, although English-language books are very expensive.

Books critical of China could still be found on the shelves in 1999, but it remains to be seen how much an issue censorship will become in the next few years.

At present, some of Hong Kong's notable bookshops include:

Bookazine Company (☎ 2523 1747) Basement, Jardine House, 1 Connaught Place, Central
Cosmos Books (☎ 2866 1677) 30 Johnston Rd, Wanchai
Hong Kong Book Centre (☎ 2522 7064) On Lok Yuen Building, 25 Des Voeux Rd, Central
Swindon Book Co (☎ 2366 8001) 13-15 Lock Rd, Tsimshatsui
Dymocks Booksellers (☎ 2522 1012) Star Ferry terminal, Central
Times Books (☎ 2504 2383) Shop P315-316, 3rd floor, World Trade Centre, 280 Gloucester Rd, Causeway Bay

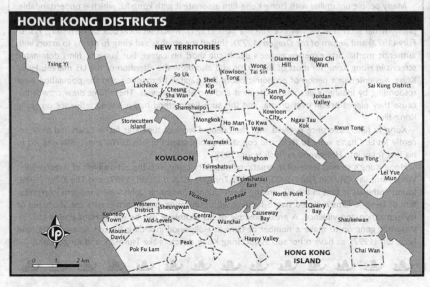

HONG KONG DISTRICTS

For used books, try Flow, at 40 Lyndhurst Terrace in Central. The Bookworm Café on Lamma Island also has used books at reasonable prices.

Cultural Events

The HKTA can give you the latest schedule of events, or check out the upcoming events in *bc magazine* or *HK Magazine*. You can pick up free copies at the Hong Kong Book Centre in Central or Swindon Books in Tsimshatsui and in various expat gathering places around town.

You can reserve tickets by calling the URBTIX hotline (☎ 2374 9009) and pick them up from any URBTIX outlet within three days. A convenient way to book and pay for movie tickets by credit card is by phoning Cityline (☎ 2317 6666).

Media

Hong Kong has two local English-language daily newspapers, the *South China Morning Post* and the *Hong Kong Standard*. Also printed in Hong Kong are the *Asian Wall St Journal*, the *International Herald Tribune* and *USA Today International*. Imported news magazines are readily available.

There are two English-language and two Cantonese TV stations. Star TV, a satellite

From Kung Fu to Cannes

The swashbuckling Hong Kong film industry has developed into reputedly the third largest outside Hollywood and Bombay. It has churned out thousands of films, predominantly action-packed kung fu dramas, and has spawned some successful international stars.

During the early years of film production in Hong Kong, films tended to mirror the traditions and conventions of the more classical Shànghǎi cinema, but amid a relatively free business environment and few political constraints, Hong Kong film gradually developed into a specific genre.

The unique feature of the cinema of Hong Kong is the successful combination of Hollywood-style audience appeal with high technical standards and the particular circumstances of Hong Kong's urban culture. Instead of being merely derivative, Hong Kong movies are infused with a distinct life of their own that strikes a chord with local viewers.

Many people unfamiliar with Hong Kong film associate it with kung fu, which is understandable, given that the first splash on the non-Asian market was via the awesome talent of Bruce Lee. Lee's phenomenal success in movies like *The Big Boss* (1971), which set local box office history, *Fist of Fury* (1972) and *Return of the Dragon* (1972), shifted the emphasis of kung fu drama to actors with authentic martial arts experience. Lee's death cut short his career, but kung fu films dominated screens in Hong Kong for most of the 1970s and also drew the attention of the US market. Hong Kong was entering a period of economic boom and capitalist expansion and the population were responding by indulging in some excitement and fun at the movies. These films drew crowds because they placed action over drama, and this sure-fire method had a lasting influence on Hong Kong film.

Kung fu films have since evolved with the talented work of superstar Jackie Chan and more recently Jet Li. Chan's kung fu flicks and cop stories dominated the late 1970s and 1980s and led to his first foray into Hollywood in *Rush Hour* (1998).

Hong Kong's second wave of international notoriety came with the action films of director John Woo. Films like *City On Fire* (1987), *A Better Tomorrow I & II* (1986, 1987) and *The Killer* (1989) found enthusiastic fans in the US, among them Quentin Tarantino. John Woo's modern interpretation of kung fu films replaced sword-fighting with gun-toting and he achieved a specific brand of stylised action and violence. A great example of his technique can be see in *Hard Boiled* (1972). Woo has gone on to make a number of films in Hollywood including *Broken Arrow* (1995) and *Face/Off* (1997), as have other successful Hong Kong directors like Tsui Hark and Ringo Lam.

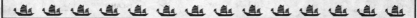

TV broadcaster, has some English programming. There's also a variety of English radio stations from which to choose.

Medical Services

There are some excellent private hospitals in Hong Kong, but their prices reflect the fact that they are required to operate at a profit. Some of the better private hospitals include Canossa (☎ 2522 2181), Grantham (☎ 2518 2111), Hong Kong Central (☎ 2522 3141), Matilda & War Memorial (☎ 2849 0111) and St Paul's (☎ 2890 6008).

Public hospitals are cheaper, although foreigners pay more than Hong Kong residents. Public hospitals include Queen Elizabeth Hospital (☎ 2958 8888), Queen Mary Hospital (☎ 2819 4111) and Prince of Wales Hospital (☎ 2632 2211).

Emergency

The general emergency phone number for ambulance, fire and police is ☎ 999. You can dial this without a coin.

ACTIVITIES

For a jog with spectacular views, nothing beats the path around Victoria Peak on Harlech and Lugard Rds. Part of this is a fitness trail with various exercise equipment.

From Kung Fu to Cannes

The essence of Hong Kong cinema lies in more than kung fu and shoot-em-up gangster films. There's a remarkable flexibility between genres, not only between films, but within films and among directors and performers. For example, Chow Yun-fat, Leslie Cheung and Jackie Chan can perform across styles in comedic, romantic and heroic roles. Hong Kong also has a very strong crop of women actors, such as Maggie Cheung, Anita Mui and Michelle Yeoh, and interesting and diverse roles are available for women.

During the early 1980s a prominent theme of cinema in Hong Kong was the imminent handover of power to China. The rise of films featuring ghost stories, demons and fantastical scenarios expressed a sense of uncertainty about the future.

The Hong Kong film industry has achieved great success and notoriety through its comedies. There's no other place in Asia that comes close to matching the quality of Hong Kong's humorous and zany flicks. Examples include: *Aces Go Places 1, 2, 3, 4* and 5 from the 1980s; *God of Gamblers 1, 2* and *3* from the early 1990s; *Golden Girls* (1995); *Haunted Cop Shop 2* (1988); *Love on Delivery* (1994); and *Mack the Knife* (1995). These films exude a wacky, manic energy, expressing a surprisingly quirky worldview that shows a side of Hong Kong that is unfamiliar to most foreigners.

There's also an evident tradition of work outside the commercial mainstream. Directors like Ann Hui, Clara Law, Jacob Cheung, Peter Chan and Stanley Kwan are known for their introspective and critical films, whether it's exploring the subject of mainland immigrants in *Comrades, Almost a Love Story* (1996); social issues in *Cageman,* (1992); or the effects of the Vietnam War in *The Story of Woo Viet,* (1981) and *Boat People* (1982). More recently, the international festival circuit has been beguiled by the lush, dream-like films of Wong Kar-wai, such as *Chungking Express* (1994) and *Happy Together* (1997), which won him Best Director at Cannes.

Today the Hong Kong film industry is in a dangerous slump. There has been a decrease in the number of productions and poor box office returns. In response to this, formal training courses have been established for crews with a general aim to produce fewer films, but of a higher quality, in an attempt to win back audience confidence.

Along with its successes Hong Kong, similar to Hollywood, produces a lot of garbage as well, much of which seems to end up as videos on that seven-hour bus ride you're taking in mainland China. Ultimately, the best Hong Kong films are like a good dim sum lunch: not too heavy, lots of variety and full of tantalising flavours to tickle the mind.

Sporting buffs should contact the South China Athletic Association (☎ 2577 6932) at 88 Caroline Hill Rd, Causeway Bay. The SCAA has numerous indoor facilities for bowling, tennis, squash, ping-pong, gymnastics, fencing, yoga, judo, karate, billiards and dancing. Outdoor activities include golf, and there is also a women's activities section. Visiting memberships are HK$50.

Another excellent place you can contact is the Hong Kong Amateur Athletic Association (☎ 2504 8215), Room 1017, Sports House 1, Stadium Path, So Kon Po, Causeway Bay. All sorts of sports clubs have activities here or hold members' meetings.

Windsurfing has become very popular in Hong Kong, especially after local athlete, Lee Lai-San, won Hong Kong's first Olympic gold medal in 1996. Some popular places to windsurf are Stanley, Shek O, Cheung Chau Island and other beaches in the New Territories. On Cheung Chau Island, the Windsurfing Centre (☎ 2981 8316) rents boards for HK$60 to HK$120. Phone the Hong Kong Windsurfing Association (☎ 2504 8255) for more information.

Hong Kong has a growing community of surfers, but surfing is not officially sanctioned. There were still discussions going on at the time of writing about whether to ban surfing completely or let it continue on a beach-sharing basis with swimmers.

The main area of contention is Big Wave Bay on Hong Kong Island. Bear in mind that you could be fined, although this has not as yet been strictly enforced. Check with the Hong Kong Surfing Association (☎ 2540 6781).

Hong Kong doesn't usually come to mind when you think of wildlife, but bird enthusiasts might consider visiting **Mai Po Marsh**, a protected wetland near the mouth of the Shenzhen River at Hau Hoi Wan (Deep Bay). Tours to the marsh are HK$345 and are booked through Gray Line Hong Kong (☎ 2368 7111). The **Hong Kong Dolphinwatch** (☎ 2984 1414) offers cruises in the waters around Hong Kong to observe Chinese white dolphins, an endangered species. Half-day and full-day cruises are available for HK$280 and HK$350.

Walking & Hiking Trails

There are numerous trails on Hong Kong Island, the New Territories and the outlying islands and there are some beautiful views from the peaks, although they can get crowded on weekends. The best place to get information on trails is at the Government Publications Centre (☎ 2537 1910, fax 2523 7195), on the ground floor of the Queensway Government Offices, 66 Queensway; the HKTA sometimes has pamphlets as well if you ask for them.

The three main trails in the region are the Hong Trail (50km), which runs through the four country parks of Hong Kong Island. A good place to start is the Peak and then head west. The Wilson Trail (78km) begins above Stanley and goes across Hong Kong Island to Quarry Bay, picks up again in Lam Tin in Kowloon, and continues to Nam Chung in the New Territories.

The Friends of Country Parks publishes a good pamphlet on the route. It's an organisation run out of the office of Tam Wing Kun Holdings (☎ 2377 2967), Room 4010, China Resources Centre, 26 Harbour Rd, Wanchai.

The longest trail is the MacLehose Trail (100km) that runs east-west across the New Territories. From Pak Tam, it traverses the Sai Kung Peninsula, heads west across the ridge of hills, and ends up in Tuen Mun.

ORGANISED TOURS

There are dozens of these, including boat tours. All can be booked through the HKTA, travel agents, large tourist hotels or directly from the tour company.

GETTING THERE & AWAY
Air

Hong Kong is a good place to buy discounted air tickets, but watch out – there are swindlers in the travel business. The most common trick is a request for a non-refundable deposit on an air ticket. So you pay a deposit for the booking, but when you go to pick up the tickets they say the flight is no longer available, but there is another flight at a higher price, sometimes 50% more! On the other hand, many travel agencies will simply not make a booking until you've paid a deposit. That's why it pays to go with a reputable agency.

The best way is not to pay a deposit, but rather to pay for the ticket in full and get a receipt clearly showing that there is no balance due and that the full amount is refundable if no ticket is issued.

Tickets are normally issued the next day after booking, but for the really cheapie tickets (actually group tickets) you must pick these up yourself at the airport from the 'tour leader' (whom you will never see again once you've got the ticket).

One note of caution: when you get the ticket from the tour leader, check it carefully. Occasionally there are errors, such as being issued a ticket with the return portion valid for only 60 days when you paid for a ticket valid for one year.

You can generally get a good idea of what fares are available by looking in the classified section of the *South China Morning Post*, where courier trips are also advertised. Some budget fares available in Hong Kong follow, but please note that these are discounted fares and may have various restrictions upon their use:

destination	one way (HK$)	return (HK$)
Auckland	3320	3920
Bangkok	1250	1650
Běijīng	1910	2850
Darwin	3310	3620
Frankfurt	2550	4400
Jakarta	1680	2120
Kathmandu	1880	3300
London	2600	4100
Los Angeles	2800	4400
Manila	950	1450
New York	3320	5220
Seoul	1970	2270
Singapore	1550	1920
Sydney	3320	3920
Taipei	1070	1320
Tokyo	2070	3300
Vancouver	2720	4520

If you're planning to fly to a destination in China, you can also book tickets in Hong Kong leaving from Guǎngzhōu or Shēnzhèn that are cheaper than flying out of Hong Kong. Domestic Chinese airlines run numerous direct flights between Hong Kong and every major city in China. Many of these flights are technically called 'charter flights'. Such tickets are usually refundable, but it's always a good idea to check.

The table in this section shows one-way fares between China and Hong Kong on domestic flights; those marked with an asterisk are 'charters'.

You can purchase a ticket from a travel agent, or The Civil Aviation Administration of China (CAAC), though you can sometimes get better rates from travel agents especially for popular routes like Hong Kong-Shànghǎi and Hong Kong-Běijīng. The most convenient CAAC ticketing offices in Hong Kong are in the airline list later in this section.

It's possible to buy all of your domestic airline tickets from a CTS office in Hong Kong (both international and domestic) and even from some non-Chinese airlines that have reciprocal arrangements with CAAC. While this should work OK for international flights, there can be occasional snags with domestic flights if your travel plans change. It can sometimes take a long time to get a refund on tickets that have been issued outside China.

Dragonair typically charges HK$100 less than CAAC on one-way tickets, and double that amount for return tickets, although again it's wise to check around. Dragonair has flights from Hong Kong to 16 cities in China: Běijīng, Chángshā, Chéngdū, Chóngqìng, Dàlián, Fúzhōu, Guìlín, Hǎikǒu, Hángzhōu, Kūnmíng, Nánjīng, Qīngdǎo, Shànghǎi, Tiānjīn, Xiàmén and Xī'ān.

In Hong Kong, any travel agent with a computer can book you onto a Dragonair flight, but you can contact the ticketing offices of Dragonair directly (see the airline list following). Within China, Dragonair tickets can be bought from CITS or a number of Dragonair representatives listed in this book.

Airport departure tax is HK$70, sometimes it's included in your ticket. If departing

Air Fares to Hong Kong

One-way air fares from major Chinese cities to Hong Kong include:

destination	fare (HK$)
Běihǎi*	880
Běijīng	1910
Chángchūn	2630
Chángshā	1200
Chéngdū	2150
Chóngqìng	1950
Dàlián	2340
Fúzhōu	1130
Guǎngzhōu	280
Guìlín	980
Guìyáng	1280
Hǎikǒu	1150
Hángzhōu	1230
Hāěrbīn	2660
Héféi	1360
Huángshān*	1600
Jǐ'nán	1590
Kūnmíng	1350
Lánzhōu	1462
Meixian*	1150
Nánchāng	1130
Nánjīng	1280
Nánníng*	1200
Níngbō	1330
Qīngdǎo	1850
Sānyà	1310
Shànghǎi	1320
Shàntóu	1080
Shěnyáng	2620
Wǔhàn	1250
Wǔyíshān*	1250
Xī'ān	1050
Zhànjiāng*	1000
Zhèngzhōu*	1800

*charter flight

by ship, departure tax is HK$26, but it's included in the purchase price of the ticket.

You need to reconfirm your onward or return flight if you break your trip in Hong Kong. This can be accomplished at one of the following airline offices:

Air Canada (☎ 2522 1001) Room 1002, Wheelock House, 20 Pedder St, Central
Air France (☎ 2524 8145) Room 2104, Alexandra House, 7 Des Voeux Rd, Central
Air India (☎ 2522 1176) 10th floor, Gloucester Tower, The Landmark, 11 Pedder St, Central
Air New Zealand (☎ 2524 9041) 17th floor, Li Po Chun Chambers, 189 Des Vouex Rd, Sheungwan
All Nippon Airways (☎ 2810 7100) Room 2512, Tower 2, Pacific Place, 88 Queensway, Central
Ansett Australia (☎ 2527 7883) 17th floor, Li Po Chun Chambers, 189 Des Vouex Rd, Sheungwan
Asiana Airlines (☎ 2523 8585) Gloucester Tower, The Landmark, 11 Pedder St, Central
British Airways (☎ 2868 0303; 2868 0768 for information) 30th floor, Alexandra House, 7 Des Voeux Rd, Central
CAAC (☎ 2973 3666) Ground floor, 10 Queen's Rd, Central; (☎ 2739 0022) Ground floor, 1 Mody Rd, Tsimshatsui
Canadian Airlines International (☎ 2867 8111) Ground floor, Swire House, 9-25 Chater Rd, Central
Cathay Pacific Airways (☎ 2747 1888) 10th floor, Office Tower, Peninsula Hotel, Middle Rd, Tsimshatsui
China Airlines (Taiwan) (☎ 2868 2299) 3rd floor, St George's Bldg, Ice House St, Central
Dragonair (☎ 2590 1188) Room 601-603, 6th Floor, Wheelock House, 20 Pedder St, Central
Garuda Indonesia (☎ 2840 0000) 7th floor, Henry Bldg, 5 Queen's Rd, Central
Japan Airlines (☎ 2523 0081) 20th floor, Gloucester Tower, 11 Pedder St, Central
Korean Air (☎ 2368 6221) Ground floor, Tsimshatsui Centre, 66 Mody Rd, Tsimshatsui East
Malaysia Airlines (☎ 2521 8181) 23rd floor, Central Tower, 28 Queen's Rd, Central
Northwest Airlines (☎ 2810 4288) 29th floor, Alexandra House, 7 Des Voeux Rd, Central
Qantas Airways (☎ 2842 1438) Room 3701, Jardine House, 1 Connaught Rd, Central
Singapore Airlines (☎ 2520 2233) 17th floor, United Centre, 95 Queensway, Central
South African Airways (☎ 2877 3277) 30th floor, Alexandra House, Central
Thai Airways International (☎ 2876 6888) 24th floor, United Centre, 95 Queensway, Central
United Airlines (☎ 2810 4888) 29th floor, Gloucester Tower, The Landmark, 11 Pedder St, Central

Vietnam Airlines (☎ 2810 6680) 10th floor, United Centre, 95 Queensway, Central
Virgin Atlantic (☎ 2532 6060) 27th floor, Kinwick Centre, 32 Hollywood Rd, Central

Bus

Shēnzhèn is the city just across the border from Hong Kong where you can get buses (and trains) to other points in Guǎngdōng. The border checkpoint is open daily from 6 am to midnight.

A new superhighway connects Hong Kong to Guǎngzhōu (Canton) – the bus journey takes three hours and there are a number of different bus companies making the trip.

In Kowloon, Citybus (☎ 2736 3888) has frequent departures to Guǎngzhōu from the bus station on the ground floor of China Hong Kong City in Tsimshatsui. Tickets are HK$150. Departures are at 7.30, 8.45, 9.30, and 10.30 am. Buses to Shēnzhèn leave at 2 pm and are HK$65 (HK$85 on weekends). There are also departures from City One in Shatin (New Territories). From Guǎngzhōu, Citybuses depart from the Garden Hotel.

Guangdong Tours Transportation (☎ 2576 9995) leaves from the New Cathay Hotel at 17 Tung Lo Wan Rd, Causeway Bay. Tickets are HK$150 and there are frequent departures in the morning until 10 am and at 2.30 pm. It also stops in Mongkok, at Exit A of the Prince Edward MTR station. In Guǎngzhōu, passengers are let off at the Liúhuā Bīnguǎn opposite the Guǎngzhōu train station.

CTS has information on other bus companies, but most of it is only available in Chinese. It also runs a bus from Hong Kong International Airport to Guǎngzhōu for HK$230.

Train

The KCR train takes 30 minutes to run from Hunghom station in Kowloon to the border checkpoint at Lo Wu. You walk across the border to the city of Shēnzhèn, and from there you can take a local train or bus to Guǎngzhōu and beyond.

Alternatively, there are express trains straight through between Hunghom station in Kowloon and Guǎngzhōu east station.

Tickets are HK$190, though a couple (not all) of trains also offer a premium-class fare of HK$230 and 2nd-class fare of HK$180. You can pick up a brochure at the Hunghom station. Trains depart for Guǎngzhōu at 8.50 am and 12.05, 1.23 and 4.08 pm. There is also a Kowloon-Foshan-Zhàoqìng train. You pass through immigration and customs at the point of departure – therefore, you must arrive at the train station at least 30 minutes before departure or you will not be allowed to board. The staff are very strict about enforcing this. You can book tickets by telephone (☎ 2947 7888).

In May 1997 the new express route from Shànghǎi and Běijīng to Kowloon opened and it offers one of the cheapest ways to head up north directly from Hong Kong. The trains leave alternate days to Běijīng (28 hours) and Shànghǎi (28 hours). To Běijīng, deluxe soft sleepers are HK$1191, soft sleepers HK$934 and middle hard sleepers HK$587. The train also stops in Chángshā, Wǔchāng and Zhèngzhōu.

To Shànghǎi, deluxe soft sleepers are HK$1089, soft sleepers HK$825 and middle hard sleepers HK$519. There are no hard seats. Phone KCR (☎ 2947 7888) for inquiries. You can book tickets at the Hunghom, Mongkok, Kowloon Tong and Shatin KCR stations, CTS or other travel agencies. You can also book return tickets.

Boat

Hong Kong has one of the most spectacular harbours in the world, so departing or arriving this way can be fun. Luxury cruise liners frequently visit Hong Kong. Unfortunately, except for Xiàmén and Wúzhōu, coastal slow boats between Hong Kong and other cities in China have largely been phased out because of competition from other forms of transportation. Keep in mind these services may also be cancelled by the time you read this. Coastal ferries leave from the China Hong Kong City ferry terminal in Kowloon.

Jet-powered catamarans and hovercrafts, however, go between Hong Kong and destinations on the Zhū Jiāng (Pearl River) Delta, as well as to Zhūhǎi and Macau. You

HONG KONG 香港

can book tickets at the ferry terminals or at CTS, who usually charges a HK$12 service fee. Boats depart from both the China Hong Kong City ferry terminal and the Hong Kong Macau ferry terminal in the Shun Tak Centre in Sheungwan.

Hong Kong – Macau There are three separate companies running rapid boat services to Macau, with frequent departures from both the Shun Tak Centre and Kowloon. See the Getting There & Away section of the Macau chapter for details.

Hong Kong – Guǎngzhōu Hovercrafts go between Guǎngzhōu and Hong Kong from the China Hong Kong City ferry terminal in Kowloon. There are two daily departures at 8.15 am and 1.30 pm. Tickets are HK$189 for economy class and HK$198 for 1st class. The trip takes just over two hours and passengers can take a shuttle bus to the Garden Hotel in Guǎngzhōu from the Húangpǔ ferry terminal.

Catamarans also leave from the China Hong Kong City ferry terminal in Kowloon for Guǎngzhōu. Departure times are 7.50 am and 1.45 pm and the trip takes 2½ hours. Tickets are HK$198/293. Shuttle buses transport passengers from the Píngzhōu ferry terminal to the White Swan Hotel and Hotel Landmark Canton in Guǎngzhōu.

Hong Kong – Shékǒu Jet-powered catamarans frequently go to Shékǒu, on the eastern side of the Shēnzhèn Special Economic Zone, departing both from Kowloon and the Shun Tak Centre. Tickets are HK$115/$150.

Hong Kong – Shēnzhèn Airport Jet-powered catamarans depart six times daily in each direction leaving from Kowloon. The trip takes about an hour and tickets are HK$189/289. The trip from Shēnzhèn airport to Kowloon is HK$18 cheaper.

Departure times are 7.30, 9 and 10.30 am, and 12.45, 2.30 and 3.45 pm.

Hong Kong – Taiping (Opium War Museum) Fast boats take at least two hours to complete the journey. Departures

from Kowloon are daily at 8.45 am, and 2.20 and 4.45 pm. Departures from Taiping are at 9.30 am, and 2.15 and 4.30 pm.

Fares from Hong Kong are for 1st class and HK$186/226.

Hong Kong – Zhàoqìng Jet-powered catamarans from Kowloon go to Zhàoqìng once a day at 8.20 am and do the journey in four hours. Fares are HK$266/HK$276 for 1st class.

Hong Kong – Zhūhǎi This is another way to get to Macau if you want to take a look at Zhūhǎi, or go into China from there. Jet-powered catamarans leave frequently from both Kowloon and the Shun Tak Centre. The trip takes about 70 minutes. Tickets are HK$177, HK$187 and HK$217 for VIP.

Coastal Ferries

Hong Kong – Wúzhōu Wúzhōu is the gateway to Guìlín. The boat journey takes eight hours, and departures from Hong Kong are at 8 am every other day. Departures from Wúzhōu are at 8 am. The fare is HK$310.

Hong Kong – Xiàmén The journey takes 20 hours. Boats leave every Tuesday at 2 pm, but it's best to phone CTS to confirm times. Departures from Xiàmén are at 3 pm. Tickets range from HK$578 for 1st class to HK$428 for 3rd class.

Hong Kong – Shàntóu Boats leave once a week and the trip takes about 14 hours. Tickets range from HK$212 for 1st class to HK$150 for 3rd class.

GETTING AROUND
To/From the Airport

Hong Kong's new airport at Chep Lap Kok opened in July 1998 (with a few glitches) and while some travellers are nostalgic for the thrill of flying over apartment buildings into the former airport at Kai Tak, Chep Lap Kok is certainly a spacious and spotless improvement (especially the public bathrooms). The massive passenger terminal has extensive services such as restaurants, travel and transport agencies (in the arrivals hall), left luggage, ATMs, banks and shops. If you're just passing through, the *Plaza Premium Lounge* (☎ 2261 2618) has an Internet service, comfy chairs and hot showers, all for HK$200. For more complete accommodation, there's the state of the art *Regal Airport Hotel* (☎ 2286 8888, fax 2286 8686), which has standard rooms starting at HK$1050.

Even though it's located off the north side of Lantau Island, there's an efficient rail service, the Airport Express, to and from Central, as well as a whole host of different bus services. The Airport Express rail line runs from Hong Kong station in Central, to Kowloon station across the harbour, to Tsing Yi station and the airport. Altogether the trip takes 23 minutes and trains depart every 10 minutes. From Central, fares are HK$70, but if you are just in Hong Kong for a day, you can return on the same fare within that day. The Airport Express stations also have free shuttle buses that go to major hotels, the ferry terminals for boats to China and Macau, and KCR Hunghom station. There are baggage check-in services at the Hong Kong and Kowloon Airport Express stations, but you can only check-in baggage two hours before your flight, so you don't save that much on convenience. From Hong Kong station, you can connect to the MTR. Tickets for the Airport Express are at the exit to the Arrivals Hall, and you can also use an Octopus card (see information on Octopus later under Mass Transit Railway).

The Airbus services to the airport run by Citybus are cheaper than the train. The A series runs from 6 am to midnight. The N series of buses follows roughly the same route, running after midnight, if you happen to come in on a very late flight.

Bus A21 (HK$33) runs from the airport and heads down Nathan Rd passing through Mongkok, Yaumatei, Jorden and Tsimshatsui then terminating at Hunghom Station.

Bus A12 (HK$45) goes to Central then through Wanchai and Causeway Bay finally terminating in Chai Wan.

Bus A11 (HK$40) goes from the airport to the Hong Kong Macau Ferry terminal, on to Central, along Hennessey Rd through Wanchai, Causeway Bay, terminating at the Tin Hau MTR station.

Buses also go to Lantau Island and destinations in the New Territories. Kiosks in the public arrival hall have brochures on all the bus services available.

A taxi from the airport to Central will cost about HK$330.

Bus

Before setting out to travel anywhere by bus, ensure you have a good pocketful of small change – the exact fare normally must be deposited in a cash box and nobody has change. Some buses, such as those run by Citybus, take the multipurpose Octopus card that can be used on the MTR and some ferries. There are plenty of buses with fares starting from HK$2.70 and going up to HK$34.20 for the fancy ones going to the New Territories. Air-con bus fares are slightly more.

Most services stop around 11 pm or midnight, but the Cross-Harbour Tunnel buses Nos 121 and 122 operate from 12.45 to 5 am. Bus No 121 runs from the Hong Kong Macau ferry terminal on Hong Kong Island, then through the tunnel to Chatham Rd in Tsimshatsui East before continuing on to Choi Hung.

Bus No 122 runs from North Point on Hong Kong Island, through the Cross-Harbour Tunnel, to Chatham Rd, the northern part of Nathan Rd and on to Laichikok in the north-western part of Kowloon.

There are three bus companies in Hong Kong – Citybus (☎ 2873 0818), New World First Bus (☎ 2136 8888) and Kowloon Motor Bus (☎ 2745 4466). The HKTA offices also have leaflets on major bus routes.

Minibus & Maxicab

Small red and yellow minibuses supplement the regular bus services. They cost HK$3 to HK$7 and you pay as you exit. They generally don't run such regular routes, but you can get on or off almost anywhere.

Maxicabs are just like minibuses except they are green and yellow and they run regular routes. Two popular ones are No 6 from the car park in front of the Star Ferry terminal in Central to Ocean Park, or No 1 from HMS Tamar (east of the Star Ferry terminal) to Victoria Peak.

Train
Mass Transit Railway The MTR (☎ 2881 8888) operates from Central across the harbour and up along Kowloon Peninsula. It is very fast and convenient, but fairly pricey. The ticket machines do not give change (available from the ticket windows or change machines) and single-journey tickets are valid only for the day they are purchased. Once you go past the turnstile, you must complete the journey within 90 minutes or the ticket becomes invalid. The MTR operates from 6 am to 1 am.

If you use the MTR frequently, it's very useful to buy a stored value Octupus card, which can also be used on the KCR, Airport Express and some buses and ferries. You can buy them at the MTR station (minimum HK$150, including deposit) and add value to them at automated machines. Seniors (65 and older) get discounted rates with the Octopus card.

Smoking, eating and drinking are not allowed in the MTR stations or on the trains (which makes you wonder about all those Maxim's Cake Shops in the stations). The fine for eating or drinking is HK$1000, while smoking on the MTR will set you back HK$2000. Busking, selling and soliciting are also forbidden.

Kowloon-Canton Railway The KCR runs from Hunghom station in Kowloon to Lo Wu, where you can walk across the border into Shēnzhèn. Apart from being a launch pad into China, the KCR is also an excellent alternative to buses for getting into the New Territories. Octopus cards can be used on the KCR, but for Lo Wu station you have to get it zapped at one of ticket booths at KCR stations.

Tram
There is just one major tram line, running east-west along the northern side of Hong Kong Island. As well as being ridiculously picturesque and fun to travel on, the tram is quite a bargain at HK$2 for any distance. You pay as you get off.

There is also a spur route off to Happy Valley. Some trams don't run the full length of the line, but basically you can just get on any tram that comes by. They pass frequently and there always seem to be half a dozen trams actually in sight.

Light Rail Transit
The LRT (☎ 2468 7788) operates only on routes in the western part of the New Territories, running between the Tuen Mun ferry pier and Yuen Long. Fares are HK$4 to HK$5.80.

Taxi
On Hong Kong Island and Kowloon, the flag fall is HK$15 for the first 2km then HK$1.40 for every 200m. In the New Territories, flag fall is HK$12.50, thereafter HK$1.20 for every 200m. There is a luggage fee of HK$5 per bag, but not all drivers insist on this.

If you go through either the Cross-Harbour Tunnel, Eastern or Western Harbour Tunnel, or any other tunnels with fees, you'll be charged double the toll. The driver is allowed to assume that he won't get a fare back so you have to pay.

Note: Taxis cannot pick up or put down passengers where there's a painted yellow line on the road.

Bicycle
Bicycling in Kowloon or Central would be suicidal, but in quiet areas of the islands or the New Territories a bike can be quite a nice way of getting around. The bike-rental places tend to run out early on weekends.

Some places where you can rent bikes and ride in safety include: Shek O on Hong Kong Island; Shatin and Tai Mei Tuk (near Tai Po) in the New Territories; Mui Wo (Silvermine Bay) on Lantau Island; and on the island of Cheung Chau.

The Flying Ball Bicycle Shop (☎ 2381 5919, @ cflying@netvigator.com) at 201 Tung Choi St (near Prince Edward MTR station) in Mongkok offers both hardware and information about cycling in China.

Boat

With such a scenic harbour, commuting by ferry is one of the great pleasures of Hong Kong. You have a wide choice of boats, although the one most familiar to tourists is the Star Ferry.

Star Ferry There are three routes on the Star Ferry, but by far the most popular one shuttles between Tsimshatsui and Central. The boats cost a mere HK$1.70 (lower deck) or HK$2.20 (upper deck), except for the Hunghom ferry, which is HK$2.20 and HK$2.70. Seniors ride for free on the Star Ferry. The schedule for all three ferries is as follows:

Tsimshatsui – Central:
    every five to 10 minutes from 6.30 am until 11.30 pm
Tsimshatsui – Wanchai:
    every 10 to 20 minutes from 7.30 am until 11 pm
Hunghom – Central:
    every 12 to 20 minutes (every 20 minutes on Sunday and holidays) from 7 am to 7.20 pm

Hovercrafts These are operated by the Hong Kong & Yaumati Ferry Company and the Hong Kong & Kowloon Ferry. The schedule for hovercrafts is as follows:

Tsimshatsui East – Central:
    (Queen's Pier, beside Star Ferry terminal); every 20 minutes from 8 am to 8 pm
Tsuen Wan – Central:
    (Outlying ferry pier area, Pier 6); every 20 minutes from 7 am to 7 pm
Tuen Mun – Central:
    (Outlying ferry pier area, Pier 5); every 10 to 20 minutes from 6.45 am to 7.40 pm

Smaller Boats A *kaido* is a small to medium-sized ferry that can make short runs on the open sea. Few kaido routes operate on regular schedules, preferring to adjust their supply according to demand. There is sort of a schedule on popular runs like the trip between Aberdeen and Lamma Island. Kaidos run most frequently on weekends and holidays when everyone tries to get away from it all.

A sampan is a motorised launch that can accommodate only a few people. A sampan is too small to be considered seaworthy, but can safely zip you around typhoon shelters like Aberdeen Harbour.

Bigger than a sampan, but smaller than a kaido, is a *walla walla*. These operate as water taxis on Victoria Harbour. Most of the customers are sailors living on ships anchored in the harbour.

Outlying Island Ferries The HKTA can supply you with schedules for these ferries or phone the Hong Kong & Yaumati Ferry Company (☎ 2542 3081) or the Hong Kong & Kowloon Ferry (☎ 2815 6063) for Lamma. Fares are higher on weekends and holidays and the boats can get crowded. From Central, most ferries go from the Outlying Islands piers just west of the Star Ferry terminal on Hong Kong Island. Besides the ordinary ferries, there are also hovercrafts to Lantau, Cheung Chau and Peng Chau.

Kowloon 九龙

Kowloon, the peninsula pointing out towards Hong Kong Island, is packed with shops, hotels, bars, restaurants, nightclubs and tourists. Nathan Rd, the main drag, has plenty of all.

Start your exploration from Kowloon's southern tip, the tourist ghetto known as Tsimshatsui. Adjacent to the Star Ferry terminal is the **Hong Kong Cultural Centre** with its controversial windowless facade facing one of the most spectacular views in the world. Just next door is the **Museum of Art**, open Monday to Saturday (closed Thursday) from 10 am to 6 pm and Sunday and holidays from 1 to 6 pm; admission is HK$10.

Adjacent to the Hong Kong Cultural Centre is the **Hong Kong Space Museum**, which has several exhibition halls and a Space Theatre (planetarium). The exhibition halls are open weekdays (except Tuesday) from 1 to 9 pm and from 10 am to 9 pm on weekends and holidays. The Space Theatre has about seven shows each day. Check times with the museum (☎ 2734 2722). Tickets are HK$10 for the exhibition halls and HK$32 for the Space Theatre.

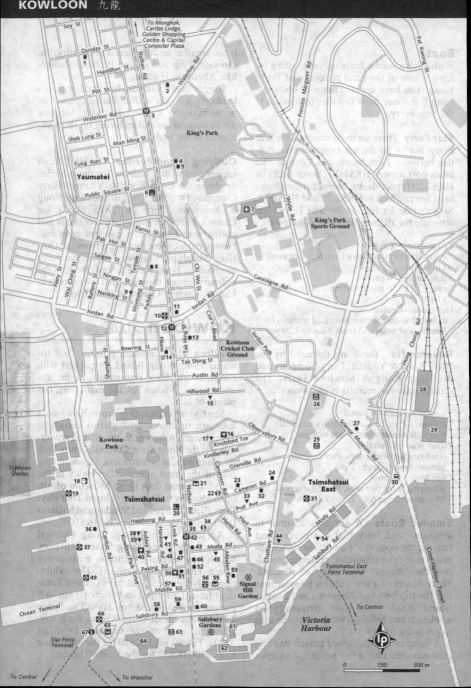

KOWLOON

PLACES TO STAY

1 STB Hostel
2 YMCA International House
4 Booth Lodge
   卜廙廬
5 Caritas Bianchi Lodge
   明愛白英奇
8 Evergreen Hotel
   萬年青
11 Hakkas Guesthouse;
   New Lucky House;
   Light Vegetarian Restaurant
   華豐大廈
13 Rent-A-Room
14 Shamrock Hotel
   新樂酒店
23 Star Guesthouse
24 Park Hotel
   百樂酒店
32 Lee Garden Guesthouse
35 Golden Crown Court
   Wah Tat Guesthouse;
   Banana Leaf Curry House;
   金冠
36 Omni Marco Polo Hotel
   香港馬哥孛羅酒店
43 Mirador Arcade
   美麗都
46 Holiday Inn Golden Mile
   金域假日酒店
47 Hyatt Regency Hotel
   香港凱悅酒店
52 Chungking Mansions
   重慶大廈
53 Mariners' Club
   海員之家
57 Kowloon Hotel
   九龍酒店
58 YMCA Salisbury
   香港基督教青年會
59 Peninsula Hotel
   半島中心
60 Sheraton Hotel
   香港喜來登酒店
62 Regent Hotel;
   Harbourside
   麗晶酒店

PLACES TO EAT

9 Temple St Night Market
   (Southern Section)
   廟街夜市（南部）
15 Tai Woo
17 Gatorfan Restaurant
33 Canton Court
38 Singapore Restaurant
   新加坡餐廳
39 Gaylord
   爵樂餐廳
41 Java South East Asian
   Restaurant
   爪哇東南亞餐廳
44 Woodlands
45 Koh-I-Noor
48 Wing Wah Restaurant
54 Tsimshatsui Centre;
   Harbour View Seafood
   尖沙嘴中心

OTHER

3 Yaumatei MTR Station
   油麻地站
6 Tin Hau Temple
   天后廟
7 Queen Elizabeth Hospital
   伊利莎伯醫院
10 Yue Hwa Chinese
   Products
   天后廟
12 Jordan MTR Station
   佐敦站
16 Bahama Mama's
18 China Hong Kong City Ferry
   Terminal; Bus Station
   中港城（客運站）
19 Gateway
   港威大廈
20 Kowloon Mosque
   清真寺
21 Post Office
   郵局
22 Hang Seng Bank
   恒生銀行
25 Hong Kong Science Museum
   香港科學館

26 Hong Kong Museum
   of History
   香港歷史博物館
27 New East Ocean Centre
   海洋中心
28 Hunghom Train Station
   紅磡車站
29 Hong Kong Coliseum
   香港體育館
30 Cross-Harbour Bus Stop
   過海隧道車站
31 Peninsula Centre
   半島中心
34 Wing Lung Bank
   永隆銀行
37 Harbour City; Eastern Palace
   海港城
40 Ned Kelly's Last Stand
   力嘉利絲餐廳
42 Tsimshatsui MTR Station
49 Ocean Centre
   海洋中心
50 Delaney's
   愛爾蘭餐廳酒吧
51 China Travel Service
   中國旅行社
55 Post Office
   郵局
56 Hong Kong Telecom
   香港電訊
61 New World Centre
   新世界中心
63 Hong Kong
   Space Museum
   香港太空館
64 Hong Kong
   Cultural Centre;
   Museum of Art
   香港文化中心；
   香港藝術館
65 Kowloon Star Ferry Bus
   Terminal
   天星碼頭巴士總站
66 Star House
   星光行
67 HKTA Information Centre
   香港旅遊協會

The lower end of Nathan Rd is known as the **Golden Mile**, a reference to both the price of its real estate its ability to suck money out of tourist pockets. At the north end of Nathan Rd are the Chinese business districts of Yaumatei and Mongkok.

Halfway up Nathan Rd between Salisbury Rd and Jordan Rd is **Kowloon Park**, which every year seems to become less of a park and more of an amusement ground. The swimming pool is perhaps the park's finest attribute – it's even equipped with waterfalls.

The **Kowloon Mosque** stands on Nathan Rd at the corner of Kowloon Park. It was opened in 1984 on the site of an earlier mosque constructed in 1896. Unless you are Muslim, you must obtain permission to go inside. You can inquire by ringing ☎ 2724 0095.

The **Hong Kong Science Museum** is in Tsimshatsui East on the corner of Chatham and Granville Rds. This multi-level complex houses more than 500 exhibits. Opening hours are 1 to 9 pm Tuesday to Friday, and 10 am to 9 pm on weekends and holidays; entry is HK$25. The museum is closed on Monday. The **Museum of History** is nearby, at 100 Chatham Rd South, in a new, larger building that was scheduled to open in late 2000. It covers Hong Kong's existence from prehistoric times (about 6000 years ago, give or take a few) to the present and contains a large collection of old photographs. The museum is open Monday to Saturday (closed Friday) from 10 am to 6 pm, and Sunday and public holidays from 1 to 6 pm; admission is HK$20.

The most exotic sight in the Mongkok district is the **Bird Market** on Yuen Po St, between the Mongkok Stadium and Kowloon-Canton Railway (KCR) railway tracks off Prince Edward Rd. It's a short walk east of the Prince Edward MTR station, which will also take you through the deliciously sensual **Flower Market**, on Flower Market Rd.

The **Wong Tai Sin Temple** is a very large and active Taoist temple built in 1973. It's right near the Wong Tai Sin MTR station in North Kowloon. The temple is open daily from 7 am to 5.30 pm. Admission is free, but a donation of HK$1 (or more) is expected.

PLACES TO STAY

For budget travellers, the situation is grim – accommodation in Hong Kong is expensive. Solo backpackers may want to seek out dormitories, some of which are very basic. There are a few YHA dormitories, which charge only HK$45 to HK$100 per bed, but all are very inconveniently located. The same is true for camp sites – they exist, but you'll spend an hour or two commuting to the city.

Guesthouses are the salvation for most budget travellers. Some guesthouses (not many) have dormitories where beds go for HK$40 to HK$100, with discounts for long-term (one week or more) rentals.

Private rooms the size of closets are available for as little as HK$160, but you can easily spend twice that. It definitely pays for two people to share a room, as this costs little or no more.

After the economic slump of 1997, the prices for many of Hong Kong's 'mid-range' hotels dropped to reasonable levels, as low as HK$350 in some cases. It's worth checking around for discounts, as the hotels are usually more comfortable than guesthouses.

At mid-range and top-end hotels you can get sizeable discounts (up to 30%) by booking through some travel agencies. One such place is Traveller Services (☎ 2375 2222). You can book discounted rooms via the Internet at www.asiatravel.com and www.asia-hotels.com.

At the airport there is a hotel reservation desk where it's possible to get discounts on mid-range hotels. You'll always get a better price if you book at this desk rather than straight through the hotels. Even budget travellers can use their free courtesy phone to call around and see who has vacancies.

The majority of cheap accommodation is on the Kowloon side. With few exceptions, the places on Hong Kong Island are mid-range to top-end hotels. Rentals are about 20% cheaper if you pay by the week, but stay one night first to make sure that the room is acceptable – noisy neighbours and rats will not be obvious at first glance.

PLACES TO STAY – BUDGET

The *STB Hostel* (☎ *2710 9199, fax 2385 0153, 2nd floor, Great Eastern Mansion, 255-261 Reclamation St, Mongkok*) is run by the Student Travel Bureau and is always a reliable place to stay. Dorm beds are HK$100, doubles are HK$300 and triples are HK$380. To get there, go to Yaumatei MTR station and take the Pitt St exit.

The *YMCA Salisbury* (☎ *2369 2211, fax 2739 9315, 41 Salisbury Rd, Tsimshatsui*) has very pricey rooms, but is attractive to travellers because of the four-person dorms on the 5th floor. At HK$190 per person, it's more than you'd pay for a bed on Nathan Rd, but the extra money is well worth it. Each room has its own bathroom and it's very clean. You can book a bed by fax or phone, but there are restrictions; guests can only stay for seven consecutive nights and it will not accept people who have already been in Hong Kong for 10 days. There's also a 10% service charge.

The *Hakkas Guesthouse* (☎ *2771 3656, 300 Nathan Rd*) is recommended for its clean rooms and friendly management. Singles/doubles/triples with bath are HK$200/250/300. It's located in the New Lucky House, at the intersection with Jordan Rd. Also in this neighbourhood, the unpretentious *Rent-A-Room* (☎ *2366 3011, fax 2366 3588, Flat A, 2nd floor, Knight Garden, 7-8 Tak Hing St*) is very good value. Singles/doubles are HK$250/350. Thomas Tang, the manager, even has a Web site at www.rentaroomhk.com that's packed with information.

Near the south end of Kowloon Park, the *Wah Tat Guesthouse* (☎ *2366 6121, fax 2311 7195, 5th floor, Golden Crown Court, 66-70 Nathan Rd, Tsimshatsui*) is spotlessly clean and highly recommended. Rooms with shared bath are HK$150 and with bath are HK$250. It's hidden in the back part of the building.

Also in this neighbourhood, down Cameron Rd, the *Star Guesthouse* (☎ *2723 8951, fax 2311 2275, 6th floor, 21 Cameron Rd*) is immaculately clean. *Lee Garden Guesthouse* (☎ *2367 2284, 8th floor, D Block, 36 Cameron Rd*) is closer to Chatham Rd. Both guesthouses are run by the same owner, the charismatic Charlie Chan. Rooms with shared bath are HK$250 and with private bath they jump to HK$300 and HK$350.

Chungking Mansions

There is probably no other place in the world like *Chungking Mansions* (*30 Nathan Rd*), the budget accommodation ghetto of Hong Kong. It's a huge high-rise dump at in the heart of Tsimshatsui with approximately 80 guesthouses. It's divided into five blocks labelled A to E, each with its own derelict lift.

If you stand around the lobby with your backpack, chances are that the touts from the guesthouses will find you before you find them.

With few exceptions, there is little difference in prices for private rooms, but dormitories are of course significantly cheaper. The price range for a private room is roughly HK$150 to HK$250, while dormitory beds go for about HK$40 to HK$100, although more dormitories are available in the Mirador Arcade further up Nathan Rd.

Dormitories are getting harder to find in the Chungking Mansions, but they are still available at the ever-popular *Travellers' Hostel* (☎ *2368 7710, 16th floor, A block*), which has beds for HK$40; it also has female-only dorm rooms and double rooms for HK$80.

Cheaper guesthouses in the Chungking Mansions include the friendly *Park Guesthouse* (☎ *2368 1689, 15th floor, A Block*) with single and double rooms with bath for HK$120 and HK$160. Singles/doubles are HK$100/110 with shared bath. The *Peking Guesthouse* (☎ *2723 8320, A Block, 12th floor*) is another well-managed place, with singles/doubles for HK$120 and HK$180 with shared bath. Singles/doubles are HK$140/200 to $250 with bath.

A little deeper in the bowels of Chungking Mansions, the *Garden Guesthouse* (☎ *2368 0981, 16th floor, C Block,*) is an excellent place and has singles/doubles for HK$120/180 with bath.

Mirador Arcade

You can avoid the stigma of staying in Chungking Mansions by checking out *Mirador Arcade* (*58 Nathan Rd*). There are numerous places here and it's a bit cleaner and less crowded.

The **Man Hing Lung** (☎ 2722 0678, fax 2311 6669, Flat F2, 14th floor) is an old favourite. All rooms come equipped with private bath, air-conditioning and a TV. Singles are HK$150 to HK$200, doubles are HK$250 and up and dormitories are HK$80 per bed. Readers have also recommended the **New Garden** (☎ 2311 2523, fax 2368 5241, Flat F4, 13th floor). Dormitory beds are HK$60 and singles/doubles with bath are HK$150/HK$180.

Another place recommended by travellers is the **Cosmic Guesthouse** (☎ 2739 4952, fax 2311 5260, 12th floor), which is run by two women. Clean rooms with bath are HK$130/180 for singles/doubles. Nicer doubles are HK$200 and HK$220. The **Man Lee Tak Guesthouse** (☎ 2739 2717, fax 2368 1233, Flat A1, 6th floor) has newly renovated rooms. Singles with bath are HK$150 and doubles with bath range from HK$200 to HK$280.

PLACES TO STAY – MID-RANGE & TOP END

Mid-range hotels cost generally between HK$550 and HK$1200, but prices have come down in recent years, and there are often good low season discounts.

One of the best deals in Kowloon is at the **Mariners' Club** (☎ 2368 8261, fax 2366 0928, 11 Middle Rd, Tsimshatsui). Once a hostel for sailors and members only, it's now open to the public. Doubles with breakfast are HK$420. It also has singles with shared bath available for HK$270.

The **Caritas Lodge** (☎ 2339 3777, fax 2338 2864, 134 Boundary St, Mongkok) (not far from the Prince Edward MTR station) is another good deal, with singles/doubles for HK$330/385. It also has discounts during the low season. Further south, the **Caritas Bianchi Lodge** (☎ 2388 1111, fax 2770 6669, 4 Cliff Rd, Yaumatei) offers singles/doubles for HK$360/410, including breakfast, but not the 10% service charge. Nearby, **Booth Lodge** (☎ 2771 9266, fax 2385 1140, 11 Wing Sing Lane, Yaumatei) has double rooms for HK$418, including breakfast. It's run by the Salvation Army, but at these prices you can expect some comfort.

The **Shamrock Hotel** (☎ 2735 2271, fax 2736 7354, 223 Nathan Rd, Yaumatei) is in a convenient location. The rooms are a bit small but more comfortable than a guesthouse. Singles/doubles are HK$373/430. Further north off Nathan Rd, the **Evergreen Hotel** (☎ 2780 4222, fax 2385 8584, 42-52 Woosung St, Yaumatei) normally has singles/doubles for HK$600/700, but discounts of up to 40% including breakfast, make this place hard to beat.

The **YMCA International House** (☎ 2771 9111, fax 2771 5238, 23 Waterloo Rd, Yaumatei) is always reliable, with rooms ranging from HK$682 to HK$1056, including breakfast. It will offer a considerable discount for stays of more than seven days. The **YWCA Anne Black Guesthouse** (☎ 2713 9211, fax 2761 1269, 5 Man Fuk Rd, Mongkok) is inconveniently located, but the rooms are reasonably priced. It's near Pui Ching and Waterloo Rds, up a hill behind a Caltex petrol station. Singles with shared bath are HK$352 and singles/doubles with bath are HK$385/396, but expect discounts of about 20% during the low season.

You can get as much as 30% off rooms in the more expensive hotels by booking through a travel agency.

One of the most unpretentious and comfortable places to stay in the Tsimshatsui area is the **YMCA Salisbury** (☎ 2369 2211, fax 2739 9315, 41 Salisbury Rd, Tsimshatsui). Singles/doubles are HK$880/1030, while harbour view rooms are HK$1150 and HK$1270. For slightly lower prices, the equally comfortable **Park Hotel** (☎ 2366 1371, fax 2739 7259, 61-65 Chatham Rd South, Tsimshatsui) is a favourite with tour groups. Doubles are HK$900, plus 15% tax and service charge, but it offers discount specials that bring the rooms down to HK$700.

The **Kowloon Hotel** (☎ 2369 8698, fax 2301 2668, 19-21 Nathan Rd, Tsimshatsui) is also relatively reasonable, with singles/doubles for HK$850/950, plus a 13% tax and service charge. The **Omni Marco Polo Hotel** (☎ 2113 0888, fax 2113 0111, Harbour City, Canton Rd, Tsimshatsui) has rack rates of HK$1950, but was offering 50% discounts at the time of writing.

The **Sheraton Hotel** (☎ 2369 1111, fax 2368 1999, 20 Nathan Rd, Tsimshatsui) has undergone a massive renovation and was offering 50% discounts on its HK$2000 rooms. Similarly, in the wake of declining tourism and a weak economy in Hong Kong, the **Holiday Inn Golden Mile** (☎ 2369 3111, fax 2369 8016, 46-52 Nathan Rd, Tsimshatsui) has the same strategy. Double rooms listed at HK$2300 have been known to go for HK$1090. The **Hyatt Regency Hotel** (☎ 2311 1234, fax 2367 3289, 67 Nathan Rd, Tsimshatsui) is nearby and also offers special rates of HK$1000 for its standard rooms.

The best hotels in Kowloon, however, are still priced beyond the means of most mortals. The **Peninsula Hotel** (☎ 2366 6251, fax 2721 4399, Salisbury Rd, Tsimshatsui) has rooms that start at HK$2600, plus a 13% tax and service charge. Suites begin at HK$5200 and go as high as HK$38,000. Not to be outdone, the **Regent Hotel** (☎ 2721 1211, fax 2739 4546, Salisbury Rd, Tsimshatsui) charges HK$2850 for its standard rooms and HK$3700 for rooms with a view, plus a 13% tax and service charge.

PLACES TO EAT

Hong Kong offers incredible variety when it comes to food. You should try dim sum at least once, a uniquely Cantonese dish served for breakfast or lunch, but never dinner. Dim sum delicacies are normally steamed in a small bamboo basket and you pay by the number of baskets you order. The baskets are stacked up on pushcarts and rolled around the dining room. You choose whatever you like from the carts, so no menu is needed.

In Cantonese restaurants, tea is often served free of charge, or at most you'll pay HK$1 for a big pot, which can be refilled indefinitely. On the other hand, coffee is seldom available except in western restaurants or coffee shops and is never free.

There are a lot of restaurants concentrated in the tourist area of Tsimshatsui.

Breakfast

If your hotel doesn't serve breakfast, you may find it difficult to eat before 9 am, when most of the restaurants open. The window of

the **Wing Wah Restaurant** (☎ 2721 2947, 21A Lock Rd) is always filled with great-looking cakes and pastries. It's near Swindon Bookstore and the Hyatt Regency. Inexpensive Chinese food is also served and – a rare treat for a Hong Kong budget Chinese cafe – there is an English menu.

The mid-1990s brought coffee culture to Hong Kong, and you can usually find small shops and kiosks commercial areas brewing up something resembling a Starbucks concoction.

To really appreciate what Hong Kong has to offer in the morning, one of the best places to have breakfast is at the **Harbourside** (☎ 2313 2405) in the Regent Hotel. The view is splendid, but it's not cheap; the buffet is HK$225. The **Peninsula Hotel** (☎ 2366 6251) is another elegant place for breakfast, or, if you get up late, try the afternoon tea.

Chinese Cuisine

Dim sum is normally served from around 11 am to 3 pm, but a few places have it available for breakfast.

The **Canton Court** (☎ 2739 3311, Guangdong Hotel, 18 Prat Ave, Tsimshatsui) serves dim sum from 7 am to 3 pm and the **Eastern Palace** (☎ 2730 6011, 3rd floor, Omni Hongkong Hotel, Shopping Arcade, Harbour City, Canton Rd, Tsimshatsui), has dim sum from 11.30 am to 3 pm

Harbour View Seafood (☎ 2722 5888, 3rd floor, Tsimshatsui Centre, 66 Mody Rd, Tsimshatsui East) offers dim sum from 11 am to 5 pm and the **Tai Woo** (☎ 2369 9773, 14-16 Hillwood Rd, Yaumatei) serves from 11 am to 3 pm. All offer quality food and reasonable prices.

The cheapest place to enjoy authentic Chinese cuisine is at the **Temple St Night Market** in Yaumatei. It starts at about 8 pm and begins to fade at 11 pm. There are also plenty of mainstream indoor restaurants with variable prices.

Indian Cuisine

The greatest concentration of cheap Indian restaurants is in Chungking Mansions on Nathan Rd. Despite the grotty appearance of the entrance to the Mansions, many of the restaurants are surprisingly plush inside. A meal of curried chicken and rice, or curry with chapattis and dhal (lentil curry), will cost around HK$30 per person.

The mezzanine floor has a number of places from the cheaper *Nepal Fast Food* to the more upmarket *Swagat* (☎ *2722 5350*), and all are good value. The *Sher-E-Punjab* (☎ *2368 0859)* is also on this floor (as well as upstairs on the 3rd floor) and it has free delivery.

Upstairs in Chungking Mansions are many other places with better food and a more pleasant atmosphere. Prices are still low, with set meals from HK$40 or so, although these are often only available at lunch. One of the best is the *Delhi Club* (☎ *2368 1682, 3rd floor, C block),* which offers free delivery, and also worth checking out is the *Islamabad Club* (☎ *2721 5362, 4th floor, C block),* which serves good Indian and Pakistani halal food.

The *Taj Mahal Club Mess* (☎ *2722 5454, 3rd floor, B block)* is excellent with good service; and inexpensive, delicious food can be found at the *Kyber Pass* (☎ *2721 2786, 7th floor, E block).*

The more upmarket *Gaylord* (☎ *2376 1001, 1st floor, 11 Ashley Centre, 23-25 Ashley Rd)* is well known in Hong Kong and you won't be disappointed.

Asian Cuisine

The *Java South East Asian Restaurant* (☎ *2367 1230, Ground floor, Han Hing Mansion, 38 Hankow Rd, Tsimshatsui)* is a good place to enjoy a *rijsttafel*, literally meaning a rice table, for about HK$150 per person.

Japanese restaurants are pretty expensive in Hong Kong, but for some good, mid-range meals, try *Gatorfan* (☎ *2722 1555, Ground floor, Prosperous Centre, 1 Knutsford Terrace, Tsimshatsui).*

The *Singapore Restaurant* (☎ *2376 1282, 23 Ashley Rd, Tsimshatsui)* has cheap, no-nonsense meals, with a mixture of western and Malaysian-style Chinese cooking.

For something with a little more spice, try the *Banana Leaf Curry House* (☎ *2721 4821, 3rd floor, Golden Crown Court, 68 Nathan Rd, Tsimshatsui).*

Vegetarian

A popular place for locals is the *Light Vegetarian Restaurant* (☎ *2384 2833, Shop 1, Ground floor, New Lucky House, 13 Jordan Rd).* The prices are reasonable and it also has dim sum from 11 am.

In Tsimshatsui, the excellent *Koh-I-Noor* (☎ *2368 3065, 3-4 Peninsula Mansion, 16C Mody Rd)* has delicious tandoori (meat or vegetables cooked in a clay oven), as well as a vegetarian buffet. In East Tsimshatsui, *Woodlands* (☎ *2369 3718, Ground floor, Mirror Tower, 61 Mody Rd)* specialises in vegetarian dishes in a friendly atmosphere.

ENTERTAINMENT

There's as much to do in Hong Kong in the evening as during the day, but none of it comes cheap and the best places are on Hong Kong Island. It's impossible to list all the bars and clubs here and the following is only a selection: it's best to check out reviews and listings in *bc magazine* or *HK Magazine*.

Ned Kelly's Last Stand (☎ *2376 0562, 11A Ashley Rd),* open from 11 am to 2 pm, became famous as a real Australian pub complete with meat pies. They often have live music.

Delaney's (☎ *2301 3980, Basement, Mary Building, 71-77 Peking Rd)* has Irish food, live folk music and great beer.

It's also worthwhile to check out the places on Knutsford Terrace, a narrow alley north of Kimberley Rd (which is one block north of Kimberley St). The easiest way to find it is through Observatory Rd, which runs west off Chatham Rd. *Bahama Mama's* (☎ *2368 2121)* and a number of other bars and restaurants are located here.

SHOPPING

The HKTA advises tourists to shop where they see the HKTA red logo on display, although this is no guarantee. The free *Official Shopping Guide*, published by the HKTA and available at its outlets, is very useful, especially if you're looking for a specific item.

Clothing is the best buy in Hong Kong. All the cheap stuff comes from China and most is decent quality, but check zippers and stitching carefully – there is some real junk around. You'll find the cheapest buys at the street markets at Tong Choi St in Mongkok and Apliu St in Shamshuipo.

Better quality stuff is found in Tsimshatsui on the eastern end of Granville Rd. Two Chinese chain stores with Italian names, Giordano's and Bossini, offer quality clothing at reasonable prices.

Yue Hwa Chinese Products, at 301 Nathan Rd, Yaumatei (corner of Nathan and Jordan Rds), is a good place to pick up everyday consumer goods and one of the best places to get eyeglasses made. It's also a good place to pick up Chinese herbal medicine and other things Chinese you might have missed on the mainland.

Sometimes it's easier to find the quintessential Chinese product in Hong Kong than it is in mainland China. Try the Chinese Arts and Crafts stores that have branches in Kowloon and on Hong Kong Island. There's one at Star House (you can't miss the sign outside) at 3 Salisbury Rd in Tsimshatsui.

The Golden Shopping Centre, Basement, 146-52 Fuk Wah St, Shamshuipo, has the cheapest collection of desktop computers, as does the New Capital Computer Plaza at 85-95 Un Chau St. You can find these places easily from the Shamshuipo MTR station. Another good place to explore is Mongkok Computer Centre, on the corner of Nelson and Fa Yuen Sts in Mongkok.

For laptop computers, the best shopping centre in Kowloon is Star Computer City, on the 2nd floor of Star House, at 3 Salisbury Rd, near the Star Ferry terminal, Tsimshatsui.

If it's a camera you need, don't even waste your time on Nathan Rd in Tsimshatsui. But if you're in a hurry, the best seem to be Kimberley Camera Company (☎ 2721 2308) and David Chan (☎ 2723 3886), located in Champagne Court, 16 Kimberley Rd. You can also find used cameras and lenses here.

Apliu St in Shamshuipo has the best collection of electronics shops selling personal stereos, CD players and the like.

HMV (☎ 2302 0122), at 12 Peking Rd in Tsimshatsui, has the largest collection of CDs in Hong Kong. KPS is also a good chainstore for discounted CDs and tapes with branches around the city – most convenient is the shop in the basement of the Silvercord Shopping Centre on Canton Rd, Tsimshatsui.

Flying Ball Bicycle Shop (☎ 2381 5919, ✉ cflying@netvigator.com), 201 Tung Choi St (near Prince Edward MTR station), Mongkok, is the best bike shop in Asia, for both information and parts.

Hong Kong is a good place to pick up decent backpacks, sleeping bags, tents and other gear for hiking, camping and travelling. Mongkok is by far the best neighbourhood to look for this stuff, although there are a couple of odd places in nearby Yaumatei. Protrek (☎ 2332 8699), at 466-72 Nathan Rd in Yaumatei, has a good selection of gear, as well as printed information.

Hong Kong Island

The northern and southern sides of the island have very different characters. The northern side is an urban jungle, while much of the south is still surprisingly rural (but developing fast). The central part of the island is incredibly mountainous and protected from further development by a country park.

NORTHERN SIDE

Central is the bustling business centre of Hong Kong. A free shuttle bus from the Star Ferry terminal brings you to the lower station of the famous Peak Tram on Garden Rd. The tram terminates at the top of **Victoria Peak** (552m) and the ride costs HK$18 one way or HK$28 return. The tram opens at 7 am and closes at midnight.

It's worth repeating the peak trip at night as the illuminated view is spectacular if the weather cooperates. Don't just admire the view from the top – wander up Mt Austin Rd to **Victoria Peak Garden** or take the more leisurely stroll around Lugard and Harlech Rds; together they make a complete circuit of the peak. You can walk right down to Aberdeen on the southern side of the island or you can try Old Peak Rd for a

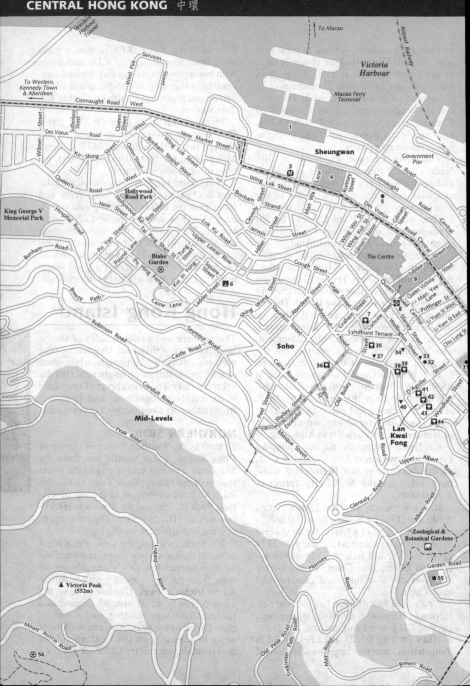

To Macau

Victoria Harbour

Western Harbour Tunnel

Airport Railway

Services

West Fire Street

West

Connaught Road West

To Western, Kennedy Town & Aberdeen

Sutherland Street

Des Voeux Road

Queen Street

New Market Street

Wilmer Street

Ko–Shing Street

Wing Lok Street

Queen Street

Bonham Strand West

Queen's Road West

New Street

Hollywood Road

Hospital Road

Bonham Road

King George V Memorial Park

Hollywood Road Park

Po Yan Street

Tai Ping Shan Street

Pound Lane

Po Hing Fong

Blake Garden

Kui In Fong

Upper Lascar Row

Ladder Street

Lok Ku Road

Hiller Street

Jervois Street

Cleverly Street

Bonham Strand

Wing Lok Street

Man Wa Lane

Rumsey Street

Des Voeux Road

Gilman's Street

Connaught Road

Sheungwan

Government Pier

Pier Road

Connaught Road Central

Jubilee Street

The Centre

Cleverly Street

Wing Wo St

Gilman's Bazaar

Queen's Road Central

Queen Victoria St

Mee Yee Lane

Pottinger Street

Man Yee Lane

Queen's Road Central

Li Yuen St West

Li Yuen St East

Chiu Lung St

Breezy Path

Robinson Road

Castle Road

Seymour Road

Shing Wong Street

Gough Street

Gage Street

Graham Street

Cochrane Street

Wellington Street

Stanley Street

D'Aguilar Street

Aberdeen Street

Hollywood Road

Peel Street

Lyndhurst Terrace

Graham Street

Soho

Caine Road

Conduit Road

Staunton Street

Elgin St

Shelley Street

Old Bailey

Escalator

Mosque Street

Arbuthnot Road

Peak Road

Upper — Albert — Road

Glenealy — Road

Wyndham Street

Lan Kwai Fong

Mid-Levels

Victoria Peak (552m)

Mount Austin Road

Lugard Road

Hornsey Road

Albany Road

Tregunter Path Road

May Road

Old Peak Road

Garden Road

Brewin Road

Zoological & Botanical Gardens

■ 56

■ 55

■ 1

■ 2

M 3

4

5

■ 6

7

7

8

9

33

32

34

35

37

36

38

39

40

41

42

43

44

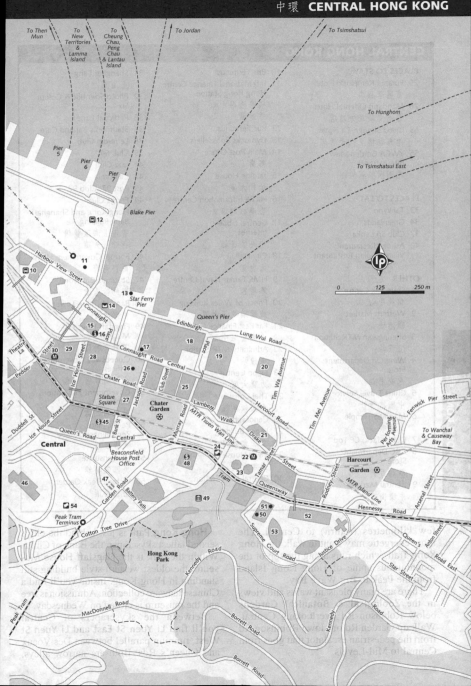

CENTRAL HONG KONG

PLACES TO STAY

25 Furama Kempinski Hotel
富麗華酒店
28 Mandarin Oriental Hotel
香港文華東方酒店
53 Island Shangri-La Hotel
港島香格里拉大酒店
55 YWCA Garden View
International
花園國際賓館

PLACES TO EAT

33 Tai Woo
34 Greenlands
37 Club Sri Lanka
40 Ashoka Restaurant;
Village Indian Restaurant

OTHER

1 Shun Tak Centre
信德中心
2 Western Market
西港城
3 Sheungwan MTR Station
上環站
4 Wing On Department
Store
永安中心
5 China Travel Service
中國旅行社
6 Man Mo Temple
文武廟
7 Dublin Jack; CE Top
8 CRC Department
Store
華潤百貨
9 Central Market
中環街市

10 Bus Terminus
11 International Finance Centre;
Hong Kong Station
國際金融中心、
香港站
12 Bus Terminus
13 Dymocks Booksellers
14 Main Post Office
郵局
15 Jardine House
怡和大廈
16 HKTA Information Centre
香港旅遊協會
17 Central Library;
Internet
中央圖書館
18 City Hall
大會堂
19 HMS Tamar Naval Centre
添馬艦
20 Prince of Wales Building
威爾斯親王大廈
21 Far East Finance Centre
遠東金融中心
22 Admiralty MTR Station
金鐘站
23 Lippo Centre
力寶大廈
24 Thai Consulate
泰國領事館
26 Cenotaph
27 Legco Building
立法會大樓
29 Swire House
太古大廈
30 Central MTR Station
中環站

31 Shanghai Tang
上海灘
32 Photo Scientific & Colour
Six
35 Petticoat Lane
36 Staunton's Bar and Cafe
38 Le Jardin Club
39 Club 64
41 Jazz Club
42 California
43 Post 97; Club 97
44 Fringe Club
45 Hong Kong and Shanghai
Bank Building
香港上海匯豐銀
行總行大廈
46 Former Government House
前督憲府
47 St John's Cathedral
聖約翰座堂
48 Bank of China Tower
中銀大廈
49 Flagstaff House
Museum
茶具文物館
50 Queensway Government
Offices
金鐘道政府大樓
51 Government Publications
Centre
政府新聞處
52 Pacific Place;
Zen Chinese Cuisine
太古廣場
54 US Consulate
美國領事館
56 Victoria Peak Garden
山頂公園

few kilometres (return) to Central. The more energetic may want to walk the **Hong Kong Trail**, which runs along the top of the mountainous spine of Hong Kong Island from the Peak to Big Wave Bay.

There are many pleasant walks and views in the **Zoological & Botanical Gardens** below Robinson Rd overlooking Central. Walk up Garden Rd or down Robinson Rd from the pedestrian escalator that goes from Central to Mid-Levels.

Hong Kong Park is just behind the city's second tallest skyscraper, the Bank of China. Within the park is the **Flagstaff House Museum**, the oldest western-style building still standing in Hong Kong. Inside you'll find a Chinese teaware collection. Admission is free and the museum is closed on Wednesday.

Between the skyscrapers of Central you'll find **Li Yuen St East** and **Li Yuen St West**, running parallel between Des Voeux and Queen's Rds. Both are narrow alleys, closed to motorised traffic and crammed with shops and stalls selling everything imaginable.

The **Hillside Escalator Link** is a mode of transport that has become a tourist attraction. The 800m moving walkway (known as a 'travelator') runs from the Vehicular ferry pier alongside the Central Market and up Shelley St to the Mid-Levels.

West of Central in the Sheungwan district is appropriately named **Ladder St**, which climbs steeply. At the junction of Ladder St and Hollywood Rd is **Man Mo Temple**, the oldest temple in Hong Kong. A bit further north near the Hong Kong Macau ferry terminal is the indoor **Western Market**, a four-storey red-brick building built in 1906 and now fully renovated.

At the Western Market you can hop on one of Hong Kong's delightfully ancient double-decker trams, which take you east to Wanchai, Causeway Bay and Happy Valley.

Just east of Central is **Wanchai**, known for its raucous nightlife, but relatively dull in the daytime. One thing worth seeing is the **Hong Kong Arts Centre** on Harbour Rd. The Pao Galleries are on the 4th and 5th floors of the centre, and international and local exhibitions are held year-round with the emphasis on contemporary art.

Wanchai's **Police Museum**, at 27 Coombe Rd, emphasises the history of the Royal Hong Kong Police Force. Opening hours are Wednesday to Sunday from 9 am to 5 pm and Tuesday from 2 to 5 pm. It's closed on Monday and admission is free.

The **Hong Kong Convention & Exhibition Centre** is an enormous building on the harbour and boasts the world's largest 'glass curtain' – a window seven storeys high. Just be glad you don't have to be the one to wash it. You can ride the escalator to the 7th floor for a superb harbour view. The new wing on the waterfront with its distinctive roof is where the handover to China took place at midnight on 30 June 1997. The building's design was meant to symbolise a bird in flight, but, as one sarcastic scribe noted, it looks more like a cockroach about to take off. Once you have that image in your mind, it kind of sticks.

On the eastern side of Causeway Bay is **Victoria Park**, a large playing field built on reclaimed land. Early in the morning it's a good place to see the slow-motion choreography of taijiquan (tai chi) practitioners.

South-east of Causeway Bay near Happy Valley is the **Tiger Balm Gardens**, officially known as the Aw Boon Haw Gardens. The gardens are three hectares of grotesque statuary that some might find to be in appallingly bad taste. Nevertheless, it's a sight to behold. Aw Boon Haw made his fortune from the Tiger Balm cure-everything medication and this was his gift to Hong Kong. He also built a similar park in Singapore. Admission is free.

SOUTHERN SIDE

With a pocketful of change you can traverse Hong Kong Island. Start in Central. You have a choice of hopping on bus No 6 at the Exchange Square bus terminal and going directly to Stanley, or taking a tram first to Shaukeiwan and changing to a bus. The bus is easier and faster, but the tram is more fun.

The tram takes you through hustling Wanchai and bustling Causeway Bay to the Sai Wan Ho ferry pier at Shaukeiwan. Look for the trams marked 'Shaukeiwan' and hop off just before the end of the line. You then take bus No 14 up and over the central hills to **Stanley**. Stanley has a decent beach, a fine market, expensive villas and a maximum-security prison.

From Stanley, bus No 73 takes you along the coast by beautiful **Repulse Bay**, which is rapidly developing into high-rises and shopping malls. The bus passes **Deep Water Bay**, which has a sandy beach, and continues to **Aberdeen**. The big attraction here is the harbour choked with boats, which are also part-time residences for Hong Kong's fishermen and their families. There will generally be several sampans (motorised launches) ready to take you on a half-hour tour of this floating city for about HK$50 per person (it's worth seeing), or bargain a whole boat for a group (about HK$150).

Floating regally amid the confusion in Aberdeen are several palace-like restaurants, the largest being the Jumbo Floating

HONG KONG 香港

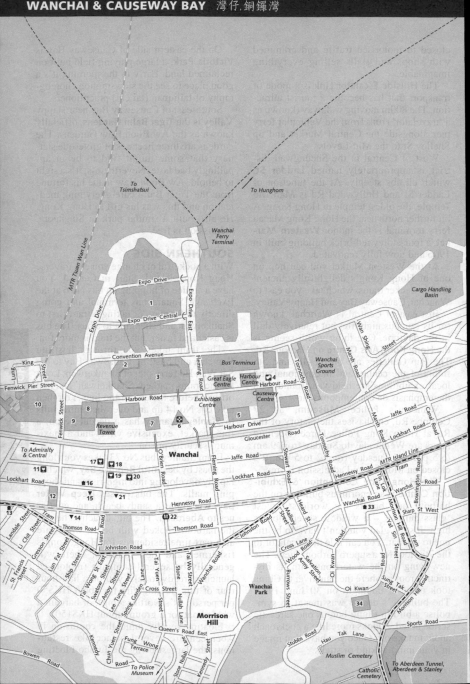

To Tsimshatsui

To Hunghom

MTR Tsuen Wan Line

Cargo Handling Basin

Wanchai Ferry Terminal

Expo Drive

Expo Drive Central

Expo Drive East

Expo Drive

1

Convention Avenue

2

3

Fleming Road

Bus Terminus

Great Eagle Centre

Harbour Centre

4

Wan Shing Street

Wanchai Sports Ground

Marsh Road

King Lung Street

Fenwick Pier Street

10

Harbour Road

Exhibition Centre

Causeway Centre

Harbour Road

5

Harbour Drive

Jaffe Road

Canal Road

Lockhart Road

9

8

Revenue Tower

7

6

Fenwick Street

Tonnochy Road

Marsh Road

Gloucester Road

Road

Stewart Road

To Admiralty & Central

17

18

Wanchai

Jaffe Road

O'Brien Road

Fleming Road

Hennessy Road

MTR Island Line

Tram

11

19

20

Lockhart Road

Heard St

Mallory St

Hennessy Road

In Lok Lane

Wanchai Road

Bowrington Road

Road

Lockhart Road

16

15

12

21

Wanchai Road

33

Sharp St West

Tram

13

14

22

Thomson Road

Luard Road

Johnston Road

Thomson Road

Johnston Road

Mallory Street

Cross Lane

Wood Road

Salvation Army Street

Yat Sin Street

Morrison Hill Road

Sung Tak Street

Thomson Road

Li Chit. Street

Cresson Street

Lun Fat Street

Ship Street

St Francis Street

Tai Wong St East

Swatow Street

Amoy Street

Lee Tung Street

Spring Garden Lane

Cross Street

Tai Yuen Street

Stone Nullah Lane

Tai Wo Street

Wanchai Road

Burrows Street

Oi Kwan

Oi Kwan Road

Wanchai Park

34

Queen's Road East

Fung Wong Terrace

Chun Yuen Street

Kennedy Road

Morrison Hill

Stone Nullah Street

Kennedy Street

Stubbs Road

Hau Tak Lane

Sports Road

Bowen Road

To Police Museum

Muslim Cemetery

Catholic Cemetery

To Aberdeen Tunnel, Aberdeen & Stanley

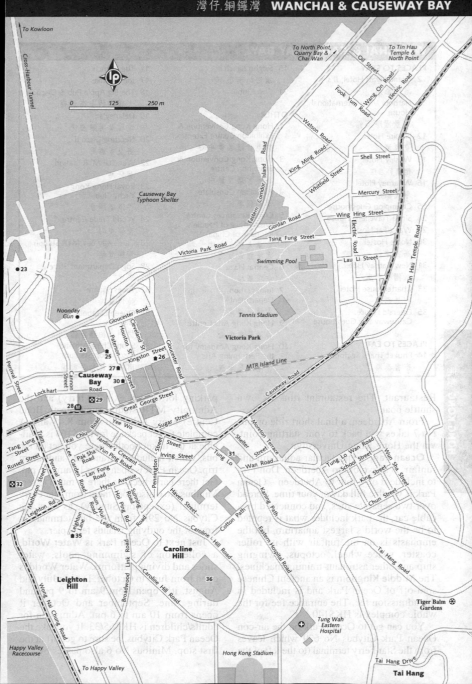

To Kowloon

Cross-Harbour Tunnel

To North Point,
Quarry Bay &
Chai Wan

To Tin Hau
Temple &
North Point

Oil Street

Wang On Road

Fook Yum Road

Electric Road

Watson Road

King Ming Road

Shell Street

Whitfield Street

Mercury Street

Wing Hing Street

Electric Road

Lau Li Street

Tin Hau Temple Road

Causeway Bay
Typhoon Shelter

Eastern Corridor Island Road

Gordan Road

Tsing Fung Street

Victoria Park Road

Swimming Pool

● 23

Noonday
Gun ●

Tennis Stadium

Gloucester Road

Houston St

Cleveland St

Paterson
St

Victoria Park

24

25

Kingston Street

Gloucester Road

27

26

Causeway
Bay
Road

30

Street

MTR Island Line

Cannon
Street

Lockhart

Causeway Road

28 M

29

Great George Street

Moreton Terrace

Shelter Street

Tung Lo Wan Road

Wun Sha Street

Yee Wo

Sugar Street

Tang Lung
Street

Kai Chiu

Jardine's Crescent

Yun Ping Road

Irving Street

Pennington Street

Tung Lo

Wan Road

School Street

King Street

Chun Street

Russell Street

Percival Street

Lee Garden Road

Pak Sha Road

Lan Fong Road

Hysan Avenue

Sunning Road

Hoi Ping Rd.

Sin Wan Road

Leighton Road

Haven Street

Kaning Path

Eastern Hospital Road

Matheson Street

32

Leighton Rd.

Leighton Line

Caroline
Hill

Caroline Hill Road

Caroline Hill Road

Broadwood Link Road

Tai Hang Road

Wong Nai Chung Road

35

Leighton
Hill

36

Tiger Balm ✿
Gardens

Happy Valley
Racecourse

Tung Wah
Eastern
Hospital

Hong Kong Stadium

Tai Hang Drive

Tai Hang

To Happy Valley

WANCHAI & CAUSEWAY BAY

PLACES TO STAY

2 Grand Hyatt Hotel; JJ's
   君悦酒店
8 Harbour View International
   House
   灣景國際賓館
12 Empire Hotel
   皇悅酒店
13 Wesley Hotel
   衛蘭軒酒店
16 Wharney Hotel
   華美酒店
25 Champion Guesthouse
26 Sinya Travellers' House
27 Wang Fat Hostel
30 Noble Hostel
   高富旅館
31 New Cathay Hotel
   新國泰酒店
33 Charterhouse Hotel
   利景酒店
35 Emerald House;
   Causeway Bay Guesthouse

PLACES TO EAT

14 Phuket Thai's Seafood
   布吉泰酒店

15 Saigon Beach
   濱海越南小館
21 Chili Club

OTHER

1 Hong Kong Convention &
   Exhibition Centre Extension
   香港會議展覽中心
3 Hong Kong Convention &
   Exhibition Centre
   香港會議展覽中心
4 Australian Consulate
   澳洲領事館
5 China Resources Centre
   (Visa Office of People's
   Republic of China)
   中華人民共和國
   大使館簽証處
6 Central Plaza
   中環廣場
7 Immigration
   Department
   入境事務處
9 Hong Kong Arts Centre
   香港藝術中心
10 Hong Kong Academy for
   the Performing Arts
   香港演藝學院

11 The Wanch
17 Joe Bananas
18 The Big Apple Pub & Disco
   大蘋果的士高酒廊
19 Delaney's
   愛爾蘭餐廳酒吧
20 Neptune Disco II
   海皇星酒廊
22 Wanchai MTR Station
   灣仔站
23 Royal Hong Kong
   Yacht Club
   香港遊艇會
24 World Trade Centre
   世貿中心
28 Causeway Bay MTR Station
   銅鑼灣站
29 Sogo Department Store
   崇光
32 Times Square
   時代廣場
34 Queen Elizabeth
   Stadium
   伊利沙柏體育館
36 South China Athletic
   Association Stadium
   南華體育會運動場

Restaurant. The restaurant runs its own shuttle boat.

From Aberdeen, a final short ride on bus No 7 takes you back to your starting point, via the Hong Kong University.

Ocean Park, a spectacular aquarium and funfair, is also close to Aberdeen. Don't try to include it on a tour to Aberdeen – Ocean Park is worth a full day of your time. Spread over two separate sites, and connected by a cable car, the park includes what is reputed to be the world's largest aquarium, but the emphasis is on the funfair with its roller coaster, space wheel, octopus, swinging ship and other astronaut-training machines. The **Middle Kingdom** is an ancient Chinese spin-off of Ocean Park and is included in the admission fee. The entrance fee for the whole complex is HK$140.

You can get to Ocean Park on the air-con Ocean Park Citybus No 629 which leaves from the Star Ferry terminal (to the left of the

parking lot as you exit the ferry) and the Admiralty MTR station (underneath Bond Centre) every half-hour from 8.45 am. A complete ticket package for HK$164 is available at the ticket booth where you get on the bus, which includes entrance fee and return trip. Ocean Park is open from 10 am to 6 pm. Get there early because there is much to see. Minibus No 6 also goes there from Star Ferry terminal (except on Sunday), as does the Citybus No 29R from the bus terminus in front of the outlying islands ferry pier.

Just next to Ocean Park is **Water World**, a collection of swimming pools, water slides and diving platforms. Water World is open from June to October. During July and August, it's open from 9 am to 9 pm and during June, September and October it opens from 10 am to 6 pm. Admission for adults/children is HK$65/33. If you take the Ocean Park Citybus, be sure to get off at the first stop. Minibus No 6 also passes by.

Shek O, on the south-eastern coast, has one of the best beaches on Hong Kong Island. Take the MTR or tram to Shaukeiwan, and from Shaukeiwan take bus No 9 to the last stop. Bus No 309 also goes to Shek O from the Exchange Square terminus.

PLACES TO STAY – BUDGET

Ma Wui Hall (☎ 2817 5715), on top of Mt Davis on Hong Kong Island, offers stunning views and is the most accessible of the YHA hostels. The drawback is that it's 'centrally located' in the relative sense only. From the Star Ferry terminal in Central it's still a good hour's journey, but travellers say it's 'almost worth it'.

Before embarking on the trek, ring up first to be sure a bed is available. The hostel runs a shuttle bus (HK$10) from the parking lot at the Hong Kong Macau ferry terminal at 9.30 am and 7, 9 and 10.30 pm. Otherwise, to get there, take bus No 5B or 47 to the 5B terminus at Felix Villas on Victoria Rd. Walk back 100m and look for the YHA sign. You've then got a 20- to 30-minute climb up the hill. Don't confuse Mt Davis Path with Mt Davis Rd! There are 112 beds here and the nightly cost is HK$65, or HK$95 for non-members. Family rooms are HK$260. You can buy a YHA card at the hostel for HK$180. The hostel is open from 7 am to 11 pm.

Most of the cheaper guesthouses on Hong Kong Island are in Causeway Bay. The friendly *Wang Fat Hostel* (☎ 2895 1015, fax 2576 7509, Flat A2, 3rd floor, 47 Paterson St) is just above the Daimaru department store. Singles/doubles with bath are HK$200/$280.

Noble Hostel (☎ 2576 6148, 2577 0847, Flat A3, 17th floor, 27 Paterson St) is spotlessly clean and very secure. Rooms with shared bath are HK$230 and singles/doubles with bath are HK$310/320.

Also on Paterson St, readers have recommended the *Champion Guesthouse* (☎ 2576 3080, fax 2576 3968, Flat B, 9th floor, 55 Paterson St). Small clean rooms with bath are HK$250 and HK$300. In the same neighbourhood, the *Sinya Travellers' House* (☎ 2915 7696, fax 2898 3106, Flat B, 5th floor, 6 Kingston St) has also got good reviews from travellers. Small doubles with bath are HK$300, larger doubles are HK$400.

On the south side of Hennessy Rd, the *Causeway Bay Guesthouse* (☎ 2895 2013, fax 2895 2355, 44 A-D Leighton Rd) has some good deals. Singles/doubles/triples with bath are HK$220/330/400. You can enter the building at Leighton Lane, around the corner, and the guesthouse is at Flat B, 1st floor. *Emerald House* (☎ 2577 2368, fax 2894 9082) is also on the 1st floor. It has clean rooms with private bath for HK$350.

PLACES TO STAY – MID-RANGE & TOP END

In terms of mid-range hotels, there's even less available on Hong Kong Island than in Kowloon. Figure on HK$500 at the minimum and up to HK$800. Again, check with travel agents for discounts.

The *New Cathay Hotel* (☎ 2577 8211, fax 2576 9365, 17 Tung Lo Wan Rd, Causeway Bay) is one of the better mid-range deals, with singles/doubles for HK$400/500, including tax. The *Harbour View International House* (☎ 2802 1111, fax 2802 9063, 4 Harbour Rd, Wanchai) has comfortable rooms for HK$639, plus 10% service charge. Sea-view rooms are more expensive at HK$1050 to HK$1450.

Closest to central, the *YWCA Garden View International* (☎ 2877 3737, fax 2845 6263, 1 MacDonnell Rd, Central) has rooms as low as HK$480, as well as suites for HK$780, plus 10% tax.

It's a good idea go through a travel agent for top-end hotels, where it is sometimes possible to get up to 30% off.

A few of the top-end hotels in Wanchai have brought down their prices which has put them closer to mid-range affordability. The *Empire Hotel* (☎ 2866 9111, fax 2861 3121, 33 Hennessy Rd, Wanchai) has singles/doubles for HK$750/830, including tax and service charges. Nearby, the *Wesley Hotel* (☎ 2866 6688, fax 2866 6613, 22 Hennessy Rd, Wanchai) has rooms for HK$800 plus a 13% tax and service charge. The *Wharney Hotel* (☎ 2861 1000, fax

2865 6023, 57 Lockhart Rd, Wanchai) is the best value, with singles/doubles for HK$760/820 including tax and service charges.

It's also worth trying the *Charterhouse Hotel* (☎ 2833 5566, fax 2833 5888, 209 219 Wanchai Rd, Wanchai). It has been known to offer a 50% discount for its HK$1200 standard rooms, not including the 13% tax and service charge. The *Furama Kempinski Hotel* (☎ 2525 5111, fax 2845 9339, 1 Connaught Rd, Central) was also offering a 30% discount for its standard rooms, normally priced at HK$1250, not including the 13% tax and service charge. Suites are also a good deal at the Furama, starting at HK$1680.

The *Mandarin Oriental Hotel* (☎ 2522 0111, fax 2530 0180, 5 Connaught Rd, Central) is the height of old-style luxury, though some people think it's starting to get a bit tattered. Standard singles/doubles start at HK$2800/3250, not including the 13% tax and service charge. The *Grand Hyatt Hotel* (☎ 2588 1234, fax 2802 0677, 1 Harbour Rd, Wanchai) is a little more modern, to say the least, and another strong contender for Hong Kong's best hotel. Rack rates for singles/doubles start around HK$2900/3200. Suites are HK$5500 to HK$25,000.

The luxurious *Island Shangri-La Hotel* (☎ 2877 3838, fax 2521 8742, Pacific Place, Supreme Court Rd, Admiralty) is not far behind. Singles/doubles are HK$2300/2500. Suites are HK$5300 and up.

PLACES TO EAT

The place to go for reasonably priced eats and late-night revelry is the neighbourhood known as Lan Kwai Fong. However, it's such a conglomeration of pubs and all-night parties that it's covered in the Entertainment section.

Breakfast

To save time and money, there are food windows adjacent to the Star Ferry terminal that open shortly after 6 am. It offers standard commuter breakfasts consisting of bread, rolls and coffee with no place to sit except on the ferry itself.

The cafeteria-style *Delifrance* has a few outlets on Hong Kong Island and serves up fresh croissants for breakfast as well as other dishes. There's one at Shop 174 on the 1st floor of the World Wide Plaza in Central. You can get good coffee at various stalls in the malls and in Lan Kwai Fong.

Of course, all the big hotels serve breakfast, often a sumptuous buffet.

Chinese Cuisine

Tai Woo (☎ 2524 5618, 15-19 Wellington St, Central) serves dim sum from 11 am to 4.30 pm and *Zen Chinese Cuisine* (☎ 2845 4555, Lower Ground 1, The Mall, Pacific Place, Phase I, 88 Queensway, Central) offers dim sum served between 11.30 am and 3.30 pm.

Indian Cuisine

Ashoka (☎ 2524 9623, 57 Wyndham St) is always popular. Next door, in the basement, the *Village Indian Restaurant* (☎ 2525 7410) is also good value. *Greenlands* (☎ 2522 6098, 64 Wellington St) is another superb Indian restaurant, though a bit more expensive, and offers great all-you-can-eat buffets.

Club Sri Lanka (☎ 2526 6559) has great Sri Lankan curries. Its fixed-price all-you-can-eat deal is a bargain compared with most Hong Kong eateries. Its in the basement of 17 Hollywood Rd, almost at the Wyndham St end.

Asian Cuisine

The *Saigon Beach* (☎ 2529 7823, 66 Lockhart Rd, Wanchai) is a popular establishment that serves up good food for under HK$100 per person.

Hong Kong also has a number of excellent Thai restaurants. In Wanchai, the *Chili Club* (2527 2872, 88 Lockhart Rd) gets rave reviews as does the *Phuket Thai's Seafood* (☎ 2527 2591, 44 Hennessy Rd).

ENTERTAINMENT
Lan Kwai Fong 兰桂坊

Running off D'Aguilar St in Central is a narrow, L-shaped alley that's closed to cars. This is Lan Kwai Fong, and along with neighbouring streets and alleys it is Hong Kong's hippest eating, drinking, dancing and partying venue. Prices range from economical to outrageous.

Club 64 (☎ *2523 2801, 12-14 Wing Wah Lane*) is an old favourite, although it has lost some of its past appeal as customers are no longer allowed to sit outdoors.

As you face the entrance to Club 64, off to your left are some stairs (outside the building, not inside). Follow the stairs up to a terrace to find *Le Jardin Club* (☎ *2526 2717, 10 Wing Wah Lane*). This is an excellent place to drink, relax and socialise.

The *Jazz Club* (☎ *2845 8477*) is next door on the 2nd floor, in the California Entertainment building, and is a good place to go after dinner. Phone first to find out what bands are playing and if there's a cover charge.

Post 97 (☎ *2810 9333, 9 Lan Kwai Fong*) is a very comfortable eating and drinking spot. During the daytime it's more of a coffee shop, and you can sit for hours to take advantage of the excellent rack of western magazines and newspapers. It can pack out at night, and the lights are dimmed to discourage reading at that time.

The *California* (☎ *2521 1345*), also in the California Entertainment building, is perhaps the most expensive bar mentioned in this book. Open from noon to 1 am, it's a restaurant by day, but there's disco dancing and a cover charge Wednesday to Sunday nights from 5 pm onwards.

Central

Just outside Lan Kwai Fong is the *Fringe Club* (☎ *2521 7251, 2 Lower Albert Rd*). It's an excellent pub known for cheap beer and an avant-garde atmosphere. Live music is provided nightly by various local folk and rock musicians.

A new area for bars and restaurants has opened up south of Hollywood Rd (thus known as Soho) and is easily accessed by the Mid-Levels escalator link. There are too many restaurants to list here (including two Nepalese restaurants if you're craving *dhal bhat*). For a cool and smooth drinking establishment, try the *Staunton's Bar & Café* (☎ *2973 6611*), at the corner of Staunton and

Shelley Sts. If you're after something a little more down to earth, head for *Dublin Jack* (☎ *2543 0081, 37 Cochrane St*), an Irish-style pub with a very comfortable interior.

Wanchai 湾仔

This Hong Kong neighbourhood once famous for its nightspots can't quite shake off its sleazy image, but at least it isn't as nauseatingly hip as Lan Kwai Fong. Most of the action is concentrated at the intersection of Luard and Jaffe Rds. Expect to pay a cover charge of HK$100 or more at most of the places mentioned below, although it's often cheaper or free for women, and may include one drink.

Joe Bananas (☎ *2529 1811, 23 Luard Rd*) has become a trendy disco nightspot and has no admission charge, but you may have to queue to get in. Happy hour is from 11 am until 9 pm (except Sunday) and the place stays open until around 5 am.

The *Neptune Disco II* (☎ *2865 2238, 98-108 Jaffe Rd*) is the place to go to for thumping tunes and has no cover charge. *The Big Apple Pub & Disco* (☎ *2529 3461, 20 Luard Rd*) has live music. Another popular dancing place with live music, but more expensive, is *JJ's* (☎ *2588 1234*) in the Grand Hyatt Hotel.

The Wanch (☎ *2861 1621, 54 Jaffe Rd*), just west of Fenwick St, is a small live venue for alternative/folk music with beer and wine at low prices, but it can get crowded. *Delaney's* (☎ *2804 2880, One Capital Place, 18 Luard Rd*) is an Irish pub that has a great atmosphere and Irish music.

Gay Pubs & Bars

Petticoat Lane (☎ *2973 0642, 2 Tun Wo Lane, Central*) is a friendly place for the local gay and lesbian scene. It's down a small lane above Lyndhurst Terrace, near the pedestrian escalator that goes up to Mid-Levels. As usual, the best dancing places in Hong Kong are part of the gay cultural scene. A fun place for everyone is *CE Top* (☎ *2544 3581, 9/F 37-43 Cochrane St, Central*). Another good place to groove to different tunes is *Club 97* (☎ *2810 9333, 9 Lan Kwai Fong, Central*).

SHOPPING

As mentioned in the Kowloon section, the HKTA advises tourists to shop where they see the HKTA red logo on display, although this is no guarantee.

Is you're shopping for clothes, the two alleys known as Li Yuen St East and Li Yuen St West in Central have some bargains. For Chinese products, Chinese Arts and Crafts stores have a branch on Hong Kong Island in the Pacific Place Mall, at 88 Queensway, Central (near the Admiralty station).

You might find cheaper mainland souvenirs at the at the Chinese products department stores such as Yue Hwa or CRC. There's a CRC in the Chiao Shang building, 92-104, Queen's Rd, Central. For Chinese retro, both pre- and post-1949, Shanghai Tang, the brainchild of maverick entrepreneur, David Tang, is one of the most fashionable (and expensive) places to shop. It's worthwhile checking out just for the decor, on the Ground floor, Pedder Building, 8 Theatre Lane, in Central.

If you're looking for the real thing, as in Mao badges and other cast-offs, try the street markets up near Hollywood Rd on Lascar Row, otherwise known as Cat Street. This is also the area to look for antiques.

Prices are generally cheaper in Kowloon, but on Hong Kong Island you can find a concentration of computer shops in Windsor House, Great George St, Causeway Bay, and at the Wanchai Computer House in the Southorn Centre at 130 Hennessy Rd, Wanchai.

For camera shopping, Photo Scientific (☎ 2522 1903), 6 Stanley St, Central, is the favourite of Hong Kong's resident professional photographers.

There's a HMV branch on the 10th floor of Windsor House, Great George St, Causeway Bay, and one on the 1st floor of the Central Building, 1-3 Pedder St, Central. Tower Records (☎ 2506 0811), 7th floor, Shop 701, Times Square, Matheson St, Causeway Bay, also has a good CD collection.

Finally, if you want to see a good shopping mall where the locals go, visit Cityplaza in Quarry Bay. Take the MTR to the Tai Koo station.

New Territories 新界

You can explore most of the New Territories by bus and train in one very busy day, assuming that you don't take time out for hiking or swimming (both worthwhile and recommended activities).

Start out by taking the MTR to the last stop at **Tsuen Wan**. The main attraction here is the **Yuen Yuen Institute**, a Taoist temple complex, and the adjacent Buddhist **Western Monastery** in Lo Wai village. The institute can be reached by taking minibus No 81 from Shiu Wo St, which is two blocks south of the MTR station. Alternatively, take a taxi, which is not expensive.

Chuk Lam Sim Yuen is another large monastery in the hills north of Tsuen Wan. To get there find Shiu Wo St and take maxicab No 85.

At Tsuen Wan you have two options. You can continue west to Tuen Mun, or north to **Tai Mo Shan** (957m), Hong Kong's highest peak. To reach Tai Mo Shan, take bus No 51 from the Tsuen Wan MTR station – the bus stop is on the overpass that goes over the roof of the station, or you can also pick it up at the Tsuen Wan ferry pier. The bus heads up Route Twisk (Twisk is derived from Tsuen Wan into Shek Kong). Get off at the top of the pass, from where it's uphill on foot. You walk on a road, but it's unlikely you'll encounter traffic. The path is part of the **MacLehose Trail**, which is 100km long. The trail runs from Tuen Mun in the west to the Sai Kung Peninsula in the east and walking the entire length would take several days.

If you choose not to visit Tai Mo Shan, from Tsuen Wan take bus No 60M or 68M to the bustling town of **Tuen Mun**. Here you can visit Hong Kong's largest shopping mall, the Tuen Mun Town Plaza. From here, hop on the LRT system to reach **Ching Chung Koon**, a temple complex smack in the middle of building estates, on the northern side of Tuen Mun.

You can then get back on the LRT and head to Yuen Long. From here, take bus No 54, 64K or 77K to the nearby walled villages at **Kam Tin**. These villages with their single stout entrances are said to date from the 16th century.

There are several walled villages at Kam Tin, but most accessible is **Kat Hing Wai**. Drop about HK$5 into the donation box by the entrance and wander the narrow little lanes. The old Hakka women in traditional gear require payment before they can be photographed.

The town of Sheung Shui is about 8km north-east on bus No 77K. Here you can hop on the KCR and go one stop south to **Fanling**. The main attraction in this town is the **Fung Ying Sin Kwun Temple**, a Taoist temple for the dead, located across from the KCR station.

At Fanling, get on the KCR and head to the Tai Po Market station. From here, you can walk 10 to 15 minutes to the **Hong Kong Railway Museum**. From the Tai Po Market station, you can take bus No 64K (from under the Uptown Plaza) to visit the **Kadoorie Farm and Botanic Garden**. The farm was set up in the early '50s by the Kadoorie brothers, a Sephardic Jewish family who made their fortune in Shànghǎi and Hong Kong. There's a fine collection of animals, including a refuge centre for injured wildlife and plants. It's better to phone prior to arriving (☎ 2488 1317). From the Kadoorie farm, you can continue on bus No 64K to Kam Tim and Yuen Long.

From Tai Po Market, the KCR goes south to the Chinese University, where there's the Art Gallery at the **Institute of Chinese Studies**. A shuttle bus takes passengers up the hill to the university. Admission is free.

The KCR will bring you to Shatin, a lively, bustling city where you can visit the huge **Shatin Town Centre**, one of Hong Kong's biggest shopping malls. Also, this is where you begin the climb up to the **Temple of 10,000 Buddhas** (which actually has over 12,000). Take the north exit from the Shatin KCR station. Look for the IKEA sign and turn right on Sheung Wo Che Rd. Do not proceed to the escalator and large ancestral complex to the north. Walk to the end of Sheung Wo Che Rd until you see the small sign for 10,000 Buddhas in English.

Go through the food stalls to where the path begins. There's also a western path, but it was closed at the time of writing.

All this should fill your day, but there are other places to visit in the New Territories. The **Sai Kung Peninsula** is one of the least spoilt areas in the New Territories – it's great for hiking and you can get from village to village on boats in the Tolo Harbour.

The best beaches in the New Territories are around the Sai Kung Peninsula, including **Clearwater Bay**. From the Choi Hung MTR station take bus No 91 to Clearwater Bay or No 92 to Sai Kung village.

To explore the eastern side of the peninsula, take bus No 94 from Sai Kung that ends at Wong Shek pier.

PLACES TO STAY

The main reason to stay in the New Territories is for camping and enjoying the outdoors. The Hong Kong Youth Hostel Association (HKYHA; ☎ 2788 1638) operates several hostels in the New Territories. All are in fairly remote locations. You'll need a YHA card – these can be bought at the hostels for HK$180 (bring a photo) – otherwise you'll have to pay the non-members' price. You are strongly advised to ring first to make sure a bed is available.

Bradbury Lodge (☎ 2662 5123, Ting Kok Rd, Tai Mei Tuk, Tai Po) is the most easily reached hostel in the New Territories. There are 80 beds costing HK$55, and HK$85 for non-members, but no camp sites. Take the KCR to Tai Po Market station, then bus No 75K to Tai Mei Tuk (last stop). Walk south for four minutes (the sea will be to your right) to reach the hostel.

Sze Lok Yuen (☎ 2488 8188, Tai Mo Shan Rd) was recently renovated. Beds cost HK$35 each and you'll need to buy a membership if you don't have one. There are 100 camp sites, costing HK$25 per site. Take bus No 51 (Tsuen Wan ferry pier-Kam Tin) at Tsuen Wan MTR station and alight at Tai Mo Shan Rd. Follow Tai Mo Shan Rd for about 45 minutes and, after passing the car park, turn on to a small concrete path on the right-hand side, which leads directly to the hostel. This is a good place from which to climb Tai Mo Shan, Hong Kong's highest peak. Because of the high elevation, it can get amazingly cold at night, so be prepared.

Pak Sha O Hostel (☎ 2328 2327, Hoi Ha Rd, Sai Kung East Peninsula) has 112 beds priced at HK$35 and HK$55 for non-members. There are 150 camp sites that are HK$16 for members and HK$20 for non-members. Take bus No 92 from the Choi Hung Estate bus station and get off at the Sai Kung station. From Sai Kung, take bus No 94 (last one is at 7 pm) towards Wong Shek pier, but get off at Ko Tong village. From there, walk 100m along Pak Tam Rd to find Hoi Ha Rd on the left. The walk along Hoi Ha Rd to the hostel is signposted and takes about 40 minutes.

Also on the Sai Kung Peninsula is *Bradbury Hall (☎ 2328 2458)* in Chek Keng. There are 100 beds in air-con rooms costing HK$45, HK$75 for non-members, plus 100 camp sites that are HK$15 and HK$25 for non-members. From Choi Hung Estate bus terminal, take bus No 92 to the Sai Kung terminal. From Sai Kung, take bus No 94 (last one is at 7 pm) to Yellow Stone Pier, but get off at Pak Tam Au. There's a footpath at the side of the road leading to Chek Keng village (a 45-minute walk). The hostel is right on the harbour just facing the Chek Keng ferry pier. An alternative route is to take the ferry from Ma Liu Shui (adjacent to the Chinese University train station) to Chek Keng ferry pier.

Outlying Islands 外島

There are 235 islands dotting the waters around Hong Kong, but only four have substantial residential communities and are thus readily accessible by ferry.

While very tranquil during the week, the islands are packed on weekends and holidays. Cars are prohibited on all of the islands except Lantau, and even there vehicle ownership is very restricted.

CHEUNG CHAU ISLAND 長洲
This dumbbell-shaped island has a large community of western residents who enjoy

the slow pace of island life and relatively low rents. Were it not for the Chinese signs and people, you might think you were in some Greek island village.

The town sprawls across the narrow neck connecting the two ends of the island. The bay on the western side of the island (where the ferry lands) is an exotic collection of fishing boats much like Aberdeen on Hong Kong Island. The eastern side of the island is where you'll find Tung Wan beach, Cheung Chau's longest. There are a few tiny but remote beaches that you can reach by foot, and at the southern tip of the island is the hideaway cave of the notorious pirate, Cheung Po Tsai.

Places to Stay
There is a solid line-up of booths when you come off the ferry pier that offer flats and rooms for rent, some of which can be very reasonable, but you'll have to bargain, and the price doubles on weekends and holidays.

Cheung Chau has one upmarket place to stay, the *Warwick Hotel (☎ 2981 0081, fax 2981 9673)* with 70 rooms. Sea-view rooms cost HK$553 on weekdays and HK$880 on weekends.

LAMMA ISLAND 南丫島
This is the second largest of the outlying islands and the one closest to the city. Lamma has good beaches and a very relaxed pace on weekdays, but on weekends it's mobbed like anywhere else. There are two main communities here – Yung Shue Wan in the north and Sok Kwu Wan in the south. Both have ferry services to Central. One of the best things to do here is hike across the island, then have something to eat in one of the many restaurants available.

Places to Stay & Eat
There are several places to stay in Yung Shue Wan. Right by the Yung Shue Wan ferry pier is the *Man Lai Wah Hotel (☎ 2982 0220, fax 2982 0349)* where rooms cost HK$350 on weekdays, rising to HK$500 on weekends.

On nearby Hung Shing Ye beach, the *Concerto Inn (☎ 2982 1668, fax 2982 0022)* is an upmarket place with rooms for

HK$448 on weekdays and HK$748 on weekends.

Both Yung Shue Wan and Sok Kwu Wan are lined with seafood restaurants, so you won't starve. The *Man Fung* (☎ 2982 1112) is close to the ferry pier in Yung Shue Wan and serves up good Cantonese dishes. The *Waterfront Bar* (☎ 2982 0914) in Yung Shue Wan is a lively place for nightlife and good food, or you can try its quieter competition, the *Island Bar*, or sit outside in front of the *Fountain Head* next to the Hongkong Bank. The *Deli Lamma* (☎ 2982 1583) has a variety of healthy food dishes, as does the *Bookworm Café* (☎ 2982 4838). *Dino's* (☎ 2982 6196) has hamburgers, and fish and chips, and *Tootchka's* (☎ 2982 0159) is another popular hang-out. Keep in mind that many restaurants on Lamma Island are closed on Monday.

LANTAU ISLAND 大屿山

This is the largest of the islands and the most sparsely populated – it's almost twice the size of Hong Kong Island, but the population is only 30,000. You could easily spend a couple of days exploring the mountainous walking trails and enjoying uncrowded beaches.

Mui Wo (Silvermine Bay) is the major arrival point for ferries. As you exit the ferry, to your right is the road leading to the beach. It passes several eateries and hotels along the way.

From Mui Wo, most visitors board bus No 2 to **Ngong Ping**, a plateau 500m above sea level in the western part of the island. It's here that you'll find the impressive **Po Lin Monastery**. It's a relatively recent construction and almost as much a tourist attraction as a religious centre. Just outside the monastery is the world's largest outdoor bronze buddha statue. It's possible to have a vegetarian lunch at the monastery dining hall and you can spend the night here. The main reason to stay overnight is to launch a sunrise expedition to climb **Lantau Peak** (934m). Another place to visit is **Tai O**, a village at the western end of the island; take bus No 1.

The 2km-long **Cheung Sha Wan** on Lantau Island is Hong Kong's longest beach. You'll have it to yourself on weekdays, but forget it on weekends.

On Lantau's northern shore is the 19th century **Tung Chung Fort**, which still has its old cannon pointing out to sea. The bad news here is that just off the coast, Hong Kong's new airport at Chek Lap Kok has transformed this part of the island, and turned the Tung Chung area into a new town development. It's connected to Tsuen Wan by the huge Tsing Ma road and rail bridge.

The railway shuttles airport passengers to Hong Kong station in front of the Exchange towers in Central. To get to Lantau via the bridge, take bus No E31 from the Tsuen Wan ferry pier and change at Tung Chung for buses to other destinations on Lantau, or take the train to Tung Chung from Hong Kong station.

A large housing development in the north-eastern part of the island, **Discovery Bay**, is serviced by jet-powered ferries to and from Central every 20 minutes. From Discovery Bay you can walk for one hour southwards along the coastline to find the **Trappist Haven Monastery**. Walking about another 1½ hours from there over a dangerously slippery trail brings you out to Mui Wo, from where you can get ferries back to Central.

Places to Stay & Eat

As you exit the ferry in Silvermine Bay, turn right and head towards the beach. Here you'll find several hotels with sea views. One of the best deals around is the *Mui Wo Inn* (☎ 2984 7225, fax 2984 1916) with rooms from HK$280 to HK$350 on weekdays, and HK$450 to HK$600 on weekends.

Top of the line is the *Silvermine Beach Hotel* (☎ 2984 8295, fax 2984 1907), which has doubles ranging from HK$600 on weekdays to HK$700 on weekends.

There are two places to stay in Ngong Ping. The *SG Davis Youth Hostel* (☎ 2985 5610) has beds for HK$45 for YHA members and HK$75 for non-members. You can buy a YHA card at the hostel for HK$180. The hostel also has a 20 camp sites, which are HK$16 for members and HK$25 for non-members. The *Tea Garden Hotel* (☎ 2985 5161) has grotty singles with shared bath for HK$180 and better double rooms with attached bath for HK$250.

There are good places to eat and drink in Lantau. *Papa Doc's Bar and Café* (☎ 2984 9003, 3 Ngan Wan Rd), in Mui Wo, is good for western food.

Further west along the road past Cheung Sha beach at Tong Fuk, *The Gallery* (☎ 2980 2582) serves up a South African-style barbecue. It's open Wednesday to Friday in the evenings, and from noon onwards on weekends.

PENG CHAU ISLAND

This is the smallest of the outlying islands that are readily accessible. It's also the most traditionally Chinese, with narrow alleys, an outdoor meat and vegetable market and a very tiny expat community. The **Tin Hau Temple** was built in 1792. A climb to the top of **Finger Hill** (95m) will reward you with a view of the entire island and nearby Lantau.

South of the main ferry pier and right along the shoreline are the two best western restaurants and pubs – the *Sea Breeze* (☎ 2983 8785) and adjacent *Forest Bar and Restaurant* (☎ 2983 8837).

Macau 澳门

☎ 0853 • pop 450,000

Sixty kilometres west of Hong Kong, on the other side of the mouth of the Zhū Jiāng (Pearl River), tiny Macau was the oldest European settlement in the east until 20 December 1999, when it was returned to the People's Republic of China. Its 16 sq km consists of central Macau, a peninsula joined to the Chinese mainland, and the islands of Taipa and Coloane, which are joined together by a causeway and linked to central Macau by two bridges.

The lure of Macau's casino gaming tables has been so actively promoted that its other attractions are almost forgotten, but it is a fascinating blend of old-world elegance and modernity. It has a very different look and feel from Hong Kong, and is well worth the one-hour boat trip to get there. Better yet, spend at least a night there – this is a place to enjoy and relax.

Portuguese galleons visited Macau in the early 16th century. In 1557, as a reward for clearing out a few pirates, China ceded the tiny enclave to the Portuguese. For centuries it was the principal meeting point for trade with China. In the 19th century, European and American traders could only operate in Guǎngzhōu (just up the Zhū Jiāng) during the trading season. During the low-season they retreated to Macau.

When the opium wars erupted between the Chinese and the British, the Portuguese stood diplomatically to one side and Macau soon found itself the poor relation of the more dynamic Hong Kong.

Macau's current prosperity is given a big boost by the Chinese gambling urge: every weekend huge numbers of Hong Kong residents shuttle off to the casinos. Although the government doesn't publicly admit it, prostitution is also a significant source of revenue. Macau suffered a blow to its tourist industry in the summer of 1997 when a number of criminal incidents related to triad gang activity kept visitors away and caused a significant drop in hotel prices. The Asian

Highlights

Population: 425,100
Area: 20 sq km

- The Ruinas de São Paulo, the symbol of Macau
- Fortaleza de Monte, with its great views
- Colonial architecture and plush casinos

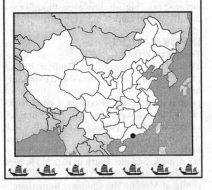

economic crisis didn't help the situation but increasing numbers of visits by mainland tour groups has boosted tourism slightly.

About 95% of Macau's people are Chinese, 3% are Portuguese and 2% are foreigners employed in what is loosely called the 'entertainment industry'. How many Portuguese and foreigners will remain now that Macau has returned to China is difficult to predict. Similar to the arrangement with Hong Kong, Macau will govern itself for a period of 50 years and Portuguese will remain as one of the official languages. Prior to the handover, Edmund Ho Hau Wah was chosen as Chief Executive.

In the meantime, Macau is pushing ahead with more reclamation projects along the waterfront, and bridge-building. The Lotus Flower Bridge, connecting China with the islands of Taipa and Coloane, was opened in December 1999 as part of the handover

MACAU 澳门

ceremonies. A 300m-high tower is being built on the Nam Van lakes and there are even nascent plans to build a 38km bridge across the Zhū Jiāng Estuary to Lantau to provide a link with Hong Kong. It may be a good idea to get there before all these projects inevitably change the face of Macau.

LANGUAGE

Portuguese may be an official language, but there's no real need to learn it for visiting Macau. Cantonese is the main language, and about half the population can speak Mandarin. Bus and taxi drivers almost never speak English, however, though they usually understand some Mandarin.

INFORMATION
Tourist Offices

The Macau Government Tourist Office (☎ 315 566) is well organised and extremely helpful. Staff have an ample supply of printed information providing a good background to various sights, as well as bilingual maps with a list of public bus routes. It's well worth following some of the routes laid out in the *Walking Tours* pamphlet. The office is at Largo do Senado, Edifício Ritz No 9, near the Leal Senado building in the square in the centre of Macau. The square is immediately recognisable for the multicoloured paving bricks arranged in a wave pattern.

Tourist information on Macau can be accessed through the Internet (one Web site is www.cityguide.gov.mo and another excellent one at www.macautourism.gov.mo).

The organisation maintains overseas tourist offices in most European and Asian countries, as well as Australia, New Zealand and the USA.

Visas

For most visitors, all that's needed to enter Macau is a passport. Everyone gets at least a 20-day stay on arrival, or 90 days for Hong Kong residents.

Visas are not required for people from the following countries: Australia, Austria, Belgium, Brazil, Canada, China, Denmark, Finland, France, Germany, Greece, Hong Kong, India, Ireland, Italy, Japan, Luxem-

bourg, Malaysia, Mexico, Netherlands, New Zealand, Norway, Philippines, Singapore, South Africa, South Korea, Spain, Sweden, Switzerland, Thailand, UK, Uruguay and the USA.

All other nationalities must have a visa, which can be obtained on arrival in Macau. Visas cost M$100 for individuals and M$50 for children under 12 and per person in a bona fide tour group (usually 10 people minimum).

Visa Extensions After your 20 days are up, you can obtain a one-month extension if you can come up with a good reason (emergency poker game?). A second extension is not possible, although it's easy enough to go across the border to China and then come back again.

The Immigration Office (☎ 725 488) is on Avenida Amizade near the Yaohan department store. There are also offices at the jetfoil pier and Barrier Gate.

Money

Costs As long as you don't go crazy at the blackjack tables or slot machines, Macau is cheaper than Hong Kong. Indeed, it's cheaper than almost anywhere else on the eastern coast of China. However, it's important to avoid weekends when hotel prices double and even the ferries charge more.

As in China, tipping is not the usual custom, although hotel porters and waiters may have different ideas. Upmarket hotels hit you with a 10% service charge and a 5% 'tourism tax'.

Most stores have fixed prices, but if you buy clothing, trinkets and other tourist junk from the street markets there is some scope for bargaining. On the other hand, if you buy from the ubiquitous pawnshops, bargain ruthlessly. Pawnbrokers are more than happy to charge whatever they can get away with – charging five times the going price for second-hand cameras and other goods is not unusual!

Currency Exchange Macau issues its own currency, the pataca, written as M$. The pataca is divided into 100 avos and is worth about 3% less than the HK dollar. HK dollars are accepted everywhere on a 1:1 basis with patacas, which means, of course, that you'll save a little by using patacas. The pataca continued to be pegged to the HK dollar after 1999 and the exchange is roughly M$8 to US$1.

Exchange Rates

country	unit		M$
Australia	A$1	=	5.23
Canada	C$1	=	5.49
euro	€1	=	8.22
France	10FF	=	1.25
Germany	DM1	=	4.20
Japan	¥100	=	7.60
New Zealand	NZ$1	=	4.14
UK	UK£1	=	13.08
USA	US$1	=	7.97
Hong Kong	HK$1	=	1.02
China	Y10	=	9.62

Although Hong Kong coins are acceptable in Macau, you'll need pataca coins to make calls at public telephones. Get rid of your patacas before leaving Macau – they are hard to dispose of in Hong Kong, although you can change them at the Hang Seng Bank.

There's a convenient moneychanger at the jetfoil pier (where most tourists arrive) and at the Chinese border, as well as a 24-hour currency-exchange machine at the airport. Banks are normally open on weekdays from 9.30 am to 4.30 pm, and on Saturday from 9.30 am until noon.

If you need to change money when the banks are closed, the major casinos (especially the Lisboa) can accommodate you 24 hours. Travellers have also recommended the moneychanger Casa de Cambio Soi Cheong, at Avenida de A Ribeiro 230 near the tourist office.

There are numerous ATMs around the city where you can easily withdraw cash using Visa, MasterCard or American Express cards.

Post & Communications

Post The main post office on Largo do Senado is open Monday to Friday from 9 am to 6 pm, and 9 am to 1 pm on Saturday.

Large hotels like the Lisboa also sell stamps and postcards and can post letters for you.

Scattered around Macau are several red-coloured 'mini-post offices', which are basically stamp-selling machines. The current postal rates are posted clearly on the machines.

Domestic letters cost M$1 for up to 20g. For international mail Macau splits the world into two zones: Zone 1 is East Asia, including Korea and Taiwan, and Zone 2 is everywhere else (although there are special rates for the rest of China and Portugal). Registration costs an extra M$12.

Telephone Companhia de Telecomunicações (CTM) runs the Macau telephone system, and for the most part the service is good. You can find public phones around the Leal Senado and most large hotels have one in the lobby.

Local calls are free from a private or hotel telephone. At a public pay phone, local calls cost M$1 for five minutes. All pay phones permit IDD. The procedure for dialling Hong Kong is totally different from all other countries. You first dial ☎ 01 and then the number you want to call – do not dial the country code.

The international access code for every country except Hong Kong is ☎ 00. To call into Macau from abroad, the country code is ☎ 853. Telephone cards from CTM are sold in denominations of M$70 and M$200. A lot of phones that accept these cards are found around Largo do Senado, the jetfoil pier and at a few large hotels. You can buy cards at the CTM office on 22 Rua Doutor Pedro José Lobo.

Some useful phone numbers in Macau include:

Directory assistance (Macau)	☎ 181
Directory assistance (Hong Kong)	☎ 101
Time	☎ 140
Emergency	☎ 999

Fax Unless you're staying at a hotel that has its own fax, the easiest way to send and receive a fax is at the EMS counter at the main post office at Largo do Senado. The

MACAU 澳门

MACAU 澳门

MACAU PENINSULA 澳門半島

Reservoir

Estrada de Ferreira do Amaral

Rua dos Pescadores

Rua Central da Areia Preta

Avenida da Ponte da Amizade

Avenida do Nordeste

Rua do Canal Novo

Rua Nova da Areia Preta

Estrada Marginal da Areia Preta

Avenida Norte do Hipódromo

Avenida Leste do Hipódromo

Avenida do Hipódromo

Estrada Marginal do Hipódromo

Avenida de Venceslau de Morais

Rua da Longevidade

Estrada da Areia Preta

Avenida da Direita do Hipódromo

Rua Direita Tao Hon

Rua Dois

Rua Um (Bairro Iao Hon)

Istmo Ferreira do Amaral

Avenida de Artur Tamagnini Barbosa

Avenida do Conselheiro Borja

Avenida do Almirante Lacerda

Avenida do Coronel Mesquita

Avenida de Horta e Costa

Avenida de Francisco Xavier Pereira

Avenida de Sidónio Pais

Rua de Ferreira do Amaral

Estrada do Repouso

Rua de Tomás Vieira

Rua da Ribeira do Patane

Camilo Pessanha

Rua de Entre Campos

Rua de São Paulo

Sun Yatsen Memorial Park

GUANGDONG
(Zhuhai Special Economic Zone)

Ilha Verde

Inner Harbour

See Central Macau Map Page 652

1
2
3
4
5
6
7
8
9
10
11
12
13
14
15
16
17
18
19
20

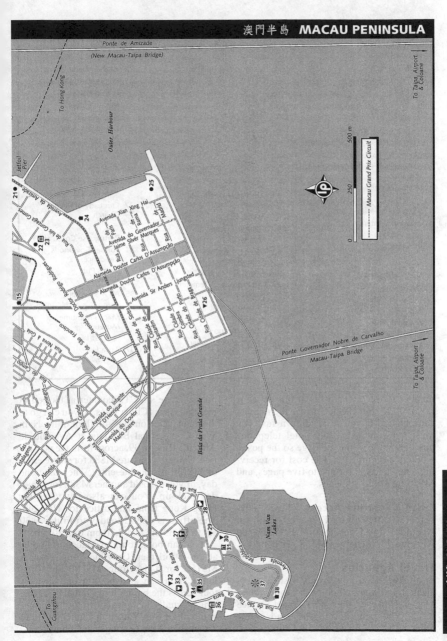

MACAU PENINSULA

PLACES TO STAY

15 Guía Hotel
   東望洋酒店
24 Mandarin Oriental;
   Embassy Bar
   澳門文華東方酒店
38 Pousada de
   São Tiago
   聖地牙哥酒店

PLACES TO EAT

26 Comida A Portuguesa
   Carlos
29 Henri's Galley
   亨利美心
30 Ali Curry House
32 O Porto Interior
   內港餐廳
34 A Lorcha;
   Barra Nova
   船屋

OTHER

1 Barrier Gate
  關閘
2 Canidrome
  跑狗場
3 Mong-Ha Fortress
  望廈古堡
4 Talker Pub

5 Kuan Iam Temple
  觀音堂
6 Macau-Seac Tin Hau
  Temple
  天后廟
7 Pak Vai Plaza
  柏蕙廣場
8 Teenager Club
  年輕人因特網吧
9 Flora Gardens
  龍喉花園
10 Lou Lim Ioc Gardens
   盧廉若花園
11 Sun Yatsen Memorial
   Home
   孫中山紀念館
12 Kiang Vu Hospital
   鏡湖醫院
13 Camões Grotto
   & Gardens
   白鴿巢賈梅士花園
14 Old Protestant Cemetery
   舊基督教墳場
16 Fortaleza de Guía
   松山燈塔
17 Jai Alai Casino
18 HK-Macau Ferry Pier;
   Tourist Office
   港澳碼頭；旅遊公司

19 Heliport
   直升機場
20 Yaohan Department Store
21 Immigration Office
   入境事務處
22 Macau Forum
   綜藝館
23 Grand Prix & Wine
   Museums
   賽車博物館；
   葡萄酒博物館
25 Cultural Centre;
   Museum of Art
   文化中心；美術館
27 Our Lady of Penha
   Church
   西望洋聖堂
28 Portuguese Consulate
31 Former Governor's
   Residence
33 King's Pub
   皇帝酒吧
35 Ah Ma Temple
   媽閣廟
36 Macau Maritime
   Museum
   海（９）暘城｜
37 Barra Hill
   媽閣山

number for receiving a fax at this office is fax 550 117, but check because the number can change. If you're sending a fax, you must put your name and hotel telephone number on top of the message so the postal workers can find you. The cost for receiving a fax is M$10 for one to five pages, and M$15 for six to 10 pages.

Email & Internet Access There's a cybercafe called the Teenager Club at Avenida do Conselheiro Ferreira de Almeida 90. It charges M$18 per hour.

Travel Agencies

In all likelihood you'll only visit a travel agent if you want to book a day tour around Macau. However, the China Travel Service (CTS; Zhōngguó Lǚxíngshè) and a few other agencies do visas for China in 24

hours. There's a CTS counter at the jetfoil pier that issues China visas, or you can go to the main office on the 14th floor of the Nam Wah Commercial Building at Avenida de Almeida Ribeiro 99, across from the post office. Chinese visas are M$88 for single entry or M$130 for double entry. They take one day, or you can add another M$88 for same-day pick-up. You can also get visas for Hong Kong from this office for HK$240. The office is open Monday to Friday 9.30 am to 11.30 am and 2.30 pm to 5.30 pm.

You can book tours of Macau at booths at the jetfoil pier. Grayline Tours charges M$150 for a day tour, M$200 including lunch. You can also book a one-day bus tour across the border into Zhūhǎi in China, which usually includes a trip to the former home of Dr Sun Yatsen in Cùihēng Cūn in Zhōngshān Xiàn (Zhongshan County).

Film & Photography

Most types of film, cameras and accessories can be found in Macau, and photo processing is of a high standard. The best store in town for all photographic services, including visa photos, is Foto Princesa (☎ 555 959), at Avenida do Infante D'Henrique 55-59, one block east of Avenida da Praia Grande.

Medical Services

Medical treatment is available at the Government Hospital (☎ 514 499, 313 731), north-east of São Francisco Garden.

Emergency

The emergency phone number is ☎ 999, and if you want the police dial ☎ 573 333.

THINGS TO SEE

Macau has far more of historical interest than Hong Kong and, unlike the rest of China, churches are a major part of the scenery. Although Buddhism and Taoism are the dominant religions, the Portuguese influence has definitely had an impact and Catholicism is very strong in Macau.

A good walk is the peninsula route outlined in the tourist office's *Walking Tour* pamphlet. Go up the hill to **São Agostinho Igreja** (St Augustine's Church) and the **Teatro Dom Pedro V**, a beautiful old theatre used for occasional special events such as music festivals and dance performances, and then continue down to **São Lourenço Igreja** (St Lawrence's Church).

From there, go down to Travessa do Padre Narciso, past the pink former **Government House**, then right, along the waterfront, turning right at Calcada da Praia to head up the hill again and into the ritzy neighbourhood of the former **Governor's Residence**. From here there are signs leading to the **Our Lady of Penha Church** on top of the hill overlooking Macau.

Ruinas de São Paulo
Ruins of St Paul's Cathedral

The facade and majestic stairway are all that remain of this old church, a symbol of Macau. It was designed by an Italian Jesuit and built in 1602 by Japanese refugees who had fled anti-Christian persecution in Nagasaki.

In 1853 the church was burned down during a catastrophic typhoon. There's a small museum at the back (down the stairs), which has some interesting artefacts and paintings from the period, as well as a relic bone (the right arm) of St Francis Xavier.

Fortaleza de Monte
Monte Fort

This fort, built by the Jesuit, overlooks the Ruinas de São Paulo and almost all of Macau from its high and central position. In 1622 a cannonball fired from the fort conveniently landed in a Dutch gunpowder carrier during an attempted Dutch invasion, demolishing most of their fleet.

It's worth visiting the **Museum of Macau** here, which features some interesting exhibits highlighting Chinese civilisation and the history of Macau. It's open Tuesday to Saturday from 10 am to 6 pm. Entry is M$15.

Kuan Iam Temple

This 400-year-old temple, the city's most historic, is dedicated to Kuan Iam, the bodhisattva of compassion. You'll find it on Avenida do Coronel Mesquita. In the study are 18 wise men in a glass case – the one with the big nose is said to be Marco Polo.

Old Protestant Cemetery

Lord Churchill (one of Winston's ancestors) and the English artist George Chinnery are buried here, but far more interesting are the graves of missionaries and their families, traders and seamen – the epitaphs often provide detailed accounts of their lives and deaths.

One US ship seems to have had half its crew 'fall from aloft' while in port. The cemetery is behind the small Protestant church, also known as the Morrison Chapel, in commemoration of Robert Morrison who translated the bible into Chinese. He is also buried here.

Camões Grotto & Gardens

This garden is a memorial to Luís de Camões, the 16th-century Portuguese poet who has become something of a local hero,

MACAU 澳門

although the claim is not all that strong. He is said to have written his epic *Os Lusíadas* by the rocks here, but there is no firm evidence that he was ever in Macau.

A bust of Camões is in the gardens, which provide a pleasant, cool and shady retreat. The gardens are popular with the local Chinese: some come to exercise, while pockets of old men sit around playing chequers.

Barrier Gate

At the most northern point of Macau, the Barrier Gate used to be of interest because you could stand 100m from it and claim that you'd seen into China. Now you can stand on the other side and claim you've seen Macau.

Leal Senado
Loyal Senate

The graceful Leal Senado building looks out over the main town square and is the main administrative body for municipal affairs. At one time it was offered (and turned down) a total monopoly on all Chinese trade! The building also houses the National Library. It's across from the main post office.

Fortaleza de Guía
Guia Fort

This is the highest point on the Macau Peninsula, and is topped with a lighthouse and 17th-century chapel. First lit up in 1865, the lighthouse is the oldest on the China coast.

São Domingo Igreja
St Dominic's Church

Arguably the most beautiful church in Macau, this 17th-century building has an impressive tiered altar. There's a small **museum** at the back, full of church regalia, images and paintings.

Lou Lim Ioc Gardens

These peaceful gardens with an ornate mansion (now the Pui Ching School) has a mixture of Chinese and European influences, with huge shady trees, lotus ponds, pavilions, bamboo groves, grottoes and odd-shaped doorways.

Ah Ma Temple

Macau means the City of God and takes its name from Ah Ma-Gau, the Bay of Ah Ma. Ah Ma Temple (Ma Kok Miu), which dates from the Ming dynasty, stands at the base of Penha Hill near the southern end of the peninsula.

According to legend, Ah Ma, goddess of seafarers, manifested as a beautiful young woman whose presence on a Guǎngzhōu-bound ship saved it from disaster. All the other ships of the fleet, whose rich owners had refused to give her passage, were destroyed in a storm. The boat people of Macau come here on a pilgrimage each year in April or May.

Macau Maritime Museum

There are a number of boats on exhibit here, including a *lorcha*, a type of sailing cargo vessel used on the Zhū Jiāng (Pearl River). Entry is M$10 and short cruises are offered for M$10. There is also a small aquarium.

The museum is on the waterfront opposite the Ah Ma Temple and is open daily except Tuesday, from 10 am to 5.30 pm.

Grand Prix & Wine Museums

These two museums are located in the same premises opposite the Kingsway Hotel. The Grand Prix exhibit has various cars that have taken part in the Macau Grand Prix since it was started in 1954, as well as simulators for any armchair racing drivers.

Across the hall, the Wine Museum has a display detailing the history of wine but is basically a promotional exhibit for Portuguese wine. You can buy and taste wine here. This strange combination celebrating both the grape and the automobile may be one of the few places in the world where you can safely drink and drive.

Bus No 3A or No 10 stops near the museum. The entry fee of M$20 includes both museums and they are open daily from 10 am to 6 pm.

Museum of Art

This is a welcome addition to Macau's growing crop of museums, located in the new Cultural Centre, which opened in 1999.

There are visiting exhibits as well as permanent exhibitions of Chinese traditional art and painting by western artists who lived in Macau, including the works of George Chinnery. The museum is open Tueday to Saturday from 10 am to 7 pm; admission is M$15.

The Islands

Directly south of the mainland peninsula are the islands of Taipa and Coloane. Two bridges connect Taipa to the mainland, and a causeway connects Taipa and Coloane.

Taipa This island seems to have become one big construction site with the Hyatt Regency Hotel and Macau University just the first of several massive projects. Long blocks of apartments now sit on reclaimed land. Taipa village, however, is pleasant and there are some fine little restaurants to sample. At the southern end of the main village street you can rent a bicycle to explore the village and further afield.

There's an **old church**, a couple of **temples** and the stately **Taipa House Museum** east of the main village street and over the hill. Entrance to the museum is free and it gives a good sense of how the Macanese middle class lived at the beginning of the 20th century.

To get to Taipa take bus No 11 from Central Macau. If you want to get to Coloane from Taipa you'll have to walk back to the roundabout north-east of the village and get onto the highway to catch the bus to Coloane.

Coloane This island has a pretty village that is nice to wander around between visits to the park or the beach.

Situated in a muddy river mouth, Macau is hardly likely to be blessed with wonderful beaches, but Coloane has a couple that are really not bad. Tiny **Cheoc Van beach** has white sand and **Hac Sa beach** has black sand. Both beaches have windsurfers, water-scooters and other sea toys for hire. Cheoc Van beach has a yacht club and Hac Sa has a horse-riding stable. Bus No 25 terminates at Hac Sa beach, and goes past the turn-off for Cheoc Van beach.

South of the causeway on Coloane, Seac Pai Van Park has a good hiking trail to the highest point in Macau, **Alto de Coloane**. It starts south of the park's entrance and is 8km long. At the top of the hill is a huge white statue of Ah Ma, the goddess of seafarers. Bus No 25 goes by the park; get off at the second bus stop after crossing the causeway.

SPECIAL EVENTS

Macau has its own collection of holidays, festivals and cultural events, including some imported from Portugal. Except for the celebration of Portugal's independence day, most Christian festivals will continue in Macau after the handover to China.

An International Fireworks Festival is held annually in mid-September and the International Music Festival is held during the third week of October. The Macau Marathon is held in late autumn.

The biggest event of the year is without doubt the Macau Grand Prix. As in Monte Carlo, the streets of the town are the race track. The race is a two-day event held on the third weekend in November – accommodation can be as scarce as a three-humped camel at this time. There's a myriad other Chinese, Portuguese and religious festivals and holidays. Some of the highlights are:

Chinese Lunar New Year As elsewhere in China, this is a three-day public holiday held in late January or early February.

Lantern Festival Not a public holiday, but a lot of fun, this festival occurs two weeks after the Chinese New Year.

Feast of the Drunken Dragon In mid-May, people who make their living by fishing close up shop and take a break to enjoy three days of drinking and feasting.

Dragon Boat Festival As in Hong Kong, this is a major public holiday held in early June.

Mid-Autumn Festival This is a major public holiday in September.

Cheung Yeung Festival This public holiday is held in October and is also celebrated in Hong Kong.

Winter Solstice This is not a public holiday, but still an interesting time to visit Macau. Many Macau Chinese consider the winter solstice more important than the Chinese New Year. There is plenty of feasting and temples are crammed with worshippers.

CENTRAL MACAU

CENTRAL MACAU

PLACES TO STAY
8 Vila Capital
  京藝賓館
9 East Asia Hotel
  東亞酒店
10 Grand Hotel
  國際酒店
11 Peninsula Hotel
  半島酒店
13 Macau Masters
  Hotel
  萬事發酒店
14 Hou Kong Hotel
  濠江酒店
15 Pensão Tai Fat
  大發酒店
17 Vila Universal
  世界迎賓館
18 San Va
  Hospedaria
  新華大旅店
19 Vila Pung Loi
  蓬萊別墅
20 Sun Sun Hotel
  新新酒店
21 London Hotel
  英京酒店
22 Pensão Kuan
  Heng
  群興賓館
24 Hotel Central
  新中央酒店
38 Metropole
  Hotel
  京都酒店
40 Vila Kimbo
43 Vila Nam Long;
  Vila Meng Meng
  南龍別墅
  明明賓館
44 Pensão Nam In
  藍茵酒店
50 Holiday Inn;
  Oskar's Pub
  假日酒店
51 Presidente
  總統酒店
52 Beverly Plaza
  Hotel
  富豪酒店

53 Vila San Vu
  珊瑚別墅
55 Lisboa Hotel & Casino;
  A Galera Restaurant
  葡京酒店
58 Sintra Hotel
  新麗華酒店

PLACES TO EAT
16 Fat Siu Lau
  佛笑樓大餐廳
25 Grand Street Café
  大街咖啡
26 Carvela Restaurante
  Vela Latina
  新帆船餐廳
29 McDonald's
  麥當勞
46 Clube Militar
  澳門陸軍俱樂部
54 Pizza Hut
  必勝客
59 Estrela do Mar
  海星餐廳

OTHER
1 Santo Antonio
  Igreja
  聖安多尼堂
2 Ruinas de São Paulo
  大三巴牌坊
3 Fortaleza de Monte
  中央大炮台
4 St Michael's
  Cemetery
  聖美基西洋墳場
5 Vasco da Gama
  Garden
  華士古達嘉馬花園
6 Government Hospital
  山頂醫院
7 Floating Casino
  (Macau Palace)
  澳門皇宮娛樂場
12 Kee Kwan Motors
  (Buses to Guǎngzhōu)
  岐關車路有限公司
23 São Domingo
  Igreja
  玫瑰堂

27 Money Changer Soi
  Cheong
28 Macau Government
  Tourist Office
  澳門旅遊司
30 Watson's Drugstore
  屈臣氏
31 Cineteatro Macau
  澳門戲院
32 Cathedral
  大教堂
33 Main Post Office
  郵電局
34 Leal Senado
  市政廳
35 CTS;
  Nam Wah
  Commercial Building
  中國旅行社
36 São Agostinho Igreja
  聖奧斯堂
37 Teatro Dom Pedro V
39 Jorge Alvares Statue
41 Foto Princesa
  公主攝影器材行
42 CTM Telephone
  Office
  澳門電訊
45 Chinese Library
  八角亭
47 Military Museum
  軍事博物館
48 Macau Exhibition
  Centre
49 Main Police Station
  正警署
56 Bank of China
  中銀大廈
57 Bus Stop to Taipa &
  Coloane
60 Former Government
  House
  澳督府
61 São Lourenco
  Igreja
  聖老楞佐堂
62 São Jose Igreja
  聖約瑟堂
63 Jazz Club
  爵士俱樂部

PLACES TO STAY

During weekends, which begin Friday night, hotel prices can double and rooms of any kind can be scarce. Some bargaining is possible during the mid-week, especially in the winter low season. All prices listed here are mid-week prices. Unless otherwise stated, guesthouse rooms have air-con.

With the mid- to top-range places you can get discounts of 30% or more by booking through a Hong Kong travel agent. The best places to do this are the numerous travel agencies in the Shun Tak Centre (Macau ferry pier) at Sheung Wan, Hong Kong Island. Top-end hotels add a 15% tax and service charge.

Places to Stay – Budget

All places listed are on the Central Macau map.

One block back from the waterfront and a couple of blocks south of Avenida de Almeida Ribeiro is an alley called Rua do Bocage. At No 28 on the 3rd floor there's the *Vila Pung Loi* (☎ 574 292), which has simple rooms for M$140 with shared bath and M$160 with bath.

A block north, at Rua da Caldeira 43, the *Pensão Tai Fat* (☎ 933 908) is a bit more expensive, but very good value with rooms for M$250. South again, near the covered market, the *Pensão Kuan Heng* (☎ 573 629, 937 624, Rua Ponte E Horta 3-4) has clean rooms with bath for M$150 and twins/triples for M$250/350.

Also down at the bottom end price-wise, the *San Va Hospedaria* (☎ 573 701) is a funky old building on the corner of Rua de Felicidade and Travessa de Felicidade, which has rooms with shared bath ranging from M$50 to M$120, although the cheaper ones don't have any windows or air-con.

Near the corner with Travessa Auto Novo, the *Vila Universal* (☎ 573 247) has singles/twins with bath for M$190/260.

Moving to the eastern side of the peninsula, the area between the Lisboa Hotel and Avenida da Praia Grande has some very cheap rooms. Intersecting with Avenida da Praia Grande is a small street called Rua do Doutor Pedro José Lobo, where there's a dense cluster of guesthouses, including the compact *Vila Meng Meng* (☎ 715 241, 2nd floor, Rua do Doutor Pedro José Lobo 24). If you don't mind a shared bathroom you can get a room for M$80; M$100 with bath.

Next door at No 30-C is the *Vila Nam Long* (☎ 712 573), where singles without a window start at M$75 doubles with attached bath cost M$140.

Just above Foto Princesa, at Avenida do Infante D'Henrique 55-59, the *Vila Kimbo* (☎ 710 010) has rooms with shared bath/ bath for M$100/150.

Running off Avenida de Dom João IV is an alley called Travessa da Praia Grande. At No 3 you'll find *Pensão Nam In* (☎ 710 024), where singles are M$100 with shared bath and M$150 with bath. The doubles with bath are more pleasant and go for M$230.

Behind the Lisboa Hotel on Avenida de Lopo Sarmento de Carvalho is a row of pawnshops and a couple of guesthouses. The *Vila San Vu* (☎ 780 779) has good rooms for M$210. There's also a sign outside in English with its translated name, the Vila Coral. This place seems a little sleazy, however – maybe it's the proximity to the Lisboa Casino.

Probably one of the nicest places to stay if you can get a bed is the *Pousada de Juventude* at Cheoc Van beach on Coloane Island. It's at the top of the driveway down to the beach, but you can't just arrive and get a bed. First you'll have to book a room at the Youth Hostel Booking Office (☎ 344 340) in Macau. You'll also need to have an International Youth Hostel Federation card (see the Hong Kong chapter for details). Mid-week prices for beds are M$40.

Places to Stay – Mid-Range

For the sake of definition, a mid-range hotel in Macau is anything priced between M$200 and M$500. Unless otherwise noted, all places are on the Central Macau map.

The *East Asia Hotel* (☎ 922 433, fax 922 430, Rua da Madeira 1-A) has gotten a bit sleazy in recent years. One traveller reports it is 'now literally overrun with prostitutes', but it's still one of the city's classic colonial buildings. The outside maintains its traditional facade, while the inside has been fully re-modelled. Clean singles/doubles start at M$230/360 with bath. The dim sum restaurant on the 2nd floor serves good breakfasts.

Almost next door to the East Asia Hotel is the **Vila Capital** (☎ 920 154, Rua Constantino Brito 3) with singles/doubles for M$200/220.

The **Hotel Central** (☎ 373 888, fax 332 275, Avenida de Almeida Ribeiro 264) is, true to its name, centrally located at a short hop west of the main post office. The hotel looks better on the outside than it does on the inside – go upstairs and look at the rooms before you decide to stay. It has a mind-boggling variety of rooms costing M$173 for singles without windows or M$210 for doubles (with windows and bath).

The **London Hotel** (☎ 937 761, Praça Ponte e Horta 4), two blocks east of the waterfront, has some remarkably good deals. Singles with bath are M$120 and doubles range from M$200 to M$240. Rooms are comfortable and clean. Next door, the **Sun Sun Hotel** (939 393, fax 938 822; in Hong Kong ☎ 2517 4273) is more upmarket, but still affordable with doubles for M$280.

Closer to Avenida de Almeida Ribeiro and a block from the waterfront is an alley called Travessa das Virtudes. On your left as you enter the alley off the waterfront is the **Hou Kong Hotel** (☎ 937 555, fax 338 884), which has singles/doubles for M$260/280. Nearby, at No 146 on the northern side of Avenida de Almeida Ribeiro, the **Grand Hotel** (☎ 921 111; fax 922 397) has singles/twins for M$242/276.

A couple of blocks south of the intersection where Avenida de Almeida Ribeiro meets the waterfront, the multistorey **Peninsula Hotel** (☎ 318 899 fax 344 933, Rua das Lorchas, Ponte Cais 14) has singles and doubles starting at M$350 and M$400. This hotel is large, clean and popular. Just down the street, the **Macau Masters Hotel** (☎ 937 572, fax 937 565, Rua das Lorchas 162) has doubles starting at M$250.

Up one of the hills overlooking Macau near the Guía lighthouse, the **Guía Hotel** (☎ 513 888, fax 559 822, Estrada do Eng Trigo 1-5) (see the Macau Peninsula map)

has standard doubles starting at M$470. Deluxe rooms are M$570 and suites start at M$750.

The **Metropole Hotel** (☎ 388 166, fax 388 553, Avenida da Praia Grande 493-501) has a prime location but is borderline mid-range. Singles are M$460 and doubles are M$600.

Places to Stay – Top End

One novel place to stay is the **Lisboa Hotel** (☎ 577 666, fax 567 193, Avenida da Lisboa 2-4; in Hong Kong ☎ 2546 6944) the wonderfully tacky facade of which is one of the best examples of the American postwar aesthetic this side of Las Vegas. Standard doubles start at M$900, but discounts are available through travel agencies in Hong Kong.

Another place with a little more traditional Macanese character is the **Pousada de São Tiago** (☎ 378 111, fax 552 170, Avenida da República; in Hong Kong ☎ 2739 1216). A small hotel with swimming pool and terrace garden, double rooms start at M$1460. Formerly the site of a Portuguese fortress, it's below Barra Hill in a pleasant location. See the Macau Peninsula map.

Otherwise, most of Macau's hotels are rather large, soulless places, much as you would expect in a casino town. At the cheaper end of the scale, the **Sintra Hotel** (☎ 710 111, fax 567 769, Avenida Dom João IV; in Hong Kong ☎ 2546 6944) is west of the Lisboa Hotel and run by the same company. Standard doubles start at M$680 and suites start at M$1480.

Similarly, the **Presidente** (☎ 553 888, fax 552 735, Avenida da Amizade; in Hong Kong ☎ 2857 1533) is a reasonable top-end option east of the Lisboa Hotel. Standard doubles start at M$620.

The **Beverly Plaza Hotel** (☎ 782 288, fax 780 684, Avenida do Doutor Rodrigo Rodrigues; in Hong Kong ☎ 2739 9928) is a large four-star hotel that often offers good discounts. Standard doubles start at M$740.

Also in this neighbourhood, the **Grandeur** (☎ 781 233, fax 781 211, Rua de Pequim 199; in Hong Kong ☎ 2857 2846) is a slightly more upmarket option. Run by CTS, standard doubles are M$1000. Nearby, the *Holiday Inn* (☎ 783 333, fax 782 321, Rua de Pequim 82-86; in Hong Kong ☎ 2810 9628) has doubles starting at M$1000, but discounts of more than 50% are available during mid-week and the low season.

Top accommodation in central Macau can be found at the *Mandarin Oriental* (☎ 567 888, fax 594 589 Avenida da Amizade; in Hong Kong ☎ 2881 1988). Double rooms begin at M$1150 and suites range from M$3500 to M$18,000 (see the Macau Peninsula map).

For rest and relaxation in a resort setting, the private and luxurious *Westin Resort* (☎ 871 111, fax 871 122; in Hong Kong ☎ 2803 2015) is at the far end of Hac Sa beach on Coloane Island. Double rooms start at M$1625 and facilities include a golf course and childcare centre.

The more prosaic *Pousada de Coloane* (☎ 882 143, fax 882 251) is at the smaller Cheoc Van beach on Coloane Island. Perched on the hillside above the beach, this older hotel has a certain faded charm. Double rooms start at M$680 and there's a small swimming pool and terrace garden.

PLACES TO EAT

Given its cosmopolitan past, it's not surprising that the food of Macau is an exotic mixture of Portuguese and Chinese. It also speaks of a far greater appreciation and integration of food culture on the part of the Portuguese compared with the British in Hong Kong. There are also influences from other European countries and Africa.

The most famous local speciality is African chicken baked with peppers and chillies. Other specialities include *bacalhau*, which is baked, grilled, stewed or boiled cod. Sole, a flatfish, is another Macanese delicacy. There's also ox tail and ox breast, rabbit prepared in various ways, and soups like *caldo verde* and *sopa à alentejana* made with vegetables, meat and olive oil.

The Brazilian contribution is *feijoadas*, a stew made of beans, pork, spicy sausages, potatoes and cabbage. The contribution from the former Portuguese enclave of Goa on the western coast of India is spicy prawns.

The Portuguese influence is visible in the many fine imported Portuguese red and white wines, port and brandy. Mateus Rosé is the most famous, but even cheaper are bottles of red or white wine. A long, lazy Portuguese meal with a carafe of red to wash it down is one of the most pleasant aspects of a Macau visit. The menus are often in Portuguese, so a few useful words are *cozido* (stew), *cabrito* (kid), *cordeiro* (lamb), *carreiro* (mutton), *galinha* (chicken), *caraguejos* (crabs), *carne de vaca* (beef) and *peixe* (fish).

Another Macau pleasure is to sit back in one of the many little *pastelarias* (cake shops) with a glass of *chá de limão* (lemon tea) and a plate of cakes – very genteel! Of course, this is the home of the famous Portuguese custard tart, which is famous in Hong Kong and is now even making headway into the mainland. The cakeshops are good places for a cheap breakfast. Not surprisingly, there's delicious bread to be found in Macau, another legacy of its Portuguese heritage.

People eat their evening meal early in Macau – you can find the chairs put away and the chef gone home around 9 pm.

The following eateries are marked on the Macau Peninsula map.

Henri's Galley (☎ 556 251, 4 Avenida da República 4) is on the waterfront on the southern end of the peninsula. The adjacent *Ali Curry House* (☎ 555 865) is also worth a visit.

You can find a couple of nice restaurants and cafes near the Maritime Museum. *A Lorcha* (☎ 313 193, Rua Almirante Sergio 289) is an old favourite, serving some of the best Portuguese food in Macau at very reasonable prices. The *O Porto Interior* (☎ 967 770) down the street at 259-B, is another good place.

The following places are marked on the Central Macau map.

Near the Largo do Senado, *Fat Siu Lau* (☎ 573 580) serves Portuguese and Chinese food. It's at Rua de Felicidade 64, the former red-light Street of Happiness, which has recently undergone a face-lift. The speciality at Fat Siu Lau is roast pigeon.

Across the street from the square, the **Carvela Restaurante Vela Latina** (☎ 356 888, 2nd floor, Avenida Almeida Ribeiro 201-209) is a good place for lunch. Set meals of Portuguese-style food are M$55.

A good place for coffee and snacks is the **Grand Street Café**, located on a side street off Avenida Almeida Ribeiro opposite Rua dos Mercadores.

Comida a Portuguesa Carlos (☎ 751 838, Rua Cicade de Braga) is a friendly and unpretentious place serving Portuguese food for very reasonable prices.

In Taipa village, Rua do Cunha and its sides streets are full of restaurants. Some Portuguese-style places to try are **Pinocchio's** (☎ 827 128, Rua do Sol 4), **Restaurante Panda** (☎ 827 338, Rua Carlos Eugenio 4-8) – don't be misled by the name, it's a *very* Portuguese restaurant – and **Galo Restaurant** (☎ 827 318, Rua dos Clerigos 47). **Estrela do Mar** (☎ 827 843, Rua Carlos Eugenio 12) is highly recommended for its African chicken, seafood and reasonable prices. There's also a branch at 11 Travessa do Paiva, off Avenida da Praia Grande.

For very elegant dining, the **Clube Militar Restaurant** (☎ 714 009, Avenida da Praia Grande 795) has buffets for lunch and dinner. Readers have also recommended the **A Galera Restaurante** (☎ 577 666), in the Lisboa Hotel, for Macanese food (particularly the appetiser of stuffed crab).

At Hac Sa beach on Coloane Island, the legendary **Fernando's** (☎ 882 264, Praia Hac Sa 9) has long had a reputation of serving up some of the best food and atmosphere in Macau. It's directly opposite the No 25 bus stop at the end of the line. In Coloane village try the **Restaurante Cacarola** (☎ 882 226, Rua das Gaivotas 8), just east of the village park roundabout.

Besides these places, of course, Macau has its fair share of cheap Chinese restaurants and fast food outlets.

ENTERTAINMENT
Gambling
Even if gambling holds no interest for you, it's fun to wander the casinos at night. The largest and most fun arena for losing money is the Lisboa Hotel, which houses the Lisboa Casino. The *Crazy Paris Show* at the hotel also features Las Vegas-style dancing shows every night, but the ticket price is steep at over M$300. Most casinos require ID and reasonably proper attire, so bring your passport and don't wear shorts. Cheating at gambling is a serious criminal offence, so don't even think about it

There is horse racing on Taipa Island at the *Jockey Club*. Dog races are held at the *Canidrome* (yes, they really call it that) in the north of Macau starting at 8 pm on Monday, Thursday, Saturday and Sunday.

Prior to Macau's handover to China, bullfights were occasionally held in Macau, every 10 years or so. In the late 1990s the event was gaining some popularity with Hong Kong residents and two bullfights were held consecutively for two years, but at the time of writing none were scheduled for the near future.

Pubs
The nightlife in Macau is decidedly lacking compared to Hong Kong. If you need a drink there are hotel bars, such as **Oskar's Pub** in the Holiday Inn or the **Embassy Bar** in the Mandarin Oriental. A gathering place for locals is the **Talker Pub** (☎ 528 975, Rua de Pedro Coutinho 102-104), near the Kuan Iam Temple (see Macau Peninsula map). It's open on Friday and Saturday nights and doesn't really get going until after 9 pm. The **King's Pub** (Rua Almirante Sergio 261 C), near the O Porto Interior and A Lorcha restaurants opens at 8 pm.

For good music, try the **Jazz Club** (☎ 596 014, Rua Alabardas 9) near São Lourenço's Igreja. It's open on Friday and Saturday night only and live music is normally performed here between 11 pm and 2 am. Go to the back of the church and turn left down Rua George Chinnery and turn right at the street at the bottom. Look for the small red-and-white-tiled facade.

At the pubs, keep an eye out for a new local beer produced by the *Macau Brewing Company*, started up by an American and two locals in 1999.

SHOPPING

Pawnshops are ubiquitous in Macau, and it is possible to get good deals on cameras, watches and jewellery, but you must be prepared to bargain without mercy. Here is one place where the nasty reputation of pawnbrokers is well deserved!

St Dominic's Market, in the alley behind the Hotel Central, is a good place to pick up cheap clothing. If you are looking for reproductions of antique Chinese furniture, it's much cheaper to buy it in Macau than Hong Kong, and the price will include shipping to Hong Kong. The shops are concentrated in the tourist area on Rua da Palha and Rua de São Paulo near the Ruinas de São Paulo.

If you've got the habit, Macau is cheap for Portuguese wine, imported cigarettes, cigars and pipe tobacco. However, Hong Kong's customs agents only allow you to bring in 1L of wine and 50 cigarettes duty free.

GETTING THERE & AWAY

Air

Macau's controversial new airport opened in December 1995. There were serious doubts that the airport would ever generate enough passengers to pay for itself, but traffic has increased in the last four years and the two million mark was reached for passenger activity in May 1997, although it doesn't seem like much when you consider that nearly 24 million air passengers went through Hong Kong in the same year.

The main airline is Air Macau, but there are also a few regional and international airlines that fly to Macau. There are flights to cities in China and Taiwan, as well as to Bangkok, Kuala Lumpur, Manila, Singapore, Seoul, P'yŏngyang and Lisbon. Departure tax for destinations in mainland China is M$80 and for international destinations is M$130.

For Hong Kong residents in a hurry to lose their money, East Asia Airlines runs a helicopter service. Flying time from Hong Kong is 20 minutes at a cost of HK$1206 on weekdays, or HK$1310 on weekends – quite an expense just to save the extra half hour required by boat. There are up to 22 flights daily.

If you're flying out of Macau from Hong Kong, you can check your baggage at the Shun Tak ferry terminal on Hong Kong Island. Shuttle buses from the Macau ferry terminal take passengers to the airport.

Bus

Macau is an easy gateway into China. You simply take a bus to the border and walk across. Buses Nos 3, 10B and AP1 run between the jetfoil pier and the Barrier Gate at the Macau-China border.

You can also catch a bus directly from Macau to Guăngzhōu. Tickets for the Guăngzhōu bus are sold at Kee Kwan Motors (☎ 933 888) beside the Macau Masters Hotel at Rua das Lorchas 12. Buses leave from there roughly every half to 1½ hours between 8 am and 6.30 pm. Tickets cost M$40 and the journey, after going through immigration, takes approximately three hours.

Boat

The vast majority of visitors to Macau make their arrival and departure by boat. If you're coming from Hong Kong, be prepared for a long wait at Macau immigration if you're stuck behind one of the tour groups from the mainland. It's wise to sprint ahead to avoid standing in line.

The jetfoil pier in Macau has left luggage lockers if you're just doing a day visit on the way to or from China.

Hong Kong-Macau Macau is separated from Hong Kong by 65km of water. Three companies do the route: Far East Hydrofoil (☎ 790 7039; in Hong Kong ☎ 2859 3333), Turbo Cat (☎ 790 3211; in Hong Kong ☎ 2921 6688) and Hong Kong & Yaumati Ferry Company (HYFCO; ☎ 726 301; in Hong Kong ☎ 2516 9581). There are departures about once every half hour during the day and about once every hour in the evening up to midnight. Far East Hydrofoil has departures every 15 minutes during the day and operates boats all night, with less frequent departures after midnight.

The Jetfoil takes 55 minutes. Turbo Cat boats come in two varieties of jet-powered catamarans: so-called jumbo-cats, which take 65 minutes, and tri-cats, which take 55 minutes. The HYFCO catamarans take about 70 minutes.

Going to Macau, jetfoils and turbocats depart from the Hong Kong and Macau ferry pier next to Shun Tak Centre (☎ 2559 9800) at 200 Connaught Rd, Sheung Wan, Hong Kong Island – this is easily reached by Hong Kong's MTR subway system to Sheung Wan station. The HYFCO catamarans leave from the China Hong Kong City ferry terminal in Kowloon, though it also has a couple of runs from the Shun Tak Centre as well. In Macau all boats to Hong Kong depart from the jetfoil pier (☎ 727 288).

Luggage space is limited to what you can carry. You'll be OK just carrying a backpack or one suitcase, but oversized baggage will need to be checked in as it would on an aircraft.

On weekends and holidays you'd be wise to book your return ticket in advance because the boats are sometimes full. Even Monday morning can be difficult for getting seats back to Hong Kong, but there is normally no problem on weekdays.

There's not much difference between the boats, though some travellers express a preference for the turbo cats. On the turbocats there are economy, 1st and VIP classes. The jetfoils have two classes (economy and 1st) and the HYFCO boats have one standard class only. The economy price to Hong Kong from the Macau ferry terminal is HK$137. Tickets from the Shun Tak Centre to Macau are HK$130. Boats to and from Kowloon are slightly cheaper. The Hong Kong government charges HK$26 departure tax, which is included in the price of your ticket. Macau charges M$22 departure tax, also included in the ticket price. Seniors and children are given discounts. All fares go up on the weekend.

Besides booking tickets by telephone, you can also buy tickets at MTR outlets in Hong Kong, as well as at the ferry terminals and most travel agencies.

Shékŏu-Macau Ferries leave once a day from the wharf behind the Peninsula Hotel to Shékŏu in the Shēnzhèn Special Economic Zone. The boat leaves Macau at 2.30 pm and arrives in Shékŏu at 4 pm. Tickets are M$100.

GETTING AROUND

Macau is fairly compact and it's relatively easy to walk almost everywhere, but you'll definitely need motorised transport to visit Taipa and Coloane.

To/From the Airport

Taxis and AP1 buses take passengers to the major hotels and the jetfoil pier, and terminate at the border. The price is M$6 and buses leave the airport every 15 minutes. A taxi from the airport to central Macau will cost about M$40.

Bus

There are minibuses and normal buses, and both offer air-con and frequent services. They operate from 7 am until midnight. Buses on the Macau Peninsula cost M$2.50 and M$4.50 for longer rides out to the islands.

Arguably the most useful bus to travellers is the No 3, which takes in the China border crossing, the jetfoil pier and the central area near the main post office. Bus No 10 also takes you into the centre of town, and bus No 10B goes directly from the jetfoil pier to the border. Bus No 11 goes from the square and the Lisboa Hotel to Taipa and No 25 goes to Coloane. The map handed out by the tourist office also has a list of bus routes. Unlike Hong Kong, however, minibuses take as many passengers as possible, and can get very crowded.

Car

The mere thought of renting a car for sightseeing on the Macau Peninsula is ridiculous – horrendous traffic and lack of parking space make driving more of a burden than a pleasure. However, car rental might make sense for a group exploring Taipa and Coloane.

As in Hong Kong, driving is on the left-hand side of the road. Another local driving rule is that motor vehicles must always stop for pedestrians at a crossing if there is no traffic light. It's illegal to beep the horn. An

International Driver's Permit is usually required, as well as a deposit of M$4000.

Happy Mokes (☎ 726 868) is in the jetfoil pier on Level 1 at counter 1025. Weekday rentals for 24 hours are M$480, M$500 on weekends. Morning to evening rentals are M$300.

Avis Rent A Car (☎ 336 789) at the Mandarin Oriental rents out Korean compacts for M$500 on weekdays and M$690 on weekends.

Taxi

Macau taxis all have meters, and drivers are required to use them. Flag fall is M$10 for the first 1.5km; M$1 every 250m thereafter. There is a M$5 surcharge to go to Coloane, but there's no surcharge on return trips.

Not many taxi drivers speak English, so it's useful to have a map with both Chinese

and either English or Portuguese. If you hire a taxi for the day or half a day, it's better to agree on a price beforehand.

Pedicab

The pedicabs are essentially for touristy sightseeing and photo opportunities. The vehicles have to be bargained for and it's hardly worth the effort – if there are two of you make sure the fare covers both. Typical pedicab hire fees are M$25 for a short photo opportunity, or about M$100 per hour. Don't worry about finding them; they'll find you.

Bicycle

You can hire bicycles out on the islands of Taipa. On the peninsula there are no places to hire bikes and, anyway, it wouldn't be pleasant riding in the insane traffic.

Guǎngdōng 广东

Guǎngdōng's proximity to Hong Kong has made it a major gateway into China and the country's most affluent province. In 1979, Guǎngdōng was only the 10th most affluent, but the high level of economic integration between Guǎngdōng's Zhū Jiāng (Pearl River) Delta and Hong Kong has led to record economic growth – some economists refer to the area as Greater Hong Kong.

The Cantonese, as the people of Guǎngdōng are called, are regarded with a mixture of envy and suspicion by many in the rest of China. Guǎngdōng's topography, unique dialect (Cantonese) and remoteness from traditional centres of authority, coupled with long-standing contact with 'foreign barbarians', has created a strong sense of autonomy and self-sufficiency.

The Cantonese also spearheaded Chinese emigration to the USA, Canada, Australia and South Africa in the mid-19th century, spurred on by the gold rushes in those countries and by the wars and growing poverty in their own country. Bustling Chinatowns around the world are steeped in the flavours of Guǎngdōng cuisine and ring with the sounds of the Cantonese dialect and Cantopop melodies. Hong Kong heroes such as Bruce Lee and Jackie Chan are as famous in Guǎngdōng as they are in Hong Kong.

The province has basked in the healthy regional economic climate encompassing Hong Kong, becoming the target for investment by overseas Chinese. Indeed, the manufacturing industries that Hong Kong was once famous are now located in Guǎngdōng.

Supping at the same table as Hong Kong has both fattened the province and cultivated a regional idiosyncrasy that finds vigorous expression in the burgeoning media industries. When China-watchers worry (or rub their hands in glee) about the possible decentralisation of power in China and the rise of regionalism, it is Guǎngdōng that they look to first. After all, Guǎngdōng was a latecomer to the Chinese empire. While it

Highlights

Capital: Guǎngzhōu
Population: 69.6 million
Area: 186,000 sq km

- The decaying colonial ambience of Guǎngzhōu's Shāmiàn Dǎo
- Fear and loathing: the bizarre range of produce for sale in Guǎngzhōu's Qīngpíng Shìchǎng
- Zhàoqìng, offering the nearby beauty of Dǐnghú Shān and scenery that is reminiscent of Guìlín

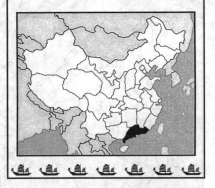

was integrated in 214 BC (during the Qin dynasty), it was not until the mid-12th century that large numbers of Han settlers (propelled by the Jurchen invaders) emigrated to the province from northern China.

Until then, Guǎngdōng was considered to be a barbaric borderland fit only for exiled officials. In subsequent years, the province was the site of many rival national governments, which earned it a reputation for unruliness and revolt.

Today Guǎngdōng is an economic powerhouse rather than a sightseeing destination. Most foreigners visiting the province are there on business, or in transit to less developed parts of China.

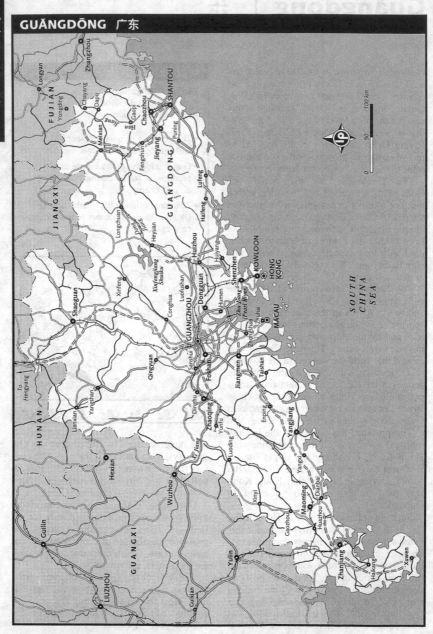

GUǍNGDŌNG 广东

Despite all its successes, the provincial capital Guăngzhōu lacks the originality, facilities and modernity of Shànghăi. Hellbent on copying Hong Kong, the city is in danger of becoming too derivative and is for the most part a traffic-locked sprawl with appalling air pollution, and a skyline crenellated with huge advertisements and building projects.

GUĂNGZHŌU 广州

☎ 020 • pop 6,664,900

Also known as Canton, Guăngzhōu is the capital of Guăngdōng and one of the most prosperous cities in China. There may not be much in the way of sights, but wandering the streets of Guăngzhōu is an interesting insight into the extremes of poverty and wealth in China.

Over the last decade Guăngzhōu has epitomised this transformation. Busy casting off the yoke of recent history, the city is eager to catch up with the late 20th century. There are a few interesting temples and parks, but most of the city's charm lingers on in the streets and alleys on Shāmiàn Dăo (Shamian Island), a foreign concession that is being gracefully gentrified.

History

The first town to be established on the site of present-day Guăngzhōu dates back to the Qin dynasty (221–207 BC). The first foreigners to come here were the Indians and Romans, who appeared as early as the 2nd century AD. By the Tang dynasty (500 years later) Arab traders were visiting, and a sizeable trade with the Middle East and South-East Asia had grown.

The Portuguese arrived in the 16th century hunting for porcelain and silk, and providing Guăngzhōu with its first contact with a modern European nation; they were allowed to set up base downriver in Macau in 1557. Then the Jesuits came in and in 1583 were allowed to establish themselves at Zhàoqìng, a town to the west of Guăngzhōu, and later in Běijīng.

The first trade overtures from the British were rebuffed in 1625, but the imperial government finally opened Guăngzhōu to foreign trade in 1685. In 1757, by imperial edict, China's foreign trade was restricted to Guăngzhōu, and the Co Hong, a Guăngzhōu merchants' guild, gained exclusive rights to it. Foreigners were restricted to Shāmiàn Dăo. Their lives there were rule-bound and the Co Hong saw to it that trade flourished in China's favour.

In 1773 the British decided to shift the balance of trade by unloading 1000 chests of Bengal opium at Guăngzhōu. The import proved popular and soon became a drain on China's silver reserves.

In 1839 opium was still the key to British trade in China. The emperor appointed Lin Zexu commissioner of Guăngzhōu with orders to stamp out the opium trade once and for all. Despite initial successes (the British surrendered 20,000 chests of opium), the Chinese war on drugs led to a British military reaction, the first Opium War. The conflict was ended by the Treaty of Nanjing (1942), which ceded Hong Kong Island to the British. A later treaty ceded the island and a piece of Kowloon 'in perpetuity'.

In the 19th century, Guăngzhōu became a cradle of revolt. The leader of the anti-dynastic Taiping Rebellion, Hong Xiuquan (1814–64), was born at Huaxian, north-west of Guăngzhōu, and the early activities of the Taipings centred on this area.

Guăngzhōu was also a stronghold of the republican forces after the fall of the Qing dynasty in 1911. Sun Yatsen, the first president of the Republic of China, was born at Cùihēng village south-west of Guăngzhōu. In the early 1920s, Sun headed the Kuomintang (Nationalist Party) in Guăngzhōu, from where the republicans mounted their campaigns against the northern warlords. Guăngzhōu was also a centre of activities for the fledgling Communist Party.

Contemporary Guăngzhōu, however, swings to the tinkle of cash registers rather than the drum roll of protest and revolt. In recent times the Cantonese have usually left the turbulence of politics to their northern compatriots.

Orientation

Central Guăngzhōu is bounded by a circle road (Huanshi Lu – literally 'circle-city road') to the north and the Zhū Jiāng (Pearl River) to the south. Most hotels, commercial areas and places of interest lie within this boundary. A larger ring road (the Huancheng expressway) and numerous inner-city overpasses are still under construction.

Accommodation tends to be clustered around the train station (in the north), on Huanshi Donglu (in the north-east), and in and around the old foreign concession of Shāmiàn Dǎo (in the south). If you don't want to leave with the impression that Guǎngzhōu is one huge construction site, seek sanctuary on Shāmiàn Dǎo, which is by far the quietest and most appealing sector of the city.

According to Chinese convention, Guǎngzhōu's major streets are usually split into numbered sectors (Zhongshan Wulu, which could also be written Zhongshan 5-Lu etc). Alternatively they are labelled by compass points: *bĕi* (north), *dōng* (east), *nán* (south) and *xī* (west) – as in Huanshi Donglu, which will sometimes be written in English as Huanshi East Road.

Guǎngzhōu's first subway line opened in July 1999 and runs from the Guǎngzhōu East train station in the north-east to across the Zhū Jiāng in the south-west.

Information

A monthly entertainment guide, *Clueless in Guangzhou*, is produced by foreigners living in the city and is an invaluable resource for what's happening in town and around. It's available at most of the major hotels and international-style bars. Check out the Web site at www.clueless.nu.

The Public Security Bureau (PSB; Gōngānjú; ☎ 8311 6253) is at 863 Jiefang Beilu, just south of the Nányuèwáng Hànmù.

Travel Agencies There's an office of the China International Travel Service (CITS; Zhōngguó Guójì Lǚxíngshè; ☎ 8666 6279) at 185 Huanshi Lu, next to the main train station, which will book tickets and has a bevy of English speakers. For more friendly service, however, try the China Foreign Trade Guangzhou Travel Service (Guǎngjīaohùi Piàowù Zhōngxīn; ☎ 8667

8000) at 117 Liuhua Lu, opposite McDonald's. The China Travel Service (CTS; Zhōngguó Lǚxíngshè) in the lobby of the Hotel Landmark Canton also runs tours and books tickets. Most hotels can help with travel needs as well.

Consulates There are several consulates that can issue visas and replace stolen passports.

Australia (☎ 8335 0909, fax 8335 0718) Room 1509, Main Building, GITIC Plaza, 339 Huanshi Donglu
Canada (☎ 8666 0569, fax 8667 2401) Room 801, China Hotel
France (☎ 8330 3405, fax 8330 3437) Room 803, GITIC Plaza, 339 Huanshi Donglu
Germany (☎ 8192 2566, fax 8192 2599) 103 Shamian Beijie, Shāmiàn Dǎo
Japan (☎ 8334 3090) 1st floor, Garden Hotel, 368 Huanshi Donglu
Thailand (☎ 8188 6968, fax 8186 1188) Room 316, White Swan Hotel, Shāmiàn Dǎo
(☎ 8335 1354, fax 8333 6485) 2nd floor, GITIC Plaza, 339 Huanshi Donglu
USA (☎ 8188 8911, fax 8186 2341) 1 Shamian Nanjie, Shāmiàn Dǎo
Vietnam (☎ 8647 7908, fax 8647 7808) 4th floor, 92 Huashi Xilu

Money There are numerous Bank of China branches around town that change travellers cheques, and also a number of ATMs that take Cirrus, MasterCard, Visa, Plus etc. There's one on the ground floor of the GITIC Plaza, one at the Bank of China near the Yǒuyì Bīnguǎn (see Places to Stay later), and another at the Bank of China on Changdi Malu.

If you're coming from Hong Kong, be warned that Guǎngzhōu's residents are all too happy to receive Hong Kong dollars from you, but they will give you change in RMB; change your dollars first to RMB at the bank or at your hotel.

Guǎngzhōu's American Express office (☎ 8331 1771, fax 8331 3535) is on the 8th floor of the GITIC Plaza Hotel.

Post & Communications The major tourist hotels have post offices where you can send letters and packets containing printed matter.

Adjacent to the train station is the main post office, known locally as the Liúhuā post office (Liúhuā yóujú). Overseas parcels can be sent from here.

DHL (☎ 8664 4668) has an office in Guǎngzhōu, as does UPS (☎ 8775 5778). Federal Express (☎ 8386 2026) is in Garden Hotel, Room 1356-7, Garden Tower.

The China Telecom office is opposite the train station on the eastern side of Renmin Beilu. Most hotels have International Direct Dialling (IDD) – calls to Hong Kong are very cheap. All the main tourist hotels have 'business centres' offering domestic and international telephone, fax and telex facilities.

The Meet Internet Coffee House (☎ 8731 1060) at the intersection of Dongfeng Lu and Nonglin Xialu has terminals for hire for Y15 per hour. It's open from 10 am to 1 am daily. Most of the major hotels also offer Internet access, but range from Y30 to Y50 for 15 minutes. At the time of writing, public terminals were being set up on the 2nd floor of the China Telecom office as well.

Bookshops The Foreign Languages Bookstore at 326 Beijing Lu is a bit difficult to find, located above a jewellery shop. There's not much available except the usual classics, but then travelling in China is a fine opportunity to brush up on your Dickens.

Most major hotels have small bookshops with a smattering of popular novels, as well as current issues of *Time*, *Newsweek*, the *Economist*, *Far Eastern Economic Review*, *Asiaweek* and even some French and German publications.

Medical Services The Guangzhou Red Cross Hospital has an emergency number (Hóngshízìhuì Yīyuànl ☎ 8441 2035), but the operator may not speak English. For general treatment of non-emergencies, try the medical clinic for foreigners at the Guangzhou No 1 People's Hospital (Dìyī Rénmín Yīyuàn; ☎ 8108 3090 ext 681) at 602 Renmin Beilu. For serious emergencies requiring an English-speaking doctor, it's best to call the Pioneer International Clinic (☎ 8384 8911), located at Room 3003, Peace World Plaza, 352 Huanshi Donglu.

If you're staying on Shāmiàn Dǎo or the riverfront, a nearby hospital is the Sun Yat-sen Memorial Hospital (Sūn Yìxiān Jìniàn Yīyuàn; ☎ 8188 2012) at 107 Yanjiang Xilu, opposite the Àiqún Dàjiǔdiàn (see Places to Stay later). Not much English is spoken here, but the medical facilities are pretty good and the prices low.

Next to Shāmiàn Dǎo and the Qīngpíng Shìchǎng (Bright Peace Market) is the Guangzhou Hospital of Traditional Chinese Medicine (Zhōngyī Yīyuàn; ☎ 8188 6504) at 16 Zhuji Lu. If you want to try acupuncture and herbs, this is the place to go. Many foreigners come here to study Chinese medicine.

Shāmiàn Dǎo 沙面岛
Sand Surface Island

This island is a blessed retreat from the bustle of Guǎngzhōu's streets. Everything is conducted in low gear – pedestrians saunter rather than walk, cars sidle rather than drive, birds sing and lazy tennis matches stretch out into the late afternoon. With its serenity and crumbling history, it's an ideal place to wander around and inhabit the past.

Shāmiàn means 'sand surface', which is all this island was until foreign traders were permitted to set up their warehouses here in the middle of the 18th century. Land reclamation has increased its area to its present size: 900m from east to west, and 300m from north to south. The island became a British and French concession after these nations defeated the Chinese in the Opium Wars, and is covered with decaying colonial buildings that housed trading offices and residences.

The French Catholic church **Our Lady of Lourdes Chapel** (Tiānzhǔjiào Loùshèngmǔ Táng) has been restored and stands on the main boulevard. The boulevard itself is a gentle stretch of gardens, trees and birdsong. Just to the west of White Swan Hotel is the Church of Christ, which is an active church, and is managed by the Guangdong Christian Council. Today most of the buildings are used as offices or apartment blocks – some with their front doors flung open to reveal old wooden staircases climbing into cavernous interiors.

SHĀMIÀN DǍO 沙面岛

Slowly but surely the island is being gentrified as new sidewalk cafes, bars and the occasional boutique open to cater to tourists and residents.

Liùróngsì Huātǎ 六榕寺花塔
Temple of the Six Banyan Trees

The six banyan trees of the temple's name are no longer standing, but the temple remains a popular attraction for its octagonal **Huā Tǎ** (Flower Pagoda). The banyan trees were celebrated in a poem by Su Dongpo, a renowned poet who visited the temple in AD 1100.

At 55m, the pagoda is the tallest in the city – from the outside it appears to have only nine storeys, but inside it has 17. The pagoda was constructed in AD 1097. It's worth climbing, although if you are tall you might end up with a collection of bruises as the doorways on the way up are very low. The admission cost is Y5.

The temple, which may date as far back as AD 537, was originally associated with Hui Neng, the sixth patriarch of the Zen Buddhist sect. Today it serves as the headquarters of the Guangzhou Buddhist Association. It is an active temple – be sensitive

about taking photographs of monks and worshippers. Inside the Guanyin Temple is a huge golden effigy of Guanyin (the goddess of compassion), to whom women burn incense and pray.

Liurong Lu, outside the temple, has a colourful array of souvenir shops selling ceramics, jade and religious ornaments. There is also a bustling fruit and meat market on Ruinan Lu, on the right just before you reach the temple itself.

Guǎngxiào Sì 光孝寺
Bright Filial Piety Temple

Guǎngxiào Sì is one of the oldest temples in Guǎngzhōu. The earliest Buddhist temple on this site possibly dates to the 4th century AD and may have even existed before the city of Guǎngzhōu was established. The temple has particular significance for Buddhists because Hui Neng of the Zen Buddhist sect was a novice monk here during the 7th century.

The temple buildings are much more recent, the original buildings having been destroyed by fire in the mid-17th century. The main temple is an impressive construction equipped with golden figures.

SHĀMIÀN DĂO

PLACES TO STAY

4 Shènglì Bīnguǎn
(New Annexe)
胜利宾馆（新楼）

6 Shènglì Bīnguǎn
胜利宾馆

10 Guangzhou Youth Hostel
省外办招待所

11 Shāmiàn Bīnguǎn
沙面宾馆

12 Qiáobaō Huódòng
Zhōngxīn
侨胞活动中心

16 White Swan Hotel
白天鹅宾馆

PLACES TO EAT

8 Lìqúnyǐnshídiàn
利群饮食店

14 Jade Garden
卒洲花园餐厅酒吧

15 Lucy's
露丝酒吧餐厅

OTHER

1 Hospital of Traditional
Chinese Medicine
中医医院

2 Qīngpíng Shìchǎng
清平市场

3 Our Lady of
Lourdes Chapel
天主教露圣母堂

5 Post Office
邮局

7 German
Consulate
德国领事馆

9 Polish Consulate
波兰领事馆

13 Bank of China
中国银行

17 US Consulate
美国领事馆

Wǔxiān Guàn 五仙观
Five Genies Temple

This Taoist temple is held to be the site of the appearance of the five rams and celestial beings in the myth of Guǎngzhōu's foundation (see the entry on Yuèxiù Gōngyuán later in this chapter for the story).

The large hollow in the rock in the temple courtyard is said to be the impression of a celestial being's foot; the Chinese refer to it as Rice-Ear Rock of Unique Beauty. The 5-tonne bell was cast during the Ming dynasty – it's 3m high, 2m in diameter and about 10cm thick, and is probably the largest in Guǎngdōng. It's known as the 'calamity bell', since the sound of the bell, which has no clapper, is a portent of calamity for the city.

At the rear of the main tower stand life-size statues with archaic Greek smiles; these appear to represent four of the five genies. In the temple forecourt are four statues of rams, and embedded in the temple walls are inscribed steles.

The temple is just south of Huáishèngsì Guāngtǎ at the end of an alley off Huifu Xilu. It's open daily from 9 am to noon and from 1.30 to 5 pm; entry is Y1.

Qīngpíng Shìchǎng 清平市场
Bright Peace Market

This market came into existence in 1979. Although such private (capitalist) markets are a feature of all Chinese cities today, it was one of Deng Xiaoping's more radical economic experiments at that time.

The market is like a takeaway zoo. Near the entrance you'll find the usual selection of medicinal herbs and spices, dried starfish, snakes, lizards, deer antlers, dried scorpions, leopard and tiger skins, bear paws, semi-toxic mushrooms, tree bark, and unidentifiable herbs and plants. Further up you'll find the live ones waiting to be butchered. Sad-eyed monkeys rattle at the bars of their wooden cages, tortoises crawl over each other in shallow tin trays, owls sit perched on boxes full of pigeons, and fish paddle around in tubs aerated with jets of water. There are also bundles of frogs, giant salamanders, pangolins (anteaters), dogs and raccoons, alive or contorted by recent violent death – which may just swear you off meat. This market will definitely upset the more sensitive traveller.

The market is north of Shāmiàn Dǎo, on the north side of Liu'ersan Lu and spills out into Tiyun Lu, which cuts east-west across Qingping Lu.

Sacred Heart Church 石室教堂

The impressive twin-spired Sacred Heart Church (Shí Shì Jiàotáng) is built entirely of granite. Started in 1863 and completed in 1888 (during the reign of Guangxu), it was designed by the French architect Guillemin. The church is an imitation of a European Gothic cathedral and its spires tower to a height of 58m. Four bronze bells suspended in the building to the east of the church were cast in France; the original coloured glass was also made in France, but almost all of it is gone. It's on the northern side of Yide Xilu, west of Haizhu Circle.

The **Zion Christian Church** (Xīān Táng), at 392 Renmin Zhonglu, is another church that may be of interest. The building is a hybrid, with a traditional European Gothic outline and Chinese eaves. It's an active place of worship.

Huáishèngsì Guāngtǎ 怀圣寺光塔
Remember the Prophet Mosque
The original mosque on this site is said to have been established in AD 627 by the first Muslim missionary to China. By all accounts the original mosque was the first Islamic building in China, which illustrates the level of early communication between the two cultures.

The present buildings were built in the Qing dynasty (1644–1911) as the original mosque was destroyed in a fire in 1343. The mosque was named in memory of the Prophet. Inside the grounds of the mosque is a minaret, which because of its even appearance is known as the Guang Tǎ (Smooth Tower). It's on Guangta Lu, which runs eastwards off Renmin Zhonglu.

Hǎizhuàng Gōngyuán
This park, south of the river, would be unremarkable but for the remains of what was once Guǎngzhōu's largest monastery, the **Hǎizhuàng Sì**. It was founded by a Buddhist monk in 1662, and in its heyday the monastery grounds covered 2.5 hectares. After 1911 the monastery was used as a school and soldiers' barracks. It was opened to the public as a park in the 1930s.

Religious services stopped at the temple during the Cultural Revolution, but have resumed today. The temple is home to three huge golden buddhas and in the rear courtyard incense burning and prayers are conducted by lay visitors. An adjacent building houses thousands of miniature shrines, each with a photograph of the deceased.

The temple, the gate to the park and other fixtures are being slowly restored, and the area gradually prettified. During the day the grounds are full of old men chatting, playing cards and chequers, and airing their pet birds.

Bus No 10 from Haizhu Circle goes to the park.

Yuèxiù Gōngyuán 越秀公园
This is the biggest park in Guǎngzhōu, covering 93 hectares, and includes the Zhènhai Lóu, the Wǔyáng Shíxiàng, a few artificial lakes and a huge swimming pool.

The **Wǔyáng Shíxiang** (Sculpture of the Five Rams), erected in 1959, is the symbol of Guǎngzhōu. It's said that long ago five celestial beings wearing robes of five colours came to Guǎngzhōu riding through the air on rams. Each carried a stem of rice, which they presented to the people as an auspicious sign from heaven that the area would be free from famine forever. Guǎngzhōu means Broad Region, but from this myth it takes its other name, City of Rams, or just Goat City.

The **Zhènhai Lóu** (Zhenhai Tower), also known as the Five-Storey Pagoda, is the only part of the old city wall that remains. From the upper storeys it commands a view of the city to the south and the Báiyún Shān (White Cloud Hills) to the north. The present tower was built during the Ming dynasty upon the highest portion of the northern city wall.

Because of its strategic location it was occupied by the British and French troops at the time of the Opium Wars. The 12 cannons in front of the tower date from this time. The tower now houses the City Museum, with exhibits that describe the history of Guǎngzhōu from Neolithic times until the early part of the 20th century.

Bus Nos 5, 24 and 101 all go to the park.

Wénhuà Gōngyuán 文化公园
Cultural Park
Just north-east of Shāmiàn Dǎo, this park was opened in 1956. There's a whole medley of attractions, including dodgem cars, a miniature funfair, a big wheel, a weights room, dolphin acts at Ocean World, a theatre and even a flight simulator. Entrance to the park is Y15 and about Y5 per ride.

Nányuèwáng Hànmù 南越王汉墓
Southern Yue Tomb Museum

This is also known as the Museum of the Western Han Dynasty of the Southern Yue King's Tomb. It stands on the site of the tomb of Emperor Wen, the second ruler of the Southern Yue kingdom dating back to 100 BC. The Southern Yue kingdom is what the area around Guǎngzhōu was called during the Han dynasty (AD 206–220).

The tomb was originally 20m under Xiànggǎng Shān (Elephant Hill) and was discovered in 1983; inside were 15 funerary bodies and more than 1000 sacrificial objects made of jade. It's an excellent museum, with a great layout and interesting English explanations. More than 500 rare artefacts are on display.

The museum is open daily from 9.30 am to 5.30 pm. Tickets are Y12. It's near the China Hotel and can be reached by taking bus No 5, 24 or 101.

Zhūjiāng Yóulǎnchuán 珠江游览船
Pearl River Cruises

The northern bank of the Zhū Jiāng is one of the most interesting areas of Guǎngzhōu – filled with people, markets and dilapidated buildings. By contrast, the southern side takes its inspiration from Victoria Harbour in Hong Kong – a growing forest of huge neon advertisements.

A tourist boat ride (☎ 8333 0397) down the Zhū Jiāng has two daily runs at 8 am and 1.30 pm. Boats leave from the Xīdī pier just east of Rénmín Qiáo (People's Bridge) and head down the river as far as Èrshā Dǎo (Ersha Island) and then turn around and head back to Rénmín Qiáo. Night cruises depart at 7.30 pm. The trips take about three hours and cost Y38.

For more upmarket evening cruises with dinner, check at the White Swan Hotel.

Other Sights

At 42 Zhongshan Silu the Nóngmín Yùndòng Jiǎngxísuǒ (Peasant Movement Institute) is a former training ground for communist aspirants to copy the good examples set by peasants; the institute is now a revolutionary museum.

Further up Zhongshan Sanlu, the Lièshì Língyuán (Memorial Garden to the Martyrs) commemorates the unsuccessful communist uprising of 11 December 1927; the garden is laid out on Hónghuāgǎng (Red Flower Hill), on Zhongshan Sanlu. North of Huanshi Donglu, Húanghūagǎng Gōngyuán (Yellow Flower Park) is the site of the Qīshíèr Lièshì Mù (Mausoleum of the 72 Martyrs)

The Chénjiā Cí (Chen Clan Academy) is a family shrine housed in a large compound built between 1890 and 1894. The compound encloses 19 traditional-style buildings along with numerous courtyards, stone carvings and sculptures. Bus Nos 102 and 104 pass by and it's within walking distance of the Chénjiācí station.

Liúhuāhú Gōngyuán (Liuhua Lake Park) is an enormous park containing the largest artificial lake in Guǎngzhōu. Ornithologists may be interested in one of the islands, which is home to thousands of birds.

It was built in 1958, a product of the ill-fated Great Leap Forward. The entrance to the park is on Renmin Beilu and can be reached on bus Nos 103 and 107.

Also built in 1958, Guǎngzhōu Dòngwùyuán is one of the largest and best zoos in China, although that's not saying much. It's on Xianlie Zhonglu in the north-east of the city; take bus No 6.

Special Events

The invitation-only, 20-day Guangzhou Trade Fair or Chinese Export Fair (Zhōngguó Chūkǒu Shāngpǐn Jiāoyì Huì) is held twice yearly, usually in April and October. Apart from the Chinese New Year, this is the biggest event in Guǎngzhōu. This fair is important to travellers because accommodation becomes a real problem while it's on and many hotels double room prices.

The city is unbearably crowded at the best of times, but during the Chinese New Year, usually in February, Guǎngzhōu is even more packed out.

Places to Stay – Budget

Guǎngzhōu is not a great place for budget hotels, but prices have dropped from the

To Beijing
(2478km)

To Baiyun
Airport
(5km)

Under
Construction

Xiwan Lu

Sanyuanli

Guangyuan Lu

Zengbu He

5

1
2
3
4
6
7
8
9
10

Lan Pu
(Orchid Garden)

TV Tower

Zhangqian Lu

六花路

Renmin Beilu

Huanshi Xilu

Xicun

Liuhua Lu

11
12
13
14
15
16
17
18
19

Yuexiu
Gongyuan

Liuhuahu
Gongyuan

Liuhua
Hu

解放北路

20

Dongfeng Xilu

41

Dongfeng Zhonglu

Jiefang Beilu

40
42

Yuehua Lu

39

Renmin
Gongyuan

Ertong
Gongyuan

To
Foshan
(28km)

Zhongshan Balu

49

Zhongshan Qilu

48

Renmin Beilu

中山六路

Zhongshan Liulu

S3

47
S4
43
44
45
46

5
38
37

Huifu Xilu

Wenchang Beilu

Longjin Xilu

Dahe Lu

Renmin Zhonglu

Jiefang Zhonglu

北京路

Wende Lu

Liwan
Gongyuan

50

Baoyuan Lu

Xiguan

Huifu Xilu

Beijing Lu

Changshou Lu

M

S2

Wenchang Nanlu

Duobao Lu

Haizhu Nanlu

Dade Lu

Enning Lu

Bauhua Lu

Daxin Lu

54

Haizhu
Circle

55

Datong Lu

Dishipu Lu

51
52
53

Xia Jiu-Shang JiuLu

Renmin Nanlu

Yide Xilu

57

Tianzi Pier

Haizhu
Qiao

Huangsha Dadao

Changdi Da Malu

58
59
60
61
62
63
64
65
66

Yanjiang Xilu

沿江西路

Jiangnan Dadao

Wenhua
Gongyuan

S1
M

Shamian
Dao

Xidi Pier

Binjiang Xilu

Tongfu Donglu

Under
Construction

See Shamian Dao Map Page 666

Renmin
Qiao

67

Zhu Jiang

Fangcun

Haizhuana
Gongyuan

Zhoutouzui
Wharf

To Bayun Shan

To Bayun Shan

Huancheng Expressway

0   400   800 m

Xiatang Xilu

Luhu
Gongyuan

Luhu Lu

Hengfu Lu

Taojin Lu

To
Shenzhen
(161km)

Guangzhou Dadao

Xianlie Zhonglu

Guangzhou
Dongwuyuan

21
22

32

23
24 25
27 28
29
26
30 31

Ouzhuang

Shuiyin Lu

To
Guangzhou
East Train
Station

Yuexiu Beilu

Tianshe Lu Malu

33 34

Nongjin Xilu

Huanshi Donglu 环市东路

35

To
Shenzhen
(166km)

东风中路

Dongfeng Donglu

Lieshi
Lingyuan

36
S6

Zhongshan
Lu

S7

Dongfeng Donglu

Zhongshan Lu

S8

S9

Guangzhou Dadao

Wenming Lu

Donghua Xilu

Dongshan

Wanfu Lu

Baiyun Lu

56

Dashatou

Dongshanhu
Gongyuan

To Lianhua Shan

Dashatou
Wharf

New
Pier

Haiyin Bridge

Dongxiao Lu

Ersha Dao

Qianjin Lu

Zhu Jiang

GUĂNGZHŌU

PLACES TO STAY
4 Liúhuā Bīnguăn
   流花宾馆
6 Guăngdōng Lǚyóu
   Dàshà
   广东旅游大厦
9 Yǒuyì Bīnguăn;
   Yìshù Bīnguăn
   友谊宾馆;
   艺术宾馆
14 Dōngfāng
   Bīnguăn
   东方宾馆
15 China Hotel;
   Hard Rock Cafe
   中国大酒店;
   硬石俱乐部
22 GITIC Plaza
   Hotel
   广东国际大酒店
24 Báiyún Bīnguăn
   白云宾馆
29 Garden Hotel
   花园酒店
30 Guótài Bīnguăn
   国泰宾馆
31 Holiday Inn
   文化假日酒店
55 Hotel Landmark
   Canton
   华厦大酒店
57 Furama Hotel
   富丽华大酒店

59 Aìqún Dàjiǔdiàn
   爱群大酒店
62 Xīnhuá Dàjiǔdiàn
   新华大酒店
63 Xīnyà Jiǔdiàn
   新亚酒店
64 Báigōng Jiǔdiàn
   白宫酒店

PLACES TO EAT
21 Banana Leaf
   Restaurant
   蕉叶风味屋
23 Elephant and
   Castle Pub
   大象堡酒吧
26 Kathleen's;
   360° Bar
   嘉芙莲
27 Cave Bar
   墨西哥餐厅酒吧
33 L'Africain
35 Cafe Elles
   本字吧
43 Tsai Ken Hsiang
   Restaurant
   菜根香素菜馆
47 Wǔyáng Huímín
   Fàndiàn
   五羊回民饭店
50 Pànxī Jiǔjiā
   泮溪酒家

51 Fóyǒuyuán
   Sùshíguăn
   佛有缘素食馆
52 Guăngzhōu Jiǔjiā
   广州酒家
53 Táotáojū
   陶陶居
60 Dàtóng Jiǔjiā
   大同酒家

OTHER
1 Long-Distance
   Bus Station
   广东省汽车客运站
2 Main Liúhuá
   Post Office
   邮政总局
   (流花邮局)
3 Liúhuá Bus Station
   流花车站
5 Main Train Station
   广州火车站
7 CITS;
   CAAC
   中国国际旅行社;
   中国民航
8 China Telecom
   国际电话大楼
10 Zion Christian Church
   锡安堂
11 China Foreign Trade
   Guangzhou Travel Service
   广交会票务中心

dizzy heights of former years. Although a bit risky, if you're getting off the train it might be worth checking out what's offered from the galaxy of touts. They will come rushing at you as you exit the station, waving photo books or simple placards advertising inexpensive rooms. Some of these places are Chinese-only, but some don't seem to care who they take.

A convenient new place has opened up beside the main train station. *Guăngdōng Lǚyóu Dàshà (Guangdong Tourist Hotel;* ☎ *8666 6889 ext 3812, fax 8667 9787, 179 Huanshi Xilu)* has clean singles/doubles with air-con and shared bath for Y108/168. Singles/doubles with bath are Y148/238. The main appeal of this place, however, is

it claims to offer a 40% discount for International Youth Hostel members, surely a first in mainland China!

Shāmiàn Dǎo, however, is a quieter and more attractive area to be; you are much more likely to meet other travellers and the bars are better.

On Shāmiàn Dǎo, near the massive White Swan Hotel, is the *Guangzhou Youth Hostel (Shěngwàibàn Zhāodàisuǒ;* ☎ *8188 4298, fax 8188 4979, 2 Shamian Sijie)*. By default, this place wins the title of 'backpackers headquarters' in Guăngzhōu since there is little else in this price range that is open to foreigners. Many travellers have complained about the service here, but it appears to have improved. The cheapest dorm

12 Jǐnhàn Bus Station
锦汉车站

13 Guangzhou Gymnasium
广州体育场

16 Nányuèwáng Hànmù
南越王汉墓

17 PSB
公安局外事科

18 Wǔyáng Shíxiàng
五羊石像

19 Zhènhǎi Lóu
镇海楼

20 Sun Yatsen Monument
孙中山纪念碑

25 Nanfang International
Plaza
南方国际商厦

28 Peace World Plaza;
Pioneer International Clinic
好世界广场

32 Húanghuāgǎng Gōngyuán;
Qīshíèr Lièshì Mù
黄花岗七十二烈士墓

34 Meet Internet Coffee
House
网吧音乐咖啡室

36 Nóngmín Yùndòng
Jiǎngxísuǒ
农民运动讲习所

37 Foreign Languages
Bookstore
外文书店

38 Guangzhou Department
Store
广州百货大楼

39 Buses to Báiyún Shān
开往白云山的汽车站

40 Liùróngsì Huātǎ
六榕寺花塔

41 Guangzhou No 1 People's
Hospital
第一人民医院

42 Guāngxiào Sì
光孝寺

44 Huáishèngsì Guāngtǎ
怀圣寺光塔

45 Wǔxiān Guàn
五仙观

46 Bank of China
中国银行

48 Chénjiā Cí
陈家祠

49 Guǎngfó Bus Station
(for Fóshān)
广佛汽车站

54 Sacred Heart Church
石室教堂

56 Train Ticket Booking Office
火车售票处

58 Bank of China
中国银行

61 Sun Yatsen Memorial
Hospital
孙逸仙纪念医院

65 Nanfang
Department Store
南方百货

66 Topshow Disco
演舞台

67 Guangzhou Red Cross
Hospital
市红十字会医院

METRO STATIONS

S1 Huángshā Dìtiězhàn
黄沙地铁站

S2 Chángshòu Dìtiězhàn
长寿地铁站

S3 Chénjiāci Dìtiězhàn
陈家祠地铁站

S4 Xīmén Kǒu Dìtiězhàn
西门口地铁站

S5 Gōngyuán Qián
Dìtiězhàn
公园前地铁站

S6 Nongjiang Suo
Dìtiězhàn
农讲所地铁站

S7 Lièshì Língyuán
Dìtiězhàn
烈士陵园地铁站

S8 Dōngshān Kǒu
Dìtiězhàn
东山口地铁站

S9 Yángjī Dìtiězhàn
杨箕地铁站

beds are Y50 and singles/doubles/triples with air-con and shared bath are Y100/170/210. Doubles/triples with bath are Y190/240.

Also on Shāmiàn Dǎo, the small but friendly **Qiābǎo Huódōng Zhōngxīn** (*Overseas Chinese Activity Centre;* ☎ *8188 5913, fax 8186 8690, 31-33 Shamian Dajie*) has claustrophobic doubles/triples with bath and air-con for Y190/250.

Places to Stay – Mid-Range
The vast number of Guǎngzhōu hotels open to foreigners belong to the mid- and top-end price ranges, but room surpluses have forced many places to offer discounts of 20% to 30%.

Train Station Area *Yǒuyì Bīnguǎn* (*Friendship Hotel;* ☎ *8667 9898, fax 8667 8653, 698 Renmin Beilu*) is a reliable mid-range hotel with doubles for Y380. One of the best mid-range deals in this neighbourhood, however, is the newly renovated *Yìshù Bīnguǎn* (*Art Hotel;* ☎ *8667 9898 ext 2101*) located directly behind Yǒuyì Bīnguǎn. Standard doubles start at Y238 and it was offering a 50% discount (*zhékòu*) at the time of writing.

Liúhuā Bīnguǎn (☎ *8666 8800, fax 8666 7828, 194 Huanshi Xilu*) is a large building opposite the train station. Service is a bit complacent because of its prime location, and rooms are a little overpriced at Y380. Nevertheless, the lobby is a great place to recuperate after stumbling off a 36-hour train ride.

Zhū Jiāng (Pearl River) Area *Shāmiàn Bīnguǎn* (☎ 8191 8359, fax 8191 1628, 50 Shamian Nanjie) has doubles that start at Y275. This is an attractive, charming and popular hotel just up from Shāmiàn Gōngyuán.

Also on Shāmiàn Dǎo are two branches of *Shènglì Bīnguǎn* (*Guangdong Victory Hotel;* ☎ 8186 2622, fax 8186 2413). Both are fairly upmarket, though the branch at 54 Shamian Beijie is the cheaper of the two and has rooms from HK$360 upwards. The branch at 53 Shamian Beijie (despite the consecutive number both hotels are on the same side of the road, around five minutes' walk from each other) has standard doubles/triples for HK$530/600 (they also accept RMB), but ask for discounts.

The *Aìqún Dàjiǔdiàn* (☎ 8186 6668, fax 8188 3519, 113 Yanjiang Xilu) is a grand old hotel from the thirties that overlooks the Zhū Jiāng. Singles are a good deal at Y250 and doubles start at Y320, with the more expensive deluxe options with a view of the river.

Three smaller hotels clustered on Renmin Nanlu cater to Hong Kong visitors and are good value, but the street and overpass above make things very noisy. *Báigōng Jiǔdiàn* (☎ 8188 2313, fax 8188 9161, 13-17 Renmin Nanlu) is a pleasant and friendly place, with singles/doubles starting at Y218/238. Opposite the Báigōng, *Xīnyà Jiǔdiàn* (*New Asia Hotel;* ☎ 8188 4722) has singles from Y210 to 240 and doubles from Y250 to 300. South of the Xīnyà Jiǔdiàn, *Xīnhuá Dàjiǔdiàn* (☎ 8188 9788, fax 8188 8809) is the best of the bunch, since it has been newly renovated. Singles/doubles are reasonably priced at Y198/288, and triples are Y398. There are also Chinese-style suites with outside terraces for Y880.

Although normally considered a top-end hotel, *Furama Hotel* (*Fùlìhuá Dàjiǔdiàn;* ☎ 8186 3288, fax 8186 3388, 316 Changdi Lu) has standard doubles for Y350, as well as more expensive rooms.

Places to Stay – Top End
Train Station Area *China Hotel* (*Zhōngguó Dàjiǔdiàn;* ☎ 8666 6888, fax 8667 7014) has long been a favourite with international business travellers and is also a hub for buses heading to Hong Kong and Macau. Doubles start at US$148 (plus a 20% service and tax charge). Next door *Dōngfāng Bīnguǎn* (☎ 8666 2946, fax 8666 2775) is a little more glitzy than it was in the days when it used to offer Y6 dormitory beds. The cheapest rooms these days are US$90, but it was offering up to 60% discounts at the time of writing.

Zhū Jiāng Area The best hotel in this area is the *White Swan Hotel* (*Báitiān'é Bīnguǎn;* ☎ 8188 6968, fax 8186 2288, 1 Shamian Nanjie), which has an excellent range of facilities, including 11 restaurants and bars, Rolls-Royce rental and a complete shopping arcade. There's a range of rooms with standard/deluxe doubles at US$140/160 and executive suites at US$230 (plus a 20% service and tax charge).

Hotel Landmark Canton (*Huáshà Dàjiǔdiàn;* ☎ 8335 5988, fax 8333 6197), conveniently located by Haizhu Circle, is very comfortable and has a wide range of facilities. Standard rooms start at Y650, plus 20% service and tax charge. Inquire about discounts.

North-Eastern Area The north-eastern part of the city has the highest concentration of top-end hotels and is probably the best area for business travellers to be based. For the tourist it's a bit bland. The five-star *GITIC Plaza Hotel* (*Guǎngdōng Guójì Dàjiǔdiàn;* ☎ 8331 1888, fax 8331 1666, 339 Huanshi Donglu) has all the trappings of an international hotel, including top-notch business services, but lacks character. Standard rooms start at Y1400 plus a 20% service and tax charge. Further east along Huanshi Donglu, *Garden Hotel* (*Huāyuán Jiǔdiàn;* ☎ 8333 8989, fax 8335 0467), is more elegant and spacious. Standard rooms start at Y1160.

On the opposite side of the street, *Báiyún Bīnguǎn* (☎ 8333 3998, fax 8334 3032) is a little easier on the wallet, with a wide range of rooms. Singles can go as low as Y398, while the standard double starts at Y508. Similarly, the smaller *Guótài Bīnguǎn (Cathay Hotel;* ☎ *8386 2888, fax 8384 2606, 376 Huanshi Donglu)* is a pleasant place with standard doubles for Y500. Because these two hotels are locally owned, the service and tax charge is only 15%.

Finally, a little further east along Huanshi Donglu, *Holiday Inn (Wénhuà Jiàrì Jiǔdiàn;* ☎ *8776 6999, fax 8775 3126)* has rooms starting at US$130 (plus 20% service and tax charge).

Places to Eat

The Chinese have a saying that to enjoy the best in life, one should 'be born in Sūzhōu, live in Hángzhōu, eat in Guǎngzhōu and die in Liǔzhōu'. Sūzhōu is renowned for beautiful women, Hángzhōu for scenery and Liǔzhōu for its coffins. Liǔzhōu can be given a miss, but Guǎngzhōu is certainly one of the best places in China to eat.

The city is famous for its old, established restaurants. However, travellers on a budget will be better off tracking down the many inexpensive eats that line the streets and back alleys.

Chinese Most budget travellers still head for the old favourite, the *Lìqúnyǐnshídiàn* on Shāmiàn Dǎo. It's built around a tree that emerges through the roof and the food is cheap and tasty. Try the *làchǎo dòugān* (spicy fried dried bean curd) and the *tángcù jīkuài* (sweet and sour chicken).

Dàtóng Jiǔjiā (☎ *8188 8988, 63 Yanjiang Xilu)* is by the river and a local favourite for dim sum. The restaurant is an eight-storey building and can seat 1600 customers so don't worry about space. Specialities are *dàtóng cuìpíjī* (crisp-fried chicken) and *kǎo rǔzhū* (roast suckling pig).

Probably the most famous eatery in the city is *Guǎngzhōu Jiǔjiā (*☎ *8188 8388, 2 Wenchang Nanlu)*. Specialities include shark fin soup with shredded chicken, chopped crabmeat balls and braised dove. This is an expensive restaurant and reservations are sometimes necessary.

For excellent Muslim-Chinese cuisine, check out *Wǔyáng Huímín Fàndiàn (Five Rams Muslim Restaurant; 325 Zhongshan Liulu)*. It's not as big as it used to be but the food is still good. Try the *shuàn yángròu* (boiled mutton slices) and the *cuìpí huóé* (crispy goose).

In the west of Guǎngzhōu, *Pànxī Jiǔjiā (*☎ *8181 5718, 151 Longjin Xilu)* is noted for its dumplings, stewed turtle, roast pork, chicken in tea leaves and a crabmeat-shark-fin consomme. Its famed dim sum is served daily from about 5 to 9.30 am, at noon and again at night.

A very popular restaurant is *Táotáojū (*☎ *8181 5769, 20 Dishipu Lu)*. Originally built as a private academy in the 17th century, it was turned into a restaurant in the late 19th century. Dim sum is the speciality here; you choose sweet and savoury snacks from the trolleys that are wheeled around the restaurant. Other specialities include the trademark *táotáo jiāngcōng jī* (Taotao ginger and onion chicken). Taotaoju mooncakes are very popular at the time of the mid-autumn Moon Festival.

Vegetarian *Tsai Ken Hsiang Restaurant (Càigēnxiāng Sùcáiguǎn;* ☎ *8334 4363, 167 Zhongshan Liulu)* is one of the few places in Guǎngzhōu where you don't have to worry about accidentally ordering dog, cat or monkey brains.

Closer to Shāmiàn Dǎo, another vegetarian option is the *Fóyǒuyuán Sùshíguǎn (*☎ *8188 7157, 74 Shangjiu Lu)*.

Pub Grub Guǎngzhōu has a quickly shifting number of international-style bars where you can scoff pizza or burgers, sink a chilled imported beer and put a few yuán into the jukebox. The trouble is keeping up with them – they come and go with annoying regularity.

For American-style food and draught beer for Y18 a pint, a good place to go on Shāmiàn Dǎo is *Lucy's (*☎ *8187 4106, 5Shamian Nanjie)*. The food is excellent. Nearby, located inside Cùizhōu Gōngyuàn, the *Jade Garden (*☎ *8410 1821, 7 Shamian Nanjie)* is another international-style restaurant bar with outdoor seating.

The *Hard Rock Cafe (Yìngshí Jùlèbù;* ☎ 8666 6888)* can be found in the basement of the China Hotel, dishing up the usual buffalo wings, steak and chips fare, albeit with hefty price tags for the experience.

Another place is *Kathleen's (Jiāfúlián;* ☎ 8359 8045, 60 Taojin Lu)* on the north side of Huanshi Donglu. More of the light music variety, this cafe bar serves up international food and is a good place for a quiet dinner. Next door, the *360° Bar* is a good place to head for some serious beer drinking. Tucked in behind Taojin Lu, these places can be difficult to find. Keep your eye out for the Guangzhou Commercial Bank sign and turn right at the first lane off Taojin Lu.

The *Cave Bar (Mòxīgē Cāntīngjǐubā;* ☎ 8386 3660, 360 Huangshi Donglu)*, which serves Tex-Mex food as well as drinks, and the *Elephant and Castle Pub (Dàxiàngbǎo Jǐubā;* ☎ 8359 3309, 363 Huanshi Donglu)*, across the street, are bars that are popular with foreigners.

If you're looking for more of a European atmosphere try *Cafe Elles (Mùzǐ Bā;* ☎ 8761 9909)* on the 2nd floor of the Huaxin Building at the corner of Shuiyin Lu and Huanshi Lu. The French owner even has an authentic crepe-making machine. Another popular place with foreigners is the *Banana Leaf Restaurant (Jiāoyè Fēngwèi Wū;* ☎ 8359 1288 ext 3118, 8 Luhu Lu)*, which is part of the same chain in Hong Kong and elsewhere. It serves up delicious South-East Asian curries and is a pleasant place to eat.

Guǎngzhōu's major international hotels are also stocked with some excellent restaurants and bars that often have good food.

Entertainment
The entertainment scene in Guǎngzhōu is moving fast, with a burgeoning rave and live music scene, but it is difficult to pin down venues. Check *Clueless in Guangzhou* for the latest spots. The large hotels offer a range of late-night drinking holes and nightclubs, but it's all pretty mundane stuff. Try any of the bars listed in the Pub Grub section of Places to Eat for darts, pool, jukebox music and imported beers.

If it's dancing you want, then try *L'Africain (Feīzōu Bā;* ☎ 8778 2433 ext 623)* near the corner of Dongfeng Donglu and Nonglin Xialu. It has dancing until 2 am on weekdays and until 4 am at weekends. It's a popular gay venue.

Hard Rock Cafe (☎ 8666 6888)*, in the basement of the China Hotel, has a disco from 10 pm to 2 am from Sunday to Thursday and from 10.30 pm to 3 am at weekends. The cover charge, (for men; women get in free) is Y60, but the beer is pricey. Sometimes it also has live music. Down by the river the *Topshow Disco (Yánwǔtái;* ☎ 8188 8489, 109 Yanjiang Xilu)* has no cover charge and is popular with locals.

Shopping
You can hardly walk anywhere in central Guǎngzhōu without stumbling over shop after shop, selling everything under the sun.

The intersection of Beijing Lu and Zhongshan Lu, north-east of Haizhu Circle, was traditionally the principal shopping area in the city and is still a good place to buy clothes and shoes if you can find the right size. Near Qīngpíng Shìchǎng, there are more clothing shops on Xiajiu Lu and Shangjiu Lu, which are closed off to vehicles on the weekends, but it can get incredibly crowded.

Not surprisingly, the large hotels have well-applied tourist shops, but bear in mind that their prices are astronomical compared to local shops, often 10 times the price on the streets, so it's worth spending some time looking around.

North of Qingping Lu there's an antique and jade market near the corner of Wenchang Lu and Changshou Lu. At the western end of Shāmiàn Dǎo, on Shamian Sijie, is a string of souvenir shops selling paintings, clothes and calligraphy. The road leading up to the Liùróngsì Huātǎ (Temple of the Six Banyan Trees) is also chock-a-block with souvenir shops bursting with ceramics and jade.

Getting There & Away
Air The Civil Aviation Administration of China (CAAC; Zhōngguó Mínháng; 24-hour hotline ☎ 8668 2000) has an office

represented by China Southern (probably China's most well-run airline) at 181 Huanshi Lu, to your left as you come out of the train station. The office is open from 8 am to 8 pm daily. You can also book air tickets at various locations around town.

China Southern has five daily flights to Hong Kong (Y590 one way; 35 minutes).

The airline also has direct flights between Guǎngzhōu and a number of foreign cities, including Amsterdam, Bangkok, Ho Chi Minh City, Jakarta, Kuala Lumpur, Los Angeles, Manila, Melbourne, Osaka, Penang, Singapore and Sydney. International airport tax is Y80.

Foreign airlines in Guǎngzhōu include:

Garuda Indonesia (☎ 8332 5484) Room 1009, Peace World Plaza, 352 Huanshi Donglu
Japan Airlines (8669 6688) Room A201, China Hotel, Liuhua Lu
Malaysia Airlines (☎ 8335 8828) Shop M04-05, Garden Hotel, 368 Huanshi Donglu
Singapore Airlines (☎ 8335 8868) Mezzanine floor, Garden Hotel, 368 Huanshi Donglu
Vietnam Airlines (☎ 8382 7187) Room 924, East Bldg, Garden Hotel, 368 Huanshi Donglu

You can fly virtually anywhere in China from Guǎngzhōu. Flights to Shànghǎi are Y1020 and Běijīng, Y1360. Domestic airport tax is Y50.

Bus Bus services in Guǎngzhōu are very well developed. A small sample of what's on offer is covered in this section.

The hassle-free way to get to Hong Kong is by the deluxe buses that ply the Guǎngzhōu-Shēnzhèn super-highway, which can get you there in just over three hours. Most of the major top-end hotels have services, and tickets range between HK$100 to HK$150. Frequent buses also depart from the Jǐnhàn bus station (Jǐnhàn zhàn) located across from the China Hotel on Liuhua Lu. Customs procedures are fairly routine, but you have to take all your luggage off the bus.

Direct buses to Macau via Zhūhǎi (Y50; three hours) leave from the China and Garden Hotels, as well as the Jǐnhàn bus station. At Zhūhǎi you have to walk across the border where shuttle buses will take you to the centre of town.

Deluxe buses to Shēnzhèn (Y55; two hours) leave frequently from the Jǐnhàn station and the main long-distance bus station (shěng qìchēzhàn), west of the train station on Huanshi Xilu. They leave every 30 minutes from 7 am to 9 pm. Economy buses (Y27) and minibuses (Y30) depart from the Liúhuā bus station (Liúhuā chēzhàn) that straddles the chaotic mess of vehicles across Huanshi Xilu in front of the train station.

Similarly, economy buses (Y35; 2½ hours) depart every half an hour for Zhūhǎi from the Liúhuā bus station, while deluxe buses (Y55; 2½ hours) leave from the long-distance and Jǐnhàn bus stations. They terminate in Gǒngběi District just on the border with Macau.

Buses to Zhàoqìng (Y30; 1¼ hours) leave from the long-distance bus station. Buses for Guìlín (Y100, sleeper; 13 hours), Nánníng (Y100; 15 hours), Hǎikǒu (Y140, air-con sleeper; 16 hours), Shàntóu (Y90; eight hours), Fóshān (every half hour, Y10; 45 minutes) and Zhōngshān (Y25; two hours) leave from the Liúhuā station. Deluxe buses also leave for Shàntóu (Y180; seven hours) from the Jǐnhàn station.

Train The Guǎngzhōu train station is a constant, seething mass of humanity, gaping road repairs and vehicular traffic that seems to defy all logic. In comparison, the Guǎngzhōu East train station, though still under construction at the time of writing, is a model of efficiency. Ticketing at East station is fairly straightforward, with separate booths for Kowloon (Hong Kong) and Shēnzhèn, on the border with Hong Kong. Signs are in English.

Trains to Kowloon and high-speed trains to Shēnzhèn that do the journey in 55 minutes depart from here. Travel to the Guǎngzhōu East train station has been vastly improved by the opening of the subway line. Bus No 272 also goes between the two stations, as does bus No 271, which departs from the Liúhuā bus station.

Booking train tickets departing from the main Guǎngzhōu station to other parts of China is a lot more painless than it used to be. Ticket touts swarm around the station area and zero in on foreigners, but it's not worth the risk of being ripped off. There are two separate ticket places at the station itself. Ticket issuing that is open 24 hours a day is in the hall to the left of the large clock as you face the station. It's open 24 hours a day and is usually more crowded. Current, next-day and two-day advance tickets are sold in the pink building just east of the station and is open daily from 5.30 am to 10.30 pm.

The CITS nearby will book train tickets up to five days in advance for a service charge of Y20. In town, other travel agencies will book train tickets (see the Information section earlier) for similar charges. You can also book train tickets at the train ticket issuing office at 185 Baiyun Lu, which is open daily from 8 am to noon and 1 to 5 pm. There's no English sign, but look for the China railway logo.

Trains head north from Guǎngzhōu to Běijīng (24 hours; arrival at Běijīng's West train station), Shànghǎi (27 hours) and every province in the country except Hǎinán Dǎo (Hainan Island) and Tibet.

The express train between Hong Kong and Guǎngzhōu is comfortable and convenient. It covers the 182km route in a shave under two hours; tickets cost Y209 for ordinary soft-seat class. You'll save more than half that by taking a hard seat to Shēnzhèn, crossing the border and taking the KCR to Hong Kong. Trains departing from Guǎngzhōu's East train station to Hong Kong follow:

train No	departs	arrives
3	8.55 am	10.53 am
1	1.53 pm	3.25 pm
7	3.55 pm	5.37 pm
9	5.25 pm	7.22 pm

The timetable for trains travelling from Hong Kong to Guǎngzhōu follows:

train No	departs	arrives
8	8.50 am	10.48 am
4	12.05 pm	2.03 pm
6	1.23 pm	3.05 pm
2	4.08 pm	5.40 pm

The local train from Shēnzhèn to Guǎngzhōu is cheap and reasonably fast (two hours). Tickets from the main station are Y42 for hard seat. Five daily high-speed trains do the trip in 55 minutes from the Guǎngzhōu East station and tickets are Y80. Trains to Zhàoqìng (Y26; two hours) leave from the main train station.

Boat Guǎngzhōu is the major port on China's southern coast. It offers high-speed catamaran services to various destinations, but overnight ferries have almost disappeared as road services improve. Former overnight services to Hong Kong and Macau have been discontinued and the boat to Hǎikǒu may soon follow suit. Coastal ferries to Shànghǎi and beyond are also the victim of improved land transportation.

The two main departure and ticketing locations are at Zhōutóuzuǐ wharf (Zhōutóuzuǐ kèyùnzhàn; ☎ 8444 8218), on the southern arm of the Zhū Jiāng, and Dàshātóu wharf (Dàshātóu kèyùnzhàn; ☎ 8383 3691) on the north shore, east of Beijing Lu.

Zhōutóuzuǐ is easily reached by taxi from the Zhū Jiāng area or take bus No 31 from Wénhuà Gōngyuàn and ask the driver to let you off at the road leading to the wharf. Bus No 7 goes from the main train station to Dàshātóu.

Hong Kong Jet-cats (jet-powered catamaran) make twice daily trips from the wharf at Píngzhōu, located about 20 minutes south-west of Guǎngzhōu. The trip takes 2½ hours and there are two classes of tickets for Y180 and Y220. You can buy tickets at Zhōutóuzuǐ wharf and a free shuttle bus departs for Píngzhōu. Tickets are also available at the White Swan Hotel and Hotel Landmark Canton, both of which also have shuttle buses.

A hovercraft service also makes the trip to Hong Kong in two hours (HK$190) from Húangpǔ, departing at 10.30 am and 4.30 pm. Tickets are sold at the Garden Hotel, where there is also a shuttle bus to the wharf.

Wúzhōu/Yángzhōu Ferry services between Guǎngzhōu and Wúzhōu have improved in recent years. It is possible to buy a combined bus/boat ticket, but there are plenty of buses available in Wúzhōu for Yángzhōu and Guìlín, and many of them are timed with the arrival of boats from Guăngzhōu.

The quickest way to get to Wúzhōu is the rapid ferry service, which takes around five hours and costs Y80. The boat departs from Dàshātóu Wharf at 12.30 pm and stops at Zhàoqìng along the way. Tickets are sold at the wharf.

The overnight boat was still running at the time of writing and takes 16 hours, departing at 5 pm. The ticket price includes a sleeper for Y50.

Zhàoqìng Wúzhōu-bound ferries (see the previous entry) stop at Zhàoqìng. The slow ferries take around eight hours to get there (Y28), while the rapid service (Y40) takes just two hours.

Hăikŏu Ferries for Hăikŏu leave from Zhōutóuzuĭ wharf every other day. The service was still operating at the time of writing, but it's probably a good idea to give the wharf a call before trooping out there to buy tickets. Tickets range from Y301, for 2nd class, to Y134, for 5th class. The trip takes 24 hours.

Getting Around
Guăngzhōu proper extends for 60 sq km, with most of the interesting sights scattered throughout, so seeing the place on foot is impractical. The subway line goes by many of the city's major sights along Zhōngshān Lu, and is also a convenient way to get to Shāmiàn Dăo. Otherwise the only alternative to riding wedged against someone's armpit on one of the public buses is to take a gridlocked taxi and inch through the streets.

Guăngzhōu's traffic conditions are in a state of mob rule. Be careful when crossing the road and use 360° vision as vehicles come from all directions.

To/From the Airport Guăngzhōu's Báiyún airport is 12km out of town near the Báiyún Shān (White Cloud Hills). There is

a regular airport bus that runs from the CAAC office near the train station to the airport (Y3), departing every 20 minutes.

Just outside the entrance to the airport is a taxi ramp. Taxis leaving from here are metered. Don't go with the taxi touts unless you want to be ripped off. When you get into a taxi, tell the driver *dă biăo* (turn on the meter). The cost should be between Y30 and Y40 depending on the size of the taxi and where you are headed in town.

Subway Guăngzhōu's new subway runs from the Guăngzhōu East train station down Tiyudong Lu, then heads west along Zhongshan Lu to the city's western district. The line then runs south along Baohua Lu to the northwest tip of Shāmiàn Dăo and under the Zhū Jiāng. At the time of writing, sixteen stations were in operation. Tickets are Y6 for nine or more stations, Y4 for trips between three to eight stations, and Y2 for two or less stations.

Bus Guăngzhōu has an extensive network of motor and electric trolley-buses, which will get you just about anywhere you want to go. Unfortunately the network is still overstretched, though the subway will ease things a bit.

It's worth getting a detailed map of the city (for the bus routes) from one of the hawkers outside the train station or at one of the hotels. Exiting the train station, you'll find a huge cluster of buses (and line-ups) on the right (with your back to the station). There are too many bus routes to list them all here, but a few of the important routes are:

No 31 Runs along Gongye Dadao Bei, east of Zhōutóuzuĭ wharf, crosses Rénmín Qiáo and goes straight up Renmin Lu to the main train station at the north of the city.

No 30 Runs from the main train station eastwards along Huanshi Lu before turning down Nonglin Xialu to terminate in the far east of the city. This is a convenient bus to take if you want to go from the train station to the Báiyún Bīnguăn and the Garden Hotel.

No 5 Starting from the main train station, this bus takes a similar route to No 31, but instead of crossing Rénmín Qiáo (People's Bridge) it turns west along Liu'ersan Lu, which runs past the northern side of Shāmiàn Dăo. Get off here and walk across the small bridge to the island. It terminates at the Huangsha terminal across from the north-west tip of Shāmiàn Dǎo.

Taxi Taxis are abundant on the streets of Guǎngzhōu, but demand is great, particularly during the peak hours: from 8 to 9 am and during lunch and dinner hours. When taking a taxi from the main train station avoid the touts; look for the row of Pepsi ads to find the taxi line-up amid the chaos that defines the Guǎngzhōu train station and tell the driver to turn on the meter (dǎ biǎo).

Taxis are equipped with meters and at the time of writing were starting at Y7. Rates may be even lower by the time you read this. Depending on the vehicle, a trip from the train station to Shāmiàn Dǎo should cost between Y15 and Y20.

Bicycle Shāmiàn Dǎo usually has a place where you can rent a bike. The shifting sands of the bike-rental world on Shamian move outlets around, so ask at your hotel for details. Usually rental is Y2 per hour or Y20 per day, plus a large deposit (Y400).

A look at the traffic in Guǎngzhōu might deter you from cycling here. Before hiring a bike, check the brakes to make sure it's not a death-trap.

AROUND GUĂNGZHŌU
Báiyún Shān 白云山
White Cloud Hills
These hills, in the north-eastern suburbs of Guǎngzhōu, are an offshoot of Dàyǔ Lǐng, the chief mountain range of Guǎngdōng. There are more than 30 peaks that were once dotted with temples and monasteries, although none of any historical significance remains. The brochure describes it as 'the first spectacular scene of Guǎngzhōu' (the lawless traffic conditions are a close second), and it's really not bad in fair weather. It's a good hike up to the top or leisurely walk down, as well as being a temporary respite from the polluted atmosphere below.

The highest peak in the Báiyún Shān is **Mōxīng Lǐng** (Star Touching Peak). On a clear day, you can see a panorama of the city – the Xīqiáo Shān to one side, the Běi

Jiāng (North River) and the Fayuan Hills on the other side, and the sweep of the Zhū Jiāng. Unfortunately, clear days are becoming a rarity in Guǎngzhōu.

Locals rate the evening view from Báiyún Wǎnwàng (the White Cloud Evening View; formerly known as Cheng Precipice) as one of the eight sights of Guǎngzhōu. The precipice was formerly the site of the oldest monastery in the area.

Famous as a resort since the Tang and Song dynasties, the area is being thematically restored to attract Hong Kong tourists and now sports water slides, a golf course, botanical gardens and a sculpture park, among other sights. One of the more interesting among these is the **Míngchūngǔ** (Mingchun Valley Aviary), which features a wide variety bird species. It's a pleasant place to walk around, though you might want to skip the talking parrot performance. Entry is Y15. The restored **Néngrén Sì** (Nengren Temple) is also worth visiting. The serenity here gives some idea of what the area might once have been like, if you can ignore the cable car overhead. The temple is a short walk down from the top. Entry is Y5.

Getting There & Away The Báiyún Shān are about 15km from Guǎngzhōu and make a good half-day excursion. Express buses leave every 20 minutes from the south side of Yuehua Lu at Jixiang Lu, a small street running north off Zhongshan Wulu beside Rénmín Gōngyuán. The trip takes between half and one hour, depending on traffic, and goes all the way up to the top. The bus stops at the park entrance for the Y5 admission fee.

Bus No 24 can take you from Dongfeng Zhonglu, just north of the Rénmín Gōngyuán, to the cable car at the bottom of the hill near the lake Lù Hú.

Liánhuā Shān 莲花山
Lotus Mountain
This mountain is an old Ming dynasty quarry site, 46km south-east of Guǎngzhōu. It's a possible day trip from Guǎngzhōu, though it may be of more interest to Guǎngzhōu residents than to travellers with a busy itinerary.

The stone-cutting at Liánhuā Shān ceased several hundred years ago and the cliffs have eroded to a state where it looks almost natural. On the mountain is an assortment of temples and pagodas, including the Liánhuā Tǎ (Old Lotus Tower) that was built in 1664. During the Opium Wars, Liánhuā Shān served as a major line of defence against the British forces.

Getting There & Away Boats to Liánhuā Shān depart from Xīdī pier (☎ 8333 0397) just south of the Nanfang department store on Yanjiang Xilu.

There's an individual service that leaves from Xīdī pier at 8 am and 1.30 pm for Y25, but probably the best option is to get the earlier, luxury one-day tour that leaves the same pier at 8 am and returns from Liánhuā Shān at 3.15 pm. Tickets are Y38 and can be bought at Xīdī pier. The trip takes about one hour.

Theoretically there should also be a bus to Liánhuā Shān, but good luck finding it! The major hotels in Guǎngzhōu also run tours to Liánhuā Shān, as does CTS in Hong Kong. Naturally it is cheaper to do it yourself.

Fóshān 佛山

☎ 0757 • pop 3,209,600

Fóshān, just 28km south-west of Guǎngzhōu, is remarkable mainly for its Ancestor Temple, which has emerged as a popular destination for local and overseas Chinese tourists.

Like all tourist attractions worth their salt in China, there is a legend connected with Fó Shān (Buddha Hill). In this case, the story involves three buddha statues that mysteriously disappeared only to be rediscovered hundreds of years later in the Tang dynasty (AD 618–907).

Fóshān also has a reputation as a handicrafts centre.

Zǔ Miào (Ancestor Temple) Fóshān's No 1 tourist attraction, this is one of those temples that has been rebuilt so many times that its name and function have drifted apart from each other.

The original 11th-century temple may have been a place of ancestor worship, but from the mid-14th century it has enshrined a 2.5-tonne bronze statue of Beidi, the Taoist god of the water and all its denizens, especially fish, turtles and snakes.

Because southern China is prone to floods, people often tried to appease Beidi by honouring him with temples and carvings of turtles and snakes. Outside the temple is a statue of 'the casted iron beast of flood easing' – a one-horned buffalo. Statues like this were placed near the river at times of flood to hold back the waters.

Among other historical fragments are some caricatures of British imperialists on the stone plinths outside the temple, some examples of ineffectual local cannons cast here during the Opium War and a huge ridge tile covered with a whole galaxy of ceramic figures. The temple is open daily from 8.30 am to 4.30 pm; entry is Y10. Bus No 1 passes by the temple from the train station.

Getting There & Away Fóshān is easily visited as a day trip from Guǎngzhōu. There are frequent minibuses from the west bus station (Guǎngfó qìchē zhàn) on Zhongshan Balu. Tickets are Y8.

Frequent minibuses also leave from the Liúhuā bus station near the train station for Y12. If you are in the Shāmiàn Dǎo area of Guǎngzhōu, just wait on Liu'ersan Lu and you will see minibuses heading west, many of which are going to Fóshān (Y10). Put your hand out and they'll stop.

Minibuses take about an hour, but can take longer in Guǎngzhōu's horrific traffic.

Minibuses arrive and depart from the Zǔmiào bus station (Zǔmiào chē zhàn) on Jianxian Lu, which is within walking distance from the temple. Buses also depart here for other destinations in Guǎngdōng such as Zhūhǎi (Y27.50/42 with/without air-con), Shēnzhèn (Y50) and Hong Kong (HK$150). The main long-distance bus station is north of town on Fenjiang Beilu. Five buses daily also leave for Hong Kong (3½ hours) from the Fóshān Bīnguǎn and the Fóshān Huáqiáo Dàshà. Buses to the

Xīqiáo Shān (Y10) depart from the main long-distance bus station on Fenjiang Beilu.

Train services between Guăngzhōu and Fóshān (Y16) are faster than the buses (half hour) but are only really worth it if you are living in the train station area. If you add on the time getting to the station and queuing for a ticket, it could take a lot longer. There are also direct express trains to/from Hong Kong. There is one service from Fóshān to Kowloon that leaves at 10.43 am, and takes three hours (HK$210). Going the other way, the train departs from Kowloon at 2.45 pm.

The CTS in Fóshān, at the Fóshān Huáqiáo Dàshà, 14 Zumiao Lu, provides a free shuttle to the Píngzhōu wharf for high-speed catamarans to Hong Kong (see the earlier Guăngzhōu Gettting There and Away section).

Getting Around You won't have to look too hard for the two-wheeled taxis – they will be looking for you. Negotiate a fare in advance. A ride from the temple to the train station will be about Y5.

Shíwān 石湾

Two kilometres south-west of Fóshān, Shíwān township is known mostly for its porcelain factories. Although there's nothing of outstanding scenic interest here, you might want to take a look if you have an interest in pottery. Bus Nos 9 and 1 go to Shíwān from the train station, via the Zǔ Miào. From the Zǔ Miào, a brisk walk would get you to Shíwān in about half an hour.

Xīqiáo Shān 西樵山

Another scenic area, made up of 72 crags and peaks (basically hills) with caves, lakes and waterfalls, Xīqiáo Shān is 62km south-west of Guăngzhōu and 28km south-west of Fóshān.

At the foot of the hills is the small market town of Xīqiáo and around the upper levels of the hills are scattered several centuries-old villages, as well as a recently built statue of Guanyin, the buddhist goddess of mercy, that is visible from the highway. Popular sights among visitors include a waterfall called **Fēiliú Qiānchǐ** (Water Flies 1000

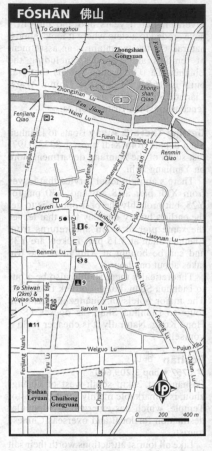

Feet) and **Báiyún Dòng** (White Cloud Cave). Most of the area is made accessible by stone paths. It's popular with local tourists, but foreigners of any kind are rare.

Getting There & Away Buses to the hills depart from the Fóshān long-distance bus station on Fenjiang Beilu. Ask at your hotel in Guăngzhōu about a day tour of Guăngzhōu, Fóshān, Shíwān, Xīqiáo Shān and back to Guăngzhōu. These tours are usually very good value and are certainly less hassle than doing it all yourself, but the commentary will undoubtedly be delivered

FÓSHĀN

1 Train Station
火车站
2 Long-Distance Bus Station
长途汽车站
3 Renmin Athletic Field
人民体育场
4 Post Office
邮电局

5 CTS
中国旅行社
6 Rénshòu Sì
仁寿寺
7 Market
莲花市场
8 Bank of China; New Stadium
中国银行；新广场

9 Zǔ Miào
祖庙
10 Zǔmiào Bus Station
祖庙汽车站
11 Fóshān Bīnguǎn; CITS
佛山宾馆；中国国际旅行社

in Chinese. The Fóshān CTS in the Fóshān Huáqiáo Dàshà, 14 Zumiao Lu, also has tours for Y60 per person, but you will need a group of 10 or more people.

SHĒNZHÈN 深圳

☎ 0755 • pop 1,094,600

'You think you're brave until you go to Manchuria, you think you're well read until you reach Běijīng and you think you're rich until you set foot in Shēnzhèn', goes an oft-coined maxim of today's China.

The locals of China's north-east have always been a rough-and-ready lot and Běijīng's residents have a long history of learning, but you can give the knives and broken bottles a miss, forgo the books and the erudition and head straight for Shēnzhèn if you want to be rolling in it.

The name 'Shēnzhèn' refers to three places: Shēnzhèn Shì (Shenzhen City; opposite the border crossing at Lo Wu); Shēnzhèn Special Economic Zone (SEZ); and Shēnzhèn County, which extends several kilometres north of the SEZ. The majority of foreigners who come here are on business. If you are coming from the north, Shēnzhèn Shì will seem like a tacky introduction to Hong Kong and if you are coming from the south, it may seem like a tacky prologue to China. Most travellers give the place a wide berth, but it is a useful transportation hub if you're coming from Hong Kong.

The northern part of the SEZ is walled off from the rest of China by an electrified fence to prevent smuggling and to keep back the hordes of people trying to emigrate illegally into Shēnzhèn and Hong Kong. There is a checkpoint when you leave the SEZ. You don't need your passport to leave, but you will need it to get back in, so don't leave it in your hotel if you decide to make a day trip outside Shēnzhèn.

History

Shēnzhèn was no more than a fishing village until it won the equivalent of the National Lottery and became an SEZ in 1980. Developers added a stock market, glittering hotels, office blocks and a population of two million. Like many fortune winners, the city attracted a lot of unwanted friends (beggars throng the streets and two-thirds of its residents have no permit to live there) and its morals have gone soft, with prostitution and sleaze endemic. A surging crime rate is another of its less appealing statistics: it jumped by 66% in the mid-90s.

These days, Shēnzhèn is becoming an extended shopping mall for Hong Kong residents, much to the chagrin of Hong Kong retailers. Shēnzhèn has no doubt been a fabulous commercial success, but it's a place without culture or spirit. In other words, if it's high-rises and the high life you want, stay in Hong Kong and if you want history, anywhere else is an improvement.

Information

Visas It is possible to cross the border from Hong Kong to Shēnzhèn without a visa to China but you are limited to a five-day stay within Shēnzhèn only. The cost is Y100 at the Shēnzhèn border check-point. At the time of writing, this option was not available to British passport holders because of an immigration dispute. British citizens who arrive at the checkpoint without a Chinese

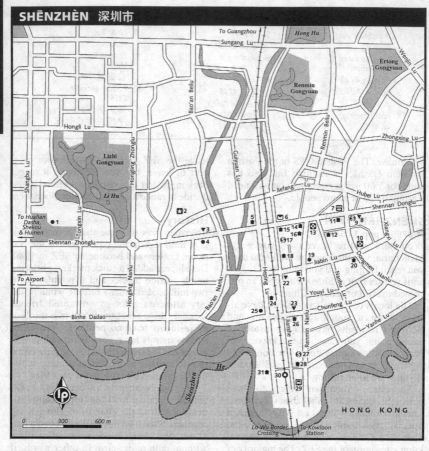

SHĒNZHÈN 深圳市

visa will be fined HK$1000 and sent back to Hong Kong. Check with the British consulate in Hong Kong for updates.

The border is open daily from 6.30 am to 11.30 pm.

Money Shēnzhèn effectively operates with a dual currency system – Chinese yuán and Hong Kong dollars. If you pay in HK dollars, you will get RMB as change and will effectively lose out on every transaction, so change some of your dollars into RMB.

There is a branch of the Hong Kong and Shanghai Bank in the Century Plaza Hotel.

The Bank of China is at 23 Jianshe Lu as well as a branch on the mainland side when you cross the border. Both the Bank of China and the Industrial and Commercial Bank (ICBC) have ATMs that take most international bank cards (Visa, Cirrus etc).

Post & Communications The main post office is at the northern end of Jianshe Lu. Telecommunications facilities are in a separate building on Shennan Donglu. An Internet service there charges Y18 per hour and is open Monday to Friday from 9 am to

SHĒNZHÈN

PLACES TO STAY

5 Rìhuá Bīnguǎn
日华宾馆

11 Hángkōng Dàjiǔdiàn
航空大酒店

12 Landmark Hotel
富苑酒店

14 Wah Chung International
Hotel; CTS
华中国际酒店；
中国旅行社

15 Shēnzhèn Jiǔdiàn
深圳酒店

16 Zhōngyóudàhuá Jiǔdiàn;
中游大花酒店

18 Nányáng Jiǔdiàn
南洋酒店

20 Sunshine Hotel; JJ's;
Polka Club
阳光酒店

21 Guǎngxìn Jiǔdiàn；CITS
广信酒店、
中国国际旅行社

24 Shēntiě Dàshà;
Tiěchéng Jiǔjiā
深铁大厦；铁城酒家

26 Century Plaza Hotel
新都酒店

28 Shangri-La Hotel;
Henry J Bean Bar and Grill
香格里大酒店

31 Forum Hotel
富临大酒店

PLACES TO EAT

3 Hard Rock Cafe;
Xīnxīng Guǎngchǎng
硬石俱乐部；信兴广场

8 Café de Coral
大家乐快餐

22 Hǎishàng Huáng Jiǔjiā
海上皇酒家

23 Luóhú Dàjiǔjiā
罗湖大酒家

OTHER

1 Shenzhen City Hall
深圳市政府

2 PSB
公安局外事科

4 Book City
书城

6 Post Office
邮局

7 Telecommunications
Building
电信大楼

9 Bank of China
中国银行

10 Seibu Department Store
东方新世界百货

13 Oriental New World
Department Store
东方天虹商场

17 Bank of China (Main
Branch)
中国银行

19 International
Trade Centre
国贸大厦

25 Wellcome Supermarket
惠康超市

27 Bank of China
中国银行

29 Long-Distance Bus Station;
Luóhú Shāngyè Chéng
汽车站；罗湖商业城

30 Train Station
火车站

5 pm, from 10 am on weekends. The entrance is on Dongmen Nanlu.

For express delivery of packages, phone DHL (☎ 339 5592) for details.

Travel Agencies There are two branches of CITS. The more convenient one for arriving travellers is the office in the train station. Otherwise there is a branch (☎ 217 6615) in the lobby of the Guǎngxìn Jiǔdiàn on Renmin Nanlu that sells train and plane tickets, while inquiries of a tourist nature are dealt with in Room 1102 (☎ 218 2660) of the same building.

CTS has a branch at the Wah Chung International Hotel (☎ 225 5888).

PSB The Foreign Affairs Branch of the PSB (☎ 557 6355) is at 174 Jiefang Lu.

Dangers & Annoyances Shēnzhèn has had a bad reputation as a mecca for beggars from all over the country, though they are swept off the streets periodically when officials visit Shēnzhèn. Beggars mainly congregate on Jianshe Lu and Renmin Nanlu and tenaciously follow foreigners in search of alms. If you do give them money, this is generally the green light for the rest to pursue you.

Places to Stay – Mid-Range

There is no real budget accommodation in Shēnzhèn. *Rìhuá Bīnguǎn* (☎ 558 8530), located just west of the train tracks on Shennan Donglu, is one exception. The outside looks a bit tattered, but the rooms are large, bright and cost Y150 for singles or doubles with bath and air-con. Otherwise, most of the cheaper hotels have rates that start at Y250 for a standard double and there's usually a 10% or 15% service charge. Always try to push for a discount. You can try your luck with the hotel touts at the train station; but they usually take you to cheap and tacky sleaze joints.

On the west side of the tracks, the *Shēntiě Dàshà* (☎ 558 4248, fax 556 1409, 63 Heping Lu) has standard doubles starting at Y258 and often offers a 20% discount. *Nányáng Bīnguǎn* (☎ 222 4968, fax 223 8927) is conveniently located on Jianshe Lu and has doubles starting at Y298, with a 20% discount available. North of here at the intersection with Shennan Donglu, *Shēnzhèn Jiǔdiàn* (☎ 223 8000, fax 222 4922) isn't much to look at from the outside but has a newly renovated interior. Standard doubles start at Y258.

Guǎngxīn Jiǔdiàn (☎ 223 8945, fax 225 5849) on Renmin Nanlu is a popular place with overseas Chinese travellers on a budget. Double rooms start at Y280 and it also has five-person rooms for Y465, as well as family suites for Y350. A 20% discount was available at the time of writing.

Another cheap option is *Zhōngyoǔdàhuá Jiǔdiàn* (CTS Dawa Hotel; ☎ 220 2828, 40 Renmin Nanlu) with singles/doubles for Y238/310, as well as a 30% discount. *Wah Chung International Hotel* (*Huázhōng Guójì Jiǔdiàn;* ☎ 223 8060, fax 222 1349) is a little faded and more pricey with singles/doubles going for Y300/380.

Hángkōng Dàjiǔdiàn (Airlines Hotel; ☎ 223 7999, fax 223 7866, 3027 Shennan Donglu) is an attractive, newly renovated hotel with friendly staff. Its starting rates for singles/doubles were Y480/638, but it was also offering a 40% discount.

Places to Stay – Top End

There's no shortage of luxurious accommodation in Shēnzhèn and competition has brought some of the prices down. *Shangri-La Hotel* (*Xiānggélǐlā Dàjiǔdiàn;* ☎ 223 0888, fax 223 9878) is a prominent landmark near the train station, with overpriced singles/doubles for Y1523/1680. Check for discounts. In the luxury hotel category, *Century Plaza Hotel* (*Xīndū Jiǔdiàn;* ☎ 222 0888, fax 223 4060) is a better deal and has more comprehensive facilities. Doubles start at Y1320, and it was offering a 50% discount at the time of writing.

The best value, however, is *Landmark Hotel* (*Shēnzhèn Fùyuàn Jiǔdiàn;* ☎ 217

2288, fax 229 0473, 3018 Nanhu Lu), which has enthusiastic English-speaking staff and rooms starting at Y650. Check for discounts that include an international-style breakfast and free Citybus transportation to Hong Kong.

Two other five-star options include: *Forum Hotel* (*Fùlín Dàjiǔdiàn;* ☎ 558 6333, fax 556 1700, 67 Heping Lu) with standard rooms starting at US$142, with a discount of up to 40%; and *Sunshine Hotel* (*Yángguāng Jiǔdiàn;* ☎ 223 3888, fax 222 6719), where rack rates are Y1633 for a standard double, and a similar discount.

Places to Eat

Shēnzhèn has a thriving upmarket dining scene, but there are also cheap eats available around town. The train station has a number of affordable restaurants on its 3rd floor.

The *Tiěchéng Jiǔjiā* beside the Shēntiě Dàshà has reasonable dim sum from 6.45 am to 5 pm. An outdoor restaurant next door also has cheap dishes.

Dim sum breakfast is available in almost all of the hotels and can usually be found in the restaurants on the 2nd and 3rd floor. Prices are slightly lower than in Hong Kong.

One of Shēnzhèn's best restaurants is the *Hǎishàng Huáng Jiǔjiā* (☎ 223 9000, 1116 Jianshe Lu). Opposite the Century Plaza Hotel is the *Luóhú Dàjiǔjiā*, which is one of the most popular restaurants in the city centre. At night it's noticeable a long way off for its decorations and bright lights.

Shēnzhèn is fast-food city and all the usual names are represented. Cantonese fast-food is also available at *Café de Coral*. For those on the run from noodles, rice and Canto-pop, the *Hard Rock Cafe* (☎ 246 1671) is at hand. You can find it in the huge Xìnxīng Guǎngchǎng building on Shennan Donglu.

For self-catering, there's a *Wellcome Supermarket* (*Huìkāng Chāoshí*) on Heping Lu, south of Shēntiě Dàshà.

Entertainment

Hard Rock Cafe (see Places to Eat previously) flings open its doors at 11.30 am, but the dancing doesn't start until 10.30 pm. Last dancers are thrown out at 3 am. Entry is Y50 on Monday to Thursday, and Y70 on weekends. Soft drinks will set you back Y20 and beer is a cool Y40.

Most of the top-end hotels have international-style bars. The *Henry J Bean Bar and Grill* is on the 2nd floor of the Shangri-La Hotel. There are two discos, *JJ's* (☎ 223 3888) and *Polka Club* (☎ 223 3911) flanking the entrance to the Sunshine Hotel. The cover charge is Y30.

For more sedate entertainment, one of the best venues is the revolving restaurant on the 31st floor of the Shangri-La Hotel. It serves meals and afternoon tea, but unfortunately when we visited the food was terrible. Better to order the cheapest drink and watch the vista of one of the most intriguing borders in the world unfold below you.

Shopping

On the flyovers to the east of the train station and around the Luóhú Shāngyè Chéng (Luohu Commercial City) are whole avenues of stalls selling ceramics and curios for souvenir and antique hunters. Don't expect to find trophies from the Summer Palace in Běijīng here, but it's a colourful and varied selection.

The shops in the Luóhú building also sell cheap bedding materials and there are some good deals on running shoes. On Youyi Lu near the intersection with Nanhu Lu are a number of small boutiques selling a nice assortment of clothing.

There are also art and antique shops at the western end of Chunfeng Lu, near the Century Plaza Hotel, with a varied if pricey selection. If you see anything that sparks your interest, either haggle hard or look around for cheaper versions.

Getting There & Away

Air Shēnzhèn's airport (☎ 777 6789 airport hotline) is rapidly becoming one of China's busiest. There are flights to most major destinations around China, but it is often significantly cheaper to fly from Guǎngzhōu.

Air tickets can be purchased from most of the larger hotels, including Shēntiě Dàshà (☎ 558 4248) and various agencies around town, including CITS.

Bus Services from Hong Kong to Shēnzhèn are run by Citybus, the Motor Transport Company of Guangdong & Hong Kong, and CTS. They depart from the Landmark Hotel four times a day and terminate at China Hong Kong City in Kowloon.

Shēnzhèn has a comprehensive and efficient long-distance bus system that makes it one of the best ways to head to other destinations in Guǎngdōng or Fújiàn. Deluxe buses leave from the Luóhú bus station (Luóhú qìchēzhàn) located underneath the Luóhú Shāngyè Chéng (see Shopping earlier). There are frequent departures to Shàntóu (Y150; four hours), Cháozhōu (Y170; five hours), Hǔmén (Y35; one hour), Guǎngzhou (Y55; two hours) and Xiàmén (Y300; nine hours). Economy buses and minibuses to various destinations are slightly cheaper.

Train The Kowloon-Canton Railway (KCR) offers the fastest and most convenient transport to Shēnzhèn from Hong Kong. See the Hong Kong chapter for more details.

There are frequent local trains (Y42; two hours) and high-speed trains (Y80; 55 minutes) between Guǎngzhōu and Shēnzhèn. The former goes to the Guǎngzhōu east train station. It's probably just as quick to take a bus.

Boat There are 11 jet-cat departures daily between Shékǒu (a port on the western side of Shēnzhèn) and Hong Kong. Four of these go to the China Hong Kong City ferry terminal in Kowloon, while the rest go to the Macau ferry terminal on Hong Kong island. Ticket prices are HK$90 and the trip takes one hour.

There are six departures daily to the China Hong Kong City ferry terminal from the Shēnzhèn Fúyǒng ferry terminal (Shēnzhèn Fúyǒng kèyùnzhàn) at the airport. The trip takes one hour and 10 minutes; ticket prices are Y161 (economy) and Y261 (1st class).

There is one jet-cat departure daily from Shékǒu to Macau. It departs from Shékǒu at 11 am and arrives at noon. Tickets are

M$100. Ferries leave every 15 minutes for Zhūhăi from Shékŏu, take one hour and cost Y65.

There's a daily boat to Hăikŏu from Shékŏu that takes 18 hours and ranges in price from Y453 to Y113.

Getting Around

To/From the Airport Shēnzhèn's airport is 36km west of the city past Shékŏu. Airport buses leave from the Huálián Dàshà (Hualian Building) on Shennan Zhonglu. Tickets are Y20 and the trip takes about 40 minutes. Bus No 101 goes to the Huálián Dàshà from the train station. A taxi to the airport will cost about Y130.

Bus Shēnzhèn has some of the best public transport in China. The city bus services are dirt cheap and not nearly as crowded as elsewhere. From the large terminus on the north side of the Luóhú Shāngyè Chéng (see Shopping earlier), bus Nos 12 and 101 from the train station pass by Lychee Park. Bus No 204 to Shékŏu leaves from just south of the intersection of Jianshe Lu and Jiabin Lu. The trip takes about 15 minutes, depending on traffic.

Taxi Taxis are abundant, but not cheap, starting at Y12.50. Insist on the driver using the meter. Payment can be made either in RMB or Hong Kong dollars.

AROUND SHĒNZHÈN

At the western end of the SEZ, grouped together near Shēnzhèn Bay, are a collection of tacky attractions possibly of interest if you are stuck in Shēnzhèn.

Shenzhen – Splendid China (Jĭnxiù Zhōnghuá) is an assembly of China's sights in miniature; famous monuments of the world get the same treatment at **Window of the World** (Shìjiè Zhī Chuāng); while the **China Folk Culture Villages** (Zhōngguó Mínzú Wénhuà Cūn) recreates 24 life-sized ethnic minority villages.

They are all clumped together not far from the Shékŏu ferry terminal and can be reached either by bus No 101 (Y4) or the purple double-decker sightseeing buses

(Y10) that leave from the terminus on the north side of the Luóhú Shāngyè Chéng (see Shopping earlier). If you are entering Shēnzhèn by way of Shékŏu, then you could take a taxi.

HŬMÉN 虎门

Also known as Taiping, the small city of Hŭmén on the Zhū Jiāng (Pearl River) is of interest only to history buffs curious about the Opium Wars that led directly to Hong Kong's creation as a British colony.

At the end of the first Opium War, after the Treaty of Nanjing, there was a British Supplementary Treaty of the Bogue, signed on 8 October 1843. The Bogue Forts (Shājiăo Pàotái) at Hŭmén is now the site of an impressive museum. There are numerous exhibits, including large artillery pieces and other relics, and the actual ponds in which Commissioner Lin Zexiu had the opium destroyed.

Economy buses to Hŭmén leave from the entrance to the Dàshàtóu wharf in Guăngzhōu. Tickets are Y20 and the trip takes about two hours. From Shēnzhèn, minibuses leave from the Luóhú bus station (Y35; one hour). Boats from Hong Kong make the trip in two hours and cost HK$186, departing from the China Hong Kong City ferry terminal in Kowloon.

ZHŪHĂI 珠海
☎ 0756 • pop 673,400

Like Shēnzhèn to the east, Zhūhăi is doing very well out of the South China Gold Coast. In true rags to riches style, Zhūhăi was built from the soles up on what was recently farmland.

Travellers from the 1980s (even *late* 1980s) remember Zhūhăi as a small agricultural town with a few rural industries and a quiet beach. Well, that's all gone – the Zhūhăi of today not only has the usual SEZ skyline of glimmering five-star hotels and big-name factories, it has its own 'aerotropolis' to boot (servicing a spotless ultra-modern airport).

Zhūhăi is mainly a business destination offering little in the way of interest to the independent traveller though its size and relaxed atmosphere makes it more attractive than Shēnzhèn. The city is so close to the border with Macau that a visit can be arranged as a day trip; alternatively, you can use Zhūhǎi as an entry or exit point for the rest of China.

Orientation

Zhūhǎi is divided into three main districts. The area nearest the Macau border is called Gǒngběi, the main tourist zone. To the north-east is Jídà, the eastern part of which has Zhūhǎi's harbour Jiǔzhōu Gǎng. A mountainous barrier separates these two sections from northern Xiāngzhōu – an area of worker flats and factories. The rest of Zhūhǎi SEZ is to the east and harbours the airport, tacky holiday resorts and infrastructure projects. In anticipation of Macau's return to China at the end of 1999, a huge new complex was being built at the south end of Yingbin Dadao. By the time you read this, it will be the site of the new checkpoint.

Information

The most useful post office is on Qiaoguang Lu, in Gǒngběi. You can make IDD calls from your own room in most hotels. The Bank of China beside Yíndū Jiǔdiàn changes travellers cheques, as does another branch on Lianhua Lu. There is a helpful CTS office (☎ 335 3338 ext 8877) next door to Huáqiáo Bīnguǎn (not to be confused with Huáqiáo Dàjiǔdiàn). The PSB (☎ 222 2211 ext 22528) is in the Xiāngzhōu District on the south-western corner of Anping Lu and Kangning Lu.

It is possible to get a 72-hour visa (limited to Zhūhǎi) at the Gǒngběi border checkpoint or Zhūhǎui's harbour if you arrive by boat.

Dangers & Annoyances Zhūhǎi's pavements are full of gaping holes that could potentially disable you if you fell in one. Out of familiarity, the locals can steer around them at night like bats, but if you've had one tequila slammer too many, tread carefully.

Things to See

North of the Gǒngběi district is a monumental symbol of where China's tourist industry is headed. The first phase of the **Yuánmíng Xīnyuán** (New Yuan Ming Palace) was completed at a cost of Y600 million. This is a reproduction of the original imperial Yuan Ming Palace in Běijīng that was torched by British and French forces during the Second Opium War.

The very impressive entrance gives way to a huge adventure playground of reproduction scenic sights from around China and the world, including the Great Wall of China, Italian and German castles, halls, restaurants, temples and a huge lake.

The colossal scale of the project is reflected in the ticket price – Y90. Depending on your taste, you're probably better off spending your money somewhere else. Opening hours are from 9 am to 5.30 pm. Bus Nos 1, 2, 4 and 13 go there from the Gǒngběi area.

The area around the **Jiǔzhōu Chéng** shopping centre in Jídà may be worth a trip. The shopping centre itself is a huge reproduction of classical Chinese architecture opposite the duty-free shopping centre.

Hǎibin Gōngyuán, just up the road and facing the sea, makes for a pleasant walk with hills on both sides, palms, statues and a windmill. For an overall view of the area, visit **Shíjīngshān Gōngyuán** and climb the hill of the same name.

The bustling **markets** and side streets of the Gǒngběi area, close to the Macau border, offer a colourful diversion. Lianhua Lu is a lively area of hairdressers, restaurants and family-run stores.

Places to Stay – Mid-Range

As in Shēnzhèn, very few travellers stay in Zhūhǎi. Most of the accommodation is clustered close to the Macau-Zhūhǎi border, an area with some charm. Budget accommodation was elbowed out of Zhūhǎi a long time ago and prices are mid-range to top end.

One of the cheapest is *Huáqiáo Dàjiǔdiàn (Overseas Chinese Great Hotel;* ☎ *888 5183)*, not to be confused with Huáqiáo Bīnguǎn, listed later. It's centrally located on Yuehua Lu and singles and doubles go for Y280, but 40% discounts are possible. Similarly, *Gǒngběi Dàshà*

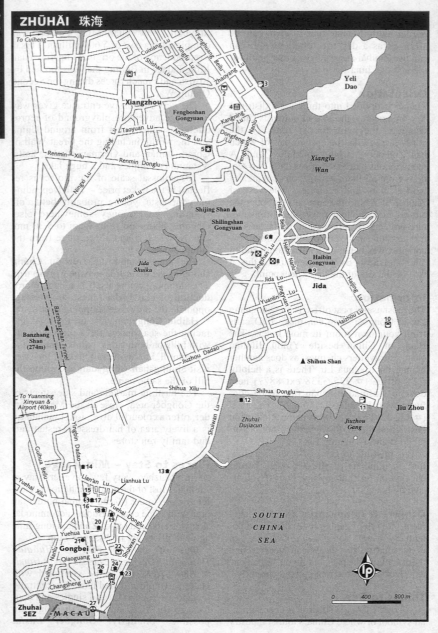

ZHŪHĂI 珠海

To Cuiheng

Cuixiang Lu
Shishan Lu
Xingfu Lu
Fenghuang Beilu
Zhaoyang Lu

1

Xiangzhou

Fengboshan
Gongyuan

2
3

Yeli
Dao

Taoyuan Lu

Zijing Lu

Anping Lu

Kangning Lu

4

Dongfeng Lu

Fenghuang Nanlu

Xianglu
Wan

Renmin Xilu
Ningxi Lu
Renmin Donglu

5

Huwan Lu

Shijing Shan ▲

Shilingshan
Gongyuan

Haijing Beilu

6

Jingshan Lu

7
8

Haibin Gongyuan

Haibin Nanlu

9

Jida
Shuiku

Jida Lu

Jingyuan Lu

Jida

Banzhang
Shan
(274m)

Banzhangshan Tunnel

Yuanlin Lu

Haibin Lu

Haizhou Lu

10

To Yuanming
Xinyuan &
Airport (40km)

Jiuzhou Dadao

Shihua Xilu

Shihua Shan ▲

Shihua Donglu

11

Jiu Zhou

Yingbin Dadao

Shuiwan Lu

12

Zhuhai
Dujiacun

Jiuzhou
Gang

Cuihua Beilu

14

13

Lian'an Lu

Lianhua Lu

Yuehai Xilu

15
16 17
18
19 20

Yuehai Donglu

SOUTH
CHINA
SEA

Yuehua Lu

Gongbei

21

22

Shuiwan Lu

Cuihua Nanlu

Qiaoguang Lu

26 24
25 23

Changsheng Lu

Zhuhai
SEZ

27

M A C A U

0   400   800 m

ZHŪHĂI

PLACES TO STAY
6 Paradise Hill Hotel
石景山旅游中心
12 Zhūhǎi Dùjiàcūn
珠海度假村
13 Grand Bay View Hotel
珠海海湾大酒店
14 Huáqiáo Bīnguǎn;
CTS
华侨宾馆;
中国旅行社
15 Yíndū Jiǔdiàn
银都酒店
17 Gōngbēi Dàshà; Máojiā
Càiguǎn
拱北大厦;毛家菜馆
18 Hǎoshìjiè Jiǔdiàn
好世界酒店
19 Guangdong International
Hotel
粤海酒店

20 Huáqiáo Dàjiǔdiàn
华侨大酒店
23 Jiǔzhōu Jiǔdiàn
九州酒店
24 Jiāotōng Dàshà
交通大厦
26 Yǒuyì Jiǔdiàn
友谊酒店

OTHER
1 Bus Station
香州汽车站
2 Post Office
邮局
3 Xiāngzhōu Harbour
香州码头
4 Lièshì Língyuán
(Martyrs' Memorial)
烈士陵园
5 PSB
公安局

7 Jiǔzhōu Chéng
九州城
8 Duty-Free Shopping
Centre
珠海免税商场
9 Zhuhai Amusement Park
珠海游乐场
10 Helicopter Pad
直升机场
11 Jiǔzhōu Harbour
九州港
16 Bank of China
中国银行
21 CAAC
中国民航
22 Post Office
邮局
25 Bus Station
长途汽车站
27 Border/Customs
海关

(Zhuhai Quzhao Hotel; ☎ *888 6256, fax 888 5351),* has singles/doubles starting at Y198/298 and are a good deal with a 40% discount.

Yǒuyì Jiǔdiàn (Friendship Hotel; ☎ *888 6683, 888 7107, 2 Youyi Lu)* is close to the border crossing and has singles and doubles starting at Y210. Also within walking distance of the border, *Jiǔzhōu Jiǔdiàn (*☎ *888 6851, fax 888 5254, 19 Shuiwan Lu)* is a friendly place with doubles starting at Y268, with the possibility of a 40% discount. Across the street, *Jiāotōng Dàshà (Traffic Hotel;* ☎ *888 4474)* has doubles for Y278 and up.

Huáqiáo Bīnguǎn (Overseas Chinese Hotel; ☎ *888 6288, fax 888 5119)* is a large place complete with restaurants and an international-style coffee shop. Adequate doubles start at Y286.

Places to Stay – Top End

Most top-end accommodation in Zhūhǎi includes tax of 10% to 15%, and sometimes a further tax of 10% to 15% for weekends and holidays.

The best place within striking distance of the border is *Yíndū Jiǔdiàn (*☎ *888 3388, fax 888 3311),* which has all the amenities you expect from a five-star hotel. Its services include a coffee shop, bar, shopping arcade, massage centre, sauna and bowling alley. Standard rooms are Y860, but at the time of writing it was offering discounts of 30%. *Guangdong International Hotel (Yuèhǎi Jiǔdiàn;* ☎ *888 8128, fax 888 5063, 30 Yuehai Donglu)* is another option in this range with standard doubles for Y730 and a 30% discount. Across the street, *Hǎo Shìjiè Jiǔdiàn (Good World Hotel;* ☎ *888 0222, fax 889 2061)* is a bit more downmarket, but good value with doubles for Y300.

Further north on Shuiwan Lu facing the South China Sea is one of Zhūhǎi's finest, *Grand Bay View Hotel (Zhūhǎi Hǎiwān Dàjiǔdiàn;* ☎ *887 7998, fax 887 8998).* Standard rooms are Y830, with a substantial discount on weekdays. The Harbour Cafe is a western restaurant in the hotel with a good view. Competing with this, the elegant *Paradise Hill Hotel (Shíjǐngshān Lǚyǒu Zhōngxīn;* ☎ *333 7388, fax 333 3508)* is a new place nestled beneath Shíjǐng Shān (Paradise Hill). Rooms are tastefully done, each with a veranda; doubles start at Y788. The hotel has three international-style restaurants, a swimming pool and tennis courts.

Finally, if you're looking for a resort in Zhūhǎi with everything from a shooting gallery to go-karts, then *Zhūhǎi Dùjiàcūn (Zhuhai Holiday Resort;* ☎ *333 2038, fax 333 2036)* is the place to go. Some of the rooms can be very good value, with doubles normally at Y788 going for half-price during the low season. Villas start at Y2288.

Places to Eat
Zhūhǎi is brimming with places to eat. The Gǒngběi area is the best place to seek out restaurants. Try Lianhua Lu for *bakeries* and a couple of restaurants serving cheap Cantonese cuisine. In warm weather many restaurants set up tables outside. There's a collection of these places opposite Huáqiáo Bīnguǎn up on Yingbin Dadao – most of them sell seafood. Most of the top-end hotels in Zhūhǎi have great bakeries.

At the *Maójiā Càiguǎn (Mao Restaurant)*, beside the entrance to Gǒngběi Dàshà, spicy Hunanese food is served by staff dressed as Red Guards. There's no English sign or menu, but you can't miss the portrait of the Chairman.

There's a cluster of fast food places at the corner of Yuehai Lu and Yingbin Dadao.

Getting There & Away
Air Zhūhǎi's glimmering new airport has domestic flights to most major cities in China. CAAC (☎ 889 5494) is located on the Ground floor of the Zhongzhu Building opposite McDonald's. Zhuhai Airlines has an office opposite Gǒngběi Dàshà. Fares to Běijīng are Y1550 and Shànghǎi, Y1120.

Bus There are connections with Guǎngzhōu, Fóshān, Zhàoqìng, Zhànjiāng and Shàntóu. Buses leave from the main bus station on Youyi Lu near the Yǒuyì Bīnguǎn. Buses from Zhūhǎi to Guǎngzhōu depart regularly through the day from 6.30 am to 6.30 pm, and air-con services cost Y50. Buses to Zhōngshān are Y16. You can also book train tickets originating from Guǎngzhōu at the bus station. Hard-sleeper bookings incur a Y40 service charge.

Buses to Hong Kong (Y130; 2½ hours) leave from the Guangdong International Hotel at 3 pm daily and pass the major hotels.

Boat Jet-cats between Zhūhǎi and Hong Kong do the trip in about 70 minutes. There are five departures a day from Zhūhǎi's harbour to the China Hong Kong City ferry terminal on Canton Rd and three a day to Central. Tickets are Y150.

A high-speed ferry operates between the port of Shékǒu in Shēnzhèn and Zhūhǎi's harbour. There are departures every 15 minutes between 7.30 am and 6 pm. The cost is Y65 and the journey takes one hour. Bus Nos 3, 25, 4 and 12 go to Zhūhǎi's harbour.

Zhūhǎi to Macau Simply walk across the border. In Macau, bus Nos 3 and 10B lead to the Barrier Gate, from where you make the crossing on foot. Taxis from the Hong Kong ferry area cost around HK$22. The Macau-Zhūhǎi border is open from 7.30 am to midnight.

Getting Around
To/From the Airport Zhūhǎi's airport is about 43km from the city centre. A taxi will be expensive (more than Y100), so the best option is a CAAC shuttle bus that runs reasonably frequently from the CAAC office near McDonald's (Y25).

Bus Zhūhǎi has a clean and efficient bus system. The buses are new and the routes are clearly marked on the Zhūhǎi city map. Minibuses ply the same routes and cost Y2 for any place in the city.

Taxi You are most likely to use taxis to shuttle between your hotel and the boats at Zhūhǎi's harbour. Taxi drivers cruising the streets use their meters. From the customs area to Zhūhǎi's harbour costs around Y20.

AROUND ZHŪHǍI
In **Cuìhēng Cūn** (Cuiheng Village), 33 km north of the city limits of Zhūhǎi, is **Sūn Zhōngshān Gùjū** (Dr Sun Yatsen's Residence). Republican, enemy of the Qing dynasty and China's most famous revolutionary, Dr Sun Yatsen was born in a house on this site on 12 November 1866. That house was torn down after a new home

was built in 1892. This second house is still standing and open to the public. Entry is Y5.

Bus No 10 goes there from the public bus stop at the south end of Yingbin Dadao.

ZHŌNGSHĀN 中山市

The administrative centre of the county by the same name, this city is also known as Shíqí. An industrial city, there is little to see or do here. If you get stranded here for an hour or so, the one and only scenic spot in town is **Zhōngshān Gōngyuán**, which is pleasantly forested and dominated by Yāndūn Shān, a large hill topped with a pagoda. It's visible from most parts of the city so it's easy to find.

AROUND ZHŌNGSHĀN

The **Zhōngshān Wēnquán** (Zhongshan Hot Springs) resort has indoor hot springs and a golf course. If you're a real enthusiast of either activity, you might want to spend a night here. Otherwise, you'll probably just want to look around briefly and then head back to Gǒngběi. It's about 25km north of Zhūhǎi, near the town of Sānxiāng.

Accommodation is available at the **Zhōngshān Wēnquán Bīnguǎn** (*Zhongshan Hot Springs Hotel; ☎ 668 3888, fax 668 3333*) from Y462 for doubles, plus a 10% service charge. Buses to Zhōngshān can drop you by the entrance to the resort, then it's a 500m walk to the hotel. For a couple of yuán you can hire someone to carry you on the back of a bicycle. You won't have to look for them as they'll be looking for you. To get back to Gǒngběi, flag down any minibus you see passing the resort entrance.

ZHÀOQÌNG 肇庆
☎ 0758 • pop 3,683,400

Zhàoqìng, home to some craggy limestone rock formations similar to those around Guìlín, is rated highly among the attractions of Guǎngdōng. Despite not having the appeal of Yángzhōu, Zhàoqìng is an attractive city with far more character than Guǎngzhōu or Fóshān. The mountainous Dǐnghú Shān area nearby is well worth visiting and features some nice walks among temples, pools, brooks and lush scenery.

Orientation & Information

Zhàoqìng, 110km west of Guǎngzhōu on the Xī Jiāng, is bounded to the south by the river and to the north by the lakes and crags that make up Qīxīng Yán Gōngyuán (Seven Star Crags Park). The main attractions can be easily seen on foot.

There's a post office on Jianshe Lu and the main Bank of China is on Duanzhou Lu east of Renmin Lu.

There is a branch of CTS (☎ 222 9908) next to the Texas Cowboy Fastfood on Duanzhou Wulu. The Xinghu Travel Agency (☎ 226 7872) also books tickets and is more friendly. It's a small office squeezed in the corner of Tianning Lu and Duanzhou Lu. The major hotels will book tickets as well.

Things to See

Zhàoqìng's premier attraction, the **Qīxīng Yán** (Seven Star Crags), is a group of limestone towers – a peculiar geological formation abundant in the paddy fields of Guìlín and Yángzhōu.

The crags are home to myriad inscriptions and limestone caves that you can explore. A boat can take you from Páifáng Guǎngchǎng (Gateway Square) at the southern tip of Xīng Hú and speed you across to a bridge that crosses over to the crags. At this point

Divine Inspiration

Legend has it that the Qīxīng Yán (Seven Star Crags) were actually seven stars that fell from the sky to form a pattern resembling the Big Dipper. Another legend dates from Ming dynasty times:

It was said that if you stood under Shíshì Yán (Stone House Crag) on a clear moonlit night, you could hear the celestial strains of music played by the Jade Emperor, the supreme god of Taoism, as he gave a banquet for the rest of the gods and goddesses.

Furthermore, a tablet known as Horse Hoof Tablet, one of many inscribed tablets in the area, was dented by the hoof of an inquisitive celestial horse as he alighted on the shores of Xīng Hú (Star Lake).

ZHÀOQÌNG 肇庆

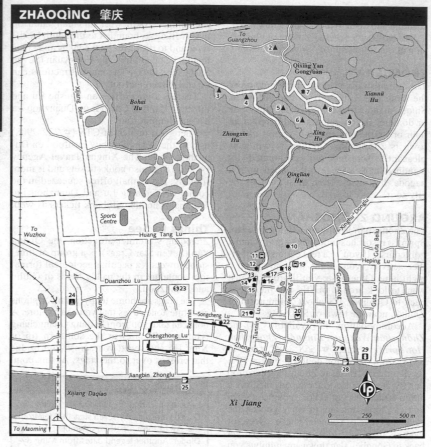

you have to pay an entrance fee or you can just turn right and keep walking in a big circle (no charge) among the willows and kapok trees all the way around the lake, looking out across at the view.

On Tajiao Lu in the south-east, the nine-storey pagoda **Chóngxī Tǎ** was in a sad state after the Cultural Revolution, but was restored in the 1980s. On the opposite bank of the river are two similar pagodas.

Yuèjiāng Lóu (River View Pavilion) is a restored building about 30 minutes' walk from Chóngxī Tǎ, just back from the waterfront at the eastern end of Zheng Donglu.

Places to Stay

Zhàoqìng is not the place to stay for budget accommodation. The only budget place is, however, in a great location within the crags. *Qīxīngyán Xuésheng Lǚguǎn (Seven Star Crags Student Youth Hostel; ☎/fax 222 4112)* has dormitory beds for Y38 and doubles/triples with air-con and bath for Y138/180. It's part of the same complex as *Xīngyán Bīnguǎn (Star Crag Hotel; ☎/fax 222 4112)*, which was under renovation at the time of writing. Doubles/triples with bath and air-con are expected to cost Y168/198. These two offer

ZHÀOQÌNG

PLACES TO STAY
7 Xīngyán Bīnguǎn;
   Qīxīngyán Xuésheng
   Lǚguǎn
   星岩宾馆;七星
   岩学生旅馆
13 Huáqiáo Dàshà
   华侨大厦
15 Duānzhōu Dàjiǔdiàn
   端州大酒店
16 Jīnbì Dàjiǔdiàn
   金碧大酒店
18 Star Lake Hotel
   星湖大酒店

OTHER
1 Zhàoqìng Train Station
   肇庆火车站
2 Āpō Yán (Crag)
   阿坡岩
3 Xiānzhang Yán
   (Fairy-Hand Crag)
   仙掌岩
4 Chánchú Yán (Toad Crag)
   蟾蜍岩

5 Tiānzhù Yán
   (Pillar of Heaven Crag)
   天柱岩
6 Shíshì Yán
   石室岩
8 Yùpíng Yán
   (Jade Curtain Crag)
   玉屏岩
9 Làngfēng Yán (Crag)
   阆风岩
10 Star Lake Amusement
   Park
   星湖游乐园
11 Bus Station (to
   Dǐnghú Shān)
   公共汽车站
   (往鼎湖山)
12 Páifáng Guǎngchǎng
   牌坊广场
14 Texas Cowboy
   Fastfood; CTS
   德州牛仔快餐;
   中国旅行社
17 Xinghu Travel Agency
   星湖国际旅行社

19 Long-Distance Bus Station
   长途汽车站
20 Post Office
   邮局
21 Xinhua Bookstore
   新华书店
22 Night Market
   夜市
23 Bank of China
   中国银行
24 Méi Ān
   (Plum Nunnery)
   梅庵
25 Passenger Ferry Terminal
   肇庆港客运站
26 Yuèjiāng Lóu
   阅江楼
27 Boat Ticketing Office
   for Hong Kong
   去香港船运售票处
28 Zhàoqìng Pier
   (Boats to Hong Kong)
   肇庆码头(去香港)
29 Chóngxǐ Tǎ
   崇禧塔

the nicest area to stay, but you'll have to hire a motorbike to get you there.

Duānzhōu Dàjiǔdiàn (☎ 223 2281, fax 222 9228, 77 Tianning Beilu) has singles/doubles/triples for Y198/228/348. A 30% discount makes this place very good value. Across the street, *Jīnbì Dàjiǔdiàn* (☎ 222 2888, fax 222 3328, 76 Tianning Beilu) is an uninspired place with standard doubles/triples at Y238/328, though a 30% discount is also available.

Nearby, *Huáqiáo Dàshà* (☎ 223 2952, fax 223 1197, 90 Tianning Beilu) is a little more upmarket and has adequate doubles for Y308 and Y363.

Star Lake Hotel (Xīnghú Dàjiǔdiàn; ☎ 222 1188, fax 223 6688, 37 Duanzhou Silu) is the nicest place to stay if you can afford it. There's a full range of near international-class services with rooms starting at Y500.

Places to Eat

A number of restaurants spill out onto the sidewalks of Wenming Lu, just west of the bus station. You can find some better restaurants on Jianshe Lu around the *KFC*. Or if you're craving other fast food, try the *Texas Cowboy Fastfood* (Dézhōuniúzǎi Kuàicān), next to Huáqiáo Dàshà (see Places to Stay earlier), which serves up fried chicken, pizza, hamburger, French toast and Chinese food.

Shopping

There is a lively night market *(yè shìchǎng)* in front of the old city walls on Songcheng Lu. Items on display include: curios, antiques, old watches, Qing dynasty water pipes, woodcarvings, jade ornaments and ceramics. It gets going after 7 pm.

Getting There & Away

Bus Frequent air-con buses to Zhàoqìng (Y30) leave from Guǎngzhōu's long-distance bus station near the train station. The trip, most of it by freeway, takes 1½ hours. Minibuses also leave from Guǎngzhōu's west bus station at Zhongshan Balu for Y15.

Zhàoqìng's bus station is conveniently located within walking distance of the lake; buses to Guǎngzhōu leave every half hour.

A deluxe bus to Hong Kong leaves daily at 4 pm from Huáqiáo Dàshà (HK$160; four hours).

Train The train is a little inconvenient compared to the bus, though marginally quicker if your bus runs into one of Guǎngzhōu's horrendous traffic jams. The fastest train to Guǎngzhōu takes two hours and hard seat tickets are Y26. You can book tickets at CTS, Xinghu travel and the Star Lake Hotel, but there's a Y15 service charge (Y30 for sleepers if you're head east to Zhànjiāng).

There's a daily train to and from Hong Kong (HK$235; 4½ hours).

Boat A good way to get to Zhàoqìng is by the daily high-speed ferry (two hours) from the Dàshātóu ferry terminal in Guǎngzhōu. Tickets are Y40. Slow boats from Guǎngzhōu leave from Dàshātóu and take eight hours. Both these boats continue on to Wúzhōu. All departures from Zhàoqìng are from the wharf at the south end of Renmin Lu.

Jet-cats speed from Zhàoqìng to Hong Kong at 2 pm, take four hours and cost Y250 for ordinary class. Boats leave from Zhàoqìng pier and tickets can be bought just up the road on Gongnong Nanlu.

Getting Around

The local bus station is on Duanzhou Lu, a few minutes' walk east of the intersection with Tianning Lu and next to Páifáng Guǎngchǎng. Bus No 1 runs to the ferry dock on the Xī Jiāng.

The train station is a long haul, but can be reached on bus No 2, which goes from the local long-distance bus station. A taxi will set you back Y12.

AROUND ZHÀOQÌNG
Dǐnghú Shān 鼎湖山

Twenty kilometres north-east of Zhàoqìng is Dǐnghú Shān, one of the most attractive scenic spots in Guǎngdōng and a protected reserve. This easy-to-reach mountainous area offers myriad walks among pools, springs, ponds, temples, nunneries and charming scenery. You can easily spend half the day or more here as there is a lot to cover. Dǐngyún Sì is the most famous temple on Dǐnghú Shān. Like many sightseeing spots in China, every geographical feature has been named in a manner to enhance the viewer's imagination. These include Yuèlóng Tan (Leaping Dragon Pool) and Xiānrén Qí'hè (Immortal Riding a Crane).

Entry to reserve is Y30. About 300m up from the main gate there's a reserve office where, for a fee of Y20, you can request permission to hike up the west trail that follows the river. You'll need to show your passport. The hike takes about four hours and eventually ends up at Qìngyún Sì. Guides are available, varying in price from Y100 to Y200, but not really necessary. Otherwise it's possible to hike up the road, or take a taxi or motorbike to the top, roughly 7km from the entry gate.

If you get stranded on the mountain, you can crash the night in the nearby *Qìngyún Dùjiàcūn (Qingyun Resort)*. Prices are Y150 to Y250. There are a few places to swim (as Sun Yatsen did back in the early '20s, though it was probably more inviting then).

Bus No 15 goes to Dǐnghú Shān from the southern tip of the lake Zhōngxīn Hú in Zhàoqìng. It takes you past the entry gate to a parking lot about 1km into the reserve.

ZHÀNJIĀNG 湛江
☎ 0759 • pop 6,273,200

Zhànjiāng is a major port on the southern coast of China, and the largest Chinese port west of Guǎngzhōu. It was leased to France in 1898 and remained under French control until WWII.

Today the French are back, but this time Zhànjiāng is a base for their oil-exploration projects in the South China Sea. Very few foreigners come to Zhànjiāng, and when they do they are usually travelling en route to Hǎinán Dǎo.

Orientation & Information

Zhànjiāng is split into two districts – Chìkǎn to the north and Xiáshān to the south. The harbour, bus station and most of

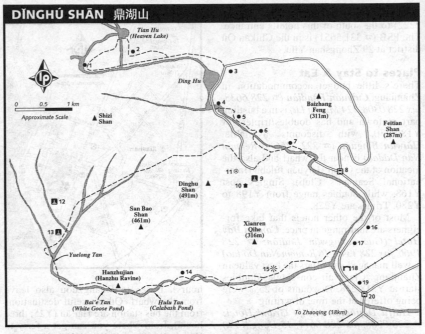

DĪNGHÚ SHĀN 鼎湖山

DĪNGHÚ SHĀN

1 Liántiānzhàndào
   (Cliff-Face Plank Path)
   连天栈道
2 No 1 Hydroelectric
   Station
   水电一站
3 No 2 Hydroelectric
   Station
   水电二站
4 Shuānghóngfēiqiàn
   (Twin Rainbow Bridge)
   双虹飞堑
5 Tīngpù Tíng (Pavilion)
   听瀑亭
6 Sun Yatsen Swimming
   Area
   孙中山游泳处

7 Bànshān Tíng
   (Half Mountain Pavilion)
   半山亭
8 Bus Station
   鼎湖山汽车站
9 Qìngyún Sì
   庆云寺
10 Qìngyún Dùjiàcūn
   庆云渡假村
11 Gǔlóng Quán (Spring)
   古龙泉
12 Báiyún Sì
   (White Cloud Temple)
   白云寺
13 Yuèlóng Ān
   (Leaping Dragon Nunnery)
   跃龙庵

14 Shīhǒu Shí
   (Lion's Roar Rock)
   狮吼石
15 Wànghè Tíng
   (Crane Viewing Pavilion)
   望鹤亭
16 Reserve Office
   树木园
17 Archway
   牌楼
18 Main Gate
   山门
19 Kēngkǒu Store
   坑口商店
20 Kēngkǒu Bus
   Station
   坑口汽车站

the hotels are conveniently close together in the southern part of town.

The Bank of China on Hongwu Lu at the corner with Renmin Nan Dadao changes cash and travellers cheques on the second floor. It's open daily from 8.30 am to 7 pm.

There's a CITS office (☎ 227 0688) north of Guǎngdōngwān Huáqiáo Bīnguǎn (see

Places to Stay later) and a CTS (☎ 222 2222) to the south of this hotel's entrance. The PSB (☎ 331 5651) is in the Chìkǎn Qū district at 29 Zhongshan Yilu.

Places to Stay & Eat

There's little budget accommodation in Zhànjiāng. *Cuìyuán Fàndiàn (☎ 228 6633, fax 228 0308, 124 Minzhi Lu)* is in a bustling part of town and has doubles/triples for Y180/230, with discounts available. *Hǎiwān Bīnguǎn (☎ 222 2266, 6 Renmin Nan Dadao)* is near the wharf and also the location of the Guójì Hǎiyuán Jùlèbù (International Seamen's Club). Singles cost Y168, while doubles range from Y198 to Y280. Triples are Y228.

Most of the other hotels that take foreigners are mid-range in price. *Canton Bay Hotel (Guǎngdōngwān Jiǔdiàn; ☎ 228 1966, fax 228 1347, 16 Renmin Nan Dadao)* is well managed and offers the best value in Zhànjiāng. Clean air-con singles/doubles start at Y218/238. Discounts of 25% were being offered at the time of writing *Hǎifù Dàjiǔdiàn (Haifu Grand Hotel; ☎ 228 0288, fax 228 0614, 15 Dongdi Lu)* tries to masquerade as a fancy hotel, but even the rooms with a view don't make up for the smelly carpets. Doubles are Y220.

There's a number of small restaurants on Renmin Dadao north of the Guǎngdōngwān Huáqiáo Bīnguǎn. Opposite the hotel the *Coffee Language Cafe (Kāfēi Yǔchá)* has some international-style meals and an English menu, as well as Chinese food, and coffee and tea.

Getting There & Away

Air The CAAC office (☎ 338 0439) is at 29 Renmin Dadao Zhonglu, in the northwestern section of the city. Tickets are easily booked at CTS.

Flights from Zhànjiāng go directly to Guǎngzhōu (Y530) and Běijīng (Y2180). Flights to Shànghǎi (Y1630) go via Guǎngzhōu.

Bus The long-distance bus station, southeast of the train station, has services to Guǎngzhōu three times daily (Y120; seven

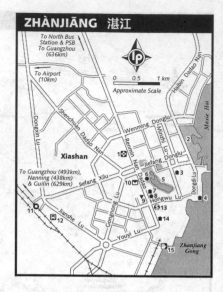

ZHÀNJIĀNG 湛江

hours). Buses to Guǎngzhōu also leave from the wharf. Other useful destinations from the bus station are Hǎi'ān (Y25; three hours), from where you can get a ferry to Hǎinán Dǎo, and Guìlín (Y100; 10 hours).

Air-con Iveco buses travel directly to Hong Kong from the CTS office, daily at 9 am, and arrive in Hong Kong 10 hours later. Tickets are Y340.

Train Trains to Guìlín, Nánníng, Fóshān and Guǎngzhōu leave from the southern train station. Overnight air-con fast trains connect with Guǎngzhōu for Y212 (sleeper) and take 10 hours. From Zhànjiāng to Guìlín takes about 13 hours. As well as at the train station, you can purchase tickets outside the customs building at the ferry terminal. CTS and hotels will also book sleepers for a Y20 service charge. Buses going to the train station meet boat arrivals at Zhànjiāng Gǎng (Zhanjiang Harbour).

Boat There are combination bus-boat tickets to Hǎikǒu on Hǎinán Dǎo on sale at the bus station. However, it is more convenient – and not much more expensive – to take the express boat to Hǎikǒu (Y100; four hours);

ZHÀNJIĀNG

PLACES TO STAY & EAT	OTHER	10 Post Office
3 Cuìyuán Fàndiàn	1 Shopping	邮电局
翠园饭店	Centre	11 Southern Train
4 Hǎifù Dàjiǔdiàn	百货大厦	Station
海富大酒店	2 Hǎibīn	湛江火车站
7 Canton Bay Hotel;	Gōngyuán	12 Long-Distance
Southwest Airlines	海滨公园	(Southern) Bus
广东湾酒店；西南航空	5 Qīngshàonián	Station
9 Coffee Language Cafe	Gōngyuán	汽车客运南站
咖啡语茶	青少年公园	13 Bank of China
14 Hǎiwān Bīnguǎn;	6 CITS	中国银行
Guójì Hǎiyuán Jùlèbù	中国国际旅行社	15 Zhànjiāng Harbour
海湾宾馆;	8 CTS	Passenger Terminal
国际海员俱乐部	中国旅行社	湛江港客运站

tickets are on sale at the harbour. The express boats leave at 9 am and 2.30 pm.

There's also a slow boat that leaves at 9.30 pm and arrives at Hǎikǒu's Xiuying wharf seven hours later. For ticket prices see the Getting There & Away section for Hǎikǒu.

Getting Around

Zhànjiāng's airport is 10km north-east of the city centre. A taxi will cost about Y20.

There are two train stations and two long-distance bus stations, one each in the northern and southern parts of town, but most travellers will only need the southern stations.

Bus No 1 runs between the two districts and bus No 10 travels along Renmin Nan Dadao from the train station. Taxis cost about Y10 for destinations anywhere in the Xiashan area. There are many motorcycles, some with side cars, cruising the streets; Y5 is enough for trips of a couple of kilometres.

Pedicabs also swarm after foreigners – Y10 will get you almost anywhere on one of these (maybe even to Guǎngzhōu).

SHÀNTÓU 汕头

☎ 0754 • pop 4,130,900

Shàntóu is one of China's four original Special Economic Zones (SEZ) along with Shēnzhèn, Zhūhǎi and Xiàmén. It's a little-visited port with a unique culture.

The local dialect is known as *chaoshan* in Mandarin – a combination of Cháozhōu and Shàntóu – or *taejiu* by the people themselves and is the language of many of the Chinese who emigrated to Thailand. The language is completely different from Cantonese. Overseas Chinese from Thailand have started to return, and it's not unusual to see Thai script in hotels and on business signs.

Unfortunately, Shàntóu shows all the signs of an SEZ damp squib, with little to recommend it. Evidence of Shàntóu history is also seriously deficient here (although there are a few pockets of interest), and the city is basically a transit point on the little-travelled haul between Guǎngzhōu and Fújiàn.

History

Shàntóu was previously known to the outside world as Swatow. As early as the 18th century, when the town was little more than a fishing village on a mudflat, the East India Company had a station on an island outside the harbour.

The port was officially opened to foreign trade in 1860 with the Treaty of Tianjin, which ended another Opium War. The British were the first foreigners to establish themselves here, although their projected settlement had to relocate to a nearby island due to local hostility.

Before 1870 foreigners were living and trading in Shàntóu town itself. Many of the old colonial buildings still survive, but in a state of extreme dilapidation.

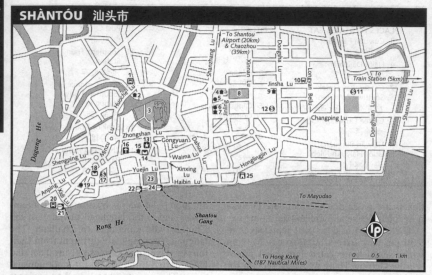

SHÀNTÓU 汕头市

Orientation

Most of Shàntóu lies on a peninsula, bounded in the south by the ocean and separated from the mainland in the west and the north by a river and canals. Most tourist amenities are in the western part of the peninsula.

Information

There are numerous Bank of China branches, but the one at the intersection of Changping Lu and Donxia Lu changes travellers cheques.

The post and telecommunications building on Waima Lu just east of Xīnhuá Jiǔdiàn has Internet services on the 2nd floor. At the time of writing it was about Y20 per hour with the first half hour free.

The CTS office (☎ 862 6646) is located beside Huáqiáo Dàshà. It sells bus, boat and air tickets.

The PSB (☎ 842 3592) is at 60 Gongyuan Lu, north of Waima Lu.

Things to See

There's not much in the way of sights in Shàntóu. However, the roundabout at the point where Shengping Lu and Anping Lu converge is interesting for its colonial remains, and it's worth looking at the architecture while it's still there.

Places to Stay

The cheapest place for foreigners is the one-star *Qiáolián Dàshà* (☎ 825 9109) perched right on the corner of Shanzhang Lu and Changping Lu. There's no English sign. It's basic but clean. Singles/doubles/triples with fan and shared bath are Y48/68/98. These are actually better value than the doubles/triples with air-con and bath for Y160/180. Next door, *Huáqiáo Dàshà* (*Overseas Chinese Hotel;* ☎ 862 9888, fax 825 2223) is a huge rambling place with clean singles for Y172 and doubles for Y160. Rooms with carpets are more expensive, but less attractive.

Xīnhuá Jiǔdiàn (☎ 827 3710, fax 827 1070, 121 Waima Lu) is an older hotel with clean tiled rooms. Doubles range from Y150 to 170 and triples from Y220 to 250. Opposite the bus station, the overpriced *Huálián Jiǔdiàn* (☎ 822 8389, fax 822 7548) has doubles/triples for Y240/290. Even a 30% discount doesn't make this place attractive.

SHÀNTÓU

PLACES TO STAY
2 Huálián Jiǔdiàn
   华联酒店
4 Swatow Peninsula
   Hotel
   鮀岛宾馆
7 Huáqiáo Dàshà;
   Qiáolián Dàshà
   华侨大厦、侨联大厦
9 International Hotel
   国际大酒店
15 Xīnhuá Jiǔdiàn
   新华酒店

OTHER
1 Long-Distance Bus Station
   汽车客货运站
3 Zhōngshān Gōngyuán
   中山公园
5 CAAC
   民航售票处

6 CTS
   中国旅行社
8 Jīnshā Gōngyuán
   金沙公园
10 CAAC Airport Bus
   (New Century Hotel)
   机场办车 (新世纪
   大酒店)
11 Bank of China
   (Main Branch)
   中国银行
12 Bank of China
   中国银行
13 PSB
   公安局
14 Post and
   Telecommunications
   Building
   电信楼
16 Shantou
   Christian Church
   市西堂

17 Bank of China
   中国银行
18 Post Office
   邮电局
19 Xinhua Bookstore
   新华书店
20 Xīdī Bus Station
   西堤客运站
21 Xīdī Passenger Ferry
   西堤客运码头
22 Shàntóu Wharf
   Passenger Terminal
   汕头港客运站
23 Rénmín
   Guǎngchǎng
   人民广场
24 Guǎngchǎng Wharf
   Passenger Terminal
   广场码头
25 Shípào Tái
   (Stone Fort)
   石炮台

The *Swatow Peninsula Hotel (Túodǎo Bīnguǎn;* ☎ *831 6668, fax 825 1013)* on Jinsha Lu is newly renovated with the cheapest rooms starting at Y388. Discounts of 40% were available.

The best top-end hotel is the glitzy *International Hotel (Guójì Dàjiǔdiàn;* ☎ *825 1212, fax 825 2250)* on Jinsha Zhonglu. It also has a western restaurant. Doubles start at Y980, including a buffet breakfast.

Places to Eat

Street markets set up at night on many streets and this is where you'll find the cuisine Shàntóu is famous for. Rice noodles (called *kwetiaw* locally) are also a speciality. Minzu Lu has a number of stalls specialising in delicious *húndùn* (wonton).

For more upmarket cuisine, try the revolving restaurant on the 23rd floor of the International Hotel, which does reasonable western food at an affordable price. You'll also find western fast-food around town.

Getting There & Away

Air Shàntóu airport, about 20km from the city centre, has flights to Bangkok and

Hong Kong (twice daily). Domestic flights are available to Běijīng, Guǎngzhōu, Fúzhōu, Guìlín, Hǎikǒu, Nánjīng, Shànghǎi and other cities.

The CAAC office (☎ 860 4698) is at 46 Shanzhang Lu, a few minutes' walk south of the intersection with Jinsha Lu. CTS is also a convenient place to get air tickets.

Bus Deluxe buses leave from the car park behind the CTS office, heading to Guǎngzhōu (Y180; seven hours), Shēnzhèn (Y150; four hours), Xiàmén (Y100; five hours) and Hong Kong (Y210; five hours). Buses to Hong Kong also leave from the International Hotel. Economy buses to other destinations leave from the main bus station. Frequent minibuses to Cháozhōu (Y12; one hour) leave from the north exit of the station.

Train There are overnight services between Shàntóu and Guǎngzhōu (Y230 hard sleeper; 10 hours) and trains to Cháozhōu, but it's easier to take the bus.

Boat Weekly boats go between Hong Kong and Shàntóu. In Hong Kong, departures are from the China Hong Kong City ferry terminal in Tsimshatsui, Kowloon.

In Shàntóu, departures are from Shàntóu wharf passenger terminal (Shàntóu gǎng kèyùnzhàn; ☎ 827 1513). At the time of writing, boats were leaving every Friday at 5 pm and arriving in Hong Kong at 7 am the next day. Tickets range from Y80 to Y140 for seats and Y190 to Y290 for a cabin shared by four to six people. Two-person VIP cabins are Y575. Tickets are available at the passenger terminal.

Getting Around
To/From the Airport Buses to Shàntóu airport (Y4; 20 minutes) leave from the New Century Hotel at the intersection of Jinsha Lu and Longyan Beilu. A taxi will cost Y40 to Y50.

Bus Nos 2 and 6 make the 10-minute trip along Jinsha Lu to the train station. Motorbikes are plentiful and cost about Y5 a ride.

AROUND SHÀNTÓU
Not far out of the city is **Māyǔ Dǎo** (Mayu Island), which makes a good day trip. A boat leaves from the Guǎngchǎng wharf (Guǎngchǎng mǎtou) at 9.30 am daily and returns at 2.30 pm (Y20 return). Speedboats do the trip in about 15 minutes for Y60 per person.

On an ordinary weekday the boat is filled with people toting bags of food and sacrificial offerings. Follow the crowd from the landing to the **Tiānhòu Miào** (Temple of the Mother of the Heavenly Emperor), built in 1985 with funds supplied by overseas Chinese.

The site has apparently always been holy to this deity, and this is where the fisherfolk burn incense before they leave in the morning. Evidently the island has been developed to keep pace with the worshippers' enthusiasm; there are hotels and restaurants, as well as marked trails for getting around. There are no cars, and the beaches and views are refreshing after the large Chinese cities.

According to the villagers, the island was settled mainly during the Japanese occupation, although there were a few people living here before then.

CHÁOZHŌU 潮州
☎ 0768 • pop 2,362,400
Cháozhōu is an ancient commercial and trading city dating back 1700 years. It is situated on the Hán Jiāng and surrounded by the Jīn Shān (Golden Hills) and Húlu Shān (Calabash Hills). It can be explored in a couple of hours and is best visited as a day trip from Shàntóu.

The chief sight is the **Kāiyuán Sì**, which was built during the Tang dynasty to house a collection of Buddhist scriptures sent here by Emperor Qian Long. This temple was reduced almost to rubble during the Cultural Revolution, but now houses three large buddhas flanked by 18 golden arhats. Noted for its colourful roof ornaments and decorations, this is an active temple and many monks are usually present at prayer.

Cháozhōu's old city wall still runs along next to the Hán Jiāng; preserved sections like the **Guǎngjǐ Mén** (Guangji Gate) area are attractive (this is also an area full of

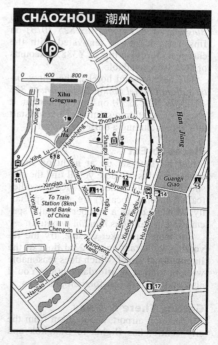

CHÁOZHŌU 潮州
0   400   800 m

CHÁOZHŌU

1 Hánbì Lóu
   (Hanbi Building)
   涵碧楼

2 Xǔfùmǎ Fǔ
   (Prince Xu's Palace)
   许驸马府

3 Zhōngjiéfáng
   (Loyalty Arch)
   忠节坊

4 Jīnshān
   Gǔsōng
   金山古松

5 City Hall
   市政府

6 Bówùguǎn
   博物馆

7 Prime Minister
   Huang's Residence

8 Bank of China
   中国银行

9 West Bus Station
   西汽车站

10 Cháozhōu Bīnguǎn
   潮洲宾馆

11 Kòuchǐ Ān
   (Nunnery)
   叩齿庵

12 Kāiyuán Sì
   开元寺

13 East Bus
   Station
   东门汽车站

14 Passenger Wharf
   客运码头

15 Hánwéngōng Cí
   韩文公祠

16 Huáqiáo Dàshà
   华侨大厦

17 Fènghuáng Tǎ
   凤凰塔

cheap food stalls). The Xī Hú (West Lake) area is also a pleasant place to stroll, particularly in the early morning or evening. The park extends up the hill behind the lake.

It's also pleasant to walk in the area around the Jīnshān Gǔsōng (Jinshan Ancient Pine) at the north end of the city wall. Crossing the river, the Guǎngjǐ Qiáo (Guangji Bridge) was first built in the Song dynasty and was originally joined in the middle by a floating span of boats that could open for barges and other vessels. The present structure dates from 1958, but you can still see remnants of the old bridge. ON the west side of the river, the Hánwén Gōng Cí (Hanwen Temple) commemorates the Tang dynasty poet and philosopher Han Yu, who was exiled to Guǎngdōng for his outspoken views against Buddhism.

South-east of Cháozhōu is the seven-storey **Fènghuáng Tǎ** (Phoenix Pagoda), built in 1585.

Places to Stay

It is worthwhile to stay in Cháozhōu a day or two. The *Cháozhōu Bīnguǎn* (☎ 226 1168, fax 226 4298) is conveniently located opposite the West bus station. Dingy but adequate doubles with bath and air-con are Y270, but bargaining is possible.

Closer to the old part of town, the *Huáqiáo Dàshà (Overseas Chinese Hotel; ☎ 222 8899, fax 222 3123, 34 Huancheng Xilu)* has similar rates plus suites for Y378.

Getting There & Away

Minibuses go to Cháozhōu (Y12; one hour) from Shàntóu's main bus station. Buses leave from Cháozhōu's West bus station to various destinations around Guǎngdōng and Fújiàn.

There are six trains a day to Guǎngzhōu. The train station in Cháozhōu is 8km west of the town centre. Minivan taxis are cheap, starting at Y6 and will cost about Y15 to the train station.

An interesting way to head into Fújiàn is to take a speedboat up the Hán Jiāng to Gāopí (Y50; three hours), then make your way by local bus to Yǒngdìng in Fújiàn via the towns of Dàpǔ and Cháyáng. The route passes through some nice country. Speedboats leave from the wharf opposite the East bus station, but there are no fixed departure times.

Hǎinán Dǎo 海南岛

Hǎinán Dǎo is a large tropical island off the southern coast of China. It was administered by the government of Guǎngdōng until 1988, when it became the province of Hǎinán.

With its acres of beaches in the south, dense vegetation, balmy winds and lilting palm trees, Hǎinán is popular as a winter refuge; unless you wish to spend the Yuletide season cheek-by-jowl with the rest of China in pricey hotels, however, miss the rush and go between March and November when you can expect large discounts on hotel accommodation.

Despite mainly catering to tour groups, Hǎinán still manages to tempt with some of the trappings of an island paradise: golden beaches, the promise of a deep tan and the thud of falling coconuts.

HISTORY

Historically, Hǎinán was a backwater of the Chinese empire, a miserable place of exile and poverty. When Li Deyu, a prime minister of the Tang dynasty, was exiled to Hǎinán he dubbed it 'the gate of hell'. According to historical records, only 18 tourists came to Hǎinán of their own volition during the entire Song, Yuan and Ming dynasties (about 1000 years)! That's about the rate per second during winter nowadays.

Times are changing – the entire island of Hǎinán was established as a Special Economic Zone (SEZ) in 1988 and quickly emerged as an enclave of free-market bedlam operating on the periphery of the law. Despite the once heady economic climate, Hǎikǒu's skyline today is punctuated with the shells of unfinished construction, testament to the fickleness of investors and financial overreaching.

Heavy industry is virtually absent, and some 80% of the island's economy is washed ashore by tourism.

CLIMATE

Hǎinán is the southernmost tip of China (Sānyà, in the south, is roughly on the same

Highlights

Capital: Hǎikǒu
Population: 7.1 million
Area: 34,000 sq km

- Li and Miao minority villages around Tōngzhá – for the intrepid, Chinese-speaking traveller
- Yàlóng Wān, to the east of Sānyà, a 7km-stretch of beautiful sand and sun

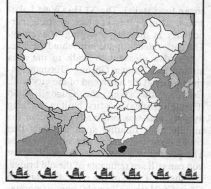

latitude as the southern reaches of Hawaii), and can be relied on to be warm even when the rest of China is freezing.

At the height of China's frigid winter, average temperatures of 21°C (69.8°F) prevail; the yearly average is 25.4°C (77.7°F). From as early as March through to November, the weather becomes hot and humid.

Typhoons can play havoc with a tight itinerary, crippling all transport and communication with the mainland for several days at a time. They usually descend on the island between May and October and there has been at least one every year for the last 50 years.

POPULATION & PEOPLE

Thirty-nine minority groups live on Hǎinán Dǎo, including the original inhabitants of the island, the Li and Miao, who live in the

The Spratly Spat

If it was not such a contentious piece of real estate, very few people would have heard of the Spratly Islands, and their near neighbours the Paracel Islands. To find them on a map, look for a parcel of dots in the South China Sea hemmed in by Malaysia, Brunei, the Philippines, Vietnam and China way to the north. They all claim the islands as their own.

It is tempting to ask what all the fuss is about. After all, this is a collection of 53 specks of land, many of which are reefs and shoals rather than islands. The answer is oil. Not that any oil has been discovered in the region, and some experts dispute that any will ever be found. Yet the very possibility that there might be oil in the Spratly Islands has set all the countries in the region at loggerheads with each other.

China, the most distant of the claimants, sees its territorial rights to the area as being validated by a historical relationship with the islands that dates back to the Han dynasty. The ruins of Chinese temples can still be found on some of the islands. Vietnam has for long been a disputant to this claim, and in 1933 the colonial French government of Vietnam annexed the islands. They lost them to Japan in 1939. With Japan's WWII defeat, the question of the Spratly Islands was left unaddressed. It was not until a Philippine claim in 1956 that the Taiwan-based Kuomintang government reasserted the traditional Chinese claim over the island group by occupying the largest of the islands, Taiping, where they remain. Vietnam followed by hoisting a flag over the westernmost of the islands. The Chinese struck back in 1988 by sinking two Vietnamese ships and forcibly occupying the islands. In 1996, the Philippine navy destroyed a small Chinese-built radar base on Mischief Reef in the Spratlys. But the Chinese refuse to be dislodged and continue to build more permanent structures on Mischief Reef.

With all the countries of the region embarking on programs of updating their military capabilities, the Spratly Islands remain one of the most potentially destabilising issues in the Asian region.

dense tropical forests covering the mountains, Límǔlǐng Shān (Mother of the Li Mountain Range), that stretch down the centre of the island. The Li probably settled on Hǎinán 3000 years ago after migrating from Fújiàn.

Although there has been a long history of rebellion by the Li against the Chinese, they aided the communist guerrillas on the island during the war with the Japanese. Perhaps for this reason the island's centre was made an 'autonomous' region after the communists came to power.

Until recently the Li women had a custom of tattooing their bodies at the age of 12 or 13. Today, almost all Li people except the elderly women wear standard Han dress. However, when a member of the Li dies, traditional Li costume is considered essential if the dead are to be accepted by ancestors in the afterworld.

The Miao (Hmong) people spread from southern China across northern Vietnam, Laos and Thailand. In China they moved south into Hǎinán as a result of the Chinese emigrations from the north, and now occupy some of the most rugged terrain on the island.

The coastal areas of the island are populated by Han Chinese. Since 1949, Chinese from Indonesia, Malaysia and, later, Vietnam have settled here. Hǎinán has a population of around 7.1 million, of which about one million are Li and 60,000 are Miao.

ORIENTATION

Hǎikǒu, the capital of Hǎinán, and Sānyà, a port with popular beaches, are the two major urban centres. They are at opposite ends of the island.

Three highways link the towns: the eastern route via Wànníng (the fastest route); the central route via Túnchāng and Tōngzhá (also known as Tōngshí); and the less popular western route via Dānzhōu (also known as Nàdà), Bāsǔo (Dōngfāng) and Yīnggēhǎi.

HĂINÁN DĂO 海南岛

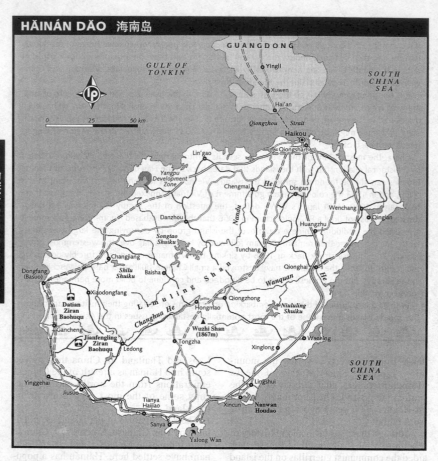

Most visitors to Hǎinán take the eastern freeway route from Hǎikǒu to Sānyà. The freeway may be completed all the way to Bāsǔo by the time you read this. A highway is also planned to replace the road that cuts across the centre of the island.

The central route takes you through the highlands of Hǎinán and past local villages of the Li and Miao minority groups. However, showcase minority villages for tour groups are not the real thing; the genuine articles lie hidden far away from convenient transport links and take a fair amount of effort to reach.

The best mountain scenery on the island is between Sānyà and Qióngzhōng, but there's little of interest beyond that. This route tunnels through what remains of the mountainous forest regions of Hǎinán; the island was the scene of mass deforestation between 1950 and 1980, when up to half of the natural forest cover was felled to make way for rubber plantations.

To get some idea of what the forested regions of Hǎinán Dǎo used to be like, it's worth making a trip to the nature reserve, Jiānfēnglǐng Zìrán Bǎohùqū, which is near the town of Sānyà.

HǍIKǑU 海口
☎ 0898 • pop 514,100

Hǎikǒu, Hǎinán's capital, lies on the northern coastline at the mouth of the river Nándù Jiāng. It's a port town and handles most of the island's commerce with the mainland.

For most travellers, Hǎikǒu is merely a transit point on the way to Sānyà. The city is quite pretty, but there's little to see and accommodation is pricey. Apart from a sprinkling of temples, and decaying colonial charm in the Sino-Portuguese architecture around Xinhua Nanlu, there's not much to keep you from hopping on a bus and heading for the surf and sun in the south.

Orientation
Hǎikǒu is split into three fairly separate sections. The western section is the port area. The centre of Hǎikǒu has all the tourist facilities. The district on the southern side of the former airport is of little interest to travellers.

Information
Money The Bank of China is outside the International Financial Centre at 33 Datong Lu. Moneychangers throng the entrance. The branch opposite the Hǎinán Huáqiáo Dàshà (see Places to Stay) and the one beside the Dōnghú Jiāfēng Dàjiǔdiàn also change travellers cheques.

Post & Communications The post and telecommunications building is south of the long-distance bus station on Daying Lu. Just up from the post office on Nanbao Lu is an Internet cafe. It's open 24 hours a day and charges Y10 per hour. There's another post and telecommunications centre on Jiefang Xilu, near the Xinhua Bookstore. Opposite the telecom on the 2nd floor of the Haikou Worker's Cinema (Gōngrén Yǐngjù Yuàn) there's another Iternet cafe with the same rates.

Travel Agencies The main China Travel Service (CTS; Zhōngguó Lǚxíngshè; ☎ 675 6266, fax 670 6281) is beside the Hǎinán Huáqiáo Dàshà. Some of the staff speak English and are quite helpful. It's worth asking about tours around the island, as these can work out much cheaper than tackling it all yourself. The tour group leader will speak Chinese, unless you are a sizeable group, in which case CTS will supply an interpreter.

There are one- to four-day tours ranging in price from Y400 to Y1780 depending on the duration and what level of comfort you're looking for. The usual package is three days and four nights, taking in Xīnglóng, Sānyà, Tōngzhá and back to Hǎikǒu via the odd minority village. Prices include transport, accommodation and meals (ticket prices for sights not included).

Take the time to shop around if CTS is too pricey. Hǎikǒu is bursting with travel agencies.

PSB The Public Security Bureau (PSB; Gōngānjú; ☎ 626 6587) is at 23 Heping Dadao in the north part of the city. The easiest way to get there is by taxi for Y15.

Things to See
Hǎikǒu is quite a pleasant city, sporting palm-tree-lined boulevards and a picturesque old quarter.

The city's crumbling colonial remains can be absorbed by strolling down Xinhua Lu. Take a couple of detours along Zhongshan Lu and then back to the city centre through the lively market street of Bo'ai Beilu.

The **Wǔgōng Cí** (Five Officials Memorial Temple) is an attractive temple dedicated to five officials who were banished to Hǎinán in earlier times. The famous Song dynasty poet, Su Dongpo, was also banished to Hǎinán and is commemorated here. The temple was first built in the Ming dynasty, restored in the Qing dynasty and is home to a collection of ponds, bridges and palm trees. It can be found at 169 Haifu Dao; take bus No 1 or 11 and get off at the stop after the East bus station. The temple is open from 8 am to 6 pm daily; tickets are Y10.

The **Hǎiruì Mù** (Tomb of Hairui) was mostly torn down during the Cultural Revolution, but has since been repaired. Hairui was a compassionate and popular official who lived in the 16th century; the temple has been fully restored and painted in vibrant colours. The ceiling is particularly attractive. The tomb is in western Hǎikǒu, off Haixiu Dadao; take bus No 2 and watch for the turn off marked by a blue sign in English and Chinese. From there it's a 1km-walk along the road heading south. Entry is Y5.

Hǎikǒu Gōngyuán (Haikou Park) has a Y2 entry charge. It's a pleasant place, except for the small zoo at the south end of the park that houses a sad collection of monkeys and bears.

Places to Stay – Budget

Prices aren't quite as bad in Hǎikǒu as they used to be, but there's not a lot to choose from for budget travellers. The **Wǔhàn Dàshà** (☎ 622 6522) has grubby, cheap singles with fan and shared bathroom for Y40. Doubles/triples are Y90/120 with air-con and bath. Look for the white-tiled building on the east side of the parking lot of the **Xīngǎng** passenger ferry terminal. The reception is on the 2nd floor.

Other budget options are available during the low season when many hotels offer discounts. Down an alley off Gongyuan Lu, the **Hǎidōng Bīnguǎn** (☎ 677 5638) offers a 50% discount for its dismal rooms. Non-discount rates for singles/doubles/triples with air-con and bath are Y158/198/268. Nearby, the **Qiáoyǒu Dàshà** (☎ 676 6852) is more pleasant and has singles for Y100 and doubles with air-con and bath for Y120.

One of the best discount deals is the **Hǎiyáng Dàshà** (Ocean Hotel; ☎ 678 1645, fax 672 4728, 2 Jichang Donglu). Clean singles/doubles with tile floors, air-con and bath are Y120/Y150. The hotel will shave off Y30 during the low season. Down the road, the **Shǔhǎi Jiǔdiàn** (☎ 535 1905, 19 Jichang Donglu) has less appealing doubles with air-con and bath for Y100 and Y150.

Places to Stay – Mid-Range

Most of Hǎikǒu's hotels are middle to top end, but push for discounts (zhékòu) wherever you go; if you avoid the winter months, you can hammer the price down.

The **Hǎinán Huáqiáo Dàshà** (Overseas Chinese Hotel; ☎ 670 8430, fax 677 2094,

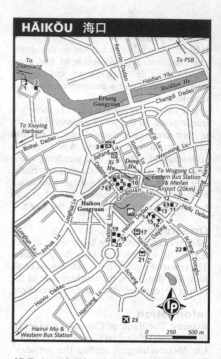

HAIKŎU 海口

17 Datong Lu) is a good mid-range option. Singles are Y248 and Y276, with air-con and bath; standard doubles are Y360. A bit more pricey but very good value is the newly renovated **Hǎinán Mínháng Bīnguǎn** (Hainan Civil Aviation Hotel; ☎ 677 2608, fax 677 2610, 9 Haixiu Dadao). Clean doubles with air-con and bath start at Y488 with 50% discounts in the low season.

Places to Stay – Top End

The **Dōnghú Jiāfēng Dàjiǔdiàn** (East Lake Hotel; ☎ 535 3333, fax 535 8827, 8 Haifu Dadao) has a pool and adequate, if somewhat overpriced, standard doubles for Y550.

Close by, the **Hǎikǒu Bīnguǎn** (☎ 535 0221, fax 535 0232) is a bustling, noisy place that is often fully booked with tour groups. Maybe they come for the dazzling video arcade strategically located off the lobby, which appears to have usurped the once sleazy coffee shop. The cheapest rooms start at Y588.

HǍIKǑU

PLACES TO STAY
2 Wǔhàn Dàshà
  武汉大厦
6 Huáqiáo Dàshà
  华侨大厦
9 Qiáoyǒu Dàshà
  侨友大厦
10 Hǎidōng Bīnguǎn
  海东宾馆
11 Dōnghú Jiāfēng Dàjiǔdiàn
  东湖嘉丰大酒店
13 Hǎikǒu Bīnguǎn
  海口宾馆
15 Hǎiyáng Dàshà; Kuàihuólín
  海洋大厦；快活林
18 Hǎinán Mínháng Bīnguǎn;
  CAAC Ticket Office
  海南民航宾馆
  民航售票处

19 Haikou International
  Financial Centre
  国际金融大厦；
  中国银行
20 Haikou International
  Commercial Centre
  海口国际商业大厦
22 Shǔhǎi Jiǔdiàn
  蜀海酒店

OTHER
1 Xīngǎng Passenger
  Ferry Terminal
  海口新港
3 Xinhua Bookstore
  新华书店
4 Telecom Building
  中国电信
5 Haikou Workers' Cinema
  海口工人影院院

7 Bank of China
  中国银行
8 CTS
  中国旅行社
12 Bank of China
  中国银行
14 Dānyòuxīn
  丹佑仙
16 Ueshima Coffee Shop
  上岛咖啡
17 Long-Distance
  Bus Station
  长途汽车站
21 Post Office;
  Internet
  邮局；网吧
23 Former Hǎikǒu
  Airport
  海口机场

Hǎikǒu's prime location is the *Haikou International Commercial Centre (Hǎikǒu Guójì Shāngyè Dàshà;* ☎ 679 6999, fax 677 4751), a modern structure catering to business travellers that offers a health club, tennis courts, banks, shops and restaurants. Standard rooms start at Y580 and for an extra Y100 you can get a room with a kitchenette. The reception is on the 3rd floor and run by an efficient and friendly staff.

The *Hǎikǒu International Financial Centre (Hǎikǒu Guójì Jīnróng Dàshà;* ☎ 677 3088, fax 677 2113, 29 Datong Lu) is similar to the Commercial Centre next door. Amenities include everything from a swimming pool to a bowling alley. Standard doubles are Y798 but the rooms are a bit cramped. Larger doubles are Y928.

Places to Eat

In response to the phalanxes of tour groups that trundle through Hǎikǒu, most restaurants tend to be hotpot affairs. They can be a lot of fun, but you may feel they are more suited to Mongolia than the tropics. A number of them spill out onto the sidewalk on Jichang Donglu, and at the north end of Xinhua Lu. Many hotpot restaurants feature dog meat and snake, besides the usual ingredients

of *pángxiè* (crab), *mógu* (mushroom), *qīngcài* (cabbage), tofu, sliced pork and lamb, and congealed duck's blood. Expect to pay about Y50 to Y60 for a hearty meal.

A well-known dish from Hǎinán and common in East and Southeast Asia is *wénchāng jī* (succulent chicken raised on a rice diet). Despite the cornucopia of tropical ingredients available in the market, food in Hǎinán isn't much different from the rest of south China. The best places for cheap, delicious meals are the informal establishments at the Xīngǎng passenger ferry terminal.

There are street *fruit sellers* offering bananas, mangoes, sugar cane. Green coconuts, with their tops chopped off and straws poked in, are delicious and plentiful as a refreshing drink for Y2. *Dānyòuxīan*, a small shop on the corner of Jichang and Xiuying Lu, offers a wide variety of freshly squeezed fruit and vegetable juices, as well as snacks.

There's a number of cheap restaurants on Jichang Donglu. *Kuàihuólín* is next door to the *Hǎiyáng Dàshà* (see Places to Stay) on Jichang Donglu. Pick and choose your dishes from the servers wheeling around trolleys for about Y15 per item. Further down Jichang Donglu *Ueshima Coffee Shop (Shàngdǎo Kāfēi)* has good set meals of rice, meat and vegetables for Y30. There's an English menu and, of course, coffee.

Entertainment

Hǎikǒu's wild reputation has been somewhat tamed in the last couple of years. Crime rates are down and prostitution isn't quite as visible as it was before. Karaoke parlours are popular and larger hotels have nightclubs and tacky floor shows. There's a disco beside the Dōnghú Jiāfēng Dàjiǔdiàn (see Places to Stay), near the Bank of China, but for more bizarre fare, check out the small arena on Jichang Donglu adjacent to the Ueshima Coffee Shop, which sometimes has live dance shows.

Getting There & Away

Air The Civil Aviation Administration of China (CAAC; Zhōngguó Mínháng; ☎ 676 3166) is in a large building that also houses the CAAC Hotel on Daying Houlu. Just a few doors down is the China Southwest Airlines office. Between them they have regular flights between Hǎikǒu and many cities including Běijīng, Guǎngzhōu, Hāěrbīn, Kūnmíng, Nánníng, Shànghǎi and Shēnzhèn.

Daily flights travel between Hǎikǒu and Hong Kong (HK$1150) on CAAC and Dragonair; China Southern has flights once a week to Bangkok (Y2060). Dragonair (☎ 677 3088 ext 743) has a representative in Room 201 at the International Financial Centre.

Bus The long-distance bus station has departures to all major destinations on the island, as well as offering combination ferry/bus journeys to many destinations on the mainland; sleeper buses go to Guǎngzhōu (Y157/Y177 without/with air-con; 16 hours) and to Zhànjiāng (Y72; six hours). Sleek air-con buses depart for Sānyà (Y70; three hours), leaving roughly every half hour between 7 am and 6.30 pm. The ordinary bus (Y45) takes five hours.

Buses for the above destinations leave from all three of Hǎikǒu's bus stations. Frequent buses leave from the East bus station for Wénchāng (Y10/Y13 without/with air-con; 1½ hours). Buses to Tōngzhá

(Y30/Y40 without/with air-con; 5½ hours) depart from the West bus station.

Boat Hǎikǒu has two harbours but most departures are from the Xīngǎng passenger ferry terminal (Hǎikǒu Xīngǎng). Minibuses No 218 and 212 got to the harbour from the stop opposite the Hǎikǒu Bīnguǎn. A taxi costs around Y15. Bus No 3 goes to Xiuying harbour.

Ferries depart roughly every 1½ hours from Xīngǎng for the 1½ hour trip to Hǎi'ān on the Léizhōu Peninsula, where there are bus connections to Zhànjiāng (Y30; three hours) and Guǎngzhōu (Y130; 13 hours), though it's easier to take a boat directly to Zhànjiāng.

Tickets for the slow ferry to Zhànjiāng (Y33; seven hours) are sold at the Hǎikǒu harbour passenger ferry ticket office opposite the Dōnghú Jiāfēng Dàjiǔdiàn (see Places to Stay), directly under the pedestrian overpass, or at the Xiuying harbour, where the boat departs from. There are two boats daily, leaving at 9 am and 9 pm. Seat prices range from Y44 to Y123. Alternatively, take one of the fast boat services from Xīngǎng, which leave for Zhànjiāng at 9.30 am and 1.30 pm (Y105; four hours).

Both harbours have an overnight boat for Běihǎi in Guǎngxī departing at 6 pm. Tickets are sold at both harbours and cost between Y58 for a seat and Y153 for a VIP cabin.

Boats leave every two days to Guǎngzhōu from Xiuying harbour and the journey takes 25 hours. Tickets are available from the Hǎikǒu harbour passenger ferry ticket office and at Xiuying starting at Y135 for the bottom class and up to Y303 for a two-person cabin in 2nd class. There's also a daily boat to Shékǒu, the harbour port near Shēnzhèn, which takes 18 hours. Tickets are Y113 for a seat to Y453 for VIP class.

There's no passenger train service on Hǎinán, but it's possible to book tickets originating from Zhànjiāng at the ticket booth inside the Xīngǎng passenger ferry terminal, on your immediate right as you enter. These include useful trains to Guǎngzhōu and Guìlín. On the ground floor of the Wǔhàn Dàshà (see Places to

Stay) another office books tickets originating from Guǎngzhōu.

Getting Around

Hǎikǒu's new Meilan airport opened in May 1999 and is located 25km south-east of the city centre. At the time of writing, transportation services were uncertain, but check with CAAC to see if there is an airport bus. A taxi will cost about Y40.

The central area of Hǎikǒu is small and easy to walk around, but there is also a workable bus system. The fare is Y1 for any destination in the city.

Taxis are reasonably abundant in Hǎikǒu and operate on a meter system. Fares start at Y10 for the first 3km.

WÉNCHĀNG 文昌
☎ 0898

Wénchāng has the distinction of being the homeland of a famous chicken dish and the Soong sisters, Meiling and Qiling, the wives of Chiang Kaishek and Sun Yatsen. For the traveller, however, it's the Dōngjiāo Yēlín and Jiànhuáshān Yēlín coconut plantations, with their cool, inviting pathways, and glorious beaches that make Wénchāng attractive.

Minibuses heading to Gālōngwān depart from the riverside in Wénchāng and pass by the turn off to the harbour Qīnglán Gǎng. It's a five-minute motorbike ride to the harbour, where you can take a ferry and motorbike to the stands of coconut palms and mile after mile of beach. Another way to get to here is to take the direct bus to Dōngjiāo (Y16) from Hǎikǒu's East bus station.

The beaches in this area have been developed as resorts and accommodation prices can be high during the holiday season.

Frequent buses leave for Wénchāng from Hǎikǒu's East bus station between 7 am and 7 pm. Tickets are Y10 and Y13 for air-con.

XĪNGLÓNG 兴隆

Since 1952 more than 20,000 Chinese-Vietnamese and overseas Chinese refugees (mostly from Indonesia or Malaysia) have settled at the Xīnglóng Huáqiáo Cūn (Xinglong Overseas Chinese Farm). Tropical agriculture, rubber and coffee are important cash crops here and Xīnglóng coffee is famous all over China. Many of the residents speak English and may be able to organise transport to Miao villages. The Xīnglóng Rèdài Zhíwùyuán (Xinglong Tropical Botanical Garden) is also worth a visit, located 3km south of the town.

Otherwise, Xīnglóng is fairly unattractive place and the nearby hot spring resort east of town is a good reminder of just how ugly tourist resort developments in China can be. The baths at the hotels are typically swimming pool-sized, open-air and separated into hot and cool, but unless you're in need of such therapy, Xīnglóng is not a place to linger.

From the bus stop to the hotels costs Y3 on the back of a motorbike, or Y5 for a motor-tricycle. Trips out to the farm and botanical garden are a little more.

XĪNCŪN 新村

Xīncūn is populated almost solely by Danjia (Tanha) minority people, who are employed in fishing and pearl cultivation. The main attraction here is Nánwān Hóudǎo (see following), home to a population of Guǎngxī monkeys *(Macaca mulatta)*. It makes a pleasant day trip from Sānyà. Buses travelling the eastern route will drop you off at a fork in the road about 3km from Xīncūn. It should then be easy to get a lift on a passing minibus, or hitch or walk into Xīncūn. Frequent minibuses run to Xīncūn directly from Língshuǐ (15km away) and Sānyà.

NÁNWĀN HÓUDǍO 南湾猴岛
Monkey Island

About a thousand monkeys live on this narrow, hilly peninsula near Xīncūn. The area is under state protection and a special wildlife research centre has been set up to investigate all the monkey business.

The animals are tame and anticipate tourist arrivals for snacks of peanuts. It's all right to feed them (there are bags of peanuts for sale at the park entrance) but don't try to touch the monkeys.

A shack on the beach at the harbour in Xīncūn functions as a booking office selling

Dǎo: island

The unsimplified version of this character is readily identifiable as a bird sitting atop a mountain, with its feet tucked under its body. One can imagine the mountain being partly submerged under water, its peak forming an island in the sea. (The modern character leaves out even more details of the bird.)

return ferry tickets (Y20). The ferry putt-putts from Xīncūn to Nánwān Hóudǎo in 10 minutes, where a bus takes you to the park entrance. Tickets are Y15. Unfortunately, a cable car is under construction that will replace the pleasant ferry ride.

For best contact with the monkeys, visit in the morning or evening, otherwise you might have trouble spotting them in the foliage; occasionally a wild, woolly head pops out of the top branches to see what's happening or to scream at you.

The mating season is a much more active time (from February to May), however, and the monkeys are, shall we say, over-hospitable and you may have to crowbar them off your leg.

SĀNYÀ 三亚

☎ 0899 • pop 440,600

Sānyà's harbour area is protected to the south-east by the hilly Lùhuítóu Peninsula. Except for the harbour area crammed with fishing boats, however, there's not much to see in Sānyà itself. The main reason to come here is for the surrounding beaches.

On the western outskirts of Sānyà there's a community of around 5000 Hui, the only Muslim inhabitants of Hǎinán.

Information

There's a convenient Bank of China in Dàdōnghǎi that changes travellers cheques, and another one in Sānyà near the Phoenix Hotel (see Places to Stay). It's open daily from 8.30 am to 5.30 pm.

The post and telecommunications building is on Xinfeng Lu in Sānyà and there's another one at the east end of Yuya Lu in Dàdōnghǎi. The lobby of the Jíyá Dàjiǔdiàn has Internet services for Y20 per hour, though by the time you read this the China Telecom office may have set up its own terminals.

The Dàdōnghǎi Hǎitān (Dadonghai Beach) area of Sānyà is full of travel agencies. For tickets and information, try the ticketing office (☎ 821 3224) associated with the Yùlìnwān Dùjiàcūn (see Places to Stay) located at Haiyun and Haihua Lu. The Dragon Travel Agency (☎ 821 3526) on Luling Lu can also arrange tickets and tours and may even be able to rustle up a couple of bicycles.

Things to See

The popular beaches are Yàlóng Wān (Asian Dragon Bay), Dàdōnghǎi, the Lùhuítóu Peninsula and Tiānyá Hǎijiǎo. The sun is very intense at this latitude from March onwards and if you intend going to the beach, take high sun-factor lotion; sunburn is common.

The best of the lot is Yàlóng Wān, to the east of Sānyà, a great beach that features a 7km strip of sand (much longer than the longest beach in Hawaii). The views here are excellent and you can roam about for hours.

The crescent-shaped beach at Dàdōnghǎi is around 3km south-east of Sānyà and is easily reached by minibuses Nos 2 and 4 (Y2) that shuttle between Sānyà and the beach. Dàdōnghǎi is a good place to base yourself, but the beach is smaller, more developed and crowded with all the accoutrements of a resort, boat, scuba and snorkelling hire and, of course, trinket-sellers.

The beaches on the Lùhuítóu Peninsula are poor, but they make for pleasant enough walks.

The beach at Tiānyá Hǎijiǎo (literally 'edge of the sky, rim of the sea'), about

24km west of Sānyà, is not bad, but is of great interest to local tourists who crowd around the stone immortalised on the back of the Y2 note to have their photo taken. Entry to the beach is Y37. Catch any minibus (Y2; ¾ hour) heading north along the coast road from the No 2 or 4 terminus.

Places to Stay – Budget

Even though it's been inundated with foreign students studying in China for years, Sānyà hasn't quite yet grasped the idea of budget travel. Most of the hotels in and around Sānyà cater mainly to package tourists. Always try to bargain for a discount.

If you want to keep costs to a minimum in a good location, the best bet is the *Bīnhǎi Dùjiàcūn (Seaside Holiday Inn Resort;* ☎ *821 3898, fax 821 2081)*, in Dàdōnghǎi. Standard doubles are Y320 but come down to Y180 in the low season. Nearby the *Chuānyà Bīnguǎn* (☎ *821 2901, fax 821 3568)* has doubles/triples for Y298/335 and offers 50% discounts. Down the lane opposite the Chuānyà Bīnguǎn in an unlikely looking building, the *Sānyà Qīhuàn Zhāodàisuǒ* (☎ *821 5770)* has small rooms with air-con and shared bath for Y100 and rooms with bath for Y150, but expect this to double during the holiday season. There's no English sign but it's located 20m down the lane.

Places to Stay – Mid Range

A good mid-range option is the *Yùlínwān Dùjiàcūn (Yulin Bay Holiday Resort;* ☎ *821 3698, fax 821 2536)*. Clean singles/doubles go for Y300/Y410, but try bargaining for a 50% discount during the low season.

There are many other hotels in the Dàdōnghǎi area (in fact there is really nothing but hotels in Dàdōnghǎi) with room rates hovering around Y350 for a double. The *South China Hotel (Nánzhōngguó Dàjiǔdiàn;* ☎ *821 3888, fax 821 4005)* is one of the better hotels along with the *Pearl River Garden Hotel (Zhūjiāng Huāyuán Jiǔdiàn;* ☎ *821 1888, 821 1999)*. The South China Hotel has standard doubles starting at Y780 and the Pearl River Garden Hotel is more pricey at Y900.

Finding a hotel in Sānyà itself will bring costs down slightly, but it's not a very pleasant place to stay. The *Sānyà Bīnguǎn* (☎ *827 4819)* is in the centre of town on Jiefang Lu, and has singles/doubles from Y130/Y180 but will give a 30% discount in the high season. In the southern part of town, the *Phoenix Hotel (Jīnfèng Jiǔdiàn;* ☎ *825 2760)* is a decrepit place, but the staff are friendly. Doubles/triples with air-con and bath are Y100/188.

Places to Stay – Top End

There are two five-star international-style resorts, *Gloria (Sānyà Kǎlái Dùjia Jiǔdià;* ☎ *856 8855, fax 856 8533)* and *Resort Horizon (Tiānyù Dùjìa Jiǔdiàn;* ☎ *856 7888, fax 856 7890)* which offer a great escape for those looking for a little high-priced luxury. There's a couple of cheaper places around as well, but Yàlóng is fairly accessible from Sānyà. See later for details on how to get there.

Places to Eat

Sānyà and its environs are swarming with restaurants. In Dàdōnghǎi, the small enterprises are cheap and tasty and seem exclusively run by Sichuanese migrants. Seafood is big, with live wares displayed in basins along the street. There's plenty of fruit for sale, but sharpen your bargaining skills. *Bīngláng* (betel nut) abounds, as it does everywhere in Hǎinán, and is worth trying if you want to walk around with a bright red mouth and a peculiar sensation in your gums. The *Peace Supermarket (Hépíng Chāoshì)* has a good supply of items for self-catering.

By far one of the best restaurants in Dàdōnghǎi is the delicious and reasonable *Dōngběiwáng Jiǔdiàn (King of the Northeast Restaurant)*. It features dishes from north China and great service. There's no English sign or menu, but it's beside the Kodak shop on Yuya Lu.

The *Coconut Restaurant* is up from the Pearl River Garden Hotel and serves western-style meals, including breakfast. Unfortunately it only seems to operate in the high season. The South China Hotel also has a good coffee shop and small bakery.

HAINÁN DǍO 海南岛

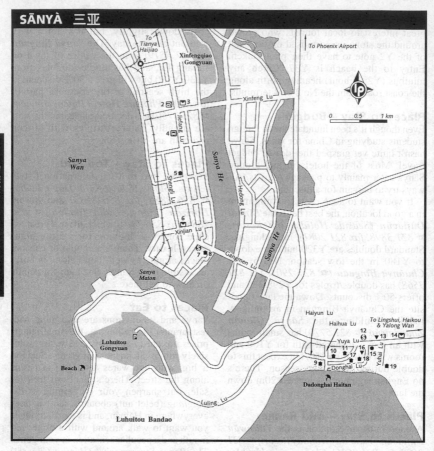

SĀNYÀ 三亚

To Tianya Haijiao

Xinfengqiao Gongyuan

To Phoenix Airport

Xinfeng Lu

Sanya Wan

Sanya He

Jiefang Lu

Shengli Lu

Hedong Lu

Sanya He

Xinjian Lu

Gangmen Lu

Sanya Matou

Luhuitou Gongyuan

Beach

Haiyun Lu

Haihua Lu

To Lingshui, Haikou & Yalong Wan

Yuya Lu

Yuhai Lu

Donghai Lu

Dadonghai Haitan

Luling Lu

Luhuitou Bandao

0   0.5   1 km

Shopping

Southern Hǎinán is famous for its cultured pearls, but watch out for fakes. Tourists have been known to pay 100 times the going price for authentic-looking plastic. Other knick knacks and souvenirs fill the shops in Dàdōnghǎi and, for some peculiar reason, they are snapped up by local tourists.

Getting There & Away

Phoenix airport is open for domestic flights including Shēnzhèn (Y710), Guǎngzhōu (Y640), Běijīng (Y1850) and Shànghǎi (Y1510).

Dàdōnghǎi is full of travel agencies and the major hotels can also book plane tickets.

From Sānyà bus station there are frequent buses and minibuses to most parts of Hǎinán. Deluxe buses to Hǎikǒu (Y70; three hours) depart frequently and you can also wave them down on Yuya Lu in Dàdōnghǎi. Buses to Tōngzhá leave roughly every 2½ hours (Y12; 2½ hours) and there are three departures daily for Qióngzhōng (Y23; five hours).

There are no direct minibuses to Yàlóng Wān. Hail any minibus heading east and see if it goes to Tiándú. From there, hire a motorcycle sidecar for Y10 out to Yàlóng.

SĀNYÀ

PLACES TO STAY

5 Sānyà Bīnguǎn
三亚宾馆

8 Phoenix Hotel
金凤酒店

9 Yúlínwān Dùjiàcūn
榆林湾度假村

10 Bīnhǎi Dùjiàcūn
滨海度假村

11 Chuānyà Bīnguǎn
川亚宾馆

17 Sānyà Qīhuán
Zhāodàisuǒ
三亚七环招待所

18 Pearl River
Garden Hotel
珠江花园酒店

19 South China Hotel
南中国大酒店

PLACES TO EAT

13 Dōngběiwáng
Jiǔdiàn
东北王酒店

16 Coconut
Restaurant
川菜馆

OTHER

1 Train Station
火车站

2 Internet at
Jíyà Hotel
(网吧)吉亚大酒店

3 Post &
Telecommunications
Office
邮电局

4 Sānyà Bus Station
三亚汽车站

6 Post & Telephone Office
邮电局

7 Bank of China
中国银行

12 Bank of China
中国银行

14 Post Office
邮电局

15 Peace
Supermarket
和平超市

The railway line is used for hauling freight and does not have a passenger service. There are currently no boat services operating from Sānyà; all boat services operate from Hǎikǒu.

Getting Around

The airport is 18km north of Sānyà and the only way there is by taxi. Expect to pay about Y50.

Motorcycle sidecars cruise the streets all day. The real fare is usually half the asking price (Y5 to most places).

Given that Sānyà's attractions are so widely spread out, it is worth getting together with a few people and hiring a vehicle and driver. The minibuses down by the long-distance bus station charge Y200 for a full day, six-destination excursion.

AROUND SĀNYÀ

Two islands, **Xīmaò Zhoū** and **Dōngmaò Zhoū** are visible off the Sānyà coastline. Only Xīmaò Zhoū is open to visitors. At 2.6 sq km, it's fairly small, but you can hike around or go snorkelling. The Peace Supermarket in Dàdōnghǎi hires out a boat for Y280 return and the trip takes about two hours. Speedboats from the beach take 30 minutes, but are very expensive. A small homestay on the island offers basic accommodation for Y80 per night.

The **Jiānfēnglǐng Zìrán Bǎohùqū** (Jianfengling Nature Reserve) is 115km from Sānyà. This lush area is located high above the humidity of the coastal plain and is home to many different species of plants and insects. To really get a feel for the place, it's best to stay overnight and spend the day walking in the reserve and surrounding area. The *Tiānchí Shānzhuāng* has basic accommodation in folksy huts in the middle of the man-made lake for Y80 with bath. Nestled up in the hill west of the lake, the other *Tiānchí Bìshǔ Shānzhuāng* (☎ 572 0162) has pristine rooms for Y120 and Y180.

Getting to Jiānfēng by public transport is a little tiresome. Buses going to Bāsuǒ from the Sānyà bus station will drop you off at the turn-off (there's an English sign). Tickets are Y15, or Y25 for air-con. From the turn-off it's a rough 10km-ride by motorcycle sidecar (Y10) or a public mini-truck (Y1) to the town of Jiānfēng, 16km from the reserve. From there a public bus leaves in mid-morning (Y5) to go up the horrendous road to the mountain. Unfortunately, if you miss the bus you'll have to hire a vehicle for about Y70.

TŌNGZHÁ
☎ 0899

Tōngzhá, also known as Tōngshí, is the capital of the Li and Miao Autonomous Prefecture. It's a pleasant place, somewhat

HĂINÁN DĂO 海南岛

cooler than the humid coast, with a lively market on Jiefang Lu, an impressive-looking university and a museum with exhibits of Li and Miao artefacts. For intrepid travellers, it's a good place to start for trips further into the highlands to seek out real Li and Miao villages.

For hikes around Tōngzhá, head out to the north-east past the Tōngzhá Lǚyoú Shānzhuāng (Tōngzhá Resort Hotel), at the head of Shanzhuang Lu, or start climbing some of the hills behind the university above the bus station.

There's a Bank of China near the intersection of Jiefang Lu and Xinhua Lu and the post office is just across the main bridge, on the north-east side of the river.

Places to Stay

There are a few hotels in Tōngzhá. One of the cheapest that accepts foreigners is the *Tōngzhá Mínzú Bīnguǎn* (☎ 662 3082, fax 662 2870), perched on the hill near the museum and above the bus station. It's a nice setting, and doubles/triples with bath and fan are Y55/Y65. Doubles/triples with aircon are Y100/Y150. It also has an outdoor hotpot restaurant off the parking lot, which overlooks the town.

On the the north-east fringe of town, the *Tōngzhá Lǚyoú Shānzhuāng* (Tongza Resort Hotel; ☎ 662 3188, fax 662 2201) is more upmarket and very pleasant. Doubles start at Y388 and rooms with rattan furniture and verandas start at Y488. Discounts of 50% are available.

Getting There & Away

Minibuses depart regularly from the Sānyà bus station (Y12; 2½ hours). Frequent buses travel on to Qióngzhōng (Y11; two hours) and Hǎikǒu (Y30; 5½ hours) from Tōngzhá. Air-con buses to Hǎikǒu travel a bit quicker and cost Y40.

To head deep into the highlands, catch the bus to Báishā (Y13; three hours), 94km north-west of Tōngzhá.

AROUND TŌNGZHÁ

Near Tōngzhá, at 1867m, is **Wǔzhǐ Shān** (Five Fingers Mountain), Hǎinán's highest mountain. Climbing the mountain takes about three to four hours, but it's a bit of a scramble. It's possible to stay at the bottom at the *Wǔzhǐshān Bīnguǎn*. Rooms cost between Y100 and Y200, depending on demand.

Buses leave at 10 am and 2 pm from the parking lot opposite the entrance to the main bridge on the north-east side of the river in Tōngzhá. Tickets are Y4 to the town of Wǔzhǐ Shān, 60km north-east of Tōngzhá. From there it's another 5km to the base of the mountain by motorcycle (Y10).

QIÓNGZHŌNG 琼中
☎ 0898

The route between Tōngzhá and Qióngzhōng passes through forested hills and small villages. It's worthwhile starting off early in the day and getting off the bus at one of the villages, such as Hóng-máozhèn, taking a look around, then catching the next bus going through. Qióngzhōng is a small, rather ugly hill town but the surrounding countryside is beautiful. The nearby waterfall at Báihuā Shān drops more than 300m and is about 7km from town. Motorcycles go up for about Y15, and it's a nice walk back.

In Qióngzhōng, there are two hotels on the main street on either side of the bus station. The *Jiāotōng Dàshà* (Traffic Building; ☎ 622 2615) has singles/doubles with fan and shared bath for Y40/Y60. Standard doubles with bath are Y80 and with air-con are Y120. A few stores down to the west, the *Hòngxiāo Dàshà* (☎ 622 1446) has similar rates.

Besides the road through the central highlands linking Qióngzhōng and Hǎikǒu to the north, and Tongza and Sānyà to the south, you can also take a bus to the coast to Xīnglóng (Y11; two hours) and hook up to the coastal freeway.

Guǎngxī 广西

Guǎngxī's best-known attraction is Guìlín, perhaps the most eulogised of all Chinese sightseeing areas. While most travellers spend some time in the nearby town of Yángshuò, few make it to other parts of Guǎngxī. Yet rich minority regions, some accessible only by water, border Guìzhōu in the north, and there are less touristed rock paintings on the Zuǒ Jiāng (Left River), not far from Nánníng. Guǎngxī also has an easily accessible border crossing with Vietnam near the town of Píngxiáng.

Guǎngxī first came under Chinese sovereignty when a Qin dynasty army was sent southwards in 214 BC to conquer what is now Guǎngdōng and eastern Guǎngxī; two earlier attempts by Emperor Qin Shi Huang had wrested little effective control from the Zhuàng people.

The situation was complicated in the northern regions by the Yao (Mien) and Miao (Hmong) people, who had been driven there from their homelands in Húnán and Jiāngxī by the advance of the Han Chinese settlers. Unlike the Zhuàng, who easily assimilated Chinese customs, the Yao and Miao remained in the hill regions, often cruelly oppressed by the Han. There was continuous conflict with the tribes, with uprisings in the 1830s and again during the Taiping Rebellion, which began in Guǎngxī.

Today the Zhuàng are China's largest minority, with well over 15 million people (according to a 1990 census) concentrated in Guǎngxī. Although they are virtually indistinguishable from the Han Chinese (the last outward vestige of their original identity being their linguistic links with the Thai people), in 1955 Guǎngxī Province was reconstituted as the Guǎngxī Zhuàng Autonomous Region. Besides the Zhuàng, Miao and Yao minorities, Guǎngxī is home to smaller numbers of Dong, Maonan, Mulao, Jing (Vietnamese Gin) and Yi peoples. Until recently, more than 75% of Guǎngxī's population was non-Han.

Highlights

Capital: Nánníng
Population: 45.9 million
Area: 236,300 sq km

- Yángshuò, a backpackers' mecca, famed for its gorgeous scenery and laid-back rural atmosphere
- Guìlín, overrated and pricey, but still one of China's most attractive cities
- Lóngshèng/Sānjiāng, mountain towns and gateways to many minority villages, spectacularly terraced fields and beautiful scenery
- Běihǎi, a sleepy seaside town boasting white-sand beaches

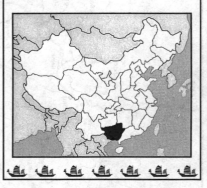

China's first canal was built in Guǎngxī after the emperor gained a foothold in the Qin dynasty. However, the scattered Han had little ability to use the canal to much economic advantage and the province remained comparatively poor until the 20th century. The first attempts at modernising Guǎngxī were made during 1926–27 when the 'Guǎngxī Clique', who were the main opposition to Chiang Kaishek within the Kuomintang, controlled much of Guǎngdōng, Húnán, Guǎngxī and Húběi. After the outbreak of war with Japan, the

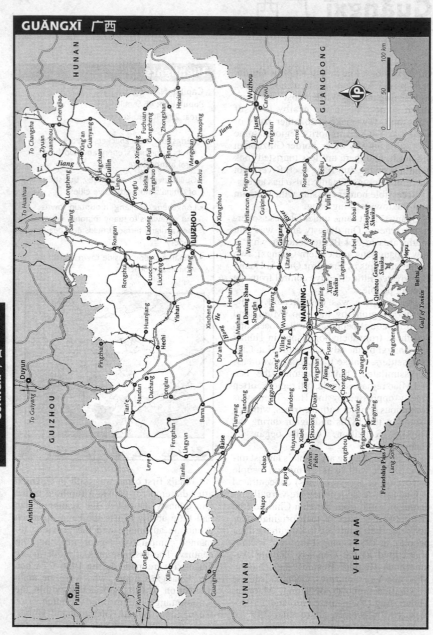

GUǍNGXĪ 广西

province was the scene of major battles and substantial destruction.

Guǎngxī remains one of China's less affluent provinces, although you might not realise this if you only visit the major centres of Nánníng, Liǔzhōu, Wúzhōu and Guìlín.

NÁNNÍNG 南宁

☎ 0771 • pop 2,812,000

Nánníng is one of those provincial centres that provide an insight into just how fast this once-backwater region of China is developing, the neon of new affluence leaping out at the visitor from every store front. It doesn't have a plethora of sights, but it's a worthwhile day-walk.

A mere market town at the turn of the century, Nánníng has grown to become the capital of Guǎngxī. Apart from the urban expansion that the post-1949 railway induced in the south-west, Nánníng became an important staging post for shipping arms to Vietnam in the 1960s and 1970s. It's now reprising that role, this time in the thriving border trade that has sprung from Běijīng's increasingly friendly ties with Hanoi.

The railway line to the border town of Píngxiáng was built in 1952, and was extended to Hanoi, giving Vietnam a lifeline to China. The link was cut in 1979 with the Chinese invasion of Vietnam; today the line is open again. Nánníng is an oft-ignored transit point for travellers moving on to Vietnam; you can even arrange a Vietnam visa here. With the appropriate paperwork, you can travel to Hanoi by train once again. Since the opening of the Nánkūn Railway in 1998, more visitors are circumventing Guìlín on the congested Kūnmíng-Yángshuò route.

Despite the region's rich patchwork of 30 minorities, the only colourful minorities you're likely to encounter in town are the occasional Miao and Dong people selling silver bracelets and earrings on the pedestrian overpasses near the train station.

Orientation

Nánníng city maps are available at shops and stalls near the train and long-distance

bus stations; better ones will have a provincial map on the back and colour-coded bus lines. At the time of writing there were no English-language maps available.

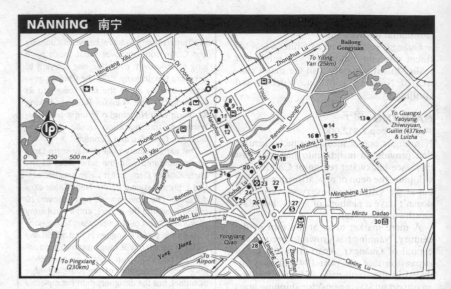

NÁNNÍNG 南宁

GUĂNGXĪ 广西

Information

Money The Bank of China is on Minzu Dadao, just east of the intersection with Chaoyang Lu. Hours are 8.30 am to noon and 3 to 5.30 pm weekdays, though summer hours fluctuate. Bus No 6 runs along Minzu Dadao from Chaoyang Lu.

Post & Communications A post office is close to the train station but you can't make international calls from here. It's open from 8.30 am to 8 pm daily. The main post office is on Minzu Dadao, east of the Bank of China.

Travel Agent The China International Travel Service (CITS; Zhōngguó Guójì Lǚxíngshè; ☎ 281 6197) is at 40 Xinmin Lu, across from the Jinyue and Xiángyún hotels. The Family and Individual Traveller (FIT) department here has English-speaking staff who can help you get the formerly elusive Vietnam visa (Y760 for a one month visa for many nationalities, a staggering sum). It takes 10 (yes, 10!) working days.

FIT also offers individual group tours throughout Vietnam but for the moment these are for Chinese travellers only. The office is open from 8.30 am to noon and from 3 to 5 pm, Monday to Friday.

Bookshops There is a foreign-languages bookshop near the corner of Renmin Donglu and Minzhu Lu, hidden amid CD and VCD shops on the 3rd floor.

PSB The regional Foreign Affairs office of the Public Security Bureau (PSB; Gōngānjú; ☎ 383 4606) is at 37 Hengyang Xilu, one large block north of the train station along Di Donglu, then west a similar distance.

Guǎngxī Shěng Bówùguǎn 广西省博物馆

Guangxi Provincial Museum

Down on Minzu Dadao, the provincial museum offers a peaceful browse through 50,000 years of Guǎngxī history up to the opium wars. There's a good deal of minority costumes and artefacts, including the world's largest bronze drum collection (not much is actually displayed). To get there, take bus No 6, which runs along Chaoyang Lu from the train station. Opening hours are from 8.30 to 11.30 am and 2.30 to 5.30 pm daily; admission is Y3.

NÁNNÍNG

PLACES TO STAY

5 Tiědaò Fàndiàn
韩文公祠

7 Yíngbīn Fàndiàn
迎宾饭店

8 Yínhé Dàjiŭdiàn
银河大酒店

11 Tiānhú Jiŭdiàn
天湖饭店

12 Fènghuáng Bīnguăn
凤凰宾馆

15 Majestic Hotel
明圆饭店

16 Xiángyún Dàjiŭdiàn;
Jinyue Hotel
翔云大酒店

PLACES TO EAT

18 Mayflower Restaurant
美丽花饭店

22 Xiaŏdúlái Shìjiè
南宁饭店

25 Qīngzhēn Fàndiàn
清真饭店

OTHER

1 PSB
公安局

2 Train Station
火车站

3 Bus Passenger Service
Centre
公路客运中心

4 Post Office
邮局

6 City No 2 Bus Station
市第二公路客运站

9 CAAC
中国民航

10 Long-Distance
Bus Station
南宁汽车站

13 Exhibition Hall
展览馆

14 CITS
中国国际旅行社

17 Foreign Languages
Bookstore
外文书店

19 Chaóyáng
Guăngchăng
朝阳广场

20 Electronics Store
(Friendship Store)
南宁友谊商店

21 Nightmarket Area
夜市

23 Nanning Department
Store
南宁百货大楼

24 Xinhua Bookstore
新华书店

26 Bicycle Hire
出租单车

27 Bank of China
中国银行

28 Dock (Tour Boat)
客运码头

29 Main Post Office
电信大楼

30 Guăngxī Shěng
Bówùguăn
广西省博物馆

Báilóng Gōngyuán 白龙公园
White Dragon Park

Also known as Rénmín Gōngyuán (People's Park), this park is pleasant enough for a stroll and has a lake, a couple of pagodas, a viewing platform for the surrounding area, a restaurant and boat hire. Entrance to the park is Y2, and it's open until 10.30 pm daily.

Qīngxiùshān Fēngjĭngqū
清秀山风景区
Beautiful Green Hill Scenic Area

South-east of the city centre is this largish 'scenic area' of lakes and ponds, pavilions, cable cars, viewing platforms, and lots of tour groups. Bus No 10 goes to the main gate and a tour bus (Y3) leaves from the Renmin Donglu side of Chaóyáng Guăng-chăng (Chaoyang Square) at 7.10 am.

Guăngxī Yàoyòng Zhíwùyuán
广西药用植物园
Guangxi Medicinal Herb Botanical Garden

Far on the eastern outskirts of town, this fascinating garden is the largest of its kind in China, with over 2400 species of medicinal plant – and more being planted all the time (Guăngxī alone has 5000 species). If you're lucky enough to tag along with one of the centre's few English speakers, or you can read Chinese, you'll be amazed. Admission is Y5. To get there, take bus No 7 from the train station all the way to its terminus, then walk along the road north-east another 15 minutes or so.

Organised Tours

The *Star Island* departs at 9.30 am from a pier off Linjiang Lu, south of the Yōngjiāng Qiáo (Yong River Bridge), and occasionally at 9.30 pm for two-hour river tours (Y25). The pier is at the head of a lovely new river walk with river-view tea houses and an excellent 500m-long mural depicting Guăngxī's history and attractions.

Places to Stay – Budget

Most cheap stand-bys are renovating themselves out of backpacker status, but the options left are quite good.

GUĂNGXĪ 广西

Top choice is the well-run, friendly *Tiědaò Fàndiàn (Railway Hotel;* ☎ *243 8600, fax 242 2572, 84 Zhonghua Lu)*, just west of the train station along Zhonghua Lu. Beds start at Y25; a bed in a spiffy double with private bath is worth the Y45 price.

Opposite the train station is the *Yíngbīn Fàndiàn* (☎ *282 8223)*, which has no English sign. This longtime stand-by has raised its prices, with beds in decent rooms – take a peek at several – from around Y40; the Y16 dorm beds will likely be unavailable.

The *Fènghuáng Bīnguǎn (Phoenix Hotel;* ☎ *283 2400, 63 Chaoyang Lu)* sits forlornly up the road and is best used as a last resort. A dank single or double with bathroom and satellite TV starts at Y80. The hotel has a gym open to the public.

Places to Stay – Mid-Range & Top End

There are many options available for Y150 and up, though most are not even remotely close to a bargain. In the train station area the *Yínhé Dàjiǔdiàn (Milky Way Hotel;* ☎ *242 8223, fax 242 0303, 84 Chaoyang Lu)* has somewhat threadbare doubles/triples for Y150/180 (likely booked out) and, what you'll be shown, OK rooms for nearly twice that much. The *Tiānhú Jiǔdiàn* (☎ *243 8423, fax 243 3398, 3 Hangzhou Lu)* nearby has doubles with air-con and satellite TV from Y280. There is a disco on the 4th floor.

Less conveniently located, the three-star *Xiángyún Dàjiǔdiàn* (☎ *282 2888, fax 283 3106, 59 Xinmin Lu)* has singles/doubles/triples starting at Y320/380/520. All are clean and good; this hotel has offered steep discounts. Next to the Xiángyún is the *Jinyue Hotel* (☎ *280 2338, fax 283 3106, 59 Xinmin Lu)*, with slightly lower-quality rooms, though not lower prices. Multi-person rooms – uncommon in a three-star hotel – might be a draw here.

Forget about the *Majestic Hotel (Míngyuán Xīndù Fàndiàn;* ☎ *283 0808, fax 283 0811, 39 Xinmin Lu)*, across the road from the Xiángyún Dàjiǔdiàn, unless you're set to bleed cash. This five-star monster has rooms starting at Y858 and topping out at a cool Y11,880.

Places to Eat

Nánníng, like Guìlín and Liǔzhōu, is famous for its *gǒuròu huǒguō* (dog hotpot). The *canine cuisine district* (just over the stream Cháoyáng Xī, south of Chaoyang Lu) teems nightly with stalls serving dog-flavoured dishes. The most raucous *food* street, rife with open-air stalls serving cuisine other than dog, is probably Zhongshan Lu.

For some excellent food and cheap beer try the *Qīngzhēn Fàndiàn (Muslim Restaurant)*. It has a limited English menu, and the staff are friendly.

A great new eatery is the wildly popular *Mayflower Restaurant (Měilìhuā Fàndiàn)*, run by a gregarious Taiwanese-American. The specialities are Taiwanese hotpot – cast-iron griddle with a cauldron of broth in the centre – and Taipei hamburgers, a burger topped with a fried egg.

Nánníng's best culinary experience is *Xiǎodúlái Shìjiè*, run by and located 100m east of the Nánníng Hotel (look for the elephant statue outside). This cacophonous, multi-tiered place serves every conceivable variety of Chinese cuisine. Be careful – this point-and-serve place is fairly cheap dish by dish (around Y5 per), but it's easy to get caught up in the feeding frenzy and things add up.

Getting There & Away

Air Domestic airlines fly daily from Nánníng's spanking-new Wuxi airport to Guǎngzhōu (Y580), Shànghǎi (Y1330), Shēnzhèn (Y710), Kūnmíng (Y500), Wǔhàn (Y870), Guìyáng (Y380), Zhūhǎi (Y550), Chéngdū (Y710), Guìlín (Y460), Hǎikǒu (Y490) and Běijīng (Y1640). There are also flights to Hong Kong (Y980) on Tuesday, Friday and Sunday and Hanoi (Y810; leaving Monday and Thursday). A charter flight leaves on Thursday to Bangkok.

The efficient Civil Aviation Administration of China (CAAC; Zhōngguó Mínháng; ☎ 243 1459) is at 82 Chaoyang Lu and is open daily from 8.30 am to noon and from 2.30 to 5 pm.

Bus Nánníng has three bus stations. The main long-distance bus station is south of the train station along Chaoyang Lu; everything you need should be here. However, you may be dropped off at stations along Zhonghua Lu or Youai Lu.

The main long-distance bus station now has many super luxury Korean buses whipping along provincial routes. Expresses leave for Guìlín at 8 and 9.30 am and 3.30 pm (Y78; five hours); regular sleepers cost Y33 and take six hours. Wúzhōu expresses (Y80; seven hours) leave at 8.50 am and 10 and 11 pm, regular buses (Y51) leave between 7.10 am and 9 pm. Expresses to Běihǎi (Y45; 3½ hours) leave six times between 8.30 am and 3.30 pm; regular and sleeper buses (Y25) leave every ½ hour and take pretty much forever. Expresses also leave hourly to Liǔzhōu (Y50; 3½ hours) and twice daily to Píngxiáng (Y45; 4½ hours). Expresses leave twice daily for Guìpíng (Y45; four hours).

Sleepers to Guǎngzhōu are Y105 and take 15 to 20 hours. A rigorous option is the sleeper berth bus service to Yúnnán's capital of Kūnmíng via Guǎngnán. Tickets are around Y175. Sleeper buses leave to Guǎngnán, just over the Guǎngxī-Yúnnán border. The roads are being rebuilt but are still bad and the whole journey can take up to 36 hours, although some have made it in 28.

Train Trains bound for Běijīng (Y497, hard-sleeper; 31 hours) allow for connections with Chángshā, Guìlín, Liǔzhōu, Wǔhàn and Zhèngzhōu. Other major destinations with direct rail links with Nánníng are Guǎngzhōu, Xī'ān and, finally as of 1998, Kūnmíng. You can also get to Hanoi now.

Direct trains run to Zhànjiāng, a coastal town in Guǎngdōng with ferry connections to Hǎinán Dǎo. The 9.25 am No 602 train is the fastest (Y55; eight hours).

Direct trains from Nánníng to Guìlín take six to seven hours and cost Y63 for a hard seat. Most direct trains also pass through Liǔzhōu. There are trains of all sorts to Liǔzhōu throughout the day. Hard-seat tickets for the four-hour trip cost Y20 to Y39, depending on the class (and speed).

To Kūnmíng, the new Nánkūn train, No 501, departs Nánníng (Y120, hard sleeper; 19 hours) at 5.51 pm. You can also break

this trip up in Xīngyì, but the train arrives at 4 am! The No 615 train departs Nánníng for Xīngyì (Y53); at 7.18 am, takes 11 hours and costs Y53.

There are two trains daily for Píngxiáng. The faster one (Y15) leaves at 8 am and arrives at 12.10 pm. The slower train takes all day. Another alternative for travel to Vietnam is the international K5 train, which departs Běijīng's west station every Monday and Friday, arrives in Nánníng the following day, and then Hanoi the third day; this alternative, however, involves train switches and much waiting.

Two trains leave daily for Běihǎi (Y20; four hours) at 5.52 am and 9.10 am; the latter also train has soft seats for Y33.

Getting Around

An airport bus (Y10) departs regularly from the CAAC office on Chaoyang Lu; it takes an hour. Oddly, bus No 301 also makes this enormous run of 30km.

Taxi rides usually start at Y10, the motorcycle taxis around Y5. A bicycle-hire place can be found along Chaoyang Lu, north of the Yōngjiāng Qiáo; rentals are available from 7 am to 11 pm for Y0.60 per hour.

AROUND NÁNNÍNG
Yīlǐng Yán & Wǔmíng
伊岭岩与武鸣

Yīlǐng Yán, a group of caves with stalagmites and galactic lights, is 25km to the north-west of Nánníng. About 15 minutes is enough for the caves themselves, but the surrounding countryside is worth exploring.

Wǔmíng is 45km from Nánníng, on the same road that leads to Yīlǐng Yán. A few kilometres further up is **Lingshui Springs**, which is a big swimming pool.

Buses depart for from the bus station along Youai Lu. Minibuses to Yīlǐng Yán are seasonal and sporadic. They leave from Chaóyáng Guǎngchǎng, where Chaoyang Lu and Renmin Lu intersect.

Dàmíng Shān
Great Shining Mountain
Some 80km north-east of Nánníng is Dàmíng Shān, an impressive mountain that

most Nánníng residents consider their summer getaway spot, escaping the heat at an average elevation of over 1200m. Its flora and fauna are diverse enough for it to form a provincially protected zone. Tour buses leave for Dàmìng Shān at 10 am from the bus stop 300m east of Chaóyáng Guăngchăng along Renmin Donglu.

Détīan Pùbù
Detian Waterfall
Guăngxī tourist powers-that-be like to rattle off the superlative: Détīan Pùbù is the world's second-largest transnational cataract. While anyone who's seen Niagara Falls may snicker at this, Détīan is still an arresting sight.

Located at the 53rd boundary marker between China and Vietnam, the waterfall is only 40m high but makes up for it by a more than modest breadth. The best time to visit is July, and water levels will be fairly high from May to late August. Show up in November or December and be thoroughly underwhelmed. Admission is Y10.

There is a new *guesthouse* with a restaurant on a rise above the falls, and it does have a great view. Beds are Y90 for a clean single/double/triple.

Getting There & Away If you're coming from Nánníng, or even from Píngxiáng, you'll probably have to first get to Dàxīn and arrange transport there. Dàxīn has a handful of good, cheap hotels. From Dàxīn, there are infrequent minibuses from a travel agency on the left as you come out of the bus station, but these are usually only on Saturday morning, if at all. Quicker is to hop on a bus to Xiàléi and get off in Shùolóng; the 47km ride costs Y6 and takes 1½ hours. Here rattletrap minibuses run the final lovely 14km for Y2. If you do wish to leave in the evening, you can never really be sure when buses to/from Shùolóng stop running.

From Shùolóng you stand by the road and wait for a bus to pass. There is a semi-regular service toward Dàxīn and thus Nánníng, but if you want to go toward Jìngxī, the best thing to do is leapfrog villages. First take a Y2 minibus to Xiàléi, and then another

Y2 minibus to Húyuān (pronounced *fuyuan* here), from where you can get a proper bus for the hour-long ride to Jìngxī. All told, from the minute you get on the minibus in Shùolóng, it should take around two hours though three isn't unheard of. South of Jìngxī is the Jiuzhou Pagoda and the friendly town has a few cheap places to stay.

From Jìngxī, take one of many buses to Bǎisè, the largest city in north-west Guăngxī; it has one good museum detailing a communist uprising and one of south-west China's largest man-made lakes. From Bǎisè it's easy to head into Guìzhōu via Xīngyì or Kūnmíng.

Lónghú Shān
Dragon Tiger Mountain
Located approximately 65km west of Nánníng, north of the road to Dàxīn and Détīan Pùbù, this mountain could make for an interesting stop-off on the way to Détīan Pùbù. Of course no public transport goes directly there. You could theoretically hop off in the tiny village of Píngshān and arrange local transport. From late spring to late summer there have been occasional minibus tours departing from the Chaóyáng Guăngchăng Saturday and Sunday at 8.30 am (Y30) and returning around 4.30 pm.

Guìpíng 桂平 & Jīntiáncūn 金田村
☎ 0775
Midway between Nánníng and Wúzhōu is this smallish, friendly town known for its mountains and its famed Xīshān tea. Most tourists come to Xīshān Gōngyuán (Western Hill Park), with a modest mountain climb of 580m. Lōngtán Gúijīa Sēnlín Gōngyuán (Dragon Pool National Forest & Park) is 20km north-west of town. It is incredibly rustic – the site of Guăngxī's only extant old-growth forest – and also nearly impossible to get to without a group tour from CITS. The CITS office is at the *Guìpíng Fàndiàn* east of the town square, the best lodging of an unimpressive array with beds in doubles from Y30.

Just 25km north of Guìpíng is Jīntiáncūn, the birthplace of Hong Xiuquan. Hong was a schoolteacher who declared himself a brother of Jesus Christ and eventually led an army of over a million followers against the Qing dynasty in what came to be known as the Taiping Rebellion, one of the bloodiest civil wars in human history.

Minibuses run every 10 minutes from Guìpíng's square for the 25km, one-hour trip. The return fare is Y4. From the village it's approximately 4km to the site, which now houses a museum.

Zuǒjiāng Fēngjǐngqū 左江风景区
Left River Scenic Area

The Zuǒjiāng Fēngjǐngqū, around 190km south-west of Nánníng, provides the opportunity to see **karst rock formations**, with the added attraction of around 80 groups of Zhuàng minority **rock paintings**. The largest of these is in the area of Huāshān Bìhuà (Flower Mountain), which has a fresco 45m high and 170m across depicting some 2000 figures of hunters, farmers and animals. Admission to the paintings is Y12; to get there takes three hours by boat.

Nánníng's FIT department offers two-day tours for around Y550 per person. Alternatively, take the morning express Píngxiáng train as far as Níngmíng. There are a couple of tour operators along Níngmíng's main street. Tours start at Y80 for one or two people; add Y50 if you want to stay overnight halfway in Pānlóng, the site of a rough, explorable **nature reserve** and the only home of the rare white leaf monkey.

The *Huāshān Mínzúshānzhài Dùjiàcūn* (*Huashan Ethnic Culture Village;* ☎ 728 1951) in Pānlóng offers rooms in Dong-style wooden cabins, but at tourist prices of around Y120 for a single/double/triple/quad.

Píngxiáng 凭祥
☎ 0771

Píngxiáng is the staging post for onward transport to Vietnam. It's basically a border trading town rife with bustling markets. Foreigners have recently been accepted at the *Yǒuyì Zhaōdàisuǒ* (*Friendship Guesthouse*) near the train station on Nanda Lu, with beds from Y10. The *Xiángxīng Bīnguǎn* on Beida Lu has doubles for Y120.

There's no real need to stay in Píngxiáng though. An early-morning bus or train from Nánníng will get you into Píngxiáng around midday, and at this point you should be able to hitch a lift to the Friendship Pass (Yǒuyì Guān) on the Vietnamese border.

There are minibuses and private transport running from around the long-distance bus station – you shouldn't have to pay more than Y5 for a ride. From the Friendship Pass it's a 10-minute walk to Vietnam. Onward transport to Hanoi by train or bus is via the Vietnamese town of Lang Son. Ensure you get to the correct crossing point; some travellers have found themselves at the 'local' crossing point and have had to purchase Y2 tickets to get to the right one. You'll probably have to take a motorcycle taxi to get to the border. Some travellers report being charged a 'departure tax' of Y10. Also remember that Vietnam is one hour behind China.

Běihǎi 北海
☎ 0779 • pop 1,364,900

This friendly, tree-lined port community 229km south of Nánníng is best-known for its ferry to Hǎinán Dǎo and its ribbony beach, touted as the best in China. The harbour area, a few kilometres west of the bus station, is full of eye-catching century-old architecture and thousands of Chinese-Vietnamese refugees still here from the 1979 Sino-Viet conflict, many of whom offer boat rides to tourists.

A major node on the 2000-year-old 'Marine Silk Route', Běihǎi flourished under the Han dynasty; pearl production later cemented its reputation.

Yíntān Southern Thailand it is not, but Yíntān (Silver Beach), which lies about 6km south-east of Běihǎi city, does have sparkling white sands and fairly clean water. A national tourist site, the beach and the road leading to it are also home to some of the oddest resort villas you're likely to see in China – Swiss chalets, German castles, French villas and the obligatory concrete hulk hotels all vie for space along the shoreline.

GUĂNGXĪ 广西

Troubled Waters

Quintessential uneasy neighbours, China and Vietnam have been at odds, if not actually skirmishing, for over 2100 years. Han dynasty armies conquered the first Vietnamese patriot, Tire Da, in the 2nd century BC, making Vietnam one of many countries devoured by China as it tried to expand its commercial influence. This had a significant cultural and social impact on Vietnam: the introduction of a patriarchal Confucian social and governmental system was a double-edged sword. It made Vietnamese elites more inclined to tolerate Chinese rule, but later also gave the Vietnamese the framework to encourage revolt. Vietnam eventually threw off the yoke of imperialism in the 10th century AD, after dozens of revolts.

After WWII, western forces sent a 200,000-strong force of Chinese Nationalists to northern Vietnam to demobilise Japanese troops. The two nations have regularly been at war ever since, apart from when China supported Vietnam during the (American) Vietnam War.

In 1979 open war broke out after years of sporadic skirmishes. The Chinese crossed the border for several reasons. In 1978 the Vietnamese had rebuffed China and signed a treaty with (and accepted military and monetary support from) the Soviet Union – another border country with a Chinese love-hate relationship. Vietnam had also invaded Cambodia to topple the Khmer Rouge and, most importantly, had seized the assets of and deported (or forced out) up to 250,000 *huaqiao* (overseas Chinese), most of them to the Chinese provinces of Yúnnán and Guǎngxī.

The Chinese say Vietnamese forces crossed the border first, necessitating their own incursion. The Vietnamese of course deny this (most western sources back their version). Over 16 days scores of people were killed and five provincial border towns in Vietnam were heavily damaged. Both sides claimed to have won this battle.

It didn't end there, though. The border was sealed and major battles erupted again in 1984 in Láoshān, Zheyoushan, and Balihedong in Yúnnán and along much of Guǎngxī's border. This time the Vietnamese used up to 10 expanded divisions to attack Chinese border forces. They shelled the Chinese with up to 10,000 rounds per day and, while they didn't seize any land in this conflict, they did inflict a humiliating lesson on China. It's not uncommon to meet China's own Vietnam veterans when travelling around the south-west provinces.

Things have long since cooled down; border points at Hékǒu in Yúnnán and the Friendship Pass (Yǒuyì Guān) in Píngxiáng, Guǎngxī, hardly show any lingering effects, and the only disagreements for a decade have been between haggling Vietnamese and Chinese traders. All is not exactly cosy, however. In 1997 Vietnam took its protests over China's selling of oil exploration rights in its waters to ASEAN (which sided with Vietnam), and in January 1998 the Vietnamese daily newspapers ran front-page banner headlines screaming about major Chinese border transgressions. The focal point was a 1km-long river embankment in Guǎngxī, which the Vietnamese said the Chinese had deliberately built 10m into Vietnamese territory and which now floods the Vietnamese side of the river.

The Chinese initially laughed off the accusations. Then, to everyone's surprise, made a concession, agreeing to clear landmines from 10 sq km (at a cost of US$10 million) in Vietnam as a goodwill gesture. Cynics argue China did this as much to facilitate further trade – which had quadrupled from 1992 to 1997 along the border – as to encourage friendly relations. As of May 1998, Chinese troops had cleared three sq km by removing 21,600 mines. The first high-level contingent of Vietnamese since 1990 then travelled to Běijīng to try to stabilise relations. Later that year historic sites in Dongxing (Guǎngxī) dating Sino-Viet ties to the 19th century were restored and opened to the public. Perhaps most symbolic: in mid-1999 direct postal links – they had previously gone through Singapore – were finally restored through Guǎngxī.

To get here from Běihǎi, walk west from the bus station, bear right at Woping Lu (which branches off behind the Běihǎi Yíngbīnguǎn – see Places to Stay) and catch a minibus at Jiefang Lu. The ride takes about 20 minutes and costs Y1.50 by day, Y2 at night.

Places to Stay

West of the long-distance bus station, approximately five minutes, is the *Nánzhú Bīnguǎn* (☎ 202 8157, fax 202 4414), with cheaper quads from Y80; standard rooms are closer to Y200. Directly opposite the bus station and down an alley is the *Taóyuán Dàjiǔdiàn* (☎ 202 0919), with doubles for Y98, a steal at this price. Next to the Hǎinán Dǎo ferry terminal is the *Haiyáng Zhaōdaisuǒ*, with fish-smelling but OK rooms for as little as Y12 per bed. The *Yíntān Zhaōdaisuǒ (Silver Beach Guesthouse)*, down an alley near the beach entrance, has beds for Y15.

For a more upmarket stay, try the *Běihǎi Yíngbīnguǎn* (32 Beibuwan Zhonglu), the favourite hangout of Chinese cadres. Singles/doubles start at Y180/240, but this place is clean, quiet and well run. Top-end hotels can literally be found every 50 feet or so.

Places To Eat

A five-minute walk west of the bus station is a pleasant *restaurant* with some outdoor seating (look for the white sign with red letters). There's no English menu, but you can get *dānghuā rìbèn dòufǔ* (sweet-and-sour beancurd) and great *hóngshāo dòufǔ* (braised beancurd). East of the bus station, cross one intersection and you'll come to arguably the town's most favourite eatery, the *Dōngfāng Shíjiē (East Restaurant)*. One block south of the bus station near the stadium is the *Xiánglóng Bīnguǎn* (☎ 203 3588), famous for its fast-food restaurant in which the servers dress in traditional garb for floor shows. For fresh seafood in outdoor restaurants, head to the harbour area, especially Wàishā, a spit of land across from the ferry terminal. In winter, steaming hotpot can be had along Changqing Lu; be careful, some dog is served.

Getting There & Away Express buses to Nánníng (Y45; four hours) leave roughly hourly; a regular sleeper bus costs around Y29. There are sleeper buses to Guǎngzhōu for Y120; express sleepers with air-conditioning are Y138. Both take 12 hours. Other sleepers, some express versions, regularly serve Wúzhōu, Zhūhǎi, Guìlín, Liǔzhōu and even Kūnmíng.

Boats for the 11-hour journey to Hǎikǒu on Hǎinán Dǎo leave daily at 6 or 6.20 pm from the Běihǎi ferry terminal (Běiháng kèyùnzhàn). Cabins for two are Y153 per head, while dorm-style beds are Y78. A seat will cost you Y48.

Běihǎi is served by flights to and from Guǎngzhōu (Y550; daily), Shēnzhèn (Y640; daily except Monday and Thursday), Hǎikǒu (Y310; daily), Hong Kong (Y1080; Monday and Friday), Běijīng (Y1650; daily), Chéngdū (Y950; Tuesday and Friday), Guìlín (Y320; daily), Chángshā (Y990), Chóngqìng (Y850; Wednesday and Sunday), Kūnmíng (Y620; daily except Thursday) and Shànghǎi (Y1270; daily except Monday and Thursday).

The train station has one train departing at 11.30 am for Nánníng, and another at 2.40 pm for Chéngdū, which also passes through Nánníng, Liǔzhōu, Guìyáng and Chóngqìng. Hard-seat fares are Y20 to Nánníng and Y45 to Liǔzhōu. The early train has soft seats for Y33 to Nánníng.

For any tickets head a few minutes west of the bus station to the new city ticket office (☎ 202 8618). Its hours are 8 am to 4 pm and it sells boat, bus and plane tickets, with train tickets to be phased in eventually.

Getting Around The CAAC office (☎ 305 1899) along Beibu Xilu, far west of the bus station, has an airport bus (Y10) departing regularly for the 17km trip to the airport.

GUÌLÍN 桂林

☎ 0773 • pop 1,342,000

Since its founding as the most beautiful spot in 'the world', Guìlín has been eulogised in innumerable literary works, paintings and inscriptions – though cynics note most photographs of 'Guìlín' are really of the countryside near Yángshuò, one hour south by bus. Rapid economic growth and a booming tourist trade have pared some of Guìlín's charm – a maddening, seemingly permanent haze hovers here as many photographers soon discover – but it's still one of China's greener, more scenic cities and it can be fun for a day or two.

If you can handle the hectic traffic, most of Guìlín's limestone karst peaks and parks are a short bicycle ride away. Unfortunately, touts won't leave you alone, some tourist sights levy exploitative entry fees for foreigners, and many travellers tell of being grossly overcharged at restaurants throughout town. All this means you'll hear plenty of 'best of/worst of' tales about Guìlín.

The city was founded during the Qin dynasty and developed as a transport centre with the building of the Líng Qú canal, which linked the important Zhū Jiāng and Cháng Jiāng river systems. Under the Ming it was a provincial capital, a status it retained until 1914 when Nánníng became the capital.

During the 1930s, and throughout WWII, Guìlín was a communist stronghold, and its population expanded from about 100,000 to over a million as people sought refuge here. Today it's home to around 600,000 people.

Orientation

Most of Guìlín lies on the western bank of the Lì Jiāng. The main artery is Zhongshan Lu, which runs roughly parallel to the river on its western side. At the southern end of this street – that is, Zhongshan Nanlu – is Guìlín train station, the only station you should need. From the train station north is a rapidly gentrifying zone of hotels, restaurants and shops.

Closer to the centre of town is Róng Hú (Banyan Lake), to the west of Zhongshan Lu, and Shān Hú (Fir Lake) on the eastern side. Around here you'll find the CITS office, the PSB and places to hire bicycles, as well as one of Guìlín's original upmarket hotels and landmarks, the Li Jiang Hotel.

Jiefang Lu runs east over Jiěfàng Qiáo (Liberation Bridge) to the large Qīxīng Gōngyuán (Seven Star Park), one of the town's chief attractions. For the best views of the surrounding karst formations you either have to climb up the hills here, or get to the top of the Lí Jiāng or Hong Kong hotels, which give you 360-degree vistas.

Information

Money The main branch of the Bank of China is on Shanhu Beilu and this is where you have to go if you want a cash advance on your credit card. For changing money and travellers cheques, there is a branch opposite the train station and another at Zhongshan Lu near Yinding Lu. More expensive tourist hotels also have foreign-exchange services though not always for non-guests.

Post & Communications The post and China Telecom building is on Zhongshan Lu. There is a second post office just north of the train station. Both have reasonably efficient international direct dialling, though no email. A new post office is being built along Zhongshan Lu and this will likely be the spot for email. Some of the large hotels, such as the Lí Jiāng, have post offices.

Internet access can be found at a small Internet cafe (Kāiyuán Wăngmí Jùlèbù) along Xinyi Lu, south of the Holiday Inn hotel – it's Y25 per hour and the place is open till midnight. Sunny's Bookstore (Tàiyáng Shūdiàn) is just east of the Holiday Inn and also has email, along with books on Chinese culture in English, German and French.

Travel Agencies The CITS office (☎ 282 7254) is north of the Lì Jiāng ticket office on Binjiang Lu. The staff are friendly and are now better equipped to serve both independent travellers and tours. They'll still try to push you into the Y200 half-day city tour or the Y550 Lì Jiāng cruise. You can send email from this office. The China Travel Service (CTS; Zhōngguó Lǚxíngshè; ☎ 383 5623) just south of here is also reportedly helpful.

PSB The office is on Sanduo Lu, a side street running west off Zhongshan Lu between Róng Hú and Jiefang Lu.

Dangers & Annoyances In Guìlín it's always hunting season, and your wallet is the quarry. Stay alert to potential rip-offs and calmly negotiate prices first, particularly in restaurants and pedicabs. And keep the word 'calm' in mind, no matter what, because it's easy to lose your cool and that makes things worse.

Be wary of students wanting to practise English on you. While most are sincere, some travellers have lost money to smooth-talking 'English students' selling art or offering to act as guides or arrange train tickets. Also, watch out for pickpockets, especially around the train station. Guys, a newer hassle may be encountered in the bus/train station area where slimy pimps offer evening escorts.

Dúxiù Fēng　独秀峰
Solitary Beauty Peak
This 152m pinnacle is at the centre of the town. The climb to the top is steep, but there are good views of the town, the Lì Jiāng and the surrounding hills. The nephew of a Ming emperor built a palace at the foot of the peak in the 14th century, but only the gate remains. The site of the palace is now occupied by a teachers' college. A Y4 entrance fee is charged.

Bus No 1 goes up Zhongshan Lu past the western side of the peak. Alternatively, take bus No 2, which goes past the eastern side along the river. Both buses leave from Guìlín train station.

Fúbō Shān　伏波山
Wave-Subduing Hill
Close to Dúxiù Fēng and standing beside the western bank of the Lì Jiāng, Fúbō Shān offers a fine view of the town. Its name is variously said to be derived from how the peak descends into the river, blocking the waves, and from a temple that was established here for a Han dynasty general who was called Fubo Jiangjun, the wave-subduing general.

On the southern slope of the hill is **Huánzhū Dòng** (Returned Pearl Cave). The story goes that the cave was illuminated by a single pearl and inhabited by a dragon.

One day a fisherman stole the pearl, but he was overcome by shame and returned it.

Near this cave is **Qiānfó Dòng** (Thousand Buddhas Cave), which has over 400 statues – some partly damaged – dating from the Tang and Song dynasties. Entrance to this peak costs a rather outrageous Y10, although some think it's worth it. Bus No 2 runs past the hill.

Other Hills
North of Dúxiù Fēng is **Diécǎi Shān** (Folded Brocade Hill). Climb the stone pathway that takes you through the cooling relief of **Wind Cave**, with walls decked with inscriptions and Buddhist sculptures. Some of the damage to faces on the sculptures is a legacy of the Cultural Revolution. There are great views from the top of the hill, which can be skirted by taking Bus No 1.

From Fúbō Shān there's a good view of **Lǎorén Shān** (Old Man Hill), a curiously shaped hill to the north-east. The best way to get there is by bicycle as buses don't go past it. At the southern end of town, one of Guìlín's best-known sights is **Xiàngbí Shān** (Elephant Trunk Hill), which actually does resemble an elephant dipping its snout into the Lì Jiāng. Another entry fee of Y10 is charged here, and the authorities have done a good job of blocking any views with fences.

Qīxīng Gōngyuán　七星公园
Seven Star Park
One of China's nicer city parks, Qīxīng Gōngyuán is on the eastern side of the Lì Jiāng. Cross Jiěfàng Qiáo (Liberation Bridge) and continue to the end of Jiefang Donglu to get there.

The park takes its name from its seven peaks, which are supposed to resemble the star pattern of the Ursa Major (Big Dipper or Great Bear) constellation. There are several caves in the peaks, where visitors have inscribed graffiti for centuries, including a recent one which says, 'The Chinese Communist Party is the core of the leadership of all the Chinese People'. Back outside, there are lots of trails in and around the hills, and sprawling lawns to sit or picnic on.

GUĂNGXĪ 广西

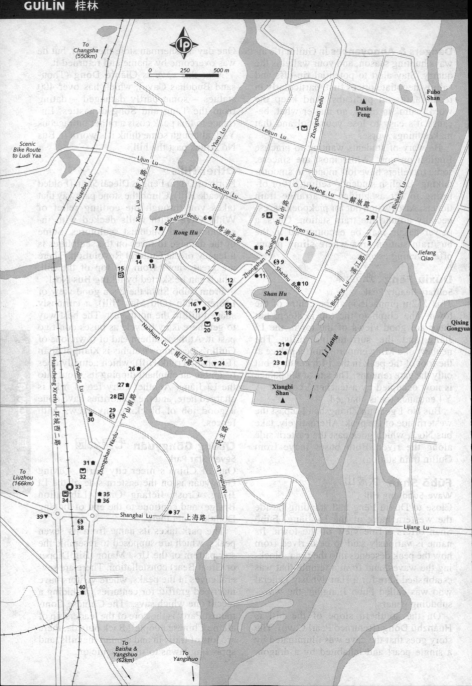

To
Changsha
(550km)

Scenic
Bike Route
to Ludi Yaa

Fubo
Shan

Duxiu
Feng

Zhongshan Beilu

Legun Lu

Yihu Lu

Huanbei Lu

Ljun Lu

Sanduo Lu

Jiefang Lu 解放路

Xinyi Lu

新义路

Ronghu Beilu

Ronghu Lu

榕湖北路

6

7

Rong Hu

14   13

15

Nanhuan Lu

Yinding Lu

Huancheng Xi'erlu

环城西一路

Zhongshan Nanlu

中山南路

16   17

18

19

20

12

11

Zhongshan

Shanhu Beilu

Shan Hu

9

10

8

5

中山中路

Zhongshan Zhonglu

Yiren Lu

4

2

3

Binjiang Lu

漓江路

Jiefang
Qiao

Qixing
Gongyua

Li Jiang

21

22

23

Xiangbi
Shan

To
Liuzhou
(166km)

33

34

31

32

35

36

37   上海路

Shanghai Lu

Lijiang Lu

30

29

28

27

26

25   24

前环路

民主路

Minzhu Lu

39

38

40

To
Baisha &
Yangshuo
(62km)

To
Yangshuo

0   250   500 m

GUÌLÍN

PLACES TO STAY

2 Universal Hotel
环球大酒店

3 Sheraton Guilin Hotel
桂林大宇大饭店

7 Rónghú Fàndiàn
榕湖饭店

8 Húbīn Fàndiàn
湖滨饭店

10 Li Jiang Hotel
漓江饭店

14 Holiday Inn Guilin
桂林 喆

23 Yùguì Bīnguǎn
玉桂宾馆

26 Osmanthus Hotel
丹桂大酒店

27 Tàihé Fàndiàn
泰和饭店

30 Xīngguì Fàndiàn
新桂饭店

31 Yǐnshān Fàndiàn
隐山饭店

35 New City Hotel
新城市酒店

36 Nánxī Fàndiàn
南溪饭店

40 Huáqiáo Dàshà
华侨大厦

PLACES TO EAT

12 Aìfēntē Kuaìcaì
爱芳特餐厅

16 Taìwān Niúroùmiàn Dàwàng
台湾牛肉面大王

19 Táilián Jiǔdiàn
台联酒店

24 Yíyuán Fàndiàn
怡园饭店

25 Dàjiāfājiǔjiā
大家发酒家

39 Hong Kong Hotel
香江饭店

OTHER

1 Post Office
邮电局

4 Xinhua Bookstore
新华书店

5 PSB
公安局

6 Nán Mén
古南门

9 Bank of China
中国银行

11 Xinhua Bookstore
新华书店

13 Sunny's Bookstore
太阳书店

15 Internet Cafe
开元网迷俱乐部

17 Shanghai Airlines
上海航空公司

18 Guilin Department Store
桂林百货大楼

20 Post Office
邮电局

21 CITS
中国国际旅行社

22 Boat Tickets
船售票处

28 Long-Distance Bus Station
长途汽车站

29 Bank of China
中国银行

32 Post Office
邮电局

33 Guilin Train Station
火车站

34 Guilin South Bus Station
城南站

37 CAAC
中国民航

38 Bank of China
中国银行

GUǍNGXĪ 广西

To get to the park take bus No 9, 10 or 11 from the train station. From the park, bus No 13 runs back across the Lì Jiāng, past Fúbō Shān and down to Lúdí Yán.

Lúdí Yán 芦笛公园
Reed Flute Cave

Some of the most extraordinary scenery Guìlín has to offer is underground at Lúdí Yán. Here multicoloured lighting and fantastic stalactites and stalagmites resemble a set from *Journey to the Centre of the Earth*.

One grotto, the Crystal Palace of the Dragon King, can comfortably hold about 1000 people, although many more crammed in here during the war when the cave was used as an air-raid shelter. The dominant feature of the cave is a great slab of white rock hanging from a ledge like a cataract, while opposite stands a huge stalactite said to resemble an old scholar. The story – one of many – goes that a visiting scholar wished to write a poem worthy of the cave's beauty. After a long time he had composed only two sentences and, lamenting his inability to find the right words, turned to stone.

Although the cave is worth visiting, some travellers may be put off by the laughably high entrance fee of Y44 (Y16 for locals) or the aggressive 'hello-postcard' hawkers. The cave is on the north-western outskirts of town. Take bus No 3 from the train station to the last stop. Bus No 13 will take you to the cave from Qīxīng Gōngyuán. Otherwise, it's a pleasant bike ride. Follow the route of bus No 3 along Lijun Lu, which runs into Taohua Jiang Lu. The latter parallels a small river and winds through fields and karst peaks, avoiding the traffic of Zhongshan Lu.

Other Sights

At the southern end of Guìlín, **Nán Gōngyuán** (South Park) is a pretty place. You can contemplate the mythological immortal said to have lived in one of the caves here; look for his statue.

There are two lakes near the city centre, Róng Hú (Banyan Lake) on the western side and Shān Hú (Fir Lake) on the eastern side. Róng Hú is named after an 800-year-old banyan tree on its shore. The tree stands by the restored **Nán Mén** (South City Gate), which was originally built during the Tang dynasty. This is one of the nicer neighbourhoods in town.

Places to Stay – Budget

The lower end of the market is served primarily by Yángshuò; keep pecking away at other hotels – they may crack and take foreigners. The old backpackers' stand-by, the *Huáqiáo Dàshà (Overseas Chinese Hotel;* ☎ *383 3573, 39 Zhongshan Nanlu)*, has decided it's now a classier establishment, but it still has the cheapest beds in town. OK dorms are Y40 and usually are not full. From here things jump to the Y280 range for a standard double.

Across from the train station, the *Nánxī Fàndiàn (South Stream Hotel)* has singles/doubles for Y60 to Y100 and triples for Y150. This place has cleaned up its act immensely since previous editions. Just north of the train station *Yǐnshān Fàndiàn (Hidden Hill Hotel)* isn't all that great but it's the only other cheapie, with singles/doubles for Y120/150.

To the north on Ronghu Lu, the *Húbīn Fàndiàn (*☎ *282 2837)* has downmarket but decent singles/doubles for Y90/100 and 'better' rooms for up to Y200.

Places to Stay – Mid-Range

Most of the low-end places mentioned earlier also have nicer rooms for Y100 to Y200, but there are also a couple of mid-range spots for those setting their sights a bit higher.

The *Xīngguì Fàndiàn*, off Zhongshan Lu, a five-minute walk north of the train station, has renovated its rooms – and prices now start at Y250 for a standard single/double.

Quite close to the long-distance bus station is the *Tàihé Fàndiàn (*☎ *383 5504)*. Newly redone doubles with air-con and TV cost Y320.

Similarly priced is the *Yùguì Bīnguǎn (*☎ *282 5499)*, which has clean singles/doubles with all the features from Y200/300. Some of the rooms also have nice views of the Lì Jiāng and Xiàngbí Shān. This place was in the middle of remodelling and may ratchet prices up dramatically.

Places to Stay – Top End

There's no shortage of choice here in terms of price, but only some of the expensive spots are worth it. One new place that several readers have rated highly is the *New City Hotel (Xīnchéngshì Jiǔdiàn;* ☎ *343 2511, fax 383 3340)*, which is just across from the train station. Its immaculate singles and doubles start at Y540 and the service is quite good. This place also has offered enticing discounts.

Just to the north of the long-distance bus station on Zhongshan Lu, the *Osmanthus Hotel (Dānguì Dàjiǔdiàn;* ☎ *383 4300, 451 Zhongshan Nanlu)* is one of the better longstanding top-end deals, with nicely furnished doubles from US$70. There are rooms for half that, but it's likely you won't get in.

The *Li Jiang Hotel (*☎ *282 2881, 1 Shanhu Beilu)* was once the main tourist hotel in Guìlín. It's right in the middle of town and the roof provides a panoramic view of the encircling hills. Standard doubles are US$80 and deluxe rooms are closer to US$150; there are no singles available. It has the full works: post office, barber, bank, restaurants, tour groups and bellboys in monkey suits.

In about the same price and value range, the *Rónghú Fàndiàn (*☎ *282 3811, 17 Ronghu Lu)* has singles and doubles from US$65 to $180. Looking out over Róng Hú, it's in a nice part of town, although a bit inconvenient unless you have a bicycle.

Up the road from the Rónghú Fàndiàn, the four-star *Holiday Inn Guilin (Guìlín Bīnguǎn; ☎ 282 3950, 14 Ronghu Lu)* has doubles posted at US$110, but when occupancy is low it offers a 20% discount, which offsets the 15% 'service charge' attached to everything. The only swimming pool in town is here as well.

The *Universal Hotel (Huánqiu Dàjiǔdiàn; ☎ 282 8228, fax 282 3868, 1 Jiefang Lu)* is a fairly new luxury hotel with rooms for US$80 to US$100, some with nice river views.

The five-star *Sheraton Guilin Hotel (Guìlín Dàzì Fàndiàn; ☎ 282 5588, fax 282 5598, 9 Binjiang Lu)* asks a minimum of US$110 for a double, although some guests have opined that a star should be pared from its ranking.

Places to Eat

Guìlín is traditionally noted for its snake soup, wild cat or bamboo rat, washed down with snake-bile wine. You could be devouring some of these animals into extinction, and we don't recommend that you do. The pangolin (a sort of Chinese armadillo) is a protected species, but still crops up on restaurant menus. Other protected species include the muntjac (Asian deer), horned pheasant, mini-turtle, short-tailed monkey and gem-faced civet. Generally the most exotic stuff you should come across is eel, catfish, pigeon and dog.

For a quick bite of more down-to-earth fare, there are a couple of places between the train station and the long-distance bus station on Zhongshan Lu with reasonable prices and limited English menus. Don't worry too much about finding these places; the staff will let you know where they are.

At night, on Zhongshan Lu north of Nanhuan Lu, the street comes alive with *food stalls* serving all sorts of wok-fried goodies. Just point at what you want, and the staff will do the rest. But make sure you set prices first: too many travellers have had a fine meal ruined by a bill for over Y100 when Y25 would do. There's also a few places that only Guìlín (or Las Vegas) could support, with cowboys in full glitter, duded up Elvises, or costumed little people lounging about the outside.

Candle-lit dinners for two are rare in Guìlín. Virtually every restaurant in town is *rè nào* (hot and noisy) and wide-eyed backpackers may find themselves placed at huge tables with boisterous tourists.

There's an outstanding and inexpensive Sìchuān restaurant on Nanhuan Lu called the *Yíyuán Fàndiàn*. Although there is no English sign, you'll easily spot the place by its tasteful, all-wood exterior. The owner speaks excellent English and will be happy to help you choose dishes. She imports all her spices from Sìchuān, and you can taste the difference. It serves from 11.30 am to 2.30 pm and again from 5.30 to 9.30 pm. Just west of this restaurant are a couple of splashy new restaurants, one of which – *Dàjiāfājiǔjiā (Everybody Rich)* – has no English sign but does sport an English menu.

Fast-food places are sprouting up. *Aìfēntē Kuàicaì (8 Elephant)* along Zhongshan Lu has burgers and fried chicken. South-west a few blocks from here is *Taìwān Niúroùmiàn Dàwàng (Taiwan Beef Noodles)* with good noodles and fried rice.

For an excellent view of Guìlín, try the revolving restaurant on the 19th floor of the *Hong Kong Hotel* (but don't get the abysmal western breakfast). For pizza at Y30, try the pizzeria at the *Universal Hotel*.

For dim sum, the *Táilián Jiǔdiàn* is considered by locals and overseas Chinese to be the best place in town, as long as you get there early, around 8 am.

Getting There & Away

Guìlín is connected to many places by air, bus, train and boat. Give some serious thought to flying in or out of this place: train connections are not particularly convenient.

Air CAAC has an office (☎ 384 4007) on the corner of Shanghai Lu and Minzhu Lu. Go in through the doorway on the corner and head up to the 2nd floor. Hours of operation are 7.30 am to 8.30 pm. Shanghai Airlines (☎ 282 7046) is at 93 Zhongshan Lu, and Dragonair (☎ 282 5588 ext 8895) has an office in the Sheraton Guilin Hotel.

Guìlín is well connected to the rest of China by air and destinations include: Běihǎi (Y520), Běijīng (Y1430), Chángshā (Y530), Chéngdū (Y780), Chóngqìng (Y580), Fúzhōu, Hǎikǒu (Y670), Hángzhōu, Hong Kong, Macau, Guǎngzhōu (Y470), Guìyáng (Y390), Lànzhōu, Nánníng (Y460), Nánjīng (Y890), Qīngdǎo (Y1380), Shànghǎi (Y1040), Shàntóu (Y630), Shēnzhèn (Y530), Ürümqi, Xiàmén (Y690), Wǔhàn (Y670) and Xī'ān (Y870). Whatever destination you have in mind you should purchase in advance: Guìlín is one of China's most popular tourist spots and with a billion people competing for seats no amount of airlines can handle the load.

Probably the most useful travellers' air option is the Guìlín-Kūnmíng flight, which can save considerable mucking about trying to get tickets on a train that is frequently booked out. To Kūnmíng it costs Y540 to Y670, depending on the day and the airline.

Bus For short local runs (ie Yángshuò, Xīng'ān), minibuses depart regularly from the train station. Buses to Yángshuò should set you back Y5, no matter what anyone says, along with Y1 or Y2 per backpack, and the trip takes just over an hour.

The long-distance bus station is north of the train station on Zhongshan Lu. Buses to Lóngshèng (Y10.50) leave approximately every 20 minutes from 6 am to 4 pm; eight luxury express buses depart from 7.40 am to 6.20 pm and cost Y15.

Buses leave for Sānjiāng eight times daily from 6 am to 4 pm and cost Y17. There is one bus daily for Xīng'ān at 11.40 am.

Regular sleeper buses do leave for Liǔzhōu (Y32) but bus station staff will tell you you're daft to take them, as they will likely take local roads and turn it into a six-hour ordeal. Instead, treat yourself to the best of the station's new sybaritic Daewoo express service. Buses depart constantly from 7 am to 8.30 pm; the trip costs Y40 and takes two hours along the Guiliu Expressway, and the attendants give highlights in (fractured and condensed) English!

Other luxury express buses include: Nánníng (Y90; 5½ hours) hourly from 8 am to 11.30 pm; Wúzhōu (Y70; eight hours) at 8.20 am (this stops in Yángshuò); Běihǎi (Y138; eight hours) at 9 am. Sleepers also ply all these routes for much less money but taking much more time.

You can also catch sleepers for Guǎngzhōu (Y100; 13 hours), which depart from 3 to 6.30 pm, and one for Zhūhǎi (Y125; 18 hours), which leaves at 1.25 pm. Sleepers leave about the same time for Shēnzhèn (Y130).

Behind the train station is the Guìlín south bus station. It's from here that buses and minibuses depart on a fairly regular basis for Lóngshèng and other relatively local destinations.

Train There are useful train connections to Guìlín, but some of these (such as the Kūnmíng-Guìyáng-Guìlín-Shànghǎi route) tend to involve long hauls on unbelievably crowded carriages. Newer trains are being used, but it's still tough to get a ticket. If you're headed to Kūnmíng, consider going to Nánníng and taking the new Nánkūn train; you can arrange this in Guìlín.

If you're booking on the day of departure you can forget about getting a hard sleeper for the highly-populated routes; be prepared to wait an extra day. You may be able to swing a hard-sleeper ticket from the cafes and travel outfits in Yángshuò, but this is definitely not something to count on. If you're in Yángshuò, you should consider a day trip to Guìlín to book your own ticket. The Yángshuò CITS can always get you a ticket, but on the most recent trip, some travellers were paying shockingly high 'service charges' (as high as 75% above face value).

A tip: if tickets are *méi yǒu* (literally 'don't have') request a ticket for a destination one or two stops *after* your intended stopping point. If it does work, you'll have to get the ticket seller to write an explanation on the back of the ticket, or you may have trouble getting the ticket conductor on the train to return it so you can disembark.

There are two trains a day to Kūnmíng: one starts from Shànghǎi and arrives at the *north* station at 1.40 am; the other starts from Guǎngzhōu and arrives at 4.40 am at the main station. Hard sleeper tickets from Guìlín to Kūnmíng range from Y187 to Y287.

Other direct trains out of Guìlín include those to Běijīng (Y265 to Y416; up to 31 hours), Chángshā (11 hours), Guǎngzhōu (Y180 to Y230; 15 hours), Guìyáng (Y118, hard sleeper; 18 hours), Liǔzhōu (four hours), Nánníng (Y40 hard-seat; seven hours), Shànghǎi (Y340; 35 hours), Xī'ān (Y221; 36 hours), and Zhànjiāng. For Chóngqìng, change trains at Guìyáng.

Getting Around

To/From the Airport Guìlín's sleek new international airport is 30km west of the city. CAAC runs buses from the Shanghai Lu office to the airport (Y20), leaving on an indecipherable schedule between 6.30 am and 7.30 pm. A taxi will cost at least Y80.

Bus & Taxi Most of the city buses leave from the terminal at Guìlín train station and will get you to many major sights, but a bicycle is definitely better, especially in the searing summer heat.

Taxis are available from the major tourist hotels for about Y20 per trip, depending on the distance. On the street, the flag fall is supposed to be Y9, with an additional Y1.40 per kilometre. Pedicabs charge Y5 to Y10 per trip.

Bicycle Bicycles are the best way to get around Guìlín. There are a few bicycle-hire shops – just look along Zhongshan Lu for the signs. Most charge between Y10 and Y15 per day, and require Y200 or your passport as security (try to avoid handing over your passport).

AROUND GUÌLÍN

The Líng Qú is a canal in Xīng'ān County, about 70km north of Guìlín. It was begun in about 200 BC during the reign of the first Qin emperor, Qin Shihuang, to transport supplies to his army. The canal links the Xiāng Hé – which flows into the Cháng Jiāng (Yangzi River) – and the Tan River – which flows into the Zhū Jiāng (Pearl River) – thus connecting two of China's major waterways.

You can see the 34km Líng Qú at Xīng'ān, a market town of about 30,000 people two hours by bus from Guìlín. A daily bus departs from the long-distance bus station at 11.40 am. Minibuses to Xīng'ān also leave from in front of the train station. The town is also connected to Guìlín by train. Two branches of the canal flow through the town, one at the northern end and one at the southern end.

Lí Jiāng 漓江

The Lí Jiāng is the connecting river between Guìlín and Yángshuò and is one of the main tourist attractions of the area.

A thousand years ago a poet wrote of the scenery around Yángshuò, 'The river forms a green gauze belt, the mountains are like blue jade hairpins'. Well, the 83km stretch between the towns is hardly that, but you do see some extraordinary peaks, sprays of bamboo lining the riverbanks, fishers in small boats and picturesque villages. As is the Chinese habit, every feature along the route has been named.

A popular tourist trip is the boat ride from Guìlín down the Lí Jiāng to Yángshuò, although low-budget travellers have been put off by the exorbitant ticket prices, which presently come in at around Y500, including lunch and the bus trip back to Guìlín from Yángshuò. This is one of Guìlín's worst cases of price gouging, as the most luxurious local trip costs only Y145. Please – laugh at them, then complain to local tourism officials; the official 'complaint line' is ☎ 280 0315. Then bus to Yángshuò and give locals your business.

Tour boats (Y500) depart from Guìlín at a jetty across the road from the Yùguì Bīnguǎn each morning at around 8 am, although when the water is low you have to take a shuttle bus to another pier downriver. For trips booked through hotels, buses usually pick you up at around 7.30 to 8 am and take you to the boat. Otherwise, the ticket office for the trip is across the road from the park entrance, on the same side of the street as the Yùguì Bīnguǎn. The trip lasts all day, and some people find the time dragging towards the end. It's probably not worth it if you're going to be spending any length of time in Yángshuò, where you can organise local boat trips.

YÁNGSHUÒ 阳朔
☎ 0773

Just an hour from Guìlín by bus, Yángshuò has, along with Dàlǐ in Yúnnán, become one of those legendary backpacker destinations that most travellers hear about long before they even set foot in China. Set amid gorgeous limestone pinnacles, it's not as quaint as it once was, but Yángshuò is still a great laid-back base from which to explore small villages in the nearby countryside.

With its Western-style cafes, Hollywood movies, Bob Marley tunes and banana pancakes, Yángshuò may not seem like the 'real China', but who cares? It's a great spot to relax, see the scenery and grab a good cup of coffee – the perfect antidote to weeks or months on the road. Don't make this your first or second stop coming from Hong Kong. Save it for after knocking around Guǎngzhōu or Guǎngxī for a spell.

And either way, for sheer scenic beauty, it's hard to top a leisurely bike ride around Yángshuò and its surrounding villages. A lot of people have even stayed overnight in the villages, and if you want to go camping in the mountains you shouldn't have any problem. It's not permitted to camp out, but who's going to climb a 200m peak to bring you down?

Information

Money The Bank of China on Binjiang Lu will change cash and travellers cheques, as well as receive wire transfers.

Post & Communications The post office, on the main road (Pantao Lu) across from Xi Jie, has English-speaking staff and long-distance phone services that are cheaper than those offered by the cafes and hotels and, depending on the clerk, may allow you to use a home-country calling card. Its operating hours are from 8 am to 5 pm.

Email & Internet Access Plenty of Internet spots – including every cafe in town – have sprouted up along all the main thoroughfares. Y25 per hour is pretty standard though Y20 is possible.

Travel Agent There is a CITS office along Xi Jie, not far from the intersection with

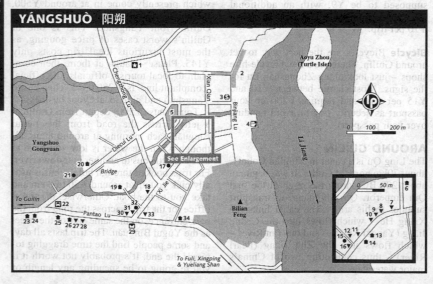

YÁNGSHUÒ 阳朔

Pantao Lu, with a larger one near Xi Jie's intersection with Chengzhong Lu. Both are generally open from 8.30 am to noon and 2.30 to 5.30 pm.

The staff are helpful and friendly, although travellers seldom avail themselves of their services – enterprising locals working from the cafes are generally more in touch with the needs of independent travellers, and definitely levy decidedly lower service charges.

Things to See

The main peak in Yángshuò is **Bìlián Fēng** (Green Lotus Peak), which stands next to the Lì Jiāng in the south-eastern corner of the town. It's also called Tóngjìng Fēng (Bronze Mirror Peak) because it has a flat northern face that is supposed to look like an ancient bronze mirror.

Yángshuò Gōngyuán is in the western part of the town, and here you'll find **Xīláng Shān** (Man Hill), which is meant to resemble a young man bowing and scraping to a shy young girl represented by Xiǎogū Shān

(Lady Hill). You may just want to look from the outside – it now costs Y5 to enter the park. Other hills nearby are named after animals: Shìzìqí Lǐyú Shān (Lion Riding Carp Hill), Lóngtóu Shān (Dragon Head Hill) and the like.

It's amazing how many travellers come to Yángshuò and don't see Yángshuò itself, being so preoccupied by the karst peaks (along with Pantao Lu's beer and movies). To the north and west of Pantao Lu there's great small-town trekking: back alleys, small markets and throngs of tourists poking about tonnes of shops.

Places to Stay

Despite the seeming plethora of local guesthouses and hotels, tourist numbers are increasing faster than lodging infrastructure can go up, and it can at times take a fair bit of walking to nail down a room. Weekly rates are pretty universally available and you can even use credit cards at many of the cheapies now.

GUǍNGXĪ 广西

YÁNGSHUÒ

PLACES TO STAY	8	Blue Lotus	OTHER
6 Hotel California		丁丁饭店	1 PSB
加州饭店	9	Brothers Bar & Cafe	公安局
13 Lisa's Cafe		兄弟酒吧	2 Market
加州饭店	10	Minnie Mao's	市场
14 Sihai Fàndiàn	11	Méi Yǒu Cafe	3 Bank of China
四海饭店		没有饭店	中国银行
19 Yangshuo Resort Hotel	12	Susanna's	4 Wharf
阳朔度假饭店		苏珊娜咖啡店	码头
20 Jīnlóng Fàndiàn	16	Cafe Under the Moon	5 Market Area
金龙饭店		月亮下咖啡馆	市场
23 Yangshuo Youth Hostel	18	Night Food Market	15 Sunny's Bookstore
花园酒店		夜间摊子	17 Merry Planet
24 Jīnyè Fàndiàn	27	Hard Seat Cafe	Language Club
金叶饭店		莲城饭店	快乐星球外语俱乐部
25 Fawlty Towers Guesthouse	28	Ebo's Hard	21 CITS; Bookshop
宝泉饭店		Rock Cafe	中国国际旅行社;
26 Good Companion Holiday		红硬石饭店	书店
Inn	30	Green Lotus Cafe	22 Long-Distance Bus Station
农资招待所		碧莲酒楼	汽车总站
34 Zhūyáng Fàndiàn	31	Paris Cafe	29 Post Office
珠阳饭店		星辰酒店	邮电局
	33	MC Blues	32 CITS
PLACES TO EAT		Bar & Cafe	中国国际旅行社
7 Anne's Art Cafe		黎仕酒店	

Often full are the clean rooms at *Lisa's Cafe* (Lìshā Fàndiàn; ☎/fax 882 0217, 71 Xi Jie) smack in the centre of town. A bed in a triple costs Y20; good singles/doubles with private bath cost Y60. Many other types of rooms exist, including suites.

Recently opened is the *Hotel California* (Jiāzhōu Fàndiàn), with beds in a very clean seven-bed dorm for Y15, and singles/doubles with shared bath for Y40/50; rooms with private bath start at Y100.

The *Sìhǎi Fàndiàn* (☎ 882 2013), next door to Lisa's, is also popular, and, apart from the noise in the evenings and the dampness of the rooms in the winter months, it's a good spot. The Sìhǎi has dorm beds as low as Y10 and myriad other rooms up to around Y200.

The *Yangshuo Youth Hostel* (Huāyuán Fàndiàn; ☎ 882 2347) – not really a hostel – has beds for Y15 in a five-bed dorm and for Y25 in a three-bed dorm, both with attached bath. Dorm beds in rooms without attached bath are Y10. Beds in singles and doubles with bath range from Y30 to Y60. Despite rather recent upgrades, this place seems a tad tired, but most travellers find it just fine.

Just up the street, the *Good Companion Holiday Inn* (Nóngzī Zhaōdaìsuǒ; ☎ 882 2766) still offers dorm beds for Y10 and beds in singles/doubles/triples for Y30, all with shared bath. Rooms with baths are Y40 to Y80, and they've just finished some excellent new doubles for Y60. Rooms in the back are quiet. Overall this place has improved markedly since previous editions. Next door and up some steps is the cheery *Fawlty Towers Guesthouse* (Baòquán Fàndiàn; ☎ 882 4309, 32 Pantao Lu), only open for a couple of years and well worth Y70/80 for singles/doubles.

On the main road toward the eastern end of town lies the friendly, clean *Zhūyáng Fàndiàn*. It's renovated the rooms, which now feature cosy all-wood flooring, air-conditioning, and TV; singles/doubles cost Y120/250. There are triples for Y150 and very threadbare quads for Y80, both of which have a shared bath.

Several formerly Chinese-only hotels are OK but tend to charge more while offering less than cheaper competition. The *Jīnlóng Fàndiàn* (Golden Dragon Hotel; ☎ 882 2674) has singles and doubles for Y150 with freshly finished all-wood interiors and small balconies. Well run is the *Jìnyè Fàndiàn* (Golden Leaves Hotel; ☎ 882 2860, fax 882 2853), along Pantao Lu, which even smells antiseptically clean. The spotless rooms all have air-con, attached bath, and 24-hour hot water. Rates are Y100/150 a single/double.

The offspring of a Sino-Malaysian joint venture, the *Yangshuo Resort Hotel* (Yángshuò Dùjiā Fàndiàn; ☎ 882 2109, fax 882 2106), replete with swimming pool, bar, and three-star rating has doubles starting at US$100! Nice rooms and a serious slate of amenities include a fitness centre, satellite TV, pool tables, a business centre, restaurants and lounges, and lots more. You knew it was only a matter of time ...

Places to Eat

Xi Jie teems with cafes offering interesting Chinese/western crossovers as well as perennial travellers' favourites such as banana pancakes, muesli and pizza. For anyone who's been wandering around China for a while it's a good chance to have a break from oily stir-fried vegetables and grab a cup of coffee. Movie junkies are in heaven, since some cafes woo travellers with Hollywood flicks over dinner.

A good newer eatery is *Cafe Under the Moon*, which has not only the most copious menu – all well done – but also wonderful 2nd-floor balcony seating, not unlike dining in antebellum New Orleans. Another good new cafe is *Blue Lotus* – it's got the best sound system in town too. *Drifters*, opened by an Australian, should be open by the time you read this.

One popular cafe is *Lisa's*. Local fame has made Lisa a tad cheeky, but she and her staff are all smiles, and the food is generally top-notch. Across from Lisa's, the *Méi Yǒu Cafe* promises 'méi yǒu bad service, méi yǒu warm beer', and it delivers – the service is good and the beer is cold. Just up the street, *Minnie Mao's* has won travellers' praise for tasty dishes and some of the most attentive service in town. **Brothers Bar & Cafe** nearby was reputedly the original Yángshuò cafe; it's run by a kung fu master. A few shops away is the very friendly family at **Anna's Art Cafe** – away from the madding crowds. Run by a third-generation artist from a famed family of artists, the place has food as lovely as the available artwork.

Heading toward the main road, on a small side street, **Susanna's** also draws a steady stream of customers. Its claim to fame is that it was the first western restaurant in town and Jimmy Carter ate there in 1987!

Other popular places include the cluster of cafes up on the corner of Xi Jie and the main road: **Green Lotus Cafe**, **Paris Cafe** and especially **MC Blues Bar & Cafe**. They all have outdoor seating and are good places to sit and watch the world go by. MC Blues has the added attraction of more than 150 tapes.

The places on the main road are where some of Yángshuò's original cafes started. They don't enjoy the popularity of some of the places on Xi Jie, but cafes like **Ebo's Hard Rock Cafe** and **Hard Seat Cafe** are friendly spots for a meal or a cup of coffee.

If you get tired of the 'international' spots, along Xi Jie a huge, boisterous open-air **night food market** appears at night; don't forsake Diecui Lu and smaller alleys, all of which have local offerings.

Shopping

Yángshuò is a good place to do some souvenir shopping. Good buys include silk jackets (at much cheaper prices than in Hong Kong), hand-painted T-shirts, scroll paintings and batiks (from Guìzhōu). Name chops cost Y10 to Y60 on average. Everything on sale should be bargained for. The paintings available in Yángshuò, for example, are generally of poor quality (even if you think they look good) and a starting price of Y150 can easily go below Y100.

If you are in the market for a chop, bear in mind that it is not the size of the stone that is important in determining a price, but the quality of the stone itself. Often the smaller pieces are more expensive than the hefty chunks of rock available.

Don't forget, too, that Yángshuò is not simply Xi Jie. Wander around the backstreets, especially north along Binjiang Lu around the Bank of China. There are tonnes of places; they're not especially better, but offer the shopper lots more comparison shopping.

Student Cards Several places around Yángshuò, most notably Merry Planet Language Club and Minnie Mao's, offer brief courses in Chinese language, *taijiquan* or medicine. Don't do it just to get a student ID card, gleefully thinking you'll nab Chinese prices – Chinese and foreign prices are getting more and more similar all the time, and it would take a long time to recoup your Y30.

Getting There & Away

Air The closest airport is in Guìlín. Cafes can drum up tickets for you, along with taxi rides from Yángshuò directly to the airport.

Bus There are frequent buses and minibuses running to Guìlín throughout the day. The best option is the minibus service that operates from the square in front of the long-distance bus station. Buses leave as soon as they fill up, which could be anywhere from five to 15 minutes, and the trip takes a little over an hour. It costs Y5 per person, and Y1 or Y2 per piece of luggage.

Only one sleeper bus per day departs Yángshuò for Guǎngzhōu; this 3.30 pm bus costs Y80 and takes 11 to 12 hours. However, buses from Guìlín to Guǎngzhōu roar along Pantao Lu all day until early evening; just flag one of them down – you can probably get on for Y65 or Y70.

If you're heading to Guǎngzhōu you can also take a bus/boat combination from Yángshuò for around Y115; buses to Wúzhōu leave in the morning and evening. The morning 9.30 am express bus from Guìlín (Y51.50; seven hours) allows you to (barely) connect with the evening boat leaving Wúzhōu. The evening bus is less convenient as it leaves you to sit out in the wee small hours of the morning. Tickets for the five-hour, high-speed ferry ride to Guǎngzhōu also must be booked in Wúzhōu.

You can arrange the Wúzhōu-Hong Kong high-speed ferry in Yángshuò. Combined bus/boat tickets are available from CITS and most cafes/travel outfits for around Y500, though doing it yourself is much cheaper. You'll probably have to get a room in Wúzhōu since the evening bus arrives at 2 am; accommodation is not included in the price of the ticket.

To get to Liǔzhōu, go to Guìlín and catch an express; you'll save lots of time. Other epic journeys include a 16- to 18-hour travail to Shēnzhèn for Y120. For Zhūhǎi, head to Guìlín and line up a bus.

Train The nearest train station is in Guìlín. Almost any cafe or travel outfit around Yángshuò will organise train tickets, and some offer hard sleepers for high-demand routes like Guìlín to Kūnmíng. Bear in mind that locals usually have to go through 'the back door' in Guìlín to get the tickets; you may have to pay through the nose. This also means that sometimes a 'guaranteed' hard-sleeper ticket can turn into a less-than-enticing hard seat, which has led some travellers to make the day-trip up to the Guìlín train station just to be sure.

To get any of these tickets you'll probably have to book at least two to three days in advance.

Getting Around

Yángshuò itself is small enough to walk around without burning up too many calories, but if you want to get further afield hire a bicycle. Just look for rows of bikes and signs near the intersection of Xi Jie and the main road. The charge is Y5 to Y10 per day and a few places now don't bother securing a deposit. Check out the bike fully before you ride away; many ugly situations have arisen over bikes being returned 'broken', and the PSB will not side with you.

AROUND YÁNGSHUÒ

The highway from Guìlín turns southward at Yángshuò and after a couple of kilometres crosses the river Jīnbǎo Hé. South of this river and just to the west of the highway is **Yuèliàng Shān** (Moon Hill), a limestone

pinnacle with a moon-shaped hole. To get to Yuèliàng Shān by bicycle, take the main road out of town towards the river and turn right on the road about 200m before the bridge. Cycle for about 50 minutes – Yuèliàng Shān is on your right and the views from the top (some 1251 steps, so reports one focused Frenchman) are incredible! You can espy Yuèliàng Shān village – itself worth checking out – and the ancient Big Banyan Tree (ask the hawkers to point it out). The hill costs Y5.

There are weeks and weeks of possible exploration out there for travellers on bike, boat, foot or any combination thereof. Some intrepid travellers have even hefted their bikes on to a boat and ridden back from elsewhere. One sure-fire trip involves the local roads through Báishā town to Fùlǐ Qiáo and Yùlóng Qiáo (Dragon Bridge). Locals say the scenery along here beats the Lì Jiāng. Báishā is 9km to the north of Yángshuò – the highway is terribly busy

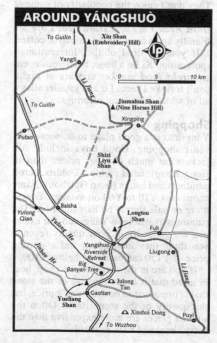

AROUND YÁNGSHUÒ

here though – and probably another 4km to 5km to the bridges beyond that. All told, it'd be a whole day's trek so be sure you know where you're going first.

A series of caves have been opened up not far from Yuèliàng Shān: the Hēifó Dòng (Black Buddha Caves), Xīnshuǐ Dòng (New Water Caves) and Jùlóng Tán (Dragon Cave). If you head out to Yuèliàng Shān, you will undoubtedly be intercepted and invited to visit the caves. Tours cost around Y25 per head, although prices can drop if there are more of you. You go through the caves and then climb down a steep chimney via a rope and ladder to an underground pool fed by a river. You can walk along the river through the mountain for a few hours and come out on the other side. Jùlóng Tán demands an outlandish Y46: not cheap for a damp and muddy trek.

In Yángshuò there are also several locals offering guided tours of Yuèliàng Shān, the caves and other famous spots, as well as their home villages. Some now cook lunch as well. These mini-tours have garnered rave reviews from some travellers and may be worth a try, although you usually need to get at least three people together to make it worth your guide's while. Prices vary wildly for these tours – but figure Y40 to Y50 for a full day.

River Excursions

There are many villages close to Yángshuò that are worth checking out. Evening cormorant fishing trips are popular; they usually take place at 6 or 7 pm and cost Y25 to Y30.

A popular river-boat trip is to the picturesque village of Fùlǐ, a short distance down the Lì Jiāng, where you'll see stone houses and cobbled lanes. There are a couple of boats a day to Fùlǐ from Yángshuò for around Y40 (foreigners' price), although most people tend to cycle there – it's a pleasant ride and takes around an hour.

An alternative mode of transport to Fùlǐ is by floating down the river in an inner tube. Inner-tube hire is available for about Y5 per day. It takes around three or four hours to get to Fùlǐ this way. Several places also offer rafting trips and kayak hire – both are popular options in the warm summer months.

On market days in Fùlǐ be very careful of pickpockets; young men work in groups of three or four, brushing up against travellers in the press of the crowd and relieving their pockets of valuables.

A host of cafes and local travel agents also organise boat trips to Yángtí (Y110) and Xīngpíng (Y70); the best scenery is between these two places.

About three hours upstream from Yángshuò, the mountain scenery around Xīngpíng is breathtaking, and there are many caves. People living in some of the caves make gunpowder for a living.

Many travellers take their bicycles out to Xīngpíng by boat and cycle back – it's a picturesque ride of about three hours, and the whole package costs Y30 to Y50 depending on how many of you there are. Any number of cafes can organise boat tickets for you.

It's possible to spend the night in Xīngpíng. One small *hotel* sits on a point that juts out into the river; basic rooms are Y20 per person. A couple of doll's house *restaurants* with bilingual menus keep everyone fed (take care that they don't overcharge).

If you're keen on a river trip, the best thing to do, as always, is shop around. Talk to lots of travellers and cafes.

Markets

Villages in the vicinity of Yángshuò are best visited on market days, and these operate on a three-day, monthly cycle. Thus, markets take place every three days starting on the first of the month for Báishā (1, 4, 7, 11, 14, 17, 21, 24, 27), every three days starting on the second of the month for Fùlǐ (2, 5, 8 etc), and every three days starting on the third of the month for Yángshuò and Xīngpíng (3, 6, 9 etc; Yángshuò is on the same cycle as Xīngpíng). There are no markets on the 10th, 20th, 30th and 31st of the month. Buses to Xīngpíng cost Y3.

LÓNGSHÈNG 龙胜
☎ 0773

Lóngshèng's main attraction is definitely not the town – a cluster of concrete hulks that clash with the mountain backdrop. Not far out of town, however, are the Lóngjǐ

Tītián (Dragon's Backbone Rice Terraces) and a nearby *wēnquán* (hot spring). The hot spring is a tacky tourist highlight and can be safely missed, although local buses running out there pass through rolling hills sculpted into precipitous rice terraces and studded with Yao minority villages. The area is reminiscent of Banaue in northern Luzon, Philippines. It's possible to dessert the bus around 6km to 7km from the hot spring and take off into the hills for some exploring. When you return from the day's outing, Lóngshèng at least offers cheap accommodation and even cheaper food at its lively night market.

Lóngjǐ Tītián
Dragon's Backbone Rice Terraces
In a region covered with terraced rice fields, Lóngjǐ Tītián sees these feats of farm engineering reach all the way up a string of 800m peaks. A half-hour climb to the top delivers an amazing vista.

The nearby village of Píng Ān is rapidly becoming a small travellers centre and within a few years may have accumulated a host of guesthouses, bars, restaurants and email cafes.

LÓNGJǏ TĪTIÁN

Approximate three-hour walk from Heping to Ping An
Rice Fields
Footpath ---
Ridge ——

0 1 2 km
Approximate Scale

Zhonglou
Tomb
Uhlong
Waterfall
Lawai
Tong Lou
Goldmine
To Longsheng
Ping An
Heping
Huang Lo
To Guilin
Tonga
Long Ji
Covered Bridges
Tomb
Tea Plantation
Jing Jiang
River Road
Entry Gate

Sadly, part of the reason for this sudden change is the construction of a road from the riverside along the bottom of the valley to Píng Ān. To make the 6km zigzag road an amazing number of terraces beyond Píng Ān had to be blasted away and serious environmental damage has resulted. In any case, you don't need to use the road as the village is only an hour's walk up a beautiful stone path.

Despite the tourist development Píng Ān is still a very attractive and traditional-looking village (not a tin roof in sight).

There's a Y20 entry charge to the terraces, collected on the main road along the valley bottom and checked just before the beautiful covered bridge at the entrance to Píng Ān village. Walking possibilities include the one-hour circuit walk from the village to the clearly marked Viewpoint 1 and Viewpoint 2 (see map).

Buses to the terraces leave from 7 am to 5.30 pm from opposite the Jīnhuí Fàndiàn (see Places to Stay). Although the trip is only about 20km, some of the buses stop midway at the town of Hépíng to try and pull in more passengers, which can make the ride last up to 1½ hours! Locals pay Y3, but you'll probably have a tough time getting your fare below Y5. A few *guesthouses* can be found near the entrance.

There are some other tourist sights around Lóngshèng, including **forest reserves**, **Dong** and **Yao villages** and unusual **stone formations**.

Places to Stay
Lóngshèng has oodles of hotels – and virtually every one is a musty pit.

Downhill from the bus station, just before the bridge, is the *Kǎikǎi Lǚshè (Riverside Hotel)*. It's run by an English teacher who has information on getting to the local sights. She's even made up a map of the surrounding area for her guests. Spartan rooms with shared bath (with hot water 24 hours) cost Y10 per bed but you'll be shown better Y40 doubles. The Kǎikǎi Lǚshè has the added attraction of night-time cormorant fishers: you can look down on them from the balcony or the roof terrace.

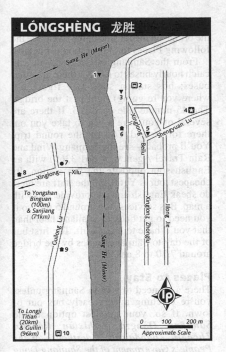

LÓNGSHÈNG 龙胜

To Yongshan
Bīnguǎn
(100m)
& Sanjiang
(71km)

To Longji
Titian
(20km)
& Guilin
(96km)

0   100   200 m
Approximate Scale

LÓNGSHÈNG

PLACES TO STAY
6 Wàimào Bīnguǎn
   外贸宾馆
8 Yínshān Bīnguǎn
   银杉宾馆
9 Kǎikǎi Lǚshè
   凯凯旅社

PLACES TO EAT
1 Floating Restaurants
   外贸宾馆
3 Jīnhuī Fàndiàn
   金徽饭店
5 Noodle Shops
   面馆

OTHER
2 Minibus Station
   小公共汽车站
4 PSB
   公安局
7 Jiāotōng Dàlóu
   交通大楼
10 Bus Station
   汽车站

Trust us on this one – the best value around for mid-range lodging is definitely the *Wàimào Bīnguǎn (Foreign Trade Hotel;* ☎ 751 2078), set back in an alley off the main roads. Lots of rooms are available, and a largish, clean, mid-range double with private bath costs just Y35 per bed (the staff often let you take the whole room for that), with good mosquito nets and ceiling fans. Dorm rooms are available from Y20. The staff have been very helpful on two visits.

The only hotel approaching anything resembling a star status is the *Yínshān Bīnguǎn* west of the bridge on the road to Sānjiāng. The Y128/150 singles/doubles are OK, but that's not saying much. You don't even get hot water 24 hours here.

The mid-range *Yongshan Bīnguǎn* (☎ 8602 75562) is a newish place run by the Forestry Department, hence its name, which means Pine Trees. Since it's 10 storeys high, all pink tiles and mirror glass, it's hard to miss. Rooms range from Y100 to Y180,

but in summer be sure any price quoted includes turning on the air-con.

Places to Eat
Lóngshèng is no culinary wonderland, but within recent years plenty of restaurants have opened up. The problem is that none has any English menus or speakers.

The downstairs *restaurant* at the Kǎikǎi Lǚshè has an English menu. Just below the bridge there are *floating restaurants*, popular with raucous office party groups.

The *Jīnhuī Fàndiàn* doesn't look like much, but serves up some decent dishes and has an English menu, albeit one pinched from a hotel in Guìlín. Negotiate the prices. Just past the bridge on Xinglong Xilu, *street stalls* appear around 8 pm, offering point-and-choose meals by lantern light. There are also some *noodle shops* on Xinglong Beilu.

Getting There & Away
From Guìlín, you can catch buses and minibuses to Lóngshèng from the long-

GUǍNGXĪ 广西

distance bus station and the south bus station (behind the train station). Buses to Lóngshèng (Y10.50) leave the long-distance bus station approximately every 20 minutes from 6 am to 4 pm; eight luxury express buses depart from 7.40 am to 6.20 pm and cost Y15. Barring landslides, the trip should take around three to four hours, an hour less in an express bus.

From Lóngshèng to Guìlín, buses leave the bus station every 15 to 20 minutes from 6 am to 5.30 pm. The fare is Y10.50. The express buses depart from the side of the Jiāotōng Dàlóu (Traffic Building), five minutes west of the bridge on the road toward Sānjiāng.

There is also a daily Lóngshèng-to-Liǔzhōu bus (Y27) which leaves at 7 am.

Buses and minibuses leave from the Lóngshèng bus station for Sānjiāng approximately every hour from 6.30 am to 5 pm. You can also catch these on the corner of Guilong Lu and Xinglong Xilu, down the road from the bus station. The fare is Y7 and the bumpy but scenic journey takes up to three hours. Oddly enough, even sleepers are making this run now, for the same price.

SĀNJIĀNG 三江
☎ 0772
If arriving in Sānjiāng leaves you wondering why you made the trip, don't worry. Like Lóngshèng, the idea is to get out and about. About 20km to the west of town, Chéngyáng Qiáo (see following) and the surrounding Dong villages are as peaceful and attractive as Sānjiāng is not.

Chéngyáng Qiáo
Rain & Wind Bridge
More than 80 years old, this elegant covered bridge is considered by the Dong to be the finest of the 108 such structures in Sānjiāng County, and took the local villagers 12 years to build. It looks out over a lush valley dotted with Dong villages and water wheels. The inevitable minority women hawking wares are there as well. An admission fee of Y5 is charged.

If you want to really enjoy and explore the area, you can stay at the Chéngyáng

Qiáo Zhāodàisuǒ, which is just to the left of the bridge on the far side of the river. See the following Places to Stay section for details.

From the Sānjiāng bus station, you can catch hourly buses to Lín Xī (there are other buses; bus station staff may figure out where you're going) right past the bridge. The 45-minute ride costs Y3. If there are several of you, hire a van to take you out there for around Y60 for the round trip. You'll probably see the Sanjiang Wind and Rain Travel Agency (☎ 861 3369) with an English sign opposite the bus station. Its cheapest tour is Y160, but the staff are nice, do speak English and can provide you with a map. Bus services stop around 5 pm, so if you need to get back to Sānjiāng later than that you'll have to hitch a lift. The first bus of the day to Sānjiāng passes by the bridge around 7.30 to 8 am.

Places to Stay
There's no need to stay in Sānjiāng unless you're catching a very early bus out of town. If so, your quietest option is the *Sānjiāng Dòngzú Zìzhìxiàn Rénmín Zhèngfǔ Zhāodàisuǒ (Guesthouse of the People's Government of the Sanjiang Dong Autonomous County)*. Singles and doubles start at Y35, or Y60 with bathroom attached. There are cheaper beds but you may not be allowed one. To get there, follow the road that runs between the Sānjiāng Bǎihuò Zhāodàisuǒ and the bus station uphill, and turn left. Walk about 10 minutes and it's on your right, across from a Dong drum tower.

Right in town on the opposite corner of the long-distance bus station, the *Sānjiāng Bǎihuò Zhāodàisuǒ (Hostel of the Department Store)* has cacophonous three/four-bed dorm beds for Y5/7, and singles/doubles with attached bathroom for Y20 per bed. There's every chance that the staff will tell you no cheap rooms are available.

Further down the street, the *Chéngyáng Qiáo Bīnguǎn (Chengyang Bridge Hotel)*, not to be confused with the National Hostel at the bridge itself, has slightly more upmarket singles/doubles starting at about Y90, though it can't overcome an annoying habit of adding foreign surcharges.

The *Chéngyáng Qiáo Zhāodàisuǒ* (*Chengyang Bridge National Hostel;* ☎ *861 2444*) is an all-wood Dong-style building with balconies overlooking the river. Beds are Y20 and nice doubles with shared bath are Y60, and staff speak some English. It closes seasonally and it's not always easy to figure out the seasons. Some travellers have opined that the hostel's service is sliding; if so, not far away is the *Dong Village Hotel* with beds from Y10 and showers.

Getting There & Away

The Sānjiāng bus station has several buses to Guìlín between 7.10 am and 2.30 pm (Y16.50 to Y18.50) and a handful of buses to Liǔzhōu (Y19 to Y27) between 6 am and 4.10 pm. Buses to Lóngshèng (Y7; 2½ to three hours) leave every 40 to 50 minutes between 6.30 am and 4.30 pm.

Sānjiāng to Kǎilǐ If you have time on your hands, it's worth considering entering Guìzhōu through the backdoor, by local bus. From Sānjiāng take the 2 pm bus to Lóng'é (Y9.90), which is just across the Guìzhōu border. Although the journey is only about three hours, you'll almost certainly have to stay overnight in Lóng'é, as the onward bus to Lìpíng leaves at 6 am. The hotel on the square where the buses stop has beds in triples for Y5 to Y10. There may be a bus all the way to Lìpíng from Sānjiāng at 6.30 am, costing Y27.

The five- to six-hour journey to Lìpíng costs Y15, and passes through some beautiful mountains and the town of Dìpíng – nice but reportedly nowhere to stay now. The highlight is the incredible town of Zhàoxīng, where the surrounding countryside may be the most beautiful you ever see (it has places to stay). From Lìpíng there is one bus to Kǎilǐ daily at 6 am, and sometimes buses run in the afternoon as well.

Another possibility is to take a train to Tōngdào in Húnán and from there travel onwards by bus to Lìpíng (there are minibuses running to the train station west of Sānjiāng half-hourly throughout the day).

You could also take a bus from Sānjiāng to Cónjiāng (Y15; five hours on an improved dirt road), an ugly little town, and leapfrog villages back to Kǎilǐ, but the scenery of the Lìpíng-Kǎilǐ route is better. One as yet untested option might be to take a bus to Fùlù, from where you should be able to get on a boat to Cónjiāng. Cónjiāng has connections to Róngjiāng and Kǎilǐ.

LIǓZHŌU 柳州

☎ 0772 • pop 1,752,900

Liǔzhōu is the largest city on the Liǔ Hé (Willow River) and an important railway junction in south-west China. The place dates back to the Tang dynasty, when it was a dumping ground for disgraced court officials. The town was largely left to its mountain wilds until 1949, when it was transformed into a major industrial city. It isn't as up-and-coming as other cities in south-western China, but it thinks it is, judging by the absurd number of banks around.

Liǔzhōu is akin to a poor cousin of Guìlín, with similar but less impressive karst scenery. (Most mornings eagle-eyed travellers can witness *taijiquan* (tai chi) practice sessions atop the peaks ringing the outskirts of town.) It sees few foreigners, so the locals are far from jaded in their dealings with travellers.

Information

The Bank of China is on Feie Lu. The post office, south of Liǔzhōu Guǎngchǎng, is open from 8 am to 8 pm. Email should be available at the post office by the time you read this.

Things to See

Along Feie Lu near the long-distance bus station is **Yúfēng Shān**, or (Fish Peak Mountain), in Yúfēng Gōngyuán (Fish Peak Park). It's very small as mountains go (33m), and derives its name from its resemblance to a 'standing fish'. Climb to the top for a smoggy vista of Guǎngxī's foremost industrial city.

Next door to Yúfēng Shān is **Mǎ'ān Shān** (Horse Saddle Mountain), which provides similar views.

Liǔhóu Gōngyuán is a more pleasant park in the north of the city. It has a lake and a small temple erected to the memory of Liu Zongyuan (AD 772–819), a famous scholar and poet. Bus No 2, 5 or 6 will get you to the park, or you can walk there from the long-distance bus station in around 20 minutes.

Places to Stay

Liǔzhōu is another Chinese city with a lack of budget lodging options. There is a new, lower-price (although not exactly budget) option to the east along Feie Lu. The *Tiědào Fàndiàn* (☎ 361 1140) is across the street and east of the Liuzhou south bus station. It's set back a bit off the street so keep a sharp eye. The interiors sport the classic China weariness, but the rooms are kept up decently. A single or double will set you back Y88.

Near the main train station down Feie Lu is the large *Nánjiāng Fàndiàn* (☎ 361 2988), which will take foreigners. Rooms with hard beds, your own TV and mouldy bathroom start at Y50 for a bed in a triple. Other rooms have increased dramatically after yet another 'face lift' to the reception area. A single or double will set you back Y120 now, although you can probably bargain it down.

Taking a step up in price, there is a nearby mid-range hotel taking foreigners. The *Yùfēng Dàshà* (☎ 383 8177) has decent, if a bit cramped, rooms starting at Y188 for a double. There is hot water 24 hours here.

The *Liǔzhōu Fàndiàn* (☎ 282 8336, fax 282 1443) is the longtime mid-range to top-end stand-by, now a three-star entity that denies any cheaper rooms. It charges Y390 to Y480 for TV and air-con. To get there take bus No 2 to Liǔhóu Gōngyuán, turn right into Youyi Lu and look out for the hotel on the left.

Places to Eat

Your best bet may be the lively *night market* across from the Foreign Language Bookstore. Starting around 8 pm, it has numerous stalls serving up tasty dumplings and noodles fried with your choice of fresh ingredients. The train station area also has

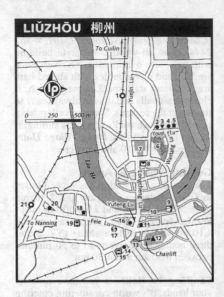

dumpling and noodle places. The *Liǔzhōu Fàndiàn* has a few restaurants, but the prices will probably put you off.

Off Liǔzhōu Guǎngchǎng towards the Liǔzhōu Fàndiàn is Liǔzhōu's first foray into western-style bars, the *Old Place (Lǎo Dìfāng; ☎ 286 9128)*. It serves up a few decent western dishes, well-prepared simple noodle and rice dishes, lots of local snacks, and draught beer!

Getting There & Away

Air The CAAC booking office (☎ 383 1604 or 382 0449) is on Feie Lu. For all its purported economic importance, Liǔzhōu isn't that easy to fly into or out of; it is simpler to go via Guìlín, an easy two-hour express bus ride away (they stop at the airport). You may have no choice – for example, to get to Běijīng you must go through Guìlín (Y1430 for both segments).

Bus The Liǔzhōu south bus station is actually north of the long-distance station cartographically, but let's not quibble. The long-distance station is an amazing place, fully computerised and with a staggeringly enormous schedule. Nearly all express

LIǓZHŌU

PLACES TO STAY & EAT
3 Old Place
   老地方酒吧
5 Liǔzhōu Fàndiàn
   柳州饭店
11 Yùfēng Dàshà
   鱼蜂大厦
18 Tiědào Fàndiàn
   铁道饭店
20 Nánjiāng Fàndiàn
   南疆饭店

OTHER
1 North Train
   Station
   火车北站

2 Xinhua Bookstore
   新华书店
4 CITS
   中国国际旅行社
6 Liǔhóu Gōngyuán
   柳侯公园
7 Liuzhou Guǎngchǎng
   柳州广场
8 Post Office
   邮电局
9 Ferry Dock
   航运码头
10 Riverside Park
   江滨公园
12 Mǎ'ān Shān
   马鞍山

13 Yúfēng Gōngyuán
   鱼峰公园
14 Foreign Language
   Bookstore; Night Market
   外文书店；夜市
15 Long-Distance Bus Station
   汽车总站
16 CAAC
   民航售票处
17 Bank of China
   中国银行
19 Liuzhou South
   Bus Station
   柳州南站
21 Main Train Station
   火车站

buses depart from here, though a couple do depart from the south bus station. From the long-distance station one can even depart for Guìzhōu, Guǎngdōng, Fújiàn and Húnán. An expressway is completed to Guìlín, and eventually four-lane highways will link Guìlín to Nánníng and Běihǎi in the south, and Wúzhōu in the east.

Express buses leave the long-distance station for Nánníng (Y50; 3½ hours) from 7 am to 8 pm, for Guìlín (Y40; two hours) from 7 am to 8.30 pm, and also to Wúzhōu (Y90), Sānjiāng (3.10 pm) and Guìpíng (Y45; 8.30 am). If you're heading for Yángshuò, avail yourself of the Guìlín express, which would get you into Yángshuò in three hours, whereas a regular sleeper could take six hours and you wouldn't save that much money! Sleepers to Yángshuò would cost Y24 to Y32.

Other destinations, almost all of which are sleeper buses, include Běihǎi (Y62), Fángchéng (Y39; regular bus), Guǎngzhōu (Y117; sleeper bus, though even private share taxis are available!), Guìpíng (Y33), Lóngshèng (Y25), Nánníng (Y34), Píngxiáng (Y45), Sānjiāng (Y19 or Y27, sleeper bus), Shēnzhèn (Y144), Wúzhōu (Y38 regular; Y64 sleeper) and Zhūhǎi (Y145).

Train Virtually all major trains into or out of Guǎngxī – including nearly all from Nánníng and Běihǎi – pass through Liǔzhōu,

and you could hook up with any one of these to get to a number of major destinations. Possibilities – prices given are middle hard sleeper – include Běijīng (Y441), Chángshā, Chéngdū (Y215), Kūnmíng (Y168), Guìyáng (Y97) and Xī'ān. Trains originate here for Shànghǎi (Y377; 3.37 pm) and Guǎngzhōu (Y247; 2.53 pm).

Many trains pass through on the way to Guìlín, fewer to Nánníng. The hard-seat fare from Liǔzhōu to Guìlín is around Y15 for slow trains, and the trip takes approximately four hours; faster trains cost up to Y28. Trains pass through to Nánníng between 7.25 am and 12.26 pm and hard-seat tickets for the five-hour trip range from Y20 for the glacial trains to Y39 for the K5 express.

Boat Nightly boats for Guǎngzhōu via Wúzhōu stopped in 1997 and officials in Liǔzhōu say that's not likely to change. However, Liǔzhōu has been building up a spiffy new wharf complex replete with restaurants, parks and river walks, and a few tour boats reportedly will soon offer river tours.

Getting Around

Liǔzhōu is a bit large for walking around, particularly at the height of summer when the place is like a blast furnace! There is now a bike rental place almost directly across from the Nánjiāng Fàndiàn; bikes

GUǍNGXĪ 广西

can be rented for Y0.80 per hour or Y4 per day. Pedicabs, motor-tricycles, motorcycle taxis and taxis are absolutely ubiquitous.

Bus No 2 will take you to the Liǔzhōu Fàndiàn, and bus No 11 links the long-distance bus station to the main train station. Bus maps – no English – can be bought from hawkers at both train stations.

WÚZHŌU 梧州
☎ 0774 • pop 2,758,500

For most travellers, Wúzhōu is a pit stop on the road between Yángshuò and Guǎngzhōu or Hong Kong. Although it's not one of Guǎngxī's major attractions, Wúzhōu has some pleasant parks and interesting street life. Not enough travellers check this place out; give it an overnight, as it's either a somewhat tame first mainland city off the boat from Hong Kong, or a calming influence after Guǎngzhōu.

In 1897 the British dived into this trading town, setting up steamer services to Guǎngzhōu, Hong Kong and later Nánníng. A British consulate was established, and the town was also used by British and US missionaries as a launching pad for the conversion of the 'heathen' Chinese.

During the period after 1949, a paper mill, food-processing factories, and machinery and plastics manufacturing plants, among other industries, were established.

During the Cultural Revolution parts of Guǎngxī appear to have become battlegrounds for Red Guard factions claiming loyalty to Mao. In something approaching a civil war, half of Wúzhōu was reportedly destroyed.

Today, Wúzhōu has some fine street markets (absolutely everywhere you walk, in fact), tailors, tobacco, herbs, roast duck and river life to explore. Wúzhōu also has one of Guǎngxī's more unusual sights: the Snake Repository.

A note: a new bridge was being constructed in Wúzhōu and as it inches along,

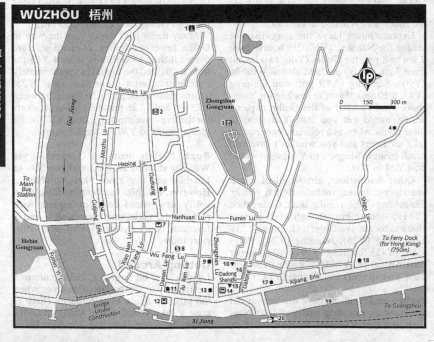

WÚZHŌU 梧州

the whole downtown area – streets and buildings – will likely change.

Information

CITS has an office along Dazhang Lu, north of the Nanhuan Lu main drag; it's down an alley – next to a Christian church that doesn't look like one – and upstairs.

The post and China Telecom offices are also located on Nanhuan Lu, east of the bridge; it's open from 8 am to 9 pm. Email facilities are only located at the Xingyi Lu branch post office (Héxīyóudiàn Júfēnjú), near the intersection with Rihua Lu, far west of the central part of town. Good maps of the city, with bus routes but again no English, are available at shops adjacent to the long-distance bus station ticket office along Xijiang Erlu.

Wúzhōu Shécáng 梧州蛇园

Wuzhou Snake Repository

Wúzhōu has what it claims is the world's largest snake repository, a major drawcard for overseas Chinese tourists and a sight that pulls in the occasional western traveller. More than one million snakes are transported each year to Wúzhōu (from places like Nánníng, Liǔzhōu and Yúlín) for export to the kitchens of Hong Kong, Macau and other snake-devouring parts of the world. To get there, walk along Shigu Lu from next to the Wúzhōu Dàjiǔdiàn (see

Places to Stay); it's about 2km away. Snake and cat fights are sometimes staged for visiting groups of tourists – something you may wish to avoid. The repository is open daily from 8 am to 6 pm. Entry is Y2.

Zhōngshān Gōngyuán

Sun Yatsen Park

Just north of the river up Zhongshan Lu, which then turns into Wenhua Lu, Zhōngshān Gōngyuán is worth a look as the site of China's earliest memorial hall for the founder of the Republic of China. The hall was constructed in 1928 and commemorates an important speech given by Sun Yatsen in Wúzhōu. Entry is Y1.

Xīzhú Yuán 西竹园

Western Bamboo Temple

Just north of town bordering Zhōngshān Gōngyuán is the Xīzhú Yuán, where around 40 Buddhist nuns live. The vegetarian restaurant, open for breakfast and lunch, is highly rated by travellers who have taken the time to wander up here. You can walk to the temple by taking Wenhua Lu into Zhōngshān Gōngyuán. From the park gate walk for about 10 minutes until you reach an old brick building with an English sign saying 'temple' on the left-hand side. The restaurant doesn't keep regular hours, but it seems the earlier you get there, the better.

GUĂNGXĪ 广西

WÚZHŌU

PLACES TO STAY & EAT	19	Underground Hotpot Stalls	7	Post Office
6	Wŭfēng Dàjiǔdiàn		地下市场		邮电局
	五丰大酒店			8	Bank of China
9	Xīnjiè Dàjiǔdiàn	**OTHER**			中国银行
	新世界大酒店	1	Xīzhú Yuán	12	Local Bus Station
10	Cháxiāngfāng		西竹园		客运站
	茶仙坊	2	Museum	14	Long-Distance Bus Station
11	Xīnxī Lǚdiàn		博物馆		客运站
	新西旅店	3	Sun Yatsen	16	Market
13	Jīnshān Jiǔdiàn		Memorial Hall		市场
	金山酒店		中山纪念堂	17	High-Speed Ferry Tickets
15	Kuàicān Jiāzhōng Cāntīng	4	Wúzhōu Shécáng		(to Guǎngzhōu)
	快菜家中餐厅		梧州蛇园		梧港客运站
18	Wúzhōu Dàjiǔdiàn	5	CITS	20	Ferry Dock (to Guǎngzhōu)
	梧州大酒店		中　　　事睐猩		客轮码头

Places to Stay

The steady flow of Hong Kong Chinese into Wúzhōu has pushed hotel prices up, and in several places room rates are quoted in Hong Kong dollars.

The great new *Jìnshān Jiǔdiàn (☎ 282 4914, 1 Zhongshan Lu)* is approximately 70m west of the Guăngzhōu boat dock, across the street from the bus station ticket office. Superb 'ordinary' singles/doubles for Y65/70 including bath are spotless, so no need to jump up to 'standard' prices. It also has triples and a couple of quads (Y140), both with bath.

Close by, the somewhat forlorn but still basically OK *Xīnxī Lǚdiàn* offers even lower rates. Spartan singles and doubles start as low as Y20, and go up to Y90 (though four times the price isn't apparent in the quality of the rooms).

The *Wúzhōu Dàjiǔdiàn (☎ 202 2193)* is also showing signs of wear and tear, and isn't much of a bargain either. Rooms range from Y120 to Y880, but the staff will likely push you toward doubles costing around Y200; there are a few diminutive Y80 doubles with private bath.

The *Xīnjiè Dàjiǔdiàn (New World Hotel; ☎ 282 8333, fax 282 4895)* north of the Jìnshān Jiǔdiàn doesn't seem worth the Y288/388 (up to Y2380!) it charges for a standard single/double. Instead, the best top-end place overlooks the river along Guijiang Erlu. The *Wǔfēng Dàjiǔdian (☎ 282 3888, fax 282 8898, 38 Guijiang Lu)* has superb singles/doubles from Y328/388 and the best service in town.

Places to Eat

There's a great underground grouping of *hotpot places*, but it's also a bit tough to find. Walk east of the ferry docks along Xijiang Erlu until you see steps leading down to the right. Dadong Shanglu is filled with point-and-shoot outdoor wok places in the evenings. Sit-down fast food is found at the very friendly and good *Kuàicān Jiāzhōng Cānfīng (House of Fast Food)* – no English sign, look for the statue of the little boy in red out front – along Wufang Lu. There is a hip little teahouse, *Cháxiāngfáng (Cele-*

stial Tea) along Wufang Lu. Owned by a bunch of friendly young guys, it serves snacks, good teas and ice-cold beers.

Don't forget about the vegetarian restaurant at the *Xīzhú Yuán*.

Getting There & Away

Air Wúzhōu has daily flights to Shēnzhèn (Y430) and Hǎikǒu (Y550).

Bus Wúzhōu has a new long-distance bus station far in the western part of town; the erstwhile bus station diagonally opposite the Guăngzhōu ferry dock on Zhongshan Lu still sells tickets. If you do purchase a ticket here, you get a free ride on a rickety old bus that acts as a shuttle to the new station – if it runs at all. It's quicker to hike two blocks north along Zhongshan Lu to the bus stop for bus No 2, which terminates near the long-distance bus station. A taxi will cost Y20 minimum.

Express non-sleeper luxury buses depart for most provincial cities. One leaves for Guìlín via Yángshuò at 8.40 am, takes eight hours and costs Y60; Y51.50 to Yángshuò. Sleepers along the same route depart from 7.15 am to 9.30 pm and cost Y50.50 to Yángshuò. Expresses leave twice in the morning and twice around 11 pm for Nán-níng (Y80; seven hours); regular sleepers cost Y68. There are six expresses and about a million sleepers per day to Guǎngzhōu; an express costs Y80, a sleeper costs Y55, and both take around five hours. Express buses also depart for Zhūhǎi (Y75), Shēnzhèn (Y150) and Liǔzhōu (Y90).

Another bus station has departures from just west of the Xīnxī Lǚdiàn on the river side of Xijiang Erlu; it has mostly local bus departures, though some go to Nánníng.

Boat There's a high-speed ferry service between Wúzhōu and Hong Kong on odd days of the month (1, 3, 5, 7 etc), leaving at 8 am and arriving in Hong Kong at around 4 pm on the same day. (From Hong Kong, boats leave at 8 am on even dates.) Tickets are pegged at Y290 and the staff showed no interest in a foreign friend surcharge. From Yángshuò, CITS and several local hotels can arrange tickets for the trip; for more details see the Yángshuò Getting There & Away section earlier in this chapter.

The dock for this ferry has relocated to the east end of Wúzhōu, approximately 15 minutes by foot east of the Wúzhōu Dàjiǔdiàn along Xijiang Erlu.

High-speed ferries now make the trip to Guǎngzhōu in around five hours. A boat leaves at 1 pm. Tickets are Y70.

Due to lack of demand, most of the slower ferries to Guǎngzhōu have suspended service. The one remaining ferry leaves at 5 pm, and the cheapest tickets are for the crowded (but bearable) dorm-style accommodation atop the boat at Y53. Two- and four-bed cabins are probably going to be phased out. Boats leave from the docks just east of the old long-distance bus stations. Tickets for the high-speed boats can be bought at a ticket office east of the docks on the opposite side of the road from the dock, or for all boats at the docks themselves.

Boats no longer serve Shēnzhèn or Zhūhǎi at all.

Guìzhōu 贵州

Pity poor Guìzhōu. A Chinese newspaper once described it as 'a place of sunless sky, endless hills, and penniless people'. The 'South-West Coal Sea' (as it's also known) sounds more benign, but is no less ugly. Until recently Guìzhōu was both a backwater and backward. It has always been one of the most sparsely populated and poverty-stricken areas in China. Statistics continue to paint a grim picture. Eight million of the province's population live below the national poverty line. Between 60% and 70% of the population are illiterate and nearly 30% of the villages are inaccessible by road.

Guìzhōu is also one of the most rewarding provinces to visit. Mountains and plateaus make up some 87% of its topography, which has an average altitude of 1000m above sea level, presenting many opportunities for hiking and stumbling around some of China's least visited villages.

About 65% of Guìzhōu's population is Han and the rest a mixture of minorities such as Miao, Bouyei, Dong, Yi, Shui, Hui, Zhuang, Bai, Tujiao and Gelao. In all, over 80 non-Han groups populate the province. Among them these minorities celebrate nearly 1000 festivals each year, which preserve fascinating customs and elaborate skills in architecture, dress and handicrafts.

Despite this, Guìzhōu is surprisingly neglected by most travellers. The south-east of Guìzhōu, in particular, deserves more attention from adventurous travellers, especially since almost all counties and towns are now open to foreigners. Miao, Dong and a mixture of other minorities make up around 72% of the population in this region.

Transport *can* be rough – if it exists at all – but certainly no rougher than, say, northern Sìchuān.

HISTORY

Although Chinese rulers established an administration in the area as early as the Han dynasty, Chinese settlement was confined to the north and east of the province. Western

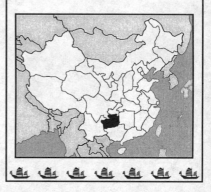

Highlights

Capital: Guìyáng
Population: 35.6 million
Area: 170,000 sq km

- Huángguǒshù Dàpùbù, China's highest waterfall at 74m, scenic countryside and minority villages
- The south-east region, home to several minority groups, offering village-hopping and festival-watching
- Caǒ Haǐ, a birdwatcher's paradise in Guìzhōu's wild west

parts were not settled until the 16th century, when the native minorities were forced out of the most fertile areas.

When the Japanese invasion forced the Kuomintang to retreat to the south-west, the development of impoverished Guìzhōu began; roads to the neighbouring provinces were constructed, a train link was built to Guǎngxī and industries were set up in Guìyáng and Zūnyì. These languished after WWII until well into communist rule and only revived when the railroads were built.

FESTIVALS

Festivities among the minorities in Guìzhōu offer much scope for exploration. Festivals

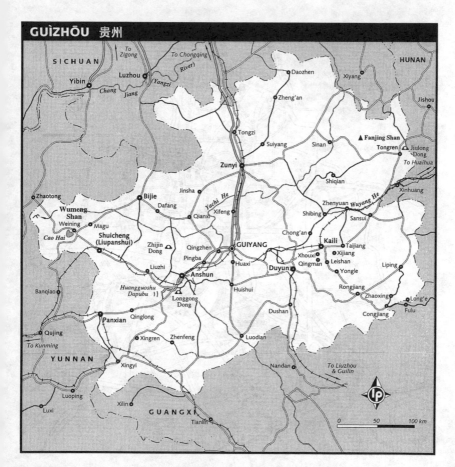

GUÌZHŌU 贵州

take place throughout the lunar calendar at specific sites and are technicolour spectaculars that can feature bullfighting, horse racing, pipe playing, comic opera, singing contests and gigantic courting parties.

Several festivals take place in Guìyáng during the first lunar month (usually February or March), fourth lunar month (around May) and sixth lunar month (around July). Some of these occur in Huāxī.

A good starting point for festival forays is Kǎilǐ, which is on the train line east of Guìyáng. A profusion of festivals is held in nearby minority areas such as Léishān,

Xījiāng, Zhōuxī, Qīngmàn and Panghai. The town of Zhijiāng, about 50km from Kǎilǐ, is also a festival centre.

About 10km further east on the train line is Zhènyuán, which is renowned for its festivals between April and July. This town was once an important staging point on the ancient post road from central China to South-East Asia.

GUÌYÁNG 贵阳

☎ 0851 • pop 3,114,300

Guìyáng, the under appreciated capital of Guìzhōu, has a mild climate all year round.

GUÌYÁNG 贵阳

Its name means 'precious sun', which may be a reference to the fact that the sun rarely seems to shine through the grey clouds and drizzle.

A few of the original neighbourhoods and temples remain, fighting for their existence amid the mushrooming high-rise towers. With some effort the place can be appreciated for the funky conglomeration of city and village that it is.

Guìyáng is a jumping-off point for the falls at Huángguǒshù Dàpùbù or, if you travel via Kǎilǐ, the minority areas of the south-east.

Orientation

Guìyáng is a sprawling kind of place that at first glance seems to lack a centre of any kind. It doesn't take long to get on top of things, however.

Zunyi Lu heads up from the train station and links up with Zhonghua Lu, the road that cuts through the centre of town and is home to Guìyáng's main shopping area. Yan'an Lu intersects Zhonghua Lu, and it is along this road that you will find the Bank of China, CITS, the expensive Guiyang Plaza Hotel (Guìyáng Jīnzhù Dàjiǔdiàn) and, at the other end, the long-distance bus station.

GUÌYÁNG

PLACES TO STAY
1 Bājiǎoyán Fàndiàn
八角岩饭店
2 Guìzhōu Fàndiàn
贵州公园饭店
3 Yúnyán Bīnguǎn
云岩宾馆
6 Gōnglù Dàshà
公路大厦
13 Guiyang Plaza Hotel
金筑大酒店
23 Jīnqiáo Fàndiàn
金桥饭店
33 Tǐyù Bīnguǎn
体育宾馆
36 Míngzhū Fàndiàn
明珠饭店

PLACES TO EAT
11 Juéyuán
Cāntīng
觉园餐厅
34 Guìzhōu Běijīng
Kǎoyādiàn
贵州北京烤鸭店

OTHER
4 Guìzhōu Shěng
Bówùguǎn
贵州省博物馆

5 Bank of China
中国银行
7 Long-Distance Bus
Station
贵阳汽车站
8 Xinhua Bookstore
新华书店
9 Guizhou Overseas
Travel Company GOTC)
贵州海外旅
行总公司
10 CITS
中国国际旅行社
12 Post & Telecom
Office
邮电局
14 Bank of China
中国银行
15 Foreign Languages
Bookstore
外文书店
16 Huájiā Gé
华家阁
17 Shìchǎng
Market
市场
18 Wénchāng Gé
文昌阁
19 Night Market
夜市

20 PSB
公安局
21 Train Ticket Office
火车票预售处
22 Department Store
百货大楼
24 Telecommunications
Business Centre
电信商场
25 Post &
Telecommunications
Building
邮电大楼
26 Jiǎxiù Lóu
甲秀楼
27 Qiánmíng Sì
黔明寺
28 Mao Statue
毛主席像
29 CAAC
中国民航
30 Guizhou Exhibition
Centre
省展览馆
31 Chaoyang Cinema
朝阳影剧院
32 Guizhou Gymnasium
省体育馆
35 Train Station
贵阳站

Information

Money The Bank of China has several branches around town that will change money: on Yan'an Donglu, near the Guiyang Plaza Hotel; across from the CAAC ticket office; and the main branch on Ruijin Beilu, where you can arrange credit card withdrawals and wire transfers.

Post & Communications The post and telecommunications building is on the intersection of Zunyi Lu and Zhonghua Nanlu. It's posted as 24 hours, but was closed on at least one morning visit. You can make international phone calls from the international and long-distance hall, to the left of the main doors. There's also the post and telecommunications office at the intersection of Zhonghua Lu and Yan'an Lu.

Email & Internet Access Internet access is available at the post and telecommunications building and costs Y10 per hour. Across the road and short walk north, Internet access at Y8 per hour is also available on the fourth floor of the Telecommunications Business Centre (Diànxìn Shāngchéng).

Travel Agencies China International Travel Service (CITS; Zhōngguó Guójì Lǚxíngshè; ☎ 582 5873), 20 Yan'an Zhonglu, is one of China's more helpful and friendly. The staff have maps and info on minority areas. The staff at Guizhou Overseas Travel Company (GOTC; Guìzhōu Hǎiwài Lǚxíng; ☎ 582 5328), a few doors down, aren't as sociable but are reliable for travel bookings.

Bookshops There's a branch of the Foreign Languages Bookstore on Yan'an Donglu, but it's not particularly well stocked. Several employees of the shop hold an English language and lecture session there every Sunday morning and they welcome foreign visitors warmly.

PSB The Public Security Bureau (PSB; Gōngānjú; ☎ 682 1231) is in a white-tiled building complex on Zhongshan Xilu, quite close to the intersection with Zhonghua Lu. This is the place to report thefts or seek visa extensions. Save for the extreme northwest, there shouldn't be any need to get permits for travel within the province.

Dangers & Annoyances Guìyáng has a reputation among Chinese as one of China's most dangerous cities for theft – the Chinese even say 'in Guìyáng they'll rob you under the sun'. Travellers have reported problems in the train station, which is a favoured haunt of pickpockets. Animated motorcycle taxi drivers may be more of a problem.

Things to See

The distinctive architectural characteristics of Guìyáng's handful of Soviet-era buildings are the columns, like the ones at the Guìzhōu Shěng Bówùguǎn (Guizhou Provincial Museum). The main street leading north from the train station, Zunyi Lu, harbours one of the largest glistening white statues of Mao Zedong in China.

Qiánlíng Gōngyuán is a park worth a visit for its forested walks and for the late Ming dynasty Hóngfú Sì, the monastery perched near the top of 1300m-high Qiánlíng Shān. It's an hour on foot or you can take the cable car for Y12 one way. The monastery has a vegetarian restaurant in the rear courtyard that's open from 11 am to around 4 pm. From the Jīnqiáo Fàndiàn or the train station area take a No 2 bus. The park is open from 8 am to 10.30 pm and admission is Y2.

Not far from the CAAC office is Hébīn Gōngyuán (Great Future Park), a park with benches under shade trees along the river and a Ferris wheel offering good views of Guìyáng for Y6.

Guìyáng's two other park attractions, Huāxī Gōngyuán (Flower Mountain Stream Park) and Nánjiāo Gōngyuán, are nothing to get particularly excited about. Both have caves and strolling areas.

Guìyáng is a pleasant enough place to stroll around (if it's not raining), and there are a few pavilions and pagodas scattered around town. These include the Wénchāng Gé, Jiàxiù Lóu, Húajié Gé and the temple Qiánmíng Sì. Check the map for their locations.

In the northern part of town, along Beijing Lu, there is the Guìzhōu Shěng Bówùguǎn (Guizhou Provincial Museum) with decent displays on Guìzhōu's minorities – their clothing, festivals and customs – along with some geological artefacts. It's open Tuesday to Sunday, 9 am to 5 pm; entry is Y10.

Places to Stay – Budget

Budget accommodation is in short supply in Guìyáng. Just east of the train station is the good *Míngzhū Fàndiàn*, where beds in a double with communal bath start at Y40. Rooms with private bath start at Y110.

A longtime trusty, cheap option is the *Jīnqiáo Fàndiàn* (☎ 582 9951, fax 581 3867) on Ruijin Zhonglu, a good 30-minute walk from the train station. Beds in a pleasant six-person dorm room cost Y40. It's a steep jump in price if you want your own bathroom. Doubles start at Y218 and don't seem a particularly good deal at that price. Bus Nos 1 and 2 run from the train station past the hotel; or take minibus No 77 from the long-distance bus station. You can dump bags for free here.

The *Gōnglù Dàshà* (Highway Department Building; ☎ 599 2524, 12 Ruijin Beilu) is walking distance east of the long-distance bus station and has two basic guesthouses, either of which *may* take you. The cheaper one is on the 13th floor, with beds for Y25 (communal bath), but you may get directed to the other one on the 5th floor, which has good doubles/triples from Y148/165 with private bath. Note that there's no elevator after 11 pm.

The **Bājiǎoyán Fàndiàn** (☎ 682 2651) is near the corner of Zhonghua Beilu and Beijing Lu. It has clean doubles with bathroom for Y138, and suites from Y168. Although somewhat of a concrete hulk, it's a quiet place and not a bad deal for the price.

Places to Stay – Mid-Range & Top End

Most of Guìyáng's accommodation is mid-range in standard, even if some of the prices quoted for rooms are definitely top end. Pick of the bunch in terms of value for money is the **Tǐyù Bīnguǎn** (*Sports Hotel*; ☎ 579 8777), on the grounds of the Guizhou Gymnasium just north of the train station. Enormous and very clean doubles with TV and bathroom start at Y150. If you are in need of a night of comfort, they're well worth the money.

The **Yúnyán Bīnguǎn** (☎ 682 3324), a cadre-style place, has singles and doubles starting at Y176, and triples at Y240. Staying here does give you access to a swimming pool in front of the hotel, although actually swimming there will cost you extra.

The **Guìzhōu Fàndiàn** (*Guizhou Park Hotel*; ☎ 682 2888, fax 682 4397) is the lap of luxury, with standard doubles ranging from Y320 to Y580.

Places to Eat

Guìyáng, like Kūnmíng, is a great city for snack tracking. Just follow Zunyi Lu up to Zhonghua Nanlu and peer into the side alleys for noodle, dumpling and kebab *stalls*. North of Zhongshan Donglu, Fushui Lu is a bustling street of outside *restaurants* – lots serving hotpot in all its incarnations, but plenty of others as well, including grill-your-own.

Next door to the Tǐyù Bīnguǎn on the grounds of the Guizhou Gymnasium is a good *Chinese restaurant* with fairly reasonable prices. Try the *gōngbǎo jīdìng* (chicken and peanuts dish). There's no English menu, but give other forms of communication a try as this place is a treat. There are literally dozens of extremely attentive staff and it's loads of fun trying to stop them doing things for you. You'll also

get the traditional form of *Bābǎo Chá* (Eight Treasures Tea), with the server swirling hot water from a long-stemmed copper kettle.

For a special night out, try the **Guìzhōu Běijīng Kǎoyādiàn** (*Guizhou Beijing Duck Restaurant*), across the road from the Tǐyù Bīnguǎn near the train station. Although you'll be looking at around Y60 for a whole duck it's money well spent since the duck here is excellent.

Vegetarians should head for the **Juéyuán Cāntīng** (*Awakening Palace Restaurant; 51 Fushui Beilu*). The building housing this Buddhist restaurant dates to 1862 and forms part of the adjacent temple. The restaurant promises food 'free of worldly dust'. Opening hours are from 11.30 am to 2.30 pm and from 4.30 to 7 pm daily.

Kebabs & Raisins

On many street corners in Guìyáng, and many other towns in the south-west, you see (and smell) the occasional hard-nosed entrepreneur grilling delicious mutton kebabs over a crackling rack of coals. On the other side of the street there will often be another swarthy-looking guy lovingly piling Turpani raisins into a conical mound, and tossing a few into his mouth every now and again.

These are Uyghur people, Turkic-speaking Muslims from Xīnjiāng in Chinese Central Asia, recognisable by their Mediterranean or Middle Eastern appearance, their black or green skullcaps and the knife that hangs perennially by their side.

On Saturday, keep an eye out for *matang*, a wonderful chewy walnut and fruit nougat loaf that some Uyghurs sell near the Penshuichi Fountain. It's a bit pricey at Y15 for 500g, but worth its weight in gold.

Most Uyghurs know about as much Chinese as you do. If you really want to impress, try out the Muslim greeting *a salaam aleikum* ('May peace be upon you') or the Turkic *yakshimisis?* ('How are you?'). If that doesn't get you cheap kebabs, nothing will.

Bradley Mayhew

Unfortunately, Guìzhōu isn't known for its beers; most are putrid, so be forewarned.

Getting There & Away

Air Guìyáng opened its shiny new airport 7km east of town in 1997. The CAAC office (☎ 584 4534 to book, ☎ 581 2138 to reconfirm) is at 170 Zunyi Lu. The staff are cheerful and helpful, and a spot check found all flights with tickets available for the following morning. The office is open daily from 8.30 am to 9 pm. Flights from Guìyáng include: Běijīng (Y1380), Chángshā, Chéngdū (Y500), Guǎngzhōu (Y690), Guìlín (Y380; twice weekly), Hǎikǒu (Y740), Kūnmíng (Y350), Shànghǎi (Y1280), Shēnzhèn (Y750), Wǔhàn (Y670), Xiàmén, Zhūhǎi (Y690), Chóngqìng (Y310), Nánníng (Y380) and Xī'ān.

China Southwest has two flights a week to Hong Kong for HK$1795 or US$216.

Bus The long-distance bus station is a long way from the train station. If you want to get out of Guìyáng quickly you're better off using the bus services that operate from in front of the train station. From there buses to Xīngyì (from where there are onward buses to Kūnmíng) run between 8 am and 6 pm for Y55; the trip takes 10 to 12 hours.

Buses to Ānshùn leave every half hour (or whenever they fill up) from 7 am to 6 pm, although some may leave later if demand warrants it. The journey takes two hours and costs Y10 to Y15. For the five-hour (if you're very, very lucky) trip to Kǎilǐ, there are buses approximately hourly from 6.30 am to 5.30 pm. The fare is Y25 to Y30. Buses to Zūnyì leave every 30 minutes between 7 am and 9 pm. The ride along the new expressway takes 2½ hours and costs Y15 to Y20. The travel times to Kǎilǐ should improve gradually as extensive roadwork is completed.

Another bus station sits at the first intersection north of the train station and might be a better option for Ānshùn, Zūnyì and Kǎilǐ, as some luxury buses do the routes. Buses depart constantly to Ānshùn and cost Y12 to Y20. Buses to Kǎilǐ leave hourly (at least) and cost Y27 to Y30. To Zūnyì, buses

cost Y15 to Y28. Sleepers also serve Róngjiāng (Y70; 12 to 14 hours) leaving at 4 pm, and other Guìzhōu destinations.

The long-distance bus station is the closer, better option if you stay overnight at the Jīnqiáo Fàndiàn. The new ticket office inexplicably has no schedules so just exit, walk the absolutely endless gauntlet of buses, and bargain. Buses to Ānshùn depart between 7 am and 6 pm; the cheapest minibuses go for Y10. After 6 pm, there is a variety of sleeper buses to Xīngyì; with bargaining, the fare is Y55.

To Zūnyì, buses leave more or less every half hour from 6.20 am to 5 pm; the trip takes 2½ hours and costs Y15 to Y25. To get to Kǎilǐ, head to the train station.

It's also possible to take tour buses (don't expect much of a 'tour' though) to Huángguǒshù Dàpùbù and the Lónggōng Dòng (Dragon Palace Caves) from the train station (bargain hard here), the long-distance bus station and most of the hotels. Buses generally depart at 6 or 7 am (7 am in the case of the bus station, and additional buses run in summer) and cost Y55 to Y68. Entry fees aren't included in this price. You may also have to take in some 'sights' you don't want to, but a good tour will make the trip painless in that you won't have to tramp around Huángguǒshù Dàpùbù looking for a cheap room.

Train Foreigners technically can use any of the computerised ticket windows, but if lines are long you might try the erstwhile foreigners' ticket office upstairs. You might even be met in the hall by a friendly retired railway official who speaks great English and keeps himself busy helping travellers.

Direct trains run to Kǎilǐ, Kūnmíng, Shànghǎi, Guìlín, Liǔzhōu, Nánníng, Zhànjiāng, Běijīng and Chóngqìng. Soft-seat trains to Zūnyì are the way to go, but they leave around 5.40 pm; seats cost Y30 and the trip is three hours. Do *not* take a local train unless you've got all day to kill. To Kǎilǐ the train is still preferable to the bus. The best option could be train No 352, which leaves at 10 am, takes three hours and costs Y14 for a hard seat. Alternatively, take train No 248 at 7.50 am, which takes a bit longer.

Some sample hard sleeper fares for foreigners from Guìyáng are: Kūnmíng (Y94; 11½ hours, cheapest hard sleeper on train No 525), Chéngdū (Y144; hours), Chángshā (Y126), Běijīng (Y488; 36 hours) and Guìlín (Y118; 18 hours). See the Ānshùn Getting There & Away section later in this chapter for fares and departure times to Ānshùn.

Getting Around

If you want to do a city-loop tour, then across the square from the train station are two round-the-city buses, Nos 1 and 2. They follow the same route, but No 2 goes clockwise while No 1 goes anticlockwise.

These buses will get you to most places; the round trip from the train station costs Y0.80 and takes about 45 minutes. Double-decker buses also ply the route.

The main shopping street is on the No 1 bus route heading north, but this area is more fun to explore on foot. Note that minibuses with route numbers on the windscreen do not follow the same routes as larger buses bearing the same numbers; minibus No 77 runs between the train and long-distance bus stations, via the Jīnqiáo Fàndiàn, for Y1.

Taxi Taxis charge a flat Y10 rate anywhere in the city.

ĀNSHÙN 安顺
☎ 0853

Spending a day or two in Ānshùn isn't the worst of fates. The karst valley setting is pleasant and some of the narrow streets are lined with interesting old wooden houses. It is also the best place from which to visit Huángguǒshù Dàpùbù and Lónggōng Dòng.

Once an opium-trading centre, Ānshùn remains the commercial hub of western Guìzhōu, but is now known for its batiks. The town's main attraction is the **Wén Miào**, a temple north-west of the train station. This temple, which dates back to the Ming dynasty, underwent restoration work in 1668. It was undergoing another renovation at the time of writing. Entrance is Y3.

Information

Post & Communications The main post office is at the corner of Zhonghua Nanlu and Tashan Donglu. Another is north at the intersection of Zhonghua Donglu and Zhongua Nanlu. The former is supposed to offer 24-hour service, but it was shut tight at 6 am on the last check.

Travel Agent The China Travel Service (CTS; Zhōngguó Lǚxíngshè; ☎ 322 4379) has an office at the northern end of Tashan Donglu on the 3rd floor of the Mínzú Fàndiàn (see Places to Stay). It organises trips to Huángguǒshù Dàpùbù (see the Around Ānshùn section later) and the surrounding area, and has information on minor attractions in the region.

Places to Stay & Eat

The *Xīxiùshān Bīnguǎn* (☎ 322 3900 ext 2800, 63 Nanhua Lu), near the bus station, used to be the only choice in town but it has now reinvented itself as a two-star joint with rooms starting at Y98. Better for the budget-conscious is the *Huáyóu Bīnguǎn* (☎ 332 9164, 15 Tashan Xilu), to the north-west along Tashan Xilu, whose friendly staff have recently begun taking foreigners. Rooms with communal bath start at Y25/40/45 for a single/double/triple in an old wing; rooms with private bath start at Y50/60 single/double. Minibus No 2 runs here from the long-distance bus station.

On the eastern side of town, near the highway to Guìyáng, the *Mínzú Fàndiàn* (☎ 322 2621, 67 Tashan Donglu) used to have cheap rooms, but has renovated and now has doubles costing around Y180 and triples for around Y240. There's a *Muslim restaurant* on the 2nd floor.

For cuisine, expect nothing other than rows of forgettable, if friendly, point-and-choose places surrounding the bus station area. But be warned – lots of dog meat is served in these parts; one local sign reads 'Lunch of Dog Counter'.

Getting There & Away

Bus In Anshùn just stick out your arm and chances are a Guìyáng-bound bus of some

GUIZHOU 贵州

ĀNSHÙN 安顺

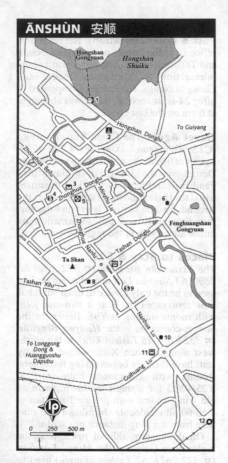

Hongshan Gongyuan
Hongshan Shuiku
Zhonghua Beilu
Hongshan Donglu
To Guiyang
Zhonghua Donglu
Minzhu Lu
Zhonghua Nanlu
Tashan Donglu
Ta Shan
Fenghuangshan Gongyuan
Tashan Xilu
Nanhua Lu
To Longgong Dong & Huangguoshu Dapubu
Guihuang Lu
0   250   500 m

ĀNSHÙN

1 Dock
   码头
2 Wén Miào
   文庙
3 Post Office
   邮电局
4 Bank of China
   中国银行
5 Department Store
   百货大楼
6 Mínzú Fàndiàn; CTS
   民族饭店；
   中国旅行社
7 Telecommunications Building
   邮电大楼
8 Huáyóu Bīnguǎn
   华油宾馆
9 Bank of China
   中国银行
10 Xīxiùshān Bīnguǎn
   西秀山宾馆
11 Long-Distance Bus Station
   长途汽车站
12 Train Station
   火车站

sort will screech to a halt. From Guìyáng to Ānshùn, minibuses and bigger express buses depart from in front of the train station or from a station one block north. They leave every 30 minutes or when full and cost Y12 to Y20, depending on the disposition of the driver. Alternatively, you can head out to the long-distance bus station, from where buses run approximately every hour between 7 am and 6 pm. The trip takes about two hours along the Guihuang Expressway, Guìzhōu's first real highway. Returning to Guìyáng the long-distance bus station has up to 10 express minibuses or luxury buses leaving between 6.40 am and 4 pm; costs range from Y18 to Y20, compared with a local minibus costing Y10. Another station along Tashan Xilu, catering for local routes, also has express buses all day for the same price as well as buses to more remote Guìzhōu villages.

From Ānshùn, Huángguǒshù Dàpùbù and Lónggōng Dòng are 46km and 32km away, respectively. See Around Ānshùn for transportation details.

Buses to Lónggōng are occasional at best, so you may have to join up with one of the local tours running from the bus station or a hotel – if you can get on.

If you don't feel like heading back to Guìyáng to book a train sleeper, you could consider travelling onwards from Ānshùn to Kūnmíng by bus. From Ānshùn there are direct buses that leave at 5 pm, arriving in Kūnmíng around 8 am, roads permitting. A regular bus costs Y55, a sleeper Y90.

GUIZHOU 贵州

More interesting might be travelling from Ānshùn or Huángguǒshù to Wēiníng in the west or Xīngyì in the south-west of Guìzhōu. Xīngyì is worth a visit in itself (see the entry later in this chapter), and there are direct buses from there to Kūnmíng (12 hours). Minibuses run hourly from 8.30 am to 3.30 pm. The ride takes eight to 10 hours and costs Y32 for a regular minibus, Y50 for a sleeper.

Train Most of the trains running between Guìyáng and Ānshùn currently depart from Guìyáng and arrive in Ānshùn in the evening (usually the late evening). On the other hand, if you're going to Guìyáng from Ānshùn, most trains leave during the day. Either way, most folks opt for the bus.

If you're thinking of travelling onwards from Ānshùn to Kūnmíng by train, bear in mind that it's almost impossible to get hold of hard-sleeper tickets in Ānshùn itself for same-day or even next-day travel, though we inexplicably managed to do it on the most recent trip.

Getting Around

From town, the bus station and the train station are 3km and 4km away, respectively. The No 1 minibus will take you into town for Y0.50 to Y1, depending on where you alight.

AROUND ĀNSHÙN
Huángguǒshù Dàpùbù 黄果树大瀑布
Yellow Fruit Trees Falls

Located 46km south-west of Ānshùn, China's premier cataract reaches a width of 81m, with a drop of 74m into the **Rhinoceros Pool**, and is the foundation of Guìzhōu's fledgling tourist industry. Huángguǒshù also provides an excellent chance to go rambling through the superb rural minority areas on foot. Although transportation is quite easy, not many travellers get here, so you'll probably be as much the attraction as anything.

Once there, you'll have no transport problems as everything you need is within walking distance. Take a raincoat if going to the waterfalls and a warm jacket or sweater if descending into caves, which can be chilly.

The thunder of Huángguǒshù Dàpùbù can be heard from some distance during rainy season, which lasts from May to October. March and April aren't good times to go. The falls are at their most spectacular about four days after heavy rains.

The main falls are the central piece of a huge waterfall, cave and karst area covering some 450 sq km. It was explored by the Chinese only in the 1980s as a preliminary to harnessing the hydroelectric potential. They discovered about 18 falls, four subterranean rivers and 100 caves, many of which are now gradually being opened up to visitors.

At the edge of the falls is **Shuǐlián Dòng** (Water Curtain Cave), a niche in the cliffs that is approached by a slippery (and dangerous) sortie wading across rocks in the Rhinoceros Pool – from the cave you'll get an interior view of the gushing waters through six 'windows'.

One kilometre above the main falls is **Dǒupō Pùbù** (Steep Slope Falls), which is easy to reach. Steep Slope Falls is 105m wide and 23m high and gets its name from the crisscross patterning of sloping waters. Eight kilometres below Huángguǒshù Dàpùbù are the **Tiānxīng Qiáo** (Star Bridge Silver Chain Falls), known as the 'potted landscape', for which there are occasional minibuses (Y10 with haggling) leaving from Huángguǒshù village.

The ridiculous entrance fee of Y30 is only the start: be prepared for many other arbitrary levies, including Y10 to enter Shuǐlián Dòng, Y5 to use the cable car, and yet another Y30 to get into Tiānxīng Qiáo.

Lónggōng Dòng 龙宫洞
Dragon Palace Caves

About 32km from Ānshùn is a spectacular series of underground caverns called Lónggōng (Dragon Palace), which form a network through some 20 mountains. Charter boats tour one of the largest water-filled caves, often called the Dragon Cave. The caverns lie in Ānshùn County, at the Bouyei settlement of Lóngtán Zhài (Dragon Pool).

The Bouyei People of Huángguǒshù

Huángguǒshù (Yellow Fruit Tree) is in the Zhenning Bouyei and Miao Autonomous County. The Miao are not in evidence around the falls, but for the Bouyei, who favour river valleys, this is prime water country.

The Bouyei are the 'aboriginals' of Guìzhōu. The people are of Thai origin and are related to the Zhuangs in Guǎngxī. The population, which numbers two million, lives mostly throughout the southwestern sector of Guìzhōu. Traditional Bouyei dress is dark and sombre with colourful trimmings; 'best' clothes come out on festival or market days. The Bouyei marry early, usually at 16, but sometimes as young as 12. Married women are distinguished by headgear symbols.

Batik (cloth wax-dyeing) is one of the skills of the Bouyei. The masonry at Huángguǒshù is also intriguing – houses are composed of stone blocks, but no plaster is used; the rooves are finished in stone slates.

There is a Bouyei festival in Huángguǒshù lasting 10 days during the first lunar month (usually February or early March). The attendance is estimated at around 10,000 people.

Other scenic caves in the vicinity include Dàjī Dòng, Chuān Dòng and Linlang Dòng. Admission is Y30.

Places to Stay & Eat At the bus park near the Huángguǒshù Dàpùbù are some *food stalls*. Farther away from the bus park is *Huángguǒshù Bīnguǎn*, which has actually become two hotels. The 'new' Huángguǒshù Bīnguǎn is up a driveway to the right and is where you'll be pointed. Rooms here start at Y190 for a standard double. The old guesthouse, which doesn't look very different from the new one, has doubles for Y140, although the staff may try to tack on a 30% 'service charge' for foreign friends. The old guesthouse also has five- to seven-bed dorms for Y86, but these are almost always fully booked out.

Some travellers have managed to get beds for Y10 in the *Chinese hotels*, while others have been turned away. If you try, go for a hotel on the waterfall side: one has a little pathway that gives you free access to the waterfall viewing area!

Along the town's main road there are several *restaurants* that have verandas at the back where you can eat, sip a cold beer and enjoy a great view of the falls.

Getting There & Away You can get to Huángguǒshù Dàpùbù and Lónggōng Dòng from either Guìyáng or Ānshùn. There are

a few direct buses – they claim to be tour buses – to the falls leaving from the Guìyáng long-distance bus station or the train station at around 7 am, although the trip takes three to four hours. These buses take in both the falls and Lónggōng Dòng for Y55 to Y60, depending on the type of bus, but not including entry fees. Tours also run from nearly all the hotels listed in the Guìyáng Places to Stay section. These buses will get you to Huángguǒshù in around two to three hours, as opposed to five hours if you take public transport.

Otherwise, catch a bus or a train to Ānshùn and catch a minibus there. Minibuses and regular buses run every 30 minutes from Guìyáng train station to Ānshùn.

From the Ānshùn long-distance bus station there is one direct bus to Huángguǒshù around 8 am. The fare is Y8. Buses to Zhēnfēng, Xīngyì and Qínglóng all pass through Huángguǒshù. There are also seven-seater microbuses running from the bus station from 8 am to 5 pm for around Y10. However, with solo travellers in particular, drivers will try for whatever fare they can get, so be prepared. (Complaints about traumatic hassles are not infrequent.) Both buses and minibuses take the local road to Huángguǒshù rather than the expressway, so the 46km ride takes around 1½ hours. However, it does pass through some interesting small towns. If you take a local bus, it may drop you along the highway instead of at the bus park by the park entrance, which requires a steep, but pretty, 15-minute walk.

Minibuses run from Huángguǒshù to Ānshùn and on to Guìyáng from 7 am to 7 pm. Buses leave as soon as they are full. Try to get one that takes the Guihuang Expressway rather than a local bus.

WESTERN GUÌZHŌU

This part of Guìzhōu is the area most recently opened to tourists and much of it is still officially off-limits. If you go you'll know why – it's a rough, forbidding place, best described by one author as 'Guìzhōu's wild west'. Still, it paves the way for a rough but fascinating access into Yúnnán via Zhāotōng – from here head for the train line in Xīchàng (Sìchuān) between Chéngdū and Kūnmíng – or Xuānwēi. Even better, along the way is Guìzhōu's other gem, the bird-watching paradise of Caǒ Haǐ (Grass Sea).

Wēiníng 威宁

Caǒ Haǐ's entry point is the town of Wēiníng, some 300km west of Guìyáng. This moderately interesting town is home to various minority peoples, particularly the Miao, grand **markets** every few days and a daily market in the eastern part of town. Note that villages surrounding Wēiníng are officially off-limits, so expect hassles the farther off-track you get.

Ten minutes south of town, Caǒ Haǐ is a 20 sq km freshwater wetland, which became a national nature reserve in 1992 (after millennia of cyclical ecological devastation and recovery). Its most famous resident is the fabulous black-necked crane.

Environmental problems remain and the government is enlisting locals in its attempts to protect the lake; ecotourism is high on the government's plans. Trails wrap around the shore of the lake, but most tourists take 'punts', many of whose operators will make you aware of their presence when you arrive. The best time to visit the lake is December to March, when the birds are wintering. Bring warm clothes.

Places to Stay The *Caǒhaǐ Bīnguǎn (Grass Sea Hotel)*, by the lake, has beds for Y30 in doubles with private hot bath. It's not a great place but the view is good; at least the restaurant, 200m away, is nice. Lots of better, cheap options exist in town, the best is probably the *Jiangong Hotel,* east of the main bus station, which has rooms from Y50.

Getting There & Away First take a train from Guìyáng to Liupanshui station, which is actually the station at the forgettable Shuicheng city. A few trains a day to/from Guìyáng run via Ānshùn and cost Y23 hard seat, Y40 soft seat. Shuicheng has but two places to stay, the better being the *Zhōngshān Bīnguǎn (☎ 223285)*, where OK doubles cost Y70 and up. From Shuicheng to Wēiníng you can take a comfortable postal bus (Y10, two to three hours) every day at 7 am from the main post office. Other buses depart from the bus station.

Leaving Wēiníng you can backtrack to Guìyáng or take a minibus from north of town to Zhāotōng in Yúnnán; they cost Y25 and take five hours. From there you can hop over to Xīchàng in southern Sìchuān to connect with the Kūnmíng-Chéngdū train line. A few minibuses also depart for Xuānwēi in Yúnnán; sleepers run to Guìyáng as well.

Xīngyì 兴义
☎ 0859

Underappreciated Xīngyì is mainly a stopover in the far south-west of Guìzhōu for those travelling between Guìyáng or Nánníng and Kūnmíng. However, it is an interesting town to wander around, and the sights include a good minorities museum.

The main attraction in the area is the 12km-long Mǎlínghé Xiágǔ (Maling Gorge), which some travellers say is more interesting than Huángguǒshù Dàpùbù. However, ongoing construction had closed some trails at the time of writing. You can also take a Y88 kayak tour. It's a good idea to bring along a torch to light your way through some of the caves that the path passes through. You can hire a motorcycle to take you out to the trailhead 6km from town for Y5.

GUÌZHŌU 贵州

The *Pánjiāng Bīnguǎn* (☎ *322 3456 ext 8118*) is the only hotel that officially takes foreigners but many places will now let you stay. The Pánjiāng has good singles/doubles/triples for Y18/38/48 with communal bath; they also have more expensive rooms. Keep an eye (and nose) out for the tasty warm cinnamon bread sold fresh in the mornings from street stalls and bakeries.

Getting There & Away Sleeper buses to Xīngyì (Y55) leave approximately hourly from in front of Guìyáng train station and the long-distance bus station between 8 am and 6 pm. The journey to Xīngyì takes 10 to 12 hours. Return sleeper buses depart every 20 minutes.

From Ānshùn, buses run hourly between 8.30 am and 3.30 pm. The ride takes eight to 10 hours and costs Y32 for a minibus, Y50 for a sleeper.

From Xīngyì, buses leave the bus station at 6 and 7 pm for the nine-hour ride to Kūnmíng (Y65); daytime minibuses (Y48) leave at 6 and 7 am; consider hopping off early at the Shí Lín (Stone Forest). Small, private companies also have buses to Kūnmíng. From Kūnmíng's long-distance bus station there are morning buses to Xīngyì.

Xīngyì is now served by the train line between Nánníng and Kūnmíng, though the train station is 10km away. If you're coming from Nánníng, the No 615 train gets you in at 6.12 pm, but from Kūnmíng or Nánníng on the Nánkún line you arrive in the middle of the night.

KǍILǏ 凯里
☎ 0855

About 195km almost directly east of Guìyáng, Kǎilǐ is the gateway to the captivating minority areas of south-eastern Guìzhōu. The bus journey between there and Lìpíng in the far south-east of Guìzhōu takes you through some of the most fascinating minority regions in this part of China. The PSB shouldn't hassle you no matter where you go here, but may be interested in you since you may find yourself in some pretty isolated spots.

Particularly recommended towns are Léishān, Róngjiāng, Zhàoxìng and Táijiāng. Lìpíng is a good base for exploring nearby Dong villages. Buses also run from Kǎilǐ to the Miao area of Shībǐng to the north, from where there are cruises on the Wǔyáng Hé, something that the local tourist authorities are promoting heavily. This whole area sees few western travellers.

Information
The Kǎilǐ CITS office (☎ 822 9441, fax 822 2506) is located in the compound of the Yìngpànpō Mínzú Bīnguǎn and is quite possibly the most helpful in China. That said, its 'minority tours', at Y600 for a kitschy day trip, are outrageously pricey. Even if you don't book the tour, the staff will still offer information on local villages and boat tours.

Things to See
There's a pagoda in the Dàgé Gōngyuán (Big Pagoda Park), which is not surprising considering the park's name. The only other thing to check out is the drum tower in Jīnquánhú Gōngyuán (Golden Spring Lake Park), the park at the very southern end of town. The moderately interesting Guìzhōu Mínzú Bówùguǎn (Minorities Museum), open as far as we can tell whenever anyone's around, is also south of the town centre. Admission is Y10.

Kǎilǐ also has a good **Sunday market** which swamps the streets with traders from nearby villages.

Festivals
Kǎilǐ and the areas around it are host to a large number of minority festivals – over 130 annually, according to CITS. One of the biggest is the Lusheng Festival, held from the 11th to the 18th of the first lunar month. The *lusheng* is a reed instrument used by the Miao people. Activities include playing the lusheng (of course), dancing, drumming, bull fighting and horse racing. Participants are said to number 30,000. The festival is held in Zhōuxī.

A similar festival is held midway through the seventh lunar month in Qīngmàn, to

KĂILĬ 凯里

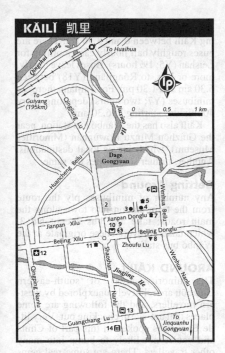

To Huaihua

Qingshui Jiang

To Guiyang (195km)

Qingjiang Lu

Jiuzhan He

0   0.5   1 km

Dage Gongyuan

Huancheng Beilu

Wenhua Beilu

Beijing Beilu

6
5
2
3 4
Jianpan Xilu

Jianpan Donglu
10 9
Beijing Donglu

Beijing Xilu
11
Zhoufu Lu

12

Shaoshan Lu

Jingjing He

Qingjiang Nanlu

Wenhua Nanlu

13

To Jinquanhu Gongyuan

Guangchang Lu
14

KĂILĬ

1 Train Station
火车站

2 Night Market
夜市

3 Minorities Souvenir Shop
民族商店

4 CITS
中国国际旅行社

5 Yíngpànpō Mínzú Bīnguǎn
营盘坡民族宾馆

6 Long-Distance Bus Station
长途汽车站

7 Shíyóu Bīnguǎn
石油宾馆

8 Lǐxiǎngmiàn Shídiàn
理想面食店

9 Bank of China
中国银行

10 Post Office
邮电局

11 Lántiān Jiǔdiàn
篮天酒店

12 PSB
公安局

13 Wànbó Bus Station
万博汽车站

14 Guìhóu Mínzú Bówùguǎn
贵州民族博物馆

which 20,000 are said to turn up. The Miao new year is celebrated on the first four days of the 10th lunar month in Kǎilǐ, Guàdīng, Zhōuxī and other Miao areas by some 50,000 people. CITS in Kǎilǐ should be able to provide you with a list of local festivals and their dates. After that, you're probably better off on your own.

Places to Stay & Eat

None of the dirt-cheap stand-bys now accept foreign guests; it's still worth giving the cheaper-looking ones a shot, but don't expect much. The best bargain in town currently is the *Lántiān Jiǔdiàn (Blue Sky Hotel;* ☎ 823 4570 ext 2100), on the main roundabout, where you can get a bed in a three-bed room for Y35. Rooms are cosy and the clean, communal showers have 24-hour hot water. Doubles with private bath start at Y168. For Y5 you can stash your bags here.

South of the long-distance bus station is the *Shíyóu Bīnguǎn,* which has singles/

doubles/triples from Y56/50/68 – you'll be shown the Y68 doubles. A few five-bed rooms from Y12 per bed and cheaper triples and quads are available, but usually full. Note that in this place you pay for the whole room regardless of whether or not it's fully occupied.

Not far from there is the *Yìngpànpō Mínzú Bīnguǎn,* which has somewhat overpriced doubles for Y60 to Y80 and triples from Y75. You can't pay for less than a full room here either. Unadvertised Chinese-priced rooms at Y50 aren't much to talk about. More upmarket doubles in a new wing go for Y218, although you might be able to bargain them down. Some quads go for Y120 to Y160.

Surprise, surprise: a backpacker-friendly place had just opened prior to our last visit. Near the intersection of Wenhua Beilu and

GUIZHOU 贵州

Běijīng Donglu the *Lǐxiǎngmiàn Shídiàn* is run by a friendly woman who has an English menu with pictures. You'll find good basic staples, along with creative local varieties, including a Chinese 'pizza' (*qiāncéng cōngbǐng*) that will stick to your ribs for Y2.20.

On the north side of Shaoshan Nanlu there is a smallish **night market** where you can find any number of critters on skewers and grills. A departure from the point-and-choose tedium are the *shā guō*, convex coal-fired grills atop which you can roast your own dinner. Beancurd is available, along with lots of greens.

Getting There & Away

Many trains departing Guìyáng pass through Kǎilǐ (Y14, hard seat), including up to four between 7 am and noon. From Kǎilǐ to Guìyáng your choices are more limited: both the No 193 at 7.22 am and the No 635 at 8.25 am trains should take around four hours; other trains, which are faster, depart in the afternoon and arrive late. The trip either way should average around three hours, although it sometimes takes up to five. For longer distances, you can't secure a sleeper in Kǎilǐ so pray for intervention or backtrack to Guìyáng.

Any train is preferable to the horrendous road and buses between Guìyáng and Kǎilǐ. Authorities are planning to have an 'expressway' finished by 2001. Presently, buses to Kǎilǐ leave frequently from in front of Guìyáng train station and from a station one block north between 6.30 am and 5.30 pm. The journey costs Y20 to Y30 and takes five to seven hours – although 10 is not unheard of. If you get there in less than six hours consider yourself blessed.

The Kǎilǐ long-distance bus station has frequent buses to Guìyáng between 6.30 am and 2.30 pm, including eight air-con express buses between 7 am and 2.30 pm for Y30. If you are headed for Tóngrén, Shībǐng or Zhènyuán, bus station staff will point you to the train station even though there are buses. Lìpíng (Y30/45 regular/sleeper; 10 hours) and Cóngjiāng (Y35/51 regular/sleeper; nine to 12 hours)

are served by one or two buses daily, leaving Kǎilǐ between 6 and 8.30 am; There are buses roughly half hourly each morning for Léishān (Y5; 1½ hours). Buses leave hourly, more or less, to Róngjiāng (Y18) between 6.30 am and 1.30 pm. For Táijiāng there are minibuses (Y7; two hours) departing every 40 minutes starting at 6.30 am.

Kǎilǐ also has the Wànbó bus station, near the Guìzhōu Mínzú Bówùguǎn (Minorities Museum), which serves local destinations. Another, further south, does the same.

Getting Around

Any number of minibuses ply the route from the train station into town along the main roads; take any bus except No 3, which takes forever. These originate at the Wànbó bus station.

AROUND KǍILǏ

The minority areas of south-eastern Guìzhōu are relatively unexplored by western travellers, and the following are some places that are worth checking out. Very little English is spoken in this part of China and you're not likely to bump into many other travellers. There are some real gems to be found if you poke around enough.

Shībǐng 施秉 & Zhènyuán 镇远
☎ 0855

Shībǐng is basically an overgrown Miao village that offers the opportunity for walks in the surrounding countryside and visits to even smaller Miao villages. The major attraction in the area are cruises on the **Wǔyáng Hé**, a river that pass through karst rock formations reminiscent of Guìlín. The dock is 9km east of town.

You can take a tour of the river from Shībǐng or Zhènyuán, but you can't travel between these towns.

Places to Stay & Eat Basic accommodation is available in Shībǐng at the *Zhēngfǔ Zhāodàisuǒ* (*Government Guesthouse*). The *Mínfù Bīnguǎn*, which has a CITS office, is more upmarket. In Zhènyuán, the *Lèróng Bīnguǎn* has beds from Y15 (Y30 in better rooms).

CHÓNG'ĀN 重安

Lying about two hours north of Kǎilǐ by bus, this hamlet's claim to fame is its Friday market. Travellers who have seen it say it's one not to miss. There are also some good walks along the river and into the Miao villages nearby. The *Jianxinlou Bīnguǎn* has cosy beds from Y8 and friendly owners; the *Xiǎojiāngnán Lǚyóu Fàndiàn* has interesting lodging options and can arrange local tours. Buses to Shībǐng pass through Chóng'ān.

KǍILǏ TO LÌPÍNG

Lìpíng, in the far south-east of Guìzhōu, is a fairly uninteresting town, but the stretch of road between it and Kǎilǐ covers some beautiful countryside and passes some impressive sights.

Ideally, get off the bus and spend at least a couple of hours in some of the minority villages like **Léishān, Táshí, Chéjiāng, Róngjiāng, Maógòng** and **Gāōjìn**. Accommodation in these small spots is usually limited to a hotel attached or next to the bus station. If you wander around looking lost, someone will either put you on the next bus or take you to the local hotel. Most of these towns have Dong wind and rain bridges and drum towers, many of which you can see from the bus.

If you decide to head straight to Lìpíng, the bus ride takes around 10 hours and costs Y30; more for an overnight sleeper. Lìpíng has basic accommodation at the *Lìpíng Zhāo-Dàisuǒ* – but at last check the hotel had stopped taking foreigners. Another *no-name place*, 500m left out of bus station, has rooms from Y30.

LÌPÍNG TO GUÌLÍN

This is really an option only for travellers with time to kill. Buses in this part of the world are very infrequent and travel at a snail's pace over roads that barely qualify as such. Buses run from Lìpíng to **Dìpíng** via Lóng'é, at *around* 7 am. To Dìpíng it takes around four hours, passing through the town of **Zhàoxīng**, an incredible Dong minority village with a total of five drum towers. A stop in the village would require

you stay in the old *wooden hotel* as there is only one bus a day travelling between Zhàoxīng and Dìpíng.

Dìpíng, another Dong village, requires another overnight stop, as the buses on to Sānjiāng in Guǎngxī don't leave till the next morning. However, at last report, the only hotel in Dìpíng had closed, leaving travellers to arrange transport 10km north to Lóng'é for spartan accommodation. New roads are being built along this stretch so traffic patterns are likely to change. From Sānjiāng there are buses on to Lóngshèng or direct to Guìlín. See the Sānjiāng section of the Guǎngxī chapter for more information.

ZŪNYÌ 遵义

☎ 0852 • pop 6,693,600

Around 163km north of Guìyáng, somewhat drab but friendly Zūnyì is worth a mention and even possibly a visit for those who have a particular interest in Chinese Communist Party (CCP) history.

On 16 October 1934, hemmed into the Jiāngxī soviet by Kuomintang forces, the communists set out on a Herculean one-year, 9600km tramp from one end of China to the other. By mid-December, having reached Guìzhōu, they marched on Zūnyì, a prosperous mercantile town. Taking the town by surprise, the communists were able to stock up on supplies and take a breather. From 15 to 18 January 1935, the communist leadership took stock of their situation in the now-famous conference at Zūnyì. The resolutions taken largely reflected the views of Mao Zedong, who was elected a full member of the ruling Standing Committee of the Politburo and chief assistant to Zhou Enlai in military planning. This was a crucial turn of events in Mao's rise to power.

Things to See

Located around 5km south-west of the train station, the **Zūnyì Huìyì Huìzhǐ** (Conference Site) is home to a collection of CCP memorabilia. The meeting rooms and living quarters are also open to the public. It is open from 8.30 am to 4.30 pm daily and

GUIZHOU 贵州

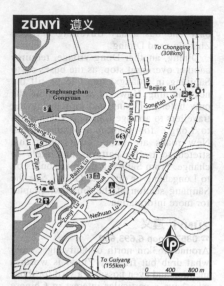

ZŪNYÌ 遵义

To Chongqing
(308km)

Fenghuangshan
Gongyuan

Beijing Lu

Songtao Lu

Fenghuang Lu

Xima Lu

Jijun Lu

Zhonghua Beilu

Yanan Lu

Waihuan Lu

Baisha Lu

Xinhua Lu – Zhonghua Nanlu

Neihuan Lu

Zunyi Lu

To Guiyang
(155km)

0   400   800 m

ZŪNYÌ

1 Train Station
   火车站
2 Lántiān Bīnguǎn
   蓝天宾馆
3 Zūntiě Dàshà
   遵铁大厦
4 Long-Distance Bus Station
   长途汽车站
5 Hotpot Stalls
   火锅摊
6 Bank of China
   中国银行
7 Hotpot Stalls
   火锅摊
8 Hóngjūn Lièshì Língyuán
   红军烈士陵园
9 Zūnyì Bīnguǎn
   遵义宾馆
10 Hóngjūn Zǒngzhèngzhibù Jiùshì
   红军总政治部旧址
11 Zūnyì Huìyì Huìzhǐ
   遵义会议会址
12 Catholic Church
   天主教堂
13 Workers' Cultural Palace
   工人文化宫
14 Báiyún Sì
   白云寺

costs Y5. More interesting is the **Hóngjūn Zǒngzhèngzhibù Jiùshì** (Old General Political Department), approximately 150m away, which has excellent displays on the Long March. Entrance costs Y2.

Zūnyì Gōngyuán is the park across the road from the conference site. Nearby, **Fènghuángshān Gōngyuán** (Phoenix Hill Park) houses the **Hóngjūn Lièshì Língyuán** (Mausoleum of the Red Army Martyrs).

Places to Stay & Eat

Across from the train station on Beijing Lu is the **Zūntiě Dàshà** (☎ 822 3266), a basic, friendly place with good singles/doubles/triples with common bath for Y50/50/45. Singles/doubles with en suite start at Y35. Opposite and set back from the street is the **Lántiān Bīnguǎn** (☎ 862 2916, 99 Beijing Lu), equally good, with beds starting at around Y25. Near the conference site the plush **Zūnyì Bīnguǎn**, the official tourist abode, has doubles from Y120.

Beijing Lu has some groupings of alfresco hot-pot restaurants come dinnertime. South on Zhonghua Beilu there are more, along with some grill-your-own places – all for devoted carnivores.

Getting There & Away

Zūnyì is on the main northern train line that connects Guìyáng with Chóngqìng, Chéngdū, Shànghǎi and, basically, the rest of China. It could be used as a stopover on any of these routes. A hard/soft-seat ticket from Guìyáng is Y10/30 (no smoking!) and takes three hours. Up to 26 trains per day make the run. The ride from Zūnyì to Chóngqìng costs Y24/47 for hard/soft seat.

Alternatively, buses leave Guìyáng's long-distance bus station every half hour between 6.20 am and 5 pm. You can also catch buses to Zūnyì in front of Guìyáng train station or at a station one block to the north. The buses depart about every half hour between 7 am and 9 pm. Prices for the 2½-hour trip range from Y15 to Y28, depending on the size and quality of the vehicle.

Zūnyì's long-distance bus station is next door to the Zūntiĕ Dàshà. There are minibuses and larger express buses leaving for Guìyáng throughout the day starting at 7 am, although they start to thin out around 6 pm. This is the only bus service to a larger destination – at the moment no buses run to Chóngqìng or Chéngdū. The government has plans to link Guìyáng with Chéngdū via Chóngqìng with new expressways.

Yúnnán 云南

Yúnnán is without doubt one of the most alluring travel destinations in China. It's the most geographically varied of all of China's provinces, with terrain as widely diverse as tropical rainforest and icy Tibetan highlands. It is also the sixth-largest province in China and home to a third of all China's ethnic minorities (nearly 50% of the province is non-Han) and half of all China's plant and animal species. If you could only go to one province, this might well be it.

Yúnnán is also well known for its mild climate year-round – its name, referring to this reputation, means 'South of the Clouds'. The provincial capital, Kūnmíng, is similarly referred to as the 'Spring City'.

Despite the best government efforts, numerous pockets of the province have successfully resisted Chinese influence and exhibit strong local identities. Even Kūnmíng has a flavour all its own that seems more than half a world away from Běijīng, although this gap is in danger of being bridged by rapid economic growth. (Yúnnán's mammoth agricultural tallies account for nearly one third of the Gross National Product.)

Nicknames are affixed to everything in China, and Yúnnán holds the vast majority. Since the province contains the nation's highest number of species of flora and fauna – including 2500 varieties of wild flowers and plants – it has been given monikers such as 'Kingdom of Plants (or Animals)', 'Garden of Heavenly Marvellous Flowers', and 'Hometown of Perfume'. Officials are less thrilled with the new tag: 'Treasure House of Crude Drugs'.

HISTORY

When Qin Shihuang and the Han emperors first held tentative sway over the southwest, Yúnnán was occupied by a large number of non-Chinese aboriginal peoples who lacked cohesive political organisation.

By the 7th century AD, however, the Bai people had established a powerful kingdom,

Highlights

Capital: Kūnmíng
Population: 40.4 million
Area: 394,000 sq km

- Kūnmíng, with its intriguing backstreets, great food and good sights (despite increasing modernisation)
- Lìjiāng's old town, the narrow stone streets of which give a fascinating glimpse into Naxi culture and history
- Hǔtiào Xiá, a multi-day gorge trek amid dramatic cliffs and waterfalls
- Zhōngdiàn/Déqīn, the next best thing to Tibet
- Dàlǐ, one of China's best places to kick back and relax surrounded by wooden buildings and flagstone streets
- Téngchōng, a quaint town with nearby hot springs and dormant volcanoes
- Ruìlì, a sometime wild border town surrounded by plenty of temples, villages and forests
- Xīshuāngbǎnnà, a taste of tropical South-East Asia and home to the Dai people

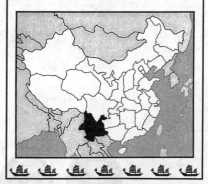

Nanzhao, south of Dàlǐ. Initially allying itself to the Chinese against the Tibetans, this kingdom extended its power until, in the

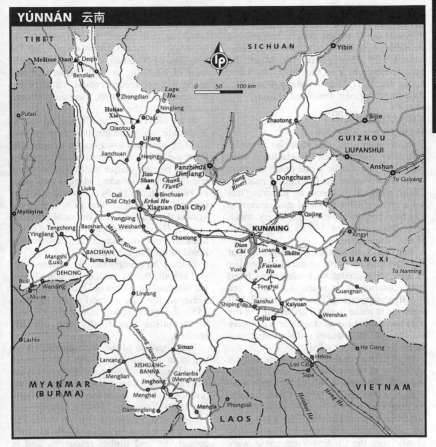

YÚNNÁN 云南

middle of the 8th century, it was able to challenge and defeat the Tang armies. It took control of a large slice of the south-west and established itself as a fully independent entity, dominating the trade routes from China to India and Burma.

The Nanzhao kingdom fell in the 10th century and was replaced by the kingdom of Dàlǐ, an independent state which lasted until it was overrun by the Mongols in the mid-13th century. After 15 centuries of resistance to northern rule, this part of the south-west was finally integrated into the empire as the province of Yúnnán.

Even so it remained an isolated frontier region, with scattered Chinese garrisons and settlements in the valleys and basins, a mixed aboriginal population occupying the highlands, and various Dai (Thai) and other minorities along the Láncāng Jiāng (Mekong River).

Like the rest of the south-west, Yúnnán was always one of the first regions to break with the northern government. During China's countless political purges, fallen officials often found themselves exiled here, which added to the province's rebellious character.

Today, however, Yúnnán looks to be firmly back in the Chinese fold. It is a province of 40 million people, including a veritable constellation of minorities (25 registered): the Zhuang, Hui, Yi, Miao, Tibetans, Mongols, Yao, Bai, Hani, Dai, Lisu, Lahu, Wa, Naxi, Jingpo, Bulang, Pumi, Nu, Achang, Benglong, Jinuo and Dulong.

KŪNMÍNG 昆明

☎ 0871 • pop 3,838,200

Once you get off the wide boulevards, Kūnmíng and its funky roads lined with pine trees can still be a fine place to spend some days wandering. But like so much of China, a big caveat comes in: Kūnmíng has been under the buzz saw of modernisation like no other south-west Chinese city, much of it thrown up for 1999's International Horticultural Expo.

For the locals this spells 'progress', but for travellers in search of the old Kūnmíng it means the quaint back alleyways lined with fascinating wooden buildings are rapidly disappearing. There are enough still standing to make it worth getting lost in the backstreets, but the next decade will likely see the last remnants of old Kūnmíng succumb to the wrecking ball.

Of Kūnmíng's total population, only a million or so inhabit the urban area. At most, minorities account for 6% of the city's population, although the farming areas in the outlying counties are home to some Yi, Hui and Miao groups. There are also a fair number of Vietnamese refugees-turned-immigrants from the Chinese-Vietnamese wars and border clashes that started in 1977.

At an elevation of 1890m, Kūnmíng has a milder climate than most other Chinese cities, and can be visited at any time of year. Light clothes will usually be adequate, but it's wise to bring some woollies during the winter months when temperatures can suddenly drop, particularly in the evenings – there have even been a couple of light snowfalls in recent years. There's a fairly even spread of temperatures from April to September. Winters are short, sunny and dry. In summer (from June to August) Kūnmíng offers cool respite, although rain is more prevalent.

History

The region of Kūnmíng has been inhabited for 2000 years. Until the 8th century the town was a remote Chinese outpost, but the kingdom of Nanzhao, centred to the northwest of Kūnmíng at Dàlǐ, captured it and made it a secondary capital. In 1274 the Mongols came through, sweeping all and sundry before them.

In the 14th century the Ming set up shop in Yunnanfu, as Kūnmíng was then known, building a walled town on the present site. From the 17th century onwards, the history of this city becomes rather grisly. The last Ming resistance to the invading Manchu took place in Yúnnán in the 1650s and was crushed by General Wu Sangui. Wu in turn rebelled against the king and held out until his death in 1678. His successor was overthrown by the Manchu emperor Kangxi and subsequently killed himself in Kūnmíng in 1681.

In the 19th century the city suffered several bloodbaths, as the rebel Muslim leader Du Wenxiu, the Sultan of Dàlǐ, attacked and besieged the city several times between 1858 and 1868; it was not until 1873 that the rebellion was finally and bloodily crushed.

The intrusion of the West into Kūnmíng began in the middle of the 19th century when Britain took control of Burma (Myanmar) and France took control of Indochina, providing access to the city from the south. By 1900 Kūnmíng, Hékǒu, Sīmáo and Měngzì were opened to foreign trade. The French were keen on exploiting the region's copper, tin and timber resources, and in 1910 their Indochina train, started in 1898 at Hanoi, reached the city.

Kūnmíng's expansion began with WWII, when factories were established here and refugees fleeing the Japanese poured in from eastern China. In a bid to keep China from falling to Japan, Anglo-American forces sent supplies to nationalist troops entrenched in Sìchuān and Yúnnán. Supplies came overland on a dirt road carved out of the mountains in 1937–8 by 160,000 Chinese with virtually no equipment. This was the famous Burma Road, a 1000km haul from Lashio to Kūnmíng. Today, the western extension of Kūnmíng's Renmin Lu, leading in the direction of Heilinpu, is the tail end of the road.

In early 1942 the Japanese captured Lashio, cutting the supply line. Kūnmíng continued to handle most of the incoming aid during 1942–5 when US planes flew the dangerous mission of crossing the 'Hump', the towering 5000m mountain ranges between India and Yúnnán. A black market sprang up and a fair proportion of the medicines, canned food, petrol and other goods intended for the military and relief agencies were siphoned off into other hands.

The face of Kūnmíng has been radically altered since then, with streets widened and office buildings and housing projects flung up. With the coming of the trains, industry has expanded rapidly, and a surprising range of goods and machinery available in China now bears the 'made in Yúnnán' stamp. The city's produce includes steel, foodstuffs, trucks, machine tools, electrical equipment, textiles, chemicals, building materials and plastics.

Orientation

The jurisdiction of Kūnmíng covers 6200 sq km, encompassing four city districts and four rural counties (which supply the city with fruit and vegetables). The centre of the city is the traffic circle at the intersection of Zhengyi Lu and Dongfeng Xilu. Surprisingly, it is still possible to find a few rows of old wooden houses in nearby neighbourhoods, although these are being levelled with alarming regularity. Kūnmíng's tree-lined Jinbi Lu, the last bastion of original architecture, fell in its entirety to the wrecking ball in late 1997.

East of the intersection is Kūnmíng's major north-south road, Beijing Lu. At the southern end is the main train station, the long-distance bus station and the Kūnhú Fàndiàn, one of the few cheap places to stay in Kūnmíng. At about the halfway point Beijing Lu is intersected by Dongfeng Donglu.

Maps Shop around as there's a great variety of maps, some with a smattering of English names. The *Kunming Tourist Map* has street and hotel names in English and shows bus lines, while the *Yunnan Communications and Tourist Map* has the names of nearly every town in the province – along with bordering countries – written out in English.

Information

At hotels or western cafes try to pick up a copy of *KMS – Kunming Scene*, a free quarterly guide to restaurants and nightspots which also has interesting local titbits.

Consulates Thailand, Laos and Myanmar (Burma) now all have visa-issuing consulates in Kūnmíng – but (sigh) still not Vietnam. When we last checked, exit permits were still not needed to go into Laos. Visa details for each country follow.

Laos The Lao consulate (☎ 316 6623) is on the 2nd floor of Building 3 at the Cháhuā Bīnguǎn. For a brief window of opportunity in 1998 some folks may have been able to talk their way into three-day visas at the Laos border in Xīshuāngbǎnnà but don't count on that happening again. You'll need to get a visa in Kūnmíng and unless you have a sponsor in Laos (doesn't everyone?) you'll probably only be able to get a seven-day transit visa, five days if you arrive by plane. This is just enough time to cross the border at Měnglà, make your way down to Vientiane and on to Thailand. The seven-day visa costs US$35 and takes four or five days to process; if you can wangle a 15-day visa it's US$40. You must bring three photos.

In the past, you needed to already have a visa from a third country stamped in your passport, but this had been waived at the time of writing. Even though Thailand grants most nationalities a grace period of 30 days before requiring a visa, you may have to get one stamped in your passport anyway, just to satisfy the Lao officials.

Also note that these regulations seem to change from month to month in recent years, so by the time you read this you may be able to show up at the border and get a 45-day visa. Or not. Office hours are Monday to Friday, 8.30 to 11.30 am and 2.30 to 4.30 pm.

Myanmar (Burma) The office (☎ 316 3000/
3004) is just above the Lao consulate, on
the 3rd floor of Building 3 at the Cháhuā
Bīnguǎn (see Places to Stay later). Myanmar seems to be really gearing up for
tourists: the consulate can grant you a four-
week visa in 24 hours for Y265, although
don't count on such speed; in three working
days it's Y165. There are two catches: first
you are required to change US$300 into
Myanmar kyat at the government's scan-
dalously low rate; and second the visas are
not good for land crossings – you must fly
in via Yangon (Rangoon) only. The consulate is open Monday to Friday from 8.30
am to noon and 1 to 4.30 pm.

Thailand The Thai consulate (☎ 316 2063/
62105, fax 316 6891) is in a building on the
Kunming Hotel grounds and can arrange
two-month visas for Y110 in three working
days. Travellers from most countries won't
need one unless they plan to spend more
than 30 days in Thailand (which actually is
not all that hard to do). It's open from 8.30
am to noon.

Money The main Bank of China is at 448
Renmin Donglu and is open from 9 am to
noon and from 1.30 to 5.30 pm. A branch
recently opened near the Golden Dragon
Hotel a block off Beijing Lu.

There are still one or two hopeful moneychangers in front of the Kunming Hotel, but
be very careful of rip-offs, which occur frequently by sleight of hand.

Post & Communications There is an international post office on the east side of
Beijing Lu. It's halfway between Tuodong
Lu and Huancheng Nanlu and has a very efficient poste restante and parcel service –
poste restante mail can be picked up here;
you must show ID first. You can also make
telephone calls here.

There is another post office to the north
of this one, at the intersection of Beijing Lu
with Dongfeng Donglu. The postal service
hours here are from 8 am to 8 pm, and the
telecommunication service operates from 8
am to 5 pm.

Email & Internet Access The Telecommunication Business Centre on the corner of
Beijing Lu and Dongfeng Donglu has fast
hook-ups and cheap rates – Y10 per hour.
Most cafes frequented by travellers also
offer email, albeit at slightly higher rates.
The area around Yunnan University is a
good spot, with many Internet cafes, including Dove Email (☎ 536 9789) at 47 Wenlin
Jie, which has access at Y16 per hour and
can help with foreign language translations.

Travel Agencies The China International
Travel Service (CITS; Zhōngguó Guójì
Lǚxíngshè; ☎ 314 8308) is just east of Beijing Lu in a large white-tiled building at 220
Huancheng Nanlu. This office emphasises
group tours and is not able to offer a lot of
assistance to individual travellers. Another
office (☎ 313 3452) can be found on
Dongfeng Donglu, near the Kunming Hotel.

Better for independent travellers would
be CITS' Family and Independent Traveller
(FIT) with offices at the King World Hotel
on Beijing Lu (☎ 313 8888/3104); and at
the Holiday Inn (☎ 316 5888/6212).

PSB The Foreign Affairs Branch of the Public Security Bureau (PSB; Gōngānjú) is a little way down an alley off 93 Beijing Lu and
is open from 8 to 11.30 am and 2.30 to 5.30
pm, and until 4.30 pm on Friday. On weekends it's posted as closed, but there's usually
someone about. It's a tiny office with a small
plaque in English on the wall outside. The
officers often speak some English. While
they happily reply *doūkěyǐ* ('everywhere is
OK!') when asked about open areas, when
pressed further they tell you that those endless rumours of the road into Tibet from
Yúnnán opening up are still greatly exaggerated, though you can get achingly close
(Déqīn). (Despite the PSB's claims, you cannot go north from Zhōngdiàn into Sìchuān.)
Visa extensions are fairly routine now.

Medical Services The Yan'an Hospital
(Yán'ān Yīyuàn), on Renmin Lu, has a foreigners' clinic (☎ 317 7499, ext 311) on the
1st floor of Building 6, at the back of the
compound.

Tang Dynasty Pagodas

To the south of Jinbi Lu are two Tang pagodas. **Xīsì Tǎ** (West Pagoda), is the one worth visiting. **Dōngsì Tǎ** (East Pagoda) was, according to Chinese sources, destroyed by an earthquake; western sources say it was destroyed by the Muslim revolt. It was rebuilt in the 19th century, but there's little to see.

The more interesting Xīsì Tǎ is on Dongsi Jie, a bustling market street. Xīsì Tǎ has a compound that is a popular spot for old people to get together, drink tea and play cards and mahjong. You can even get a haircut and a shave at the base of the pagoda.

It's a bit tricky to find. Look out for a red gateway hidden among the trees and karaoke signs: the pagoda is about 20m in along a narrow corridor. The temple is open from 9 am to 9 pm and admission is Y2.

Yúnnán Shěng
Bówùguǎn 云南省博物馆
Yunnan Provincial Museum

This museum, on Wuyi Lu, houses an exhibition centred on Yúnnán's minorities, and a collection of artefacts from tomb excavations at Jìnníng on the southern rim of Diān Chí. At the time of writing, the museum was closed for renovation – no doubt for the international expo in 1999 – and staff promised it would be an excellent museum when finished. The museum is open Tuesday to Sunday from 9 am to 5 pm and costs Y5.

Kūnmíngshì
Bówùguǎn 昆明市博物馆
Kunming City Museum

Located along Tuodong Lu, the Kūnmíngshì Bówùguǎn focuses on the history of the Diān Chí area. Only one room has English, but a few rooms, despite the language barrier, offer fascinating looks at the history of Kūnmíng, and one room peeks into Kūnmíng's leap into the millennium. The museum is open Wednesday to Sunday from 10 am to 4 pm; admission is Y5.

Yuántōng Sì 圆通寺

Yuántōng Sì, north-east of the Cuìhú Bīnguǎn, is the largest Buddhist complex in Kūnmíng and a target for pilgrims. It is over 1000 years old and has seen many renovations. Leading up to the main hall from the entrance is an extensive display of flowers and potted landscapes. The central courtyard holds a large square pond intersected by walkways and bridges, and has an octagonal **pavilion** at the centre.

To the rear of the temple a new hall has been added, enshrining a **statue of Sakyamuni**, a gift from the king of Thailand. There's a great vegetarian restaurant west of the temple entrance (open lunch and dinner).

The temple is open from 8 am to 5 pm; admission is Y2. Watch out for pickpockets outside the temple.

Kūnmíng
Dòngwùyuán 昆明动物园
Kunming Zoo

Close to Yuántōng Sì is the zoo. The grounds are pleasantly leafy and high up, and provide a bird's-eye vista of the city, but most travellers find the animals' living conditions depressing.

Cuìhú Gōngyuán 翠湖公园
Green Lake Park

A short distance south-west of the zoo, Cuìhú Gōngyuán is good for a stroll. Sunday sees the park at its liveliest, when it is host to an English Corner, colourful paddleboats and hordes of families at play. Admission is Y2.

Mosques

Kūnmíng's Buddhist shrines, devastated during the Cultural Revolution, have been mostly 'rehabilitated' and now hum with tourist trade. Now the local officials have focused on the left-out Muslim community and their mosques *(qīngzhēn sì)*. The oldest of the lot, the 400-year-old **Nánchéng Qīngzhēn Gǔsì** (Nancheng Muslim Ancient Mosque) was ripped down in 1997 in order to build a larger version.

Completed in 1998, the new mosque sits immediately north of the Kunming department store at 51 Zhengyi Lu. Looking vaguely like a Las Vegas casino, it has the appearance of a typical white-tiled office building (it does have office space) topped

Yúnnán's Muslims

Unlike Muslims in other parts of China, who generally formed settlements at the terminus of trade routes used by Arab traders, Yúnnán's sizable Muslim population dates back to the 13th century, when Mongol forces swooped into the province to outflank the Song dynasty troops. They were followed by Muslim traders, builders, and craftsmen. Yúnnán was the only region to have been put under a Muslim leader immediately after Kublai Khan's armies arrived, with Sayyid Ajall named governor in 1274.

All over China mosques were simultaneously raised with the new Yuan dynasty banner. A Muslim was entrusted to build the first Mongol palace in Běijīng. An observatory based on Persian models was constructed in Běijīng, and later copied by the Ming emperor. Dozens of Arabic texts were translated and consulted by Chinese scientists, influencing Chinese mathematics more than any other source. The most famous Yúnnán Muslim was Cheng Ho, the famed eunuch admiral who opened up the Chinese sea lanes to the Middle East.

Ethnically indistinguishable from the Han Chinese, the huí, as Muslims are known, have had an unfortunate history of repression and persecution, a recent low point being the years of the Cultural Revolution. The Cultural Revolution failed to spark off a revolt of any kind, though unsuccessful protests were registered in Běijīng. The turbulent years of the mid-19th century, which witnessed the massive Taiping and Nian rebellions, were another matter. Heavy land taxes and disputes between Muslims and Han Chinese over local gold and silver mines triggered a Muslim uprising in 1855, which lasted until 1873.

The Muslims made Dàlǐ the centre of their operations and laid siege to Kunming, overrunning the city briefly in 1863. Du Wenxiu, the Muslim leader, proclaimed his newly established kingdom Nanping Guo, or the Kingdom of the Pacified South, and he took the name Sultan Suleyman. But the Muslim successes were short-lived. In 1873 Dàlǐ was taken by Qing forces and Du Wenxiu was captured and executed, having failed in a suicide attempt. Up to a million people died in Yúnnán alone, the death toll rising to 18 million including Gānsù and Qīnghǎi provinces. The uprisings were quelled, but they also had the lasting effect of eliciting sympathy from Burma and fomenting a passion for culture among many of South-West China's ethnic minorities, most of whom had supported the Hui.

by bluish domes. Not too far away is a lively strip of lots and lots of Muslim restaurants. To get there, walk north-west past the Chūnchéng Jiǔlóu and then bear left a half-block to a small alley.

There's another mosque nearby, wedged between Huguo Lu and Chongyun Jie; it too had a friendly army of workers renovating it at last check.

Organised Tours

Several tour outfits cover Kūnmíng and its surrounding sights faster than public minibuses would, but you must be prepared to pay for them. They generally feature a lot of sights that most travellers find rather boring, like Hēilóng Tán (see later) and various caves. More central sights like Yuántōng Sì are just a short bicycle ride away – it hardly makes sense to join a tour to see them.

Some tour operators refuse to take foreigners on their tours, claiming the language barrier causes too much trouble.

For details on tours to Shí Lín (Stone Forest) from Kūnmíng, see the Shí Lín section later.

Yunnan Exploration (☎ 531 2283, fax 531 2324, ✉ travelguide@km.col.com.cn), at 73 Renmin Xilu, can organise jeep tours, hiking, backcountry skiing, bicycle trips and other more exotic outdoor activities, most of which take place far away from Kūnmíng. What's on offer looks interesting, although probably beyond the budgets of many travellers.

Places to Stay – Budget

Long frequented by budget travellers, the *Cháhuā Bīnguǎn (Camellia Hotel;* ☎ *316 3000 or 316 2918, fax 316 1879, 154*

Dongfeng Donglu) is still a grand bargain, with beds for Y30. Building 3 is in a quiet location and has three floors of dorms – some OK, some great, which are among the cheapest such rooms in Kūnmíng.

The Cháhuā has bicycle hire, a foreign-exchange counter, poste restante, a decent Y20 breakfast buffet, massage-quality pressure in the public showers, and the cheapest laundry service you'll find. Maybe best of all – 2 pm checkout is available. The staff do a pretty good job with the steady stream of backpacker guests. To get there from the train station, take bus Nos 2 or 23 to Dongfeng Lu, then change to bus No 5 heading east and get off at the second stop.

Near the train and bus stations on Beijing Lu, the *Kūnhú Fàndiàn (☎ 313 3737)* has beds in quads for Y25, which attract many backpackers. Unfortunately the dorm rooms look out onto Beijing Lu, so they're quite noisy. The hotel also has singles/doubles with common bath for Y60/68. Beyond this, rooms aren't quite worth the price – dingy doubles with attached bath go for Y120. Some travellers have been more than a bit unnerved by the unisex washrooms *and* showers; but the common bathrooms are fairly clean. Next door to the hotel are several cafes. Considering the extraordinary number of travellers that pass through, this place holds up pretty well. The hotel is two stops from the train station on numerous buses, though it's an easy walk as well.

Slightly higher in price but thoroughly worth it are the Y100 doubles with private bath (you may find a cheaper double with common bath) at *Yúndà Zhaōdaìsuǒ (Yunnan University Chinese Language Center for Foreign Students; ☎ 503 3624, fax 514 8513)*. Rooms are clean and come with TV.

Places to Stay – Mid-Range

The *Cháhuā Bīnguǎn* (see Places to Stay – Budget) has decent doubles from Y220 but take a look at the Y140 doubles with bath and TV in the older wing, as they've all been recently been spruced up and are a great bargain.

A trusty stand-by has always been the *Chūnchéng Jiǔlóu (☎ 316 3271, fax 316*

4191) on Dongfeng Xilu. It has spacious clean doubles with attached bathroom from Y150 to Y175 and triples from Y214 – take a look at a few rooms, as we've seen some clunkers as well as some of prime value. There are also doubles with common washroom for Y82, which are not such a good deal. Friendly, attentive service is the norm here. The restaurant gets great reviews too.

Right next to the main train station, the *Tiělù Lǚxíngshè (Railroad Travel Service; ☎ 351 2166, fax 351 3421)* has doubles with bath for Y180. There are much cheaper rooms, but they're not for you. The hotel is fairly new, so it's not a bad place to stay as long as you don't mind wading through the train station crowds on your way in and out of the building.

Places to Stay – Top End

Owing to Kūnmíng's hosting of a 1999 international expo an astonishing number of new hotels dot the central area and several former proletarian stand-bys have received luxury face-lifts, so there is plenty to choose from in this category.

The *Kunming Hotel (Kūnmíng Fàndiàn; ☎ 316 2063, fax 316 3784 or 313 8220, 145 Dongfeng Donglu)* once had a cheaper wing but no longer; standard rooms start at US$120. The hotel has some useful facilities: airline ticket bookings, poste restante, post office, photocopying, a snooker room, bike hire, several high-end restaurants, including Korean and Cháozhōu eateries, and a couple of shops. To get there from the main station, take bus No 23 to the intersection of Dongfeng Lu and Beijing Lu, and then take a bus east or walk. From the west bus station (Xīzhàn) take bus No 5.

Diagonally opposite the Kunming Hotel is Kūnmíng's super-luxury monster: the *Holiday Inn Kunming (Yínghuā Jiǎrì Jiǔdiàn; ☎ 316 5888, fax 313 5189)*, sporting some excellent restaurants (Thai and South-West US/Mexican along with a popular breakfast/lunch buffet), a western-style pub, and a super-chic disco. You can expect the usual Holiday Inn rates (US$137 to US$154 for a double, and then into the stratosphere at US$250 to US$888 for a

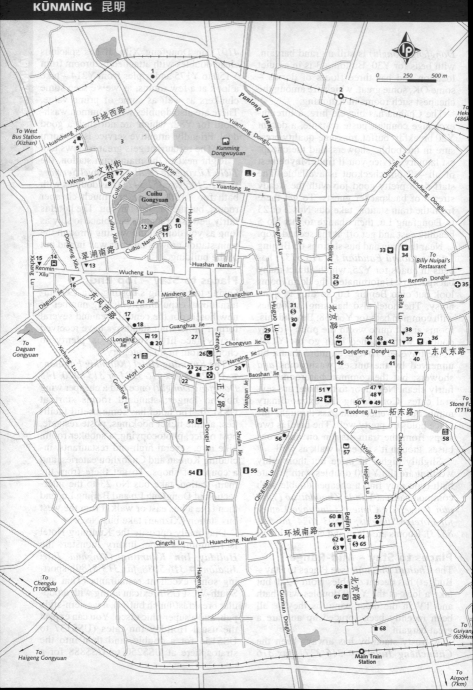

To West
Bus Station
(Xizhan)

环城西路
Huancheng Xilu

To Heko
(486k

Panlong Jiang

Yuantong Donglu

Kunming
Dongwuyuan

Chuanjin Lu

Huancheng
Donglu

文林街
Wenlin Jie

Qingyun Jie

Cuihu Beilu

Cuihu
Gongyuan

Yuantong Jie

Huashan Xilu

Cuihu Xilu

Cuihu Nanlu

Huashan Nanlu

Taoyuan Jie

Qinglian Lu

Beijing Lu

To
Billy Nuipai's
Restaurant

Renmin Donglu

Baita Lu

Dongfeng Xilu

Renmin
Xilu

Wucheng Lu

Xichang
Lu

Minsheng Jie

Changchun Lu

Hugou Lu

Ru An Jie

Daguan Jie

东风西路

To
Daguan
Gongyuan

Guanghua Jie

Longjing
Jie

Chongyun Jie

Nanping Jie

Dongfeng Donglu

东风东路

Zhengyi Lu

Wuyi Lu

Guofong Lu

Xichang Lu

Baoshan Jie

Xiangyan Jie

正义路

Jinbi Lu

Tuodong Lu

拓东路

Chuncheng Lu

To
Stone Fo
(111k

Dongsi Jie

Shulin Jie

Qingnian Lu

Wujing Lu

Heping Lu

To
Chengdu
(1100km)

Qingchi Lu

Huancheng Nanlu

Haigeng Lu

Guannan Donglu

环城南路

Beijing Lu

北京路

To
Haigeng Gongyuan

Main Train
Station

To
Guiyang
(639km

To
Airport
(7km)

0   250   500 m

PLACES TO STAY

4 Yúndà Zhāodàisuǒ
云大招待所

10 Cuìhú Bīnguǎn
翠湖宾馆

20 Yúnnán Fàndiàn
云南饭店

24 Chūnchéng Jiǔlóu
春城酒楼

36 Cháhuā Bīnguǎn;
Lao Consulate;
Myanmar Consulate
茶花宾馆;
老挝领事馆;
缅甸领事馆

41 Holiday Inn Kunming
樱花酒楼

42 Kunming Hotel;
Royal Thai Consulate
樱花假日酒店;
泰王国总领事馆

60 Kūnhú Fàndiàn
昆湖饭店

64 Golden Dragon Hotel
金龙饭店

66 King World Hotel
锦华大酒店

68 Tiělù Lǚxíngshè
铁路旅行社

PLACES TO EAT

5 Journey to the East Cafe
往东方旅行

7 Teresa's Pizzeria

8 Rum Bar;
Golden Sun Italy Cafe

12 Lǎozhīqīng Shíguǎn
老知青食馆

13 Bluebird Cafe

15 Mengzi Across-the-Bridge
Noodles Restaurant
蒙自过桥米线

16 Yúnnán Fēngwèi
Kuàicān
云南风味快餐

17 Shànghǎi Miànguǎn
上 C㕂

22 Muslim Restaurants
清真饭店

28 Běijīng Fàndiàn
北京饭店

38 Ma Ma Fu's 2
马马付2

39 Gēnxīng Fàndiàn
根兴饭店

40 Xuéchú Fàndiàn
学厨饭店

47 Báitǎdǎiwèi Cāntīng
白塔傣味餐厅

48 Wei's Place – La Piazzetta
哈哈餐厅

50 Yuánlóng Fēngwèichéng
元龙风味城

51 Mengzi Across-the-Bridge
Noodles Restaurant
蒙自过桥米线

61 Yuèlái Píjiǔguǎn; Mr Ball's
悦来啤酒馆

63 Dicos
得卡斯

ENTERTAINMENT

11 Yoko Ono Bar

18 Arts Theatre
艺术剧院

33 Camel Bar
骆驼酒吧

34 Back Street Bar

37 Camel Bar 2
骆驼酒吧2

56 Upriver Club
上河会馆

THINGS TO SEE

1 Yunnan Minorities Institute
云南民族学院

9 Yuántōng Sì
圆通寺

21 Yúnnán Shěng Bówùguǎn
云南省博物馆

26 Nánchéng Qīngzhēn Gǔsì
南城清真古寺

27 Flower & Bird Market;
Hot Spot
花鸟市场

29 Mosque
清真寺

53 Mosque
清真寺

54 Xīsì Tǎ
西寺塔

55 Dōngsì Tǎ
东寺塔

58 Kūnmíngshì Bówùguǎn
昆明市博物馆

TRANSPORT

2 North Train Station
火车北站

14 Xiǎoxīmén Bus Station
小西门汽车客运站

19 Buses to Xi Shān &
Qióngzhú Sì
往西山、筇竹寺的车

23 Kunming United Airlines
昆明联合航空公司

44 China Southern &
Shanghai Airlines
上海航空公司

46 China Southern Airlines
西南航空公司

49 Yunnan Airlines; CAAC
云南航空公司;
中国民航

62 China Southwest Airlines
西南航空公司

67 Long Distance Bus Station
长途汽车总站

OTHER

3 Yunnan University
云南大学

6 Dove Email

25 Kunming Department Store
昆明百货商店

30 Foreign Languages
Bookstore
外文书店

31 Bank of China
中国银行

32 Bank of China
(Main Branch)
中国银行

35 Yan'an Hospital
延安医院

43 CITS
中国国际旅行社

45 Post Office; Telecom
Business Centre
邮电局;电信营业厅

52 PSB
公安局

57 International Post Office
国际邮局

59 CITS
中国国际旅行社

65 Bank of China
中国银行

suite) but on our visit the room we were shown was obviously and embarrassingly in need of a paint job – for US$140. Rooms come with a western buffet breakfast.

The *Cuìhú Bīnguǎn (Green Lake Hotel;* ☎ *515 8888, fax 515 3286, 6 Cuihu Nanlu)* is in an older section of Kūnmíng overlooking Cuìhú Gōngyuán. It used to be quiet and quaint, but has lost some of its character with the construction of a 20-floor, four-star addition in the back. It's something of a stretch to charge Y280 for doubles in the old wing; we've had some reader complaints about these and keep in mind that equivalent rooms for Y100 less can be found in town. Much spiffier rooms can be found for US$100 in the new section. The hotel has a bar, a coffee shop and both western and Chinese restaurants that serve good food.

Down on Beijing Lu, the *Golden Dragon Hotel (Jīnlóng Fàndiàn;* ☎ *313 3015, fax 313 1082575 Beijing Lu)* has held up admirably and is good value for the price range. Only doubles are on offer and these start at US$88, while suites start at US$140 and reach the giddy heights of US$600 (plus 10% service charge); prices include breakfast. Rooms come with a breakfast; checkout time is 1 pm. A 15% discount is sometimes available on request. Dragonair has an office here and there is a business centre on the premises also. A shuttle is offered to the airport.

Down the road from the Golden Dragon is another luxury hotel, the *King World Hotel (Jīnhuá Dàjiǔdiàn;* ☎ *313 8888, fax 313 1910).* Doubles start at Y950, plus 15% service charge. The hotel features an expensive revolving restaurant (the highest above sea level in China, the hotel proudly points out) on the top floor. Rooms come with fruit baskets and a complimentary breakfast. The best rooms even have computer modules, some of the first in China. A shuttle is offered to the airport.

The *Yúnnán Fàndiàn (*☎ *361 3888)* on Dongfeng Xilu, near the Yúnnán Shěng Bówùguǎn, was Kūnmíng's first tourist hotel. It recently made a break with its humble beginnings and now its cheapest rooms are Y288. Go through to the back and Y60 rooms are still there, if you can get anybody to acknowledge their existence. For the pricier rooms, if you can get one that even resembles the brochures, then go for it; otherwise, there's better value in town.

Places to Eat

Chinese Cuisine There are several eating places near the Kūnmíng and Cháhuā Hotels on Dongfeng Donglu that have bilingual menus. The *Xuéchú Fàndiàn (Cooking School)* specialises in local fish and vegetable dishes, but it must save its novice chefs for the foreigners; it gets mixed reviews. On the other hand, the *Gēnxīng Fàndiàn (Yunnan Typical Local Food Restaurant)* has a good range of dishes, including across-the-bridge noodles, and gets good reviews on its food from both locals and foreigners.

If you want real Yúnnán food real fast, an outstanding new option is *Yúnnán Fēngwèi Kuàicān (Yunnan Flavour Fast Food)*, east of the Xiaoximen bus station and set back a bit off Renmin Xilu (look for Yúnnán's first US-based Wal-Mart store (as if you could ever miss one); it's opposite that enormous place. It's also known as Xīngfùyǔ (Happy Fish) and displays an oversized piscine fibreglass statue outside. You pay first, then just wander along a pan-Yúnnán line of food stations, point, and drool as chefs prepare it in front of you. You can get dishes for as little as Y5. A similar venture just west of Yunnan Airlines, the *Yuánlóng Fēngweìchéng (King Dragon Food Village)*, is a bit harder to deal with since the cooks are set far back behind high counters.

Several small restaurants in the vicinity of Yunnan University's main gate are quite good. Coming out of the Yunnan University gate, go left on the main road and then take the first left onto a small back street. There's a slew of little *restaurants* on this street, most of which have outdoor seating and are overflowing with happy diners. They're worth a try as well. This area is about 15 minutes' walk north of the Cuìhú Bīnguǎn.

Two of the better-known places for steampot chicken are the *Chūnchéng*

Kūnmíng Food

Kūnmíng has some great food, especially in the snack line. Regional specialities are *qìguōjī* (herb-infused chicken cooked in an earthenware steampot), *xuānwēi huǒtuǐ* (Yúnnán ham), *guòqiáo mǐxiàn* (across-the-bridge noodles), *rǔbǐng* (goat's cheese) and various Muslim beef and mutton dishes. Some travellers wax lyrical about toasted goat's cheese, another local speciality. It probably depends on how long you've been away from home – the cheese is actually quite bland and sticks to your teeth.

Gourmets with money to burn may perhaps be interested in a whole banquet based on Jizhong fungus (mushrooms) or 30 courses of cold mutton, not to mention fried grasshoppers or elephant trunk braised in soy sauce.

The chief breakfast in Kūnmíng, as throughout most of Yúnnán, is noodles (choice of rice or wheat), usually served in a meat broth with a chilli sauce.

Yúnnán's best known dish is across-the-bridge noodles. You are provided with a bowl of very hot soup (stewed with chicken, duck and spare ribs) on which a thin layer of oil is floating, along with a side dish of raw pork slivers (in classier places this might be chicken or fish) and vegetables, and a bowl of rice noodles. Diners place all of the ingredients quickly into the soup bowl, where they are cooked by the steamy broth.

Across-the-bridge noodles is the stuff of which fairy tales are made, as the following story proves:

Once upon a time there was a scholar at the South Lake in Mēngzǐ (southern Yúnnán) who was attracted by the peace and quiet of an island there. He settled into a cottage on the island, in preparation for official examinations. His wife, meanwhile, had to cross a long wooden bridge over the lake to bring the bookworm his meals. The food was always cold in winter by the time she got to the study bower. Oversleeping one day, she made a curious discovery. She'd stewed a fat chicken and was puzzled to find the broth still hot, though it gave off no steam – the oil layer on the surface had preserved the temperature of the broth. Subsequent experiments showed that she could cook the rest of the ingredients for her husband's meal in the hot broth after she crossed the bridge.

It is possible to try across-the-bridge noodles in innumerable restaurants in Kūnmíng. Prices generally vary from Y5 to Y15 depending on the side dishes provided. It's usually worth spending a bit more, because with only one or two condiments it lacks zest.

Jiǔlóu (see Places to Stay), on Dongfeng Xilu, and the *Dōngfēng Fàndiàn*, around the corner of Wuyi Lu and Wucheng Lu, in the direction of the Cuìhú Bīnguǎn.

Several small, private *restaurants* on Beijing Lu, opposite the long-distance bus station, sell cheaper versions of steampot chicken. Steampot chicken is served in dark-brown Jiànshuǐ County casserole pots, and is imbued with medicinal properties depending on the spicing – *chóngcǎo* (caterpillar fungus) and pseudo-ginseng are two favourite local ingredients.

Sadly, lots of places specialising in Kūnmíng's favourite noodles are disappearing. A few options have held out. The

Mengzi Across-the-Bridge-Noodles Restaurant (Mēngzǐ Guòqiáo Mǐxiàn) has noodles from Y5 to Y20. You'll find one on Beijing Lu near the PSB office; another is on Renmin Xilu west of the Xiaoximen bus station.

A more recent phenomenon in Kūnmíng is the discovery of ethnic cuisines. At present there are at least two Dai minority restaurants in Kūnmíng. The food is spicy and uses sticky rice as its staple. Popular with overseas students studying in Kūnmíng is the *Lǎozhīqīng Shíguǎn*, adjacent to the entrance to Cuìhú Gōngyuán; dishes start at Y6 but rise precipitously from there.

The *Báitǎdǎiwèi Cāntīng*, nestled down an alley opposite the Kunming Hotel, has tasty food, an English menu and cold draught beer. The prices are a bit high, but it's a good place to try Dai cuisine – an opportunity you won't get again unless you head down to Xīshuāngbǎnnà.

There is a string of eateries on Xiangyan Jie between Jinbi Lu and Nanping Jie. At the Nanping end is the *Běijīng Fàndiàn*, which offers northern-style seafood, chicken and duck. Further down are lots of street vendors and small private restaurants.

Pick of the basic restaurants is the *Shànghǎi Miànguǎn* in a yellow-fronted building along Dongfeng Xilu. To the left side you'll get cheap noodles; to the right are steampot chicken, cold cuts and dumplings.

Vegetarian Apart from the various temples in and around town, most of the restaurants near the Kūnhú and Cháhuā hotels that cater to westerners also have vegie selections. The *Chūnchéng Jiǔlóu* has a dim sum with good vegie items. West of the Yuántōng Sì, a few doors down, is an amazing *vegetarian restaurant* which takes copying meat-based dishes with vegie alternatives to new heights. This place is pricey but has dishes from Y6. The fungus dishes are some of the best in China; the staff recommends the duck in fermented beancurd.

Snacks Kūnmíng used to be a good place for bakeries, but many of these seem to be disappearing. Exploration of Kūnmíng's backstreets might turn up a few lingerers, however.

In the vicinity of the long-distance bus station and in many of the side streets running off Beijing Lu are *roadside noodle shops*. Generally you get a bowl of rice noodles for around Y2 and a bewildering array of sauces with which to flavour the broth – most of them are hot and spicy.

Another place to go snack hunting is Huguo Lu. The intersection of Changchun and Huguo yields lots of *small eateries*. Also try Shuncheng Jie, an east-west street running south of Dongfeng Xilu near the Chūnchéng Jiǔlóu. Here you'll find literally dozens of *Muslim restaurants*, *dumpling shops* and *noodle stands*.

Heping Nanlu runs north-south from just west of CITS along Huancheng Nanlu; here in the evenings you'll find dozens and dozens of small *outdoor eateries*.

Other Cuisines Literally dozens of friendly western-style cafes are found near the Cháhuā and Kūnhú hotels, and especially the new up-and-coming areas surrounding Yunnan University. *Ma Ma Fu's 2 (Māmáfù Cāntīng)*, a legendary Lìjiāng cafe, recently opened up around the corner east of the Cháhuā Bīnguǎn and is now run by the original Mama and Papa; it's still got the same to-die-for fresh breads and apple pie. The Kūnhú Fàndiàn has about a half a dozen options right outside its doors, including the *Yuèlaí Píjiǔguǎn*, which has good food. Right next door is the very new and very popular *Mr Ball's* (it's got a few names actually) – with excellent food, good service, and a budget-conscious menu.

The environs of Yunnan University (and nearby Cuìhú Gōngyuán) show the most promise for the future. Between the university and park along Wenlin Jie is the delightful *Teresa's Pizzeria*, with excellent pizzas, calzones, salads and a great atmosphere. Wenlin Jie and its tiny alleys house a host of other restaurants, bars, Internet cafes, a real French bakery, and even *Paul's*, a grocery specialising in western gourmet and hard-to-find imports. To the north of here adjacent to Yunnan University is the town's original western cafe, *Journey to the East Cafe (Wàngdōngfāng Lǚxíng)*, with good food, email, and tons of books – this place is a good place to mingle with travellers brimming with local knowledge.

Branching off Wenlin Jie to the southwest is Cuihu Beilu, another row of pubs and cafes. The *Rum Bar* has Mexican fare, pizza and pub grub; then there is the *Golden Sun Italy Cafe* (☎ 536 2502, 16 Cuihi Beilu) – the name says it all. Continuing all the way along this road to Cuihu Nanlu and turn right, you'll come to the *Bluebird Café* (☎ 531 4071, 150 Cuihu Nanlu), another quaint eatery equally popular with locals.

Kūnmíng hasn't as yet experienced the invasion of KFC a la Chéngdū, but an excellent local approximation – *Dicos* (*Dékèshì Huòjī*) – has outlets in front of the Kunming department store and just south of the Kūnhú Fàndiàn.

A few swank steakhouses have opened in Kūnmíng. Tucked away in the north-eastern Xinying Xiaoqu district is the original, *Billy Niupai's* (*Bǐlì Niúpái;* ☎ *331 1748, 47 Tianyuan Lu*), where you can get steaks, burgers, pasta and even tacos that should successfully satisfy a homesick appetite. Figure on around Y50 for a full western meal, much of it made with imported ingredients. The decor is strictly American cowboy, but pleasant for all that. It's probably best to take a taxi, if for no other reason than you'll definitely need the cab driver to help you find the place. The ride should cost around Y15 from the Kūnhú Fàndiàn, less from the Cháhuā Bīnguǎn.

The big hotels all sport coffee shops. For a no-holds-barred breakfast buffet, head down to the *Holiday Inn Kunming*, where you can eat as much as you can stuff in for Y70. If you're a caffeine addict you'll love its coffee deal – Y20 for as many refills as you can stomach, and the coffee is excellent. The ground-floor coffee shop in the *Golden Dragon Hotel* is not quite in the same league, but the coffee is also good. The *Cháhuā Bīnguǎn* has a breakfast buffet for Y20; it's bare-bones compared with the two above, but it's great value for the low price.

A giant block south of the Cháhuā Bīnguǎn is a cafe with outstanding food and pleasant eclectic western music called *Wei's Place – La Piazzetta*. It is located off Tuodong Lu in a small alley. In addition to the dense menu of believable Italian food, the wood-fired pizzas are unspeakably good, even with pizza now popping up all over China. You can also get Chinese dishes, such as good medicinal-herb chicken in a pot. Frosted mugs of beer top off the effect. There are plenty of magazines and newspapers to peruse as well. It's open from 8 am (theoretically) to midnight, but the breakfasts don't match the dinners.

Entertainment

Once restricted to dismal karaoke bars, Kūnmíng is exploding with night-time options, most of the boozing rather than dancing variety. Any of the western-style cafes mentioned above double as drinking holes. One unique place is the *Upriver Club* (*Shànghé Huìguǎn*), a coffee/tea shop-cum-art gallery west of the river Pánlóng Hé, south of Jinbi Lu along Houxin Road. It's got a pleasant outdoor area, Internet access and books.

The *Camel Bar* (*Lùotuō Jiǔbā;* ☎ *337 6255, 274 Baita Lu*) is north of the Cháhuā Bīnguǎn along Baita Lu. Run by Li Du, a local rocker of some repute, it's got cheap Tsingtao beer and live music on weekends. The Camel is so popular that a new version, *Camel Bar 2* (*72 Donfeng Lu*), recently opened just west of the Cháhuā Bīnguǎn along Dongfeng Donglu; this incarnation also has Internet access and bike rentals. North of the original is another lively joint, the *Back Street Bar* (*377 Baita Lu*).

Not far from the western-style cafes on Cuihu Beilu and opposite the south entrance of Cuìhú Gōngyuán is the new *Yoko Ono Bar* (*88 Cuihu Nanlu*), with Y10 mixed drinks and a fairly eclectic CD collection.

Adjacent to the Huāniǎo Shìchǎng (Flower and Bird Market), east of the Yúnnán Fàndiàn, is perhaps the hippest place. The *Hot Spot* (*Shifu Dongjie Caimao Julebu*) opens at 3 pm, has cheap beer, a good happy hour, and rocking parties every Friday. This is Kūnmíng's most likely place to hear trip-hop and gangsta rap on the same night. It's tough to find, too. At last check a nearby store had a prominent yellow sign out front, but note that landmarks in Kūnmíng come and go.

The most happening disco for local wannabes at the moment is *Top One* at the Cháhuā Bīnguǎn.

Over at the Holiday Inn, *Charlie's* bar is frequented by Kūnmíng's expat community, but prices are considerably higher – stick to beer, since a mixed drink will cost you around Y80.

You might be able to chase up minority dancing displays (more often held for the benefit of group tours), travelling troupes or Yúnnán Opera. CITS sometimes has information on these events. The *Arts Theatre*, on Dongfeng Xilu, is a likely venue.

Shopping

You have to do a fair bit of digging to come up with inspiring purchases in Kūnmíng. Yúnnán specialities are jade, marble (from the Dàlǐ area), batik, minority embroidery (also musical instruments and dress accessories) and spotted brass utensils.

Some of the basic utilitarian items that are part of everyday Yunnanese life make good souvenirs: large bamboo water pipes for smoking angel-haired Yúnnán tobacco, *qìguō* (ceramic steampots) and local herbal medicines such as *yúnnán báiyào* (Yúnnán white medicine), which is a blend of over 100 herbs and highly prized by Chinese throughout the world.

Yunnanese tea is also an excellent buy and comes in several varieties, from bowl-shaped bricks of smoked green tea called *tuóchá*, which have been around since at least Marco Polo's time, to leafy black tea that rivals some of India's best.

One of the main shopping drags is Zhengyi Lu, which has numerous department stores. Other shopping areas are Jinbi Lu by the Zhengyi Lu intersection (lots of small speciality shops), and Dongfeng Donglu, between Zhengyi Lu and Huguo Lu (here renamed Nanping Jie).

The Huāniǎo Shìchǎng (Flower and Bird Market) is definitely worth a visit. It's tucked away on Tongdao Jie, one of numerous little streets and alleys lying between Zhengyi Lu and Wuyi Lu, just north of the Kunming department store. Pet supplies, fishing gear and flowers dominate the cramped rows of tiny stalls, but there is a bizarre assortment of other items such as old coins, wooden elephants, tacky wall murals and so-called 'antiques'. Just walking around here is rewarding: if you actually find something you want to buy, consider it an added bonus. Animal lovers beware – you're apt to see lots you don't like.

For antiques it's better to look among the privately run shops on Beijing Lu and

Dongfeng Donglu. Outside the Kunming Hotel you will probably be ambushed by women flogging their handiwork – bargain if you want a sane price. Both the Cuìhú and Kunming hotels sell batik which you can also find in Dàlǐ. For Yúnnán herbal medicines, check the large pharmacy on Zhengyi Lu (on the east side, several blocks up from the Kunming department store). There are also a few herbal medicine shops at the southern end of Beijing Lu.

Getting There & Away

Air The Civil Aviation Administration of China (CAAC; Zhōngguó Mínháng; ☎ 558 1466, 312 1223) supposedly shares office space with Yunnan Airlines (☎ 316 4270, 312 1223) along Tuodong Lu, but Yunnan Airlines gets all the business. Try the ticket offices of the other airlines mentioned later in this section if you can't get on Yunnan Airlines' flights. It's open from 8.30 am to 7.30 pm and the airport shuttle bus leaves from here starting at around 8 am. Yunnan Airlines has a 'Peacock Card' which costs Y300 but also gets you 20% off any of its flights. If you take the Kūnmíng-Bangkok flight, it pays for itself!

China Southern Airlines (☎ 317 4682) has its main office on the other side of the Kunming Hotel, as well as a number of branches around the city, including a new one (☎ 310 1831 or 310 1832) off the corner of Beijing Lu and Dongfeng Donglu. The main branch is open from 8.30 am to 8 pm. Thai Airways International (☎ 313 3315) is adjacent to the King World Hotel and is open weekdays from 9 am to 5 pm, and until noon Saturdays.

For internal flights, other alternatives include Shanghai Airlines (☎ 316 3687), on Dongfeng Donglu, Kunming United Airlines (☎ 316 4590), on Dongfeng Xilu, and China Southwest Airlines (☎ 317 9696), at 36 Beijing Lu, open from 8 am to 7 pm.

Kūnmíng is well connected by air to the rest of China, and most flights (even within Yúnnán) are on Boeing 737 and 757 jets. The most popular destinations include: Běijīng (Y1450), Chéngdū (Y560), Chóngqìng (Y570), Guǎngzhōu (Y1010), Guìlín (Y670),

Guìyáng (Y400), Hǎikǒu (Y900), Lánzhōu (Y1510), Nánjīng (Y1680), Nánníng (Y500), Qīngdǎo (Y2000), Shànghǎi (Y1520), Shàntóu (Y1300), Shēnzhèn (Y1300), Wǔhàn (Y1200), Xiàmén (Y1440) and Xī'ān (Y1000).

Within the province you can reach Bǎoshān (Y400), Jǐnghóng (Y520), Lìjiāng (Y390; up to four times per day), Mángshì (Déhóng) (Y530), Xiàguān (Dàlǐ; Y320), Zhōngdiàn (Y560; three times weekly) and Zhāotòng (Y400).

Several carriers have flights to Hong Kong (Y1710; daily) and to international destinations such as Bangkok (Y1590; daily), Chiang Rai (four times per week), Yangon (Y2800; weekly), Vientiane (Y1290; twice weekly), Singapore (Y3480; twice weekly), Macau (Y1310; twice weekly), Osaka (Wednesday) and Kuala Lumpur (Y1900; Friday).

Bus The bus situation in Kūnmíng can be a little confusing at first. There seem to be buses leaving from all over the place. However, the long-distance bus station on Beijing Lu is the main centre of operations, and this is the best place to organise bus tickets to almost anywhere in Yúnnán or further afield. Exceptions to this are more local destinations like Diān Chí.

The most popular bus routes from Kūnmíng are to Dàlǐ, Lìjiāng and Jǐnghóng (to the south, in Xīshuāngbǎnnà), and Déhóng (to the west). The long distances to the last two destinations make sleeper buses a popular if not necessary option. The long-distance bus station now has super-fast Korean luxury buses for many destinations.

For information on Dàlǐ, see the Dàlǐ Getting There & Away section.

Once an unspeakably horrible trip of up to 30 hours, Lìjiāng (Y155; departs 7.30 am) is now just 10 hours away on the Korean express buses. Expresses also depart for Hékǒu (Y109; departs 9.30 am) and Zhōngdiàn, though even the bus station staff says you're nuts to break the trip to the latter in Dàlǐ or Lìjiāng.

To Lìjiāng on regular buses it'll take 12 to 15 hours, new highways notwithstanding; sleepers depart four times daily and cost Y106 to Y126 depending on the bus.

With road and vehicle improvements, the marathon trip to Jǐnghóng in Xīshuāngbǎnnà now takes only 18 to 24 hours, depending on the length of the numerous meal breaks and various unscheduled but inevitable stops. The trip used to include an overnight stop, but now nearly all buses drive straight through. Sleepers to Jǐnghóng cost Y137 and leave often. Many more sleeper buses to Jǐnghóng are found in front of the train station and negotiation can at times enter in here. These operators also have a few sleepers which bypass Jǐnghóng and go straight to Měnglà (Y157), the jump-off point for Laos.

Both options for getting to the Déhóng region involve long hauls, so it's worth considering doing at least one leg of the trip by air (to Mángshì). Sleeper buses leave for Bǎoshān (Y114; 15 to 18 hours) from the long-distance bus station three times a day between 4 and 6.30 pm. Buses – all sleepers via Mángshì – direct to Ruìlì (Y156; 22 to 26 hours) leave six times daily between 9.20 am and 7.40 pm. More options are found outside the train station. To Nínglàng (for Lúgū Hú) there is a bus (Y101) at 11.40 am.

If you're headed to Vietnam, there are night sleeper buses to the Chinese border town of Hékǒu (Y90 to Y98; 12 hours), leaving at 8.30 am, and 6.40 and 7.15 pm. Travellers looking to go overland to Laos can either go to Jǐnghóng and then Měnglà, though some sleepers from in front of the train station do it in one shot (see earlier).

It is possible to travel by bus to several destinations in neighbouring provinces from the long-distance bus station, including Guìyáng (Guìzhōu) and Nánníng (Guǎngxī); Xīngyì (Guìzhōu; Y48 to Y65; 10 hours) is the closest.

For more information see the Shí Lín section later in this chapter.

Train Rail options (all prices listed are hard sleeper) include trains to Shànghǎi (Y349; via Guìyáng, Zhūzhōu, Nánchāng and Hángzhōu), Běijīng (Y576; via Guìyáng, Chángshā and Zhèngzhōu), Chóngqìng (Y162; via Guìyáng), Guǎngzhōu (Y426;

via Guìlín), Xī'ān, Éméi and Chéngdū (Y255).

You can also take a train down the narrow-gauge line to the border crossing with Vietnam at Hékǒu; this now continues on to Hanoi (trains depart Friday and Sunday at 2.30 pm and take 30 hours). New rail links have finally been established with Xiàguān (Dàlǐ) and Nánníng, the latter of which has dramatically eased the stress on trying to train it to Guǎngxī. Tourist trains also roar to Shí Lín (see the Shí Lín section later in this chapter).

The main station sells both hard-sleeper and hard-seat tickets from 8.30 am, up to three days in advance. At peak times, especially holidays, you may need to book this far ahead. The train station ticket office is open from 6.30 am to 11.10 pm. The good news is that the station seems to have more hard sleeper tickets available closer to departure days, sometimes even next morning (though not for Guìlín).

If you're going to Guìlín, consider the impressive new Nánkún railway to Nánníng. Train No 502 departs at 2.10 pm (Y120 hard sleeper; 20 hours). To Xiàguān the bus is probably faster but trains depart at 10.10 pm (Y51 hard seat; 10 to 11 hours).

Getting Around

Most of the major sights are within a 15km radius of Kūnmíng. Local transport to these places is awkward, crowded and time-consuming; it tends to be an out-and-back job, with few crossovers for combined touring. If you wish to take in everything, it would take something like five return trips, which would consume three days or more.

You can simplify this by pushing Hēilóng Tán, Ānníng Wēnquán and Jīn Diàn to the background, and concentrating on the trips of high interest – Qióngzhú Sì and Xī Shān, both of which have decent transport connections with special express buses in the mornings. (See following section, Around Kūnmíng.) Diān Chí presents some engrossing circular-tour possibilities on its own. Better still, buy a map, hire a good bicycle and tour the area on two wheels (although there are some steep hills lurking out there ...).

To/From the Airport A super-efficient shuttle (Y5) departs to and from Kūnmíng airport and the Yunnan Airlines office. Service is supposed to be from 6 am to 8 pm, but these times aren't to be taken too seriously. Buses run from the airport when full, and every 15 minutes from the airlines office.

Alternatively, you can exit the airport, walk past the taxis, a traffic roundabout and a hotel to the main road. Bus No 52 runs along this road, terminating near the airport entrance.

Better still, treat yourself to a taxi (approximately Y15) – this is one of the few cheap airport taxi rides in China.

Bus The best option for getting out to Qióngzhú Sì and Xī Shān is to head over to the Yúnnán Fàndiàn – buses and minibuses leave from in front of the hotel in the morning. Departure times depend on how fast the bus fills up: afternoon buses can sit around for hours.

Public buses run out to most of the other major sights. Options include: No 10 to Jīn Diàn and No 9 to Hēilóng Tán, both from the north train station; No 44 from Kūnmíng train station to Hǎigěng Gōngyuán; and No 4 from the zoo to Dàguān Gōngyuán (Grand View Park).

Bicycle The Cháhuā Bīnguǎn carries a decent selection of bikes for hire (and requires large deposits of between Y200 and Y400!); the Camel Bar 2 nearby also has some. The Kūnhú also has had a few bikes for hire, but they're dwindling in number. A new bike shop at 33 Qianjue Jie, just off Cuihu Nanlu, has superb equipment and organises Sunday morning bike rides – you need to make reservations ahead of time.

AROUND KŪNMÍNG
Jīn Diàn 金殿
Golden Temple

This Taoist temple is perched in a pine forest on Phoenix Song Mountain, 11km north-east of Kūnmíng. The original Jīn Diàn was carted off to Dàlǐ; the present one dates from the Ming dynasty and was enlarged by General Wu Sangui, who was dispatched by the Manchus in 1659 to quell the uprisings in the region. Wu Sangui turned against the Manchus and set himself up as a rebel warlord, with Jīn Diàn as his summer residence.

The pillars, ornate door frames, walls, fittings and roof tiles of the 6m-high temple are all made of copper; the entire structure, laid on a white Dàlǐ marble foundation, is estimated to weigh more than 300 tonnes. In the courtyard are ancient camellia trees. At the back is a 14-tonne bronze bell, cast in 1423.

To get there, take bus No 10 from Kūnmíng's north train station. Many travellers ride hired bikes to the temple – it's fairly level-going all the way to the base of the hill. Once you get there, you'll have to climb an easy hill path to the temple compound. You may or may not think the Y20 entrance fee (just the beginning of these) is worth it.

Hēilóng Tán 黑龙潭
Black Dragon Pool
Eleven kilometres north of Kūnmíng is Hēilóng Tán, a rather mediocre garden with old cypresses, dull Taoist pavilions and no bubble in the springs. But the view of the surrounding mountains from the garden is inspiring. Within walking distance is the **Kunming Botanical Institute**, where the flora collection might be of interest to specialists. Take bus No 9 from the north train station; admission is Y1.

Qióngzhú Sì 筇竹寺
Bamboo Temple
Twelve kilometres north-west of Kūnmíng, Qióngzhú Sì dates back to the Tang dynasty. Burned down and rebuilt in the 15th century, it was restored from 1883 to 1890 when the abbot employed master Sìchuān sculptor Li Guangxiu and his apprentices to fashion 500 *luohan* (arhats or noble ones). These life-size clay figures are stunning – either very realistic or very surrealistic – a sculptural tour de force. Down one huge wall come the incredible surfing buddhas, some 70-odd, riding the waves on a variety

of mounts – blue dogs, giant crabs, shrimp, turtles and unicorns.

The statues have been constructed with the precision of a split-second photograph – a monk about to chomp into a large peach (the face contorted almost into a scream), a figure caught turning around to emphasise a discussion point, another about to clap two cymbals together, yet another cursing a pet monster. The old, the sick, the emaciated – nothing is spared; the expressions of joy, anger, grief or boredom are extremely vivid.

So lifelike are the sculptures that they were considered in bad taste by Li Guangxiu's contemporaries (some of whom no doubt appeared in caricature), and upon the project's completion he disappeared into thin air.

By far the easiest way to get there is to take a bus from in front of the Yúnnán Fàndiàn. Buses run from 7 am to around 4.30 pm (although the last often goes at around 10 am) leaving as soon as they are full. The ride takes 30 minutes and costs around Y8 one way. Admission to the temple is Y3 and it is generally considered to be worth it.

Ānníng Wēnquán 安宁温泉
Anning Hot Springs
Most travellers sensibly give this place, 44km south-west of Kūnmíng, a wide berth. The hot springs and the surrounding area (which includes some Miao minority villages) are not particularly interesting.

There are various hotels and guesthouses here that pipe the hot spring water into the rooms, but reports have it that couples are not accepted in some of them – this rule may have changed.

Nearby, and possibly worth a look, is the **Caoxi Sì**. This temple is over the river and a couple of kilometres or so to the south in a bamboo grove on Cong Hill.

Buses to the springs run approximately every hour from the Xiaoximen bus station between 8 am and 6 pm; the trip costs Y4. Returning, the last bus is at 5 pm. There is another bus station west of Xiaoximen which may also have buses.

YÚNNÁN 云南

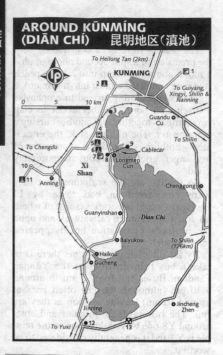

AROUND KŪNMÍNG (DIĀN CHÍ) 昆明地区（滇池）

To Heilong Tan (2km)

KŪNMÍNG

To Guiyang,
Xingyi, Shilin &
Nanning

0   5   10 km

To Chengdu

Guandu
Cu

To Shilin

Xī
Shān

Cablecar

Longmén
Cun

Anning

Chenggong

Guanyinshan

Dian Chi

Baiyukou

To Shilin
(126km)

Haikou

Gucheng

Jincheng
Zhen

Jinning

To Yuxi

AROUND KŪNMÍNG

1 Jīndiàn
   金殿
2 Qióngzhú Sì
   筇竹寺
3 Dàguān Gōngyuán
   大观公园
4 Gāoyáo Bus Station
   高峣汽车站
5 Huátíng Sì
   华亭寺
6 Tàihuá Sì
   太华寺
7 Sānqīng Gé
   三清阁
8 Lóng Mén
   龙门
9 Hǎigēng Gōngyuán
   海埂公园
10 Ānníng Wēnquán
   安宁温泉
11 Cáoxī Sì
   曹溪寺
12 Zhènghé Gōngyuán
   郑和公园
13 Stone Village Hill

Diān Chí 滇池
Dian Lake

The shoreline of Diān Chí, to the south of Kūnmíng, is dotted with settlements, farms and fishing enterprises; the western side is hilly, while the eastern side is flat country. The southern end of the lake, particularly the south-east, is industrial.

The lake is elongated – about 40km from north to south – and covers an area of 300 sq km. Plying the waters are *fanchuan*, pirate-sized junks with bamboo-battened canvas sails. It's mainly for scenic touring and hiking, and there are some fabulous aerial views from the ridges at Lóng Mén (Dragon Gate) in Xī Shān (see Xī Shān section).

Dàguān Gōngyuán 大观公园
Grand View Park

Dàguān Gōngyuán is at the northernmost tip of Diān Chí, 3km south-west of the city centre. A Buddhist temple was originally constructed there in 1862. It covers 60

hectares and includes a nursery, a children's playground, row boats and pavilions. **Dàguān Lóu** (Grand View Tower) provides good views of Diān Chí. Its facades are inscribed with a 180-character poem by Qing poet Sun Ranweng, rapturously extolling the beauty of the lake. Bus No 4 runs to Dàguān Gōngyuán from Yuántōng Sì, bus No 52 departs near the Kunming Hotel.

At the north-eastern end of the park is a dock where you can get boats (40 minutes; Y5) to Lóngmén village and Hǎigēng Gōngyuán. From Lóngmén village you can hike up the trail to Lóng Mén and Xī Shān, and catch a minibus back into town near the summit at the Nièěr Zhīmù (Tomb of Nie Er). From Hǎigēng, take bus No 44 to Kūnmíng's main train station.

Xī Shān 往西山
Western Hills

Xī Shān spreads out across a long wedge of parkland on the western side of Diān Chí;

it's also known as the 'Sleeping Beauty Hills', a reference to the hills' undulating contours, which are thought to resemble a reclining woman with tresses of hair flowing into the sea. The path up to the summit passes a series of famous temples – it's a steep approach from the north side. The hike from Gāoyáo bus station, at the foot of Xī Shān, to Lóng Mén takes 2½ hours. If you're pushed for time, there's a connecting bus from Gāoyáo to the top section, or you could take a minibus direct from in front of the Yúnnán Fàndiàn to Lóng Mén. Alternatively, it is also possible to cycle to Xī Shān in about an hour – to vary the trip, consider doing the return route across the dykes of upper Diān Chí.

At the foot of the climb, about 15km from Kūnmíng, is **Huátíng Sì**, a country temple of the Nanzhao kingdom believed to have been constructed in the 11th century, rebuilt in the 14th century, and extended in the Ming and Qing dynasties. The temple has some fine statues, a Buddhist scripture library, and excellent gardens. There is a Y3 entry fee.

The road from Huátíng Sì winds from here up to the Ming dynasty **Tàihuá Sì**, the courtyard of which houses a fine collection of flowering trees, including magnolias and camellias. Entry here costs Y3.

Between Tàihuá Sì and Sānqīng Gé Taoist temple near the summit is **Nièěr Zhīmù** (Tomb of Nie Er). Nie Er was a talented Yúnnán musician (1912–36) who composed the national anthem of the PRC before drowning in Japan en route for further training in the Soviet Union. From here you can catch a chairlift (Y20) if you want to skip the fairly steep ascent to the summit. If you decide to visit the restaurant at the top, watch that you are not overcharged.

The **Sānqīng Gé**, near the top of the mountain, was a country villa for a prince of the Yuan dynasty, and was later turned into a temple dedicated to the three main Taoist deities.

Further up is **Lóng Mén** (Dragon Gate), a group of grottoes, sculptures, corridors and pavilions hacked from the cliff between 1781 and 1835 by a Taoist monk and co-workers, who must have been hanging up there by their fingertips. At least that's what the locals do when they visit, seeking out the most precarious perches for views of Diān Chí. The tunnelling along the outer cliff edge is so narrow that only one or two people can squeeze by at a time, so avoid public holidays and weekends! Entry to the Lóng Mén area (which includes Sānqīng Gé) costs Y10.

From Kūnmíng to Xī Shān the most convenient mode of transport is minibus (Y8; half hour). These leave as they fill up from outside the Yúnnán Fàndiàn between 8.30 am and 1 pm (although they're posted as running until 4.30 pm); some folks have been stuck waiting after 10 am.

Alternatively, you can use the local bus service to get there. Take bus No 5 (Y0.74) from the Kunming Hotel to the terminus at Liǎngjīahé, and then change to bus No 6 (Y1), which will take you to Gāoyáo bus station at the foot of the hills. Buses to the Kūnmíng steel plant *(kūngāng)* also run past Gāoyáo, and leave from in front of the arts theatre (near the Yúnnán Fàndiàn), or from Xiaoximen bus station.

From the Xī Shān to Kūnmíng you can either take the bus or scramble down from the Lóng Mén area directly to the lake side along a zigzag dirt path and steps that lead to Lóngmén Cūn (Longmen Village), also known as Sānyì Cūn (Sanyi Village). When you reach the road, turn right and walk about 100m to a narrow spit of land which leads across the lake. Continuing across the land spit, you arrive at a narrow stretch of water and a small bridge. (You could also take a new cable car across to Hǎigěng Gōngyuán for Y30.) Proceed by foot through this area along the lake side road that runs back to Hǎigěng Gōngyuán, where you can catch bus No 44 to Kūnmíng train station.

The tour can easily be done in reverse; start with bus No 44 to Hǎigěng Gōngyuán, walk to Lóngmén village, climb straight up to Lóng Mén, then make your way down through the temples to Gāoyáo bus station, where you can get bus No 6 back to Xiaoximen bus station. Alternatively, bus No 33 runs along the coast through Lóngmén village, or you can take a boat from Dàguān Gōngyuán. Other public bus options exist from near the train station or Xiaoximen.

Hǎigěng Gōngyuán 海埂公园 & Yúnnán Mínzúcūn 云南民族村
Haigeng Park & Yunnan Nationalities Village

The local tourist authorities have thrown together a string of model minority villages on the north-eastern side of the lake with the aim of finally representing all 25 of Yúnnán's minorities.

It's a rather expensive cultural experience for the visitor, with a Y35 general entry fee and even more surcharges in each village. There are also various song-and-dance performances throughout the day, some of which also cost extra. If you're at all averse to tourist-board fabrications of ethnic cultures, give the place a miss and spend an extra day in Xīshuāngbǎnnà or Déhóng, where you can see the real thing. However, with the advent of the Yúnnán Mínzúcūn, what little remains of Hǎigěng Gōngyuán – a narrow strip of greenery along the lakefront – has become a good place to escape the crowds and enjoy the scenery. The roller coaster is covered with weeds and most of the lakefront restaurants are shuttered, giving the place a ghost town feel.

Bus No 44 runs to Haigeng Lu from one street north of the Kūnmíng train station.

Zhènghé Gōngyuán 郑和公园
Zhang He Park

At the south-west corner of the Diàn Chí, this park commemorates the Ming dynasty navigator Zheng He (known as Admiral Cheng Ho throughout most of the world). A mausoleum here holds tablets describing his life and works. Zheng He, a Muslim, made seven voyages to more than 30 Asian and African countries in the 15th century in command of a huge imperial fleet.

From Xiaoximen bus station take the bus to Kúnyáng; the park is on a hill overlooking the town. For a change of pace, take a train from the north train station to Hǎikǒu and then a local bus to Kúnyáng. You can complete a full circuit by catching a bus on to Jìnchéngzhèn and Chénggòng. There's

also accommodation in Kúnyáng for around Y20 per bed if you feel like moving at a more relaxed pace.

Jìnníng Xiàn 晋宁县
Jinning County

This is the site of archaeological discoveries from early Kūnmíng, and you'll find it at the southern end of the lake. Bronze vessels, a gold seal and other artefacts were unearthed at Stone Village Hill, and some items are displayed at the Yúnnán Shěng Bówùguǎn in Kūnmíng.

The bus to Kúnyáng runs via Jincheng to Jìnníng.

Chénggòng Xiàn 呈贡县
Chenggong County

This is an orchard region on the eastern side of the lake Diàn Chí. Flowers bloom all year round, with the 'flower tide' in January, February and March. This is the best time to visit, especially diminutive Dòunán village near Chénggòng. Once one of Yúnnán's poorest villages, it now sells more than 400,000 spray of flowers *each day*. The village's per capita income went from US$13 to US$415 in four years (even Yunnan Airlines has opened an office to expedite international deliveries).

Many western varieties of camellia, azalea, orchid and magnolia derive from south-west Chinese varieties. They were introduced to the west by adventuring botanists who carted off samples in the 19th and 20th centuries. Azaleas are native to China – of the 800 varieties in the world, 650 are found in Yúnnán.

During the Spring Festival (February/March) a profusion of blooming species can be found at temple sites around Kūnmíng – notably the Tàihuá, Huátíng and Jīn Diàn temples, as well as Hēilóng Tán and Yuántōng Shān.

Take bus No 5 east to the terminus at Juhuacun, and change there for bus No 12 to Chénggòng.

SHÍ LÍN 石林
Stone Forest ☎ 0871

Shí Lín, around 120km south-east of Kūnmíng, is a massive collection of grey

SHÍ LÍN (STONE FOREST) 石林

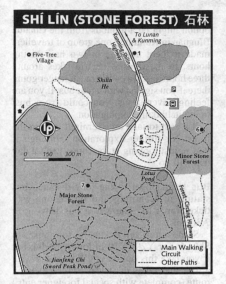

To Lunan & Kunming

Kunming-Shilin Highway

Five-Tree Village

Shilin He

Minor Stone Forest

Lotus Pond

Major Stone Forest

Forest-Circling Highway

Jianfeng Chi (Sword Peak Pond)

0   150   300 m

- - - Main Walking Circuit
········ Other Paths

SHÍ LÍN (STONE FOREST)

1 Truck Stop
   卡车站
2 Bus Departures
   汽车站
3 Local Handicraft
   Stalls
   工艺摊
4 Yúnlín Bīnguǎn
   云林宾馆
5 Shílín Bīnguǎn; CITS
   石林宾馆;
   中国国际旅行社
6 Inscription of Mao
   Zedong's poem 'Ode
   to the Plum Blossom'
   咏梅石
7 Sweet Water Well
   甜水井

limestone pillars, the tallest 30m high, split and eroded by wind and rain water into their present fanciful forms. Marine fossils found in the area suggest that it was once under the sea. Legend has it that the immortals smashed a mountain into a labyrinth for lovers seeking privacy – picnicking couples heed the myth (it can get busy in there!).

The maze of grey pinnacles and peaks, with the odd pond, is treated as an oversized rockery, with a walkway here, a pavilion there, some railings along paths and, if you look closely, some mind-bending weeds.

There are actually several 'stone forests' in the region – the section open to foreign tourists covers 80 hectares. Twelve kilometres to the north-east is a larger (300-hectare) rock series called Fungi Forest, with karst caves and a large waterfall.

Some travellers find Shí Lín somewhat overrated on the scale of geographical wonders. The important thing, if you venture there, is to get away from the main tourist area – within a couple of kilometres of the centre you will find some idyllic, secluded walks and by moonlight it's otherworldly.

The villages in the Lùnán County vicinity are inhabited by the Sani branch of the

Yi tribespeople. Considering that so many other 'ethnic' areas of Yúnnán are now open, you could be disappointed if you make the trip just to see the tribespeople who live in this area. Their craftwork (embroidery, purses, footwear) is sold at stalls by the entrance to the 'forest', and Sani women act as tour guides for groups.

Off to the side is **Five-Tree Village**, which is an easy walk and has the flavour of a Mexican pueblo, but the tribespeople have been swayed by commercialism.

For those keen on genuine village and farming life, well, Shí Lín is a big place – you can easily get lost. Just take your butterfly net and a lunch box along and keep walking and you'll get somewhere eventually.

There is a Y55 entry fee into the main stone forest for foreigners.

Special Events

The Shílín and Yúnlín hotels (see Places to Stay) put on Sani song-and-dance evenings when there are enough tourists around. Surprisingly, these events generally turn into good-natured exchanges between Homo Ektachromo and Sani Dollari, and neither seems to come off the worse for wear. The hotels usually charge a fee of around Y25 for the performances, which start around 7.30 to 8 pm.

The Torch Festival (wrestling, bullfighting, singing and dancing) takes place on 24 June at a natural outdoor amphitheatre by Hidden Lake.

Places to Stay

The **Shílín Bīnguǎn** (☎ 771 1405), near the main entrance to the stone forest, is a villa-type place with a souvenir shop and dining hall. A double room costs Y250 (Y200 in the off season), and triples are Y300. Before you despair, wait: there's a 'Common Room Department' *(pǔtōng kèfáng)* at the rear section of the hotel compound, with dormitory accommodation for Y30 per bed. It's on the other side of the hill, across from a restaurant and a couple of souvenir shops.

Rates are a bit cheaper at the **Yúnlín Bīnguǎn**, which is a little less than a kilometre down the road that forks to the right after you cross the bridge. In addition to Y150 doubles and Y200 triples, the Yúnlín has one concrete cell with four soft beds for Y80 – but they won't give the cheapies to foreigners.

Near the bus terminal are several *smaller hotels* with basic rooms for Y20 to Y30 per person: these have similar bathing facilities to the dorm rooms at the Shílín and Yúnlín, but are not as clean. They may or may not accept foreign guests.

Places to Eat

Several *restaurants* next to the bus terminal specialise in duck roasted in extremely hot clay ovens with pine needles. A whole duck costs Y40 to Y50 and takes about 20 minutes to cook – have the restaurant staff put a beer in their freezer and it'll be just right when the duck comes out. Near the main stone forest entrance is a cluster of *food vendors* that purvey a variety of pastries and noodles from dawn to dusk. The Shílín Bīnguǎn and Yúnlín Fàndiàn offer fixed-price meals that aren't bad. Western breakfasts are available at both hotels.

Getting There & Away

Express tourist trains to Shí Lín were introduced in 1998 and may be kept if demand warrants it; see the Kūnmíng Train section. If the trains are no longer running your fastest option might be a minibus from the Cháhuā Bīnguǎn in Kūnmíng; one group of travellers made it there nonstop in two hair-raising hours. In most cases the trip takes around three hours one way – it's much longer going there if you sign on with a tour bus. If you are feeling adventurous, you could try a bus/train/hitchhiking combination.

It's best to take an overnight stop in the forest for further exploration, although if you're just looking at the forest itself a day trip will do.

Bus Head down to the long-distance bus station in Kūnmíng and buy a one-way ticket for Y16. There is a bus leaving at 7.30 am.

Some hotels sell tickets for tour buses to Shí Lín for Y20 (Y10 in low periods), but if you take this option you'll be stuck with a tour that takes in at least three caves en route (complete with special foreigner entry fees); once you've pigged out on the obligatory lunch, you'll be lucky to have had two hours wandering around the forest. The street adjacent to the King World Hotel is lined with Shí Lín tour buses. They will swear on their ancestors' graves that they don't stop at any caves. Take these claims with large grains of salt. These buses also cost Y20 one way, although they may be flexible in low tourist periods.

The Cháhuā Bīnguǎn runs a minibus that goes straight to Shí Lín. The bus leaves at 8 am and costs Y40 for a return trip, but the catch is that there must be at least six people, or you pay Y240 regardless of the number. Although you escape the caves, there is a stop at an awful jade market along the way, ostensibly for you to use the bathroom.

Getting back from Shí Lín to Kūnmíng is fairly simple. There are usually minibuses waiting along the road outside the entrance, and once they're full, they tend to go straight back to Kūnmíng. There are also local buses leaving at 7 am and between 2.30 and 3.30 pm, but these can be cancelled if they don't look like filling up. You could also try hitching back to Kūnmíng from Shí Lín.

Train The old French narrow-gauge line that runs all the way from Kūnmíng to Hanoi has a stop at the town of Yíliáng, which is only 45 minutes by bus from Shí Lín. Stations along the way sport steep roofs and painted shutters in the French style. Unfortunately, no trains are all that convenient and buses from Yíliáng are infrequent (be prepared for a wait of a couple of hours), and often only go as far as Lùnán, from where you will have to hitch to Shí Lín.

In 1998 new tourist express trains were put on the new Nánkún railway line. One departs Kūnmíng at 8 am, returning at 2.32 pm; the other departs at 9.20 am and returns at 3.34 pm. Either way the trip takes 1½ hours and costs Y30 to Y40 return, depending on hard or soft seat. Pray that demand warrants their continuance. Regular trains also ply the route; they're much slower at 2½ hours and may have bad arrival hours but cost only Y6.

LÙNÁN 路南
☎ 0871

Lùnán is a small market town about 10km from Shí Lín. It's not really worth making a special effort to visit, but if you do go, try and catch a market day (Wednesday or some Saturdays), when Lùnán becomes a colossal jam of donkeys, horse carts and bikes. The streets are packed with produce, poultry and wares, and the Sani women are dressed in their finest.

To get to Lùnán from Shí Lín, head back towards Kūnmíng and turn left at the first major crossroads. Go straight on at the second crossroads, but veering to the right. You'll have to hitch a truck or hire a three wheeler (Y5 for a 20-minute ride). Plenty of trucks head that way on market day, some from the car park near the forest.

XIÀGUĀN 下关
☎ 0872

Xiàguān lies at the southern tip of Ěrhǎi Hú (Ear-Shaped Lake), about 400km west of Kūnmíng. It was once an important staging post on the Burma Road and is still a key centre for transport in north-west Yúnnán. Xiàguān is the capital of Dàlǐ Prefecture and

is also referred to as Dàlǐ Shì (Dàlǐ City). This confuses some travellers, who think they are already in Dàlǐ, book into a hotel and head off in pursuit of a banana pancake only to discover they haven't arrived yet. (See the Dàlǐ & Ěrhǎi Hú Region map later in this chapter.) Nobody stays in Xiàguān unless they have an early bus the next morning.

There are two bus stations on the road to Dàlǐ; between the two on the corner, diagonally opposite the Dali Hotel, is the station for local bus No 4, which runs to the real Dàlǐ (half hour; Y1.20). If you want to be sure, ask for Dàlǐ Gǔchéng (Dàlǐ Old City).

Things to See
Xiàguān has developed into an industrial city specialising in tea processing, cigarette making and the production of textiles and chemicals. There is little to keep you here other than transport connections.

There are good views of the lake and mountains from **Ěrhǎi Gōngyuán** (Ear-Shaped Lake Park). You can reach the park on foot or by motor-tricycle for around Y3.

Local travel agents around the bus station also sell tickets for day trips up and down Ěrhǎi Hú, taking in all the major sights. Prices for the all-day tours range from Y60 to Y80. Bus No 6 runs to the park.

Places to Stay
Some travellers end up staying a night in Xiàguān in order to catch an early-morning bus from the long-distance bus station. The **Dàlǐ Bīnguǎn** (☎ 217 9888), near No 4 bus stop, has transformed itself into a three-star monster for Y128/168 single/double.

Right next to the bus station is the cheaper and mildly chaotic (but worth it) **Kèyùn Fàndiàn** (☎ 212 5286). It has basic beds ranging from Y8 in an eight-person room to Y24 in a single, all with shared bath. More upmarket rooms are available for Y128 single/double.

Almost directly opposite is the **Xiàguān Bīnguǎn** (☎ 212 5579), the most upmarket of the cheap hotels. Basic triples are available for Y72 per bed and doubles with bathroom are Y198. These rooms are all right for the price.

Getting There & Away

Air Xiàguān's new airport is 15km from town. Frequent flights depart during the day and the one-way fare from Kūnmíng is Y320. CAAC buses meet incoming flights.

Bus Xiàguān has two bus stations on the main road to Dàlǐ, which also throws some travellers. Luckily, they are both on the same side of the street, approximately two blocks apart. You might get dropped off at either one. If you appear to be at a huge, newish-looking one with big schedule boards, turn *right* to the local bus to Dàlǐ; otherwise, turn left. Both have departures throughout the province, so if the main station doesn't have a good departure time for you, wander over to the other one.

Unfortunately there's now a third station, just off the new expressway to Kūnmíng. If you get dropped off here, exit and look for a traffic roundabout. Walk west from there, a 20-minute hike; a taxi should cost Y5 or bus No 1 runs along the road.

Unless you're heading for one of the typical traveller's destinations (eg Kūnmíng or Lìjiāng) you'll probably have to head into the Xiàguān long-distance bus station to organise your onward transport. You can buy just about any ticket in Dàlǐ, but you have to catch the bus for many destinations in Xiàguān. Other bus options include Bǎoshān (Y25 to Y43), Téngchōng (Y50 to Y82), Lijiāng (Y44.20), Ruìlì (Y60) and Zhōngdiàn (Y67).

There's also a new sleeper bus direct – more or less – to Chéngdū (Y210), leaving at 6 pm daily and taking two nights and one day. Once the train line is completed this will probably stop running.

For the interesting possibility of buses from Xiàguān to Xīshuāngbǎnnà, you can try getting a 6.10 am bus via Jingdong, which should put you into Jǐnghóng the following night for a total of some 32 hours. Roads are very bad along this route, and travel times have been known to stretch to three or four days. A sleeper should cost around Y145.

For Jīzú Shān, buses run from the east entrance of the smaller bus station to Bīnchúan (two hours; Y10).

AROUND XIÀGUĀN
Jīzú Shān 鸡足山
Chicken-Foot Mountain

Jīzú Shān is a major attraction for Buddhist pilgrims – both Chinese and Tibetan. At the time of the Qing dynasty there were approximately 100 temples on the mountain and somewhere in the vicinity of 5000 resident monks. The Cultural Revolution's anarchic assault on the traditional past did away with much that was of interest on the mountain, although renovation work on the temples has been going on since 1979.

Today it is estimated that more than 150,000 tourists and pilgrims clamber up the mountain every year to watch the sun rise. Jīndīng, the Golden Summit, is at a cool 3240m so you will need some warm clothing.

Sights along the way include the temple **Zhùshèng Sì**, about an hour's walk up from the bus stop at Shazhi. This is the most important temple on the mountain. **Zhōngshān Sì** (Mid-Mountain Temple), about halfway up the mountain, is a fairly recent construction and holds little of interest.

Just before the last ascent is the **Huáshǒu Mén** (Magnificent Head Gate). At the summit is the **Lengyan Pagoda**, a 13-tier Tang dynasty pagoda that was restored in 1927, and there is basic accommodation at *Jīndīng Sì* (Golden Summit Temple) next to the pagoda – a sleeping bag might be a good idea at this altitude.

A popular option for making the ascent is to hire a pony. The ponies were originally used to carry up supplies until a local hit on the idea of hiring them out to the big noses with the bulging wallets. Travellers who have done the trip claim it's a lot of fun. A cable car to the summit is a good way to cheat.

Places to Stay & Eat Accommodation is available at the base of the mountain, about halfway up and on the summit. Prices average Y10 to Y15 per bed. Food gets fairly expensive once you reach the summit so you may want to consider bringing some of your own.

If you wish to stay overnight in Bīnchúan, there are a few hotels around with dorm beds for as low as Y5.

Getting There & Away To reach Jīzú Shān from Xiàguān you should first take a bus to Bīnchuán, which is 70km east of Xiàguān. Buses leave at 8 am from the long-distance bus station. From Bīnchuán take another bus or minibus to the foot of the mountain. If you turn up in Bīnchuán, the locals will probably guess your destination.

Some travellers have hiked from Wāsè, on the east shore of Ěrhǎi Hú, to Jīzú Shān. It is certainly a possibility, but it isn't recommended and should only be undertaken by experienced hikers. Locals in Dàlǐ claim that it is easy to get lost in the mountainous terrain and in bad weather the hike could turn into a bad experience. Take care, and talk to locals in Dàlǐ about your plans before you go.

Wēishān 魏山

Wēishān is famous for the Taoist temples on nearby **Wēibǎo Shān** (Towering Treasure Mountain). There are reportedly some fine Taoist murals here. It's 61km due south of Xiàguān, so it could be done as a day trip.

Yǒngpíng 永平

Yǒngpíng is 103km south-west of Xiàguān on the old Burma Road. **Jīnguāng Sì** is the attraction here.

DÀLǏ 大理
☎ 0872

Dàlǐ is a perfect place to tune out for a while and forget about trains, planes and bone-jarring buses. The stunning mountain backdrop, Ěrhǎi Hú, the old city, cappuccinos, pizzas and the herbal alternative to cheap Chinese beer (you can pick it yourself) make it, along with Yángshuò in Guǎngxī, one of the few places in China where you can well and truly take a vacation from travelling.

Dàlǐ lies on the western edge of Ěrhǎi Hú at an altitude of 1900m, with the imposing Cāng Shān (Jade Green Mountains; average height 4000m) behind it. For much of the five centuries in which Yúnnán governed its own affairs, Dàlǐ was the centre of operations, and the old city still retains a historical atmosphere that is hard to come by in other parts of China.

The main inhabitants of the region are the Bai, who number about 1.5 million, according to a 1990 census. The Bai people have long-established roots in the Ěrhǎi Hú region, and are thought to have settled the area some 3000 years ago. In the early 8th century they grouped together and succeeded in defeating the Tang imperial army before establishing the Nanzhao kingdom.

The kingdom exerted considerable influence throughout south-west China and even, to a lesser degree, South-East Asia, since it controlled upper Burma for much of the 9th century. This later established Dàlǐ as an end node on the famed Burma Road. In the mid-13th century it fell before the invincible Mongol hordes of Kublai Khan.

At last check Dàlǐ was dust-choked from a radical renovation along the south edge, hoping to recreate the 'old' Dàlǐ image, replete with original gate. Locals were worried the wrecking balls would begin to creep closer and closer to the centre.

Orientation

Dàlǐ is a miniature city that has some preserved cobbled streets and traditional stone architecture within its old walls. Unless you are in a mad hurry (in which case use a bike), you can just get your bearings just by taking a walk for an hour or so. It takes about half an hour to walk from Nán Mén (South Gate) across town to Běi Mén (North Gate). Many of the sights around Dàlǐ couldn't be considered stunning on their own, but they do provide a destination towards which you can happily dawdle even if you don't arrive. Huguo Lu is the main strip for cafes – locals call it 'foreigner's street' *(yángrén jiē)* – and this is where to turn to for your cafe latte, burritos, ice-cold beer and other treats.

Maps of Dàlǐ and the Ěrhǎi Hú area are available at street stalls near the corner of Huguo Lu and Fuxing Lu. None of them is all that useful.

Information

PSB The PSB office is between No 3 and No 4 Guesthouses on Huguo Lu. Previous goodwill has been overtaxed by some travellers, so this is no longer an automatic place to get a second or third visa extension (though first extensions are OK).

Money The Bank of China is in the centre of town, near the corner of Huguo Lu and Fuxing Lu. The new Industrial and Commercial Bank, right on Huguo Lu, changes cash and travellers cheques. Both are open till 9 pm and have Saturday (and some Sunday) hours – so you really don't have to keep track of what day it is in Dàlǐ.

Post & Communications The post office is on the corner of Fuxing Lu and Huguo Lu. This is the best place to make international calls, as it has direct dial and doesn't levy a service charge. However, you can't use an international calling card. It's open till 8.30 pm.

Email & Internet Access A number of cafes offer Internet access and most are expensive – Y25 to Y30 per hour; they're not ripping you off, as the post office controls the system and levies heavy charges. If you're a regular customer of a cafe, they often allow you to read/write offline.

Dangers & Annoyances The hike up to Zhōnghé Sì and along the mountain ridges is super, but there have been instances of robbery of solo walkers, and in 1997 one German traveller was killed. Try to find a partner.

Dàlǐ Bówùguǎn 大理博物馆
Dali Museum
This small collection of archaeological pieces relating to Bai history has some moderately interesting exhibits on marble handicrafts; a number of marble steles grace one wing. The museum is open from 8.30 am to 5 pm and admission is Y5.

Sāntǎsì 三塔寺
Three Pagodas
Standing on the hillside a couple of kilometres north-west of Dàlǐ, the Sāntǎsì look pretty, particularly when reflected in the nearby lake. They are among the oldest standing structures in south-western China.

The tallest of the three, Qianxun Pagoda, has 16 tiers that reach a height of 70m. It was originally erected in the mid-9th century by Xī'ān engineers. It is flanked by two smaller 10-tiered pagodas, which are each 42m high.

The temple behind the pagodas, **Chongsheng Temple**, is laid out in the traditional Yunnanese style, with three layers of buildings lined up with a sacred peak in the background. The temple has been recently restored and converted into a museum chronicling the history, construction and renovation of the pagodas. Also on exhibit are marble slabs that have been cut and framed so that the patterns of the marble appear to depict landscapes. Admission is Y10.

Organised Tours
Numerous travel agencies on Huguo Lu have tours to sights around Dàlǐ. A newer activity includes horse riding at Y20 per hour or Y70 per day without a guide

DÀLĬ

PLACES TO STAY

8 Jīnhuā Dàjiŭdiàn
   金花大酒店
10 Dì'èr Zhāodàisuŏ
   第二招待所
18 Sāngní Yuán
   第三招待所
   （桑尼园）
20 Yú'ān Yuán
   第四招待所
   （榆安园）
22 Jímŭ Hépíng
   Fàndiàn
   吉姆和平饭店
23 Sìjì Kèzhàn
   大理四季客栈
24 Dàlĭ Bīnguăn
   大理宾馆
27 MCA
   Guesthouse

PLACES TO EAT

2 Yunnan Cafe
   云南咖啡馆
3 Earth Cafe
5 Marley's Cafe
   马丽咖啡馆
6 Tibetan Cafe
   西藏餐厅
7 Old Wooden House
   如意饭店
11 Cafe de Jack
   樱花阁
13 Sunshine Cafe
14 Happy Cafe
15 Sister's Cafe
17 Mr China's Son Café

OTHER

1 Bĕi Mén
   北门

4 Post Office
   邮电局
9 Bank of China
   中国银行
12 Dàlĭ Passenger
   Service Ticket
   Office
   大理客运站售票处
16 Dàlĭ Passenger
   Service Ticket
   Office
   大理客运站售票处
19 PSB
   公安局
21 Local Buses to Shāpíng
   往沙平的公共汽车
25 Dàlĭ Bówùguăn
   大理博物馆
26 Nán Mén
   南门

(though many want you to have one). Some of the cafes also offer trips, mostly in the form of boat outings across Ěrhăi Hú to Wāsè, which has an open-air market every five days, or to festivals. Private entrepreneurs run cruises around the lake daily if there is enough demand.

Special Events

If you don't mind crowds, the best time to be in Dàlĭ is probably during the Third Moon Fair (Sānyuè Jiē), which begins on the 15th day of the third lunar month (usually April) and ends on the 21st day. The origins of the fair lie in its commemoration of a fabled visit by Guanyin, the Buddhist goddess of mercy, to the Nanzhao kingdom. Today it's more like an extra festive market, with people from all over Yúnnán arriving to buy, sell and make merry.

The Three Temples Festival (Ràosān-Líng) is held between the 23rd and 25th days of the fourth lunar month (usually May). The first day involves a trip from Dàlĭ's Nán Mén to the Xīzhōu Shèngyuán Sì (Sacred Fountainhead Temple) at the foot of Wŭtái Shān. Here travellers stay up until dawn, dancing and singing, before moving on to Jīngùi Sì on the shore of Ěrhăi

Hú. The final day involves walking back to Dàlĭ by way of Majiuyi Temple.

The Torch Festival (Huŏbă Jié) is held on the 24th day of the sixth lunar month (normally July). Flaming torches are paraded at night through homes and fields. Other events include fireworks displays and dragon-boat racing.

Markets Markets follow the lunar calendar, but shrewd local operators have co-opted it into a regular scheme so tourists know where to go. See Around Dàlĭ for information on the Monday Shāpíng market. Markets then take place around Ěrhăi Hú in Shuāngláng (Tuesday), Yousuo (Friday, the largest in Yúnnán) and Jiangwei (Saturday). Lots of biking between villages is available. Mr. China's Son cafe (see Places to Eat) has a good outline and maps.

Places to Stay

The addition of several new, low-budget hotels has greatly improved the accommodation situation in Dàlĭ. Even so, places tend to fill up quickly, and those visiting during the peak summer months may find themselves trekking around town in search of that perfect bed on their first day.

A popular place to see and be seen on the backpacker circuit Dàlǐ stop is the *MCA Guesthouse* (☎ 267 3666, 700 Wenxiang Lu) south of Nán Mén. The owner's brother runs the Dongba House in Lìjiāng and they hope to establish a 'Tibetan culture route' for travellers all the way to Lhasa. This self-contained little community has spacious dorms with hardwood floors. Beds are Y10 or Y20 for 'softer' mattresses. (The only very minor down side is that the OK bathrooms are across the compound; the showers at least have 24-hour hot water.) Good doubles with private bath cost Y100, but also face the popular pool area. The bar/restaurant is a pleasant place to hang out in.

The guesthouse also has book rental, laundry service (and a washing machine), poste restante (Y5), bikes for rent and email; weekends feature a Tibetan brunch.

The newest and without question the most interesting place to stay is the *Sìjì Kèzhàn (Old Dali Four Seasons Inn; No 5 Guesthouse)*; ☎ 267 0382). This one makes use of one of the street's oldest and most distinctive old-style buildings, a former school. Two wings of the two-storey complex face a flower-laden courtyard, which has a gazebo and lots of greenery. A cafe serves good food. The bathrooms are clean and showers have reliable hot water 18 hours per day (supposedly). Dorm rooms start at Y10 per hard bed in clean quads; for an extra Y5, you can get the 'luxury dorm', which means a soft bed. Singles/doubles with common bath cost Y40. There are also doubles with private bath for around Y120. Bicycles can be rented here.

Dàlǐ, like Lìjiāng, also has a few other traditional-style inns sprinkled around town; one is currently being remodelled around a *mosque*! These are often reluctant to take foreigners though this is changing slowly.

Still popular and rated highly by travellers is the old favourite *Yú'ān Yuán (Yu'an Garden; No 4 Guesthouse)*; ☎ 267 2093). Perched at the top of Huguo Lu, this idyllic little spot has it all – bamboo pavilions, 24-hour hot water, a lovely Thai-style cafe, washing machines, a score of laundry lines, friendly staff and dorm beds for Y10

to Y15, as well as singles/doubles for Y30/50 (although these tend to suffer from poor ventilation). Look at a few options, since there's a wide variety. The only problem with the Yú'ān Yuán is that the best rooms always seem to be full.

Just down from the Yú'ān Yuán, the *Sāngní Yuán (Sunny Garden; No 3 Guesthouse)*; ☎ 267 0213) is crammed into an area about half the size of Yú'ān Yuán. It's also gone downhill quite a bit at recent checks and should be used as a last resort.

Jímǔ Hépíng Fàndiàn (Jim's Peace Guesthouse) is down the street from the Sāngní Yuán, and offers a single room with an awesome bathtub for Y50, a double for the same price, and a slightly less inspiring triple and even a rooftop room. Jim's a longtime entrepreneur in town and is always cooking something up; he's currently creating a Tibetan massage and medicine twist on the guesthouse.

Closest to the action on Huguo Lu, *Dì'èr Zhāodàisuǒ (New Red Camelia Hotel; No 2 Guesthouse*; ☎ 267 0423) has long been Dàlǐ's old stand-by. Though a bit lacking in charm, it's actually not a bad place to stay, especially if you get a room on the 2nd or 3rd floor of the old wing. First floor rooms tend to be damp and dark. Singles/doubles/triples with common washroom are Y25/25/30. There are also doubles with attached bath in the old wing for Y80, but these are mostly on the 1st floor, and not really worth the money unless you're a pair. The Dì'èr Zhāodàisuǒ also has standard doubles, with 24-hour hot water, in the new building for Y140 to Y180; for two they're decent value.

The *Dàlǐ Bīnguǎn* (☎ 267 0386) is a bit farther away, on Fuxing Lu, but the exercise of walking the 10 minutes or so to Huguo Lu may give you the illusion of having earned your banana pancake. It has triples with private bath for Y150 – an acceptable option if all the other places are booked. Basic doubles with attached bath start at Y110 – there's a bit of variety so check a few – while standard doubles with all mod cons are Y220. They have offered steep discounts on a few occasions, indicating a bit of desperation.

Sticking out like a sore thumb on the *Jīnhuā Dàjiǔdiàn* (☎ *267 3343, fax 267 0573*) probably won't see much in the way of backpacker traffic. Standard doubles/triples with air-con, satellite TV and all the rest start at Y168/198. Sporting red-capped door-men and a marble staircase, and hostesses with colourful and ill-fitting headgear, the Jīnhuā definitely seems out of sync with the rest of Dàlǐ. But if you're in the mood for luxury, or are toting the kids around, this might be a good choice. A few readers have written to complain, two using the word 'surly' to describe the service.

Places to Eat

There are many more restaurants than those listed here, but truthfully many restaurants in places like Dàlǐ (and Yángshuò in Guǎngxī) are nothing more than cookie-cutter tedium – not bad, simply unremarkable. So many restaurants have opened up that some reported a 10-fold drop in business from one summer to the next. The rule is: spread your patronage; you'll eventually find one you really like.

Many little local places, way off the main drag, have English menus, but you'd never know it without some exploring. So get around and experiment.

One place that seems certain to keep drawing a steady crowd is *Marley's Cafe*, in a great new building. The mostly wooden interiors are tastefully decorated with art, and Marley's has a tome of a menu with western and Chinese food; particularly popular is the Sunday Bai food group dinner (make reservations). A new deck on the roof will give you a great excuse to while away the day, and the outdoor seating here is very popular. Marley herself is a great source of local information and she also gets kudos for having one of the few places in town with a bathroom. (She's pondering relocating to Fuxing Lu to avoid tourists gawking at her customers.)

Long popular also is the *Tibetan Cafe*, almost next door to Marley's. Across the street, the *Star Cafe* is dark but cosy and has good Japanese food. Around the corner to the north is the new *Oriental Cafe*, with a modest menu but cheery staff. A little way west, don't miss the friendliest folks in town at the *Sunshine Cafe* where the smiles never end. They've got a couple of good Tibetan dishes and whip up the best brownies in Dàlǐ. Their couch, placed under a nice skylight, is extremely comfortable! Near there, the *Old Wooden House* has good outside seating and its bolognese is definitely worth trying – a roving Italian gave them the recipe.

The *Yunnan Cafe* is about five minutes' walk down Huguo Lu. Formerly called the Coca Cola Restaurant (until the long arm of Coca-Cola Inc sniffed out the use of its name and dispatched warnings to Dàlǐ), it serves consistently good food. On the last couple of visits, service was way down in quality if not attitude from previous years, but hopefully that's an aberration. Travellers routinely plant themselves on the rooftop sun deck until the night-time chill or closing time drives them away. Xiangxia, who runs the place, is a fluent English speaker and a mine of useful information on Dàlǐ. Not far away, the *Earth Cafe* has a varied menu and rates a mention for starting the movie-and-meal trend, a la Yángshuò.

Back up on Boai Lu, the number one choice for hip music and a congenial atmosphere is *Cafe de Jack*, known for its amazing chocolate cake with ice cream; it also has good pizza and another couch seating arrangement worth a mention. For an interesting afternoon of conversation, you can try *Mr China's Son*, a cafe opened by an old gentleman who has penned an English-language account of his trials and tribulations during the Cultural Revolution. Do visit here for the most thorough collection of maps and tips on Dàlǐ and environs – it's got a minor guidebook of its own. During festivals, the place has lots of cultural tours.

If you're a fan of Japanese food, try the *Happy Café* – it serves the Japanese travellers' market. The food is rivalled by that of *Sister's Cafe*. Nearby the *Yak Cafe* also doubles as an impressive art gallery.

Shopping

Dàlǐ is famous for its marble, and while a slab of the stuff in your backpack might slow you down a bit, local entrepreneurs produce everything from ashtrays to model pagodas in small enough chunks to make it feasible to stow one or two away.

Huguo Lu has become a smaller version of Bangkok's Khao San Rd in its profusion of clothes shops. It won't take you long to decide whether the clothes are for you or not – you could outfit yourself for a time-machine jaunt back to Woodstock here, but bear in mind that the shopkeepers can also make clothes to your specifications, so you're not necessarily just stuck with the ready-made hippie stuff. Prices are very reasonable.

Most of the 'silver' jewellery sold in Dàlǐ is really brass. Occasionally it actually is silver, although this will be reflected in the starting price. The only advice worth giving, if you're in the market for this kind of thing, is to bargain hard. For those roving sales ladies badgering you incessantly, don't feel bad to pay *one-fifth* of their asking price – that's what locals advise. For marble from street sellers, 40% to half price is fair. In shops, two-thirds of the price is average. And don't fall for any 'expert' opinions; go back later on your own and deal.

Batik wall hangings also have become popular in Dàlǐ. Several places near the Dì'èr Zhāodàisuǒ on Huguo Lu have a good collection, but don't believe the proprietors when they tell you they make the stuff themselves and start justifying the extortionate prices they charge by telling how many hours they worked on a piece. Most of the batik, as in Yángshuò, comes from Guìzhōu where it can be bought for a song. Check with cafe owners and other locals about prices before you set out shopping. In general, Huguo Lu is about 20% higher than elsewhere in town.

Getting There & Away

Xiàguān's new airport has brought Dàlǐ to within 45 minutes' flying time from Kūnmíng. Flights run daily, usually many times per day. You can also get daily flights directly to Jínghóng in Xīshuāngbǎnnà. The one-way fare to Kūnmíng is Y320.

A new expressway from Kūnmíng to Xiàguān, the link to Dàlǐ, was (finally) completed in 1998; travel time has been cut to seven to nine hours on either frequent daytime minibuses (Y54) or sleeper buses (Y71). The latter depart from north of the train station a few times a day from 6.30 am, or at 8.30 pm (though this puts you into Xiàguān at an ungodly hour – they let you sleep aboard the bus till daybreak). Some buses do go direct to the old city. Although some buses are technically 'direct', travellers have reported some operators taking a few side roads to add passengers.

Xiàguān (Y95; six hours) is also one of the routes served, eight times daily, by the Kūnmíng long-distance bus station's super-luxury express Daewoo buses.

Leaving Dàlǐ, the best thing to do is *shop around*. Plenty of tour and travel agencies means plenty of options and competitive prices. Most buses for Lìjiāng and Kūnmíng depart right in Dàlǐ; for other destinations, you can buy tickets in Dàlǐ, but must return to Xiàguān to get on the bus.

Buses to Kūnmíng generally leave from next to whatever agency sells the tickets; some may pick you up. Most of these are middle-sized buses which leave during the morning. Claims vary wildly – four to 10 hours – with about eight being right, depending on traffic and whether it *is* truly a direct bus or not. All agencies have big sleeper buses, generally leaving in the evening. Prices are flexible to say the least; in one six-month period, prices dropped 20% due to competition. Buses are usually cheaper *returning* to Kūnmíng and are a few yuán more expensive than hopping the bus in Xiàguān.

Buses to Lìjiāng leave between 7 am and mid-afternoon and travel along a newly expanded and faster highway. Tickets for the three-hour trip range from Y25 to Y48 depending on comfort level, and can be bought at whatever agency sponsors them. You can also catch any one of numerous buses to Lìjiāng that originate in Xiàguān along the highway, or flag down the bus to Zhōngdiàn here (Y40; seven to eight hours).

To catch buses to other points, such as Bǎoshān, Ruìlì or Jínghóng, you'll have to go to Xiàguān, although there is rumoured to be a bus to Jínghóng originating in Dàlǐ,

Descreet news and advertising, Guǎngzhōu-style

In-your-face advertising, Hong Kong–style

CHRIS MELLOR

Guǎngzhōu, Guǎngdōng

DIANA MAYFIELD

The rippling rice terraces of Guǎngxī

CHRIS MELLOR

Junks jostle for space on the waters of Hǎinán Dǎo.

and stopping in Xiàguān on the way. To Zhōngdiàn, walk up to the highway around 7 or 7.30 am and flag down the Xiàguān-Zhōngdiàn bus.

Tickets for most of these routes can be bought in Dàlǐ. Local bus No 4 to Xiàguān (Y1.20 to Y1.50; ½ hour) starts up early enough – around 6 am – runs every 10 minutes, and stops along Boai Lu. If your bus from Xiàguān leaves earlier than 7 am, you'll have to overnight in Xiàguān.

Xiàguān's train station finally opened in 1999. To get there from Kūnmíng, train No 212 departs at 10.10 pm (Y51 hard seat; 10½ hours).

Getting Around

A taxi to the airport should take around 45 minutes and cost around Y60 to Y70. Airport buses do meet incoming flights.

Bikes are the best way to get around. Prices average Y5 per day for clunky Chinese models, Y2 per hour and Y10 for better mountain bikes. There is no shortage of selection around town.

AROUND DÀLǏ
Ěrhǎi Hú 洱海湖
Ear-Shaped Lake

This lake is a 50-minute walk from town or a 10-minute downhill zip on a bike. You can watch the large junks or the smaller boats with their queue of captive fishing cormorants perched on the edge of the boat. A ring placed around their necks stops them from guzzling the catch.

From Caicun, a pleasant little lake-side village east of Dàlǐ (Y3 in a horse cart), there's a ferry at 4.30 pm to **Wāsè** on the other side of the lake. You can stay overnight and catch a ferry back at 6 am. Plenty of locals take their bikes over.

Ferries crisscross the lake at various points, so there could be some scope for extended touring. Close to Wāsè is **Pǔtuó Dǎo** (Putuo Island) with **Xiǎopǔtuó Sì** (Lesser Putuo Temple). Other ferries run between Longkan and Haidong, and between Xiàguān and Jīnsuō Dǎo (Golden Shuttle Island). Ferries appear to leave early in the morning (for market) and return around 4

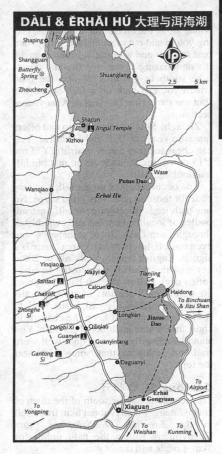

DÀLǏ & ĚRHĂI HÚ 大理与洱海湖

pm; timetables are flexible. Plenty of cafes can arrange a horse-and-carriage ride to the lake, then a boat ride to **Tiānjing Gé** and **Luoquan Gé** temples, then Jīnsuō Dǎo or whatever you dream up, for around Y30 per day.

Zhōnghé Sì 中和寺
Peace & Justice Temple

Zhōnghé is a long, steep hike up the mountainside behind Dàlǐ. When you finally get there, you might be received with a cup of tea and a smile. Smile or no, it's Y2 per person. Restaurants here serve up some interesting local concoctions. Branching out from either side of the temple is a trail that winds along the face of the mountains, taking you in and out of steep lush valleys and past streams and waterfalls. From Zhōnghé it's an amazing 11km-long (up-and-down) hike south to Gǎntōng Sì and the road where you can pick up a Dàlǐ-bound bus (but see the earlier Dangers & Annoyances section).

Zhōnghé Sì is a great day trip and offers fantastic vistas of Dàlǐ and Ěrhǎi Hú. You can cheat and take a new chairlift (Y35 up, Y15 down) up Zhōnghé Shān, that big hill overlooking Dàlǐ.

You could also hike up the hill, a sweaty hour for those in relatively good shape. No one path leads directly up the hill; instead, oodles of local paths wind and switchback through farm fields, local cemeteries, and even one off-limits military area (there is a sign in English here!). Walk about 200m north of the chairlift base to the riverbed (often dry). Follow the left bank for about 50m and you'll see lots of ribbony trails leading up. Basically, all roads lead to Rome from here, just keep the chairlift in sight and when in doubt, bear left. You should eventually come upon a well-worn trail and, following that, some steps near the top.

Gǎntōng Sì 感通寺
This temple is not far south of the town of Guānyīntáng, which is about 6km from Dàlǐ in the direction of Xiàguān. From Guānyīntáng follow the path uphill for 3km. Locals will direct you.

Guānyīn Táng 观音堂
Goddess of Mercy Temple
Guānyīn Táng is built over a large boulder said to have been placed there by the goddess of mercy to block the advance of an invading enemy. It is 5km south of Dàlǐ.

Qīngbì Xī 清碧溪
This scenic picnic spot near the village of Qiliqiao is 3km from Dàlǐ in the direction of Xiàguān. After hiking 4km up a path running close to the river, you'll reach three ponds.

Xǐzhōu 喜洲
Among the 101 things to do while you're in Dàlǐ, a trip to Xǐzhōu would have to rate fairly high. It's an old town around 18km north of Dàlǐ, with even better preserved Bai architecture than Dàlǐ. A local bus would be the easiest option for getting there, but a bicycle trip with an overnight stop in Xǐzhōu (there's accommodation in town) is also a good idea. From here, Zhoucheng is 7km farther north and is also outstanding; it too has basic accommodation.

A few intrepid travellers have leap-frogged these lovely villages, then made it for Shāping's market, then continued all the way around the lake for other markets, including Wāsè's, before boating themselves and their bicycles back to Dàlǐ. From Dàlǐ to Wāsè it's around 58km.

Shāpíng Gǎnjí 沙坪赶集
Shaping Market
Every Monday the town of Shāpíng, about 30km north of Dàlǐ, is host to a colourful market. The market starts to rattle and hum at 10 am and ends around 2.30 pm. You can buy everything from tobacco, melon seeds and noodles to meat, pots and wardrobes. In the ethnic clothing line, you can look at shirts, headdresses, embroidered shoes and moneybelts. Expect to be quoted ridiculously high prices on anything you set your eyes on, so get into a bargaining frame of mind, and you should have a good time.

Getting to Shāpíng market from Dàlǐ is fairly easy. Some of the hotels and cafes in town run minibuses out there on market day. Usually they leave at 9 am, although it's a good idea to ask around and book the day before. Most places charge Y11; some travellers think it's worth it, others don't. Alternatively you can walk up Huguo Lu to the main road and catch a local bus from there, although bear in mind that market day is not going to be the ideal time to take a spin on the local buses. A ticket should be around Y6.

DÀLǏ TO LÌJIĀNG
Most travellers take a direct route between Dàlǐ and Lìjiāng. However, a couple of

places might make interesting detours. Transport could be a case of pot luck with buses or hitching.

Jiànchuān 剑川

This town is 92km north of Dàlǐ on the Dàlǐ-Lìjiāng road. Approaching from the direction of Dàlǐ, you'll come to the small village of Diànnán, about 8km before Jiànchuān. At Diànnán, a small road branches south-west from the main road and passes through the village of Shāxī (23km from the junction). Close to this village are the **Shíbǎoshān Shíkū** (Stone Treasure Grottoes). There are three temple groups at the grottoes: Shí Zhōng (Stone Bell), Shīzi Guān (Lion Pass) and Shādēng Cūn (Shadeng Village).

Hèqìng 鹤庆

About 46km south of Lìjiāng, Hèqìng is on the road that joins the main Dàlǐ-Lìjiāng road just above Ěrhǎi Hú at Dèngchúan. In the centre of town is the Yunhe Pavilion, a wooden structure built during the Ming dynasty.

LÌJIĀNG 丽江
☎ 08891

North of Dàlǐ, bordering Tibet, the town of Lìjiāng is set in a beautiful valley and makes another great spot to while away a few days or weeks. Your initial response when you pull into town and roar toward the bus station will not likely be positive. It's not until you get into the old town – a delightful maze of cobbled streets, rickety old wooden buildings, gushing canals and the hurly-burly of market life – that you realise Lìjiāng is more than a boring urban sprawl in the middle of nowhere.

There are a number of interesting sights around Lìjiāng, some of which can be reached by bicycle. You can also use a bike to get out of town to the mountains, where you can hike around, although you may need time to acclimatise to the altitude (2400m).

Yúnnán was a hunting ground for famous foreign plant-hunters such as Kingdon Ward and Joseph Rock. Rock, an Austro-American, lived almost continuously in Lìjiāng between 1922 and 1949. 'Hef', as

he was known, is still remembered by some locals. A man of quick and violent temper, he commissioned local carpenters to build special chairs and a desk to accommodate his stocky frame. He burdened his large caravans with a gold dinner service and a collapsible bathtub from Abercrombie & Fitch. He also wrote a guide to Hawaiian flora before devoting the rest of his life to researching Naxi culture and collecting the flora of the region.

The Ancient Nakhi Kingdom of Southwest China is Joseph Rock's definitive work; the two volumes are heavy-duty reading. For a lighter treatment of the man and his work, take a look at *In China's Border Provinces: The Turbulent Career of Joseph Rock, Botanist-Explorer* by JB Sutton.

Another venerable work on Lìjiāng that's worth reading if you can find it is *The Forgotten Kingdom* by Peter Goulart. Goulart

---

Building 'Em Like They Used To

Lìjiāng can consider itself lucky. In February 1996 an earthquake measuring over 7 on the Richter scale rocked the Lìjiāng area, killing over 300 – including one international tourist – and injuring many times that number. Damage was estimated at over half a billion US dollars. The Chinese government took note and today is sinking millions of yuan into rebuilding most of Lìjiāng County with traditional Naxi architecture: cobblestone and wood will replace cement on streets and bridges. (Modern necessities such as sanitation and sewage treatment will also be factored in.) This isn't simply a cynical attempt to lure tourists – while much of newer Lìjiāng was levelled, the old-style architecture was largely unscathed. (But it is true that the local government had been destroying much local architecture for years, ignoring the uproar it caused.) The UN was so impressed by the survival of Lìjiāng that it has placed all of Lìjiāng County on the World Heritage Site list. Another earthquake – this one measuring 5.3 on the Richter scale – hit the area in October 1997, causing no deaths but moderate damage.

was a White Russian who studied Naxi culture and lived in Lìjiāng from 1940 to 1949.

Orientation

Lìjiāng is separated into old and new towns that are starkly different. The approximate line of division is **Shīzī Shān** (Lion Hill), the bump in the middle of town that's topped by a radio mast and Wànggǔ Lóu (Looking at the Past Pavilion), a new pagoda. Everything west of the hill is the new town, and everything east of the hill is the old town.

The easiest way into the old town is to head up to the cinema, turn east into a small square that also serves as the town's night market, and head south. The old town is a delightful maze of twists and turns – although it's small, it's easy to get lost in, which, of course, is part of the fun. Enjoy!

Information

It was only a matter of time before Chinese cities got their own Web site addresses too. Check out Lìjiāng's Web site at www .lijiang.com.

Money The Bank of China is on Xin Dajie almost opposite the intersection of the road that leads off to the Lìjiāng Bīnguǎn and the PSB. This is where to go for a credit card advance.

There is also a small branch just next to the entrance of the Lìjiāng Bīnguǎn. It is possible to change travellers cheques at both branches.

Post & Communications The Post and China Telecom office is on Xin Dajie, just south of the turn to get to the old town. It's open from 8.30 am to around 8 pm. You can't make reverse-charge calls or use a calling card. Another post office is in old town along Dong Dajie.

Email & Internet Access The 2nd floor of the post office has Internet access for Y15 per hour until 8 pm. Few cafes in town do, but this should change.

Travel Agencies Cafes and backpacker inns are your best source of information.

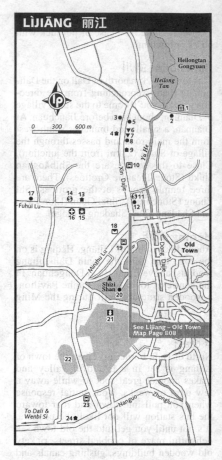

The CITS main office and FIT department, across the street from the Gǔlùwān Bīnguǎn, are worth a visit. The staff at the Lìjiāng office are generally helpful, but no, they still cannot get you that train ticket for Jīnjiāng.

PSB The PSB is opposite the Lìjiāng Bīnguǎn and the official in charge of visa extensions has been one of the most helpful in all of China. Let's hope he keeps his job. It's open Monday to Friday from 8 am to noon though somebody's usually around anytime.

LÌJIĀNG

PLACES TO STAY
4 Gǔlùwān Bīnguǎn
古路湾宾馆
9 Hóngtàiyáng Jiǔdiàn
红太阳酒店
13 Lìjiāng Bīnguǎn
丽江宾馆
24 Yúnshān Fàndiàn
云杉饭店

PLACES TO EAT
6 Ali Baba's Cafe
阿里巴巴餐厅
7 Peter's Café

OTHER
1 Dōngbā Bówùguǎn
& Shop
东巴博物馆

2 Dōngbā Wénhuà
Yánjiūshì
东巴研究所
3 Yunling Theatre
云岭剧场
5 CITS/FIT
中国国际旅行社
8 Máo Zhǔxí
Guǎngchǎng
毛主席广场
10 Lìjiāng Bus
Station
丽江客运站
11 Bank of China
中国银行
12 Xinhua Bookstore
新华书店
14 Bank of China
中国银行

15 PSB
公安局
16 Hospital
门诊所
17 CAAC
民航售票处
18 Post & China Telecom
Office
邮电局
19 Buses to Báishā &
Yùlóng Xuě Shān
20 Radio Mast
狮子山
21 Wànggǔ Lóu
望古楼
22 Sports Ground
体育场
23 Long-Distance Bus Station
长途汽车站

Dangers & Annoyances In recent visits two solo female travellers were robbed at knifepoint in separate incidents atop Xiàng Shān (Elephant Hill) in Hēilóngtán Gōngyuán. Both attacks occurred in broad daylight in the early afternoon, so keep your eyes sharp for people lurking behind you. It would obviously be a good idea to pair up with at least one other traveller.

Some rather inept pickpockets have also appeared north of the old town near the square.

Old Town
☎ 0888

Criss-crossed by canals and a maze of narrow streets, the old town is not to be missed. Arrive by mid-morning to see the market square full of Naxi women in traditional dress. Parrots and plants adorn the front porches, women sell griddle cakes in front of teahouses, men walk past with hunting falcons proudly keeping balance on their gloved fists, and players energetically slam down the trumps on a card table in the middle of the street. Embroidery and lengths of cloth are sold in shops around the market.

For all the controversy regarding what to preserve in the town and how, for now it is extraordinary.

Above the old town is a beautiful park which can be reached on the path leading past the radio antenna. Sit on the slope in the early morning and watch the mist clearing as the old town comes to life.

Now acting as sentinel of sorts for the town is the Wànggǔ Lóu, a pagoda raised at a cost of over one million yuán. It's famed for a unique design using dozens of four-storey pillars, but unfortunately these were culled from northern Yúnnán old-growth forests. A path (with English signs) leads from the Sìfāng Jiē (Old Market Square). Admission is Y15.

Hēilóngtán Gōngyuán 黑龙潭公园
Black Dragon Pool Park

Hēilóngtán Gōngyuán is on the northern edge of town. Apart from strolling around the pool – its view of Yùlóng Xuěshān is the most obligatory photo shoot in southwest China – you can visit the **Dōngbā Wénhuà Yánjiūshì** (Dongba Research Institute), which is part of a renovated complex on the hillside. The **Dōngbā Bówùguǎn** (Dongba Museum) displays Dōngbā scrolls and artefacts. Admission is Y2.

At the far side of the pool are renovated buildings used for an art exhibition, a pavilion with its own bridge across the water and

The Naxi

Lìjiāng is the base of the Naxi (also spelt Nakhi and Nahi) minority, who number about 278,000 in Yúnnán and Sìchuān. The Naxi are descended from Tibetan nomads and lived until recently in matrilineal families. Since local rulers were always male it wasn't truly matriarchal, but women still seem to run the show, certainly in the old part of Lìjiāng.

The Naxi matriarchs maintained their hold over the men with flexible arrangements for love affairs. The *azhu* (friend) system allowed a couple to become lovers without setting up joint residence. Both partners would continue to live in their respective homes; the boyfriend would spend the nights at his girlfriend's house but return to live and work at his mother's house during the day. Any children born to the couple belonged to the woman, who was responsible for bringing them up. The father provided support, but once the relationship was over, so was the support. Children lived with their mothers, and no special effort was made to recognise paternity. Women inherited all property, and disputes were adjudicated by female elders. The matriarchal system appears to have survived around Yongning, north of Lìjiāng.

There are strong matriarchal influences in the Naxi language. Nouns enlarge their meaning when the word for 'female' is added; conversely, the addition of the word for 'male' will decrease the meaning. For example, 'stone' plus 'female' conveys the idea of a boulder; 'stone' plus 'male' conveys the idea of a pebble.

Naxi women wear blue blouses and trousers covered by blue or black aprons. The T-shaped traditional cape not only stops the basket always worn on the back from chafing, but also symbolises the heavens. Day and night are represented by the light and dark halves of the cape; seven embroidered circles symbolise the stars. Two larger circles, one on each shoulder, are used to depict the eyes of a frog, which until the 15th century was an important god to the Naxi. With the decline of animist beliefs, the frog eyes fell out of fashion, but the Naxi still call the cape by its original name: 'frog-eye sheepskin'.

The Naxi created a written language over 1000 years ago using an extraordinary system of pictographs. The most famous Naxi text is the Dongba classic *The Creation*, and ancient copies of it and other texts can still be found in Lìjiāng, as well as in the archives of some US universities. Dongba were Naxi shamans who were caretakers of the written language and mediators between the Naxi and the spirit world. The Dongba religion eventually absorbed itself into an amalgam of Lamaist Buddhism, Islam and Taoism. The Tibetan origins of the Naxi are confirmed by references in Naxi literature to Lake Manasarovar and Mt Kailas, both in western Tibet.

the Wǔfèng Sì (Five Pheonix Temple) which dates from the Ming dynasty.

Trails lead straight up Xiàng Shān to a dilapidated gazebo and then across a spiny ridge past a communications centre and back down the other side, making a nice 45-minute (if you push it) morning hike. Entry to the park costs Y8.

Xūan Kē Zhùsuǒ 宣科住所
Xuan Ke Museum

Xuan Ke, a Naxi scholar who spent 20 years in labour camps following the suppression of the Hundred Flowers movement, has turned his Lìjiāng family home into a small repository for Naxi and Lìjiāng cultural items. Besides clothing and musical instruments (including an original Persian lute that has been used in Naxi music for centuries), his home displays Dr Joseph Rock's large, handmade furniture and has a small library of out-of-print books on Lìjiāng. Dr Rock was a close family friend.

Xuan Ke speaks English and is always willing to discuss his original ideas about world culture (for example, that music and dance originated as rites of exorcism).

His home is in the old town, at 11 Jishan Alley, just west of the Dongba House (see Places to Stay).

Festivals

The 13th day of the third moon (late March or early April) is the traditional day to hold a Fertility Festival. July brings the Torch Festival (Huǒbǎ Jié), also celebrated by the Bai in the Dàlǐ region. The origin of this festival can be traced back to the intrigues of the Nanzhao kingdom, when the wife of a man burned to death by the king eluded the romantic entreaties of the monarch by leaping into a fire.

Places to Stay

Lìjiāng now has half a dozen guesthouses with traditional Naxi architecture. Stroll around – there will be more by the time you read this – and compare.

The first place you're likely to come across when you arrive in town is the **Yúnshān Fàndiàn** (☎ 512 1315), next to the south bus station. There's not much reason to stay here: even if you're catching an early bus you can usually board at the north bus station. The Yúnshān has three-bed dorms for Y75, and two-bed dorms for Y70. Doubles with attached bathroom are Y160.

Adjacent to Máo Zhǔxí Guǎngchǎng (Mao Square), the **Hóngtàiyáng Jiǔdiàn** (Red Sun Hotel; ☎ 512 1018) has beds in six- to eight-bed dorms for Y20, while those in doubles without bath are Y35. The hotel also has doubles/triples with attached washroom for Y200. There are more higher-priced choices. The dorms are large and bright, and the facilities are fine, although a few travellers have reported ear-shattering karaoke or disinterested staff.

The **Lìjiāng Bīnguǎn** (☎ 512 1911), also known as No 1 Hotel (Dìyī Zhāodàisuǒ), is no longer budget. Nicely furnished doubles/triples with attached bath cost Y160 in the more luxurious block at the back.

For more upmarket accommodation, two options are centrally located. The **Gǔlùwān Bīnguǎn** (☎ 512 1446) is north of Máo Zhǔxí Guǎngchǎng and doubles as the car park for the northern bus station. Standard doubles now start at Y200, triples are available for Y180. The Gǔlùwān has a small travel agency on the grounds, as well as an air ticket booking office (check to see how

much their commission is – it might be better to try CITS across the street). It's recently re-opened its budget lodging for foreigners. Decent and quiet (due to location) rooms start at Y10 in a quad; the cheapest rooms with private bath are Y30.

Old Town Coming south from the square into the old town, the first place you'll stumble across is the well-done **Gǔchéng Kèzhàn** (Old Town Inn; ☎ 518 9000), with slightly more upmarket rooms with beds in common doubles for Y75; cosy singles/doubles/triples/quads with bath are Y150/250/330/360. Staff are pleasant here.

Farther south and around the corner is the recently renovated **Sānhé Nà'xī Bīnguǎn** (☎ 512 0891, fax 512 3281), which has a multi-person dorm with bunk beds for Y20, and then beds in singles/doubles/triples/quads for Y40/35/30/25. They also have standard rooms for Y220. After the renovation the place has a good atmosphere. You'll also find ethnic artworks, a painting gallery and the odd traditional dance performance.

Still farther south is the new **Dongba House** (Dōngbā Haúsī aka Holiday Inn; ☎/fax 517 5431), a very well-run place with dorm beds for Y20, and singles/doubles/triples with common bath for Y50/50/75. The only down side is the bath/shower – there's only one and it's in the kitchen. The place has an attractive sunlit sitting cafe, Internet (Y20 per hour), bike rental and international phone calls. The owner, a government bureaucrat and a Tibetan (his brother owns the MCA Guesthouse in Dàlǐ), is extremely helpful. He hopes to establish genuine Tibetan guesthouses from Lìjiāng through Zhōngdiàn, western Sìchuān, and into Tibet. This is a good place to book a bus to Dàjù.

The first-rate **Dìyīwān Kèzhàn** (First Bend Inn; ☎ 518 1688) is a favourite with travellers and one of the old city's most distinctive and well-preserved buildings. It features rooms on two levels around an attractive courtyard. Little touches include travel information, cheap laundry and even motion-sensor lights for late-night trips to use the facilities. Rooms are comfortable and bathrooms are quite clean. Showers have reliable hot water in the evenings *and* mornings (usually from 8 to 10 am). Doubles/triples/quads are Y80/Y90/Y100; all rooms have common bath. The staff are attentive and friendly and are full of information on local sights.

Lìjiāng now has many other traditional-style inns. Immediately to the rear of Sìfāng Jiē (Old Market Square) is perhaps the best new option, the *Sìfāng Kèzhàn (Square Inn)*, with very clean singles/doubles/triples for Y60. Take a look at a few rooms. The facilities are excellent and the proprietors were wonderful on a first experience. South and east of here along the warren of alleys are two additional options – the *Rénhéyuán* and the *Nà'xī Sìhéyuán Jiudìan (Naxi Quad Inn)*, neither of which approaches the Sìfāng Kèzhàn for ambience.

The *Lijiang Grand Hotel (Gélán Dàjiǔdiàn;* ☎ *512 8888, fax 512 7878)*, at the northern edge of the old town, is a hulking luxury monster with facilities and prices (US$60 for a double) that seem completely at odds with the rest of Lìjiāng (there have been no complaints however). The hotel is a Chinese-Thai joint venture managed in part by several Europeans.

Places to Eat
Like Dàlǐ, Lìjiāng has a legion of small, family-operated restaurants catering to backpackers. The following run-down is by no means exhaustive.

There are always several 'Naxi' items on the menu, including the famous 'Naxi omelette' and 'Naxi sandwich' (goat's cheese, tomato and fried egg between two pieces of local *baba* flatbread; the *yumi baba*, corn *baba* on a husk, is delicious). Try locally produced *yinjiu*, a lychee-based wine with a 500-year history – it tastes like a decent semi-sweet sherry.

Máo Zhǔxí Guǎngchǎng Most people stumble across the restaurants lining Máo Zhǔxí Guǎngchǎng (Mao Square) first. *Peter's Café*, a former favourite with travellers, has taken a nose dive. The food is acceptable, but the place is now gloomy if not

LÌJIĀNG – OLD TOWN
丽江市中心

fly-ridden and all traces of personality seem to have been surgically removed.

At the northern edge of the square, *Ali Baba's Café* is a better bet, with good food and friendly people.

Old Town The *Old Market Inn (Nà'xī Cāntīng)* is often mentioned for its atmosphere. Seats downstairs look out onto the market square, allowing you to take in the market sights and sounds over a cold beer or hot Yúnnán coffee.

Walking along Xinyi Jie into the old quarter you will come across *Din-Din's Restaurant (Dīngdīng Cāntīng)*, a long-established cafe which does a fairly steady trade despite the competition from the market square cafes.

The *Well Bistro (Jǐngzhǔo Cānguǎn)*, around the corner and down from the Dìyīwān Kèzhàn (see Places to Stay earlier), will likely capture your fancy. The cosy all-wood interiors and tastefully understated decor add to the superb food. Everything is made from scratch, including the bread and to-die-for desserts, which change daily. The pizza here without a doubt rivals any in south-west China. Lots

LÌJIĀNG – OLD TOWN

PLACES TO STAY
2 Lijiang Grand Hotel
格兰饭店
5 Gǔchéng Kèzhàn
古城客栈
7 Sānhé Nà'xī Bīnguǎn
三合纳西酒店
8 Dongba House
东巴豪斯
10 Dìyīwān Kèzhàn
第一湾客栈
22 Sìfāng Kèzhàn
四方客栈
23 Nà'xī Sìhéyuán Jiǔdiàn
纳西四合园酒店
24 Rénhéyuán
人和院

PLACES TO EAT
6 Din Din's
Restaurant
叮叮餐厅
11 Well Bistro
井卓餐馆
12 Blue Page
14 Sakura Cafe
15 Delta Cafe
16 Ma Ma Fu's
马马付餐厅
21 Old Market Inn
纳西餐厅

OTHER
1 Cinema
电影院

3 Yùlóng Qiáo
玉龙桥
4 Night Market
Area
夜市
9 Xuān Kē Zhùsuǒ
宣科住所
13 Naxi Music
Performances
纳西音乐
17 Post Office
邮电局
18 Dàshí Qiáo
大石桥
19 Sìfāng Jiē
四方街
20 CC Bar

of good vegetarian options are on the menu as well. Hip, eclectic music echoes quietly throughout the day. You'll probably spend lots of time here reading its books and making your collect calls. Across the alley is the *Blue Page*, outstanding for vegie food and for set-meal options (none with MSG); they also have good Hǔtiào Xiá (Tiger Leaping Gorge) information and Internet access.

In perhaps the loveliest old town location is the recently relocated *Ma Ma Fu's* (*Māmāfù Cāntīng*), right along a stream. Now run by a younger Mama Fu, it's still got grand home-baked breads and pies, and an excellent array of foods.

West of here along the west branch of the Yù Hé is perhaps the best recent addition. *Sakura Cafe* has excellent Korean and Japanese food (the cook is Korean and is married to a Lìjiāng local) – the outstanding *bibimbap* set meal is enough for two. Close to here is the *Delta Cafe* (*Hòujiē Wǔhaò Xīcāntīng*) which has good food and better music, heavy on the reggae.

Other Places to Eat Elsewhere around Lìjiāng and off the travellers' circuit, look out for places serving *baba*, the Lìjiāng local speciality – thick flatbreads of wheat, served plain or stuffed with meats, vegetable

or sweets. Morning is the best time to check out the baba selection.

In the old town, you can buy baba from street vendors. In the southern section of the old town is a string of grubby but charming little hole-in-the-wall *eateries* so desperate for your business that they've Anglicised their signs to read *Old Town Small Eat* and the like, although they haven't gotten around to translating the menu yet. A couple have completely remade their interiors and are very enticing.

There are several smaller restaurants just before the entrance to the Hēilóngtán Gōngyuán on Xin Dajie. Nearby are restaurants with 'medicinal herb chicken in steampot' and a few pastry shops.

Entertainment
One of the few things you can do in the evening in Lìjiāng is attend performances of the **Naxi Orchestra**. Performances are given every night in a beautiful old building inside the old town, usually from 8 to 10 pm.

Not only are all 20 to 24 members Naxi, but they play a type of Taoist temple music that has been lost elsewhere in China. The pieces they perform are supposedly faithful renditions of music from the Han, Song and Tang dynasties, played on original instruments (in most of China such instruments didn't survive the Cultural Revolution; several of this group hid theirs by burying them underground). They also play plenty of Han Chinese music, so don't be surprised.

This is a rare chance to hear Chinese music as it must have sounded in classical China. Xuan Ke usually speaks for the group at performances – talks too much, some say – explaining each musical piece and describing the instruments. There are taped recordings of the music available; a set of two costs Y30. If you're interested, make sure you buy the tape at the show – tapes on sale at shops around town, and even in Kūnmíng, are pirated copies.

You can usually turn up on your own and watch a performance, but you might want to arrive 15 minutes early to ensure a good seat. Tickets are Y35. Co-opted versions have sprouted around town; give them a miss.

Getting There & Away

Air Lìjiāng's airport is 25km to the east of town. Yunnan Airlines now flies from Kūnmíng to Lìjiāng a few times daily (Y370; 45 minutes). Most days there are also multiple direct flights to Jǐnghóng in Xīshuāngbǎnnà (Y610). In Lìjiāng, tickets can be booked at the CAAC ticket office (☎ 512 0289), which closes from 11.30 am to 2 pm; and the Gǔlùwān Bīnguǎn and CITS, which both levy a service charge. Direct flights to Guǎngzhōu and Guìlín are rumoured but not yet existent.

Bus Lìjiāng has a northern and southern bus station; many, but not all, buses make stops at both. The ticket window for the northern station is just south of the Hóngtàiyàng Jiǔdiàn, though buses depart from the Gǔlùwān Bīnguǎn car park. Note that schedules on the wall are mostly wrong at both.

Buses for Xiàguān (Y23.50 to Y43.80; three hours) depart either bus station generally from 7.30 am to 5.30 pm and pass by Dàlǐ along the highway (if not into town itself). The expresses should serve both bus stations – check to be sure.

Few cheaper minibuses make the run to Kūnmíng now. You're mostly left to sleeper buses (Y115 to Y124) and new luxury express buses (Y155); either version will get you there in around 10 hours on the express buses, a time which would have been unthinkably fast just a couple of years ago (but regular sleepers are still coming in at around 25 hours on real bad days). The first bus departs at 3.30 am, the last one at 6 pm. A private company operates luxury express buses for similar prices from in front of the Lìjiāng Bīnguǎn.

To Jīnjiāng (in Sìchuān, for rail connections with Chéngdū) six buses serve either station from 6.30 am to 4 pm and range in price from Y43 to Y62; the nine-hour trip can get you into Jīnjiāng in time for the evening Chéngdū train (No 206/203) if you leave early enough. During the rainy season (July to September) the Lìjiāng-Jīnjiāng road is often washed out and Chéngdū-bound travellers have no option but to return to Kūnmíng to catch a train or plane onward.

Buses to Zhōngdiàn (Y21 to Y29; five hours) depart regularly from 7.30 am to 1.30 pm.

Other buses include: Shígǔ at 12.50 pm (Y7); Dàjù at 8 and 8.30 am (Y25; three to five hours); and Nínglàng at 7.10, 8 and 9 am (Y32 to Y37; seven hours). The southern bus station was also planning to have a minibus travel along the new road through Hǔtiào Xiá; it was to leave at 8.30 am.

Getting Around

Yunnan Airlines has a bus service to and from the airport for Y10.

Taxis start at Y6 flag fall in town. The old town, however, is best seen on foot. Bike hire is readily available around town at Máo Zhǔxí Guǎngchǎng or Dongba House. Bikes should cost around Y15 for the day.

Lìjiāng (nicknamed 'Land of Horses') is famous for its easily trained horses, which are usually white or chestnut with distinctive white stripes on the back. It may be possible to arrange an excursion on horseback.

AROUND LÌJIĀNG

It is possible to see most of Lìjiāng's environs on your own, but a few agencies do offer half- or full-day tours, starting from

Y150; it might be worth it if you take one in which admission fees are included.

Monasteries

Lìjiāng's monasteries are Tibetan in origin and belong to the Karmapa (Red Hat) sect. Most of them were extensively damaged during the Cultural Revolution and there's not much monastic activity nowadays. Nevertheless, it's worth hopping on a bicycle and heading out of town for a look.

Around 5km north-west of Lìjiāng (on a trail that passes the two ponds to the north of town) are a few monks at the **Pǔjí Sì**, who are usually happy to show the occasional stray traveller around.

Fùguó Sì Not far from the town of Báishā lies what was once the largest of Lìjiāng's monasteries. Much of it was destroyed during the Cultural Revolution. In the monastery compound look out for the **Hufa Hall**; the interior walls have some interesting frescoes.

Yùfēng Sì (Jade Peak Temple) This is a small lamasery is on a hillside about 5km past Báishā. The last 3km of the track requires a steep climb. If you decide to leave your bike at the foot of the hill, don't leave it too close to the village below – the local kids have been known to let the air out of the tyres!

The monastery sits at the foot of Yùlóng Xuěshān and was established in 1756. The monastery's main attraction nowadays is the **Wànduǒ Shānchá** (Camellia Tree of 10,000 Blossoms). Ten thousand might be something of an exaggeration, but locals claim that the tree produces at least 4000 between February and April. A monk on the grounds risked his life to keep the tree secretly watered during the years of the Cultural Revolution.

Wénbǐ Sì To get to Wénbǐ Sì requires a fairly steep uphill ride to the south-west of Lìjiāng. The monastery itself is not that

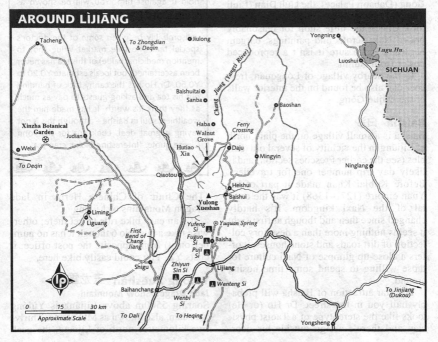

AROUND LÌJIĀNG

Tacheng
Jiulong
To Zhongdian & Deqin
Yongning
Lugu Hu
Luoshui
SICHUAN
Baishuitai
Sanba
Chang Jiang (Yangzi River)
Baoshan
Xinzha Botanical Garden
Judian
Weixi
Haba
Walnut Grove
Ferry Crossing
Hutiao Xia
Daju
Mingyin
Ninglang
To Deqin
Qiaotou
Heishui
Baishui
Yulong Xueshan
Liming
Liguang
First Bend of Chang Jiang
Yufeng Si
Fuguo Si
Yuquan Spring
Baisha
Puji Si
Shigu
Zhiyun Sin Si
Lijiang
Baihanchang
Wenten Si
Wenbi Si
To Jinjiang (Dukou)
To Dali
To Heqing
Yongsheng

0   15   30 km
Approximate Scale

interesting, but there are some good views and pleasant walks in the near vicinity.

Frescoes

Lìjiāng is famed for its temple frescoes. Most travellers are probably not going to want to spend a week or so traipsing around seeking them out, but it may be worth checking out one or two of them.

For the most part the frescoes were painted during the 15th and 16th centuries by Tibetan, Naxi, Bai and Han artists. Many of them were subsequently restored during the Qing dynasty. They depict various Taoist, Chinese and Tibetan Buddhist themes and can be found on the interior walls of temples in the area. Experts say the best example is the fresco in Báishā's **Dàbǎojī Gōng**. However, the Red Guards came through here slashing and gouging during the Cultural Revolution, so there's not that much to see.

In Báishā ask around for the **Dàbǎojī Gōng** (Dabaoji Palace), the **Liúlí Diàn** (Liuli Temple) or the **Dàdìng Gé** (Dading Pavilion). Check the little shop for reasonably priced Naxi scrolls and paintings; bargain hard and make sure it isn't a reproduced poster from Guìlín.

In the nearby village of Lóngquán, frescoes can also be found on the interior walls of the **Dàjué Gōng**.

Báishā 白沙

Báishā is a small village on the plain north of Lìjiāng in the vicinity of several old temples (see the earlier Frescoes section) and is likely day trip number one for travellers. Before Kublai Khan made it part of his Yuan empire (1271–1368) it was the capital of the Naxi kingdom. It's hardly changed since then and though at first sight it seems nothing more than a desultory collection of dirt roads and stone houses, it offers a close-up glimpse of Naxi culture for those willing to spend some time nosing around.

The star attraction of Báishā will probably hail you in the street. Dr Ho (or He) looks like the stereotype of a Taoist physician and there's a sign outside his door:

The Dr Ho Phenomenon

Dr Ho gets extremely mixed reports from travellers, and it's worth bearing in mind before you head out to Báishā that the majority of these reports are negative.

It's not entirely the venerable doctor's fault. Bruce Chatwin, a travel writer who was among the first to stumble across and mythologise Dr Ho as the 'Taoist physician in the Jade-Dragon Mountains of Lijiang', is at least partly responsible. Chatwin did such a romantic job on Dr Ho that he was to subsequently appear in every travel book (including this one) with an entry on Lijiang; journalists and photographers turned up from every corner of the world; and Dr Ho, previously an unknown doctor in an unknown town, had achieved worldwide renown.

If you visit, the doctor's son will drag you off the street for your obligatory house call on Dr Ho. Unfortunately the attention has gone to the doctor's head somewhat – try not to hold it against him. You will be shown as many press clippings proving his international fame as your attention span allows, and you will probably be given some of the doctor's special tea. The true market value (not to mention medicinal value) of this tea has never been ascertained, but locals estimate Y0.20 to Y0.50. Dr Ho has the canny trick of handing out his tea and asking guests to pay as much as they think it's worth. It has made him the wealthiest soul in Báishā – although this is not saying a great deal. Look out for the John Cleese quote: 'Interesting bloke; crap tea'.

'The Clinic of Chinese Herbs in Jade Dragon Mountains of Lijiang'

It's an easy bike ride to get there; otherwise take a bus (No 6 though it has no number on it) from opposite the post office; it costs Y2. You could easily bike here.

Yùlóng Xuěshān 玉龙雪山
Jade Dragon Snow Mountain

Soaring 5500m above Lìjiāng is Yùlóng Xuěshān, also known as Mt Satseto. Thirty-five kilometres north of Lìjiāng, the peak was climbed for the first time in 1963 by a research team from Běijīng.

A chairlift has recently opened which brings you about halfway up a nearby slope, from where you can rent horses which will take you to a large meadow. You can choose to keep going up to a stunning 4506m along the second chairlift segment, completed in 1999 after nearly four years of construction. It's now the highest in Asia and you'll believe it when you pass by the glaciers.

At the meadow, if the weather is clear, you will be greeted by a stunning view of Yùlóng Xuěshān. This meadow is the spot of a legendary couple's suicide pact.

A bus does depart from Lijiāng once daily at 8.15 am for Yùlóng Xuěshān from the bus stop opposite the post office; it costs Y25 return. Hiring your own van for around Y150 is also possible. Otherwise, hitching is the only way to get here.

Local tour operators in Lìjiāng have prohibitively priced tours taking in the mountain; a couple are located on Máo Zhǔxí Guǎngchǎng. Once there, there's a Y40 entrance. The first chairlift ride will cost you Y80 return, and the horse rental (not necessary) another Y20.

Alternatively, you can reach the snow line on one of the adjoining peaks if you continue along the base of the hillside near Báishā but ignore the track to Yùfēng Sì. On the other side of the next obvious valley, a well-worn path leads uphill to a lake. It might be a good idea to ask locals about conditions in this area before setting out.

Shígǔ 石鼓 & Chángjiāng Dìyīwān 长江第一湾
Shígǔ & First Bend of the Yangzi River
The small town of Shígǔ sits on the first bend of China's greatest river. Shígǔ means 'Stone Drum', referring to the marble plaque shaped like a drum that commemorates a 16th-century Naxi victory over a Tibetan army. The other plaque on the river's edge celebrates the People's Army crossing here in 1936 in the Great March to the north. Lodging is all grotty here, but reportedly first bend fish are the tastiest in the region.

Buses to Shígǔ leave at 12.50 pm from Lìjiāng's north bus station, and take three hours. This would probably require an overnight stay since the last bus back is usually at 4 or 5 pm. Alternatively, try buses bound for Jùdiàn or get a bus as far as BáihànchÁng and hitch from this point.

Hǔtiào Xiá 虎跳峡
Tiger Leaping Gorge
After making its first turn at Shígǔ the mighty Cháng Jiāng (at this point known as the Jinsha River) surges between the mountains of the Hābā Shān and the Yùlóng Xuěshān, through what is one of the deepest gorges in the world – Hǔtiào Xiá. The entire gorge measures 16km, and from the waters of the Cháng Jiāng to the mountaintops is a giddy 3900m.

Within five years the hike through the gorge went from obscure to the can't-miss experience of northern Yúnnán, although you'll probably only encounter several other travellers on the trail. All up, plan on spending three days minimum away from Lìjiāng doing the hike. Ideally you can do the walk in two days – one superhero American walked it in a day – although some travellers, enchanted with Walnut Grove, have lengthened it to over a week.

Dangers & Annoyances The gorge trek is not to be taken lightly. Half a dozen people – including a few foreign travellers – have died in the gorge. Most perished because they wandered off the trail, got lost and/or were unable to return to the trail, or fell. One hiker was buried while trying to scramble over a landslide. Two solo travellers have also reported being assaulted on the trail by locals, although this couldn't (or wouldn't) be officially confirmed.

The newest danger is just as serious: dynamite. Though the road is finished, follow-up engineering could result in continued blasting along the lower route.

On a less severe note, several travellers have reported becoming ill after eating in Qiáotóu or from drinking water along the trek. Speaking of water, one litre of water is *not* enough on this trek.

The other major annoyance is soon to come: development. New construction has sadly diminished the appeal of the gorge somewhat. After three years of dynamite blasting and Herculean building, a road now stretches from Qiáotóu to Walnut Grove, and will eventually bend north all the way to Zhōngdiàn on a tourist loop. A ski hill and theme park are just two of the first proposals for the area. The effects are just starting to be felt.

Gorge Trek The first thing to do is to check with cafes in Lìjiāng for the latest gossip on the mini trek, particularly the weather and its possibly lethal effects on the trail.

Transport is easier than it once was, but this also can still be where problems arise. Finishing in Qiáotóu allows for quicker transport back to Lìjiāng, but transport to Dàjù is tricky and you might get stuck in Dàjù overnight before you've even begun. Most people take a Zhōngdiàn-bound bus early in the morning, hop off in Qiáotóu, and hike quickly to overnight in Walnut Grove.

In Qiáotóu you'll find five places to stay. Really the only good choice is the *Gorge Village Hotel*, in front of the bridge leading to the trail. Here, beds in older rooms are Y10, Y12 with a TV, or Y25 in a new wing. Facilities are clean and the family is friendly. Nothing upmarket exists, and the other cheap versions are adequate at best.

Across from the bridge in Qiáotóu is the nerve-centre of trail information, the *Backpacker Cafe*, with an English menu, passable English spoken, and backpack storage. Just north of here, a *Muslim Restaurant* has a few English translations.

There is a new admission fee of Y20 at the gorge, which many people have avoided simply by walking through at 5 am. The following description starts at Qiáotóu.

There are now two trails – the higher (the older route, known as the 24-bend path, although it's more like 30), and the lower, the new road, replete with belching tour buses. One traveller aptly points out, 'Remember the high road leaves less time for drinking beer in Walnut Grove'. You could walk both trails, one going and one returning the

next day, avoiding Dàjù altogether, or even combine the two roads in an extremely ambitious and hair-raising day trip. There are now yellow arrows – a godsend – pointing you along the upper path. To get to the high road, after crossing through the gate, cross a small stream and go 150m. Take a left fork, go through the schoolyard, and from there follow the yellow arrows. Via the upper path, it's a strenuous eight to 10 hours; via the new path it'll be four to six hours. Along the high road is the great *Halfway Lodge* in Ben Di Wan village. A few years back the owner, a traditional medicine practitioner, was so regularly interrupted by exhausted, dehydrated travellers panicking in the dark outside his modest home that he just opened up a room. He and his ad hoc medicinal herb and plant tours proved so popular that he's now had to expand with additional rooms and showers/toilets; he can't keep up with demand so don't count on a bed.

Both roads can be dangerous during the rainy months of July and August – or any time it rains really – when landslides and swollen waterfalls can place themselves in your path. Ask locals in Lìjiāng or at the Backpacker Cafe about conditions.

Walnut Grove is the overnight point, a bit beyond the halfway mark, and there are two hotels nestled among the walnut trees. The *Spring Guesthouse*, which incorporates *Sean's Cafe*, is the spot for more lively evenings and socialising. *Chateau de Woody*, the other option, is considered the quiet alternative. Both places have dorm beds for Y7 (perhaps less in low season), doubles for Y10 per person, and 24-hour hot water, and both have won praise from travellers. Food and beer are also available here. Supplies of bottled water can be chancy; it's probably best to bring your own. Be aware that in peak times – particularly late summer – up to 100 people a day can make the trek, so bed space is short. Both hotels are planning to expand, but be prepared to sleep in a back room somewhere.

The next day's walk is slightly shorter at four to six hours. Note that due to landslides this path has changed from previous years. Walk 1½ hours from the Grove to the river – Woody's or Sean's will have guides – and take the ferry across. It's a flat fee of Y10 to cross ... ridiculous, but what can you do? From here it's an additional two hours, or less. The *Snowflake Hotel*, Dàjù's premier vacationer's residence, costs Y10 a bed. Another hotel is in town.

If you're doing the walk the other way round and heading for Qiáotóu, walk north through Dàjù, aiming for the white pagoda at the foot of the mountains.

Hǔtiào Xiá to Báishuǐtái Both guesthouses in Walnut Grove are trying to figure out how to circumvent the proposed tour buses and kitschy tourist traps. They've set new trails through the hills and can line up camping and horseback trips. Perhaps most intriguing is the trek from here north to Báishuǐtái or even Zhōngdiàn. From Walnut Grove to Hābā village (Lisu and Naxi) is eight hours, six if you tough it out. From here to Sānbā (Yi) would be four hours (Sānbā has a county guesthouse with beds for Y20), and from here Báishuǐtái is close. All of this is done via old trails and a rough road; at the time of writing, a sturdy high-clearance vehicle could make it from Hābā to Sānbā. From Báishuǐtái you can take a bus to Zhōngdiàn, or continue another two days via Jiǔlóng (stay with Yisu villagers) to Bìtǎ Hǎi – Jiǔlóng to Bìtǎ Hǎi has no road at all – and again then bus to Zhōngdiàn. Even some hardy mountain bikers have made the trail, but you can only do it from north to south, elevations being what they are. Eventually public buses will make this run but for now it's true roughing it.

If you plan to continue on foot from Hǔtiào Xiá, prepare before you go. Assume you'll need all provisions and equipment for all extremes of weather. Ask for local advice before setting out.

Getting There & Away Buses run to Zhōngdiàn (Y11) via Qiáotóu daily from the main long-distance bus station in Lìjiāng from 7.30 am. Buses to Dàjù (Y25; five hours) leave at 8.30 am and 1.30 pm; you can easily book these tickets at Dongba

House in Lìjiāng. These buses return to Lìjiāng – although don't count on that second one going – and the trip costs Y30. (Some travellers insist that the Dàjù hotels are in a conspiracy with the bus drivers.) In any event be prepared to get out and push in adverse weather; buses pass through Heīshuǐ, often mentioned by Joseph Rock.

Returning to Lìjiāng from Qiáotóu, buses start running from Zhōngdiàn around 7 am, though 9 am is more like it; just plop yourself on a chair in front of the Backpacker Cafe and stick your arm out. It'll cost you around Y11, though Y15 isn't unheard of and you're in no position to argue. The last one headed toward Lìjiāng should be around 4.30 pm though they say 7 pm. Qiáotóu at times has direct buses to Lìjiāng but these are rare.

Eventually the new road will link Qiáotóu, Walnut Grove and Dàjù, then bend north through Hābā, Báishuǐtái, and eventually Zhōngdiàn. Public transport will likely be available on one or more of these segments by the time you read this.

Lúgū Hú 泸沽湖

This remote lake overlaps the Yúnnán-Sìchuān border and is a centre for several Tibetan, Yi and Mosu (a Naxi subgroup) villages. The Mosu still practise matriarchy, and many of the Naxi customs now lost in Lìjiāng are still in evidence here. The lake itself is fairly high at 2685m and is usually snowbound over the winter months. The best times to visit are April to May and September to October, when the weather is dry and mild. A road was completed in 1999 from here to Nínglàng, the jump-off point. Later, roads will run from here to Dàjù and Hǔtiào Xiá, bending north to Zhōngdiàn. Eventually south-west Sìchuān will be linked too.

Things to See You can visit several islands on the lake via large dugout canoes, which the Mosu call 'pig troughs' (*zhūcáo*). The canoes, which are rowed by Mosu who also serve as guides, generally take you out to **Lǐwùbǐ Dǎo** (Liwubi Island), the lake's largest island. From here you can practically wade across to a spit of land in Sìchuān, or throw a stone, or both. Out to the island and back is around Y15 per person, Y30 if you want to be rowed around the island as well. The canoes can hold around seven people, but the price should be the same regardless of how many of you there are. At those prices you should stretch it into a whole day of picnicking. Canoes leave from near the Mósuōyuàn hotel.

Many travellers are put off by the crowds and crass disregard of minority culture. You could stay with a family on **Lǐgēn Daò** (Ligen Island) on the opposite side of the lake. To get there, don't stop in Luòshuǐ Cūn, but continue toward Yǒngníng, 18km north. Tell the driver to let you off where the road branches; from here it's 2km, though it's tough to find at night. A taxi is really expensive.

In Yǒngníng itself is **Yǒngníng Sì**, a lamasery with at least 20 lamas in residence. There is also a hot spring (wēnquán) up around here; a private bus costs Y15 a head for the half-hour ride and entry is Y1. A bus passes through Luòshuǐ to Yǒngníng for Y5; you could opt to walk the 20km or so through pleasant scenery.

Places to Stay & Eat In Luòshuǐ you can stay in Mosu homes for around Y10 per bed. Most of the homes are equipped to take guests, so you won't be short of options. There are no showers. Food is cooked up for you by the Mosu: little fish, potatoes and barbecued hard-boiled eggs are the order of the day. Average prices are Y5 to Y10, depending on how well you want to eat. The *Móānyuán (Peace Garden)* is good and far away from the clutter for Y15.

There are also three guesthouses in Luòshuǐ, all very similar (triples/quads are Y45/Y40). There is no running water: you can wash up from a cistern in the courtyard. Of the three, the *Mósuōyuán* seems to be the centre of action: occasional Mosu song-and-dance performances are held here, and morning buses to Nínglàng leave from in front of the hotel.

There are also several guesthouses in Yǒngníng. These make good bases from which to hike out to the nearby hot spring. Beds average around Y20.

If you have to stay overnight in Nínglàng, the changeover point between Lìjiāng and Lúgū Hú, probably most convenient is the *Kèyùn Zhāodàisuǒ (Bus Station Guesthouse)*, with singles/doubles/triples for Y40/30/30. More expensive options are found to the right out of the station. Travellers used to frequent the *Zhèngfǔ Zhāodàisuǒ (Government Guesthouse)*, which has dorms beds for Y15 and standard doubles for Y160. The problem here is that the hotel is about 1km from the bus station up a fairly steep hill; transport links are not convenient and there's not much in the way of places to eat nearby.

Getting There & Away From Lìjiāng it's a nine-hour bus trip to Nínglàng – with road construction it should be less by the time you read this. From Nínglàng it's another two hours by bus to Lúgū Hú and minibuses should meet you at the bus station in Nínglàng. If you take the 7.10 am bus from Lìjiāng's north station (Y32 to Y37), you should have no problem hooking up with a minibus immediately. The three-hour ride to Yǒngníng costs Y20. Back to Lìjiāng, buses leave from 7.10 to 11 am.

If you don't get a minibus meeting you in Nínglàng, the town has two bus stations on the main street quite close to one another. Check in both for the next bus to Lúgū. There may also be an English speaker in the Zhèngfǔ Zhāodàisuǒ happy to provide information. Coming back from Lúgū Hú, buses (Y20) to Nínglàng leave in the morning from in front of the Mósuōyuàn hotel or along the main road. The first one usually leaves around 9 am. Going this way you will probably have to overnight in Nínglàng as there is no afternoon connection to Lìjiāng.

Some travellers have tried hiking from Yǒngníng on to Mùlǐ in Sìchuān, from where there is bus transport to Xīchàng on the Kūnmíng-Chéngdū line. But be warned: it's a dangerous route with no accommodation. You'll need to bring a tent, a warm sleeping bag and all your own provisions. There's also no reason to expect the Tibetan tribespeople (all armed) you come across en route to be friendly. One Canadian traveller we met had a frightening experience with locals while hiking this route and headed back to Yǒngníng. (Though another had a challenging but rewarding experience.) Most travellers head back to Lìjiāng the same way they came.

ZHŌNGDIÀN 中甸

☎ 0887

Zhōngdiàn, 198km north-west of Lìjiāng, used to be the last stop in Yúnnán for more hardy travellers looking at a rough five- or six-day journey to Chéngdū via the Tibetan townships and rugged terrain of western Sìchuān. The PSB choked off this route in 1997 and at last check travel had been opened from Sìchuān into Yúnnán, but not the other way around, despite what officials in Kūnmíng or Lìjiāng may tell you.

It is not even the last stop in Yúnnán any more; in 1998 Déqīng, 10 hours by bus to the north-west, was opened.

At 3200m, Zhōngdiàn, a principally Tibetan town with a heavy Han overlay and a sprinkling of Hui (Muslim), Bai and Naxi, is definitely worth a look. One thing you'll notice is that Zhōngdiàn has become perhaps the supreme example of a Chinese construction zone. By the time you read this, there should be all kinds of new stuff around. Not to worry – Zhōngdiàn still had an interesting old section.

In mid-June Zhōngdiàn plays host to a horse racing festival that sees several days of dancing, singing, eating and, of course, horse racing. Another new festival – usually in September – features minority artists of south-west China. Accommodation can be a bit tight around these times, so you may want to arrive a day or two early in order to secure a room.

Dangers & Annoyances

Be careful in Zhōngdiàn's bus station, particularly on the early morning Lìjiāng buses; there's been a spell of push-and-slash bandit bands.

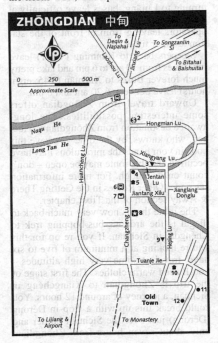

ZHŌNGDIÀN 中甸

To Deqin & Napahai
To Songzanlin Si
To Bitahai & Baishuitai
Lacohou Lu
Jinxiang Lu
0   250   500 m
Approximate Scale
Naqu He
Hongmian Lu
Long Tan He
Huancheng Lu
Xiangyang Lu
Jentan Lu
Jiantang Xilu
Jianglang Donglu
Changzheng Lu
Heping Lu
Tuanje Jie
Old Town
To Lijiang & Airport
To Monastery

ZHŌNGDIÀN

1 Long-Distance Bus Station
   汽车站
2 Bank of China
   中国人民银行
3 Tibetan Art Cafe & Coffee Shop
   金丝咖啡室
4 CITS
   中国国际旅行社
5 Dìqìng Bīnguǎn
   迪庆宾馆
6 Central Long-Distance Bus Station
   汽车总站
7 Post Office
   邮局
8 PSB
   公安局
9 AAA Cafe
10 Tibet Hotel
    永生旅馆
11 Zànggōng Táng
    藏公堂
12 Zhōngdiànshān Gōngyuán
    中甸山公园

Things to See

About an hour's walk north of town is Sōngzànlín Sì, a 300-year-old Tibetan monastery complex with several hundred monks. It sits upon a hill surrounded by mountains, and is without question worth the trip to Zhōngdiàn. Entrance is Y10. Bus No 3 runs there from anywhere along Changzheng Lu (Y1).

Much closer to the centre of things, over-looking the old town district, is another monastery with exceedingly friendly monks.

Close to the Tibet Hotel are Zhōng-diànshān Gōngyuán (Y3), a park that has nice views, and Zànggōng Táng (Y5), a memorial hall to the Red Army's Long March.

Places to Stay & Eat

There has always been the cheery and help-ful *Tibet Hotel (Yǒngshēng Fàndiàn; ☎ 822 3263)*, a clean and friendly spot. Despite big renovations, it's remained backpacker friendly. Dorm beds here cost Y17, and there are doubles for Y50; all come with satellite television and electric blankets. More upmarket Y180 doubles are usually booked out by tour groups. Twenty-four hour hot water is a godsend in January. The hotel also has money exchange, interna-tional calls and a laundry service, all of which are available on a hit-or-miss basis. Getting there is easy: exit the bus station to the right. Keep going all the way until the first major intersection. Turn left and keep walking two giant blocks.

The *Díqìng Bīnguǎn (☎ 822 7599)* is ap-proximately opposite the bus station, set back a bit, and looks pretty opulent to be of-fering dorm rooms. Don't get excited, as the rooms are in a dilapidated wing out back. Beds range from Y20 in a dorm to Y250 for standard doubles. Lots of more expensive hotels can be found on this road.

One giant block from the bus station in the direction of the Tibet Hotel is the *AAA Café* – the owner's the original cafe owner in Zhōngdiàn. Ten minutes to the left of the AAA Cafe is the *Tibetan Art Cafe and Cof-fee Shop*, run by a Tibetan woman who speaks good English. There are also a few

Tibetan and Naxi restaurants south of the bus station.

The brother owners of the MCA Guest-house in Dàlǐ and Dongba House in Lìjiāng were planning to open the *Tibet* Café some-where in the vicinity of the Tibet Hotel, fol-lowed up perhaps by a guesthouse in the future.

Getting There & Away

On the day we visited, Zhōngdiàn cut the ribbon on a new airport, unofficially dubbed 'Shangri-La Airport', making use of the catchy provincial tourism nickname for the Zhōngdiàn and Díqìng regions. Cur-rently flights leave Kūnmíng Tuesday, Thursday and Saturday for Y560; these will likely become more frequent.

Buses to Zhōngdiàn (Y21 to Y29; five hours) depart each of Lìjiāng's bus stations regularly from 7.30 am to 1.30 pm. Buses to Zhōngdiàn pass through Qiáotóu, at the southern end of the Hǔtiào Xiá trek. Re-turning to Lìjiāng, buses leave officially at 7 am and 1.30 pm but there are independent operators leaving from in front of the sta-tion at other times.

Sleepers back to Kūnmíng (Y141) leave four times from 10 am to 6 pm and take pretty much forever Buses to Xiàguān (Y45; eight hours) leave between 6.20 am and 8 pm.

Onward travel from Zhōngdiàn offers some interesting possibilities. The long-awaited destination from Zhōngdiàn is Tibet and, who knows, by the time you have this book in your hands the miraculous may have occurred and this route may be open – don't count on it, though. For more information see under Other Routes in the Getting There & Away section of the Tibet chapter.

The route that is now very much back to illegal is the arduous bus-hopping trek to Chéngdū, in Sìchuān. If you're up for this you're looking at a minimum of five to six days' travel at some very high altitudes – you'll need warm clothes. The first stage of the trip is Zhōngdiàn to Xiāngchéng in Sìchuān, a journey of around 12 hours. You could break this up with a stop in Déróng (Dêrong) just over the Sìchuān border and only about seven hours from Zhōngdiàn.

From Xiāngchéng, head to Lǐtáng (10 hours); however, if roads are bad you may be forced to stay overnight in Dàochéng. From Lǐtáng it's 12 hours to Kāngdìng and another 12 hours on to Chéngdū. Accommodation on the way is rough and your fellow passengers are likely to be chain-smoking phlegm removalists whose idea of fun is leaving the windows open and letting the sub-zero mountain breezes ruffle their hair. Have fun!

Warning The route to Lǐtáng via Xiāngchéng was definitely closed at the time of writing. Despite Chéngdū PSB's insistence that Xiāngchéng was open – and the fact that travellers were not being hassled – the Zhōngdiàn bus station was denying tickets to foreigners. For the record, the Zhōngdiàn bus station has a bus leaving at 7.30 am daily for Xiāngchéng; the rattletrap trip costs Y45.

One way to thumb your nose at the PSB would be to try and get a ticket to Déróng, just over the border with Yúnnán, which has a bus departing to it every other day at 8 am. Otherwise, many people have arrived, discovered the route closed, and been stuck since they've already seen Dàlǐ, Lìjiāng, and Kūnmíng.

Your best bet from Zhōngdiàn then would be to take the 10.30 am sleeper bus (Y98) directly to Jīnjiāng in Sìchuān, via Lìjiāng; it takes 15 to 16 hours and if you miss the last train some nice bus drivers may let you sleep on the bus.

AROUND ZHŌNGDIÀN

Approximately 10km south-east of Zhōngdiàn is the **Tiānshēng Qiáo** (Tiansheng Bridge), a natural limestone formation, and farther south-east, a subterranean **hot spring**. If you can arrange transport, nearby is the **Dàbǎo Sì** (Great Treasure Temple), one of the earliest Buddhist temples in Yúnnán.

Nàpà Hǎi 纳帕海

North-west of Zhōngdiàn some 10km is this lake – part of a nature reserve – surrounded by a large grass meadow. Budding ornithologists will love the myriad rare species, including the black-necked crane.

Báishuǐtái & Bìtǎ Hǎi 白水台与碧塔海

Báishuǐtái is a limestone deposit plateau 108km to the south-east of Zhōngdiàn with some breathtaking scenery and Tibetan villages en route. The terraces are resplendent in sunlight, but can be tough to access if rainfall has made trails slippery.

On the way, some 25km east of Zhōngdiàn, the bus can drop you along the highway for Bìtǎ Hǎi (Emerald Pagoda Lake), 8km down a trail; it's famous for its white-lipped deer. Admission is Y20 and basic cabins cost Y15 to Y30. Lots of hiking options on foot or ponies can be arranged at the lake. Leaving Bìtǎ Hǎi you can wait (sometimes forever) for a bus; or, hike to the road by 9.30 am and wait for taxis dropping off tourists – these guys need fares back to Zhōngdiàn so bargain hard.

A couple of guesthouses at Báishuǐtái have rooms with beds from Y10 to Y15.

A bus for Báishuǐtái leaves Zhōngdiàn daily in summer at 8.30 am, every other day in winter; it costs Y20 from the bus station, Y30 if you get on along the way.

One intriguing idea floated by locals is to trek all the way from Bìtǎ Hǎi or Báishuǐtái to Hǔtiào Xiá on foot, three-wheeled tractor, or even pony (one guy used a mountain bike). The Tibet Hotel can't help with details but it should know someone who can. See the Hǔtiào Xiá section for information.

DÉQĪN 德钦

Some 168km north-west of Zhōngdiàn is the new (opened in 1998) last outpost of Yúnnán on the way to Tibet – Déqīn (Dêqên), seat of the northern-most county in Yúnnán. (Both are subsumed by Díqìng Zàng Autonomous Prefecture.) The county has an average elevation of 3550m and is 80% Tibetan, though a dozen other minorities are found here, including one of the few settlements of non-Hui Muslims in China. For borderholics, east is Sìchuān, west Tibet, and Myanmar lies south-west. Chinese authorities have christened Déqīn 'Shangri La' and claim James Hilton's classic *Lost Horizon* used the area for inspiration; they've decided to pump millions of yuan into tourism in coming years.

Getting here is possible on a bus but you're crossing some serious ranges along this route and at any time from mid-October to late spring heavy snows can close the road. The mountain town is inaccessible from Zhōngdiàn at these times. Pack sensibly if you go.

Tibet beckons, to be sure. Be warned that even if you find a jeep driver to sneak you into Tibet, more than a few travellers have paid half of the fare only to have the driver disappear.

Places to Stay & Eat
Any place in Déqīn will let you stay (there are a half dozen); none is a particular treat. From the bus station exit left; the place at the end is the *Déxīn Lǚshè*. It's got newer looking interiors and, they claim, reliable hot water (though we had none). Five-person rooms are Y150, doubles/triples are Y120.

The *Shěngzhèngfǔ Zhaōdàisuǒ (Deqin Government Guesthouse)* has beds from Y20, no hot water, but amazingly clean bathrooms. If you need creature comforts, down by the river a new three-star monster *hotel* has rooms for around Y220.

Not much is here for foodies. The *Shuǐyuán Cāntīng (Tax Office Restaurant)* has decent food, including a good local noodle soup. Look for a billiard table; the entrance has a colourful canopy.

Getting There & Away
Buses leave Zhōngdiàn for Déqīn (Y28) at 6.50 and 8 am. Any bus south will pass through Zhōngdiàn; buses start at 6 am.

AROUND DÉQĪN
Approximately 10km north-west of Déqīn is Feīláí Sì, actually the remnants of a temple and not much to look at. They also charge Y15 admission. You'll need to hire a taxi (Y30).

On the road back to Zhōngdiàn, you bypass Baímángxuě Shān (Vast White Snow Mountains), a mountain nature reserve and

another sacred mountain range. Approximately halfway to Zhōngdiàn is Bēnzílán, the only settlement between the two towns and where you'll eat lunch. North of here is the fantastic Dōngzhúlín Sì – one of the most impressive temples in Yúnnán – set down in a valley off the road.

Meílǐxuě Shān 梅里雪山
Straddling the Yúnnán-Tibet border Meílǐxuě Shān is Yúnnán's highest and most magnificent peak. The Mekong River runs along the eastern base, eventually linking up with the Cháng Jiāng in a remarkable narrow valley after a drop of 4000m.

The summit is sacred Kagbo Peak, also called 'Virgin Peak'. At 6740m it is Yúnnán's highest and most challenging climb – it still hasn't been scaled and has cost dozens of lives. For millennia it's been a pilgrimage site, but today's travellers come to visit the temples, waterfalls and glaciers.

Minyang Glacier is one of the lowest glaciers in China and affects the local climate enough that the fog it creates permeates homes in surrounding villages.

You can get a glimpse of Meílǐxuě Shān – weather permitting – just outside of Déqīn on the road to Zhōngdiàn; just look for the white stupa and prayer flags. September proffers the best views. To actually get to the glacier you'll need to charter a vehicle – the cheapest is around Y350 for a five-person van. It takes two hours to get to the nearest village, then two hours up; horses are a good idea but cost around Y80 up and down. You may have to overnight with villagers.

Xīshuāngbǎnnà Region 西双版纳

The region of Xīshuāngbǎnnà (usually called Bǎnnà) is in the deep south of Yúnnán, next to the Myanmar and Lao borders. The name is a Chinese approximation of the original Thai name, *Sip Sawng Panna* (12 Rice-Growing Districts). The place has a laid-back South-East Asian feel and it's easy to watch the weeks slip by as you make your way around small villages, tropical forests and the occasional stupa.

In recent years Xīshuāngbǎnnà has become China's own mini-Thailand, and tourists have been heading down in droves for the sunshine, Dai minority dancing, water-splashing festivals (held daily nowadays), as well as the ubiquitous tour group lures, such as the Dúshù Chénglín (Forest of one Tree), the King of Tea Trees and other trees with names suggesting something less prosaic than a mere tree. But it's easy to get away from the crowds and explore the surrounding countryside and villages.

Xīshuāngbǎnnà Dai Autonomous Prefecture, as it is known officially, is subdivided into the three counties of Jǐnghóng, Měnghǎi and Měnglà.

The region has wet and dry seasons. The wet season is between June and August, when it rains ferociously almost every day. From September to February there is less rainfall, but thick fog descends during the late evening and doesn't lift until 10 am or even later at the height of winter. Between May and August there are frequent and spectacular thunderstorms.

Between November and March temperatures average about 19°C (66.2°F). The hottest months of the year are from April to September, when you can expect an average of 25°C (77°F).

Like Hǎinán Dǎo, Xīshuāngbǎnnà is home to many unique species of plant and animal life. Unfortunately, recent scientific studies have demonstrated the devastating effect of previous government policies on land use; the tropical rainforest areas of Hǎinán and Xīshuāngbǎnnà are now as acutely endangered as similar rainforest areas elsewhere on the planet. Studies have indicated that since 1960 the average temperature of Xīshuāngbǎnnà has risen 1°C, and rainfall has dropped off 10% to 20%.

The jungle areas that remain still contain dwindling numbers of wild tigers, leopards,

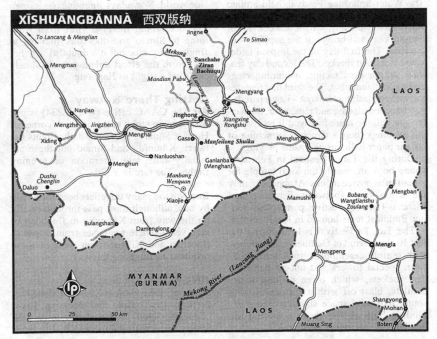

XĪSHUĀNGBǍNNÀ 西双版纳

elephants and golden-haired monkeys, although sadly the only elephants you're likely to see are the ones chained by the foot to the trees under the tourist lodges built into the triple (now double) thick canopies (see Sānchàhé Zìrán Bǎohùqù later). To be fair, the number of elephants has doubled to 250, up 100% from the early 1980s; the government now offers compensation to villagers whose crops are destroyed by elephants, or who assist in wildlife conservation. In 1998 the government banned hunting or processing of animals in toto, though poaching is notoriously difficult to control.

About one-third of the 800,000-strong population of this region are Dai; another third or so are Han Chinese and the rest is made up of minorities which include the Miao, Zhuang, Yao and lesser-known hill tribes such as the Aini, Jinuo, Bulang, Lahu and Wa.

SPECIAL EVENTS

The Water-Splashing Festival, held around mid-April (usually from the 13th to the 15th) washes away the dirt, sorrow and demons of the old year and brings in the happiness of the new. The first day of the festival is devoted to a giant market. The second day features dragon-boat racing, swimming races and rocket launching. The third day features the water-splashing freakout – be prepared to get drenched all day, and remember, the wetter you get, the more luck you'll receive. In the evenings there's dancing, launching of hot-air paper balloons and game playing.

During the Tanpa Festival in February, young boys are sent to the local temple for initiation as novice monks. At approximately the same time (between February and March), Tan Jing Festival participants honour Buddhist texts housed in local temples.

The Tan Ta Festival is held during the last 10-day period of October or November, with temple ceremonies, rocket launches from special towers and hot-air balloons. The rockets, which often contain lucky amulets, blast off with a curious droning sound like mini-space shuttles before exploding high above; those who find the amulets are assured of good luck.

The farming season (from July to October) is the time for the Closed-Door Festival, when marriages or festivals are banned. Traditionally, this is also the time of year that men aged 20 or older ordain as monks for a period of time. The season ends with the Open-Door Festival, when everyone lets their hair down again to celebrate the harvest.

During festivals, booking same-day airline tickets to Jǐnghóng can be extremely difficult – even with 17 flights a day! You can try getting a flight into Sīmáo, 162km to the north, or take the bus. Hotels in Jǐnghóng town are booked solid, but you could stay in a nearby Dai village and commute. Festivities take place all over Xīshuāngbǎnnà, so you might be lucky further away from Jǐnghóng.

SĪMÁO 思茅

☎ 0879

Sīmáo, an uninteresting little town, used to be Xīshuāngbǎnnà's air link with the outside world. Nowadays Jǐnghóng has its own airport and very few travellers stop here. The occasional traveller flies from Kūnmíng to Sīmáo and does the final leg to Jǐnghóng by bus, but it's doubtful whether it's worth the effort unless you absolutely can't get a flight to Jǐnghóng.

Getting There & Away

Air The CAAC office (☎ 223 234) is just off the main street at the northern corner of Hongqi Square. There are daily flights between Kūnmíng and Sīmáo but these are usually late, late afternoon or evening flights. The fare is Y320.

Bus Not too many travellers head for Sīmáo by bus, although most pass through briefly on the way from Kūnmíng to Jǐnghóng or vice versa. There are buses from Sīmáo to Bǎoshān and Xiàguān, but most of these originate in Jǐnghóng anyway.

JǏNGHÓNG 景洪

Jǐnghóng, the capital of Xīshuāngbǎnnà Prefecture, lies beside the Mekong River (Láncāng Jiāng). It's a sleepy town with streets lined with palms, which help mask the Chinese-built concrete boxes until they merge with the stilt-houses in the surrounding villages. It's more a base for operations than a place to hang out, although it's not without a certain laid-back charm that somehow endures despite the tourists. Given its slow but steady sprawling growth, eventually it will be as neon-laden as any other Chinese regional big town; the karaoke shriekers have taken over a few tourist streets, and the discos can't be far behind.

Information

Money The Bank of China is on Jinghong Nanlu, next door to the Banna Mansion Hotel. It's open Monday to Friday from 8 to 11.30 am and from 3 to 6 pm. The China Agricultural Bank is east of the PSB and also takes care of travellers cheques and credit card advances during similar working hours.

Post & Communications The post office is in the centre of town at the intersection of Jǐnghóng west and south roads (Xilu and Nanlu). You can also direct dial from most of the hotels, but as usual their rates are noticeably higher. Postal service is available from 8 am to 8.30 pm, with telecommunication services slightly longer.

Email & Internet Access Along Manting Lu is E-Scape Cafe, which charges Y18 per hour.

Travel Agencies CITS (☎ 213 3271/0460) has an office across from the entrance to the Xīshuāngbǎnnà Bīnguǎn. The staff are friendly, and can provide information on several one-day tours from Y50 to Y100 per person that generally take in one to two towns and sights en route.

PSB The PSB is opposite Kǒngquèhú Gōngyuán in the centre of town. Staff there are polite enough; visa extensions are fairly straightforward. The office is open from 8 to 11.30 am and from 2 pm to 5.30 pm.

Dangers & Annoyances There have been two reports (unconfirmed) from travellers regarding drug-and-robbings (one successful, one not) on the Kūnmíng-Jǐnghóng bus trip. If true, it marks the first time it's appeared in Yúnnán. Like other countries in South-East Asia, be careful who your friends are on buses, accept nothing, and leave nothing unattended when you hop off on breaks.

Chūnhuān Gōngyuán
Auspicious Spring Park
Chūnhuān Gōngyuán, in the south of Jǐnghóng, is not particularly inspiring. The park has a couple of replica stupas, Dai dancing girls (you'll probably get to see a water-splashing festival now held daily by popular demand) and a pitiful elephant in chains. All this for just Y12. Just before you get to the park entrance is the **Màntíng Fósì** (Manting Buddhist Temple). It's claimed to date back 1100 years.

Rèdài Zuòwù Yánjiùsuǒ
热带作物研究所
Tropical Plant Research Institute
Rèdài Zuòwù Yánjiùsuǒ, west of the town centre, is one of Jǐnghóng's better attractions. A modest entry fee of Y5 gets you into the institute's inner sanctum, where you can view over 1000 different types of plant life. Unless you're a botanist, telling them all apart could be tricky – the only English is scientific. Still, it's easy to get a feel for the impressive variety of plants that make up Yúnnán's tropical forests, and the grounds make for a pleasant stroll. The Y5 admission also gets you into the **Zhou Enlai Memorial** (Zhōu Sīlái Zǒnglǐ Jìniànbēi) a 2001-like sculpture commemorating a 1961 visit by China's best loved premier. (It sounds better than it is.) There may or may not be a shop selling agricultural products grown on the premises, including tea, Chinese medicine and ground coffee – it was closed up and contained few items on last check.

A little way back towards town and on the opposite side of the road is the **Yàoyùng Zhíwùyuán** (Medicinal Botanical Gardens). Staff at the gate might try to deter you from entering by telling you it's boring. It's not a trick to keep you out – they're telling the truth. Entry is Y4, and a stroll around the gardens could kill half an hour.

Kǒngquèhú Gōngyuán 孔雀湖公园
Peacock Lake Park

This artificial lake in the centre of town isn't much, but the small park next to it is pleasant. There's also a zoo, but it's not for the squeamish. The English Language Corner takes place here every Sunday evening, so this is your chance to exchange views or practise your English with the locals.

Mínzú Fēngqíng Gōngyuán
民族风情公园
National Minorities Park

If you come in to Jǐnghóng by plane, you'll pass the Mínzú Fēngqíng Gōngyuán on the way into town. It's not that far south of the CAAC booking office. On some maps of Jǐnghóng it's mysteriously referred to as the 'Minority Flirtation Expression'. Intrigued? If so, head down on Friday or Saturday when, from 8 to 10 pm, there are minority dances, crocodile shows and so on. Entry is Y20.

Láncāng Qiáo 大桥
Mekong Bridge

The original bridge is no technical wonder, and the views of the river from it are not even that good, but it's there and it is a bridge over the Mekong after all. If rumour is correct, there was an attempt some years ago by a member of a disaffected minority to blow up the bridge. Jǐnghóng is such a splendidly torpid town, it's hard to imagine the excitement. The hills above the town on the other side make for some pleasant walks.

South of here toward Gǎnlǎnbà one can't help but notice the new massive bridge being built as part of a major new highway to Laos via Jǐnghóng and Měnglà. It should be finished by the time you read this, and allow for alternate bicycle routes into the villages around Jǐnghóng.

Places to Stay

Jǐnghóng does not lack hotel space, although most places have little to set them apart from their rivals. Former Chinese-only hotels are wavering; give them all a shot.

The *Xīshuāngbǎnnà Bīnguǎn* (☎ 212 3679/3559, fax 212 6501, 11 Ganlan Lu),

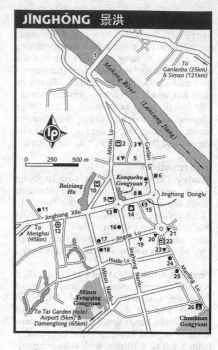

also known as the Bǎnnà Bīnguǎn, is in the centre of town. It used to be one of those exceedingly rare Chinese hotels that travellers reminisced about after they had left. It's not quite that idyllic any more, but it's still generally solid. The staff are usually very attentive and friendly, even to the cheapskate travellers. It's also got 24-hour hot water. Doubles with balcony, bathroom and TV in building Nos 6 and 7 are not a bad deal at Y80; similar triples are Y90. Doubles and triples in the Bamboo House are more worn, but cost the same. After that it's Y150 to Y300 for standard doubles in the Riverview Buildings which already seem to be falling apart. If you get a dorm room on the ground floor you may want to leave any valuables with the front desk, as some travellers have had possessions stolen here.

If you're in the market for basic accommodation with a Dai flavour, head down to Manting Lu. It's a long walk from the bus station (around 25 minutes), in the south of town.

JĬNGHÓNG

PLACES TO STAY

6 Xīshuāngbǎnnà Bīnguǎn
版纳宾馆

8 Jǐngyǒng Fàndiàn
景咏宾馆

13 Banna Mansion Hotel;
Bank of China; Mengyuan
Travel Service
版纳大厦；中国银行

24 Dǎijiā Huāyuán Xiǎolóu
傣家花苑小楼

25 Dǎizhaōdaìsuǒ
傣招待所

PLACES TO EAT

3 Xīnngǔang Jiǔjiā
星光酒家

4 Myanmar Cold
Drinks Shop
缅甸风味冷饮店

19 Yǎhú Píjiǔdiàn
雅壶啤酒店

20 Mei Mei Cafe
美美咖啡厅

21 Forest Cafe
森林咖啡厅

23 Wǎnlì Dǎiwèilóu Cāntīng
婉丽傣味楼

OTHER

1 Láncāng Qiáo
澜沧桥

2 Long-Distance Bus Station
长途汽车站

5 Market
市场

7 CITS
中国国际旅行社

9 Post Office
邮电大楼

10 No 2 Bus Station
第二客运站

11 Rèdài Zhíwùyuán
热带植物园

12 Yàoyùng Zhíwùyuán
药用植物园

14 PSB
公安局

15 China Agricultural Bank
中国农业银行

16 Workers' Cultural Palace
工人文化宫

17 DDDisco
迪士高广场

18 CAAC
民航售票处

22 E-Scape Cafe

26 Mántíng Fósì
曼听佛寺

At the far end of this road, top pick is the **Dǎijiā Huāyuán Xiǎolóu** (*Dai Building Hotel*) – one of the first signs you see upon entering the courtyard is 'Cold Beer'. All accommodation is in separate bamboo bungalows on stilts. Clean beds cost Y25 in doubles/triples. The bathrooms are extremely clean and a new solar-heated hot shower has been installed. The owner, John, speaks good English as he was once an assistant manager of a Holiday Inn in Běijīng. When he came to Jǐnghóng to open this hotel, he contracted only Dai designers and workers.

Another place on the opposite side of the street bills itself as Dai's Bamboo House. Don't believe it – they don't take foreigners. The **Wǎnlì Dǎiwèilóu Cāntīng** (*Wǎnlì Dai Restaurant*) also says guesthouse on the sign but that's a remnant of the old days. Now run by the owner of James' Cafe, it may or may not reopen its rooms.

For the cheapest lodging on Manting Lu, just south of Dǎijiā Huāyuán Xiǎolóu is the decidedly non-Dai style but cheery **Dǎizhaōdaìsuǒ** (*Dai Guesthouse*; ☎ 212 8151). A hard bed in a spartan triple costs Y10. The toilets are passable, but make sure you wear shower sandals. The shower has very passive solar-heated water.

Manting Lu has some formerly Chinese-only places which will accept foreigners, so you may wish to shop around.

A more centrally located place with dormitory accommodation is the **Jǐngyǒng Fàndiàn** (*12 Jinghong Donglu*). It's Y40 for a bed in a triple. Clean doubles with fan and attached bath are available for Y80. If it's air-conditioning you're after, it will cost you Y190 for a double. This hotel is one of the few in China which freely mixes Chinese and foreigners in dorm rooms.

Finally, right in the heart of town, the **Banna Mansion Hotel** (*Bǎnnà Dàshà;* ☎ 212 2049, fax 212 7021) is Jǐnghóng's original luxury option – there are literally dozens now – with air-con doubles for Y238, and triples for Y316. Probably the top option is the **Tai Garden Hotel** (*Tǎiyuán Jiǔdiàn;* ☎ 212 3888, fax 212 6060) south of town toward the airport. On quiet grounds replete with its own island on a pond, it has singles/doubles for US$70/80 and a full list of amenities. Non-guests can use exercise facilities.

Places to Eat

As with accommodation, Manting Lu is the place for Dai-style food. The road is lined

The Dai

The Dai people are concentrated in this pocket of Yúnnán and exercise a clear upper hand in the economy of Xīshuāngbǎnnà. During the Cultural Revolution many Dai people simply voted with their feet and slipped across the border to join their fellow Dai who are sprinkled throughout Thailand, Laos, Myanmar and Vietnam. Not only the Dai but also most of the other minorities in these areas display a nonchalant disregard for borders and authority in general.

The Dai are Buddhists who were driven southwards by the Mongol invasion of the 13th century. The Dai state of Xīshuāngbǎnnà was annexed by the Mongols and then by the Chinese, and a Chinese governor was installed in the regional capital of Jinglan (present-day Jǐnghóng). Countless Buddhist temples were built in the early days of the Dai state and now lie in the jungles in ruins. During the Cultural Revolution, Xīshuāngbǎnnà's temples were desecrated and destroyed. Some were saved by serving as granaries, but many are now being rebuilt from scratch. Temples are also recovering their role, with or without official blessing, as village schools where young children are accepted for religious training as monks.

To keep themselves off the damp earth in the tropical rainforest weather, the Dai live in spacious wooden houses raised on stilts in the classic style, with the pigs and chickens below. The common dress for Dai women is a straw hat or towel-wrap headdress; a tight, short blouse in a bright colour; and a printed sarong with a belt of silver links. Some Dai men tattoo their bodies with animal designs. Betel-nut chewing is popular and many Dai youngsters get their teeth capped with gold; otherwise they are considered ugly.

Ethno-linguistically, the Dai are part of the very large Thai family that includes the Siamese, Lao, Shan, Thai Dam and Ahom peoples found scattered throughout the river valleys of Thailand, Myanmar, Laos, northern Vietnam and Assam. The Xīshuāngbǎnnà Dai are broken into four subgroups, the Shui Dai, Han Dai, Huayai Dai and Kemu Dai, each distinguished by variations in costume. All speak the Dai language, which is quite similar to Lao and northern Thai dialects. In fact, Thai is often as useful as Chinese once you get off the beaten track, and those with a firm linguistic background might have fun with a Thai phrasebook. The written language of the Dais employs a script which looks like a cross between Lao and Burmese.

Around Dai temples, the same rules apply as elsewhere: dress appropriately (no tank tops or shorts); take off shoes; don't take photos of monks or interior shots without permission; leave a donation if you take any photos and consider a token donation even if you don't since, unlike Thailand, these Buddhists receive no government assistance. Like Thailand it is polite to *wai* the monks and remember never to touch anyone's head, raise yourself higher than a Buddha figure, or point your feet at anyone.

In the temple courtyard, look for a cement structure looking like a letterbox; this is an altar to local spirits, a combination of Buddhism and indigenous spirit worship. Some 32 separate spirits exist for humans.

Zhang khap is the name of solo narrative opera, for which the Dai have a long tradition. Singers are trained from childhood to perform long songs accompanied by native flute or *erhu*, usually at all-night parties. Performances are given at monk initiations, when new houses are built, at weddings, and on the birthdays of important people. Westerners generally find it monotonous and even if you do understand Dai, the lyrics are complex if not fully improvised in a polite language. At the end, the audience shouts *Shuay! Shuay!* which is close to 'Hip, hip, hooray!' Even courtship is done via this singing.

Some Dai Phrases

Hello.	*doūzaŏ lī*
Thank you	*yíndii*
Goodbye	*goīhán*

YÚNNÁN 云南

with *restaurants*, most of which are pretty similar. One drawback (or bonus, depending on how you view it) is that the majority of these restaurants dish up Dai dance performances along with their culinary specialities. This explains why the words 'singing and dancing hall' are tacked on to a lot of restaurant names. These places have bored-looking Dai women thumping drums at the entrance and are filled nearly every night with tourists whooping it up, hollering, playing drinking games and generally being festive. Once is worth a try.

In these places, try the roast fish, eel or beef cooked with lemon grass or served with peanut-and-tomato sauce. Vegetarians can order roast bamboo shoot prepared in the same fashion. Other mouth-watering specialities include fried river moss (sounds rather unappetising but is excellent with beer) and spicy bamboo-shoot soup. Don't forget to try the black glutinous rice.

The original – at least the first to have an English menu – was *Wǎnlì Dǎiwèilóu Cāntīng* along Manting Lu, which closed briefly in 1997 but reopened in 1998. It sports the same menu as James' Cafe, as it should since James now owns it. (There's not that much Dai fare on the menu.) Manting Lu has many other Dai restaurants.

If you want Dai food in an unpretentious atmosphere, north of the market area on Ganlan Lu is the *Xīngūang Jiǔjiā*, run by one of Xīshuāngbǎnnà's best-known traditional singers (you may see her out front roasting animals). The place is packed at lunch.

Elsewhere around town is pretty much standard Chinese fare. Walk up from Manting Lu and turn left in the direction of the CAAC booking office and you will find a host of tiny *Chinese restaurants*; most of them are pretty good for lunch. Next to the bus station there are also some good restaurants – look out for the place specialising in dumplings.

Street markets sell coconuts, bananas, papayas, pomelos (a type of grapefruit) and pineapples. The pineapples, served peeled on a stick, are probably the best in China. The market north of the Bǎnnà Bīnguǎn has the *Myanmar Cold Drinks Shop* (*Miǎndiàn Fēngweì Lěngyǐndiàn*), with great milk tea and simple fried rice dishes.

Manting Lu and environs has western-style cafes which come and go. For good food, strong coffee, really cold beer and (you guessed it) banana pancakes, stop by the *Mei Mei Cafe* (*Měiměi Kafeītīng*) on Manting Lu, a pleasant little Akha hole in the wall just down from the intersection with Jingde Lu. You'll be greeted with a smile, and usually find fellow travellers with whom to swap tall tales. Mei Mei was the first cafe to cater to foreigners and is still the most popular. Azhu, the owner, and her staff are delightful and great fun to while away an evening with. You can also get your laundry done and this is the spot to rent a bicycle.

Another one definitely meriting your attention is the *Forest Cafe* (*Sēnlín Kafeītīng*) with food equal to the Mei Mei Cafe. The Forest Cafe has unquestionably the greatest hamburger found in China, along with home-baked speciality breads, good juices, the hippest music, and more books than anywhere else. They have bicycles for rent here.

Note that both the Mei Mei Cafe and Forest Cafe had been notified by the city planners that they may be moved to facilitate massive new road construction which may level entire blocks of downtown.

Around the corner in the other direction and up a block is the open air *Yǎhú Píjiǔdiàn* (*Yahu Beer Hall*), which brews

The Hani (Akha) People

The Hani (also known in adjacent countries as the Akha) are of Tibetan origin, but according to folklore they are descended from frogs' eyes. They stick to the hills, cultivating rice, corn and the occasional poppy. At weekly markets the Dai obviously dominate the Hani, who seem only too keen to scamper back to their mountain retreats.

Hani women wear headdresses of beads, feathers, coins and silver rings. Some of the coins include French (Vietnamese), Burmese and Indian coins from the turn of the century.

its own. You can get a pitcher for around Y38. It's also a restaurant specialising in mediocre hotpot.

The Tai Garden Hotel has a decent breakfast buffet for Y25, with OK coffee.

Entertainment

On Jingde Lu near CAAC is the *DDDisco*. The somewhat dated music is at least loud, the floor shows aren't silly, and the beer's reasonably priced. Admission is Y15.

Getting There & Away

Air More flights and bigger planes (737s) mean that it's a lot easier to fly to Jǐnghóng from Kūnmíng than it used to be. It's usually even possible to book the day before if not same day. If one travel agent in Kūnmíng says the flights are all full, check with another place: travel agencies tend to snap up large blocks of seats ahead of time, and often fail to fill them all. In April (Water-Splashing Festival), however, you may need to allow for several days' advance booking, as this is a very popular time for tourists to visit. And always be careful if you want to change your flight date on or around a weekend. There are normally several flights daily to Jǐnghóng; at peak seasons up to 17 per day. The flight takes 50 minutes and the one-way fare is Y520. Flights also go directly to Lìjiāng and Dàlǐ each a few times a day. A Wednesday flight to Bangkok stops in Jǐnghóng and there are rumours another to Chiang Rai (Thailand) will start. Shanghai Airlines has a flight from Shànghǎi, with a stop in Kūnmíng. Eventually, flights to Myanmar and Laos will begin. Flights can be booked at the CAAC booking office (☎ 212 4774) in Jǐnghóng. It's open from 8 to 11.30 am and from 3 to 5 pm.

Bus There are daily buses from Kūnmíng to Jǐnghóng (see the Kūnmíng Getting There & Away section for details).

Buses back to Kūnmíng are available from the long-distance bus station, and the No 2 bus station. From the main bus station, sleepers leave each day from 6.30 am to 6 pm and cost Y137. Sleepers depart the No 2

bus station hourly from 7 am to 6.30 pm for similar prices. Private companies may offer more options with more creature comforts.

If you're torn between the bus and the plane, don't worry about missing the scenery on the flight. There are some good views from the bus window, but nothing that won't stop you nodding off to sleep and certainly nothing much that will make you sit up and decide that the 24 hours of inhaling second-hand smoke and bouncing up and down in lieu of sleep were worth it.

The Jǐnghóng long-distance bus station also has buses running epic journeys to Xiàguān, Bǎoshān and Ruìlì. The PSB has decided to stop discouraging travellers from making this arduous journey (though they may still think you're crazy to do so, since foreigners *must* have enough money to fly). The trips to Xiàguān and Bǎoshān shouldn't require any overnight stays if on a sleeper, but don't count on it. If so, the bus to Xiàguān will overnight in Zhenyuan, while en route to Bǎoshān the town of Líncāng plays midway host to frazzled passengers. Sleepers to Xiàguān (Y152; 28 to 36 hours) leave the long-distance station at 6.20 and 7.30 am and from the No 2 bus station at 12.30 pm; ordinary buses – if any are still running – cost Y80. Buses to Bǎoshān cost about the same but take 36 hours – and these routes are served by minibuses at times!

Going to Ruìlì, bus station staff will sell you a ticket to Bǎoshān, expecting any sane person to break up the trip there.

Roads are quite poor on these routes, and the buses, even the new sleepers, not much better. If you choose this option, don't do it to save time – many travellers have found their two-day trip stretch to three and even four days due to landslides, floods and bus breakdowns. At least this is where the scenery can be gorgeous.

The Jǐnghóng long-distance bus station has buses running to towns around Xīshuāngbǎnnà, but it is mainly useful for more distant destinations. The best place to get out of Jǐnghóng and explore other parts of Xīshuāngbǎnnà is the No 2 bus station, which has frequent buses, minibuses and minivans from 7 am to around 5 pm.

Timetables are flexible to say the least. See the Around Jǐnghóng section for details on these buses.

Getting Around
The airport is 5km south of the city; CAAC buses (Y4) leave from next to the booking office about an hour before scheduled departures.

Jǐnghóng is small enough that you can walk to most destinations, but a bike makes life easier. Mei Mei Cafe and Forest Cafe hire out bikes for Y10 a day, Y18 for mountain bikes.

AROUND JǏNGHÓNG
The possibilities for day trips and longer excursions out of Jǐnghóng are endless. Some travellers have hiked and hitched from Měnghǎi to Dàměnglóng, some have cycled up to Měnghǎi and Měngzhē on mountain bikes (it's almost impossible on bikes without gears), and one French photographer hitched up with a local medicine man and spent seven days doing house calls in the jungle.

Obviously, it's the longer trips that allow you to escape the hordes of tourists and get a feel for what Xīshuāngbǎnnà is about. But even with limited time there are some interesting possibilities. Probably the best is an overnight (or several nights) stay in Gǎnlǎnbà (also known as Měnghǎn). It's only around 27km from Jǐnghóng, and not that hard to cycle to, even on a local bike. The trip takes two to three hours.

Most other destinations in Xīshuāngbǎnnà are only two or three hours away by bus, but generally they are not much in themselves – you need to get out and about. Note that to get to many villages, you'll often first have to bus to a primary village and overnight there, since only one bus a day – if that – travels to the tinier villages.

If you're a serious collector of local market experiences, there are plenty to be found in the region. Like anything else, markets are a subjective thing, but most people seem to prefer the Thursday market in Xīdìng, then Měnghùn, followed up by Měnghǎi. Note that Xīdìng has no accommodation.

The best advice is to get yourself a bike or some sturdy hiking boots, pick up a map, put down this book, and get out of town.

Nearby Villages
Before heading further afield, there are numerous villages in the vicinity of Jǐnghóng that can be reached by bicycle. Most of them you will happen upon by chance, and it's difficult to make recommendations.

On the other side of the Mekong are some small villages, and a popular jaunt involves heading off down Manting Lu – if you go far enough you'll hit a ferry crossing point on the Mekong.

Sānchàhé Zìrán Bǎohùqù
三岔河自然保护区
Sanchahe Nature Preserve
Sānchàhé, north of Jǐnghóng, is one of four enormous forest preserves in southern Yúnnán, this one totalling nearly 1.5 million hectares. It is possible to strike off into dense jungle, usually following the river, and rough it. (Take a local who knows his or her way around.) However, most travellers won't have time to get past the

---

The Jinuo People

The Jinuo, sometimes known as the Youle, were officially 'discovered' as a minority in 1979. The women wear a white cowl, a cotton tunic with bright horizontal stripes and a tubular black skirt. Ear-lobe decoration is an elaborate custom – the larger the hole and the more flowers it can contain the better. The teeth are sometimes painted black with the sap of the lacquer tree, which serves the dual dental purpose of beautifying the mouth and preventing tooth decay and halitosis.

Previously, the Jinuo lived in long houses with as many as 27 families occupying rooms on either side of the central corridor. Each family had its own hearth, but the oldest man owned the largest hearth, which was the first at the door. Long houses are rarely used now and it looks like the Jinuo are quickly losing their distinctive way of life.

tourist-oriented part of the preserve – over-priced canopy tree-house rooms (Y180 per night), and pitiful elephants chained to trees or giving 'wild' elephant performances for throngs of shutterbug tourists.

Just about any bus travelling north will pass the preserve, or you can inquire at one of the local cafes on minibus departures from the No 2 bus station. Minibuses should cost Y10. Admission is Y15, Y8 students.

Měngyǎng 勐养

Měngyǎng is 34km north-east of Jǐnghóng on the road to Sīmáo. It's a centre for the Hani, Lahu and Floral-Belt Dai. Chinese tourists stop here to see the **Xiàngxíng Róngshù** – a banyan tree shaped like an elephant.

From Měngyǎng it's another 19km to Jīnuò, which is home base for the Jinuo minority. Travellers have reported that the Jinuo are unfriendly, so you'll probably have to stay in Měngyǎng. Some minorities dislike tourists, and if this is the case with the Jinuo they should be left alone.

Gǎnlǎnbà 橄榄坝 (Měnghǎn)

Gǎnlǎnbà, or Měnghǎn as it's sometimes referred to, lies on the Mekong south-east of Jǐnghóng. In the past the main attraction of Gǎnlǎnbà was the boat journey down the Mekong from Jǐnghóng. Unfortunately, improved roads sank the popular boat trip (locals prefer to spend an hour on a bus to three hours on the boat), and the only way to travel down the river now is to charter a boat at special tourist prices that most tourists can't afford.

However, Gǎnlǎnbà remains a wonderful retreat from hectic Jǐnghóng. The town itself is fairly forgettable, but if you come on a bike (it is also possible to hire one in Gǎnlǎnbà) there is plenty of scope for exploration in the neighbourhood.

Check the visitors' book in the Dai Bamboo House or the Sarlar Restaurant for some ideas.

Places to Stay The family-run *Dai Bamboo House* is a house on stilts with a dorm for Y10 per bed and small doubles for Y25; all beds are on the floor in the traditional Dai style. The family serves Dai food on tiny lacquered tables; just give them notice several hours before dinner. It costs Y25, so be warned. Search out the visitors' books, which have several helpful maps of the area drawn by previous guests. You can also rent bikes here for Y10. Recent reports have been extremely mixed. The house is sort of under new management – the previous owner's son took it over. The Bamboo House is on the right-hand side of the main road that runs through town (heading away from Jǐnghóng).

Alternatively, the friendly *Sarlar Restaurant* has garnered most business recently. The capacious restaurant has three small but cosy rooms (Y20) off to one side, with mats on the floor in the traditional Dai style. The bathrooms and shower room are clean. Mountain bikes can be rented here for Y10 per day. To get here, continue past the Dai Bamboo House until just before the road begins to bend to the right. Carved dragons grace the entrance.

More lodging and Dai food can be found a block south of the main road. The Dai restaurant with an English menu has received mixed reports; the *Liánwǎn Jiǔjiā* is on the second floor of a building. It has great Dai food, down to the minced brain cooked in leaves.

Getting There & Away Minivans leave from behind Jǐnghóng's No 2 bus station as they fill up; you can also catch a bus at the long-distance bus station (Y7; 45 minutes). Vans from Gǎnlǎnbà depart from a small bus station found by walking on the main road in the direction of Jǐnghóng, and then turning right at the last intersection of any size and walking one block. It's possible to cycle the distance in a brisk two hours or a leisurely three hours, and it's a pleasant enough ride.

Getting Around The only way to do this is by bicycle or hiking. If you didn't bring your own bike, you can rent one at the Sarlar Restaurant or Dai Bamboo House. If they're out, nearby on the same side of the road is a place where you can hire bicycles for around Y20 a day.

Around Gǎnlǎnbà

The stately **Wat Ban Suan Men**, south-west of town, is said to be 730 years old and is one of the best surviving examples of Dai temple architecture in Yúnnán. Follow the road closest to the river southwards out of town and then take a path that follows the river. Check at the Dai Bamboo House or Sarlar Restaurant for information before you leave.

There are numerous temples and villages in the area that are worth exploring. From one block south of the main road you can head a couple of kilometres out to some local **minority parks** and a gorgeous **Dai temple**, the renovation of which is partly sponsored by the government of Thailand. There's an old decaying temple on the road into town from Jǐnghóng, and to the south of this, over-looking the Mekong, is a white stupa.

Most travellers who have spent any time here recommend striking off aimlessly on day trips and seeing what turns up.

Měnglún 勐伦

Měnglún is the next major port of call east of Gǎnlǎnbà. The major attraction for Chinese visitors is the Rèdài Zhíwùyuán (Tropical Plant Gardens). It's a pleasant enough place, although concrete pathways and guides toting bullhorns dash any hopes of communing with nature. But the gardens are nicely laid out, and the tour groups give it a somewhat festive atmosphere.

After going about two-thirds of the way into town, you'll come to a road leading downhill on the right-hand side. Follow this until you reach a footbridge across the Mekong. The ticket booth is just in front of the bridge. The entry fee is Y20 and the park is supposedly open until midnight.

Places to Stay For dirt-cheap lodging outside the park entrance there is the friendly *Chūnlín Lǚshè* (☎ 871 7172), with dorm beds for Y10 and a wide variety of rooms starting at Y30 for a single/double.

There is also budget accommodation within the gardens. After crossing the bridge, follow the main path for about 15 minutes until you arrive at a group of buildings and

a fork in the road. Take the left fork and you'll find a grungy *hostel* with dorm beds for around Y15. For a more upmarket stay, take the right fork, go over the hill and to the left of the pond, where there is a damp but clean Chinese hotel with doubles and attached bath for Y88. Another wing has upmarket Y300 doubles.

Getting There & Away From Jǐnghóng's No 2 bus station there are buses to Měnglún (Y17) approximately every 45 minutes between 6.30 am and 3 pm, most between 10 am and 1 pm. The long-distance station has a minivan leaving at 4 pm (Y17). Any Měnglà-bound bus will pass through Měnglún and also Gǎnlǎnbà. Minivans occasionally leave from the main street of Gǎnlǎnbà to Měnglún, and also charge Y10.

Some travellers have also cycled here from Gǎnlǎnbà. When the weighty restrictions on foreigners hiring motorbikes have finally eased, this will be prime touring country (read, lots of hilly areas).

Měnglà 孟腊

Měnglà may not be a very inspiring town, but it does see an increasing number of travellers passing through en route to Laos via the border crossing at Mòhān. As the bus journey from Jǐnghóng, or even Měnglún, will take the better part of the day, you will probably have to overnight here.

A couple of the cheap places here have unisex showers. Downhill from the bus station, the *Bīnyà Bīnguǎn* has hard dorm beds for Y20. Across the street from the square, the *Suìfēng Bīnguǎn* has competitive prices and is every bit nicer.

CITS has an office with at least one or two English-speaking staff at the *Měnglà Bīnguǎn*, which is about 2km uphill from the bus station. The Měnglà has dorm beds for around Y20, and doubles with bath and TV for Y60. The location is inconvenient, but a pedicab should get you there for Y3 to Y4.

A day trip from Měnglà might include a stop at the *Bǔbàng Wàngtiānshù Zǒuláng* (Aerial Skyway), a 45-minute bus ride. It has walks along raised wooden pathways through the forest canopy but unfortunately sparse facilities. It also costs Y30 to enter.

Getting There & Away There are four or five direct buses a day between Jǐnghóng's No 2 station and Měnglà, leaving between 6.30 am and 4.30 pm. The long-distance bus station also has departures five times a day between 6.40 am and 5.30 pm. The 200km ride takes anywhere from five to seven hours and the fare is Y25 to Y31, depending on the size of the bus. If you scout around the vicinity of Kūnmíng's long-distance bus station, you can find sleepers which go directly to Měnglà. Měnglà has two bus stations. The first one on the left coming from Jǐnghóng is the short-distance station.

Laos Border Crossing

First off, do *not* expect to show up and obtain a visa; it's officially impossible and even slick talkers are finding it a long haul back to Kūnmíng to get a visa. This crossing sees a fair amount of traffic. From Měnglà, there are buses to Mòhān (Y9.50). *Double check all stamps!* No matter what anyone says, there should be no 'charge' to cross. Once your passport is stamped and you've waved goodbye to the border guards, you can jump on a tractor or truck to take you into Laos for around Y3. If you can't find a bus to Mòhān, get on one to Shàngyǒng, from where it should be relatively easy to arrange another ride. Whatever you do, go early. Things often wrap up for good around noon on the Laos side (and don't forget they're an hour ahead) and you won't find a truck if you go later. Guesthouses are on the Chinese side but the Lao side is busy building some; change money on the Lao side.

DÀMĚNGLÓNG 大勐龙

Dàměnglóng (written just 'Měnglóng' on buses) is about 70km south of Jǐnghóng and a few kilometres from the Myanmar border. It's another sleepy village that serves well enough as a base for hikes around the surrounding hills. The village itself is not much (it rouses itself somewhat for the Sunday market), but the surrounding countryside, peppered with decaying stupas and

little villages, is worth a couple of days' exploration. You can hire bikes at the Dàměnglóng Zhāodàisuǒ for Y15 a day.

The town's laid-back feel may change in the next few years, however. The border crossing point with Myanmar (poetically named 2-4-0) has been designated as the entry point for a planned highway linking Thailand, Myanmar and China. The road is due to open sometime around 2000, although at last check things were certainly far from complete on the Chinese side. If and when it does, things should definitely pick up in Dàměnglóng.

Mànfēilóng Tǎ 曼飞龙塔
White Bamboo Shoot Pagoda

This pagoda, built in 1204, is Dàměnglóng's premier attraction. According to legend, the temple was built on the spot of a hallowed footprint left by Sakyamuni, who is said to have once visited Xīshuāngbǎnnà – if you're interested in ancient footprints you can look for it in a niche below one of the nine stupas. Unfortunately, in recent years a 'beautification' job has been done on the temple with a couple of cans of white paint – it probably sounded like a good idea at the time, but now that the paint has started to flake off it creates a very tacky effect.

If you're in Xīshuāngbǎnnà in late October or early November, check the precise dates of the Tan Ta Festival. At this time Mànfēilóng Tǎ is host to hundreds of locals whose celebrations include dancing, rockets, paper balloons and so on.

Mànfēilóng is easy to get to: just walk back along the main road towards Jǐnghóng for 2km until you reach a small village with a temple on your left. From here there's a path up the hill; it's about a 20-minute walk. There's a Y5 entrance fee, but plenty of times no-one's around anyway.

Hēi Tǎ 黑塔
Black Pagoda

Just above the centre of town is a Dai monastery with a steep path beside it leading up to the Hēi Tǎ, which you can't help but notice when you enter Dàměnglóng.

The glittering golden turrets of a Dai temple in Gǎnlǎnbà, Yúnnán

The sun sets on another business day across Hong Kong's harbour.

Old town old timers in Líjiāng, Yúnnán

A nurse in Kūnmíng, Yúnnán, takes a break.

The orchestra of the Naxi people play up a storm in Líjiāng, Yúnnán.

Trekking in Xīshuāngbǎnnà

Treks around Xīshuāngbǎnnà used to be among the best in China – you'd certainly be invited into a local's home to eat, sleep, and drink *baijiu* for free. Increasing numbers of visitors have changed this in places. Don't automatically expect a welcome mat and a free lunch just because you're a foreigner. (But don't go changing the local economy by throwing money around either.) Also – it is jungle out there, so know before you go, go prepared, and make sure somebody knows where you are and when you should return.

Dàměnglóng–Bulangshan Trek

The most popular walk, and the only one which even neophytes shouldn't need a guide, is a long two-day-or-more, 48km trek to Bulangshan through Dai, Habi, Bulang and Lahu villages from Manguanghan, via Dàměnglóng. This is a much poorer area but the folks are still friendly and the jungle more pristine than other more deforested areas. If you do get invited in, leave an offering – usually around Y5–10 – even though the family may insist on nothing. Start by taking a bus to Dàměnglóng (see Dàměnglóng's Getting There & Away section). From there it's a 10km-or-so walk or a hitch on a tractor (haggle the fare) to the Dai village Manguanghan; one bus a day should leave Dàměnglóng at noon but this is neither certain nor necessary. Then it's another 10–12km or three or so hours at a steady but not killer pace to Manpo, a Bulang village; 200m beyond the end of Manguanghan take the path to the right. You cross through Guangmin, an Aini village, en route and at one point espy a temple. After overnighting in Manpo – you'll have to locate a local's home – the next day is a walk to Weidong via Nuna (Bulang), Sóngéer (Lahu), and Bannankan, some 24km in all; in Manpo just ask for the right path to Weidong (the path goes down). There are three or four places where you may get off the track and have to backtrack a few kilometres but that's part of the fun. Overnight in Weidong and the next day is another leisurely 10km to Bulangshan via a real road. In Bulangshan you'll probably have to overnight again since the only bus, to Měnghùn, leaves at 8 am. There is a truck stop/karaoke hellhole in town with beds, but it's raucous and you don't sleep a wink. It would be preferable to try and find a local to put you up. If you're short of time, there's no reason why the second day you couldn't get to Bulangshan from Manpo without overnighting in Weidong; it's an epic day of trekking

Guides

At present one travel agency catering to these treks is the *Mengyuan Travel Service* (☎ 212-5214 or 213-2234), directly next to the Bank of China on Jinghong Nanlu in Jīnghóng. It may be willing to cook something special up as well. Mei Mei Cafe and Forest Cafe can line you up with a local English-speaking guide.

The pagoda itself is not black at all – it's covered in cheap gold paint. Take a stroll up, but bear in mind that the real reason for the climb is the superb views of Dàměnglóng and the surrounding countryside. An English-speaking Malaysian monk is said to spend most of his time around here, although we didn't run into him.

Places to Stay & Eat

Plenty of cheap options are available for foreigners. One place that usually isn't is the *bus station guesthouse*; too bad, since it has quite pleasant-looking rooms. A cheap place sits at the base of the Hēi Tǎ.

Formerly the only place for foreigners was the low-key *Dàměnglóng Zhàodàisuǒ*. To get there, walk uphill from the main highway to where the local government building sits. The hotel is in the grounds to the left, just past some ornamental frogs. Basic dorm beds are Y10. Bathrooms are fragrant but passable. Bicycles can be rented here for Y3 per hour, Y15 per day.

Down from the bus station, near the steps leading up to the Hēi Tǎ, are a couple of decent *restaurants*. The Chinese signs proclaim them to be Dai restaurants – and in fact many Chinese in Jǐnghóng swear by the Dai food here – but it's the old story of going out the back, pointing to your vegies and getting them five minutes later in a little pool of oil. Dàměnglóng specialises in *shaōkaŏ*, skewers of beast or bird or pork wrapped in banana leaves grilled over wood fires.

Getting There & Away

There are buses to Dàměnglóng (Y13; 2½ hours) every half hour (or less) between 7 am and 5 pm (occasionally until 7 or 8 pm) from Jǐnghóng's No 2 bus station. Purchase your tickets on the bus – just walk through the station and across the car park to the far left corner, where they congregate. Remember that the 'Da' character won't be painted on the bus window. Buses for the return trip are on a similar schedule, although the last bus tends to leave a bit earlier.

AROUND DÀMĚNGLÓNG

The village of Xiaŏjīe, about 15km before Dàměnglóng, is surrounded by Bulang, Lahu and Hani villages. Lahu women shave their heads; apparently the younger ones aren't happy about this any more and hide their heads beneath caps. The Bulang are possibly descended from the Lolo in northern Yúnnán. The women wear black turbans with silver decorations; many of the designs are of shells, fish and marine life.

There's plenty of room for exploration in this area, although you're not allowed over the border.

Měnghǎi 勐海

This uninspiring place serves as a centre for trips into the surrounding area. The Sunday market attracts members of the hill tribes and the best way to find it is to follow the early-morning crowds.

There are a couple of drab *hotels*. One near the old bus station at the centre of town has beds for Y10. About 1km further down the street, near the smaller but more active

bus station, the *Liángyuán Bīnguǎn* has doubles/triples for Y60.

Buses and minibuses (seven small, eight large) run from Jǐnghóng's No 2 bus station to Měnghǎi approximately every 20 minutes between 7 am and 5.30 pm. The fare is Y10 and the trip takes about 90 minutes. Minibuses to Jǐnghóng, Měnghùn and Jǐngzhēn leave from a smaller bus station, at the western end of Měnghǎi.

Měnghùn 勐混

This tiny village is about 26km south-west of Měnghǎi. Some prefer the Sunday market here to that of Měnghǎi. It all begins buzzing around 7 am and lingers on through to noon. The swirl of hill tribes and women sporting fancy leggings, head-dresses, earrings and bracelets alone makes the trip worthwhile. Although the market seems to be the main attraction, a temple and footpaths that wind through the lush hills behind the Báitǎ Fàndiàn are also worth an extra day or two.

Places to Stay & Eat Right at the centre of town where the buses let you off, the *Yúnchuān Fàndiàn* is nothing to get excited about, but the rooms are (barely) acceptable. It has rooms for around Y10. Further down on the right-hand side of the street, the *Fènghuáng Fàndiàn (Phoenix Hotel)* is cheaper (Y5 a bed), but very noisy and better off given a miss.

The more secluded *Báitǎ Fàndiàn (White Tower Hotel)* is roomier, quieter and looks out over a lily pond. Beds in doubles here cost Y10, but you can probably talk the price down. From the main intersection, take the road uphill, walk through the archway, then bear left along a small path heading downhill. These directions are only approximate; everyone has trouble finding the place, so you'll probably have to ask locals.

There are several good *Dai restaurants* along the main street, some of which have English menus.

Getting There & Away Buses from Jǐnghóng to Dǎluò pass through Měnghùn, and leave Jǐnghóng's No 2 bus station every half hour between 7 am and 4.30 pm. The fare to Měnghùn is Y15. Going back you just have to wait on the side of the road until a bus passes by. Normally you shouldn't have to wait too long.

Unless you have a very good bike with gears, cycling to Měnghǎi and Měnghùn is not a real option. The road up to Měnghǎi is so steep that you'll end up pushing the bike most of the way.

Intrepid travellers have hitched and hiked all the way from here to Dàměnglóng. This should be no problem, providing you don't inadvertently stray over the Myanmar border at some point. A mountain bike would be the best way to do it. Hitching and walking should take a leisurely seven days.

Jǐngzhēn 景真

In the village of Jǐngzhēn, about 14km north-west of Měnghǎi, is the **Bājiǎo Tíng** (Octagonal Pavilion), first built in 1701. The original structure was severely damaged during the Cultural Revolution, so the present renovated building isn't all that thrilling. Take a close look at the new paintings on the wall of the temple. There are some interesting scenes which appear to depict People's Liberation Army (PLA) soldiers causing death and destruction during the Cultural Revolution; adjoining scenes depict Buddha vanquishing PLA soldiers, one of whom is waving goodbye as he drowns in a pond. Unfortunately, the pavilion is usually closed except for special days; when you can talk your way in it's Y10.

Jǐngzhēn is a pleasant rural spot for walks along the river or the fish ponds behind the village. Frequent minibuses from the minibus centre in Měnghǎi go via Jǐngzhēn.

Nánlúo Shān 南罗山

Nánlúo Shān lies south of the road between Jǐnghóng and Měnghǎi (17km from Měnghǎi). It's best done as a day trip from Měnghǎi, providing you start early and return to the main road before dusk. The bus will drop you off close to a bridge; cross the bridge and follow the dirt track about 6km uphill until you join a newly constructed main road.

About 1km before the junction, you'll round a bend in the road and see a fence with a stile and stone benches beyond. This is the turn-off for the steps down to the overrated **Cháwáng** (King of Tea Trees) – the name says it all! According to the Hani, their ancestors have been growing tea for 55 generations and this tree was the first one planted. The tree is definitely not worth descending hundreds of steps to see; it is half dead and covered with moss, graffiti and signs forbidding graffiti. A crumbling concrete pavilion daubed with red paint completes the picture. (If you want a real King of Tea Trees, in the Bādá district, Hesongzhai Village, some 55km south-west of Měnghǎi, is a wild tree 1700 years old.) You can get to the tree for Y4 by motorcycle taxi, and an admission of Y2 is charged.

A highway has been bulldozed out of the mountain for the comfort of tourists who can now visit the hill tribes further up the mountain. Repeated exposure to tour buses is certain to cause changes among the Hani and Lahu villagers there. If you leave the main road, there's some pleasant hiking in the area, but don't expect villagers to automatically give you a bed for the night. A Hani villager did invite us into his stilt house for an excellent meal and some firewater that left us wobbling downhill.

Bǎoshān Region

Travellers who pass through the Bǎoshān area (Bǎoshān dìqū) tend to do so quickly, generally staying overnight in Bǎoshān city on the way to or from Ruìlì and Wǎndīng, but the area is worth a bit more time than that. There are some worthwhile historical sights, the old quarters of Téngchōng and Bǎoshān make for some good browsing, distinctive minority groups are in abundance (as in other parts of southern Yúnnán), and the Téngchōng area is rich in volcanic activity, with hot springs and volcanic peaks.

As early as the 4th and 5th centuries BC (two centuries before the northern routes through central Asia were established), the Bǎoshān area was an important stage on the southern Silk Road – the Sìchuān-India route. The area did not really come under Chinese control until the time of the Han dynasty when, in AD 69, it was named the Yongchang Administrative District.

BǍOSHĀN 保山
☎ 0875

Bǎoshān is a small city that's easily explored on foot. There are pockets of traditional wooden architecture still standing in the city area and some good walks on the outskirts of town. It has innumerable speciality products, ranging from coffee (which is excellent) and pepper to leather boots and silk. Tea aficionados might like to try the Reclining Buddha Baoshan Tea, a brand of national repute.

Information
Shops in the long-distance bus station sell maps of Bǎoshān Prefecture, which includes Bǎoshān city and Téngchōng as well as regional sights, with some explanations in English. Otherwise you're pretty much on your own. The Bank of China is next to the Yíndū Dàjiǔdiàn, and the post office is not far away. You can go online at the Kele Computer Company (Kèlè Diànnǎogōngsī), which has Internet access for Y10 per hour.

Things to See
Bǎoshān is an interesting city to wander aimlessly in. The streets are lively and, in many areas, lined with old traditional homes. The major sight within easy walking distance of the centre of town is the park Tàibǎo Gōngyuán. It's flanked to the south by the Wénbǐ Tǎ (Writing Style Pagoda) and to the east by the Yùhuáng Gé (Jade Emperor Pavilion). All three are worth a look. The Yùhuáng Gé dates back to the Ming dynasty and has a small museum next door to it. The small viewing pagodas in the park provide good views of Bǎoshān, Wénbǐ Tǎ and Yìluó Chí (Yiluo Pool).

There are paths in the park striking off to the north, west and south. The northern path doubles back to the south and eventually takes you past a very mediocre zoo (keep walking). Continuing to the south you will reach Yìluó Chí, also known as Lóngquán Chí (Dragon Spring Pond). The best thing about the latter are the views of the 13-tiered Wénbǐ Tǎ. An entrance fee of Y4 is charged to Yìluó Chí.

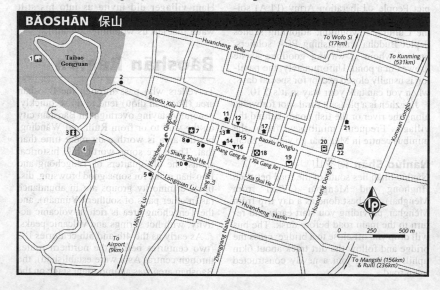

Places to Stay

There are plenty of inexpensive places to stay in Bǎoshān. Really good value is the *Huāchéng Bīnguǎn* (☎ 212 2037), two or three minutes north of the long-distance bus station on the other side of the road. Doubles/triples cost Y40/45 with common bath. But the best deal may be the doubles with attached bathroom for Y40 to Y50. Rooms are clean, bright and airy and, depending on who your neighbours are for the night, quiet. Deals for stays of three or more nights are available.

Along Baoxiu Xilu are a few sprawling Chinese-style hotels with little to separate them. The first is the *Yǒngchāng Bīnguǎn* (☎ 212 2802), which is OK but best used as a last resort. Not far up the road is the *Lánhuā Bīnguǎn* (☎ 212 2803), which has three-bed dorms for Y24. Doubles/triples with attached bathroom start at Y60 and deluxe singles at Y120.

Bǎoshān's premier accommodation is nearby, the *Lándù Fàndiàn* (☎ 212 1888, fax 212 1990), with fine rooms and slavish service for Y400, though they promptly went down to Y280 at the mere idea of bargaining.

The erstwhile posh place, brought to you by the Bank of China, is the *Yíndū Dàjiǔdiàn* (☎ 212 0948), a money-making venture set up by the bank. It offers standard doubles for Y80 to Y180, but if you're en route to Téngchōng, hold out a bit longer: you can get a comparable room there for half the price.

A block south, the pleasant *Bǎoshān Bīnguǎn* (☎ 212 2804) is where the pedicab drivers will probably take you if you stumble off the bus looking dazed and confused. It has not good doubles with common bath for Y60; from there it goes to slightly up-market but diminutive doubles for Y120 (bathroom attached). This place is better used for its great outdoor restaurant.

Places to Eat

Baoxiu Lu and the road running parallel to the south of it are good places to seek out cheap *restaurants*. Next door to the Bǎoshān Bīnguǎn is an outdoor *across-the-bridge noodles restaurant* that is worth checking out, although it closes quite early. Near the intersection of Baoxiu Xilu and Huancheng Xilu is a handful of *Muslim, Dai,* and *Burmese restaurants*.

As in Kūnmíng there are plenty of *roadside snacks* available. There's a tiny *coffee shop* across from the Yǒngchāng Bīnguǎn. While its coffee is very sweet and very instant, it's only Y3 per cup. Cold drinks are

BĂOSHĀN

PLACES TO STAY
11 Lándù Fàndiàn
　　兰都饭店
13 Lánhuā Bīnguǎn
　　兰苑宾馆
14 Bǎoshān Bīnguǎn
　　保山宾馆
15 Yǒngchāng Bīnguǎn
　　永昌宾馆
17 Yíndū Dàjiǔdiàn;
　　Bank of China
　　银都大酒店；
　　中国银行
21 Huāchéng Bīnguǎn
　　花城宾馆

PLACES TO EAT
6 Dai, Burmese Restaurants
　　傣缅风味饭店

12 Coffee Shop
　　咖啡冷饮
16 Across-the-Bridge
　　Noodle Restaurant
　　过桥园

OTHER
1 Zoo
　　动物园
2 Yùhuáng Gé
　　玉皇阁
3 Wénbǐ Tǎ
　　文笔塔
4 Yìluó Chí
　　易罗池
5 CAAC
　　中国民航售票处
7 PSB
　　公安局

8 Workers' Cultural
　　Palace
　　工人文化宫
9 Kele Computer
　　Company
　　科乐电脑公司
10 Youth Palace
　　青少年宫
18 Department
　　Store
　　百货大楼
19 Post Office
　　邮电局
20 Long-Distance
　　Bus Station
　　汽车总站
22 City Bus
　　Station
　　市车站

also served. *A Splendid Tea House* in the long-distance bus compound is best left on its own.

Getting There & Away

You can fly in and out of Bǎoshān, although very few western travellers do. The Bǎoshān CAAC office (☎ 216 1747) is rather inconveniently located at the intersection of Longquan Lu and Minhang Lu. Look for a large yellow-tiled building. The ticket office is on the 1st floor, facing Longquan Lu. There are four flights weekly (Wednesday, Thursday, Friday and Sunday) to Kūnmíng, and tickets cost Y370. The airport is around 9km south of town.

The Bǎoshān long-distance bus station has buses running to a host of destinations around Yúnnán. Some private companies have offices around the corner on Baoxiu Donglu. There are numerous late-afternoon sleeper buses from 3 to 7 pm making the 13- to18-hour haul to Kūnmíng. Fares are Y110 for sleepers.

Buses for ride to Xiàguān (Dàlǐ) leave four times between 6.50 and 11 am the (Y21 to Y27; five to six hours). Buses to Téngchōng (Y27; six hours) leave daily at 6.50, 9.30 and 11 am. Buses on to Yíngjiāng, past Téngchōng, leave at 7.30 am and take pretty much forever. There are three buses to Ruìlì (Y30 to Y35; seven to eight hours) between 8 and 9.30 am, which pass through Mángshì and Wǎndīng. Other morning buses go as far as Mángshì. There is also a bus once daily to Jǐnghóng in Xīshuāngbǎnnà, although most travellers opt to take the direct Dàlǐ-Jǐnghóng bus now. If you take it from Bǎoshān it's still a two-day travail, with an overnight stay, usually in Líncāng.

Across the street at the city bus station you can catch a bus to most of the same destinations as from the long-distance station. To Ruìlì via Mángshì the first bus departs at 8 am. Kūnmíng sleepers depart from 4.30 pm for Y100. Buses go to Xiàguān (Y25) from 8.30 am to 1 pm. Note that the schedule on the wall of this station is woefully out of date.

Getting Around

Bǎoshān can comfortably be explored on foot, which is probably why there is no evidence of bicycle-hire stands around town. This is a pity because a bicycle would be the ideal way to get to some of the sights around Bǎoshān.

AROUND BǍOSHĀN

Just 17km north of town, Wòfó Sì (Reclining Buddha Temple) is one of the most important historical sights in the vicinity of Bǎoshān. The temple dates back to the Tang dynasty, with a history of some 1200 years. The reclining buddha itself, in a cave to the rear of the temple area, was severely damaged during the Cultural Revolution and has only recently been restored.

The only problem is getting there: there are no local buses or minibuses. A motorcycle with sidecar can take two people there and back for Y40. Taxis ask around Y70 to Y80. It would be a fairly comfortable bicycle trip if you could get hold of a bike.

TÉNGCHŌNG 腾冲
☎ 0875

Not many travellers get to this town on the other side of the Gāolígòng Shān mountain range, but it's an interesting place. There are about 20 volcanoes in the vicinity and lots of hot springs. It's also prime earthquake territory, having experienced 71 earthquakes measuring over five on the Richter scale since AD 1500.

The town has preserved, on a larger scale, the kind of traditional wooden architecture that has survived only in pockets in Kūnmíng and Bǎoshān. It's not exactly Dàlǐ, but there's a definite charm to some of the narrow backstreets. At an altitude of 1650m, the town can get chilly on winter evenings.

Information

Téngchōng has a small travel office at the front gate of the Téngchōng Bīnguǎn. The staff don't speak much English, but can provide you with maps of the county, and maybe some assistance. Maps are also sold at the shop in the hotel courtyard.

The post office is on Fengshan Lu. The Bank of China, which dominates the town's main intersection, won't change travellers cheques, so you'll have to come to Téngchōng armed with enough cash to get you through your visit.

Things to See

There's not exactly a wealth of sights in town, but it's worth taking a look at the **Frontier Trade Bazaar of Tengchong** – yes, that's the English sign at the head of the market. It's not as lively as the markets in Ruìlì, but there's plenty of colour and activity in the mornings.

The best street for **old buildings** is Yingjiang Lu – both the east and west sections. The backstreets running off the western section of Yingjiang Lu make for some good exploring and photographs.

About 2km south-west of town is **Láifēng Sì** (Come Wind Temple). The temple is nothing to get excited about, especially as foreigners are charged Y5 to get in (as opposed to Y0.5 for locals), but the walk up to and around the temple takes you through lush pine forests. The temple also borders the **Fēngshān Guójiā Sēlín Gōngyuān** (Fengshan Forest Reserve) which offers further hiking possibilities and also gives an idea of what this part of China may have been like before the trees gave way to farms.

Places to Stay

Téngchōng's accommodation options are fairly spread out. South of the bus station, the **Gōnglù Zhāodàisuǒ** has beds for Y10 in a triple and other options starting at Y15. It's a noisy place, but it's the closest place to the bus station. The hotel has no English sign – look for the ubiquitous bus steering wheel logo at the top of the entry gate. Across the street is a newly opened better option, the **Tōnglìdá Bīnguǎn** (☎ 518 7787). Beds in spartan but fine multi-person concrete rooms go for Y20 to Y25; shared showers and toilets are clean. Fine double rooms start at Y80, and are worth it for two people. Hot water is available all day.

Close to the centre of town, the **Téngyún Bīnguǎn** is well into the process of dilapi-

dation, but still has dorm beds for Y10 in pleasant old wooden buildings, and doubles/triples in the (somewhat) newer wing for Y30. None of the rooms have bathrooms – the common ones are OK, the showers (Y2) aren't. You can pick out the entrance by looking for the little Burmese teahouse on the right-hand side.

Around the corner on Fengshan Lu look for an English sign saying 'Check in at a Hotel' – the spartan but decent **Fúzhuāng-chǎng Zhāodàisuǒ** also has beds from Y12 in doubles; showers are clean.

The sprawling **Téngchōng Bīnguǎn** is in a quiet location, though far from the bus station. Beds in clean, spacious dorms range from Y15 to Y20, and there are singles/doubles with attached bath from Y60. The more you pay from here, the better the room. It's not exactly the Hilton – the lights in the entire hotel dim when anyone uses the only elevator – but for the money it's great value.

Places to Eat

There are scores of tiny, inviting *eateries* housed in Téngchōng's wooden buildings; you can also find some excellent *fruit shakes stalls*. Along Fengshan Lu on the corner with Yingjiang Xilu is a great *stall* for freshly steamed *bǎozi*.

For sweet coffee, excellent samosas, Mekong whisky, and the likely chance of chatting with some of Téngchōng's itinerant Burmese jewellery peddlers, stop by the **Burmese Teahouse & Cafe** at the entrance to the Téngyún Bīnguǎn. There is an English sign out the front, and usually at least one English speaker within.

Not far away from here to the west is the clean **Nánbeǐfēngweì Xiǎochī** (*South-North Snacks*) with excellent steamed and fried dumplings.

Getting There & Away

Téngchōng's long-distance bus station must be the only bus station in the whole of the south-west that has a board with English information about bus times and prices. Ignore it – it's completely out of date, although it's a nice thought.

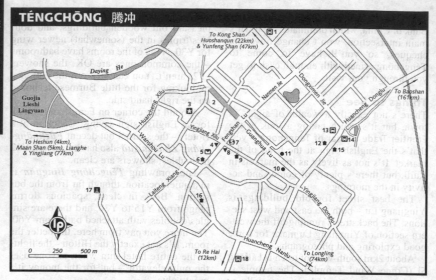

TÉNGCHŌNG 腾冲

Buses leave hourly from the long-distance bus station to Bǎoshān (Y27; five to six hours) from 7.30 am to 4 pm. Directly to Xiàguān (Dàlǐ) there is an overnight bus leaving at 7 pm (Y60), but it would make sense to overnight in Bǎoshān.

Some buses to Ruìlì run via Yíngjiāng and Zhāngfēng (Y30; six to eight hours). Alternatively, if you have time on your hands, travel to Yíngjiāng (stopping to have a browse in Liánghé on the way), stay overnight there and travel on to Ruìlì by bus the next day. A bus leaves for Yíngjiāng Y18; three to four hours) at 10.30 am. There is also a bus to Mángshì at 7.30 am (Y20; five hours) and a sleeper to Kūnmíng (Y130 to Y140; around 24 hours) at 10.30 am.

Another bus station is located a short way south, on the opposite side of the street. It has a less complicated detailed schedule, but you may find something to your liking if your bus from the long-distance station has just left without you.

Getting Around

Téngchōng is small enough to walk around, but a bicycle would be useful for getting to some of the closer sights outside town – the surrounding scenery alone justifies a ride. If you're interested, there is a bicycle shop on Guanghua Lu that rents bikes for Y1 per hour, with a deposit of Y200. There's a sign in fractured English out the front, but just look for a mass of bicycles parked in front of a yellow wooden building.

AROUND TÉNGCHŌNG

There's a lot to see around Téngchōng but, as in Bǎoshān, getting out to the sights is a bit tricky. Catching buses part of the way and hiking up to the sights is one possibility, while some of the closer sights can be reached by bicycle.

Your other option is a hired van, which may be affordable if there are several of you. The Five Continent Travel Service (Wǔzhōu Lǚxíngshè), located just outside the Téngchōng Bīnguǎn compound, cannot arrange such transport, but it does have nice maps. You can then make your way down to the minibus stand further south (take a right at the large roundabout), where van drivers often sit around puffing cigarettes and waiting for some business to walk their way.

TÉNGCHŌNG

PLACES TO STAY

6 Fúzhuāngchǎng
Zhāodàisuǒ
服装厂招待所

9 Téngyún Bīnguǎn;
Burmese Teahouse &Cafe
腾云宾馆，
缅甸咖啡厅

12 Gōnglù
Zhāodàisuǒ
公路招待所

15 Tōnglìdá
Bīnguǎn
通利达宾馆

16 Téngchōng Bīnguǎn
腾冲宾馆

PLACES TO EAT

4 Bāozi Stall
包子摊

8 Nánběifēngwèi Xiǎochī
南北风味小吃

OTHER

1 Mǎzhàn Buses
往马站的汽车

2 Frontier Trade Bazaar of
Tengchong
腾冲边境货物商场

3 PSB
公安局

5 Post Office
邮电局

7 Bank of China
中国银行

10 Workers' Cultural
Palace
工人文化宫

11 Bicycle Shop
自行车出租

13 Long-Distance
Bus Station
长途汽车站

14 Bus Station
客运站

17 Láifēng Sì
来凤寺

18 Minibuses
中巴车站

Héshùn Xiāng 和顺乡

Just 4km outside of town is the village of
Héshùn. It's worth hiking or cycling back to
take a closer look. It has been set aside as a
kind of retirement village for overseas Chinese, but for the average western visitor it's
likely to be of more interest as a quiet, traditional Chinese village with cobbled
streets. There are some great old buildings
in the village, providing lots of photo opportunities. You may also get a chance to
meet some older English-speaking locals.
You could take a minibus from a stand
along Wanshou Lu, but it's a fair hike and
the road was slated for reconstruction, so
these have probably relocated.

Yúnfēng Shān 云蜂山
Cloudy Peak Mountain

Yúnfēng Shān is a Taoist mountain dotted
with temples and monastic retreats, 47km
north of Téngchōng. The temples were built
in the early 17th century, and the best example is Yúnfēng Sì, at the summit.

Getting there is not so easy. The only
budget option is to take a bus to Ruìdiàn.
One bus leaves the long-distance bus station
daily at noon and costs Y10. After passing
through the town of Gúdōng (Y7), you will
come to a turn-off for the mountain. After
getting off here you will have to either walk
or hitch the remaining 9km to 10km to
reach the base of the mountain. Hiring a ve-

hicle to take you there and back will cost
around Y300.

Volcanoes

Téngchōng County is renowned for its volcanoes (huǒshānqún), and although they
have been behaving themselves for many
centuries the seismic and geothermal activity in the area indicates that they won't always continue to do so. The closest one to
town is Mǎān Shān (Saddle Mountain),
around 5km to the north-west. It's just south
of the main road that runs to Yíngjiāng.

Around 22km to the north of town, near
the village of Mǎzhàn, is a cluster of volcanoes: the Kōng Shān Huǒshānqún (Hollow
Mountain Volcanoes). Buses to Gúdōng run
past Mǎzhàn. A minibus station north along
Dongximen Lu has buses to the north. From
Mǎzhàn you can either walk or take a
motor-tricycle (Y5) to the volcano area. Alternatively, hire a van from Téngchōng to
take you there and back for around Y150.

Rè Hǎi 热海
Sea of Heat

Rè Hǎi is a cluster of hot springs, geysers
and streams around 12km south-west of
Téngchōng. In addition to the usual indoor
baths, there is an outdoor hot spring as well
as a warm-water pool, sitting above a river.

Two hotels at the entrance to the springs
have simple doubles for Y30 to Y50 and

restaurants serving up local specialities, so it's easy to make this a relaxing overnight trip. However, in summer a fairly active mosquito community can wreak havoc with sleep – you may wish to opt for just a day's sojourn if the weather is hot.

No travel agencies in Téngchōng have scheduled charters, so you'll have to head for the Huancheng Nanlu turn-off to the hot springs; look for the big roundabout, then head south. Minibuses generally leave anytime from 8 am, with the last returning around 8 pm (but don't count on it). Depending on your bargaining skills, you can generally line up a van to the hot springs for around Y5 per person or Y25 for a whole van. At the springs there is a Y5 entrance fee; it's another Y5 to actually swim, and it is recommended.

Déhóng Prefecture
德洪地区

Déhóng Prefecture, like Xīshuāngbǎnnà, borders Myanmar and is heavily populated by distinctive minority groups, but for some reason it doesn't seem to have captured the imagination of travellers to the extent that Xīshuāngbǎnnà has. It's in the far west of Yúnnán and is definitely more off the beaten track than Xīshuāngbǎnnà – you're unlikely to see the bus loads of tourists who have overrun Xīshuāngbǎnnà in recent years.

Most Chinese tourists in Déhóng are there for the Myanmar trade that comes through the towns of Ruìlì and Wǎndīng. Burmese jade is a commodity that many Chinese have grown rich on in recent years, but there are countless other items being spirited over the border that separates China and Myanmar, some of them illicit.

Many minority groups are represented in Déhóng, but among the most obvious are the Burmese, Dai and Jingpo (known in Myanmar as the Kachin, a minority long engaged in armed struggle against the Myanmar government).

In Déhóng it is possible to see signs in Chinese, Burmese, Dai and English. It is a border region getting rich on trade – in the markets you can see Indian jewellery, tinned fruits from Thailand, Burmese papier-mache furniture, young bloods with wads of foreign currency, and Chinese plain-clothes police trying not to look too obvious.

YÍNGJIĀNG   盈江

Yíngjiāng is a possible stopover if you're heading to Ruìlì from Téngchōng. It's not really worth a special effort, but the locals are friendly and, even though there's not a damn thing to do, it's a good place to break up the bus ride.

Things to See
There's nothing much to see really. Take a minibus out to **Jiùchéng** (Old Town) to see an old Chinese town. It's only a 20-minute ride, and it's fairly picturesque. Back on the road to Ruìlì, a couple of kilometres out of town, is an old stupa named **Lǎomiǎn Tǎ** (Old Burmese Stupa). Locals claim it's a nice place to visit in the evenings 'with someone you care about' – see if you can find the local PSB and invite one of the boys in green along.

Places to Stay & Eat
Opposite the long-distance bus station is the drab *Guóyíng Lǚshè (State Guesthouse)*. Locals claim it's a den of iniquity, but unfortunately we didn't find any. It's Y4 for a bed in a three- or five-bed dorm, Y16 for a double and Y10 for a single. None of the rooms have showers. You also need to take a bit of a hike if you want to use the toilet.

Better still, give the State Den of Iniquity a miss and walk towards town (turn right after you exit the bus station) for the *Yíngqīng Lǚshé*. It's on the right-hand side of the road, on the corner of the first large intersection. This clean and friendly place has singles/doubles for Y15/20 and singles with bathroom and TV for Y40.

Yíngjiāng's answer to the Hilton is the *Chángchéng Bīnguǎn (Great Wall Hotel)*, where the cheapest rooms cost Y60 and the most expensive are a shocking Y600. All rooms have their own TVs and bathrooms. To get there, keep walking from the

Yíngqīng Lǔshé and turn right at the first major intersection; the Chángchéng is on the corner of the next intersection. Turning left at that second intersection brings you to the *Míngzhū Dàjiǔdiàn (Bright Pearl Hotel)*, which has similar standards and rates. It's got a clean and popular restaurant with good food and service, despite the fact that it served up a nasty bug on a recent visit.

Yíngjiāng is not a gastronomical experience, but the cheap *noodle stores* over near the bus station will keep you alive for another day.

Getting There & Away

From Ruìlì, buses leave twice in the mornings to Yíngjiāng (Y18; five hours). Buses to Ruìlì leave at 7 and 9 am. Buses at 8 and 9.30 am go to Mángshì via Ruìlì; tickets cost Y37.

From Téngchōng, buses leave three times daily for Yíngjiāng (Y18). Up to around 4 pm you may be able to catch a minibus across from the bus station to Zhāngfēng, where you can connect with buses to Ruìlì. The whole journey should cost Y25 and take around five hours.

Going the other way, there are four buses to Téngchōng between 7 am and 2 pm (Y18 to Y20; three to four hours). Bǎoshān connections are spotty, and you'll probably have to go through Téngchōng. You can even get a sleeper bus from here to Kūnmíng, departing daily at 7 am. The 29-hour odyssey costs Y185.

RUÌLÌ 瑞丽
☎ 0692

Ruìlì is without a doubt one of the more interesting towns in south-western China. It's just a few kilometres from Myanmar and has a real border-town feel. There's a great mix of Han Chinese, minorities and ubiquitous Burmese traders hawking jade, and travellers tend to linger longer than they intended just for the atmosphere. The place is getting dustier with all the new construction, but it's worth giving it a couple of days.

Compared with the rest of China, Ruìlì seems unrestricted, like people get away with a lot more here. That this atmosphere is generated by proximity to Myanmar and it's repressive military junta makes Ruìlì all the more interesting. There are some interesting minority villages nearby; the stupas are in much better condition than those in Xīshuāngbǎnnà, and it's worth travelling onwards to Wǎndīng and Mángshì, either as day trips or as overnight stops.

Hopefully, Myanmar will lighten up on border-crossing restrictions for foreigners in the future. By the early millennium new highways laid to facilitate border trade should stretch all the way from Jiěgào, on the border, to Mandalay, making much more sane what had been a hellish five-day journey. One day travellers may be able to recreate the 'Southern Silk Route', of which Ruìlì and Mandalay were a part.

Information
Money The Bank of China is not far from the long-distance bus station. In case you're headed to Myanmar, the bank will let you cash travellers cheques for US dollars, which would come in handy if you could get across the border. This Bank of China branch also garners kudos for speed and efficiency.

Post & Communications Off the corner of Renmin Lu and Mengmao Lu is the China Telecom, from where you can make direct-dial international calls. A new post office complex was going up. The post office is open from 8 am to 6 pm, the telecommunications office till 10 pm.

Travel Agencies The shop next to the reception area of the Ruìlì Guesthouse has maps and a few brochures on Ruìlì, but there's very little else in the way of information. The bookshop on the corner of Nanmao Jie and Renmin Lu has good maps.

PSB The PSB, when anybody's around, is just up the road from the Ruìlì Bīnguǎn.

Dangers & Annoyances You'll hear incessantly of Ruìlì's image problems, for which there is some empirical evidence. The town's pubs and discos – many simply fronts for an enormous prostitution industry – have always had a rough reputation. And though most of the populace are simple traders, a significant share of the local commerce is of the poppy-derived variety, Ruìlì being an entry point for Burmese opium headed to Hong Kong. This has resulted in a serious IV drug use problem in the Déhóng region, along with its pernicious sibling – HIV. Apparently, since 1990 virtually all of China's new HIV cases were reported in Ruìlì and its vicinity, and by 1995 70% of the nation's cases were in Yúnnán, most in Ruìlì. The province, with Běijīng's help, has poured over 125 million yuan into anti-drug efforts along the border of Myanmar with Yúnnán; yet in the first three months of 1999 alone 1.18 tons of heroin were seized. (The strong yuan has hindered efforts to curb the trade, as it makes Yúnnán an attractive place to smuggle.)

Myanmar Border Crossing More rumours fly about regarding the Ruìlì border crossing than anything in the Déhóng or Bǎoshān regions. Everyone had hoped that once Myanmar had been admitted into ASEAN in 1997, it would have to crack its borders a bit. Not even close. At present absolutely *nobody* gets into Myanmar's border town of Mùsè, not even on a day trip. (Japanese or Koreans might be able to sneak across as locals, but definitely not westerners.) The friendly enough Chinese border guards will wince if you approach – so many foreigners have arrived and pleaded for a day pass that the commander and some of his underlings are planning to study English!

The Chinese government is perfectly willing to OK transit, but the Myanmar government doesn't really have a handle on corruption and lawlessness in the region and claims it doesn't want foreign tourists wandering through that lethal cocktail. The Chinese have actually tried to facilitate border crossings. Whatever the case, this is a rapidly expanding area and, who knows, by the time you have this book in your hand things may have done an about face and hordes of tourists will be piling over the border.

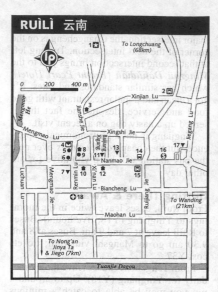

Things to See

There is really not a lot to see in Ruìlì itself, although it's a great town to wander around, and is small enough that you can cover most of it in an hour or so. The **market street** in the west of town is the most colourful by day, especially in the morning, while by night the **market street** just around the corner from the Ruìlì Bīnguǎn is the liveliest place to hang out. Most of Ruìlì's sights are outside town, and you'll need a bicycle to get out and see them.

Nobody really comes to Ruìlì for the *day*life, though. Ruìlì doesn't even crack a somnolent eye until 10 pm, at which point it transforms itself into an entirely different city altogether. The candlelight power from the neon and flashing lights could probably be viewed from the Mir space station – hundreds of sidewalk restaurants spring open, tourists get taken everywhere to look at cheap jade while their friends scream into karaoke microphones. Others take potshots in the ever-present electronic rifle ranges. The population of Ruìlì seems to triple at night. All this fun madness is lasting until later and later; it still isn't a city that never sleeps, but it's getting there.

RUÌLÌ

PLACES TO STAY
3 Ruìlì Bīnguǎn
   瑞丽宾馆
8 Yǒngchāng
   Dàjiǔdiàn
   永昌大酒家
10 Limín Bīnguǎn
   利民宾馆
12 Nányáng Bīnguǎn
   南洋宾馆

PLACES TO EAT
7 Burmese
   Restaurants
   缅甸餐厅

11 Jo Jo's Cold Drinks Shop
   觉觉冷饮店
13 Noodle Stalls
   面条店
17 Burmese Restaurants
   缅甸餐厅

OTHER
1 PSB
   公安局
2 Buses to
   Zhāngfēng
   往章凤的汽车
4 Post Office
   邮电大楼

5 Xinhua Bookstore
   新华书店
6 Cinema
   电影院
9 Yunnan Airlines
   云南航空公司
14 Minibus Stand
   小型车站
15 Long-Distance
   Bus Station
   长途汽车站
16 Bank of China
   中国银行
18 Hospital
   医院

Places to Stay

The well-run **Limín Bīnguǎn** has triples with common washroom for Y60. Similar doubles are Y40, while standard doubles with attached bath are Y120. One other place that takes foreigners and has dormitory accommodation is the **Ruìlì Bīnguǎn**. Being a bit further away from the main strip, it offers refuge from the blaring discos and evil roadside karaoke stands. Beds in basic quads and doubles are Y20 each. Bathrooms and showers are on the 1st floor. There are also doubles for Y120 – some are OK value.

Across the street, the Mingrui Hotel was for a long time the budget hotel for foreigners. No longer: the PSB closed it down in 1999, reportedly after a spate of questionable room thefts.

The **Yǒngchāng Dàjiǔdiàn** (☎ 414 1808) attracts fewer travellers, but is also a comfortable and clean place to stay; look at a few rooms. Standard singles/doubles here are Y120 to Y360 though they've been amenable to negotiation. Back on the main strip, the **Nányáng Bīnguǎn** (☎ 414 1768) has doubles/triples for Y100/90. Though this place doesn't look like much at first, some of the rooms aren't that bad at all, and it has the pluses of 24-hour hot water and a management amenable to price negotiation.

If all of the above are full (not likely) or not to your taste, there are many other **hotels** to choose from, including several down

on Biancheng Lu. Standard doubles at these places all share a sense of shabby luxury, and usually cost between Y100 and Y130.

Places to Eat

Reports concerning the existence of decent curries in Ruìlì are the result perhaps of wishful embellishment, but some food is good. Take a stroll up the market street around the corner from the Ruìlì Bīnguǎn in the evening and check out all the hotpot stands (as always with hotpot, confirm prices before you order and eat).

For good Burmese food, there are several **restaurants** in a small alley off Jiegang Lu. The one at the top of the north-western corner is particularly good, and sees a lot of Burmese patrons. This is also the spot to go for Thai Mekong whisky, served Thai style with soda water and ice. More **Burmese places**, with outdoor seating in the evenings, can be found just south of the cinema on Renmin Lu. The **noodle stalls** on the street off Nanmao Jie just west of the bus station are also very good.

For nice iced coffee and fruit juice drinks, or something stronger, try **Jo Jo's Cold Drinks Shop** (Juéjué Léngyǐndiàn). The shop is on the corner of Nanmao Jie and Baijiang Xigang. Burmese ales cost Y10 a pop but are twice the strength of Chinese beers. You can also get fried noodles or other basic dishes. A proliferation of other 'beer/coffee/tea/ice cream/juice' places

– many actually incorporate all those in their names – have cropped up along the main and side drags.

Take the opportunity to try a freshly squeezed lime juice from one of the numerous stands dotting the town. At Y5 a glass it costs a bit more than your average drink, but the taste is superb.

Entertainment

Ruìlì may only be a small town, but by Chinese standards it packs a lot of punch on the entertainment level. For the Chinese, Ruìlì has a reputation as one of *the* happening places in Yúnnán, and young people with money head down here just for a few nights out. But where discos used to be the venue of choice, now massage parlours have taken over. Prostitution is rampant in Ruìlì, and it's difficult to find a sleaze-free bar or dance hall. This is, of course, still China, and things are much tamer than Bangkok or Manila. Everything closes down around 1 to 2 am, and you needn't worry about being flagged down in the street by pimps. Still, be aware if you get adventurous and duck into a dark bar for a drink.

The discos are still in action, although they tend to slow down even earlier, around midnight on a slow night. There is also a dance hall opposite the Burmese restaurants on Renmin Jie that has a live band playing most nights. There is usually an entrance fee of Y20 or so, depending on where you go, but it's worth it for an insight into China's jiving nightspots.

Getting There & Away

Ruìlì has daily flight connections to Kūnmíng via Mángshì (Y530; 50 minutes). Yunnan Airlines (☎ 414 8275; in Mángshì ☎ 212 1492) has an office next to the Yǒngchàng Dàjiǔdiàn. You can also use the ticket office to book and reconfirm return flights.

As always, the Chinese government is supposedly hard at work 'improving' roads between Déhóng region and Kūnmíng. Although things are much improved these days, it's still a long, long haul. Sleeper buses for the 22- to 24-hour ride (god will-ing) to Kūnmíng leave from the long-distance bus station eight times daily from 7 am to 7 pm. The trip costs Y150 to Y160.

Sleeper buses to Xiàguān (Dàlǐ) leave at 4, 6, and 7 pm (Y90; 10 hours).

There are 10 buses between 6.50 am and 2 pm to Bǎoshān (Y35; seven to nine hours). This ride should become shorter as work progresses on a new primary-grade road linking Ruìlì and Bǎoshān.

Buses for Téngchōng leave at 6.30, 7 and 9 am (one small and one large, Y25); the trip takes anywhere between five and seven hours. There are two buses for Yíngjiāng (Y18). On a good day, the ride takes four to five hours, but there are few good days on this rainy route.

Buses leave for Mángshì frequently between 8 am and 3 pm from a driveway just east of the long-distance bus station. The two-hour ride costs Y15 to Y20. Private entrepreneurs advertise lots of destinations from just a few steps to the west of the bus station's ticket window, so check the signs for more convenient departures or prices.

Minibuses and vans leave for more local destinations from opposite the long-distance bus station.

Getting Around

To/From the Airport Minibuses leave daily for the two-hour trip to the airport; check that day's flight schedule to see what time they leave.

Other Transport Ruìlì itself is easily explored on foot, but all the most interesting day trips require a bicycle.

A flat rate for a route inside the city should be Y5.

AROUND RUÌLÌ

Most of the sights around Ruìlì can be explored easily by bicycle. It's worth making frequent detours down the narrow paths that lead off the main roads to visit minority villages. The people are friendly, and there are lots of photo opportunities. The shortest ride is left at the corner near the post office and then out of the town proper into a little village. There are half a dozen Shan temples scattered about, and it's a great trip first finding them all, and then looking inside the unique interiors.

Nóng'ān Jīnyā Tǎ
Golden Duck Temple

A short ride to the south-west of town, Nóng'ān Jīnyā Tǎ is an attractive stupa in a courtyard. It is said to have been established to mark the arrival of a pair of golden ducks that brought good fortune to what was previously an uninhabited marshy area.

Jiěgào Border Checkpoint
姐告边检点

Continue straight ahead from the Nóng'ān Jīnyā Tǎ, cross the Myanmar bridge over the Ruìlì River and you will come to Jiěgào, a little thumb of land jutting into Myanmar that serves as the main checkpoint for a steady stream of cross-border traffic (see the Myanmar Border Crossing section earlier for more details). There's not a lot to see. But you can still marvel at how laid-back everything seems on both sides of the – quite literally – bamboo curtain and indulge the perennial fascination with illicit borders. Wildly popular casinos and other sordid dens of iniquity line the streets of both sides of the border, and in one case apparently right on the border.

Jiěgào is about 7km from the Ruìlì long-distance bus station. Locals pay Y4 for a ride before 10 pm, and Y5 after that, but you'll likely have to pay Y5 anyway. If there are four or five of you, bargain them down to Y3.

Temples

Just after the Nóng'ān Jīnyā Tǎ is a crossroads. The road to the right leads to the villages of Jiěxiàng and Nóngdǎo, and on the way are a number of small temples, villages and stupas worth a look. Most of them are not particularly noteworthy and the village life nearby is more interesting – there are often small market areas near the temples.

The first major temple is the **Hánshāzhuāng Sì** (Hansha Temple), a fine wooden structure with a few resident monks. It's set a little off the road, but is easy to find.

Another 15 minutes or so down the road, look out for a white stupa on the hillside to the right. This is **Léizhuāngxiāng**, Ruìlì's oldest stupa, dating back to the middle of the Tang dynasty. There's a nunnery in the grounds of the stupa and fantastic views of the Ruìlì area. Once the stupa comes into view, take the next path to the right that cuts through the fields. There are signs in Chinese and Dai pointing the way, which leads through a couple of Dai villages. You'll need to get off your bicycle and push for the last ascent up to the stupa.

A couple of kilometres past the town of Jiěxiàng is **Dēnghánnóngzhuāng Sì**, a wooden Dai temple with pleasant surroundings. Like the other temples in the area, the effect is spoiled somewhat by the corrugated tin roof.

Nóngdǎo 弄岛

Around 29km south-west of Ruìlì, the small town of Nóngdǎo is worth an overnight trip (or not as some have opined). The locals (mainly Burmese and Dai) don't get all that many foreign visitors and are a friendly lot. There's a solitary hotel in town (you can't miss it) which has cheap doubles with beds and a few ants from Y10. It would be possible to cycle here, stopping off at some of the temple sights along the way, or take a minibus from Ruìlì – they leave fairly frequently through the day.

Jiělè Jīntǎ 姐勒金塔
Golden Pagoda

A few kilometres to the east of Ruìlì on the road to Wāndīng is the Jiělè Jīntǎ, a fine structure that dates back 200 years.

WĀNDĪNG 畹町

Many travellers don't make it to Wāndīng, or do it only as a day trip. It's not as interesting as Ruìlì, but there's cheaper accommodation here and it's a nice laid-back place to spend a day or so. Part of the attraction is that the town is on the Myanmar border – the Wāndīng Bīnguǎn and the Yùfēng Dàlóu both provide good views of the hills, small township and occasional stupas over on the Myanmar side.

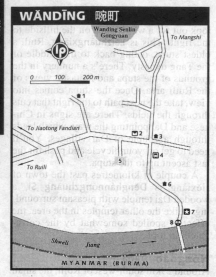

WĂNDĪNG 畹町

WĂNDĪNG

1 Wǎndīng Bīnguǎn
畹町宾馆
2 Post Office
邮局
3 Yùfēng Dàlóu
裕丰大楼
4 Minivans to Ruili &
Mángshi
芒市、
瑞丽小型汽车站
5 Cooperative Border
Market
中缅友谊市场
6 Zhōngyín Bīnguǎn
中银宾馆
7 PSB
公安局
8 Myanmar Border
Checkpoint
缅甸边界

Information

The post office, where you can make international phone calls, is next door to the Xinhua Bookstore on the same road.

Staff at the foreign affairs office of the PSB, just across from the Chinese border checkpoint, seem quite easygoing and, despite the fact they won't help you sneak into Myanmar, they are otherwise quite accommodating.

Things to See & Do

The new **Cooperative Border Market** is a vast multi-storey affair complete with atrium and skylights, and hundreds of stalls for would-be border traders. At the time of writing, occupants numbered only several dozen, and the empty, echoing hallways seemed to be waiting for a vast surge of business that was still nowhere in sight. You might want to stop by to see if things have picked up.

A two-minute walk down from the Yùfēng Dàlóu will see you in Myanmar. The only giveaway is the dilapidated customs office. Apparently a Belgian couple did a day trip into Myanmar for US$20 several years ago (the proceeds were shared by those who failed to notice them crossing the

bridge), but the guards were not interested in allowing a repeat performance when we were in town.

It's worth climbing up to the north of town to take a look at the **Wǎndīng Sēnlín Gōngyuán** (Wanding Forest Reserve). There's a Y2 entry charge and some pleasant walks. Avoid the absolutely pathetic zoo, home to three psychotic monkeys, a couple of peacocks and an unidentifiable ball of fur that was either fast asleep or dead.

Local places to stay can provide information on river trips which include a barbecue lunch in a minority village. Prices vary depending on the number of participants, but you should be able to do it for around Y50 per person.

Places to Stay & Eat

The cheapest place to stay is the slightly decayed *Yùfēng Dàlóu*. If you can get them, dorm beds here are Y15. They'll likely as not push you into basic doubles for Y60.

The better-kept and friendly *Wǎndīng Bīnguǎn* is in a rambling building up on the hill with good views of Myanmar. Comfortable doubles with attached bathroom and satellite TV are Y80. Look for the alabaster statue of a frolicking maiden holding what looks to be a miniature UFO in her hand at the front entrance.

Just up the street from the border, the **Zhōngyín Bīnguǎn** is another budget choice in Wǎndīng, with singles/doubles from Y50/60.

A brand-new hulking thing – the **Jiāotōng Fàndiàn** (*Traffic Hotel*) – has opened on the west side of town. Upmarket doubles start at Y120 here.

The area around the Yùfēng Dàlóu is best for *cheap restaurants*. Most of them are of the pick-and-choose variety, and all are much the same. In the mornings try the **dumpling stands** opposite the turn-off for the Wǎndīng Bīnguǎn.

Getting There & Away

Minibuses run to Ruìlì for Y10 to Y15 and to Mángshì for Y15 to Y25; they should be on the lower end of the price range. They leave throughout the day whenever they are full. You shouldn't have to wait more than 15 minutes for a bus to Ruìlì; buses to Mángshì are less frequent.

MÁNGSHÌ 芒市 (LUXI)

Mángshì is Déhóng's air link with the outside world. If you fly in from Kūnmíng there are minibuses running direct from the airport to Ruìlì and most people take this option. But Mángshì has a casual south-east Asian feel to it – despite the fact that it went from somnolent to buzzing in one edition – and there are a few sights in and around the town that make dallying here a day or so worthwhile if you have the time.

Things to See

It's interesting just to take a wander round. There are a couple of markets in town and a number of **temples** in the vicinity of the Déhóng Bīnguǎn. Around 7km to 8km south of town are the **Fǎpà Wēnquán** (Fapa Hot Springs), which get good reports from travellers.

One block south of the main road along Qingnian Lu is the **Mínzú Wénhuà Gōng** (Mangshi Nationalities Palace), which is more like a large park/plaza full of elderly Chinese practising their *taijiquan* (tai chi).

MÁNGSHÌ

1 Buses to Wǎndīng & Ruìlì
   往畹町,瑞丽的汽车站
2 CAAC
   中国民航
3 Buses to Wǎndīng & Ruìlì
   往畹町,瑞丽的汽车站
4 Nánjiāng Fàndiàn
   南疆饭店
5 Bank of China
   中国银行
6 Post Office
   邮局
7 Market
   市场
8 Long-Distance Bus Station
   客运中心
9 Táiwān Dòujiāng Dàwáng
   台湾豆浆大王
10 Mángshì Tángchǎng Dàjiǔjiā
   芒市糖厂大酒家
11 Temples
   寺庙
12 Déhóng Zhōu Mángshì Bīnguǎn
   德宏州芒市宾馆
13 Mínzú Wénhuà Gōng
   民族文化宫

It has small exhibits on nationalities and lots of ersatz water-splashing festivities daily in a mock Dai village. It recently relocated here, so perhaps more will be added. There is a Y3 main gate entrance fee. It's posted as open from 7.30 am to midnight, but it's rarely open these long hours.

Places to Stay & Eat

The most popular place to stay is the peaceful, friendly and very well-run *Déhóng Zhōu Mángshì Bīnguǎn (Dehong State Mangshi Guesthouse)*, set back a bit off the road (you have to go under a gate of sorts). To get there from the main road, head south down a bizarre-looking block completely redone in Miami Beach Art Deco pastels. Doubles/triples with bath, TV and fan are Y100/110, an excellent deal. Upmarket doubles range from Y140 to Y180. They're often willing to bargain. *Don't confuse this place with a similarly named place one large block north-east.*

Two blocks west of here is the *Mángshì Tángchǎng Dàjiǔjiā*, and though it's called a restaurant it's got immaculate rooms with doubles from Y40 to Y60.

On the main road, the *Nánjiāng Fàndiàn* (☎ 212 1641) has dorm beds from Y10. Standard doubles/triples go for Y80/90. The place is nothing to rave about, but it's conveniently situated if you're catching an early bus or booking plane tickets.

There are also numerous pick-and-choose *restaurants* around town. Along the block leading to the main road from the Déhóng Zhōu Mángshì Bīnguǎn is the *Taíwān Dòujiāng Dàwáng (Taiwan Doujiang King)*, king of the tasty soybean drink. It also has Taiwan-style ice desserts along with basic stir-fried entrees and noodles. Another version is found north of the long-distance bus station, where a couple of the Burmese employees speak a modicum of English. One block west of the Déhóng Zhōu Mángshì Bīnguǎn at the first intersection is a smattering of *cold drink vendors*.

Getting There & Away

There are daily Boeing 737 flights between Mángshì and Kūnmíng (Y530; 50 minutes).

Mángshì has many private bus stations – at least four on an east-west stroll of the downtown area. Shop around. Minibuses connect Mángshì proper with Wǎndīng for Y15 to Y25 depending on your bargaining skills. Most of the minibuses to Wǎndīng troll the main road back and forth until full; be prepared for a half hour of circling. All stations except the long-distance station have scheduled daily buses for the ride to Ruìlì from 7 am to 1 pm (Y20 to Y25; two hours).

There are buses to Bǎoshān every day between 7 am and noon (Y30, Y60 in a sleeper; five hours). Buses to Téngchōng (Y22; five hours) leave at 8.30 and 11 am. The Nánjiāng Fàndiàn also runs a minibus there.

There is one sleeper bus daily to Xiàguān at 8 am (Y90; 11 hours) and sleeper buses to Kūnmíng from 10.30 to 5 pm (Y120; 18 hours).

Getting Around

Buses leave from the airport to Mángshì (Y2) after the Kūnmíng flight arrives. Buses depart the Mángshì CAAC office for the airport around an hour before flight departures. It is possible to book or reconfirm flights here, or you could wait until you get to Ruìlì, which most travellers do. A fleet of minibuses to Ruìlì (Y30) awaits incoming flights.

Chóngqìng 重庆

CHÓNGQÌNG CITY 重庆
☎ 0811

Perched on steep hills overlooking the confluence of two rivers, Chóngqìng is one of China's more unusual cities. Dusty grey tenements and shining office towers cling to the precipitous hillsides that make up much of the city centre.

Another unique aspect is the absence of bicycles. There's barely a cyclist to be found, as the hill climbs make it coronary country for any would-be rider. In 1997 the city *banned* outright the use of car horns to improve noise pollution on the congested peninsula. Traffic laws are enforced somewhat more rigorously here in general.

Chóngqìng is quite pleasant to stroll around and although it's not exactly brimming with 'sights' there's a certain picturesque quality to this grey city. For tourists the 'sights' are usually connected with the communist revolution, most being linked to the city's role as the wartime capital of the Kuomintang from 1938 to 1945.

Though it plays second fiddle to Chéngdū, Chóngqìng is hardly a backwater. It is rated as the chief industrial city of south-western China, with its production amounting to a fifth of Sìchuān's total industrial output. The total metropolitan area has a population of some 14 million; of these around three million live in the city proper.

With all this, the city long lobbied for a special status akin to that of Shànghǎi. In 1997 what it got was not quite province status, but the 30-odd million residents of the three county area (now the largest in China by most statistical methods) separated from Sìchuān and became a 'special' municipality directly under the control of the central government, like Běijīng, Tiānjīn and Shànghǎi.

China's economic boom has infected Chóngqìng with a severe case of skyscraper fever: at every turn there seems to be either a tower going up or a vast hole in the ground awaiting a foundation.

Highlights

Population: 30.4 million
Area: 82,400 sq km

- Dàzú Xiàn, the site of some of China's most celebrated Buddhist cave sculptures and grotto art
- Hóngyán Cūn, the WWII headquarters of the communist representatives to the Kuomintang

Within China, Chóngqìng is famous for its searing summers, when temperatures can exceed 40°C (104°F). This pleasant climate has earned the city a place among the country's 'three furnaces' – the other two being Wǔhàn and Nánjīng.

History
In 1996 stone tools unearthed along the Cháng Jiāng (Yangzi River) valleys showed that hominids were found in this region two million years ago, a million years earlier than had been thought.

Chóngqìng (known in pre-Pinyin China as 'Chungking') was opened as a treaty port in 1890, but not many foreigners made it up the river to this isolated outpost, and those who did had little impact.

An industrialisation program started in 1928, but it was in the wake of the Japanese

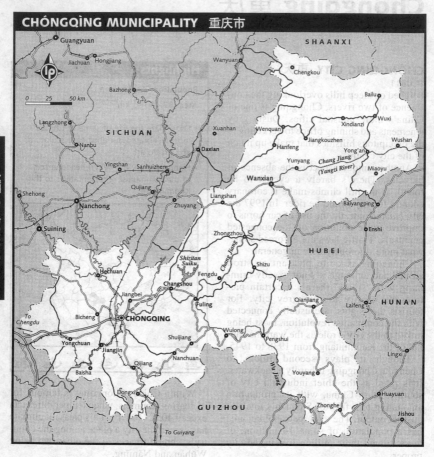

CHÓNGQÌNG 重庆

In more modern times, in the shadow of
strutting Kuomintang military leaders, representatives of the Chinese Communist
Party (CCP), including Zhou Enlai, acted as
'liaisons' between Chóngqìng and the communists' headquarters at Yán'ān, in
Shaanxi.

invasion that Chóngqìng really took off as a
major centre, after the Kuomintang retreated
to set up its wartime capital here. Refugees
from all over China flooded in, swelling the
population to more than two million.

The irony of this overpopulated, over-
strained city with its bomb-shattered houses
is that the name means 'double jubilation'
or 'repeated good luck'. Emperor Zhao Dun
of the Song dynasty ascended to the throne
in 1190, having previously been made the
prince of the city of Guǎngzhōu; as a celebration of these two happy events, he renamed Guǎngzhōu as Chóngqìng.

Repeated efforts to bring the sides together in a unified front against the Japanese largely failed due to mutual distrust and
Chiang Kaishek's obsession with wiping
out the communists, even at the cost of
yielding Chinese territory to an invading
army.

Orientation

The heart of Chóngqìng spreads across a hilly peninsula of land wedged between the Jiālíng Jiāng (Jialing River) to the north and the Cháng Jiāng (Yangzi River) to the south. They meet at the tip of the peninsula at the eastern end of the city.

For most visitors the central focus of this congested peninsula of winding streets is the now neon-shrouded **Jiěfàng Bēi** (Liberation Monument), which is within walking distance of most accommodation.

Chóngqìng is easy to explore on foot. The distances are manageable, and there's always an interesting alley to duck into. Between the Jiěfàng Bēi and **Cháotiānmén Dock** (Cháotiānmén Mǎtóu) are a number of steep, laddered alleyways, usually lined with little shops. Also of interest, and within walking distance of the Jiěfàng Bēi, are the cable cars over the Jiālíng and Cháng Rivers.

Maps Good maps in Chinese and much less detailed ones in English are available from street vendors around the Jiěfàng Bēi area or surrounding the bus stations.

Information

Money The main Chóngqìng branch of the Bank of China is on Minzu Lu, up the road from the Huìxiānlóu Bīnguǎn (see Places to Stay). The branch right next door to the Huìxiānlóu Bīnguǎn also has a window for changing money on the 2nd floor. Most hotels have foreign-exchange counters.

Post & Communications There's a post office on Minzu Lu, which is within walking distance of the Chóngqìng Fàndiàn and Huìxiānlóu Bīnguǎn, and purports to have 24-hour services. Basic postal services are available at most of the top-end hotels.

PSB The Public Security Bureau (PSB; Gōngānjú; ☎ 383 1830) has an office on Linjiang Lu. Bus No 103 from the front of the Rénmín Bīnguǎn will take you there. If you're after permits for the wilds of northern or western Sìchuān, wait until you get to Chéngdū, where the PSB are more used to dealing with this kind of thing.

Edgar Snow

In 1939 Edgar Snow arrived in Chóngqìng to find a city living in fear of Japanese raids. It was, he said:

... a place of moist heat, dirt and wide confusion, into which, between air raids, the imported central government ... made an effort to introduce some technique of order and construction. Acres of buildings had been destroyed in the barbaric raids of May and June.

The Japanese preferred moonlit nights for their calls, when from their base in Hankow they could follow the silver banner of the angzi River up to its confluence with the Jialing River, which identified the capital in a way no blackout could obscure.

The city had no defending air force and only a few anti-aircraft guns ... Spacious public shelters were being dug, but it was estimated that a third of the population still had no protection. Government officials, given advance warning, sped outside the city in their motor cars – cabinet ministers first, then vice-ministers, then minor bureaucrats.

The populace soon caught on; when they saw a string of official cars racing to the west, they dropped everything and ran. A mad scramble of rickshaws, carts, animals and humanity blew up the main streets like a great wind, carrying all before it.

Luóhàn Sì 罗汉寺
Arhat Temple

'Luohan' is the Chinese rendering of the Sanskrit 'arhat', which is a Buddhist term referring to people who have released themselves from the psychological bondage of greed, hate and delusion.

Built about 1000 years ago, the Luóhàn Sì has a long entrance flanked by rock carvings, a hall of painted terracotta arhat sculptures and a hall containing a large gold buddha figure. Behind the buddha altar is an Indian-style jataka mural depicting Prince Siddhartha in the process of cutting his hair to renounce the world.

CHÓNGQÌNG 重庆

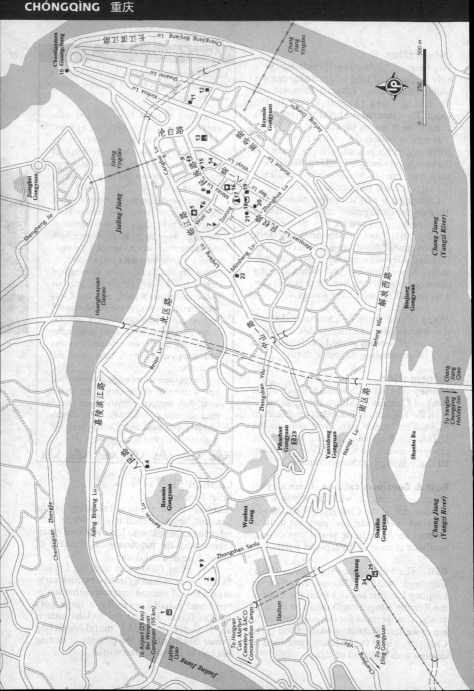

Chaotianmen 朝天门
10 Guangchang

长江滨江路 Changjiang Binjiang Lu

Chang Jiang Yingdao 长江英岛

Shaanxi Lu 陕西路

Xinhua Lu 新华路

11 12

Renmin Dongiu 人民东路

Jiefang Beilu 解放北路

Renmin Gongyuan 人民公园

沧白路 Cangbai Lu

13

9
15
14

Jiebei Lu 五一路

Xinhua Lu 新华路

Jiefang Beilu 解放北路

Jiefang Beilu

Jiefang Beilu

Jialing Yingdao 嘉陵英岛

Jialing Jiang 嘉陵江

临江路 Linjiang Lu

5
8

16
17

Wusi Lu 五四路

6

7

Zourong Lu 邹容路

21
18 19
20

Zhonghua Lu 中华路

Minsheng Lu 民生路

Wenhua Lu 文化路

Chang Jiang (Yangzi River) 长江

Binjiang Gongyuan 滨江公园

Jiangbei Gongyuan 江北公园

Shengheng Jie 胜恒街

Chenjiaguan Zhengjie 陈家馆正街

22

Mincheng Lu 民成路

Huanghuayuan Daqiao 黄花园大桥

Beiqu Lu 北区路

Jiefang Xilu 解放西路
Jiefang Xilu

Zhongshan Yilu 中山一路

Chang Jiang Qiao 长江桥

To Yangtze Chongqing Holiday Inn

北区路 Beiqu Lu

嘉陵滨江路 Jialing Binjiang Lu

Zhongshan Yilu 中山一路

Nanqu Lu 南区路

Shanhu Ba 珊瑚坝

Pibashan Gongyuan 枇杷山公园
23

Yanzidong Gongyuan 燕子洞公园

To Airport (25 km) &
Bei Wenquan
(55 km)

Jialing Qiao 嘉陵桥

Jialing Binjiang Lu 嘉陵滨江路

4

Renmin Gongyuan 人民公园

Renmin Lu 人民路

Wenhua Gong 文化宫

Zhongshan Sanlu 中山三路

3

2

To Hongyan
Cun, Martyrs'
Cemetery & SACO
Concentration Camps

1

Stadium

Zhongshan Sanlu 中山三路

Shanhu Gongyuan 珊瑚公园

Yilu

Eling Gongyuan 鹅岭公园

To Zoo &
Eling Gongyuan

Guangchang 广场

24
25

Jialing Jiang 嘉陵江

Chang Jiang (Yangzi River) 长江

N
500 m
250
0

CHÓNGQÌNG

PLACES TO STAY

4 Rénmín Bīnguǎn
人民宾馆

8 Huìxiānlóu Bīnguǎn
会仙楼宾馆

11 Chóngqìng Fàndiàn
重庆饭店

12 Chóngqìng Shípǐn Dàshà
重庆食品大厦

19 Yúdū Bīnguǎn
渝都宾馆

22 Chóngqìng Bīnguǎn
重庆宾馆

PLACES TO EAT

3 Dōngnányà Cānyǐnzhōngxīn
东南亚餐饮中心

6 California Beef Noodles
加州牛肉面

7 Yízhīshí Dàjiǔdiàn
颐之时大酒店

14 Lǎo Sìchuān Fàndiàn
老四川饭店

15 Yángròu Guǎn
羊肉馆

OTHER

1 Buses to SACO Concentration Camps
至中美合作所汽车站

2 CAAC
中国民航

5 PSB
公安局外事科

9 Bank of China
中国银行

10 Cháotiānmén Dock (Booking Hall)
朝天门码头（售票处）

13 Luóhàn Sì
罗汉寺

16 Jiǔkù Jiǔbā
酒库酒吧

17 Jiěfàng Bēi
解放碑

18 Post Office
邮电局

20 Foreign Languages Bookstore
外文书店

21 Xinhua Bookstore
新华书店

23 Chóngqìng Bówùguǎn
博物馆

24 Train Station
火车站

25 Long-Distance Bus Station
长途汽车站

CHÓNGQÌNG 重庆

During its peak, Luóhàn Sì was home to some 70 monks; these days there's around 18 in residence. The temple is popular with local worshippers who burn tonnes of fragrant incense. Try and make an effort to call into this temple, even just to take a quick look at the incredibly lifelike arhats. You can't miss the place now – there's actually a sign out front advertising rooms and the temple's vegetarian restaurant via a winking monk!

The vegetarian restaurant is excellent and very cheap, but it's only open for lunch (approximately 11.30 am to 1.30 pm). The temple itself is open from 8 am to 5 pm and admission is Y3. Follow Minzu Lu northeast from Jiěfàng Bēi, turn right into Canghai Lu, then right down a small alley.

Hóngyán Cūn 红岩村
Red Cliff Village

During the tenuous Kuomintang-communist alliance against the Japanese during WWII, Hóngyán Cūn, outside Chóngqìng, was used as the offices and living quarters of the communist representatives to the Kuomintang.

Among others, Ye Jianying, Zhou Enlai and Zhou's wife Deng Yingchao lived here. After the Japanese surrender in 1945, it was also to Chóngqìng that Mao Zedong – at the instigation of US ambassador Patrick Hurley – came in August of that year to join in the peace negotiations with the Kuomintang. The talks lasted 42 days and resulted in a formal agreement, which Mao described as 'words on paper'. The museum on site now has a large collection of photos, although none of the captions is in English.

A short walk from the museum is the building that housed the South Bureau of the Communist Party's Central Committee and the office of the representatives of the Eighth Route Army – although there's little to see except a few sparse furnishings and photographs.

To get to Hóngyán Cūn, take bus No 104 from its station on Beiqu Lu, just north of the Jiěfàng Bēi. However, locals insist the best one to take is the No 215.

Hóngyán Cūn is open daily from 8 am to 5.30 pm and admission is Y6. At the time of writing the museum was not accessible due to renovation; you may only be able to view the Eighth Army Route office.

Concentration Camps

In 1943, the USA and Chiang Kaishek signed a secret agreement to set up the Sino-American Cooperation Organisation

(SACO), under which the USA helped to train and dispatch secret agents for the Kuomintang government.

The chief of SACO was Dai Li, the notorious head of the Kuomintang military secret service; its deputy chief was a US Navy officer, Commodore ME Miles. The SACO prisons were set up outside Chóngqìng during WWII. The Kuomintang recognised, though never tolerated, the Communist Party as a legal political entity, though in theory it recognised its army as allies in the struggle against the Japanese invaders.

Civilian communists remained subject to the same repressive laws and, although these were not enforced at the time, they were not actually rescinded. Hundreds of political prisoners were kept captive by the Kuomintang in these prisons and others; documents exist showing many were executed. Unfortunately, the absence of English captions makes this a fairly uninteresting sight for most western visitors. The **US-Chiang Kaishek Criminal Acts Exhibition Hall**, or **Zhōngměi Hézuòsuǒ Jízhōngyíng Jiùzhǐ**, has lots of photos on display; there are manacles and chains, but nothing too ghoulish. The hall is open daily from 8 am to 7 pm and admission is Y2.

To get there take bus No 215 or 217 (45 minutes) from the terminus just south of Zhongshan Sanlu, not far from the Jiālǐng Qiáo (Jialing Bridge). Make sure that the driver knows where you want to get off, as the place is not obvious. The prisons are a long hour's walk from the hall.

Alternatively, if you are really keen to see these sights, there are Chinese tour buses leaving from the Cháotiānmén Dock and the train station. Tours are a pricey Y60 for four hours and should include everything. They take in both the hall and the prisons and throw in some other revolutionary sights as well.

Temple Parks
Chóngqìng's two temple parks get neglected by many visitors, but they are a pleasant enough way to while away an afternoon. **Píbǎshān Gōngyuán**, at 345m, marks the highest point on the Chóngqìng peninsula. The **Hóngxīng Gé** (Hongxing

Pavilion), at the top of the park, provides good views of Chóngqìng. The park is open from 6 am to 10 pm and costs Y5 with another Y3 admission for the park's temple.

The **Élíng Gōngyuán** (Goose Mountain Park), at the neck of the peninsula, is more of a hike and contains the Liangjiang Pavilion.

Bridges
Worth checking out are the enormous Jiālǐng and Cháng Jiāng Bridges. The **Jiālǐng Qiáo**, which crosses the river west of central Chóngqìng, was built between 1963 and 1966. It is 150m long and 60m high and for 15 years was one of the few means of access to the rest of China.

The **Chángjiāng Qiáo**, to the south, was finished in 1981. In 1989 the new Shímén Qiáo over the Jiālǐng Jiāng was completed.

Cable-Car Trips
There are cable cars spanning both the Jiālǐng Jiāng and Cháng Jiāng. The rides provide stunning views of precipitously stacked housing and environment-unfriendly industrial estates. The ride over the Cháng Jiāng actually links up to a series of lifts and Chiang Kaishek's old domicile. Both are within walking distance of the Jiěfàng Bēi (Liberation Monument).

The Jiālǐng Jiāng cable car starts from Cangbai Lu, and the Cháng Jiāng cable car starts from near Xinhua Lu. Both run daily from 6.30 am to 9.30 pm and cost Y1.

Chóngqìng Bówùguǎn 博物馆
Chongqing Museum

The dinosaur skeletons on display at this museum were unearthed at Zígòng, Yangchuan and elsewhere in Sìchuān between 1974 and 1977. The museum is at the foot of Píbǎshān Gōngyuán in the south of town; its open daily from 9 am to 5 pm; entry is Y10 and Y10 for the dinosaur exhibits.

Běi Wēnquán Gōngyuán
北温泉公园
Northern Hot Springs Park

Fifty-five kilometres north-east of the city, overlooking the Jiālǐng Jiāng, the Běi Wēnquán (Northern Hot Springs) are in a

Quán: spring, fountain
The modern character is a simple combination of the characters for pure (above) and water (below), since the water from a spring is likely to be drinkable.

large park that is the site of a 5th-century Buddhist temple.

The springs have an Olympic-size swimming pool where you can bathe to an audience. There are also private rooms with big hot baths. Water temperature averages around 32°C (89.6°F). Swimsuits, coloured red to symbolise happiness, can be hired here. Twenty kilometres south of Chóngqìng is another group of springs with hotter waters, but the Běi Wēnquán are better.

To get to Běi Wēnquán Gōngyuán, hop on bus No 306 at the Jiěfàng Bēi.

Places to Stay – Budget & Mid-Range

Chóngqìng has a serious shortage of budget accommodation, which means that most travellers get out of town as quickly as possible.

Near Cháotiānmén Dock, for a brief period in early 1999, a couple of cheap Chinese hotels accepted foreigners for as little as Y30 per double. Just as swiftly the long arm of the law put a stop to it. One or two will still accept foreigners but the cheapest beds you'll find are in Y150 triples with common bath.

The only dorms in the central part of the city are the seven-bed rooms at the **Huìxiānlóu Bīnguǎn** (☎ 638 45101, fax 638 44234), close to the Jiěfàng Bēi, where a bed will set you back Y70. It's expensive,

but the hotel is in a good location and the remodelled, air-conditioned dorms are quite nice. From the train station, walk up to Zhongshan Lu and take bus No 405 to the Jiěfàng Bēi.

Another option is **Chóngqìng Shípǐn Dàshà** (☎ 6384 76775, 72 Shaanxi Lu) (look for the 'Food Hotel' sign), near the Cháotiānmén Dock. This place has unremarkable but decent (best described by one traveller as 'cleanish') singles/doubles/triples with bath and air-con for Y130/150/180. The hotel also has doubles and triples with common bath for Y60/90, but you probably won't have much luck getting in. It'll also help you book boat and train tickets here.

Places to Stay – Top End

Most hotels in Chóngqìng charge ridiculous amounts of money. If you don't mind an expensive stay, the **Rénmín Bīnguǎn** (☎ 638 51421, fax 638 52076) is one of the most incredible hotels in China, and if you don't stay here you have to at least visit the place. It's quite literally a palace, with a design that seems inspired by the Temple of Heaven and the Forbidden City in Běijīng. Singles are priced at Y600, while doubles range from Y600 and Y1700. There's also a presidential suite that commands a cool US$460 a night.

An enormous circular concert hall, 65m high and seating 4000 people, sits amid the splendour; technically it isn't part of the hotel but it sure adds to the glamour of the place.

From the train station, the best way to get to the hotel is to head up to Zhongshan Lu and catch bus No 401 or 405 to the traffic circle and walk east down Renmin Lu. Alternatively, if you are spending this kind of money for a room, catch a taxi for Y12.

The **Chóngqìng Fàndiàn** (☎ 638 38888, fax 638 43085, 41-43 Xinhua Lu), a three-star joint-venture operation on Xinhua Lu near the Cháotiānmén Dock area, has singles and doubles for Y270. Facilities include a small gift shop (with a few English books), currency exchange, post and telecommunications, a taxi service and a clinic.

The **Chóngqìng Bīnguǎn** (☎ 638 45888, fax 638 30643), on Minsheng Lu, has transformed itself into a four-star Chinese-style luxury hotel. Singles/doubles in the old wing are US$50/60, and singles and doubles in the new VIP wing start at US$105, which includes breakfast.

Close to the Jiěfàng Běi, the *Yúdū Jiǔdiàn* (☎ *638 35215, fax 638 18168*) boasts a good location and the rooms cost Y280/360/420 for a single/double/triple.

Finally, a fair trudge from all the action on the southern side of the Cháng Jiāng (Yangzi River), is the *Yangtze Chongqing Holiday Inn (Yángzǐjiāng Jiàrì Jiǔdiàn;* ☎ *638 03380)*, with all the services that you would expect of the Holiday Inn chain. Room rates start at US$115, although discounts are possible when the hotel isn't flooded with tour groups.

Places to Eat

The central business district, in the eastern section of the city near the docks, abounds with small *restaurants* and *street vendors*. For tasty noodles and *baozi* (steamed buns), check out Xinhua Lu and Shaanxi Lu towards Cháotiānmén Dock. There are some good *night markets* behind the Huìxiānlóu Bīnguǎn, in the vicinity of Luóhàn Sì and near the Yúdū Jiǔdiàn.

Chóngqìng's number one speciality is *huǒguō*, or hotpot. Skewers of pre-sliced meat and vegetables are placed in boiling hot, spiced oil. Hotpot is usually priced by the skewer and, while it's usually cheap, it's a good idea to check prices as you go along.

Although hotpot can be found wherever there are street vendors or small restaurants, Wuyi Lu has the greatest variety and is locally known as *huǒguō jiē*, or 'hotpot street'. Wuyi Lu runs off Minzu Lu, parallel to Xinhua Lu, a couple of blocks away from the Huìxiānlóu Bīnguǎn and Chóngqìng Fàndiàn (see Places to Stay). Bayi Lu is also a great street for snack hunting.

Zourong Lu is a good street for larger, sit-down restaurants when you have a group and feel like feasting on Sìchuānese main courses. Among them is the well known *Yīzhīshí Cāntīng*, which serves Sìchuān-style pastries in the morning and local specialities like tea-smoked duck and

dry-stewed fish at lunch and dinner. The 2nd floor has full-course meals; go up to the 3rd floor and Y25 will buy you a sampler course of famous Chóngqìng snacks. Draught beer and special *bābǎochá* (eight-treasure tea) do a fine job of washing it all down.

The area around Huìxiānlóu Bīnguǎn is teeming with restaurants. Carnivores can try the *Yángròu Guǎn (Lamb Restaurant)*, just up the road from the hotel. All the lamb dishes here are *hot*, but the kebabs aren't too punishing on the taste buds.

Also not far away is the *Lǎo Sìchuān Fàndiàn*, which is going on 80 years old and is considered Chóngqìng's most famous Sìchuān eatery. Prices are reasonable, but get there early: it closes at 9 pm.

Around the corner from the Huìxiānlóu Bīnguǎn on Wusi Lu is *California Beef Noodles (Jiāzhōu Níuròu Miàn)*, one of seemingly dozens of Chinese restaurants employing the name 'California' for no apparent reason. Nothing Californian about it – the noodles are Chóngqìng hot!

Of the hotel restaurants, Chóngqìng Fàndiàn has the best food. It's expensive by Chinese standards, but moderately priced for most foreigners. Opened shortly after Liberation, this place is another favourite with locals, who just call it 'the old restaurant'. The dishes are nicely presented and accompanied by live Chinese music at night. The hotel's coffee shop serves western breakfasts.

In the western part of the peninsula, opposite the CAAC office, is the slightly up-market *Dōngnányà Cānyǐnzhōngxīn (South-East Asian Restaurant)*, offering a pan-Asia bounty and an English menu. Noodle dishes start at Y10 but most are rather more expensive.

A couple of entertainment options have sprouted up in the Huìxiānlóu Bīnguǎn area. Near the Jiěfàng Běi, the *Jiǔkù Jiǔba (Wine Cellar Bar)* has great views and cosy interiors. New nightspots are opening all the time so ask around.

Getting There & Away

Transport from Chóngqìng to Chéngdū is much easier with the completion of the new expressway. Plans are also underway to link Lèshān with both Chóngqìng and Chéngdū by another high-speed thoroughfare, creating a commerce-friendly triangle of transportation.

Air Chóngqìng's new Jiangbei airport is 25km north of the city. You can buy tickets at the Civil Aviation Administration of China (CAAC; Zhōngguó Mínháng; ☎ 386 2970). Its office, near the corner of Zhongshan Sanlu and Renmin Lu, can be accessed from either street. You can also book flights at the Chóngqìng Fàndiàn, and there are numerous ticket offices around the Jiěfàng Bēi.

Chóngqìng has daily flights to Běijīng (Y1250), Guǎngzhōu (Y940), Shànghǎi (Y1190), Kūnmíng (Y570) and Xī'ān (Y630). Other destinations include Ürümqi (Y2310), Guìlín (Y580), Nánjīng (Y1020) and Hong Kong (Y2250). Services to Bangkok, Taipei and Kaohsiung in Taiwan are planned.

Bus Bus travel in and out of Chóngqìng has become much more convenient with the opening of a new multistorey long-distance bus station next to the train station. It features two ticket halls, two waiting halls and dozens of gates, and the station can process 800 to 1000 buses daily, or so the management claims. If you can't get a bus here, take the pedestrian underpass to the other side of the road along the Cháng Jiāng (Yangzi River), where there's another station. At the time of writing, yet *another* station was being built right at the Cháotiānmén Dock.

To Chéngdū, there are official buses running from 5.45 am to 9.10 pm virtually all the time. Regular minibuses take four to six hours and cost Y59; these are waning in number. Express buses – much more comfy – take three to four hours and cost Y98 plus Y4 for insurance. From Chéngdū to Chóngqìng, the Wuguiqiao bus station has the fastest express buses; see the Chéngdū Getting There & Away section in the Sìchuān chapter.

To Lèshān, buses of all sorts depart hourly from 7 am to 4 pm and cost Y61 to Y91 for the six- to eight-hour trip.

Minibuses to Dàzú (Y29; 2½ hours) depart from the 2nd floor of the main bus station from 6 am to 6 pm every 15 minutes.

Train From Chóngqìng there are direct trains to Shànghǎi, Xī'ān, Guìyáng, Nánníng, Chéngdū, Zhèngzhōu, Guǎngzhōu, Běijīng and Kūnmíng.

There are at least three trains from Chóngqìng to Dàzú between 7.46 am and 12.45 pm. The 7.46 am train (No 204) gets in to Dàzú (it's actually Yóutíng, although schedules say Dàzú) at around 11.50 am. Almost no other trains between Chóngqìng and Chéngdū actually stop in Dàzú.

Trains to Nánníng go via Guìyáng and Liŭzhōu (two hours by bus from Guìlín) and take around 32 hours; a hard sleeper could cost Y159. Trains to Guìyáng take eight to 12 hours and cost Y76 for a hard sleeper.

Trains to Shànghǎi also take in Guìyáng, before making a long haul through the sticks to Hángzhōu and on to the final destination. The journey takes around 44 hours in the fastest train and costs Y488 for a hard sleeper, or Y269 if you're desperate enough to hard seat it.

To Chéngdū, it takes around 11 hours and costs Y86 for a hard sleeper, or Y49 for a hard seat. Trains to Kūnmíng and Panzhihua (for Líjiāng and Dàlǐ) go via Chéngdū, and it makes a lot of sense to break your trip at this point.

If you want to get to Guìlín in a hurry you will have to fly; travelling by train requires that you change in Guìyáng. Alternatively, you might consider travelling to Liŭzhōu by train (Y145 for a hard sleeper) and go on direct to Yángshuò or Guìlín by bus.

Boat The ride from Chóngqìng down the Cháng Jiāng (Yangzi River) to Wǔhàn is a popular tourist trip – a good way of getting away from the trains and an excellent way to get to Wǔhàn. Consider doing it before the Chinese government finishes its massive dam project and floods the Three Gorges (Sānxiá). For details, see the special section on Cháng Jiāng cruises in this chapter.

Another boat option, and one that very few travellers use, is the service to Lèshān.

Sorting out just when the boats leave is a bit of a hassle. Due to river level fluctuations in recent years, service has been sporadic.

When boats are running, it's much, much easier to do the float downstream *from* Lèshān, since most return trips are for freight only. The trip is for hard-core river rats only. Boats leave from the dock in Chóngqìng; third-class tickets are around Y131.

Getting Around

The Airport CAAC runs shuttle buses between the airport and the ticket office, timed to coincide with flights. Buses to the airport leave 2½ hours before scheduled flight times; the fare is Y15.

Bus Buses in Chóngqìng can be tediously slow, and since there are no bicycles they're even more crowded than in other Chinese cities. Useful routes include No 401, which runs between the Cháotiānmén Dock and the CAAC office at the intersection of Renmin Lu and Zhongshan Sanlu; No 405, running the length of Zhongshan Lu up to the Jiěfàng Bēi; and No 102, which connects the train station and Cháotiānmén Dock. Many minibuses shuttle between the dock and train station as well for Y1.

Taxi Nowadays, as in most other Chinese cities, flagging down a taxi is no problem. Flag fall starts at Y5 for the smallest of taxis, depending on the size of the car. Expect to pay around Y15 for all runs on the peninsula. Note that the plethora of one-way and 'no entrance' streets makes for some circuitous routing.

DÀZÚ XIÀN 大足县

The grotto art found in Dàzú Xiàn, 160km north-west of Chóngqìng, is rated alongside China's other great Buddhist cave sculptures at Dūnhuáng, Luòyáng and Dàtóng. Historical records for Dàzú are sketchy. The cliff carvings and statues (with Buddhist, Taoist and Confucian influences) amount to thousands of pieces, large and small, scattered over the county in some 40-odd places. (Ān Yuè has been recommended to see carvings.)

The main groupings are at Běi Shān and the more interesting Bǎodǐng Shān. They date from the Tang dynasty (9th century) to the Song (13th century).

The town of Dàzú is a small, unhurried and languid place. Although not hilly, there's a conspicuous absence of bicycles. It's one community which definitely makes use of piped-in social propaganda from every corner. It's also relatively unvisited by westerners – though this is gradually changing. The only problem is the budget accommodation: there isn't any.

Běi Shān 北山
North Hill

Běi Shān is about a 30-minute hike from Dàzú town – aim straight for the pagoda visible from the bus station. There are good overall views from the top of the hill. The dark niches hold small statues, many in poor condition; only one or two really stand out.

Niche No 136 depicts Puxian, the patron saint (male) of Éméi Shān (Emei Mountain), riding a white elephant. The same niche has the androgynous Sun and Moon Guanyin. Niche 155 holds a bit more talent, the Peacock King. According to inscriptions, the Běi Shān site was once a military camp and the earliest carvings were commissioned by a general.

At Běi Shān there's a Y5 entry fee for the park area and a further Y40 entry fee for the sculptures. The park is open from 8 am to 5 pm.

Bǎodǐng Shān 宝顶山
Treasured Summit Hill

About 15km north-east of Dàzú town, the Bǎodǐng Shān sculptures are definitely more interesting than those at Běi Shān (although anyone who's seen Dàtóng's grottoes may be slightly underwhelmed).

The founding work is attributed to Zhao Zhifeng, a monk from an obscure Yoga sect of Tantric Buddhism. On the lower section of the hill below a monastery is a horse-shoe-shaped cliff sculpted with coloured figures, some of them up to 8m high.

The centrepiece is a 31m-long, 5m-high reclining buddha, depicted in the state of entering nirvana, the torso sunk into the cliff face.

Statues around the rest of the 125m horseshoe vary considerably: buddhist sages and teachers, historical figures, realistic scenes (on the rear of a postcard one is described as 'Pastureland – Cowboy at Rest') and delicate sculptures a few centimetres high. Some erosion is apparent but generally there is a remarkable survival rate (some fanatical Red Guards did descend on the Dàzú area bent on defacing the sculptures, but were stopped – so the story goes – by an urgent order from Zhou Enlai). You'll note, however, that the ones in the best condition are not to be photographed – gotta keep that postcard business humming ...

Bǎodǐng Shān differs from other grottoes in that it was based on a preconceived plan, which incorporated some of the area's natural features – a sculpture next to the reclining buddha, for example, makes use of an underground spring.

The sculptures are believed to have taken 70 years to complete, between AD 1179 and 1249. Inside a small temple on the carved cliff is the goddess of mercy with a spectacular gilt forest of fingers (1007 hands if you care to check). Each hand has an eye, the symbol of wisdom.

Minibuses to Bǎodǐng Shān leave the Dàzú bus station every 30 minutes or so (or as soon as they fill up) throughout the day, although they start to thin out by about 4 pm. The price for foreigners is Y5 – many times more than local price – and they're very insistent about it. The trip takes anywhere from 30 to 45 minutes.

For a splurge (and a much quicker ride) it's a pretty, winding journey on the back of a motorcycle taxi, which you can bargain down to Y15. The last bus departs Bǎodǐng Shān for Dàzú at around 6 pm. The sites are open from 8 am to 5 pm, and there's a Y85 entry fee; yes, it's a whopping amount, but it does also get you into Běi Shān (you may be able to wangle separate entrances, but it's still Y50). As you pass by in the bus, keep an eye on the cliff faces for solo sculptures that may occasionally pop up.

Places to Stay & Eat

The local PSB has done a good job of cowing most hotels into refusing foreigners, leaving you with only two options in Dàzú, neither of which is cheap.

The **Běishān Bīnguǎn** (☎ 437 22888), near the base of Běi Shān, is a pleasant though somewhat unkempt place aimed at the less affluent tour-group traveller. Standard doubles cost Y260 (they may be all right if you get a garden view), but it also has doubles/triples with attached bath for Y180 that are a tad weary but fine when you consider they're the cheapest in town. To get there, turn left out of the bus station, cross the bridge and proceed past the roundabout straight up the main road through town. After about 500m the road ends in a three-way intersection. Turn right; the hotel is on the left-hand side of the street. One good point about the Běishān Bīnguǎn is that it's close to the Běi Shān stone carvings. Facing the hotel, the road up to the statues is on the left, just next to the indoor sports arena.

The **Dàzú Bīnguǎn**, like so many other hotels in Chinese tourist towns, has been reborn as a three-star hotel, which means you won't be able to get a room for under US$50. Should the urge for luxury grab you, turn left out of the bus station, cross over the bridge and bear right at the roundabout. The hotel is about 500m up the road on the left.

Finding a bite to eat in Dàzú is no problem. At night the main road, from the bus station all the way to the Běishān Bīnguǎn, comes alive with dozens of *street stalls* serving noodles, dumplings, hotpot and wok-fried dishes.

There are also a few point-and-choose *restaurants* along the way, although the selection at these is decidedly more meagre than in other places. You might try wandering down the first street on the right up from the roundabout. You have to walk about 500m before the restaurants start appearing, but along the way are street vendors selling everything from raw handmade noodles to fresh spices to black lace lingerie. The restaurant at the Běishān Bīnguǎn is best left to its own devices.

CHÓNGQÌNG 重庆

Getting There & Away

Bus Dàzú is much easier to reach from Chóngqìng than from Chéngdū. Minibuses to Dàzú (Y29; 2½ hours) from Chóngqìng's new long-distance bus station run from 6 am to 6 pm, although most run from 8.15 am to 4.15 pm, more or less every half hour; the buses depart from the 2nd floor on the left-hand side and you buy tickets at the window by the gate.

Buses from Chéngdū to Dàzú are more problematic. Most stations don't have departures, and if they do, they get you in late at night. Chéngdū's Wuguiqiao express bus station has departures but not that many. What the staff may do is put you on a fast bus bound for Yóutíng, roughly halfway to Chóngqìng. Just north of the expressway here is a bustling crossroads bus station, and from here there are dozens of buses to Dàzú. From Dàzú there are onward buses to Chóngqìng and Chéngdū. Buses to

Chóngqìng (Y29; two hours) leave from the bus station every hour between 6 am to 6 pm. For Chéngdū there are five buses between 7.30 and 9.30 am using the expressway. The best option is to take an express (and theoretically non-stop) Iveco van at either 8.30 am or 2.30 pm (Y51; four hours).

Train To get to Dàzú by train, you should get off the Chéngdū-Chóngqìng railway line at Yóutíng town (five hours from Chóngqìng, seven hours from Chéngdū), which is the nearest stop to Dàzú.

Despite the fact that the town is around 30km from Dàzú, train timetables refer to it as Dàzú station. See the Chóngqìng Getting There & Away section earlier and the Chéngdū Getting There & Away section in the Sìchuān chapter for more information on trains to Dàzú. There are frequent minibuses running from the train station to Dàzú.

CRUISING DOWNRIVER
The Cháng Jiāng (Yangzi River) from Chóngqìng to Shànghǎi

The dramatic scenery and rushing waters of China's greatest river may have been inspirational to many of China's painters and poets, but there was very little in the way of inspiration for those charged with the task of negotiating the twists and turns of this dangerous stretch of water.

There was also sheer hard work. A large boat pushing upstream often needed hundreds of coolies (trackers) who lined the riverbanks and hauled the boat with long ropes against the surging waters. Even today smaller boats can still be seen being pulled up the river by their crews.

The Cháng Jiāng is China's longest river and at 6300km is the third longest in the world. The river originates in the snow-covered Tanggula Shān in south-west Qīnghǎi and cuts its way through Tibet and seven Chinese provinces before emptying into the East China Sea just north of Shànghǎi. Between the towns of Fengjie in Sìchuān and Yíchāng in Húběi lie three great gorges, regarded as one of the great scenic attractions of China. Well, for now anyway: by 2009 when the mega-project Three Gorges (Sānxiá) Dam is completed, the famed Three Gorges will have been completely submerged, 1.5 million people will have been dislocated, and south-west China will never be the same. See the boxed text in the Húběi chapter for more information. For the moment, tour boats are running constantly to take care of tourists and their last-ditch efforts to see it all.

The steamer ride from Chóngqìng to Wǔhàn is a popular tourist trip and the scenery is pleasant, but don't expect to be dwarfed by mile-high cliffs! A lot of people find the trip a bit of an antii-climax after their high expectations. You might be able to line up a hydrofoil from Chóngqìng to Wànxiàn and try to hook up with a ferry there; this depends a lot on what boats are running at the time. From Yíchāng you could also take direct trains to Běijīng, Wǔhàn, and Xī'ān or Huáihuà to connect to trains south. There are also a few boats that go beyond Wǔhàn, including one all the way to Shànghǎi, which is 2400km downriver – a week's journey.

Tickets

It's good to book two or three days ahead of your intended date of departure, although a rapid expansion in the number of Cháng Jiāng cruise operators means tickets are usually ready for same day travel. CITS adds a service charge of Y15 to the price of the tickets. Budget travellers take note: if you book tickets with CITS, make sure you're not being put on one of the luxury liners reserved solely for foreigners – the price could inflict mortal damage on your cash reserves. A 50% surcharge was once normal for foreigners' tickets, but you shouldn't have to pay these any longer.

Most boats leave in the evening, but on the off chance you get a morning departure, it's sometimes possible to sleep on board the night before for a nominal charge (Y25 to Y35).

Once you've boarded, a steward will exchange your ticket for a numbered, colour-coded tag that denotes your bed assignment. Hang on to the tag, since it must be exchanged for your ticket at the end of the voyage – without it they may not let you off the boat.

Classes

In a sign of the changing times in what was once egalitarian China, some boats now boast 1st-class cabins. These come with two beds, a private bathroom, a television and air-con.

Second-class cabins have two to four berths, with soft beds, a small desk and chair, and a washbasin. Third class usually has from six to 12 beds depending on what boat you're on. Fourth class usually has eight to 12, but on older vessels can have over 20 beds. Fifth class can be anything from 15 beds to deck-space. Toilets and showers are communal, although you should be able to use the toilets and showers in 2nd class. In any event, upkeep on some boats is minimal.

In addition to the above tour boats, there are also several vessels for well-heeled foreign tour groups. CITS and some of the independent booking agents around the Cháotiānmén Dock area in Chóngqìng can arrange tickets for these luxury liners.

Fares

It is advised that you shop around. Prices will be higher if you book through CITS or one of the independent operators.

Note that there are also 1st and 5th classes – the former most travellers won't go for, with their 100% price mark-up over 2nd class, and the latter is dirt-cheap but not always easy to get.

Chóngqìng (downriver) to:	2nd class (Y)	3rd class (Y)	4th class (Y)
Yíchāng	464	218	155
Yuèyáng	618	289	206
Wǔhàn (Hankou)	684	320	229
Nánjīng	920	429	305
Shànghǎi	1031	480	339

Food

There are usually a couple of restaurants on the boat. Those on the lower decks cater for the masses and can be pretty terrible. If there's a restaurant on the upper deck chances are it's a bit better, but how much you're charged seems to vary from boat to boat. It's a good idea to bring some of your own food with you. When the boat stops at a town for any length of time, passengers may disembark and eat at little restaurants near the pier.

The Route

Boats stop frequently during the cruise to visit cities, towns and a slew of tourist sights. Most boats stop between the first and second gorge for six hours for tours of the Xiǎo Sānxiá (Little Three Gorges) (see the Wànxiàn to Yíchāng section below). For travellers who want to avoid this, there are some boats that pass directly through, but you'll have to ask around.

Chóngqìng to Wànxiàn

For the first few hours the river is lined with factories, although this gives way to some pretty, green terraced countryside with the occasional small town.

One of the first stops is usually the town of **Fúlíng**. It overlooks the mouth of the Wū Hé, which runs southwards into Guìzhōu and controls the river traffic between Guìzhōu and eastern Sìchuān.

Near Fúlíng, in the middle of the Cháng Jiāng, is a huge rock called Baihe Ridge. On one side of the rock are three carvings known as 'stone fish' which date back to ancient times and are thought to have served as watermarks – the rock can be seen only when the river is at its very lowest.

The next major town is **Fēngdū**. Nearby is Pingdu Shān which is said to be the abode of devils. The story goes that during the Han dynasty two men, Yin Changsheng and Wang Fangping, lived on the mountain, and when their family names were joined together they were mistakenly thought to be the Yinwang, the King of Hell. Numerous temples containing sculptures of demons and devils have been built on the mountain since the Tang dynasty, with heartening names like 'Between the Living and the Dead', 'Bridge of Helplessness' and 'Palace of the King of Hell'.

The boat then passes through **Zhōngxiàn County**. North-east of the county seat of Zhongzhou is the **Qian Jinggou** site, where primitive stone artefacts, including axes, hoes and stone weights attached to fishing nets, were unearthed.

Soon after comes the **Shibaozhai** (Stone Treasure Stronghold) on the northern bank of the river. Shibaozhai is a 30m-high rock which is supposed to look something like a stone seal. During the early years of Emperor Qianlong's reign (1736–97) an impressive red wooden temple, the Lanruo Dian (Orchid-like Temple), shaped like a pagoda and 11 storeys high, was built on the rock. It houses a statue of Buddha and inscriptions which commemorate its construction.

Next is the large town of **Wànxiàn**, where most morning boats tie up for the night. It's a neat, hilly town and a great place to wander around for a few hours while the boat is in port.

Wànxiàn to Yíchāng

Boats staying overnight at Wànxiàn generally depart before dawn. Before entering the gorges the boat passes by (and may stop at) the town of **Fengjie** (Yong'an). This ancient town was the capital of the state of Kui during the Spring and Autumn and Warring States periods from 722 to 221 BC.

The town overlooks the Qútáng Xiá, the first of the three Cháng Jiāng gorges. Just east of Fengjie is a 1km-long shoal where the remains of stone piles could be seen when the water level was low. These piles were erected in the Stone and Bronze ages, possibly for commemorative and sacrificial purposes, but their remains were removed in 1964 since they were considered a danger to navigation.

Another set of similar structures can be found 7.5km east of Fengjie outside **Báidìchéng**. At the entrance to the Qútáng Xiá, Báidìchéng, or White King Town, is on the river's northern bank. The story goes that a high official proclaimed himself king during the Western Han dynasty, and moved his capital to this town. A well was discovered which emitted a fragrant white vapour; this struck him as such an auspicious omen that he renamed himself the White King and his capital 'White King Town'.

The spectacular **Three Gorges** (Sānxiá), Qútáng, Wū and Xīlíng, start just after Fengjie and end near Yíchāng, a stretch of about 200km. The gorges vary from 300m at their widest to less than 100m at their narrowest. The seasonal difference in water level can be as much as 50m.

Qútáng Xiá is the smallest and shortest gorge (only 8km long), although the water flows most rapidly here. High on the northern bank, at a place called Fengxiang Xiá (Bellows Gorge), are a series of crevices. There is said to have been an ancient tribe in this area whose custom

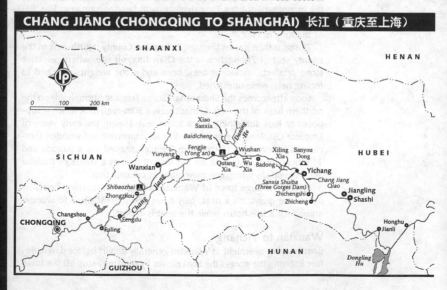

CHÁNG JIĀNG (CHÓNGQÌNG TO SHÀNGHǍI) 长江（重庆至上海）

was to place the coffins of their dead in high mountain caves. Nine coffins were discovered in these crevices, some containing bronze swords, armour and other artefacts, but they are believed to date back only as far as the Warring States Period.

Wū Xiá is about 40km in length and the cliffs on either side rise to just over 900m. The gorge is noted for the Kong Ming tablet, a large slab of rock at the foot of the Peak of the Immortals. Kong Ming was prime minister of the state of Shu during the period of the Three Kingdoms (AD 220–80). On the tablet is a description of his stance upholding the alliance between the states of Shu and Wu against the state of Wei. Badong is a town on the southern bank of the river within the gorge. The town is a communications centre from which roads span out into western Húběi.

In between the Qútáng and Wū gorges, most boats will stop for five to six passengers can shift to smaller boats for tours of the **Xiǎo Sānxiá** (Little Three Gorges). Flanking the Daning Hé, these gorges are much narrower than their larger counterparts and, some travellers say, more dramatic. The tour usually costs Y50 to Y60, and a foreigner surcharge may still exist. Though some travellers have complained of the cost, many enjoy the chance to get out and view the rock formations up close.

On the way to the Xiǎo Sānxiá the boats usually stop at several gratuitous tourist traps, most of which are not worth the entry fee. For example, one stop promises views of a mysterious mountain cave coffin on high, which turns out to mean a brief look through a pair of binoculars.

长江（重庆至上海）CHÁNG JIĀNG (CHÓNGQÌNG TO SHÀNGHĂI)

Xīlíng Xiá, at 80km, is the longest of the three gorges. At the end of the gorge everyone crowds out onto the deck to watch the boat pass through the locks of the huge Gezhou Dam.

The next stop is the industrial town of **Yíchāng**, which is regarded as the gateway to the upper Cháng Jiāng and was once a walled city dating back at least as far as the Sui dynasty. Near the Yíchāng train station you can take bus No 10 to **Báimǎ Dòng** (White Horse Cave), where for a fee you can boat and walk through caverns with impressive stalactites and stalagmites. Five minutes walk from the other end is the equally impressive **Sānyóu Dòng** (Three Visitors Cave), along with a cliff trail that overlooks the Cháng Jiāng.

Yíchāng to Wǔhàn

After leaving Yíchāng, the boat passes under the immense **Cháng Jiāng Qiáo** (Yangzi River Bridge) at the town of **Zhicheng**. The bridge is 1700m in length and supports a double-track railway with roads for trucks and cars on either side. It commenced operation in 1971.

The next major town is **Shashì**, a light-industrial town. As early as the Tang dynasty, Shashì was a trading centre of some importance, enjoying great prosperity during the Taiping Rebellion when trade lower down the Cháng Jiāng was largely at a standstill. About 7.5km from Shashì is the ancient town of **Jīngzhōu**, to which you can catch a bus.

After Shashì there's not much to look at: you're out on the flat plains of central China, the river widens immensely and you can see little of the shore. The boat continues down the river to pass by (and possibly stop at) the town of **Chénglíngjī**, which lies at the confluence of Dòngtíng Hú and the Cháng Jiāng.

East of Dòngtíng Hú is the town of **Yuèyáng**. Another nine hours will bring you to Wǔhàn, at which point most travellers are quite ready to part ways with their boat.

Wǔhàn to Shànghǎi

Wǔhàn more or less marks the halfway point in the long navigable stretch of the Cháng Jiāng from Chóngqìng down to Shànghǎi. The journey to the sea is far more mundane than the trip upriver to Chóngqìng; the Cháng Jiāng broadens and most of the towns and cities are industrial in character.

Heading downriver on leaving Wǔhàn, you pass through **Huangshi** in eastern Húběi. This town lies on the southern bank of the river and is being developed as a centre for heavy industry. Nearby is an ancient mining tunnel dating back to the Spring and Autumn Period; it contained numerous mining tools, including bronze axes.

Near the border with Jiāngxī, on the northern bank, is the town of **Wuxue**, noted for the production of bamboo goods.

The first major town you come to in Jiāngxī is **Jiǔjiuāng**, the jumping-off point for nearby Lúshān. The mouth of Bōyáng Hú is situated on the Cháng Jiāng and at this point on the southern bank of the river is Stone Bell Mountain, noted for its numerous Tang dynasty stone carvings. This was also the place where Taiping troops were garrisoned for five years defending Jinling, their capital.

The first major town you approach in Ānhuī is **Ānqìng**, on the northern bank, in the foothills of the Dabie mountains. Next comes the town of **Guichi**, from which you can get a bus to Jiǔhuá Shān (Nine Brilliant Mountains) and the spectacular Huáng Shān (Yellow Mountains).

The town of **Tónglíng** lies in a mountainous area in central Ānhuī on the southern bank, west of Tongguan Shan. Tongling has been a copper-mining centre for 2000 years and is a source of copper for the minting of coins. Still in Ānhuī, and at the confluence of the Cháng and Qingyi rivers, is **Wúhú**, also a jumping-off point for Huáng Shān. Just before Ānhuī ends is the city of **Manshan**, the site of a large iron and steel complex.

In Jiāngsū the first large city you pass is **Nánjīng**, followed by **Zhèjiāng**, then the port of **Nantong** at the confluence of the Tongyang and Tonglu canals. The ferry then proceeds along the Cháng Jiāng and turns down the Huangpu Hé to **Shànghǎi**. The Cháng Jiāng empties into the East China Sea.

Sìchuān 四川

Sìchuān is one of the largest provinces in China, and the most heavily populated. In the eastern region of the province, the great Chūanxī plain supports one of the densest rural populations in the world, while the regions to the west are mountainous and sparsely populated, principally by Tibetans. Sìchuān is roughly the size of France and is rich in natural resources.

Wild, mountainous terrain and fast rivers kept it relatively isolated until recent times, and much of the western fringe is still remote. This inaccessibility has made it the site of a number of breakaway kingdoms throughout Chinese history, and it was here that the beleaguered Kuomintang Party spent its final days before fleeing to Taiwan.

The Chinese often refer to Sìchuān as the 'Heavenly Kingdom' (Tiānfǔ Zhīguó), a reference to its resources and rich cultural heritage. The name Sìchuān means 'four rivers' and refers to four of the 80-plus mighty rivers that tumble through the province.

Sìchuān became famous during the Warring States Period when engineer Li Bing somehow corralled the Dū Hé (Du River) on the Chūanxī plain with his weir system, allowing Sìchuān some 2200 continuous years of irrigation and prosperity.

Zhao Ziyang soared from the post of First Party Secretary of Sìchuān to General Secretary of the Communist Party before his fall from grace in the wake of the Tiānānmén massacre in 1989. His reputation was made by the pioneering agricultural reforms he instituted in the province. Under the so-called 'responsibility system', plots of land were let out to farmers for individual use on the condition that a portion of the crops be sold back to the government. By 1984 the reforms had spread throughout China and were later applied to the industrial sector.

A less fortunate result of these reforms is job-loss; Sìchuān has the lion's share of China's 130 million-strong 'surplus labour

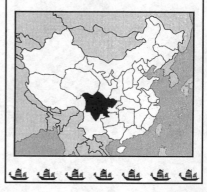

force', and minor skirmishes between police and unemployed workers took place in 1997.

Meanwhile, worlds away from urban renewal and economic reform, the remote mountains of Sìchuān, bordering Gānsù and Shaanxi, are the habitat of the giant panda, the animal westerners automatically associate with China thanks to its role of 'little ambassador' for the Chinese government.

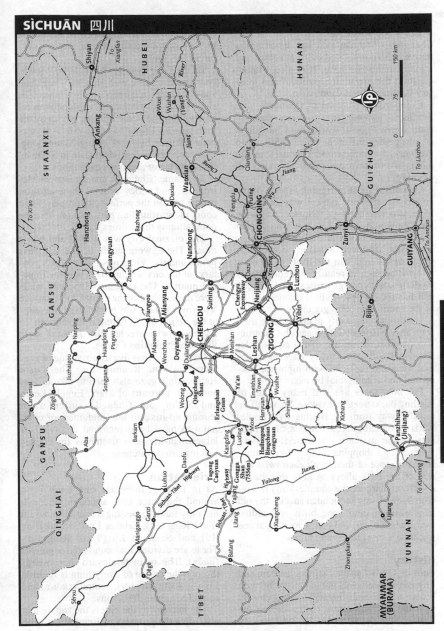

CHÉNGDŪ 成都

☎ 028 • pop 9,891,900

Chéngdū is Sìchuān's capital, its administrative, educational and cultural centre and a major industrial base. It is also without question the economic, political and military linchpin of the south-west.

Comparisons between Chéngdū and Běijīng are tempting (the same city-planning hand seems to be at work), but Chéngdū is an altogether different place, with more greenery, looming wooden houses in the older parts of town and a very different kind of energy.

One of the most intriguing aspects of the city is its artisans: basket-weavers, cobblers, itinerant dentists, tailors, house-ware merchants and snack hawkers who swarm the streets and contribute to its bustling energy. Here affluence blends in – nowhere in south-west China can the fruits of China's reforms be seen so readily – but despite its modernisations and gentrification, Chéngdū still has the highest 'hello!' quotient of all of the south-west's bigger cities.

Unfortunately, if city planners have their way, this will probably mean the destruction of most, if not all, of the city's older wooden buildings – many have been demolished and replaced with high-rise residential and commercial blocks.

For now there are still many miles of bustling backstreets to explore. Strike off on a walk away from the Běijīng-style boulevards; free markets, flea markets, black markets, pedlar markets, commercial districts, underground shopping malls – you'll stumble over more of them with each twist and turn of the back alleys. Add to this the indoor food markets, the countless tiny restaurants specialising in Sìchuān snacks, the old men walking their song birds or huddled over a game of go, and you're looking at one of China's most intriguing cities.

History

Built in 316 BC as the Dūjiāngyàn dam and irrigation system was put in place, Chéngdū boasts a 2300-year history. Linked closely with the arts and crafts trades, during the Eastern Han dynasty (AD 25–220) the city was often referred to as Jǐnchéng (Brocade City) due to its thriving silk brocade industry. A modern localism for the city is a synonym for 'lotus'.

By the Tang dynasty (AD 618–907) it was considered – along with Handan, Fangzhan, and Changan – a cornerstone of Chinese society. It was devastated by the Mongols in retaliation for the fierce fighting put up by the Sichuanese. From 1644 to 1647 it was presided over by rebel Zhang Xiangzhong, who set up an independent state in Sìchuān, ruling by terror and mass executions.

The name 'Chéngdū' means Perfect Metropolis, and today around three million people inhabit the perfect city proper; if you count the surrounding metropolitan area the population is three times that.

The original city was walled and had a moat. There were gates at the compass points and the Viceroy's Palace (14th century) at the city's heart. This was the imperial quarter. The remains of the city walls were demolished in the early 1960s, and the Viceroy's Palace was blown to smithereens at the height of the Cultural Revolution. In its place was erected the Russian-style Sichuan Exhibition Centre.

Outside, a massive Mao statue waves merrily down Renmin Lu. The Great Helmsman's gaze also used to take in four enormous portraits of Marx, Engels, Lenin and Stalin, but Chéngdū suffers from chronic ad-itis and the forefathers of communism have been removed in favour of larger-than-life advertisements for cognac and imported watches.

Orientation

As in Běijīng, there are ring roads right around the outer city, although Chéngdū has only three to Běijīng's four: Yihuan Lu (First Ring Rd), Erhuan Lu (Second Ring Rd) and Sanhuan Lu (Third Ring Rd). These are divided into numbered segments (*duàn*). The main boulevard that sweeps through the centre of everything is Renmin Lu – in its north (*běi*), central (*zhōng*) and south (*nán*) manifestations.

The nucleus of the city is the square that interrupts the progress of Renmin Lu, with administrative buildings, the Sichuan Exhibition Centre, a sports stadium and, at its southern extent, the colossal Mao presiding over a city long oblivious to his presence.

The area where Renmin Nanlu crosses the Jǐn Jiāng (Brocade River), near the Jǐnjiāng and Traffic Hotels, has become the city's tourist ghetto. This is where you'll find most of the restaurants, arts and crafts shops catering to foreigners, and even a couple of pubs.

Finally, Chéngdū is a true Asian city in its nonchalant disregard of systematic street numbering and naming. It's not unusual for street numbers going in one direction to meet another set coming the other way, often leaving the poor family in the middle with five sets of numbers over their doorway. Street names, also, seem to change every 100m or so, with very little apparent logic. Bear this in mind when you're looking for places, and rely more on nearby landmarks and relative locations on maps than on street numbers and names.

Maps City bus maps can be found at train and bus stations, the Traffic Hotel and Xinhua Bookstore. Three different maps in Chinese provide excellent detail of the city and surrounding regions. *Chengdu – the Latest Tourist Map* available from the Foreign Languages Bookstore has English but it's not as new as it claims. Even the best ones cannot hope to fully capture the insanity that is Chéngdū's street naming.

Information
Consulates The US consulate (☎ 558 3992) is in a small fortress at 4 Lingshiguan Lu, just off Renmin Nanlu between the first and second ring roads.

Money Many of Chéngdū's hotels have foreign-exchange counters. There is a Bank of China branch on Renmin Nanlu next to the Jǐnjiāng Bīnguǎn.

The main branch of the Bank of China is in a huge yellow building on Renmin Donglu. Credit card withdrawals are available here and banking hours are 8.30 to 11.30 am and 2 to 5 pm.

Post & Communications The main post office is housed in what looks like a converted church on the corner of Huaxingzheng Jie and Shuwa Beijie, close to the Cultural Palace in the centre of town. It's open from 8.30 am to 6 pm daily.

Numerous other small post offices are scattered throughout the central part of town. Poste restante mail is no longer picked up from the main post office; you need to go to the post office (the EMS building) on Shawan Rd, near the intersection of Bei Yihuan Lu. To get there, take bus No 48 to the second-last stop. Walk east along the ring road until you see a statue, and turn right. It'll be ahead on the left.

More convenient might be the poste restante service at the Traffic Hotel, which holds letters and parcels for 15 days. Send items to the Traffic Hotel, 77 Linjiang Road, Xinnanmen, Chengdu 610041.

The best place in town for making collect calls is the Telecommunications Business Centre (Diànxìn Shāngche'ng) east of the Sichuan Exhibition Centre. You can also make direct-dial overseas calls and faxes from here. Public phones which take home-country calling cards are along a wall to the left after entering. The service is posted as 24 hours, but that's dubious.

Email & Internet Access Any western-style cafe will have email access for around Y20 per hour. One of south-west China's hippest places is the Telecommunications Business Centre. On the 2nd storey a real Internet cafe – a coffee lounge with computers – offers good access for Y20 per hour.

Travel Agencies Staff in the main China International Travel Service office (CITS; Zhōngguó Guójì Lǚxíngshè; ☎ 667 5578), on Renmin Nanlu opposite the Jǐnjiāng Bīnguǎn, are friendly but can't book train tickets and have been trained to say 'Tibet is closed'. If you want to avail yourself of its services, the office is open daily from 8.30 am to 5 pm.

For the kind of help that individual travellers need, try the small outfits in and around the Traffic Hotel.

SÌCHUĀN 四川

PSB You'll probably do best to start at the Foreign Affairs section (☎ 630 1454) of the Public Security Bureau (PSB; Gōngānjú) – a single-storey building at 40 Wenmiaohou Jie, which is off Nan Dajie to the west of the Jǐnjiāng Bīnguǎn.

To get there from the Traffic Hotel, walk up Renmin Lu to Hongzhao Bijie and turn left. Follow it as it bears south-west for a long block or so until it meets up with a road. Turn right and it'll be on the right-hand side. Some members of the staff speak excellent English. This office is open from 8.15 to 11.30 am Monday to Friday and from 2.45 to 4.30 pm on Tuesday and Thursday. Some travellers have managed to badger guards into tracking down somebody official on Saturday and after hours.

Dangers & Annoyances There have been several reports of foreigners becoming targets for rip-offs and theft in Chéngdū. In particular there have been a couple of incidents (one foreigner was stabbed) on the riverside pathway between the Jǐnjiāng and Traffic Hotels. Take care late at night – it's best not to walk alone.

To avoid getting ripped off by pedicab drivers and restaurants, always get the price at the start. Pickpockets are common around bus and train stations and post offices; watch out for gangs who use razors to slit your bags on buses. If you want to play it safe with train tickets, make a note of the ticket numbers: if the tickets are stolen you'll be given replacements, providing you can supply the numbers of the old ones.

Wénshū Yuàn 文殊院
God of Wisdom Temple

Wénshū Yuàn, a monastery which dates back to the Tang dynasty, is Chéngdū's largest and best-preserved Buddhist temple. Originally known as Xinxiang Temple, it was renamed after a Buddhist monk who lived there in the late 17th century. It is believed that his presence literally illuminated the monastery. Many of the buildings in the complex are decorated with exquisite relief carvings.

Perhaps the best thing about the monastery is the noisy, bustling crowds of worshippers who flock to the place. It's a fairly active place of worship and as such is well worth the trip.

The alley off Renmin Zhonglu, on which Wénshū is located, is a curiosity in itself, with joss-stick vendors, foot-callus removers, beggars, blind fortune-tellers with bamboo spills, and flower and fireworks sellers. Check out the teahouse and vegetarian restaurant in the monastery area. The teahouse is one of the largest you'll see, with what seem like acres of tables, and is always full; tea costs Y6. The monastery is open daily from 6 am to 8.30 pm, and there's an entry charge of Y1. Some travellers have reported not being able to enter until 8 am.

Wángjiàn Mù 王建墓
Tomb of Wang Jian

In the north-west of town, the Wángjiàn Mù was, until 1942, thought to be Zhuge Liang's music pavilion (see Wǔhòu Cí in the following Temple Parks section). The tomb in the central building is surrounded by statues of 24 musicians all playing different instruments, and is considered to be the best surviving record of a Tang dynasty musical troupe.

Wang Jian (AD 847–918) was a Tang general who established the Former Shu kingdom in the aftermath of the collapse of the Tang in 907. Also featured are relics taken from the tomb itself, including a jade belt, mourning books and imperial seals. The tomb is open daily from 8.30 am to 5.30 pm.

Temple Parks

There are a couple of worthwhile temple parks in the city area, all within cycling distance of the Jǐnjiāng and Traffic Hotels, and all open seven days a week.

West of the Mao statue on the western section of the circular road is Wénhuà Gōngyuán (Wenhua Park), home to **Qīngyáng Gōng** (Qingyang Temple). This is the oldest and most extensive Taoist temple in the Chéngdū area and it houses a vegetarian restaurant.

The story goes that Laotzu, the high priest of Taoism, asked a friend to meet him there. When the friend arrived he saw only a boy leading two goats on a leash – and in a fabulous leap of lateral thinking realised the boy was Laotzu. The goats are represented in bronze in the rear building on the temple grounds.

If the one-horned goat looks slightly un-goat-like, it is because it combines features of all the Chinese zodiac animals. The solitary horn was borrowed from a dragon. And if you're wondering whether the goat has any goatish qualities at all, take a look at the beard. The other goat can vanquish life's troubles and pains if you stroke its flank. The park is open from 6 am to 8 pm and costs Y1.50 to enter. Entry to the temple is Y2.

Qīngyáng Gōng can be combined with a visit to nearby **Dùfǔ Cǎotáng** (Du Fu's Cottage), erstwhile home of the celebrated Tang dynasty poet. Something of a rover, Du Fu (AD 712–70) was born in Hénán and left his home province to see China at the tender age of 20. He was an official in Chang'an (the ancient capital on the site of modern-day Xī'ān) for 10 years, and was later captured by rebels after an uprising and fled to Chéngdū, where he stayed for four years. He built himself a humble cottage and penned more than 200 poems on simple themes around the lives of the people who lived and worked nearby.

The present grounds – 20 hectares of leafy bamboo and luxuriant vegetation – are a much enlarged version of Du Fu's original poetic retreat. It's also the centre of the Chéngdū Du Fu Study Society, and several halls display examples of the poet's work.

Du Fu's statue is accompanied by statues of two lesser poets: Li You and Huang Tingjian. From the time of his death in exile (in Húnán), Du Fu acquired a cult status, and his poems have been a major source of inspiration for many Chinese artists. Dùfǔ Cǎotáng is open from 7 am to 11 pm. The entry fee is Y5 to the grounds, Y15 to the cottage.

To the west of the Jǐnjiāng Bīnguǎn and next to Nánjiāo Gōngyuán (Southern Outskirts Park) is **Wǔhòu Cí**. Wǔhòu might be translated as 'Minister of War'. That was the title given to Zhuge Liang, a famous military strategist of the Three Kingdoms Period (AD 220–80) immortalised in one of the classics of Chinese literature, *The Tale of the Three Kingdoms*. Curiously, Zhuge Liang is not the main attraction of the temple. The front shrine instead is dedicated to Liu Bei, Zhuge Liang's emperor. Liu's temple, the Hanzhaolie Temple, was moved here and rebuilt during the Ming dynasty, but the Wǔhòu Cí name stuck.

Liu is a common Chinese surname and many overseas Chinese with the surname make a point of visiting the temple while they are in Chéngdū on the glorious off-chance that the emperor is a distant ancestor. Admission is Y15 although this seems to be fluid – some have had to pay only Y5 and a few Y2 or Y3 separate admissions inside.

In the south-east of town, near Sichuan University, is **Wàngjiānglóu Gōngyuán** (River Viewing Pavilion Park). The pavilion itself is a four-storey wooden Qing structure overlooking the Jǐn Jiāng. The park is famous for its lush forests, boasting over 150 varieties of bamboo from China, Japan and South-East Asia. They range from bonsai-sized potted plants to towering giants, creating a shady retreat in the heat of summer (and a cold, damp retreat in winter).

The Wàngjiāng Lóu was built in the memory of Xue Tao, a female Tang dynasty poet with a great love for bamboo. Nearby is a well where she is believed to have drawn water to dye her writing paper. The park is open from 6 am to 9 pm and the entry fee is Y2.

Rénmín Gōngyuán 人民公园
People's Park

This is one Chinese park that travellers either love or loathe. It's to the south-west of the city centre. The teahouse here is excellent (see the Places to Eat section later in this entry) and it's a perfect perch for people-watching and whiling away a lazy afternoon.

The park also holds a bonsai rockery, a playground, swimming pools, and the Monument to the Martyrs of the Railway Protection Movement (1911). Decorated with shunting manoeuvres and train tracks, this commemorates an uprising of the people against officers who siphoned funds meant for the construction of the Chéngdū-Chóngqìng line. Since Rénmín Gōngyuán was also at the time a private officers' garden, it was fitting to erect the structure here.

Across the lake from the teahouse is the entry to an underground museum/funhouse that must count as one of the weirder experiences in Chéngdū. An entry fee of Y10 buys you a tour through a converted air-raid shelter that houses, among other things: models of New York, Sydney, Rome and the Taj Mahal (the latter two complete with copies of Moscow's St Basil's Cathedral thrown in for good measure), a life-size statue of Saddam Hussein, and a miniature subway that takes you through 'outer space', 'the rainforest', 'undersea', 'hell' and several other choice locales. The point of all this is anyone's guess, but it makes for an entertaining visit.

Rénmín Gōngyuán opens at 6.30 am and stays open until 2 am to allow free access to patrons of a disco dance hall located on the park grounds. Admission is Y2.

Sìchuān Shěng Bówùguǎn 四川省博物馆
Sichuan Provincial Museum

The Sìchuān Shěng Bówùguǎn is the largest provincial museum in China's south-west, with more than 150,000 items, although not nearly that much are on display. For historians, the displays of tiled murals and frescoes taken from tombs are of great interest.

The museum is open on weekdays from 9 am to 5 pm, and on weekends from 10 am to 5 pm. Admission is Y10 and many have come away disappointed. It's down Renmin Nanlu in the direction of the south train station, but still within cycling distance of the Jǐnjiāng Bīnguǎn.

Sìchuān Dàxué Bówùguǎn 四川大学博物馆
Sichuan University Museum

Founded in 1914 by US scholar DS Dye, the Sìdà Bówùguǎn underwent several closings and name changes before reopening under its current name in 1984. The four exhibition rooms display more than 40,000 items on a rotating basis. The collection is particularly strong in the fields of ethnology, folklore and traditional arts.

The ethnology room exhibits artefacts from the Yi, Qiang, Miao, Jingpo, Naxi and Tibetan cultures. The Chinese painting and calligraphy room displays works from the Tang, Song, Yuan, Ming and Qing dynasties. Some exhibits have English labels.

The museum is open Monday to Friday from 8.30 to 11.30 am and 2.40 to 5.30 pm; you definitely need over an hour to appreciate the place. Entrance is Y10. From the university's main gate, enter and go straight until the road ends at a 'T' intersection. The museum is the first building on the right.

Chéngdū Dòngwùyuán 动物园
Chengdu Zoo

Although now upstaged by the nearby Dàxióngmāo Fánzhí Yánjiū Zhōngxīn (Giant Panda Breeding Research Base), the Chéngdū Dòngwùyuán still has a respectable collection of six pandas, although they're not very active during the hottest summer months.

The zoo is about 6km from Chéngdū city centre, and is open from 7.30 am to 8 pm daily. Admission is Y3. The best way to get there is by bicycle (around half an hour from the Traffic Hotel). There are also minibuses running directly to the zoo from the north train station.

Zhàojué Sì 照觉寺

Next door to the zoo, Zhàojué Sì is a Tang dynasty temple dating from the 7th century. It underwent extensive reconstruction during the early Qing under the supervision of Po Shan, a famous Buddhist monk, with waterways and groves of trees established around the temple. This temple has served as a model for many Japanese and South-East Asian Buddhist temples.

It went through hard times during the Cultural Revolution and has only been restored in the last 10 years. There's a vegetarian restaurant on the grounds that serves lunch from 11 am to 2 pm and a teahouse next door. The temple is open from 7 am to 7 pm; admission is Y1.

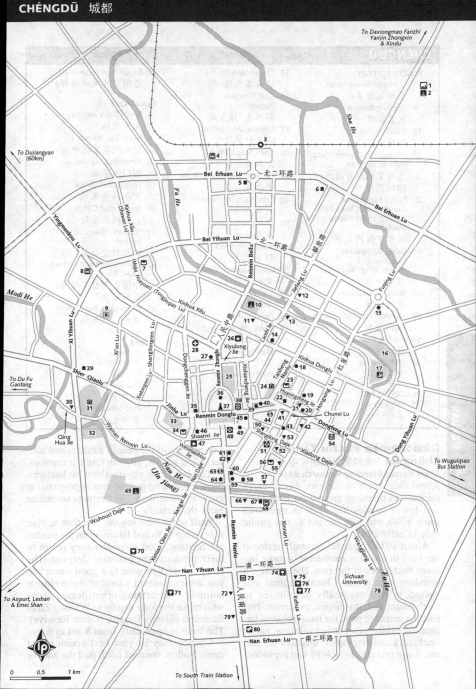

To Daxiongmao Fanzhi
Yanjin Zhongxin
& Xindu

Shu He

1
2

To Dujiangyan
(60km)

Fu He

Bei Erhuan Lu   北二环路
5

6

Bei Erhuan Lu

Xinhua Xilu
(Shawan Lu)

Bei Yihuan Lu   北一环路

北
一
环
路

Renmin Beilu

Jiefang Lu

Fuqing Lu

Yingmenkou Lu

8

Modi He

9

Xi Yihuan Lu

7

(Mijia Huayuan)

Xinhua Xilu   (Tongjinqiao Lu)

10

11

12

Caoshi Jie

13

15

Xi'an Lu

Xifan Lu

Chengzhong Lu   成中路

26

28

27

Xiyulong
Jie

14

16

17

To Du Fu
Gaotang

29

Shier Qiaolu

Xiulongren Lu—Shangtongren Lu

Dongchengen Lu

Renmin Zhonglu   人民中路

25

Xihuncheng Jie

24

Taicheng
Nanlu

Xinhua Donglu

18

红星路

23

22

Huaxingzheng Jie

19

20

Chunxi Lu

21

Hongxing Lu

30

31

Jinhe Lu

35

36

37

Renmin Donglu

39

40

41

44

50

42

Dongfeng Lu

43

53

54

33

34

Shaanxi Jie

46

47

48

49

45

52

Shangdong Dajie

Xiadong Dajie

32

Wainan Renmin Lu

Qing
Hua Jie

Wenmiaohou
Jie

Nan He
(Jin Jiang)

61

62

63

64

60

59

58

57

55

56

To Wuguiqiao
Bus Station

65

Jiangnan Jie

Jiangxi Jie

66

67

68

Wuhouci Dajie

69

Renmin Nanlu

Xinnan Lu

Dong Yihuan Lu

70

71

72

Nan Yihuan Lu   南一环路

74

75

76

77

Sichuan
University

Wangjiang Lu

To Airport, Leshan
& Emei Shan

79

Kehua Lu

78

Tu He

80

Nan Erhuan Lu   南二环路

0   0.5   1 km

To South Train Station

CHÉNGDŪ

PLACES TO STAY

5 Chengdu Grand Hotel
成都大酒店

6 Jīngróng Bīnguǎn
京蓉宾馆

14 Jīndì Fàndiàn
金地饭店

22 Holiday Inn Crowne Plaza;
Sìchuān Bīnguǎn
总府皇冠假日酒店；
四川宾馆

29 Sam's Backpacker
Guesthouse; Chengdu
College of Traditional
Medicine
成都中医药大学

46 Sam's Backpacker
Guesthouse 2
(Róngchéng Fàndiàn)
蓉成饭店

58 Bīnjiāng Fàndiàn
滨江饭店

60 Mínshān Fàndiàn
岷山饭店

64 Jǐnjiāng Bīnguǎn
锦江宾馆

67 Traffic Hotel
交通饭店

PLACES TO EAT

11 Restaurants
餐厅

12 Chén Mápó Dòufu
陈麻婆豆腐

13 Guō Tāngyuán;
Pùgàimiàn
郭汤元；铺盖面

21 Shìměixuān Cāntīng
市美轩餐厅

30 Chén Mápó Dòufu
陈麻婆豆腐

41 Taiping Department Store
太平洋百货

42 Lido Plaza; Ito Yokado
利都广场

50 Chéngdū Cāntīng
成都餐厅

52 Yàohuá Fàndiàn
耀华饭店

53 Lóngchāoshǒu Cāntīng
龙抄手餐厅

55 Gàn Bāozi
干包子

57 Paul's Cafe

66 Carol's by the River
卡罗西餐

69 Highfly Cafe
高飞咖啡厅

72 Wild Goose Cafe
鸿咖啡厅

75 Red Brick Cafe Pub
& Pizzeria
红砖西餐厅

79 Bāguó Bùyī Fēngwèijiǔbù
巴国布衣风味酒部

TRANSPORT

3 North Train Station
火车北站

4 North Bus Station
城北汽车客运中心

8 Xīmén Bus Station
西门汽车站

15 Train Ticket Office
火车站售票处

49 Train Ticket Office
火车站售票处

61 Sichuan Provincial
Airlines
四川航空公司

62 China Southwest Airlines;
CAAC Buses
中国西南航空公司；
民航班车

68 Xīnnánmén Bus Station
新南门汽车站

OTHER

1 Chéngdū
Dòngwùyuán
动物园

2 Zhàojué Sì
照觉寺

7 Post Office/EMS
市邮电局

Dàxióngmāo Fánzhí Yánjiū Zhōngxīn 大熊猫繁殖研究中心
Giant Panda Breeding Research Base

About 6km north of the zoo, this research station and breeding ground for both giant and lesser pandas has been in operation since 1990, but was opened to the public only in early 1995.

About 10 to 12 pandas currently reside at the base in quarters considerably more humane than those at the zoo. There is also a breeding area where China's animal ambassadors will eventually be allowed to freely roam and, it is hoped, procreate. Just past the entrance gate, the base museum has detailed exhibits on panda evolution, habits (including rather graphic displays on the, um, more private physiology and reproduc-tive aspects of the bears), habitats and conservation efforts, all with English captions.

The base now covers about 36 hectares, but the breeding ground area is projected to grow to more than 230 hectares sometime early this century.

Staff at the base say the best time to visit is between 8.30 and 10 am when the pandas are feeding; soon thereafter they return to their predominant pastime, sleeping. The entry fee of Y10 goes to a good cause and you are guaranteed a look at these elusive animals – something often denied those who make the long trip up to Wòlóng Zìrán Bǎohùqū (Sleepy Dragon Nature Reserve). The base is open daily from 8 am to 6 pm.

Cycling may be your best option to get there. Follow the road north past the zoo for

CHÉNGDŪ

9 Wángjiàn Mù
王建墓

10 Wénshū Yuàn
文殊院

16 Recreation Park
市游乐园

17 Mengzhuiwan Swimming Pool
猛追湾游泳池

18 Telecom Business Centre
电信营业厅

19 Jinjiang Theatre
锦江剧院

20 Foreign Languages Bookstore
省外文书店

23 Main Post Office
市电信局

24 Cultural Palace
文化宫

25 Municipal Sports Stadium
市体育场

26 PSB
公安局

27 Tape & CD Shop
音像书店

28 No 3 Hospital
三医院

31 Qīngyáng Gōng
青羊宫

32 Bǎihuátán Gōngyuán
百花潭公园

33 Rénmín Gōngyuán
人民公园

34 Post Office
邮电局

35 Sichuan Fine Arts Exhibition Hall
四川美术展览馆

36 Sichuan Exhibition Centre
省展览馆

37 Mao Statue
毛主席像

38 Telecom Business Centre
电信营业厅

39 PICC Office
中国人民保险公司

40 Hongqi Market
红旗商场

43 Chunxi Commercial District
春熙路商业区

44 Bank of China
中国银行

45 Rénmín Shìchǎng
人民商场

47 PSB
省公安局外事科

48 Chengdu Department Store
成都百货大楼

51 Friendship Store
友谊商店

54 Sichuān Shěng Bówùguǎn
市博物馆

56 Post Office
邮电局

59 CITS
中国国际旅行社

63 Bank of China
中国银行

65 Wǔhòu Cí; Nánjiāo Gōngyuán
武侯祠; 南郊公园

70 Black Ant Pub
黑蚂蚁酒馆

71 Red Flamingo
火烈鸟

73 Sichuān Shěng Bówùguǎn
四川省博物馆

74 Jurassic Park Pub & Disco
侏落撕克酒吧

76 The Pub Same as Before Old Pub

77 Noble Bowling

78 Wàngjiānglóu Gōngyuán
望江楼公园

80 US Consulate
美国领事馆

SÌCHUĀN 四川

about 2.5km, keeping an eye out for an overhead road sign with a panda on it. At the sign, turn right onto Xiongmao Dadao (Panda Avenue) and keep going for another 3km.

The base is not served by any bus routes, so your other options are to take a taxi all the way there, or to bicycle to the zoo and from there take a taxi or motor-tricycle (the one-way fare should be Y10). Travel outfits at the Traffic Hotel also offer tours for Y80 per person, and since a taxi would be Y85 anyway it'd make sense to take this option.

English Corner

On the northern side of the Jǐnjiāng Qiáo (Jin River Bridge) along Renmin Nanlu local English speakers congregate for an English Corner Wednesday and Friday evenings around 7.30 pm.

Places to Stay – Budget

Chéngdū is that rarest of big cities – a budget traveller's paradise.

Sam's Backpacker Guesthouse (☎ 777 2593), located on the grounds of the Chengdu College of Traditional Medicine (Chéngdū Zhōngyīyào Dàxué), fills a need for cheap lodging not far from the Ximen bus station. Beds in triples with private bath are only Y25 and decent singles/doubles are Y60; more expensive rooms are available. Each room has a small tiled balcony and fan. Sam also has a travel service, email access, and a book exchange; there's also a decent cafe. Be careful, there's another guesthouse on the campus grounds, not nearly so backpacker friendly. To get there from Ximen bus station, exit right out of the station, turn right at the first intersection, and continue south for about 15 or 20 minutes, until you pass a gate with a big statue inside. Continue to the street corner (it should be Shier Qiaolu) and turn left into the gate. Turn right and follow this road 200m as it veers left.

Sam recently opened **Sam's Backpacker Guesthouse 2** by leasing a wing inside the Róngchéng Fàndiàn (☎ *612 2529, fax 613 5532, 130 Shanxi Jie*). It's up an alley west of Renmin Nanlu, and is easily accessed from Xinannmen bus station. Beds in clean rooms with private bath start at Y35 and go up to Y70. If no one is in Sam's office, look across the street for Lynne of her eponymous cafe; she's the one to go through. If you ask the hotel staff for help, they'll sell you the same rooms at twice the price or just show you the Y260 Garden Wing rooms, which actually are quite nice, especially since they'll probably be more than willing to deal on the rate. The latter rooms surround an absolutely lovely traditional Chinese courtyard – though most rooms don't actually overlook it.

The **Traffic Hotel** (Jiāotōng Fàndiàn; ☎ *555 1017, fax 558 2777*), next to Xinnanmen bus station, has for a long time been the main hang-out for backpackers. Though no longer the cheapest in town, it's still an amazing spot for the money. This oasis is clean, comfortable, fairly quiet and close to a number of good dining spots. A bed in a triple with satellite TV and fan is Y40, with immaculate showers and toilets down the hall. Doubles/triples with satellite TV and private bathroom cost Y220/210. All prices include a decidedly uninspiring although filling breakfast; go for the Chinese version. The staff are mostly friendly and there's a notice board just outside the foyer with travel information. Another useful service here is the baggage room where you can leave heavy backpacks for a few days while you head off to Éméi Shān or Jiǔzhài Gōu (Y1 per day). To get here from the north train station, take bus No 16

across the bridge just south of the Jǐnjiāng Bīnguǎn and walk east along the south bank of the river to the hotel.

Places to Stay – Mid-Range
The **Bīnjiāng Fàndiàn** (☎ *665 6009, fax 662 2193*), not far from the Traffic Hotel, used to be a popular mid-range option, but it has gone for a major face-lift, jacked up its prices and for all that still looks not quite worth its Y196 doubles or Y270 triples. Some Y140 doubles – much like the more expensive rooms – are usually not available unless you get a local travel agent to intercede.

Another option is the friendly **Jīndì Fàndiàn** (☎ *691 5339, ext 281, fax 662 7778, 89 Desheng Lu*), which has modest singles and doubles from Y130 to Y180; it also has standard rooms for Y230. Some of the cheaper doubles are in amazingly good condition for the price. The hotel is in a good location for visiting sights in northern Chéngdū.

Up north by the train station, the **Jīngróng Bīnguǎn** (☎ *333 7878*) has doubles with all mod cons for Y298.

Places to Stay – Top End
The **Jǐnjiāng Bīnguǎn** (☎ *558 2222, fax 558 1849, 80 Renmin Nanlu*) was once the headquarters for all travellers who made it to Chéngdū. Now it has become a four-star giant with standard doubles starting at Y1000, while a cheaper wing has doubles from Y780. There are good views to be had from the rooftop Chinese restaurant here, but at a high price.

Opposite the Jǐnjiāng Bīnguǎn on Renmin Nanlu is the newer, 21-storey **Mínshān Fàndiàn** (☎ *558 3333, fax 558 2154*), which does a brisk tour-group business. Modern doubles start at Y800 and suites are Y1400. The Mínshān has a couple of bars, a coffee shop and five restaurants.

Opposite the north train station is the **Chengdu Grand Hotel** (Chéngdū Dàjiǔdiàn; ☎ *317 3888*), a plush place designed to attract the roving business account. Prices vary according to demand (they will double when conferences are held in town), but you can reckon on a minimum of Y288 for a standard double; some older rooms go for half this.

Just east of the Sichuan Exhibition Centre, the **Holiday Inn Crowne Plaza** (*Zǒngfǔ Huángguàn Rì Jiǔdiàn;* ☎ 678 6666, fax 678 6599) is a new top-end place with all the trappings of a Holiday Inn. In addition to the numerous restaurants, it has a laundry list of amenities, including one of the few exercise facilities you'll find in China. You can pick up a copy of the *International Herald Tribune* here as well. All this for a mere US$108 base rate, although they'll likely trim it by 30% since it's never full. Before you book a room, wander to the next building to the west. This, the **Sìchuān Bīnguǎn** (☎ 675 9147, fax 674 5263, 31 Zongfu Jie) has its most luxurious rooms for Y800, where the Holiday Inn starts. The Sìchuān Bīnguǎn also has a Dragonair office.

Places to Eat

Chinese Restaurants The **Chéngdū Cāntīng** (*134 Shangdong Dajie*) is one of Chéngdū's most famous and authentic Sìchuān restaurants and a favourite with travellers. It combines a good atmosphere, decent food and reasonable prices. Downstairs serves set courses of Sìchuān appetisers, while full meals can be had upstairs. Try to assemble a party of vagabonds before sallying forth; tables are large and you get to sample more with a bigger group. It's about a 20-minute walk along a side alley opposite the Jǐnjiāng Bīnguǎn. Arrive early: the place starts shutting down at around 8.30 pm.

For *guoba roupian* (crispy rice in pork and lychee sauce), you can't beat the **Shìmějixuān Cāntīng** opposite the Jinjiang Theatre (see the Entertainment section) on Huaxingzheng Jie. A large plate costs around Y10, which is plenty for two. The restaurant has lots of other great dishes, and the proprietors don't seem to mind if you walk through the kitchen and point out what you want. Large, clean dining rooms with wooden tables and ceiling fans make eating here even more enjoyable.

Another main-course restaurant in the heart of the city is the **Yàohuá Fàndiàn**

(☎ 672 9518), on the corner of Chunxi Lu and Changsha Dongdajie. A visit by Mao himself in 1958 clinched the restaurant's reputation; today it's as likely to have a Cindy Crawford photo on the walls. The restaurant also has passable western food. You can get a set meal for around Y15.

Bāguó Bùyī Fēngweìjiǔbù, along Renmin Nanlu just north of the intersection with the road to the US consulate, takes its name from the traditional cotton clothing worn by peasants in an ancient state of eastern Sìchuān. Best-described as down-home country Sìchuān, the food is prepared all over the bi-level place; you wander and point. Be careful – it ain't cheap.

Many food stall areas are also known for having the nickname 'Catfish' (*lián yú*). The name comes from Qíuxī Hé (Qiuxi River) catfish, a speciality of the Chéngdū-Chóngqìng corridor. Qíuxī town has literally hundreds of catfish and silver carp restaurants, and many chefs relocate to the bright lights of Chéngdū.

The healthfulness of eating river fish is debatable, but if you're brave you can find little restaurants specialising in a hot-fired wok stew with hot pepper, ginger, garlic and fresh chopped fish, sprinkled with green onion and parsley.

Vegetarian Restaurants A special treat for ailing vegetarians is to head out to the Wénshū Yuàn, where there's an excellent **vegetarian restaurant** with an English menu. The Zhàojué Sì also serves up vegie dishes for lunch, but the menu is only in Chinese. If you're really keen, you might ride out to the **Bǎoguāng Sì** (Monastery of Divine Light) in Xīndū, 18km north of Chéngdū, in time for lunch (11 am to noon). For details of the bus service, see the Around Chéngdū section later in this chapter.

Snack Bars Many of Chéngdū's specialities originated as *xiǎo chī* or 'little eats'. The snack bars are great fun and will cost you next to nothing. In fact, the offerings can be outdone in no other Chinese city – and if you line up several of these places you will get yourself a banquet in stages.

Unfortunately many of Chéngdū's best-known snack places are falling prey to the massive reconstruction work that is tearing down whole neighbourhoods. This is particularly true of the Dongfeng Lu district, although a few places are still hanging in there. We can't promise that all the places marked on the map and mentioned here will still be there by the time you set out in search of them. Take a look anyway – it's worth the effort. At the first major intersection east of Wénshū Yuàn sits the provincially recognised *Guō Tāngyuán (Guo Soup Balls Restaurant)*; the name pretty much says it all. Virtually next door is *Pùgaìmiàn (Pugai Noodles)*, with the freshest, thickest, most delectable hand-sliced noodles in town for around Y2 per bowl.

To the north of here, *Chén Mápō Dòufu (Pock-marked Grandma Chen's Bean Curd)* serves *mápō dòufu* with a vengeance. Soft bean curd is served up with a fiery meat sauce (laced with garlic, minced beef, salted soybean, chilli oil and nasty little peppercorns). The story goes that the old lady with the pock-marked face set up shop here (reputed to be the same shop as today's) a century ago, providing food and lodging for itinerant peddlers. The bean curd is made on the premises and costs around Y3 a bowl. Beer is served to cool the fires. Don't worry about the grotty decor – those spices should kill any lurking bugs. Also served are spicy chicken and duck, and plates of tripe.

Situated along Jiefang Lu north of the Fǔ Hé (Fu River), the shop has a vertical sign, the outside edge of which has the name in Pinyin. Be sure to sit downstairs: the 2nd floor has been redone to look like a typical Chinese banquet hall and carries a Y5 'seating charge'. This place is no longer an unknown cubbyhole – it is spiffier than it is greasy and it appears to have franchised, opening a *branch* across from Wénhuà Gōngyuán.

North of the Traffic Hotel along Hongxing Lu is the famed *Gàn Bāozi (Gan Dumplings; 20 Hongxin Lu, Section 4)*, serving up legendary *baōzi* (dumplings) for over 80 years – you can get six to 10 dumplings for Y4.50 depending on the ingredients. At 5.30 pm this place has a line out the door for takeaway.

Another place that is still going strong is *Lóngcháoshǒu Cāntīng*. The beauty of this little restaurant is that it has sampler courses that allow you to dip into the whole gamut of the Chéngdū snack experience. The Y5 course gives you a range of sweet and savoury items, while the Y10 and Y15 courses are basically the same deal on a grander and more filling scale. It's on the north-eastern corner of Chunxi Lu and Shangdong Dajie.

Hotpot Although it is said to have originated in Chóngqìng, *huǒguō*, or hotpot, is very popular in Chéngdū. You'll see lots of sidewalk hotpot operations in the older section of town near the Chunxi Lu market, as well as along the river.

Big woks full of hot, spiced oil (not to be confused with the mild Mongolian version, which employs simmering soup broth) invite passers-by to sit down, pick out skewers of raw ingredients and make a do-it-yourself fondue. You pay by the skewer – it's best to ask the price of a skewer before you place it in the oil.

During the winter months the skewered items on offer tend to be meat or 'heavy' vegetables like potatoes. In the summer months lighter, mostly vegetarian fare is the norm. This stuff is *very* hot and many non-Sichuanese can't take it. If this is the case, try asking for *báiwèi*, the hotpot for wimps. Chinese (and some travellers) will turn their noses up at this, claiming that it's not the real thing – just ignore them.

Teahouses The *Rénmín Cháguǎn* in Rénmín Gōngyuán is a leisurely tangle of bamboo armchairs, sooty kettles and ceramics, with a great outdoor location by a lake. It's a family-type teahouse and is crowded on weekends. In the late afternoon workers roll up to soothe factory-shattered nerves, and some are known to doze off in their armchairs. You can do the same. A most pleasant afternoon can be spent here in relative anonymity over a bottomless cup of stone-flower tea at a cost so ridiculous it's not worth quoting. When enough tea freaks appear on the terrace, the stray earpicker, with Q-tips at the ready, roves through, and paper-profile cutters with deft scissors also make the rounds.

A charming indoor family-type *teahouse* is also to be found in Wénshū Yuàn, with an amazingly crowded and steamy ambience.

Another place definitely worth checking out is in the *Jǐnjiāng Jùyuàn* (see the Entertainment section), not far from the post office. This place also has performances of Sìchuān opera.

Western & Japanese Food The *Taiping department store (Taìpíngyáng Baíhuà)*, near the KFCs on Renmin Donglu, has a pan-Cathay fast-food place and a to-die-for (though pricey) pizza joint. East of here off Hongxing Lu the Lidu Plaza (Lìdù Guǎngchǎng) has *Ito Yokado*, a good Japanese restaurant.

For much better western food head south of the Xinnanmen bus station along Xinnan Lu. Cross Nan Yihuan Lu and continue for five minutes along Kehua Lu. On the left-hand side is the *Red Brick Cafe Pub & Pizzeria (Hóng Zhuān Xīcāntīng)*. The proprietor, who speaks English, and staff, who

mostly don't, are a friendly lot. The offerings include two set meals daily (Y38) and the food includes moderately priced appetisers, decent burgers and fries, excellent pastas, pizzas, and chicken dishes, and even some pan-Asian and African dishes.

Otherwise, western food cafes have absolutely exploded in number in the vicinity of the Traffic Hotel. Almost directly across the river sits *Paul's Cafe*, perhaps best described as an island surrounded by reality. The food's good, the beer's *ice* cold, and the proprietor is a cultural ambassador bar none. This place generally has travellers moving the furniture outside and dancing till the wee hours. Directly west of the Traffic Hotel sits *Carol's by the River (Kǎluó Xīcàn, 2 Linjiang Lu)*, where you can find good food with south-western US and Mexican overtones (and airy interiors). Carol's has another version nearer Sichuan University. West of the original Carol's, then south along Renmin Nanlu sits *Highfly Cafe (Gāofēi Kāfēitīng, 658 Renmin Nanlu)*, owned by Felix, whose sister Claudia runs the Sunshine Cafe in Dàlǐ (Yúnnán). Farther south is the *Wild Goose Cafe (Hóngkāfēitīng)* where you can get access to western media, attend Chinese cultural lectures, or see live music on Friday.

Taking Tea and More in Chéngdū

The teahouse, or *chádiàn*, has always been the equivalent in China of the French cafe or the British pub – or at least it was prior to 1949. Activities you might have encountered range from haggling over a bride's dowry to fierce political debate (and sometimes tea drinking). The latter was especially true of Sìchuān, which historically has been quick to rebel and slow to come to heel.

Chéngdū's teahouses are thus somewhat special. As in other Chinese cities, they were closed down during the Cultural Revolution because they were thought to be dangerous assembly places for 'counter-revolutionaries'. With factional battles raging in Sìchuān as late as 1975, the re-emergence of what was once a part of daily life has been slow – but you can't keep an old tea addict down! In the back alleys teahouses sprawl over Chéngdū's pavements.

In the past, Chéngdū teahouses also functioned as venues for Sìchuān opera – the plain-clothes variety, performed by amateurs or retired workers. However, the advent of VCRs and karaoke has dealt a blow to such live performances; a local may be able to direct to you any that remain.

Other kinds of entertainment include storytelling and musical performances, while some teahouses seem given over entirely to chess. Most Chinese teahouses cater to the menfolk, young and old (mostly old), who come to meet, stoke their pipes or thump cards on the table. But the women are increasing and can often be found piling up winnings at the mahjong table.

Entertainment

There is some entertainment to be had in Chéngdū, but you will have to hunt. If you don't speak Chinese, ask around among the English-speaking staff at the Traffic Hotel or the travel outfits nearby.

If something strikes your fancy, get it written down in Chinese and get a good map location – these places are often hard to find, especially at night. If you have more time, try and get advance tickets. Offerings include teahouse entertainment, acrobatics, cinema, Sìchuān opera, Běijīng opera, drama, traditional music, shadow plays, art exhibits and storytelling.

Chéngdū is the home of Sìchuān opera, which has a 200-year tradition and features slapstick dress-ups, men dressed as women, eyeglass-shattering songs and occasional gymnastics. There are several opera houses scattered throughout the older sections of town. As attendances continue to fall, most have cut back performances to only once or twice per week.

One of the easier Sìchuān opera venues to find is the *Jinjiang Theatre (Jǐnjiāng Jùyuàn)*, on Huaxingzheng Jie, which is a combination of teahouse, opera theatre and cinema. High-standard Sìchuān opera performances are given here every Sunday afternoon.

Lots of local English-speaking tour guides touting their stuff around the Traffic Hotel or Sam's Backpacker Guesthouse(s) will organise tours, usually for Y40 to Y50 per person, and most travellers have found the experience well worth it.

Pubs Most of Chéngdū's boozing options are of the karaoke variety. These places tend to be expensive and of limited interest to most westerners. However, the area around the Traffic Hotel has the first forays into serious western-style pubs. A caveat: these places come and go with a frustrating regularity; the ones here may be gone, but there surely will be others.

Two fairly durable places for imbibing and dancing are the *Black Ant Pub (Hēi Máyǐ Píjiǔguǎn)* on Nan Yihuan Lu, and the *Red Flamingo (Huǒlièniǎo)*, east of there along Nan Yihuan Lu, then south on a smaller side street.

A whole slew of pubs has recently sprouted south of the Traffic Hotel on Kehua Lu. Walk south of the Xinnanmen bus station on Xinan Lu to Nan Yihuan Lu. Cross the road and start the pub run. A half-dozen pubs include *Jurassic Park Pub & Disco (Zhūluōsīkè Jiǔbā)*, *Noble Bowling* (you really can bowl) and the intriguingly named *The Pub Same as Before Old Pub*.

Most of these places have draught beer for around Y20, the cheaper ones have jugs *(zhāzā píjiǔ)* for around Y50. Open until the wee hours – from 7 pm to 7 am usually – these spots can make for an entertaining evening, but can also play havoc with early-morning travel plans (did I say I was catching the 7 am bus to Lèshān?).

Shopping

Chéngdū is home to a host of commercial and shopping districts: the Qingyang Palace Commercial Street, the Shudu Boulevard Commercial Street, the Chenghuang Miao Electronic Market, the Chunxi Lu Commercial Street and even, as one locally produced English map indicates, 'Electronic Brain (ie 'Computer') Street – No 1 Ring Road'.

Let's assume, however, that you don't want to splurge in Chéngdū's commercial streets; therefore, the pick of the bunch for a stroll and a few purchases is Chunxi Lu. It's the main shopping artery, lined with department stores, art dealers, second-hand bookshops, stationers, spectacle shops and photo stores. At No 10 is the Arts & Crafts Service Department Store (Chéngdū Měishùpǐn Fúwùbù), dealing in most of the Sìchuān specialities including lacquer ware, silver work and bamboo products.

The best advice for Chunxi Lu is just to stroll around and dive into any shop that looks interesting. You are almost bound to come up with something you couldn't possibly do without. Look out for the Derentang Chemist, the oldest and largest of all Chéngdū's Chinese pharmacies, at the bottom end (south) of the road on the left.

The Sichuan Antique Store, which used to be on the northern end of Chunxi Lu, has now moved to a huge new building opposite the Sichuan Fine Arts Exhibition Hall (Sìchuān Meǐshù Zhǎnlǎn Guǎn) on Renmin Donglu. It's worth a visit and, while a lot of the stuff is quite overpriced, there are usually still a few bargains to be had.

For other antiques along with lots of scrollwork and other 'traditional' Chinese souvenirs, go north past the Mínshān Fàndiàn on Renmin Donglu and take the first right, then the first left. A whole string of shops lines both sides of the street. If you take the *second* left you'll come to what is known as Qīngshíqiáo Shìcháng, a nice old market chock-full of fish, flowers, birds and such.

Rénmín Shìchǎng (People's Market) is a maze of daily necessity stuff – worth poking your nose into, but not of great interest for purchases.

Getting There & Away

The transport connections in Chéngdū are more comprehensive than in other parts of the south-west. Transport between Chóngqìng and Chéngdū is much improved with the completion of the high-speed expressway; another expressway linking Lèshān with Chéngdū, cutting travel time to perhaps two hours, should be completed by early 2000. (This will be followed by another highway from Lèshān to Chóngqìng, forming a high-speed triangle.)

Air Shuangliu airport is 18km west of the city. Major destinations (most flights are daily) include Běijīng (Y1150), Guǎngzhōu (Y1040), Guìlín (Y780), Guìyǎng (Y540), Kūnmíng (Y560), Lhasa (Y1900 to Y3200!), Nánjīng (Y1230), Xī'ān (Y500), Ürümqi (Y1820) and Shànghǎi (Y1290). There was even a service planned to Jǐnghóng (Xīshuāngbǎnnà, Yúnnán, Y1080). Several flights a week also go to Hong Kong (Y2510), Singapore (Y3050) and Bangkok (Y1480). Service to Chóngqìng was close to being suspended. Chéngdū's airport has great dim sum, if you have to leave too early for the hotel's breakfast, but give the coffee a miss.

China Southwest Airlines (☎ 666 5911) is diagonally opposite the Jǐnjiāng Bīnguǎn, and is a good place to purchase tickets for destinations all across China. The smaller Sichuan Provincial Airlines (☎ 664 7196) also has an office nearby; once a frightening airline, it's recently upgraded its fleet with a few airbuses.

The most frequently asked question in Chéngdū must be 'Can I fly to Lhasa?' If you're on your own, the official answer is 'No'. To get around this, travel agents can sign you on to a 'tour', which usually includes a one-way ticket to Lhasa, the two-hour transfer from Gonggar airport to Lhasa and your first night's accommodation there. The fact that members of the tour group have never seen each other prior to the flight, and split up immediately after, is overlooked by the authorities. These packages cost as much as Y3200 on our last check, although this had risen quite arbitrarily from Y1900 in a three-week period. You can always try picking up a ticket from one of the airlines yourself: some travellers occasionally – no, rarely – get lucky. Just make sure you have the cash on hand to snatch up the ticket before the airline has a change of mind. Another trick is to ask for a 1st-class ticket.

Bus The main bus station, Xinnanmen, sells tickets to most destinations around Sìchuān, but not to the north. For northern destinations you need to head over to the Ximen bus station in the north-west of the city. A third bus station is near the north train station. To get to Chóngqìng, Dàzú, Zígòng or Nèijiāng, it's best to go to the Wuguiqiao express bus station 7km from the city centre in south-east Chéngdū, near Tázìshān Gōngyuán (Pagoda Park) and the start of the expressway to Chóngqìng; bus No 49 runs between the Traffic Hotel and here or a taxi costs Y12. Chóngqìng is also served by the north bus station.

Getting to western Sìchuān generally induces most headaches from officialdom; see the boxed text 'Warning'. Day buses to Kāngdìng (Y65) and Lúdìng may attempt to cross the notoriously dangerous Èrlangshān Guān (Erlang Mountain Pass), which is often subject to landslides that stretch the 10-hour trip to 18 or 20 hours. Some don't,

SÌCHUĀN 四川

Warning

Travellers may be required to purchase insurance from the People's Insurance Company of China (PICC) for bus travel in Sìchuān and Gānsù provinces. If you're just headed to Jiǔzhài Gōu and back you'll be OK, but for anything north of that you might want to scout out insurance first: the whole of western Sìchuān requires it. The ticket office at the Ximen bus station in Chéngdū used to require foreigners to present a PICC card, but now says that insurance is factored into the cost of foreigners' double-priced bus tickets.

However, to get to western Sìchuān the Xinnanmen station requires you to purchase your own insurance. The card costs Y15 per day of coverage and is available from the PICC office on Shudu Dadao (Renmin Donglu) in Chéngdū. Look for the building with the green banner running down its west face (it's on the corner with Goutou Xiang). Ask for *shuù dàshà*. Monthly rates weren't being offered last visit (though they're supposed to be). Buying just enough to get to Kāngdìng or Lǐtáng is OK, but now travellers are finding hassles from ticket sellers and bus drivers on the return from western Sìchuān to Chéngdū, and there are no PICC offices out there. If you're stuck, you may have to trudge to the edge of town, hold up your hand, and wait for a sympathetic driver who'll look the other way on the insurance beef.

Travellers in Zöigê and towns in Gānsù have also been sent to PICC branch offices to pick up insurance cards before being allowed to board their buses, which often leave without them anyway. Don't bother telling the staff you have travel insurance already: non-PICC coverage is not recognised. This policy apparently follows from a lawsuit brought upon the Chinese government by the family of a Japanese tourist who was killed in a bus crash in the Jiǔzhài Gōu area.

hours), but is more likely to get you there on time. Sleepers depart around 4 or 4.30 pm and cost Y108; regular hardcore buses cost Y63. Road upgrades are incessantly begun, then shelved, then begun again, so these travel times may change by the time you read this. To Yǎ'ān the road is good.

Travellers going to western Sìchuān must purchase insurance, which jacks prices up Y15 per day of coverage. You can't even buy it at the station, but must trudge to the People's Insurance Company of China (PICC; Zhōngguó Rénmín Bǎoxiǎn Gōngsī) office. Travel agents adjoining the station or around the Traffic Hotel could also scare up a ticket and insurance for you, saving you the legwork.

The Ximen bus station is for travellers heading up to Jiǔzhài Gōu or taking the overland route to Xiàhé in Gānsù by way of northern Sìchuān. This place also has special foreigners' prices (a surcharge of 70%) for northern routes and it's quite insistent.

There are buses to Sōngpān (Y63; 10 hours on a new road), Jiǔzhài Gōu, Nánpíng and Màoxìan. Consider taking a Nánpíng-bound sleeper bus at 7.20 am and hopping off in Jiǔzhài Gōu, then backtracking to Sōngpān; you could do it this way and get sleeper buses the whole route – on a new highway it's now only 12 hours to Jiǔzhài Gōu. For tickets to Sōngpān, again travel agents around the bus station or Traffic Hotel could do the work for you.

Other buses from Ximen (not requiring insurance) include those to Dūjiāngyàn (Y5 to Y8; every 10 minutes), Qīngchéng Shān (Y9 to Y11), Lèshān, (Y17 to Y24), Bàoguó Sì (Y17) and Éméi Shān (Y16).

The north bus station is west of the train station and has buses to Dūjiāngyàn (Y7), Bàoguó Sì (Y17) and Lèshān (Y18 to Y26). Note that none go to Qīngchéng Shān from here.

Train Getting train tickets out of Chéngdū is no easy feat, though it's far easier today than in years past. Many travellers simply give up on the idea and get locals around the Traffic Hotel to fix tickets up for them. This is fine if you don't mind paying extra for

and the road's often closed, so ask first. All-night sleeper buses now skirt Èrláng Shān by taking a southern route via Yǎ'ān and Shímían. It's longer at 18 hours (on a good day – one poor bloke enjoyed it for 38

their services. (But even then success isn't guaranteed – remember, everyone and their sister is trying to get to Xī'ān and Kūnmíng.)

You'll usually need to arrange tickets 1½ days in advance. Don't bother with CITS, but do give the advance-booking office a try first, as it has been easier and easier to reserve tickets. Even so, hard-sleeper tickets for popular destinations almost never get done on the same day. The advance-booking office is open from 8 am to noon and 1.30 to 6 pm.

For those wanting to travel to Lìjiāng and Dàlĭ there are five trains a day to Pānzhīhūa (across from Jǐnjiāng) on the Chéngdū-Kūnmíng route (Y120). The trip averages 16 hours.

You can use any of the trains headed for Kūnmíng or Pānzhīhūa to get to Éméi Shān. Express trains take just under two hours, while fast trains take around three hours. A hard seat should cost Y7. Trains to Kūnmíng take either 21 hours or 26 hours, depending on whether they are express or fast, and the cost is around Y255 for a hard sleeper.

There are three trains daily to Chóngqìng (Y82 hard sleeper) and same-day tickets are possible, or at least much more so than for Kūnmíng or Xī'ān. If you're headed to Dàzú, your best bet is train No 537, which leaves around 7.20 am and arrives at Yóutíng at 4 pm. There you can catch a minibus to Dàzú, 30km to the north.

Other rail options include Běijīng, Guǎngzhōu, Guìyáng, Héféi, Lánzhōu, Shànghǎi, Tàiyuán, Ürümqi and Xī'ān, the last of which is easily the most popular destination after Kūnmíng. You'll definitely need to hang out in Chéngdū for a day and a half waiting for a ticket, although at least you can get one yourself. Hard sleepers cost Y117.

Getting Around

Airport Civil Aviation Administration of China (CAAC; Zhōngguó Mínháng) runs a bus every half-hour between the ticket office on Renmin Nanlu, near the China Southwest Airlines ticket office, and Shuangliu airport. The fare is Y10. A taxi should cost around Y40 on the meter.

If there aren't enough passengers the CAAC bus won't run; in that case, you'll be put four to a Speed Racer taxi and the fare should still be Y10.

Bus The most useful bus is No 16, running from the north train station to the south train station along Renmin Nanlu. Regular buses cost Y0.60, and double-deckers cost Y1.

Bus maps have colour-coding for electric and ordinary buses – bus Nos 2, 4 and 5 can also be electric buses bearing the same number. Ordinary bus No 4 runs from the Ximen bus station (north-western end of town) to the south-eastern sector, and continues services until 1 am (most others cease around 9.30 to 10.30 pm).

Minibuses also carry numbers, but the routes differ from those of the big buses. Minibus No 12 circles the city along Yi-huan Lu, starting and ending at the north train station.

Bicycle Many of Chéngdū's old bicycle-hire shops have disappeared, and most travellers hire their bikes these days from the Traffic Hotel or Sam's Backpacker Guesthouses, all of which do a fairly good job of bicycle maintenance. The Traffic's rate is around Y10 per day; Sam's is slightly cheaper.

The only problem with the Traffic is the shop opens rather late and if you want to see the pandas before they retire you have to pedal like mad.

The usual rules apply – check your bike before you cycle off; some of them are death traps. Also make an effort to park your bike in a designated parking area. Bicycle theft is a problem here as in most Chinese cities.

Taxi Taxis have a flag fall of Y4.8, plus Y1.2 to Y1.4 per kilometre. Chéngdū takes the cake for the Chinese obsession with mobile phones; even taxis have them. For Y1 per minute you too can show off. By the time you read this, you should be able to make domestic and even international calls.

From the Traffic Hotel to the Ximen bus station, the straight route is around Y12, although most will take the left fork and thus the tourist route for up to Y16.

SÌCHUĀN 四川

AROUND CHÉNGDŪ
Bǎoguāng Sì 宝光寺
Monastery of Divine Light

Bǎoguāng Sì, in the north of Xīndū County, is an active Buddhist temple. It comprises five halls and 16 courtyards, surrounded by bamboo. Pilgrims, monks and tourists head for Xīndū, which makes for a lively atmosphere and attracts a fine line-up of hawkers.

Founded in the 9th century, the temple was subsequently destroyed before being reconstructed in the 17th century. Among the monastery treasures are a white jade buddha from Myanmar (Burma), Ming and Qing paintings and calligraphy, a stone tablet engraved with 1000 Buddhist figures (AD 540) and ceremonial musical instruments. Unfortunately, most of the more valuable items are locked away and require special permission to view them – you may be able to get this if you can find whoever's in charge.

The **Arhat Hall**, built in the 19th century, contains 500 2m-high clay figurines of Buddhist saints and disciples – well, not all saints: among this spaced-out lot are two earthlings, the emperors Kangxi and Qianlong. They're distinguishable by their royal costumes, beards, boots and capes. One of the impostors, Kangxi, is represented with a pockmarked face, perhaps a whim of the sculptor.

About 1km from the monastery is **Osmanthus Lake** and its bamboo groves, lotuses and osmanthus trees. In the middle of the lake is a small **memorial hall** for the Ming scholar Yang Shengan.

Bǎoguāng Sì has an excellent vegetarian restaurant where a huge array of dishes is prepared by monastic chefs. The restaurant's opening hours are from 10 am to 3 pm, although it is best to be here around lunch time, when there is more available. The monastery itself is open daily between 8 am and 5.30 pm.

Getting There & Away Xīndū is 18km north of Chéngdū; a round trip on a bicycle would be 40km, or at least four hours cycling time on a Chinese bike. Alternatively, buses to Xīndū run from in front of the north train station and from the north bus station from around 6 am to 6 pm. The trip takes just under an hour.

Qīngchéng Shān 青城山
Azure City Mountain

For those with limited time, Qīngchéng Shān (1600m), a holy Taoist mountain some 65km west of Chéngdū, is a good alternative to the more rigorous climb at Éméi Shān.

There are numerous Taoist temples en route to the summit. The **Jiànfú Gōng**, at the entrance to the mountain area, is probably the best preserved. Of the 500 or so Taoist monks in residence on the mountain prior to the revolution, there are now thought to be around 100 left.

Most people ascend by way of Tiānshī Dòng and descend via Sìwàng Guǎn (Siwang Pavilion) and Bànshān Tíng (Halfway Pavilion).

The climb to the top is a four-hour hike, making Qīngchéng Shān a pleasant (al-

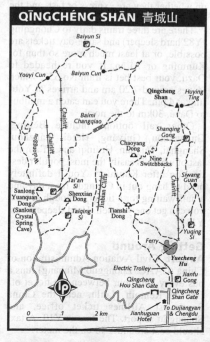

QĪNGCHÉNG SHĀN 青城山

though fairly long) day trip from Chéngdū. Be careful, because there are numerous slippery spots, the steps seem designed for baby feet, and the whole system is poorly marked.

It might be more relaxing to set off around noon, stay overnight at Shàngqīng Gōng (see Places to Stay & Eat later) and hike up to the summit for the sunrise. This leaves time to walk down and head over to Dūjiāngyàn for the afternoon. There's a Y25 entry charge for the mountain area.

To avoid the hike, you can take a cable car/boat/chairlift combination up to Shàngqīng Gōng, requiring about an hour all told, including the walk. The combined one-way cost of around Y30 keeps most people on the trail.

Places to Stay & Eat Accommodation and food are available at three spots on the mountain: at the base at *Jiànfú Gōng*, about halfway up at *Tiānshī Dòng* (Heavenly Master Cave) and at the summit at *Shàngqīng Gōng*. For budget prices reckon on around Y15 per person, or Y20 to Y30 if you want your own bathroom. Unfortunately, most temples now sport freshly painted English signs whose prices don't happen to jibe with the Chinese. You'll be politely pressured to go for Y50/75/100 doubles which certainly aren't worth the price – we encountered China's largest rat in one on our last trip. There are also some smaller privately run hostels along the way, but many of these are overly reluctant to take foreigners.

If you miss the last bus back to Dūjiāngyàn and don't feel like hiking back up the mountain to a temple, up the road towards Dūjiāngyàn from Qīngchéng Shān Gate is the *Jiànfúguǎn Hotel* (no English sign), with very basic doubles from Y50 to Y70. This is a last resort only, judging by the look and smell of the toilets. The rooms themselves are spartan, but OK. It might be the time for a splurge at one of the nicer lodging options nearby.

Getting There & Away There are minibuses to Qīngchéng Shān (and Qīngchéng Hòu Shān, so be sure you know which one) leaving from the Chéngdū

Ximen bus station every half-hour between 7 am and noon. You may find a few buses from Chéngdū's north station but don't bet on it. The fare direct to the mountain from both stations is Y9 to Y11, Y5 to Y8 to Dūjiāngyàn. From Dūjiāngyàn you can catch a minibus at the city bus station for Y3: they leave as soon as they fill up.

From the entrance to the mountain there are buses running back to Chéngdū and also to Dūjiāngyàn. The last bus for Chéngdū leaves around 5 pm, although you might get lucky until as late as 7 pm. It might be quicker to go to Dūjiāngyàn and transfer there.

Qīngchéng Hòu Shān 青城后山
Azure City Black Mountain

In a bid to bolster tourism, local authorities have also recently opened up the Qīngchéng Hòu Shān, the base of which lies about 15km north-west of the base of Qīngchéng Shān proper. With more than 20km of hiking trails, the back mountain offers a more natural alternative to the temple-strewn slopes of Qīngchéng Shān. Locals especially recommend the Wǔlónggōu (Five Dragon Gorge) for its dramatic vistas. There is a cable car to help with part of the route, but climbing the back mountain will still require an overnight stay, either at the mountain itself or in nearby Dūjiāngyàn; doing it as a day trip from Chéngdū isn't really practical.

There's accommodation at the base in the *Tài'ān Sì (Great Peace Temple)* or halfway up at *Yòuyī Cūn* village, at around Y15 to whatever you'll pay for a dorm bed.

Dūjiāngyàn 都江堰

The Dūjiāngyàn irrigation project, some 60km north-west of Chéngdū, was undertaken in the 3rd century BC by the famed prefect and engineer Li Bing to divert the fast-flowing Mín Hé (Min River) into irrigation canals.

The Mín was subject to flooding at this point, yet when it subsided droughts could ensue. A weir system was built to split the force of the river, and a trunk canal was cut through a mountain to irrigate the Chéngdū plain.

SICHUĀN 四川

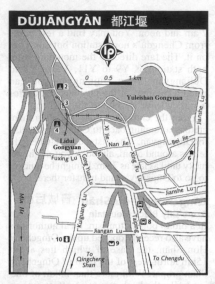

0   0.5   1 km

Yuleishan Gongyuan

Lidui Gongyuan

Fuxing Lu

Nan Jie

Bei Jie

Xi Jie

Xing Fu Lu

Jianshe Lu

Gong Yuan Lu

Min He

Taiping Jie

Jiangan Lu

Jianshe Lu

To Qingcheng Shan

To Chengdu

DŪJIĀNGYÀN

1 Ānlán Cable Bridge
  安澜索桥
2 Èrwáng Miào
  二王庙
3 Chairlift
  索道
4 Fúlóng Guàn
  伏龙观
5 Nán Qiáo
  南桥
6 Dūjiāngyàn Bīnguǎn
  都江堰宾馆
7 City Bus Station
  市客运站
8 County Bus Station
  县客运站
9 Post Office
  邮电大楼
10 Kuíguāng Tǎ
  奎光塔

Li Bing's brilliant idea was to devise an annual maintenance plan to remove silt build-up. Thus the mighty Mín was tamed, and a temple was erected to commemorate the occasion in AD 168. **Fúlóng Guàn** (Dragon-Subduing Temple) can still be seen in Líduī Gōngyuán (Solitude Park). A small-ish, pleasant place, it has a tame gallery of self-congratulatory propaganda photographs showing, among many others, Jimmy Carter visiting the site. Admission to the park is Y4.

The irrigation project is ongoing. It originally fed more than a million hectares of land, and since the revolution this has expanded to three million hectares. Most of the present dams, reservoirs, pumping stations, hydroelectric works, bridgework and features are modern; a good overall view of the outlay can be gained from **Èrwáng Miào** (Two Kings Temple), which dates from AD 494. The two kings are Li Bing and his son, Er Lang.

Inside is a shockingly lifelike statue of Li Bing, and in the rear hall is a standing figure of his son holding a dam tool. There's also a Qing dynasty project map, and behind the temple there is a terrace saying, in effect, 'Mao was here' (1958).

A chairlift runs from Líduī Gōngyuán to Èrwáng Miào and to Yùlěi Shān Gōngyuán (Jade Wall Hall Park), but the Y16 to Y25 *per segment* cost puts off most travellers.

Dūjiāngyàn receives mixed reports from travellers. Some people love the place, others find the whole idea of visiting a massive mocha-coloured irrigation project boring. There's not a great deal of local flavour, although there are small teahouses lining the river around the funky **Nán Qiáo** (South Bridge), near the Líduī Gōngyuán entrance, and visiting the nearby temples is not a bad way to while away an afternoon. The streets lined with canopies of trees make for some nice walks as well. You could also get lost for a spell in Yùlěishān Gōngyuán (open from 8 am to 6 pm).

Places to Stay Dūjiāngyàn is easy to do as a day trip. Should you decide to stay overnight, perhaps to tackle Qīngchéng Shān the next day, the *Dūjiāngyàn Bīnguǎn*, about 15 minutes' walk from the city bus station, has beds in triples for as low as Y40, and air-con doubles for Y120. If you're solo, you can usually bargain a bed for around Y60, but not much less.

Don't bother with the *China Travel Service Hotel*, a shabby-looking two-star nearby. The management labours under the illusion that some wayward foreigner will consider shelling out US$33 for a mouldy double.

Getting There & Away Buses to Dūjiāngyàn run between 7 and 6 pm from Ximen bus station in Chéngdū. There are also hourly buses leaving the Chéngdū north bus station from 7.30 am to 6 pm. The trip costs from Y5 to Y8 and takes 1½ hours.

From the Dūjiāngyàn city bus station it's not a bad idea to catch another bus to Èrwáng Miào and work your way back. It's also possible to hook up with buses here going to Qīngchéng Shān. Returning to Chéngdū, there are frequent minibuses departing from along Taiping Jie, in the area of the city bus station. The last one leaves at around 8 pm.

Be aware that a monstrous new bus station has been erected south of town, off the map. If you get dropped off here, just look for the big statue and walk past it to the right. Bearing right, you hook up with Kuangfeng Loulu and take a left. Walk about 300m and you should be at Jiangan Lu. There's no need to come to this station to go back to Chéngdū, but for the record, buses to Chéngdū's north station leave frequently from here from 6.30 am to 6.30 pm and cost Y7.

Wòlóng Zìrán Bǎohùqū 卧龙自然保护区
Sleepy Dragon Nature Reserve
Wòlóng Zìrán Bǎohùqū lies 140km northwest of Chéngdū, about an eight-hour trip on rough roads by bus (via Dūjiāngyàn).

It was set up in the late 1970s and is the largest of the 16 reserves set aside by the Chinese government especially for panda conservation. Of these 16 reserves, 11 are in Sìchuān. The United Nations has designated Wòlóng as an international biosphere preserve.

Before setting out for Wòlóng be forewarned: there is very little chance of seeing a panda in the wild. Dr George Schaller, invited by China to help with panda research

and conservation efforts, spent two months trekking in the mountains before he saw one.

To see a live panda in something resembling its natural habitat, your best bet is the Dàxióngmāo Fánzhí Yánjiū Zhōngxīn (Giant Panda Breeding Research Base) in Chéngdū (see the earlier entry under Chéngdū).

The opening of the research base and improved access to the northern areas of Sìchuān has dampened demand for tours of the Wòlóng reserve. Although most travel outfits at the Traffic Hotel have dropped this tour, one or two still offer packages that include transportation, entry to the reserve and one night's accommodation in Wòlóng town for Y350 per person, with a four-person minimum.

Your other option is to catch a bus to Dūjiāngyàn, where there is a bus to Wòlóng, though times change with the wind. The latter trip takes about four hours and costs Y14. From here you can theoretically link up with buses all the way to Kāngdìng. Entry to the nature reserve is Y50.

In Wòlóng, the *Wòlóng Zhāodàisuǒ (Sleepy Dragon Hostel)* has doubles for around Y100.

ÉMÉI SHĀN 峨眉山
Climate
The best season to visit is from May to October. Winter is not impossible, but will present some trekking problems – iron soles with spikes can be hired to deal with encrusted ice and snow on the trails. It's mind-numbingly cold at nights in winter, so be prepared.

At the height of summer, which is scorching elsewhere in Sìchuān, Émèi presents cool majesty. Temperate zones start at 1000m. Cloud cover and mist are prevalent, and will most likely interfere with the sunrise. If you're (very) lucky, you'll see Gònggà Shān to the west; if not, you'll have to settle for the telecom tower 'temple' and the meteorological station. Some monthly average temperatures in degrees Celsius are:

	Jan	Apr	Jul	Oct
Émèi Town	7	21	26	17
Summit	-6	3	12	-1

Pandas & Conservation

There are an estimated 1000 giant pandas separated into 30 isolated groups, most in 28 counties of north and north-western Sìchuān. (Other protected animals in this region are the golden monkey, golden langur, musk deer and snow leopard.) The Wòlóng Zìrán Bǎohùqū (Sleepy Dragon Nature Reserve), set aside for panda conservation, covers 200,000 hectares. To the north-west is Siguniang Shān (6240m) and to the east the reserve drops as low as 155m. Pandas like to dine in the zone from 2300m to 3200m, but range lower in winter.

The earliest known remains of the panda date back 600,000 years. It's stoutly built, rather clumsy and has a thick pelt of fine hair, a short tail and a round, white face with eyes set in black patches. Although it staggers when it walks, the panda is a good climber, and lives on a mostly vegetarian diet of bamboo and sugar-cane leaves. Mating season has proved a great disappointment to observers at the Wòlóng reserve, since pandas are rather particular. Related to the bear and the raccoon, pandas can be vicious in self-defence. In captivity they establish remarkable ties with their keepers and can be trained to do tricks.

Chinese literature has references to pandas going back more than 3000 years, but it wasn't until 1869 that the west found out about the animal, when a French missionary brought a pelt back with him to Paris. Now the giant panda, a target of poachers, is headed for extinction. Part of the problem is the gradual diminution of its food supply: In the mid-70s more than 130 pandas starved to death when one of the bamboo species on which they fed flowered and withered in the Mín Shān of Sìchuān. Pandas consume enormous amounts of bamboo, although their digestive tracts get little value from the plant (consumption is up to 20kg of bamboo a day in captivity). They are carnivorous, but they're slow to catch animals. Other problems are genetic defects, internal parasites and a slow reproductive rate (artificial insemination has been used at Beijing Zoo).

In a rare move, the Chinese invited the World Wide Fund for Nature (whose emblem is the lovable panda) to assist in research. In 1978 the research centre was set up at Wòlóng and eminent animal behaviourist Dr George Schaller has paid several visits to the area to work with Chinese biologist Professor Hu Jinchu.

Some animal-rights activists decry such captivity as another threat to the pandas. Artificial insemination in research bases is intended to preserve pandas, but pandas are also 'rented' to overseas zoos, which brings in tons of cash, and these money-generating ventures ultimately cross from panda preservation to crass commercialisation.

However, things are looking up. One of Schaller's research tasks was to fit wild pandas with radio-monitoring devices. In early 1983 the *People's Daily* reported that Hanhan, one of the very few pandas tagged, was caught in a steel wire trap by a Wòlóng local. The man strangled the panda, cut off its monitoring ring, skinned it, took it home and ate it. The meal earned the man two years in jail. Since then penalties have increased in severity: In 1990 two Sìchuān men who were found with four panda skins were publicly executed and in January 1999 a Sichuanese was sentenced to 20 years in prison for killing three pandas.

Laws are now in place strictly forbidding locals to hunt, fell trees or make charcoal in the mountainous habitats of the panda. Peasants in the areas are being offered rewards equivalent to double their annual salary if they save a starving panda. And despite a constant battle with budget deficits, China's central government has established the Dàxióngmāo Fánzhí Yánjiū Zhōngxīn (Giant Panda Breeding Research Base) in Chéngdū, which is looking at ways to preserve pandas and their habitats.

What to Bring

Éméi Shān is high at 3099m, so the weather is uncertain and you'd be best advised to prepare for sudden changes without weigh-ing yourself down with a huge pack (the steps can be steep).

No heating or insulation exist in the monasteries, but blankets are provided (a couple of places have electric blankets nowadays), and you can hire heavy overcoats at the top. Drenching rain can be a problem, calling for a good pair of rough-soled shoes or boots so you don't go head-over-heels on the smooth stone steps further up. Flimsy plastic raincoats are sold by enterprising vendors on the slopes – these will last about 10 minutes before you get wet. A fixed-length umbrella would be most useful – for the rain, and as a walking stick, and cost from around Y30 to Y45. If you want to look more authentic you can get yourself a handcrafted walking stick and, while you're at it, a fan and a straw hat too. A torch would be handy. Food supplies are not necessary, but a pocket of munchies wouldn't hurt. Bring toilet paper with you.

More than one traveller has reported coming down with a serious case of conjunctivitis in guesthouses. About the only way to avoid this is by covering pillows with towels (and then washing them in the morning). Some travellers have become sick from contaminated water supplies on the mountain, so you might consider carrying bottled water.

Ascending the Heights

You can dump your bags at the Teddy Bear Cafe (see Places to Stay & Eat); it's unnecessary to leave them in Chéngdū if you don't wish to backtrack, since the cafe can now handle most onward transport arrangements from Éméi Shān, including train tickets.

Most people start their ascent of the mountain at Wànnián Sì (Myriad Years Monastery) and come down through Qīngyīn Gé (Pure Sound Pavilion). From Bàoguó Sì (Declare Nation Monastery) there are minibuses running to car parks in the vicinity of Wànnián Sì and Qīngyīn Gé between 7 am and 3 pm. Buses leave as soon as they fill up, so it's better to go in the early morning when there are more passengers about.

The fare is Y6 to Wànnián Sì, though if you catch the bus at the intersection of the road up the mountain with the road to Éméi town it costs Y2. Returning from Wànnián, buses start running around 8 am and stop at 4 pm. To Jiēyǐn Dián the bus costs Y20.

Buses back to Bàoguó Sì depart from Jiēyǐn Dián and Qīngyīn Gé and Wànnián Sì. Miss the last bus of the day and you're left to negotiate with local minivan drivers. If you're stuck for connections you may be able to hitch back to Bàoguó, otherwise it's a 15km hike.

For a 'softer' combination, take a minibus to Qīngyīn Gé and then walk along the more scenic route via Hóngchūnpíng and Yùxīan up to Jiēyǐn Dián, from where you can catch a cable car (Y40; Y70 return) up to the Jīndǐng Sì. From there you can descend the 6km back to Jiēyǐn and take a bus back down. If you want to 'cheat' in earnest, see the Cheating section later.

One thing to watch out for: Éméi Shān levies a Y60 entry fee for foreigners, good for one entry only. So if, for instance, you catch a bus at Jiēyǐn Dián, and take it down to Wànnián Sì, you will be required to buy another entry ticket. Take this unpleasant little fact into account when planning your route. If you're hiking the entire way, this won't be a problem. This high price is reputedly temporary – levied to pay for one-time maintenance and road construction – but don't count on it. At least you get your photograph printed right onto the ticket – talk about a souvenir!

Routes Most people ascend Éméi Shān via Wànnián Sì, Chu Sì, Huáyán Dǐng (Huayan Summit), Xǐxiàng Chí (Elephant Bathing Pool) and on to the summit, and descend from the summit via Xǐxiàng Chí, Xiānfēng Sì, Hóngchūnpíng (Venerable Trees Terrace) and Qīngyīn Gé. (Almost everyone says the descent is superior in sights.) The paths converge just below Xǐxiàng Chí.

Duration Two to three days on site is enough. You usually need one day up and one day down. Enough time should be left for a slow-paced descent, which can be more punishing for the old trotters. A hardy Frenchman made it up and down on the same day, but he must have had unusual legs. Chinese and western sources have some wildly misleading figures on the length and difficulty of the Éméi Shān climb.

ÉMÉI SHĀN 峨眉山

APPROXIMATE WALKING TIMES

Ascent
Qingyin Ge to Wannian Si - 1 hour
Wannian Si to Xixiang Chi - 4 hours
Xixiang Chi to Jieyin Dian - 3 hours
Jieyin Dian to Jinding - 1 hour
Jinding Si to Wanfo Ding - 1 hour

Descent
Wanfo Ding to Jinding Si - 45 mins
Jinding Si to Jieyin Dian - 45 mins
Jieyin Dian to Xixiang Chi - 2½ hours
Xixiang Chi to Xianfeng Si - 2 hours
Xianfeng Si to Qingyin Ge - 3½ hours

Assuming that most people will want to start climbing from Qīngyīn Gé or Wànnián Sì, buses from Bàoguó Sì run close to these points, which knocks off the initial 15km. Wànnián Sì is at 1020m elevation, and Jīndǐng Sì is at 3077m. With a healthy set of lungs, at a rate of 200m elevation gain per hour, the trip up from Wànnián Sì could be done in 10 hours if foul weather doesn't interfere.

Starting off early in the morning from Wànnián Sì, you should be able to get to a point below Jīndǐng Sì by nightfall, then continue to the Jīn Dǐng (Golden Summit) and Wànfó Dǐng (Ten Thousand Buddha Summit) summits the next day, before descending to Bàoguó Sì. Some people prefer to take two days up and two days down, spending more time exploring along the way. If you have time to spare, you could meander over the slopes to villages hugging the mountainsides.

A number of readers have written to dispute our estimated walking times; half

thought they were overly conservative, and half thought we assumed all readers were expert alpinists! (They were intended to be on the conservative side.) So for whatever it's worth, on the main routes described above, in climbing time you'd be looking at:

Ascent Qīngyīn Gé (one hour), Wànnián Sì (four hours), Xǐxiàng Chí (three hours), Jiēyín Dián (one hour), Jīndǐng Sì (one hour), Wànfó Dǐng
Descent Wànfó Dǐng (¾ hour), Jīndǐng Sì (¾ hour), Jiēyín Dián (2½ hours), Xǐxiàng Chí (two hours), Xiānfēng Sì (3½ hours), Qīngyīn Gé

Cheating 'Cheating' is a popular option on Éméi: old women are portered up – and especially down – on the sturdy backs of young men (as are healthy-looking young men and women!). Official rates should be posted along the way by the time you read this. (A hint: if you come down late, late afternoon, when the porters have to go down anyway, they'll be much more amenable to steep discounts.)

If this mode of transport isn't your cup of tea, there are also minibuses leaving from the square in front of Bàoguó Sì between 8 am and 5 pm, although the wait can get long once the morning rush of tourists has passed. The minibuses run along a recently surfaced road around the back of the mountain up to Jiēyīn Diàn (2540m). From there, it's only 1½ hours to the top. The ride takes around two hours and costs Y20.

If you don't feel up to the Jiēyīn Diàn – Jīndǐng Sì climb, a cable car will haul you up there in about 20 minutes for Y40 one way or Y70 return. Lines can get very long, particularly just before sunrise.

If for some reason you wish to do the whole mountain in one day, most hotels can book you on a bus leaving at 3.30 am. This is *supposed* to get you to the summit in time to see the sunrise, and is a popular option. There is, however, a huge drawback – so many buses make this early-morning run that there is usually an immense traffic jam at the entrance gate (up to a 45-minute wait) and then the clog of tourists up the mountainside slows to a snail's crawl. The result is that very, very few people make it to Jīndǐng Sì for a proper sunrise. There's also only one good vantage point for photographs about half an hour below the summit, and it's generally crowded with other shutterbugs.

The buses head down from Jiēyīn Diàn around mid-morning, stopping at various temples along the way and finally bringing you back to Bàoguó at around 5 pm. The return trip costs about Y40 and will probably leave your head spinning. It's best to just do it in segments – buy your ticket (Y15) up at the Teddy Bear Cafe the day before. Once you're up there you can decide if, when and how you return.

Bàoguó Sì 报国寺
Declare Nation Temple
This monastery was built in the 16th century, enlarged in the 17th century by Emperor Kangxi and has undergone numerous renovations since. Its 3.5m **porcelain buddha**, made in 1415, is housed near the Sutra Library. To the left of the gate is a **rockery**

for potted miniature trees and rare plants. Admission is Y4.

A **museum** is diagonally opposite the monastery. Give it and its meagre desiccated taxidermy displays, not to mention roaming chickens, a miss – it's a waste of Y4.

Fúhǔ Sì 伏虎寺
Crouching Tiger Monastery
Fúhǔ Sì is sunk in the forest. Inside is a 7m-high **copper pagoda** inscribed with Buddhist images and texts.

Wànnián Sì 万年寺
Temple of 10,000 Years
Wànnián Sì is the oldest surviving Éméi monastery (reconstructed in the 9th century). It's dedicated to the man on the white elephant, the Bodhisattva Puxian, who is the protector of the mountain. The **statue of Puxian** – 8.5m high, cast in copper and bronze, and weighing an estimated 62,000kg – is in Brick Hall, a domed building with small stupas on it. The statue was made in AD 980. There is a **graveyard** to the rear of the temple.

Qīngyīn Gé 清音阁
Pure Sound Pavilion
Named Qīngyīn Gé because of the sound produced by water coursing rapidly around the area's rock formations, the temple is built on an outcrop in the middle of a fast-flowing stream.

There are small **pavilions** from which to observe the waterworks and appreciate the natural music, and it is also possible to swim here.

Jīndǐng Sì 金顶寺
Golden Summit Temple
To paraphrase a Chinese sage: Expect nothing. At 3077m, the magnificent Jīndǐng Sì is as far as most hikers get. Covered with glazed tiles and surrounded by white marble balustrades, it has been entirely rebuilt since being gutted by fire several years ago. The original temple had a bronze-coated roof, which is how it came by the name Jīn Dǐng (which means Gold Top as well as Golden Summit). However, it's overrun

SÌCHUĀN 四川

with tourists, pilgrims and monks, so expect to be bumped and jostled. The sun will rarely force its way through the mists, and your photos will have a TV tower in them.

From Jīn Dǐng it was once possible to hike to Wànfó Dǐng but pilgrims now take a monorail – a one-hour return costs Y50. Back down the mountain at the base of the cable car from the bus park to Jīn Dǐng you can now even go skiing for Y30 per hour.

Places to Stay & Eat

The old monasteries offer food, shelter and sights all rolled into one, and, while spartan, are a delightful change from the regular tourist hotels. Plumbing and electricity are primitive; candles are supplied. Wherever you stay rats are a problem, particularly if you leave food lying around.

You may well be asked to pay some ridiculous prices, so be prepared to bargain. You can pretty much safely disregard all posted dormitory or private room rates (as low as Y5 for Chinese). It would take the intervention of Buddha for foreigners to get local prices, if they can get in at all. Jīndǐng Sì and Bàoguó Sì are particularly known for pumping up prices for the big-noses; locals have even intervened, asking them to go easy. You can find beds for around Y20 to Y30 with some haggling (but in high season it's difficult); generally Y40 is where the monks will start. If they quote you Y200 – not unthinkable – laugh and head to one of the private guesthouses, where you can generally get a room and possibly hot water for Y30 to Y40.

There are eight monastery guesthouses: Bàoguó Sì (at the foot of Éméi Shān), Qīngyīn Gé, Wànnián Sì, Xǐxiàng Chí, Xiānfēng Sì, Hóngchūnpíng, Fúhǔ Sì and Leíyín Sì. Locals recommend Hóngchūnpíng or Xiānfēng Sì. There's also a host of smaller lodgings: Chu Sì, Jiēyǐn Dián, Yùxiān, Báilóngdòng, Jīndǐng Sì and Huáyán Dǐng, for instance.

The smaller places will accept you if the main monasteries are overloaded. Failing those, you can kip out virtually anywhere, at a teahouse or wayside restaurant. Hotel prices get steep once you reach the summit,

except for Jīndǐng Sì (see On the Mountain following). There are some cheap spots, but many may refuse to accept foreigners. Expect to pay a minimum of Y30 for a bed and the places will have rank facilities.

A good rule of thumb here: the earlier, the better. Be prepared to backtrack or advance under cover of darkness, as key points are often full of pilgrims – old women two to a bed, camped down the corridors, or camping out on the floor of the hallowed temple itself. Monasteries usually have halfway-hygienic restaurants with monk-chefs serving up the vegetarian fare; Y10 should cover a meal. There is often a small retail outlet selling peanuts, biscuits, beer and canned fruit within the monastery precincts. Smaller restaurants with surprisingly plentiful choices can be found at points along the route; establish prices before you eat and shop around as not all are exorbitant. Food gets more expensive and less varied the higher you mount, due to cartage surcharges and difficulties. Be wary of teahouses or restaurants serving 'divine water' (shénshuǐ), or any type of tea or food said to possess mystical healing qualities. While you're very unlikely to witness a miracle, you'll definitely end up being charged Y10 for a cup of tea.

On the Mountain Most of the following monasteries are located at key walking junctions and tend to be packed out. If you don't get in, do check out the restaurant and its patrons.

Fúhǔ Sì has been completely renovated, with the addition of beds for 400 and a restaurant seating 200. At Y30 to Y40 for a bed in a double, a stay here costs a bit more than at the average Éméi Shān monastery, but is well worth it if you can get in.

Accommodation in the *Wànnián Sì* area is Y25 to Y30 per person, with good vegetarian food. If it's full, go towards Qīngyīn Gé to *Báilóngdòng*, a small guesthouse. Rooms at *Qīngyīn Gé* are also available and start at Y30.

According to legend, *Xǐxiàng Chí* (Elephant Bathing Pool) is the spot where Puxian flew his elephant in for a big scrub, but there's not much of a pool to speak of today. Almost at the crossroads of both major trails, it is something of a hang-out and beds are scarce, unless you get here in the early afternoon. New extensions to the accommodation haven't completely solved the problem of pilgrim overload, so be prepared to move on. Beds are around Y20 here.

Jǐndǐng Sì is one of the noisiest places to stay, but also one of the cheapest. A bed in a large dorm with seven to 10 beds is Y10, if you can get it (which you won't). Otherwise there are beds in five-person dorms for Y20 and quads/doubles for Y30/50. Coming from the trail leading up to the summit, the rooms are located in a big building just before you reach the temple itself.

A short walk down from Jǐndǐng Sì are a handful of *smaller guesthouses* with rates from Y25 to Y100, many with heating and hot water.

The surroundings are wonderful, backed onto rugged cliffs, and the *Xiānfēng Sì* (Magic Peak Monastery) has loads of character. Try and get a room at the rear, where the floors give pleasant views. It's off the main track so it's not crowded. Nearby is Jiǔlǎo Dòng (Jiulao Cave), inhabited by edible-nest swifts.

If you are in the mood for (relative) luxury, the *Wòyún Hotel*, located just under the cable-car station, is the summit's only hotel that can boast 24-hour hot water. Standard doubles are Y180.

Around the Base At *Bàoguó Sì* beds in a seven-person dorm start at Y5; staff will likely deny the existence of these rooms and you'll be shown something in the Y30 to Y40 range. There's also a nice *teahouse* and a *vegetarian restaurant*.

Two old, cheap stand-bys within 50m of the monastery have closed in order to renovate to two-star status; they may be open by the time you read this.

Éméi Shān trekkers generally report directly to the *Teddy Bear Cafe (Wánjùxióng Cānguǎn)*, a few hundred metres from Bàoguó Sì toward Éméi town. Not only is this the friendliest place in town with great food, loads of information, train/bus/boat

tickets, baggage storage and laundry, but they've now leased a wing of the Post Office Guesthouse across the street and opened the – appropriately enough – *Teddy Bear Guesthouse (Wánjùxióng Zhāodàisǔo)*, with beds starting at Y20 and rising to Y60 for a bed in a double with air-con.

At the cafe you may bump into Zhang Guangyui, a local English teacher who seems happy to give advice on places to stay and hike around; in fact, he may meet you off the bus in Éméi town. The whole staff is extremely friendly and helpful. If you're pressed for time, ask at the Teddy Bear for interesting day-hike options in the vicinity of Bàoguó Sì.

East of the monastery, located at an intersection, is the *Qīnggōng Bīnguǎn* with standard singles/doubles for Y70 per bed (you can split the cost) and triples for Y120. With air-con, TV and evening hot water, it's not bad.

Past the Qīnggōng the *Hóngzhūshān Bīnguǎn* also lacks cheap accommodation. The cheapest rooms are the Y198 'villa-style' rooms (at least that is what they'll tell you). This place does have Internet access for Y30 per hour.

Along the trim, landscaped road leading to Éméi town are scattered a number of hotels, a few of which may accept foreigners, depending on their mood. Prices are generally high, but you may be able to scare up some dorm rooms. This area also has a slew of small restaurants lining both sides of the street.

Near Bàoguó Sì is a new *minorities folk customs park*. Some travellers have found it worthwhile; others are put off either by the Y40 admission or the regular horse fights. Be aware that participation in dances and the like inside requires additional payments.

Getting There & Away

The hubs of the transport links to Éméi Shān are Bàoguó village and Éméi town. Éméi town itself is best skipped, although it does have markets, some cheap hotels, restaurants and a long-distance bus station.

From Chéngdū you can get morning buses from the north or Ximen bus stations to Bàoguó, and any bus station has countless departures throughout the day to Éméi town. Cheapest and slowest buses cost Y15; express vans cost Y30 and up.

Éméi town lies 3.5km from the train station. Bàoguó is another 6.5km from there. Buses to town from Éméi train station are few and far between; when they run, it's Y1 in a local bus. A taxi to Éméi town (not Bàoguó) is Y10 to Y20 depending on your bargaining skills. To Bàoguó from Éméi town, frequent microbuses (Y2) depart from the first intersection exiting the bus station to the left.

These microbuses return to Éméi, where you can go to Lèshān (Y4; one hour) or back to Chéngdū. See Lèshān for more information. You may also find occasional direct buses between Éméi and Qīngyīn Gé.

Because of tourist fleecing, authorities were planning to eliminate all Chéngdū-bound buses from Bàoguó Sì and put them at a new bus station along the road near the Teddy Bear Cafe, but at last check only one morning bus was departing from the new bus station. You can get a bus to Chóngqìng from here also.

Éméi train station is on the Chéngdū-Kūnmíng line and the three-hour journey to Chéngdū costs Y9 (hard seat, Chinese price). The Teddy Bear Cafe can book sleeper tickets for you while you're on the mountain – that's the best development in Éméi in years.

Trains bound for Chéngdū depart from Éméi station at 5.55 am (No 622), 6.36 am (No 203/206), 8.31 am (No 108) 12.18 pm (No 166) and 7.48 pm (No 118). To Pānzhīhuā (Jīnjiāng), there are five departures a day: 1.38 am and 12.14, 6.41, 7.56 and 10.18 pm. The trip takes 12 hours.

LÈSHĀN 乐山
☎ 0833 • pop 3,433,500

Once a sleepy counterpart to Éméi Shān, Lèshān has taken off as China's newly affluent tourists flock to see the city's claim to fame, the towering Dà Fó (Grand Buddha).

Old brick and plaster homes are increasingly giving way to apartment towers, and the city centre is rife with neon signs for imported electronics, Coca-Cola and stock brokerages. For all that, Lèshān has a great feel to it. The hotel situation is pretty good, decent food can be unearthed and it's a good resting spot for those Éméi-weary legs.

Information

The Bank of China is on Renmin Lu, north of Baita Lu. The local PSB office, at 29 Shanxi Jie, is one of China's best places for a visa extension. The post office has Internet access (Y18 per hour) on the 3rd floor; it's open daily from noon to midnight.

Things to See

The 71m-high Dà Fó (Grand Buddha) is carved into a cliff face overlooking the confluence of the Dàdù Hé and Mín Hé. Even sitting down it qualifies as the largest buddha in the world, followed by the one at Bamian, Afghanistan. Dà Fó's ears are 7m long, insteps 8.5m broad, and a picnic could be conducted on the nail of his big toe, which is 1.5m long – the toe itself is 8.5m long.

This mammoth project was begun in AD 713 by a Buddhist monk called Haitong, who organised fund-raising and hired workers. It was completed 90 years later. Below the buddha was a hollow where boatmen used to vanish – Haitong hoped that the buddha's presence would subdue the swift currents and protect the boatmen, and Dà Fó did do a lot of good, as the surplus rocks from the sculpting filled the river hollow.

Haitong gouged out his own eyes in an effort to protect funding from disappearing into the hands of officials, but he died before the completion of his life's work.

Inside the body, hidden from view, is a water-drainage system to prevent weathering, although the stone statue has seen its fair share. Dà Fó is so old that foliage is trying to reclaim him – flowers growing on the giant hands, a bushy chest, ferns in his topknots, and weeds winding out of his ears. He gazes down, perhaps in alarm, at the drifting pollutants in the river that presumably come from the paper mill at the industrial end of town (which started large-scale operation in 1979).

Officials are worried about the possibility of a collapse due to soil erosion; one suggestion that has not met with an enthusiastic response is to cover the buddha with a huge transparent shell.

It's worth making several passes at Dà Fó, as there are all kinds of angles on him. You can go to the top, opposite the head, and then descend a short stairway to the feet for a Lilliputian perspective. Tour boats pass by for a frontal view, which reveals two guardians in the cliff side that are not visible from land.

To make a round tour that encompasses these possibilities, take a tour boat from the Lèshān pier, across from the Táoyuán Bīnguǎn. Boats and speedboats leave approximately every ½ hour from 7 am to 5 pm and cost Y10 to Y30; sit on the upper deck facing the dock and get ready to snap like mad when the boat turns and races its engine to battle the current. There are also smaller ferries which cost all of Y1 but they only pass Dà Fó once. To return, there are local ferries departing from jetties north along Lingyun Lu; the service is sporadic

and the last runs are awfully early – around mid-afternoon sometimes. The cost is Y1.

On the way over you pass close by Dà Fó, and the first stop is Wūyōu Sì. The monastery, like Dà Fó, dates from the Tang dynasty with Ming and Qing renovations – it's a museum piece containing calligraphy, painting and artefacts, and commands panoramic views.

Wūyōu Sì also has a hall of 1000 arhats, terracotta monks displaying an incredible variety of postures and facial expressions – no two are alike. The temple's vegie restaurant is famed for its imitation meat dishes: spare ribs and beef strips that look like the real thing. The taste, however, is another matter, and you'll probably be better off with straight vegetables.

If you want you can get off the boat here, go cross-country over the top of Wūyóu Shān, and down to a small bridge linking it to Língyún Shān (Towering Cloud Hill). Here you will find the entrance to Dōngfāng Fódū Gōngyuán (Oriental Buddha Park), a newly assembled collection of 3000 buddha statues and figurines from all around Asia. The centrepiece is a 170m-long reclining buddha, said to be the world's longest. Although touted by local tourist authorities as a major attraction, the park seems more a hasty effort to cash in on buddha-mania – the Hong Kong and Chinese sculptors raced to knock off the reclining buddha in a mere two years. Still it makes for an interesting walk, albeit a pricey one at Y30.

Nearby is the Máhàoyá Mù Bówùguǎn (Mahaoya Tomb Museum) which has a modest collection of tombs and burial artefacts dating from the Eastern Han dynasty (AD 25–220).

Continuing past Dōngfāng Fódū and up Língyún Shān you come to the semi-active Dà Fó Sì (Grand Buddha Temple), which sits near Dà Fó's head. From here you can catch views of the head and walk down a narrow staircase to reach the feet. To get back to Lèshān walk west to the small ferry going direct across the Mín Hé.

This whole exercise can be done in less than 1½ hours from the Lèshān dock; however, it's worth making a day of it. If you want to avoid the crowds, you should consider doing this route in reverse, that is, starting with Dà Fó Sì and Dà Fó in the morning and on to Wūyōu Sì in the afternoon.

It would be a mistake to think of Lèshān as one big buddha, for the area is steeped in history. North of Lèshān, 2.5km west of the train station at Jiājiāng, are the **Jiājiāng Qiānfóyán** (Thousand Buddha Cliffs). For once, the name is not an exaggeration: more than 2400 buddhas dot the cliffs, dating back as far as the Eastern Han dynasty. The statues are said to be in fairly good shape, despite the ravages of time and the Cultural Revolution. Entrance is Y10.

There are some pleasant walks to be had in Lèshān itself. By the remains of the town ramparts is an older section of town where you can still find some cobbled streets and green, blue- and red-shuttered buildings. The area around the ferry docks and the old town buzzes with market activity.

Farther out, by the Jiāzhōu Bīnguǎn, are teahouses with bamboo chairs spilling onto the street. Lèshān used to be known for its Dà Fó cableway spanning the river. Many advertisements still use it and the structures still stand; unfortunately it has been shut down and probably won't operate again.

There are fantastic day trips to villages outside Lèshān, including Lúochéng, famed for its old 'boathouse' architecture, and Wǔtōngqiáo. Mr Yang of Yangs' restaurant (see Places to Stay & Eat later) offers tours for around Y120, transportation and food included.

Entry Fees The Dà Fó park used to pester travellers to death with a surcharge every 50 feet or so. Officials finally tired of complaints and just lumped everything together into a Y40 entrance fee. There are still one or two extra fees lurking out there, and temples still charge around Y2 to get in. Some travellers get very irate about all these hidden costs, but rules is rules!

Places to Stay & Eat

Around the corner from the long-distance bus station, the *Lèshān Jiàoyù Bīnguǎn*

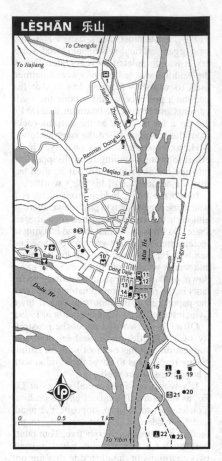

LÈSHĀN 乐山

(Leshan Education Hotel; ☎ *213 4257, 156 Liren Jie)* used to be a dirt-cheap guesthouse but painted its front desk area and now bills itself as a hotel. Beds in passably clean singles/doubles/triples with common bath are Y30/50/60. Somewhat damp and shabby doubles with bath attached are considerably more expensive at Y100; definitely not good value. Take a look at more than one room, since consistency is not a virtue around here.

Just south of the Lèshān Jiàoyù Bīnguǎn, on the corner of Jiading Zhonglu and Renmin Donglu, stands the *Jiādìng Fàndiàn*

LÈSHĀN

PLACES TO STAY & EAT	OTHER	13 Ferry Ticket Office
2 Lèshān Jiàoyù Bīnguǎn	1 Long-Distance Bus Station	渡轮售票处
乐山教育宾馆	长途汽车站	15 Tour Boat Dock
3 Jiādìng Fàndiàn	6 Newcastle Arms Pub	(Lèshān Pier)
嘉定饭店	7 PSB	短途码头
4 The Yangs' Restaurant	公安局外事科	16 Dà Fó
杨家餐厅	8 Bank of China	大佛
5 Jiāzhōu Bīnguǎn	中国银行	17 Dàfó Sì
嘉州宾馆	9 Workers' Cultural Palace	大佛寺
14 Táoyuán Bīnguǎn	劳动人民文化宫	20 Dōngfāng Fódū
桃源宾馆	10 Post Office	Gōngyuán
18 Nánlóu Bīnguǎn	邮电局	东方佛都公园
南楼宾馆	11 Central Bus Company	21 Máhàoyá Mù
19 Jiùrìfēng Bīnguǎn	省汽车客运中心站	Bówùguǎn
就日峰宾馆	12 Ferries to Chóngqìng,	麻浩崖墓博物馆
23 Xiāndǎo Bīnguǎn	Yíbīn	22 Wūyóu Sì
仙岛宾馆	长途码头	乌尤寺

(☎ 212 4079), which is decidedly more pro-letarian, but still better than the Lèshān Jiàoyù Bīnguǎn in most respects. The staff do seem to try here. Beds in doubles/triples without bath cost Y30/15 (the washrooms are nothing to write home about, but will do), while singles/doubles with bath start at Y40/60, with some possibility of shaving a few yuán off this. Bus No 8, which links Lèshān pier with the Lèshān long-distance bus station, passes near both hotels.

The *Táoyuán Bīnguǎn* (☎ 212 7758, fax 212 9904) is in a much better location down by the Lèshān pier and offers excellent views of the Dà Fó. The staff – mostly students – tries really hard to make things work, but it's been getting mixed reports. Common doubles/triples cost Y25 per bed; with a private bathroom, doubles/triples start at Y120. A whole range of rooms is available, up to a Y360 deluxe suite. The hotel offers a fax service, laundry, international dialling, and sauna.

Over on the buddha's side of the Mín Hé are a couple of pricey but pleasant places to stay. Close to the Wūyōu Sì is the friendly *Xiāndǎo Bīnguǎn* (☎ 213 3268) which has upmarket doubles for Y218. Triples are a bit more affordable at Y188. There appear to be several good restaurants here, and the hotel has a sauna.

There are two hotels in the area above the head of Dà Fó, *Nánlóu Bīnguǎn* and *Jiùrìfēng Bīnguǎn.* Perhaps due to the buddha's drainage system, the cliff around here is wet, and the dampness can extend to the rooms. The Nánlóu, set right next to the Dà Fó Sì, is definitely out of budget range, only offering standard doubles for around Y450.

The Jiùrìfēng is only slightly cheaper and not quite as nice, so the former may be the better choice if you're in the mood to spend. If you do stay at the Jiùrìfēng, go for rooms in the upper building, with commanding views. A standard double costs Y290.

Top-of-the-line is the three-star *Jiāzhōu Bīnguǎn* (☎ 213 9888, fax 213 3233), which has become rather expensive. Doubles and triples start at Y360 and suites at Y480; both include breakfast. The hotel is in a pleasant area; to get there take bus No 1 from the corner of Jiading Nanlu and Dong Dajie to the end of the line.

The area between the Jiāzhōu Bīnguǎn and the pier is good for small *restaurants* and *street stalls*. For a home-style meal and good conversation, wander over to another of those oases of English menu and Chinese prices – *The Yangs' Restaurant* (49 Baita Jie), a wooden hole-in-the-wall. The engaging owner, Mr Yang, speaks English and has an exceedingly interesting history.

SÌCHUĀN 四川

Travellers have raved about his all-in tours to small villages around Lèshān, and he's also able to make travel arrangements, including train tickets. He also acts as representative for a Cháng Jiāng (Yangzi River) cruise boat company and can often get you tickets for one classer higher than you paid.

Back towards the centre of town and across from – but not affiliated with – the Jiāzhōu Bīnguǎn is the *Newcastle Arms Pub*, a branch of a Chéngdū pub.

Getting There & Away

Construction is under way on an expressway between Chéngdū and Lèshān, which should shave travel time down to two hours (and no doubt swell the numbers on Éméi Shān). It should be finished by the time you read this.

Following that road's completion, Lèshān and Chóngqìng are set to be linked with a similar expressway. The result will be a triangular transportation conduit second to none in south-west China.

Plans are also being finalised for an enormous new airport 20km outside Lèshān; when finished (no exact date for this yet) it will be larger than Chéngdū's.

Bus There are two bus stations in Lèshān. The main one for travellers is the Lèshān long-distance bus station, somewhat inconveniently located in the northern reaches of the city. It may get worse – city officials want to relocate all buses far, far out on the northern side of town, beyond the first bridge, although at the time of writing there was no timetable to do this.

A variety of regular minibuses, non-stop 11-passenger vans, or even Korean Daewoo express buses to Chéngdū, leave every 15 to 30 minutes from 7 am to 6 pm and cost Y15 to Y31. Depending on traffic and your driver, it's a three- to four-hour trip. The bigger buses have air-con, smiling hostesses, souvenirs, and a Hong Kong flick to boot; book these ahead of time.

One thing to watch out for is the bus' Chéngdū destination. Most of the buses run to the Xinnanmen bus station next to the Traffic Hotel, but several run to the north

bus station or train station. From Chéngdū, all bus stations have the same variety of options to get to Lèshān.

From Lèshān to Éméi Shān is 30km; minibuses run every 10 to 15 minutes to Éméi town (Y4; one hour) between 6.20 am and 6 pm from the main long-distance station or from the Central Bus Company (Shěngqìchēkèyuǎn Zhōngxīnzhàn) station just up the street from the Táoyuán Bīnguǎn.

To Chóngqìng regular buses, express buses, and sleepers depart pretty much hourly from the main long-distance bus station from 7.10 am to 5 pm and range in price from Y61 to Y91. With road improvements, sleepers are slowly being phased out and luxury expresses coming in, so try and book ahead. The trip takes six to eight hours.

Buses for Jiājiāng train station or Jiājiāng Qiānfóyán (Thousand Buddha Cliffs) depart all day and cost Y3.

Boat At one time there was regular boat service between Lèshān and Yíbīn, with further service to Chóngqìng. River fluctuations and bad management doomed it and normal boats were no longer running at last check. (Yíbīn to Chóngqìng is more consistent.)

Plans are under way to manipulate water levels and allow a more stable service. Better today is the high-speed boat to Yíbīn (Y80; 2½ hours), departing Lèshān daily at 2.30 pm when running (June to August). Tickets can be bought at the ticket office across the street from Lèshān pier.

Getting Around

Bus Nos 1 and 8 run the length of Jiading Lu and connect the pier area with the long-distance bus station, and the Jiādìng and Lèshan Jiàoyù hotels. Buses runs from 6 am to 6 pm, at roughly 20-minute intervals.

On foot, it's about an hour's walk from one end of town to the other. A pedicab from the bus station to the Táoyuán Bīnguǎn should cost Y5; to the Jiādìng Fàndiàn it's Y2; from the pier to the Jiāzhōu Bīnguǎn is also Y2. You can bargain a ride from Dà Fó all the way back to the Táoyuán

Bīnguǎn for as little as Y10, although this takes some effort. Pedicab operators in Lèshān all split up the fare, so don't be paranoid when one of them stops halfway and tells you to get on his buddy's pedicab. Just pay him half (or whatever) and pay the remainder when you arrive. Unfortunately, there doesn't seem to be any bicycle hire.

MÉISHĀN 眉山

Méishān, 90km south-west of Chéngdū by road or train (it's on the Kūnmíng-Chéngdū line), is largely appealing to those with an interest in Chinese language, literature and calligraphy.

It was the residence of Su Xun and his two sons, Su Shi and Su Zhe, the three noted literati of the Northern Song dynasty (960–1126). Their residence was converted into a temple in the early Ming dynasty, with renovations under the Qing emperor Hongwu (1875–1909).

The mansion and pavilions now operate as a museum for the study of the writings of the Northern Song period. Historical documents, relics of the Su family, writings, calligraphy – some 4500 items all told – are on display at the Sānsù (Three Sus Shrine).

Western Sìchuān & the Road to Tibet

Literally the next best thing to Tibet is the Sìchuān mountains to the north and west of Chéngdū – heaps of whipped cream that rise above 5000m, with deep valleys and rapid rivers.

Tibetans and Tibetan-related peoples (Qiang) live by herding yaks, sheep and goats on the high-altitude Kangba Plateau Grasslands to the far north-west. Another zone, the Zöigê Grassland (north of Chéngdū, towards the Gānsù border) is more than 3000m above sea level.

Closer to Chéngdū, the Tibetans have been assimilated, speak Chinese and are less bound by tradition, although they're regarded as a separate minority and are exempt from birth control quotas. Farther out,

Tibetan customs and clothing are much more in evidence.

Towns on the Kangba Plateau experience cold temperatures, with up to 200 freezing days per year; summers are blistering by day and the high altitude invites particularly bad sunburn. Lightning storms are frequent from May to October and cloud cover can shroud the scenic peaks. On a more pleasant note, there appear to be sufficient hot springs in these areas to have a solid bath along the route.

Ancient Chinese poetry has it that the road to Sìchuān is harder to travel than the road to heaven. Nowadays, with the province more accessible by road, we can shift the poetry to Tibet and the highway connecting it with western Sìchuān. The Sìchuān-Tibet Highway, begun in 1950 and finished in 1954, is one of the world's highest, roughest, most dangerous and most beautiful roads. The highway has been split into northern and southern routes, forking 70km west of Kāngdìng.

The northern route (2412km) runs via Kāngdìng, Gānzī and Dégé before crossing the boundary into Tibet. The southern route (2140km) runs via Kāngdìng, Lǐtáng and Bātáng before entering Tibet (see the Gānzī and Lǐtáng sections later in this chapter).

Whether you are able to actually enter Tibet is an open question. The land route between Chéngdū and Lhasa is still to all intents closed to foreigners for reasons of safety and political security. Some palefaces have succeeded and arrived intact in Lhasa, usually by hitching rides on trucks. The PSB has cracked down on this now, however, and it's reportedly getting harder to find rides.

It is possible to do the trip to the Tibet border by local buses, but foreigners will definitely encounter problems near the Tibetan border, and may even have trouble buying tickets for Bātáng or Dégé. A few travellers have reportedly managed to bribe their way across, but at a cost that makes flying from Chéngdū to Lhasa more economical.

Years ago there was a legendary crate, the Chéngdū-Lhasa bus, which suffered countless breakdowns and took weeks to arrive. In 1985 a monumental mudslide on the southern route took out the road for dozens of kilometres and the service was discontinued.

Trucks are the only transport travelling consistently long hauls on this highway. The major truck depots are in Chéngdū, Chamdo and Lhasa. Trucks usually run from Lhasa or from Chéngdū only as far as Chamdo, where you have to find another lift. However, police keep an eye out for truckers giving lifts to foreigners and it's not likely you'll slip past the checkpoints at Dégé or Bātáng. If drivers are caught, they could lose their licences or receive massive fines. Foreigners caught arriving from Chéngdū are sometimes fined and always sent back. However, if you're arriving from Tibet nobody gives a damn.

Incessant rumours persist that the Chinese government will 'improve' the condition of highways to Tibet, probably to facilitate transport of goods, if not tourists. Don't believe it. Instead, in 1997 the Chinese government decided to disregard the advice of international consultants and will attempt to sink Y500 million into a project worthy of Sisyphus – tunnelling highways westward all the way to Tibet, part of the way through solid ice. Whether or not it's possible is debatable, but if it is, it's a *long* way off – and even then they still may not permit foreigners in.

In sum, the odds are stacked much higher against you when travelling into, rather than out of, Tibet. Whatever you do, bear in mind the risk and equip yourself properly with food and warm clothing. And remember, accidents can happen. Some years back a group of Americans and Australians were on the back of a truck which overturned close to Dégé; one member of the group lost half an arm and another member sustained multiple injuries to her back. It took several days for medical help to be sent and even longer before the injured could be brought back to Chéngdū.

Bus services on the Sìchuān-Tibet Highway will take you all the way to the border, and at the time of writing it was not difficult to buy tickets to Bātáng, Gānzī and Dégé and other towns in the Gānzī (Garzê)

Autonomous Prefecture. Having said that, the Exit-Entry Administration Office of Chéngdū's PSB was definitely not keen to give out permits to these places, so clampdowns are always a possibility.

All towns west of Kāngdìng were officially open at last check.

For information on Tibet and Qīnghǎi see the separate chapters in this book.

KĀNGDÌNG   康定
Dardo ☎ 0836

Kāngdìng (2560m) is a fairly large town nestled in a steep river valley. Swift currents from the rapids of the Zheduo River provide Kāngdìng with hydroelectric power, the town's source of heating and electricity.

The town itself is nothing special, but you must stop here en route to anywhere in western Sìchuān. The surrounding scenery is beautiful, and there are a few sights worth walking to in the area. Chinese know the town from a popular Chinese love song inspired by the local scenery.

Towering above Kāngdìng is the mighty peak of Gōnggà Shān (7556m) – 'to behold it is worth 10 years of meditation', says an inscription in a ruined monastery by the base. The mountain is apparently often covered with cloud so patience is required for the beholding.

Gōnggà Shān sits in a mountain range, with a sister peak just below it towering to 5200m. Pilgrims used to circle the two for several hundred kilometres to pay homage. Gōnggà Shān is on the open list for foreign mountaineers – in 1981 it buried eight Japanese climbers in an avalanche. Known conquests of this awesome 'goddess' include those by two Americans in 1939, and by six Chinese in 1957.

Information
The PSB office is a five-minute walk south of the Gōnggà Shān Hostel but is fairly useless.

Kangding Travel Agency (Kāngdìng Lǚxíngshè; ☎ 282 4032) is a semi-private agency that has information on possible day hikes or tours of the area; however, the fees are quite high.

Things to See

There are several lamaseries in and around Kāngdìng. Just behind the Gōnggà Shān Hostel, **Ānjué Sì** is a fairly quiet lamasery, with several monks and a few prayer wheels. To get there, walk to the right from the bus station along the main road to where the town is divided by the Zheduo River. Cross the third bridge: the monastery is on the right.

With some 70 to 80 lamas, the **Nánwù Sì** is the most active lamasery in the area. Set in the western part of the town on the northern bank of the river, it affords good views of Kāngdìng and the valley. Walk along the main road and follow its bend to the left for 2km, cross the bridge at the end of town and go another 300m. Next to a walled Han Chinese cemetery you will find a dirt path leading uphill along a stream which leads to the lamasery.

For spectacular views of Kāngdìng and (if the weather obliges) nearby snow-capped mountains, try the 500m hike to the top of **Pǎomǎ Shān**. The ascent takes you past oodles of prayer flags, several Buddhist temples and up to a white stupa and another temple (with cows munching grass all over).

From there, if you're lucky, you may even catch a glimpse of Gònggà Shān. Bear left at the fork in the road just up from the bus station and walk for about 10 minutes until you reach a concrete stairway on the left-hand side of the road. The Walking Around the Mountain Festival (Zhuànshān Jié) takes place on Pǎomǎ Shān on the eighth day of the fourth lunar month to commemorate the birthday of Sakyamuni (the historical Buddha).

Places to Stay & Eat

The first option to confront you is the *Chēzhàn Jiāotōng Lǚshè (Bus Station Hotel)*. The place is a noisy, filthy dump, but it is convenient. Beds start from Y20 at foreigner prices.

Next to Ānjué Sì, the *Gònggàshān Lǚshè* is much better with triples for Y30 per bed. It's quieter, cleaner and a hell of a lot more pleasant. The only drawback is a grim squat toilet and *no* washing facilities.

There's no English sign: look for the balcony that looks out over the river. Ask the nice folks at the stand beneath a public phone sign.

Immediately behind this, the chaotic *Kāngdìng Bīnguǎn (☎ 282 3153)* was once the best hotel in town, but no longer. Weary-looking rooms start at Y40 per bed in a triple for foreigners; with a student card it's only Y20. Solo travellers have to bargain them down to around Y50 or Y60 for a room. At least there's hot water at nights; it comes on together with the rousing karaoke sessions.

For more upmarket rooms, just up the street is the *Pǎomǎ Bīnguǎn*. Its cheapest option is a bed in a quad/triple with attached bath for Y70/80. Doubles are Y200, which is amazingly expensive for this part of the world.

For a rousing cup of yak butter tea, try the *teahouse* adjacent to the Gònggà Shān Hostel. Its noodles are also quite tasty. Otherwise, there are numerous point-and-choose *restaurants* along Kāngdìng's main drag along with a few *shuǐjiǎo* (dumpling) places. The Pǎomǎ Bīnguǎn has a nice restaurant attached.

Getting There & Away

Kāngdìng is a long haul from anywhere, so be prepared. If you're not particularly gung ho for long, rough journeys, it might make some sense to leave from Chéngdū or even Lèshān and stop for a night in Yǎ'ān.

There's no particular reason to see Yǎ'ān other than to rest your bones, but there are connections to Kāngdìng and Lèshān. If you wish to break up the journey here, do not take the afternoon sleepers from Kāngdìng or Chéngdū, as either one gets you in around 2 or 3 am.

There are daily buses to Kāngdìng departing from Chéngdū's Xinnanmen bus station at 6.30 (and sometimes 7.30) am and 4 pm. This route is troubled by pesky Sìchuān insurance hassles and landslides, and is covered in detail in Chéngdū's Getting There & Away section.

Returning to Chéngdū from Kāndìng, there are sleeper buses at 7.30 am and 2 pm;

these should cost Y108, but you probably won't get to pay these Chinese prices. Regular buses leave sporadically from the bus station from 7 am onwards – going over Èrlangshān Guān every other day – but these are intermittent and for hard-core riders; a few travellers have scored the Chinese price of Y63 on these rattletrap rides.

Buses to Lúdìng (Y8) are scheduled to leave at 7 am and 2, 3.30, 4.30 and 5.30 pm. There are more unofficial departures than this. Just walk past the ticket window in the bus station and bear right. Down the stairs in the car park, minibuses and vans sit, waiting to fill up. You can usually get out within 20 minutes. These are all slower than shared taxis (Y10) which congregate at the northern end of town where the two rivers converge.

There was one bus daily to Móxī (Y16) at 6 am, but it has been on and off for the past few editions. If you're headed to Hǎiluógōu Bīngchuān Gōngyuán (Couch Gully Glacier Park) this bus (if it's running) will save you having to mess around or spend the night in Lúdìng. It takes five hours and is always crowded so get there early. It would be advisable to not always trust the timetable on the wall; ask the clerks. If this bus isn't running, just get an *early* bus to Lúdìng and line something up from there.

Going west from Kāngdìng, there are buses daily to Lǐtáng at 6.40 am (Y65; 12 hours), Bātáng (Y95 to Y180; 7 am; two days) and Gānzī (Y97; 14 hours). Kāngdìng (not Lúdìng) has a bus to Dégé departing every third day, starting on the third day of each month, although this isn't set in stone around here; if it does go, it leaves at around 7 am and costs Y114.

There is also a bus to Xiāngchéng (Y98), which departs at 6.40 am on odd days of the month, and overnights in Lǐtáng en route. PSB officials insisted this route was open so you shouldn't suffer any arbitrary fines; then again, don't be surprised if this all changes.

For more information see the Northern and Southern Route sections later in this chapter.

AROUND KĀNGDÌNG

About 110km north-west of Kāngdìng lies the **Tǎgōng Cǎoyuán** (Tagong Grasslands), a vast expanse of green meadow surrounded by snow-capped peaks and dotted with Tibetan herdsmen and tents. Nearby is the **Tǎgōng Sī**, a lamasery that blends Han Chinese and Tibetan styles and dates back to the Qing dynasty. An annual horse racing festival (*saìmǎhuì*) features thousands of local Tibetan herdsmen and perhaps Tibetan opera. Despite promotion from local tourism officials, this place is relatively untrampled.

There are daily buses from Kāngdìng to Tǎgōng (Y18; four hours) at 6, 7 and 10 am, which return in the afternoon; without enough demand only the latter one leaves. Locals will assure you there are up to six buses a day, but this is only around festival time.

There are several mountain lakes and hot springs in the vicinity of Kāngdìng. **Mùgécuò** (3700m), 21km to the north of town, is one of the highest lakes in north-west Sìchuān. Locals also boast it's one of the most beautiful, although there are likely to be many such spots in this superb part of China. There is actually a series of lakes here, some connected by trails. Be careful not to stray too far off the paths – there are wolves and other wild beasts in these parts. Besides, the meaning of the name in Tibetan is 'Wild Men's Lake'. The *Mùgécuò Bīnguǎn* has simple rooms with beds from Y30; other lakes have small hotels and camping should be no problem.

There is no bus service to Mùgécuò, so you pretty much have to hire a vehicle. Van drivers seem to while away their hours in front of the shops in Kāngdìng, so hiring a vehicle shouldn't be too difficult. Getting to Mùgécuò and back should cost around Y150 to Y200. Kāngdìng Travel Agency can arrange a vehicle for you for around Y250; the trip takes around 1½ hours.

MÓXĪ 磨西

Nestled in the mountains around 50km south-west of Lúdìng, this peaceful one-street town is the gateway to the Hǎiluógōu Bīngchuān Gōngyuán (see later for details).

Buses generally stop near the Catholic church (you can't miss it – it's the multicoloured one with a steeple and cross on top). The church's main claim to fame is that Mao slept in it during the Long March. The main road leads uphill past the Hǎiluógōu Bīnguǎn to a junction. The left branch continues 400m to the park's reception office.

Places to Stay

There are several very basic hotels, two of which flank the main bus stop. To the left, bearing an English sign which says 'Reception Center' is the *Lǚyóu Fàndiàn,* which has beds in quiet, all-wood rooms for Y12. Hot showers cost Y2. Private *houses* nearby offer simple rooms from Y8

About 500m up the road, near the entrance to Hǎiluógōu, is the hulking *Hǎilín Bīnguǎn*, which wasn't open at last check.

There are more upmarket rooms at the *Hǎiluógōu Bīnguǎn*, which has beds from Y60/50 in nice doubles/triples. It's on the right-hand side along the road to the park off the main road.

Getting There & Away

There should be one bus daily from Kāngdìng to Móxī which leaves at 6 am and costs Y16. It wasn't running at last check, so you may have to go to Lúdìng first. If it is running get there very early, since this crate is always crowded. From Lúdìng there are three to four buses daily between 6 am and 2.30 pm. The 54km trip takes nearly three hours and costs Y8. It should also get your pulse racing: roads are generally awful but even on the good stretches there are several cliff-side sections where the road seems to disappear from under your bus, which will almost certainly be bulging with passengers, just to add to the excitement.

From Móxī there are usually several buses back to Lúdìng from 6 am to noon. One may go on to Kāngdìng. The early-morning bus is usually jam-packed with locals heading down to Lúdìng, so if you want a seat you should walk up to where the bus starts, near the Hǎilín Bīnguǎn, at around 5.45 or 6.45 am.

Many travellers who come to visit Hǎiluógōu set out by way of Kāngdìng, and return via Lúdìng, which has direct regular buses to Chéngdū at 6 and 7 am, and 3 pm. No sleepers depart from Lúdìng; you'll have to flag down a bus from Kāngdìng.

Another option is to continue south and loop around to Éméi Shān and Lèshān or even continue south through the Yi minority areas to Xīchàng. Take the 7 am bus to Lúdìng, but tell the driver to let you off at Māozǐpíng; you could also take a Y10 minivan there. Cross the scary suspension bridge to the other side of the river and the main road linking Lúdìng with Shímían. From here you can flag down a bus to Shímían (Y10) or Wūsīhé (Y6), which is on the Chéngdū-Kūnmíng train line. Motorcycles may ply the route for Y20. For more details, see the Lúdìng-Wūsīhé-Lèshān section under Lúdìng.

HǍILUÓGŌU BĪNGCHUĀN GŌNGYUÁN 海螺沟冰川公园
Conch Gully Glacier Park

Magnificent Hǎiluógōu Bīngchuān Gōngyuán is part of Gònggà Shān and is one of the lowest glaciers in Asia. The main glacier (No 1 Glacier) is 14km long and covers an area of 16 sq km. It's relatively young as glaciers go: around 1600 years.

Guides from the town of Móxī lead inexpensive three- to seven-day pony treks along glacier trails. The top of Hǎiluógōu can offer incredible vistas of Gònggà Shān (Tribute Mountain), but how much you actually see is entirely up to Mother Nature. If you are after spectacular views it will probably pay to build a couple of extra days into your schedule. The rainy season for this area spans July and August, and some travellers have found heavy cloud cover and drizzle take a lot of fun out of the trip. Locals say the best time to visit is during late September and October, when skies are generally clear though at this time No 3 Camp can be fairly brisk.

The trek has become much more accessible over recent years, but it's still a good idea to come prepared. Bring warm clothing and good sunglasses with you as a minimum. There is food and drink available en route, but it's worth bringing some high-calorie food with you. Camping is great – you'll probably be invited to sit with other local trekkers around a roaring bonfire, while listening to workers sing Tibetan songs.

If you are on a pony (they can be hired from the park reception office) you can do the entire trip through to the No 3 Camp in around seven to eight hours. On foot you would be better off doing the trip over two days, although it's probably possible to make it to the No 3 Camp in one day if you keep up a brisk pace.

The guides are likely to push you toward the three-day, two-night trek. This usually consists of spending the first night at No 1 Camp, riding up to No 3 Camp the next day for lunch and glacier viewing, and then heading back down to spend the second night at the No 2 Camp. Pony rental is Y30 to Y35 per day.

If you opt to hike, you can also rent a pack horse for Y30 per day which can carry up to three bags. You can even rent ponies for just the ride up (Y15 to No 1 Camp, Y35 to No 3), and then walk back on your own. Maps with English are available at the park reception office in Móxī.

From Móxī the path, which is marked in English, follows the Yanzigou River. Just after Móxī you'll be stopped at the park gate, where you will be charged a Y57 entry fee, which includes a guidebook and map (both in Chinese), along with guide fee for the glacier beyond No 3 Camp. From here it's a straightforward walk or ride (if you are on a pony) around 11km to the No 1 Camp (Yīhào Yíngdì; 1940m). En route you'll cross a rickety bridge over the river. The distance to the next camp is around 6km.

Note that construction is ongoing and thorough, often marring the scenery. A new hotel appears to be under construction and paved roads now lead to No 1 Camp and will keep inching upward.

At the No 2 Camp (Èrhào Yíngdì; 2620m) the path leaves the river valley and passes through lush rainforest for around 5km. No 2 Camp has the best hot springs and best culinary options. Lots of new building pops up after this. At the No 3 Camp (Sānhào Yíngdì; 2940m) there is a sign notifying visitors that you should take a guide to the glacier itself. Pony guides from Móxī do not qualify, but the hire of a glacier guide is included in the park entry fee, so you shouldn't have to pay any extra. If you bypassed the entrance earlier, the current guide fee is Y11. Guides won't depart after 2 pm.

From the No 3 Camp the first stop is the **Glacier Viewing Platform** (Bīngchuān Guānjǐngtái) at 3000m. From here you can see the **Glacier Tongue** to the left and to the right the **No 2 Glacier**.

From the platform it is possible to continue for 2.5km on a path that runs alongside the glacier to the **Bīngchuān Pùbù Guānjǐngtái** (Glacier Waterfall Viewing Platform). There is also an ice cave another half-hour's walk beyond that. Just how far you get from the No 3 Camp will depend entirely on weather conditions.

Places to Stay & Eat

Accommodation in damp and dirty lodges is around Y30 per bed at each of the camps en route to the glacier, and service can be glacial as well. On the brighter side, both the No 1 and No 2 camps have hot springs – those at No 2 are particularly nice – if you are in need of a soak; they cost Y10. New hotels are being built.

Some people do the walk slowly (three or four hours a day), overnighting at each of the camps. But it is possible to head straight up to the No 3 Camp, where there is chalet-style accommodation, albeit a bit run down.

Park authorities appear to frown on camping, and there isn't a great deal in the way of flat ground on the way up in any case. Naturally you can't expect any showering facilities up here – save your dirt for the hot springs lower down.

The camps all sell some food and drinks. Mineral water, soft drinks and beer are all usually available. Food is uniformly miserable – consisting of a steady diet of cabbage soup and green peppers fried with pork fat. You'd better bring some of your own munchies along.

Getting There & Away

Hǎiluógōu is accessible via the town of Móxī, which in turn can be reached by bus from Kāngdìng and Lúdìng. There's a travel agency at the Yagudu Hotel in Lúdìng which organises trips in high tourist seasons. See the following entry on Lúdìng for details.

LÚDÌNG 泸定

Lúdìng is around halfway between Kāngdìng and Móxī, and is possibly worth a brief stop en route to either destination or on the way back to Chéngdū.

Lúdìng is famous throughout China as the site of what is commonly regarded as the most glorious moment of the Long March. The key element in this is the Lúdìng Qiáo, a chain suspension bridge high over the Dàdù Hé (Big Ferry River).

On 29 May 1935 the communist troops were approaching Lúdìng Qiáo, only to discover that Kuomintang troops had beat them to it, removed the planks from the bridge and had it covered with firepower. In response, 20 communist troops crossed the bridge hand-over-hand armed with grenades and then proceeded to overcome the Kuomintang troops on the other side. This action allowed the Long March to continue before the main body of the Kuomintang forces could catch up with them.

The Lúdìng Qiáo is in the south of town. The original bridge was first constructed in 1705 and was an important link in the Sìchuān-Tibet road; its entrance fee is Y1. On the main street in town you might want to look out for the Lúdìng Qiáo Gémìng Wénwù Chénlièguǎn (Luding Bridge Revolutionary Artefacts Museum), which houses a collection of some 150 items left behind by members of the Long March.

You can also get a gander at some of Mao's calligraphy on a shelter near the Buddhist Temple on the hillside above town.

Places to Stay

There are a few hotels in Lúdìng. Off the main road down south of the bus station, the Xiàn Zhāodàisuǒ (Luding County Government Guesthouse) has beds in triples for Y20, and beds in acceptable doubles with bath for Y50. Confusingly, the guesthouse is also referred to as the Lúdìng Bīnguǎn – there's English vertically on the (broken) sign, but you can't see it from the main road.

The Chēzhàn Lǚguǎn (Bus Station Hotel), near the southern bus station, has beds in triples for Y12, but you won't get them to give you a bed for less than Y22, so walk out, turn right and go about 40m and look for the Lu He Guesthouse – there are three Chinese signs and one in English which says 'State Operated Hotel' in small letters. Friendly owners operate this place and there are decent rooms for Y20, with TV and facilities as clean as anything in these parts.

The best rooms in town come south of the Lúdìng Qiáo along the main road at the Yagudu Hotel. Good doubles cost Y50 and rooms include TV, private bath and evening hot water. There is a tiny English sign which says 'Check in'.

Getting There & Away

Lúdìng has two bus stations; the local bus station is on the main road from Kangdìng, at the northern edge of town. It's near a basketball court, just near where the road bends. Don't trust the schedule on the wall and be prepared for a blood-from-stone ordeal getting the clerks to offer up departure times.

From here you can get buses to Móxī (Y8), Kāngdìng (Y8) and even direct to Chéngdū (Y58). Buses to Chéngdū – no sleepers – leave at 6 and 7 am and take 12 to 18 hours barring landslides and depending on whether they try to brave Èrlangshān Guān or skirt it via Shímían.

Buses to Kāngdìng run more or less hourly between 6 am and 4 pm. There are only a couple of buses to Móxī, at 6 and 8.30 am. In peak seasons you can also organise trips to the Hǎiluógōu Bīngchuān Gōngyuán from the travel agency in the Yagudu Hotel. Several buses each morning depart for Shímían, where you can switch to a bus bound for Wūsīhé, which is on the Chéngdū-Kūnmíng train line.

At the southern part of town, one street uphill from the main road, is the southern bus station. From here you can also get buses to Chéngdū, Kāngdìng (Y8), Yǎ'ān (Y37) and Shímían (Y17). This station has no sleeper buses, even though the schedule says it does; the 3 pm departure is a regular rattletrap bus which should make for an excruciatingly bouncy evening. All of this fun costs Y58 (Chinese price) to Chéngdū and tickets were being sold to foreigners at last check. If you need a sleeper to Chéngdū, you'll need to flag one down as it roars through from Kāngdìng; don't expect a berth.

Lúdìng-Wūsīhé-Lèshān

If you're headed to Lèshān, Émeǐ Shān or Kūnmíng, and don't feel like doubling back to Chéngdū, you can try heading down to the railhead at Wūsīhé. There are usually one or two buses daily from Lúdìng to Wūsīhé, but if you miss these, just jump on a bus to Shímían (meaning 'asbestos'!), where there are frequent onward buses. One rather decent bus leaves Lúdìng at 11.30 am and takes six hours.

Buses from Shímían to Wūsīhé stop for an hour or so at Hànyúan, one of many such halts you're likely to encounter en route. Altogether the 210km journey requires most of the day, but it does take you through some impressive gorge and river scenery.

Trains from Wūsīhé to Émeí and Lèshān generally leave in mid- to late-afternoon, so you should be able to make one without overnighting in Wūsīhé. There are several hotels clustered around the train station, all with beds for around Y10. The one just off the road that leads into the station is not bad. Some travellers have reported being denied rooms at cheaper hotels; others have had no problem.

A hard-seat ticket to either Émeí or Lèshān should cost around Y8. The ride to both is about 3½ hours on most trains. One does leave at 6.25 am, with tickets on sale at 5.50 am.

If you're headed south to Pānzhīhūa (where you connect with buses to Lìjiāng in Yúnnán) or Kūnmíng, be advised that you can only buy hard-seat tickets at the Wūsīhé train station, and most trains don't stop there anyway.

SÌCHUĀN-TIBET HIGHWAY – NORTHERN ROUTE

Of the two routes to Tibet from Sìchuān, this is less heavily travelled, probably because it's nearly 300km longer than the southern route.

One added advantage for travellers is that if you are turned back at the Tibet border, you may be able to work your way up to Qīnghǎi via Sêrxu (Shíqú). However, even getting this far could be a problem; at the time of writing the PSB was doing a good job of closing this route off to foreigners.

If you do make it up here, remember that bus service is sparse and erratic: this is no place to be if you're in a hurry.

Gānzī 甘孜

Gānzī, the capital of the Gānzī (Garzê) Autonomous Prefecture, sits at 3800m in the Chola Shān mountain valley 385km northwest of Kāngdìng, and is populated by mostly Tibetans and Khampas.

Very few westerners have sojourned here, in part because the PSB, suspecting you are Tibet-bound, will do its best to stop you from doing so. As the Xīníng-Chéngdū route between Qīnghǎi and Sìchuān becomes more popular it may yet get its due, and it's easier to get here if you're headed toward Chéngdū.

For now it's little more than an intermediate stop between Sêrxu and Kāngdìng for travellers in a hurry to reach 'civilisation' after the rigours of the Xīníng-Sêrxu road.

Gānzī Sì, just north of the town's Tibetan quarter, is worth a visit for its views of the Gānzī valley, although it's not a particularly spectacular structure.

The *Gānzīxiàn Zhāodàisuǒ* has beds for Y10 to Y20, a decent dining room, friendly staff and plenty of hot water.

For details on the trip north to Xīníng via Sêrxu, see the Xīníng section in the Qīnghǎi chapter.

Getting There & Away Buses to Gānzī (Y96; 14 hours) leave Kāngdìng daily at 7 am. From Gānzī, there should also be one bus daily to Kāngdìng, leaving around daybreak. Expect sleeper buses to ply the route as well.

There are buses every third day to Dégé which originate in Kāngdìng, stay over night in Lúhùo and pass through Gānzī at around 10 am.

Under ideal conditions the 200km ride from Gānzī to Dégé takes eight hours. Similarly, buses to Sêrxu originate in Kāngdìng every third day or so, overnight in Dàofú and stop over in Gānzī around 1 pm before resuming their drive.

Dégé 德格

Dégé (Dêgê) is the last town on the northern route before it enters Tibet proper. As such, it's reportedly well patrolled and it may be difficult to slip past the checkpoint. Guards are said to keep a sharp lookout for foreigners trying to sneak through on the backs of trucks, and a fair number of travellers have been turned back at this point. Apparently the best option is to find a postal truck – they're not checked as often – and stay hidden in the back until Qamdo.

Dégé is home to the 250-year-old **Bakong Scripture Printing Lamasery**, housing an extensive collection of Tibetan scriptures of the five Lamaist sects which are revered by followers the world over.

Built in the Qing dynasty by the 42nd prefect of Dégé, along with others in Shigatse and Lhasa, it was one of the three most important. There are 300 workers under the direction of the abbot, in a monastery which houses more than 215,000 hardwood printing plates. Texts include ancient works on astronomy, geography, music, medicine and Buddhist classics, including two of the most important Tibetan sutras. One history of Indian Buddhism comprising 555 woodblock plates (written in Hindi, Sanskrit and Tibetan) is the only surviving copy in the world.

Half of the interior is taken up by block collections; you can also examine storage chambers, paper-cutting and binding rooms, block-cleaning platforms, and a statue hall. Protecting the monastery from fire and earthquake is a guardian goddess, a green Avalokitesvara.

Accommodation in Dégé is very basic: no showers and hard wooden beds at the *bus station hotel* for Y10.

Getting There & Away There is a direct bus to Dégé from Kāngdìng. At the time of writing departures were every three days starting on the third of the month (3, 6, 9 etc) but this schedule is 'flexible' to say the least. Often there won't be a bus for a week.

The bus leaves Kāngdìng around 7 or 7.30 am, overnights in Lúhùo, passes through Gānzī around 10 am and arrives in Dégé that same evening, barring any inevitable delays; tickets are Y114.

Buses to Gānzī and on to Kāngdìng leave Dégé every third day starting on the second of the month (2, 5, 8 etc).

SÌCHUĀN-TIBET HIGHWAY – SOUTHERN ROUTE

This route has considerably more traveller traffic – mostly because the Kāngdìng-Lǐtáng-Xiāngchéng- Zhōngdiàn route into Yúnnán is a great way to experience Tibet without actually making it into Tibet.

PSB officials in Chéngdū smilingly claim that the road all the way to Bātáng – including Bātáng – was open to foreigners. However, this changes like the wind (Bātáng has always been off-limits) so play it cool if the local PSB hassles you.

Between Kāngdìng and the border town of Bātáng lies more than 500km of dirt roads, 4000m mountain passes, stunning scenery and occasional landslides.

Lǐtáng 理塘

At over 4000m Lǐtáng is one of the highest towns in China, and even a short hike around here may have you wondering where the oxygen went. The town rests at the edge of a vast grassland and is the watering hole for neighbouring Tibetan herdsmen, who can be seen kicking up a trail of dust through town at dusk.

Some travellers have found great bargains here on yak-skin boots, cloaks and other Tibetan clothing. A trading fair and festival lasting 10 days and sponsored by the Panchen Lama is held here annually beginning on the 13th day of the sixth lunar month.

Lǐtáng also has a **lamasery** that is said to have been built by the Third Dalai Lama and contains a buddha statue that locals claim was brought over from Lhasa by foot. Friendly monks are apparently happy to pull in any wandering foreigners for extensive tours of the lamasery.

Places to Stay The *hotel* at the bus station, in the southern part of town, has dorm beds for Y10. Like so many of these charming places, you share the bathroom with any and all bus passengers.

Up the road about 150m on the righthand side is a small *guesthouse* with cleaner, quieter dorm beds for Y11. Neither place has showers, but around 15 minutes' walk from the bus station is a public bath where you can get all the hot water your heart desires for Y4. The people at the bus station can point you in the right direction.

Getting There & Away There is one bus daily from Kāngdìng to Lǐtáng, leaving at 6.40 am. The fare is Y54 and the 284km journey, which crosses several high passes, takes at least 12 hours. Even in summer months it would be best to have some warm clothing to fend off the arctic blasts that live above 4000m.

From Lǐtáng, there are buses to Kāngdìng at 6.30 am, although if the bus that day originates from Bātáng, then you may not leave until later in the morning. There is a mad scramble for seats, so get there early (or before the bus arrives) if you don't wish to stand for 12 hours of bone-jarring dirt-road travel.

Buses for Bātáng leave every morning; how early depends on whether the bus, which originates in Kāngdìng, overnights in Lǐtáng or in Yǎjiāng, 136km east of Lǐtáng. There are also buses to Xiāngchéng. See the 'Lǐtáng to Zhōngdiàn' section following.

Lǐtáng to Zhōngdiàn: The Back Door to Yúnnán

Formerly the favourite route for travellers with time on their hands and Tibet on the brain, this route was cut off by the PSB in May 1997, then reopened in 1999. Sort of. At the time of writing, it was possible to go from Sìchuān into Yúnnán – but not the other way around (no matter what officials may tell you in Lìjiāng).

The 400km trip takes you over several breathtaking passes and past fields of Tibetan nomads, semi-submerged Tibetan cabins and endless mountain vistas.

Xiāngchéng is a pretty riverside village of square stone houses with wooden roofs, Tibetan monasteries and the occasional passing nomad. Monks at the monasteries have welcomed foreign visitors and given them guided tours of the premises. Surrounding Xiāngchéng is Dàochéng County, which has some of the most isolated but incredibly gorgeous and sacred mountain ranges in China. Eventually a road is planned to link Xiāngchéng with Lúgú Hú (Lugu Lake), Bìtǎhǎi (Zhōngdiàn) and Dàochéng County.

The *bus station hotel* in Xiāngchéng has beds in quads for Y10. There's a chance that the local PSB will only let you stay one or two nights here, depending on which day your bus is leaving.

Getting There & Away Like the rest of western Sìchuān, bus service in the region is limited to one run daily at most, and in many cases buses only leave every other day. But if you're taking this route this shouldn't matter too much: it's a fascinating region that deserves a closer look. And if you can't get to Tibet, this is undoubtedly the next best thing.

Buses leave Lǐtáng for Xiāngchéng in the morning on even days of the month. The exact departure time varies, as the bus originates in Kāngdìng and may have overnighted in Yǎjiāng. The ride is 200km of rough gravel, single-lane track, takes 10 hours and costs around Y45.

If you're headed in the opposite direction, north to Lǐtáng, buses leave Xiāngchéng on odd days of the month at 6.30 am.

Heading to Zhōngdiàn, buses leave daily from Xiāngchéng at 6 am (Y45; 12 hours).

The vehicles are some of the most haggard in China, so don't expect much.

Coming the other way, buses leave Zhōngdiàn for Xiāngchéng daily at 7.30 am. For details on Zhōngdiàn, see the Yúnnán chapter.

Bātáng 八塘

Lying 32km from the Tibet border, Bātáng is not much more than a glorified truck park and bus station. But this one-street town is reportedly quite friendly and populated almost completely by Tibetans.

Most of the activity centres around the steady stream of truck traffic heading into Tibet. Several Tibetan truckers separately offered one traveller here a ride to Lhasa for Y500, so it may be possible to sneak across here. Just don't pay in advance, in case you are dragged out of your hiding place at the border crossing and sent back to Chéngdū.

Though purportedly open to westerners now, for a long time most travellers who made it to Bātáng were fined and asked to turn back within 24 hours. One traveller reports:

I heard a knock on my door, and opened it to find two PSB officers there. They were really quite polite, and said they were sorry, but I was not supposed to be here, and could I please leave the next day. They then reluctantly fined me Y130, but when I showed them a student card, they gave me a discount of Y95!

Places to Stay Coming from Lǐtáng, the *bus station hotel* is halfway into town on the right-hand side and has beds for Y5. Coming out of the bus station, about 50m up the street to the right is a small, two-storey white building with yellow trim. There's no sign or reception area, but the place is a *hotel* all the same, with friendly staff and beds in fairly clean, quiet rooms for Y8.

Getting There & Away There is one bus leaving Bātáng for Lǐtáng daily in the early morning. The trip takes 12 to 14 hours and crosses the 4675m Haizishan Pass.

From Kāngdìng you can get a bus at 7.20 am, but this stops off in Lǐtáng anyway. For more details on getting to Bātáng, see the Lǐtáng Getting There & Away section.

Northern Sìchuān

The Ābà (Tibet & Qiang) Autonomous Prefecture of northern Sìchuān is one of the most Tibetan areas of the province and doesn't require any special permits from the Chéngdū PSB, at least for now.

With its dense alpine forests and wide grasslands, it is also a great place to get out and commune with nature. Pony treks around Sōngpān and hiking in the nature preserve of Jiǔzhài Gōu have made this area increasingly popular with travellers, many of whom pass through here on their way up to Lǎngmùsì, Xiàhé and other destinations in Gānsù.

Most of northern Sìchuān lies between 2000m and 3000m in altitude, so make sure you take warm clothing: even in summer, temperatures can drop to 15°C (59°F) at night. The rainy season lasts from June to August. While you're getting prepared, also bear in mind that there are few places to change money in this region, so bring sufficient cash.

Roads in the region are improving but still dangerous so don't expect more than minimum standards of vehicle, driver or road maintenance except on the main road to/from Chéngdū. Roads are particularly hazardous in summer when heavy rains prompt frequent landslides, and you might want to consider planning this trip for the spring or autumn, when the weather is better anyway.

Several foreigners were killed in the summer of 1995 when their bus was caught in a landslip and plunged into a river. Because of the hazards, travellers are required to purchase insurance – Chinese insurance only – for travel in the north. This is simple enough to do if coming from Chéngdū, since it's built into the cost of a bus ticket.

Once you're in the wilds of northern Sìchuān, however, you may run into the old Catch-22 of not getting on an onward bus without insurance, but since there's no insurance office in town ...

Many towns have two bus stations, of which one is an officially designated tourist ticket dispenser. It's getting easier to get on local buses, but still don't be surprised if you get stuck for a day, even if a local bus is leaving in 10 minutes.

SŌNGPĀN 松潘

Although largely viewed as a stopover point on the road to Jiǔzhài Gōu or as a base to take a guided horse trek, this bustling, friendly town merits a visit of its own. A good number of its old wooden buildings are still intact, as are the ancient gates that date from when Sōngpān was a walled city.

Farmers and Tibetan cattle herders clop down the cobblestone streets on horseback, street artisans peddle their wares in the market area, and several kilometres out of town there's idyllic mountain forests and emerald-green lakes.

Those great thick Tibetan overcoats are a bit cheaper here than other places. And, whatever you do, take a torch (flashlight): Sōngpān goes long stretches without electricity.

Horse Treks

Although Sōngpān is nice, the surrounding mountain scenery is better still. One of the best ways to experience it is by joining up with a horse trek.

Guides take you out for anywhere from two to seven days, bringing you through valleys and forests that are pristine and peaceful. And don't worry – the horses are tame enough for anyone. Too tame, some people say.

There are two horse trek operators in Sōngpān – Shun Jiang Horse Treks (Shùn-jiāng Lǚyóu Mǎduì) and Happy Trails (Kuàilède Xiǎolù Qímǎlǚyóu; ☎ 723 1064) – which run out of little offices down the road from the bus station. Both have been long established but the only problem is that internecine turf battles can sometimes get you caught in the middle. At the time of writing, the young dudes of the latter operation were gaining most of the business but that isn't necessarily to say the other one isn't all right; don't be pressured by either

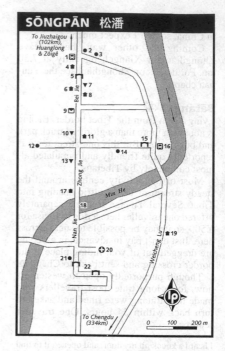

side and tell them to take a hike while you make up your mind. The manager of the Happy Trails outfit definitely speaks the best English in town. Talk to all the other foreigners in town and ask how their trip was. You will probably be met by operators from both companies while you're still on the bus, usually an hour out of town. Although facing a sales pitch is not the perfect way to cap off the10-hour ride up from Chéngdū, try not to be put off. What they're selling is well worth it.

For Y40 to Y70 per day – it can vary wildly depending on season and demand – you get a horse, three meals a day, tents, bedding and even warm jackets in case you get chilly. The guides take care of everything – you won't touch a tent pole or a cooking pot unless you want to. They usually speak no English unless you count 'yak' and 'potato', but communicate admirably nonetheless. It's not necessary to tip them, but they work their tails off for

SŌNGPĀN

PLACES TO STAY

4 Tàiyáng Dàjiǔdiàn
   太阳大酒店
6 Sōngzhōu Bīnguǎn
   松州宾馆
8 Xiànzhèngfǔ Zhāodàisuǒ
   县政府招待所
11 Huánglóng Bīnguǎn
   黄龙宾馆
17 Sōngpān Fàndiàn
   松潘宾馆
19 Sōngpān Bīnguǎn
   松潘宾馆

PLACES TO EAT

7 Xīnxīn Fàndiàn
   忻忻饭店

10 Yùlán Fànguǎn
   玉兰饭店
13 Mùsīlín Fàndiàn
   穆斯林饭店

OTHER

1 Main Bus Station
   汽车北站
2 Happy Trails
   快乐的小路骑马旅游
3 Shun Jiang Horse
   Treks
   顺江旅游马队
5 Běi Mén (North Gate)
   北门
9 Post Office
   邮局

12 Cinema
   电影院
14 National Store of Xue Yu
   雪域民族商店
15 Dōng Mén (East Gate)
   东门
16 East Bus Station
   汽车东站
18 Covered Bridge
   古松桥
20 Hospital
   医院
21 Public Showers
   公共洪浴
22 Nán Mén (South Gate)
   南门

you, so an occasional beer might be a nice idea. Alternatively, take their picture and offer to send them a copy.

The basic three-day trip takes you to a series of mountain lakes and a hot spring at Erdao Hai, and then on the next day to the Zhaga Waterfall. Trek operators will, however, tailor a trip to your wishes; it's an awesome way to experience Hǎiluógōu Bīngchuān Gōngyuán. There are entry fees of Y33 at both areas: the money goes directly to park maintenance.

Food consists mainly of potatoes, some green vegetables and bread. Bring some extra snacks along if you want more variety. If you want beer, you'll have to supply that too. If you've been itching to really get out and enjoy China's beautiful scenery, this is a great opportunity to view it up close.

Places to Stay

Many travellers report a hot water dodge from local hotels. They promise evening hot water before you check in, but *voila*, come 8 pm, suddenly there's no hot water. Or the next night, or the next. (This is particularly vexing if you're coming in from three days on a trek.) If it is a local conspiracy, it's a complicated one, since every lodging is in on it.

Actually, the problem generally is that the town constantly loses electricity and –

supposedly – the water pumps can't operate. Whatever the case, be prepared to stay grimy. You can find *public showers* near the South Gate, on the west side of the street inside the gate; they cost Y2 or whatever they think is appropriate that day. In addition to the lodging listed below, there are numerous flyspeck-sized 'guesthouses' that are good as last resorts only, many of them grungy even by bus station hotel standards.

On the main street, *Xiànzhèngfǔ Zhāodàisuǒ (Songpan County Government Guesthouse)* used to be a dump but travellers have said to go easier on them since they've got new showers (Y2). Dorm beds in filthy rooms are priced at Y10 to Y15, and triples go from Y120. The bathrooms are disgusting and the service frigid. The staff know it's bad – they're bargaining the price down immediately you've set your eyes on the room. Visa extensions can be obtained in the same complex.

Across the street, the *Sōngzhōu Bīnguǎn* has similar prices, with beds from Y20, but is more pleasant. It even has rooms with attached bath, although the Y160 price tag is a bit steep. It *never* has hot water.

A bit further down the street to the south, the *Huánglóng Bīnguǎn* was closed for renovation but should be open by the time you read this. Even farther south, the *Sōngpān Fàndiàn* is truly dilapidated and dusty, but for Y15 the beds actually aren't that bad and at least the sheets are changed for you.

The **Sōngpān Bīnguǎn** is farther out of town and has standard doubles/triples for Y260/360. Its main drawback is the price – not worth it when there's often no electricity or hot water. If better rooms are what you need, the **Tàiyáng Dàjiǔdiàn** (Sunshine Hotel) is the newest hotel around and has doubles/triples from Y260/270.

Places to Eat

In the morning, check out the dumpling stalls lining the main street. Lots of places sell the local breakfast speciality, dense bread patties heated atop metal drums – they'll stick to your ribs all day and can't be beaten on cold mornings.

Sōngpān is gradually coming to grips with foreign visitors, and there are a fair number of small restaurants with English signs and menus. The **Xīnxīn Fàndiàn** has average fare but sports the catchy 'Chinese food, English prices' sign. The place immediately next door has good food, but no English.

The local absolute favourite now is the **Yùlán Fànguǎn** – it's gone to calling itself the 'Pancake House' – on Bei Jie north of the east gate road intersection. It also has an English menu, with translations of pertinent phrases such as 'I'm a vegetarian' and the like. But its owners, an irrepressibly cheery couple, are the real draw. The menu has muesli, cafe au lait and other western items to satisfy cravings. Another plus is the tiny coal stoves under the tables for heat.

Down near the covered bridge and market area, the **Mùsīlín Fàndiàn** (Muslim Restaurant) is very clean and has great food. Prices are a bit higher – particularly for chicken and fish – and there's no English menu, but you can easily pick out what you want in the kitchen. The yúxiāng qiézi (fish-flavoured eggplant) is outstanding.

Getting There & Away

Although it's a fairly small town, Sōngpān has two bus stations. The one near the north gate is technically the one that sells tickets to foreigners and includes the cost of insur-

ance in your ticket. However, the freeze out is thawing, and some north-bound travellers have used the east bus station. Check out where your bus originates, so you get a seat.

A bus leaves Chéngdū's Ximen bus station each day at 7 am for Sōngpān; it costs Y63 and takes 10 hours along a new, winding, sometimes lovely 335km road. Going back to Chéngdū, the north gate station has a bus leaving daily at 5 – gulp! – am. There is a later bus but it's more of a rattletrap and there's more of a chance you'll get in way late. You could also try to flag down one of the two buses en route from Nánpíng (at around 10.30 am), although one of these will theoretically be Chinese-only and there's no guarantee you'll get a ticket. To Chéngdū costs Y75 and yes we know this conflicts with what you paid in Chéngdū but remember where you are.

From Sōngpān there are buses to Jiǔzhài Gōu (Y44) at 9 am which continue to Nánpíng. For you can experience a lovely trip of three to four hours on a spiffy new road.

Buses to Zöigê (Y45; six to seven hours) leave on even-numbered days between 6 and 7 am, although check this as it's flexible at best. Find out for sure which station it departs from as it fills up before it reaches the city limits.

HUÁNGLÓNG 黄龙

This valley, studded with terraced, coloured ponds (blue, yellow, white and green) and waterfalls, is about 56km from Sōngpān, on the main road to Jiǔzhài Gōu.

Huánglóng Sì (Yellow Dragon Temple) and the surrounding area were designated a national park in 1983. The most spectacular terraced ponds are behind the temple, about a two-hour walk from the main road.

An annual miao hui (temple fair) is held here around the middle of the sixth lunar month (roughly mid-August); it attracts large numbers of traders from the Qiang minority.

Huánglóng is almost always included on the itinerary for one of the seven-day Jiǔzhài Gōu tours run out of Chéngdū, but some people find it disappointing and prefer an extra day at Jiǔzhài Gōu.

In the national park there are several small guesthouses with beds for Y10 or less – no frills, just hard beds and maybe a coal burner in the winter. The *Huánglóng Zhāodàisuǒ* has slightly more upmarket accommodation, with beds in triples with attached bath for Y30 and standard doubles for Y80. It's down at the entrance to the park. There is a hefty admission fee of Y140 now, which makes up many travellers' minds for them.

There is no public bus service to Huánglóng, and it will be difficult to get here unless you've signed up with a tour; if conditions are benign, Sōngpān's horse trek operators offer four-day tours. With improved roads, a bus between Sōngpān and Píngwǔ may begin to run once a day or every other day and get you within hitching distance, but then you're dead stuck for transport inside the park.

JIǓZHÀI GŌU 九寨沟
Nine Stockade Gully

In northern Sìchuān, close to the Gānsù border, is Jiǔzhài Gōu, which was 'discovered' in the 1970s and is now being groomed for an annual influx of 300,000 visitors.

In 1984 Zhao Ziyang made the famous comment which all Sichuanese tourism officials love to quote: 'Guìlín's scenery ranks top in the world, but Jiǔzhài Gōu's scenery even tops Guìlín's'. In 1992 Unesco declared it a World Heritage Site, and in 1997 it became part of the Man and Biosphere Network.

Jiǔzhài Gōu, which has several Tibetan settlements, offers a number of dazzling features – it is a nature reserve area (with some panda conservation zones) with North American-type alpine scenes (peaks, hundreds of clear lakes and forests). Scattered throughout the region are Tibetan prayer wheels and *chortens*, Tibetan stupas.

The remoteness of the region and the (until recently) chaotic transport connections have kept it clean and relatively untouristed. Despite the good intentions of the authorities, all this is changing fast. A helicopter landing pad was built even though the mountain ranges between Chéngdū and Jiǔzhài Gōu are not ideal terrain for helicopters. And Chinese resort-style hotels, though as yet largely empty, line the road leading to the park entrance.

You should calculate between a week and 10 days for the return trip by road. It takes from two to three days to get there and you can easily spend three or four days in spectacular scenery of waterfalls, ponds, lakes and forests – it's just the place to rejuvenate polluted urban senses.

You'll even get the chance to nose around the Tibetan temple Zārú Sì just inside the entrance; the monks are a friendly lot and seem pleased to see foreign tourists.

One downside is that most forest trails have been placed off-limits, and even a number of boardwalks for admiring the scenery have been pulled up, though they may still be marked on local maps. There's little in the way of alpine back-country trekking, but that shouldn't dissuade you from visiting.

The entrance to **Jiǔzhài Gōu Gúojìají Zìrán Bǎohùqū** (Nine Stockade Gully National Nature Preserve) is close to the Yángdōng Bīnguǎn, where the bus will likely drop you off. Here lies probably the most painful part of the trip: a park entry fee of Y102. This is exceedingly high for China (even locals must pay it), and there's no real way around it. Student cards don't work, unless you can back them up with a legitimate residence or work certificate. At least the money goes toward a national park, rather than into the pockets of some shady hotel or tour operator. The entry fee includes one night's stay at one of the three lodging areas – Héyè Cūn (Heye Village), Shùzhēng Zhài (Shuzheng Stockade) or Zécháwā Zhài. Note that in the off-season – and there's no real schedule for this – your lodging is limited to Héyè Cūn for the duration.

From the park entrance to the first hotels within the park it's about 5km along a surfaced road, and 14km to the bifurcation of the road. You can arrange rides from local drivers hanging around the entrance gate. Up to Nuòrìlǎng should cost Y10 to Y20 per person, although they'll likely try to charge more. Bargain hard with these guys.

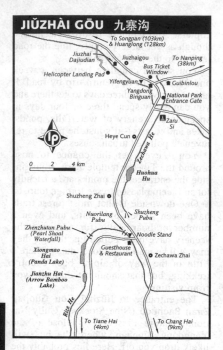

JIǓZHÀI GŌU 九寨沟

To Songpan (103km)
& Huanglgou (128km)
Jiuzhai
Dajiudian
Jiuzhaigou
To Nanping
(38km)
Helicopter Landing Pad
Bus Ticket
Window
Yifengyuàn
Guibinlou
Yangdong
Binguan
National Park
Entrance Gate
Zaru
Si
Heye Cun
Huohua
Hu
Shuzheng Zhai
Nuorilang
Pubu
Shuzheng
Pubu
Zhenzhutan Pubu
(Pearl Shoal
Waterfall)
Noodle Stand
Xiongmao
Hai
(Panda Lake)
Guesthouse
& Restaurant
Zechawa Zhai
Jianzhu Hai
(Arrow Bamboo
Lake)
To Tiane Hai
(4km)
To Chang Hai
(9km)
0 2 4 km
Zéchawa Hé
Rìze Hé

With the low level of traffic – just the occasional blitzkrieg tour bus – it's actually a lovely walk, if you're looking for exercise. An ambitious itinerary: each day walk to the next settlement, with gorgeous scenery along the whole way, and spend the day exploring the immediate area. On the fourth day hike/hitch towards Tiānè Hǎi (Swan Lake) and back (though traffic is sparse). Save the ride for the last day.

If you're crunched for time, your group can get a van driver to take you everywhere; bargaining starts at Y300 or whatever they think you'll stomach for the one-day trip.

After passing Nuòrìlǎng Pùbù (Promising Bright Bay Waterfall) the road splits: branch right for Tiānè Hǎi, and left for Cháng Hǎi (Long Lake). Cháng Hǎi is 18km, Nuòrìlǎng Rìzé is 9km and Nuòrìlǎng Rìzé to Tiānè Hǎi is 8km. Cháng Hǎi generally has fewer tourists, though this is changing with a surfaced road.

Organised Tours

During summer, a number of companies in Chéngdū operate tours to Jiǔzhài Gōu. Some include side trips in the general region. These tours take a lot of the hassle out of travelling in a region where roads and transport links are quite poor. Of course, they also dictate your schedule, which could be a problem if you decide you want to spend some more time in Jiǔzhài Gōu or Sōngpān, for example.

Most of the trips are advertised for a certain day, but the bus will only go if full. If you are unlucky you may spend days waiting. Find out exactly how many days the trip lasts and which places are to be visited. If you're not sure about the tour company, avoid paying in advance. If there's a booking list, have a look and see how many people have registered. You can register first and pay before departure.

A standard tour includes Huánglóng and Jiǔzhài Gōu, lasts six to seven days and costs a minimum of Y300 to Y500 per person. Hotels, food and entry fees are not included. There are longer tours which include visits to the Tibetan grassland areas of Barkam and Zöigê.

Chéngdū travel agencies in the Traffic Hotel, the Ximen bus station, the Jǐnjiāng Bīnguǎn and CITS all offer tours. The latter two are the most expensive. Check around and compare prices. A word of warning: several tour operators in Chéngdū have been blacklisted by travellers for lousy service, rip-offs and rudeness. Ask around among travellers to pinpoint a reliable agency.

Places to Stay & Eat

Unless you're catching an early bus the next day, you're better off staying inside the park. Lodging is found in three places – Héyè Cūn, Shùzhēng Zhài and Zéchǎwà Zhài. All feature a choice between funky wooden Tibetan-style rooms with the smell of pine still lingering or concrete-block 'guesthouse' rooms.

All three areas are set up a bit oddly – you have to locate the 'central service desk', which will be located somewhere in the middle of the village; your first night you'll be issued a voucher, and after that you're left to your own devices. Some places try to tack on an extra foreign-friend surcharge, but a few places don't, so check out a few places if you have time. You can often negotiate a deal on multi-night stays. Facilities are primitive, and don't even ask about showers.

The Tibetan-style rooms obviously ooze more character and the owners of some of these are quite friendly, although this may mean sitting through cups of yak butter tea – definitely an acquired taste.

Just above Nuòrìlǎng Pùbù, *Zéchǎwā Zhài* has a few more upmarket rooms but is the hardest lodging area to suss out. You'll likely as not wander about trying to find out where the hell anyone is. One hotel has great three-bed wooden rooms with common bath for Y22, although it may get you for Y35 for being a foreigner. It also has quite nice doubles with evening hot water and TV for Y90 per room. Further uphill are more forgettable guesthouse options along with the only *restaurant* in this village.

Héyè Cūn is the place where most travellers *don't* stay, since it's the furthest from the local sights (but closest to the park entrance). If you do stay there, rates for standard spartan rooms are around Y30 per person.

Just past Huǒhuā Hǎi (Sparkling Lake), *Shùzhēng Zhài* has rooms with what may be the best view in the country, overlooking spectacular turquoise pools, white baby cascades and dense verdancy. Simple rooms are Y22; go for the wooden ones if they're available, since the buildings are the newest. There are no longer any hotels along the road to Tiānè Hǎi – local authorities ordered them closed to preserve the natural environment.

Just outside the park entrance, the *Yángdóng Bīnguǎn* offers a more upmarket stay, with standard doubles with attached bath and TV for Y120. It's barely worth it. If you have the resources, near the park entrance and aside a stream is the new *Guìbīnlóu*, with all-wood interiors, private heaters, and clean private baths. Doubles/triples are Y300/350.

All the cheaper Tibetan-style lodgings left out of the park entrance along the road to Jiǔzhài Gōu village have been razed for new three-star hotels. Any of these when finished will gladly take you. For a cheaper option, the new *Jiǔzhài Dàjiǔdiàn* (something of an exaggeration to say 'hotel') is found in the village, approximately 10 minutes' walk from the park entrance. The elderly proprietress loves to rail in disgust against the garish hotels fleecing tourists; she offers simple but comfortable doubles with bath for Y50 and for groups of three or four she's amenable to negotiation. If this holds, it's good news for travellers.

Near the park entrance is a number of OK restaurants. The *Yīfēngyuán* is the last one on the south side of the road. (Look for Christmas lights around the sign.) The owner – the one with the beard – speaks a bit of English and is traveller friendly.

The local *làmiàn* is particularly good. Two small *noodle shops* in Zéchǎwā serve up this outstanding vegie noodle soup with hand-rolled noodles for Y5. One is just uphill from where the road splits, on the right side. The other is next door to the middle hotel. Otherwise, dining options are limited, so it would be wise to bring some of your own food. Chéngdū would be a good place to stock up.

Shùzhēng and Zéchǎwā stockades have the only two *eating halls* resembling anything like a restaurant. Prices are about 15% higher than you're used to paying for similar dishes – not to mention the fact that they lack many items – but you don't have much choice if you haven't packed in sustenance.

Neither place seems to mind you wandering through the kitchen to indicate your choice; there are plenty of local specialities the staff will point out. Héyè Cūn is limited to snack vendors and Pepsi.

Getting There & Away

Until local authorities get desperate, level a mountain or two and build an airport, the local bus remains the best means of transport. It can be taken in one dose or as part of a bus/train combination.

If you're coming down from Gānsù via Zöigê, you'll have to go through Sōngpān.

With a new road from Sōngpān to Jiǔzhài Gōu, the once horrid ride from Chéngdū can be done in 12 relatively painless hours; take the Nánpíng sleeper bus (Y100) in the morning from Chéngdū's Ximen station. From Sōngpān to Jiǔzhài Gōu (Y44; four hours) the road goes up and over and is gorgeous in parts.

If you nod off and miss the entrance to Jiǔzhài Gōu, you will have to overnight in Nánpíng and then backtrack the next day.

Bus/train combinations are more troublesome, but can be done. The most popular option is to travel north on the Chéngdū-Bàojī train line as far as Zhāohuá, where you will have to stay overnight.

From Zhāohuá there are usually tour buses to both Jiǔzhài Gōu and Huánglóng in the height of the tourist season, but if this isn't the case you can either bus to Nánpíng and overnight there before doing the final 41km the next morning or take a Chéngdū-bound bus to Jiǔzhài Gōu.

Buses for Chéngdū from Zhāohuá go via Nánpíng and Jiǔzhài Gōu (check to be certain). It's a good idea to book your onward bus ticket as soon as you get into Zhāohuá. The road between Zhāohuá and Nánpíng is notoriously dangerous – this is not a trip for those with no stomach for adventurous travel.

Another train/bus option is to take a train or bus to either Miányáng or Jiāngyóu, both north of Chéngdū. Then take a bus to Píngwǔ, where you can change for a bus to Jiǔzhài Gōu. This road is reportedly superior to the one between Zhāohuá and Nánpíng.

Between October and April snow often cuts off access to Jiǔzhài Gōu for weeks on end. Even at the best of times, transport is not plentiful. Hitching on tour buses has supposedly happened, but it's a rare occurrence indeed. To maximise your chances of a seat on a bus out of Jiǔzhài Gōu, it's best to try and book your ticket in advance at the entrance to the reserve. There are two buses daily from the park to Chéngdū (Y100). Tickets can be purchased at the ticket office on the opposite side of the main road from the park entrance.

Theoretically this ticket office has six berths reserved daily on the Chéngdū sleeper, but it's generally chaos anyway. To *guarantee* a seat, pick up the bus where it begins in Nánpíng (see the Nánpíng section following); you can pick up a handful of buses headed towards Nánpíng from the main road at the park entrance. You can get onto a small bus or van for Y15 to Y20 per person. It takes an hour and the road is paved, although rife with landslides.

NÁNPÍNG 南坪

Nánpíng has little of interest for travellers unless you like the surreal experience of hearing Alanis Morissette followed by social propaganda booming through loudspeakers throughout the town.

Some people head here either to guarantee a seat on a Chéngdū-bound bus, or to take the more scenic side routes via Zhāohuá and Jiāngyóu. Buses will probably drop you off right in the town centre.

Places to Stay

The bus station for foreigners (see Getting There & Away) has cheap beds at Y10 and hot showers. The *Yínyuán Bīnguǎn* (☎ 232 2799) is centrally located and the best hotel you'll find in town. It's also the only one willing to negotiate on the ridiculous local practice of charging foreigners an 80% mark-up on room rates. You can get a triple for Y150, with some arm-twisting. Other places are a few yuán cheaper, but are not as clean – one or two at least have 24-hour hot water.

Getting There & Away

The bus stations are a bit complicated. There are two of them, both on the same road, and both far from the centre of town. One is for locals and one is for foreigners. To get there from the Yínyuán Bīnguǎn, bear left after leaving the hotel until you cross a small bridge (there's likely to be no water). Take a right and walk along the opposite embankment for approximately 100m until it becomes a small road. Follow this uphill until it finishes. Turn right and walk *past* the first station, and continue to the second. Here you can get a ticket for Chéngdū (6 am; Y100) after filling out a registration form – you may have to lie and say you also have your own insurance.

Trying to get to Jiāngyóu or Zhāohúa is more problematic – the roads, already in horrid shape, wash out with an alarming regularity, so you may be stuck for a spell. Both of these buses also leave at 6 am.

CHÉNGDŪ TO XIÀHÉ

This journey has emerged as a popular backdoor route into Gānsù for many travellers. Those who have done it in the winter months don't recommend it. The roads often become impassable and temperatures plummet way past the tolerance levels of most mere mortals.

Even in good weather you need to give yourself at least five days to do the trip, more if you want to poke around some monasteries or make a side trip to Jiǔzhài Gōu.

The first leg is from Chéngdū to Sōngpān (see Getting There & Away in the Sōngpān section earlier in this chapter). Most travellers take a side trip from Sōngpān to Jiǔzhài Gōu at this point. From Sōngpān you can travel 168km north-west to your next overnight stop in Zöigê (Ruòěrgài), a dusty little town surrounded by sweeping grasslands. There is some confusion as to the status of Zöigê for individual travellers. There is an apparently under-used 'Foreigners Registration Office' near the main bus station. Some travellers have successfully ignored it, while others have had to pay for a travel permit. Don't worry about it too much – the PSB will find you if they think it's important.

From the cinema in town it is possible to walk up the hills and visit a couple of monasteries. There are superb views from up here.

There are a couple of hotels in Zöigê which take foreigners. The *Liángjú Bīnguǎn (Grain Bureau Guest House)* is probably the best choice, with beds in very

clean triples for Y12 (Y22 with TV); doubles are Y50 (all have electric blankets). There are common showers and toilets on each floor. To get there, turn right out of the main bus station, and take the first left. You'll come to a three way intersection. Turn right: the hotel is on the left-hand side of the street.

Further down the street, also on the left, the *Ruòěrgài Xiànzhèngfǔ Zhāodàisuǒ (Zöigê County Government Hostel)* is a little bit cheaper at Y10 per bed in a triple, but the rooms are filthy and the toilets putrid. Doubles at the back of the building for Y30 are a bit cleaner.

There are a few *restaurants* – some expensive so be careful – and lots of cheap *noodle places* near the Liángjú Bīnguǎn. You can also get public showers in town (Y3).

Getting There & Away

Zöigê has two bus stations (one at either end of town) with buses back to Sōngpān and on to Lǎngmùsì and Hézuò on alternating days. If you can't get an onward ticket for the next day at one bus station, try the other. Buses in the direction of Lǎngmùsì leave at 7 am (Y24; two to 3½ hours); some buses do not go to Lǎngmùsì and you'll need to hop off at a police checkpoint and walk or hitch 13km to get there. Direct buses to Hézuò (Y43; eight hours) leave at 6.20 am.

Lǎngmùsì is worth a stopover. It's an attractive Tibetan village nestled in the mountains, and travellers have had great visits with the monks at the local lamasery.

From Lǎngmùsì it's easy to catch a bus to Hézuò. It is by all accounts a dump, but is only a few hours from Xiàhé, so you may not have to overnight there. From Xiàhé you have the option of travelling on to Lánzhōu or taking the more unusual option of travelling on to Xīníng in Qīnghǎi via Tóngrén.

Xīnjiāng 新疆

In Xīnjiāng vast deserts and arid plains stretch for thousands of kilometres before ending abruptly at the foot of towering mountain ranges. The ruins of Buddhist cities pepper the deserts as reminders of the past, while newer Islamic monuments point the way to the future.

Xīnjiāng is a huge, geopolitically strategic area, four times the size of Japan. It shares an international border with eight other nations and is the largest province in China, comprising 16% of the country's land surface.

The province was made an autonomous region in 1955 and named after the majority Turkic-speaking Muslim Uyghurs (Wéiwúěr) at a time when more than 90% of the population was non-Chinese. The north has traditionally consisted of nomadic pastoralists, such as the Kazakhs, while the Uyghurs are settled in the south in fertile oases scattered along the ancient Silk Road. With the building of the railway from Lánzhōu to Ürümqi and the development of industry in the region, the Han Chinese now form a majority in the northern area, while the Uyghurs continue to predominate in the south.

For travellers, the region is one of the most interesting in China, packed with history, archaeological remains, ethnic variety, superb landscapes and a vibrant Central Asian culture. Memories of a cold Xīnjiāng beer under the grape trellises of Turpan, of wandering the bustling bazaars of Hotan or Kashgar, and of the poplar-lined Uyghur villages will remain long after the end of most peoples' trips.

History

Han dynasty China had already pioneered its new trade routes (later named the Silk Road) through this region by the 1st century BC. The first Chinese conquest of Xīnjiāng, led by the brilliant Chinese general Pan Zhao (AD 32–102) was between AD 73 and 97. In AD 138 the Chinese envoy Zhang Qian passed through the region in his search

Highlights

Capital: Ürümqi
Population: 16.9 million
Area: 1,600,000 sq km

- Tiān Chí, a chunk of alpine scenery that looks like a Swiss postcard
- Kashgar, the fabled oasis of the ancient silk road that still retains its exotic eastern feel
- Travelling the Sino-Pakistani Karakoram Highway, one of the most beautiful road journeys in the world
- Turpan, a desert oasis, the lowest and hottest spot in China, graced with grape vines, mosques and abandoned ancient cities
- Hānàsī Hú, a beautiful lake surrounded by alpine wilderness and semi-nomadic Kazakhs

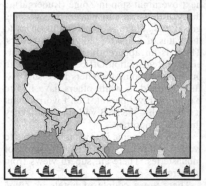

for potential allies against the Xiongnu tribes who were ceaselessly harassing the Chinese heartland. Despite the expenditure of vast resources in policing the 'Western Region', it eventually succumbed to northern nomadic warrior tribes, Mongols and later, Turks.

At the time that the Buddhist pilgrims Fa Xian and Xuan Zang visited the region in

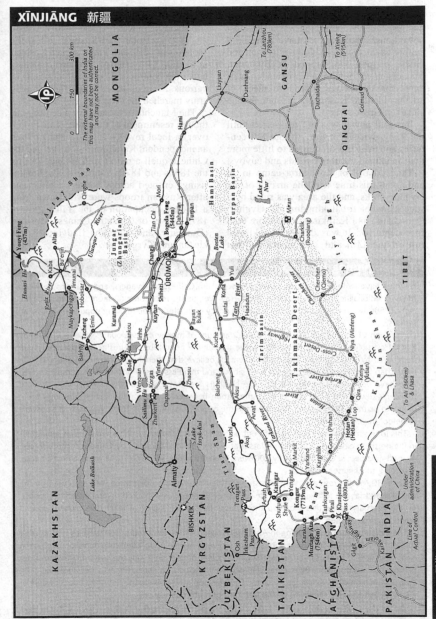

XĪNJIĀNG 新疆

search of Buddhist scriptures, in AD 400 and 644 respectively, the region was a Buddhist powerhouse. Ruined cities have revealed a culture where red-haired Indo-European and Altaic peoples worshipped at Buddhist, Manichaeist or Nestorian Christian temples, expressing themselves in beautiful pieces of art that blended Kashmiri, Tibetan, Indian and even Greek styles.

Imperial power was not reasserted until the Tang dynasty in the 7th and 8th centuries and even this amounted to little more than an annual tribute of goods and envoys.

Tang control of Kashgaria came to an end about this time with the arrival of the Uyghur Turks, and the area was ruled by a succession of tribal kingdoms – Uyghur, Qarakhanid and Karakitay – for more than four centuries. It was during Qarakhanid rule in the 11th and 12th centuries that Islam took hold here. Qarakhanid tombs are still standing in Kashgar and nearby Artush.

Yīlí (Ili), Hotan and Kashgar fell to the Mongols in 1219, and Timur sacked Kashgar in the late 14th century. The area remained under the control of Timur's descendants or various Mongol tribes until the Manchu army marched into Kashgar in 1755.

The Manchus remained for a century, although resentment of their rule often boiled over in local revolts. In 1847 Hunza, then an independent Karakoram state, helped the Chinese quell a revolt in Yarkand. During the 1860s and 1870s a series of Muslim uprisings erupted across western China, and after Russian troops were withdrawn from a 10-year occupation of the Yīlí region in 1871, waves of Uyghurs, Chinese Muslims (Dungans) and Kazakhs fled into Kazakhstan and Kyrgyzstan.

The Beginning or the End?

Uyghurs have, with good reason, always viewed Han Chinese as invaders, and relations between the two nationalities have never been good. However, ties have become far more strained since the early 1950s, when communist China began its policy of bolstering the Xīnjiāng population with Han settlers.

Although China has actually invested a fair amount of money in developing Xīnjiāng's economy and infrastructure, Uyghurs frequently argue that all the good jobs and business opportunities are dominated by Han Chinese. The more vehement believe that the Chinese regard Uyghurs as little more than 'animals, suitable only for hard labour and mindless jobs'. For their part, some Han Chinese have been heard to remark that the Uyghurs are 'not a very bright race'. A look through Xīnjiāng's towns and cities shows little integration between the two nationalities, although there seems to be more Han-Uyghur interaction in the capital, Ürümqi. Even there, however, it's possible to detect the underlying tension.

This long simmering Uyghur resentment boiled over in February 1997 when Muslim separatists in the northern city of Yīníng started riots that led to a swift crackdown by Chinese security forces. At least nine people died and nearly 200 were injured, making the protest the most violent to date, according to Chinese media.

Some 30 Muslim residents were arrested for their roles in the riots: three were executed on the day of their trial, the rest were given life sentences. These arrests sparked several deadly responses. In late February separatists blew up three buses in Ürümqi, killing at least nine passengers and wounding many others.

The violence returned to Yīníng in April 1997, when a mob attacked prison vehicles transporting some of the convicted February rioters. Again, several people were killed or wounded. Uyghurs in exile have vowed to continue the campaign of violent protest until Xīnjiāng gains its freedom from Běijīng. At the same time, Běijīng has clamped down heavily on separatist activities and is keeping a close watch on all of Xīnjiāng's Muslims. The question now is: were the February riots the start of a long march towards secession or the last gasp of a hopeless cause?

In 1865 a Kokandi officer named Yaqub Beg seized Kashgaria, proclaimed an independent Turkestan and made diplomatic contacts with Britain and Russia. A few years later, however, a Manchu army returned, Beg committed suicide and Kashgaria was formally incorporated into China's newly created Xīnjiāng (New Dominions) Province.

With the fall of the Qing in 1911, Xīnjiāng came under the rule of a succession of warlords, over whom the Kuomintang had very little control. The first of these warlord-rulers was Yang Zhengxin, who ruled from 1911 until his assassination in 1928 at a banquet in Ürümqi.

Yang was followed by a second tyrannical overlord who, after being forced to flee in 1933, was replaced by a still more oppressive leader named Sheng Shicai. The latter remained in power almost until the end of WWII, when he too was forced out.

The only real attempt to establish an independent state was in the 1940s, when a Kazakh named Osman led a rebellion of Uyghurs, Kazakhs and Mongols. He took control of south-western Xīnjiāng and established an independent eastern Turkestan Republic in January 1945.

The Kuomintang convinced the Muslims to abolish their new republic in return for a pledge of real autonomy. This promise wasn't kept, but Chiang Kaishek's preoccupation with the civil war left him with little time to re-establish control over the region.

The Kuomintang eventually appointed a Muslim named Burhan as governor of the region in 1948, unaware that he was actually a communist supporter.

A Muslim league opposed to Chinese rule was formed in Xīnjiāng, but in August 1949 a number of its most prominent leaders died in a mysterious plane crash on their way to Běijīng to hold talks with the new communist leaders. Muslim opposition to Chinese rule collapsed, although the Kazakh Osman continued to fight until he was captured and executed by the Chinese communists in early 1951.

Since 1949 Běijīng's main goal has been to keep a lid on minority separatism while flooding the region with Han settlers. Xīnjiāng's minorities, notably the Uyghurs, make little secret of their dislike of China's policies and have staged sporadic protests over the past decades, some of them violent.

ÜRÜMQI 乌鲁木齐

The capital of Xīnjiāng, Ürümqi (Wūlǔmùqí) has little to distinguish itself other than the claim to being the furthest city in the world from the ocean (2250km).

The drab white-tile and concrete-block architecture has been imported lock, stock and barrel from eastern China, and Ürümqi essentially looks little different from the smokestack cities 2000km east. There are few 'sights' as such, but it's an important crossroad and is interesting for all the various nationalities you see on the streets: Uyghurs, Kazakhs, Pakistanis, Russians and Uzbeks (and of course Han Chinese and foreign tourists).

Orientation

Most of the sights, tourist facilities and hotels are scattered across the city, although they're all easily reached on local buses.

The train and long-distance bus stations are in the south-western corner of the city.

Which Time Is It?

Xīnjiāng is several time zones removed from Běijīng, which prefers to ignore the fact. While all of China officially runs on Běijīng time (běijīng shíjián), most of Xīnjiāng runs on an unofficial Xīnjiāng time (xīnjiāng shíjián), two hours behind Běijīng time. Thus 9 am Běijīng time is 7 am Xīnjiāng time. Almost all government-run services such as the bank, post office, bus station and Xinjiang Airlines run on Běijīng time. To cater for the time difference, government offices (including the post office and CITS) generally operate from 10 am to 1.30 pm and from 4 to 8 pm. Unless otherwise stated, we use Běijīng time in this book. To be sure, though, if you arrange a time with someone make sure you know which, as well as what, time.

XĪNJIĀNG 新疆

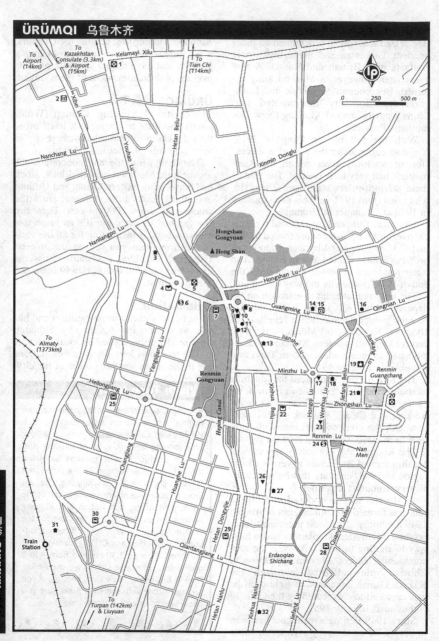

ÜRÜMQI 乌鲁木齐

To Airport (14km)

To Kazakhstan Consulate (3.3km) & Airport (15km)

Kelamayi Xilu

To Tian Chi (114km)

0   250   500 m

Xibei Beilu

Youhao Lu

Hetan Beilu

Nanchang Lu

Xinmin Donglu

Nanliangpo Lu

Hongshan Gongyuan

▲ Hong Shan

Hongshan Lu

Guangming Lu

Qingnian Lu

To Almaty (1373km)

Yangzijiang Lu

Jianshe Lu

Jiankang Lu

Renmin Guangchang

Heilongjiang Lu

Minzhu Lu

Jiefang Beilu

Renmin Gongyuan

Heping Canal

Xinhua Beilu

Hongqi Lu

Wenhua Lu

Zhongshan Lu

Changjiang Lu

Renmin Lu

Nan Men

Huanghe Lu

Hetan Dongyilu

Erdaoqiao Shichang

Quanyin Dadao

Train Station

Qiantangjiang Lu

Hetan Nanlu

Xinhua Nanlu

Jiefang Lu

To Turpan (142km) & Liuyuan

ÜRÜMQI

PLACES TO STAY
3 Huádū Dàfàndiàn
华都大饭店
8 Hóngshān Bīnguǎn; CYTS
红山宾馆
10 Holiday Inn
假日大酒店
13 Xīnjiāng Xīyù Dàjiǔdiàn
新疆西域大酒店
14 Bógédá Bīnguǎn
博格达宾馆
18 Xīnjiāng Diànlì Bīnguǎn
新疆电力宾馆
21 Hoi Tak Hotel
海德酒店
27 Huálián Bīnguǎn
华联宾馆
31 Yà'ōu Bīnguǎn
亚欧宾馆
32 Huáqiáo Bīnguǎn; CTS
华侨宾馆; 中国旅行社

PLACES TO EAT
9 John's Information Cafe
约翰咖啡厅

17 Dōng Nán Wèi
东南味
23 Yǔqīng Fàndiàn
雨青饭店
26 Měishēng Yànhuìtīng
美生宴会厅

OTHER
1 Youhao Department Store
友好商场
2 Xīnjiāng Uygur Zizhiqu Bówùguǎn
新疆维吾尔自治区博物馆
4 Main Post Office
总邮局
5 Hongshan Department Store
红山
6 Bank of China
中国银行
7 Buses to Tiān Chí
往天池和白杨沟汽车站
11 Lǚyou Hotel; CITS
旅游宾馆; 中国国际旅行社

12 Kyrghyzstan & Uzbekistan Airlines Office; Yingjisha Hotel
15 Galaxy 169 Internet Bar
银宇电脑网吧
16 Xinjiang Airlines Booking Office
中国新疆航空公司售票处
19 PSB
公安局
20 Tianshan Department Store
22 Post & Telephone Office
邮电局
24 Bank of China
中国银行
25 Long-Distance Bus Station
长途汽车站
28 Buses to Turpan
吐鲁番汽车站
29 Altai Regional Bus Station
阿勒泰地区汽车站
30 Kashgar Bus Station
喀什办事处

The city centre revolves around Minzhu Lu, Zhongshan Lu and Jianshe Lu, location of government offices, fancier hotels and department stores. In the north of town are Youhao and Hóngshān, major intersections that are popular shopping areas; the latter is an important local transport hub.

Information

Consulates Kazakhstan has a consulate (Hāsàkèsītǎn Lǐngshìguǎn; ☎ 383 2324) in the northern section of the city, just off Beijing Lu. It issues a three-day transit visa to those who have an onward visa for a neighbouring country, not including China. The visa takes a week to be issued and costs US$15, plus a Y65 processing fee. It is theoretically possible to obtain a three-day transit visa on arrival at Almaty airport, however Chinese customs won't let you on a plane without a Kazakhstan visa.

The visa section is only open Monday to Thursday from 10.30 am to 1.30 pm.

Before you head to the consulate, give it a ring. A taxi there will cost about Y15.

Money The main Bank of China is at 343 Jiefang Nanlu, next to the Nán Mén (South Gate). Another branch is opposite the main post office at Hóngshān. Both are open daily. Credit card cash advances are available here.

Post & Communications The main post office is in the north of the city at Hóngshān. This is the only place that handles international parcels and is open daily from 10 am to 8 pm. There is also a post and telephone office on Zhongshan Lu, near the corner of Xinhua Nanlu.

The Galaxy 169 Internet Bar (Yínyǔ Diànnǎo Wǎngbā) is just next door to the Bógédá Bīnguǎn on Guangming Lu. The bar is on the 2nd floor and is open 24 hours a day and charges a reasonable Y10 an hour (Y5 for students) to surf the Net.

XĪNJIĀNG 新疆

Travel Agencies The Lǚyóu Hotel (just behind the Holiday Inn) is home to several tourist and travel agencies. On the ground floor is the China International Travel Service (CITS; Zhōngguó Guójì Lǚxíngshè; ☎ 282 6719, fax 281 0689).

A more useful place is the China Youth Travel Service (CYTS; Zhōngguó Qīngnián Lǚxíngshè; ☎ 282 4761 ext 130), in the Hóngshān Bīnguǎn, that seems relatively efficient at organising reasonably priced tickets and tours. CITS also has an office here that is a bit more helpful than the one in the Lǚyóu Hotel.

The China Travel Service (CTS; Zhōngguó Lǚxíngshè; ☎ 652 1440) is in the grounds of the Huáqiáo Bīnguǎn. Most of Ürümqi's hotels have travel agents offering similar deals for trips around Xīnjiāng. Agents from both the Hóngshān Bīnguǎn and Yǎ'ōu Bīnguǎn have been recommended by readers.

If you encounter any problems with the quality of tourism services in Xīnjiāng, there is a tourist complaint hotline (☎ 283 1902).

PSB The foreign affairs office of the Public Security Bureau (PSB; Gōngānjú) is on Jiankang Lu, just north of Minzhu Lu: look out for the sign that reads 'Aliens Reception Room'. It is open Monday to Friday from 9.30 am to 2 pm and from 4 to 8 pm.

Xīnjiāng Zìzhìqū Bówùguǎn
新疆维吾尔自治区 博物馆
Xinjiang Autonomous Region Museum
This museum is worth a look as it contains some interesting visual exhibits relating to Xīnjiāng minority groups. There are at least 13 different ethnic groups in Xīnjiāng, and facets of daily existence of each group are on special display. There is a fascinating collection of minority clothing, musical instruments, textiles, jewellery, cooking and farming utensils, and tools for hunting.

Another wing of the museum has a section devoted to the history of early settlements along the Silk Road, which include a fine collection of ceramics, tools, tapestries and bronze figures. Prime exhibits are the preserved bodies of nearly a dozen men, women and babies discovered in tombs in Xīnjiāng: it can get a bit creepy if you're there alone. There are very few English explanations, but the museum's exhibits are a rich visual experience.

The distinctive green domed Soviet-style building is on Xibei Lu, about 20-minutes walk from Hóngshān. The museum is open weekdays from 9.30 am to 6.30 pm and 10 am to 4.30 pm on weekends. During winter, opening hours are reduced and the museum is closed on the weekends. Admission is Y12. From Hóngshān take bus No 7 for four stops and ask to get off at the museum (bówùguǎn).

Rénmín Gōngyuán 人民公园
People's Park
This scenic, tree-shaded park is about a kilometre in length and can be entered from either the northern or southern gates. The best time to visit is early in the morning when many locals exercise here. There are plenty of birds in the park, a few pavilions and a lake where you can hire rowing boats. The park is open from 7.30 am to 10 pm and admission is Y5.

Hóngshān Gōngyuán
This is Xīnjiāng's premier amusement park, complete with a Ferris wheel, bumper cars and those swinging gondolas designed to bring up your lunch. Other attractions include an eight-storey pagoda and sweeping views of the city. Entry is Y3.

Places to Stay
Ürümqi has a good variety of hotels, offering reasonably priced rooms, however be warned that during the peak summer months (June to October) most hotel rooms double in price.

Places to Stay – Budget
The Hóngshān Bīnguǎn (☎ 282 4761) is a good base in the centre of town and is popular with budget travellers. Dorm beds cost Y40 in a three-bed dorm with private bath. However, it also has unhelpful desk staff and discriminates against foreigners by charging them more than Chinese customers.

The Karakul Lake area in Xīnjiāng is dotted with Mongolian yurts, homes of the local Tajiks.

Kashgar's famous bazaar sells everything from livestock to musical instruments.

Reading the Koran in Kashgar, Xīnjiāng

The intricate tile-work of the Abakh Hoja Tomb in Kashgar

Instead, try the nearby two-star *Bógédá Bīnguǎn* (☎ 282 3910), which has five-bed dorms for Y45 per person and beds in a triple with bath for Y60. Nice twins cost a reasonable Y144 or Y288 during the high season. Just next door to the train station is the *Yǎ'ōu Bīnguǎn* (☎ 585 6699), where basic dorm beds start at Y12 in an eight-person room and beds in triples/quads with attached bath are Y50/40. Its singles/twins are a little overpriced at Y130/158, but you should be able to bargain them down. The other advantage to this hotel is that train tickets can be purchased for guests, free of service charge.

For relatively cheap twins, there's the *Huáqiáo Bīnguǎn* (*Overseas Chinese Hotel;* ☎ 286 0793, fax 286 2279, 51 Xinhua Nanlu), which charges Y100 for compact rooms in the older, Russian-style building and Y180 in the newer wing.

The *Huálián Bīnguǎn* is also on Xinhua Nanlu, but is a little closer to the city centre. It has unexciting twins for Y80, even worse ones for Y100 and surprisingly good value twins for Y150. The latter can be bargained down to Y120. The staff are friendly and inquisitive, if not a little intrusive.

Places to Stay – Mid-Range

In the city centre, the *Xīnjiāng Diànlì Bīnguǎn* (*Xīnjiāng Electric Power Hotel;* ☎ 282 2911, fax 282 6031) is actually a pretty good place, despite the silly name. Comfortable twins range from Y250 to Y366. Breakfast is included and the staff collect and deliver guests to the airport and train station for free.

The *Xīnjiāng Xīyù Dàjiǔdiàn* (☎ 282 6788, fax 283 3613, 84 Xinhua Beilu) has singles/twins for Y280/200, including breakfast and dinner. The hotel is quite new, but is already showing signs of poor maintenance standards.

The *Huádū Dàfàndiàn* (☎ 452 9922, fax 452 2708), at the Hóngshān intersection, has nice twins for Y180.

Places to Stay – Top End

The *Hoi Tak Hotel* (*Hǎidé Jiǔdiàn,* ☎ 232 2828, fax 232 1818, @ hthxjbc@mail.wl.xj .cn) has five-star services and facilities.

Standard rooms are Y665 and superior rooms are Y735, plus a 15% service charge and 3% tax.

Even if you can't afford to stay here, it has great coffee and an excellent breakfast/lunch/dinner buffet.

The *Holiday Inn* (*Jiàrì Dàjiǔdiàn,* ☎ 281 8788, fax 281 7422, @ holiday@mail.wl.xj .cn) is a popular choice with western tour groups. Standard rooms range from Y680 to Y935, while singles are Y580, plus a 15% service charge. There is a cake shop on the 1st floor that sells a good range of pastries and after 8pm everything is discounted by 25%. During the summer months it also offers a number of deals on the buffets and barbecues.

Places to Eat

Ürümqi is not a bad spot to try Uyghur foods, such as *náng* (shish kebab with flatbread). Another local speciality is *lāmiàn* (noodles with spicy vegetables, beef or lamb). There is a row of *restaurants* on Jianshe Lu where you can sample both of these dishes as well as Han Chinese food.

The *Měishēng Yànhuìtīng* is a large Uyghur restaurant that is popular with the locals. Both Uyghur and Chinese food is on offer and there are traditional dancing and singing performances most nights, usually starting after 10 pm. Most of the dishes are very generous, so you may prefer asking for an entrée serving (*bàn pán*).

The restaurant is on the 2nd floor of the large building adjacent to the Huálián Bīnguǎn on Xinhua Nanlu. The entrance is just to the left of the Bank of China.

For cheap and tasty Chinese fare, the *Yǔqīng Fànguǎn*, on Wenhua Lu, hits the spot. Its *làzi jīdīng* (spicy chicken) and *riben hongshao doufu* (Japanese-style caramel tofu) are worth trying. There is no English menu or sign, just look out for the white writing on a green sign.

Honqi Lu, in the city centre, is another good street to go restaurant hunting, it has lots of noodle and dumpling shops and other small eateries. One place that locals speak highly of is *Dōng Nán Wèi*. It's little more than a hole in the wall, but has a good reputation for its *huángyú* (fish) and *páigǔ* (spare rib) dishes. There's no English to be found anywhere, though you can always resort to pointing at meals on other people's tables.

John's Information Cafe is inside the small park opposite the Hóngshān Bīnguǎn. It has Chinese food as well as some reasonably priced western fare, and is a good place to meet up with other travellers and down a few beers.

If you're craving western food, then head for either the Hoi Tak Hotel or the Holiday Inn. Its all-you-can-eat breakfast and lunch buffets may do the trick, but at more than Y100 per person you'd want to be hungry.

At night the sidewalk areas along Minzhu Lu and around the Youhao and Hóngshān intersections become bustling *night markets* with fresh handmade noodle dishes, shish kebab skewers and a whole range of point-and-choose fried dishes. They're definitely worth a look around.

During July and August the markets are packed with delicious fruit, both fresh and dried. The best market is the **Èrdàoqiáo Shìchǎng**, in the southern end of the city, not too far from the Turpan bus station.

Getting There & Away

Air Ürümqi is well served by domestic services and even has a few international flights, especially to neighbouring Central

---

Uyghur Food

Uyghur cuisine includes all the trusty Central Asian standbys such as kebabs, *pulau* (plov) and dumplings (*chuchura*), but has benefited from Chinese influence to make it the most enjoyable region of Central Asia in which to eat.

Uyghurs boast endless varieties of laghman (*lāmiàn* in Chinese), though the usual topping is some combination of mutton, peppers, tomatoes, eggplant, green beans and garlic. *Suoman* are noodle squares fried with tomatoes peppers garlic and meat. *Suoman goshsiz* are the vegetarian variety. Suoman can be quite spicy so ask for *lazasiz* (without peppers) if you prefer a milder version.

Kebabs are another staple and are generally of a much better standard than the ropey shashlyk of the Central Asian republics. *Jiger* (liver) kebabs are the low-fat variety. *Tonur kebabs* are larger and baked in an oven *tonor* – tandoori style.

Breads are a particular speciality, especially when straight out of the oven and sprinkled with poppy seeds, sesame seeds or fennel. They make a great plate for a round of kebabs. Uyghur bakers also make wonderful bagels (*girde nan*).

Other snacks include *serik ash* (yellow meatless noodles), *nokot* (chickpeas with carrot), *pintang* (meat and vegetable soup) and *gangpen* rice with fried vegetable and meat. Most travellers understandably steer clear of *opke*, a nauseating broth of bobbling goat's heads and coiled, stuffed intestines.

Samsas (baked envelopes of meat) are available everywhere but the meat-to-fat ratio varies wildly. Hotan and Kashgar offer huge meat pies called *daman* or *gosh girde*. You can even get *balyk* (fried fish), as far away from the sea as it is humanly possible to be.

For dessert you can try *maroji* (vanilla ice cream churned in iced wooden barrels), *matang* (walnut fruit loaf), *kharsen meghriz* (fried dough balls filled with sugar, raisins and walnuts) or *dogh* (sometimes known as durap), a delicious, though potentially deadly, mix of shaved ice, syrup, yoghurt and iced water. *Tangzaza* are triangles of glutinous rice wrapped in bamboo leaves covered in syrup.

Xīnjiāng is justly famous for its fruit, whether it be *uruk* (apricots), *uzum* (grapes), *tawuz* (watermelon), *khoghun* (sweet melon) or *yimish* (raisins). The best grapes come from Turpan; the sweetest melons from Hami.

Meals are washed down with beer or *kok chai* (green tea), often laced with nutmeg. Uyghur restaurants usually provide a miniature rubbish bin on the table in which to dispose of the waste tea after rinsing out the bowl.

Asian countries. International departures include flights to Almaty (Kazakhstan), Bishkek (Kyrgyzstan), Islamabad (Pakistan), Novosibirsk (Russia) and Moscow. It's not uncommon for these flight to be suspended, especially during the winter months.

There are several international airline offices in town. Siberia Airlines (☎ 286 2326) has an office in the Huáqiáo Bīnguǎn; Kazakhstan Airlines (☎ 382 5564) has an office next to the Kazakhstan consulate; Kyrghyzstan Airlines and Uzbekistan Airways (☎ 231 6333) share an office on the 1st floor of the Yingjisha Hotel.

Domestic flights connect Ürümqi with Běijīng (Y1930), Chéngdū (Y1350), Chóngqìng (Y1460), Lánzhōu (Y1040), Guǎngzhōu (Y2270), Hong Kong, Shànghǎi (Y2240), Xī'ān (Y1330) and most other major cities.

Within Xīnjiāng there are regular flights from Ürümqi to Aksu (Akesu), Hotan (Hetian), Karamai (Kelamayi), Kashgar (Kashi), Korla (Kuerle), Tǎchéng and Yīníng. Information on some of these flights can be found in the Getting There & Away sections of the relevant destinations.

The Xīnjiāng Airlines booking office (☎ 264 1826) is at 2 Xinmin Lu, near the Běi Mén (North Gate) on the 1st floor of the China Construction Bank building.

It's also possible to purchase tickets through most hotels.

Bus The long-distance bus station is on Heilongjiang Lu. There are buses for most cities in Xīnjiāng, the notable exception being Turpan, and many destinations have there own bus station scattered across town.

Large public buses and more comfortable minibuses to Turpan run from near the Héngyuán Hotel on Quanyin Dadao, in the southern part of the city. The best way to get there is to hop in a taxi: just tell the driver you want to go to the tǔlǔfān qìchēzhàn. The ride shouldn't cost more than Y10 to Y15 from anywhere within the city.

If you're heading to Kashgar, you can get a sleeper bus from either the main station or the Kashgar bus station, which is just east of the train station. Departure times and

fares are listed in the Getting There & Away sections for the relevant destinations.

An interesting option is the Almaty (Ālāmùtú) bus service. The 1052km trip takes 24 hours with three stops for meals, and costs Y450.

At the time of writing buses to Almaty were leaving the long-distance bus station once daily at 6 pm; check at window No 8 for the latest on this service. Crossing the border shouldn't really be a problem, but you should prepare yourself for possible bureaucratic delays.

Train The schedule of daily departures from Ürümqi is as follows:

destination	train	departs	duration (hours)
Běijīng	70	9.25 pm	60
Chéngdū	314	11.52 am	58
Lánzhōu	508	11.58 pm	34½
Shànghǎi	54	11.02 pm	56
Xī'ān	344	2.59 pm	48

Getting tickets can still be a hassle; hard sleepers on special express trains to places like Běijīng and Shànghǎi sell out quickly, so it's good to book as far in advance as possible.

You might also try going to the station at more irregular hours, such as after 8 pm Běijīng time; it's far less crowded and you *may* have luck getting a ticket, although maybe not for the exact departure time you want.

The new rail link between Ürümqi and Kashgar via Kùchè began in December 1999. The journey takes 31 hours and takes you through an interesting mix of desert and mountain scenery.

There are trains running Monday and Saturday from Ürümqi to Almaty, Kazakhstan. The journey takes a very slow 35 hours, eight of which is spent at both the Chinese and Kazakh customs, and the fare is Y409. At the Ürümqi train station there's a special ticket window for these trains, inside the large waiting room in the main building. It's only open Monday, Thursday, Friday and Saturday, from 10 am to 1 pm and 3 to 7 pm. You will, of course, need a visa for Kazakhstan.

Getting Around
To/From the Airport Minibuses (Y8) head out to the airport half-hourly from 6 am and depart from the Xinjiang Airlines office and pass through the Hóngshān intersection. The same minibuses also greet all incoming flights.

The airport is 16km from the Hóngshān intersection. A taxi should cost between Y40 and Y50. If you're in no hurry, bus No 51 runs between Hóngshān and the airport gate, but takes about an hour.

Bus Ürümqi's public buses are packed to the roof and beyond. It's better to spend an extra few jiǎo for a minibus.

Some of the more useful bus routes include No 7, which runs up Xinhua Lu to the Youhao intersection, linking the city centre with the main post office; and No 2, which runs from the train station, past the main post office and way up along Beijing Lu, past the Kazakhstan consulate.

AROUND ÜRÜMQI
Tiān Chí 天池
Heaven Pool
Halfway up a mountain in the middle of a desert is Tiān Chí, a small, deep-blue lake surrounded by hills covered with fir trees and grazed by horses. Scattered around are the yurts (circular tents) of the Kazak people who inhabit the mountains; in the distance are the snow-covered peaks of the Tiān Shān (Heavenly Mountains), and you can climb the hills right up to the snow line. It's a heavily touristed spot, especially in the high season, but is beautiful nonetheless.

The lake is 115km east of Ürümqi at an elevation of 1980m. Nearby is the 5445m **Bógédá Fēng** (Peak of God), which can be climbed by well-equipped mountaineers with permits (see CITS for information). The lake freezes over in Xīnjiāng's bitter winter and the roads up here are open only in the summer months.

The best way to spend your time is to hike around the lake and even up into the hills. The surrounding countryside is quite beautiful. Follow the track skirting the lake for about 4km to the far end where there is a small nursery and PSB office. From here you can just choose your valley. From personal experience, avoid trying a circuit of the lake as a day trip.

During the summer, Kazakhs set up yurts in this area for tourist accommodation at Y40 per person, with three meals. This is not a bad option; during the day the area can get quite cramped with day-trippers, but you'll pretty much have the place to yourself after 4 pm and in the morning. Readers recommend **Rashits Yurt**, which is about half-way around the lake and has an English-speaking owner. Some people have also brought their own tents and gear and camped here.

Admission to the lake area costs Y24. It is possible to hire horses for treks around the lake, a trip to the snow line costs about Y80. The return trek takes between 8 and 10 hours, depending on where the snowline is.

Buses to Tiān Chí leave Ürümqi from 9 to 9.30 am from the north gate of Rénmín Gōngyuán (see section earlier) and return between 5 and 6 pm. Tickets are sold from the desks to the left of the park entrance. The return fare is between Y25 and Y50, depending on the size and quality of the bus. The trip takes about 2½ hours. There are also usually private buses leaving from in front of the Hóngshān Bīnguǎn, and return fares from there are about Y30. Buses back to Ürümqi leave between 4 and 5 pm.

DÀHÉYÀN 大河沿
The jumping-off point for Turpan is a place on the train line signposted 'Turpan Zhan' (Tǔlǔfān Zhàn). In fact, you are actually in Dàhéyàn, and the Turpan oasis is a 58km drive south-east across the desert. Dàhéyàn is not really a place where you'll want to hang around.

The bus station is a five-minute walk from the train station. Walk up the road leading from the train station and turn right at the first main intersection; the bus station is a few minutes' walk ahead on the left-hand side of the road.

Minibuses run from here to Turpan (Y5; 1½ hours) about once every 30 minutes throughout the day.

Although Dàhéyàn train station is rarely crowded, it can be difficult to get hard-sleeper tickets, as most of these will have already been sold from Ürümqi. The best option is to board the train and try your luck with an upgrade.

Most travellers are interested in the trains heading east or west, since people going northwards from Turpan usually opt for the bus to Ürümqi, which is much faster than trekking up here to catch a train. There are daily trains to Běijīng, Chéngdū, Lánzhōu (30 hours), Xī'ān and Kashgar (29 hours). Trains also go to Liǔyuán (10 hours) and Jiāyùguān (16 hours).

TURPAN 吐鲁番

East of Ürümqi the Tiān Shān split into a southern and a northern range, and between the two lie the Hami and Turpan basins. Both are below sea level and receive practically no rain so summers are searingly hot.

Part of the Turpan Basin is 154m below sea level – it's the lowest spot in China and the second lowest depression in the world (after the Dead Sea).

Turpan (Tǔlǔfān) holds a special place in Uyghur history, since nearby Gāochāng was once the capital of the Uyghurs. It was an important staging post on the Silk Road and was a centre of Buddhism before being converted to Islam in the 8th century. During the Chinese occupation it served as a garrison town.

Turpan is also the hottest spot in China – the highest recorded temperature here was 49.6°C (121.3°F). Fortunately, the humidity is low – so low that your laundry is practically dry by the time you hang it out! To compensate, Turpan is famous for its grapes and is an important producer of sultanas and wine.

Turpan County is inhabited by about 240,000 people – just over half are Uyghurs and the rest mostly Han. The centre of the county is the Turpan oasis, a small city set in a vast tract of grain fields and grape vines. Despite the concrete-block architecture of the city centre, it's a pleasant, relaxing place. Some of the smaller streets have pavements covered with grapevine trellises, which are a godsend in the fierce heat of summer.

Moving further out of town, the narrow streets are lined with mud-brick walls enclosing thatch-plaster houses. Open channels with flowing water run down the sides of the streets; the inhabitants draw water from these and use them to wash their clothes, dishes and themselves.

Some of Turpan's hotels provide good spots to sit underneath the vine trellises and contemplate the moon and stars. The living is relatively cheap, the food is good, the people friendly, and there are numerous interesting sights scattered around to keep you occupied.

Orientation

The centre of the Turpan oasis is called **Lǎo Chéng** (Old City) and the western part is called **Xīn Chéng** (New City). Lǎo Chéng is where you'll find the tourist hotels, shops, market, long-distance bus station and restaurants – all within easy walking distance of each other. Most of the sights are scattered on the outskirts of the oasis or in the surrounding desert.

Information

The Bank of China has two branches that can change cash and travellers cheques. Both are open daily.

The main post office is west of the bus station and is also a small post office inside the Oasis Hotel that handles parcels.

CITS (☎ 852 1352) has a branch on the grounds of the Oasis Hotel and can help book train and plane tickets, as well as arrange tours of local sights.

The PSB is on Gaochang Lu, in the north of town.

Shì Màoyì Shìchǎng 市贸易市场
Bazaar

While this market is fun to poke around, it's nothing like its more exotic counterpart in Kashgar. At the front you'll find a few stalls selling brightly decorated knives, Muslim clothing and some other interesting items, but as you move towards the back it's mainly household goods and synthetic fabrics.

Qīngzhēn Sì 清真寺
City Mosque

There are several mosques in town. The Qīngzhēn Sì, the most active of them, is on the western outskirts about 3km from the town centre. Take care not to disturb the worshippers. You can get here by bicycle.

Émǐn Tǎ 额敏塔
Emin Minaret

Also known as Sūgōng Tǎ, this tower and adjoining mosque is just 3km from Turpan on the eastern edge of town. It's designed in a simple Afghani style and was built in 1777 by the local ruler, Emin Hoja.

The minaret is circular, 44m high and tapers towards the top. The temple is bare inside, but services are held every Friday and on holidays. The surrounding scenery is nice, and from the roof of the mosque you can get a good view of the Turpan oasis. You can't climb the minaret: it was closed off to tourists in 1989 to help preserve the structure.

You can walk or bicycle here, although many people stop on a minibus tour. The mosque is open during daylight hours and entry is Y12.

Places to Stay

All hotels in Turpan increase their already inflated prices during the hot summer months. During this period the first thing you will probably be looking for, other than a pool, is air-con in working order.

Right next to the bus station, the *Jiāotōng Bīnguǎn* (☎ 853 1320) is pretty noisy, but is definitely the cheapest spot in town. It has very basic dorms with fans from Y8 to Y18 per person. Twins with attached bath and air-con cost Y40 or Y80.

The most popular abode of backpackers is the *Oasis Hotel* (Lǚzhōu Bīnguǎn, ☎ 852 2491). Beds in a quad with air-con and common showers cost Y27. Twins, including a Uyghur-style room, are a ridiculous Y350. The hotel enjoys a quiet location and has a fairly nice courtyard with grapevine

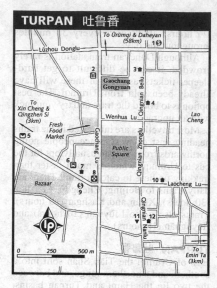

TURPAN 吐鲁番

trellises and tree-lined walkways. They have a Web site at www.the-silk-road.com.

The *Xīnhuá Bīnguǎn* (☎ 852 0169) is just north of the Oasis Hotel and has clean dorms in triples/quads for Y35/30. Good value singles are Y80 and a bed in a twin costs Y60. The only drawback are the common toilets, which are often filthy.

The *Tǔlǔfān Bīnguǎn* (☎ 852 1416, fax 852 3262) has a nice vine-trellised courtyard, a beer garden, quiet rooms and even a swimming pool. It has air-con dorms for Y30, triples for Y220 and over-priced twins for Y350 (although CITS will book you into these for Y200). The *Liángmào Bīnguǎn* (Grain Trade Hotel; ☎ 852 4301) is an uninteresting but friendly place that has dorm beds from Y20 and twins for Y160, although it should be easy to bargain them down.

Places to Eat

There is a string of small *restaurants* along Laocheng Lu, between Gaochang Lu and Qingnian Lu. Quite a few have English menus, and the food is generally good and reasonably priced. Most of the places serve Sìchuān and other Han-style dishes, but you can also get Uyghur food on request.

TURPAN

PLACES TO STAY
3 Xīnhuá Bīnguǎn
新华宾馆
4 Oasis Hotel; CITS
绿洲宾馆
中国国际旅行社
7 Jiāotōng Bīnguǎn
交通宾馆
10 Liángmào Bīnguǎn
粮贸宾馆

12 Tǔlǔfān Bīnguǎn
吐鲁番宾馆

OTHER
1 Bank of China
中国银行
2 Turpan Museum
吐鲁番博物馆
5 Post Office
邮局

6 Long-Distance
Bus Station
长途汽车站
8 Department
Store
吐鲁番百货大楼
9 Bank of China
中国银行
11 John's Information Cafe
约翰中西餐厅

Opposite the Tǔlǔfān Bīnguǎn is *John's Information Cafe*. This is the only place in town that does good western food, but there are Chinese meals available too. The menu is in English, prices are reasonable and you can even get cold drinks with ice (much appreciated in Turpan's heat!).

Entertainment

A traditional Uyghur music, song and dance show is staged in the *courtyard* of the Tǔlǔfān Bīnguǎn under the trellises almost nightly in the high season. In the low season, performances take place on the 2nd floor of the hotel restaurant building. It's possible to order a decent meal here prior to the performance.

During the summer the shows are held almost every night from around 10 pm. They're fun nights that usually end up with the front row of the audience being dragged out to dance with the performers. Tickets are Y20.

Getting There & Away

The bus station is near the bazaar. Buses to Ürümqi (Y23; 2½ to three hours) via the new freeway leave between 8 am and 6 pm.

Minibuses to Dàhéyàn (Y6; 1½ hours) run approximately every 30 minutes between 8 am and 6 pm.

The nearest train station is at Dàhéyàn, 58km north of Turpan. (See the Dàhéyàn section for information.)

Getting Around

Public transport around Turpan is by minibus, pedicab, bicycle or donkey cart. Bicycles are most convenient for the town itself.

John's Information Cafe and the Tǔlǔfān Bīnguǎn also have bicycle rental. Pedicab drivers usually hang around the hotel gates – negotiate the fare in advance. Donkey carts can be found around the market, but this mode of transport is gradually fading.

AROUND TURPAN

There are many sights in the countryside around Turpan, and it requires at least a day to see everything of importance.

The only way to see the sights is to join a tour or hire a minibus for a full day (about 10 hours). You won't have to look for them – the drivers will come looking for you. They will find other travellers to share the expense. Figure on paying between Y40 and Y60 (depending on your bargaining skills) each. Both the tours organised by the Oasis Hotel and Tǔlǔfān Bīnguǎn include an English guide and are cheap, reliable and recommended by readers.

Make sure it's clearly understood which places you want to see. Practically no drivers speak English, but many speak fluent Japanese.

Don't underestimate the weather. The desert sun is hot – damn hot – and it can bake your brain in less time than it takes to make fried rice. Essential survival gear includes a water bottle, sunglasses and a straw hat. Some sunscreen and vaseline (or chapstick) for your lips will prove useful.

Āsītǎnà Gǔmùqū 阿斯塔那古墓区
Astana Graves
These graves, where the dead of Gāochāng are buried, lie north-west of the ancient city.

XĪNJIĀNG 新疆

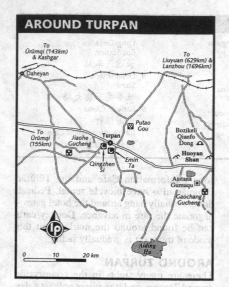

AROUND TURPAN

To Ūrūmqi (143km) & Kashgar
Daheyan
To Liuyuan (629km) & Lanzhou (1696km)
To Ūrūmqi (155km)
Putao Gou
Jiaohe Gucheng
Turpan
Bozikeli Qianfo Dong
Huoyan Shan
Qingzhen Si
Emin Ta
Asitana Gumuqu
Gaochang Gucheng
Aiding Hu
0   10   20 km

Only three of the tombs are open to tourists, and each of these is approached by a short flight of steps that lead down to the burial chamber about 6m below ground level.

One tomb contains portraits of the deceased painted on the walls, while another has paintings of birds. The third tomb holds two well-preserved corpses like those in the museums at Ūrūmqi and Hángzhōu (one mummy from the original trio seems to have been removed to Turpan's museum).

Some of the artefacts date back as far as the Jin dynasty, from the 3rd to 5th centuries AD. The finds include silks, brocades, embroideries and many funerary objects, such as shoes, hats and sashes made of recycled paper. The last turned out to be quite special for archaeologists, since the paper included deeds, records of slave purchases, orders for silk and other everyday transactions. Admission is Y10.

Gāochāng Gùchéng 高昌故城
Gaochang Ruins
About 46km east of Turpan are the ruins of Gāochāng, the capital of the Uyghurs when they moved into the Xīnjiāng region from Mongolia in the 9th century.

The town was founded in the 7th century during the Tang dynasty and became a major staging post on the Silk Road. The walls of the city are clearly visible. They stood as thick as 12m, formed a rough square with a perimeter of 6km, and were surrounded by a moat. Gāochāng was divided into an outer city, an inner city within the walls, and a palace and government compound.

A large monastery in the south-western part of the city is in reasonable condition, with some of its rooms, corridors and doorways still preserved. The entry fee is Y10.

Huǒyàn Shān 火焰山
Flaming Mountains
North of Gāochāng lie the aptly named Huǒyàn Shān – they look like they're on fire in the midday sun. Purplish-brown in colour, they are 100km long and 10km wide. The minibus tours don't usually include a stop here, but they drive through on the way to Bózīkèlǐ Qiānfó Dòng (Bezeklik Thousand Buddha Caves).

The Huǒyàn Shān were made famous in Chinese literature by the classic novel *Journey to the West*. The story is about the monk Xuan Zang and his followers who travelled west in search of the Buddhist sutra. The mountains were a formidable barrier which they had to cross.

Bózīkèlǐkè Qiānfó Dòng
柏孜克里克千佛洞
Bezeklik Thousand Buddha Caves
On the north-western side of the Huǒyàn Shān, on a cliff face fronting a river valley, are the remains of these Buddhist cave temples. All the caves are in dreadful condition, most having been devastated by Muslims or robbed by all and sundry.

The large statues that stood at the back of each cave have been destroyed or stolen, and the faces of the buddhas ornamenting the walls have either been scrapped or completely gouged out. Particularly active in the export of murals was a German, Albert von Le Coq, who removed whole frescoes from the stone walls and transported them back to the Berlin Museum – where Allied bombing wiped most of them out during WWII.

Today the caves reveal little more than a hint of what these works of art were like in their heyday, those that remain are usually tacky replicas. Fortunately, the scenery just outside the caves is fine. Admission is Y12.

Pútao Gōu 葡萄沟
Grape Valley

This small paradise, a thick maze of vines and grape trellises, is surrounded by stark desert. Most of the minibus tours stop here for lunch; the food isn't bad, and there are plenty of grapes in season (late August to early September is best).

There is a winery (*guǒjiǔchǎng*) near the valley and lots of well-ventilated brick buildings for drying grapes – wine and raisins are major exports of Turpan. CITS runs an annual 'grape festival' in August, featuring dancing singing, wine-tasting and, of course, a lot of grape eating.

Tempting as it might be, don't pick the grapes here or anywhere else in Turpan. There is a Y15 fine if you do. Considerable effort goes into raising these grapes and the farmers don't appreciate tourists eating their profits. There's a Y10 entry fee for the Pútao Gōu.

Jiāohé Gùchéng 交河故城
Jiaohe Ruins

During the Han dynasty, Jiāohé was established by the Chinese as a garrison town to defend the borderlands. The city was decimated by Genghis Khan's 'travelling road show' and there's little left to see.

The buildings are rather more obvious than the ruins of Gāochāng though, and you can walk through the old streets and along the roads. A main road cuts through the city, and at the end is a large monastery with figures of Buddha still visible.

The ruins are around 7km to 8km west of Turpan and stand on an island bound by two small rivers – thus the name Jiāohé, which means 'confluence of two rivers'. During the cooler months you can cycle out here without any problem. Entry costs Y12.

Àidīng Hú 艾丁湖
Aydingkol Lake

At the very bottom of the Turpan depression is Àidīng Hú, 154m below sea level. The 'lake' usually has little water – it's a huge, muddy evaporating pond with a surface of crystallised salt, but technically it's the second lowest lake in the world, surpassed only by the Dead Sea in Israel and Jordan.

Most of the tours don't stop here. If you want to see Àidīng Hú, tell your driver and expect to pay extra for the additional distance. And be forewarned that it's a pretty rough ride.

Foreign Devils on the Silk Road

Adventurers on the road to Xīnjiāng might like to reflect on an earlier group of European adventurers who descended on Chinese Turkestan, as Xīnjiāng was then known, and carted off early Buddhist art treasures by the tonne at the turn of the century.

The British first began to take an interest in the Central Asian region from their imperial base in India. They heard from oasis dwellers in the Taklamakan Desert of legendary ancient cities buried beneath the sands of the desert. In 1864 William Johnson was the first British official to sneak into the region, visiting one of these fabled lost cities in its tomb of sand close to Hotan. He was soon followed by Sir Douglas Forsyth, who made a report on his exploits: *On the Buried Cities in the Shifting Sands of the Great Desert of Gobi*. Not long afterwards, the race to unearth the treasures beneath the desert's 'shifting sands' was on.

By 1914, expeditions by Swedes, Hungarians, Germans, Russians, Japanese and French had all taken their share of the region's archaeological treasures. While these explorers were feted and lionised by adoring publics at home, the Chinese today commonly see them as robbers who stripped the region of its past. Defenders point to the wide-scale destruction that took place during the Cultural Revolution and to the defacing of Buddhist artworks by Muslims who stumbled across them. Whatever the case, today most of Central Asia's finest archaeological finds are scattered across the museums of Europe.

Karez

The *karez* is a peculiarly Central Asian means of irrigation that can be found in Xīnjiāng, Afghanistan and Iran. Like many dry, arid countries Xīnjiāng has great underground reservoirs of water, which can transform otherwise barren stretches of land – if you can get the water up. This subterranean water is often so far underground that drilling or digging for it, with primitive equipment, is virtually impossible.

Long ago the Uyghurs devised a better way. They dig a karez, known as the 'head well', on higher ground, where snowmelt from the mountains collects (in Turpan's case the Bogda Mountains). A long underground tunnel is then dug to conduct this water down to the village farmland. A whole series of vertical wells, looking from above like giant anthills, are dug every 20m along the path of this tunnel to aid construction and provide access. The wells are fed entirely by gravity, thus eliminating the need for pumps. Furthermore, having the channels underground greatly reduces water loss from evaporation.

Digging a karez is skilled and dangerous work and the *karez-kans* are respected and highly paid workers. The cost of making and maintaining a karez was traditionally split between a whole village and the karez was communally owned.

The city of Turpan owes its existence to these vital wells and channels, some of which were constructed over 2000 years ago. There are over a thousand wells, and the total length of the channels runs to an incredible 5000km, all constructed by hand and without modern machinery or building materials.

KÙCHĒ 库车

The oasis town of Kùchē (Kuqa) was another key stop on the ancient Silk Road. Scattered around the area are eight **Qiānfó Dòng** (Thousand Buddha Caves), which rival those of Dūnhuáng, Dàtóng and Luòyáng. There are also at least four ancient ruined cities in the area.

The Buddhist cave paintings and ruined cities in the area are remains of a pre-Islamic Buddhist civilisation. When the 7th century Chinese monk Xuan Zang passed through Kùchē he recorded that the city's western gate was flanked by two enormous 30m-high buddha statues, and that there was a number of monasteries in the area decorated with beautiful Buddhist frescoes; 1200 years later, the German archaeologist-adventurers Grünwedel and Le Coq removed many of these paintings and sculptures and took them to Berlin.

Sadly, modern-day Kùchē retains little, if any, of its former glory. There is still some traditional architecture remaining, and traffic jams of donkey-cart taxis add some appeal. But for most people, it's the sights outside the town that would justify a stop here.

Orientation & Information

There is no real town centre as such, but the main thoroughfare is Renmin Lu, which connects the new and old parts of town. The bus station is in the east of town and the train station is an isolated 5km south-east of here.

CITS (☎ 712 2005) is located in the Qiūcī Bīnguǎn, a hotel in the west of town on Tianshan Lu.

Qiūcī Gùchéng 龟兹故城
Qiuci Ancient City Ruins

These ruins are all that is left of the ancient capital of Qiūcī. Qiūcī was one of several ancient feudal states in what was once loosely called the Western Region of China.

Qiūcī has had several name changes. During the Han dynasty it was named Yancheng, but in the Tang era (when Xuan Zang dropped in) it was called Yiluolu. The ruins are along the main road, about a 10-minute walk west of the Qiūcī Bīnguǎn.

Lǎochéng Bāzā & Qīngzhēn Dàsì
老城巴扎与清真大寺
Bazaar & Great Mosque

Every Friday a large bazaar is held about 2.5km west of town, next to a bridge on Renmin Lu. Traders come in from around the countryside to ply their crafts, wares and foodstuffs. While the local tourism offices are trying to make it a sightseeing draw, the bazaar is thus far largely a local affair, and is worth a visit.

About 150m farther west from the bazaar is the Qīngzhēn Dàsì (Great Mosque), Kùchē's main centre for Muslim worship. Though large in size, the mosque is a fairly modest affair, but some of the carvings around the main gateway are quite elaborate.

Places to Stay & Eat
The cheapest spot in town, without question, is the *Jiāotōng Bīnguǎn* (☎ 712 2682), which is next door to the bus station. Dorm beds in quads/twins are Y10/20, while twins with attached bath are Y60. There is usually hot water after 10 pm. If you are staying in the dorms and need a shower, there are public showers next door for Y1 a wash.

The *Kùchē Xiǎo Bīnguǎn* (☎ 712 2844) offers nicer surroundings with a large courtyard. Simple, clean twins go for Y40 a bed, however it may try and add a foreigners' surcharge. Be polite but firm and the staff may back down. If not, go elsewhere. Hot showers are available in the evenings or on demand. The hotel is in the north-west of town, just off the end of Jianshe Lu, look for the small sign.

The *Kùchē Fàndiàn* (☎ 712 0285) is a little out of town, but offers the best value accommodation. In addition to spacious twins and triples for Y80/100, it also has a swimming pool, sauna, spa and a beauty salon the size of a cinema. You will probably need a guided tour to avoid getting lost. Bus No 6 from the train station travels here, or it's a 10-minute walk east from the bus station.

The *restaurant* at the Kùchē Fàndiàn serves tasty Chinese food, but the best place to get a bite to eat is at one of the *stalls* in the market. There are the usual kebabs, noodles and breads available for a few yuán. If you would prefer to eat indoors, then try the *Mùsīlín Cāntīng*, on Wenhua Lu, near the corner of Jiefang Lu. It has cheap and tasty kebabs, lāmiàn noodles and cold beer.

Getting There & Away
Air When we last visited the weekly flight to Ürümqi had been cancelled indefinitely.

Bus Since the completion of the train line to Kashgar in late 1999, the bus station will be of minor consequence for most travellers. If you prefer the rattle and bump of bus travel, then there is a daily sleeper to Kashgar (Y120), which takes around 16 hours, barring breakdowns and bad weather.

From Kùchē there are four bumpy sleeper buses to Ürümqi (Y120; 22 hours) daily. There is also one daily bus to Yīníng (Y56; 22 hours): a spectacular trip crossing the Tianshan Range.

Train The best way to visit Kùchē is by train from either Kashgar or Turpan. If you want to purchase sleeper tickets, then it would be best to get to the train station at least 10 minutes before it opens at 10.30 am on the day of departure. There is also a ticket office at the bus station that sells tickets for trains that depart from Korla and Ürümqi.

Getting Around
Taxi Kùchē's sights are scattered around the surrounding countryside, and the only way to get to see them is to hire a vehicle. CITS can arrange jeep or car hire for the day, however taxi drivers will offer better rates.

Within town, taxi rides are a standard Y10 per trip, while horse or donkey carts are generally Y2 to Y3, depending on the distance.

AROUND KÙCHĒ
Kèzīěr Qiānfó Dòng 克孜尔千佛洞
Kizil Thousand Buddha Caves
There are quite a lot of Qiānfó Dòng (Thousand Buddha Caves) around Kùchē, but the most important site is this one, 72km to the west of Kùchē in Bàichéng Xiàn (Baicheng County). The caves date back to the 3rd century AD and are believed to have taken over 500 years to complete.

Although there are more than 230 caves here, only 24 are generally open to the public. Sadly, most of the caves have been damaged by both religious attacks and the elements over the centuries. The caves are divided into eastern and western sections. In the eastern section the caves are more general in style and include many depictions of the Buddhist legends. The western caves contain paintings that depict the life of Sakyamuni (the 'historical Buddha').

Entry to each of the sections costs Y25. Access to additional caves can cost up to Y150 per cave! More caves are planned to be open to the public in the near future. If you visit during the summer months, you are compensated with delicious berries and grapes that can be freely picked from the orchard in front of the caves. The caves are open daily from 9.30 am to 8 pm.

The easiest way to get to the caves is to hire a vehicle. CITS charges Y300 for the return trip, while private taxi drivers offer rates of around Y150 to Y200. It is also possible to catch the Bàichéng bus from Kùchē and get off at the turn off to the caves. It is still another 11km along a dirt track, so you will need to hitch the rest of the way.

Other Buddhist cave sites around Kùchē include **Kumtura** and **Kizilgaha**. Kumtura is theoretically closed, but CITS can arrange exclusive visits. The catch: Y450 for the privilege of viewing the caves here. Considering that it takes most of the day to get there and back, most travellers opt to forgo this particular trip.

The one-way journey to Kèzǐěr or Kazilgaha takes 1½ hours, and to Kumtura around four hours.

Gùchéng 故城
Ancient City Ruins
Aside from Qiūcí (in Kùchē itself), there are several other ruined cities in the region. Around 23km to the north-east of Kùchē is the ancient city of Sūbāshí Gùchéng. About 20km to the south of Kùchē is the ancient city of Wushkat.

About 60km south-west of Kùchē is Tonggusibashi, one of the largest and best preserved of the ruined cities. Again you'll need to hire a vehicle to get to these spots; rates are similar to those for the Kèzǐěr Qiānfó Dòng.

South-West Xīnjiāng – Kashgaria

Kashgaria is the historical name for the western Tarim Basin. Despite its present isolation, Kashgaria was a major hub of the Silk Road and has bristled with activity for over 2000 years. A ring of oasis lined with poplar trees and centred around weekly bazaars remain a testament to the mercantile tradition. The region remains the heartland of the Uyghur.

KASHGAR 喀什
Even as the 20th century draws to a close, the name Kashgar (Kāshí) still sparks images of a remote desert oasis, the sole outpost of civilisation leading from the vast deserts of Xīnjiāng to the icy peaks of the Karakoram. Desert brigands, exotic bazaars and colourful silks spring to mind at the mention of China's westernmost city.

Kashgar is no longer so remote, and the modern age has certainly taken its toll (emphatically symbolised by the statue of Chairman Mao – one of the largest in China). Kashgar is only 1½ hours by plane from Ürümqi, or less than two days by sleeper bus. The old town walls have been torn down, flashy red taxis with blaring horns congest the sidewalks and Chinese super freeways encircle the beleaguered old town. In October 1999 the railway link from Ürümqi was formally opened, sounding what many fear will be the death-knell for traditional Kashgar.

Even so, Kashgar retains an intoxicating air of the exotic, mainly due to its fascinating ethnic mix of Uyghurs (who comprise the majority of the population), Tajiks, Kyrgyz, Uzbeks and a growing number of Han Chinese. Some things haven't changed since medieval times – blacksmiths, carpenters and cobblers use hand tools in the old quarter and the Id Kah Mosque draws the town's faithful as it has since 1442. Markets with rows of shimmering silks, knives and jewellery vie for your attention and narrow backstreets lined with earthenwalled homes beckon for exploration.

Kashgar has been a Silk Road trading centre for two millennia and traders from Kazakhstan, Kyrgyzstan, Pakistan and even Russia (along with travellers from around the globe) continue to fuel the city with impromptu street-corner negotiations, perpetual bazaars, and hotel-room deals with Gilgit traders. Shifting geopolitics have reopened lines of communication and it's not hard to imagine a new high-tech Silk Road recrossing the Tarim Basin one day. Kashgar's future, it seems, lies firmly rooted in its past.

With all the trading activity, one couldn't call Kashgar 'laid-back', but it has a great atmosphere and it is a fine place to settle back for a week or so. The town is also a good launching pad for trips along the southern Silk Road to Hotan, over the Torugart Pass to Kyrgyzstan or south to beautiful Karakul Lake and the stunning Karakoram Highway to Pakistan.

Kashgar experiences blistering hot summers, although at 1290m above sea level it's cooler than Turpan, Kùchē and other stops along the Xīnjiāng section of the Silk Road.

Orientation

Official (Chinese) street names are given here. The town centre is a Tiānānmén-style square north of Rénmín Gōngyuán (People's Park), dominated by a statue of Mao Zedong. The Uyghur old town lies just north of here, bisected by Jiefang Beilu. The budget travellers' enclave is on the west side. The grounds of the Sunday Market are on the east side.

Information

John's Cafe (☎/fax 282 4186, ✉ Johncafe@public.qd.sd.cn) organises bookings, transport and excursions and can link you up with other budget-minded tourists to share costs. The cafe is a good place in town to meet travellers and swap information.

At some point in your stay you are bound to bump in to Ablimit Ghopor (aka 'Elvis'). Elvis' main business is buying and selling carpets but he also takes tourists on offbeat tours of the old town to visit anything from

a local *pir* or holy man, to a traditional Uyghur house or local teahouse, where he can act as translator and cultural interpreter. This is a great chance to find out about traditional Uyghur life in Kashgar. He can normally be found at the Oasis Cafe (see Places to Eat) between 4 and 6 pm.

Money The central Bank of China, at 239 Renmin Xilu, can change travellers cheques and cash and can also give quick cash advances on major credit cards. Bank summer hours are weekdays from 9.30 am to 1.30 pm and 4 to 8 pm, and weekends from 11 am to 3 pm. You can also sell RMB back into dollars at the bank's foreign exchange desk if you have exchange receipts; a good idea if you are headed to Tashkurgan, where the bank hours are erratic.

Post & Communications The post office at 40 Renmin Xilu is open daily from 10 am to 8 pm.

Across the road is China Telecom, open daily from 9.30 am to 8 pm.

Email & Internet Access New Century, at 243 Seman Lu, offers Internet access for Y30 an hour, as well as a copier service and some travel information.

New Era, in the plaza outside the Chini Bagh Gate, also charges Y30 an hour. Both are theoretically open 24 hours. Try going online early in the morning or late at night to avoid slow downloads. John's Cafe has Internet access at Y40 an hour.

Travel Agencies The main CITS office (☎ 282 8473, fax 282 3087) is up two flights of stairs in a building inside the Chini Bagh. However, the more useful CITS Foreign Independent Traveller branch is just inside the gate. CTS (☎ 283 2875, fax 282 2552) is up two more flights in the same building, but it also has an independent office for small groups and individuals in the plaza facing Shengli Lu, outside the Chini Bagh Gate. CTS is consistently cheaper than CITS.

The Kashgar Mountaineering Association or KMA (*takka chkesh* in Uyghur;

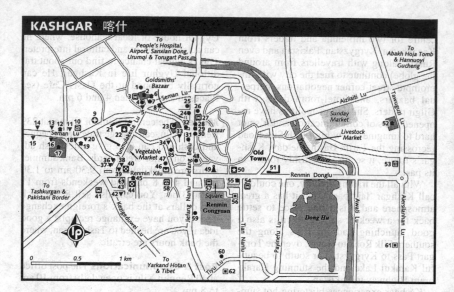

KASHGAR 喀什

dengshān xiéhuì in Chinese) is a government liaison office for expeditions and group sports travel and will help individuals with guides or vehicles, though both are scarce in the high season. The office (☎ 282 3680, fax 282 2957) is far away at 45 Tiyu Lu, off Jiefang Nanlu beyond the CAAC.

PSB The PSB is at 111 Yunmulakexia Lu. A friendlier office is located at 67 Renmin Donglu, north-east of Rénmín Gōngyuán. Alien Travel Permits (Wàibīn Tōngxíng Zhèng), for areas not freely open to foreigners, cost Y50 a pop.

You can get a month-long visa extension here too; price depends on nationality. The office is open weekdays from 9.30 am to 1.30 pm and 4 to 8 pm.

Medical Services The main Chinese hospital is People's Hospital (Rénmín Yīyuàn) on Jiefang Beilu, north of the river. There's a Hospital of Traditional Uyghur Medicine on Seman Lu about 500m east of the Sèmǎn Bīnguǎn, though it is reportedly none too clean. A small clinic under the CITS building in the Chini Bagh compound can

administer first aid and medicines; some staff speak English.

Dangers & Annoyances Travellers have lost money or passports to pickpockets at the Sunday Market, in the ticket scrum at the bus station, and even on local buses, so keep yours tucked away.

Some foreign women walking the streets alone have been sexually harassed, by both locals and visiting Pakistanis. The Muslim Uyghur women dress in long skirts and heavy stockings like the Uyghur women in Ürümqi and Turpan, but here one sees more female faces hidden behind veils of brown gauze. It's wise for women travellers to dress as would be appropriate in any Muslim country, covering arms and legs. This should be second nature for travellers who have come from Pakistan but it may come as a surprise if you've come from Kyrgyzstan, Kazakhstan or eastern China.

Sunday Market

Once a week Kashgar's population swells by 50,000 as people stream in to the Sunday Market (Xīngqīrì Shìchǎng) – surely the most mind-boggling bazaar in Asia, and not

KASHGAR

PLACES TO STAY

- 2 Chini Bagh Hotel
  其尼瓦克宾馆
- 6 Kashgar-Gilgit International
  Hotel
  友谊宾馆
- 8 Noor Bish Hotel
  脑北西旅社
- 12 Huáqiáo Bīnguǎn
  喀什华侨宾馆
- 17 Sèmǎn Bīnguǎn
  色满宾馆
- 19 Sèmǎn Bīnguǎn No.3
  Building
  色满宾馆第3号
- 45 Qiánhǎi Bīnguǎn
  前海宾馆
- 52 Kashgar Hotel
  喀什噶尔宾馆
- 55 Tiānnán Fàndiàn
  天南饭店

PLACES TO EAT

- 5 Yùhuāyuàn Cāntīng;
  New Era Internet
  御花苑餐厅
  新纪元
- 11 Bakery & Teahouse
- 13 Oasis Cafe
- 14 Teahouse
  茶馆
- 15 Bakery
- 16 Pútaojià Cāntīng
  葡萄架餐厅
- 18 John's Cafe
- 20 Noor Look Kebab House
  烤肉大排挡
- 33 Night Food Market
  夜市场

- 34 Teahouse
  茶馆
- 36 Lao Shāndōng Shuǐjiǎo
  老山东水饺
- 37 Taoyuan Cānguǎn
  桃园餐厅
- 38 Chinese Food Stalls
- 39 Restaurant
  餐馆
- 42 Chinese Food Stalls

OTHER

- 1 Former British Consulate
  老英国领事馆
- 3 Buses to Pakistan
  去巴基斯坦的班车
- 4 CITS & CTS
  中国国际旅行社
- 7 CITS FIT Branch
- 9 Hospital of Traditional
  Uyghur Medicine
- 10 New Century
  新世纪打字复印店
- 21 Old Town Walls
- 22 PSB
  公安局
- 23 Id Kah Mosque
  艾提尔清真寺
- 24 Bicycle Shop
- 25 Kashgar City Traditional
  Minority Handicraft and
  Souvenir Shop
- 26 Bicycle Shop
- 27 Buses and Tuk-tuks to
  Sunday Market
- 28 Hat Bazaar
- 29 Cloth Bazaar
- 30 Dried Fruit & Nut Bazaar
- 31 Cinema
  电影院

- 32 Clocktower
- 35 Musical Instrument Shops
- 40 Caohu Department Store
  草湖商场
- 41 Regional Bus Stop
- 43 Bank of China
  中国银行
- 44 Huanjiang Shangmaocheng
  Department Store
  环疆商贸城
- 46 Post Office
  邮局
- 47 Copper & Brass Shops
- 48 Xinhua Bookstore
  新华书店
- 49 Mao Statue
  毛泽东塑像
- 50 PSB
  公安局
- 51 Old Town Walls
- 53 Kāshí Dìqū Bówùguǎn
  喀什地区博物馆
- 54 Long-Distance Bus Station
  长途汽车站
- 56 Ak Mazar
- 57 Local & Regional Bus Stand
- 58 China Telecom
  电信局
- 59 Xinjiang Airlines (CAAC)
  中国新疆航空公司
  售票处
- 60 Kashgar Mountaineering
  Association (KMA)
  喀什登山协会
- 61 Tomb of Ali Arslan Khan
  赛衣提艾里艾斯
  拉罕墓
- 62 Tomb of Yusuf Has Hajib
  玉素甫哈斯哈吉
  甫陵墓

to be missed. By sunrise the roads east of town are a sea of pedestrians, horses, bikes, motorcycles, donkey carts, trucks and belching tuk-tuks, everyone shouting *boish-boish!* (coming through!).

In arenas off the livestock market, men 'test-drive' horses or peer into sheep's mouths. A wonderful assortment of people sit by their rugs and blankets, clothing and

boots, hardware and junk, tapes and boomboxes – and, of course, hats. In fact the whole town turns into a bazaar, with hawkers everywhere. It's wonderfully photogenic so bring twice as much film as you think you might need and get there early to avoid the tour groups.

The grounds are on Aizilaiti Lu, a 30 or 40-minute walk from the Chini Bagh Gate or Sèmǎn Bīnguǎn. You can take a bike and park it in the bike-lot in front of the entrance to the carpet pavilion. Taxis are plentiful outside tourist hotels on market day, cost should be about Y10 from the Sèmǎn, less from Chini Bagh. You might catch a donkey cart outside the city centre, but negotiate a price beforehand. You can also get a minibus or passenger tuk-tuk from the east side of Id Kah Square. Ask for the Yekshenba bazaar (Sunday market). In July and August John Hu offers a free one-way minibus shuttle from his cafe after breakfast.

If the tourist crush gets to you, try the Sunday Market at Hotan (see the Southern Silk Road section).

Id Kah Mosque

The big yellow-tiled Id Kah Mosque (Ài Tígǎ'ér Qīngzhēn Sì) is one of the largest in China, with a courtyard and gardens that can hold 20,000 people during the annual Qurban Baiyram celebrations. It was built in 1442 as a smaller mosque on what was then the outskirts of town. During the Cultural Revolution Id Kah suffered heavy damage, but has since been restored. There are also more than 90 tiny neighbourhood mosques throughout the city.

It's acceptable for non-Muslims to go into Id Kah; there's a Y3 fee. Local women are rarely seen inside but western women are usually ignored if they're modestly dressed (arms and legs covered and a scarf on the head). Take off your shoes if entering carpeted areas, and be discreet about photos. In front of the mosque is Id Kah Square, which on sunny days swarms with a diverse array of locals.

At night the square comes alive with exotic food vendors and blaring televisions surrounded by dozens of onlookers.

Other Tombs

There are numerous other interesting tombs in and around Kashgar, including: Abakh Hoja Tomb (Xiāngfēi Mù), Tomb of Yusup Has Hajip (Yùsùfǔ Hāsī Hājífǔ Mù), Tomb of Ali Arslan Khan (Aīěrsīlánhǎn Qīngzhēnsì) and Ak Mazar (Bái Mázā).

Gùchéng 故城
Old Town

Sprawling all around Id Kah are roads full of Uyghur shops and narrow passages lined with adobe houses that seem trapped in a time warp.

At the east end of Seman Lu stands a 10m-high section of the old town walls, at least 500 years old. Another rank of them are visible from Yunmulakexia Lu opposite the vegetable market. Construction around, on and in them makes access impossible, and there's clearly no interest in preserving them.

Kāshí Dìqū Bówùguǎn
喀什地区博物馆
Kashgar Regional Museum

At the time of research a new 'Silk Road Cultural Relic Show' was due to open at this museum, which is out on the eastern edge of Kashgar. The museum is open daily from 9.30 am to 1.30 pm and 4 to 8 pm; entry costs Y10.

Sānxiān Dòng 三仙洞
Three Immortals Caves

Twenty kilometres north of Kashgar is one of the area's few traces of the flowering of Buddhism, the Sānxiān Dòng, three grottoes high on a sandstone cliff, one of which has some peeling frescoes. Unfortunately, the cliff is too sheer to climb, so it's a bit of a disappointment. Watch for them if you enter Kashgar via the Torugart Pass.

Hànnuòyī Gùchéng & Mù'ěr Fótǎ
Ha Noi Ruins & Mor Pagoda

At the end of a jarring 35km drive northeast of town are the ruins of Ha Noi, a Tang dynasty town built in the 7th century and abandoned in the 12th century. Little remains except a great solid pyramid-like structure and the huge Mor Pagoda or stupa.

CITS will take you to Ha Noi for Y200 per Land Cruiser, or hire a car from CTS for Y63 per person. John Hu, at John's Cafe, charges Y350 per car.

Places to Stay – Budget

Accommodation is tighter on the days preceding the Sunday Market than afterward.

Low season, or for stays of more than a few days, you may be able to coax out some discounts. Except at very budget places, Chinese-style squat loos are rare.

The *Chini Bagh Hotel* (*Qíníwāké Bīnguǎn;* ☎ 282 2084, fax 282 3842, 93 Seman Lu) is a five-storey tower where the British consulate's front gate used to be, located conveniently close to the old town. Spartan but clean triples/quads with hot shower are Y25/20 per bed. Clean doubles with hot shower in the main building are Y120; very nice carpeted singles/doubles with TV in the Jingyuan annex are Y120/180, however at the time of research the annex was being renovated and prices may have gone up. All rooms are discounted by Y20 without breakfast. The complex has Chinese and Uyghur restaurants, souvenirs, travel agencies and a coffee shop.

The *Sèmàn Bīnguǎn* (☎ 282 2147, fax 282 2861, 170 Seman Lu) dominates the courtyard of the old Russian consulate, and is probably the most popular place for backpackers, due more to the good amenities nearby than the quality of the rooms. The 500-bed complex has three buildings, a restaurant, a laundry service, shady gardens and enough overpriced souvenir shops to occupy days.

Dorms of two to six beds with common bathroom are Y15 per person. Spartan doubles with common bath cost Y30 per person, while small, musty and overpriced doubles with private bathroom in No 2 block go for Y60 per person. Rooms on the 2nd floor are dangerously close to the hotel's karaoke bar. Better doubles in No 1 block go for Y280.

Building No 3 is actually across the street above John's Cafe. Compact but carpeted doubles cost Y30 per person and come with a bathroom and hot water. Standards vary, so check more than one room. The place is particularly popular with Pakistani traders.

The *Huáqiáo Bīnguǎn* (*Overseas Chinese Hotel;* ☎ 283 3262), across the road (on the site of a building bombed by militants in 1993), has hot, decaying rooms with medieval plumbing for a negotiable Y30 per person.

The *Tiānnán Fàndiàn*, near the bus station, has dreary doubles for Y30, Y50 or Y90 per bed, depending on the building. Building No 1 also has grim triples and quads for Y20/16 per bed. Showers are communal except for the most expensive doubles; hot water is available in the evening only.

The *Noor Bish Hotel* (*Nǎobèixī Lǔshé;* ☎ 282 3092) is a small Uyghur guesthouse just off the road that connects the Chini Bagh to the Id Kah Square. Basic rooms set around a pleasant courtyard cost between Y10 and Y20, though you might well get unwelcome attention from the PSB for staying here.

Places to Stay – Mid-Range

The *Kashgar Hotel* (*Kāshí Gě'ěr Bīnguǎn;* ☎ 261 4954, fax 261 4679), also called the Kashgar Guesthouse, has seen better days. The spacious, dusty 200-room compound has Chinese and Uyghur restaurants and a beer garden. Carpeted doubles with telephone and hot shower are Y200, or Y250 with TV and bathtub. Quads with bath and TV are better value at Y200. The drawback is that it's 3km east of the centre, although taxis (about Y5 to the centre) linger at the gate. Bus No 10 goes to the Id Kah Mosque and Rénmín Gōngyuán, or you can rent a bike from the hotel for Y3 an hour.

The *Qiánhǎi Bīnguǎn* (☎ 282 2922, 48 Renmin Xilu), tucked back about 50m from the street, is aimed squarely at the mobile phone-toting Chinese nouveaux riche. Plush but smoky air-conditioned doubles are a decent Y240, or larger suites for Y500. The hotel has two restaurants, a business centre, a meeting hall, and some basic exercise facilities.

Kashgar-Gilgit International Hotel (*Yǒuyì Bīnguǎn;* ☎ 282 4173, fax 282 3842), the high-rise tower in the Chini Bagh's front yard, is a joint venture between CITS and Gilgit's Northern Areas Trading Cooperative. It's poor value for tourists; comfortable but damp doubles with bath are an undeserving Y280 with breakfast, but Y700 gets you an alarmingly large, plush suite. The friendly staff accept all major credit cards and there's a branch of the Bank of China here.

The former Russian consulate at the back of the **Sèmǎn Bīnguǎn** (see Places to Stay – Budget) has been converted into five standard rooms (Y400) and two suites (Y600). Nicely decorated and oozing atmosphere this is the must-stay choice of the well-heeled

Great Game aficionado (see the boxed text 'Listening Posts of the Great Game').

Places to Eat

Uyghur Food The best way to sample Uyghur food is at the *food stalls* outside Id Kah Mosque. Vendors sell noodles, chickpeas, poached eggs, kebabs, breads, boiled

---

Listening Posts of the Great Game

The British and Russian rivalry across the Pamir Range was matched by personal rivalries across town – for information, influence and even Silk Road antiquities. The Russian and British consulates in Kashgar quickly became listening posts on the front line of the Great Game. While opening up mountain routes and expanding trade, the consul-generals kept an anxious ear open for news of political alliances and military manoeuvres.

In 1890, 24-year old George Macartney arrived with Francis Younghusband to set up the British office (Chini Bagh) in Kashgar. Younghusband left a year later; Macartney remained for the next 28. Eventually George was joined by wife Catherine, who gradually turned the Chini Bagh into an island of European civility, with cuttings from English gardens, exotic flowers, and pear and apple trees. Ping-pong tables were set up indoors and tennis courts were built nearby. Brahms records provided melodious lullabies and eventually a piano was shipped over the mountain passes. Explorers such as Aurel Stein and Albert Von le Coq called at the Chini Bagh on their way to the sandy wastes of the Taklamakan Desert, and Peter Fleming enjoyed his first bath and coffee there for over five months. Subsequent consuls included Percy Etherton, Clarmont Skrine (1922), George Gillan, Thompson Glover, and Eric Shipton (1940-42 and 1946-48).

Across town the Russian consuls made similar attempts at introducing luxuries, vying for the company of passing westerners and gaining the favour of information. The Russian consul Nikolai Petrovsky once gave Macartney a much-coveted pane of glass, only to demand it back (secured by his Cossack guard) after a sensitive issue involving a political cartoon. Following the incident the two didn't speak to each other for 2½ years. Subsequent Russian consuls included Mestchersky, who later fled the Bolshevik revolution in Russia and ended up in Paris, working as a waiter while his wife became a chambermaid. Ironically, the Russian consulate in Kashgar became a safe haven for White Russians, including Paul Nazarov, who sought refuge here for four years, until the Bolshiviks took the consulate in 1925.

Both consulates were closed down in 1949, though the Chini Bagh functioned as a British representative office to India and Pakistan for a while. The consulates remain today as the Chini Bagh and Sèmǎn Hotels.

The Chini Bagh Hotel is built right smack in front of the old consulate, whose main floor is now a Chinese banquet hall. The upper three-room suite, finished in 1913, is awaiting renovation, but you may be able to talk your way upstairs to the living quarters and enjoy the view from the flat roof, where one consul's wife was shot through the shoulder during the Dungan rebellion of 1934.

The Russian consulate has fared better than the Chini Bagh and remains in the form of atmospheric suites in the courtyard behind the Sèmǎn Bīnguǎn. The well-appointed suites cost Y400 and Y600 and are a must for Great Game buffs and romantics.

To recreate a flavour of these lost times try reading Diana Shipton's *The Antique Land* (wife of Eric Shipton) or Catherine Macartney's *An English Lady in Chinese Turkistan*.

---

goat heads, chicken and fried fish; bring your own fork. For desert you can try watermelon by the slice, vanilla ice cream, *tangzaza* (triangles of glutinous rice covered in syrup), *kharsen meghriz* (fried dough balls filled with sugar, raisins and walnuts), or just a glass of hot milk and a pastry.

The *Yùhuāyuàn Cāntíng (Imperial Garden Restaurant)*, in the plaza outside the Chini Bagh Gate, has good, cheap Uyghur food, quick service and clean surroundings. Recommended is the *suoman* (spicy noodles) or *suoman goshsiz* (spicy noodles without meat) for Y4.

The *Noor Look Kebab House (Kăoròu Dàpái)*, inside a cool courtyard at 285 Seman Lu, specialises in kebabs, but the staff will cook up anything if you can explain it.

The Chini Bagh Hotel, Sèmăn Bīnguăn and Kashgar Hotel each have clean, but boring, Muslim dining halls where you can eat fixed Uyghur meals during limited hours.

Chinese Food Chinese fast food stalls serve up oily but cheap lunches in an alley off Renmin Xilu, behind the Bank of China. This is a good option for vegetarians; just point and pay, a tray of ready-cooked food costs about Y5. Go at noon when the food is hot.

At night, tables are set up outside the Chinese restaurants on Yunmulakexia Lu, north of Renmin Xilu, selling beer and cheap snacks. Among the snails and chicken's feet are more appealing offerings such as *shāguō* (vegetables, tofu and mushroom broth in an earthenware pot), *shuǐjiǎo* (ravioli) and *húndun* (wanton soup). The nearby *Lao Shāndōng Shuǐjiǎo* is recommended for shuijiao – order by the bowl or the *jin* (500g is enough for two).

The *Taoyuan Cānguăn* is one of several alongside the night market that offer good value authentic Chinese food.

The *Chinese Restaurant* at the Chini Bagh Hotel and the *Pútaojià Cāntíng (Grapevine Restaurant)*, inside the courtyard of the Sèmăn Bīnguăn, serve decent Chinese at mid-range prices. Both *John's Cafe* and the *Oasis Cafe* offer large quasi-Chinese menus in English, from which you can satisfy a raging hunger for under Y15

(it also serves chips and an adequate western breakfast in a 'street cafe' atmosphere).

Shopping

Souvenirs For serious shopping go to the old town; Sunday Market prices tend to be higher. The citizens of Kashgar have been selling things for 2000 years, so be ready to bargain. It helps to listen in on what local people pay (a good reason to learn Uyghur numbers).

Look for hats, teapot sets, copper/brass ware and handicrafts along the south side of Id Kah Mosque. A better place for hats is behind the cloth bazaar. A big favourite with tourists are Uyghur knives, which have colourfully inlaid handles, but don't try to fly out of Kashgar with them in your hand luggage!

There are a couple of high-quality but pricey handicraft stores on the east side of the Id Kah Mosque. These and the bazaar have a depressing line-up of snow leopard pelts. Aside from the moral issues of buying the skins of endangered species, bear in mind that you may not be able to import such items into your own country.

Hotel gift shops have convenient selections of overpriced Chinese souvenirs.

Musical Instruments Beautiful long-necked stringed instruments run the gamut from junk to collector's items. They include the bulbous two-string *dutar*, larger three-string *khomuz*, small *tambur* and elaborately shaped *rabap*, which has five strings and a snake or lizard-skin sounding board. The small reed horn is a *sunai* or *surnai*. A *dab* is a type of tambourine. The friendly Ababekry Seley shop, on the street north from the post office, sells these plus miniature tourist versions. Try to negotiate a carrying case if you buy an instrument as this will greatly increase the chances of it getting home in one piece.

Gold An arcade of goldsmiths is just southwest of Id Kah Mosque. At the rear of some you can see young apprentices at work making jewellery. Typically heavy and ornate, the jewellery is designed for dowry pieces.

Carpets There are a few dealers in the bazaar and some bargains in small shops, but most have moved out to the Sunday Market pavilion. Do some carpet homework if you plan to buy one in Kashgar. A small carpet factory is located in the 'Kashgar City Traditional Minority Handicrafts and Souvenir Shop' at the far end of the goldsmiths' arcade. Regionally, the best carpets are said to be in Hotan.

Getting There & Away

Air The only place you can fly to/from is Ürümqi (Y980; daily flights in summer, four flights weekly in winter). These flights are sometimes cancelled because of wind or sandstorms. If so, just show up for the next flight and you get priority; there's no need to change the ticket (but you must change any ticket for a connecting flight out of Ürümqi).

You should try to book at least a week ahead in summer. The China Xīnjiāng Airlines/CAAC ticket office (☎ 282 2113), at 95 Jiefang Nanlu on the ground floor of a blue four-storey building, opens daily from 10 am to 1 pm and 4.30 to 8 pm. You can buy tickets here for other domestic flights.

Bus to Kyrgyzstan There are public buses to Kyrgyzstan over the Torugart Pass but at time of writing foreigners were not allowed to take these services.

For the record, a Chinese sleeper bus runs from the Chini Bagh Hotel to Bishkek every Monday and Friday and a normal Kyrgyz bus runs every Thursday at 9.30 am for US$50. Another Kyrgyz bus runs to Naryn every Friday for Y205. There are also services to Bishkek and Naryn from nearby Artux.

Both bus companies are more than happy to sell you a ticket for these buses but without a permit you'll be thrown off the bus at the customs post. (See the boxed text 'Over the Torugart Pass'.)

Bus to Pakistan The terminus for buses to/from Sost (Y270; two days) in Pakistan is the customs shed beside the Chini Bagh Hotel. From June to September it lays on as

XĪNJIĀNG 新疆

Over the Torugart Pass

Officially the Torugart Pass is a 'second grade' pass and therefore for local not international traffic. Except of course that it is. What you require on the Chinese side is a *xŭkĕzhèng* permit from the PSB entry-exit section in Ürümqi. Most agents in Kashgar can get this (CTS claim in two working days), though no-one would arrange a permit without transport.

You can hire a 4WD Land Cruiser (holding four to six passengers) or minibuses (holding eight to 12) from the Kashgar Mountaineering Association, CTS, CITS or John Hu at John's Café. At the time of research a Land Cruiser to meet or drop you off at Torugart was about Y1000 to Y1200, plus from Y200 to Y300 per person to arrange the requisite permits. CTS was offering the cheapest rates, while John Hu was charging Y2000 for a car (up to four people). Land Cruiser rates with CTS all the way to Bishkek were around US$430 for four people, plus US$30 per person for permits.

It's unclear whether you can get into Kyrgyzstan without booking Kyrgyz transport. Officially the Chinese won't let you leave the arch without onward transport into Kyrgyzstan and Chinese travel agencies are reluctant to take you without booking onward transport – but it looks likely that the Chinese guards will let you cross if you can find a lift from the arch to the Kyrgyz border post. If you do manage to get to the Kyrgyz border post you will need to find onward transport to Naryn or Bishkek. Taxi sharks may open the bidding at US$200 or more to Bishkek (and may lead you to think that's for the vehicle, then later tell you it's per person), though US$50 for the car is a more realistic amount.

There are public buses to Kyrgyzstan over the Torugart Pass, but at time of writing foreigners were not allowed to take these services. Without a permit you'll most likely be thrown off the bus at the customs post. You must of course already have a Kyrgyzstan visa. There are local buses from Kashgar to the customs post but this doesn't help much.

many buses as needed, so you needn't book very far ahead. Earlier or later in the season there may not be buses on some days. Landslides can cancel departures even in summer.

The bus leaves about noon Běijīng time. The 500km trip takes two days, with an overnight at Tashkurgan. Bring water and snacks and warm clothes as nights can be cold in any season. Sit on the left side for the best views.

Customs procedures are conducted at Tashkurgan. Drivers like luggage to go on the roof, though most people load up the back seats if there aren't too many passengers.

If buses have stopped for the season but you're desperate to cross the border, Pakistani traders may have space in a truck or chartered bus. You can also hire a 4WD; see Renting a 4WD in this section.

Bus to Ürümqi You can now make the 1480km trip to Ürümqi in a non-stop, soft-seat or sleeper coach in around 30 hours, for Y210 (upper berth) or Y240 (lower). You can also go in an ordinary bus for about Y138.

All of these depart from the long-distance bus station three times daily – the regular and soft-seat buses at 1 pm and 6 pm and the sleepers at 9 am and 9 pm.

Other Bus Destinations Other buses use the long-distance bus station (aptoos biket). There have been instances of theft at the bus station, especially in the early-morning crush, sometimes with packs cut open, so keep a close watch on your bags.

Local buses to Tashkurgan leave daily except Sunday at 9 am (Y37) and charge the full fare to drop you off in Karakul. There are also sleeper buses to Toksun (for Turpan) for Y188 or Y213.

Overnight buses leave for Hotan (Y51; 10 hours) daily at 8 pm. Buses and minibuses to Yengisar, Yarkand (Y19; 3½ hours) and Karghilik (Y24; five hours) depart every half hour or so until 8 pm.

Train A daily train to Ürümqi departs at noon (Běijīng time) and takes 31 hours. Hard seat tickets cost Y93; hard sleepers range from Y185 to Y199 and soft sleepers are Y306.

Renting a 4WD You can hire 4WD Land Cruisers (holding four to six passengers) and minibuses (holding eight to 12) from the Kashgar Mountaineering Association, CTS, CITS or John Hu at John's Cafe. At the time of research a Land Cruiser to meet/drop you off at Torugart was about Y1200, plus Y250 to Y300 per person to arrange the requisite permits. A Land Cruiser to Sost (Pakistan border) was Y5000. Food and lodging are extra, and the driver pays for his own. Book ahead, a week or more in the high season. Just because you are paying through the nose, don't expect high standards – our driver was so exhausted when he arrived that we had to drive ourselves all the way from the Torugart Pass to the customs post!

Hitching You might hitch a lift to Tashkurgan but from there to Pakistan you'll probably have to wait for an empty seat on the bus. There are plenty of goods trucks crossing the Torugart Pass to Kyrgyzstan but you'll probably have problems getting past the customs post.

Getting Around

To/From the Airport A CAAC bus (Y4) leaves from the China Xinjiang Airlines/CAAC ticket office, on Jiefang Nanlu, 2½ hours before all flight departures, and one meets all incoming flights. The airport is 12km north-east of the centre. A taxi there will cost Y30.

Bus A local bus stand at the west end of the square, opposite the Mao Statue, is the terminus for bus No 2 (to the airport), bus No 10 (to the Kashgar Hotel), bus No 20 (to the Abakh Hoja Tomb) and bus No 9 (to the Sèmǎn Bīnguǎn, Chini Bagh Gate, People's Hospital and Artush).

Taxis A new fleet of noisy, red taxis clog every street and alley way, honking and congesting the city. About Y5 to Y10 should get you anywhere within the city.

Donkey-Carts The traditional Kashgar 'taxis' are getting scarce. They're not allowed in the centre in the daytime, so routes tend to be roundabout. If you hire your own, set the price and destination before you go. Don't pay until you get there, and make sure you have exact change.

Bicycle Rental A bike is the cheapest and most versatile way to get around Kashgar. One-gear clunkers can be hired by the hour (Y2) or the day at many hotels and John's Cafe. A deposit is required; don't leave your passport with them, as some ask you to do. You can negotiate a daily rate with most hotels.

KARAKORAM HIGHWAY 中巴公路

The Karakoram Highway (Zhōngbā Gōnglù) over the Khunjerab Pass (4800m) is the gateway to Pakistan. For centuries this route was used by caravans plodding down the Silk Road. Khunjerab means 'valley of blood', a reference to local bandits who took advantage of the terrain to plunder caravans and slaughter the merchants.

Nearly 20 years were required to plan, push, blast and level the present road between Islamabad and Kashgar and more than 400 road-builders died in the process. Facilities en route are being steadily improved, but take warm clothing, food and drink on board with you – once stowed on the roof of the bus your baggage will not be easily accessible.

Even if you don't wish to go to Pakistan, it's worth doing the trip up to Tashkurgan from Kashgar – there's plenty to see. From Kashgar, you first cross the Pamir Plateau (3000m), passing the foothills of Kongur Mountain (Gōnggé'ér Shān), which is 7719m high, and nearby Muztagh-Ata Mountain (Mùshìtágé Shān) at 7546m. In between the two lies Karakul Lake, one of the most scenic spots on the Chinese side of the highway.

The journey continues through stunning scenery – high mountain pastures with grazing camels and yaks tended by Tajiks who live in yurts. The last major town on the Chinese side is Tashkurgan at 3600m.

Officially, the border opens 15 April and closes 31 October. However, the border can open late or close early depending on conditions at Khunjerab Pass. Travel formalities are performed at Sust, on the Pakistan border; the Chinese border post is at Tashkurgan.

At the time of writing travellers could get a seven-day Pakistan transit visa at the border, though it wouldn't be wise to plan your trip around the possibility of this happening. If you're coming in from Pakistan, make sure you have enough cash on hand – the bank in Tashkurgan doesn't change travellers cheques.

Kashgar to Karakul

As you leave Kashgar the main attraction, rising up from the plain to the west, is the luminous rampart of the Pamir. An hour down the road is **Upal** village (Wùpà'ér in Chinese), where the Kashgar-Sost bus normally stops for lunch. There's an interesting weekly market here every Monday. About 3km off the road from here is the small tomb of Mahmud al-Kashgari, an 11th century Uyghur scholar (born at Barskoön in Kyrgyzstan) famous for writing the first comparative dictionary of Turkic languages. Most settlements as far as Karakul are Kyrgyz.

Two hours from Kashgar you enter the canyon of the Ghez river (Ghez Darya in Uyghur), with wine-red sandstone walls at its lower end. **Ghez** itself is just a checkpost; photographing soldiers or buildings here can result in confiscated film. Upstream the road is cut into sheer walls or inches across huge boulder fields. At the top of the canyon, 3½ hours above the plain, is a huge wet plateau ringed with sand dunes, aptly called the Kumtagh, or Sand Mountain by locals.

Southern Silk Road

The Silk Road east of Kashgar splits into two threads in the face of the huge Taklamakan Desert. The northern thread follows the course of the modern road and railway to Kùchē and Turpan. The southern road charts a more remote course between the desert sands and the huge Pamir and Kunlun ranges. The ancient route is marked by a ring of abandoned cities deserted by retreating rivers and encroaching sands. Some cities, like Niya, Miran and Yotkan, remain covered by sand, others, like Yarkand and Khotan, remain important Uyghur centres.

From Kashgar you can visit the southern towns as a multi-day trip from Kashgar, en route to Ürümqi or as part of a rugged backdoor route into China's Qīnghǎi or Gānsù provinces.

YENGISAR 阳霞

The sleepy town of Yengisar (Yīngjíshā), 58km south of Kashgar, is synonymous with knife production. The are dozens of knife shops here (though prices are not much better than in Kashgar) and it's possible to visit the knife factory (xiǎodāochǎng in Chinese; pichak chilik karakhana in Uyghur) in the centre of town to see the knives actually being made. Each worker makes the blade, handle and inlays himself, using only the most basic of tools. Try not to time a visit between noon and 4 pm when most workers head off for lunch. From the main highway walk south past the Yīngjíshā Bīnguǎn then turn left to the bazaar. The factory is just north of the bazaar.

Buses pass through the town regularly en route to Yarkand (Y13; 2½ hours) and Kashgar (Y7; 1½ hours). Shared taxis wait at the main crossroads to speed passengers to the Kashgar bus station for Y10 per person, whenever there are three passengers or more.

Places to Stay

There's no real need to stay overnight at Yengisar but if you decide to, the Yīngjíshā Bīnguǎn (☎ 3622 390) is a pretty good choice. Building No 1 has beds in a triple/double with hot shower for Y40/50. Building No 2 is more spartan, with beds in a quad/triple/double for Y20/25/30, with solar heated hot water. There's no English sign so look out for the 'Handicraft of National Store' at the entrance gate.

Alternatively, the Yīngjíshā Dàjiǔdiàn is on the main road from Kashgar. Beds in a quad/triple/double cost Y25/30/40.

Getting There & Away

Buses pass through the town regularly en route to Yarkand (Y13; 2½ hours) and Kashgar (Y7; 1½ hours). Shared taxis wait at the main crossroads to speed passengers to the Kashgar bus station for Y10 per person, whenever there are three passengers or more.

YARKAND 莎车

Yarkand (Shāchē) is one of those Central Asian towns, like Samarkand and Kashgar, whose name still resonates deeply with Silk Road romance. At the end of a major trade route from British India, over the Karakorum Pass from Leh, Yarkand was for centuries an important caravan town and centre of Hindu tradesmen and moneylenders. Robert Shaw, Francis Younghusband's uncle, visited the town in 1868 and dreamed of opening up China to the joys of British tea.

Today Yarkand is dominated by its large Chinese New Town, which is little more than a single street of department stores and Sichuanese restaurants. The Old Town, to the east, is of far more interest, and is an excellent place to explore traditional Uyghur life.

Things to See

Yarkand's main 'sight' is the Altyn Mosque complex. In the central courtyard of the mosque, near to where worshippers carry out their pre-prayer ablutions, is the newly-built Tomb of Aman Isa Khan (1526–60), musician, poetess and wife of the Khan of Yarkand. From here you can gain access to the Tombs of the Kings of Yarkand. The complex has an entry fee of Y10. Across from mosque is the solitary gateway, or orda darvaza, all that remains of the former citadel.

The huge sprawling cemetery behind the mosque is a fascinating place to visit, especially at dawn when mourners are out in force. Amid the endless graves are the blue tilework and the Yeti Sultan Mosque and Mazar at the back of the cemetery. There should be no charge to visit the cemetery.

If you turn left out of the mosque and then left again after 30m, this road takes you down into the centre of the traditional old town and the back of Wénhuà Gōngyuán, a park where there is a small bazaar and several traditional Uyghur teahouses.

Other tombs out of town include Hajiman Deng Mazar, Sud Pasha Mazar and Hayzi Terper Mazar. There's plenty of scope here to take many interesting walks around the surrounding countryside.

Yarkand also has a large **Sunday Market**, untouristed but smaller than Kashgar or Hotan's. The market is held a block north of the Altyn mosque.

Places to Stay & Eat
Finding a cheap place to stay can be a problem in Yarkand. The only hotel that officially accepts foreigners is the *Shāchē Bīnguǎn* (☎ *851 2365*), where comfortable triples/doubles cost Y120/160. This is particularly bad value for single travellers who must pay for all the beds in the room. Rooms in the old block are laughably overpriced at Y100, without a bathroom.

Yarkand's other hotels include the *Jiāotōng Bīnguǎn*, by the bus station, with beds in a quad/triple/double for Y15/20/35 and the *Gǔlèbāgé Bīnguǎn*, with beds in doubles for Y50, but neither takes foreigners.

The only place we found willing to take in a cash-starved foreigner was the *Hèdū Bīnguǎn* (☎ *851 4850*), one block left of the bus station, which has beds in a clean and spacious double for Y45, with private hot water bathroom. There are also cheaper triples and quads with shared facilities. The more Chinese you speak the more willing the staff will be to take you in.

There are Uyghur *foodstalls* in front of the bus station and on most street corners. For Chinese snacks there are several places just west of the Shāchē Bīnguǎn. The *Ali Baba Restaurant*, on the main road, looks interesting.

Getting There & Around
Buses leave hourly for Kashgar (Y19; four hours) and Yengisar (Y12.50; 2½ hours). Buses leave at 11 am for Hotan (Y30; six hours) and at 9.30 am to Ürümqi (Y205; 36 hours).

From the bus station it's about 1.5km to the Shāchē Bīnguǎn and the same again to

the start of the Old Town. Cycle rickshaws cost Y1 or Y2.

KARGHILIK 哈尔里克
Karghilik (Yèchéng) is a convenient place to break the long trip to Hotan. There are decent places to stay and you could enjoyably spend several hours exploring the interesting Uyghur old town. Karghilik is also of importance to travellers as the springboard for the long overland trip to Tibet.

The main thing to see in town is the 15th-century **Jama Masjid** (Friday Mosque). The mosque is surrounded by an interesting covered bazaar, while the traditional mud-walled backstreets of the old town spread south behind the mosque.

The town of Charbagh, 10 minutes' drive towards Yarkand has an interesting market on Tuesday.

Places to Stay & Eat
The *Jiāotōng Bīnguǎn* (☎ *728 5540*), right by the bus station, has comfortable carpeted doubles for Y80 per person, though the staff will probably take Y50 if it's late. Hot water can be temperamental on the upper floors.

Next door to the main hotel is a cheaper *Jiāotōng Zhàodàisuǒ*, where beds in a quad/triple/double with common bathroom cost Y20/26/30.

The other main choice is the *Dēngshān Bīnguǎn* (Mountaineering Hotel), one block south and 2½ blocks east from the bus station, where beds start at Y30.

There are some busy 24-hour food stalls across the main road from the bus station and some good Uyghur places in front of the mosque.

Getting There & Away
There are buses every two hours to Hotan (Y23; five hours) and to Yarkand/Kashgar every half hour until 8 pm (Y6/23). There are also daily sleeper buses to Korla (Y154) and Ürümqi (Y216).

To Tibet The 1100km long road to Ali, in western Tibet, branches off from the main Kashgar-Hotan road 6km east of Karghilik. There are no buses along this road so you'll have to hitch a ride with a truck. This is a very tough road with several passes over 5400m and several foreigners have died, either from exposure or in traffic accidents. You should come equipped with warm clothes and enough food for a week (though the trip to Ali can take as little as three days). In addition, the route is officially off-limits to foreigners and there are numerous checkpoints en route (though surprising numbers of travellers have been making it through in recent years). See Lonely Planet's guide to *Tibet* for more details.

Getting Around

Pedicabs charge a flat Y1 anywhere in town.

HOTAN 和田

About 1980km south-west of Ürümqi by road, dusty Hotan (Hétián), or Khotan, is one of the most remote parts of Xīnjiāng, sitting at the southern boundary of the Taklamakan Desert.

The main reason to haul yourself all the way out here is to catch the fantastic Sunday Market, but Hotan is also renowned for its silk, carpets and jade, which are considered the finest in China. You can even see deposits of white jade along the Jade Dragon Kashgar River, which passes to the east of town. You can check out the local selection at the rows of stores and stalls along the town's main street.

For those setting off on the infrequently explored southern Silk Road, via Keriya (Yútián), Cherchen (Qiěmò), Charklik (Rùoqiāng) and on to Golmud, this is the last place to take care of important errands like changing money, stocking up on supplies or extending your visa.

Information

Hetian International Travel Service (Hétián Guójì Lüvxíngshè; ☎ 202 8994, in Room 228 of the Hetian City Guest House, can arrange a car and guide to the ruins at Yuètègān and Málìkèwǎtè for Y350 for three people, or to the Silk Factory for Y150. It also offers an adventurous (and expensive) week-long trip into the Mushi

Mountains, 150km south of Hotan, and trips into the Yengi Eriq Desert to the north.

The Bank of China cashes travellers cheques and is open Monday to Friday, 9.30 am to 1.30 pm and 4 to 8 pm.

Sunday Market

Hotan's biggest draw is its traditional weekly market, which rivals Kashgar's in both size and interest. The market swamps the old town and reaches a pitch between noon and 2 pm Xīnjiāng time. The most interesting parts to head for are the *gillam* (carpet) bazaar, which also has a selection of *atlas* silks, the *doppi* (skullcap) bazaar, and the livestock bazaar.

Hotan Cultural Museum

Also known as the Historical Relics Ancient Corpses Exhibit, this small museum is worth a brief visit. The main attractions are two mummies, a 10-year-old girl and 35-year-old man, both of whom are now over 1500 years old. There's a useful map showing the location of the region's buried cities. It's open daily from 9 am to 7 pm; closed weekdays from 2 to 4 pm. Entry is Y7.

Ancient Cities

The deserts around Hotan are peppered with the faint ruins of abandoned cities. Ten kilometres to the west of town are the **Yuètègān Yízhǐ** (Yotkan Ruins), the ancient capital of a pre-Islamic kingdom dating from the 3rd to 8th centuries AD.

The **Málìkèwǎtè Gùchéng** (Melikawat Ruins) are 25km south of town, and there are some temples and pagoda-like buildings a further 10km to the south. Visiting any of these places will require hiring a taxi, which can be arranged at the hotels, through the museum, or with any taxi driver who knows the way. The two sites theoretically charge Y5 for entry and Y5 for photos.

Other ruins such as the Rawaq Pagoda and city of Niya (Endere) have been put off limits due to the high fees charged.

Silk and Carpet Factories

Jíyǎxiāng, a small town 3km east and then 8km north of Hotan, is a traditional centre for atlas silk production. Look around the small but fascinating workshop (*karakhana* in Uyghur) to see how the silk is spun, dyed and woven using traditional methods. A taxi from Hotan to the village costs Y10.

En route to the village, on the eastern bank of the Jade Dragon Kashgar River, is a small **carpet factory** (gillam karakhana in Uyghur), which is also worth a quick look around. Take minibus No 2 from in front of the Hétián Shì Bīnguǎn and then change to No 3 or walk 20 minutes over the bridge.

The **Hétián Sīchóu Chǎng** (Hotan Silk Factory) uses a less traditional form of silk production, employing over 2000 workers. Staff at the office will give you a tour of the plant to see the boiling of cocoons and spinning, weaving, dyeing and printing of silk. The factory is open Monday to Friday from 9 am to 1.30 pm and 3.30 to 7.30 pm, though if you don't speak at least some Chinese you are better off arranging a visit through Hetian Travel Service. No photos are allowed in the factory. To get there, take minibus No 1 from outside the bus station to the end of the line and then walk back 150m.

None of the above factories charges for a look around, though all have shops that you are expected to at least look in.

Places to Stay

The cheapest reliable accommodation for foreigners is the **Hétián Yínbīnguǎn** (☎ 202 2203). The north building has beds in a quad/triple with shared bath for Y15/20, and comfortable doubles with hot shower for Y45 per bed. More upmarket rooms in the new block cost Y180 and up. Prices include a miserable breakfast.

The **Hétián Wài Bīnguǎn** (☎ 202 3564), on the western edge of town, is somewhat fancier, with comfortable but smoky doubles/triples for Y240/260. They offer beds in carpeted six-bed dorms for Y30 – the bathrooms are grim but if you are the only foreigner you'll get the room to yourself.

The **Hétián Shì Bīnguǎn** (☎ 204 6101), by the central crossroads, has beds in a quad/triple with shared bath for Y15/20, or in smoky doubles with private bathroom for Y40.

The **Jiāotōng Bīnguǎn** (☎ 203 2700), right next to the bus station, has comfortable, carpeted doubles for Y60 per bed. The cheaper hostel (*lǚshé*) next door doesn't take foreigners.

A basic Uyghur-style alternative is the **Xìngfú Lǚshé (Happy Hotel)**, a couple of minutes' walk to the right from the bus station. Rooms are a little grimy but there are hot showers. The owner asks around Y30 per bed but will take less. The 100% Uyghur **Silk Town Guest House** is ultra-basic but ultra-cheap at Y5 per bed.

Places to Eat

There are plenty of standard Chinese restaurants in the New Town and Uyghur restaurants in the Old Town, though few places speak English. One to recommend is the hole-in-the-wall **Jīnyǒu Cāntīng**. There's no English spoken here but everything on the menu costs a flat Y6. There's also a more expensive menu available. The **Chéngdū** restaurant, nearby, is of a similar standard.

The **Yíyuàn Kuàicān** is another good, cheap Chinese place 60m south of the Hétián Yínbīnguǎn gate (not the fancy looking place to the left).

Getting There & Away

Air There are four flights weekly between Hotan and Ürümqi (Y1000). The CAAC /Xinjiang Airlines office (☎ 202 2178) is on Positan Nanlu. The airport is 10km south of town and the taxi ride from town costs Y20.

Bus Buses from Ürümqi to Hotan now travel along the recently opened Cross-Desert Highway, which spans 500km of almost completely deserted land between Luntai and Niya (Mínfēng). The roadway is actually built on a raised roadbed to help prevent sandstorms from building up dunes on the tarmac. Sleeper buses leave Hotan twice a day at 4 and 7 pm (Y290; 30 hours). Express sleeper buses (Y340 to Y360; 22 hours) leave at noon on Tuesday, Thursday and Saturday. There are also plenty of sleeper buses to Aksu (Y146; 15 hours).

There are two daily buses between Hotan and Kashgar – one in the morning and one in the evening. The 530km trip takes around 10 hours and seats cost Y34 for the morning bus, or Y55 for the 'luxury' overnight bus. At the time of writing, the sleeper bus service had been discontinued due to insufficient demand. There are also several buses daily to Yarkand (Y21) via Yecheng (Y17 to Y28).

Getting Around

Donkey carts take you to and from the Sunday Market (Y0.50 a trip). Taxis cost a flat Y5; there are also three-wheeler motorbikes.

HOTAN TO GOLMUD
和田至格尔木

To continue along the southern Silk Road into China proper catch an early-morning bus to Qiěmò (Cherchen), 580km to the east. The trip generally takes two days and costs Y55 and goes via the Uyghur towns of Keriya (Yútián) and Niya (Mínfēng).

From Qiěmò buses continue another 320km east to Ruòqiāng (Charklik). The trip takes anywhere from 13 to 16 hours under good conditions, and tickets are around Y35. From Ruòqiāng you may be able to get a bus to Golmud, although some travellers have had to resort to private jeep services that take you the nine hours to the border with Qīnghǎi. From there you can reportedly take a series of buses on to Dachaidan in Qīnghǎi, and from there connect with buses to Golmud. This route requires a few overnight stops, and roads in this area are plagued by washouts and landslides, so don't try this route if you're in a hurry.

Northen Xīnjiāng

This part of Xīnjiāng is positively stunning, a land of thick evergreen forests, rushing rivers and lakes. The highlight of the area is beautiful Hānàsī Hú (Hanas Lake) and the surrounding mountainous valleys.

Until recently, the area was a quiet backwater of China's far north-west and closed off to foreigners due to the proximity of the Russian, Mongolian and Kazakhstan borders.

The area is rich in ethnic minorities and despite constant Han migration, continues to remain predominantly Kazakh. Tourism and its related industries are just starting to take off and the region remains relatively untouched by pollution.

BÙ'ĚRJĪN 布尔津

Bù'ěrjīn, meaning dark green water in Mongolian, is named after the nearby river Bù'ěrjīn Hé, which is a tributary of the Ertix River. The Ertix is the only river in China to flow into the Arctic Ocean. Bù'ěrjīn, 620km north of Ürümqi, marks the end of the desert and the beginning of the grasslands and mountains to the north. The town's population of 60,000 is mainly Kazakh (57%), but there are also Han, Uyghurs, Tuwa Mongolians and Russians.

There isn't much to see in Bù'ěrjīn, but it is a convenient transit stop if your heading for Hānàsī Hú or Kaba.

Information

CITS (☎ 652 2652), at 4 Huancheng Xilu, can arrange jeeps, guides and permits, but it would be cheaper and quicker to deal through one of the drivers that greet you at the bus station.

The PSB is on the corner of Xiangyang Lu and Xinfu Lu. This is where you come to pick up a permit for Hānàsī Hú.

There is nowhere to change travellers cheques in Bù'ěrjīn, but the local Industrial & Commercial Bank (ICBC) can change major currencies.

Places to Stay

The most convenient place to stay is the *Jiāotōng Bīnguǎn*, at the bus station. It has beds in triples/quads for Y17/9 and singles for Y40. The rooms are nothing special and there is often no hot water, but the staff are friendly.

A more pleasant option is the *Bù'ěrjīn Lǚyóu Bīnguǎn* (☎ 652 1325). It has comfortable twins for Y58 per person and 24-hour hot water. There are also dorms in triples/quads for Y30/20 and singles for Y88.

Another reasonable option is the *Jiākèsī Jiǔdiàn* (☎ 652 1716), on Xiang Nanlu. It has dorm beds for Y20 and a bed in a twin with attached bath for Y55. The hot water is turned on from 10 pm to 1 am.

Places to Eat

The best freshly baked *nang* in Xīnjiāng is at the *Wénmínglù Kǎonángdiàn*, just north of the bus station on Wenmin Lu.

Just next door is the *Yínchuān Húimín Fàndiàn*, which serves up a tasty bowl of spicy *niuroumian* noodles.

A good plate of *banmian* noodles can be found opposite the bus station at the *Nánqiáo Dì'ěrhúimín Shítáng*.

Getting There & Away

Buses from Ürümqi leave in the evening and take around 15 hours to get to Bù'ěrjīn. Seats on a regular rattletrap bus cost Y50, while a berth on a sleeper is Y108. Tickets can be bought at either the main bus station or the alternative bus station for the Altai region (Ālètài Bànshìchù), which is on Hetan Dongyijie, just after the overpass and north of Qiantangjiang Lu. Heading back to Ürümqi there are departures at 4, 5 and 6 pm.

There are two daily buses to Chōnghū'ăr (Y10.20; two hours) at 4 and 5 pm. There are regular buses to Kaba (Y6.70; one hour) and to Jímǔnǎi (Y11; two hours).

Hānàsī Hú Zìrán Bǎohùqū

Hanas Lake Nature Reserve

The most splendid sight in the Altai region is Hānàsī Hú, an alpine lagoon surrounded by pines, boulders and mountains. In the autumn, the aspen and maple trees provide a scenic backdrop of riotous colour.

The whole area has a diverse range of flora and fauna. In addition to the camels, cattle, horses, sheep, and goats, there are also eagles, brown bear, lynx, snow leopard, black stork and lots of squirrels. The forests are dominated by spruce, birch, elm, poplar, Korean pine and Siberian larch.

The trip up to Hānàsī Hú is stunning, with beautiful vistas that range from desert, to grasslands, to alpine wilderness. Along the way you pass hundreds of semi-nomadic Kazakhs, who are either on their way up or down the valley, depending on the

season. The latter half of the road runs along next to the roaring Hānàsī Hé. As the road slowly winds its way up to Hānàsī Hú, 1370m elevation, there are many scenic spots along the road that are worth stopping at to take in the beauty.

There are many possibilities for hiking in and around the lake. In fact, there is even more incredible scenery in the neighbouring valley of **Hemu Hanas** (Hémù Kānàsī) and **Bai Kaba** (Báihābā) village. For those who want more content with day hikes, then there are a couple of paths that lead out from the tourist village of Hānàsī.

A popular day walk is the trip up to **Guānyú Tíng** (2030m), the peak on the other side of the lake. It's a 1½-hour walk from the river up the steps to the pavilion. From the top you are rewarded with panoramic views of the lake, the mountains and surrounding grasslands. It is possible to return to Hānàsī via a circuitous scenic route down the eastern slope by following the dirt road. The round walk takes a lazy five hours.

It's also possible to climb the mountains behind the tourist camp or even partly around the lake to some nearby rock paintings.

Boats also leave from the pier to **Shuāng Hú** (Twin Lakes) and up to the head waters of the lake.

When is the best time to visit? It all depends on what you enjoy. The area is really only easily accessible from June to early October, with ice and heavy snow closing the road between October and May. There isn't really any summer up here, more a

BÙ'ĚRJĪN

PLACES TO STAY & EAT
1 Yínchuān Huímín Fàndiàn
银川回民饭店
2 Wénmínglù Kǎonángdiàn
文明路烤馕店
3 Jiāotōng Bīnguǎn
交通宾馆
5 Nánqiáo Dìèr Huímín
Shítáng
南桥第二回民食堂

9 Jiākèsī Jiǔdiàn
嘉客思酒店
12 Bù'ěrjīn Lǚyóu Bīnguǎn
布尔津旅游宾馆

OTHER
4 Bus Station
客运站
6 PSB
公安局外事科

7 Xinhua
Bookstore
新华书店
8 Post & Telephone
Office
邮电局
10 ICBC Bank
中国工商银行
11 CITS
中国国际旅行社

gradual transition from autumn to spring, with the temperature remaining pleasant throughout.

During June and July a blanket of alpine flowers accentuates the beauty of the region. In August wild berries litter the ground. In September and October the first snow starts to fall and the forests begin to turn a brilliant red and yellow. Winter trips are also possible by trekking in on horseback, on skis or for the well endowed, snow jet skis.

Places to Stay
An accommodation construction boom is currently underway and no doubt the area will undergo some dramatic changes. Hopefully the impact on the environment can be minimised.

Officially, the only option for foreigners is the tourist bureau's cabins and yurts. Most of these are located in the northern section of the tourist village. Rates range from Y25 per person in a yurt to Y200 for a twin room with bathroom. During the peak summer months, there are nightly barbecues around the yurts accompanied by Kazakh and Mongolian dancing and a roaring bonfire.

The best accommodation up here is either staying in a yurt with some Kazakhs and Mongolians, or bringing your tent with you and heading out into the great wilderness. Some of the best places for camping are actually along the route up to Hānàsī Hú after the town of Chōnghū'ěr. Chinese tourists are already doing this, but the officials are still bit nervous about foreigners making

their own plans. If you do head off, make sure you are equipped to deal with freezing temperatures and heavy rain, both of which are common throughout the year.

Getting There & Away
The lake is a 145km stunning journey from Bù'ěrjīn. During July and August there are tourist buses (Y50) that head up to the lake from Bù'ěrjīn's bus station. A more flexible option is to hire a 4WD (Y400/Y500 one way/return), which allows you to stop and take photos along the way. The drive takes about five to six hours.

The road from Bù'ěrjīn passes through Chōnghū'ěr, Hāliútán, and Jiādè Dēngyù before reaching the tourist town of Hānàsī. All of these towns have restaurants and small supply shops. The main road is sealed to just past Chōnghū'ěr, but there are plans to widen and seal the road all the way to the lake. In fact, the tourist bureau also plans to construct a runway up here, but hopefully this will take a bit longer.

Entrance to the Hānàsī Hú Zìrán Bǎohùqū costs Y40, but foreigners are also expected to pay an extra Y6 per day to ensure the ongoing protection of the area. You will only pay this fee if you are unfortunate enough to bump into an environmental bureau officer. They usually hang around the pier area on the other side of the lake.

Before you head up to Hānàsī Hú, drop into Bù'ěrjīn's PSB to arrange a permit (tōngxíngzhèng). The permit costs Y52, plus an extra Y50 deposit, which the staff give back to you when you return from your trip. If you are interested in visiting other areas or villages, then make sure you include them on the permit. There are a number of checkpoints throughout the whole region, where you will be asked to hand over your permit and sometimes your passport. This regimentation will probably fade away as time goes on and more and more foreigners make their way up here.

Yǒuyì Fēng 友谊峰

Friendship Peak

At 4374m, this is the highest summit in this mountainous area. Standing on the glacier-covered summit allows you to be in three nations at once. Presumably you won't need a visa for each one, but you will need a climbing permit, a guide, an ice axe, crampons and other appropriate mountaineering paraphernalia.

JÍMǓNǍI 吉木乃

The only reason you would want to visit this forlorn little town is if you are heading for Kazakhstan. The border checkpoint is 18km from town. The border here has become more popular in recent years due to the irregularity of the crossing at Tǎchéng, but border guards are still not used to foreigners and you should come armed with a plan B in case you don't get through. The first major town in Kazakhstan is Maykipcha-gay, from where you can catch a taxi to Zaysan and then a bus to Semey (12 hours).

There are a couple of buses that depart from the bus station and the main intersection for Ürümqi between 4 and 5 pm daily. The trip takes 14 hours and costs Y52 for a seat or Y100 for a sleeper, although prices are negotiable with the private operators. There are four daily buses that make the dusty trip to Bù'ěrjīn (Y11; two hours).

There is no reliable public transport to the border, but you can catch a taxi there for Y25. Coming the other way you can share a taxi to Jímǔnǎi for Y5.

TǍCHÉNG 塔城

Located in a lonely corner of north-west Xīnjiāng, Tǎchéng is a relatively obscure border crossing into neighbouring Kazakhstan. Life here is usually pretty slow and relaxed, but things have dropped a tempo in recent years due to the closure of the Kazakh side of the border. Locals report that the Kazakh customs are a little erratic in charging duties and were therefore shutdown. However, now and then the gates are opened and a rush of trade starts to flow through the main streets again. If you do make it here and discover the border closed, don't despair, Tǎchéng is a pleasant enough place to relax before catching a bus south to Alashankou or north to Jímǔnǎi.

Information

The post and telephone office in the centre of town, on the corner of Xinhua Lu and Ta'er Bahetai Lu. The PSB is on Jianshe Jie

The Bank of China is south of here on Guangming Lu and can handle both cash and travellers cheques.

Places to Stay & Eat

The *Tǎchéng Bīnguǎn* (☎ 622 2093) is tucked away in the north-west of town on Youhao Jie. It has dorm beds in a Russian-style building for Y20 and Y30. The rooms come complete with cracked ornate plaster, broken windows, peeling paint and wet carpet. If the place smelt of vodka it would be the authentic Russian experience. More comfortable twins in the main hotel range from Y80 to Y160. All rooms have attached bathroom and 24-hour hot water.

The *Tǎchéngshì Kèyùn Bīnguǎn* (☎ 622 2544) is the cheapest option in town, with dorm beds from Y10 to Y18 with common shower. A bed in a simple twin is Y25 or Y50 in a triple with a large sofa. There is hot water from 10 pm to 2 am.

The *Yínxiáng Bīnguǎn* (☎ 622 2222 ext 2666) is the most upmarket option, with standard twins for Y124 or suites for Y188, complete with living room and a large double bed. It has 24-hour hot water and can usually offer a bit of a discount on all rooms. You can't miss this place, as it is the biggest white tile and blue reflective glass building in town.

There is a great *night market* in front of the cinema on Xinhua Lu, just opposite the Yínxiáng Bīnguǎn. It has an amazing array of dishes for all budgets and tastes.

The *Yuèliangchéng* restaurant has a good range of cheap and tasty Chinese dishes. The restaurant is adjacent to the post office on Ta'er Bahetai Lu, look for the pink characters on the window.

Getting There & Away

Air There are flights on Tuesday and Saturday between Ürümqi and Tǎchéng (Y310). Tickets can be purchased from CAAC (☎ 622 3428). The shuttle bus to the airport also departs from here.

Bus There are three daily buses to Tǎchéng (Y52; 15 hours) from Ürümqi, departing at 6, 8 and 9 pm. The first of these is a sleeper (Y84/97). From Tǎchéng to Ürümqi the times and prices are similar.

Getting Around

Taxi Tǎchéng is small enough to get around on foot. Taxis cost Y5 to get around town or Y20 if you want to head down to the border checkpoint. If you have come from Kazakhstan, then you can share a taxi for Y5 into town.

YĪNÍNG 伊宁

Also known as Gulja, Yīníng lies close to the Kazakhstan border, about 390km west of Ürümqi. It is the centre of the Ili Kazak Autonomous Prefecture.

The Yīlí Gǔ (Ili Valley) has, in times past, been an easy access point for invaders, as well as for the northern route of the Silk Road. The Russian influence has probably been the most influential, not counting the obvious Han influence. Yīníng was occupied by Russian troops in 1872 during Yakub Beg's independent rule of Kashgaria. Five years later, the Chinese cracked down on Yakub Beg and Yīníng was handed back by the Russians. In 1962 there were major Sino-Soviet clashes along the Yīlí Hé (Ili River).

Today Yīníng has little to show for this influence: a few faded remnants of Russian architecture and street names. Overall there's not much to the town itself, other than enjoying the surrounding scenery. The best of which can be seen along the roads from Ürümqi and Kùchē that pass through some spectacular desert, grassland and alpine landscapes.

More recently, Yīníng was the scene of violent riots started by Uyghur separatists, resulting in a number of deaths. Although the riots were swiftly quelled, underlying tension and resentment continues. Despite this, there is little trace today of a turbulent past. The people of Yīníng are a pretty friendly bunch and at night during the warmer months the streets are often bustling with night markets and small eateries.

Information

The PSB is opposite the Yīlítè Dàjiǔdiàn (Yilite Grand Hotel) on Stalin Jie. The Bank of China is opposite the bus station on Jiefang Lu and the post and telephone office is right on the big traffic circle in the centre of town. There is also another post and telephone office east of the bus station on Jiefang Lu. Internet access is available on the 2nd floor of this office. Xinhua Bookstore is just next door to the bus station, on the 2nd floor of the department store. You can pick up a city map here.

Things to See

Just to the south of town is the **Yīlí Hé** (Ili River), a popular recreational area with the locals. Down by the river are some pleasant restaurants, teahouses and bars – it's a good place to relax and enjoy the river passing you by. To get there, hop on bus No 2 and get off at the last stop, just before the bridge over the river.

Places to Stay & Eat

Budget travellers can try the *Yǒuyì Bīnguǎn (Friendship Hotel;* ☎ *802 3901)*, which has dorm beds in triples for Y32. Twins start at Y90. It's about a 10-minute walk south-east of the bus station, but isn't that easy to find – it's down an obscure side street and the only sign pointing the way is in Chinese.

Nearby to here is the *Yàxīyà Bīnguǎn (Asia Hotel;* ☎ *803 6077)*, which offers beds in twins/triples for Y40/32 and doubles for Y88.

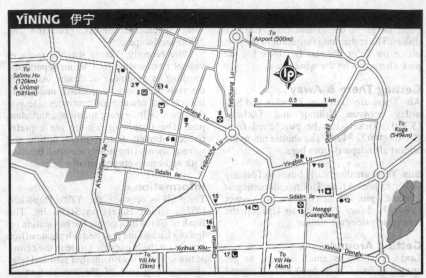

YĪNÍNG 伊宁

YĪNÍNG

PLACES TO STAY & EAT
2 Market
市场
6 Yǒuyì Bīnguǎn
友谊宾馆
7 Yàxīyà Bīnguǎn
亚西亚宾馆
9 Yīlí Bīnguǎn
伊犁宾馆
10 Jiāhé Měishílín
嘉禾美食林
15 Market
市场

16 Tiānmǎ Bīnguǎn
天马宾馆

OTHER
1 Xinhua Bookstore
新华书店
3 Bus Station
长途汽车站
4 Bank of China
中国银行
5 Post & Telephone
Office; Internet
邮电局；因特网

8 Department Store
民贸商场
11 PSB
公安局外事科
12 CAAC Booking Office;
Yīlítè Dàjiǔdiàn
民航售票处；
伊犁特大酒店
13 Yining Department Store
伊宁商场
14 Post and Telephone Office
邮局
17 Mosque
清真寺

The **Tiānmǎ Bīnguǎn** (☎ 802 2662) is a nine-storey white tiled building on Qingnian Lu. A bed in a quad with common bath is Y18 and a twin room costs Y80. Other than the cigarette burns in the carpet, the rooms are clean and good value. Look out for the small English sign that reads 'Fixed Hotel for overseas visitors'.

Closer to all the action (such as it is), is the **Yīlí Bīnguǎn** (☎ 802 3799, fax 802 4964), where a bed in a clean triple is Y40.

Twins range from Y150 in the older wing to Y360 in the brand new three-star wing. The hotel has very pleasant tree-shaded grounds, in fact you almost need a map to find your way around. If you are looking for some remnants of Soviet architecture, this is where you will find it, complete with a bust of Lenin at the entrance.

There are plenty of **street markets** that set up stalls in the evenings around town. The **Jiāhé Měishílín** is a popular local restaurant

Cups of Eight Auspicious Tea on the banks of the Huáng Hé (Yellow River); Lánzhōu, Gānsù

Pilgrims at the Labrang Monastery in Xiàhé, Gānsù

Welcoming the Tibetan New Year at the Labrang Monastery in Xiàhé, Gānsù

Sìchuān opera is performed for some homesick Sichuanese in a local teahouse in Xīníng, Qīnghǎi.

adjacent to the entrance of the Yīlí Bīnguǎn. It serves a pretty tasty *dapanji* (a whole chicken cut up and stir-fried with potatoes, herbs and vegetables and served on a bed of noodles) as well as lots of snacks.

Getting There & Away

Air There are daily flights between Ürümqi and Yīníng for Y590. There is a CAAC office inside the Yīlítè Dàjiǔdiàn, opposite Hóngqí Guǎngchǎng. A taxi to the airport costs Y7.

Bus Buses leave every hour from Ürümqi between 9 am and 6 pm. The 581km ride takes 14 to 20 hours. Departures from Yīníng start at around 8 am. Regular buses cost Y56 and sleepers Y87/97. There is a spectacular bus ride to Kùchē in the south, which passes over the Tianshan Ranges and through the small Mongolian village of Bayanbulak: a good place to break the journey. A daily bus leaves at 10.30 am and seats costs Y56 for the 22-hour trip.

It is possible to travel by bus from Yīníng to Almaty in Kazakhstan. Buses leave Yīníng on Monday, Wednesday, Thursday and Saturday between 3.30 and 4 am. The ticket office is in the main waiting hall, next to the customs office. Tickets cost US$30.

AROUND YĪNÍNG
Yīlí Gǔ 伊犁谷
Ili Valley

About 6km south of the town centre is a bridge over the Yīlí Hé. The Yīlí Gǔ is pretty – the roads are lined with tall birch trees and there are farms everywhere. This is dairy country and home to some 20,000

Xibe people, who were dispatched to safeguard the region by the Manchus. They have proudly retained their own language and writing system and continue to live in a relatively closed community.

Sàilǐmù Hú 赛里木湖
Sayram Lake

The large and beautiful Sàilǐmù Hú is 120km north of Yīníng, and offers some nice hiking opportunities. The lake is especially colourful during June and July, when alpine flowers blanket the ground.

A very yurty village has sprung up on the main road to cater for the influx of tourists during July and August. The first signs of inadequate management are already revealing themselves in the form of scum along the shore of the lake. If you would prefer peace and tranquillity rather than *kok* (karaoke) and traffic, then just hop off the bus anywhere along the lake and set off. If you need a quick getaway then there are horses and speedboats for hire from the yurty village.

If you want to spend some time exploring this alpine lake area, then bring a tent. There is food up here, but the selection is limited and prices expensive, so bring what you need. Otherwise there are plenty of Kazakh yurts around the lake willing to take a boarder. The usual fee is Y30 per night including meals.

Buses from Yīníng to Sàilǐmù Hú take about three hours. From Kyutun it takes 6½ hours and costs Y30. All buses between Ürümqi and Yīníng pass by the lake, so there is usually no problem with transport. Just stand by the road and wave a passing bus down.

Gānsù 甘肃

A rugged, barren province consisting mostly of mountains and deserts, Gānsù has long been a poor and forgotten backwater controlled only loosely by Běijīng. Nonetheless it has played an important role in Chinese history. Threading its way through Gānsù was the famed Silk Road, the ancient highway along which camel caravans carried goods in and out of China.

Travellers and merchants from as far as the Roman Empire entered the Middle Kingdom via this route along the Silk Road using a string of oasis towns as stepping-stones through the barren landscape. Buddhism was also carried into China along the Silk Road, and the Buddhist cave temples that are found all the way from Xīnjiāng through Gānsù and up through northern China are reminders of the influx of ideas that were made possible by the Silk Road. The Great Wall also ends here near the town of Dūnhuáng.

Traditionally the towns of Gānsù have been established in the oases along the major caravan route where agriculture is possible. With the arrival of modern transport, some industrial development and mining has taken place. The 1892km Lánzhōu-Ürümqi railway line, completed in 1963, was one of the greatest achievements of the early communist regime, and it has done much to relieve the isolation of this region. Today, tourism is an important cash cow, especially in Lánzhōu, Dūnhuáng and Jiāyùguān.

Over 25 million people now inhabit Gānsù. The province is home to a considerable variety of minority peoples, including the Hui, Mongols, Tibetans and Kazaks, although the Han people are now in the vast majority.

LÁNZHŌU 兰州
• pop 2,804,600

The capital of Gānsù, Lánzhōu has been an important garrison town and transport centre since ancient times. Its development as

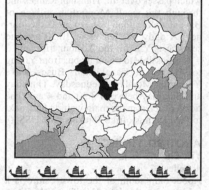

an industrial centre began after the communist victory and the city's subsequent integration into China's expanding national rail network. The city's population increased more than tenfold within little more than a generation. China's economic reform policies have spurred further growth, and office towers and new housing blocks are sprouting up throughout the city.

Although Lánzhōu is not a major tourist drawcard in itself, there are some interesting sights in the surrounding area. Lánzhōu's strategic location also makes it an important transport hub for travellers heading into western China.

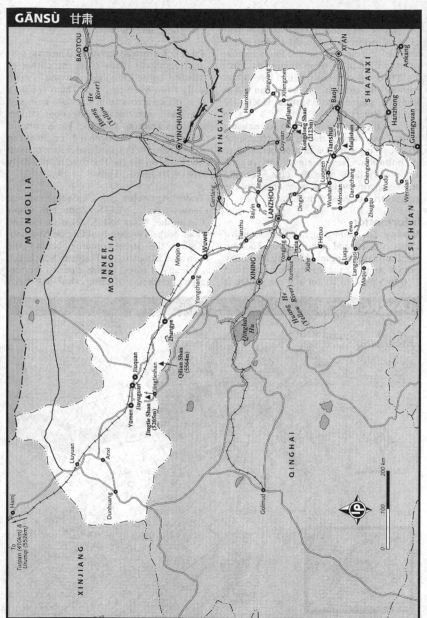

GĀNSÙ 甘肃

BAOTOU

Huáng He (Yellow River)

YINCHUAN

MONGOLIA

INNER MONGOLIA

NINGXIA

Huanxian

Qingyang

Xifengzhen

Qingyang

Guyuan

Pingliang

Kongdong Shan (2123m)

Baiyin

Jingyuan

LANZHOU

Dingxi

Gantang

Wuwei

Tianzhu

Minqin

Yongchang

Yongdeng

XINING

Yongjing

Linxia

Xunhua

Xiahe

Qinghai Hu

Zhangye

Jiuquan

Jiayuguan

Jingtieshan

Qilian Shan (5564m)

Jingtie Shan (5205m)

Yumen

Anxi

Liuyuan

Dunhuang

Hami

To Turpan (410km) & Ürümqi (553km)

XINJIANG

QINGHAI

Golmud

XI'AN

Baoji

SHAANXI

Hanzhong

Ankang

Guangyuan

Tianshui

Maijishan

Luomen

Wushan

Minxian

Dangchang

Chengxian

Wudu

Wenxian

Hezuo

Tewo

Luqu

Langmusi

Maqu

Zhugqu

SICHUAN

Huáng He (Yellow River)

200 km

0 100

Orientation

Geography has conspired to make Lánzhōu a city of awkward design. At 1600m above sea level, the city is crammed into a narrow valley walled in by steep mountains, forcing it to develop westwards in a long urban corridor that extends for more than 20km along the southern banks of the Huáng Hé (Yellow River).

The valley is a perfect trap for exhaust fumes from motor vehicles and chimneys, often burying Lánzhōu in a perpetual haze of pollution. Nevertheless, the rugged topography does give the city a certain unique charm, which is augmented by the general friendliness of the locals.

Information

Money The main branch of the Bank of China is in a brand new tower on Tianshui Lu. Banking hours are Monday to Friday from 9 am to 12 pm and on Saturday from 2.30 to 5 pm and 10 am to 4 pm. There is

another branch on the southern side of Dōngfānghóng Guǎngchǎng.

Post & Communications The main post and telephone office is on the corner of Minzhu Lu and Pingliang Lu and is open daily from 8 am to 7 pm. There is also a post office across from Lánzhōu train station and another near the west bus station.

China Telecom's Internet bar is north of Dōngfānghóng Guǎngchǎng, on Jinchang Lu, just next to the plant and flower market. The bar is on the 2nd floor and is open daily from 9.30 am to 10 pm.

Travel Agencies The China International Travel Service (CITS; Zhōngguó Guójì Lǚxíngshè; ☎/fax 881 3222) is on the 2nd floor of the Tourism Building on Nongmin Xiang, the street running behind the Lánzhōu Bīnguǎn (see Places to Stay later).

Heaps of travel agents cater to the foreign market, offering one-day and

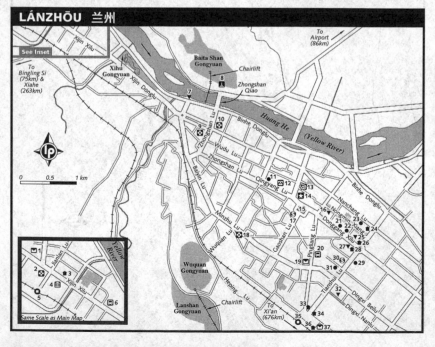

overnight tours to scenic spots in the Lánzhōu vicinity.

One place worth checking out is the reliable Western Travel Service (☎ 841 6321 ext 8638, fax 841 8608), located in the west wing of the Lánzhōu Bīnguǎn (see Places to Stay later). It readily gives out information regardless of whether you bring it business, and its prices for tours and ticket bookings are competitive.

PSB The Public Security Bureau (PSB; Gōngānjú; ☎ 882 7961 ext 8820) is at 38 Qingyang Lu, near the square, Dōngfānghóng Guǎngchǎng. The office is on the left before you go through the main gate, look for the 'Reception Room' sign. It's open Monday to Friday from 9 to 11.30 am and 3 to 5 pm.

Gānsù Shěng Bówùguǎn
省博物馆
Gansu Provincial Museum
If you're into museums, you should quite enjoy this one, which is located directly across the street from the Yǒuyì Bīnguǎn (see Places to Stay later).

The 'Cultural Relics of the Silk Road' exhibition features Neolithic painted pottery taken from a site 300km south-east of here at Dadiwan. Dadiwan culture existed at least 7000 years ago and is thought by some archaeologists to predate the better known Yangshuo culture.

Exhibits from the Han dynasty include inscribed wooden tablets used to relay messages along the Silk Road and an outstanding 1.5m-high Tang dynasty warrior made from glaze-coloured earthenware. Also interesting

LÁNZHŌU

PLACES TO STAY
3 Yǒuyì Bīnguǎn 友谊宾馆
24 Jīnchéng Fàndiàn 金城饭店
26 Lánzhōu Bīnguǎn; Western Travel Service 兰州饭店;西部旅行社
28 Lánzhōu Fēitiān Dàjiǔdiàn 兰州飞天大酒店
33 Lánzhōu Dàshà 兰州大厦
34 Lánshān Bīnguǎn 兰山宾馆
36 Xīnshìjì Jiǔdiàn 新世纪酒店

PLACES TO EAT
7 Snack Tents 帐篷
16 Nóngmín Xiàng (Street Food Stalls) 农民巷
25 Bǎisùjī 百岁鸡
27 Bakery 面包店
32 Dingxī Nánlù Day Market 定西南路市场

OTHER
1 Post & Telephone Office 邮电局
2 Huangjin Shopping Centre 黄金大厦
4 Gānsù Shěng Bówùguǎn 省博物馆
5 West Train Station 火车西站
6 West Bus Station 汽车西站
8 Báitǎ Sì 白塔寺
9 Jinda Shopping Centre 金达商厦
10 Asia-Europe Shopping Centre 亚欧商厦
11 PICC Office 中国人民保险公司
12 Telephone & Telegram Office 电信大楼
13 Wǎngbā (Internet Cafe) 网吧
14 PSB 公安局
15 Dōngfānghóng Guǎngchǎng 东方红广场

17 Bank of China 中国银行
18 Department Store 民百大楼
19 Post & Telephone Office 邮电局
20 East Bus Station 汽车东站
21 Train Booking Office (ICBC Bank) 火车站售票处
22 China Northwest Airlines Booking Office (CAAC) 中国西北航空公司;售票处
23 CITS 中国国际旅行社
29 Lanzhou University 兰州大学
30 Bank of China (Main Branch) 中国银行
31 Xinhua Bookstore 新华书店
35 Main Train Station 火车总站
37 Post & Telephone Office 邮电局

is a 2nd century BC gilded silver plate depicting Bacchus, the Greek god of wine, from the eastern Roman Empire. It was unearthed in 1989 at Jīngyuán, 120km north-east of Lánzhōu, and is evidence of significant contact between the two ancient civilisations.

The museum is open Tuesday to Saturday from 9 am to 12 pm and 2.30 to 5 pm; it's closed on Sunday and Monday. Admission is Y15.

Lánshān Gōngyuán

The mountain range of Lán Shān rises steeply to the south of Lánzhōu. The temperature at its 2100m-high summit is normally a good 5°C cooler than in the valley, so it's a good retreat in summer.

The quickest and easiest way up is by chairlift (lánshān lǎnchē) from behind the Wǔquán Gōngyuán (Five Springs Park). The chairlift takes about 20 minutes to make the diagonal climb to the upper terminal. On the summit you'll find the pavilion Sāntái Gé, refreshment stands and a fun park. A paved trail zigzags its way back down to Wǔquán Gōngyuán, although it's a long walk.

Getting there can take some effort. From the train station take bus No 31 or 34 five stops to Wǔquán stop, get off and walk back until you reach Wuquan Lu. Turn right here and walk about 500m to the Wǔquán Gōngyuán ticket office. You can access the chairlift by going through the park (Y6). Otherwise, you can catch a taxi to the chairlift terminus. The park and chairlift are open from 9 am to 10 pm and admission to the park is Y2. For foreigners, the chairlift costs Y10 for the ride up or Y18 return. During summer the locals usually head up to the peak of Lán Shān to enjoy the sunset and the city's night lights.

Báitǎ Shān 白塔山
White Pagoda Hill

This pleasant, well-managed park is on the northern bank of the Huáng Hé (Yellow River), near the Zhongshan Bridge. The steep slopes are terraced, with small walkways leading through the forest to pavilions, teahouses and a plant nursery on a secluded hillside.

On top of the hill is the Báitǎ Sì (White Pagoda Temple), originally built during the Yuan dynasty, from where you get a good view across the city. There are several mosques on the park periphery. It's possible to catch a chairlift (Y12/16 one way/return) across the Huáng Hé to the park. The terminal is just to the west of Zhongshan Bridge and the last chairlift departs at 7 pm. In summer the park is open from 6.30 am to 10 pm; admission is Y6. Minibus No 101 goes there from in front of the train station on Tianshui Lu.

Places to Stay

The *Lánzhōu Dàshà* (☎ 841 7210, fax 841 7177), opposite the train station, charges Y23 for beds in a triple without bath, or Y25 with a bath. Twins with private bath range from Y100 to Y120, which is not such a bad deal for Lánzhōu. The main advantage of staying here is that it's close to the train station.

The *Lánshān Bīnguǎn* (☎ 861 7211) is a very humble abode that has beds in twins/triples for Y26/22, but the staff would prefer you took the whole room. Its singles are not bad value for Y66. Hot water is available from 8 to 11 pm.

The *Lánzhōu Bīnguǎn* (☎ 841 6321, fax 841 8608) is a large, fully renovated Sino-Stalinist edifice, which is a pleasant place to stay. It offers clean, comfortable triples with attached bath for Y50 per bed – this is at the higher end of the budget range, but is decidedly worth it. Twins range from Y120 to Y230 in the older wings (also a good price for Lánzhōu) and cost Y480 in the main building. The staff are usually open to a bit of friendly bargaining on most rooms. The hotel is a 20-minute walk from the train station or you can take bus No 1 or 7 for two stops.

The *Xīnshìjì Jiǔdiàn* (New Century Hotel; ☎ 861 5888, fax 861 9133) is a new hotel next to the train station with mid-range prices and very comfortable rooms. Twins range from Y280 to Y380 and its suites start at Y580. All rates include a buffet breakfast. It was offering 40% off these prices when we last checked, so maybe drop in to see if it has any deals going.

Nearby, the three-star *Jīnchéng Fàndiàn* (☎ *841 6638, fax 841 8438*) has two separate wings. There are basic twins/triples for Y102/123 in the south building of the hotel, but the staff would prefer you take one of the standard twins for Y380 in the new building. If you want to stay in the south building then head down there to check in.

Opposite the Lánzhōu Bīnguǎn, but on the same traffic circle, is the four-star *Lánzhōu Fēitiān Dàjiǔdiàn (Lanzhou Legend Hotel; ☎ 888 2876, fax 888 7876, ✉ legend@public.lz.gs.cn)*. This is the most upmarket place in town. Discounted rates for twins range from Y623 to Y690 and include a delicious buffet breakfast.

The *Yǒuyì Bīnguǎn (Friendship Hotel; ☎ 233 3051, fax 233 0304)* is a fairly upmarket place on the western side of town. It's only useful if you're catching the early bus to Xiàhé from the west bus station or visiting the Gānsù Shěng Bówùguǎn. Dorm beds in the east building range from Y30 to Y50, and twins range from Y94 in the old wing to Y380 in the three-star building at the back.

Places to Eat

One of the best spots for street food is Nongmin Xiang. The street is lined with small *restaurants* and *food stalls*. At the east end, across from CITS, are a few good places that have tasty, inexpensive dishes.

Both Dingxi Beilu and Dingxi Nanlu, just south of Lanzhou University, have rows of *restaurants* and *street stalls*. Prices here are a bit cheaper, to cater to the student clientele. Several typical Lánzhōu specialities are sold on the streets. One is called *ròujiābǐng*, which is lamb or pork fried with onion, capsicum and a dash of paprika, served inside a 'pocket' of flat bread.

Just 50m to the west of the Lánzhōu Bīnguǎn is *Bǎisùijī* or literally '100-year-old chook', which is a chain of hotpot spicy chicken restaurants. The chicken is cooked in a large wok at your table in a broth of carrots, zucchini, celery, onion, coriander and mushrooms. You will need a minimum of two people to finish the smallest serving (*xiǎo xiǎo guō*). Try adding *tǔdòu* (potato),

dòufu (tofu) and *fěntiáo* (noodles) and wash it all down with a cold draft beer (Y5).

Lánzhōu is famous for its *niúròumiàn* (beef noodles served in spicy soup) – if you don't want the chillies, say '*búyào làjiāo*'. There are a number of fine places to try this around town.

Down by the Huáng Hé, near Zhongshan Bridge, are dozens of *tents* serving tea, beer and snacks. It's possible to sit back in a banana chair and sink some beers, shoot some pool and watch the sun go down over the murky waters of China's No 2 river. For the more active, there are horse riding, speed boats and balloon shooting.

Just next to the Lánzhōu Fēitiān Dàjiǔdiàn (see Places to Stay earlier) is a small *bakery* that makes a delicious banana cake loaf that is great for day hikes.

Getting There & Away

Air China Northwest Airlines has a booking office (☎ 882 1964) on Donggang Xilu, a five-minute walk north-west of the Lánzhōu Bīnguǎn. It's open from 8 am to 9 pm.

There are daily flights to Běijīng (Y1070), Chéngdū (Y750), Guǎngzhōu (Y1510), Ürümqi (Y1040) and Xī'ān (Y430). Other destinations include Kūnmíng, Shànghǎi, Shēnzhèn, Fúzhōu, Hángzhōu, Nánjīng, Qīngdǎo, Shěnyáng, Xiàmén and Wǔhàn.

Bus The west bus station (qìchē xīzhàn) on Xijin Xilu handles departures to Liújiāxiá, near Bǐnglíng Sì, Línxià, Xiàhé, Hézuò, Zhāngyè and Dūnhuáng. Foreigners are charged double for all bus fares unless they purchase PICC insurance (see the boxed text 'Travel Insurance' for more details). For more information see the relevant Getting There & Away sections.

Many travellers have reported that the private bus operators that tout at the bus station are unreliable and prone to ripping travellers off. Many claim to be going to Xiàhé, but instead terminate at Línxià or drop you off at the Xiàhé turn-off. It's always best to purchase tickets from the ticket office inside, unless you are able to broker a reasonable deal in Chinese with a driver.

Travel Insurance

A regulation requires that foreigners who travel by public bus in Gānsù must be insured with the People's Insurance Company of China (PICC), regardless of whether they have taken out their own travel insurance or not.

Some long-distance bus stations may refuse to sell you a ticket unless you can show them your PICC insurance, or else they will charge you double for an 'insurance fee' on the spot (no receipt issued though).

The requirement is currently being enforced mainly on routes in and out of Lánzhōu and in eastern Gānsù. Ironically, you couldn't actually collect anything from this insurance policy if you were involved some sort of accident – it is there to insure the government bus company against lawsuits.

You can buy insurance at most bus stations throughout Gānsù. If they don't sell it, then they probably don't need to see it. It costs Y30 for 20 days; after that it's possible to renew it. CITS and some of the hotels charge an additional Y5 to Y10 commission. Sadly, it's worth buying the insurance, just to avoid further hassles on buses and at the bus station.

The east bus station on Pingliang Lu has departures for mainly eastern destinations. Unlike their west station counterparts, staff here aren't as quick to check foreigners for insurance. There is one nightly sleeper to Xī'ān (Y105; 15 hours) and morning and evening buses for Yínchuān (Y37.20, Y69 sleeper; 10 hours) and Tiānshuǐ (Y27, Y54 sleeper; nine hours). There are buses every hour to Píngliáng (Y31.80; seven hours) and one bus daily to Gùyuán (in Níngxià) leaving at 6.30 am.

Train Trains run to: Ürümqi; Běijīng via Hohhot and Dàtóng; Golmud via Xīníng; Shànghǎi via Xī'ān and Zhèngzhōu; and Běijīng via Xī'ān and Zhèngzhōu. You can also go south to Chéngdū. Heading west, it takes 10½ hours to reach Jiāyùguān, 20 hours to Liǔyuán, 30 hours to Turpan and 32 hours to Ürümqi.

Tickets can be bought from the train station or at the train booking office inside the Industrial Commercial Bank of China (ICBC) on Donggang Xilu, just next door to the CAAC office. Tickets can be bought up to five days in advance, especially sleeper tickets for trains starting from Lánzhōu. It's open daily from 8.30 am to noon and 1 to 4.30 pm.

Getting Around
The airport is at Zhongchuan, almost 90km north of the city. Airport buses (Y25; 1¼ hours) leave from the CAAC office three hours before scheduled flight departures.

The most useful bus routes are Nos 1 and 31 running from the main train station to the west bus station and the Yǒuyì Bīnguǎn. Bus Nos 7 and 10 run from the train station up the length of Tianshui Lu before heading west and east, respectively. Public buses cost between Y0.30 and Y1.

AROUND LÁNZHŌU
Bǐnglíng Sì
Thousand Buddha Caves Temple
Located 75km south-west of Lánzhōu, this set of Buddhist grottoes carved into the cliffs of a 60m-high gorge is one of the more unusual sights in Gānsù. Isolated by the waters of the reservoir Liújiāxiá Shǐkù on the Huáng Hé (Yellow River), the grottoes were spared the vandalism of the Cultural Revolution.

The reservoir itself at one time actually threatened to inundate the caves, but a levy now protects the area from flooding during high-water periods.

Bǐnglíng Sì is also called the **Qiān Fó Dòng** (Thousand Buddha Caves), although in fact the total number of caves is only 183. The setting is spectacular, with soaring cliffs composed of eroded and porous rock with numerous natural cavities. The creators of these grottoes dangled from ropes while carving their masterpieces into the face of the cliffs – one has to wonder how many artisans fell to their deaths.

The oldest caves have been repaired and added to on numerous occasions since they were built during the Western Qin dynasty.

They contain 694 statues, 82 clay sculptures and a number of frescoes. Cave 169, containing a buddha and two bodhisattvas, is one of the oldest (AD 420) and best preserved in China. Most of the other caves were completed during the prosperous Tang period. The star of the caves is the 27m-high seated statue of Maitreya, the future Buddha (cave 172).

Depending on which caves you want to see, entry costs Y20 to Y300. The cheaper tickets are for the unlocked caves, while the Y300 ticket gives you a complete guided tour including the magnificent caves 169 and 172.

Getting There & Away

From Lánzhōu to the caves is a 12-hour round trip – half of that time on a bus and half on a boat. The caves are inaccessible in winter because the water level in the river is too low and ice may also block the boats.

Western Travel Service (in the Lánzhōu Bīnguǎn) and CITS all run tours to the caves whenever they have enough people; the usual tour price is Y250, which only includes transport. If there are two people, Western Travel and CITS charge Y300 per person.

If you're going on to Línxià or Xiàhé, you can avoid backtracking to Lánzhōu by catching a bus to Línxià. The trip from Liújiāxia to Línxià takes about 4½ hours, via an interesting high route east of the Huáng Hé (Yellow River) through areas settled by the Dongxiang ethnic minority. Another alternative is the Western Travel tour, which instead of returning to the port of Liújiāxia after visiting Bǐnglíng Sì, the staff drop passengers off at the small port of Lianhuatai. From there it is possible to catch a bus to Línxià (40 minutes) and then on to Xiàhé. You can also arrange this trip with the private boat operators at Liújiāxia.

A bus from Lánzhōu to Liújiāxia leaves the west bus station at 7.30 am (Y5.60; one hour). It often arrives just in time to catch one of the boats to Bǐnglíng Sì. The last bus back to Lánzhōu from Liújiāxia usually leaves between 5 and 6 pm, but if there are not enough passengers it waits until the next day.

The boat trip costs Y30 and takes three hours each way; boats only stay at the caves

for one hour, so don't mess about! Alternatively you could charter a speedboat for Y400, which gets there in one hour and carries up to eight people.

LÍNXIÀ 临夏

Línxià was once an important stop on the Silk Road between Lánzhōu and Yáng Guān. The town has a decidedly Muslim Hui character, with a large mosque in the centre of town.

In the markets you'll see carved gourds, daggers, saddlery, carpets, wrought iron goods and a thriving trade in spectacles made with ground crystal lenses and metal frames.

Línxià is also a regional centre for the Dongxiang minority. The Dongxiang minority speak their own Altaic language and are believed to be descendants of 13th-century immigrants from central Asia who were moved forcibly to China after Kublai Khan's conquest of the Middle East. Some have greenish-blue eyes, high cheekbones and large noses.

Places to Stay

The friendly *Shuǐquán Bīnguǎn* (☎ 621 4968) is 50m along on your right as you leave the south bus station. It offers beds in three-person dorms for Y10 and twins with bathroom for Y40 and Y80.

Getting There & Away

Buses to Línxià (Y12.50; three hours) leave Lánzhōu's west bus station every 30 minutes between 7 am and 2 pm. Private minibuses also make the trip frequently and run until 6 pm.

In the opposite direction, buses leave Línxià for Lánzhōu approximately every 20 minutes from 6.30 am to 5 pm. There have been lots of reports of bus driver scams recently. Drivers are telling travellers that they are going to Xiàhé, but they instead terminate in Línxià. They are apparently demanding extra fares halfway through the journey and threatening travellers. You can avoid this by buying your tickets through the bus stations and holding onto your ticket.

From Línxià, buses to Xiàhé (Y9; two hours) leave approximately every 40 minutes between 6.30 am and 4.40 pm. Buses to Hézuò (Y8; 3½ hours) leave about every half hour from 6.30 am to 5 pm.

There are two long-distance bus stations in Línxià. For services to Qīnghǎi and Yǒngjìng as well as extra services to Xiàhé and Línxià, use the west bus station on Minzhu Xilu. An interesting option are the buses to Xúnhuā and Dahejia (Mèngdá Tiānchí) in Qīnghǎi. There are four daily buses to Xúnhuā (Y12; 3½ hours) via Hanjie and Daowei. There is only one bus to Xīníng (Y25; 11 hours) at 5.40 am, which runs via Yǒngjìng (Bǐnglíng Sì).

You can buy insurance at both of the long-distance bus stations.

XIÀHÉ 夏河

Set in a beautiful mountain valley, Xiàhé is most definitely worth a visit, especially if you can't get to Tibet. It's the leading Tibetan monastery town outside of Lhasa and many Tibetans come here on pilgrimage dressed in their finest, most colourful clothing. Outside of town there are hiking opportunities in nearby grasslands and the surrounding mountains.

Religious activity centres on the Lābǔlèng Sì (Labrang Monastery), one of the six major Tibetan monasteries of the Gelukpa (Yellow Hat sect of Tibetan Buddhism). The others are Ganden, Sera and Drepung Monasteries in the Lhasa area; Tashilhunpo Monastery in Shigatse; and Ta'er (Kumbum) Monastery near Xīníng, Qīnghǎi.

Walking through the warrens and alleys of this huge monastery, side by side with pilgrims and monks, feels like you've entered another world.

Xiàhé is a microcosm of south-western Gānsù, with the area's three principal ethnic groups represented. In rough terms, Xiàhé's population is 50% Tibetan, 40% Han and 10% Hui.

Orientation

At 2920m above sea level, the Xià Hé flows for several kilometres east-to-west along the valley of the Dàxià Hé. The Lābǔlèng Sì (Labrang Monastery) is roughly halfway along, and marks the division between Xiàhé's mainly Han and Hui Chinese eastern quarter and the overwhelmingly Tibetan village to the west.

A 3km pilgrims' way, with long rows of prayer wheels (1174 of them!) and Buddhist shrines, encircles the monastery. There are some 40 smaller monasteries affiliated with Lābǔlèng Sì (Labrang Monastery) in the surrounding mountains (as well as many others scattered across Tibet and China) and the area is a great place for hiking in clean, peaceful surroundings. Take warm clothing and rain gear.

You can follow the river up to Sāngkē or head up into the surrounding valleys, but carry a stick or a pocket full of rocks, as wild dogs can be a problem.

Information

It is possible to change US dollars at the banks or otherwise try some of the small antique shops along the main street who will give you a reasonable rate.

The post and telephone office is in the east of town, near the bus station. There is an Internet bar in the Chinese section of town. Look out for the large ad (Intranet Club) on the 2nd floor of the terraced building. It charges a hefty Y32 per hour, so you may prefer waiting until you return to a larger city.

The PSB is just opposite the Yǒuyì Bīnguǎn (see Places to Stay later)

Lābǔlèng Sì 拉卜楞寺
Labrang Monastery

The monastery was built in 1709 by E'angzongzhe, the first-generation Jiamuyang (living Buddha), who came from the nearby town of Ganjia. It is home to six institutes (Institute of Esoteric Buddhism, Higher & Lower Institutes of Theology, Institute of Medicine, Institute of Astrology and Institute of Law). There are also numerous temple halls, 'living buddha' residences and living quarters for the monks.

At its peak the monastery housed nearly 4000 monks, but their ranks were decimated during the Cultural Revolution, when monks and buildings took a heavy beating. The numbers are gradually recovering, and there are about 1200 monks today, drawn from Qīnghǎi, Gānsù, Sìchuān and Inner Mongolia.

In April 1985 the main Prayer Hall of the Institute of Esoteric Buddhism was razed in a fire caused by faulty electrical wiring. The fire is said to have burnt for a week and destroyed some priceless relics. The hall's reconstruction was completed at great cost in mid-1990, but the monks remain reluctant to allow the use of electricity in most parts of the monastery.

Entry to the main temple is by tour only. One of the monks (some speak English well) will show you around. Tours generally include the Institute of Medicine, the Ser Kung Golden Temple, the Prayer Hall and the museum. The ticket office and souvenir shop are on the right-hand side of the monastery car park. The office is open from 8 am to 12 pm and from 2 to 6 pm. Admission is Y23 for foreigners. There are English tours of the monastery leaving the ticket office at 10, 10.30 am and 3 pm daily.

Access to the rest of the monastery area is free, and you can easily spend several hours just walking around and taking in the atmosphere. Try to make friends with a monk or two: they'll probably be happy to invite you into their living quarters, which always makes for an interesting house call.

Festivals

These are important not only for the monks, but also for the nomads who stream into town in multicoloured splendour from the grasslands. Since the Tibetans use a lunar calendar, dates for individual festivals vary from year to year.

The Monlam (Great Prayer) Festival starts three days after the Tibetan New Year, which is usually in February or early March. On the 13th, 14th, 15th and 16th days of this month there are some spectacular ceremonies.

On the morning of the 13th a *thangka* (sacred painting on cloth) of Buddha, measuring over 30m by 20m, is unfurled on the other side of the Dàxià Hé from the hillside facing

the monastery. This event is accompanied by processions and prayer assemblies.

On the 14th there is an all-day session of Cham dances performed by 35 masked dancers, with Yama, the lord of death, playing the leading role. On the 15th there is an evening display of butter lanterns and sculptures. On the 16th the Maitreya statue is paraded around the monastery all day.

During the second month (usually starting in March or early April) there are several interesting festivals, especially those held on the seventh and eighth days. Scriptural debates, lighting of butter lamps, collective prayers and blessings take place at other times during the year to commemorate Sakyamuni, Tsong Khapa or individual generations of the 'living buddhas'.

Places to Stay

The best place in town, without a doubt, is *Tara Guesthouse (Cáiràng Zhuōmǎ Lǚshè; ☎ 712 1274)*, which straddles the border between the Tibetan and Han parts of town. All the rooms are Tibetan style and are very clean and comfortable. Beds in cosy four-bed dorms are Y15 and twins with shared bath are Y40 and Y50. There is hot water from 6 am to noon and then again from 6 pm to midnight. The owner, Tsering Dolma, speaks fluent English, is a fine host and is quite knowledgeable about the area.

The next best choice in the budget category is probably the *Overseas Tibetan Hotel (Huáqiáo Bīnguǎn; ☎ 712 2642, 77 Renmin Xijie)*, which has clean beds in dorms from Y7 to Y15 or in twins for Y25. It has common showers with hot water usually available in the evenings. It also has well-maintained bicycles for hire and a laundry service.

The cheapest option is the *Lābǔlèngsì Zhāodàisuǒ (Labrang Monastery Guesthouse)*, a quiet place nestled inside a small courtyard with authentic yak butter 'scented' beds from Y10. It doesn't have showers, but there's always plenty of hot water from the boiler.

A more comfortable option is the *Lābǔlèng Bīnguǎn (Labrang Hotel; ☎ 712 1849)*, by the river a few kilometres up the

GĀNSÙ 甘肃

XIÀHÉ & LĀBŬLÈNG SÌ (LABRANG MONASTERY) 夏河、拉卜楞寺

valley from the village. It's a friendly, tranquil place, and one of the few hotels in China where you can wake to the gentle sound of a rushing stream. The only drawback is the 'hot' water, which seems to only get lukewarm at best. In the rear building, beds in triples with private bath are Y20, and twins are Y120 – both fairly good value for the money. More expensive twins in the main building (Y280) and in Tibetan-style concrete 'tents' (Y360) are not such a good deal. Some of their more interesting rooms are being returned to the monastery who may turn them into a school. You can get there by motor-tricycle for about Y5, or walk there in 45 minutes. The hotel rents bicycles for Y5 per hour or Y15 a day.

In the Chinese quarter are a few standard Chinese-style hotels that offer cheap rooms, but very little in the way of personality. The **Dàshà Bīnguǎn** (☎ 712 1546) is a simple place with dorm beds from Y21 and twins with bathroom for Y82. It also has bikes for hire. Nearer the bus station, the **Yǒuyì Bīnguǎn** (*Friendship Hotel*) offers dorm beds in quads/triples for Y10/15 and decent twins for Y70. Both these hotels have hot water in the evening, generally after 9 pm.

Places to Eat
For Tibetan food, locals say the two best places in town are the **Restaurant of the Labrang Monastery** (*Lābǔlèngsì Fàndiàn*) and the **Snowland Restaurant** (*Xuěyù Cāntīng*). Both are just west of Tara Guesthouse and have authentic Tibetan dishes such as yak-milk yoghurt and *tsampa*: a

mixture of yak butter, cheese, barley and sugar mixed into a dough with the fingers and eaten uncooked. A bit bland, but worth trying at least once. The Lābǔlèngsì Fàndiàn also has a rear courtyard where tables are set up during the summer months.

Next door to the Overseas Tibetan Hotel is the **Everest Restaurant**, a rather sterile looking affair that dishes up some surprisingly delicious Nepali vegetable, mutton or chicken curries.

For Chinese or Hui food, there is a row of small places east of Tara Guesthouse along the main road.

Shopping
You can pick up some Tibetan handicrafts in the shops along the main street, including yak-butter pots, daggers, fur-lined boots, colourful Tibetan shawls, tiny silver teapots and Tibetan *laba* trumpets. Prices in the tourist shops are negotiable, but the Tibetan household goods shops have set prices: don't annoy the staff by trying to bargain.

Getting There & Away
Xiàhé is accessible only by bus. Some travellers arrive from Lánzhōu, while others come from Sìchuān.

From Lánzhōu, there is only one direct daily bus departing from the west bus station at 7.30 am (Y19). It's a six-hour ride, including a stop for lunch near Línxià. If you can't get a direct ticket from Lánzhōu to Xiàhé, then take a morning bus to Línxià and change there (see the Línxià section for more details).

XIÀHÉ & LĀBŬLÈNG SÌ (LABRANG MONASTERY)

1 Lābŭlèng Bīnguǎn; CITS
拉卜楞宾馆；
中国国际 眯猩

2 Monastery Ticket Office
售票处

3 Restaurant of Labrang Monastery
拉卜楞寺饭店

4 Snowland Restaurant
雪域餐厅

5 Lābŭlèngsì Zhāodàisuǒ
拉卜楞寺招待所

6 Tara Guesthouse
卓玛旅社

7 Overseas Tibetan Hotel
华侨宾馆

8 Everest Restaurant

9 Intranet Club
网吧

10 Mosque
清真寺

11 Dàshà Bīnguǎn
大厦宾馆

12 Post & Telephone Office
邮电局

13 Yǒuyì Bīnguǎn
友谊宾馆

14 PSB
公安局

15 Bus Station
汽车站

From Xiàhé the direct bus to Lánzhōu (Y20) leaves at 7.20 am, turn up a bit earlier to get a good seat and store your luggage on the roof. Don't worry if this is too early as there are plenty of buses to Línxià, from where you can change to a Lánzhōu bus.

Buses to Línxià (Y9; 2½ hours) run once or twice an hour between 6 am and 6 pm. The schedule is similar for buses to Hézuò (Y6.50; 1½ hours).

There is also one bus daily to Tóngrén, in Qīnghǎi (Y12; 6 hours). From Tóngrén you can get a connecting bus to Xīníng or Xúnhuā.

You can buy insurance at the bus station.

Getting Around

Most hotels and restaurants rent bikes for about Y10 per day. Share taxis and the motor-tricycles charge about Y2 for a short trip.

AROUND XIÀHÉ
Sāngkē & Gānjiā Cǎoyuán
桑科与甘加草原

Around and beyond the village of Sāngkē, 14km up the valley from Xiàhé, is a small lake surrounded by large expanses of open grassland where the Tibetans graze their yak herds. In summer these rolling pastures are at their greenest and have numerous wildflowers. It's a lovely place for walking.

The Lābŭlèng Bīnguǎn has some nomad-style tents on the grasslands where you can stay overnight for around Y40 per bed. The road from Xiàhé rises gradually and you can bicycle up in about one hour. You can

also get there by taking a bus from Xiàhé to Sāngkē village (Sāngkē Gōngshè) or hire a motor-tricycle for about Y20 return.

Around 34km outside Xiàhé, the **Gānjiā Cǎoyuán** (Ganjia Grasslands) feature rolling hills and even nicer views than Sāngkē. Buses run here; ask for Gānjiā Gōngshè.

HÉZUÒ 合作

This town is mainly used as a transit point for travellers plying the route between Gānsù and Sìchuān provinces. It's not too exciting, but certainly has some character – traders walk around with fur pelts slung over their shoulders, Tibetan monks make their way through narrow backstreets and white-capped Chinese Hui Muslims are busy running shops, restaurants and other small businesses.

About 2km from the bus station along the main road in the direction of Xiàhé is the **Mǐlāerbā Fógé** (Ando Hezuo Mila Riba Palace). Built in 1777, this 14-storey temple was razed by Red Guards during the Cultural Revolution and was rebuilt in 1988. The inside furnishings are quite elaborate and a climb to the top rewards you with views of the beautiful grasslands surrounding Hézuò.

Places to Stay & Eat

If you time your buses, then you won't have to spend the night here. If not, then the *Jīndū Bīnguǎn* is to the left as you exit the bus station and it's 100m on your right. A bed in a triple with shared bath is Y30 and in a twin with attached bath is Y50. Hot water is available from 8.30 to 11 pm.

In the unlikely event that all the beds are full, then jump in a share taxi (Y2) and head over to *Bāyī Bīnguǎn*. It has beds in clean twins for Y30 with attached bathroom. The lukewarm water comes on at 9.30 pm.

Getting There & Away

There are two bus stations in Hézuò, one government-run, the other private, and their schedules are much the same. Buses from both stations often annoyingly roam the streets of Hézuò for an hour before they depart, although the private buses are surprisingly more reliable. The private bus station can be reached by walking east from the main bus station along Maqu Donglu for 10 minutes.

Hézuò is the place where buses from Zöige (Sìchuān) and Xiàhé meet. There are frequent buses to Xiàhé (Y8; 2½ hours) and to Línxiá (Y8; 3½ hours) from 7.30 am to 5 pm.

Going south is a different story. There is only one bus a day to Zoigê, leaving at 7.30 am (Y27; nine hours). Buses to Lǎngmùsì leave between 6.30 and 10.50 am (Y15; six hours).

You can buy insurance at the bus station.

LĀNGMÙSÌ 朗木寺

This attractive little village has two large Tibetan Buddhist monasteries, each with around 600 monks. There's mountainous scenery on all sides, which provide ample opportunity for some great day walks. It's one of the most Tibetan places outside of Tibet, and a relaxing place to while away a few days.

Accommodation in Lǎngmùsì is pretty basic. The *Lǎngmùsì Fàndiàn* has comfortable dorm beds in triple rooms for Y15. There are showers after 9 pm and inside toilets.

The *Lǎngmùsì Bīnguǎn* is under the archway just next door and has a little more atmosphere. Dorm beds start at Y10 and there were plans afoot to have indoor showers and toilets in the near future.

There are several small restaurants in town, including two with English signs and menus, the *Lǎngmùsì Restaurant* and *Leisha's Cafe*, otherwise known as The Little Restaurant. Leisha's Cafe is the most

popular option – no doubt due to the delicious apple pie and excellent meat and vegie dumplings, not to mention the fact that it has a comfy sofa to relax on.

Getting There & Away

Unless you take a direct bus to Lǎngmùsì from Hézuò, you can get there on one of the Hézuò-Zoigê buses, which drop you off at an intersection about 4km from the village. Motor-tricycles that usually wait there will take you into town for Y1 or Y2.

To get to Zoigê you'll need to catch one of the buses from Hézuò, which means catching a motor-tricycle out to the intersection with the main road to Sìchuān. Buses to Zoigê generally pass by between 11.30 am and 2 pm. From Lǎngmùsì there are two daily buses to Hézuò departing at 7 am and 8.30 am (Y15). From Hézuò it is easy to travel on to Xiàhé, Línxià and Lánzhōu.

Hexi Corridor

JIĀYÙGUĀN 嘉峪关

☎ 0947 • pop 130,900

Jiāyùguān is an ancient Han Chinese outpost. The Great Wall once extended beyond here, but in 1372, during the first few years of the Ming dynasty, a fortress was built. From then on Jiāyùguān was considered both the western tip of the wall and the western boundary of the empire.

The city itself lacks soul. However, it's not an unfriendly place, and the snow-capped mountains provide a dramatic backdrop when the weather is clear.

Although a mandatory stop for tour groups, Jiāyùguān and its surrounding sights are not so amazing as to merit a special visit. However, if you're moving east or west through the Hexi Corridor at a leisurely pace, a stop here should prove interesting enough.

Information

Money The main Bank of China, on Xinhua Nanlu, is the only place that changes travellers cheques and is open Monday to

Friday from 9.30 am to 5.30 pm weekends from 10 am to 4 pm.

Post & Communications The post and telephone office is diagonally opposite the Jiāyùguān Bīnguǎn and is open from 8.30 am to 7 pm. Just next door is China Telecom's Internet bar. It's open from 10 am to 10 pm and charges Y10 per hour. The Jiāyùguān Bīnguǎn also has Internet access for Y12 per hour.

Travel Agent Xiongguan Travel Service in the Jiāyùguān Bīnguǎn is allied with CITS. It's mainly directed at tour groups and can't do much to help individual travellers.

PSB The PSB office is in the south of the city and has a roving foreign affairs officer who visits the hotels. If you need a visa extension, contact the front desk of your hotel and the staff will arrange for the foreign affairs officer to come by.

Chángchéng Bówùguǎn
长城博物馆
Great Wall Museum
Built to resemble the towers and turrets of the Great Wall, this museum has some mildly interesting displays on the history, construction and current state of China's most famous tourist attraction. However, there are no English descriptions, making it pretty dull if you can't read Chinese.

The museum is south of the centre and is open Monday to Friday from 8.30 am to 12 pm and 2.30 to 6 pm and weekends from 10 am to 5 pm; admission is Y12.

Places to Stay
The *Xióngguān Bīnguǎn* (☎ 622 5115, fax 622 5399), on Xinhua Nanlu, is the best deal in town. Dorm beds range from Y12 to Y16 and twins with private bath are Y80

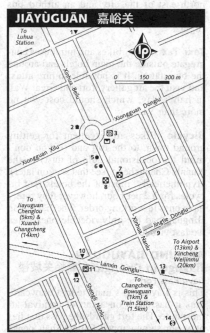

JIĀYÙGUĀN 嘉峪关

To Luhua Station
Xinhua Beilu
Xiongguan Donglu
Xiongguan Xilu
0   150   300 m
To Jiayuguan Chenglou (5km) & Xuanbi Changcheng (14km)
Xinhua Nanlu
Jingtie Donglu
Lanxin Gonglu
Shengli Nanlu
To Airport (13km) & Xincheng Weijinmu (20km)
To Changcheng Bowuguan (1km) & Train Station (1.5km)

JIĀYÙGUĀN

1 Night Market
   夜市
2 Jiāyùguān Bīnguǎn;
   Xiongguan Travel Service
   嘉峪关宾馆；雄关旅行社
3 Internet Bar
   网吧
4 Post & Telephone Office
   邮电局
5 CAAC
   民航售票处
6 Xinhua Bookstore
   新华书店
7 Department Store
   百货商店
8 Renmin Department Store
   人民商城
9 Vegetable Market
   市场
10 Línyuàn Jiǔjiā
   林苑酒家
11 Bus Station
   汽车站
12 Wùmào Bīnguǎn
   物贸宾馆
13 Xióngguān Bīnguǎn
   雄关宾馆
14 Bank of China
   中国银行

and Y100. The staff are friendly and speak a little English.

On the traffic circle at the centre of town is the upmarket *Jiāyùguān Bīnguǎn* (☎ 622 6983, fax 622 7174). It has beds in unexciting dorms in the old wing for Y12, Y18 and Y26. Twins are Y280 in the new wing or Y120 in the old wing, however, these can be bargained down to Y220 and Y80 respectively. All the rooms are fairly reasonable value given the facilities and service.

If the other places are full then you could try the *Wùmào Bīnguǎn*, which is just by the bus station and has basic dorm beds for Y15. Due to a foreigners surcharge its other rooms are not great value.

Places to Eat

Restaurants are few and far between in Jiāyùguān and tend to close by around 10 pm.

For cheap and tasty food try the area in front of the Renmin department store, off Xinhua Beilu, or the *night market*, which is crammed with stalls selling ròujiāmó (grilled lamb and chicken skewers), *liáng miàn* (spicy cold noodles), yoghurt, and plenty of draft beer, which unfortunately tends to be rather flat.

Just opposite the bus station is a collection of competing restaurants. One of the most popular is the *Línyuàn Jiǔjiā*, which does spicy Sìchuān food. It has a Romanised sign that says 'Linyuan Jiujia' and one or two of the staff speak a little English.

Getting There & Away

Air Jiāyùguān's airport only operates from July to the end of October when it offers a thrice-weekly flight to Dūnhuáng (Y400) and Lánzhōu (Y730).

The CAAC booking office is on Xinhua Nanlu, just south of the Jiāyùguān Bīnguǎn.

Bus There are three direct daily buses between Dūnhuáng and Jiāyùguān (Y29; six hours). There are four departures to Lánzhōu, two of which are sleeper coaches. The trip takes 16 hours and should only cost Y57 for the hard seat and Y127 for the sleeper. There are numerous buses to Zhāngyè (Y19; five hours).

The bus station attempts to charge an extra foreigners fee, regardless of whether you have PICC insurance or not, for all buses heading east to Zhāngyè and Lánzhōu. Take the staff up on the issue and they might back down.

Train Jiāyùguān lies on the Lánzhōu-Ürümqi railway line. From here it's five hours to Liǔyuán, less than four hours to Zhāngyè, 26 hours to Xī'ān, and 10½ hours to Lánzhōu. Sleeper tickets on train No 206 to Lánzhōu and No 507 to Ürümqi are the most readily available. Other destinations include Běijīng, Chéngdū, Zhōngwèi, Shànghǎi and Zhèngzhōu.

The train station is 5km south of the town centre. Minibuses run down Xinhua Nanlu to the station and charge Y1. A taxi there should cost no more than Y10.

Getting Around

To/From the Airport The airport is 13km north-east of the city and an airport bus (Y10) from the CAAC office meets all flights.

Taxi Taxis, motorbikes and minibuses congregate outside the main hotels and around the bus station. It is possible to hire a taxi and visit the art gallery, fort and Great Wall in half a day, which should cost you no more than Y150.

Bicycle Bikes are excellent for getting around town, to the fort and (if you don't mind the occasional gulp of dust) to the Xuánbì Chángchéng (see that section later). Hypothetically, most of the hotels rent bicycles fŏr Y2 per hour, however they rarely have ones in working order. The Jiāyùguān Bīnguǎn had the only rideable ones when we last visited.

AROUND JIĀYÙGUĀN
Jiāyùguān Chénglóu 嘉峪关城楼
Jiayu Pass Fort

This is Jiāyùguān's main tourist drawcard, thus it has taken on a sort of carnival atmosphere. The fort guards the pass that lies between snow-capped Qílián Shān peaks and **Hēi Shān** (Black Mountain) of the Mazong Range.

Built in 1372, the fort was dubbed the 'Impregnable Defile Under Heaven'. Although the Chinese often controlled territory far beyond Jiāyùguān, this was the last major stronghold of the empire to the west.

At the eastern end of the fort is the **Guānghuà Mén** (Gate of Enlightenment) and in the west is the **Róuyuǎn Mén** (Gate of Conciliation). Over each gate stand 17m-high towers with upturned flying eaves. On the inside of each gate are horse lanes leading up to the top of the wall. However, the entire complex has been renovated, which makes it a bit hard to get a feel for its history.

The fort is 5km west of Jiāyùguān. It is possible to cycle out here in about half an hour, or otherwise take a taxi. The fort is open from 8 am to 8 pm and entry costs Y15, plus another Y3 to go up to the main viewing tower.

Xuánbì Chángchéng 悬壁长城
Overhanging Great Wall

Linking Jiāyùguān with Hēi Shān, the wall is believed to have been constructed in 1539. It had since pretty much crumbled to dust, but was reconstructed in 1987. Students were brought in to do the work and were paid one fen for each brick laid.

From the upper tower high on a ridge you get a sweeping view of the desert, the oasis of Jiāyùguān and the glittering snow-capped peaks in the distance.

The wall is 6km north of Jiāyùguān Chénglóu via the shortest route (a rough dirt road leading north towards the mountains) or 10km on the surfaced road. A walk along the wall costs Y8.

Xīnchéng Wèijìnmù
Art Gallery

This is not really an art gallery, but ancient tombs with original wall paintings. There are literally thousands of tombs in the desert 20km east of Jiāyùguān, but only one is currently open to visitors. The tombs date from approximately AD 220 to 420 (the Wei and Western Jin periods).

The brick-paintings vividly depict various social activities including hunting, farming, fruit picking and banqueting. The contents of some of these tombs, including the wooden coffins, are held in an exhibition room opposite the ticket office.

The gallery is open daily from 8 am to 8 pm and admission is Y30.

Qīyī Bīngchuān
July 1st Glacier

The glacier sits at 4300m, high up in the Qílián Shān mountains. The glacier is about 90km south-west of Jiāyùguān and is best reached via train No 953 to the iron ore town of Jìngtiěshān, which departs from Jiāyùguān's Luhua station at 8.30 am. It's a scenic three-hour train trip to Jìngtiěshān, where you can hire a taxi to the glacier. It is a further 20km to the glacier and the return trip should cost about Y120. Hikers can walk a 5km trail alongside the glacier, but at that elevation it gets cold even in summer, so come prepared.

The return train to Jiāyùguān leaves Jìngtiěshān at 1.38 pm, so as the incoming train doesn't arrive into town until 11.30 am, you will need to stay the night in Jìngtiěshān in order to get to the glacier. This leaves you with enough time the next morning to hire a taxi (Y50 return) up to Tiān'é Hú and the Tibetan village Qíqīng. This same bumpy road eventually ends up in Qīnghǎi, but there is no public transport past Jìngtiěshān. There is a cheap and basic hostel (*zhāodàisuǒ*) in town.

LIǓYUÁN 柳园
☎ 0937

Liǔyuán, a forlorn little town on the Lánzhōu-Ürümqi railway line, is the jumping off point for Dūnhuáng, 130km and 2½ hours south by bus.

Unless you're catching an early morning train, there should be no need to stay here. But if you must, the only place that takes foreigners when we last visited was the ***Liǔyuán Bīnguǎn*** (*☎557 2340*), which has dorms for Y15 and Y25 with common showers and twins from Y80 to Y120.

There are six trains daily in each direction. Going east, it takes five hours to reach

Jiāyùguān and 20 hours to Lánzhōu. To the west, it's 12 hours to Turpan and 15 hours to Ürümqi. The overnight tourist train (No 205) runs between Ürümqi and Liǔyuán and takes 12 hours. This is a good option if you are heading for Turpan, as tickets are easier to purchase. Tickets can be purchased up to three days in advance, otherwise turn up in Liǔyuán a bit earlier on the day of departure. There are also daily departures to Běijīng, Chéngdū, Korla, Shànghǎi, Xī'ān and Zhèngzhōu.

Minibuses for Dūnhuáng depart from in front of the train station when trains arrive. If there are enough passengers you will leave immediately; if not be prepared to wait until the bus fills up. The one-way fare is Y10, plus Y5 for each bag placed on the roof. A share taxi is not a bad option if the bus isn't moving. They generally charge between Y25 and Y30 per person.

If you're coming back from Dūnhuáng to catch a train, check the weather: if sand storms are blowing, the ride could take as long as four hours.

On the way to Dūnhuáng, the road passes some crumbling remains of the Great Wall that were built during the Han dynasty. The sections are visible from the road between the 85km and 90km markers.

DŪNHUÁNG 敦煌
☎ 0937

After travelling for hours towards Dūnhuáng, the flat, barren desert landscape suddenly gives way to lush, green cultivated fields with mountainous rolling sand dunes as a backdrop. The area has a certain haunting beauty, especially at night under a star-studded sky. It's not so much the desert dunes and romantic nights that attract so many tourists to Dūnhuáng, but the superb Buddhist art at the nearby Mògāo Kū (Mogao Caves).

During the Han and Tang dynasties Dūnhuáng was a major point of interchange between China and the outside world – a stopping-off post for both incoming and outgoing trading caravans. Despite a surge in tourism-related development, the town still has a fairly relaxed feel to it, and it's

easy to kick back here for a few days. There are several sights worth visiting in the surrounding area, and the town is just lively enough to keep you entertained, but not overwhelmed.

Information
Money A small branch of the Bank of China, on Yangguan Zhonglu, is open daily and can change cash and travellers cheques. The larger bank opposite doesn't close for lunch, but is closed on weekends.

Post & Communications The post and telephone office is on the north-western side of the main traffic circle. There is an Internet cafe just west of the post office. It charges Y12 per hour and is open from 8 am to 11 pm, but closes for a couple of hours over lunch.

Travel Agencies CITS has a branch inside the Dūnhuáng Bīnguǎn. There are other travel agents scattered about town, sequestered in various hotels. Most can book train and air tickets, as well as tours to surrounding sights such as Yáng Guān and Yùmén Guān.

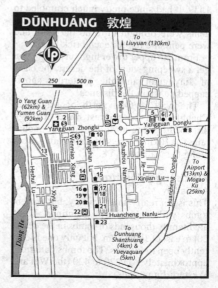

GĀNSÙ 甘肃

PSB The PSB foreign affairs office is in the main PSB building on Yangguan Zhonglu, near the Bank of China.

Xiàn Bówùguǎn 县博物馆
County Museum
The museum is on Yangguan Donglu, east of the main traffic circle, and makes for a pleasant browse.

Exhibits include some of the Tibetan and Chinese scriptures unearthed from Cave No 17 at Mògāo, sacrificial objects from the Han to Tang dynasties, and relics such as silks, brocades and reed torches for the beacons from Yáng Guān and Yùmén Guān. For the curious, the incongruously placed MiG-15 fighter jet in the front courtyard was originally destined for the town park, but before it could be moved the museum built a main gate. Today there's no moving the thing unless the wings are shorn off.

Museum hours are 8 am to 12 pm and 2.30 to 6 pm; admission is Y10.

Places to Stay
Most hotels in Dūnhuáng vary the rates by season. The tourist season is from June to September and hotel rates rise by about 50% or more at that time. The rates quoted in this section are for the low season.

Places to Stay – Budget
Almost directly opposite the bus station, the two-star *Fēitiān Bīnguǎn* (☎ 882 2337, fax 882 2311) offers reasonable rates and a good location. Beds in clean, multi-bed dorms start at Y15 and comfortable twins are Y160. The Fēitiān is also home to *John's Information Cafe*.

Opposite the Fēitiān Bīnguǎn, the *Wǔhuán Zhāodàisuǒ (Five Rings Olympic Hotel;* ☎ 883 2147) may have an awkward name, but it's clean and staff are eager to please. Dorm beds range from Y10 to Y25 and twins with bath are Y80. To top things off, it has 24-hour hot water.

The simple *Yǒuhǎo Bīnguǎn* (☎ 882 2678) has dorm beds for Y20 and beds in a twin/triple with bathroom for Y40/35.

The *Shāzhōu Fàndiàn* (☎ 882 2380) is at the top end of Mingshan Lu and is the newest place in town. The staff are friendly and the rooms and toilets are all very clean. A dorm bed in a triple/quad is Y20 or in a twin Y25. Very comfortable air-con twins are Y180, while standard twins are only Y120.

The *Míngshān Bīnguǎn* (☎ 882 2122) is an old-style place, but for the money it's not a bad deal and it's conveniently located. Dorm beds start at Y20 in a quad or more comfortable twins with private bath are Y80.

DŪNHUÁNG

PLACES TO STAY
8 Dūnhuáng Bīnguǎn; CITS
敦煌宾馆; 中国国际旅行社
10 Shāzhōu Fàndiàn
沙洲饭店
11 Míngshān Bīnguǎn
鸣山宾馆
15 Dūnhuáng Fàndiàn
敦煌饭店
17 Jīnmào Fàndiàn
金贸饭店
20 Wǔhuán Zhāodàisuǒ
五环招待所
21 Fēitiān Bīnguǎn; John's Information Cafe
飞天宾馆

23 Yǒuhǎo Bīnguǎn
友好宾馆

PLACES TO EAT
9 Night Market
敦煌夜市
18 Charlie Johng's Cafe
风味餐馆
19 Shirley's Cafe
风味餐馆

OTHER
1 PSB
公安局
2 Bank of China
中国银行
3 Internet Cafe
网吧

4 Post & Telephone Office
邮电局
5 Xiàn Bówùguǎn
县博物馆
6 Xinhua Bookstore
新华书店
7 CAAC Booking Office
民航售票处
12 Bank of China
中国银行
13 Day Market
农副市场
14 Minibus Stop
小公共汽车站
16 Bike Rental
22 Long-Distance Bus Station
长途汽车站

The *Jīnmào Fàndiàn* (☎ 883 3106, 18 Mingshan Lu) lacks charm, but the friendliness of the staff and the eagerness to please fills the gap. Dorm beds range from Y10 to Y40 and singles are Y120.

There are two places in town calling themselves the 'Dunhuang Hotel' in English, but they have different Chinese names. The budget alternative is the *Dūnhuáng Fàndiàn* (☎ 882 2413), near the bus station. Rates are cheap and all rooms have been recently renovated. Beds in quads/triples with shared bath are Y20/25. Twins with attached bath are Y60 per person and suites with air-con are Y200.

Places to Stay – Mid-Range

On the eastern side of town, the larger *Dūnhuáng Bīnguǎn* (☎ 882 2415, fax 882 2309) is a three-star place aimed at tour groups and visiting cadres. The staff are friendly and the hotel's gardens are quite pleasant, but the catch is the overpriced rooms. Comfortable twins with a fridge range from Y580 to Y650, including breakfast. Although rates are negotiable, it still isn't really worth the money.

Places to Stay – Top End

Four kilometres to the south of town, near the Míngshā Shān sand dunes, is the *Dūnhuáng Shānzhuāng (Silk Road Dunhuang Hotel;* ☎ 888 2088, fax 888 2086), a Chinese-Hong Kong joint venture. Standing out from the desert trying to resemble a Ming dynasty palace, this place is definitely the most luxurious in the area, as reflected by the prices. Nicely decorated twins are US$100 and stylish suites start at US$150. A 15% service charge is added to all rates. During the low season, prices drop by 50% to 80% and there is no service charge. Although expensive, it is a tastefully designed place and, being only a kilometre from the sand dunes, it enjoys great sunrise and sunset views.

Places to Eat

Charlie Johng's Cafe, just north of the Fēitiān Bīnguǎn, has good western and Chinese food at cheap prices, plus an English menu and nice background music (you can bring your own tapes if you wish). Across the street Charlie's sister operates *Shirley's Cafe*, which is also pretty good.

Inside the grounds of the Fēitiān Bīnguǎn is the Dūnhuáng branch of *John's Information Cafe*. It has a nice outdoor location (for those evening beers) and friendly staff who can also help with travel arrangements and information.

On this same block there are numerous Chinese restaurants – most have English menus, reasonable prices and are worth trying. A popular local dish speciality is *dàpánjī*, a whole chicken cut up and stir-fried with potatoes, herbs and vegetables and served on a bed of noodles. It usually costs between Y35 to Y50, but you'll need three people at the very least to finish the thing, so it's not that pricey and certainly worth a try.

Dūnhuáng's *night market* is an extremely lively scene and worth a visit. Mostly contained within a large courtyard off Yangguan Donglu, it houses scores of restaurants and small tables surrounded by lawn chairs and a drinking hostess. The tables are rented out by entrepreneurs, who charge fairly steep prices for beer, soft drinks, tea and the pourer. Instead, you might prefer a tasty *ròujiāmó* (kebab) and yoghurt from one of the nearby barbecue vendors.

Getting There & Away

Air In the summer high season from June to September there are regular flights to Lánzhōu (Y820), Xī'ān (Y1340), Běijīng (Y1500) and Ürümqi (Y570). Flights to Jiāyùguān (Y400) only operate from July to September. Flight frequency is cut during the winter months to just Lánzhōu and Xī'ān. Seats can be booked at the CAAC office (☎ 882 2389) on Yanguan Donglu, which is open from 8.30 to 11.30 am and 3 to 6 pm.

Bus Minibuses to Liǔyuán depart when full from the bus station. The last bus usually leaves around 8 pm. The fare is Y10, plus Y5 for each bag that needs to be placed on the roof. The trip takes 2½ hours, but up to four hours if there's a sand storm blowing.

There are four to five buses to Jiāyùguān leaving between 6.30 am and 1 pm. There is also a more comfortable air-con bus that departs at 8.30 am (Y42; five hours).

Departures to Lánzhōu are at 8.30 and 10.30 am each day. The latter is a sleeper bus and costs Y171. Regular buses cost Y102. The 1148km trip takes at least 24 hours.

The regular bus to Golmud (Y45) leaves at 7.30 am, and takes 12 hours via a rugged but scenic route that crosses the snow-capped Altunshan. There is also a sleeper bus (Y78.30) in the evening. Arrive early enough to store your luggage on the roof. It's chilly up in the mountains, so keep some warm clothing handy regardless of how hot it may be in Dūnhuáng itself.

Other daily departures include buses to Xīníng, Hāmì and Ürümqi.

Train The closest station is at Liǔyuán, on the Lánzhōu-Ürümqi railway line (see the Liǔyuán section for more details).

Getting Around
Dūnhuáng's airport is 13km east of town. In addition to the CAAC bus (Y6), you can hire a minibus to the airport for about Y30.

Dūnhuáng is small enough that you can easily cover it on foot, but taxis and minivans can be chartered for trips to sights outside town. The minibus stop near the Dūnhuáng Fàndiàn is the place to go to start the negotiations.

The Fēitiān Bīnguǎn (see Places to Stay earlier) has modern and well-maintained bikes for a reasonable Y2 per hour. Otherwise, just across the street are a number of stalls that rent bikes for Y1 per hour. A bit of exploratory pedalling around the oasis is fine, and getting to some outlying sights is also possible, although maybe not such a great idea during the height of summer.

AROUND DŪNHUÁNG
Yuèyáquán 月牙泉
Crescent Moon Lake
The lake is 6km south of the centre of Dūnhuáng at the Míngshā Shān (Singing Sand Mountains), where the oasis meets the desert. Spring water trickles into a depression between huge sand dunes, forming a small, crescent-shaped pond (not to be confused with the concrete storage pool nearby).

More impressive than the lake are the incredible sand dunes that tower above (the highest peak reaching 1715m). The climb to the top of the dunes is sweaty work, but the dramatic view across the rolling desert sands towards the oasis makes it worthwhile.

Out here the recreational activities include camel rides, 'dune surfing' (sand sliding) and paragliding (jumping off the top of high dunes with a chute on your back). There is also a tow-gliding operation closer to the entry gate: continue past it if you want to jump off a dune.

The admission fee to the lake and dunes area is Y20 and includes admission to the Dūnhuáng Folk Arts Museum.

Most people head out to the dunes at around 5 pm when the weather starts to cool down. You can ride a bike out there in around 20 minutes. Minibuses cost Y3 and make the run whenever full. Taxis cost Y15 one way and motorised pedicabs are Y10.

Mògāo Kū 莫高窟
Mogao Caves
Most of the Dūnhuáng art dates from the Northern and Western Wei, Northern Zhou, Sui and Tang dynasties, although examples from the Five Dynasties, Northern Song, Western Xia and Yuan can also be found. The Northern Wei, Western Wei, Northern Zhou and Tang caves are in the best state of preservation.

The caves are generally rectangular or square with recessed, decorated ceilings. The focal point of each is a group of brightly painted statues representing buddha and the bodhisattvas, or buddha's disciples.

The smaller statues are composed of terracotta coated with a kind of plaster surface so that intricate details could be etched into the surface.

The walls and ceilings were also plastered with layers of cement and clay and then painted with watercolour. Large sections of the murals are made up of decorative patterns using motifs from nature, architecture or textiles.

Many of the caves have been touched up at one time or another.

Northern Wei, Western Wei & Northern Zhou Caves The Turkic-speaking Tobas, who invaded and conquered the country in the 4th century, inhabited the region north of China and founded the Northern Wei dynasty around AD 386.

Friction between groups who wanted to maintain the traditional Toba lifestyle and those who wanted to assimilate with the Chinese eventually split the Toba empire in the middle of the 6th century.

The eastern part adopted the Chinese way of life and the rulers took the dynasty name of Northern Qi. The western part took the dynasty name of Northern Zhou and tried in vain to revert to Toba customs. By AD 567, however, they had managed to defeat the Qi to take control of all of northern China.

The fall of the Han dynasty in AD 220 sent Confucianism into decline. This, plus the turmoil of the Toba invasions, made Buddhism's teachings of nirvana and personal salvation highly appealing to many people. Under the patronage of the new rulers, the religion spread rapidly and made a new and decisive impact on Chinese art which can be seen in the Buddhist statues at Mògāo.

The art of this period is characterised by its attempt to depict the spirituality of those who had achieved enlightenment and transcended the material world through their asceticism. The Wei statues are slim, ethereal figures with finely chiselled features and comparatively large heads, and clearly show the influence of Indian Buddhist art and teachings.

Sui Caves The Sui dynasty began when a general of Chinese or mixed Chinese-Toba origin usurped the throne of the Northern Zhou dynasty. Prudently putting to death all the sons of the former emperor, he embarked on a series of wars which by AD 589 had reunited northern and southern China for the first time in 360 years.

The Tobas simply disappeared from history, either mixing with other Turkish tribes from central Asia or assimilating with the Chinese.

The Sui dynasty was short-lived, and very much a transition between the Wei and Tang periods. This can be seen in the Sui caves: the graceful Indian curves in the buddha and bodhisattvas figures start to give way to the more rigid style of Chinese sculpture.

Tang Caves During the Tang period, China pushed its borders forcefully westward as far as Lake Balkhash in today's Kazakhstan. Trade expanded and foreign merchants and people of diverse religions streamed into the Tang capital of Chang'an.

Buddhism became prominent and Buddhist art reached its peak; the proud bearing of the Buddhist figures in the Mògāo Kū reflects the feelings of the times, the prevailing image of the brave Tang warrior, and the strength and steadfastness of the empire.

This was also the high point of the cave art at Mògāo. Some 230 caves were carved, including two impressive grottoes containing enormous seated buddha figures. The statue residing in cave 96 is a towering 34.5m tall – a slightly shorter (26m) counterpart in cave 130 is no less impressive.

The portraits of Tang nobles are considerably larger than those of the Wei and Sui dynasties, and the figures tend to occupy important positions within the murals. In some cases the patrons are portrayed in the same scene as the buddha.

Later Caves The Tang period marked the ultimate development of the cave paintings. During later dynasties, the economy around Dūnhuáng went into decline and the luxury and vigour typical of Tang painting began to be replaced by simpler drawing techniques and flatter figures. However, there were some masterpieces in the post-Tang era, notably the 16m-long reclining buddha (cave 158), attended by rows of disciples, all bearing different expressions that show you how close they are to achieving the state of nirvana.

Admission A general entrance ticket costs Y50, which entails entrance to about 15 caves and a Chinese-speaking guide.

For an extra Y5, you can visit the museum (highly recommended), and for an additional Y20 per person, you are provided with an English-speaking guide (best Y20 spent at Mògāo). It doesn't matter if you want one or not – the guide has the keys to doors protecting all of the caves you'll be seeing. Guides are usually available for French, Italian, Spanish, German, Korean and Japanese speakers. Paying the extra for the foreign language guide is really rewarding. As the groups are much smaller, you can choose which caves you would like to visit (within reason), you have much more time to browse and you can ask more questions (the guides are usually very helpful and informative).

In addition to the 30 caves that are open to the public, it is possible to visit some of the 'closed' caves for an 'additional fee'. Some, like cave 465, contain Tantric art whose explicit sexual portrayals have been deemed too corrupting for the public to view. (However, you can check them out if you ask special permission and pay an extra Y60 to Y200.)

The grottoes are theoretically open from 8 am to 5 pm, but guides are generally only available between 8.30 and 10 am and again at 2 pm. The 15-cave tour usually takes between one hour (Chinese tours) and two hours or more (foreign tours). After visiting the caves you could visit the interesting museum, which is opposite the ticket office.

Photography is strictly prohibited everywhere within the fenced-off caves area, although photos are sometimes permitted after payment of an appropriately large sum of money. Cameras and hand luggage must be deposited at an office near the entrance gate (for a fee of Y2).

Most caves are lit only by indirect sunlight from outside, often making it hard to see detail, particularly in the niches. Heavy but low-powered torches (flashlights) can be hired outside the gate (Y3); if you have your own, bring it.

Despite the high fee and the inconvenience of the guide system, don't be discouraged – entering your first cave will make it all seem worthwhile. And it helps to know that at least some of the money sustains the excellent preservation efforts here.

Getting There & Away The Mògāo Kū are 25km and half an hour by bus from Dūnhuáng. Minibuses leave at around 8 am from the Dūnhuáng Fàndiàn and also across the street from the Fēitiān Bīnguǎn. The one-way fare is Y5.

At other times you can hire a minibus for around Y60 to Y80 return, depending on your bargaining skills. If you go in the afternoon, don't bother heading out before 2 pm, as you won't be able to get in to see the caves until at least 2.30 pm.

Some people ride out to the caves on a bicycle, but be warned that half the ride is through total desert – hot work in summer.

Xī Qiānfó Dòng 西千佛洞
Western Thousand Buddha Caves
These caves, 35km west of Dūnhuáng, are cut into the cliff face of the scenic Dang River gorge. Many travellers skip these caves due to the popularity of the impressive caves at Mògāo, however the paintings are in fact in good condition and a visit is very rewarding.

There are currently 16 caves still intact here, 10 of which are open to the public. The earliest caves date back to the Northern Wei dynasty (AD 386–534) and the most recent were constructed during the Tang dynasty (AD 618–907). Many of the images and stories depicted in the paintings are similar to those at Mògāo. Entrance to the caves should cost Y12, however the staff attempt to charge foreigners Y22. The extra charge is for an English-speaking guide, who it seems prefers the pay at Mògāo. Therefore, unless you have a strong appreciation of Buddhism, hiring a guide from Dūnhuáng is recommended.

The caves are best reached by hire vehicle and can be included in a day trip to Yáng Guān and Yùmén Guān. Alternatively catch a public bus from the intersection of Xihuan Jie and Xida Jie in Dūnhuáng which goes to Shāzǎoyuán. Just ask the driver to drop you off at the turn-off to the caves. It's a five-minute walk down to the caves.

Yáng Guān & Yùmén Guān
阳关与玉门关
South Pass & Jade Gate Pass

Some 62km south-west of Dūnhuáng is Yáng Guān. Here, Han dynasty beacon towers marked the caravan route westwards and warned of advancing invaders, but what remains has now largely disappeared under the shifting sands.

Nearby are the ruins of the ancient Han town of Shouchang. Yùmén Guān, 98km north-west of Dūnhuáng, is also known for its ancient ruins.

Caravans leaving China would travel the Hexi corridor to Dūnhuáng; Yùmén Guān was the starting point of the road which ran across the north of what is now Xīnjiāng; Yáng Guān was the start of the route that cut through the south of the region.

The road to Yùmén Guān should be complete by the time you read this, therefore making it more accessible and a lot cheaper to visit. An interesting day trip could include the two passes, a visit to the Xī Qiānfó Dòng (Western Thousand Buddha Caves), as well as a trip to the village of Shazaoyuan and the nearby Wowa Reservoir. To hire a Santana taxi for this sort of trip would cost between Y200 and Y300. There are also a couple of buses a day to Shazaoyuan that pass by the caves and Yáng Guān.

Eastern Gānsù

PÍNGLIÁNG 平凉

Since the completion, in 1996, of the Bǎojī-Zhōngwèi railway line, Píngliáng has become a lot more accessible to the outside world. Despite this, it remains a quiet town tucked away in the foothills of the Liùpánshān Range and a good base for exploring the nearby Taoist mountain, Kōngdòng Shān.

Orientation & Information

The train station is in the north-east of town and the bus station in the far west. The two stations are connected by Dajie, the main thoroughfare and home to the town's major hotels, restaurants and shops.

The Bank of China is on Dong Dajie in the east of town opposite the Kōngdòngshān Bīnguǎn. CITS is in the same grounds as the Píngliáng Bīnguǎn. The PSB is on Xi Dajie, west of Xinmin Beilu, and the post and telephone office is opposite.

Places to Stay & Eat

The *Píngliáng Bīnguǎn* (☎ 821 2921) is in a central location and has clean rooms and friendly staff. It has beds in twins and triples with common showers for Y22 and Y20. Comfortable twins are Y63 and large doubles are Y100. All rates include breakfast. From either the bus or train station you can catch bus No 1 to the hotel or it will cost Y5 in a taxi.

The *Huámíng Diànlì Bīnguǎn* (☎ 821 3922, 71 Xidajie) is a new and clean place with a good range of inexpensive rooms. Beds start at Y25 in a triple or quad and singles are Y50. Large twins are Y120 and doubles Y160. The hotel is adjacent to the Píngliáng Bīnguǎn.

Just opposite the bus station are a couple of cheap and smelly hotels. Most have dorm beds in triples/quads from Y15 to Y25.

The *Huámíng Cāntīng* is a good place to eat and is surprisingly cheap. The restaurant is just next door to the Huámíng Diànlì Bīnguǎn.

The *Yěwèi Diàn (Game Restaurant; 32 Dong Dajie)* is a small family restaurant that serves up very tasty game meat dishes including rabbit, deer and dog. Some of its dishes are a bit expensive, but you can always ask for a smaller serving.

Getting There & Away

Bus From Xī'ān, there are half-hourly buses to Píngliáng leaving from 6 am to 2.30 pm (Y26; eight hours). Heading the other way, buses depart from Píngliáng at 6.20, 6.40, 7 and 7.40 am. There is one daily bus to Yán'ān at 6 am (15 hours) that passes through some pleasant rural countryside on the way.

There are regular buses to Gùyuán (Níngxià) throughout the day. Buses to Lánzhōu mostly leave in the morning and take eight hours.

Train The best way to visit Píngliáng is by train, although you do seem to miss most of the surrounding scenery. There is an overnight train to Lánzhōu (No 211) and an evening train to Xī'ān (No 396).

The ticket office at the station is reluctant to sell sleepers for trains that don't originate in Píngliáng. Instead, the staff send you to the Kōngdòngshān Bīnguǎn, on Dong Dajie, where you can line up at 9 am.

Getting Around
Bus No 1 runs from the train station to the bus station along Dajie. The town is small enough to walk to most destinations, otherwise hop in a taxi for Y5.

AROUND PÍNGLIÁNG
Kōngdòng Shān   崆峒山
Sitting on the border of Níngxià, in the Liupanshan Range, Kōngdòng Shān is 11km to the west of Píngliáng and is regarded as China's number one sacred Taoist mountain. The highest peak is over 2100m and there are numerous small paths that lead to the dozens of temples and pagodas that are scattered across the mountain. Many of the buildings date back to the Tang dynasty and contain valuable frescoes.

There is simple accommodation and food on the mountain. The *Kōngtóng Shānzhuāng* (☎ 860 0099) has dorms in quads for Y20 and in triples for Y30. It even has a suite for Y180. Showers are available in the evening.

Getting There & Away
There are regular buses from Píngliáng that depart from opposite the bus station and head up to the base of the mountain (Y3) or up to the car park (Y8) near the summit. A taxi to the base costs Y20/40 one way/return, including waiting time. Admission is Y18. Try to head back early as there are not many buses after 5 pm.

If you interested in exploring the Liupanshan Range further, then there are a couple of buses that pass the main entrance heading for Jīngyuán in Níngxià. Jīngyuán is only 36km away and is a good base from which to explore the surrounding mountains.

MÀIJĪ SHĀN 麦积山 &
TIĀNSHUǏ 天水
Haystack Mountain & Tiānshuǐ
● pop (Tiānshuǐ) 3,253,800
Màijī Shān, a small mountain south of Tiānshuǐ town in south-eastern Gānsù, is the site of some impressive Buddhist cave art.

The mountain bears some resemblance to a haystack, hence the name Màijī Shān. The scenery is also quite nice: a lush valley dotted with fields and surrounded by green hills that offers some pleasant hiking opportunities.

Orientation
Tiānshuǐ has two sections – the railhead, known as Běidào, and the main city area 16km to the east, known as Qínchéng. Bus Nos 1 and 6 run frequently between the two districts (Y2; 20 minutes). However, unless you have some business with CITS or need to catch a long-distance bus, there's no compelling reason to go to Qínchéng.

Màijī Shān is 35km south of Běidào. There are no direct public buses to Màijī Shān, but minibuses leave when full from in front of the train station (Y5; 1½ hours). You can also hire a taxi for Y100 return.

Information
In Běidào you can change both cash and travellers cheques at the Bank of China branch on Beihe Nanlu, about 500m south of the intersection with Weibin Nanlu. There's also a branch on Minzhu Donglu in Qínchéng. Opening hours are 8.30 am to 12 pm and 2.30 to 5.30 pm.

CITS (☎ 821 4463) is in an obscure building in Qínchéng's Luoyu district (Lúoyù Xiǎoqū).

Màijī Shān Shíkū
Haystack Mountain Grottoes
The grottoes are one of China's four largest temple groups; the others are at Dàtóng, Lùoyáng and Dūnhuáng. The caves date back to the Northern Wei and Song dynasties and contain clay figures and wall paintings.

It's not certain just how the artists managed to clamber so high; one theory is that they piled up blocks of wood to the top of

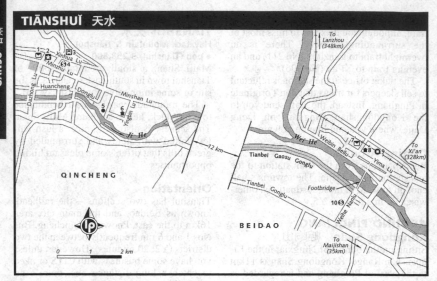

TIĀNSHUǏ 天水

QINCHENG

BEIDAO

To Lanzhou (348km)
To Xi'an (328km)
To Maijishan (35km)

Tianbei Gaosu Gonglu

Tianbei Gonglu

Footbridge

Wei He
Ji He
Weibin Beilu
Yima Lu
Weihe Nanlu

Minzhu Lu
Xinhua Lu
Donglu
Minshan Lu
Huancheng Lu
Dazhong Lu
Yingbin Lu

0   1   2 km

the mountain before moving down, gradually removing blocks of wood as they descended. Stone sculptures were evidently brought in from elsewhere, since the local rock is too soft for carving, as at Dūnhuáng.

Earthquakes have demolished many of the caves in the central section, while murals have tended to drop off due to damp or rain. Fire has also destroyed a large number of the wooden structures. Parts of the rock wall have now been stabilised with sprayed-on liquid cement.

Catwalks and steep spiral stairs have been built across the cliff face, so while the art is not as amazing as that at Dūnhuáng, getting to it is more fun. Most of the remaining 194 caves can only be seen through wire netting or barred doors – bring a torch (flashlight).

Apart from the Qifo Pavilion and the huge buddha statues that are easily accessible, it's hard to get a rewarding peek into many of the caves unless you take a guide. CITS has English-speaking guides for Y100 (excluding transport and entry fees) – you'll need to go to CITS in Qínchéng to meet up before heading to the caves. There are guides available at Màijī Shān (ask at the ticket office) for a fee, but getting an English-speaking one at short notice is not always possible.

The ticket office is about a five-minute walk uphill from where the bus lets you off. Cameras and bags may not be taken into the caves area – the office has a left-luggage section (Y2 per item) for this purpose. The caves are open from 9 am to 5 pm and admission costs Y30 or Y40 with a guide (minimum of six). You may also get charged an Y11 'area fee' if you catch a taxi or the minibus stops at the outermost gateway.

The area behind Màijī Shān has been turned into a botanical garden (sēnlín gōngyuán). There are some nice hiking opportunities accessing the high ridge behind Màijī Shān, which offers fine views of the grottoes. To get to the park, take the stairs to the right just as the road turns sharply left toward the Màijī Shān ticket office and upper parking lot. If you come across the main entrance, there is a steep entrance fee of Y30.

Places to Stay & Eat
The *Tiělù Zhāodàisuǒ* (☎ 273 5154) has simple but cheap dorm beds ranging from Y10 to Y36. Showers are on the 1st floor

TIĀNSHUĬ

1 Post & Telephone Office
邮电大楼
2 PSB
公安局
3 Long-Distance Bus Station
长途汽车站
4 Bank of China
中国银行
5 CITS
中国国际旅行社
6 Tiānshuǐ Bīnguǎn
天水宾馆
7 Post Office
邮电局
8 Tiělù Zhāodàisuǒ
铁路招待所
9 Train Station
火车站
10 Bank of China
中国银行

and there is hot water between 8 and 10.30 pm. To get there, turn left as you leave the square in front of the train station and continue for about 50m.

The *Tiānshuǐ Bīnguǎn* (☎ 821 4542, 5 *Yingbin Lu*) is a clean and friendly midrange option in Qínchéng. Buses from the train station can drop you off at the corner just up from the hotel. Twins/doubles are Y186/158 and twins with common showers are Y136. The hotel's restaurant is not bad.

If you have some time on your hands, you could try the *Màijī Shānzhuāng* (☎ 272 2277 ext 2100), a quiet, slightly worn-down place about 500m before the main car park. Beds in triples/quads with common shower are Y31/26 or twins/triples with attached bath are Y122/169. Staying here will give you a chance to do some hiking in the surrounding area. The hotel has a small *restaurant*, and there are also *food stalls* and cheap *restaurants* closer to Màijī Shān.

Getting There & Away

Bus From the long-distance bus station in Qínchéng, there are three daily buses to Lánzhōu: a regular bus at 6 and 8 am (Y29; 10 hours) and a sleeper at 6.30 pm

(Y54.50). There are also buses to Lánzhōu that depart at similar times from in front of the train station at Běidào.

Other long-distance destinations from the Qínchéng bus station include a 6.30 am bus to Línxià (Y32: 13 hours) and a 5 pm sleeper bus to Yínchuān in Níngxià (Y85; 15 hours). There are also daily buses to Gùyuán (Níngxià) and Píngliáng (Kōngdòng Shān).

Train Tiānshuǐ is on the Xī'ān-Lánzhōu railway line; there are dozens of daily trains in either direction, all of which stop here. If you arrive early you can visit Màijī Shān as a day trip, avoiding the need to stay overnight in Tiānshuǐ.

There are westbound departures approximately hourly from 7 pm to 7 am. Heading east, trains leave about once an hour between 12.45 pm and 7 pm and again from 11 pm to 7 am. From Tiānshuǐ it's about seven hours to either Lánzhōu or Xī'ān.

LUÒMÉN 洛门

In the Wǔshān Ranges outside Luòmén, a small town 250km south-east of Lánzhōu, are the **Shuǐlián Dòng** (Water Curtain Thousand Buddha Caves), which contain the temple **Lāshāo Sì**. The temple is a quaint old building nestled in a shallow cave on the

Shíkū: grotto
The top of the character *shí* (stone, rock) is like the corner of a rock or a cliff, whereas the bottom half is a cake of rock. The top of *kū* means a cave or an earth room. The bottom half sees someone bending to carry something into or out of the cave or room, which would usually have a very low ceiling.

nearby forested mountainside. The temple, cave paintings and rock carvings date back to the early Northern Wei dynasty (AD 386–534). Carved onto a rock face is a remarkable 31m-high figure of Sakyamuni, made during the Northern Wei period.

The Shuǐlián Dòng and Lāshāo Sì are in a remote and spectacular gorge, which is accessible in good weather via a 17km makeshift road up the dry river bed. You can charter a minibus from Luòmén and back for around Y60. Entrance is Y5. A *Hostel*

(zhāodàisuǒ) is directly opposite the Luòmén train station and has dorm beds for Y15.

Luòmén is on the Lánzhōu-Xī'ān railway line, but it's a small station and only a few trains stop here. If your'e coming from Lánzhōu, most trains arrive in the afternoon, whereas from Tiānshuǐ they are mostly morning trains.

You can also get a bus to Luòmén from Tiānshuǐ; buses leave from in front of the train station throughout the morning (Y9; 3½ hours).

Níngxià 宁夏

Níngxià is part of the arid north-west of China and much of its landscape suffers a harsh climate. Plummeting temperatures mean winters are hard, and blistering summers make irrigation a necessity. The province would be virtually uninhabitable if it were not for the Huáng Hé (Yellow River), Níngxià's lifeline. Most of the population lives near the river or the irrigation channels that run off it. These channels were created in the Han dynasty, when the area was first settled by the Han Chinese in the 1st century BC.

About a third of Níngxià's people are Hui, living mostly in the south of the province, and the rest are Han Chinese. The Hui minority are descended from Arab and Iranian traders who travelled to China during the Tang dynasty. Immigrants from Central Asia increased their numbers during the Yuan dynasty. Apart from their continued adherence to Islam, the Hui have been largely assimilated into Han culture.

The completion of the Bāotóu-Lánzhōu railway in 1958 helped to relieve the area's isolation and develop industry in this otherwise almost exclusively agricultural region.

YÍNCHUĀN 银川

☎ 0951 ● pop 928,300

Sheltered from the deserts of Mongolia by the high mountain ranges of the Hèlán Shān to its west and abundantly supplied with water from the nearby Huáng Hé (Yellow River), Yínchuān occupies a favoured geographical position in otherwise harsh surroundings.

This city was once the capital of the Western Xia, a mysterious kingdom founded during the 11th century. Today it's one of China's more pleasant, relaxed provincial capitals, with a few interesting sights and a lively market atmosphere.

Orientation

Yínchuān is divided into two parts. The new industrialised section is close to the train station and is simply called Xīn Chéng

(New City). The Lǎo Chéng (Old City) is about 8km to the west and has most of the town's sights, hotels, restaurants and shops, as well as the long-distance bus station.

Information

Money The main branch of the Bank of China is on Jiefang Xijie and there is another branch on Xinhua Dongjie, just west of Minzu Nanjie. Both can change cash and travellers cheques and are open Monday to Friday from 8 am to noon and 2.30 to 5 pm.

Post & Communications The post and communications office is in the centre of town on Jiefang Xijie, next to the Hóngqiáo Dàjiǔdiàn (see Places to Stay later). The

NÍNGXIÀ 宁夏

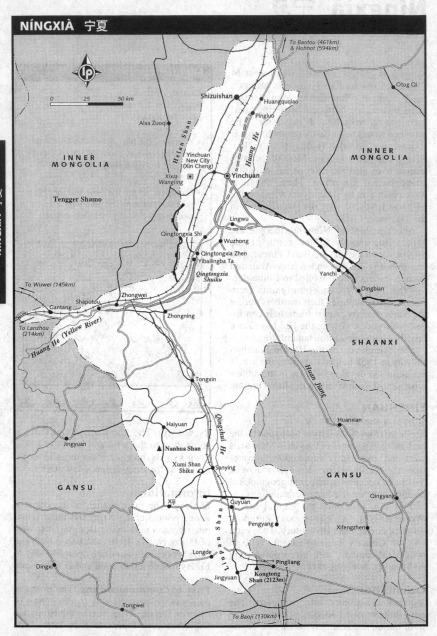

NÍNGXIÀ 宁夏

To Baotou (461km)
& Hohhot (594km)

Otog Qi

Shizuishan
Huangquqiao
Pingluo

Alxa Zuoqi

INNER
MONGOLIA

Helan Shan

Huang He

INNER
MONGOLIA

Tengger Shamo

Yinchuan
New City
(Xin Cheng)

Xixia
Wangling

Yinchuan

Lingwu

Qingtongxia Shi

Wuzhong

Qingtongxia Zhen

Yibailingba Ta

Qingtongxia
Shuiku

Yanchi

To Wuwei (145km)

Dingbian

Gantang

Shapotou

Zhongwei

To Lanzhou
(214km)

Huang He (Yellow River)

Zhongning

SHAANXI

Tongxin

Huan Jiang

Haiyuan

Huanxian

Jingyuan

▲ Nanhua Shan

Xumi Shan
Shiku

Sanying

Qingshui He

GANSU

GANSU

Qingyang

Xiji

Guyuan

Pengyang

Xifengzhen

Dingxi

Longde

Liupan Shan

Pingliang

Jingyuan

Kongtong
Shan (2123m)

Tongwei

To Baoji (130km)

telephone office is on the 2nd floor and is open daily from 8 am to 6 pm.

There are two China Telecom Internet bars in town. One is on Zhongshan Beijie and the other is on the 5th floor of the Xinhua department store (Xīnhuá Bǎihuò Shāngdiàn). Both are open from 8 am to 7 pm and charge Y9 per hour.

Travel Agencies China International Travel Service (CITS; Zhōngguó Guójì Lǚxíngshè; ☎ 504 8006) has an office on the 3rd floor of the building at 150 Jiefang Xijie. It's a pretty friendly group and will arrange tours of the surrounding sights as well as some more interesting trips. A two-day camping trip to the nearby grasslands and desert costs Y585 per person (minimum four people).

PSB The foreign affairs section of the Public Security Bureau (PSB; Gōngānjú) is in a small office on Limin Jie, just south of Jiefang Xijie.

Hǎibǎo Tǎ 海宝塔
Haibo Pagoda
Hǎibǎo Tǎ, also called Běi Tǎ (North Pagoda), stands out prominently in the north of the city. Records of the structure date from the 5th century. In 1739 an earthquake toppled the lot, but it was rebuilt in 1771 in the original style.

It's set in the pleasant gardens of a working monastery, but you can still climb up the pagoda for an extra Y7. The structure is some nine storeys high and offers fine views of the Hèlán Shān to the west and the Huáng Hé (Yellow River) to the east. Behind the pagoda are several interesting temples, including one housing a hefty reclining buddha. It's open daily from 7 am to 6 pm and entry is Y2.

There is no public transport out there, so you'll either have to bicycle or take a taxi (Y7). It's a little over 3.5km from the Yínchuān Fàndiàn.

Níngxià Shěng Bówùguǎn
宁夏博物馆
Ningxia Provincial Museum
The museum is on Jinning Nanjie in the old Chéngtiān Sì monastery. Its collection includes Western Xia and Northern Zhou historical relics, as well as material covering the Hui culture.

Within the leafy courtyard is the pagoda Chéngtiānsì Tǎ, also known as Xī Tǎ (West Pagoda), which you can climb via 13 tiers of steepish stairs. The museum is open from 9 am to noon and 2 to 5 pm. Admission is Y1 for the park, and an extra Y3 and Y5 for the pagoda and museum, respectively.

Perhaps of more interest is the small **Cānkǎo Yuèlǎnshì** (Reading Room) at the eastern gate of the museum on Limin Jie. It has a good variety of magazines in English and also some French and German material.

Nánguān Qīngzhēnsì 南关清真寺
Nanguan Mosque
The mosque is a modern Middle Eastern-style structure that shows little Chinese architectural influence, with Islamic arches and dome roofs covered in green tiles. This is Yínchuān's main mosque and is an active place of worship. Entry costs Y5 and it's open daily from 7 am to 7.30 pm.

Places to Stay
Lǎo Chéng (Old City) The *Yínchuān Fàndiàn* (☎ 602 3053), on Jiefang Xijie, is the best bet for budget backpackers. The cheapest beds are Y24 in a twin or Y29 for a single room, and both rooms have common showers. Beds in a twin with a bathroom range from Y48 to Y108. It's in a good, central location, but maintenance has long been absent from the hotel and so the time has arrived for an extensive renovation. If you're coming from the train station hop on either bus No 1 or 11 (Y0.70) and get off at the post office stop (*yóudiàn dàshà*). There's no English sign, just a brass plaque that reads 'Foreign Nationals Hotel'.

The friendly *Guǎngcháng Fàndiàn* (☎ 410 8472) is just opposite the bus station on Shengli Beijie. It has beds in a clean triple for Y23 and singles with a bathroom for Y58. A suite is a cheap Y98. The hotel is not officially allowed to take foreigners, but seems willing to do so.

The *Níngxià Bīnguǎn* (☎ 503 1229, fax 504 4338) is a peaceful place set among

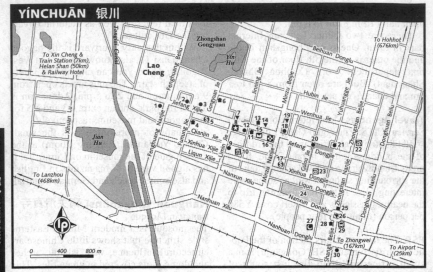

YÍNCHUĀN 银川

pleasant gardens. It has small twins for
Y178 and standard twins for Y218, both of
which are good value.

Another good mid-range option is the
Zhōngyín Bīnguǎn (☎ 501 1918, fax 504
7545, 53 Funing Jie), which has very clean
and new singles/twins for Y200/238 and
suites from Y580. Breakfast and saunas are
free and all rooms have air-con. The hotel
is just off Jiefang Xijie.

The three-star **Hóngqiáo Dàjiǔdiàn** (Rainbow Bridge Hotel; ☎ 691 8888, fax 691
8788) is at the top end of Yínchuān's hotel
scene. It has large and comfortable singles for
Y382 and twins from Y276 to Y339. The
cheapest suite comes with an extra bathroom
and costs Y615. The hotel usually offers 20%
off these prices outside of July and August.

Xīn Chéng (New City) The most convenient place for making a quick getaway is
the **Tiědào Bīnguǎn** (Railway Hotel; ☎ 306
9119), just a short walk from the train station. Beds in a quad cost Y35 with attached
bath, or Y25 without a bathroom, while
twins/triples with private bath are Y250 for
the room. The staff are usually willing to
take 20% off these prices.

Places to Eat

Good for street food are the *stalls* in the
backstreets around the long-distance bus
station or the *night market* nearby on Xinhua Dongjie.

The **Yíngbīnlóu Qīngzhēn Fànzhuāng**
(Yingbinlou Islamic Restaurant), next to the
Yínchuān Fàndiàn, is a raucous spot, popular with the locals. The restaurant on the
2nd floor has some tasty dishes and the 1st
floor offers yoghurt, ice cream and beer.

At either end of the Nán Mén (South
Gate) are two **Qīngzhēn Niúròu Lāmiàn**
(Muslim Noodle Restaurants) that serve up
cheap (Y2) and tasty noodles.

The speciality of the **Shāojīgōng** restaurant is a spicy chicken stew. You cook it
yourself and you can add various vegetables
and noodles to this tasty meal. A small serving (Y36) is enough for two people. Look
for the pecking rooster.

Ālǐ Xībǐng (Aile Cakeshop) is a pleasant
place to sit down and write a few postcards.
It has basic cakes and instant coffee.

Over in the new city there is a lively *market*, just across from the Tiědào Bīnguǎn
(Railway Hotel), where you can warm your
tummy with a bowl of spicy noodles.

YÍNCHUĀN

PLACES TO STAY
4 Zhōngyín Bīnguǎn
中银宾馆
6 Níngxià Bīnguǎn
宁夏宾馆
11 Hóngqiáo Dàjiǔdiàn
红桥大酒店
13 Yínchuān Fàndiàn
银川饭店
28 Guǎngchǎng Fàndiàn
广场饭店

PLACES TO EAT
7 Shāojīgōng
烧鸡公
14 Yíngbīnlóu Qīngzhēn Fànzhuāng
迎宾楼清真饭庄
19 Āǐ Xǐbǐng
A里西饼
26 Qīngzhēn Niúròu Lāmiàn
清真牛肉拉面

OTHER
1 CITS
中国国际旅行社
2 Train Ticket Office
银川火车站售票处
3 Xinhua Bookstore
新华书店
5 Bank of China
中国银行
8 PSB
公安局
9 Cānkǎo Yuèlǎnshì
参考阅览室
10 Níngxià Shěng Bówùguǎn; Chéngtiānsì Tǎ
宁夏博物馆、承天寺塔
12 Foreign Languages Bookstore
外文书店
15 Post & Telephone Office
邮电大楼
16 Yinchuan Department Store
银川百货大楼

17 Bank of China
中国银行
18 Bike Rental
20 Gǔ Lóu
鼓楼
21 Yùhuáng Gé
玉皇阁
22 Wǎng Bā
网吧
23 Wǎng Bā
网吧
24 Indoor/Outdoor Market
商城
25 Nánmén Lóu
南门楼
27 Nánguān Qīngzhēnsì
南关清真寺
29 Bus Station
银川汽车站
30 CAAC
民航售票处

Getting There & Away

Air The main ticket office of the Civil Aviation Administration of China (CAAC; Zhōngguó Mínháng; ☎ 691 3455) is south of the bus station on the corner of Nanhuan Donglu and Shengli Beijie. The office is open daily from 8 am to 5.30 pm. There are flights connecting Yínchuān with Běijīng (Y870), Chéngdū (Y810), Guǎngzhōu (Y1510), Shànghǎi (Y1080) and Xī'ān (Y430).

Bus The long-distance bus station is in the south-eastern part of town on the square near the Nán Mén. There are six buses to Zhōngwèi (Y13.20; four hours) that leave between 7 am and 4.30 pm.

Buses to Gùyuán (Y25; seven hours) leave every half hour from 6 am to 1 pm.

There are four daily buses leaving in the afternoon for the 17-hour trip to Xī'ān – at least one of which is a sleeper (Y85). There are two buses a day to Yán'ān (Shaanxi) at

6 am and 6 pm; the latter is a sleeper. The trip takes at least 13 hours and costs Y38 for the regular bus and Y75 for the sleeper.

Train Yínchuān is on the Lánzhōu-Běijīng railway line, which also runs via Bāotóu, Hohhot and Dàtóng. Express trains from Yínchuān take nine hours to Lánzhōu, 11 hours to Hohhot, 17 hours to Xī'ān and 22 hours to Běijīng. If you're heading for Lánzhōu or Xīníng, there is a convenient overnight tourist train (No 203). The train station is in the Xīn Chéng (New City), about 13km from the Lǎo Chéng (Old City) centre.

There's a train booking office in the Lǎo Chéng, at 57 Jiefang Xijie, where tickets can be bought at least four days in advance. The office is on the ground floor at the eastern end of a five-storey building, next door to a flashy red and white hotpot restaurant. It's open daily from 9.30 am to noon and 2 to 5 pm.

Getting Around

The airport is 25km from town and a CAAC shuttle bus (Y15) meets all flights. A taxi to the airport will cost around Y40.

Bus No 1 runs from the bus station in the Lǎo Chéng, along Jiefang Jie and then on to the train station in the Xīn Chéng. The fare is just Y0.70. Minibuses cover the same route faster, but charge Y3.

Taxis are fairly cheap, with flag fall at Y5 to Y6 depending on the vehicle. A taxi between the train station and the Lǎo Chéng will cost around Y25.

AROUND YÍNCHUĀN
Hèlán Shān 贺兰山

The mountains of the Hèlán Shān range are clearly visible from Yínchuān. The range forms an important natural barrier against desert winds and invaders alike, with the highest peak reaching 3556m. Along the foothills of the Hèlán Shān lie some interesting sights.

About 54km north-west of Yínchuān's Xīn Chéng is the historic pass village of **Gūnzhōngkǒu**, where there are walking trails up into the surrounding hills. No buses travel here, the only way to reach it is by taxi or by hiring a vehicle through CITS or another travel agency.

North of Gūnzhōngkǒu are the **Báisìkǒu Shuāngtǎ** (Twin Pagodas of Báisìkǒu), which are 13 and 14 storeys high and decorated with buddha statuettes. These are accessible only by jeep, bicycle or on foot, so don't expect taxis to be able to get you here.

South of Gūnzhōngkǒu lie the **Xīxià Wánglíng** (Western Xia Tombs), the main tourist destination in this area. According to legend, the founder of the Western Xia kingdom, Li Yuanhao, built 72 tombs. One was for himself, others held relatives or were left empty. The Western Xia kingdom lasted for 190 years and 10 successive emperors, and had its own written language and a strong military.

Again, you'll need to cycle or hire a vehicle to get here. Hiring a minivan taxi for half a day should cost Y80 or Y150 for the full day. In half a day you could visit Hèlán Shān and the Xīxià Wánglíng. For a full day

add the twin pagodas at Báisìkǒu Shuāngtǎ and Gūnzhōngkǒu.

CITS asks considerably more, but it throws in an English-speaking guide for 'free'.

Yībǎilíngbā Tǎ 一百零八塔
108 Dagobas

These mysterious Buddhist dagobas, or stupas, are 83km south of Yínchuān by the Huáng Hé, near the town of Qīngtóngxiá Zhèn. The 12 rows of dagobas are arranged in a large triangular constellation on the banks of the Huáng Hé. The dagobas date from the Yuan dynasty and it's still not known why they were erected here. The white vase-like shape contrasts strikingly with the surrounding arid landscape. A visit to the Yībǎilíngbā Tǎ can be a very relaxing day trip from Yínchuān. You may even stumble across an isolated stretch of the Great Wall not far from the town.

It is possible to visit this site independently by catching a train or bus from Yínchuān. Only a few buses go directly to the smaller town of Qīngtóngxiá Zhèn, but you can catch a local bus or taxi from Qīngtóngxiá Shì to the Yībǎilíngbā Tǎ. From town there are sometimes tourist buses; otherwise hire a taxi or even walk.

ZHŌNGWÈI 中卫
☎ 0953

Zhōngwèi lies 167km south-west of Yínchuān on the Lánzhōu-Bāotóu railway line, sandwiched between the sand dunes of the Tengger Shāmò (Tengger Desert) to the north and the Huáng Hé to the south. In addition to its unusual setting, Zhōngwèi has a fairly relaxed pace – a nice change from the rush of most Chinese cities.

Information

Zhōngwèi Travel Service (☎ 701 2620), in the foyer of the Yìxīng Dàjiǔdiàn, can arrange some interesting trips to sights out of town (see the Around Zhōngwèi section for details). Across from the drum tower roundabout is the Bank of China, open Monday to Friday from 8 am to noon and 2.30 to 6 pm.

Gāo Miào 高庙
Gao Temple

The main attraction in town is the Gāo Miào, an eclectic, multipurpose temple that serves Buddhism, Confucianism and Taoism. Built during the 15th century and flattened by an earthquake during the 18th century, it was later rebuilt and expanded several times until being virtually razed again by fire in 1942.

The present wooden structure's dozens of towers and pavilions look like parts of a jagged wedding cake. But rather than cream and pastry in the basement, the Gāo Miào has a showcase *hell*. Mind you, this is no ordinary hell.

During the Cultural Revolution the temple's basement was converted into a bomb shelter. To try and rake in a bit more cash, the eerie shelter has become a neon-light torture chamber hell, complete with patrons being sawn in half and having their tongues cut off by devils for committing various offences. The prize goes to the chamber of grated heads or officially called 'waster of grain room'. A subtle reminder to all those kiddies who leave that last grain of rice in their bowl.

A sneak preview of hell will set you back Y5, which includes a torture chamber map on the back of the ticket. We recommend asking for a guide, as it's not the sort of place you would want to get lost in. The Gāo Miào is open daily from 8 am to 6 pm and admission is Y5.

Places to Stay & Eat

The *Zhōngtiě Bīnguǎn (Railway Hotel; ☎ 703 1948)*, to the left as you exit the train station, has beds in triples/quads with common bath for Y28/25 and twins for Y80. The rooms are fairly comfortable and breakfast is free, so this is not a bad deal.

The *Zhōngwèi Fàndiàn (☎ 710 2219)*, on Gulou Beidajie, has beds in dusty

ZHŌNGWÈI 中卫

1 Train Station
火车站
2 Tiělù Bīnguǎn
铁路宾馆
3 Minibuses to Shāpōtóu
去沙坡头的中巴
4 Gāo Miào
高庙
5 Zhōngwèi Fàndiàn
中卫饭店
6 Night Food Market
夜市
7 Yìxīng Dàjiǔdiàn;
Zhongwei Travel Service
逸兴大酒店;
中卫旅行社
8 Gǔ Lóu
鼓楼
9 Bank of China
中国银行
10 Gulou Department Store
鼓楼百货大楼
11 Post Office
邮局
12 PSB
公安局
13 Minibuses to Shāpōtóu
去沙坡头的中巴
14 Night Market
夜市

twins/triples with breakfast and attached bath for Y35/32. It also has very basic dorm beds for Y10 and Y15.

The *Yìxīng Dàjiǔdiàn* (☎ *701 7666, fax 701 9993*) is the most upmarket place in town. Surprisingly, it has a good range of prices and all rooms include breakfast. Beds in triples/twins are Y35/45 and singles are Y56. More comfortable triples/twins are Y150/168 and suites cost Y388.

There's a nice guesthouse at Shāpōtóu (20km from Zhōngwèi) that's worth considering as an alternative to staying in town (see the Around Zhōngwèi section for details).

In Zhōngwèi there are lots of small restaurants along Bei Dajie. The best place in town is the *night market*, on Gulou Beijie; it's a happening spot with all different types of local specialities. Two favourites are *ròujiāmó* (fried pork or beef stuffed in pita bread, sometimes with green peppers and cumin) and *shāguō* (a mini-hotpot). Otherwise there are always kebabs (Y0.20 each) and draft beer (Y2.50).

Getting There & Away

Bus The long-distance bus station is about 1km east of the Gǔ Lóu (Drum Tower), on the southern side of Dong Dajie. Buses to Yínchuān (Y13; four hours) leave every half hour from 6.30 am to 4.30 pm. A sleeper bus to Lánzhōu (Y40; seven hours) leaves at 10.30 pm.

Train From Zhōngwèi you can catch trains heading north, south, west and south-east. By express it's 2½ hours to Yínchuān (No 44), six hours to Lánzhōu (No 43), 11 hours to Xī'ān (No 395) and 23 hours to Ürümqi (No 197). Other destinations include Běijīng, Chéngdū, Píngliáng, Shànghǎi and Hohhot.

AROUND ZHŌNGWÈI

The best thing about exploring this area is seeing the abrupt convergence of desert sand dunes and lush farm fields.

Shāpōtóu, 20km west of Zhōngwèi, lies on the fringe of the Tengger Desert. It's based around the **Shāpōtóu Shāmò Yánjiùsuǒ** (Shapotou Desert Research Centre), which was founded in 1956 to find a way to keep drifting sand dunes from covering the railway line.

Shāpōtóu has become a bit of a Chinese playground, with camel rides, speed boats, a castle, cable cars, sheep skin rafts, sand sleds and desert walks. It is a scenic spot next to the Huáng Hé and it's not a bad place to spend the night. There are two entrances to the area, one at the guesthouse and the other at the top of the sand dunes. From the top entrance it is possible to rent a sand sled (Y5) and skid across the sand dunes almost all the way to the front gate of the guesthouse. Entrance to the main area is Y10 and Y5 to the botanical gardens and neighbouring desert.

Water wheels (*shuǐ chē*) used to be a common sight in Níngxià. Mechanical pumps have now taken over, but there is still one operational water wheel upstream from Shāpōtóu at Beichangtai, a small mountain village some 70km south-west of Zhōngwèi. It's best reached by boat.

At Shāpōtóu you may also see some leather rafts (*yángpí fázi*) in action. A traditional mode of transport on the Huáng Hé for centuries, the rafts are made from sheep or cattle skins soaked in oil and brine and then inflated. An average of 14 hides are tied together under a wooden framework to make a strong raft capable of carrying four people and four bikes. Touts at Shāpōtóu offer rides down to Shaheyuan (10km west of Zhōngwèi) for Y150 per person, including transport back to Shāpōtóu. For Y40 you can hop on a raft for a short stretch of the river, but you have to make your own way back.

To the north of Zhōngwèi in the Tengger Desert, there's a few scattered remains of the **Great Wall** dating from the Ming dynasty. There isn't much left of the wall, but getting there is quite interesting.

Organised Tours

Zhongwei Travel Service offers several interesting river and desert trips. Examples include a two-day journey into the Tengger Desert that includes a visit to the Great Wall and camping in the dunes. Transport (including camels), guide and accommodation cost around Y200 per person per day, as long as there are at least three of you. Desert trips of up to seven days are available.

Another option is a one-day leather raft trip down the Huáng Hé, starting at Shāpōtóu and ending at Zhōngwèi. With three people this should cost around Y150, including transport to Shāpōtóu from Zhōngwèi.

Places to Stay

A pleasant option would be a night or two at the *Shāpō Shānzhuāng* (☎ 768 1481), a guesthouse built around a garden courtyard on the banks of the Huáng Hé. It has beds from Y25 to Y40 in twins/triples with attached bath. There's also a small bar/restaurant on the premises; however, cold beers are rare.

Getting There & Away

From Zhōngwèi there are regular minibuses to Shāpōtóu (Y4; one hour). The frequency increases during the peak tourist months of June, July and August, when buses run as often as every half hour. At other times you may have to wait an hour or two. The first bus departs Zhōngwèi at 7 am and the last bus departs from the Shāpōtóu main entrance, near the Shāpō Shānzhuāng, at 6.30 pm.

In Zhōngwèi minibuses leave from in front of the long-distance bus station, stop first at the intersection of Gulou Beijie and Changcheng Xilu, pause again at the corner of Gulou Xijie and Xihuan Lu, and then head off to Shāpōtóu.

Train No 773, heading for Wuwei, stops at Shāpōtóu for half an hour after leaving Zhōngwèi at 3.15 pm. You can also hire a motor-tricycle to take you there for Y30/40 one way/return.

GÙYUÁN 固原
☎ 0954

Gùyuán is located in the south of Níngxià, about 460km from Yínchuān. There is an interesting set of **Shíkū** (Buddhist Grottoes) at Xūmí Shān (Treasure Mountain), which is about 50km north-west of Gùyuán. Xūmí is the Chinese version of the Sanskrit word *sumeru*, which translates as 'treasure mountain'.

Cut into five adjacent peaks are 132 caves containing more than 300 Buddhist statues dating back 1400 years, from the Northern Wei to the Sui and Tang dynasties. The finest statues are in caves 14, 45, 46, 51, 67 and 70. Cave 5 contains the most famous statue on Xūmí Shān: a colossal Maitreya buddha, standing 19m high. It remains remarkably well preserved even though the protective tower has long since collapsed and left it exposed and vulnerable to the elements.

There is no regular transport to the caves, but you can catch a bus from Gùyuán directly to Sānyíng. Sānyíng is on the main road 40km north of Gùyuán near the Xūmíshān turn-off. From Sānyíng you can hop on a minibus to **Huangduobao** and then jump on a tractor (Y2) up to the caves. Alternatively you can hire a taxi from Sānyíng for about Y50 return.

Places to Stay

The *Dōngyuè Bīnguǎn* (☎ 203 4131) is to the left as you exit the train station. It has beds in twins/triples for Y35/30 and singles for Y80. It also has good dorm beds for Y20, but there are no common showers.

The *Gùyuán Bīnguǎn* (☎ 203 2479), on Zhengfu Jie south-east of the bus station,

The Wrath of Khan

According to legend, Genghis Khan saw the Xia kingdom as a potential vassal/ally, but the Xia baulked at the thought of bowing to another ruler.

Genghis Khan mounted six separate campaigns against the Xia, all of which failed. During the sixth campaign, Xia archers sneaked down to Khan's war camp, near present-day Gùyuán, and fatally wounded the military leader with poison-tipped arrows.

Enraged even at death's door, Genghis Khan gave his final order: the total annihilation of the Western Xia kingdom. Looking at the site today, one must conclude that Khan's subordinates carried out his command with a vengeance.

has nice twins for Y136, as well as beds in triples with attached bath for Y33.

Getting There & Away

Gùyuán is on the Zhōngwèi-Baoji railway line and is served by trains from Xī'ān (eight hours), Zhōngwèi (3½ hours) and Yínchuān (six hours).

Buses to Gùyuán (Y25; seven hours) leave every half hour between 6 am and 1 pm from the Yínchuān long-distance bus station. There are buses running once daily from Lánzhōu (Y27; 11 hours) and Tiānshuǐ (Y20; seven hours), which are both in Gānsù. There are also regular buses to Jīngyuán.

Inner Mongolia 内蒙古

For most foreigners, the big attractions of Inner Mongolia (Nèi Ménggǔ) are the grasslands, the horses and the Mongolian way of life.

Just how much you can see of the Mongolian way of life in China is dubious, but the grasslands are indeed perfect horse country, and horse-drawn carts seem to be a common form of transport on the communes (a Hohhot tourist leaflet shows foreigners riding in a decorated camel cart with suspension and truck tyres). However, the small Mongolian horse is being phased out – herders can now purchase motorcycles (preferred over bicycles because of strong winds), and on some of the large state-run farms, helicopters and light aircraft are used to round up steers and spot grazing herds.

It's important to distinguish between Inner Mongolia (the Chinese province) and Mongolia, the independent country to the north, formerly called Outer Mongolia. For more information on the country of Mongolia, see Lonely Planet's *Mongolia* guide.

HISTORY
The nomadic tribes to the north of China have always been a problem for China's rulers. The first emperor of the Qin dynasty, Qin Shihuang, started building the Great Wall for the express purpose of keeping them out.

Inner Mongolia is only one part of what was originally the Mongol homeland, a vast area that also encompasses all of Outer Mongolia and a large slice of Siberia.

The Mongols endured a rough life as shepherds and horse breeders in the grasslands beyond the Great Wall and the Gobi Desert. They moved with the seasons in search of pastures for their animals, living in tents known as yurts (a Russian word) or *gers* (the Mongolian word). The yurts were made of animal hide usually supported by wooden rods, and could be taken apart quickly to pack onto wagons.

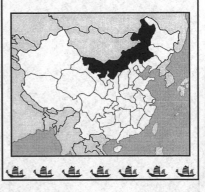
At the mercy of their environment, the Mongols based their religion on the forces of nature: moon, sun and stars were all revered, as were the rivers. The gods were virtually infinite in number, signifying a universal supernatural presence. Mongol priests could speak to the gods and communicate their orders to the tribal chief, the khan.

Mongol Empire
United by Genghis Khan (see History in the Facts about China chapter) and later led by his grandson Kublai Khan, the Mongols went on to conquer not only China but most of the known world, founding an empire that stretched from Vietnam to Hungary.

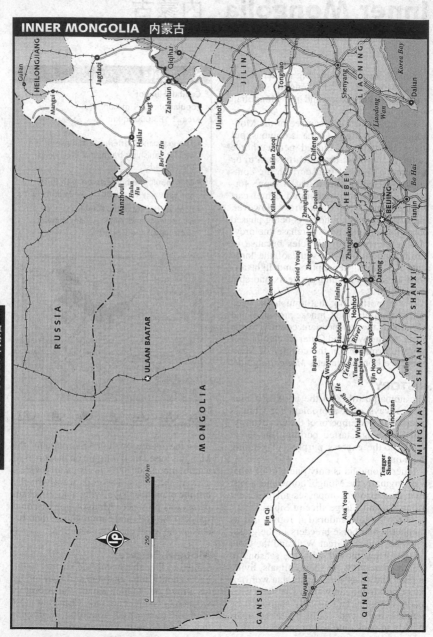

INNER MONGOLIA 内蒙古

It was an empire won on horseback: the entire Mongol army was cavalry and this allowed rapid movement and deployment of the armies. The Mongols excelled in military science and were quick to adopt and improve on Persian and Chinese weaponry. But their cultural and scientific legacy was meagre.

Once they abandoned their policies of terror and destruction, they became patrons, but not practitioners, of science and art. Influenced by the people they had conquered, they also adopted the local religions – mainly Buddhism and Islam.

The Mongol conquest of China was slow, delayed by campaigns in the west and by internal strife. Secure behind their Great Wall, the Chinese rulers had little idea of the fury the Mongols would unleash in 1211, when the invasion began.

For two years the Great Wall held them back, but the Mongols eventually penetrated through a 27km gorge into the northern Chinese plains. In 1215 a Chinese general went over to the Mongols and led them into Běijīng. Nevertheless, the Chinese stubbornly held out, and the war in China was placed under the command of one of Genghis' generals so the Khan could turn his attention to the west.

Despite the death of Genghis Khan in 1227, the Mongols lost none of their vigour. Genghis had divided the empire into separate domains, each domain ruled by one of his sons or other descendants. Ogadai was given China and was also elected the Great Khan in 1229 by an assemblage of princes. Northern China was subdued, but the conquest of the south was delayed while the Khan turned his attention to the invasion and subjugation of Russia. With the death of Ogadai in 1241, the invasion of Europe was cancelled and Mangu Khan, a grandson of Genghis, continued the conquest of China.

He sent his brother Kublai to attack the south of China, which was ruled by the Song emperors. Mangu died of dysentery while fighting in China in 1259 and Kublai was elected Great Khan. Once he had swept away a challenge to his rule by his brother Arik-Boko and opposition from his enemies in the 'Golden Horde' (the Mongol faction that controlled the far west of the empire), Kublai was able to complete the conquest of southern China by 1279. It was the first and only time that China had been ruled in its entirety by foreigners.

The Mongols established their capital at Běijīng, and Kublai Khan became the first emperor of the Yuan dynasty. Kublai's empire was the largest nation the world has ever known. The Mongols improved the road system linking China with Russia, promoted trade throughout the empire and with Europe, instituted a famine relief scheme and expanded the canal system, which brought food from the countryside to the cities. It was into this China that Marco Polo wandered, and his book *Description of the World* revealed the secrets of Asia to an amazed Europe.

Kublai died in 1294, the last Khan to rule over a united Mongol empire. He was followed by a series of weak and incompetent rulers who were unable to contain the revolts that spread all over China.

The entire Mongol Empire had disintegrated by the end of the 14th century, and the Mongol homeland returned to the way of life it knew before Genghis Khan. The Mongols once again became a loose collection of disorganised roaming tribes, warring among themselves and occasionally raiding China, until the Qing emperors finally gained control over them in the 18th century.

Mongolia Today

Mongolians make up only about 15% of the total population of Inner Mongolia – the other 85% are mostly Han Chinese with a smattering of minority Huis, Manchus, Daurs and Ewenkis.

Since 1949 the Chinese have done their best to assimilate the Mongolians, though the Mongolians have been permitted to keep their written and spoken language. Tibetan Buddhism, the traditional religion of the Mongolians, has not fared so well.

The Mongolians are scattered throughout China's north-eastern provinces, as well as through Qīnghǎi and Xīnjiāng. Altogether there are about 3.5 million of them living in China, and another half a million in Russia.

Today, the 'Inner Mongolia Autonomous Region' enjoys little or no autonomy at all. Since the break-up of the Soviet Union in 1991, Outer Mongolia has been free of Soviet control and is reasserting its nationalism. This has the Chinese worried – nationalistic movements like those in Tibet and Xīnjiāng do not please Běijīng. As a result, the PSB keeps a tight lid on potential real or imagined independence activists.

Much of the Inner Mongolia region comprises vast areas of natural grazing land. However, the far north is forested – the Greater Hinggan range contains about one-sixth of the country's forests and is an important source of timber and paper pulp. Inner Mongolia is also rich in minerals such as coal and iron ore, as you see if you visit Bāotóu.

The Mongolian climate tends towards extremes. Siberian blizzards and cold currents rake the plains in winter (from December to March) – forget it! In winter you'll even witness snow on the desert sand dunes. Summer (from June to August) brings pleasant temperatures, but it can get scorchingly hot during the day in the western areas.

From May to September is the recommended time to visit, but pack warm clothing for the Inner Mongolian spring or autumn.

HOHHOT 呼和浩特

☎ 0471 • pop 2,003,700

Hohhot (Hūhéhàotè) was founded in the 16th century and, like other towns, grew around its temples and lamaseries, which are now in ruins. It became the capital of Inner Mongolia in 1952.

Hohhot means Blue City in Mongolian, although many Chinese-speaking locals mistakenly claim it means 'green city'. Perhaps the name refers to the crisp blue skies – this is one of the sunniest parts of China outside of the western deserts.

Hohhot is a relatively prosperous and cosmopolitan city that serves as the main entrance point for tours of the grasslands. Both the China International Travel Service (CITS; Zhōngguó Guójì Lǚxíngshè) and China Travel Service (CTS; Zhōngguó Lǚxíngshè) turn on the culture in Hohhot,

from the grasslands tour to the equestrian displays at the horse racing ground. Horse racing, polo and stunt riding are put on for large tour groups, if you latch onto one; otherwise, they take place only on rare festive occasions. It's the same with song and dance soirees.

Information

Money The Bank of China is on Xinhua Dajie. There are also money changing facilities inside the Nèi Ménggǔ (Inner Mongolia) and Zhāojūn hotels.

Post & Communications The main post and China Telecom office is on Zhongshan Xilu. There is an Internet bar on the 2nd floor of the telephone section. It costs just Y8 an hour and drinks are available. There is a more convenient post office on the left-hand side of the square as you exit the train station. The entrance closest to the station is the place to make long-distance phone calls.

Travel Agencies CTS (☎ 696 4233 ext 8123) has a small office at Nèi Ménggǔ Fàndiàn and is a good source of information. In addition to grasslands tours, it can also book discounted accommodation. The CITS can also be found here.

PSB For visa extensions and other inquiries the Public Security Bureau (PSB; Gōngānjú; ☎ 696 8148) is at 39 Zhongshan Xilu, on the northern side of the street near the corner of Xilin Guole Lu. The foreigner office is just inside the gate on the left; look for the English plaque.

Nèi Ménggǔ Bówùguǎn
内蒙古博物馆
Inner Mongolia Museum

Well presented and definitely worth a visit, the Nèi Ménggǔ Bówùguǎn is the biggest attraction in town. The collection includes a large mammoth skeleton dug out of a coal mine near Mǎnzhōulǐ, dinosaur exhibits, a yurt and a fantastic array of Mongolian costumes, artefacts, archery equipment and saddles. The top floors of the museum are sometimes closed.

The museum is on the western side of Hulunbei'er Lu at the intersections of Xinhua Dajie and Zhongshan Xilu. Entry is Y8 for foreigners.

Xílètú Zhào 席勒图召

This is the stomping ground of the 11th Grand Living Buddha, who dresses in civvies and is apparently active. There's nothing special to see though. The original temple burned down and the present one was built in the 19th century; the Chinese-style building has a few Tibetan touches. The swastika symbols on the exterior have long been used in Persian, Indian, Greek and Jewish cultures – they symbolise prosperity and have no relation to their mirror image, the Nazi reverse swastika. Entry is Y6.

Qīngzhēn Dàsì 清真大寺

Great Mosque

North of the temple, Xílètú Zhào, on Tongdao Jie is Qīngzhēn Dàsì. Built in Chinese style, with the addition of a minaret, it dates from the Qing dynasty (with later expansions). It is an active place of worship for the Hohhot Muslim community, holding prayers five times a day. You can wander around, as long you don't enter the prayer area. There is no entrance fee.

Naadam

The summer festival known as Naadam features traditional Mongolian sports such as competition archery, wrestling, horse racing and camel racing. Prizes vary from a goat to a fully equipped horse. The fair has its origins in the ancient Obo-Worshipping Festival (an *obo* is a pile of stones with a hollow space for offerings – a kind of shamanistic shrine).

The Mongolian clans make a beeline for the fairs on any form of transport they can muster, and create an impromptu yurt city. For foreigners, Hohhot is a good place to see the Naadam festivities. Horse racing, camel racing, wrestling and archery take place at the horse racing grounds (*sàimǎchǎng*) in the northern part of the city on bus route No 13.

The exact date of Naadam varies in China, but is usually between mid-July and mid-August. Apparently it depends on when the grass is at its greenest. It's worth knowing that Naadam is celebrated at a different time in Outer Mongolia – always from 11 to 13 July, which corresponds to the date of Mongolia's 1921 revolution.

Places to Stay

The ***Běiyuán Fàndiàn*** (☎ 696 6211, fax 696 4642, 28 Chezhan Xijie) is the best value in Hohhot and it's very convenient to both the bus and train station. It has singles/twins/triples for Y30/60/75 with common bath. Twins with attached shower are Y100. Its best suite is a very reasonable Y180. To top it off, all rooms come with free bicycle hire.

If the Běiyúan is full, try the ***Hūhéhàotè Tiělù Bīnguǎn*** (Huhehot Railway Hotel; ☎ 693 3377, fax 695 4746). Twins with common bath go for Y52/62 and with attached bathroom are Y116 and Y152. The hotel also has a gym, library and billiards room.

The ***Xīnchéng Bīnguǎn*** (☎ 629 2288, fax 693 1141) is on spacious, well-treed grounds. Triples and quads in building No 10 cost Y120 for the room, but you may be able to talk the staff into giving you just a bed. Doubles range from Y120 to Y430. There's no bus from the train station to the hotel. Bus No 20 stops near the hotel, but to catch this bus you must turn left as you exit the train station and walk a long block to Hulunbei'er Lu. A taxi ride (Y6) is recommended, as the hotel's reception is a long way from the bus stop.

The ***Nèi Ménggǔ Fàndiàn*** (Inner Mongolia Hotel; ☎ 696 4233, fax 696 1479) is around the corner from the Xīnchéng Bīnguǎn. A 14-storey high-rise on Wulanchabu Xilu, this is the home of CITS and CTS, and although the standard is three star, the plumbing and the western restaurant aren't the greatest. Standard twins range from Y280 to Y340.

Places to Eat

A popular place with the locals is the ***Wángshì Huǒguōchéng*** on the north side of Hongqi Jie, a mall running west off Xilin Guole Lu. Tables are set up out the front where you can have your Sìchuān hotpot and watch the crowds watch you. Food vendors also set up tables on summer nights at the corner in front of the Zhāojūn Dàjiūdiàn.

The *Mǎlāqìn* (meaning 'horseman') *Fàndiàn*, on Julong Changjie is recommended for Mongolian and Chinese food. Try the Mongolian hotpot, roasted lamb and kebab. Tasty vegetarian dishes include: *sùhézǐ* (an egg, spinach and noodle patty) and *chǎoxiānnǎi* (fried milk and egg with pine nuts). Prices are moderate and the friendly staff speak some English.

Shopping
The Minority Handicraft Factory is on the southern side of Shiyangqiao Xilu, near the intersection with Nanchafang Jie. It's in the southern section of town on the bus No 1 route and has a retail outlet for tourists. It only carries a limited selection of stock, but wares include inlaid knife and chopstick sets, saddles, daggers, boots, embroidered shoes, costumes, brassware, blankets and curios.

You'll actually find a better selection and lower prices on the 2nd floor of the Minzu department store (Mínzú shāngchǎng). It's on Zhongshan Xilu where the pedestrian bridge crosses the road. Other good buys in this section of the store are the very cheap silver earrings, necklaces and bracelets.

Many of the souvenir shops have selections of jewellery as well, and the small shop beside the Nèi Měnggǔ Bówùguǎn has some nice items.

Getting There & Away
Air The Civil Aviation Administration of China (CAAC; Zhōngguó Mínháng; ☎ 696 4103) has an office on Xilin Guole Lu. There are regular flights to Běijīng (Y400), Guǎngzhōu (Y1500), Shànghǎi (Y1180) and many other major cities.

There are also flights to Ulaan Baatar in Outer Mongolia on Monday and Thursday with Mongolian Airlines (☎ 430 2026) for Y640 one way.

Bus There are bus connections between Hohhot and Dàtóng (Y22; seven hours).

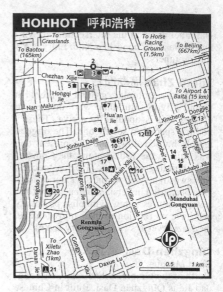

Buses to Bāotóu (Y14; three hours) leave about every half hour or you can catch the twice-daily freeway bus (Y25; 1½ hours). There are five daily buses to Dōngshèng (Y25; five hours), starting at 7.30 am.

Train Hohhot is on the Běijīng-Lánzhōu railway line that cuts a long loop through Inner Mongolia. About 2½ hours out of Běijīng you'll pass the crumbled remains of the Great Wall (it looks like little more than a dirt embankment).

Express trains go to Běijīng (11 hours), Dàtóng (4½ hours), Bāotóu (2½ hours), and Yínchuān (11 hours).

Windows 9 and 10 sell tickets up to four days in advance. Otherwise many hotels and travel agencies sell sleepers for a service fee of Y30.

Getting Around
Hohhot airport is about 15km east of the city. The airport bus (Y5) leaves from the CAAC booking office or you can catch a taxi for around Y30.

Bus No 1 runs from the train station to the old part of the city in the south-western corner, via Zhongshan Xilu.

HOHHOT

PLACES TO STAY

5 Běiyuán Fàndiàn
北原饭店

8 Hūhéhàotè Tiělù
Bīnguǎn
呼和浩特铁路宾馆

14 Xīnchéng Bīnguǎn
新城宾馆

15 Nèi Ménggǔ Fàndiàn;
CITS; CTS
内蒙古饭店;
中国国际旅行社;
中国旅行社

PLACES TO EAT

6 Wángshì Huǒguōchéng
王市火锅成

13 Mǎlāqìn Fàndiàn
马拉沁饭店

OTHER

1 Bus Station
汽车站

2 Train Station
火车站

3 Bike Rental

4 Post Office
邮局

7 Bike Rental

9 Zhāojūn Dàjiǔdiàn
昭君大酒店

10 Foreign Language
Bookstore
外文书店

11 Bank of China
中国银行

12 Nèi Ménggǔ Bówùguǎn
内蒙古博物馆

16 Main Post Office;
China Telecom
邮局;中国电信

17 CAAC
中国民航

18 PSB
公安局外事科

19 Minzu Department Store
民族商场

20 Qīngzhēn Dàsì
清真大寺

21 Xílètú Zhào
席勒图召

Hohhot is reasonably small and there are quite a few stalls hiring bicycles for a pittance.

There are two bike rental places near the train station. One is in the small rectangular building to the left as you exit the train station and the other is at the corner of Xilin Guole Lu and Hua'an Jie. Both are ridiculously cheap, about Y2 for the day.

Bicycle rental is also available from the Běiyuán, Xīnchéng and Nèi Ménggǔ hotels.

AROUND HOHHOT

About 20km west of Hohhot is the Sino-Tibetan monastery **Wusutu Zhao** is hardly worth looking at, but the surrounding arid landscape is impressive. A taxi will cost about Y50 to take you there from the train station.

About 15km east of Hohhot, just past the airport, is the **Bái Tǎ** (White Pagoda), a seven-storey octagonal tower. The pagoda can be reached by a 20-minute train ride on No 752 that leaves at 8.02 am; buy your tickets on the train. You'll probably have to get a taxi (Y25) back though, because the train only makes the return journey in the evening.

THE GRASSLANDS

The Grasslands (Cǎoyuán) is what most travellers come to see in Inner Mongolia,

but if you are after a more authentic experience of the grasslands, consider a trip to Hǎilāěr or Mǎnzhōulǐ (or better still, the nation of Mongolia).

Organised Tours

Cashing in on the magic draw of 'Mongolia' is the name of the game here. As for visions of the descendants of the mighty Khan riding the endless plains, the herds of wild horses and the remnants of Xanadu, remember that this is China and most of the population is now Han Chinese. Nevertheless, CTS and CITS are only too happy to organise tours to give you a glimpse of the traditional Mongolian lifestyle, which now seems to be an anachronism in Inner Mongolia.

The real country for seeing Mongolians in their own environment is Outer Mongolia, but getting there is both expensive and difficult. Grasslands and yurt dwellings can be seen in other parts of China, such as Xīnjiāng. Remember that grass is only green in summer – the verdant pasturelands can turn a shrivelled shade of frost-coated brown from November to April. Take warm, windproof clothing – there's a considerable wind-chill factor even in the middle of summer.

There are three grasslands areas targeted by most tours: **Xilamuren** (two hours from Hohhot), **Gegentala** (2½ to three hours

INNER MONGOLIA 内蒙古

Grasslands Tour Prices

no of people	cost per person (Y)		
	1 day	2 days	3 days
To Xilamuren			
1	690	840	985
2-4	440	560	690
5-10	405	465	550
11-15	250	340	450
16-20	200	350	400
over 21	188	268	300
To Gegentala			
1	-	958	1185
2-4	-	585	680
5-10	-	525	630
11-15	-	495	570
16-20	-	460	500
over 21	-	310	400
To Huitengxile			
1	-	920	1140
2-4	-	595	695
5-10	-	480	560
11-15	-	425	520
16-20	-	380	410
over 21	-	246	320

from Hohhot) and **Huitengxile** (three to 3½ hours from Hohhot), which is the most beautiful but least visited.

There are some fledgling private travel agents who try to solicit business in the lobbies of the tourist hotels – you can talk to them and discuss prices. You can get to Xilamuren independently on one of the twice-daily buses to Zhaohe (Y11). Just ask the driver to drop you off at the grasslands. There are also taxi drivers around the train station who do self-styled grasslands tours for around Y300 per person (extra if you stay overnight). The trip may consist of staying in a yurt belonging to the driver's family. There is a general Grasslands management fee of Y30 for all designated areas.

The name of the game is 'bargain'. Be aware that these unofficial tours get very mixed reviews. One traveller was served a wretched meal in a yurt – cooked over a cow-dung fire – and got food poisoning. As you'll discover if you explore the Mongolian hinterland, sanitation is not a strong point, so watch what you eat and drink. Others have reported that the so-called 'Mongolians' are just Hans dressed up in Mongolian costume. But if you still feel like going on a tour, the table above has prices for tours quoted by CTS.

BĀOTÓU 包头
☎ 0472 • pop 1,989,200

The other large city in Inner Mongolia, Bāotóu lies on the bleak northernmost reaches of the Huáng Hé (Yellow River), to the west of Hohhot. The name means 'land with deer' in Mongolian, and although there is still a deer farm outside of Bāotóu you are only likely to encounter these creatures on the dinner plate in some of the upmarket restaurants around town.

Previously set in an area of undeveloped semi-desert inhabited by Mongol herders, Bāotóu underwent a radical change when the communists came to power in 1949. Over the next decade, a 1923 railway line linking the town with Běijīng was extended south-east to Yínchuān, and roads were constructed to facilitate access to the region's iron, coal and other mineral deposits.

Today, Bāotóu is an industrial community of about two million people. Despite the showcase street signs in Mongolian, nearly the entire population is Han Chinese. While West Bāotóu has undergone a major facelift, East Bāotóu remains an unpleasant urban area. Not highly endowed with scenic places, Bāotóu is definitely a city for specialised interests – a couple of nearby monasteries, a steel mill, a steam locomotive museum, sand dunes and a mausoleum dedicated to Genghis Khan. Most of these sights are not in the city itself, but a couple of hours outside town.

Overall, Bāotóu is a useful transit point and you can keep yourself amused here for a day or so, but if you miss it, don't lose any sleep. The best thing we can say for the place is that the people are friendly.

Orientation
Bāotóu is a huge town – 20km of urban sprawl separate the eastern and western

EAST BĀOTÓU (DŌNGHÉ)
包头东河区

Huancheng Lu

To Wudang
Zhao (67km)

Gongye Beilu

▼1

0   250   500 m   2■

3
▼

Bayan Tala Xidajie

To West
Baotou
(6km)

Nanmenwai Dajie

■4

Bayan Tala Dajie

Gongye Lu

5🕔 🕛6 7   8
To Lanzhou   ■▼   ☐
(996km)   Zhanbei Lu

O
9

To Airport (3km)

To Beijing
(817km)

EAST BĀOTÓU (DŌNGHÉ)

PLACES TO STAY & EAT
1 Péngláigé Cāntīng
   蓬莱阁餐厅
2 Dōnghé Bīnguǎn;
   CAAC
   东河宾馆；
   中国民航
3 Hóngguāng Cāntīng
   红光餐厅
4 Xīhú Fàndiàn
   西湖饭店
6 Jiāotōng Dàshà
   交通大厦
7 Dàdùzi Jiǎozi
   大肚子饺子

OTHER
5 Bank of China
   中国银行
8 Bus Station
   汽车站
9 Bāotóu East Train Station
   包头东站

parts of the city. It's the eastern area that most travellers visit because it's useful as a transit hub – the western area has the steel mill and locomotive museum.

The station for the western area is Bāotóu train station (Bāotóu Zhàn); for the eastern area it's Bāotóu East train station (Bāotóu Dōng Zhàn). The eastern district is called Dōnghé; the western area is subdivided into two districts – Qingshan and Kundulun.

Information
Money In Dōnghé the Bank of China is on the left as you exit the train station. It only does currency exchange. To change travellers cheques you have to go to the branch in West Bāotóu.

Post & Communications In west Bāotóu there is a night telephone office just next door to the main post & telephone office. There is an Internet bar on the 2nd floor.

Travel Agencies CITS (☎ 515 4615) is inconveniently located at 9 Qingnian Lu, north of the Bāotóu Bīnguǎn in West Bāotóu. The offices are on the 4th floor. There is a friendly and more helpful China

Youth Travel Service (CYTS; Zhōngguó Qīngnián Lǚxíngshè; ☎ 511 0920) on the 3rd floor of the west building in the Bāotóu Bīnguǎn (see Places to Stay).

PSB The PSB is at 59 Gangtie Dajie, near the Baotou department store. The foreigner affairs office is behind the main building; just follow the lane to the right.

Zhēngqì Huǒchē Bówùguǎn
蒸汽火车博物馆
Steam Locomotive Museum
The Zhēngqì Huǒchē Bówùguǎn is fairly small and tours have to be organised through CITS or CYTS. The latter is a bit cheaper and will do a tour for Y50, not including car hire.

Keep in mind that steam trains offer a more dramatic spectacle in the winter time. This is when most people visit the museum and it might be easier to hook up with a tour then.

Places to Stay
East Bāotóu The *Jiāotōng Dàshà* is opposite the train station and doesn't officially

WEST BĀOTÓU 包头西部

take foreigners, but seems willing to accept the odd backpacker. It has dorm beds for Y17 and reasonable twins with bath from Y66 to Y112.

The *Dōnghé Bīnguǎn* (☎ 417 2266, fax 417 2541, 14 Nanmenwai Dajie) is about 10 minutes' walk (or take bus No 5) from the Bāotóu East train station. Singles/doubles go for Y60/70 and twins range from Y70 to Y90. There are cheaper rooms in the south building for Y50, but they were looking a little worse for wear. All rooms have bathrooms and include breakfast.

The *Xīhú Fàndiàn (West Lake Hotel;* ☎ 417 2288, fax 416 8181) is a reasonably new Sino-US joint venture. It has basic twins with attached bath for Y116 and suites with air-con, fridge and a balcony for Y418. It also has dorm beds in triples or quads for Y30. Try a bit of friendly bargaining on the standard rooms.

West Bāotóu Unfortunately, none of the hotels near the train station will take foreigners. The best option for budget accommodation is the *Bāotóu Bīnguǎn* (☎ 515 6655, fax 515 4641) on Gangtie Dajie. It has a range of rooms in three buildings, from Y38 for a bed in a twin without bath in the west building, to Y160 for twins in the more comfortable newer high-rise. If you're arriving by train, get off at Bāotóu train station. The station is 8km from the hotel – take bus No 1, a taxi or a motor-tricycle. If arriving by bus from Hohhot, you can ask the driver to drop you off right in front of the hotel.

The *Xīngyuàn Dàjiǔdiàn* (☎ 512 8888, fax 513 6408, 28 Gangtie Dajie) is just to the west of the Bank of China. It has good twins and doubles from Y298 to Y368.

Places to Eat

The *Hóngguāng Cānfīng (10 Nanmenwai Jie)* is just across from the Dōnghé Bīnguǎn and has tasty food at reasonable prices. It specialises in Mongolian hotpot with sliced mutton *(shuàn yángròu)*, but there are plenty of other dishes available.

The *Pénglàigé Cānfīng*, in the north of town on Gongye Beilu, is one of the most popular restaurants serving a whole assortment of delicious food.

Just opposite the train station is the *Dàdùzi Jiǎozi (Big Tummy Dumpling Restaurant)*, a large canteen that serves a good range of staple Chinese breakfast dishes, like congee and buns. Its dumplings are not bad, but nothing worth writing home about.

If you're visiting in the summer, tables and foodstalls are set up for a lively **night market** just to the north of the Dōnghé Bīnguǎn, at the intersection of Huancheng Lu and Nanmenwai.

In western Bāotóu, the *Tiānjīn Gǒubùlì Bāozidiàn* is very popular with locals for reproducing the famous Tianjin dumplings. Just about everyone eats the dumplings, so ordering them is easy.

Shopping

The hotel gift shops offer a small selection of tourist-oriented minority handicrafts, but Hohhot is a better place to buy this stuff. As

WEST BĀOTÓU

PLACES TO STAY & EAT

1 Tiānjīn Gǒubùlì Bāozidiàn
 天津狗不里孢子店

5 Bāotóu Bīnguǎn; CYTS
 包头宾馆;
 中国青年旅行社

6 Xīngyuàn Dàjiǔdiàn
 兴苑大酒店

OTHER

2 PSB
 公安局

3 Post & Telecom Office
 邮电局

4 CITS
 中国国际旅行社

7 Bank of China
 中国银行

8 CAAC
 中国民航

9 TV Tower
 电视塔

China's mineral capital, Bāotóu would be a good place to find bargains on iron ore, cobalt and lignite, in case you need to stock up.

Getting There & Away

Air The CAAC ticket office (☎ 513 5492) is at 26 Gangtie Dajie beside the Bank of China. Another is at the Bāotóu Bīnguǎn; you can book tickets at the Dōnghé Bīnguǎn and pick them up at the airport. There are flights connecting Bāotóu with Běijīng (Y470), Guǎngzhōu (Y1510), Wǔhàn (Y970), Shànghǎi (Y1080) and Xī'ān (Y640).

Bus Buses go from in front of the long-distance bus station to Hohhot for Y15 and the trip takes three hours or 1½ hours via the freeway. Regular buses to Dōngshèng take two hours and cost Y11.5. There are also buses to Yúlín (Y50; 10 hours) and Yán'ān (Y87; 18 hours) in Shaanxi.

From west Bāotóu, buses leave from the intersection of Tuanjie Dajie and Baiyun E'bo Lu.

Train There are frequent trains to and from Hohhot to Bāotóu that stop in both the eastern and western sections. The journey takes just under two hours on the fast trains.

There are also trains to Běijīng (13½ hours), Yínchuān (eight hours), Tàiyuán (14½ hours) and other major cities to the south.

Getting Around

While East Bāotóu is easy to get around on foot, west Bāotóu is a sprawling expanse of long boulevards, necessitating the use of public buses.

To/From the Airport The airport is 2km south of Bāotóu East train station. In spite of the short distance, taxis ask around Y20 for the one-way journey. If you are coming from west Bāotóu, an airport bus leaves from the CAAC ticket office; tickets are Y10.

Bus Bus Nos 5 and 10 stop close to the Bāotóu Bīnguǎn and shuttle between the western and eastern sections of Bāotóu in 45 minutes. The double-decker buses are the most comfortable.

There are also minibuses (zhōngbā), which cost Y2.5 – you board these at the regular bus stops.

AROUND BĀOTÓU
Wǔdāng Zhào 五当召

The main tourist attraction near Bāotóu is the large monastery Wǔdāng Zhào, about 2½ hours from the city by bus.

This monastery of the Gelukpa (Yellow Hat) sect of Tibetan Buddhism was built around 1749 in typical Tibetan flat-roofed style. It once housed 1200 monks. The ashes of seven reincarnations of the monastery's 'living buddha' are kept in a special hall and there is a collection of Buddhist wall paintings dating from the Qing dynasty. Today all religious activity is restricted to a handful of pilgrims and doorkeeper-monks who collect the admission fee.

The lighting is a bit dim so you might want to take a torch if you want to see anything inside the monastery. Entrance is Y10.

INNER MONGOLIA 内蒙古

The crowds of day-tripping, camera-clicking tourists make this no place for religion. Try to walk into the hills away from the pandemonium; the site has a peculiar strength in its secretive, brooding atmosphere.

Getting There & Away The monastery is 67km north-east of Bāotóu. A direct bus to Wǔdāng Zhào (Y5.50) leaves at 7 am – or whenever it's full – from east Bāotóu's long-distance bus station.

Otherwise, bus No 7 (Y4; one hour), at the far left of the parking lot as you exit the long-distance bus station, goes to Shiguai, 40km north-west of Bāotóu. From Shiguai there are infrequent buses that can do the second leg of the journey. If your time is limited, you'd be better off hiring a taxi from Shiguai to the monastery and back for about Y70.

Měidài Zhào 美岱召

This monastery is much smaller than Wǔdāng Zhào and though easier to get to is little visited. Měidài Zhào is halfway between Bāotóu and Hohhot, a 10-minute walk north of the main highway. As long as they take the old highway and not the freeway, buses on the Bāotóu-Hohhot route can drop you off here. From Hohhot the fare is Y8 and from Bāotóu Y7. Like Wǔdāng Zhào, the monastery belongs to the Gelukpa sect. Admission is Y5.

Yīméng Xiǎngshāwān 伊盟响沙湾
Resonant Sand Gorge

The Gobi Desert starts just to the south of Bāotóu. Some 60km south of Bāotóu and a few kilometres west of the Bāotóu-Dōngshèng highway is a gorge filled to the brim with sand dunes.

Although the gorge has long been known to locals as a barren place to be avoided (no grass for the sheep), it has recently been turned into a money-spinner by CITS. Japanese tour groups in particular come here to frolic in the sand. To spice up the romance of such frolicking, the area has been named Yīméng Xiǎngshāwān, a reference to the swooshing sound made by loose sand when you step on it. The highest dunes are about 90m high.

The Bāotóu to Dōngshèng bus passes by the turn-off to the new chairlift that shuttles visitors from the main road.

Prior to the completion of the chairlift entry to the sands was Y10. It is also possible to ride a camel (Y10) to the top of the dunes or you can try para-sailing (Y20), if sliding around in the sand isn't enough for you.

DŌNGSHÈNG 东胜
☎ 0477

Dōngshèng lies south-west of Bāotóu and serves as the stage for Genghis Khan's Mausoleum. Dōngshèng itself is not blessed with scenic attractions, though it's smaller and more attractive than Bāotóu.

Of interest is the **Mínshēng Shìchǎng** (Minsheng Indoor Market), where you can buy practical things such as clothing (not Mongolian style).

If you get an early start it's possible to reach Dōngshèng in the morning, visit Genghis Khan's Mausoleum, then return to Dōngshèng to spend the night, or even travel all the way back to Bāotóu the same day (though this would be exhausting).

Places to Stay & Eat

The *Yíngbīn Fàndiàn* (☎ 832 1575), on Hangjin Beilu adjacent to the long-distance bus station, has beds in twins with bath for Y28, or with common shower for Y18. The price is right, but the sanitation leaves something to be desired.

The *Dōngshèng Dàjiǔdiàn* (☎ 832 7333) is down the other end of Hangjin Lu on the corner of E'erduosi Jie. It's a lot more comfortable, with twins/triples with attached bath for Y122/138. In the new building twins range from Y186 to Y198.

The *Yīkè Zhāoméng Bīnguǎn* (*Ih Ju League Hotel*), usually just called the Yīméng Bīnguǎn, was not accepting foreigners when we last visited, but it may later. The hotel is on E'erduosi Jie at the corner of Dala'te Lu (one block east of the Dōngshèng Dàjiǔdiàn).

Food-wise there's not a lot available in Dōngshèng, but the restaurant in the Dōngshèng Dàjiǔdiàn serves up reasonable food.

Getting There & Away

Bus Most travellers take the bus directly from Hohhot. It departs at 7.40 am, takes five hours and costs Y25. Sit on the right-hand side of the bus for mountain views along the way (or the left on the way back). The bus goes via Bāotóu, but doesn't stop there. Just to the south of Bāotóu, the bus crosses the Huáng Hé (Yellow River). There are three buses daily departing Dōngshèng for Hohhot, the last one leaving at 12.30 pm.

Another route is to go from Bāotóu. Catch a bus to Dōngshèng from the long-distance bus station (eastern Bāotóu). Buses run every 20 minutes from 6.20 am. The journey from Bāotóu to Dōngshèng takes about 2½ hours. There is also a bus to Xī'an (18 hours) from Dōngshèng, departing in the early afternoon and arriving late the next morning.

AROUND DŌNGSHÈNG
Genghis Khan's Mausoleum
成吉思汗陵园

Genghis Khan's Mausoleum (Chéngjí Sīhán Língyuán) is a bus trip away from Dōngshèng in the middle of nowhere. What are said to be the ashes of the Khan were brought back from Qīnghǎi (where they had been taken to prevent them from falling into the hands of the Japanese) in 1954, and a large Mongolian-style mausoleum was built near Ejin Horo Qi.

The Cultural Revolution did enough damage to the mausoleum to keep the renovators busy for eight years. Since the collapse of Soviet domination in 1991, Mongolia has been whipping itself into a nationalistic fervour and Genghis Khan has been elevated to god-like status. As a result, holy pilgrimages to the mausoleum have become the sacred duty of both Inner and Outer Mongolians. If you would like to meet any true Mongolians, this is probably one of the best places in China to do it.

Ceremonies are held four times a year at the mausoleum to honour his memory. Butter lamps are lit, *khatas* (ritual scarves) presented and whole cooked sheep piled high before the Khan's stone statue while chanting is performed by Mongolian monks and specially chosen Daur elders.

On the embankment beside the entrance there is an obo festooned with prayer flags in commemoration of Genghis Khan.

Inside are displays of the Khan's martial gear and a statue. Various yurts contain the biers of Genghis and his close relatives. The huge frescoes around the walls are rendered in cartoon style to depict important stages in the Khan's rise – all that's missing is bubble captions with 'pow' or 'zap'.

Buy your ticket at the booth to the right of the parking lot as you enter before you head up the steps to the mausoleum entrance, otherwise the staff will send you down again to buy a ticket. Entry is Y25.

After you've taken a look at the mausoleum you can visit the temporary residence of the Khan on the same ticket. It's 1km down the dirt road to the right of the parking lot (when facing the mausoleum).

Nearby is a compound (open only in summer) with nice grasslands, horses, cows, sheep and goats, plus some interesting buildings with traditional clothing, warrior outfits and riding equipment inside – all ready for the Naadam tourist carnival.

Places to Stay

There is a tourist yurt camping ground, the *Chéngjísīhán Bīnguǎn* (*Ghenghis Khan Hotel*), and yurts (*ménggǔbāo*) to stay in at the right of the parking lot as you enter. The cost is Y20 per person. However, most visitors elect to stay in Dōngshèng or Bāotóu and go to the mausoleum on a day trip.

Getting There & Away

Several buses depart from Dōngshèng each day heading towards the mausoleum; the first one leaves at 6.20 am and the last one at 12.30 pm. Tickets cost Y7. The driver will let you off, but you won't be able to miss the blue-tiled dome of the museum as it comes into view. It's about a two-hour ride, but if the road is being repaired it can take up to four hours.

HǍILĀĚR 海拉尔
☎ 0470

The northernmost major town in Inner Mongolia, Hǎilāĕr has very little to offer visitors beyond being a useful transit point to nearby Mănzhōulǐ. In fact, unless you fly here, there is no compelling reason to stop here as there are direct trains to Mănzhōulǐ.

You can visit the surrounding Hūlúnbèi'ěr Grasslands from here though, and both CITS and CTS in Hăilāěr offer tours, but they are mainly geared towards larger tour groups and consist of tourist 'yurt camps' rather than places where Mongolians actually live.

Information
The main Bank of China branch is also in Hédōng at 5 Shengli Lu. It's about a five-minute walk north from the roundabout at Shengli Jie and is the only place to change travellers cheques.

The main post and telephone office is on Zhongyang Dajie, just north of the main square.

CITS (☎ 822 4017) is located inside the Běiyuàn Bīnguăn on Shengli Jie in the eastern section (called *hédōng*, 'east of the river') of the town. The PSB is opposite at 10 Shengli Jie.

Places to Stay & Eat
The rather dilapidated but friendly *Mínzú Fàndiàn* (☎ 833 0548) has a central location on Qiaotou Dajie, just opposite the CAAC office. Bed and breakfast costs between Y25 and Y40 in a twin room with attached bath. The rooms are OK, but the bathrooms are filthy.

The *Yǒuyì Dàjiǔdiàn* (Friendship Hotel; ☎ 833 1040) on Qiaotou Dajie is a good place to stay for mid-range prices. Twins /triples with attached bathrooms cost Y180 and include a free breakfast. The entrance is on the right of the market lane, near the main intersection, and the reception desk is hidden on the 2nd floor. The hotel also sells train tickets for a Y5 commission.

The *Hǎizhàn Dàjiǔdiàn* is just behind the train station and offers reasonable and cheap beds in twins for Y40 or dorm beds for Y15. As you exit the train station turn left and cross the footbridge. The hotel is to the left just on the other side of the bridge.

Most of the hotels have decent *restaurants*, with the restaurant of the Yǒujì

Dàjiǔdiàn winning the praise of the locals. There's also a *night food market* in front of the hotel.

Getting There & Away
Air The CAAC office (☎ 833 1010) is on Qiaotou Dajie beside the bridge and diagonally opposite the Mínzú Fàndiàn. There are direct flights between Hăilāěr and Běijīng (Y920) five times a week, and also twice a week to Hohhot (Y1050).

Train You can reach Hăilāěr by train from Hāěrbīn (12 hours), Qíqíhā'ěr (nine hours) and Běijīng (27 hours). There are also four trains a day to Mănzhōulǐ (three hours), all in the morning. The station is in the northwestern part of town. If you arrive by train, it's better to cross the train tracks using the footbridge to the left of the station as you exit and get a bus, taxi or motor-tricycle from there.

Bus The long-distance bus station is on Chezhan Jie, south-east of the train station. There are half-hourly buses to Mănzhōulǐ (four hours), but it's cheaper and easier to take the train.

Getting Around
The airport bus leaves from the booking office; tickets are Y3. A taxi costs about Y20.

Bus No 1 runs from Hédōng to the train station, although all buses are marked No 3; best to ask first. In fact, it's just as easy to walk.

MĂNZHŌULǏ 满洲里
☎ 0470
The border town where the Trans-Siberian Railway crosses from China to Russia, Mănzhōulǐ was established in 1901 as a stop for the train, although the area has long been inhabited by Mongolians and other nomads. There are huge coal deposits in the vicinity, including the open pit mine in nearby Zālàinuò'ěr that was first developed by the Russians early in the 20th century. The Russians have played a major role in Mănzhōulǐ's history, as evidenced in the old buildings and log houses with their filigree

windows dotting the town. Recently they've returned, crossing the border by bus and private car from Siberia to buy Chinese goods. The place feels more Russian than Chinese and there's a special kind of laissez-faire bordertown ambience that can make for some interesting encounters.

Orientation

Mănzhōulĭ is small enough to get around on foot and the grid lay out of the streets makes this easier. The town centre sits between the train station in the south and Beihu Park in the north.

Information

The Bank of China is at 16 Erdao Jie. The post and telephone office is on the corner of Sidao Jie and Haiguan Jie. Xinhua Bookstore is on the corner of Sidao Jie and Xinhua Lu. It has Internet access and sells maps of Mănzhōulĭ.

CITS (☎ 622 4241) is next door to the Guójì Fàndiàn (International Hotel) at 121 Erdao Jie on the 4th floor. If you're heading for Moscow you can purchase tickets here for the Trans-Siberian Railway. The PSB is also in this building, on the 2nd floor.

Places to Stay

One of the best-value places to stay is the Diànlì Bīnguǎn (☎ 622 2549). Beds in pleasant and comfy twins with attached bath are Y35 and Y45. It's at the intersection of Sandao Jie and Shulin Lu in the eastern part of town.

The Yóudiǎn Bīnguǎn (☎ 622 3351, 14 Haiguan Lu), just next door to the post office, has dorm beds from Y22.50 and clean beds in singles/triples with attached bathroom for Y82.50/47.50.

Another good option is the Mănzhōulĭ Fàndiàn (☎ 622 4855) on the corner of Sandao Jie and Zhongsu Lu. It has twins/doubles for Y120/100, but it can be bargained down to Y100/70. There are also clean dorm beds for Y18.

Most of the Russians stay at the Míngzhū Fàndiàn (☎ 622 7418), which makes it a lively place. Comfortable twins range from Y140 to Y240. It's on the corner of Xinhua Lu and Yidao Jie. For entertainment you can't beat sitting in the lobby and watching the world go by.

The Guójì Fàndiàn (☎ 622 2225, fax 622 2976) has twins from Y160 to Y220, including breakfast. It's beside the CITS building on Erdao Jie.

Places to Eat

There are many Russian restaurants around town, but by far the best place to eat is at Mockba Neon Lights, a Russian-style restaurant just east of the Míngzhū Fàndiàn. Just look for the neon lights. It has a Russian menu and even Russian dancers: the action starts about 9 or 10 pm. Try the sūbā tāng with bread, a delicious vegetable and broth soup.

For breakfast, drop into the western restaurant at the Míngzhū Fàndiàn, where it has Russian tea and nǎibǐng (pancakes) with cream and jam.

On the other side of town, opposite the Diànlì Bīnguǎn on Shulin Lu, is Shèngquàn Xiǎochī (Shengquan Snacks), which serves up some tasty local dishes.

The southern end of Haiguan Lu has several reasonable budget Chinese restaurants. There are also numerous Mongolian and Korean barbecue restaurants around town, just look out for the different scripts outside the restaurants.

Getting There & Away

The best way to reach Mănzhōulĭ is by train from Hǎilāěr (three hours), Hāěrbīn (15 hours) or Qíqíhā'ěr (11 hours); better yet, get off the Trans-Siberian.

Most of the Russians drive over the border, which is 9km from town, in private vehicles and you might be able to organise a lift across. A taxi to the checkpoint costs Y10. Naturally, you will need a Russian visa.

The train to Moscow from Běijīng passes through town early on Monday morning. It's possible to purchase tickets here for Moscow at CITS or otherwise if you want to make a stopover. Confirm it when you buy your ticket in Běijīng or Moscow.

If you arrive by train you can easily walk (10 minutes) to the town centre. Turn right as you exit the station and cross the footbridge.

Regular buses leave all day for Hǎilǎěr (four hours) from the long-distance bus station on Yidao Jie, three blocks west of the Míngzhū Fàndiàn.

AROUND MǍNZHŌULǏ

The main reason for visiting Mǎnzhōulǐ, other than to see the Russians, is Hūlún Hú (Hulun Lake), also known as Dálài Hú. One of the largest lakes in China, it unexpectedly pops out of the Mongolian grasslands like an enormous inland sea. It's a prime venue for fishing and bird-watching. Slightly further south is the lake Bèiěr Hú, which straddles the border with Outer Mongolia.

The easiest way to get to Dálài Hú is to hire a taxi or try to hitch a ride with one of the Russian or Chinese tour buses that are often parked on Xinhua Lu or in the parking lot by the CITS building. The lake is 39km south-east of Mǎnzhōulǐ and the return trip by taxi will cost about Y80. Entrance to the lake is Y3 and Y10 per vehicle.

The vast grasslands are another feature of Mǎnzhōulǐ and they surround the town in verdant splendour. If you're looking for big sky country, this is the place to come to. It's possible to arrange taxi or jeep excursions to the grasslands with overnight stops in yurts, tea-tasting and campfires. Should you strike a Mongolian living traditionally, you might get a cup of their milk tea. It's made of horse's milk and salt, and tastes revolting; it's also most impolite to refuse. CITS can also arrange a stay in a yurt with a Mongolian family, which can include horseback riding and a Mongolian banquet.

The other big feature is for train buffs – the steam locomotive storage and repair yards in Zālàinuò'ěr some of the more impressive in China, as is the mine that still uses steam engines to haul out the coal.

Unfortunately, to visit the steam train repair yards and open pit mine at Zālàinuò'ěr you'll also need to go through CITS, but it's cheaper to hire your own taxi than use its transport.

XANADU 元上都
☎ 0479

About 320km north of Běijīng, tucked away near Duōlún in Inner Mongolia, are the remains of Xanadu (Yuánshàngdū), the great Kublai Khan's palace of legendary splendour. In the 19th century, Samuel Taylor Coleridge (who never went near the place) stoked his imagination with some opium and composed *Kubla Khan,* a glowing poem about Xanadu that has been on the set menu for students of English literature ever since.

Over the centuries the deserted palace has crumbled back to dust and the site has been visited by very few foreigners. Hardly anything remains of the ancient city.

Getting There & Away

Unfortunately, foreigners can only visit Xanadu legally by going on a very expensive CITS tour, but perhaps this might change in the future. Check with the PSB (☎ 696 8148) in Hohhot.

The best way to get there would be to bus directly to Duōlún or Zhenglanqi and proceed to Xanadu from there, but these are closed areas at present.

If you want to go, first you have to travel to Xilinhot and arrange it through the CITS office (☎ 822 4448), which is on the 3rd floor of the Báimǎ Fàndiàn.

Tibet 西藏

'Shangri-La', 'the Land of Snows', 'the Rooftop of the World': locked away in its mountain fortress of the Himalayas, Tibet (Xīzàng) has long exercised a unique hold on the imagination of the west. Tibet is mysterious in a way few other places are.

Until recently, few outsiders had laid eyes on the holy city of Lhasa and the other secrets of Tibet. It is more the pity that when Tibet finally opened to tourism in the mid-1980s, it was no longer the magical Buddhist kingdom that had so intoxicated early western travellers.

Tibetans have never had it easy. Their environment is harsh, and human habitation has always been a precarious proposition. By necessity, Tibetans have become a tough and resilient people. Yet despite what appears to be a continuous grim struggle against nature and misfortune, Tibetans have not only survived, but have managed to retain a remarkably cheerful outlook on life.

Most of Tibet is too arid and cold to support human life and the place is still very thinly populated. With a geographical area more than twice that of France, Tibet still manages only a total population of 2.3 million. There are, however, estimated to be some four million more Tibetans spread out over Qīnghǎi, Sìchuān, Gānsù and Yúnnán.

Most of Tibet is made up of an immense plateau that lies at an altitude of 4000m to 5000m. The Qamdo region in the east is a somewhat lower section of plateau, drained by the headwaters of the Salween, Mekong and upper Cháng (Yangzi) rivers. It's an area of considerably greater rainfall than the rest of Tibet and the climate is less extreme. Most of the Tibetan population lives in the valleys of this area. On the uplands surrounding these valleys, the inhabitants are mainly semi-nomadic pastoralists who raise sheep, yaks and horses.

Since full-scale coverage of Tibetan regions would take a whole book, Lonely Planet has published a separate *Tibet* guide.

Highlights

Capital: Lhasa
Population: 2.4 million
Area: 1,220,000 sq km

- Lhasa, home of the Potala Palace, the Jokhang Temple and the Barkhor
- Shigatse, Tibet's second city and site of Tashilhunpo Monastery, the traditional home of the Panchen Lama
- Magnificent views from Rongphu Monastery
- Mt Kailash, a three- or four-day pilgrim circuit around the auspicious holy mountain

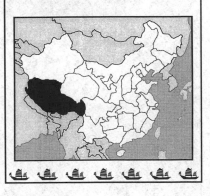

HISTORY

Recorded Tibetan history begins in the 7th century AD when the Tibetan armies were considered as great a scourge to their neighbours as the Huns were to Europe. Under King Songtsen Gampo, the Tibetans occupied Nepal and collected tribute from parts of Yúnnán.

Shortly after the death of Gampo, the armies moved north and took control of the Silk Road, including the great city of Kashgar. Opposed by Chinese troops, who occupied all of Xīnjiāng under the Tang dynasty, the Tibetans responded by sacking

TIBET 西藏

TIBET 西藏

the imperial city of Chang'an (present-day Xī'ān).

It was not until 842 that Tibetan expansion came to a sudden halt with the assassination of the king, and the region broke up into independent feuding principalities. Never again would the Tibetan armies leave their high plateau.

As secular authority waned, the power of the Buddhist clergy increased. When Buddhism reached Tibet in the 3rd century, it had to compete with Bon, the traditional animistic religion of the region. Buddhism adopted many of the rituals of Bon, and this, combined with the esoteric practices of Tantric Buddhism (imported from India) provided the basis from which Tibetan Buddhism evolved.

The religion had spread through Tibet by the 7th century; after the 9th century the monasteries became increasingly politicised, and in 1641 the Gelukpa (the Yellow Hat sect) used the support of the Buddhist Mongols to crush the Red Hats, their rivals.

The Yellow Hats' leader adopted the title of Dalai Lama, or Ocean of Wisdom; religion and politics became inextricably entwined, presided over by the Dalai Lama, the god-king. Each Dalai Lama was considered the reincarnation of the last. Upon his death, the monks searched the land for a newborn child who showed some sign of embodying his predecessor's spirit.

With the fall of the Qing dynasty in 1911, Tibet entered a period of independence that was to last until 1950.

One point needs to be made clear – Tibet during this time was not the liberal democracy that many westerners contend. Tibet was a highly repressive theocracy based on serfdom. In 1950 China seized on this fact as a justification to invade (the invasion was labelled a 'liberation') and to make good a long-held Chinese claim on the strategically important high plateau.

It made no difference that the Chinese claim was based on highly dubious historical grounds: between 1950 and 1970 the Chinese 'liberated' the Tibetans of their independence, drove their spiritual leader and 100,000 of Tibet's finest into exile, caused 1.2 million Tibetan deaths and destroyed most of the Tibetans' cultural heritage.

Despite Chinese efforts to paint a rosy picture of life on the roof of the world, the general picture is of a country under occupation. The Dalai Lama continues to be worshipped by his people, and his acceptance in late 1989 of the Nobel Peace Prize marked a greater sympathy on the part of the western world for the plight of the Tibetan people.

The Dalai Lama himself has referred to China's policies as 'cultural genocide' for the Tibetan people. Unfortunately, China's great potential as a trading nation and as a market for western goods makes many world leaders wary of raising the Tibet issue with China. Those who believe that pressure from western governments will eventually force China to grant Tibet independence or true autonomy are probably being unduly optimistic.

For their part, the Chinese can't understand the ingratitude of the Tibetans. As they see it, China has built roads, schools, hospitals, an airport, factories and a budding tourist industry. The Chinese honestly believe that they saved the Tibetans from feudalism and that their continued occupation is a mission of mercy.

The Tibetans, who cannot forgive the destruction of their monasteries and attacks on their religion and culture, see it differently. Nor do the Tibetans get much joy from the continuous heavy-handed presence of the Chinese police and military. Certainly the Chinese are not winning any friends in Tibet with their policy of stealthy resettlement: a massive influx of Han settlers from surrounding provinces threatens to make Tibetans a minority in their own 'autonomous region' and to swamp Tibetan culture with that of the Han Chinese.

The present Chinese policy on individual tourism in Tibet seems to be one of extorting as much cash as possible from foreigners, but not so much as to scare them off completely.

TREKKING
Trekking is not officially approved in Tibet; the local Public Security Bureau (PSB;

Gōngānjú) officials will tell you that it is only possible with an approved tour group.

Independent trekking is feasible for the experienced walker, providing you are prepared to be self-sufficient in food, fuel and shelter. There are now supplies of most trekking goods available in Lhasa, but it is still recommended to bring equipment suitable for subzero temperatures, such as a high-quality down sleeping bag, thermal underwear, ground mat, four-season tent, stove and fuel.

TRAVEL RESTRICTIONS
The current regulations (which could change tomorrow) say that all foreigners wanting to visit Tibet must be part of a 'tour group' (minimum of five people). In addition, every foreigner should have a Tibetan Tourism Bureau permit (TTB), Chinese insurance, a minimum three-day tour, and also a return ticket to a choice of three destinations (Kathmandu, Chéngdū or Golmud). If you want to stay longer, you are told that you have to pay an extra Y100 per day.

In reality, most people either pay up and then cancel or extend their return tickets when they arrive in Lhasa, or they try to independently hitch in. In Lhasa there doesn't seem to be anyone checking to see who has or hasn't a travel permit. However some travellers have reported that they have been fined (Y100) when flying out of Tibet because they lacked 'adequate papers'.

Once in Tibet, there are some places that actually require you to procure a travel permit (namely the Everest Base Camp, Samye, Tsetang and Mt Kailash etc). The cost of the permit varies, but expect to pay between Y50 and Y100. Getting the permits yourself is a nonstarter – the PSB insists you go through an authorised travel agency and that you be a member of a tour group.

Not surprisingly, Lhasa has a large number of travel agencies catering to this market. At the time of writing, permits were being strictly enforced and travel agencies were only issuing permits for members of valid groups.

Despite all the regulations and paperwork, some travellers have successfully slipped past road blocks and avoided the PSB.

It's worth bearing in mind that Tibet (much more than the rest of China) is effectively a police state, and political discussions with local Tibetans can have serious consequences. Incidentally, many of the secret police are ethnic Tibetans.

WHAT TO BRING
Figuring out what type of clothing to bring is tricky, due to the extremes of the climate. Department stores in Chéngdū, Xīníng, Golmud and Lhasa have a wide selection of warm clothing and it is also advisable to bring sun protection gear.

Food is no problem in Lhasa, but remote areas offer little to eat beyond lichen, dust and rocks. If you are considering a long journey, like Mt Kailash, then it would be wise to stock up before heading off.

There are several medications that are particularly useful in Tibet, and you should bring them from abroad rather than rely on local supplies. Drugs to consider carrying include Diomox, Tiniba and Flagyl. For more information see the Health section in the Facts for the Visitor chapter at the beginning of the book.

DANGERS & ANNOYANCES
Health Risks
The greatest dangers to travellers' health are acute mountain sickness (AMS) and giardiasis. For a full discussion of prevention and treatment, see the Health section in the Facts for the Visitor chapter at the beginning of the book.

Not Shangri-La
Tibetans are among the friendliest, most hospitable people in the world. At the same time, however, there is little point in pretending that visiting the Land of Snows is a Disneyland holiday.

Most Tibetans are only too happy to have foreign visitors in their country, but do not expect smiles all the way. Travellers who have poked their noses into Tibetan funerals and other personal matters have quite rightly received a very hostile reception.

Stories abound of surly monks, of aggressive Tibetans at checkpoints and of rip-offs. Tibetan tour operators can be just as rapacious as their Chinese counterparts. Some foreigners have had a few bad experiences and come away disillusioned.

Dogs

Tibetan dogs are even more xenophobic than the PSB. They (the dogs) roam in packs around monasteries and towns, and seem to have a particular antipathy to foreigners who look and smell different from the locals. Keep your distance during the day, and watch your step in the dark.

GETTING AROUND

Transport can be a major hurdle if you want to explore the backwaters. The main types of vehicle are bus, minibus, truck and 4WD.

So-called public 'pilgrim buses' to monastery attractions have become more widespread in recent years, but are generally restricted to the major monastic sites in the Lhasa region.

On some routes there are modern Japanese buses; other routes are covered by battered wrecks, which gasp over each high pass as if it's their last. Trucks are often more comfortable, more fun and faster than the bus. Land Cruisers are pricey, but not impossible for non-budget travellers willing to split the cost among several people.

In Tibet, 'road safety' is just a slogan. Potential hazards include bad roads, vehicle breakdowns, icy weather and reckless drivers (not necessarily your driver, but the other maniacs on the road). Road accidents are frequent and foreigners have been injured or killed in the past. Tibetans take their minds off these variables by praying, and you'd be wise to follow their example unless you want to end up a gibbering bag of nerves.

Be prepared for the cold, which can easily go below zero at night even during summer. All buses have heaters, although these are sometimes broken. More seriously, a mechanical breakdown could have fatal consequences if you have no warm clothing.

As for bicycling – it is possible, but is not without its hazards. Aside from hassles with the PSB, cyclists in Tibet have died from road accidents, hypothermia and pulmonary oedema (pneumonia). Tibet is not the place to learn the ins and outs of long-distance cycling – do your training elsewhere.

Despite the odds, a number of experienced cyclists have individually travelled around Tibet without too many problems.

LHASA 拉萨

☎ 0891

Lhasa (Lāsà) is the heart and soul of Tibet, the abode of the Dalai Lamas and an object of devout pilgrimage. Despite the large-scale encroachments of Chinese influence, it is still a city of wonders.

As you enter the Kyi Chu Valley, either on the long haul from Golmud or from Gonggar airport, your first hint that Lhasa is close at hand is the sight of the Potala Palace, a vast white and ochre fortress soaring over one of the world's highest cities. It is a sight that has heralded the marvels of the holy city to travellers for three centuries.

The Potala Palace dominates the Lhasa skyline. The site of the tombs of previous Dalai Lamas, it was once the seat of Tibetan government and the winter residence of the Dalai Lama. While the Potala Palace serves as a symbolic focus for Tibetan hopes for self-government, it is the Jokhang Temple, some 2km to the east of the Potala, that is the spiritual heart of the city.

The Jokhang Temple, a curious mix of sombre darkness, wafting incense and prostrating pilgrims, is the most sacred and active of Tibet's temples. Encircling it is the Barkhor, the holiest of Lhasa's devotional circumambulation circuits. It is here that most visitors first fall in love with Tibet. The medieval push and shove of crowds, the street performers, the stalls hawking everything from prayer flags to jewel-encrusted yak skulls, and the devout tapping their foreheads to the ground at every step is an exotic brew that few newcomers can resist.

Orientation

Modern Lhasa divides clearly into a Chinese section in the west and a Tibetan section in the east. For travellers who have arrived from other parts of China, the Chinese part of town harbours few surprises.

Nestled at the foot of the Potala Palace and extending a couple of kilometres westward is an uninspired muddle of restaurants, karaoke bars, administrative blocks and department stores.

The Tibetan part of town, which begins west of the Jokhang Temple, is altogether more colourful and the better area to be based in.

Information

The best place for the latest on Tibetan individual travel these days is in the courtyards of one of the popular Tibetan hotels, or a table in Tashi's restaurants. The information boards in some of the hotels can be very useful if you're looking for a travel partner or a used travel book.

Consulate The Nepalese consulate (☎ 682 2881, fax 683 6890) is on a side street just south of the Lhasa Hotel and north of the Norbu Lingka. Visa application hours are Monday to Saturday from 10 am to 12.30 pm. Visas are issued in 24 hours.

The fee for a 15-day visa is Y135 and Y225 for a 30-day visa. Remember to bring a visa photo. It is also possible to obtain visas for the same cost at Kodari, the Nepalese border town, although it would be sensible to check that this has not changed.

Money The most convenient place for travellers is a branch of the Bank of China located between the Banak Shol and Kirey Hotels. The main Bank of China is behind the Potala Palace – turn right at the yak statues and look for it on the left. Come here for credit card advances and foreign exchange on Saturday. Its opening hours are 9.30 am to 12.30 pm and 2 to 6 pm weekdays, and 9.30 am to 12.30 pm on Saturday.

Post & Communications The main post office is adjacent to the Potala Palace on Beijing Donglu. It is open Monday to Saturday from 9 am to 8 pm and Sunday from 10 am to 6 pm.

The telephone office is next door and is open from 8 am till midnight. There is another post and telecommunications centre in

the east of Lhasa on the corner of Linkuo Donglu and Linkuo Beilu.

Internet access is available at the Barkor Café, the Yak Hotel and the Pentoc Guesthouse.

Travel Agencies If you want to do any official trekking or visit remote areas, you need to visit a travel agency in order to secure a permit, motorised transport (usually a jeep) and (possibly) a guide.

Most travellers use the budget agencies scattered around the old Tibetan part of town, around the Yak and Banak Shol Hotels. All can provide limited information and offer reasonably cheap deals on vehicle rental, but most are fairly disorganised and are dedicated more to relieving you of the contents of your wallet than to providing reasonable levels of service.

There has been a recent proliferation of travel services in Lhasa; proceed with caution. First talk to other travellers and shop around.

PSB There are two PSB offices in Lhasa, although it's doubtful that either will prove to be of much use. The one on the eastern end of Beijing Donglu issues travel permits, but the staff are unwilling to issue these to individual travellers and will instead refer you to a travel agency.

The other PSB office on Linkuo Beilu has been more helpful with information and is granting seven-day visa extensions. If you require a longer extension contact one of the travel agencies.

Medical Services In the case of an emergency you will probably be taken or directed to the People's Hospital on Linkuo Beilu. Expect minimal hygiene standards, but the staff are competent.

There are also a number of clinics along Beijing Donglu that will provide medication for minor ailments. Take along a Tibetan or Chinese phrasebook.

Potala Palace 布达拉宫

The most imposing attraction of Lhasa is the Potala Palace (Bùdálāgōng), once the centre of the Tibetan government and the winter residence of the Dalai Lama. Each day a stream of chanting pilgrims files through this religious maze to offer *khata* (ceremonial scarves) or yak butter at one of the innumerable chapels and shrines.

One of the architectural wonders of the world, this immense construction is 13 storeys tall and contains thousands of rooms, shrines and statues. Construction of the present structure began during the reign of the fifth Dalai Lama in 1645 and it took more than 50 years to complete. The first recorded use of the site dates from the 7th century AD, when King Songtsen Gampo built a palace here.

The general layout of the Potala includes the White Palace (the main part of the building), for the living quarters of the Dalai Lama, and the Red Palace (the central building rising above), for religious functions. The Red Palace contains many halls and chapels – the most stunning chapels house the jewel-bedecked tombs of previous Dalai Lamas. The apartments of the 13th and 14th Dalai Lamas, in the White Palace, offer an insight into the high life. The roof gives marvellous views of Lhasa and the region – don't forget your camera (although be prepared for a hefty Y50 charge to bring it into the palace).

The Potala Palace is open every day from 9 am to 1 pm only. Foreigners pay Y45 admission or Y22 with a student card. Avoid the weekends, as the entrance charge goes up to Y85. The long climb to the entrance is not recommended on your first day in town; do something relaxing at ground level until you acclimatise.

Barkhor

The Barkhor is essentially a pilgrim circuit (*kora*) that is followed clockwise round the periphery of the Jokhang Temple. It is also a hive of market activity, an astounding jamboree, and a wonderful Tibetan-style stock exchange.

All around the circuit are shops, stalls, teahouses and hawkers. There's a wide variety of items to gladden a Tibetan heart – prayer flags, block prints of the holy scrip-

tures, earrings, Tibetan boots, Nepalese biscuits, puffed rice, yak butter and incense. Whether you buy from a shop or a hawker, many of the Tibetan goods on sale have been imported from Nepal and many of the 'antiques' are not genuine. Be prepared to bargain hard.

People who roll up from remote parts of Tibet include Khambas from eastern Tibet, who braid their hair with red yarn and stride around with ornate swords or daggers, and Goloks (Tibetan nomads) from the north, who wear ragged sheepskins. Golok women display incredibly ornate hairbands down their backs.

Jokhang Temple 大昭寺

The golden-roofed Jokhang Temple is 1300 years old and is one of Tibet's holiest shrines. It was built to commemorate the marriage of the Tang princess Wencheng to King Songtsen Gampo, and houses a pure gold statue of the Buddha Sakyamuni brought to Tibet by the princess.

Here, too, hundreds of pilgrims prostrate themselves in front of the temple entrance before continuing on their circuit.

Follow the pilgrims through a labyrinth of shrines, halls and galleries containing some of the finest and oldest treasures of Tibetan art. Some originals were destroyed during the Cultural Revolution and have been replaced with duplicates.

The Jokhang Temple is best visited early in the morning; after noon, you will have to enter via the side door to the right of the entrance. Entry is free, unless you're with a guide (Y25).

Norbu Lingka 罗布林卡

About 3km west of the Potala Palace is the Norbu Lingka (Jewel Park), which used to be the summer residence of the Dalai Lama. The pleasant park contains small palaces, chapels and a zoo. The best time to visit is during festivals or on public holidays.

The Norbu Lingka is open daily from 9 am to midday and 3.30 to 5.30 pm. Entry is Y25 or Y1 for monks. Entry on Sunday costs Y1 but only the gardens are open.

Bus No 2 will take you there for Y2.

TIBET 西藏

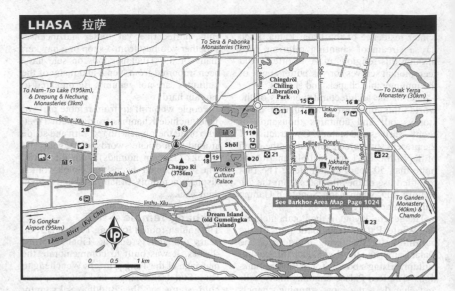

LHASA 拉萨

Festivals

If it is at all possible, try and time your visit to Lhasa with one of the city's festivals. Pilgrims often flock to Lhasa at these times and the city's pilgrim circuits take on a colourful party atmosphere. The Losar and Saga Dawa festivals are particularly exciting as thousands of pilgrims flood into town.

Tibetan festivals are held according to the Tibetan lunar calendar, which usually lags at least a month behind our Gregorian calendar. The following are a brief selection of Lhasa's major festivals:

Losar Festival (New Year Festival) Taking place in the first week of the first lunar month, Losar is a colourful week of activities. There are performances of Tibetan drama, pilgrims making incense offerings and the streets are thronged with Tibetans dressed in their finest.

Lantern Festival Held on the 15th of the first lunar month; huge yak-butter sculptures are placed around Lhasa's Barkhor circuit.

Mönlam Festival Known also as the Great Prayer Festival, this is held mid-way through the first lunar month (officially culminating on the 25th). An image of Maitreya from Lhasa's Jokhang Temple is borne around the Barkhor circuit, attracting enthusiastic crowds of locals and pilgrims.

Tsurphu Festival *Cham* dancing and *chang* drinking are the order of the day at this festival on the 10th day of the fourth lunar month. The highlight is the dance of the Karmapa.

Saga Dawa (Sakyamuni's Enlightenment) The 15th day of the fourth lunar month (full moon) is an occasion for outdoor operas and also sees large numbers of pilgrims at Lhasa's Jokhang Temple and on the Barkhor circuit.

Worship of the Buddha During the second week of the fifth lunar month, the parks of Lhasa, in particular the Norbu Lingka, are crowded with picnickers.

Shötun Festival (Yoghurt Festival) This is held in the first week of the seventh lunar month. It starts at Drepung Monastery and moves down to the Norbu Lingka. Operas and masked dances are held, and locals take the occasion as another excuse for more picnics.

Onkor Festival In the first week of the eighth lunar month Tibetans get together and party in celebration of this traditional Harvest Festival.

Palden Lhamo The 15th day of the 10th lunar month has a procession around the Barkhor bearing Palden Lhamo, protective deity of the Jokhang Temple.

Places to Stay – Budget

During the last few years most budget hotels have provided showers and also included a

LHASA

PLACES TO STAY	7 Yak Statues 牦牛像	14 Ramoche Temple 小昭寺
1 Grand Hotel	8 Bank of China (Main Branch) 中国银行	15 PSB (Visa Extensions) 公安局外事科
2 Lhasa Hotel 拉萨饭店		17 Main Telecom Office; Post Office 邮电局
16 Yínqiáo Fàndiàn 银桥饭店	9 Potala Palace 布达拉宫	18 Yeti Mountaineering
23 Himalaya Hotel 喜玛拉亚宾馆	10 Vegetable Market 市场	19 Potala Square 布达拉广场
OTHER	11 CAAC; Airport Bus Departures 中国民航; 机场班车发车处	20 Photographic Stores
3 Nepalese Consulate 尼泊尔领使馆		21 New Century Department Store 新世纪百货
4 Zoo 动物园	12 Main Post Office; Telecom Office 邮电局	22 PSB (Travel Permits) 公安局
5 Norbu Lingka 罗布林卡	13 People's Hospital 人民医院	
6 Bus Station 汽车站		

mid-range option with the construction of new rooms. These rooms are often better value than staying at the more expensive hotels.

The **Banak Shol Hotel** (Bālángxuě Lǚguǎn; ☎ 632 3829) is a popular abode in Lhasa with a charming Tibetan-style courtyard, a free laundry service, bicycles for hire and a very good information board. Four-bed dorms are Y25. Pokey single rooms cost Y35 and all face onto the noisy main road. Doubles are better at Y60.

The **Kirey Hotel** (Jírì Lǚguǎn; ☎ 632 3462), close to the Banak Shol, is a quieter place that charges Y25 for beds in a triple, while beds in a comfortable twin cost Y35. It has reliable hot showers, a free laundry service and super-friendly staff.

The **Yak Hotel** (Yàkè Lǚshè; ☎ 632 3496), on Beijing Donglu, has a range of options, with dark dorms from Y25 to excellent twins with Tibetan-style decor for Y250. Hot showers are available in the morning and the evening.

Snowlands Hotel (Xuěyù Lǚguǎn; ☎ 632 3687), close to the Jokhang Temple, is a friendly place with rooms arranged around a courtyard. Dorm beds with a locker are Y25 and double rooms cost Y60.

The **Pentoc Guesthouse** (☎ 632 6686 fax 633 0700, ✉ pentoc@public.east.cn.net) is

across the road from Snowlands Hotel and is friendly, clean and stylish. Beds in clean but very small six-bed dorms cost Y30. Singles/doubles cost Y80/120. It has 24-hour showers and hiking gear for rent.

Places to Stay – Mid-Range

Most of Lhasa's mid-range places are constructed in the Chinese style that you may be familiar with from elsewhere on your trip. All of the budget hotels mentioned earlier offer mid-range doubles with private attached bathroom, carpet, a TV etc. The Kirey Hotel has the best value doubles for Y120.

Hotel Kechu (Lāsàjìqū Fàndiàn; ☎ 633 8824, fax 632 0234) is a friendly and well-run choice west of Tashi's Restaurant (see Places to Eat). Room rates are Y180/280 for a carpeted single/double and Y350 for a well-furnished four-bed room.

One of the older Chinese-style places to stay is the one-star **Himalaya Hotel** (Xīmǎlāyǎ Fàndiàn; ☎ 632 2293), which is located near the Lhasa River. Glum doubles are available from Y275. A new block of three-star rooms should be available from sometime in 2000.

The **Yínqiáo Fàndiàn** (☎ 633 0663) is a two-star Chinese hotel on Linkuo Beilu. Clean triples cost from Y220 to Y300.

TIBET 西藏

Places to Stay – Top End

The *Lhasa Hotel* (*Lāsà Fàndiàn;* ☎ *683 2221, fax 683 5796, 1 Minzu Lu*) is just north of the Norbu Lingka. Rates for economy twins are around Y700, while standard doubles weigh in at around Y1147. Standards have dropped considerably since the Holiday Inn pulled out in 1997.

For cheaper rates and better service and amenities try the *Grand Hotel* (☎ *682 6096*), on Beijing Xilu, which used to serve as the government guesthouse but now operates as a plush and comfortable three-star option with standard rooms for Y420.

Places to Eat

Food can be mighty scarce out on the high plateau, but Lhasa offers Chinese, western, Tibetan and even some Nepalese and Indian cuisine.

The staple diet in Tibet is *tsampa* (roasted barley meal) and butter tea. *Momos* (dumplings filled with vegetables or meat) and *thukpa* (noodles with meat) are usually available at small restaurants. Tibetans consume large quantities of *chang*, a tangy alcoholic drink derived from fermented barley.

Tashi's Restaurant deserves a special mention. This place has been running for a while now, and despite increased competition continues to be a favourite and serves good food with a smile. *Tashi's II*, in the Kirey Hotel, has the same menu and the same friendly service. Special praise is reserved for the *bobis* (chapatti-like unleavened bread), which most people order with seasoned cream cheese and fried vegetables or meat. Tashi's cheesecakes are to die for.

Probably the most popular place in town is the *Kailash Restaurant*, on the 2nd floor of the Banak Shol Hotel. Prices are definitely higher than at the Tashi restaurants but dishes on offer include vegetarian lasagne and yak burgers.

On the south-eastern corner of the Barkhor circuit is the popular *Makye Ame*. This foreign-run restaurant serves decent western and Nepalese cuisine plus treats like great brownies and Kahlúa coffee.

Snowlands Restaurant, attached to the Snowlands Hotel, is a slightly more upmar-

BARKHOR AREA 八角街

ket place that serves a mixture of Tibetan and Nepalese food in civilised surroundings. Most dishes are around Y25 to Y35.

Next door to the Yak Hotel is the *Crazy Yak Saloon*. It isn't as popular as it perhaps deserves to be. The food might be a little expensive and the menu a bit short, but what it has is very good. The Tibetan-style interior is also probably the best in this part of town and there's live music whenever a group is passing through. The food is mainly Chinese with a couple of Tibetan items thrown in.

The *Barkhor Café* is down in the Barkhor Square area and has roof-top dining areas, which provide great views of the Jokhang Temple and Barkhor Square.

The *Friend's Corner Restaurant*, on Beijing Donglu not far from Tashi's Restaurant, currently has the best Chinese food in this part of town, though it's owned and run by a Tibetan couple.

Entertainment

For many Tibetans a night on the town usually involves a visit to a friend's house for some serious consumption of chang and lots of laughter. Alternatively, many Tibetan restaurants around town entertain their customers with karaoke or video shows, and you would be more than welcome to venture in and pull up a pew.

If karaoke isn't your idea of entertainment, then the Makye Ame, Kailash, Crazy Yak and Tashi's restaurants sometimes have impromptu parties where travellers guzzle beers and share tales of their exploits.

BARKHOR AREA

PLACES TO STAY	PLACES TO EAT	
2 Yak Hotel 亚客旅社	1 Friend's Corner Restaurant	13 Minibus Stop 小型车站
4 Hotel Kechu 拉萨吉曲饭店	3 Crazy Yak Saloon	14 Tibetan Hospital 藏医院
7 Pentoc Guesthouse	6 Tashi's Restaurant	15 Minibuses to Drepung, Ganden, Samye &
8 Kirey Hotel; Tashi's II Restaurant 吉日旅馆	11 Snowlands Restaurant 雪域饭馆	Tsetang Monasteries 17 Jokhang Temple 大昭寺
10 Banak Shol Hotel; Kailash Restaurant 八郎学旅馆	16 Barkhor Café 19 Makye Ame 情人饭店	18 Ganden Monastery Bus Tickets 汽车售票处
12 Snowlands Hotel 雪域旅馆	OTHER 5 Mount Green Trekking 9 Bank of China 中国银行	20 Main Mosque 清真寺

Shopping

Whether it's prayer wheels, daggers, rings or muesli, then you shouldn't have a problem finding it in Lhasa. The Barkhor circuit is especially good for buying souvenirs to fill up your pack.

Mount Green Trekking and Yeti Mountaineering have down jackets, fleeces and gloves; Mount Green's stock are made in Nepal while Yeti's are China made.

It is still a good idea to come with your own film supplies, but slide film is now relatively easy to find in Lhasa. A profusion of photographic shops are clustered around the entrance to the Workers' Cultural Palace, just east of the Potala square.

Getting There & Away

Air Lhasa has air connections to Kathmandu (Y1850) on Tuesday, Thursday and Saturday; to Chéngdū (Y1200) twice daily; to Chóngqìng (Y1300) on Tuesday; and Xī'ān (Y1320) on Wednesday.

Flights between Kathmandu and Lhasa operate twice weekly in the low season (departing Tuesday and Saturday) and three times a week in the high season.

No matter whether you fly in from Chéngdū, Běijīng, Xī'ān, Chóngqìng or Kathmandu, all tickets to Lhasa have to be purchased through a travel agency. At the time of writing, the cheapest of tours from Kathmandu was a three-day tour for around US$360. This included the flight ticket (US$228), airport transfer to Kathmandu and Lhasa, TTB permits and dormitory accommodation for three nights in Lhasa.

Leaving Lhasa is a lot simpler, as tickets can be purchased from the Civil Aviation Administration of China (CAAC; Zhōngguó Mínháng) office at 88 Niangre Lu. Preferably purchase your ticket several days in advance of your intended departure date. CAAC is open daily from 9 am until 9 pm.

Bus The bus station is a deserted monstrosity 3km from the main post office, near the Norbu Lingka.

Tickets for buses from Lhasa to Golmud can be bought at the main bus station south of the Lhasa Hotel. Prices are Y424 for a Japanese sleeper bus or Y244 for a clapped-out Chinese bus. There are also sleeper buses that continue all the way to Xīníng, the capital of Qīnghǎi. Hard-core masochists might be attracted by the epic nonstop 3287km sleeper bus to Chéngdū (three days and four nights), though most sane people will take the plane.

There are three daily departures to Tsetang (Y60), and daily departures to Shigatse (Y80), Chamdo (Y302) and Bayi (Y310), though foreigners might have problems getting on the last two buses. All prices quoted are foreigners' prices, which are double local price.

TIBET 西藏

Few foreigners use the bus station's Shigatse service as there are minibuses departing from in front of the Kirey Hotel from 7 am. They do the trip quicker than the public buses and cost only Y38. Since the completion of the Lhasa-Shigatse Highway, there is no public transport direct to Gyantse. It is necessary to travel to Shigatse first and then change to a private minibus or a public bus.

Buses to Ganden (Y8; 2½ hours), the Samye ferry crossing (Y23) and Tsetang (advertised as Shannan, the name of the county; Y30) leave every morning from the west side of Barkhor Square.

There are no longer buses to the Nepalese border (Zhangmu), though the private agencies in the Tibetan quarter advertise weekly minibuses to Zhangmu, departing Thursday. Seats cost between Y250 and Y350 for the two-day trip.

Rented Vehicles   Rented vehicles have emerged as the most popular way to travel away from Lhasa in recent years. The most popular route is a leisurely and slightly circuitous journey down to Zhangmu on the Tibetan-Nepalese border, taking in Yamdrok-tso Lake, Gyantse, Shigatse, Sakya, Tingri and Everest Base Camp on the way. A six- to seven-day trip of this sort in a 4WD costs around Y6000, including all necessary permits, driver, guide and car.

Other popular trips include Mt Kailash (Kangrinpoche 6714m), Nam-tso Lake and eastern Tibet.

Although there are five major road routes to Lhasa, foreigners are officially allowed to use only the Nepal and Qīnghǎi routes.

Nepal Route   The 920km road connecting Lhasa with Kathmandu is known as the Friendship Highway. It's a spectacular trip over high passes and across the Tibetan plateau, the highest point being La Lungla Pass (5200m).

If the weather's good, you'll get a fine view of Mt Everest from the Tibetan village of Tingri. Accommodation en route is generally basic with fairly reasonable prices (Y15 to Y25), and there's no great hardship involved, as long as you don't mind doing without luxuries (such as a shower) for the duration of your trip. The food situation has also improved greatly in recent years.

By far the most popular option for the trip is renting a 4WD through a hotel or travel agency, and sorting out a private itinerary with the driver. A five-day trip to the Nepalese border, via Shigatse, Everest Base Camp and Tingri, will cost about Y1200 each in a 4WD. A direct run to the Nepalese border costs from Y250 to Y400 per person, depending on the numbers and the type of vehicle. The trip normally takes two days to Zhangmu.

When travelling from Nepal to Lhasa, foreigners must arrange transport through tour agencies in Kathmandu. If you already have a Chinese visa, you could try turning up at the border and organising a permit in Zhangmu. Although, this is a gamble as the rules and regulations change hourly. The occasional traveller slips through (even a couple on bicycles). At Zhangmu you can hunt around for buses, minibuses, 4WDs or trucks heading towards Lhasa.

Qīnghǎi Route   The 1754km road that connects Xīníng with Lhasa via Golmud crosses the desolate, barren and virtually uninhabited Tibetan Plateau. The highest point is Tanggula Pass (5180m), but despite the altitude, the surrounding scenery is not very interesting.

Theoretically, local Chinese buses and decidedly more comfortable 'Japanese' buses (made in China) do the run. However, the 'Japanese' buses are often not available, so you get to ride budget class at five-star prices.

Reckon on a minimum 35 hours from Golmud to Lhasa by bus and remember to take warm clothing, food and water on the bus, since baggage is not accessible during the trip.

Other Routes   Between Lhasa and Sìchuān, Yúnnán or Xīnjiāng provinces are some of the wildest, highest and most dangerous routes in the world; these are not officially open to foreigners.

The lack of public transport on these routes makes it necessary to hitch, but that is also prohibited. At the time of writing there were a few travellers hitching into Tibet from Kashgar, via Ali with minimal hassles. However, the authorities have come down very heavily on truck drivers giving lifts to foreigners, particularly on the Yúnnán and Sìchuān routes in or out of Tibet.

Getting Around

To/From the Airport Gonggar airport is 95km (1½ hours by bus) from Lhasa. Buses leave from the car park behind the CAAC office every hour from 6 am and cost Y30. Tickets are sold on the bus, so show up early to guarantee yourself a seat. If you need to get to the airport more quickly, you could share a taxi for about Y25 per person, but this is usually a bit of a squeeze.

CAAC buses greet incoming flights, so getting into town is no problem.

Minibus Privately run minibuses are frequent on and around Beijing Lu. There is a flat Y2 charge. This is a quick and convenient way to get across town. From the minibus station near Barkhor Square there are jeeps and minibuses running up to the Drepung and Sera Monasteries.

Bicycle The best option is to hire a bike and peddle around yourself. They can be hired from the Yak, Banak Shol, Pentoc and Snowlands Hotels.

AROUND LHASA
Drepung Monastery 哲蚌寺

Drepung Monastery (Zhébàng Sì) dates back to the early 15th century and lies about 7km west of Lhasa. In its time it was the largest of Tibet's monastic towns and, some maintain, the largest monastery in the world. Drepung, Sera and Ganden Monasteries functioned as the three 'pillars of the Tibetan state'.

Prior to 1959 the number of monks in residence here was around 7000. During the Cultural Revolution there was a concerted effort to smash the influence of the major monasteries and much of the monastic

population was wiped out. Today around 700 monks reside here and in nearby Nechung. Around 40% of the monastery's structures have been destroyed.

The monastery is open daily from early morning until 4 pm and entry is Y30. Try and catch the lunch break when the monks feast on tsampa and yak butter tea. You can wander into the kitchen and check out the incredible wood-fired stoves and massive pots.

Drepung Monastery is easily reached by bike, although most people take minibus No 3 for Y2 from the minibus stand near Barkhor Square.

Sera Monastery 色拉寺

About 5km north of Lhasa, Sera Monastery (Sèlā Sì) was founded in 1419 by a disciple of Tsong Khapa.

About 600 monks are now in residence, well down from an original population of around 5000, after the Cultural Revolution attempted to destroy the monasteries' power. Debating takes place from 3.30 pm in a garden next to the Jepa Duchen, the assembly hall in the centre of the monastery. Sera Monastery is open daily from 9 am to 4.30 pm, and admission is Y30. An hour's walk will get you up to the monastery, or catch minibus No 5 for Y3.

From Sera Monastery it's possible to continue up the valley for another hour to **Pabonka Monastery**. Built in the 7th century by King Songtsen Gampo, this is one of the most ancient Buddhist sites in the Lhasa region and is well worth the effort.

Ganden Monastery 甘丹寺

About 40km east of Lhasa, Ganden Monastery (Gāndān Sì) was founded in 1417 by Tsongkhapa. During the Cultural Revolution the monastery was subjected to intense shelling, and monks were made to dismantle the remains.

Some 400 monks have now returned and extensive reconstruction work is taking place. The monastery is still well worth visiting and remains an important pilgrimage site.

Pilgrim buses leave for Ganden Monastery at 6.30 am and tickets can be bought the day before or on the bus. The ticket office is on the Barkhor circuit, 100m to the right of the main entrance to the Jokhang Temple. Look out for the tin shed. Tickets are sold from 2.30 to 7 pm. The cost is Y16 for a return ticket. If you decide to buy the ticket on the bus, try to arrive in Barkhor Square by 6 am.

Nam-tso Lake 纳木错

An overnight stay at Nam-tso Lake (Nàmùcuò), 195km north of Lhasa, has become a popular trip in recent years. The sacred, turquoise-blue lake is surrounded by mountains with peaks of over 7000m and the scenery is breathtaking.

Accommodation is available at **Tashi Dor Monastery** (4718m), which is on the edge of the lake, or you can camp nearby. It costs Y15 to enter the area and another Y15 a night for a bed at the Tashi Dor Monastery. The closest public transport to Nam-tso Lake takes you to Damxung (Dāngxióng), a small town with a couple of Sichuanese restaurants and a military base, but the lake is still another 40km or more. The best option would be to organise a 4WD in Lhasa, which should cost between Y1100 and Y1500 for a two-day trip.

Permits and guides are not necessary for the area; however, do not underestimate the rapid ascent of 1100m.

It would be preferable to be in Lhasa at least a week before heading up to Nam-tso Lake, so as to avoid AMS (see the Health section in the Facts for the Visitor chapter).

YARLUNG VALLEY 雅鲁流域

About 170km south-east of Lhasa, the Yarlung Valley (Yǎlǔ Liúyù) is considered to be the birthplace of Tibetan culture. Near the town of Tsetang, which forms the administrative centre of the region, are several sites of religious importance.

Samye Monastery

Located about 30km west of Tsetang, on the opposite bank of the Yarlung Zangbo (Brahmaputra) River, Samye Monastery (Sāngyī Sì) was the first monastery in Tibet. It was founded in AD 775 by King Trisong Detsen. Getting there is quite complicated, but it commands a beautiful, secluded position.

To reach Samye Monastery, catch one of the morning buses from opposite the Kirey Hotel in Lhasa or from the bus stop just to the west of Barkhor Square. Buses leave at 7.30 am and cost Y23. There is a police check at the ferry crossing for valid permits. When we last visited, it was possible to pay the PSB officers Y50 and cross without any problems. Before you leave Lhasa, ask around about the current situation.

The bus will drop you at the ferry, which will take you across the river whenever it's full. From there, a lift in the back of a truck will carry you the 5km to Samye Monastery. The ferry crossing is Y10 and then it's another Y10 for the bumpy truck ride. The local cost for both trips is Y3.

Simple accommodation is available at the **Monastery Guesthouse** from Y10 to Y25 and tasty Amdo momos are served up at **Gompo's Restaurant**.

Yumbulagang

About 12km south-west of Tsetang on a dirt road, Yumbulagang (Yōngbùlākǎng) is the legendary first building in Tibet. Although small in scale, it soars in recently renovated splendour above the valley. Get there by hiring a bike or 4WD in Tsetang, or hitch on a tractor. The roof provides wonderful views of the surrounding valley.

On your way to Yumbulagang consider stopping at **Trandruk Monastery**, one of Tibet's oldest Buddhist monasteries and a popular destination for pilgrims. It is a lively monastery with friendly monks and is well worth it to stop for a brief visit en route to Yumbulagang.

Tsetang 泽当

The rather uninteresting town of Tsetang (Zédāng), 183km from Lhasa, is mainly used as a jumping board for exploration of the Yarlung Valley area. Officially you need to organise a permit for the surrounding area, which can only be done through the local CITS. The office is located in the back of the Tsetang Hotel, and can be worth a visit if there is a group of you. Otherwise, if you keep a low profile, you might be able to avoid the PSB altogether.

Accommodation for foreigners is a sad affair. The cheapest official option is the **Regional Guesthouse**, on Naidong Lu, about a 15-minute walk south from the traffic circle. Beds in twins start at Y100, but it may let you stay in one of its Y50 beds. Like everything in Tsetang, that's still double the local price.

Further south is the new **Gold Grain Hotel** with comfortable singles/twins for Y180/200.

The **Tsetang Hotel** is the town's premier lodging, but is best avoided.

Getting There & Away Buses for Tsetang leave Lhasa regularly from Lhasa's Barkhor Square. Buses heading back to Lhasa depart hourly from the traffic circle in Tsetang until about 2 pm.

YAMDROK-TSO LAKE

On the old road between Gyantse and Lhasa, the dazzling Yamdrok-tso Lake (4488m) can be seen from the summit of the Ganbala Pass (4794m). The lake lies several hundred metres below the road, and in clear weather is a fabulous shade of deep turquoise. Far in the distance is the huge massif of Mt Nojin Kangtsang (7191m).

Nangartse, a small town along the way, has basic accommodation and a restaurant.

A 20- to 30-minute drive or a two-hour walk from Nangartse brings you to **Samding Monastery**, a charming place with scenic views of the surrounding area and lake.

GYANTSE 江孜

Gyantse (Jiāngzī) is one of the least Chinese-influenced towns in Tibet and is worth a visit for this reason alone. It's also one of southern Tibet's principal centres, although it's more like a small village.

Things to See

The **Pelkhor Chöde Monastery**, founded in 1418, is notable for its superb **Kumbum Stupa** (10,000 Images Stupa), which has nine tiers and, according to the Buddhist tradition, 108 chapels. The monks may not

allow you to complete the pilgrim circuit to the top, but the lower tiers contain excellent murals. Take a torch (flashlight).

The **Dzong** (Old Fort), which towers above Gyantse, offers an amazing view of the neighbouring sights and surrounding valley. Entry (Y20) to the Dzong is via an alley that runs from the left of the eastbound road from the roundabout.

Places to Stay & Eat

One good place is the **Hostel of Gyantse Town Furniture Factory**, on the main junction. Decent, clean rooms run at around Y30 per person. There are toilets and a nice sitting area with great views of the fort, but no washing facilities. There's also a Tibetan teahouse next door, visible from the sitting area.

The **Foodstuffs Hotel**, just opposite the Furniture Factory Hostel, is a Chinese-style hotel but it's better than it looks from the outside. Again there are no showers but rooms have a basin and a TV – not bad for the money. Beds in a single/double are Y40/30.

The **Canda Hotel (Chan Da)** is a new mid-range hotel that opened in 1998. At the time of writing it was great value with spotless doubles with private bathroom going for Y150.

Gyantse's dining options have improved immensely in recent years, largely due to Sichuanese and Muslim Chinese immigration. Restaurants are concentrated on the stretch of road opposite the Gyantse Hotel.

Getting There & Away

All public transport to Gyantse is by way of Shigatse. Minibuses from Lhasa arrive in Shigatse around 3 pm and there are usually minibuses on to Gyantse (Y25; two hours) from the minibus stand in front of the Shigatse bus station until around 5 pm. Minibuses from Gyantse back to Shigatse leave on an irregular basis through the day from the main intersection.

SHIGATSE 日喀则

elevation 3900m

Shigatse (Rìkāzé) is the second largest town in Tibet and the traditional capital of Tsang. Shigatse has long been an important trading town and administrative centre. The Tsang kings exercised their power from the once imposing heights of the Shigatse Dzong – the present ruins only hint at its former glory – and the fort later became the residence of the governor of Tsang. Since the Mongol sponsorship of the Gelugpa order, Shigatse has been the seat of the Panchen Lama, who is traditionally based in Tashilhunpo Monastery. The monastery is Shigatse's foremost attraction.

Once the sun goes down packs of dogs take over the streets and it is advisable to avoid a late evening stroll.

Information

The Bank of China is next door to the Shigatse Hotel and is open on weekdays from around 9 am to 1 pm and 4 to 7 pm, and from 10 am to 4 pm on weekends. Travellers cheques and cash in most currencies can be changed with a minimum of fuss.

The main post office is open 9 am to 8 pm. You can make international phone calls and send faxes, though it may take some time.

PSB If you want to travel without the cost of a tour and 4WD then ask for a permit at the Shigatse PSB. This PSB has probably the most useful officials in Tibet. At the time of writing this was the only place where you could get a travel permit without being part of an organised tour. If you are hitching or cycling it would pay to be vague about your means of transportation. The cost of a permit is Y50 per person. Recent travellers have reported that the situation has changed and Shigatse is again off-limits. Your best advice is to ask other travellers, as the rules change like the wind.

Tashilhunpo Monastery
扎什伦布寺

The main attraction in Shigatse is Tashilhunpo Monastery (Zhāshílúnbù Sì), the seat of the Panchen Lama. Built in 1447 by a nephew of Tsong Khapa, the monastery once housed over 4000 monks, but now there are only 600.

Apart from a giant statue of the Maitreya Buddha (nearly 27m high) in the Temple of

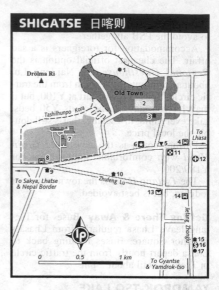

the Maitreya, the monastery is also famed for its Grand Hall, which houses the opulent tomb (containing 85kg of gold and masses of jewels) of the fourth Panchen Lama. The monastery is open from 9 am to 5 pm and is closed for two hours from noon for lunch. Admission costs the standard Y30 or Y15 with a Chinese student card.

Shigatse Fortress 日喀则宗

Very little remains of the old Shigatse Fortress (Rìkāzé Zōng), but the ruins on the skyline are imposing all the same. It's possible to hike up to the fortress from the pilgrim circuit for good views of the town.

Places to Stay & Eat

In the middle of town is the *Tenzin Hotel* (*Tiānxīn Lǚguǎn;* ☎ 882 2018), a friendly and busy place. Beds cost Y25 in the dorm rooms, Y30 in nicer four-bed rooms and modern doubles with a view of the fort range from Y60 to Y100. Hot water is off and on and off again 24 hours a day. Wear ear muffs if you don't like listening to the dogs howl all night long.

The *Orchard Hotel* (*Guǒyuán Lǚguǎn*) is just across the road from the main entrance

SHIGATSE

PLACES TO STAY	OTHER	
3 Tenzin Hotel; Tiānfù Restaurant 天新旅馆、天富餐	1 Shigatse Fortress 日喀则宗	8 Minibuses to Lhatse
9 Orchard Hotel 果园旅馆	2 Market 农贸市场	11 Department Store 商场
10 Everest Hotel 主峰宾馆	4 Minibuses to Lhasa	12 People's Hospital 人民医院
15 Shigatse Hotel 日喀则宾馆	6 PSB 公安局	13 Post Office 邮局
	7 Tashilhunpo Monastery 扎什伦布寺	14 Bus Station 汽车站
PLACES TO EAT		16 Bank of China 中国银行
5 Gongkar Tibetan Restaurant		17 CITS 中国国际旅行社

to the Tashilhunpo Monastery. It's a simple Chinese-style hotel with cheap dorm beds for Y15 or Y30/40 with a TV. Doubles are also available. The manager will normally open up one of the suites and let you use the hot shower there.

A newer hotel is the ***Everest Hotel*** (*Zhǔfēng Bīnguǎn*; ☎ 882 3383), a five-minute walk south-east of the Orchard Hotel. Doubles come with a private bathroom and hot water, and are excellent value at Y50 per person.

Shigatse Hotel (*Rìkāzé Fàndiàn*; ☎ 882 2525, fax 882 1900) is a three-star palace in the south of town. Chinese- or Tibetan-style standard twins with attached bathrooms (24-hour hot water!) cost Y450, economy triples cost Y480 and singles are available for Y430. If you want to feel important for the night, the presidential suite is Y1540.

The most convenient place to eat if you are staying at the Tenzin Hotel is the ***Tiānfù Restaurant***, which is on the ground floor of the hotel. It has a wide range of food, including a number of vegetarian options.

Worth a try is the ***Gongkar Tibetan Restaurant***, which is Chinese-run but has an English menu.

Getting There & Away

Bus Between Lhasa and Shigatse most travellers use the minibus service. Minibuses for Lhasa (Y38; seven hours) leave between 7.30 and 8 am from a cross-roads at the eastern edge of town.

Buses to Gyantse (Y25, Y50 on a government bus; two hours) depart from the main bus station whenever full from around 10 am until 5 pm. There is also a bus that departs at 8 am and travels to Yatung, passing within 5km of Gyantse, though you'll have to persuade the bus driver to let you on the bus as Yatung itself is officially off-limits to foreigners.

From the main bus station there are also buses every other day at 8.30 am for Sakya (Y54). These return to Shigatse the next day so you get either an afternoon or 2½ days at Sakya – neither one ideal. An alternative is to take the daily bus to Lhatse, get off at the Sakya turn-off and hitch the remaining 25km. You'll most likely have to pay the full fare to Lhatse though. Private mini-buses depart daily at around 8 am to Lhatse (Y30).

Those heading out to the Nepal border or Tingri have very few options. Hitching is one possibility, or you could inquire at the Shigatse Hotel for minibuses or Land Cruisers heading out to the border to pick up tour groups. However, the cost for hooking up with one of these varies and the service is unreliable.

Rented Vehicles Renting vehicles in Shigatse is more difficult than in Lhasa and prices are not as competitive. The few agencies operating in town have a reputation for ripping travellers off and should be treated with caution.

TIBET 西藏

CITS has a branch near the Shigatse Hotel. Prices are not cheap, but surprisingly this is probably the most reliable outfit around. Sample prices are Y3400 for a three-day trip to Rongphu Monastery or Y3800 to Rongphu Monastery and the Nepalese border (Y4400 return).

SAKYA 萨迦
elevation 4280m
The monastic town of Sakya (Sàjiā) is one of Tsang's most important historical sights and, even more than Gyantse, is very Tibetan in character, making it an interesting place to spend a day or so. Sakya's principal attractions are its northern and southern monasteries on either side of the Trum Chu. The fortress-like southern monastery is of most interest. The original, northern monastery has been mostly reduced to picturesque ruins, though restoration work is ongoing.

Places to Stay & Eat
The *Sakya Guesthouse* has basic rooms with dirt floors and no electricity but it's bearable if you have a sleeping bag. There's a certain timeless feel about the place. Beds should cost Y8 per person but foreigners are asked to pay anything from Y10 to Y20 (one group was asked Y50!). The scenic pit toilets offer great views of the northern monastery.

A popular place to eat is the *Sichuan Flavour Restaurant*, just outside the Sakya Guesthouse. Recommended dishes are *gōngbào jīdīng* (spicy chicken with peanuts) or *yúxiāng qièzi* (fried eggplant).

Another good choice is the *Red Sun Restaurant*, opposite the County Guesthouse.

Getting There & Away
Sakya is the last stop for foreigners using public transport. The bus leaves Shigatse every two days and is a slow journey. Buy your ticket the day before.

Most people arrange to see Sakya as an overnight stop when they hire a 4WD to the border or to the Everest Base Camp. It's also possible to hitch, as there is enough transport on the road to Sakya.

RONGPHU MONASTERY & EVEREST BASE CAMP
Before heading down to the border, many travellers doing the Lhasa-Kodari trip take in Rongphu Monastery and the Everest Base Camp (also known as Mt Qomolangma Base Camp).

The road to Rongphu Monastery is a bumpy one to say the least and it takes at least four hours from the Chay checkpoint. It is here that all vehicles pay a Y400 entrance fee and every passenger Y65.

Most 4WD drivers are not keen on driving all the way to the base camp. If you want to go all the way make sure that you mention it in your itinerary.

The walk from Rongphu Monastery to the base camp takes about two hours, or 20 minutes in a 4WD. Everest Base Camp (5200m) is at the far edge of this plain. The site has a couple of permanent structures and there are usually tents belonging to various expeditions. Endowed with springs, Everest Base Camp was first used by the 1924 British Everest expedition.

There is *dorm accommodation* at Rongphu Monastery for Y25 a bed and there is a small *restaurant* with simple supplies nearby.

TINGRI 定日
elevation 4390m
Tingri (Dìngrì) is a huddle of Tibetan homes that overlooks a sweeping plain bordered by the towering Himalaya Range, is where most travellers spend their last night in Tibet en route to Nepal, or their first night en route to Lhasa from Kathmandu

Ruins on the hill overlooking Tingri are all that remain of the Tingri Dzong. This is a fort that was not blown up by Red Guards but rather destroyed in a late 18th-century Nepalese invasion. Many more ruins on the plains between Shegar and Tingri shared the same fate and can be seen from the Friendship Highway.

Most budget travellers passing through in rented vehicles stay in the *Everest View Hotel* (or the 'Lao Dhengre Haho Everest Veo Hotel & Restaurant' as the sign cryptically advertises), a shabby little place

青海

arranged around a compound. Beds are Y20 and basic food is available.

The nicest place by far is the ***Everest Snow Leopard Hotel***, about 400m east of the other hotels. The all-brick rooms are spotlessly clean, very cosy and there are some nice touches like unsolicited buckets of hot and cold water and views of Cho Oyu from most of the rooms. There's also a nice restaurant and sitting area, which doubles as reception. Rates are officially Y60 per bed but this normally crumbles to around Y30 if you don't arrive in a flashy Land Cruiser.

From Tingri it's four or five spectacular hours to the border – up, up, up and then down, down, down.

ZHANGMU 樟木
elevation 2300m

Zhangmu (Zhāngmù), also known as Khasa in Nepali and Dram in Tibetan, is a remarkable town that hugs the rim of a seemingly never-ending succession of hairpin bends down to the customs area at the border of China and Nepal. After Tibet, it all seems incredibly green and luxuriant, the smells of curry and incense in the air are smells from the subcontinent and the babbling sound of fast-flowing streams that cut through the town is music to the ears.

CITS has an office just next to the Zhangmu Hotel. It arranges transport and occasionally organises Tibetan Tourism Bureau (TTB) permits for travellers who turn up from Nepal without prearranged transport or a guide.

The ***Gang Gyen Hotel*** (☎ 2188) is just up from Chinese customs and has twins for Y70 or beds in a five-bed dorm for Y50, but the latter normally slides down to around Y30. The dorms are nice and spotlessly clean, though the communal bathrooms are

a little grim. Hot showers are available on the roof.

ZHANGMU TO KODARI

Access to Nepal is via the Friendship Bridge and Kodari, around 8km below Zhangmu. Traffic on the stretch of no-man's land between the two countries has increased over the last couple of years and it has now become quite easy to hitch a lift, though you will probably have to pay. Around Y15 should do the trick, but the amount depends entirely on who is giving the lift.

If you decide to walk, it takes a couple of hours down to the bridge. There are porters at both customs points who will carry your pack for a few rupees or yuan. Look out for short cuts down between the hairpin bends of the road. They save quite a bit of time if you find them, though they put a real strain on the knees.

It is possible to get a Nepali visa at the border for the same price as in Lhasa, though it would be sensible to get one in Lhasa just in case. There are a couple of hotels on the Nepalese side, which offer rooms for around Rs 80. For those looking at continuing straight on to Kathmandu, there are a couple of buses a day from Kodari that leave whenever they are full. If you can't find a direct bus you'll have to change halfway at Barabise. The other option is to hire a vehicle. There are usually touts for vehicles to Kathmandu in front of the hotels on the Nepalese side. The cost is around Rs 1500 to Rs 2000. Most of the vehicles are private cars, and small ones at that; you will be hard pressed to fit more than three people into one, especially if you have big packs. Depending on the condition of the road, it should take around four to five hours from Kodari to Kathmandu.

Nepal is 2¼ hours behind Chinese time.

Qīnghǎi 青海

Qīnghǎi lies on the north-eastern border of Tibet and is one of the great cartographic constructions of our time.

For centuries this was part of the Tibetan world; these days it's separated from the Tibetan Autonomous Region by nothing more than the colours on a Chinese-made map.

With the exception of the eastern area around the provincial capital Xīníng, Qīnghǎi (formerly known as Amdo) was not incorporated into the Chinese empire until the early 18th century. Since 1949 the province has served as a sort of Chinese Siberia, where common criminals, as well as political prisoners, have been incarcerated. These prisoners have included former Kuomintang army and police officers, 'rightists' arrested during the late 1950s harvesting of the Hundred Flowers, victims of the Cultural Revolution, former Red Guards arrested for their activities during the Cultural Revolution, supporters of the Gang of Four, and opponents of the present regime.

Eastern Qīnghǎi is a high grassy plateau rising between 2500m and 3000m above sea level, slashed by a series of mountain ranges with peaks rising up to 5000m. It's also the source of the Huáng Hé (Yellow River).

Most of the agricultural regions are concentrated in the east around Xīníng, but the surrounding uplands and the regions west of Qīnghǎi Hú (Qinghai Lake) have good pasturelands for sheep, horses and cattle.

North-western Qīnghǎi is a great basin consisting mainly of barren desert surrounded by mountains. It's littered with salt marshes and saline lakes and afflicted by harsh, cold winters.

Southern Qīnghǎi is a high plateau sitting 3500m above sea level. It's separated from Tibet by the Tanggulashan Range, which has peaks rising to more than 6500m; both the Cháng Jiāng (Yangzi River) and the Mekong River have their source here. Most of the region is grassland

Highlights

Capital: Xīníng
Population: 4.9 million
Area: 720,000 sq km

- Tǎ'ěr Sì, one of the six great monasteries of the Yellow Hat sect of Tibetan Buddhism
- Qīnghǎi Hú, China's largest lake, renowned for its breathtaking scenery and abundant birdlife
- The rough but stunning overland trip into Tibet via Golmud
- Mèngdá Tiān Chí, a peaceful nature reserve by the Huáng Hé (Yellow River)

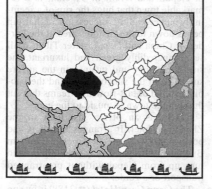

and the population is composed almost entirely of semi-nomadic Tibetan herders rearing goats, sheep and yaks.

The population of Qīnghǎi is a mixture of minorities, including the Kazakhs, Mongols and Hui. Tibetans are found throughout the province and the Han settlers are concentrated around the area of Xīníng.

Although a train line stretching as far as Golmud has helped improve Qīnghǎi's economy, it still remains one of China's poorest provinces. Unemployment is high, and those rural residents that have jobs often earn as little as Y300 per month.

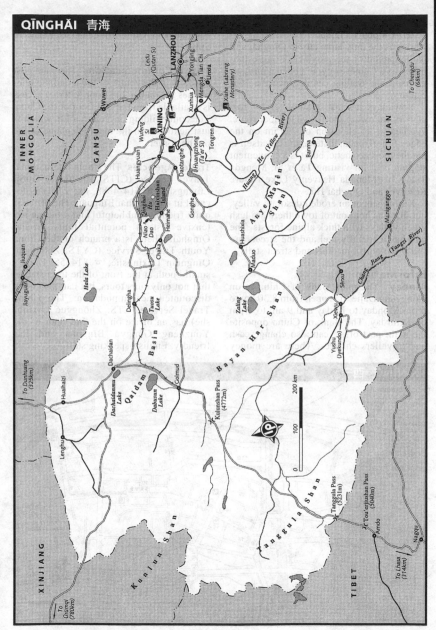

QĪNGHǍI 青海

INNER MONGOLIA

GANSU

XINJIANG

TIBET

SICHUAN

LANZHOU

Ledu (Qutan Si)

Yongjing

Linxia

Mengda Tian Chi

Xiahe (Labrang Monastery)

Wuwei

Xining

Wutong Si

Huangyuan

Daotanghe

Huangzhong (Tǎ ěr Sì)

Tongren

Xunhua

Huang He (Yellow River)

Banma

Anye Maqên Shan

Gonghe

Heimahe

Chaka

Niao Dao

Qinghai Hu

Haixinshan Island

Huashixia

Maduo

Zaling Lake

Bayan Har Shan

Hala Lake

Jiayuguan

Jiuquan

Delingha

Tuosu Lake

Qaidam Basin

Dachaidamu Lake

Dabusun Lake

Dachaidan

Golmud

Kunlunshan Pass (4772m)

Huaihaizi

Lenghu

To Dunhuang (325km)

To Ürümqi (780km)

Kunlun Shan

Chang Jiang (Yangzi River)

Sêrxu

Manganggo

Xiewu

Yushu (Jyekundo)

To Chengdu (68km)

Tanggula Pass (5231m)

Tanggula Shan

Toul'erjiushan Pass (5040m)

Ando

Nagqu

To Lhasa (314km)

0   100   200 km

XĪNÍNG 西宁

☎ 0971 • pop 1,112,600

Xīníng is the only large city in Qīnghǎi and is the capital of the province. Long established as a Chinese city, it's been a military garrison and trading centre since the 16th century.

Nowadays it's also a stopover for foreigners following the Qīnghǎi-Tibet route. Perched at an elevation of 2275m on the edge of the Tibetan Plateau, the city itself is not the most aesthetic, but it is a convenient staging post for visiting Tǎ'ěr Sì, Mèngdá Tiān Chí (Mengda Heavenly Lake Nature Reserve) and Qīnghǎi Hú.

Xīníng sits in an eroded desolate valley, but just one hour out of town there are lush green valleys with thick alpine forests. The city has a friendly feel and the streets are full of colourful markets and street stalls.

Information

Money The main Bank of China is on Dongguan Dajie. It is open from 8.30 am to 6 pm Monday to Friday and 9 am to 4 pm on Saturday. The Bank of China opposite the main post office can also change cash and travellers cheques. There are money changing facilities at both the Qīnghǎi Bīnguǎn and Xīníng Bīnguǎn (see Places to Stay).

Post & Communications The main post office is in the centre of town and the telephones are on the 2nd floor. Internet access is available from the 2nd floor of the China Telecom building on Tongren Lu, which is just next door to the main telephone office on the corner.

Travel Agencies The China International Travel Service (CITS; Zhōngguó Guójì Lǚxíngshè; ☎ 614 4888, ext 2471) is located in the Qīnghǎi Bīnguǎn. The office is quite friendly and helpful and it has an extensive list of potential tours around Qīnghǎi. There is a branch of the China Youth Travel Service (CYTS; Zhōngguó Qīngnián Lǚxíngshè; ☎ 814 5514) in a small booth at the front of the train station that not only runs tours, but can also book discounted accommodation. The China Travel Service (CTS; Zhōngguó Lǚxíngshè) has an office on the 2nd floor of the Yóuzhèng Gōngyù Bīnguǎn and has friendly, English-speaking staff.

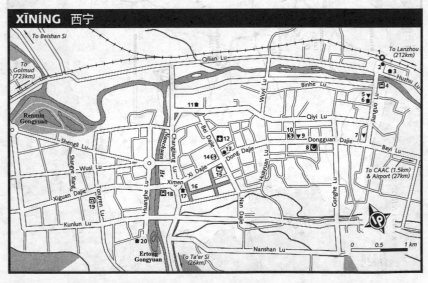

XĪNÍNG 西宁

PSB The Public Security Bureau (PSB; Gōngānjú) alien affairs section is at 35 Bei Dajie and is a good place to extend your visa.

Běishān Sì 北山寺
North Mountain Temple
The temple is about a 45-minute walk up the mountainside north-west of the Xīníng Bīnguǎn. The hike is pleasant and you'll be rewarded with a good view over Xīníng. Admission is Y6.

Qīngzhēn Dàsì 东关清真大寺
Great Mosque
This mosque is one of the largest in China's north-west and attracts large crowds of worshippers. It was built during the late 14th century and recently restored.

Shuǐjǐng Xiàng Shāngchǎng
水井巷商场
The Shuǐjǐng Xiàng Shāngchǎng is the most colourful market in town. It's an enjoyable place just to browse and watch the crowds watch you. There is a good supply of munchies here if you need stocking up. The market is near Xī Mén (West Gate).

There are lots of other markets around town, namely along Shangye Xiang and in the park on Nánchuān Hé (Nanchuan River).

Places to Stay
The best budget bargain in town lies only a few minutes' walk east of the train station at the *Yóuzhèng Gōngyù Bīnguǎn* (☎ 814 9484 ext 2751, 138 Huzhu Lu). It's a friendly, fairly clean place with dorm beds from Y16 to Y24 and singles with private bath for Y46. One drawback is the noise, you have a choice of rooms, either with hooting cars or tooting trains. There are a couple of other budget options around the train station that will take foreigners, but only if you can speak Chinese.

Another inexpensive option close to the train station is the *Xīníng Tiědào Bīnguǎn*, which has dorm beds ranging from Y25 to Y50, or a bed in a twin with attached bath for Y50. The hotel is quite new, but the water dripping from the ceiling and running down the walls is not such a good omen. The hotel is just five minutes' walk from the train station and is next to a lane that usually functions as a fruit market. When we last visited they were processing an application to receive foreigners.

The *Jiànyín Bīnguǎn* (☎ 826 1885, fax 826 1551, 55 Xi Dajie) is probably the fanciest hotel in town. They have good twins from Y218 to Y298 and comfortable doubles for Y258. All rates include breakfast and there is a classy restaurant on the top

---

XĪNÍNG

PLACES TO STAY	7 Food Tents 帐篷食摊	10 Bank of China 中国银行
3 Yóuzhèng Gōngyù Bīnguǎn; CTS 邮政公寓宾馆、中国旅行社	9 Xiǎoyuánmén Shìfǔ 小圆门食府	12 PSB 公安局
6 Xīníng Tiědào Bīnguǎn 西宁铁道宾馆	OTHER	13 Xinhua Bookstore 新华书店
11 Xīníng Bīnguǎn 西宁宾馆	1 Train Station 火车站	14 Bank of China 中国银行
17 Jiànyín Bīnguǎn 建银宾馆	2 CYTS 中国青年旅行社	15 Post & Telephone Office 邮电局、邮政大楼
20 Qīnghǎi Bīnguǎn; CITS 青海宾馆、中国国际旅行社	4 Long-Distance Bus Station 长途汽车站	16 Shuǐjǐng Xiàng Shāngchǎng 水井巷商场
PLACES TO EAT	8 Qīngzhēn Dàsì 东关清真大寺	18 Buses to Huángzhōng; Tǎ'ěr Sì 去湟中、塔尔寺
5 Xī'ān Mǎjiá Pàomó 西安马家泡馍		19 China Telecom; Internet 中国电信、网吧

floor which serves both western and Chinese food.

Although not in a convenient location, the *Xīníng Bīnguǎn (☎ 823 8798, fax 823 8701)* is a peaceful place with some nice gardens. It's a typical Chinese three-star operation, with twins ranging from Y198 to Y520. There are a few triples with attached bath available for Y30 per bed, which are good value. All rooms include a free breakfast, the only drawback is the hotel charges foreigners an extra 10%. The reception is in the building at the rear, behind the pleasant gardens where people play golf and sip tea. Take bus No 9 from opposite the train station and get off at the 7th stop.

The *Qīnghǎi Bīnguǎn (☎ 614 4888)*, a towering pink monolith in the western part of town, is Xīníng's most upmarket hotel. This is reflected in the rates, which start at Y268 for a twin. Staying here is probably not worth the money, although staff try to do their best.

Places to Eat

Just a couple of doors down from the Xīníng Tiědào Bīnguǎn is the *Xī'ān Mǎjiǎ Pàomó*, a good little restaurant that serves a heart-warming bowl of lamb *pàomó* (Y5–10). Break up the bread yourself and then hand the bowl back, but remember your peg number.

The area around the Xīníng Tiědào Bīnguǎn and Yóuzhèng Gōngyù Bīnguǎn has a good selection of *food tents* in the evening; check out the kebab stalls and the places selling *shā guō* (a mini-hotpot of beef, mutton, vegetables, tofu and noodles). It's very filling and costs only Y5, including a bowl of rice.

The *Xiǎoyuánmén Shífǔ*, a Muslim place on Dongguan Dajie, has a good reputation among locals. The only English signage is the word 'Qingzhen', a transliteration of the Chinese word for Muslim.

Out near the Shuǐjǐng Xiàng Shāngchǎng there is also are a number of excellent eating options.

Getting There & Away

Air Xīníng has flights to Běijīng (thrice weekly, Y1630), Chéngdū (twice weekly, Y1060), Guǎngzhōu (twice weekly, Y1950), and one flight a week to Shànghǎi (Y1970), Ürümqi (Y1400) and Xī'ān (Y710).

There is also a twice-weekly flight to Lhasa for Y1300, but you'll still need to go through CITS to purchase your ticket. The same rules apply here, in that you have to wait for another five passengers before they will process the 'Tibet permit'. In Xīníng, it could take a while before another four people turn up. For interest's sake, the whole deal should cost about Y2000 per person.

The Civil Aviation Administration of China (CAAC; Zhōngguó Mínháng; ☎ 817 4616) has a booking office on the eastern edge of town at 34 Bayi Xilu, which is open daily from 8.30 am to noon and 2 to 5.30 pm. To get there take the eastbound bus No 9 from the corner of Jianguo Lu and Dongguan Dajie, get off at the second stop and walk east another 50m. You can also purchase tickets through almost any travel agency or hotel.

Bus The main bus station serves all destinations except Tǎ'ěr Sì. Sleeper buses to Golmud (Y72; 20 hours) leave daily between 4 and 6 pm. Buses to Lánzhōu (Y20.2; five to six hours) leave every 20 minutes from 7.30 am to 5 pm. There is also a sleeper bus to Dūnhuáng (Y160; 20 hours plus) in Gānsù that leaves every second day at 10 am.

Between 7.30 am and 3 pm there are buses every 30 minutes to Tóngrén (Y18.4; five hours). From Tóngrén it is possible to take onward buses to Xiàhé in Gānsù. Heading towards Mèngdá Tiān Chí, there are three morning buses prior to 8.30 am to Xúnhuà (Y16.5; four hours). There are also several buses to Hēimǎhé (Y19), near Qīnghǎi Hú (see the Qīnghǎi Hú entry below).

Some travellers looking for an off-beat Tibetan experience have made the journey from Xīníng to Chéngdū in Sìchuān by bus. The scenery is stunning and very Tibetan, but it's a rough trip that takes nearly a week. The route to Chéngdū is as follows: Xīníng to Mǎduō; Mǎduō to Xiēwǔ; Xiēwǔ to Sêrxu (Shíqú); Sêrxu to Kāngdìng; and Kāngdìng to Chéngdū.

All along the way there are cheap places to stay – the bus company will either put you up at its own hostels or direct you to another hotel. Another option would be to take a bus to Banma (two days), where you could then get a bus to Zoigê (one day), then to Sōngpān (eight hours) and on to Chéngdū (14 hours).

From Xīníng, buses to Mǎduō (Y73) leave daily at 1 and 3 pm; those to Banma (1½ days) depart only on the 4th, 10th, 14th, 20th, 24th and 30th of each month.

Train Xīníng has frequent rail connections to Lánzhōu (4½ hours). A special tourist train, No 202, offers soft seats (Y42) and does the trip in a rapid 3½ hours. It leaves Xīníng daily at 8 am. Other train connections include Běijīng, Shànghǎi, Qīngdǎo, Xī'ān and Golmud.

There are two trains to Golmud and the trip takes either 18 or 24 hours.

Getting Around
To/From the Airport The airport is 27km outside the city. A CAAC shuttle bus meets all flights and costs Y10; a taxi fare there should be around Y50.

AROUND XĪNÍNG
Tǎ'ěr Sì 塔尔寺
One of the six great monasteries of the Yellow Hat sect of Tibetan Buddhism, Tǎ'ěr Sì (or Kumbum in Tibetan) is found in the town of Huángzhōng, a mere 26km south of Xīníng. It was built in 1577 on sacred ground – the birthplace of Tsong Khapa, founder of the Yellow Hat sect.

The monastery is noted for its extraordinary sculptures of human figures, animals and landscapes carved out of yak butter. The art of butter sculpture probably dates back 1300 years in Tibet and was taken up by the Tǎ'ěr Sì in the last years of the 16th century.

It's a pretty place and very popular with local tourists. An earthquake in 1990 and subsequent heavy snows threatened to destroy many of the buildings, and the Chinese government eventually forked out Y70 million for a major restoration project. Despite the damage, the place still maintains its historical atmosphere.

Go hiking in the surrounding area or follow the pilgrims clockwise on a scenic circuit round the monastery. Six temples are open; admission tickets (Y21) are sold at the building diagonally opposite the row of stupas. Photography is prohibited inside the temples.

Places to Stay & Eat
The *Tǎ'ěr Sì Bīnguǎn* (☎ 232 452) is outside the monastery wall, opposite the ticket office, and has beds in a triple for Y35 and twins with attached bath for Y120 and Y180.

Just behind the row of stupas is a sign saying 'Kumbun Motel', but when we last visited, the monastery was not taking guests. Instead, there's a small *restaurant* in the courtyard that has a few Tibetan dishes and reasonably priced Chinese food.

For some variety, take a stroll down the hill towards town and try some noodles in one of the many *Muslim restaurants*.

Getting There & Away
If you are on a tour you may visit the monastery as a stopover on the way to or from Qīnghǎi Hú. However, this probably means that your trip to Qīnghǎi Hú won't visit Niǎo Dǎo (Bird Island) (see the Qīnghǎi Hú section below for details).

Minibuses and taxis to Huángzhōng (Y3; 45 minutes) leave every ten to 20 minutes from the lane next to the Xining Sports Arena (Xīníng Tǐyùguǎn). A minivan taxi costs Y30, not a bad option if there are several of you.

Buses first stop at the Huángzhōng bus station, but most will continue on to the monastery.

Catch the return bus or minibus to Xīníng from the square in Huángzhōng; 500m down the road from the monastery. The last buses leave at around 8 pm. To get to the Xining Sports Arena from the train station, take bus No 1 for seven stops to Xī Mén.

MÈNGDÁ TIĀN CHÍ
Mengda Heavenly Lake Nature Reserve
Mèngdá Tiān Chí is a beautiful nature reserve situated by the Huáng Hé (Yellow River), 190km south-east of Xīníng. The

highlight of the reserve is Tiān Chí (Heavenly Lake), a sacred lake for the both the local Sala Muslims and Tibetan buddhists. The lake is a scenic 2½-hour walk up from the Huáng Hé along a dirt track through a lush valley of verdant alpine forest.

At the top it is possible to walk around the lake, when the water level is low enough, or head up to most of the surrounding peaks.

The bus will drop you off at the turn-off to Tiān Chí, from where it is a 4km (one hour) walk to the ticket office. All the way up from the turn-off to the park entrance people will try and offer you horses and accommodation in their homes. Entry to the reserve is Y12. From the ticket office, the road continues on for a couple more kilometres until the car park. From the car park it's a sweaty one hour walk up to the lake.

Places to Stay & Eat

There is plenty of accommodation available on the way up to and at the lake itself. Most people lodge at one of the two *hostels*, the first by the lake and the other at the ticket office. Both are very basic and have dorm beds for Y15. Both places are reasonably clean, claim the owners, with rooms and sheets cleaned at least weekly!

When we last visited, the guesthouse on the other side of the lake was to be moved back down the mountain to the car park. They were forced to move due to their negative impact on the environment. In any case their rooms were basic and overpriced. If their style and price haven't changed then just keep on walking.

There is a *Hui restaurant* at the lake which serves up some tasty mushroom and noodle dishes. The two hostels also serve a few basic dishes.

In the nearby town of **Xúnhuà**, there are two basic options. The *Jiāotōng Bīnguǎn* (☎ 812 615) is just next door to the bus station and has good dorms from Y10 to Y30. Twins are Y90 and their suite is Y130. They might try and charge you double, but be insistent and they will probably back down. If not, turn left out the door and head down the road 500m until you get to a small market

street. The building on the left-hand corner is the *Zhèngfǔ Zhāodàisuǒ (Government Hostel)*. It has dorms from Y8 to Y16 and beds in twins for Y25. Both hotels have hot water from 9 pm.

Getting There & Away

Mèngdá Tiān Chí is 1½ hours by bus from Xúnhuà (27km) along a road cut into the cliffs of the Huáng Hé (Yellow River). This is a spectacular drive along a precipitous cliff face. The road passes through a couple of peaceful rural towns as it slowly descends to **Mèngdá**, passing fields of barley, rape, corn and wheat. All this time the Huáng Hé slurps its way through the gorge below. There are four daily buses that pass Mèngdá Tiān Chí on their way to Dàhéjiā, from where it is possible to continue on to Línxià in Gānsù.

From Xúnhuà there are four daily buses to both Línxià (Y12; four hours) and Xīníng (Y16.5; four hours).

QĪNGHǍI HÚ 青海湖
Qinghai Lake

Qīnghǎi Hú (Koko Nor), known as the Western Sea in ancient times, is a somewhat surreal-looking saline lake to the west of Xīníng. It's the largest lake in China and contains huge numbers of fish.

The main attraction is **Niǎo Dǎo** (Bird Island), on the western side of the lake, about 300km from Xīníng. It's a breeding ground for thousands of wild geese, gulls, cormorants, sandpipers, extremely rare black-necked cranes and many other bird species. Perhaps most interesting of them are the bar-headed geese. These hardy birds migrate high over the Himalayas to spend winter on the Indian plains, and have been spotted flying at altitudes of 10,000m. You will see birds in quantity only during the breeding season – between March and early June.

Despite its name, Niǎo Dǎo is not an island, but used to be before the lake shore receded and made it part of the mainland. There is one small island, Hǎixīnshān, and for Y45 you can take a boat trip from Niǎo Dǎo around the lake that takes in this and other sights.

It gets chilly at night so bring warm clothing. The lake water is too salty to drink, so be sure to carry a sufficient water supply if you intend to do any hiking. There are nomads around the lake – most are friendly and may invite you in for a cup of tea in their tents. There is a Y35 entry fee to the Niǎo Dǎo area, plus Y5 for entry to Qīnghǎi Hú

Organised Tours

Between May and early September tour buses run almost daily to Niǎo Dǎo. Xīníng has a plethora of travel agents offering tours to the lake and most of them offer the same deals. CITS, located in the Qīnghǎi Bīnguǎn, and CYTS, housed in the small booth in front of the train station, both charge Y120 (transport) for a very long day excursion.

The bus usually departs at around 6 am and returns after 9 pm, with much of the day sitting in the bus. Therefore it might be a better option to join their two-day tour (Y240), which stays overnight at Niǎo Dǎo. Prices don't include accommodation, food or entry fees. These tours often include trips to Tǎ'ěr Sì and a brief stop at Rìyuè Shānkǒu (Sun Moon Mountain Pass) for some photo opportunities. Most tours will visit either Tǎ'ěr Sì or Niǎo Dǎo, but check with the operators first.

Places to Stay & Eat

If you're not content with a day trip, you can stay overnight at the *Niǎo Dǎo Bīnguǎn*, which offers dorm beds for Y20 and twins from Y120. The restaurant in the hotel is surprisingly good.

Getting There & Away

Bus Unfortunately there are no public buses to Niǎo Dǎo. The closest you can get to is to the small settlement of Hēimǎhé, which is 50km from Niǎo Dǎo. Getting from Hēimǎhé to Niǎo Dǎo will probably cost you another Y50 for a taxi or less if you hitch. From Xīníng there are three departures to Hēimǎhé near Qīnghǎi Hú (Y18; five hours) between 7.30 and 9 am and the return schedule is similar.

GOLMUD 格尔木
☎ 0979

For travellers, the only reason to visit this forlorn outpost in the oblivion end of China is to continue into Tibet. While not a terrible place, you probably wouldn't want to stay around Golmud (Gé'ěrmù) more than a day or two, and few visitors do. The town owes its existence to mining and oil drilling. It's inhabited mostly by Chinese, but there are a few Tibetans around.

The eerie moonscape of the Tibetan Plateau can be an inhospitable place – come prepared! At 2800m elevation, summer days can be very warm, but the nights are always cool. The daytime sun is incredibly bright – sunglasses and sunblock lotion are de rigueur. Winters are brutally cold.

Message from a Reader
A Winter's tale

Winter simply makes Golmud even more depressing than LP's description. Many shops and restaurants are shut. If you want reassurance that Golmud is among the most utterly depressing places in China, go to Ertong Park ... the amusement rides probably dates back before communist rule, every single blade of grass has clearly found somewhere more exciting to go to and the undoubted highlight has to be the caged pile-of-rocks. OK, so some animal probably once 'lived' in here but it obviously didn't need permission from CITS to leave.

Richard Middleton

Information

CITS (☎/fax 413 003) has an office in the Golmud Hotel. If you're planning to go to Lhasa according to the rules of the 'Tibet game', you'll almost certainly have to visit this office (see Getting to Tibet later in this section).

The PSB is on Chaidamu Lu, east of the post office. The Bank of China is on the corner of Kunlun Lu and Chaidamu Lu.

Places to Stay & Eat

There's only one place accepting foreigners, the *Golmud Hotel* (Gé'ěrmù Bīnguǎn; ☎ 412 061, 160 Kunlun Lu). The place is divided into two sections – the upmarket hotel (bīnguǎn) and the hostel (zhāodàisuǒ). Beds in a six-person dorm with shared bath

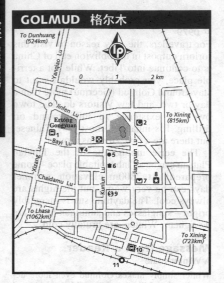

GOLMUD 格尔木

To Dunhuang
(524km)

Yangqiao Lu

0   1   2 km

Jinfen Lu

Ertong
Gongyuan

Bayi Lu

Xizang Lu

Chaidamu Lu

Kunlun Lu

Jiangyuan Lu

To Xining
(815km)

To Xining
(723km)

To Lhasa
(1062km)

GOLMUD

1 Tibet Bus Station
西藏汽车站
2 Mosque
清真寺
3 Nongken No 1
Department Store
农垦一商场
4 Bǎisuìjī
百岁鸡
5 Market
格尔木集贸市场
6 Golmud Hotel;
CITS
格尔木宾馆、
中国国际旅行社
7 Post Office
邮局
8 PSB
公安局
9 Bank of China
中国银行
10 Bus Station
长途汽车站
11 Train Station
火车站

in the hostel are Y16 and those in a triple are Y28. Hot water is available 24 hours. There are reasonable twins in the hotel for Y150

Minibuses meet all arriving trains and can take you to the hotel for 'free' (CITS probably doesn't know about it yet).

If you're getting hungry waiting for that fifth person, then head over to *Bǎisuìjī (21 Zhongshan Lu)*, which literally means '100-year-old chook'. The restaurant specialises in a spicy chicken stew, which is cooked on the table in front of you. The chook is cooked in a broth of carrots, zucchini, celery, onion, coriander and mushrooms. You will need a minimum of two people to finish their smallest serving *(xiǎo xiǎo guō)*. Try adding *tǔdòu* (potato) or *fěntiáo* (tofu and noodles) and wash it all down with a cold draft beer (Y5).

It's pretty easy to find, just look out for the green uniformed staff loitering in the entrance.

Getting There & Away

Bus The Golmud bus station is just opposite the train station. The journey from Golmud to Dūnhuáng is 524km (13 hours) and

there are two buses, a regular one at 7.30 am (Y50) and a sleeper bus at 8 pm (Y80). It's a scenic trip through the desert and mountains, but take a jacket as it can get cold at night.

There are also daily buses to Xīníng, but it makes little sense to go this way, as the train is smoother and faster.

Train Express trains (Nos 603 and 604) on the Xīníng–Golmud route take just 18¼ hours, while the local trains (Nos 759 and 760) chug along for 24 hours.

An attempt to build a railway from Golmud to Lhasa was abandoned after it was discovered that it would be necessary to bore a tunnel through an ice-filled mountain. The Chinese consulted the Swiss (the world's best tunnel builders), who concluded that it was impossible.

GETTING TO TIBET

CITS has an iron grip on foreign bus tickets from Golmud to Lhasa – all travellers must buy their tickets through the travel agency, and they pay dearly for it.

The situation is increasingly frustrating for travellers. CITS says it is required by the Tibet Tourism Bureau to ensure every foreigner has not only a Tibet Tourism Bureau permit (TTB), insurance and a minimum three-day tour, but also a return ticket to a choice of three destinations (Kathmandu, Chéngdū or back to Golmud). For all this, you will have the pleasure of handing over a minimum of Y1660, which includes the return bus fare to Golmud; this is the cheapest and most popular option. In comparison the Chinese pay either Y120 (seat) or Y160 (sleeper) for a ticket to Lhasa. If you would like to stay in Tibet for more than three days, then you have to pay an extra Y100 per day. In reality, most people either pay up and then throw their return ticket away when they arrive in Lhasa or they try one of the numerous touts offering lifts.

Of course travellers try to get around this by going directly to the Tibet bus station to purchase a ticket to Lhasa – the staff at the station politely tell them to go to CITS. Others try to hitch rides on trucks, but the local PSB are wise to this, and drivers have been cowed by the threat of a heavy fine if caught.

You won't have to go looking for the guys offering seats on a bus to Tibet, they will find you. They generally ask for between Y600 and Y1000 to Lhasa. It's assumed that this price includes a bribe to the PSB along the way. There is no way to guarantee that you will get to Lhasa or that you won't be fined and sent back. Some travellers have encountered problems, whilst others have made it to Lhasa hassle free.

This scheme is crying out for reform and is only serving to reinforce foreign travellers' negative attitude towards the Chinese bureaucracy.

If the situation doesn't improve and your not willing to risk hitching, then the cheapest option is to buy your return ticket with a minimum three-day tour. When you purchase your ticket, make sure that CITS provides you with the ticket, not just a receipt. In Lhasa you should be able to extend the date of departure at either the bus or CAAC office. Otherwise cancel the ticket. Either way you'll probably lose 10% of the ticket price. Once you're in Lhasa there doesn't seem to be anyone telling foreigners to leave, although this could also change.

For those who wish to avoid this aggravating scenario, remember that there are many areas outside the Tibetan Autonomous Region (TAR) in Qīnghǎi, Gānsù, Sìchuān and Yúnnán, where foreigners are free to visit.

There are buses to Lhasa from the main bus station, as well as a number of private operators around town. CITS-approved buses for Lhasa leave from the Tibet bus station on Xizang Lu at around 5 pm. Foreigners are usually picked up at the Golmud Hotel and taken by CITS to the station. The road to Lhasa has vastly improved in recent years, and the trip can take anywhere from 26 to 63 hours. The latter time is usually a result of breakdowns or traffic hold-ups (both highly possible). Some travellers were buying oxygen from the Golmud Hotel for Y30 a canister to try to avoid the altitude sickness.

It would be wise to stock up on a few necessities for the trip. Toasty-warm People's Liberation Army (PLA) overcoats are available for around Y65 in town – consider getting one even if you wind up giving it away in Lhasa. It can easily get down to –10°C or lower in those mountain passes at night; although the buses are heated, you could be in serious trouble if you are ill equipped and there is a breakdown. Keep an eye on your possessions as there have been a couple of reports of thieves on the buses.

Language

MANDARIN

The official language of the PRC is the dialect spoken in Běijīng. It is usually referred to in the west as 'Mandarin', but the Chinese call it Putonghua – common speech. Putonghua is variously referred to as the 'Han language' *(hànyǔ)*, the 'national language' *(guóyǔ)* or simply 'Chinese' *(zhōngwén* or *zhōngguóhuà).*

Spoken

Dialects Discounting ethnic minority languages, China has eight major dialect groups: Putonghua (Mandarin), Yue (Cantonese), Wu (Shanghainese), Minbei (Fuzhou), Minnan (Hokkien-Taiwanese), Xiang, Gan and Hakka. These dialects also divide into many more sub-dialects.

With the exception of the western and southernmost provinces, most of the population speaks Mandarin, although regional accents can make comprehension difficult.

Grammar Chinese grammar is much simpler than that of European languages. There are no articles ('a'/'the'), no tenses and no plurals. The basic point to bear in mind is that, like English, Chinese word order is subject-verb-object. In other words, a basic English sentence like 'I (subject) love (verb) you (object)' is constructed in exactly the same way in Chinese. The catch is mastering the tones.

Writing System

Chinese is often referred to as a language of pictographs. Many of the basic Chinese characters are in fact highly stylised pictures of what they represent, but most Chinese characters (around 90%) are compounds of a 'meaning' element and a 'sound' element.

So just how many Chinese characters are there? It's possible to verify the existence of some 56,000 characters, but the vast majority of these are archaic. It is commonly felt that a well-educated, contemporary Chinese

person might know and use between 6000 and 8000 characters. To read a Chinese newspaper you will need to know 2000 to 3000 characters, but 1200 to 1500 would be enough to get the gist.

Writing systems usually alter people's perception of a language, and this is certainly true of Chinese. Each Chinese character represents a spoken syllable, leading many people to declare that Chinese is a 'monosyllabic language.' Actually, it's more a case of having a monosyllabic writing system. While the building block of the Chinese language is indeed the monosyllabic Chinese character, Chinese words are usually a combination of two or more characters. You could think of Chinese words as being compounds. The Chinese word for 'east' is composed of a single character *(dōng),* but must be combined with the character for 'west' *(xī)* to form the word for 'thing' *(dōngxī).* English has some compound words too (although not nearly as many as Chinese), examples being 'whitewash' and 'backslide'.

Theoretically, all Chinese dialects share the same written system. In practice, Cantonese adds about 3000 specialised characters of its own and many of the dialects don't have a written form at all.

Simplification

In the interests of promoting universal literacy, the Committee for Reforming the Chinese Language was set up by the Běijīng government in 1954. Around 2200 Chinese characters were simplified. Chinese communities outside China (notably Taiwan and Hong Kong), however, continue to use the traditional, full-form characters.

Over the past few years – probably as a result of large-scale investment by overseas Chinese and tourism – full-form characters have returned to China. These are mainly seen in advertising (where the traditional characters are considered more attractive) and on restaurant, hotel and shop signs.

Chinglish

Initially you might be puzzled by a sign in the bathroom that reads 'Please don't take the odds and ends put into the nightstool'. In fact this is a warning to resist sudden impulses to empty the contents of your pockets or backpack into the toilet. An apparently ambiguous sign with anarchic implications like the one in the Lhasa Bank of China that reads 'Question Authority' is really just an economical way of saying 'Please address your questions to one of the clerks'.

On the other hand, just to confuse things, a company name like the 'Risky Investment Co' means just what it says. An English-Chinese dictionary proudly proclaims in the preface that it is 'very useful for the using'. And a beloved sign in the Liangmao Hotel in Tài'ān proclaims:

Safety Needing Attention!
Be care of depending fire
Sweep away six injurious insect
Pay attention to civilisation

If this all sounds confusing, don't worry. It won't be long before you have a small armoury of Chinglish phrases of your own. Before you know it, you'll know without even thinking that 'Be careful not to be stolen' is a warning against thieves; that 'Shoplifters will be fined 10 times' means that shoplifting is not a good idea in China; that 'Do not stroke the works' (generally found in museums) means 'No touching'; and that you 'very like' something means that you 'like it very much'.

The best advice for travellers in China grappling with the complexities of a new language is not to set your sights too high. Bear in mind that it takes a minimum of 15 years of schooling in the Chinese language and a crash course in English to be able to write Chinglish with any fluency.

Pronunciation

Most letters are pronounced as in English, with the exception of the following:

Vowels

a	as in 'father'
ai	as in 'high'
ao	as the 'ow' in 'cow'
e	as the 'u' in 'fur'
ei	as the 'ei' in 'weigh'
i	as the 'ee' in 'meet' (or like the 'oo' in 'book' after c, ch, r, s, sh, z or zh)
ian	as in 'yen'
ie	as in the English word 'yeah'
o	as in 'or'
ou	as the 'oa' in 'boat'
u	as in 'flute'
ui	as in the word 'way'
uo	like a 'w' followed by 'o'
yu	as in the German 'ü' – pucker your lips and try saying 'ee'
ü	as the German 'ü'

Consonants

c	as the 'ts' in 'bits'
ch	as in 'chop', but with the tongue curled back
h	as in 'hay', but articulated from farther back in the throat
q	as the 'ch' in 'cheese'
r	as the 's' in 'pleasure'
sh	as in 'ship', but with the tongue curled back
x	as in 'ship'
z	as the 'dz' in 'suds'
zh	as the 'j' in 'judge' but with the tongue curled back

The only consonants that occur at the end of a syllable are n, ng and r.

In Pinyin, apostrophes are occasionally used to separate syllables in order to prevent ambiguity, eg the word píng'ān can be written with an apostrophe after the 'g' to prevent it being pronounced as pín'gān.

Pinyin

While there are many dialects across China, the one thing all Chinese speakers have in common is their written language. Efforts have been made over the last 100 years to reform the written language, and a system called Pinyin (literally meaning 'spell sound') was invented this century as the standard for spelling Chinese characters. While Pinyin started its life as a communist ploy to unite the peoples and popularise Mandarin within China, in its short life it has become the United Nations standard for 'spelling' Chinese characters, and to transliterate the names of people, places and scientific terms. Taiwan initially promulgated a different system of Romanisation, but recently announced that it was switching to the communist-designed Pinyin system, falling into line with the rest of the world.

Pinyin was not the first foray into spelling out Chinese characters. As early as the 17th century, foreign missionaries sought effective ways to spread the word and various spelling systems arose; even the Bible was reproduced in such scripts. In the late 19th century the Chinese themselves started to explore the problem of phonetic spelling systems. In 1933 the communists worked with a Russian and designed what they called Latinised New Script. This was based on Mandarin pronunciation and in 1958 the communist government implemented this as the official system, coinciding with its decision to adopt Mandarin as the official language of China. This new script came to be known as Pinyin and the government's prime purpose in writing an alphabet pronunciation of Chinese characters was to promote Mandarin throughout the nation. Although it was the the language of government, Mandarin was previously at the same level as numerous other dialects spoken in China. A secondary purpose was to enable non-Chinese ethnic groups in China to create or reform their languages with a common base.

Another, less important, aim of Pinyin was to assist foreigners to learn Chinese. As foreign language learners will tell you, Pinyin is a fantastic tool particularly at the beginning of a quest on the road to fluency. Unlike English, once you learn the Pinyin pronunciation system it is completely phonetic – every time you see a word in Pinyin, the pronunciation is phonetic and consistent. However, once the pronunciation system is learnt, problems start to arise: for one, Pinyin does not itself indicate tones (mandarin has four tones) and there may be dozens of characters represented by a Pinyin word: for example there are about 80 dictionary entries for the word pronounced and written *yi*. Luckily, combinations with other sounds to make compound words, as well as context and grammatical structures, usually give a few clues as to which *yi* is meant. To assist travellers, this book has used tones throughout for towns, cities, sights, hotels, restaurants and entertainment venues.

Pinyin has permeated some groups in Chinese society, however most ordinary Chinese cannot use it very effectively, and some people argue that Pinyin is for foreigners. For those travelling in China using either this book or the Lonely Planet *Mandarin Phrasebook*, the ability to use Pinyin and the government's regulation that all signs be in Pinyin and characters, will be a blessing.

Charles Qin

Tones

Chinese is a language with a large number of words with the same pronunciation but a different meaning; what distinguishes these 'homophones' is their 'tonal' quality – the raising and lowering of pitch on certain syllables. Mandarin has four tones – high, rising, falling-rising and falling, plus a fifth 'neutral' tone which you can all but ignore. To illustrate, look at the word ma which has four different meanings according to tone:

high	mā	'mother'
rising	má	'hemp' or 'numb'
falling-rising	mǎ	'horse'
falling	mà	'to scold' or 'swear'

Mastering tones is tricky for newcomers to Mandarin, but with a little practice it can be done.

Gestures

Hand signs are frequently used in China. The 'thumbs-up' sign has a long tradition as an indication of excellence. An alternative way to indicate excellence is to gently pull your earlobe between your thumb and index finger.

The Chinese have a system for counting on their hands. If you can't speak the language, it would be worth your while at least to learn Chinese finger counting. One of the disadvantages of finger counting is that there are regional differences. The symbol for number 10 is to form a cross with the index fingers, but many Chinese just use a fist.

Phrasebooks

Phrasebooks are invaluable, but it's a better idea to copy out the appropriate phrases in Chinese rather than show someone the book – otherwise they may take it and read every page! Reading place names or street signs isn't difficult since the Chinese name is usually accompanied by the Pinyin form; if not you'll soon learn lots of characters just by repeated exposure. A small dictionary with English, Pinyin and Chinese characters is also useful for learning a few words.

For a more comprehensive guide to Mandarin, get a copy of the new edition of Lonely Planet's *Mandarin phrasebook*.

Pronouns

I
  wǒ   我
you
  nǐ   你
he, she, it
  tā   他/她/它
we, us
  wǒmen   我们
you (plural)
  nǐmen   你们
they, them
  tāmen   他们

Greetings & Civilities

Hello.
  Nǐ hǎo.   你好
Goodbye.
  Zàijiàn.   再见
Thank you.
  Xièxie.   谢谢
You're welcome.
  Búkèqi.   不客气
I'm sorry.
  Duìbùqǐ.   对不起

Small Talk

May I ask your name?
  Nín guìxìng?   您贵姓?
My (sur)name is ...
  Wǒ xìng ...   我姓 ...

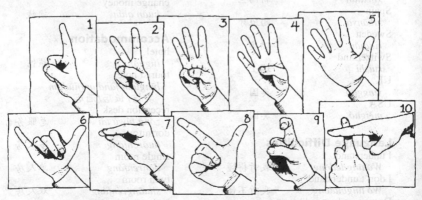

The Chinese system of finger-counting

Where are you from?
Nǐ shì cōng nǎr láide?
你是从哪儿来的？

I'm from ...
Wǒ shì cōng ... láide. 我是从 ... 来的

No. (don't have)
Méi yǒu. 没有

No. (not so)
Búshì. 不是

I'm a foreign student.
Wǒ shì liúxuéshēng. 我是留学生

What's to be done now?
Zěnme bàn? 怎么办？

It doesn't matter.
Méishì. 没事

I want ...
Wǒ yào ... 我要

No, I don't want it.
Búyào. 不要

Countries

Australia
àodàlìyà 澳大利亚

Canada
jiānádà 加拿大

Denmark
dānmài 丹麦

France
fǎguó 法国

Germany
déguó 德国

Netherlands
hélán 荷兰

New Zealand
xīnxīlán 新西兰

Spain
xībānyá 西班牙

Sweden
ruìdiǎn 瑞典

Switzerland
ruìshì 瑞士

UK
yīngguó 英国

USA
měiguó 美国

Language Difficulties

I understand.
Wǒ tīngdedǒng. 我听得懂

I don't understand.
Wǒ tīngbudǒng. 我听不懂

Do you understand?
Dǒng ma? 懂吗？

Could you speak more slowly please?
Qīng nǐ shuō màn yīdiǎn, hǎo ma?
请你说慢一点，好吗？

Visas & Documents

passport
hùzhào 护照

visa
qiānzhèng 签证

visa extension
yáncháng qiānzhèng 延长签证

Public Security Bureau (PSB)
gōng'ān jú 公安局

Foreign Affairs Branch
wàishì kē 外事科

Toilets

toilet (restroom)
cèsuǒ 厕所

toilet paper
wèishēng zhǐ 卫生纸

bathroom (washroom)
xǐshǒu jiān 洗手间

Money

How much is it?
Duōshǎo qián? 多少钱？

Is there anything cheaper?
Yǒu piányi yìdiǎnde ma?
有便宜一点的吗？

That's too expensive.
Tài guì le. 太贵了

Bank of China
zhōngguó yínháng 中国银行

change money
huàn qián 换钱

Accommodation

hotel
lǚguǎn 旅馆

tourist hotel
bīnguǎn/fàndiàn/jiǔdiàn
宾馆/饭店/酒店

reception desk
zǒng fúwù tái 总服务台

dormitory
duōrénfáng 多人房

single room
dānrénfáng 单人房

twin room
shuāngrénfáng 双人房

bed
chuángwèi 床位

economy room (no bath)
pǔtōngfáng 普通房
standard room
biāozhǔn fángjiān 标准房间
deluxe suite
háohuá tàofáng 豪华套房
book a whole room
bāofáng 包房
Is there a room vacant?
Yǒu méiyǒu kōng fángjiān?
有没有空房间?
Yes, there is.
Yǒu. 有
No, there isn't.
Méi yǒu. 没有
Can I see the room?
Wǒ néng kànkan fángjiān ma?
我能看看房间吗?
I don't like this room.
Wǒ bù xǐhuan zhèijiān fángjiān.
我不喜欢这间房间
Are there any messages for me?
Yǒu méiyǒu liú huà? 有没有留话?
May I have a hotel namecard?
Yǒu méiyǒu lǚguǎn de míngpiàn?
有没有旅馆的名片?
Could I have these clothes washed, please?
Qǐng bǎ zhè xiē yīfú xǐ gānjìng, hǎo ma?
请把这些衣服洗干净,好吗?

Post

post office
yóujú 邮局
letter
xìn 信
envelope
xìnfēng 信封
package
bāoguǒ 包裹
airmail
hángkōng xìn 航空信
surface mail
píngyóu 平邮
stamps
yóupiào 邮票
postcard
míngxìnpiàn 明信片
aerogramme
hángkōng xìnjiàn 航空信件
poste restante
cúnjú hòulǐnglán 存局候领栏
express mail (EMS)
yóuzhèng tèkuài zhuāndì
邮政特快专递

registered mail
guà hào 挂号

Telecommunications

telephone
diànhuà 电话
telephone office
diànxùn dàlóu 电讯大楼
telephone card
diànhuà kǎ 电话卡
international call
guójì diànhuà 国际电话
collect call
duìfāng fùqián diànhuà
对方付钱电话
direct-dial call
zhíbō diànhuà 直拨电话
fax
chuánzhēn 传真
computer
diànnǎo 电脑
email (often called 'email')
diànzǐyóujiàn 电子邮件
Internet
yīntèwǎng 因特网
online
shàng wǎng 上网
Where can I get online?
Wǒ zài nǎlǐ kěyǐ shàng wǎng?
我在哪儿可以上网?

Directions

map
dìtú 地图
Where is the ...?
... zài nǎlǐ? ... 在哪里?
I'm lost.
Wǒ mílùle. 我迷路了
Turn right.
Yòu zhuǎn. 右转
Turn left.
Zuǒ zhuǎn. 左转
Go straight ahead.
Yìzhí zǒu. 一直走
Turn around.
Wàng huí zǒu. 往回走
alley
hútong 胡同
lane
xiàng 巷
road
lù 路
boulevard
dàdào 大道

section
duàn 段
street
jiē, dàjiē 街，大街
No 21
21 hào 21号

Bicycle

bicycle
zìxíngchē 自行车
I want to hire a bicycle.
Wǒ yào zū yíliàng zìxíngchē.
我要租一辆自行车
How much is it per day?
Yìtiān duōshǎo qián? 一天多少钱?
How much is it per hour?
Yíge xiǎoshí duōshǎo qián?
一个小时多少钱?
How much is the deposit?
Yājīn duōshǎo qián? 押金多少钱?

Time

What's the time?
Jǐ diǎn? 几点?
... hour ... minute
... diǎn ... fēn ... 点 ... 分
3.05
sān diǎn wǔ fēn 3点5分
now
xiànzài 现在
today
jīntiān 今天
tomorrow
míngtiān 明天
day after tomorrow
hòutiān 后天
three days from now
dàhòutiān 大后天
yesterday
zuótiān 昨天
Wait a moment.
Děng yīxià. 等一下

Transport

I want to go to ...
Wǒ yào qù ... 我要去 ...
I want to get off.
Wǒ yào xiàchē. 我要下车
luggage
xínglì 行李

left-luggage room
jìcún chù 寄存处
one ticket
yìzhāng piào 一张票
two tickets
liǎngzhāng piào 两张票
What time does it depart?
Jǐdiǎn kāi? 几点开?
What time does it arrive?
Jǐdiǎn dào? 几点到?
How long does the trip take?
Zhècì lǚxíng yào huā duōcháng shíjiān?
这次旅行要花多长时间?
buy a ticket
mǎi piào 买票
refund a ticket
tuì piào 退票
taxi
chūzū chē 出租车
dīshì 的士
microbus ('bread') taxi
miànbāo chē, miàndī 面包车，面的
Please use the meter.
Dǎ biǎo. 打表

Air

airport
fēijīchǎng 飞机场
CAAC ticket office
zhōngguó mínháng shòupiào chù
中国民航售票处
one-way ticket
dānchéng piào 单程票
return ticket
láihuí piào 来回票
boarding pass
dēngjī kǎ 登机卡
reconfirm
quèrèn 确认
cancel
qǔxiāo 取消
bonded baggage
cúnzhàn xínglì 存栈行李

Bus

bus
gōnggòng qìchē 公共汽车
minibus
xiǎo gōnggòng qìchē 小公共汽车
long-distance bus station
chángtú qìchē zhàn 长途汽车站

When is the first bus?
Tóubān qìchē jǐdiǎn kāi?
头班汽车几点开?
When is the last bus?
Mòbān qìchē jǐdiǎn kāi?
末班汽车几点开?
When is the next bus?
Xià yìbān qìchē jǐdiǎn kāi?
下一班汽车几点开?

Train

train
huǒchē 火车
ticket office
shòupiào chù 售票处
railway station
huǒchē zhàn 火车站
hard-seat
yìngxí, yìngzuò 硬席, 硬座
soft-seat
ruǎnxí, ruǎnzuò 软席, 软座
hard-sleeper
yìngwò 硬卧
soft-sleeper
ruǎnwò 软卧
platform ticket
zhàntái piào 站台票
Which platform?
Dìjǐhào zhàntái? 第几号站台?
upgrade ticket (after boarding)
bǔpiào 补票
subway (underground)
dìtiě 地铁
subway station
dìtiě zhàn 地铁站

Emergency

emergency
jǐnjí qíngkuàng 紧急情况
hospital emergency room
jízhěn shì 急诊室
police
jǐngchá 警察
Fire!
Zhǎohuǒ le! 着火了!
Help!
Jiùmìng a! 救命啊!
Thief!
Xiǎotōu! 小偷!
pickpocket
páshǒu 扒手
rapist
qiángjiānfàn 强奸犯

Health

I'm sick.
Wǒ shēngbìngle. 我生病了
I'm injured.
Wǒ shòushāngle. 我受伤了
hospital
yīyuàn 医院
laxative
xièyào 泻药
anti-diarrhoea medicine
zhǐxièyào 止泻药
rehydration salts
shūwéizhì dīnà fāpàodìng
舒维质低钠发泡锭
aspirin
āsīpǐlín 阿斯匹林
antibiotics
kàngjùnsù 抗菌素
condom
bìyùn tào 避孕套
tampon
wèishēng mián tiáo 卫生棉条
sanitary napkin (Kotex)
wèishēng mián 卫生棉
sunscreen (UV) lotion
fáng shài yóu 防晒油
mosquito coils
wénxiāng 蚊香
mosquito pads
diàn wénxiāng 电蚊香

Numbers

0	*líng*	零
1	*yī, yāo*	一, 幺
2	*èr, liǎng*	二, 两
3	*sān*	三
4	*sì*	四
5	*wǔ*	五
6	*liù*	六
7	*qī*	七
8	*bā*	八
9	*jiǔ*	九
10	*shí*	十
11	*shíyī*	十一
12	*shí'èr*	十二
20	*èrshí*	二十
21	*èrshíyī*	二十一
100	*yìbǎi*	一百
200	*liǎngbǎi*	两百
1000	*yìqiān*	一千
2000	*liǎngqiān*	两千
10,000	*yíwàn*	一万

LANGUAGE

20,000	*liǎngwàn*	两万
100,000	*shíwàn*	十万
200,000	*èrshíwàn*	二十万

CANTONESE

What a difference a border makes. Cantonese is still the most popular dialect in Hong Kong, Guǎngzhōu and the surrounding area. It differs from Mandarin as much as French differs from Spanish. Speakers of both dialects can read Chinese characters, but a Cantonese speaker will pronounce many of the characters differently from a Mandarin speaker. For example, when Mr Ng from Hong Kong goes to Běijīng the Mandarin-speakers will call him Mr Wu. If Mr Wong goes from Hong Kong to Fújiàn the character for his name will be read as Mr Wee, and in Běijīng he is Mr Huang.

Romanisation

Unfortunately, several competing systems of Romanisation of Cantonese script exist and no single one has emerged as an official standard. A number have come and gone, but at least three have survived and are currently used in Hong Kong: Meyer-Wempe, Sidney Lau and Yale. In this language guide we use the Yale system. It's the most phonetically accurate and the one generally preferred by foreign students.

Pronunciation

The following pronunciation guide is designed to help you pronounce the Cantonese words and phrases in this book with as little anxiety as possible. Note that the examples given reflect British pronunciation.

a	as in 'father'
ai	as the 'i' in 'find', but shorter
au	as the 'ou' in 'bout'
e	as in 'let'
ei	as the 'a' in 'say'
eu	as 'e' + the 'ur' in 'urn' (with pursed lips)
i	as the 'ee' in 'see'
iu	similar to the word 'you'

o	as in 'got'; as in 'go' when word-final
oi	as the 'oy' in 'boy'
oo	as in 'soon'
ou	as the word 'owe'
u	as in 'put'
ue	as in 'Sue'
ui	as 'oo' + 'ee'

Consonants are generally pronounced as in English. Some that may give you trouble are:

j	as the 'ds' in 'suds'
ch	as the 'ts' in 'tsar'
ng	as in 'sing'; practise using this sound at the beginning of a word

Tones

In the Yale system six basic tones are represented: three 'level' tones which do not noticeably rise or fall in pitch (high, middle and low) and three 'moving' tones which either rise or fall in pitch (high rising, low rising and low falling). The following examples show the six basic tones – note how important they can be to your intended meaning:

high tone	represented by a macron above a vowel, eg *fōo* (husband)
middle tone	represented by an unaccented vowel, eg *foo* (wealthy)
low tone	represented by the letter 'h' after a vowel, eg *fooh* (owe); note that when 'h' appears at the beginning of a word it is still pronounced, elsewhere it signifies a low tone
middle tone rising	represented by an acute accent, eg *fóo* (tiger)
low falling tone	represented by a grave accent followed by the low tone letter 'h', eg *fòoh* (to lean)
low rising tone	represented by an acute accent and the low tone letter 'h', eg *fóoh* (woman)

Useful Phrases

Even if you never gain fluency, knowing a few simple Cantonese phrases can be useful. The following phrase list should help get you started. For a more in depth guide to Cantonese, with loads of information on grammar and pronunciation plus a comprehensive phraselist, get hold of the new edition of Lonely Planet's *Cantonese phrasebook*.

Pronouns

I
  ngóh   我
you
  néhìh   你
he/she/it
  kúhìh   佢
we/us
  ngóh dēìh   我们
you (pl)
  néhìh dēìh   你们
they/them
  kúhìh dēìh   他们

Greetings & Civilities

Hello, how are you?
  néhìh hó ma?   你好嗎？
Fine.
  Géìh hó.   幾好
Goodbye.
  Bāahìh baahìh./Joìh gin.   拜拜／再見
Thanks. (making a
  request or purchase)
  M gōìh.   唔該
You're welcome.
  M sáìh haàhk hēìh.   唔駛客氣
Excuse me. (calling
  someone's attention)
  M gōìh.   唔該
What is your surname? (polite)
  Chéng mahn gwaìh sìng?
  請問貴姓？
My surname is ...
  Síuh sìng ...   小姓 ...
Do you speak English?
  Néhìh sìk m sìk góng yìng mán a?
  你識唔識講英文呀？
I don't understand.
  Ngóh m mìhng.   我唔明

Getting Around

airport
  gēìh chèhùhng   機場
bus stop
  bā sí jahàhm   巴士站
pier
  máh tàhùh   碼頭
subway station
  dēìh tit jahàhm   地鐵站
north
  bāk   北
south
  nàhàhm   南
east
  dūng   東
west
  sāìh   西
I'd like to go to ...
  Ngóh séuhng huìh ... 我想去 ...
Where is the ...?
  ... háìh bìn doh a?   邊度呀？
Does this (bus, train etc) go to ...?
  Huìh m huìh ... a?   去唔去 ... 呀？
How much is the fare?
  Géìh dōh chín a?   幾多錢呀？

Accommodation & Food

Do you have any rooms
  available?
  Yáhùh mó fóng a?   有冇房呀？
How much per night?
  Géìh dōh chín yāt máhàhn a?
  幾多錢一晚呀？
Do you have an English menu?
  Yáhùh mó yīng mán chāàhn páàhìh a?
  有冇英文餐牌呀？
Can you recommend any dishes?
  Yáhùh māt yéh hó gaàhìh sìuh a?
  有好介紹呀？
I'm a vegetarian.
  Ngóh sihk jāàhìh.   我食齋

Shopping

How much is this?
  Nī goh géìh dōh chín a?
  呢個幾多錢呀？
That's very expensive.
  Hó gwaìh.   好貴
Can you reduce the price?
  Pèhng dī dāk m dāk a?
  平得唔得呀？

LANGUAGE

Numbers

0	*lìhng*	零
1	*yāt*	一
2	*yih (léhùhng)*	二(兩)
3	*sāàhm*	三
4	*sēih*	四
5	*ng*	五
6	*luhk*	六
7	*chāt*	七
8	*baàht*	八
9	*gáùh*	九
10	*sahp*	十
11	*sahp yāt*	十一
12	*sahp yih*	十二
20	*yih sahp*	二十
21	*yih sahp yāt*	二十一
30	*sāàhm sahp*	三十
100	*yāt baàhk*	一百
101	*yāt baàhk lìhng yāt*	一百零一
110	*yāt baàhk yāt sahp*	一百一十
112	*yāt baàhk yāt sahp yih*	一百一十二
120	*yāt baàhk yih sahp*	一百二十
200	*yih baàhk*	二百
1000	*yāt chīn*	一千
10,000	*yāt mahàhn*	一萬
100,000	*sahp mahàhn*	十萬

Emergencies

Help!
   Gaùh mēng a!   救命呀！
I need a doctor.
   Ngóh yiùh táih yī sāng.   我要睇醫生
Call an ambulance!
   Giùh gaùh sēùhng chē!   叫救傷車！
Call the police!
   Giùh gíng chaàht!   叫警察！
Watch out!
   Síùh sām!   小心！
Thief!
   Chéùhng yéh a!   搶呀！

PORTUGUESE

Like French, Italian, Spanish and Romanian, Portuguese is a Romance language (one closely derived from Latin). It's spoken in Portugal, Brazil, several African states and Macau.

Pronunciation

Pronunciation of Portuguese is difficult; like English, vowels and consonants have more than one possible sound depending on position and stress. Moreover, there are nasal vowels and diphthongs in Portuguese with no equivalents in English.

Vowels   Single vowels should present relatively few problems. Nasalisation is represented by an 'n' or an 'm' after the vowel, or by a tilde (eg **ã**) over it. The nasal 'i' exists in English as the 'ing' in 'sing'. For other nasal vowels, try to pronounce a long 'a', 'ah', 'e' or 'eh' while holding your nose, so that you sound as if you have a cold.

  Vowel combinations (diphthongs) are relatively straightforward. For nasal diphthongs, try the same technique as for nasal vowels. To say *não*, pronounce 'now' through your nose.

Word Stress   Word stress is important in Portuguese, as it can affect the meaning of a word. Many Portuguese words have a written accent which indicates the syllable to be stressed.

Greetings & Civilities

Hello.
   Bom dia/Olá/Chao.
Good morning.   *Bom dia.*
Good evening.   *Boa tarde.*
Goodbye.   *Adeus/Chao.*
See you later.   *Até logo.*
How are you?   *Como está?*
I'm fine, thanks.
   Bem, obrigado/a.
Please.
   Se faz favor/Por favor.
Thank you.   *Obrigado/a.*
You're welcome.   *De nada.*
Sorry. (forgive me)   *Desculpe.*
Yes.   *Sim.*
No.   *Não.*
Maybe.   *Talvez.*
What's your name?
   Como se chama?
My name is ...   *Chamo-me ...*

Getting Around

I want to go to …
Quero ir a …

What time does the next … leave/arrive?
A que horas parte/chega o próximo …?

boat	*barco*
bus (city)	*autocarro*
bus (intercity)	*camioneta*

Where is … the bus stop?
Onde é … a paragem de auto carro?
Is this the bus to …?
E este o autocarre para … ?
I'd like a one-way ticket
Queria um bilhete simples/de ida.
I'd like a return ticket.
Queria um bilhete de ida e volta.
left-luggage office
o depósito de bagagem

platform	*cais*
timetable	*horário*

I'd like to hire …	*Queria alugar …*
a car	*um carro*
a motorcycle	*uma motocicleta*
a bicycle	*uma bicicleta*

How do I get to …?
Como vou para …?

What … is this?
O que … é isto/ista?

street/road	*rua/estrada*
town	*cidade/vila*
north/south	*norte/sul*
east/west	*este/oeste*

Around Town

Where is …?	*Onde é …?*
a bank	*um banco*
an exchange office	*um câmbio*

the city centre
o centro da cidade/da baixa

the hospital	*o hospital*
my hotel	*do meu hotel*
the post office	*dos correios*

the public toilet
sanitários/casa de banho pública
telephone centre
da central de telefones
the tourist office
do turismo/posta de turismo

What time does it …?	*A que horas …?*
open	*abre*
close	*fecha*

I'd like to make a telephone call.
Quero usar o telefone.

I'd like to change …	*Queria trocar …*
some money	*dinheiro*

travellers cheques
cheques de viagem

Accommodation

I'm looking for …	*Procuro …*

a youth hostel
uma pousada de juventude/
albergue de juventude

a guesthouse	*uma pensão*
a hotel	*uma hotel*

Do you have any rooms available?
Tem quartos livres?

I'd like to book …
Quero fazer una reserva para …

a bed	*uma cama*

a single room
um quarto individual
a double room/with twin beds
um quarto de casal/duplo
a dormitory bed
cama de dormitório

May I see the room?
Posso ver o quarto?
How much is it per night/per person?
Quanto é por noite/por pessoa?
Is breakfast included?
O pequeno almoço está incluído?
Where is the toilet?
Onde ficam os lavabos?

Time & Dates

What time is it?	*Que horas são?*
When?	*Quando?*
today	*hoje*
tonight	*hoje à noite*
tomorrow	*amanhã*
yesterday	*ontem*
morning	*manhã*
afternoon	*tarde*

Health

I need a doctor.
  Preciso um médico.

Where is a ...?   *Onde é um ...?*
hospital   *hospital*
medical clinic   *centro de saúde*

I'm allergic to ...
  Sou alérgica/o a ...
antibiotics   *antibióticos*
penicillin   *penicilina*

Numbers

1	*um/uma*
2	*dois/duas*
3	*três*
4	*quatro*
5	*cinco*
6	*seis*
7	*sete*
8	*oito*
9	*nove*
10	*dez*
100	*cem*
1000	*mil*

Emergencies

Help!   *Socorro!*
Call a doctor!
  Chame um médico!
Call the police!
  Chame a polícia!
Go away!
  Deixe-me em paz!
I've been robbed.   *Fui roubado/a.*
I'm lost.
  Estou perdido/a.

TIBETAN

Tibetan belongs to the Tibeto-Burman family of languages. It differs in many ways from Chinese, having a different written language, a different grammar and being nontonal. Lhasa dialect, which is the standard form of Tibetan, does employ a system of rising and falling tones, but the differences are subtle and meaning is made clear by context. Beginners need not worry about it.

Pronunciation

Like all foreign languages Tibetan has its fair share of tricky pronunciations. There are quite a few consonant clusters, and Tibetan is a language (like Korean and Thai) that makes an important distinction between aspirated and unaspirated consonants.

Naturally, the best way to approach these difficulties is to work through a phrasebook with a native speaker or with a tape. Lonely Planet's *Tibetan phrasebook* would be useful if you plan on learning the language in greater depth.

Vowels

The following pronunciation guide is based on standard British pronunciation (North Americans beware).

a	as in 'father'
ay	as in 'play'
e	as in 'met'
ee	as in 'meet'
i	as in 'big'
o	as in 'go'
oo	as in 'soon'
ö	as the 'ur' in 'fur'
ü	as in 'flute'

Consonants

With the exception of the ones listed below, Tibetan consonants should be pronounced as in English. Where consonants are followed by an 'h', it means that the consonant is aspirated (accompanied by a puff of air).

An English example might be 'kettle', where the 'k' is aspirated and the 'tt' is unaspirated. The distinction is fairly important, but in simple Tibetan the context should make it clear what you are talking about even if you get the sounds muddled up a bit.

ky	as the 'kie' in 'Kiev'
ng	as the 'ng' in 'sing'
r	produced with a slight trill
ts	as the 'ts' in 'bits'

Pronouns

I	*nga*
you	*kerang*
he, she	*khong*
we	*nga-tso*
you all	*kerang-tso*
they	*khong-tso*

Useful Phrases

Hello. *Tashi dele.*
Goodbye. (to person leaving)
  Kale phe.
Goodbye. (by person leaving)
  Kale shoo.
Thank you. *Thoo jaychay.*
Yes, OK. *La ong.*
I'm sorry. (forgive me) *Gonda.*
I want ... *Nga la ... go.*
Do you speak English?
  Injeeke shing gi yö pe?
Do you understand?
  Ha ko song-ngey?
I understand. *Ha ko song.*
I don't understand. *Ha ko ma song.*
How much? *Ka tsö ray?*
It's expensive.
  Gonzg chenpo ray
What's your name?
  Kerang gi ming la kary zer gi yö?
My name is ... *Ngai ... ming la.*
... And you?
  ... A ni kerang zer gi yö?
Where are you from?
  Kerang ka-ne ray?

Getting Around

I want to go to ...
  Nga ... la drondö yö.
I'm getting off. *Nga phap gi yin.*
What time do we leave?
  Ngatso chutsö katsö la dro gi yin?
What time do we arrive?
  Ngatso chutsö katsö la lep gi yin?
Where can I rent a bicycle?
  Kanggari kaba ragi ray?
How much per day?
  Nyima chik la ray?
Where is the ...? *Kaba yo ray?*
I'm lost.
  Nga lam khag lag song.

airport	*namdrutang*
bicycle	*kanggari*
bus	*lamkhor*
right	*yeba*
left	*yönba*
straight ahead	*shar gya*
north/south	*chang/lo*
east/west	*shar/noop*
porter	*dopo khur khen*
pack animal	*skel semchen*

Accommodation

hotel *dhönkhang*
Do you have a room? *Kang mi yöpe?*
How much is it for one night?
  Tsen chik la katsö ray?
I'd like to stay with a Tibetan family.
  Nga phöbe mitsang nyemdo dendö yö.

Geographical Terms

cave	*trapoo*
hot spring	*chuzay*
lake	*tso*
mountain	*ree*
river	*tsangpo*
road/trail	*lam*
valley	*loong shon*
waterfall	*papchu*

Health

I'm sick.
  Nga bedo mindu.
Please call a doctor.
  Amjee ke tangronang.

altitude sickness	*lâdu na*
diarrhoea	*troko she*
fever	*tsawa*
hospital	*menkang*

Time

What's the time?
  Chutsö katsö ray?

hour/minute	*chutsö/karma*
When?	*kadü?*
now	*thanda*
today	*thiring*
tomorrow	*sangnyi*
yesterday	*kesa*
morning	*shogay*
afternoon	
nying gung gyab la	
evening/night	*gonta*

Numbers

Note: the word in brackets is added before *chik*, 'one' etc to make the compound numbers.

1	*chik*
2	*nyi*
3	*sum*
4	*shi*
5	*nga*
6	*troo*
7	*dün*
8	*gye*
9	*gu*
10	*chu*
20	*nyi shu (tsa)*
30	*sum shu (so)*
40	*shi chu (zhe) chig*
50	*nga chu (nga)*
60	*troo chu ray*
70	*dun chu don*
80	*gye chu gya*
90	*gu chu go*
100	*chik gya*
1000	*chik tong*

Glossary

adetki mashina – (Uyghur) ordinary bus

ali mashina – (Uyghur) soft seat coach

amah – a servant, usually a woman, who cleans houses and looks after the children. Older Chinese women from the countryside used to find work as amahs, but in Hong Kong the job is mostly done by Filipinos and other South-East Asian migrant workers

antiphonal – a form of singing involving echoing refrains, duets and choruses

apsaras – Buddhist celestial beings, similar to angels

aptoos biket – (Uyghur) long-distance bus station

arhat – Buddhist, especially a monk who has achieved enlightenment and passes to nirvana at death

báijiǔ – literally 'white alcohol', a type of face-numbing rice wine served at banquets and get-togethers

bāozi – steamed savoury buns with tasty meat filling

běi – north

běicái – quarry

biānjiè – border

biéshù – villa

bīnguǎn – tourist hotel

Bodhisattva – one worthy of nirvana but who remains on earth to help others attain enlightenment

Bön – The pre-Buddhist indigenous faith of Tibet, pockets of which survive in western Sìchuān

bówùguǎn – museum

CAAC – The Civil Aviation Administration of China

cadre – Chinese government bureaucrat

cāntīng – restaurant

cǎoyuán – grasslands

catty – unit of weight, one catty (jīn) equals 0.6kg

CCP – Chinese Communist Party, founded in Shànghǎi in 1921

cham – a ritual Tibetan dance peformed over several days by monks and lamas

chang – a Tibetan brew made from fermented barley

Chángchéng – Great Wall

chau – (Cantonese) land mass, such as islands

chéng – labyrinth

cheongsam – (Cantonese) originating in Shànghǎi, a fashionable tight-fitting Chinese dress with a slit up the side. Often worn on special occasions, it's also the favoured gown for a bride departing on her honeymoon

chí – lake, pool

chim – (Cantonese) sticks that are used to divine the future. They're shaken out of a box onto the ground and then 'read'

chops – see name chops

chörten – Tibetan stupa

CITS – China International Travel Service; deals with China's foreign tourists

congee – watery rice porridge

CTS – China Travel Service; originally set up to handle tourists from Hong Kong, Macau, Taiwan and overseas Chinese

cūn – village

CYTS – China Youth Travel Service

dàdào – boulevard

dàfàndiàn – large hotel

dàjiē – avenue

dàjiǔdiàn – large hotel

dānwèi – work unit, the cornerstone of China's social structure

dǎo – island

dàpùbù – large waterfall

dàqiáo – large bridge

dàshà – hotel, building

dàshèngtǎ – great sacred pagoda

dàxué – university

dōng – east

dòng – cave

dòngwùyuán – zoo

értóng – children

fàndiàn – a hotel or restaurant

fēn– one tenth of a jiǎo

fēng – peak

fēngjǐngqū – scenic area

fēngshuǐ – geomancy, literally 'wind and water', the art of using ancient principles to maximise the flow of *qì*, or universal energy

Fifth Generation – a generation of film directors who trained after the Cultural Revolution and whose political works revolutionised the film industry in the 1980s and 1990s

fó – buddha

Fourth Generation – a generation of film directors whose careers were suspended by the Cultural Revolution

gǎng – harbour

Gang of Four – members of a clique, headed by Mao's wife, Jiang Qing, who were blamed for the disastrous Cultural Revolution

gé – pavilion, temple

godown – a warehouse, usually located on or near the waterfront; in Guǎngzhōu, Hong Kong

gompa – (Tibetan) monastery

gōng – palace

gōngshēng – unit of measure, roughly equivalent to 1L or 0.22 gallons

gōngyuán – park

gōu – gorge, valley

gù – previous, earlier

gǔ – valley

guān – pass

guānxì – advantageous social or business connections

guānyú – pond

gùchéng – ruins

gǔmùqū – graves

gùjū – old house/home/residence

gwailo – (Cantonese) a foreigner; literally meaning 'ghost person' and interpreted as 'foreign devil'

hǎi – sea

hǎitān – beach

Hakka – a Chinese ethnic group

hé – river

hong – (from Cantonese) a company, usually engaged in trade. Often used to refer to Hong Kong's original trading houses, such as Jardine Matheson or Swire

hú – lake

Huí – ethnic Chinese Muslims

huǒshānqún – volcano group

hútòng – a narrow alleyway

jiāng – river

jiǎo – one-tenth of a yuán

jiàotáng – church

jiē – street

jié – festival

jīn – unit of meaure, roughly equivalent to 0.6kg or 1.1 lb

jìniànbēi – memorial

jìniànguǎn – memorial hall

jìniàntǎ – monument

jiǔdiàn – hotel

jū – residence, home

junk – originally referred to Chinese fishing and war vessels with square sails. Now applies to various types of boating craft

kadimi shahr – (Uyghur) old part of towns

kaido – (Cantonese) a small to medium-sized ferry that makes short runs on the open sea, usually used for non-scheduled service between small islands and fishing villages

kǎoyādiàn – roast duck restaurant

karakhana – (Uyghur) workshop, factory

karst – denotes the characteristically eroded landscape of limestone regions, eg the whimsical scenery of Guìlín and Yángshuò

KCR – Kowloon-Canton Railway; in Hong Kong

Kham – traditional name for eastern Tibet, encompassing western Sìchuān

kinju – a regional form of classical opera developed in the cities of Sūzhōu, Hángzhōu and Nánjīng

KMB – Kowloon Motor Bus; in Hong Kong

kuài – colloquial term for the currency, yuan

Kuomintang – Chiang Kaishek's Nationalist Party, the dominant political force after the fall of the Qing dynasty. Now Taiwan's major political party

lǎobǎixìng – common people, the masses

lama – a Buddhist priest of the Tantric or Lamaist school

lǐ – unit of meaure, roughly equivalent to 500m or 0.31 miles
lín – forest
líng – tomb
lìshǐ – history
lóu – tower
LRT – Light Rail Transit; in Hong Kong
lù – road
lǚguǎn – hotel
lúshēng – a reed pipe that features in many festivals in Guìzhōu

mahjong – popular Chinese card game played among four persons with tiles engraved with Chinese characters
Mandate of Heaven – a political concept where heaven gives wise leaders a mandate to rule and removes power from those who are evil or corrupt
máo – colloquial term for the *jiǎo*, 10 of which equal one *kuài*
mǎtou – dock
mén – gate
Miáo – Chinese ethnic group
miào – temple
motor-tricycle – an enclosed three-wheeled vehicle with a driver at the front, a small motorbike engine below and seats for two passengers in the back
MTR – Mass Transit Railway; in Hong Kong
mù – tomb

name chop – a carved name seal that acts as a signature
nán – south

obo – (Inner Mongolia) a pile of stones with a hollow space for offerings, a kind of shaman shrine
oolong – (from Cantonese) high-grade Chinese tea, partially fermented
overseas Chinese – Chinese people who have left China to settle overseas

pedicab – pedal-powered tricycle with a seat to carry passengers
píng – unit of area, one píng equals 1.82 sq metres
Pīnyīn – the official system to transliterate Chinese script into roman characters
pípa – a plucked stringed instrument

PLA – People's Liberation Army
Politburo – the 25-member supreme policy-making authority of the CCP
PRC – People's Republic of China
PSB – Public Security Bureau; the arm of the police force set up to deal with foreigners
pùbù – waterfall
Pǔtōnghuà – the standard form of the Chinese language used since the beginning of this century, based on the dialect of Běijīng

qarvatlik mashina – (Uyghur) sleeper coach
qì – vital energy (life force) or cosmic currents manipulated in acupuncture and massage
qiáo – bridge
qìgōng – exercise that channels *qì*
qīngzhēnsì – mosque
quán – spring

Red Guards – a pro-Mao faction who persecuted rightists during the Cultural Revolution
rénmín – people, people's
Rénmínbì – literally 'people's money', the formal name for the currency of China. Shortened to RMB
ROC – Republic of China; also known as Taiwan

sampan – (from Cantonese) a motorised launch that can accommodate only a few people and is too small to go on the open sea
SAR – Special Administrative Region
savdo dukoni – (Uyghur) commercial shops
shān – mountain
shāngdiàn – shop, store
shěng – province, provincial
shì – city
shí – rock
shìchǎng – market
shìjiè – world
shíkū – grotto
shuǐkù – reservoir
sì – temple, monastery
sìhéyuàn – traditional courtyard house
special municipality – the name given to centrally administered regions such as Běijīng, Tiānjīn, Chóngqìng and Shànghǎi
stele – a stone slab or column decorated with figures or inscriptions

GLOSSARY

tă – pagoda

tael – unit of weight, one tael *(liăng)* equals 37.5g and there are 16 taels to the catty

tàijíquán – slow motion shadow boxing, a form of exercise. The graceful, flowing exercise that has its roots in China's martial arts. Also known, particularly in the west, as taichi

taipan – (from Cantonese) boss of a large company

tán – pool

Tanka – a Chinese ethnic group who traditionally live on boats

tíng – pavilion

triads – secret societies. Originally founded to protect Chinese culture from the influence of usurping Manchurians, their modern-day members are little more than gangsters, involved mainly in drug-running, prostitution and protection rackets

tripitaka – Buddhist scriptures

wān – bay

wēnquán – hot springs

xī – west

xĭ – small stream or brook

xiá – gorge

xiàn – county

xiàng – statue

xuěshān – snow mountain

yá – cliff

yán – rock or crag

yangi shahr – (Uyghur) new part of towns, usually Han-dominated

yēlín – coconut plantation

yuán – the Chinese unit of currency; also referred to as RMB

yuán – garden

yurt – abodes found in Inner Mongolia, a type of circular tent made with animal skin or felt

zhāodàisuŏ – basic lodgings, a hotel or guesthouse

zhēng – a 13- or 14-stringed harp

zhíwùyuán – botanical gardens

zhōng – middle

zìrán băohùqū – nature reserve

zŭjū – ancestral home

People

An Lushun – (703–57) general in command of 180,000 troops and three northern provinces; he led a rebellion against emperor Xuanzong in 755 (Tang dynasty)

Ba Jin – a popular and prolific anarchist writer of the 1930s and 1940s, Li Feigan (his real name) is probably best known for his 1931 novel *Jiā (The Family)*

Chen Kaige – a Fifth Generation director whose films, characterised by their strong political comment, include *Bàwáng Biéjī (Farewell my Concubine)*, the joint winner of the Palme d'Or at the 1993 Cannes Film Festival

Chiang Kaishek – (1887–1975) leader of the Kuomintang, anticommunist and head of the nationalist government from 1928 to 1949

Chuangtzu – (c. 369–286 BC) leading Taoist thinker who built on the teachings of Laotzu

Cixi – Empress Dowager 1834–1908; concubine who became ruler of the Qing dynasty

Confucius – (551–479 BC) Legendary scholar who developed the philosophy of Confucianism, which defines codes of conduct and patterns of obedience in society

Cui Jian – classical trumpet player turned rock star whose music was adopted by the protesters during the 1989 Tiānānmén Square demonstration

Deng Xiaoping – (1904–97) considered to be the most powerful political figure in China from the late 1970s until his death; Deng's reforms resulted in economic growth, but he is also remembered for harsh social policies and for authorising the military force that resulted in the Tiānānmén Massacre

Ding Ling – (1904–86) popular Marxist author who earned the ire of Mao for her criticism of the CCP and, in particular, its treatment of women

Du Fu – (712–70) poet skilled in all poetic forms of his time

Fang Lizhi – dissident blamed by the CCP for the 1989 Tiānānmén Square protests

Feng Jicai – noted Chinese author

Ge You – actor

Genghis Khan – uniter of the roaming Mongol tribes, his armies took Běijīng in 1215

Gong Li – internationally acclaimed and awarded actor who burst onto the screen in 1988; her works have included *Bàwáng Biéjī (Farewell, My Concubine)*, which won the 1993 Palme d'Or at the Cannes Film Festival

Guo Baosheng – dissident

He Jianjun – film director

Henry YH Zhao – writer

Hong Xiuquan – (1814–64) leader of the Taiping Rebellion and self-proclaimed second son of God

Hu Feng – writer, sparked Hundred Flowers

Hu Yaobang – (1915–89) a veteran of the Long March, Hu, along with his mentor Deng Xiaoping, returned to favour in the late 1970s and rose to the position of CCP chairman in 1981

Hua Guofeng – Mao's protege, premier 1976–80 and CCP chairman 1976–81

Huang Chao – leader of a 10-year rebellion that debilitated the Tang dynasty and led to its downfall

Huang Jianxin – Fifth Generation film director

Hui Neng – (638–713) sixth patriarch of the Zen Buddhist sect who renounced traditional Buddhism and founded the Southern school, which became influential throughout China and Japan

Jiang Qing – Mao's wife and leader of the Gang of Four, she was blamed for the Cultural Revolution

Jiang Wen – film director

Jiang Zemin – current state president and Communist Party general secretary

Kangxi – (1662–1722) expansionist Qing emperor

Kublai Khan – Grandson of Mongol Genghis Khan and founder of the Yuan dynasty (1271–1368), the world's largest empire

Lao Gui – writer

Lao She – (1899–1966) writer of humorous short stories and novels and head of the All-China Anti-Japanese Writers Federation during the Sino-Japanese War and WWII

Laotzu – a philosopher whose beliefs, inscribed in the slim volume the *Tao Te Ching (The Way & Its Power)*, inspired the birth of Taoism as a religion

Lee Tenghui – the first Taiwan-born president of Taiwan, Lee was appointed in 1988 and later won Taiwan's first direct presidential election (in 1996)

Li Bai – poet

Li Dazhao – (1888–1927) Mao Zedong's mentor and joint founder of the CCP

Li Jie – rock star

Lin Biao – (1907–71) military commander and CCP leader whose roles included Minister of Defence; Lin's death, which came shortly after he plotted to kill Mao Zedong, remains a mystery

Lin Zexu – (1785–1850) Qing dynasty official who tackled the illegal opium trade

Li Peng – Chinese premier from 1988 to 1998, Li continues to be an influential figure in the CCP and government

Liu Bang – a commoner who became emperor after his army defeated the Qin and founded the Han dynasty

Liu Binyan – dissident

Liu Shaoqi – (1898–1969) PRC chairman 1959–68

Li Wenming – dissident

Li Yuan – (566–635) the Tang dynasty's first emperor and founder

Li Yuanhong – (1864–1928) army commander who, in 1911, led a military uprising against the Qing and, alongside Sun Yatsen, established a republican government

Lu Xun – (1881–1936) acclaimed writer whose works tackled Confucian culture

Mao Zedong – (1893–1976) leader of the early communist forces, he founded the PRC and was party chairman until his death

Mencius – (372–289 BC) a scholar who raised Confucian ideals into the national consciousness

Mingdi – (c. AD 29–76) Han emperor whose reign saw Buddhism introduced

Ning Ying – film director

Peng Dehuai – (1898–1974) military commander and defence minister from 1954 to 1959 who was deposed when he criticised the Great Leap Forward

Peng Mingmin – Taiwanese politician

Polo, Marco – Italian merchant who (supposedly) visited China and the Far East in the 13th century

Puyi – (1906–67) last emperor of the Qing dynasty who took the throne aged three only to abdicate three years later after a republican revolt; Puyi also reigned as emperor of Manchuria (1934–45) in Japan's puppet state

Qianlong – (1711–99) Qing dynasty's fourth emperor

Qin Shihuang – first emperor of the Qin dynasty (reigned 221–207 BC), remembered for his cruelty

Ricci, Matteo – (1552–1610) Italian missionary appointed director of Jesuit activities in China in 1597

Ruggieri, Michele – Jesuit missionary who, with compatriot Matteo Ricci, brought Christianity to China in the 16th century

Shen Congwen – (1902–1988) fiction writer whose works focussed on rural life

Stilwell, Joseph – (1883–1946) WWII commanding general who led US and Chinese forces against the invading Japanese

Su Dongpo – (1036–1101) one of China's poetic greats, known for his optimism and for bending poetic conventions

Sun Tzu – (c. 4th century BC) author of *Ping-fa (The Art of War)*, a Chinese classic and the first known narrative on war

Sun Yatsen – (1866–1925) first President of the Republic of China. A revolutionary loved by republicans and communists alike

Taizong – (600–49) second emperor of the Tang dynasty and Gaozu's son

Tian Zhuangzhuang – contemporary, controversial film producer

Wang Dan – a leader of the 1989 Tiānānmén Square democracy movement who was jailed for six years before being exiled to the USA

Wang Hongwen – member of the Gang of Four (responsible for the Cultural Revolution)

Wang Meng – (1308–85) famous painter of the Yuan era

Wang Shuo – contemporary fiction writer

Wei Jingsheng – dissident who spent 18 years in prison for his antigovernment writings, and who has since been exiled to the USA

Wu Wenguang – film director who was the first to make a documentary-style video (in 1988), sparking a new era in Chinese cinema

Wu Zetian – (625–705) China's only female empress (Tang dynasty)

Wu Ziniu – Fifth Generation film director

Xuan Zang – (600–64) pilgrim whose wanderings included a 16-year journey to India to collect Buddhist scriptures

Xuanzong – (685–762) the 'Radiant Emperor' was the sixth emperor of the Tang dynasty, which flourished under his rule (712–56)

Yangdi – (569–618) second Sui dynasty emperor said to have murdered his father, Yang Jian (Wendi)

Yang Guifei – Xuanzong's consort

Yang Jian – (541–604) Wendi, the 'Cultured Emperor' and founder of the Sui dynasty

Yao Wenyuan – member of the Gang of Four (responsible for the Cultural Revolution)

Yongcheng – Qin emperor

Yongle – (1360–1424) third Ming emperor

Yuan Shikai – (1859–1916) the Republic of China's first president

Zhang Chunqiao – member of the Gang of Four (responsible for the Cultural Revolution)

Zhang Qian – early Han explorer who established links with the peoples of Central Asia

Zhang Xianliang – writer

Zhang Yimou – highly acclaimed Fifth Generation actor and director

Zhang Yuan – director who made underground films before breaking onto the world stage in 1992

Zhao Kuangyin – established Song dynasty

Zhao Ziyang – Deng's protege, Chinese premier 1980–87 and CCP general secretary 1987–89; Zhao's relatively liberal economic policies boosted agricultural and industrial production

Zheng He – (1371–1433) diplomat and explorer who forged relationships, on behalf of China, with over 35 countries

Zhou Enlai – an early comrade of Mao's, Zhou exercised the most influence in the day-to-day governing of China following the Cultural Revolution. His death triggered the 1976 Tiānānmén Incident

Zhu De – a Communist army leader who, together with Mao and Zhou Enlai, led the 1927 Nanchang Uprising and the Long March

Zhu Rongji – premier since 1998

Zhu Yuanzhang – established Ming dynasty, became Hongwu

Historical Events

Boxer Rebellion – A fanatical anti-foreign and anti-Christian movement that emerged from Shāndōng in 1898

Cultural Revolution – a brutal and devastating purge of the arts, religion and the intelligentsia by Mao's Red Guards and later the PLA from 1966–70

Great Leap Forward – failed socioeconomic program that resulted in a devastating famine in the early 1960s

Hundred Flowers – short-lived campaign of Mao's to allow 'freedom' in the arts and sciences

Long March – the 9500km march in 1934 from Jiāngxī to Shǎnxī by communist armies besieged in the south

Taiping Rebellion – A 1.1 million-strong rebellion that attempted to overthrow the Qing dynasty from 1850–64

Tiānānmén Incident (1976) – a 1976 protest sparked by anger against Jiang Qing and sorrow over the death of Zhou Enlai. Police broke up the protest on the orders of Mao and the politburo

Tiānānmén Incident (1989) – the quelling of pro-democracy demonstrators in Tiānānmén Square by government troops in 1989, echoing the Tiānānmén Incident of 13 years before

Wuchang Uprising – A joint 1911 rebellion by disaffected Chinese troops and Sun Yatsen's republican movement that resulted in the end of dynastic rule in China

This Book

This book was taken through production at Lonely Planet's Melbourne office by coordinators Leanne Peake (mapping and design) and Lara Morcombe (editorial). Leanne was assisted in mapping by Kieran Grogan, Pablo Gastar, Jack Gavran, Meredith Mail, Neb Milic, Chris Love and Chris Thomas. The book was edited by Lucy Williams and Bruce Evans with assistance from Kate Daly, Julia Taylor, Tony Davidson, Martin Heng and Cherry Prior. Lucy Williams and Tim Uden took the book through layout, and layout checks and assistance were provided by Glenn Beanland, Tim Fitzgerald, Martin Heng and Kristin Odijk. Valerie Tellini and Lonely Planet Images provided the photographs, and Kieran Grogan and Enjarn Lin provided the illustrations. Leonie Mugavin researched various factual questions, Mark Germanchis gave assistance during layout and Isabelle Young gave health advice. Chris Lee Ack and Paul Piaia provided mapping advice. Quentin Frayne worked tirelessly on the Language chapter, and Charles Qin and Alex English mastered the Chinese script. Maria Vallianos produced the cover, and Megan Fraser and Nikki Anderson handled the rights.

Thanks to Kui Hua Wang of Deakin University for updating the Legal Matters section.

Special thanks to: Suzanne Possehl and the Lonely Planet *Russia, Ukraine & Belarus* team for their work on the Trans-Siberian Railway section; Leonie Mugavin for writing the Getting There & Away chapter; Kieran Grogan for writing the Architecture section and various parts of the Arts section; Graham Fricke for writing the Senior Travellers section; Alex English for writing the Travelling with Children section and for working on the map keys; Charles Qin for writing the special asides on Pinyin and researching the stories behind various Chinese pictographs; Martin Heng for writing the Cuisine special section; Chang Enlai for providing the menu lists in the Cuisine special section; Lucy Williams for compiling the Highlights special section; and Cherry Prior for compiling the glossary.

Acknowledgments

THANKS

Many thanks to the travellers who used the last edition and wrote to us with helpful hints, useful advise and interesting anecdotes:

A C Hopps, A C Steenbeek, A Smithee, A Thorlby, Adam Aziz, Adam Dunnett, Adi Bloom, Adrian Gallardo, Agatha Li, Aine Ni Chonaill, Al Moore, Alan Butterworth, Alan Garretson, Alan Okinaka, Alastor Coleby, Alessandro Arduino, Alex Cockain, Alex Forsyth, Alex Lauder, Alex Williams, Alfred Bust, Alice Baer, Alice Buchtova, Alison Battisson, Alison Griffin, Alison Johnston, Alison McShanag, Allan Lightman, Allen Rose, Allison Watkins, Alvin Wong, Amanda Buster, Amanda Martin , Amy Leckie, Amy Zelmer, Anders Blichferdt, Anders McCarthy, Andre du Plessis, Andrea Hampton, Andrea Rogge, Andreas Rindler, Andrew Beale, Andrew Cave, Andrew Glassner, Andrew Musgrave, Andrew Ray, Andrew Tamblyn, Andrew Turner, Andy Bodge , Andy Field, Andy Heiskell, Andy Holloway, Andy Kennedy, Andy Kinlay, Andy Nicholson , Angela Bischoff, Angela Murray, Ann Ez El Din, Ann Hogan, Ann Krumboltz, Anna Del Franco, Anna Noelle, Annabel Battersby, Anne Brosnahan, Anne Pyke, Anneke Kooijman, AnneMarie, Annette Watson, Annmarie Owen, Anonda Bell, Anson Yu, Antoine Seillan, Antony Dapiran, Ariel Minkman, Arved Gintenreiter, Asbjoern Berge, Audrey Dauchy, Audrey Turner, Avi Rafilovich, Aydin Bulgen, B Ward, Bahout Claude, Bailliu Sarlet, Barbara Ann Berkley, Barbara Emmerson, Batsu, Bay Corbishley, Becca Wiley, Ben Oei, Ben Roberts, Benjamin Satterfield, Berian Griffiths, Berna Gerce, Bernadette Mergeay, Bernard Phelps, Bernd Mayer, Bernd Schmidt, Bertrand Manhe, Beth Poad, Bethanne Gennette, Bianca Haushern, Billy, Bjorn Burss, Bob, Bob Davis, Bob Garner, Bob Kurkjian, Bobby Meyer, Bonnie Braga, Boya Bockman, Bradley Mayhew, Bram Verweij, Brenda Soffe, Brett Mandel, Brett Montgomery, Brett Prowse, Brian Gibel, Brian Nomi, Brit Lehrmann Nielsen, Britta Hensen, Bruce Furner, Bruce Williams, Bryan Allen, C H Pearce, Caley Johnson, Camilla Van Christensen, Carl Jokisch, Carla Van Diest, Carlos Costa, Carlos Costa Recuero, Carlos Garza, Carol Wiley, Caroline Chandler, Caroline Clark, Carolyn Courtman, Carolyn Towell, Carolynn Fischer, Carrie Kirby, Catherine E A Kusske, Catherine Gallagher, Catherine Mole, Cathy Cardillo, Cecial Meys, Cedric Rimaud, Celia Smith, Chad Yoneda, Charles Lort-

Phillips, Charlie Strick van Linschoten, Charlotte Lee, Chirs Bauer, Choo Hwee Miang, Chris Ashmore, Chris Bowling, Chris Consilvio, Chris Dieckmann, Chris Hauserman, Chris Jackson, Chris Lee, Chris Mitchell, Chrishtoph Sporri, Christa-Maria Dinkelman, Christina Chan, Christine Jones, Christine Smith, Christine Wenyansong, Christine Zimmerli, Christopher Lynn, Christopher Reed, Christy Lanzl, Christy Su, Chyono Flynn, Cladia Roeder, Claire Jorrand, Claire Rudd, Clare Ashwin, Clare Bateson, Clare Egan, Claude Vigneault, Claudia Riquelme, Claudia Roeder, Clyde A Goodrum, Collin Hoondert, Connie, Conrad Paulson, Cor van Marion, Cornelia Vronaues, Corrie Rob, Craig, Craig Cottrell, Craig Mandsager, Crystal Wong, Dan Brake, Dan Carmi, Dan Michaelis, Dan Schar, Dan Shingleton, Daniel Dawson, Daniel Olds, Daniel Say, Daniel Yuen, Danny, Daria Vyncke, Darren Pepperell, Darren Schwab, Darren Spowart, Dave Lam, Dave McCullough, Dave Nicel, Dave Quinn, David Cole, David Fischer, David Flack, David Fregona, David G Atwill, David Hughes, David Jinwei, David Leung, David Loiter, David New, David Pullman, David Reid, David Smith, David Tilley, Dawn Metcalfe, Dean Moore, Debbie Nicholson, Deborah McCulloch, Denise, Derek B Moir, Derek Emmerson, Diana Lavarini, Diana X Jing, Dick Cijffers, Dieter Kapp, DJ She, Dominique Grandchamp, Donald Yap, Doreen Manning, Doris Woo, Dory Gardner, Doug Cooper, Doug Francis, Doug Howich, Douglas Raupach, Duncan Touch, Ebbe Lavendt, Eddie Settle, Eden Winnacott, Edoardo Rege, Edward J Kormondy, Edwin Bronsteede, Edwin Feiler Jr, Edwina Crawfrod, Elain Genser, Elena Potapova, Eli Teicher, Eliane Cavalcante de Almeida, Elisa Fung, Elisabeth Hooghe, Elizabeth Cox, Elizabeth Henry, Ellen Lommerse, Elsie Harrison, Elvira Hautvast, Elvis Ablimit, Emanuel Vahid Towfigh, Emma Smith, En Sai Mok, Enrico Giacoletto, Ep Heuvelink, Eric Horton, Eric Lynn, Eric Sarlet, Eric Taylor, Erica T Jolly, Erik Iliff, Erik Laridon, Erik Palin, Erik Shapiro, Erik Van Maasdijk, Erik Wienese, Erika McNamara, Ernst J Derra, Esteban Botero, Estelle Bentall, Eva Marie Lindsgaardvig, Eva Muenich, Evan Berry, Evan Owens, Evelyn Koh, Ezra Cohen-Yashar, Fabrice Mathieu, Fabrice Poulin, Fan Weihong, Felicity Poyner, Fernando Greco, Fili Lou, Filip Crombez, Fiona Clarkson, Fiona Gibbons, Florian Pfahler, Floriau Deib, Flouis Bylsma, Fox Wong, Francesca Camisoli, Francis Dix, Francois, Francois Carstens, Frank A Doonan, Frank Langfitt, Frank Sanders, Frank Wheby, Freark de Vries, Fred H, Frederiek de Rijke-Hoondert, Freerk Nienhuis, Fusen Hu, G D Jarvis, G Sinclair, Gabi Drechsel, Gail Swatt, Gareth Pearson, Gary Glazner, Gary Glazner, Gary Heatherington, Gary Shapcott, Gary Shepherd, Genevieve Touzel, Geoff Brown, Geoff Payne, George D Davis, George Xu, Georgiana Moreton, Gerard Ferlin, Germano Rollero, Gerrit Schmidt, Gez Collins, Gil Zioni, Gill Teicher, Gillian Austin, Gillian M Long, Gina Green, Ginny Eley, Giueseppe Gabusi, Glenn Burnside, Glenn Reynolds, Goncalo Magalhaes, Gordon Hutton, Gordon O'Connor, Grace Gao, Grace Tin, Graham Hodden, Graham Todd, Grant Daniel, Greg Wan, Gregory S Pun, Grgor Sucharowski, Griet Daled, Guillaume Dougados, Gunnar Bohne, Guntram Herda, Guy Kelman, Guy Sarlett, Gwen Chesnais, H G Harman, H J S Dorren, Hakan Widerstrom, Hamish Martin, Hanne Finholt, Hans Hayden, Harald Penkert, Harry, Hayes H Wei, Heath Watts, Heather Cox, Helen Finch, Helen Keffelon, Helen Tse, Helene Strauss, Henriette Buist, Henrik Hansson, Herb Helmstaedt, Hester Dolleman, Hillary Munro, Holger Bruning, Hon Leng Ee, Hong Xiu Ping, Hubert Peres, Iain Mackay, Ian Mclaughlin, Ian Pullin, Iftach Warshavsky, Inge Santosa, Ingeborg Dalheim, Ingeborg van Eerden, Ishay Nadler, Itai Michaelson, Iva C Tref, J Brice Guariglia, J Broscombe & S Rogers, J M Chalet, Jac, Jack Babbage, Jack Wright, Jackie Sheehan, Jacques Van Gelder, Jakub Hrncir, James Downey, James Manley, James Martin, James Murray, James Parker, James Whitlow Delano, Jamie Balliu, Jan, Jan Hanley, Jan Willem Roks, Janet Tang, Janet Koop, Janet Sweeney, Jarek Rudnik, Jasmine Why, Jason Cameron, Jasper Woodcock, Javier Galan, Jay K, Jay Martin, Jean Kahe, Jean Louis Rallu, Jeanette Hamber, Jeanie Paxton, Jean-Jacques Braun, Jean-Luc Widlowski, Jeanne Liogier, Jean-Philippe Fargeaud, Jean-Yves Massiot, Jeff Bakker, Jeff Kruse, Jeff Miller, Jeff Ruffolo, Jeffrey Lee, Jeffrey Mahn, Jeffrey van Hout, Jen Makin, Jenine Hilton, Jennie Challender, Jennifer Chen, Jennifer Choo, Jennifer West, Jenny Berg, Jenny Jing, Jens Behrens, Jeremy Dowdell, Jeremy Keays, Jeremy Stevens, Jerome Martelecque, Jerome Ottenwaelter, Jerry Wagman, Jerzy Dyczkowski, Jessica Thomas, Jimmy Qin, Joachim Kehren, Jo-Ann Lim, Joanna Furniss, Joanna Vibert, Joe Brock, Joe Marks, Joe Scheier-Dolberg, Joel Emond, Joel Matsuda, Joerund Buen, Johan G Borchert, Johan Nilsson, John Bower, John Cox, John Edwards, John Gartland, John Gould, John Hogan, John Macdonald, John Robinson, John Roy, John Steingraeber, Joktan Cohen, Jolanda Trouwee, Jon Aldridge, Jonathan Harris, Jonathan Meltz, Jonathan Smith, Jonathon Braman, Jonathon Cheng, Jonathon Fenby, Jono Feldman, Jos Lommerse, Josep Giro, Joseph C Kolars, Josephine Loo, Josh Ngu, Joszefina Cimbalova, Joyce

Morse, Judith Scott, Judy Kendall, Judy Pex, Julie Gaw, Julie Langfitt, Julie Lim, Julie Poirier, Julie Razkallah, Justin Nobbs, Justin Reed, JWJ van Dorp, K Macknight, Kai Gronlund, Kai Portmann, Kaj Heydorn, Kam-Wing Pang, Kara Jenkinson, Karl-Koenig Koenigsson, Kasom Skultab, Kate Crossan, Kate Frost, Kate Lynn, Kate Pearson, Kate Wadnizak, Katherine Barlow, Kathryn Kellogg, Kees Kooijman, Kees Van Boven, Keith Davies, Keith Potter, Ken Fernie, Ken Lee, Ken Leong, Ken Owen, Kevin O'Grady, Kieron Flynn, Kim Bayes, Kim Young, Kirsten Lueders, Kirsten Wilson, Kitana, Kjartan Jonsson, Knut Magne Arnesen, Korey Hartwich, Kris North, Kris Tuuttila, Kristen Nutile, Kristen Vogel, Kristyn Wilson, Krzysztof Pawlik, Krzysztof Rapala, Krzysztof Rybak, Kumar Narayanan, Kyril Dambuleff, Kyril Pamburg, L E Butler, Lamarque Paule, Larry James, Larry McClay, Lars H Young Mogensen, Laszlo Wagner, Laura Lu Hedrick, Laura Steinert, Laurens den Dulk, Laurie Stott, Le Anne Kion, Lee Henn, Lee Sau Dan, Lejeune Vincent, Les Charters, Leslie Wang, LH van Keijzerswaard, Li Nan, Li Jie, Liliane Bailliu, Linda Mack, Linda Przibilla, Linda Stevens, Lisa Blumhagen-Anderson, Lisa Mackenzie, Lisbeth Rochlitz, Livio Rolle, Llion Iwan, Lo, Lori Shemanski, Louise Choy, Louise Gaudry, Louise Simon, Lu Jin, Luca Dall'Olio, Lucia Yu, Luis Moreton Achsel, luke Dornan, Lyn Rowley, Lynda Hinds, M Evans, M Gunter, M Sweeney, Ma Dao Yun, Maarten Derksen, Madeline McCloskey, Madeline Rainer, Mae Rethers, Magda Zupancic, Marjorie Atkinson, Mal North, Manuela Mueller, Manuela Sporri, Mara Byrne, Marc Reusch, Marcel Horman, Marcel van der lem, Marcin Wodzinski, Marco Del Corona, Marcus Hennecke, Marcus Hiller, Marcus Jansson, Margaret Glazner, Margaret Scott, Margo Carter, Maria A Benavides, Maria Haanpaa, Maria Siow, Maria Sovensen, Maria Yatano Roche, Marie-Helene Faures-Mons, Marischa Withaar, Marjorie Atlinson, Mark Aksoy, Mark Bryant, Mark Kowalsky, Mark Nicholls, Mark Patton, Mark Russell, Mark Shrime, Mark Simon, Mark Tinker, Mark Wadnizak, Mark Wang, Marketa Hyksova, Marshall Burgess, Martha Mahoney, Martin Mortensen, Martin Sulev, Martin Voon, Mary Welch, Massimo Triberti, Mathias Muller, Matin Voon, Matt Sexton, Matthew Perrement, Matthew Tagney, Matthew Tyler-Jones, Matthew Weerden, Matthieu Schegg, Matti Minkman, Matyn Mieke, Maureen Kolkka, Maurice Conklin, Max Fette, Max Mergeay, Mayte De La Torre, Melanie Cheng, Melissa Fehrman, Merry Batten, Merry Ewing, Michael Berg, Michael Cahng, Michael Connelly, Michael Eckert, Michael Estermann, Michael Fackler, Michael Hay, Michael Hoare, Michael Jensen, Michael Kohn, Michael Krieg, Michael Pershern, Michael Summers, Michael Wu,

Michel Smit, Micheline Reusch, Michelle Chow, Michelle Kane, Michelle Lee, Michelle Sutherland, Michiel, Mikael Johansson, Mike Hagen, Mike Krosin, Mike Moran, Mike Roberts, Mike Saito, Mike Sovensen, Milan Vigil, Mimi Locher, Minta-Maria Hirvonen, Mitch Joe, Mitch Smith, Moira Rehmer, Molly Merson, Monica Salyer, Monica Wojtaszewski, Muira Katsuo, Murray Bailey, N Baker, Nad Tabit, Nan Burgess, Nantawan Hansomburnana, Nanthana P, Natacha Beeckman, Natalie Marshall, Nathanial Pulsifer, Neil F Clancy, Nena Joy, Nick Picton, Nicolaas Cuperus, Nicole Mathers, Nicole McGaffney-Lee, Nicole Schuchardt & E Derra, Nikki Singh, Nilesh Korgaokar, Nilza Homma, Noel Flor, Norman Mah, Nuno Andre Gomes, Nuno Martins, Nynhe Deinema, Odar, Oliver Hagemann, Oliver Picton, Olivier Delaby, Ong Hong Quan, Ong Seow Chong, Oplatek Blanka, Orchid, Orit Reiss, Othmar Zendron, Ovorkhangai Aimag, Pam Riley, Pamela Hines, Pascal Vanhove, Pat McDonald, Patricia Neale, Patrick, Patrick Alexander, Patrick Chon, Patrick Connolly, Patrick Fischer, Patrick Jennings, Patrick McAloon, Patrick Tyler, Patrick Yee, Paul Bearpark, Paul Clements, Paul Crick, Paul Daniels, Paul Durham, Paul Famador, Paul Futcher, Paul Futcher, Paul Gaylard, Paul Kahe, Paul Oxenham, Paul Przibilla, Paul Robinson, Paul White, Paul Witteman, Paula Golden, Penny Bayfield, Penny Turner, Per Jensen, Pete Birch, Peter Boers, Peter Dryden, Peter Fellows, Peter Hardie, Peter Hruska, Peter Kisby, Peter McIndoe, Peter Thornton, Peter Turner, Peter W Choo, Peter Yam, Peter Yau, Phil Koester, Phil Manson, Phil Soffe, Philip Billingsley, Philip Davis, Philip Mason, Philip Senn, Philipp Greiner, Philippa Collins, Phillip Molzer, Pierre Wong, Piers Touzel, Pip Batten, Pter Leykam, Qing Zhang, R Gunter, Rachael McDouall, Rachel Core, Rachel Smith, Randy Brooks, Randy Davis, Ray Gard, Ray Hilsinger, Ray Palmer, Raymond Ang, Ren Yanqing, Rene Folle, Rene Reinhardt, Ria Smith, Ric Phillips, Ricard Vilata, Richard Baker, Richard Bullock, Richard Grassi, Richard Graves, Richard Gregg, Richard Groom, Richard King, Richard Lee Eng Kit, Richard Middleton, Richard N Gottfried, Richard Reay, Richard Sanford, Richard Selby, Rick Graves, Rick Rabern, Ricky Shum, Rita Brons, Rob McIlwaine, Rob Minnee, Rob Snodgrass, Robert Collins, Robert Cousland, Robert Evangelisti, Robert Fowler, Robert Hooghe, Robert James Olajos, Robert Lenard, Robert Webster, Robin Cheung, Robin Deal, Robin Thirtle, Robin Tudge, Rod Gerstenhaber, Roderick O'Brien, Roger Broad, Roger Phillips, Roland Beutler, Rolf Lienekogel, Rolf Walther, Romano Sambo, Ron Keehn, Rosana C Sialong, Rose Kerlin, Rosemarie Nunning, Roy Peleg, Rupert Chesman, Russell Hall, Russell Menyhart, Ruth Crampton, Ruth Harper, Ryan Houk, Ryann Thomas, Sabine Verhelst, Sam De Laender, Samantha Harrison, Samuel Yue, Sander Ouwerkerk, Sandra Van Heyste, Sandy, Sara Cherlin, Sarah Bland, Sarah Bonner, Sarah Dettwiler, Sarah O'Neill, Sarah Squire, Sarie Gilbert, Saskia Lieshout, Satish Bhatnagar, Scott Ackiss, Scott Smith, Sean, Sebastian F Buechte, Seung Beom Kim, Shahida Akram, Shane A Heyden, Shari Aubrey, Sharon Smith, Sheba, Shenaz Malik, Sheridan Pettiford, Shin-yi Chao, Shlomo Hasson, Si, Sigrid Seel, Silvie Dobke, Simon Bristow, Simon Evans, Simon Li, Simon Lynch, Simon Pedersen, Simon Wilson, Simone, Sivan, Slate Evans, Soeren Stub Rasmussen, Sonja Henne, Soren Roschmann, Stefan C Otte, Stefano Scagliola, Stefany Lepoutre, Stephane Morichere-Matte, Stephanie Born, Stephanie Howarth, Stephanie Kirschnick, Stephen B Long, Stephen Barker, Stephen Capen, Stephen Jones, Stephen McFarlane, Stephen Winterstein, Steve Cook, Steve Drake, Steve Drodge, Steve Jones, Steve Marcus, Stevn Coxhead, Stuart Johen, Stuart Kelly, Suellen Zima, Sung Ho Park, Susan Blick, Susan Ruttenber, Susana Poulin, Susanne Beal, Susanne Ritz, Suzanne Auer, Suzanne Freeman, Suzanne Zyla, Svenja Klotzbucher, T Baker, T K Chang, Talya Rabern, Tam Chiwai, Tamara Herrmann, Tamara Shie, Tan Cheng Ling, Tan Meng Shern, Tanja Schirmann, Tasneem Hussain, Tatjana, Tchin Vo Giao, Ted Bongiovanni, Ted Gordon, Ted Pei, Tess Johnston, Teung Sze Wing, Therese Bodin, Thomas Digeser, Thomas Genssler, Thomas Hodges, Thomas Rau, Thorsten Bick, Tianyuan, Tim Boole, Tim McMillan, Tim Morton, Tim Woodward, Timothy Dugdale, Tina, Tini Twischmann, Tjasa, Tobias Baumann, Todd Lundgren, Tom Feser, Tom Jorgen Martinussen, Tom Rasmussen, Tom Trewartha, Tom van Dillen, Tom Weller, Tomas Beranek, Toni Roeder, Tony Brasunas, Tony Burgess, Tony Burgess, Tony Roeder, Tooker, Tooker Gomberg, Tove Hagman, Tracey Furner, Tracey Sutherland, Tracy Hennige, Tracy Hudson, Treharne Lynn, Trevor Liss, Tricia Jacobson, Tze On Chu, Ulrich Fischer, Ulrik Skibsted, Ursula Fruehwirt, Vanessa Landry-Claverie, Vanessa Smith Holburn, Vera Binder, Vibeke Cohe, Vicky, Vicky Tian, Victor, Viveca Moritz, Vivian Rutgers, Vivienne Ling, Vladimir Benes, Wan Lin, Wayne Brabin, Wei Wu, Wendy E Shepard, Wesley Chiang, Wesley J Hayter, Wilbert Yee, Will Fairey, Will Harper, William Corr, William Francis, William Lee, William McDowall, Willy Eriz, Wilma O'Sullivan, Wim Pannecoucke, Wolf Kadavanich, Wong Wei Ming, Wu Wei, Wyn Ingham, Wynne Cochran, Yan Wong, Yang Huai Kuo, Yannick Littoux, Yasmin Tan, Yewah Lau, Yin Yi, Yiqun Chen, Yoav Perlman, Yuval Shafir, Yvonne Kwakernaak, Zac Savage, Zac Shepherd, Zai Jian, Zak Hofman, Zane Ritchie, Zarina Marsh, Ze Do Rock, Zeke, Zene Dickson, Zoe Ash

LONELY PLANET

Guides by Region

L onely Planet is known worldwide for publishing practical, reliable and no-nonsense travel information in our guides and on our web site. The Lonely Planet list covers just about every accessible part of the world. Currently there are fifteen series: travel guides, Shoestrings, Condensed, Phrasebooks, Read This First, Healthy Travel, Walking guides, Cycling guides, Pisces Diving & Snorkeling guides, City Maps, Travel Atlases, Out to Eat, World Food, Journeys travel literature and Pictorials.

AFRICA Africa on a shoestring • Africa – the South • Arabic (Egyptian) phrasebook • Arabic (Moroccan) phrasebook • Cairo • Cape Town • Cape Town city map • Central Africa • East Africa • Egypt • Egypt travel atlas • Ethiopian (Amharic) phrasebook • The Gambia & Senegal • Healthy Travel Africa • Kenya • Kenya travel atlas • Malawi, Mozambique & Zambia • Morocco • North Africa • Read This First Africa • South Africa, Lesotho & Swaziland • South Africa, Lesotho & Swaziland travel atlas • Swahili phrasebook • Tanzania, Zanzibar & Pemba • Trekking in East Africa • Tunisia • West Africa • Zimbabwe, Botswana & Namibia • Zimbabwe, Botswana & Namibia Travel Atlas • World Food Morocco**Travel Literature:** The Rainbird: A Central African Journey • Songs to an African Sunset: A Zimbabwean Story • Mali Blues: Traveling to an African Beat

AUSTRALIA & THE PACIFIC Auckland • Australia • Australian phrasebook • Bushwalking in Australia • Bushwalking in Papua New Guinea • Fiji • Fijian phrasebook • Healthy Travel Australia, NZ and the Pacific • Islands of Australia's Great Barrier Reef • Melbourne • Melbourne city map • Micronesia • New Caledonia • New South Wales & the ACT • New Zealand • Northern Territory • Outback Australia • Out To Eat – Melbourne • Out to Eat – Sydney • Papua New Guinea • Pidgin phrasebook • Queensland • Rarotonga & the Cook Islands • Samoa • Solomon Islands • South Australia • South Pacific • South Pacific Languages phrasebook • Sydney • Sydney city map • Sydney Condensed • Tahiti & French Polynesia • Tasmania • Tonga • Tramping in New Zealand • Vanuatu • Victoria • Western Australia
Travel Literature: Islands in the Clouds • Kiwi Tracks: A New Zealand Journey • Sean & David's Long Drive

CENTRAL AMERICA & THE CARIBBEAN Bahamas, Turks & Caicos • Bermuda • Central America on a shoestring • Costa Rica • Cuba • Dominican Republic & Haiti • Eastern Caribbean • Guatemala, Belize & Yucatán: La Ruta Maya • Jamaica • Mexico • Mexico City • Panama • Puerto Rico • Read This First Central & South America • World Food Mexico
Travel Literature: Green Dreams: Travels in Central America

EUROPE Amsterdam • Amsterdam city map • Andalucía • Austria • Baltic States phrasebook • Barcelona • Berlin • Berlin city map • Britain • British phrasebook • Brussels, Bruges & Antwerp • Budapest city map • Canary Islands • Central Europe • Central Europe phrasebook • Corfu & Ionians • Corsica • Crete • Crete Condensed • Croatia • Cyprus • Czech & Slovak Republics • Denmark • Dublin • Eastern Europe • Eastern Europe phrasebook • Edinburgh • Estonia, Latvia & Lithuania • Europe on a shoestring • Finland • Florence • France • French phrasebook • Germany • German phrasebook • Greece • Greek Islands • Greek phrasebook • Hungary • Iceland, Greenland & the Faroe Islands • Ireland • Italian phrasebook • Italy • Krakow • Lisbon • The Loire • London • London city map • London Condensed • Mediterranean Europe • Mediterranean Europe phrasebook • Munich • Norway • Paris • Paris city map • Paris Condensed • Poland • Portugal • Portugese phrasebook • Portugal travel atlas • Prague • Prague city map • Provence & the Côte d'Azur • Read This First Europe • Romania & Moldova • Rome • Russia, Ukraine & Belarus • Russian phrasebook • Scandinavian & Baltic Europe • Scandinavian Europe phrasebook • Scotland • Slovenia • Spain • Spanish phrasebook • St Petersburg • Sweden • Switzerland • Trekking in Spain • Tuscany • Ukrainian phrasebook • Venice • Vienna • Walking in Britain • Walking in Ireland • Walking in Italy • Walking in Spain • Walking in Switzerland • Western Europe • Western Europe phrasebook • World Food Ireland • World Food Italy • World Food Spain
Travel Literature: The Olive Grove: Travels in Greece

INDIAN SUBCONTINENT Bangladesh • Bengali phrasebook • Bhutan • Delhi • Goa • Hindi & Urdu phrasebook • India • India & Bangladesh travel atlas • Indian Himalaya • Karakoram Highway • Kerala • Mumbai (Bombay) • Nepal • Nepali phrasebook • Pakistan • Rajasthan • Read This First: Asia & India • South India • Sri Lanka • Sri Lanka phrasebook • Trekking in the Indian Himalaya • Trekking in the Karakoram & Hindukush • Trekking in the Nepal Himalaya
Travel Literature: In Rajasthan • Shopping for Buddhas • The Age Of Kali

LONELY PLANET

Mail Order

onely Planet products are distributed worldwide. They are also available by mail order from Lonely Planet, so if you have difficulty finding a title please write to us. North and South American residents should write to 150 Linden St, Oakland CA 94607, USA; European and African residents should write to 10a Spring Place, London, NW5 3BH; and residents of other countries to PO Box 617, Hawthorn, Victoria 3122, Australia.

ISLANDS OF THE INDIAN OCEAN Madagascar & Comoros • Maldives • Mauritius, Réunion & Seychelles

MIDDLE EAST & CENTRAL ASIA Bahrain, Kuwait & Qatar • Central Asia • Central Asia phrasebook • Dubai • Hebrew phrasebook • Iran • Israel & the Palestinian Territories • Israel & the Palestinian Territories travel atlas • Istanbul • Istanbul City Map • Istanbul to Cairo on a shoestring • Jerusalem • Jerusalem City Map • Jordan • Jordan, Syria & Lebanon travel atlas • Lebanon • Middle East • Oman & the United Arab Emirates • Syria • Turkey • Turkey travel atlas • Turkish phrasebook • World Food Turkey • Yemen
Travel Literature: The Gates of Damascus • Kingdom of the Film Stars: Journey into Jordan • Black on Black: Iran Revisited

NORTH AMERICA Alaska • Backpacking in Alaska • Baja California • California & Nevada • California Condensed • Canada • Chicago • Chicago city map • Deep South • Florida • Hawaii • Honolulu • Las Vegas • Los Angeles • Miami • New England • New Orleans • New York City • New York city map • New York Condensed • New York, New Jersey & Pennsylvania • Oahu • Pacific Northwest USA • Puerto Rico • Rocky Mountain • San Francisco • San Francisco city map • Seattle • Southwest USA • Texas • USA • USA phrasebook • Vancouver • Washington, DC & the Capital Region • Washington DC city map
Travel Literature: Drive Thru America

NORTH-EAST ASIA Beijing • Cantonese phrasebook • China • Hong Kong • Hong Kong city map • Hong Kong, Macau & Guangzhou • Japan • Japanese phrasebook • Japanese audio pack • Korea • Korean phrasebook • Kyoto • Mandarin phrasebook • Mongolia • Mongolian phrasebook • North-East Asia on a shoestring • Seoul • South-West China • Taiwan • Tibet • Tibetan phrasebook • Tokyo
Travel Literature: Lost Japan • In Xanadu

SOUTH AMERICA Argentina, Uruguay & Paraguay • Bolivia • Brazil • Brazilian phrasebook • Buenos Aires • Chile & Easter Island • Chile & Easter Island travel atlas • Colombia • Ecuador & the Galapagos Islands • Healthy Travel Central & South America • Latin American Spanish phrasebook • Peru • Quechua phrasebook • Rio de Janeiro • Rio de Janeiro city map • South America on a shoestring • Trekking in the Patagonian Andes • Venezuela
Travel Literature: Full Circle: A South American Journey

SOUTH-EAST ASIA Bali & Lombok • Bangkok • Bangkok city map • Burmese phrasebook • Cambodia • Hanoi • Healthy Travel Asia & India • Hill Tribes phrasebook • Ho Chi Minh City • Indonesia • Indonesia's Eastern Islands • Indonesian phrasebook • Indonesian audio pack • Jakarta • Java • Laos • Lao phrasebook • Laos travel atlas • Malay phrasebook • Malaysia, Singapore & Brunei • Myanmar (Burma) • Philippines • Pilipino (Tagalog) phrasebook • Read This First Asia & India • Singapore • South-East Asia on a shoestring • South-East Asia phrasebook • Thailand • Thailand's Islands & Beaches • Thailand travel atlas • Thai phrasebook • Thai audio pack • Vietnam • Vietnamese phrasebook • Vietnam travel atlas • World Food Thailand • World Food Vietnam

ALSO AVAILABLE: Antarctica • The Arctic • Brief Encounters: Stories of Love, Sex & Travel • Chasing Rickshaws • Lonely Planet Unpacked • Not the Only Planet: Travel Stories from Science Fiction • Sacred India • Travel with Children • Traveller's Tales

LONELY PLANET

You already know that Lonely Planet produces more than this one guidebook, but you might not be aware of the other products we have on this region. Here is a selection of titles which you may want to check out as well:

South-West China
ISBN 0 86442 596 1
US$19.95 • UK£12.99 • 160FF

Healthy Travel Asia & India
ISBN 1 86450 051 4
US$5.95 • UK£3.99 • 39FF

Hong Kong, Macau & Guangzhou
ISBN 0 86442 584 8
US$15.95 • UK£9.99 • 120FF

Karakoram Highway
ISBN 0 86442 531 7
US$17.95 • UK£11.99 • 140FF

Beijing
ISBN 1 86450 144 8
US$14.99 • UK£8.99 • 109FF

Read this First Asia & India
ISBN 1 86450 049 2
US$14.99 • UK£8.99 • 99FF

Chasing Rickshaws
ISBN 0 86442 640 2
US$34.95 • UK£19.99 • 220FF

Cantonese phrasebook
ISBN 0 86442 645 3
US$6.95 • UK£4.50 • 50FF

Mandarin phrasebook
ISBN 0 86442 652 6
US$7.95 • UK£4.50 • 50FF

Hong Kong city map
ISBN 1 86450 007 7
US$5.95 • UK£3.99 • 39FF

Hong Kong condensed
ISBN 1 86450 253 3
US$11.99 • UK£6.99 • 69FF

Tibet
ISBN 0 86442 637 2
US$17.95 • UK£11.99 • 140FF

Available wherever books are sold.

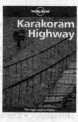

Index

Abbreviations

Anh – Ānhuī
Bej – Běijīng
Chq – Chóngqìng
Fuj – Fújiàn
Gan – Gānsù
G'dong – Guǎngdōng
Gui – Guìzhōu
G'xi – Guǎngxī
Hain – Hǎinán Dǎo
Heb – Héběi
Heil – Hēilóngjiāng

HK – Hong Kong
Hen – Hénán
Hub – Húběi
Hun – Húnán
In Mon – Inner Mongolia
J'su – Jiāngsū
J'xi – Jiāngxī
Jil – Jílín
Lia –Liáoníng
Mac – Macau
Nin – Níngxià

Qin – Qīnghǎi
Shaa– Shaanxi
S'dong – Shāndōng
S'hai – Shànghǎi
S'xi – Shānxī
Sic – Sìchuān
Tia – Tiānjīn
Tib – Tibet
Xin – Xīnjiāng
Yunn – Yúnnán
Zhe – Zhèjiāng

Text

A

accommodation 132-6
Àidīng Hú (Aydingkol Lake)
  (Xin) 937
air travel 150-6, 168-9
  airlines 150
  airports 150
  to/from China 151-6
  within China 168-9
Akha people, see Hani (Akha)
  people
Ānhuī 357-69, **358**
Ānníng Wēnquán (Anning Hot
  Springs) (Yunn) 787
Ānshùn (Gui) 759-61, **760**
antiques 137-8
Ānyáng (Hen) 544-5
architecture 65-7
Army of Terracotta Warriors
  (Shaa) 519-21
arts 60-9
  architecture 65-7
  bronze vessels 62
  calligraphy 69
  ceramics 60-2
  film 67-8
  funerary objects 62-3
  jade 62
  literature 63-5
  music 60
  painting 69
  theatre 68

Asītànà Gǔmùqū (Astana
  Graves) (Xin) 935-6
Aydingkol Lake (Àidīng Hú)
  (Xin) 937
Azure City Black Mountain
  (Qīngchéng Hòu Shān) (Sic)
  889
Azure City Mountain
  (Qīngchéng Shān) (Sic) 888-9

B

Bādálíng Great Wall (Bei) 228-9
Bai people 752, 770
Báishā (Yunn) 812
Báishuǐtái (Yunn) 815
Báiyún Shān (White Cloud
  Hills) (G'dong) 680
banks, see money
Bànpō Bówùguǎn (Banpo
  Neolithic Village) (Shaa) 522
Bǎodǐng Shān (Treasured
  Summit Hill) (Chq) 860-1
Bǎoguāng Sì (Monastery of
  Divine Light) (Sic) 888
Bǎoshān (Yunn) 836-8, **836**
Bǎoshān Region (Yunn) 835-42
Bāotóu (In Mon) 1006-9,
  1007, 1008
Barkhor (Tib) 1021
Bātáng (Sic) 913
Běi Líng (North Tomb) (Lia) 442
Běi Shān (North Hill) (Chq) 860
Běidàihé (Heb) 269-72, **270,
  271**

Běihǎi (G'xi) 725-7
Běijīng (Bei) 183-241, **185,
  194-5, 204-5**
  entertainment 217-20
  Forbidden City 188-9
  getting around 224-8, **227**
  getting there & away
    222-4
  Great Wall 228-38
  history 183-6
  information 186-8
  museums & galleries 200-1
  national buildings &
    monuments 188-98
  orientation 186
  parks & gardens 198-200
  places to eat 213-7
  places to see 203-8
  places to stay 208-13
  shopping 220-2
  Summer Palace 193-7
  temples & mosques 201-3
  Tiānānmén Square 190-1
Běijīng Opera 218
Bezeklik Thousand Buddha
  Caves (Bózīkèlǐkè Qiānfó
  Dòng) (Xin) 936-7
bicycle travel 176-8
  in Běijīng 192
Bīnglíng Sì (Thousand Buddha
  Caves Temple) (Gan) 968-9
Bīngyù Gōu (Bingyu Valley)
  (Lia) 456
Bird Island (Niǎo Dǎo) (Qin)
  1040-1

Bold indicates maps.

bird-watching
  Caŏ Haĭ (Gui) 763
  Niăo Dăo (Qin) 1040-1
  Zhălóng Zìrán Băohùqū
    (Heil) 488-90
Bìshŭ Shānzhuāng (Imperial
  Summer Villa) (Heb) 266
Black Dragon Pool (Hēilóng
  Tán) (Yunn) 787
Black Dragon River Borderlands
  (Hēilóngjiāng Biánjìng) (Heil)
  486-8
boat travel
  to/from China 164-5
  within China 179
boat trips
  Cháng Jiāng (Yangzi River)
    863-9, **866**
  Huángpǔ Jiāng (S'hai) 387
  Yángshuò (G'xi) 741
books, see also literature
  general 94-5
  history & politics 93-4
  travel tales 93
border crossings 156-60
  Kazakhstan 958
  Laos 832
  Myanmar 844
  North Korea 457
  Vietnam 725
Bouyei people 752, 762
Boxer Rebellion 28, 278
Bózhōu (Anh) 361-6
Bózīkèlĭkè Qiānfó Dòng
  (Bezeklik Thousand Buddha
  Caves) (Xin) 936-7
British in China 27, 242,
  946
bronze vessels 62
Buddhism 75-6, 506
Bù'ěrjīn (Xin) 955-8, **956**
Bund, The (S'hai) 377-8
bus travel 169-71
  local buses 179-80
  within China 169-71
business hours 124-5

C

calligraphy 69
camping, see accommodation
Canton, see Guăngzhōu
Cāngyán Shān (Heb) 263
capitalism 251

Bold indicates maps.

car & motorcycle travel
  175-6
  driving licence 84-5
caves
  Bīnglíng Sì (Gan) 968-9
  Bózīkèlĭkè Qiānfó Dòng
    (Xin) 936-7
  cave dwellings 536
  Dàzú Xiàn (Chq) 860-2
  Gōngyì Shíkūsì (Hen) 542
  Jiǔtiān Dòng (Hun) 598
  Lónggōng Dòng (Gui) 761-3
  Lóngmén Shíkū (Hen) 543-4
  Lúdí Yán (G'xi) 731-2
  Màijī Shān Shíkū (Gan) 985-6
  Mògāo Kū (Gan) 981-3
  Sānxiān Dòng (Xin) 944
  Shíhuī Yándòng (J'su) 334-5
  Shuĭlián Dòng (Gan) 987-8
  Xī Qiānfó Dòng (Gan) 983
  Yīlīng Yán (G'xi) 723
  Yúngāng Shíkū (S'xi) 505-7
CCP 30-46, 576, 767
  religion & communism 77-8
  site of the 1st National
    Congress of the CCP
    (S'hai) 379
ceramics 60-2, 571-2, 682
  Dīngshān (J'su) 335-41
  Yíxīng teapots 336
Cháng Jiāng (Yangzi River) 47,
  863-9, **866**
Chāng'ān (Shaa), see Xī'ān
Chángbái Shān (Ever White
  Mountains) (Jil) 468-72, **469**
Chángchéng, see Great Wall
Chángchūn (Jil) 460-5, **462**
Chángshā (Hun) 581-92, **584**
Cháozhōu (G'dong) 702-3,
  702
Chéjiāng (Gui) 767
Chéngdū (Sic) 872-87, **877**
  getting around 887
  getting there & away 885-7
  history 872
  information 873-4
  places to eat 881-3
  places to stay 879-81
  things to see 874-9
Chéngdé (Heb) 263-9, **264**
Chénggòng Xiàn (Yunn) 790
Chiang Kaishek 30, 419, 855
Chicken-Foot Mountain (Jīzú
  Shān) (Yunn) 794-5
children, travel with 117
China International Travel
  Service, see CITS

China Travel Service, see CTS
China Youth Travel Service, see
  CYTS
Chinese Communist Party, see
  CCP
Chinese New Year 125
Chóng'ān (Gui) 767
Chóngqìng 851-62, **852**
Chóngqìng City (Chq) 851-60,
  854
Chóngwǔ (Fuj) 437
Christianity 77
Chún'ān Xiàn (Zhe) 422
Chungking (Chq), see
  Chóngqìng
cinema 96, 610-1
Cípíng (J'xi), see Jīnggāng Shān
circus 386
CITS 181
Cixi, Dowager Empress 28
climate 48-50
Cloud Ridge Caves (Yúngāng
  Shíkū) (S'xi) 505-7
Cloudy Peak Mountain
  (Yúnfēng Shān) (Yunn) 841
Communism 526-8, 583-5
Conch Gully Glacier Park
  (Hăiluógōu Bīngchuān
  Gōngyuán) (Sic) 907-9
conduct 70-2
Confucianism 74-5, 294
Confucius 291-7, 465
  Qūfù (S'dong) 291-7
consulates, see embassies
costs 87
courses 131
credit cards 88
Crescent Moon Lake
  (Yuèyáquán) (Gan) 981
crime 118
cuisine, see food
CTS 181-2
Cultural Revolution 40-2
cultural events, see festivals
currency 88
customs 86-7
CYTS 182

D

Dà Fó (Grand Buddha) (Sic)
  898-900
Dàguān Gōngyuán (Grand
  View Park) (Yunn) 788
Dàgū Shān (Lonely Mountain)
  (Lia) 459
Dàhéyàn (Xin) 932-3

Dai people 826
Dai (Yunn) 821
Dalai Lama 76, 1017-21
Dàlǐ (Yunn) 795-801, **796**, **801**
Dàlián (Lia) 448-55, **452**, **456**
  getting around 455
  getting there & away 454-5
  information 449
  places to eat 453-4
  places to stay 449-53
  things to see 449
Dāndōng (Lia) 456-9, **458**
dangers, see safe travel
Dàměnglóng (Yunn) 832-4
Dardo (Sic), see Kāngdìng
Dàtóng (S'xi) 502, **502**
Dàxióngmāo Fánzhí Yánjiū
  Zhōngxīn (Giant Panda
  Breeding Research Base)
  (Sic) 878-9
Dàzú Xiàn (Chq) 860-2
Dégé (Dêgê) (Sic) 911
Déhóng Prefecture (Yunn)
  842-50
Dēngfēng (Hen) 538-9
Deng Xiaoping 37, 41, 42-3
departure tax 151
Déqīn (Yunn) 819-20
Détiān Pùbù (Detian Waterfall)
  (G'xi) 724
Diān Chí (Dian Lake) (Yunn)
  788, **788**
diarrhoea 106
disabled travellers 116
Dǐnghú Shān (G'dong) 696, **697**
Dīngshān (J'su) 335-41
Divine Rock Temple (Língyán
  Sì) (S'dong) 291
Dong people 717, 752, 767
Dōng Shān (J'su) 350
Dōngběi Hǔlín Yuán (Siberia
  Tiger Park) (Heil) 477-9
Dōngshèng (In Mon) 1010-1
Dongxiang people 969
Dragon Gate Grottos (Lóng-
  mén Shíkū) (Hen) 543-4
Dragon Palace Caves (Lóng-
  gōng Dòng) (Gui) 761-3
Dragon's Backbone Rice
  Terraces (Lóngjǐ Tītián)
  (G'xi) 742, **742**
Drepung Monastery (Zhébàng
  Sì) (Tib) 1027
drinks 148-9
drugs 123-6
Du Fu 875
Dūjiāngyàn (Sic) 889-91, **890**

Dūnhuáng (Gan) 978-81, **978**
dynasties 21-9

E
Ear Shaped Lake (Ěrhǎi Hú)
  (Yunn) 801, **801**
Eastern Qing Tombs (Qīng
  Dōng Líng) (Bei) 239
ecology 50-2
economy 56
electricity 98-9
email 92-3
embassies
  Chinese 85
  consulates 86-7
  foreign 85-6
Éméi Shān (Sic) 891-8, **894**
energy use 50-1
entertainment 136
environment 50-2
Ěrhǎi Hú (Ear Shaped Lake)
  (Yunn) 801, **801**
eunuchs 188
Ever White Mountains (Chángbái Shān) (Jil) 468-72, **469**
Everest Base Camp (Tib) 1032

F
fauna
  cruelty to animals 53
  endangered species 53-4
fax services 92-3
Fènghuáng Shān (Phoenix
  Emperor Mountain) (Lia) 459
fēngshuǐ 70-1
festivals 125-6
  Dàlǐ (Yunn) 797
  Guìzhōu 752-3
  Haerbin Music Festival (Heil)
    480
  Ice Lantern Festival 467, 480
  Kǎilǐ (Gui) 764-5
  Lhasa (Tib) 1022
  Lìjiāng (Yunn) 807
  Macau 651
  Naadam (In Mon) 1003
  Xiàhé (Gan) 971
  Xīshuāngbǎnnà (Yunn) 822
film 67-8, 96, see also cinema
Five Dynasties 25
Five Large Connected Lakes
  (Wǔdàlián Chí) (Heil) 485-6
Five-Terrace Mountain (Wǔtái
  Shān) (S'xi) 499-502, **499**
Flaming Mountains (Huǒyàn
  Shān) (Xin) 936

flora 52-3
food
  chinese cuisine 139-49
  eastern school 141-2
  etiquette 146-7
  Kūnmíng (Yunn) 781
  northern school 140
  southern school 145
  Uyghur 147, 757, 930
  western school 143-4
Forbidden City (Bei) 188-9
foreign concessions 378, 379
Fóshān (G'dong) 681-2, **682**
Four-Gate Pagoda (Simén Tǎ)
  (S'dong) 283
French in China 242, 378, 379
Friendship Peak (Yǒuyì Fēng)
  (Xin) 958
Fújiàn 423-39, **424**
Fukkien, see Fújiàn
funerary objects 62-3
Fúróngzhèn (Hun) 599
Fúzhōu (Fuj) 423-8, **426**

G
Gǎnlǎnbà (Yunn) 830
Ganden Monastery (Gāndān
  Sì) (Tib) 1027-8
Gang of Four 40, 42
Gānjiā Cǎoyuán (Ganjia Grass-
  lands) (Gan) 973
Gānsù 962-88, **866**
  Eastern Gānsù 984-8
  Hexi Corridor 974-84
Gānzī (Sic) 910-1
Gāochāng Gùchéng (Gaochang
  Ruins) (Xin) 936
Gāojīn (Gui) 767
gardens
  Sūzhōu (J'su) 346
gay & lesbian travellers 115-6
Géěrmù (Qin), see Golmud
Gegentala (In Mon) 1005
Gelao people 752
Genghis Khan 25, 997, 999-1001
  mausoleum 1011
geography 46-8
Germans in China 276-302
Giant Panda Breeding Research
  Base (Dàxióngmāo Fánzhí
  Yánjiū Zhōngxīn) (Sic) 878-9
ginseng 475
glaciers
  Hǎiluógōu Bīngchuān
    Gōngyuán (Sic) 907-9
  Minyang Glacier (Yunn) 820
  Qīyī Bīngchuān (Gan) 977

golf 130-1
Golmud (Qin) 1041-2, **1042**
Gōngyì Shì (Hen) 542
Gōngyì Shíkūsì (Gongyi Buddhist Caves) (Hen) 542
government 54-5
  political dissidence 55
Grand Buddha (Dà Fó) (Sic) 898-900
Grand Canal 330, 350
Grand View Park (Dàguān Gōngyuán) (Yunn) 788
Grape Valley (Pútao Gōu) (Xin) 937
grasslands
  Gānjiā Cǎoyuán (Gan) 973
  Inner Mongolia 1005-6
  Sāngkē Cǎoyuán (Gan) 973
  Tǎgōng Cǎoyuán (Sic) 906
Great Leap Forward, The 39-40
Great Wall 228-38, 258
  Bādálíng (Bei) 228-9
  conservation of 230
  Huánghuā (Bei) 231-9, **232**
  Jīnshānlǐn (Heb) 267-8
  Jīnshānlǐng (Bei) 231
  Jūyōng Guān (Bei) 230
  Mùtiányù (Bei) 229-30
  Shānhǎiguān (Heb) 272-3
  Sīmǎtái (Bei) 230-1
  Tengger Desert (Nin) 996
  walking the wild wall 232-8, **232**
  Xuánbì Chángchéng (Overhanging Great Wall) (Gan) 977
  Yellow Cliff Pass (Huángyá Guān) (Tia) 258
grottoes, see caves
Guǎngdōng 661-703, **662**
Guǎngxī 717-51, **718**
Guǎngzhōu (G'dong) 663-80, **670**
  getting around 679-80
  getting there & away 676-9
  history 663
  information 664-5
  places to eat 675-6
Guǎngzhōu (G'dong) continued
  places to stay 669-75
  Shāmiàn Dǎo 665-6, **666**
  things to see 665-9
Guānyīn Táng (Goddess of Mercy Temple) (Yunn) 802

Bold indicates maps.

Guìchí (Anh) 369
Guìlín (G'xi) 727-35, **730**
Gūishān Hànmù (Han Dynasty Tomb) (J'su) 353-4
Guìpíng (G'xi) 724-5
Guìyáng (Gui) 753-9, **754**
Guìzhōu 752-69, **753**
Gǔlàng Yǔ (Gulang Island) (Fuj) 429-34, **430**
Gulja (Xin), see Yīníng
Gùyuán (Nin) 997-8
Gyantse (Tib) 1029

H

Hāěrbīn (Heil) 473-83, **478**
Hǎikǒu (Hain) 707-11, **708**
Hǎilāěr (In Mon) 1011-2
Hǎiluógōu Bīngchuān
  Gōngyuán (Conch Gully Glacier Park) (Sic) 907-9
Hǎinán Dǎo 704-16, **706**
Hakka people 434
Han dynasty 22-3
Han Dynasty Tomb (Gūishān Hànmù) (J'su) 353-4
Hānàsī (Xin) 957
Hānàsī Hú Zìrán Bǎohùqū (Hanas Lake Nature Reserve) (Xin) 956-7
handover to China
  Hong Kong 44
  Macau 44
Hanging Monastery (Xuánkōng Sì) (S'xi) 505-7
Hángzhōu (Zhe) 401-10, **404**
  getting around 410
  getting there & away 409-10
  history 402-3
  information 403
  places to eat 408
  places to stay 407-8
  things to see 405-7
Hani (Akha) people 827
Haystack Mountain (Màijī Shān) (Gan) 985-7
Haystack Mountain Grottoes (Màijī Shān Shíkū) (Gan) 985-6
health 99-114
  acupuncture 107
  herbal medicine 108-9
  women's health 113-4
Heaven Pool (Tiān Chí) (Jil) 469, 471, **469**
Heaven Pool (Tiān Chí) (Xin) 932

Heavenly Terrace Mountain (Tiāntái Shān) (Zhe) 422
Héběi 259-75, **260**
Héféi (Anh) 357-361, **360**
Hēilóng Tán (Black Dragon Pool) (Yunn) 787
Hēilóngjiāng 473-90, **474**
Hēilóngjiāng Biānjìng (Black Dragon River Borderlands) (Heil) 486-8
Hèlán Shān (Nin) 994
Hénán 531-50, **532**
Héng Shān (Hun) 595-6
Héngyáng (Hun) 594-5
Hèqíng (Yunn) 803-4
Hétián (Xin), see Hotan
Hezhen people 486, 488
Hézuò (Gan) 973-4
highlights in China 31-6
hiking 126-8
history 21-46
hitching 178-9
Hmong, see Miao people
Hohhot (In Mon) 1002-5, **1004**
Hokkien, see Fújiàn
holidays 125-6
Hong Kong 601-42, **606, 609**
  activities 611-2
  Cheung Chau Island 640-2
  entertainment 626, 636-7
  getting around 616-9
  getting there & away 612-6
  handover to China 604
  history & politics 601-3
  Hong Kong Island 627-38, **628, 632**
  information 603-11
  Kowloon 619-27, **620**
  New Territories 638-40
  Outlying Islands 640-2
  places to eat 625-6, 636-7
  places to stay 622-5, 635-6, 639-40
  shopping 626-7, 638
  things to see 619-22, 627-35, 638-9
Hong Kong film 610-1
Hong Xiuquan 663
Hóngyán Cūn (Red Cliff Village) (Chq) 855
horse treks
  Sōngpān (Sic) 914-5
Hotan (Xin) 953-5
Huáihuà (Hun) 596
Huáng Hé (Yellow River) 47
  Shāndōng 276
  Hénán 533-4

Huáng Shān (Yellow Mountain) (Anh) 361-6, **363**
Huángguǒshù Dàpùbù (Yellow Fruit Trees Falls) (Gui) 761
Huánglóng (Sic) 916-7
Huángshān Shì (Anh), see Túnxi
Huángshízhài (Hun) 598
Huángyá Guān (Yellow Cliff Pass) Great Wall (Tia) 258
Huáqíng Chí (Hanging Pool) (Shaa) 521
Huá Shān (Shaa) 524-6, **525**
Húběi 551-65, **552**
Hu Feng 39
Hūhéhàotè (In Mon), see Hohhot
Hui 989, 1034
Hui people 752, 772
Huitengxile (In Mon) 1006
Hūlún Hú (Hulun Lake) (In Mon) 1014
Hǔmén (G'dong) 688
Húnán 581-600, **582**
Hundred Flowers 39
Húnyuán (S'xi) 505
Huǒyàn Shān (Flaming Mountains) (Xin) 936
Hǔtiào Xiá (Tiger Leaping Gorge) (Yunn) 813-5

I
Id Kah Mosque (Ài Tígǎ'ér Qīngzhēn Sì) (Xin) 944
Ili Valley (Yīlí Gǔ) (Xin) 961
Imperial Summer Villa (Bìshǔ Shānzhuāng) (Heb) 266
Imperial Tombs (Shaa) 522-3
Inner Mongolia 999-1014, **1000**
insurance
  travel 84, 968
intellectual revolution 29-30
Internet
  email 92-3
  resources 95-6
Islam 76-7, 776
islands
  Cheung Chau Island (HK) 640-2
  Gǔlàng Yǔ (Fuj) 429-4, **430**
  Hǎinán Dǎo (Hain) 704-16, **706**
  Hong Kong's outlying islands (HK) 640-2
  Māyǔ Dǎo (G'dong) 702

Méizhōu (Fuj) 437
Nánwān Hóudǎo (Hain) 711-2
Pǔtuóshān (Zhe) 416-9, **418**
Spratly Islands 705
itineraries 81-2

J
jade 62
Jade Gate Pass (Yùmén Guān) (Gan) 984
Japanese invasion 37-8
Japanese in China 314, 853
  Rape of Nánjīng 314, 319
Jiang Qing 41-2
Jiang Zemin 45
Jīgōng Shān (Rooster Mountain) (Hen) 546
Ji people 717
Jiànchuān (Yunn) 803
Jiāngsū 310-56, **311**
Jiāngxī 566-80, **567**
Jiāohé Gùchéng (Jiaohe Ruins) (Xin) 937
Jiāyùguān (Gan) 974-6, **975**
Jiāyùguān Chénglóu (Jiayu Pass Fort) (Gan) 976-7
Jílín 460-72, **461**
Jílín (City) (Jil) 465-8, **466**
Jímǔnǎi (Xin) 958
Jíměi Xuéxiào Cūn (Jimei School Village) (Fuj) 433
Jì'nán (S'dong) 278-83, **280**
Jìncí Sì (Jinci Temple) (S'xi) 495-6
Jin dynasty 25
Jing people 717
Jǐngdézhèn (J'xi) 571-3, **572**
Jǐnggāng Shān (J'xi) 578-80
Jǐnghóng (Yunn) 822-9, **824**
Jìngpò Hú (Mirror Lake) (Heil) 483-4
Jǐngzhēn (Yunn) 835
Jìnníng Xiàn (Yunn) 790
Jīnshānlǐng Great Wall (Bei) 231
Jīntiáncūn (G'xi) 724-5
Jinuo people 829
Jiǔhuá Shān (Nine Brilliant Mountains) (Anh) 367-9
Jiǔjiāng (J'xi) 574-6, **574**
Jiǔtiān Dòng (Jiutian Cave) (Hun) 598
Jiǔzhài Gōu (Nine Stockade Gully) (Sic) 917-20, **918**
Jìxiàn (Tia) 257-8
Jīzú Shān (Chicken-Foot Mountain) (Yunn) 794-5

Jokhang Temple (Tib) 1021
Judaism 77, 546
July 1st Glacier (Qīyī Bīngchuān) (Gan) 977

K
Kāifēng (Hen) 546-50, **548**
Kāilǐ (Gui) 764-6, **765**
Kāngdìng (Sic) 904-6
Karakoram Highway (Zhōngbā Gōnglù) (Xin) 950
Karakul (Xin) 950
karaoke 136, 219
karez 938
Karghilik (Xin) 952-3
Kashgar (Kāshí) (Xin) 940-50, **942**
Kazakhs 922, 1034
Kèzīěr Qiānfó Dòng (Kizil Thousand Buddha Caves) (Xin) 939-40
Khotan (Xin), see Hotan
King Yu 411
Kizil Thousand Buddha Caves (Kèzīěr Qiānfó Dòng) (Xin) 939-40
Kodari (Tib) 1033
Koko Nor (Qin), see Qīnghǎi Hú (Qinghai Lake)
Kōngdóng Shān (Gan) 985
Korean Autonomous Prefecture (Yánbiān Cháoxiǎn) (Jil) 472
Koreans in China 472
Kublai Khan 25, 999, 1001, 1014
Kùchē (Xin) 938-9
Kumbum (Qin), see Tǎ'ěr Sì
Kūnmíng (Yunn) 772-86, **778**
  getting around 786
  getting there & away 784-6
  history 772-3
  information 773-4
  places to eat 780-3
  places to stay 776-80
  things to see 775-6
Kuomintang 30-8, 717, 855
Kuqa (Xin), see Kùchē

L
Lahu people 822, 830, 835
Labrang Monastery (Lābǔlèng Sì) (Gan) 970-3, **972**
Lābǔlèng Sì (Labrang Monastery) (Gan) 970-3, **972**
lakes
  Àidīng Hú (Xin) 937
  Diān Chí (Yunn) 788, **788**

Ěrhǎi Hú (Yunn) 801, **801**
Hānàsī Hú (Xin) 956-7
Hēilóng Tán (Yunn) 787
Huáqīng Chí (Shaa) 521
Hūlún Hú (In Mon) 1014
Jìngpò Hú (Heil) 483-4
Mèngdá Tiān Chí (Qin)
  1039-41
Nam-tso Lake (Tib) 1028
Qīnghǎi Hú (Qin) 1040-1
Sàilǐmù Hú (Xin) 961
Tiān Chí (Jil) 469, 471, **469**
Tiān Chí (Xin) 932
Wǔdàlián Chí (Heil) 485-6
Yamdrok-tso Lake (Tib) 1029
Yuèyáquán (Gan) 981
Lǎngmùsì (Gan) 974
language 1044-58
  Cantonese 1052-4
  Mandarin 1044-51
  Pinyin 1046
  Portuguese 1054-6
  Tibetan 1056-8
Laotzu 72-74
Láncāng Jiāng, see Mekong River
Lánzhōu (Gan) 962-8, **964**
laundry 99
Left River Scenic Area (Zuǒjiāng
  Fēngjǐngqū) (G'xi) 725
legal matters 121-3
legal system 121-2
Léishān (Gui) 764
Lèshān (Sic) 898-903, **900**
Lhasa (Lāsà) (Tib) 1019-27, **1022**
  Barkhor 1021, **1024**
  getting around 1027
  getting there & away 1025-7
  places to eat 1024
  places to stay 1022-4
  Potala Palace 1020-1
  things to see 1020-1
Lí Jiāng (G'xi) 735-6
Li people 704
Liánhuā Shān (Lotus Mountain)
  (G'dong) 680
Liányúngǎng (J'su) 355-6
Liáoníng 440-59, **441**
Lìjiāng (Yunn) 803-10, **804**,
  808, 811
  monasteries 811-2
Lin Biao 37, 41
Língyán Shān (J'su) 350
Língyán Sì (Divine Rock Tem-
  ple) (S'dong) 291

Língyǐn Sì (Temple of the Soul's
  Retreat) (Zhe) 405-6
Línxià (Gan) 969-70
Línzī (S'dong) 297
Lìpíng (Gui) 767
Li Qingzhao 280, 282
  poetry 282
literature 63-5, see also books
Liu Shaoqi 37
Liǔyuán (Gan) 977-8
Liǔzhōu (G'xi) 745-8, **746**
Lonely Mountain (Dàgū Shān)
  (Lia) 459
Long March 37
Lónggōng Dòng (Dragon
  Palace Caves) (Gui) 761-3
Lóngjǐ Tītián (Dragon's Back-
  bone Rice Terraces) (G'xi)
  742, **742**
Lóngmén Shíkū (Dragon Gate
  Grottos) (Hen) 543-4
Lóngshèng (G'xi) 741-4, **743**
Lotus Mountain (Liánhuā Shān)
  (G'dong) 680
Lǐtáng (Sic) 911-2
Lúdí Yán (Reed Flute Cave)
  (G'xi) 731-2
Lúdíng (Sic) 909-10
Lúgū Hú (Yunn) 815-7
Lùnán (Yunn) 793
Luòmén (Gan) 987-8
Luòyáng (Hen) 539-43, **540**
Lúshān (J'xi) 576-8, **576**
Luxi, see Mángshì

M
Macau (Mac) 643-60, **646, 652**
  entertainment 657
  getting around 659-60
  getting there & away
    658-9
  information 644-9
  places to eat 656-7
  places to stay 654-6
  special events 651
  things to see 649-51
magazines 96-7
Màijī Shān (Haystack Mountain) (Gan) 985-7
Màijī Shān Shíkū (Haystack
  Mountain Grottoes) (Gan)
  985-6
malaria 101
Mǎlínghé Xiágǔ (Maling
  Gorge) (Gui) 763-4
Mandate of Heaven 22

Mángshì (Luxi) (Yunn) 849-50,
  849
Mǎnzhōulǐ (In Mon) 1012-4
Mao Zedong 37, 42, 590-1
  birthplace (Hun) 587-92
  Mao mania 221
  Mao Zedong Mausoleum 191
  Maoist pilgrimage spots
    (Hun) 583
Máogòng (Gui) 767
Maonan people 717
maps 79
martial arts 127-9
  Shàolín Sì (Hen) 536-7
Marco Polo 423
May Fourth Incident 30
May Fourth Movement 30
Māyǔ Dǎo (Mayu Island)
  (G'dong) 702
Meílǐxuě Shān (Yunn) 820
Méishān (Sic) 903
Méizhōu (Fuj) 437
Mekong River (Láncāng Jiāng)
  (Yunn) 822
Mencius 74
Mèngdá Tiān Chí (Mengda
  Heavenly Lake Nature
  Reserve) (Qin) 1039-41
Měngdònghé (Hun) 599-600
Měnghǎi (Yunn) 834
Měnghǎn (Yunn), see
  Gǎnlǎnbà
Měnghùn (Yunn) 834-5
Měnglà (Yunn) 831-2
Měnglóng (Yunn), see
  Dàměnglóng
Měnglún (Yunn) 831
Měngyǎng (Yunn) 830
Miao 766, 787
Miao people 717, 752, 762, 772
Ming dynasty 26
Ming Tombs (Bei), see Shísān
  Líng (Thirteen Tombs)
Mirror Lake (Jìngpò Hú) (Heil)
  483-4
Mògāo Kū (Mogao Caves)
  (Gan) 981-3
monasteries, see temples &
  monasteries
Monastery of Divine Light
  (Bǎoguāng Sì) (Sic) 888
money 87-9
  costs 87
  currency exchange 88
Mongol Reign 25-6
Mongolia, see Inner Mongolia
Mongols 999-1001, 1034

Monkey Island (Nánwān Hóudǎo) (Hain) 711-2
monkeys (Sic) 897
Morning of Birds Temple (Qīxiá Sì) (J'su) 326
motorcycle travel, see car & motorcycle travel
Mount Everest Base Camp (Tib) 1032
mountains
Chángbái Shān (Jil) 468-72, **469**
Éméi Shān (Sic) 891-98, **894**
Hèlán Shān (Nin) 994
Héng Shān (Hun) 595-6
Huá Shān (Shaa) 524-6, **525**
Huáng Shān (Anh) 361-6, **363**
Huōyàn Shān (Xin) 936
Liánhuā Shān (G'dong) 680
Jīgōng Shān (Hen) 546
Jǐnggāng Shān (J'xi) 578-80
Jiǔhuá Shān (Anh) 367-9
Kōngdóng Shān (Gan) 985
Màijī Shān (Gan) 985-7
Pán Shān (Tia) 256-8
Qiān Shān (Lia) 447-8
Qīngchéng Hòu Shān (Sic) 889, **888**
Qīngchéng Shān (Sic) 888-9, **888**
Qīngyuán Shān (Fuj) 436
Sōng Shān (Hen) 536-9
Tài Shān (S'dong) 283-8, **284**
Tiāntái Shān (Zhe) 422
Wǔdāng Shān (Hub) 560-1
Wǔtái Shān (S'xi) 499-502, **499**
Wǔyí Shān (Fuj) 437-9
Yǒuyì Fēng (Xin) 958
Yúnfēng Shān (Yunn) 841
Móxī (Sic) 906-7
Mǔdānjiāng (Heil) 483
Mùgécuò (Sic) 906
Mulao people 717
music 60, 61
Muslims, see Islam
Mùtiányù Great Wall (Bei) 229-30
Mùyúpíng (Hub) 561

N

Nahi (Kakhi), see Naxi people
Nam-tso Lake (Nàmùcuò) (Tib) 1028
Nánchāng (J'xi) 566-73, **568**

Nándàihé (Heb) 271
Nánjīng (J'su) 310-26
getting around 326
getting there & away 325-6
history 311-3
orientation 313
places to eat 324-5
places to stay 323-4
things to see 315-23
Nánkūn Railway 719
Nánlúo Shān (Yunn) 835
Nánníng (G'xi) 719-23, **720**
Nánpíng (Sic) 920-21
Nánwān Hóudǎo (Monkey Island) (Hain) 711-2
national parks, see reserves
Nationalist Party, see Kuomintang
Naxi people 806
newspapers 96-7
Niǎo Dǎo (Bird Island) (Qin) 1040-1
Nine Brilliant Mountains (Jiǔhuá Shān) (Anh) 367-9
Nine Stockade Gully (Jiǔzhài Gōu) (Sic) 917-20, **918**
Níngbō (Zhe) 413-6, **414**
Níngxià 989-98, **990**
Nóngdǎo (Yunn) 847
Norbu Lingka (Tib) 1021
Norman Bethune 260
North Hill (Běi Shān) (Chq) 860
North Tomb (Běi Líng) (Lia) 442
Northern dynasties 23
Northern Expedition 30

O

Old Summer Palace (Beij) 197-8
one-child policy 58
opera 218
Opium Wars 27, 313, 428, 663, 688
organised tours 165-7
Oroqen people 487
Overhanging Great Wall (Xuánbì Chángchéng) (Gan) 977

P

painting 69-70
Pán Shān (Tia) 258
Panchen Lama 1030
pandas 892
Dàxióngmāo Fánzhí Yánjiū Zhōngxīn (Giant Panda Breeding Research Base) (Sic) 878-9

Peace & Justice Temple (Zhōnghé Sì) (Yunn) 801-2
Peking, see Běijīng
Peking Man Site (Bei) 240
Pénglái (S'dong) 308
People's Liberation Army, see PLA
Phoenix Emperor Mountain (Fènghuáng Shān) (Lia) 459
photography & video 97-8
Píngliáng (Gan) 984-5
Píngxiáng (G'xi) 725
Píngyáo (S'xi) 496-8
PLA 257
planning 79-80
poetry 282
police, see PSB
politics 54-5
pollution 50-1
Polo, Marco 423
population 56-9
porcelain, see ceramics
Portuguese in China 27, 413-4, 643-4, 663
postal services 89-90
Potala Palace (Tib) 1020-1
pottery, see ceramics
PSB (Public Security Bureau)123-4
Pǔdōng Xīnqū (Pudong New Area) (S'hai) 385
Pure Water Source Mountains (Qīngyuán Shān) (Fuj) 436
Pútāo Gōu (Grape Valley) (Xin) 937
Pǔtuóshān (Zhe) 416-9, **418**

Q

Qiān Shān (Lia) 447-8
Qiang (Sic) 903
Qin dynasty 22
Qín Shǐhuáng Líng (Tomb of Qín Shǐhuáng) (Shaa) 521
Qīngdǎo (S'dong) 298-304, **300**
Qīng Dōng Líng (Eastern Qing Tombs) (Bei) 239
Qing dynasty 26-9
Qīngchéng Hòu Shān (Azure City Black Mountain) (Sic) 889, **888**
Qīngchéng Shān (Azure City Mountain) (Sic) 888-9, **888**
Qīnghǎi 1034-43, **1035**
Qīnghǎi Hú (Qinghai Lake) (Qin) 1040-1

Qīngpíng Shìchǎng (Qingping Market) (G'dong) 667
Qīngyuán Shān (Pure Water Source Mountains) (Fuj) 436
Qínhuángdǎo (Heb) 272, **270**
Qióngzhōng (Hain) 716
Qíqíhā'ěr (Heil) 488
Qiūcī Gùchéng (Qiuci Ancient City Ruins) (Xin) 938
Qīxiá Sì (Morning of Birds Temple) (J'su) 326
Qīxīng Yán (Seven Star Crags) (G'dong) 693-4
Qīyī Bīngchuān (July 1st Glacier) (Gan) 977
Quánzhōu (Fuj) 434-5, **436**
Qūfù (S'dong) 291-7, **292**

R

racism 120
radio 97
rafting 599
rail travel, see train travel
Railway Protection Movement 29
Rè Hǎi (Sea of Heat) (Yunn) 841-2
Red Cliff Village (Hóngyán Cūn) (Chq) 855
Reed Flute Cave (Lúdí Yán) (G'xi) 731-2
religion 72-8
  Buddhism 75-6, 506
  Christianity 77
  Confucianism 74-5, 294
  Islam 76-7, 776
  Judaism 77, 546
  Taoism 72-4, 309
reserves
  Chángbái Shān (Jil) 468-72, **469**
  Hǎiluógōu Bīngchuān Gōngyuán (Sic) 907-9
  Hānàsī Hú Zìrán Bǎohùqū (Xin) 956-7
  Jiǔzhài Gōu (Sic) 917-20
reserves continued
  Mèngdá Tiān Chí (Qin) 1039-41
  Sānchàhé Zìrán Bǎohùqù (Yunn) 829-30
  Wòlóng Zìrán Bǎohùqū (Sic) 891
  Wǔdàlián Chí (Heil) 485-6

Wǔlǐngyuán Fēngjǐngqū (Hun) 596-9, **597**
Wǔyí Shān (Fuj) 437-9
Zhālóng Zìrán Bǎohùqū (Heil) 488-90
Zhāngjiājiè (Hun) 596-9
Zuòjiāng Fēngjǐngqū (G'xi) 725
Resonant Sand Gorge (Yīméng Xiāngshāwān) (In Mon) 1010
river trips, see boat trips
Róngjiāng (Gui) 764
Rongphu Monastery (Tib) 1032
Rooster Mountain (Jīgōng Shān) (Hen) 546
Ruìchéng (S'xi) 498
Ruìlì (Yunn) 843-6, **844**
Russians in China 473, 946, 1012-3
Sino-Soviet split 40

S

safe travel 118-9
Sàilǐmù Hú (Sayram Lake) (Xin) 961
Sakya (Tib) 1032
Samye Monastery (Sāngyī Sì) (Tib) 1028
Sānchàhé Zìrán Bǎohùqù (Sanchahe Nature Preserve) (Yunn) 829-30
Sāngkē Cǎoyuán (Sangke Grasslands) (Gan) 973
Sānjiāng (G'xi) 744-5
Sānxiá (Hub), see Three Gorges
Sānxiān Dòng (Three Immor-tals Caves) (Xin) 944
Sānyà (Hain) 712-5, **714**
Sayram Lake (Sàilǐmù Hú) (Xin) 961
Sea of Heat (Rè Hǎi) (Yunn) 841-2
sea travel, see boat travel
senior travellers 116-7
Sera Monastery (Sèlà Sì) (Tib) 1027
Seven Star Crags (Qīxīng Yán) (G'dong) 693-4
Shaanxi 508-30, **509**
Shāchē (Xin), see Yarkand
Shang dynasty 21
Shang dynasty (Hen) 531, 533
Shànghǎi 370-400, **372, 374, 380**
Bund, The 377-8
economy 372-3

entertainment 393-5
French concession 378-9
getting around 399-400
getting there & away 397-9
government 371-2
history 370-1
information 374-7
orientation 373-4
Pǔdōng Xīnqū (Pudong New Area) 385
places to eat 391-3
places to stay 387-91
shopping 395-7
things to see 378-87
Shāmiàn Dǎo (Shamian Island) (G'dong) 665-6, **666**
Shàntóu (G'dong) 699-702, **700**
Shāndōng 276-309, **277**
Shānhǎiguān (Heb) 272-5, **270, 273**
Shānxī 491-507, **492**
Shānxī see Shaanxi
Shàolín Sì (Hen) 536-7
Sháoshān (Hun) 587-92, **588**
Shàoxīng (Zhe) 410-3, **412**
Shāpíng Gǎnjí (Shaping Mar-ket) (Yunn) 802
Shāpōtóu (Nin) 996
Shénnóngjià (Hub) 561
Shěnyáng (Lia) 440-7, **444**
Shēnzhèn (G'dong) 683-8, **684**
Shíhuī Yándòng (Karst Caves) (J'su) 334-5
Shèxiàn (Anh) 367
Shí Lín (Stone Forest) (Yunn) 790-3, **791**
Shídù (Bei) 240-1
Shígǔ (Yunn) 813
Shigatse (Rìkāzé) (Tib) 1029-32, **1030**
Shíjiāzhuāng (Heb) 259-62, **261**
Shísān Líng (Thirteen Tombs) (Bei) 238-9
Shíwān (G'dong) 682
Shībǐng (Gui) 766-7
shopping 1378
  antiques 137-8, 244
  Běijīng (Bei) 220-2
  ceramics 335-41
  Hong Kong 626-7, 638
  Shànghǎi (S'hai) 395-7
Shuānglín Sì (Shuanglin Monastery) (S'xi) 496
Shui people 752
Shuǐlián Dòng (Water Curtain Thousand Buddha Caves) (Gan) 987-8

Bold indicates maps.

Siberia Tiger Park (Dōngběi
  Hǔlin Yuán) (Heil) 477-9
Sìchuān 870-921, **871**
  Northern Sìchuān 913-21
  Western Sìchuān 903-13
Silk Road 922, 937, 950-5
Silver Beach (Yíntān) (G'xi) 725
Sīmáo (Yunn) 822
Sīmǎtái Great Wall (Bei) 230-1
Sìmén Tǎ (Four Gate Pagoda)
  (S'dong) 283
Sino-Japanese War 440, 450-1
skiing 130
  ski resorts 468, 483
Sleepy Dragon Nature Reserve
  (Wòlóng Zìrán Bǎohùqū)
  (Sic) 891
snake repository, Wúzhōu
  (G'xi) 749
Song dynasty 25
Sòng Líng (Song Tombs) (Hen)
  542
Sōng Shān (Hen) 5369
Sōngpān (Sic) 914-6, **914**
South Pass (Yáng Guān) (Gan)
  984
Southern dynasties 23
special events, see festivals
sport 136-7
Spratly Islands 705
Stone Forest (Shí Lín) (Yunn)
  790-3, **791**
study 131
Sui dynasty 23
Suífēnhé (Heil) 484-5
Summer Palace (Bei) 193-7,
  see also Old Summer Palace
Sun Yatsen 29, 692-3
  mausoleum 322
  Sūn Zhōngshān Gùjū (Sun
    Yatsen's Residence)
    (S'hai) 384
Sūzhōu (J'su) 341-50, **342, 350**
  gardens 345-6

T

Tǎchéng (Xin) 958-9
Tǎ'ěr Sì (Qin) 1039-41
Tǎgōng Cǎoyuán (Tagong
  Grasslands) (Sic) 906
Tài Hú (J'su) 336-41, **185**
Tài Shān (S'dong) 283-8, **284**
Tài'ān (S'dong) 288-91, **288**
Táihuái (S'xi) 499-502, **500**
Táijiāng (Gui) 764
Taiping, see Hǔmén

Taiping Rebellion 28, 312
  Tàipíng Tiānguó Lìshǐ
    Bówùguǎn (Taiping
    Heavenly Kingdom History
    Museum) (J'su) 318
Táshí (Gui) 767
Taiwan 44-5
Tàiyuán (S'xi) 491-5, **494**
Tang dynasty 23-4
Tánggǔ (Tia) 255-7, **256**
Tāngkǒu (Anh) 361-4
Tánzhè Sì (Cudrania Pool
  Temple) (Bei) 239-40
Taoism 72-4, 309
Tashilhunpo Monastery
  (Zhāshílúnbù Sì) (Tib) 1030
Tashkurgan (Xin) 249-50
teahouse (chádiàn) 883
telephone services 91-3
temples & monasteries
  Bǎoguāng Sì (Sic) 888
  Bīnglíng Sì (Gan) 968-9
  Drepung Monastery (Tib)
    1027
  Ganden Monastery (Tib)
    1027-8
  Guānyīn Táng (Yunn) 802
  Jìncí Sì (S'xi) 495-6
  Labrang Monastery (Gan)
    970-3, **972**
  Lìjiāng monasteries (Yunn)
    811-2
  Língyán Sì (S'dong) 291
  Língyīn Sì (Zhe) 405-6
  Norbu Lingka (Tib) 1021
  Rongphu Monastery (Tib)
    1032
  Samye Monastery (Tib) 1028
  Shàolín Sì (Hen) 536-7
  Shuānglín Sì (S'xi) 496
  Tǎ'ěr Sì (Qin) 1039-41
  Tánzhè Sì (Bei) 239-40
  Tashilhunpo Monastery (Tib)
    1030
  Xuánkōng Sì (S'xi) 505-7
  Zhōnghé Sì (Yunn) 801-2
Temple of Heaven Park (Bei)
  199-200
Temple of the Soul's Retreat
  (Língyīn Sì) (Zhe) 405-6
Ten Kingdoms 25
Téngchōng (Yunn) 838-40,
  840
Tengger Desert (Nin) 996-7
Terracotta Warriors, see Army
  of Terracotta Warriors
theatre 68

Thousand Buddha Caves
  Temple (Bīnglíng Sì) (Gan)
  968-9
Three Gorges 866-7
Three Gorges (Hub) 561-2
Three Gorges Dam (Hub) 562,
  564
Three Immortals Caves
  (Sānxiān Dòng) (Xin) 944
Tibet 1015-33, **1016**
  getting around 1019
  history 1015-7
  information 1020
  Sichuān to Tibet 910-1
  travel restrictions 1018
  trekking 1017-8
  Qīnghǎi to Tibet 1042-3
Tiān Chí (Heaven Pool) (Jil)
  469, 471, **469**
Tiān Chí (Heaven Pool) (Xin) 932
Tiānānmén Incident (1976) 42
Tiānānmén Incident (1989) 43-4
Tiānānmén Square (Bei) 190-1
Tiānjīn 242-58, **243, 244, 246**
  entertainment 252
  getting around 254-6
  getting there & away 253-4
  Gǔwán Shìchǎng (antique
    market) 245-7
  history 242-3
  information 245
  orientation 243-5
  places to eat 250-2
  places to stay 249-50
  shopping 252-3
  things to see 245-9
Tiānshuǐ (Gan) 985-7, **986**
Tiāntái Shān (Heavenly Terrace
  Mountain) (Zhe) 422
Tiāntán Gōngyuán (Bei) 199-200
Tiger Leaping Gorge (Hǔtiào
  Xiá) (Yunn) 813-5
tigers
  Dōngběi Hǔlin Yuán (Siberia
    Tiger Park) (Heil) 477-9
time 98, 925
Tingri (Dìngrì) (Tib) 1032-1033
toilets 114-5
Tomb of Qín Shǐhuáng (Qín
  Shǐhuáng Líng (Shaa) 521
tombs
  Běi Líng (Lia) 442
  Gùshān Hànmù (J'su) 353-4
  Imperial Tombs (Shaa) 522-3
  Ming Tombs (Bei), see
    Shísān Líng
  Qīng Dōng Líng (Bei) 239

Shísān Líng (Bei) 238-9
Sòng Líng (Hen) 542
Tomb of Qín Shǐhuáng
(Shaa) 521
Xīxià Wánglíng (Nin) 994
Tóngjiāng (Heil) 487-8
Torugart Pass (Xin) 948
tourist offices, see travel agents
tours 165-7, 181-2
train travel 160-4, 171-5
Nánkūn Railway (G'xi) 719
Trans-Siberian Railway 160-4
within China 171-5
travel agents 166-7
Trans Siberian Railway 160-4
travel insurance 968
Treasured Summit Hill (Bǎodǐng
Shān) (Chq) 860-1
Treaty of Nanjing 318-9, 602
Nánjīng Tiáoyuē Shǐliào
(Nanjing Treaty History
Museum) (J'su) 318-9
Treaty of Shanghai 581
Treaty of Tianjin 242
trekking
Xīshuāngbǎnnà (Yunn) 833
Tsetang (Zédāng) (Tib) 1028-9
Tujiao people 752
Tǔlǔfān Zhàn (Xin), see
Dàhéyàn
Túnxī (Anh) 366-7
Turpan (Tǔlǔfān) (Xin) 933-5,
934, 936
TV 97
Tōngzhá (Tōngshí) (Hain) 715-6

U

Ūrümqi (Xin) 925-32, **926**
Uyghur
people 922, 924, 938
food 757, 930

V

video 97-8
video systems 97
Vietnam, relations with 726
visas 82-4
volcanoes 841

W

Wǎndǐng (Yunn) 847-9, **848**
weights & measures 99

Bold indicates maps.

Wēihǎi (S'dong) 309
Wēiníng (Gui) 763
Wēishān (Yunn) 795
Wénchāng (Hain) 711
Wēnzhōu (Zhe) 420-2, **420**
Western Hills (Xī Shān) (Yunn)
788-90
Western Thousand Buddha
Caves (Xī Qiānfó Dòng)
(Gan) 983
Western Xia Tombs (Xīxià
Wánglíng) (Nin) 994
White Cloud Hills (Báiyún
Shān) (G'dong) 680
Wòlóng Zìrán Bǎohùqū (Sleepy
Dragon Nature Reserve)
(Sic) 891
women travellers 115
women's health 113-4
work 131-2
Wuchang Uprising 29
Wǔdàlián Chí (Five Large
Connected Lakes) (Heil)
485-6
Wǔdāng Shān (Hub) 560-1
Wǔdāng Zhào (In Mon)
1009-10
Wǔhàn (Hub) 551-60, **554**
getting there & away
559-60
information 553-5
places to stay 557-8
things to see 555-7
Wúhú (Anh) 369
Wǔlíngyuán Fēngjǐngqū
(Wulingyuan Scenic Area)
(Hun) 596-9, **597**
Wūlǔmùqí (Xin) 925-32, **926**
Wǔmíng (G'xi) 723
Wǔqīng (Tia) 258
Wusutu Zhao (In Mon) 1005
Wǔtái Shān (Five-terrace
Mountain) (S'xi) 499-502,
499
Wǔyí Shān (Fuj) 437-9
Wúxī (J'su) 336-41, **338, 340**
Wúzhōu (G'xi) 748-51, **748**
Wúzhōu Shécáng (Wuzhou
Snake Repository) (G'xi) 749

X

Xanadu (In Mon) 1014
Xī Qiānfó Dòng (Western Thousand Buddha Caves) (Gan) 983
Xī Shān (Western Hills) (Yunn)
788-90

Xia dynasty 21
Xī'ān (Shaa) 508-19, **514, 520**
getting around 519
getting there & away 518-9
history 510-1
information 511
places to eat 517-8
places to stay 516-7
things to see 512-6
Xiàguān (Yunn) 793-4
Xiàhé (Gan) 970-3, **972**
Xiàmén (Fuj) 428-33, **430**
Xiāngchéng (Sic) 912
Xiányáng (Shaa) 522-6
Xīkǒu (Zhe) 419
Xilamuren (In Mon) 1005
Xīncūn (Hain) 711-2
Xīnglóng (Hain) 711
Xīngyì (Gui) 763-4
Xīníng (Qin) 1036-9, **1036**
Xīnjiāng 922-61, **923**
Northen Xīnjiāng 955-61
Southern Silk Road 950-5
South-West (Kashgaria)
940-50
Xīqiáo Shān (G'dong) 682-3
Xīshuāngbǎnnà Region (Yunn)
820-35, **821**
Xīzhōu (Yunn) 802
Xīxià Wánglíng (Western Xia
Tombs) (Nin) 994
Xuánbì Chángchéng (Overhang-
ing Great Wall) (Gan) 977
Xuánkōng Sì (Hanging
Monastery) (S'xi) 505-7
Xúzhōu (J'su) 353-5, **354**

Y

Yamdrok-tso Lake (Tib) 1029
Yán'ān (Shaa) 526-9, **528**
Yánbiān Cháoxiǎn (Korean
Autonomous Prefecture) (Jil)
472
Yáng Guān (South Pass) (Gan)
984
Yángshān Bēicái (Yanshan
Quarry) (J'su) 327
Yángshuò (G'xi) 736-40, **736,
740**
Yángzhōu (J'su) 329-34, **332**
Yangzi (Yangtze) River 47, see
Cháng Jiāng
Yangzi River cruises, see boat
trips
Yāntái (S'dong) 305-8, **306**
Yao people 717, 742

Yarkand (Xin) 951-2
Yarlung Valley (Yǎlǔ Liúyù)
  (Tib) 1028
Yèchéng (Xin), see Karghilik
Yellow Cliff Pass (Huángyá
  Guān) Great Wall (Tia) 258
Yellow Fruit Trees Falls
  (Huángguǒshù Dàpùbù)
  (Gui) 761
Yellow Mountain (Huáng Shān)
  (Anh) 361-6, **363**
Yellow River, see Huáng Hé
Yengisar (Xin) 951
Yi people 752, 772
Yíchāng (Hub) 561-5, **562**
Yíhéyuán, see Summer Palace
Yílí Gǔ (Ili Valley) (Xin) 961
Yīméng Xiǎngshāwān (Resonant
  Sand Gorge) (In Mon) 1010
Yínchuān (Nin) 989-94, **992**
Yíngjiāng (Yunn) 842-3
Yīngjíshā (Xin), see Yengisar
Yīngtán (J'xi) 578
Yíníng (Xin) 959-61, **960**
Yíntān (Silver Beach) (G'xi) 725
Yíxiàn (Anh) 367
Yíxīng Xiàn (J'su) 334-5
Yōngbùlākāng (Tib), see
  Yumbulagang
Yǒngdìng (Fuj) 434
Yǒngpíng (Yunn) 795
Youle people, see Jinuo people

Yǒuyì Fēng (Friendship Peak)
  (Xin) 958
Yuan dynasty 25-6
Yuan Shikai 29
Yuánshàngdū (In Mon), see
  Xanadu
Yuèyáng (Hun) 592-4, **592**
Yuèyáquán (Crescent Moon
  Lake) (Gan) 981
Yúlín (Shaa) 529-30
Yumbulagang (Tib) 1028
Yùmén Guān (Jade Gate Pass)
  (Gan) 984
Yùnchéng (S'xi) 498
Yúnfēng Shān (Cloudy Peak
  Mountain) (Yunn) 841
Yúngāng Shíkū (Cloud Ridge
  Caves) (S'xi) 505-7
Yúnnán 770-850, **771**
Yùquán (Heil) 483

Z
Zhālóng Zìrán Bǎohùqū (Zha-
  long Nature Reserve) (Heil)
  488-90
Zhāngjiājiè (Hun) 596-9
Zhangmu (Zhāngmù) (Tib) 1033
Zhànjiāng (G'dong) 696-9, **698**
Zhàoqing (G'dong) 693-6, **694**
Zhàoxìng (Gui) 764
Zhàozhōu Qiáo (Zhaozhou
  Bridge) (Heb) 263

Zhèjiāng 401-22, **402**
Zhèngdìng (Heb) 262
Zhèngzhōu (Hen) 532-6, **534**,
  537
Zhènjiāng (J'su) 327-9, **328**
Zhènyuán (Gui) 766-7
Zhōngdiàn (Sic) 912-3
Zhōngdiàn (Yunn) 817-9, **817**
Zhōnghé Sì (Peace & Justice
  Temple) (Yunn) 801-2
Zhōngshān (G'dong) 693
Zhōngwèi (Nin) 994-6, **995**
Zhou dynasty 21-2
Zhou Enlai 37, 38, 41, 403, 411
  Zhōu Ēnlái Zǔjū (Zhou
  Enlai's ancestral home)
  (Zhe) 411
  Zhōu Ēnlái Jìniànguǎn (Zhou
  Enlai Memorial) (Tia) 247
Zhōuzhuāng (J'su) 351-2, **352**
Zhu De 37
Zhuàng people 717, 752
Zhūhǎi (G'dong) 688-92, **690**
Zhūzhōu (Hun) 592
Zǐjìn Chéng, see Forbidden City
zodiac 73
Zöigê (Sic) 918-21
Zōuxiàn (S'dong) 297
Zūnyì (Gui) 767-9, **768**
Zuǒjiāng Fēngjǐngqū (Left River
  Scenic Area) (G'xi) 725

Boxed Text

Acupuncture 107
Air Fares to Hong Kong 614
Beginning or the End?, The 924
Beware of the Border 470
Běijīng Music Scene 61
Běijīng Opera 218
Bodhisattvas, Dragons &
  Celestial Beings 506
Bouyei People of
  Huángguǒshù, The 762
Broken as Jade 314
Building 'Em Like They Used To
  803
Capitalist Road 251
Cathay Hotel, The 389
Cave Dwellings 536
Chen Liyan 443
Chinese Circus, The 386
Chinese Martial Arts 127-9
Chinese Zodiac 73

Chinglish 1045
Close Shave, A 403
Confucianism 294
Conserving the Great Wall 230
Dai, The 826
Divine Inspiration 693
Dr Ho Phenomenon, The 812
Edgar Snow 853
Fēngshuǐ 70
Fists of Righteousness &
  Harmony, The 278
Foreign Devils on the Silk Road
  937
From Kung Fu to Cannes 610-1
Future Train 719
Gǒngyì Shì 542
Gender Games 115
Grand Canal, The 330
Grasslands Tour Prices 1006
Hani (Akha) People, The 827

Heavenly Kingdom of the
  Taiping, The 312
Huáng Shān – A Tradition of
  Tranquillity and Inspiration 362
Immortal Eight, The 309
Jinuo People, The 829
Judging a Yíxīng Teapot 336
Kūnmíng Food 781
Karaoke Phenomenon, The 219
Karez 938
Kebabs & Raisins 757
Kǎifēng's Israelites 547
Kill the Rooster to Frighten the
  Monkey 124
Life After the Handover 604
Listening Posts of the Great
  Game 946
Magical Root, The 475
Mao Mania 221
Mao Zedong 590-1

Monkey Etiquette 897
More Than Meets the Eye ... 138
Myths and Mists of Tiān Chí 471
Navigating Cities on Foot 169
Naxi, The 806
Northern Warlords 450-1
On Your Bike 192
Oroqen, The 487
Over the Torugart Pass 948
Paging Passenger Li 156
Pandas & Conservation 892
Paper Propaganda 97
Pedicabs Versus Rickshaws 181
Pinyin 1046
Power of Eunuchs, The 188
Rare Cranes Find Sanctuary 489

Sūzhōu's Gardens 346
Shànghǎi Bówùguǎn (Shanghai Museum) 379
Sherry Liu 57
Song Poet, The 282
Species under Threat 477
Spratly Spat, The 705
Stunt Driving 175
Taking Tea and More in Chéngdū 883
Tale of Two Rivers, A 47
Therapeutic Massage 130
Thousand Lotuses Mountain 447
Three Gorges Dam, The 564
Travel Insurance 968
Travel Times & Train Fares from Běijīng 225

Trekking in Xīshuāngbǎnnà 833
Trips to Traumatise 170
Troubled Waters 726
Unequal Treaties 602
Up in Smoke 119
Uyghur Food 930
Visiting the Basic People's Court 121
Walking the Wild Wall 232-8
Which Time Is It? 925
Wives for Sale 59
Wrath of Khan, The 997
Xiao Liangyu 184
Yúnnán's Muslims 776
Zhou Peikun 320

MAP LEGEND

CITY ROUTES

Freeway	Freeway
Highway	Primary Road
Road	Secondary Road
Street	Street
Lane	Lane
	On/Off Ramp
Unsealed Road	
One Way Street	
Pedestrian Street	
Stepped Street	
Tunnel	
Footbridge	

REGIONAL ROUTES

Tollway, Freeway	
Primary Road	
Secondary Road	
Minor Road	

BOUNDARIES

International	
State	
Disputed	
Fortified Wall	

HYDROGRAPHY

River, Creek	Dry Lake; Salt Lake
Canal	Spring; Rapids
Lake	Waterfalls

TRANSPORT ROUTES & STATIONS

Train	Ferry
Underground Train	Walking Trail
Metro	Walking Tour
Tramway	Path
Cable Car, Chairlift	Pier or Jetty

AREA FEATURES

Building	Market	Beach
Park, Gardens	Sports Ground	Cemetery
		Campus
		Plaza

POPULATION SYMBOLS

✪ CAPITAL — National Capital	● CITY — City	⊙ Village — Village	
◉ CAPITAL — State Capital	● Town — Town		Urban Area

MAP SYMBOLS

♠ Place to Stay	▼ Place to Eat	● Point of Interest
✕ Airport	⌐ Gate	Telephone
$ Bank	✚ Hospital	Temple (Confucian)
Bird Sanctuary	Internet Cafe	Temple (Other)
Border Crossing	❋ Lookout	Temple (Taoist)
Bus Terminal, Stop	Monument, Ruins	Tomb
Cave	Mosque	Tourist Information
Church	Mountain, Range	Transport
Embassy	Museum, Theatre	Zoo
	National Park	
	Pagoda	
	Pass	
	Police Station	
	Post Office	
	Pub or Bar	
	Shopping Centre	
	Stately Home	

Note: not all symbols displayed above appear in this book

LONELY PLANET OFFICES

Australia
PO Box 617, Hawthorn, Victoria 3122
☎ 03 9819 1877 fax 03 9819 6459
email: talk2us@lonelyplanet.com.au

USA
150 Linden St, Oakland, CA 94607
☎ 510 893 8555 TOLL FREE: 800 275 8555
fax 510 893 8572
email: info@lonelyplanet.com

UK
10a Spring Place, London NW5 3BH
☎ 020 7428 4800 fax 020 7428 4828
email: go@lonelyplanet.co.uk

France
1 rue du Dahomey, 75011 Paris
☎ 01 55 25 33 00 fax 01 55 25 33 01
email: bip@lonelyplanet.fr
www.lonelyplanet.fr

World Wide Web: www.lonelyplanet.com *or* AOL keyword: lp
Lonely Planet Images: lpi@lonelyplanet.com.au